SMITH and ROBERSON'S
BUSINESS LAW

By

LEN YOUNG SMITH

Chairman of the Department of Business Law
Northwestern University

and

G. GALE ROBERSON

Professorial Lecturer in Business Law
Northwestern University

Uniform Commercial Code Edition
Second Edition

ST. PAUL, MINN.
WEST PUBLISHING CO.
1966

PREFACE

This Second Edition incorporates the relevant provisions of the Uniform Commercial Code in a presentation of the fundamental concepts, rules and principles of law in those areas commonly embraced within the field of Business Law. It covers the subjects of Contracts, Agency, Bailments, Carriers, Sales, Products Liability, Commercial Paper, Bank Deposits and Collections, Partnerships, Corporations, Unfair Competition and Trade Regulation, Bankruptcy, Secured Transactions, Property, Insurance, and Wills, and contains narrative text, court decisions, problems, and statutes.

This is a revision of the One Volume Uniform Commercial Code Edition of Smith and Roberson's Business Law published in 1962 at which time 18 States had adopted the Code. During the past four years an additional 31 jurisdictions have adopted the Code, bringing the total to 49, including 47 States, the District of Columbia, and the Virgin Islands. The three remaining States which have not yet adopted the Code are Arizona, Idaho, and Louisiana. A list of the adopting jurisdictions appears in Chapter 1 and also at the beginning of Appendix A which contains all ten Articles of the Code.

This widespread acceptance of the Code has made revision necessary. The present volume presents and discusses the Code almost exclusively in its treatment of the subject matter of Sales, Documents of Title, Bulk Sales, Commercial Paper, Bank Deposits and Collections, Transfer of Shares of Corporations, and Secured Transactions.

It is the intention of the authors to furnish a complete, current, and adaptable vehicle of instruction for the study of Business Law. This Edition should also be useful to schools offering combined short courses or review courses in the preparation of students for C.P.A. examinations. In addition, colleges of liberal arts and sciences may find it adaptable for use in an elective course designed to afford the students a background of knowledge of basic legal principles and precepts and of the nature of the judicial process.

The division of the chapters into text, selected cases, problems, and statutory materials is regarded as desirable both from the standpoint of the teacher and the student of Business Law. The text discusses the general rules of law which find application in the specific factual situations presented by the cases. The text precedes the cases in order to give the students an understanding of what they are looking for and what may be expected.

The cases have been carefully selected and edited, not only to fulfill fundamental teaching requirements but also to present the type of litigation current in modern business which illustrates commercial problems of particular interest to students of business. Wherever feasible, recent modern cases have replaced older ones.

PREFACE

To reduce the burden of reading unnecessarily long statements of fact, editing of the cases has consisted, in large measure, of summarizing the essential facts. The cases have been compressed to present an adequate factual statement and the reasons of the court in reaching its decision upon the points of substantive law involved. In certain cases the facts are briefly summarized and presented within brackets immediately preceding the opinion of the court. To keep the cases within reasonable space limitations, portions of the courts' opinions are omitted as indicated by asterisks. The word "Citation" or "Citations," where inserted in brackets in the cases, indicates omission of the titles of cases and references thereto by the court as supporting authorities.

The authors have long been of the opinion that the fundamental principles of law in the various subjects comprising the field of Business Law may be more readily learned from text and reported cases which possess a degree of human interest. The authors regard more recent applications of basic principles preferable to older cases covering the same points. Study of the cases reveals that the law is not static, but develops and changes to meet the social and economic needs of a dynamic politically organized society. It is important not only to know the rules of law but also the reasons underlying these rules as expressed by the courts. With changes in the needs of the business community, the reasons for the old rules lose validity and the law inevitably changes.

The text reflects the extended and extensive experience of the authors as teachers of Business Law. Their constant aim and object has been to state concisely and accurately the basic principles and rules of law with which students in schools of business and commerce should be familiar without sacrificing a view of the comprehensiveness of each subject.

The problems at the end of the chapters should be of assistance to the men and women who teach Business Law. We have found them extremely helpful in developing the analytical talents of the students and in the application of rules presented in the particular chapter. The problems promote classroom discussion and a more thorough understanding of the principles covered in the text and case materials.

In order that the student of Business Law may become familiar with statutory material we have included as appendices the entire Uniform Commercial Code, the Uniform Partnership Act, the Uniform Limited Partnership Act and the Model Business Corporation Act. These statutes should be used extensively from the beginning of the study of the particular subjects to which they apply.

One definite, positive, benefit which a student should receive from a course in Business Law is learning to use words properly as a medium of expressing his thoughts precisely and in a manner not unfamiliar with legal terminology. Definitions of terms are of utmost importance in paving the way to understanding and in many cases to the solution of a problem. It is therefore recommended that at the commencement of the study of a given subject matter, the students be instructed to learn the particular definitions that are applicable. The Uniform Commercial Code is most

PREFACE

helpful in this respect, and students should be especially required to read Sections 1–201, 1–204, 2–103, 2–104, 2–105, 2–106, 3–102, 4–104, 4–105, 5–103, 6–102, 7–102, 8–102, 9–105, 9–106, and 9–107. If the student forgets the substance of the other sections of the Code that he has studied, as he probably will in the course of time, but remembers the substance of these definitions, he will nevertheless find the capacity of his mind enlarged and its powers strengthened.

This volume is designed to accommodate the amount of time and the type and content of courses in Business Law generally offered in universities, colleges, and schools of business and commerce. By reason of its broad coverage, including new chapters on Products Liability, Bank Deposits and Collections, and Unfair Competition and Trade Regulation, it is readily adaptable to specially designed courses in Business Law by the assignment of different combinations of the subject matter. Schools which provide a program of study with substantial emphasis upon Business Law will probably offer instruction in each of the fields included in this book. Where curriculum requirements and time available make necessary a reduction in the content or scope of the course or courses to be given, the materials may be adapted to particular objectives. Thus, a course may be given to include only the chapters on Contracts, Agency, Partnerships, and Corporations, or the chapters on Sales, Products Liability, Commercial Paper, Bank Deposits and Collections, and Secured Transactions, or any of numerous other combinations of assigned subject matter to meet the desired coverage.

In the Preface to the 1962 edition we acknowledged with gratitude the assistance of Professor William D. Hawkland, now Dean of the School of Law, State University of New York at Buffalo, of Ray David Henson, Jr., Lecturer in Business Law at Northwestern University, and of G. Gale Roberson, Jr., of the Chicago Bar. We acknowledge the able assistance of J. Gordon Henry, of the Illinois and New York Bars, and Attorney, The Northern Trust Company, Chicago, in the preparation of certain chapters of the text material in the present edition; and of James Allan III of the Chicago Bar in the preparation of the Index.

LEN YOUNG SMITH
G. GALE ROBERSON

Chicago, Illinois
July, 1966

*

TABLE OF CONTENTS

PART ONE. CONTRACTS

TABLE OF CONTENTS

PART FIVE. COMMERCIAL PAPER

PART SIX. PARTNERSHIPS

PART SEVEN. CORPORATIONS

PART EIGHT. UNFAIR COMPETITION, BANKRUPTCY, SECURED TRANSACTIONS

PART NINE. PROPERTY

TABLE OF CONTENTS

PART NINE. PROPERTY—Continued

PART TEN. TRUSTS, MORTGAGES, INSURANCE, WILLS

APPENDICES

INDEX

*

TABLE OF STATUTES

TABLE OF STATUTES

TABLE OF STATUTES

TABLE OF STATUTES

TABLE OF STATUTES

TABLE OF STATUTES

TABLE OF STATUTES

TABLE OF STATUTES

XVIII

TABLE OF STATUTES

TABLE OF STATUTES

TABLE OF STATUTES

TABLE OF STATUTES

TABLE OF STATUTES

*

TABLE OF CASES

Cases in italics are those cited in text.

References are to pages.

TABLE OF CASES

TABLE OF CASES

TABLE OF CASES

TABLE OF CASES

†

TABLE OF CASES

BUSINESS LAW

PART ONE

CONTRACTS

CHAPTER 1

INTRODUCTION TO LAW—CONTRACTS

The Function of Law. No part of a social mechanism is fully understood apart from the whole. A study of business law, which is a branch of the "law", is not complete without some appreciation of the "law" generally.

Law is readily identifiable as an instrument of social control. It is possible to view law as a systematic statement of the legal consequences of specific conduct. If a man steals, he will, under certain circumstances, go to prison. Thus, law regulates, within certain limitations, human conduct and relationships. We recognize, however, that much of human conduct is regulated by considerations above the law, i. e., by ethical determinants. This distinction is sometimes ignored by critics of the law who believe that the law moves too slowly in meeting the challenge of a changing society.

In our society the function of the law is not that of a causative agent. Its purpose is not to promote or prevent change but to keep society moving along in a civilized manner. Our law has historically taken a middle road, responding to man's aspirations rather than inspiring them. Society creates laws with a view to conclusions already reached, often after much groping.

The function of law and its contrast to ethics may be easily illustrated. If Smith, a private citizen, while walking along a pier, sees Jones drowning in deep water only ten feet from the pier, the law generally imposes no legal duty on Smith to attempt a rescue. If Smith is an excellent swimmer, the mores of the community may prompt the rescue. But until such time as society insists on the rescue attempt, the law will not require it.

Oliver Wendell Holmes wrote: "The life of the law has not been logic; it has been experience". The law is fashioned out of the experience of mankind and is the result of the development of society. The conservatism of the law is not designed to make it an opponent of change. The law is not to be regarded as the primary instrument of reform or progress; instead, it should be viewed as the expression of such change. It has been correctly observed that the law has never

1

been able in the long run to resist successfully a social or economic need that was strong and just.

The law is not precise, exact and certain in application. It is a social science. A Federal judge once observed: "The law works with blunt tools". Admittedly, society has not yet been able to formulate a completely just or scientific social system. "General rules," continued the judge, "applicable to the majority of cases, but sometimes having an oppressive bearing upon particular ones, make up the principles upon which, of necessity, she (the law) founds her decisions, for the law must be workable." As society progresses, the law will progress.

Law Defined. There is no one generally accepted definition of the term "law." Roscoe Pound, a famous American legal scholar, has described three distinct meanings of the term:

"1. Historically, the oldest and longest continued use of 'law' * * * is to mean the aggregate of laws, the whole body of legal precepts which obtain in a given politically organized society. * * * In this sense, jurists speak of 'systems of law' and 'justice according to law'. * * *

"2. In another sense the term 'law' is used to mean the legal order. It is used to mean the regime of ordering human activities and adjusting human relations through the systematic application of the force of a politically organized society. * * The legal order is a specialized phase of social control. * * * The word 'law' is used in the sense of the legal order when we speak of 'respect for law', or 'the end of law'. Thus, when we speak of respect for law, we mean respect for the legal order. One might, for example, respect the legal order and yet object to some particular item of the body of legal precepts. * * *

"3. In still another sense, many who write of 'law' mean what Mr. Justice Cardozo has taught us to call 'the judicial process'. In this sense law is used to mean the process of determining controversies whether as it actually takes place or as it is conceived it ought to take place." Pound, Jurisprudence, vol. I, pp. 12–14.

The first of these three definitions is the one generally in mind when we speak of the "law." We think of the body of rules or principles, derived from judicial opinions and legislative enactments and enforced by the courts as constituting the law of a particular jurisdiction.

Blackstone, the English jurist whose famous Commentaries influenced the development of the Anglo-American law, defined law as "A rule of civil conduct prescribed by the supreme power in a state, commanding what is right, and prohibiting what is wrong." Blackstone's definition rightly asserts the imperative character of the law. The law stems from sovereignty, i. e., the supreme and exclusive political power in a state. A state is sovereign when it exercises undivided authority over all persons and property within its border and is independent of direct control by any other power. It is from this sovereign authority of the state that the law of the state emanates.

Laws without sanctions would be meaningless. Sanctions are the means of enforcing the law. Sanctions are most apparent in criminal law, which provides fines, imprisonment or death for certain proscribed conduct. Sanctions are also a vital part of our civil law. A contract would be meaningless in our society if a breach of the contract would afford the innocent party a remedy which was unenforceable. The state provides a means of enforcing that remedy. For example, if money damages are awarded in a breach of contract action, it is possible in the event of failure on the part of the wrongdoer to pay the judgment, to have the appropriate legal officer seize and sell his property in order to satisfy the judgment. In short, to say that the law has sanction is simply another way of saying that law is based on the physical force of the state.

Sources of Law. What we speak of as law, legal rules and principles, derive ultimately from a multitude of sources; e. g., customs of a community, religious doctrines, moral and philosophical ideas. However, these are formalized in two principal ways and appear as the immediate sources of law: (1) decisions of courts (case law); (2) enactments of the legislative bodies (legislation or statutory law).

In our legal system, the case law is the common law of England, supplemented by equity jurisprudence which paralleled the growth of the common law, and decisions of American courts. The statutory law is that of Federal and State legislative bodies, augmented by written constitutions and Federal treaties. These sources are considered in the subsections which follow.

(a) The Common Law. The last of the Roman legions left Britain in 411, and for at least another 700 years there was nothing resembling a nationally administered system of law. Judicial power was vested in local bodies, such as shire (county) courts and manorial courts. It was not until after the advent of William the Conqueror in 1066, and particularly after the ascendancy to the throne of Henry II in 1154 that we observe the beginning of a common law. As the kings undertook to consolidate the administration of their realm, they brought into being a system of law administered by their own justices, a system known as the common law. The history of the common law of England is the history of the expansion of royal justice, administered by courts of the king, at the expense of the local judicial bodies which had theretofore adjudicated controversies. This transition was abetted by the advantages litigants had in the king's courts, including trial by jury.

One seeking redress in the king's courts applied for a "writ." Originally, a writ was merely a written command given by the king or in his name. Later, it came to be a command to the defendant to appear in court to answer the charges of the plaintiff. It was thus the manner in which a legal action could be started in a royal court. But the litigant had to find a writ which would fit his case. If there were no writ suitable to the claim he was asserting, his only recourse would be to local tribunals. There was no general law of contract or of tort, administered in the king's courts; rather, there were certain legal remedies, corresponding to the recognized writs. Each writ was the foundation of a separate form of action, such as "covenant" (action on a promise under seal), "debt" (action for a liquidated debt), or "replevin" (action to recover a chattel wrongfully taken or withheld by another). Most of the early writs, as might be expected, pertained to land disputes, so-called "real actions." One of the oldest was the "writ of right," used to try title to land.

One of the most important writs at common law was "trespass," which made its appearance in the thirteenth century and came to be used to obtain redress for certain civil wrongs; viz., trespass to person (trespass vi et armis), trespass to land (trespass quare clausum fregit), and trespass to goods (trespass de bonis asportatis). In each instance there was involved a breach of the peace (the "king's peace"), justifying intervention by the king and his tribunals. The writ of trespass developed further, all the while bringing more matters within the jurisdiction of the king's justices. Later, about the turn of the fifteenth century, there appeared another writ, "trespass on the case" or simply "case," which brought within the purview of the royal courts additional types of cases where the wrong complained of was tortious in character. Indeed, the two writs, trespass and case, form the basis for the modern law of torts.

The writ of "assumpsit" appeared around 1500, as an offshoot of "case." It is from the law that developed with respect to assumpsit that our law of contracts traces its ancestry.

The common-law courts were three in number: Court of Exchequer, Court of Common Pleas, and Court of King's Bench. The Court of Exchequer originally handled only tax matters, but later became a regular law court. The Court of Common Pleas, also called Common Bench, decided ordinary civil actions. The Court of the King's Bench had sole criminal jurisdiction.

Utilizing the writ system, these courts began to build up a body of law, of decided cases, which came to serve as precedent in the future determination of controversies. The principle of stare decisis (to stand by the decisions), whereby past decisions are adhered to and relied upon in the solution of present disputes, is a hallmark of the common law as articulated by these English tribunals. And, so it is with courts today in this country.

Judicial decisions have two uses: first, to determine with finality the case decided; and, second, to indicate to the public how similar cases, will be decided if and when they arise. Stare decisis is a guiding principle whereby a court is bound by precedent in deciding the case before it, to follow and apply the rules, principles, and precepts announced and applied by it in its former decisions. It is the instrument of stability in our legal system. It furnishes certainty, predictability and reliability. It assures all persons of equality and uniformity of treatment. Its strength proceeds from its devotion to the preservation of well-accepted doctrine rather than a blind persistence in tradition. A court may rightly interpret new factors, social or economic, or interpret new conditions in such a way as to effect a change in the case law while adhering to the basic legal principles involved.

In this country stare decisis does not preclude correction of erroneous decisions or judicial choice of conflicting precedents. The proper American conception comprehends stare decisis as a flexible doctrine, functioning approximately as follows:

1. The United States Supreme Court has never held itself to be rigidly bound by its own decisions, and other Federal and State courts have followed that course in reference to their own decisions.

2. A decision of the Supreme Court is binding on Federal matters on all other courts, Federal or State.

3. While a decision of a Federal court, other than the Supreme Court, may be persuasive in a State court on a Federal matter, it is, nevertheless, not binding since the State court owes obedience insofar as it has jurisdiction over a case involving Federal law to only one Federal court, namely, the Supreme Court. The converse is also true; a decision of a State court may be persuasive in the Federal courts but it is not binding, except where Federal jurisdiction is based on diversity of citizenship, in which case the Federal courts are required to apply local State law.

Decisions of the Federal courts (other than the Supreme Court) are not binding upon other Federal courts of coordinate rank, or of inferior rank, unless the latter owe obedience to the court rendering the decision.

(b) *Equity.* As the common law developed, it had a tendency to become overly rigid, beset with technicalities. As a consequence, for many wrongs no remedies were provided, the judges insisting that a claim be within the scope of one of the recognized writs. Moreover, in practically every case the only relief obtainable was a money judgment. There could be nothing like the injunction, for example, to prevent future wrongs and obviate a multiplicity of suits. Disappointed subjects began to petition to the king directly for justice. He, in turn, came to delegate these petitions to his Chancellor, a member of his Council who in the early period was always a bishop. Gradually, there evolved what was in effect a new and supplementary system of needed judicial relief to those who had no adequate remedy at law. It was called Equity and was administered by the Court of Chancery presided over by the Chancellor. The latter, deciding cases on "equity and good conscience," afforded relief in many instances where the common-law judges refused to act, or "where the remedy at law was inadequate." Thus, there grew up, side by side, two systems within the framework of the law administered by different tribunals, the common-law courts and courts of equity. Actually, the fusion of the two did not occur, either in England or this country, until comparatively recent times.

Equity jurisdiction, in some cases, recognized rights which were enforceable at common law as well, but provided more efficacious remedies. For example, for breach of a land contract a litigant could obtain specific performance in a court of equity, but only a judgment for money damages in a court of law. The defendant seller would be commanded to perform his part of the contract by conveying title to the land. A hallmark of the Court of Chancery was the injunction, a device to prevent future wrongs. No comparable remedy was available in the common-law courts. There were other remedies in equity, which were not available elsewhere, among them the remedy of reformation, whereby upon the ground of mutual mistake, an action could be brought to reform or change the language of a written agreement to conform to the actual intention of the contracting parties. Another was an action for rescission of a contract by the party who was induced to enter into it because of the fraud or duress of the other party. Equity opened up altogether new fields, including those untouched by the common-law courts. The most notable was the recognition and enforcement of trusts.

Equity courts over the years formulated many general legal principles which were called "maxims." A few of these familiar maxims of equity are as follows: Equity will not suffer a wrong to be without a remedy. Equity regards the substance rather than the form. Equity abhors a forfeiture. Equity delights to do justice and not by halves. He who comes into equity must come with clean hands. He who seeks equity must do equity.

Today, in nearly every jurisdiction there has been a union of law and equity; the same courts administer both systems of law. However, remnants of the old division continue. For our purpose, it is sufficient to note that the early decisions of the equity courts, as well as those of the common-law courts, are a part of our legal heritage which effectively continue to shape the law of today, as attention is paid to older judicial precedents in deciding present controversies.

(c) *Legislation.* As indicated, the two main sources of law are judicial decisions (case law) and legislative enactments (statutory law). Whereas case law evolves from the judicial determination of particular controversies, statutory law is the product of a legislative body and, in general, operates only prospectively.

In considering the history of legislation, Roscoe Pound observed five stages of development. (Pound, Jurisprudence, vol. III, pp. 579–84.) The first is the "unconscious legislation in the period of customary law." Although historically courts were established before legislatures, from an early time the laws enforced are regarded as having always existed.

The next stage is "declaratory legislation in the period when the traditional law is reduced to writing." Many ancient codes are of this kind. They do not purport to be declarations of new laws, but a written memorial of laws already recognized and observed.

The third is the "selection and amendment when by the political union of peoples having in some particulars divergent customs it becomes necessary to choose in declaring the custom of the new whole." Choices must be made between conflicting traditions.

The next development leads to "conscious constructive lawmaking as an occasional expedient at first to meet political exigencies, but gradually to effect important changes here and there in the legal system in emergencies." At this point there is the de-emphasis of law as being declarative of that which already exists in the customs of the people and a corresponding emphasis upon changing the law theretofore regarded as immutable.

Finally, there is "habitual legislation as an ordinary agency of legal development, often culminating in codification of the entire legal system." This, of course, brings us to the present, a period in which legislative bodies assume an ever increasing share of the lawmaking. Indeed, a large part of a court's work today is interpretative, given over to construing and applying law promulgated by the legislature.

Constitutional Law. Underlying all our law in the United States, whether case law or statutory law, is the Federal constitution, which is the "supreme law of the land." No law, Federal or State, is valid if it violates the Federal constitution. The final arbiter as to constitutionality is the Supreme Court of the United States.

One of the fundamental principles upon which the government is founded is that of separation of powers, a doctrine which can be traced back to Baron Montesquieu and to John Locke. As incorporated into our Constitution it means that there are to be three distinct and independent branches of government, of which the Federal judiciary should be one. The principle of judicial review is thus one of the basic ideas incorporated in that document which William Gladstone once characterized as the greatest ever struck off at one time by the brain and purpose of man.

The Constitution in Article III states "The judicial power shall extend to all cases, in law and equity, arising under this Constitution, the laws of the United States, and treaties made, or which shall be made, under their authority." This provision together with the one in regard to the judicial power of the United States being vested in the courts unmistakably gives the courts the power to test the validity of Acts of Congress. Alexander Hamilton forcefully expressed the idea when he contended that "The interpretation of the laws is the proper and peculiar province of the courts. A constitution is, in fact, and must be regarded by the judges, a fundamental law. It therefore belongs to them to ascertain its meaning, as well as the meaning of any particular act or proceeding from the legislative body. If there should happen to be an irreconcilable variance between the two, that which has the superior obligation and validity ought, of course, to be preferred; or, in other words, the Constitution ought to be preferred to the statute, the intention of the people to the intention of their agents." (The Federalist, No. 78, Lodge Ed., pp. 485–6.)

The constitution also provides that treaties made under the authority of the United States shall be the supreme law of the land. Federal treaties are, therefore, paramount to State constitutions and statutes. Federal legislation is, of course, of major significance as a source of law. The importance and complexity of new bills enacted at each Congressional session results from the tremendous economic and social forces within this great nation. Federal legislative activity is also manifest in the promulgation of executive orders by the President and in the rules and regulations of Federal administrative officials and agencies.

Leaving the Federal sphere, we see virtually the same pattern in every State. The highest law of each State is contained in its written constitution. Subordinate to this is the myriad of statutes passed by the legislatures of the various States. Likewise, State administrative agencies issue rules and regulations having the force of law. In addition, cities, towns and villages have limited legislative powers within their respective municipal areas. Taken together, the annual volume of legislative law is enormous; it is small wonder that society supports a professional class of lawyers, one of whose primary concerns it is to keep abreast of these matters.

Classification of law. (a) Substantive Law and Adjective Law. A common classification divides substantive law from adjective or procedural law. The former includes laws which create, define and regulate legal rights and obligations. Thus, the rule in contracts that an offer must be communicated to the offeree is a statement of substantive law. Adjective law, also called procedural or remedial law, prescribes the methods of enforcing rights which exist by reason of the substantive law. One turns to adjective law, found for the most part in codes of procedure, to ascertain the method by which he is to obtain redress in court. In the standard law school curriculum, contracts, torts, property and agency, are all substantive law courses; adjective law courses are those dealing with civil, criminal, and administrative procedure, and evidence.

(b) Public Law and Private Law. Public law is that branch of law which deals with the rights and powers of the state, in its political or sovereign capacity, in its relation to individuals or groups. Public law comprises constitutional, administrative and criminal law. Private law is that which governs private individuals in their relations with one another, or law which is administered between citizen and citizen. Business law is primarily of a private law nature.

(c) Tort Law. A tort is a legal wrong consisting of the violation of a right not created by contract. Tort law is concerned with compensation for losses suffered by individuals whose legally protected interests in property, personalty, or relations with others, have been invaded, either by physical means, misappropriation, defamation or in some other manner by the misconduct of others. Among the more common torts are the following: assault, battery, false imprisonment, trespass to land or chattels, conversion, negligence, libel, slander, invasion of the right of privacy, and business wrongs.

In a tort action the injured party sues to recover compensation for damage he has suffered. The purpose of tort law is to compensate the aggrieved party, not to punish the wrongdoer, as is the case with criminal law. Of course, the same conduct may, and often does, constitute both a crime and a tort. But something may be criminal without being tortious, and by the same token, an act may amount to a tort and not be a crime. The closest that tort law comes to an implementation of objectives of the criminal law is in certain cases where courts may award what are called "punitive" or "exemplary" damages. Where the defendant's tortious conduct has been intentional and deliberate, exhibiting "malice" or a fraudulent or evil motive, most courts will permit a jury to award damages over and above the amount necessary to compensate the plaintiff. The allowance of punitive damages is designed to punish the defendant and deter others from doing what he did. For the most part, however, the sole purpose is to compensate those whose loss or damage has resulted from the violation of a duty by the defendant, such as the duty not to cause intentional harm, the duty to use reasonable care, and the duty not to trespass.

The law of torts is an active area of the law. A large part of all civil litigation is devoted to the trial of negligence actions. In a later section, "Journey of a Case through the Courts", a tort action is traced from its inception, to culmination with an appeal to a reviewing court.

(d) *Criminal Law.* Criminal law is that branch of law which treats of crimes and their punishment. It thus encompasses substantive criminal offenses such as murder, larceny, burglary, and robbery, and the administration of criminal justice, the procedure by which the substantive criminal law is enforced.

A crime is any act or omission prohibited by public law in the interest of protection of the public and made punishable by the state in a judicial proceeding brought by it. Crimes are prohibited and punished upon the ground of public policy, which may include the protection and safeguarding of government (as in treason), human life (as in murder), private property (as in larceny), or other valued institutions and interests. Within recent years the scope of the criminal law has increased substantially. The traditional crimes have been augmented by a multitude of regulations and laws to which are attached criminal penalties. These pertain to nearly every phase of modern living. Typical examples in the business law field are those respecting the licensing and conduct of a business, and the so-called "Blue-Sky Laws" governing the sale of securities.

Having regard to the seriousness of the offense, crimes are usually classified as felonies or misdemeanors. A felony at common law was any crime which occasioned the forfeiture of lands and goods. It was usually a capital offense as well. Among the common-law felonies were homicide (later classified into murder and manslaughter), mayhem, arson, rape, robbery, burglary, and larceny. The term "misdemeanor" came to be applied to all crimes other than those which were felonies, and which carried lighter punishments than felonies. This classification persists to this day, with the word "felony" used to denominate crimes of a more serious nature which permit of capital punishment or

imprisonment in the penitentiary. Misdemeanors are relatively minor offenses, usually punished by fine only or by imprisonment other than in a penitentiary.

In general, two elements must be present for a crime: (1) the wrongful act; (2) the criminal intent. For example, it is not enough for a larceny prosecution to show that the defendant appropriated another's goods; it must be established that he intended to steal the goods. The mens rea (guilty mind), as it is called, is a requisite of most crimes. Moreover, as is well known, criminal guilt must be established beyond a reasonable doubt. Under Anglo-American law, guilt is never presumed. Indeed, the law presumes the innocence of the accused, and this presumption is not affected by a failure to testify in his own defense. The State still has the burden of affirmatively proving the guilt of the accused, and this is not met until proof is adduced to show guilt beyond a reasonable doubt.

Typically, a criminal prosecution is begun by the issuance of a "warrant" and the "arrest" of the defendant. The warrant, which states the offense with which the person to be arrested is charged, is issued by a judge at the behest of a "complainant." In many instances, an arrest may be made without a warrant, usually by a police officer. An officer may arrest a person or persons to stop the commission of a criminal offense or to apprehend one whom he reasonably believes has committed a crime. An ordinary citizen also has powers of arrest, but this power is much more circumscribed and is, in fact, rarely exercised.

After arrest, the accused is brought before a judge, or magistrate. If the offense is of a minor nature, such as disorderly conduct or an ordinary traffic violation, the magistrate can dispose of the matter in a summary trial. If the charge is more serious, the magistrate does not have jurisdiction to try the case, but conducts what is called a "preliminary examination." He does not adjudge the guilt or innocence of the accused, but simply determines whether there is probable cause to "bind over" the defendant for further proceedings. The magistrate will set and approve "bail," determining the amount of the "bond" and conditions thereof which the defendant must post to secure his release from custody pending further developments in the matter.

The next step, where the crime is a serious one, is a proceeding before the grand jury, a body whose function is to decide, upon a showing by the State's Attorney, whether the accused ought to be prosecuted. If the grand jury decides in the affirmative it returns what is called a "true bill" and an "indictment" is issued. The grand jurors do not determine guilt or innocence, but only whether a criminal action should be brought against the accused. They hear only witnesses presented by the State, and upon the subsequent trial of the case before a petit jury or judge without a jury the grand jury's determination is not evidence of the defendant's guilt. In this example, the grand jury considered the matter on a bind-over from the magistrate; it can also initiate action on its own. In that event, the proceeding is called a "presentment," and the warrant of arrest is called a "bench warrant."

In some States, an alternative method to that of indictment by a grand jury, as a method of instituting criminal proceedings, is the "information." The prosecutor can avoid the necessity of presenting the case to a grand jury, and simply bring an information, a statement drawn by him setting forth the facts and the charge in much the same way as the indictment. Ordinarily, this method is limited, however, to crimes of a less serious nature.

After the foregoing steps have been taken, the defendant is brought before the court which will ultimately try him, for an "arraignment." He is informed of the charge against him, and he enters his "plea." If his plea is "not guilty," he must stand trial. He is entitled to a jury trial, but if he chooses, he may have his guilt or innocence determined by the court sitting without a jury, a "bench trial." In either case, he has a right to be represented by counsel, to adduce evidence in his own defense, to cross-examine witnesses for the State, and to refuse to testify. In short, he is entitled to all those procedural safeguards necessary to assure a fair trial, a right guaranteed under the due process clauses of both State and Federal constitutions.

At the conclusion of the testimony, the jury is instructed as to the applicable law, and they retire to arrive at their "verdict." In most States the verdict must be unanimous. If the verdict is "not guilty," the matter ends there. The State has no right to appeal from an "acquittal," and the accused having been placed in "jeopardy," cannot be tried a second time for the same offense. If the verdict is "guilty" and judgment is entered thereon, the defendant has further recourse. He may make a "motion for a new trial," asserting that prejudicial error occurred at the trial, necessitating a retrial of the cause. Or he can assert that the evidence was insufficient upon which to predicate guilt and ask for his discharge. He may perfect an "appeal" to a reviewing court, alleging error in the trial court and asking either his discharge or a remandment of the case for a new trial. There may, of course, be other proceedings in a criminal cause, including for example, a request for probation, but the foregoing, in the main, illustrates the typical course of a criminal cause as it proceeds from the initial arrest to review by an appellate court.

(e) *Administrative Law.* This branch of public law deals with various functions and activities of the government in its executive capacity as performed, supervised, and regulated by public officials, departments, and boards and commissions, and with controversies arising in connection therewith between individuals and such public officials and agencies. Administrative functions and activities concern such matters of national and social safety, welfare, and convenience, as the establishment and maintenance of military forces, police, citizenship and naturalization, coinage of money, highways and watercourses, elections, and, in general, public health, safety, and welfare. Administrative law is both Federal and State law. There are, however, certain governmental functions, such as those concerning the military forces, coinage of money, and the regulation of interstate commerce, which can be performed only by the Federal government.

Because of the increasing complexity of the social, economic, and industrial life of the nation, the scope of administrative law has expanded enormously in the last few decades. This is evidenced by the great increase in the number and activities of Federal government boards, commissions and other agencies. The first important agency of this group was the Interstate Commerce Commission created in 1887. This was followed by the Federal Trade Commission in 1914. In more recent years, beginning in 1934, the following Federal agencies, among others, have been created: National Railroad Retirement Board, Federal Communications Commission, Securities and Exchange Commission, Social Security Administration, National Labor Relations Board, Federal Power Commission, Maritime Commission, and the Civil Aeronautics Board. Among the more important boards of commissions in the several States are those supervising and regulating banking, insurance, and public utilities, and Workmen's Compensation Boards for the administration of employers' liability laws.

So extensive and numerous have become the activities of these boards and commissions that, in their entirety, such activities are referred to as the administrative process.

This term is used in contradistinction to the term "judicial process." The former term implies the administration of law by non-judicial agencies; the latter, the administration of law by judicial bodies or courts. Since these boards are not judicial bodies, but only quasi-judicial, an appeal from their rulings or orders can be taken to the courts.

(f) *Business or Commercial Law.* The whole body of laws pertaining to commercial dealings is commonly referred to as business or commercial law. The broad scope of this category appears from the mere naming of the legal subjects considered in detail in this text on business law: contracts, agency, bailments, carriers, sales, products liability, partnerships, corporations, unfair competition, property, commercial paper, insurance and bankruptcy.

Before the advent of common-law courts, a system of mercantile courts existed in England which administered a law known generally as Lex mercatoria, the "law merchant." This law, predicated on the customs of the merchants, was not completely brought within the common-law tradition until the eighteenth century.

The law merchant was important particularly at the time of a fair, when men came with their merchandise from all over Europe. In the Magna Charta (1215) special provisions were made respecting merchants, including Section 41 which provided that all merchants "shall have safe and secure conduct, to go out of, and to come into England, and to stay there, and to pass as well by lands as by water, for buying and selling by the ancient and allowed customs."

A characteristic of the merchant courts was the dispatch with which they adjudicated disputes. Adapted to the needs of the litigants, the courts sought to prevent undue delay for the itinerant merchants. The law merchant courts were in operation from hour to hour, and one common type of mercantile courts, known as the Piepoudre Courts,

courts of record incident to every fair and market and having jurisdiction over all commercial injuries and minor offenses committed at that particular fair or market, took its name from this characteristic of rendering immediate decisions. The words "pied poudre" are of French derivation, and mean "dusty feet." The designation indicates that justice was rendered so swiftly that the suits of wandering merchants were tried before the dust could fall from their feet.

Eventually, the law merchant was absorbed into the common law, and thus it became a part of American law. A significant development in this country has been the codification of large parts of commercial law. The impetus for this movement came from the National Conference of Commissioners on Uniform State Laws, which from time to time drafted uniform statutes and recommended their adoption by State legislatures. The first was the Negotiable Instruments Act, approved in 1896. This was followed in 1906 by the Uniform Sales Act and the Uniform Warehouse Receipts Act. The Uniform Stock Transfer Act and the Uniform Bills of Lading Act were first promulgated in 1909. The Uniform Conditional Sales Act was approved in 1918, and in 1933 the Conference recommended the Uniform Trust Receipts Act. In 1952 a Uniform Commercial Code embracing the subject matter and superseding and repealing these Uniform Acts and certain other statutes was submitted to the States and within 14 years had been adopted by 45 of them.

THE UNIFORM COMMERCIAL CODE

The Uniform Commercial Code has been prepared under the sponsorship and direction of the National Conference of Commissioners on Uniform State Laws and the American Law Institute with the assistance of hundreds of practicing lawyers, judges, law teachers, bankers, and business men.

The effort to obtain desirable uniformity in the laws of the several States especially in the field of commercial law dates back to the 1890's when the National Conference was established composed of commissioners appointed by the governors of the States. The only way in which uniformity among the laws of the several States may be achieved is to have the legislature of each State enact identical statutes on a given subject matter. The preparation of such statutes has been the task of the National Conference of Commissioners.

The American Law Institute was organized in 1923 for the purpose of making a thorough study and restatement of general common-law principles in the form of specific rules. Its membership includes leading members of the bar, judges, and members of law school faculties. It has prepared and published Restatements of the Law in the fields of contracts, property, torts, agency, trusts and other subjects. While the rules of the Restatements are not authoritative or binding on the courts, their careful drafting, clarity of expression, and sound foundation in the common law has resulted in their widespread use by lawyers and judges and their frequent citation in judicial opinions.

The need for a new statute to replace the earlier uniform Acts arose from the numerous changes in business methods which have developed in the twentieth century. The separate acts were based upon nineteenth century concepts of law many of which had become inadequate for modern commercial practices. The courts nevertheless were compelled to apply the older concepts to the rights and obligations of parties in types of transactions which were unknown at the time the earlier uniform Acts were adopted.

Rather than amend the separate uniform Acts on a piecemeal basis, in 1940 it was proposed at the annual meeting of the Commissioners on Uniform State Laws that a code be prepared to bring the statutory commercial law up to date which would repeal and supersede the earlier commercial acts.

Work on drafting the Article on Sales began in 1942 and on the entire project in 1945. An official draft of the Code was first published in 1952, and an Official Text in 1958 which contained amendments to comply with suggestions of the New York Revision Committee. Subsequently, a 1962 Official Text was published which is the form in which the Code has been adopted by most of the States. The 1962 Official Text is set forth in Appendix A of this book.

In 1961 the American Law Institute and the National Conference of Commissioners of Uniform State Laws jointly established a Permanent Editorial Board for the Uniform Commercial Code consisting of eleven members. The function of this Permanent Board is to keep abreast of the manner and extent to which the Code, as reflected in judicial decisions and amendments by legislative bodies, is fulfilling its avowed purposes, to suggest from time to time clarifying amendments where necessary, and to discourage amendments which are merely a change in language and not of substance, but which may introduce doubt and uncertainty. The Board will also be required to keep informed on new commercial practices which may cause provisions of the Code to become obsolete or make new provisions desirable.

Forty-nine jurisdictions, including 47 States, the District of Columbia, and the Virgin Islands, have adopted the Code. Pennsylvania in 1953 was the first adopting State. The largest number of adoptions in any year occurred in 1965 in which there were 14 additional adoptions.

The jurisdictions in which the Uniform Commercial Code has been adopted, and the year of adoption, are:

Pennsylvania	1953
Massachusetts	1957
Kentucky	1958
Connecticut	1959
New Hampshire	1959
Rhode Island	1960
Wyoming	1961
Arkansas	1961
New Mexico	1961
Ohio	1961
Oregon	1961
Oklahoma	1961
Illinois	1961
New Jersey	1961
Georgia	1962
Alaska	1962
New York	1962
Michigan	1962
Indiana	1963
Tennessee	1963
West Virginia	1963
Montana	1963
Maryland	1963
California	1963
Wisconsin	1963
Maine	1963
Nebraska	1963
Missouri	1963
District of Columbia	1963
Virginia	1964
Virgin Islands	1965
Utah	1965
North Dakota	1965
Iowa	1965
Washington	1965
Nevada	1965
Hawaii	1965
Kansas	1965
Colorado	1965
Florida	1965
Texas	1965
North Carolina	1965
Minnesota	1965
Alabama	1965
South Dakota	1966
Vermont	1966
South Carolina	1966
Delaware	1966
Mississippi	1966

The Code consists of ten Articles, namely:

1. General Provisions
2. Sales

3. Commercial Paper
4. Bank Deposits and Collections
5. Letters of Credit
6. Bank Transfers
7. Documents of Title
8. Investment Securities
9. Secured Transactions
10. Effective Date and Repealer

The Code repeals numerous statutes, some of long standing, including the Uniform Negotiable Instruments Law, Uniform Sales Act, Uniform Conditional Sales Act, Uniform Bills of Lading Act, Uniform Warehouse Receipts Act, Uniform Trust Receipts Act, Uniform Stock Transfer Act, Bulk Sales Act, and Factors Lien Act. The substantive provisions of these statutes are replaced by the Code.

As stated in Section 1–102 the underlying purposes and policies of the Code are:

(a) to simplify, clarify and modernize the law governing commercial transactions;

(b) to permit the continued expansion of commercial practices through custom, usage and agreement of the parties;

(c) to make uniform the law among the various jurisdictions.

The basic principles of commercial law are not overhauled or radically changed by the Code. These principles are expanded and significant changes are made in the manner in which they are implemented in order to clarify and liberalize the rules and state definitely the legal relationships of the parties in various types of modern commercial transactions. The Code is transaction oriented rather than legal concept oriented. It defines the rights and duties of parties as they develop in commercial situations and describes what events or acts of the parties will alter or modify them. To illustrate, unlike the Sales Act the Code does not treat title to goods as determining risk of loss absent agreement of the parties, but places risk of loss upon the seller or buyer depending on the situation and the agreement as the goods move in the process of marketing and distribution.

The great detail of the Code is manifest from its 401 sections many of which contain subsections, and its emphasis upon precision from the 168 definitions of terms and language employed. The large number of terms defined, many of them well known to business men but heretofore not defined by statute, illustrates the purpose of the Code to conform the rules to modern commercial usages and understandings.

The Code applies a higher standard of conduct to merchants than to those not engaged in business. It defines a "merchant" as a person who deals in goods of the kind involved in the transaction or who by his occupation holds himself out as having knowledge or skill with reference thereto, including one who employs an agent or broker having such knowledge or skill. Certain sections of the Code prescribe different rules for transactions with a merchant and for transactions between merchants. "Good faith" is defined as honesty in fact in the conduct or transaction concerned. However, in the case of a merchant "good faith" means in addition to such honesty the observance of reasonable commercial standards of fair dealing in the trade. Every contract or duty within the Code imposes an obligation of good faith in its performance or enforcement. The Code should have the long term effect of improving the morals of the market place.

The importance of the Code cannot be overemphasized with respect to those branches of commercial law to which it applies. The change in fundamental principle may be slight, but the legal effect of failure to act within a prescribed time may produce a complete change in practical result.

By and large the Code is designed to aid in ascertaining the intention of the parties to a contract and when ascertained, or if a contract was intended, to give force and effect to the agreement. Numerous sections are prefaced by the preservative phrase "Unless otherwise agreed." The Code therefore endeavors to uphold the agreement as made by the parties. The instances of the Code specifically forbidding certain provisions in contracts as a matter of public policy are relatively few. In ten instances, however, the Code expressly declares certain specific types of provisions in contracts to be ineffective in order to preserve the purpose and intendment of the Code from erosion by private contract. These specific instances which serve to demonstrate the enlightened character of the Code are:

(1) The obligations of good faith, diligence, reasonableness, and care prescribed by the Code may not be disclaimed by agreement, although standards may be agreed upon if not manifestly unreasonable. Section 1–102.

(2) Unconscionable clauses in contracts may be denied enforcement. Section 2–302.

(3) A contract may not prohibit the assignment of a right to damages for breach of the whole contract or a right arising out of the due performance by the assignor of his entire obligation under the contract. Section 2–210(2).

(4) A seller of goods may not exclude or limit the extension of his express or implied warranties to a member of the family or household of the buyer or a guest in the buyer's home. Section 2–318.

(5) A bank may not disclaim responsibility for its own lack of good faith or failure to exercise ordinary care, or limit the measure of damages for such lack or failure. Section 4–103(1).

(6) A warehouseman may not insert in his receipt for goods any term which impairs his obligation of delivery or his duty of care of the goods. Section 7–202(3).

(7) A warehouseman may not limit his liability for conversion of the goods to his own use. Section 7–204(2).

(8) A carrier may not exempt itself from liability for accurate count of packages received for shipment or for accurate description in the bill of lading of the kind and quantity of bulk freight. Section 7–301(2) and (3).

(9) A carrier may not limit its liability for conversion of the goods for its own use. Section 7–309(2).

(10) A contract may not contain a provision which prohibits the assignment of an account or of a contract right. Section 9–318(4).

Many areas of commercial law are untouched by the Code. This book does not attempt to present the Code in its entirety but only within certain areas in sufficient depth to acquaint the student with its more important provisions and to enable him to develop an understanding of its purpose and general content. The Uniform Commercial Code is referred to herein as the U.C.C. or simply "the Code."

Judicial Systems. Federal Courts. The Federal constitution provides for a system of Federal courts. Article III, Section 1, states that "the judicial Power of the United States, shall be vested in one supreme Court, and in such inferior Courts as the Congress may from time to time ordain and establish". Section 2 of article III sets forth the jurisdiction of these courts, as follows: "The judicial Power shall extend to all Cases, in Law and Equity, arising under this Constitution, the Laws of the United States, and Treaties made, or which shall be made, under their Authority;—to all Cases affecting Ambassadors, other public Ministers and Consuls;—to all Cases of admiralty and maritime Jurisdiction;—to Controversies to which the United States shall be a party;—to Controversies between two or more States;—between a State and Citizens of another State; —between Citizens of different States;— between Citizens of the same State claiming Lands under Grants of different States, and between a State, or the Citizens thereof, and foreign States, Citizens or Subjects."

The nation's highest judicial tribunal is the Supreme Court of the United States. There are nine members of the Court, and they receive lifetime appointments from the President, subject to confirmation by the United States Senate. "In all Cases affecting Ambassadors, other public Ministers and Consuls, and those in which a State shall be a Party, the supreme Court shall have original Jurisdiction. In all other Cases before mentioned, the supreme Court shall have appellate Jurisdiction, both as to Law and Fact, with such Exceptions, and under such Regulations as the Congress shall make." Article III, Section 2.

The next highest courts in our Federal system are the Courts of Appeals. The United States is divided into eleven Federal judicial circuits, and each circuit has a Court of Appeals. The seventh circuit, for example, comprises the States of Wisconsin, Illinois and Indiana. The second circuit includes Vermont, Connecticut and New York. These courts exercise appellate jurisdiction, mainly the reviewing of cases on appeal from Federal District Courts, but also decisions of Federal administrative agencies.

The Federal trial courts are called District Courts. There are 93 of these, one for each Federal judicial district. These include, in addition to the 88 district courts in the 50 States, a district court in the District of Columbia, Guam, the Canal Zone, the Virgin Islands, and Puerto Rico. Their jurisdiction is extensive. They have exclusive jurisdiction of all Federal criminal prosecutions. Where there is "diversity of citizenship" and the amount in controversy exceeds $10,000, an action between private litigants may be filed in a Federal District Court or removed there from a State court. These courts also have exclusive jurisdiction of bankruptcy, anti-trust, patent, trademark and copyright cases.

In addition to the foregoing Federal courts, sometimes referred to as "constitutional courts," the following are also in the Federal judicial system: Court of Claims, Tax Court, Customs Court, and Court of Customs and Patent Appeals.

State Courts. In addition to the system of Federal courts existing in the United States, every State has its own judicial system. The judicial structure of each State varies slightly from that of the others, but a common pattern can be discerned.

At the summit is the State's highest tribunal, a reviewing court which is generally called the Supreme Court of the State. In New York, however, it is called the Court of Appeals. In some States the large volume of cases in which review is sought has necessitated the creation of intermediate appellate courts. This has been true, for example, in California, Illinois, Louisiana, New York, Ohio and Pennsylvania. In general, appellate courts do not hear witnesses. Their function is to examine the record of a case on appeal and to determine whether the trial court committed prejudicial error, and, if so, to reverse the judgment of the lower court, otherwise to affirm it.

Below the appellate courts are the trial courts of general or original jurisdiction. They are called by various names: Circuit Courts (Illinois, Indiana, Michigan); Superior Courts (California, Massachusetts); District Courts (Iowa, Minnesota, Oklahoma, Wyoming); Courts of Common Pleas (Ohio, Pennsylvania). In addition to these trial courts there are usually special courts having a limited jurisdiction such as the Probate or Surrogate Court, which has jurisdiction over the administration of the estates of decedents, minors and the mentally incompetent.

At the lowest level are various courts of inferior jurisdiction. Perhaps the best known are the Justice of the Peace Courts. Such local judicial bodies have limited power. Their jurisdiction in civil actions is limited to small claims where the amount in controversy does not exceed a few hundred dollars. Their criminal jurisdiction is limited to misdemeanors. The procedure in this type of court is informal, and an appeal may be taken from this court to a court of general jurisdiction or trial court, where the entire case is tried anew.

JOURNEY OF A CASE THROUGH THE COURTS

To acquaint the student with the procedure of cases in the courts, it will be helpful to carry a hypothetical action at law through the trial court to the highest court of review in the State. Assume that A, a pedestrian, while crossing a street in Chicago, is struck by an automobile driven by B. A suffers serious personal injuries, incurs heavy medical and hospital expenses, and is unable to work for several months. Naturally, A desires damages from B. Attempts at settlement failing, he brings an action at law against B. Both A and B are represented by counsel. When reference is made to A filing a pleading, it is understood that the pleading is actually filed by his lawyer. In Illinois, where A sustained his injuries, there is no limitation on the amount recoverable. A commences his action against B by filing with the clerk of the circuit court of Cook county his complaint containing a statement of his cause of action. A is referred to as the plaintiff. The sheriff of the county, or one of his deputies, serves a summons upon B, the defendant, commanding him to file his appearance and answer in the circuit court within thirty days of the day of service of the summons. A's complaint sets forth in considerable detail the facts attending his injuries, alleges that he was in the exercise of due and reasonable care for his own safety at the time he was struck by B's automobile, and that, on the other hand, B's negligent driving of his automobile was the proximate cause of A's injuries, and asks damages in the amount of $35,000. B must reply to A's complaint by filing an answer or motion challenging the legal sufficiency of A's statement of a cause of action. In this particular case, we assume that B interposes an answer to A's complaint. By his answer, he categorically denies the allegations of A's pleading and avers, on the other hand, that he, B, was driving his car carefully and in the exercise of caution for the safety of others, but that A dashed across the street without looking in any direction to see whether cars or other vehicles were approaching, and that, in short, A's injuries were occasioned by his own negligence and, accordingly, that he should not be permitted to recover any damages. An issue of fact is thus made by the pleadings as to whether A and B, respectively, were exercising reasonable care or, instead, were negligent. Reference has been made to the pleadings of A and B as the complaint and answer. In some States A's pleading still bears the common-law designation of declaration, and B's reply is called a plea. An issue of fact having been made, the cause is now ready for trial.

In the course of preparing for the trial, the attorneys for A and B may each decide to take the depositions of the adverse party and of other occurrence witnesses. A deposition consists of the sworn testimony of a person taken upon interrogatories propounded by counsel in the presence of a notary public or other official. The taking of depositions is an effective pre-trial discovery procedure which permits the parties to evaluate their cases and, possibly, to settle their dispute before trial. The testimony taken in the course of the deposition is of further value for impeachment purposes, i. e., the testimony given by a deponent may be used to contradict any conflicting story he may tell from the witness stand during the trial of the case. Modern rules of procedure provide for the taking of depositions as well as other pre-trial discovery procedures, e. g., demand for admissions of fact, and written interrogatories. Implementing these procedural rules of discovery is the pre-trial conference held before one of the trial judges of the court. At this conference the attorneys seek to further narrow the disputed issues to expedite the trial of the case and, again, an effort to settle the case may be made.

In due course, absent any intervening settlement, the case will be assigned for trial. When the day of the trial arrives, the attorneys, the parties, and the witnesses are all present in the courtroom ready to proceed. The case is called by name, and if either party has at the initiation of the suit demanded a trial by jury, their attorneys first examine prospective jurors. Upon the selection of a jury, the attorneys make an opening statement of what they expect to prove upon the trial. Plaintiff and his witnesses then testify upon direct examination. Each is subject to cross-examination by defendant's attorney. Plaintiff and his witnesses all testify to the fact that A looked in every direction before proceeding across the street at the time of his injury. Defendant and his witnesses then testify, also upon direct and cross-examination. In each instance there may be redirect examination and further re-cross-examination. Defendant and his witnesses testify that he was in the exercise of reasonable care and was driving his car at a low rate of speed when it struck and injured A. When the parties and their witnesses have concluded their testimony, the plaintiff's attorney makes his final argument to the jury, reviewing the evidence and urging a verdict in favor of his client. Defendant's attorney next argues to the jury, summarizing the evidence in the light most favorable to his client. A short rebuttal is then available to plaintiff's attorney. The attorneys now tender instructions on the law of the case to the trial judge. The judge gives those instructions to the jury which he deems correct and refuses to give those

which he considers incorrect. The judge may also give the jury instructions of his own choosing. These instructions (called "charges" in some States) are for the purpose of aiding the jury in reaching its conclusion upon the conflicting testimony. They cover such matters as credibility of the witnesses, the weight of the evidence and the fact that a greater number of witnesses testified for one party is not to be considered unfavorably against the other party. The jury then retires to the jury room to deliberate and to reach its decision on the facts. This decision is its verdict. If it finds the issues in favor of the defendant, its verdict is "not guilty." If, however, it finds the issues in favor of the plaintiff, it finds the defendant guilty and fixes the plaintiff's damages at a specified amount, in this case, let us say, $25,000. The jury returns to the jury box, and the foreman announces the verdict. Most likely, the defendant's attorney will ask permission to file a written motion for a new trial in which he will assign many grounds of error, among others, that the verdict is manifestly against the weight of the evidence, that erroneous instructions were given, and that proper instructions were refused. If this motion be denied, a motion in arrest of judgment may be made, a motion predicated on the same grounds as the previous motion. Upon the denial of this second motion, the judge enters judgment on the verdict for $25,000.

If the defendant does not prosecute an appeal to a court of review, the task of collecting the judgment remains. Briefly, an execution is issued to the sheriff who, in turn, demands payment of the judgment and, if it is not paid, proceeds to seize or levy upon property belonging to B, the defendant, and causes it to be sold to pay or satisfy the judgment. If, however, the sheriff finds no property belonging to B, he returns the execution unsatisfied. Plaintiff's (A's) attorney may then bring the defendant into court in a supplementary proceeding in an attempt to locate money or other property belonging to him, in an effort to find a means of collecting the judgment. If these efforts fail, and if A knows of money owing to B by C or property belonging to B in the hands of C, a third party, he may institute a garnishment proceeding against C in an attempt to collect his judgment.

Thus far we have proceeded on the assumption that B did not appeal his case. Assume instead that B directs his attorney to appeal. An appeal lies to the intermediate court of review, the Illinois Appellate Court. A notice of appeal is filed with the clerk of the trial court within the prescribed time. Later, within the time fixed, a transcript of the record is filed in the reviewing court. This record contains the pleadings previously described, a transcript of the testimony, the arguments of counsel to the jury, the instructions, the verdict, the motions thereafter, and the judgment rendered on the verdict. B, who files this record, is required to prepare a condensation of it, known as an abstract. He is required to file his brief and abstract with the Appellate Court. His brief contains a statement of the facts, the pleadings, the progress of the case through the trial court, the reasons why he claims the verdict and judgment are erroneous, a statement of the law applicable to the facts, and his argument applying the law to the facts. B, the unsuccessful party, is now designated as the appellant. A, the successful party, is the appellee. He files a brief answering B's brief. If A deems the abstract supplied by B inaccurate or insufficient, he may file an additional abstract of the record. B may, but is not required to, file a reply brief. The case is now ready for the consideration of the Appellate Court. This court does not hear any evidence. It takes the case upon the record, abstracts and briefs. The court may also have the benefit of oral argument by the attorneys. The court then assigns the

case to one of its members to prepare a written opinion. If the opinion which the judge submits meets with the approval of the majority of the court, it is filed as the opinion of the court. The opinion states the essential facts, the questions of law presented, and the judgment of the Appellate Court. This judgment may be an affirmance of the judgment of the trial court. On the other hand, if the court finds that the verdict is against the weight of the evidence, or that certain instructions given were prejudicial to B, the appellant, or that certain instructions which were refused should have been given to the jury, the judgment will be reversed and the cause remanded for a new trial.

If the Appellate Court affirms, B, the defeated appellant, may decide to seek a reversal of the judgments of the circuit court and of the Appellate Court by appealing the case to the Supreme Court of Illinois. B may file a petition for leave to appeal with the Supreme Court. His petition contains a copy of the Appellate Court opinion, a short statement of the facts, and the alleged errors of the Appellate Court. The abstract, with a supplementary abstract covering the proceedings in the Appellate Court, is also filed with the Supreme Court. A petition for leave to appeal, which corresponds to a petition for a writ of certiorari in the United States Supreme Court and some State Supreme Courts, must be filed within the time prescribed. A may, if he so elects, file an answer to the petition for leave to appeal. The Supreme Court will first decide, upon the basis of B's petition and A's answer, whether to permit a further review. The great majority of petitions are denied, and the litigation thus comes to an end. If the Supreme Court decides to allow the petition for leave to appeal, B, the petitioner, again becomes the appellant and A the appellee. The parties file new briefs with the Supreme Court. These briefs are of the same character as those filed in the Appellate

Court, but usually are somewhat enlarged both in the statement of the facts and of the law. Oral argument is permitted if the parties desire it, and the case is then taken under advisement, as in the Appellate Court. The case is assigned to one of the justices to prepare a written opinion and, if the opinion written by him meets with the approval of a majority of the court, it is adopted and filed as the court's opinion. If the Supreme Court concludes that the judgment of the Appellate Court was correct, it affirms that judgment. If, however, it reaches the conclusion that the Appellate Court judgment was erroneous, a judgment is entered reversing the judgments of both the Appellate Court and the circuit court, and, in some instances, remanding the cause for a new trial. In either event, the unsuccessful party may file a petition for a rehearing. The assumption will be made here, as in the Appellate Court, that a petition was filed and denied. Barring the remote possibility of an application for a still further review to the United States Supreme Court, the case of A against B has reached its terminus upon an affirmance, or is about to start, upon a remand, its second journey through the courts, beginning, as originally, in the trial court.

While the foregoing illustration of the trial and appeal of a case has been centered in the courts of Illinois, it will serve to give the student some general understanding of the trial and appeal of cases generally. It is true that there are some technical differences in trial and appellate procedure in different States. For example, in many of the less populous States, there are no intermediate courts of appeal, and appeals are taken directly from the trial court to the Supreme Court. On the whole, however, this story of a law suit should serve to give some knowledge of the technique of the litigation of a case from the beginning of the cause of action (B's automobile striking A) to its final disposition by the Supreme Court.

Writ of Error. A common method of review is by writ of error. The suing out of a writ of error from the court of review to the trial court or intermediate appellate court, as the case may be, is technically the beginning of a new action. The party suing out the writ of error assigns errors and his assignment of errors, for all practical purposes, corresponds to a complaint or declaration in the trial court. Where a review is by writ of error, the party who sues out the writ is known as the plaintiff in error and his adversary becomes the defendant in error. A writ of error was originally a writ directed to the judge or judges of a court of record commanding that the record of an action in which final judgment had been rendered be sent to a court of appellate jurisdiction for the purpose of correcting alleged errors in the proceeding. In statutory proceedings, it is sometimes provided that a review of the proceedings of the trial court be by writ of error. Again, where a review by an appellate tribunal is a matter of grace, the application for a review is captioned "petition for writ of error," thus corresponding to the petition for leave to appeal in other cases.

CASES AND LEGAL ANALYSIS

Since a large part of our law is developed by promulgating and applying legal precedents in particularized fact situations, it is apparent that decided cases should be reported and their legal principles clearly stated, understood, and applied.

As might be expected, trial court decisions are not ordinarily reported, i. e., published. The weight of the precedent set by a trial court is generally not sufficient to warrant permanent reporting for, as has been observed, stare decisis does not make the decision of a trial court binding upon the reviewing courts of that or any other jurisdiction nor, indeed, any other trial court within the same jurisdiction. Except for the Federal courts, New York, and a few other States, wherein selected opinions of trial courts are published, decisions in trial courts are simply filed in the office of the clerk of the court where they are available for public inspection.

The reported decisions are published in volumes called "reports" which are numbered consecutively. Most State court decisions are found in the State reports of that particular State. In addition, the State reports are published in a regional reporter published by West Publishing Company and called the National Reporter System, comprised of the following: Atlantic (Atl. or A.); Southeastern (S.E.); Southwestern (S.W.); New York Supplement (N.Y.S.); North Western (N.W.); North Eastern (N.E.); Southern (So.); Pacific (Pac. or P.). The volumes containing these reports are currently designated as Second Series, or 2d. There are also several systems of selected case reports publishing opinions considered to be of special significance. An opinion of a State reviewing court in most instances will be published in at least two sets of books. After they are published, these opinions or "cases" are referred to ("cited") by giving the name of the case, the volume, name and page of the official State report, if any, in which it is published; the volume, name and page of the particular set and series of the National Reporter System; and the volume, name and page of any other selected case series. For instance, the case of Lefkowitz v. Great Minneapolis Surplus Store, Inc., 251 Minn. 188, 86 N.W.2d 689 (1957) (page 40 of this book) indicates that the opinion in this case may be found in Volume 251 of the Official Minnesota Reports at page 188; and in Volume 86 of the Northwestern Reporter Second Series, at page 689. The Federal court decisions are found in the Federal Reporter (Fed. or F.); Federal Supplement (F.Supp.); Federal Rules Decisions (F.R.D.); and United States Supreme Court Reports (U.S.), Supreme Court Reporter (S.Ct.) Lawyers Edition (L.Ed.).

Reading these reported cases requires an understanding and application of legal analysis. Normally, the reported opinion in a case sets forth (a) essential facts, the nature of the action, the parties, what happened to precipitate the controversy, what happened in the court or courts below, and what pleadings are material to the issues; (b) the issues of law or fact; (c) the legal principles involved; (d) the application of these principles; and (e) the decision.

HOW TO BRIEF A CASE

A serviceable method of analyzing and briefing an opinion after a careful reading and comprehension of it, is to write a concise statement of (a) the facts; (b) the issue or question; (c) the decision; and (d) the reasons for the decision.

INTRODUCTION TO THE LAW OF CONTRACTS

What promises ought the courts to enforce? This is the basic inquiry of contract law. For every issue regarding the legal enforcement of a promise is properly a contracts issue. The law of contracts relates to a promise or "undertaking, however expressed, either that something shall happen, or that something shall not happen, in the future." Restatement of the Law of Contracts, Section 2.

The scope of this subject will appear as its study is pursued. But as a beginning consider a typical transaction, a contract for the sale of land. At a minimum, the vendor promises to convey title to the land, and the purchaser promises to pay the purchase price. In addition, the vendor may promise to pay certain accrued taxes or assessments, the purchaser may promise to assume a mortgage or other indebtedness on the premises, or may promise to reconvey the property to the vendor upon the occurrence of a certain contingency, or the purchaser may promise to pay the purchase price to a certain creditor of the vendor. There may be the assignment of a fire insurance policy, which itself is a contract, involving a promise by the insurance company to pay not to exceed a certain amount in the event of loss by fire. A portion of the purchase price might be given in the form of the purchaser's promissory note, which is a type of contract containing the purchaser's written promise. If the parties are represented by counsel they will very likely have contracts with their respective attorneys. If, after consummation of the sale, the vendor deposits the proceeds in the bank, a contractual relationship arises between him and the bank. If, later on, the vendee leases the property to another, he thereby enters into a contract. Indeed, even when one of the parties leaves his car in a parking lot to attend to any of these matters, he has assumed a contractual relationship with the proprietor of the lot. In short, nearly every business transaction is based upon contract, and many other transactions, involving as they do promises of individuals, have contractual implications.

Definition of Contract. Many definitions of contract have been advanced over the years. A common definition is that of Blackstone, who defined a contract as "an agreement, upon sufficient consideration, to do or not to do a particular thing." But since a contract may come into being without "agreement" in the sense of an actual subjective assent of two parties, it is deemed better to define contract in the terms of that element which is common to all contracts, the promise. Hence, a brief but acceptable definition is "a promise enforceable by law." The Restatement of the Law of Contracts, Section 1, gives the following definition: "A contract is a promise or a set of promises for the breach of which the law gives a remedy, or the performance of which the law in some way recognizes as a duty."

The Restatement, Section 2, defines a promise:

(1) A promise is an undertaking, however expressed, either that something shall happen or that something shall not happen, in the future.

(2) Words which in terms promise the happening or failure to happen of something not within human control, or the existence or non-existence of a present or past state of facts, are to be interpreted as a promise or undertaking to be answerable for such proximate damage as may be caused by the failure to happen or the happening of the specified event, or by the existence or non-existence of the asserted state of facts.

The U.C.C. definition of a contract is:

"Contract" means the total legal obligation which results from the parties' agreement as affected by this Act and any other applicable rules of law. Section 1–201(11).

The U.C.C. definition of agreement is:

"Agreement" means the bargain of the parties in fact as found in their language or by implication from other circumstances including course of dealing or usage of trade or course of performance as provided in this Act. Whether an agreement has legal consequences is determined by the provisions of this Act, if applicable; otherwise by the law of contracts. Section 1–201(3).

It is clear from the Restatement that a promise may be binding or not binding, and from the Code that an agreement may be contractual or non-contractual. The word "agreement" has a much broader scope and meaning than "contract."

But what precisely is *the* contract? In common speech the document or writing containing the parties' promises is spoken of as the contract. But this is obviously inadequate, since contracts may be oral as well as written. Again, the contract might be regarded as those events leading up to the formation of the contract, such as the offer and the acceptance. Yet while these are requisites for the formation of the ordinary contract and are evidence of the contract, they can hardly be said to be the contract itself. Rather, the contract is the *legal relationship*, in terms of the rights and duties of the contracting parties. Thus, in the land contract the vendor has a duty to convey and a right to receive the money, while the purchaser has a duty to pay the price and a right to the conveyance. These are correlative rights and duties, and the relationship establishing them is, strictly speaking, the contract.

Classification of Contracts. Contracts have been classified from various standpoints, as for example, their method of formation, their content, and their legal effect. In the subsections which follow, these standard classifications are considered: (1) Formal and Informal Contracts; (2) Express and Implied Contracts; (3) Unilateral and Bilateral Contracts; (4) Void, Voidable and Unenforceable Contracts; (5) Executed and Executory Contracts.

(1) Formal and Informal Contracts. A formal contract depends upon a particular form, or mode of expression, for its legal efficacy. For example, at common law a promise under seal was enforceable without anything more. Another formal contract is the negotiable instrument, where the note or other instrument has certain legal attributes because of the special form in which it is cast. Recognizances, formal acknowledgments of indebtedness made in court, are other examples of formal contracts. All other contracts are called informal contracts, since as we shall see they do not depend upon mere formality for their legal existence. Our study is confined to informal contracts.

(2) Express and Implied Contracts. At times contracting parties manifest their willingness to enter a certain bargain by express language; at other times they do not. For instance, a man might pick up an item at a drug store, simply show it to the clerk and walk out. Yet this may be a perfectly valid contract. The clerk knows from the customer's conduct that the latter is buying the item at the stipulated price and wants it charged to his account. His actions speak as well as his words. A contract in which the parties manifest assent in words is called an express contract; the other type is an implied contract, or more accurately, implied-in-fact contract. Both are genuine contracts. In each the assent is manifested differently.

To be distinguished, however, from the foregoing are so-called implied-in-law contracts or quasi contracts. It may happen that one is benefited at the expense of another under circumstances where it is inequitable to retain the benefit without making restitution. Still there may be no contract. Suppose, for example, that by mistake A delivers to B an envelope containing $100 intended for C. It does not belong to B, yet B is under no contractual obligation to return it. Historically, however, A could obtain redress through the use of a legal remedy, assumpsit, used for the enforcement of contracts. For this reason, for a long time the courts were inclined to regard B's obligation as contractual in nature. Hence, it was said he was bound by a quasi (or "as if") contract. To distinguish this from the implied-in-fact contract discussed above, the quasi contract is called an implied-in-law contract. Quasi contract is still an extremely important concept, and applications of it will be discussed at various appropriate places in the text which follows. But a quasi contract is not strictly a contract, for the reason that no promise has been made, either expressly or impliedly. The situation is simply that the law recognizes an obligation in order to prevent an unjust enrichment, and this obligation is quasi contractual.

(3) Unilateral and Bilateral Contracts. In the typical contractual transaction, each

party makes at least one promise. The vendor promises to convey title, and the purchaser promises to pay the price. These are mutual promises, both parties undertaking to do something. When the contract comes into existence, at the time of the exchange of promises, each is under a duty to the other. This kind of contract is called bilateral (or two-sided). Each party is both a promisor and a promisee, and is under a duty to render a performance, and enjoys the right to receive a performance.

But suppose that at the time the contract comes into existence, there is only one promise outstanding. Suppose A says to B "If you will mow my lawn, I will give you five dollars." A contract will be formed when B mows the lawn. At that point there is an enforceable promise, the promise of A to pay the five dollars. There are, be it noted, no mutual promises. For assuming that A requested the act of mowing the lawn as the acceptance of his offer, no contract would arise by B merely promising to mow it. Rather, A wanted the act and was not bound on his promise until the act was performed. Similarly, B was under no duty to mow the lawn. This is a unilateral (one-sided) contract. In a unilateral contract only one of the parties makes a promise, a promise that is exchanged for a performance by the other. And there is no contract at all until the requested performance is rendered.

A bilateral contract results from the exchange of a promise for a promise. A unilateral contract results from the exchange of a promise for an act or a forbearance to act.

(4) *Void, Voidable and Unenforceable Contracts.* A "void contract" is no contract. By definition a contract is enforceable. If we say there is no legal effect whatever, there can be no contract. This is a common classification, supported by wide usage, to denominate those transactions in which abortive efforts are made to contract, but for some reason no legal effects are produced.

A voidable contract, on the other hand, is not wholly lacking in legal effect. It is a contract but because of the manner or method in which it was brought about, one of the parties is permitted to avoid his duties thereunder. For instance, A through fraud induces B to enter into a certain contract. In such case B may, upon discovery of the fraud, avoid any liability under the contract. A contract induced by fraud is not void, but is voidable at the election of the defrauded party. A minor's contracts are also voidable, since the minor may at his option disaffirm them.

A contract may be neither void nor voidable in the usual sense and still be unenforceable. For example, a contract may be unenforceable because of a failure to satisfy the requirements of the Statute of Frauds which requires certain kinds of contracts to be in writing in order to be enforceable. A later writing, signed by the party to be charged, would make the contract enforceable as against him. A necessary prerequisite of enforceability would then have occurred. Contracts upon which a right of action has been lost, as by the running of the Statute of Limitations which requires actions to be brought within prescribed time limits, are also commonly referred to as unenforceable, rather than void or voidable.

(5) *Executed and Executory Contracts.* If a contract has been fully performed on both sides it is an "executed contract." Strictly, an executed contract is no contract in the present tense, as all duties under it have become discharged, but it is useful to have a term for the completed or fully performed contract. The term "executory contract" applies to the situations where there are one or more unperformed promises on one side, that is, a contract which is wholly performed on one side, but unperformed or

executory on the other side, or unperformed on both sides in whole or in part.

Essentials of a Contract. The four essential ingredients of a binding promise are:

(1) Manifestation of mutual assent.

(2) Consideration.

(3) Legality of object.

(4) Capacity of the parties.

If all of these essentials are present, the promise is contractual. If any of them is lacking, the promise is not binding. Each of them will be separately considered in succeeding chapters.

CHAPTER 2

MANIFESTATION OF MUTUAL ASSENT

Agreement of the Parties. While each requirement for the formation of a contract is essential to its existence, mutual assent is so basic that frequently a contract is referred to as the agreement between the parties. When the contract is enforced, it is the agreement that is enforced. The agreement between the parties is the very core of the contract.

To effect the formation of a contract the agreement must be objectively manifested. The Restatement of the Law of Contracts, Section 3, has this definition: "An agreement is a manifestation of mutual assent by two or more persons to one another." The important thing is what the parties made manifest to one another by spoken or written words or by conduct. The law applies an objective standard and is concerned only with the assent, agreement, or intention of a party as it reasonably appears from his words and actions. The law of contracts is not concerned with what a party may have actually thought or the meaning that he intended to convey, that is, his subjective understanding or intention insofar as it differs from the meaning objectively manifested. If A offers to sell to B his white horse but intends to offer and believes that he is offering his black horse, and B accepts the offer reasonably believing it to be for the white horse, a contract has been formed for the sale of the white horse. Subjectively, there is no agreement as to the subject matter, but objectively there is a manifestation of agreement, and this is sufficient.

The concept of agreement is much broader than that of contract. An agreement may be contractual or non-contractual. It may consist of a promise to have dinner with someone at a certain time and place, or to attend a theater party, or may merely amount to reaching an accord with respect to the details of some past event. A contractual agreement always involves either a promise exchanged for a promise, or a promise exchanged for an act or forbearance to act, as manifested by what the parties communicated to one another.

Offer and Acceptance. The manner in which parties usually manifest a mutual assent is by offer and acceptance. An offer is a definite proposal or undertaking made by one person to another which by its terms is conditional upon an act, forbearance or return promise being given in exchange. The person making the proposal is the offeror. The person to whom it is made is the offeree. An offer is always a promise. Upon communication it creates in the mind of the offeree a sense of expectancy that upon his expressing a willingness to comply with the terms of the offer, that is, by giving the promise or performance requested in exchange, he will obtain or realize whatever has been promised to him by the offeror. The expression of such willingness is an acceptance of the offer. To form a contract it must be unequivocal and must accept all of the terms and conditions contained in the offer.

Invitations Seeking Offers. A business man desirous of selling merchandise is interested in informing potential customers about the goods, the terms of sale, and price. But if he makes widespread offers to sell to each person on his mailing list, it is conceivable that the number of acceptances and resulting contracts might exceed his ability to perform as seller. Consequently, he refrains from making offers by merely announcing that he has goods for sale, describing the goods, and quoting prices. He thereby invites his customers, and in the case of published adver-

25

tisements, the public, to become interested by making offers to him to buy the goods. The responses to his advertisements, circulars, quotation sheets, and display of merchandise, are not acceptances because no promise or offer to sell has been made. A quotation of prices is not an offer because (1) it does not contain a promise, and (2) it leaves unexpressed many terms which would be necessary to the making of a contract. It is important to distinguish language which constitutes an offer from that which merely solicits or invites offers.

Communications between the parties in many cases take the form of preliminary negotiations. The parties are either requesting or supplying the terms of an offer which may or may not be given. A statement which may indicate a willingness to offer is not itself an offer. If A writes to B "Will you buy my new automobile for $2000?", and B replies "Yes.", there is no contract. A has not made an offer to sell his new automobile to B for $2,000.

Proposals in Jest. Occasionally, a person exercises his sense of humor by speaking or writing words which taken literally and without regard to context or surrounding circumstances could be construed as an offer. However, the promise is intended as a joke, and the promisee as a reasonable man understands it to be such. Therefore it is not an offer. It does not create a sense of reasonable expectancy in the mind of the person to whom it is made because of his realization that it is not being made in earnest. There is no contractual intent on the part of the promisor, and the promisee is or reasonably ought to be aware of that fact. However, the success of a joke or prank is measured by the extent to which it deceives the one upon whom it is practiced. The words in jest must be spoken with a straight face or appearance of seriousness, else they are fatuous. If the intended jest is so successful that the promisee as a reasonable man under all the cir-

cumstances reasonably believes that it has been made as an offer, and so believing accepts, the objective standard applies and the parties have entered into a contract.

Likewise, a promise made under circumstances of excitement or unusual strain is not an offer. For example, A, whose wife is trapped in his burning house, cries out that he will give a million dollars to anyone who will save her. B, a bystander, hears A, and at the risk of his life, rescues A's wife. Even if A could pay a million dollars, B could not recover that amount. Under the circumstances, A's statement was not an offer.

Essentials of an Offer. The contract which is formed upon the acceptance of an offer must be definite and certain, as otherwise it would be impossible to describe the obligations created thereby in terms which would permit a court to determine whether or not a breach had occurred, and if so, the measure or extent of the damages resulting from the breach. To enforce a contractual obligation the court must be able to ascertain exactly its terms and limitations in order to adjudge the extent to which it has been performed or unperformed. For this reason, the terms of an offer, which upon acceptance become the terms of the contract, must be definite and certain. With respect to agreements for the sale of goods, the Code provides standards by which essential omitted terms may be ascertained and such deficiency supplied, provided the parties intended a binding agreement which affords a reasonably certain basis for granting an appropriate remedy. Section 2–204(3).

Definiteness of Offer. To be definite an offer must define or describe its subject matter, whether property or services, and set forth material terms such as quantity and price or refer to some standard whereby these terms may be ascertained and made certain. A reference to the market value on a specific date by which to determine the price, if there is a market, or to reasonable value if there is no ready market, is a sufficient standard by which to determine the price. A statement in the offer that the price shall be determined by appraisers or a designated third person is also a sufficient standard. A reference to the amount of goods or supplies which a certain industrial plant requires for its operations during a stated period of time is sufficient for determination of the quantity offered. The offer is also sufficiently definite if it contains a minimum and a maximum and requires the offeree to state in his acceptance an amount within these limits. Thus, A writes to B that he will sell to B between 2,000 and 3,000 tons of steel at $80 per ton. B replies that he accepts for 2,400 tons of the steel. A contract is formed for 2,400 tons.

The Code provides built-in standards and permits an offer, otherwise fatally indefinite because one or more of its terms are left open, to ripen into a contract if the parties intended to make a contract. Sections 2–204, 2–305, 2–311.

An offer for the purchase or sale of goods may leave open particulars of performance to be specified by one of the parties. The indefiniteness of such offer is cured by the requirement of the Code that "Any such specification must be made in good faith and within limits set by commercial reasonableness." Section 2–311(1).

"Good faith" is defined as "honesty in fact in the conduct or transaction concerned." Section 1–201(19).

"Commercial reasonableness" is a standard measured by the business judgment of reasonable men under the facts and circumstances of the case.

A contract formed by acceptance of an offer which in certain respects is indefinite is re-inforced by the obligation of good faith which the Code makes generally applicable in Section 1–203: "Every contract or duty within this Act imposes an obligation of good faith in its performance or enforcement."

Commercial standards and reasonable practices of business men supply those terms omitted by parties who have reached an agreement intended by them to be mutually binding. An agreement sufficient to constitute a contract of sale may exist even though it is impossible to determine the exact moment that the contract was made. Section 2–204(2).

Open Price Terms. The parties may enter into a contract for the sale of goods even though they have reached no agreement on the price. A contract for the sale of goods may contain an open price term. Under Section 2–305, the price is a reasonable one at the time for delivery where the agreement (a) says nothing as to price, or (b) provides that the parties shall agree later on the price and they fail to so agree, or (c) fixes the price in terms of some agreed market or other standard or as set by a third person or agency, and the price is not so set. An agreement that the price is to be fixed by the seller or buyer means that it must be fixed in good faith. If the price is to be fixed otherwise than by agreement and is not so fixed through the fault of one of the parties, the other party has an option to treat the contract as cancelled or himself fix a reasonable price for the goods. However, where the parties intend not to be bound unless the price is fixed or agreed upon as provided in the agreement, and it is not so fixed or agreed upon, the Code provides that there is no contractual liability. In such case the seller must refund to the buyer any portion of the price received, and the buyer must return the goods to the seller or if unable to do so, pay the reasonable value thereof. Section 2–305(4).

Offers in the Alternative. An offer is not uncertain or indefinite because it is in the alternative. Thus, A offers to sell to B a certain radio for $25 or a certain television set for $200. B accepts the offer. The resulting contract obligates A to sell and B to buy either the radio for $25 or the television set for $200. B has the election to determine which of the two he will take. If he refuses to take either, after having accepted the offer, he is liable to A in damages measured by his refusal to take the radio and pay for it, as the law will hold a contracting party only for the least that he has promised if performance thereof would constitute full performance under the contract. By taking and paying for the radio B would have completely fulfilled his contractual obligation, and the damages resulting from his failure to do so are therefore the most that A would be entitled to recover.

Output, Requirements, and Exclusive Dealings. An agreement of a buyer to purchase the entire output of a seller's factory for a stated period, or an agreement of a seller to supply a buyer with all his requirements of certain goods used in his business operations, may appear to lack definiteness and mutuality of obligation. The exact quantity of goods is not specified, and the seller may have some degree of control over his output, and the buyer over his requirements. However, such agreements are enforceable by the application of an objective standard based upon good faith of both parties. The seller cannot operate his factory twenty-four hours a day and insist upon the buyer taking all of the output where he did not do so before the agreement was made. Nor can the buyer expand his business abnormally and insist that the seller supply all of his requirements. The Code expresses this standard of good faith in Section 2-306(1):

> A term which measures the quantity by the output of the seller or the requirements of the buyer means such actual output or requirements as may occur in good faith, except that no quantity unreasonably disproportionate to any stated estimate or in the absence of a stated estimate to any normal or otherwise comparable prior output or requirements may be tendered or demanded.

An agreement between buyer and seller for an exclusive dealing in a certain kind of merchandise creates implied obligations upon both parties which are stated in the Code, Section 2-306(2), as follows:

> A lawful agreement by either the seller or the buyer for exclusive dealing in the kind of goods concerned imposes unless otherwise agreed an obligation by the seller to use best efforts to supply the goods and by the buyer to use best efforts to promote their sale.

Auction Sales. The auctioneer at an auction sale does not make offers to sell the property which is being auctioned, but invites offers to buy. The classic statement by the auctioneer is "How much am I offered?" The persons attending the auction may make progressively higher bids for the property, and each bid or statement of a price or a figure is an offer to buy at that figure. If the bid is accepted, which is customarily by the fall of the hammer in the hands of the auctioneer, a contract results. A bidder is free to withdraw his bid at any time prior to its acceptance. The auctioneer is likewise free to withdraw the goods from sale unless the sale is advertised or announced to be without reserve.

If the auction sale is advertised or announced in explicit terms to be without reserve, the auctioneer may not withdraw an article or lot put up for sale unless no bid is made within a reasonable time. Unless so advertised or announced the sale is with reserve. Whether with or without reserve, a bidder may retract his bid at any time prior to acceptance by the auctioneer. Such retraction does not revive any previous bid.

Unless the seller has given notice that he reserves the right to bid at the auction sale, any such bid by or on behalf of the seller gives the bidder to whom the goods are sold an election either (1) to avoid the sale, or (2) to take the goods at the price of the last good faith bid before the sale. Section 2-328.

Types of Offers. (1) An offer may be in the form of a promise for a promise. For instance A offers to sell and deliver to B his horse Dobbin for $500. By accepting this offer, B gives A a promise to pay $500 in exchange for A's promise to sell and deliver Dobbin. This exchange of mutual promises forms a bilateral contract and each is bound by his promise to the other. (2) An offer may be a promise for an act. An illustration is the offer of a reward. This offer may be accepted only by the offeree doing that which is requested in the offer, and upon doing so, a unilateral contract is formed. A promise by the offeree to do the act will not create a contract, as the offer requested performance and not a promise. (3) An offer may be an act for a promise. Thus, A ships to B a box of cigars with a note that B may keep and smoke them and that if he does, the price is $10. By keeping and smoking the cigars, B has accepted the offer, and an inverted unilateral contract has been formed.

An Offer Must be Communicated. In order to have the mutual assent requisite to a contract, which in practically every case is manifested by an offer and an acceptance, the offeree must have knowledge of the offer, and the offer must have been communicated by the offeror. An offeree cannot possibly agree to something of which he has no knowledge.

Assume that A writes and signs a letter containing an offer to B, but leaves it on top of the desk in his office. Later that day, B, without prearrangement, goes to A's office, discovers that A is away, notices the letter on A's desk, reads it, and then writes thereon an acceptance of the offer which he dates and signs. No contract is formed because the offer never became effective for the reason that it was never communicated by A to B. If A had mailed the letter, and it had gone astray in the mails, the offer contained therein would likewise never have become effective. The offer must be communicated to the offeree and the communication must be made or authorized by the offeror. If Jones tells Black that he is going to offer $400 to White for the latter's piano, and Black promptly informs White of this expressed intention of Jones, no offer has been made. There was no authorized communication of any offer by Jones to White. By the same token, if X should offer to sell to Y his diamond ring, an acceptance of this offer by Z would be ineffective, as X made no offer to Z.

Expressions by the parties of a willingness to the same terms do not form a contract unless made with reference to one another. Thus, if C says to A "Are you willing to sell your color television set to B for $250?", and A answers "Yes"; and C promptly goes to B and says to him "Are you willing to buy A's color television set for $250?", and B replies "Yes," there is no contract between A and B. Neither A nor B had made a promise or manifested any assent to the other. However, if the parties were together when C interrogated them, and upon receiving their affirmative answers C announced to them "I hereby pronounce that you have entered into a contract," A and B would be bound to one another unless one of them immediately disclaimed that he was entering into such contract. A promise from the one to the other would be implied from their failure to deny the pronouncement of C made in their presence.

An offer need not be stated or communicated by words. Conduct from which a reasonable person may infer a promise in return for an act will amount to an offer. For example, A owns a house which is enclosed by a picket fence sadly in need of paint. One day B applied a coat of fresh white paint to the picket fence. A is not obligated to pay B for this paint job, as he did not order it. If, however, A were present, observed B painting the fence, knew that B's occupation was that of a painter, and said nothing to B, he would then be obligated to pay B the reasonable value of the paint job. Under the circumstances, A as a reasonable man ought to have known that B in doing the work expected to be compensated for it. A's liability would be based upon an implied contract.

An offer may be made generally or to the public. However, no person can accept such an offer until and unless he has knowledge that the offer exists. If a person, without knowledge of the existence of an advertised reward for information leading to the arrest of a particular criminal, gives information which leads to such arrest, he is not entitled to the reward. His act was not an acceptance of the offer because he could not accept something of which he had no knowledge.

Duration of Offers. An offer confers a power upon the offeree to create rights and duties by merely manifesting his acceptance, which power continues until the offer terminates. Upon termination the offeree no longer has such power, that is, the offer may not thereafter be accepted. The ways in which an offer may be terminated, other than by acceptance, are: (1) Expiration of the time specified in the offer, or if no time is specified, the expiration of a reasonable time; (2) Revocation; (3) Rejection; (4) Death of the offeror; (5) Death of the offeree; (6) Insanity of the offeror; (7) Insanity of the offeree; (8) Destruction of the specific subject matter to which the offer relates; and (9) Legislation enacted subsequent to the offer which makes illegal and unenforceable the type of contract contemplated by the offer.

The duration or life of an offer is measured by the time between the effective moment of its communication to the offeree and the moment of its termination in any of the ways described above. If A writes an offer to B dated April 15 and states "This offer is open ten days," the ten-day period commences as of April 15, the day of the writing, although the offer is not effective until B receives it which may be a day or two later. If through a delay in the mails the letter containing the offer were not delivered to B until April 26, the offer would never have become effective. However, if A writes an offer to B and states that B can have ten days in which to accept, the ten-day period commences on the day that B receives the offer, not on the day that the letter containing the offer was written or mailed. Assume that A in Chicago mails an offer on May 1 to B in Boston, in which A allows B ten days in which to accept. If sent by regular mail, this offer would normally reach B on May 3. In such case, the ten-day period would commence on May 3 and expire on May 12. Assume, however, that A's letter is delayed in some way and that it is not delivered to B until May 7. Does B still have ten days in which to accept, or only five days? The rule on this point is given in the Restatement of the Law of Contracts, Section 51, as follows:

> If communication of an offer to an offeree is delayed, the period in which a contract can be created is not thereby extended if the offeree knows or has reason to know of the delay, though it is due to the fault of the offeror; but if the delay is due to the fault of the offeror or to the means of transmission adopted by him, and the offeree neither knows nor has reason to know that there has been delay, a contract can be created by acceptance within the period which would have been permissible if the offer had been dispatched at the time that its arrival seems to indicate.

Accordingly, if B knew or had reason to know of the delay, even though it was due to A's fault, in that, for example, A addressed the envelope incorrectly, then B has only five days in which to accept. However, if B neither knew nor had reason to know that there had been a delay, then B has ten days in which to accept.

Assume that A mailed his offer on May 1, and that it was duly delivered to B's office on May 3; that B was then ill at home or out of town; and that he did not return to his office until May 8, when he first learns of A's offer. For the purpose of computing the time in which B may effectively accept this offer, it began on May 3, when the offer was delivered to B's office. The delay here was in no way attributable to A, but wholly to B.

Lapse of Time. The offeror may specify the time within which the offer is to be accepted, just as he may specify any other term or condition in the offer. Unless otherwise terminated, the offer remains open during the time fixed by the offeror. After the expiration of that time, the offer no longer exists and cannot be accepted.

If no time is stated in the offer within which the offeree may accept, the acceptance must be within a reasonable time. Section 40 of the Restatement of the Law of Contracts, provides:

> "40. (1) The power to create a contract by acceptance of an offer terminates at the time specified in the offer, or, if no time is specified, at the end of a reasonable time.
>
> "(2) What is a reasonable time is a question of fact, depending on the nature of the contract proposed, the usages of business and other circumstances of the case which the offeree at the time of his acceptance either knows or has reason to know.
>
> "(3) In the absence of usage or a provision in the offer to the contrary, and subject to the rule stated in § 51, an offer sent by mail is seasonably accepted if an acceptance is mailed at any time during the day on which the offer is received."

Revocation. Prior to acceptance, the offeror, except a merchant who has made a written offer to buy or sell goods (Section 2–205), maintains the power of life or death over the offer which he has freely made. He may cancel or revoke it at any time. If the offeror originally stated that the offer would be open for twenty days or thirty days, but after five days wishes to terminate it, he may do so by giving the offeree notice that he is withdrawing the offer. This notice may be given by any means of communication, but is effective to terminate the offer only when received by the offeree. It is regarded as received when it arrives at the place to which the offer was addressed. An offer to the public may be revoked by giving equivalent publicity to a notice of revocation.

Notice of revocation may be indirectly communicated to the offeree, as where he receives reliable information from a third person that the offeror has disposed of the goods which he has offered for sale or has otherwise placed himself in a position which indicates an unwillingness or inability to perform the promise contained in the offer. Suppose that A offers to sell his portable television set to B and tells B that he has ten days in which to accept. A week later B observes the television set in C's house and is informed that C has bought it from A. The next day B sends to A an acceptance of the offer. There is no contract, as A's offer was effectively revoked when B learned of A's unwillingness and inability to sell the television set to B by reason of his having sold it to C.

Revocation of Offer for Unilateral Contract. Where the offer contemplates a unilateral contract, that is, a promise for an act, injustice to the offeree may result if revocation is permitted after he has started to perform the act requested by the offer and has substantially but not completely accomplished it. Certainly the offer is not accepted and a contract is not formed until the offeree has completed the requested act. No promise has been requested of the offeree, and he has made none. By commencing to perform he does not thereby bind himself to continue, and he may therefore stop at any time without incurring liability. Some courts have attempted to solve the difficulty by treating it as though it were an offer for a bilateral contract, that is, a promise for a promise, which is accepted by the offeree's commencing performance. Such construction may do violence to the terms of the offer, and causes the offeree to become bound as well as the offeror which may not have been within the contemplation of the parties. Other courts have held that where the performance of the requested act necessarily requires time and effort to be expended by the offeree, an obligation not to revoke the offer for a reasonable time arises by implication in consideration of the offeree commencing performance. The Restatement of the Law of Contracts, Section 45, provides:

> "If an offer for a unilateral contract is made, and part of the consideration requested in the offer is given or tendered by the offeree in response thereto, the offeror is bound by a contract, the duty of immediate performance of which is conditional on the full consideration being given or tendered within the time stated in the offer, or, if no time is stated therein, within a reasonable time."

The above rule does not require any notice to the offeror that performance has been commenced or is being given by the offeree. Where the offeror is not informed or notified that performance has been undertaken by the offeree, the situation is one in which the offeree knows that a contract has been formed, but the offeror does not know. To alleviate this hardship upon the offeror, the Code provides, Section 2–206(2):

> (2) Where the beginning of a requested performance is a reasonable mode of acceptance an offeror who is not notified of acceptance within a reasonable time may treat the offer as having lapsed before acceptance.

The Code also provides that an order or offer to buy goods for prompt shipment may be either accepted by a promise to ship the goods or by the prompt shipment of conforming or non-conforming goods. If the seller promptly ships conforming goods, a unilateral contract is formed; if he promises to ship or ships non-conforming goods, a bilateral contract is formed. If the goods shipped do not conform to the order, the seller has both accepted the offer and become liable for breach of contract. However, the seller may protect himself upon shipment of non-conforming goods if he notifies the buyer that they are offered only as an accommodation to the buyer. Section 2–206(1)(b).

Suppose B telegraphs A: Please ship at once carload No. 1 Blue nut-size coal. A promptly ships No. 1 Blue lump-size coal. At common law A has made no promise to ship and his shipment of non-conforming goods is not an acceptance of the offer. Thus, as no contract has been formed A cannot be liable for breach of contract. This result defeats the reasonable expectation of the buyer as it gives no legal significance to the act of shipping. It unfairly benefits the seller who can ship non-conforming goods with impunity. Under the Code, the shipment of non-conforming goods by A to B is an acceptance of the offer and A would be liable for breach of contract. If the seller desires to make a counter-offer by shipping goods different from those ordered and at the same time not bind himself to ship conforming goods, by notifying the buyer that the goods are being shipped only as an accommodation his shipment of non-conforming goods is not an acceptance.

Irrevocable offers. An ordinary offer by one private individual to another is always revocable. An offeror may find himself paralyzed or cut off from channels of communication so that he is physically unable to communicate to the offeree a withdrawal of the offer. In a practical sense, physical impossibility to give notice of revocation might be considered as making the offer irrevocable. However, the term is not used in this sense. An irrevocable offer is one which the offeror has made a binding promise not to revoke, or which is irrevocable by virtue of a statute. If, in consideration of $100 paid to A by B, A gives B an option to buy Blackacre at a price of $10,000 exercisable at any time within thirty days, this is an offer to sell Blackacre which A is not at liberty to revoke. The option is a unilateral contract to keep the offer open for thirty days. A is therefore bound to do so, and any communication by A to B of notice of withdrawal of the offer would be legally ineffective. B is not bound to accept the offer, but the option contract entitles him to thirty days in which to consider acceptance. Certain offers are made irrevocable by statute, such as bids for the construction of a building or some public work made to the State, a municipality, or other governmental corporation. Another illustration is pre-incorporation stock subscription agreements which are irrevocable under certain statutes for a period of six months.

Firm Offers. The Code imposes a stricter standard upon merchants than upon non-merchants with respect to firm offers to buy or sell goods. Such an offer in writing and signed by the merchant offeror may not be withdrawn, as provided in Section 2–205:

> "An offer by a merchant to buy or sell goods in a signed writing which by its terms gives assurance that it will be held open is not revocable, for lack of consideration, during the time stated or if no time is stated for a reasonable time, but in no event may such period of irrevocability exceed three months; but any such term of assurance on a form supplied by the offeree must be separately signed by the offeror."

Rejection. Just as the acceptance of an offer is a manifestation of the willingness of the offeree to accept, a rejection of an offer is a manifestation by the offeree of his unwillingness to accept. The power of acceptance is terminated by a communicated rejection. From and after the effective moment of rejection, the offeree may no longer accept the offer. Rejection by the offeree may consist of express language, or may be implied from language or from conduct.

To be effective to terminate the offer, a rejection must be communicated by the offeree to the offeror. For example, A in New York sends by air mail to B in San Francisco an offer which is expressly stated to be open for one week. On the fourth day B sends to A by air mail a letter of rejection which is delivered on the morning of the sixth day. At noon on the fifth day B dispatches a telegram of acceptance which is received by A before the close of business on that day. Because of the prior letter of rejection, the sending of the telegram of acceptance did not form a contract. A contract was formed at the time B's telegram was received by A, and the letter of rejection never became effective, because of the prior receipt by the offeror of the telegram of acceptance. The Restatement of the Law of Contracts, Section 39, provides:

> "Rejection by mail or telegram does not destroy the power of acceptance until received by the offeror, but limits the power so that a letter or telegram of acceptance started after the sending of the rejection is only a counter-offer unless the acceptance is received by the offeror before he receives the rejection."

Counter-offer. A counter-offer moves from the offeree to the offeror and indicates a willingness to contract with reference to the subject matter of the offer but upon terms or conditions different from those contained in the offer. It is not an acceptance, and, because by implication it indicates an unwillingness to agree to the terms of the offer, it operates as a rejection. Assume that A writes B a letter offering to sell to B a second-hand color television set for $300 and stating that the offer is open for two weeks. B replies that he will pay A $250 for the set. This is a counter-offer and a rejection which immediately terminates A's offer to sell for the reason that it manifests B's unwillingness to pay $300 for the television set. However, if B in his reply states that he wants to consider the $300 offer for the two weeks period but is willing to pay $250 at once for the set, this is a counter-offer which does not reject A's offer. In the first instance, if A rejects the counter-offer, B may not thereafter accept the $300 offer. In the second instance he may do so, as the counter-offer was stated in such a way as not to indicate an unwillingness to accept the original offer and therefore did not terminate it.

Death or Insanity of Offeror or Offeree. The death or insanity of either the offeror or the offeree terminates the ordinary offer. An open offer embodies the continuing willingness of the offeror to enter into a contract upon the terms stated in the offer. Upon his death or insanity the offeror no longer has a mind or legal capacity to enter into a contract. His willingness to contract is thereby terminated. Death or insanity of the offeree likewise terminates the offer, because an ordinary offer is not assignable and can be accepted only by the person to whom it was made. When the offeree ceases to be a person or ceases to have legal capacity to enter into a contract, there is in effect no one who can accept the offer which therefore necessarily terminates.

The death or insanity of the offeror or offeree does not terminate an offer contained in an option for the reason that an option is a contract, a promise binding on the offeror to keep the offer open for a stated period of time. Death does not discharge this type of contractual obligation. If A should give B a sixty-day option to buy Blackacre for $25,000 and die before the expiration of the sixty days, B could exercise the option within the stated period by giving written notice of his acceptance to the personal representative of A, deceased. If during the period B, not having exercised the option, should die, his personal representative, the executor of his will or administrator of his estate, could validly exercise it within the time remaining.

Destruction of Subject Matter. Mutual mistake of the parties as to the existence of the subject matter, or destruction of the subject matter, terminates an offer with respect thereto. Such destruction, as well as the death of a specified person whose continued existence was essential to the performance of a contract, would operate as an excuse for non-performance and be effective as a discharge of contractual duty if it occurred subsequent to the formation of the contract. For the same reason, based upon prospective impossibility of performance, an offer to buy, sell, lease, pledge, or mortgage is terminated upon the destruction of the subject matter of such offer; and, likewise, an offer with respect to personal services which contemplates the continued existence of a specific person is terminated upon the death of such person.

Subsequent Illegality. One of the four essential ingredients of a contract, as previously mentioned, is legality of purpose or subject matter. If performance of a valid contract is made illegal by a subsequently enacted statute, the obligations of the parties thereunder are discharged. Illegality taking effect after the making of an offer has the same effect upon the offer prior to acceptance as subsequent illegality would have upon a contract. In certain situations, a statute may apply prospectively only as in the case of a usury statute reducing the permissible rate of interest on loans of money. The higher rate would still be lawful on contracts made before the effective date of the statute, although payable subsequently. However, an offer to lend or to borrow at a rate higher than that permitted by the statute would be terminated upon the effective date thereof.

Acceptance. The acceptance of the offer is essential to the creation of a contract. Acceptance is some overt act by the offeree which manifests his assent to the terms of the offer, such as speaking, sending a letter, telegram, or other communication to the offeror, or performing the requested act or forbearance with the intention of accepting, if the offer is for a unilateral contract. Since the overt act, or manifestation of assent, indicates the agreement of the offeree to the terms of the offer, the offeree prior to acceptance must necessarily have knowledge of the offer.

Acceptance is both a matter of intention and an overt act of manifestation. If A publishes an offer of a reward to anyone who finds the diamond ring which he has lost, and B with knowledge of the offer finds and returns the ring to A but in doing so disclaims the reward and says that he does not accept the offer, there is no contract. Merely doing the act requested by the offeror is not sufficient to form a contract where it is not done with the intention of accepting the offer.

An acceptance must be positive and unequivocal. It may not change any of the terms of the offer, nor add to, subtract from, or qualify in any way, the provisions of the offer. Any communication by the offeree which attempts to do so is not an acceptance. If the offer is for a bilateral contract, the acceptance must contain a promise directly or by implication. Once an acceptance has been given, the contract is completely formed and subsequent communications do not affect it unless amounting to a mutual agreement to rescind.

An acceptance must strictly comply with the terms of the offer. If the offer requests a promise, the acceptance must unequivocally contain or imply the exact promise requested. If the offer requests an act or a forbearance, the precise act or forbearance must be performed by the offeree in order to constitute an acceptance. An acknowledgement of an order stating that it will receive prompt attention is not an acceptance unless accompanied by words or conduct from which a promise to fulfill the order will be implied. In one case an offeree who had solicited bids for certain work sent the following telegram to an offeror: "You are low bidder. Come on morning train." This was held not to constitute an acceptance of the bid, as the telegram did not contain a promise.

Where an offer is made and accepted in the course of a telephone conversation, the contract is formed at the time and place where the offeree speaks the words of acceptance into the transmitter.

The above-stated requirements of an acceptance are modified by the Code with respect to transactions in goods, as provided in Section 2–207(1) (2):

> (1) A definite and seasonable expression of acceptance or a written confirmation which is sent within a reasonable time operates as an acceptance even though it states terms additional to or different from those offered or agreed upon, unless acceptance is expressly made conditional on assent to the additional or different terms.

> (2) The additional terms are to be construed as proposals for addition to the contract. Between merchants such terms become part of the contract unless:
>
> (a) the offer expressly limits acceptance to the terms of the offer;
>
> (b) they materially alter it; or
>
> (c) notification of objection to them has already been given or is given within a reasonable time after notice of them is received.

An offer is not assignable and therefore can be accepted only by the offeree, the person or persons to whom it was made. If A makes an offer to B, and performance is tendered to A by C, A may refuse the tendered performance. If A accepts the tendered performance under the belief that it comes from B, upon learning the truth he may surrender it and thereby avoid liability or, if he chooses, he may retain it. The tender of performance by C was, in effect, a new offer and A by accepting the performance accepted C's offer.

Where the offer contemplates the formation of a bilateral contract, the offeree must communicate his acceptance to the offeror or at least place it in the ordinary channels of communication in order to form a contract. In this manner the offeror is informed of the existence of the contract. However, where the offer consists of a promise for an act, the performance of the act may be out of the presence of the offeror or without his knowledge. A contract is therefore formed of which one of the parties, and the only party who has become bound, is uninformed. Usually the offeror has means of knowing whether the act requested by the offer has been performed, but the formation and existence of the contract does not depend upon notice thereof being given to him. In the case of a guaranty contract, suppose A writes a letter to B stating that if B will extend a line of credit to C not to exceed $5,000, A will make good any default in payment by C. B thereupon and from time to time on C's order ships a total of $5,000 of merchandise to C on credit. A is not advised that B has accepted his offer of guaranty. However, a unilateral contract was formed between A and B when B sold the merchandise to C on credit and thereby accepted A's offer. In this type of case the law imposes notice to the offeror within a reasonable time as a condition subsequent to the continued existence of the contract. That is, the contractual duty of A will be discharged unless B within a reasonable time after commencing to extend the line of credit to C notifies A that he is doing so. The Restatement of the Law of Contracts, Section 56, provides:

"Where forbearance or an act other than a promise is the consideration for a promise, no notification that the act or forbearance has been given is necessary to complete the contract. But if the offeror has no adequate means of ascertaining with reasonable promptness and certainty that the act or forbearance has been given, and the offeree should know this, the contract is discharged unless within a reasonable time after performance of the act or forbearance, the of-feree exercises reasonable diligence to notify the offeror thereof."

Effective Moment of Acceptance. As pointed out above, an offer becomes effective when it is communicated, that is, when received by the offeree. A notice of revocation is also effective when received by the offeree. A rejection is effective when received by the offeror. By effective moment is meant the precise time when a particular communication, placed in the channels of transmission, has its intended effect. The effect of an acceptance is to create a contract. If the parties are corresponding by mail, is the acceptance effective, and the contract formed, the moment the offeree deposits a letter of acceptance in the mail, or the moment the offeror receives it?

The law is well settled that if in reply to an offer by mail, the offeree places in the mail a letter of acceptance properly stamped and addressed to the offeror, a contract is formed at the time and place that the offeree mails the letter. This assumes, of course, that the offer at that time was open and had not been terminated by any of the methods previously discussed. The reason for this rule is that the offeror by using the mail, impliedly authorized the offeree to use the same channel of communication and his mailing of an acceptance is an overt act of manifestation of assent. The use of the mails is so common today that this authorization also applies to an offer handed to the offeree or delivered to him by messenger. If the offer is by telegram, a telegraphic acceptance is effective when dispatched. It is immaterial if the telegram of acceptance is delayed in transmission, or if the letter of acceptance goes astray in the mails and is never received. Likewise, if the offeree after mailing a letter of acceptance, succeeds in withdrawing it from the mails by complying with postal regulations, a contract has been formed by the act of mailing, even though the offeror may not in due course learn about it.

When the medium of communication used by the offeree is different from that adopted by the offeror, the question whether it is authorized is one of fact, and depends upon whether it was a medium which might reasonably be expected to be used in view of the position of the parties, business usages, and surrounding circumstances.

The Code provides that where the language in the offer or the circumstances do not otherwise clearly indicate, "an offer to make a contract shall be construed as inviting acceptance in any manner and by any medium reasonable in the circumstances." Section 2–206(1) (a). The Code therefore substitutes the requirement that the offeree use a reasonable rather than an authorized medium or means of communication of the acceptance. Thus, the telegraph is a reasonable medium of communication, and therefore an acceptance by telegram in response to an offer by mail would be effective when dispatched.

If the offeree uses an unauthorized means of communicating his acceptance, or if under the Code, an unreasonable medium of communication, a contract is not formed when the acceptance is dispatched. The acceptance, however, is effective when and if received by the offeror, provided that the offer at the time of receipt is still open. The Restatement of the Law of Contracts, Section 68, provides:

> "An acceptance inoperative when despatched only because the offeree uses means of transmission which he was not authorized to use is operative when received, if received by the offeror within the time within which an acceptance sent in an authorized manner would probably have been received by him."

The rule that an acceptance is effective when dispatched or sent does not apply to the case where the offer provides that the acceptance must be received by the offeror. If the offeror states that a reply must be received by a certain date or that he must hear from the offeree, or uses other language indicating that the acceptance must be received by him, the effective moment of the acceptance is when it is received by the offeror and not when it is sent or dispatched by the offeree.

A late acceptance does not create a contract. After the offer has expired there can be no acceptance of it. However, a late or defective acceptance does manifest a willingness on the part of the offeree to enter into a contract and therefore constitutes a new offer. The offeror who receives a late or defective acceptance may not by silence or inaction regard it as effective. In order to create a contract the original offeror must accept the new offer by manifesting his assent to the original offeree.

Silence of Offeree as Acceptance. An offeree is generally under no legal duty to reply to an offer. His silence or inaction is therefore no acceptance of the offer. However, he may be under a duty to speak if he does not wish to accept, as where services are performed for his benefit and with his knowledge under circumstances which indicate to a reasonable man that they are being performed with the expectation of compensation. A failure to reject the offered services in this type of situation is an acceptance.

Salesmen employed by a manufacturing company to solicit orders for its merchandise from its customers usually have no authority to bind their employer by contract. The order forms expressly recite that no contract is formed until the order of the buyer is accepted at the home office of the manufacturer. Upon receipt of purchase orders, the manufacturer is under a duty to notify the customer within a reasonable time of the non-acceptance in the event the manufacturer is unable or unwilling to ship the goods ordered. Silence or inaction of the manufacturing company is an acceptance of the order.

The Restatement of the Law of Contracts, Section 72, provides:

"(1) Where an offeree fails to reply to an offer, his silence and inaction operate as an acceptance in the following cases and in no others:

(a) Where the offeree with reasonable opportunity to reject offered services takes the benefit of them under circumstances which would indicate to a reasonable man that they were offered with the expectation of compensation.

(b) Where the offeror has stated or given the offeree reason to understand that assent may be manifested by silence or inaction, and the offeree in remaining silent and inactive intends to accept the offer.

(c) Where because of previous dealings or otherwise, the offeree has given the offeror reason to understand that the silence or inaction is intended by the offeree as a manifestation of assent, and the offeror does so understand.

"(2) Where the offeree exercises dominion over things which are offered to him, such exercise of dominion in the absence of other circumstances showing a contrary intention is an acceptance. If circumstances indicate that the exercise of dominion is tortious the offeror may at his option treat it as an acceptance, though the offeree manifests an intention not to accept."

When the offeror requests in his offer silence of the offeree as a manifestation of assent, and the offeree upon receiving and reading the offer remains silent, the difficulty is that the offeree's silence is ambiguous. The offeree may remain silent intending to accept, or he may remain silent intending not to accept. If the latter, no contract is formed by his silence. However, assume that A by letter offers to sell to B for $450 a certain automobile belonging to A, but in B's possession. The letter also states that unless A hears from B to the contrary within ten days it will be understood that B has accept-

ed the offer. Upon receipt of A's offer, B decides to accept it, and in reliance upon A's statement in the offer does not notify A of his acceptance. B's silence while ambiguous is nevertheless the type of manifestation of assent requested by the offeror A who should not complain of being taken at his word. According to the Restatement, Section 72 above, in such case B's silence operates as an acceptance and a contract is formed.

Contract Formed by Conduct. Under the Code an express contract for the sale of goods may be made by conduct of the parties. There may be no definite offer and acceptance, or definite acceptance of an offer, yet a contract exists if both of the parties have acted in a manner which manifests a recognition by each of them of the existence of a contract. Recognition may result from the cumulative effect of a number of occurrences or incidents which bespeak reliance of both parties upon the existence of a contract. It may be impossible to determine the exact moment when a contract formed by conduct was made. Section 2–204 provides:

(1) A contract for sale of goods may be made in any manner sufficient to show agreement, including conduct by both parties which recognizes the existence of such a contract.

(2) An agreement sufficient to constitute a contract for sale may be found even though the moment of its making is undetermined.

(3) Even though one or more terms are left open a contract for sale does not fail for indefiniteness if the parties have intended to make a contract and there is a reasonably certain basis for giving an appropriate remedy.

The Code further provides in Section 2–207(3):

(?) Conduct by both parties which recognizes the existence of a contract is sufficient to establish a contract for sale although the writings of the parties do not otherwise establish a contract. In such case the terms of the particular contract consist of those terms on which the writings of the parties agree, together with any supplementary terms incorporated under any other provisions of this Act.

Credit Cards. The widespread use of credit cards reflects their convenience to the customer in reducing his immediate cash requirements, and the promotion of sales of the products and services by issuers of the cards. The card is usually made of plastic upon which is embossed the name and address of the person to whom issued and an account number. Hotels, department stores, oil companies, railroads, and airlines are only a few of the suppliers of credit who issue such cards.

Credit cards serve a useful purpose in identifying and enabling a person whose credit is established with the issuer to use this credit promptly at any time or place. No problem is created when the use is by the person to whom the card is issued or by him authorized.

If a credit card is lost or stolen and used by an unauthorized person to purchase goods or services, a question arises as to the liability of the person to whom the card was issued for such purchases. Although sometimes stated as a guaranty, a frequent provision on the reverse side of the card is that the person whose name is imprinted or embossed thereon, by retaining or using the card, agrees to pay for all purchases by any one using the card until the card has been surrendered to the issuer or written notice given the issuer that the card has been lost or stolen.

The issuance of the card containing such provision is an offer to the person named thereon to extend credit by the issuer to any one using the card in consideration of the promise of the offeree to make payment. The retention or use of the card is an acceptance of the offer. It is of course essential that the terms of the offer be communicated to the offeree and that he have knowledge of the terms and conditions on the reverse side of the card. A New York statute requires that the provision imposing liability after loss or theft of the card be conspicuously written or printed on the card in at least eight point bold type.

The courts enforce credit card contracts, and it is therefore important that the holder keep it safely in his possession or under his control at all times, that he maintain a record of his credit card account number, and promptly report to the issuer any loss or theft of the card.

Existing Impossibility Known to Promisor. The non-existence of the subject matter unknown to both parties will prevent the formation of a contract on the ground of mutual mistake. Destruction of the specific subject matter will terminate an offer to buy or to sell, and such destruction occurring after the offer has been accepted will afford a valid excuse for non-performance of the contract.

However, the situation may arise where one of the parties may know or have reason to know that the subject matter is not existing and that performance of the contract on his part is therefore impossible, whereas the other party having no such knowledge enters into the contract with complete faith and expectation of performance on both sides. In such case, a contract is formed although its performance is impossible. The promisor who knows, or under the circumstances ought to know of his inability to perform, becomes bound where the promisee in such case is not so informed.

This rule does not pertain to supervening impossibility which is discussed in the chapter on Discharge of Contracts, but applies only to impossibility existing at the time of the formation of the contract which is or should be known to the promisor but is unknown to the promisee.

An application of this rule is found in the Australian case of McRae v. Commonwealth Disposals Commission, 84 Commonwealth Law Rep. 377 (1951). After World War II, the defendant Commission in that case had the function of disposing of wrecked and stranded ships and other war surplus property in the South Pacific. The defendant advertised for sale and solicited bids for "an oil tanker on Jourmand Reef approximately one hundred miles north of Samarai (New Guinea)." In response to the advertisement the plaintiff made a bid of £285, which defendant duly accepted. Upon plaintiff asking the defendant for a more definite location of the stranded oil tanker, the defendant defined the location by latitude and longitude. Plaintiff paid the full amount of the purchase price to defendant, outfitted a salvage ship, and proceeded to the designated location for the purpose of taking possession of the oil tanker. The defendant had expressly made no warranties of any kind as to the condition of either the ship or its contents. When the plaintiff arrived at the specified location, he discovered that there was no ship answering the description of the tanker either there or anywhere in the area. The evidence indicated that the agents of defendant may have been confused and possibly had in mind a wrecked oil barge, a vessel not designed or constructed to be self-propelled, which was lying 11 miles from the designated location. The High Court of Australia held that the defendant was guilty of the "grossest negligence" in advertising for sale a ship which it ought to have known did not exist. The Court held that there was a contract for the purchase of the non-existing oil tanker which was breached by the defendant, and allowed the plaintiff a recovery of £3000 in damages and £285 as refund of the purchase price.

CASES

LEFKOWITZ v. GREAT MINNEAPOLIS SURPLUS STORE, INC.

(1957) 251 Minn. 188, 86 N.W.2d 689.

MURPHY, J. This is an appeal from an order of the Municipal Court of Minneapolis denying the motion of the defendant for amended findings of fact, or, in the alternative, for a new trial. The order for judgment awarded the plaintiff the sum of $138.50 as damages for breach of contract.

This case grows out of the alleged refusal of the defendant to sell to the plaintiff a certain fur piece which it had offered for sale in a newspaper advertisement. It appears from the record that on April 6, 1956, the defendant published the following advertisement in a Minneapolis newspaper:

"Saturday 9 A.M. Sharp
3 Brand New
Fur
Coats
Worth to $100.00
First Come
First Served
$1
Each"

On April 13, the defendant again published an advertisement in the same newspaper as follows:

"Saturday 9 A.M.
2 Brand New Pastel
Mink 3-Skin Scarfs
Selling for $89.50
Out they go
Saturday. Each....$1.00
1 Black Lapin Stole
Beautiful,
worth $139.50....$1.00
First Come
First Served"

The record supports the findings of the court that on each of the Saturdays following the publication of the above-described ads the plaintiff was the first to present himself at the appropriate counter in the defendant's store and on each occasion demanded the coat and the stole so advertised and indicated his readiness to pay the sale price of $1. On both occasions, the defendant refused to sell the merchandise to the plaintiff, stating on the first occasion that by a "house rule" the offer was intended for women only and sales would not be made to men, and on the second visit that plaintiff knew defendant's house rules. * * *

The defendant contends that a newspaper advertisement offering items of merchandise for sale at a named price is a "unilateral offer" which may be withdrawn without notice. He relies upon authorities which hold that, where an advertiser publishes in a newspaper that he has a certain quantity or quality of goods which he wants to dispose of at certain prices and on certain terms, such advertisements are not offers which become contracts as soon as any person to whose notice they may come signifies his acceptance by notifying the other that he will take a certain quantity of them. Such advertisements have been construed as an invitation for an offer of sale on the terms stated, which offer, when received, may be accepted or rejected and which therefore does not become a contract of sale until accepted by the seller; and until a contract has been so made, the seller may modify or revoke such prices or terms. [Citations.] * * *

On the facts before us we are concerned with whether the advertisement constituted an offer, and, if so, whether the plaintiff's conduct constituted an acceptance. * * *

The test of whether a binding obligation may originate in advertisements addressed to the general public is "whether the facts show that some performance was promised in positive terms in return for something requested." 1 Williston, Contracts (Rev. ed.) § 27. * * *

Whether in any individual instance a newspaper advertisement is an offer rather than an invitation to make an offer depends on the legal intention of the parties and the surrounding circumstances. [Citations.] We are of the view on the facts before us that the offer by the defendant of the sale of the Lapin fur was clear, definite, and explicit, and left nothing open for negotiation. The plaintiff having successfully managed to be the first one to appear at the seller's place of business to be served, as requested by the advertisement, and having offered the stated purchase price of the article, he was entitled to performance on the part of the defendant. We think the trial court was correct in holding that there was in the conduct of the parties a sufficient mutuality of obligation to constitute a contract of sale.

The defendant contends that the offer was modified by a "house rule" to the effect that only women were qualified to receive the bargains advertised. The advertisement contained no such restriction. This objection may be disposed of briefly by stating that, while an advertiser has the right at any time before acceptance to modify his offer, he does not have the right, after acceptance, to impose new or arbitrary conditions not contained in the published offer. [Citations.]

Affirmed.

SHUEY v. UNITED STATES

(1875) 92 U.S. 73, 23 L.Ed. 697.

Henry B. Ste. Marie filed his petition in the Court of Claims to recover the sum of $15,000, being the balance alleged to be due him of the reward of $25,000 offered by the Secretary of War, on the 20th of April, 1865, for the apprehension of John H. Surratt, one of Booth's alleged accomplices in the murder of President Lincoln.

The court below found the facts as follows:—

1. On the 20th April, 1865, the Secretary of War issued, and caused to be published in the public newspapers and otherwise, a proclamation, whereby he announced that there would be paid by the War Department "for the apprehension of John H. Surratt, one of Booth's accomplices," $25,000 reward, and also that "liberal rewards will be paid for any

information that shall conduce to the arrest of either of the above-named criminals or their accomplices;" and such proclamation was not limited in terms to any specific period, and it was signed "Edwin M. Stanton, Secretary of War." On the 24th November, 1865, the President caused to be published his order revoking the reward offered for the arrest of John H. Surratt. 13 Stat. 778.

2. In April, 1866, John H. Surratt was a zouave in the military service of the Papal government, and the claimant was also a zouave in the same service. During that month he communicated to Mr. King, the American minister at Rome, the fact that he had discovered and identified Surratt, who had confessed to him his participation in the plot against the life of President Lincoln. The claimant also subsequently communicated further information to the same effect, and kept watch, at the request of the American minister, over Surratt. Thereupon certain diplomatic correspondence passed between the government of the United States and the Papal government relative to the arrest and extradition of Surratt; and on the 6th November, 1866, the Papal government, at the request of the United States, ordered the arrest of Surratt, and that he be brought to Rome, he then being at Veroli. Under this order of the Papal government, Surratt was arrested; but, at the moment of leaving prison at Veroli, he escaped from the guard having him in custody, and, crossing the frontier of the Papal territory, embarked at Naples, and escaped to Alexandria in Egypt. Immediately after his escape, and both before and after his embarkation at Naples, the American minister at Rome, being informed of the escape by the Papal government, took measures to trace and rearrest him, which was done in Alexandria. From that place he was subsequently conveyed by the American government to the United States; but the American minister, having previously procured the discharge of the claimant from the Papal military service, sent him forward to Alexandria to identify Surratt. At the time of the first interview between the claimant and the American minister, and at all subsequent times until the final capture of Surratt, they were ignorant of the fact that the reward offered by the Secretary of War for his arrest had been revoked by the President. The discovery and arrest of Surratt were due entirely to the disclosures made by the claimant to the American minister at Rome; but the arrest was not made by the claimant, either at Veroli, or subsequently at Alexandria.

3. There has been paid to the claimant by the defendants, under the act of 27th July, 1868 (15 Stat. 234, sect. 3), the sum of $10,000. Such payment was made by a draft on the treasury payable to the order of the claimant, which draft was by him duly indorsed.

The court found as a matter of law that the claimant's service, as set forth in the foregoing findings, did not constitute an arrest of Surratt within the meaning of the proclamation, but was merely the giving of information which conduced to the arrest. For such information the remuneration allowed to him under the act of Congress was a full satisfaction, and discharges the defendants from all liability.

The petition was dismissed accordingly: whereupon an appeal was taken to this court.

Ste. Marie having died *pendente lite*, his executor was substituted in his stead.

STRONG, J. We agree with the Court of Claims, that the service rendered by the plaintiff's testator was, not the apprehension of John H. Surratt, for which the War Department had offered a reward of $25,000, but giving information that conduced to the arrest. These are quite distinct things, though one may have been a consequence of the other. The proclamation of the Secretary of War treated them as different; and, while a reward of $25,000 was offered for the apprehension, the offer for information was only a "liberal reward." The findings of the Court of Claims also exhibit a clear distinction between making the arrest and giving the information that led to it. It is found as a fact, that the arrest was not made by the claimant, though the discovery and arrest were due entirely to the disclosures made by him. The plain meaning of this is, that Surratt's apprehension was a consequence of the disclosures made. But the consequence of a man's acts are not his acts. Between the consequence and the disclosure that leads to it there may be, and in this case there were, intermediate agencies. Other persons than the claimant made the arrest,—persons who were not his agents, and who themselves were entitled to the proffered reward for his arrest, if any persons were. We think therefore, that at most the claimant was entitled to the "liberal reward" promised for information conducing to the arrest; and that reward he has received.

But, if this were not so, the judgment given by the Court of Claims is correct.

The offer of a reward for the apprehension of Surratt was revoked on the twenty-fourth day of November, 1865; and notice of the revocation was published. It is not to be doubted that the offer was revocable at any time before it was accepted, and before any thing had been done in reliance upon it. There was no contract until its terms were complied with. Like any other offer of a contract, it might, therefore, be withdrawn before rights had accrued under it; and it was withdrawn through the same channel in which it was made. The same notoriety was given to the revocation that was given to the offer; and the findings of fact do not show that any information was given by the claimant, or that he did any thing to entitle him to the reward offered, until five months after the offer had been withdrawn. True, it is found that then, and at all times until the

arrest was actually made, he was ignorant of the withdrawal; but that is an immaterial fact. The offer of the reward not having been made to him directly, but by means of a published proclamation, he should have known that it could be revoked in the manner in which it was made.

Judgment affirmed.

DREW v. JOHN DEERE COMPANY OF SYRACUSE, INC.

(1963) 19 A.D.2d 308, 241 N.Y.S.2d 267.

HALPERN, J. This is an appeal from an order denying the plaintiff's motion to strike out the answer of the defendants as sham and frivolous and for summary judgment.

The theory of the complaint is that a contract by the corporate defendant to sell a certain tractor to the plaintiff had come into existence as the result of an auction sale conducted by the defendant and that the defendant breached the contract by refusing to deliver the tractor upon the tender of the purchase price.

The corporate defendant was the assignee of a conditional sales contract covering the tractor, which it had repossessed upon the vendee's default. More than 50% of the purchase price having been paid, the defendant was required to resell the repossessed tractor at public auction (Personal Property Law, § 79). The defendant advertised the auction sale, stating that the property would be sold to the highest bidder at the sale. The plaintiff bid $1500 at the sale but the auctioneer did not accept the bid; instead he announced that the defendant itself had bid $1600 and accordingly the property was struck down to the defendant.

The plaintiff claims that the defendant was disqualified to bid because it had not announced in advance that it intended to bid pursuant to section 102, subdivision 4, of the Personal Property Law. Hence, the plaintiff argues, his bid was the highest lawful bid and therefore a contract of sale came into existence between the plaintiff and the defendant for the sale of the tractor at the price bid.

The plaintiff's whole case rests upon the theory that the auction was one "without reserve". At such an auction, the owner of the property has no right to withdraw the property after bidding has commenced. It is also necessarily implicit in an auction "without reserve", that the owner of the property may not himself bid in the property, as this would be equivalent to withdrawing it from sale (Restatement of Contracts, § 27). Various legal theories have been advanced for the holding that the announcement that the auction would be "without reserve" imposes a binding legal obligation upon the owner, but the best view seems to be that the owner, by making such an announcement, enters into a collateral contract with all persons bidding at the auction that he will not withdraw the property from sale, regardless of how low the highest bid might be [citations]. Therefore, the highest bona fide bidder at an auction "without reserve" may insist that the property be sold to him or that the owner answer to him in damages [citations].

On the other hand, in an auction sale not expressly announced to be "without reserve", the owner may withdraw the property at any time before it is actually "knocked down" to a bidder by the auctioneer. There is no contract until the offer made by the bidder is accepted by the auctioneer's "knocking down" the property to him (Personal Property Law, § 102, subd. 2). "An auction 'with reserve' is the normal procedure" (Comment 2 to section 2–328, Uniform Commercial Code).

In our case, there was no express statement that the auction would be "without reserve". The statement that the sale would be made to the highest bidder is not the equivalent of an announcement that the auction would be "without reserve" (cf. Personal Property Law, § 102(2); Uniform Commercial Code, § 2–328, subd. 3). "An announcement that a person will sell his property at public auction to the highest bidder is a mere declaration of intention to hold an auction at which bids will be received" [citations].

Corbin writes that the auctioneer at an auction sale in asking for bids, does not make an operative offer. "This is true even though the seller or his representative has issued advertisements or made other statements that the article will be sold to the highest bidder, or is offered for sale to the highest bidder. Such statements are merely preliminary negotiation, not intended and not reasonably understood to be intended to affect legal relations. When such is the case, the seller or his representative is as free to reject the bids, highest to lowest, as are the bidders to withdraw them. The seller may at any time withdraw the article from sale, if he has not already accepted a bid. He need give no reasons; indeed, he rejects all bids by merely failing to accept them—by doing nothing at all. It is not necessary for him to say that 'the privilege is reserved to reject any and all bids.' Such a statement is merely evidence that the goods are not being offered 'without reserve'" (1 Corbin on Contracts, § 108, pp. 338–340).

Since, upon the present record, the auction sale appears to have been "with reserve", no contract of sale came into existence, even if we assume that the plaintiff was the highest lawful bidder [citation]. Concededly, the plaintiff's bid was never accepted. Therefore, the plaintiff's papers upon his motion for summary judgment fail to make out a cause of action for breach of contract.

In view of this conclusion, it is unnecessary to decide the legal questions discussed by the parties as to the meaning and effect of sections 79 and 102(4) of the Personal Property Law. Section 79 specifically authorizes the conditional vendor to bid at the sale of the repossessed article. It is argued by the defendant that this specific authority overrides the requirement of section 102(4) of the Personal Property Law that at any auction sale the owner of the property must expressly reserve the right to bid by announcement in advance, if he desires to bid. The soundness of this argument may well be doubted, although it is supported by a decision by the Supreme Court of Michigan (Toy v. Griffith Oldsmobile Co., 342 Mich. 533, 536, 70 N.W.2d 726, 727–728). Section 79 is designed to remove any disqualification of the conditional vendor or his assignee, vis-a-vis the original vendee. Section 102(4) is designed to protect the prospective bidders at an auction sale so that they will not be forced up in their bidding by secret bids on behalf of the owner. Section 102 specifically provides that if the owner has bid without an announcement in advance of his intention to do so, the successful bidder may, if he wishes, avoid the sale on the ground that it was fraudulent. It will be noted that in the Uniform Commercial Code, to go into effect September 27, 1964 (L.1962, ch. 553), it is expressly provided that a sale of repossessed goods shall be conducted in accordance with the article on Sales which contains a provision similar to section 102 (4) [U.C.C., §§ 9–504; 2–328(3)].

But even if section 102(4) is held to be applicable to a conditional vendor's auction sale of repossessed goods, it does not help the plaintiff in this case. The plaintiff was not the successful bidder and he is not seeking to avoid a sale because he was misled into bidding a higher sum than he otherwise would have bid. The only remedy provided in the section, for a violation thereof, is the right of the successful bidder to nullify the sale. There is nothing in the statute which compels the owner to sell to the second highest bidder at an auction sale "with reserve", if the owner himself bid in the property without having announced his intention to bid.

We thus are brought back to the original point that the plaintiff's case depends upon a showing that the auction was one "without reserve". It is only in that type of auction that he could claim to be entitled to the purchase of the property at the amount bid by him, if his bid was the highest bona fide bid and was improperly topped by a bid by the owner (Restatement of Contracts, § 27, Illustration No. 4). If the auction was "without reserve", there was no need for the plaintiff to invoke section 102(4) to bar the defendant from bidding; if the auction was not one "without reserve", section 102(4) does not help the plaintiff. The plaintiff has failed to show that the sale was one "without reserve".

The plaintiff's motion for summary judgment was therefore properly denied. The defendant asks us to go further and to grant a summary judgment in favor of the defendant. We do not believe that this should be done. The plaintiff relied upon the announcement that the sale would be to the highest bidder as showing that the auction sale was to be "without reserve". As we have seen, the announcement was insufficient of itself for that purpose but the plaintiff should be given an opportunity to produce any other evidence he may have on that subject. For that reason, summary judgment for the defendant should be denied.

The order appealed from should be affirmed.

MORRISON v. THOELKE

(1963, Fla.) 155 So.2d 889.

ALLEN, C. J. * * * A number of undisputed facts were established by the pleadings, including the facts that appellees are the owners of the subject property, located in Orange County; that on November 26, 1957, appellants, as purchasers, executed a contract for the sale and purchase of the subject property and mailed the contract to appellees who were in Texas; and that on November 27, 1957, appellees executed the contract and placed it in the mails addressed to appellants' attorney in Florida. It is also undisputed that after mailing said contract, but prior to its receipt in Florida, appellees called appellants' attorney and cancelled and repudiated the execution and contract. Nonetheless, appellants, upon receipt of the contract caused the same to be recorded. Additional factual allegations concerning demand for performance, tender of the purchase price and payment of taxes were disputed.

On the basis of the foregoing facts, the lower court entered summary decree for the appellees, quieting title in them. The basis of this decision was, in the words of the able trial judge:

"[T]he contract executed by the parties hereto * * * constituted a cloud on the title of Plaintiffs. * * * The Court finds said contract to have been cancelled and repudiated by Plaintiffs prior to its receipt by Defendants * * * and that on this basis there was no legal contract binding on the parties * * *."

Turning to the principal point raised in this appeal, we are confronted with a question apparently of first impression in this jurisdiction. The question is whether a contract is complete and binding when a letter of acceptance is mailed, thus barring repudiation prior to delivery to the offeror, or when the letter of acceptance is received, thus permitting repudiation prior to receipt. Appellants, of course, argue that posting the acceptance creates the contract; appellees contend that only receipt of the acceptance bars repudiation.

* * *

A near identical statement of the general rule is found in 1 Williston, Contracts § 81 (3rd ed. 1957):

"Contracts are frequently made between parties at some distance and therefore it is of vital importance to determine at what moment the contract is complete. If the mailing of an acceptance completes the contract, what happens thereafter, whether the death of either party, the receipt of a revocation or rejection, or a telegraphic recalling of the acceptance, though occurring before the receipt of the acceptance, will be of no avail; whereas, if a contract is not completed until the acceptance has been received, in all the situations supposed no contract will arise.

"It was early decided that the contract was completed upon the mailing of the acceptance. The reason influencing the court was evidently that when the acceptance was mailed, there had been an overt manifestation of assent to the proposal. The court failed to consider that since the proposed contract was bilateral, as is almost invariably any contract made by mail, the so-called acceptance must also have become effective as a promise to the offeror in order to create a contract. The result thus early reached, however, has definitely established the law not only in England but also in the United States, Canada and other common law jurisdictions. It is, therefore, immaterial that the acceptance never reaches its destination."

The same work, in Section 86, negatives the possible effect of a power to recall an acceptance after mailing. In the author's words:

"By the United States Postal Regulations, the sender of a letter may regain it by complying with certain specified formalities, and yet a contract is completed by mailing an acceptance in the authorized channel. Since the acceptance is binding when it is mailed, the fact that the sender of a letter may regain possession of it should have no effect on the validity of the acceptance. * * *"

A second leading treatise on the law of contracts, Corbin, Contracts §§ 78 and 80 (1950 Supp.1961), also devotes some discussion to the "rule" urged by appellants. Corbin writes:

"Where the parties are negotiating at a distance from each other, the most common method of making an offer is by sending it by mail; and more often than not the offeror has specified no particular mode of acceptance. In such a case, it is now the prevailing rule that the offeree has power to accept and close the contract by mailing a letter of acceptance, properly stamped and addressed, within a reasonable time. The contract is regarded as made at the time and place that the letter of acceptance is put into the possession of the post office department."

Like the editor of Williston, Corbin negates the effect of the offeree's power to recall his letter:

"The postal regulations have for a long period made it possible for the sender of a letter to intercept it and prevent its delivery to the addressee. This has caused some doubt to be expressed as to whether an acceptance can ever be operative upon the mere mailing of the letter, since the delivery to the post office has not put it entirely beyond the sender's control.

"It is believed that no such doubt should exist. * * * In view of common practices, in view of the difficulties involved in the process of interception of a letter, and in view of the decisions and printed discussions dealing with acceptance by post, it is believed that the fact that a letter can be lawfully intercepted by the sender should not prevent the acceptance from being operative on mailing. If the offer was made under such circumstances that the offeror should know that the offeree might reasonably regard this as a proper method of closing the deal, and the offeree does so regard it, and makes use of it, the contract is consummated even though the letter of acceptance is intercepted and not delivered."

Significantly, Corbin expressly distinguishes cases involving bank drafts or bills of exchange from cases involving bilateral contracts. He writes:

"It should be borne in mind that whenever the receipt of the letter is necessary to produce some legal effect, the interception, and resulting nondelivery of the letter will prevent that effect. For almost all purposes, other than the acceptance of an offer, the mere mailing of a letter is not enough to attain the purpose. Unless it is clearly otherwise agreed, the mailing of a letter is not a sufficient notice to quit a tenancy, it is not actual payment of money that is inclosed, it does not transfer title to a check or other document; it will not ordinarily be sufficient notice required by a contract as a condition precedent to some contractual duty of immediate performance."

    *   *   *

The rule that a contract is complete upon deposit of the acceptance in the mails, hereinbefore referred to as "deposited acceptance rule" and also known as the "rule in Adams v. Lindsell," had its origin, insofar as the common law is concerned, in Adams v. Lindsell, 1 Barn. & Ald. 681, 106 Eng.Rep. 250 (K.B. 1818). In that case, the defendants had sent an offer to plaintiffs on September 2nd, indicating that they expected an answer "in course of post." The offer was misdirected and was not received and accepted until the 5th, the acceptance being mailed that day and received by defendant-offerors on the 9th. However, the defendants, who had expected to receive the acceptance on or before the 7th, sold the goods offered on the 8th of September. It was conceded that the delay had been occasioned by the fault of the defendants in initially misdirecting the offer.

    *   *   *

The justification for the "deposited acceptance" rule proceeds from the uncontested premise of Adams v. Lindsell that there must be, both in practical and conceptual terms, a point in time when a contract is complete. In the formation of contracts *inter praesentes* this point is readily reached upon expressions of assent instantaneously communicated. In the formation of contracts *inter absentes* by post, however, delay in communication prevents concurrent knowledge of assents and some point must be chosen as legally significant. The problem raised by the impossibility of concurrent knowledge of manifest assent is discussed and a justification for the traditional rule is offered in Corbin, Contracts § 78 (1950).

"A better explanation of the existing rule seems to be that in such cases the mailing of a letter has long been a customary and expected way of accepting the offer. It is ordinary business usage. More than this, however, is needed to explain why the letter is operative on mailing rather than on receipt by the offeror. Even though it is business usage to send an offer by mail, it creates no power of acceptance until it is received. Indeed, most notices sent by mail are not operative unless actually received.

"The additional reasons for holding that a different rule applies to an acceptance and that it is operative on mailing may be suggested as follows: When an offer is by mail and the acceptance also is by mail, the contract must date either from the mailing of the acceptance or from its receipt. In either case, one of the parties will be bound by the contract without being actually aware of that fact. If we hold the offeror bound on the mailing of the acceptance, he may change his position in ignorance of the acceptance; even though he waits a reasonable time before acting, he may still remain unaware that he is bound by contract because the letter of acceptance is delayed, or is actually lost or destroyed, in the mails. Therefore this rule is going to cause loss and inconvenience to the offeror in some cases. But if we adopt the alternative rule that the letter of acceptance is not operative until receipt, it is the offeree who is subjected to the danger of loss and inconvenience. He can not know that his letter has been received and that he is bound by contract until a new communication is received by him. His letter of acceptance may never

have been received and so no letter of notification is sent to him; or it may have been received, and the letter of notification may be delayed or entirely lost in the mails. One of the parties must carry the risk of loss and inconvenience. We need a definite and uniform rule as to this. We can choose either rule; but we must choose one. We can put the risk on either party; but we must not leave it in doubt. The party not carrying the risk can then act promptly and with confidence in reliance on the contract; the party carrying the risk can insure against it if he so desires. The business community could no doubt adjust itself to either rule; but the rule throwing the risk on the offeror has the merit of closing the deal more quickly and enabling performance more promptly. It must be remembered that in the vast majority of cases the acceptance is neither lost nor delayed; and promptness of action is of importance in all of them. Also it is the offeror who has invited the acceptance."

* * *

In short, both advocates and critics muster persuasive argument. As Corbin indicated, there must be a choice made, and such choice may, by the nature of things, seem unjust in some cases. Weighing the arguments with reference not to specific cases but toward a rule of general application and recognizing the general and traditional acceptance of the rule as well as the modern changes in effective long-distance communication, it would seem that the balance tips, whether heavily or near imperceptively, to continued adherence to the "Rule in Adams v. Lindsell." This rule, although not entirely compatible with ordered, consistent and sometime artificial principles of contract advanced by some theorists, is, in our view, in accord with the practical considerations and essential concepts of contract law. [Citation.]

* * *

In choosing to align this jurisdiction with those adhering to the deposited acceptance rule, we adopt a view contrary to that of the very able judge below, contrary to the decisions of other respected courts and possibly contrary to the decision which might have been reached had this case been heard in a sister court in this State. However, we are constrained by factors hereinbefore discussed to hold that an acceptance is effective upon mailing and not upon receipt. Necessarily this decision is limited in any prospective application to circumstances involving the mails and does not purport to determine the rule possibly applicable to cases involving other modern methods of communication. Cf. Entores v. Miles Far East Corp., 2 Q.B. 327 (1955) (rejecting the application of Adams v. Lindsell to a case involving instantaneous communication). Restatement, Contracts § 65 (1932).

In the instant case, an unqualified offer was accepted and the acceptance made manifest. Later, the offerees sought to repudiate their initial assent. Had there been a delay in their determination to repudiate permitting the letter to be delivered to appellant, no question as to the invalidity of the repudiation would have been entertained. As it were, the repudiation antedated receipt of the letter. However, adopting the view that the acceptance was effective when the letter of acceptance was deposited in the mails, the repudiation was equally invalid and cannot alone, support the summary decree for appellees.

The summary decree is reversed and the cause remanded for further proceedings.

PETERSEN v. PILGRIM VILLAGE

(1950) 256 Wis. 621, 42 N.W.2d 273.

FRITZ, C. J. On this appeal the defendant states that it is concerned with solely the adjudication that plaintiff is entitled to recover $8000 on his fourth cause of action. As his first cause of action plaintiff alleged that he was in the employ of defendant as superintendent of its construction of houses and in charge of the maintenance and operation of its enterprise during 1947 until September 1, 1947; that for his services defendant agreed to pay him a salary of $4600 per year, making $3066.67 due to him for eight months of 1947, and that he was paid $2400, leaving $666.67 due to him for such services; and the jury assessed plaintiff's damages at $666.67 on the first cause of action. Defendant does not appeal from the judgment in this respect.

As his fourth cause of action plaintiff alleged: He entered the employ of defendant about ten years ago, and it agreed with plaintiff that he would share in the profits of the corporation, and in reliance thereon he took charge of all building construction for defendant, and all maintenance of its enterprises throughout the term of his employment, and continued in the employment of defendant throughout said term of years, and was repeatedly promised that he would be paid for such services, in addition to his regular stated salary, a share in the profits of the corporation; and that he believes defendant has made profits of at least $200,000, and the reasonable amount of his share of such profits is at least ten per cent thereof, or $20,000, and no part thereof has been paid.

In relation to that cause of action defendant, at the commencement of the trial, entered a demurrer ore tenus, which the court overruled; and subsequently defendant moved for nonsuit and finally for a directed verdict on the ground that the fourth cause of action failed to allege, and the evidence on the trial failed to establish, facts sufficient to constitute a legal cause of action. Defendant's motions were denied by the court.

* * *

As stated in Restatement of the Law on Contracts, sec. 32, pp. 40, 41,

"An offer must be so definite in its terms, or require such definite terms in the acceptance, that the promises and performances to be rendered by each party are reasonably certain.

"Comment:

"a. Inasmuch as the law of contracts deals only with duties defined by the expressions of the parties, the rule stated in the Section is one of necessity as well as of law. The law cannot subject a person to a contractual duty or give another a contractual right unless the character thereof is fixed by the agreement of the parties. A statement by A that he will pay B what A chooses is no promise. A promise by A to give B employment is not wholly illusory, but if neither the character of the employment nor the compensation therefor is stated, the promise is so indefinite that the law cannot enforce it, even if consideration is given for it.

"b. Promises may be indefinite in time or in place, or in the work or things to be given in exchange for the promise. In dealing with such cases the law endeavors to give a sufficiently clear meaning to offers and promises where the parties intended to enter into a bargain, but in some cases this is impossible."

* * *

Consequently, as at the conclusion of the trial the evidence in respect to plaintiff's damages on the fourth cause of action was merely that he was to be paid "some share of the profits", and as the parties never came to any definite agreement as to what that percentage of the profits was to be, the court erred in denying defendant's motion for a directed verdict, because at that time there had been no application for leave to amend the complaint. Instead the court, on plaintiff's motion for leave to amend his complaint, allowed him to add an allegation that "a reasonable value of the services of the plaintiff rendered to the defendant corporation from May 28, 1942, through August 31, 1947, in addition to the payments made to the plaintiff in the form of cash and notes, is

at least $10,000." As there was no evidence whatever of any promise or agreement by defendant to pay plaintiff "a reasonable value" of additional services rendered by him, there was no basis for granting plaintiff's motion for leave to amend his complaint in that respect. * * *

Judgment reversed and cause remanded.

LUCY v. ZEHMER

(1954) 196 Va. 493, 84 S.E.2d 516.

BUCHANAN, J. This suit was instituted by W. O. Lucy and J. C. Lucy, complainants, against A. H. Zehmer and Ida S. Zehmer, his wife, defendants to have specific performance of a contract by which it was alleged the Zehmers had sold to W. O. Lucy a tract of land owned by A. H. Zehmer in Dinwiddie county containing 471.6 acres, more or less, known as the Ferguson farm, for $50,000. J. C. Lucy, the other complainant, is a brother of W. O. Lucy, to whom W. O. Lucy transferred a half interest in his alleged purchase.

The instrument sought to be enforced was written by A. H. Zehmer on December 20, 1952, in these words: "We hereby agree to sell to W. O. Lucy the Ferguson Farm complete for $50,000.00, title satisfactory to buyer," and signed by the defendants, A. H. Zehmer and Ida S. Zehmer.

The answer of A. H. Zehmer admitted that at the time mentioned W. O. Lucy offered him $50,000 cash for the farm, but that he, Zehmer, considered that the offer was made in jest; that so thinking, and both he and Lucy having had several drinks, he wrote out "the memorandum" quoted above and induced his wife to sign it; that he did not deliver the memorandum to Lucy, but that Lucy picked it up, read it, put it in his pocket, attempted to offer Zehmer $5 to bind the bargain, which Zehmer refused to accept, and realizing for the first time that Lucy was serious, Zehmer assured him that he had no intention of selling the farm and that the whole matter was a joke. Lucy left the premises insisting that he had purchased the farm. * * *

Mrs. Zehmer testified that when Lucy came into the restaurant he looked as if he had had a drink. When Zehmer came in he took a drink out of a bottle that Lucy handed him. She went back to help the waitress who was getting things ready for next day. Lucy and Zehmer were talking but she did not pay too much attention to what they were saying. She heard Lucy ask Zehmer if he had sold the Ferguson farm, and Zehmer replied that he had not and did not want to sell it. Lucy said, "I bet you wouldn't take $50,000.00 cash for that farm," and Zehmer replied, "You haven't got $50,000 cash." Lucy said, "I can get it." Zehmer said he might form a company and get it, "but you haven't got $50,000.00 cash to pay me tonight." Lucy asked him if he would put it in writing that he would sell him this farm. Zehmer then wrote on the back of a pad, "I agree to sell the Ferguson Place to W. O. Lucy for $50,000.00 cash." Lucy said, "All right, get your wife to sign it." Zehmer came back to where she was standing and said, "You want to put your name to this?" She said "No," but he said in an undertone, "It is nothing but a joke," and she signed it. * * *

In his testimony Zehmer claimed that he "was high as a Georgia pine," and that the transaction "was just a bunch of two dog-goned drunks bluffing to see who could talk the biggest and say the most." That claim is inconsistent with his attempt to testify in great detail as to what was said and what was done. It is contradicted by other evidence as to the condition of both parties, and rendered of no weight by the testimony of his wife that when Lucy left the restaurant she suggested that Zehmer drive him home. The record is convincing that Zehmer was not intoxicated to the extent of being unable to comprehend the nature and consequences of the instrument he executed, and hence that instrument is not to be invalidated on that ground. [Citations.] It was in fact conceded by defendants' counsel in oral argument that under the evidence Zehmer was not too drunk to make a valid contract. * * *

The mental assent of the parties is not requisite for the formation of a contract. If the words or other acts of one of the parties have but one reasonable meaning, his undisclosed intention is immaterial except when an unreasonable meaning which he attaches to his manifestations is known to the other party. Restatement of the Law of Contracts, Vol. I, § 71, p. 74.

" * * * The law, therefore, judges of an agreement between two persons exclusively from those expressions of their intentions which are communicated between them. * * *." Clark on Contracts, 4 ed., § 3, p. 4.

An agreement or mutual assent is of course essential to a valid contract but the law imputes to a person an intention corresponding to the reasonable meaning of his words and acts. If his words and acts, judged by a reasonable standard, manifest an intention to agree, it is immaterial what may be the real but unexpressed state of his mind. [Citations.]

So a person cannot set up that he was merely jesting when his conduct and words would warrant a reasonable person in believing that he intended a real agreement. [Citations.]

Whether the writing signed by the defendants and now sought to be enforced by the complainants was the result of a serious offer by Lucy and a serious acceptance by the defendants, or was a serious offer by Lucy and an acceptance in secret jest by the defendants, in either event it constituted a binding contract of sale between the parties. * * *

The complainants are entitled to have specific performance of the contract sued on. The decree appealed from is therefore reversed and the cause is remanded for the entry of a proper decree requiring the defendants to perform the contract in accordance with the prayer of the bill.

Reversed and remanded.

ROTO–LITH, LTD. v. F. P. BARTLETT & CO., INC.

(1962 C.A.1) 297 F.2d 497.

ALDRICH, J. Plaintiff-appellant Roto-Lith, Ltd., is a New York corporation engaged *inter alia* in manufacturing, or "converting," cellophane bags for packaging vegetables. Defendant-appellee is a Massachusetts corporation which makes emulsion for use as a cellophane adhesive. This is a field of some difficulty, and various emulsions are employed, depending upon the intended purpose of the bags. In May and October 1959 plaintiff purchased emulsion from the defendant. Subsequently bags produced with this emulsion failed to adhere, and this action was instituted in the district court for the District of Massachusetts. At the conclusion of the evidence the court directed a verdict for the defendant. This appeal followed.

* * *

On October 23, 1959, plaintiff, in New York, mailed a written order to defendant in Massachusetts for a drum of "N–132–C" emulsion, stating "End use: wet pack spinach bags." Defendant on October 26 prepared simultaneously an acknowledgment and an invoice. The printed forms were exactly the same, except that one was headed "Acknowledgment" and the other "Invoice," and the former contemplated insertion of the proposed, and the latter of the actual, shipment date. Defendant testified that in accordance with its regular practice the acknowledgment was prepared and mailed the same day. The plaintiff's principal liability witness testified that he did not know whether this acknowledgment "was received, or what happened to it." On this state of the evidence there is an unrebutted presumption of receipt. [Citations.] The goods were shipped to New York on October 27. On the evidence it must be found that the acknowledgment was received at least no later than the goods. The invoice was received presumably a day or two after the goods.

The acknowledgment and the invoice bore in conspicuous type on their face the following legend, "All goods sold without warranties, express or implied, and subject to the terms on reverse side." In somewhat smaller, but still conspicuous, type there were printed on the back certain terms of sale, of which the following are relevant:

"1. Due to the variable conditions under which these goods may be transported, stored, handled, or used, Seller hereby expressly excludes any and all warranties, guaranties, or representations whatsoever. Buyer assumes risk for results obtained from use of these goods, whether used alone or in combination with other products. Seller's liability hereunder shall be limited to the replacement of any goods that materially differ from the Seller's sample order on the basis of which the order for such goods was made.

"7. This acknowledgment contains all of the terms of this purchase and sale. No one except a duly authorized officer of Seller may execute or modify contracts. Payment may be made only at the offices of the Seller. *If these terms are not acceptable, Buyer must so notify Seller at once.*" (Ital. suppl.)

It is conceded that plaintiff did not protest defendant's attempt so to limit its liability, and in due course paid for the emulsion and used it. It is also conceded that adequate notice was given of breach of warranty, if there were warranties. The only issue which we will consider is whether all warranties were excluded by defendant's acknowledgment.

The first question is what law the Massachusetts court would look to in order to determine the terms of the contract. Under Massachusetts law this is the place where the last material act occurs. [Citations.] Under the Uniform Commercial Code, Mass. Gen.Laws Ann. (1958) ch. 106, § 2–206, mailing the acknowledgment would clearly have completed the contract in Massachusetts by acceptance had the acknowledgment not sought to introduce new terms. Section 2–207 provides:

"(1) A definite and seasonable expression of acceptance or a written confirmation which is sent within a reasonable time operates as an acceptance even though it states terms additional to or different from those offered or agreed upon, unless acceptance is expressly made conditional on assent to the additional or different terms.

"(2) The additional terms are to be construed as proposals for addition to the contract. Between merchants such terms become part of the contract unless:

"(a) the offer expressly limits acceptance to the terms of the offer;

"(b) they materially alter it; or

"(c) notification of objection to them has already been given or is given within a reasonable time after notice of them is received."

Plaintiff exaggerates the freedom which this section affords an offeror to ignore a reply from an offeree that does not in terms coincide with the original offer. According to plaintiff defendant's condition that there should be no warranties constituted a proposal which "materially altered" the agreement. As to this we concur. See Uniform Commercial Code comment to this section, Mass.Gen.Laws annotation, supra, paragraph 4. Plaintiff goes on to say that by virtue of the statute the acknowledgment effected a completed agreement without this condition, and that as a further proposal the condition

never became part of the agreement because plaintiff did not express assent. We agree that section 2–207 changed the existing law, but not to this extent. Its purpose was to modify the strict principle that a response not precisely in accordance with the offer was a rejection and a counteroffer. [Citations.] Now, within stated limits, a response that does not in all respects correspond with the offer constitutes an acceptance of the offer, and a counteroffer only as to the differences. If plaintiff's contention is correct that a reply to an offer stating additional conditions unilaterally burdensome upon the offeror is a binding acceptance of the original offer plus simply a proposal for the additional conditions, the statute would lead to an absurdity. Obviously no offeror will subsequently assent to such conditions.

The statute is not too happily drafted. Perhaps it would be wiser in all cases for an offeree to say in so many words, "I will not accept your offer until you assent to the following: * * *" But businessmen cannot be expected to act by rubric. It would be unrealistic to suppose that when an offeree replies setting out conditions that would be burdensome only to the offeror he intended to make an unconditional acceptance of the original offer, leaving it simply to the offeror's good nature whether he would assume the additional restrictions. To give the statute a practical construction we must hold that a response which states a condition materially altering the obligation solely to the disadvantage of the offeror is an "acceptance * * * expressly * * * conditional on assent to the additional * * * terms."

Plaintiff accepted the goods with knowledge of the conditions specified in the acknowledgment. It became bound. [Citations.] Whether the contract was made in Massachusetts or New York, there has been no suggestion that either jurisdiction will not give effect to an appropriate disclaimer of warranties. [Citations.] * * *

[Judgment for defendant affirmed.]

HILL'S, INC. v. WILLIAM B. KESSLER, INC.

(1952) 41 Wash.2d 42, 246 P.2d 1099.

MALLERY, J. The plaintiff, Hill's, Inc., ordered thirty-four men's suits from the defendant, using a printed form supplied by defendant through its salesman.

The printed form provided that the order would not become a binding contract until it had been accepted by an authorized officer of the defendant at its office in Hammonton, New Jersey.

The defendant's salesman procured the order on May 16, 1950, and on May 23, 1950, the defendant, by form letter, advised the plaintiff that "You may be assured of our very best attention to this order." What occurred next is shown by the trial court's finding of fact:

" * * * but notwithstanding, on or about July 18, 1950, defendant intentionally and deliberately, at the instigation of a large retail store selling defendant's clothing in the downtown Seattle area, wrongfully cancelled said order and breached its agreement with plaintiff to deliver said suits as ordered, or at all. That at the time defendant cancelled said order and breached its agreement, the period for placing orders for delivery of fall suits had passed, and it was impossible for plaintiff to thereafter procure comparable suits from any other source to meet its fall trade. * * * "

Thereupon, plaintiff brought this action for loss of profits in the amount of a 66⅔ per cent markup aggregating $815.83.

From a judgment in favor of the plaintiff, the defendant appeals.

The defendant contends that its letter of May 23, 1950, in which it said "You may be assured of our very best attention to this order," was not an acceptance of the plaintiff's order.

In Bauman v. McManus, 75 Kan. 106, 89 P. 15, 18, 10 L.R.A.,N.S., 1138, the court said:

" * * * The promise that the order shall receive prompt and *careful* attention seems to imply something more than that the manufacturers will quickly and cautiously investigate the advisability of accepting it. The care they might expend in that direction—in looking up the defendants' financial standing, for instance—is not presumably a matter in which any one but themselves would be greatly interested. The engagement to use care seems more naturally to relate to the manner of filling the order than to the settling of a doubt whether to fill it at all. The expression of thanks for the favor has some tendency in the same direction. We incline strongly to the opinion that the latter standing by itself was as effectual to close a contract as though in set phrase it had said that the goods would be shipped; that to permit any other construction to be placed upon it would be to countenance the studied use of equivocal expressions, with a set purpose, if an advantage may thereby be derived, to keep the word of promise to the ear and break it to the hope."

Notwithstanding that the Bauman case is exactly in point, it is not necessary to rely upon it exclusively, for the reason that the intention of the defendant to accept the offer is shown by subsequent correspondence with the plaintiff in this case.

On July 18, 1950, defendant wrote plaintiff the following letter:

"This is to inform you we find it will be impossible to ship the Fall order which you placed with Mr. Jacobus on May 16, order #8585. We dislike very much having to inform you of this, but we trust that you will understand when we say that because of previous commitments to other stores in town it is necessary to *cancel* this order.

"We are certainly sincerely sorry if this action on our part inconveniences you at all." (Italics ours.)

This letter recognizes the existence of a contract, which it undertakes to cancel. * * *

The defendant contends that the court erred in allowing loss of profits as the measure of damages, in this case, and complains that the plaintiff made no effort to procure similar suits elsewhere by way of mitigating the damages. The plaintiff, however, showed that the cost of going east to fill such an order would have been greater than his lost profits, and, hence, would not have been justified.

We think that the defendant understood that the plaintiff was purchasing the thirty-four suits for resale at a 66⅔ per cent markup; that the order was specifically placed for the plaintiff's fall trade; and that the suits, of the defendant, were of a quality that was unobtainable in the west. Loss of profits, in such a case, is a correct measure of damages. [Citations.]

The judgment is affirmed.

TEXACO, INC. v. GOLDSTEIN

(1962) 34 Misc.2d 751, 229 N.Y.S.2d 51.

WAHL, J. The plaintiff seeks to recover a judgment against the defendant predicated upon purchases made pursuant to the terms and conditions of a credit card issued by the plaintiff to the defendant on or about June 11, 1959.

The plaintiff is a major oil company engaged in the production and distribution of petroleum and related products throughout the United States. Dealers operating gas stations and engaged in private enterprise, retail the petroleum products of the plaintiff in the operation of their stations and by means of dealer agreements with the plaintiff are authorized to vend products of the plaintiff.

Texaco, Inc., as a device to stimulate sales, issued a credit card enabling the holder to purchase its products at any authorized Texaco station. The practice is that the party to whom the card issues thereafter receives a monthly statement covering all purchases made in prior months.

The credit card issued by the plaintiff is made of plastic and measures 3⅜ inches by 2⅓ inches. Plaintiff's name appears conspicuously upon the face of the card and the name of the customer appears embossed on the face of the card in prominent raised letters.

The face of the card also contains a signature block in which the customer is to sign his name. Directly above the customer's signature block, the words "Issued subject to conditions on reverse side, Texaco, Inc." are inscribed.

On the reverse side of the card the agreement between the customer and the company is contained and the relevant portion appears as follows:

"This credit card confirms the authorization of credit during the period shown, to the person, corporation or firm whose name is embossed on the reverse side thereof. Such person, corporation or firm assumes full responsibility for all purchases made hereunder by any one through the use of this credit card prior to surrendering it to the company or to giving the company notice in writing that the card has been lost or stolen. Retention of this card or use thereof constitutes acceptance of all the terms and conditions thereof."

Upon the defendant's application, a card was issued to him by the plaintiff, bearing a certain number with an expiration date of the last day of May, 1961.

Thereafter the defendant was deprived of the card by theft, but failed to report the loss to the plaintiff. A dealer marketing plaintiff's products picked up the card on or about December 23, 1960 at Chicago, Illinois, where it had been tendered by an illicit possessor, for the purpose of purchase of petroleum products. The dealer then notified the plaintiff that the card had been reclaimed, and plaintiff in turn notified the defendant that his card was being used by another in the Chicago area. The plaintiff then confirmed a telephone conversation with the defendant by a letter dated January 23, 1961.

Written communications were received by plaintiff from defendant in connection with the loss of the credit card, but all of said communications were subsequent to the last charge made upon the credit card.

From the date the card was missing to the date of the telephone notification by plaintiff to defendant of its recovery, some $569.98 in charges were made with the said credit card, which charges constitute the subject of this action.

The issues raised here are whether the defendant is liable pursuant to the terms and conditions as set forth on the reverse side of the credit card, for the unauthorized purchases made by another person, prior to notification to the plaintiff by the defendant of the loss of the credit card.

* * *

The questions raised in the case now at issue were discussed at great length in the case of Union Oil v. Lull (supra, p. 416 of 220 Or., 349 P.2d p. 245). In that case, the words "The customer * * * guarantees payment * * * to anyone presenting this card, guaranty to continue until the card is surrendered or written notice is received by the company that it is lost or stolen" are used.

We recognize a distinction between the case at bar and the Lull case supra, in that the agreement between the parties is not one of "guaranty" as the same is used in the Lull case, but that of an original undertaking in which the defendant made it his own responsibility for any use of the card. In the Lull case the Court held that the credit card transaction created a suretyship contract between the parties, making the issuee a gratuitous indemnitor, with the only consideration moving to him the convenience of the use of the credit card. It further stated that the company benefited to the extent of getting a new user of its products. The "responsibility" portion of the card was therefore to be interpreted in this light, bearing in mind the further hazard that the indemnitor had no control over the user of the lost card, and would impress upon the Company the duty to use reasonable diligence in the transactions where the credit card is used.

The agreement expressed in the provisions of the credit card in the case at bar, are not unreasonable. The plaintiff assumes the risk of all loss after it receives notice of the loss or theft of the credit card; the defendant assumes the risk of loss prior to such notice.

With the increasing use of the credit card and its growing importance to the economy, the imposition of a high duty of diligence upon the major oil companies in general, most of whom use the same or similar systems of credit card transactions would result in an impairment of an important segment of our economic structure. We must take into consideration that for the most part, the dealers to whom the cards are presented are independent contractors engaged in private enterprise. The plaintiff undertakes to honor credit card purchases by persons presenting them to the individual dealers for credit. In each such transaction however, the plaintiff is in no way involved; it had previously agreed to purchase from the dealer, such charges at par and the plaintiff has no control of either the dealer or the purchaser using the card, until the credit charge invoice actually reaches the company for payment to the dealer on presentation by him. Accordingly, the negligence of the card holder becomes most important. The intent of the parties is that in the event of the issuee's or obligor's loss of his card, or it having been stolen, that he be required to treat his credit card with at least the same importance, or perhaps greater importance than he would with his currency. Assuming the defendant were to have lost some currency, he, alone bears the risk of loss, and his loss is fixed by the amount of currency he lost. Should he, however, lose his credit card, the amount of loss would not be fixed, and the risk of loss is not only borne by him, but also by the Company when he actually complies with the conditions of the issuance of the card to him. This is a risk the company is apparently willing to assume, and the only requirement by the company is that the card holder exercise a proper degree of care in the handling of his card. Unless actual notice of loss is given to the company, it can have no way of knowing of such loss, and to require some thirty thousand dealers to suspect the loss of any particular credit card and use diligence against its abuse, is not within the requirements of plaintiff as the issuer of the credit card. Unlike credit cards used in the restaurant and hotel fields, where personal use to the issuee is usually restricted, any holder of the credit card can use the same.

The Legislature of the State of New York took cognizance of the problem presented by the issuance and use of credit cards, by the enactment of sections 511, 512, and 513 of the General Business Law, as amended effective January 1st, 1962. Section 512 provided in part as follows:

"A provision to impose liability on an obligor for the purchase or lease of property or services by the use of a credit card after its loss or theft is effective only if it is conspicuously written or printed in a size at least equal to eight point bold type either on the card, or on a writing accompanying the card when issued or on the obligor's application for the card * * *."

The Legislature acknowledged the validity of the agreement between the parties to the action as it existed on the date when the credit card was issued by the plaintiff to the defendant, and imposed a condition on subsequent credit cards that the said condition be printed in eight point bold type which is the equivalent of newspaper print.

It is the opinion of this Court that the application to the plaintiff, by the defendant, for the issuance to him of a credit card, and the acceptance by him and use thereafter of the card, constitutes the offer and acceptance resulting in an entire contract.

The liability of the defendant to the plaintiff arises out of the contract contained on the credit card itself.

* * *

Judgment for the plaintiff in the sum of $569.98.

Affirmed unanimously. Texaco, Inc. v. Goldstein, 241 N.Y.S.2d 495 (1963).

PROBLEMS

1. Ames, seeking business for his lawn maintenance firm, posted the following notice in the meeting room of the Antlers, a local lodge: "To the members of the Antlers—Special this month. I will resod your lawn for 25 cents per square foot using Fairway brand sod. This offer expires July 15."

The notice also included Ames's name and address, his signature and specified that the acceptance was to be in writing.

Bates, a member of the Antlers, and Cramer, the janitor, read the notice and became interested. Bates wrote a letter to Ames saying he would accept the offer if Ames would use Putting Green brand sod. Ames received this letter July 14, and wrote to Bates saying he would not use Putting Green sod. Bates received Ames's letter on July 16, and promptly wrote Ames that he would accept Fairway sod. Cramer wrote to Ames on July 10, saying he accepted Ames's offer.

By July 15, Ames had found more profitable ventures and refused to resod either lawn at the specified price. Bates and Cramer brought an appropriate action against Ames for breach of contract. Decision as to the respective claims of Bates and Cramer?

2. In which, if any, of the following four situations described was a contract formed?

(a) A owned four speedboats named Porpoise, Priscilla, Providence and Prudence. On April 2, A made written offers to sell the four boats in the order named, for $2,200 each to C, D, E and F, respectively, allowing ten days for acceptance. Five days later, C received notice from A that he had contracted to sell Porpoise to M. The next day, April 8, C notified A that he accepted A's offer.

(b) On the third day, April 5, D mailed a rejection to A which reached A on the morning of the fifth day. At 10:00 A.M., on the fourth day, D sent an acceptance by telegram to A who received it at noon on the same day.

(c) E, on April 3, replied that he was interested in buying Providence but declared the price asked appeared slightly excessive and wondered if, perhaps, A would be willing to sell the boat for $1,900. Five days later, having received no reply from A, E, by letter, accepted A's offer and enclosed a certified check for $2,200.

(d) F was accidentally killed in an automobile accident on April 9. The following day, the executor of F's will mailed an acceptance of A's offer to A.

3. Alpha Rolling Mill Corporation, by letter dated June 8 offered to sell Brooklyn Railroad Company 2,000 to 5,000 tons of 50-pound iron rails upon certain specified terms adding that, if the offer was accepted, Alpha Corporation would expect to be notified prior to June 20. Brooklyn Company, on June 16, by telegram, referring to Alpha Corporation's offer of June 8, directed Alpha Corporation to enter an order for 1,200 tons of 50-pound iron rails on the terms specified. The same day, June 16, Brooklyn Company, by letter to Alpha Corporation, confirmed the telegram. On June 18, Alpha Corporation by telegram, declined to fulfill the order. Brooklyn Company, on June 19, telegraphed Alpha Corporation: "Please enter an order for 2,000 tons rails as per your letter of the eighth. Please forward written contract. Reply." To Brooklyn Company's repeated inquiries whether the order

for 2,000 tons of rails had been entered, Alpha denied the existence of any contract between Brooklyn Company and itself. Thereafter, Brooklyn Company sues Alpha Corporation for breach of contract. Decision?

4. Bill Gulley received through the mail a book and a box of condolence cards. Both packages were unsolicited. A notice with the book said: "The book is sent for ten days' free examination. If, after 10 days you wish to keep it, just send us $3.95; if you do not wish to keep it, just return it." Except for a difference in price, a similar notice arrived with the cards. Bill gave the cards to his wife, who immediately sent two of them to acquaintances. He put the book away with no intention of reading it or returning it. In neither case did he remit the requested purchase price. Both sellers sue Bill for the purchase price of their goods. What results?

5. Zenith Motors, Inc., an automobile manufacturer, announced on its nationwide television show on January 1, 1965, that, if it should sell 700,000 cars during 1965, it would give every retail buyer of a new Zenith during that year a stated share of its net profits for 1965. Beyer, having heard of the announcement from one of his employees who had seen and heard the program, purchased seven new Zeniths for his business on February 1. Neither his contract with the local dealer nor his bill of sale in any way referred to the manufacturer's announced proposition. By the end of the year, 854,321 new Zeniths had been sold at retail.

Beyer demanded from Zenith Motors, Inc., his stated share of the profits and, upon the corporation's refusal to pay it, he brought an action for its recovery on the theory of breach of contract. Zenith Motors, Inc., interposed the following defenses: (a) No offer had been made to Beyer; (b) Even if an offer had been made to him, it was not properly accepted; and (c) Even if an offer had been made, it had been effectively revoked by a full-page announcement in the January, 1965, issue of a well-known national magazine.

Are all or any of these defenses valid?

6. On October 1, T, the owner of a small tobacco store, wrote to three reputable manufacturers of neon signs, A, B and C asking each to quote a price for a sign of described specifications. By return mail, A offered to sell such a sign to T for $900 and a few days later, B offered the same sign for $920. On October 15, T received a telegram from C offering to sell such

a sign for $91. T immediately sent a telegram to C: "I accept your offer. Ship sign as soon as possible. T." On November 16, C delivered the sign and it was then discovered that the telegraph company had erroneously transmitted $91 instead of the correct price, $910, in C's offer to T. T insists that he is entitled to the sign for $91. C contends that T must take the sign and pay $910 for it. What are the rights and liabilities of T, C and the telegraph company?

7. A offered, by mail, to sell his farm to B for $10,000. A's letter was mailed on July 5, and received by B on July 8.

(a) Assume that B wrote to A on July 9, inquiring, "Will you take less?" A replied by letter of July 13, "No, I will not take a penny less." B then mailed a letter to A on July 17, saying, "I accept your offer of July 5." A refused to convey the property to B. Is there a contract between A and B for the sale of the farm?

(b) Assume that B wrote to A on July 9, and said, "I shall meet you with the money in a few days and be ready to arrange particulars." A in his written reply mailed on July 13, said, "I have decided not to sell my farm and hereby withdraw my offer to sell." Is there a contract between A and B?

(c) Assume that B was not interested in A's offer and gave A's letter to C telling C to accept if he were interested. C sent a letter to A in which he said, "I accept your offer." A refused to convey the land to C. Is there a contract between A and C?

8. Shaw, a resident of Chicago, was the owner of a valuable painting known as "The Lavender Lady." On February 1, Shaw wrote to Arnold, in St. Louis, offering to sell him the painting for $10,000 payable thirty days after delivery. Arnold received the letter the next morning. On the morning of February 3, Otello, an Italian count, visited Shaw in Chicago. Otello saw the painting and told Shaw he would buy it from him for $15,000, payment and delivery to be made on February 5. Shaw said, "I accept your offer," and they shook hands on the deal.

At 4:00 p. m. on February 3, Shaw sent a telegram to Arnold in St. Louis, revoking his offer to sell the painting. Arnold received this telegram at 6:30 p. m. on the same day. However, at 5:00 p. m. that afternoon Arnold had received a telephone call from Shaw's grandson, a confirmed alcoholic, who said that he had heard that Shaw had sold the painting to some foreign count. Shortly after receiving the call, Arnold wrote Shaw a letter accepting his offer. Arnold mailed the letter, properly addressed, from St. Louis at 6:00 p. m., February 3. Shaw received Arnold's letter on the morning of February 4.

What are the respective rights and liabilities of Shaw, Arnold and Otello?

9. Eyestrain, Inc., a television manufacturer, sent a circular letter to Adams, an electrical appliance dealer, stating: "We have prepared and are sending herewith a price list setting forth in detail the terms and conditions upon which Eyestrain TV Receivers will be supplied to dealers. Hereafter, no order will be filled except on the terms set forth in the enclosed price list." Adams sent in an order for 10 receivers on the exact terms stated, but the manufacturer refused to fill the order. What can Adams do?

10. On January 15, A published in the Chicago Daily News a quarter page advertisement stating that he would pay $5,000 for information leading to the arrest and conviction of the person or persons who set fire to his manufacturing plant on the night of January 5. B, a resident of Omaha, Nebraska, while passing through Chicago, saw this advertisement in the paper. On June 15, A published in the Chicago Daily News a quarter page ad stating that he was withdrawing the offer of a reward published on January 15. B did not see this ad or otherwise hear of the revocation. On November 1, B overheard a conversation in a tavern in Omaha to the effect that X and Y had set fire to A's plant. B obtained the number of the automobile license plate on X's car and notified the police in Omaha and also the prosecuting authorities in Illinois. X and Y were arrested. They confessed the crime, waived extradition, and were returned to Chicago where they were indicted and convicted of arson. B brings an action against A to recover the $5,000 reward. Decision?

CHAPTER 3

REALITY OF CONSENT

Introductory. A contract is a consensual transaction; each party must give unqualified approval or assent to the terms. But, as a general rule, the existence of this requisite mutual assent is judged by an objective standard; that is, whether it appears that the parties assented, not whether they did in actual fact. There need be no subjective "meeting of minds," but only the appearance of agreement. For it is not what the parties intend that is critical, but what they lead each other reasonably to believe that they intended. If A has in mind offering to sell his Ford automobile to B, but mistakenly offers to sell his Chevrolet, B's acceptance is valid and a contract is concluded if B reasonably believed that A had offered to sell him the Chevrolet. The objective approach is deemed essential to the formation of contractual relationships since one may thereby act in reliance upon what reasonably appears to be the other's state of mind. He need not worry that the other did not mean what he said. However, there are vast areas where there may be an apparent manifestation of assent but the contract fails altogether or is subject to avoidance by one of the parties, because of what is regarded as a lack of "real consent." The problems are traditionally considered under the headings of duress, undue influence, fraud and mistake.

Duress. It is obvious that one should not be held to a bargain which he does not enter voluntarily but because of wrongful force or threats exerted by the other party. If B physically takes A's hand and forces him to sign a note, or puts a gun to A's back and threatens to shoot unless he signs, A can repudiate the signature. The foregoing are rather extreme examples of duress, which has been defined as follows: "(a) any wrongful act of one person that compels a manifestation of apparent assent by another to a transaction without his volition, or (b) any wrongful threat of one person by words or other conduct that induces another to enter into a transaction under the influence of such fear as precludes him from exercising free will and judgment, if the threat was intended or should reasonably have been expected to operate as an inducement." Restatement of the Law of Contracts, Section 492.

What if the act or threat is not such as would affect a person of average strength and intelligence, but it does put the particular person in fear and induces an action against his will? Is the test here to be subjective or objective? This problem was considered in a Massachusetts case, Silsbee v. Webber, 171 Mass. 378, 50 N.E. 555 (1898) and the view there enunciated prevails today. In favoring a subjective test, Mr. Justice Holmes said in the course of his opinion:

> "If a party obtains a contract by creating a motive from which the other party ought to be free, and which in fact is and is known to be sufficient to produce the result, it does not matter that the motive would not have prevailed with a differently constituted person, whether the motive be a fraudulently created belief or an unlawfully created fear."

The case also shows the extent to which courts will go in vitiating a contract because of duress. The defendant was the employer of the plaintiff's son, whom he accused of stealing money. He threatened the plaintiff that if she did not execute an assignment of a share in her father's estate to make good the losses, he would tell her husband (the boy's father) of the theft. The plaintiff feared that this would be very detrimental to her husband, who was in a weakened condition because of illness, all of which was known to the defendant. The trial court directed a verdict for the defendant, but the Supreme Judicial Court of Massachusetts said a jury would have been warranted in finding that the defendant obtained the assignment by duress, "solely by inspiring the plaintiff with fear of what he threatened to do."

In a Missouri case a son-in-law obtained a deed to certain property by threatening his deceased wife's parents, at a time when they were both in an enfeebled condition because of typhoid fever. The mother-in-law interpreted his threat that he would make it "hotter than hell" for them as meaning he intended to burn their house down while they lay ill in bed. The court ordered the deed cancelled. The rule and its rationale are summarized as follows by the Restatement of the Law of Contracts:

> "The test of what act or threat produces the required degree of fear is not objective. The threat need not be such as would put a brave man, or even a man of ordinary firmness, in fear. The question is rather, did it put one entering into the transaction in such fear as to preclude the exercise by him of free will and judgment. Age, sex, capacity, relation of the parties, attendant circumstances, must all be considered. Persons of a weak or cowardly nature are the very ones that need protection. The courageous can usually protect themselves; timid persons are generally the ones influenced by threats, and the unscrupulous are not allowed to impose upon them because they are so unfortunately constituted." Restatement of the Law of Contracts, Section 492, Comment a.

Ordinarily, the acts or threats constituting duress are themselves crimes or torts. But this is not true in all cases. For they need not necessarily be criminal or tortious in order to be "wrongful"; they may otherwise be contrary to public policy or morally reprehensible. An example is the Massachusetts case discussed above. It would not have been an actionable wrong for the employer to have told the woman's husband of the son's theft. But, under the circumstances

of the case, the court did consider it wrongful to so threaten, since the employer knew of the husband's weakened condition and knew that this threat would induce the woman to execute the assignment regardless of her belief in the merits of his claim.

Stated somewhat differently, duress may be occasioned by threats of criminal prosecution and imprisonment against one who has committed an unlawful act as well as against one who has not committed an unlawful act. As observed in Motor Equipment Co. v. McLaughlin, 156 Kan. 258, 133 P.2d 149: "Although the authorities even now remain somewhat divided, we think the better reasoned cases and the modern rule is that although the State might successfully prosecute a person for the commission of an unlawful act, such fact does not destroy the coercive character and compelling force of threats of imprisonment which result in the threatener obtaining an advantage. [Citations.] The important question in cases of this character is not whether there was ground for the threatened arrest or imprisonment but whether the party threatened was, by such threats, deprived of his free will. [Citations.]"

Numerous cases have permitted a party to recover payments made in response to a threat of criminal prosecution. In the Montana case of Clifford v. Great Falls Gas Co., 68 Mont. 300, 216 P. 1114 (1923), the plaintiff had been taking gas from the defendant company's line through the use of a device which allowed the gas to circumvent the meter. Upon the discovery of this, the manager of the company threatened: "I have got the goods on you now. You are stealing gas. I will send you over the road to the penitentiary. * * * You have burned it all winter and I want $200." The plaintiff paid the defendant the $200 demanded "for the purpose of avoiding prosecution or being sent to the penitentiary or jail." The court held that the threats of prosecution "were not made for the mere purpose of calling to his attention the fact that he was liable to prosecution under the penal statutes of the state, but were made solely to compel the payment of a debt alleged to be due to the defendant from the plaintiff." The court recognized the plaintiff's right to recover the $200. To be distinguished are threats to resort to ordinary civil remedies in order to recover a debt due from another. It would not have been wrongful in the foregoing case for the defendant's manager to have threatened to sue the plaintiff for what he believed to be owing the company. It is the inducement of the payment by the threat to use criminal prosecution that is proscribed. Referring to this, Justice Cardozo, while a judge on the New York Court of Appeals, wrote as follows:

> "The principle thus vindicated is simple and commanding. There is to be no traffic in the privilege of invoking the public justice of the state. One may press a charge or withhold it as one will. One may not make action or inaction dependent on a price." Union Exchange Nat. Bank of New York v. Joseph, 231 N.Y. 250, 131 N.E. 905 (1921).

A threat is usually an expression of intention to harm the other party. But it might also be a threat to harm one close to him (his wife, a child, a close relative) or even to injure or deprive him of property. The latter is referred to as "duress of goods." Hence, if A, in possession of a chattel belonging to B, wrongfully retains possession on a claim of money due, B's promise to pay the asserted claim in order to reacquire lawful possession is not enforceable. The modern tendency is to expand the area of "economic duress," those forms of compulsion and coercion aimed at a man's property (his trade, or business) rather than his person.

The applicable law has been succinctly summarized by Professor Corbin, as follows:

"One who has been injured by the criminal act of another, as when his money has been embezzled or goods stolen, may lawfully threaten prosecution for the offense. Nor is a bargain for the settlement of the civil claim for damages made illegal by the mere fact that prosecution was threatened, or by the fact that the wrongdoer agreed to the settlement with the hope that prosecution would be avoided thereby, or by the fact that prosecution did not in fact follow. The settlement agreement is made illegal only when a consideration is given in exchange for actual forbearance to prosecute or for a promise of such forbearance.

"Nevertheless, it is not safe to threaten prosecution as a means of inducing settlement of a civil claim. This is especially true when the settlement is made, not by the guilty party himself but by the parent or other close relative. When threats have been made it is easy to infer that the settlement was in exchange for forbearance or a promise thereof; and the bargain is just as illegal when the agreement is implied as when it is express. Moreover, the threats readily shade into improper duress; and if it turns out that the threatened party was in fact innocent, the transaction may have the appearance of blackmail. Even if the threatened party was guilty, threats to prosecute as a means of collecting money justly due may be a statutory offense." Corbin on Contracts, Section 1421, pp. 701–703.

Undue Influence. The law has traditionally scrutinized very carefully contracts between those in a relationship which is likely to permit unfair persuasion being exerted by one upon the other. Examples are the relationships of guardian and ward, trustee and beneficiary, principal and agent, husband and wife, parent and child, attorney and client, physician and patient, and pastor and parishioner. "Where one party is under the domination of another, or by virtue of the relation between them is justified in assuming that the other party will not act in a manner inconsistent with his welfare, a transaction induced by unfair persuasion of the latter, is induced by undue influence and is voidable." (Restatement of the Law of Contracts, Section 497.) The ultimate question in undue influence cases is whether the transaction was induced by influencing a freely exercised and competent judgment, or by dominating the mind or emotions. Obviously, the weakness or dependence of the person persuaded is a strong circumstance tending to show the persuasion may have been unfair.

Undue influence seldom arises outside the context of the aforementioned relationships in which one is in a position of dominance over the other, or is likely to be. Indeed, the concept, originated by courts of equity, is in a sense an extension of the principle affording relief from duress to require more upright conduct from those whose powers for depriving another of his free agency are greater. Where such a relationship exists at the time of the transaction and it appears that the dominant party has gained at the expense of the dependent party, the transaction is presumptively fraudulent. For example, in a contract between a guardian and his ward, the law presumes that advantage was taken by the guardian. It is, therefore, incumbent upon the guardian to rebut this presumption. Important factors in determining whether the contract is fair are (1) whether the guardian made a full disclosure of all relevant information known to him, (2) whether the consideration was adequate, and (3) whether the ward had competent and independent advice before completing the transaction.

Apart from the standard fiduciary relationships (guardian and ward, trustee and beneficiary, attorney and client), most cases of undue influence have arisen out of family relationships, as between husband and wife or parent and child, typical situations where trust and confidence are reposed. But there is no arbitrary limit to the parties who might be affected; if, in fact, a confidential relationship exists, applying generally to all persons who occupy a relation of trust and confidence, the dominant party is held to utmost good faith in his dealings with the other.

Fraud. Another factor which bears upon the quality of the consent manifested by a contracting party is fraud. If a merchant procures a sale by knowingly misrepresenting a material attribute of his product, the contract is voidable at the buyer's option. The purchaser in reliance upon the misrepresentation has assented to something which he would not otherwise have agreed to but for the merchant's fraudulent conduct. The purchaser's contractual consent has been obtained by "fraud in the inducement." This is the most frequent type of fraud, although there is another species of fraud which is called "fraud in the execution." For example, A secures B's signature to a document which A represents is a simple letter of introduction but knows to be a promissory note payable to himself. B has been reasonably led to believe that the act which he is performing is something altogether different than it actually is. In cases of fraud in the execution, often perpetrated through the surreptitious substitution of one document for another, the transaction is absolutely void, not merely voidable at the option of the defrauded party. The reason why fraud in the execution results in no contract at all, while fraud in the inducement results in a voidable contract is that the former is a type of fraud which precludes the requisite contractual assent, whereas the latter induces a genuine consent.

Courts are reluctant to advance an all-encompassing definition of fraud. This is understandable, since the type of proscribed conduct regarded as fraudulent can assume many forms, and the courts do not want to foreclose the possibility of relief because of an apparent definitional limitation. The following definition, however, will cover most cases of fraud in the inducement: "A false representation of a material fact made with knowledge of its falsity or culpable ignorance of its truth with intention that it be acted on by the party deceived and inducing him to contract to his injury." 17 Corpus Juris Secundum, Contracts, Section 153.

In some instances fraud may consist of the concealment or non-disclosure of a fact. It may be possible for one to avoid liability on a contract which he has been induced to enter through the innocent misrepresentation of another. These questions are treated in subsequent sections. The present discussion pertains to the typical fraud case where the defrauded party has been induced to enter into the contract in reliance upon the other party's misrepresentation of a material fact, and is therefore permitted either to rescind the transaction or to sue for damages in a tort action of deceit. Problems in this area will be discussed under the following headings: (a) False representation of fact; (b) Materiality; (c) Knowledge of falsity; intention to deceive; (d) Reliance; injury.

(a) False Representation of Fact. The basic element of fraud is the misrepresentation of a material *fact*; actionable fraud can rarely be predicated upon what is merely a statement of opinion. The line between fact and opinion is not an easy one to draw, and in close cases is an issue for the jury. Suppose that A induces B to purchase shares in a company unknown to the latter at a price of $100 per share, by representing that he had the preceding year paid $150 per share for them, when in fact he had paid but $50 each. This is a representation of a past event, definitely ascertainable and verifiable; he either paid $150 per share or he did not. If, on the other hand, A said to B that the shares were "a good investment," he is merely stating his opinion, and in the usual case B ought to regard it as no more than the statement of an opinion. Suppose, however, that A said the company "had a good year last year," when in fact it failed to show a profit. Is this opinion or fact? It is difficult, if not impossible, to decide without additional

evidence. The solution will often turn upon the character of the person making the statement and the information available to the other party. If A is a professional broker advising a client, the courts would be more likely to regard the statement as fraudulent. This might even be true of the statement that the purchase was "a good investment." Despite its being an expression of opinion, it is the opinion of one holding himself out as having expert knowledge, and the tendency is to grant relief to those who reasonably rely upon such expert evaluation in taking action.

Additional problems of distinguishing between statements of fact and opinion are considered in the materials on Sales where, for example, the difference between "sales talk" and factual representations is drawn with respect to ascertaining the existence and extent of a seller's warranties. Suffice it to say that, ordinarily, statements of "value" ("This is the best car for the money in town;" "This deluxe model will give you twice the wear of a cheaper model,") are not grounds for the avoidance of a contract. Such exaggerations and commendations of articles offered for sale are to be expected from dealers, and the customer is not reasonable if he relies upon the statement of a seller who is merely puffing his wares.

Also to be distinguished from a representation of fact is a prediction of what will happen in the future. Predictions are closely akin to opinions, as one cannot know with certainty what will happen in the future, and they should not be regarded as factual statements. It is also said that promissory statements cannot form the basis of fraud. But, while it is true that the mere breach of contract or breaking of a promise does not constitute fraud, by the majority view in this country a promise which the promisor has no intention of keeping does amount to a misrepresentation of a fact and may justify a rescission. Most courts take the position that the state of one's mind, which is there misrepresented, is as much a fact as anything else—as the state of one's digestion, so one court put it. If a dealer promises "I will service the machine free for the next year," but has no intention of doing so, his conduct is fraudulent if the promise of such service was a material inducement for the customer's making the purchase.

Suppose that the vendor of land induces a sale by misrepresenting that a certain zoning classification will, properly construed, permit the type of commercial activity contemplated by the purchaser, or that the zoning ordinance is unconstitutional as applied to the property. Has he made a misrepresentation of fact? Practically all courts will agree that he has not. Rather, he has misrepresented the state of the law, and since everyone is presumed to know the law the purchaser is not justified in relying upon the vendor's representation of this type and cannot assert fraud. There are, however, a few exceptions to this rule. If the vendor occupied a fiduciary or confidential relationship with respect to the purchaser, the latter would be able to avoid the transaction. A misrepresentation by one who is learned in the law, as for example a practicing attorney, may, under certain circumstances, be fraudulent. It is not unreasonable to rely upon the expert's statement of the law. It is generally held that misrepresenting the law of a foreign jurisdiction, including the law of sister States, is tantamount to a misrepresentation of fact and gives the defrauded party a cause of action.

(b) Materiality. In addition to the requirement that the representation be one of fact it is necessary that it be material. It must relate to something of substance, something that induces the other to act as he did. In the sale of a race horse it may not be material whether the horse was ridden by a certain jockey his last time out, but the running time for the race probably would be. In determining the materiality of the representa-

tion, courts look to the impression made upon the mind of the other party. It is always material if, but for the representation, he would not have entered into the transaction. Many courts deem the representation to be material if in any substantial degree it influenced the other's decision, even though it was not the decisive factor.

(c) Knowledge of Falsity; Intention to Deceive. To establish fraud it is not enough to show that the representation of fact was false; generally speaking, the misrepresentation must have been known by the speaker to be false and made with an intention to deceive. If he acts reasonably and in good faith, fraud cannot be imputed to him, even though he is in error. But in most jurisdictions, good faith alone will not protect him; he may be honest in his belief, but unreasonable in so believing He may, for example, have taken at face value what was reported to him from a very unreliable source. In such case, fault or culpability can be ascribed to him, and he may be liable to the other party. An aspect of this problem is considered in a subsequent section dealing with the effect of innocent misrepresentation.

(d) Reliance; Injury. One is not entitled to relief unless he has justifiably relied upon the misrepresentation, to his detriment or injury. Thus, courts speak of the requirement that the misrepresentation be the proximate cause of the action or change of position. If, for example, the complaining party knew that the representation of the defendant was untrue, but still entered into the contract, he is in a weak position to argue liability. If his decison was in no way influenced by the misrepresentation, he must abide by the terms of the contract. He is not deceived if he does not rely. Moreover, it may turn out that even though fraud was perpetrated, the bargain is a most advantageous one for the defrauded party, and there is no occasion for judicial relief. He may have purchased a painting in reliance upon the seller's state-

ment that it was the work of a certain famous artist, only to discover later that it was the work of another equally famous artist, worth a great deal more than the purchase price. In legal contemplation he has not been injured; accordingly, he would not be entitled to recover a judgment for damages, although he would be entitled to a rescission and a return of the price. The fraudulent seller presumably would be pleased to rescind and receive back the painting upon a refund of the price.

Silence: Non-disclosure and Concealment. As a general rule, silence alone does not amount to fraud. There is no obligation on the part of a seller, for example, to tell a purchaser everything he knows about the subject of the sale, particularly if it is something which is reasonably apparent anyway. But there are exceptions. Many cases hold that if there is a latent (or hidden) defect of a substantial character, one that would not be discovered by an ordinary examination, the seller is obliged to reveal it. Moreover, one may have a duty of disclosure because of prior representations innocently made but not in accord with existing facts. The Restatement of the Law of Contracts gives this illustration: "A, in conversation with B, states that A's land Blackacre contains thirty acres. A supposes this statement to be true, and makes it with no expectation of selling the land. Subsequently A discovers that the land contains only twenty-three acres, and after acquiring this knowledge, and having in mind his previous conversation, contracts with B to sell him the land. A's lack of disclosure is fraud, and it is immaterial that A shows B the boundaries of the land before the contract is made." Restatement of the Law of Contracts, Section 472, Illustration 1.

The dominant party in a confidential or fiduciary relationship owes it to the other party to make a full disclosure of all facts relevant to the transaction. His duty in this respect exceeds that of one who is dealing with another at "arm's length."

It is everywhere recognized that active concealment can form the basis for fraud, as where one puts heavy oil or grease in an engine to conceal a knock. Truth may be suppressed by concealment quite as much as by active misrepresentation, and one must answer truthfully if asked a question by the other party. A denial of knowledge of a fact which one knows to exist, or the statement of a misleading half-truth, can form the basis for fraud.

Effect of Innocent Misrepresentation. At common law it was necessary for a successful party in a fraud action, whether asking rescission or damages in tort, to prove an intention to deceive. Hence, the necessity for showing knowledge of the falsity or at least culpable ignorance. The absence of an honest belief was essential; the misrepresentation alone was insufficient. An English court expressed the general view of the common-law judges when it stated that "a charge of fraud is such a terrible thing to bring against a man that it cannot be maintained in any Court unless it is shown that he had a wicked mind." LeLievre v. Gould, 1 Q.B. 491, 498 (1893). However, this view was later modified by courts of equity, which allowed a rescission even if the false statement was innocently made. The rationale was that it is unjust to permit one who has made false representations, albeit innocently, to retain the fruits of the bargain so induced. A Minnesota court put the matter this way: "The injury suffered by the defrauded party may be just as great, whether the fraud was intentional or unintentional." Jacobson v. Chicago, M. & St. P. R. Co., 132 Minn. 181, 156 N.W. 251 (1916). Today a majority of courts will permit a rescission, which results in a restoration of the status quo, for innocent misrepresentation, provided, of course, that it was with respect to a material fact inducing the plaintiff to enter into the contract. Although some courts have departed from the strict view in actions for damages as well, the majority still insist upon proof of scienter (knowledge) in establishing a cause of action for deceit.

Legal Remedies of Defrauded Party. At common law there are two courses open to a party who has been induced to enter into a contract by the fraudulent representations of another; i. e., he may either affirm or disaffirm (rescind) the contract. These remedies are mutually exclusive.

Affirmation occurs where the defrauded party, with full knowledge of the facts, either declares his intention to proceed with the contract or takes some other action from which such intention may reasonably be inferred. Thus, suppose that A was induced to purchase a ring from B through the latter's fraudulent misrepresentation. If, after learning the truth, A undertakes to sell the ring to C or otherwise does something which is consistent only with his ownership thereof, he may no longer rescind the transaction.

If the defrauded party does not desire to go through with the contract, and it is still executory, he may assert the fraud as a defense to an action by the other. If the contract is executed, he may rescind the contract, and, upon restoring the consideration that he has received, reacquire that which he parted with —be it money, goods, or other property. If the defrauded party, in lieu of a rescission, desires to retain the consideration which he has received, he may do so and maintain an action in tort for the damages sustained.

There are important limitations upon the right of the defrauded party to rescind. First, the power of avoidance is lost if after acquiring knowledge of the fraud he unreasonably delays in giving notice to the other party of his intention to avoid the transaction. To illustrate, a defrauded purchaser of stock cannot wait unduly to see if the market price or value of the stock appreciates suffi-

ciently to justify his retention of it. Second, in order to rescind, the defrauded party must restore everything that he has received under the contract. If he cannot make this restoration, as where the goods are destroyed or consumed, he cannot rescind. The purpose of this limitation is expressed as follows in an English case: "Though the defendant has been fraudulent, he must not be robbed, nor must the plaintiff be unjustly enriched, as he would be if he both got back what he had parted with and kept what he had received in return. The purpose of the relief is not punishment but compensation." Spence v. Crawford, 3 All E.R. 271, 288–9 (1939). This requirement prompted one judicial wit to give the example of one fraudulently induced to buy a cake. He said the buyer could return it and recover the price, but "cannot both eat your cake—and return your cake." Clarke v. Dickson (1858), E. B. & E. 148, 152. Third, if a third party good-faith purchaser acquires an interest in the subject matter of the contract before the defrauded party shall have elected to rescind, no rescission is permitted. In the ordinary case of fraud in the inducement, the transaction is voidable. A fraudulent buyer therefore acquires a voidable title to the goods. Upon a sale of the goods by him to a third person who is a purchaser in good faith and for value, the latter having obtained title is allowed to keep the goods. Since both the defrauded seller and the good-faith purchaser are innocent, the law will not disturb the title in the good-faith purchaser. In this case, as in all cases where rescission is not available to a defrauded party, his only recourse is to recover damages against the fraudulent party in the tort action of deceit.

The Code changes the common-law rule with respect to contracts for the sale of goods by not restricting the defrauded party to an election of remedies. He may have his cake and eat it too. That is, he may both rescind the contract by restoring the status quo and, in addition, recover damages, if any, resulting from the fraud. The defrauded party is entitled to all of the remedies which he would have in the case of a non-fraudulent breach of the contract by the other party. The remedies available to the seller and the buyer for breach of contract are discussed in Chapter 22. Section 2–721 of the Code provides:

> Remedies for material misrepresentation or fraud include all remedies available under this Article for non-fraudulent breach. Neither rescission or a claim for rescission of the contract for sale nor rejection or return of the goods shall bar or be deemed inconsistent with a claim for damages or other remedy.

Mistake. An elusive branch of the law is that which is concerned with the effect of "mistake" upon the formation of a contract. Certain problems have been settled, but many have not been. There is, however, one concept that runs through the cases and which will at least help to place the issues in a meaningful context as well as assist in predicting results. In the chapter on "Manifestation of Mutual Assent" attention was given to the standard by which the assent of the parties is to be tested. The courts favor an objective approach. A person is bound by the reasonable impression which he has created in the mind of the other party, even if this differs from his own subjective intention. Thus, in the first illustration in this chapter, where A, by mistake, offers to sell B his Chevrolet automobile rather than his Ford as he intended, A is bound. This view is even carried forward by most courts where the mistake is made by an independent intermediary chosen by the offeror. In one case, the following message was given to a telegraph company for transmission: "Will sell 800 M. laths, delivered at your wharf, two ten net cash. July shipment. Answer quick." The telegraph company, by mistake, omitted the word "ten" in the message as delivered to the offeree. Unaware of the mistake, the recipient wired an acceptance, and the court held that a contract was concluded upon the terms expressed in the message as it was delivered by the telegraph company. The offeree relied upon what was manifested to him. The problem is how far can the objective theory be extended in mistake cases? At what point is there a lack of "real consent"?

(a) Mistake as to Existence or Identity of Subject Matter. Suppose A offers to sell B a certain boat, but unknown to both parties the boat has been destroyed. If B accepts, is he entitled to damages upon A's failure to deliver the boat as promised? He is not. Section 2–613 of the Code provides: "Where the contract requires for its performance goods identified when the contract is made, and the goods suffer casualty without fault of either party before the risk of loss passes to the buyer, or in a proper case under a 'no arrival, no sale' term (Section 2–324) then (a) if the loss is total the contract is avoided; and (b) if the loss is partial or the goods have so deteriorated as no longer to conform to the contract the buyer may nevertheless demand inspection and at his option either treat the contract as avoided or accept the goods with due allowance from the contract price for the deterioration or the deficiency in quantity but without further right against the seller."

The rationale of these rules is based upon the presumed intention of the parties in ordinary transactions; that is, no subject matter, no contract. To be distinguished from the case in which the parties are mutually mistaken, is the contract which contemplates an assumption of the risk. For instance, a ship at sea may be sold "lost or not lost." In such case the buyer is liable whether the ship was lost or not lost at the time of the making of the contract. "There is no mistake; instead, there is conscious ignorance." Corbin on Contracts, Section 600.

Possibly the most famous decision involving mutual mistake is Raffles v. Wichelhaus,

2 Hurlstone & Coltman 906 (1864), popularly known as the "Peerless Case." A contract of purchase was made for "certain goods, to-wit, 125 bales of Surat Cotton * * * to arrive ex Peerless from Bombay." It happened, however, that there were two ships by the name of "Peerless," each sailing from Bombay, one in October and the other in December. The buyer had in mind the ship that sailed in October, while the seller reasonably believed the agreement referred to the Peerless sailing in December. Neither party was culpable, but believed in good faith that a different ship was intended. The English court held that no contract existed. The Restatement of the Law of Contracts, Section 71 is in accord: " * * * (a) If the manifestations of intention of either party are uncertain or ambiguous, and he has no reason to know that they may bear a different meaning to the other party from that which he himself attaches to them, his manifestations are operative in the formation of a contract only in event that the other party attaches to them the same meaning. (b) If both parties know or have reason to know that the manifestations of one of them are uncertain or ambiguous and the parties attach different meanings to the manifestations, this difference prevents the uncertain or ambiguous manifestations from being operative as an offer or an acceptance. (c) If either party knows that the other does not intend what his words or other acts express, this knowledge prevents such words or other acts from being operative as an offer or an acceptance." Hence, if blame can be ascribed to either party, he is responsible. If neither is to blame, or both are to blame, there is no contract at all. One writer in discussing this has said: "Where an offer couched in ambiguous language is accepted, it cannot be said that the parties have objectively manifested their assent at all as to which meaning is to be attached to the ambiguous term. In such case, the result of contract or no con-

tract must depend upon their subjective agreement or disagreement." Simpson on Contracts, Section 30.

(b) Mistake as to Nature of Subject Matter. If B contracts to purchase A's automobile under the belief that he can sell it at a profit to C, he obviously is not excused from liability if he is mistaken in this belief. Nor can he rescind the agreement simply because he was mistaken as to his estimate of what the automobile was worth. These are the ordinary risks of business, and courts do not undertake to relieve against them. But suppose that the parties contract upon the assumption that the automobile is a 1966 Cadillac, with 15,000 miles use, when, in fact, the engine is that of a cheaper model and has been run in excess of 50,000 miles? Here, a court would likely allow a rescission because of mutual mistake respecting a material fact. Another example of mutual mistake of fact was presented in a California case where a noted violinist purchased two violins from a collector for $8,000, the bill of sale reading: " * * * I have on this date sold to Mr. Efrem Zimbalist one Joseph Guarnerius violin and one Stradivarius violin dated 1717." Actually, unknown to either party, neither violin was genuine. Taken together they were worth no more than $300. The purchaser was successful in contesting the seller's suit for the balance due. In a New Zealand case, the plaintiff purchased a "stud bull" at an auction. There were no express warranties as to "sex, condition or otherwise." Actually, the bull was sterile. Rescission was allowed, the court observing that it was a "bull in name only."

The foregoing cases are to be contrasted with situations where the parties are aware that they do not know the character or value of the item sold. For example, the Supreme Court of Wisconsin refused to rescind the sale of a stone for which the purchaser paid one dollar, but subsequently discovered was an uncut diamond valued at $700. The parties did not know at the time of sale what the stone was, and knew they did not know. Each consciously assumed the risk that the value might be more or less than the selling price.

It is frequently stated that relief will not be given for mistake unless the mistake is "mutual." This can be misleading. By way of illustration, suppose a building contractor submits a bid for a job that is one-half of what it should be, because he made a serious error in his computations. If the other party knows that he made such an error, or reasonably should have known of it, he cannot, as a general rule, take advantage of the other's mistake and "snap up" the offer. In an Oregon case, Rushlight Automatic Sprinkler Co. v. City of Portland, 189 Or. 194, 219 P.2d 732 (1950), the plaintiff, in computing his bid on a city sewer project, by mistake omitted the cost of one item, the steel. Accordingly, his bid was substantially lower than the others. He bid $429,444.20; the next higher bid was $671,600. All other bids were even higher. An estimate made by the city engineers, undisclosed to the bidders prior to the submission of the bids, was $632,000. The plaintiff received a sympathetic ear from the Court, which stated in the course of its opinion: "It is our belief that although the plaintiff alone made the mistake, the City was aware of it. When it accepted the plaintiff's bid, with knowledge of the mistake, it sought to take an unconscionable advantage of an inadvertent error." Some courts refer to a case of this type as one of "palpable unilateral mistake," to distinguish it from the situation where the other had no suspicion, nor any good reason to suspect that an error had been committed. In the latter type of case no judicial relief from the contract is available.

(c) Mistake by Failure to Read Document. As a general proposition, a party is held to what he signs. His signature authenticates the writing, and he cannot repudiate that which he has voluntarily approved. As a Louisiana court expressed it: "Signatures to obligations are not mere ornaments." Hence, "One who makes a written offer which is accepted, or who manifests acceptance of a writing which he should reasonably understand to be an offer or proposed contract, is bound by the contract, though ignorant of the terms of the writing or of its proper interpretation." Restatement of the Law of Contracts, Section 70. This view has been stated as follows by the Court of Appeals of New York: "When a party to a written contract accepts it as a contract he is bound by the stipulations and conditions expressed in it whether he reads them or not. Ignorance through negligence or inexcusable trustfulness will not relieve a party from his contractual obligations. He who signs or accepts a written contract, in the absence of fraud or other wrongful act on the part of another contracting party, is conclusively presumed to know its contents and to assent to them." Metzger v. Aetna Ins. Co., 227 N.Y. 411, 125 N.E. 814 (1920). However, there are instances where one is relieved of obligations to which he has thus apparently assented; namely, where the character of the writing was misrepresented by the other or where the writing was such that a reasonable person would not think it contained contractual provisions. An example of the latter would be a hatcheck stub containing in fine print a limitation of the proprietor's liability in case of loss or damage to the item checked. Ordinarily, stubs of this type are used for identification purposes only; hence, in the usual case one is not held to have assented to the limitation of proprietor liability merely by accepting the stub.

Mistake of Law. One cannot obtain a release from contract liability upon the ground that he did not understand the legal effect of the contract. Courts will not relieve from a mistake of law. By the majority view in this country, one paying money to another under a mistake of law cannot recover that money even though it was not legally due, provided the payee's claim was asserted in good faith. There are, however, some exceptions. Payments made by governmental agencies or payments made to a court or court official under mistake of law are recoverable. Where the mistake is one of foreign law, including the law of sister States, the general rule does not apply. The general reluctance to grant relief for mistake of law has been subjected to serious criticism, and has been abrogated by statute in a few States. In these States relief for mistake of law is placed upon the same basis as mutual mistake of fact.

CASES

GREAT AMERICAN INDEMNITY CO. v. BERRYESSA

(1952) 122 Utah 243, 248 P.2d 367.

WADE, J. The Great American Indemnity Company, appellant herein, brought this suit against Frank Berryessa and W. S. Berryessa, the obligors on a joint promissory note. Frank Berryessa was not served with summons and did not participate in the trial. W. S. Berryessa pleaded as defenses duress and lack of consideration and also counterclaimed for the return of $1,500 paid by him and the cancellation of a personal check given by him and not cashed at time of suit. This appeal is from a jury verdict and judgment thereon in favor of respondent W. S. Berryessa.

Viewing the evidence in the light most favorable to respondent, as we must, the jury having found in his favor, it discloses that Frank Berryessa, a son of W. S. Berryessa, misappropriated some funds of his employer the Eccles Hotel Company, which operates the Ben Lomond Hotel in Ogden, Utah. When the father first learned of this, it was thought that the sum involved was approximately $2,000 and he agreed to repay this amount if the bonding company would not be notified and no publicity given to the matter, and gave the hotel his promissory note for $2,186 to cover the shortage. Before this note became due, it was discovered that the shortage would probably be over $6,000 and therefore the manager of the hotel called W. S. Berryessa in for a conference. W. S. Berryessa knew he couldn't pay this larger sum and it was decided that the bonding company, the appellant herein, should be advised of the shortages. The hotel didn't try to collect the note for $2,186 after the bonding company was notified apparently expecting that company to reimburse the hotel for the entire shortage discovered. After the bonding company was notified, its agent had several conferences with the Berryessas and the hotel management in which there was ascertained that the total shortage amounted to $6,865.28 and Frank Berryessa signed a statement that he had misappropriated that amount. Frank Berryessa had stated that he had given a brother-in-law some of the money he had embezzled and it was suggested that he sign a note along with the Berryessas. The brother-in-law did not sign the note and at a further meeting of the Berryessas with the agent W. S. Berryessa indicated that he did not think his son Frank would be able to make the payments of $250 quarterly suggested and that he was sure that he personally would not be able to do so and therefore did not want to sign the note. Mr. Berryessa then testified, although this was denied by the agent, that the agent thereupon swore, pounded his fists on his desk, and told him, "You can't come here and tell me what you will do." and then told them that if W. S. Berryessa would pay $2,000 in cash and sign a note with Frank Berryessa for $4,865.20, payable at the rate of $50 a month, that Frank would not be prosecuted but that if he did not sign Frank would have to be prosecuted. Thereupon, W. S. Berryessa agreed to do this and a couple of days later signed the note sued upon herein and about a month later, having secured a loan by mortgaging his home, gave the agent a cashier's check in the amount of $1,500 and a personal check in the amount of $500 as payment for the $2,000 cash agreed upon. Mr. Berryessa asked the agent not to cash the $500 check for about a month until he could get some more funds to pay it. This is the check which was never presented for payment by the appellant.

At the conclusion of the trial, appellant moved for a directed verdict in its favor and for a dismissal of the counterclaim because there was insufficient evidence of duress or lack of consideration. The court refused to grant its motion and this refusal is relied upon by appellant for reversal in this case.

It is appellant's contention that there was insufficient evidence of duress to present that question to the jury and that the court erred in giving its instructions numbered 1 and 6 because it gave the jury the idea that there were two separate and distinct defenses to the validity of the transaction. Respondent pleaded both duress and illegal consideration as defenses. The court in its Instruction No. 1 told the jury:

"You are instructed that the defendant, W. S. Berryessa, admits signing the note sued upon but raises two defenses to his liability thereon. The first defense is that his signature was obtained as a result of the duress upon him of the plaintiff's agent, J. G. Hagman Jr., that if defendant, W. S. Berryessa, did not sign the note his son, Frank Berryessa, would be criminally prosecuted and sent to jail. The second defense is that even if it should be determined that such duress has not been proven, nevertheless the only consideration for his signing the note

was the promise of plaintiff's agent, J. G. Hagman, Jr., that if he would sign Frank Berryessa would not be criminally prosecuted, and that such consideration is illegal and insufficient to support the note. You are instructed that either of these defenses, if established by preponderance of the evidence is a sufficient and adequate defense to plaintiff's action against the defendant, W. S. Berryessa."

In Instruction No. 6, the jury were told:

"You are instructed that the note sued upon by the plaintiff is invalid against the defendant, W. S. Berryessa, if not supported by a valuable consideration. A promissory note given for the suppression of a criminal prosecution is against public policy and cannot be enforced between the parties, and it is immaterial whether the individual as to whom the criminal prosecution is suppressed was guilty or innocent. Accordingly, if you believe from a preponderance of the evidence that the defendant, W. S. Berryessa, signed the note sued upon by the plaintiff in consideration of plaintiff's promise through its agent, J. G. Hagman, Jr., that Frank Berryessa would not be criminally prosecuted for his defalcations, the note is invalid as to the defendant, W. S. Berryessa, and you must so find.

"The burden of proof is on the defendant in this case to prove that the consideration for which the defendant signed the note was the suppression of a criminal prosecution against defendant's son."

It will be noted that these instructions correctly placed the burden of proving their defenses of duress or illegal consideration upon the Berryessas.

It is well settled that a note given to suppress a criminal prosecution is against public policy and is not enforceable between the parties. See 10 C.J.S., Bills and Notes, § 154, pages 630–631 and Simon Newman Co. v.

Woods, 85 Cal.App. 360, 259 P. 460, on pages 462, 463, wherein the court said:

"It is conceded that a note or mortgage given on promise to refrain from the prosecution of a person for a felony, or under threats of arrest or prosecution, would be void as against public policy; * * *."

In this case respondent relied on two separate defenses, duress and illegal consideration, either one of which is sufficient to nullify this note. So if the jury found that the note was the result of duress or that respondent signed the note because appellant promised to refrain from criminal prosecution of his son, either one would be sufficient to invalidate the note and would constitute a defense thereto.

The uncashed check and the payment of $1,500 cash, present a different problem. Respondent had given the hotel a note for slightly over $2,000 to pay for the son's defalcations. At the time this note was given, there can be no question that no coercion was exercised against respondent and that his act was voluntary and at his own suggestion. There is nothing in the record to indicate that this note was given under duress or a promise to suppress prosecution. When appellant as surety paid the hotel the entire amount embezzled, it was entitled to be subrogated to the rights of the hotel and to an assignment of the note which respondent had given it. Respondent knew he had signed the note and was liable thereon. He, therefore, substituted for his promise to pay the hotel a promise to pay $2,000 to the Indemnity Company. In conformity to that promise, he paid $1,500 and gave his check for $500. This should be regarded as the extinguishment of a pre-existing, valid debt, which the appellant had a right to collect. Under such circumstances, the court erred in submitting the issue of duress and illegal consideration to the jury on respondent's counterclaim.

The judgment against appellant on its complaint is affirmed. The judgment in favor of the respondent on his counterclaim is reversed.

PEACOCK v. DU BOIS

(1925) 90 Fla. 162, 105 So. 321.

TERRELL, J. Some time in 1921 Anna Du Bois Robie, aged 57, moved from Albany, New York, to Fort Lauderdale, Florida, where she purchased certain real estate on which she resided as her home. She left surviving her in the state of New York one son, Kenneth H. DuBois, and one daughter, Grace Du Bois Whitcomb, all of whom are appellees here.

Anna Du Bois Robie died intestate in a hospital in Miami September 13, 1922. On May 31, George L. Peacock, aged 28, appellant in this case, took board and lodging with Mrs. Robie and remained in her home up to the time of her death. It appears that Peacock was very attentive to Mrs. Robie these three months or more he roomed and boarded with her and about four weeks prior to her death she executed a deed to him conveying her home place; the same being lots 5 and 6 of block 6 of Rio Vista subdivision as the same appears of record in the public records of Broward county, Fla. She also made him a bill of sale to her automobile.

This suit was brought by appellees [plaintiffs] in the court below to cancel and set aside the deed from Mrs. Robie to Peacock on the ground of fraud and undue influence. Issue was made on the answer and cross-bill to the amended bill of complaint. Testimony was taken by a special master, and on final hearing the chancellor entered his decree in favor of appellees. Appeal is taken from this decree.

* * *

It is conceded by all counsel engaged in this case that the sole question presented for review here is the sufficiency of the testimony to sustain the decree of the chancellor. This court has repeatedly held that in equity as in law every presumption is in favor of the correctness of the ruling of the trial court and a decree based largely or solely on questions of fact will not be disturbed unless clearly erroneous. [Citations.]

Does the testimony show fraud and undue influence? Fraud and undue influence are not strictly speaking synonymous, though undue influence has been classified as either a species of fraud or a kind of duress and in either instance is treated as fraud in general. [Citations.]

* * *

In Myatt v. Myatt, 149 N.C. 137, 62 S.E. 887, the court said that: To constitute "undue influence," it is unnecessary that moral turpitude or improper motive should exist, and if one, from the best of motives, having obtained a dominant influence over a grantor's mind, induces him to execute a deed or other instrument materially affecting his rights, which he would not have otherwise executed, so exercising the influence obtained that the grantor's will is effaced or supplanted, the instrument is fraudulent.

* * *

The rule seems to be well settled that undue influence justifying the setting aside of the will, deed, or other contract must be such as to dethrone the free agency of the person making it and rendering his act the product of the will of another instead of his own. The character of the transaction, the mental condition of the person whose act is in question, and the relationship of the parties concerned to each other are all elements that may be taken in consideration in applying the rule. [Citations.]

In Appeal of Worrall, 110 Pa. 349, 1 A. 380, 385, 765, it was held that, where a conveyance was made by a weak and sickly young man to a woman older than himself, and who had been to him as a mother, a presumption arose that such conveyance was obtained by undue influence.

In the case at bar a woman in her late fifties, physically infirm, knowing that she was soon to undergo an operation which might and in fact did prove fatal, conveyed her home and other property valued at approximately $15,000 to a young man in his late twenties. The record discloses that the money represented by this property had been recently inherited from an uncle, and that the woman was a novice in business, could be readily influenced and easily became the dupe and tool of anyone with whom she came in contact. She had no sense of moral values, was greatly lacking in knowledge and business experience, and while it is not conclusively shown that she was a woman of enfeebled mentality in the common acceptance of that term, it is shown that she was possessed of a mind unbalanced, that she knew no distinctions among men or women and as easily became the victim of the good or honest as she did the bad or the dishonest.

The property involved in this litigation is virtually all that Mrs. Robie owned, and it is repulsive to every rule of law and right and love of justice to argue that she would uninfluenced deed this property for a nominal consideration to a young man who was a stranger to her, that she had known hardly two months, and who it is not shown had any claims whatever on her bounty, thereby disinheriting the children she had mothered and to whom she was bound by all the ties of love and affection. The fact of the execution of the deed on the showing made by the record, we think, imposes on the appellant the duty of showing that the transaction was bona fide and that it was not secured by undue influence. The testimony is entirely inadequate to show this. [Citations.]

* * *

For reasons announced in this opinion the decree of the Chancellor was properly entered and is affirmed.

SMITH v. AGAN

(1965) 111 Ga.App. 536, 142 S.E.2d 291.

PANNELL, J. The often announced rule that one having the capacity and opportunity to read a written contract and who signs it, not under any emergency, and whose signature is not obtained by any trick or artifice of the other party, but solely on the representations of the other party as to its contents, cannot afterwards set up fraud in the procurement of the signature of the instrument, [citations], is but another statement of the rule that one cannot claim to be defrauded by the false representations of another, where, by the exercise of ordinary diligence, such person could have discovered the falsity of the representations before acting thereon; and, while there is a wide difference between that class of cases in which one can read and those where one, from illiteracy or ignorance, is unable to read, the writing he is induced to sign, and has to rely upon the representations made by the draftsman, [citation] to the extent that one who cannot read "may ordinarily rely upon the representation of the other party as to what the instrument is or as to what it contained; and his mere failure to request the other party or someone else to read it to him will not generally be such negligence as will make the instrument binding upon him," [citations]; yet, one not having the capacity to read a written contract is not relieved from his obligation of exercising ordinary diligence, [citation] to ascertain the contents of the writing, where, as in the present case, there are no representations made as to its contents, but only a representation as to why the signature on the instrument is desired and such reason is true and is not inconsistent with the actual contents and purpose of the instrument, and the party dealing with such person does not know that he cannot read, and such person, before signing, looks at the instrument as if reading the same and does not inquire as to its contents. [Citation.]

Where, as in the present case, an agreement of accord and satisfaction of a claim for damages is entered into between the parties in the form of a release signed by the plaintiff claimant and reciting a cash consideration to the claimant, and such signed release is delivered to the other party with no demand for the cash or for immediate payment, and later a check in payment is received by the claimant and the claimant attempts to return the check and refuse the same solely on the ground that his signature to the same was obtained by fraud, and under the undisputed facts there was no fraud in procuring his signature to the release, the refusal to accept the check in payment on that ground alone was a waiver of the time of payment and the medium of payment. [Citations.]

The trial judge did not err in granting the defendant's motion for summary judgment upon the grounds indicated above, and it is unnecessary to determine whether his ruling was correct upon any other grounds of the motion.

Judgment affirmed.

WILLIAMS v. JOSLIN

(1965) 65 Wash.2d 674, 399 P.2d 308.

ROSELLINI, C. J. The sellers of a parcel of real estate appeal from a judgment of the trial court rescinding the contract. The court found that the buyer had been induced to purchase the property by fraudulent representations of the sellers concerning the income which they had derived from the property during their ownership of it. There was no finding, and no contention, that the property was worth less than the amount which the buyer had agreed to pay for it.

The appellants maintain that there is no clear, cogent, and convincing evidence to support the trial court's finding of fraud. It is well settled, of course, that such evidence must be produced if fraud is to be established, and the evidence must show the following elements:

   (1) A representation of an existing fact;

   (2) Its materiality;

   (3) Its falsity;

   (4) The speaker's knowledge of its falsity;

   (5) His intent that it shall be acted upon by the person to whom it is made;

   (6) Ignorance of its falsity on the part of the person to whom the representation is addressed;

   (7) The latter's reliance on the truth of the representation;

   (8) His right to rely upon it; and

   (9) His consequent damage.

[Citation.]

It is first urged that the evidence conclusively showed that no misrepresentation of fact was made. The respondent testified that the appellants, who were real estate agents, told him that the motel property grossed over $1,000 every two months. He did not deny their testimony that they showed him the deposit slips covering their period of ownership, and the trial court found in its memorandum decision that these evidences of receipts had been exhibited to him at his request. They showed that the business grossed less than $400 per month. However, the trial court was entitled to believe, as it evidently did, that the oral representation had been made, even though it was not borne out by the written evidence which was exhibited to the respondent.

However, we think the appellants are correct in their contention that the evidence did not support a finding that the respondent relied upon the representation. The rule is that such reliance must be reasonable under the circumstances, that is, a party may not be heard to say that he relied upon a representation when he had no right to do so.

*   *   *

The parties to this action dealt at arms length; the appellant asked to be shown the record of receipts and was shown them,

and they revealed that the oral representation was false. Since the evidence of the actual receipts was before the respondent, he had no right to rely upon any oral representation that contradicted it.

*   *   *

The judgment is reversed and the cause remanded.

SUNDERHAUS v. PEREL & LOWENSTEIN

(1965 Tenn.) 388 S.W.2d 140.

HOLMES, J. The Chancellor sustained a demurrer to the original bill in this case as amended. The appellant, Virgina Sunderhaus, has perfected an appeal to this Court.

The original bill alleges that on February 10, 1958 complainant purchased a diamond ring from the defendant, Perel & Lowenstein, for the sum of $699.25 and received from the defendant a written warranty guaranteeing to complainant the perfection of the ring, its value, style, and trade-in value. This written warranty is made an exhibit to the original bill.

It is further alleged in the original bill that thereafter complainant desired to trade this ring for another ring and found that one jeweler appraised the ring as having a value of $300.00, and another jeweler appraised the ring at a value of $350.00.

The original bill prays for rescission of the contract, or, in the alternative, that complainant have a judgment against defendant for the difference between the price paid by her for the ring and the actual value of the ring. The original bill was filed on December 31, 1963. The defendant demurred to the original bill.

Thereafter, on January 24, 1964, the original bill was amended so as to allege that complainant discovered the discrepancy between the warranty made an exhibit to the original bill and the actual character of the ring on or about November 8, 1963. By this amendment it was further alleged that the diamond sold complainant was not a perfect diamond as warranted by the defendant.

Later, on April 10, 1964, a further amendment to the original bill was filed in which complainant alleged that at the time of the purchase of this ring from the defendant the defendant's agent, David L. Richman, represented to her that the diamond was worth the amount of money she paid, that the defendant's agent misrepresented to her the true value of the diamond and that this representation was a fraudulent representation, that she was unfamiliar with the value of diamonds and relied upon the statement made by the agent of the defendant as to value, that the defendant's agent knew at the time of the sale that the price she paid was not the true retail value of the diamond which she purchased, that this amounted to a fraud on the purchaser, and that the defendant through its agent took advantage of complainant's trust in his statements. This amendment prays for rescission of the contract, or, in the alternative, for a judgment for the difference between the sale price and the actual retail value of the ring. In this amendment, complainant abandons the allegations theretofore made as to the imperfection of the diamond.

* * *

The alleged false representations of the appellee's agent relate to the value of the diamond purchased by appellant. We find the general rule to be that ordinarily representations of value made by one seeking to dispose of property commercially are to be regarded as expressions of opinion or commendatory trade statements not constituting a basis of fraud. There are, however, a number of exceptions to this general rule. In 23 Am.Jur., Fraud and Deceit, § 59, at Page 830, it is stated:

" * * * Likewise, a statement of value may be of such a character, so made and intended, and so received, as to constitute fundamental misrepresentation; and if it is made as an assertion of fact, and with the purpose that it shall be so received, and it is so received, it may amount to a fraud. Moreover, a statement of value involving and coupled with a statement of a material fact is fraud.

"Value is frequently made by the parties themselves the principal element in a contract; and there are many cases where articles possess a standard commercial value, in which it is a chief criterion of quality among those who are not experts."

Further, in this same work, the rule is stated, as follows:

"Under various circumstances, it has been held that representations as to market price or market value are not mere statements of opinion, but are representations of fact which, if false, will support an action for fraud or deceit. Thus, it has been held that a false representation as to the market value of bank stock, which has an ascertainable market value, is not the mere expression of an opinion, but a misrepresentation of fact on which fraud may be based to sustain an action for deceit. The relief sought by the party to whom the alleged misrepresentations as to market value were made has usually been based upon the assertion of a right on his part to rescind the contract, on the ground of fraud, and the misrepresentation as to market value or market price, as a rule, has been held to constitute a proper basis for fraud." 23 Am.Jur., Fraud and Deceit, § 62, Page 834.

The rule is stated as follows in 3 Pomeroy, Equity Jurisprudence, § 878b (5th ed. 1941):

"There is still another and perhaps more common form of such misrepresentation. Wherever a party states a matter, which might otherwise be only an opinion, and does not state it *as the mere expression of his own opinion*, but affirms it *as an existing fact* material to the transaction, so that the other party may reasonably treat it as a fact, and rely and act upon it as such, then the statement clearly becomes an affirmation of fact within the meaning of the general rule, and may be a fraudulent misrepresentation.

"Value. The statements which most frequently come within this branch of the rule are those concerning value."

* * *

Of necessity, in the purchase of a diamond or other precious stone, the purchaser must rely upon the integrity of the jeweler from whom he purchases. The layman is in no position to weigh the stone and make his own determination as to its true value, but must rely upon statements of value made to him by the jeweler. Here, the bill charges the agent of the appellee falsely represented the value of the diamond to the complainant, knowing the falsity of the representation, that the appellant was not familiar with the value of the diamond and relied upon the false representation of the appellee's agent. These averments contain all of the elements necessary to state a cause of action for fraud and deceit.

* * *

In our judgment it cannot be said that the bill as amended fails to state a cause of action for fraud and deceit. Therefore, the decree of the Chancery Court is reversed and the cause is remanded for further proceedings.

———

LOGHRY v. CAPEL

(1965 Iowa) 132 N.W.2d 417.

THORNTON, J. Plaintiffs, purchasers of a duplex from defendants, bring this action for fraud in failing to disclose the duplex was constructed on improperly compacted filled ground.

Plaintiffs are husband and wife, ages 32 and 26. Defendants are husband and wife, the husband's age is 41. The husbands are the principal actors.

The jury returned a verdict for plaintiff for the amount of repairs and incidental expenses due to the settling and cracking of the duplex claimed to be caused by the defective fill.

Defendant appeals urging the evidence is insufficient to prove representation, knowledge, scienter, intent to deceive, reliance and consequent damage. Defendant in his argument bearing on representation reaches the question of whether a latent soil defect, known to the seller of a house built on such soil, creates a duty of disclosure in the seller. That such is the seller's duty has been held or recognized in Cohen v. Vivian, 141 Colo. 443, 349 P.2d 366, 80 A.L.R.2d 1448. [Citations.] A contrary view is expressed in Polson v. Martin, 228 Md. 343, 180 A.2d 295, particularly where the purchaser has equal opportunity to know of the soil defect by ordinary inspection.

Defendant purchased Lot 4, in Vergamini's Second Addition to Council Bluffs, Pottawattamie County, Iowa, which he later sold to plaintiff, from the developer in early 1958. Defendant built the duplex on Lot 4 in July of 1958. Defendant rented both sides of the duplex for a year and seven months before selling it to plaintiff in January of 1960. This sale was made through a real estate broker. Plaintiff and defendant did not meet at that time. Plaintiff did not know defendant was the builder of the duplex for about two years after the sale. Plaintiff rented both sides of the duplex until he moved into one side in July, 1962.

The cracking in the basement and walls of the duplex was first called to plaintiff's attention in 1961. In 1961 plaintiff called defendant relative to this condition. Later defendant employed an engineer from the Omaha

Testing Laboratories to make soil tests. From the engineer's testimony the jury could properly find the lot was defectively filled to a depth of from 12 to 13 feet below the surface level and five to six feet below the footings and that the cracked condition of the duplex was due to such defective fill. From the testimony of the contractor who repaired the damage the jury could also properly find the duplex was placed on defectively filled ground, that the fill was approximately 17 feet below the outside grade, and such defective fill was the cause of the damage.

I. Defendant's contention relative to representation is that there is no evidence defendant made any representation in the nature of a nondisclosure in order to induce plaintiff to enter into the sale and no evidence of any mistake on the part of plaintiff induced by defendant's nondisclosure. Defendant cites Restatement of the Law of Contracts, Section 471:

" 'Fraud' in the Restatement of this Subject unless accompanied by qualifying words, means * * * (b) concealment, or (c) nondisclosure where it is not privileged, by any person intending or expecting thereby to cause a mistake by another to exist or continue, in order to induce the latter to enter into or refrain from entering into a transaction; * * *."

And Section 500 of the Restatement of the Law of Contracts, " * * * mistake means a state of mind that is not in accord with the facts."

Defendant's contention is the record shows plaintiff had no state of mind concerning the subsoil. Plaintiff made no inquiry about the subsoil. He did examine the house briefly on two occasions. He dealt solely with the realtor. The offer signed by plaintiff stated he had not examined the property and accepted the same in its present condition and stated upon acceptance would like to look at said property.

Also defendant contends there is a distinction between this case and those where there is an affirmative duty to disclose by reason of a confidential or fiduciary relationship or a relationship of principal and agent.

The latter argument denies the existence of the rule of law expressed in the cases first above cited. The rule of law there expressed is simply one who sells real estate knowing of a soil defect, patent to him, latent to the purchaser, is required to disclose such defect. It is evident such defect is material to the sale and will substantially affect the structure on the land or to be constructed on the land. The doctrine is sound and we adopt it. We have long recognized that fraud may consist of concealment of a material fact. [Citations.]

The former argument that the evidence shows plaintiff had no state of mind relative to the subsoil fails to consider plaintiff wife did testify directly to her state of mind. She said, "I did not think it was filled ground." Both plaintiffs testified they would not have purchased the duplex if they knew it was on filled ground. The circumstances of the general appearance of the lot would also show plaintiffs were in no way alerted to the soil defect. They had a right under the rule here expressed to rely on such appearance until advised to the contrary. The jury could properly find that by his nondisclosure defendant caused plaintiffs to believe the soil was as it appeared to be on the surface, and plaintiffs' state of mind was not in accord with the fact.

Defendant does not contend he did in fact disclose the condition of the soil to plaintiff.

II. In this action prior knowledge of the defective soil condition is evidence of scienter and intent to deceive. [Citations.] * * *

From the nature of Lot 4, its location in the subdivision being developed, the excavation and building carried on by defendant husband and under his direction, coupled with his experience and knowledge of building and his assumption of one-half the cost of the testing expense, the jury could properly find it was more probable he knew of the defective soil condition than he did not know of it.

* * *

III. When the jury, as here, has found defendant's knowledge of the defective soil condition, and defendant does not disclose this fact, the only result to follow is the natural consequence of such nondisclosure, and that is that plaintiffs were allowed to assume the lot was what it appeared to be. The plaintiffs were thereby deceived. Defendant cannot be heard to say he did not intend the natural consequences of his failure to disclose, his intent to deceive is presumed. [Citation.]

IV. We have pointed out both plaintiffs testified they would not have purchased the property if they knew it was filled. This is direct evidence that they relied on the appearance of the lot and duplex. The representation made by the nondisclosure is material. Under such circumstances courts permit inferences of inducement and reliance. [Citations.]

V. The testimony of the testing engineer and repairing contractor is substantial evidence the defective fill caused the damage to the duplex.

Affirmed.

RAFFLES v. WICHELHAUS

The Court of Exchequer (England)
(1864) 2 Hurlstone and Coltman Reports 906.

To a declaration for not accepting Surat cotton which the defendant bought of the plaintiff "to arrive ex Peerless from Bombay," the defendant pleaded that he meant a ship called the "Peerless" which sailed from Bombay in October, and the plaintiff was not ready to deliver any cotton which arrived by that ship, but only cotton which arrived by another ship called the "Peerless," which sailed from Bombay in December. Held, on demurrer, that the plea was a good answer.

DECLARATION. For that it was agreed between the plaintiff and the defendants, to wit, at Liverpool, that the plaintiff should sell to the defendants, and the defendants buy of the plaintiff, certain goods, to wit, 125 bales of Surat cotton, guaranteed middling fair merchant's Dhollorah, to arrive ex "Peerless" from Bombay; and that the cotton should be taken from the quay, and that the defendants would pay the plaintiff for the same at a certain rate, to wit, at the rate of 17¼d. per pound, within a certain time then agreed upon after the arrival of the said goods in England.—Averments: that the said goods did arrive by the said ship from Bombay in England, to wit, at Liverpool, and the plaintiff was then and there ready and willing and offered to deliver the said goods to the defendants &c., Breach: that the defendants refused to accept the said goods or pay the plaintiff for them.

Plea. That the said ship mentioned in the said agreement was meant and intended by the defendants to be the ship called the "Peerless," which sailed from Bombay, to wit, in October; and that the plaintiff was not ready and willing and did not offer to deliver to the defendants any bales of cotton which arrived by the last-mentioned ship, but instead thereof was only ready and willing and offered to deliver to the defendants 125 bales of Surat cotton which arrived by another and different ship, which was also called the "Peerless," and which sailed from Bombay, to wit, in December.

Demurrer, and joinder therein.

Milward, in support of the demurrer. The contract was for the sale of a number of bales of cotton of a particular description, which the plaintiff was ready to deliver. It is immaterial by what ship the cotton was to arrive, so that it was a ship called the "Peerless." The words "to arrive ex 'Peerless,'" only mean that if the vessel is lost on the voyage, the contract is to be at an end. (POLLOCK, C. B. It would be a question for the jury whether both parties meant the same ship called the "Peerless.") That would be so if the contract was for the sale of a ship called the "Peerless;" but it is for the sale of cotton on board a ship of that name. (POLLOCK, C. B. The defendant only bought that cotton which was to arrive by a particular ship. It may as well be said that if there is a contract for the purchase of certain goods in warehouse A., that is satisfied by the delivery of goods of the same description in warehouse B.) In that case there would be goods in both warehouses; here it does not appear that the plaintiff had any goods on board the other "Peerless." (MARTIN, B. It is imposing on the defendant a contract different from that which he entered into. POLLOCK, C. B. It is like a contract for the purchase of wine coming from a particular estate in France or Spain, where there are two estates of that name.) The defendant has no right to contradict by parol evidence a written contract good upon the face of it. He does not impute misrepresentation or fraud, but only says that he fancied the ship was a different one. Intention is of no avail, unless stated at the time of the contract. (POLLOCK, C. B. One vessel sailed in October and the other in December.) The time of sailing is no part of the contract.

Mellish (Cohen with him), in support of the plea. There is nothing on the face of the contract to show that any particular ship called the "Peerless" was meant; but the moment it appears that two ships called the "Peerless" were about to sail from Bombay there is a latent ambiguity, and parol evidence may be given for the purpose of showing that the defendant meant one "Peerless"

and the plaintiff another. That being so, there was no consensus ad idem, and therefore no binding contract. He was then stopped by the Court.

PER CURIAM. There must be judgment for the defendants.

BOYD v. AETNA LIFE INS. CO.

(1941) 310 Ill.App. 547, 35 N.E.2d 99.

STONE, P. J. This suit grows out of the cancellation and surrender of a life insurance policy issued by the Aetna Life Insurance Company, appellee (hereinafter designated as defendant), on the life of one Jimmie Boyd, who, at the time the policy was issued, was the husband of Christine Boyd, appellant (hereinafter designated as plaintiff). The policy insured against permanent total disability at the rate of $50 per month during the life of the insured, beginning six months after the beginning of such permanent total disability, together with abatement of premiums and $5,000 to be paid in the event of death, with no deduction from the face of the policy on account of payments made under the total disability clause. Plaintiff was designated as beneficiary, both for the total disability benefits and the death benefit.

After the policy had been in force for a number of years, plaintiff and her husband separated. Plaintiff continued to live in Carmi, Illinois, but her husband left there and traveled as advance agent for shows that were traveling about the country, so that it was impossible for plaintiff to keep informed as to his whereabouts or his state of health.

Following their separation plaintiff paid the premiums on the insurance policy, up until about the month of August, 1938, when, owing to her financial circumstances, she felt that she could no longer afford to pay the premiums and notified the insurance company that she desired to surrender the policy and receive its cash surrender value. A loan had previously been made on this policy, which, with accrued interest, amounted to the sum of $1,039, so that when plaintiff surrendered the policy she received but $4.19 in money, that being the balance of the cash surrender value above the loan and interest.

Shortly after the policy had been surrendered and cancelled, plaintiff learned the insured had been permanently and totally disabled more than six months before the surrender of said policy. Neither plaintiff nor defendant knew of the physical condition of the insured at the time the policy was surrendered. Upon learning of the permanent total disability of the insured, plaintiff requested the reinstatement of the insurance policy she had surrendered, and the payment of the disability benefits provided therein. Afterwards, on April 8, 1939, the insured, Jimmie Boyd, died and plaintiff then requested of defendant, the payment of the death benefit, in addition to the disability benefits, claimed to have previously accrued. This was not paid, whereupon suit was instituted.

The amended complaint filed by plaintiff, set forth in substance the above facts, and prayed that defendant be required to produce the surrendered policy in court; that an accounting be had, and that defendant be required to pay plaintiff whatever sum might be found to be due her upon such accounting. Defendant filed a motion to dismiss the amended complaint which was allowed by the court. Plaintiff elected to stand upon her amended complaint, whereupon the court dismissed said cause for want of equity and rendered judgment against plaintiff for costs, from which action of the Court, plaintiff prosecutes her appeal to this court.

Plaintiff alleges as error the action of the court in dismissing the case for want of equity, upon motion of defendant, and it is argued in her behalf that equity has jurisdiction to relieve against the consequences of a mutual mistake of fact and the cancellation or rescission of the insurance policy in question was made under such mutual mistake of fact.

It is defendant's earnest contention that at the time plaintiff decided to surrender the policy and asked for the cash surrender value, she knew that she did not know the condition of health of her husband, the insured. It is stressed that there was no unconscious ignorance on the part of plaintiff as to the health of insured, so it is claimed that the allegations of the amended complaint failed to show any mistake of fact in the legal sense upon her part; that notwithstanding her conscious want of ignorance of the condition of health of her husband she had elected to surrender the policy in question and take the cash surrender value thereof, in lieu of paying any further premiums on the policy and by such action waived any rights she had under the policy of insurance.

* * *

In the instant case, the question of the state of health of insured was not a collateral matter, nor a matter calculated to merely enhance the damages. It was not a compromise, comparable to the case of parties entering into a contract based upon uncertain or contingent events, purposely as a compromise of some doubtful claim arising from them, in which case, in the absence of bad faith no rescission can be had, though the facts turn out differently from the expectation of both parties. In such agreements the parties are presumed to calculate the chances and to assume the risks. * * *

We believe that the case of Duncan v. New York Mutual Insurance Company, 138 N.Y. 88, 33 N.E. 730, 731, 20 L.R.A. 386 is very much in point. In that case defendant issued a policy of insurance for $5,000 upon a vessel for one year from August 8, 1888. The policy contained a provision that defendant would "return pro rata premium for every thirty days of unexpired time, if the policy be canceled upon arrival." On November 22, the vessel sailed on a voyage, the ordinary length of which was seven days. At the request of plaintiff, then agent of the owner of the vessel, the policy was cancelled at and from December third, and the unearned premium, $233.33, returned. At that time neither party had heard from the vessel since it sailed. Plaintiff supposed it had arrived. The vessel never reached her port of destination, but was lost prior to December third. There the court held that the cancellation looked to the future, not the past, and if binding, it did not absolve defendant from liability already incurred; that as at the time of the cancellation an absolute obligation existed to pay the amount of the policy, it was not discharged by the cancellation and payment made; also that as the cancellation was made under a mistake of fact, it could be rescinded if necessary. * * *

The case of Riegel v. American Life Insurance Co., 153 Pa. 134, 25 A. 1070, 1072, 19 L.R.A. 166 is another case that seems to be very much in point. In that case a creditor who held a policy for $6,000, on the life of her debtor, whose whereabouts was unknown, finding it difficult to pay the premium, made an arrangement with the insurance company, under which the policy was surrendered. At the time of the transaction both parties acted on the supposition, that the assured was alive but as a matter of fact, he had been dead for ten days. The court held that the contract was not in the nature of a compromise of a doubtful claim, but an agreement made under the influence of a mutual mistake of fact and that plaintiff was entitled to have the original policy reinstated as of the date of its surrender. The court there said: "The case presented on these facts was that of a contract entered into under the influence of a mutual mistake * * *. The mistake was in relation to the fact of Leisenring's [the insured's] death. Both parties evidently supposed and acted

on the supposition that he was alive, and that the annual premiums upon his life, which had become burdensome to Mrs. Riegel, must be continued indefinitely until his death should take place. * * * This was the contract she made while in ignorance of Leisenring's death. At the time she made it she was already relieved from the burdensome premiums, and the entire amount of the policy was honestly due her from the company. These facts seem to us to present a clear and a strong case for equitable relief, so strong, indeed, that a mere statement of them is the only argument necessary for its support. * * *."

The decisive and practically sole question for the consideration of this court is whether the facts alleged in the amended complaint, set forth a sufficient mistake of fact, in the legal acceptation of the term, as to justify the intervention of a court of equity, and relieve against the consequences of that alleged mistake of fact, in the entering into the contract of rescission.

"Mistake of fact" has been defined to be a mistake, not caused by the neglect of a legal duty on the part of the person making the mistake, and consisting in an unconscious ignorance or forgetfulness of a fact past or present material to the contract, or belief in the present existence of a thing material to the contract which does not exist, or in the past existence of a thing which has not existed. [Citations.] It has also been defined as that which gives rise to a right of recovery, existing either when some fact which really exists is unknown or when some fact is supposed to exist, which really does not exist. [Citation.]

* * * It is not contended that plaintiff had any claim at the time of cancellation or supposed that she had one. There was in no sense a compromise. As a matter of fact, at the time of cancellation plaintiff had a perfectly valid claim, but she and the com-

pany were both at that time, according to the allegations of the amended complaint, ignorant of the fact that there was a claim in existence, due to the total permanent disability of insured. The supposed element of doubt as to the health of Boyd never entered into the contemplation of either party, nor did it form any part of the consideration for the cancellation and surrender of the policy. It would be quite natural that they would assume as they evidently did, that the insured was in good health. As a matter of fact such is the express allegation of the amended complaint.

* * *

In the instant case, the insured's state of health was not merely incidental, nor was it a matter that would merely enhance the amount of damages. The subject matter of the mistake was intrinsic to the transaction. As set forth in plaintiff's amended complaint, "if she had known the true facts as to said Jimmie Boyd's total permanent disability * * * she would not have surrendered same (the policy) to the defendant." This policy was in full force and effect at the time of total permanent disability. Upon that contingency coming to pass the liability of defendant was fixed. The cancellation was not intended to reach back and absolve defendant from any liability which it had already incurred. Even as in the Duncan case the parties believed the vessel insured was still in existence; and as in the Riegel case, the parties believed the insured alive, in the instant case both parties believed Jimmie Boyd in good health, and contracted with reference to that supposed state of facts. We are of the opinion, therefore, that the facts alleged show ground for equitable relief, and that the court erred in dismissing the amended complaint for want of equity.

The order and judgment of the Circuit Court will be reversed and the cause remanded with directions to overrule the motion to dismiss, and for further proceedings in accordance with the views herein expressed.

Reversed and remanded with directions.

————

PROBLEMS

1. A and B were negotiating and A's attorney prepared a long and carefully drawn contract which was given to B for examination. Five days later and prior to its execution, B's eyes became so infected that it was impossible for him to read. Ten days thereafter and during the continuance of the illness A called upon B and urged him to sign the contract, but without in any way misrepresenting the contents of it, and B signed without reading it. In a subsequent action by A, B claimed that the contract was not binding upon him because he had not and could not have read it prior to his signing it. Decision?

2. (a) A tells B that he paid $25,000 for his farm back in 1945 and that it is worth twice that today. Relying on these statements, B buys the farm from A for $40,000. Actually, while A did pay $25,000 for the farm in 1945, its value has increased only slightly since then and it is not worth $50,000 now. On discovering this, B offers to reconvey the farm to A and sues for the return of his $40,000. Result?

(b) Modify (a) above, by assuming that A had actually paid only $15,000 for the property in 1945, what result?

3. On September 1, A in Portland, Oregon, wrote a letter to B in New York City offering to sell to B 1,000 tons of chromite at $48 per ton, f. o. b. New York City, to be shipped by S. S. Malabar sailing from Portland, Ore., to New York City via the Panama Canal. Upon receiving the letter on September 5, B immediately mailed to A a letter stating that he accepted the offer. There were two ships by the name of S. S. Malabar sailing from Portland to New York City via the Panama Canal, one sailing in October, and the other sailing in December. At the time of mailing his letter of acceptance B knew of both sailings and further knew that A knew only of the December sailing. Is there a contract? If so, to which S. S. Malabar does it relate?

4. On March 1, A sold to B 50 acres of land in Oregon which A at the time represented to be fine, black loam, high and dry, and free of stumps. B paid A the agreed price of $5,000, and took from A a deed to the land which B subse-

quently discovered to be low, swampy, and not entirely free of stumps. B nevertheless undertook to convert the greater part of the land into cranberry bogs. After one year of cranberry culture, B became entirely dissatisfied, tendered the land back to A, and demanded from A the return of the $5,000. Upon A's refusal to repay the money, B brings an action at law against him to recover the $5,000. What judgment?

5. A owes B, a police captain, $500. A threatens B that unless B gives him a discharge from the debt, A will disclose the fact that B has on several occasions become intoxicated and has been seen in the company of certain disreputable persons. B, induced by fear that such a disclosure would cost him his position, and in any event lead to social disgrace, gives A a release, but subsequently sues to set it aside and recover on his claim. Decision?

6. A owned a farm which was worth about $60 an acre. By false representations of fact, A induced B to buy the farm at $100 an acre. Shortly after taking possession of the farm, B discovered oil under the land. A, on learning this, sues to have the sale set aside on the ground that it was voidable because of fraud. Decision?

7. On February 2, A induced B to purchase from him fifty (50) shares of stock in the XYZ Corporation for $10,000, representing that the actual book value of each share was $200. A certificate for fifty (50) shares was delivered to B. On February 16, B discovered that the book value was only $50 per share on February 2. Thereafter, B sues A. Decision?

8. A, in attempting to sell to B a small used airplane for $2,000, stated (a) that it had been flown only 80 hours; (b) that it was worth at least $2,000; and (c) that he was the original owner. Actually, the plane had been flown 200 hours; was worth only $1,000; and had been purchased second hand by A. All this was known to A. B knew that A was not the original owner. B bought the plane for $1,800. When he learned that the other statements were false, he offered to return the plane and sued to recover the $1,800 he had paid. Discuss each of A's statements and state their legal effect.

9. Jones, a farmer, found an odd-looking stone in his fields. He went to Smith, the town jeweler, and asked him what he thought it was. Smith said he did not know but thought it might be a ruby. Jones asked Smith what he would pay for it and Smith said $50; whereupon Jones sold it to Smith for $50. The stone turned out to be an uncut diamond worth $2,000. Jones brought an action against Smith to recover the stone. On trial, it was proved that Smith actually did not know the stone was a diamond when he bought it, but thought it might be a ruby. Decision?

10. John, a salesman for International Woolens, takes Jack to lunch, and after two cocktails, John induces Jack to buy 500 yards of woolens for $700, after he has represented to Jack that the woolens have cost him $1,000, but that he is willing to take a loss because he needs cash. John knows at the time of the statement that he has misrepresented the cost, having paid only $600 for the cloth. Later, Jack, through other commercial friends, finds that the value of the woolens is not as stated and refuses to complete the order. John brings an appropriate action to enforce the contract. Decision?

CHAPTER 4

CONSIDERATION

Definition of Consideration. A legally sufficient consideration is one of the requirements of a binding promise. There are exceptions such as promises under seal, promises to pay a debt barred by the Statute of Limitations or by a discharge in bankruptcy, and those made under circumstances amounting to a promissory estoppel, which will be considered later in this chapter. We are at this point dealing with consideration as a requirement.

Consideration is basically whatever is given in exchange for something else. Consideration is present therefore only when the parties intend an exchange, whether it be a promise exchanged for a promise, a promise for an act, or a promise exchanged for a forbearance to act. The central idea is that the parties have bargained with one another. They have each traded something and have both given and received a quid pro quo. Thus, a promise to give someone a birthday present is without consideration, as the promisor received nothing in exchange for his promise of a present. A promise to give someone a new suit of clothes if he will accompany the promisor to a certain clothing store is likewise without consideration, even though the promisee accompanies the promisor to the designated clothing store. It is a promise of a gift on condition. It is no less a gift promise because the promisee performed an act which would have been legally sufficient consideration if there had been an agreed upon exchange. The reason that it is a gift promise is that the promisor intended to make a gift at the time he made the promise and a reasonable person in the position of the promisee would have understood that such was the intention of the promisor and that neither of them intended the act of walking as something bargained

for and exchanged for the promise of a suit of clothes.

Section 75 of the Restatement of the Law of Contracts defines consideration for a promise as (a) an act other than a promise, or (b) a forbearance, or (c) the creation, modification, or destruction of a legal relation, or (d) a return promise bargained for and given in exchange for the promise. The consideration may be given to the promisor or to some other person. It may be given by the promisee or by some other person.

Legal Sufficiency of Consideration. It is not enough that consideration exist, that is, that the promisor merely receive something bargained for in exchange for his promise. The consideration found to exist must meet the test of legal sufficiency. The definition of legal sufficiency is technical, and in certain cases its application produces a result which is artificial. To be legally sufficient, the consideration for the promise must be either a legal detriment to the promisee or a legal benefit to the promisor. In most cases where there is legal detriment to the promisee, a legal benefit to the promisor will also be found. However, the presence of either one is sufficient. Legal detriment is not necessarily actual detriment, nor does legal benefit necessarily mean actual benefit. These terms are words of art and have specific technical meanings.

Legal detriment means the doing or undertaking to do that which the promisee was under no prior legal obligation to do, or the refraining from doing or undertaking to refrain from doing that which he was previously under no obligation to refrain from doing. On the other hand, legal benefit means the obtaining by the promisor of that which he had no prior legal right to obtain. The law does not regard the performance of a legal duty as either a legal detriment to the obligor or a legal benefit to the obligee. Thus, if A owes B the sum of $100, the payment of this debt involves no legal detriment to A, although it may have been actually difficult and laborious for A to obtain the money with which to make the payment. Likewise, the receipt of the $100 is no legal benefit to B, although he may have been in necessitous circumstances and in dire need of the money.

Legal sufficiency has nothing to do with adequacy of consideration. The subject matter which the parties respectively have exchanged need not have approximately the same value. The law will treat the parties as having considered them adequate by reason of having freely agreed to the exchange. The requirement of legally sufficient consideration is therefore not at all concerned with whether the bargain was good or bad, or whether one party received disproportionately more or less than what he gave or promised in exchange for it. Such an inquiry might be relevant if a question of fraud, duress, or undue influence were involved. However, the instant requirement is simply (1) that the parties have agreed to an exchange; and (2) that with respect to each promise the subject matter exchanged therefor, or promised in exchange therefor, either imposed a legal detriment upon the promisee or conferred a legal benefit upon the promisor.

To illustrate that legal detriment is not the same as actual detriment, or legal benefit the same as actual benefit, suppose that A promises B, a high school graduate, that if B will attend the XYZ College and graduate therefrom, A will pay to B upon graduation the entire cost of his college education. B enters XYZ College and duly graduates therefrom. The college education which he received is undeniably an actual benefit to B, but legally he suffered a detriment in graduating from XYZ College in that he gave up his freedom to attend any other college or to not attend college at all in consideration for A's promise. Consequently, the consideration which B gave for A's promise although not actually detrimental was legally detrimental to the promisee B. It is therefore legally sufficient and A's promise is enforceable by B. Furthermore, A may have received no actual benefit from B having obtained a college education at XYZ College, yet A received a legal benefit in that he obtained from B something that he had no previous right to have, namely, B's attendance at XYZ College and his graduation therefrom. This legal benefit may be of no value or usefulness to A, but nevertheless A's promise resulted in A obtaining a performance from B which A was not otherwise entitled to have.

The payment of a sum of money in consideration of a promise of discharge of a fully matured liquidated undisputed debt in an amount larger than the sum paid is legally insufficient to support the promise of discharge. Assume that B owes A $100, and in consideration of B paying A $50, A agrees to accept the lesser sum in full satisfaction of the debt. B pays A $50, and A writes "paid in full" on an invoice for $100 and signs and delivers this receipt to B. In a subsequent suit by A against B to recover the remaining $50 at common law, A is entitled to a judgment for $50 on the ground that the promise of discharge is not binding for the reason that B's payment of $50 was no legal detriment to the promisee B as he was obligated to pay that much and more. By the same token the receipt of $50 was no legal benefit to the promisor A. Consequently, the consideration for A's promise of discharge was legally insufficient, and A is not bound on his promise. However, if A had accepted from B the sum of $40 and a fountain pen worth $10 or less, or even the fountain pen with no payment of money, in full satisfaction of the $100 debt, the consideration moving from B would be a legal detriment to him inasmuch as he was under no prior obligation to give a fountain pen to A. It would also be a legal benefit to the promisor A for the reason that in receiving a fountain pen from B he obtained something that he had no prior right to obtain from B. Hence, this consideration would be legally sufficient and the entire $100 debt discharged.

Consideration Distinguished from Condition. As will be seen in a subsequent chapter on Discharge of Contracts, a condition is an operative event. It is not a promise, but an event the happening of which qualifies the duty of performance of a promise. If the promise in an offer is made subject to a condition, the requested consideration, that is, the sought for exchange, is not the happening or the non-happening of the event which is the condition. The consideration is either a return promise if the offer was for a bilateral contract, or an act or forbearance if for a unilateral contract. Thus, if A offers to pay B $1,000 for B's horse, provided that A receives such amount as distributee of the estate of his deceased uncle, and B accepts the offer and delivers the horse to A, the duty of A to pay $1,000 to B is conditioned upon his receiving $1,000 from his deceased uncle's estate. The consideration moving from B to A is the transfer of title to the horse. The consideration moving from A to B is the promise of $1,000 subject to the condition. The contract is complete, definite and certain. Although it may be uncertain whether B will receive $1,000, his right to it is not uncertain. It is definite, but conditional.

A gratuitous promise made on condition that the promisee do something is not any the less gratuitous because made upon a condition, where the condition is not reasonably regarded by the parties as part of the bargained for exchange. If A invites his friend B to come to A's home for Sunday dinner, B's going to A's home at the appointed time is a legal detriment to the promisee B. He is

doing something that he is not legally obligated to do. It is also a legal benefit to the promisor A, who had no legal right that B make the visit to his home. However, detriment to the promisee or benefit to the promisor are tests only of the legal sufficiency of consideration. If no consideration in fact exists, it is idle to look for legal sufficiency, the quality of something which does not exist. The reason that no contract is formed is that there is no consideration in fact for A's promise of a Sunday dinner. The act of B in going to A's home was not regarded by either party as something either requested or given in exchange for A's promise. It was a necessary condition to A's promise that B go to A's home in order to avail himself of the offered hospitality. If the parties had in fact bargained for B making a visit to A's home in exchange for the Sunday dinner, there would be consideration in fact. If consideration in fact is found to exist, it is clearly legally sufficient as both detriment to the promisee B and benefit to the promisor A are present, as shown above, and a contract would be formed upon B's acceptance of A's offer of the Sunday dinner.

Past Consideration. The element of exchange is absent where a promise is given for a past transaction. Hence, past consideration is no consideration. A promise made on account of something which the promisee has already done is not enforceable. Thus, on June 1, A sells B a horse for $300 payable on July 1. On June 15 B asks A if he warrants the horse to be sound, and A tells B that he so warrants it. There is no consideration for B's warranty. At common law it would be unenforceable. Under the Code, as a modification of the contract of sale, it would be binding without consideration. Section 2–209(1).

Consideration in Unilateral Contracts. In a unilateral contract, a promise is exchanged for an act or a forbearance to act. The test of consideration is whether the exchange is of a quid pro quo. Unilateral contracts are the most simple and earliest recognized form of contract. If the promisor or offeror requests a forbearance, such as non-smoking, non-drinking, or withholding the filing of a suit, and the offeree accepts the offer by forbearing as requested, there is no question of consideration in fact. The exchange of the offeror's promise for the offeree's forbearance is the consideration. There may be a question whether the forbearance is a legal detriment to the promisee. A forbearance to pursue a course of conduct which may be physically harmful or morally detrimental, such as drinking or gambling, may be actually beneficial to the promisee. But, since he is free to indulge in gambling or drinking, forbearance is legally a detriment to him.

The situation may arise where the promisee is under a duty to a third person to give a certain requested performance and is not under a duty to the promisor. Thus, B having contracted with the X Fair Grounds to ascend in a balloon as high as the balloon will go, receives a promise by A to pay him $500 if he ascends beyond 50,000 feet. The promisee B suffers no legal detriment by ascending 52,000 feet. However, the promisor A receives a legal benefit, as he had no prior right that B ascend at all. A is bound by his promise to pay $500 to B, as the consideration furnished by B is legally sufficient because of the legal benefit to the promisor A.

Consideration in Bilateral Contracts. When the promisor in an offer requests only a promise in exchange, the courts look at the substance of the promise requested. A person is under no legal obligation to promise to perform an existing duty. If he gives such promise, it subjects him to no greater obligation than does the pre-existing duty. Therefore, looking to the substance rather than the shadow, a new promise of an obligor to perform a pre-existing duty is not a legal detriment. However, if the offeror obtains the promise of a third person to perform a pre-existing duty owing to him by the offeree, it is legally sufficient consideration. Thus, if B owes A $100, as we have seen, neither a promise to pay nor payment by B of $50 which A accepts in full satisfaction, will discharge the $100 debt. However, an assignment by B to A of a claim for $50 which B has against a third party C, or a transfer by B to A of C's promissory note for $50, would discharge the $100 debt if accepted by A in full payment.

Illusory Promises. It is fundamental to the formation of a bilateral contract that if one party is not bound, neither party is bound. A promise by its literal terms may impose no obligation upon the promisor. Thus, a promise to purchase such quantity of goods as the promisor may "desire" or "want" or "wish to buy" imposes no obligation as it is indefinite and uncertain. The promisor may wish or desire to buy none of the goods, and in buying none would exactly fulfill his promise. For this reason an offer containing such a promise, although accepted by the offeree, does not create a contract because the promise is illusory.

Output and Requirement Contracts. An agreement to sell the entire production of a particular plant, factory, or mine, is called an output contract. It affords the seller an assured market for his goods. An agreement to purchase all materials of a particular kind for a particular use is called a requirements contract. It assures a buyer of a ready source of inventory or supplies. These contracts when made may or may not be accompanied by an estimate of the quantity to be sold or to be purchased.

Assume that A promises to supply B who promises to buy from A at an agreed price per ton all of the coal which may be required to operate B's factory for one year. These promises are not illusory. The amount of coal which B has agreed to buy is not subject to his whim or caprice. His promise is not to buy such coal as he may desire or wish to buy, but to buy such coal as is needed for a given purpose, namely, the operation of his factory. The contract is valid although B may decide not to operate the factory in which event he would need no coal and would not be required to take or pay for any. B's promise involves at least two alternatives, each of which is a detriment to him. The alternative of not operating the factory whereby he requires no coal involves a legal detriment to B, as he is free to operate or not operate it. The alternative of operating and buying all coal needed from A is also a legal detriment. The possibility that B may change the type of fuel to oil or gas, or even convert his factory to electricity, does not change the result as each of these alternatives would also involve a legal detriment to him.

The Code imposes a good faith limitation upon the quantity to be sold or purchased under an output or requirements contract, as provided in Section 2–306(1):

> (1) A term which measures the quantity by the output of the seller or the requirements of the buyer means such actual output or requirements as may occur in good faith, except that no quantity unreasonably disproportionate to any stated estimate or in the absence of a stated estimate to any normal or otherwise comparable prior output or requirements may be tendered or demanded.

Exclusive Dealing Contracts. Where a manufacturer of goods grants an exclusive franchise or license to a distributor to sell his products in a designated territory, unless otherwise agreed, an implied obligation is imposed on the manufacturer to use his best efforts to supply the goods and on the distributor to use his best efforts to promote their sale. As Justice Cordozo stated in Wood v. Lucy, Lady Duff-Gordon, page 100, the exclusive privilege is "instinct with an obligation." The Code provides, Section 2–306(2):

> (2) A lawful agreement by either the seller or the buyer for exclusive dealing in the kind of goods concerned imposes unless otherwise agreed an obligation by the seller to use best efforts to supply the goods and by the buyer to use best efforts to promote their sale.

Settlement of a Liquidated Undisputed Debt. A liquidated debt is an obligation to pay a sum certain in money, or to pay an amount which by computation can be reduced to a sum certain in money. If the debtor has made an express promise to pay a specific sum of money, i. e. $100, or has signed a promissory note, the debt is liquidated. If he has agreed to pay $3 per bushel for apples delivered, and 50 bushels of apples have been delivered, the debt is liquidated in the amount of $150. An unliquidated debt also involves a definite obligation to pay, but the amount of money to be paid has not been agreed upon by the parties. Implied contracts frequently create obligations to pay unliquidated amounts. Where a person has requested professional services from a doctor or a dentist and no agreement was made with respect to the amount of the fee to be charged, the doctor or dentist is entitled to receive from his patient a reasonable fee for the services which he has rendered. As no definite amount of compensation has been agreed upon, the debt is unliquidated. The legal obligation of the patient is to pay the reasonable worth of the services according to the standards of reasonableness at the time and place that they were performed. When the doctor or dentist sends the patient a bill for his services, the amount stated in the bill is his estimate of the reasonable value of the services, but the debt does not in this manner become liquidated until and unless the patient agrees to pay the amount of the bill.

Payment or Security Differing from the Debtor's Legal Obligation. If a debtor pays any sum of money to his creditor before it is due he incurs a legal detriment. Thus, if, before maturity of the debt, the creditor accepts from the debtor a lesser sum offered in full satisfaction, a contract results which discharges the entire debt. Similarly, if the debt is unsecured, and the creditor agrees to accept in full payment a lesser sum secured by a chattel mortgage or some type of collateral as security, the giving of such security is something which the debtor is not legally bound to do and, therefore, amounts to a legal detriment to the debtor promisee and sufficient consideration for the creditor's promise.

Settlement of a Disputed Debt. If the claim is unliquidated, or the debtor honestly disputes the amount that is owing and tenders in full settlement an amount less than that claimed by the creditor, acceptance of the lesser amount by the creditor discharges the debt. This is usually accomplished by the debtor sending to the creditor a check for the lesser amount marked "payment in full." The creditor may accept the check only upon the terms upon which it is offered. By cashing it, he accepts the offer of the debtor. By holding the check beyond a reasonable time, without rejecting the offer, the creditor is deemed to have accepted it, because the debtor sustains a detriment in being obligated to keep in his account at the bank at all times an amount sufficient to pay the check upon presentation.

In case the debtor admits that he owes a part of an unliquidated claim or disputed debt and pays in full satisfaction only the part which he admittedly owes, some courts have held that the entire claim or debt is not discharged by the creditor's acceptance of such lesser amount. The reason is that payment of a sum admittedly due is no more legal detriment than doing what one is obligated to do. The majority of courts, however, consider the unliquidated or disputed claim as a whole, and hold that acceptance by the creditor in this type of case would discharge the entire claim or debt.

In order for the giving up of a disputed claim to constitute legally sufficient consideration, the dispute, whether with respect to the existence or the amount of the asserted debt, must have been honest and not frivolous. Where the dispute is based upon contentions which are non-meritorious or not made in good faith, the giving up of such contentions by the debtor is no legal detriment to him. The dispute must have been a reasonable one and made in good faith. The reasonableness of a certain contention or dispute is not measured by the level of intelligence or legal competence of the average lawyer, but by the standard of intelligence and information possessed by the average reasonable layman, a person who has no special knowledge of the rules of law.

The problem of discharging a liquidated and undisputed debt by payment of a lesser sum in full settlement, and of the enforcement of a new promise to pay additional consideration for performance due under a pre-existing contract, may be handled under the Code by means of a written waiver or renunciation. The creditor or the promisor of the new promise merely signs and delivers to the debtor or promisee a written waiver or renunciation of his claim or rights under the prior contract. No consideration is necessary to make this binding. The Code provides, Section 1–107:

> Any claim or right arising out of an alleged breach can be discharged in whole or in part without consideration by a written waiver or renunciation signed and delivered by the aggrieved party.

It may be noted that while consideration is necessary in order to create a valid obligation, it is not necessary under the Code in order to discharge one in whole or in part.

Moral Obligation as Consideration. A promise made in order to satisfy or make good a pre-existing moral obligation is generally unenforceable for lack of consideration. Instances involving such moral obligation are promises to pay for board and lodging previously furnished to a needy relative of the promisor, promises to pay debts contracted by the father or by a husband of the promisor, and promises of an employer to pay a completely disabled former employee a sum of money in addition to the amount of an award made under a Workmen's Compensation statute. In many cases the moral obligation may be strong by reason of the particular facts and circumstances, yet no liability attaches to the promise solely by reason thereof. A few States have statutes which provide that a moral or natural obligation constitutes a sufficient consideration, but these are definitely in the minority. Where the promisor has received a direct benefit by reason of some prior act or conduct of the promisee the courts are inclined to treat a subsequent promise to pay therefor as binding.

Promises to pay a debt barred by the Statute of Limitations or to pay a debt discharged in bankruptcy, which are hereinafter discussed, are enforceable without consideration and may be regarded as based upon a moral obligation. However, the moral obligation in these instances has as its antecedent a definite legal obligation. The moral obligation does not apply with respect to a new promise to pay a debt that has been voluntarily released by the creditor or settled and discharged by an accord and satisfaction. In such case in order to be binding, the new promise to pay a debt which has been voluntarily released or settled must be supported by a fresh consideration.

New Promise to Pay a Debt Barred by the Statute of Limitations. Every State has in effect statutes which provide that suits to enforce debts must be commenced within a prescribed period of time after the debts become due. Suits not commenced within the time limited may be dismissed. The periods of time vary among the States, and also vary with the nature of the claim sought to be enforced. In some states the period is five years on oral contracts, and ten years on written contracts. These statutes are known as Statutes of Limitations.

A new promise by the debtor to pay the debt extends the period of limitation for the statutory period. This new promise requires no consideration. In most States the new promise must be in writing. An unqualified acknowledgment of the debt by making part payment implies a promise to pay, and thereby extends the statutory period. The new promise to pay or acknowledgment is sufficient whether made before or after the statute has run.

The question sometimes arises whether the new promise is itself the binding obligation or whether it merely revives the old debt. The better view would seem to be that the new promise constitutes a new obligation inasmuch as the obligation thus created is measured by the terms of the new promise. If A's indebtedness to B in the amount of $500 is barred by the Statute of Limitations, and A makes a new promise to B to pay only $250, B can recover from A only the sum of $250. Furthermore, if B promises to pay $250 at the rate of $10 per month, B can only recover the amount which has accrued at this monthly rate. If A's new promise is conditional, such as a promise to pay $250 when he is able to do so, B's right to recover $250 is subject to proof of A's ability to pay this sum of money. Thus the scope and extent and conditions imposed by the new promise measure the creditor's rights thereon.

New Promise to Pay a Debt Discharged in Bankruptcy. The Federal Bankruptcy Act contains no provision relating to the effect of a new promise to pay a debt which has been discharged in bankruptcy. However, the courts uniformly hold that such a promise is binding without consideration. The promise must be clear and definite, although it may be conditional. A mere expression of good intentions by the discharged bankrupt is not sufficient. A new promise will not be implied merely from a part payment or from a mere acknowledgment of liability.

By statute in a few States the new promise of the bankrupt must be in writing in order to bind him. An oral promise is sufficient in the absence of such a statute. A new promise prior to the bankruptcy proceedings is ineffectual, as such promise would itself be subject to the discharge obtained in the proceedings, as well as contrary to public policy.

The new promise by the discharged bankrupt is the measure of his liability, as in the case of a new promise to pay a debt barred by the statute of limitations.

Charitable Subscription Promises. Numerous churches, memorials, college buildings, stadia, hospitals, and other structures used for religious, educational and charitable purposes have been built with the assistance of contributions made through fulfillment of pledges or promises to contribute to the particular worthwhile cause. These pledges are usually in the form of subscriptions, and the promisor agrees in writing to subscribe or pay the specific amount set forth above his signature. The intent of the subscriber is generally donative. He regards himself as making a gift for a charitable purpose. Gift promises are not enforceable, yet the courts universally enforce charitable subscription promises. Various reasons and theories have been advanced in support of holding liable a subscriber who refuses to pay. The most generally accepted and valid reason is that the subscription has induced a change of position by the promisee, the church, school, or charitable organization, in reliance on the promise. As a result of the total pledges and

the amount pledged, the promisee has employed architects, made plans, entered into building contracts, and in other ways changed its position. This is held either to be the equivalent of consideration, or a substitute for consideration. Some courts have held that the acceptance of the subscription by the trustees of the charity implies a promise to carry on to completion the proposed charitable undertaking. The subscriber, however, requested no such promise. Other courts have held that the promise of each subscriber is given in exchange for the promises of the other subscribers and that these promises mutually support one another. The difficulty with this theory is that it does not accord with the facts. The subscribers do not in fact bargain with each other. The requirement of consideration has been stretched and pulled in many ways by the courts which, impelled by the desirability of enforcing this type of promise, have found various ways of holding charitable subscriptions binding without expressly abrogating the doctrine of consideration.

Promissory Estoppel. A promise may be binding even though the promisor may have received nothing by way of an agreed upon exchange for it where made under circumstances which should lead the promisor reasonably to expect that the promisee will be induced thereby to take definite and substantial action in reliance thereon and the promisee does take such action. The basis of the promisor's liability is promissory estoppel, and consideration for the promise is not required. The promisor is estopped from pleading a lack of consideration for his promise where it has induced the promisee to make a substantial change of position in reliance thereon.

The rationale of promissory estoppel is similar to that underlying the principle of a true waiver. The terms "waive" and "waiver" are frequently misused. A person waives a condition upon which his liability depends when he tells a person who has the power and capacity to bring about the happening of the condition that it will be unnecessary to do so. A party waives the defense of the statute of limitations when he induces his creditor to forbear bringing an action by a promise of payment or a promise not to plead the statute as a defense. In these cases the condition or defense is waived because of the justifiable reliance upon the statement which induced a forbearance to act or a change of position.

Section 90 of the Restatement of the Law of Contracts provides:

> A promise which the promisor should reasonably expect to induce action or forbearance of a definite and substantial character on the part of the promisee and which does induce such action or forbearance is binding if injustice can be avoided only by enforcement of the promise.

Promissory estoppel does not mean that every gratuitous promise is binding simply because it is followed by a change of position on the part of the promisee. The promisor must have known or had reason to believe that a definite and substantial change of position by the promisee was likely to occur as a result of the promise. The liability is created by the change of position in justifiable reliance on the promise.

Promises under the Code which Require No Consideration. The U.C.C. expressly provides that no consideration is required in certain instances, as follows:

(1) Any claim or right arising out of an alleged breach of contract can be discharged in whole or in part without consideration by a written waiver or renunciation signed and delivered by the aggrieved party. Section 1–107.

(2) A written offer signed by a merchant offeror to buy or sell goods is not revocable for lack of consideration, during the time stated that it is open, not to exceed three months, or if no time is stated, for a reasonable time. Section 2–205.

(3) An agreement modifying a contract for the sale of goods needs no consideration to be binding. Section 2–209(1).

(4) The holder of a promissory note or draft or check may discharge any party to the instrument without consideration by (1) intentional cancellation of the instrument; (2) striking out the signature of the party on the instrument; (3) renunciation of rights on the instrument in a writing signed and delivered; or (4) surrender of the instrument to the party to be discharged. Section 3–605.

(5) No consideration is necessary to establish a letter of credit or to enlarge or otherwise modify its terms. Section 5–105.

Contracts under Seal. In the early days of the common law, before the development of the law of contracts, many important persons of means and substance could neither read nor write. In the middle ages, reading and writing was an art confined mostly to the monasteries and to men of learning in universities. When a person desired to bind himself by bond, or deed, or solemn promise, he executed his promise under seal. He did not have to sign the document. His delivery of a document to which he had affixed his seal was sufficient. No consideration for his promise was necessary. It is still the law today, except where changed by statute, that a promise under seal is binding without consideration.

A seal was originally an impression on a piece of wax, wafer, or other substance, affixed to the paper or other material on which was written the promise, release, conveyance, or covenant. Later, by statutes, the requirements of a seal were relaxed so that any impression or mark on a writing intended as a seal is sufficient. The written or printed word "Seal", or the initials "L.S." (Locus Sigilli, place of the seal) following the signature on a document, is the most common form of seal used today.

A contract under seal is known as a specialty, a bond, or a deed. It is also called a formal contract. Contracts made orally or in writing but not under seal are known as informal contracts. A contract under seal is a more solemn obligation, and in certain States the Statute of Limitations provides a longer period of time for such contracts than for those not under seal.

In many States the distinction between contracts under seal and written unsealed contracts is abolished by statute. Some statutes provide that a promise under seal shall be presumed to have been made for sufficient consideration, which presumption is rebuttable by evidence to the contrary. Other statutes do not even create such a presumption, and consideration for a promise under seal must be proved as in the case of any informal contract.

The Code, Section 2–203, in line with the modern viewpoint that seals are obsolete, provides that with respect to offers or contracts for the sale of goods seals are inoperative:

> The affixing of a seal to a writing evidencing a contract for sale or an offer to buy or sell goods does not constitute the writing a sealed instrument and the law with respect to sealed instruments does not apply to such a contract or offer.

CASES

DEVECMON v. SHAW & DEVRIES

(1888) 69 Md. 199, 14 A. 464, 9 Am.St.Rep. 422.

[Plaintiff brings action against the executors of the will of his deceased uncle to recover money paid by the plaintiff to defray the expenses of a trip to Europe which the plaintiff took at the instance and request of his uncle. From a judgment for defendant executors, plaintiff appeals.]

BRYAN, J. John Semmes Devecmon brought suit against the executors of John S. Combs, deceased. The evidence consisted of * * * testimony that the plaintiff was a nephew of the deceased, and lived for several years in his family, and was in his service as clerk for several years. The plaintiff then made an offer of testimony, which is thus stated in the bill of exceptions: "That the plaintiff took a trip to Europe in 1878, and that said trip was taken by said plaintiff, and the money spent on said trip was spent by the said plaintiff at the instance and request of said Combs, and upon a promise from him that he would reimburse and repay to the plaintiff all money expended by him in said trip; and that the trip was so taken and the money so expended by the said plaintiff, but that the said trip had no connection with the business of said Combs; and that said Combs spoke to the witness of his conduct in being thus willing to pay his nephew's expenses as liberal and generous on his part." On objection, the Court refused to permit the evidence to be given, and the plaintiff excepted.

It might very well be, and probably was the case, that the plaintiff would not have taken a trip to Europe at his own expense. But whether this be so or not, the testimony would have tended to show that the plaintiff incurred expense at the instance and request of the deceased, and upon an express promise by him that he would repay the money spent. It was a burden incurred at the request of the other party, and was certainly a sufficient consideration for a promise to pay. Great injury might be done by inducing persons to make expenditures beyond their means, on express promise of repayment, if the law were otherwise. It is an entirely different case from a promise to make another a present; or render him a gratuitous service. It is nothing to the purpose, that the plaintiff was benefited by the expenditure of his own money. He was induced by this promise to spend it in this way, instead of some other mode. If it is not fulfilled, the expenditure will have been procured by a false pretense.

As the plaintiff, on the theory of this evidence, had fulfilled his part of the contract, and nothing remained to be done but the payment of the money by the defendant, there could be a recovery in indebitatus assumpsit; and it was not necessary to declare on the special contract. * * *

Judgment reversed, and new trial ordered.

INTERNATIONAL SHOE CO. v. HERNDON

(1926) 135 S.C. 138, 133 S.E. 202, 45 A.L.R. 1192.

[Plaintiff brought an action to recover $467.59 for merchandise sold and delivered to defendant. Defendant did not contest the plaintiff's claim but set up a counterclaim in the amount of $2,500 for breach by plaintiff of an alleged exclusive agency contract. Plaintiff's demurrer to the counterclaim was overruled by the trial court, and plaintiff appeals.]

COTHRAN, J. * * * The defendant in his answer admitted the sale and delivery of the goods as alleged, and set up a counterclaim in substance as follows: That in March, 1915, he bought a bill of shoes from the plaintiff, in consideration of which the plaintiff "entered into a parol agreement with the defendant, C. H. Herndon, trading as Herndon Clothing Store, wherein it contracted and agreed that the defendant should have the exclusive sale of plaintiff's shoes at Walterboro, and should be the only person, firm, or corporation to handle said line of shoes at said place, said parol agreement further providing that the defendant should have the exclusive agency as long as he would handle said

shoes and as long as he wished to handle same"; that acting upon said agreement the defendant bought bills of goods from the plaintiff from year to year, up to June, 1923, and paid for them, aggregating more than $15,000, and expended in advertising the plaintiff's shoes not less than $1,500; that in May, 1923, the plaintiff violated said agreement by selling its shoes to two or more merchants in Walterboro, all to his damage in loss of profits and injury to his reputation as a merchant, in the sum of $2,500.

The plaintiff interposed a demurrer to the counterclaim upon the general ground, specifying: "That under the alleged contract there was no mutuality of interest (obligation?), and no allegation that the defendant was under any obligation to buy goods from the plaintiff under the terms of the contract, and, therefore (it) was without consideration."

The matter came on to be heard by his Honor, Judge Johnson, who filed a decree, dated December 5, 1924, in which he held, "I am satisfied that the agreement set up in the counterclaim is supported by a consideration, and that the contract as alleged does not lack mutuality," and overruled the demurrer. The plaintiff has appealed, raising the same question as in the demurrer.

The contract set up in the counterclaim is not declared upon as a unilateral contract, but as a bilateral one—a contract by which the defendant agreed to buy a certain bill of goods, and in consideration thereof the plaintiff agreed to give him the exclusive sale of the shoes at Walterboro, S. C.

It is very true that mutuality of obligation is not an essential element in unilateral contracts, such as option contracts, contracts evidenced by a subscription paper, contract of offers of rewards or a guaranty, or in many other instances readily put in ordinary business affairs. The nonrequirement of mutuality in such contracts, however, does not dispense with the necessity of a valuable consideration. But in bilateral contracts, where the consideration is sought to be sustained upon mutual promises, the contract consists of the several engagements of the parties; the engagement of one being the consideration for the engagement of the other, and the combined engagements constituting the contract. In order to accomplish this result, it is manifest that the promise or engagement of one of the parties, which is sought to be held as the consideration for the promise or engagement of the other, must be an absolute engagement of such party; for if it is not, the contract is lacking in mutuality, notwithstanding the absolute character of the engagement of the other party.

The rule is thus stated in Elliott on Contracts, Vol. 1, par. 231:

"A promise may constitute the consideration for another promise. But a promise is not a good consideration for a promise unless there is absolutely mutuality of the engagements, so that each party has the right to hold the other to a positive agreement. In case the promise of one of the parties imposes no legal duty upon the party making it, such promise furnishes no consideration for a promise."

Thus, in the case at bar, the defendant seeks to hold the plaintiff to the alleged contract of March, 1915, by which he engaged to buy a bill of shoes from the plaintiff, and the plaintiff engaged to give him the exclusive sale of its shoes at Walterboro. There is no question as to the absolute character of the defendant's engagement; but if the plaintiff's engagement was not an absolute enforceable one, it is clear that the contract, which must consist of an absolute enforceable engagement on each side, is lacking in mutuality, and, therefore, wanting in consideration. So the question of the validity of the alleged contract is to be resolved by the further question of the validity of the

plaintiff's alleged engagement to give to the defendant the exclusive sale of its shoes.

It will be observed that this alleged engagement is not only indefinite as to time, quantity, price and terms, but it is accompanied by no corresponding engagement on the part of the defendant; he binds himself to nothing; he could, under it, order one or a thousand pairs of shoes, or none at all; at a price unknown, not agreed upon, and upon indefinite terms.

Under such circumstances, it cannot be considered as partaking of any of the elements of an absolute, binding, enforceable engagement, such as will constitute the consideration for defendant's engagement, the essential element of a valid contract. * * *

We think, therefore, that the alleged contract, for the breach of which the defendant asks damages, was lacking in consideration and mutuality, and that the plaintiff's demurrer should have been sustained.

The judgment of this Court is that the order of the Circuit Court overruling the plaintiff's demurrer to the defendant's counterclaim be reversed, and that the case be remanded to that Court with direction to enter an order sustaining the same, and of judgment in favor of plaintiff upon the amount sued upon admitted by the answer.

DEDEAUX v. YOUNG

(1965) 251 Miss. 604, 170 So.2d 561.

RODGERS, J. The issue in this case is twofold. First, it is the contention of appellee K. L. Young that appellant Curtis O. Dedeaux agreed to pay him a broker's fee of five percent on the sale of property from William B. Bosworth, Jr. to appellant. Appellant admits that he agreed to pay expenses that Young might have incurred because of the transaction but denied that he intended to pay a five percent commission on the sale price. This is an issue of fact, and we are of the opinion that there is ample evidence in the record to substantiate the finding of the chancellor on this issue. The finding of the chancellor on disputed issues of fact will not be disturbed on appeal unless it appears that his finding is manifestly wrong. [Citation.]

Second, it is the contention of appellant Dedeaux that, assuming he promised to pay appellee Young a small commission, the promise was not a contract because there was no consideration moving to Dedeaux, therefore such a promise, if made, was not binding. The testimony shows, however, that at the time appellant made the promise to pay the commission, he did so to prevent appellee from filing a suit, which could have prevented the culmination of the sale of the property. The chancellor held, as a matter of law, that Young's agreement not to file suit was sufficient consideration moving from Young to Dedeaux to make the contract binding. A request to forbear to exercise a legal right has been generally accepted as sufficient consideration to support a contract, by this and other Supreme Courts, for many years. [Citations.]

We are of the opinion that the chancellor was correct in his ruling on both questions of law and fact, and that this case should be, and is, affirmed.

Affirmed.

———

CHESTER v. STATE OF FLORIDA

(1965 Fla.) 176 So.2d 104.

WIGGINTON, J. Appellant has appealed a final decree rendered by the Circuit Court of Leon County, In Chancery, which denied him any share of the reward offered by the State of Florida for information leading to the arrest and conviction of the party or parties responsible for the disappearance of Judge C. E. Chillingworth. It is contended that the chancellor misconceived the legal effect of the evidence and applied thereto an incorrect principle of law in finding and holding that appellant was not entitled to all or a portion of the reward.

This interpleader action was instituted by the State of Florida, through its proper officials, for the purpose of seeking an adjudication as to the person or persons entitled to the above-mentioned reward of $100,000.00. All persons, including appellant, who were known to have or assert any claim to the reward, or any portion thereof, were joined as defendants in the action. The amount of reward was deposited in the court registry and the State of Florida was discharged from any further obligation or responsibility with respect to the subject matter of the cause. The various claimants filed their claims asserting entitlement to all or such part of the reward fund as the court may deem them entitled. Upon consideration of the evidence adduced during the trial the chancellor entered his decree finding that three of the claimants were entitled to receive the entire reward in the proportions fixed in the decree. It was further decreed that appellant Chester was not entitled to any part of the reward, and his claim was therefore disapproved and rejected.

On June 15, 1955, Honorable C. E. Chillingworth, a distinguished jurist of the State of Florida, together with his wife, mysteriously disappeared from their home in Palm Beach County. An extensive investigation surrounding their disappearance was instituted and carried forward by the law enforcement officers of Palm Beach County and the State of Florida. As a result of this investigation it became evident that Judge Chillingworth and his wife had been murdered, and that three men were primarily responsible for the crime, to wit: Joseph A. Peel, Jr., Floyd A. Holzapfel, and George David (Bobby) Lincoln. The evidence reveals that despite the complete information obtained by the law enforcement officials regarding the facts and circumstances surrounding the murder event, and the complicity of the three above-named men in the perpetration of the crime, the State nevertheless continued its investigation without charging or arresting any of the suspects awaiting the time when further evidence might be developed which would assure a successful prosecution and conviction.

* * *

It was while the investigation of this case was in progress that appellant Chester, a duly licensed and practicing attorney of West Palm Beach, was employed to represent the interest of the above-mentioned Lincoln who was then incarcerated in the Federal Correctional Institution at Tallahassee. Appellant visited Lincoln at the latter's request in reference to the Chillingworths' disappearance and murder. On this occasion Lincoln made a full and complete disclosure to appellant of the facts and circumstances surrounding the murder of Judge and Mrs. Chillingworth, and of his participation in that crime. Lincoln further disclosed to appellant Holzapfel's and Peel's participation in the murder and thereupon requested appellant to take this information and do with it what he could for Lincoln's best interest. Appellant agreed to the request made of him by his client, and stated that he would contact the state attorney at West Palm Beach regarding the matter. It was agreed at that conference that if it were not inconsistent with his duty as a lawyer, appellant would claim the reward offered by the State in connection with the Chillingworth murder. Following the conference appellant promptly conferred with the state attorney on two or more occasions on behalf of his client Lincoln with the result that an agreement was reached whereby Lincoln would turn State's evidence and testify fully, fairly and truthfully on behalf of the State in the prosecution of Holzapfel and Peel for the murder of Judge and Mrs. Chillingworth, in exchange for immuni-

ty from prosecution for either of said crimes and also for the crime of having murdered a third person. Lincoln was subsequently transferred to Palm Beach County where he made a full and complete written disclosure of the facts surrounding the crime. Lincoln's testimony as an eyewitness was the final link of evidence needed by the State to assure the successful prosecution and conviction of Peel and Holzapfel for the Chillingworth murders. After the latter two suspects were arrested and Holzapfel learned of Lincoln's confession, Holzapfel likewise confessed his complicity in the crime and pleaded guilty to the indictment brought against him charging murder in the first degree. It was upon the testimony of both Lincoln and Holzapfel that Peel was subsequently tried and convicted of murder in the first degree, with the recommendation of mercy.

Based upon the foregoing evidence the trial court reached the following finding and conclusions, to wit:

"It seems clear that the information furnished by claimant Chester, as reflected in Lincoln's confession and turning of state's evidence, was not furnished in response to the reward offer but furnished in response to his sacred and solemn duty to his client, Bobby Lincoln. Irrespective of the reward, it was the duty of claimant to 'use every endeavor in his power' in behalf of his client. Apparently, the information furnished by Chester was furnished in an effort to save Lincoln from evident doom. As a matter of law, the reward in nowise could have influenced, changed or altered the effort, duty or responsibility of Chester to his client and was, therefore, no inducement and no consideration for the information furnished by him. Moreover, the state has already paid in full and to the utmost extent for such information by granting Lincoln immunity against prosecution in three separate and distinct murder cases.

"It follows, therefore, that Chester did nothing beyond the scope of his legal duty in the defense of his client Lincoln and is, therefore, not entitled to participate in the reward offered by the state for which he has made claim in this proceeding."

* * *

It is clear from this record that the only knowledge of the Chillingworth crime possessed by appellant was divulged to the law enforcement officers in the discharge of his duty to his client, Lincoln, which duty he was ethically bound to discharge regardless of whether a reward had been offered by the State. It is equally clear that the availability of the reward provided by the statute had no effect on spurring the individual initiative and diligence of appellant in the premises. He owed his client all of the initiative and diligence which he possessed in rendering the legal services he was obligated to perform irrespective of whether the possibility existed for him to share in the reward. We are of the view that the conclusion reached by the chancellor was the correct one, and the decree should not be disturbed.

For the reasons above stated the decree appealed is affirmed.

OTIS F. WOOD v. LUCY, LADY DUFF-GORDON

(1917) 222 N.Y. 88, 118 N.E. 214.

CARDOZO, J. The defendant styles herself "a creator of fashions." Her favor helps a sale. Manufacturers of dresses, millinery and like articles are glad to pay for a certificate of her approval. The things which she designs, fabrics, parasols and what not, have a new value in the public mind when issued in her name. She employed the plaintiff to help her turn this vogue into money. He was to have the exclusive right, subject always to her approval, to place her indorsements on the designs of others. He was also to have the exclusive right to place her own designs on sale, or to license others to market them. In return, she was to have one-half of "all profits and revenues" derived from any contracts he might make. The exclusive right was to last at least one year from April 1, 1915, and thereafter from year to year unless terminated by notice of ninety days. The plaintiff says that he kept the contract on his part, and that the defendant broke it. She placed her indorsement on fabrics, dresses and millinery without his knowledge, and withheld the profits. He sues her for the damages, and the case comes here on demurrer.

The agreement of employment is signed by both parties. It has a wealth of recitals. The defendant insists, however, that it lacks the elements of a contract. She says that the plaintiff does not bind himself to anything. It is true that he does not promise in so many words that he will use reasonable efforts to place the defendant's indorsements and market her designs. We think, however, that such a promise is fairly to be implied. The law has outgrown its primitive stage of formalism when the precise word was the sovereign talisman, and every slip was fatal. It takes a broader view to-day. A promise may be lacking, and yet the whole writing may be "instinct with an obligation," imperfectly expressed (Scott, J., in McCall Co. v. Wright, 133 App.Div. 62, 117 N.Y.S. 775. Moran v. Standard Oil Co., 211 N.Y. 187, 198, 105 N.E. 217). If that is so, there is a contract.

The implication of a promise here finds support in many circumstances. The defendant gave an *exclusive* privilege. She was to have no right for at least a year to place her own indorsements or market her own designs except through the agency of the plaintiff. The acceptance of the exclusive agency was an assumption of its duties. [Citations.]

We are not to suppose that one party was to be placed at the mercy of the other. [Citations.] Many other terms of the agreement point the same way. We are told at the outset by way of recital that "the said Otis F. Wood possesses a business organization adapted to the placing of such indorsements as the said Lucy, Lady Duff-Gordon has approved." The implication is that the plaintiff's business organization will be used for the purpose for which it is adapted. But the terms of the defendant's compensation are even more significant. Her sole compensation for the grant of an exclusive agency is to be one-half of all the profits resulting from the plaintiff's efforts. Unless he gave his efforts, she could never get anything. Without an implied promise, the transaction cannot have such business "efficacy as both parties must have intended that at all events it should have" (Bowen, L. J., in The Moorcock, 14 P.D. 64, 68). But the contract does not stop there. The plaintiff goes on to promise that he will account monthly for all moneys received by him, and that he will take out all such patents and copyrights and trademarks as may in his judgment be necessary to protect the rights and articles affected by the agreement. It is true, of course, as the Appellate Division has said, that if he was under no duty to try to market designs or to place certificates of indorsement, his promise to account for profits or take out copyrights would be valueless. But in determining the intention of the parties, the promise *has* a value. It helps to enforce the conclusion that the plaintiff *had* some duties. His promise to pay the defendant one-half of the profits and revenues resulting from the exclusive agency and to render accounts monthly, was a promise to use reasonable efforts to bring profits and revenues into existence. For this conclusion, the authorities are ample. * * *

Judgment reversed.

JAFFRAY v. DAVIS

(1891) 124 N.Y. 164, 26 N.E. 351, 11 L.R.A. 710.

[Plaintiff Davis and others sued defendant Jaffray and others to recover the amount claimed to be due and unpaid on a certain debt. The defendants pleaded that the entire original debt was discharged by an agreement whereby the plaintiffs accepted in full satisfaction three promissory notes in a lesser amount executed by the defendants and secured by a chattel mortgage of certain personal property, all of which notes were paid. Judgment for plaintiffs was entered for the amount of the balance of the original indebtedness. Defendants appeal.]

POTTER, J. The facts found by the trial court in this case were agreed upon. They are simple and present a familiar question of law. The facts are that defendants were owing plaintiffs on the 8th day of December, 1886, for goods sold between that date and the May previous at an agreed price, the sum of $7,714.37, and that on the 27th of the same December, the defendants delivered to the plaintiffs their three promissory notes amounting in the aggregate to $3,462.24 secured by a chattel mortgage on the stock, fixtures and other property of defendants, located in East Saginaw, Michigan, which said notes and chattel mortgage were received by plaintiffs under an agreement to accept same in full satisfaction and discharge of said indebtedness. "That said notes have all been paid and said mortgage discharged of record."

The question of law arising from these facts and presented to this court for its determination is whether such agreement, with full performance, constitutes a bar to this action, which was brought after such performance to recover the balance of such indebtedness over the sum so secured and paid.

One of the elements embraced in the question presented upon this appeal is, viz., whether the payment of a sum less than the amount of a liquidated debt under an agreement to accept the same in satisfaction of such debt forms a bar to the recovery of the balance of the debt. This single question was presented to the English court in 1602, when it was resolved (if not decided) in Pinnel's case (5 Coke 117), "that payment of a lesser sum on the day in satisfaction of a greater, cannot be any satisfaction for the whole," and that this is so, although it was agreed that such payment should satisfy the whole. This simple question has since arisen in the English courts and in the courts of this country in almost numberless instances, and has received the same solution, notwithstanding the courts, while so ruling, have rarely failed, upon any recurrence of the question, to criticize and condemn its reasonableness, justice, fairness or honesty. * * *

The steadfast adhesion to this doctrine by the courts in spite of the current of condemnation by the individual judges of the court, and in the face of the demands and conveniences of a much greater business and more extensive mercantile dealings and operations, demonstrate the force of the doctrine of stare decisis. But the doctrine of stare decisis is further illustrated by the course of judicial decisions upon this subject, for while the courts still hold to the doctrine of the Pinnel [5 Coke 117] and Cumber v. Wane [1 Strange 426] cases, supra, they have seemed to seize with avidity upon any consideration to support the agreement to accept the lesser sum in satisfaction of the larger, or in other words to extract if possible from the circumstances of each case a consideration for the new agreement, and to substitute the new agreement in place of the old and thus to form a defense to the action brought upon the old agreement. It will serve the purpose of illustrating the adhesion of the court to settled law and at the same time enable us perhaps more satisfactorily to decide whether there was a good considera-

tion to support the agreement in this case, to refer to the consideration in a few of the numerous cases which the courts have held to be sufficient to support the new agreement.

Lord Blackburn said in his opinion in Foakes v. Beer L.R. (9 App.Cas.) 605, and while maintaining the doctrine "that a lesser sum cannot be a satisfaction of a greater sum," "but the gift of a horse, hawk or robe, etc. in satisfaction is good" quite regardless of the amount of the debt. And it was further said by him in the same opinion "that payment and acceptance of a parcel before the day of payment of a larger sum would be a good satisfaction in regard to the circumstance of time" "and so if I am bound in twenty pounds to pay you ten pounds at Westminster, and you request me to pay you five pounds at the day at York, and you will accept it in full satisfaction for the whole ten pounds, it is a good satisfaction." * * *

It was held in Bull v. Bull, 43 Conn. 455, "and although the claim is a money demand liquidated and not doubtful, and it cannot be satisfied with a smaller sum of money, yet if any other personal property is received in satisfaction, it will be good no matter what the value." * * *

It was held in LePage v. McCrea, 1 Wend., N.Y., 164, 19 Am.Dec. 469 and in Boyd v. Hitchcock, 20 Johns. 76, that "giving further security for part of a debt or other security, though for a less sum than the debt and acceptance of it in full of all demands, make a valid accord and satisfaction."

That "if a debtor gives his creditor a note indorsed by a third party for a less sum than the debt (no matter how much less), but in full satisfaction of the debt, and it is received as such, the transaction constitutes a good accord and satisfaction." [Citation.] And so it has been held "where by mode or time of part payment, different than that provided for in the contract, a new benefit is or may be conferred or a burden imposed, a new consideration arises out of the transaction and gives validity to the agreement of the creditor" [citation], and so if "payment of less than the whole debt, if made before it is due or at a different place from that stipulated, if received in full, is a good satisfaction." [Citations.] * * *

It has been held that a partial payment made to another, though at the creditor's instance and request, is a good discharge of the whole debt. [Citation.] "The reason of the rule is that the debtor in such case has done something more than he was originally bound to do or at least something different. It may be more or it may be less, as a matter of fact." * * *

It has been held that a payment in advance of the time if agreed to is full satisfaction for a larger claim not yet due. [Citation.]

These cases show in a striking manner the extreme ingenuity and assiduity which the courts have exercised to avoid the operation of the "rigid and rather unreasonable rule of the old law," as it is characterized in Johnston v. Brannan (5 Johns. 268–272), or as it is called in Kellogg v. Richards (14 Wend. 116), "technical and not very well supported by reason," or as may be more practically stated, a rule that "a bar of gold worth $100 will discharge a debt of $500, while 400 gold dollars in current coin will not." [Citations.] The general doctrine in Cumber v. Wane, and the reason of all the exceptions and distinctions which have been engraved on it, may perhaps be summed up as follows, viz.: "That a creditor cannot bind himself by a simple agreement to accept a smaller sum in lieu of an ascertained debt of larger amount, such an agreement being nudum pactum. But if there be any benefit or even any legal possibility of benefit to the creditor thrown in, that additional weight will turn the scale and

render the consideration sufficient to support the agreement." [Citations.]

In the case at bar the defendants gave their promissory notes upon time for one-half of the debt they owed plaintiff, and also gave plaintiff a chattel mortgage on the stock, fixtures and other personal property of the defendants under an agreement with plaintiff, to accept the same in full satisfaction and discharge of said indebtedness. Defendants paid the notes as they became due, and plaintiff then discharged the mortgage. Under the cases above cited, and upon principle, this new agreement was supported by a sufficient consideration to make it a valid agreement, and this agreement was by the parties substituted in place of the former. * * *

Judgment reversed.

GROVES v. SAWYER

(1964 Tex.Civ.App.) 384 S.W.2d 193.

GRISSOM, C. J. J. G. Groves sued N. C. Sawyer for $542.63, alleged to be the balance due for work and material furnished by Groves in constructing a motel for defendant. Sawyer answered that after Groves had completed his contract and presented Sawyer with said claim, which Sawyer disputed, Sawyer executed and delivered to Groves his check for $269.25, writing on the reverse side above the place for Groves' endorsement: "Payment in full for all labor and material and in full settlement for contract performed by me on the property known as Sands Motel * * *. The acceptance of this check acknowledges settlement in full"; that (1) the check was tendered to Groves in full settlement of his disputed claim and that Groves accepted and cashed the check in full satisfaction and discharge of his cause of action; (2) that Groves retained the check for nearly five months and then on October 28, 1963, returned it to

Sawyer, who sent it back to Groves on the day he received it, stating that it was being returned because Sawyer had tendered it in full payment of Groves' claim and Groves had accepted and retained it for nearly five months and, therefore, there was an accord and satisfaction; that plaintiff again, on November 1st returned the check to defendant, who promptly returned it to plaintiff with the statement that it was not being returned to him as part payment of Groves' claim but that it had theretofore been tendered to and accepted by plaintiff in full settlement by retaining the check for five months and, further, that thereafter Groves endorsed the check, scratched out the condition placed thereon by Sawyer, cashed it and kept the money, and there was an accord and satisfaction of plaintiff's claim.

Sawyer filed a motion for summary judgment supported by affidavits and correspondence between the parties showing the facts alleged by him. Plaintiff answered that there was a genuine issue as to a material fact; that Groves had delivered the uncashed check to his attorney with the instruction that he would not accept it as full payment of his claim and that the correspondence attached to defendant's motion showed that the check was cashed only as part payment, not in full settlement, of plaintiff's claim and that the question whether plaintiff accepted the check in satisfaction of plaintiff's entire claim was one of fact. The court sustained defendant's motion and entered judgment accordingly. Groves has appealed.

Appellant contends the court erred in holding there was an acceptance of the check by retention thereof for five months. This point will not be further noticed because, although it was alleged as one of appellee's defenses, Sawyer concedes that it merely raised a question of fact and therefore, of itself, is insufficient to support the summary judgment. But, appellee says summary judg-

ment was required because it is undisputed that Groves cashed the check tendered to him upon condition that he accept it as full payment of his claim.

Defendant's motion, the attached correspondence and affidavits disclose a bona fide dispute as to the correctness and liability of defendant for plaintiff's unliquidated claim, a tender of defendant's check for a lesser amount than claimed by plaintiff upon condition that it be accepted as full payment and that, knowing that condition, plaintiff accepted the check, cashed it and retained the proceeds. [Citations.] Groves thereby bound himself to accept the money he obtained by cashing appellee's check as full payment of his claim. It is immaterial that at the time he cashed the check he scratched out the condition placed thereon by appellee to the effect that it was full payment of all appellee owed appellant. Appellant could not avoid being bound by scratching out such condition when he cashed the check. Where " * * * there is a bona fide dispute as to the correctness of an account, and the debtor tenders his check to the creditor on condition that it be accepted in full payment, the creditor must either refuse to receive the check, or accept it burdened with its attached condition." [Citations.] * * *

We conclude that all prerequisites for application of the stated rule are apparent in the record. The court correctly held that appellant, by cashing appellee's check, knowing it was tendered upon condition that it be accepted as full payment of appellant's claim, is bound thereby and he cannot maintain this suit for the balance claimed to be due. [Citation.]

The judgment is affirmed.

HOWARD v. ZILCH

(1963) 343 Mass. 33, 190 N.E.2d 77.

SPIEGEL, J. This is an action of contract in which the plaintiff seeks to recover $3,-

833.47, with interest thereon. The case was submitted to the Superior Court under a statement of agreed facts. The case is here on the plaintiff's appeal from the order of a judge in the Superior Court that judgment be entered for the defendant.

We summarize the agreed facts. In April of 1956 the plaintiff became an accommodation cosigner on a note payable by the defendant Zilch to a bank. On or about December 3, 1956, the defendant was adjudicated a bankrupt in the United States District Court for the District of Massachusetts. The plaintiff, as cosigner of the note, "was called upon by the bank for payment of the balance then due." The plaintiff paid the bank $3,558.07, plus interest. In the bankruptcy proceedings the defendant listed the plaintiff as a creditor and listed the claim in his schedule of debts. The plaintiff filed a proof of claim in the bankruptcy proceedings totaling $3,598, which was duly allowed. No dividends were paid to any of the creditors and on June 12, 1958, the defendant was ordered discharged from all debts and claims in the bankruptcy proceedings. During those proceedings and after his discharge, he orally promised to reimburse the plaintiff for all payments which the plaintiff made on the defaulted note. The reimbursement was to be made "out of the proceeds of a motor vehicle tort action" in which the defendant was represented by a Mr. George W. Dana. The defendant orally directed and authorized Mr. Dana to determine the amounts paid by the plaintiff on the defaulted note and "to make arrangements" for reimbursement of that amount out of the defendant's funds in the possession of Mr. Dana. On or about December 30, 1958, Mr. Dana and the plaintiff met, whereupon Mr. Dana drew a check payable to the defendant and the plaintiff in the sum of $3,833.47. Mr. Dana then mailed the check to the defendant who held it until "the end of February or the first of March 1959," when he

went to the plaintiff. The defendant signed his name on the reverse side of the check and gave it to the plaintiff "without instructions." The plaintiff understood that he "might cash the same and retain the proceeds." This meeting occurred in the evening after business hours. About 1 A.M. the next morning, the defendant called Mr. Dana and requested him to stop payment on the check. At 9 A.M. of that same day, Mr. Dana ordered payment stopped on the check. He called the plaintiff advising him that he had done so at the defendant's request. "As a result, the plaintiff did not endorse the check or present it for payment." Mr. Dana represented the defendant during all of these transactions and at no time did he represent the plaintiff. No payment has been made on the check and the plaintiff still has it in his possession.

In order to recover on the underlying obligation, the plaintiff must show that the provisions of G.L. c. 259, § 3, have been met. This section states: "No promise for the payment of a debt, made by an insolvent debtor who has obtained his discharge from such debt under proceedings in bankruptcy or insolvency, shall be evidence of a new or continuing contract whereby to deprive the debtor of the benefit of relying upon such discharge in bar of the recovery of a judgment upon such debt, unless such promise is made by or contained in some writing signed by him, or by some person thereunto by him lawfully authorized." The promise must be "definite and unequivocal" and yet "[a]s the statute does not extend beyond the requirement of evidence of a continuing promise in some writing signed by the debtor, or by his authority, no precise form of statement is necessary and the intention and obligation of the debtor must be gathered from the phraseology he chooses to use." [Citation.] Assuming a sufficient promise in writing, no consideration other than the discharged debt is necessary to bind the debtor. [Citations.]

The issue before us is whether the check drawn by Mr. Dana, who is conceded to have been the authorized representative of the defendant, constitutes a promise "contained in some writing" within the ambit of G.L. c. 259, § 3. We believe it does. The Uniform Commercial Code, G.L. c. 106, § 3–413 (2), provides: "The drawer engages that upon dishonor of the draft and any necessary notice of dishonor or protest he will pay the amount of the draft to the holder or to any indorser who takes it up. The drawer may disclaim this liability by drawing without recourse." The check involved in this case is a "draft" drawn on a bank and payable on demand. G.L. c. 106, § 3–104(2) (b). The drawer, Mr. Dana, by his order to stop payment caused the check to be dishonored within the meaning of § 3–507 (1), which states: "An instrument is dishonored when * * * (b) presentment is excused and the instrument is not duly accepted or paid." * * * A check is a "contract in writing." [Citation.] Thus, the drawer, Mr. Dana, made a promise in writing to pay the amount on the face of the check. Since it is undisputed that the face amount was determined by the discharged debt and that Mr. Dana was a "person * * * lawfully authorized" by the defendant, the end result is that the defendant has made a promise "contained in some writing" sufficient to satisfy G.L. c. 259, § 3. This result comports with reason and commercial feasibility. An opposite conclusion would give less legal significance to a check than to a letter in which the discharged debtor made a promise to pay. [Citations.] In equating a check with such a letter for purposes of G.L. c. 259, § 3, the danger of a bankrupt thoughtlessly yielding the benefit of his discharge or of "vexatious" suits being brought against him is sufficiently inhibited. [Citation.] Indeed, we believe a debtor is far less likely to draw a check, or to authorize its drawing, than to make a promise to pay in a personal letter if he

lacks a real intention to pay and merely intends the recognition of a moral obligation.

In deciding that the plaintiff is entitled to recover from the defendant on the underlying obligation, evidenced by the check, we do not reach the question raised by the plaintiff, as to whether there could have been recovery on the instrument against the defendant on a contract of indorsement. See § 3–802(1) (b). Whether there could be recovery against the drawer, who is not a party defendant in this action, is not before us. Either theory would raise issues under § 3–116(b) and other sections, which we need not here decide. The order that judgment be entered for the defendant is reversed and judgment is to be entered for the plaintiff.

So ordered.

IN RE ESTATE OF LOUIS LIPSKY, DECEASED

(1965) 45 Misc.2d 320, 256 N.Y.S.2d 429.

Di Falco, Surrogate. The facts are not in dispute. On or about June 30, 1959 the decedent during a fund raising campaign conducted by the respondent charity made an oral pledge to contribute $500 to it. On or about November 29, 1959 he paid $250 on account of this pledge. On or about September 14, 1960 the decedent requested that the unpaid balance of his 1959 pledge be considered as his pledge towards the 1960 United Jewish Appeal campaign and on June 6, 1961 he further pledged the sum of $250 to the respondent charity. By a letter dated June 28, 1961 signed by its treasurer, the United Jewish Appeal of Greater New York acknowledged receipt of the pledge and expressed its gratitude to the decedent for his support of its charitable aims. The decedent died on May 27, 1963 without making any further payments on account of his pledges, leaving a balance of $500 unpaid with respect thereto. The statute of frauds has not been pleaded as a defense and the only issue presented for determination is whether the oral pledges concededly made by the decedent are binding upon his estate or must fail for want of consideration.

The United Jewish Appeal of Greater New York is a New York membership corporation organized and operated exclusively for charitable purposes. Its objective generally is to raise funds for the relief, rehabilitation and resettlement of Jews in need or in danger in various parts of the world. The funds raised by the respondent are distributed to various charitable organizations engaged in relief, rehabilitation and settlement work and by agreement these beneficiary agencies designate the respondent as their sole fund raising agency and refrain from engaging in any fund raising activities.

It is alleged and undisputed that the respondent charity could not function or carry out its charitable works without reliance upon the pledges and the contributions received as the result of such pledges. During the years 1959, 1960 and 1961 the United Jewish Appeal of Greater New York, in order to carry out its charitable functions, borrowed the aggregate sum of $60,000,000 from seven different banks in anticipation of and in advance of collection of the contributions pledged to it. Its contract with the banks required it to furnish on the fifteenth day of each month a certificate setting forth the aggregate amount of pledges outstanding as of the end of the preceding month which it had received from its fund raising campaigns during the two years next preceding. There can be little doubt that great reliance is placed upon the subscription pledges by both the banks and the United Jewish Appeal in preparing its budgets and estimating the funds that will be available to it and the beneficiary agencies during the year ahead.

A review of the authorities would indicate that the trend of judicial decision during the last century has been towards the en-

forcement of charitable pledges almost as a matter of public policy [citations]. In discussing the trend and the gradual expansion of the strictures of the "moulds of consideration" as applied to charitable subscriptions, Judge Cardozo stated: "Very likely, conceptions of public policy have shaped, more or less subconsciously, the rulings thus made. Judges have been affected by the thought that 'defenses of that character' are 'breaches of faith towards the public, and especially towards those engaged in the same enterprise, and an unwarrantable disappointment of the reasonable expectations of those interested.' * * *." [Citation.]

In an effort to free charitable pledges or subscriptions from the traditional requirement that an enforceable promise must be supported by consideration our courts have resorted to various theories. In some instances the decisions are predicated upon the existence and consummation of either a bilateral or uni-lateral contract [citations], and in others the subscriptions have been upheld by application of the equitable principle of estoppel often referred to as promissory estoppel [citations]. As the Court of Appeals so clearly stated in Metropolitan Life Ins. Co. v. Childs Co., 230 N.Y. 285, at pp. 292, 293, 130 N.E. 295, at p. 298, 14 A.L.R. 658: "An estoppel rests upon the word or deed of one party upon which another rightfully relies, and, so relying, changes his position to his injury. When this occurs it would be inequitable to permit the first to enforce what would have been his rights under other circumstances".

In many of the cited cases it is difficult to ascertain the precise theory relied upon to sustain the charitable subscriptions or pledges but the end result has invariably been the same. Sound public policy would appear to dictate these results and this court is in agreement with the efforts made to sustain charitable pledges by our courts. The philanthropic work carried on by organized charities, made possible through voluntary subscriptions, is a distinguishing and distinguished feature of our free society. It is a demonstration of the human sympathy, mercy, consideration and goodwill borne by those more fortunately endowed towards their less fortunate fellowmen. The agreed facts submitted in the case at bar establish that the respondent charity entered into contracts and incurred liability in reliance upon the pledge made by this decedent and others.

Under the authorities hereinabove cited the court finds, therefore, that the charitable pledges made by the decedent are binding upon his estate. Submit decree on notice.

PROBLEMS

1. Jones had a $10,000 life insurance policy in which his wife, Agnes, was the named beneficiary. The policy provided that if the named beneficiary predeceased the insured, the proceeds would be paid to his estate. Subsequently, Agnes died and later Jones married Jane. Jane later induced Jones, while on his death-bed, to sign a document naming her as the beneficiary of the policy.

A week after Jones's death, Jones's children by his first wife, Agnes, advised Jane that they planned to contest the validity of the change of beneficiary. They contended that, because of his illness, Jones lacked the necessary mental capacity to effect the change of beneficiary. Jane then promised to pay $2,000 to the children from the proceeds of the policy if they would refrain from contesting the change. She collected the proceeds of the policy but refused to pay the $2,000, as agreed. The children bring an appropriate action to recover the $2,000. Decision?

2. B signed an agreement granting an option to A which recited that it was "In consideration of the sum of $1 in hand paid." Upon B refusing to comply with the option, A brought an action for specific performance. At the trial, it was shown that the consideration of $1 mentioned in the writing was not in fact paid, and A did not claim that it was. What decree?

3. A owed $500 to B. The debt was due on June 30, 1965. In March of 1966, the debt was still unpaid. B was in urgent need of ready cash and told A that if he would pay $150 on the debt at once, B would release him from the balance and give him a receipt in full. A paid $150 and received a receipt from B which stated that all claims had been paid in full. In August, 1966, B demanded the unpaid balance and subsequently sued A for $350. Decision?

4. A owed B $800 on a personal loan. Neither the amount of the debt nor A's liability to pay the $800 was disputed. B had also rendered services as a carpenter to A without any agreement as to the price to be paid. When the work was completed, an honest and reasonable difference of opinion developed between A and B with respect to the value of B's services. Upon receiving B's bill for $800, A mailed his check for $800 to B with the following notation on its face: "This check is in full satisfaction of all accounts." In an accompanying letter, A stated that the enclosed check was in full settlement of both claims. B indorsed and cashed the check. Thereafter, B unsuccessfully sought to collect from A an alleged unpaid balance of $800. B then sued A for $800. Decision?

5. Carter engaged Hughes to do plumbing work for him without any agreement with respect to the price or amount to be charged for the services. Upon completion of the work, Hughes submitted a bill for $325, to which Carter objected as being excessive. He requested an itemized bill, and thereafter received such a bill for $345.-67. Carter again protested, stating that $175 would be a reasonable price. Although Hughes told Carter he would not accept a proffered check for $175 in settlement of his claim, Carter sent a check for $175 to Carter, payable to his order, bearing the legend on both the face and back "Payment in full for services rendered." Hughes struck out the quoted words on the back of the check and deposited it. The check was paid. Hughes then sued Carter to recover $170.67 for work performed. Decision?

6. The Snyder Mfg. Co. being a large user of coal, entered into separate contracts with several coal companies, in each of which it was agreed that the coal company would supply coal during the year 1965 in such amounts as the manufacturing company might desire to order, at a price of $7.50 per ton. In February, 1965, the Snyder Company ordered 1,000 tons of coal from Union Coal Company, one of the contracting parties. Union Coal Company delivered 500 tons of the order and then notified Snyder Company that no more deliveries would be made and that it denied

any obligation under the contract. In an action by Union Coal to collect $7.50 per ton for the 500 tons of coal delivered, Snyder files a counterclaim, claiming damages of $1,500 for failure to deliver the additional 500 tons of the order and damages of $2,500 for breach of the agreement to deliver coal during the balance of the year. Decision?

7. On February 5, D entered into a written agreement with P whereby P agreed to drill a well on D's property for the sum of $5000 and to complete the well on or before April 15. Before entering into the contract, P made test borings and had satisfied himself as to the character of the subsurface. After two days of drilling P struck hard rock. On February 17, P removed his equipment and advised D that the project had proved unprofitable and that he would not continue. On March 17, D went to P and told P that he would assume the risk of the enterprise and would pay P $100 for each day required to drill the well, as compensation for labor, the use of P's equipment and P's services in supervising the work, provided P would furnish certain special equipment designed to cut through hard rock. P said that the proposal was satisfactory. The work was continued by P and completed in an additional 58 days. Upon completion of the work D failed to pay and P brought an action to recover $5800. D answered that he had never become obligated to pay $100 a day and filed a counterclaim for damages in the amount of $500 for the month's delay based on an alleged breach of contract by P. Decision?

8. Discuss and explain whether there is valid consideration for each of the following promises:

(a) Where A and B had entered into a binding contract for the purchase and sale of goods, A subsequently promised to pay a higher price for the goods upon B's refusal to deliver at the lower price.

(b) A promised in writing to pay a debt, which was due from B to C, upon C's agreement to extend the time of payment for one year.

(c) A executed a promissory note to his son, B, solely in consideration of past services rendered to A by B, for which there had been no agreement or request to pay.

(d) A agrees to sell, and B agrees to buy, all of the medicine cabinets, which B may want during the year 1966, at a price of $25 per cabinet, F.O.B.

9. A, an accountant, sent B a bill for $1,000 for personal services. There had been no agreement as to the price to be paid. B, on receiving the bill, sent a letter to A questioning the reasonableness of the amount charged but did not dispute the service, enclosing a check for $500 which he stated was in full satisfaction of A's claim. A made no reply but retained and deposited the check in the bank. The first of the following month, A sent another bill to B for $500 for services rendered, crediting the $500 represented by the check, and requested payment of the balance. B refused to pay the $500 and A sued B to recover the $500 as the balance due. Decision?

10. A purchased shoes from B on open account. B sent A a bill for $10,000. A wrote back that 200 pairs of the shoes were defective and offered to pay $6,000 and give B his promissory note for $1,000. B accepted the offer and A sent his check for $6,000, and his note conformably to the agreement. B cashed the check, collected on the note and, one month later, sued A for $3,000. Decision?

CHAPTER 5

ILLEGAL BARGAINS

Introductory. When the formation or performance of an agreement is criminal, tortious or otherwise opposed to public policy, the bargain is illegal and unenforceable. In this connection, it is preferable to use the terms "illegal bargain" or "illegal agreement" rather than an "illegal contract," for the reason that the word "contract," by definition, implies a legal and enforceable agreement. Discussion of this subject will be in terms of agreements (a) contrary to legislative enactment, and (b) violative of public policy.

Illegal Bargains: Violations of Statute. An agreement declared illegal by statute will not be enforced by the courts. For example, "wagering contracts" are often expressly declared unenforceable. But what if there is no express prohibition of this type, but the formation or performance of the agreement involves a statutory violation? For the most part, the rule still obtains that the courts will deny enforcement. Due recognition of the statute is held to call for such judicial non-recognition of the agreement. Yet it is not always evident from a statute how far proper implementation and respect require the sanction of depriving a guilty party of a remedy in contract.

(a) *Criminal Statutes: In General.* In a leading New York case the plaintiff sued for the purchase price, $1555.81, of certain hosiery and wrappers delivered to the defendant, owner of a department store. The latter defended upon the ground that the order for the goods was obtained through the bribing of defendant's purchasing agent, the plaintiff paying the agent five per cent of the purchase price. This act of the plaintiff was clearly in violation of the New York Penal Code which made this type of commercial bribery a misdemeanor punishable by fine and/or imprisonment. There was no showing that the price of the goods was excessive, nor did the defendant return them or offer to do so. Under these circumstances, is there an enforceable contract of sale between the plaintiff and the defendant? There is certainly no question but that an agreement between A and B to bribe C is unenforceable. The same is true of an agreement to commit any criminal act—murder, larceny, embezzlement, forgery. But there is nothing illegal about the sale of hosiery and wrappers, and the defendant urged that voiding the contract would result in the imposition of a penalty not prescribed by the legislature. The majority of the court held there could be no recovery. Taking account of the purpose of the statute to stop commercial bribery, it said that the refusal to aid the plaintiff who obtained the contract by a secret bribe of the defendant's employee would contribute to that end. The court stated that as it is the province of the legislature to declare the public policy of the State, it is the duty of the court to be guided thereby in administering the law.

(b) *Licensing Statutes.* In every jurisdiction there are laws requiring a license of those who engage in certain trades, professions or businesses. Common examples are licensing statutes which apply to lawyers, doctors, teachers, accountants, brokers, plumbers and contractors. Can one recover for services rendered if he has not complied with a licensing provision? Can an unlicensed lawyer or doctor recover for professional services rendered? Can an unlicensed plumber enforce a plumbing contract to which he is a party?

The courts commonly distinguish between those statutes or ordinances which are *regulatory* in character and those which are en-

110

acted merely to raise *revenue*. If the statute is regulatory, there can be no recovery in contract; if the law is for revenue purposes only, the contracts are enforceable.

A regulatory measure is one designed for the protection of the public against unqualified persons, such as statutes prescribing standards for those who seek to practice law or medicine. A revenue measure, on the other hand, does not seek to protect against the incompetent or unqualified, but to furnish revenue. An example is a statute requiring a license of plumbers but not establishing standards of competence for those who seek to follow the trade. It would be regarded as a taxing measure and lacking in any expression of legislative intent to preclude plumbers from enforcing their business contracts.

These licensing requirements sometimes trap the unwary. Some real estate brokers have negotiated sales only to find they cannot recover their fees. In one case a broker who was licensed in Illinois undertook to sell Illinois land, but the brokerage contract was executed in New York, where he was not licensed. The Illinois Supreme Court denied a recovery in his action to collect the promised fee. In the course of its opinion, the court said: "The rule is that when a statute declares that it shall be unlawful to perform an act, and imposes a penalty for its violation, contracts for the performance of such acts are void and incapable of enforcement. * * * The object of the statute is to promote the public welfare by permitting only persons with the necessary qualifications to act as real estate brokers and salesmen. The location of the land outside the State of New York does not affect the policy of the statute, since it is the vendor and the purchaser who are sought to be protected. The statute does not in any way seek to regulate the sale of Illinois real estate, but operates only on the brokerage contract." Frankel v. Allied Mills, Inc., 369 Ill. 578, 17 N.E.2d 570 (1938). The

result was that the plaintiff lost a $17,000 fee. Some statutes affecting real estate brokers expressly provide that an unlicensed person cannot enforce his brokerage contracts. But in a few instances where there was no such express prohibition, and none could reasonably be implied, the broker has been able to collect, the courts holding the statutes to be revenue measures only.

In what has been widely interpreted as a significant withdrawal from the strict view of denying recovery where the statute is regulatory in nature, an unlicensed milk dealer in New York was permitted to recover for milk sold despite the fact that his conduct constituted a misdemeanor. The court considered the statutory penalties of fine and imprisonment as sufficient. While it recognized that the law was not a revenue measure, it said that the violation did not "endanger health or morals" and "such additional punishment should not be imposed unless the legislative intent is expressed or appears by clear implication." John E. Rosasco Creameries, Inc. v. Cohen, 276 N.Y. 274, 11 N.E.2d 908, 118 A.L.R. 641 (1937). The "additional punishment" would be depriving the plaintiff of $11,000, the price of the milk sold. This case suggests an argument in support of recovery of compensation despite the fact that the statute is of a regulatory character, but, with very few exceptions, the courts have rejected this argument.

(c) Gambling Statutes. All States have legislation pertaining to gambling, and it is common for wagering and gambling contracts to be declared illegal by statute. Even without such a statute, American courts have refused to recognize the enforceability of a gambling contract. Thus, if A makes a bet with B upon the outcome of a ball game, the agreement is void. The loser need not pay, and in a few States may recover back any payments he has made.

In a wager the parties stipulate that one shall win and the other lose depending upon the outcome of an uncertain event in which they have no "interest" other than that arising from the possibility of such gain or loss. To be distinguished, therefore, are ordinary insurance contracts in which the insured having an "insurable interest" pays a certain sum of money or premium in exchange for a promise of the company to pay a larger amount upon the occurrence of some uncertain event such as a fire or the occurrence of a certain event at an uncertain time as, for example, death. Here, the agreement is one which transfers an existing risk, rather than creates a wholly new risk. In a wager the parties contemplate gain through mere chance, whereas in an insurance contract they seek to distribute possible loss by reason of mischance.

Obviously, the mere existence of the risk element in a business contract does not make it a gambling contract. For example, a "futures contract" is legal, provided a bona fide sale is intended, with actual delivery if required. The fact that the seller does not have the merchandise at the time of the sale does not render such an agreement illegal, nor does the transaction become a wager because one or both of the parties do not believe actual delivery will ever be demanded. Usually, a settlement is made by the payment of the difference in prices.

Lotteries are generally prohibited by statute. A common statutory definition of lottery is as follows: "a scheme for the distribution of property by chance, among persons who have paid or agreed to pay a valuable consideration for the chance, whether called a lottery, a raffle, a gift enterprise, or by some other name."

(d) *Usury Statutes*. All States have provided by statute the "legal rate" of interest, e. g., the amount of interest to be charged when the parties have agreed to the payment of interest but have not specified the rate. The legal rate is also applied in cases where the law allows interest without the assent of the debtor but no specific rate is set, as where a statute provides that a court judgment shall bear interest until satisfied. The most commonly expressed legal rate of interest is 6% per annum. North Dakota provides for 4% per annum; several States provide for 7% per annum.

Almost every State has a "usury law," a statute establishing a maximum rate of permissible interest which may be contracted for in a loan. Maximum rates permitted range from 4% per annum in North Dakota to 30% per annum in Rhode Island. In the majority of States the established maximum rate varies between 6 and 8% per annum. These statutes are general in their application, and only those arrangements or parties specifically exempted are exempt from compliance. Almost half of the States, including Illinois, New Jersey, New York, Ohio and Pennsylvania, set no limit on the rate of interest which may be charged on loans to corporations. Some States, e. g., Illinois, permit the parties to contract for any rate of interest on business loans (loans made to individual proprietorships or partnerships for the purpose of carrying on the business).

The legal effect to be given a usurious loan, e. g., a loan in which the stated interest rate exceeds the maximum prescribed by statute, varies from State to State. In a few States, (e. g., Iowa, Minnesota and New York) both principal and interest are forfeited. In some jurisdictions (e. g., California, Michigan and New Jersey) the lender can recover the principal but forfeits all interest. In other States (e. g., Delaware, Indiana, Maryland, Missouri and Pennsylvania) only that portion of interest exceeding the maximum permitted is forfeited. In a few States the amount forfeited is a multiple (double or treble) of the interest charged. Disposition of usurious interest already paid also varies. In a number of States, the interest paid may be recovered by the debtor and applied to the principal. In Alaska the debtor may recover double all usurious interest paid; but in Connecticut recovery of usurious interest paid is not permitted. In Illinois the debtor may recover by means of an action or defense an amount equal to twice the total of all interest, discount and charges determined by the loan contract or paid by him, whichever is greater, plus reasonable attorney's fees and court costs. An action to recover usurious interest paid is required to be filed within a certain time limit, ranging from one year to four years from date of payment.

The acquisition of consumer goods and services on credit has been a phenomenon of this century. Prior to the early part of this century wage earners sought credit only in cases of emergency or necessity. Interest and usury laws were then directed to commercial lending and borrowing. Initially, wage earners were unable to obtain loans through regular credit institutions which considered the established interest ceilings insufficient to cover the cost of making these small and apparently more risky loans. The individual borrowers soon became victims of loan sharks. The situation prompted passage of small loan acts, originally permitting licensed lenders to charge interest up to 3% per month on the unpaid balance of loans up to $300. Small loan laws today are in force in all States except Arkansas. They permit the licensed lender, now commonly referred to as a personal loan company or consumer finance company, to make a maximum loan ranging from $200 in some States to as high as $5,000 in other States, at interest rates higher than the rate set in the usury law. Most of the States provide graduated rates. For example, in Illinois the maximum rate is 3% per month on the first $150 of the loan, 2% per month on the amount from $150 to $300, and 1% per month on the amount from $300 to $800. Frequently, the small loan laws will allow the lender to make additional charges for specific items, such as fees for filing, recording or releasing instruments;

court costs and attorney's fees; delinquency and deferral charges; charges for insurance covering property taken as security for the loan; charges for life, accident or health insurance on the person of the borrower.

Special statutory treatment has been accorded other, particularly designated institutions, e. g., credit unions, industrial banks, savings and loan associations, and pawnbrokers. They may, under applicable law, and subject to regulation, charge rates of interest higher than the generally permitted maximum.

In addition to the exceptions accorded certain designated lenders, about four-fifths of the States have enacted installment loan laws, which permit eligible lenders a higher return on installment loans than would otherwise be permitted under the applicable general interest statute. Wherever effective, installment loan laws are applicable to banks. In about one-half of the States having such laws, only banks are eligible to make loans under the law. A few States expand the eligible group by including selected, supervised, financial institutions, e. g., savings and loan associations. Only about one-third of the States having such laws authorize any person or organization to make loans in accordance with the provisions of such laws. These laws vary greatly. Under the most simple type of statute, an eligible lender is authorized to calculate charges on an installment loan at the maximum contract rate authorized under the general interest and usury law as though the loan were a single payment loan which matured in its entirety at the time that the final installment of the loan is due. The lender is also authorized to deduct in advance the charges so computed. The described method of computation, even if charges are not deducted in advance, produces a greater return for the lender than he would be able to realize if the charges were calculated at the maximum rate authorized by the general interest statute on the declining unpaid principal balance of the loan. A typical illustration involves the financing over a 30-month period of an automobile which costs $2,400 (principal). At 5% interest, the purchaser-borrower is required to pay $300 interest for the whole term of the loan. The total amount of $2,700 is payable in 30 equal installments of $90. Taking into account the monthly payments to apply on principal, e. g., the declining principal balance, it is seen that the effective rate of interest is almost 10% per annum. Some States have gone further and established special maximum rates of charge for installment loans.

The credit extended by a seller in connection with the sale of goods or services has traditionally been characterized as something other than a loan of money. The entire structure of statutory limitations on interest, including the exceptions, has not been considered applicable to vendor credit even when the seller imposes a special charge for the credit extended. The courts traditionally have required the following factors before finding the transaction usurious: (a) a loan or forbearance; (b) of money; (c) which is repayable absolutely and in all events; (d) for which something is exacted in excess of and in addition to the interest allowed by law. The traditional view that the general usury laws do not apply to credit sales has been reached by use of the time-price doctrine, which holds that a seller may, at his discretion, set one price for a cash sale and any other price he chooses for a time-sale. This has been justified on the theory that a person finding it necessary to borrow money is in a disadvantageous bargaining position and deserving of statutory protection, whereas a purchaser's position is not analogous since, should he find the price unsatisfactory, he can always refrain from making the purchase. This distinction arose before the advent of large scale installment sales of automobiles and household goods and appliances. Although the distinction dis-

regards the facts of present day economic life, the traditional view that a credit sale is not subject to the usury statutes is still followed in most jurisdictions.

Courts unanimously agree that transactions which, in fact, are loans may not be clothed with the trappings of a sale for the purpose of avoiding the usury laws. One court noted that the "shifts and devices of usurers to evade the statute against usury have taken every shape and form that the wit of man could devise." The court could have added that for the most part they have been successful.

Some recent decisions, however, have eroded the time-price doctrine by curtailing its applicability in cases involving (a) cooperation between the dealer and the finance company, (b) contact prior to the sale between the buyer and the finance company, (c) improper or misleading itemization of charges, indicating the lack of a genuine time-price, or (d) refinancing. In these situations a court may find that a transaction which purported to be a sale was in fact a loan and thus subject to the usury laws.

Only two States, Arkansas and Nebraska, hold that for the purpose of applying interest and usury prescriptions, credit sales will be considered loans. In Hare v. General Contract Purchase Co., 220 Ark. 601, 249 S.W.2d 973 (1952), the purchaser of a used truck brought an action against the finance company to which the seller had sold the contract, alleging usury. The conditional sales contract showed a cash price of $1,750, a down payment of $600, and a finance charge (designated as "time price differential") of $289.13, consisting of $148.24 for insurance and $140.89 as a general service charge. The amount owed was to be paid in 21 months, resulting in an effective interest rate of 11.5 per cent per annum, which exceeded the 10% per annum maximum authorized by the Arkansas constitution. Under Arkansas law if the purchaser prevailed in his claim, the contract would be void; the money he had paid would be returned to him; and he would be permitted to retain the truck. The court held that the finance company had made a usurious loan to the buyer but affirmed a decision for the finance company on the basis of a series of older Arkansas cases which it then prospectively overruled by caveat, warning the public that it would not follow them in the future. The court stated:

"We * * * give this caveat to the public generally:

"(1) We leave unimpaired the doctrine that a seller may, in a bona fide transaction, increase the price to compensate for the risk that is involved in a credit sale. But there may be a question of fact as to whether the so-called credit price was bona fide as such, or only a cloak for usury.

"(2) If the seller, whether he has quoted two prices to the purchaser or not, subsequently transfers the title documents to an individual or company which is engaged in the business of purchasing such documents, at a price which permits the transferee to obtain more than a return of 10% on its investment, then a question of fact arises as to whether the seller increased his cash price with the reasonable assurance that he could so discount the paper to such individual or finance company. If that reasonable assurance existed, then the transaction is in substance a loan, and may be attacked for usury.

"(3) When finance companies or purchasers of title paper supply dealers with a set of forms and a schedule for credit price increases, such will tend to show that the dealer had reasonable assurance that such finance company or purchaser of the paper would take the paper at such discount.

"What we are trying to do is, to keep the spirit of the constitutional mandate against usury abreast of present day commercial transactions. We give this caveat prospectively, so as not to entrench on property rights acquired by reason of our previous opinions, and this caveat applies to all transactions entered into after this opinion becomes final."

As a result of the Hare case and subsequent decisions, the vendor-creditor in Arkansas must now comply with the interest requirements set forth in the Arkansas constitution, i. e., consumer lender credit and vendor credit are treated the same.

States which follow the traditional time-price doctrine regulate or control, by statute, some aspects of consumer installment credit sales contracts. These statutes, retail installment sales acts, apply to credit sales contracts made between a buyer and a seller for the purchase of goods and services to be used by the buyer for consumer purposes and to be paid by him in installments over a specified period of time. These acts differ widely. Some cover only contracts for the sale of motor vehicles; some cover only contracts for goods other than motor vehicles; and some cover both types of contracts. Some acts regulate only the format and style of contract forms, evidencing an intent to require full disclosure of information to the buyer rather than control of the substance of the terms of the contract. Most acts now, however, specify maximum rates of credit charges.

Assuming that it is established that the arrangement is a loan, not a sale, what expenses or charges may be exacted in addition to the maximum legal interest? "Payments made by a borrower to the lender for expenses incurred, or for services rendered in good faith in making a loan or in obtaining security for its repayment are not included in determining whether the loan is usurious, but payments made to the lender or from which he derives an advantage if they exceed the reasonable value of services actually rendered are included." Restatement of the Law of Contracts, Section 533. Ordinary expenses by the lender which are permissible include costs of examining title, investigating the character of the borrower, drawing necessary documents and inspecting the property. If not excessive, they are not considered in determining the issue of usury. The question of reasonableness of the charges is frequently a question of fact for the jury, and in ascertaining the good faith of the lender, courts will look beyond the mere form of the transaction.

In a genuine loan situation the amount of interest actually received may exceed the maximum rate without being usurious provided the payment is subject to the happening of a contingent event. For example, if X loans $25,000 to Y, repayable in one year, with interest at twenty-five per cent only if Y realizes a certain profit from a new business venture, the loan is not usurious. The contract is said to be "aleatory." X runs the risk of receiving no interest at all if the business venture is not profitable. However, such a transaction must not have been entered into for the purpose of avoiding the effect of usury laws; the courts will inquire into the good faith of the parties.

(e) Sunday Statutes. At common law a valid contract could be entered into on Sunday, the same as on any other day. Many States have legislation modifying this common-law view in some respects. The laws differ, but a few generalizations are possible. Works of "necessity" and "charity" are ordinarily excepted. Moreover, a contract is not illegal because of preliminary negotiations on Sunday, and the modern tendency is to permit week-day "ratification" or "adoption" of a contract executed on Sunday. Even in a State which prohibits contracts on Sunday, a court would enforce a subsequent week-day promise to pay a loan made on Sunday or to pay the price of goods sold and delivered on Sunday. This promise need not be express, but may be "implied" from the retention and enjoyment of the money or goods.

Illegal Bargains: Violations of "Public Policy." We have seen that the reach of a statute may extend beyond its language, since courts by analogy use the statute and the policy sought to be served thereby as a guide in determining the private contract rights of one in violation of the statute. The present discussion relates to situations where legislation plays at most a subsidiary role, and the court is called upon to articulate the "public policy" of a jurisdiction without significant help from statutory sources. This judicially declared public policy is very broad in scope, it often being said that agreements which have "a tendency to be injurious to the public or the public good" are contrary to public policy. Examples to be considered are agreements in restraint of trade, or which have a tendency to obstruct the administration of justice, or tend to corrupt public officials or impair the legislative process.

(a) Common-Law Restraint of Trade. Suppose A, a grocer, sells his business, including the good will, to B, and as part of the sales agreement promises not to engage in the grocery business in the area for the ensuing five years? Or, suppose that X, a clothing store manager, promises as a part of his employment contract with Y Company not to enter the employment of any of the company's competitors within five years from the termination of the employment? Are the promises enforceable? Are these agreements contrary to public policy?

At early common law any restraint upon an individual's right to exercise his trade or calling was illegal. The restraints were viewed with disfavor because of the belief that they would diminish the individual's means of earning a living, deprive the public of useful services, adversely affect competition, and otherwise be harmful to society. But this strict view was subsequently modified so that the courts enforced what were regarded as *reasonable* restraints.

Thus, in the sale of a business, it was recognized that the purchaser had a legitimate property interest to protect, and a reasonable self-imposed restriction upon the seller's right to compete was upheld. Today, an agreement to refrain from a particular trade, profession or business is enforceable if (1) the purpose of the restraint is to protect a property interest of the promisee and (2) the restraint is no more extensive than is reasonably necessary to protect that interest.

The purchaser of a business is commonly regarded as having a property interest entitled to protection. In order to protect the good will, an asset which he has purchased, it is necessary that he be allowed to enforce a covenant not to compete agreed upon by the vendor. Most of the litigation has centered around the second requirement, that the restraint be no greater than is reasonably necessary. The promise of one selling a service station business in Detroit not to enter the service station business in Michigan for the ensuing 25 years is unreasonable, both as to area and time. The business interest to be protected would not be co-extensive with the State, so it is not necessary to the protection of the purchaser that the seller be precluded from engaging in business in the entire State, or perhaps for that matter, the entire city of Detroit. Limiting the area to the neighborhood, or within a radius of a mile or two, would probably be adequate. If the business were a city-wide business, such as a laundry or cleaning establishment with neighborhood outlets, a covenant restraining competition anywhere in the city would be reasonable. The same type of inquiry must be made with respect to time limitations. In the service station sale, 25 years would be unreasonable, but three years probably would not. Each case must be considered on its own facts, with the court determining what is reasonable under the particular circumstances.

Salesmen, management personnel, and other employees are frequently required to sign employment contracts prohibiting them from competing with their employers during the time of employment and for some additional stated period after termination. The courts readily enforce the covenant not to compete during the period of employment. The promise not to compete after termination of employment is subjected to the same tests of reasonableness applied to covenants not to compete which are ancillary to the sale of a business but the courts apply these tests more rigidly in the employment contract cases. Since application for injunctive relief, e. g., a court order prohibiting the employee from competing in a described territory for a stated period of time, is the usual method by which the employer seeks enforcement of the covenant by the employee, it is understandable that the courts insist that the employer demonstrate the restriction is necessary to protect his legitimate interests. Issuance of the injunction has the practical effect of placing the defendant out of work. In short, the courts must balance the public policy giving the employer the right to protect his business interests vis-a-vis the public policy against unemployment of individuals.

Often a professional partnership agreement, as between lawyers or doctors, will contain a covenant not to compete upon retirement or separation from the partnership. These covenants are enforceable, provided that the area and time limitations are reasonable.

(b) *Obstructing the Administration of Justice.* Agreements which are harmful to the administration of justice are illegal and void. For example, a promise by an employer not to press criminal charges against an embezzling employee who restores the stolen funds is not enforceable. "Compounding a felony" is a crime at common law, and any agreement to stifle a criminal prosecution is contrary to public policy. Similarly, a promise to conceal evidence or to give false testimony tends to obstruct the administration of justice and for that reason is illegal and unenforceable.

At common law the courts dealt strictly with those who "supported" the litigation of another, as by paying costs and attorney's fees, whether or not there was agreement for sharing the proceeds. This officious intermeddling in the lawsuit of another, as it was regarded, is "maintenance," and when coupled with a bargain for sharing proceeds, is "champerty." Both maintenance and champerty are common-law crimes, and it follows, of course, that a "champertous bargain" is void.

The strict view has been modified. Today, "A bargain for maintenance, though the bargain includes an agreement to pay the expense of litigation, is not illegal if entered into from charitable motives and without an intention to make a profit, or in order to determine a question on which a right or duty of the maintaining party depends; but if such a bargain is entered into for the purpose of annoying another it is illegal." Restatement of the Laws of Contracts, Section 541. A contingent fee contract, whereby a lawyer agrees to conduct litigation for a client and to receive as compensation a certain percentage of the amount recovered, is permissible.

At one time arbitration agreements, under which parties agreed to submit to arbitration all future disputes arising out of a certain transaction were unenforceable. But here, too, the older view has been relaxed. Practically every State now has a statute respecting arbitration agreements, the general effect of which is to recognize their validity. In some States, however, agreements to arbitrate future disputes have been adjudged unenforceable.

(c) *Corrupting Public Officials or Impairing the Legislative Process.* Agreements which have a tendency to affect adversely the public interest through the corruption of public officials or the impairment of the legislative process are unenforceable. Examples are agreements to influence legislation, secure some official action, or procure a government contract through the exercise of improper political pressure.

The "five per-centers," lobbyists who are paid a percentage of the gain acquired for the client, principally in the government contract field, have run into collection difficulties because of this declared public policy. If a scrutiny of the employment arrangement convinces the court that improper means were contemplated, there is no hesitation in holding the agreement void. The fact that the compensation is contingent on success, however, does not of itself conclusively establish that improper means were contemplated.

A bargain by a candidate for public office to make a certain appointment is illegal, as is an agreement to induce a public official to do so. In addition, an agreement to pay a public officer something extra for performing his official duty, as a promise to a policeman if he will strictly enforce the traffic laws on his beat, is illegal. The same is true of an agreement whereby a citizen promises to perform, or to refrain from performing, duties imposed upon him by citizenship. A promise by X to pay five dollars to Y if he will register and vote is opposed to public policy and will not be enforced by the courts.

Effect of Illegality: No Remedy Available. Assuming that an agreement is illegal, what are the consequences? With but few exceptions, neither party can sue the other for breach nor recover for any performance rendered. The statement is often made that where parties are in pari delicto (in equal fault) a court will leave them where it finds them. The law will provide neither with a remedy.

The rationale is contained in the following classic statement of Lord Mansfield: "The objection, that a contract is immoral or illegal as between plaintiff and defendant, sounds at all times very ill in the mouth of the defendant. It is not for his sake, however, that the objection is ever allowed; but it is founded in general principles of policy, which the defendant has the advantage of, contrary to the real justice, as between him and the plaintiff, by accident, if I may so say. The principle of public policy is this: *Ex dolo malo non oritur actio.* [From fraud a right of action does not arise.] No Court will lend its aid to a man who founds his cause of action upon an immoral or an illegal act. If, from the plaintiff's own stating or otherwise, the cause of action appears to arise *ex turpi causa* [from a base cause], or the transgression of a positive law of this country, there the Court says he has no right to be assisted. It is upon that ground the Court goes; not for the sake of the defendant, but because they will not lend their aid to such a plaintiff. So if the plaintiff and the defendant were to change sides, and the defendant was to bring his action against the plaintiff, the latter would then have the advantage of it; for where both are *equally* in fault, *potior est conditio defendentis.* [The condition of a defendant is better.]" Holman v. Johnson, 1 Cowp. 341, 343 (1775).

A striking application of this doctrine is contained in a Federal court case involving the city of Kansas City, Kansas. The State of Kansas had a criminal statute prohibiting "the business of pool selling and book making." The city passed an ordinance to the effect that any person might carry on the business of book making and pool selling in Kansas City for an annual license fee of $5,-000. The plaintiff purchased such a license, but two days later was arrested by the city for doing the very things supposedly authorized by the city license. The plaintiff sued to recover the $5,000 paid for the license, but the court denied a recovery. Pointing out that the business was prohibited by a State penal statute, the court stated it would not lend its aid to parties to recover money or property lost through transactions in which they were guilty of the violation of a general law enacted to carry into effect the public policy of the State or nation. It said that the controlling issue in the case was the legal-

ity and righteousness of the acts of the plaintiff; those of the defendant had little materiality.

This strict, orthodox rule is subject to some exceptions, which are discussed in the subsections that follow.

(a) Exception: Party Withdrawing Before Illegal Performance—Locus Poenitentiae. Under some circumstances one who is party to an illegal agreement may, prior to performance, withdraw from the transaction and recover whatever he has contributed. He is said to have a locus poenitentiae, an opportunity or time within which to repent before consummation of the illegal venture. The Restatement of the Law of Contracts, Section 605, states this exception as follows: "Where money has been paid or goods have been delivered under a bargain containing illegal provisions the money or the value of the goods can be recovered so long as the illegal part of the bargain is wholly unexecuted, unless entering into the bargain involves serious moral turpitude on the part of the plaintiff." A common illustration is recovering money left with a stakeholder pursuant to a wager, but the doctrine has been applied in more serious situations as well. For example, despite the statement that locus poenitentiae is unavailable where the bargain involves serious moral turpitude, courts have permitted the recovery of money turned over to another for use in bribing a government official where the action was timely rescinded.

(b) Exception: Party Protected by Statute. It often happens that where an agreement is illegal because of a statutory violation, the law in question is designed to protect people in the position of one of the parties. For example, State "Blue Sky Laws," which prohibit the sale of unregistered securities, are designed primarily for the protection of purchasers. If the rule denying recovery to either party to an illegal agreement were to prevail, a purchaser of such securi-

ties would have no recourse against the seller, even to recover any payments which have been made. But this result would tend to thwart the very purpose of the statute, so the general rule is not applied and the statute usually expressly gives the purchaser a right to recover the payments.

(c) *Exception: Party Not In Pari Delicto.* Suppose one is induced to enter an illegal bargain through the fraud, duress or undue influence of the other. Here the courts are inclined to regard the parties as not in pari delicto and the general rule as inapplicable. While each is blameworthy to an extent, if they regard the plaintiff as not guilty of serious wrong (moral turpitude) courts will permit him to repudiate the bargain, and, if he has rendered any performance recover it or its value. Otherwise, it is felt that the one who ought most to suffer would be unjustly enriched. The following is illustrative: A, who is indebted to a number of persons, and who fears judgment will go against him for a large amount, is induced by his counsel, B, to make a fraudulent transfer of a large part of his property to B, who agrees to transfer it back when A's financial troubles are over. B subsequently refuses to perform his promise. Although generally a debtor who makes a fraudulent transfer subject to an agreement to retransfer cannot enforce the agreement, in this case A can do so.

(d) *Exception: Party Ignorant of Facts Making Bargain Illegal.* An illegal agreement may appear regular on its face, and one of the parties may be completely unaware of the facts rendering it illegal. For example, a man and woman make mutual promises to marry, but unknown to the woman, the man is already married. In such case the courts again mitigate the harshness of the orthodox rule and permit the party who is ignorant of the vitiating fact to sue the other for damages. The exception was recognized in a Massachusetts case where an employee sued successfully to recover for services rendered in a business which was unlawful by reason of the employer's failure to procure a license, the plaintiff being justifiably ignorant of the fact. The party must be careful, however, not to continue performing after knowledge of the fact is acquired; in such event, the excuse would be lost and no recovery allowed.

(e) *Exception: Partial Illegality.* Ordinarily, the entire agreement is void and unenforceable if any part of the consideration for a promise is illegal or any part of the entire promise is illegal. For example, a promise to pay $1,000 for the delivery of two types of goods, one type legal and the other illegal, is unenforceable. The seller could not even recover payment for the legal items. But, if the facts are altered slightly he may prevail. If within the same agreement there is a separate price allocation for the different types of goods, as $250 for the legal and $750 for the illegal, he could probably maintain a successful action for the $250. Even though the agreement is tainted with illegality, there is a tendency to disregard this if the legal and illegal portions can be "severed" and the ends of justice seem to require the recognition of at least a partial recovery. Certainly, there would be no objection to enforcing a legal contract because of the fact that the same parties have also entered into a separate illegal transaction. It may be viewed as but a slight extension of this to separate the parts of the same contract and grant enforcement of the legal part.

CASES

WOMACK v. MANER

(1957) 227 Ark. 786, 301 S.W.2d 438.

ROBINSON, J. The complaint in this case alleges: "From time to time, and at various intervals, * * * the plaintiff has paid to the defendant the sum of $1,675 * * * for the consideration of the defendant, as the Judge of the Circuit Court of Saline County giving to the plaintiff whatever protection was necessary to prevent the plaintiff from being prosecuted or suffering punishment in said court for engaging in the unlawful business of gambling in Saline County which the plaintiff was engaged in with the full knowledge, consent and approval of the said defendant as the Judge of said Court. Plaintiff alleges, that the consideration for his paying to the defendant the said sum of money as herein above set forth is void and unlawful and was void and unlawful when said money was paid by him to defendant, * * *. Wherefore, plaintiff prays, that he have judgment against the defendant for his cause of action herein stated, in the sum of Sixteen Hundred and Seventy Five Dollars; for his costs herein expended, and for all proper relief."

The defendant demurred to the complaint on the ground that a cause of action is not stated. The demurrer was sustained by the trial court, presided over by a judge on exchange. The plaintiff, Womack, has appealed.

The appellant relies on Lane v. Alexander, 168 Ark. 700, 271 S.W. 710, 712, as authority for his alleged right to recover. In that case, Alexander filed suit to replevy bonds valued at $20,100. As a defense, Lane alleged that he had won the bonds from Alexander at the gaming table. Chief Justice McCulloch said: "The answer tendered no valid defense, for the statutes of this state expressly authorize the maintenance of an action for the recovery of money or property lost at any game or gaming device or on any bet or wager." Crawford & Moses Digest, § 4899, Ark.Stats. § 34–1601.

But, we have no statute authorizing the recovery of money alleged to have been paid as a bribe. It is firmly established that in a situation such as is set out in the complaint

the law will not aid either party to the alleged illegal and void contract. According to the allegations in the complaint the parties are *pari delicto*, hence, plaintiff cannot recover.

In Edwards v. Randle, 63 Ark. 318, 38 S.W. 343, 344, 36 L.R.A. 174, this court said: "The transaction, taken altogether, plainly shows that the sale and purchase of the office of postmaster was the main thing, * * *. This court cannot lend its aid to either party in respect to any claim or thing involved in such a contract."

"The general rule is that, where an illegal contract has been made, neither courts of law nor of equity will interpose to grant any relief to the parties, but will leave them where it finds them, if they have been equally cognizant of the illegality." Shattuck v. Watson, 53 Ark. 147, 13 S.W. 516, 517, 7 L.R.A. 551.

"Where the ground of a promise on one part, or the thing promised to be done on the other part, is unlawful, the courts will not enforce the contract for either party." Neece v. Joseph, 95 Ark. 552, 129 S.W. 797, 798, 30 L.R.A.,N.S., 278.

"Any contract, therefore, the consideration of which is to conceal or withhold evidence of a crime or to abstain from the prosecution therefor, is void, * * *." Goodrum v. Merchants & Planters Bank, 102 Ark. 326, 144 S.W. 198, 202.

In Patterson v. Hamilton, 42 S.W. 88, 19 Ky.L.Rep. 825, it was held that there can be no recovery of money paid as a bribe.

The United States Supreme Court said, in Clark v. United States, 102 U.S. 322, 26 L.Ed. 181 "Clearly this was bribery, and placed the claimants and the man they corrupted *in pari delicto*. They could not recover back from him the money they paid, * * *."

And, in United States v. Galbreath, D.C., 8 F.2d 360, it was said: "Petitioner therefore was guilty at least of an attempt to commit bribery, if not of that crime itself. It is of course unthinkable that a court of justice will assist in the recovery of property voluntarily surrendered under such circumstances."

Affirmed.

McCONNELL v. COMMONWEALTH PICTURES CORPORATION

(1960) 7 N.Y.2d 465, 166 N.E.2d 494.

DESMOND, C. J. The appeal is by defendant from so much of an Appellate Division, First Department, order as affirmed that part of a Special Term order which struck out two defenses in the answer.

Plaintiff sues for an accounting. Defendant had agreed in writing that, if plaintiff should succeed in negotiating a contract with a motion-picture producer whereby defendant would get the distribution rights for certain motion pictures, defendant would pay plaintiff $10,000 on execution of the contract between defendant and the producer, and would thereafter pay plaintiff a stated percentage of defendant's gross receipts from distribution of the pictures. Plaintiff negotiated the distribution rights for defendant and defendant paid plaintiff the promised $10,000 but later refused to pay him the commissions or to give him an accounting of profits.

Defendant's answer contains, besides certain denials and counterclaims not now before us, two affirmative defenses the sufficiency of which we must decide. In these defenses it is asserted that plaintiff, without the knowledge of defendant or of the producer, procured the distribution rights by bribing a representative of the producer and that plaintiff agreed to pay and did pay to that representative as a bribe the $10,-000 which defendant paid plaintiff. The courts below (despite a strong dissent in the Appellate Division) held that the defenses were insufficient to defeat plaintiff's

suit. Special Term's opinion said that, since the agreement sued upon—between plaintiff and defendant—was not in itself illegal, plaintiff's right to be paid for performing it could not be defeated by a showing that he had misconducted himself in carrying it out. [The following question was certified "Did the Appellate Division correctly affirm the order of Special Term?"] The court found a substantial difference between this and the performance of an illegal contract. We take a different view. Proper and consistent application of a prime and long-settled public policy closes the doors of our courts to those who sue to collect the rewards of corruption.

New York's policy has been frequently and emphatically announced in the decisions. " 'It is the settled law of this State (and probably of every other State) that a party to an illegal contract cannot ask a court of law to help him carry out his illegal object, nor can such a person plead or prove in any court a case in which he, as a basis for his claim, must show forth his illegal purpose', Stone v. Freeman, 298 N.Y. 268, 271, 82 N.E. 2d 571, 572, 8 A.L.R.2d 304, citing the leading cases. The money plaintiff sues for was the fruit of an admitted crime and 'no court should be required to serve as paymaster of the wages of crime'. Stone v. Freeman, supra, 298 N.Y. at page 271, 82 N.E.2d at page 572. And it makes no difference that defendant has no title to the money since the court's concern 'is not with the position of the defendant' but with the question of whether 'a recovery by the plaintiff should be denied for the sake of public interests', a question which is one 'of public policy in the administration of the law'. [Citations.] That public policy is the one described in Riggs v. Palmer, 115 N.Y. 506, 511–512, 22 N.E. 188, 190, 5 L.R.A. 340: 'No one shall be permitted to profit by his own fraud, or to take advantage of his own wrong, or to found any claim upon his own iniquity, or to acquire property by his own crime. These maxims are dictated by public policy, have their foundation in universal law administered in all civilized countries, and have nowhere been superseded by statutes'." [Citation.]

We must either repudiate those statements of public policy or uphold these challenged defenses. [Citations.] To allow this plaintiff to collect his commissions would be to let him "profit by his own fraud, or to take advantage of his own wrong, or to found [a] claim upon his own iniquity, or to acquire property by his own crime" (Riggs v. Palmer, 115 N.Y. 506, 511, 22 N.E. 188, 190, 5 L.R.A. 340). The issue is not whether the acts alleged in the defenses would constitute the crime of commercial bribery under section 439 of the Penal Law, Consol.Laws, c. 40, although it appears that they would. "A seller cannot recover the price of goods sold where he has paid a commission to an agent of the purchaser (Sirkin v. Fourteenth Street Store, 124 App.Div. 384, 108 N.Y.S. 830); neither could the agent recover the commission, even at common law and before the enactment of section 384–r of the Penal Law (now section 439)" [Citation.] In unmistakable terms it [the Sirkin opinion] forbids the courts to honor claims founded on commercial bribery.

We are not working here with narrow questions of technical law. We are applying fundamental concepts of morality and fair dealing not to be weakened by exceptions. So far as precedent is necessary, we can rely on Sirkin v. Fourteenth Street Store, 124 App.Div. 384, 108 N.Y.S. 830, supra, and Reiner v. North American Newspaper Alliance, 259 N.Y. 250, 181 N.E. 564, 83 A.L.R. 23, supra. Sirkin is the case closest to ours and shows that, whatever be the law in other jurisdictions, we in New York deny awards for the corrupt performance of contracts even though in essence the contracts are not illegal. Sirkin had sued for the price of goods sold and delivered to defendant. Held to be good was a defense which charged that plaintiff seller had paid a secret commission to an agent of defendant purchaser. There cannot be any difference in principle between that situation and the present one where plaintiff (it is alleged) contracted to buy motion-picture rights for defendant but performed his covenant only by bribing the seller's agent. In the Reiner case (supra), likewise, the plaintiff had fully performed the services required by his agreement with the defendant but was denied a recovery because his performance had involved and included "fraud and deception" practiced not on defendant but on a third party. It is beside the point that the present plaintiff on the trial might be able to prove a prima facie case without the bribery being exposed. On the whole case (again assuming that the defenses speak the truth) the disclosed situation would be within the rule of our precedents forbidding court assistance to bribers.

It is argued that a reversal here means that the doing of any small illegality in the performance of an otherwise lawful contract will deprive the doer of all rights, with the result that the other party will get a windfall and there will be great injustice. Our ruling does not go as far as that. It is not every minor wrongdoing in the course of contract performance that will insulate the other party from liability for work done or goods furnished. There must at least be a direct connection between the illegal transaction and the obligation sued upon. Connection is a matter of degree. Some illegalities are merely incidental to the contract sued on. [Citations.] We cannot now, any more than in our past decisions, announce what will be the results of all the kinds of corruption, minor and major, essential and peripheral. All we are doing here is labeling the conduct described in these defenses as gross corruption depriving plaintiff of all right of access to the courts of New York

State. Consistent with public morality and settled public policy, we hold that a party will be denied recovery even on a contract valid on its face, if it appears that he has resorted to gravely immoral and illegal conduct in accomplishing its performance.

Perhaps this application of the principle represents a distinct step beyond Sirkin and Reiner (supra) in the sense that we are here barring recovery under a contract which in itself is entirely legal. But if this be an extension, public policy supports it. We point out that our holding is limited to cases in which the illegal performance of a contract originally valid takes the form of commercial bribery or similar conduct and in which the illegality is central to or a dominant part of the plaintiff's whole course of conduct in performance of the contract.

*   *   *

The order appealed from should be reversed, with costs, the certified question answered in the negative, and plaintiff's motion, insofar as it attacks the sufficiency of the two separate defenses, should be denied.

SPIVAK v. SACHS

(1965) 16 N.Y.2d 163, 953 N.Y.S.2d 263, 211 N.E.2d 329.

DESMOND, C. J. Plaintiff, a California attorney not admitted to the Bar of New York State (or of Connecticut), has an affirmed judgment against defendant for the reasonable value of legal services (plus traveling and other expenses) rendered to defendant in New York City where defendant resided. Defendant appeals here, arguing that plaintiff cannot recover since what he did amounted to the illegal practice of law in this State in violation of section 270 of the Penal Law, Consol.Laws, c. 40.

Both courts below held—and it is not really disputed or disputable—that these were legal services. The Trial Term and the Ap-

pellate Division majority decided, however, that what plaintiff did in New York was not the "practice" of law within the meaning of section 270 of the Penal Law which, as all agree, states the basic law, but was a mere "isolated situation". The Appellate Division dissent, however, pointed (21 A.D.2d 348, pp. 350–351, 250 N.Y.S.2d 666, pp. 668, 669) to the undisputed fact that the services consisted of "advice and assistance rendered to defendant and her attorneys * * *, including litigation pending in Connecticut and the proposed drafts of a settlement agreement", also legal advice as to "the matter of the proper jurisdiction for the matrimonial litigation, the advisability of the dismissal of the Connecticut proceedings with the institution of a new action in New York, the matter of property settlements * * * the custody of the infant son of the parties" as well as the giving of plaintiff's opinion "as to the nature of the representation defendant was receiving at the hands of her present counsel in New York with a recommendation that she retain a certain other attorney here".

The dissent below emphasized that the advice given by plaintiff was in part based on his knowledge or claimed knowledge of New York law. The dissenting Justices concluded that all this showed that plaintiff had practiced law illegally in New York. With that conclusion we agree.

We summarize the facts as found below. Plaintiff had never represented defendant before but had met her and her husband socially in California, Connecticut and New York. In 1959 defendant's husband sued her for a divorce in Connecticut and she retained attorneys in New York and Connecticut to represent her in the litigation and to negotiate a separation agreement. In November of that year defendant telephoned from New York to plaintiff in California. She told him that she was being pressed into a property settlement, that one child had been taken from her and she feared she might lose the custody of the other child and that she was confused and wanted plaintiff to come to New York to talk to her about her affairs. There were two other such telephone conversations during which defendant explained the details of the proposed agreements and again urged plaintiff to come to New York. He agreed to do so, informing her that he would advance his own expenses, then charge them to her plus a reasonable fee for his services. He told her that he was not licensed in New York and could do no more than consult with her, advise her and recommend New York counsel. Flying to New York, he spent about fourteen days there on defendant's affairs. During several meetings with defendant he examined various drafts of separation agreements as proposed by defendant's Connecticut counsel and discussed her problems as to financial arrangements and custody of the children. Based on his knowledge of both New York and California law, so he testified, he expressed his opinion that the suggested financial provisions for her were inadequate and that "she wasn't being adequately represented". Later defendant arranged meetings of plaintiff with defendant's New York attorney and plaintiff told that New York attorney that Connecticut was not the "proper jurisdiction" for the divorce suit. After several more meetings with the New York lawyer at some of which defendant was present, plaintiff tried without success to persuade defendant to discharge her New York counsel and retain a different New York lawyer named by plaintiff. For these services plaintiff demanded a fee of $10,575 but was awarded judgment for $3,-500 as his fee at the rate of $250 per day, plus about $1,600 in travel, hotel, telephone and incidental expense.

It is settled that the practice of law forbidden in this State by section 270 of the Penal Law to all but duly licensed New York attorneys includes legal advice and counsel as well as appearing in the courts and hold-ing oneself out as a lawyer [citations]. All this plaintiff concedes but he argues here, as he did successfully below, that although not admitted to the New York Bar he may still collect a fee for legal services performed here, since what he did was a "single, isolated incident" and not the "practice" of law. We think this is a misreading of the statute and a misapplication of the holdings in People v. Alfani, 227 N.Y. 334, 125 N.E. 671, and People v. Goldsmith, 249 N.Y. 586, 164 N.E. 593, particularly the latter.

Alfani and Goldsmith were both laymen and both were prosecuted and convicted for alleged violations of section 270. Alfani's conviction was upheld since he had made it his regular business to draw legal papers for hire. Goldsmith's conviction was reversed upon the ground that there was no evidence that he "held himself out to the public as being entitled to practice law within the meaning of section 270 of the Penal Law. (See People v. Alfani, 227 N.Y. 334, 125 N.E. 671.)" This court followed the Appellate Division's dissent in Goldsmith's case and agreed with it that the drawing by a layman of one single document for a small fee without any "holding out" was not the "practice" of law. The contrast was with Alfani who made such work his regular business. The exculpation of Goldsmith was consistent with People v. Title Guar. & Trust Co. (227 N.Y. 366, 125 N.E. 666) where a corporation which abstracted titles and guaranteed mortgages was held not to have violated section 280 of the Penal Law by drawing a single document without giving any legal advice.

The Alfani, Goldsmith and Title Guarantee cases (supra), laying down the rule that drawing a single document for a small fee or no fee is not law practice, have no relevance to the case at hand. Here we have a California lawyer brought to New York not for a conference or to look over a document but to advise directly with a New York resident as to most important marital rights and problems. Not only did he give her legal counsel as to those matters but essayed to give his opinion as to New York's being the proper jurisdiction for litigation concerning the marital res and as to related alimony and custody issues, and even went so far as to urge a change in New York counsel. To say that this falls short of the "practice of law" in New York is to defeat section 270 and the policy it represents. The statute aims to protect our citizens against the dangers of legal representation and advice given by persons not trained, examined and licensed for such work, whether they be laymen or lawyers from other jurisdictions.

This is not answered by pointing to rules permitting out-of-State lawyers to appear in our courts on occasion or even to be admitted to practice here. The first is by express permission of the court and always on recommendation of a member of our Bar. As to admission here of a lawyer from another jurisdiction, that comes about only after the fulfillment of certain express requirements.

There is, of course, a danger that section 270 could under other circumstances be stretched to outlaw customary and innocuous practices. We agree with the Supreme Court of New Jersey (Appell v. Reiner, 43 N.J. 313, 204 A.2d 146) that, recognizing the numerous multi-State transactions and relationships of modern times, we cannot penalize every instance in which an attorney from another State comes into our State for conferences or negotiations relating to a New York client and a transaction somehow tied to New York. We can decide those cases when we get them but they are entirely unlike the present one.

This was an illegal transaction and under our settled rules we refuse to aid in it but leave the parties where they are [citations].

The order should be reversed and the complaint dismissed.

Order reversed, etc.

LEW BONN CO. v. HERMAN

(1965) 271 Minn. 105, 135 N.W.2d 222.

MURPHY, J. This is an appeal from a judgment in favor of Virgil L. Hillstrom, doing business as F. N. Hurd Company, F. N. Hurd, and Hurd Electric Company, Inc., against Alen Herman and Tony L. Ferrara, individually and as partners under the trade name of Calhoun Terrace Company, hereinafter referred to as the Calhoun Company. The action grows out of extended lien claim litigation following the construction of an apartment building in Minneapolis. On appeal here the issue is reduced to the question of whether the failure of Hillstrom to file plans and specifications with the city building inspector as required by ordinance is sufficient ground to deny to him recovery for work performed as an electrical contractor.

From the record it appears that the Calhoun Company entered into an agreement with Hillstrom to perform the electrical work in the construction of the building. The basic plans for the building drawn by architects for the owners did not contain plans and specifications for electrical installations. The Calhoun Company did not employ an electrical engineer. Hillstrom performed this function as best he could. He secured a copy of the architect's plans, superimposed his proposed electrical layout on them, and had sepia copies made of the sheet as the electrical plans and specifications. The contract was entered into on the basis of a condensed bill of materials. It was agreed that the work was to be installed in accordance with the city and state building codes. Section 4½ (a) and (c) of the Electrical Ordinance of the city of Minneapolis, in effect when the contract was made, required that plans and specifications for new electrical installations in new buildings "for which plans and specifications are required for obtaining a building permit shall be submitted to the Department of Buildings for checking in every case where there is a combined electrical load of 30 KVA or over, or when requested by the Department of Buildings" so as to enable the Department of Buildings to check them for "safety, adequacy, and code compliance."

After Hillstrom began work on April 14, 1959, he applied for and was issued a building permit. It does not appear, however, that he filed the plans and specifications of the electrical installations as required by the ordinance. It is contended that this failure renders the contract illegal so as to deny Hillstrom and his associates recovery of the sum of $10,435.18, the amount awarded by the trial court.

*   *   *

We conclude that the asserted breach relates entirely to a matter collateral to the agreement and that noncompliance under the circumstances of this case does not require that recovery be denied.

The trial court found that although the electrical plans and specifications were not filed, they were nevertheless available to the city electrical inspector and that the work was performed in full compliance with the electrical code and that the contract "was not an illegal contract." The record established that one of the city electrical inspectors was on the premises from time to time while the job was in progress for the purpose of inspecting the installations and that he had an opportunity to examine the plans and specifications. *   *   *

The trial court was of the view that Hillstrom's failure to file plans and specifications did not under the circumstances deny to the other party benefits or protection which the ordinance was intended to give

him and did not conflict with a public policy which would justify denial of recovery.

Although the general rule is that a contract entered into in violation of a statute which imposes a prohibition and a penalty for the doing of an act, such as the pursuit of a business, profession, or occupation without procuring a license or permit required by law for the protection of the public, is void, such rule is not to be applied without first examining the nature and circumstances of the contract in light of the applicable statute or ordinance. In construing such a statute or ordinance, courts will infer that the legislature did not intend that an instrument executed in violation of its terms should be void unless that be necessary to accomplish its purpose. [Citation.] The general rule has been applied in this state with varying results. In Ingersoll v. Randall, 14 Minn. 400, Gil. 304, and Leuthold v. Stickney, 116 Minn. 299, 133 N.W. 856, contracts in violation of law were held to be unenforceable under circumstances where the violations offended important public policy with respect to health and safety of the public. However, in De Mers v. Daniels, 39 Minn. 158, 39 N.W. 98, and In re Estate of Peterson, 230 Minn. 478, 42 N.W.2d 59, 18 A.L.R. 2d 910, the holdings indicate that the breach of a provision of law as it bears upon the performance of a contract will not necessarily render the agreement unenforceable where the legislative intent to be found in the act would not indicate that its sanction should apply where the violation is slight, not seriously injurious to the public order, and where no wrong has resulted from want of compliance.

Appellants in their reply brief rely on 6 Williston, Contracts (Rev. ed.) § 1761, and Tocci v. Lembo, 325 Mass. 707, 92 N.E.2d 254. They neglect, however, to refer to the more recent Massachusetts decision of Buccella v. Schuster, 340 Mass. 323, 164 N.E.2d 141, in which both of the above authorities are discussed. The latter case, by which we are persuaded, involved an action to recover for labor performed and equipment rented pursuant to a contract for blasting a ledge on the defendant's premises. The plaintiff did the work without securing a permit or filing a bond as required by statute. There, as here, there was no evidence of the presence of evils which the statute or ordinance was intended to guard against, nor was there a possibility of damage from the happening of any event which the statute sought to prevent. There, as here, the failure to obtain the bond and permit was "only an incidental part of the performance of the contract." 340 Mass. 325, 164 N.E.2d 142. In holding that the failure to comply with the statute did not void the contract, the Massachusetts court said that the contractor's performance without the required bond and permit was not so repugnant to public policy "that the defendant should receive a gift of the plaintiff's services" and pointed out that the defendant "received all to which he was entitled under his contract." 340 Mass. 326, 164 N.E.2d 143.

The language of Mr. Justice Holmes, speaking for the Massachusetts court in Fox v. Rogers, 171 Mass. 546, 547, 50 N.E. 1041, 1042, is appropriate here. He said:

"We shall not trouble ourselves about the construction of the statute and ordinances, because it does not follow that the plaintiff cannot recover if he broke them. There is no policy of the law against the plaintiff's recovery unless his contract was illegal, and a contract is not necessarily illegal because it is carried out in an illegal way."

The contentions of appellants come down to the proposition that they are entitled to a windfall of more than $10,000 because of the failure of their creditor to comply strictly with the provisions of a city ordinance. It could hardly be said that such a decision would be consonant with principles of justice where there is nothing in the record to indicate that when the contract was entered into there was any intention to violate the law, or to indicate bad motives or a design to deny the protection of law to one of a class for whose benefit the statute or ordinance was enacted. We do not think that the legislature intended that a slight violation relating to failure to comply with a collateral duty in the filing of plans and specifications should result in the forfeiture of a just debt. [Citations.] We fully agree with the trial court that the Calhoun Company has received the benefit of Hillstrom's contributions to the construction of its property, that the work was performed in "compliance with the code in all material respects," and that it should be required to pay the judgment.

Affirmed.

BANKERS GUARANTEE TITLE & TRUST CO. v. FISHER

(1964) 2 Ohio Misc. 18, 31 O.O.2d 115, 204 N.E.2d 103.

ROSSETTI, J. The plaintiff filed a law suit against the defendants claiming that there is due the plaintiff from the defendants Fisher the sum of Eighty-nine hundred ninety-eight dollars and ninety-six cents ($8998.96) with interest from February 1, 1962. Defendants Fisher filed an answer requesting that the interest of the plaintiff and the defendants be determined.

The plaintiff filed a motion for summary judgment and affidavit in support of said motion. Stipulations were agreed to between the parties herein and this matter now comes on for the hearing of the motion for summary judgment.

The defendants, Daniel Arthur Fisher and Dorothy L. Fisher, entered into a written contract with William J. Savage and Mildred E. Savage to purchase certain premises in Louisville, Ohio. The plaintiff loaned the Fisher defendants Ninety-one hundred and fifty dollars ($9150.00) and accepted a note and mortgage for that amount.

A closing of this transaction was held in the office of the plaintiff and certain costs were paid by the Fisher defendants, among which was Item F in the fourth stipulation in the amount of Ninety-one dollars and fifty cents ($91.50) designated as "origination charge", which is one percent of the loan.

Another cost item paid by the Fisher defendants is the so-called loan discount fee of Eight hundred twenty-three dollars and fifty cents ($823.50) which is nine (9) percent of the face amount of the loan. This was authorized to be deducted from the sales price by the sellers of the property.

The item of Eight hundred twenty-three dollars and fifty cents ($823.50) has been referred to as a loan discount fee, and again in the plaintiff's brief it has been referred to as "points". Whatever it is called, the simple fact is that nine (9) percent of the loan was deducted and retained by the plaintiff bank, amounting to Eight hundred twenty-three dollars and fifty cents ($823.50). However, as between the plaintiff bank and the defendant borrowers this sum or item was not deducted which means that the bank received in addition to the regular interest charged on the loan of Ninety-one hundred and fifty dollars ($9150.-00) the sum of Eight hundred twenty-three dollars and fifty cents ($823.50), plus the origination charge.

The Fisher defendants claim that they should not pay any more to the plaintiff than what plaintiff paid out, and consequently the plaintiff bank is only entitled to recover the sum of Eighty-three hundred twenty-six dollars and fifty cents ($8326.50) plus interest and less any payments made.

One of the questions in this case is as follows:

"When the payee of a promissory note in the amount of Nine thousand one hundred fifty dollars ($9,150.00) pays to and disburses for the maker of said note the sum of Eight thousand three hundred twenty-six dollars and fifty cents ($8,326.50), how much can the payee recover from the maker?"

It is to be noted that the parties to this law suit are the original maker and payee on said note. * * *

It is well established as a rule that, as between the original parties to an instrument, the consideration may be inquired into.

* * *

The next question is whether the transaction in this case was a shift or device to evade the usury law. The evidence shows that the only contract was between the plaintiff and the Fisher defendants and that was as a result of the note and mortgage. The note and mortgage clearly indicates that the subject of the loan was the property in question.

The Court must, therefore, examine all disbursements made by the plaintiff and deductions held by the plaintiff to determine whether or not the plaintiff violated the usury statute and whether or not the plaintiff collected more than the legal rate of interest allowed in Ohio.

The evidence shows that the plaintiff received the following for making the loan to the Fisher defendants:

1. Origination charge, $91.50 or 1 per cent.

2. Interest on the $9150.00 note or 5¼ per cent.

3. Loan discount fee of $823.50 or 9 per cent.

Thus we find that the plaintiff bank actually disbursed the sum of Eighty-three hundred twenty-six dollars and fifty cents ($8326.50) of the Ninety-one hundred fifty dollar loan for the Fisher defendants. That simply means the plaintiff bank realized an additional profit of Eight hundred twenty-three dollars and fifty cents ($823.50) for making a loan to these defendants in addition to the interest and origination charge.

* * *

The law against usury was made necessary and originated by reason of evil practices that prevailed to a large degree in the loaning of money, and out of that condition came the prohibition by express statute, Section 1343.01, Ohio Revised Code, which reads as follows:

"The parties to a bond, bill, promissory note, or other instrument of writing for the forebearance of payment of money at any future time, may stipulate therein for the payment of interest upon the amount thereof at any rate not exceeding eight per cent per annum payable annually."

Referring to Item F of the closing costs of this case the evidence does not show the purpose of the so-called origination charge of Ninety-one dollars and fifty cents ($91.50) which is exactly one (1) per cent of the face amount of the note. There is no explanation of what value or benefit is rendered to the Fisher defendants by this charge. This Court must consider this charge as interest on the loan.

Again the evidence does not show the purpose of the loan discount fee which was a matter between the plaintiff bank and the seller of the property. It appears to this Court that this is a matter of the seller of the property reducing the sales price of the property, and in that event the purchaser is entitled to receive the full benefit of the reduction of the sales price.

The question is not what the parties called the transaction herein, but what does the transaction require the Court to call it. It, therefore, is necessary for this Court to scan the transaction carefully to ascertain its real substance with a purpose of determining whether it is a disguised loan or something else.

The question in this case is not what price the Fisher defendants paid for their house, but rather what did the plaintiff receive for making this loan to the Fisher defendants. Therefore, is the plaintiff lender exacting an interest rate greater than eight (8) per cent in making this loan to the borrowers? What is the plaintiff receiving for making the loan in this case? There can be no question but what the plaintiff is receiving 15¼ per cent of the loan which is in excess of the legal rate of eight (8) per cent.

Having in mind, therefore, the purposes of the statute in its inception and the need for a rule understandable by laymen as well as the courts the Court expresses the following rule for determination of usury:

"If the total amount contracted to be paid by a borrower before or after the use of money actually received as a loan for the period of time it is used, regardless of the names used for the various charges, is in excess of eight per cent per annum, then the excess is usurious."

This was the purpose and intent of the law. This is a rule easily followed and understood by all.

* * *

The Court cannot close its eyes to the pretense between lenders and the sellers of real estate who agree on circumstances which will result in a lender's receipt of interest in an amount greater than its legal rate of eight (8) per cent. This Court cannot approve a transaction which is merely a shift or device to evade the usury law.

The evidence in this case fails to show that plaintiff rendered any additional service to the Fisher defendants which would justify the plaintiff retaining the sum of Eight hundred twenty-three dollars and fifty cents ($823.50).

The Court finds that the plaintiff only disbursed or paid out for the Fisher defendants on the Ninety-one hundred and fifty dollar ($9150.00) note, the sum of Eighty-three hundred twenty-six dollars and fifty cents ($8326.50).

The Court finds that the Fisher defendants paid interest to the plaintiff on Ninety-one hundred fifty dollars ($9150.00).

The Court finds from the evidence that the note and mortgage provides a rate of interest within the law; however, the Court further finds that the plaintiff did receive a bonus, points, or loan discount fee of Eight hundred twenty-three dollars and fifty cents ($823.50), which together with the rate of interest constituted a usurious transaction in violation of the law.

The motion of the plaintiff for summary judgment is sustained. Judgment is rendered to the plaintiff for Eighty-three hundred twenty-six dollars and fifty cents ($8326.50), plus interest, and less any credits or payments made on said note.

EXTINE v. WILLIAMSON MIDWEST, INC.

(1964) 176 Ohio St. 403, 200 N.E.2d 297.

Glenn Extine, appellant herein, instituted this action in the Court of Common Pleas of Williams County. In his petition he prays for a declaratory judgment to determine his rights under the following provisions of a written agreement entered into with his employer, appellee herein.

"Agreement between Glenn Extine hereinafter called 'Employee,' and Williamson & Company, including Williamson Engineering Corp., Caldwell Compounding Corp., Williamson Midwest, Inc., Williamson Pacific, Inc., and Williamson Southern, Inc., which together with the parent company are hereinafter collectively called 'Employer';

"Witnesseth:

"In consideration of his employment by Employer, Employee agrees that on the termination for any cause whatsoever of his said employment, he will not, within two years after such termination, directly or indirectly, engage in the same or similar or competitive line of business to that now carried on by Employer, either on his own account or through or for or in behalf of any former employee of Employer and that he will not, within said period of employment and two years thereafter, in any way, directly or indirectly, divert or attempt to divert from Employer any business whatsoever and particularly not by influencing or attempting to influence any of the customers with whom he may have had dealings.

"In witness whereof, Employee has hereunto set his hand and seal, and Employer has caused these presents to be executed by a duly authorized officer this day of Feb. 13, 1961.

"[Sig.]   Glenn Extine   L.S.
          Employee
"[Sig.]   Thomas P. Cullahen
          Authorized signer for Employer."

This action was commenced in December of 1962 after appellant had terminated his employment with appellee.

The Court of Common Pleas entered judgment for the appellee-employer. Upon appeal on questions of law, the Court of Appeals affirmed the judgment. The Court of Appeals * * * ordered that the record be certified to this court for review and final determination.

HERBERT, J. The basic question presented here is whether the agreement, supra, is valid in whole or in part. The courts both here and in England have definitely modified the early English rule of rigid construction of agreements, in restraint of trade to meet an ever growing and expanding economy.

Originally it was held that all agreements in restraint of trade were void as being against public policy. [Citation.]

In the course of a century and a quarter, a second rule was evolved wherein *general* restraints were considered void as being against public policy, while *partial* restraints were judged according to their "reasonableness" as a restraint of trade. [Citation.] The early American judiciary adopted this second rule, with the validity of the restraint dependent upon the existence of certain limitations as to time and space of the restraint. [Citation.] The time and space rule was strictly applied at its inception, although its inequities were apparent. Every restraint, limited in time and space, was deemed *partial* and, therefore, valid, although patently unreasonable. The courts have also favored the rule of construction that illegal promises, if severable, may be stricken from an otherwise valid agreement in order to avoid the harshness of the time and space rule. [Citation.] Under the majority view this "blue pencil" test, or the doctrine of partial validity, requires that the terms be severable or the entire agreement fails. [Citation.] A growing minority view does not require divisibility of terms; the agreement is held enforceable as to a reasonable restraint providing the agreement is not so unreasonable so as to preclude modification. [Citations.]

For the time being, at least, we believe that the "blue pencil" or partial validity test should apply. [Citation.] The near unanimous view recognized by the courts today concerning trade restraints is embodied in the following statement of principle:

"An agreement in restraint of trade is reasonable if, on consideration of the subject matter, the nature of the business, the situation of the parties and the circumstances of the particular case, the restriction is such only as to afford fair protection to the interests of the covenantee and not so large as to interfere with the public interests or impose undue hardship on the party restricted." 17 C.J.S. Contracts § 247, p. 1124 (1963).

In addition to the absence or presence of limitations as to time and space, when attempting to decide the reasonableness of the restraint, the courts have considered the following factors: Whether the employee represents the sole contact with the customer; whether the employee is possessed with confidential information or trade secrets; whether the covenant seeks to eliminate competition which would be unfair to the employer or merely seeks to eliminate ordinary competition; whether the covenant seeks to stifle the inherent skill and experience of the employee; whether the benefit to the employer is disproportional to the detriment to the employee; whether the covenant operates as a bar to the employee's sole means of support; whether the employee's talent which the employer seeks to suppress was actually developed during the period of employment; and whether the forbidden employment is merely incidental to the main employment. [Citations.]

The agreement in the case at bar lends itself to the "blue pencil" or partial validity test. The agreement in effect provides that the appellant will refrain from participating in four distinct activities within a two-year period after termination of employment, to wit: (1) He will not engage in the same or similar competitive line of business on his own account; (2) he will not engage in the same or similar or competitive line of business for or in behalf of any former employee of the employer; (3) he will not divert or attempt to divert from employer any business whatsoever; and (4) he will not divert or attempt to divert from the employer any business whatsoever by influencing or attempting to influence any of the customers with whom he may have been dealing. Restraints Nos. (1) and (2) upon the employee-appellant have no limitation whatsoever as to space. These restraints, if enforced, would apply to areas in the world where the employer-appellee has no activity whatsoever and may never intend to engage in any activity in such a location. Consequently, it follows that restraints Nos. (1) and (2) are unreasonable and being severable are stricken from the agreement and are inoperative.

Restraints Nos. (3) and (4) are plainly for the protection of the employer in its own legitimate occupation and enterprise, and, therefore, are valid and enforceable. [Citation.]

It follows, therefore, that appellant is not subject to and is freed from restraints Nos. (1) and (2) and that he is subject to restraints Nos. (3) and (4) as herein indicated.

The judgment of the Court of Appeals is, therefore, affirmed in part and reversed in part as herein set out.

Judgment affirmed in part and reversed in part.

BAUER v. SAWYER

(1956) 8 Ill.2d 351, 134 N.E.2d 329.

SCHAEFER, J. All of the parties to this action are doctors. Prior to March 31, 1954, they were associated together in a medical partnership known as the Kankakee Clinic. On that date Dr. P. W. Sawyer, the principal defendant, withdrew from the partnership and in May of 1954 he opened offices for the practice of medicine and surgery in the city of Kankakee. Five of the eleven remaining partners instituted this action, alleging that the partnership agreement prohibited a retiring partner from practicing medicine in the city of Kankakee and seeking an injunction to restrain Dr. Sawyer from violating the agreement. The other six remaining partners were joined as defendants. They admitted the allegations of the complaint, but sought no relief against Dr. Sawyer. Dr. Sawyer also admitted the allegations of the complaint, but defended on the ground that the partnership agreement contemplated that a withdrawing partner had the alternative right to perform the agreement or to pay

liquidated damages. The case was submitted upon the pleadings and a stipulation of facts. The circuit court entered a decree dismissing the complaint. The Appellate Court reversed, 6 Ill.App.2d 178, 126 N.E.2d 844, and we granted leave to appeal.

The partnership agreement provides that the interest of an individual partner may be terminated by retirement based on physical incapacity, by voluntary withdrawal, or by expulsion for unprofessional conduct or for failure to carry out the provisions of the agreement. In each instance the remaining partners are to purchase the interest of the outgoing partner at a stated percentage of its value as shown on the partnership books: 100 per cent in case of retirement for incapacity, 80 per cent in case of voluntary withdrawal, and 75 per cent in case of expulsion. By the agreement each partner covenants that after the termination of his interest he will not engage in the practice of medicine, surgery or radiology within a radius of 25 miles of Kankakee for a period of five years. The agreement also provides that if the former partner violates this covenant, he shall forfeit any unpaid portion of the purchase price of his interest. In the case of a partner withdrawing voluntarily, one half the purchase price is payable 30 days after withdrawal and the other half is to be evidenced by notes payable in one year which are to be delivered to an escrow agent, who is directed to cancel the notes upon certification by the remaining partners that the former partner has resumed practice. At the time of his withdrawal from the firm Dr. Sawyer was paid 40 per cent of the value of his partnership interest, and a note for the remaining 40 per cent was turned over to an escrow agent in accordance with the agreement.

Although Dr. Sawyer admits that he resumed practice in Kankakee in violation of the contract, he contends that the contract ought not to be specifically enforced against him, (1) because it is an unreasonable restraint of trade and contrary to public policy, and (2) because it contains a provision for liquidated damages which bars specific enforcement.

The principles governing cases of this kind were stated in Ryan v. Hamilton, 205 Ill. 191, 197, 68 N.E. 781, 783, in which a contract by a physician not to engage in practice in a specified community was enforced by injunction: "That contracts in general restraint of trade are generally held to be illegal is beyond controversy. But the rule admits of well-defined exceptions, and among the exceptions are contracts of the kind and character presented in this case. Contracts of this class, where the limitation as to territory is reasonable, and there exists a legal consideration for the restraint, are valid and enforceable in equity, and in such cases relief by injunction is customary and proper." [Citations.] In determining whether a restraint is reasonable it is necessary to consider whether enforcement will be injurious to the public or cause undue hardship to the promisor, and whether the restraint imposed is greater than is necessary to protect the promisee. [Citations.]

In this case the interest of the public is in having adequate medical protection, and it is of course true, as suggested by Dr. Sawyer, that if the injunction is granted the number of doctors available in the Kankakee community will be reduced. A stipulation entered into by the parties, however, shows that there are now 70 doctors serving the area. We are unable to say that the reduction of this number by one will cause such injury to the public as to justify us in refusing to enforce this contract. In any case, there is no reason why Dr. Sawyer cannot serve the public interest equally well by practicing in another community. No special hardship to Dr. Sawyer appears which would justify the denial of relief in this case. He may resume practice in Kankakee after five years and in the meantime he may practice

elsewhere. The territorial limitation to the city of Kankakee and the surrounding area is not, we think, unreasonable in the light of modern methods of transportation and communication. [Citation.] Agreements unlimited in time have heretofore been enforced, [citations] although other authorities hold that the restraint must be limited in time as well as space. [Citations.] We need not here consider whether a time limitation is essential, because in any event the present five-year period does not appear unreasonable. [Citation.]

It thus appears that the agreement is not contrary to public policy by the tests that have heretofore been employed. Dr. Sawyer contends, however, that the prior cases decided by this and other courts are distinguishable because they involve either the sale of an established practice or the taking of a newcomer into an established practice, as employee or partner. Pointing out that in this case there was no express sale of the practice of any of the partners, and each of the partners was a practicing physician when the agreement was entered into, he argues that "If there is no established practice sold and no newcomer as a potential usurper, there is no need for the restraint being enforced by injunction."

With this contention we do not agree. No case is cited which holds that the members of a partnership may not by their agreement reasonably protect themselves against the competition of an outgoing partner. Indeed such agreements are classic illustrations of reasonable restraints of trade. "A legitimate method of enhancing the good will of continuing partners in professional, as well as commercial, partnerships is to secure forbearance from competition by a retired partner. He may agree not to compete, within reasonable limits as to time and space, and such an undertaking will be enforced by injunction." Crane on Partnerships, sec. 84. "The contract of a partner not to compete with the partnership either directly or indirectly is not opposed to public policy; but such an agreement must be ancillary to the relation of contract of partnership or to a contract by which a partner disposes of his interest." 5 Williston on Contracts, sec. 1644; Restatement of the Law, Contracts, sec. 516, comment (f). Our own decision in Storer v. Brock, 351 Ill. 643, 184 N.E. 868, enforced an agreement, entered into between two doctors upon the dissolution of their partnership, which restricted the future practice of the retiring partner. The distinction attempted to be drawn is without merit.

* * *

We conclude that the provision is a penalty and that the partners therefore remain liable to Dr. Sawyer in the amount of the outstanding unpaid balance. Plaintiffs' conduct was not, we think, inequitable or inconsistent with their theory of recovery and does not bar injunctive relief. * * *

Judgment affirmed.

PAUL JONES & CO. v. WILKINS

(1916) 135 Tenn. 146, 185 S.W. 1074,
Ann.Cas.1918B, 977.

WILLIAMS, J. This suit was commenced by Paul Jones & Co., a wholesale liquor concern of Louisville, Ky., to recover the sale price of thirty-five cases of whisky sold to Wilkins and shipped to Memphis. The defense was based on the ground that the liquor was sold to Wilkins to be by him retailed in Shelby county, in violation of the prohibition laws of this State in force in that city. The trial judge and the court of civil appeals have concurred in a denial of a remedy to plaintiff in the suit [judgment for defendant]; and the cause is before us for review on a petition for certiorari.

* * *

The general rule is that in case of the sale of intoxicating liquors mere knowledge

on the part of the seller that the purchaser intends illegally to resell such liquors will not render the contract void so as to bar the seller's action for the purchase price. [Citations.]

However, if the seller participates or contributes to the intention of the purchaser to sell in violation of law, or does any act, however slight, to facilitate or in furtherance of the design to transgress, or has an interest therein, the right to recover for the price is lost. The participation in the illegal purpose or act must be in some manner other than the mere act of making the sale. [Citations]

We are of opinion that the facts in this case show such a participation on the part of the plaintiff vendor as to bar him of any remedy. The plaintiff knew through its local solicitor in Memphis that Wilkins was running a "wide-open" retail liquor saloon; the solicitor had bought drinks for himself and others over the bar. The shipment represented by the account in suit was not made to Wilkins as consignee, but to the Lewis Transfer Company for delivery—so agreed in order that the public would not know to whom it was to be delivered. The cases were not marked with the name of T. B. Wilkins, but with the initials, "T. B. W."

The manager of the vendor company testifies that the shipment to the transfer company as consignee was for the purpose of insuring delivery to Wilkins. We fail to see how that end could have been more safely attained by the marking of the outside of the cases with mere initials, rather than with the name and street address of the purchaser, even though it was desirable thus to use the transfer company.

In Gaylord v. Soragen, 32 Vt. 110, 76 Am. Dec. 154, it was held that an action by the seller could not be maintained when, at the defendant's request, the plaintiff marked the packages in a peculiar way, omitting the defendant's name so as to enable the defendant with greater facility to save them from seizure.

Particular pertinency is given to these authorities by the fact that we have in this state a statute (Act Extra Session 1913, chapter 1) that requires common carriers to cause all consignees of liquors to sign, before delivery of goods, an affidavit setting out his name, address, the fact of consignment to affiant, the use to be made of the liquors, etc. It is manifest that the manipulation resorted to by the plaintiff was to circumvent the object sought to be attained by the legislature in the passage of this act.

A correct result has been reached in this case. Writ denied.

PROBLEMS

1. A and B were the principal shareholders in XYZ Corporation located in the city of Jonesville, Wisconsin. This corporation was engaged in the business of manufacturing paper novelties which were sold over a wide area in the Middle West. The corporation also was in the business of binding books. A purchased B's shares of the XYZ Corporation and, in consideration thereof, B agreed that for a period of five years he would not: (a) manufacture or sell in Wisconsin any paper novelties of any kind which would compete with those sold by the XYZ Corporation, (b) engage in the book binding business in the city of Jonesville. Discuss the validity and effect, if any, of his agreement.

2. Wilkins, a resident of, and licensed by, the State of Texas as a certified public accountant, rendered service in his professional capacity in Louisiana to Coverton Cosmetics Company. He was not registered as a certified public accountant in Louisiana. His service under his contract with the cosmetics company was not the only occasion on which he had practiced his profession in that State. The company denied liability and refused to pay him relying upon a statute declaring it unlawful for any person to perform or offer to perform services as a CPA for compensation until he has been registered by the designated agency of the State and holds an unrevoked registration card. Provision is made for issuance of a certificate as a CPA without examination, to any applicant who holds a valid unrevoked certificate as a CPA under the laws of any other State. The statute provides further that rendition of services of the character performed by Wilkins, without registration, is a misdemeanor punishable by a fine or imprisonment in the county jail, or by both fine and imprisonment. Wilkins brought an action against Coverton seeking to recover a fee in the amount of $1,500 as the reasonable value of his services. Decision?

3. A solicitor was hired by a corporation to develop its business by procuring new customers, his compensation to consist of commissions. The contract specified that the employment was for ten years and could be terminated by either party on one week's notice and that in the event of termination by either party the solicitor was not to solicit for himself or for any other business organization in competition with the corporation within the county or within any adjoining county during a period of four years thereafter. Is the four-year provision valid?

4. A is interested in promoting the passage of a bill in a State legislature. He agrees with B, an attorney, to pay B for his services in drawing the required bill, procuring its introduction in the legislature and making an argument for its passage before the legislative committee to which it will be referred. B renders these services. Subsequently, upon A's refusal to pay B, B sues A for damages for breach of contract. Decision?

5. A desired to borrow $1,000 from B for one year. B gave A $930 and took his note for $1,000 payable in one year. The note also provides that if the $1,000 is not paid when due, it shall bear interest after maturity at the rate of 7% per annum. One year after the note has become due and unpaid, B brings suit against A who claims that the note is usurious. How much if anything, may B recover on this note under the laws of the State of X which provide that an interest charge in excess of 7% is usurious?

6. (a) A sells his grocery business to B, and as part of the bargain promises not to engage in business of any kind within the city.

(b) A sells his business to B, and as part of the bargain promises not to engage in a business of the same kind within a hundred miles. The scope of neither A's nor B's business extends so far.

(c) A sells his grocery business to B, another grocer, and as part of the agreement promises not to engage in that business within a radius of fifteen miles. B's business covers that extent of territory. A's business covered only a portion of it.

Subsequently, the validity of each of the three agreements is attacked. Decision as to (a), (b) and (c), respectively?

7. The XYZ Company was engaged in the business of making and selling harvesting machines. It sold everything pertaining to the business to the ABC Company agreeing "not again to go into the manufacture of harvesting machines anywhere in the United States." The seller had a national and international good will in its business. It now begins the manufacture of such machines contrary to its agreement. Should the court enjoin it?

8. A employed B to work in his factory pursuant to a written contract of employment which provided in part: "All risks of loss or injury to person, of any and all kinds and however caused, and whether or not caused by the employer, his agents or servants, are hereby assumed by the employee." B was injured while at work through the negligence of his employer A, and brings an action at law to recover damages. By way of defense A relies on the contract of employment. What judgment?

9. A Dairy and B Dairy, the only dairies in Centerville, a town of 6,000 population, entered into an agreement which provided that A Dairy would solicit only customers who lived on the north side of Main Street, and B Dairy would solicit only customers who lived on the south side of Main Street. The agreement contained no provisions with respect to prices. B Dairy, in violation of the agreement, began to solicit customers who lived on the north side of Main Street at prices less than those quoted by A Dairy. A Dairy sues to enjoin B Dairy from so doing. Result?

10. Sharpie, a would-be poker player, contacted Jones, stating that he needed $2,000 to pay for his losses in recent poker games and that he felt that with a stake of $1,000 he could recoup his losses and more. Therefore, he offered to borrow $3,000 from Jones, repayable in 90 days with interest at the maximum non-usurious rate. Jones agreed and loaned Sharpie the money. As it developed, Sharpie lost the $1,000 playing poker and was soon destitute. When the time for repayment had passed and Sharpie did not pay, Jones brought an action against Sharpie to recover $3,000. Decision?

CHAPTER 6

CONTRACTUAL CAPACITY

Introductory. Not all persons have the ability or capacity to make a valid contract. For various reasons, such as minority, insanity or intoxication, an individual may have only limited contractual capacity. Similarly, the contracting power of so-called artificial persons, such as corporations, may be circumscribed by law. The persons whose capacity to contract is limited in some essential respect will be discussed in the following order: (1) minors; (2) insane persons; (3) intoxicated persons; (4) aliens; (5) convicts; (6) married women; (7) private corporations; (8) public corporations.

(1) Minors: Contractual Incapacity. A minor (or infant) at common law was one who had not attained the age of twenty-one years, and he could, at his option, avoid liability upon contracts to which he purported to be a party. Today the age limit has been changed in some jurisdictions by statute, as in Illinois where a girl attains her majority at eighteen, but minors still do not have full contractual capacity. Almost without exception, a minor's contract is voidable at his option. Even an "emancipated" minor, one who by reason of marriage or otherwise is no longer subject to strict parental control, is able to avoid contractual liability in most jurisdictions.

Thus, if a minor makes a contract to purchase a motorcycle or automobile from an adult, he need not go through with the deal. However, the adult is bound to honor the agreement provided the minor wishes to consummate the sale. The minor can avoid the contract; the adult cannot. Moreover, a like privilege is given the minor after the sale has been concluded by payment and delivery. If the minor accepts delivery of the motorcycle or automobile, he may while still a minor return the vehicle and recover the purchase price. By the majority view, this is true even if he has wrecked the machine; he need simply return the damaged vehicle and demand a return of the consideration paid.

This extraordinary privilege which the law accords to minors is deemed necessary in order to protect them from improvident and unjust bargains. In general, therefore, businessmen deal with minors at their peril.

Liability for Necessaries. Contractual immunity does not excuse a minor from an obligation to pay for necessaries, those things which suitably and reasonably supply his personal needs, such as food and clothing. But even here the supplier does not recover the agreed price but, instead, the reasonable value of the items furnished. That is, recovery is not based upon contract, but is quasi-contractual. If a clothier sells a minor a suit which the latter needs, he can successfully sue the minor and recover the reasonable value of the suit. But he is limited to this amount even if it is substantially less than the selling price and deprives him of all profit on the sale.

Determining what are necessaries is a difficult problem. That minors are liable for necessaries is a rule of law; whether particular items are necessaries is essentially a question of fact. In general, those things are regarded as necessary which the minor needs to maintain himself in his particular station in life. Items necessary for subsistence and health are obviously included, such as food, lodging, clothing, medicine and medical services. But others less essential may be included as well, such as text books, school instruction, and legal advice.

Each case must be decided on its own facts, having regard for the age, state and condition in life of the minor and the extent of need. For example, a new suit of clothing for one who is already adequately supplied, whether by his parents or others, is not a necessary. Nor is an exceptionally expensive suit a necessary for one whose social standing or duties do not call for such expensive apparel. Legal treatises may be necessary for a law student, but not for a high school student or an apprentice plumber. In all events, the articles furnished must pertain to the person of the minor, not his property. Fire insurance on a building owned by a minor is not viewed as a necessary, and the same is true of repairs or improvements on the property.

Ordinary luxury items seldom qualify as necessaries. This would normally exclude such items as cameras, tape recorders, phonographs, television sets, and motor boats. Although earlier cases uniformly denied that an automobile was a necessary, some recent decisions have recognized that under certain circumstances an automobile might be found a necessary. In Bancredit, Inc. v. Bethea, 65 N.J.Super. 538, 168 A.2d 250 (1961) the court observed:

> "While an automobile has not generally been classed as a necessary, in accordance with the principle that articles used for pleasure or for business advantage are not bodily or mental essentials [citations], recent decisions have espoused the more realistic view that an occupational accessory may well be a link in the chain of physical survival. * * We are in accord with the recognition * * that modern transportation habits and the definitional flexibility of 'necessary,' dependent as the term is upon the social position and situation in life of the minor [citation], may well combine to dictate that, under certain circumstances, an automobile is sufficiently indispensable to bind an infant who contracts for one".

In the same vein, the Kentucky Court of Appeals, in Williams v. Buckler, 264 S.W.2d 279 (1954), holding farm machinery as a necessary, noted: "We realize the general rule to be that an infant should not be encouraged to go into business and articles purchased by him for business purposes are not usually regarded as necessaries. * * * But * * * 'an infant must live as well as a man.' In the case at bar these farm tools are necessaries for the infant to support himself and family." Recovery has been allowed for services in providing an elementary school education. While no reported case appears to have found a college education a necessary as a matter of law, the question has been termed a factual one, i. e., circumstances may be such as to warrant the factual conclusion by judge or jury that a college or professional education is a necessary. Perhaps today a more expansive interpretation would be forthcoming respecting the need for more advanced education. A statute enacted in 1959 provides that any student who has been accepted for admission to an institution in the State approved by the State Superintendent of Public Instruction as an institution of higher education shall be permitted to execute a legally binding promissory note for a loan necessary to attend or to continue in attendance at an institution of higher education, subject to approval by the institution attended. Illinois Revised Statutes, 1965, Chapter 29, § 43.

Life insurance has traditionally been viewed as not a necessary, and the general rule is that an insurance contract of a minor is voidable by him, although subject to ratification after attaining his majority. In some jurisdictions, however, a minor, at varying ages, may contract for life, health and accident insurance on his own life, and cannot, by reason of his minority, rescind, avoid, or repudiate his contract. Money as such, will seldom be viewed as a necessary. At the very least the money must be expended for necessaries, and it is probably incumbent upon the lender to see personally that the money is so spent. Since a man is legally obligated to support his wife, a minor is accountable for necessaries furnished her. The same is true of necessaries furnished a minor's child.

It is apparent that a business man must be wary of dealing with a minor, even with respect to those items traditionally classified as necessaries. There can be no recovery against a minor for breach of an executory contract, even for necessaries; it is only where the items are already furnished that a possibility of successful suit exists. And even then the seller has the burden of establishing that the goods were actually necessaries for the particular person in question. Even though his chances of success are good, his claim may still be contested and expensive litigation may eventuate. In addition, other unanticipated pitfalls may appear. If it turns out that the minor's parents were able and willing to provide the items, they were not necessaries for this person and the merchant cannot recover. Similarly, if the minor was already adequately supplied they were not necessaries. Where recovery is allowed, the supplier is likely to realize no profit from the transaction, for the recovery is not the selling price but the reasonable value of the goods or services furnished, as determined by the court. As a practical matter, of course, it may be sound business practice for one to advance credit to certain minors or otherwise contract with them, even though they can avoid liability. It may be the experience of the merchant that, on the average, the probabilities of recovery are very good and justify taking the legal risk of non-collectibility.

Ratification and Disaffirmance. A minor's contract is not entirely void and of no legal effect, but it is voidable at the minor's option. He has a power of avoidance. His exercise of this power is called a disaffirmance, and he is thereby released outright from liability on the contract. On the other hand, after the minor becomes of age he may choose to adopt or ratify the contract, in which case he becomes bound.

(*a*) *Ratification.* Suppose that a minor, seventeen years of age, makes a contract to buy land from an adult. The contract is voidable by the minor and he can escape liability. But, suppose that after reaching his twenty-first birthday, he promises to go through with the purchase. His promise is binding, and the adult can sue for breach upon his failure to perform. He has expressly ratified the contract entered into when he was a minor.

But a ratification need not be express, it may be implied from the minor's conduct. If, for example, the minor should, after attaining his majority, go into possession of the property, or undertake to sell it to someone else, or perform other acts showing an intention to affirm the contract, he may not thereafter disaffirm but is liable on the contract.

Ordinarily, mere silence after becoming of age will not amount to a ratification. Yet this is not always so, since it might appear that, under the circumstances, the minor had a duty to speak. For instance, suppose the minor is the vendor of land or a chattel, of which the purchaser has taken possession. If, after becoming of age, he stands by knowingly while the purchaser makes improvements on the property, he will be estopped to disaffirm the contract.

Perhaps the most common form of implied ratification occurs when the minor, after attaining his majority, continues to use the property which he purchased as a minor. This use is obviously inconsistent with the nonexistence of the contract, and whether the contract is executed or still partly executory, it will amount to a ratification and preclude a disaffirmance by the minor. Although there is a split of authority, payments by the minor either upon principal or as interest, standing alone, have been held to amount to a ratification. Some courts state that it is necessary that there be some additional evidence of an intention to abide by the contract, such as an express promise to that effect or the use of the subject matter of the contract. Mere retention of the goods for an unreasonable time after attaining majority has been construed as a ratification.

It should be noted that a minor has no power to ratify a contract while he remains a minor. A ratification cannot be predicated upon words or conduct occurring while he is still under age, for his ratification at that time would be no more effective than his original contractual promise. The ratification must take place after the individual has acquired complete contractual capacity by attaining his majority.

(b) *Disaffirmance.* As stated, a minor's contract is voidable at his option, thereby conferring upon him a power to avoid liability. He exercises his power to disaffirm through words or conduct manifesting an intention not to abide by the contract, or as it is stated, an intention to disaffirm. Aspects of this power will be considered in the following order: (1) When can the minor disaffirm? (2) How can he disaffirm? (3) What, if anything, must he do upon a disaffirmance?

In general, a minor may disaffirm a contract at any time, either before or after he becomes of age. A notable exception is that a conveyance of land by a minor cannot be disaffirmed until after he reaches his majority. But need his disaffirmance come immediately upon his becoming an adult? In the case of a deed to land, there is strong authority for a view that the minor may wait until the expiration of the period of the Statute of Limitations. It is otherwise with an executed contract for the sale of a chattel or other types of contracts. There the disaffirmance must come within a reasonable time after reaching majority, the precise period varying with the circumstance and the local law. In some States there are stat-

utes requiring a minor to disaffirm all his contracts within a reasonable time after coming of age or lose the right to so avoid liability.

As is true of ratification, the disaffirmance may be either express or implied. No particular form of words is essential, so long as they show an intention not to be bound. This intention may be manifested by acts or by conduct, e. g., where the minor-vendor sells the property forming the subject matter of the contract to a third person.

A troublesome and at the same time very important problem in this area pertains to the minor's duty of restitution upon a disaffirmance. For example, if the minor-purchaser still has the motorcycle or automobile in his possession when sued by the merchant, must he return it upon disaffirming the contract? If he has sold it to another, must he give the merchant the proceeds of the sale or the equivalent? Suppose the vehicle has been destroyed through his own fault; must he pay the merchant the depreciated value or an amount necessary to put it in proper repair? In any case where he has received the beneficial enjoyment of the chattel, must the disaffirming minor pay the seller an amount equal to the value of the benefit enjoyed?

There is no unanimity of opinion on these questions. By the majority view, it is only necessary that the minor return the chattel itself, provided he has it in his possession at the time of disaffirmance. Nothing more. If the vehicle has been wrecked, he need only return the wrecked vehicle. His only duty is one of restoration in specie. A few States, either by statute or judicial opinion, recognize a duty upon the part of the minor to make restitution, i. e., return an equivalency of what has been received in order to place the seller in approximately the same position he would have occupied had the sale not occurred. Others not going so far require at least the payment of a reasonable amount for the use of the property, or to cover the depreciation while in the hands of the minor.

Finally, can a minor disaffirm and recover property which has been transferred by his buyer to a bona fide purchaser for value without notice? At one time he could avoid the contract and recover the property, despite the fact that the third person gave value for it and had no notice of the minority. This has been changed by Section 2–403 of the Uniform Commercial Code, which provides that a person with voidable title, e. g., the person buying goods from a minor, has power to transfer a good title to a good faith purchaser for value. In Jones v. Caldwell, 216 Ark. 260, 225 S.W.2d 323, 16 A.L.R.2d 1416 (1950), a minor sold his car to an individual who resold it to a used car dealership, an innocent purchaser for value. The court, construing a statutory provision to the effect that any seller of goods who has voidable title could pass good title to a good faith purchaser for value, found no exception in favor of a minor and concluded that the used car dealership had good title. On the other hand, in the case of the sale of real estate, a minor's deed of conveyance may be rescinded even as against a good faith purchaser of the land who did not know of the minority.

Effect of Misrepresentation of Age. What if a minor misrepresents his age in acquiring goods from the seller? Suppose he says he is twenty-one years of age and actually looks that old or even older? By the prevailing view in this country the minor can still disaffirm the contract. In a minority of States the courts hold that the minor is estopped under these circumstances to assert his minority.

An example of the predominant opinion on this issue is a New York case, Sternlieb v. Normandie Nat. Securities Corp., 263 N.Y. 245, 188 N.E. 726, which involved the purchase in September, 1929, of five shares of bank stock by a minor just under twenty years of age at a price of $990. In Septem-

ber, 1932, at which time the stock was worthless, he notified the seller that he was ready to return the stock and sued to recover the purchase price. The vendor alleged that the minor represented himself to be over twenty-one, but the court held this to be an insufficient reason to deny disaffirmance and recovery. The court was not altogether happy with the result which it felt compelled to reach by virtue of past decisions. The following is an excerpt from its opinion:

"Like so many questions of policy, there is much to be said upon both sides, and the necessities of one period of time are not always those of another. The law, from time out of mind, has recognized that infants must be protected from their own folly and improvidence. It is not always flattering to our young men in college and in business, between the ages of eighteen and twenty-one, to refer to them as infants, and yet this is exactly what the law considers them in their mental capacities and abilities to protect themselves in ordinary transactions and business relationships. That many young people under twenty-one years of age are improvident and reckless is quite evident, but these defects in judgment are by no means confined to the young. There is another side to the question. As long as young men and women, under twenty-one years of age, having the semblance and appearance of adults, are forced to make a living and enter into business transactions, how are the persons dealing with them to be protected if the infant's word cannot be taken or recognized at law? Are business men to deal with young people at their peril? * * * Some States have met the situation by legislation."

The New York opinion referred to statutes of Iowa, Kansas, Utah and Washington. Since the date of the opinion, other States have joined the growing minority which has modified the older rule either by legislation or judicial opinion. Michigan, for example, eliminates the defense in a number of transactions where the minor has wilfully misrepresented himself to be over twenty-one years, provided "such representation shall have been made in writing in a separate instrument containing only the statement of age, date of signing and the signature." Mich. Statutes Annotated, Vol. 21, sec. 27A, 1403. New York, incidentally, has since mitigated the hardship to adults to some extent, by a statute providing that a minor over eighteen years may not disaffirm a contract made in the course of his business if it is found to have been provident and reasonable when made.

Even where the other party to the contract cannot successfully argue that the minor is estopped, he may not be altogether without a remedy. An argument often advanced by sellers caught in this type of predicament is that the minor committed the tort of fraud and deceit, and thereby caused the seller to part with the goods. It is well settled that minors are, as a general proposition, liable for their torts, including assault, battery, libel, fraud, and negligence. In this type of case many courts reason that the tort and contract are distinct, and contractual immunity is no ground for excusing the tort. It is pointed out that were it not for the prior tort there would never have been a contract. In a Missouri case the court supported its position as follows:

> "The protection of adults against depredations by minors knowingly employing fraudulent methods outweighs the interests of such minors, and adults should have available the remedies not founded on contract for their protection. Every case involving a contract to which a minor is a party should not necessarily be forced into the Procrustean bed of the rule that allows a minor to escape responsibility for his other acts upon exercising the privilege of rescinding his contract at his will. Plaintiff was not a toddler, or a teen-ager, but an 'old' infant, cunning enough to conceive and perpetrate a fraud upon experienced adults. * * * Liability ex delicto and liability ex contractu are based on different principles and involve different measures of recovery. If an infant is liable for his torts generally, the better reasoned decisions hold he is liable for his deceit in misrepresenting his age. His deceit induces

the contract. It does not involve the subject matter of the contract. The recovery is the damage resulting to the defrauded person and not the contract consideration. He is not held liable on the contract in form or substance." Byers v. Lemay Bank & Trust Co., 365 Mo. 341, 282 S.W.2d 512 (1955).

Nonetheless, there are some courts which are reluctant to recognize a tort action where there has been a misrepresentation of age inducing an adult to contract with a minor. For, it is said, this would amount to the indirect enforcement of a minor's contract and the overturning of precedents and policies of contract law.

As noted, those courts which recognize a tort liability on the part of the minor because of his fraudulent misrepresentation of age emphasize that the tort is independent of the contract. There is a general doctrine in the law that if the tort and the contract are so connected or "interwoven" that to enforce a tort action the court must enforce the contract, the minor is not liable in tort. Thus, if a minor rents an automobile from an adult, he enters into a bailment relationship (a type of contract) obliging him to exercise reasonable care and diligence to protect the property from injury. By negligently damaging the automobile, he breaches that contractual undertaking. But his contractual immunity protects him from an action by the adult predicated on this theory. However, can the adult sue for damages on a tort theory? By the majority view, he cannot. For, it is reasoned, a tort recovery would, in effect, be an enforcement of the contract. This rationale has been stated by the Supreme Court of New Jersey as follows:

> "The general liability of infants for their torts does not take from them their special immunity from liability for their contracts; each rests upon a policy of the law. When these two policies come into conflict they cancel each other to the extent that they deal with the same subject matter. If this cancellation be complete, so that all that is claimed as the foundation of the infant's

tort is covered by the breach of his contract, nothing remains upon which to found an action of tort independently of the contract." La Rosa v. Nichols, 92 N.J.L. 375, 105 A. 201 (1918).

What if, however, the minor departs from the terms of the bailment, as by using the automobile for an unauthorized purpose, and in so doing negligently causes the damage complained of? In that event most courts would hold that the tort is independent and there should be a recovery. This would not involve the breach of a duty flowing from the contractual status, but, rather, the commission of a tort during the course of an activity which is a complete departure from the bailment. When the minor departs from the object of the bailment and puts the property to an unauthorized use, the bailment has terminated and he is guilty of a conversion of the property to the same extent as if his original possession were without permission.

(2) *Insane Persons*. Since a contract is fundamentally a consensual transaction, it is, of course, necessary to a valid contract that the parties have requisite mental capacity. If one is lacking in such capacity, or mentally incompetent, he may avoid liability under the agreement.

A person who is lacking in sufficient mental capacity to enter into a contract is one unable to comprehend the subject of the contract, its nature and probable consequences. To vitiate the contract it is not necessary that he be proved permanently insane, still less that he be so adjudged by a court. If, indeed, he has been so adjudged, his contracts are void and of no legal effect whatever. On the other hand, it must be something more than a weakness of intellect or a lack of average intelligence. In short, a person is competent unless he is unable to understand the effect and nature of his act.

As in the case of a minor, an insane person is liable for necessaries furnished on a theory of quasi contract, the measure of recovery being the reasonable value of the goods or services. Moreover, an insane person's voidable contract can be ratified or disaffirmed by him when sane, or by his guardian during insanity, or by his representative after his death.

The predominant view in this country respecting an insane person's responsibility upon disaffirmance varies somewhat from that of a minor. Although a few cases can be found upholding an insane person's contract where the other party did not reasonably suspect the mental impairment and did not take advantage of him, the majority permit a disaffirmance here if there is a return of the consideration received (restoration in specie) or an equivalence in money (restitution). If the merchant does in fact have knowledge of the insanity and takes advantage of the mentally incompetent, no duty of restitution rests with the insane person, or his representative upon a rescission. The merchant's conduct is tantamount to fraud.

(3) *Intoxicated Persons*. If, at the time of the asserted contract, a party is so intoxicated as not to be able to comprehend the nature and effect of the transaction, it is voidable at his option. It does not matter that the intoxication was due to his own voluntary conduct; he may still avoid liability. Slight intoxication will not, of course, destroy his contractual capacity, but neither is it essential that he be so drunk as to be totally without reason or understanding.

In general, the same effects follow in these cases where one lacks contractual capacity because of drunkenness as where his contract is voidable because of insanity. The options of ratification or disaffirmance remain. And the courts are even more strict with respect to the requirement of restitution upon disaffirmance than they are in the area of an insane person's agreements. The rule is only relaxed where the person dealing with the intoxicated person fraudulently took advantage of him. As with insane persons, intoxicated persons are liable in quasi contract for necessaries furnished during their incapacity.

(4) Aliens. While some States undertake to prohibit aliens from owning land, no effective effort has been made to substantially impair an alien's contractual power in other areas. An alien lawfully in this country can, therefore, contract freely and utilize the courts for enforcement of contractual obligations. Aliens illegally in this country have, however, been denied access to our courts for the purpose of asserting contract rights. And enemy aliens, citizens or subjects of a country with which the United States is at war, will not be able to enforce their contracts in this country if such action will afford aid to the enemy country.

(5) Convicts. At one time the common law deprived convicted felons of all right to sue on a contract. But this view never obtained in the United States, where for the most part convicts have been accorded full contractual capacity. While limited in several respects as regards the exercise of civil rights (e. g., right to vote and hold public office,) the imprisoned party has not been denied the right to make contracts and to use the courts for their enforcement.

(6) Married Women. The common law denied to married women the power to make contracts. Refusing to recognize the wife as a separate legal entity from the husband, the older courts imposed several rules limiting the legal status of married women. These rules were modified by courts of equity, and it is likely that they never applied in the earlier English law administered by the various local courts which were superseded by the common-law courts. And today, by virtue of State statutes, usually called Married Women's Property Acts, substantially all of the old disabilities have been removed. Consequently, a married woman is free to contract the same as a single woman or a man. Only slight remnants of the older views remain, as in some States where married women are not permitted to enter into contracts with their husbands.

(7) Private Corporations. A private corporation is a creature of the State in which it is incorporated, and its powers, including that of contracting, are limited to those which have been delegated to it by law. In its corporate charter will be found express grants of power from the State, but, in addition, a corporation has implied powers, those which are reasonably necessary and incidental to the accomplishment of its corporate purposes. If it purports to act beyond the scope of its powers, its action is nugatory. Contracts exceeding its corporate powers are said to be ultra vires. There are some variations in the treatment of ultra vires contracts by the courts. In some jurisdictions, there can only be a recovery for the benefit conferred, on a quasi contractual theory. In a greater number, the corporation is held to the terms of its undertaking and is denied the defense of ultra vires. This is the rule under Section 6 of the Model Business Corporation Act. See Appendix D.

(8) Public Corporations. Public corporations, such as cities, villages, towns, school districts, sanitary districts, and other municipal corporations, may not contract in excess of the power granted them by their parent authority, the State. And while in some instances there may still be redress against a private corporation acting *ultra vires*, there can be no recovery against a public corporation which exceeds its legal limitations. Hence, caution should be exercised by those contracting with such units, to ascertain that the corporation has the power to enter into the proposed contract and that those who act on its behalf have the lawful authority to bind the municipal corporation. Typically, public contracts are subject to detailed laws and regulations respecting authorized terms; only by careful perusal of these may one safely proceed to contract with public corporations.

CASES

ROBERTSON v. KING

(1955) 225 Ark. 276, 280 S.W.2d 402.

ROBINSON, J. The principal issue here is whether appellant, a minor, may rescind a contract to purchase a pick-up truck. On the 20th day of March, 1954, L. D. Robertson, a minor, entered into a conditional sales agreement whereby he purchased from Turner King and J. W. Julian, doing business as the Julian Pontiac Company, a pick-up truck for the agreed price of $1,743.85. On the day of the purchase, Robertson was 17 years of age, and did not have his 18th birthday until April 8th. Robertson traded in a passenger car for which he was given a credit of $723.85 on the purchase price, leaving a balance of $1,020 payable in 23 monthly installments of $52.66 plus one payment of $52.83. He paid the April installment of $52.66.

It appears that Robertson had considerable trouble with the wiring on the truck. He returned it to the automobile dealers for repairs, but the defective condition was not remedied. On May 2nd, the truck caught fire and was practically destroyed. He notified the automobile concern and they stated that they would send the insurance man to see him. It appears that the insurance representative, upon finding out that Robertson was only 17 years of age, refused to deal with him.

On June 7th, appellees filed suit to replevy the damaged truck from Robertson. By his father and next friend, Robertson filed a cross-complaint in which he alleged that he is a minor and asked that the contract of purchase be rescinded and sought to recover that part of the purchase price he had paid, which he alleges is the amount of $723.85, allowed by the dealers on the car traded in, plus the one monthly payment of $52.66, totalling $776.51. A jury was waived and the cause was submitted to the court. There was a judgment for King and Julian on the complaint and the cross-complaint. On appeal, Robertson contends that he was 17 years of age at the time of the alleged purchase and that he has a right under the law to rescind the contract and to recover the portion of the purchase price he has paid.

Appellees contend that the judgment should be sustained because Robertson did not return the damaged truck to the automobile dealers. However, the judgment of the court states: "The court further finds the proof to be that the plaintiff has possession of the said GMC pick-up truck." Hence, there is no merit to this contention. * * *

Appellees further contend that the minor is bound by the contract because the automobile was a necessary. The record does not contain any substantial evidence to support this contention. The only evidence on this issue is that the boy quit school in 1951 and has been earning his own living since that time, and that he has been working for a construction company and traveling around the country to different jobs with his father in his father's truck. The boy lives at home with his parents and there is no showing whatever that he needed the truck in connection with any work he was doing. One of the witnesses for the appellees testified that the boy stated he wanted to use the truck in a farming operation. The record contains no evidence that he was engaged in farming at any time. Another witness for the appellees testified that the boy stated that he wanted to purchase the truck on the "farmer's plan", but there is no showing that the car was sold to him on a "farmer's plan". He was allowed a sum on the car which he traded in, amounting to more than one-third of the purchase price of the new truck, and he was to make substantial monthly payments for the balance. Just what the "farmer's plan" is does not appear in the record, but it is a matter of common knowledge that the plan under which the boy bought the truck is the usual method of making purchases of automobiles. In a suit by a minor to rescind a contract the burden is on the defendant to show that the article was a necessary. [Citation.]

It is our conclusion that the evidence does not sustain a finding that the truck was a necessary to Robertson. In that respect, this case is distinguishable from Sykes v. Dickerson, 216 Ark. 116, 224 S.W.2d 360, where the court said: "It was contemplated that he would use the truck in hauling lumber, and for some months he did so, as an aid to self-support." The law is settled in this State that a minor may rescind a contract to purchase where the property involved is not a necessary. [Citations.]

The automobile dealers have disposed of the car they received in the trade, and cannot restore it to the minor. In a situation of this kind, the weight of authority is that the actual value of the property given as part of the purchase price by the minor is the correct measure of damages. Neither side is bound by the agreement reached as to the value of the car at the time the trade was made. This is true because the contract has been rescinded and there is no contract fixing the value. It is said in 43 C.J.S., Infants, § 47, p. 117: "While it is generally held that, where property traded in by the infant as part of the price is beyond reach of the seller, the infant is entitled to the reasonable value of the property at the time of the purchase, rather than the value fixed in the purchase agreement, it has also been held that he is entitled to receive the value fixed in the agreement."

In support of the rule that a reasonable value of the property at the time of purchase governs, C.J.S. cites Collins v. Norfleet-Baggs, Inc., 197 N.C. 659, 150 S.E. 177, 178, where the court said: "Where the infant parts with personal property, he may, upon disaffirmance, recover the value of such property, as of the date of the contract, but he is neither bound by, nor entitled to be awarded, the price fixed by the contract, for its real value may be more or less than the amount so stipulated." However, in Lockhart v. National Cash Register Co., 66 S.W.2d 796, the Court of Civil Appeals in Texas held the fixed trade in value prevailed. In 27 Am.Jur. 790, it is said: "Where upon an infant's disaffirmance of a purchase of an automobile in exchange for his note and an old automobile, the old automobile cannot be restored, he is entitled to recover the value thereof, which is presumably the valuation at which the defendant took it." Cited as authority is Schoenung v. Gallet, 206 Wis. 52, 238 N.W. 852, 854, 78 A.L.R. 387. In that case there was no showing that the automobile traded in by the infant had any value other than that mentioned in the purchase agreement. The court said: "As plaintiff's former automobile has been wrecked and cannot be restored by defendant, he is liable for the value thereof, which is, presumably, the sum of $50 at which he valued it when he obtained it from plaintiff."

In the case at bar, although the minor was allowed over $700 on his car in the trade, there is evidence to the effect that it was actually worth about $350. Although there is conflict among the authorities as pointed out above, we believe the better rule holds that the value of an article given in trade by a minor as a part of the purchase price is the reasonable market value of the article at the time of the purchase, and that neither party is bound by the value fixed in the purchase agreement.

Young Robertson is a minor; the truck was not a necessary. * * * Hence, the court erred in finding for the automobile dealers, and the cause is therefore reversed and remanded for a new trial.

BRUNHOELZL v. BRANDES

(1917) 90 N.J.Law 31, 100 A. 163.

This was an action in tort brought to recover damages for injury to the plaintiff's automobile resulting from the unskillful manner in which it was driven by the defendant, who was an infant.

The amended state of demand set forth that the plaintiff at the request of the defendant lent to the latter an automobile for use on the evning of June 29, 1916, and that on that same evening the defendant reported to plaintiff that the automobile had upset and was damaged. There was no testimony by the plaintiff as to the cause of the accident, which by the testimony of the defendant and those who were in the car with him, while possibly attributable to poor judgment or lack of caution, was not occasioned by recklessness, wantonness, or gross negligence. At the close of the evidence the defendant's attorney moved for a direction upon the ground that the defendant was an infant, and that the testimony showed merely a breach of his contract of bailment, which motion was denied.

GARRISON, J. The appellant's motion for judgment should have been granted. The general liability of infants for their torts does not take from them their special immunity from liability for their contracts; each rests upon a policy of the law. When these two policies come into conflict they cancel each other to the extent that they deal with the same subject-matter. If this cancellation be complete, so that all that is claimed as the foundation of the infant's tort is covered by the breach of his contract, nothing remains upon which to found an action of tort independently of the contract. The practical test therefore would seem to be not whether the tort arose out of or was connected with the infant's contract, but whether the infant can be held liable for such tort without in effect enforcing his liability on his contract.

In the present case the promise of the infant as bailee was that he would exercise reasonable care in driving the borrowed car. If injury came to the car because of the failure of the bailee to exercise such care, he cannot be held liable therefor in tort without being in effect held liable for a breach of his promise. The facts that constitute the breach of such promise cancel all of the facts that constitute the alleged tort, leaving nothing over and above the breach of the contract upon which to found an action. This result which harmonizes the two policies of the law cannot be frustrated by allowing a plaintiff to elect to sue in tort rather than in contract, as he might do in the case of an adult where no similar policy was involved.

This, in somewhat more extended form, was the ratio decidendi of a very early case in this state. Schenck v. Strong, 4 N.J. Law, 97.

The facts in that case were that the plaintiff had let the defendants have his riding chair (whatever that may be) to go a certain journey in consideration of which they agreed to employ it for no different journey and to use it with moderation and care, notwithstanding which they did go a different journey and did carelessly and improperly break the chair in different parts. It being admitted that the defendants were infants, it was held that the plaintiff should have been non-suited. The opinion delivered by Chief Justice Kirkpatrick goes much further than it is necessary for us to go in the present case, in which there was no departure from the stipulated use of the car, whereas in the decided case a different journey was taken. Without expressing any opinion upon this point, we consider the case an authority, as to the soundness of which upon the question involved we have no doubt.

* * *

The judgment of the Paterson district court is reversed, and, upon the facts stipulated in the agreed state of the case, judgment of no cause of action is ordered to be entered.

BYERS v. LEMAY BANK & TRUST CO.

(1955) 365 Mo. 341, 282 S.W.2d 512.

[Action by Byers, a minor, to recover the sum of his deposits in defendant bank which were applied by the bank upon an indebtedness incurred by the minor under contract entered into during minority. The bank filed counterclaims for outstanding notes executed by the minor. The trial court entered judgment denying the minor's claim and granting the bank's counterclaims. The minor appeals.]

BOHLING, COMMISSIONER. Russell Byers, plaintiff, appeals from a judgment in favor of the Lemay Bank and Trust Company, a corporation, on plaintiff's claim for $4,452 against defendant, and from a judgment of $3,780.40 on defendant's counterclaims against plaintiff. The litigation involves the disaffirmance by a quondam infant of contracts entered into while a minor. The trial was to the court without a jury. Plaintiff contends the judgment on each claim should have been in his favor. * * *

In plaintiff's petition plaintiff pleaded his minority, admitted his indebtedness to defendant as evidenced by his $6,500 note of February 19, 1952, and his renewal note of March 21, 1952, therefor; alleged the application by defendant of $4,452 ($4,440 as established by the evidence) of his deposits on said indebtedness on March 25 and 26, 1952, and sought the recovery of the moneys so applied by defendant, plaintiff alleging he desired to invoke his rights and immunities as a minor and had notified defendant on July 23, 1952, "of his intention of repudiating, rescinding and avoiding" his said written obligation.

Defendant's answer charged plaintiff fraudulently represented that he was 23 years of age, and that defendant, being deceived and entrapped thereby, loaned to plaintiff $6,500 for which plaintiff executed to defendant his said note of February 19, 1952, and, as security therefor, his chattel mortgage on five automobiles, representing to defendant that he was the sole owner of said automobiles, and that plaintiff disposed of said automobiles without the knowledge or consent of defendant.

Defendant's two counterclaims are based on plaintiff's unpaid notes. In its first counterclaim defendant sought judgment on a $1,900 note, dated July 1, 1952, which represented the then balance due on the original $6,500 indebtedness of February 19, 1952. In its second counterclaim defendant sought judgment on a $1,590 note of February 21, 1952. Defendant prayed judgment on each note for the respective balance due, with interest and an attorney's fee of ten per cent in accord with the terms of each of said notes.

Plaintiff, for his defense to defendant's counterclaims, pleaded his infancy. These were all the pleadings in the case.

The clear preponderance of the evidence established the facts alleged by defendant. Plaintiff was 21 years old August 19, 1952. He worked at many places and bought and sold automobiles. He banked with defendant. When he applied for his first loan in November, 1950, he talked to Edgar P. Crecelius, president of defendant, and wanted to know if defendant would "floor plan" automobiles for him. Mr. Crecelius asked plaintiff his age and plaintiff answered that he was 23 years old. The cashier and assistant cashier of defendant corroborated this testimony of Mr. Crecelius. Thereafter a number of loans were made to plaintiff by defendant, each note being secured by a chattel mortgage, and plaintiff paid the notes in due course.

On February 19, 1952, plaintiff borrowed $6,500 from defendant, executed his note therefor and secured its payment by a chattel mortgage on five automobiles. The note was payable on demand or, if no demand, on March 19, 1952. It was not paid and Mr. Crecelius called on plaintiff at his car lot. Plaintiff informed Mr. Crecelius that the automobiles had been disposed of; that he did not know where they were; that he did not have the money; and that he could not help it that they were subject to defendant's mortgage. Mr. Crecelius told plaintiff he would give him a few days to meet his obligation but plaintiff would have to come to the bank and renew the loan. Plaintiff, on March 24, 1952, executed a new note for $6,500 and a chattel mortgage on the five automobiles.

Plaintiff had a balance in the bank to his credit of $6.17. He deposited $4,134 in the bank on March 25, 1952. Mr. Crecelius applied $4,140 on plaintiff's $6,500 note on March 25th. Plaintiff made another deposit of $300 on March 26, 1952, and it also was applied by defendant against the loan. The note was renewed several times and plaintiff made several payments thereon. The last renewal note, for $1,900, was executed July 1, 1952. It has not been paid.

Plaintiff also borrowed $1,590 from defendant on February 21, 1952, executing an installment note, payable in eighteen monthly payments, and, as security, gave a chattel mortgage on a 1952 sedan. Plaintiff paid $265.02 on this note, but the sedan was disposed of without defendant's knowledge, and the note has not been paid.

The judgment, as stated, was against plaintiff on his claim and for defendant on its counterclaims, the court finding defendant entitled on defendant's first counterclaim to $1,900, with interest of $133 and attorney's fees of $190, total $2,223; and on defendant's second counterclaim $1,325, with interest of $99.90 and attorney's fees of $132.50, total $1,557.40, a grand total of $3,780.40.

Defendant does not contend that the case falls within any of the acts of ratification set forth in Section 431.060 RSMo 1949, V. A.M.S., which provides: "No action shall be maintained whereby to charge any person upon any debt contracted during infancy, unless such person shall have ratified the same by some other act than a verbal promise to pay the same", and specifies the acts constituting a ratification after the infant becomes of full age.

Protecting those lacking in experience and of immature mind from designing adults developed in the common law of feudal England. Y. B. 21 Edw. I, p. 318 (1292). The purpose is to shield minors against their own folly and inexperience and against unscrupulous persons, but not to give minors a sword with which to wreak injury upon unsuspecting adults. With the advancement of civilization, the spread of education, and modern industrial conditions minors attain a high state of sophistication. Many earn their own livelihood and are more worldly-wise than their parents. Plaintiff's father testified plaintiff never came to him for fatherly advice. The common law is said to be a growing institution, keeping pace with social and economic conditions. [Citation.] * * *

Different results have been reached in different jurisdictions and in some instances within the same jurisdiction on the responsibility of a minor who, as an inducement for an adult to contract with him, misrepresents that he is of age and deceives the adult by his false statement to the adult's resulting injury. Some jurisdictions tend to uncompromisingly permit minors to rescind their contracts. A number of jurisdictions hold that the minor is not estopped by misrepresentations as to his age in actions at law and a lesser number where the suit is in equity; but other jurisdictions hold estoppel is available in an action at law and a greater number apply estoppel where the suit is in equity. [Citations.] An apparently increasing number of jurisdictions hold the infant liable in tort for inducing the contract by misrepresentations that he is of age. [Citations.] Liability ex delicto and liability ex contractu are based on different principles and involve different measures of recovery. If an infant is liable for his torts generally, the better reasoned decisions hold he is liable for his deceit in misrepresenting his age. His deceit induces the contract. It does not involve the subject matter of the contract. The recovery is the damage resulting to the defrauded person and not the contract consideration. He is not held liable on the contract in form or substance.

Plaintiff argues that he was only asked his age, and that since defendant did not ask him to show his service card, or ask him where he was born, or ask him for his birth certificate, defendant did not exercise reasonable diligence and may not successfully assert it was misled by plaintiff's statement. We do not agree. The misrepresentation is the vital fact. All the elements of a deceit are present. Plaintiff stated his age was 23. Plaintiff knew this was untrue. Plaintiff made the statement with the intent that defendant act upon it. Defendant acted upon the statement in the manner contemplated by plaintiff. Defendant suffered actual damage by reason of plaintiff's misrepresentation as to his age, and the damage was the natural and probable consequences of plaintiff's fraud. * * *

Broadly stated, we have considered minors responsible for their marriage, [citations] for their crimes [citations] and for their torts. [Citations.]

The effect of plaintiff's claim is to rescind his contract and recover the money defendant applied to the discharge of his obligation. We hold the trial court correctly ruled plaintiff's claim.

Defendant's counterclaims are suits on the two notes executed by plaintiff while a

minor, and the judgment, which includes interest and attorney fees, is a judgment on said notes. Defendant's counterclaims are not in tort. Section 431.060, supra, provides that, in the circumstances here of record, "no action shall be maintained whereby to charge any person upon any debt contracted during infancy." * * *

In defendant's case of Swoboda v. Nowak, 213 Mo.App. 452, 255 S.W. 1079, 1082 [7, 8, 13], it was held that an infant was liable on a note given in settlement of his tort, since he was liable for the tort; but the consideration for the note was held to be as fully open to inquiry as though the suit were on the original tort. The instant case does not present that situation. Defendant's notes were not given in settlement of a tort. On its presentation, defendant is not entitled to hold the judgment on its counterclaims.

The judgment for defendant on plaintiff's claim is affirmed, but the judgment against plaintiff on defendant's counterclaims is reversed and the cause as to said counterclaims remanded for such action as defendant may properly take.

HURWITZ v. BARR

(1963 D.C.Court of Appeals) 193 A.2d 360.

QUINN, ASSOCIATE JUDGE. Appellee, (Barr) an infant, purchased a motor scooter for $240 from appellant, (Hurwitz) also an infant. Approximately one week later, appellee sought to rescind the contract on the ground that the motor scooter was defective. Appellee tendered back to appellant the scooter, but appellant refused to return the purchase price. Thereafter suit was brought and judgment entered for appellee ordering the return of the purchase price upon tender to appellant of the scooter. This appeal followed.

The question presented is whether the general rule that the contracts of an infant are voidable at his option [citation] applies to an executed contract between two infants. Appellant contends the rule is inapplicable. We disagree.

The law renders an infant's contracts unenforceable to protect infants from improvident bargains and injustice. It seeks to restore the infant to his position prior to contracting. [Citation.] We feel these rules are equally applicable when both parties to the contract are infants. To hold otherwise would convert the privilege of infancy, which the law intends as a shield to protect the infant, into a sword to be used to the possible injury of others. [Citations.] Indeed, appellant is apparently trying to use the privilege of infancy to enforce the contract because it is appellee who made the improvident bargain. While appellant as an infant has the option of affirming the contract, this option cannot nullify any rights or privileges which appellee, also an infant, is capable of asserting. Hence appellant cannot destroy appellee's right to rescind, and the contract was therefore voidable by appellee. [Citations.]

Appellant also contends that there is no evidence that he is still in possession of the consideration and is capable of restoring it to appellee. He cites two cases in which the courts refuse to rescind a contract between two infants because the defendant had spent the money before the plaintiff sought to avoid the contract. [Citations.] Apparently, appellant seeks alternatively to use the privilege of infancy to disaffirm the contract and take advantage of the rule that an infant will not be held responsible for an inability to restore the consideration if it is spent or otherwise lost. [Citation.] Nevertheless, such is not the case at bar.

Rule 8(c) of the Court of General Sessions provides: "In pleading to a preceding pleading, a party shall set forth * * * any * * matter constituting an avoidance or affirmative defense." An examination of the record discloses that appellant's answer failed to raise the defense of inability to restore the consideration. Further, where in an executed contract the consideration can be restored, in whole or in part, equity will treat the infant as a trustee for the other party and require restoration, on the ground that the infant is in possession of property which, in good conscience, he will not be permitted to retain when he has elected to disaffirm. [Citation.] The record before us is devoid of any indication that appellant cannot return the purchase price upon tender by appellee of the scooter. The judgment is therefore

Affirmed.

EHRSAM v. BORGEN

(1959) 185 Kan. 776, 347 P.2d 260.

WERTZ, J. Eldon Ehrsam, plaintiff (appellant), brought this action against Charles Borgen, defendant (appellee), to recover damages for personal injuries sustained in a collision while riding in defendant's automobile.

The petition, insofar as is pertinent to the issue involved herein, alleged that defendant was the owner and operator of the automobile in which plaintiff was riding on the day in question; that both plaintiff and defendant, residents of Lawrence, were employees of the DuPont Construction Company located between Lawrence and Topeka, and that plaintiff was riding as a passenger pursuant to an arrangement with defendant whereby they exchanged rides every other day in going to and from work. Plaintiff then alleged that due to enumerated acts of negligence on the part of defendant his automobile collided with another vehicle and plaintiff sustained serious injuries for which he sought damages.

The defendant, by way of answer, alleged that he was a minor twenty years of age at the time of the accident and if there was any share-the-ride arrangement between him and plaintiff he disaffirmed any and all such arrangement, contract or agreement; that at the time of the collision plaintiff was riding as a guest without payment in defendant's automobile.

The issues were joined and a pre-trial conference was had pursuant to G.S.1949, 60–2704 and 60–2902, at which time the trial court was requested to determine the legal effect of defendant's disaffirmance of the exchange of ride agreement and the degree of proof required of plaintiff in establishing his right to recover damages.

The learned trial judge found:

"I think it is clear that but for the alleged exchange of ride agreement, plaintiff would have been riding in defendant's automobile as a gratuitous guest at the time of the collision in question. This of course means that if plaintiff is to recover from defendant on proof of ordinary negligence only, as distinguished from the degree of proof required under the Guest Statute (G.S.1949, 8–122b), he must in effect do so by enforcing defendant's liability on the alleged exchange of ride agreement. Since defendant has disaffirmed whatever exchange of ride or share the ride arrangement or agreement that plaintiff alleges was in effect at the time of the collision, plaintiff is left in the same position relative to defendant's alleged tort as would have been the case had no such arrangement ever been entered into, unless defendant may not under the circumstances be permitted to disaffirm."

The trial court concluded that in view of defendant's disaffirmance plaintiff was bound by the degree of proof required by the guest statute. To support his conclusion, the trial judge in his opinion chiefly relied on Brown v. Wood, 293 Mich. 148, 291 N.W. 255, 127 A.L.R. 1436. It is from this order that plaintiff appeals.

Brown v. Wood, supra, seems to hold that if the tort with which an infant is charged is so connected with his voidable contract that commission of the tort constitutes a breach of the contract or if the tort is predicated on a transaction with the infant so that to hold the infant liable in tort would in effect enforce his liability arising out of such contract, then the infant cannot be held liable for his tort, since he cannot be held liable under his contract.

Our statute with reference to contracts of infants [citation] was passed in 1868. It provides that a minor is bound not only by contracts for necessaries but also by his other contracts, unless he disaffirms them within a reasonable time after he attains his majority and restores to the other party all money or property received by him by virtue of the contract and remaining within his control at any time after his attaining his majority. It is apparent that under the statute a minor's contract is never void, unless it is void for some other reason than minority. It can never be more than voidable for minority alone, and, even then, it is valid unless disaffirmed within a reasonable time after majority is attained. If the contract is for necessaries, it may not be disaffirmed. [Citation.]

At the time plaintiff and defendant entered into the share-the-ride agreement, defendant was over twenty years of age, he was an employee of the DuPont Construction Company, he was performing a man's job and was apparently supporting himself, and he owned his own automobile. We will take judicial notice of the fact that the distance from Lawrence to Topeka is approximately twenty-five miles and the distance from Lawrence to the DuPont Construction Company, the place of employment of both parties, is approximately twenty miles; that in order for defendant to hold his job and earn a livelihood, he had to get to and from work and, under such conditions, the arrangement made between the parties was necessary insofar as defendant was concerned. As early as the year 1680, in the case of Barber v. Vincent, Freeman's King Bench Reports, p. 530, it was held that a horse was a necessity to a minor for carrying out his necessary affairs.

It might be said that earlier in the history of our country, when industry was centralized in cities or industrial communities where housing was adequate and public transportation, by way of the streetcar, the bus or the community train, was available to all, private transportation was not necessary for one getting to and from his work. However, since World War II there has been a tremendous growth in our country's population, and in this highly industrial age, where industry has the tendency to decentralize and move to less populated or rural communities within which there is a shortage of housing and very little, if any, public transportation available, the worker is, as a result, required to commute long distances to and from his place of employment. We are, therefore, of the opinion that private transportation for the worker is now a necessity and an agreement made by a minor for such transportation is binding and not subject to disaffirmance for the reason of minority alone.

Our guest statute, [citation] provides that no person who is transported by the *owner or operator* of a motor vehicle as his guest without payment for such transportation shall have a cause of action for damages against such owner or operator for injury, unless such injury or damage shall have resulted from the gross and wanton negligence of the *operator* of such vehicle.

There can be no question but what our guest statute was passed in order to cure certain well-known evils that existed prior to its passage, and that it was passed for the purpose of protecting the owner or operator of an automobile. By the same token, the guest statute should not be extended beyond correction of the evils which it may be assumed were the motivating reasons for its enactment, and, certainly, it was never intended to create a greater evil than that which it attempted to correct. It may be noted that the statute applies to any owner or operator of a motor vehicle and makes no exception as to minors. The statute is plain and clearly reveals that if such owner or operator, whether adult or minor, transports his guest without payment, then such owner or operator shall not be liable in damages for injury to the guest, unless the owner or operator is guilty of gross and wanton negligence. However, if such owner or operator accepts payment or benefits from the passenger, then the act has no application [citation], and this is true whether the owner or operator is an adult or a minor.

In order to take a person riding in an automobile out of the guest status, it is not necessary that the compensation for the ride be a strict contractual consideration or that an enforceable contract relation relative to the ride should exist between the parties. Where the trip is not purely social, any substantial benefit to the owner or operator of the automobile is sufficient to take the case out of the statute. [Citation.] The legislature, when using the word "guest," did not intend to include persons who are being transported for the mutual benefit of both the passenger and the owner or operator of the car. The person transported is not a guest within the meaning of the statute if the transportation is for the mutual benefit of both parties, and in determining whether it was for their mutual benefit, the relationship between the parties to which it was an incident may be considered.

The guest statute, which was passed in 1931, is applicable to the specific circumstances to which it relates. We have held that a statute relating to a specific thing takes precedence over a general statute which might be construed to relate to it. [Citation.]

In the instant case, defendant, by the share-the-ride agreement, accepted payment from plaintiff by way of benefits received and plaintiff thereby became a passenger for payment in defendant's vehicle, with the result that the guest statute was no longer available to defendant as a defense. It is clear that in passing the guest statute the state legislature established the policy of protecting the owner or operator of an automobile, whether adult or minor, from liability for damages under certain specified conditions. It is not the purpose of the act to furnish to the owner or operator of an automobile an escape route for his common-law negligence in carrying passengers for payment. In using a trite expression, we may say that our guest statute was passed to serve as a shield, and not as a sword, for the owner or operator of an automobile.

In view of what has been said, the case of Brown v. Wood, supra, relied on by the trial court, has no application to the facts in this case and it follows that the judgment of the trial court is reversed.

GREEN v. COOK

(1955) 45 Wash.2d 888, 278 P.2d 402.

[Action by Green, guardian of an incompetent person, for rescission of an exchange of realty. Judgment for Green, and defendant appeals.]

MALLERY, JUSTICE. On May 18, 1953, John Elmer Clark, a man eighty-eight years of age, was adjudicated to be incompetent, in an *ex parte* proceeding. The plaintiff herein was appointed as his guardian and authorized to bring this action for rescission of an exchange of real estate made with defendants about sixty days previously on March 19, 1953.

The trial court found that, at the time of the exchange, Clark "was suffering from mental and physical deterioration, which made him incompetent and unable to know or comprehend the nature or the consequences of his act and deed."

The trial court found that the home Clark traded to Cook had a value of $12,500, and was subject to a first mortgage in the sum of $4,734 and a second mortgage in the sum of $300, giving it a net worth of $7,466; and that the house Cook traded to him was worth $3,500, subject to a mortgage in the approximate amount of $1,500, giving it a net worth of $2,000.

The trial court decreed a rescission of the exchange and allowed defendants $850 for betterments made to the Clark home while in their possession. From this decree the defendants appeal.

We are satisfied from the record that John Elmer Clark was incompetent at the time of the transaction in question, and we are satisfied that the record sustains the disparity in value of the two houses, as found by the trial court.

We can agree with appellants that old age is not a ground for rescission of a contract. However, the trial court based its decree upon Clark's incompetence, not his old age.

The gravamen of appellants' appeal, aside from challenging the trial court's findings of incompetence and the values of the houses, is that respondent failed to prove fraud. This contention involves Clark's desire for an old age pension. He was willing to do almost anything to secure one. The defendant Cook told him that he knew the governor, and that, if the exchange of properties was made, he would help Clark secure an old age pension and help him repair his house. It is appellants' position that these statements were not false and, hence, could not constitute clear and cogent proof of fraud.

We think it is immaterial whether the statements were true or not, since they were made for the purpose of inducing an incompetent person to make an improvident exchange of properties having a great disparity in value. Equity will protect incompetent persons against such improvident transactions. [Citations.]

The judgment is affirmed.

PROBLEMS

1. M, a minor, operates a one-man automobile repair shop. A, having heard of M's good work on other cars, takes his car to M's shop for a thorough engine overhaul. M, while overhauling A's engine, carelessly fits an unsuitable piston ring on one of the pistons, with the result that A's engine is seriously damaged. M offers to return the sum which A paid him for his work, but refuses to make good the damage. A sues M in tort for the damage to his engine. Decision?

2. On March 20, Andy Small became 19 years old, but he appeared to be at least 24. On April 1, he moved into a rooming house in Chicago where he orally agreed to pay the landlady $100 a month for room and board, payable at the end of each month for services and room during that month. On April 4, he went to Honest Hal's Carfeteria and signed a contract to buy a used car on time with a small down payment. He made no representation as to his age, but Honest Hal represented the car to be in A–1 condition, which it subsequently turned out not to be. On April 7 Andy sold and conveyed to Adam Smith a parcel of real estate which he owned. On April 30, he refused to pay his landlady for his room and board for the month of April, he returned the car to Honest Hal and demanded his down payment be given back, and he demanded that Adam Smith reconvey the land although the purchase price, which Andy received in cash, had been spent in riotous living. Decision as to each claim?

3. A, age 19, and B, age 20, were brothers. A was the owner of Whiteacre and entered into a written contract to sell Whiteacre to C for $10,-000. B entered into a written contract to purchase Blackacre from C for $10,000. A and B told C that they were both of age. A refused to convey Whiteacre, when properly requested and upon his refusal, C refused to convey Blackacre to B.

C brings an appropriate action against A to obtain Whiteacre. B brings an appropriate action against C to obtain Blackacre. What decisions?

4. Jones, 20 years of age, owned a 1965 automobile. He traded it to Stone for a 1966 car. Jones went on a three-week trip and found that the 1966 car was not as good as the 1965 car. He asked Stone to return the 1965 car but was told that it had been sold to Tate. Jones thereupon sued Tate for the return of the 1965 car. Decision?

5. On May 7, Roy, 20 years of age, a resident of Smithton, purchased an automobile from Royal Motors, Inc., for $1,750 in cash. On the same day he bought a motor scooter from Marks, also 20 years of age, for $450 and paid him in full. On June 5, two days before his twenty-first birthday, Roy disaffirmed the contracts and offered to return the car and the motor scooter to the respective sellers. Royal Motors, Inc., and Marks each refused the offers. On June 16, Roy brought separate appropriate actions against Royal Motors, Inc., and Marks, to recover the purchase price of the car and the motor scooter. By agreement, on July 30, Royal Motors, Inc., accepted the automobile. Royal filed a counterclaim against Roy for the reasonable rental value of the car between June 5 and July 30. The car was not damaged during this period. Royal knew that Roy lived 25 miles from his place of employment in Smithton and that he would probably drive the car, as he did, to provide himself necessary transportation.

Decision as to (a) Roy's action against Royal Motors, Inc., and its counterclaim against Roy; (b) Roy's action against Marks?

6. M, a minor 17 years of age, contracted to purchase a bicycle at the price of $65. He paid $20 and the bicycle was turned over to him; and he agreed to pay weekly installments of $1.50. After using the bicycle 6 months, M, in the meantime having failed to pay the weekly installments agreed upon, returned the bicycle and demanded back the $20 paid. The seller accepted the bicycle and refused to return the initial payment, whereupon M sued to recover. Decision?

7. George Jones on October 1, being then a minor 20 years of age, entered into a contract with the Johnson Motor Company, a dealer in automobiles, to buy a car for $1,800. He paid

$800 down and, under the agreement, was to make monthly payments thereafter of $100 each. After making the first payment on November 1, he failed to make any more payments. Jones was 20 years old at the time he made the contract. He represented to the company that he was 23 years old and the reason he made the representation was because he was afraid that if the company knew his real age, it would not sell the car to him. His appearance was that of a man of 23 or 24 years of age. On December 15, the company repossessed the car under the terms provided in the contract. At that time, the car had been damaged and was in need of repairs. On December 20, George Jones became of age and at once disaffirmed the contract and demanded the return of the $900 paid on the contract. On refusal of the company to do so, George Jones brought an action to recover the $900 and the company set up a counterclaim for $1,000 for expenses to which it was put in repairing the car. Decision?

8. The Climax Corporation was organized in May, 1962, with a capital stock of $9,000. Bell, a minor, subscribed and paid $3,000 for thirty shares of stock. He was elected secretary and treasurer of the corporation, and also was employed as salesman and bookkeeper at a salary of $125 per week. In December, 1965, while still a minor, Bell became dissatisfied with the conduct of the business. He brought an appropriate action charging mismanagement of the corporation, repudiating, on account of his minority, his contract for the purchase of the stock, and offered to return the certificates of stock. Decision?

9. A entered into a written contract to sell certain real estate to M, a minor for $10,000, payable $2,000 upon the execution of the contract, and $200 on the first day of each month thereafter until paid. M paid the $2,000 down payment and 8 monthly installments before attaining his majority. Thereafter, M made two additional monthly payments, and caused the contract to be recorded in the county in which the real estate was located. M was then advised by his attorney that his contract was voidable. Immediately upon being so advised, M tendered the contract to A, together with a quit claim deed reconveying all of M's interest in the property to A. Also, M demanded that A return to him the money which he had paid under the contract. A refused the tender and declined to repay any portion of the money paid to him by M. M then brought an action to cancel the contract and recover the amount paid to A. Decision?

10. A sold and delivered a horse to B, a minor. B during his minority, returned the horse to A, saying that he disaffirmed the sale. A accepted the horse and said he would return the purchase price to B the next day. Later in the day, without A having paid B, he (B) changed his mind, took the horse without A's knowledge and sold it to C. Upon what theory, if any, can A recover from B?

CHAPTER 7

STATUTE OF FRAUDS

Introductory. Except as otherwise provided by statute, an oral contract, i. e., one made by word of mouth and not evidenced by any writing, is in every way as enforceable as a written contract. Recently, a barge line was awarded $200,000 in damages for breach of an oral contract by which the defendant agreed to furnish certain barge equipment for a season. An oral agreement to pay $750,000 to a writer for a new movie script to be written by him, the employment by oral agreement of a public relations firm for an indefinite period at a monthly rate of $1,000, an oral agreement to purchase a household appliance for $80, are common examples of some commercial contracts which are completely valid and enforceable notwithstanding they are not evidenced by a writing.

The requirement that certain kinds of contracts must be in writing to be enforceable is traced back to 1677, when the English Parliament passed legislation requiring that certain classes of contracts be in writing, "signed by the party to be charged," before an action could be brought on them. This was part of a comprehensive statute, entitled "An Act for Prevention of Frauds and Perjuries," designed to prevent fraud and perjury in the proof of various kinds of legal transactions. Sections 4 and 17 of this "Statute of Frauds," as it came to be called, pertained to contracts, and these provisions have been substantially reenacted in almost every State in this country. Although the word "Frauds" is contained in the commonly accepted name of the Statute, it should be borne in mind that the Statute does not directly pertain to fraud, but only to formal requirements necessary to the enforceability of certain types of contracts.

Section 4 of the original Statute of Frauds provides as follows:

> "No action shall be brought (1) whereby to charge any executor or administrator upon any special promise, to answer for damages out of his own estate; (2) or whereby to charge the defendant upon any special promise to answer for the debt, default or miscarriage of another person; (3) or to charge any person upon any agreement made upon consideration of marriage; (4) or upon any contract or sale of lands, tenements or hereditaments, or any interest in or concerning them; (5) or upon any agreement that is not to be performed within the space of one year from the making thereof * * * unless the agreement upon which such action shall be brought, or some memorandum or note thereof, shall be in writing, and signed by the party to be charged therewith or some other person thereunto by him lawfully authorized."

Section 17 is as follows:

> "No contract for the sale of any goods, wares and merchandizes, for the price of ten pounds sterling or upwards, shall be allowed to be good, except the buyer shall accept part of the goods so sold, and actually receive the same, or give something in earnest to bind the bargain, or in part payment, or that some note or memorandum in writing of the said bargain be made and signed by the parties to be charged by such contract, or their agents thereunto lawfully authorized."

In addition to those contracts specified in the original statute, some modern statutes require that others be written; for example, a contract to make a will, to authorize an agent to sell real estate, or to pay commission to a real estate broker. If there is no statute in the jurisdiction requiring a contract to be in writing, it remains true today that an oral contract will be enforced.

Contracts of a type or class governed by the Statute of Frauds are said to be "within" the Statute. Those contracts to which the provisions of the Statute do not apply are "not within" the Statute of Frauds.

Scope of the Statute of Frauds: Section 4 *(1)—Promise by Executor or Administrator.* This clause applies to promises of an executor of a decedent's will or the administrator of his estate if he dies without a will to pay debts of the estate he is administering out of his own funds. If an executor or administrator promises to pay, out of his own funds, a debt of the decedent the promise is unenforceable unless in writing. The substance of this section is included within Section 4(2) relative to promises to answer for the debt of another. The "other" is the estate which the executor or administrator is administering.

Section 4(2)—Promise to Answer for the Debt of Another. Often called the "Suretyship Section," this provision applies typically to contracts wherein a promise is made to a creditor to pay the debts or obligations of a third person, the debtor. Thus, if a father tells a merchant to extend credit to his son, and says "If he doesn't pay, I will," the promise must be in writing to be enforceable. The factual situation can be reduced to the simple "If X doesn't pay, I will." The promise is said to be "collateral," in that the promisor is not the one who is primarily liable. He does not promise to pay in any event; his promise is to pay only upon the default of the one primarily obligated.

It is sometimes difficult to ascertain whether a promise is "collateral" ("I'll pay if X doesn't"), as above, or whether the promisor undertakes to become primarily liable, or, as the courts say, makes an "original" promise ("I'll pay"). For example, a father tells a merchant to deliver certain items to his son, and says "I will pay for them." The Statute of Frauds does not apply, and the promise may be oral. Here, the father is not promising to answer for the debt of another; he is making the debt his own. It is to the father, and to the father alone, that the merchant extends credit and looks for payment. Similarly, where the son, without authority from the father, secures credit from the merchant upon the assurance that "if father does not pay, I will," the son's promise is enforceable, though oral, for here there is no underlying debt of another which the son is promising to pay. The father is not indebted for these goods, and the son's promise is regarded as an original promise.

A situation where the included format is observed (i. e., where one promises to answer for the debt of another,) but where the promise might be held not to be within the Statute of Frauds involves the application of a judicially declared "main purpose doctrine" or "leading object rule." Suppose that a supply company has refused to furnish materials upon the credit of a building contractor. Faced with a possible slow-down which he is desirous of avoiding, the owner promises the supplier that if he will extend credit to the contractor, the owner will pay if the contractor does not. Here, a court would be likely to view this as a situation where the purpose of the promisor was to subserve a pecuniary interest of his own, even though the performance of the promise would discharge the debt of another. The intent to benefit the contractor was at most incidental, and courts will uphold oral promises of this type by a judicial interpretation which does not follow the literal language of the statute. The courts regard this type of transaction as one against which Section 4 of the Statute of Frauds was not aimed. Another application of the rule is shown in the following excerpt from the Restatement of the Law of Contracts: "D owes C $1000. C is about to levy an attachment on D's factory. S, who is also a creditor of D's, fearing that the attachment will ruin D's business and thereby destroy his own chance of collecting his claim, orally promises C that if C will forbear to take legal proceedings against D for three months, S will pay D's debt if D fails to do so. S's promise is enforceable." Restatement of the Law of Contracts, Section 184, Illustration 2.

Finally, courts do not regard promises made to a *debtor* as being within the Statute. For example, D owes a debt to C. S promises D to pay this debt. Courts do not hold that the "debt of another" which the promisor undertakes to pay can be the promisee's own debt. Accordingly, the promise may be oral. For this reason also, contracts of "indemnity," as where S says to D, "Buy goods from C and I will indemnify you against loss," are not required to be in writing.

Section 4(3)—Agreement upon Consideration of Marriage. The notable feature of this section is that it does not apply to the one case where there is perhaps the most danger of fraud and perjured testimony, namely, mutual promises to marry. The consideration is not the marriage but the promise to marry. The section does apply to the ordinary "marriage settlement" or antenuptial contract, as for example, where the groom promises his bride to convey title to a certain farm if the latter accepts his proposal of marriage. The bride accepts, and they are married. Unless the groom's promise to convey the farm is evidenced by a writing, it is not enforceable.

The following are illustrative of the promises which are within this section of the Statute of Frauds: "In consideration of a woman's promise to marry him, a man promises to make a settlement of money or other property in trust for her. In consideration of Mary's promising to marry or actually marrying John, John promises to pay her an allowance or to execute a will leaving Mary some or all of John's property at death. In consideration of Mary's marrying John, Peter promises to convey property or to pay an

annuity. John and Mary mutually agree that their marriage shall not affect the existing property rights of each. Mary marries John in return for John's promise to give Sarah a share in his estate, or to adopt and care for Sarah. Mary promises to release a money judgment against John in consideration of his marrying her." Corbin on Contracts, Section 462.

Section 4(4)—Contract for Sale of Land or any Interest Therein. It is not surprising that the drafters of the Statute of Frauds included land contracts within its provisions. A contract involving the sale of land is likely to be an important contract, with the attendant temptations to fraud and perjury accentuated. But this is not always true, since some land transactions might involve "property" of very little value, or the sale of an interest in land which is quite insignificant. For example, an "easement" to cross certain property is an interest in land, but may be of small value from an economic standpoint.

To ascertain the subject matter covered by this section, "land or an interest therein," courts consider precedents taken from the law of property. A distinction is made between real property (land) and personal property (goods, chattels). In addition to the ordinary "estates in land," real property includes leases, mortgages, and easements. A contract for the sale of timber, minerals or the like, or a structure or its materials to be removed from the land is considered a contract for the sale of personal property if they are to be severed by the seller. Section 2–107(1), U.C.C. If the buyer is to sever, such contracts are considered contracts affecting land. A contract for the sale apart from the land of growing crops or other things not enumerated in the preceding sentence capable of severance without material harm to the land is deemed to be a contract for the sale of personal property, irrespective of whether the buyer or seller is to sever the goods from the land. Section 2–107(2).

Assume that a seller and a purchaser make an oral contract for the sale of a certain tract of land. In reliance upon this contract the purchaser takes possession of the property, pays a part of the purchase price and erects valuable improvements. If the seller refuses to go through with the deal, asserting the Statute of Frauds land clause, may the purchaser obtain redress in the courts? Upon the basis of the literal language of the Statute, he clearly could not. There are no exceptions—for "hardship" or anything else. However, there is a "part performance doctrine," developed in courts of equity which sometimes grants relief to a buyer under these and similar circumstances. Simply expressed, the courts deem it inequitable and unjust to permit the Statute to be interposed by the seller after such reliance by the purchaser. Often it is said that the seller is "estopped" to assert the defense of the Statute of Frauds.

Courts differ from one jurisdiction to another respecting the degree of reliance that must be established to entitle a purchaser to relief. The Restatement of the Law of Contracts, Section 197, states the rule as follows: "Where, acting under an oral contract for the transfer of an interest in land, the purchaser with the assent of the vendor (a) makes valuable improvements on the land, or (b) takes possession thereof or retains a possession thereof existing at the time of the bargain, and also pays a portion or all of the purchase price, the purchaser or the vendor may specifically enforce the contract."

Section 4(5)—Agreements Not to be Performed within One Year. One approaching this section for the first time might be surprised by the manner in which it has been interpreted by the courts. The test is not whether the agreement is one which is likely to be performed within one year from the date of the making of the contract, or whether the parties contemplate that performance will be within the year, but whether it is *possible* for the contract to be performed within a year. Thus, if A agrees to support B for life, the contract is not within the Statute of Frauds. It is possible that B may die within the year, in which case the contract would be completely performed. The contract is therefore one which is *fully performable* within a year. However, an oral contract to support another person for thirteen months is not possible of performance within a year and is unenforceable.

It should be observed in these cases that the year runs from the time the agreement is made, not from the time when the performance is to begin. Hence, a contract for a year's performance which is to begin three days from the date of the making of the contract is within the Statute, and if oral is unenforceable. If, however, the performance is to begin the following day, or consistently with the terms of the agreement could have begun the following day, it is not within the Statute, and need not be in writing, as the one year's performance would be completed on the anniversary date of the making of the contract, and the law disregards fractions of a day.

As simple as the foregoing test might appear, it is sometimes difficult to apply. In Sinclair v. Sullivan Chevrolet Co., 45 Ill.App. 2d 10, 195 N.E.2d 250 (1964), affirmed 31 Ill.2d 507, 202 N.E.2d 516 (1964), an action was brought on an alleged oral agreement between plaintiff and defendant made on May 30, 1960, whereby plaintiff was to start work for defendant on June 6, 1960, for at least one year as sales manager of defendant corporation. It was alleged that acting upon the defendant's promises to pay a stipulated salary, to pay a bonus based on profits but not to be less than a fixed amount each year, to pay plaintiff's costs of re-locating his home, to provide plaintiff with a car, and to reduce the agreement to writing, plaintiff resigned a good job in St. Louis and moved to Champaign. Plaintiff worked until March

18, 1961, then left defendant, alleging that he left because of defendant's failure to keep its promises. In holding the Statute of Frauds applicable, the Illinois Appellate Court observed:

> "Plaintiff argues that the contract could have been concluded by many conditions, all occurring within one year. Other than the death of plaintiff, we find nothing within the record and nothing is brought to the court's attention to show the contract could have been 'performed' within one year. In every employment contract the contract is subject to termination at the death of the employed party, but this does not mean the contract has been performed in full. If we were to hold termination and performance synonymous, the act would be rendered useless. * * * Where the contract extends to a point in time, be it death or some other circumstance, at which time the full service contemplated will have been rendered, and that point in time could occur within one year, the Statute of Frauds will not be a bar to enforcement of the action."

The courts have at times developed a rule to "take cases out of the Statute of Frauds," as, for instance, the "part performance doctrine" in the land contract cases and the "main purpose doctrine" in promises to answer for the debt of another. A judicially constructed exception has been engrafted upon this one-year section as well. Where a bilateral contract has been fully performed on one side, most courts hold that the promise of the other party is enforceable even though by its terms its performance was not possible within the period of a year. For example, A orally promises to pay B $600, in three annual installments of $200 each, in consideration for a boat owned by B which B delivers to A at once. A's promise is enforceable notwithstanding the one-year clause, because B has fully performed. On the other hand, the court in the Sinclair case, discussed above, refused to find that plaintiff's move from St. Louis to Champaign and partial performance estopped the defendant from invoking the Statute of Frauds.

In certain instances of fraud or material misrepresentation, the guilty party may be estopped to assert the defense of the Statute of Frauds. In order to invoke the doctrine of equitable estoppel, there must appear words or conduct by the guilty party amounting to a misrepresentation or concealment of material fact, i. e., the false representation must relate to an existing or past event and not to a promise or prognostication concerning a future happening. In the Sinclair case the court refused to find that the defendant was estopped to assert the defense of the Statute since the oral promises concerned only future performances which the law did not regard as binding.

Sales of Goods. Section 17 of the original Statute of Frauds relates to the sale of goods. In a revised form it has become Section 2–201 of the Uniform Commercial Code applicable to sales of goods for a price of $500 or more.

Section 2–201 of the Code provides:

> (1) Except as otherwise provided in this Section a contract for the sale of goods for the price of $500 or more is not enforceable by way of action or defense unless there is some writing sufficient to indicate that a contract for sale has been made between the parties and signed by the party against whom enforcement is sought or by his authorized agent or broker. A writing is not insufficient because it omits or incorrectly states a term agreed upon but the contract is not enforceable under this paragraph beyond the quantity of goods shown in such writing.
>
> (2) Between merchants if within a reasonable time a writing in confirmation of the contract and sufficient against the sender is received and the party receiving it has reason to know its contents, it satisfies the requirements of subsection (1) against such party unless written notice of objection to its contents is given within 10 days after it is received.
>
> (3) A contract which does not satisfy the requirements of subsection (1) but which is valid in other respects is enforceable

(a) if the goods are to be specially manufactured for the buyer and are not suitable for sale to others in the ordinary course of the seller's business and the seller, before notice of repudiation is received and under circumstances which reasonably indicate that the goods are for the buyer, has made either a substantial beginning of their manufacture or commitments for their procurement; or

(b) if the party against whom enforcement is sought admits in his pleading, testimony or otherwise in court that a contract for sale was made, but the contract is not enforceable under this provision beyond the quantity of goods admitted; or

(c) with respect to goods for which payment has been made and accepted or which have been received and accepted.

Section 2–201 covers a contract for the sale of "goods." Section 2–105 of the Code defines "goods" to include all things, including specially manufactured goods, which are movable at the time of identification to the contract for sale. It expressly includes growing crops and unborn animals. It expressly excludes investment securities which are separately covered by Article 8 of the Code.

Sales of Securities. Section 8–319 of the Code is a separate Statute of Frauds applicable to contracts for the sale of securities (stocks and bonds). Such contracts are not enforceable without a signed writing sufficient to indicate that a contract has been made and stating the parties, the quantity, the price, and a description of the securities.

Every contract for the sale of securities is within the Statute as no minimum amount in terms of price is excluded. Delivery and acceptance of the security or payment of the price satisfies the Statute, but the contract is enforceable only to the extent of such delivery or such payment.

The Statute is also satisfied if within a reasonable time a sufficient confirmatory writing is sent by one party to the other who fails to object to its contents within ten days after receipt. This method of compliance is effective although the oral contract is not between merchants, unlike the comparable provision with reference to a contract for the sale of goods.

An admission in a pleading, testimony, or otherwise in court will also satisfy the requirements of the Code and make the contract enforceable.

Sales of Other Kinds of Personal Property. Section 1–206 of the Code is a catch-all Statute of Frauds applicable to contracts for the sale of personal property, other than goods, securities or security agreements in amount or value beyond $5,000. That section makes such contracts unenforceable by way of action or defense unless there is some writing which indicates that a contract for sale has been made between the parties at a defined or stated price, reasonably identifies the subject matter, and is signed by the party against whom enforcement is sought or by his authorized agents. This section of the Code covers rights under bilateral contracts, royalty rights, patent rights, and "general intangibles," as defined in Section 9–106.

Methods of Compliance—The Writing or Memoranda. Section 4 of the original Statute of Frauds requires that the agreement upon which the action is brought, or some memorandum or note thereof, be in writing signed by the party to be charged or by his agent. The note or memorandum should specify the parties to the contracts, the subject matter, and any material or special terms and conditions, all with reasonable certainty. As to a statement of consideration, this is required by the statute in some States, and is dispensed with by the statute in other States, where it can be proved by parol evidence. In States where the statute is silent on this matter, some courts require the consideration to be stated, and some do not. The note or memorandum may be extremely informal, and may be written in ink or pencil or be typewritten. All that is necessary is that it describe or identify the parties and the subject matter (e. g., the land, the debt of a third person) with reasonable certainty, and specify such other terms, if any, as are material.

The memorandum may be such that the parties view it as having no legal significance whatever, as for example, a personal letter between the parties or a third person, an inter-departmental communication, an advertisement, or handbill, or the minutes or record books of a business. The writing need not have been delivered to the party who seeks to take advantage of it, and it may even contain a repudiation of the oral agreement. It may consist of several papers or documents, not one of which would be sufficient by itself. Section 208 of the Restatement of the Law of Contracts provides: "The memorandum may consist of several writings, (a) if each writing is signed by the party to be charged and the writings indicate that they relate to the same transaction, or (b) though one writing only is signed if (i) the signed writing is physically annexed to the other writing by the party to be charged, or (ii) the signed writing refers to the unsigned writing, or (iii) it appears from examination of all the writings that the signed writing was signed with reference to the unsigned writings." Illustrating the final clause is the following: "A and B enter into an oral contract within the Statute. A memorandum of the contract is made on two sheets of paper which are not attached to one another. If the sheets can be read together the memorandum contains all requisites. They may be read together if the second sheet indicates that it is a continuation of the first, as where an incomplete sentence on the first sheet is finished on the second, or where the contract partially disclosed by the first sheet is evidently the same contract as that partially disclosed by the

second sheet." Restatement of the Law of Contracts, Section 208(b), Illustration 3.

The Statute of Frauds provisions under the Code tend to be even more liberal. The Code requires merely some writing sufficient to indicate that a contract has been made between the parties and signed by the party against whom enforcement is sought or by his authorized agent or broker. The writing is not insufficient because it omits or incorrectly states a term agreed upon but the contract can in such case be enforced only to the extent of the quantity of goods shown in the writing. Its non-insistence that the writing contain all of the terms, other than quantity, is consistent with other provisions of the Code that contracts may be enforced, although material terms are omitted, as in Section 2–305 (Open Price Contracts), Section 2–306 (Output, Requirements, and Exclusive Dealing Contracts), and Section 2–311 (Particulars of Performance to be specified by one of the parties). Given proof that a contract was intended and a signed writing describing the goods, the quantity thereof, and names of parties, the Court, under the Code, can supply omitted terms such as price, terms and place of payment, time and place of delivery, and warranties, if any.

Concerning the signature of "the party to be charged," or "the party against whom enforcement is sought" (Section 2–201(1)), most courts hold that both parties need not have signed, only the one against whom the contract is sought to be enforced. The party "to be charged" is always the defendant. Moreover, the "signature" may be by initials, or even typewritten or printed, so long as the party intended thereby to authenticate the writing. Furthermore, it need not be at the bottom of the page or at the customary place for a signature. "The signature to a memorandum under the Statute may be written or printed and need not be subscribed at the foot of the memorandum, but must be made or adopted with the declared or apparent intent of authenticating the memorandum as that of the signer". Restatement of the Law of Contracts, Section 210.

Other Methods of Compliance Under the Code. An oral contract for the sale of goods may comply with the requirements of the Code in the following instances: (1) where written confirmation of a contract between merchants is sent and no objection is made within ten days; (2) where the party defending against the contract admits it by pleading, testimony or otherwise in court; (3) under certain circumstances, where the goods are to be specially manufactured; and (4) where there has been payment or delivery and acceptance.

The Code provides relief to a merchant who has confirmed an oral agreement for the sale of goods by letter or signed writing to the other party if he, too, is a merchant. Prior to the Code, if A and B, both merchants, had entered into a contract by telephone for the sale of goods and A had written a confirming letter, the Statute of Frauds would have been satisfied with respect to the enforcement of the contract against A, although the contract would not be enforceable against B, since B had not signed any note or memorandum. B thus was placed in the unfairly advantageous position of being able to play the market against the contract price. He could either seek to enforce the contract or avoid it, whichever course was to his advantage. The Code does not permit this advantage, since it provides that as between merchants the written confirmation, if sufficient against the sender is also sufficient against the recipient of the confirmation unless the recipient gives written notice of his objection within ten days after receiving the confirmation. Section 2–201(2).

The Code permits an oral contract for the sale of goods to be enforced against a party who in his pleading, testimony, or otherwise in court, admits that a contract was made, but limits enforcement to the quantity of goods so admitted. Section 2–201(3) (b). This is unique. Prior to the Code, the defendant could plead the Statute of Frauds by referring to the contract as an "alleged agreement" within the Statute, and thereby admit nothing. Under the Code, a careful lawyer could similarly plead the Statute. But testimony is oral and compulsory, and the language "otherwise in court" may include compulsory pre-trial discovery depositions of the defendant. This section may considerably restrict the protection heretofore afforded by the Statute of Frauds with respect to oral contracts for the sale of goods and securities.

Prior to the Code a contract for goods to be manufactured especially for the purchaser, upon his special order, was not within the statute. The Code permits enforcement of an oral contract for such special order goods only if there is extrinsic evidence indicating that the goods were made for the buyer and only if the seller can show that he has made a substantial beginning of their manufacture or commitments for their procurement prior to receipt of any notice of repudiation. If the goods, although manufactured on special order, are readily marketable in the ordinary course of the seller's business, the contract is within the statute. If B brings an action against A alleging that, pursuant to a contract A ordered from B three million balloons with A's trademark imprinted thereon at a price of $30,000, the action is not subject to the defense of the statute, unless A can show (1) that the balloons are suitable for sale to other buyers, which is highly improbable in view of the trademark, or (2) that notice of repudiation was received by B before he had made a substantial start on the production of the balloons or had otherwise substantially committed himself for their procurement. If, for example, B had completed the manufacture of 200,000 balloons, the alleged contract could be proved by parol testimony. Or, if B had executed a written contract with C pursuant to which C was to manufacture part or all of the three million balloons, the alleged contract between A and B would fall outside the statute and could be established by parol evidence.

Prior to the Code delivery and acceptance of part of the goods or payment of part of the price made enforceable the entire oral contract against the buyer who had received part payment. Under the Code, such "partial performance," as a substitute for the required memorandum, validates the contract only for the goods which have been accepted or for which payment has been made and accepted. Receipt and acceptance either of the goods or of the price constitutes an admission by both parties that some contract exists between them. If the court can make a just apportionment, the agreed price of any goods actually delivered can be recovered without a writing; or, if the price has been paid, the seller can be forced to deliver an apportionable part of the goods. The overt actions of the parties make admissible evidence of the other terms of the contract necessary to reach a just apportionment.

If the parties to a contract agree to modify its terms, the contract, as modified, is within the Statute of Frauds and to be enforceable must comply with its requirements. Section 2–209(3). Thus, if the parties enter into an oral contract to sell an automobile for $450 to be delivered to the buyer and later, prior to delivery, orally agree that the seller shall paint the car and install new tires and the buyer pay a price of $550, the modified contract is unenforceable and the original contract will probably be held to be rescinded. Similarly, if the parties have a written contract for the sale of 500 bushels of wheat at a price of $1.50 per bushel and later upon oral agreement increase the quantity to 1,000 bushels at the same price per bushel, the agreement, as modified, is unenforceable.

Where the parties have entered into a "sale or return" type of contract which permits the buyer to return conforming goods and be relieved of his duty to pay the price, the "or return" portion of the agreement is treated as a separate contract within the Statute of Frauds. Section 2–326(4).

Effect of Noncompliance with the Statute of Frauds. The original statute provided that "no action shall be brought" upon a contract to which the Statute of Frauds applied and which did not comply with its requirements. Most State statutes still retain this terminology, although a few declare the contracts "void" or "invalid." The Code states that the contract "is not enforceable by way of action or defense." Despite the difference in language the basic legal effect is the same: a contracting party has a defense to an action by the other for enforcement of an oral contract which is within the Statute and which does not comply with the Statute. In short, the oral contract is unenforceable.

If A, a painter, and B, a home owner, make an oral contract whereby B is to give A a certain tract of land in return for the painting of B's house, the contract is unenforceable under the Statute of Frauds. It is a contract for the sale of an interest in land. Either party can repudiate and has a defense to an action by the other to enforce the contract.

If the painter has already performed a part of the work is he completely without a remedy? Clearly, he cannot sue for breach of contract, but courts may still permit a recovery in quasi contract to prevent an unjust enrichment. This type of restitutory remedy allows the painter to recover damages equal to the amount of the benefit that he has conferred upon the home owner. Thus, all may not be lost to a party unable to enforce an oral contract. However, this possibility should impel a contracting party to use the utmost caution to assure compliance with the Statute. Only by complying with the Statute of Frauds can one be reasonably certain of obtaining the benefit of the bargain that has been made.

CASES

PETERSON v. ROWE

(1957) 63 N.M. 135, 314 P.2d 892.

COMPTON, J. Appellee brought this action to recover for professional services rendered appellants' father. Issue was joined by a general denial. The cause was tried to the court and the judgment went against appellants, M. H. Rowe and William W. Rowe, and they appeal. The pertinent findings are:

"(2) That between the approximate dates of July 26, 1955, and September 11, 1955, plaintiff provided hospital care, laboratory facilities and medication to patient William H. Rowe at the special instance and request of his sons, M. H. Rowe and William W. Rowe.

"(3) That the statement for services rendered totaled $3,144.25, but defendants, M. H. Rowe and William W. Rowe paid on account $245.00, and the Southwest Blood Bank credited $160.00 to this account, leaving a balance of $2739.25.

"(4) That defendants, M. H. Rowe and William W. Rowe, made direct, independent, unqualified and unconditional promises to pay for the hospital services rendered by plaintiff to William H. Rowe.

"(5) That plaintiff, in reliance upon the promises of defendants M. H. Rowe and William W. Rowe, did perform his part of the agreement."

Appellants contend (a) that the findings are not supported by substantial evidence, and, (b) that the contract, being oral, is within the statute of frauds. These contentions require a determination whether appel-

lants are original promisors or mere guarantors. If the former, they are liable; if the latter, the statute is a complete defense. A review of the evidence convinces us that appellants are original promisors and not guarantors. It follows, both contentions must be rejected.

On July 26, 1955, when William H. Rowe was admitted to appellee's hospital, he was suffering from the effects of a severe gastric hemorrhage. He was first given emergency treatment, and later prepared for surgery, which was performed July 31, 1955. He was discharged from the hospital September 11, 1955. The hospital services medicines, treatments, laboratory facilities, etc., amounted to $3,144.25, which amount was later reduced to $2,739.25 by appellants and Southwest Blood Bank.

The evidence discloses at least four conversations between the parties concerning payment for services to be furnished the patient. Appellants were at the hospital the day after William H. Rowe was admitted, and while there, discussed with appellee the matter of making financial arrangements. Appellee explained to appellants that the patient was very ill and would require extensive treatment. Appellants informed appellee that their father had no financial means, nevertheless, appellant, M. H. Rowe, stated that appellants themselves would pay for such services. His exact statement was: "You go right ahead and give him whatever is necessary to save his life and I will pay for it." Subsequently on July 29, appellants, accompanied by their wives, came to the hospital, and again appellant, W. H. Rowe, stated to appellee: "Well, we want you to do everything you can to save his life and we don't want you to spare any expense because whatever he needs, doctor, you go ahead and get it and I will pay you." On July 31, the date of the operation, appellants were at the hospital, and again the question of payment of expenses was renewed. At that time, M. H. Rowe voluntarily authorized the services of special nurses, stating: "because whatever he needs, I want him to have it and I will pay you for it." To which appellant William W. Rowe assented as follows: "That is correct, anything that—any expense." "Do not spare any expense on my father and I will pay you for it." The testimony of both Dr. Kinne and Dr. Andrews lends strong support to appellee. This evidence is substantial. Further, some three weeks later, the business manager of the hospital phoned appellants and advised them that the expenses were continuing to mount, and asked them to come in and discuss the matter. They did, but stated they were just then short of cash. Appellant, M. H. Rowe, said: "We will pay you $200 now and then we will pay you $200 every month." He stated further: "My father has some property back in Missouri and we will put it on the market for sale and that when we sell the property why we will pay the entire balance off in full." Appellant, William W. Rowe, spoke up, saying, "that is correct". They then paid $200 and $45 later when threatened with litigation.

Of course, in the absence of an expressed contract, appellants would have been under no legal obligation to pay for the services rendered to their father. [Citations.] But it was at appellants' request, and for their benefit, that the services were furnished; hence, the promise to pay was an original undertaking and is without the statute. [Citations.]

Appellants argue the point that appellee did not release the patient, William H. Rowe, from liability. True, but that is not important. Appellants, having contracted for the services, are in no position to complain that the father had not been released. [Citations.]

The judgment will be affirmed and remanded with direction to enter judgment against appellants and the sureties upon their supersedeas bond, and it is so ordered.

MID–ATLANTIC APPLIANCES v. MORGAN

(1952) 194 Va. 324, 73 S.E.2d 385.

SPRATLEY, J. On April 11, 1951, plaintiff in error, Mid-Atlantic Appliances, Inc., a corporation, filed the following notice of motion for judgment against John W. Morgan:

"The plaintiff, Mid-Atlantic, Appliances, Inc., a corporation, moves the Court for judgment against the defendant John W. Morgan for Four Thousand Twenty-nine Dollars and Forty Cents ($4,029.40) due the plaintiff upon defendant's contract, for that:

"On or about the 21st day of March, 1951, defendant, President and a Director of Grant's, Inc., a Virginia corporation, 3536 Mt. Vernon Avenue, Alexandria, Virginia, promised and agreed to assume and pay in full the plaintiff's open account claim against said Grant's, Inc., in the amount of Four Thousand Twenty-nine Dollars and Forty Cents ($4,029.40) for and in consideration of the following:

"1. that plaintiff withhold suit against Grant's, Inc., upon its, the plaintiff's open account claim, suit then being imminent.

"2. that defendant be given voting control of said Grant's, Inc., through transfer to him of the share holding in said corporation of Margaret Grant. The condition of defendant's promise was that he, the defendant, would assume voting control of Grant's, Inc., and assume personally and pay the existing obligation to the plaintiff, if after ten days from said 21st day of March, 1951, a purchaser had not been found who would buy defendant's entire interest in Grant's, Inc.

"Pursuant to the agreement and understanding, said share holding of Margaret Grant was deposited in escrow to be delivered to defendant at the end of ten days, in order that defendant might assume voting control in the event that he had not in that time sold his interest. And further pursuant thereto, plaintiff corporation refrained from instituting legal action against Grant's, Inc. Defendant has not however accepted delivery of said share holding, or assumed voting control of Grant's, Inc., nor has he paid the plaintiff corporation's claim as he had promised to do, nor has any purchaser, in said ten day period or thereafter, purchased the interest of defendant in Grant's, Inc. And defendant has refused, and still refuses, to pay or personally endorse the obligation of the said Grant's, Inc., to plaintiff."

On the same day plaintiffs in error, Washington Wholesalers and Southern Wholesalers, Inc., filed separate notices of motion for judgment against Morgan, based upon exactly similar causes of action. The only difference was in the names of the respective plaintiffs and the amounts sought to be recovered.

In response, Morgan filed in each case a plea of the statute of frauds, setting out that the promise and undertaking alleged in the notice of motion was a promise to answer for the debt of another, and that "no promise, contract, agreement, representation, assurance, or ratification in respect of or relating to the said supposed cause of action in the said notice of motion for judgment mentioned, nor any memorandum or note thereof, was or is in writing, or was or is signed by the said defendant or his agent." Code of Virginia 1950, § 11–2(4).

It was stipulated by counsel for the parties that the alleged promise of Morgan was not in writing, and "that the defendant would admit that there was a promise solely for the purpose" of considering the issue raised by his plea. Since the same question of law was involved in each proceeding, the cases were heard together under an agreement that they were to be subject to like determination.

Upon consideration of the notice of motion, the plea of the statute of frauds, and the terms of the stipulation, the trial court held that since the notice failed to "allege that the original liability was extinguished by a novation, or that, as a result of any promise by Morgan, the parties released Grant's, Inc., from its liability," it was of opinion that "The pleadings set up cases based upon collateral and not original promises, and, therefore, come within the statute of frauds." It accordingly sustained the plea of the statute of frauds, and dismissed the three cases.

The sole error assigned was that the court erred in its ruling and judgment.

Plaintiffs in error contend that defendant's promise was an original independent undertaking on his part and given with the objective of direct benefit to himself as a consideration of the promise, and was, therefore, not within the statute of frauds. * * *

Numerous cases coming within that branch of the statute of frauds here under consideration have been before this court and the courts of other jurisdictions. The broad statements and general expressions used in the various decisions with reference to the particular facts involved in the individual case, and the subtle distinctions sometimes made, present a lack of uniformity of views as to the effect of a new consideration on a promise to answer for the debt of another. However, in Virginia, we have consistently followed the basic rule stated in Noyes v. Humphreys, 11 Gratt. 636, 52 Va. 636, 643: "Every collateral promise to answer for the debt, default or misdoings of another person, is within the statute, and void if not in writing; but original undertakings need not be in writing, not being within the statute. The difficulty is in determining under which head the undertaking in any particular case is to be classed."

Reviewing the above case and a number of other cases, Judge Burks, in Way v. Baydush, 133 Va. 400, 408, 112 S.E. 611, in considering the difference between a collateral and an original undertaking, said this:

"In Noyes v. Humphreys, 11 Gratt. 636, 52 Va. 636, the prior cases in this jurisdiction are cited and it appears from them that the holding in this jurisdiction is that if the original contractor remains liable and the undertaking of the new party is merely that of surety or guarantor, the undertaking of the latter is collateral and within the statute of frauds. We do not purpose to depart from that holding in this case."

* * *

"According to the better view, the fact that there is an independent consideration for a promise is not conclusive that the promise is not one to answer for the debt of another within the statute of frauds. A promise is collateral and within the statute where the primary purpose of the promisor is to secure the debt of another, although a benefit actually inures to him because of his promise." 49 Am.Jur., Statute of Frauds, sec. 74, p. 426. * * *

In 37 C.J.S., Frauds, Statute of, § 24, page 533, this is said:

"Generally speaking, an oral undertaking by a person not previously liable, for the purpose of securing the debt or performing the same duty for which the person for whom the undertaking is made remains liable, is within the statute and must be in writing, and if the liability of the debtor is extinguished the promise is original. The continuance of liability of the original debtor is frequently used as a test in determining whether the contract is collateral or original."

In view of the rule established in Virginia, it is unnecessary to cite decisions from other States. However, in Richardson Press v. Andrew Albright, 224 N.Y. 497, 121 N.E. 362, 8 A.L.R. 1195, it was held that a stockholder of a publishing company, beneficially interested in having its publication continue without interruption, was not liable upon his oral promise to pay an overdue printing bill and to pay cash for future issues, when the creditor continued to regard the publishing company as the principal debtor and attempted to collect the bills from it. * * *

Measured by the rule long established in Virginia, the promise alleged in the notice of motion under review was a collateral and not an original independent undertaking by the defendant. He did not assume an independent duty of payment which made the debt his own, irrespective of the liability of the principal debtor. This, we think, is made clear by the language of the notice.

Analyzing the notice of motion under review, it will be observed that the promise is conditional. It is alleged, in paragraph number 2, that "the defendant *would* assume voting control of Grant's, Inc., and *assume personally and pay the existing obligation* to the plaintiff, *if after ten days* * * * a purchaser had not been found who would buy defendant's entire interest in Grant's, Inc." (Italics added). All that the notice charged was that the defendant failed to carry out a promise that he would, at some later time, if a certain event occurred, assume the debt of another, not that he made a positive promise to answer for the said debt. Again, it is further alleged that "defendant has refused, and still refuses, to pay or personally endorse *the obligation of the said Grant's Inc., to plaintiff.*" (Italics added). This is a clear recognition of the continued liability of Grant's, Inc. That debt was not extinguished or released. There was no novation. The circumstances alleged in the notice of motion do not make out an original independent undertaking by the defendant. * * *

For the foregoing reasons, we are of opinion to affirm the judgment of the trial court, sustaining the plea of the statute. Accordingly, its judgment is affirmed in each of the three proceedings under review.

Affirmed.

ZUPAN v. BLUMBERG

(1957) 2 N.Y.2d 547, 141 N.E.2d 819.

VAN VOORHIS, J. The sole question presented is whether a contract of employment whereby plaintiff was to secure advertising accounts for defendants in return for a percentage commission was within the Statute of Frauds, Personal Property Law, Consol. Laws, c. 41, § 31. Plaintiff, a free-lance advertising solicitor, testified that in oral negotiations with defendants in 1946 and again in 1949, he was asked to get accounts for them and that he was to receive 25% commission on any account that he brought in for so long as the account was active. Plaintiff testified that in 1950 he brought in the account of the firm in question, and that defendants paid him commissions thereon until May, 1951, but not thereafter, although they continued to handle the account. Plaintiff's Exhibit 1 (Summary Commission Statement) shows conclusively that he is suing for commissions on orders claimed to have been placed with defendants by this customer after the lapse of one year from the date when the contract to pay commissions to plaintiff is claimed to have been made. * * *

A service contract of indefinite duration, in which one party agrees to procure customers or accounts or orders on behalf of the second party, is not by its terms performable within a year—and hence must be in writing under the Cohen and Martocci cases—since performance is dependent, not upon the will of the parties to the contract, but upon that of a third party. In Cohen v. Bartgis Bros. Co., 264 App.Div. 260, 35 N.Y.S.2d 207, * * * an oral contract to employ a salesman and pay him commissions "upon all orders placed by" a named customer "at any time, whether or not plaintiff was in defendant's employ" when the orders were placed, was deemed unenforcible under the Statute of Frauds. To the argument that a termination of the contract within a year might result if defendant's business were dis-

solved or otherwise ended, the Appellant Division's answer was, * * * " 'termination is not performance, but rather the destruction of the contract * * * where there is no provision authorizing either or both of the parties to terminate as a matter of right.' [Citation.]"

Similarly, in Martocci v. Greater New York Brewery, 301 N.Y. 57, 92 N.E.2d 887, this court decided that an oral agreement to pay the plaintiff commissions on sales to prospective customers whom he introduced to defendant was within the statute. In reaching that conclusion, Judge Froessel wrote, * * * "If the terms of the contract here had included an event which might end the contractual relationship of the parties within a year, defendant's possible liability beyond that time would not bring the contract within the statute. Since, however, the terms of the contract are such that the relationship will continue beyond a year, it is within the statute, even though the continuing liability to which defendant is subject is merely a contingent one. The endurance of defendant's liability is the deciding factor."

The case before us is very similar to Cohen and Martocci, supra, involving as it does an oral employment contract of indefinite duration to procure business on a commission basis. The lower courts, however, and respondent, take the view that, because of the testimony of defendant Blumberg that the contract was "at will", the case falls within the ambit of Nat Nal Service Stations v. Wolf, 304 N.Y. 332, 107 N.E.2d 473, which held that the Statute of Frauds was inapplicable in a situation where there was a continuing offer to contract, which could be withdrawn at any time and could never eventuate in a contract unless and until both parties mutually agreed thereafter. Thus, in Nat Nal Service Stations v. Wolf, the alleged oral agreement was that "defendants promised and agreed to and with the plaintiff that so long as plaintiff purchased from Socony Vacuum Oil Company or the Standard Oil Company or either or both, its requirements for gasoline at its place of business through the defendants and the defendants accepted the same, the defendants would pay to the plaintiff an amount equal to the discount allowed to defendants by said Socony Vacuum Oil Company and Standard Oil Company or either or both of them, on each gallon of gasoline so purchased." After declaring the statute inapplicable because, "if performance be possible within the year, however unlikely or improbable that may be, the agreement does not come within the proscription of the statute", we held that the alleged agreement "was clearly one at will and for no definite or specific time and thus by its terms did not of necessity extend beyond one year from the time of its making. * * * We are confronted with an alleged contract by the terms of which neither party was bound to do anything at any time, and consequently there is nothing in its terms to bring it within the Statute of Frauds." The court distinguished the Cohen and Martocci cases, supra, on the ground that there *"the plaintiff salesmen had executed their parts of the respective contracts. * * * The plaintiffs' right to commissions in those two cases was not dependent upon any act of the plaintiffs or the defendants, as here, but was wholly dependent upon the act of the third party, the procured customer."*

The present case is not like Nat Nal Service Stations v. Wolf, supra, where performance depended solely upon the will and desires of the two parties and could rightfully be terminated at any time by either of them. In other words, plaintiff might or might not place orders with defendant and defendant might or might not accept them. Here, however, the contract was, on plaintiff's part, to procure accounts and—on defendants' part— to pay to plaintiff a percentage for so long as business from those accounts was forth-coming. It was within the contemplation of the parties to the contract that the customer might give orders for years, as actually occurred. Indeed, plaintiff is here suing for commissions based on orders accepted several years after this contract is claimed to have been made. The contract was not, then, one which might be *performed* within a year, but rather one which could only be *terminated* within that period by a breach of one or the other party to it. The possibility of such wrongful termination is not, of course, the same as the possibility of performance within the statutory period.

The testimony of defendant Blumberg that the employment was "at will" can hardly mean that, once plaintiff procured an account for defendants, they might immediately terminate plaintiff's employment, retain the customer and collect their fees. It can only mean that defendants might cease at any time to employ plaintiff to procure further accounts for them and, similarly, that plaintiff might decide to quit defendants' employ. But, as long as they handle the Tifford account, defendants would be obligated to pay commissions to plaintiff.

The judgment appealed from should be reversed and the complaint dismissed, with costs in all courts.

NEWTON v. ALLEN

(1965) 220 Ga. 681, 141 S.E.2d 417.

GRICE, J. The validity of an instrument purporting to lease timber for turpentine purposes is controlling upon this review. Miriam Newton Allen filed a petition against Jack C. Newton, Jr., and W. L. Sparks in the Superior Court of Jenkins County charging the invalidity of the timber lease which they rely upon for the right to work the turpentine on her land. The instrument is as follows: "I, Mrs. Miriam N. Allen, do lease all of my workable timber for turpentine on all lands owned or controlled by me to Jack C. Newton, Jr., for a period of five years for a percentage of 30% of each and every dipping. Plus payment for cups all ready up. To include government payment of timber already cut. Signed this 6th day of January, 1964. Witness by Georgia M. Newton this 6th day of January 1964. /s/ Miriam N. Allen (L.S.) /s/ Jack C. Newton, Jr."

The petition as amended made, insofar as material here, the allegations which follow. The plaintiff, owner of certain described lands, entered into the above quoted agreement with the defendant Newton for the working of turpentine on her lands. Both defendants are using her timber thereon for turpentine purposes although she has advised them that she does not recognize the agreement as legal and binding and has demanded that they desist from further trespasses. She has offered to make restitution and to reimburse them for any expenses they have incured in working the turpentine, but they have not responded to her offer and are continuing the trespasses and damage to her timber. The prayers included temporary and permanent injunction from going upon and using her land, accounting for gum taken and monetary damages.

To the foregoing petition, the defendants urged their general demurrer asserting that the petition did not set out a cause of action since it showed upon its face that the instrument is valid. The assignment of error here is to the overruling of such demurrer.

The plaintiff's right to the relief she seeks depends upon the validity of the purported lease agreement. As we view it, the sufficiency of the description of the land on which the timber stands is determinative of that issue.

The instrument provides that "I * * * do lease all of my workable timber for turpentine on all lands owned or controlled by me * * * for a period of five years for a percentage of 30% of each and every dipping * * * "

This writing purports to lease, for a period of five years, all of the plaintiff's timber suitable for turpentine purposes. The parties evidence no intent to pass a lesser interest so it will be presumed that they intended to convey an estate for years. [Citations.] The fact that the use is limited to turpentine purposes does not reduce the interest transferred to a mere usufruct where there is no indication that the parties so intended. [Citations.]

This instrument, then, purported to convey an estate for years in standing timber, which is realty. [Citations.] Code § 85–801 provides that if an estate for years " * * is in lands, it passes as realty."

Our Code, § 20–401(4), requires, in order to bind the promisor, that "Any contract for sale of lands, or any interest in, or concerning them" must be in writing. Lease contracts which convey an estate for years fall within this section. [Citations.] Such leases of standing timber must describe the land upon which the timber stands, with sufficient certainty for identification or give a key by which it may be identified. [Citations.]

Thus, the question is whether the description "all lands owned or controlled by me" meets these requirements.

We hold that it does not. It fails to describe any particular land or to furnish any key to make certain the identification of lands owned by plaintiff. Nor does it identify in any manner the lands "controlled" by her.

We are mindful that this court has held a devise of "all of my lands" to be a sufficient description to operate as color of title by will. Harriss v. Howard, 126 Ga. 325, 55 S.E. 59 (one Justice absent). However, the opinion (at page 330, 55 S.E. at page 61) was at pains to state that "We recognize, of course, the difference between a will and a deed, and the great liberality allowed in making wills and passing title by them."

In Sarmon v. Liles, 150 Ga. 338, 103 S.E. 797, a timber lease description quite similar to the one here was adjudged by this court (one Justice dissenting) to be insufficient. The record in that case disclosed the wording there to have been "the standing cypress timber on the lands of the party of the first part."

In Blue Ridge Apartment Company, Inc. v. Telfair Stockton & Company, Inc., 205 Ga. 552, 560 (one Justice dissenting), 54 S.E.2d 608, this court held that the descriptive language "*all* the assets, tangible and intangible, *property, real,* personal and mixed, business and good will of the company * * *" was not sufficient to pass title to land. (Emphasis ours.) In that opinion a thorough history was provided as to descriptions in conveyances in the light of the blanket "all."

We regard the above cited decisions as controlling upon the description issue here and therefore hold that the language in the instant document was insufficient to convey any interest to the defendant Newton.

There is no merit in the defendants' contention that the instrument here purported to lease or sell only the turpentine itself and thus constituted a contract for the sale of personalty under the Uniform Commercial Code (Ga.L.1962, p. 156 et seq.; Code Ann. Title 109A). This writing purported to lease the *trees* themselves, not merely the product thereof, and therefore was a lease of realty. This court held in Adcock v. Berry, 194 Ga. 243 (2a, 2b), 21 S.E.2d 605 that Code § 85-1901, declaring that all crops, matured and unmatured are personalty, and Code § 85-1902, providing that the word "crops" includes crude gum from a living tree, apply only to the fruits and products of plants, trees and shrubs and do not refer to the plants, trees and shrubs themselves. The Uniform Commercial Code does not purport

to change the law relating to instruments which transfer an interest in land.

The petition shows that the purported lease agreement under which the defendants claim the right to take turpentine from plaintiff's timber, is void for lack of adequate description of the land. Therefore, the plaintiff is entitled to the relief she seeks. The judgment overruling the general demurrer to the petition is

Affirmed.

MONTANARO v. PANDOLFINI

(1961) 148 Conn. 153, 168 A.2d 550.

MURPHY, ASSOCIATE JUSTICE. The plaintiff brought this action for specific performance to compel the defendant to carry out the terms of a written agreement to sell to the plaintiff a ten-family house on Albany Avenue, Hartford, which the defendant owned. The plaintiff also sought damages. The defendant demurred to the complaint on the ground that the agreement did not comply with the requirements of the Statute of Frauds and, more specifically, that the terms of the purchase money mortgage provided for in the agreement were uncertain and indefinite. The trial court overruled the demurrer. Thereupon the defendant filed an answer in which he set up in a special defense his claim as to the interpretation of the agreement. Upon trial, the issues were found for the plaintiff and judgment was rendered in his favor. The defendant has appealed. We shall take up the assignment of error relating to the overruling of the demurrer.

The plaintiff in his complaint alleged the execution by the parties on February 24, 1958, of the agreement, a copy of which was attached to the complaint and marked exhibit A. He alleged also that on May 1, 1958, in accordance with the terms of the agreement, he tendered the balance of the cash payment to the defendant, together with an executed purchase money mortgage in the amount and on the terms specified in the agreement, and demanded a conveyance of the premises. Upon the defendant's refusal to convey, he instituted this suit. It is unnecessary to recite all of the provisions of exhibit A. The parties are named, the property is described, the price is stated and the agreement is signed. Suffice it to say that while the demurrer is addressed to the entire complaint, only the portion of the agreement providing for the purchase money mortgage is under attack. It reads as follows: "By executing purchase money mortgage to Seller in the amount of Eighteen Thousand Dollars ($18,000.00) payable monthly for 15 yrs at 5%. Said mortgage to contain usual clauses for default (30 days) an anticipation clause, etc." The trial court in its memorandum of decision on the demurrer concluded that the agreement provided for the principal of the mortgage to be paid with interest at the rate of 5 per cent in equal monthly instalments for a period of fifteen years and that the contract was definite, certain and not in violation of the Statute of Frauds.

That the provision in question is susceptible to at least two interpretations is evidenced by the construction which has been placed upon it by each of the parties. The plaintiff claims that the $18,000, together with interest at the rate of 5 per cent per annum, was payable in successive equal monthly payments of $142.35, starting one month after title passed and continuing over a period of fifteen years. Under this construction, the amount of the total monthly payment would be constant, but the allocation of it to principal and interest would vary. The allotment to principal would increase progressively each month from $67.35 the first month to $139.74 on the final payment, whereas the allotment to interest would decrease each month from $75 the

first month to 58 cents the last month. The defendant claimed that the principal of $18,000 was payable in equal monthly instalments of $100 each for a period of fifteen years with interest on the unpaid balance at the rate of 5 per cent per annum payable monthly. Under this construction, the amount of the total monthly payment would not be constant, though the instalments on the principal would. The interest payments would decrease each month as the unpaid balance of the principal became less.

It is to be noted that the mortgage provision in the agreement does not specify when the monthly payments are to commence, nor does it state the amount of each payment. It does not state that the payments have to be equal in amount, either as to the payments on principal or as to the combined payments on principal and interest. In addition to the constructions placed upon the provision by the parties, it could also be construed as permitting monthly payments in different amounts so long as the payments on principal totaled $18,000 spread over a period of fifteen years, together with interest on the unpaid balance computed at the rate of 5 per cent per annum, payable annually, semiannually, monthly, or otherwise.

* * * From Nichols v. Johnson, 10 Conn. 192, through Garre v. Geryk, 145 Conn. 669, 145 A.2d 829, we have had occasion to review numerous cases in which it has been maintained that a written agreement for the sale of real estate was not enforceable because it did not conform to the requirements established under the Statute of Frauds. We have uniformly held that such an agreement must state the contract with such certainty that its essentials can be known from the memorandum itself, without the aid of parol proof, or from a reference contained therein to some other writing or thing certain; and these essentials must at least consist of the subject of the sale, the terms of it and the parties to it, so as to furnish evidence of a complete agreement. In Sullivan v. Ladden, 101 Conn. 166, 168, 125 A. 250, we held that a written agreement which provided for a purchase money mortgage but did not specify the length of time it was to run failed to satisfy the Statute of Frauds. In Gendelman v. Mongillo, 96 Conn. 541, 545, 114 A. 914, the sufficiency of the memorandum so far as it related to the purchase money mortgage was in issue, and it was held that it was impossible from the memorandum to determine with any degree of certainty what the parties intended as to the method and terms of payment and that the memorandum did not meet the statutory requirements. With respect to a lease, we said in Handy v. Barclay, 98 Conn. 290, 296, 119 A. 227, that a definite contract of lease must contain, besides the names of the parties, a description of the property let, the term of the lease, the amount of the rent and the terms of payment of the rent.

All of the material terms and conditions of the contract must be embodied in the written agreement in order to satisfy the statute. [Citations.] All of the terms and conditions of payment of the principal sum of the mortgage over the period of fifteen years during which it was to run should have been set out in the agreement in the instant case. Otherwise parol evidence would be required to establish the undertaking of the parties. The agreement, so far as the provision relating to the purchase money mortgage is concerned, fails to meet the requirements of the statute. It is ambiguous, indefinite and uncertain. The demurrer to the complaint should have been sustained.

There is error, the judgment is set aside and the case is remanded with direction to sustain the demurrer.

In this opinion the other Judges concurred.

GULF LIQUID FERTILIZER CO. v. TITUS
(1962) 163 Tex. 260, 354 S.W.2d 378.

GREENHILL, J. The Statute of Frauds states, among other things, that no action shall be brought in any court to charge any person upon a promise to answer for the debt, default, or miscarriage of another unless the promise be in writing. In this case, James Titus was sued by Gulf Liquid Fertilizer Company for merchandise which he purchased for the "Titus & Stracner Farm," a partnership, and also on his oral promise to pay a pre-existing debt of his partner, Lonzo Stracner. Lonzo Stracner was also sued, but he filed no answer and did not appear. The trial court, sitting without a jury, rendered judgment against Titus and Stracner, jointly and severally, for the merchandise Titus had purchased and also for the debt of Stracner. Titus alone appealed. The El Paso Court of Civil Appeals, in effect, reversed and rendered that judgment as to Titus on the Statute of Frauds point. It held that Titus's oral promise to pay the debt of his partner Stracner was unenforceable under the Statute of Frauds, and that the payments on the Stracner note out of the funds of the Titus and Stracner partnership were invalid.

The facts are these: Lonzo Stracner accumulated an indebtedness of $7,183.58 with Gulf Liquid Fertilizer Company, for merchandise purchased in connection with his 1957 crop. On January 29, 1958, he gave his note to Gulf Liquid to evidence this debt. The note was payable in four installments of $1,500 on the 15th of each month, beginning in July, 1958. The fifth and last payment, in an odd amount, was due on November 15, 1958.

Early in 1958, Stracner and Titus entered into a farming partnership. On March 15, 1958, a check was drawn from the account of the "Titus & Stracner Farm" (the partnership) for $1,500. It was prepared by

Titus's wife who kept the books for the partnership, and was signed by Stracner. The only notation on the check was that it was for "fertilizer." On June 5, 1958, a second check, in the amount of $1,303, was sent to Gulf Liquid. It was signed by Titus. The check bore a notation that it was for "fertilizer and poison for June." Up to this point, the partnership had made no purchases. The amounts of these checks were credited as received by Gulf Liquid on the note of Stracner.

On June 24, 1958, the partnership made its first purchase of $339.60 on account from plaintiff, Gulf Liquid, doing business as Western Chemicals.

On July 9, 1958, a third check was sent to Gulf Liquid. It was drawn on the "Titus & Stracner Farm" account for $1,500 and was executed by Titus. The only notation on the check was that it was for "fertilizer and poison." It likewise was credited on the Stracner note.

After June 24, 1958, Titus made various purchases on open account from Gulf Liquid for fertilizer and poisons. The total amount purchased on credit in 1958 was $5,000.80. This account forms part of the amount in litigation, but there is no dispute as to the amount purchased or the charges made thereon. At least a part of this sale on credit in 1958 was made before Titus's oral promise to pay the Stracner note. Titus contends that the two checks for $1,500 and the third check for $1,303 should not have been credited on Stracner's note, but should have been applied on the debt created by the open account purchases on and after June 24, 1958. He concedes that there was no agreement to pay in advance for 1958 purchases. Ferguson, assistant manager of Gulf Liquid, testified that there was no agreement that the partnership would pay in advance; that no one told him or his company to do otherwise than to credit the payments on the Stracner note.

During 1958 Stracner disappeared, and Titus was left to run the farm and the partnership. The time of his departure was not fixed with certainty. Titus admitted that Stracner was not back when he had his conversation with Ferguson. It was during this conversation that the oral promise was made by Titus. Titus testified that this conversation took place on or about July 15, 1958. Ferguson testified that it was earlier, at least as early as July 9, 1958 (by which time the partnership had purchased $725 of goods on credit).

Ferguson testified that in this conversation Titus specifically agreed to pay the Stracner note; that the promise was made in return for a continuation of credit by Gulf Liquid for the Titus & Stracner partnership for the 1958 crop year and for an extension of additional credit at the end of 1958 if needed. He also testified that Gulf Liquid would not have continued credit except for Titus's promise to pay the Stracner note, and at that time he had to decide whether to file suit. At another place in his testimony, Ferguson testified that Titus agreed "to take care of" the Stracner debt; that "he would pay that [note] out * * * and * * * if he needed additional credit, I agreed to give it to him." At another place, Ferguson testified that Titus promised that he would "see that the note was paid." Then again on direct examination, Ferguson said Titus said "I will pay" the note.

Titus testified that he agreed only to see that the Stracner note was paid, and that he meant by this that he would see that Stracner himself paid it; that he, Titus, was not going to get himself obligated, but that he would see that Stracner paid his debt. He also testified that he had no discussion with the officers of Gulf Liquid concerning credit for the partnership's 1958 crop or of credit being stopped if the promise to pay the Stracner note was not given; that he had no knowledge of the Stracner note until it was showed to him by Ferguson in mid-July of 1958, when he had already started buying on credit from Gulf Liquid; that it was not necessary for him to establish credit with Gulf Liquid because the financing of the 1958 crop had already been arranged with Western Cotton Oil Company which had advanced money to the partnership for the 1958 crop, and that a budget for fertilizer and insecticides and a bank account had already been set up.

* * *

One of the problems here is the meaning of the trial court's finding of fact Number 6, that Titus "agreed to pay to plaintiff the indebtedness represented by the said note * * * *or* to see that same was paid." The trial court's "conclusion of law" was that Titus agreed unconditionally *to pay* the note. Nevertheless, the Court of Civil Appeals treated the trial court's findings of fact as a finding of a "collateral" and "conditional" promise, and therefore barred by the Statute of Frauds. * * * We have concluded, however, that there is evidence to support the finding of the trial court that Titus intended to accept primary responsibility for the Stracner note and that the consideration he received in return for his promise satisfied the "leading object" or "main purpose" rule. We therefore hold that his promise is outside the Statute and enforceable.

* * *

In reading the cases and the texts, it appears to us that most cases have turned upon two or more of the following inquiries which are made to determine whether an oral promise to pay the debt of another is without the Statute and enforceable. * * *

I. Was there a promise of primary responsibility to pay, or was there a promise of suretyship?

* * *

We have a fact finding by the trial court that Titus agreed to pay or to see that the debt was paid. The Court of Civil Appeals has treated the character or nature of Titus's promise as "conditional" and "collateral," and based its decision upon an emphasis on the portion of the trial court's finding of fact that Titus agreed "to see that same was paid." In effect, that Court concluded that the words used evidence an intent not to assume primary responsibility but rather to be a surety.

There is, however, evidence that Titus agreed "to pay." Those words indicate an intention to accept primary responsibility. There is also evidence that he agreed "to see that the debt was paid." These words are subject to several interpretations as to intent. The additional words, "or see that the debt was paid," particularly when accompanied by other words of promise to pay, could be interpreted to mean that he, Titus, would arrange for payment if he were unable to pay the note as he had promised. This is still a promise of the nature or character of one to accept primary responsibility.

* * *

We think the words used by Titus, in the context in which they were used, are not so clear as to be capable of only one construction. The trial court concluded that the promise of Titus was "an unconditional promise to pay" and that "the promise of Titus to pay was an original obligation." While we think reasonable minds could differ on the meaning and intent of Titus, we cannot say as a matter of law that the trial court was wrong in its interpretation.

II. Was there sufficient consideration to support the promise to pay?

The next inquiry is whether there was sufficient consideration to support Titus's promise to pay Stracner's note. [Citation.] There must of course be sufficient consideration to make any promise a binding and enforceable one. [Citation.] The Court of Civil Appeals held that the consideration passing to Titus was not sufficient. We conclude that it was.

* * *

III. Was the consideration such as to remove the promise from the Statute of Frauds?

There is a difference between adequacy of consideration in law and the sort of consideration which the courts say is necessary to take the promise out of the Statute. Professor Corbin explains this difference:

"It should be noted in the beginning that a consideration may be sufficient to satisfy the requirements of the common law of contracts without being sufficient to satisfy the 'leading object' rule and take the promise out of the statute of frauds. A promise is not out of the statute merely because there is a consideration for it. * * * The statute is applicable to promises to answer for the debt of another for which there is some sufficient consideration. It appears, however, that certain kinds of consideration will prevent a promise from being one 'to answer for the debt of another' and will make the promisor a debtor on his own account." 2 Corbin, Contracts, (1950 ed.) 279, § 367.

Corbin continues:

"The 'leading object' that is sufficient to take a promise out of the statute must be found in the consideration for the promise and not in the promise itself or in the result of its performance. The promise is itself a promise to a creditor to pay a debt due to him from a third party; if it is not such a promise, it is certainly not within the statute. The performance of the promise will clearly benefit the creditor; and it will benefit the debtor too by discharging his duty to that creditor. * * * The *promisor* is not in the least benefited by the performance of his own promise. *In order to take his promise out of the statute, he must be bargaining for a consideration that is beneficial to him-*

self and that constitutes his primary object of desire." (Emphasis added.) Ibid., 284.

The "leading object" or "main purpose" rule has been adopted by the American Law Institute in its Restatement of the Law of Contracts, Section 184. This rule was announced by this court in Lemmon v. Box, 20 Tex. 329 (1857), where it said:

" * * * that wherever the main purpose and object of the promisor is, not to answer for another, but to subserve some purpose of his own, his promise is not within the statute, although it may be in form a promise to pay the debt of another, and although the performance of it may incidentally have the effect of extinguishing the liability of another."

"Here the leading object of the plaintiff (as charged in the plea) was not to guarantee or to secure the debt of the Carpenters * * * but it was to subserve some purpose of his own." [p. 333]

* * *

We now apply the "main purpose" doctrine to this case. Assuming as we have that Titus, for a consideration, made a promise to pay the debt of Stracner, was his main purpose and object to subserve some purpose of his own? The trial court found as a fact that the promise was made "in order to obtain credit for the partnership of Stracner and Titus." The trial court also concluded that the promise was supported by a new and independent consideration, the sale of merchandise on credit during 1958, but for which the credit would not have been extended. We find no evidence that the promise was made for Stracner's benefit. The fact that Stracner had left him and that Titus was trying to produce a crop in 1958 without his partner is evidence that he gave the promise primarily to benefit himself. Assuming as we have that he made the promise to obtain the credit, the crucial point is that the consideration necessarily benefited him as a member of the partnership because he shared in the partnership's ultimate profits, if any, and the benefit he received as a member of the partnership is considered sufficient to satisfy the "main purpose" rule. We think there are facts to support the findings and conclusions of the trial court. We therefore hold that the oral promise of Titus is enforceable and is not barred by the Statute of Frauds.

* * *

The judgment of the Court of Civil Appeals is reversed and that of the trial court is affirmed.

COOK GRAINS, INC. v. FALLIS

(1965) 239 Ark. 962, 395 S.W.2d 555.

ROBINSON, J. Appellant, Cook Grains, Inc., filed this suit alleging that it entered into a valid contract with appellee, Paul Fallis, whereby Fallis sold and agreed to deliver to Cook 5,000 bushels of soybeans at $2.54 per bushel. It is alleged that Fallis breached the alleged contract by failing to deliver the beans, and that as a result thereof Cook has been damaged in the sum of $1,287.50. There was a judgment for Fallis. The grain company has appealed.

Appellant introduced evidence to the effect that its agent, Lester Horton, entered into a verbal agreement with appellee whereby appellee sold and agreed to deliver to appellant grain company 5,000 bushels of beans; that delivery was to be made in September, October, and November, 1963. Fallis denied entering into such a contract. He contends that although a sale was discussed, no agreement was reached. He also contends that the alleged contract is barred by the statute of frauds.

Following the discussion or sale, whichever it was, between Horton and Fallis, appellant grain company prepared and mailed to Fallis a proposed contract in writing which provided that Fallis sold to the grain company 5,000 bushels of beans. The instrument was signed by the grain company and it would have been bound thereby if Fallis had signed the paper, but Fallis did not sign the instrument and did not return it to the grain company. Later, Fallis refused to deliver the beans and the grain company filed suit.

The appellant grain company concedes that ordinarily the alleged cause of action would be barred by the statute of frauds, but contends that here the alleged sale is taken out of the statute of frauds by the Uniform Commercial Code. Ark.Stat.Ann. § 85–2–201 (1961 Addendum) is relied on. It is as follows:

"Formal requirements—Statute of frauds. —(1) Except as otherwise provided in this section a contract for the sale of goods for the price of $500 or more is not enforceable by way of action or defense unless there is some writing sufficient to indicate that a contract for sale has been made between the parties and signed by the party against whom enforcement is sought or by his authorized agent or broker. A writing is not insufficient because it omits or incorrectly states a term agreed upon but the contract is not enforceable under this paragraph beyond the quantity of goods shown in such writing.

"(2) Between merchants if within a reasonable time a writing in confirmation of the contract and sufficient against the sender is received and the party receiving it has reason to know its contents, it satisfies the requirements of subsection (1) against such party unless written notice of objection to its contents is given within ten [10] days after it is received. * * *"

Thus, it will be seen that under the statute, if appellee is a merchant he would be liable on the alleged contract because he did not, within ten days, give written notice that he rejected it.

The solution of the case turns on the point of whether the appellee Fallis is a "merchant" within the meaning of the statute. Ark.Stat.Ann. § 85–2–104 (1961 Addendum) provides:

" 'Merchant' means a person who deals in goods of the kind or otherwise by his occupation holds himself out as having knowledge or skill peculiar to the practices or goods involved in the transaction or to whom such knowledge or skill may be attributed by his employment of an agent or broker or other intermediary who by his occupation holds himself out as having such knowledge or skill. * * * "

There is not a scintilla of evidence in the record, or proferred as evidence, that appellee is a dealer in goods of the kind or by his occupation holds himself out as having knowledge or a skill peculiar to the practices of goods involved in the transaction, and no such knowledge or skill can be attributed to him.

The evidence in this case is that appellee is a farmer and nothing else. He farms about 550 acres and there is no showing that he has any other occupation. In Vol. 16, Words and Phrases, beginning at page 401 there are many cases cited giving the definition of a farmer, such as:

"A 'farmer' is one devoted to the tillage of the soil, such as an agriculturalist. Sohner v. Mason, 136 Cal.App.2d 449, 288 P.2d 616, 617. * * *

"The term 'farmer' means a man who cultivates a considerable tract of land in some one of the usual recognized ways of farming. O'Neil v. Pleasant Prairie Mut. Fire Ins. Co., 71 Wis. 621, 38 N.W. 345, 346."

Our attention has been called to no case, and we have found none holding that the word farmer may be construed to mean merchant.

If the General Assembly had intended that in the circumstances of this case a farmer should be considered a merchant and therefore liable on an alleged contract to sell his commodities, which he did not sign, no doubt clear and explicit language would have been used in the statute to that effect. There is nothing whatever in the statute indicating that the word "merchant" should apply to a farmer when he is acting in the capacity of a farmer, and he comes within that category when he is merely trying to sell the commodities he has raised.

Notes 1 and 2 under Ark.Stat.Ann. § 85–2–104 (1961 Addendum), (Uniform Commercial Code) defining merchant indicate that this provision of the statute is meant to apply to professional traders. In Note 1 it is stated: "This section lays the foundation of this policy defining those who are to be regarded as professionals or 'merchants', * * * " It is said in Note 2: "The term 'merchant' as defined here roots in the 'law merchant' concept of a professional in business. * * * "

The following are some definitions of the word merchant taken from Vol. 27, Words and Phrases, p. 136:

"A merchant is defined to be, in one sense, a trader, by Webster, and by Burrill and Bouvier in their Law Dictionaries, and a person who is engaged in farming and stock raising is not a merchant. In re Ragsdale, 20 Fed.Cas. 175. * * *

" 'The term "merchants" includes those only who traffic, in the way of commerce, by importation or exportation, who carry on business by way of emption, vendition, barter, permutation, or exchange and who make it their living to buy and sell by a continued vivacity or frequent negotiations in the mystery of merchandise, and does not include a farmer who sells what he makes.' Dyott v. Letcher, 29 Ky. (6 J.J.Marsh.) 541, 543."

In construing a statute its words must be given their plain and ordinary meaning. [Citations.]

The judgment is affirmed.

HARRY RUBIN & SONS, INC. v. CONSOLIDATED PIPE CO.

(1959) 396 Pa. 506, 153 A.2d 472.

BENJAMIN R. JONES, J. This is an appeal from the action of the Court of Common Pleas No. 1 of Philadelphia County, which sustained, in part, the appellees' preliminary objections to the appellants' complaint in assumpsit.

Rubin-Arandell, in their complaint, alleged that on three different dates—August 22nd, 25th and 28th, 1958—they entered into three separate oral agreements, all for the sale of goods in excess of $500, with one Carl Pearl, an officer and agent of Consolidated-Lustro, for the purchase of plastic hoops and materials for use in assembling plastic hoops, and that Consolidated-Lustro failed to deliver a substantial portion of the hoops and material as required by the terms of the oral agreements. The court below, passing upon Consolidated-Lustro's preliminary objections, held that two of the alleged oral agreements violated the statute of frauds provision of the Uniform Commercial Code and were unenforceable. Rubin-Arandell contend that certain memoranda [1] (attached as exhibits

---

1.   "Purchase Order . . .
"Lustro Plastic Tile Company   No. 2859
      General Office & Warehouse
         1066 Home Avenue
         AKRON 10, OHIO
         POrtage 2-8801
"Ordered From
      Consolidated Tile Co.

		Date Ship to			
Ship when		Route Via		FOB	
Quantity	Number			Description	Price
30,000				Hoops Te-Vee	36½¢

Red, Green, Blue
as per sample
From Lengths 8'–10"
to 9'–3"   So they can
nest
                              "Lustro Plastic Tile Co.
                    By /s/ Harry Rubin & Sons Inc.
                              Leonard R. Rubin, V. Pres."

———————◆———————

"Consolidated Pipe Co.   "August 25, 1958
1066 Homes Ave.
Akron, Ohio.
Att: Mr. Carl Pearl
"Dear Carl,
      "As per our phone conversation of today kindly enter our order for the following:
            60,000 Tee-Vee Hoops made of rigid polyethylene
            tubing from lengths of 8' 10" to 9' 2"; material to
            weigh 15 feet per lb., colors red, green and yellow
            packed 2 Dozen per carton
            39¢ each
      "It is our understanding that these will be produced upon comp[l]etion of
the present order for 30,000 hoops.
                              "Very truly yours,
                              Harry Rubin & Sons, Inc.
                    /s/ Leonard R. Rubin, Vice-pres."

to the complaint) were sufficient to take both oral agreements out of the statute of frauds. * * *

The statute of frauds provision of the Uniform Commercial Code, supra, states: "§ 2–201. Formal Requirements: Statute of Frauds (1) Except as otherwise provided in this section a contract for the sale of goods for the price of $500 or more is not enforceable by way of action or defense unless there is some writing sufficient to indicate that a contract for sale has been made between the parties and signed by the party against whom enforcement is sought or by his authorized agent or broker. A writing is not insufficient because it omits or incorrectly states a term agreed upon but the contract is not enforceable under this paragraph beyond the quantity of goods shown in such writing. (2) Between merchants if within a reasonable time a writing in confirmation of the contract and sufficient against the sender is received and the party receiving it has reason to know its contents, it satisfies the requirements of subsection (1) against such party unless written notice of objection to its contents is given within ten days after it is received."

As between merchants, the present statute of frauds provision (i. e. under Section 2–201 (2), supra) significantly changes the former law by obviating the necessity of having a memorandum signed by the party sought to be charged. The present statutory requirements are: (1) that, within a reasonable time, there be a writing in confirmation of the oral contract; (2) that the writing be sufficient to bind the sender; (3) that such writing be received; (4) that no reply thereto has been made although the recipient had reason to know of its contents. Section 2–201 (2) penalizes a party who fails to "answer a written confirmation of a contract within ten days" of the receipt of the writing by depriving such party of the defense of the statute of frauds.

The memoranda upon which Rubin-Arandell rely consist of the purchase order on the Lustro form signed by Rubin stating the quantity ordered as 30,000 hoops with a description, the size and the price of the hoops listed and the letter of August 25th from Rubin to Consolidated requesting the entry of a similar order for an additional 60,000 hoops at a fixed price: "As per our phone conversation of today." This letter closes with the significant sentence that: "It is our understanding that these [the second order for 60,000 hoops] will be produced upon completion of the present order for 30,000 hoops."

Consolidated-Lustro's objection to the memoranda in question is that by employment of the word "order" rather than "contract" or "agreement", the validity of such memoranda depended upon acceptance thereof by Consolidated-Lustro and could not be "in confirmation of the contract[s]" as required by Section 2–201 (2). We believe, however, that the letter of August 25th sufficiently complies with Section 2–201 (2) to remove both oral contracts from the statute of frauds. The word "order" as employed in this letter obviously contemplated a binding agreement, at least, on the part of the sender, and, in all reason, should have been interpreted in that manner by the recipient. The sender in stating that "It is our understanding that these will be produced upon completion of the present order for 30,000 hoops," was referring to the initial order as an accomplished fact, not as an offer depending upon acceptance for its validity. Any doubt that may exist as to the sender's use of the word "order" is clearly dispelled by its use in the communication confirming a third contract.[2] This letter of August 28th, 1958, states: "Pursuant to our phone conversation of yesterday, *you may enter our order* for

2. As to this alleged oral contract, the court below held Consolidated-Lustro's defense of the statute of frauds provision was without merit.

the following [number, description and price]. * * * *This order is to be entered* based upon our phone conversation, in which you *agreed* to ship us your entire production of this Hoop material at the above price * * *." (Emphasis supplied.) The letter of August 25th was a sufficient confirmation in writing of the two alleged oral contracts, and, in the absence of a denial or rejection on the part of the recipient within ten days, satisfied the requirements of Section 2–201 (2) of the Uniform Commercial Code.

Under the statute of frauds as revised in the Code "All that is required is that the writing afford a basis for believing that the offered oral evidence rests on a real transaction." Its object is the elimination of certain formalistic requirements adherence to which often resulted in injustice, rather than the prevention of fraud. The present memoranda fulfill the requirement of affording a belief that the oral contracts rested on a real transaction and the court below erred in holding otherwise. Nor are Consolidated-Lustro harmed by such a determination since Rubin-Arandell must still sustain the burden of persuading the trier of fact that the contracts were in fact made orally prior to the written confirmation.[3]

* * *

The order of the court below, as modified, is affirmed and the record remanded for proceedings consistent with this opinion.

PROBLEMS

1. A was the principal shareholder in X Corporation, and, as a result, he received the lion's share of X Corporation's dividends. X Corporation was anxious to close an important deal for iron ore products to use in its business. A writ-

----

[3]. Appellees also argue that parties not named in the communications cannot be bound. Oral testimony to establish that the addressee of the letter was an agent of the unnamed appellees is admissible and does not violate the Statute of Frauds. See Penn Discount Corp. v. Sharp, 125 Pa.Super. 171, 189 A. 749.

----

ten contract was on the desk of Z Corporation for the sale of the iron ore to X Corporation. Z Corporation, however, was cautious about signing the contract, and it was not until A called Z Corporation on the telephone and stated that if X Corporation did not pay for the ore, he would, that Z Corporation signed the contract. Business reverses struck X Corporation and it failed. Z Corporation sues A. What defense, if any has A?

2. Green was the owner of a large department store. On Wednesday, January 26, he talked to Smith and said, "I will hire you to act as sales manager in my store for one year at a salary of $15,000, the year to begin next Monday." Smith accepted and started work on Monday, January 31. At the end of three months, Smith was discharged by Green. On May 15, Smith brings an action against Green to recover the unpaid portion of the $15,000 salary. Decision?

3. A, while driving, ran into B, injuring B and rendering him unconscious. There was some doubt as to who was at fault. A took B to a hospital, where he remained unconscious for twenty-four hours. On arriving at the hospital, A told the official in charge to treat B for his injuries, and stated that he would pay the bill. B was duly treated and cured by the hospital, but A refused to pay the bill. On being sued by the hospital, A pleads the fourth section of the Statute of Frauds as a defense. Decision?

4. Consider the following situations in the light of the Statute of Frauds: (a) B delivers some goods to S after S tells B "charge them to A, and if he does not pay for them, I will." A does not pay for the goods. Can B enforce S's oral promise to pay? (b) A owes B $10,000. B is about to levy attachment on A's factory. S, who is a creditor of A's, fearing that the attachment will ruin A's business and so destroy his own, (S's) chance of collecting his claim, orally promises B that if B will forbear the attachment, he (S) will pay A's debt if A does not. A does not. Can B enforce S's oral promise to pay?

5. On May 1, Green received a letter from Brown in which Brown offered to buy Green's store building and lot for $200,000. Green immediately called Brown on the telephone and said, "I received your letter today and I accept your offer to purchase my store building and lot and I will have the deed ready for you at any time." Green then wrote a letter to a friend, Black, in which he said, "I am tired of this business, so I have just made arrangements to sell my building and lot to Brown for a good price." The

following day Brown tendered the $200,000 to Green but Green refused to deliver the deed. Brown brings an appropriate action against Green. What decision?

6. Ames, Bell, Cain and Dole each orally ordered color television sets from Marvel Radio Company which accepted the orders. Ames's set was to be specially designed and encased in an ebony cabinet. Bell, Cain and Dole ordered standard sets described as "Alpha Omega Theatre." The price of Ames's set was $1,500 and of the sets ordered by Bell, Cain and Dole, $600 each. Bell paid the radio company $75 to apply on his purchase; Ames, Cain and Dole paid nothing. The next day, Marvel Radio Company sent Ames, Bell, Cain and Dole written confirmations captioned "Purchase Memorandum," numbered 12345, 12346, 12347 and 12348, respectively, containing the essential terms of the oral agreements. Each memorandum was sent in duplicate with the request that one copy be signed and returned to the company. No one of the four purchasers returned a signed copy, as requested. Ames promptly sent the radio company a repudiation of the oral contract which it received before beginning manufacture of the set for Ames or making commitments to carry out the contract. Cain sent the radio company a letter reading in part, "Referring to your Contract No. 12347, please be advised I have cancelled this contract. Yours truly, (Signed) Cain." The four television sets were duly tendered by Marvel Radio Company to Ames, Bell, Cain and Dole, all of whom refused to accept delivery. Marvel Radio Company brings four separate actions against Ames, Bell, Cain and Dole for breach of contract.

Decide each claim.

7. A orally promises B to sell him five crops of potatoes to be grown on Blackacre, a farm in Minnesota, and B promises to pay a stated price for them on delivery. Is the contract enforceable?

8. A and B enter into an oral contract by which A promises to sell and B promises to buy Blackacre for $5,000. A repudiates the contract by writing a letter to B in which he states accurately the terms of the bargain, but adds "our agreement was oral. It, therefore, is not binding upon me, and I shall not carry it out." Thereafter, B sues A for specific performance of the contract. A interposes the defense of the Statute of Frauds, averring that the contract is within the Statute and, hence, void and unenforceable. Decision?

9. A claims that B fraudulently misrepresented a material fact and thereby fraudulently induced A to make a certain contract. Can A rely upon the Statute of Frauds in support of his claim?

10. On March 1, Jameson called Bushmill on the telephone and offered him $25,000 for a house and lot which Bushmill owned. The offer was accepted at once on the telephone. Later in the day, Jameson told Mary that if she would marry him, he would convey to her the house and lot then owned by Bushmill and which had been the subject of the earlier agreement. Still later in the day, Jameson called Peggy and offered her $6,000 if she would work for him for the year beginning March 15 and she agreed. When Bette Davies, who had worked for Jameson for some years, heard of this, she threatened to quit and only agreed to remain when he promised to pay her a bonus of $1,500 if she would stay with him until the next Christmas.

By August, Jameson and Mary had become married; Bushmill had refused to convey the house and lot to Jameson; Jameson had renounced his promise of the house and lot to Mary; Peggy had duly gone to work for Jameson but had been fired without cause on July 5; Bette had quit working for Jameson on January 7 after Jameson failed to pay her the bonus; and Mary had left Jameson and instituted divorce proceedings.

What rights have: (a) Jameson against Bushmill for failure to convey the house and lot? (b) Mary against Jameson for failure to convey the house and lot to her? (c) Peggy against Jameson for firing her before the end of the agreed term? (d) Bette against Jameson for failure to pay the promised bonus?

CHAPTER 8

PAROL EVIDENCE RULE—INTERPRETATION
OF CONTRACTS

Introductory. A contract reduced to writing and signed by the parties is frequently the culmination of numerous conversations, conferences, proposals, counter proposals, letters and memoranda, and sometimes the result of negotiations conducted, or partly conducted, by agents of the parties. At some stage in the negotiations tentative agreements may have been reached on a certain point or points which were superseded, or so regarded by one of the parties, by subsequent negotiations. Offers may have been made and withdrawn, either expressly or by implication, or lost sight of, in the give and take of negotiations which have continued for a period of time. Ultimately a final draft of the written contract is prepared and signed by the parties. It may or may not include all of the points which have been discussed and agreed upon in the course of the negotiations. However, by signing the written agreement, the parties have solemnly declared it to be their contract, and the terms as contained therein represent the contract which they have made. As a rule of substantive law, neither party is permitted subsequently to show that the contract which they made is different from the terms and provisions as they appear in the written agreement.

The word "parol" means literally "speech," or "words." It is a term applied to contracts which are made either orally or in writing not under seal, which are called parol contracts, in order to distinguish such contracts from those which are under seal and are known as deeds or specialties. The term "parol evidence" refers to any evidence, whether oral or in writing, which is extrinsic to the written contract.

The parties may differ as to the proper or intended meaning of language contained in the written agreement, where such language is ambiguous or susceptible of different interpretations. To ascertain the proper meaning requires a construction of the contract. This does not involve any change, alteration, modification, addition to, or elimination, of any of the words, figures, or punctuation, in the written agreement, but merely a construing of the language in order to ascertain its meaning. While the parol evidence rule precludes either party from introducing any evidence in any lawsuit involving the written agreement which would change, alter, or vary the language or provisions thereof, rules of interpretation or construction permit the introduction of evidence in order to resolve ambiguity and to show the meaning of the language employed and the sense in which both parties used it.

Statement of the Rule. The parol evidence rule applies only to an integrated agreement or contract, that is, one in which the parties have assented to a certain writing or writings as the statement of the agreement or contract between them. When there is such an integration of an agreement or contract, no parol evidence of any other agreement will be permitted to vary, change, alter, or modify any of the terms or provisions of the written agreement.

Reason for the Rule. The reason for the rule is that the parties, by reducing their agreement to writing, are regarded as having intended the writing which they signed to include the whole of their agreement. The terms and provisions contained in the writing are there because the parties intended them to be in their contract. Any provision not in the writing is regarded as having been omitted because the parties intended that it should not be a part of their contract. The rule excluding evidence which would tend to change, alter, vary, or modify the terms of the written agreement is therefore a rule which safeguards the contract as made by the parties.

Situations to Which the Rule Does Not Apply. The parol evidence rule, in spite of its name, is not an exclusionary rule of evidence, nor is it a rule of construction or interpretation. It is a rule of substantive law which defines the limits of a contract. Bearing this in mind, as well as the reason underlying the rule, it will be readily understood that the rule does not apply to any of the following:

1. A contract which is partly written and partly oral. Where a written offer is accepted orally, there is no integration of the contract in a writing.

2. A receipt for goods or merchandise. This is not a contract.

3. A gross clerical or typographical error which obviously does not represent the agreement of the parties. Where a written contract for the services of a skilled mining engineer provides that his rate of compensation is to be $1.00 per day, a court of equity would permit reformation of the contract to correct the mistake upon a showing that both parties intended the rate to be $100 per day.

4. The lack of contractual capacity of one of the parties, by proof of minority or insanity. Such evidence would not tend to vary, change, or alter any of the terms of the written agreement, but merely to show that the written agreement was voidable or void.

5. A defense of fraud, duress, undue influence, or illegality. Evidence establishing any of these defenses would not purport to vary, change, or alter any of the terms of the written agreement, but merely to show such agreement to be voidable or unenforceable.

6. A condition agreed upon orally at the time of the execution of the written agreement and to which the entire agreement was made subject. If A signs a subscription agreement to buy stock in a corporation to be formed, and delivers it to B with the understanding that the agreement is not to be operative unless ten other responsible persons shall each agree to buy at least an equivalent amount of such stock, A is permitted to show by parol evidence this condition. Such evidence does not tend to vary, alter, or change any of the terms of the stock subscription, but merely to show that the entire written agreement, unchanged and unaltered, never became effective.

7. A subsequent oral mutual rescission or agreed modification of the written contract. Parol evidence of a later agreement does not tend to show that the integrated writing did not represent the contract between the parties at the time it was made. If the contract is one which the Statute of Frauds requires to be in writing, a subsequent mutual rescission or modification must also be in writing.

8. Usage and custom. Parol evidence of usage and custom which is not inconsistent with the terms of the written agreement is admissible to define the meaning of the language in the agreement, where both parties knew or should have known of the existence of the usage or custom in the particular trade or locality. Such evidence does not alter, change, or vary any of the terms or language of the written contract, but simply shows the meaning which the parties attached to the particular language.

Supplemental Evidence. Under the Code, although a written agreement may not be contradicted by evidence of a prior agreement or of a contemporaneous oral agreement, a written contract for the sale of goods may be explained or supplemented by (1) course of dealing between the parties, (2) usage of trade, (3) course of performance, or (4) evidence of consistent additional terms unless the writing was intended by the parties as a complete and exclusive statement of their agreement.

The Code defines "course of dealing" and "usage of trade" in Sections 1–205(1) and 1–205(2):

> (1) A course of dealing is a sequence of previous conduct between the parties to a particular transaction which is fairly to be regarded as establishing a common basis of understanding for interpreting their expressions and other conduct.
>
> (2) A usage of trade is any practice or method of dealing having such regularity of observance in a place, vocation or trade as to justify an expectation that it will be observed with respect to the transaction in question. The existence and scope of such a usage are to be proved as facts. If it is established that such a usage is embodied in a written trade code or similar writing the interpretation of the writing is for the court.

"Course of performance" refers to evidence of the manner and extent to which the respective parties to a contract have accepted repeated occasions of performance by the other party without objection.

The introduction of evidence of an oral agreement to establish terms of the contract which are not inconsistent with the terms of the written agreement represents a departure from the common law rule which does not admit oral proof of any addition to a written contract in which the language is unambiguous.

Section 2–202 permitting such supplemental evidence is contained in Article 2 of the Code. The question therefore arises whether this rule admitting oral evidence of consistent terms applies to contracts other than those for the sale of goods. If not, the rule at common law continues to apply to such other contracts.

Section 2–102 provides: "Unless the context otherwise requires, this Article applies to transactions in goods."

"Goods" are defined in Section 2–105(1):

> (1) "Goods" means all things (including specially manufactured goods) which are movable at the time of identification to the contract for sale other than the money in which the price is to be paid, investment securities (Article 8) and things in action. "Goods" also includes the unborn young of animals and growing crops and other identified things attached to realty as described in the section on goods to be severed from realty (Section 2–107).

Section 1–109 states that "Section captions are parts of this Act." The caption of Section 2–102 is: "Scope; Certain Security and Other Transactions Excluded From This Article." The caption and the text of Section 2–102 do not exclude employment contracts or real estate contracts; nor do they include them. Under the general scope and purpose of the Code, such contracts would seem to be excluded from its operation. The Code does not expressly apply its parol evidence rule to contracts for the sale of securities. However, it is possible for Code concepts to become engrafted by judicial decision upon common-law rules. The answer to the question must await development of the law by the Courts.

INTERPRETATION OF CONTRACTS

Fundamental Rules of Interpretation. While the written words or language in which the parties embodied their agreement or contract may not be changed by parol evidence, the ascertainment of the meaning to be given to the written language is outside the scope of the parol evidence rule. The written words are sacrosanct. They are the terms of the contract. However, words are but symbols. If their meaning is not clear, it may be made clear by the application of rules of interpretation or construction, and by the use of extrinsic evidence for this purpose where necessary. As stated in one case:

"The great object of construction is to collect from the terms or language of the instrument, the manner and extent to which the parties intended to be bound. To facilitate this, the law has devised certain rules, which are not merely conventional, but are the canons by which all writings are to be construed, and the meaning and intention of men to be ascertained. These rules are to be applied with consistency and uniformity. They constitute a part of the common law, and the application of them, in the interpretation and construction of dispositive writings, is not discretionary with courts of justice, but an imperative duty." Johnson County v. Wood, 84 Mo. 489 (1884).

Section 226 of the Restatement of the Law of Contracts defines interpretation as follows:

"Interpretation of words and of other manifestations of intention forming an agreement, or having reference to the formation of an agreement, is the ascertainment of the meaning to be given to such words and manifestations."

Where the language in a contract is clear and unambiguous, extrinsic evidence tending to show a meaning different from that which the words clearly import will not be received by a court. It is the function of the court to interpret and construe written contracts and documents. Rules of interpretation are adopted in order to apply a legal standard to the words contained in the agreement by which to determine their sense or meaning.

Section 230 of the Restatement of the Law of Contracts provides:

"The standard of interpretation of an integration, except where it produces an ambiguous result, or is excluded by a rule of law establishing a definite meaning, is the meaning that would be attached to the integration by a reasonably intelligent person acquainted with all operative usages and knowing all the circumstances prior to and contempo-

raneous with the making of the integration, other than oral statements by the parties of what they intended it to mean."

In Section 235, the Restatement sets forth the following rules which aid in the application of the standard above quoted:

"(a) The ordinary meaning of language throughout the country is given to words unless circumstances show that a different meaning is applicable.

"(b) Technical terms and words of art are given their technical meaning unless the context or a usage which is applicable indicates a different meaning.

"(c) A writing is interpreted as a whole and all writings forming part of the same transaction are interpreted together.

"(d) All circumstances accompanying the transaction may be taken into consideration, subject in case of integrations to the qualifications stated in § 230.

"(e) If the conduct of the parties subsequent to a manifestation of intention indicates that all the parties placed a particular interpretation upon it, that meaning is adopted if a reasonable person could attach it to the manifestation."

Secondary rules aiding the application of this standard of interpretation are set forth in the Restatement of the Law of Contracts, Section 236:

"(a) An interpretation which gives a reasonable, lawful and effective meaning to all manifestations of intention is preferred to an interpretation which leaves a part of such manifestations unreasonable, unlawful or of no effect.

"(b) The principal apparent purpose of the parties is given great weight in determining the meaning to be given to manifestations of intention or to any part thereof.

"(c) Where there is an inconsistency between general provisions and specific provisions, the specific provisions ordinarily qualify the meaning of the general provisions.

"(d) Where words or other manifestations of intention bear more than one reasonable meaning an interpretation is preferred which operates more strongly against the party from whom they proceed, unless their use by him is prescribed by law.

"(e) Where written provisions are inconsistent with printed provisions, an interpretation is preferred which gives effect to the written provisions.

"(f) Where a public interest is affected an interpretation is preferred which favors the public."

In an action for breach of a written sales contract the subject matter was described as "Season's output of cotton linters for season 1915–1916, about four hundred (400) bales." The defendant seller shipped to the plaintiff buyer 155 bales of linters which was the total output of its mill for the season. The buyer sued for failure to deliver 245 bales. Cotton linters were a by-product of defendant's cottonseed oil mill. The Court construed the contract as one for season's output and not for 400 bales, upon the ground that the specific language controlled the general, and held for defendant. Kenan, McKay & Spier v. Yorkville Cotton Oil Co., 109 S.C. 462, 96 S.E. 524 (1917).

Course of Performance. To the above rules of interpretation should be added the Code provisions applicable to contracts for the sale of goods, namely, course of performance, course of dealing between the parties, and usage of trade, where these are not inconsistent with the express terms of the agreement.

By their actions in performing under the contract their respective duties the parties manifest a practical interpretation and indicate the meaning which they attribute to the terms of the contract. Course of performance is therefore an active recognition by conduct of the parties of the import of the contract and controls both course of dealing and usage of trade. It does not control a clear express term of the contract. Section 2–208 provides:

(1) Where the contract for sale involves repeated occasions for performance by either party with knowledge of the nature of the performance and opportunity for objection to it by the other, any course of performance accepted or acquiesced in without objection shall be relevant to determine the meaning of the agreement.

(2) The express terms of the agreement and any such course of performance, as well as any course of dealing and usage of trade, shall be construed whenever reasonable as consistent with each other; but when such construction is unreasonable, express terms shall control course of performance and course of performance shall control both course of dealing and usage of trade (Section 1–205).

(3) Subject to the provisions of the next section on modification and waiver, such course of performance shall be relevant to show a waiver or modification of any term inconsistent with such course of performance.

A course of performance acquiesced in by the parties which differs from the express terms of the contract may result in a waiver of such express terms. A waiver of the express requirements of a contract to the extent that it remains unperformed may be retracted by reasonable notice provided that the party in whose favor the waiver would operate has not changed his position materially in reliance upon the waiver. Section 2–209 (5) provides:

(5) A party who has made a waiver affecting an executory portion of the contract may retract the waiver by reasonable notification received by the other party that strict performance will be required of any term waived, unless the retraction would be unjust in view of a material change of position in reliance on the waiver.

Through the application of the parol evidence rule, where it is properly applicable, and the above rules of interpretation and construction, it may be observed that the law not only enforces a contract but in doing so exercises great care that the contract being enforced is the one which the parties made, and that the sense and meaning of the manifested intentions of the parties is carefully ascertained and given effect.

CASES

MITCHILL v. LATH

(1928) 247 N.Y. 377, 160 N.E. 646,
68 A.L.R. 239.

[The plaintiff brought an action seeking to compel specific performance by the defendants of an alleged oral contract to remove an ice house. The trial court entered a decree for the plaintiff. Defendants appeal.]

ANDREWS, J. In the fall of 1923 the Laths owned a farm. This they wished to sell. Across the road, on land belonging to Lieutenant-Governor Lunn, they had an ice house which they might remove. Mrs. Mitchill looked over the land with a view to its purchase. She found the ice house objectionable. Thereupon "the defendants orally promised and agreed, for and in consideration of the purchase of their farm by the plaintiff, to remove the said ice house in the spring of 1924." Relying upon this promise, she made a written contract to buy the property for $8,400, for cash and a mortgage and containing various provisions usual in such papers. Later receiving a deed, she entered into possession and has spent considerable sums in improving the property for use as a summer residence. The defendants have not fulfilled their promise as to the ice house and do not intend to do so. We are not dealing, however, with their moral delinquencies. The question before us is whether their oral agreement may be enforced in a court of equity.

This requires a discussion of the parol evidence rule—a rule of law which defines the limits of the contract to be construed. * * * It applies, however, to attempts to modify such a contract by parol. It does not affect a parol collateral contract distinct from and independent of the written agreement. It is, at times, troublesome to draw the line. Williston, in his work on Contracts (sec. 637) points out the difficulty. "Two entirely distinct contracts," he says, "each for a separate consideration may be made at the same time and will be distinct legally. Where, however, one agreement is entered into wholly or partly in consideration of the simultaneous agreement to enter into another, the transactions are necessarily bound together. * * * Then if one of the agreements is oral and the other is written, the problem arises whether the bond is sufficiently close to prevent proof of the oral agreement." That is the situation here. It is claimed that the defendants are called upon to do more than is required by their written contract in connection with the sale as to which it deals.

The principle may be clear, but it can be given effect by no mechanical rule. As so often happens, it is a matter of degree, for as Professor Williston also says where a contract contains several promises on each side it is not difficult to put any one of them in the form of a collateral agreement. If this were enough written contracts might always be modified by parol. Not form, but substance is the test.

In applying this test the policy of our courts is to be considered. We have believed that the purpose behind the rule was a wise one not easily to be abandoned. Notwithstanding injustice here and there, on the whole it works for good. Old precedents and principles are not to be lightly cast aside unless it is certain that they are an obstruction under present conditions. * * *

Under our decisions, before such an oral agreement as the present is received to vary the written contract, at least three conditions must exist. (1) The agreement must in form be a collateral one; (2) it must not contradict express or implied provisions of the written contract; (3) it must be one that parties would not ordinarily be expected to embody in the writing; or put in another way, an inspection of the written contract, read in the light of surrounding circumstances must not indicate that the writing appears "to contain the engagements of the parties, and to define the object and measure the extent of such engagement." Or again, it must not be so clearly connected with the principal transaction as to be part and parcel of it.

The respondent does not satisfy the third of these requirements. It may be, not the second. We have a written contract for the purchase and sale of land. The buyer is to pay $8,400 in the way described. She is also to pay her portion of any rents, interest on mortgages, insurance premiums and water meter charges. She may have a survey made of the premises. On their part the sellers are to give a full covenant deed of the premises as described, or as they may be described by the surveyor if the survey is had, executed and acknowledged at their own expense; they sell the personal property on the farm and represent they own it; they agree that all amounts paid them on the contract and the expense of examining the title shall be a lien on the property; they assume the risk of loss or damage by fire until the deed is delivered; and they agree to pay the broker his commissions. Are they to do more? Or is such a claim inconsistent with these precise provisions? It could not be shown that the plaintiff was to pay $500 additional. Is it also implied that the defendants are not to do anything unexpressed in the writing?

That we need not decide. At least, however, an inspection of this contract shows a full and complete agreement, setting forth in detail the obligations of each party. On reading it one would conclude that the reciprocal obligations of the parties were fully detailed. Nor would his opinion alter if he knew the surrounding circumstances. The presence of the ice house, even the knowledge that Mrs. Mitchill thought it objectionable, would not lead to the belief that a separate agreement existed with regard to it. Were such an agreement made it would seem most

natural that the inquirer should find it in the contract. Collateral in form it is found to be, but it is closely related to the subject dealt with in the written agreement—so closely that we hold it may not be proved. * * *

[Judgment reversed.]

SPITZ v. BRICKHOUSE

(1954) 3 Ill.App.2d 536, 123 N.E.2d 117,
49 A.L.R.2d 673.

ROBSON, J. Alexander H. Spitz and Warren E. Spitz, doing business as Spitz & Spitz, plaintiffs, brought this action to recover $2,675 as their architects' fee under a written contract with Jack Brickhouse, the defendant. Defendant in his answer charges that plaintiffs breached their contract by failing to design a home costing no more than $25,-000, and counterclaims for the return of $250 he had paid plaintiffs. The court tried the issues without a jury, found for the defendant and entered judgment on his counterclaim. Plaintiffs appealed.

Two points are cited by plaintiffs as error. 1. The admission of parol testimony to prove, vary and change the terms. 2. The findings of the court are not supported by, but are contrary to the evidence.

The record discloses that plaintiffs and defendant entered into a standard A. I. A. form contract on June 12, 1950. It provides that defendant agrees to pay plaintiffs for their professional services "a fee of Ten (10) per cent of the cost of the work * * * said percentage being hereinafter referred to as the 'basic rate.'" Enumerated thereafter are the architect's services, consisting of necessary conferences, preparation of preliminary studies, working drawings, specifications, etc. * * *

Plaintiffs prepared the plans, specifications, made detail drawings and conferred with the defendant about them. Plaintiffs took bids in conformity with the specifications. The lowest bid received was $39,000. Defendant contends that the parties orally agreed that the maximum cost of the home would not exceed $25,000, and on this basis rejected the bid and refused to proceed with the work. The court admitted evidence of the oral agreement, to which plaintiffs objected.

The law is well established that where a written contract is uncertain, ambiguous, or incomplete, evidence of a contemporaneous oral agreement to prove the entire contract is admissible. [Citation.] Whether it was intended to be their complete and final agreement is to be determined from the circumstances of the case. [Citation.] If it is silent in essential particulars, parol evidence is admissible to establish the missing parts, although inadmissible to contradict those unambiguous terms expressed in the document. [Citations.]

The form contract in the instant case is silent as to the style of the house to be designed, the number of its rooms, its dimensions, the quantity and quality of the materials to be used in erecting it, and so on. In Bair v. School Dist. No. 141 of Smith County, 94 Kan. 144, 146 P. 347, the court said: "There must be something outside the contract to determine these questions. The architect must have had instructions outside the contract with which to undertake to comply, in the preparation of his plans." [Citation.] One of those instructions must have concerned the cost of the building. [Citations.] As in these cases, so in the following —all involving similar or substantially identical A. I. A. form contracts—parol evidence to prove an agreement as to maximum cost where the form contract was silent was held admissible: [Citations.]

Furthermore, to sustain plaintiffs' contention that the cost is to be determined by the lowest bona fide bid, it would be necessary to hold that no matter how large the bid for

doing the work, the owner would be obligated to pay an architectural fee based on that amount. As Warren Spitz, one of the plaintiffs, testified, "Under our understanding the theory of this contract, if we were to design a house after we had procured his signature on that written contract, a five room house could cost anywhere from $10,000 to half a million." The written language of the contract renders this testimony of doubtful credibility. In paragraph 5 it is provided that upon completion of the preliminary studies the architect should be paid 25% of the basic rate "computed on a reasonable estimated cost." Unless some "reasonable estimated cost" had been agreed upon, it would render meaningless the "basic rate" for the determination of the architect's fee. [Citations.] There is nothing in the contract, nor anything in the circumstances of this case, to buttress plaintiffs' contention. Expression of their intention could have been made clear. They provided the form contract. It is to be construed most strongly against them and any ambiguity resolved favorably to the defendant. [Citations.]

It was not error for the trial court to admit testimony to explain the ambiguities and any incomplete portions of the contract.

Plaintiffs cite Mitterhausen v. South Wisconsin Conference Ass'n, 245 Wis. 353, 14 N.W.2d 19, involving an identical standard A. I. A. contract, where parol evidence was held inadmissible. That case is not in conflict with any of the cases we have cited [citation] nor with our holding in the instant case. Viewing the contract through the prism of different circumstances, the court in the Mitterhausen case concluded that the contract contained the complete agreement of the parties. There was evidence of "extensive negotiations" culminating in the contract, and the owner's approval bottomed on sketches, drawings, plans and specifications rather than on some specific price. That is, the owner was not so much concerned with cost, as such, but concerned more that the structure to be erected conform to the sketches, drawings, plans and specifications which had been agreed upon. Under these circumstances, while there are points of variance, our views are not incompatible with those expressed in the Mitterhausen case.

* * * The record reveals that defendant and his wife at all times insisted that the maximum cost of the house should not exceed $25,000. Defendant testified that in May 1950, he and his wife and plaintiff Warren Spitz went to the lot upon which they desired to build and asked Warren Spitz if he could build a five and a half or six-room house, ranch style, if defendant provided the lot, for $25,000. Spitz answered, "I believe so, yes; and we can make it a beauty." In June 1950, at their second conference with Warren Spitz, he informed defendant that he would like a retainer of $250. When asked how he arrived at that figure, he informed them that it was ten per cent of their fee. A check for $250 was given at that time. Warren Spitz presented a contract. He said it was the standard form of agreement. Defendant asked him what it meant. Warren Spitz said, "It means that when you build a house, we are your architects; this is to keep you from changing horses in the middle of the stream." The agreement as prepared by plaintiffs was signed without any changes. Defendant repeated that the cost of the house was not to exceed $25,000. He was informed that this figure was correct and "when your home is put up, our fee will be $2,500," and the $250 was ten per cent of the cost. Defendant and his wife both testified that when they were informed that the house would cost from $39,000 to $44,000 they told plaintiffs they could not finance such a home. The lot had cost them $5,000. The furnishings would run $10,000 to $12,000. All this would bring the total close to $60,000.

* * *

Judgment affirmed.

AGAR PACKING & PROVISION CO. v. WELDON

(1956) 42 Tenn.App. 175, 300 S.W.2d 51.

BEJACH, J. This cause involves an appeal by the defendant, Cliff Weldon, d/b/a Argo-Collier Truck Lines, from a decree against him in the sum of $206.82.

For convenience the parties will be styled as in the lower court, complainant and defendant, the appellant in this Court, Cliff Weldon, having been the defendant in the lower court, and the appellee, Agar Packing and Provision Company, the complainant there.

Complainant, a wholesale dealer in Chicago, Illinois, on or about August 7, 1950 delivered to the agent of defendant for shipment to the Russell Company at Jackson, Mississippi a number of cartons of refined lard, smoked meat, and cooked meat. Defendant's agent delivered to complainant a bill of lading which evidenced receipt of this shipment. The bill of lading correctly identified all of the shipment except the cases of cooked meats which contained prepared hams. With reference to these cases of cooked meats, the bill of lading showed 15 cases of cooked meats weighing 1,263 pounds. This was an error, as 20 cases of cooked meats weighing 1,263 pounds were, in fact, delivered to defendant for shipment. The complainant's proof consisted of depositions taken on interrogatories. The defendant's proof consisted of the testimony of witnesses examined orally in open court before the Chancellor.

* * * The proof also establishes that when the shipment was delivered to Russell and Company in Jackson, Mississippi, there were on the truck five additional cases of hams which were not delivered, the driver of the truck refusing to deliver same because not called for by the bill of lading or delivery ticket. The driver in question, as is shown by the proof, was not a regular employee of

defendant, and his whereabouts could not be ascertained at the time of the trial. Neither this driver nor the five cases of hams have been heard from since the delivery of the remainder of the shipment to the Russell Company in Jackson, Mississippi.

The defendant, as appellant, has filed five assignments of error in this Court. These five assignments, however, present only two questions for determination by this Court, viz.:

1st. Whether or not complainants are bound by the recital in the bill of lading that only 15 cases of hams were shipped. * * *

Defendant's counsel contends that the bill of lading here involved is a contract which cannot be varied by oral testimony; and that, as this case involves an interstate shipment, it must be controlled by the federal statutes and decisions construing same. * * *

So far as the bill of lading involved in this cause is considered or treated as a contract, the authorities cited by defendant are applicable and in point; but the bill of lading is not only a contract, it is also a receipt; and, with reference to that aspect of the situation, these authorities are not controlling.

On this subject, 9 Am.Jur., Carriers, Sec. 425, p. 680, is as follows:

"So far as a bill of lading is a receipt, it has the same character as other receipts and is subject to the same principles of law. There is no more solemnity in its execution nor any more importance to be attached to it than to other instruments of a like character. It may be stated generally that the receipt clauses in a bill of lading are subject to explanation, variation, or contradiction by parol evidence, as the general rule applicable to the admissibility of parol evidence to vary a written contract is not applicable to such clauses. The fact that both a contract and a receipt are embodied in the same instrument forms no reason why they should be regarded

as differing in effect from similar instruments executed in an independent form."

* * *

On the same subject, discussing the matter with more particularity, 9 Am.Jur., Carriers, Sec. 426, p. 681, says:

"As between the shipper and the carrier, in the absence of any express stipulation between the parties affecting the conclusiveness of the bill of lading, parol evidence is ordinarily admissible to show that there is a mistake in the statement in the bill as to the quantity of goods received, and that the quantity specified in the bill is greater than the quantity actually received. Especially is this rule true where a bill of lading acknowledges the receipt of a certain quantity of goods, which is in sealed packages when delivered to the carrier, or where a bill of lading by its terms indicates that there is some uncertainty as to the quantity."

* * *

We think all of the equities are with the complainant in this cause. For the reasons hereinabove stated, the decree of the Chancellor will be affirmed, and a decree will be entered here in favor of complainant and against the defendant for the amount decreed by the Chancellor, together with interest thereon from June 8, 1956, the date on which the decree was entered in the lower court.

JESS FISHER & CO. v. DARBY

(1953 Mun.App.D.C.) 96 A.2d 270.

QUINN, J. This was a suit for a real estate broker's commission. Appellant, plaintiff in the trial court, obtained from the defendant a thirty-day exclusive authorization to offer her apartment building for sale, agreeing to pay a 5% commission if a sale were consummated. Plaintiff claimed that he complied with the conditions set forth in the sales agreement within the thirty-day period but that the defendant refused to sign the contract. Trial was before the court, and a finding was entered for defendant.

On appeal plaintiff contends that the court erred in permitting defendant to testify relative to an alleged condition precedent, in the absence of a pleading to that effect, and that the variance between the pleading and proof was fatal. Defendant testified that she had expressly informed the plaintiff that she would not sell her property until he had obtained for her another building in which she could live and which would produce for her a higher income than her present building. She stated further that she signed the listing agreement with the distinct understanding that no sale would be consummated until this condition had been fulfilled. She further stated that the plaintiff had agreed to this condition at the time the listing agreement was signed. Her testimony was corroborated by that of her daughter and by a letter from her to the plaintiff dated October 11, 1948, which was approximately two weeks after the listing agreement had been signed and which letter was offered in evidence by plaintiff. This letter stated:

" * * * You will recall that my immediate reaction to your suggestion was that I would have no other source of income and no place to live if I sold this property, as I am solely dependent on the income from the small apartment house and small income from a savings account, which represent my only assets. You stated that you understood my situation, and that you would like to have permission to sell my building, with the understanding that you would secure for me another piece of property which would provide me with more income and a place for my family to live.

"Although you were able to locate a purchaser for my property without any delay, you have made no apparent effort to satisfy the prime condition on which I consented to sign the listing with you; thus, you have not placed me in a position to consummate the sale, in that you have not located an income-producing property for me, in which I can move with my family."

* * *

It is next contended that the court erred in receiving parol testimony which modified the terms of the written listing agreement. The agreement stated that the plaintiff was to have the exclusive right for thirty days to sell the defendant's property at a given price and that he was to receive a specified commission if a purchaser was found during the thirty-day period. He now argues that he was entitled to a directed verdict as a matter of law as he had produced a purchaser able, ready, and willing to buy on the seller's terms and that under the parol evidence rule the written agreement could not be modified by parol testimony of a condition precedent. But such is not the law. In this jurisdiction there is no question that a written contract may be conditioned on an oral agreement and that the contract will not become binding until some condition precedent resting in parol shall have been performed. As an exception to the parol evidence rule, it is entirely permissible to allow parol testimony to prove such a condition when the written agreement is silent on the matter, the testimony does not contradict nor is it inconsistent with the writing, and if under the circumstances it may properly be inferred that the parties did not intend the writing to be a complete statement of the entire transaction between them.

In the instant case the listing agreement was silent as to any conditions. The intention of the parties as to whether the writing was meant to be a complete statement of their agreement was a question of fact, and there was ample evidence that the writing was not a complete statement of the agreement. Moreover, the parol testimony was not inconsistent with nor did it contradict the listing agreement, but was offered to prove the circumstances under which it was given. It was a condition or contingency which never happened and therefore did not contradict the written listing. In Ellis v. Morgan, D.C.Mun.App., 65 A.2d 797, we had a similar factual situation. There the real estate broker had induced the owner of a rooming house business to sign a listing agreement and a contract of sale for her business. She was allowed to testify that both contracts were signed on a condition that she need not sell until she had found a new place. We held there that such testimony did not contradict the written contracts and was therefore admissible. The trial court did not err in admitting the testimony in question.

Affirmed.

————

GANLEY BROS., INC. v. BUTLER BROS. BUILDING CO.

(1927) 170 Minn. 373, 212 N.W. 602,
56 A.L.R. 1.

[The defendant had three contracts for highway construction. It sublet all of the work in one of the contracts to the plaintiff who brought an action to recover damages for fraud. The contract between the plaintiff and defendant provided:

"The contractor [plaintiff] has examined the said contracts of December 7, 1922, and the specifications and plans forming a part thereof, and is familiar with the location of said work and conditions under which the same must be performed, and knows all the requirements, and is not relying upon any statement made by the company in respect thereto."

The trial court sustained a motion by defendant for judgment on the pleadings holding in effect that the plaintiff would not be permitted to prove fraud by reason of the above quoted provision in the contract. From an order denying its motion for a new trial, plaintiff appeals.]

WILSON, C. J. * * * Parol evidence is admissible to show that the making of the contract was procured by fraudulent representations. This does not vary the terms of the contract. It is merely to show the presence of fraud which permits an avoidance of the contract. Established fraud impeaches its validity. A contract resting on fraud, when under attack, cannot stand. The fact that the contract has been reduced to writing does not change the rule. The contract as written was induced by the fraud. The evidence in proof of the fraud establishes the inducing or influencing cause and in no way varies or contradicts the terms of the contracts. This rule cannot be curtailed or destroyed by writing in the contract: "This contract was not procured by fraud." If so, a party could take advantage of his own fraud if he could succeed, by fraud if necessary, in getting into the instrument a clause negativing fraud. The evidence relates to an inducing cause, which is entirely distinct from the terms of the contract which are in no sense varied or modified. [Citations.]
* * *

The authorities will not permit a distinction so as to allow the contract to be valid and binding to the extent that the defrauded party has agreed and unalterably committed himself to the fact that he has not relied upon any statements or representations of his adversary, but upon his own knowledge and information. Moreover this limitation would effectually destroy the general rule because in the absence of reliance there is seldom actionable fraud. Such theory would permit a party to do indirectly what he could not do directly. The contract as written may be an important factor to be considered in the determination of the facts.

The law should not and does not permit a covenant of immunity to be drawn that will protect a person against his own fraud, Such is not enforceable because of public policy. [Citation.] Language is not strong enough to write such a contract. Fraud destroys all consent. It is the purpose of the law to shield only those whose armor embraces good faith. Theoretically, if there is no fraud the rule we announce is harmless. If there is fraud the rule we announce is wholesome. Whether the rule is effective depends upon the facts. Public interest supports our conclusion. 2 Williston, Contr. par. 811, says:

"It seems clear that no agreement of the parties can preclude this defense, for fraud in the inception of the agreement renders voidable the very agreement not to set up fraud, and, aside from this technical but sound argument, such an agreement would obviously be against public policy." * * *

Judgment reversed.

FRIEDMAN v. VIRGINIA METAL PRODUCTS CORP.

(1952 Fla.) 56 So.2d 515.

MATHEWS, J. The appellee sued the appellants in the Circuit Court of Dade County on a written guarantee which reads as follows: "I hereby personally guarantee the account of Shore Equipment & Supply Co. of Florida, Inc., located at 3164 North Miami Avenue, Miami, Florida; this guarantee to cover all materials purchased by Shore Equipment & Supply Co. of Florida, Inc., from Virginia Metal Products Corporation."

* * * The Amended Declaration alleged in Count I: "Defendants did guarantee the Plaintiff payment for all materials purchased from Plaintiff by Shore Equipment & Supply Co. of Florida, Inc., and that said guarantees were *intended* to guarantee payment to Plaintiff of all materials purchased by Shore Equipment & Supply Co. of Florida, Inc., from Plaintiff *in the past* and all materials *to be purchased* by Shore Equipment & Supply Co. of Florida, Inc., from Plaintiff *in the future.*" (Italics supplied.) * * *

* * *

At the trial of the cause the construction of the written guarantee above set forth became the material issue. It was contended by the appellants that the guarantee properly construed, meant that it was limited to "all materials purchased" at the time of the execution and delivery of the written guarantee.

It was contended by the appellees, as shown by Counts I and II of the Amended Declaration above set forth, that "said guarantees were intended to guarantee payment to plaintiff of all materials purchased * * from plaintiff in the past and all materials to be purchased * * * from plaintiff in the future". * * *

The trial judge determined that the word "purchased" was clear, definite and unambiguous, and included all materials "purchased in the past" and all materials to be "purchased in the future", and would not permit parol testimony about the contract on the theory that it would change, alter or vary the terms of a written instrument.

It is a cardinal rule, that the construction of all written instruments, is a question of law and belongs to the courts, provided: "the language used is clear, plain, certain, undisputed, unambiguous, unequivocal, and not subject to conflicting inferences". [Citations.]

The important question to be determined here is whether or not the word "purchased" under the circumstances developed in this case, is clear, plain, certain, undisputed, unambiguous, unequivocal, and not subject to conflicting inferences.

The trial judge was correct in excluding parol testimony to vary or change the terms of a written instrument if the terms of that instrument were clear and unambiguous. On the other hand, if the word "purchased" was not clear and unambiguous, then parol testimony was admissible for the purpose, not of changing or varying the terms of the written instrument, but to elucidate, explain or clarify the words used. [Citations.]

The appellants strongly contend that the word "purchased" has a definite meaning and that it is unambiguous. Their contention is that the word "purchased" is in the past tense and can have no meaning other than goods "purchased" up to the time of the execution and the delivery of the guarantee. In their brief they have quoted extensively from dictionaries and standard works on grammar to the effect that the word "purchased" applies only to purchases made up to the time of the execution and delivery of the contract and in order for the word to apply to future purchases, it would have been necessary to supply some prefix to the word. If these definitions from standard dictionaries and works on grammar were to be used alone and without reference to the facts and circumstances of this case and without reference to decided cases, we would be inclined to agree with the appellants.

*   *   *

A word or phrase in a contract is "ambiguous" only when it is of uncertain meaning, and may be fairly understood in more ways than one. [Citation.]

The term "ambiguous" means susceptible of more than one meaning. [Citation.]

"Language is ambiguous where it is susceptible of interpretation in opposite ways." [Citation.]

Where either general language or particular words or phrases used in insurance contracts are "ambiguous", that is, doubtful as to meaning, or, in the light of other facts, reasonably capable of having more than one meaning so that the one applicable to the contract in question cannot be ascertained without outside aid, extrinsic evidence may be introduced to explain the ambiguity. [Citation.]

A contract is ambiguous when it is reasonably or fairly susceptible to different constructions. [Citation.]

We, therefore, hold that the word "purchased" in this contract and under the circumstances of this case is ambiguous, and that parol testimony may be received, not to vary or change the terms of the contract, but to explain, clarify or elucidate the word "purchased" with reference to the subject matter of the contract, the relation of the parties, and the circumstances surrounding them, when they entered into the contract and for the purpose of properly interpreting, or construing, the contract. It was error to exclude parol testimony for this purpose.

Having reached the above conclusion, and as there must be another trial of this cause, it is unnecessary for us to pass upon the other assignments of error.

[Judgment reversed].

———

SMITH v. ELIZA JENNINGS HOME

(1964) 176 Ohio St. 351, 199 N.E.2d 733.

[The Court of Common Pleas determined that plaintiff is entitled to recover from the Home the sum of $5,601.31 (the admission fee and the amount received by the Home as cash dividends and from the sale of stock rights) less the reasonable value of the board, shelter and care furnished plaintiff's decedent in the amount of $1,524 and her funeral expenses in the amount of $242.25. The court also ordered the Home to assign, transfer and deliver forthwith to the plaintiff the securities and any and all dividends not accounted for. Upon appeal, the Court of Appeals affirmed the judgment for the plaintiff.]

GIBSON, J. There being no dispute over the amount allowed as the reasonable value of the board, shelter and care furnished or the amount of the funeral expenses paid by the Home for plaintiff's decedent, the sole problem before the court is to determine who is entitled to the property transferred and delivered to the Home by the plaintiff's decedent. The answer to this problem is to be found from the fact that certain moneys and securities were delivered and transferred to the Home and from the admission agreement executed by plaintiff's decedent in 1956. This agreement provides in pertinent part:

"In consideration of my being admitted as a patient to the care of, and to share the benefits of the Eliza Jennings Home, as such *to continue until my death, withdrawal or expulsion* for the reasons below, I agree:

" *   *   *

"(b) That the terms of my admission and my right to continue to share the benefits of a patient shall be subject in all respects to the rules and regulations of said Home.

"(c) That my right to continue as a patient and *the obligation of the Home to care for me, shall cease if:*

"1. I shall be at any time adjudged insane by proper public authorities.

"2. The Board of Trustees shall find at its discretion that I can be better cared for by some other person or institution.

"3. The Board of Trustees shall find that I have failed to abide by the rules and regulations of the Home, or shall find that for any other cause or reason I am unfitted to continue as a resident of the Home or to be entitled to its care and benefits.

"(d) That I will pay or cause to be paid to the Home at the time of my admission an admission fee *   *   *.

"(e) That I will forthwith give, transfer and convey to the said Home, by proper documents, all money and all property of every kind which I now own or may hereafter acquire; it being understood that so long as I live I shall have the use of the income of such money and property, and that *at my death such money and property shall become the property of the Home to use as the Board of Trustees may direct.*

" *   *   *

"I further understand and agree that, if my application is granted, I am to be admitted to the Home *on probation for a period of not less than six months from date of admission;* and that at any time during such six months period, the Home may, in its sole discretion, refuse to accept me as a patient if for any reason it shall deem my admission inadvisable. *During such probation period only,* I am to have the right at my sole discretion to withdraw my application for admission, and in the event I withdraw during my probation period, the Home shall return to me all property which I have turned over to it, including fees, *less a reasonable charge for my board, shelter, and care for the period during which I have lived in the Home."* (Emphasis added.)

As far as pertinent to the case at hand, the rules and regulations of the Home, which were incorporated by reference in the admission agreement, are:

"A resident admitted to the Home will receive board, lodging and care during her lifetime. However, the Home shall have the right, at any time within six months from the date of admission *to terminate the residency* of any person who does not meet its requirements.

" *   *   *

"A Resident of the Home shall have the right at any time within six months from date of admission *to terminate her residency* by giving the Board of Trustees thirty days' notice of her desire to do so. All money, securities and property, or their equivalent, held in the Resident's Trust Fund for her benefit, in excess of the Admission Fee, shall be returned to her and thereupon the Home will be discharged of all further obligations. The Board of Trustees may, however, at its discretion charge a reasonable amount for board in lieu of retaining the Admission Fee, which amount will be deducted from the Admission Fee or other funds held for her benefit." (Emphasis added.)

The admission agreement and the rules and regulations of the Home, which are incorporated by reference, were drawn by the Home. A careful examination of the relevant provisions, as quoted above, will reveal several conflicting provisions. Further, other provisions, which would appear to be relevant to such a contract, are absent. Specifically, there is no express provision concerning disposition of the admission fee or the property held in the resident's trust fund in the event a resident dies during the probationary period, which, although not entirely clear, appears to be the six-month period following the date of admission. Under such circumstances, the well-established rule that where there is doubt or ambiguity in the language of a contract it will be construed strictly against the party who prepared it is applicable. [Citations.]

The agreement entered into by the Home and the plaintiff's decedent is divisible according to the length of the residence. There is an agreement *in praesenti* for temporary support, and a contract *in futuro* for permanent support which comes into existence only after the fulfillment of the condition precedent. Until the probationary period had passed each party reserved the right to determine whether to be bound by a lifetime contract. The passage of this six-month period is a condition precedent to the coming into existence of the permanent contract.

On the date of the decedent's death, the agreement to furnish board, shelter and care during the remainder of decedent's lifetime was subject to two conditions precedent, which had not been met. At that time, the decedent was not obligated to accept such care on the terms offered nor was the Home obligated to furnish such services. Only upon the completion of the probationary period would a permanent contractual relationship between the parties come into existence. Until the completion of the probationary period, the only contract in existence was that the resident would pay the reasonable value

of the services rendered by the Home during her temporary period of residency.

The Home having prepared the admission agreement and having failed to make express provision for retaining the money paid and property transferred by plaintiff's decedent as a permanent residency fee, it would be unreasonable to construe such contract as justifying the Home's retention of the money and property, where decedent died during the period of her status as a probationary resident. We believe that a reasonable person in the position of the decedent at the time of the execution of the admission agreement would have understood, in the absence of an express provision to the contrary, that unless and until she attained the status of a permanent (life) resident in the Home she, or her estate, would be entitled to a return of the money and property given for such right, less the reasonable value of the services rendered during the temporary period of her residence. This conforms with the view of the majority of jurisdictions that have considered this question. Such jurisdictions have held that a charitable home may not retain an applicant's property on the ground that the death of the applicant has made it impossible to determine whether he would have become a permanent (life) resident at the end of the probationary period. [Citation.]

Judgment affirmed.

ASSOCIATED HARDWARE SUPPLY CO. v. BIG WHEEL DISTRIBUTING CO.

(1965 D.C.W.D.Pa.) 236 F.Supp. 879.

DUMBAULD, D. J. * * *

Plaintiff creditor seeks to recover $40,185.-62 as the balance of an open unpaid account for merchandise sold and delivered, together with interest. * * *

When the voluminous verbiage with which this case has been surrounded is penetrated and disentangled, the issue is seen to be one of price. Defendant contends that the goods were to be sold at cost plus 10 per cent, whereas plaintiff billed them at dealers' catalogue price (representing a 20 per cent markup) less 11 per cent. * * *

What was the contract between the parties, as shown by the undisputed facts in the record?

Plaintiff in a letter of February 9, 1962 [Ex. A to Complaint] made an offer, subject to a volume of $5,000 per week at catalogue price less 11 per cent discount. * * *

Defendant ordered, received, retained, and paid for a large volume of merchandise, billed at catalogue price less 11 per cent discount.

As calculated in plaintiff's brief, defendant's purchases from February 1962 through May 1964 aggregated $860,000. This figure apparently includes the unpaid amount of $40,185.62, to collect which the present suit was brought. Over $800,000 of merchandise was thus bought and paid for under billings computed under plaintiff's method.

What effect did these dealings of the parties have upon their legal rights, in the light of the Uniform Commercial Code?

We conclude as a matter of law, after consideration of numerous provisions of the Code, that there was a contract between the parties, and that the price was governed by plaintiff's formula.

* * *

Obviously, to say that cost plus 10 per cent is the same as catalogue price less 11 per cent is to indulge in approximation, and the mathematical relationships were as obvious to defendant as to plaintiff. We compute the price on defendant's theory as 1.1 times plaintiff's costs, whereas under plaintiff's system the price would be 1.068 times plaintiff's costs. * * *

Turning to the Code provisions involved, we begin with 12A P.S. § 1–103 that "Unless displaced by the particular provisions of this Act, the principles of law and equity, including * * * the law relative to * * * fraud, misrepresentation, duress, coercion, mistake * * * or other validating or invalidating cause shall supplement its provisions". This section merely invites us to look to more specific provisions of the Code to determine whether a contract arose between the parties, and what its terms were.

Section 1–201(3) defines "Agreement" as "the bargain in fact as found in the language of the parties or in course of dealing or usage of trade or course of performance or by implication from other circumstances."

Section 1–201(11) defines "Contract" as "the total obligation in law which results from the parties' agreement as affected by this Act and any other applicable rules of law."

Section 1–205(1) says: "A course of dealing is a sequence of previous conduct between the parties to a particular transaction which is in fact fairly to be regarded as establishing a common basis of understanding for interpreting their words and conduct."

Section 1–205(3) provides: "The parties to a contract are bound by any course of dealing between them."

Section 1–205(4) (a) declares that "Unless contrary to a mandatory rule of this Act: (a) A course of dealing * * * gives particular meaning to and supplements or qualifies terms of the agreement."

Section 2–104(1) and (3) defines "merchants" and "between merchants", and we consider both parties to this litigation as knowledgeable merchants.

Section 2–106(2) defines "goods or conduct including any part of a performance" as "conforming" when in accordance with the obligations under the contract.

Section 2–201(1) reads: "Except as otherwise provided in this section a contract for the sale of goods for the price of $500 or more is not enforceable by way of action or defense unless there is some writing sufficient to indicate that a contract for sale has been made between the parties and signed by the party against whom enforcement is sought".

Section 2–201(2) provides that: "Between merchants if within a reasonable time a writing in confirmation of the contract and sufficient against the sender is received and the party receiving it has reason to know its contents, it satisfies the requirements of subsection (1) against such party unless written notice of objection to its contents is given within ten days after it is received."

Section 2–201(3) (c) provides: "A contract which does not satisfy the requirements of subsection (1) but which is valid in other respects is enforceable (c) with respect to goods for which payment has been made and accepted or which have been received and accepted."

Section 2–202(a) provides that a writing "may be explained or supplemented * * * by course of dealing."

Section 2–204(1) says: "A contract for sale of goods may be made in any manner sufficient to show agreement."

Section 2–204(2) provides that: "Conduct by both parties which recognizes the existence of a contract is sufficient to establish a contract for sale even though the moment of its making cannot be determined."

Section 2–204(3) provides: "Even though one or more terms are left open a contract for sale does not fail for indefiniteness if the parties have intended to make a contract and there is a reasonably certain basis for giving an appropriate remedy."

Section 2–206(1) says: "Unless the contrary is unambiguously indicated by the language or circumstances (a) an offer to make a contract shall be construed as inviting acceptance in any manner and by any medium reasonable in the circumstances."

Section 2–206(3) provides that "The beginning of a requested performance can be a reasonable mode of acceptance."

Section 2–208 provides: "Where the contract for sale involves repeated occasions for performance by either party with knowledge of the nature of the performance and opportunity for objection by the other, any course of performance accepted without objection shall be relevant to determine the meaning of the agreement or to show a waiver or modification of any term inconsistent with such course of performance."

Review of the foregoing Code provisions shows that the Code attaches great weight to the course of dealing of the parties, even in the absence of a written agreement with respect to every term of the contract. Weighing in the light of the Code the conduct of the parties here, it seems clear that the mode of calculating price set forth in plaintiff's letter of February 9, 1962, although not accepted formally by signature of a copy, was adhered to by both parties during an extensive course of dealing, during which defendant received, accepted, and paid for over $800,000 worth of merchandise. This course of dealing must be held applicable and governing with respect to the remaining merchandise which has been received and accepted but not paid for. Judgment should be rendered for plaintiff for the amount due.

* * *

[Judgment for plaintiff in the amount of $40,185.62, plus interest and costs.]

PROBLEMS

1. On March 1, A entered into a written contract with B whereby A agreed to sell to B not less than 1,000 pounds of menhaden per week at a price of five cents per pound during the six months period beginning May 1. A

delivered to B 1,000 pounds of menhaden per week for four weeks beginning May 1, and thereafter refused to sell or deliver to B any further menhaden under the contract. In an action by B against A for breach of contract, A offers in evidence certain proof that B was packing and reselling the menhaden as mackerel by means of misleading labels and false advertising. B objects to the offer of any such proof on the ground that it is not permitted by the parol evidence rule. What decision?

2. A executes a written contract with B for the sale of A's building to B. Just before the parties sign the contract the parties agree orally that B will retain A as janitor for six months at a salary of $200 per month. One month later after B has taken possession of the building he discharges A. In an action by A against B, B raises the parol evidence rule to exclude evidence of the contract. Discuss B's defense. Decision?

3. A and B made a written contract for the sale of A's car to B. Just before the contract was signed, A orally agreed to rent his garage to B for the next six months at $10 a month. The sale of the car was duly made, but A refused to allow B to use his garage. B sues A for breach of contract. Point involved? Decision?

4. On June 1, A entered into a written contract with B for the sale to B of A's entire cotton crop at thirty-five cents per pound. On September 1, A, B, and C orally agreed that C would be the buyer of A's cotton crop at a price of thirty-five cents per pound in lieu of B. C did not perform this agreement. In an action by A against B for breach of the contract of June 1, does the parol evidence rule exclude B's defense of the oral agreement of September 1?

5. A leased an apartment to B for the term May 1, 1965, to April 30, 1966, at $150 a month "payable in advance on the first day of each and every month of said term". At the time the lease was signed, B told A that he received his salary on the 10th of the month, and that he would be unable to pay the rent before that date each month. A replied that that would be satisfactory. Thereafter B paid his rent regularly on the 10th of each month through November 10, A making no complaint. On December 2, B not having paid the December rent A sued B for such rent. At the trial, B offered to prove the oral agreement as to the date of payment each month, and also that he had paid his rent regularly on the 10th of the month for the preceding seven months without any complaint by A. Decision?

6. A bought a car from the B Used Car Agency under a written contract. He purchased the same in reliance on B's agent's oral representations that the car had never been in a wreck and could be driven at least 2,000 miles without adding oil. Thereafter A discovered that the car had, in fact, been previously wrecked and rebuilt, that it used excessive quantities of oil, and that B's agent was aware of these facts when the car was sold. A brings an action to rescind the contract and recover the purchase price. B objects to the introduction of oral testimony concerning representations of its agent, contending that the written contract alone governed the rights of the parties. Decision on the objection and reason?

7. A, a restaurant owner, entered into a written contract with Air Conditioning Company to purchase an air conditioning system and to have it installed in his restaurant. So far as material here, the written contract speaks of sale and installation of "air conditioning apparatus" described as "one G. E. warm air conditioning L. B. 4; one complete set of duct work; all controls for heating; complete installation for winter air conditioning; one oil tank." After the Company had installed the system, A refused to pay the agreed price. Air Conditioning Company sued A for the agreed price and A defended upon the ground that he signed the contract after being assured by the Company's agents that the installation would remove smoke, kitchen odors, purify the air and heat the premises, and that it had failed to do this. Air Conditioning Company contended that A was not permitted to prove what its agents may have told him, under the parol evidence rule. The contract recited: "This contract contains the entire agreement of the parties, and no representations or promises or warranties of any kind have been made except as contained in this written agreement." What are the rights of the parties?

8. In a contract drawn up by X Company, it agreed to sell and Y Contracting Company agreed to buy wood shingles at $3.25. After the shingles were delivered and used, X Company billed Y Company at $3.25 per bunch of 900 shingles. Y Company refused to pay because it thought the contract meant $3.25 per thousand shingles. X Company brought an action to recover on the basis of $3.25 per bunch. The evidence showed that there was no applicable custom or usage in the trade and that each party held its belief in good faith. Decision?

CHAPTER 9

ASSIGNMENTS—CONTRACTS FOR BENEFIT OF THIRD PARTIES

Introductory. Previous chapters have considered situations in which essentially only two parties were involved. This chapter deals with the rights of third parties arising by way of (1) assignments, and (2) contracts for the benefit of third parties.

ASSIGNMENTS

Choses in Action Not Assignable at Early Common Law. A chose in action is the intangible right which the owner of a debt or contract has to bring an action at law against his obligor, reduce the debt or claim to judgment, and proceed to enforce the judgment. The words literally mean "thing in action." It is an asset. If A has $100 which he lends to B upon B's oral promise to repay, A has exchanged cash for a chose in action. A merchant selling goods on credit exchanges them for accounts receivable which are choses in action.

At early common law, the obligee of a chose in action could not assign it. At that time the law regarded the personal relationship between the obligor and the obligee as a vital part of the obligation. It could not be changed any more than any other term of the obligation. This view prevails today with respect to a revocable offer.

Because the assignees of choses in action had no remedy at law, courts of equity began to enforce assignments. Such courts were created in England for the purpose of providing relief where the remedy at law was inadequate or unavailable, and granting relief to assignees was one of the early tasks of courts of equity. Relief was allowed in equity so consistently that ultimately courts of law began to enforce assignments and for the past century or more actions by assignees to recover money have been exclusively in courts of law.

Definition of Assignment. An assignment is generally considered as the transfer of a right. However, it is unlike the transfer of title to goods, merchandise, or tangible personal property. It is more in the nature of an irrevocable power of attorney to collect a debt or claim with the right of the assignee to retain the proceeds when collected.

As defined in the Restatement of the Law of Contracts, Section 149:

"(1) An 'assignment' of a right is a manifestation to another person by the owner of the right indicating his intention to transfer, without further action or manifestation of intention, the right to such other person or to a third person.

"(2) An 'assignor' is a person who assigns a right, whether or not he is the original owner thereof.

"(3) An 'assignee' is a person to whom a right is assigned, whether or not the assignor is the original owner thereof.

"(4) A 'sub-assignee' is an assignee to whom a right is assigned by one who is himself a previous assignee thereof."

The Restatement, Section 150, defines an effective assignment:

"(1) An 'effective assignment' is one by which the assignor's right to performance by the obligor is extinguished and the assignee acquires a right to such performance.

"(2) An assignment is not ineffective because it is conditional, revocable or voidable by the assignor for lack of consideration or for other reason, or because it is within the provisions of a Statute of Frauds."

What Amounts to Assignment. No special form or particular words are necessary to an assignment. Any words which fairly indicate an intention to make the assignee the owner of the claim are sufficient, and the assignment may be oral or written. A distinction must be drawn between an assignment and a promise to assign. An assignment effectively extinguishes the obligee's right to receive performance from the obligor where a promise to assign does not. The promise of a creditor to pay a collection agency, or broker, or attorney, a percentage or portion of the monies collected by the promisee from the debtor is not an assignment. It may give the promisee a contract right, but does not make him the owner of any part of the claim or debt. Likewise, a check which is a written order drawn upon a bank for the payment of money is not an assignment of any of the funds which the drawer may have to his credit in the drawee bank. The order is not made payable out of a particular fund, and is a general order on the bank to pay irrespective whether money is owing by the bank to the drawer.

An Option Contract is Assignable. An option is a contract whereby an offeror is bound to keep an offer open for a stated period of time. Ordinarily, only the offeree may accept an offer. However, if performance by any person is equivalent to performance by the offeree, as in a contract which does not involve personal service or credit, an irrevocable offer to enter into such type of contract is assignable. Thus, if A gives B a thirty-day option to buy Blackacre for $25,000, B may assign this option to C who, upon timely acceptance of the offer, enters into a contract with A for the purchase of Blackacre.

Distinction between Assignment of Rights and Delegation of Duties. Only rights under a contract are assignable. Duties may never be assigned, but their performance may be delegated to a third person if they are not of a type which involves the personal service or individual attention of the obligor, an attribute known as delectus personae (choice of person). Thus, contracts for personal

services are never assignable. An assignment is also ineffective where performance to the assignee would be different in extent than performance to the assignor and would therefore change the duty of the obligor. Thus, a public liability automobile policy issued to A is not assignable by A to B. The risk assumed by the insurance company was liability for A's negligent operation of the automobile. Liability for operation of the same automobile by B would be an entirely different risk and one which the insurance company had not assumed. However, a bilateral contract for the purchase of coal in which no credit is extended to the buyer, may be assigned by either seller or buyer to a third person. If by the former, the seller assigns the right to the price and delegates the duty of delivering the coal. If by the latter, the buyer assigns the right to receive the coal and delegates the duty to pay the price. The respective performances, namely, delivery of the coal and payment of the price are essentially the same whether performed by the seller or buyer, or by a third person.

The Code particularly distinguishes between assignment of rights and delegations of duties in Section 2–210, as follows:

(1) A party may perform his duty through a delegate unless otherwise agreed or unless the other party has a substantial interest in having his original promisor perform or control the acts required by the contract. No delegation of performance relieves the party delegating of any duty to perform or any liability for breach.

(2) Unless otherwise agreed all rights of either seller or buyer can be assigned except where the assignment would materially change the duty of the other party or increase materially the burden or risk imposed on him by his contract, or impair materially his chance of obtaining return performance. A right to damages for breach of the whole contract or a right arising out of the assignor's due performance of his entire obligation can be assigned despite agreement otherwise.

(3) Unless the circumstances indicate the contrary a prohibition of assignment of "the contract" is to be construed as barring only the delegation to the assignee of the assignor's performance.

(4) An assignment of "the contract" or of "all my rights under the contract" or an assignment in similar general terms is an assignment of rights and unless the language or the circumstances (as in an assignment for security) indicate the contrary, it is a delegation of performance of the duties of the assignor and its acceptance by the assignee constitutes a promise by him to perform those duties. This promise is enforceable by either the assignor or the other party to the original contract.

(5) The other party may treat any assignment which delegates performance as creating reasonable grounds for insecurity and may without prejudice to his rights against the assignor demand assurances from the assignee (Section 2–609).

Where the rights and duties under a contract are of a highly personal nature, such rights cannot be assigned. An extreme example of such contract is a contract of two persons to marry each other. Obviously, the rights under such contract cannot be assigned by either party. A more common example of contracts of a personal character is a contract for the personal services of one of the parties. Whether the service is simple manual labor or is highly skilled or professional, the party having the right to the other's service cannot assign such right to another. One has the right to serve or work for whom he will, and cannot have another thrust upon him without his consent. Nor can the party who is under the duty to perform the service delegate his duty to another, no matter how competent that other may be.

An obligor may never rid himself of the duties under a contract without the consent of the obligee. Any delegation of a duty to a third person nevertheless leaves the obligor bound to perform it. If the obligor desires to be discharged of the duty, it may be possible for him to enter into a third-party contract and obtain the consent of the obligee to substitute a third person in his place. This is a novation whereby the original obligor is discharged and the third party becomes directly bound upon a new promise to the obligee.

Assignment of Future Rights. An assignment of rights expected to accrue in the future under a contract is enforceable to the extent that the rights arise. It is not operative as an assignment at the time of execution as the rights sought to be assigned do not then exist.

Wage Assignments. A wage-earner may assign future wages or salary as security for the payment of an existing debt, or as part of the consideration for a loan, or to secure payment of the price of goods purchased. Assignments of future wages are subject to statutes, some of which prohibit them altogether while others require them to be in writing and subject to certain restrictions. In Illinois, they must be in a writing which is signed by the wage-earner and states his social security number, the name of his employer, the amount of money secured, the interest rate, and dates when payments are due. The wage assignment must be a separate document and not part of any conditional sales contract or other instrument, must be headed by the words "Wage Assignment" printed or written in bold face letters not less than one-quarter inch in height, and an exact copy must be furnished the wage-earner at the time of its execution. A proper wage assignment does not become invalid by reason of cessation of the employment, and is valid as against any future employer of the wage-earner for a period of two years from date of execution. If a wage-earner has executed more than one assignment, the assignees shall collect in the order of priority of service of demand upon the employer, subject to the limitation that the total of all collections shall not exceed 15% of the gross wages of the wage-earner covering any period. The statute further provides that no wage assignment shall be valid for any purpose after three years from date of execution.

Rights of the Assignee. The assignee of a chose in action or claim stands in the shoes of the assignor. He acquires no new rights by reason of the assignment and takes the assigned claim with all of the defenses, defects, and infirmities to which it would be subject in a suit against the debtor by the assignor. This distinguishes an assignment from the negotiation of a negotiable instrument whereby new rights may be acquired by a transferee of the instrument. In a suit by the assignee against the debtor, the latter may plead fraud, duress, no contract, failure of consideration, breach of contract, or any other defense which he may have against the assignor. The debtor may also assert rights of set-off or counterclaim arising out of entirely separate matters which he may have against the assignor provided they arose prior to his obtaining notice of the assignment. The debtor may also set off claims which he has against the assignee for the reason that the latter is before the court as plaintiff in the suit.

The Code permits the buyer under a contract of sale to agree as part of the contract that he will not assert against an assignee of the seller any claim or defense which he may have against the seller. Such provision in an agreement affords greater marketability to the rights of the seller which thereby become analogous to the rights of a holder in due course of a negotiable instrument. Section 9–206.

An assignee will lose his rights against the debtor if the latter pays the assignor without notice of the assignment. The right of the assignee is essentially equitable and it would be unfair to compel a debtor to pay a claim a second time where he has paid it once to the only person whom he knew to be entitled to receive payment.

Under the Code even after notice of an assignment has been given to an account debtor, the debtor and assignor may in good faith effect modification of or substitution for the contract where the right of payment thereunder has not already matured into an account receivable. Section 9–318.

Standing in the shoes of the assignor permits the assignee to have the benefit of any outstanding securities for the claim, even though not expressly assigned. If the claim has any right of priority in the hands of the assignor, such as a wage claim in bankruptcy, the assignee is entitled to the same priority as he is enforcing the right of the assignor.

At common law the mere assignment of a contract right does not impose upon the assignee any duty of performance. He is regarded as having an irrevocable power of attorney to collect the proceeds of the assigned claim or right and to retain them for himself. Unless he expressly assumed the obligations of the assignor, he would not be liable for any breach of the contract out of which the assigned right arose.

Under the Code, an assignment of "the contract" or of "all my rights under the contract" or an assignment in similar broad general terms is also a delegation of performance of the duties under the contract, and unless the language or circumstances indicates the contrary an acceptance of the rights under the assignment constitutes a promise by the assignee to perform such duties. This promise may be enforced either by the assignor or by the debtor under the original contract. Section 2–210(4).

Express Prohibition against Assignment. At common law a contract may contain an express prohibition against any assignment of the rights created under it. The promisor may make his promise as narrow as he pleases and if the language in the contract clearly limits the rights thereunder solely to the promisee, an assignment by the promisee is ineffectual. The assignee of such a promise has a remedy only against the assignor for failure of consideration and breach of implied warranty. This narrowing of the right created by the terms of promise is to be distinguished from a contract which merely provides that the promisee agrees not to assign. In the latter case, an assignment gives the assignee rights against the obligor who may, however, hold the assignor liable for breach of contract.

The rights of an insured under a policy of fire or liability insurance, before loss occurs, are not assignable, and the policy may even provide for a forfeiture in the event of an attempted assignment. However, after loss has occurred, the duty of the insurance company to pay the amount of the loss has become fixed, and the right of the insured to recover such amount is assignable. The law favors assignability in the interest of free alienability of rights, thus permitting a person to sell or transfer something of value which he has. The law, however, will not re-make a contract or change the character or extent of a right or duty from that which the contract created.

Under the Code, a promise in a contract which prohibits assignment of an account receivable or a contract right (as defined in Article 9) is ineffective. Section 9–318(4). Such a provision in a contract for the sale of goods, while ineffective to prohibit the assignment of rights, is construed, unless the circumstances indicate the contrary, as prohibiting delegation to the assignee of the assignor's performance under the contract. Section 2–210(3).

A right of action arising out of the breach of an entire contract or out of complete performance by the assignor is assignable, notwithstanding an agreement to the contrary. Section 2–210(2). Under the Code a different result might be reached in Allhusen v. Caristo Construction Corp., page 214.

Partial Assignments. The owner of a claim may assign portions thereof or fractional interests therein to different assignees. He thereby makes partial assignments of his claim. An assignee of a part of a claim has no right to sue the debtor in an action at law. The debtor or obligor is not required to perform in installments unless he has expressly or impliedly agreed to do so. Where his promise is to render a single performance, breaking it into piecemeal parts imposes a greater duty than he undertook. However, a partial assigneee may sue in equity by naming as defendants not only the debtor or obligor but also all other partial assignees or persons having an interest in the claim. In such suit, the court of equity may enforce the liability of the obligor upon the entire claim as it has before it all parties in interest. It would be an undue hardship on the debtor to cause him to raise the same defenses in a number of suits brought in different courts by partial assignees.

Sub-Assignments. A chose in action or contract claim may be reassigned by the assignee. This is known as a sub-assignment. The sub-assignee may, in turn, become a sub-assignor and make a further reassignment of the claim. Every assignee or sub-assignee seeking to enforce the claim is subject to all of the defenses and rights of set-off which the obligor may assert against the assignor. In this respect, the position of any sub-assignee is similar to that of the original or first assignee. Assume that B owes A $500. A assigns the debt to C for value. C sub-assigns it to D in reliance upon a fraudulent statement by D. D later sub-assigns the claim to E, a bona fide purchaser for value who has no notice of the fraud. May E enforce the claim against the debtor B, or does C have a superior right upon learning of the fraud and rescinding the transfer to D. It should be noted that both the rights of C and E are equitable rights. If E were regarded as having a legal ownership of the debt, the latent equity of C would be cut off. The majority view of the courts is that C would prevail and that his latent equity is not cut off by the equitable interest subsequently acquired by E. A minority view protects the rights of E as against C. The Restatement of the Law of Contracts, Section 174, appears to support the minority view:

> "If an assignor's right against the obligor is voidable by some one other than the obligor or is held in trust for such a person, an assignee who purchases the assignment for value in good faith without notice of the right of such person cannot be deprived of the assigned right or its proceeds."

Successive Assignments of Same Right. The owner of a claim may conceivably make successive assignments of the same claim to different persons. Although morally reprehensible, the question is what are the rights of the successive assignees. Assume that B owes A $1,000. On June 1, A for value assigns the debt to C. Thereafter, on June 15, A for value assigns it to D, a bona fide purchaser who has no knowledge of the prior assignment by A to C. The first assignee C is in a position to give the debtor notice of the assignment before the second assignee D may do so. However, it is possible that the debtor B may receive notice of the second assignment before being notified of the first. At common law the majority rule in the United States is that the first assignee in point of time prevails over subsequent assignees. In England, and in a minority of the States, priority of notice of the assignment to the obligor determines which assignee prevails. Even under the majority rule whereby the first assignee C prevails, if the second assignee D in good faith collects the amount of the claim from the obligor B, he will be allowed to retain the money thus collected; and if the second assignee D, acting in good faith, obtains judgment against the obligor B, he may enforce the judgment and retain the money collected

thereon, even though after the entry of the judgment but before collection he and the obligor were notified of the prior assignment to C. In any case payment by the obligor to the assignor, without notice of the assignment, completely discharges the obligor.

The Restatement of the Law of Contracts, Section 173, adopts the majority American rule and provides that a prior assignee is entitled to the assigned right and its proceeds, to the exclusion of a subsequent assignee, except where (1) the prior assignment is revocable or voidable by the assignor; or (2) the subsequent assignee obtains payment or satisfaction of the obligor's duty; or (3) the subsequent assignee obtains judgment against the obligor; or (4) a new contract is entered into between the subsequent assignee and the obligor by means of a novation; or (5) the subsequent assignee obtains delivery of a tangible token or writing the surrender of which is required by the obligor's contract for its enforcement.

Gift Assignments. A gift of property is ineffective without delivery of the property to the donee. An intangible contract right cannot be delivered in the sense that tangible property may be physically delivered. Nevertheless, the gift of a contract right may be accomplished by assignment, the donee acquiring a power of attorney to collect. A gift assignment, however, is revocable by the assignor, and is revoked by the death of the assignor. Revocation is ineffective if prior thereto the gift assignee has received payment of the claim from the debtor or has obtained judgment against the debtor. Where a contract right is identified with a document, such as a savings bank book, a policy of life insurance, a negotiable note of a third person, or a certificate of stock, a delivery of the document to the donee with the intention of making a gift is an irrevocable effective assignment of both the document and the rights represented thereby.

Implied Warranties of Assignor. In the absence of an expressed intention to the contrary, an assignor who receives value makes certain implied warranties to the assignee with respect to the assigned claim. The assignor does not guarantee that the debtor will pay the assigned debt or that the obligor will perform, but he does warrant that the right exists and is free of defenses except these which are disclosed to the assignee. The Restatement of the Law of Contracts, Section 175, provides:

(1) An assignor of a right by assignment under seal or for value warrants to the assignee, in the absence of circumstances showing a contrary intention,

(a) that he will do nothing to defeat or impair the value of the assignment;

(b) that the right, as assigned, actually exists and is subject to no limitations or defences other than those stated or apparent at the time of the assignment;

(c) that any token, writing or evidence of the right delivered to the assignee as part of the transaction of assignment, or exhibited to him as an inducement to accept the assignment, is genuine and what it purports to be.

(2) An assignor does not by the mere fact of assigning warrant that the obligor is solvent or that he will perform his obligation.

(3) An assignor is bound by affirmations and promises to the assignee with reference to the right assigned, in the same way and to the same extent that one who transfers chattels is bound under like circumstances.

(4) An assignee's rights under his assignor's warranties are not assigned to a subassignee by the mere assignment of the right against the obligor, to which the warranties relate, but the rights under such warranties may be expressly assigned.

THIRD PARTY BENEFICIARY CONTRACTS

Types of Beneficiaries. A contract in which a party promises to render a certain performance not to the promisee but to a third person is called a third party beneficiary contract. The third person is not a party to the contract but is a beneficiary of the promise. Such contracts may be divided into three types: (1) donee beneficiary; (2) creditor beneficiary; and (3) incidental beneficiary. A great majority of courts enforce both the donee beneficiary and the creditor beneficiary type of third party contract, but no court enforces the incidental beneficiary type.

Donee Beneficiary. A third person is a donee beneficiary if the purpose of the promisee in bargaining for and obtaining the promise was to make a gift to the beneficiary. The ordinary life insurance policy is an illustration. The insured makes a contract with an insurance company which promises, in consideration of premiums paid to it by the insured, to pay upon the death of the insured a stated sum of money to a beneficiary named in the policy. The beneficiary need not even know of the existence of the policy in order to have rights under it. If the policy does not reserve to the insured the right to change the beneficiary, the beneficiary has vested rights under the policy of which he may not be deprived without his consent. In most policies a reservation by the insured of the right to change the beneficiary is a standard provision.

The desirability of allowing donee beneficiaries to recover on contracts made for their benefit is manifest. The promisee has no pecuniary interest in performance by the promisor and in case of a breach by the promisor and a suit against him by the promisee, the damages which could be established by the promisee would be nominal. Unless the donee beneficiary is given the right to recover against the promisor, even though he furnished no consideration and is not in privity of contract with the promisor, the purpose of the parties to the contract is defeated and the content of the promisor's consideration has lost its value. The donee beneficiary clearly has no right of action against the promisee, who is his donor, and a denial of his right of recovery against the promisor would frustrate the agreement between the promisee and promisor.

Creditor Beneficiary. A third person is a creditor beneficiary if no intention to make a gift appears in the contract and the performance of the promise will satisfy a duty owing by the promisee to the beneficiary. In this type of case the beneficiary is a creditor of the promisee, and the contract involves consideration moving from the promisee to the promisor in exchange for the promise to pay some debt or discharge some obligation of the promisee to the third person. The making of the contract does not in any way change or affect the obligation of the promisee to the beneficiary as it previously existed. Where the contract is enforceable, as it is by the weight of authority, the creditor beneficiary has both his rights against the promisee, based upon the original obligation, and rights against the promisor based upon the third party contract. If neither performs, the third person can maintain separate suits against both and obtain judgments against both, although he can obtain satisfaction of only one of the judgments.

The sale of real estate upon which there is an outstanding mortgage may be made to a purchaser who expressly assumes to pay the mortgage or to one who merely acquires title to the land subject to the mortgage. Thus, A the owner of Blackacre which is encumbered by a mortgage securing A's note to B in the amount of $15,000, sells Blackacre to C who assumes the mortgage debt. B is a third party creditor beneficiary of the contract between A and C and has a right to enforce payment from C. A remains liable on the mortgage note but as surety because C should pay the debt and save A harmless.

If C, instead of assuming the mortgage, had merely accepted a deed subject to the mortgage, he would not have become personally liable to pay B, and although C may lose his investment in Blackacre by a foreclosure sale, he is not in such case liable for any deficiency in the event the proceeds of such sale are not sufficient to pay the amount due on the mortgage.

Third Party Beneficiaries Under the Code. In a contract for the sale of goods the seller's warranty, whether express or implied, extends to any member of the family or household of the buyer or guest in the buyer's home, if it is reasonable to expect that such person may use, consume, or be affected by the goods. The Code extends this warranty only to personal injuries of the third party resulting from breach of the warranty.

The seller may disclaim any warranty in his contract with the buyer, and of course if there is no warranty, there can be no third party beneficiary. But the seller may not by contract, or otherwise, exclude or limit the applicability of any warranty to this designated class of statutory third party beneficiaries. Section 2–318 provides:

> A seller's warranty whether express or implied extends to any natural person who is in the family or household of his buyer or who is a guest in his home if it is reasonable to expect that such person may use, consume or be affected by the goods and who is injured in person by breach of the warranty. A seller may not exclude or limit the operation of this section.

Rescission of the Contract. With respect to a rescission or discharge or variation of the contract between the promisor and promisee, and the effect thereof upon the rights of the third party beneficiary, as to donee beneficiaries generally the majority rule is that a right vests in the beneficiary at the time of the making of the contract, whether he has knowledge of it or not, of which right he may not be divested without his consent. As to creditor beneficiaries, the general rule is that the parties to the contract may rescind or make a variation in the contract if the creditor beneficiary has not learned of it or assented to it. If the creditor beneficiary has not brought suit upon the promise nor otherwise changed his position in reliance upon it before the parties to the contract have rescinded or altered it by agreement, such rescission or variation of the contract is effective as to the beneficiary. Where the third party beneficiary contract is executory on both sides a mutual rescission by the parties to the contract may be made at any time, and the beneficiary has no ground for complaint.

In an action by the beneficiary of a third-party contract, the defendant promisor may assert any defense which would be available to him if the plaintiff in the action were the promisee. The rights of the third party are based upon the defendant promisor's contract. Any defense which seeks to show that no contract existed, such as illegality, or lack of capacity, mutual consent, or consideration, would be permitted. The defenses of fraud, duress, or failure of consideration, may also be pleaded by the defendant promisor.

Incidental Beneficiary. A third person who may be incidentally benefited by the performance of a contract to which he is not a party has no rights under such contract. It was not the intention of either the promisee or the promisor that the third person be benefited. Assume that for a stated consideration B promises A that he will purchase and deliver to A a brand new Buick automobile of the latest model. A performs. B does not. C, the local exclusive Buick dealer, has no rights under the contract although performance by B would produce a sale from which C would derive a profit. C is only an incidental beneficiary.

CASES

GINSBURG v. BULL DOG AUTO FIRE INS. ASS'N OF CHICAGO

(1928) 328 Ill. 571, 160 N.E. 145,
56 A.L.R. 1387.

PARTLOW, COMMISSIONER. Defendant in error, the Bull Dog Auto Fire Insurance Association of Chicago, a mutual and reciprocal insurance company, issued a policy of insurance to Nick D'Alassandro against loss by theft of an automobile. On January 17, 1920, the automobile was stolen and was never recovered. D'Alassandro assigned his claim under the policy to plaintiff in error, Elkin Ginsburg. The policy provided that "no assignment of interest under this policy shall be or become binding upon the association unless the written consent of the attorney is endorsed thereon and an additional membership fee is paid." Plaintiff in error began suit in the circuit court of Cook county against defendant in error upon the assignment. * * *

There was a verdict and judgment against defendant in error for $1,195.75. An appeal was prosecuted to the Appellate Court for the First District, where the judgment was reversed, and the case is brought to this court on a writ of certiorari.

The entire defense was based upon the failure to comply with the terms of the policy above quoted with reference to the assignment. There is a distinction between the assignment of a policy of insurance before loss and the assignment of a claim for loss after the loss has occurred. In the case of an executory contract, whether it be a policy of insurance or any other contract, the rule is well settled that the contract generally is not assignable without the consent of both parties thereto, where the personal acts and qualities of one of the parties form a material and ingredient part of the contract. [Citations.] This is upon the doctrine that every one has a right to select and determine with whom he will contract, and he cannot have another person thrust upon him without his consent. In the familiar phrase of Lord Denman, "You have the right to the benefit you anticipate from the character, credit and substance of the party with whom you contract." * * *

After the contract has been fully executed and nothing remains to be done except to pay the money a different rule applies. The element of the personal character, credit and substance of the party with whom the contract is made is no longer material, because the contract has been completed and all that remains to be done is to pay the amount due. The claim becomes a chose in action, which is assignable and enforcible under section 18 of the Practice act, Smith-Hurd Stats.1927, c. 110, § 18. In Sloan v. Williams, 138 Ill. 43, on page 46, 27 N.E. 531, 12 L.R.A. 496, it is said: "It is true, that after the contract has been executed by the person agreeing to perform such personal services or exercise such personal skill he may assign the right to recover compensation.—3 Pomeroy's Eq. Jur. sec. 1275, note 2 supra." * * * In May on Insurance (vol. 2, sec. 386,) it is said: "An assignment after loss is not the assignment of the policy but the assignment of a claim or debt—a chose in action. * * * An assignment after loss does not violate the clause in the policy forbidding a transfer even if the clause reads before or after loss. The reason of the restriction is, that the company might be willing to write a risk for one person of known habits and character and not for another person of less integrity and prudence, but after loss this reason no longer exists." * * *

When the automobile was stolen and defendant refused to pay, a cause of action arose in favor of the insured. It became a chose in action and the policy became the evidence of the debt. The insured had the right to assign this debt, and when he did so, plaintiff in error had a right to begin this suit. Defendant in error offered no evidence of any claim against either the insured or plaintiff in error, as provided in section 18 of the Practice act. In fact, the evidence shows no defense of any kind or character.

The Appellate Court was in error in reversing the judgment of the trial court, and the judgment of the Appellate Court will be reversed and the judgment of the circuit court will be affirmed.

ALLHUSEN v. CARISTO CONST. CORP.

(1952) 303 N.Y. 446, 103 N.E.2d 891.

FROESSEL, J. Defendant, a general contractor, subcontracted with the Kroo Painting Company (hereinafter called Kroo) for the performance by the latter of certain painting work in New York City public schools. Their contracts contained the following prohibitory provision: "The assignment by the second party [Kroo] of this contract or any interest therein, or of any money due or to become due by reason of the terms hereof without the written consent of the first party [defendant] shall be void." Kroo subsequently assigned certain rights under the contracts to Marine Midland Trust Company of New York, which in turn assigned said rights to plaintiff. These rights included the "moneys due and to become due" to Kroo. The *contracts* were not assigned, and no question of improper delegation of contractual duties is involved. No written consent to the assignments was procured from defendant.

Plaintiff as assignee seeks to recover, in six causes of action, $11,650 allegedly due and owing for work done by Kroo. Defendant answered with denials, and by way of defense set up the aforementioned prohibitory clause, in addition to certain setoffs and counterclaims, alleged to have existed at the time of the assignments. It thereupon moved for summary judgment under rule 113 of the Rules of Civil Practice, and demanded dismissal of plaintiff's several causes of action on the sole ground that the prohibitory clause constituted a defense sufficient as a matter of law to defeat each cause of action. Special Term dismissed the complaint, holding that the prohibition against assignments "must be given effect." The Appellate Division affirmed, one Justice dissenting on the ground that the "account receivable was assignable by nature, and could not be rendered otherwise without imposing an unlawful restraint upon the power of alienation of property." [Citation.]

Whether an anti-assignment clause is effective is a question that has troubled the courts not only of this State but in other jurisdictions as well. [Citations.]

Our courts have not construed a contractual provision against assignments framed in the language of the clause now before us. Such kindred clauses as have been subject to interpretation usually have been held to be either (1) personal covenants limiting the covenantee to a claim for damages in the event of a breach [citations], or (2) ineffectual because of the use of uncertain language. [Citation.] But these decisions are not to be read as meaning that there can be no enforcible prohibition against the assignment of a claim; indeed, they are authority only for the proposition that, in the absence of language clearly indicating that a contractual right thereunder shall be nonassignable, a prohibitory clause will be interpreted as a personal covenant not to assign.

* * *

In the light of the foregoing, we think it is reasonably clear that, while the courts have striven to uphold freedom of assignability, they have not failed to recognize the concept of freedom to contract. In large measure they agree that, where appropriate language is used, assignments of money due under contracts may be prohibited. When "clear language" is used, and the "plainest words * * * have been chosen", parties may "limit the freedom of alienation of rights and prohibit the assignment." [Citations.] We have now before us a clause embodying clear, definite and appropriate language, which may be construed in no other way but that any attempted assignment of either the contract or any rights created thereunder shall be "void" as against the obligor. One would have to do violence to the language here employed to hold that it is merely an agreement by the subcontractor not to assign. The objectivity of the language precludes such a construction. We are therefore compelled to conclude that this prohibitory clause is a valid and effective restriction of the right to assign.

Such a holding is not violative of public policy. Professor Williston, in his treatise on Contracts, states (Vol. 2 § 422, p. 1214): "The question of the free alienation of property does not seem to be involved." The New York cases do not hold otherwise. [Citations.] Plaintiff's claimed rights arise out of the very contract embodying the provision now sought to be invalidated. The right to moneys under the contracts is but a companion to other jural relations forming an aggregation of actual and potential interrelated rights and obligations. No sound reason appears why an assignee should remain unaffected by a provision in the very contract which gave life to the claim he asserts.

Nor is there any merit in plaintiff's contention that section 41 of the Personal Property Law, Consol. Laws, c. 41, requires that the prohibitory clause be denied effect. Because the statute provides that a person may transfer a claim, it does not follow that he may not contract otherwise. Countless rights granted by statutes are voluntarily surrendered in the everyday affairs of individuals.

*   *   *

Judgment affirmed.

FEDERAL FINANCE CO. v. HUMISTON

(1965) 66 Wash.2d 648, 404 P.2d 465.

HALE, J. Evanescent as the moonmist from which it was named, the household china Captain Neal A. Humiston bought from Lyle L. Sparber vanished before it materialized. Sparber promised the china, but failed to deliver. Federal Finance Company, Sparber's assignee, demanded payment. Captain Humiston said he would not pay for something he did not receive—and thereby hangs this case.

Neal Humiston and Lyle Sparber were boyhood chums in Potlatch, Idaho; they played football on the same high school team and visited back and forth in each other's home. After high school, they separated and went off to war. Eventually Sparber took a job selling china under the name of Winfield Sales; Humiston renewed his military career and became a Captain in the Air Force. Their paths crossed ten years later in Spokane when Sparber sold Humiston a goodly quantity of china.

Sparber sold Humiston two 97-piece sets of the Moon Mist pattern and 24 coffee mugs at a price of $1,114.88. A $4 fee for "filing and credit report" plus $236 to cover what the contract called "time charges" brought the total price to $1,354.88. Captain Humiston made a down payment of $88.88, leaving a balance of $1,266. Sparber told Humiston the china would be delivered in about six weeks.

They executed a written agreement dated October 4, 1962, on a printed form labeled "Conditional Sale Contract" which designated Winfield Sales, by Lyle L. Sparber, as seller and Neal A. Humiston as purchaser. It declared that "The purchaser shall pay to Federal Finance Co., Inc. the deferred balance of $1266.00 in 23 installments of $52.75 each, and a final installment of $52.75 commencing Nov. 18, 1962." The contract also said that "The Purchaser, after thorough examination, buys and accepts delivery of the above described chattels on date hereof and promises to pay to the order of the Seller the said Time Balance in accordance with payment schedule set forth above."

Winfield Sales, by Lyle L. Sparber, owner, signed and delivered to Federal Finance Company a separate printed instrument demominated "Assignment and Guarantee," dated October 5, 1962, assigning and transferring to Federal all of the seller's rights in the Humiston contract, and guaranteeing that the purchaser would make all of the payments and fully perform the contract. The assignment provided also that the assignor would perform the contract if the purchaser failed to do so. Humiston was not a party to the assignment nor was there evidence that he had knowledge of this assignment to Federal Finance.

Captain Humiston commenced making the payments to Federal Finance. The china did not arrive. Humiston demanded both an explanation and return of his money from Sparber. Sparber gave him the first, explaining that he had several big deals pending and had been compelled to divert delivery to other customers; as to return of the money, Sparber gave Humiston a check December 20, 1962, for $45.70 and another January 29, 1963, for $104.85, each of which was dishonored by the bank.

Humiston continued making the payments to Federal Finance despite failure of delivery. He says Sparber promised to reimburse him. In May and June, 1963, he received checks from Sparber in the amount of $52.75 each, both of which were dishonored by the bank. Each time Humiston chided Sparber, Sparber promised an early delivery, so, according to Humiston, the best way out of the fiasco was to make the payments in the hope of getting the china.

Robert L. Lobdell, a former manager of Federal Finance, testified that the company did not usually advance money to the seller on assigned contracts until they received a delivery and acceptance receipt, but could not explain in this instance Federal's failure to require such an instrument. He remembered that one time he had called the Humistons (November 20, 1962), to inquire about the tardiness of the November payment. Captain Humiston promised a payment by November 26th and the promise was kept; again, on January 2, 1963, he talked to Captain Humiston by telephone. In neither conversation did the purchaser protest nondelivery. Then, Lobdell remembered talking to Mrs. Humiston during late December, 1962, and asking her how she liked the china. He recalled her saying that they enjoyed it very much and used it a lot for entertaining. The trial court attached little significance to this reported conversation.

Humiston continued his payments to Federal Finance until September 30, 1963 (ten payments in all), relying, he says, on reimbursement by Sparber from time to time and on Sparber's promises that delivery would soon be made. When Humiston finally refused to make further payments, Federal Finance, as assignee of the conditional sales contract, brought this action for the principal balance of $749.06, for late charges of $5.28, and for an attorney's fee of $200. Humiston defends on the ground of total failure of consideration.

* * *

The conditional sales contract recited delivery of the china, but the overwhelming evidence showed no delivery had been made by Sparber or anyone else. The buyer never received the goods. Although the written agreement between the vendor and vendee acknowledged delivery, parol evidence was admissible to prove no delivery had ever been made. [Citation.] A party to contract is not bound by a false recital of fact, and parol evidence is admissible to prove the recital erroneous. [Citation.] Failure to deliver the subject matter of a contract to purchase merchandise represents a total failure of consideration—unless, of course, the contract provides otherwise. Captain Humiston, not having received the china, had a right to rescind his contract with Sparber and then and there terminate his liability under the contract. The Restatement confirms this view:

A total failure to receive the agreed exchange for the performance of a promisor's contractual duty discharges that duty; but if the failure is due to the promisor's fault he becomes subject to a duty to render compensation. 2 Restatement, Contracts § 399 (1) (1932).

Federal Finance, as Sparber's assignee—at no time undertaking to carry out his promise to deliver the china—took the contract subject to any defenses the purchaser had against the seller. [Citation.]

(1) An assignee's right against the obligor is subject to all limitations of the obligee's right, to all absolute and temporary defenses thereto, and to all set-offs and counterclaims of the obligor which would have been available against the obligee had there been no assignment, provided that such defenses and set-offs are based on facts existing at the time of the assignment, or are based on facts arising thereafter prior to knowledge of the assignment by the obligor.

(2) Except as stated in Subsection (3), an assignee's right against the obligor is subject to all set-offs and counterclaims which would have been available against the assignee if he were the original obligee.

(3) A sub-assignee's right against the obligor is not subject to the set-off or coun-

terclaim of a right of the obligor against a prior assignee unless the obligor's right was acquired prior to any sub-assignment by the prior assignee, nor even in that case if the sub-assignee claiming under such prior assignee is a bona fide purchaser for value of the assigned right, without notice of the existence of the obligor's right. 1 Restatement, Contracts § 167 (1932).

The assignee of a nonnegotiable instrument acquires no greater rights against the obligor than the assignor had against him at the time of the assignment unless, of course, an equitable estoppel may be interposed to prevent the obligor from setting up such defenses. [Citation.] One of the essentials to such an estoppel is that the assignee has acted to his detriment because of the actions of the obligor. Other than accepting the payments it would not otherwise have received, the record shows no steps that Federal Finance would or could have taken to recover against Sparber had the payments been earlier discontinued.

*   *   *

Judgment for defendant affirmed.

_____

NASSAU DISCOUNT CORP. v. ALLEN

(1965) 44 Misc.2d 1007, 255 N.Y.S.2d 608.

HELLER, J. This is an action by an assignee of an instalment contract for the purchase price of goods sold and delivered. The parties have stipulated to the following facts: On April 22, 1963, a salesman representing the seller, Educational Guild, Inc., presented himself to the defendant at defendant's home. Claiming to be connected with the Board of Education and emphasizing his official position, he convinced the buyer that she was required to purchase certain books for the use of her school-age child. In reality, the seller was in no way connected with the Board of Education but because of these misrepresentations the defendant was induced to enter into an instalment sales con-

tract for the purchase of the books. The books covered by the contract were never delivered to defendant.

On April 30, 1963, the plaintiff, Nassau Discount Corp., took an assignment of the contract for value. The reverse side of the contract contains several conditions one of which directly relates to the assignment and states:

"Buyer will settle all mechanical, service and other claims of whatsoever character with respect to the sale evidenced hereby, directly with Seller (and not with any such Assignee) and will not set up any such claim(s) as a defense or counterclaim to any action for payment or possession which may be brought by an Assignee who acquires this Contract in good faith and for value * *."

Thereafter, on May 5, 1963, plaintiff mailed to defendant a Notice of Assignment in conformance with Section 403, subdivision 3(a) of the Personal Property Law requesting the buyer to notify the assignee in writing within ten days from the date of the mailing of the notice of any defense that she might have arising out of the sale or otherwise be barred from asserting such defense in an action by the assignee. Plaintiff received no written response to its Notice of Assignment. However, defendant upon receipt of the notice immediately returned plaintiff's coupon payment book by mail. Defendant has since refused to pay any instalments of the contract and thereupon plaintiff instituted this law suit.

The broad issue presented for determination by this court is whether defendant is barred by the waiver of defenses clause contained within the contract from asserting her defenses of fraud and non-delivery against plaintiff assignee. Subsidiary to the determination of this broad issue is whether the fraud alleged is fraud in factum, the real defense of fraud, or fraud in the inducement, and furthermore, whether plaintiff takes subject to the real defense of fraud.

Fraud in the factum exists where one is induced to sign an instrument of a different nature or character than that he was led to believe was before him. [Citations.] In the present case defendant does not assert that she was deceived as to the nature of the paper she was signing but rather that she was *induced* to sign the contract through the fraudulent misrepresentations of the salesman. Therefore, the fraud involved in this case is fraud in the inducement of the contract and we need not decide whether plaintiff takes subject to the real defense of fraud.

More accurately phrased, the issue is whether defendant has waived her defenses of fraud in the inducement of the contract and non-delivery. The controlling statute in the resolution of this issue is Section 403, subdivision 3(a) of the Personal Property Law which provides in substance that no contract shall contain any provision whereby the buyer agrees not to assert against an assignee a claim or defense arising out of the sale, but it *may* contain such a provision as to an assignee who acquires the contract in good faith and for value and to whom the buyer has not mailed written notice of the facts giving rise to a claim or defense within ten days after the assignee has mailed notice of the assignment to the buyer. Subdivision 3(a) further provides stringent requirements for the contents of the notice of assignment, all of which have been complied with by plaintiff.

* * *

Good faith necessarily requires that the assignee be "not so identified with the seller, to an extent that it could fairly be said that the dealings of one are inextricably interwoven with that of the other." Public National Bank and Trust Co. of New York v. Fernandez, Mun.Ct., 121 N.Y.S.2d 721, 724. The court further stated:

"Certain unmistakable indicia point inevitably that this plaintiff, far from being a bona fide assignee of a chosen action, was in fact a principal in the transaction * *." It was pointed out that the contract provided that all instalments be paid to the plaintiff assignee; that the title to the merchandise was to be retained by the holder, who was defined as either the seller or the assignee; that the assignment was made even before the goods were delivered to the buyer and that the sale and assignment were physically encompassed within the same document. The court concluded:

"From all the above it would appear that the bank, rather than being a bona fide purchaser of the contract in question, was to all intents and purposes a party to the original agreement."

* * *

When contracts are supplied by an assignee, complete with the assignee's name printed thereon, it is obvious that the assignee is a specific assignee, vitally interested in the sale, so closely related that it is almost as if the assignee were "looking over the parties' shoulders when the sale was consummated." [Citation.] Form contracts supplied by a specific assignee containing waiver of defenses clauses inescapably point to the conclusion of a pre-formed intention upon the part of the assignee to defeat the rights of the buyer so as to negate the requirement of good faith. [Citation.]

It can fairly be said that assignee and seller in the circumstances of this case were so inextricably intertwined as to impugn plaintiff's good faith status. This court, therefore, finds as an ultimate fact that an implied agency existed under the terms of the contract and that plaintiff is subject to the defenses of fraud in the inducement and non-delivery.

Defendant is entitled to judgment dismissing the complaint. * * *

BEAM v. JOHN DEERE CO. OF ST. LOUIS

(1966) 240 Ark. 98, 398 S.W.2d 218.

WARD, J. On July 21, 1964 The John Deere Company of St. Louis (appellee herein) filed a complaint in circuit court against Neal Beam, d/b/a Beam Construction Company (appellant herein), containing in substance the following allegations material on this appeal: (a) On February 9, 1962 appellant executed a title retaining note in the sum of $9,284.44 in part payment of a used John Deere Tractor purchased from the Pulaski Implement Company, hereafter referred to as "Pulaski"; (b) said note was negotiated, before maturity, to appellee who is the bona fide holder thereof; (c) appellant has failed and refused to pay said note according to its terms, and there is a balance due of $3,271.-39; (d) appellant is now in possession of said tractor and refuses to surrender same to appellee; (e) the tractor is of the value of $6,500; (f) appellee is entitled to the immediate possession of said tractor; (g) *The prayer was for the recovery of the tractor,* and all other proper relief. (Similar allegations were also made regarding another tractor which raises no new issue and need not be considered on appeal). Filed in connection with the complaint was an affidavit and bond to obtain delivery, and also a Writ of Replevin.

To the above complaint appellant filed an answer, set-off, and Cross-Complaint. *Answer:* Admits buying the tractor from Pulaski, which was represented to be a 1962 model, as used equipment, and purported to have a cash value of $11,750; (b) admits paying $4500, leaving a balance of $8,225; (c) Pulaski did not know the tractor was a 1962 model—it being in fact a 1958 model—having a market value of only $5,600; (d) appellee knew the tractor was sold to Pulaski for twice its worth, and Pulaski was an agent of appellee—therefore appellee was not a bona fide purchaser of the conditional sales contract; (e) admits he is in possession of said tractor and refuses to surrender possession to appellee; (f) denies all other allegations in the complaint, and; (g) claims his right under Ark.Stat.Ann. § 51-1102 (1947), i. e. the right to pay any judgment against him and keep the tractor.

Set-Off and Cross-Complaint: (a) Pulaski was an agent of appellee in making the sale and therefore a necessary party to this action; (b) Pulaski knew the tractor was older and less valuable than was represented; (c) he is entitled to judgment against Pulaski and appellee for $_____, and appellee is entitled to nothing.

Order and Judgment: The cause was submitted to the trial court on appellee's Motion for Summary Judgment, the pleadings, and interrogatories. The court found that "there is no genuine issue as to any material fact", and entered judgment in favor of appellee as prayed, including possession of the tractor, with appellant having the right to redeem the equipment.

For a reversal, appellant relies on the three separate points discussed hereafter.

After both sides had rested, and the matter had been submitted to the court on appellee's motion for a summary judgment, appellant moved the court to reopen the case to allow him to show the tractor was sold by appellee to Pulaski for $500. This motion was denied by the court, and, we think, correctly so. In the first place there was offered no substantial proof of the allegation. In the second place it appears that appellant had not used due diligence to discover the asserted fact sooner. Also, there was undisputed proof that the tractor had been extensively repaired or rebuilt by Pulaski before it was sold to appellant. This fact having been established, the price Pulaski paid for the tractor was no proof of its value when sold to appellant.

* * *

It would serve no useful purpose to attempt to set forth the dozens of letters, exhibits, pleadings and interrogatories found in the voluminous record in this case. It appears that appellant's principal contention, to show a fact issue is involved, may be fairly summarized in his own statement that there is a material issue of fact "as to the actual value of the equipment when sold, Beam claiming it was worth less than half what Deere claimed it was". It may be conceded that there is much testimony in the record to indicate that perhaps appellant has a right of action against Pulaski, but when he signed the conditional sales contract upon purchasing the tractor from Pulaski he waived all claims against appellee to whom the contract was assigned. In part the contract reads:

"I (we) will settle all claims of any kind against seller directly with seller and if seller assigns this note, I (we) will *not* use any such claim as a defense, set-off or counter-claim against an effort by the holder of this note to collect the amount due on this note or to repossess the goods * * *." (Emphasis ours.)

The above language clearly falls within the purview of the Uniform Commercial Code (§ 85–9–206) which reads in part:

"Subject to any statute or decision which establishes a different rule for buyers of consumer goods, an agreement by a buyer that he will not assert against an assignee any claim or defense which he may have against the seller is enforceable by an assignee who takes an assignment for value, in good faith * *." There is not, and could not be, any contention or valid claim that the machinery here involved constitutes consumer goods. The recent case of Morgan v. John Deere Company of Indianapolis, Inc., (Ky.), 394 S.W.2d 453, is very much in point here to sustain the action of the trial court in this case. In that case the Court said:

"The contract of sale contained a waiver of defenses in the following language:

'I will settle all claims of any kind against Seller directly with Seller and if Seller assigns this note, I will not use any such claim as a defense, setoff or counterclaim against any effort by the holder of this note to collect the amount due on this note or to repossess the Goods.' "

  *   *   *   *   *   *   *

"Morgan contends that the case was not a proper one for summary judgment. However, on the key point in the case, namely, the waiver clause, there was no genuine issue of a material fact, so we thing [think] summary judgment was proper.

"The judgment is affirmed."

Likewise, there is no contention here that appellant did not sign the waiver clause.

The judgment of the trial court is, therefore, affirmed.

Affirmed.

BOULEVARD NAT. BANK OF MIAMI v. AIR METALS INDUS.

(1965 Fla.) 176 So.2d 94.

WILLIS, CIR. J. * * * The "question" which was passed upon by the certifying court is whether the law of Florida requires recognition of the so-called "English" rule or "American" rule of priority between assignees of successive assignments of an account receivable or other similar chose in action. Stated in its simplest form, the American rule would give priority to the assignee first in point of time of assignment, while the English rule would give preference to the assignment of which the debtor was first given notice. Both rules presuppose the absence of any estoppel or other special equities in favor of or against either assignee. The English rule giving priority to the assignee first giving notice to the debtor is specifically qualified as applying "unless he takes a later assignment with notice of a previous one or without a valuable consideration". [Citations.]

* * *

The American rule for which petitioner contends is based upon the reasoning that an account or other chose in action may be assigned at will by the owner; that notice to the debtor is not essential to complete the assignment; and that when such assignment is made the property rights become vested in the assignee so that the assignor no longer has any interest in the account or chose which he may subsequently assign to another. [Citations.]

* * *

It is undoubted that the creditor of an account receivable or other similar chose in action arising out of contract may assign it to another so that the assignee may sue on it in his own name and make recovery. Formal requisites of such an assignment are not prescribed by statute and it may be accomplished by parol, by instrument in writing, or other mode, such as delivery of evidences of the debt, as may demonstrate an intent to transfer and an acceptance of it. * * *

It seems to be generally agreed that notice to a debtor of an assignment is necessary to impose on the debtor the duty of payment to the assignee, and that if before receiving such notice he pays the debt to the assignor, or to a subsequent assignee, he will be discharged from the debt. 6 Am.Jur.2d 278 (Assignments, Sec. 96). To regard the debtor as a total non-participant in the assignment by the creditor of his interests to another is to deny the obvious. An account receivable is only the right to receive payment of a debt which ultimately must be done by the act of the debtor. For the assignee to acquire the right to stand in the shoes of the assigning creditor he must acquire some "delivery" or "possession" of the debt constituting a means of clearly establishing his right to collect. The very nature of an account receivable renders "delivery"

and "possession" matters very different and more difficult than in the case of tangible personalty and negotiable instruments which are readily capable of physical handling and holding. However, the very principles which render a sale of personal property with possession remaining in the vendor unexplained fraudulent and void as to creditors applies with equal urgency to choses in action which are the subject of assignment. It would seem to follow that the mere private dealing between the creditor and his assignee unaccompanied by any manifestations discernable to others having or considering the acquiring of an interest in the account would not meet the requirement of delivery and acceptance of possession which is essential to the consummation of the assignment. Proper notice to the debtor of the assignment is a manifestation of such delivery. It fixes the accountability of the debtor to the assignee instead of the assignor and enables all involved to deal more safely.

* * *

We thus find that the so-called English rule which the trial and appellant court approved and applied is harmonious with our jurisprudence, whereas the so-called American rule is not. * * *

LAWRENCE v. FOX

(1859) 20 N.Y. 268.

[Action by plaintiff against defendant to recover $300 and interest. The evidence showed that one Holly, in November, 1857, at the request of defendant, loaned and advanced to him $300, stating at the time that he, Holly, owed that sum to plaintiff, and had agreed to pay it to plaintiff next day; that the defendant, in consideration thereof, at the time of receiving the money promised Holly to pay it to plaintiff next day. Defendant failed to pay plaintiff. From a judgment for $344.66 for plaintiff, defendant appeals.]

H. GRAY, J. * * * In Hall v. Marston, 17 Mass. 575, the court say: "It seems to have been well settled that if A promises B for a valuable consideration to pay C, the latter may maintain assumpsit for the money;" and in Brewer v. Dyer, 7 Cush. 337, the recovery was upheld, as the court said, "Upon the principle of law long recognized and clearly established, that when one person, for a valuable consideration, engages with another, by a simple contract, to do some act for the benefit of a third, the latter, who would enjoy the benefit of the act, may maintain an action for the breach of such engagement; that it does not rest upon the ground of any actual or supposed relationship between the parties as some of the earlier cases would seem to indicate, but upon the broader and more satisfactory basis, that the law operating on the act of the parties creates the duty, establishes a privity, and implies the promise and obligation on which the action is founded." * * *

Affirmed.

SAYLOR v. SAYLOR

(1965 Ky.) 389 S.W.2d 904.

PALMORE, J. This is a declaratory judgment action to determine the ownership of a bank savings account. The facts are stipulated. The contest is between the administrator and the widow of Adrian M. Saylor. The trial court found in favor of the widow, and the administrator appeals.

The account was opened by Mr. Saylor on March 19, 1962, with the deposit of $6,540.-65 derived from the sale of government bonds owned exclusively by him. The pass book issued by the bank to Mr. Saylor on March 19, 1962, was made out in the names of "Mr. or Mrs. Adrian M. Saylor," and the bank's ledger card for the account was established and thenceforth maintained in the names of "Adrian M. Saylor or Kathleen B. Saylor." Kathleen is the widow.

At the time the account was established Mr. Saylor signed an "authorized signature" card made out in the names of "Mr. & Mrs. Adrian M. Saylor." Two check marks below indicated that two signatures were contemplated, but Mrs. Saylor never signed the card. The form of the card was designed for an individual account.

On June 15, 1963, Mr. Saylor deposited $2,132.60 of his own money in the account, and the deposit was entered in the pass book. There were no other deposits, and for purposes of this opinion it may be assumed that there were no withdrawals whatever, prior to the death of Mr. Saylor on May 15, 1964.

The question is whether the balance of the account at Mr. Saylor's death is payable wholly to the administrator, wholly to the widow, or half to each. The trial court held it was a survivorship account, passing wholly to the widow.

It is recognized in this state that a person may by depositing his own money in the names of himself and another create the equivalent of a tenancy in common or a tenancy by the entirety, depending upon his intent. [Citations.] As in the case of other intangibles such as bonds or stock certificates, the right gratuitously conferred on the other party is recognized and is enforceable on the theory of third party beneficiary contract. It is not necessary that such a contract be supported by a consideration moving from the beneficiary, and it is not necessary that a "gift" be proved. [Citation.]

"The prevailing modern view is that a donee-beneficiary has a right of action to enforce a promise made for his benefit. In this respect, the courts so holding have rejected any requirement of consideration, privity, or obligation as between the promisee and the third person." [Citation.]

"In this jurisdiction a party beneficiary of a contract may look to the promisor directly and sue him in his own name to enforce a promise made for plaintiff's benefit, even though he is a stranger, it being sufficient that there is a consideration between the parties who made the agreement for the benefit of the third party." Traylor Brothers, Inc. v. Pound, Ky., 338 S.W.2d 687, 688 (1960). See also Restatement of Contracts, §§ 113, 135.

"It is not essential, in order to enable a third person to recover on a contract made and intended for his benefit, that he knew of the contract at the time it was made." 17 Am.Jur.2d 741 (Contracts, § 314). A fortiori, that Mrs. Saylor did not sign the signature card or otherwise participate in the establishment of the account is immaterial.

By his deposit of money a contract was created between Mr. Saylor and the bank. By causing the account to be established and maintained in the names of himself and his wife, in the absence of evidence to the contrary there is a rebuttable presumption that Mr. Saylor intended to and did make his wife a third party beneficiary of the contract. * * *

In this case the pass book made out in names of "Mr. or Mrs. Adrian M. Saylor" outweighs the signature card bearing the names of "Mr. & Mrs. Adrian M. Saylor" for the simple reason that as between the two the pass book is the one Mr. Saylor is more likely to have noticed, since he kept it in his possession. That he did have it in possession, and used it in making a subsequent deposit, without suggesting a change in the manner in which the names appeared on it is the best evidence of how he intended them to appear. From the evidence stipulated the trial court came to the only reasonable conclusion, which is that Mr. Saylor intended the account to be in the names of "Mr. or Mrs. Adrian M. Saylor."

That Mr. Saylor did not have Mrs. Saylor sign the signature card may indicate that he did not wish her to make any withdrawals. If so, that circumstance is consistent with a purpose to give her the right of survivorship, because otherwise there would have been no reason at all for him to establish a joint account.

The judgment is affirmed.

EXERCYCLE OF MICHIGAN, INC. v. WAYSON

(1965 C.A.7th) 341 F.2d 335.

KILEY, C. J. Plaintiff, suing as third party beneficiary, had judgment for $22,324.50 in this diversity suit for an accounting, based on claims of breach of defendants' contract and of malicious interference with plaintiff's business and contract rights. Defendants appeal, and we affirm the judgment.

Exercycle Corporation of New York sells its machines through a national system of territorial distributorships. During the period in question here, each contract between Exercycle Corporation and the various distributors, including those of plaintiff and defendants, granted the distributor an exclusive right to sell exercycles within a specified area and each contract contained a provision similar to that of clause 11 of defendants' contract. In that clause the distributor agreed "Not to sell Exercycles in any territory other than that assigned to him by the Company under clause 1."

Defendants' contract, entered into on December 21, 1955, giving them the exclusive distributorship in Greater Chicago and nearby cities, was, with modifications not material here, in effect from that time until the trial. From time to time defendants were given non-exclusive rights to sell and advertise in other territories, but never in plaintiff's territory, which included the state of Michigan and the area within a fifty mile radius of Toledo, Ohio. Plaintiff's contract was in effect from October 15, 1955, until the franchise was surrendered pending suit.

The district court found, on conflicting evidence, that early in January 1958 plaintiff protested to defendants about the latter's invasion of plaintiff's territory, that in November 1958 Exercycle Corporation "reminded" defendants that Michigan was plaintiff's exclusive territory in which no other distributor could sell exercycles, but that defendants continued selling in Michigan, and that beginning in 1957 defendants sold 123 exercycles in that state. The court found also that clause 11 in defendants' contract was for the purpose of protecting plaintiff's exclusive territorial rights.   *   *   *

Defendants claim that plaintiff failed to prove its case because plaintiff's president and principal witness, Donald Harris, was impeached. Any inconsistencies in the testimony of the witness were a matter of credibility for the district court to resolve. On the findings made, the district court concluded that defendants' sales in plaintiff's territory were in violation of plaintiff's third party rights in clause 11 of defendants' contract with Exercycle Corporation.

We are not persuaded by defendants' argument that the contract did not contemplate third party benefits, and that they were unaware of the terms of other distributorship contracts. Since they knew of the national scope of Excrcycle Corporation's business and the territorial limitation of their own franchise, they knew, or should have known, that beyond the limits of their own was another's territory and that they transgressed these boundaries at their peril.

The clause prohibiting defendants from selling in other than their assigned territory, as the district court found, was intended for the protection of other distributors, including plaintiff. This purpose was primary, and not merely incidental. [Citations.]

Defendants contend that the proof of damages was speculative and legally insufficient to support the judgment. We think there was substantial proof of damages. Simply because the loss of profits cannot be shown with precision, defendant, who caused the damages, may not be heard to say that no damages may be awarded. [Citations.] The district court found that if the 123 sales had not been made in plaintiff's exclusive territory it would have had increased sales of at least 123 exercycles; that the gross selling price of the 123 exercycles was $56,715.00; that the cost of sales would have been $34,390.50; and that plaintiff's lost profits were accordingly $22,324.50—the amount of the judgment.   *   *   *

Judgment affirmed.

BURNS v. WASHINGTON SAVINGS

(1965) 251 Miss. 789, 171 So.2d 322.

RODGERS, JUSTICE. This is a suit brought to recover damages for the breach of certain alleged contracts claimed by the complainant Lee Burns to have been made for his benefit. In short, this is an action to enforce a contract for the benefit of a third party beneficiary.

*   *   *

The original bill of complaint alleges that appellant is a building contractor, doing business under the trade name of B & E Construction Company. Certain individuals (hereafter called homeowners) entered into written contracts with appellant to build separate residences upon land owned by them; that they desired to obtain loans to finance the construction of their residences; and that appellant directed them to Washington Savings. The homeowners filed their application with Washington Savings requesting loans as follows: W. F. Blair $8,500; A. J. Cothren $9,000; Clifton C. Jackson $4,500; J. C. Jones $4,700. Appellant aided in obtaining surveys, credit reports, title insurance and plans and specifications which were filed with Washington Savings. It is alleged that Washington Savings gave written commitments to make the loans requested by letters addressed to B & E Construction Company. It is charged that the application for loans, and letters addressed to appellant in regard to each homeowner's loan constituted a written contract entered into between the homeowners and Washington Savings in each case. It is charged that the contracts were sufficiently broad to include appellant as a third party beneficiary. It is charged that Washington Savings refused to make the loans to the homeowners and appellant was forced to take mortgages upon their property and sell them at a loss. Appellant charges that he has been damaged as a result of the breach of the various contracts in the total sum of $19,849.15. Suit was therefore instituted by appellant upon the theory that he was a third party beneficiary under the contract, and thus had a right to sue in his own name. Defendants filed general demurrers to the original bill of complaint. The demurrers were sustained, and when appellant failed to amend his bill of complaint the case was dismissed. Appellant has appealed.

In the outset, we bypass the obvious issue as to whether or not the written applications for loans, taken together with letters addressed to the B & E Construction Company stating that loans would be made, are in fact legally sufficient to constitute contracts. We assume, without deciding, that such writings constituted contracts with the various loan applicants. We go directly to the real issue as to whether or not appellant Lee Burns can maintain an action to recover damages for the breach of the various contracts.

It is a general rule of the law of contracts that in order to maintain an action to enforce the breach of a contract, or to recover damages growing out of the breach, or for failure to carry out the terms of the contract, it is ordinarily a necessary prerequisite that the relationship of privity of contract exist between the party damaged and the party sought to be held liable for the breach of the contract. [Citations.]

An exception has been engrafted on this rule and stated succinctly, it is as follows: A third person may sue on a contract made for his benefit between others to the consideration of which he is a stranger. Or stated differently, "a third person may in his own right and name, enforce a promise made for his benefit even though he is a stranger both to the contract and the consideration." [Citations.]

In England, it was originally held that where the person to be benefited was the child of the promisee, the child could maintain an action against the promisor upon the contract. [Citations.] This rule has been reiterated in later cases and has become a firm, established doctrine in England. The rule is nevertheless regarded as a special case controlled by the relationship of the parties. [Citation.] The English rule is strictly adhered to and no exception is made in case of parties closely related to each other. [Citations.]

The early cases establishing the rule in the United States appear to have arisen in New York where the doctrine was broadly established; that where one person makes a promise to another for the benefit of a third person, the third person may maintain an action on such promise. [Citations.] This principle of law has been recognized by most of the states of the United States, although some states have modified the rule. [Citations.]

The historical development of the rule giving the third party beneficiary the right to maintain an action for the breach of the contract has not been entirely satisfactory to the courts so they have repeatedly declared that the rule is to be confined to its original limits. Thus, it has been established that an incidental benefit to a third party is not a sufficient legal ground to give him a right of action upon a contract. It is said: "The principle that one not a party or privy to a contract but who is the beneficiary thereof is entitled to maintain an action for its breach is not so far extended as to give to a third person who is only indirectly and incidentally benefited by the contract the right to sue upon it. A mere incidental, collateral, or consequential benefit which may accrue to a third person by reason of the performance of the contract, or the mere fact that he has been injured by the breach thereof, is not sufficient to enable him to maintain an action on the contract. Where the contract is primarily for the benefit of the parties thereto, the mere fact that a third person would be incidentally benefited does not give him a right to sue for its breach." [Citations].

In order for the third person beneficiary to have a cause of action, the contracts between the original parties must have been entered into for his benefit, or at least such benefit must be the direct result of the performance within the contemplation of the parties as shown by its terms. There must have been a legal obligation or duty on the part of the promisee to such third person beneficiary. This obligation must have been a legal duty which connects the beneficiary with the contract. In other words, the right of the third party beneficiary to maintain an action on the contract must spring from the terms of the contract itself. [Citation.]

Mississippi adopted the so-called American rule early in our judicial history. In the case of Lee v. Newman, 55 Miss. 365, at p. 374 (1877), this Court said: "It has been held from very early times, though not always without question, that where a contract not under seal is made with A to pay B a sum of money, B may maintain an action in his own name; and in America it has been held that such promise is to be deemed made to the third party, if adopted by him, though he was not cognizant of it when made." This

rule has been reiterated many times. [Citations.]

* * * Taking the leading among those cases, as, for instance Smyth v. City of New York, 203 N.Y. 106, 96 N.E. 409, and searching through them for a more definite or a more tangible statement of the rule, we think it will be found that the best considered of these cases reason the matter down to this: (1) When the terms of the contract are expressly broad enough to include the third party either by name as one of a specified class, and (2) the said third party was evidently within the intent of the term so used, the said third party will be within its benefits, if (3) the promisee had, in fact, a substantial and articulate interest in the welfare of the said third party in respect to the subject of the contract." [Citation.]

In what category then, does the B & E Construction Company fit into the rule as the third party beneficiary?

We find no expression or words in the alleged contract *expressly* including appellant, either by *name* or as one of the *specified class*. We find no *terms used* in the contract showing the *intent* of the parties to include appellant as a beneficiary. We find no substantial and articulate interest of the promisee in the welfare of the B & E Construction Company.

It now becomes apparent that the only beneficial interest the B & E Construction Company had in the carrying out of the alleged contracts between the homeowners and Washington Savings was that appellant would have been benefited, in that the homeowners would have obtained funds with which to have paid appellant, building contractor. However, all persons who advanced funds, materials, labor, insurance premiums, engineers' fees, and attorneys' fees were also interested in the carrying out of the contracts since they too would have benefited by loans to the homeowners. It is apparent, however, that they were merely incidental beneficiaries and not third party beneficiaries within the intent, terms and meaning of the contract. In the case of Hartford Acc. & Indem. Co. v. Hewes, 190 Miss. 225, 199 So. 93, 199 So. 772 (1940–1941) this Court said: "But the controlling principle of law here involved is that one not a party to a contract can sue for a breach thereof only when the condition which is alleged to have been broken was *placed in the contract for his direct benefit*. A mere incidental beneficiary acquires by virtue of the contractual obligation no right against the promisor or the promisee." (Emphasis supplied.)

We have reached the conclusion that appellant was not a third party beneficiary within the terms of the alleged contract between the homeowners and the lending agency, Washington Savings. Appellant therefore could not maintain an action against the lending agency because of its alleged failure to carry out an alleged agreement with the homeowners. Thus the Chancellor was correct in sustaining the demurrer filed by appellee.

* * *

Affirmed and remanded for further proceedings not inconsistent with this opinion.

PROBLEMS

1. On December 1, A, a famous singer, contracted with B to sing at B's theatre on December 31st for a fee of $3,000 to be paid immediately after the performance. (a) A, for value received, assigns this fee to C. (b) A, for value received, assigns this contract to sing to D, an equally famous singer. (c) B sells his theatre to E, and assigns his contract with A to E.

State the effect of each of these assignments.

2. The Smooth Paving Company entered into a paving contract with the city of Chicago. The contract contained the clause "contractor shall be liable for all damages to buildings resulting from the work performed." In the process of construction one of the bulldozers of the Smooth Paving Company struck a gas main, breaking the main causing an explosion and a fire which destroyed the house of John Puff. Puff brought an appropriate action against the Smooth Paving Company to recover damages for the loss of this house. Decision?

3. A, who was unemployed, registered with the X Employment Agency. A contract was then made whereby A, in consideration of such position as the Agency would obtain for A, agreed to pay the Agency one-half of his first month's salary. The contract also contained an assignment by A to the Agency of one-half of such first month's salary. Two weeks later, the Agency obtained a permanent position for A with the B Co. at a monthly salary of $600. The Agency also notified the B Co. of the assignment by A. At the end of the first month, the B. Co. paid A his salary in full. A then quit and disappeared. The Agency now sues the B Co. for $300 under the assignment. Decision?

4. B owned 50% of the stock of the X Co. A written contract was made between B and X Co., whereby B surrendered his stock to the X Co., the X Co., agreeing to pay B $100,000 cash, the sum of $5,000 each year as long as he lived, and after his death the sum of $2,500 each year to his wife until her death. Upon B's death several years later, his wife surviving, X Co. refused to pay her anything upon the ground that she was not a party to the contract. The wife sues X Co. Decision?

5. A, a municipality, employs B, a teacher, for the school year 1965–1966. B, in the expectation of being employed by C, another municipality, during the school year 1966–1967, assigned to D the salary for the first month of service which he might render as a teacher to the municipality of C. B was subsequently employed by C, as anticipated, and B's salary for the first month became due. D made demand upon C for payment of the salary. C refused and paid B. D sues C. Decision?

6. A owed B $600 on an open book account. B owed C $800 on an open book account. B assigned A's obligation to C in partial payment for the $800 that he owed C. B owed A $100 at the time that B assigned A's obligation of $600 to C. Subsequent to B's assignment of A's account, B ran up a $500 bill with A. C then started action against A on the assigned obligation. How much can he recover from A? From B?

7. P contracts to sell to A, an ice cream manufacturer, the amount of ice A may need in his business for the ensuing three years, to the ex-

tent of not more than 250 tons a week at a stated price per ton. A makes a corresponding promise to B to buy such an amount of ice. A sells his ice cream plant to C and assigns to C all A's rights under the contract with B. Upon learning of the sale, B refused to furnish ice to C. C sues B for damages. Decision?

8. Brown enters into a written contract with Ideal Insurance Company whereby, in consideration of the payment of the premiums, the Insurance Company promises to pay XYZ College the face amount of the policy, $100,000, on Brown's death. Brown pays the premiums until his death. Thereafter, XYZ College makes demand for the $100,000 of Insurance Company, which refuses to pay upon the ground that there is no privity of contract and that XYZ College was not a party to the contract. Decision?

9. A and B enter into a contract binding A personally to do some delicate cabinet work. A assigns his rights and delegates performance of his duties to C. On being informed of this, B agrees with C in consideration of C's promise to do the work that B will accept C's work, if properly done, instead of the performance promised by A. Later, without cause, B refuses to allow C to proceed with the work, though C is ready to do so, and makes demand on A that A perform. A refuses. Can C recover damages from B? Can B recover from A?

CHAPTER 10

DISCHARGE OF CONTRACTS

Introductory. The subject of discharge of contracts pertains to the termination of the duty or duties created upon the formation of a contract. In earlier chapters, we have seen how parties may become bound by contract and have discussed the four essential elements of a binding promise. It may be as desirable for a person to know how he may become unbound, as it is for him to know how he may become bound by contract. When a contract is made, it is not intended by either party that the duties thereby created shall exist forever. Contractual promises are made for a purpose and the parties reasonably expect this purpose to be fulfilled by performance. However, performance of a contractual duty is only one method of discharge. It is important to know the others, which are numerous.

Whatever causes a binding promise to cease to be binding is a discharge of the contract. In general, there are two types of discharge, (a) by act of the parties, and (b) by operation of law, and there are various methods of discharge of each type. Closely allied to discharge is an excuse for non-performance of a contractual duty. This makes necessary a brief discussion of the subject of conditions.

Conditions. A condition is any operative event the happening or non-happening of which either limits, modifies, prevents, or precedes the duty of immediate performance under a contract, or terminates an existing obligation under a contract. A condition is therefore the natural enemy of a promise. It is inserted for the protection and benefit of the promisor. The more conditions to which a promise is subject, the less content the promise has. A promise to pay $1,000 provided that such sum is realized from the sale of an automobile, provided the automobile is sold within 60 days, and provided that the automobile which has been stolen can be found, is manifestly different from and worth considerably less than an unconditional promise by the same promisor to pay $1,000.

A fundamental distinction exists between the breach or non-performance of a promise, and the failure or non-happening of a condition. A breach of contract subjects the promisor to liability. It may or may not, depending upon its materiality, excuse non-performance by the other party, the promisee, of his duty under the contract. The happening or non-happening of a condition prevents the promisee from acquiring a right, or deprives him of a right, but subjects him to no liability, as he has made no promise that the condition will or will not occur.

Conditions may be either (1) express, (2) implied in fact, or (3) implied in law. They are also classified as (1) conditions precedent, (2) conditions concurrent, and (3) conditions subsequent.

These conditions are not external to the contract, that is, they do not relate to the formation or existence of the contract, but are either part and parcel of the contract as entered into between the parties, or arise by reason of events occurring subsequent to its formation. Consequently, none of the four essentials to the existence of a contract, discussed in earlier chapters, are treated as conditions.

Express Conditions. A condition is express when it is set forth in language usually preceded by such words as "provided that," "on condition that," "while," "after," "upon," or "as soon as". While no particular form of words is necessary to create an express condition, the operative event to which

230

the performance of the promise is made subject is in some manner clearly expressed.

An illustration is the provision frequently found in building contracts to the effect that before the owner is required to pay the price, or the final installment thereof, the builder shall furnish a certificate of the architect that the building has been constructed according to plans and specifications. The price is being paid for the building, not for the certificate, yet before the owner is obliged to pay, he must have both the building and the certificate, as the duty of immediate payment was made expressly conditional upon the presentation of the certificate. This condition is excused if the architect dies or becomes insane, or capriciously refuses to give a certificate, or if there is collusion between the owner and the architect.

Satisfaction as an Express Condition. The parties to a contract may agree that performance by one of them shall be to the satisfaction of the other who shall not be obligated to pay for it unless he is satisfied. This is an express condition precedent to the duty to pay for the performance. It is a valid condition. Assume that a tailor A contracts to make a suit of clothes to B's satisfaction, and that B promises to pay A $250 for the suit, if he is satisfied with it when completed. A completes the suit, using materials ordered by B. The suit fits B beautifully, but B tells A that he is not satisfied with it and refuses to accept or pay for it. A is not entitled to recover $250 or any amount from B by reason of the non-happening of the express condition precedent. This is so, even if the dissatisfaction of B, although honest and sincere, is unreasonable. Where satisfaction relates to a matter of personal taste, opinion or judgment, the law applies the subjective standard, and the condition has not occurred if the promisor is actually dissatisfied. The condition relates to the individual satisfaction of B and to no one else, including a reasonable man. However, if the contract were one for

the sale of coal, steel, road building equipment, or items of everyday merchandise, the condition of satisfaction would be regarded as applying to the marketability, utility, or mechanical fitness of the subject matter, and the law would apply an objective standard. In such case, the question would not be whether the promisor was actually satisfied with the performance tendered to him by the other party, but whether as a reasonable man, he ought to be satisfied. Applying the objective standard, if the promisor reasonably ought to be satisfied, he is liable.

Conditions Implied in Fact. Such conditions are similar to express conditions, in that they are understood to be part of the agreement, although not found in express language. They are necessarily inferred from the promise contained in the contract, and therefore must have been intended in order to give effect to the promise. Thus, if A for $750 contracts to paint B's house any color desired by B, it is necessarily implied in fact that B will inform A of the desired color before A shall commence to paint. The notification of choice of color is an implied in fact condition, an operative event which must occur before A is subject to the immediate duty of painting the house. Likewise, a promise to do plumbing or repair work at another's house is subject to the implied in fact condition that the promisor be given access to the house.

Conditions Implied in Law. A condition implied in law differs from an express condition and a condition implied in fact in that it is not contained in the language of the contract, or necessarily implied therefrom, but is imposed by law in order to make the performance of each party dependent upon performance or tender of performance by the other party, where such mutual dependency would not be inconsistent with the terms of the contract.

If A contracts to sell a certain horse to B for $200, and the contract is silent as to the time of delivery of the horse and payment of the price, the law will imply that the respective performances are not independent of one another. The law will treat the promises as mutually dependent, and therefore that a delivery or tender of the horse by A to B is a condition to the duty of B to pay the price and, conversely, that payment or tender of $200 by B to A is a condition to the duty of A to deliver the horse to B. If the contract specified a sale on credit, and A gave B 30 days after delivery within which to pay the price, these conditions would not be implied as the parties by their contract have made their respective duties of performance independent.

The rationale of conditions implied in law is based upon the idea of doing fairness between the parties. Unless the parties have agreed otherwise, it is unfair that one party should be required to perform unless the other party performs. Conditions implied in law are imposed in order to do justice between the parties and to relieve against hardship. Where the performance by one party requires time, as in a contract by B to build a house for A, unless otherwise agreed, A is not obligated to make any payment to B until the house is completed. This is in fairness to A, as he should not be compelled to perform until B has performed. However, if B has substantially performed, that is, has completed the entire house except for one window in the bathroom, and sues A for the price, the court will not treat this failure of completion as ground for defeating B's action. B will recover the agreed price less an amount equal to the cost of installing the window and completing the house. It would be unjust to deny any recovery to B where he has substantially performed, and the law in such case will not impose complete performance by B as a condition to A's liability. It is more fair that A pay the price reduced by the cost of the window. B is allowed to recover because the condition, in this case

satisfied by substantial performance, was implied by law and not created by the agreement between the parties. If the contract required an architect's certificate as a condition to A's duty to pay the price, and the architect refused to certify because of the missing window, by virtue of which he would be derelict if he did certify, B could not recover anything in his action against A. Such is the difference in effect between an express condition and a condition implied in law.

Conditions Precedent. A condition precedent is an operative event the happening of which precedes the creation of a duty of immediate performance under a contract. Where the immediate duty of one party to perform is subject to the condition that some event must first occur, such event is a condition precedent. A fire insurance policy usually provides that in the event of a loss by fire, the insured shall furnish the insurer with notice of the loss and a statement of the damage within 60 days from the date of the fire, and that a failure to give such notice will excuse the insurer from any liability for such loss. The required notice is an express condition precedent.

Concurrent Conditions. Where the proposed reciprocal and agreed performances of two mutual promisors are to take place at the same time, such performances are concurrent conditions. Such conditions can only exist where complete performance by both promisors can take place simultaneously. If A has contracted to sell B a watch for $100, with delivery and payment to take place concurrently, neither party may maintain an action against the other without first performing on his side or tendering performance. The party who is suing must have first placed the other party in default. In this respect concurrent conditions operate in the same manner as conditions precedent. However, where the conditions are concurrent, a tender of performance need not be absolute but may be made conditional upon receiving performance by the other party.

Conditions Subsequent. A condition subsequent is an operative event which terminates an existing duty of immediate performance under a contract. Where goods are sold under terms of "sale or return," the buyer has the right to return the goods to the seller within a stated period, but is under an immediate duty to pay the price unless credit has been agreed upon. The duty to pay the price is terminated by a return of the goods which thereby operates as a condition subsequent. Insurance policies often contain a provision that in the event of loss and after due notice thereof has been given to the insurer, the insured must bring suit on the policy within twelve months from the date of the loss or be barred from recovery. The giving of proper notice is a condition precedent, and upon its occurrence the insurer is under an immediate duty to pay the amount of the loss, which duty will terminate by lapse of time unless suit is brought within twelve months. The failure to bring suit within the stated period is an express condition subsequent to the liability of the insurer.

Methods of Discharge. The Restatement of the Law of Contracts, Section 385, enumerates the following methods of discharge:

"(1) * * *

(a) performance of the duty;

(b) occurrence of a condition subsequent;

(c) breach by the other party or failure of consideration, or frustration;

(d) release or contract not to sue;

(e) rescission by agreement of the parties;

(f) renunciation, rejection of tender or executed gift;

(g) accord and satisfaction;

(h) account stated;

(i) assignment, novation or contract for the benefit of a third person;

(j) exercise of the power of avoidance if the duty is voidable;

(k) cancellation or surrender, if the contract is formal;

(l) alteration of a written contract;

(m) merger;

(n) res judicata;

(o) incapacity of the parties to retain the right-duty relation;

(p) acquisition by the debtor of the correlative right;

(q) the rules governing joint debtors;

(r) the rules governing sureties;

(s) impossibility;

(t) illegality of a contract or of its enforcement;

(u) bankruptcy.

"(2) The failure of a condition precedent to exist or to occur may discharge a contractual duty, but that method of discharge is not applicable to a duty to make compensation.

"(3) Remedial rights for breach of a contractual duty may be barred or suspended, by

(a) bankruptcy;

(b) Statute of Limitations;

(c) impossibility or illegality of enforcement."

Performance. Undoubtedly, this is the most frequent method of discharge. If a promisor exactly performs his duty under the contract, he is no longer subject to that duty. Less than exact performance, such as substantial performance, does not fully discharge him, although it may provide him with rights against the other party to the contract by depriving such other party of an excuse for nonperformance on his side.

Where the contract is bilateral, a tendered or offered performance by one party to the other which is refused or rejected may be treated as a repudiation which excuses or discharges the tendering party from further duty of performance under the contract.

A tender of payment of a debt past due does not discharge the debt if the creditor refuses to accept the tender. The effect of such refusal is to stop further accrual of interest on the debt and to deprive the creditor of court costs in a subsequent suit by him to recover the amount due.

If a debtor owes money on several accounts and tenders to his creditor less than the total amounts due, the debtor has the right to designate the account or debt to which the payment is to be applied. This direction by the debtor must be accepted by the creditor. If the debtor does not direct the application of the payment, the creditor may apply it to any account owing to him by the debtor or distribute it among several such accounts. Once the debtor has made payment without specifying its application, he may not thereafter direct its application. The payment was unconditionally made by him and may not thereafter become conditional. The application of payment may be a matter of importance, as where one of several debts is secured and the others not, or where one is barred by the Statute of Limitations and the others not barred.

Prevention of Performance. If one party to a contract substantially interferes with or prevents performance by the other, such other party may be discharged. Prevention is usually asserted in connection with the non-occurrence of a condition. If a promisor whose duty of performance is subject to the happening of a certain operative event prevents the event from happening, he may not thereafter assert the condition as an excuse for his non-performance. For instance, A prevents an architect from giving a certificate which is a condition to A's liability to pay B a certain sum of money. A may not set up B's failure to produce a certificate as an excuse for A's nonpayment. Likewise, if A has contracted to grow a certain crop for B and after A has planted the seed, B plows the field and destroys the seedling plants, his interference with A's performance discharges A from his duty under the contract. It does not, however, discharge B from his duty under the contract.

Condition Subsequent as a Discharge. A condition subsequent is defined as an operative event, the happening of which terminates an existing duty of performance. Thus, a fire insurance policy may provide that upon the failure of the insured to notify the insurance company of a loss by fire within 60 days of the occurrence of the loss, the insurance company shall not be liable for such loss. This is a condition precedent to the company's liability. However, the policy further provides that if suit is not filed against the company within one year from the date of the loss, the company shall not be liable. This is a condition subsequent. Upon the happening of a fire and the giving of proper notice, the duty of the company to pay the amount of the loss becomes fixed. The happening of the condition subsequent, i. e., the failure to sue within one year, discharges this duty.

Breach by One Party as a Discharge of the Other. Breach of contract always gives rise to a cause of action by the aggrieved party. It may, however, have a more important effect. Because of the rule that one party need not perform unless the other party performs, a breach by one party operates as an excuse for non-performance by the other party, and if the breach is material and goes to the essence of the contract, it discharges the other party from any further duty under the contract.

A slight breach, such as a three-day delay by a seller of goods in delivery to the buyer of the tenth installment under a twelve-installment contract, operates as a dilatory excuse for non-performance. The buyer may rightly take the position that he will not pay for or accept any more goods until the seller's breach is cured. He may not for such trivial breach take the position that he refuses to accept any more goods under the contract. However, if the seller fails to deliver the first installment, or completely misses two or three consecutive installments, the breach is more serious. This would be a material breach, and the buyer may assert it as an absolute excuse for non-performance discharging him from any duty to accept further deliveries of goods under the contract. The seller, however, would not be discharged from his duty to make compensation to the buyer for breach of the entire contract.

The Code uses the term "cancellation" in connection with an excuse for non-performance by one party as the result of a material breach by the other party, and distinguishes between "cancellation" and "termination" in Section 2–106(3) and (4) as follows:

> (3) "Termination" occurs when either party pursuant to a power created by agreement or law puts an end to the contract otherwise than for its breach. On "termination" all obligations which are still executory on both sides are discharged but any right based on prior breach or performance survives.

> (4) "Cancellation" occurs when either party puts an end to the contract for breach by the other and its effect is the same as that of "termination" except that the cancelling party also retains any remedy for breach of the whole contract or any unperformed balance.

It is to be noted that termination discharges the executory portion of the contract on both sides and is permitted for a cause otherwise than a breach, whereas cancellation which is permitted by reason of a breach discharges the cancelling party but not the breaching party from the executory portion of the contract. Neither termination nor cancellation discharges a right or remedy based upon a prior breach or performance.

Anticipatory Breach. A breach of contract is simply a failure to perform it. It is logically and physically impossible to fail to perform a duty in advance of the date that performance is due. A party may announce prior to such date that he will not perform.

This is a repudiation of the contract, informing the other party that a breach is in prospect. However, it cannot be an immediate breach, for if the repudiating party should later change his mind and fully perform on the appointed date, the contract would be both breached and performed. A repudiation of a contract prior to the date fixed by the contract for performance is called an anticipatory breach. The courts allow it to be treated as a breach and permit the non-repudiating party to bring suit immediately as if it were a breach. This rule was first clearly announced in Hochster v. De La Tour (page 247) in which Lord Campbell reasoned that since the defendant's repudiation prior to the date for performance gave the plaintiff an excuse for non-performance and enabled the plaintiff to change his position and plans, and since a breach by the defendant would have the same effect, the plaintiff may, therefore, treat the repudiation as a breach. This is not logic, but it is the law. It should be noted that Hochster v. De La Tour involved an executory bilateral contract. If the contract had been unilateral, Lord Campbell could never have confused an excuse for non-performance with a breach, as the plaintiff would not have had a duty of performance to be excused. The doctrine of anticipatory breach has never been applied to unilateral contracts. If B owes A $500 on a note which will become due on January 1, no repudiation, threat, or statement by B prior to the maturity date that he is not going to pay the note will enable A to commence suit upon the note until after January 1.

The Code provides that an anticipatory repudiation of a contract for the sale of goods entitles the aggrieved party to suspend performance on his part and to maintain an action for breach although he has urged retraction of the repudiation. Section 2–610 provides:

> When either party repudiates the contract with respect to a performance not yet due

the loss of which will substantially impair the value of the contract to the other, the aggrieved party may

    (a) for a commercially reasonable time await performance by the repudiating party; or

    (b) resort to any remedy for breach (Section 2–703 or Section 2–711), even though he has notified the repudiating party that he would await the latter's performance and has urged retraction; and

    (c) in either case suspend his own performance or proceed in accordance with the provisions of this Article on the seller's right to identify goods to the contract notwithstanding breach or to salvage unfinished goods (Section 2–704).

The retraction of a repudiation before the aggrieved party has cancelled the contract by reason thereof or has materially changed his position reinstates the rights of the repudiating party under the contract as provided in Section 2–611, as follows:

(1) Until the repudiating party's next performance is due he can retract his repudiation unless the aggrieved party has since the repudiation cancelled or materially changed his position or otherwise indicated that he considers the repudiation final.

(2) Retraction may be by any method which clearly indicates to the aggrieved party that the repudiating party intends to perform, but must include any assurance justifiably demanded under the provisions of this Article (Section 2–609).

(3) Retraction reinstates the repudiating party's rights under the contract with due excuse and allowance to the aggrieved party for any delay occasioned by the repudiation.

A retracted repudiation does not eliminate the effect of having impaired the expectation of the other party of receiving due performance. His confidence is shaken and he feels insecure. Unless he receives adequate assurance of due performance demanded by him in writing, he may suspend any further performance on his part. When other rea-

sonable grounds for insecurity exist with respect to performance of a contract for the sale of goods, a written demand for adequate assurance of due performance may be made by the insecure party and failure of the other party to provide such assurance within a reasonable time, not in excess of 30 days, is a repudiation. Section 2–609 provides:

(1) A contract for sale imposes an obligation on each party that the other's expectation of receiving due performance will not be impaired. When reasonable grounds for insecurity arise with respect to the performance of either party the other may in writing demand adequate assurance of due performance and until he receives such assurance may if commercially reasonable suspend any performance for which he has not already received the agreed return.

(2) Between merchants the reasonableness of grounds for insecurity and the adequacy of any assurance offered shall be determined according to commercial standards.

(3) Acceptance of any improper delivery or payment does not prejudice the aggrieved party's right to demand adequate assurance of future performance.

(4) After receipt of a justified demand failure to provide within a reasonable time not exceeding 30 days such assurance of due performance as is adequate under the circumstances of the particular case is a repudiation of the contract.

Release and Covenants not to Sue. A release is technically a discharge under seal of an existing obligation. The term is also applied to any formal writing supported by sufficient consideration which recites a present relinquishment and termination of the rights therein described. A covenant or promise not to sue does not effect a discharge of the obligation, as does a release. It may be interposed as a bar to any suit brought in violation of the covenant and to this extent has the effect of a release. Covenants not to sue are usually employed where an obligee of joint obligors makes a settlement with one of them and wishes to preserve his rights against the others. A release of one joint obligor releases all of them. A covenant not to sue one or more but less than all obligors does not release the remaining ones.

Mutual Rescission. A rescission is an agreement between the parties to a contract to terminate their respective duties under the contract. It is a contract to end a contract. All of the essentials of a contract must be present. Each party furnishes consideration in giving up his rights under the contract in exchange for the other party's relinquishment of his rights therein. An oral agreement of mutual rescission is valid and will discharge a written contract unless the contract to rescind involves the retransfer of a subject matter which is within the Statute of Frauds, or unless under the Code the written contract provides that it cannot be modified or rescinded except by a signed writing. Section 2–209(2). In such case, under the Code, an oral rescission or modification would be ineffective. A contract containing a provision which is contrary to or inconsistent with a provision in a prior contract between the same parties is a mutual rescission of the inconsistent provision in the prior contract. Whether the later contract completely supersedes and discharges all of the provisions of the prior contract is a matter of interpretation.

Renunciation. A duty to make compensation in unliquidated damages for breach of a bilateral contract which is unperformed on both sides may be discharged by a manifestation of the obligee to treat his excuse for non-performance as a termination of the contract. Thus, if A contracts to employ B to work for one year at an agreed salary commencing July 1, and B on June 25 repudiates the contract by informing A that he will not work for him, A has an excuse for non-performance and may promptly fill the job by employing C. If this is all that happens, B would remain liable to A for breach of the contract. However, if when B repudiates, A tells B that he is satisfied and will regard the contract as terminated, both B and A are discharged by this act of renunciation.

The Restatement of the Law of Contracts, Section 415, provides:

"A duty under a unilateral or independent contractual obligation other than one to transfer land or to pay money, is discharged by a manifestation by the obligee to the obligor, at or before the time when performance is due, of unwillingness to receive the performance when due or of assent to its omission, if the manifestation is not withdrawn before the expiration of a reasonable time after performance becomes due and before any material change of position by the obligor in reliance on the manifestation."

Accord and Satisfaction. An accord is a contract between an obligee and his obligor whereby the former agrees to accept and the latter agrees to render a substituted performance in satisfaction of the original obligation. Thus, if B owes A $500, and the parties agree that B shall paint A's house in satisfaction of the debt, the agreement is an executory accord. The debt is not discharged by the accord. However, when B has performed the accord by painting A's house, the $500 debt is discharged by accord and satisfaction.

Account Stated. Where two parties have engaged in various transactions creating the relationship of debtor and creditor, a promise by the debtor to pay a stated sum of money which the parties had agreed upon as the amount due is an account stated. This agreement discharges the obligations arising under the prior transactions. A submission of a statement of account by a creditor to his debtor who retains it without objection for an unreasonably long time is an account stated as the silence of the debtor is taken as a manifestation of implied assent. The rule of an account stated applies only where a debtor-creditor relationship exists. A debt is an obligation to pay a liquidated sum of money, that is, an amount which is fixed and certain or by mathematical computation can be reduced to certainty. Restatement of the Law of Contracts, Section 422.

Novation. A novation involves three parties and an agreement between them to substitute a new obligee in place of an existing obligee, or to replace an existing obligor with a new one. The effect is to discharge the old obligation by the creation of a new one in which there is either a new obligee or a new obligor. Thus, if B owes A $100 and A, B, and C agree that C will pay the debt and B will be discharged, the novation is the substitute of the new debtor C for B. If the three parties agree that B will pay $100 to C instead of to A, the novation is the substitution of a new creditor C for A. In each instance the debt owing by B to A is discharged.

Exercise of a Power of Avoidance in a Voidable Contract. If a contract has been induced by fraud or duress, it is voidable at the instance of the defrauded party or the party upon whom the duress was exercised. The contract of an infant is also voidable at the option of the infant. A voidable contract is of two kinds. In one, the party having the power of avoidance need take no action in order to exercise his power. He may sit back and wait until he is sued and then successfully plead his defense. The other kind of voidable contract requires affirmative action by the party having the power of avoidance in order to be relieved of a duty of performance. Thus, if A fraudulently induces B to purchase goods which A delivers to B, the contract and the sale is voidable by B. But if B after learning of the fraud does not within a reasonable time take affirmative action to rescind the contract, he may not thereafter disaffirm it. He may sue A and receive damages as a result of the fraud, or he may assert such damages defensively if A sues him. However, in order to avoid any and all duty under the voidable contract, he must take affirmative action. The taking of this action is a discharge of his duties under the contract.

Cancellation or Surrender of Formal Contract. A contractual duty which is embodied in a contract under seal, or formal document, or negotiable instrument, may be discharged by a cancellation or surrender of the document or writing or instrument. Cancellation at common law refers to an act of the obligee which physically destroys or mutilates the document or consists in writing the word "cancelled" or a similar word on the face of the document. Surrender means a redelivery of the document by the obligee to the obligor or to someone on his behalf with the intention of relinquishing all rights therein.

An agreement of "cancellation" or "rescission" of a contract, under the Code, as in the case of "termination" or "cancellation" by unilateral action, applies only to the executory or unperformed part of the contract, and unless the contrary intention clearly appears, does not discharge any claim for damages for prior breach of the contract. Section 2–720 provides:

> Unless the contrary intention clearly appears, expressions of "cancellation" or "rescission" of the contract or the like shall not be construed as a renunciation or discharge of any claim in damages for an antecedent breach.

Material Alteration. An alteration or change of any of the material terms or provisions of a written contract or document is a discharge of the entire contract. The alteration to operate as a discharge must be material and must be the act of a party to the contract or someone acting on his behalf. An unauthorized change in the terms of a written contract by one who is a stranger to the contract is not an alteration but a spoliation which does not discharge the contract.

A material alteration is defined in Section 435 of the Restatement of the Law of Contracts, as follows:

> "An alteration of a written contract or of a memorandum of an oral contract within

the Statute of Frauds is material with reference to any party to the contract if such an alteration duly authorized by him, would vary his rights against or duties to the party making the alteration or injuriously affect his legal relations with third persons."

Merger. Where a contractual duty or a duty to make compensation is replaced by an obligation of a different and higher degree, the former is merged into the latter and is discharged. A contract under seal, or formal contract, is an obligation of higher degree than one which arises informally such as a promise of the buyer to pay for goods delivered to him. If, after such a debt has arisen, the buyer should execute and deliver to the seller or creditor a promise under seal to pay the amount of it, the debt would be discharged by merger in the contract under seal. An account payable or informal debt may be discharged by merger in a negotiable instrument executed by the debtor and delivered to the creditor.

Res Judicata. A judgment entered by a court imposes an obligation of a higher degree than the contractual duty or duty to make compensation upon which it is based. Hence, such duty is discharged by a merger in the judgment. No further action may be taken with respect to such duty, and the rights of the obligee are confined to the judgment. If the adjudication by the court is in favor of the defendant, any obligation of the defendant asserted by the plaintiff and within the issues determined by the court is discharged and the plaintiff may not thereafter bring a new action to enforce any such obligation. The matter is *res judicata.*

Incapacity of Parties to Retain the Right-Duty Relation. At common law a husband and wife could not contract with one another, and a contract existing between them before their marriage became unenforceable upon the marriage. This rule has been changed in many States by statute. Section 450 of the

Restatement of the Law of Contracts provides:

> "The marriage of a person subject to a contractual duty or to a duty to make compensation, with the person having the correlative right, discharges the duty, unless the right is held for the benefit of a third person."

Acquisition by Debtor of Correlative Right. A person cannot have a right against himself or owe a legal duty to himself. Therefore, when a person who is under a duty acquires the correlative right in the same capacity, the duty is discharged. Thus, B owes his father A $1,000. A dies without a will leaving B his only next-of-kin who inherits all of A's property. B's duty is discharged. However, if A had died leaving a will by which he bequeathed all of his property to C and named B as executor, B's duty is not discharged. He owes the money to himself in a different capacity, namely that of executor.

Discharge of Joint Debtors. A joint obligation is the single obligation of several obligors. It cannot be released or discharged in part, and, therefore, a release of one of several joint debtors releases all of them.

Discharge of Sureties. A surety is one who is contractually bound together with another party known as the principal to pay a sum of money or render a certain performance to a creditor or obligee. The surety, unlike a guarantor, does not promise to pay if the principal does not pay. The promise of the surety makes him a primary obligor along with the principal. However, the relationship between the surety and principal is such that the latter should pay the creditor the whole amount that is due and save the surety harmless. Any change in the obligation of the principal by agreement between the creditor and principal, such as an extension of the maturity of the debt or a change in the terms of the contract, discharges the surety.

Subsequent Illegality. Performance of a contract which was legal when formed may become illegal by reason of a subsequently enacted law. In such case, the duty of performance is discharged. Thus, A contracts to sell and deliver to B ten cases of a certain whiskey each month for one year. A subsequent prohibition law makes unlawful the manufacture, transportation, or sale of intoxicating liquor. The contract, to the extent unperformed by A, is discharged. War is another illustration of supervening illegality. If a contract for the sale of goods is made between citizens of two countries which subsequently are at war with one another, each country prohibits trading with the enemy. This discharges the contract either upon the ground of subsequent illegality or impossibility.

Impossibility. It may be impossible for a promisor to perform his contract because he is financially unable or because he personally lacks the capability or competence. This is subjective impossibility and does not excuse the promisor from liability for breach of contract. On the other hand, performance may be impossible not because the particular promisor is unable to perform, but because no one is able to perform. This is objective impossibility which in a great number of situations will be held to excuse the promisor or discharge his duty to perform. The death or illness of a person who has contracted to render personal services is a discharge of this contractual duty. If a jockey contracts to ride a certain horse in the Kentucky Derby and the horse dies prior to the Derby, the contract is discharged. It is objectively impossible for any one to perform this contract. Also, if A contracts to lease to B a certain ballroom for a party on a scheduled future date, destruction of the ballroom by fire before the scheduled event discharges the contract. Destruction of the subject matter or means of performance of a contract is excusable impossibility.

Where the purpose of a contract has been frustrated by fortuitous circumstances which deprive the performance of the value attached to it by the parties, although performance is not impossible, the courts generally regard the frustration as a discharge. This rule developed from the so-called "coronation cases." When Edward VII became king of England upon the death of his mother Queen Victoria, impressive coronation ceremonies were planned including a procession along a designated route through certain streets in London. Contracts were made by owners and lessees of buildings along the route to permit the use of rooms with a view on the date scheduled for the procession. The king became ill and the procession did not take place. The purpose for using the rooms having failed, the rooms were not used. Numerous suits were filed, some by landowners seeking to hold the would-be-viewers liable on their promises, and some by the would-be-viewers seeking to recover back money paid in advance for the rooms. The principle involved was novel, but from these cases evolved the frustration of purpose doctrine whereby a contract is discharged if the supervening circumstances destroy the purpose which both parties to the contract had in mind.

Bankruptcy. The subject of bankruptcy is treated in Chapter 43. It is a method of discharge of a contractual duty by operation of law available to one who is adjudicated bankrupt and who by compliance with the requirements of the Bankruptcy Act obtains an order of discharge in bankruptcy. It is applicable only to those obligations which the statute provides are dischargeable in bankruptcy.

Statute of Limitations. At common law a plaintiff was subject to no time limitation within which to bring a suit. All States now have statutes which provide such a limitation. The courts hold that the running of the period of the Statute of Limitations does not operate as a discharge but merely bars the remedy. The debtor is not discharged, but the creditor cannot maintain an action against him after the Statute has run. This distinction may be important, as in a situation where the creditor applies a payment by the debtor to a barred debt. The period of time begins to run from the day that a suit could have been filed, that is, when the remedial right accrues. The statute which governs is that of the State in which the suit is filed. However, if the cause of action arose in another State, the law of the forum may apply the law of such other State.

CASES

PEACOCK CONSTRUCTION COMPANY v. WEST

(1965) 111 Ga.App. 604, 142 S.E.2d 332.

[Action by sub-contractor against prime contractor to recover for work performed on hospital construction project. The trial court entered judgment for the plaintiff. On appeal by defendant, judgment reversed.]

BELL, P. J. * * * The construction contract for breach of which plaintiff seeks to recover is attached as an exhibit to the petition. It sets out an agreement that plaintiff would perform certain work "in strict accordance with" plans prepared by a firm denominated as "Architect." Other provisions of the contract especially material to a consideration of the defendants' general demurrers are: "All work shall be done under the direction of the Architect and his decisions as to the true construction and meaning of the drawings and specifications shall be final * * *. Contractor agrees to pay sub-contractor for said work the sum of [$36,180.00] * * * subject to additions and deductions as hereinbefore provided, payable as the work progresses, based upon estimates of the Archi-

tect and payment by Owner to Contractor * * * Final payment shall be made within 30 days after the completion of the work included in this subcontract, written acceptance by the Architect, and full payment therefor by the Owner." Plaintiff's amended petition omits to allege facts showing or excusing written acceptance by the architect and full payment by the owner.

If the language quoted from the contract is construed as conditions precedent, the petition is fatally defective. Where the existence of a condition precedent affirmatively appears from the petition and exhibits to the petition, the failure to allege fulfillment of the condition precedent or legal justification for nonfulfillment render the petition subject to general demurrer. [Citations.] "Conditions may be precedent or subsequent. In the former, the condition must be performed before the contract becomes absolute and obligatory upon the other party." Code § 20–110.

Plaintiff contends that the defendants' promise to pay was unconditional and that the above quoted portion of the contract merely specified the time when payment should be made. We cannot agree with that contention, for as we construe the plain and unambiguous language of the agreement, there are clearly expressed conditions precedent to defendants' liability for the final payment of the contract price.

* * *

The contract evinces the parties' intentions that plaintiff's work should conform absolutely to the specified architectural standards: Plaintiff was to perform "in strict accordance with" plans drawn by the architect; all work was to be done under the direction of the architect; plaintiff was to be paid in installments according to progress of the work (in conformity with the required standards) as estimated by the architect. These provisions lend emphasis to our conclusion that the contract contained conditions precedent to liability for final payment to the plaintiff that the payment be made "within 30 days after the completion of the work included in this sub-contract, written acceptance by the Architect and full payment by the owner." Written acceptance by the architect in itself is one condition precedent to liability for final payment. [Citations.]

In addition, the contract is open to the construction that * * * the owner's payment to the prime contractor for the subcontractor's work is yet another condition precedent to defendants' liability, so that the plaintiff's failure to allege the owner's payment to the prime contractor renders his petition further defective.

The trial court erred in overruling the renewed general demurrers to plaintiff's petition. This ruling being determinative of the case it is not necessary to consider the remaining assignments of error.

Judgment reversed.

BRADLEY v. WESTERFIELD

(1965) 1 Ariz.App. 319, 402 P.2d 577.

Hathaway, J. Hugh A. Westerfield, the plaintiff below, filed suit in Superior Court against Elizabeth K. Bradley, defendant below, to recover a real estate commission allegedly earned by the plaintiff. The case was tried to the court sitting without a jury, judgment was rendered for the plaintiff and defendant appeals.

The sequence of events which gave rise to this lawsuit is as follows: Defendant entered into a business listing agreement with the plaintiff authorizing the plaintiff to procure a purchaser for defendant's business, the Rio Rita Bar. The listing described the business as a bar with a full liquor license.

* * *

The sole question to be resolved in this appeal is whether the plaintiff was entitled to a commission despite the fact that the sale was not consummated.

Generally speaking, a real estate broker has earned his commission when he has brought to the vendor a purchaser who is ready, willing and able to buy the property on the terms authorized or on any terms acceptable to the seller, when the seller has entered into a written contract with a purchaser produced by the broker. [Citations.] It is not a condition precedent to payment of commission, under the foregoing rule, that the sale be consummated.

Through the listing agreement, the defendant-seller employed the broker to effect a sale of the described business which included, inter alia, a No. 6 Liquor License. The defendant had nothing to sell in the way of an operating business, namely a bar, unless the sale included the liquor license. On the other hand, one purchasing a bar would certainly require a transfer of the liquor license as he could not lawfully operate without a license duly issued by the Superintendent of Liquor Licenses and Control. 2 A.R.S. § 4–244.

In the instant case, the defendant contracted to sell a business, including a liquor license, and the plaintiff procured a purchaser who agreed to the terms set forth in the listing agreement. The parties entered into a binding contract of sale, providing for excuse of performance if the necessary approval of the license transfer was not obtained. The record discloses that the buyer was qualified to hold the license and that the sole impediment to the license transfer was the refusal of the second chattel mortgagee to consent.

The defendant had not provided for this contingency nor made it a condition of the sale. The defendant had warranted that the title was merchantable, indicating that she could produce all necessary transfers and conveyances. If through her own fault or inability the defendant became unable to deliver that which she had contracted to sell, that would not excuse her performance of the contract of sale. [Citation.]

If an employed broker procures a purchaser ready, willing and able to buy the property on the terms specified by the seller, the broker is entitled to compensation for his services, even though the sale should fall through because the seller who employed the broker is unable to convey good title to the property. [Citations.]

It is the view of this court that the instant case falls within the oft repeated rule of law laid down by our Supreme Court in Lockett v. Drake, 43 Ariz. 357, 31 P.2d 499 (1934), at page 500:

" * * * It is the almost universally accepted rule of law that, in the absence of a specific contract to the contrary, when a real estate broker has brought together the parties to a sale or exchange of real estate, and they have agreed fully on the terms and entered into a binding contract for such sale or exchange, his duties are at an end and his commission is fully earned, and it is immaterial that the parties to the contract rescind mutually or that one or the other thereof defaults and the sale or exchange is not fully effected."

The defendant knew, or should have known that there existed a restriction on the transfer of the license in favor of the second chattel mortgagee. In order to deliver merchantable title, the duty to obtain his consent devolved upon her. Her inability or neglect to procure this consent did not relieve her from the obligation to pay to plaintiff the realty commission. This obligation she incurred when she listed the Rio Rita Bar for sale.

Judgment affirmed.

ACOSTA v. COLE

(1965 La.) 178 So.2d 456.

BAILES, J. The plaintiff brings this action to recover the sum of $11,894.55 allegedly paid by her to the defendants for the purchase of 1205 hours of dancing lessons. Additionally, plaintiff seeks to recover the sum of $98.08 paid to defendants, Cullen E. Cole and Ethel R. Cole, as a deposit on a certain allegedly unconsummated dancing lessons contract. The defendants are Cullen E. Cole and Ethel R. Cole, the original licensees of Arthur Murray Inc., Arthur Murray Inc., the licensor, and Charles L. Miller, Jr., and Jerri A. Miller who purchased the Arthur Murray Studio of Baton Rouge from defendants, Cullen E. Cole and Ethel R. Cole, on or about November 1, 1960. After trial, the lower court awarded judgment in favor of plaintiff and against all defendants in solido in the sum of $98.08, but rejected all other demands of the plaintiff. Plaintiff appealed.

* * *

It was also stipulated that the plaintiff had paid to the Arthur Murray Studio the sum of $98.08; that the plaintiff "has received a total of 140½ hours of instruction covering the period from 10–31–58 through March 7, 1959, thus leaving a balance of 1064½ hours presently reflected on the books of the Arthur Murray Studios of Baton Rouge, which are paid for but unused, not considering the check for $98.08 dated March 6, 1959 and the lessons represented by said payment if any."

* * * Here the agreement provided that Mrs. Acosta:

" * * * shall not be relieved of my obligation to pay said tuition herein agreed upon, and that no deduction allowed or refunds for tuition paid and due under this agreement shall be made by reason of my absence or withdrawal. I understand that no refunds will be made under the terms of this contract.'

* * *

We find that the trial court did not pass on the probative value of the evidence introduced by the plaintiff for the purpose of showing physical and mental inability to perform her obligations under the contract, that, of taking the dancing lessons contracted for with the defendants. As shown supra, the trial court ruled that the quoted condition of the contract prohibited any refunds of money paid under the contracts.

On the question of physical and mental disability of the plaintiff, we find the proof clear and convincing that she is, in fact, unable to continue to receive dancing instructions. The plaintiff offered the testimony of four doctors, these being a gynecologist, an internist, and two psychiatrists; however, only one psychiatrist, Dr. Sparkman Wyatt, testified as to any mental illness affecting performance of this contract.

Dr. Edward G. Cailleteau, physician and gynecologist, who has treated the plaintiff since 1948, testified that plaintiff was suffering from inactive tuberculosis, hypertension and emotional depression.

* * *

In addition to the three expert medical witnesses, the plaintiff testified to her own inability to physically and emotionally withstand the exertions of the dancing lessons, and introduced the testimony of six lay witnesses who have known her for a number of years and who testified that plaintiff was physically and mentally ill. Their testimony, in the main, corroborated the expert medical opinion.

We find that the plaintiff has clearly demonstrated her physical and mental illness and inability to perform her part of the contract and to further pursue the dancing instructions contracted for with the defendants.

We find it worthy to note that the record is barren of any medical testimony introduced by defendants to rebut or refute the medical evidence of physical and mental disability of the plaintiff.

* * *

Conceding the validity of the principles that legal agreements have the effect of law as between the parties thereto, and the courts cannot concern themselves with the wisdom or folly of the contractual provisions, we are, nevertheless, of the opinion that the contracts here involved are personal and must be so interpreted both as to the obligor and obligee. Under the specific provisions of LSA–C.C. Article 2000 the obligation on the part of defendant must be construed to be purely personal since she undertook to perform specific services that required her personal skill and attention.

"Similarly, under the plain wording of LSA–C.C. Article 2001, the obligation is personal as to plaintiff because of its nature which was designed for her personal gratification.

"Although the codal articles above noted particularly refer to the inability to perform by reason of death, there is no reason to consider that they should not be applied to cases involving the total and permanent disability of either of the parties to perform the obligations imposed by the contract.

* * *

In 17A C.J.S. § 465, p. 623, we find the rule affecting resolution of a personal contract expressed in the following language:

" * * *

"Contracts to perform personal acts are considered as made on the implied condition that the party shall be alive and capable of performing the contract, so that death or disability, including sickness, will operate as a discharge, termination of the contract, or excuse for nonperformance; contracts resting on the skill, taste, or science of a party, that is, those contracts wherein personal performance by the promisor is of the essence and the duty imposed cannot be done as well by others as by the promisor himself, are personal and do not survive his death. Each case must be decided on its peculiar facts, including a consideration of the language of the contract in the light of the surrounding circumstances; and contract, regardless of its subject matter, may be made personal so as to be brought within the operation of the rule. * * * "

We have here the plaintiff and defendants who entered into a perfect synallagmatic contract, a contract in which each personally bound himself to perform a certain act for the benefit of the other. There is implied in such a contract the resolutory condition that in the event either is rendered incapable of performing the conditions imposed upon him for the benefit of the other, the contract will be dissolved and the parties restored to the positions formerly occupied by each, as perfectly as possible. Thus, translated into the facts before us, this means that the plaintiff obligated herself to receive from the defendants 1205 hours of dancing lessons and to pay the defendants therefor the total sum of $11,894.55, and the defendants obligated themselves to provide for and furnish to the plaintiff the contracted for 1205 hours of dancing lessons. Both conditions or the mutual conditions of the contract required the personal performance of the conditions by both parties thereto. Therefore, in the event of the fulfillment or the occurrence of the resolutory condition, the inability of the plaintiff to receive the dancing lessons, the plaintiff is entitled to be restored to the condition that existed prior to the confection of the contract, to be relieved of the obligation to receive the dancing lessons and to a refund of the unearned portion of the contract price thereof.

Accordingly, the plaintiff is entitled to judgment dissolving the contract she entered into with defendants and to a refund of the unearned portion of the contracts. It was stipulated that she had used 140½ hours of dancing lessons. These 140½ hours of instruction will be deducted from the first 140½ hours contracted for by her. The defendants are entitled to retain the price plaintiff paid for the first 140½ hours of instruction, which means that the contract entered into on October 31, 1958 for five hours of instruction at a cost of $14.50, and the contract entered into on November 8, 1958 for 104 hours at a cost of $1,112.80 will be considered as completed contracts. This leaves a total of 32½ hours of instruction to be paid for from the contract entered into on November 19, 1958 wherein 315 hours of instruction were contracted for at a cost of $3,638.25, or an hourly instruction rate of $11.55. Thirty-two and one-half hours of instruction at $11.55 per hour equals $375.38. The plaintiff is entitled to a refund of the total amount of the contracts entered into on November 21, 1958 for $2,981.45 and January 9, 1959 for $4,147.55, plus the contract entered into on November 19, 1958 for $3,638.25, less the sum of $375.38, or the sum of $10,328.87.

For the foregoing reasons the judgment appealed from is amended and increased to the sum of Ten Thousand Four Hundred Twenty-six & 95/100 ($10,426.95) Dollars, together with legal interest thereon from date of judicial demand until paid, and in all other respects the judgment appealed from is affirmed. Defendants to pay all court costs.

Amended and affirmed.

––––––––––

NEW ERA HOMES CORPORATION
v. FORSTER

(1949) 299 N.Y. 303, 86 N.E.2d 757.

DESMOND, J. Plaintiff entered into a written agreement with defendants, to make extensive alterations to defendants' home, the reference therein to price and payment being as follows:

"All above material, and labor to erect and install same to be supplied for $3,075.00 to be paid as follows:

$ 150.00 on signing of contract,
$1,000.00 upon delivery of materials and starting of work,

$1,500.00 on completion of rough carpentry and rough plumbing,

$ 425.00 upon job being completed."

The work was commenced and partly finished, and the first two stipulated payments were made. Then, when the "rough work" was done, plaintiff asked for the third installment of $1,500 but defendants would not pay it, so plaintiff stopped work and brought suit for the whole of the balance, that is, for the two last payments of $1,500 and $425. On the trial plaintiff stipulated to reduce its demand to $1,500, its theory being that, since all the necessary "rough carpentry and rough plumbing" had been done, the time had arrived for it to collect $1,500. It offered no other proof as to its damages. Defendants conceded their default, but argued at the trial, and argue here, that plaintiff was entitled not to the $1,500 third payment, but to such amount as it could establish by way of actual loss sustained from defendants' breach. In other words, defendants say the correct measure of damage was the value of the work actually done, less payments made, plus lost profits. The jury, however, by its verdict gave plaintiff its $1,500. The Appellate Division, Second Department, affirmed the judgment, and we granted defendants leave to appeal to this court.

The whole question is as to the meaning of so much of the agreement as we have quoted above. Did that language make it an entire contract, with one consideration for the doing of the whole work, and payments on account at fixed points in the progress of the job, or was the bargain a severable or divisible one in the sense that, of the total consideration, $1,150 was to be the full and fixed payment for "delivery of materials and starting of work", $1,500 the full and fixed payment for work done up to and including "completion of rough carpentry and rough plumbing", and $425 for the rest. We hold that the total price of $3,075 was the single consideration for the whole of the work, and

that the separately listed payments were not allocated absolutely to certain parts of the undertaking, but were scheduled part payments, mutually convenient to the builder and the owner. That conclusion, we think, is a necessary one from the very words of the writing, since the arrangement there stated was not that separate items of work be done for separate amounts of money, but that the whole alteration project, including material and labor, was "to be supplied for $3,075.00". There is nothing in the record to suggest that the parties had intended to group, in this contract, several separate engagements, each with its own separate consideration. They did not say, for instance, that the price for all the work up to the completion of rough carpentry and plumbing was to be $1,500. They did agree that at that point $1,500 would be due, but as a part payment on the whole price. To illustrate: it is hardly conceivable that the amount of $150, payable "on signing of contract" was a reward to plaintiff for the act of affixing its corporate name and seal.

We would, in short, be writing a new contract for these people if we broke this single promise up into separate deals; and the new contract so written by us might be for all we know, most unjust to one or the other party.

We find no controlling New York case, but the trend of authority in this State, and elsewhere, is that such agreements express an intent that payment be conditioned and dependent upon completion of all the agreed work. [Citations.] We think that is the reasonable rule—after all, a householder who remodels his home is, usually, committing himself to one plan and one result, not a series of unrelated projects. The parties to a construction or alteration contract may, of course, make is divisible and stipulate the value of each divisible part. But there is no sign that these people so intended. [Citation.] It follows that plaintiff, on defendants' default, could collect either in quantum meruit for what had been finished, Heine v. Meyer, 61 N.Y. 171, or in contract for the value of what plaintiff had lost—that is, the contract price, less payments made and less the cost of completion. [Citations.]

The judgments should be reversed, and a new trial granted.

MERRICK v. ALLSTATE INSURANCE CO.

(1964 D.C.E.D.Mo.) 236 F.Supp. 451.

HARPER, CHIEF JUDGE. * * * Plaintiff's claim is based on a policy of insurance with the defendant and under which plaintiff has been receiving disability payments of $50.00 per week. Plaintiff has previously brought three separate suits against the defendant in order to obtain her payments. At the time this suit was filed there was pending in the Magistrate Court of the City of St. Louis, Cause No. 52691, the third suit referred to.

Plaintiff contends in this action that defendant's refusal to pay constitutes a total and complete repudiation of the contract of insurance and prays for the payment of all future installments due based upon the period of plaintiff's life expectancy. * * *

The Missouri courts have repeatedly held that when a contract remains executory on one side only, such as where money is to be paid regularly to the other contracting party, then in the event of default in performance, suit may be brought to collect only the amount due at the time of the suit. [Citations.]

Thus, the complaining party may sue immediately for each payment as it becomes due, or elect to wait until such time as complete performance is due and then collect the total amount owed. The Allen case (228 Mo.

App. 450, 67 S.W.2d 534), is very similar to the case before the court and recovery was only permitted for payments due when the suit was filed, and recovery was denied for benefits not due at the time the suit was filed, but based on life expectancy. * * *

Accordingly, defendant's motion for summary judgment will be sustained and the clerk will prepare and enter the proper order to that effect.

HOCHSTER v. DE LA TOUR

Court of Queen's Bench (England).
(1853) 2 Ellis and Blackburn Reports 678.

[Plaintiff brought an action against defendant on May 22, 1852, for breach of a contract of employment whereby the plaintiff was to enter the service of defendant in the capacity of a courier and travel with defendant on the continent of Europe for three months commencing June 1, 1852, at an agreed salary. The contract was made on April 12, 1852, and on May 11, 1852, defendant notified the plaintiff that he had changed his mind and declined plaintiff's services. The defendant refused to pay any compensation to the plaintiff. The plaintiff between the date of commencing the action, May 22, and June 1, obtained an engagement to act as courier for Lord Ashburton, on equally good terms, but not commencing until July 4. The jury returned a verdict for the plaintiff. Defendant made a motion in arrest of judgment.]

LORD CAMPBELL, C. J. On this motion in arrest of judgment, the question arises, Whether, if there be an agreement between A. and B., whereby B. engages to employ A. on and from a future day for a given period of time, to travel with him into a foreign country as a courier, and to start with him in that capacity on that day, A. being to receive a monthly salary during the continuance of such service, B. may, before the day, refuse to perform the agreement and break and renounce it, so as to entitle A. before the day to commence an action against B. to recover damages for breach of the agreement; A. having been ready and willing to perform it, till it was broken and renounced by B. The defendant's counsel very powerfully contended that, if the plaintiff was not contented to dissolve the contract, and to abandon all remedy upon it, he was bound to remain ready and willing to perform it till the day when the actual employment as courier in the service of the defendant was to begin; and that there could be no breach of the agreement, before that day, to give a right of action. But it cannot be laid down as a universal rule that, where by agreement an act is to be done on a future day, no action can be brought for a breach of the agreement till the day for doing the act has arrived. * * *

If the plaintiff has no remedy for breach of the contract unless he treats the contract as in force, and acts upon it down to the 1st June, 1852, it follows that, till then, he must enter into no employment which will interfere with his promise "to start with the defendant on such travels on the day and year," and that he must then be properly equipped in all respects as a courier for a three months' tour on the continent of Europe. But it is surely much more rational, and more for the benefit of both parties, that, after the renunciation of the agreement by the defendant, the plaintiff should be at liberty to consider himself absolved from any future performance of it, retaining his right to sue for any damage he has suffered from the breach of it. Thus, instead of remaining idle and laying out money in preparations which must be useless, he is at liberty to seek service under another employer, which would go in mitigation of the damages to which he would otherwise be entitled for a breach of the contract. It seems strange that the defendant, after renouncing the contract, and absolutely declaring that he will never

act under it, should be permitted to object that faith is given to his assertion, and that an opportunity is not left to him of changing his mind. If the plaintiff is barred of any remedy by entering into an engagement inconsistent with starting as a courier with the defendant on the 1st June, he is prejudiced by putting faith in the defendant's assertion: and it would be more consonant with principle, if the defendant were precluded from saying that he had not broken the contract when he declared that he entirely renounced it. * * * The man who wrongfully renounces a contract into which he has deliberately entered cannot justly complain if he is immediately sued for a compensation in damages by the man whom he has injured: and it seems reasonable to allow an option to the injured party, either to sue immediately, or to wait till the time when the act was to be done, still holding it as prospectively binding for the exercise of this option, which may be advantageous to the innocent party, and cannot be prejudicial to the wrongdoer. An argument against the action before the 1st of June is urged from the difficulty of calculating the damages: but this argument is equally strong against an action before the 1st of September, when the three months would expire. In either case, the jury in assessing the damages would be justified in looking to all that had happened, or was likely to happen, to increase or mitigate the loss of the plaintiff down to the day of trial. * * *

Judgment for plaintiff.

CHRISTY v. PILKINTON

(1954) 224 Ark. 407, 273 S.W.2d 533.

GEORGE ROSE SMITH, J. This is a suit for specific performance, brought by the appellee as vendor in a contract for the sale of real property. In appealing from a decree for the plaintiff the defendants contend only that the court erred in ordering them to perform a promise which the proof shows to be beyond their financial resources.

It is conceded that the parties executed a valid written contract by which the Christys agreed to buy an apartment house from Mrs. Pilkinton for $30,000. The vendor's title is admittedly good. When the time came for performance the purchasers, although not insolvent, were unable to raise enough money to carry out their contract. Mrs. Pilkinton, after having tendered a deed to the property, brought this suit. At the trial the defendants' evidence tended to show that, as a result of a decline in Christy's used car business, they do not possess and cannot borrow the unpaid balance of $29,900.

Proof of this kind does not establish the type of impossibility that constitutes a defense. There is a familiar distinction between objective impossibility, which amounts to saying, "The thing cannot be done," and subjective impossibility—"I cannot do it." Rest., Contracts, § 455; Williston on Contracts, § 1932. The latter, which is well illustrated by a promisor's financial inability to pay, does not discharge the contractual duty and is therefore not a bar to a decree for specific performance.

Much of the appellants' brief is devoted to a discussion of the difficulty that the chancellor may have in enforcing his decree; but that problem is not now before us. By the decree the defendants were allowed a period of twenty days in which to perform their obligation. If their default continues it will of course be for the chancellor to say whether further relief should be granted, as by a foreclosure of the vendor's lien or by other process available to a court of equity. At present it is enough to observe that foreseeable obstacles to the enforcement of a judgment are not a sufficient reason for denying the relief to which the plaintiff is entitled.

Affirmed.

WOOD v. BARTOLINO

(1944) 48 N.M. 175, 146 P.2d 883.

BRICE, JUSTICE. The appellant leased a building to appellees "for use solely as a filling station and not for restaurant or lunch counter purposes," at a rental of $100 per month for a term of five years commencing June 1, 1939. It was operated by sub-lessees until February 1, 1941, and thereafter until July 1, 1942 by appellees, when the latter ceased its operation and offered to restore possession of the premises upon the alleged ground that the lease contract had been terminated because of "commercial frustration" resulting from government rules, regulations, and orders freezing automobiles, tires and tubes and rationing the sale of gasoline, so that it was "impossible and impracticable to use or operate the leased premises as a filling station" at any time after the first of December, 1942; and that such "impossibility and impracticability" still continued and would continue throughout the term of the lease. * * *

Of the facts found by the court, which we deem necessary to a decision, the following is the substance:

The filling station in question is located near the center of the business district of Raton, New Mexico, on the main highway passing through that city. Appellees' customers were mainly tourists and commercial travellers who used this highway. Ordinarily tourist travel is heavy, beginning in May and continuing through the summer and autumn. The Federal rules and regulations which limited and restricted the sale of tires, tubes and automobiles became effective about the first of 1942 and have since continued in effect. These regulations so seriously reduced the operation of motor vehicles that the travel of tourists and commercial travellers practically and abruptly ceased.

As a direct and proximate consequence of the governmental rules, regulations and orders concerning the "freezing" of tires, tubes and automobiles, it became and was impossible and impracticable to use or operate the leased premises as a filling station during the months of July, August, September, October and November, 1942, and by reason thereof, and of the rationing of gasoline, it became and was impossible and impracticable to use or operate the leased premises as a filling station during the months of December, 1942, January, 1943, or any time thereafter, and that such impossibility and impracticability still continues and will continue throughout the term of the lease contract.

* * *

The parties, at the time the lease contract was entered into, did not contemplate, and could not reasonably have contemplated, that such laws, rules and regulations would be enacted, promulgated or enforced, or that they would materially and substantially change the conditions of the business operated in the leased premises. * * *

The doctrine of "commercial frustration," or, as more often called by the courts of this country, the doctrine of "implied condition," has been developed by a process of evolution from the rules: (1) a party to a contract is excused from performance if it depends upon the existence of a given person or thing, if that person or thing perishes. [Citation.] (2) A party to a contract is excused from performance if it is rendered impossible by act of God, the law, or the other party. [Citation.] The rules are otherwise stated, as follows:

"(1) Impossibility due to domestic law;

"(2) Impossibility due to the death or illness of one who by the terms of the contract was to do an act requiring his personal performance.

"(3) Impossibility due to fortuitous destruction or change in character of some-

thing to which the contract related, or which by the terms of the contract was made a necessary means of performance." 6 Williston on Contracts, Sec. 1935.

Regarding a fourth and a fifth class, Williston states:

"The fourth class of cases, to which allusion was made above as standing on more debatable ground, comprises cases where impossibility is due to the failure of some means of performance, contemplated but not contracted for.

"The fifth class does not strictly fall within the boundaries of impossibility. Performance remains entirely possible, but the whole value of the performance to one of the parties at least, and the basic reason recognized as such by both parties, for entering into the contract has been destroyed by a supervening and unforeseen event. This does not operate primarily as an excuse for the promisor, the performance of whose promise has lost its value, but as a failure of consideration for the promise of the other party, not in a literal sense it is true, since the performance bargained for can be given, but in substance, because the performance has lost its value. The name 'frustration' has been given to this situation. Until recently, it had received little clear recognition, but its adoption seems involved in some decisions, and their justice is plain." Id. Sec. 1935.

Regarding the meaning of "impossibility" as used in the rules that excuse the non-performance of contracts, it is stated:

"As pointed out in the Restatement of Contracts, the essence of the modern defense of impossibility is that the promised performance was at the making of the contract, or thereafter became, impracticable owing to some extreme or unreasonable difficulty, expense, injury, or loss involved, rather than that it is scientifically or actually impossible. * * * The important question is whether an unanticipated circumstance has made performance of the promise vitally different from what should reasonably have been within the contemplation of both parties when they entered into the contract. If so, the risk should not fairly be thrown upon the promisor." Id. Sec. 1931.

* * *

The courts of this country, Federal and State, have cited with approval, and generally followed, the decisions of the English courts on the doctrine of "commercial frustration," involving commercial transactions. It is held by the English courts that the doctrine has no application to an ordinary lease of real property. * * *

Professor Williston was of the opinion that it is difficult to apply the doctrine of commercial frustration to leases of real property. He states:

"There is obviously no impossibility or illegality in paying the rent, and the landlord, by making and delivering the lease, has conveyed to the tenant the estate for which rent was promised. * * * The fact that a lease is a conveyance and not simply a continuing contract and the numerous authorities enforcing liability to pay rent in spite of destruction of the leased premises, however, have made it difficult to give relief * * *. Even more clearly with respect to leases than in regard to the ordinary contracts the applicability of the doctrine of frustration depends on the *total or nearly total destruction* of the purpose for which, in the contemplation of both parties, the transaction was entered into." (Our emphasis.) 6 Williston on Contracts, Rev.Ed., Sec. 1955. * * *

There are no Federal regulations prohibiting the sale of gasoline, oil, tires, tubes and other merchandise ordinarily sold at filling stations, though the enforcement of such regulations has drastically reduced appellees' income, which before was less than operating expenses; nor has any Federal law, rule or regulation deprived appellees of the use of the premises as a filling station.

It follows that the trial court erred in denying recovery of rent by appellant.

It is just, and no doubt to the best interest of landlords, for them to voluntarily shoulder a portion of the burden, and that it is being done generally, we are advised. But the appellant may enforce the covenant to pay her rent. In such cases relief lies only in the conscience of the landlord, to which in this case, it appears, fruitless appeals for relief have been made.

The judgment of the district court is reversed and cause remanded with instructions to the district court to set aside its judgment and enter judgment for the appellant.

It is so ordered.

HIPSKIND HEATING & PLUMB. CO. v. GENERAL INDUSTRIES

(1965) — Ind. —, 204 N.E.2d 339.

[Contractor brought action against owner for the foreclosure of a mechanic's lien. The Superior Court entered judgment for the owner, and the contractor appealed. The Appellate Court, 194 N.E.2d 733, affirmed the judgment. A petition was filed in the Supreme Court to transfer from the Appellate Court. The Supreme Court, Arterburn, C. J., held that contractor, which was originally obligated to perform contract with reference to repairs on building that was destroyed by fire, could not recover on quantum meruit for partial work done.]

ARTERBURN, C. J. * * * In this case a building in the process of repairs by the installation of a sprinkler system was destroyed by fire. The destruction of a building which is the subject of the contract for repairs excuses the performance of the remainder of the contract as to each party. The majority rule is that an event unforeseen which creates an impossibility of performance by reason of the destruction of the subject matter of the contract will excuse the performance thereof by each of the parties. 6 Williston, Contracts § 1975, at 5549 (rev. ed. 1938).

However, that is not the exact question here. The question here is: may a contractor who was originally obligated to perform a contract with reference to repairs on a building which has been destroyed by fire recover for partial work done not on the expressed contract but on quantum meruit? The authority on the latter question is divided in this country. 6 Williston, Contracts §§ 1975, 1977, at 5551–5557 (rev. ed. 1938).

However, in Indiana it seems under the authority of Krause v. Board, etc. (1904), 162 Ind. 278, 70 N.E.2d 264, 65 L.R.A. 111, this Court has said that it leaves both parties as it finds them in a case such as this and that neither can recover from the other if each is "equally blameless and irresponsible for the accident by which the property is destroyed."

Petition to transfer is denied.

————

SECHREST v. FOREST FURNITURE CO.

(1965) 264 N.C. 216, 141 S.E.2d 292.

[Action by plywood drawer bottom seller against buyer for value of bottoms manufactured to buyer's specifications. From dismissal of action plaintiff appeals.]

Higgins, J. The plaintiff alleged a contract, its performance, defendant's breach, and the amount of plaintiff's damage resulting from the breach. The complaint stated a cause of action. The defendant admitted the contract but by way of defense alleged the factory, in which it intended to use the drawer bottoms, burned without its fault; and that the purposes of the contract were frustrated by the fire; and the defendant should be released from performance for that reason.

* * *

In this case the defendant and the court have misconstrued the applicability of the frustration of purpose doctrine as recognized by this Court. The subject of the contract was the special manufacture of plywood drawer bottoms. They were not burned. The doctrine of frustration would be available to the defendant if it had contracted to sell the factory and it burned before the execution of the deed. In that event the defendant properly could plead frustration in a claim for failure to convey the factory. The doctrine of frustration is clearly stated in Sale v. State Highway and Public Works Comm., supra: " 'Where parties contract with reference to specific property and the obligations assumed clearly contemplate its continued existence, if the property is accidentally lost or destroyed by fire or otherwise, rendering performance impossible, the parties are relieved from further obligations concerning it. * * * Before a party can avail himself of such a position, he is required to show that the property was destroyed, and without fault on his part.' "

* * *

The plaintiff was in nowise responsible for the fire that destroyed defendant's building. The defendant is bound by its contract. The destruction of its factory does not relieve it of liability for its debts. At the trial the parties will have opportunity to contest the amount due under the contract.

The defendant's factual allegations are insufficient to support its plea of frustration. The plaintiff's motions to strike should have been allowed. The trial court committed error in sustaining the demurrer *ore tenus*. The judgment in the court below is

Reversed.

————

PROBLEMS

1. A agrees to construct, completely, a dwelling for B, A to furnish all labor and materials necessary. While the building is being shingled

it is struck by lightning and burned to the ground. B demands that A build a new building, which A refuses to do, and sues B for the value of the labor and materials put into the burned building. Judgment for whom?

2. A company enters into a contract with B agreeing to manufacture and deliver to him, at an agreed price, 5,000 ladies' sweaters, deliveries to be made in equal quantities over a five months' period. Before any deliveries can be made the company's employees go out on a strike which remains unsettled for a period of two or three months beyond the last delivery date. B is compelled to buy his sweaters in the open market and brings suit to recover damages for the failure of the company to carry out its contract. Can he recover? If so, could the company have protected itself in the contract against such a liability?

3. The Perfection Produce Company entered into a written contract, dated March 21, 1966, with Hiram Hodges for the purchase of 200 tons of potatoes to be grown on Hodges's farm in Maine, at a stipulated price per ton. The land would ordinarily produce 1,000 tons. Although the planting and cultivation were properly done, Hodges was able to deliver only 100 tons because of a partial crop failure owing to an unprecedented drought. Hodges sued the produce company to recover an unpaid balance of the agreed price for 100 tons of potatoes. The produce company, by an appropriate counterclaim against Hodges, sought damages for his failure to deliver the additional 100 tons. Decision?

4. A was a dealer in automobiles and contracted with B to deliver to B a fleet of 10, 1966 Model Z Buicks, no particular lot being specified, at $3,600 per car. A had 10 such cars on hand but unknown to either party 5 were completely destroyed by a fire before the contract was made. A delivered the remaining 5 cars to B. B demanded delivery of 5 more cars but A refused stating B was only entitled to the 5 already delivered because the contract was divisible, and delivery of the balance was excused. Who is right and why?

5. S dealt in automobile accessories at wholesale. Although manufacturing a few items in his own factory, among them windshield wipers, S purchased most of his supplies from a large number of other manufacturers. In January, S entered into a written contract to sell B 2,000 windshield wipers for $900, delivery to be made June 1.

In April, S's factory burned to the ground and S failed to make delivery on June 1. B, forced to buy windshield wipers elsewhere at a higher price, brings an action against S for breach of contract. Decision?

6. On May 15, the Hughes Electric Company and the Moss Coal Company entered into a written contract whereby the coal company agreed to sell and deliver to the electric company 500 tons of coal at a stipulated price, on or before November 1. By September 1, the market price of coal had increased considerably and, on the day named, the coal company notified the electric company that it would not make delivery of the coal, as agreed. By its reply, mailed on September 2, the electric company notified the coal company that it would expect performance in full by the coal company on November 1. On September 30, the electric company closed its plant temporarily because of a slump in the sales of electric equipment. On November 1, the coal company delivered 500 tons of coal to the electric company. The electric company refused to accept any part of the coal delivered. Thereafter, the coal company sues the electric company for damages for breach of contract. Decision?

7. On January 2, A entered into a written contract with B whereby B in consideration of $25,000 agreed to sell and deliver to A on June 15 a certain race horse by the name of Sunrise County. In the meantime, on February 15, A repudiated the contract and gave notice to B of his intention not to perform it. On February 18, B brought an action against A seeking specific performance of the contract. What decree?

8. Winston owned and operated a local daily newspaper in southern Ohio. On November 30, 1964, Winston sold the paper to Acme Press Company under a contract which provided, among other things, that Winston was to be employed as managing editor for one year at a salary of $10,000. At the end of the year, Winston, at his option, could elect to continue for an additional year at the same salary. On October 15, 1965, Acme suspended publication of the newspaper because of decreased circulation and increased labor costs. Acme paid Winston through November 30, 1965. Winston properly notified Acme that he elected to continue as managing editor for another year, but Acme refused to recognize any obligation beyond November 30 upon the ground that the position of managing editor no longer existed. Winston brings an action against

Acme to recover damages under the contract. Decision?

9. A agreed in writing to work for B for three years as superintendent in B's business as a manufacturer and dealer in clothing, and to devote himself entirely to the business, giving his whole time, attention and skill thereto, for which he was to receive $12,000 per annum, in monthly instalments of $1,000 each month. A worked and was paid for the first twelve months, when through no fault of his own or B's, he was arrested and imprisoned for one month. It became imperative for B to employ another and he treated the contract with A as breached and abandoned, refusing to permit A to resume work upon his release from jail. What rights, if any, does A have under the contract?

10. The Park Plaza Hotel awarded the valet and laundry concession to Larson for a three-year term. The contract contained the following provision: "It is distinctly understood and agreed that the services to be rendered by Larson shall meet with the approval of the Park Plaza Hotel, which shall be the sole judge of the sufficiency and propriety of the services." After seven months, the hotel gave a month's notice to discontinue services based on the failure of the services to meet its approval. Larson brought an action against the hotel, alleging that its dissatisfaction was unreasonable. The hotel defended upon the ground that subjective or personal satisfaction may not be the sole justification for termination of a contract. Assume that the hotel's dissatisfaction was not reasonable. Decision?

CHAPTER 11

REMEDIES FOR BREACH OF CONTRACT

Introductory. Each party to a contract has a primary right to receive the exact performance promised by the other party. Upon breach, or failure to perform, by one of the parties, the other party will never receive that to which his primary right entitles him. If a promisee is entitled to receive money, goods, or services on June 1, payment or delivery by the promisor subsequent to June 1, or the entry of judgment against the promisor, may be the equivalent of the promised performance, but it is not the same.

Upon a breach of contract, the injured party acquires secondary rights and the breaching party becomes subject to secondary duties, which the law substitutes for the duty of exact performance. These secondary rights are remedial in nature. The law endeavors to give the injured party a remedy which will as nearly as possible compensate him for the loss he has sustained by the breach. These remedies are (1) recovery of compensatory money damages; (2) restitution; and (3) specific performance.

Right of Action for Damages. The right to recover compensatory money damages for breach of contract is always available to the injured party, except in one situation. The Restatement of the Law of Contract, Section 327, provides:

> "Except in the case stated in § 197, a judgment for damages will be given for any breach of contract, unless the right of action has been suspended or discharged."

The situation in which damages will not be permitted, as stated in Section 197, is:

> "Where, acting under an oral contract for the transfer of an interest in land, the purchaser with the assent of the vendor
> (a) makes valuable improvements on the land, or

> (b) takes possession thereof or retains a possession thereof existing at the time of the bargain, and also pays a portion or all of the purchase price,
> the purchaser or the vendor may specifically enforce the contract."

Compensatory Damages. The purpose in allowing damages is to provide compensation to the plaintiff which will place him in as good a position as if the defendant had performed under the contract. In the case of a unilateral contract which has become wholly executed by the plaintiff, the measure of damages is the value of the performance promised by the defendant. In the case of a bilateral contract which is either wholly or partly unperformed by the plaintiff, that is, executory on both sides, the measure of damages is the value of defendant's promised performance less the cost of completing the plaintiff's performance.

If the plaintiff is a seller of goods and the defendant buyer has received title to the goods, with or without possession, the plaintiff is entitled to recover the contract price of the goods. This is subject, however, to the rules with respect to risk of loss under the U.C.C. See Chapter 18. If title to the goods has not passed to the buyer who is in default, the measure of the seller's damages is the difference between the contract price and the market value of the goods at the time and place fixed by the contract for their delivery. In an action for damages by a buyer of goods against a seller for breach of an executory contract of sale, the measure of damages is also the difference between the contract price and the market value of the goods at the time and place of delivery.

A leading case on the subject of compensatory damages is Hadley v. Baxendale, decided in England in 1854. In this case the plaintiffs operated a flour mill and conducted an extensive milling business at Gloucester. Their mill was compelled to cease operating because of a broken crank shaft attached to the steam engine which furnished power to the mill. It was necessary to send the broken shaft to a foundry located at Greenwich so that a new shaft could be made that would fit the other parts of the engine. The plaintiffs delivered the broken shaft to the defendants, who were common carriers, for transportation from Gloucester to Greenwich and informed defendants at the time that the mill was stopped and that the shaft must be sent immediately. The defendants received the shaft, collected the freight charges in advance, and promised the plaintiffs to deliver the shaft at Greenwich the following day. The defendants neglected to make prompt delivery as promised, and as a result the resumption of the operation of the mill was delayed for several days and the plaintiffs lost profits which they otherwise would have received. The defendants contended that the loss of profits was too remote to be recoverable. In awarding damages to the plaintiffs, the jury was permitted to take into consideration the loss of these profits. The Court of Exchequer ordered a new trial on the ground that the special circumstances which caused the loss of profits, namely, the continued stoppage of the mill while awaiting the new crank shaft, had never been communicated by the plaintiffs to the defendants. Unless given express notice of these circumstances, a common carrier would not reasonably foresee that the plaintiffs' mill would be shut down as a result of delay in transporting the broken crank shaft. The opinion in this case contains a classic statement of the rule by Baron Alderson whereby reasonable foreseeability of the kind and extent of loss is made the measure of damages:

"Where two parties have made a contract which one of them has broken, the damages which the other party ought to receive in respect of such breach of contract should be such as may fairly and reasonably be considered either arising naturally, i. e., according to the usual course of things, from such breach of contract itself, or such as may reasonably be supposed to have been in the contemplation of both parties, at the time they made the contract, as the probable result of the breach of it. Now, if the special circumstances under which the contract was actually made were communicated by the plaintiffs to the defendants, and thus known to both parties, the damages resulting from the breach of such a contract, which they would reasonably contemplate, would be the amount of injury which would ordinarily follow from a breach of contract under these special circumstances so known and communicated. But, on the other hand, if these special circumstances were wholly unknown to the party breaking the contract, he, at the most, could only be supposed to have had in his contemplation the amount of injury which would arise generally, and in the great multitude of cases not affected by any special circumstances, from such a breach of contract."

Mr. Justice Holmes expressed the substance and rationale of the rule in Hadley v. Baxendale in an opinion of the Supreme Court in which he stated:

"It is true that, as people when contracting contemplate performance, not breach, they commonly say little or nothing as to what shall happen in the latter event, and the common rules have been worked out by common sense, which has established what the parties probably would have said if they had spoken about the matter. But a man never can be absolutely certain of performing any contract when the time of performance arrives, and, in many cases, he obviously is taking the risk of an event which is wholly, or to an appreciable extent, beyond his control. The extent of liability in such cases is likely to be within his contemplation, and, whether it is or not, should be worked out on terms which it fairly may be presumed he would have assented to if they had been presented to his mind." Globe Refining Co. v. Landa Cotton Oil Co., 190 U.S. 540, 543, 23 S.Ct. 754, 775.

The Restatement of the Law of Contracts, Section 330, expresses the rule as follows:

> "In awarding damages, compensation is given for only those injuries that the defendant had reason to foresee as a probable result of his breach when the contract was made. If the injury is one that follows the breach in the usual course of events, there is sufficient reason for the defendant to foresee it; otherwise, it must be shown specifically that the defendant had reason to know the facts and to foresee the injury."

Nominal Damages. An action to recover damages for breach of contract may be maintained even though the plaintiff has not sustained or cannot prove any injury or loss resulting from the breach. In such case he will be permitted to recover nominal damages, such as $1.00 and costs. Because of his inability to show a loss, the plaintiff is not entitled to compensatory damages.

Exemplary or Punitive Damages. The usual purpose in allowing damages is to compensate the plaintiff for the loss which he has sustained by reason of the defendant's breach of contract or wrongful conduct. In a contract case this involves an award of money sufficient to place the plaintiff in the position in which he would have been if the defendant had not breached the contract. In a tort case the objective is to compensate the plaintiff in an amount commensurate with the injury sustained based upon his condition and position prior to the injury.

In certain situations involving willful, wanton, malicious or negligent torts, the courts have allowed exemplary or punitive damages, sometimes referred to as "smart money." The purpose is to punish the defendant and thereby discourage him and others from similar wrongful conduct. Damages assessed by way of punishment to the wrongdoer are in addition to the amount of compensation to the plaintiff measured by the harm suffered and are imposed to make an example of the defendant.

The Restatement of the Law of Contracts, Section 342, provides: "Punitive damages are not recoverable for breach of contract." Even in actions against public service companies for failure to perform a public utility service to a customer, punitive damages are not allowed.

In an action to recover damages for persistent and repeated wrongful conduct in the operation of a business, if the defendant is merely required to make restitution, or part with his ill-gotten gains, or pay compensatory damages to the plaintiff, he may regard such damages in an occasional lawsuit as not too high a price to pay for continuing his unlawful profitable practices. He is not sued by every customer and in the event of a lawsuit, merely loses what he had no right to gain. He may, however, be discouraged from engaging in such practices by punishment in the form of punitive damages.

An illustration of punitive damages of $40,000 allowed to the plaintiff by reason of defendant's fraudulent business practices is the case of Syester v. Banta, p. 269.

A willful breach of fiduciary duty may also result in the imposition of punitive damages where the defendant has held himself out to the public as experienced and competent in some business or professional field of activity, and has grossly violated the trust reposed in him by the plaintiff. In one case, the defendant, a licensed real estate broker, suggested to the plaintiff that he enter into an "exchange contract" whereby he would sell his old house and purchase a new one with the proceeds of the sale. To accomplish this, the broker obtained a conveyance to himself of the old house in which the plaintiff had an equity of $9,000. The broker thereupon obtained for plaintiff a new house with no equity value. When the plaintiff hesitated entering into this transaction and suggested that he obtain a lawyer, the broker advised him that he was a lawyer and would take care of him. The Court sustained a jury finding of compensatory damages of $7,000 and punitive damages of $7,500. Brown v. Coates, 102 U.S.App. D.C. 300, 253 F.2d 36, 67 A.L.R.2d 943 (C.A. D.C.1958).

Special Damages. A seller of goods who expressly or impliedly warrants the goods to have a certain quality may be liable for special damages sustained by the buyer which are the readily foreseeable consequences of a breach of the warranty. Unwholesome food sold for human consumption may involve the seller in extensive liability. A seller of livestock who warrants the animals to be sound when, in fact, they are diseased and they communicate the disease to other animals belonging to the buyer, is liable not only for the expense of a veterinarian and medicine, but for all of the damages inflicted upon the other animals. If the seller of a horse expressly warrants it to be gentle, as he may have reason to believe, and the horse, when hitched to a buggy, runs away with the buyer causing the buggy to overturn and to break the buyer's leg, the special damages recoverable against the seller, including the medical and hospital expenses of the buyer and the property damage to the buggy, are far in excess of the value or price of the horse. Where a farmer buys seeds with a warranty, he may recover the loss or diminished value of the crop resulting from a breach of the warranty.

The above instances of special damages are to be distinguished from the ordinary measures of damages in the case of a breach of warranty which is the difference between the value of the goods if they had been as warranted and the value of the goods in their actual condition when received by the buyer.

Liquidated Damages. A contract may contain a provision whereby one of the parties promises to pay to the other a fixed sum of money, or a fixed rate for each day of delayed performance, in the event of his breach. Such a provision for liquidated damages is not to be considered as an alternative promise of performance. If it amounts to a reasonable forecast of just compensation for the loss which may result from a breach, it will be enforced. If, however, the sum agreed upon as liquidated damages does not bear a reasonable relationship to the amount of the probable loss which may result from a breach, it will be treated as a penalty and not enforced. The law abhors a penalty and will look at the substance of the provision, the nature of the contract, and extent of probable harm to the promisee which may reasonably be expected to be caused by a breach, in order to determine whether the agreed amount is proper as liquidated damages or unenforceable as a penalty. It is immaterial what name or label the parties to the contract attach to the provision. A reasonable provision for liquidated damages whereby the parties substitute their concept of the amount of loss for that of a court or jury may be especially useful in a situation where the harm caused by a breach is one which may be extremely difficult of accurate estimation.

Damages for Breach of Alternative Promises. A contract may contain alternative promises. The promisee may be given the election as to which of these promises he desires the promisor to perform. If the contract is silent as to which party has the election, the promisor has the right to determine which of the alternative promises he will perform. In such event his failure to perform either promise will cause him to be liable for the lesser of his promises, that is, the one which will result in the smallest recovery by the promisee. Thus, A contracts to build for B either a boat for $2,000 or a barge for $1,000, each according to stated specifications. In the event of a breach, A is liable to B for the damages which result from his failure to build the barge, assuming this to be the lesser of the alternative promises and subjects him to the least liability.

The Restatement of the Law of Contracts, Section 344, provides:

> "The damages for breach of an alternative contract are determined in accordance with that one of the alternatives that is chosen by the party having an election, or, in case of breach without an election, in accordance with the alternative that will result in the smallest recovery."

Mitigation of Damages. Where a breach of contract occurs, the injured party is required to take such steps as may be reasonably calculated to lessen or mitigate the damages that he may sustain. Where a buyer receives inferior goods furnished to him under a contract, he may not enhance his damages by continuing to use the goods after learning of their unfitness. Similarly, a buyer who does not receive goods or services promised to him under a contract cannot recover damages resulting from his doing without such goods or services where it is possible for him to substitute other goods or services which he can obtain elsewhere. Where A is under a contract to manufacture goods for B who repudiates the contract after A has commenced performance, A will not be allowed to recover loss which he sustains by continuing to manufacture the goods, if to do so would increase the amount of his damages. If the goods were almost completed when B repudiated, the completion of the goods might mitigate the damages as the finished goods may be resalable whereas the unfinished goods may not. If A contracts to work for B for one year for a weekly salary and after two months is wrongfully discharged by B, A must use reasonable efforts to mitigate his damages by seeking other employment. If he cannot obtain other employment of the same general character, he is entitled to recover full pay for the contract period that he is unemployed. He is not obliged to accept a radically different type of employment or to accept work at a distant place. A person who is employed as a school teacher or accountant and is wrongfully discharged is not obliged in order to mitigate damages to accept available employment as a chauffeur or truck driver.

Restitution. One of the remedies which may be available to a party to a contract for a breach by the other is restitution. This remedy is an alternative to recovery of damages for breach of contract. A party may not have both restitution and damages. Restitution is a return to the aggrieved party of the consideration, or its value, which he gave to the other party. An action for damages seeks to recover the value of the performance promised by the defendant. The object of restitution is to restore the injured party to the position he was in before the contract was made. Restitution, or restoration of the status quo, is not available to a plaintiff who has fully performed on his part and the only obligation of the defendant is to pay a sum of money to the plaintiff. Thus, the seller of goods on credit, upon failure of the buyer to pay for them, is not permitted to rescind the sale and sue the buyer either to recover the possession of the goods or their value. However, a seller who has transferred to the buyer a parcel of real estate or a unique chattel, or exclusive privileges such as patents or copyrights, in the event of total failure of consideration by the buyer, may rescind the sale and obtain a cancellation of the deed of conveyance, a return of the unique chattel, or a reassignment of the patents or copyrights, provided the buyer has not transferred them to a bona fide purchaser for value.

Restitution in Favor of a Plaintiff Who is in Default. A person who is in default for failure to perform or tender performance on his side of the contract is not ordinarily entitled to recover for a breach by the other party. If the plaintiff having only partially performed is permitted to recover, the court is enforcing a contract different from that which the parties made in allowing the plaintiff to sell his partial performance at a value fixed by a court or jury to a defendant who has agreed to pay only for a complete performance. However, in certain situations, a denial of recovery to the plaintiff would result in the defendant receiving more than fair compensation for the plaintiff's breach and would impose a forfeiture on the plaintiff. The doctrine of substantial performance, as applied to a building contract, is an illustration of the principle involved. Where a seller of goods is unable to perform fully, or is prevented by circumstances beyond his control and not attributable to the buyer from making full delivery of the merchandise to the buyer he is permitted to recover the value of the goods which he has delivered and which the buyer has not returned, on the theory of unjust enrichment.

Specific Performance. While in most cases an action at law to recover money damages for breach of contract is both an adequate remedy and the only one available to the plaintiff, there are certain contracts in which the promised performance is specifically enforceable. Only a court of equity may decree specific performance. Contracts to buy and sell land are specifically enforceable, as each parcel of land is unique and by location and nature differs from every other parcel. Money damages are inadequate relief to a buyer of land who needs the specific land for a home or for the location or expansion of a business. Contracts for the purchase of personal property may be specifically enforced if the property is unique, such as a particular painting by Rembrandt, a famous race horse, a patent, or an invention. To be specifically enforceable, the promise must be clear, unambiguous, and relate to a specific identifiable item. A court of equity will not enter a decree which is impossible of performance or which would involve the court in the supervision of details of performance. The decree of specific performance is an order requiring the defendant to perform a certain act or to refrain from certain conduct, and the court has power to enforce compliance with its decree by finding the

defendant in contempt of court for non-compliance and by imprisoning him for such contempt. The court will not decree specific performance of a building contract, as enforcement of the decree would require minute supervision of the details and the progress of construction. A court will also not decree specific performance of a contract for personal services. However, a court of equity will enforce negative covenants in a contract for personal services where damages for a breach would be inadequate. If a concert pianist has contracted that he will not perform publicly during a certain period of time in order to provide added attractiveness to an advertised and scheduled performance, the court will enforce this promise specifically by an injunction. It is much easier for the court to enforce a negative covenant, a promise to refrain from doing something, by enjoining the defendant from doing that which would constitute a breach, than to enforce a promise of affirmative performance. A court would not decree that the concert pianist must appear at a certain time and place and play a certain program.

Election of Remedies. A party who is aggrieved by breach of contract may be required to choose between the remedies available to him. An action to recover damages and a suit for restitution are inconsistent with one another, and by filing one the plaintiff is barred from seeking the other type of relief. Specific performance and restitution are likewise inconsistent remedies. However, specific performance and compensation in money are not inconsistent remedies and may both be sought in the same suit.

The Restatement of the Law of Contracts, Section 384, provides:

"(1) Damages and restitution are alternative remedies, only one of which will be given as a remedy for a breach of contract.

(2) Specific performance and compensation in money are not alternative remedies, and both forms of relief may be given in the same proceeding; but compensation will not

be awarded for an injury that an existing decree is intended to prevent, and specific performance will not be decreed for the prevention of an injury for which there is an existing award of compensation."

Section 381 of the Restatement provides:

"(1) When the alternative remedies of damages and restitution are available to a party injured by a breach, his manifested choice of one of them by bringing suit or otherwise, followed by a material change of position by the other party in reliance thereon, is a bar to the other alternative remedy.

(2) The bringing of an action for one of these remedies is a bar to the alternative one unless the plaintiff shows reasonable ground for making the change of remedy."

Section 382 of the Restatement further provides:

"The bringing of a suit either for specific performance or for compensation in money is not such an election of the remedy sued for as to operate as a bar to a later suit or to an amendment asking for the other remedy with respect to the same breach; but a material change of position by the defendant in reasonable reliance upon the plaintiff's first choice of remedy may operate as such a bar."

Remedies for Breach of Sales Contracts. The subject of sales of personal property is a specialized branch of the law of contracts covered in Article 2 of the Code. The remedies of sellers and buyers of goods are too particularized under the Code to warrant a general discussion at this point. They are treated in Chapter 22 of this book.

CASES

CHRISTENSEN v. HOSKINS

(1964) 65 Wash.2d 417, 397 P.2d 830.

SHORETT, J. The respondents Christensen purchased a home which had been constructed by the appellants Hoskins. As the Federal Housing Administration insured the financing of the house, the builder delivered to the purchaser a written warranty that the house had been constructed in substantial compliance with the FHA approved plans and specifications. After the FHA had approved the original plans, the builder added a shower in the utility room and finished the wall with enamel paint, which was not waterproof, as required by the approved specifications. Because of the defective waterproofing, water seeped through the wall, causing extensive dry rotting in the floor and supporting beams of the living room. Thus, it was necessary to replace 5 feet of the supporting beam, the floor joists, the oak floor and some wall studding.

The trial court found a breach of the warranty and entered judgment for $8,000 against the Hoskinses. This was the sum asked for in the Christensens' complaint, and found by the trial court to be the difference between the value of the house, if there had been no dry rot, and the value with the dry rot condition.

Upon this appeal, the Hoskinses contend that the warranty does not apply because the shower was added after FHA approval of the plan; that no proper notice of breach of warranty was given; that the Christensens should have mitigated damages; and, even if the warranty does apply, the proper measure of damages is the cost of repair.

We are satisfied that the warranty covered additions such as the utility room shower by explicitly guaranteeing that the house "is constructed in substantial conformity with the plans and specifications (including any amendments thereof, or changes and variations therein)."

The warranty required notice of any defect within 1 year, and the respondents complied by written notice saying "Plaster is cracking in several rooms in the home. The half-bath and utility room are in bad condition." We regard this as adequate notification to the appellants and the FHA of the visible defects. The respondents could not be expected to know the consequences of such defects. Such matters would more likely be within the knowledge and competency of the builder and the FHA.

We come next to the question of damages. Mr. Hoskins testified that the defects could be corrected for $500. Mr. Christensen testified that he had completed the repairs on the building, had done much of the work himself and had had a carpenter work with him, gave no estimate of the cost of repair, but estimated that the house would have been worth at least $8,000 more if there had been no dry rot. There was no other testimony on damages. * * *

With such unsatisfactory alternatives in the evidence, the trial court selected Mr. Christensen's testimony as the more believable, and entered findings of fact to the effect that the house would have been worth $8,000 more if it were not for the damages caused by the dry rot.

In our opinion, the damages properly to be allowed are the cost of repair and such other damages as are proved to be the direct result of the breach of warranty.

* * *

In Baldwin v. Alberti, 58 Wash.2d 243, 245, 362 P.2d 258, 260, this court reviewed many authorities on the subject and approved the following from 1 Restatement, Contracts, § 346:

" '§ 346. Damages for Breach of a Construction Contract. (1) For a breach by one who has contracted to construct a specified product, the other party can get judgment for compensatory damages for all unavoidable harm that the builder had reason to foresee when the contract was made, less such part of the contract price as has not been paid and is not still payable, determined as follows:

" '(a) For defective or unfinished construction he can get judgment for either.

" '(i) the reasonable cost of construction and completion in accordance with the contract, if this is possible and does not involve *unreasonable economic waste;* or

" '(ii) the difference between the value that the product contracted for would have had and the value of the performance that has been received by the plaintiff, if construction and completion in accordance with the contract would involve *unreasonable economic waste.*' (Italics ours.)

" '*Comment on Subsection* (1a),' following the above-quoted section of the Restatement, states:

" ' * * * Sometimes defects in a completed structure cannot be physically remedied without tearing down and rebuilding, at a cost that would be imprudent and unreasonable. The law does not require damages to be measured by a method requiring such economic waste. *If no such waste is involved, the cost of remedying the defect is the amount awarded as compensation for failure to render the promised performance.*' (Italics ours.)"

In the instant case, the facts demonstrate that the defects could be repaired without "unreasonable economic waste."

The appellants' contention that the respondents did not minimize their damages by making earlier repairs cannot be considered because it was neither raised by the pleadings nor properly presented to the trial court.

Since an incorrect measure of damages was applied and there is an insufficiency of testimony under the proper rule, the cause is remanded for a new trial on the question of damages.

WILLIAMS v. ROBINSON

(1923) 158 Ark. 327, 250 S.W. 14, 28 A.L.R. 734.

[The plaintiff Robinson brought an action to recover wages alleged to be due under a contract of employment. The wages had accrued subsequently to an alleged wrongful discharge of plaintiff by the employer defendant. From a judgment for plaintiff, defendant appeals.]

SMITH, J. Appellee alleged that she was employed by appellants to take charge of their kitchen and to do all the baking and to make salads at the summer hotel which appellants ran at Winslow, Ark. The contract was made by letters exchanged between the parties, and these very clearly establish an agreement on the part of appellants to pay appellee $25 per week during the "season." At the time the parties began to correspond, appellee resided in Amarillo, Tex., and it was necessary, of course, for her to report to Winslow to perform her duties under the contract; but there is nothing in the correspondence to obligate appellants to pay appellee anything except $25 per week for her services. Appellee was discharged July 9th, and the season for summer visitors closed September 14th, so there was a period of nine weeks and four days during which appellee was not furnished employment under the contract. The compensation for this time at $25 per week is $239.28 * * *

Over appellants' objection an instruction was given in which the jury was told that, if they found appellee was entitled to recover, she should recover the whole of the wages due her by the terms of the contract, less what she had an opportunity to earn by like services after her dismissal. The objection to the instruction was that the jury was required to take into account only such sum as appellee might have earned by like services, appellants having testified that they had offered appellee other employment at $10 per week. This employment was in a more me-

nial capacity, and appellee declined to accept it. This she had the right to do. It was her duty to seek and accept other like employment; but she was not required to seek or accept employment of a different character; and the instruction, therefore, correctly declared the law. [Citations.]

Appellee testified that she sought similar employment, but could not obtain it, but that she did obtain employment for 5½ days as a waitress at a cafe, and also secured 16 days' employment as a nurse at $1 per day, but that she was unable to obtain any other employment except that offered by appellant.

* * *

Appellee testified that she expended $21.48 coming to Winslow, and it was, of course, a necessary expenditure to enable her to perform the service specified in the contract; but there is nothing in the contract which obligated appellants to pay this expense. Their agreement was to pay $25 per week, and they cannot be held liable for an expense which appellee had to incur to earn this money in the absence of an agreement to pay that expense.

* * * Appellee was not required to accept employment as a waitress or as a nurse, but she did so, and the $21.50 thus earned is to be credited upon her recovery. Assuming that the jury, under the erroneous instruction, allowed the item of $21.48, it, too, must be deducted to render the instruction nonprejudicial. These two items total $42.98; but, when that total has been deducted from the $239.28, there remains $196.30, for which the verdict should have been rendered, whereas the verdict returned was for only $180. The jury may have thought that some credit should be allowed on account of appellee's failure to accept the refused employment notwithstanding the court's instruction to the contrary.

At any rate, after appellants are allowed all the credits which they could claim under the testimony, there remains due appellee a sum in excess of the jury's verdict, if it be assumed that she was wrongfully discharged, and, as we have said, that question is concluded by the verdict of the jury.

* * *

Judgment affirmed.

WRIGHT v. BAUMANN

(1965) 239 Or. 410, 398 P.2d 119.

O'CONNELL, J. Plaintiffs seek to recover for a breach of agreement under which plaintiffs agreed to erect an office building and defendant, a dentist, agreed to enter into a lease of one of the offices after the building was constructed. Both parties waived a jury trial. Defendant appeals from a judgment for plaintiffs.

Defendant's principal assignments of error are directed at the trial court's rejection of evidence tending to show that plaintiffs had the opportunity to mitigate damages but refused to do so. Plaintiffs' objections to defendant's questions relating to mitigation were sustained by the trial court, apparently on the ground that the instrument signed by the parties was a lease rather than a contract and that, being a lease, the lessor had no obligation to mitigate damages. Defendant contends that the rule relied upon by plaintiffs is inapplicable because the "Agreement" in question is not a lease but is a contract to make a lease, and that therefore plaintiffs are required to mitigate as in any other contract case. * * *

Defendant's offer of proof clearly indicates that he made a reasonable effort to mitigate the damages resulting from his refusal to take possession of the part of the premises intended for his occupancy. The offer of proof showed that plaintiffs notified defendant on August 27, 1956, that the building would be ready for occupancy on September 24, 1956. On September 6, 1956, defendant notified plaintiffs that he did not desire to enter into a lease of any part of the building. It was further shown that defendant informed two doctors that the space allotted to him was available and that during September, 1956, the two doctors had offered to lease the space allotted to defendant on the terms and conditions specified in the "Agreement" in question but that plaintiffs refused to lease the office space to them, giving no reasons for the refusal to do so.

A majority of the courts, including Oregon, hold that a lessor is not required to mitigate damages when the lessee abandons the leasehold. In a few states it is incumbent upon the lessor to use reasonable means to mitigate damages. If the transaction is a contract to make a lease rather than an executed lease, it is universally recognized that the landowner has an obligation to mitigate damages upon a breach of the contract by the promisor.

The majority view, absolving the lessor from any obligation to mitigate is based upon the theory that the lessee becomes the owner of the premises for a term and therefore the lessor need not concern himself with lessee's abandonment of his own property. That view might have some validity in those cases where there is simply a lease of the land alone with no covenants except the covenant to pay rent. But a modern business lease is predominantly an exchange of promises and only incidentally a sale of a part of the lessor's interest in the land. * * *

The covenants in the instrument in the present case relate to the continuing obligations of the respective parties. The transaction is essentially a contract. There is no reason why the principle of mitigation of damages should not be applied to it. "* * * [I]t is important that the rules for awarding damages should be such as to discourage even persons against whom wrongs have been committed from passively suffering economic loss which could be averted by reasonable efforts   *   *   *." McCormick, Damages, p. 127 (1935).

Lessors as well as contract promisors should be made to serve this salutary policy. To borrow again from McCormick, "the realities of feudal tenure have vanished and a new system based upon a theory of contractual obligations has in general taken its place." He reminds us that in disregarding the contractual nature of modern leases we have "neglected the caution of Mr. Justice Holmes, 'that continuity with the past is only a necessity and not a duty.'" Writing in 1925, McCormick predicted that eventually "the logic, inescapable according to the standards of a 'jurisprudence of conceptions' which permits the landlord to stand idly by the vacant, abandoned premises and treat them as the property of the tenant and recover full rent, will yield to the more realistic notions of social advantage which in other fields of the law have forbidden a recovery for damages which the plaintiff by reasonable efforts could have avoided." We believe that it is time for McCormick's prediction to become a reality.

It does not seem that the burden imposed upon a lessor in mitigating damages would ordinarily be any greater than that imposed upon promisees of contracts not relating to the occupancy of land. However, if it could be said that it is unreasonable to require the lessor to seek out other tenants, plaintiffs in the present case would not be benefited by that argument because defendant presented a willing and, we may assume, suitable substitute tenant. If defendant had entered into possession and thereafter had offered the landlord a person willing to sublet the premises, plaintiffs under the terms of the "Agreement" could not have refused to accept the new tenant without reasonable grounds for doing so. The situation is essentially the same when the proposed new tenant is offered for the purpose of reducing the tenant's damages.

Even if we were to perpetuate the distinction between a lease and a contract in the application of the principle of mitigation of damages, we would reach the same result. The agreement in question is a contract to make a lease rather than a lease. At the time the agreement was entered into the office building had not been constructed, and the office which was to constitute defendant's leasehold could not then be identified. Consequently, there was nothing that could constitute the subject matter of a conveyance at that time. Conceding that one may make a present demise of a term to begin in the future, it is difficult to conceive of the present transfer of the title (or a part of it in the case of a lease) when that which is to be transferred has no existence.   *   *   * In his motion for a new trial defendant admitted that the question of the character of the instrument was not "squarely" presented to the court. But there was nothing to suggest that defendant was not relying upon the theory that the transaction was a contract to make a lease. On the contrary, it might be said that since all but three states have refused to require a lessor to mitigate damages defendant's offer of proof on the point of mitigation indicated that he was proceeding on the assumption that the transaction was a contract only.

The judgment is reversed and the cause is remanded for a new trial.

BETHLEHEM STEEL CO. v. CITY OF CHICAGO

(1964 D.C.N.D.Ill.) 234 F.Supp. 726.

ROBSON, DISTRICT JUDGE. Defendant has moved for summary judgment and plaintiff has filed a countermotion for the same relief. Plaintiff has also moved to strike portions of the defendant's answer, as amended. The suit involves the parties' rights and liabilities under a written construction contract of December 21, 1961, governing plaintiff's furnishing and erecting for $1,734,200 the steel work for a section of the South Route Superhighway known as Section S–2424.3–2HF.

The critical provision of the contract here involved is that which provides for $1,000 "liquidated damages" for each day of delay. The work was originally to have been completed on or before July 29, 1962, but that date was extended by the City to September 20, 1962. The work was actually completed November 21, 1962—52 days late—giving rise to the City's claim of the right to deduct $52,000 from the contract price.

The court concludes that there is no genuine issue of fact, and that the defendant's motion for summary judgment should be granted as to the $52,000 item.

*   *   *

Bethlehem contends it is entitled to the $52,000 on the ground that the City actually sustained *no* damages in that the Superhighway was *timely completed.* If the contract were construed otherwise the provision would be a penalty.

> Defendant's answer points out that " *   *   * [Where] *   *   * a contractor for construction of public work on a highway *   *   * is one of several contracts executed for the purpose of carrying out the project, and the planned coordination of all work under the various contracts then make it difficult if not impossible, to determine what actual damage would result if delays are encountered in construction under the contract, the circumstances are appropriate for the inclusion of a liquidated damage provision in such construction contract. *   *   *"

And also that

> " *   *   * [A] liquidated damages provision in a contract for construc-

tion is to be judged as of the time of making the contract, and the fact that actual damages suffered are shown to be greater or less than the liquidated damages fixed by the parties is not determinative of the unreasonableness of the stipulated damages nor fatal to their validity."

*   *   *

The decisions involving contract provisions for liquidated damages or penalties are legion. The consensus seems to be in favor of upholding and enforcing such provisions, even absent proof of any actual damages, where it was *reasonable at the time of making the contract* to so contract. Thus it was said in Rex Trailer Co. v. United States, 350 U.S. 148, at page 151, 76 S.Ct. 219, at page 221, 100 L.Ed. 149 (1956):

> " *   *   * Liquidated damages are a well-known remedy, and in fact Congress has utilized this form of recovery in numerous situations. In all building contracts, for example, Congress has required the insertion of a liquidated-damage clause which 'shall be conclusive and binding upon all parties' *without proof of 'actual or specific damages sustained* *   *   *.' " (Italics supplied.)

A complete study of this problem appears in the article, Liquidated Damages in Illinois, 31 Illinois Law Review 879, 880. It is there said:

> "The validity of liquidated damage clauses is traditionally determined by the application of three primary tests, which may be referred to as the intent test, the reasonableness test, and the uncertainty test.

> " *   *   * [T]he intent and reasonableness tests must be applied with reference to the time when the

contract was made, and before the breach occurred."

Especially pertinent is the observation made in the above cited article, at pages 885, 887:

> *"In principle it can make no difference whether or not actual loss followed from the breach for which stipulated damages are sought, because the validity of the stipulation must be judged as of the time when the contract was entered into.*
>
> * * *"

* * * * * *

> "Considered as a whole, *the Illinois cases support the view that the stipulation will be upheld although no loss be shown, if a loss in the amount stipulated, and legally compensable, was to have been anticipated.*" (Italics supplied.)

* * *

The Illinois Uniform Commercial Code, Ill.Rev.Stat.1961, Ch. 26, which became effective after this contract, similarly provides:

> "Damages for breach by either party may be liquidated in the agreement but only at an amount which is reasonable in the light of the anticipated or actual harm caused by the breach, the difficulties of proof of loss, and the inconvenience or nonfeasibility of otherwise obtaining an adequate remedy. A term fixing unreasonably large liquidated damages is void as a penalty." [Sec. 2–718(1).]

Viewing this contract from the time it was entered into, it is evident that the provision for $1,000 for a day's delay was a reasonable provision and that it was the parties' intent that that be the sum recoverable for each day's delay in order to forestall legal proceedings for a determination of the pre-

cise amount of damages. Further, as the court reads the correspondence, it is evident that in some measure at least, Bethlehem's delay gave rise to real problems to the City in the expeditious consummation of the work, because of complaints of hindrance to the prosecution of other contractors' work, with necessary laying off of employees, greater danger of accidents, et-cetera.

Bethlehem argues that the fact that the route was timely opened *ipso facto* proves there could be no damage. However, it is surmisable that if Bethlehem were the only contractor who delayed, this route could have been opened far earlier due to the evident expedition of the other contractors, with consequent beneficial earlier use of the route.

SECURITY SAFETY CORP. v. KUZNICKI

(1966) — Mass. —, 213 N.E.2d 866.

WILKINS, C. J. The defendants, Edmund and Rachel Kuznicki, signed a written contract with the plaintiff for the installation of a fire detection system on their premises in Blandford for the sum of $498. Their cancellation presents the question of the validity of a provision that "In the event of cancellation of this agreement * * * the owner agrees to pay 33⅓% of the contract price, as liquidated damages." The trial judge held that the provision was unreasonable and void as a penalty. He found for the plaintiff in the amount of $1, and reported the correctness of his finding to the Appellate Division, which dismissed the report. The plaintiff appealed.

The case was submitted on agreed facts. The contract was signed the evening of March 25, 1964. The defendants made a deposit of $1 and agreed to pay the balance in "cash Sept. 15th." About nine o'clock on the morning following the signing of the contract the defendants cancelled "before the plaintiff did anything in respect to the work it was to perform." "No evidence was agreed upon or offered as to the actual damage suffered by the plaintiff."

There was no error. The case is governed in all respects by A–Z Servicenter, Inc. v. Segall, 334 Mass. 672, 138 N.E.2d 266. For aught that appears, the damages in event of breach were not going to be difficult of ascertainment. [Citations.] Time was lacking for an opportunity for the plaintiff to incur much expense of performance. The stipulated sum is unreasonably and grossly disproportionate to the real damages from the breach. In these circumstances, the aggrieved party will be awarded no more than his actual damage. [Citations.] Compare the rule for the sale of goods in the Uniform Commercial Code. G.L. c. 106, § 2–718(1). Of actual damage there was no evidence.

Order dismissing report affirmed.

––––––––

MULLINIX v. MORSE

(1965) 81 Nev. 451, 406 P.2d 298.

ZENOFF, D. J. In this action for restitution of premises for the breach of a contract for the sale of real and personal property, the buyers, Gerald J. and Marie S. Mullinix, appeal from a decision of the Sixth Judicial District Court awarding Leo V. and Dorothy R. Morse, sellers, $6,278.73 damages, plus costs.

On June 1, 1960, buyers entered into a written contract for the purchase of Rodeo Lanes, a bowling alley in Winnemucca, and various equipment contained therein. The purchase price of $179,000 was to be paid as follows:

a. $10,000 upon execution of the contract.

b. $10,000 on before 60 days from date of the contract.

c. Appellants assumed the payments on several promissory notes.

d. The balance of $70,031.62 was to be paid in $500 monthly installments until June 1, 1962; thereafter, in $800 monthly installments at 6% interest.

Buyers further agreed to assign to the sellers the principal due on two promissory notes, one for $10,000 executed by James J. Branscom and the other for $7,000 executed by John H. and Lorraine C. Small. These payments were to be applied to the unpaid purchase price. Buyers agreed to pay taxes on the real and personal property received under this contract and to keep in force fire, public liability and property damage insurance on the premises, and to keep the property free of liens.

Under the forfeiture clause of the contract, buyers agreed to relinquish all rights under the contract and the money paid was to be considered rent for the use of the property and as liquidated damages. If buyers failed to comply with the agreement, and this failure continued for 15 days after written notice of default, they were to vacate and surrender the premises on demand. Time was of the essence. The bill of sale, the assumed notes, and the Branscom and Small promissory notes were all placed in escrow with instructions that in the event of the buyers' default, after 15 days notice, the documents were to be delivered to the sellers.

On May 20, 1963, sellers served notice of default upon buyers, citing a delinquency in the May 1, 1963, $800 installment payment; $200 on the Acree note; and $528.26 on the May 1, 1963 payment to the First National Bank of Nevada. They also claimed a failure to pay insurance premiums, taxes and for repairs which caused liens to be placed on the premises for material and labor.

On June 6, 1963, an action for restitution of the premises was commenced at which time the buyers surrendered possession of the property. The stipulated sole issue before the trial court, after restitution had been voluntarily given, was the ownership of the Branscom and Small promissory notes. Below this stipulation agreement, an additional clause was placed which read, "Defendants (Appellants here) having hereby voluntarily surrendered possession of the premises may put at issue in this action other matters of counter-claim or set-off." At the time of default, buyers had paid $80,861.62 on the contract.

The lower court held that (1) the Branscom and Small promissory notes were to be returned to the buyers, but the $1,000 paid thereon to the buyers was to be turned over to the sellers; (2) that the sellers should be reimbursed for the payments, totaling $5,278.73, which became due while the buyers were in possession, but remained unpaid at the time of default. The buyers, Gerald J. and Marie S. Mullinix, appeal from this money judgment of $6,278.73 for the sellers.

The issue presented to the court is: Was the award of $6,278.73 by the lower court a recovery in damages on breach of the contract of sale and, therefore, precluded by an election of the remedy of restitution.

The law is clear that damages and restitution are alternative remedies and an election to pursue one is a bar to invoking the other in a suit for breach of contract. [Citations.] The Restatement of Contracts, § 381, is in accord.

"Election Between Damages and Restitution. (1) When the alternative remedies of damages and restitution are available to a party injured by a breach, his manifested choice of one of them by bringing suit or otherwise, followed by a material change of position by the other party in reliance thereon, is a bar to the other alternative remedy. (2) The bringing of an action for one of these remedies is a bar to the alternative one unless the plaintiff shows reasonable ground for making the change of remedy."

* * *

The sellers elected the remedy of restitution, filed suit therefor, and secured immediate possession by temporary writ. By stipulation, the litigation was restricted to the ownership of the Branscom and Small promissory notes. Thus, the sellers chose restitution and rejected any claim for damages. The buyers had a right to rely on this fact and did so.

The sellers' choice of remedy precludes an award of damages. Damages, in addition to restitution, are limited to those cases where the damages arise during the period when the property is being wrongfully withheld from those who have the right of possession. [Citations] * * *.

In this case, there is no issue of rents for illegal withholding. Rather, the sellers are seeking the payment of certain installments, due under the contract of sale, which they claim were items constituting breaches of contract. As they have elected the remedy of restitution, they cannot now ask for damages in the form of a refund for these payments as well.

* * *

The decision of the lower court, awarding $6,278.73 to the sellers, is reversed. Judgment will be entered for the buyers, Gerald J. and Marie S. Mullinix, who were defendants below.

Judgment reversed.

———

SYESTER v. BANTA

(1965) — Iowa —, 133 N.W.2d 666.

SNELL, J. This is a law action seeking damages, actual and exemplary, for allegedly false and fraudulent representations in the sale of dancing instruction to plaintiff. From the final judgment entered after a jury verdict for plaintiff in a substantial amount [$14,300 actual damages and $40,000 punitive damages] defendants have appealed.

Plaintiff is a lonely and elderly widow who fell for the blandishments and flattery of those who saw some "easy money" available.

Defendants are the owners of the Des Moines Arthur Murray Dance Studio. They have a legitimate service to sell but when their selling techniques transcend the utmost limits of reason and fairness they must expect courts and juries to frown thereon. In this case the jury has done so.

Since the beginning of recorded history men and women have persisted in selling their birthrights for a mess of pottage and courts cannot protect against the folly of bad judgment. We can, however, insist on honesty in selling. The old doctrine of caveat emptor is no longer the pole star for business.

* * *

Plaintiff is a widow living alone. She has no family. Her exact age does not appear but a former employee of defendants and a favorite dancing instructor of plaintiff testified "that during the period from 1957 through the fall of 1960 she was 68 years old."

After her husband's death plaintiff worked at Bishops as a "coffee girl." She first went to the Arthur Murray Studio in 1954 as a gift from a friend. On the first visit there was no attempt to sell her any lessons but she was invited to return a few days later. When she returned she was interviewed by the manager and sold a small course of dancing lessons. From that time on there appears to have been an astoundingly successful selling campaign.

* * *

On May 2, 1955 when plaintiff bought 1200 additional hours of instruction for $6,000 she had already bought 2022 hours and had used only 261 hours.

Included in the courses offered were lifetime memberships. With the purchase of 1,000 or 1,200 hours of instruction it was the policy of defendants to give free attendance to weekly dances for life and two hours of instruction or practice a month to keep active on what had been learned. Included in plaintiff's purchases were three lifetime memberships. Plaintiff attended the weekly dances and incidental entertainments and admitted having fun.

Plaintiff testified that defendants' manager sold her the first lifetime membership. She testified "He promised me all the privileges of the studio and I would be a professional dancer." To make such a promise to a lady plaintiff's age was ridiculous. The fact that she was so gullible as to be an easy victim does not justify taking over $29,000 of her money. She may have been willing and easily sold but nevertheless a victim.

The members of defendants' staff were carefully schooled and supervised in the art of high-powered salesmanship. Mr. Carey, a witness for plaintiff, testified at length as to methods and as to his contact with plaintiff. * * *

Defendants' studio occupies seven rooms consisting of a grand ballroom and six private studios. Each private studio is wired for sound so the manager could monitor conversations between instructor and student and without the student's knowledge correct the instructor's sales technique.

Mr. Carey had received two months training including a course on sales technique taught by the manager. Plaintiff's Exhibit H is a revised edition of defendants' "Eight Good Rules For Interviewing." It is an exhaustive set of instructions, outlines and suggested conversations covering twenty-two typewritten pages. A few pertinent parts are:

"1. How to prevent a prospect from consulting his banker, lawyer, wife or friend.

"2. Avoid permitting your prospect to think the matter over.

"3. Tell the prospect that has never danced before that it is an advantage and tell the prospect that has danced before that it is an advantage.

"4. To dance with the prospect and then tell the prospect that the rhythm is very good, their animation or self confidence is good, that their natural ability is very good. That they will be an excellent ballroom dancer in much less time and that if they didn't have natural ability it would take twice as long.

"5. To summarize the prospects ability to learn as follows: 'Did you know that the three most important points on this D.A. are: rhythm, natural ability and animation? You've been graded Excellent in all three.'

"6. In quoting the price for various courses, the instructor is supposed to say 'the trouble with most people is that they dance lifelessly, but as I told you on your analysis, you have animation—vitality in your dancing. No matter what course you decide on you're going to be a really smooth dancer (men would rather be a smooth dancer—women would rather be a beautiful, graceful dancer.)'

"7. To use 'emotional selling' and the instructor is tutored as follows: 'This is the warm-up period and is a very important part of your interview. You have proved to him by now that he can learn to dance; now you must appeal to his emotions in such a way that he will want lessons regardless of the cost.' "

Theoretically, for advancing proficiency in dancing (the jury must have thought that $29,000 had something to do with it), plaintiff was awarded a Bronze Medal, then a Silver Medal and then a Gold Medal. These awards were given plaintiff all in the same year although defendants' manager testified that it takes approximately two to four years to qualify for a Bronze Medal, five to seven years for a Silver Medal and anytime after 1200 hours a student could qualify for the Gold Medal. Finally after considerable thought about new incentives for plaintiff to buy something more she was shown a film on Gold Star dancing. This is a difficult professional type of dancing. "The dancers on the film were brought in from Europe by Mr. Murray. The dancing is English quick step and is the type of dancing done by Ginger Rogers and Fred Astaire only about twice as difficult." This film had been studied 15 to 20 times to determine what parts to stress with plaintiff.

Plaintiff was easily sold a Gold Star course of 625 hours for $6,250. A few days later she came into the ballroom, handed Mr. Carey an envelope and said "Well, it took some doing but here is the money." The money was delivered to the manager.

The Gold Star course was started although even the instructor was "faking it" and had no idea what he was doing.

Mr. Carey testified that from 1957 through the fall of 1960 plaintiff's dancing ability did not improve. "She was 68 years old and had gone as far as she would ever go in dancing, thereon it would be merely repetitious." In his opinion "it would take 200 to 400 hours of instructions to teach her to dance in the manner she was dancing in 1960." He also testified that while he was at the studio none of his students ever failed to qualify for any of the medals. When he questioned plaintiff's ability to do the advanced type of dancing she was being sold he was reminded by defendants' manager that he was an employee and that the manager made the rules.

Mr. Carey testified at length as to the attentions, inducements, promises and lies (he said they were) lavished on plaintiff. He became plaintiff's regular instructor. He was about twenty-five years old and apparently quite charming and fascinating to plaintiff. She gave him a diamond ring for his birthday in 1960.

The testimony is rather fantastic but it would unduly extend this opinion to set it forth in greater detail. It was in our opinion sufficient for the jury to find that plaintiff was the victim of a calculated course of intentional misrepresentations.

The charge for instruction varied somewhat up to $10 per hour. After some refunds, and, according to defendants' computation, plaintiff paid approximately $6.75 per hour for 3425 hours of instruction or about $23,000.

If Mr. Carey's estimate of plaintiff's ability and possibility of progress is accepted plaintiff was knowingly overcharged for 3025 hours or a total sum of $20,418.75.

Mr. Carey was discharged by defendants in the fall of 1960. Plaintiff quit the studio shortly thereafter. She still had 1750 hours of unused time that she had purchased. She testified that she did so because she "was unhappy because things didn't go right and I was through with dancing, and that was the only reason I quit." Defendants' manager testified that plaintiff "became unhappy over the dismissal of Mr. Carey and left the studio." Another witness for defendants said plaintiff complained mostly about losing her instructor, Mr. Carey.

* * *

Defendants argue that there was no evidence from which the jury could find the fair and reasonable value of the instruction received other than the amount paid by plaintiff. Defendants' manager testified that plaintiff still has 899 hours of unused lessons. Mr. Carey's testimony would support a finding that plaintiff was knowingly overcharged for 3025 hours or the sum of $20,418.75. The jury's verdict for $14,300 actual damages was within the evidence. We have no means of knowing just how the jury computed the damage. It was for more than the charge for the unused time according to defendants,

but less than would be due for unproductive instruction. In argument defendants have stressed the value of plaintiff's enjoyment. That may have entered into the jury's computation.

The verdict was not beyond the scope of the evidence or the instructions.

In addition to actual damages plaintiff asked for exemplary or punitive damages. The claim was submitted to the jury and a verdict for $40,000 punitive damages was returned.

Defendants argue that the record will not support an award of punitive damages in any amount and that the issue should not have been submitted, but do not challenge the accuracy of the instructions relative thereto.

Defendants argue that in the absence of actual damages, punitive damages cannot be awarded. That proposition is well established and needs no extended discussion here for we have said in Division III, supra, that there was support for an award of actual damages. The rule is stated in 17 Iowa Law Review, 413, 414, as follows:

"It is a well settled and almost universally accepted rule in the law of damages that a finding of exemplary damages must be predicated upon a finding of actual damages. The reason for the rule lies in the theory behind exemplary damages, and this theory is ordinarily utilized by the courts in supporting their statements. As indicated by its synonyms, 'exemplary' damages are a species of punishment. They are awarded to the plaintiff in the discretion of the jury as a means of retaliation against the defendant for his antisocial conduct, as a means of preventing him from acting similarly in the future, and as a means of deterring others who might be so inclined. It is argued effectively, therefore, that if no actual damages have been sustained, the defendant merits no harsh treatment, and that there is no foundation on which exemplary damages may be based. * * *"

In the absence of malice, punitive damages cannot be awarded. The problem of what constitutes malice and the evidence necessary to support a finding has been considered in many decisions. * * *

Judge Graven in Amos v. Prom, 115 F. Supp. 127 thoroughly analyzed the rules and supporting authorities incident to exemplary damages. We quote and adopt, but need not repeat the supporting citations for that opinion.

"[T]here is no mathematical ratio and exemplary damages may considerably exceed compensatory damages in some cases." loc. cit. 131.

"Under Iowa law exemplary damages are not a matter of right but rest in the discretion of the jury." (Citations) loc. cit. 133.

"Exemplary damages may be awarded where it appears that the defendant is guilty of fraud." loc. cit. 133.

"Such exemplary damages are permitted on the theory that they serve as a deterrent to wrongdoers and as punishment for wrongdoing." loc. cit. 134.

Malice or wanton conduct is imputable to the principal. loc. cit. 134.

"While it is not entirely clear whether the Iowa decisions regard 'malice in fact' as a descriptive term for 'legal malice' or as a synonym for 'express malice,' it is apparent that the 'malice' required to permit an award of exemplary damages is something less than actual ill-will or express malice and may be termed 'legal malice' for want of a better expression."

"It is finally said that the intentional doing of a 'wrongful act' without justification will permit an inference of the wicked state of mind. Yet it is apparent that many wrongful or illegal acts may be intentionally committed from motives wholly apart from any malice or evil intent directed toward the person who happens to suffer by the action, as where defendant is motivated by a desire for gain and has no feeling at all for those injured by him.

"Therefore, when the law reaches this last stage, as it has in Iowa, it is no longer 'malice' which is required but the 'something else' from which malice is said to be presumed. (Citations) 'It is enough (for legal malice) if it be the result of any improper or sinister motive and in disregard of the rights of others.' [Jenkins v. Gilligan, 131 Iowa 176] 108 N.W. at page 238 [9 L.R.A.,N.S., 1087]. The rule would seem to be: exemplary damages may be awarded where defendant acts maliciously, but malice may be inferred where defendant's act is illegal or improper; where the nature of the illegal act is such as to negative any inference of feeling toward the person injured, and is in fact consistent with a complete indifference on the part of defendant, liability for exemplary damages is not based upon the maliciousness of the defendant but is based, rather, upon the separate substantive principle that illegal or improper acts ought to be deterred by the exaction from the defendant of sums over and above the actual damage he has caused."

The jury award of $40,000 was large. However, the evidence of greed and avariciousness on the part of defendants is shocking of our sense of justice as it obviously was to the jury.

The allowance of exemplary damages is wholly within the discretion of the jury where there is a legal basis for the allowance of such damages. We may interfere only where passion and prejudice appear and then only by reversal.

* * *

We think the question of exemplary damages was properly submitted to the jury; that there was evidence to support a verdict; that there is no indication of such passion and prejudice as to require a reversal and that the case should be and hereby is

Affirmed.

FELCH v. FINDLAY COLLEGE

(1963) 119 Ohio App. 357, 200 N.E.2d 353.

GUERNSEY, J. This is an appeal on questions of law and fact from a judgment of the Common Pleas Court for the defendant, Findlay College, a private nonprofit corporation.

Plaintiff, William E. Felch, alleges, among other things, that he was employed by the defendant as a member of its faculty on a continuing basis and that contrary to and without compliance with the provisions for dismissal contained in administrative memoranda purporting to require certain hearings the board of trustees of defendant on August 22, 1961, approved the action of its president on July 20, 1961, dismissing the plaintiff effective August 11, 1961. Plaintiff prays that "defendant be enjoined from carrying into effect the dismissal of this plaintiff as a member of the faculty * * * and that the defendant may be ordered to continue plaintiff as such member of the faculty of Findlay College, Findlay, Ohio, and that defendant be ordered to pay to this plaintiff the salary therefore agreed upon."

In essence and in legal effect plaintiff seeks by injunction the specific performance of an employment contract. There are no Ohio statutes which purport to entitle plaintiff to the relief prayed for, and plaintiff's rights must be determined by general equitable principles.

The first and primary issue before this court is as to the remedy which plaintiff seeks and to determine this issue we will assume, without deciding, that a binding contract has existed between the plaintiff and defendant purporting to give plaintiff continuing employment status with a covenant by the defendant that plaintiff should not be dismissed for cause without a hearing conducted at the place, time, and in the manner provided by such covenant, and we will further assume, without deciding, that the defendant has breached this contract of employment by dismissing plaintiff without compliance with the hearing provisions of said covenant. * *

In 81 C.J.S. Specific Performance § 82, p. 591, the rule is stated as follows:

"In general, specific performance does not lie to enforce a provision in a contract for the performance of personal services requiring special knowledge, ability, experience, or the exercise of judgment, skill, taste, discretion, labor, tact, energy, or integrity, *particularly where the performance of such services would be continuous over a long period of time.* This rule is based on the fact that mischief likely to result from an enforced continuance of the relationship incident to the service after it has become personally obnoxious to one of the parties is so great that the interests of society require that the remedy be denied, and on the fact that the enforcement of a decree requiring the performance of such a contract would impose too great a burden on the courts. * * *

However, it is claimed by the plaintiff and the *amicus curiae* herein that the provisions of the plaintiff's contract require a hearing before dismissal and that the same constitutes a negative covenant, i. e., that the defendant has agreed not to dismiss the plaintiff without following such dismissal procedure. It is recognized under the law of injunctions and specific performance that notwithstanding that a personal service contract may not ordinarily be ordered specifically performed a negative covenant in such contract may, under some circumstances, be enforced by injunction. However, there are limitations on such enforcement. As stated in 2 Restatement of the Law of Contracts, 704, Section 380:

"(1) An injunction against the breach of a contractual duty that is negative in character may be granted either

"(a) to prevent harm for which money damages are not an adequate remedy caused by the breach of the negative promise itself, even though there are accompanying affirmative promises by either party that will not be specifically enforced, *unless such partial enforcement will lead to unjust or harmful results*; or

"(b) as an indirect mode of specifically enforcing an accompanying affirmative promise, if it is likely to be effective for that purpose *and if the affirmative promise is itself one that would be enforced by affirmative decree* except for the mere practical difficulties of such enforcement." (Emphasis added.)

Thus, even if the provisions for a hearing are, as claimed by plaintiff, a negative covenant, the enforcement of same would still lead to the same "unjust or harmful results" which constitute reasons for denying specific performance of the affirmative promise to employ plaintiff, and the enforcement of the negative covenant may not be used indirectly to specifically enforce the accompanying affirmative promise to employ for the reason that the affirmative promise is *not* "itself one that would be enforced by affirmative decree."

For these reasons it is the opinion and judgment of this court that the remedy of specific performance, either in itself or by means of the injunctive process, is not available to the plaintiff to enforce the provisions of the employment contract which he claims to exist between himself and defendant private college.

Judgment affirmed.

MADISON SQUARE GARDEN CORPORATION, ILL. v. CARNERA

(1931 C.C.A.2d) 52 F.2d 47.

Suit by plaintiff, Madison Square Garden Corporation, against Primo Carnera, defendant. From an order granting an injunction against defendant, defendant appeals.

CHASE, CIRCUIT JUDGE. On January 13, 1931, the plaintiff and defendant by their duly authorized agents entered into the following agreement in writing:

"1. Carnera agrees that he will render services as a boxer in his next contest (which contest, hereinafter called the 'First Contest,' shall be with the winner of the proposed Schmeling-Stribling contest, or, if the same is drawn, shall be with Schmeling, and shall be deemed to be a contest for the heavyweight championship title; provided, however, that, in the event of the inability of the Garden to cause Schmeling or Stribling, as the case may be, to perform the terms of his agreement with the Garden calling for such contest, the Garden shall be without further liability to Carnera,) exclusively under the auspices of the Garden, in the United States of America, or the Dominion of Canada, at such time, not, however, later than midnight of September 30, 1931, as the Garden may direct. * * *

"9. Carnera shall not, pending the holding of the First Contest, render services as a boxer in any major boxing contest, without the written permission of the Garden in each case had and obtained. A major contest is understood to be one with Sharkey, Baer, Campolo, Godfrey, or like grade heavyweights, or heavyweights who shall have beaten any of the above subsequent to the date hereof. If in any boxing contest engaged in by Carnera prior to the holding of the First Contest, he shall lose the same, the Garden shall at its option, to be exercised by a two weeks' notice to Carnera in writing, be without further liability under the terms of this agreement to Carnera. Carnera shall not render services during the continuance of the option referred to in paragraph 8 hereof for any person, firm or corporation other than the Garden. Carnera shall, however, at all times be permitted to engage in sparring exhibitions in which no decision is rendered and in which the heavyweight championship title is not at stake, and in which Carnera boxes not more than four rounds with any one opponent. * * *"

Thereafter the defendant, without the permission of the plaintiff, written or otherwise, made a contract to engage in a boxing contest with the Sharkey mentioned in paragraph 9 of the agreement above quoted, and by the terms thereof the contest was to take place before the first contest mentioned in the defendant's contract with the plaintiff was to be held.

The plaintiff then brought this suit to restrain the defendant from carrying out his contract to box Sharkey, and obtained the preliminary injunction order, from which this appeal was taken. Jurisdiction is based on diversity of citizenship and the required amount is involved.

The District Court has found on affidavits which adequately show it that the defendant's services are unique and extraordinary. A negative covenant in a contract for such personal services is enforceable by injunction where the damages for a breach are incapable of ascertainment. [Citations.]

The defendant points to what is claimed to be lack of consideration for his negative promise, in that the contract is inequitable and contains no agreement to employ him. It is true that there is no promise in so many words to employ the defendant to box in a contest with Stribling or Schmeling, but the agreement read as a whole binds the plaintiff to do just that, providing either Stribling or Schmeling becomes the contestant as the result of the match between them and can be induced to box the defendant. The defendant has agreed to "render services as a boxer" for the plaintiff exclusively, and the plaintiff has agreed to pay him a definite percentage of the gate receipts as his compensation for so doing. The promise to employ the defendant to enable him to earn the compensation agreed upon is implied to the same force and effect as though expressly stated. [Citations.] The fact that the plaintiff's implied promise is conditioned, with respect to the contest with the winner of the Stribling-Schmeling match, upon the consent of that performer, does not show any failure of consideration for the defendant's promise. [Citation.]

As we have seen, the contract is valid and enforceable. It contains a restrictive covenant which may be given effect. Whether a preliminary injunction shall be issued under such circumstances rests in the sound discretion of the court. [Citations.] The District Court, in its discretion, did issue the preliminary injunction and required the plaintiff as a condition upon its issuance to secure its own performance of the contract in suit with a bond for $25,000 and to give a bond in the sum of $35,000 to pay the defendant such damages as he may sustain by reason of the injunction. Such an order is clearly not an abuse of discretion.

Order affirmed.

PROBLEMS

1. A contracted to buy and B to sell to A, 1,000 barrels of sugar. B failed to deliver and A could not buy any sugar in the market, so that he was compelled to shut down his candy factory. (a) What damages is A entitled to recover? (b) Would it make any difference if B had been told by A that he wanted the sugar to make candies for the Christmas trade and that he had accepted contracts for the delivery by certain dates?

2. A agreed to erect an apartment building for B for $75,000, A to suffer deduction of $100 per day for every day of delay. A was twenty days late in finishing the job, losing ten days because of a strike and ten days by reason of delay on the part of the material men in furnishing A with material. A claims that he is entitled to payment in full (a) because the agreement as to $100 a day is a penalty; (b) because B had not shown that he has sustained any damage. Discuss each contention and decide.

3. A contracted with B, a shirtmaker, for 1,-000 shirts for men. B manufactured and delivered 500 shirts which were paid for by A, who at the same time notified B that he could not use or dispose of the other 500 shirts and directed B not to manufacture any more under the contract. B proceeded to make up the other 500 shirts, tendered them to A, who refused to accept, and B then sued for the purchase price. Decision?

4. A contracts to act in a comedy for B and to comply with all theater regulations for four seasons. B promises to pay A $50 for each performance and to allow A one benefit performance each season. It is expressly agreed that "if either party shall fail to perform as agreed in any respect he will pay $5,000 as liquidated damages and not as a penalty." After two seasons A refused to further perform. Thereafter, B sues A for $5,000 for breach of contract. Decision?

5. A leases a building to B for five years at a rental of $1,000 per month, commencing July 1, 1965, B depositing $10,000 as security for performance of all his covenants in the lease, to be retained by A in case of any breach on B's part, otherwise to be applied in payment of rent for the last ten months of the term of the lease. B defaulted in the payment of rent for the months of May and June, 1966. After proper notice to B of the termination of the lease for non-payment of rent, A sued B for possession of the building and recovered a judgment for possession. Thereafter, B sues A to recover the $10,000 less the amount of rent due A for May and June, 1966. Decision?

6. (a) A and B enter into a written agreement under which A agrees to sell and B agrees to buy 100 shares of the capital stock of the Infinitesimal Steel Corporation, whose shares are not listed on any exchange and are closely held, for $10 per share. A refused to deliver when tendered the $1000 and B sues in equity for specific performance, tendering the $1,000. Decision?

(b) Modifying (a) above, assume that the subject matter of the agreement is stock of the United States Steel Corporation, which is listed and readily available. Decision?

(c) Modifying (a) above, assume that the subject matter of the agreement is undeveloped farm land of little commercial value. Decision?

*

PART TWO
AGENCY

CHAPTER 12

PRINCIPAL AND AGENT RELATIONSHIP

Definition of Agency. Agency is a relationship between two persons whereby one of them is authorized to act for and on behalf of the other. The person who is so authorized and consents to act is the agent. The one for whom he acts is the principal. The authorized acts of the agent bind the principal and create legal rights and duties with respect to third persons. The acts of the agent may also result in the principal acquiring or transferring ownership in property. The creation of contract rights and obligations, the existence of tort duties, and the transfer of title to property, are changes in the legal position of the principal which may be produced by the acts of an agent on his behalf.

In its legal sense, the term "agency" applies to contractual or commercial dealings between two parties by or through the medium of another.

Utility of Agency Concept. If the law should require that each party to a contract or business transaction must personally and directly participate in making the contract or effecting the transaction, the ability of any person to conduct a given business enterprise would be limited by the number of contracts or sales which he could personally negotiate. This would seriously curtail the size and operation of every business unit. It would make impossible the conduct of business by a corporation which is an artificial legal entity that can act only through its agents, officers, and employees. It would

radically change the fundamental rule of the law of partnerships whereby every partner is both an agent and a principal of his co-partners with respect to the conduct of the business of the partnership. The agency concept is indispensable to trade and commerce in modern society. Through the use of agents, one person may enter into 100 or 500 business transactions, with the same effect as if done by him personally, in no greater an amount of time than required by him to negotiate personally a single contract. A person may thus multiply and ramify his business activities. If the law of agency were to be abolished, a substitute would have to be devised and made effective immediately in order for modern business to continue to exist.

Qui Facit per Alium, Facit per Se. This ancient maximum literally translated is: He who acts through another, acts himself. It expresses the basic principle of the law of agency that the authorized act of the agent is the act of the principal.

Creation of Agency. An agency may be created by contract or agreement between the principal and agent, by operation of law, by estoppel, or by ratification. Agency may result from a direction given by one person to another to act for or on his account with or without a promise by such other to act or any understanding that he is to receive compensation for his services if he acts. The relationship of principal and agent may exist although the element of consideration is lacking. However agency by contract or agreement is the most usual method of creating the relationship and requires a manifestation of consent by both the principal and the agent. Agency by operation of law is commonly by statute, such as the non-resident motorist statute which has been adopted in a majority of the States. This statute provides that the operation of a motor vehicle upon the highway of a State amounts to the appointment of the Secretary of State as the agent of the nonresident for service of process in any action arising out of the operation of the motor vehicle in the State. Estoppel exists where a person by his conduct clothes another with apparent authority which reasonably induces a third person in reliance thereon to deal with such person as an agent. Ratification is an affirmance of the unauthorized act of an agent or of the act of a purported agent which relates back to the commission of the act with the same effect as if the act were originally authorized.

Scope of Agency Purposes. As a general rule, whatever a person may do personally he may do through an agent, and conversely, whatever he cannot legally do himself, he cannot authorize another to do for him. An exception to the first statement exists with respect to the performance of acts which are so peculiarly personal that their performance may not be delegated to another, as in the case of a contract for personal services. A person may not validly authorize another to commit on his behalf an illegal or unlawful act, or crime. Any such agreement is void, and all parties participating in the planning or commission of a crime or unlawful act are, in effect, principals.

Capacity to be Principal. The capacity to act through the instrumentality of an agent depends upon the capacity of the principal to do the act himself. Thus, contracts entered into by an infant or an insane person are voidable. Similarly, the appointment of an agent by an infant or insane person is

voidable. At common law, the appointment of an agent by a married woman is void. By statute in every State a married woman may validly contract and, consequently, she may appoint an agent who may bind her by contract. War terminates commerce and trade between the belligerent countries, and therefore a citizen of one of the warring countries cannot appoint an agent in the enemy country.

Capacity to be Agent. As the act of the agent is the act of the principal, the incapacity of a person acting as an agent to bind himself by contract does not disqualify him from making a contract which is binding on his principal. Thus, infants may act as agents, as may insane persons and married women. As between the principal and the agent, the contract of agency may be voidable or void, but as between the principal and the third person who dealt with the agent, the contract is valid. Some mental capacity is necessary in an agent and, therefore, infants of tender years, lunatics, and imbeciles, under certain fact situations, may be held incompetent to act as agents. A person having an interest adverse to that of the principal is not permitted to act as his agent. Thus, under the Statute of Frauds a party to a contract is not allowed to execute a note or memorandum as agent for the other party.

Other Relations Distinguished from Agency. It is well to distinguish the relationship of master and servant from that of principal and agent. Generally, a servant performs duties of a ministerial nature and has limited, if any, authority to enter into contracts on behalf of his master.

The relationship of a person to an independent contractor is not that of principal and agent. This relationship depends on the nature of the work performed or services rendered by one person for another and the extent to which control is or may be exercised over it by such other.

The Restatement of the Law of Agency, 2d, Section 2, defines these relationships as follows:

(1) A master is a principal who employs another to perform service in his affairs and who controls or has the right to control the physical conduct of the other in the performance of the service.

(2) A servant is an agent employed by a master to perform service in his affairs whose physical conduct in the performance of the service is controlled or is subject to the right to control by the master.

(3) An independent contractor is a person who contracts with another to do something for him but who is not controlled by the other nor subject to the other's right to control with respect to his physical conduct in the performance of the undertaking. He may or may not be an agent.

Classes and Kinds of Agents. Agents may be actual or ostensible. An actual agent is one to whom the principal has given express or implied authority to act. An ostensible agent is one to whom the principal has given no authority but by conduct has induced others to believe reasonably that he has authority to act.

Agents may also be classified as general or special. A general agent is one employed to transact all of the business of his principal or all of the principal's business of a particular kind or in a particular place. A special agent is one employed to act for his principal only in a specific transaction or only for a particular purpose or class of work. The special agent is not given entire control over a particular business but is given only authority to do certain acts.

A subagent is a person employed by an agent, with the knowledge and consent of the principal, to assist the agent in transacting the affairs of the principal. The subagent is not a mere servant of the agent but possesses authority to bind the principal.

Ratification. The adoption or confirmation by one person of an act which has been performed on his behalf by another without his authority is a ratification of such act and binds the ratifying person as well as the third person as if the act had initially been authorized.

As defined in the Restatement of the Law of Agency, 2d, Section 82:

"Ratification is the affirmance by a person of a prior act which did not bind him but which was done or professedly done on his account, whereby the act, as to some or all persons, is given effect as if originally authorized by him."

The Restatement, 2d Section 83, defines affirmance:

Affirmance is either

(a) a manifestation of an election by one on whose account an unauthorized act has been done to treat the act as authorized, or

(b) conduct by him justifiable only if there were such an election.

Ratification may relate to the acts of an agent which have exceeded the authority granted to him, as well as to the acts of a stranger who is without any authority. However, the third person who deals with the agent or purported agent must be ignorant of his lack of authority at the time of the doing of the act; and when the act is brought to the attention of the purported principal, he may elect either to confirm or to repudiate it. In order to make this election, the purported principal must have knowledge of the facts with respect to the unauthorized act. To effect a ratification, he must manifest in some way an intent to do so, although it is not necessary that the intent to ratify be communicated either to the purported agent or to the third person. The manifestation may be in the form of express language, or may be implied from the conduct of the principal or by his acceptance of the benefits of the transaction.

A ratification relates back to the time of the performance of the unauthorized act. For example, on June 1, B acting without authority from A represents to C that he is A's agent and enters into a bilateral executory contract with C on behalf of A. Since B had no authorization, A is not bound by this contract. It is a fundamental rule of the law of contracts that where one party to a purported bilateral contract is not bound, the other party is not bound. Hence, C is not bound to A. If, on June 15, A ratifies the act of B, then both A and C become bound by contract as of June 1. The June 15 ratification relates back to June 1. However, suppose that on June 12 C learns that B acted without authority and promptly notifies A that he withdraws from the contract. Thereafter, on June 15, A ratifies the act of B. The doctrine of relation back is a rule of the law of agency. To permit its application in a situation where C has withdrawn prior to A's ratification would run counter to the law of contracts because at the time of the withdrawal neither A nor C were bound and therefore C should be permitted to withdraw. Consequently, the ratification after the withdrawal is not effective.

The Restatement of the Law of Agency, 2d Section 88, provides:

> "To constitute ratification, the affirmance of a transaction must be before the third person has manifested his withdrawal from it either to the purported principal or to the agent, and before the offer or agreement has otherwise teminated or been discharged."

Duties of Agent to Principal. The several duties of an agent to his principal, in addition to the fiduciary duties discussed hereafter, are defined in the Restatement of the Law of Agency, 2d, as follows:

Section 379. Duty of Care and Skill.

(1) Unless otherwise agreed, a paid agent is subject to a duty to the principal to act with standard care and with the skill which is standard in the locality for the kind of work which he is employed to perform and, in addition, to exercise any special skill that he has.

(2) Unless otherwise agreed, a gratuitous agent is under a duty to the principal to act with the care and skill which is required of persons not agents performing similar gratuitous undertakings for others.

Section 380. Duty of Good Conduct.

Unless otherwise agreed, an agent is subject to a duty not to conduct himself with such impropriety that he brings disrepute upon the principal or upon the business in which he is engaged. If the service involves personal relations, he has a duty not to act in such a way as to make continued friendly relations with the principal impossible.

Section 381. Duty to Give Information.

Unless otherwise agreed, an agent is subject to a duty to use reasonable efforts to give his principal information which is relevant to affairs entrusted to him and which, as the agent has notice, the principal would desire to have and which can be communicated without violating a superior duty to a third person.

Section 382. Duty to Keep and Render Accounts.

Unless otherwise agreed, an agent is subject to a duty to keep, and render to his principal, an account of money or other things which he has received or paid out on behalf of the principal.

Section 383. Duty to Act Only as Authorized.

Except when he is privileged to protect his own or another's interests, an agent is subject to a duty to the principal not to act in the principal's affairs except in accordance with the principal's manifestation of consent.

Section 384. Duty Not to Attempt the Impossible or Impracticable.

Unless otherwise agreed, an agent is subject to a duty to the principal not to continue to render service which subjects the principal to risk of expense if it reasonably appears to him to be impossible or impracticable for him to accomplish the objects of the principal and if he cannot communicate with the principal.

Section 385. Duty to Obey.

(1) Unless otherwise agreed, an agent is subject to a duty to obey all reasonable di-

rections in regard to the manner of performing a service that he has contracted to perform.

(2) Unless he is privileged to protect his own or another's interests, an agent is subject to a duty not to act in matters entrusted to him on account of the principal contrary to the directions of the principal, even though the terms of the employment prescribe that such directions shall not be given.

Section 386. Duties after Termination of Authority.

Unless otherwise agreed, an agent is subject to a duty not to act as such after the termination of his authority.

Fiduciary Duties of Agent. A fiduciary duty is one which arises out of a position of trust and confidence. It is a duty imposed by law which a trustee owes to a beneficiary of the trust, an officer or director of a corporation owes to the corporation and its shareholders, a lawyer owes to his client, an employee owes to his employer, and an agent owes to his principal. Fiduciary duties are not limited to these situations but exist in every relationship where one person is induced to repose trust and confidence in another.

The fiduciary duty is one of utmost loyalty and good faith. An agent must act solely in the interest of his principal, and not in his own interest or in the interest of another. An agent may not enter into any transaction in which he has a personal interest, nor may he take a position in conflict with the interest of his principal, unless the principal, with full knowledge of all of the facts, consents. The agent owes his principal at all times the duty of full disclosure. He does not deal with his principal at arm's length.

The fiduciary duty of an agent prevents him from competing with his principal concerning the subject matter of the agency, or acting on behalf of a competitor or for persons whose interests conflict with those of the principal. An agent who is employed to buy may not buy from himself. An agent who is employed to sell may not become the purchaser, nor may he act as agent for the purchaser. The agent's loyalty must be undivided and his actions devoted exclusively to represent and promote the interests of his principal.

An agent may not use for his own benefit, and contrary to the interest of his principal, information obtained in the course of the agency. For example, if an agent in the course of his employment discovers a defect in his principal's title to certain property, he may not use the information to acquire the title for himself. Or, if an employee prior to the expiration of his employer's lease, secretly obtains a lease of the property for his own benefit, he may be compelled to transfer it to his employer.

An agent is not permitted to make a secret profit out of the subject matter of the agency. He is entitled to receive the agreed salary or commission, or reasonable compensation where the amount was not fixed by agreement. All profits belong to the principal to whom the agent must account. Thus, if an agent who is authorized to sell certain property of his principal for $1,000, sells it for $1,500, he may not secretly pocket the additional $500. If a real estate broker who is employed to sell certain land for a commission of five per cent of the sales price, knowing that the owner is willing to sell the land for $20,000, agrees secretly with a prospective buyer who is willing to pay $22,000 for the land that he will endeavor to obtain the consent of the owner to sell for $20,000, in which event the buyer will pay the broker $1,000, or one-half of the amount which the buyer believes that he is saving on the price, the broker by making this agreement with the buyer violates his fiduciary duty to his principal, the seller. The dishonest broker is not allowed to retain the secret profit of $1,000 but must pay it to his principal. Furthermore, he loses the right to any commission or compensation in handling the sale.

The result is that the seller who was willing to sell and did sell the land for $20,000 and expected to pay a commission of $1,000 and thereby net $19,000, receives $21,000 for the land free of commission. The breach of fiduciary duty by the broker has produced an unexpected windfall for the seller. However, this is incidental to the enforcement of the obligation of the fiduciary.

Duties of the Principal to the Agent. The duties of a principal to his agent may be either in contract or in tort. The tort duties generally arise out of an employer-employee relationship and are discussed hereafter. The contractual duties of the principal as set forth in the Restatement of the Law of Agency, 2d, are as follows:

Section 432. Duty to Perform Contract.

A principal is subject to a duty to an agent to perform the contract which he has made with the agent.

Section 433. Duty to Furnish Opportunity for Work.

A principal does not, by contracting to employ an agent, thereby promise to provide him with an opportunity for work, but the circumstances under which the agreement for employment is made or the nature of the employment may warrant an inference of such a promise.

Section 434. Duty Not to Interfere with Agent's Work.

A principal who has contracted to afford an agent an opportunity to work has a duty to refrain from unreasonably interfering with his work.

Section 435. Duty to Give Agent Information.

Unless otherwise agreed, it is inferred that a principal contracts to use care to inform the agent of risks of physical harm or pecuniary loss which, as the principal has reason to know, exist in the performance of authorized acts and which he has reason to know are unknown to the agent. His duty to give other information depends upon the agreement between them.

Section 436. Duty to Keep and Render Accounts.

Unless otherwise agreed, a master has a duty to keep and render accounts of the amount due from him to a servant; whether principals of other agents have such a duty depends upon the method of compensation, the fact that the agent operates or does not operate an independent enterprise, the customs of business and other similar factors.

Section 437. Duty of Good Conduct.

Unless otherwise agreed, a principal who has contracted to employ an agent has a duty to conduct himself so as not to harm the agent's reputation nor to make it impossible for the agent, consistently with his reasonable self-respect or personal safety, to continue in the employment.

Section 439. When Duty of Indemnity Exists.

Unless otherwise agreed, a principal is subject to a duty to exonerate an agent who is not barred by the illegality of his conduct to indemnify him for:

(a) authorized payments made by the agent on behalf of the principal;

(b) payments upon contracts upon which the agent is authorized to make himself liable, and upon obligations arising from the possession or ownership of things which he is authorized to hold on account of the principal;

(c) payments of damages to third persons which he is required to make on account of the authorized performance of an act which constitutes a tort or a breach of contract;

(d) expenses of defending actions by third persons brought because of the agent's authorized conduct, such actions being unfounded but not brought in bad faith; and

(e) payments resulting in benefit to the principal, made by the agent under such circumstances that it would be inequitable for indemnity not to be made.

Section 441. Duty to Pay Compensation.

Unless the relation of the parties, the triviality of the services, or other circumstances, indicate that the parties have agreed otherwise, it is inferred that a person promises to pay for services which he requests or permits another to perform for him as his agent.

Section 443. Amount of Compensation.

If the contract of employment provides for compensation to the agent, he is entitled to receive for the full performance of the agreed service:

(a) the definite amount agreed upon and no more, if the agreement is definite as to amount; or

(b) the fair value of his services, if there is no agreement for a definite amount.

Section 450. Duty Not to Terminate Employment.

A principal has a duty not to repudiate or terminate the employment in violation of the contract of employment.

Section 458. Liability of Principal to Subagent.

The authorized employment of a subservant or other subagent does not thereby subject the principal to contractual liability to the subagent but the principal is subject to the same tort and liability and has the same duty of indemnity to him as to agents directly employed.

Duties and Liability of Employer. In addition to the contractual duties mentioned above, an employer owes certain tort duties to his employees. Among these is the duty to provide reasonably safe conditions of employment, and to warn the employee of any unreasonable risk involved in the employment, if the employer should realize that it exists and that the employee is likely not to become aware of it. An employer is also liable to his employees for damage caused by the tortious conduct of other employees who are not fellow servants, and of other agents or persons doing work for him, to the same extent as he is to third persons. The fellow servant rule will be discussed later.

The duty of an employer as to working conditions for his employees extends to the maintenance, inspection, and repair of the premises under his control and of the tools or implements which his employees use. He is also under a duty to supply competent supervisors of the operative details of the business where this is reasonably necessary to prevent undue risk of harm to the employees. Where work is dangerous to employees unless rules are made for its conduct, the employer is also under a duty to promulgate and enforce suitable rules. The employer is under a duty to provide his employees with a reasonably safe place in which to work, and if the employee comes into a position of imminent danger of serious harm which is or should be known to the employer or to the person having the duties of management, the employer is liable for a failure to exercise reasonable care to avert the threatened harm.

In an action by an injured employee against his employer to recover damages resulting from the breach of any of the employer's tort duties, the employer has several well-established defenses available to him at common law. These include the defense of (1) lack of negligence of the employer; (2) contributory negligence on the part of the employee; (3) the fellow servant rule; and (4) the doctrine of assumption of risk by the employee.

(1) The basis of most tort actions by an employee against his employer is the failure of the employer to use reasonable care under the circumstances for the safety of the employee. The failure to measure up to this standard of due care is negligence. If the facts in a given case show that the employer was not negligent, he is not liable.

(2) In addition to proving negligence of the employer, the employee plaintiff must also prove in an action at common law that he was not guilty of any negligence which contributed to his injury or damage. If the employer and employee were both negligent, the employer is not liable.

(3) A third common-law defense is the fellow servant rule whereby an employer is not liable for injuries sustained by an employee if the injuries were caused by the negligence of a fellow servant, that is, a co-employee of the injured party. Fellow servants are employees of the same employer

who are engaged upon the same piece of work and are subject to special risks from the negligence of each other.

(4) At common law an employer is not liable to an employee for harm or injury caused by the unsafe condition of the premises, if the employee, with knowledge of the facts and understanding of the risks, voluntarily enters into or continues in the employment. This is a voluntary assumption of the risk by the employee.

Workmen's Compensation Acts. In order to provide speedier and more certain relief to employees, most States have adopted Workmen's Compensation Acts. These statutes create commissions or boards which determine whether an injured employee is entitled to receive compensation and, if so, how much. The common-law defenses discussed above are not available to employers in proceedings under these statutes. Such defenses are abolished, and the only requirement is that the employee be injured and that the injury arise out of and in the course of his employment. The amounts recoverable are fixed by statute for each type of injury, and are on a scale which is less than a court or jury would probably award in an action at common law. However, actions at law are not permitted to injured employees who come within the Workmen's Compensation Acts. The courts do not have jurisdiction over such cases except to review decisions of the board or commission, and then only to determine whether such decisions are in accordance with the statute.

Shop Right of Employer. A person possessing technical skills or scientific training may be employed in the research department of an employer for the purpose of making discoveries or inventions for the employer. The contract of employment in such cases invariably provides that the employee will assign to the employer all rights to such discoveries or inventions and to all patents which may be issued thereon.

On the other hand, a person may not be employed to make inventions but having an inventive mind and disposition may develop and perfect an invention through the use of materials and help furnished by the employer, and the use of the facilities in the shop of the employer. This invention may be sufficiently novel that upon application by the employee a patent is issued to him. The employer does not own this patent, and the employee is not required to assign it to the employer. However, the employer does have a license or shop right to use the invention in connection with the business conducted by the employer. The employer has a non-exclusive right to use the invention without paying royalty or license fees to the holder of the patent. This is called a shop right.

CASES

BASINGER v. HUFF

(1958) 98 Ga.App. 288, 105 S.E.2d 362.

CARLISLE, J. "The relation of principal and agent arises wherever one person, expressly or by implication, authorizes another to act for him, or subsequently ratifies the acts of another in his behalf." Code, § 4–101. Where, in an action by a landowner for the negligent burning of an outbuilding, pasture land, and personal property thereon, alleged to have been caused by the defendant through his agents, servants, or employees, the evidence shows that the defendant's fiancee went to his property which adjoined that of the plaintiff's to clean up around the house, and while so doing started a trash fire which she allowed to spread from the defendant's property to the plaintiff's, causing the damage sued for; and, where, from the only evidence introduced, it appeared that she did this while the defendant was at work and without his instructions, knowledge, or consent, and that the defendant had no notice of her actions until he was notified at his place of employment of the fire, and that all this took place two days prior to their wedding, such evidence was insufficient to show the relation of principal and agent between the defendant and his fiancee so as to charge the defendant with her negligence in the burning of the plaintiff's property. This is so notwithstanding the fact that the defendant testified in effect that though he did not know at the time that his fiancee was out at his place, had he known it, it would have been all right with him and he would have consented for her to go out there and clean up. [Citations.] Furthermore, the action of the defendant and his wife a few days thereafter, in going to the plaintiff and expressing regret for the damage and offering to pay the plaintiff for it, was not such a ratification of her acts as would charge him with her negligence as his agent. [Citation.] Since the plaintiff utterly failed to prove that the relationship of principal and agent, or master and servant, or employer and employee existed between the defendant and his fiancee at the time of the occurrence, the evidence demanded a verdict for the defendant and the trial court erred in denying the motion for judgment notwithstanding the verdict.

Judgment reversed.

On Motion for Rehearing

In the motion for rehearing, counsel for the defendant in error states that the evidence shows that the defendant and his fiancee went to his place in the country to see what cleaning up had to be done, and that a day or so later, his fiancee went out and started "this work" and let the fire get out and cause the damage; that the work that she did followed definite plans that they had jointly made. It is contended that this evidence showed that the defendant's fiancee was his agent and that he accepted the benefits of her work and thus ratified her act. An examination of the record and the brief of the evidence in this case fails to reveal any testimony supporting this contention. The testimony in the brief of evidence shows simply that the defendant's fiancee went out to the defendant's place to clean up his place without his knowledge, and there is not one word of evidence in the record before this court which would authorize the conclusion that she went out to his place pursuant to a prearranged plan between her and the defendant for her to do so. Furthermore, under the facts of this case, if it can be said that the defendant accepted whatever benefits accrued to him as a result of his fiancee's efforts, such acceptance could not constitute a ratification of her tort.

Rehearing denied.

GRAHAM v. McCORD

(1964 Tex.) 384 S.W.2d 897.

POPE, J. Fred McCord, while repairing an automobile in the service department of Goad Motor Company in San Antonio, was injured when Mrs. Walter Graham drove her car into the rear of the vehicle upon which he was working. McCord brought suit in Bexar County against both Mrs. Graham and her husband, Walter Graham, who reside in Randall County, Texas. After suit was filed but before service upon her, Mrs. Graham passed away. The venue hearing proceeded against Walter Graham as sole defendant, and the court overruled his plea * * *.

To hold defendant, Graham, in Bexar County, plaintiff had to prove, under Sec. 9a, Art. 1995, three things. One of them is "That such act or omission was that of the defendant, in person, or that of his servant, agent or representative acting within the scope of his employment." With Graham left in the case as the sole defendant, plaintiff had to prove that Mrs. Graham's tort was in law Mr. Graham's tort. This means that plaintiff had to prove that Graham was liable under principles of respondeat superior.

While a wife is not a general agent of her husband [citation], a husband can make his wife his agent. [Citations.] It is not mere agency, however, which fixes tort liability upon a principal. Only an agent whose principal has the right of control over the agent's physical movements in the performance of the thing authorized can hold his principal liable for torts. Principals are liable for the torts of only those agents who are subject to that kind of control which also establishes the master-servant relationship. * * *

* * * The wording of Sec. 9a shows that it was plainly intended that only those agents who fall within a master-servant relationship can bind their principals for torts. This is so because of the requirement that the servant, agent or representative must be shown to be "acting within the scope of his employment." The phrase, "scope of his employment" carries with it the requirement of control inherent in the master-servant relationship which will invoke the respondeat superior doctrine. The plaintiff, therefore, had the burden to prove that the husband had the right to control the physical conduct of his wife at the time and in respect to the very thing which caused the injury.

The evidence is that defendant, Graham, came to San Antonio from Happy, Texas, in Randall County, for the purpose of buying some cattle. His wife came with him so she could shop. She did all the driving. About nine o'clock on the morning of the accident, she drove Mr. Graham from the San Antonio hotel to the cattle sale several miles away. She told her husband to page her at Frost Brothers, where she planned to shop, if he wanted her to return and pick him up earlier than expected. He did not page her during the day and she went back for him about five in the afternoon. In the meantime, after she left him in the morning, she drove to Goad Motor Company to have some minor repairs made to the Cadillac car she was driving. When she drove in, she rammed the rear of the car that plaintiff was working on. Goad Motor checked the door hinges on the Cadillac, corrected a door vent, removed a rattle in the dash and adjusted the automatic dimmer. Mr. Graham did not know his wife was going to have any repairs made to the car and, from the record, there is nothing to show that he knew any repairs were needed. He had given her no instructions and had never heard of Goad Motor Company. He had asked her to do nothing for him except pick him up. There is no evidence of such measure of control over the wife's actions as inheres in a master-servant relationship unless we can find it supplied in some way from the marriage relationship.

The marriage relationship did not make defendant's wife his agent in the sense that he controlled her physical conduct. Marriage confers upon the wife an agency to purchase and contract for necessities. [Citation.] That, however, is not the test in the case of torts. Authority to make binding contracts does not supply the tort test for respondeat superior. In the case of torts one must have the right of control over another's physical conduct.

* * *

In our opinion, there is no evidence that the wife's tort was her husband's tort so that the husband can be held in an action which names him as the sole defendant. The judgment must be reversed.

(Judgment for defendant.)

McCARTY v. GREAT BEND BOARD OF EDUCATION

(1965) 195 Kan. 310, 403 P.2d 956.

FONTRON, J. * * * The evidence is not seriously in dispute and may be summarized briefly. The claimant, an elderly gentleman of some 72 years, is a plasterer by trade. On June 23, 1963, either the director or the secretary of the recreation commission called the claimant about patching some plaster in the building occupied and used by the commission. Claimant agreed to do the work but said that, although he would use his own hand tools, the commission would have to furnish the scaffold, the mortar box and the helpers. This was agreeable and claimant appeared for work the next morning, at which time the scaffold was not built, nor were the helpers there. The claimant then went home but returned later after receiving a call that everything was ready. At this time, Carl Soden, the director of the commission, showed claimant the work to be done upstairs and said he had some more in the downstairs hallway. Claimant thereupon began work, using the scaffold which had been put up and being assisted by two commission employees who mixed the mortar and carried it to the scaffold for claimant's use. Soon after commencing work, the claimant fell from the scaffold and sustained severe injuries, the extent of which is not material to this appeal.

* * *

In general, it may be said that an independent contractor is one who, in the exercise of an independent employment, contracts to do a piece of work according to his own methods and who is subject to his employer's control only as to the end product or final result of his work. [Citation.] On the other hand, an employer's right to direct and control the method and manner of doing the work is the most significant aspect of the employer-employee relationship, although it is not the only factor entitled to considera-

tion. An employer's right to discharge the workman, payment by the hour rather than by the job, and the furnishing of equipment by the employer are also indicia of a master-servant relation. [Citation.]

It is our opinion that, when measured by the foregoing standards, the recorded evidence sufficiently supports the findings adopted by the trial court. The record discloses, in addition to the facts already related, that claimant was being paid on an hourly basis; that Soden had the right to discharge claimant if the latter's work was unsatisfactory; and that Soden could have told claimant how he wanted the work done and claimant would have followed his directions. These are all circumstances indicating that claimant was an employee of the recreation commission.

The respondents suggest that claimant's employment was not covered by the act because the work being performed was not in pursuance of the commission's principal business. This suggestion, we believe, is without merit. An employer may not come within the provisions of the act as to some of its employees and not as to others. [Citation.] Furthermore, we cannot say that the repair and maintenance of a building occupied and used by the commission is unrelated to its business of furnishing recreational facilities for the people of Great Bend.

* * *

The judgment of the lower court is affirmed.

[Claimant held to be an employee, and entitled to workmen's compensation.]

———

MARTIN v. CLINTON

(1965) 239 Or. 541, 398 P.2d 742.

O'CONNELL, J. This is an action brought by a real estate broker to recover a commission claimed to have been earned in procuring a purchaser for defendant's restaurant. The case was tried without a jury. Plaintiff appeals from a judgment in favor of defendant.

Under a written contract executed by the parties, defendant agreed to pay plaintiff a commission for finding a buyer "ready and willing to enter into a deal for said price and terms, or such other terms and price as I may accept." We construe this language as an agreement to procure a purchaser ready, willing and *able* to purchase the property offered for sale.

The only question on appeal is whether there was sufficient evidence to support the trial court's finding that the prospective purchasers procured by defendant were not financially able to pay the purchase price, which was $52,000 of which $10,000 was to be paid down and the balance to be paid in installments. The trial court found as follows:

"That the said Klapperiches were not ready, willing and able to purchase the property of the defendant at the terms prescribed by the seller in that the Klapperiches did not have the experience or knowledge and primarily the financial ability to purchase the property upon the terms of the seller, in that the said Henry J. Klapperich was indebted to the extent that there were several unpaid judgments against him; that he had not sufficient capital to sustain the payments as required under the seller's terms and that he himself did not feel he could meet the requirements of the proposed terms of the contract."

There was sufficient evidence to support the foregoing finding. Plaintiff must show that the proposed purchasers had the ability not only to make the down payment but the installment payments as well. There was evidence from which the trial court could have reasonably concluded that the propective purchasers would not be able to make the deferred payments. There was a reasonable doubt as to whether the purchasers would be able to make the installment payments out of the operation of the restaurant and there was also reason to believe that if the purchasers could not make the payments from that source they might not be able to borrow money to meet the installments.

The judgment is affirmed.

DAVID v. SERGES

(1964) 373 Mich. 442, 129 N.W.2d 882.

SOURIS, J. When an agent purporting to act for his principal exceeds his actual or apparent authority, the act of the agent still may bind the principal if he ratifies it. The Restatement of Agency 2d, § 82, defines ratification thusly:

"Ratification is the affirmance by a person of a prior act which did not bind him but which was done or professedly done on his account, whereby the act, as to some or all persons, is given effect as if originally authorized by him."

"Affirmance" is defined in § 83 of the Restatement:

"Affirmance is either

"(a) a manifestation of an election by one on whose account an unauthorized act has been done to treat the act as authorized, or

"(b) conduct by him justifiable only if there were such an election."

Although Michigan cases in which ratification has been discussed usually have involved receipt of direct benefits by the ratifying principal evidence of receipt of benefits, while it lends plausibility to an allegation of ratification and, indeed, may in itself constitute ratification, is not a *sine qua non* of ratification. Paragraph (d) of the comment to § 82 of the Restatement, supra, discusses the matter in these terms:

"That the doctrine of ratification may at times operate unfairly must be admitted, since it gives to the purported principal an election to blow hot or cold upon a transaction to which, in contract cases, the other party normally believes himself to be bound. But this hardship is minimized by denying a power to ratify when it would obviously be unfair. See §§ 88–90. Further, if the transaction is not ratified normally the pseudo-agent is responsible; if not, it is because the third party knew, or agreed to take the risk, of lack of authority by the agent. In many cases, the third person is a distinct gainer as where the purported principal ratifies a tort or a loan for which he was not liable and for which he receives nothing. This result is not, however, unjust, since although the creation of liability against the ratifier may run counter to established tort or contract principles, the liability is self-imposed. Even one who ratifies to protect his business reputation or who retains unwanted goods rather than defend a law suit, chooses ratification as preferable to the alternative. * * * "

In this case the only testimony taken was plaintiff's, who testified that defendant's managing agent had borrowed from him $3,500 upon defendant's behalf and for use in defendant's business a retail meat market. Plaintiff further testified that defendant subsequently had paid to him $200 on the alleged loan and had upon several occasions stated to plaintiff that the full sum would eventually be paid. With this testimony in the record plaintiff rested his case and defendant, without likewise resting, moved for a judgment of no cause on the theory that plaintiff had failed to prove a *prima facie* case.

The trial court erred in granting defendant's motion. * * *

Even if borrowing money were not within the agent's actual or apparent authority, plaintiff's evidence, viewed favorably, was legally sufficient to establish defendant's liability for the alleged loan upon a theory of ratification. Thus, plaintiff's evidence was sufficient to require defendant to be put to his proofs.

Reversed and remanded. Costs to plaintiff.

FARM BUREAU MUTUAL INSURANCE CO. v. COFFIN

(1962) — Ind.App. —, 186 N.E.2d 180.

PFAFF, J. This action was begun by the appellee, Bonnie Eugene Coffin, to recover on an alleged oral contract of insurance between the appellee and the appellant through its employee, James R. Pierson, in which contract appellee's liability and property damage insurance was transferred to a new car and comprehensive and collision coverages were added to the policy. The appellant's answer denied that appellee had his automobile insured with the appellant except for bodily injury and property damage.

The issues having been formed, a trial was held and evidence was heard before the court without a jury, which resulted in a finding and judgment for the appellee in the sum of $1760.00, plus costs. A motion for a new trial and later an amended motion for a new trial were filed and overruled. * * *

The evidence discloses that the appellee, Bonnie Eugene Coffin, who was an assigned risk to the appellant, Farm Bureau Mutual Insurance Company, called the appellant's home office on December 13, 1955. When a girl answered the telephone, appellee stated that he wanted to transfer the insurance on his car. The call was switched to a second girl who in turn stated that she would connect appellee with Dick Pierson (James R. Pierson). When the appellee told James R. Pierson that he wanted to transfer the liability and property damage insurance on his 1953 Chevrolet to a new 1956 Buick and get additional collision and comprehensive insurance, the reply was: "O. K. you are covered." Pierson has a different version of this conversation, but in view of the fact that the appellee was successful he is entitled to the testimony most favorable to him.

Pierson also told the appellee that his application papers would be in the morning mail and the appellee should fill them out and return them. In completing these forms appellee, Coffin, did not properly mark the application to indicate that he desired the comprehensive and collision coverages.

The testimony indicates that James R. Pierson was not an insurance agent. At the time in question, he was Typing Supervisor in the Auto Underwriters Department. Transfers of insurance were routine matters; however evidence revealed the home office would only give additional coverage on written directives. The usual practice was to deal through an agent. There is no contrary testimony to the statements that Pierson had no authority to give collision coverage to an assigned risk.

The appellee had an accident one day after he talked to Pierson, that is, on December 14, 1955. This action was begun to recover for damage to the appellee's car which damage was caused by that accident.

* * *

The problem is whether the law applicable to special agents or that applicable to general agents should be followed in this case.

"The distinction between a general and special agent is very accurately and correctly stated by Mr. Wait, in his work on Law and Practice, vol. 1, p. 215, where it is said: 'A general agent is one who is authorized to transact all the business of his principal, or all his business of some particular kind, or at some particular place. The principal will be bound by the acts of a general agent, if the latter acted within the usual and ordinary scope of the business in which he was employed, notwithstanding he may have violated the private instructions which the principal may have given him, provided the person dealing with such agent was ignorant of such violation and that the agent exceeded his authority. [Citations.] The authority of an agent being limited to a particular business does not make it special; it may be as general in regard to that, as though its

range were unlimited. [Citation.] A special agent is one who is authorized to do one or more specific acts, in pursuance of particular instructions or within restrictions necessarily implied from the act to be done. The principal is not bound by the acts of a special agent, if he exceeds the limits of his authority. And it is the duty of every person who deals with a special agent to ascertain the extent of the agent's authority before dealing with him. If this is neglected, such person will deal at his peril, and the principal will not be bound by any act which exceeds the particular authority given.' " [Citations.]

* * *

Since the trial judge below found for the appellee and entered judgment, he must have concluded that Pierson was clothed with such authority that the appellee was justified in assuming that Pierson was a general agent. The question then is whether sufficient evidence was presented from which the trial judge could find that James R. Pierson had apparent authority to enter into an oral contract for the transfer of the appellee's liability insurance and the addition of comprehensive and collision insurance to the policy. The appellee called the appellant's home office and stated that he desired to transfer his insurance. He talked to two different girls who did not have authority to make such a transfer. Finally he was connected was James R. Pierson, who told the appellee that he had collision coverage as of that moment. We think that these facts are sufficient to sustain a finding that James R. Pierson had apparent authority to transfer the appellee's liability and property damage insurance and to add collision coverage.

When one has the appearance of a general agent the law is clear that a third person dealing with him is not bound to inquire into his specific authority, nor is the principal protected by secret limitations upon the authority of such an agent. The reason for the rule is that where one of two innocent persons must suffer because of the betrayal of a trust reposed in a third, the one who is most at fault should bear the loss. Since the principal put the agent in the position of trust, he is the one who should suffer the detriment. [Citations.] * * *.

Even if the trial court concluded that said James R. Pierson was a special agent, it appears, nevertheless, upon the record herein, that the evidence was amply sufficient to support the finding that he was clothed with the apparent authority of a general agent authorized to enter into the contract now in question on behalf of the appellant. The appellant has failed to show error by the record; therefore the judgment must be affirmed.

Judgment affirmed.

WASHINGTON BROADCASTING CO. v. GOOZH GIFTS

(1955 D.C.Mun.App.) 118 A.2d 392, 53 A.L.R.2d 1136.

CAYTON, C. J. This was a suit for advertising services rendered Goozh Gifts, Inc., by radio station WOL, owned by Washington Broadcasting Company. The defense was that Goozh had never contracted with WOL but had dealt with an advertising agency operated by one Shane and had paid Shane, and that after Shane had become bankrupt WOL demanded payment from Goozh. The trial judge found that plaintiff had not borne its burden of proving that Shane was the agent of Goozh, that there was no contractual relationship between WOL and Goozh, and that the evidence established that Shane was the agent of WOL. On this appeal plaintiff challenges these findings.

Testimony for plaintiff tended to show that the Goozh account was brought to WOL by Shane, that all the station's dealings were with Shane; that there was no formal contract between them, but simply an understanding under which all bills were sent to Shane. The president of WOL testified that he relied on the credit of Goozh, but admitted that he had never investigated Goozh directly. He admitted that on other occasions his station had in the usual course of business sued advertising agencies for monies owing on advertising accounts placed by them. He also admitted that the Shane agency was an "accredited agency" at the time the account was placed, that one of the factors of such accreditation was the agent's financial responsibility. It was also admitted that no one at WOL ever had any direct dealings with Goozh in connection with the account until after they learned of Shane's impending bankruptcy, and then for the first time they demanded payment of defendant.

* * * It was incumbent on plaintiff to establish that Shane was the agent of Goozh and contracted with WOL in Goozh's behalf. There was no written contract between any of the parties and there was only a loose method of dealing between WOL and Shane, based on trade practices and their earlier verbal understandings.

In view of the vague nature of the contractual arrangement, the surest criterion of liability is to be found in the intention of the parties. [Citations.] Granting that Shane was authorized to place advertising for Goozh, there was no evidence whatever of any intention that Goozh was to be liable to WOL. On the contrary it seems to have been established that WOL never intended to hold Goozh, but relied on Shane as its direct contracting party. And there was no evidence from which it could even be inferred that if Goozh paid Shane it would be doing so at its peril. It follows that plaintiff was not entitled to prevail.

There are not many decisions dealing with the particular relationship here involved, but those which have come to our attention seem to establish that the circumstances of each case and the agreements arrived at will determine whether an advertising agency is to be considered the agent of the advertising medium or of the advertiser. [Citations.]

Affirmed.

WASHINGTON v. COURTESY MOTOR SALES, INC.

(1964) 48 Ill.App.2d 380, 199 N.E.2d 263.

MURPHY, P. J. This is an action of fraud and deceit. The trial court struck the amended complaint and dismissed the action as to defendant Ford Motor Company, on the ground that the amended complaint, as to Ford, was "substantially insufficient in law." Plaintiff appeals.

In substance, the fraud alleged is that while plaintiff negotiated and paid for a new car, the automobile which was delivered to her had been previously used, and its speedometer had been set back. Charging fraud and deceit in the sale, plaintiff seeks damages totaling $50,018—being $1,018 compensatory and $49,000 exemplary.

The determinative question is whether the amended complaint alleges sufficient facts in law to support plaintiff's allegation that, for the purpose of selling a new Ford automobile to plaintiff, defendant Courtesy Motor Sales was an agent of the defendant Ford Motor Company.

The amended complaint alleges that defendant Courtesy is a "duly authorized franchised dealer for selling and distributing the products of Defendant, Ford Motor Company" and "acting as a franchised agent of the Ford Motor Company * * * executed a contract of sale and purchase with the Plaintiff on Courtesy Motor Sales New Car Division order blanks. * * * upon delivery of the automobile, Ford Motor Company, by and through its franchised agent, Courtesy Motor Sales, warranted the 1962 Ford Fairlane * * * to be new by giving Plaintiff a New Car Warranty."

* * *

After examining the amended complaint and all of its exhibits, we are not persuaded that it alleges sufficient facts to establish that an "authorized franchised Ford Dealer" is the agent of Ford Motor Company for the purpose of selling new cars. With the exception of "D" and "E," all of the exhibits clearly identify the seller of the automobile in question, defendant Courtesy Motor Sales, as an independent dealer. As the other exhibits refer only to defendant Courtesy, plaintiff asserts exhibits "D" and "E" are sufficient to establish the agency between defendants and to justify reliance by plaintiff on the acts of the alleged agent.

We believe that Exhibit "D" makes it clear that it is "your Ford Dealer," defendant Courtesy, which was making, on its own behalf, any warranties contained in the form. Exhibit "E" nowhere refers to defendant Ford Motor Company and continuously refers to "Ford Dealer."

We think it is a matter of common knowledge that the term "Authorized Ford Dealer" is in the nature of a trade-mark sign, which is used by independent dealers [citation] and means nothing more than a dealer who sells products which have a trade name carrying substantial good will. As stated in Westerdale v. Kaiser-Frazer Corp., 6 N.J. 571, 80 A.2d 91, 94 (1951):

"Nor does the fact that when a sale is made by a dealer to the ultimate purchaser a manufacturer's warranty goes with the automobile spell out the dealer as the agent of the manufacturer. It is merely incidental to the sale and in no wise by itself gives apparent authority or agency to the dealer. * * * The owner's service policy simply provided that defective material or workmanship would be replaced free by an authorized Frazer dealer or distributor without charge. This was an undertaking of the distributor, not the Kaiser-Frazer Corporation, and spelled out no agency existing between them."

We conclude that, absence the pleading of other facts which directly or circumstantially establish an agency relationship, plaintiff has failed to allege facts to show in law that an "authorized" or "franchised" dealer, in the sale of a new car, is an agent of the manufacturer rather than an independent merchant. [Citations.]

For the reasons given, the order of the trial court is affirmed.

BERENSON v. NIRENSTEIN

(1950) 326 Mass. 285, 93 N.E.2d 610.

QUA, C. J. Material allegations of the amended bill may be summarized as follows: The plaintiff lives in Newton and does business in Boston. The defendant Nirenstein lives and does business in Springfield. In January, 1949, Nirenstein called on the plaintiff in Boston, stated that all the shares of Bowles Lunch, Inc., which had its principal business in Springfield, could be purchased, and offered "to act as agent and broker for the plaintiff in seeking to buy" these shares. The plaintiff expressed interest. Nirenstein handed to the plaintiff detailed audits of Bowles Lunch, Inc., and "represented that he was peculiarly in a position to negotiate a purchase of these shares of stock on behalf of the plaintiff because of his knowledge of the situation and his acquaintance with the parties" in Springfield. The plaintiff then "retained the defendant [Nirenstein] as his broker and agent to effect a purchase of the shares of stock at an agreed commission of Five Dollars ($5.00) per share, to be paid by the plaintiff to the defendant [Nirenstein] at the time when such purchase was consummated, and the defendant [Nirenstein] agreed to act as such broker and agent on behalf of the plaintiff and to use his best efforts to purchase said shares of stock for him." After further conferences and some negotiations by Nirenstein, the plaintiff authorized that defendant to make a firm offer

of $70 a share for four thousand seven hundred four shares held by certain trustees. Thereafter Nirenstein, while still representing to the plaintiff that he was acting in the plaintiff's behalf, entered into a written agreement with the trustees for the purchase of the shares himself at $70 a share.

* * *

The trial judge sustained demurrers to the bill and stated, not without considerable justification, that he did so in reliance upon Salter v. Beal, 321 Mass. 105, 71 N.E.2d 872, and the cases there cited.

In Salter v. Beal the defendant had been employed by the plaintiff to appraise certain machinery which the plaintiff contemplated buying, and had bought the machinery for himself. This court held that no fiduciary obligation was shown. We do not intend to cast doubt upon the correctness of that decision on the facts. But we reached our conclusion in that case largely, though not wholly, because of a line of cases which appeared to be "authority for the proposition that a mere engagement to buy in behalf of another without more is not deemed in this Commonwealth to create a fiduciary relation." [Citation.] * * * On the other hand, it is established by a long line of decisions here and elsewhere that the relation of principal and broker is a fiduciary one involving trust and confidence. And a fiduciary is ordinarily chargeable as constructive trustee for the benefit of one rightfully entitled to property acquired by the fiduciary in breach of trust. Restatement: Restitution, §§ 190, 194.

So far as we are aware this is the first time when possible conflict between these two lines of cases has been squarely brought to the attention of this court by the issues and the argument in any case, and it has become necessary to consider them in relation to each other. The fiduciary obligation toward his principal of one who is acting in the full sense as a broker in the sale or purchase of property rests upon fundamental principles of business morality and honor which are of the highest public interest, and which it is the bounden duty of courts to preserve unimpaired. * * *

We think that the amended bill in this case sufficiently alleges the existence of a full and complete relation of principal and broker between the plaintiff and the defendant Nirenstein, out of which arose all the fiduciary obligations incident to such a relation, and that the bill sufficiently shows a breach of such obligations by the defendant Nirenstein at the instigation and to the profit of the defendant Bowles. The bill can therefore stand on the theory of a constructive trust in the shares of stock and their proceeds.

* * * The final decree dismissing the bill is reversed, with costs to the plaintiff.

WELLINGTON PRINT WORKS, INC. v. MAGID

(1965 D.C.E.D.Pa.) 242 F.Supp. 614.

WOOD, D. J. * * * The law is clear that "absent a contrary understanding the mere existence of an employer-employee relationship does not entitle the employer to ownership of an invention of the employee even though the employee uses the time and facilities of the employer * * *." [Citation.] However, if the employee does use his employer's time and facilities, the employer is entitled to a shop right in the invention. [Citations.] Such a shop right "passes from the employee to his employer *immediately* upon the making of the invention by the employee * * *." (Emphasis Supplied) [Citation.] A shop right is limited to a non-exclusive right in the employer to practice the employee's invention. [Citation.] * * *

The record in this case compels the conclusion that no agreement either express or implied existed between the plaintiff and the defendant, whereby the defendant was obligated to assign his inventions to the plaintiff. We found no *credible* evidence which reflects that the plaintiff had any arrangement whatsoever with the defendant.

However, we do conclude that because the defendant used his employer's time and facilities in developing these inventions that the plaintiff does have a non-exclusive license to practice them.

We reject the defendant's contention that because he experimented primarily on the late shifts that he was working on his own time and not Wellington's. When an employee receives a large salary of $25,000.00 a year and is an officer of a corporation his obligations do not cease at the close of normal business hours. Particularly is this true in a situation where the employer functions 24 hours a day. The method of production employed by Wellington in operating around the clock made the defendant's inventions possible.

PROBLEMS

1. A, the owner of certain unimproved real estate in Chicago, employed B, a real estate agent, to sell the property for a price of $5,000 or better and agreed to pay B a commission of 5% for making a sale. B negotiated with C who was greatly interested in buying the property and who was willing to pay as much as $6,000 for it. B made an agreement with C that if B could obtain A's signature to a contract to sell the property to C for $5,000, C would pay B a bonus of $500. B prepared and A signed a contract to sell the property to C for $5,000. C refuses to pay B the $500 as promised. A refuses to pay B the 5% commission. In an action by B against both A and C, what judgment?

2. In October, 1961, Black, the owner of the Grand Opera House, and Harvey entered into a written agreement leasing the Opera House to Harvey for five years at a rental of $30,000 a year. Harvey engaged Day as manager of the theatre at a salary of $175 per week plus 10 per cent of the profits. One of the duties of Day was to determine each night the amount of money taken in and, after deducting ex-

penses, to divide the profits between Harvey and the Manager of the particular attraction which was playing at the theatre. In September, 1966, Day went to Black and offered to rent the Opera House from Black at a rental of $37,500 per year, whereupon Black entered into a lease with Day for five years at this figure. When Harvey learned of and objected to this transaction, Day offered to assign the lease to him for $60,000 per year. Harvey refused, and brought an appropriate action seeking to have Day declared a trustee of the Opera House on behalf of Harvey. Decision?

3. X upon learning that Z, without any authority, entered into a contract with King Co. for the purchase of goods for X, said to Y "that was a good contract that Z made for me with King Co." Later, King Co. brought suit on the contract against X. Is X liable?

4. P, the owner of land, employs A, a real estate broker, to sell the land at a price of $15,-000, A to receive the usual commission for the sale. A discovers that the land is actually worth $25,000 so he furnishes his wife with $15,000 and she purchases the land under the name of Sadie Stone. A accepts his commission from P and then directs his wife to sell the land to Z for $25,000 which she does and turns over the money to A. P later learns of the transaction and sues A for (a) return of the commission paid; (b) $10,000. Decision?

5. X Department Store advertises from time to time that it maintains a barber shop in its store in charge of Y. Actually, Y is not an employee of the store but merely rents space in the store. Y, while shaving Z in the barber shop, negligently cut off one of Z's ears. Z sues X Department Store for damages. Decision?

6. P employed A to sell a parcel of real estate at a fixed price without knowledge that D had previously employed A to purchase the same property for him. P gave A no discretion as to price or terms and A entered into a contract of sale with D, upon the exact terms authorized by P. After accepting a partial payment P discovered that A was employed by D and brought an action to rescind. D resisted on the ground that admittedly P had suffered no damage for the reason that A had been given no discretion and the sale was made upon the exact basis authorized by P. Decision?

7. A, the owner of Blackacre, lists the property with B, a real estate broker, for the purpose of selling it. A tells B that he will sell the property for $10,000 cash. B finds a buyer C who is willing to pay $10,000 cash. B prepares a contract for the sale of Blackacre for $10,000 which C signs. Upon presenting this to A for signature, A refuses to sign the contract unless the buyer C agrees to pay the real estate broker's commission of 5%, or unless the price is changed to $10,500. C refuses to pay an additional $500, and the property is therefore not sold. In an action by B against A to recover a real estate broker's commission of 5%, or $500, what judgment?

8. An agent makes a contract in the name of his principal, by whom he represents he is authorized. The third person discovers that the agent has no authority and notifies the principal promptly by mail that he withdraws from the agreement. The principal replies at once that he authorizes the act. Should the withdrawal be permitted? What are the rights of the parties?

9. B made a written agreement with A, a real estate broker, whereby he made A his sole selling agent for a period of two years of a certain house and lot owned by B. The agreement fixed the minimum selling price of $10,000 and provided that A should receive for his services all over $10,000 which he could obtain for the property. Six months later, A tendered B $10,000 for the property and demanded the execution and delivery of a deed to him. B refused on the ground that A had no legal right to sell the house and lot to himself. Is A entitled to a deed?

10. Pluto Company employed two research engineers, A and B, for terms of five years "to make or cause to be made, improvements in the Pluto garden-type tractor, such improvements when made to belong to Pluto." Later C was hired orally for six months with the general understanding that he was to make garden-tractor improvements. During such employment, using the facilities and material of Pluto, A and C made garden tractor improvements and B invented a corn planting machine. After some controversy, Pluto brought actions against A, B and C to compel each to assign pending patent applications to Pluto or, in the alternative, to give Pluto irrevocable, royalty-free licenses for the use of the improvements. What results, as to each, A, B and C?

CHAPTER 13

LIABILITY OF PRINCIPAL TO THIRD PERSONS

Introductory. The ability of the principal to manifest his will through an agent imposes liability upon the principal to third persons for the acts or omissions of the agent. The agent possesses a power to cause his principal to become bound to third persons. A power may be defined as the ability of a person to produce a change in legal relations, and whether used rightfully or wrongfully, results in the creation of new rights and new duties.

The liability of a principal to third persons is based either upon contract or tort. The agent has the power to subject his principal to either or both types of liability.

Contractual Liability of the Principal. A principal is liable to third persons on contracts made in his behalf by his agent acting within the scope of his actual or apparent authority. Actual authority may be defined as the power of the agent to affect the legal relations of his principal by acts in accordance with the consent manifested by the principal to the agent. Apparent authority is the power of an agent or supposed agent to affect the legal relations of the principal with respect to a third person by acts in accordance with such principal's manifestations of consent to such third person as to an agency relationship. To the extent that things are as represented to be, apparent authority is actual authority. But apparent authority need not be actual, and the term is commonly used to distinguish this type of authority from that which is real or actual.

A fundamental rule of the law of agency is that the principal is not liable in contract for the unauthorized acts of an agent. To bind the principal, an agent must act strictly within the limits of the authority conferred upon him by the principal.

The authority of an agent is the power to create and affect legal relations of the principal with third persons. It is essential to the relationship of principal and agent and stems from the principal. There are two basic types of authority: actual, and apparent. Actual authority, which may be either express or implied, is real and genuine. Apparent authority may or may not be genuine. It is ostensible authority, and where things are what they appear to be it is genuine. However, apparent authority generally refers to a situation of no real authority, but one in which conduct, facts, and circumstances mislead third persons into reasonable reliance that authority exists. Whether the authority of the agent is express, implied, or apparent, it is effective to bind the principal in contract by acts of the agent or supposed agent within its scope.

Express Authority of Agent. The express authority of an agent is found in words of the principal, spoken or written. It is actual authority embodied in language directing or instructing the agent to do something specific. If A orally or in writing requests his agent B to sell A's automobile for $1500, B's authority to sell the car for this sum is express.

Implied Authority of Agent. Implied authority, like express authority, is real or actual. It is based upon the consent of the principal manifested to the agent. However, it is not found in express or explicit words of the principal, but is inferred from words or conduct manifested to the agent by the principal. Authority granted to an agent to accomplish a particular end necessarily includes authority to employ all means reasonably necessary for its accomplishment. Thus A authorizes B to manage his twelve-apartment building at a commission of five per cent of the rentals collected, and nothing more is said by A. In order to manage the building, B must employ a janitor, purchase fuel for heating, arrange for the painting and repair of screens, when needed, and occasionally redecorate an apartment. The authority of B to do these things and to incur reasonable maintenance and decorating expenses, while not expressly granted, is implied because these acts are necessarily incidental to the proper management of the building. Whatever may be reasonably inferred as necessary to complete the task assigned to the agent is impliedly authorized. Thus, if A merely instructs his agent B to drive A's new car from Detroit to San Francisco and says nothing further, B has implied authority to buy enough oil and gasoline to enable him to drive the car from Detroit to San Francisco.

Apparent Authority of Agent. Apparent authority is ostensible authority manifested by the principal to the third person with whom the agent deals. This manifestation may be by words or conduct. If A writes a letter to B authorizing him to sell A's automobile, and sends a copy of the letter to C, a prospective purchaser, B has express authority to sell the car, and as to C, apparent authority. If, A on the following day writes a letter to B revoking the authority to sell the car, but does not send a copy of the second letter to C who is not otherwise informed of the revocation, while B has no actual authority to sell the car, as to C he continues to have apparent authority. Or, suppose that B in the presence of A tells C that he is A's agent to buy lumber. A does not deny B's statement. C in reliance upon the statement ships lumber to A on B's order. A is bound to C, although in fact B had no actual authority. However, if B ordered lumber from D or E, A would not be liable to D or E, as no actual authority existed and as to D or E, there was no apparent authority.

Delegation of Authority. If an agent is authorized to appoint or select other persons, or subagents, to perform or assist in the performance of the agent's duties, or his act in doing so is ratified by the principal, the acts of the subagent are binding on the principal to the same extent as if they had been performed by the agent.

The appointment of an agent usually reflects confidence and reliance by the principal upon his personal skill, integrity, or other qualifications. The agent has been selected because of his supposed fitness to perform the task assigned to him by the principal. Therefore, an agent ordinarily has no power to delegate his authority or to appoint a subagent. This is the basis of the legal maxim, Delegata potestas non potest delegari, (delegated authority cannot be delegated). Thus, A employs or retains B to collect his accounts. B may not delegate this authority to C. A reposed trust and confidence in B, not in C. Likewise, if A retains Doctor B to remove his appendix, Doctor B may not delegate the performance of the operation to Doctor C without A's consent.

However, in certain situations, it is clear that the principal intended to permit the agent to delegate the authority granted to him, as where the authority contains an express power of substitution. Such an intention may also be gathered from the character of the business, the usages of trade, or the prior conduct of the parties. If a check is deposited in a bank for collection at a distant place, authority to the bank to employ another bank at the place of payment is necessarily implied.

If no authorization exists to delegate the agent's authority, but the agent nevertheless proceeds to do so, the acts of the subagent do not impose any obligation or liability whatever upon the principal to third persons. Likewise, the principal acquires no rights by reason of the acts of the subagent, except by his ratification of such acts. The subagent is responsible only to the agent who is his employer. The agent in turn is responsible to the principal for the acts or omissions of the subagent.

Where the agent appoints a subagent by authority of the principal, the subagent, with respect to the rights and duties of third persons, is the agent of the principal. The agent may have been authorized to employ a subagent on the principal's behalf, in which case a privity of contract is created between the principal and the subagent. Or the agent may have been authorized only to employ a subagent on his own responsibility in which case there is no privity of contract between the principal and the subagent. Insofar as the rights of third persons are concerned, it makes no difference so long as the employment of the subagent is authorized whether or not there is privity of contract between the principal and the subagent. Privity of contract is important only as to rights and duties as between the principal, the agent, and the subagent. If there is privity of contract between the principal and the subagent, the agent completely discharges his duty to the principal by the exercise of reasonable care in the selection of the subagent, and the agent is not liable for the acts or defaults of the subagent. However, if there is no privity of contract between the principal and subagent, but only as between the agent and subagent, the agent remains responsible to the principal for the acts and defaults of the subagent.

Agency of Necessity. In certain legal relations, under circumstances of necessity or emergency, the law confers authority upon an agent which he otherwise would not possess. Persons who are employed as railway conductors, station agents, or ordinary employees of a railroad company, who have no express, implied, or apparent authority to employ physicians or surgeons, may, in the event of a railroad accident in some remote area, become by operation of law authorized to employ a local physician or surgeon to attend an injured employee. The railroad company has no other person present who is authorized to obtain the needed medical or surgical attention. Hence, the authority to do so by reason of the emergency devolves upon the employee at the scene of the accident. As a general rule, any unforeseen contingency in which the interests of the principal require protection and where it is not practicable for an agent to communicate with his principal confers upon the agent the requisite authority to appoint another agent to act on behalf of the principal.

Admissions of Agent. The admission of a fact by a party to a lawsuit is always usable against him. The admission of a party's agent is admissible against the principal if within the scope of the agent's authority. However, an agency relationship may not be proved by a statement of the agent. In order that the statement of an agent against the principal be admitted into evidence, the relation of principal and agent must first be proved. It must appear that the person making the statement was acting as an agent in order that an admission of such person will bind the principal. A statement by a railway detective that he was an employee of the railroad company would not be admissible to prove his employment. However, once the employment was established, a statement made by such detective to the police that a porter employed by the railroad company absconded with certain baggage belonging to a passenger would be admissible against the company.

Notice to Agent. When, in the course of his employment, an agent acquires knowledge, or receives notice, of any fact which is material to the business in which he is employed, the principal is thereby deemed to have notice of such fact. This is generally true even though the agent acquires the knowledge while acting in some other transaction or for some other principal. However, such notice is not imputed to the principal if acquired by the agent confidentially for another principal under circumstances that it would be a breach of his duty to the other principal to disclose it. Nor is it imputed to the principal if the agent is engaged in perpetrating an independent fraud on his own account, or where the agent is openly acting adversely to his principal.

Scope of Particular Agencies. Certain well-established rules have developed with reference to particular types of agencies.

No authority to sell is to be inferred from the mere possession by an agent of the principal's goods, unless the agent is a factor, one engaged regularly in the business of selling the goods of others for a commission. A factor of goods is distinguished from a broker in that the broker does not have possession of the goods whereas the factor does have possession. A further exception is the entrusting of the possession of goods to a dealer whose business is the selling of goods of that description, that is, the voluntary creation of a peculiarly deceptive bailment situation within Section 2–403(2) of the Code.

Authority to sell land normally includes only authority to obtain a prospective buyer and does not include authority or power to bind the principal by a contract to sell. An agent who is expressly authorized in writing to convey title to land is thereby authorized to receive any part of the purchase price which is payable at the time, but is not authorized to receive deferred payments of the purchase price.

Authority to sell personal property confers authority to sell for cash and not for credit, and at a private sale and not at auction, unless expressly consented to by the principal. Authority to buy, however, impliedly confers authority upon the agent to buy at an auction sale.

Unless otherwise agreed, authority to buy or to sell property for the principal includes authority to agree upon the terms, to demand or make the usual representations and warranties, to receive or execute the instruments usually required, to pay or receive so much of the purchase price as is to be paid at the time of the transfer, and to receive possession of the goods if a buying agent, or to surrender possession of them if a selling agent.

An agent authorized to buy or sell has no implied authority to rescind or modify the terms of the sale after its completion except to correct for fraud or obvious mistake. An agent employed to carry on repeated dealings with customers, as in the course of selling at retail, may have authority to make adjustments. However, this situation is to be distinguished from that of the agent employed to conduct a single transaction. His authority terminates upon the completion of the transaction.

Authority of an agent to receive payment due to his principal will be implied whenever it is a necessary and usual incident of the business transacted and usually accompanies it. Thus, as agent in possession of his principal's goods, or entrusted with documents representing title to the goods, with authority to sell them is impliedly authorized to receive payment upon delivery of the goods or transfer of the documents. This is not true of a salesman who merely solicits and takes orders for goods which are shipped by the principal directly to the customer.

Authority given an agent merely to purchase goods does not include authority to pay for them unless the agent receives possession of the goods or of the documents representing title to the goods.

An agent is not impliedly authorized to borrow money on behalf of his principal unless such borrowing is an incident to the performance of the acts which he is authorized to perform. Thus, A employs B as a paymaster whose duty is to verify invoices and to pay them. B usually makes prompt payment of invoices and thereby takes advantage of the discount allowed. An invoice is presented to B at a time when the funds in A's bank account are insufficient to pay it. Without consulting A, B borrows money at the bank in A's name in order to pay the invoice. B's act in borrowing the money is not authorized. However, if the principal A were away on a business trip and telegraphed B to send him $2,000 immediately by Western Union, B's borrowing of this sum at the bank in A's name would be authorized.

Authority of an agent to draw, accept, make, or indorse bills of exchange or promissory notes is not implied unless necessarily incident to the performance of the acts which the agent is authorized to perform for his principal. Where the agent is managing a business in which it is customary to accept notes or checks of customers in payment for goods or services, the agent has authority to indorse the checks or discount the notes on behalf of the principal. However, this power is confined to the business of the agency and the agent is not authorized to execute commercial paper in the name of the principal for the benefit of the agent or to execute accommodation paper.

An agent has no implied authority to make warranties of the goods that he is authorized to sell except warranties that are usual and customary. Thus, A authorizes B to sell a certain quantity of A's flour. It is a customary trade usage in the community for the seller of flour to warrant that it is freshly milled. In selling the flour to C, B warrants (1) the flour is freshly milled, and (2) the flour will retain its mill freshness after a sea voyage in the tropics. The first warranty is authorized, but the second one is not.

General authority to manage or conduct business transactions for the principal, unless otherwise agreed, impliedly confers authority upon the agent to buy property for the principal and to sell property of the principal to the extent that such purchases or sales are usual and customary in such transactions or reasonably necessary to their accomplishment. In such case, the authority is to buy or sell at the market price, if any, otherwise at a reasonable price.

The interpretation of authorization to manage a business as set forth in Section 73 of the Restatement of the Law of Agency, 2d, is:

> Unless otherwise agreed, authority to manage a business includes authority:
> (a) to make contracts which are incidental to such business, are usually made in it, or are reasonably necessary in conducting it;
> (b) to procure equipment and supplies and to make repairs reasonably necessary for the proper conduct of the business;
> (c) to employ, supervise, or discharge employees as the course of business may reasonably require;
> (d) to sell or otherwise dispose of goods or other things in accordance with the purposes for which the business is operated;
> (e) to receive payment of sums due the principal and to pay debts due from the principal arising out of the business enterprise; and
> (f) to direct the ordinary operations of the business.

Tort Liability of Principal. A principal may authorize his agent to commit a tortious act with respect to the person or property of a third person. In such case the principal is clearly liable to the third person by application of the maxim que facit per alium, facit per se. Thus, if A directs his agent B to enter upon C's land and cut timber, and neither A nor B have any right to do so, the cutting of the timber is a trespass and A is liable to C for having committed the trespass. Or, suppose that A instructs his agent B to make certain representations as to A's property which B is authorized to sell. A knows that the representations are false, but B does not. The making of such representations by B to C who in reliance thereon buys the property is a deceit practiced by A upon C. For this tort A is liable to C in damages.

The Doctrine of Respondeat Superior. A principal may be liable for a tort committed by his agent which he did not authorize, even one which is in flagrant disobedience of his instructions to the agent, where the tort was committed by the agent in the course of his employment. This is a form of liability without fault and is based upon the doctrine of respondeat superior, i. e., let the superior respond. The rationale of this doctrine is that one who multiplies his business activities through the use of agents and employees, is liable for their negligence in carrying out the business purposes for which they were employed. It is the price which the employer pays for thus enlarging the scope of his business activities. It does not matter how carefully the employer selected the employee, if in fact the latter negligently injured a third person while engaged in the business of the employer.

The wrongful act of the agent or employee must be connected with the employment and within the scope of the employment in order that the principal be held liable for resulting injuries or damage to third persons.

The Restatement of the Law of Agency, 2d, gives two illustrations under the comment to section 235, at page 522:

A is delivering gasoline for P. He lights his pipe and negligently throws the blazing match into a pool of gasoline which has dripped upon the ground during the delivery and which ignites. For the resulting harm, P is subject to liability.

A, while driving as chauffeur for P, negligently throws his lighted cigarette from the window of the car into a passing load of hay, not intending to ignite it, but careless as to where the cigarette falls. P is not liable for this act.

The difference in result in these two situations is that the negligence of the employee delivering the gasoline relates directly to the manner in which he is handling the goods in his custody and his conduct with respect to the gasoline which is under his control, whereas the negligence of the cigarette smoking chauffeur is unrelated to his management or control of the car he is driving and is not a part of or incident to the services of a chauffeur. If the chauffeur while driving his employer's car on an errand for his employer suddenly decided that he would use his pistol and shoot at pedestrians on the sidewalk for target practice, the employer would not be liable to the pedestrians. This willful and intentional misconduct is not related to the performance of the services for which the chauffeur was employed. The same rule applies to unrelated negligent misconduct of an employee.

If A employs B to deliver merchandise in a given city to A's customers, and while driving a delivery truck in going to or returning from a place of delivery B negligently causes the truck to hit and injure C, A is liable to C for the injuries sustained. But if, after making the scheduled deliveries, B drives the truck to a neighboring city to visit a friend and while so doing negligently causes the truck to hit and injure C, A is not liable. In such case, B is said to be on a "frolic of his own." He has deviated from the purpose of his employment and was using A's truck to accomplish purposes of his own and not the business of his employer. Of course, in all of these situations the wrongdoing agent B is personally liable to C as a tortfeasor.

In addition to the liability of a principal or employer based upon the rule of *respondent superior*, a principal may be held liable in damages for his own negligence or recklessness in carrying on an activity by means of servants or agents. The Restatement of the Law of Agency, 2d, Section 213 provides:

> *Principal Negligent or Reckless.* A person conducting an activity through servants or other agents is subject to liability for harm resulting from his conduct if he is negligent or reckless:
>
> (a) in giving improper or ambiguous orders of in failing to make proper regulations; or
>
> (b) in the employment of improper persons or instrumentalities in work involving risk of harm to others;
>
> (c) in the supervision of the activity; or
>
> (d) in permitting, or failing to prevent, negligent or other tortious conduct by persons, whether or not his servants or agents, upon premises or with instrumentalities under his control.

Criminal Liability of Principal. A principal is not ordinarily liable for the unauthorized criminal acts of his agents. One of the elements of a crime is a guilty mind, and this element is not present where the act of the agent was not authorized, so far as criminal responsibility of the principal is concerned. The act of an agent may be both tortious and criminal. If connected to and committed in the course of the agent's employment, the principal will be liable civilly in damages but not criminally. However, as to certain offenses, a principal may be liable criminally for the acts of his agent as in the case of the publication of a criminal libel in a newspaper, or with respect to certain statutory crimes relating to a subject matter as to which a person is compelled at his peril to see that the law is not disobeyed, such as the sale of liquor to minors or to intoxicated persons, or the sale of unwholesome or adulterated food.

Torts of Independent Contractor; Non-Delegable Duty. An independent contractor is not the agent or servant of the person for whom he is performing work or rendering services. Hence, the doctrine of respondeat superior does not apply to torts committed by an independent contractor. Nevertheless, certain duties imposed by law are non-delegable and a person may not escape the consequences of their non-performance by contract with an independent contractor. A landowner who permits an independent contractor to maintain a dangerous condition on his premises, such as an excavation adjoining a public sidewalk which is unprotected by a guard rail or lights at night, is liable to a member of the public who is injured as a result of falling into the excavation. Or, in the case of the erection of a faulty or defective scaffolding on a building by an independent contractor, the owner of the building is liable by statute in certain States for injuries to employees of the independent contractor who are injured as a result of using the defective scaffolding.

Automobile Guest Statutes. A majority of the States have enacted statutes which relieve the operator of an automobile from civil liability for injuries sustained by a guest where the operator has been guilty only of ordinary negligence, that is, merely failing to use due care under the circumstances. At common law, a guest in an automobile may recover damages resulting from the ordinary negligence of the operator. Under automobile guest statutes, a guest, that is, one who is a non-paying passenger in the automobile, is not permitted to recover unless the misconduct of the operator was wilful, wanton, or grossly negligent. A principal is protected by the statute to the extent that his agent is protected where the agent operates an automobile for the purpose of the principal and his ordinary negligence results in injury to a non-business guest.

Typical of these statutes is Chapter 95½, Section 9–201 of the Illinois Revised Statutes, as follows:

> *"Liability for Bodily Injury to or Death of Guest.* No person riding in or upon a motor vehicle or motorcycle as a guest without payment for such ride, or while engaged in a joint enterprise with the owner or driver

of such motor vehicle or motorcycle, nor his personal representative in the event of the death of such guest, shall have a cause of action for damages against the driver or operator of such motor vehicle or motorcycle, or its owner or his employee or agent for injury, death or loss, in case of accident, unless such accident shall have been caused by the wilful and wanton misconduct of the driver or operator of such motor vehicle or motorcycle or its owner or his employee or agent and unless such wilful and wanton misconduct contributed to the injury, death or loss for which the action is brought.

Nothing contained in this section shall be construed to relieve a motor vehicle or motorcycle carrier of passengers for hire of responsibility for injury or death sustained by any passenger for hire."

CASES

IN RE UNION CITY MILK CO.

(1951) 329 Mich. 506, 46 N.W.2d 361.

CARR, J. The facts disclosed by the record in this case appear in certain exhibits, and in statements prepared by counsel representing the parties to the case which were submitted on stipulation to the circuit judge for his consideration. On November 19, 1947, James W. Patterson and Frances C. Patterson, his wife, negotiated a loan from E. Hill & Sons State Bank, Colon, Michigan, in the sum of $7,231.82. A note evidencing the obligation was executed, payable in installments with interest at 6% per annum. By way of security Mr. and Mrs. Patterson gave a chattel mortgage on two described trucks and two milk routes of the Union City Milk Company, a corporation herein referred to as the milk company. An assignment was executed by Mr. Patterson authorizing the milk company to make certain payments to the bank out of

his bimonthly pay checks. Payments substantially reducing the amount of the indebtedness were made on the note.

At the time of the transaction referred to the manager of the milk company was R. K. Cooney, the father of Mrs. Patterson. Presumably for the purpose of enabling his son-in-law and daughter to obtain the loan from E. Hill & Sons State Bank, he executed the following instrument:

"Colon, Michigan
Nov. 19th, 1947

"We hereby declare ourselves to guaranty both Principal and Interest of the Loan of James W. Patterson and Frances M. Patterson for $7231.82 to E. Hill & Sons State Bank, Colon, Michigan dated November 19th, 1947 for 37 months.

"It is our understanding that on notice of default from said Bank that we will pay up said loan within 30 days after receipt of notice of default. In case that guaranty is exercised it is understood that we are to take the place of the mortgagee and take over what security is offered in this case a 1947 Ford Truck with Milk Body and Milk Route No. 600 and a 1944 Chevrolet 1½ Ton Truck with Milk Body and Route #1400.

"This guaranty is signed by an Officer having legal right to bind the Company thru authorization of the Board of Directors.

"Union City Milk Co.
"S/R. K. Cooney, Mgr."

Before the loan was finally closed an officer of the bank telephoned the president of the milk company, who was also a director, and was, it appears, "given to understand" that Mr. Cooney was authorized to execute the guaranty above quoted. There is nothing in the record to indicate that the other members of the board of directors had any knowledge whatever of the guaranty, or that the board had ever authorized the manager to execute any such undertaking. The books of the corporation did not show the existence of the potential liability.

* * *

It does not appear that the manager of the company had at any time been authorized by its board of directors to execute a contract of guaranty in connection with its business. Neither does it appear that he had previously undertaken to exercise any such authority.

* * *

Attention is called by appellant to the declaration in the contract of guaranty as to the authority of the manager to execute it, such statement being in effect that he had such right because of authorization by the board of directors. Such statement indicates a recognition that the parties at the time considered express authority requisite to a binding guaranty. Appellant was not entitled to rely on the statement of the manager with reference to the authority granted to him. Agency may not be established by proof of declarations by the supposed agent. [Citation.] Nor may the extent of the authority of an agent be shown by testimony as to his acts and conduct not within the actual or implied scope of the powers granted to him by his principal. [Citation.]

Authority to bind the principal by a contract of guaranty or suretyship is not ordinarily to be implied from the existence of a general agency. In 2 C.J.S., Agency, § 106, p. 1269 it is said:

"* * * such a contract is extraordinary and unusual and so not normally within the powers accruing to an agent by implication, however general the character of the agency; ordinarily the power exists only if expressly given. Consequently a manager, superintendent, or the like, of business or property cannot ordinarily bind his principal as surety for third persons.

"In the absence of special authority actually or ostensibly empowering him so to do, an agent may not pledge the principal's credit for the debts of others who have assumed to buy or otherwise contract on the principal's credit.

"Where the agent in so contracting exceeds his instructions or the limitations of his authority, of which other party has knowledge or notice, the latter cannot hold the principal as a surety upon any asserted implication or appearance of authority."

In the case at bar it is apparently assumed by counsel that the purpose of the loan to Mr. and Mrs. Patterson was to enable them to purchase the milk routes and the trucks covered by the chattel mortgage, and that Mr. Patterson thereafter operated the routes for some time. It may be inferred that he used the trucks in connection with such operation. However, it does not appear that there was any agreement between himself and the milk company in any way obligating him to do so. Insofar as this record discloses, he might have discontinued hauling milk. Neither does it appear that the company was actually benefited by the use of property purchased with the proceeds of the loan. Even if such were the case, the fact still remains that appellant failed to show before the trial court that the board of directors had knowledge of the existence of the contract of guaranty.

* * *

The order of the trial court is affirmed.

PORSHIN v. SNIDER

(1965) — Mass. —, 212 N.E.2d 216.

SPALDING, J. This is an action of contract in two counts. One is against the Universal Shoe Corporation (Universal); the other is against Hyman Snider individually.

The evidence most favorable to the plaintiff is as follows. In April, 1945, Snider "negotiated with the plaintiff * * * to come to work in Sanford, Maine * * * [for Universal] at * * * ($125.00) per week, plus board and room valued at * *

($30.00) per week." At this time the plaintiff was employed as a stitching room foreman in a shoe factory in Haverhill at $100 per week. The plaintiff had been in the shoe business since 1905 and was "interested in his future security." Snider told the plaintiff "he would have a permanent job with [Universal] 'as long as it was in business' and if the * * * [plaintiff] 'wouldn't be able to work * * * [Snider] would take care of * * * [him]' * * *. 'You got security as long as the factory exists, you will work with me.'" Relying on this arrangement, the plaintiff gave up his job in Haverhill and worked with Universal in Sanford, Maine, for thirteen years. Snider was general manager of Universal at the time of the hiring "with authority to hire and fire." He had been general manager for over twenty years and continued as such throughout the period of the plaintiff's employment. In 1957 the plaintiff had a stroke but came back to work after seven weeks. In 1958 Snider offered the plaintiff $600 if he would resign from his job but the plaintiff refused. On the following day "Snider fired him." Motions for directed verdicts presented by the defendants were allowed by the judge subject to the plaintiff's exceptions.

1. Apart from the question of Snider's authority, we assume that a contract of this sort would be enforceable to the extent indicated in Carnig v. Carr, 167 Mass. 544, 46 N.E. 117, 35 L.R.A. 512. However, no evidence was offered which could support a finding of either express or implied authority in Snider to bind the corporation by this type of contract. The mere fact that he was general manager of Universal, with authority to hire and fire, cannot be said to clothe him with ostensible authority to make a contract for permanent employment. [Citations.] Nor was there any evidence which would warrant a finding of ratification by Universal. The direction of the verdict, therefore, in favor of Universal on the first count reveals no error.

2. The direction of the verdict in favor of Snider on the second count was likewise proper. It is plain that he was attempting to contract on behalf of Universal. "Unless otherwise agreed, a person making or purporting to make a contract for a disclosed principal does not become a party to the contract." Restatement 2d: Agency, § 320 and comment a. [Citations.] Exceptions overruled. [Judgment for defendants affirmed.]

MAGENAU v. AETNA FREIGHT LINES

(1958 C.A.3d) 257 F.2d 445.

GOODRICH, J. This is an appeal from the District Court for the Western District of Pennsylvania upon a judgment entered in a death by wrongful act case in favor of the administrator of Norman Ormsbee, Jr. The recovery was based on the alleged negligence of the defendant and there was also a finding by the jury that the defendant was guilty of "wanton conduct." The defendant attacks the verdict and judgment on several grounds. The case is in federal court by diversity only and we look to the relevant Pennsylvania decisions.

The first question involves points of tort and agency law. The driver of the truck which was leased to the defendant, Aetna Freight Lines, Inc., had been encountering difficulties while enroute to Midland, Pennsylvania. A day or two prior to the accident there had been brake trouble which defendant's superintendent at Buffalo had endeavored to adjust. On the afternoon of the day in question the driver, Schroyer, stopped at Jones's Tavern at Waterford, Erie County, Pennsylvania. There he complained to the proprietor that he was having trouble with his brakes. Shortly thereafter the decedent, Ormsbee, and a man named Herbert Brown, entered the tavern. Schroyer offered Brown

$25 if he would accompany him on the remainder of the trip to Midland stating that he, Schroyer, was afraid he was going to run into trouble. Brown declined the offer. Schroyer thereupon asked Ormsbee to accompany him and he agreed to for the price of $25. The two men got into the tractor. This was the last time they were seen alive. Later that evening state police received a call and in answer thereto found the tractor-trailer off the highway over an embankment and both men dead. This is all the evidence we have except further details of the difficulties which the driver had had with this truck in the earlier part of his trip and the result of a post accident investigation.

The jury was given forthright interrogatories on this phase of the case. They are, with the answers thereto, as follows:

1. "Under the evidence in this case, do you find that an unforeseen contingency arose which made it reasonably necessary for the protection of the defendant's interests that the driver Charles Schroyer engage the decedent Norman Ormsbee, Jr. to accompany him for the remainder of the trip?" Answer: "Yes."

2. "Was the defendant Aetna Freight Lines, Inc. negligent in the maintenance of the equipment or in the operation of the vehicle by the driver Charles Schroyer, either or both, which negligence was the proximate cause of the death of Norman Ormsbee, Jr.?" Answer: "Yes."

3. "Do you find that the braking equipment upon the vehicle in question, considering its size and load and road conditions prevailing, was in proper working order on March 20, 1956?" Answer: "No."

* * *

The rule of law governing the situation is not so difficult. It is stated in the Restatement as follows:

"If a servant is authorized or apparently authorized to invite persons upon the vehicle

* * * of the master, a person so invited is a guest of the master and if the entry is for business purposes, he is a business visitor." 1 Restatement, Agency 2d § 242, com. b (Tent. Draft No. 4, 1956) (not in 1st ed.).

"Unless otherwise agreed, an agent is authorized to appoint another agent for the principal if:

"* * *

"(d) an unforeseen contingency arises making it impracticable to communicate with the principal and making such an appointment reasonably necessary for the protection of the interests of the principal entrusted to the agent." 1 Restatement, Agency 2d § 79(d) (Tent. Draft No. 3, 1955) (same as in 1st ed.).

The Pennsylvania cases emphasize the necessity of the "emergency." [Citations.]

* * *

The jury's finding is a forthright answer to a forthright question. The trial judge who heard all the testimony was satisfied with it. We do not think on this state of the record that we would be justified in setting it aside.

[Judgment reversed, upon the ground that the sole remedy of the plaintiff is under the Pennsylvania Workmen's Compensation Act.]

REGO v. THOMAS BROTHERS CORPORATION

(1960) 340 Mass. 334, 164 N.E.2d 144.

COUNIHAN, J. In this action of tort the plaintiff seeks to recover damages for personal injuries sustained on May 20, 1957, as the result of an altercation between the plaintiff and one Clark, an employee of the defendant. The action comes here upon the exception of the defendant to the denial of its motion for a directed verdict. There was no error.

The evidence, in its aspects most favorable to the plaintiff, showed that Clark was employed by the defendant as superintendent of construction work on a public highway in the city of New Bedford, known as Phillips Road. During the course of the work several large boulders had rolled onto land of a Mrs. Sylvia abutting the highway. She was a niece of the plaintiff who lived with her in a house on this land.

On the morning of the day of the assault Mrs. Sylvia met Clark and ordered him to remove the boulders from this land. Upon his refusal to do so, she complained to the State engineer in charge of the job. He thereupon ordered Clark to remove the boulders and carry them off to a dump. As a result Clark returned to Mrs. Sylvia's land with two other employees of the defendant and began the work of removing the boulders.

Mrs. Sylvia appeared and told Clark that she had changed her mind and to stop. While she and Clark were arguing about it, the plaintiff came onto the land and ran up to Clark and in a loud voice told Clark to leave the boulders where they were. An altercation followed during which Clark struck the plaintiff two severe blows on his face breaking his jaw. Clark was forty-eight years old, about six feet in height, and weighed one hundred ninety pounds. The plaintiff was sixty-five years old, about five feet five inches in height, and weighed one hundred twenty-two pounds. The plaintiff testified that he never struck or attempted to strike Clark.

It was early said in Levi v. Brooks, 121 Mass. 501, at page 505, "The test of the liability of the master is, that the act of the servant is done in the course of doing the master's work, and for the purpose of accomplishing it. If so done it is the act of the master, and he is responsible 'whether the wrong done be occasioned by negligence, or

by a war.ton and reckless purpose to accomplish the master's business in an unlawful manner." [Citations.]

Exceptions overruled.

[Judgment for plaintiff upheld.]

HEIMS v. HANKE
(1958) 5 Wis.2d 465, 93 N.W.2d 455.

WINGERT, J. Appellant contends that there was no evidence of actionable negligence on his part, that William's negligence, if any, could not properly be imputed to defendant, that no nuisance was established, that plaintiff's negligence was the sole cause of the accident, and that the trial court erred in excluding certain evidence.

The finding that the icy condition of the sidewalk was caused by the negligence of the defendant is supported by sufficient evidence.

The court could properly find that William, the nephew, was negligent in spilling water on the sidewalk in freezing weather and doing nothing to prevent the formation of ice or to remove or sand it, or to warn pedestrians of it. While the day was not too cold for washing a car bare-handed, the car was in the bright sunlight while the sidewalk where the water was spilled was then or soon would be in the shade of the house. The court could well infer that one in the exercise of ordinary care would have foreseen the formation of a slippery condition and would have done something to protect users of the sidewalk.

It was also permissible to conclude from the evidence that defendant was liable for injuries resulting from William's negligence, on the principle respondeat superior. Probably William was defendant's servant in carrying the water. A servant is one employed to perform service for another in his affairs and who, with respect to his physical conduct in the performance of the service, is subject to the other's control or right to control. Restatement 1 Agency, 2d sec. 220. The evidence permits the inference that William was in that category, although he was an unpaid volunteer. One volunteering service without any agreement for or expectation of reward may be a servant of the one accepting such services. Restatement 1 Agency, 2d Sec. 225. The illustration given in Comment a under that section is pertinent:

"A, a social guest at P's house, not skilled in repairing, volunteers to assist P in the repair of P's house. During the execution of such repair, A negligently drops a board upon a person passing upon the street. A may be found to be a servant of P."

If William was not the employee or servant of the defendant in the strict sense, he was certainly defendant's agent in fetching water from the faucet, although he received no compensation. [Citations.] A principal is subject to liability for physical harm to the person of another caused by the negligence of an agent who is not a servant, where the principal is under a duty to have care used to protect others and he confides the performance of the duty to the agent. [Citations.]

When defendant sent his agent to carry water across the sidewalk in freezing weather, he was under a duty to have care used to protect users of the sidewalk from ice, and since he confided the performance of that duty to William, he was responsible for William's negligence in the premises.

Defendant relies on Walley v. Patacke, 271 Wis. 530, 74 N.W.2d 130, for the proposition that owners of property abutting a city street are not responsible for injuries resulting from failure to remove accumulations of snow and ice from the sidewalk. The proposition and the case cited relate only to natural accumulations of snow and ice. One who negligently creates an artificial accumulation of ice on a public sidewalk may be liable to one injured thereby. [Citations.]

Since the finding of negligence attributable to defendant is sustainable, there is no need to consider whether the condition constituted a nuisance.

* * *

Judgment affirmed.

GREENBAUM v. BROOKS

(1964) 110 Ga.App. 661, 139 S.E.2d 432.

[Action to recover damages for false imprisonment. Judgment for plaintiff.]

BELL, P. J. * * * There is evidence to the effect that plaintiff was taken into a defendant's office, the door was closed and the interrogator placed a chair against the door and sat in the chair. The plaintiff was then questioned regarding stolen money. At least twice during the interrogation the plaintiff asked to leave. Plaintiff testified he was afraid to leave and was at the time physically afraid of the interrogator. On one occasion plaintiff stood up to leave but was shoved back and told that "You're not through yet." This evidence alone, although contradicted, was sufficient to create a jury issue on the false imprisonment of the plaintiff's person and to support their affirmative finding that he was illegally restrained.

* * *

The defendants contend they are not liable for any illegal restraint of the plaintiff's person since the interrogator was an independent contractor and not the defendants' agent.

While there is evidence in the record showing that the interrogator was an investigator for a detective agency with whom the defendants had contracted to conduct "purchase tests" in the defendants' store, there is nothing specific in the written contract between the defendants and the detective agency relating to oral interrogations. For this reason the contract is not at all inconsistent with a finding that at the time of plaintiff's detention the investigator was acting no longer as agent of the independent contractor, but instead as defendants' agent. Add to this the following uncontradicted facts shown by the evidence: (1) One of the defendants, together with the investigator, planned the "mutually suggested" interrogation of plaintiff. (2) One defendant provided his private office on the defendants' premises as the place for conducting the interrogation. (3) One defendant made plaintiff available for the interrogation during working hours and initiated it by directing plaintiff into the office and presenting him to the interrogator. (4) One defendant determined when the interrogation should cease. Obviously the plaintiff could not have been interrogated at all without having at least the cooperation of the defendants and the facts are susceptible to the inference that the defendants actually exercised a power of direction and control over the interrogator at the time of plaintiff's detention.

The agency relationship may arise *by implication* as well as by express authority. [Citations.] "[A] claim of agency may be proved, as any other fact, by circumstantial evidence. * * * 'The fact of agency may be established by proof of circumstances, apparent relations, and the conduct of the parties.'" [Citation.] The test to be applied in determining the relationship of the parties is whether the contract gives, *or the employer assumes*, the right to control the time and manner of executing the work, as distinguished from the right merely to require results in conformity to the contract. [Citation.] "The employer is liable for the negligence of the contractor * * * If the employer retains the right to direct or control the time and manner of executing the work; or interferes and assumes control, so as to create the relation of master and servant * * *." [Citations.] "A principal may be liable for the willful tort of his agent, done in the prosecution and within the scope

of his business, although it is not expressly shown that he either commanded the commission of the willful act or assented to it. Since the determinative question in the case is whether the act is done 'in the prosecution and within the scope of' the principal's business * * * either command or assent can properly be implied * * *." [Citations.]

Under the foregoing principles the evidence authorized the inference that at the time of plaintiff's illegal detention the interrogator was acting as the defendants' agent and within the scope of his authority.

* * *

Judgment affirmed.

COUNCELL v. DOUGLAS

(1955) 163 Ohio St. 292, 126 N.E.2d 597.

[At the trial, the undisputed evidence disclosed that at about 5 p. m. on January 6, 1951, defendant, a resident of Utica, Ohio, drove his automobile to the Pure Oil Service Station in that village to have it lubricated and washed, the oil changed and the tires switched. While making arrangements for this work with Cooksey and Hunter, who were apparently employees at this service station, defendant requested that someone ride home with him and drive his automobile back to the service station for this work. Thereupon, Cooksey rode home with defendant and then undertook to return defendant's automobile to the service station. While doing so, Cooksey collided with a car in which plaintiff was riding.

Defendant's motion for a directed verdict was overruled, the jury returned a verdict for plaintiff against defendant for $3,280.50, defendant's motion for judgment notwithstanding the verdict was overruled, judgment was rendered on the verdict for plaintiff against defendant and defendant's motion for a new trial was overruled.]

TAFT, J. * * *

In the opinion by the court in Miller v. Metropolitan Life Ins. Co., 134 Ohio St. 289, 291, 16 N.E.2d 447, 448, it is said:

"The fundamental rule generally recognized is that the doctrine of *respondeat superior* is applicable to the relation of master and servant or of principal and agent, but not to that of employer and independent contractor. * * *

"The relation of principal and agent or master and servant is distinguished from the relation of employer and independent contractor by the following test: Did the employer retain control, or the right to control, the mode and manner of doing the work contracted for? If he did, the relation is that of principal and agent or master and servant. If he did not but is interested merely in the ultimate result to be accomplished, the relation is that of employer and independent contractor."

* * *

In the instant case, it is clear that, after defendant delivered his car to Cooksey to be driven back to the service station, he had relinquished any right "to control the mode or manner of doing the work" for which he had contracted, and that "work" included the driving of his car from his home to the service station. The fact, that thereafter he might further direct with respect to the redelivery of his car or the quantity of the work to be done or the condition of the work when completed, was not, as pointed out in paragraph four of the syllabus of the Hughes case, "a right to control the mode or manner of doing the work," within the rule stated in that syllabus for determining whether the relationship between the parties was that of principal and agent or of master and servant.

In the instant case, it would hardly be contended that, in rendering the service ar-ranged for with respect to defendant's automobile, the service station and its employees would be either agents or servants of defendant. There is nothing in the evidence tending to prove that the riding home with defendant and the driving of his car back to the service station were not done merely as incidents to rendering the services to his automobile and as a part of the result for which defendant had contracted. There certainly would have been no occasion for defendant to request anyone to ride home with him and drive his car back if he had not wanted the service station to render the services on his automobile for which he had contracted.

* * *

Our conclusion is that, where the owner of an automobile arranges with a service station for the servicing of his automobile and at the time of making such arrangements it is agreed that an employee of the station will ride home with him and drive his automobile back to the station for the servicing, and where the owner does drive home and surrenders his car to such employee to be driven back to the station for servicing, the owner will not be responsible for negligence of such station employee in driving his automobile back to the service station. We believe that this conclusion is supported by the overwhelming weight of authority. [Citations.]

Judgment reversed and final judgment for defendant.

JOEL v. MORISON

(1833) Court of Exchequer (England),
6 Carrington & Payne Reports 501.

The declaration stated, that, on the 18th of April, 1833, the plaintiff was proceeding on foot across a certain public and common highway, and that the defendant was possessed of a cart and horse, which were under the care, government, and direction of a servant of his, who was driving the same along the said highway, and that the defendant by his said servant so carelessly, negligently, and improperly drove, governed, and directed the said horse and cart, that, by the carelessness, negligence, and improper conduct of the defendant by his servant, the cart and horse were driven against the plaintiff, and struck him, whereby he was thrown down and the bone of one of his legs was fractured, and he was ill in consequence, and prevented from transacting his business, and obliged to incur a great expense in and about the setting the said bone, &c., and a further great expense in retaining and employing divers persons to superintend and look after his business for six calendar months. Plea—Not guilty.

From the evidence on the part of the plaintiff it appeared that he was in Bishopsgate-street, when he was knocked down by a cart and horse coming in the direction from Shoreditch, which were sworn to have been driven at the time by a person who was the servant of the defendant, another of his servants being in the cart with him. The injury was a fracture of the fibula.

On the part of the defendant witnesses were called, who swore that his cart was for weeks before and after the time sworn to by the plaintiff's witnesses only in the habit of being driven between Burton Crescent Mews and Finchley, and did not go into the City at all.

Thesiger, for the plaintiff, in reply, suggested that either the defendant's servants might in coming from Finchley have gone out of their way for their own purposes, or might have taken the cart at a time when it was not wanted for the purpose of business, and have gone to pay a visit to some friend. He was observing that, under these circumstances, the defendant was liable for the acts of his servants.

PARKE, B. He is not liable, if, as you suggest, these young men took the cart without leave; he is liable if they were going extra viam in going from Burton Crescent Mews to Finchley; but if they chose to go of their own accord to see a friend, when they were not on their master's business, he is not liable.

His Lordship afterwards, in summing up said—This is an action to recover damages for an injury sustained by the plaintiff, in consequence of the negligence of the defendant's servant. There is no doubt that the plaintiff has suffered the injury, and there is no doubt that the driver of the cart was guilty of negligence, and there is no doubt also that the master, if that person was driving the cart on his master's business, is responsible. If the servants, being on their master's business, took a detour to call upon a friend, the master will be responsible. If you think the servants lent the cart to a person who was driving without the defendant's knowledge, he will not be responsible. Or, if you think that the young man, who was driving took the cart surreptitiously, and was not at the time employed on his master's business, the defendant will not be liable. The master is only liable where the servant is acting in the course of his employment. If he was going out of his way, against his master's implied commands, when driving on his master's business, he will make his master liable; but if he was going on a frolic of his own, without being at all on his master's business, the master will not be liable. As to the damages, the master is not guilty of any offence, he is only responsible in law, therefor the amount should be reasonable.

Verdict, for the plaintiff—damages, 30£.

PROBLEMS

1. Stone was the authorized agent to sell stock of the X Company at $10, per share, the par value,

and was authorized, in case of sale, to fill in the blanks in the certificates with the name of the purchaser, the number of shares and the date of sale. He sold 100 shares to Barrie, and without the knowledge or consent of the company and without reporting the same, he endorsed on the back of the certificate the following:

> "It is hereby agreed that X Company shall, at the end of three years after the date, re-purchase the stock at $11.00 per share on thirty days' notice. X Company, by Stone."

After three years, demand was made on X Company to re-purchase, which was refused and the company repudiated the agreement on the ground that the agent had no authority to make the agreement for re-purchase. Barrie sued X Company. Decision?

2. A meat packing company employed A as its salesman and collector. A called on a local butcher about once a week and took his orders for meat and mailed them to the packing company. The packing company then sent statements of the butcher's account to A, whose duty it was to present the statements to the butcher and collect the amount due. After A had continued this practice with the butcher for about three months, he altered a certain statement and raised the amount, and presented the altered statement to the butcher, who paid it. The amounts falsely added to the statement totalled $159.00. Upon discovery of this, the butcher demanded payment of the $159.00 from the packing company, and upon refusal of the packing company to pay it, brought suit against the packing company for $159.00. Decision?

3. A kept his car in B's public garage and paid $30 a month for housing the car. B had an employee, C, whose duty it was to come to the garage at 6:00 p. m., when the other attendants quit work, and stay through the evening and in-to the night as long as necessary to do the work of washing cars and letting patrons in and out with their cars. His quitting time was generally from midnight to 4:00 a. m. While on duty he was the only attendant. Generally, he kept the door locked, but opened it from time to time to accommodate customers. On leaving, it was his business to lock the door. One night he finished his work at 1:00 a. m., left the garage, locked the door, and went to a lunch counter where he met a friend and they conceived the idea of going back to the garage and taking a ride in A's car. No one had the right to take out A's car without A's consent. C and his friend took the car out

and while using it damaged the car. A sued B for the damage to his car. Decision?

4. B & Company, rug manufacturers, em-ployed Jones as a traveling salesman and fur-nished him with samples to use in calling upon the retail trade. Jones had authority from the company to accept orders for merchandise but no authority to collect payment for goods sold. Jones went to the X Furniture Company, showed them the samples and stated that he had authori-ty to sell the samples and receive payment. The X Furniture Company purchased the samples and paid Jones for them by check payable to B & Company or bearer, and Jones delivered the samples. Jones did not deliver the check to B & Company, but cashed it himself. B & Com-pany never received payment. The X Furniture Company had no notice of the lack of authority of Jones to collect payment for goods sold. Jones reported the sale to B & Company which made out and sent a bill for the goods to the X Furni-ture Company which returned the bill with notice that it had paid Jones. B & Company then brought suit against the X Furniture Company for the price of the goods. Decision?

5. A was P's traveling salesman. A called on T, from whom he had previously received an order, to solicit another order. A left his car engine running while he went into T's store, and somehow the car got into gear, ran on the sidewalk, and injured X. T did not give A another order, but at A's request paid A the purchase price of the previous order. A ab-sconded with the money. (a) X sues P for dam-ages for personal injuries. Decision? (b) P sues T for the price of T's previous order. Decision?

6. R was general manager of a telephone company. In August, the bank account of the company was insufficient to meet the payroll and R arranged with the bank for an over-draft. In September R executed a note for $350 in the company's name, discounted the note at the bank, and left town with the pro-ceeds. The company contested liability on the overdraft and the note. Decision?

7. P was in the business of buying and sell-ing bonds and other securities. A was his gen-eral manager, and had authority to sell bonds for P. A was negotiating the sale of five X Corporation $1,000 bonds to T, and to induce T to buy the bonds stated that P would guarantee the payment of the bonds. T thereupon pur-chased the bonds, and also received from A a written guaranty of the payment of the bonds,

signed "P, by A, General Manager." X Corporation defaulted on the bonds at maturity. T thereupon sues P on the guaranty, which was unknown to P. Decision?

8. Brown owns an automobile which he occasionally allows his son, Junior (a licensed operator), to drive. On Saturday, Junior borrows the car with his father's permission to go to a dance. The only request made of Junior is that he leave the dance by 11:30 p.m. so that he can pick up his parents at a party. On his way to the dance, Junior injures Jones, a pedestrian, who sues Brown. Decision?

(b) On the following Wednesday, Junior borrows the car to pick up some groceries ordered by his mother, and on his way to the store, injures Smith, a pedestrian. Junior's use of the car was without permission of his father, a physicial fitness faddist, who would never have given his permission to take the car for this kind of errand. Smith sues Brown. Decision?

9. The Cherokee Hockey Corporation owned a professional ice hockey team which finished last in the league standings for several years because of the lack of aggressive defense players. In an attempt to strengthen the team and increase gate receipts, the corporation purchased "Wild Joe" Scraggs who had a national reputation for rough and colorful defense tactics. During a heated game, Scraggs intentionally swung his stick at an opponent and struck a spectator seated in the front row of the arena, dislodging several teeth. The spectator sued the Cherokee Hockey Corporation. During the course of the trial, it was proved that about fifteen persons reported to the first-aid station at the arena during each hockey season for injuries sustained from flying pucks or from hockey sticks. Decision?

10. (a) A and B, conductors of XYZ Railroad Company, get into an argument over national politics and A attacks B, injuring him seriously. B sues the railroad company. Decision? (b) A, a conductor of WRS Railroad Company, gets into a similar argument with C, a passenger, and attacks C, injuring him seriously. C sues WRS Railroad Company. Decision?

CHAPTER 14

RELATIONSHIP OF AGENT AND THIRD PERSONS; AGENCY TERMINATION

Introductory. The function of an agent is that of a conduit of the will of the principal. The agent is not a party to the contract which he makes with a third person on behalf of a disclosed principal. The third person is aware of the fact that he is dealing with an agent, that the agent is acting on behalf of an identified principal, and that the authority of the agent is limited to the extent conferred upon him by the principal. The resulting contract, if within the agent's authority, is between the third person and the principal. The agent is not liable for the nonperformance of the contract by either party.

An agent, however, may be liable to the third person in certain situations such as acting on behalf of an undisclosed principal or partially disclosed principal, acting without authority or exceeding the scope of the authority granted, entering into the contract in a personal capacity, guaranteeing performance by the principal, or committing a tortious or wrongful act. Under certain circumstances, an agent may acquire rights against a third person.

Liability of Agent to Third Person. The liability of an agent to a third person may be either in contract or in tort. The liability in contract will be first considered.

Undisclosed or Partially Disclosed Principal. An agent acts for an undisclosed principal when he appears to be acting in his own behalf and the third person with whom he is dealing has no knowledge that he is acting as an agent. The instructions of the principal to the agent are not only to conceal the identity of the principal but also not to disclose the agency relationship. Ostensibly, the third person is dealing with the agent as

though he were a principal. A partially disclosed principal is one whose existence is known but whose identity is unknown. The third person is aware that the agent is acting on behalf of another but he is not informed of the name or identity of the principal.

The agent is personally liable upon a contract which he enters into with a third person on behalf of an undisclosed principal or a partially disclosed principal, unless the third person after discovery of the existence and identity of such principal elects to hold the principal to the contract. The reason for the liability of the agent is that the third person has placed reliance upon the agent individually and has accepted the agent's personal undertaking to perform the contract. Obviously where the principal is wholly undisclosed the third person does not know of the interest of anyone in the contract other than himself and the agent. The reason for the liability of the undisclosed or partially disclosed principal is that he authorized the agent to act, and having received the benefits of the agent's acts should assume and be responsible for the burdens thereof.

After the third person has discovered the identity of the undisclosed principal, he may hold either the principal or the agent to performance of the contract, but he cannot hold both. He has the choice of disregarding the undisclosed principal and demanding performance only by the agent or of requiring performance by the undisclosed principal. Having once made an election, he is irrevocably bound by it. What constitutes an election is a question of fact. Some courts hold that a failure of the third person to demand performance by the principal within a reasonable time after discovery of his identity is a waiver of the right to hold the principal to the contract. If the third person should demand performance by both the agent and the principal, merely bringing suit against both would not be an election, but before the entry of judgment he would be compelled to make an election as he would not be entitled to a judgment against both.

Rights of Undisclosed Principal. An undisclosed or partially disclosed principal acquires rights and may maintain an action against the third person with whom the agent entered into a contract in his own name, except in two instances, namely, (1) where the contract between the agent and the third person is under seal, and (2) where the agent is a party to a negotiable instrument.

A contract under seal is a formal document, and at common law no one except parties to sealed instruments could have rights or be subject to duties thereunder. The only way in which a principal could acquire rights in such a contract executed by his agent would be by the agent signing the name of the principal on the line where the seal appears. If this were done, of course, there would no longer be an undisclosed principal. If the agent were to add the word "agent" after signing his own name, this would give the partially disclosed principal no rights on the contract under seal. The party to the contract would be the agent, and the addition of the word "agent" to his signature would be merely descriptio personae, a description of the person. It would have no more effect than if the agent were to sign his name "John Jones, Janitor," or "John Jones, Philosopher," or "John Jones, Balloonist." The contractual undertaking would be that of John Jones.

A bill of exchange or negotiable promissory note is also a formal instrument, and no one is liable upon such an instrument whose name does not appear thereon as a signer of the instrument. An agent may execute a negotiable instrument in the name of his principal, but if the identity of the principal does not appear, the agent is individually liable and the principal is not liable on the instrument.

The undisclosed principal is not prevented by the parol evidence rule from establishing his rights under a written contract entered into by his agent. The agent is not excused from liability by the subsequent disclosure of the principal, and evidence of the agency relationship merely introduces another person, the principal, who is bound by the contract. However, if the agent represents to the third person that he is not acting on behalf of another but solely for himself as principal, the undisclosed principal would have no rights upon the contract.

Where the Statute of Frauds requires the contract to be in writing, or a memorandum thereof reduced to writing, and signed by the party to be charged, a signature of the agent without indicating either in the body of the writing or in the signature that he is acting on behalf of another, or the identity of such other, is nevertheless sufficient to bind the undisclosed principal. A signature of the third person or of an agent in his behalf satisfies the requirements of the Statute of Frauds so as to make the contract enforceable by the undisclosed principal. It is possible for both parties to a contract to be acting as agents for their respective undisclosed principals.

The undisclosed principal not only has rights upon the contract, but is also subject to duties. After his identity and interest have been discovered, the third person may hold him liable for nonperformance of the agent's contract. In such an action against him, the principal may assert as defenses those which would be available to the agent if he were being sued, such as fraud, duress, or failure of consideration, and any or all of four additional defenses: (1) that the contract was under seal; (2) that the action is based upon a negotiable instrument which is not signed by or on behalf of the principal; (3) that the third person has elected to hold the agent to the contract; and (4) that before discovery by the third person of the existence of the undisclosed principal, the principal had made a settlement of his accounts with the agent in reasonable reliance upon conduct of the third person.

The common law rule that an undisclosed principal is not liable upon a contract executed by his agent under seal has been held to be abrogated by Section 2–203 of the Uniform Commercial Code with respect to contracts for the sale of goods. This Section provides that the affixing of a seal to a written contract for the sale of goods or to an offer to buy or sell goods does not make the writing a sealed instrument, and the law with respect to sealed instruments does not apply to such a contract or offer. Commonwealth Bank and Trust Co. v. Keech, 201 Pa.Super. 285, 192 A.2d 133 (1963).

The Restatement of the Law of Agency, Second, provides: Section 208,

> An undisclosed principal is not discharged from liability to the other party to a transaction conducted by an agent by payment to, or settlement of accounts with, the agent, unless he does so in reasonable reliance upon conduct of the other party which is not induced by the agent's misrepresentations and which indicates that the agent has settled the account.

Agent's Implied Warranty of Authority. A person who undertakes to contract as agent impliedly warrants that he is in fact authorized to make the contract on behalf of the party whom he purports to represent. If the agent does not have authority to bind the principal, the agent is bound by the contract unless the principal ratifies it. However, no implied warranty exists if the contract expressly provides that the agent shall not be responsible for any lack of authority, or if the agent, acting in good faith, discloses to the third person all of the facts upon which his authority rests. For example, agent B has received a power of attorney or letter of instructions from his principal A which is ambiguous. He shows it to C stating that it represents all of the authority that he has to act, and both B and C rely upon its sufficiency. In this case, there is no implied warranty or any warranty by B to C of his authority. The interpretation of the letter of instruction may present a question of law, but the agent did not assume the risk that it was sufficient to bind the principal.

If a purported agent falsely represents to a third person that he has authority to make a contract on behalf of a principal whom he has no power to bind, he is liable in a tort action of deceit to the third person for the loss sustained in reliance upon such misrepresentation.

Agent of Partially Incompetent Principal. An agent does not impliedly warrant the capacity of his principal to contract. The mere fact that the third person is willing to contract with the principal, even though the latter is acting through an agent, indicates some knowledge of the principal. Thus, an agent for an infant or for an insane person does not impliedly warrant the contractual capacity of his principal, and the agent is not liable for nonperformance in the event his principal should exercise the right of disaffirmance. However, if the agent expressly warrants the legal capacity of his principal, he may become liable to the third person upon such express warranty. If the agent has knowledge of his principal's lack of capacity and knows also that the third person is ignorant thereof, he is liable to the third person for loss resulting from the principal's disaffirmance.

Liability of Agent Where Principal is Non-Existent. A person who professes to act as agent for a fictitious or non-existent principal is personally liable on a contract entered into with a third person on behalf of such principal. A promoter of a corporation who enters into contracts with third persons in the name of a corporation to be organized is personally liable on such contract. The corporation is not liable as it did not authorize the contracts. It could not ratify them as it was not in existence when the contracts were made. If the corporation after coming into existence affirmatively adopts a pre-incorporation contract made in its behalf, it thereupon becomes bound and the liability of the promoter is terminated. This, in effect, is a novation.

An agent who enters into a contract with a third person on behalf of a principal who died prior to the making of the contract is personally liable on such contract, unless the third person had knowledge of the principal's death at the time of making the contract. Where the agent was ignorant of his principal's death at the time of making the contract, the courts give weight to circumstances which indicate an intention of the parties that the agent would not be held to the contract if the principal were dead. For instance, if both the agent and the third person knew that the principal at the time of the contract was abroad on a hazardous expedition or was in a combat zone in time of war, the courts would probably hold that the existence of the principal was an implied condition to the contract.

Agent's Liability for Money or Things Received from Third Persons. If an agent with authority to collect money owing to his principal receives payment from a third person but fails to remit to the principal, the third person has no right of action against the agent. The debt of the third person to the principal is discharged by payment to the agent. However, if the third person pays the agent more than the amount due to the principal, or by mistake pays the agent without realizing that the debt has been previously paid, the agent is under a duty to repay to the third person the excess, or the amount of the second payment, if demand for repayment is made upon the agent before he has settled his accounts with the principal or made remittance to the principal.

Assume that A owns a building which he has insured against loss by fire with the C Company. Following a fire, B, as agent for A, collects from C the amount of the loss resulting from the fire. Before making remittance to A, B learns that A had deliberately set fire to the building in order to collect the insurance. B is under a duty to refund the money to the C Company, and if, after ascertaining the facts as to the origin of the fire, he remits to his principal A, he remains liable to C. However, if B settles his accounts with A before learning of the origin of the fire, B is not liable to C.

An agent who receives possession of property from his principal which be believes in good faith to belong to the principal, is not liable for conversion of the property where, under instructions from the principal and with no knowledge of its true ownership, he transports the property, disposes of it, or returns it to the principal. For example, Y steals a horse belonging to X and sells it to A who pays value and purchases the horse without knowledge that it is stolen property. A later delivers the horse to his agent B with instructions to sell it to C. B has no knowledge that the horse was stolen and in good faith sells it to C who is a bona fide purchaser. B collects from C the price of the horse and remits it to A. Under these facts, B is not liable for conversion of the horse, although A is liable and C is liable. If X should discover the facts and make demand upon the agent B when B had in his possession either the horse or the proceeds of the sale received from C, B would be liable to X for refusal to deliver to him the horse or the proceeds of the sale.

Rights of Agent against Third Person. An agent who makes a contract with a third person on behalf of a disclosed principal has no right of action against the third person for breach of the contract. The agent is not a party to the contract nor a promisee of the third person. However, an agent for an undisclosed principal or partially disclosed principal may maintain in his own name an action against the third person for breach of contract. In such case, the agent is also individually liable on the contract. Where such contract is breached by the third person, an action by the agent is not prohibited by statutes which require every action to be brought by the real party in interest, as exception is made in the case of a trustee of an express trust, and suit by the agent is permitted upon the theory that he sues and recovers as trustee for his principal.

An agent, such as a factor or auctioneer, has a lien on goods to secure advances made by the agent on behalf of the principal, and may assert this lien as against the rights of a third person to the goods.

An agent may also recover from the third person money paid by him to the third person under a mistake of fact, or money paid or goods delivered to the third person upon a fraudulent inducement. In the case of fraud, the agent may rescind the voidable contract and recover in an action in his own name the consideration paid to the third person. The principal also has a right of rescission, and the agent may not rescind if the principal elects not to avoid the contract.

An agent in possession of goods of his principal, such as a factor or auctioneer, may maintain in his own name a tort action against a third person who has converted the goods. The third person has committed a trespass for a wrongful taking or detention of the goods and has invaded the ownership rights of the principal and the possessory rights of the agent. Either the principal or the agent may sue. The agent, in bringing suit against the third person, is entitled to recover the full amount of the reasonable value of the goods.

An agent has the right to maintain in his own behalf a tort action against a third person who assaults him while protecting his principal's goods, or who defames him because of his relationship with the principal. An agent or employee also has a right to recover damages against a third person who maliciously and without justifiable cause induces his employer to discharge him.

Tort Liability of Agent. An agent is personally liable for his wrongful acts which cause damage to third persons, regardless of whether such acts are authorized or unauthorized by the principal. The agent is liable for his negligence or failure to use due care under the circumstances for the safety of others. This is true whether the principal may or may not also be liable.

An agent who commits a wrong at the direction or under instructions of his principal is personally liable therefor. An agent is personally liable if he converts the goods of a third person to his principal's use. However, if goods which have been previously converted by the principal are delivered to the agent, mere possession of the goods on behalf of the principal does not make the agent liable to the true owner of the goods, unless the agent upon demand by the true owner refuses to deliver to him the goods, or unless the agent transfers possession of the goods to the principal or to any person, except the true owner, with notice of the claim of the true owner.

An agent is liable to a third person for fraudulent representations which he makes to such person, including an untrue statement of his authority to act on behalf of the purported principal as well as any other false statement upon which the third person relies. However, an agent acting with authority has whatever privilege the principal may have. Thus, in negotiating with a third person, an agent is privileged to make such misrepresentations, generally regarded as "seller's talk," as the principal would be permitted to make. For example, A, who is interested in buying C's automobile, tells his agent B to endeavor to buy the car for approximately $2,750 and to advise C that A will absolutely pay no more than $3,000 for the car, but that if C offers the car for $3,500 to accept the offer on A's behalf. B tells C that A's absolute top price is $3,000. C sells the car to A at this price. C has no action of deceit against either B or A.

An agent is not liable under the doctrine of respondeat superior for injury to third persons caused by the tortious acts of employees of the principal who are under his control. Thus, A employs B as general manager of a factory. C, who has been employed by B to work in the factory and is under B's immediate supervision, negligently operates a machine thereby injuring D, a business visitor. B is not liable to D.

An agent incurs no liability to a third person merely because of his failure to perform a duty which he owes to his principal. Thus, if A gives $1,000 to his agent B with instructions to pay it to C to whom it is owing, and B fails to pay the money to C, there is no liability of B to C. This is so, even if A subsequently becomes insolvent and C is unable to collect the debt.

The courts frequently state that an agent is not liable for injuries sustained by third persons which result from the agent's nonfeasance, but is liable where the injuries result from his misfeasance or malfeasance. In certain situations, the distinction may be one which is difficult to make. For instance, A places his agent B in charge and control of certain real estate with the duty to cause all necessary repairs to be made. C, who is lawfully on the premises, is injured by the sudden collapse of a stairway. Some courts hold that the failure of B to have repaired the staircase, while a violation of his duty to A, is merely nonfeasance as to C, and therefore B is not liable to C. Other courts regard B's neglect as misfeasance and hold him person-

ally liable to C. If B had undertaken to repair or replace the stairway and had done so negligently, there would be no question of his personal liability to a business invitee injured by reason of the defective condition of the repaired or replaced staircase. In this instance, B would clearly be guilty of misfeasance.

Termination of Agency. The distinction between the authority and the power of an agent is important in dealing with the termination of the agency relationship. The principal may revoke the authority by notice to the agent. However, the power of the agent to bind the principal by contract to third persons will continue until the third persons have knowledge of the termination. When the agent's authority is terminated, he is not entitled to compensation for services rendered thereafter, his fiduciary duties are ended, and he is free to deal with the subject matter of his former agency for his individual profit. When the agent's power is terminated, third persons can no longer obtain rights against the principal by dealing with the agent.

Termination of the agent's authority may take place by: (1) mutual agreement of the parties; (2) fulfillment of the purpose of the agency; (3) revocation by the principal; (4) renunciation by the agent; (5) bankruptcy of the principal; (6) bankruptcy of the agent; (7) death of the principal; (8) death of the agent; (9) insanity of the principal; (10) insanity of the agent; (11) change in business conditions; (12) loss or destruction of the subject matter; (13) loss of qualification of principal or agent; (14) disloyalty of the agent; (15) change of law whereby the exercise of the authority is illegal; (16) outbreak of war where the principal and agent are citizens of belligerent countries.

Mutual Agreement of the Parties. The agency relationship is created by agreement. Except for agency by estoppel, or conduct of the principal giving rise to apparent authority of the agent, no person is a principal without his consent. Likewise, no person is an agent without his consent. This voluntary relationship may be terminated at any time by mutual agreement of the principal and agent.

Fulfillment of Purpose. The authority of an agent to perform a specific act or to accomplish a particular result is terminated when the act is done or the result is accomplished by the agent. If it is accomplished by some one other than the agent, the authority terminates when the agent receives notice thereof.

If A authorizes B to sell or lease A's land, and B leases the land to C, his authority is terminated and he may not thereafter sell the land.

Revocation of Authority. The principal may at any time by notice to the agent revoke or withdraw the authority that he has given to the agent. This revocation may be for cause or without cause. It may be justified and consistent with a reservation to revoke, or it may be wrongful and a breach by the principal of his contract with the agent. It is, however, an effective termination of the agent's authority.

Renunciation by the Agent. As the principal may revoke the agency at any time, the agent also has the power to put an end to the agency by notice to the principal that he renounces the power conferred upon him by the principal. Where the agency was for an indefinite period of time, the agent by giving the principal reasonable notice of his renunciation incurs no liability to the principal. Where the parties had contracted that the agency continue for a specified time, renunciation by the agent prior to the expiration of the time specified subjects him to liability for damages sustained by the principal.

Bankruptcy of the Principal. The bankruptcy or substantial impairment of the assets of the principal, of which the agent has notice, terminates the agent's authority with respect to transactions which the agent should realize the principal is no longer willing to undertake. The assets of a bankrupt pass to the trustee in bankruptcy who administers them for the benefit of the creditors. A principal who becomes bankrupt and is thus stripped of his assets may be in no position to undertake commitments which his agent is authorized to make on his behalf. Knowledge by the agent of the principal's bankruptcy is necessary to terminate the authority. Notice of the bankruptcy does not terminate the authority where the bankruptcy creates no inference that the principal may desire discontinuance of it. For example, A, a stock broker, becomes bankrupt. His housekeeper B continues to buy food and supplies for A's household. No inference is created by A's bankruptcy that B's authority to purchase such supplies is terminated.

Bankruptcy of the Agent. The bankruptcy or insolvency of an agent terminates his authority to act on behalf of his principal where the agent should infer that the state of his credit would so affect the interests of the principal that the latter, if he had knowledge of the facts, would no longer consent that the agent act on his behalf. Thus, A employs B, a factor, to sell A's goods. The practice is for the factor after selling the goods to deposit the proceeds of the sale in his bank and remit by check to the principal. B becomes bankrupt or insolvent. It is a reasonable inference that A would no longer authorize B to mingle the proceeds of the sale with B's funds and thereby cause B to become a debtor to A. This terminates the authority of the agent B.

Death of the Principal. As a dead person cannot act, no one can act for him. The rationale of agency is that the agent is manifesting the will of the principal, and that the principal acts through the agent. Death of the principal terminates the authority of the agent.

There is a conflict among the authorities as to whether notice or knowledge of the principal's death is necessary to terminate an agency that is not coupled with an interest. Certain jurisdictions hold that notice is not required and that payment made to an agent in ignorance of the death of the principal does not discharge the obligation of the payor to the deceased principal's estate. Other authorities hold that where the third party acts in good faith and in ignorance of the principal's death, payment to the agent discharges his obligation to the estate of the deceased principal. Some authorities hold that the agency is deemed revoked as of the time the agent receives notice of the death of his principal.

Death of the Agent. The authority given by the principal to the agent is personal to the agent. Upon his death it does not vest in his executors or administrators. Death of the agent, therefore, terminates the agent's authority. The death of an agent also terminates the authority of a subagent unless there is privity of contract between the subagent and the principal.

Insanity of the Principal. The insanity of the principal affects his capacity to contract. The manifestation of assent necessary to a contract implies the existence of a mind or a will. If a person is so mentally deranged that he is completely bereft of mind or will, he is incompetent to contract. The loss of capacity to contract by the principal terminates the authority of the agent. If the principal is formally adjudged insane by a court which appoints a conservator for his assets, his lack of capacity is judicially established whereby the authority of the agent is terminated.

Insanity of the Agent. It may be observed that mental derangement is a matter of degree. A person is not required to have capacity to contract on his own behalf in order to be capable of acting as agent for another. However, if an agent should become a raving lunatic or imbecile, or be adjudicated insane in a court proceeding, his authority to act on behalf of the principal is terminated.

As in the case of death of the principal or death of the agent, notice to or knowledge by the agent of the insanity of the principal, or to the principal of the insanity of the agent, is not required to terminate the agency.

Change in Business Conditions. The authority of an agent is terminated by notice to him of a change in the value of the subject matter or a change in business conditions from which he should infer that the principal, if such changes were known to him, would not consent to the exercise of the authority. Thus, A authorizes his agent B to sell his 80 acres of farm land for $200 per acre. Subsequently, oil is discovered on nearby land which causes A's land to become worth $800 per acre. B knows of this, but A does not. B's authority to sell the land is terminated.

Loss or Destruction of the Subject Matter. Where the authority conferred upon the agent relates to a specific subject matter which becomes lost or destroyed, the authority of the agent is terminated. Thus, A delivers his horse Dobbin to his agent B with instructions to sell it for not less than $300. Dobbin dies. B's authority to sell the horse is terminated.

Loss of Qualification of Principal or Agent. When the authority given the agent relates to the conduct of a certain business the operation of which requires a license from the government or a regulatory agency, the failure to acquire, or the loss or revocation of such license, terminates the authority of the agent. Thus, A, who holds a retail liquor license, employs B to sell liquor at retail in A's store. A's license is revoked. B's authority to sell A's liquor at retail is terminated.

Disloyalty of Agent. If an agent, without the knowledge of his principal, acquires interests which are adverse to those of the principal or is otherwise guilty of a serious breach of his duty of loyalty to the principal, his authority to act on behalf of the principal is terminated. Thus, A employs B, a realtor, to sell A's land. Unknown to A, B has been authorized by C to purchase this land from A. B is not authorized to sell the land to C.

Change of Law. Subsequent to the employment of the agent, a change in the law may cause the performance of the authorized act to be illegal or criminal, or may impose sanctions which the agent should realize would be unwanted by the principal. Such a change in the law terminates the authority of the agent. Thus, A directs his agent B to ship young elm trees from State X to State Y. In order to control elm disease, a quarantine is established by State X upon the shipment into any other state of any elm trees, and any such shipment is punishable by fine. B's authority to ship the elm trees is terminated.

Outbreak of War. Where the outbreak of war places the principal and agent in the position of alien enemies, the authority of the agent is terminated because its exercise is illegal. Where the principal and agent are citizens of the same country and the outbreak of war or a revolution makes the originally authorized transaction unexpectedly hazardous or impracticable, as the agent knows or should know, the agent's authority is terminated.

Irrevocable Agencies. In the foregoing discussion of the various ways in which the authority of an agent may be terminated, the agency relationship was assumed to be the ordinary one in which the agent does not have a security interest in the power conferred upon him by the principal. Where the agency is coupled with an interest of the agent in the subject matter, as where the agent has advanced funds on behalf of the principal and his power to act is given as security therefor, the authority of the agent is irrevocable by the principal. In such case, neither the death, insanity or bankruptcy of the principal terminates the authority or the power of the agent. The Restatement of the Law of Agency, 2d, Section 139, provides:

Termination of Powers Given As Security. (1) Unless otherwise agreed, a power given as security is not terminated by:

(a) revocation by the creator of the power;

(b) surrender by the holder of the power, if he holds for the benefit of another;

(c) the loss of capacity during the lifetime of either the creator of the power or the holder of the power; or

(d) the death of the holder of the power, or, if the power is given as security for a duty which does not terminate at the death of the creator of the power, by his death.

(2) A power given as security is terminated by its surrender by the beneficiary, if of full capacity; or by the happening of events which, by its terms, discharges the obligations secured by it, or which makes its execution illegal or impossible.

CASES

GOLDFINGER v. DOHERTY

(1934) 153 Misc. 826, 276 N.Y.S. 289.

SHIENTAG, J. The plaintiff sued the defendant Doherty, disaffirming certain purchases of stock, made in her behalf by her duly authorized agent, alleging that she was an infant at the time of the transactions, and that she now elected to rescind and offered to return the stock, together with the stock and cash dividends received thereon. The defendant Doherty thereupon obtained an order permitting him to serve a supplemental summons and complaint on the agent Samuel Goldfinger. * * * The supplemental pleading alleged, in substance, that the agent purchased the stock from Doherty on behalf of the alleged infant "without disclosing the infancy of his principal." It further alleged that, if plaintiff should recover against Doherty, then the defendant Goldfinger, plaintiff's agent, will be liable to defendant Doherty for damages sustained through the rescission of the contracts by plaintiff, "on the ground that defendant Samuel Goldfinger has breached his implied warranty that he was authorized to enter into binding contracts for the plaintiff."

The supplemental pleading was dismissed below for insufficiency, no opinion being rendered. From that determination, the defendant Doherty has appealed to this court.

The fair inference to be drawn from the pleading is that at the time of the transactions in suit the infant was at least sixteen years old; that she has disaffirmed, not the authority of the agent to act in her behalf, but the transactions entered into by her duly authorized agent. The relationship between the infant and the agent is not disclosed by the pleading, nor is there any allegation that, at the time of the transaction, the agent knew, or had reasonable cause to know, of his principal's infancy, or that the other contracting party, Doherty, was in ignorance thereof. * * *

An infant's appointment of an agent is not void; it is merely voidable, like any other contract he makes. "Notwithstanding numerous general statements in the books, sound principles compel the conclusion that no satisfactory distinction can be drawn between a sale and delivery by the infant and a sale and delivery by an agent for him. * * * Dicta and general statements to the contrary are no longer respectable authori-

ty." Casey v. Kastel, 237 N.Y. 305, 311, 142 N.E. 671, 673, 31 A.L.R. 995.

There is, therefore, no basis for the contention of the appellant that disaffirmance by the infant of a contract entered into on his behalf by his agent renders the transaction void ab initio, so that the agent is deemed to have acted without any authority. The infant, without questioning the authority of his agent, may disaffirm the contract entered into on his behalf, in the same manner as if he had made the contract directly. The infant may disaffirm the contract of agency; he may disaffirm the contract entered into by his agent. Either contract is voidable; neither is void.

The general rule is that, if, in making a contract in the name of his principal, the agent acts without authority or beyond it, he becomes liable. As the agent assumes to represent the principal he cannot be heard to say that he had no authority, or that there was, in fact, no principal to be bound; he impliedly warrants that there is a principal, and that he is authorized to act for him.

"The agent does not warrant the capacity of the principal." Hall v. Lauderdale, 46 N.Y. 70, 75. "An agent does not warrant that his principal has full contractual capacity, any more than he warrants that his principal is solvent. Thus an agent for one not of legal age is not necessarily liable if the infant avoids the obligation of the contract made on his account." Comment (a) on section 332, Restatement of the Law of Agency. An agent who misrepresents the capacity of his principal to contract is liable as for any other misrepresentation, and this whether he misrepresents tortiously or innocently.

In the absence of misrepresentation, under what circumstances, if any, is an agent acting for an infant, who subsequently disaffirms, not the agency, but the transaction of the agent, liable to the other contracting party? It must appear that the agent knew or had reason to know of his principal's lack of full capacity, and it must further appear that the other contracting party was in ignorance thereof. The theory of breach of warranty of authority is that one dealing with an agent has been misled by him. This could hardly be deemed to have occurred, if all the facts are known. "It is material, in these cases, that the party claiming a want of authority in the agent should be ignorant of the truth touching the agency." Thilmany v. Iowa Paper Bag Co., 108 Iowa 357, 361, 79 N.W. 261, 262, 75 Am.St.Rep. 259. If the agent "acts within his instructions, and in good faith, especially when the facts are equally known to both parties, he is not personally responsible, although it may happen that the authority itself is void." Hall v. Lauderdale, 46 N.Y. 70, 75.

Assuming that the agent knows or has reason to know of his principal's lack of full capacity, and of the other party's ignorance thereof, what, if any, is the agent's liability? * * *

The basis of the liability of an agent, in a situation such as we are here considering, is that he has produced "a false impression upon the mind of the other party; and, if this result is accomplished, it is unimportant whether the means of accomplishing it are words or acts of the defendant, or his concealment or suppression of material facts not equally within the knowledge or reach of the plaintiff." Stewart v. Wyoming Cattle Ranche Co., 128 U.S. 383, 388, 9 S.Ct. 101, 103, 32 L.Ed. 439. We believe that the correct rule is that set forth in the Restatement of the Law of Agency as follows: "par. 332. Agent of partially incompetent principal. An agent making a contract for a disclosed principal whose contracts are voidable because of lack of full capacity to contract, or for a principal who, although having capacity to contract generally, is incompetent to enter into the particular transaction, is not thereby liable to the other party. He does not be-

come liable by reason of the failure of the principal to perform, unless he contracts or represents that the principal has capacity or unless he has reason to know of the principal's lack of capacity and of the other party's ignorance thereof." * * *

If, therefore, the liability of the agent is to be based on his failure to disclose facts in connection with his principal's lack of full capacity to the other contracting party, it must appear (1) that the agent knew or had reason to know the facts indicating his principal's lack of full capacity; (2) that the other contracting party was in ignorance thereof and the agent had reason so to believe; and (3) that the transaction is one in which lack of full capacity was a material fact.

Drawing the most favorable inferences from the pleading under consideration, we find that it fails to set forth enough facts to constitute a cause of action. We feel, however, that the defendant Doherty should have an opportunity to amend, if he be so advised, so as to conform his pleading to the requirements herein set forth.

The order dismissing the supplemental complaint is affirmed, * * * with leave to the defendant to serve an amended supplemental complaint.

MORTGAGE INVESTMENT CO., INC. v. TOONE

(1965) 17 Utah 2d 152, 406 P.2d 30.

CROCKETT, J. Plaintiff Mortgage Investment Co., Inc., assignee of a uniform real estate contract sued to recover $7,596.22 delinquent payments thereon, plus attorney fees and costs, against the defendant Spencer W. Toone, the purchaser named in said contract. The trial court granted plaintiff's motion for summary judgment. Defendant appeals.

In December, 1962, the Northwestern Investment Company and Spencer W. Toone entered into a uniform real estate contract by which the former agreed to sell and the latter agreed to buy the real property known as 3324 West 3540 South, Salt Lake City. Later in the same month, plaintiff purchased and took an assignment of the contract from Northwestern. It provides for semi-annual payments of $3,925 to be made in May and October of each year. When the first payment, for May, 1963, was not made, plaintiff brought this action for that amount and subsequently, by amendment, included the October payment. At the pretrial conference it was made to appear to the court that the amount stated was delinquent and unpaid, and that the defendant had no meritorious defense thereto.

In its brief plaintiff points to three defenses asserted by defendant: (1) lack of consideration, (2) another outstanding agreement covering the same property between the parties, and (3) that defendant signed the contract only as agent for another; and makes the following colorful characterization of them: as to (1) "ridiculous," as to (2) "preposterous," and as to (3) "unsupportable by the wildest stretch of the imagination." We are in accord with the view of the trial court as to the lack of merit in the asserted defenses, though not in the terms chosen by the plaintiff.

As to (1), this is a contract duly executed by the parties containing mutual obligations which are consideration for each other. As to (2), it is not made to appear what the claim of another contract between the parties on this property has to do with the instant one, nor how the former could affect the validity of the latter. As to (3), the contract names the defendant as purchaser, and he personally signed it without indicating that he was an agent acting for a principal. He is therefore personally bound by the contract which he signed in his individual capacity. [Citation.]

Judgment affirmed.

COOK v. SAFEWAY STORES INC.

(1958 Okl.) 330 P.2d 375.

CORN, VICE C. J. Bobby Cook brought this action against Safeway Stores Incorporated, a corporation, and William P. Roderick to recover damages sustained by reason of the consumption by his sons of certain unwholesome foodstuffs, a meat product known as bologna, cheese, lettuce, milk, bread and a cereal known as "Wheaties", within an hour after such foodstuffs had been purchased from said store, resulting in the serious illness of both sons. He alleged that the defendant, Safeway Stores Incorporated, was engaged in the business of selling foodstuffs; that the defendant Roderick was its agent, servant and employee, and while acting within the scope of his authority sold the aforementioned foodstuffs to the plaintiff and his wife; that the defendant corporation and its agents, servants and employees impliedly warranted such food to be wholesome, fit for human consumption, harmless and pure and containing no harmful or injurious substance; that plaintiff relied upon such warranties in his purchase and furnishing the food to his sons to consume; that the defendants, and each of them, in breach of the warranties, sold to him the aforementioned unwholesome food. He prayed damages in the total sum of $2,650.

The defendant Roderick filed his separate general demurrer to the petition on the grounds that it failed to state cause of action against him.

The trial court sustained the demurrer of defendant Roderick. The plaintiff elected to stand on the petition and the court dismissed the petition as to defendant Roderick. He has duly perfected his appeal to this court.

The defendant corporation filed its answer to the petition. No question is here presented as to it.

Plaintiff takes the position that the trial court erred as a matter of law in holding that an agent of a disclosed principal is not liable for the breach of an implied warranty to sell food fit for human consumption.

Unquestionably the general rule, as well as the rule adopted by this court, is that where a dealer sells foods for immediate human consumption, purchaser may rely on implied warranty that such food is wholesome and not deleterious, and in the event he sustains injury from the consumption thereof he may maintain his cause of action upon such implied warranty. This implied warranty in favor of the consumer in such a case extends to the manufacturer, packer, processor and each intermediate dealer as well as the retail seller. [Citations.]

However the agent, servant and employee of the retailer who actually makes the sale, ordinarily cannot be held liable on such implied warranty unless such agent assumes to personally undertake to warrant the food as fit for human consumption. Thus a retail store clerk, merely passing out articles of food sold and receiving price for principal, does not individually impliedly warrant the same, unless he has actual knowledge of its unfitness or unless he assumes the responsibility placed upon sellers of food or unless he owes some particular duty to the purchaser. [Citation.]

The petition in the case at bar does not allege that the agent had knowledge of the unfit condition of the food or that he assumed the responsibility placed upon his employer, a retailer of food, or that he owed a particular duty to the plaintiff. The petition merely contained general allegation that the defendant store and its agents, servants and employees impliedly warranted the fitness for human consumption, and that plaintiff relied thereon. Unless particular circumstances exist, protection of the buyer of food by implied warranty of fitness for human consumption by the seller thereof does not re- quire the extension thereof to the clerk of the seller who actually delivers the article and takes the money therefor.

Judgment affirmed.

PORETTA v. SUPERIOR DOWEL COMPANY

(1957) 153 Me. 308, 137 A.2d 361, 71 A.L.R.2d 898.

Dubord, J. * * * The issue thus raised presents a problem of novel impression in this State. The issue is:

"Is an undisclosed principal absolved from liability to his agent's vendor who has sold goods to the agent upon the credit of the agent who has received payment or advances or a settlement of accounts, from his undisclosed principal before discovery of the undisclosed principal by the agent's vendor?"

There are two different rules bearing upon the issue. The first one, which appears to be supported by the weight of authority is that an undisclosed principal is generally relieved of his liability for his agent's contracts to the extent that he has settled with his agent prior to the discovery of the agency. The other rule is, that an undisclosed principal is discharged only where he has been induced to settle with the agent by conduct on the part of the third person leading him to believe that such person has settled with the agent.

The decisions appear to be in a state of hopeless confusion.

"The rule that an undisclosed principal, when discovered, may be held liable upon a contract made in his behalf will not be enforced for the advantage of a third party, if it will work injustice to the principal. An undisclosed principal may be relieved from liability by reason of a changed state of accounts between him and the agent, the rule formerly laid down in England and now very generally followed in the United States being that, where the principal, acting in good faith, has settled with the agent so that he would be subjected to loss were he compelled to pay the third person, he is relieved from liability to the latter, and this doctrine is, in at least one jurisdiction, in effect prescribed by statute. This doctrine is now held in England, and in a few cases in the United States, to be too broad, and the better rule is stated to be that the principal is discharged only where he has been induced to settle with the agent by conduct on the part of the third person leading him to believe that such person has settled with the agent or has elected to hold the latter. In any event the principal is relieved from liability, where he has been induced by the conduct of the third person to settle with the agent." [Citations.]

"It is often said that persons dealing in their own names are presumed to deal for themselves as principals, yet if one authorized by another to act as his agent, in acting on behalf of the principal, fails to disclose the principal to the third person, or to disclose that he is acting as agent, the principal, when discovered, may become liable for the acts done in his behalf, and may be sued thereon just as if, at the time the transaction was entered into, the agent had disclosed the fact of his agency and the identity of the principal, unless the principal and the agent have so adjusted their accounts that to hold the principal liable would work an injustice to him." [Citation.]

The expression "unless the principal and the agent have so adjusted their accounts that to hold the principal liable would work an injustice to him," is qualified by 2 Am. Jur. § 399, which reads as follows:

"The general rule which allows a third person to have recourse against an undisclosed principal is subject to the qualification that the principal shall not be prejudiced by being made personally liable because he has in good faith relied upon the conduct of the third person and has paid or settled with the agent; conversely, the rule is that a third person who deals with the agent of an undisclosed principal can, upon discovering the principal, resort to the latter for payment, unless by his conduct he has led the principal in the meanwhile to pay or settle with the agent. The comparable expression of the American Law Institute is that an undisclosed principal is discharged from liability to the other party to the contract if he has paid or settled accounts with his agent, reasonably relying upon conduct of the other party, not induced by the agent's misrepresentations, which indicates that the agent has paid or otherwise settled the accounts. Thus, if the principal has settled with his agent on the basis of receipts or other documents furnished the agent by the seller, the principal cannot be held liable for the price."

The American Law Institute, as of May 4, 1933, adopted and promulgated the following rule:

"An undisclosed principal is discharged from liability to the other party to the contract if he has paid or settled accounts with an agent reasonably relying upon conduct of the other party, not induced by the agent's misrepresentations, which indicates that the agent has paid or otherwise settled the account." 1 Am.Law Inst. Restatement of Agency, § 208.

*   *   *

The Restatement may be regarded both as the product of expert opinion and as the expression of the law by the legal profession.

The Committee on Agency which prepared the Restatement of the Law of Agency was composed of outstanding representatives of the leading law schools of the country. It was headed by Mr. Floyd R. Mechem, who at the time was regarded as the foremost living authority on the subject of agency. Its rule as set forth in § 208 promulgated on May 4, 1933 expounds the thinking of some of the best legal minds in the country.

The purpose of the Institute in the promotion of clarification of the law can be applied to no more needy situation than that of the question before us for determination. It is our opinion that the reasoning of Mr. Mechem in support of the doctrine promulgated in the Restatement is sound. The adoption of this doctrine by this court will establish a clear cut and explicit rule of law free from the confusion, complications and perplexities which have existed throughout the years.

We, therefore, adopt the rule as laid down in the Restatement of the Law of Agency.

COSTELLO v. KASTELER

(1958) 7 Utah 2d 310, 324 P.2d 772.

WADE, J. This is an appeal from a judgment in favor of M. S. Costello, plaintiff below and respondent herein, for the reasonable value of services rendered by him to appellants in loading trucks with materials from a mine.

Appellants contend the court erred in allowing an amendment to respondent's amended complaint which in effect changed the complaint from one on an express contract to one for quantum meruit without granting the requested time to be able to prepare to meet evidence in this new cause of action. There is no merit to this contention. The amended complaint alleged in one paragraph thereof in its First Cause of Action against Kasteler a claim on an express contract and in another paragraph thereof that "the agreed value and the reasonable value of said services is the sum of $1,155.00" and the same averments were made in his Alternative First Cause of Action against the Uranium-Chemical Corporation. The amendment by interlineation which the court allowed was in the prayer of the complaint which before the amendment prayed for judgment in the amount of $1,155.00 and after the amendment prayed for that sum "or the reasonable value of said services." It is apparent from the allegations in the complaint that respond-

ent was claiming payment both on an express contract and on a quantum meruit basis and appellant should have been prepared to meet both issues. The court therefore did not err in allowing the amendment.

Appellants further contend that the court erred in granting judgment against both of them since the court found that at the time of the negotiations for the services appellant Kasteler did not disclose to respondent that he was acting as the agent for the appellant Uranium Chemical Corporation and the law is well settled that where a contract is entered into with the agent of an undisclosed principal for the use and benefit of the principal an election must be made as to whether the agent or the principal will be held liable, but a judgment cannot be obtained against both. As authority appellant cites Love v. St. Joseph Stock Yards Co., 51 Utah 305, 169 P. 951. That case does contain a dictum to that effect and respondent concedes that the majority rule in the United States is to the effect that after discovery of an undisclosed principal a judgment cannot ordinarily be obtained against both the principal and the agent. As stated in 118 A.L.R., page 704, note 111:

"It has generally been held that where the agent and undisclosed principal are joined, the plaintiff may not have judgment against both, but must, prior to judgment, elect to hold one or the other."

Ordinarily plaintiff would not be entitled to judgment against both. However, appellants did not demand or move for an election by respondent as to whether the principal or agent should be held and the failure to do so was a waiver. See note 111(b), 118 A.L.R. page 707 and cases therein cited. Since respondent in his brief has stated that if this court should find that he is not entitled to judgment against both appellants then he requests that he be allowed to make his election in this court and chooses to hold the agent

Kasteler. We deem it proper to grant this request.

Affirmed with instructions to vacate the judgment against appellant Uranium Chemical Corporation.

COMMERCIAL NURSERY CO. v. IVEY

(1932) 164 Tenn. 502, 51 S.W.2d 238.

GREEN, C. J. This is a suit against an administratrix and her surety to recover against them on account of matters hereinafter set out. There was a decree against both defendants by the chancellor, from which decree the surety alone appealed. * *

The complainant is a partnership engaged in the general nursery business. Ben W. Ivey, deceased, was employed as an agent by complainant to sell nursery stock. Under the contract between the complainant and Ivey, complainant would make Ivey a price on the stock. Ivey would sell to customers procured at an advanced price. When Ivey would make a sale to a customer, he would secure from him an order specifying the particular varieties of trees, shrubs, or plants purchased by the customer, and appended to this order, and a part thereof, was a promissory note whereby the customer undertook upon delivery of the stock to pay to the Commercial Nursery Company, or order, the sum agreed upon between the customer and Ivey as the sale price of such stock.

All such orders and notes appear to have been forwarded by Ivey to the Commercial Nursery Company and later turned back to Ivey for collection, when the stock had been shipped. Under the agreement between the parties, it seems that it was Ivey's duty, from his collections generally, to remit to the nursery company the balance of its account against him. That is, an amount equivalent to the price at which the nursery company had quoted all stock shipped on his orders. After this was done, the notes remaining in Ivey's hands, or the proceeds of the remaining notes, belonged to him.

When Ivey died, he had quite a batch of these notes in his hands, the exact amount of which is not important. It is agreed that there was due to the complainant, out of the proceeds of these notes, $755.05. The defendant Josie Ivey qualified as administratrix of her husband with the United States Fidelity & Guaranty Company on her bond. She took over the notes referred to and appears to have collected from them something over $1,300. She has not, however, made any settlement with complainant, and complainant accordingly sued.

The surety defends on the theory that these notes were no part of the estate of Ivey; that Ivey's administratrix had no authority to take said notes into her possession and collect them; and that, as such surety, it cannot be held to account for assets unlawfully taken over by the administratrix.

* * *

The sureties on the bond of an administrator are only liable for a due accounting by their principal for assets of the estate, and the principal cannot extend their liability by taking possession of property which is not properly assets of the estate. [Citations.]

It is, of course, the general rule that the death of either principal or agent terminates the relation. An exception to this rule is that if the authority or power of the agent be coupled with an interest in the subject-matter of the agency, then the power is not revocable either by death or by the act of the principal. [Citations.]

A power so coupled with an interest will survive to the personal representative of an agent upon the death of the latter. [Citations.]

It is urged that the agent here had such an interest in these notes as preserved his powers respecting them to his administratrix. But this contention is not maintainable in view of the allegations of complainant's bill. It is repeatedly therein averred that the decedent Ivey had no interest in the notes until payment in full was made to complainant for the trees. Since $755.05 was due to complainant on account of the stock sold at the time of decedent Ivey's death, according to further averments in the bill, it follows that by complainant's own allegations Ivey had no interest when he died in the subject-matter of the agency.

It is set out in the bill: "That such order, order blank or note, so signed by the purchaser of the nursery stock, was made payable to the complainant and was the property of complainant until all indebtedness due from the agent to complainant was paid in full. * * * Said notes were never transferred by complainant to any agent until after all indebtedness due the complainant by the agent was paid in full, after which time all notes in the hands of an agent became the property of such agent and was the compensation received by the agent as his profit. * * * That said notes in the possession of said B. W. Ivey as aforesaid, at the time of his death, taken in the name of complainant, as aforesaid, were the exclusive property of complainant until their account against said Ivey should be paid in full."

* * * As the contract sued upon is averred by the complainant, decedent's only interest attached to the notes remaining after complainant was paid. He had no interest in the notes as a whole.

It results that the decree of the lower courts must be reversed in so far as they held the surety liable.

Reversed.

PROBLEMS

1. P's agent A bought goods from T on credit in his (A's) name and delivered the goods to P. Not being paid, T sued A and recovered a judgment against him. A had no assets and the judgment remained unpaid. Thereafter, T learned that P was A's principal and brought suit against P for the purchase price of the goods. Decision?

2. P authorizes A to buy goods for him. A buys them in his own name from T, not disclosing that he is buying for a principal. T gives A a bill of the goods marked "paid" by mistake. A delivers the goods to P and asks P for the money exhibiting the bill as evidence of payment. P thereupon pays A. A does not pay T, who sues P. What are the rights of the parties?

3. Oldham owned and operated a store in Centerville under the name of the Fair Store. Sims was the manager of this store. On June 28, 1965, Oldham sold the store to Sims. While Sims was manager he ordered merchandise from Brice-Burton Dry Goods Company for the account of Oldham, and after he purchased the store he continued to order goods from Brice-Burton for the account of Oldham. Beginning in December, 1965, Betz, a salesman in the employ of Brice-Burton sold goods to the Fair Store. Sims made the purchases and the goods were billed to Oldham. No notice was given to Brice-Burton Company or Betz of the sale of the store to Sims. There was no difference in the operation of the store before June 28, 1965, and thereafter. When Brice-Burton learned of the sale of the Fair Store, it discontinued selling its merchandise to Sims, and unsuccessfully attempted to collect from Oldham the balance of $2,856 due on its merchandise account. Thereafter, Brice-Burton Company sued Oldham for $2,856 for merchandise sold subsequent to June 28, 1965. Decision?

4. P owned and operated a fruit cannery in Southton, Illinois. He stored a substantial amount of finished canned goods in a warehouse in East St. Louis, Illinois, owned and operated by A in order to have goods readily available for the St. Louis market. On March 1, he had 10,000 cans of peaches and 5,000 cans of apples on storage with A. On the day named, he borrowed $5,000 from A, giving A his promissory note for this amount due June 1 together with a letter authorizing A, in the event the note was not paid at maturity, to sell any or all of his goods on storage, pay the indebtedness and account to him for any surplus. P died on June 2, without having paid the note. On June 8, A told T, a wholesale food distributor, that he had for sale as agent of the owner, 10,000 cans of peaches and 5,000 cans of apples. T said he would take the peaches and would decide later about the apples.

A contract for the sale of 10,000 cans of peaches for $6,000 was thereupon signed. "A, agent for P, seller; T, buyer." Both A and T knew of the death of P. Delivery of the peaches and payment therefor were made on June 10. On June 11, A and T signed a similar contract covering the 5,000 cans of apples, delivery and payment to be made June 30. On June 23, P's executor, having learned of these contracts, wrote A and T stating that A had no authority to make the contracts, demanding that T return the peaches and directing A not to deliver the apples. Discuss the correctness of the contentions of P's executor.

5. A entered into a contract with B whereby B agreed to construct a house according to certain specifications. In making this contract, A was acting as the agent of P, an undisclosed principal. B constructed the building and after its completion discovered for the first time that A was merely the agent of P. Thereafter, B brought suit to hold A liable on the contract. Subsequently B brought suit against P on the contract. What judgment in each suit?

6. B made a valid contract with A whereunder A was to sell B's goods on commission during the period from January 1 to June 30. A made satisfactory sales up to May 15, and was then about to close an unusually large order when B suddenly and without notice revoked A's authority to sell. Can A continue to sell B's goods during the unexpired term of his contract?

7. A sold T 600 bags of grain and made certain warranties as to the quality of the grain. The warranties were not true, and T started suit against A. After he had gone to judgment in the suit, he discovered for the first time that A was acting for P, who ran a chain of grain stores. What remedy, if any, does T have against P? If he has a remedy what would determine whether or not he would use it in this case?

8. A was P's traveling salesman, and was also authorized to collect accounts. Prior to the agreed termination of the agency, P wrongfully discharged A. A then called on T, an old customer, and collected an account from T. He also called on X, a new prospect, as P's agent, secured a large order, collected the price of the order, sent the order to P, and disappeared with the collections. P delivered the goods to X as per the order.

(a) P sues T for his account. Decision?

(b) P sues X for the agreed price of the goods. Decision?

9. T owed P $150. A, P's agent, called on T, and an agreement was made, without any authority on A's part, that the debt was to be settled in full by T mailing to P a bond with a face value of $100, then having a market value of $100. T mailed the bond to P, stating that it was sent in full payment of his account, as per the agreement made with A. P replied that he repudiated the agreement made by A and would not be bound thereon, but would credit T's account with $100, and would look to T for the remaining $50. Can P hold T for the remaining $50? Decision?

10. (a) P instructed A, his agent, to purchase a quantity of hides. A bought the hides from T in his own (A's) name and delivered the hides to P. T, learning later that P was the principal, sends the bill to P, who gives A the money to pay to T. A absconds with the money. T sues P. Decision?

(b) Assume instead, that on discovering that P is A's principal, T sues A and P for the purchase price. Decision?

*

PART THREE
BAILMENTS AND CARRIERS

CHAPTER 15
BAILMENTS

Introductory. A bailment commonly involves delivery of possession, without transfer of title, by the owner called the bailor, to a person called the bailee for the accomplishment of a certain purpose, whereupon the property is to be returned by the bailee to the bailor or to a person designated by the bailor. But neither ownership in the bailor nor actual delivery to the bailee is essential to the bailment relation. Thus A, who merely has possession of personal property may deliver such possession to B and retain the right to have the property returned to him or returned to a person he designates, and the relation between A and B is one of bailment although it is possible that C, the true owner, may intervene and assert a better right to possession than either A or B may have. So also, B may obtain lawful possession of personal property without delivery, as by finding, and A may have the right to have the property returned to him either because A is the owner of the property or because he has a better right to possession than anyone else who claims it, and the relation between A and B is again that of bailment.

Essential Elements of a Bailment. The essential elements of a bailment include the following: (I) there must be lawful possession without title in the bailee (II) for a determinable time (III) of personal property (IV) which the bailee must restore when his lawful possession comes to an end (V) to the bailor who is either the owner or a person who has the superior right to possession.

Why a Law of Bailments? Before discussing some of the elements of a bailment, it is helpful to consider why there is a law of bailments at all. What are the sort of things the bailor and bailee might do or fail to do which will require intervention by the law? The bailor might (a) deliver defective personal property to the bailee causing the bailee to be injured; (b) fail to recompense the bailee for his services in keeping, transporting or working on the property bailed. The bailee might (a) fail to return the property to the bailor or to the person designated by him at the proper time, or altogether; (b) damage the property or permit it to be damaged while in his possession. The foregoing indicates why the subject matter of the law of bailments is not covered by the law of contracts and negligence.

The law of contracts is of a later origin than the law of bailments. Apart from this fact, there are good reasons why the bailment relationship has not been left to contract law, alone. Contract law would not cover cases where a person becomes a bailee through finding or some mistaken delivery. In many cases there would be additional problems of consideration. But the overriding reason why the bailment relationship was not left to contract law, alone, is that this would have impossibly complicated everyday business transactions. A person storing a car in a public garage, leaving personal property to be repaired or cleaned, or checking a hat or overcoat at a theater or restaurant, would have to enter into an elaborate contract each time in order to be assured of minimum safety for his property.

The law of negligence is closer both in fact and historically to the law of bailments than is the law of contract. But the law of negligence which requires that one take reasonable care not to injure another in his person or property has not been accepted as controlling in the relationship between bailor and bailee in several important respects. This will appear more fully when we discuss the duties of the bailee, and it will be seen that where the bailee is an innkeeper or a common carrier his duties are not governed by the law of negligence in any respect. We now consider some of the elements of a bailment:

I. *Possession.* The concept of possession is an elusive one at common law chiefly because it has been grafted on from the Roman law and the graft has not taken too well. But for purposes of the law of bailments, possession which will constitute a person a bailee may be said to involve: (1) physical control and (2) an intention to control on the part of the bailee, or instead of (2), (2a) an awareness on the part of the bailee that the rightful possessor has lost physical control of the personal property.

Thus, where a customer in a restaurant hangs his hat or coat on a hook furnished for this purpose, the hat or coat is within an area which is under the physical control of the restaurant owner, but the restaurant owner is not a bailee of the hat or coat unless he clearly signifies that he intends to exercise control over the hat or coat. On the other hand, where a clerk in a store helps a customer remove his coat in order to try on a new one, it is generally held that the owner of the store becomes a bailee of the old coat through the clerk, his employee. Here, the clerk has signified an intention to exercise control over the coat by taking it from the customer and a bailment results. Traditionally, the courts have spoken of delivery in

such cases. They have said that the customer in the restaurant does not "deliver" the coat or hat to the restaurant owner when he hangs it on a hook while the customer in the store "delivers" his coat to the clerk. But the concept of delivery does not account for many cases where a bailment is said to exist. Suppose that the customer in the restaurant hangs his hat on a hook and then forgets and leaves it behind. If now, while he is gone, the restaurant owner notices the hat and realizes that it has been left behind by one of his customers, he becomes a bailee of the hat. What has happened here is not that some mythical delivery has suddenly taken place, but the restaurant owner having physical control of the area in which the hat is found, is aware that the rightful possessor has lost physical control of it, and, according to our definition of possession, now has possession of the hat. This is really the position of all finders of personal property. A finder on the street is not a bailee merely because he has observed a billfold lying there. But he becomes a bailee as soon as he picks up the billfold. The reason for the difference between the finder in the street and the restaurant owner is that the finder on the street does not have physical control of the area in which the billfold is found, therefore he must assume physical control of the billfold before he can become a bailee. Pursuing our inquiry into the meaning of possession for purposes of bailment we come to several troublesome situations.

Parking Lot Transactions. The general rule is what we would expect it to be, namely, when an owner leaves his car in a parking lot, pays a charge and receives a claim check, but locks the car and takes the keys away, the parking lot attendant is not left with enough physical control of the car to constitute him a bailee. The courts have generally held that where the owner keeps the keys there is no bailment. But the amount of free access permitted by the parking lot operator is also material. Thus, where a parking lot is so constructed and manned by the parking lot operator that it is clearly impossible for anyone not authorized to enter and leave except through the parking lot operator's failure to carry out the obvious scheme of his operations, this may be sufficient to constitute him a bailee. The question is really how much control does the parking lot operator hold himself out to the public to be exercising? If by the physical structure of the parking lot, and by the way it appears to be manned, the parking lot operator holds himself out to be exercising a very high degree of control, the fact that the owner is not required to leave the car unlocked and the keys behind, should not prevent the transaction from becoming a bailment. This is not inconsistent with what has been said about possession. The significance of the keys is that, without them, the car cannot be moved, in theory. When a thief demonstrates that this is not true in practice, the parking lot operator may not be able to say that he did not have sufficient control of the car because he could not *cause* it to move, where it appears, by the physical structure of the lot and the way it was manned, that he had assumed sufficient control to *prevent* it from being moved.

Safe Deposit Companies. Normally, when a person rents a safe deposit box, the bank or safe deposit company will retain a guard or master key and the renter's access to the box is dependent upon the simultaneous use of both his own key and the key retained by the bank or safe deposit company. It should be fairly clear from what has been said about the parking lot operator, that the bank or the safe deposit company is a bailee. The conceptual difficulty experienced is due to the fact that what the depositor is concerned about is not the safe deposit box but its contents.

Things Within Things. The problem of the safe deposit box is that of things within things. It would never have existed at common law if it had not been for the influence of the Roman law concept of possession. Early common law knew no such concept. Carrier's Case, 1473, Y.B.Edw. IV fo. 9, Pasch.Pl. 5. The Roman law taught the common law that possession of the container implies possession of the contents. A strict application of this learning might have meant that a bailee of the container must be held liable for the safety of contents which he cannot reasonably be expected to know are there. But this did not become the rule at common law. Thus, the present rule is that a bailee is not liable for the contents of a closed container, or, to put it more correctly, for things which are not visible when the container is bailed to him, unless, from the nature of the container itself or from the surrounding circumstances, he ought, as a reasonable man, to have anticipated the presence of such contents, or unless he had express notice of what the contents were. This rule strictly pertains to the question of the bailee's liability and not to his possession, but it is discussed here because of its bearing upon the safe deposit situation. The safe deposit company is liable as bailee for the contents of the safe deposit box regardless of the value of the things contained therein, because it has a high degree of control in *preventing* unauthorized access and because, in view of the circumstances, it ought to anticipate that a safe deposit box might contain *any* kind of valuable thing which will fit into it.

The applicable law is well stated in National Safe Deposit Company v. Stead, 250 Ill. 584, 95 N.E. 973 (1911): "We think it clear that where a safety deposit company leases a safety deposit box or safe, and the lessee takes possession of the box or safe and places therein his securities or other valuables, the relation of bailee and bailor is created between the parties to the transaction as to such securities or other valuables, and that the fact that the safety deposit company does not know, and that it is not expected it shall know, the character or description of the property which is deposited in such safety deposit box or safe does not change that relation, any more than the relation of a bailee who should receive for safekeeping a trunk from a bailor would be changed by reason of the fact that the trunk was locked and the key retained by the bailor, although the obligation resting upon the bailee with reference to the care he should bestow upon the property in the trunk might depend upon his knowledge of the contents of the trunk. Obviously, the bailee would be in possession of the trunk and its contents, and no amount of argument would demonstrate that while the trunk was in possession of the bailee its contents were in the possession of the bailor, solely by reason of the fact that the bailor of the trunk retained the key and the bailee did not have access to the trunk. We are of the opinion that the relation of bailee and bailor exists between the appellant [National Safety Deposit Company] and its lessees, and that the deposit of the securities and valuables by its lessees in rented safety deposit boxes or safes is a bailment, and that the law applicable to bailments, generally, applies to such transactions and to such property."

Servants. Servants are not bailees of their masters' personal property because it is said that they do not have possession of such property but merely custody. Thus, a servant may exercise the degree of control over such property which would be sufficient to constitute one a bailee and he may have the required intention to exercise such control and yet he is not a bailee. A person in possession of property could not, at common law, be held for its theft. This did not please mediaeval masters and so it was early said that servants do not have possession but only custody. But the rule is not so much of an anomaly as would appear. A servant is under the complete control of his master and so it can be said that the control which he exercises over the master's personal property is not his own but the master's. So today, the question whether an agent, as opposed to a servant, is a bailee depends upon the degree of control which the principal assumes over him.

"Lawful" Possession. The requirement that the possession be lawful will be discussed more fully under the heading Rights and Duties of Bailor and Bailee.

II. *Possession for a Determinable Time.* To say that a bailment will only arise where the bailee has possession for a determinable time is merely to say that the bailee must be under a duty to return the personal property and must not have title to it. This brings us to the distinction between bailments and sales, and other transfers of title.

Sales. A sale always involves a transfer of title to the buyer. If the identical property is to be returned, even though in altered form, the transaction is a bailment, but if other property of equal value, or the money value, may be returned, there is a transfer of title and the transaction is a sale. Whether a particular transaction constitutes a bailment or a sale must be determined by the particular factual situation presented. The substance of the agreement, and its form or the particular expressions employed in it, is controlling.

The buyer does not always obtain title on delivery of the goods to him. Thus, in a sale "on approval" or on trial or on satisfaction, the buyer will obtain possession of goods but he will not obtain the property in them until he signifies his approval or acceptance to the seller. In one sense, therefore, a buyer on approval is a bailee of the goods until he signifies his approval. He will be charged with the same duty of care, before approval, as that required of a bailee. But his position is different from that of the bailee in several important respects. If the goods are destroyed while in his possession, due to his negligence, he will be liable for the contract price and not for the market value of the goods. If the buyer resells the goods to a third party before signifying his approval to the seller, he is regarded as thereby approving of the goods, and title passes to him and through him to the third party. A bailee would be guilty of conversion if he sold the bailed property, and he would pass no better title to the third party than he himself had.

Conditional Sales. In a conditional sale, usually on the installment plan, the contract expressly reserves the title to the goods in the seller until the purchase price is paid in full. But title is reserved in the seller for security purposes only. For all other purposes, including risk of loss, beneficial ownership is in the buyer. The position of the buyer under a conditional sales contract is not the same as that of a bailee in any respect. He has no option to return the goods, but must pay the contract price. The fact that the goods are damaged or destroyed without his fault will not relieve him from payment of the contract price because the goods are at his risk.

Other Transfers of Title. Whenever a person intentionally abandons all his interest in certain personal property, the relation between him and a person who takes possession of the property will not be that of bailor and bailee. A loser and finder are bailor and bailee because, although the loser may abandon hope that he will ever find the property, he does not abandon his interest in it. One who intentionally throws his property away, however, cannot be bailor because he has abandoned his interest in it. Likewise, one who gives his property to another is not a bailor. The finder of intentionally abandoned property and the donee of a gift are not bailees.

III. *Personal Property.* The bailment relation can only exist with respect to personal property. It is not necessary that the property be tangible. Such choses in action as promissory notes, and corporate bonds, being evidenced by written instruments and so capable of delivery, may be and frequently are the subject matter of bailments. This is also true of such documents of title as warehouse receipts and bills of lading.

IV. *The Bailee Must Restore the Possession of the Property When His Lawful Possession Comes to an End.*

V. *The Bailor to Whom the Goods are Restored Must be Either the Owner or a Person Who Has the Superior Right to Possession.* These two elements of the bailment relationship will be discussed under the next heading, Rights and Duties of Bailor and Bailee.

Rights and Duties of Bailor and Bailee.

Bailee Must Exercise Care. The bailee must exercise care not to injure or destroy the property bailed, and must exercise care not to permit injury or destruction of it by others.

Bailments are commonly classified as bailments for mutual benefit or for hire, bailments for the sole benefit of the bailee, and bailments for the sole benefit of the bailor. Ordinarily, a bailee is not an insurer of the subject of the bailment. Since negligence in the care of property is the basis of his liability, in the absence of negligence, the bailee is not liable where the goods are lost, or stolen, or destroyed by fire.

In the context of a commercial bailment, from which both parties derive a benefit, the law requires the bailee to exercise the care which a reasonably prudent person would exercise under the same circumstances. Where the bailment is one which benefits the bailee alone, as in the case of one who gratuitously borrows a truck from another, the law has required more than reasonable care of him. On the other hand, where the bailee accepts the goods to accommodate the bailor, without himself deriving any economic benefit from this, the law has required only slight care upon his part. These distinctions are still preserved in a judge's instructions to the jury. Thus, in the case of a bailment for the bailee's sole benefit, the jury will be instructed that the law requires the bailee to exercise greater care than that of a reasonably prudent person, while in the case of a commercial bailment, the jury will be told that the bailee was required to exercise the care of a reasonably prudent person.

It should be remembered, however, that the amount of care required to satisfy any of the standards will vary with the character of the property. A bailee required to take only slight care under the foregoing general rules may be liable if he does not take greater care of a $500 bracelet than he would have of a $10 watch. In practice, therefore, the distinctions are blurred by the fact that whatever degree of care is required in the abstract, a bailee must respond to the magnitude of the consequences which reasonably ought to have been foreseen if the property were lost or destroyed.

Limitation of Liability. As we shall see, the law does not permit certain bailees, namely, common carriers, public warehousemen and innkeepers, to limit their liability except as provided by statute. Other bailees, however, are free to vary their duties and liabilities in whatever manner they deem fit by contract with the bailor. There is, of course, a limit in what the market will stand. However, the law requires that any such limitation be properly brought to the attention of the bailor before the goods are bailed by him. A variation or limitation in writing contained in a check or stub given to the bailor or posted on the walls of the bailee's place of business will not ordinarily bind the bailor unless (a) the bailee draws his attention to the writing and (b) informs him that

it contains a limitation or variation of liability, although the bailee is not required to read and interpret the limitation or variation to the bailor.

Burden of Proof as to Bailee's Negligence. When the goods are lost, damaged or destroyed while in the possession of the bailee, it is often impossible for the bailor to obtain enough information to show that the loss or damage was due to the bailee's negligence. The law aids the bailor in this respect by setting up a presumption that the bailee was negligent. The bailor is merely required to show that certain goods were delivered to the bailee and that the bailee has failed to return them or that they were returned in damaged condition. Upon introduction of this proof, the law raises a presumption that the loss or damage was due to the bailee's negligence and the burden then rests upon the bailee to prove that he exercised the care required of him or that he is unable to return the goods for some other reason which constitutes an adequate defense to an action for failure to return.

Bailee Must Return Bailed Property to Bailor or Person Designated by Bailor at Proper Time and Place. The very nature of a bailment requires a bailee to return the goods when the purpose of the bailment has been accomplished. The bailee must return the goods to the bailor or to a person designated by the bailor at the proper time or place. The bailee has a very strict duty to return the goods to the correct person. Normally, the bailee is required to return the identical goods bailed although the goods may be in a changed condition due to the work which the bailee was required to perform upon them. However, there is a necessary exception to this rule in the case of fungible goods, such as grain, where, for all practical purposes, every particle is precisely like every other particle, and when the bailee is required or expected to mingle with other such goods during the bailment. In such a case, obviously the bailee cannot be required to return the identical goods bailed. His obligation is simply to return goods of the same quality and quantity out of the common mass. Where fungible goods belonging to several bailors are properly stored in a common mass, for example, grain in an elevator, and a portion of the common mass is destroyed without fault upon the part of the bailee, each of the bailors whose goods make up the common mass will bear the loss in proportion to his share of the common mass.

Exception to Bailee's Duty to Return Bailed Property. The bailee is excused from the duty to return the bailed property in undamaged condition if he has exercised the degree of care required of him under the particular bailment, while the property was within his control. To this general rule there are certain important exceptions.

(a) Where the bailee has an obligation by express agreement with the bailor or by custom to insure the goods against certain risks, but fails to do so and the goods are destroyed or damaged by such risk, he is liable for the damage or non-delivery, notwithstanding that he has exercised due care.

(b) Where the bailee uses the bailed property in a manner not authorized by the bailor or by the character of the bailment, and during the course of such use the property is damaged or destroyed, without fault on the part of the bailee, the bailee is absolutely liable for the damage or destruction. The reason for this is that wrongful use by the bailee automatically terminates his lawful possession, and he becomes a trespasser as to the property. That is what we have earlier referred to as the requirement that the possession must be "lawful" to constitute a bailment. A trespasser is not a bailee, and he is absolutely liable for all damage resulting to the property which would not have occurred but for his trespass, regardless of fault. To illustrate the last rule, suppose a garage mechanic, after repairing A's car, takes it out for a road test, and the car is damaged in an accident which is solely the fault of someone other than the mechanic. The proprietor of the garage will not be liable as bailee for such damage, a road test being a normal incident to this type of bailment. But where the mechanic takes A's car for a joy ride, and the car is damaged solely through the fault of someone other than the mechanic, the proprietor will be liable as bailee for such damage. The better modern opinion is that the garage operator cannot escape liability upon the ground that his mechanic was acting outside the scope of his employment.

(c) A bailee has an absolute duty to return the property to the right person. The classical rule is that he is not excused from delivering the property to the wrong person by mistake, even where such mistake was induced by negligence on the part of the bailor. But it is doubtful whether modern opinion would render the bailee liable for misdelivery without some slight fault on his part. A mistake generally involves lack of sufficient attention on the part of the mistaken party. But where the bailor loses a claim check to his coat, and the bailee delivers the coat to the finder of the claim check, under circumstances where it is impossible for the bailee to know that the finder is not the true bailor, it is doubtful that the bailee would be liable, although, under the classical view, he would not be excused. With this possible exception, the bailee is liable for misdelivery, regardless of fault, except: (1) Where the person to whom he delivers the property is better entitled to its possession than the bailor. It is not sufficient that the bailee thinks that such person is so entitled. (2) Where the property is taken from the bailee under valid legal process, as by a sheriff under a writ of execution. But, in all such cases, the bailee must take care to notify the bailor before he surrenders the property, and if he fails to do so, and the bailor is thereby deprived of some legal remedy to avert the seizure of the property, the bailee will be liable to the bailor. The legal process must be formally valid, and as we shall see when we come to Documents of Title, the bailee is not justified in surrendering the property unless any outstanding negotiable document of title to the property is surrendered to him, or its further negotiation is enjoined.

The fact that the bailee may be excused for misdelivery where he delivers to the person best entitled to possession brings out the point that a bailor is not always the owner. A person having lawful possession of property for the time being may validly bail the property to another. Thus, an agent may bail his principal's property, if he is authorized to do so. A person having lawful right to possession under some agreement with the owner may bail the property, if he does not thereby violate the agreement. If such an agent or other person having lawful possession bails the property in violation of his authority from, or agreement with, the owner, he loses his right to possession and the best right to possession will vest in the owner. The bailee then is justified in delivering the property to the owner instead of to the bailor. But the bailee is not justified in delivering the property to the owner if the bailor has not exceeded his authority or violated any agreement with the owner, and where, by the terms of his authority from, or agreement with, the owner he continues to be entitled to the possession of the property as against the owner. Thus, a bailee may assume a risk when he delivers property to its owner merely because he happens to be the owner. That is why we have said earlier that the two last elements of a bailment relationship are that the bailee must restore the possession of the property, when his lawful possession comes to an end, to the bailor, who

is either the owner or a person who has the superior right to possession.

It is an old rule that the bailee is estopped to deny the bailor's title to the property. What is meant is that the bailee may not set up a better right to possession in someone other than the bailor as an excuse for failure to return the property to the bailor.

If the bailee, by mistake or intentionally, misdelivers the property to someone other than the bailor, someone who has no right to its possession, he is guilty of conversion and is liable to the bailor, except, possibly, in the case of an innocent mistaken delivery to the finder of a claim check.

Rights of Bailor and Bailee When Third Party Injures the Goods. If a third party negligently damages the goods, both the bailor and the bailee have a right of action against him. The law permits either the bailor or the bailee to sue alone for the entire damage. In such case, whichever one sues, he is required to account to the other for that portion of the entire recovery which represents the other's interest in the goods.

Difficult questions arise when the bailee is guilty of contributory negligence. In jurisdictions where contributory negligence is a complete bar to an action, the question arises whether the bailor may nevertheless sue the third party upon the theory that *he* was not negligent. Certainly, where the bailee has a substantial compensable interest in the goods, the bailor should not be permitted to recover the entire damages against the third party. If he were, he would be required to account to the bailee for that portion of the recovery which represents the bailee's interest. The bailee would thus be indirectly compensated by the third party despite his own contributory negligence. Most courts deny full recovery to the bailor under these circumstances. Partial recovery for the damage done to the bailor's interest in the goods is generally permitted.

Bailee's Rights to Compensation and Reimbursement for Expenses.

Compensation: A bailee who by agreement, express or implied, undertakes to perform work upon, or render services in connection with, the bailed goods is entitled to reasonable compensation therefor. In most cases, of course, the agreement between bailor and bailee fixes the amount of compensation and provides how it shall be paid. In the absence of a contrary agreement, the compensation is payable upon completion of the work or the performance of the services by the bailee. If, after such completion or performance, and before the goods are redelivered to the bailor, the goods are lost or damaged without fault upon the part of the bailee, the bailee is still entitled to compensation for his work and services. The same is true if the goods are lost or destroyed without fault of the bailee before his work has been fully completed or his services fully rendered. In such case the bailee is entitled to compensation pro tanto for the materials used and the labor bestowed upon the goods up to the moment of loss or damage. The contract between bailor and bailee may, however, specifically provide that compensation shall not be due until the goods are safely redelivered to the bailor. The mere fact that the payment is not normally due until the bailee redelivers the goods is not sufficient to prevent the bailee from recovering compensation in case the goods are lost or damaged without his fault. To have this result, the contract must clearly provide that no payment is due unless the goods are redelivered safely.

Where the bailee, in breach of his obligation, fails to complete the work or services agreed upon, the prevailing view is that he is not entitled to offset the cost of his services against the damages due to the bailor. In practice, however, particularly in jury cases, the damages assessed in favor of the bailor will probably reflect the benefit actually conferred upon the bailor by the bailee's partial performance.

Expenses: The bailee who performs work or services on the bailed chattel is, of course, entitled to compensation for those expenses which are incident to his performance. In a different type of bailment, which does not involve the performance of work or services by the bailee, the question arises as to who is to bear the expenses incident to such bailment. For instance, who is to bear the expenses incident to the bailment involved in the rental of an automobile? The rule is that, unless the agreement between the parties provides otherwise, the bailee bears all the ordinary expenses of maintenance, i. e., he has to pay for gas, oil, and for all ordinary repairs and replacements. Ordinary repairs and replacements, in this context, are such as are normally incident to the operation of an automobile of comparable age in reasonable condition. The bailor, however, bears the cost of all extraordinary repairs and replacements, i. e., such as are not normally incident to the operation of an automobile of comparable age in reasonable condition.

Bailee's Lien. Today, most bailees who are entitled to compensation for work and services performed in connection with bailed goods acquire a lien upon the goods for the payment of such compensation. Originally, under the common law, such a lien was acquired only by those who, by law, were required to accept goods in bailment. Such bailees were common carriers and innkeepers. The common-law lien, moreover, was a *possessory* lien. This meant that the lien continued only so long as the bailee retained possession of the bailed goods. Furthermore, the bailee had no right to sell the goods for the satisfaction of his charges—all that he could do was to retain the goods until payment.

By statute in most jurisdictions the bailee is given the right to obtain a judicial foreclosure of his lien and sale of the goods.

The right to acquire such lien has been extended to all who perform work or services in connection with bailed goods. A substantial number of statutes provide, also, that the bailee does not lose his lien upon redelivery of the goods to the bailor—as was the case with the common-law possessory lien. Instead, the lien continues for a specified period after redelivery. The bailee, however, must perfect his lien by recording an instrument claiming such lien with the proper authorities. Special forms for such instruments are available and the statutes provide that these must be filed within a specified time, usually six months, of the redelivery. If, after such filing, the charges are not paid the lien may be foreclosed by court action and the goods seized and sold. The bailee's lien, whether statutory or common-law, is generally a "special" lien. A "special" lien is a lien which secures only those charges which arise out of work and services performed in connection with the article subjected to the lien. A "general" lien, on the other hand, secures all debts as between the bailor and bailee without regard to the source of the debt.

Special Kinds of Bailees.

Pledgee: A pledge is a security device by which the owner gives possession of his goods to another to secure a debt or to assure the performance of some obligation. A pledge is similar to a lien, in that both the pledgee and the lienholder have no title to the goods involved but merely a special interest to secure a debt or some other obligation. However, the lienholder's interest is personal to him, and he cannot assign it to anyone else. The pledgee, however, can transfer and assign his special interest in the goods to others, even without the consent of the pledgor. Furthermore, the pledgee always had the right under the common law to sell the goods in satisfaction of his debt, whereas the lienholder had no such right until statutes specifically so provided. At the present time, most jurisdictions have statutes governing sales by the pledgee. These statutes generally withdraw from him his common-law right to sell the goods and make the statutory procedure mandatory. The statutes vary in their provisions. Some allow sale only by court order; others permit private sale by the pledgee upon compliance with the statutory requirements for notice to all interested parties. In all other respects, the pledgee's duties and liabilities are the same as those of the bailee for compensation.

Warehouseman: A warehouseman is a bailee who receives goods and merchandise to be stored in his warehouse for compensation. His duties and liabilities under the common law were in all respects the same as those of the ordinary bailee for compensation. The common law imposed very strict liability upon certain bailees such as common carriers and innkeepers because of their "common calling." Due, perhaps, to the fact that warehousing of consumer goods was not as widespread in the early days of the common law as it is today, the common law did not place warehousemen in the same category as common carriers and innkeepers. Thus, it did not impose upon the warehouseman any greater duty of care than that of the ordinary bailee for compensation. While the common carrier and innkeeper were not permitted to reject, the one, goods properly tendered for carriage, the other, unobjectionable wayfarers as guests, the warehouseman was not required, under the common law, to accept goods properly tendered for storage.

The rule that a warehouseman has no greater duty of care than the ordinary bailee for compensation still survives. However, because their activities affect the public welfare, warehousemen are today subject to extensive regulation by State and Federal authorities. Statutes changing the rule as to acceptance of goods properly tendered for storage, and imposing extensive regulations involving structural safety and health measure are in force in all jurisdictions. Similar Federal statutes govern warehousemen who store goods for interstate and foreign commerce. Warehousemen must also be distinguished from ordinary bailees in that the receipts they issue for storage have acquired a special status in commerce. These receipts are regarded as "documents of title" and are governed by rules which are codified in Article 7 of the Uniform Commercial Code.

Some State statutes provide that a warehouseman's liability may be limited by a provision in the warehouse receipt that the warehouseman's liability shall not exceed a value stated in the warehouse receipt, if the warehouseman's rates vary with value and the depositor is afforded an opportunity to declare a higher value, and also may be limited by reasonable provisions as to the time and manner of presenting claims or instituting actions against the warehouseman. No such limitation, however, is effective with respect to the warehouseman's liability for gross negligence, willful wrong or fraud.

Termination of the Bailment. A bailment for the mutual benefit of both parties ordinarily terminates when the purpose of the bailment is fully accomplished or when the time expires for which the bailment was created. Such bailment may, of course, be terminated earlier by mutual consent of the parties. A breach by the bailee of any of his obligations gives the bailor the privilege of terminating the bailment forthwith. A bailment is terminated, in a sense, by the destruction of the bailed goods. It is terminated, because there can be no bailment without the bailed goods, yet if the loss is due to the bailee's fault he, of course, continues to be liable under his bailment obligation.

Bailments for the benefit of the bailee alone or for the benefit of the bailor alone are ordinarily bailments for a definite time or purpose. Such bailments cannot be terminated by either party until the specified time expires or the purpose is accomplished. In practice, however, such bailments are often terminated at will. For example, one who has gratuitously undertaken to store his neighbor's piano for six months will most likely be able to return the piano before the expiration of that period with impunity. It is unlikely that litigation will ensue. However, if he dumps it back in the neighbor's garage before the six months expire, while his neighbor is away on vacation, and the piano is damaged he may well be liable. Similarly, one who has gratuitously borrowed a lawnmower to cut his grass will probably return it if asked to do so before his special purpose is accomplished unless he is willing to face social opprobrium by insisting that he retain possession until he shall have completed the mowing of his lawn pursuant to his rights under the bailment.

CASES

LAVAL v. LEOPOLD

(1965) 47 Misc.2d 624, 262 N.Y.S.2d 820.

BERNARD NADEL, J. Plaintiff brings this action to recover $1,725, the value of plaintiff's coat, which she claims she delivered into defendant's care and custody and which was not returned.

Defendant moves for summary judgment, asserting that there are no triable issues of fact and that plaintiff, as a matter of law, was guilty of contributory negligence and therefore may not have a recovery against him. Plaintiff cross-moves for summary judgment in her favor.

Defendant is a practicing psychiatrist, who, at the time, when plaintiff was his patient, maintained his office with two associates or colleagues, also practicing in the same field.

No receptionist or other employee attended the office.

Plaintiff claims that on one of her professional visits to defendant's office, in accordance with her usual custom she deposited her coat in a clothes closet in the office reception room. When plaintiff's professional consultation was complete and she was ready to leave defendant's office, her coat was missing.

The maintenance of the closet in defendant's office created an implied invitation to plaintiff to deposit her coat there.

In Webster v. Lane, 125 Misc. 868, 212 N.Y.S. 298, which involved the loss of a coat in a dentist's office, the court took judicial notice of the fact that patients of a dentist are not placed in a dental chair with their wraps on. This court likewise takes judicial notice that it is not the custom for a patient to lie on the couch or sit in the chair in a psychiatrist's office wrapped in her fur coat.

The plaintiff cannot be said to be contributorily negligent as a matter of law because she placed her coat in a clothes closet in defendant's reception room.

" * * * that defendant undertook voluntary custody of the coat as an accommodation to his patient, and as part of the service for which he was being paid. [Citation.]" Webster v. Lane, supra.

Implicit in the relationship between the parties, the defendant became a bailee of plaintiff's coat, and it is for the trier of the facts to determine whether under the circumstances then prevailing at the time and place of this happening, reasonable care was exercised by the defendant with reference to plaintiff's coat which was temporarily deposited in the reception room closet preliminary to treatment by the defendant.

Accordingly, the motion and cross-motion are denied.

DRYBROUGH v. VEECH

(1951 Ky.) 238 S.W.2d 996.

MILLIKEN, J. This is an appeal from an order of the trial court overruling defendant's (Drybrough's) motion for judgment notwithstanding a verdict against him for $214. The motion was made under Section 386, Civil Code of Practice, and is based on the assertion that the pleadings entitle the defendant to judgment notwithstanding the verdict. Because the pleadings and procedure in the trial court are the subjects under discussion, we shall refer to the parties as plaintiff and defendant rather than appellee and appellant.

The plaintiff, Ray F. Veech, filed her petition stating that she had parked her automobile at the parking lot of the defendant, F. W. Drybrough, on South Fourth Street, Louisville, paid fifty cents for the privilege, and that the defendant, Drybrough, "and his agents and servants so negligently managed and conducted said parking lot * * * as to cause and permit the plaintiff's fur coat to be stolen from the automobile while parked on said lot." The petition alleged that "as a direct and proximate result of said negligence" the plaintiff suffered damages amounting to the value of the fur coat.

The defendant, Drybrough, filed no demurrer to the petition, but simply filed an answer stating "that he is without knowledge or information sufficient to constitute a belief and therefore specifically denies each and every additional allegation, word, and figure of the plaintiff's petition." Upon a verdict being rendered for the plaintiff, the defendant moved the court for judgment notwithstanding the verdict upon the ground that the petition did not state a cause of action. When the trial court overruled this motion, appeal was taken directly from this ruling.

* * *

The petition in the case at bar alleges a bailment of the automobile, but no bailment of the contents of the car or the fur coat. The only way the petition can be considered adequate as imposing a duty on the bailee in regard to the fur coat is for us to conclude that the bailment of the automobile implies a bailment of the contents of the car. As stated in appellant's brief: "Here it is claimed an automobile was bailed and a coat was stolen." In the one Kentucky case upon the subject, Barnett v. Latonia Jockey Club, 1933, 249 Ky. 285, 60 S.W.2d 622, 624, we said: "Moreover, this action complains of no dereliction with reference to the automobile, but only of what happened to its contents, and the law recognizes well-settled distinctions between liability of a bailee for a bailed vehicle and liability for its contents, the latter existing only in special cases which it is the duty of the loser (the alleged bailor) to both allege and prove before recovery may be had."

There being no allegation of a bailment of the coat or its presence in the car being called to the attention of the parking lot attendants in any way, we conclude there was no duty as to the coat imposed upon the appellant or his agents at the parking lot and as a consequence they could not be negligent as to it. It is not necessary for us to discuss cases involving obligations of gratuitous bailees because here there was no bailment of the coat, gratuitous or otherwise. Where a petition fails to state a duty owed by the defendant, as in the case at bar, a judgment notwithstanding the verdict should be entered for the defendant. [Citation.]

The judgment is reversed with directions for the trial court to enter judgment for the defendant in accordance with his motion notwithstanding the verdict against him.

KERGALD v. ARMSTRONG TRANSFER EXP. CO.

(1953) 330 Mass. 254, 113 N.E.2d 53.

LUMMUS, J. This is an action of contract, begun by writ dated August 26, 1949, in which the plaintiff sues for the loss of her trunk and its contents. The defendant is an intrastate common carrier. There was evidence that the plaintiff arrived with her trunk at the South Station in Boston late in an evening in May, 1949, and went to the defendant's office there. She was not asked the value of her trunk, but was given a small pasteboard check by the defendant which was not read to her and which she did not read, but put in her purse. The trunk was to be delivered at her home in Boston. The defendant failed to deliver her trunk, and admitted that it had been lost. The small check had on one side the order number and the words "Read contract on reverse side," and on the other the words, "The holder of this check agrees that the value of the baggage checked does not exceed $100 unless a greater value has been declared at time of checking and additional payment made therefor." * * *

The judge instructed the jury, over the exception of the defendant, that the plaintiff is bound by that limitation if she had knowledge of it when she took the check, and otherwise is not. The jury returned a verdict for the plaintiff for $1,700, and the defendant brought the case here.

Where what is given to a plaintiff purports on its face to set forth the terms of a contract, the plaintiff, whether he reads it or not, by accepting it assents to its terms, and is bound by any limitation of liability therein contained, in the absence of fraud. [Citations.]

On the other hand, where as in this case what is received is apparently a means of identification of the property bailed, rather than a complete contract, the bailor is not bound by a limitation upon the liability of the bailee unless it is actually known to the bailor. [Citations.]

The cases in this Commonwealth so clearly show the law applicable to the facts of this case that we need not discuss decisions elsewhere. But we may say that our conclusions are supported by well-reasoned cases in New York as well as other jurisdictions. [Citations.] In our opinion no error is disclosed by the record.

Exceptions overruled.

MALONE v. SANTORA

(1949) 135 Conn. 286, 64 A.2d 51.

BROWN, J. The plaintiff in each of these cases sued the defendant to recover for damage to the plaintiff's automobile consequent upon its being stolen from the defendant's parking lot, where the plaintiff owner had left it and paid the required parking charge. In each case judgment was rendered for the plaintiff and the defendant has appealed.

The essential facts are undisputed and may be thus summarized: The plaintiff Johnson's car was stolen on the evening of November 22, 1946, and that of the plaintiff Malone on the evening of November 29, 1946. Each was subsequently recovered in damaged condition. The defendant's parking lot, with a capacity of 150 cars, has a frontage of 70 feet on the north side of East Main Street in Waterbury and a depth of 270 feet. It is effectively inclosed except for two entrances, one, about 14 feet wide, at a rear corner, and the other, 59 feet wide, on East Main Street. About 8 p. m. on November 22 the plaintiff Johnson drove her car into the lot, paid the defendant or one of his attendants the customary twenty-five-cent charge and left the car with him in response to his statement, "Leave your keys, I'll park the car." She left her keys

in the car and he parked it. For the purpose of identification she was given a ticket, a detached part of which he placed on the car. On it was printed: "Liability. Management assumes no responsibility of any kind. Charges are for Rental of space. From 8 A.M. to 11 P.M. Not responsible for articles left in or on the car. Agree to the within terms." She read these words and understood their purport to be that the car owner agreed to the terms stated. There was also a sign on the premises which she did not notice and which read: "Charges are for use of Parking space until 11 P.M. Not responsible for cars left open after 11 P.M. You may lock your car." She left and when she returned for her car shortly before 11 p. m. it could not be found. It had been stolen meantime. Upon her return the defendant and two attendants were there on duty. In accepting this car as he did, the defendant acted in the ordinary course of his business as a parking lot operator and in accord with his practice as to the car of the plaintiff and as to those of many others, not only upon that evening but upon other occasions also. It was his policy to insist that no one claiming a car should be allowed to drive it off the lot without first presenting the identifying ticket, unless the claimant was known to the defendant or his employees.

About 7 p. m. on November 29 the plaintiff Malone drove his car onto the parking lot, turned it over to one of the defendant's employees, paid the twenty-five-cent charge and received a ticket from the attendant, who placed the detached part of it on the car. The printing on the ticket was of the same purport as recited above. Malone put the ticket in his pocket without reading it and left. The attendant parked the car, leaving the key in the switch. Shortly before 10 p. m. Malone returned, presented the ticket to the attendant and demanded his car. It could not be found. Meantime a person had entered the lot and stated to one of the attendants that his brother was the owner of the car and that he had requested him to get the car for him. Malone had authorized no one to call for the car and the person making the request was an imposter and a thief. One of the attendants delivered the car to him and he drove it away. On that evening at least three attendants were on duty.

In each case the court concluded: There was a bailor and bailee relationship between the plaintiff and defendant; the wording on ticket and sign did not bar the plaintiff's right of recovery; on the ground of public policy the bailment was not subject to the limitation on liability therein set forth; the defendant was negligent in the discharge of his duty as bailee; the plaintiff is entitled to recover for the damage accruing to his car, that of the plaintiff Johnson being $168 and that of the plaintiff Malone $400. Whether these conclusions are justified is the question determinative of these appeals.

In recent years there have been many decisions concerning the liability of operators of parking lots for cars parked thereon by customers. As has been well observed, cases of this nature may be divided into "two types: first, those where the attendant merely collects the fee and designates the area in which to park, the driver himself doing the parking and retaining complete control over the car, locking it or not as he wishes; and second, those lots, usually enclosed, where the attendants take complete charge of the car at the entrance, park it, retain the keys and move the car about as necessary, giving the driver a check or ticket, upon presentation of which they deliver the car to him." 27 Geo.L.J. 162, 163. As this article goes on to point out, situations of the second type have usually been held to give rise to liability on the ground that the transaction is a bailment, while liability has been denied in those of the first, the courts holding that the lack of the essential element of possession in the lot

operator renders the relationship one of a license or of a privilege to park rather than of bailment. Of the large number of authorities which have recognized this basic distinction and held assumption of control the determinative factor, we cite but a few. [Citations.]

Whether a car owner merely hires a place to put his car or has turned its possession over to the care and custody of the lot operator depends on the place, the conditions and the nature of the transaction. [Citation.] Among the significant facts in each of the instant cases were these: The lot was inclosed; the defendant's attendants were present to attend to cars brought in to be parked; the plaintiff paid the parking charge to the attendant who gave him his claim ticket; the plaintiff left the switch key in the car at the request of the attendant who then took the car and parked it; no particular space for placing the car was either mentioned or contemplated. Under the principles which we have stated, it is clear that in each case these facts, without more, warranted, if in fact they did not require, the conclusion that the relationship between the plaintiff and the defendant was that of bailor and bailee.

In neither case has the defendant assigned error in the court's finding that the plaintiff's car was stolen. He does however, attack its conclusion in each that the theft of the car with the damage accruing to the plaintiff was due to the defendant's negligence. The court's conclusion was warranted on the record. The return of the car to the plaintiff in a damaged condition raised a presumption that this was due to the negligence of the bailee and prima facie established his liability; the presumption ceased to operate when the defendant had proven the circumstances of the theft of the car; and it was then for the trial court in the light of those circumstances to determine whether or not the bailee was negligent. [Citation.] The finding, interpreted in the light of the memorandum of decision, makes clear that the court did find the bailee negligent.

The defendant has assigned error in the court's conclusion that recovery was not barred by any limitation of liability in the ticket's provision or the wording of the sign. In so far as the Malone case is concerned, the fact that the plaintiff had no knowledge of the content of either shows that he did not assent to and could not have been bound by any such agreement. [Citation.] In the Johnson case also there is good reason for concluding that one purpose for which the ticket was given and accepted was to afford a means of identification for the plaintiff in claiming her car and that it did not constitute a contract exempting the defendant from liability. The language of the ticket suggests that the defendant was charging the plaintiff only rental of space and assumed no responsibility of any kind. Since the plaintiff read the ticket she knew its terms. Had she herself parked the car on the lot, left it there and paid the charge, the transaction might have been regarded as constituting a case of the first type referred to above, with consequent immunity of the defendant from liability for theft of the car. Even so, the court's conclusion that the defendant was responsible under a bailor and bailee relationship was not necessarily unwarranted. An existing contract may be modified or abrogated by a new contract arising by implication from the conduct of the parties. [Citation.] So here the defendant's subsequent assumption of control of the car, acquiesced in by the plaintiff, was totally inconsistent with an agreement of the first type and afforded reason for concluding that the contract actually made was one of bailment of which the provision exculpating the defendant from responsibility was no part. Actions may be held to speak louder than words, and the defendant's assumption of control of the car may be held to have

negatived any intent by either party that an agreement for a license upon the terms indicated by the ticket should in fact arise. Upon the facts, what was in form such a contract lacked that intent to make it effective without which no true contract could come into existence. [Citation.]

We must regard the transaction in the Johnson case as giving rise to a bailment, and the provision against liability printed on the ticket could not avail the defendant to bar recovery by the plaintiff. This is so because of "the well-recognized rule that the right of a bailee to limit his liability by special contract does not go to the extent of relieving him against his own negligence." [Citations.] The reason is that such a provision is "revolting to the moral sense, and contrary alike to the salutary principles of law and a sound public policy." Welch v. Boston & A. R. Co., 41 Conn. 331, at page 342.

* * *

There is no error in either case.

[Judgments affirmed.]

HENDERICK v. UPTOWN SAFE DEPOSIT CO.

(1959) 21 Ill.App.2d 515, 159 N.E.2d 58.

FRIEND, P. J. Plaintiff, who had rented a safe deposit box in the vault of defendant, Uptown Safe Deposit Company, a corporation, brought suit to recover damages for the alleged failure of defendant to keep safe $37,750 in cash alleged to have been placed in the box and to have disappeared. Trial by the court and jury resulted in a verdict for the amount claimed, and after the denial of post-trial motions, judgment was entered on the verdict, from which defendant appeals.

The complaint, as amended, alleges that the funds were not lost or misplaced by plaintiff but, through the carelessness and negligence of defendant in the maintenance and protection of her property, disappeared from the box leased for her use. Defendant's answer denied carelessness and negligence and, by way of affirmative defense, averred that it exercised the ordinary care and diligence required of a bailee in the preservation of any and all deposited property by plaintiff when the box was in the exclusive control of defendant and not in the use of plaintiff or the co-renters.

It is agreed that the relation between the parties was that of bailor and bailee. Within this relation, the depositary for hire was bound to exercise ordinary care and diligence in the preservation of plaintiff's property. Ordinary care in such cases has been defined to be such care as prudent men take of their own property; and ordinary diligence, as men of common prudence usually exercise about their own affairs. [Citations.] The duty of exercising such care arises from the nature of the business which the safe deposit company carries on. The obligation to discharge such duty is implied from the relation between the parties. [Citation.] However, defendant was not an insurer of the safety of the contents of plaintiff's deposit box. [Citation.] It is fundamental that in an action based on negligence the plaintiff must not only allege but also prove actionable negligence; and while plaintiff is entitled to the most favorable inferences that can be drawn from the evidence, nevertheless, in a case of this kind, there must be some competent evidence that the money had been taken from the box without the knowledge or consent of plaintiff and the co-renters, by reason of defendant's failure to exercise ordinary care in safeguarding her property.

From evidence adduced upon the hearing, as set out in a record of almost 500 pages, it appears that plaintiff was about eighty years old at the time of trial and had been a resident of Chicago since 1893. For about thirty years she and her husband Edemond had been engaged in the business of renting furnished apartments and sleeping rooms. In November 1951 they rented jointly box No. C786 in defendant's vault, in which they deposited, from time to time, cash proceeds from the income of their business enterprise. In August 1953 plaintiff was advised that her husband was incurably ill, and for that reason she wished to have his name taken off their box. Accordingly, on the fifteenth of that month she communicated her wishes to the officers of the safe deposit company, and, because her husband was too ill to accompany her to the vault and sign a surrender card, she was advised, in order to effectuate the change immediately, to surrender the jointly-held box and take out another box in her own name. In accordance with that advice, box No. 13 414 was assigned to her as the sole renter. She took both boxes to a booth in the vault, removed all the contents from the jointly-held box and transferred them to the newly assigned box held in her name only. She testified that at the time of this transfer she had cash accumulations in the safe deposit box of something over $89,000. Her husband died September 23, 1953, and shortly thereafter, on October fourteenth, her son Joseph Henderick and her daughter Helen Gehrke went to the office of the safe deposit company to sign a contract making them cotenants of box No. 13 414. A week later, on October 21, 1953, plaintiff and her daughter took the box to a booth and found in it $51,650, an amount which represented a loss, so they contended, of $37,750. In testifying as to the amount of $51,650 plaintiff consulted a memorandum on which her daughter had written that amount and which plaintiff took to the witness stand with her because, as she explained, she couldn't "remember so good any more."

Plaintiff had savings accounts totaling in excess of $40,000 and placed in five banks. Her business was conducted on a cash basis, and whenever she had more cash at home than she thought prudent, she deposited it in her safe deposit box. Evidently it was her practice to put cash in her box and then take it out from time to time to purchase bonds, generally at the Uptown National Bank. She once testified that she and Mr. Henderick counted the money in August 1953; later she stated that she could not remember when they counted it. From the record it appears that on October 21, 1953, she purchased at Uptown National Bank government bonds in the amount of $5,250, $5,-250, and $20,000 (cost price), in which she, or she and her son or daughter, were named as owners. In the aggregate they represent a cost value of $30,500, a sum not a great deal less than the $37,750 for which plaintiff is suing. Previously, on December 24, 1952, she had purchased a government bond in the amount of $3,000 in her husband's name; on March 11, 1953, she had purchased a $525 government bond in her own name; on March 12, 1953, she had purchased a $3,000 government bond, and on April 23, 1953, a $6,000 government bond, both bonds in the name of herself and her husband. All these bonds were purchased at the Uptown National Bank; from the first purchase recorded here, on December 24, 1952, to the last, on October 21, 1953, her cost price investment in government bonds totaled $43,-025—a total, one may note, not greatly in excess of the $37,750 for which plaintiff is suing. In February of 1954 she purchased a government bond in the amount of $11,625 at the First National Bank in Chicago.

Plaintiff and her daughter testified that there was but $51,650 in the box on Wednesday, October 21, 1953, when plaintiff opened it at 11:00 a. m. Plaintiff estimated, as she testified, that $37,750 was missing, and immediately reported the alleged loss to the vault authorities.

* * *

Whenever a box holder desires entry to his box, he is required to sign an entrance ticket pertaining to his box. This he presents to the counterman at the business office who checks the signature, and if it is found to be that of the renter, the ticket is initialed and time-stamped. The counterman then admits the renter to the vault by releasing the lock on the day gate at the front vault door by means of a buzzer. He is met by a custodian who examines the ticket; if it is found in proper order the custodian, using the customer's key and his own guard key, unlocks the cubicle in which the box is locked.

If a box holder takes his box to one of the booths in the booth lobby, the door of the cubicle is opened and the custodian gives him back the key with the box. The door to the booth locks behind the customer after he has entered, and when he comes out the booth door automatically locks again. The custodian then examines the booth to ascertain if anything has been left there; any articles found are turned over to the manager and returned to the owner if he can be traced. The vault is cleaned daily by a maintenance man in the presence of the manager or a custodian. The vault mechanism is inspected every two months by Diebold, Inc. It appears that during the past eighteen years no burglaries or hold-ups have occurred. * * * In the present case there was no mark on the face of the door of the cubicle which showed any tampering; the original lacquer was still on it.

The evidence discloses that the safe deposit company used care in the selection of its employees. * * *

In cases cited by plaintiff it appears that the receipt of the bailed article was either admitted or established by a fair degree of proof, as in Heyman & Bros., Inc. v. Marshall Field & Co., 301 Ill.App. 340, 22 N.E.2d 776, where a diamond brooch was admittedly received by the bailee and discovered missing from the value room; in Brenton v. Sloan's United Storage & Van Co., 315 Ill.App. 278, 42 N.E.2d 945, where the bailed articles were furniture admittedly received; in Byalos v. Matheson, 328 Ill. 269, 159 N.E. 242, where there was no question of plaintiff's having delivered the bailed automobile to bailee; in Dunne v. South Shore Country Club, 230 Ill.App. 11, where there was no question of the delivery of a fur coat to the checkroom; and in Chicago German Hod Carriers Union v. Security Trust & Deposit Co., 315 Ill. 204, 146 N.E. 135, where officers of plaintiff had counted the cash contents of the box more than once, and with the aid of their account books were able to establish a fair degree of proof as to how much cash was in the box before thieves broke in and absconded with the contents. In these cases the delivery and identity of the bailed property having either been admitted or proved, the burden of showing ordinary care in safeguarding the bailed goods was cast on defendants. * * *

Plaintiff also relies on cases where some degree of negligence was established by the bailor, as in Saddler v. National Bank of Bloomington, 403 Ill. 218, 85 N.E.2d 733, where the wife of the lessee of the box, obtaining the key, was permitted by the vault authorities, without the consent of the lessee, to enter his box, while he was away in the armed services, and take his property from it; in Kammerer v. Graymont Hotel Corp., 337 Ill.App. 434, 86 N.E.2d 383, where (as appears from the briefs, although the evidence is not set out in the opinion proper) it was shown that a master key was temporarily missing; and in Mayer v. Brensinger, 180 Ill. 110, 54 N.E. 159, where plaintiff showed that he had deposited in his safe deposit box money which had come into his hands as the result of distribution of the residue of an estate, and where an employee of the owner of the safe deposit vault, although knowing the depositor was then in a detention hospital (with a mental illness), permitted two strangers to have access to his box without identification, except that they

had the key and power of attorney purporting to be signed by the depositor.

Miles v. International Hotel Co., 289 Ill. 320, 124 N.E. 599, 602, a bailment case, contains a good statement of the guidelines to be followed: "The weight of modern authority holds the rule to be that, where the bailor has shown that the goods were received in good condition by the bailee and were not returned to the bailor on demand, the bailor has made out a case of *prima facie* negligence against the bailee, and the bailee must show that the loss or damage was caused without his fault." * * *

There is, in the instant case, nothing more than plaintiff's testimony, supported by that of her daughter (who had to depend on her mother's assessment of the amount), that $37,750 in cash was missing from her safe deposit box. Plaintiff, a woman about eighty at the time of the trial, commented herself that she couldn't "remember so good any more"; moreover, she did not employ a methodical system—perhaps it would be more accurate to say that she did not employ a system at all—in keeping a record of her cash deposits in the box. There is no evidence that the money claimed to be missing had been taken from the safe deposit box without the knowledge or consent of plaintiff or one of the co-renters. From the facts concerning the operation of the vault, plaintiff attempts to deduce the theory that one or more of the bank tellers, after checking their accounts at the close of the banking day and delivering the proceeds by truck to the vault area, may have surreptitiously gained access to plaintiff's box through some unexplained means and taken from it the cash alleged to be missing. There is no evidence that any of the tellers ever entered the area of the vault where customers' safe deposit boxes were located, or that they could have gained access to plaintiff's box if they had entered that area. * * * Plaintiff's theory is purely speculative, conjectural and without evidentiary support. One would, indeed, be forced to Procrustean efforts to conform plaintiff's evidence to the proof required in a case of bailment.

*   *   *

The principle underlying all the cases to which our attention has been called and in which the plaintiff prevailed is that the receipt of the bailed article was admitted or established by a fair degree of proof, and that the loss was occasioned through the imprudent operation of agents or agencies under the control of the bailee. [Citation.] After a careful consideration of the evidence in the instant case and the law applicable thereto, we have reached the conclusion that plaintiff did not prove negligence as charged, and that the case should not have been submitted to the jury.

Moreover, defendant's proof showed without contradiction that every reasonable precaution was employed to safeguard the property of its renters. Its employees were carefully selected, access to its vault was carefully supervised, its box keys were meticulously accounted for. Defendant was bound to use only ordinary care, and the evidence shows beyond question that such a degree of care was exercised. It would be a dangerous doctrine and an invitation to fraud to allow a renter to recover upon the mere statement that cash or securities were found missing from his box, or had in some unknown way disappeared, without requiring a fair degree of proof of negligence on the part of a safe deposit company.

*   *   *

Judgment reversed and cause remanded with directions.

WALLINGA v. JOHNSON

(1964) 269 Minn. 436, 131 N.W.2d 216.

ROGOSHESKE, J. This appeal concerns an action to recover the value of two diamond rings owned by plaintiff. They were delivered and accepted for safekeeping by the Commodore Hotel, operated by defendant partnership, and were subsequently taken from the hotel safe by robbery. Plaintiff had occupied an apartment in the hotel for some years. On July 9, 1960, having been confined in a hospital with a broken leg, she directed her son to take two rings from her apartment and deposit them with the hotel clerk for safekeeping. In accordance with customary practice in performing this service, the rings were exhibited to the clerk and placed in a sealed "safety deposit envelope" used by the hotel for depositing valuables belonging to guests. A numbered stub attached to the envelope was signed by the clerk and plaintiff's son, and a "depositor's check" containing the same number was detached from the signed stub and given to him. This "depositor's check" was to be presented when the envelope and contents were called for, at which time the depositor was required to sign it so that the signatures could be compared. The envelope containing the rings was placed in a large safe located in the hotel's front office 4 or 5 feet behind the registration desk and about the same distance from the hotel switchboard. The safe was used not only to keep the valuables of guests, but also cash for use in the hotel's cafe, bar, and coffee shop. Although it was equipped with a combination lock, during the 16 years that defendants operated the hotel the safe door, while customarily closed, was never locked. A clerk was on duty at the registration desk at all times.

On July 10 at 3:45 a. m., two armed men surprised the night clerk then on duty, rifled cash drawers in the registration desk, and took the contents of the unlocked safe, including the envelope containing plaintiff's rings. The rings have not been recovered.

The question of defendants' liability was submitted to a jury upon the sole issue of whether defendants were negligent in failing to keep the rings safely locked up and, if they were, whether such negligence was the proximate cause of the loss. The jury returned a verdict for defendants, and plaintiff appeals from an order denying her motion for a new trial.

The primary question presented is whether the court erred in refusing to hold as a matter of law that the relationship between plaintiff and defendants was that of bailor and bailee.

Bailment is the legal relation arising upon delivery of goods without transference of ownership under an express or implied agreement that the goods be returned. [Citations.] The actions of plaintiff's son and the hotel clerk—inserting the rings in the safety deposit envelope, signing the numbered stub, detaching the companion presentation stub, and placing the envelope in the safe—plainly indicate that the parties intended the rings to be kept for safekeeping until called for. This was a bailment as a matter of law.

The error at trial lay in assuming that Asseltyne v. Fay Hotel, 222 Minn. 91, 23 N. W.2d 357, applied to the facts of this case. In that case, the plaintiff was a residential guest of the defendant hotel. Her personal property, located in her rented room, was destroyed by fire. The pivotal issue was whether plaintiff's relationship to the hotel was that of a residential lodger or a transient guest. Unlike this case, the owner did not surrender exclusive possession and control of the property to the hotel. Thus, a bailment was not created and the case is inapplicable. We agree with plaintiff that Peet v. Roth Hotel Co., 191 Minn. 151, 253 N.W. 546, controls. There, plaintiff, who had no relationship to the hotel, left a ring with the hotel clerk for the purpose of delivering it to a jeweler, a guest of the hotel. We held that a bailment was established as a matter of law.

Application of the Asseltyne case and the court's refusal to find a bailment resulted in its erroneously instructing the jury that plaintiff bore the burden of proving defendants' negligence. Since Rustad v. G. N. Ry. Co., 122 Minn. 453, 142 N.W. 727, the rule in Minnesota has been that where the plaintiff has shown a bailment relationship to exist, the defendant must assume not only the burden of going forward with evidence to show lack of negligence but also the burden of ultimate persuasion. [Citations.]

The record reveals that plaintiff's proof was not wholly consistent with her theory that defendants' liability was governed by the law of bailment. In addition to proving delivery and nonreturn of the rings, she went forward with evidence tending to establish defendants' negligence. Contrary to defendants' contention, however, she did not thereby waive any right to object to the erroneous instructions. At most, she may have waived the right to have defendants assume the burden of going forward with the evidence. The error in instructing the jury as to the burden of proof is one of fundamental law and controlling principle and was properly assigned in plaintiff's motion for a new trial. [Citation.] Moreover, it appears from counsel's affidavit in support of plaintiff's motion for a new trial that he made oral requests to charge the jury on the theory of a bailment which were refused. Clearly, plaintiff is not precluded from asserting the error on appeal. [Citation.]

While the burden of proof in a bailment case rests on the defendant, the basis of his liability remains ordinary negligence. [Citation.] Failure to lock the safe, at least during the night, is very strong evidence tending to show negligence. The hotel, however, established that a clerk was on duty at all times and the unlocked door was, to some extent, a convenience for guests who wished to retrieve valuables without delay. This evidence, we believe, falls short of establishing defendants' negligence as a matter of law and the question is for the jury under proper instructions.

Since the case must be retried, defendants' contention that their actions, even if negligent, do not result in liability because the robbery was a superseding cause should be put at rest. As a general rule, a criminal act breaks the chain of causation and insulates the primary actor from liability. [Citations.] A criminal intervening force, however, cannot be a legally effective superseding cause unless it possesses the attribute of unforeseeability. [Citation.] The original actor cannot claim immunity from liability for loss when the possibility that third persons will act in a certain manner is one of the hazards he should guard against. [Citation.] The primary purpose of depositing the rings for safekeeping was to guard against theft; defendants must have, or at least should have, foreseen the possibility of their loss in the manner in which they were taken. We therefore hold that the robbery could not as a matter of law be a superseding cause.

" * * * Only when there might be a reasonable difference of opinion regarding the foreseeability of the intervening act should the question of intervening cause be submitted to the jury." [Citation.]

Reversed and new trial granted.

WILLARD VAN DYKE PRODUCTIONS v. EASTMAN KODAK CO.

(1963) 12 N.Y.2d 301, 239 N.Y.S.2d 337, 189 N.E.2d 693.

FULD, J. This case, submitted to the Appellate Division on an agreed statement of facts [citation] and here by our leave, poses the question whether the written notice accompanying the sale of film by the defendant Eastman Kodak Company is effectual to limit its liability for negligence in the subsequent processing of that same film.

In January of 1959 the plaintiff, a corporation engaged in commercial photography, purchased a number of rolls of Kodak Ektachrome Commercial 16mm film from the defendant's agent in New York. The plaintiff had contracted with the Western Electric Company to make a moving picture of certain of its facilities in Alaska and the film in question was bought for such use. Accordingly, the plaintiff took the film to Alaska and there it was properly exposed, it being admitted that a negative resulted which, if properly developed, would have resulted in prints commercially valuable and entirely satisfactory to fulfill plaintiff's contract with Western Electric. After exposure in Alaska, the plaintiff delivered the film to defendant's laboratory in New York to be developed. It was in good condition when received by the defendant for processing but during its development a substantial portion was so damaged by a deposit of foreign material and by ink marks that such portion became commercially valueless; on the basis of the submission, the inference is warranted that the defendant was negligent. [Citation.]

Although the plaintiff incurred expenses of over $1,500 in retaking certain sequences in order to fulfill its contract with Western Electric and sought reimbursement for such expenses, the defendant has repaid the plaintiff only for the cost of the damaged film and for the prorata cost of its processing. In taking this position, the defendant relies upon a "notice" set forth on a label on the box containing the film. It states rather plainly, in black type against a white background, "FILM PRICE DOES NOT INCLUDE PROCESSING" and includes, in much smaller type, black against a blue background, this recital:

"READ THIS NOTICE

"This film will be replaced if defective in manufacture, labeling, or packaging, or if damaged or lost by us or any subsidiary company. Except for such replacement, the sale or subsequent handling of this film for any purpose is without warranty or other liability of any kind. Since dyes used with color films, like other dyes, may, in time, change, this film will not be replaced for, or otherwise warranted against, any change in color."

It is conceded that the plaintiff was aware of the nature of the label's contents, and, as noted above, the question for our decision is whether it effectively limits the defendant's liability for negligence in developing the film.

The law looks with disfavor upon attempts of a party to avoid liability for his own fault and, although it is permissible in many cases to contract one's self out of liability for negligence, the courts insist that it must be absolutely clear that such was the understanding of the parties. In other words, it must be plainly and precisely provided that "limitation of liability extends to negligence or other fault of the party attempting to shed his ordinary responsibility." [Citations.]

In line with this principle, we have consistently decided that contracts will not be construed to absolve a party from, or indemnify him against, his own negligence, "unless such intention is expressed in unequivocal terms." (Thompson-Starrett Co. v. Otis Elevator Co., 271 N.Y. 36, 41, 2 N.E.2d 35, 37.) In the Thompson case (271 N.Y. 36, 2 N.E.2d 36, supra), for instance, the court concluded that an agreement to indemnify one "against all claims for damages to persons growing out of the execution of the work" was not phrased in terms sufficiently unequivocal to encompass the indemnitee's negligence. In the Kaufman case (5 N.Y.2d 1016, 185 N.Y.S.2d 268, 158 N.E.2d 128), the court held that an agreement to release the defendant "of any and all responsibility or liability of any nature whatsoever for any loss of property or personal injury occurring on this trip" lacked the requisite clarity to relieve the defendant of liability for its own negligence. And, in

the Mynard case (71 N.Y. 180), where the plaintiff agreed to "release and discharge the said company [defendant] from all claims, demands and liabilities of every kind whatsoever for or on account of, or connected with, any damage or injury to or the loss of said stock, or any portion thereof, from whatsoever cause arising", the court determined that, despite the breadth of the language employed, it was not sufficiently explicit to absolve the defendant from its own negligence.

Moreover, not only does the provision upon which reliance is placed fail to express, in the clear and unequivocal terms demanded, that the parties agreed to limit the defendant's liability for its own negligence but plaintiff could reasonably have believed that it was not intended to apply to the film's processing. As noted, the label on which the provision appears accompanied the sale of the film and expressly recited that "FILM PRICE DOES NOT INCLUDE PROCESSING". It was reasonable, therefore, to conclude that the processing of the film was to constitute a transaction entirely separate and distinct from its sale. Accordingly, as the Appellate Division aptly observed, "The provision for the limitation of defendant's liability in connection with the 'subsequent handling of this film for any purpose' would be confined to a limitation of liability in the subsequent handling of the unexposed film for any purpose in connection with the sale."

The judgment appealed from should be affirmed.

Judgment affirmed.

NORTH END AUTO PARK v. PETRINGA TRUCKING CO.

(1958) 337 Mass. 618, 150 N.E.2d 735.

SPALDING, J. This is a petition to enforce a garage keeper's lien under G.L. c. 255, §§ 25 and 26. The case was submitted on a statement of agreed facts, amounting to a case stated.

The petitioner operates a public garage in Boston. During the period from August 1, 1955, to August 2, 1956, the respondents Mary Petringa and Petringa Trucking Co., Inc., were the owners of all of the motor vehicles (consisting of trucks, trailers and tractors) on which a lien is claimed. In this period the petitioner stored the vehicles, supplied them with gasoline and oil, and repaired them. During part of this period (from August 1, 1955, to April 30, 1956) the respondents used all of the vehicles in their trucking business, taking them away each day from the petitioner's garage with its knowledge and consent. On April 30, 1956, the petitioner refused to allow the respondents to remove the vehicles, and from that date to August 2, 1956, they remained in the uninterrupted possession of the petitioner under a claim of lien. On the latter date the vehicles were sold and the proceeds, under a stipulation executed by all of the interested parties, were placed in escrow, "pending judicial determination of the rights of the petitioner in * * * [the fund] under the claim of lien."

As of April 30, 1956, the unpaid balance due the petitioner in connection with the vehicles was as follows: for gasoline and oil $3,425.21; for repairs $464.47; for storage $2,250. These charges, amounting to $6,139.68 in the aggregate, were incurred during the period from August 1, 1955, to April 30, 1956.

After the commencement of the present proceedings both respondents were adjudicated bankrupts, and their trustees in bankruptcy were substituted as parties.

The trial judge ruled that for the period up to April 30, 1956, the petitioner had no lien because it did not retain uninterrupted possession of the trucks. He further ruled that by reason of the petitioner's uninterrupted possession of the trucks for the period

between April 30, 1956, and August 2, 1956, the petitioner was entitled to have its lien established in the amount of $750, the storage charges for three months. A report to the Appellate Division was dismissed and the petitioner appealed.

The petitioner is asserting a lien for storage, gasoline, oil, and repairs. The questions for decision are whether, for the period during which the vehicles were taken daily from the garage, any lien exists, and, if so, to which of the foregoing items it extends.

1. Section 25 of c. 255 provides: "Persons maintaining public garages for the storage and care of motor vehicles brought to their premises or placed in their care by or with the consent of the owners thereof shall have a lien upon such motor vehicles for proper charges due them for the storage and care of the same." At common law the garage keeper had no lien for storage and it is only by § 25 that he acquired one. [Citation.] In this respect he was in the same situation as the agistor or keeper of animals who likewise had no lien at common law but was given one by statute. [Citation.] The agistor's lien was construed by this court in Vinal v. Spofford, 139 Mass. 126, 29 N.E. 288, and since this decision is heavily relied on by the respondents and was to a considerable extent the basis for the opinion of the Appellate Division, it merits discussion. In that case the owner of a horse boarded it at the defendant's livery stable and had become indebted to the defendant for the horse's board. The defendant, nevertheless, permitted the owner to take and use the horse every day. While this arrangement was in force, the owner, while in possession of the horse, sold it to the plaintiff, a bona fide purchaser. The plaintiff continued to board the horse at the defendant's stable (the defendant having no knowledge of the sale), taking it out each day and returning it each night. On the failure of the former owner to pay the indebtedness for the board of the horse the defend-

ant seized the horse while it was in the plaintiff's possession away from the stable. The plaintiff brought replevin to recover the horse. It was held that the defendant's lien was lost. It was said per Holmes, J., "Such a transaction would divest a common-law lien. * * * [The statute] gives no intimation that it uses the word 'lien' in any different sense from that which is known to the common law. On the contrary, it in terms supposes that the animals in question have been placed in the care—that is to say, in the possession—of the party to whom the lien is given. * * * To admit that it was intended to create a tacit hypothecation, like that enforced from necessity, but within narrow limits, in the admiralty, would be to go in the face of the whole policy of our statutes, which always strive to secure public registration when possession is not given and retained, and which expressly provide for such registration when they in terms create a lien not depending on possession" (139 Mass. at page 130, 29 N.E. at page 288). What was said in Vinal v. Spofford concerning the lien there involved is equally applicable here. In other words the lien of the garage keeper like that of the keeper of animals essentially is a possessory lien and is divested by a complete and voluntary loss of possession. Restatement: Security, § 80.

It might appear at first blush that the principles discussed in Vinal v. Spofford militate against the existence of a lien in the case at bar for the period when the trucks were daily taken out of the garage. But as Mr. Justice Lummus said in § 85 of his treatise, The Law of Liens, "The common-law rule requiring continued possession in order to keep alive a lien must, in reason, be subject to some modification in the case of livery-stable keepers, just as it is in the case of innkeepers. While a complete voluntary loss of possession would doubtless defeat the lien * * * merely allowing the owner to take the animal for use during the day, with the expectation

on the part of both parties that he was to be brought back to the stable when the temporary use has ended, according to the almost universal custom, must be held not to defeat the lien, at least as against the owner or persons having notice, or the statute giving the lien is of little value." This reasoning is equally applicable to the garage keeper's lien. While the precise question has never been decided by this court there are intimations which tend in the direction of the principle just stated. Thus in Perkins v. Boardman, 14 Gray 481, 483, it was said, "A lien may perhaps be renewed by the return and restitution of the property; but in such case it will be subordinate to any intervening incumbrance to which the property in the mean time has become subject." And concerning the closely analogous situation of a pledge it was said in Walker v. Staples, 5 Allen 34, 35, that "the doctrine that possession must be retained is held with reasonable qualifications." There is nothing to the contrary in Vinal v. Spofford. All that was actually decided in that case was that the lien was divested by the sale of the horse to a bona fide purchaser while it was out of the stable keeper's possession, and he did not regain the lien by seizing the horse while it was in the possession of the purchaser. The question whether the lien might have revived if the horse had been voluntarily restored to the possession of the stable keeper was expressly left open.

The question whether a garage keeper's lien or one of like nature is revived by a return of the property to the possession of the lienor after a temporary interruption of possession has been considered by courts elsewhere and the prevailing view is that the lien revives. * * * Commercial Acceptance Corp. v. Hislop Garage Co., 89 N.H. 45, 192 A. 627 (garage keeper's lien for repairs not lost by temporary surrender of vehicle). * * * Pacific States Finance Corp. v. Freitas, 113 Cal.App. 757, 295 P. 804 (taking automobile from garage each day and returning it at night held not to destroy lien). [Citation.] In re Carter, D.C.W.D.N.Y., 21 F. 2d 587 (garage keeper's lien not lost by surrender to owner for temporary use under agreement to return). Restatement: Security, § 80 and comment c.

We are of opinion that both on principle and authority the petitioner's lien here was not defeated by the owner taking the trucks out daily and returning them to the garage each night. A contrary conclusion would render the lien of little value; it would be limited to charges accruing after the last return of the vehicle. Except for vehicles in "dead storage" such charges would be comparatively small. We think that the Legislature in enacting § 25 intended to give the garage keeper a more substantial right.

Of course, the rule just stated is subject to the qualification that if a bona fide purchaser acquires rights in the vehicle while it is temporarily out of the garage his rights will prevail over those of the garage keeper. [Citation.] And doubtless an attaching or levying creditor who has no knowledge of the lienor's interest would have rights superior to the lienor if he acquired them while the vehicle was out of the lienor's possession. Restatement: Security, § 80.

2. The lien under § 25 is for "storage and care." We must now determine what items, beyond that of storage, are covered by these words. We are of opinion that they do not cover the items for gasoline and oil. A more difficult question is whether "care" is limited to that care which is incident to the storing of automobiles, or whether it is used in a more general sense to include repairs made to an automobile. This question, however, we need not decide, because we think that the petitioner can secure its charges for repairs with a common law lien. At common law a mechanic or artisan who, with the consent of the owner, does work upon or adds materials to a chattel has a lien. [Cita-

tions.] We are of opinion that such a lien extends to the labor and materials expended by a garage keeper in repairing an automobile. * * *

The petitioner has not claimed a common law lien; it has sought a lien only under the statute. The failure to plead a common law lien, however, is of no consequence. Where, as here, a case is submitted on a statement of agreed facts all questions of pleading are waived and the only question is whether the plaintiffs "can recover upon any form of declaration or in any form of action." [Citations.] We think that the interrupted possession here involved no more defeated the common law lien for repairs than it defeated the statutory lien for storage.

* * *

It follows that the petitioner is entitled to recover for repairs in the amount of $464.-47, and storage in the amount of $3,000, or $3,464.47 in the aggregate. Accordingly the order of the Appellate Division is reversed and judgment is to be entered for the petitioner in the sum of $3,464.47.

So ordered.

PROBLEMS

1. A was the owner of a herd of 20 highly bred dairy cows. He was a prosperous farmer, but his health was very poor. On the advice of his doctor, A decided to winter in Arizona. Before he left he made an agreement with Y, whereby Y was to keep the cows on Y's farm through the winter, pay A the sum of $800, and return to A the 20 cows at the close of the winter. For reasons that Y thought were good farming, Y sold six of the cows and replaced them with six other cows. After the winter was over, A returned from Arizona. When he saw that Y had replaced six cows out of the 20 originally given, he sued Y for the conversion of the original six cows. Decision?

2. O left his automobile at R's garage for repairs and storage, stating that he would pick it up in ten days. R agreed to park the car in the lot adjacent to his garage after the repairs were

completed. O had left a valuable wrist watch in the glove compartment, but R had no knowledge of the presence of the wrist watch. R loaned O's car to F while F's car was being repaired by R. F returned the car in three days. When O returned he found that the wrist watch was missing and also that one fender of the car was damaged. O sued R and F for damage to the car and the loss of the wrist watch. Decision?

3. Minnie Hill placed her diamond ring, valued at $300, in pawn with X, a licensed pawnbroker. She received a loan of $70 on the ring from X. X also delivered to Minnie a pawn ticket containing a description of the ring pawned, the amount loaned, the time for redemption, and the name and location of his place of business. The pawn ticket further stated that X's business was protected by the "Sure Protective Company." Before the time for redemption, X, without notice to Minnie, sold all his interest in whatever pledges he had, including Minnie's, to Y, another duly licensed pawnbroker, who was admittedly a reputable business man. Y took all of the chattels to his pawn shop. Shortly thereafter, Y's pawn shop was robbed by armed robbers who forcibly took from his safe a large number of articles, including Minnie's diamond ring, which was not recovered. Minnie sues X claiming conversion by X of her diamond ring valued at $400. Decision?

4. Hines stored his furniture, including a grand piano in Arnett's warehouse. Needing more space, Arnett stored Hines's piano in Butler's warehouse next door. As a result of a fire, which occurred without any fault of Arnett or Butler, both warehouses and contents were destroyed. Hines sues Arnett for the value of his piano and furniture. Decision?

5. B rented a safe deposit box from X Safe Deposit Company in which he deposited valuable securities and $4,000 in currency. Subsequently, B went to the box and found that $1,000 was missing. B brought an action against X and upon the trial, the company showed that its customary procedure was as follows: That there were two keys for each box furnished to each renter; that if the key was lost the lock was changed; also, that new keys were provided for each lock each time a box was rented; that there were two clerks in charge of the vault; and that one of the clerks was always present to open the box. X Safe Deposit Company also proved two keys were given to B at the time he rented his box; that his box could not be opened without the use of one of the keys in his possession, and the company had issued no other keys to B's box. Decision?

6. A, B, and C each stored 5000 bushels of yellow corn in the same bin in X's warehouse. X wrongfully sold 10,000 bushels of this corn to Y. A contends that inasmuch as his 5,000 bushels of corn were placed in the bin first, the remaining 5,000 bushels belong to him. What are the rights of the parties?

7. (a) On April 1, Mary Rich, at the solicitation of Super Fur Company, delivered a $3,000 mink coat to the company at its place of business for storage in its vaults until November 1. On the same day, she paid the company its customary charge of $10 for such storage. After Mary left the store, the general manager of the company, upon finding that its storage vaults were already filled to capacity, delivered Mary's coat to Swift Trucking Company for shipment to Fur Storage Company. En route, the truck in which Mary's coat was being transported was totally damaged by fire caused by negligence on the part of the driver of the truck, and Mary's coat was totally destroyed. Is Super Fur Company liable to Mary for the value of her coat?

(b) Would your answer be the same if Mary's coat had been safely delivered to Fur Storage Company and had been stolen from its storage vaults without negligence on its part?

8. Rich, a club member, left his golf clubs with Bogan, pro at the Happy Hours Country Club, to be refinished at Bogan's pro shop. The refinisher employed by Bogan, suddenly left town taking Rich's clubs with him. The refinisher had theretofore been above suspicion, although Bogan had never checked on the man's character references. A valuable sand wedge which Bogan had borrowed from another member, Smith, for his own use in an important tournament match was also stolen by the refinisher, as well as several pairs of golf shoes which Bogan had checked for members without charge as an accommodation. The club members concerned each make claims against Bogan for their losses. Can (a) Rich, (b) Smith and the other members compel Bogan to make good their respective losses?

9. The Drive and Fly Rental Company was in the business of renting automobiles and airplanes. Henry Limburg rented an automobile and a plane from the company. He drove to the airport and took off in the rented plane. As Limburg was returning and preparing to land,

the plane accidentally caught on fire and a forced landing was made. Limburg escaped unhurt, but the plane was destroyed. Limburg started back to the company office in the rented car to report the loss of the plane. En route to the office, Limburg overturned and wrecked the car and was instantly killed. The company brought an appropriate action against Limburg's estate to recover damages for the plane and automobile. There was no proof as to the cause of the car being wrecked. Decision?

10. (a) P went to a theater wearing a high silk hat which he had borrowed from a friend. He checked the hat and his overcoat at the cloak-room. He inadvertently left his wallet in his overcoat pocket. The checking service was gratuitous although a fee was charged for admission to the theater. A large notice over the check-room counter stated that the theater was not liable for loss of checked property. A numbered card was given for each garment checked.

(b) During the intermission, a patron of the theater faints, and the check-room girl runs to her assistance, leaving the check-room unguarded for about five minutes. When P presents his check at the end of the performance, the hat and his overcoat including the wallet can not be found.

P sues the theater to recover the value of the hat, overcoat and wallet. Decision?

CHAPTER 16

CARRIERS AND INNKEEPERS

COMMON CARRIERS OF GOODS

Introductory. Carriers which undertake to transport the goods of others from place to place are clearly bailees of the goods entrusted to them for transportation. Thus, unless the contract of carriage provides otherwise, all carriers owe to the person for whom they undertake to carry goods the duties which a bailee owes to his bailor. Among those duties, it will be recalled, is the duty to take reasonable care of the goods and the strict duty to deliver the goods to the right person.

The common law, however, has from the earliest times imposed a special liability upon the common carrier because of the public nature of his services. It is the common carrier's special position in the law which we now consider.

Common Carriers and Private Carriers Distinguished. A common carrier offers his services and facilities, whatever they may be, to the public at large upon terms and under circumstances which indicate that the offering is made indifferently to all persons and is not casual or individual in its character. One who carries the goods of another on particular isolated occasions, or one who serves a limited number of customers under individual long-term contracts without offering the same or similar contracts to the public at large, is a private or contract carrier—not a common carrier. On the other hand, a carrier consistently soliciting individual long-term contracts with the general public and accepting, within the limits of its capacity, anyone who is interested in the terms offered, may be classified as a common carrier. It is not an essential characteristic of a common carrier that he operate between fixed termini, or on regular schedules, or at uniform or fixed rates. It is sufficient that his operations indicate that he is offering his services continuously, and not on isolated occasions, to the public at large—not to a few selected individuals.

Duty to Carry. A common carrier is under a duty to serve the public to the limits of his capacity and, within those limits, to accept for carriage goods of the kind which he normally carries in his business. A private carrier has no duty to accept goods for carriage except where he is bound to do so by a contract with a particular customer.

The common carrier's duty to accept goods for carriage is subject to certain exceptions. He is not bound to accept goods beyond his capacity. Nor is he bound to accept goods of a kind which he does not normally carry and which he has no facilities to carry. Furthermore, a common carrier may reject goods which may endanger persons or property or which are injurious to health. Likewise, a common carrier may reject goods improperly prepared for transportation or improperly loaded, or goods in such a condition that their transportation will entail extraordinary care and risk.

Liability of the Common Carrier for Loss or Damage. A private carrier, in the absence of special contract terms, is liable as a bailee with respect to the goods he undertakes to carry. But the common carrier is under a stricter liability. Under the common law a common carrier is treated as an insurer of the safety of the goods, subject to five exceptions.

The common law imposes strict liability upon the common carrier in recognition of the fact that the owner of the goods has very little control over a long distance transportation with the result that it is difficult, if not impossible, for him to prove negligence. Moreover, lack of control exposes him to fraud and other forms of misdealing. Thus, at common law, if the goods are lost or damaged *during carriage* the common carrier is liable in full for the loss or damage, notwithstanding that he has exercised due care and notwithstanding that the loss or damage was due to an unavoidable cause such as fire. However, to this absolute liability the common law has recognized five exceptions.

1. *Acts of God.* The common carrier is not liable for loss or damage resulting directly from "acts of God." Acts of God, within this exception, are sudden, violent, natural phenomena such as lightning, earthquakes, floods, tornadoes or hurricanes. Unprecedented snowstorms may also fall within this category although normal winter conditions do not. The narrow scope of the exception is illustrated by the fact that fire does not come within it unless caused directly by lightning. Even fire spread by a strong wind is not regarded as an act of God.

The carrier is absolved from liability within this exception only if the loss or damage to the goods is the *direct proximate* result of an act of God. A sudden unprecedented snowstorm causing delay and spoilage of the goods will absolve the carrier from liability but if the delay is attributable even in small part to lack of adequate clearing equipment the carrier will not be absolved. Obviously, if the carrier is in any degree negligent in failing to guard against the elements he will not be absolved from liability.

2. *Acts of Public Enemy.* A carrier is not liable for loss or damage caused directly by the military forces of a hostile nation. The words "public enemy" here refer only to bodies of men organized by a hostile government and do not include the lawless acts of mobs or strikers, nor do they include the lawless acts of individuals such as burglars.

3. *Acts or Negligence of the Shipper.* A carrier is not liable for loss or damage directly attributable to the acts or negligence of the shipper himself. Thus, if he follows the directions of the shipper in every detail and loss results from faulty directions, the carrier is absolved from liability.

Defective Packing. If the goods are defectively packed by the shipper and this is not apparent or known to the carrier, the carrier is not liable for loss or damage due directly to such defective packing. But, if the loss or damage is due in some degree to the carrier's negligence in transportation he will not be absolved from liability even though the damage was greater because of the defective packing. If the carrier knows or has reason to know of the defective packing, some courts hold that he is under a duty to refuse transportation and that he is liable if he nevertheless accepts the goods and they are damaged.

Defective Loading and Description of the Goods. Where the shipper loads the goods and furnishes the description of them to be entered in the contract of carriage there is authority that the carrier is not absolved from liability if the goods are damaged on account of the defective loading or if a purchaser of the goods suffers loss because of reliance upon an inaccurate description of the goods in the contract of carriage. The normal contract of carriage is the bill of lading. A bill of lading is both a contract of carriage and a receipt for the goods, and it contains statements as to the character, condition, quantity and weight of the goods shipped. Furthermore, when the bill of lading is in negotiable form, shortly to be discussed, it is the general practice to sell and purchase the goods while in the course of transportation by selling and purchasing the bill of lading. Thus, a purchaser who buys goods in transit, by purchasing a bill of lading, places considerable reliance upon the description of the goods contained in the bill. The carrier is clearly liable to such buyer for loss due to any misdescription of the goods in the bill of lading issued by him.

However, where the shipper loads the goods and furnishes the description of them to be entered in the bill of lading, the carrier may escape liability for loss due to defective loading or misdescription by inserting the words "shipper's load, weight, and count" or words of similar import on the face of the bill of lading. Suppose, however, that the carrier knows that the loading is defective, or that the goods are misdescribed by the shipper, because his agents were present at the loading and observed the defects and inaccuracies. The question arises whether the carrier is liable for fraud to a purchaser of the bill of lading who relies upon the description of the goods, notwithstanding that the bill of lading bears the legend "shipper's load, weight, and count." The better view is that the carrier is liable.

It is clear that the carrier is liable for his own misstatements in the bill of lading. The standard form bill of lading contains the words "Received, * * * the property described below, in apparent good order, except as noted (contents and condition of contents of packages unknown) * * *." This statement is clearly the carrier's. If the carrier's agents are present at the loading or inspect the goods before issuing the bill of lading, and if they observe that the goods are not "in apparent good order," the issuance of a bill of lading containing these words is clearly a fraud upon a purchaser who suffers loss in reliance upon them. Since the statement is the carrier's the carrier should be liable to such purchaser, notwithstanding that the bill of lading bears the legend "shipper's load, weight, and count."

4. *Inherent Nature of the Goods.* The carrier is not liable for loss or damage due directly to the inherent nature of the goods. The carrier is not liable for normal natural spoilage which is not attributable to unwarranted delay, lack of adequate facilities or negligent handling during transportation. Some courts, however, have held that a carrier who knows that the goods are of the kind which may deteriorate, notwithstanding all reasonable precautions, should not accept them for transportation, and that he is liable for the loss if he does.

5. *Act of Public Authority.* While this exception is not as well defined as are the others, the carrier is generally not liable for loss or damage caused directly by the acts of properly constituted public authority. Unreasonable delay resulting in loss caused by inspections of public health officials or customs officials will not expose the carrier to liability unless the inspections were occasioned by the carrier's negligence.

Duration of Carriage. As has been stated earlier, the strict liability of the carrier continues only *during carriage.* Carriage is considered to have begun as soon as the goods are placed within the exclusive control of the carrier with nothing remaining to be done by the shipper to send the goods on their way. If the goods are placed within the area of the carrier's physical control, as when they are left on his loading dock, he is not considered to have exclusive control within this rule until he is notified that the goods are there. However, even if the goods are placed within the carrier's control and he has notice of this fact, carriage is not considered to have begun if anything remains to be done by the shipper to send the goods on their way. The carrier is not held to strict liability until the goods are ready for transportation and, until such time, the carrier is regarded as a bailee or warehouseman with respect to the goods and is held only for loss due to his negligence. Thus, if the shipper has not yet given the carrier instructions as to destination or if he is required to load the goods on the carrier's cars and has not yet done so, or if the shipment is incomplete as to the quantity agreed to be shipped, the carrier, even though he is in control of the goods, will be liable only as warehouseman for his own negligence. He will not be liable as insurer until the things required to be done by the shipper to send the goods on their way are done.

Once the liability of the carrier as insurer attaches, it continues until the carriage is completed. However, if the shipper exercises a right of stoppage in transit the carriage comes to an end and thereafter the carrier is liable only as warehouseman. In general, carriage is completed when the goods have reached destination and the carrier has unloaded the goods and notified the person to whom the goods were shipped, the consignee, of their arrival. The carrier's liability is not reduced to that of warehouseman until the goods are unloaded and put in a safe and convenient place ready to be taken by the consignee. However, in some cases the carrier is not required or expected in the usual course of business to remove the goods from the cars, as in the case of grain in bulk, coal, or lumber. In such cases, delivery of the car in a safe and convenient position for unloading at an elevator, warehouse, or other place designated by the contract or required in the usual course of business will suffice.

The courts are divided on the question whether notice of the arrival of the goods must be given before the carrier's liability as insurer comes to an end. A majority of the jurisdictions require such notice and in some jurisdictions the carrier's strict liability does not come to an end until a reasonable time has elapsed from the date of such notice. What has been said about the termination of carriage by arrival at destination, unloading and notice to the consignee, does not apply to express companies. Express companies normally undertake to carry the goods from door to door and as to them carriage is not completed until actual delivery to the consignee.

Carrier's Duty to Deliver to the Right Person. The carrier is under an absolute duty to deliver the goods to the right person. This duty is not peculiar to common carriers but extends also to private carriers. Essentially, this is the same duty which, it will be recalled, renders the bailee absolutely liable for misdelivery.

The question of the person to whom delivery must be made is controlled by the form of the bill of lading or other contract of carriage. In Chapter 19 the distinction between a negotiable bill of lading and a non-negotiable or "straight bill" is considered. For present purposes, it is sufficient to say that delivery under a non-negotiable or "straight bill," or other contract of carriage, must be made to the consignee named in the bill of lading or contract. If the goods are sold by the consignee to a third party, the carrier must make delivery to the named consignee unless he is notified of the sale and even then he delivers to the third party at his own peril unless he receives confirmation from the named consignee himself, or unless the named consignee has acted in a manner which leads the carrier to believe that the third party's claim is genuine.

The situation in the case of a negotiable bill of lading is different. Because of the form of the bill of lading, the carrier knows that the goods may have been sold and that the bill of lading may have been negotiated to a third party. He is, therefore, never justified in delivering the goods to the consignee named in the bill of lading without assuring himself that no one else has bought the goods and has become the rightful holder of the bill of lading. From this it follows that a carrier delivering goods covered by a negotiable bill of lading must demand surrender of the bill of lading before he delivers the goods to anyone and must assure himself that the person who produces the bill of lading is the person who, under the terms and indorsements of the bill, is entitled to delivery.

When is the Carrier Excused for Misdelivery? The carrier is absolutely liable if he delivers the goods to the wrong person. However, he may be excused if the shipper or consignee misleads him into making the mistake. Furthermore, the carrier may be excused under certain circumstances if he delivers the goods to the wrong person under an order of a competent court of law or to an officer of the court under valid process issued by it. However, in such cases, the carrier has a duty to inform the person entitled to delivery of the court order or process or of any proceedings instituted against the goods as soon as he has knowledge thereof. His failure to do so may deprive the rightful owner of the goods of a chance to appear in court and protect his rights and the carrier will be liable for any loss occasioned thereby.

Limitation of Liability. There are statutes in some jurisdictions prohibiting the common carrier from limiting his strict common-law liability in any way by contract with the shipper. These statutes apply only to intrastate carriage and have no application to interstate carriage. Contracts for interstate carriage are governed by the Carmack Amendment to the Interstate Commerce Act (U.S.C.A., Title 49, Section 20 (11)), and by other Federal statutes.

In most jurisdictions, the carrier is permitted to limit his liability by contract with the shipper. However, it is a well established rule in all jurisdictions that a carrier may not, by contract, absolve himself of liability for his own negligence. This is expressly provided for in Section 7–309 of the Uniform Commercial Code. Where such limitations of liability by contract are not prohibited by statute, the carrier may limit his liability by excepting particular hazards, such as fire or strikes, or he may limit his liability to a certain value of the goods agreed upon between himself and the shipper or to the value declared by the shipper. But, in order that he may avail himself of such a limitation, the carrier is required to offer to the shipper a choice between limited and unlimited liability. The carrier may, of course, charge different rates to reflect the degree of liability which he assumes. It should be noted that interstate rates and the contracts offered under them are subject to regulation and approval by the Interstate Commerce Commission and that many States have similar requirements for intrastate rates and contracts.

Requirement that Shipper Assent to Limitation. In general, in order that a carrier may avail itself of a limitation of liability it must show that the shipper knew of and assented to the limitation. This is particularly true of limitations contained in mere shipping receipts. A shipping receipt may be a contract as well as a receipt. Bills of lading are both receipts and contracts. However, in the case of a shipping receipt other than a bill of lading the carrier has the burden of showing that the shipper knew of and assented to the conditions and limitations contained therein. In the case of a bill of lading, the majority view is that acceptance by the shipper of a bill of lading is prima facie evidence that he assented to its conditions and limitations. The reason is that shippers are expected to know that bills of lading are not only receipts but contracts as well. Moreover, it is well established that a shipper is placed upon notice of limitations contained in published tariffs filed by the carrier and approved by the appropriate State or Federal agency. Pursuant to powers vested in it by Congress, the Interstate Commerce Commission has approved standard forms for bills of lading. These have come to be used by all carriers, both for their interstate and intrastate carriage. These forms are known as the "Uniform Bill of Lading." Reference has been made to "forms" in the plural because there is a uniform domestic bill of lading and a uniform export bill of lading. These I.C.C. approved forms contain a number of conditions and limitations which should be scrutinized carefully. These conditions and limitations are generally printed on the back of the forms, but this is not required. There are a number of forms currently in use which simply state on their face "SUBJECT TO TERMS AND CONDITIONS OF UNIFORM BILL OF LADING." If the bill of lading is issued for inland carriage, the reference is to the uniform domestic bill of lading; if for export, the reference is to the uniform export bill. A shipper who accepts such a form is taken prima facie to have assented to the terms and conditions of the relevant uniform bill, notwithstanding that the terms and conditions are not printed on the back of the form. The reason for this is that the terms and conditions of the uniform bill are a matter of public record.

Interstate Transportation. Limitation of a carrier's liability under contract for interstate transportation of property is governed by the provisions of the Interstate Commerce Act (U.S.C.A., Title 49, Chapter 1). Section 20(11) of Title 49 provides, in part:

> "no contract, receipt, rule, regulation or other limitation of any character whatsoever shall exempt such common carrier, railroad, or transportation company [receiving property for interstate transportation] from * * * liability * * * for the full actual loss, damage, or injury to such property caused by it."

However, Section 20(11) provides that this restriction upon carriers who attempt to limit their liability shall not apply: "first, to baggage carried on passenger trains or boats, or trains or boats carrying passengers; second, to property, except ordinary livestock, received for transportation concerning which the carrier shall have been or shall be expressly authorized or required by order of the Interstate Commerce Commission * * to establish and maintain rates, dependent upon the value declared in writing by the shipper or agreed upon in writing as the re-

leased value of the property, in which case such declaration or agreement shall have no other effect than to limit liability and recovery to an amount not exceeding the value so declared * * *."

Under this Act, therefore, the carrier may limit its liability for baggage, by contract, both as to particular hazards and as to value, and for other property only as to value by appropriate tariffs filed with the Interstate Commerce Commission where required or authorized to do so. The Civil Aeronautics Act (U.S.C.A., Title 49, Chapter 9, Section 483) provides for the filing of tariffs by air carriers with the Civil Aeronautics Board and such tariffs and regulations may limit the carrier's liability not only as to value but with respect to such things as flight cancellation, rerouting, or transshipment.

COMMON CARRIERS OF PASSENGERS

Introductory. The essential characteristics required to constitute one a common carrier of passengers are the same as those of the common carrier of goods. It must appear from the carrier's operations that he is holding himself out as willing to carry members of the public at large.

Passengers. The legal position of the common carrier of passengers may properly be discussed under the heading of tort or negligence law. It is dealt with briefly here because there are a number of special rules applicable to such carrier on account of its public calling. A common carrier of passengers is not an insurer of the safety of its passengers but, because of his public calling, is held to the highest degree of care, skill and diligence. He is required to furnish safe places to board and alight from his vehicles and is subject to extensive regulation by State and, in the case of interstate carriage, by Federal agencies, both as to the type of services he offers and as to the kind and quality of physical facilities. In addition, he is subject to regulation as to rates.

A common carrier of passengers is bound to accept for carriage, without discrimination, all proper persons who desire and properly offer to become passengers. However, he may refuse transportation to persons who may endanger the health and safety of other passengers or imperil safe transportation. The common carrier is held to the highest degree of care only with respect to those who are properly passengers.

A passenger is one who comes upon the carrier's premises with the intention to travel by the carrier's regular public conveyances under a contract express or implied as to a fare. To constitute one a passenger, it is not necessary that he have boarded a vehicle or purchased a ticket; it is sufficient that he has come upon the carrier's premises with the intention forthwith to purchase a ticket and board an appropriate vehicle. The carrier's own employees are not passengers if they render services in connection with the transportation in question. However, employees of the carrier who do not render services in connection with the transportation involved but who travel free for their own convenience or pleasure are regarded as passengers. Employees of others transported under a special contract between their employer and the carrier are passengers of the carrier. For example, an employee of a newspaper company who sells newspapers on the journey is a passenger if there is a contract between his employer and the carrier for this purpose. Absent such contract, vendors and other persons who are permitted to board the carrier's vehicles are licensees of the carrier and the carrier owes them only the minimum duty of care. This rule, however, does not apply to children of tender age and such children who are invited or permitted to ride on the carrier's vehicles are treated as passengers.

A person who refuses or fails to pay his fare and who is not invited to board the carrier's vehicles is a trespasser, and the carrier owes him no duties beyond a duty to refrain from inflicting intentional or wanton harm. The carrier is entitled to use such reasonable force as is necessary to eject persons who have no right to transportation. In this category are persons who refuse or fail to pay their fare; persons who become obnoxious or who suffer from contagious disease; and persons who otherwise endanger the health or safety of other passengers.

Baggage. A passenger presenting himself for transportation may require the carrier to accept a reasonable amount of baggage and the carrier has a duty to transport such baggage without extra charge. The carrier's liability with respect to such baggage is the same as that of a common carrier of goods. However, this liability does not apply to items retained by the passenger close to his person and within his immediate control. Nor does it apply to any items which are not properly classified as baggage.

The term "baggage" includes such articles as a passenger takes with him for his own personal use, comfort, and convenience and which accord with the habits or wants of the social group to which he belongs. The definition extends to articles to be used after the journey comes to an end as well as to articles intended for use during the journey. On the other hand, articles intended for the use of other persons or merchandise destined to be sold or exhibited for the purpose of sale do not constitute baggage. Household goods of considerable bulk or value are not regarded as baggage. Nor is jewelry in unusual quantities or of exceptional value. The same applies to money. In other words, it is felt that a carrier, being forced to accept baggage without extra charge, should be exposed to liability only in accordance with what it might reasonably expect a person to take with him for his own use and convenience. With regard to articles of exceptional value or other articles which are not properly baggage the carrier is entitled to appropriate compensation for their carriage. The duty of the carrier to transport baggage cannot be used by passengers to avoid payment of the usual freight or to throw the risk of exceptionally valuable articles upon the carrier without payment therefor. For this reason, it is generally held that with regard to articles which are not baggage but which the passenger has tendered and passed off as baggage, the carrier has only a slight duty of care. Some courts hold that it owes no duty of care whatever.

Most jurisdictions permit the carrier to limit his liability with regard to baggage to the value declared by the passenger. As previously observed, the Carmack Amendment to the Interstate Commerce Act expressly permits limitations of liability in connection with baggage carried in interstate commerce.

INNKEEPERS

With the discussion of common carriers, it is traditional to join a discussion of the liability of innkeepers. The reason for this is that, under the common law, innkeepers (today better known as hotel owners or operators), are held to the same strict liability with regard to their guests' belongings as are carriers with regard to the goods they carry. At common law, the rule of strict liability affects only those who furnish lodging to the public at large for compensation as a regular business and such liability extends only to the belongings of lodgers who are "guests." To qualify as a "guest," within this rule, one must be a transient, and persons who intend to become and are accepted as permanent lodgers are not guests.

Today, in almost all jurisdictions, the old common-law strict liability of the "innkeeper" has been substantially modified by case law and statute. The statutes vary as to detail but they all have certain features in common. They provide that the innkeeper may avoid strict liability for loss of his guests' valuables or money by providing a safe where

they may be kept and by posting adequate notice of its availability. To avoid liability, the innkeeper must comply strictly with the statutory prescribed mode of posting such notices. With regard to articles which are not placed in a safe provided for this purpose, or which are not articles of the kind normally kept in a safe, the statutes often limit recovery to a maximum figure which, while it differs from jurisdiction to jurisdiction, is generally insubstantial. However, these statutory limitations do not apply where the loss is due to the fault of the innkeeper or his employees. In the case of loss due to his own fault or that of his employees, the innkeeper is liable for the full value of the property.

CASES

VOGEL v. STATE

(1953) 204 Misc. 614, 124 N.Y.S.2d 563.

YOUNG, J. The Belleayre Mountain Ski Center is a ski resort owned by the State of New York and operated and maintained by its Conservation Department. Among its facilities is a chair lift, a device for transporting skiers upmountain. During the summer, the lift is used to carry sightseers.

* * *

On March 4, 1950, the claimant, a young lady attorney, accompanied by some friends, went to Belleayre to ski. Belleayre's particular attraction for her was the chair lift, because, even though she had skied for three years and was classed as an intermediate skier, she had never been on one.

She purchased some tickets, went to the loading platform of the chair lift, and then proceeded to practice the preachments of every attorney—extreme caution. Instead of immediately embarking on the lift, she stood at the base of the slope and watched its operation for about thirty or forty minutes. She observed how others got on and rode. She quizzed her friends about its operation and was assured by them that it was "simple". Being thus instructed and assured, she took her position in the waiting line to take her first ride. From this point on, everything she did appears to have been wrong.

When it came her turn to ride, claimant, carrying her poles in her left hand, took a seat in the moving chair. A loading attendant shouted that her poles were in the wrong hand. Looking up the slope ahead of her, she could see that the others appeared to have their poles across their laps, with the handles to the right and the points to the left. Following their example, she shifted her poles, continuing the while up the hill toward the intermediate station.

Approaching the intermediate station, she prepared to alight by opening the safety gate and calling out "Intermediate Station, please".

When claimant arrived at the platform, the attendant started to guide her chair from the left and she started to leave it to the right. Then she discovered that she had permitted her ski poles to become lodged in the chair in some manner and that she was unable to disengage them. Trying to free the poles, the chair bumping her from the rear, claimant became panicky, her coordination deserted her, and she threw herself to the right.

The attendant, seeing and appreciating her plight, pulled the cut-off switch. The chair came to a stop a few feet upmountain from the claimant *with the poles still entangled in it*. In the meantime, the claimant, having lost her balance, fell to the ground and fractured her leg, for which injury, suit is brought.

* * *

The claimant argues that the chair lift is a common carrier within the definition set forth by Anderson v. Fidelity & Casualty Co. of New York, 228 N.Y. 475, 127 N.E. 584, 9 A.L.R. 1544, in that it is a conveyance offered to the public for hire at a fixed fare for all, and that a duty exists to provide a safe place for alighting. [Citation.]

"A common carrier of personal property is one who agrees for a specified compensation to transport such property from one place to another for all persons that may see fit to employ him. [Citations.] One is not a common carrier unless he indicates to the public that he is ready and willing to do business for all that may see fit to employ him 'up to the capacity of his facilities.' Michigan Public Utilities Commission v. Duke, 266 U.S. 570, 577, 45 S.Ct. 191, 69 L.Ed. 445, 36 A.L.R. 1105; 2 Parsons on Contracts (9th Ed.) 166." Gerhard & Hey, Inc., v. Cattaraugus Tanning Co., 241 N.Y. 413, 150 N.E. 500, 501. Evolution has brought the definition to include the carrying of passengers as well as goods, [citation] and the definition has been further delineated over the years when the courts have ruled out various supposed criteria. For example, fixed termini are not essential, [citation]; nor are fixed charges, [citation]; it matters not whether the transportation be vertical or horizontal, [citation].

The factor which distinguishes the common carrier from others is that he holds himself out to the public " 'in common, that is to all persons who choose to employ him, as ready to carry for hire' ". Allen v. Sackrider, 37 N.Y. 341, 342. Even the word "all" has its exceptions. One instance is that a common carrier is not required to carry a passenger who is so intoxicated or otherwise disorderly as to endanger the safety of the other passengers or to cause them annoyance or inconvenience. [Citation.]

"It would seem that in every case of general obligation to serve, the custom of service qualifies the nature of the duty." Anderson v. Fidelity & Casualty Co. of New York,

228 N.Y. 475, 491, 127 N.E. 584, 589, quoting Columbia Law Review, Dec. 1917, pp. 710, 713. This case thus expresses recognition of the fact that every common carrier's obligation to serve all must be qualified by reasonable regulation else its service would be destroyed.

The State of New York, as part of its commendable effort to provide its people with parks and recreational areas, has developed, promoted and advertised its Belleayre Mountain Ski Center. High among its attractive features is the chair lift, which, as we have stated, was the compelling attraction for the claimant, and, we can well imagine, for many others.

The service offered by the chair lift is transportation of passengers for which a fee is charged. * * *

The service is offered to the public "in common", subject, we assume, to the reasonable qualification that, in wintertime, each passenger must be equipped for skiing, although the evidence is silent on that point.

* * *

In Burke v. State, 64 Misc. 558, 119 N.Y.S. 1089, the transportation concerned was that provided by an inclined railway running from a lower level to an upper level in a State park at Niagara Falls. It is of interest to know that there was little difference, mechanically speaking, between the railway cars suspended from and moved by the cable and the chairs suspended from and moved by the ski lift cable, except that the railroad car did not hang freely in the air but moved along a track built along or up from the ground.

In the Burke case, the Court held, at 119 N.Y.S. 1104, "The state owned and operated the inclined railway at the time of the accident. It placed placards announcing the railway, notices calling attention to it and the amount charged to ride thereon, thereby inviting the public to patronize it and to pay for the transportation. The state had ticket offices for the sale of tickets to ride on the railway, with its employes to sell the tickets, to receive the sum charged and to collect the tickets sold. The state maintained the structure, provided the cars and appurtenances and the machinery which ran the cars. Its employes operated it, and its officers had the care, control, and management of it. It received the fruits from operating it. The receipts from it were turned into the state treasury. Any person who bought and received a ticket was entitled to ride thereon as a passenger. This made and constituted the state a common carrier of passengers for hire, and subjected it to the duties and liabilities attaching to such carriers."

* * *

"With the development in traveling facilities from the post horse to the chaise, the stage coach, and to the modern railroad train or steamboat, the term 'common carrier' has been applied to each new development catering to the public generally, and the strict rules of the old law have been relaxed but little, for with the development came new dangers of a mechanical sort inherent to swiftly moving machines." Anderson v. Fidelity & Casualty Co. of New York, 228 N.Y. 475, 480, 127 N.E. 584, 585. The Court then (in 1920) forecast application of the term "common carrier" to "that most recent device for eliminating the fetters of distance, the aeroplane".

* * *

The Court can only conclude that the facts herein fit the definition and that the State of New York, in operating the chair lift, is a common carrier, and subject to the concomitant duties of care.

The duty owed by a common carrier of passengers is to use the utmost foresight as to possible dangers and the utmost prudence in guarding against them. [Citation.] This includes making provision for the passenger to safely alight. [Citation.] "The degree of care to be exercised is commensurate with the danger to be avoided". Richardson v. Nassau Electric R. R. Co., 190 App.Div. 529, 180 N.Y.S. 109, 110. "It is obvious that all of the varying circumstances must be taken into consideration. The character and mode of the conveyance is a matter playing its part." Warren's Negligence in New York Courts (1941), Vol. 2, p. 108.

* * *

It is a manifest impossibility for the operator of a ski resort to oversee and classify for his own protection the liability of every skier who may come to ski on his slope. Consequently, he must rely on each skier being a competent judge of his own abilities. Certainly, the operator cannot be responsible for the broken neck of the novice, who, overestimating his competence, scorns the gentle slopes and tries to ski jump. * * *

The Court feels the State exercised the highest degree of care. Any hazards inherent in riding the lift were obvious to all. The signs posted were not a necessary, but merely an added, precaution. The attendant service provided was as sufficient as the mode of transportation and the surrounding circumstances permitted. About the only thing not done was to stop each chair to let the skier alight. We do not feel that the State was called upon to do this as it could rely on the skier's ability to execute this simple maneuver, proof of the pudding lying in the fact that this was the first such accident in thirty thousand rides.

The proximate cause of the accident was the claimant's own negligence in permitting her poles to become entangled in the chair. Reasonable prudence should have suggested that she make certain the poles were free before she attempted to alight. If she then found she could not free them, the attendant could have, and undoubtedly would have, stopped the chair. As it happened, she apparently never gave a thought to the poles until she started to alight, and the at-

tendant took the only course of action open to him.

The claim is dismissed.

———

JOHN I. HAAS, INC. v. AMERICAN EXPORT LINES, INC.

(1964) 237 Md. 73, 205 A.2d 223.

HAMMOND, J. Suit was brought below by the importer of one hundred sixty-four bales of Styrian hops, which it had sold to breweries, against the steamship company which brought the hops to Baltimore, the Baltimore and Ohio Railroad Co., which acted both as operator of the pier at which the hops were unloaded and as the initial rail carrier, and Superintendence Co., Inc., which sampled and weighed the bales at the pier, for the value of forty-seven of the bales which, at the end of a rail journey at San Francisco, were found on inspection to have become contaminated by oil, grease and moisture and were rejected in part as to twenty bales and in whole as to twenty-seven bales by the brewery there to whom they had been consigned.

The case was heard by the court sitting without a jury, and the significant facts were presented almost entirely by depositions. The court found that the bales were delivered in good condition by the steamship company and that the importer had not proven that the oil, grease or moisture had been caused by the Superintendence Company. Judge Carter held that the railroad was not liable either as warehouseman—where it "is held to the duty of care with which a reasonable man would treat his own possessions"—or as a common carrier—where it "is held to be an insurer of the goods, and his liability can be rebutted only by a showing of inherent vice or an act of God, etc." He found as facts that the "predominant damage" to the hops was mold; the mold was caused by moisture; to prevent sweating and hence mold, hops are customarily stored or kept in cool or freezing temperature; the hops were transported from Baltimore to San Francisco in an un-refrigerated car, no request having been made for a refrigerated car, and because the hops were not refrigerated during transit they sweated and the sweating caused the damage.

There was testimony from which the trier of fact properly could have found, as he did, that there was no oil, grease or moisture on or in the bales as a result of their handling by the Superintendence Company or by the railroad as warehouseman. This included the following facts: (a) all of the one hundred sixty-four bales received the same handling at the same pier before they were delivered to a carrier and none was damaged but the forty-seven bales which were shipped to San Francisco (forty-one bales were sent in one lot to a Milwaukee brewery by motor carrier, as were twenty-seven other bales to a Baltimore brewery by another truck line, and all were undamaged and accepted by the brewery); (b) another lot of forty-nine bales were sent by rail to Los Angeles, delivered undamaged and accepted by the consignee brewery there; and (c) the freight waybill for the Los Angeles shipment bore the notation "all covers dirty" as did the waybill covering the San Francisco shipment here involved, and the testimony was that if the bales had shown signs of oil or grease or moisture, the notation would not have been "dirty" since this connoted only ordinary dirt resulting from customary handling. [Citation.]

We think, however, (a) that the evidence before the trial judge did not permit the finding he made as to the cause of the damage to the hops that were shipped to San Francisco, and that therefore his finding was clearly erroneous, and (b) that although the controlling law as to the liability of the railroad as a common carrier was correctly stated, it was not correctly applied.

Where a plaintiff proves that goods were delivered to a carrier in good condition and were in bad condition upon arrival at destination, a presumption arises that the damage occurred through the fault or negligence of the carrier, and this casts upon the carrier the burden of going forward and showing either that the goods were not in good condition when delivered to the carrier or that the damage was occasioned by some cause which excepts the carrier from absolute liability, such as inherent vice or infirmity of the goods or act of God. Accordingly, the mere proof of delivery of the goods to the carrier in good condition and of their arrival at the place of destination in damaged condition makes out a prima facie case against the carrier, so that if no satisfactory explanation is given as to how the damage occurred, the carrier may be held liable. [Citations.]

The evidence in the present case showed that the railroad as a carrier received the forty-seven bales of hops consigned to San Francisco in good condition and that they arrived at destination damaged from penetration of oil, grease and moisture. The brewery to whom the shipment was consigned was persuaded to accept twenty of the least damaged bales upon being granted an allowance for the damaged portions of the hops, but it refused to accept the remaining bales after it had sampled each one and found the damage so extensive as to make the hops therein unusable.

The testimony in the depositions of the brewmaster and assistant brewmaster of the consignee brewery and of an experienced cargo surveyor was that upon examination at San Francisco the burlap wrappings of the bales were stained with oil, with grease, with bird droppings and with colorless moisture spots and yellow stains apparently caused by some liquid. They agreed that the colorless spots and the yellow spots were still moist when they examined the bales and that the moisture had penetrated into the hops from the outside. There was no evidence of moisture damage or of mold except under the spots, and most of it was under the yellow spots. The brewmaster's testimony was that moisture did more damage than oil or grease, although both of the latter two caused extensive harm and often there were both kinds of damage to the hops in the same bale.

The railroad offered no testimony to explain how the oil, grease and moisture got into the bales or to show that it was not responsible for their presence. The forty-seven bales were loaded on November 25, 1961, from the pier in Baltimore into car number SO 272429. On November 28 a car inspector at the Locust Point yards of the railroad, not far from the pier, found a defect in that car and ordered it transferred to the repair track. There, the car department found it could not be repaired with the load in it and it was sent back to the pier, where the forty-seven bales were removed and reloaded into car number GN 12517, in which they travelled to San Francisco, arriving there on December 12. No witness was produced by the railroad to show the condition of the first car or the circumstances of the handling of the bales while in it or while they were in the process of being transferred to the second car.

To escape liability, the railroad relied below and relies here on the statements of the brewmasters that their brewery stored hops for several years, and during that time kept them under refrigeration to maintain their flavor and aroma and to prevent their sweating, which compressed hops have a tendency to do. Some breweries, it was said, keep the temperature at freezing, others at 42° to 45°.

We think this testimony does not fairly lend itself to a finding that internal sweating from lack of refrigeration caused the damage to the hops, or even that the predominant damage was from moisture. The cargo surveyor testified without controversion that at the time of the year when the hops were transported—November 25 to December 12 —no refrigeration would have been needed (and this would seem to coincide with common experience and knowledge of mankind). The testimony of the brewmasters and the cargo surveyor all but demonstrated that two kinds of moisture had descended onto the outside of the bales and that the resulting dampness penetrated within and caused the moisture damage and mold, and that such damage was not caused by internal sweating. The railroad offered no testimony that the cargo surveyor was wrong in his view that no refrigeration was needed in the late fall or early winter period of the transportation, either that the fact was to the contrary or as to unusual warm weather anywhere along the northern route from November 25 to December 12, or of heat in the car, or otherwise. Further, the testimony showed that almost as much damage occurred from oil and grease as from moisture and often the two kinds of damage overlapped. [Citations.]

Since the railroad did not meet its burden of showing it was not responsible for the harm to the hops which occurred while they were in carriage, and there is no real controversy as to the amount of the loss suffered by the importer, [citations] judgment will be entered for it against the railroad. The testimony was that the aggregate of the cost of reconditioning the twenty bales which the brewery accepted and the loss of the bad hops in these bales was $299.80 ($130.26 for labor and $169.54 for destroyed hops). The rejected twenty-seven bales contained hops of a net weight of 15,075 pounds. The brewery had agreed to pay $0.93408 per pound, or a total of $14,081.25. The extensively damaged hops were sold for $4,221.-00, leaving the claimant-importer with a net loss of $9,860.25. Adding the $299.80 makes $10,160.05, for which judgment will be entered as of July 15, 1963, the date of the entry of the erroneous judgment below.

Judgment in favor of Baltimore and Ohio Railroad Company reversed; judgment in favor of American Export Lines, Inc. and Superintendence Co., Inc., affirmed; judgment as of July 15, 1963, entered in this court in favor of John I. Haas, Inc., against the Baltimore and Ohio Railroad Company for $10,160.05, costs in this court to be paid by the Baltimore and Ohio Railroad Company.

RIO GRANDE CITY RY. CO. v. GUERRA

(1930 Tex.Civ.App.) 26 S.W.2d 360.

FLY, C. J. Horace P. Guerra and Virginia C. Guerra, doing business under the firm name of M. Guerra & Son, sued appellant to recover the sum of $2,094.01, alleged to be due as damages arising from the negligent destruction of twenty-three bales of cotton weighing 11,319 pounds in the aggregate. The cause was tried by jury, which returned a verdict for appellees in the sum of $2,-094.01.

The facts are, that appellees delivered appellant twenty-nine bales of cotton, for shipment, when seventy-one more bales were delivered, so as to constitute a shipment of one hundred bales of cotton. The remaining bales were in the possession of appellees and were to be delivered to appellant at another time.

When the twenty-nine bales were brought to the agent of appellant he instructed the employees of appellees to place them on a certain platform used for shipping purposes. The platform was not the one nearest to the depot, but was the one designated by the agent. The first night the cotton was on the platform twenty-three bales were destroyed by fire.

It is the contention of appellant that the relation of shipper and carrier had not arisen between the parties, and that, if appellant was liable, it was not as a carrier, but as a warehouseman.

When the cotton was delivered it was the distinct understanding that the delivery was not for immediate transportation, but that the bales delivered were to be held until the number delivered by appellees had reached one hundred bales, and, from the fact that only twenty-nine bales were delivered on the first day, it may be inferred or presumed that it would take at least two more days to deliver the remaining seventy-one bales. Evidently the twenty-nine bales of cotton were delivered and received for storage until the time fixed by appellees for shipment; that is when one hundred bales had been placed on the platform. It is the ordinary rule that, where goods are delivered to be held by the carrier for a certain time before shipment, the liability of the carrier is that of a warehouseman. There was an implied agreement between the parties that the cotton should be held by appellant as a warehouseman until the remaining cotton was delivered. Elliott on Railroads, Sec. 1464.

The facts of this case place appellant in the position of a warehouseman; indeed, it is not contended by appellees, in their brief, that appellant is liable other than as a warehouseman. In such case appellant was not an insurer of the cotton, and is not liable for its destruction, unless it appears that its negligence contributed to the loss of the property. It was liable as a bailee and owed the duty to exercise ordinary care and diligence in protecting the property of appellees, and unless a breach of the exercise of ordinary care and diligence is reasonably apparent from all the facts and circumstances, its liability does not attach. [Citations.]

The court instructed a verdict for appellees, whether on the assumption that appellant occupied the position of carrier to the cotton, or upon the assumption that it was incumbent upon appellant to show that it was not guilty of negligence as a warehouseman, we know not. The cotton was not delivered for immediate shipment, and for that reason the company could be held liable only as a warehouseman, and not as a common carrier. Elliott on Railroads, Sec. 1409. The shipment was not to be made at once, but depended on further acts by appellees. So it was necessary to show negligence upon the part of appellant, and if it could be held that placing the cotton on the platform, or failure to have a watchman, if there was such failure, or any other circumstances, none nor all of them constituted negligence per se, and the question of negligence, if any was shown, should have been submitted to a jury. The verdict should not have been instructed. [Citations.]

The judgment will be reversed, and the cause remanded.

BERNARD ROSCH v. UNITED AIR LINES, INC.

(1956 D.C.N.Y.) 146 F.Supp. 266.

BOLDT, DISTRICT JUDGE. Plaintiff, the owner of a racing greyhound brood matron, delivered the animal on August 9, 1954 to defendant United Air Lines, Inc. in New York City. United, an air carrier operating pursuant to the Civil Aeronautics Act, Title 49, U.S.C.A. § 401 et seq., and under tariffs filed with the Civil Aeronautics Board, accepted the shipment and issued its airbill to the plaintiff. The routing inserted in the airbill called for the shipment to go from New York City to Chicago via United, thence via Braniff International Airways, Inc. to Oklahoma City. From there it was to be transported by Railway Express Agency, Inc. to the consignee in Ardmore, Oklahoma.

At the time of the shipment, an embargo on all cargo shipments had been declared by Braniff due to the strain on its facilities re-

sulting from a pilots' strike of American Airlines. Defendant United was aware of the embargo when it accepted the shipment. As a consequence of the embargo, when the animal reached Chicago the only available means of transporting it to destination were via Railway Express. The latter transported the dog to Oklahoma City where it was found to be sick. It died a short time later. $15,000 damages for the loss of the dog are sought in this action.

The airbill contained a space for the insertion of a declared value for carriage by the shipper and provided that in the absence of such declaration, the shipment would be deemed to have the agreed value as set forth in the air carrier's tariffs. Plaintiff originally declared a value of $2,000, but upon ascertaining the excess value charges applicable thereto, caused that figure to be stricken by the air carrier's freight agent. The tariff valuation, on a weight basis, and in the absence of a greater declared value, was $50.

Plaintiff claims that the defendant air carrier deviated from the routing shown in the airbill, thereby giving rise to a course of conduct leading to the animal's death from mishandling, delay and negligence. He urges that the defendant, because of its knowledge of the embargo and the impossibility of routing the shipment via Braniff, should not have accepted the shipment with such routing; that having done so, it is bound thereby and is estopped by its conduct from invoking certain provisions of its Official Air Freight Rules Tariff No. 1–A by way of complete defense to the action; that similarly, it cannot assert, in the alternative, that its liability, if any, is limited to $50.

While there may be some individual hardship on a shipper in a case of this kind, I am of the opinion that the air carrier has the right to invoke its tariff and airbill provisions. Congress, in the interests of a sound national transportation policy, has sought to prevent all forms of unjust discrimination by interstate carriers so that shippers will be accorded equal treatment. Such policy rejects the concept of estoppel urged by plaintiff. It holds all agreements between shipper and carrier contrary to the provisions of the carrier's filed tariffs to be null and void. [Citations.] The attainment of the national public policy here requires that the plaintiff and defendant air carrier be bound by the latter's filed tariffs. [Citation.] Those tariffs and the airbill constitute the contract of carriage. [Citations.] Those tariffs, among other things, permit the carrier to deviate from any route shown on the airbill when necessary in its opinion to expedite delivery via any air carrier or other transportation agency [Rule 3.8(b)]. Plaintiff is deemed to have agreed to such proviso when he delivered his shipment to defendant for transportation by it. * * *

Accordingly, plaintiff is to have judgment against defendant air carrier in the sum of $50, and the third-party claim of the latter against third-party defendant Railway Express Agency, Inc., is withdrawn by consent.

HOPKINS v. LONG ISLAND RAILROAD CO.

(1964) 21 A.D.2d 814, 251 N.Y.S.2d 590.

MEMORANDUM BY THE COURT. In an action to recover damages for personal injury the defendant appeals, as limited by its brief, from a judgment of the Supreme Court, Nassau County, entered February 11, 1964 after trial, upon a jury's verdict in favor of the plaintiff.

Judgment reversed on the law without costs, and complaint dismissed without costs. Finding of fact implicit in the jury's verdict are affirmed.

Plaintiff was an employee, not of this defendant, but of the Pennsylvania Railroad. He was riding upon defendant's railroad on a free pass issued to him, not as part of his contract of employment, but merely as a gratuity. The reverse side of the pass contained the following condition: "The person accepting and using [the pass] thereby assumes all risk of accident to person or property * * *." Plaintiff admitted knowledge of such condition. Plaintiff was injured as a result of the ordinary negligence of defendant.

In our opinion, the pass by its expressly stated condition barred plaintiff's recovery based on the defendant's ordinary negligence, despite the fact that the stated condition did not contain a clause specifically exculpating defendant from liability "by reason of negligence". [Citations.]

We are also of the opinion that, even in the absence of the said stipulation or condition in the pass that plaintiff "assumes all risk of accident," there would be no liability in any event on the part of defendant here. When plaintiff used the pass given to him as a gratuity, plaintiff was not a "passenger" on defendant's railroad, but a mere licensee; and hence, as to the plaintiff, the defendant was not a common carrier. [Citations.] To a licensee the defendant owed the duty only of abstaining from affirmative acts of negligence or of not injuring him intentionally. [Citation.] No breach of such duty is claimed here.

SHIRAZI v. GREYHOUND CORPORATION

(1965) 145 Mont. 421, 401 P.2d 559.

CASTLES, J. The plaintiff, Ebrahim Shirazi, brought an action in the district court of the eighteenth judicial district for the loss of certain luggage he had checked with the defendant Greyhound Corporation. The court, sitting without a jury, entered judgment in favor of the plaintiff for the sum of $680.00. The defendant appealed alleging that its liability in this case was limited to $25.00.

The plaintiff is a citizen of Persia, Iran. He came to the United States in 1961 to attend school. He attended a school in Michigan where he learned to speak approximately 400 English words. Subsequently he enrolled at Montana State College in Bozeman, Montana. During the summer of 1962, the plaintiff journeyed to California. In order to return to Bozeman the plaintiff purchased a bus ticket from the defendant in San Francisco. He then traveled to Redding, California. At Redding, the plaintiff went to defendant's bus depot, checked his luggage and was given a baggage receipt. His luggage consisted of a suitcase and two pasteboard boxes. The pasteboard boxes arrived in Bozeman but the suitcase was lost.

The defendant had filed with the Interstate Commerce Commission a tariff which limited liability for lost luggage to the sum of $25.00 unless excess value was declared and a higher fare paid. At the time the plaintiff checked his luggage at the defendant's depot in Redding, there was posted at the baggage counter a printed notice that the defendant's liability for lost baggage was so limited. This same limitation of liability was also printed on the baggage receipt delivered to the plaintiff.

The lower court concluded: that the printed notice posted at the baggage counter was insufficient to inform the plaintiff of any limitation of liability for the reason plaintiff was unable to read or understand said notice; that the matter printed on the baggage check was not sufficient to inform the plaintiff of any limitation of liability because the same was not presented to the plaintiff until after his baggage was checked and in any event, the plaintiff was unable to read or understand the matter printed on said baggage check, and that the attempt by defendant to so limit its liability to $25.00 is unreasonable.

Questions relating to the limitation of liability by interstate carriers for loss of baggage checked by passengers are governed by Federal law. [Citations.] In order to ascertain the Federal law in this area the applicable statutes and cases must be examined. Title 49, § 20(11), U.S.C.A. of the Interstate Commerce Act provides:

"Any common carrier * * * receiving property for transportation * * * shall issue a receipt or bill of lading therefor, and shall be liable to the lawful holder thereof for any loss, damage, or injury to such property caused by it * * *, and no contract, receipt, rule, regulation, or other limitation of any character whatsoever shall exempt such common carrier * * * from the liability imposed; * * * notwithstanding any limitation of liability or limitation of the amount of recovery or representation or agreement as to value in any such receipt or bill of lading, or in any contract, rule, regulation, or in any tariff filed with the Interstate Commerce Commission; and any such limitation, without respect to the manner or form in which it is sought to be made is declared to be unlawful and void: * * * *Provided, however,* That the provisions hereof respecting liability for full actual loss, damage, or injury, * * * shall not apply, first, to baggage carried on passenger trains or boats, or trains or boats carrying passengers; * * *."

Title 49, § 319 of the Interstate Commerce Act provides:

"The provisions of section 20(11) and (12) of this title * * * shall apply with respect to common carriers by motor vehicle with like force and effect as in the case of those persons to which such provisions are specifically applicable."

Notwithstanding authority to the contrary [citation], it is the view of this court that section 319 of Title 49 extends the provisions of section 20(11) to baggage carried on motor vehicles or busses engaged in interstate commerce. This position is supported by ample authority from other jurisdictions. [Citations.]

The conclusion that motor carriers may limit their liability for loss or damage to baggage brings us to the chief point of conflict, that is, whether under all the facts and circumstances peculiar to this case the limitation of liability by the defendant is binding upon the plaintiff. First, we must determine whether the plaintiff was given sufficient notice of the limitation. The rule that the shipper be given notice of the limitation of liability requires that he be given a fair and reasonable opportunity to discover the limitation. [Citation.] It does not require actual knowledge of the limitation on the part of the passenger. [Citations.] * * *

Secoulsky v. Oceanic Steam Nav. Co., 223 Mass. 465, 112 N.E. 151, is a case in which the plaintiff exchanged a certificate for passage for a ticket to travel by way of steamship from England to the United States. The plaintiff was unable to read the limitation of liability printed on the ticket because he could not read the English language. The court stated that the fact he was unable to read or write of itself did not avoid the contract. It further declared:

"The plaintiff knew he could not embark or be cared for during the journey unless he obtained a ticket; and that the paper received in exchange for the certificate was a ticket; and it is of no consequence that before embarking he failed to acquaint himself with the contents."

Likewise, in the case before us, the plaintiff, Mr. Shirazi, knew that the baggage receipt presented to him by the defendant's agent was concerned with the transaction of checking and shipping his luggage. It was incumbent upon Mr. Shirazi, who knew of his own inability to read the English language, to acquaint himself with the contents of the ticket. It was not incumbent upon the defendant to discover the plaintiff's inability and then inform him of the limitation contained in the matter printed on the baggage receipt and on the notice posted at the baggage counter.

Also, the lower court's finding that the matter contained in the baggage receipt was not sufficient notice of the limitation of liability because the receipt was not presented to the plaintiff until after his baggage was checked, is error. As pointed out by the appellant there was no significant lapse of time between the checking of the baggage and the giving of the receipt. The two acts involved a single transaction. There was nothing to prevent the plaintiff from paying a higher fare for higher coverage even after the baggage receipt had been delivered to him.

The finding of the court below that it was unreasonable for the defendant to limit its liability to $25 is also error. If liability were limited to $25 without provision for obtaining greater coverage, the determination of the lower court may have been valid. However, plaintiff was given adequate notice of the opportunity to declare a higher value, pay a higher fare and obtain greater coverage. It seems only fair that the transportation company be allowed to require that the compensation paid bear a reasonable relation to the risk and responsibility assumed. The controlling factor, as seen by this court, in determining the validity of a regulation limiting liability for loss or damage to baggage is whether the shipper is given an opportunity to choose between rates on the basis of values tied to them. The plaintiff in this case had such an opportunity. [Citation.]

Further, in this regard, there is authority to the effect that if a regulation limiting liability is unreasonable it may be challenged only by proceedings contesting their reasonableness before the Interstate Commerce Commission. [Citations.]

The final argument of the plaintiff is that since defendant violated its tariff by accepting for transportation plaintiff's pasteboard boxes of books, it waived its limitation of liability and was responsible for the entire loss. The pasteboard boxes were checked along with the suitcase which was lost. The case of Neece v. Richmond Greyhound Lines, (246 N.C. 547, 99 S.E.2d 756, 68 A.L.R.2d 1341) has been cited by plaintiff in support of his final contention. In the Neece case, the carrier accepted a wardrobe bag in violation of a filed tariff. The wardrobe bag was lost and the court held the carrier to have waived its limitation of liability by violating its tariff. In the case now before us the pasteboard boxes, which were accepted in violation of the filed tariff, were delivered to the plaintiff. The suitcase, which was not in violation of the tariff, was lost. This court is not now deciding what defendant's liability would be if the lost suitcase had been accepted for carriage in violation of its filed tariff as that question is not before us. The decision of this court is that where baggage accepted for carriage in conformity with the tariff filed by the carrier is lost, an otherwise valid limitation of liability is not waived by the acceptance for carriage of other baggage in violation of the carrier's tariff and this baggage is not lost.

The judgment of the district court awarding the plaintiff $680 plus costs is reduced to $25 plus costs.

PHOENIX ASSUR. CO. OF N. Y. v. ROYALE INVESTMENT CO.

(1965 Mo.) 393 S.W.2d 43.

WOLFE, ACTING P. J. This is an action by the plaintiff, Phoenix Assurance Company of New York, to recover from Royale Investment Company the amount the "Assurance Company" paid to Roy M. Scott. The plaintiff sought recovery by right of subrogation after paying Scott $603.62 under a policy of insurance. This sum was for damages to

Scott's automobile which had been stolen from a parking lot operated by the defendant Royale Investment Company. There was a judgment for the plaintiff, and the defendant prosecutes this appeal.

The facts of the matter are that the Royale Investment Company operated the Ambassador-Kingsway Hotel in the City of St. Louis. Directly to the east of the hotel it maintained a parking lot which was generally used for hotel guests. The defendant corporation also maintained another lot about 100 feet east of the one mentioned, which was used for parking of cars belonging to persons who attended various functions at the hotel.

Roy M. Scott carried a policy of comprehensive insurance with the plaintiff Phoenix Assurance Company of New York on his 1957 Buick. He came to St. Louis with his wife on September 27, 1960 in the automobile. They stopped by the main entrance of the Ambassador-Kingsway Hotel at about ten p. m. There a doorman took over the automobile and gave Scott a claim check. Scott kept the key to his car as the Buick ignition switch was made so that it could be turned and the motor started without the use of the key.

Scott and his wife retired to their room in the hotel. At about 4:30 in the morning Scott was awakened by a phone call from a police officer who told him that his car had been involved in a wreck in south St. Louis. Scott dressed at once and went to the police station from which the call originated. The police gave him a release order to get his car, which had been taken to a parking lot. There he found his car damaged in the front end, including the hood, headlights, windshield, and right front fender. The car would still operate and he drove it away. The car was later taken to Yates Oldsmobile, Inc., and it was repaired there at a cost of $545.-09. Scott was obliged to rent a car for a week, as he was in St. Louis on business, and for this he paid $50.00. He also paid a towing charge of $8.53. His insurance company, Phoenix Assurance Company of New York, the plaintiff herein, paid the damages that he had thus sustained in the total sum of $603.62.

Scott remained at the hotel until October 4. He was charged and paid one dollar for the first night of parking. The claim check that he was given by the doorman had printed on the back of it:

"The Hotel assumes no responsibility for cars parked on this lot whether for the car or damages or contents therein.

"We do not have an attendant at all times.

"This ticket is not a receipt. It indicates our agreement concerning parking.

"All owners placing automobiles with the Hotel parking lot do so subject to the above terms and conditions."

The defendant's evidence chiefly consisted of the testimony of the bell captain of the hotel. He recalled that Scott and his wife arrived at the hotel and that he told Scott that he would park his car for him. He said that Scott kept the key, but he could operate the car without it and lock all of the doors. He said that he told Scott that he would park the car at Scott's own risk. He also said that he called Scott's attention to the "writing on the stub". He stated that he took the car, parked it on the lot, and that he closed all of the windows and locked the doors. The parking lot was lighted, but it was unattended from 1:30 a. m. to 8:00 a. m.

The first point raised by the appellant defendant is that the court erred in refusing defendant's offered instruction C. This instruction stated that the automobile was parked at the owner's own risk if the owner's attention was directed to the printed statement, set out above, on the ticket given him, and that if his attention was so directed the defendant was not liable for the damage to the car.

The respondent points out that its petition contained a general charge of negligence,

and it contends that it is against public policy to permit one serving the public to exempt oneself from liability for one's own negligence. There is some support for respondent's contention in 8 Am.Jur. (2d), paragraph 131, p. 1026, wherein it is said:

"The courts, while recognizing that an ordinary bailee may contract to exempt himself from liability for loss of or damage to the goods, occasioned by his own negligence or that of his employee, exhibit a strong tendency to hold contracts of this character, when entered into by bailees in the course of general dealing with the public to be violative of public policy and this tendency becomes more pronounced in the more recent decisions. These bailees, who are termed 'professional,' as distinguished from 'ordinary,' bailees, are those who make it their principal business to act as bailees and who deal with the public on a uniform and not an individual basis, such as owners or proprietors of parcel checkrooms, garages, parking stations, and parking lots, carriers, innkeepers, and warehousemen. The basis for denying the right of such bailees to limit their liability for their own negligence is that the public, in dealing with them, lacks practical equality of bargaining power, since it must either accede to the conditions sought to be imposed or else forego the desired service. It is said that a bailee who is performing services for which the public has a substantial need should not be permitted to use this circumstance to coerce the members of the public into contracts of this kind."

*   *   *

We do not reach the point raised by the respondent, on the facts before us, as to what public policy is or should be on the subject of such bailments. The established rule of construction of a contract containing provisions exempting one from liability will never be implied to extend to liability for one's own negligence unless such an intention is clearly and explicitly stated. [Citations.]

The general exculpatory clause does not meet the requirement set out above, and consequently cannot be construed to cover the negligence of the bailee. Nor is the bailee saved by the added statement, "We do not have an attendant at all times," for this does not exclude a conclusion that the defendant was negligent in leaving the entrance and exit of the lot open when the lot was not attended. The court therefore did not err in refusing the instruction offered by the defendant relating to the printed matter on the claim check.

As stated, the petition charges general negligence. Under the pleading the proof of damage to the automobile raised a presumption of negligence, and the burden of going forward with the evidence then shifted to the defendant. [Citations.]

The fact that the car was stolen did not absolve the defendant, for it was incumbent upon it to present evidence that it had exercised ordinary care to safeguard the automobile from theft. [Citations.]

Another point raised is that the court erred in refusing to give defendant's offered instruction "D", which limited to $200 the amount of damages which the jury might award. This was offered under the theory that the loss came under Section 419.010, RSMo 1959, V.A.M.S., which limits innkeepers' liability for certain losses to $200. The statute relates to the loss of "any money, jewelry, wearing apparel, baggage or other property of a guest." It is contended that the words "or other property" includes a guest's automobile.

Under the common law, innkeepers were liable for the loss of their guests' goods, and this was to protect travelers against dishonest practices of innkeepers and their servants. [Citation.] In so far as statutes of this nature are in derogation of the common law, they are to be strictly construed. [Citation.]

Under the rule or maxim of construction known as ejusdem generis, general words following the enumeration of particular classes of things will be construed as applyings to things of the same general nature or class of those enumerated. [Citations.] Applying that rule to the statute in question, the words "or other property" obviously applied to things carried into the hotel by the guest. It would not include the guest's automobile. For this reason and for the further reason that the defendant under the evidence was nothing more than a bailee for hire, the statute has no application. The court did not err in refusing the offered instruction.

For the foregoing reasons, we affirm the judgment of the Circuit Court.

PROBLEMS

1. P carries with him onto a train a valise containing his valuable salesman's samples. During his trip the valise is stolen from his room in the train by a fellow passenger. P sues the railroad company on the ground that it is absolutely liable for the safety of his baggage. Decision?

2. A certified public accountant completed an out-of-town engagement and returned to his home-office city by railroad. He purchased a one-way ticket with Pullman accommodations and checked a large brief case and a suitcase as baggage. There was no excess baggage charge. The brief case and the suitcase were carried on the same train with the accountant, but for some unknown reason the brief case could not be found by the carrier at the end of the journey. No questions had been asked by the railroad agent concerning the contents of either case, and the passenger had volunteered no information about them. The brief case contained working papers the replacement of which would cost more than $1,000. Is the carrier legally responsible for the loss of the brief case as baggage?

3. A common carrier accepted a shipment of goods at Chicago for delivery to a buyer in Boston, Mass. The goods were in transit between the two cities. State and explain briefly whether the carrier would be liable to the owner of the

goods if they were destroyed under the following conditions.

(a) The goods were destroyed by a fire caused by a bolt of lightning.

(b) The goods were destroyed by a riot of 100 people.

(c) A discharged employee, holding a grudge against the carrier, caused a wreck which destroyed the goods.

(d) The goods were destroyed by a fire caused by the negligence of an employee of the carrier.

(e) The goods were destroyed because of improper packing by the shipper of the goods.

4. The Midland Trucking Company was engaged in transporting drugs for the Northern Drug Company. On February 1, the truck was driven by a new driver who had no experience in operating a loaded tractor-trailer type truck. En route from Springfield to Chicago, the driver allowed the truck to travel at an excessive speed, and the truck began to weave, forcing it from the highway and to blow out a front tire. While the driver was changing the tire, a flash flood occurred with sufficient force to wash the truck from the right-of-way destroying the cargo of drugs. The Northern Drug Company brings an action against Midland Trucking Company for damage to its cargo. Decision?

5. B in New York orders 100 Grade A cowhides from S in Chicago, the goods to be shipped via N.Y.C. Railroad, f. o. b. Chicago. Indicate by letter (B for buyer, S for seller and RR for railroad) who bears the loss in each of the following cases.

(a) The goods are loaded onto a N. Y. C. railroad car and a bill of lading is received by S from the N. Y. C. R. R. Before starting on the journey a flood destroys the car and goods. (b) The goods are shipped via Erie RR but are really Grade B hides. The hides are destroyed en route by a flood. (c) The goods are shipped via N. Y. C. R. R. The bill of lading contains a clause relieving it of liability for all loss to property in transit caused by fire. A fire caused by the negligence of the carrier's agent destroyed the goods en route.

6. S, seller, in San Francisco, ships 400 cartons of tomatoes to B, buyer, in Chicago, by the Union Pacific Railroad Co. In conformity with the contract of sale, B pays a sight draft attached to the bill of lading forwarded to him by S before the tomatoes arrive. The tomatoes arrive, cartons crushed, all tomatoes squashed and mouldy. The tomatoes were loaded on board a car of the Union Pacific Railroad by S. The Railroad Company issued a uniform inland bill of lading containing the usual notation "received in apparent good order, except as noted (contents and condition of packages unknown)." There was no other notation as to the condition of the goods, but the bill of lading had been stamped "Shipper's load, count & weight." S loaded the tomatoes in the presence of John Doe, an agent of the Railroad Company. S's loading was clearly defective in that he did nothing to secure them against tumbling. John Doe did not assist in this operation, he merely observed it. He also observed that most of the cartons of tomatoes were outwardly spoiled indicating that some of the tomatoes were already squashed. What are B's rights, if any, against the Union Pacific Railroad Company?

PART FOUR

SALES

CHAPTER 17

SALES AND SALES CONTRACTS

Introductory. One of the oldest branches of the common law is that dealing with sales of personal property. Before the use of money as a medium of exchange people exchanged goods by way of barter, and even today a barter, or the exchange of goods for other goods, is a sale under the Uniform Commercial Code (Section 2–304(1)).

The importance of the law of sales is self-evident, as the selling of goods, wares, and merchandise is the chief objective of most business enterprises, and practically everyone in our economy is a purchaser of both the durable goods and consumable goods which are required or used in everyday living.

Although the common law of sales is old, the first codification of the law of Sales was the enactment in England in 1893 of the Sale of Goods Act. In 1906 the Commissioners on Uniform State Laws submitted to the States for adoption a Uniform Sales Act patterned after the English Sale of Goods Act.

The Uniform Sales Act, having been adopted in 36 States and the District of Columbia, and in effect in certain States for 50 years or more, is repealed and superseded by the Uniform Commercial Code. Article 2 of the Code contains the statutory law on the subject of Sales in all States which have adopted the U.C.C. which comprise most of the States. Appendix A.

Distinction Between a Sale and a Contract to Sell. A fundamental distinction exists between a sale and a contract to sell. A sale is the transfer of title to goods by the seller to the buyer for a consideration known as the price. A contract to sell is not a sale because it does not cause an instant transfer of title to the goods. It is a contractual promise to transfer title in the future, and at the time of making the contract the subject matter may be either goods in existence or goods which are to be manufactured or grown in the future.

This basic distinction is set forth in Section 2–106 of the Code:

> (1) In this Article unless the context otherwise requires "contract" and "agreement" are limited to those relating to the present or future sale of goods. "Contract for sale" includes both a present sale of goods and a contract to sell goods at a future time. A "sale" consists in the passing of title from the seller to the buyer for a price (Section 2–401). A "present sale" means a sale which is accomplished by the making of the contract.

Definition of Goods. The Code defines "goods" as all things, including those specially manufactured, which are movable at the time of identification to the contract for sale, excluding money, investment securities, and choses in action. "Goods" include the unborn young of animals, growing crops, and certain identified things such as timber, minerals, or a structure or its materials attached to realty and to be removed therefrom by the seller. Section 2–105(1).

Before any interest in goods can be transferred, the goods must be both existing and identified. Goods which are not both existing and identified are "future" goods. Section 2–105(2).

A purported present sale of future goods operates as a contract to sell.

Sales Distinguished from Other Transactions. In order to understand clearly what is meant by a sale of goods, it is well to distinguish it from certain other transactions, such as a gift, bailment, chattel mortgage, pledge, and conditional sale.

A gift is a transfer of title to property but differs from a sale in that the transferor neither bargains for nor receives anything in exchange for the goods. A promise to make a gift is unenforceable for lack of consideration. To be effective, a gift requires a delivery of the property to the donee with donative intent. Delivery of the property is not necessary in order to pass title by way of sale.

A bailment is a transfer of the possession of personal property without a transfer of the title. Transfer of title is essential to a sale, although transfer of possession is not.

A chattel mortgage is the transfer of title to personal property as security for the payment of a debt. The mortgagee obtains a defeasible title or, in some jurisdictions, a lien on the goods. It is not an absolute unconditional transfer of title, as in the case of a sale. The mortgagor ordinarily retains possession of the mortgaged property. To be valid against other creditors of the mortgagor, a chattel mortgage must be placed on public record in the Recorder's office.

A pledge is a transfer of the possession of personal property, but not the title, as security for the payment of a debt. Its purpose is, therefore, different from that of a sale. It is further distinguished from a sale and from a chattel mortgage in that title to the goods is not transferred.

A conditional sale is a transfer of title to goods for a consideration upon the happening of a certain operative event or condition. The parties by their contract may provide that title shall pass to the buyer upon the happening of any event or condition, but the event which is usually of the greatest interest to the seller is payment of the price. Consequently, the term conditional sale, in ordinary usage, refers to a contract whereby the seller has delivered possession of the goods to the buyer, the buyer has agreed to pay the price, and title is not to pass to the buyer until the price is completely paid. The seller thereby reserves title to the goods as security for the payment of the price. The operative event or condition precedent to the transfer of title is the payment of the price, or the final installment thereof, to the seller. When this occurs, title automatically passes to the buyer pursuant to the contract without any further act by either party.

Under the Code, a chattel mortgage, conditional sales contract, or any other agreement which creates or provides for a security interest in goods is known as a "security agreement." The transfer or location of title or possession is unimportant to the existence or enforceability of the security interest. Section 9–202. The owner of a security interest is protected against claims of third parties where required by the Code by the public filing of a "financing statement."

A sale is distinguished from a security agreement in that it transfers to the buyer all of the ownership rights of the seller in the goods, whereas under a security agreement both the creditor and the debtor have ownership rights in the goods. The right of the secured creditor in the goods is to realize upon their value in the event of default by the debtor. The right of the debtor is to use, possess, and enjoy the goods, and where specifically provided to sell them in the ordinary course of business and account for the proceeds.

No security agreement or filing of a financing statement is necessary to the enforcement of a pledge as the debtor does not have possession of the goods.

Title and Ownership. The concept of legal title is generally well understood. It is the concept of ownership, a legally protected interest in specific property good against the entire world. The law regards specific property as owned by some person or persons at all times.

Absolute ownership means that there is only one legally protected interest in the goods. However, it is possible for different ownership interests to exist in the same goods at the same time. At common law, a divided ownership in specific goods exists in the case of a chattel mortgage or a conditional sale. The legal title transferred to the mortgagee or reserved in the conditional vendor is a security interest. Its purpose is to provide tangible security for the performance of an obligation to pay a debt or to pay the price of the goods. On the other hand, the property interest of the mortgagor or conditional vendee, accompanied by possession, use, and enjoyment of the goods, is equitable or beneficial ownership.

The ascertainment of ownership of goods is important in many respects. In the event of destruction of the goods, risk of loss ordinarily falls upon the owner. A levy upon or attachment of goods by a judgment creditor is unavailing unless the judgment debtor owns the goods and is effective only to the extent of such ownership. Goods which are subject to a contract of sale may not be attached by creditors of the seller if the ownership has been transferred to the buyer, nor by creditors of the buyer if the ownership remains in the seller. The obligation to pay personal property taxes assessed against the goods rests upon the owner who may be the buyer or the seller depending upon whether title has been transferred.

The Code recognizes that several property interests may be held by different persons in the same goods, and particularizes these various interests by referring to or defining: (1) title; (2) security interest; (3) special property; (4) insurable interest; (5) right to goods, and (6) risk of loss. The Code does not attach to the concept of title all of the legal incidents of the common law, but provides for specific property rights and interests which the parties may have in the goods, as well as the right which the seller may have to recover the price for the goods, independently of transfer of title.

Certificate of Title to Motor Vehicle. As an anti-theft measure, every State has a statute which provides in essence that the Secretary of State or other proper State official shall not issue or renew the registration of any motor vehicle unless the owner thereof shall have a certificate of title to the motor vehicle duly issued to him by the State in which registration is sought or by another State in which the motor vehicle was purchased or previously registered. The statute also provides that the owner of a motor vehicle who sells or transfers his interest therein shall endorse a sworn assignment and warranty of title upon the certificate of title thereto and deliver it to the purchaser or transferee at the time of delivering to him the motor vehicle. A failure to comply with the statute is a misdemeanor and subjects the offender upon conviction to a fine or imprisonment, or both. With respect to the validity of the sale of the motor vehicle, where the owner does not comply with the certificate of title law, the provisions of the various statutes differ and the rules differ in the various jurisdictions. The majority rule is that non-compliance with the statute does not invalidate the sale.

There Can be No Sale of Goods Not in Existence. As a matter of definition, since a sale is a present transfer of the title to goods, and no one owns or can transfer goods which do not exist, it is impossible to make a sale of goods which are not in existence.

Acceptance of Goods. The word "acceptance" means a willingness to agree and includes overt acts or conduct which are a manifestation of such willingness. In contracts, acceptance is a manifestation by the offeree of willingness to abide by the terms of the offer. In sales, acceptance is a manifestation by the buyer of willingness to become owner of the goods.

The Code provides, Section 2–606, that acceptance occurs:

(1) when the buyer, after a reasonable opportunity to inspect the goods, signifies to the seller that the goods conform to the contract, or

(2) when the buyer, after a reasonable opportunity to inspect, signifies to the seller that he will take the goods or retain them in spite of their non-conformity to the contract, or

(3) when the buyer fails to make an effective rejection of the goods, after a reasonable opportunity to inspect them, or

(4) when the buyer does any act with respect to the goods which is inconsistent with the seller's ownership of them.

A buyer may upon certain conditions, by acting within a reasonable time, revoke his acceptance of nonconforming goods, as provided in Section 2–608.

Rejection of Goods. Rejection means a manifestation by the buyer of his unwillingness to become owner of the goods. It must be within a reasonable time after the goods have been tendered or delivered. It is not effective unless the buyer seasonably notifies the seller. Section 2–602(1).

Rejection of the goods may be rightful or wrongful, depending on whether the goods tendered or delivered conform to the contract.

After rejection of the goods, any exercise of ownership by the buyer with respect to them is wrongful as against the seller. If the buyer does not have a security interest in the goods he is under a duty after rejec-tion to hold them, and to exercise reasonable care with respect to their safekeeping, for a time sufficient to permit the seller to remove them. If the buyer's rejection is rightful, he has no further obligations with regard to the goods. If wrongful, the seller has remedies as provided in Section 2–703.

Contract to Sell Future Goods. Goods which are to be grown or manufactured by the seller or to be acquired by the seller after he has made a contract to sell them, are known as future goods. While it is impossible to make a present sale of future goods, it is possible to make a contract to sell them. There is no prohibition in the law against a person making a contract to sell goods which he does not own at the time of the making of the contract, or which are not then in existence.

The Code provides that goods must be both existing and identified to the contract before any interest in them can pass; and goods which are not both existing and identified are "future" goods. Section 2–105. A contract for the sale of anything not in existence at the time of making the contract is manifestly a contract for future goods. Goods which are both existing and identified are not future goods.

Doctrine of Potential Possession. At common law, where a person was the owner or lessee of land, he could by using language of present transfer make a sale of future crops grown upon the land. The same rule applied to the owner of animals with respect to future offspring. Of course, no title to the future crops or unborn animals could pass at the time the parties used language of present transfer, as the goods were not then in existence. But under this doctrine of potential possession, ownership of the crops or of the offspring was regarded as in the transferee as of the moment the crops matured or the offspring was born.

The doctrine was never applied in a case where the grantor of future crops did not have a present interest in the land upon which the crops were to be grown at the time of the grant, nor to the future offspring of animals which did not belong to the grantor at the time of the grant. The doctrine does not apply to a present transfer of fish to be caught on a prospective fishing voyage. The degree of potential or the likelihood of catching fish in the ocean is not as great as that of obtaining a crop by planting seed in the earth.

The Code does not deal with the problem of growing crops and unborn young of animals in terms of potential possession but approaches it directly and realistically by enlarging the concepts of property interests and by establishing rules to determine whether goods are identified to the contract. Growing crops and the unborn young of animals, in the absence of explicit agreement, are identified to the contract respectively when the crops are planted and when the young are conceived. (Section 2–501.) Thereupon the buyer obtains a special property and an insurable interest in these future goods. Upon becoming identified to the contract these future goods exist as planted seed, but the contract is not for planted seed. It is for matured crops and offspring of animals. Consequently, title cannot pass until the crops have fully matured and the animals are born. The Code does not change the common-law rule that title passes to the buyer at that time.

Fungible Goods. Goods of which each particle or unit of measurement is the equivalent of every other particle or like unit of the same goods, such as grain, cereals, flour, oil, and wine, are known as fungible goods. The goods just named are fungible by nature. Other goods, such as hogsheads of molasses, or bales of cotton, may be fungible by commercial usage. Each hogshead may not be exactly alike in volume to every other, nor each bale of cotton be the exact weight of every other bale, but if the par-

ties or the usage of trade so regard them they are deemed fungible. Section 1–201 of the Code contains this definition:

> "Fungible" with respect to goods or securities means goods or securities of which any unit is, by nature or usage of trade, the equivalent of any other like unit. Goods which are not fungible shall be deemed fungible for the purposes of this Act to the extent that under a particular agreement or document unlike units are treated as equivalents.

Where the subject matter of a contract of sale is the undivided portion of a mass of fungible goods, an ownership or property interest may pass to the buyer without a separation of the portion from the mass. The buyer becomes the owner of an undivided fractional interest in the mass or a tenant in common of the goods. Furthermore, a warehouseman or bailee may commingle different lots of fungible goods without violating his duty to keep separate the goods covered by each warehouse receipt.

Sale of Undivided Shares. It has long been settled law that a joint owner or tenant in common of specific personal property could sell his undivided interest in the property. The buyer becomes a tenant in common with the other owners.

Section 2–105 of the Code provides:

> (3) There may be a sale of a part interest in existing identified goods.
>
> (4) An undivided share in an identified bulk of fungible goods is sufficiently identified to be sold although the quantity of the bulk is not determined. Any agreed proportion of such a bulk or any quantity thereof agreed upon by number, weight or other measure may to the extent of the seller's interest in the bulk be sold to the buyer who then becomes an owner in common.

There is a manifest difference in being the owner of an undivided one-third interest in a horse and being the owner of an undivided one-third interest in 300 bushels of wheat. In the latter case, severance may be had and by agreement of the parties one of them may exchange his undivided interest in the 300 bushels for complete ownership of 100 bushels of the wheat which have been separated from the mass. The wheat is fungible, the horse is neither fungible nor divisible.

Assume that A owns a large pile of nut size coal of uniform quality amounting to 500 tons. A executes a bill of sale to B which recites that in consideration of $800 paid by B to A, A sells and transfers to B 100 tons of coal in the pile. It is obvious that B does not obtain title to 100 tons of the coal notwithstanding the expressed intention of the parties. The reason is that 100 tons of the coal as such does not exist. The pile of coal is specific, and the goods to which the contract refers are identified, but title to 100 tons of the coal cannot be transferred until this quantity is separated from the mass. However, since the parties intended to create in the buyer an immediate ownership interest, under Section 2–105(4) of the Code the buyer becomes a tenant in common with the seller and owns an undivided fractional interest or share in the mass of coal. This interest is measured by the fraction of which the number of tons of coal purchased is the numerator and the entire number of tons in the mass is the denominator.

Grain Elevator Cases. When grain is harvested in the fall and the grower or owner has no convenient or suitable place to store it, it is common practice for him to deliver it to a grain elevator. The owner of the elevator accepts grain of the same kind and quality from numerous persons and either buys the grain on delivery or issues a storage receipt and sells the grain later as directed by the owner. At the time of delivery the transaction becomes either a sale or a bailment depending upon the expressed intention of the parties. The grain placed in the elevator is mingled with similar grain which the elevator operator has received from other persons. The quantity of grain in the elevator con-

stantly fluctuates as additions and withdrawals are made. The grain is fungible, and the entire mass in the elevator at any one time is owned as tenants in common by the elevator operator and those who hold storage receipts from the elevator operator. A farmer who delivers to the operator 100 bushels of grain for storage no longer owns 100 bushels of grain, as his grain has lost its identity upon being placed in the elevator. However, he is still an owner of grain in that he has acquired an undivided share in all of the grain in the elevator as a tenant in common with the other owners thereof.

The storage receipt issued by the elevator operator or warehouseman may be a document of title as defined in Section 1–201(15):

"Document of title" includes bill of lading, dock warrant, dock receipt, warehouse receipt or order for the delivery of goods, and also any other document which in the regular course of business or financing is treated as adequately evidencing that the person in possession of it is entitled to receive, hold and dispose of the document and the goods it covers. To be a document of title a document must purport to be issued by or addressed to a bailee and purport to cover goods in the bailee's possession which are either identified or are fungible portions of an identified mass.

Section 7–207 of the Code provides:

Goods Must Be Kept Separate; Fungible Goods

(1) Unless the warehouse receipt otherwise provides, a warehouseman must keep separate the goods covered by each receipt so as to permit at all times identification and delivery of those goods except that different lots of fungible goods may be commingled.

(2) Fungible goods so commingled are owned in common by the persons entitled thereto and the warehouseman is severally liable to each owner for that owner's share. Where because of overissue a mass of fungible goods is insufficient to meet all the receipts which the warehouseman has issued against it, the persons entitled include all

holders to whom overissued receipts have been duly negotiated.

Statute of Frauds. A sale or contract to sell goods for a price of $500 or more must comply with the Statute of Frauds in order to be enforceable. This is a formal requirement in addition to the basic one that a contract exist.

Section 2–201 of the Code provides for enforceability if there is a signed writing sufficient to indicate that a contract for sale has been made. The writing is not insufficient if it omits terms or incorrectly states a term of the contract. It need not contain all of the essential terms of the contract, but must state the quantity of goods, and the contract is not enforceable beyond the quantity stated in the writing.

The signing of the writing may consist of any symbol or mark made or used with the intention of authenticating the writing. The use of a letter head or printed signature is sufficient. "Signed" is defined in Section 1–201(39) of the Code.

To be sufficient under the Code, the three requirements of a writing are: (1) it must evidence a contract for the sale of goods; (2) it must be signed; and (3) it must specify a quantity.

A special rule applies to contracts between merchants whereby a written confirmation of an oral agreement if sufficient to make the contract enforceable against the merchant sending it is also sufficient against the merchant receiving it unless the latter gives written notice of objection within 10 days after receipt. Section 201(2).

In addition to a signed writing or memorandum the Code provides four other methods of satisfying the requirements of the Statute of Frauds in Section 2–201(3):

(1) Where the goods are to be specially manufactured for the buyer and are not suitable for sale to others in the ordinary course of the seller's business, by the action of the seller in making a substantial beginning of their manufacture or commitments for their procurement prior to receipt of notice of repudiation.

(2) By an admission in a pleading, testimony, or otherwise in court that a contract for sale was made, limited, however, to the quantity of goods so admitted.

(3) By payment to the extent that goods have been paid for and accepted by the buyer.

(4) By receipt and acceptance of goods by the buyer to the extent of such receipt and acceptance.

Sales By and Between Merchants. A novel feature of the Code is the introduction into the law of sales of standards of commercial reasonableness which it wisely leaves undefined, and the establishment of separate rules which apply to transactions between merchants or involving a merchant as a party.

A "merchant" is defined as a person (1) who is a dealer in the goods, or (2) who by his occupation holds himself out as having knowledge or skill peculiar to the goods or practices involved, or (3) who employs an agent or broker whom he holds out as having such knowledge or skill. Section 2–104.

Fifteen sections of the Code contain special rules which apply to transactions between merchants or in which a merchant is a party. These rules do not apply to non-merchants and exact a higher standard of conduct of merchants because of their knowledgeability of trade and commerce, and because merchants as a class generally set the standards.

1. A contract for the sale of goods for the price of $500 or more requires a writing to be enforceable (Statute of Frauds). Where such a contract between merchants is oral, a confirmatory writing by one to the other satisfies the statute unless the recipient within 10 days objects in writing. Section 2–201(2).

2. A written offer by a merchant to buy or sell goods is irrevocable during the period of time it is stated to remain open, or if no time is stated, for a reasonable time, not to exceed 3 months, without consideration. Section 2–205.

3. Between merchants, terms contained in an offeree's acceptance which add to or differ from those in the offer become part of the contract unless (a) the offer expressly limits acceptance to the terms of the offer; or (b) the different terms materially alter the offer; or (c) the offeror objects to such additional or different terms within a reasonable time. Section 2–207(2).

4. A signed agreement cannot be modified or rescinded except by a signed writing where it expressly so requires. However, where the signed agreement is not between merchants such requirement on a form supplied by a merchant party must be separately signed by the non-merchant party. Where the signed agreement is between merchants such requirement on a form supplied by one of them need not be signed by the other. Section 2–209(2).

5. A seller who is a merchant impliedly warrants that goods of the kind in which he regularly deals shall be delivered free of any rightful claim of any third person by way of infringement. Section 2–312(3).

6. A seller who is a merchant impliedly warrants the merchantability of the goods that he sells, unless such warranty is expressly excluded or modified. Section 2–314(1).

7. Where goods are delivered for sale to a merchant who maintains a place of business where he deals in goods of the kind involved, under a name other than the name of the person making delivery, the goods are deemed to be on sale or return with respect to creditors of the merchant. Section 2–326(3).

8. Under a sale on approval unless otherwise agreed, a merchant-buyer after giving notice of his election to return the goods must follow any reasonable instructions of the seller in order that the return be at the seller's risk and expense. Section 2–327(1) (c).

9. Where retention of possession of goods by the seller would be fraudulent as to creditors of the seller under any rule of law, such retention by a merchant-seller in good faith and in the current course of trade for a commercially reasonable time is not fraudulent. Section 2–402(2).

10. Any entrusting of the possession of goods to a merchant who deals in goods of that kind gives him power to transfer all rights of the entruster to a buyer in the ordinary course of business. Section 2–403 (2).

11. Except where the contract requires or authorizes the seller to ship the goods by carrier, and except where the goods are held by a bailee to be delivered to the buyer without being moved, the risk of loss passes to the buyer upon his receipt of the goods if the seller is a merchant. In such case, if the seller is not a merchant, the risk of loss passes to the buyer on tender of delivery. Section 2–509(3).

12. Where a merchant-buyer has rightfully rejected goods in his possession, and the seller has no agent or place of business at the market of rejection, the merchant-buyer is under a duty to follow any reasonable instructions of the seller with respect to the goods, and in the absence of such instructions to make reasonable efforts to sell them for the seller's account if they are perishable. Section 2–603(1).

13. When a merchant-buyer sells goods pursuant to section 2–603(1), he is entitled to a selling commission and to reimbursement of his reasonable expenses out of the proceeds. Section 2–603(2).

14. Between merchants, a buyer who has rejected goods is precluded from relying upon any unstated defect to justify such rejection or to establish a breach by the seller where the seller has made a request in writing for a full and final written statement of all defects upon which the buyer proposes to rely. Section 2–605(1) (b).

15. When reasonable grounds for insecurity arise with respect to the performance of either party to a contract for the sale of goods, the other party may in writing demand adequate assurance of due performance and may suspend performance until such assurance is received. Between merchants, the reasonableness of grounds for insecurity and the adequacy of any assurance offered is determined according to commercial standards. Section 2–609(1) (2).

Casualty to Identified Goods. A purported sale of nonexistent goods is void, as in the case of a seller who purports to make a sale of specific goods which unknown to him and the buyer have been wholly destroyed.

A different situation is presented where the seller purports to sell specific or identified goods and without the knowledge of the parties a portion of them has been destroyed. Thus, A purports to make a sale to B of a specific lot of wheat containing 1,000 bushels at a price of $2 per bushel. Unknown to A, a fire had destroyed or damaged 300 bushels of the wheat. The contract is divisible. B does not have to take the remaining 700 bushels of wheat, but he has the option to do so upon paying $1,400, the price of 700 bushels.

Under the Code, the buyer in the case of a partial destruction or deterioration of the goods, has the option to avoid the contract or to accept the undestroyed or deteriorated goods with due allowance or deduction from the contract price. The rights of the buyer do not depend upon whether the contract or sale is divisible or indivisible. In fairness to the buyer where specific or identified goods are partially destroyed or damaged without the fault of either party, and he elects to accept the remaining or damaged goods, he should in no event be obliged to pay the full contract price for them. The Code provides, Section 2–613:

Casualty To Identified Goods

Where the contract requires for its performance goods identified when the contract is made, and the goods suffer casualty without fault of either party before the risk of loss passes to the buyer, or in a proper case under a "no arrival, no sale" term (Section 2–324) then

(a) if the loss is total the contract is avoided; and

(b) if the loss is partial or the goods have so deteriorated as no longer to conform to the contract the buyer may nevertheless demand inspection and at his option either treat the contract as avoided or accept the goods with due allowance from the contract price for the deterioration or the deficiency in quantity but without further right against the seller.

If the destruction or casualty to the goods, total or partial, occurs after risk of loss has passed to the buyer, the buyer has no option but must pay the contract price of the goods.

Ascertainment of the Price. The price is the consideration which the buyer pays or promises to pay to the seller for the goods. It is usually expressed in terms of money, but it may be made payable in any personal property. Section 2–304.

The terms of the sale or contract to sell usually sets forth the price of the goods, but if the buyer orders and receives goods from the seller and nothing is stated by either party as to the price of the goods, the buyer is under a duty to pay a reasonable price, such as the prevailing price in the market, or the price customarily charged by the seller for like goods.

At common law if the parties enter into an executory agreement for the sale of goods in which nothing is stated about the price, nor is there any undertaking by the buyer to pay a price, the agreement is void for indefiniteness. No contract is formed as one of the essentials is lacking, namely, consideration on the part of the buyer.

However, under the Code, the parties may enter into a contract for the sale of goods even though the agreement contains no price provision. Section 2–305 provides:

Open Price Term

(1) The parties if they so intend can conclude a contract for sale even though the price is not settled. In such a case the price is a reasonable price at the time for delivery if

(a) nothing is said as to price; or

(b) the price is left to be agreed by the parties and they fail to agree; or

(c) the price is to be fixed in terms of some agreed market or other standard as set or recorded by a third person or agency and it is not so set or recorded.

(2) A price to be fixed by the seller or by the buyer means a price for him to fix in good faith.

(3) When a price left to be fixed otherwise than by agreement of the parties fails to be fixed through fault of one party the other may at his option treat the contract as cancelled or himself fix a reasonable price.

(4) Where, however, the parties intend not to be bound unless the price be fixed or agreed and it is not fixed or agreed there is no contract. In such a case the buyer must return any goods already received or if unable so to do must pay their reasonable value at the time of delivery and the seller must return any portion of the price paid on account.

Sale at a Valuation. The seller and buyer may enter into a sale or contract to sell whereby the price of the goods or the terms of sale are to be fixed by a third person. At common law if the third person, without the

fault of the seller or the buyer, does not or cannot fix the price or terms, the contract is avoided and neither party is liable to the other. Under the Code, in such case, the price for the goods is the reasonable price at the time for delivery, and both buyer and seller are bound by contract.

If the contract for the sale of goods provides for a valuation by three persons, one selected by the buyer, one selected by the seller, and a third to be designated by the two thus selected, both the seller and the buyer have impliedly promised one another to select a valuer. A failure or refusal by either party to select a valuer is a breach of the contract.

In such case, under the Code, the party who has not committed the breach has an option either to treat the contract as cancelled or to fix a reasonable price for the goods which is binding upon both parties. He would, however, have to fix the price in good faith.

The price of the goods fixed by valuers which the parties have agreed upon is conclusive upon the parties, in the absence of fraud, collusion, or mistake.

CASES

LOW v. PEW

(1871) 108 Mass. 347, 11 Am.Rep. 357.

[Replevin by Alfred Low & Company of a lot of flitched halibut from the assignees in bankruptcy of John Low & Son. The parties stated the following case for the judgment of the court:

On April 17, 1869, as the schooner Florence Reed, owned by John Low & Son, was about to sail from Gloucester on a fishing voyage, that firm received $1,500 from the plaintiffs, and signed and gave the plaintiffs the following writing:

"We, John Low & Son, hereby sell, assign and set over unto Alfred Low & Company all the halibut that may be caught by the master and crew of the schooner Florence Reed, on the voyage upon which she is about to proceed from the port of Gloucester to the Grand Banks, at the rate of five cents and a quarter per pound for flitched halibut, to be delivered to said Alfred Low & Company as soon as said schooner arrives at said port of Gloucester at their wharf. And we, the said John Low & Son, hereby acknowledge the receipt of $1500 in part payment for the halibut that may be caught by the master and crew of said schooner on said voyage."

In July 1869 proceedings in bankruptcy were begun against John Low & Son in the district court of the United States for this district, in which they were adjudged bankrupts on August 6, and on August 20 these defendants were appointed the assignees in bankruptcy, and the deed of assignment was executed to them. On Saturday, August 14, the Florence Reed arrived at the port of Gloucester on her home voyage, and was hauled to the plaintiff's wharf; and on the morning of Monday, August 16, the United States marshal took possession of the vessel and cargo under a warrant issued to him on August 6 in the proceedings in bankruptcy, and transferred his possession to the defendants upon their appointment.

The catch of the schooner consisted of about 40,000 pounds of halibut, and of some codfish. The plaintiffs demanded the halibut of the defendants, and offered at the same time to pay the price of it at the rate of five and a quarter cents per pound, less the $1500 already paid. The defendants refused the demand; and the plaintiffs then replevied such a quantity of the halibut as represented the amount of $1500 at that rate per pound, and offered to receive the rest of the halibut

and pay for it at the same rate, but the defendants refused to acknowledge any right whatever of the plaintiffs in or to the fish.

If on these facts the plaintiffs were entitled to recover, they were to have judgment for nominal damages; but if otherwise the defendants were to have judgment for a return, with damages equal to interest at the annual rate of six per cent. on the appraised value of the fish replevied.]

MORTON, J. By the decree adjudging John Low & Son bankrupts, all their property, except such as is exempted by the bankrupt law, was brought within the custody of the law, and by the subsequent assignment passed to their assignees. [Citation.] The firm could not by a subsequent sale and delivery transfer any of such property to the plaintiffs. The schooner which contained the halibut in suit arrived in Gloucester August 14, 1869, which was after the decree of bankruptcy. If there had been then a sale and delivery to the plaintiffs of the property replevied, it would have been invalid. The plaintiffs therefore show no title to the halibut replevied, unless the effect of the contract of April 17, 1869, was to vest in them the property in the halibut before the bankruptcy. It seems to us clear, as claimed by both parties, that this was a contract of sale, and not a mere executory agreement to sell at some future day. The plaintiffs cannot maintain their suit upon any other construction, because, if it is an executory agreement to sell, the property in the halibut remained in the bankrupts, and, there being no delivery before the bankruptcy, passed to the assignees. The question in the case therefore is, whether a sale of halibut afterwards to be caught is valid, so as to pass to the purchaser the property in them when caught.

It is an elementary principle of the law of sales, that a man cannot grant personal property in which he has no interest or title. To be able to sell property, he must have a vested right in it at the time of the sale. Thus it has been held that a mortgage of goods which the mortgagor does not own at the time the mortgage is made, though he afterwards acquires them, is void. [Citation.] The same principle is applicable to all sales of personal property. [Citations.]

It is equally well settled that it is sufficient if the seller has a potential interest in the thing sold. But a mere possibility or expectancy or acquiring property, not coupled with any interest, does not constitute a potential interest in it, within the meaning of this rule. The seller must have a present interest in the property, of which the thing sold is the product, growth or increase. Having such interest, the right to the thing sold, when it shall come into existence, is a present vested right, and the sale of it is valid. Thus a man may sell the wool to grow upon his own sheep, but not upon the sheep of another; or the crops to grow upon his own land, but not upon land in which he has no interest. [Citations.]

* * *

In the case at bar, the sellers, at the time of the sale, had no interest in the thing sold. There was a possibility that they might catch halibut; but it was a mere possibility and expectancy, coupled with no interest. We are of opinion that they had no actual or potential possession of, or interest in, the fish; and that the sale to the plaintiffs was void. * * *

Judgment for the defendants.

————

PENLEY v. LITTLEFIELD & SONS CO.

(1921) 120 Me. 552, 114 A. 197.

Memorandum Decision. Action of assumpsit for the price of a hog alleged to have been sold and delivered. The plaintiff recovered a verdict. The case comes to this court on the defendant's motion. The plaintiff's agent brought a live hog and left it at the defend-ant's slaughter house in Auburn. During the following night or day the hog died, without the fault of either party.

The plaintiff claims that the animal was sold and delivered to the defendant to be paid for at the rate of twenty cents per pound dressed weight. The defendant's contention is that the hog was left at its slaughter house after some negotiations about a sale but that there was no sale. The defendant says it was expressly agreed that the hog should be left at the plaintiff's risk. The jury accepted the plaintiff's version.

If a sale and purchase were intended by the parties and the hog delivered in pursuance of such intent, it matters not that the determination of the amount to be paid was deferred until after the slaughtering and weighing. The rule as stated in Benjamin on Sales, quoted by the defendant's counsel, is not decisive. More nearly in point are the many authorities cited in Bennett's Notes to the same work, sustaining the proposition that "where the whole thing sold is delivered it is reasonable to expect that the vendee will do the weighing, measuring, etc., and the title may pass even before he has done it." Benjamin on Sales, 7 Ed., Page 297. Whether the transaction wherein personal property is delivered is a completed sale or a mere bailment is a question of fact. In this case the jury have found this fact against the defendant. The verdict is not manifestly wrong. Motion overruled.

————

KIMBERLY v. PATCHIN

(1859) 19 N.Y. 330.

[Action to recover the value of 6,000 bushels of wheat alleged to have been converted by the defendant. The plaintiffs' alleged ownership of the wheat is derived from one Dickinson. Defendant bought the wheat from one Shuttleworth who had bought it from said Dickinson. At the trial it was proved that Dickinson had in a warehouse in Wisconsin two piles of wheat amounting to 6,249 bushels. Shuttleworth proposed to buy 6,000 bushels of the wheat. Upon being shown the piles he expressed doubt that they contained 6,000 bushels. Dickinson affirmed that they did and agreed to make up the quantity if they fell short. Dickinson signed and delivered to Shuttleworth a memorandum of sale and a warehouse receipt covering 6,000 bushels of wheat. The wheat was left undisturbed in the warehouse. Shuttleworth assigned to defendant the bill of sale and warehouse receipt. Dickinson, shortly afterwards, sold the entire quantity of wheat in the two piles to a person under whom plaintiffs derived title. The defendant having obtained possession of the wheat, this action was brought. Defendant appeals from a judgment entered for the plaintiffs in the trial court.]

COMSTOCK, J. Both parties trace their title to the wheat in controversy to D. O. Dickinson, who was the former owner. * * * The defendant claims through a sale made by Dickinson to one Shuttleworth * * *. If that sale was effectual to pass the title, it is not now pretended that there is any ground on which the plaintiffs can recover in this suit. The sale to the person under whom they claim, was about two and a half months junior in point of time. * * *

The sale to Shuttleworth was by a writing in the form of a present transfer of six thousand bushels of wheat, at seventy cents per bushel. No manual delivery was then made, but instead thereof the vendor executed and delivered to the vendee another instrument, declaring that he had received in store the six thousand bushels subject to the vendee's order; of the price $2,600 was paid down, and the residue $1,600 which was to be paid at a future day, the purchaser afterwards offered to pay, according to the agreement. So far the contract had all the requisites of a perfect sale. * * *

The quantity of wheat in store to which the contract related, was estimated by the parties at about six thousand bushels. But subsequently, after Dickinson made another sale of the same wheat to the party under whom the plaintiffs claim, it appeared on measurement that the number of bushels was six thousand two hundred and forty-nine, being an excess of two hundred and forty-nine bushels. When Shuttleworth bought the six thousand bushels, that quantity was mixed in the storehouse with the excess, and no measurement or separation was made. The sale was not in bulk, but precisely of the six thousand bushels. On this ground it is claimed on the part of the plaintiffs, that in legal effect the contract was executory, in other words a mere agreement to sell and deliver the specified quantity, so that no title passed by the transaction. It is not denied, however, nor does it admit of denial, that the parties intended a transfer of the title. The argument is, and it is the only one which is even plausible, that the law overrules that intention, although expressed in plain written language, entirely appropriate to the purpose.

It is a rule asserted in many legal authorities, but which may be quite as fitly called a rule of reason and logic as of law, that in order to have an executed sale, so as to transfer a title from one party to another, the thing sold must be ascertained. This is a self-evident truth, when applied to those subjects of property which are distinguishable by their physical attributes from all other things, and, therefore, are capable of exact identification. No person can be said to own a horse or a picture, unless he is able to identify the chattel or specify what horse or what picture it is that belongs to him. It is not only legally, but logically, impossible to hold property in such things, unless they are ascertained and distinguished from all other things; and this I apprehend is the foundation of the rule that, on a sale of chattels, in order to pass the title, the articles must, if not delivered, be designated, so that possession can be taken by the purchaser without any further act on the part of the seller.

* * *

It appears to me that a very simple and elementary inquiry lies at the foundation of the present case. A quantity of wheat being in store, is it possible in reason and in law for one man to own a given portion of it and for another man to own the residue without a separation of the parts? To bring the inquiry to the facts of the case: in the storehouse of Dickinson there was a quantity not precisely known. In any conceivable circumstances could Shuttleworth become owner of six thousand bushels, and Dickinson of the residue, which turned out to be two hundred and forty-nine bushels, without the portion of either being divided from the other? The answer to this inquiry is plain. Suppose a third person, being the prior owner of the whole, had given to S. a bill of sale of six thousand bushels, and then one to D. for the residue more or less, intending to pass to each the title, and expressing that intention in plain words, what would have been the result? The former owner most certainly would have parted with all his title. If, then, the two purchasers did not acquire it no one could own the wheat, and the title would be lost. This would be an absurdity. But if the parties thus purchasing could and would be the owners, how would they hold it? Plainly according to their contracts. One would be entitled to six thousand bushels, and the other to what remained after that quantity was subtracted.

Again suppose, Dickinson having in store and owning two hundred and forty-nine bushels, Shuttleworth had deposited with him six thousand bushels for storage merely, both parties agreeing that the quantities might be mixed. This would be a case of confusion of property where neither would lose his title. In the law of bailments it is

entirely settled that S., being the bailor of the six thousand bushels, would lose nothing by the mixture, and it being done by consent, it is also clear that the bailee would lose nothing.

* * *

We are of opinion, therefore, both upon authority and clearly upon the principle and reason of the thing, that the defendant, under the sale to Shuttleworth, acquired a perfect title to the six thousand bushels of wheat. Of that quantity he took possession at Buffalo, by a writ of replevin against the master of the vessel in which the whole had been transported to that place. For that taking the suit was brought, and it results that the plaintiff cannot recover. It is unnecessary to decide whether the parties to the original sale became tenants in common. If a tenancy in common arises in such cases, it must be with some peculiar incidents not usually belonging to that species of ownership. I think each party would have the right of severing the tenancy by his own act: that is, the right of taking the portion of the mass which belonged to him, being accountable only if he invaded the quantity which belonged to the other. But assuming that the case is one of strict tenancy in common, the defendant became the owner of six thousand and the plaintiffs of two hundred and forty-nine parts of the whole. As neither could maintain an action against the other, for taking possession merely of the whole, more clearly he cannot if the other takes only the quantity which belongs to him.

* * *

Judgment reversed and new trial ordered.

OHIO CASUALTY INS. CO. v. GUTERMAN

(1954) 97 Ohio App. 237, 125 N.E.2d 350.

WISEMAN, PRESIDING JUDGE. This is an appeal on questions of law from the Common

Pleas Court of Montgomery County, which rendered judgment in favor of the plaintiff in an action to replevin an automobile.

The cause was submitted to the court on an agreed statement of facts, which is as follows:

"1. On September 19, 1950, Brady Motors, Inc., an Illinois corporation, was the owner of and held a duly issued Illinois certificate of title to, a 1950 Pontiac two-tone club coupe automobile, motor and serial No. P–8–T–H–4052.

"2. On September 19, 1950, said automobile was stolen from the lot of Brady Motors, Inc., 3738 West 63d Street, Chicago, Illinois.

"3. Pursuant to a contract of insurance with Brady Motors, Inc., the Ohio Casualty Insurance Company paid to Brady Motors, Inc., the sum of two thousand, three hundred fifty-three and 50/100ths dollars ($2,353.50) upon proof of loss of said automobile, and in consideration of that payment, Brady Motors, Inc. duly assigned its title to said automobile to the Ohio Casualty Insurance Company.

"4. Thereafter defendant in good faith purchased the same automobile from John E. Terebist, d. b. a. Veterans Auto Exchange, in Bossier City, Louisiana, who was a person other than the thief and held title through an intermediary purchaser. Defendant brought the automobile into the state of Ohio, and had issued to him an Ohio certificate of title thereto, which defendant held at the time this action was filed.

"5. The value of said automobile at the present time is one thousand, three hundred fifty dollars ($1,350)."

The defendant contends that the judgment is contrary to law. The question presented may be concisely stated as follows: Can plaintiff, holder of a valid Illinois certificate of title to an automobile, maintain an action in replevin in Ohio against defendant, who holds an Ohio certificate of title to said automobile which is derived from a person who stole the automobile from the assignor of the plaintiff?

The issue is determined by proper application of the provisions of Section 6290–4, General Code, which in part provides:

"No court in any case at law or in equity shall recognize the right, title, claim, or interest of any person in or to any motor vehicle, hereafter sold or disposed of, or mortgaged or encumbered, unless evidenced by a certificate of title or manufacturer's or importer's certificate duly issued, in accordance with the provisions of this chapter."

It is axiomatic that in a replevin action the plaintiff must rely on the strength of his own title or right to immediate possession, and not on the weakness of the title or right of possession of the defendant. [Citation.]

Which has superior title and the right of immediate possession under the facts in this case? This appears to be a case of first impression in Ohio.

At common law, no person can derive title or right of possession from a thief, as against the rightful owner. Does Section 6290–4, General Code, change the rule under the circumstances in this case? Defendant contends that, under this section of the statute, before the plaintiff can maintain the action it must show the possession of a certificate of title issued under the Ohio Law; and that since the defendant holds a certificate of title under the Ohio law, the defendant should prevail against the claim of the plaintiff.

* * *

The appellee relies on Mock v. Kaffits, 75 Ohio App. 305, 62 N.E.2d 172, where an automobile was stolen from the owner in Pennsylvania. The insurance company paid the owner for the loss and a certificate of title was issued to the insurance company. Registration papers, purporting to have been issued by the state of New York, were presented in Ohio, and, thereupon, a certificate of title was issued in the name of Randall, who assigned it to a dealer in Columbus, Ohio, which in turn sold it to the plaintiff. It appears that the motor number had been changed and that the plaintiff's certificate of title carried a false number. Plaintiff sought to replevin the automobile from the chief of police. However, the contest was between the plaintiff and the insurance company which intervened. The trial court found that the Ohio certificate of title issued to Randall was void *ab initio* and that the Pennsylvania certificate of title issued to the insurance company was valid. The Court of Appeals affirmed the judgment. In the opinion by the Court of Appeals, 75 Ohio App. on page 307, 62 N.E.2d 172, the court states that but for the presence of the Ohio certificate of title law, the problem would be promptly solved by the application of the rule that stolen property is recoverable from an innocent purchaser so long as it is susceptible to identification. In that case, the plaintiff contended, as does the defendant in this case, that the certificate of title issued under the Ohio law is conclusive evidence of ownership and right of possession. The court, 75 Ohio App. on page 308, 62 N.E. 2d on page 174, said:

"Just what is the purpose of the Certificate of Title Act? The answer is found in Automobile Finance Co. v. Munday, 137 Ohio St. 504, 521, 30 N.E.2d 1002, 1010, wherein Judge Turner stated that 'the very purpose of the law is to protect ownership against fraud.' If plaintiff's theory be adopted, it must be perceived that the avowed purpose of the act would be frustrated. It would become a shield to the thief's criminal act and would stamp with the law's approval the source of title which flows from him. It would surely follow that Ohio might be made the dumping ground for stolen cars."

On page 309 of 75 Ohio App., on page 174 of 62 N.E.2d, the court said:

"If plaintiff is to prevail he must do so on the strength of his own title. If evidence of title has been procured through fraud and deception, the title of a subsequent innocent holder for value, which arose therefrom, can have no greater solemnity than the source from which it sprang." * * *

We are satisfied to apply the reasoning in these two cases to the facts in this case. Certainly, the Ohio certificate of title law was never intended to operate as a shield to 'a thief and a sword to the innocent. * * *

In discussing the effect of Section 6290–4, General Code, the court, 112 F.Supp. on page 776, said:

"There is nothing in the Ohio Certificate of Title law which indicates an intention on the part of the legislature to make a transaction of this kind, valid under Michigan laws, void under the laws of Ohio, and the Court will not read into the statute language which is not there.

"The Supreme Court of Ohio apparently recognized the distinction above referred to, and that the law has no extra-territorial effect, in the case of State ex rel. City Loan & Savings Co. v. Taggart, 134 Ohio St. 374, 379, 17 N.E.2d 758, 760, holding the Ohio Certificate of Title Law constitutional, in which the Court said:

"'No extra-territorial scope may be given to these sections. The law must be limited in its operation to those manufacturers, etc., who are subject to the jurisdiction of Ohio, and to those persons in Ohio who are obligated to secure a certificate of title under the law of this state. If they do not present the documentary proof demanded they are not entitled to a certificate.'" (Emphasis added.)

The court cited the case of Mock v. Kaffits, supra, and in 112 F.Supp. on page 777 said:

"(2) That an out-of-state certificate of title may be recognized by the Courts of Ohio without an Ohio certificate of title being issued therefor to the owner is held in the case of Mock v. Kaffits, Franklin County, 1944, 75 Ohio App. 305, 62 N.E.2d 172."

* * *

In our opinion, the rights of the plaintiff should prevail over the rights of the defendant who bases his right of ownership and immediate possession on a prior theft.

Judgment affirmed.

———

PROBLEMS

1. A who had 100 bushel baskets of peaches in his fruit shed offered to sell them to B for $1.50 per bushel. B accepted the offer. At this time the peaches were fully packed and in the baskets. At the end of the day upon which A had received B's acceptance of his offer, A placed 50 of the baskets of peaches on a wagon which was standing inside the shed. During the night the fruit shed accidentally caught fire. A rushed to the scene and was able to pull the loaded wagon out of the burning shed and save the 50 baskets which were on the wagon but was unable to save the other 50 baskets which were destroyed with the shed. What are the rights of the parties?

2. B enters into a contract to buy from A certain specifically identified goods located in a public warehouse.

   (a) If, without the knowledge of either party, these goods had been completely destroyed by fire prior to the execution of the contract, what are the rights of the parties?

   (b) If, without negligence or fault of either party, these goods were completely destroyed by fire after the execution of the contract, what are the rights of the parties?

3. A, a New York dealer, purchased 25 barrels of specially graded and packed apples from a producer at Hood River, Oregon. These apples he afterwards resold to B under a contract which specified an agreed price on delivery at B's place of business in New York. The apples were shipped to A from Oregon but, through no fault of either A or B, were totally destroyed before reaching New York. Is there any liability resting upon A?

4. A advertises his car for sale. It is kept by A in his private garage. B calls on A in the evening, examines the car, and says, "I'll take it." It is agreed that B will call next morning, pay for the car and take delivery of it. During the night, A's garage is broken into by a thief who steals the car. Can A hold B for the agreed purchase of the car?

5. A, a trapper, made a contract with B whereby A "hereby sells and transfers title to B, for the price of 25 cents each, all the rabbits I trap during the month of October 1966." A caught 500 rabbits during that month, and sold and delivered them to the C Co. B sues the C Co. for the possession of the rabbits, claiming title to the rabbits under his contract with A. Decision?

6. A owned a quantity of corn which was contained in a corn crib located on A's farm. On March 12, A wrote a letter to B stating that he would sell to B all of the corn in this crib, which he estimated at between 900 and 1000 bushels, for $1.75 cents per bushel. B received this letter on March 13, and immediately wrote and mailed on the same day a letter to A stating that he would buy the corn. The corn crib and contents were accidently destroyed by fire which broke out about 3 o'clock a.m. on March 14. What are the rights of the parties? What difference, if any, in result if A is a merchant?

7. Price was engaged in the business of buying and selling automobiles at wholesale. In February, Price sold a used Ford sedan on a conditional sales contract to Hunt who was known to him to be a retail dealer in new and used cars. Hunt signed a note for the amount of the purchase price. The conditional sales contract provided that title was to remain in Price until the note was paid in full.

A statute in effect provides that the owner of a motor vehicle who sells the same shall supply the purchaser with a certificate of title. No certificate of title was delivered to Hunt.

Day saw this Ford in Hunt's garage and purchased it from him, paying the purchase price in full. No certificate of title was delivered to Day. Thereafter, Hunt defaulted on his conditional sales contract, and Price brings an appropriate action to recover possession of the Ford from Day, who for the first time learned of Price's claim of ownership. What decision?

CHAPTER 18

TRANSFER OF TITLE AND RISK OF LOSS

Introductory. Transfer of title is essential to a sale of goods. It is not essential to imposition of risk of loss or damage to the goods.

The Code does not regard the location of title as the principal method of resolving the rights of the parties, but treats separately and distinctly the concept of title and placement of the risk of loss.

Transfer of title is important at common law in order to permit the seller to recover the purchase price of the goods. The Code does not change this basic rule by providing that the seller may recover the price of goods which the buyer has accepted (i. e. where transfer of title to the buyer has occurred), or of conforming goods lost or damaged after risk of loss has passed to the buyer. Section 2–709(1).

Instead of permitting title to govern the rights of the parties, the Code sets forth specific rules which apply to various transactional situations covering the rights, duties, and remedies of the seller and the buyer. Risk of loss may follow ownership of the goods according to the ancient maxim *res perit domino*, but under the Code this is not necessarily so. Risk of loss may exist independently of ownership of the goods.

A determination of whether title to goods has been transferred continues to be important with respect to liability for taxes, duties created by statute, situations not covered by a specific rule, and the rights of third parties.

Transfer of Title. Under the Code title to goods which have been identified to the contract passes from the seller to the buyer in any manner and on any conditions explicitly agreed upon by the parties. Section 2–401.

The rule both at common law and under the Code is that title to the goods passes when the parties intend it to pass.

The one type of contract in which the parties clearly and explicitly agree with respect to transfer of title is the conditional sales contract which expressly recites that title is reserved in the seller until the entire purchase price is paid.

In many contracts for the sale of goods other than conditional sales, the parties do not express their intention as to the time or manner or condition upon which title is to be transferred. Title to the goods may not even be discussed in the negotiations. It is implicit, or taken for granted. The parties are more interested in reaching a satisfactory agreement on matters of price, quantity, quality, warranties, delivery schedule, credit terms, discounts, defaults, liquidated damages, and such items. They seldom concern themselves with the abstract concept of title, or an express agreement as to the particular time or manner in which title is to be transferred.

Where the parties have no explicit agreement as to transfer of title, the Code provides in Section 2–401 that title passes to the buyer:

(1) At the time and place at which the seller completes his performance with reference to delivery of the goods, despite any reservation of a security interest or any agreement that a document of title is to be delivered to the buyer at a different time or place.

(2) At the time and place of shipment, if the contract authorizes shipment but does not require the seller to deliver the goods to the buyer at destination.

(3) Upon tender of the goods to the buyer at destination, if the contract requires delivery at destination.

(4) Upon delivery of a document of title where the contract calls for delivery of such document without moving the goods.

(5) At the time and place of contracting where the goods at that time are identified to the contract, no documents are to be delivered, and delivery is to be made without moving the goods.

Title can only be transferred to existing, specific, identified goods. The Code provides that title cannot pass under a contract of sale prior to their identification to the contract.

As to goods shipped or delivered to the buyer, any retention or reservation of title in the seller is limited in effect to the reservation of a security interest. Section 2–401.

Re-transfer of Title Back to Seller. By acceptance of the goods the buyer becomes owner of them. However, prior to acceptance the buyer may obtain title to the goods under the terms of an explicit agreement or in any of the five situations set forth above under Transfer of Title.

A buyer having once accepted goods which conform to the contract may not thereafter reject them and revest title in the seller. Section 2–607. Any such attempt at rejection is wrongful.

A buyer, however, may reject goods which he has not accepted. He may also revoke his acceptance of non-conforming goods provided (1) he accepted them on the reasonable assumption that the non-conformity would be cured, and it has not been seasonably cured, or (2) his acceptance having been made prior to discovery of non-conformity was reasonably induced by the difficulty of discovery before acceptance or by the seller's assurances. Section 2–608(1).

Revocation of acceptance is not effective until the buyer notifies the seller of it. Such notice must be given within a reasonable time after the buyer has discovered or should have discovered that the goods are non-conforming, and before the condition of the goods has changed by any cause other than their inherent defects. Section 2–608(2).

A rightful revocation of acceptance of the goods by the buyer has the same effect as a rightful rejection of them. Section 2–608 (3).

Title to the goods is revested in the seller by rejection or refusal of the buyer to receive or retain them, whether the action of the buyer is justified or not justified. However, a revocation of acceptance does not revest title in the seller unless the revocation is justified. A revesting of title in the seller in the manner here discussed occurs by operation of law and is not a "sale" of the goods. Section 2–401(4).

Documents of Title. Although treated more fully in Chapter 19, documents of title are briefly mentioned here because of their important use as a means of transferring title to goods.

A document of title is a receipt or order for the delivery of goods which evidences a right to receive, hold, or dispose of the goods described in the document. Section 1–201 (15). The most frequently used documents are bills of lading issued by carriers and warehouse receipts issued by warehousemen. They are negotiable if by the terms of the document the goods are deliverable to bearer or to the order of a named person. Section 7–104. The person who is entitled to possession and delivery of the goods by the terms of a negotiable document is regarded commercially as having either title or a security interest in the goods. He also has the power to make a transfer of title to the goods by a negotiation of the document even if such transfer defeats the rights of other parties in the goods.

Special Property of the Buyer in the Goods. The Code creates a new property interest in goods which is unknown at common law. It is described as a special property which the buyer obtains by the identification of existing goods as goods to which the contract of sale refers. Sections 2–401 (1), 2–501(1).

Identification of goods to the contract may take place by agreement of the parties, by act of the seller alone, or by act of the buyer alone. Where it is accomplished by unilateral action of the seller, the buyer may acquire a special property in goods without knowledge of the fact.

Identification of the Goods to the Contract. In order for the buyer to acquire a special property in the goods it is essential that the goods be identified to the contract of sale. After formation of the contract it is normal for the seller to take steps to obtain, manufacture, prepare, or select goods with which to fulfill his obligation under the contract. At some stage in the process the seller will have identified the goods which he intends to ship or deliver or hold for the buyer. These goods may or may not conform to the contract.

This identification of goods to the contract is extremely important as it immediately creates for the buyer a special property in the goods so identified and an insurable interest in them, even though in fact they do not conform to the contract. Section 2–501(1).

Identification of the goods to the contract does not shift the risk of loss. The risk of loss provisions of the Code still apply. After identification, the seller may under the contract have duties to perform with respect to the goods and his remedies depend upon his not defaulting under the contract.

Identification may be made by either the seller or the buyer, and can be made at any time and in any manner agreed upon by the parties. In the absence of explicit agreement identification takes place, as provided in Section 2–501(1):

(1) upon the making of the contract if it is for goods already existing and identified;

(2) if the contract is one for future goods other than crops to be grown or unborn animals, when the seller ships, marks, or otherwise designates the goods as those to which the contract refers;

(3) if the contract is for crops to be grown within 12 months or the next normal harvest, or for the offspring of animals to be born within 12 months, when the crops are planted or become growing, or when the young animals are conceived. Section 2–501.

Where the goods have been identified to the contract by the seller alone he may substitute other goods for those so identified until he (a) defaults, or (b) becomes insolvent, or (c) notifies the buyer that the identification is final. Section 2–501(2).

Where the buyer commits a breach of contract the seller may proceed to identify to the contract conforming goods not already identified if when he learns of the breach they are in his possession or control. Section 2–704(1). The seller's remedy of resale applies to goods which need not be in existence or identified to the contract at the time of the buyer's breach. Section 2–706(2).

Incidents of Special Property in the Goods. This Code created interest designated as a special property in goods identified to the contract has specific incidents which give rise to the following rights in the buyer:

(1) The buyer has an insurable interest in the goods. Section 2–501.

(2) Where the buyer has paid all or part of the price of goods he may reclaim them from the seller who has become insolvent within 10 days after receiving the first installment on the price. If the identification creating the special property was made by the buyer alone he may reclaim the goods only if they conform to the contract of sale. Section 2–502.

(3) The buyer has the right to inspect identified goods at any reasonable time and place. Section 2–513(1).

(4) The buyer has the right to replevin goods identified to the contract if he is unable to effect cover for such goods. Section 2–716.

(5) The buyer may maintain an action and recover damages against a third party for conversion of identified goods or for loss or injury to the goods caused by a third party. Section 2–722.

For example, A in Chicago has a contract to sell to B in New York 1,000 cases of dog food to be delivered in New York. A stencils 1,000 cases of dog food with the name and address of B and stacks them separately from other goods in his warehouse preparatory to having them placed on a truck for shipment. Before they can be shipped a fire negligently caused by C destroys A's warehouse and contents including the 1,000 cases marked with B's name. Both A and B have separate rights of action against C to recover damages for the negligent destruction of the goods. The risk of loss with respect to the 1,000 cases at the time of their destruction was on A. Therefore, any recovery by B against C would be held in trust for A, subject however to the interest of B. Section 2–722(b).

Insurable Interest in the Goods. In order for a contract or policy of insurance to be valid the insured must have an insurable interest in the subject matter. At common law only a person with title or a lien could insure his interest in specific goods. The Code extends this right to a buyer's interest in goods which have been identified as goods to which the contract of sale refers. This interest designated as a special property enables the buyer to purchase insurance protection on goods which he does not own but which he may own upon delivery by the seller. Section 2–501(1).

The seller also has an insurable interest in the goods so long as he has title to them or any security interest in them. Section 2–501(2). This is consistent with the well established rule of common law. There is nothing to prevent both seller and buyer at the same time carrying insurance on goods in which they both have a property interest, whether it be title, security interest, or special property.

Security Interest in the Goods. A "security interest" is defined in the Code as an interest in personal property or fixtures which secures payment or performance of an obligation. Section 1–201(37). Security interests in goods are governed by Article 9 of the Code, except that so long as the debtor does not have or lawfully obtain possession of the goods (a) no security agreement is necessary, (b) no filing is required, and (c) the rights of the secured party on default by the debtor are governed by Article 2. Section 9–113.

Security interests in goods and in other property except real estate are discussed more fully in Chapter 44 entitled Secured Transactions.

Any reservation by the seller of title to goods delivered to the buyer, as in the case of a conditional sales contract, is the reservation of a security interest. Section 2–401.

A shipment of identified goods by the seller who obtains with respect thereto a negotiable bill of lading to his own order reserves a security interest in the seller. If the bill of lading is to the order of a financing agency or the buyer, the security interest is reserved with the expectation of transferring it to the person named in the bill of lading. Section 2–505(1) (a).

A non-negotiable bill of lading issued in the name of the seller or his nominee also reserves a security interest in the seller. A non-negotiable bill naming the buyer as consignee reserves no security interest in the seller even though he retains possession of the bill of lading. Section 2–505(1)(b).

A shipment of goods with reservation of a security interest in the seller which is in violation of the contract does not impair the rights of the buyer upon shipment, nor the identification of the goods, nor the seller's powers as holder of a negotiable bill of lading. Section 2–505(2).

The buyer has a security interest in goods in his possession upon rightful rejection or justifiable revocation of acceptance to the extent of payments on the price and expenses reasonably incurred in the receipt, inspection, transportation, care, and custody of the goods. Section 2–711. The buyer in such case is a "person in the position of a seller." Similarly any agent who has paid or has become responsible for the price of the goods on behalf of the buyer has a security interest in goods in his possession. Section 2–707(1).

Risk of Loss. It has been observed that according to the general rule the risk of loss or damage to goods is borne by the person who is the owner at the time of the loss or damage. This is true in every case. Even where the Code places risk of loss upon the buyer although title may be retained by the seller, it is unrealistic to state that a destruction of the goods does not involve loss to the seller. Although he may recover a judgment against the buyer for the purchase price, a judgment is not the same as the price. The buyer may be insolvent, or the judgment otherwise uncollectible. Destruction or damage to goods results in loss to every one who has an interest in them. The seller has lost his right to resell the goods upon the buyer's default, his right to reclaim them, his right to a security interest. He has lost all of the rights he might have even where both title and risk of loss were in the buyer, such as the right to stop delivery of the goods.

It is all right to ask "For Whom the Bells Toll", but the answer is that they toll for every one who had an interest in the subject matter that is lost, to the extent of his interest.

Risk of loss, as the term is used in the law of Sales, means placement of the ultimate loss upon the buyer or the seller. If placed upon the buyer, he is under a duty to pay the price for lost or damaged goods even though he never received them or became owner of them. If upon the seller, he has no right to recover the purchase price from the buyer.

The Code contains specific rules which impose risk of loss upon the buyer or the seller irrespective of title or ownership of the goods. These rules apply to particularized situations, as follows:

1. *Agreement of the Parties.* The parties by agreement may not only shift the allocation of risk of loss but may also divide the risk between them. Such agreement is controlling. Under Section 2–509(4) the rules of the Code are expressly subject to a contrary agreement of the parties. Section 2–303 provides:

> Where this Article allocates a risk or a burden as between the parties "unless otherwise agreed", the agreement may not only shift the allocation but may also divide the risk or burden.

2. *Delivery to a Carrier.* If the contract does not require the seller to deliver the goods at a particular destination, risk of loss passes to the buyer upon delivery of the goods to the carrier. If the seller is required to deliver them at a particular destination, risk of loss passes to the buyer at destination upon tender even though the goods are in the possession of the carrier. Section 2–509(1) provides:

> (1) Where the contract requires or authorizes the seller to ship the goods by carrier

(a) if it does not require him to deliver them at a particular destination, the risk of loss passes to the buyer when the goods are duly delivered to the carrier even though the shipment is under reservation (Section 2–505); but

(b) if it does require him to deliver them at a particular destination and the goods are there duly tendered while in the possession of the carrier, the risk of loss passes to the buyer when the goods are there duly so tendered as to enable the buyer to take delivery.

3. *Goods in Possession of Bailee to Be Delivered without Being Moved.* Where the goods at the time of the contract are in the possession of a bailee and the parties intend that they shall so remain, risk of loss passes to the buyer as provided in Section 2–509(2):

(2) Where the goods are held by a bailee to be delivered without being moved, the risk of loss passes to the buyer

(a) on his receipt of a negotiable document of title covering the goods; or

(b) on acknowledgment by the bailee of the buyer's right to possession of the goods; or

(c) after his receipt of a non-negotiable document of title or other written direction to deliver, as provided in subsection (4)(b) of Section 2–503.

The Code also provides in Section 2–503 (4):

(4) Where goods are in the possession of a bailee and are to be delivered without being moved

(a) tender requires that the seller either tender a negotiable document of title covering such goods or procure acknowledgment by the bailee of the buyer's right to possession of the goods; but

(b) tender to the buyer of a non-negotiable document of title or of a written direction to the bailee to deliver is sufficient tender unless the buy-

er seasonably objects, and receipt by the bailee of notification of the buyer's rights fixes those rights as against the bailee and all third persons; but risk of loss of the goods and of any failure by the bailee to honor the non-negotiable document of title or to obey the direction remains on the seller until the buyer has had a reasonable time to present the document or direction, and a refusal by the bailee to honor the document or to obey the direction defeats the tender.

4. *Goods Not to be Shipped by Carrier.* Where the goods are not to be shipped by carrier, they may be at the time of the making of the contract either future goods, or existing goods in the possession of the seller or buyer or other bailee. If they are in the possession of a third party bailee, the contract may provide for delivery to the buyer either without moving the goods or by moving them. Risk of loss as to goods held by a third party bailee and to be delivered without being moved is covered under the preceding sub-heading.

If the goods are in the possession of the buyer at the time of the making of the contract, risk of loss passes to the buyer at that time, as the buyer is in "receipt of the goods." Section 2–509(3). Title would also pass to the buyer at that time, as the seller would have no performance to complete "with reference to the physical delivery of the goods." Section 2–401(2).

However, if at the time the contract was formed, the goods were not in the possession of the buyer, were not to be shipped by carrier, and were not in the possession of a bailee, the situation is one of frequent occurrence in which a seller is required to tender or deliver the goods to the buyer. In such case, risk of loss depends upon whether the seller is a merchant. If the seller is a merchant, risk of loss passes to the buyer upon delivery and receipt of the goods. If the seller is not a merchant, it passes on tender of the goods by the seller to the buyer. Section 2–509(3).

For example, A is a dealer in furniture. B goes to A's store, selects a particular set of dining room furniture and pays A the agreed price of $800 for it upon A's agreement to stain the set a darker color and deliver it. A stains the furniture, transports it by truck to B's residence, and there tenders it to B who refuses to accept it. The furniture is then returned to A's store where shortly thereafter it is accidentally destroyed by fire. B can recover from A $800 less the amount of A's damages resulting from B's breach of contract. The risk of loss is on A.

However if X, an accountant, upon moving to a different city contracts to sell his household furniture to Y for $1000 by written agreement signed by Y, and thereafter loads the furniture on a truck which is driven to Y's residence where the goods are tendered to Y who refuses to accept or pay for them, and on the return trip the truck is smashed and the furniture damaged, X may recover from Y the $1000 purchase price. The risk of loss is on Y.

5. *Effect of Breach of Contract.* If the seller ships non-conforming goods to the buyer, the risk of loss remains on the seller until the buyer has accepted the goods, and the buyer is under no duty to accept them. Section 2–510(1) provides:

> (1) Where a tender or delivery of goods so fails to conform to the contract as to give a right of rejection the risk of their loss remains on the seller until cure or acceptance.

Where the buyer has accepted non-conforming goods, and thereafter by timely notice to the seller rightfully revokes his acceptance, he may treat the risk of loss as resting on the seller from the beginning to the extent of any deficiency in the buyer's effective insurance coverage. Section 2–510 (2).

Where conforming goods have been identified to the contract which the buyer repudiates or breaches before risk of loss has passed to him, the seller may treat the risk of loss as resting on the buyer "for a commercially reasonable time" to the extent of any deficiency in the seller's effective insurance coverage. Section 2–510(3).

6. *Effect of Agreement for Inspection.* The right of the buyer to inspect the goods is secondary. Its purpose is to enable the buyer to see that the goods comply with the contract before he pays the price. If the buyer fails to inspect, pays the seller, and receives non-conforming goods, he has remedies available and may sue the seller. However, a buyer may prefer to avoid the trouble, inconvenience, and expense of a lawsuit to recover the price paid by inspecting the goods before parting with the price. Inspection does not postpone identification or affect the place for delivery or the risk of loss. Section 2–513(4) provides:

> A place or method of inspection fixed by the parties is presumed to be exclusive, but unless otherwise expressly agreed it does not postpone identification or shift the place for delivery or for passing the risk of loss.

7. *Sale on Approval.* In a sale on approval the goods are delivered to the buyer for a stated period of time, or for a reasonable time if none is stated, during which period the buyer may use the goods to determine whether he wishes to buy them. Title and risk of loss are with the seller until "approval" or acceptance of the goods by the buyer. Section 2–326 of the Code provides:

> (1) Unless otherwise agreed, if delivered goods may be returned by the buyer even though they conform to the contract, the transaction is
>
>   (a) a "sale on approval" if the goods are delivered primarily for use, and
>
>   (b) a "sale or return" if the goods are delivered primarily for resale.
>
> (2) Except as provided in subsection (3), goods held on approval are not subject to the

claims of the buyer's creditors until acceptance; goods held on sale or return are subject to such claims while in the buyer's possession.

(3) Where goods are delivered to a person for sale and such person maintains a place of business at which he deals in goods of the kind involved, under a name other than the name of the person making delivery, then with respect to claims of creditors of the person conducting the business the goods are deemed to be on sale or return. The provisions of this subsection are applicable even though an agreement purports to reserve title to the person making delivery until payment or resale or uses such words as "on consignment" or "on memorandum". However, this subsection is not applicable if the person making delivery

     (a) complies with an applicable law providing for a consignor's interest or the like to be evidenced by a sign, or

     (b) establishes that the person conducting the business is generally known by his creditors to be substantially engaged in selling the goods of others, or

     (c) complies with the filing provisions of the Article on Secured Transactions (Article 9).

(4) Any "or return" term of a contract for sale is to be treated as a separate contract for sale within the statute of frauds section of this Article (Section 2–201) and as contradicting the sale aspect of the contract within the provisions of this Article on parol or extrinsic evidence (Section 2–202).

Section 2–327 provides:

(1) Under a sale on approval unless otherwise agreed

     (a) although the goods are identified to the contract the risk of loss and the title do not pass to the buyer until acceptance; and

     (b) use of the goods consistent with the purpose of trial is not acceptance but failure seasonably to notify the seller of election to return the goods is acceptance, and if the goods

conform to the contract acceptance of any part is acceptance of the whole; and

     (c) after due notification of election to return, the return is at the seller's risk and expense but a merchant buyer must follow any reasonable instructions.

(2) Under a sale or return unless otherwise agreed

     (a) the option to return extends to the whole or any commercial unit of the goods while in substantially their original condition, but must be exercised seasonably; and

     (b) the return is at the buyer's risk and expense.

8. *Sale or Return.* In a sale or return, the goods are delivered to the buyer with an option to return them to the seller. The risk of loss is on the buyer who has title until he revests it in the seller by a return of the goods. The return of the goods is at the buyer's risk and expense.

Under common law it is frequently difficult to determine from the facts of a particular transaction whether the parties intended a sale on approval or a sale or return. The consequences are, of course, drastically different with respect to transfer of title and risk of loss. The Code provides a test which is neat, sensible, and easily applied, namely, unless otherwise agreed, if the goods are delivered primarily for the buyer's use the transaction is a sale on approval; if they are delivered primarily for resale by the buyer, it is a sale or return. Section 2–326(1).

9. *F.O.B. and F.A.S. Shipments.* The initials F.O.B. mean "free on board;" and F.A.S. means "free alongside." Under the Code these are both delivery terms and not price terms when used in a contract of sale. Section 2–319(1) and (2) provide:

(1) Unless otherwise agreed the term F.O.B. (which means "free on board") at a named place, even though used only in con-

nection with the stated price, is a delivery term under which

   (a) when the term is F.O.B. the place of shipment, the seller must at that place ship the goods in the manner provided in this Article (Section 2–504) and bear the expense and risk of putting them into the possession of the carrier; or

   (b) when the term is F.O.B. the place of destination, the seller must at his own expense and risk transport the goods to that place and there tender delivery of them in the manner provided in this Article (Section 2–503);

   (c) when under either (a) or (b) the term is also F.O.B. vessel, car or other vehicle, the seller must in addition at his own expense and risk load the goods on board. If the term is F.O.B. vessel the buyer must name the vessel and in an appropriate case the seller must comply with the provisions of this Article on the form of bill of lading (Section 2–323).

(2) Unless otherwise agreed the term F.A.S. vessel (which means "free alongside") at a named port, even though used only in connection with the stated price, is a delivery term under which the seller must

   (a) at his own expense and risk deliver the goods alongside the vessel in the manner usual in that port or on a dock designated and provided by the buyer; and

   (b) obtain and tender a receipt for the goods in exchange for which the carrier is under a duty to issue a bill of lading.

10. *C.I.F. and C. & F. Shipments.* The initials C.I.F. mean "cost, insurance, and freight;" C. & F. means simply "cost and freight."

Under a C.I.F. contract, in consideration for an agreed unit price for the goods the seller pays all costs of transportation, insurance, and freight to destination. The amount of the agreed unit price of the goods

will, of course, reflect these costs. The unit price in a C. & F. contract is understandably less than in a C.I.F. contract as it does not include the cost of insurance.

In a C.I.F. contract the buyer is bargaining for insurance for which he is paying by reason of its inclusion in the unit price of the goods. This may be regarded as evidence of intention of the parties that title and risk of loss are to pass to the buyer upon shipment of the goods.

Under the Code, both C.I.F. and C. & F. contracts are regarded as shipment and not destination contracts. In a shipment contract, title and risk of loss pass to the buyer upon delivery of the goods to the carrier. Section 2–509. If the seller has properly performed all of his obligations with respect to the goods, title and risk of loss under either a C.I.F. or a C. & F. contract pass to the buyer upon delivery of the goods to the carrier.

Section 2–320 of the Code provides:

   (1) The term C.I.F. means that the price includes in a lump sum the cost of the goods and the insurance and freight to the named destination. The term C. & F. or C.F. means that the price so includes cost and freight to the named destination.

   (2) Unless otherwise agreed and even though used only in connection with the stated price and destination the term C.I.F. destination or its equivalent requires the seller at his own expense and risk to

      (a) put the goods into the possession of a carrier at the port for shipment and obtain a negotiable bill or bills of lading covering the entire transportation to the named destination; and

      (b) load the goods and obtain a receipt from the carrier (which may be contained in the bill of lading) showing that the freight has been paid or provided for; and

      (c) obtain a policy or certificate of insurance, including any war risk insurance, of a kind and on terms then current at the port of shipment in the usual amount, in the currency of the contract, shown to cover the same goods covered by the bill of lading and providing for payment of loss to the order of the buyer or for the account of whom it may concern; but the seller may add to the price the amount of the premium for any such war risk insurance; and

(d) prepare an invoice of the goods and procure any other documents required to effect shipment or to comply with the contract; and

(e) forward and tender with commercial promptness all the documents in due form and with any indorsement necessary to perfect the buyer's rights.

(3) Unless otherwise agreed the term C. & F. or its equivalent has the same effect and imposes upon the seller the same obligations and risks as a C.I.F. term except the obligation as to insurance.

(4) Under the term C.I.F. or C. & F. unless otherwise agreed the buyer must make payment against tender of the required documents and the seller may not tender nor the buyer demand delivery of the goods in substitution for the documents.

Section 2–321 of the Code provides:

Under a contract containing a term C.I.F. or C. & F.

(1) Where the price is based on or is to be adjusted according to "net landed weights", "delivered weights", "out turn" quantity or quality or the like, unless otherwise agreed the seller must reasonably estimate the price. The payment due on tender of the documents called for by the contract is the amount so estimated, but after final adjustment of the price a settlement must be made with commercial promptness.

(2) An agreement described in subsection (1) or any warranty of quality or condition of the goods on arrival places upon the seller the risk of ordinary deterioration, shrinkage and the like in transportation but has no effect on the place or time of identification to the contract for sale or delivery or on the passing of the risk of loss.

(3) Unless otherwise agreed where the contract provides for payment on or after arrival of the goods the seller must before payment allow such preliminary inspection as is feasible; but if the goods are lost delivery of the documents and payment are due when the goods should have arrived.

11. *C.O.D. Shipments.* These initials mean "Collect on Delivery", and are instructions to the carrier not to deliver the goods at destination until it has collected the price and transportation charges from the consignee. In this manner the seller retains control over the possession of the goods by preventing the buyer from obtaining delivery unless he pays the price. It does not prevent title from passing to the buyer upon delivery of the goods to the carrier. Under the usual rule, where the buyer pays or agrees to pay the freight, title passes upon delivery to the carrier. A shipment C.O.D., where authorized by the buyer, does not evidence any intention which would cause the usual rule not to apply. A shipment C.O.D. deprives the buyer of the right of inspection to which he would otherwise be entitled under Section 2–513(3) (a) of the Code.

12. *Delivery "Ex-Ship" Contract.* Where the contract provides for delivery "ex-ship", or from the ship, it is not only a destination contract but title and risk of loss do not pass to the buyer until the goods are off the ship at destination. Section 2–322.

13. *"No Arrival, No Sale" Contract.* Where the contract contains terms of "no arrival, no sale", the title and risk of loss do not pass to the buyer until the seller makes a tender of the goods after their arrival at destination. These terms excuse the seller from any liability to the buyer for failure of the goods to arrive, unless the seller has caused their non-arrival.

Section 2–324 of the Code provides:

> Under a term "no arrival, no sale" or terms of like meaning, unless otherwise agreed,
>
> > (a) the seller must properly ship conforming goods and if they arrive by any means he must tender them on arrival but he assumes no obligation that the goods will arrive unless he has caused the non-arrival; and
> >
> > (b) where without fault of the seller the goods are in part lost or have so deteriorated as no longer to conform to the contract or arrive after the contract time, the buyer may proceed as if there had been casualty to identified goods.

In emphasizing the location of risk of loss with definite rules for specific situations, the Code departs sharply from the common law concept of risk of loss determined by ownership of the goods which depended upon whether title was transferred. In its transactional approach, the Code is necessarily detailed, and for this reason is probably more understandable and meaningful to the intelligent and interested businessman than a more summary statement of legal principles.

CASES

CITY OF BOSCOBEL v. MUSCODA MFG. CO.

(1921) 175 Wis. 62, 183 N.W. 963.

[The court's statement of the facts is as follows:

The plaintiff city was the owner of two engines and two steam pumps and other equipment formerly used by it in connection with its municipal lighting plant. The defendant is engaged in the manufacturing business in the city of Boscobel, and on December 23 the parties entered into the following contract:

"Boscobel, Wis., 12/23, 1919.
"Sold to Muscoda Mfg. Co., Muscoda, Wis.

"The power plant formerly used by the city of Boscobel as an electric light plant, consisting of 2 boilers, 2 engines, 2 steam pumps, water heaters, and all other equipment and fittings that go with outfit.

"Muscoda Mfg. Co. agrees to pay the sum of $1,800 for the outfit, to be paid $200 cash, which is hereby paid, and the balance, $1,600, to be paid before taking out the plant, and plant is to be taken out before June 1, 1920. Muscoda Mfg. Co. is to repair buildings where boiler is to be taken out in as good shape as before.

"City of Boscobel,
"By John Scheinpflug, Mayor.
"Muscoda Mfg. Co.,
"By B. L. Marcus, Pres."

At the time of the execution and delivery of the contract and the payment of $200 the property was situated within a frame building covered with sheet iron. * * * On March 12, 1920, the building was burned and the property covered by the contract was practically destroyed, being worthless for any purpose except junk. This suit is brought by the plaintiff to recover the remainder of the purchase price, amounting to $1,600, with interest. There was judgment for the plaintiff, from which the defendant appeals.]

ROSENBERRY, J. Two principal questions are raised upon the appeal: First, Did the contract of December 23, 1919, vest the title to the property in the defendant? * * *

Whether or not the title to the goods described in the contract passed to the defendant depends upon the intention of the parties. Sec. 1684t–18, Stats. The contract itself does not in terms say when the title should pass. Recourse must be had, therefore, to rules of construction. Sec. 1684t–19 establishes the rules for ascertaining the intention of the parties as to the time at which the property in goods is to pass to the buyer where there is no specific provision in the contract. Rule 1:

"Where there is an unconditional contract to sell specific goods, in a deliverable state, the property in the goods passes to the buyer when the contract is made and it is immaterial whether the time of payment, or the time of delivery, or both, be postponed."

In this case the goods were ascertained and in a deliverable state. The buyer had the right at any time before June 1, 1920, upon payment of the remainder of the purchase price, to take the goods, and if the plaintiff had, upon tender being made to it, refused to deliver the goods, the right of the defendant to recover the same in an action of replevin would have been complete.

It is argued that the sale was conditional, that the payment of the remainder of the purchase price was a condition precedent to the right of the defendant to the possession of the property. While a sale by the terms of which the purchaser is to pay cash on delivery is in a sense conditional (35 Cyc. 323), the distinguishing feature of a conditional sale, as that term is used and understood, means a sale by which the title to the goods is to remain in the seller until the payment of the price but the possession and use of the goods are with the purchaser until there is a default in payment. Sec. 1684u-1. The facts in this case bring it squarely within the provisions of Rule 1, and it must be held that the title to the goods passed to the defendant and the risk of loss was with it. [Citations.]

*   *   *

Judgment affirmed.

MARTIN v. WHITELEY

(1965) 89 Idaho 429, 405 P.2d 963.

McFADDEN, J. * * * During 1962, Martin raised a crop of potatoes which he stored in a potato cellar located on his property. In late October, 1962, Whiteley, who was engaged in the farming and produce business discussed with Martin the purchase of the potatoes. The initial discussions were to the effect that Martin wished to sell the stored, ungraded potatoes, which he estimated to be about 31,000 cwt. (sacks). Whiteley indicated that he would purchase the lot if there were that many and requested the opportunity to examine them.

He then examined the potatoes and upon measuring them estimated the quantity to be over 32,000 cwt. At his direction his bookkeeper prepared a sales agreement, which both Martin and Whiteley executed, reading as follows:

"THIS AGREEMENT Made and entered into in triplicate this *5th* day of *November,* 1962, by and between *W. B. Whiteley* of Oakley, Idaho, hereinafter referred to as the Buyer, and *Phillip S. Martin,* of Burley, Idaho, hereinafter refere*e*d to as the Seller

WITNESSETH:

That for and in consideration of $50,000, the Buyer agrees to buy and does buy from the Seller, and the Seller agrees to sell and does sell to the Buyer the *31,000* cwt. bin run Idaho Russet potatoes, Said potatoes in storage located on Phillip S. Martin ranch, *9 miles,* South of Burley, Idaho."

The parties agreed that Martin would take a credit memorandum from Whiteley, which would be paid on demand after January 1, 1963, and such a memorandum was delivered to Martin.

Later Whiteley entered into negotiations with Eastern Idaho Packing Corporation for the purchase by it of the Martin potatoes.

*   *   *

Before Whiteley and Eastern reached any agreement, a representative of Eastern and a representative of the National Produce Distributors, a company associated with

Eastern, inspected and measured the stored potatoes.

The only written evidence of the agreement between Whiteley and Eastern is to be found in two letters: the first written by Mr. Reitman, a representative of Eastern to National Produce Distributors, Inc., under date of December 14, 1962 stated:

"Please be advised that EIPC [Eastern] now owns the potatoes that you looked at with Whiteley and myself on our last visit here. The deal is as follows:

The trade was made with the following understanding: This cellar of potatoes contains approximately 32,500 bags of field run for which we pay Whiteley $55,000 from this cellar of potatoes. For this price he is to run these potatoes over an eliminator setting back the seed, load the commercials, haul and deliver same to EIPC warehouse. The seed which remains in the cellar Whiteley has agreed to buy at $1.50 cwt. in the cellar.

* * * "

* * *

Whiteley paid Martin $28,000 on the purchase price of the potatoes. Eastern paid Whiteley $27,500.00. Eastern also gave Whiteley a check for $22,500, and Whiteley issued a check to Martin for $22,000. In March, 1963, Eastern requested Whiteley to haul the potatoes from the cellar to the warehouse, but at that time Whiteley, not having the trucks or equipment, agreed to use some of Eastern's trucks and equipment. When the trucks were being loaded, Eastern's representative observed frost damage to the potatoes, and Eastern stopped payment of its check to Whiteley, who in turn stopped payment of his check to Martin. Eastern complained of the frost damage to Whiteley, who in turn contacted Martin and discussions were had relative to the frost damage. No settlement having been reached, Martin instituted this action against Whiteley for the balance due him of $22,000.00. In turn,

Whiteley brought Eastern into the case by a third party complaint for the balance he claimed due and owing.

Eastern filed a counterclaim against Whiteley claiming an offset by reason of the frost damage to the potatoes, to be offset against the amount Whiteley claimed against Eastern, and asked for judgment for the balance.

The cause was tried before the court on issues framed on the various pleadings, and the trial court entered findings of fact, conclusions of law and judgment on Martin's claim against Whiteley; also entered separate findings of fact, conclusions of law and judgment on the third party claim of Whiteley against Eastern and the counterclaim interposed by Eastern, and judgment in favor of Martin against Whiteley for $22,000; also entered another judgment in favor of Whiteley against Eastern for $23,-500, (being balance of $27,500, less $4,000 offset which Whiteley agreed he owed Eastern). * * *

Resolution of the question as to when the title to the potatoes actually passed in the transaction between Martin and Whiteley, and between Whiteley and Eastern was the determinative issue in the lower court. Risk of loss by freezing or otherwise would follow the title. [Citation.]

Because Whiteley could convey to Eastern only such title as he had, it first becomes necessary to consider the issues presented by the Whiteley appeal.

The trial court found that Martin and Whiteley executed the written agreement whereby Martin in consideration of $50,000 sold the crop of potatoes stored in the cellar owned by a third party and rented to Martin; that the lot or crop consisted of 31,000 cwt. of field-run potatoes; that Martin was not required to deliver the crop to Whiteley, who was to remove them from the cellar himself after November 5,

1962; that Martin did not agree to perform any further acts in connection with the potatoes, including care of the potatoes after November 5, 1962, but that an employee of Martin's performed certain acts during the period of time the potatoes were in the cellar to protect the crop from frost; that the potatoes were in good condition on November 5, 1962, and remained in good condition until February, 1963; that there was no negligence or lack of reasonable care or attention by Martin or any of his employees concerning the potatoes; that it was the intention of the parties that title pass from Martin to Whiteley on November 5, 1962.

The agreement above set out is expressed in the unconditional terms that Martin sold the potatoes to Whiteley, and that Whiteley bought them from Martin; the goods involved were ascertained and identified and were in a deliverable state. The credit memorandum given by Whiteley to Martin was not qualified in any manner. Nothing appears in the record showing any intention of the parties that the title was not to pass. * * *

The circumstances surrounding this transaction, inter alia, the statement of Mr. Reitman that Whiteley was to receive $5,000 over and above the purchase price for the performance of the duties, the understanding of the transaction as testified to by Mr. Whiteley, the use of the following terms in the correspondence: "EIPC now own the potatoes" and "you finally sold us that cellar of potatoes", indicate the intent of the parties that the title to and property in the crop of potatoes passed on December 14, 1962. Eastern, however, argues that the words or phrases in a contract to sell denoting present transfer of title, such as "own" or "sold" are not conclusive as to intent of the parties, [citations]. However, these cited cases involved the sale of goods not in existence at the time of the contract, or goods that were sold on a trial basis. Although the use of the terms "own" or "sold" are not conclusive as to intent, certainly the use of such words under these circumstances is strong evidence of the intent of the parties to exercise immediate domain over the property in question.

On January 16, 1963, Eastern made a $5,000 payment to Whiteley on the potatoes, with a memorandum attached to the check which stated: "Deposit on purchase of Phil Martin lot of potatoes located in Phil Martin Cellar. Terms of purchase per letter dated December 14, 1962." Eastern wrote two additional checks to Whiteley on March 19, 1963, before discovery of the frost damage. These two checks were each in the amount of $22,500, the first deposited and paid, the second not to be deposited until April 20th, payment of which latter check was refused upon presentation. This is further evidence that it was the intent of the parties to transfer title before there was any delivery; otherwise Eastern would not have made payment until delivery. * * *

Judgments affirmed.

NEAL, CLARK & NEAL CO. v. TARBY

(1917) 99 Misc. 380, 163 N.Y.S. 675.

[Action by Neal, Clark & Neal Co. to recover the possession of a Victrola which the plaintiff had sold on approval to one Fertig, who resold and delivered it to the defendant. The plaintiff appeals from a judgment dismissing the complaint.]

WHEELER, J. The facts in this case are undisputed, and briefly stated are: That the plaintiff, among other things, deals in Victrolas. One Fertig was the solicitor of advertising, and in that capacity was accustomed to visit the plaintiff's store. On the occasion of one of his visits the subject of the purchase of a Victrola was brought up by one of plaintiff's salesmen. Fertig was asked if he had decided to purchase a Victrola, to which he replied: "No; we haven't reached a point where we will decide on it." The salesman suggested sending one out on approval, to which Fertig replied: "If you want to take a chance, and send it out on approval, with the understanding I don't have to purchase it unless I want it, all right." To this the salesman replied: "All right, I will send it out with a selection of records, and see if we can't later sell you the machine."

They then selected a Victrola of the price of $150, which seems to have been fully understood, and the machine was delivered to Fertig. The salesman testified that some time later he asked Fertig if he had decided to purchase, to which Fertig replied: "We haven't quite decided to purchase the machine." To which the salesman replied: "All right; let us know when you are ready." It further appears that Fertig moved the machine to the Lenox Hotel, where he went to live, and while there sold and delivered the Victrola to the defendant in this action, who paid Fertig $75 therefor. Fertig then left, and has not since been seen.

The plaintiff, learning the facts, and claiming to own the machine, demanded it of the defendant, who refused to deliver it up. The plaintiff then brought this action in the City Court to recover possession. The City Court dismissed its complaint, and the case now comes before this court on appeal.

The plaintiff, in substance, contends there never was any consummated sale; that the title of the property never passed to Fertig, and he could give none to the defendant; that Fertig stole or converted the Victrola to his own use, and the plaintiff should have recovered. The defendant contends he is protected as a bona fide purchaser for value under the provisions of the Personal Property Law, and that the court below did not err in dismissing the plaintiff's complaint.

The defendant stands on the provisions of section 129 of that act, as added by Laws 1911, c. 571, providing:

"The buyer is deemed to have accepted the goods when he intimates to the seller that he has accepted them, or when the goods have been delivered to him and he does any act in relation to them which is inconsistent with the ownership of the seller, or when, after the lapse of a reasonable time, he retains the goods without intimating to the seller that he has rejected them."

It seems to us that this section governs the case here presented for review. If we correctly interpret the transaction between the plaintiff and Fertig, it amounted to this: The plaintiff delivered to Fertig the Victrola in question for trial, with the option to purchase it at the price of $150. This offer was at no time canceled or recalled by the plaintiff. There was evidently, under this arrangement, no actual sale, and no transfer of title to Fertig, until he had accepted the offer, or until he did some act in relation thereto "inconsistent with the ownership of the seller." The instant Fertig undertook to sell the machine as his own, he did an act inconsistent with the ownership of the plaintiff. It was evident that he had, in fact, acted upon the plaintiff's option to sell, and, in the absence of fraud, it became a consummated sale between the parties to it. Under such circumstances, I think there can be no question but what the plaintiff would have had a perfect right to have sued and recovered from Fertig the agreed purchase price of the machine.

Section 100 of the Personal Property Law also provides:

"When goods are delivered to the buyer on approval or on trial or on satisfaction, or other similar terms, the property therein passes to the buyer—(a) When he signifies his approval or acceptance to the seller or does any other act adopting the transaction."

* * *

I am of the opinion that the judgment appealed from should be affirmed. So ordered.

WESTERN HAT & MFG. CO. v. BERKNER BROS., INC.

(1927) 172 Minn. 4, 214 N.W. 475.

[Action by a wholesaler of Milwaukee, Wisconsin, to recover the purchase price of gloves ordered by defendant buyer, a retailer, of Sleepy Eye, Minnesota. The defendant countermanded the order before the gloves were shipped. From a judgment entered for the defendant, plaintiff appeals.]

LEES, Commissioner. * * * The court found that on April 14, 1925, respondent [defendant] gave one of appellant's traveling salesmen a written order for a quantity of gloves, describing them by number, size, and name. The salesman made a memorandum, stating that the gloves were to be shipped over the Chicago & North Western Railway in August and were to be paid for in November. The order was accepted and respondent notified thereof. Appellant [plaintiff] had the gloves in stock, selected those ordered, packed them ready for shipment, set them aside in its warehouse, and attached shipping tags bearing respondent's name and address. Thereafter and on June 30, respondent countermanded the order and requested appellant to cancel it, but appellant refused. On August 12 the gloves were shipped to respondent and an invoice mailed. On receipt of the invoice respondent notified appellant that it would refuse to receive the gloves. They were tendered to respondent by the railroad company, were refused, and have remained in the hands of the railroad company ever since. Appellant's salesmen did not carry or attempt to sell gloves after June 30. They are goods usually sold by whole-salers for the fall trade and are not readily salable after June.

The court held that these facts fell short of showing that the property in the gloves had passed to the respondent before the order was countermanded, and that appellant could not recover the purchase price.

Appellant cites sections 19 and 63 of the uniform sales act in support of its contention that the court should have allowed a recovery of the purchase price. Section 19, rule 4, reads:

"(1) Where there is a contract to sell unascertained or future goods by description, and goods of that description and in a deliverable state are unconditionally appropriated to the contract, either by the seller with the assent of the buyer, or by the buyer with the assent of the seller, the property in the goods thereupon passes to the buyer. Such assent may be expressed or implied, and may be given either before or after the appropriation is made." * * *

Section 19 of the act begins with the words:

"Unless a different intention appears, the following are rules for ascertaining the intention of the parties as to the time at which the property in the goods is to pass to the buyer."

Then follows rule 4, quoted above. It thus appears that the intention of the parties controls if it is apparent, and only when it is not may resort be had to the rules. When, as here, the contract requires the seller to ship the goods to the buyer, we think it should be held, if there is nothing to show a different intention, that the parties did not intend that the property in the goods should pass prior to a delivery to a carrier for shipment. In such a case, setting the goods apart in the seller's warehouse is not an irrevocable appropriation of them to the fulfilment of the contract and will not give the seller the right to sue for the purchase price. * * *

[Judgment affirmed.]

HUNTER BROS. MILLING CO. v. KRAMER BROS.

(1905) 71 Kan. 468, 80 P. 963.

[Action by the plaintiff buyer to recover $900 as damages for the failure of defendants to deliver bran purchased from the defendants and paid for by the plaintiff. The parties had entered into a contract whereby the defendant of Wellington, Kansas, agreed to sell to the plaintiff of St. Louis, Mo., 1600 sacks of bran "delivered in East St. Louis." Defendant shipped 1600 sacks of bran to the plaintiff in four cars. Only two carloads were received by the plaintiff, the two remaining cars having been caught in a flood and the bran destroyed. From a judgment in favor of defendants, plaintiff brings the case to the Supreme Court of Kansas on a writ of error.]

JOHNSTON, C. J. * * * In this transaction the correspondence indicates with reasonable clearness that the defendants were to put the bran in sacks and lay it down in East St. Louis for a specific price. The telegrahic offer of plaintiff was to the effect that if defendants would deliver bran in one-hundred-pound sacks, without limit as to quantity, in East St. Louis, in May, the plaintiff would pay them at the rate of seventy-three cents per hundred. The offer was accepted in a telegram that, as the witness translated it, specified a delivery in East St. Louis, and fixed the quantity sold at 1600 sacks. * * *

The contract for the sale of the bran, then, determined the quantity, the quality, the price, and the place of delivery, and showed that the delivery was to be made free on board the cars at East St. Louis, and not at the place of shipment. If the contract by its terms had not expressly provided for a delivery of the bran by defendants at East St. Louis the fact that the defendants were to pay the freight and furnish the bran at that place for a specified price, without cost to the plaintiff, would be some evidence tending to prove an agreement to deliver the bran there, and that the sale was not complete until the delivery was made. In such a case the railroad company would be deemed to be the agent of the defendants, and not of the plaintiff. The case of Suit v. Woodhall, 113 Mass. 391, involved a contract for the sale of liquors, and there was testimony that the plaintiff, who was the seller, was to pay the freight to the place of destination, and the trial court refused an instruction to the jury that if they found the plaintiff was to pay the freight and deliver the property to defendants at their place of business the sale was made there. The refusal so to instruct was held to be error. The court said:

"Delivery to the carrier was a delivery to the defendants, if there was no agreement to the contrary. * * * But if the parties agreed that the goods were to be delivered in Lawrence, it would not be a completed sale until the delivery, and the laws of this state would apply to it."

In another case the same court held that one who makes and sells an article to another, agreeing to deliver it at the place of business of the buyer, is liable for any injury or loss occurring in the transportation of it, although at the time of making the contract for the article nothing was said about delivery. [Citation.] In Brewing Association v. Nipp, 6 Kan.App. 730, 50 P. 956, it was said:

"Ordinarily a delivery of merchandise to the carrier is a delivery to the purchaser; but when the seller pays the freight the carrier is his agent and the delivery is made at the place of its destination."

In this case the defendants were to pay the freight to East St. Louis, where the bran was to be delivered at a fixed price, without charge, cost or expense to the plaintiff. The rule, as stated at page 1050 of volume 24 of the American and English Encyclopedia of Law, is as follows:

"If by the terms of the contract the seller is required to send or forward or deliver the goods to the buyer, the title and risk remain in the seller until the transportation is at an end or the goods are delivered in accordance with the contract, after which time the title is vested in the buyer." * * *

In view of the correspondence and the circumstances developed by the testimony it is manifest that the contract required the defendants to make delivery in East St. Louis, and that the title to the bran would not pass until it reached that place. There was certainly evidence to take the case to the jury, and, therefore, the judgment sustaining the demurrer to plaintiff's evidence is reversed, and the cause remanded for further proceedings.

[Reversed and remanded.]

VAL DECKER PACKING CO. v. ARMOUR AND COMPANY

(1962 Ohio Comm.Pl.) 184 N.E.2d 548.

GESSAMAN, J. Plaintiff seeks to recover from the defendant the sum of $1690.49. A jury was waived and the case has been submitted to the Court upon the evidence and the briefs of counsel.

The facts are not in dispute. At about 5:00 P.M., December 26, 1956, a Mr. Irwin Busse, representing the defendant, called the plaintiff's office and talked with Mr. Louis B. Decker, Chairman of the Board of Directors of plaintiff. At the price of $8885.51, fixed by Mr. Decker, Mr. Busse ordered from plaintiff for defendant a truck load of dressed hogs to be shipped to Western Pork Packers, Inc. "C.A.F.", Worcester, Mass. Plaintiff engaged the Wilson Freight Forwarding Co., Cincinnati, Ohio, to transport the hogs in a refrigerated truck. The loaded truck left plaintiff's place of business in Piqua,

Ohio, at 12:25 P.M., December 27, 1956. On December 28, 1956, before 3:00 P.M. the driver of the truck called Mr. Ralph Cutillo, Armour and Company manager in Worcester, Mass., and stated that his truck had developed mechanical trouble and that he could not make delivery by 3:00 P.M. that day. Mr. Cutillo authorized the driver to deliver by 6:00 A.M. December 29, 1956. The truck did not arrive by that time and did not arrive until December 31, 1956, at which time defendant refused to accept the shipment. It was sold to another company for $7203.99. The condition and quality of the merchandise is not in dispute.

After the telephone conversation between Mr. Busse and Mr. Decker, plaintiff received from defendant a "Confirmation of Purchase". In addition to the provisions to which we have already referred, there are contained in this document the shipping date, "11 P.M. 12/26/56." "Payment: S.D.B.L. (sight draft bill of lading) against documents," and the following: "Note: Please show on bill of lading in large size, bright colored print or crayon that Western Pork Packers, Inc. desire to unload these hogs not later than 3:00 P.M. Friday, 12/28 and as much sooner as possible. If delayed, truck driver to please called collect, Mr. Ralph Cutillo, Mgr. Armour & Co., 219 Summit St., Worcester, Mass., tele. No. Pleasant 2–5653." This was done.

Counsel for the plaintiff contend that since the hogs were to be shipped "C.A.F." Worcester, their duty under the contract was fulfilled when the merchandise was delivered to the carrier at their place of business in Piqua, and that the risk thereafter was on the buyer, the defendant. Counsel for the defendant contend as follows:

"The defendant takes no issue with the general legal incidents of a 'C&F' or 'C.I.F.' contract, as set forth in plaintiff's brief. It is agreed that title to the goods with the attendant risk of loss passes from the seller to the buyer upon delivery to the carrier, but only if the terms of the contract to sell are fulfilled by the seller."

* * *

One of the terms of the contract, which also involves a usage of the trade, is the provision that the hogs were to be shipped "C.A.F. Worcester." To understand that term fully, we call attention to Madeirense Do Brasil S/A v. Stulman-Emrick Lumber Co., 147 F.2d 399 and specifically to the language of the Court at page 402 of the opinion:

"Plaintiff argues further that it has duly performed because a c. & f. contract requires it only to deliver, or to tender delivery of, the lumber to a carrier in Brazil. The term 'c. & f.' means that the price includes in a lump sum 'cost' and 'freight' to the named destination. [Citations.] The term 'c. & f.' thus either requires the seller to prepay the freight or permits the buyer after having paid the actual charges to deduct them from the price, in either case putting the seller under an ultimate obligation to pay for the transportation. Ordinarily where the seller pays the freight, there is an inference under Rule 5 of § 19 of the Uniform Sales Act, N. Y. Personal Property Law, Consol.Laws, c. 41, § 100, rule 5, that the parties intend no passage of title until the goods reach the destination to which freight is paid. But commercial usage, recognized by the courts and text writers, is that under a c. & f. contract the seller fulfills his duty on shipment of the goods, and that the risk thereafter is on the buyer unless other terms of the contract indicate a contrary intention. * * *"

Does the contract indicate such a contrary intention? We think not.

* * *

Therein their argument is summarized. Did the plaintiff fail to perform "an essential term" of the contract? To state it in another way, was the time of shipment (as contained in the contract) "of the essence of the agreement?" We think not.

"Time is not of the essence of the contract unless made so by its terms." [Citations.] A careful examination of the contract reveals clearly that the consignee *desired* to unload the shipment by "3:00 P.M. Friday, 12/28." Whether that date was or was not of the essence, need not now be determined but it is obvious that it was the only date in which either the defendant or Western Pork Packers, Inc. were interested. That fact is emphasized by the provision that the driver should call the defendants' manager at Worcester in case of delay and by the fact that that date was to be shown "on the bill of lading in large size, bright colored print or crayon." There is nothing in the agreement which indicates that anyone cared whether the hogs were shipped by 11:00 P.M. 12/26/56, just so they arrived by "3:00 P.M. Friday, 12/28." The latter was the important date.

The shipment actually left plaintiff's place of business on December 27, 1956, at 12:25 P.M. The evidence discloses that the driving time from Piqua, Ohio, to Worcester, Mass. was twenty-four hours. Had nothing happened to the truck, it is reasonable to assume that the hogs would have been delivered by 12:25 P.M. December 28, 1956, or two and one-half hours prior to the desired time. We refer to this only to point out that neither the defendant nor Western Pork Packers, Inc. were particularly interested in the time at which the hogs left Piqua. They were interested in the time at which they arrived at Worcester. Therefore, we feel that the time of shipment, mentioned in the contract, was not made of the essence "by its terms" nor was there anything in the conduct or acts of the parties that made it of the essence of the contract, nor was it an essential term thereof.

* * *

Our conclusions are: 1. That the agreement entered into between plaintiff and defendant was a C.A.F. or C. & F. contract; 2. that the shipping date was neither an essential term of nor was it of the essence of the contract; 3. that, therefore, plaintiff did not breach the contract by shipping the hogs on December 27, 1956; 4. that when plaintiff delivered the hogs to the carrier title passed to the defendant and the risk thereafter was on the defendant; 5. that defendant's refusal to accept the hogs when they were delivered in Worcester, Mass. did not relieve it of its duty to pay plaintiff for them and, 6. that therefore the plaintiff should recover from the defendant the difference between the contract price of the hogs and the price at which it sold them, plus $8.97 expense incurred by plaintiff by reason of defendant's refusal to accept the hogs. Our finding is that the plaintif recover from the defendant the sum of $1690.49.

Judgment for plaintiff.

GENERAL ELECTRIC CO. v. PETTINGELL SUPPLY CO.

(1964) 347 Mass. 631, 199 N.E.2d 326.

WHITTEMORE, J. The plaintiff by writ of replevin took from the defendant David S. Miller, assignee for the benefit of creditors of the defendant Pettingell Supply Company, certain large lamps that had been delivered by the plaintiff to Pettingell as "agent to sell or distribute" such lamps. Large lamps are "lamps used in commercial and industrial installations." General Electric by outline bill of exceptions presents for our review the ruling of the judgment in the Superior Court that because of the Uniform Commercial Code (G.L. c. 106, inserted by St.1957, c. 765, § 1) the plaintiff must return the replevied goods. * * *

The sole issue argued concerns the effect of G.L. c. 106, § 2–326, on the rights of the parties. That section provides in relevant part: "(1) Unless otherwise agreed, if de-livered goods may be returned by the buyer even though they conform to the contract, the transaction is * * * (b) a 'sale or return' if the goods are delivered primarily for resale. (2) * * * [G]oods held on sale or return are subject to * * * claims [of the buyer's 'creditors'] while in the buyer's possession. (3) Where goods are delivered to a person for sale and such person maintains a place of business at which he deals in goods of the kind involved, under a name other than the name of the person making delivery, then with respect to claims of creditors of the person conducting the business the goods are deemed to be on sale or return. The provisions of this subsection are applicable even though an agreement purports to reserve title to the person making delivery until payment or resale or uses such words as 'on consignment' or 'on memorandum'. However, this subsection is not applicable if the person making delivery (a) complies with an applicable law providing for a consignor's interest or the like to be evidenced by a sign; or (b) establishes that the person conducting the business is generally known by his creditors to be substantially engaged in selling the goods of others; or (c) complies with the filing provisions of the Article on Secured Transactions (Article 9)."

General Electric concedes that clauses (a), (b), and (c) of subsection 3 did not operate to exclude the arrangement between it and Pettingell from the operation of the subsection and accepts as conclusive the judge's findings and rulings to that effect. The plaintiff also concedes that if Pettingell's creditors have claims under § 2–326, Miller, who took possession of the large lamps from Pettingell, may establish these claims. See G.L. c. 106, § 1–201(12). Hence, if this is a transaction which § 2–326(3) characterizes as a "sale or return" the large lamps are subject to the claim of Miller as assignee.

The plaintiff contends that § 2–326 is applicable only to cases where the relationship between manufacturer and dealer is that of seller and buyer and that inasmuch as the contract in suit establishes only a principal-agent relationship between the plaintiff and Pettingell no part of § 2–326 is applicable.

We disagree with the contention that § 2–326(3) is inapplicable. That subsection is by its terms concerned with certain transactions which, although they may not be sales under the definition of G.L. c. 106, § 2–106(1), are nonetheless "deemed to be on sale or return" "with respect to claims of creditors of the person conducting the business * * *." The subsection specifically states that it is applicable even though the "agreement purports to reserve title to the person making delivery until payment or resale or uses such words as 'on consignment' or 'on memorandum'." The agreement between the plaintiff and Pettingell binds the former "to maintain on consignment in the custody of the agent, to be disposed of as herein provided, a stock of said General Electric large lamps."

The plaintiff relies on the wording of the second sentence of § 2–326(3) which states that the subsection applies even though there is a reservation of title "to the person making delivery until payment or *resale*" (emphasis supplied). From this the plaintiff argues that the subsection applies only where the manufacturer has sold the goods to the dealer because otherwise there could be no "resale." The second sentence gives examples of transactions to which the subsection applies and does not limit the plain meaning of the first sentence. The subsection is concerned with transactions "deemed" to be of "sale or return" and the first sentence is carefully drafted to apply to transactions which might not ordinarily be characterized as sales. * * *

The judge found that Pettingell maintained a place of business in which it dealt in goods of the kind involved, under a name other than the name of the plaintiff. The plaintiff's attack on this finding is based on

the claimed absence of evidence that Pettingell sold any General Electric large lamps in its own name without disclosing its agency. We think the finding is supported by the evidence that Pettingell sold other electrical merchandise including other items from the plaintiff. The statute in referring to "goods of the kind involved" does not restrict the relevant business to dealings in the precise kind of electrical goods. Pettingell was a wholesaler "buying and selling electrical, hardware and housewares merchandise." Its gross annual business ranged from $300,000 to $400,000, and 25% of this business was in "the sale and distribution" of General Electric large lamps. This large lamp business was its only consignment business.

General Electric put in evidence forms supplied Pettingell for use by the latter in the sale of large lamps. These forms state that they are "from" Pettingell as "serving agent for General Electric, consignor company." It is unnecessary for us to decide whether, if Pettingell sold and distributed large lamps only, these forms alone would show that Pettingell was not in business "under a name other than the name of the person making delivery" or whether, because of the concern of § 2–326(3) with the rights of creditors, Miller need have only showed that "the consignee" did not completely identify "his business name with that of the consignor." Hawkland, Consignments Under the Uniform Commercial Code, supra.

The issue under subsection (3) thus becomes the narrow one whether the "goods" were "delivered to" Pettingell "for sale."

Under the agency contract Pettingell could sell directly to certain customers who bought for their own use or who bought in small volume for resale. Pettingell was also authorized to make deliveries under contracts of sale entered into between General Electric and purchasers and to "distribute" large lamps to other agents of General Electric. The latter were retailers under agency contracts with General Electric. The retail agents would procure the lamps from Pettingell, sell them as the plaintiff's agents and remit to Pettingell in accordance with the latter's invoices. The evidence showed that over a four year period 74% of Pettingell's "sales" were to subagents and 26% were direct sales other than those which General Electric negotiated. Under the contract in suit Pettingell would not have title to the large lamps at any time.

We need not determine the ruling required if Pettingell's sole authority had been to distribute lamps to subagents. Since Pettingell had authority to sell the lamps they were "delivered" to Pettingell "for sale." Section 2–326(1) (b) does not, we think, require a different result. That section defines a "sale or return" as a sale where "goods are delivered primarily for resale." That subsection, read with § 2–326(1) (a), might require us to determine in an appropriate case whether goods were delivered to a "consignee" primarily for his own use. It does not, however, exclude a consignment of goods to be sold or to be delivered to other agents as orders may require. * * *

The plaintiff's exceptions are overruled.

Judgment for defendant (Miller) affirmed.

PROBLEMS

1. A agreed to sell and B agreed to buy at a price of $80 per M feet, all of the oak timber located in A's lumber yard amounting to approximately 500 M feet. Subsequently, A contracted to build for B an 80-foot barge out of part of this timber for a consideration of $5,000; and B contracted to build for A an oak desk of given specifications out of part of this timber, for a consideration of $175. A selected and set aside the timber for the construction of the barge. B selected and set aside the timber to be used in the construction of the desk. An accidental fire on A's premises destroyed all of the timber. What are the rights of the parties?

2. A in New York ordered from B, a Chicago radio wholesaler, 20 television sets which were to be delivered to the carrier in Chicago and payment therefor to be made on receipt in New York. After accepting the order B had the sets tagged with A's name and set aside in his warehouse. Z, who has a judgment against B, directs the sheriff to seize all B's goods to satisfy the judgment and the sheriff seizes all television sets in the warehouse including those tagged for A. A brings a replevin suit against the sheriff to recover the 20 television sets on the ground that they are his property. Decision?

3. A, of Vancouver, B. C., made a C.I.F. contract with B of San Francisco, for the sale by A to B of 1,000 cases of salmon for $8,000. A shipped the goods, but due to the captain's negligence, the ship struck a reef, and the entire cargo was destroyed.

(a) State the acts required to be performed by A under this contract.

(b) Assuming that A can prove such performance, can he hold B for the $8,000?

(c) Explain any other possible rights or liabilities of the parties involved.

4. N sold and delivered a radio to P on 10 days' approval. On the twelfth day, P without giving notice to N, sold the radio to T for cash, T to have the right to return it in 20 days. Before the expiration of the 20 days N learned of the sale to T, and not having been paid by P, he (N) sues T for recovery of the radio. Decision?

5. A in New Orleans ordered 200 bolts of cloth from B in New York, to be shipped by the next boat from New York to New Orleans. B received and accepted the order on Tuesday morning. A boat left New York for New Orleans every Monday morning. B had plenty of time to ship by the boat leaving on the following Monday morning but negligently failed to get the cloth to the wharf until the boat had left. The goods were thereupon stored in a warehouse belonging to the owners of the boat to await the sailing one week later. Two days later the warehouse burned down and the cloth was totally destroyed. B sues A for the price of the cloth. Decision?

6. A agreed to sell and deliver to B on the following day three specific used typewriters, all similar in make and value, for $150, title to pass on delivery and payment. During the night one of the typewriters was stolen from A's store. The next day, A tendered the two remaining type-

writers to B and demanded $100 payment. B refused to accept the typewriters or pay for them. A sues B. Decision?

7. On May 10, the A Company, acting through one Brown, entered into a contract with C for the installation of a milking machine at C's farm. Following the enumeration of the articles to be furnished, together with the price of each article, the written contract provided: "This outfit is subject to thirty days' free trial and is to be installed about June 1." Within thirty days after installation, the entire outfit, excepting the double utility unit, was destroyed by fire through no fault of C. The A company sued C to recover the value of the articles destroyed. Decision?

8. A, at Chicago, sells and ships, C. O. D., liquor to B, a resident of Ft. Wayne, Indiana. The liquor was destroyed in transit due to an unusual flood. A sues B for the purchase price and B defends on the ground that a sale of liquor in Ft. Wayne without a license is illegal. Decision?

9. A contracted to buy twenty cases of X Brand canned corn from B at a contract price of $600. Pursuant to the contract, B selected and set aside twenty cases of X Brand canned corn and tagged them "For A." The contract required B to ship the corn to A via T Railroad, F.O.B. Toledo. Before B delivered the corn to the railroad, the twenty cases were stolen from B's warehouse.

(a) Who is liable for the loss of the twenty cases of corn, A or B?

(b) Suppose B had delivered the corn to the railroad. After the corn had been loaded on a freight car, but before the train left the yard, the car was broken open and its contents, including the corn, stolen. As between A and B, who is liable for the loss?

(c) Would your answer in question (b) be the same if this were a C.O.D. contract, all other facts remaining the same?

CHAPTER 19

DOCUMENTS OF TITLE

Introductory. The use of documents as symbols for the ownership of goods in the possession of a bailee has been recognized by custom of merchants and by courts of law for centuries. It is a convenient way of dealing with goods which are in storage with a warehouseman or which are in the course of transportation and in the possession of a carrier. The basic requirements are a bailment and a document acknowledging receipt of the goods and stating the terms of the contract upon which they are being held or transported. The most commonly used documents of title are warehouse receipts and bills of lading.

Such documents in order or bearer form have acquired by mercantile custom, court decisions, and statutes, certain qualities of negotiability which may enable a transferee of the document to obtain greater rights to goods than his transferor could have transferred by dealing with the goods.

The form of a document of title is important in determining who has control of the goods represented thereby. The mercantile concept is that the person entitled by the form of the document to demand and receive possession of goods from the issuing bailee is the owner of the goods.

Documents of title are not fully negotiable in the same sense as negotiable instruments. They are not a substitute for the goods in the same way that negotiable instruments may be a substitute for money. Documents of title have inherent limitations. A negotiable instrument is an order or a promise to pay generally and not out of a particular fund. If the order or promise is to pay money out of a particular fund the instrument is non-negotiable. On the other hand, a document of title necessarily relates to and describes specific goods. If the goods were never received by the bailee as in the case of a document issued fraudulently, or if the goods were delivered to the bailee by a thief or unauthorized person, or if the goods were destroyed while in the possession of the bailee or if they were delivered by the bailee without a surrender of the document, it is obvious that upon or after the happening of any of these events, the document does not represent title to goods. Regardless of other consequences, a transfer of a document which has no goods behind it or which no longer represents the goods does not effect a transfer of title or any interest in goods.

Documents of title serve an important function in reserving or transferring a security interest in goods represented by the document because of the ease and facility with which they can be handled and transferred as compared to handling or transferring the goods themselves.

Applicability of the Uniform Commercial Code. The Code does not repeal or supersede all statutory regulation of documents of title. It repeals the Uniform Sales Act, the Uniform Warehouse Receipts Act, and the Uniform Bills of Lading Act (U.B.L.A.), and brings together and modernizes the subject matter of these older statutes in Article 7. However, the Code does not cover interstate shipments or foreign commerce, and is expressly subject to applicable Federal statutes including the Federal Bills of Lading Act, the Interstate Commerce Act, the Harter Act of 1893 regulating offshore ocean commerce, the Carriage of Goods by Sea Act, and the United States Warehouse Act. Section 7–103.

Definitions. The Code provides definitions of the various terms necessary to an understanding of this subject matter:

"Document" means document of title as defined in the general definitions in Article 1 (Section 1–201). Section 7–102(1) (e).

"Document of title" includes bill of lading dock warrant, dock receipt, warehouse receipt or order for the delivery of goods, and also any other document which in the regular course of business or financing is treated as adequately evidencing that the person in possession of it is entitled to receive, hold and dispose of the document and the goods it covers. To be a document of title a document must purport to be issued by or addressed to a bailee and purport to cover goods in the bailee's possession which are either identified or are fungible portions of an identified mass. Section 1–201(15).

"Bill of lading" means a document evidencing the receipt of goods for shipment issued by a person engaged in the business of transporting or forwarding goods, and includes an airbill. "Airbill" means a document serving for air transportation as a bill of lading does for marine or rail transportation, and includes an air consignment note or air waybill. Section 1–201(6).

"Warehouse receipt" means a receipt issued by a person engaged in the business of storing goods for hire. Section 1–201(45).

"Bailee" means the person who by a warehouse receipt, bill of lading or other document of title acknowledges possession of goods and contracts to deliver them. Section 7–102(1) (a).

"Warehouseman" is a person engaged in the business of storing goods for hire. Section 7–102(1) (h).

"Delivery order" means a written order to deliver goods directed to a warehouseman, carrier or other person who in the ordinary course of business issues warehouse receipts or bills of lading. Section 7–102(1) (d).

"Consignee" means the person named in a bill to whom or to whose order the bill promises delivery. Section 7–102(1) (c).

"Bearer" means the person in possession of an instrument, document of title, or security payable to bearer or indorsed in blank. Section 1–201(5).

"Purchase" includes taking by sale, discount, negotiation, mortgage, pledge, lien, issue or re-issue, gift or any other voluntary transaction creating an interest in property. Section 1–201(32).

"Purchaser" means a person who takes by purchase. Section 1–201(33).

"Holder" means a person who is in possession of a document of title or an instrument or an investment security drawn, issued or indorsed to him or to his order or to bearer or in blank. Section 1–201(20).

Warehouse Receipts. A warehouse receipt is not required to be in any particular form. Section 7–202 of the Code provides that a warehouseman is liable for damages caused to any person by reason of the failure of the receipt to contain any of the following:

(1) Location of warehouse where goods are stored.

(2) Date of issue of the receipt.

(3) Consecutive number of the receipt.

(4) Statement whether the goods will be delivered to bearer, to a specified person, or to order.

(5) Rate of storage and handling charges.

(6) Description of the goods or of the packages containing them.

(7) Signature of the warehouseman or his agent.

(8) If the receipt is for goods owned by the warehouseman, either solely or as co-owner, the facts of such ownership.

(9) Statement of advances made or liabilities incurred for which the warehouseman claims a lien or security interest.

Duties of Warehouseman. The warehouseman, or other issuer of a document of title other than a bill of lading is liable to a bona fide purchaser for value of the document for damages caused by non-receipt or misdescription of the goods, unless the document conspicuously indicates that the issuer does not know whether the goods or any part of them were in fact received or whether they conform to the description in kind, quantity, or condition. In such case the warehouseman may qualify the receipt or description of the goods by conspicuously stating on the document "CONTENTS, CONDITION AND QUALITY UNKNOWN", or "SAID TO CONTAIN", or words of similar import. Section 7–203.

A warehouseman is under the following duty of care:

> A warehouseman is liable for damages for loss of or injury to the goods caused by his failure to exercise such care in regard to them as a reasonably careful man would exercise under like circumstances but unless otherwise agreed he is not liable for damages which could not have been avoided by the exercise of such care. Section 7–204(1).

The warehouseman must keep separate the goods covered by each receipt although different lots of fungible goods may be commingled. Section 7–207 provides:

> (1) Unless the warehouse receipt otherwise provides, a warehouseman must keep separate the goods covered by each receipt so as to permit at all times identification and delivery of those goods except that different lots of fungible goods may be commingled.

> (2) Fungible goods so commingled are owned in common by the persons entitled thereto and the warehouseman is severally liable to each owner for that owner's share. Where because of overissue a mass of fungible goods is insufficient to meet all the receipts which the warehouseman has issued against it, the persons entitled include all holders to whom overissued receipts have been duly negotiated.

The warehouseman must deliver the goods to the person entitled to receive them under the terms of the warehouse receipt. If he has already delivered the goods to another, the burden is on him to establish that such delivery was rightful as against the holder of the document. Similarly, if the goods have become damaged, lost, or destroyed, the burden is on the warehouseman to prove by evidence the facts and circumstances which establish his non-liability. Section 7–403 (1). It may be noted that the optional language in Section 7–403(1) (b) changes the common-law rule as to burden of proof with respect to negligence.

If a warehouseman issues a negotiable warehouse receipt in blank, and the blank is subsequently filled in without authority, a purchaser of the receipt for value without notice of the lack of authority may treat the insertion as authorized. The warehouseman is liable to such purchaser upon the terms of the document as filled in. However, if a receipt has been altered without authority it is enforceable against the warehouseman issuer only according to its original tenor. Section 7–208.

Contractual Limitation of Liability of Warehouseman. The extent of the liability of a warehouseman may be limited by a provision in the warehouse receipt fixing a specific maximum liability per article, or item, or unit of weight. This limitation does not apply in the event of a conversion of the goods by the warehouseman to his own use. Section 7–204(2).

Bona Fide Purchaser of Fungible Goods from Warehouseman. The Code protects bona fide purchasers of fungible goods from a warehouseman-dealer in such goods. If a warehouseman is in the business of buying and selling fungible goods, a buyer of such goods from him in the ordinary course of business takes them free of any claim under an outstanding warehouse receipt even though duly negotiated. Section 7–205. The protection of the buyer of the goods as against the holders of negotiable warehouse receipts is consistent with the warehouseman's right of commingling fungible goods and the reasonable commercial expectations of bailors in this type of situation.

Thus, the owner or grower of wheat delivers it to a grain elevator either by way of sale or bailment. If it is a sale, the warehouseman becomes the owner of an undivided fractional interest in the mass of grain in the elevator as tenant in common; and if a bailment, the bailor acquires such interest in lieu of his former complete ownership of specific wheat. Where the operator of the elevator (bailee warehouseman) is also buying and selling grain on his own account, the bailor should recognize the possibility of loss by reason of a sale by the warehouseman to third parties in the ordinary course of business.

Termination of Storage. A warehouseman is not required to keep the goods indefinitely. At the termination of the period of storage stated in the document, the warehouseman may notify the person on whose account the goods are held to pay accrued storage charges and remove the goods. If no period of time is stated in the document, the warehouseman is required to give 30 days notice to pay charges and remove the goods. A shorter time, which must be reasonable, is permitted if the goods are about to deteriorate or decine in value to less than the amount of the warehouseman's lien, or if the quality or condition of the goods cause them to be a hazard to other property or to persons. Section 7–206.

Lien of Warehouseman. To enforce the payment of his charges and necessary expenses in connection with keeping and handling the goods a warehouseman has a lien on the goods which enables him to sell them at public or private sale after notice, and to apply the net proceeds of the sale to the amount of his charges.

As against the holder of a negotiable warehouse receipt to whom it has been duly negotiated, this lien is limited to charges at the rate specified in the receipt, and if none are specified, to a reasonable charge for storage of the goods subsequent to the date of the receipt. Section 7–209(1).

The Code provides a more swift and flexible procedure for enforcement of the lien of a warehouseman against goods stored by a merchant in the ordinary course of business, usually for resale, than against goods such as household furniture stored by owners for convenience or not by way of operation of a business. Section 7–210.

Bills of Lading. A bill of lading is a document issued by a carrier upon receipt of goods for transportation. It serves a threefold function: (1) as a receipt for the goods; (2) as evidence of the contract of affreightment, and (3) as a document of title.

Under the Code bills of lading may be issued not only by common carriers, but by contract carriers, freight forwarders, or any person engaged in the business of transporting or forwarding goods, and the term includes an airbill. Section 1–201(6).

Duties of Issuer of Bill of Lading. The Code treats the duties of a carrier and those of a warehouseman in separate sections. Their functions, namely, transportation and storage, are different, and in addition common carriers of goods are extraordinary bailees under the law and subject to a greater degree of liability than an ordinary bailee such as a warehouseman. See Chapter 16 on Carriers and Innkeepers.

For this reason the duties of an issuer of a bill of lading under the Code are set forth separately from those of a warehouseman. The student should note the differences.

The carrier is liable to the consignee of a non-negotiable bill who has given value in good faith or a holder to whom a negotiable bill has been duly negotiated for damages caused by misdating the bill or by non-receipt or misdescription of the goods, unless the document indicates that the issuer does not know whether the goods were in fact received or conform to the kind, quantity or condition described. In such case the carrier may qualify its obligation by stating on the document: "contents or condition of contents of packages unknown," or "said to contain", or "shipper's weight, load and count", or words of similar import. Section 7–301.

While its broad duty of care is similar to that of a warehouseman, the extraordinary liability of the common carrier at common law is preserved in Section 7–309(1):

> A carrier who issues a bill of lading whether negotiable or non-negotiable must exercise the degree of care in relation to the goods which a reasonably careful man would exercise under like circumstances. This subsection does not repeal or change any law or rule of law which imposes liability upon a common carrier for damages not caused by its negligence.

A carrier is not in the business of buying and selling goods, as a warehouseman may be, and therefore no special rule is required as to buyers of fungible goods from warehousemen, as provided in Section 7–205.

The carrier must deliver the goods to the person entitled to receive them under the terms of the bill of lading. The carrier's duty in this respect is similar to that of the warehouseman. Section 7–403(1).

Any unauthorized alteration of a bill of lading or the unauthorized filling in of a blank in a bill of lading leaves the bill enforceable only according to its original tenor. Section 7–306. The carrier thus has greater protection than the warehouseman in the case of an unauthorized filling in of a blank. Section 7–208.

Contractual Limitation of Liability of Carrier. Although carriers have for many years been permitted to limit their liability contractually with respect to interstate shipments (Interstate Commerce Act, U. S. Code, Title 49, Section 20), in many States a limitation of liability was not permitted as to intrastate shipments.

The Code allows a carrier to limit its liability by contract in all cases where its rates are dependent upon value and the shipper is given an opportunity to declare a higher value. The limitation does not apply to a conversion of the goods by the carrier to its own use. Section 7–309(2) provides:

> Damages may be limited by a provision that the carrier's liability shall not exceed a value stated in the document if the carrier's rates are dependent upon value and the consignor by the carrier's tariff is afforded an opportunity to declare a higher value or a value as lawfully provided in the tariff, or where no tariff is filed he is otherwise advised of such opportunity; but no such limitation is effective with respect to the carrier's liability for conversion to its own use.

Through Bills of Lading. A bill of lading may provide that the issuer deliver the goods to a connecting carrier for further transportation to destination. Manifestly, the carrier accepting goods for shipment does not itself provide service to every place of destination. It will endeavor to route the shipment in such manner as will give the initial carrier the longest haul on its line in order to obtain maximum freight revenue, before delivery to a connecting carrier which may or may not be the destination carrier. A bill of lading which specifies one or more connecting carriers is called a "through bill of lading."

The initial or originating carrier which receives the goods from the shipper and issues a through bill of lading, which includes transportation on other lines, is liable to the holder of the document for loss or damage to the goods caused by any connecting or delivering carrier. Section 7–302(1). A carrier, however, is not required to issue through bills of lading.

Unlike the initial carrier, the liability of the connecting carrier is limited to the period while the goods are in its possession.

The carrier issuing a through bill of lading is entitled to recover from the connecting or delivering carrier in possession of the goods when loss or damage occurred the amount of damages that it has been obliged to pay to any one entitled to recover under the document, together with the reasonable expenses of defending any action brought against it in connection with such loss or damage. Section 7–302(3).

Thus, A in Milwaukee, Wisconsin, receives an order for a carload of merchandise from buyer B in Portland, Maine. A delivers the merchandise to the Chicago and North Western Ry. Co. in Milwaukee which issues a through bill of lading routing the shipment by C. & N. W. to Chicago, thence by New York Central R. R. to New York, thence by New York, New Haven & Hartford R. R. to Boston, thence by Boston and Maine R. R. to destination. Assume that the document issued by the C. & N. W. is a straight or non-negotiable bill of lading naming B as consignee. The merchandise is damaged while moving from Boston to Portland under circumstances which make the carrier Boston and Maine R. R. liable. The consignee B is entitled to recover the entire loss from the Chicago and North Western Ry. Co. which issued the bill of lading although it had the least haul and least participation in the freight charges. The C. & N. W. may then recover from the Boston and Maine R. R. If the through bill of lading were negotiable, that is, in order form, the same result would follow with respect to liability and the holder of the bill of lading could recover from the initial carrier.

Diversion or Reconsignment of Goods. A shipment of goods may be diverted or reconsigned when in the course of transportation. This may occur when the shipper has no buyer of the goods at the time of shipment. If the goods are perishable, such as fruits and vegetables, they are usually loaded in iced cars at the local market where grown and shipped immediately to a metropolitan market. The carrier issues a shipper's order bill of lading, or a straight bill naming the shipper or his agent as consignee. While the goods are moving on the rails or on the highways, the shipper makes a contract for their

sale and accordingly instructs the carrier to reconsign them or divert them to the buyer.

Section 7–303 provides:

> (1) Unless the bill of lading otherwise provides, the carrier may deliver the goods to a person or destination other than that stated in the bill or may otherwise dispose of the goods on instructions from
>
> (a) the holder of a negotiable bill; or
>
> (b) the consignor on a non-negotiable bill notwithstanding contrary instructions from the consignee; or
>
> (c) the consignee on a non-negotiable bill in the absence of contrary instructions from the consignor, if the goods have arrived at the billed destination or if the consignee is in possession of the bill; or
>
> (d) the consignee on a non-negotiable bill if he is entitled as against the consignor to dispose of them.
>
> (2) Unless such instructions are noted on a negotiable bill of lading, a person to whom the bill is duly negotiated can hold the bailee according to the original terms.

If the carrier has issued a non-negotiable bill of lading covering the goods, a diversion of them or change in shipping instructions by the consignor whereby the carrier does not deliver the goods to the consignee defeats all rights of the consignee against the carrier. Section 7–504(3).

Destination Bills of Lading. A novel provision in the Code designed to facilitate the use of negotiable bills in connection with fast shipments permits the carrier to issue the bill at destination or any other place requested by the consignor. The carrier is under no duty to issue a destination bill.

However, such a bill may be useful where goods shipped overnight by fast truck, rail, or air service are scheduled to arrive before a document issued at place of origin could be received by mail, and the carrier has inadequate terminal facilities for holding the goods. The seller may request the carrier to issue the bill of lading to the order of a bank located in the city of destination and deliver the bill to the bank. The seller sends to the bank by telegraph a draft drawn on the buyer. Upon honoring the draft, the bank indorses and delivers the bill of lading to the buyer.

Section 7–305 provides:

(1) Instead of issuing a bill of lading to the consignor at the place of shipment a carrier may at the request of the consignor procure the bill to be issued at destination or at any other place designated in the request.

(2) Upon request of anyone entitled as against the carrier to control the goods while in transit and on surrender of any outstanding bill of lading or other receipt covering such goods, the issuer may procure a substitute bill to be issued at any place designated in the request.

Lien of Carrier. Upon goods in its possession covered by a bill of lading the carrier has a lien for its charges, including demurrage and terminal charges, and expenses necessary for preservation of the goods. As against a purchaser for value of a negotiable bill of lading this lien is limited to charges stated in the bill or in the applicable published tariff, and if no charges are so stated, to a reasonable charge. Section 7–307(1).

If the consignor had no authority of the owner of the goods to ship them or subject them to such charges and expenses, the lien is nevertheless effective unless the carrier had notice of the lack of authority. Section 7–307(2).

The enforcement of the lien of the carrier is by public or private sale of the goods after notice to all persons known to the carrier to claim an interest in them. The sale must be on terms which are "commercially reasonable", and must be conducted in a "commercially reasonable manner." Section 7–308 (1).

A purchaser in good faith of goods sold to enforce the lien takes free of any rights of persons against whom the lien was valid, even though the enforcement of the lien does not comply with the requirements of the Code. This rule applies to both carrier's and warehouseman's liens. Sections 7–308(4), 7–310 (5).

Negotiability of Documents of Title. In the prior discussion and in quoted sections of the Code reference has been made to negotiable and non-negotiable documents without defining these terms. Section 7–104 of the Code provides:

(1) A warehouse receipt, bill of lading or other document of title is negotiable

(a) if by its terms the goods are to be delivered to bearer or to the order of a named person; or

(b) where recognized in overseas trade, if it runs to a named person or assigns.

(2) Any other document is non-negotiable. A bill of lading in which it is stated that the goods are consigned to a named person is not made negotiable by a provision that the goods are to be delivered only against a written order signed by the same or another named person.

The concept of negotiability has been long established in the law and is well known to bankers and business men. It is encountered not only in connection with documents of title, but also in the field of commercial paper commonly known as negotiable instruments which are treated in Chapters 25 to 29 of this book, and in connection with investment securities which include corporate stock certificates treated in Chapter 38.

Negotiability is a characteristic which the law gives to certain instruments and documents that are in a certain prescribed form. The magic words in the form are "bearer" or "order." A promise to deliver goods to a named person is manifestly different from a promise to deliver goods to bearer or to the order of a named person. The first promise may be safely performed by delivering the goods to the person named. It is not necessary for the issuer to obtain surrender of a non-negotiable document. The second promise may not be safely performed without surrender of the document by the bearer or by the person to whom the named person ordered the goods to be delivered. The first promise is one which the issuer does not intend to have circulate freely in the market place. The second is one intended to go to market, to pass from hand to hand and to circulate freely, as indicated by the terms of the promise. The first promise does not provide negotiability to the document containing it. The second promise does. A non-negotiable document may be assigned but not negotiated. Only a negotiable document or instrument may be negotiated.

This brings us to the next question. What is the importance of negotiation? What is its effect? How is it useful to bankers and business men?

Negotiation is a form of transfer whereby the transferee acquires not merely the rights which the transferor had but also direct rights based upon the language of the promise contained in the instrument or document. Where a property right is merely assigned, the assignee takes only such rights as the assignor had. He stands in the shoes of the assignor, and his rights are subject to all defects and infirmities in the title of the assignor. However, where a document is negotiable and is transferred by due negotiation, the transferee is one to whom the promise of the issuer runs and he thereby acquires the direct obligation of the issuer. Thus, if A issues a warehouse receipt to B wherein he promises to deliver the goods to bearer, and subsequently X presents the document to A and demands the goods, X is the bearer and therefore the very person to whom A promised to deliver the goods. The same is true with respect to a properly indorsed order form warehouse receipt or bill of lading.

The effect of due negotiation is that it creates new rights in the holder of the docu-

ment. Upon due negotiation the transferee does not stand in the shoes of his transferor. Defects and defenses available against the transferor are not available against the new holder. His rights are newly created by the negotiation and free of such defects and defenses. This enables bankers and business men to extend credit upon documents of title without concern about possible adverse claims or the rights of third parties.

The form of negotiation and requirements of "due negotiation" are set forth in Section 7–501:

(1) A negotiable document of title running to the order of a named person is negotiated by his indorsement and delivery. After his indorsement in blank or to bearer any person can negotiate it by delivery alone.

(2) (a) A negotiable document of title is also negotiated by delivery alone when by its original terms it runs to bearer;

(b) when a document running to the order of a named person is delivered to him the effect is the same as if the document had been negotiated.

(3) Negotiation of a negotiable document of title after it has been indorsed to a specified person requires indorsement by the special indorsee as well as delivery.

(4) A negotiable document of title is "duly negotiated" when it is negotiated in the manner stated in this Section to a holder who purchases it in good faith without notice of any defense against or claim to it on the part of any person and for value, unless it is established that the negotiation is not in the regular course of business or financing or involves receiving the document in settlement or payment of a money obligation.

(5) Indorsement of a non-negotiable document neither makes it negotiable nor adds to the transferee's rights.

(6) The naming in a negotiable bill of a person to be notified of the arrival of the goods does not limit the negotiability of the bill nor constitute notice to a purchaser thereof of any interest of such person in the goods.

It will be observed that "due negotiation" is a term peculiar to Article 7 and requires not only that the purchaser of the negotiable document must take it in good faith without notice of any adverse claim or defense and pay value, but also that he must take it in the regular course of business or financing, and value does not include the settlement or payment of a pre-existing debt. Thus, a transfer for value of a negotiable document of title to a non-business man or non-banker, such as a college professor or playboy, would not be a due negotiation.

The rights acquired by due negotiation are set forth in Section 7–502:

(1) Subject to the following section and to the provisions of Section 7–205 on fungible goods, a holder to whom a negotiable document of title has been duly negotiated acquires thereby:

(a) title to the document;

(b) title to the goods;

(c) all rights accruing under the law of agency or estoppel, including rights to goods delivered to the bailee after the document was issued; and

(d) the direct obligation of the issuer to hold or deliver the goods according to the terms of the document free of any defense or claim by him except those arising under the terms of the document or under this Article. In the case of a delivery order the bailee's obligation accrues only upon acceptance and the obligation acquired by the holder is that the issuer and any indorser will procure the acceptance of the bailee.

(2) Subject to the following section, title and rights so acquired are not defeated by any stoppage of the goods represented by the document or by surrender of such goods by the bailee, and are not impaired even though the negotiation or any prior negotiation constituted a breach of duty or even though any person has been deprived of possession of the document by misrepresentation, fraud, accident, mistake, duress, loss, theft or conversion, or even though a previous sale or other transfer of the goods or document has been made to a third person.

The indorsement of a document of title does not make the indorser liable for any default by the bailee or by previous indorsers. Section 7–505.

If an order form document of title is transferred without a requisite indorsement, the transferee has the right to compel his transferor to supply any necessary indorsement. This right is specifically enforceable in a court of equity. The transfer becomes a negotiation only as of the time the indorsement is supplied. Section 7–506.

Rights Acquired in the Absence of Due Negotiation. If a non-negotiable document is transferred, or a negotiable document is transferred without due negotiation, the transferee acquires rights as set forth in Section 7–504:

(1) A transferee of a document, whether negotiable or non-negotiable, to whom the document has been delivered but not duly negotiated, acquires the title and rights which his transferor had or had actual authority to convey.

(2) In the case of a non-negotiable document, until but not after the bailee receives notification of the transfer, the rights of the transferee may be defeated

(a) by those creditors of the transferor who could treat the sale as void under Section 2–402; or

(b) by a buyer from the transferor in ordinary course of business if the bailee has delivered the goods to the buyer or received notification of his rights; or

(c) as against the bailee by good faith dealings of the bailee with the transferor.

(3) A diversion or other change of shipping instructions by the consignor in a non-negotiable bill of lading which causes the bailee not to deliver to the consignee defeats the consignee's title to the goods if they have been delivered to a buyer in ordinary course of business and in any event defeats the consignee's rights against the bailee.

(4) Delivery pursuant to a non-negotiable document may be stopped by a seller under

Section 2–705, and subject to the requirement of due notification there provided. A bailee honoring the seller's instructions is entitled to be indemnified by the seller against any resulting loss or expense.

Ineffective Documents of Title. It is fundamental that a thief or finder of goods may not by delivery of them to a warehouseman or carrier and issuance to the thief or finder of a negotiable document of title defeat the rights of the owner by a negotiation of the document. While such document would be genuine and its indorsement by the thief or finder not a forgery, it would in such case not represent title to the goods.

In order that a person obtain title to goods by a negotiation to him of a document, the goods must have been delivered to the issuer of the document by the owner of the goods or by one to whom the owner has delivered or entrusted them with actual or apparent authority to ship, store, or sell them. Section 7–503(1).

Protection of Warehousemen and Carriers Who Deliver Goods Pursuant to Document of Title. A warehouseman or carrier may deliver goods according to the terms of the document which it has issued, or otherwise dispose of the goods as provided in the Code, without incurring liability even though the document did not represent title to the goods. It must have acted in good faith and complied with reasonable commercial standards in both the receipt and delivery or other disposition of the goods. The bailee has no liability even though the person from whom it received the goods had no authority to obtain the issuance of the document or dispose of the goods, and even though the person to whom it delivered the goods had no authority to receive them. Section 7–404.

This protection accorded the issuer of a document of title does not apply generally to a person acting in good faith and in the ordinary course of business who resells goods which he has received or purchased from a thief or person with no authority to dispose of them. Thus, a factor who in good faith receives goods from a thief or finder and resells them in the ordinary course of business is liable to the true owner for conversion of the goods.

A carrier or warehouseman who receives goods from a thief or finder and later delivers them to a person to whom the thief or finder ordered them to be delivered is not liable to the true owner of the goods. Even a sale of the goods by the carrier or warehouseman to enforce a lien for transportation or storage charges and expenses would not subject it to liability.

Warehousemen and carriers are regarded as furnishing a service necessary to trade and commerce. They are not a link in the chain of title, and do not purport to represent the owner in transactions affecting title to the goods. Consequently, it is a sound rule which relieves them from liability upon delivery of the goods pursuant to their contract under the document of title even though the document is ineffective against the true owner of the goods.

Warranties on Negotiation or Transfer. A person who either negotiates or transfers a document of title for value, other than a collecting bank or other intermediary, assumes certain warranty obligations unless otherwise agreed, as provided in Section 7–507:

> Where a person negotiates or transfers a document of title for value otherwise than as a mere intermediary under the next following section, then unless otherwise agreed he warrants to his immediate purchaser only in addition to any warranty made in selling the goods
>
> (a) that the document is genuine; and
>
> (b) that he has no knowledge of any fact which would impair its validity or worth; and
>
> (c) that his negotiation or transfer is rightful and fully effective with

respect to the title to the document and the goods it represents.

Lost or Missing Documents of Title. If a document has been lost, stolen, or destroyed, a claimant of the goods may apply to a court for an order directing delivery of the goods or the issuance of a substitute document. Compliance of the carrier or warehouseman with the order of court relieves it of liability. Section 7–601(1).

The claimant must provide security approved by the court if the missing document is negotiable.

If the carrier or warehouseman without a court order delivers goods to a person claiming them under a missing negotiable document, it is liable to any person who is thereby injured. Delivery to such person in good faith is not a conversion of the goods if security is posted in an amount at least double the value of the goods to indemnify any person injured by the delivery who files notice of claim within one year. Section 7–601(2).

Freight Forwarder Bills of Lading. Freight forwarders are engaged in the business of consolidating less-than-carload (l.c.l.) shipments into carloads to secure the benefit of lower carload rates. They are particularly active in interstate shipments. By the Interstate Commerce Act, they are required to issue bills of lading to their shippers and a 1950 amendment to the Act defines them as "common carriers." U.S.C.A., Title 49, Section 1002(a) (5). Thus, while freight forwarders do not in fact engage in carriage, they are treated as common carriers under the Interstate Commerce Act, so that bills of lading issued by them for interstate shipments are governed by the Federal Bills of Lading Act, and their responsibilities and obligations upon such bills of lading are those of any issuing carrier.

Section 7–503 of the Code provides:

> (3) Title to goods based upon a bill of lading issued to a freight forwarder is sub-

ject to the rights of anyone to whom a bill issued by the freight forwarder is duly negotiated; but delivery by the carrier in accordance with Part 4 of this Article pursuant to its own bill of lading discharges the carrier's obligation to deliver.

Although a freight forwarder is not a bailee as not in possession of the goods, it may issue a certificate or sub-bill of lading based upon the bill of lading issued to its order by the carrier. Title to goods based upon the bill of lading issued by the carrier is subordinate to the rights of a holder of the freight forwarder's bill of lading duly negotiated.

CASES

MARCUS v. ARMER, 117 Tex. 368, 5 S.W.2d 960, 60 A.L.R. 672 (1928). *Greenwood, J.* * * * We regard as unassailable the following conclusions of Mr. Benjamin:

"If A in New York orders goods from B in Liverpool without sending the money for them, B may execute the order in one of two modes without assuming risk. B may take the bill of lading, making the goods deliverable to his own order, or that of his agent in New York, and send it to his agent, with instructions not to transfer it to A except on payment for the goods. Or B may draw a bill of exchange for the price of the goods on A, and sell the bill to a Liverpool banker, transferring to the banker the bill of lading for the goods, to be delivered to A on due payment of the bill of exchange. Now in both these modes of doing business, it is impossible to infer that B had the least idea of passing the property to A at the time of appropriating the goods to the contract. So that, although he may write to A, and specify the packages and marks identifying the goods, and although he may accompany this with an invoice, stating that these specific goods are shipped for A's account, and in accordance with A's order, making his election final and determinate, the property in the goods will nevertheless remain in B till the bill of lading has been endorsed and delivered up to A." Benjamin on Sales (6th Ed.), pp. 420, 421.

Professor Williston says:

"It follows from what has been said that if the seller takes a bill of lading in which he is named as consignee as well as consignor, the carrier is a bailee for the seller, not the buyer, and the title is retained. The practice of taking bills of lading in this form has been common for centuries in order to preserve to the seller a hold upon the goods during transit, and many cases have sustained the validity of this retention of title. This principle is applicable even though the goods are shipped on the buyer's vessel, for the captain having authority to sign bills of lading by so doing constitutes himself as an independent bailee of the goods for the shipper. It is commonly said that the seller by taking the bill of lading in his own name reserves the jus disponendi or right of disposal of the goods, and the latter expression is used in the section of the English Sale of Goods Act corresponding to that here under discussion. There seems no doubt that the seller who thus consigns the goods to himself has complete control over them, and that the so-called jus disponendi is in fact title. The seller may not only retain the goods until the buyer performs his obligation under the contract, but may, even in violation of the contract, dispose of them to third persons. If the seller does this, of course he is liable in damages to the buyer, but the second purchaser from the seller acquires an indefeasible right." 1 Williston on Sales, 2d Ed., Sec. 283, pp. 637, 638.

KORESKA v. UNITED CARGO CORP.

(1965) 23 App.Div.2d 37, 258 N.Y.S.2d 432.

PER CURIAM. Plaintiff, an Austrian manufacturer and seller of thermographic copying paper, appeals from an order denying his motion for summary judgment for the value of paper allegedly converted by defendant United Cargo Corporation. United, a carrier, having issued a negotiable order bill of lading for the goods, consisting of four large packages, delivered them to the New York purchaser without requiring or taking up the bill of lading, and before plaintiff had received his purchase price.

The substantial question presented is whether United has raised a triable issue of fact in contending that it was excused from its duty of requiring surrender of the bill of lading before delivering the goods. United urges that it was so excused by an oral waiver made by plaintiff's agent and also by a binding trade custom or course of dealing.

It is concluded that United has failed to raise any triable issue as to the alleged oral waiver, and that the order denying plaintiff's motion for summary judgment should be reversed, and his motion granted.

The material facts are as follows. Defendant United is the operator of a container delivery service between the United States and Europe. Plaintiff Koreska had either sold or had contracted to sell the goods in issue to a New York buyer, third-party defendant Parker Whitney, Ltd. Thereafter a forwarding agency, Allgemeine Land und Seetransportgesellschaft Herman Ludwig, procured from United the negotiable bill of lading, naming Koreska's collecting agent, a New York bank, as consignee. The document required that the arrival notice be sent to the New York buyer, Parker Whitney. On arrival of the goods in New York, in November, 1963, United delivered them to the buyer, Parker Whitney, without requiring the bill of lading.

* * *

It is claimed that there are contested factual issues whether the seller, Koreska, waived the requirement that United, the issuer of the negotiable document of title, take it up before delivering the goods. United's New York import manager states that in accordance with a regular course of dealing between the parties Allgemeine's New York representative, on behalf of Koreska, orally authorized United to make delivery to Parker Whitney without awaiting presentment of the bill of lading. Allgemeine's New York representative, on the other hand, denies having given such permission, denies that Allgemeine was acting as Koreska's agent, and denies knowledge of such a course of dealing or trade custom.

Although there may be factual issues with respect to the making of the oral waiver and the existence of the course of dealing, United has failed to give any evidentiary facts showing that Allgemeine was Koreska's agent for purposes of modifying the terms of the bill of lading. The evidentiary facts are to the contrary. Another bill of lading, covering a prior sale from Koreska to Parker Whitney expressly refers to Allgemeine as "agent of UCC", meaning agent of defendant United. Moreover, both this prior bill of lading and the one covering the goods in issue show the New York bank as consignee and require that the goods be delivered to its order. Thus the New York bank was known to United to be the appropriate New York representative of Koreska on all matters relating to delivery of the goods.

It is hornbook law that an agent may be one party's agent for one purpose and another party's agent for another [citation]. Thus Allgemeine may have had powers, not shown in this record, to bind United with respect to the issuance of a bill of lading and perhaps to bind Koreska with respect to receipt thereof and payment therefor. Even if such be the case, the agent's powers are limited to the particular purpose for which the agency is, or appears to be, created [citations].

* * *

Even if a factual issue had been raised with respect to Allgemeine's agency, Koreska would be entitled to summary judgment. In the case of an order, or negotiable bill of lading, as opposed to a straight, or non-negotiable bill, it is ordinarily the consignee or other holder of the negotiable bill, who alone is entitled to authorize a diversion or modification of the delivery term (cf. U.C.C. §§ 7-303 [1] [a], 7-403). Even if Allgemeine obtained possession of the bill after authorizing a waiver, as claimed by United, it was never a holder with power to divert in the absence of an actual indorsement of the bill to it (cf. U.C.C. § 1-201 [20]). Moreover the seller-shipper, Koreska, never became a consignee or holder, and therefore did not, under these rules, have the power to divert the goods without the cooperation of its collecting agent-consignee, the New York bank. It follows that its alleged agent, Allgemeine, similarly had no such power.

A further reason why United may not avail itself of the alleged waiver, is that the waiver was oral only, and would modify the express term of the bill that delivery was to be made at the order of the New York bank consignee. One of the conditions printed on the back of the bill provides:

"None of the terms of this bill of lading shall be deemed to have been waived by any person unless by express waiver signed by such person, or his duly authorized agent."

Ordinary prudence, moreover, would dictate that the carrier require that such instructions be noted on the bill itself (cf. U.C.C. § 7-303 [2]).

For similar reasons evidence of the course of dealing or trade custom is also without significance. The express term, requiring delivery in accordance with the consignee's order, is controlling, whenever the course of dealing or trade custom are inconsistent with it [citations]; cf. U.C.C. § 1–205 [4]).

In the absence of a triable issue of fact, summary judgment must be granted. Summary relief is, moreover, particularly appropriate in commercial cases, such as this, where the injured party is far away and has relied on documentary rights and evidence. If a trade custom or the oral waiver by an unknown purported agent, contrary to the plain terms of trade documents, were given the effect contended for by United, the ability of such a distant person to engage in foreign trade in reliance on negotiable documents of title would be severely and unduly handicapped. Allowance of such a practice is certainly destructive of the integrity of documents used in international trade throughout the world.

* * *

Order, entered on October 19, 1964, reversed on the law with $30 costs and disbursements to appellant and the motion for summary judgment for $13,939.72, the invoice price, in favor of plaintiff is granted.

CHRISTOFFERSEN v. MURRAY PACKING CO.

(1965) 24 A.D.2d 587, 262 N.Y.S.2d 636.

MEMORANDUM BY THE COURT. In a replevin action, the plaintiff appeals from an order of the Supreme Court, Kings County, entered November 17, 1964, which denied his motion for summary judgment striking out the answers of the three defendants: Pride Wholesale Meat & Poultry Corp., Paul Castellano and Fort Meat Wholesalers, Inc.

Order reversed, with $10 costs and disbursements payable jointly by said defendants; plaintiff's motion granted; summary judgment directed in favor of plaintiff against said defendants, with costs; and action remitted to Special Term for the entry of judgment accordingly.

Plaintiff is a California turkey grower who contracted to ship a truck load of turkeys to the defendant Murray Packing Co., Inc. in New York. Plaintiff consigned the turkeys to himself and sent the bill of lading, together with a sight draft on Murray, to a New York bank for collection. Without paying the draft and without obtaining the bill of lading, Murray obtained possession of the turkeys from the truck driver of the carrier by telling him that the payment had been "taken care of." Thereafter Murray sold the turkeys to the defendant Pride Wholesale Meat & Poultry Corp., which in turn sold them to the defendants Paul Castellano and Fort Meat Wholesalers, Inc. Pride, Castellano and Fort Meat all claim to have been ignorant of Murray's wrongdoing.

The transaction is governed by the statutory provisions (Personal Property Law, § 101, subd. [2] and § 226, subd. [b]) as they existed at the time of the transaction. Those sections, which provide that the seller may retain property in the goods by shipping them to himself, are a codification of the common law [citation]. Even if plaintiff's interest in the goods be deemed to be only for the purpose of assuring payment by the buyer, and even if those deriving title from Murray were unaware of Murray's failure to pay, they had constructive notice that the title remained, as security, in the seller [citation]. Under the circumstances here, certain perquisites of title may have passed to the buyer but they coexisted with the rights retained by the seller. As stated by a noted author with respect to these coexisting rights of the buyer and seller: "The root of the difficulty is the failure to grasp the idea that more than one person can have a property right in the same goods" (2 Williston on Sales [rev. ed.], pp. 170–171).

Plaintiff did all he could to protect his interest in the goods. It was the three defendants here who relied on the reputation of Murray; and it is these defendants who must bear the consequences of their misplaced trust.

COOPER'S FINER FOODS v. PAN AMERICAN WORLD AIRWAYS

(1965 Fla.) 178 So.2d 62.

CARROLL, J. Cooper's Finer Foods, Inc., herein referred to as Cooper, sued Pan American World Airways, Inc., herein referred to as Pan American, and The First National Bank of Miami, herein referred to as the bank, in the civil court of record in Dade County. Cooper's claim against the bank was for damages for alleged wrongful payment on a letter of credit. Recovery was sought against Pan American for alleged negligent handling of certain documents in connection with a shipment, resulting in an unauthorized payment being made by the bank.

Plaintiff and both defendants moved for summary judgment. Based on the complaint and answers, and upon evidence consisting of documents, depositions, and interrogatories and answers thereto, the trial court granted summary judgment in favor of the plaintiff against the bank, and granted summary judgment in favor of the defendant Pan American. The bank appealed from the former judgment and Cooper appealed from the latter. The appeals were consolidated.

The material facts were not in dispute. To facilitate purchase of frozen shrimp from R. J. Zappi, a dealer in Caracas, Venezuela, Cooper arranged with The First National Bank of Miami to issue a letter of credit for $35,000 under which payment could be made to Zappi on sight draft for the invoice value of shipments of frozen shrimp of a designated size at a stated price per pound when the invoice was presented to the bank's correspondent, Banco de Commerce, Caracas, Venezuela, accompanied by certain documents listed in the letter of credit as follows: "Commercial invoice in triplicate; marine and war risks insurance policy or certificate in duplicate; copy of non-negotiable airway bill's of lading showing consignment to First National Bank of Miami, Miami, Florida," (for Cooper).

A shipment of shrimp invoiced at $4,175 was delivered to Pan American at Caracas for transportation to Miami as thus authorized. Airway bill of lading was issued for the shipment. As per custom there were twelve in number, three originals and nine copies. All bore the reception stamp of the carrier. Three were designated as originals, No. 1 for the issuing carrier, No. 2 for the consignee, and No. 3 for the consignor. Each of the remaining nine was marked "Copy." The copy with which this case is concerned was copy No. 9, which also bore the notation "For Sales Agent."

Upon discovering there was a lack of space for the shipment, Pan American returned the merchandise to the consignor, as it was entitled to do, and took up the consignor's bill of lading. Pan American did not take up copy No. 9.

Thereafter the consignor submitted the invoice and other specified papers, including copy No. 9 of the air bill of lading, to the bank in Caracas and thereupon, based on the letter of credit, received the invoiced amount of $4,175.

With reference to appeal No. 65–124, which concerns the summary judgment in favor of the plaintiff and against the bank, the determinative question is whether the copy of the air bill of lading which was submitted met the requirements for such as contained in the letter of credit. The trial court was of the opinion that it did not. We conclude that in so holding the able trial judge was in error.

The appellee Cooper contends that the notation on the copy of the bill of lading that it was for the sales agent was notice to the bank it was not an appropriate copy for submission under the letter of credit. We fail to see how such a notation appearing on the copy of the bill of lading could nullify its character or efficacy. For example, in view of the wording of the letter of credit, if the shipment had been made the bank could not have refused payment because the copy of bill of lading contained a notation that it was for the sales agent.

The appellee argues further that payment by the bank should not have been made without production of one of the three designated originals of the bill of lading. In answer the appellant points out that the letter of credit did not require that an "original" of the bill of lading should be submitted, but on the contrary specified that a "copy" be produced. The copy presented contained all that was required of it under the terms of the letter of credit and bore the carrier's reception stamp.

On the facts presented payment by the bank was proper as authorized by the letter of credit, and the bank's motion for summary judgment should not have been denied. Whereupon, the summary judgment appealed from in case No. 65–124 is reversed, and the cause is remanded with directions to enter summary judgment in favor of the defendant The First National Bank of Miami.

On the issue as to negligence of the defendant Pan American, the trial judge correctly determined there were no triable issues of fact, but erred in holding that Pan American was entitled to judgment as a matter of law.

Appellants contend that failure of the carrier, on rejecting the shipment and returning it to the consignor, to take up copies of the bill of lading which it had issued with its reception stamp thereon was negligence which proximately resulted in the loss to Cooper. That contention has merit. The record discloses that the carrier's reception stamp was placed on the copy in question; that Pan American knew of the letter of credit and was aware of the Uniform Customs Brochure No. 222, under which the bank was entitled to honor a draft accompanied by a bill of lading

(and, under the letter of credit, a *copy* of bill of lading) bearing the carrier's reception stamp. It was shown in a deposition of one of its employees that it was the custom of Pan American to take up all signed or stamped copies of bills of lading when goods were turned back to a shipper.

Pan American takes the position that only those bills of lading which were designated as originals should be considered as material or effective and that it had no responsibility to take up copies, as distinguished from originals of bills of lading. That argument is without force. For one thing, it was the carrier's custom to take up all copies which were signed or bore its reception stamp, when a shipment was returned to the consignor. And a fact which may not be avoided is that the carrier placed its reception stamp on the copy in question, and allowed it to remain outstanding with knowledge of the letter of credit and of the published regulation referred to. Without a copy of the bill of lading bearing the reception stamp of the carrier and thereby signifying that shipment as per invoice had been made, the consignor could not have obtained the undeserved payment. On the facts established, the liability of Pan American seems clear.

For the reasons stated the summary judgment for the defendant Pan American which is appealed from in case No. 64–782 is reversed, and the cause is remanded with directions to enter summary judgment for plaintiff against the defendant Pan American World Airways, Inc.

It is so ordered.

[Judgment for Plaintiff].

PROBLEMS

1. Pursuant to a contract with B, A shipped one carload of eggs, from Chicago to New York, taking from the carrier a shipper's order bill of lading, notify B in New York. A indorsed the bill of lading in blank, attached to it a draft drawn

on B for the amount of the price, and mailed both the draft and the bill of lading to C, A's agent in New York. C presented the papers to B in New York who took the bill of lading and gave C a check for the price drawn upon a Chicago bank. C promptly forwarded the check to A in Chicago who discovered two days later that B had insufficient funds in the drawee bank with which to pay the check. A immediately telegraphed this information to C who promptly demanded from B the return of the bill of lading. In the meantime B had transferred the bill of lading by delivery to D, a purchaser for value. What are the rights of the parties?

2. A shipped goods to B under a straight bill of lading. Instead of sending the bill of lading to B, A sent it to a bank in B's city, attached to a sight draft drawn by A on B for $1,000, the amount of the purchase price. A then wrote to B informing him of these facts. B did not go to the bank, but went to the freight station, obtained delivery of the goods, and disappeared. What rights, if any, has A?

3. A steals B's goods and consigns them to C or order over R.R. Co. which issues a negotiable bill of lading therefor. The bill of lading is duly indorsed by C and delivered for value to X, an innocent purchaser. As against B does X have title to the goods?

4. A, in Chicago, pursuant to a contract with B in New York, ships certain goods by railroad to New York, and takes from the carrier a shipper's order bill of lading which A indorses in blank and forwards by mail to C, his agent in New York, with instructions to deliver the bill of lading to B upon receipt of payment of the price for the goods. X, a thief, steals the bill of lading from C and transfers it for value to Y, a bona fide purchaser. Before the goods arrive in New York, B is petitioned into bankruptcy. What are the rights of the parties?

5. A, in Chicago, pursuant to a contract with B in Boston, shipped a carload of eggs via Michigan Central Railroad from Chicago to Boston, taking from the Michigan Central a shipper's order bill of lading which read "Notify B in Boston." A indorsed the bill of lading in blank, attached it to a thirty-day draft drawn on B for the price, and discounted the draft at the First National Bank in Chicago. The Bank promptly forwarded the draft and bill of lading attached to the Shawmut National Bank in Boston which

delivered the bill of lading to B upon obtaining B's acceptance of the draft, and thereupon returned the accepted draft to the First National Bank in Chicago. When the eggs arrived in Boston, B discovered that a large part of them were spoiled. B refused to take the eggs, and A was compelled to dispose of them. B did not pay the draft when it became due and A, who was obliged to pay the amount of the draft to the First National Bank, brings an action against B on the draft. What judgment?

6. B, in Chicago, sold five thousand cases of canned peas to C in New York, to be delivered by rail, F.O.B. Chicago, within 90 days. In order to fulfill his contract with C, B contracted to purchase 5,000 cases of canned peas from A. A agreed to deliver and load the peas on board railroad cars in Chicago within the 90 days specified in B's contract with C, and B agreed to pay cash upon such delivery. A delivered and loaded the peas as agreed and B gave A his check for the price. B immediately obtained negotiable bills of lading from the railroad company to the order of C, and mailed them to C. B's check did not clear. Who has title to the goods?

7. B Harvester Machine Company, Chicago, Illinois, sold twenty-five machines to C, a merchant in Lincoln, Nebraska. B Company shipped the machines to C over the Chicago and Northwestern Railway and forwarded an order bill of lading therefor to C. While the machines were in transit C, who was insolvent, made an assignment of his property, including the bill of lading, for the benefit of his creditors. B Company, on being advised of the facts and before the machines were delivered, exercised a right of stoppage in transitu by proper notice to the railroad company. C's assignee claimed the machines by reason of holding the bill of lading, maintaining that the transfer to him of the document terminated B Company's right of stoppage in transitu. To whom should the machines be awarded?

8. A, a New York merchant, purchased merchandise from B in Chicago. The contract of sale provided that the merchandise was sold f. o. b. the Pennsylvania Railroad at Chicago, payment to be made 60 days after delivery. B delivered the goods to the Pennsylvania Railroad at Chicago, took an order bill of lading in the name of A and forwarded it to A. Before the goods arrived at New York, B learned that A had become insolvent, and exercised a right of stoppage in transitu by proper notice to the railroad company.

Thereafter, and before the shipment reached New York, A indorsed and delivered the bill of lading to C, an innocent purchaser for value. C claimed the goods by reason of holding the bill of lading. To whom should the goods be awarded?

9. (a) A shipped a carload of furniture over the M Railroad. The railroad issued a bill of lading to the order of A. B stole the bill, indorsed A's name on it and sold it to C, an innocent purchaser, for value. M Railroad surrendered the furniture to C when C produced the bill of lading. Did C have title to the furniture?

(b) T, an employee of X Railroad, issued an order bill of lading to his friend, B. The bill purported to cover a carload of scrap iron shipped over X Railroad. Actually, no iron was shipped, although T's duties included the issuance of bills of lading for the railroad. B indorsed the bill of lading and sold it to P, a bona fide purchaser for value. Can P hold X Railroad liable?

CHAPTER 20

SALE OF GOODS BY NON-OWNER

Introductory. Numerous sales are made by the owners of goods through their duly authorized agents. A corporation can act in no other way than through an agent. The sale of goods by the authorized agent of the owner to whom they have been entrusted for sale is not a sale by a non-owner. The act of the agent is that of the principal and the sale is by the owner of the goods. Such transactions present no problem of ownership rights acquired by the buyer and therefore are not within the scope of this chapter.

This chapter treats of sales by a person in possession of goods which he neither owns nor has authority to sell, of pledges by factors or commission agents under Factors' Acts, of resales by conditional vendees, fraudulent buyers, persons having voidable title to the goods, and by sellers who have been permitted by the buyer to retain possession of goods sold. Also treated are allied subjects not strictly involving a sale by a non-owner such as the rights of attaching creditors of a seller of goods in whose possession the goods have been left by the buyer, or of a seller who has sold goods in bulk without compliance with Article 6 of the Uniform Commercial Code which covers Bulk Transfers.

Two Competing Policies of the Law. The venerable rule of property law protecting existing ownership of goods is the starting point and background in any discussion of a sale of goods by a non-owner. It is elementary that a purchaser of goods obtains such title as his transferor had or had power to transfer, and the Code expressly so states. Section 2–403. Likewise the purchaser of a limited interest in goods acquires rights only to the extent of the interest which he purchased.

A fundamental rule of the common law is that no one can transfer what he does not have. A purported sale by a thief, or finder, or ordinary bailee of goods does not transfer title to the purchaser, even to a bona fide purchaser for value without notice or knowledge of lack of title in the transferor.

The reasons underlying the policy of the law in protecting existing ownership of goods are obvious. A person should not be required to retain possession or control at all times of all the goods that he owns in order to maintain his ownership of them. One of the valuable incidents of ownership of goods is the freedom of the owner to make a bailment of his goods as he pleases, and the mere possession of goods by a bailee does not establish any authority of the bailee to sell them.

A policy of the law in competition with that which protects existing ownership is based upon the needs of trade and commerce in protecting the security of good faith transactions in goods.

To encourage and make secure good faith acquisitions of goods it is necessary that bona fide purchasers for value under certain circumstances be protected. An entrusting by the owner of his goods to a merchant who deals in goods of that type is a bailment which is peculiarly dangerous to bona fide purchasers from the merchant. In such case the Code protects the bona fide purchaser, and the rights of the owner are defeated. Section 2–403(2).

The problems presented in this chapter and the rules for their solution should be considered in the light of these two competing policies of the law. Both policies are sound, salutary, and worthy of enforcement. One protects existing property rights; the other protects the stability of transactions in the market place. In the area of sales of goods by a non-owner, these policies come into conflict. In every such conflict only one may prevail. As between innocent parties, the law must either protect existing ownership and defeat the interests of bona fide purchasers for value, or vice versa.

Void and Voidable Title to Goods. A void title is no title. A person claiming ownership of goods by virtue of a bill of sale bearing the forged signature of the true owner has a void title. A thief or a finder of goods has no title to them, and can transfer none. Where a thief or a finder delivers the goods to a carrier or warehouseman and receives a negotiable document of title which he subsequently indorses and delivers to a bona fide purchaser for value, the bona fide purchaser of the document acquires no title to the goods. Section 7–503.

A voidable title is one acquired under circumstances which permit the former owner to rescind the transfer and re-vest himself with title. The title of a buyer may be subject to rescission by the seller, as in a case of mistake, duress, fraud in the inducement, or sale by an infant. In these situations, the buyer has acquired legal title to the goods of which he may be divested by action taken by the seller. If, before the seller has rescinded the transfer of title, the buyer should resell the goods to a bona fide purchaser for value and without notice of any infirmity in his title, the equity of rescission in the seller is cut off, and the bona fide purchaser acquires good title.

The distinction between a void and voidable title is extremely important in determining the rights of bona fide purchasers of goods. The bona fide purchaser always believes that he is buying the goods from the owner or from one with authority to sell. Otherwise he would not be acting in good faith. In each situation the party selling the goods appears to be the owner whether his title is valid, void, or voidable. As between two innocent persons, the true owner who has done nothing wrong and the bona fide pur-

chaser who has done nothing wrong, the law will not disturb the legal title but will rule in favor of the one who has it. Thus, where A transfers possession of goods to B under such circumstances that B acquires no title or a void title, and B thereafter sells the goods to C, a bona fide purchaser for value, B has nothing except possession to transfer to C. In a lawsuit between A and C involving the right to the goods, A will win because he has the legal title. However, if B acquired a voidable title from A and resold the goods to C, in a suit between A and C over the goods, C would win. In this case, B had title, although it was voidable, which he transferred to the bona fide purchaser. The title thus acquired by C will be protected. The voidable title in B is title until it has been avoided. After transfer to a bona fide purchaser, it may not be avoided.

Resale by a Fraudulent Buyer. Where the buyer of goods perpetrates a fraud upon the seller, and having obtained possession of the goods resells them to a bona fide purchaser for value, the ensuing controversy seldom involves the wrongdoing buyer. He is either in jail, insolvent, or has fled the jurisdiction.

The controversy in this type of situation over the right to recover the goods or their value is always between two innocent parties, namely, the original owner of the goods who has been defrauded and the bona fide purchaser for value from the fraudulent vendee.

Rule at Common Law. The rights of the innocent purchaser at common law depend upon whether he obtained title to the goods from the fraudulent buyer. This, in turn, depended upon the nature of the transaction between the defrauded vendor and the fraudulent buyer. The controversy between the two innocent parties, i. e., the defrauded vendor and the bona fide purchaser, was determined by the location of legal title which the court would not disturb. The transfer of legal title depended upon the intention of the parties. If the fraud induced in the defrauded vendor a consent to pass title, the fraudulent buyer obtained a voidable title. A transfer of this title to a bona fide purchaser would destroy the power of avoidance in the defrauded vendor, and the bona fide purchaser would prevail. On the other hand, if the fraud perpetrated was of the kind known as fraud in the execution, the defrauded vendor did not consent to pass title, and the fraudulent buyer received no title or a void title. Having no title he could transfer none to a bona fide purchaser.

The question of whether the fraudulent buyer obtained a void or voidable title was also present in situations where the fraudulent buyer misrepresented his identity, where the buyer gave the seller a bad check, or where the buyer obtained the goods under a "cash sale" and did not pay for them.

At common law, it has been held that the buyer of goods acquired a void title and a subsequent bona fide purchaser from him was not protected, in the following situations:

(1) Where the original owner (seller) was deceived as to the identity of the buyer, as in the case of a fraudulent buyer who obtained possession of the goods by misrepresenting himself as an agent, or by means of a forged purchase order.

(2) Where the seller delivered the goods to the buyer in exchange for a check which was subsequently dishonored.

(3) Where the transaction was a "cash sale" and the seller delivered the goods to the fraudulent buyer upon his promise to pay the price in cash immediately which he failed to do.

(4) Where fraud in the execution was employed by the fraudulent buyer, as in the case of obtaining the signature of the seller by trick such as the substitution of a different document for the one which the seller reasonably believed that he was signing.

Rule under the Uniform Commercial Code. The Code enlarges the rights of bona fide purchasers of goods by changing the common law rule in the first three of the above four situations so that the fraudulent buyer or purchaser at a "cash sale" is in the position of one having voidable title by expressly providing that such person has the "power to transfer a good title to a good faith purchaser for value." Section 2–403(1) provides that when goods have been delivered under a transaction of purchase, the purchaser has such power even though:

(a) the transferor was deceived as to the identity of the purchaser, or

(b) the delivery was in exchange for a check which is later dishonored, or

(c) it was agreed that the transaction was to be a "cash sale", or

(d) the delivery was procured through fraud punishable as larcenous under the criminal law.

The above provisions of the Code make sweeping changes in the prior law, although a minority of courts by common-law development reached the same result as the Code (e. g., Parr v. Helfrich, page 452). The Code strongly favors protection of good faith acquisition of goods.

A "good faith purchaser for value" is one who acts honestly in taking the goods by way of sale, discount, negotiation, pledge, lien, or other voluntary transaction creating an interest in the property (Section 1–201(32)); who takes without notice or knowledge of any defect or infirmity in the title of his transferor; and who gives value.

"Value" is defined to include (1) purchases in return for a binding commitment to extend credit; (2) taking the goods as security for or in total or partial satisfaction of a pre-existing claim; (3) accepting delivery under a pre-existing purchase contract; and (4) generally, any consideration sufficient to support a simple contract. Section 1–201 (44).

The Code establishes a broad rule protecting good faith acquisitions of goods in the ordinary course of business from merchants who deal in goods of that kind, where the owner has entrusted possession of the goods to the merchant. Section 2–403(2) provides:

> Any entrusting of possession of goods to a merchant who deals in goods of that kind gives him power to transfer all rights of the entruster to a buyer in ordinary course of business.

The Code defines "buyer in ordinary course of business" as "a person who in good faith and without knowledge that the sale to him is in violation of the ownership rights or security interest of a third party in the goods buys in ordinary course from a person in the business of selling goods of that kind but does not include a pawnbroker." Section 1–201 (9).

Section 2–403(2) above quoted approximates but does not adopt the English rule of market overt. The Code does not go so far as to protect the bona fide purchaser from a merchant to whom the goods have been entrusted by a thief or finder, or by a completely unauthorized person.

Market Overt. Under English law, a special doctrine has evolved from early custom whereby a buyer of goods in the open market, or market overt, who pays value and acts in good faith without notice of any defect in the title of the seller, becomes owner of the goods even though the seller had no title. Every shop wherein goods are displayed for sale to the public is market overt with respect to goods of the type or kind which the shopkeeper ordinarily sells.

The law of market overt has never been established in the United States. It is set forth in Section 22 of the English Sale of Goods Act which has no counterpart in the Uniform Commercial Code. The Sale of Goods Act has been adopted in almost all of the provinces of Canada but with the provisions of Section 22 omitted.

Estoppel of the Owner. The principle of estoppel is applied to the situation where the owner of certain goods by words or conduct represents that a person in possession of the goods is the owner, and a third party in reliance therein and in good faith purchases the goods for value from the possessor. The true owner of the goods is precluded by his conduct from denying the seller's authority to sell.

The rules discussed herein do not apply to every kind of property. They do not apply to money, negotiable instruments, negotiable documents of title, or stock certificates, to which the law attaches the attribute of negotiability permitting greater freedom of circulation in the market place. A thief or finder of money, or indorsed in blank negotiable instruments, or similarly indorsed bills of lading, warehouse receipts, or stock certificates, may transfer them to a bona fide purchaser for value who acquires good title. This is not true of goods, wares, and merchandise, which are not negotiable.

However, the owner of goods may intrust their possession, together with some evidence or indicia of title, to a person which will enable him to transfer title to a bona fide purchaser. Thus, where an owner of grain permits his agent to store the grain in an elevator in the name of the agent, and the books and records of the elevator company show apparent ownership in the agent, a bona fide purchaser from the agent relying upon this indicia of title will be protected.

Similarly, the owner of an automobile who permits registration or the issuance of an ownership certificate in the name of another, provides such person with indicia of title, and a bona fide purchaser acting in reliance thereon will be protected. The owner of a station wagon who permits his employee to paint his name thereon and to use the station wagon publicly has provided the employee with indicia of ownership. Although the employee has no authority to sell the station wagon, a bona fide purchaser from him will be protected. However, if a thief should steal the station wagon, and repaint it with only the name of the thief appearing thereon, a bona fide purchaser from the thief, although deceived by appearances just as much as a bona fide purchaser from the employee, would not be protected. The thief was not clothed by the owner with indicia of ownership, and no estoppel would apply.

Factors' Acts. A factor is a person to whom merchandise is consigned or intrusted by the owner for a purpose of sale. A factor may advance money to the owner prior to selling the goods. Occasionally, he may without authority of the owner pledge the goods or documents representing the goods as security for his individual borrowings. He may act contrary to the authority of the owner in making a sale of the goods. Certain States, but not the majority, have enacted so-called Factors' Acts the purpose of which is to protect good faith buyers and pledgees of goods from factors. Under certain statutes such a buyer or pledgee is protected even where the factor has obtained the goods from the owner by fraud. The Code does not change the rule existing under the Factors' Acts.

Resale of Goods by a Conditional Vendee. The buyer of goods under a conditional sales contract does not acquire legal title until he has paid the price in full. He has possession, control, use, and enjoyment of the goods. He has equitable ownership, and his conduct toward the goods is that of an owner. He may sell or mortgage his equitable ownership in the goods, and the purchaser or mortgagee thereby acquires the interest of the conditional vendee subject to the outstanding legal title in the conditional vendor.

If the conditional vendee attempts to sell not merely his interest in the goods but to transfer complete ownership to a bona fide purchaser, the title reserved in the conditional vendor would prevail over the interest of the bona fide purchaser. However, if the conditional sale were for purpose of resale as in the case of inventory or goods on consignment, the purchaser in the ordinary course of business would prevail.

Under the Code conditional sales contracts are secured transactions and governed by Article 9 which classifies goods as either (1) consumer goods, (2) equipment, (3) farm products, or (4) inventory. Section 9–109. See Chapter 44.

A conditional sale of consumer goods, or of farm equipment having an original purchase price not in excess of $2,500 creates a purchase money security interest which is perfected without a public filing. Section 9–302. A bona fide purchaser for value of such goods who buys them from the conditional vendee for his own personal, family, or household use, or for his own farming operations, takes free and clear of any perfected security interest unless there has been a prior public filing. Section 9–307.

Thus, A sells a television set to B under a conditional sales contract. The set is installed in B's home for family use. There is no public filing under Article 9 of the Code. B resells the set to C who pays value and buys it for his personal use without knowledge of A's security interest. Under the Code, C has title to the television set and A no longer has any security interest in it. The Code is purposive and specific. If A had sold by conditional sales contract the same television set to B, a dealer, it would be regarded as "inventory" and not as "consumer goods". A purchase of it by C from B, the dealer, in the ordinary course of business would protect C and defeat A's security interest even if there were a public filing and even if C had knowledge of A's security interest.

The Code seeks to protect good faith commercial transactions as well as to accommodate the fundamental purposes of the parties. Goods held as inventory are intended for resale. Protection of the interest of buyers of such goods is necessary to effectuate this purpose. Consumer goods, farm products, and equipment, present a different situation. The conditional vendor may always perfect and thereby protect his security interest in such goods by a public filing.

Resale by a Minor. As previously stated, a person holding voidable title to goods may transfer it to a bona fide purchaser for value who thereby obtains legal title which is good against the entire world. This is the rule under Section 2–403 of the Code.

The common law permitted an infant seller of goods to disaffirm the contract and the sale, and to recover the goods from a third person who had purchased them in good faith and for value from the immediate vendee of the infant. Thus, A, a minor, sells certain goods to B who in turn resells them to C, a bona fide purchaser for value. Upon disaffirmance, A may not recover the goods from C. The Code does not permit the minor seller to prevail over the bona fide purchaser for value, as the vendee of the minor acquired a voidable title which he had power to transfer to the bona fide purchaser. Section 2–403.

Sales by Seller in Possession of Goods Already Sold. Where the buyer of goods to whom title has passed leaves the seller in possession of the goods, a deceptive bailment situation is created. It makes no difference whether the buyer has paid the seller the price of the goods, if the seller resells and delivers the goods to a bona fide purchaser for value, this second buyer acquires good title to the goods. The Code defines "entrusting" as including "any acquiescence in retention of possession." Section 2–403(3).

The rule applies to a third purchaser of the goods where the first and second buyers have each left the seller in possession. Thus, A sells certain goods to B who pays the price but allows possession to remain with A. A thereafter sells the same goods to C who pays the price and also leaves possession with A. A then sells the goods to D, a bona fide purchaser for value without notice of the prior sales to B and C. D takes delivery of the goods. Neither B nor C have any rights against D or to the goods. If B, C, and D had each left A in possession of the goods, and after the sale to D, B had obtained delivery of them from A, neither C nor D would have any rights against B or to the goods.

Where goods have been shipped by the seller to a buyer under a non-negotiable bill of lading, and the seller while the goods are in transit changes the shipping instructions and by notifying the carrier diverts the shipment to a third party who is a buyer in the ordinary course of business, the second buyer is protected and the first buyer loses his title to the goods. Section 7–504(3).

There is nothing unusual about a diversion or reconsignment of goods or a sale of them while in transit either under a negotiable or non-negotiable bill of lading. If under the former, the sale can be accomplished only through a negotiation of the bill of lading. If the goods are under a non-negotiable bill of lading, the document is not required in order to transfer title, and the control which the shipper may exercise over the goods while in the possession of the carrier enables him readily to make a resale of them. For these reasons the bona fide purchaser in the ordinary course of business is protected. It is an extension of the rule protecting the bona fide purchaser as against a seller who has retained possession of the goods.

Rights of Seller's Creditors Against Sold Goods. Whereas Section 2–403 of the Code deals with the rights of bona fide purchasers, Section 2–402 of the Code deals with the rights of creditors of the seller in goods sold but left in the possession of the seller. Section 2–402(2) provides:

> A creditor of the seller may treat a sale or an identification of goods to a contract for sale as void if as against him a retention of

possession by the seller is fraudulent under any rule of law of the state where the goods are situated, except that retention of possession in good faith and current course of trade by a merchant-seller for a commercially reasonable time after a sale or identification is not fraudulent.

The facility with which a debtor in embarrassed or failing financial circumstances may transfer title to his property to a friend or favored person in order to defraud his creditors by trying to place the property beyond their reach has led every State to enact a Fraudulent Conveyance statute based upon the early English statute of 13 Eliz. c. 5. The early statutes provided that the retention of possession by the seller made the transfer fraudulent and void as to his creditors. The creditors, therefore, could proceed to attach and levy upon the goods as if no transfer had occurred.

It is the purpose of the Code not to change the local law as to the rights of creditors with respect to goods sold but left in the possession of the seller. The statutes in the various States contain different provisions regarding the fraudulent effect of retention of possession by the seller, and each State has well-settled rules on this subject embodied in its court decisions. Each such case involves, in addition to retention of possession by the seller, other questions of fact such as, whether the transfer was for value or gratuitous, the intent of the transferor and his financial circumstances, the intent of the transferee and his knowledge of the circumstances and of the intent of the transferor, and the standing of the particular creditor seeking to set aside the transfer.

In some States, retention of possession by the transferor is merely evidence to be considered by the court with all of the other evidence, and does not give rise to a presumption of fraud. In other States, the courts hold that retention of possession is presumptively fraudulent, that is, *prima facie* evidence of fraud which may be rebutted by other evidence tending to show that the transfer was for value and in good faith. A third rule enforced in other States is that retention of possession by the seller creates a conclusive presumption of fraud. A presumption which is conclusive is not rebutable by any amount or any quality of evidence to the contrary. These various rules of local State law are not changed by the Code.

Transfers in Bulk. In order to protect the creditors of dealers and merchants who sell all or the major part of their merchandise or inventory in bulk and not in the usual and ordinary course of business, every State in the United States has a statute which makes such sales or transfers in bulk invalid against creditors of the transferor unless certain procedures are followed and the creditors are duly notified in advance of the proposed sale or transfer. The danger to creditors is that the debtor may secretly liquidate all or a major part of his tangible assets by a bulk sale not in the ordinary course of business and conceal or divert the proceeds of the sale without paying his creditors.

Article 6 of the Code relates to such sales and defines a bulk transfer as "any transfer in bulk and not in the ordinary course of the transferor's business of a major part of the materials, supplies, merchandise, or other inventory (Section 9–109) of an enterprise subject to this Article." The transfer of a substantial part of equipment is a bulk transfer only if made in connection with a bulk transfer of inventory. The enterprises governed by Article 6 of the Code are all those whose principal business is the sale of merchandise from stock, including those who manufacture what they sell. (Section 6–102.)

Requirements of Article 6. The Code provides that a bulk transfer of assets is ineffective against any creditor of the transferor, unless four requirements are met, namely:

1. The transferor furnishes to the transferee a sworn list of his existing creditors, including those whose claims are disputed, stating names, business addresses, and amounts due and owing when known. Section 6–104(1) (a).

2. The transferor and transferee prepare a schedule or list of the property being transferred, sufficient to identify it. Section 6–104(1) (b).

3. The transferee preserve the list of creditors and schedule of property for six months and permit inspection thereof by any creditor of the transferor, or file the list and schedule with the Recorder of Deeds; (Section 6–104(1) (c)), and

4. Notice of the proposed transfer in bulk be given by the transferee to each creditor of the transferor at least 10 days before the transferee takes possession of the goods or makes payment for them, whichever happens first. Section 6–105.

If each of the above steps are taken, the transfer in bulk complies with the statute and the transferee acquires the goods free of all claims of creditors of the transferor. The transferor is responsible for the completeness and accuracy of the sworn list of his creditors. Errors or omissions in this list do not impair the validity of the bulk transfer unless the transferee has knowledge of such errors or omissions. Section 6–104 (3).

Contents of Notice to Creditors. The Code requires that the notice from the transferee to the creditors of the transferor shall state (Section 6–107):

1. That a bulk transfer is about to be made.
2. The names and business addresses of the transferor and transferee.
3. Whether all debts of the transferor are to be paid in full as they fall due as a result of the transaction, and if so, the address to which creditors should send their bills.

4. If the debts of the transferor are not to be paid in full as they fall due:

   (a) the location and general description of the property to be transferred, and estimated total of transferor's debts;

   (b) the address where schedule of property and list of creditors may be inspected;

   (c) whether the transfer is for the purpose of paying existing debts, and if so, the amount of such debts and to whom owing;

   (d) whether the transfer is for new consideration and if so, the amount of such consideration and the time and place of payment.

It will be noted that if the debts of the transferor are to be paid in full as they fall due, only a short form of notice to creditors is required as provided in Section 6–107.

Exempted Bulk Transfers. Under the Code certain transfers in bulk are exempt and need not comply with Article 6. As provided in section 6–103 the exempted transfers are:

(1) Transfers by way of security.

(2) General assignments for the benefit of all creditors of the transferor.

(3) Transfers in settlement or realization of a lien or security interest.

(4) Sales by executors, administrators, receivers, trustees in bankruptcy, or any public officer under judicial process.

(5) Sales in the course of proceedings for the dissolution or reorganization of a corporation pursuant to order of a court or administrative agency where notice is given to the creditors.

(6) Transfers to a person who maintains a known place of business in the State, who agrees to become bound to pay the debts of the transferor in full and gives public notice of that fact, and who is solvent after becoming so bound.

(7) Transfers to a new business enterprise organized to take over and continue the business of the transferor, where public notice is given, the new enterprise as-

sumes the debts of the transferor, and the transferor receives nothing from the transaction except an interest in the new enterprise which is junior to the claims of creditors.

(8) Transfers of property which is exempt from execution under exemption statutes.

Effect of Failure to Comply with Article 6. The effect of a failure to comply with the requirements of Article 6 of the Code is that the goods in the possession of the transferee continue to be subject to the claims of unpaid creditors of the transferor. These creditors may proceed against the goods by levy or attachment and by sheriff's sale, or by causing the involuntary bankruptcy of the transferor and the appointment of a trustee in bankruptcy to take over the goods from the transferee.

Where the title of the transferee is subject to the defect of non-compliance with the Code, a bona fide purchaser of the goods from the transferee who pays value in good faith and takes the property without notice of such defect acquires the goods free of any claim of creditors of the transferor. A purchaser of the property from the transferee who pays no value or who takes with notice of non-compliance with the Code acquires the goods subject to the claims of creditors of the transferor.

Optional Provisions of Article 6. In the case of bulk transfers for which new consideration is payable, except those made at auction sales, the Code imposes in optional Section 6–106 a personal duty upon the transferee to apply the new consideration to the payment of the debts of the transferor, and if it is insufficient to pay them in full, to make distribution to creditors pro rata.

In Code States which do not adopt optional Section 6–106, there is no duty on the transferee owing to the creditors of the transferor. In the event of non-compliance with the Code, except for sales at auction, the cred-

itors merely proceed to enforce their claims against the property transferred as though it belonged to the transferor. This is what is meant by the language of the Code that the bulk transfer "is ineffective against any creditor of the transferor." The transferee loses the property but does not assume any obligation to pay the debts of the transferor.

Optional subsection (4) of Section 6–106 provides that the transferee may discharge his duty to pay the creditors of the transferor out of the proceeds by payment of the consideration into court within 10 days after taking possession of the goods, and by giving notice to all of the creditors that such payment has been made and that they should file their claims with the court.

Auction Sales. The Code has special provisions with respect to auction sales of goods which represent a transfer in bulk not in the ordinary course of the transferor's business where the goods offered for sale are a major part of the materials, supplies, merchandise, or inventory used in the business. In such an auction sale Section 6–108 requires that:

1. The transferor furnish the auctioneer a sworn list of his creditors and assist in the preparation of a schedule of the property to be sold.

2. The auctioneer receive and retain the list of creditors and schedule of property for six months and permit inspection thereof by any creditor, or file the list and schedule with the Recorder of Deeds.

3. The auctioneer give notice at least 10 days before the auction to all creditors named in the list as well as all other persons known to him to have any claims against the transferor.

4. The auctioneer apply the net proceeds of the auction sale to payment of all debts of the transferor as provided in Section 6–106.

A failure of the auctioneer to perform his duties does not affect the validity of the sale or the title of the purchasers of the goods at the auction sale. The auctioneer is personally liable to creditors of the transferor as a class to the extent of the net proceeds of the auction.

Limitation of Actions and Levies. The Code provides that creditors of the transferor may not take any action or make any levy upon the goods after six months from the date on which the transferee took possession. However, if the transfer was concealed, creditors may take action or make levies within six months after its discovery. Section 6–111.

CASES

PARR v. HELFRICH

(1922) 108 Neb. 801, 189 N.W. 281.

[Replevin to recover possession of an automobile. Plaintiff, owner of the car, had sold and delivered it to two men who were unknown to the plaintiff, but who gave plaintiff a purported certified check for the price. The check was a forgery. The men later sold the car to defendant, a bona fide purchaser for value. From a judgment for the plaintiff, defendant appeals.]

MORRISSEY, C. J. This is an action of replevin. Plaintiff, a resident of Denver, Colorado, was the owner of an automobile, which he advertised for sale. The automobile was in the garage at plaintiff's residence and his wife exhibited the car for sale to all persons who called to inspect it. There was no explicit designation of plaintiff's wife as agent with authority to sell the car, but their conduct and relations were such that her authority to so act is apparent. Among others who called to inspect the car were two men unknown to plaintiff's wife. These men rep-

resented that they were desirous of buying the car, inspected it, and ascertained the sum for which it could be purchased. They later returned and delivered to plaintiff's wife a purported certified check on the First National Bank of Denver for the price theretofore agreed upon, and the car was delivered to them. These men drove the car to Bridgeport, Nebraska, and sold and delivered it to defendant. Plaintiff presented the purported certified check to the bank on which it was drawn and whose certification it was supposed to bear. The check was pronounced a forgery and payment refused. At the conclusion of the testimony the court instructed a verdict in favor of plaintiff, and defendant appeals.

From the conduct of the trial and the language of the motion made for a directed verdict it may be inferred that plaintiff questions the good faith of defendant in making the purchase and is not disposed to concede him the status of an innocent, good-faith purchaser for value. We shall not review the evidence on the question of defendant's good faith. If the bona fides of the transaction is not conclusively shown it was a question to be determined by the jury. [Citation.]

It is well settled that when property is obtained from its owner by fraud, and the facts show a sale by the owner to the fraudulent vendee, an innocent purchaser of the property from the fraudulent vendee will take good title. The inquiry is: Did the owner intend to transfer the ownership as well as the possession of the property? If he did, there was a contract of sale. The essential thing in the passing of title to personal property is that the vendor and the vendee intend that the title shall pass, and not what induced them to have that intention. But one who has been induced by fraud to part with title to his property has his remedy either in an action because of the fraud and deceit, or he may rescind the contract and recover back the property while title still remains in the fraudulent vendee, but he cannot recover it when title has passed to a bona fide purchaser for value. [Citations.] * * *

Two pertinent inquiries were presented on the trial of this cause: Did plaintiff, through his agent, transfer title to the automobile to his fraudulent vendees? Did defendant become a bona fide purchaser, without notice of the fraud? On the record presented each of these questions should have been answered affirmatively by the court, or submitted to the jury for its determination.

The judgment is reversed and the cause remanded.

PHELPS v. McQUADE

(1917) 220 N.Y. 232, 115 N.E. 441, L.R.A.1918B, 973.

[Replevin action to recover certain jewelry. The plaintiffs, in reliance upon the false representations of one Walter J. Gwynne that he was Baldwin J. Gwynne, sold the jewelry to said Walter J. Gwynne who in turn sold and delivered it to the defendant, a bona fide purchaser for value. A judgment for the plaintiffs in the trial court was reversed by the Appellate Division, from which order of reversal plaintiffs appeal.]

ANDREWS, J. One Walter J. Gwynne falsely represented to the appellants [plaintiffs] that he was Baldwin J. Gwynne, a man of financial responsibility, residing at Cleveland, Ohio. Relying upon the truth of this statement the appellants delivered to him upon credit a quantity of jewelry. Gwynne in turn sold it to the respondent [defendant], who bought it without notice express or implied of any defect in title, and for value. Learning of the deception practiced upon them, the appellants began an action in replevin to recover the goods.

The only question before us is whether under such circumstances, the vendor of personal property does or does not retain title

thereto after he has parted with possession thereof. * * * Where the vendor of personal property intends to sell his goods to the person with whom he deals, then title passes, even though he be deceived as to that person's identity or responsibility. Otherwise it does not. It is purely a question of the vendor's intention.

The fact that the vendor deals with the person personally rather than by letter is immaterial, except in so far as it bears upon the question of intent.

Where the transaction is a personal one the seller intends to transfer title to a person of credit, and he supposes the one standing before him to be that person. He is deceived. But in spite of that fact his primary intention is to sell his goods to the person with whom he negotiates.

Where the transaction is by letter the vendor intends to deal with the person whose name is signed to the letter. He knows no one else. He supposes he is dealing with no one else. And while in both cases other facts may be shown that would alter the rule, yet in their absence, in the first title passes; in the second it does not. [Citations.]

In Edmunds v. Merchants' D. Transportation Company, 135 Mass. 283, a swindler, representing himself to be one Edward Pape, personally bought goods of the plaintiff on credit. The court held that the title passed. "The minds of the parties met and agreed upon all the terms of the sale, the thing sold, the price and the time of payment, the person selling and the person buying. The fact that the seller was induced to sell by fraud of the buyer made the sale voidable, but not void. He could not have supposed that he was selling to any other person; his intention was to sell to the person present, and identified by sight and hearing; it does not defeat the sale because the buyer assumed a false name, or practiced any other deceit to induce the vendor to sell." [Citations.]

In Cundy v. Lindsay [L.R. (3 App.Cas.) 463] one Blenkarn, signing himself Blenkiron & Co., bought goods by letter of Lindsay & Co. The latter shipped the goods to Blenkiron & Co. They knew of the firm of Blenkiron & Son; believed the letter came from that firm and that the goods were shipped to it. Blenkiron & Son were the persons with whom Lindsay & Co. intended to deal and supposed they were dealing. Under these circumstances it was held that although Blenkarn obtained possession of the goods he never acquired title thereto. * * *

[Judgment for defendant affirmed.]

ILLINOIS BOND & INVESTMENT CO. v. GARDNER

(1928) 249 Ill.App. 337.

WOLFE, J. This is an action in replevin brought in the circuit court of Franklin county, at the June term, A. D. 1927, by the appellant [plaintiff], the Illinois Bond & Investment Company, against the appellees, H. F. Gardner, the Summers Motor Company and James S. Pritchard, sheriff of Franklin county, to recover the possession of a Nash automobile described in the affidavit, writ and declaration. * * *

Section 23 of the Uniform Sales Act, is as follows: "Subject to the provisions of this Act, where goods are sold by a person who is not the owner thereof, and who does not sell them under the authority or with the consent of the owner, the buyer acquires no better title to the goods than the seller had, unless the owner of the goods is by his conduct precluded from denying the seller's authority to sell."

The automobile in question was delivered to the Summers Motor Company on terms and conditions as set forth in the trust receipt; the said Summers Motor Company had for some years prior to the sale in question operated its garage in the city of Benton, Illinois, and was the distributor of Nash automobiles similar to the one involved in this case, the said automobiles being kept on display in the sales and storage room of the garage of said Summers Motor Company, all of which was so known to the appellant.

"Where the true owner of property allows another to appear as the owner of, or to have full power of disposition over the property, so that an innocent third party is led into dealing with the apparent owner, an estoppel may operate against the true owner which will preclude him from disputing the existence of a title which he has caused or allowed to appear to be vested in another." * * * Without regard to the terms of contract of sale, an innocent purchaser will be protected where the appearance of ownership is in one while the title is really in another, and if the vendor delivers the chattel to the vendee before payment of the purchase price and allows the vendee to have all the indicia of ownership, retaining a secret lien for payment, he cannot assert his right against a judgment creditor to the vendee without notice before a levy is made." Drain v. La-Grange State Bank, 303 Ill. 330, 135 N.E. 780. * * *

In the case at bar the Summers Motor Company was engaged in the business of selling the kind of automobiles that the appellant was handling. He took the automobile to his regular place of business and placed it in the display, sales and storage room where other cars were displayed and stored. A purchaser desiring to buy the automobile would be led to believe that the Summers Motor Company, which had possession of the car on display in their salesroom (without any notice of any secret agreement between Summers Motor Company and anyone else) was the owner of and had a right to sell the said automobile.

A customer going into a retail store and seeing goods on display offered to the public generally for sale, buying such goods, in good faith, should be protected against the holder or owner of any secret lien of which the purchaser has no notice. To hold otherwise would seriously interrupt business. Purchasers would hesitate before buying for fear the seller could not give good title to the goods he has for sale, because of some one having a secret lien through some trade acceptance or bill of sale for said goods.

We believe the legislature in passing this statute, Smith-Hurd Stats. c. 121½, § 23, Cahill's St. ch. 121a, par. 26, meant to protect the owner whose goods were sold without his authority or consent, but for the protection of innocent purchasers, having no reason to suspect secret liens, etc., has very wisely added, "unless the owner of the goods is by his conduct precluded from denying the seller's authority to sell."

We are of the opinion that the appellant has precluded itself from denying the seller's right or authority to sell the automobile in question. * * *

[Judgment affirmed.]

ZENDMAN v. HARRY WINSTON, INC.

(1953) 305 N.Y. 180, 111 N.E.2d 871.

FULD, J. On November 28, 1947, plaintiff Jane Zendman, bought a diamond ring for $12,500, at an auction held at the gallery of Brand, Inc., on the Boardwalk in Atlantic City, New Jersey. Harry Winston, Inc., a diamond merchant located in New York City, claims ownership of the ring.

Brand and Winston had done business together for years. It was the custom of Harold Brand, the owner and proprietor of Brand, Inc., to visit Winston's premises in New York several times a month and select articles that were later sold at the gallery in Atlantic City. In October of 1947, Brand chose the ring—later purchased by Miss Zendman—advising that he wished to show it to a customer, and, at his request, that one item was mailed to the gallery in New Jersey. Accompanying it was a memorandum, reciting that "the goods" were only for Brand's examination and that no title was to pass "until you have made your selection, notified us of your agreement to pay the indicated price [$11,000] and we have indicated our acceptance thereof by sending to you a bill of sale."

Upon the receipt of the ring, Brand placed it in one of its public show windows, such display being with the knowledge and acquiescence of the owner Winston. And there the ring remained on display until, more than a month later, it was put up at auction and, after some bidding, "knocked down" and sold to plaintiff for $12,500. She received a bill of sale from Brand and knew nothing about the written memorandum or the circumstances under which Brand had obtained possession. Sometime in January, 1948, Winston discovered that Brand had sold the ring to plaintiff and, on February 2d, demanded its return. On the following day, an involuntary petition in bankruptcy was filed against Brand.

The record established that delivery of merchandise "on memorandum" similar to that here involved, had been the regular course of dealing between Winston and Brand for some years, and "hundreds" of such memoranda were found in Brand's files. Every week or so—evidence, admitted without objection, disclosed—one of Winston's salesmen and officers, Raticoff, would visit Brand's gallery, and, after checking items that had been sent to Brand, would settle Winston's account, collecting either cash or Brand's check or the checks of those customers who had bought Winston articles.

The court at Special Term, in the exercise of its discretion, declined to grant a declaratory judgment, Rules of Civil Practice, rule 212, but rendered judgment in favor of plaintiff on defendant Winston's counterclaim for replevin. Finding that plaintiff had purchased the ring for full value and in entire good faith, the court proceeded to hold—in reliance upon the sales act provisions of New Jersey, N.J.S.A. 46:30–29,—that Winston had, by its conduct, "precluded" itself "from denying the seller's authority to sell." Upon appeal, the Appellate Division, deciding that there was no basis for an "estoppel," reversed and directed judgment for defendant.

It is the law of New Jersey—the place where the sale to plaintiff occurred and where the ring was then located—that governs our decision. [Citations.]

* * *

Generally, we seek a proper balance between the competing interests of an owner who has entrusted his property to another for purposes other than sale, and of an innocent purchaser who has in good faith bought that property from the latter without notice of the seller's lack of title or authority to sell. In resolving this conflict, the courts have evolved certain principles "akin to estoppel", 2 Williston, op. cit., § 311, p. 242, based on the maxim that "As between two innocent victims of the fraud, the one who made possible the fraud on the other should suffer." [Citation.]

Thus, on the one hand, it is settled that simply delivering possession of an article of property to another as depository, pledgee or agent "is clearly insufficient to preclude the real owner from reclaiming his property, in case of an unauthorized disposition of it by the person so intrusted. [Citations.] "Neither is it sufficient, to work an estoppel, that the person to whose possession the owner intrusts chattels is a dealer in similar merchandise." [Citations.] Nor, finally, is an estoppel created merely by the addition of the circumstance "that the possessor of the chattel is authorized by the owner to exhibit the same for the purpose of obtaining offers of purchase." [Citations.]

On the other hand, it is equally settled that "but slight additional circumstances may turn the scale" against the true owner, 2 Williston, op. cit., § 315, p. 249, and estop him from asserting title against one who has purchased the property in good faith. [Citations.] As this court noted, some eighty years ago, in McNeil v. Tenth Nat. Bank, supra, 46 N.Y. 325, 329, the rule that a vendor can convey no greater title to property than he possesses "is a truism, predicable of a simple transfer from one party to another where no other element intervenes." However, continued the court, "It does not interfere with the well-established principle, that where the true owner holds out another, or allows him to appear, as the owner of, or as having full power of disposition over the property, and innocent third parties are thus led into dealing with such apparent owner, they will be protected. Their rights in such cases do not depend upon the actual title or authority of the party with whom they deal directly, but are derived from the act of the real owner, which precludes him from disputing, as against them, the existence of the title or power which, through negligence or mistaken confidence he caused or allowed to appear to be vested in the party making the conveyance. [Citations.]"

Adopting that principle, the courts have generally acknowledged that "The rightful owner may be estopped by his own acts from asserting his title. If he has invested another with the usual evidence of title, *or an apparent authority to dispose of it*, he will not be allowed to make claim against an innocent purchaser dealing on the faith of such apparent ownership." [Citations.]

* * *

We realize, of course, that "The law takes into account not simply the deception of the subsequent buyer by the appearance of title in the possessor of the goods, but also whether this appearance of title was created by the original owner for a purpose so essential and proper that the original title must be protected irrespective of the injury to the subsequent buyer". 2 Williston, op. cit., § 312, p. 243. The task in each case is, therefore to balance the probability of deception with the necessity for adopting the particular mode of entrusting chosen. In this case, we fail to see how defendant's mode of operation is "so essential" to the conduct of its business as to warrant placing upon an innocent purchaser the burden and consequences of the very fraud which defendant made possible.

An owner must be fully aware of the potentialities for fraud created when, for purposes of sale, he entrusts merchandise to a retail dealer, regularly engaged in selling such goods, and the dangers are many times multiplied if that dealer happens to be an auctioneer. It ill behooves the owner to complain if he is not permitted to rely upon his private and secret agreement, when he himself has failed to require strict adherence to its terms and has thus become responsible for the dealer's apparent authority to sell.

The judgment of the Appellate Division should be reversed and that of Special Term affirmed, with costs in this court and the Appellate Division.

Judgment accordingly.

ASHTON v. LEYSEN

(1951 Tex.Civ.App.) 237 S.W.2d 713.

CRAMER, J. Appellee, as seller, filed this suit in the trial court against appellants, as purchasers, to recover an escrow deposit of $500 placed in connection with a written contract for the sale of a gift shop business in the City of Dallas. The parties will be designated as seller and purchasers in this opinion. The material facts are as follows: The contract of sale, although on a real estate form, is sufficient and sets out with clarity the terms of the sale. In substance purchasers agreed to pay $2,000 for the fixtures and equipment, plus actual inventory value of the stock, and to assume the lease on the rented building housing the business. Accounts receivable were to be agreed upon at date of closing; seller was to pay all outstanding obligations and, according to the contract, the transfer was to be " * * * free and clear of any and all encumbrances, except those herein named * * *." The instrument also provided for the forfeiture of the $500 escrow deposit in case of failure or refusal of purchasers to complete the contract; for proration of taxes, etc. Before completion of the sale, purchasers demanded that seller comply with the bulk sales law, Articles 4001–2–3, Vernon's Texas Civil Statutes, which seller refused to do. After such refusal, purchasers declined to go further without such compliance.

On trial before the court, without a jury, seller prevailed and was awarded judgment for the $500 deposit as against the purchasers, from which judgment purchasers duly perfected this appeal.

Purchasers assign but one point of error, in substance, error in holding that the bulk sales law was not an inherent part of the contract and they, as purchasers of bulk merchandise, were not entitled to be protected thereunder. Seller counters by asserting that the bulk sales law as amended is for the benefit of the creditors and cannot become a part of the contract between the parties as seller and purchaser of the business, unless specifically mentioned in the contract.

It is our opinion that a failure to comply with the bulk sales law would not have transferred the stock of goods free and clear of encumbrances.

The record shows that seller, at the time she offered to close, had written checks for what she testified were all of the then known accounts of such business and due by her; further, that she had $500 set aside to cover anything left over.

The testimony further shows that the books of the business which would have shown purchases and invoice prices on such purchases of merchandise were not available and that seller had not furnished such books for inspection by purchasers' auditor, although they were demanded of her, and that purchasers' auditor had to prepare the invoice in connection with the sale by taking the retail price marked on the items and dividing the same by two to get the cost price, since the only rule he had to go by was seller's statement that she had marked up the cost 100% as the sale price.

Under the bulk sales law, the sale, as between seller and purchaser, is void as to creditors unless such bulk sales law is complied with. This provision of the law, we hold, is as much a part of the contract as if it had been written into the contract verbatim. If purchasers had not made the demand for compliance with the bulk sales law, or had purchased the stock of goods without compliance, they would have held the stock of goods, not as absolute owners, free and clear of encumbrances, but as trustees for the creditors of said business, and such stock of goods would have been liable for the payment of such debts if such creditors had not thereafter been paid. Such legal consequences would result, whether the contract referred to and made the law a part of the contract or not. The fact that the evidence shows the seller had stated to purchasers that she had checks made out ready to be mailed upon the closing of the deal, and had a reserve of $500 to pay such creditors as she did not then know about, did not comply with the bulk sales law; and purchasers' acceptance of such statement would not have had the effect of wiping out any right the creditors would have had under the bulk sales law. * * *

The trial court therefore erred, in its judgment and such judgment must be here reversed and judgment here rendered in favor of Floyd P. Ashton and wife, against Edna Hunter Leysen, for the escrow deposit of $500, plus costs.

Reversed and rendered.

PROBLEMS

1. Adams Jewelry Company employed Brown as a jewelry salesman and delivered to him a sample line of watches, diamonds and rings, which he was to show to customers. He was authorized to sell for cash and on making any sale was to report it to the jewelry company and turn over the cash. Brown took one of the diamond rings which was delivered to him by the jewelry company and pawned it with a pawnbroker for $200. The jewelry company later discovered that the pawnbroker had the ring and made a demand upon him, and upon his failure to deliver the ring, brought an action against him for the value of the ring. The pawnbroker defended upon the ground that the jewelry company having put it in the power of Brown, the salesman, to represent himself as the owner of the property the jewelry company, and not he, should suffer the loss. Decision?

2. Smith was approached by a man who introduced himself as Brown of Brown and Co. Brown was not known to Smith, but Smith asked Dun & Bradstreet for a credit report and obtained a very favorable report on Brown. He thereupon sold Brown some expensive gems and billed Brown & Co. "Brown" turned out to be a clever jewel thief, who later sold the gems to Brown & Co. for valuable consideration. Brown & Co. being unaware of "Brown's" transaction with Smith. Smith sued Brown & Co. for the return of the gems or the price thereof as billed to Brown & Co. Decision?

3. Z, the owner of a 1965 Cadillac automobile, agreed to loan the car to Y for the month of February of 1966 while he (Z) went to Florida for a winter vacation. It was understood that Y, who was a small town Cadillac dealer, would merely place Z's car in his showroom for exhibition and sales promotion purposes. While Z was away, Y sold the car to B. Upon Z's return from Florida, he sued to recover the car from B. Decision?

4. A was indebted to B and also to C. On April 2, he gave B a bill of sale of certain farm implements but did not deliver possession. On April 7, he executed and delivered to C a security

agreement covering the same implements and also signed a financing statement which was duly filed with the Secretary of State. C had no prior knowledge of the bill of sale. Later, the property was sold at public auction under the provisions of the security agreement. B and C both claimed to be entitled to the proceeds of the sale. Which one was right?

5. A offered his automobile to B for $300 cash. B agreed to buy the car, gave A a check for $300, and drove away in the car. The next day B sold the car for $250 to C, a bona fide purchaser. The $300 check was returned to A by the bank in which he had deposited it for the reason that there were insufficient funds in the drawer's account in the drawee bank. A brings an action against C to recover the automobile. What judgment?

6. A, the owner of an old homestead furnished with antique furniture, leased the house furnished to B, an antique dealer, with full knowledge that B would conduct his business therein and from time to time would bring in, display and sell various antique merchandise, including furniture. While operating his business therein, B sold to C some of the furniture which belonged to A. Immediately upon discovery of the sale, A brought an action against C to replevy the various articles of furniture, which he claimed to have merely leased to B. Decision?

7. A offers to sell his horse Dobbin to B for $100. B, accepts the offer, pays A the price and leaves A in possession of Dobbin. Subsequently A sells and delivers Dobbin to C for $90. What are the rights of the parties?

8. Altman and his wife spent every winter at Miami Beach, Florida, including the period at and around January 30, which was his wife's birthday. For several years Altman had the habit of purchasing jewelry as a birthday gift from a retail store on Collins Avenue known as Malcolm of Miami. On January 28, Altman bought a diamond bracelet for his wife for $4,000. He paid Malcolm by check and received a receipt, a bill of sale and a written appraisal, valuing the bracelet at $4,775. On April 15, Altman received a letter from a jeweler in New Jersey known as Thomas of Trenton. Thomas demanded return of the diamond bracelet or its value of $4,775 in cash. He advised Altman that he was the owner of the bracelet and had sent it to Malcolm in accordance with a consignment agreement which contained the following provision: "A sale of merchandise can only be effected and title will pass only if, as and when Thomas of Trenton shall agree to such sale and a bill of sale rendered therefor by him." When Altman refused to return the bracelet or pay Thomas, Thomas brought an action against Altman. Decision?

9. On January 3, A entered into an agreement with B, whereby A agreed to purchase a grocery business owned by B in Chicago, including the stock of merchandise and all equipment and fixtures. It was agreed that the transfer would take place on February 15 and that the purchase price would be paid at that time. At A's request, B furnished to him an affidavit, setting forth the names and addresses of all of B's creditors and the amounts owing to them. On January 15, A sent registered letters to the creditors listed, notifying them that he was purchasing the business and advising them of the price, terms and conditions of the sale. On February 15 the sale was consummated and the purchase price paid. Subsequently, three business creditors of the former owner made demand upon A for payment of their indebtedness: (a) X, who was not listed in the affidavit furnished by B; (b) Y, who was listed in the affidavit, but who received no notice of the sale, because his name was overlooked by A; and (c) Z, who was listed in the affidavit, and who received the notice sent by A. What is the liability of A, if any, with respect to each of these creditors?

CHAPTER 21

PERFORMANCE OF SALES CONTRACTS

Introductory. Before commencing the study of this chapter, it is suggested that the student review Chapter 10 of this book entitled Discharge of Contracts, wherein performance is treated as a method of discharge of a contractual duty.

To understand what is required for performance by the seller and the buyer under a contract for the sale of goods, it is necessary to know the nature and extent of the duty to be discharged. This is the subject matter of the present chapter.

Delivery and Payment. The contract of sale may expressly provide whether the seller must deliver the goods before receiving payment of the price or whether the buyer must pay the price before receiving the goods. The rights of the parties are fixed by the terms of the contract which has resulted from negotiation and bargaining. If the seller has agreed to sell goods on 60 or 90 days' credit, he is required to perform his part of the contract in advance of performance by the buyer. Likewise, if the buyer has agreed to pay for the goods in advance of delivery either to the buyer or to a carrier, his duty to perform is not conditional upon performance or a tender of performance by the seller. The parties made their contract and they are each bound by its terms.

Where the contract does not expressly provide that the sale is on credit, or that one party must perform before the other performs, delivery of the goods and payment of the price are said to be concurrent conditions. In fairness to both parties, neither is required to perform until the other performs or tenders performance. This is based upon the assumption that delivery and payment

are acts which are each capable of simultaneous performance, and it is unfair that one party to a contract should be compelled to part with the consideration which he has promised unless he receives at the same time the consideration promised by the other party. These conditions are secondary and remedial as they pertain solely to performance and have nothing to do either with the formation of the contract or the effectuation of a sale or transfer of title. Section 2–301 of the Code provides:

> The obligation of the seller is to transfer and deliver and that of the buyer is to accept and pay in accordance with the contract.

Under the Code the seller must be ready and willing to deliver the goods or control of the goods to the buyer in exchange for the price, and the buyer must be ready and willing to pay the price in exchange for possession or control of possession of the goods. It is not enough for both parties merely to stand ready, able, and willing to perform. In order for either party to maintain against the other an action upon the contract, he must put the other party in default. This is accomplished either by (a) performance according to the contract, (b) tender of performance according to the contract, or (c) being excused from tender of performance.

Assume that A enters into a contract to sell to B 100 tons of coal at $9 per ton, delivery to be made on February 1, and the price to be paid by B on February 15. If A fails to deliver the coal on February 1, B may properly start an action against him on February 2, or any date up to and including February 14, to recover damages for breach of contract without first making a tender of the price. A has breached the contract, and no act is required on B's part to put A in default as the respective performances are not concurrent conditions by reason of the terms of the contract. However, when the time for B's performance arrives on February 15, he must tender the price to A, in order to maintain an action against A, unless A by words or conduct has excused tender. While originally the respective duties of performance on the part of buyer and seller were independent of one another, by lapse of time and inaction of the parties they have become mutually dependent.

The Requirement of Tender. The Code is explicit in requiring a tender of performance by one party as a condition to performance by the other party. Section 2–507 provides with respect to the seller:

> *Effect of Seller's Tender; Delivery on Condition*
>
> (1) Tender of delivery is a condition to the buyer's duty to accept the goods and, unless otherwise agreed, to his duty to pay for them. Tender entitles the seller to acceptance of the goods and to payment according to the contract.
>
> (2) Where payment is due and demanded on the delivery to the buyer of goods or documents of title, his right as against the seller to retain or dispose of them is conditional upon his making the payment due.

Section 2–511 provides with respect to the buyer:

> *Tender of Payment by Buyer; Payment by Check*
>
> (1) Unless otherwise agreed tender of payment is a condition to the seller's duty to tender and complete any delivery.
>
> (2) Tender of payment is sufficient when made by any means or in any manner current in the ordinary course of business unless the seller demands payment in legal tender and gives any extension of time reasonably necessary to procure it.
>
> (3) Subject to the provisions of this Act on the effect of an instrument on an obligation (Section 3–802), payment by check is conditional and is defeated as between the parties by dishonor of the check on due presentment.

Tender of delivery requires that the seller put and hold goods which conform to the contract at the buyer's disposition and that he give the buyer notification reasonably necessary to enable him to take delivery. (Section 2–503.)

Time, Place and Manner of Delivery. Tender must be at a reasonable hour, and the goods tendered must be kept available for the period reasonably necessary to enable the buyer to take possession of them. Unless otherwise agreed the buyer must furnish facilities reasonably suited to the receipt of the goods. (Section 2–503.)

Unless the parties so agree, a contract is not performable piecemeal or in installments with a portion of the consideration of one party due upon partial performance by the other. All of the goods called for by a contract must be tendered in a single delivery and payment is due only on such tender. However, where the circumstances give either party the right to make or demand delivery in lots, the price if it can be apportioned may be demanded for each lot. (Section 2–307.)

If the contract is silent as to the place for delivery of the goods, the place for delivery is the seller's place of business; or if he has none, his residence. If the contract is for the sale of identified goods which the parties know at the time of making the contract are located elsewhere than the seller's place of business or residence, the location of the goods is the place for their delivery. (Section 2–308.)

Example: A, a boat builder in Chicago, contracts to sell to B a certain yacht which both parties know is anchored at Milwaukee. As part of the contract, A agrees to overhaul the motor at A's shipyard in Chicago. A would have to return the yacht to Chicago, and the place of delivery would be A's ship-yard. However, if the contract did not require such overhauling of the motor but provided only that the seller should replace two deck chairs in order to put the yacht in a deliverable condition, this could readily be done at Milwaukee and the place of delivery would be there.

If no definite time for delivery is fixed by the terms of the contract, the seller is allowed a reasonable time after the making of the contract within which to deliver the goods to the buyer, or have them available for delivery at the required place. Likewise, the buyer has a reasonable time within which to accept delivery. What length of time is reasonable is a question of fact, and depends upon the facts and circumstances of each case. If the goods are capable of immediate delivery, a reasonable time would be very short. Where the goods must be constructed or manufactured, obviously a reasonable time would be longer and would depend upon the usual length of time required to make the goods, together with other factors.

Section 2–309(3) of the Code provides:

> (3) Termination of a contract by one party except on the happening of an agreed event requires that reasonable notification be received by the other party and an agreement dispensing with notification is invalid if its operation would be unconscionable.

Obligation of Payment. The terms of the contract may expressly state the time and place that the buyer is obligated to pay for the goods. If so, these terms are controlling. In the absence of agreement, payment is due at the time and place at which the buyer is to receive the goods even though the place of shipment is the place of delivery. (Section 2–310(a).)

This rule is understandable in view of the right of the buyer to inspect the goods before being obliged to pay for them, in the absence of agreement to the contrary.

Where the sale is on credit the buyer is not obligated to pay for the goods when he receives them. The credit provision in the contract will control the time of payment. Unless the contract specifies the time when the credit period commences to run, the time commences on the date of the shipment of the goods. However, post-dating the invoice or delaying its dispatch will correspondingly delay the starting of the credit period. (Section 2–310(d).)

Where the goods are in the possession of a third party, the seller does not discharge his obligation to the buyer merely by telling the buyer where the goods are located or by notifying the bailee to deliver them to the buyer. The bailee must affirmatively consent to hold the goods for the buyer or deliver them to the buyer. The distinction should be observed between what is necessary in order to constitute performance by the seller in such case, and what is necessary to protect the buyer against loss of the goods through levy of a writ of execution at the instance of the seller's creditors or through a sale to subsequent purchasers.

If A sells to B a certain piano which is stored in C's warehouse, A must obtain for B a promise from C to hold the goods as B's agent or bailee before A can maintain an action to recover the price. In the absence of such a promise by the bailee, if either A or B notify C of the sale, B is protected against a levy upon the goods by creditors of A or a resale of the goods by A to D, a bona fide purchaser. After such notice, a misdelivery of the goods by C would be a conversion of B's goods. Mere notice, however, is ineffectual where the party in possession of the goods as bailee has issued a negotiable warehouse receipt or negotiable bill of lading which is outstanding. In such case the document of title must be delivered or surrendered. Section 2–503(4).

Where the seller is required or authorized to send the goods to the buyer and the contract does not require him to deliver them at a particular destination, Section 2–504 of the Code provides that unless otherwise agreed the seller must:

(a) put the goods in the possession of such a carrier and make such a contract for their transporation as may be reasonable having regard to the nature of the goods and other circumstances of the case; and

(b) obtain and promptly deliver or tender in due form any document necessary to enable the buyer to obtain possession of the goods or otherwise required by the agreement or by usage of trade; and

(c) promptly notify the buyer of the shipment.

Failure to notify the buyer under paragraph (c) or to make a proper contract under paragraph (a) is a ground for rejection only if material delay or loss ensues.

Cure by Seller of Improper Tender or Delivery. Where the buyer refuses to accept a tender of goods which do not conform to the contract, or upon the delivery of such goods rejects them, the seller by acting promptly and within the time allowed for performance may make a proper tender or delivery of conforming goods and thereby "cure" his defective tender or performance. Section 2–508.

If the buyer refuses a tender of goods or rejects them as non-conforming without disclosing to the seller the nature of the defect, he may not assert such defect as an excuse for not accepting the goods or as a breach of contract by the seller if the defect is one which is curable. The buyer must act in good faith and state his reasons for refusing to accept the goods or be precluded from later relying upon such reasons. Section 2–605.

Installment Contracts—Materiality of Breach. As previously noted, unless the parties have otherwise agreed, the buyer does not have to pay any part of the price of the goods until the entire quantity specified in

the contract has been delivered or tendered to him. (Section 2–307). An installment contract is an instance where the parties have otherwise agreed. It expressly provides for delivery of the goods in separate lots or installments and usually for payment of the price in installments. Section 2—612.

Every breach of contract however small gives rise to a cause of action to recover a judgment in the amount of the damages thereby caused. So far as the right to recover is concerned, the size or extent of the breach bears only upon the amount of damages recoverable. Obviously, the more serious the breach, the greater the damages. If the breach is small or trivial, the amount of the judgment will be nominal.

However, a breach of contract may have an effect in addition to giving rise to a cause of action for damages. It may serve as an excuse for nonperformance on the part of the non-breaching party. This consequence may possibly be much more important than the cause of action for damages which the breach engenders.

Example: A makes a contract to deliver to B 50 tons of coal each month for one year, delivery to be made on the first day of each month commencing with January; B agrees to pay a certain price for each installment on the twentieth day of the month of delivery. A delivers to B 50 tons of coal on January 1. B does not pay for this coal on January 20. May A on January 21 treat this breach of contract by B, consisting of a one-day delay in payment of the first installment, as completely excusing A from any further duty to perform under the contract? There is no question of A's right to recover the price of the 50 tons delivered in January. The question is whether A may be permitted to treat B's breach as excusing A's non-performance of his duty to deliver coal in February and succeeding months and, if so excused from such duty, to maintain an action against B to recover damages for breach of the entire contract. A one-day delay in making payment would not have this effect. However, as this breach by the buyer is in limine, a delay at the beginning is a more material breach than would a delay of equal length after the contract had been partly or substantially performed. A delay of a week or ten days in payment of the January installment might well be a material breach going to the essence of the contract and thereby excusing the seller from any duty to perform further, whereas an equal delay in payment of the July installment, by which time the contract has been one-half performed on both sides, would probably not be a material breach.

A breach of contract, while not sufficiently serious to serve as an absolute excuse for non-performance, will nevertheless serve as a dilatory excuse. Thus, if by August 1, the buyer has not paid for the July coal, and if such breach under the circumstances is not a material breach, the seller may properly take the position that he will not deliver the August coal until the buyer pays for the July coal. This is utilizing the buyer's breach as a dilatory excuse for the seller's non-performance. If the buyer's breach continues long enough so that it becomes a material breach, the seller may then properly take the position that he will never deliver any more coal to the buyer under the contract. The buyer's material breach of contract provides the seller with an absolute excuse for non-performance.

The test is therefore the materiality of the breach. This involves a weighing of all relevant factors among which are the terms of the contract, its subject matter, the nature and extent of the breach, the reason for delay in performance, the time when the breach occurred, whether in limine or after partial or substantial performance on both sides, and the effect of the delay upon the party from whom performance has been withheld.

Conceivably, a delay in delivery of an installment of the goods might be more serious than an equal delay in the payment of an installment of the price.

It should be observed that under Section 2–612 of the Code a party to an installment contract loses his right to treat a material breach as one which entitles him to cancel the entire contract if he (1) accepts a nonconforming installment without seasonably notifying the other party of cancellation, or (2) brings an action to recover only for past installments, or (3) demands performance as to future installments. "Cancellation" occurs when either party puts an end to the contract for breach by the other, and in such case the cancelling party retains any remedy for breach of the whole contract or any unperformed balance. (Section 2–106(4).)

Courses Open to Buyer upon Improper Delivery. The buyer is not obliged to accept a tender or delivery of goods which do not conform to the contract. Upon such tender or delivery by the seller, the buyer under Section 2–601 of the Code has the choice of three alternatives. He may (1) reject all of the goods; or (2) accept all of the goods; or (3) accept any commercial unit or units of the goods and reject the rest.

The buyer's rejection of non-conforming goods is rightful. The rejection must be within a reasonable time after their delivery or tender, and to be effective the buyer must notify the seller of the rejection within such reasonable time. Upon thus effectively rejecting the goods the buyer may recover damages against the seller for nondelivery of the goods. (Section 2–711.)

Upon knowingly accepting goods which are non-conforming, the buyer may not thereafter reject them unless the acceptance was on the reasonable assumption that the non-conformity would be seasonably cured. The buyer must pay for any goods accepted at the contract rate, but upon giving the seller reasonable notice of the breach, the buyer is entitled to recover from the seller or to deduct from the unpaid price such damages as he has sustained by reason of the non-conformity of the goods to the contract. (Section 2–714; Section 2–717.)

The buyer may accept part of the nonconforming goods and reject the rest, so long as the goods accepted consist of commercial units. Section 2–105(6) defines such unit as follows:

> "Commercial unit" means such a unit of goods as by commercial usage is a single whole for purposes of sale and division of which materially impairs its character or value on the market or in use. A commercial unit may be a single article (as a machine) or a set of articles (as a suite of furniture or an assortment of sizes) or a quantity (as a bale, gross, or carload) or any other unit treated in use or in the relevant market as a single whole.

The buyer must pay at the contract rate for such commercial units as he accepts. However, upon giving the seller reasonable notice of the breach, the buyer is entitled to recover from the seller or deduct from the purchase price the amount of damages for non-conformity of the commercial units accepted and for non-delivery of the commercial units rejected. Acceptance of any part of a commercial unit is acceptance of the entire unit. (Section 2–606(2).)

Where the seller delivers or offers to deliver a larger quantity than the buyer ordered or contracted to buy, the buyer may (a) accept the entire lot, (b) accept only the quantity he ordered or contracted for and reject the rest, or (c) reject the entire lot. This last alternative may seem to give the buyer an undue advantage, as the seller's offer of performance might conceivably be considered as simply an offer to let the buyer have the quantity of goods specified in the order or contract, and more if the buyer wants them, but in any event the amount specified. However, the buyer has this election. If he does not want to take the trouble of separating the correct quantity from the remainder of the goods, he does not have to do so. Conceivably, a separation effected by the buyer might involve him in a dispute with the seller, and it is for the buyer to decide whether he wants to run the risk of such dispute.

The buyer is not required to become a tenant in common with others of goods in a mass unless trade usage, course of performance, or course of dealing between the parties would so indicate.

Where the seller delivers to the buyer goods of a different description mixed with the goods ordered or contracted for, he is in effect making an offer to sell all of the goods so delivered. The buyer may therefore accept the entire lot. He is under no obligation to do so and may with impunity reject all of the goods so delivered, if he wishes. Or the buyer may make a separation of the goods, retain the part which is in accordance with the contract, and reject the rest.

After the buyer has rejected the goods any exercise of ownership of the goods by him is wrongful as against the seller. If the buyer has possession of the rejected goods but no security interest in them, he is obliged to hold them with reasonable care for a time sufficient to permit the seller to remove them. The buyer who is not a merchant is under no further obligation with regard to goods rightfully rejected. (Section 2–602.)

A merchant buyer of goods who has rightfully rejected them is obligated to follow reasonable instructions from the seller with respect to the disposition of the goods when the seller has no agent or place of business at the market of rejection. If the goods are perishable or threaten to decline in value speedily, the merchant buyer must make reasonable efforts to sell them for the seller's account even in the absence of instructions from the seller. (Section 2–603.)

If the seller gives the buyer no instructions with respect to the rejected goods within a reasonable time after notification of the rejection, the buyer may (1) store the goods for the seller's account, or (2) reship the goods to the seller, or (3) resell them for the seller's account. The buyer is entitled to reimbursement of expenses in caring for and selling the goods as well as a reasonable selling commission in the event of resale. (Section 2–604.) Such action by the buyer is not obligatory but is permitted in order to salvage the goods and minimize loss thereby reducing the amount in dispute between the parties. The freedom of the buyer to so deal with the goods without effecting an acceptance or conversion of them exists when (1) the goods are non-conforming, (2) the buyer has given the seller due notice of rejection, and (3) the seller has failed to give instructions to the buyer. A merchant buyer, however, is obliged to follow the instructions of the seller as provided in Section 2–603.

The Buyer's Right of Inspection. The right of inspection is essentially a right which the buyer has to satisfy himself before making payment of the price that the goods tendered or delivered are what he contracted for or ordered. If the goods are not what the buyer ordered, title did not pass to the buyer upon delivery to the carrier. The buyer first discovers this upon an examination of the goods. The buyer is entitled to know that he is under a duty to pay the price before being required to make payment. An opportunity for inspection is therefore a condition precedent to the seller's right to enforce payment. If the seller ships the goods to the buyer C.O.D., the buyer may rightfully refuse to accept them unless the contract expressly provides for a C.O.D. shipment. The carrier does not permit inspection by the consignee under this form of shipment, and the effect is a denial of the right of inspection. Where the buyer, by the terms of the contract, has agreed to a

C.O.D. shipment, or to pay for the goods upon presentation of a bill of lading, no right of inspection exists because it is negatived by the agreement. Unless so negatived, it is a breach on the part of the seller to ship goods in such a way as to deprive the buyer of his right of inspection.

If goods are shipped with a reservation of security interest in the seller and tender is to be made of the document of title, the buyer may inspect the goods after their arrival before payment is due unless such inspection is inconsistent with the contract. The right would be inconsistent with a contract which provides that payment is due at the time and place where the buyer is to receive the document of title. (Section 2–310.)

The buyer is allowed a reasonable time to inspect the goods and may, if necessary to determine whether the goods conform to the contract, test or analyze them, even though such testing or analysis involves a destruction of a small portion of the goods. If the buyer makes an unnecessary test or destroys more than a reasonable quantity of the goods in testing, he loses the right to reject the goods. The buyer must bear the expense of testing, but incurs no liability for the value of the goods necessarily destroyed in making the test. If the goods do not conform to the contract and are rejected, the buyer may recover from the seller the necessary expenses of inspection. (Section 2–513(2).)

The right of inspection is independent of identification of the goods to the contract, transfer of title, or risk of loss. Section 2–513(4) provides:

"A place or method of inspection fixed by the parties is presumed to be exclusive but unless otherwise expressly agreed it does not postpone identification or shift the place for delivery or for passing the risk of loss."

Where a dispute exists as to whether the goods conform to the contract, either party upon reasonable notice to the other has the right to inspect, test and sample the goods even though the goods are in the possession of the other party. Section 2–515.

Acceptance of the Goods. As the term is used in the law of sales, acceptance means a manifestation of assent to become the owner of specific goods offered by the seller. Acceptance is therefore something independent of possession, delivery or payment for the goods. Acceptance may be indicated by the express words or presumed intention of the buyer, or by conduct of the buyer with respect to specific goods inconsistent with the seller's ownership thereof.

Section 2–606 of the Code provides:

What Constitutes Acceptance of Goods

(1) Acceptance of goods occurs when the buyer

    (a) after a reasonable opportunity to inspect the goods signifies to the seller that the goods are conforming or that he will take or retain them in spite of their non-conformity; or

    (b) fails to make an effective rejection (subsection (1) of Section 2–602), but such acceptance does not occur until the buyer has had a reasonable opportunity to inspect them; or

    (c) does any act inconsistent with the seller's ownership; but if such act is wrongful as against the seller it is an acceptance only if ratified by him.

(2) Acceptance of a part of any commercial unit is acceptance of that entire unit.

A buyer who accepts goods must within a reasonable time after he discovers or should have discovered any breach of contract or breach of warranty, notify the seller of the breach or be barred from any remedy. The burden is on the buyer to establish any breach with respect to goods which he has accepted. (Section 2–607.)

Revocation of Acceptance. Under certain circumstances and upon giving notice to the seller a buyer may revoke his acceptance of goods and upon doing so is in the same position with respect to the goods as if he had rejected them.

Section 2–608 of the Code provides:

Revocation of Acceptance in Whole or in Part

(1) The buyer may revoke his acceptance of a lot or commercial unit whose non-conformity substantially impairs its value to him if he has accepted it

    (a) on the reasonable assumption that its non-conformity would be cured and it has not been seasonably cured; or

    (b) without discovery of such non-conformity if his acceptance was reasonably induced either by the difficulty of discovery before acceptance or by the seller's assurances.

(2) Revocation of acceptance must occur within a reasonable time after the buyer discovers or should have discovered the ground for it and before any substantial change in condition of the goods which is not caused by their own defects. It is not effective until the buyer notifies the seller of it.

(3) A buyer who so revokes has the same rights and duties with regard to the goods involved as if he had rejected them.

Rights of Buyer being Sued for Breach of Warranty for which Seller is Answerable to Buyer. The buyer after making a resale of the goods may be sued by his purchaser for breach of implied warranty of merchantability. In the event of the buyer's liability to his purchaser, the seller is liable to the buyer if the same implied warranty was made in the original sale. There may also be contractual rights of the buyer under the terms of the original sale requiring the seller to indemnify the buyer.

In order to protect the buyer against the cost, inconvenience, and hazard of re-litigating the same issues in a second lawsuit, the Code permits the buyer by notice and demand to cause the seller to become bound by the determination of the lawsuit brought against the buyer by his purchaser. Section 2–607(5)(a).

Manufacturer A sells certain goods to Retailer B with a warranty. B resells the goods to Consumer C with the same warranty. The warranty is breached and C is injured. C brings an action against B. B may thereupon give written notice to A of the litigation advising A that he may come in and defend B in the suit and that if he fails to do so, he will be bound by the outcome of the suit in any subsequent action against him by B. Unless A thereupon comes in and defends B in the suit of C against B, he is so bound.

Rights of Seller and Buyer to Indemnity against Liability for Patent Infringement. It is not an uncommon provision in a contract for the sale of certain types of goods that the seller shall indemnify and hold the buyer harmless against any loss or expense, including attorneys' fees, arising out of any claim of patent infringement by a third party. Section 2–312(3) of the Code provides that a merchant seller impliedly warrants against infringement claims, and that a buyer who furnishes specifications to the seller must hold the seller harmless against such claims. In the event of an infringement suit, the party who is sued must give the indemnifying party reasonable notice of the litigation or be barred from any remedy over against such party. (Section 2–607(3) (b).)

X sells to Y certain goods upon which Z holds a patent. X agrees to indemnify Y against any loss or expense by reason of any claim or suit against Y for patent infringement. Z sues Y in an accounting action for patent infringement. X demands that Y turn over to X the control of the defense of this suit of Z against Y, including the employment of X's attorneys to represent Y in the suit. X agrees to bear all expense and to pay attorneys' fees and any judgment which may be entered against Y in the suit. Unless Y turns over to X the defense of the suit after receipt of this demand, Y may not recover from X on the indemnification agreement. Section 2–607(5) (b).

Unconscionable Contracts. Every contract of sale may be scrutinized by the court to determine whether in its commercial setting, purpose, and effect, it is unconscionable. The court may refuse to enforce an unconscionable contract or any part thereof found to be unconscionable. Section 2–302 provides:

> If the court as a matter of law finds the contract or any clause of the contract to have been unconscionable at the time it was made the court may refuse to enforce the contract, or it may enforce the remainder of the contract without the unconscionable clause, or it may so limit the application of any unconscionable clause as to avoid any unconscionable result.

The Code does not define "unconscionable". However, the Oxford Universal Dictionary (3rd ed.) definition is: "Monstrously extortionate, harsh, showing no regard for conscience."

Section 2–302 imposes a statutory limitation upon the rights of a party to demand enforcement of an unconscionable contract for the sale of goods in the interest of fairness and decency and to correct harshness in contracts resulting from unequal bargaining positions of the parties. This restriction upon freedom of contract is a departure from the 19th century doctrine of laissez-faire. Although the principle is not novel, its embodiment in a statute dealing with commercial transactions is novel.

In Henningsen v. Bloomfield Motors, Inc. (page 520) the Supreme Court of New Jersey in a pre-Code decision refused to enforce a harsh disclaimer of warranty in a contract for the purchase of an automobile, saying, "An instinctively felt sense of justice cries out against such a sharp bargain."

Section 2–302 is contained in Article 2, the express scope of which is "transactions in goods." (Section 2–102.) Application of the principle of Section 2–302 to transactions covered by other Articles of the Code, or to areas entirely outside the Code, may be based upon precepts and principles developed in courts of equity. This Section provides an undeniable stimulus to the extension of these principles.

In Campbell Soup Co. v. Wentz, 172 F.2d 80 (C.A. 3, 1948) the court denied equitable relief of specific performance of a contract whereby defendant, a farmer, had agreed to sell to plaintiff all of the Chautenay carrots to be grown on 15 acres during the 1947 season. A shortage of this type of carrots caused an increase in the market price to three times that of the contract price. Various provisions of the contract were held to be one-sided and unconscionable, among them an agreement of defendant not to sell carrots to any one else or permit any one else to grow carrots on his land, and contingencies excusing the plaintiff from any duty to purchase carrots from the defendant. The court stated that equity does not enforce unconscionable bargains.

In two cases in 1965 a referee in bankruptcy for the Eastern District of Pennsylvania held that security agreements executed by the bankrupts and governed by Article 9 of the Code were unenforceable by reason of their unconscionable provisions. The rulings of the referee were based upon established equitable principles and also upon application of Section 1–102 of the Code whereby in the opinion of the referee the prohibition of unconscionability "pervades *all* Code contractual arrangements." (Dorset Steel Equipment Co., Inc., Case No. 26532; Elkins-Dell Manufacturing Co., Inc., Case No. 26109, U.S.D.C. E.D., Pa.)

The security agreements held to be unconscionable contained provisions to the effect that:

(1) The finance company would buy only accounts of the debtor which in its sole and unlimited discretion were acceptable to it.

(2) The debtor would not borrow any money whatsoever from any source other than the finance company without its written consent.

(3) The finance company could change the terms of the loan agreement upon notice by mail to the debtor which could file a written dissent within five days.

(4) The finance company could direct the Post Office to deliver to it all mail addressed to the debtor, with the right to receive, open, and dispose of all such mail.

(5) The debtor could not suspend business without the prior written consent of the finance company.

(6) The debtor could not file a voluntary petition in bankruptcy, or for an arrangement or reorganization, without the prior written consent of the finance company.

(7) The debtor must pay the finance company a minimum of $6,000 interest charges for each year or fraction of a year the agreement is in force, regardless of the amount of its indebtedness.

The effect of these provisions which the court found unconscionable was that the entire security agreement was unenforceable.

Substituted Performance. The Code provides that where neither party is at fault and the agreed manner of delivery of the goods becomes commercially impracticable, as by reason of the failure of berthing, loading, or unloading facilities, or unavailability of an agreed type of carrier, or similar cause, a substituted manner of performance, if commercially reasonable, must be tendered and accepted. Section 2–614(1).

The goods must be delivered or tendered where reasonable, practical, commercial facilities are available for delivery. Neither seller nor buyer is excused on the ground that delivery in the express manner provided in the contract is impossible where such an alternative or substitute exists.

If the means or manner in which the buyer is to make payment becomes impossible by reason of supervening governmental regulation, the seller may withhold or stop delivery of the goods unless the buyer provides payment which is commercially substantially equivalent to that required by the contract. If delivery has already been made, payment as provided by the governmental regulation discharges the buyer unless the regulation is "discriminatory, oppressive or predatory." Section 2–614(2). The Code does not define these terms, and presumably the burden of establishing the unsavory character of the regulation would rest upon the seller.

Excuse of Performance by Non-happening of Presupposed Conditions. The ability to perform a contract for the sale of goods is subject to possible hazards, such as strikes, lock-outs, unforeseen shutdown of sources of supply, loss of plant or machinery by fire or other casualty, embargoes or other governmental regulations. Ordinarily these do not operate as an excuse on the ground of impossibility of performance, unless the contract expressly so provides. However, both parties may have understood at the time the contract was made that its performance depended upon the existence of certain facilities, or that the purpose of the contract and the value of performance depended entirely upon the happening of a certain future contemplated event, as for instance a contract for the sale of programs for a scheduled yacht regatta which is called off; or for the sale of tin horns for export to Cuba which become subject to embargo; or for the production of goods at a designated factory which becomes damaged or destroyed by fire. Due to the fault of neither party, these conditions cease to exist or do not occur.

Under these circumstances, unless the seller has expressly assumed the risk of the non-happening of the presupposed conditions, the Code provides that the seller is excused from his duty of performance. Section 2–615(a).

Allocation of Goods by Seller among His Customers. Although the seller may be relieved of his contractual duty by the non-happening of presupposed conditions, if the contingency affects only a part of the seller's capacity to perform, he must to the extent of his remaining capacity allocate delivery and production among his customers.

Where delay in delivery or non-delivery, in whole or in part, results from the happening of such contingency, the seller must give seasonable notice thereof to the buyer and in the event that allocation of goods is required must also provide the buyer with an estimate of the quota of goods which will be made available to him.

When the buyer receives notice of such delay in delivery or of an allocation of goods to him, he may by written notice to the seller where the prospective deficiency is material either (1) terminate the contract and discharge any portion of it which is executory, or (2) modify the contract by agreement to accept his quota of the goods.

If the buyer after receiving notice from the seller of such delay in delivery or of an allocation of goods fails to modify the contract by written notice to the seller within a reasonable time not exceeding 30 days, the contract is terminated with respect to any further deliveries. Section 2–616(2).

CASES

VIDAL v. TRANSCONTINENTAL & WESTERN AIR, INC.

(1941 C.A.3d) 120 F.2d 67.

GOODRICH, C. J. This action for breach of contract was tried by the court below without a jury. This appeal by the plaintiffs is from the action of the trial court in dismissing their complaint. By the terms of the contract, which bears date of April 14, 1937, the defendant agreed to sell and the plaintiff agreed to buy four used airplanes of a specified type belonging to the seller. The price was stipulated and payment was to be made by certified check upon delivery of the airplanes to the buyer at the Municipal Airport, Kansas City, Missouri. The date for delivery was stated to be June 1, 1937. As to the date of delivery, however, the seller's obligation to deliver on June 1 was qualified by saying "unless on that date we have not received a sufficient number of Douglas DC–3 or SDT airplanes to enable us to withdraw from service the airplanes to be purchased by you, in which event such airplanes shall be delivered to you and you agree to make payment within five (5) days after notice from us to you that such airplanes are ready for delivery to you." The buyers were privileged, by a following clause, to withdraw from the agreement if the seller was unable to deliver on or before July 1, 1937.

Twelve days later one of the buyers telegraphed to Mr. Frye, president of the defendant corporation (the seller), asking "Can you let us know approximate dates delivery * * *." Mr. Frye replied the same day: "Can deliver first ship June first and others by July tenth subject no further delays by Douglas." Plaintiffs did not answer this telegram. The trial court found as a fact that on June 1 the defendant was ready, able and willing to deliver one of the planes described in the contract to the plaintiffs at Municipal Airport in Kansas City, Missouri, and that after June 1 and on and prior to July 10 the defendant was ready, able and willing to deliver all of the four airplanes at the place specified. It was also found as a fact that the plaintiffs did not on June 1 or any other date either tender payment on any or all of the machines nor request delivery. Plaintiffs' action for damages was begun in the

United States District Court for the District of Delaware on October 8, 1938.

What are the respective rights and duties of the parties in a contract of this kind? Assume, for the moment, that there had been no qualifying clause with regard to time of delivery and there was a simple contract promising delivery by the seller to the buyer of specified goods at a definite time and place and neither party demanded performance from the other or tendered his own. Has either a right against the other? Payment and delivery are concurrent conditions since both parties are bound to render performance at the same time. Restatement, Contracts, § 251. In such a case, as Williston points out, neither party can maintain an action against the other without first making an offer of performance himself. Otherwise, if each stayed at home ready and willing to perform each would have a right of action against the other. " * * * to maintain an action at law the plaintiff must not only be ready and willing but he must have manifested this before bringing his action, by some offer of performance to the defendant, * * * It is one of the consequences of concurrent conditions that a situation may arise where no right of action ever arises against either party * * so long as both parties remain inactive, neither is liable * * *." This statement by the learned author not only has the force of his authority and that of many decisions from many states, but is also sound common sense. It is not an unfair requirement that a party complaining of another's conduct should be required to show that the other has fallen short in the performance of a legal obligation.

* * *

The conclusion is, therefore, that the defendant is not in default. Neither side having demanded performance by the other, neither side is in a position to complain or to assert any claim in an action of law against the other. This view of the case makes it unnecessary to examine the testimony which asserts that the buyers either abandoned or repudiated the contract prior to the time of the performance.

The judgment is affirmed.

GREATER LOUISVILLE AUTO AUCTION v. OGLE BUICK, INC.

(1965 Ky.) 387 S.W.2d 17.

PALMORE, J. The appellant, to which we shall refer as Auction or the auction company, is a corporation which during the time pertinent to this litigation conducted weekly auctions of used cars at its place of business in Louisville. On July 18, 1961, one Marion Caylor caused to be sold through the auction a group of automobiles he had purchased during the previous week from the various appellees, whom we shall call the Indiana sellers. Caylor had given the Indiana sellers checks on his bank at Franklin, Indiana, in full payment for cars so purchased. These checks, aggregating about $12,500, were rendered uncollectible by Auction's action on July 18 and 19, 1961, in stopping payment on checks it had theretofore given to Caylor as advances to finance his acquisition of vehicles to be sold through its auction, as well as the checks it gave Caylor on July 18, 1961, representing the proceeds from the cars auctioned off on that day, with the result that Auction kept the money for the cars Caylor had purchased from the Indiana sellers and the Indiana sellers got nothing. So the Indiana sellers brought this action against Auction for the amounts of their checks from Caylor which had been made cold by Auction's stop payment orders.

The trial court found in favor of the Indiana sellers, and Auction appeals.

We do not have any question in this case concerning legal title of the vehicles in question, which passed freely from the Indiana sellers through Caylor to the ultimate purchasers. Cf. § 2–403, Uniform Commercial Code (KRS Ch. 355). The question to be decided is whether the Indiana sellers had, as between them and Caylor, any rights with respect to the property which under the particular circumstances were good against Auction's seizure of the proceeds. We agree with the chancellor that they did.

It was the custom over a period of some two years for Auction and Caylor on each Tuesday to exchange checks in the amount required in order for Caylor to purchase cars during the ensuing week. The purpose of Caylor's check to Auction was to cover the advance, and it would not be deposited by Auction until a week later. Auction received a fee of $20 per car sold through it by Caylor, and Caylor received whatever profit was realized on each car. Though Caylor was a vice president of the auction company, it can be assumed for purposes of the argument that in buying cars and selling them through Auction he was acting for himself, free of any control by the company. There was no restriction or understanding to the effect that the vehicles acquired with money advanced by Auction one week would be brought to the auction the very next week. Caylor had a wholesale car lot at Franklin, Indiana, and often brought newly acquired vehicles there to be "cleaned up" before taking them to Louisville for sale.

On the eve of Tuesday, July 18, 1961, Auction had two $15,000 checks it had received from Caylor on July 11 and had not yet deposited, one $20,000 check dated June 20 which had bounced three times, and two $15,000 checks dated June 27 which had bounced once. The chief officers of Auction were greatly alarmed, and in spite of reassurances from Caylor that he had other checks coming in and also had some $10,000 worth of cars at his lot in Franklin, when their bank opened its doors on the morning of July 18 they stopped payment on about $21,000 in outstanding checks "and all others" they had given Caylor, and on the next day executed a similar order covering "all checks to Marion Caylor." These stop orders had the effect of cancelling about $36,000 worth of checks Caylor had deposited in his bank at Franklin, thus wiping out his bank account. Meanwhile, on July 18 the cars Caylor had bought from the Indiana sellers had been sold and Auction had issued Caylor checks in the amount of about $12,000 representing the proceeds.

* * *

UCC § 2–507(2) provides that when payment for goods is due and demanded on delivery, as between the parties the buyer's right to retain or dispose of the property is "conditional upon his making the payment due." Payment by check "is conditional and is defeated as between the parties by dishonor of the check on due presentment." UCC § 2–511(3). Therefore, as between Caylor and the Indiana sellers Caylor had no right either to retain or dispose of the cars. In such circumstances the UCC does not specifically reserve to the seller a right of reclamation. However, Comment 3 to UCC § 2–507 suggests that the seller's rights are the same as provided in UCC § 2–702, relating to sale on credit to an insolvent buyer, and we agree that surely the rights of an unpaid seller under UCC § 2–507(2) must be no less than in the case of a sale falling within the express terms of UCC § 2–702(2).

According to UCC § 2–702(2), if the seller discovers that the buyer has received goods on credit while insolvent (however innocently) he may reclaim them on demand within 10 days after the receipt. § 2–702(3) makes this right of reclamation subject to the rights of a buyer in ordinary course or other good faith purchaser or lien creditor. "A person is 'insolvent' who either has ceased to pay his debts in the ordinary course of business or cannot pay his debts as they become due or is insolvent within the meaning of the federal bankruptcy law." Id., § 1–201(23). Under this definition it seems obvious that Caylor

was "insolvent" when he traded with the Indiana sellers on July 14 and 15, 1961. Hence if the sales had been made "on credit" each of the sellers would have had a right of reclamation until the cars were resold within 10 days thereafter. We hold that an unpaid seller under UCC § 2–507(2) has the same right. Cf. Comment 3, UCC § 2–507.

Certainly Auction was not a lien creditor, nor could it have been a "buyer in the ordinary course of business or other good faith purchaser" from Caylor, since it did not purchase from him but merely acted as his agent in selling the cars to others. By retaining the proceeds Auction in effect took the cars from Caylor, not as a buyer but as an unsecured creditor, and applied them toward the satisfaction of its account against him. Though technically the Indiana sellers' right of reclamation ended when the cars were sold at auction to the ultimate buyers in ordinary course, we think that equity cannot allow Auction to retain the proceeds under circumstances in which it would not have been permitted to defeat the prior and superior rights of the Indiana sellers by taking the cars themselves.

* * *

All that we have said still might not justify impressing the interest of the Indiana sellers upon the proceeds of sale except that Auction knew enough of the circumstances to put it on notice of the likelihood that its actions in stopping payment of its checks would result in the dishonor of checks Caylor had issued in payment for the vehicles sold. The chancellor so found, and in our opinion that factual conclusion is supported by the evidence.

We recognize that the Indiana sellers, who had done business with Caylor on prior occasions, looked solely to his credit for their pay. Each of them took his personal check in satisfaction of the bargain and sale. Since he thought his checks would be good, he did not commit actual fraud on them. Auction had no detailed knowledge of the transactions between Caylor and the sellers. So far as it was concerned the cars belonged to Caylor and he had the unencumbered title papers. Ostensibly he could have paid cash for them, though there is nothing in the record to suggest any such custom on his part. Caylor also did an undisclosed amount of borrowing from another source. Nevertheless, Auction knew that for the past two or three weeks Cayor's checks had been bouncing like rubber balls, from which it was bound to realize that other checks given by him to other people would likewise be dishonored, particularly after the stop orders. One would ordinarily expect business of the type here in question to be done by check. Auction surely realized from the ordinary course of its business with Caylor that these automobiles probably had been purchased very recently. That they had been paid for by check also was an undeniable likelihood; that such checks would be dishonored was almost a certainty. Therefore, we agree with the chancellor that Auction's knowledge of the circumstances was sufficient to put it on notice of the rights of the Indiana sellers. "A person has 'notice' of a fact when * * * from all the facts and circumstances known to him at the time in question he has reason to know that it exists." UCC § 1–201(25).

The judgment is affirmed.

PARK COUNTY IMPLEMENT CO. v. CRAIG

(1964 Wyo.) 397 P.2d 800.

PARKER, C. J. Plaintiff sued defendants for the amount due on a purchase of a truck chassis and cab. Defendants entered a general denial, moved for a summary judgment, and thereafter plaintiff filed a similar motion. Certain affidavits and interrogatories were submitted, and the court after considering the matter entered a summary judgment for de-

fendants, from which judgment this appeal is taken.

On February 16, 1962, defendants ordered a 1962 International A–162 chassis and cab from plaintiff, which advised that one was not on hand but should be in the area. Three days later defendants were informed that such a vehicle was at the International Harvester Company in Billings, Montana, whereupon defendant Holler drove to Billings and there received the vehicle from that company, asking the International employee from whom the vehicle was received for a statement of origin, title certificate, or some evidence of title. The employee responded that the company did not have the same. The agreed selling price was approximately $3,150 delivered in Cody, Wyoming, or approximately $3,115 if defendants took delivery of the truck at Billings. According to the interrogatories and affidavit, defendants brought the vehicle to Cody, put it in their shop, and were installing a hoist and dump bed when a fire occurred March 1, destroying the chassis and cab. Defendants said they had made request of plaintiff's manager for statement of origin or other title papers to no avail, but plaintiff's manager said a statement of origin was tendered to defendants on March 2 and was refused.

* * *

Assuming that the position of the litigants has remained consistent, we review defendants' arguments here. In essence they say that there was no completed sale because either (1) the Montana law was applicable and under holdings in that jurisdiction there was no completed sale until there had been compliance with various sections of the motor vehicle code, notably, the issuance of a certificate of ownership. * * *

They say further that the Uniform Commercial Code—Sales (Article 2, Chapter 22, Title 34, W.S.1957 (1963 Cumulative Supp.)), does not apply since a motor vehicle cannot be classified as "goods." Accordingly, they assert that there was no genuine issue as to any material fact and that they were entitled to judgment as a matter of law. We examine such theses. Before deciding the applicability of Montana law, we must determine what is the law of Wyoming, that State being the residence of the parties and the scene of every activity concerning the motor vehicle in question except its having been received in Billings, Montana, by Holler, one of the defendants. At the inception of the synthesis, we note that the Uniform Commercial Code—Sales had been adopted in Wyoming January 1, 1962, and was in effect at the time of the transaction, and further that this code has been held as applicable to motor vehicles. [Citation.]

This leads us to the section of the Uniform Commercial Code dealing with the territorial application of the Act, § 34–1–105, W.S.1957 (1963 Cumulative Supp.), which provides:

"(1) Except as provided hereafter in this section, when a transaction bears a reasonable relation to this state and also to another state or nation the parties may agree that the law either of this state or of such other state or nation shall govern their rights and duties. Failing such agreement this act [§§ 34–1–101 to 34–10–105] applies to transactions bearing an appropriate relation to this state."

* * * The official Uniform Code Comment regarding revised § 1–105, which is identical with its counterpart in Wyoming, is manifest in disclosing both the problems and the desired solution:

"Where a transaction has significant contacts with a state which has enacted the Act and also with other jurisdictions, the question what relation is 'appropriate' is left to judicial decision. In deciding that question, the court is not strictly bound by precedents established in other contexts. Thus a conflict-of-laws decision refusing to apply a purely local statute or rule of law to a particular multi-state transaction may not be valid precedent for refusal to apply the Code in an analogous situation. Application of the Code in such circumstances may be justified by its comprehensiveness, by the policy of uniformity, and by the fact that it is in large part a reformulation and restatement of the law merchant and of the understanding of a business community which transcends state and even national boundaries. [Citation.] In particular, where a transaction is governed in large part by the Code, application of another law to some detail of performance because of an accident of geography may violate the commercial understanding of the parties." Uniform Commercial Code (U.L.A.) § 1–105, p. 17 (1962).

In the light of the development of the statute—its history, purposes, and objectives—and the arrangements between the parties in this case, the going to Billings for the vehicle would seem under any concept to have been a minor part of the transaction, and the portions occurring in Wyoming bear an appropriate relation to an extent that the Uniform Commercial Code applies. See Schnabel Company v. School District of Pittsburgh, 178 Pa.Super. 553, 116 A.2d 73, 75. We hold, therefore, that the transaction in this case was within the Uniform Commercial Code—Sales. The buyers accepted the goods under the provisions of § 34–2–606(1) (c), W.S. 1957 (1963 Cumulative Supp.), "Acceptance of goods occurs when the buyer does any act inconsistent with the seller's ownership," when they began installing a hoist and dump bed on the vehicle. At that time the buyer became liable under the provisions of § 34–2–607(1), "The buyer must pay at the contract rate for any goods accepted."

Even if there is merit in defendants' contention concerning the pertinency of various provisions of the motor vehicle law requiring certificates of title to be issued under certain circumstances, the rights of the parties under the code do not depend upon title. As is noted in the official comment:

"This Article [Uniform Commercial Code—Sales] deals with the issues between seller and buyer in terms of step by step performance or nonperformance under the contract for sale and not in terms of whether or not 'title' to the goods has passed. * * *" Uniform Commercial Code (U.L.A.) § 2–401, p. 190 (1962).

In the instant case, there were no issues of fact before the court except the question of whether or not the plaintiff offered statement of origin to defendants on March 2 and this point is not material. Under the admitted facts the defendants accepted the goods at an agreed price. The summary judgment granted to defendants was in error; the motion of plaintiff for summary judgment should have been granted. The cause is reversed with instructions to enter judgment for plaintiff.

Reversed.

LAMBORN v. SEGGERMAN BROS., INC.

(1925) 240 N.Y. 118, 147 N.E. 607, 38 A.L.R. 1540.

[Action by Lamborn and others, copartners, plaintiffs, (buyer) against Seggerman Brothers, defendant, (seller) to recover the purchase price of certain boxes of apples paid by plaintiffs to defendant.

The written contract of the parties provided that the plaintiffs bought and defendant sold a car of 1,200 boxes of apples, F.O.B. Pacific Coast Rail Shipping Point. Payment of the purchase price, $13,377, was made in advance by plaintiffs to defendant. Defendant later caused to be forwarded to plaintiffs at New York a car containing 1,770 boxes of apples. These apples were seized by United States government officials before reaching New York. Plaintiffs never received the 1,-200 boxes they paid for. Judgment for defendant, and plaintiffs appeal.]

LEHMAN, J. These apples have been seized. All that remains is a possible claim against some party. If the defendant has complied with its contract; if it has made delivery of the goods; if title has passed to the plaintiffs, then the plaintiffs were bound to pay the agreed price and there has been no failure of consideration for such payment and there can be no recovery under the contract. On the other hand, if the defendant's obligation to transfer title to the apples still remained open, then its contract was entirely unperformed and upon failure to perform, even though performance was frustrated without its fault, restitution of the consideration received still remains. [Citation.] * * *

The delivery to the carrier which would transfer responsibility to the buyer was only such delivery as the seller was authorized to make. * * * A delivery by a seller to a carrier, even for the purpose of transmission to the buyer, of a quantity greater than the amount called for by the contract does not constitute an appropriation of goods to the buyer's contract which constitutes a delivery to the buyer sufficient to pass property in any of the goods. "In order for the property to so pass the seller must have acted in conformity with authority given by the buyer." Williston on Sales, 2d Ed., sec. 278. Here the defendant was authorized to ship to the plaintiffs 1,200 boxes which under the contract were referred to as a "specific car of boxes." The parties contemplated a definite appropriation of a particular 1,200 boxes to the contract. The defendant never appropriated to this contract any particular 1,200 boxes; the boxes it was required to deliver still remained part of a mass and were shipped, not as a "specific car," but as a part of a carload. * * * The plaintiffs never agreed to purchase an undivided share in a mass; they never authorized shipment of 1,200 boxes of apples as part of a mass or even as part of a pool car, for their contract refers to a specific carload and to 1,200 boxes of apples to be ascertained and appropriated before shipment and no title to any apples has ever passed to the plaintiffs. * * *

Judgment reversed.

F. W. LANG CO. v. FLEET

(1960) 193 Pa.Super. 365, 165 A.2d 258.

PER CURIAM. The order of the court below is affirmed on the opinion of Judge Boyle, of the Municipal Court of Philadelphia.

The opinion of Judge Boyle follows:

This is an appeal from an order discharging a rule to open a judgment which was entered by confession.

On April 30, 1957, the defendants purchased from the plaintiff an ice cream freezer and a refrigeration compressor unit. A written installment sales contract was executed wherein the defendants agreed to pay a total sale price of $2160; the sum of $860 was to be paid as a down payment and the balance including finance charges was to be paid in 18 equal installments of $78.72.

Actually the defendants paid only the sum of $200 at the time of receiving the freezer and compressor and made no further payments. On July 30, 1959, the plaintiff caused a writ of replevin to issue in this court as of July Term, 1959, No. 3911, and the equipment was seized by the sheriff and delivered to the plaintiff. The defendants did not assert a lien for the money paid to the plaintiff and suffered judgment in replevin to be entered against them.

The plaintiff sold the equipment for $500, the highest price then obtainable and there is no averment by the defendants that this sale was not a fair and equitable resale of the equipment in accordance with accepted commercial practices. The defendants were given credit for this sum in the assessment of damages filed by the plaintiff.

The defendants filed a complaint in assumpsit in this court as of September Term, 1959, No. 3198, alleging there that the equipment was defective and was wholly unusable for the purpose intended. The defendants demanded damages for the return of the down money, the cost of maintenance of the equipment while it was in the possession of the defendants and the court costs incurred in defending the replevin action.

The plaintiff obtained judgment by confession pursuant to the written installment sales contract on January 4, 1960. The defendants filed a petition and rule to show cause "why the judgment should not be opened and defendants let into a defense and this matter consolidated with Bertram Fleet and Sidney Danowitz v. F. W. Lang Co., Municipal Court, September Term, 1959, No. 3198." The petition avers that many efforts were made by the defendants "to seek return of the equipment and a rebate of the deposit" and that the defendants have a defense to plaintiff's claim as set forth in their action in assumpsit.

The plaintiff filed an answer to the petition which avers that the defendants refused to permit the plaintiff to remove the equipment unless plaintiff refunded the deposit of $200 which made it necessary to obtain return of the equipment by an action in replevin. The answer also denies that the defendants have any defense whatsoever to plaintiff's claim and avers that the equipment was in perfect operating condition and was actually being used by the defendants up until the time when it was repossessed.

* * *

Both the petition to open judgment and the complaint in assumpsit are based on an alleged rescission of the contract by the defendants. But the depositions establish that the defendants have forfeited any right of rescission, if such right did exist in fact. About one year after the equipment was installed the defendants moved to a new location and took the equipment with them without notifying the plaintiff. In May or June of 1959 the defendants disconnected the compressor from the freezer and connected it to an air conditioner where it was used by the defendants to operate the air conditioner until the equipment was replevied by the plaintiff.

The Uniform Commercial Code, Sec. 2–602, 12A P.S. § 2–602 provides:

"(1) Rejection of goods must be within a reasonable time after their delivery or tender.

"It is ineffective unless the buyer seasonably notifies the seller.

"(2) * * * (a) after rejection any exercise of ownership by the buyer with respect to any commercial unit is wrongful as against the seller."

Section 2–606 provides:

"(1) Acceptance of goods occurs when the buyer * * *

"(c) does any act inconsistent with the seller's ownership; but if such act is wrongful as against the seller it is an acceptance only if ratified by him.

"(2) Acceptance of a part of any commercial unit is acceptance of that entire unit."

In the instant case the defendants exercised dominion over the compressor unit by using it to operate an air conditioner. This is completely inconsistent with the seller's ownership. The seller in this case by entering judgment for the unpaid balance ratified the sale as represented by the installment sales contract. The seller never accepted or agreed to a rescission by the defendants. Therefore under the cited provisions of the Commercial Code the buyer is deemed to have accepted the goods and is precluded from unilaterally asserting a rescission of the sales contract.

A rescission based on breach of warranty must be made within a reasonable time and cannot be made if the buyer exercises an act of dominion over the goods or permits the goods to be altered or changed while in his exclusive possession—[Citations].

The defendants contend that because they instituted an action in assumpsit to recover the down money paid and their expenses it is mandatory that the judgment be opened so that the claim on which the judgment was based can be litigated together with their action in assumpsit. This position is untenable. In the first place the action in assumpsit was instituted more than two years after the defendants obtained possession of the equipment. Moreover the defendants failed to assert in the action in replevin a lien based on their right to rescind the contract and receive the return of the down money paid.

The Commercial Code, Section 2–711 provides:

"(3) On rightful rejection or justifiable revocation of acceptance a buyer who has paid all or part of the price has a security interest in goods in his possession or control for the amount paid plus any expenses reasonably incurred in their inspection, receipt, transportation, care and custody."

* * *

We are convinced that there is no valid defense to the plaintiff's claim and, hence, we discharged the defendants' rule to open the judgment.

WILLIAMS v. WALKER-THOMAS FURNITURE COMPANY

(1965 C.A.D.C.) 350 F.2d 445.

WRIGHT, C. J. Appellee, Walker-Thomas Furniture Company, operates a retail furniture store in the District of Columbia. During the period from 1957 to 1962 each appellant in these cases purchased a number of household items from Walker-Thomas, for which payment was to be made in installments. The terms of each purchase were contained in a printed form contract which set forth the value of the purchased item and purported to lease the item to appellant for a stipulated monthly rent payment. The contract then provided, in substance, that title would remain in Walker-Thomas until the total of all the monthly payments made equaled the stated value of the item, at which time appellants could take title. In the event of a default in the payment of any monthly installment, Walker-Thomas could repossess the item.

The contract further provided that "the amount of each periodical installment payment to be made by [purchaser] to the Company under this present lease shall be inclusive of and not in addition to the amount of each installment payment to be made by [purchaser] under such prior leases, bills or accounts; *and all payments now and hereafter made by [purchaser] shall be credited pro rata on all outstanding leases, bills and accounts* due the Company by [purchaser] at the time each such payment is made." (Emphasis added.) The effect of this rather obscure provision was to keep a balance due on every item purchased until the balance due on all items, whenever purchased, was liquidated. As a result, the debt incurred at the time of purchase of each item was secured by the right to repossess all the items previously purchased by the same purchaser, and each new item purchased automatically became subject to a security interest arising out of the previous dealings.

On May 12, 1962, appellant Thorne purchased an item described as a Daveno, three tables, and two lamps, having total stated value of $391.10. Shortly thereafter, he defaulted on his monthly payments and appellee sought to replevy all the items purchased since the first transaction in 1958. Similarly, on April 17, 1962, appellant Williams bought a stereo set of stated value of $514.95. She too defaulted shortly thereafter, and appellee sought to replevy all the

items purchased since December, 1957. The Court of General Sessions granted judgment for appellee. The District of Columbia Court of Appeals affirmed, and we granted appellants' motion for leave to appeal to this court.

Appellants' principal contention, rejected by both the trial and the appellate courts below, is that these contracts, or at least some of them, are unconscionable and, hence, not enforceable. * * *

We do not agree that the court lacked the power to refuse enforcement to contracts found to be unconscionable. In other jurisdictions, it has been held as a matter of common law that unconscionable contracts are not enforceable. While no decision of this court so holding has been found, the notion that an unconscionable bargain should not be given full enforcement is by no means novel. * * *

Congress has recently enacted the Uniform Commercial Code, which specifically provides that the court may refuse to enforce a contract which it finds to be unconscionable at the time it was made. 28 D.C.Code § 2–302 (Supp. IV 1965). The enactment of this section, which occurred subsequent to the contracts here in suit, does not mean that the common law of the District of Columbia was otherwise at the time of enactment, nor does it preclude the court from adopting a similar rule in the exercise of its powers to develop the common law for the District of Columbia. In fact, in view of the absence of prior authority on the point, we consider the congressional adoption of § 2–302 persuasive authority for following the rationale of the cases from which the section is explicitly derived. Accordingly, we hold that where the element of unconscionability is present at the time a contract is made, the contract should not be enforced.

Unconscionability has generally been recognized to include an absence of meaningful choice on the part of one of the parties together with contract terms which are unreasonably favorable to the other party. Whether a meaningful choice is present in a particular case can only be determined by consideration of all the circumstances surrounding the transaction. In many cases the meaningfulness of the choice is negated by a gross inequality of bargaining power. The manner in which the contract was entered is also relevant to this consideration. Did each party to the contract, considering his obvious education or lack of it, have a reasonable opportunity to understand the terms of the contract, or were the important terms hidden in a maze of fine print and minimized by deceptive sales practices? Ordinarily, one who signs an agreement without full knowledge of its terms might be held to assume the risk that he has entered a one-sided bargain. But when a party of little bargaining power, and hence little real choice, signs a commercially unreasonable contract with little or no knowledge of its terms, it is hardly likely that his consent, or even an objective manifestation of his consent, was ever given to all the terms. In such a case the usual rule that the terms of the agreement are not to be questioned should be abandoned and the court should consider whether the terms of the contract are so unfair that enforcement should be withheld.

In determining reasonableness or fairness, the primary concern must be with the terms of the contract considered in light of the circumstances existing when the contract was made. The test is not simple, nor can it be mechanically applied. The terms are to be considered "in the light of the general commercial background and the commercial needs of the particular trade or case." Corbin suggests the test as being whether the terms are "so extreme as to appear unconscionable according to the mores and business practices of the time and place." [Citation.] We think this formulation correctly states the test to be applied in those cases where no meaningful choice was exercised upon entering the contract.

Because the trial court and the appellate court did not feel that enforcement could be refused, no findings were made on the possible unconscionability of the contracts in these cases. Since the record is not sufficient for our deciding the issue as a matter of law, the cases must be remanded to the trial court for further proceedings.

Reversed and remanded.

AMERICAN HOME IMPROVEMENT, INC. v. MacIVER

(1964) 105 N.H. 435, 201 A.2d 886.

This is an agreed case submitted on exhibits and certain stipulated facts. The plaintiff seeks to recover damages for breach by the defendants of an alleged agreement for home improvements. The agreement (Exhibit No. 1) was signed by the defendants April 4, 1963 and it provided that the plaintiff would "furnish and install 14 combination windows and 1 door" and "flintcoat" the side walls of the defendants' property at a cost of $1,759.

KENISON, C. J. * * * In examining the exhibits and agreed facts in this case we find that to settle the principal debt of $1,759 the defendants signed instruments obligating them to pay $42.81 for 60 months, making a total payment of $2,568.60, or an increase of $809.60 over the contract price. In reliance upon the total payment the defendants were to make, the plaintiff pay a sales commission of $800. Counsel suggests that the goods and services to be furnished the defendants thus had a value of only $959, for which they would pay an additional $1,609.-60 computed as follows:

"Value of goods and services		$ 959.00
Commission	800.00	
Interest and carrying charges	809.60	1,609.60
Total payment		$2,568.60"

In the circumstances of the present case we conclude that the purpose of the disclosure statute will be implemented by denying recovery to the plaintiff on its contract and granting the defendants' motion to dismiss. [Citations.]

There is another and independent reason why the recovery should be barred in the present case because the transaction was unconscionable. "The courts have often avoided the enforcement of unconscionable provisions in long printed standardized contracts, in part by the process of 'interpretation' against the parties using them, and in part by the method used by Lord Nelson at Copenhagen." 1 Corbin, Contracts, s. 128 (1963). Without using either of these methods reliance can be placed upon the Uniform Commercial Code (U.C.C. 2–302(1)). See RSA 382–A:2–302(1) which reads as follows: "If the court as a matter of law finds the contract or any clause of the contract to have been unconscionable at the time it was made the court may refuse to enforce the contract, or it may enforce the remainder of the contract without the unconscionable clause, or it may so limit the application of any unconscionable clause as to avoid any unconscionable result."

Inasmuch as the defendants have received little or nothing of value and under the transaction they entered into they were paying $1,609 for goods and services valued at far less, the contract should not be enforced because of its unconscionable features. This is not a new thought or a new rule in this jurisdiction. [Citation.] "It has long been the law in this state that contracts may be declared void because unconscionable and oppressive * * *."

The defendants' motion to dismiss should be granted. In view of the result reached it is unnecessary to consider any other questions and the order is

Remanded.

PROBLEMS

1. A contracted with B to manufacture, sell and deliver to B and put in running order a certain machine. A set up the machine and put it in running order. B found it unsatisfactory and notified A that he rejected the machine. He continued to use it for three months, but continually complained of its defective condition. At the end of the three months he took it down and notified A to come and get it. Has B lost his right to reject the machine?

2. Smith, having contracted to sell 30 tons of described fertilizer, consigned what he said conformed to the contract to the buyer, and tendered him the bill of lading. Nothing had been said in the contract as to the time of payment, but Smith demanded payment as a condition of handing over the bill of lading. The buyer refused to pay, unless he were given the opportunity to inspect the fertilizer. Smith then sued for breach of contract. Judgment for whom?

3. A and B entered into a contract for the sale of 100 barrels of flour. No mention was made of any place of delivery. Thereafter, B demanded that A should deliver the flour at B's place of business, and A demanded that B should come and take the flour from A's warehouse. Neither party acceded to the demand of the other. Has either one a right of action against the other? Is it important whether the contract related to specific barrels?

4. A, a manufacturer of air conditioning units, makes a written contract with B to sell and deliver to B 40 units at a price of $200 each and to deliver them at a certain apartment building owned by B for installation by B. Upon the arrival of A's truck for delivery at the apartment building, B examines the units on the truck, counts only 30 units and asks the driver if this is the total delivery. The driver replies that it is as far as he knows. B tells the driver that he will not accept delivery of the units. The next day A telephones B and inquires why delivery was refused. B states that the units on the truck were not what he ordered and that he was going to buy air conditioning units elsewhere. In an action by A against B for breach of contract, B defends upon the ground that the tender of 30 units was improper as the contract called for delivery of 40 units. Is this a valid defense?

5. S in Chicago entered into a contract to sell certain machines to B, in New York. The ma-

chines are to be manufactured by S and shipped f. o. b. Chicago not later than March 25. On March 24, when S is about to ship the machines, he receives a telegram from B wrongfully repudiating the contract. The machines cannot readily be resold for a reasonable price being of a special kind used only in B's manufacturing processes. S sues B to recover the agreed price of the machines. What are the rights of the parties?

6. A and B enter into a written contract whereby A agrees to sell and B to buy 6,000 bushels of wheat at $2 per bushel, deliverable at the rate of 1,000 bushels a month commencing June 1, the price for each installment being pay-able ten days after delivery thereof. A delivered and received payment for the June installment. A defaulted by failing to deliver the July and August installments. By August 15, the market price of wheat had increased to $2.25 per bushel. B thereupon entered into a contract with C to purchase 5,000 bushels of wheat at $2.25 per bushel deliverable over the ensuing four months. In late September, the market price of wheat commenced to decline and by December 1 was $1.90 per bushel. B brings an action against A to recover $1,250, the difference between the contract price of 5,000 bushels of wheat and the price which he paid C for this amount of wheat. What are the rights of the parties?

CHAPTER 22

REMEDIES OF SELLER AND BUYER

Introductory. The remedial rights of the seller and the buyer include both remedies for breach of contract and remedies with respect to the goods.

The performance of a contract for the sale of goods frequently involves a progression of events in stages, and at any stage one of the parties may breach or repudiate the contract, or insolvency of one of the parties may occur. At the time of the happening of such event the contract may be wholly executory, the goods may be in the possession of the seller and identified to the contract, or in transit, or in the possession of the buyer. The goods may be conforming or non-conforming to the contract. In either case they may be accepted or rejected by the buyer whose conduct may be rightful or wrongful. Remedies are therefore necessary which relate not only to a breach of the contract but to the factual situation with respect to the goods.

The several and distinct remedies of the seller and of the buyer will be separately considered.

REMEDIES OF THE SELLER

The remedies of an unpaid seller under the Code are to (1) withhold delivery of the goods; (2) identify goods to the contract notwithstanding breach; (3) stop delivery of goods by a bailee; (4) resell the goods; (5) recover damages for non-acceptance or repudiation; (6) recover the price and incidental damages; (7) recover the goods upon the buyer's insolvency; (8) cancel the contract.

(1) *To Withhold Delivery of the Goods*. The seller may withhold delivery of goods to a buyer who has wrongfully rejected or has revoked acceptance of those which have been tendered or delivered, or who has failed to make a payment due on or before delivery, or who has repudiated with respect to a part or the whole of the contract. This right applies with respect to any goods directly affected and if the breach by the buyer is of the whole contract, it applies to the whole undelivered balance of the goods. (Section 2–703.)

The Code does not refer to this right as an unpaid seller's lien upon the goods, as the right does not depend upon whether title has passed to the buyer. The right is essentially that of a seller to discontinue any further performance on his side of the contract by reason of the buyer's breach. It is one of a series of remedies which the seller has under Section 2–703 of the Code.

(2) *To Identify Goods to the Contract Notwithstanding Buyer's Breach*. Upon a breach of the contract by the buyer, the seller may proceed to identify to the contract conforming goods in his possession or control which were not so identified at the time he learned of the breach. (Section 2–704.) He may also treat as the subject of resale unfinished goods which have demonstrably been intended for fulfillment of the particular contract. With respect to such unfinished goods, the seller in the exercise of reasonable commercial judgment for the purpose of mitigating loss may either complete their manufacture and identify them to the contract or cease their manufacture and resell the unfinished goods for scrap or salvage value. (Section 2–704.) For example, if at the time of the buyer's breach or repudiation the goods in the process of manufacture are 90% finished, in order to avoid loss and obtain maximum realization of value a seller may be justified in completing their manu-

facture and reselling them as finished goods. On the other hand, if at such time the manufacturing process has only just commenced, sound business judgment may require that the manufacture be halted in order to minimize loss and damage.

(3) *To Stop Delivery of the Goods by a Carrier or Other Bailee.* When an unpaid seller discovers that his buyer is insolvent, he may order the carrier or other bailee in possession of the goods to stop delivery of the goods. He may also stop shipments of carload, truckload, planeload, or larger shipments of express or freight when the buyer repudiates or fails to make a payment that is due, or if for any other reason he has a right to withhold or reclaim the goods. This right is broader than the seller's right of stoppage in transitu as it existed at common law. It applies to goods in the possession of any bailee and not only in the event of the buyer's insolvency but also upon a repudiation or breach by the buyer. (Section 2–705.)

The right of the seller to stop delivery ceases when (1) the buyer receives the goods; or (2) the bailee of the goods, except a carrier, acknowledges to the buyer that he holds them for the buyer; or (3) the carrier acknowledges to the buyer that he holds them for the buyer by reshipment or as warehouseman; or (4) a negotiable document of title covering the goods is negotiated to the buyer.

In order to stop delivery of the goods, the seller must so notify the carrier or bailee that by reasonable diligence it may prevent delivery of the goods to the buyer. Upon such notification, the carrier or bailee must hold the goods and deliver them according to the directions of the seller who is liable to the carrier or bailee for any ensuing charges or damages. If a negotiable document of title has been issued for the goods the carrier or bailee is not obliged to obey a notice to stop

delivery until surrender of the document. A carrier who has issued a non-negotiable bill of lading is not obliged to obey a notification to stop delivery received from any person other than the consignor.

Insolvency, as it applies to the right to stop delivery and to other rights of the seller and the buyer when pertinent, is defined in Section 1–201(23) of the Code as follows:

> A person is "insolvent" who either has ceased to pay his debts in the ordinary course of business or cannot pay his debts as they become due, or is insolvent within the meaning of the federal bankruptcy law.

Insolvency is thus defined in both the equity sense and the bankruptcy sense. The equity meaning of insolvency is the inability of a person to pay his debts as they mature. The bankruptcy meaning is that his total liabilities exceed in amount the total value of all of his assets.

(4) *To Resell the Goods.* Under the same circumstances which permit the seller to withhold delivery of goods to the buyer, the seller may resell the goods concerned or the undelivered balance thereof. (Section 2–706.) The resale must be made in good faith and in a commercially reasonable manner, and the seller may recover from the buyer the difference between the resale price and the contract price, together with any incidental damages such as reasonable charges and expenses incurred in stopping delivery, in the transportation, care, and custody of the goods after the buyer's breach, and in connection with the return or resale of the goods, less expenses saved in consequence of the buyer's breach.

The resale may be at public or private sale and the goods may be sold as a unit or in parcels. The goods resold must be identified as referring to the broken contract, but it is not necessary that the goods be in existence or that they have been identified to the contract before the buyer's breach.

Where the resale is at private sale the seller must give the buyer reasonable notice of his intention to resell.

Where the resale is at public sale only identified goods can be sold except where there is a recognized market for a public sale of future goods of the kind involved. The public sale must be made at a usual place or market for public sale if one is reasonably available. The seller must give the buyer reasonable notice of the time and place of the resale unless the goods are perishable or threaten to decline in value speedily. Prospective bidders at the sale must be given an opportunity for reasonable inspection of the goods before the sale. The seller may be a purchaser of the goods at the public sale.

The seller is not accountable to the buyer for any profit made on any resale of the goods. However, "a person in the position of a seller" who resells the goods, as an agent who has paid or become responsible for the price on behalf of his principal, or a buyer who has acquired a security interest in the goods, must account for any excess realized over the amount of his security interest. (Section 2–706(6).)

A bona fide purchaser at a resale takes the goods free of any rights of the original buyer, even though the seller has failed to comply with one or more of the requirements of the Code with respect to making the resale. (Section 2–706(5).)

(5) *To Recover Damages for Non-acceptance or Repudiation.* The seller in the event of a repudiation or non-acceptance of the goods by the buyer may maintain an action at law and recover damages from the buyer measured by the difference between the market price at the time and place of tender of the goods and the unpaid contract price, plus incidental damages, less expenses saved in consequence of the buyer's breach. (Section 2–708.)

If the difference between the market price and the contract price is inadequate to place the seller in as good a position as performance would have done, the Code also provides that the measure of damages is the profit, including reasonable overhead, which the seller would have realized from full performance by the buyer, plus any incidental damages less expenses saved in consequence of the buyer's breach. (Section 2–708(2).)

(6) *To Recover the Price and Incidental Damages.* At common law, an action by the seller to recover the price depended upon a transfer of title to the buyer. The Code permits the seller to recover the price in three situations: (1) where the buyer has accepted the goods; (2) where conforming goods have been lost or damaged after the risk of loss has passed to the buyer; and (3) where the goods have been identified to the contract and there is no ready market available for their resale at a reasonable price. (Section 2–709.) A seller who sues for the price must hold for the buyer any goods which have been identified to the contract and are still in his control. If resale becomes possible, the seller may resell the goods at any time prior to the collection of the judgment and the net proceeds of any such resale must be credited to the buyer. Payment of the judgment entitles the buyer to any goods not resold.

If the buyer has wrongfully rejected or revoked acceptance of the goods or has repudiated or failed to make a payment due, a seller who is held not entitled to recover the price shall be awarded damages for non-acceptance of the goods. (Section 2–709(3).)

In addition to the price the seller may also recover in the same action his incidental damages which are defined in Section 2–710 of the Code as follows:

> Incidental damages to an aggrieved seller include any commercially reasonable charges, expenses or commissions incurred in stopping delivery, in the transportation, care and custody of goods after the buyer's breach, in

connection with return or resale of the goods or otherwise resulting from the breach.

(7) *To Recover Goods upon the Buyer's Insolvency*. At common law as well as under the Code, a seller of goods on credit has the right upon learning of the buyer's insolvency to withhold delivery except upon payment of the price in cash. The right to stoppage in transitu is an extension of this right to withhold delivery.

The Code enlarges this right of the seller by providing that he may not only stop delivery of the goods but may reclaim them from an insolvent buyer by demand made within ten days after the buyer has received the goods. Where the buyer has committed fraud by a misrepresentation in writing of his solvency within three months prior to the delivery of the goods, the ten-day limitation does not apply. In the event of such fraud the seller may reclaim the goods from the buyer at any time unless the buyer has resold them to a bona fide purchaser or the lien of a creditor has attached to them. Upon reclaiming the goods from an insolvent buyer, the seller obtains a preference over other creditors of the buyer and for this reason he is denied all other remedies with respect to the goods. Section 2–702.

(8) *To Cancel the Contract*. Where the buyer wrongfully rejects or revokes acceptance of the goods, or fails to make a payment due, or repudiates the contract in whole or in part, the seller may cancel the contract with respect to the goods directly affected, and if the breach is a material one, he may cancel the entire contract. (Section 2–703 (f).)

A material breach is one going to the essence of the contract. It is a failure to perform wholly or a partial failure of performance which substantially impairs the value of the whole contract to the aggrieved party. The materiality of a breach depends upon all of the circumstances. A breach in limine, that is, at the beginning or threshold of the performance due under an installment contract, is more serious than a breach after acceptance and payment for a number of installments.

Section 2–106 of the Code defines cancellation as the putting an end to the contract by one party by reason of a breach by the other. The obligation of the cancelling party for any future performance under the contract is discharged, although he retains any remedy for breach of the whole contract or any unperformed balance.

The seller must give the buyer notice of cancellation, and upon doing so, provided the buyer has repudiated or committed a material breach, the seller without making any tender of further performance is entitled to recover from the buyer damages for breach of the entire contract.

REMEDIES OF THE BUYER

In General. The Code greatly enlarges both in number and in scope the remedies available to a buyer. The remedies of the buyer are to (1) "cover" and also have damages for the seller's breach; (2) recover damages for non-delivery or repudiation; (3) recover damages for breach in regard to accepted goods; (4) recover both incidental and consequential damages; (5) recover identified goods upon seller's insolvency; (6) obtain specific performance of the contract; (7) replevin the goods; (8) obtain a security interest in the goods upon rightful rejection or justifiable revocation of acceptance; (9) enforce his security interest in the goods as a "person in the position of a seller"; and (10) cancel the contract.

(1) *The Right of "Cover"*. Where a seller repudiates the contract or fails to make delivery or where the buyer rightfully rejects or justifiably revokes an acceptance of the goods the buyer may protect himself by a "cover." This means that the buyer may in good faith and without unreasonable delay

proceed to purchase goods or make a contract to purchase goods in substitution for those due under the contract from the seller. This right enables the buyer to assure himself of a needed source of supply of the goods.

The buyer is not required to effect "cover" and his failure to do so does not bar him from any other remedy provided by the Code. (Section 2–712.)

Upon making a reasonable contract to purchase the goods from a third person the buyer may recover from the seller as damages the difference between the cost of cover and the contract price, plus any incidental or consequential damages, less expenses saved in consequence of the seller's breach. (Section 2–712.)

(2) *Recovery of Damages for Non-delivery or Repudiation.* In the event that the seller repudiates the contract or fails to deliver the goods, the buyer is entitled to recover damages from the seller measured by the difference between the market price at the time when the buyer learned of the breach and the contract price, together with incidental and consequential damages, less expenses saved in consequence of the seller's breach. The market price is to be determined as of the place for tender, or, in the event that the buyer has rightfully rejected the goods or has justifiably revoked his acceptance of them, the market price is to be determined as of the place of arrival. (Section 2–713.)

(3) *Recovery of Damages for Breach in Regard to Accepted Goods.* Where the buyer has accepted non-conforming goods and has given notification to the seller of the breach of contract, the buyer is entitled to maintain an action at law to recover from the seller the damages which have resulted in the ordinary course of events from the seller's breach. (Section 2–714.)

In the event of breach of warranty by the seller, the measure of damages is the difference at the time and place of acceptance between the value of the goods which have been accepted and the value that the goods would have had if they had been as warranted. Special circumstances may entitle the buyer to recover damages proximately resulting from the breach of warranty in a different amount as well as incidental and consequential damages. (Section 2–714).

(4) *Recovery of Incidental and Consequential Damages.* Section 2–715 of the Code defines the buyer's incidental and consequential damages as follows:

(1) Incidental damages resulting from the seller's breach include expenses reasonably incurred in inspection, receipt, transportation and care and custody of goods rightfully rejected, any commercial reasonable charges, expenses or commissions in connection with effecting cover and any other reasonable expense incident to the delay or other breach.

(2) Consequential damages resulting from the seller's breach include

(a) any loss resulting from general or particular requirements and needs of which the seller at the time of contracting had reason to know and which could not reasonably be prevented by cover or otherwise; and

(b) injury to person or property proximately resulting from any breach of warranty.

(5) *Recovery of Identified Goods upon the Seller's Insolvency.* Where existing goods are identified to the contract of sale, the buyer acquires a special property in the goods. (Section 2–501.) This special property exists even though the goods are non-conforming and the buyer has the right to return or reject them. Identification of the goods to the contract may be made either by the buyer or by the seller.

The Code gives the buyer a right which does not exist at common law to recover from an insolvent seller the goods in which the buyer has a special property and for which he has paid a part or all of the price.

This right exists where the seller who is in possession or control of the goods becomes insolvent within 10 days after receipt of the first installment of the price. To exercise it the buyer must tender to the seller any unpaid portion of the price. If the special property exists by reason of an identification made by the buyer, he may recover the goods only if they conform to the contract for sale. The buyer does not have the right to recover from an insolvent seller nonconforming goods which only the buyer has identified to the contract. (Section 2–502.)

(6) *Suit for Specific Performance.* In most cases, the buyer can recover only a money judgment for damages against a seller who refuses or neglects to perform. Damages are recoverable in an action at law, and ordinarily a money judgment is an adequate remedy. The remedy of specific performance of a contract is obtainable, if at all, only in a court of equity. Courts of equity will not grant specific performance where the remedy at law is adequate. However, where the subject matter of the contract is unique such as a work of art, a famous race horse, an heirloom, patent, copyright, or shares of stock in a closely held corporation, a court of equity has jurisdiction to order the seller specifically to deliver to the buyer the goods described in the contract. If a seller refuses to perform after being so ordered by a proper decree of a court of equity, he is subject to the contempt powers of the court, including the power to fine and imprison.

The Code provides that the buyer may have specific performance of a contract for the sale of goods where the goods are unique or in other proper circumstances. In addition, a decree for specific performance may include terms and conditions as to payment of the price, damages or other relief. (Section 2–716.)

(7) *Right of Replevin.* Replevin is a form of action to recover specific goods in the possession of a defendant which are being unlawfully withheld from the plaintiff.

The buyer may maintain against the seller an action of replevin for goods which have been identified to the contract where the seller has repudiated or breached the contract, if (1) the buyer after a reasonable effort is unable to effect cover for such goods, or (2) the goods have been shipped under reservation of a security interest in the seller and satisfaction of this security interest has been made or tendered. (Section 2–716.)

(8) *Buyer's Security Interest in the Goods.* A buyer who has rightfully rejected or justifiably revoked his acceptance of goods which remain in his possession or control has a security interest in these goods to the extent of any payment of the price which he has made and for any expenses reasonably incurred in their inspection, receipt, transportation, care and custody. The buyer may hold such goods and resell them in the same manner as an aggrieved seller may resell goods. (Section 2–711(3).)

(9) *The Buyer as a "Person in the Position of a Seller."* The buyer who has rightfully rejected goods for which he has made payment of the price or incurred expenses or who has justifiably revoked his acceptance of such goods has a security interest in the goods as stated above. He is desirous of obtaining from the seller a refund of the price paid and reimbursement of expenses, together with damages sustained. The Code provides that such a buyer is a "person in the position of a seller" with respect to the enforcement of his security interest in the goods. Thus, if the buyer has reshipped the goods to the seller or has placed them in the hands of a bailee for the seller, he may upon learning of the seller's insolvency stop delivery of the goods. As a person in the position of a seller he has the same rights as an unpaid seller to withhold or stop delivery of the goods or to resell them. (Section 2–706 (6).) In the event of a resale the buyer is

required to account to the seller for any excess of the net proceeds of the resale over the amount of his security interest. (Section 2–706(6).)

(10) *Cancellation of the Contract.* Where the seller fails to make delivery or repudiates the contract, or where the buyer rightfully rejects or justifiably revokes acceptance of the goods tendered or delivered to him, the buyer may cancel the contract with respect to any goods involved, and if the breach by the seller is material and goes to the whole contract, the buyer may cancel the entire contract. (Section 2–711(1).)

The materiality of a breach depends upon the same factors previously discussed in connection with the seller's right to cancel.

The buyer must give the seller notice of his cancellation of the contract and is not only excused from further performance or tender on his part but may recover damages from the seller for non-delivery of the goods. (Section 2–711(1) (b).)

Duty of Buyer as to Rightfully Rejected Goods. If the buyer is a merchant and rightfully rejects goods which are in his possession and control and located where the seller has no agent or place of business, he is under a duty to follow reasonable instructions from the seller with respect to disposition of the goods. Such instructions are not reasonable if the seller does not upon demand by the buyer indemnify the buyer for expenses. Section 2–603(1).

If the seller gives no instructions and the goods are perishable or likely to decline in value speedily, a merchant buyer is obliged to make reasonable efforts to sell the goods for the seller's account. This sale is subject to any security interest of the buyer in the goods. The buyer is entitled to reimbursement of expenses in taking care of the goods and selling them which may include a reasonable selling commission not to exceed 10% of the gross proceeds of the sale. Section 2–603 (2).

Whether or not the buyer is a merchant, he has certain salvage options with respect to disposition of rejected goods if the seller gives no instructions within a reasonable time after notice of rejection. Except for goods that are perishable, he may (1) store them for the seller's account, or (2) reship them to the seller, or (3) resell them for the seller's account. Section 2–604.

The purpose of these options is to enable the buyer by salvage of the goods to minimize the amount in controversy between the parties. In thus disposing of the goods the buyer is neither accepting them nor converting them. The Code expressly so provides in both Sections 2–603 and 2–604.

Liquidation or Limitation of Damages. The parties may provide in their contract for liquidated damages by specifying the amount or measure of damages which either party may recover in the event of a breach by the other party. The amount of such damages must be reasonable and commensurate with the anticipated or actual loss resulting from a breach. A provision in a contract fixing unreasonably large liquidated damages is void as a penalty. (Section 2–718.)

Where the seller justifiably withholds delivery of the goods because of the buyer's breach, and the buyer has made payments on the price, the buyer is entitled to restitution of the amount by which the sum of his payments exceeds the amount of liquidated damages to which the seller is entitled under the contract. In the absence of a provision for liquidated damages, the buyer may recover the difference between the amounts which he has paid on the price and 20% of the value of the buyer's performance under the contract or $500, whichever sum is smaller. (Section 2–718(2).)

The buyer's right to restitution may be offset by the seller's right to recover other damages as provided in the Code, where the contract does not provide for liquidated damages. (Section 2–718(3).)

Thus, if a buyer after depositing $1,500 with the seller on a $10,000 contract for goods, breaches the contract and the seller withholds delivery, in the absence of a provision for liquidated damages, and in the absence of the seller establishing greater actual damages resulting from the breach, the buyer is entitled to restitution of $1,000 ($1500 less $500). If the deposit were $250 on a $500 contract, the buyer would be entitled to $150 ($250 less $100 which is 20% of the price).

Modification or Limitation of Remedy by Agreement. The contract between the seller and buyer may expressly provide for remedies in addition to or in lieu of those provided in the Code and may limit or change the measure of damages recoverable in the event of breach. (Section 2–719.)

The contract may validly limit the remedy of the buyer to a return of the goods and a refunding of the price, or to the replacement of non-conforming goods or parts.

A remedy provided by the contract is optional unless it is expressly agreed to be exclusive of other remedies, in which event it is the sole remedy. However, where circumstances cause such exclusive remedy to fail of its essential purpose, resort may be had to the remedies provided by the Code. (Section 2–719(2).)

The contract may expressly limit or exclude consequential damages unless such limitation or exclusion would be unconscionable. Limitation of consequential damages for personal injuries resulting from breach of warranty in the sale of consumer goods is prima facie unconscionable, whereas limitation of such damages where the loss is commercial is not. (Section 2–719(3).) However, the seller may free himself of liability for such damages by a disclaimer of warranties as provided in Section 2–316.

CASES

JAGGER BROTHERS, INC. v. TECHNICAL TEXTILE CO.

(1964) 202 Pa.Super. 639, 198 A.2d 888.

MONTGOMERY, J. This appeal concerns the measure of damages in an action of assumpsit based on a written contract under which appellant agreed to purchase, at $2.15 per pound, 20,000 pounds of yarn to be manufactured by appellee. Appellee manufactured 3,723 pounds of the yarn and delivered it to appellant, who accepted and paid for it. The remaining 16,277 pounds were never manufactured because appellant advised appellee by letter, dated August 12, 1960, that it repudiated the contract and would refuse any future delivery of yarn.

Appellee was awarded $4,069.25 in a non-jury trial, which award was based on testimony offered by appellee that the market price of the yarn was $1.90 per pound on August 12, 1960. The award represents 16,277 times the difference between the contract price and the market price ($.25 per pound). No evidence was offered as to the cost of manufacturing the yarn.

Appellant contends that the proper measure of damages in such cases is the difference between the cost of manufacturing and the contract price; and, therefore, since appellee did not prove its cost of manufacture, it is entitled only to nominal damages.

Appellee contends that it has properly proved its damages under section 2–708 of the Uniform Commercial Code, April 6, 1953, P.L. 3, as amended October 2, 1959, P.L. 1023, § 2, 12A P.S. 2–708, which reads as follows:

"Seller's Damages for Non-Acceptance or Repudiation—(1) Subject to subsection (2) and to the provisions of this Article with respect to proof of market price (Section

2–723) the measure of damages for non-acceptance or repudiation by the buyer is the difference between the market price at the time and place for tender and the unpaid contract price together with any incidental damages provided in this Article (Section 2–710), but less expenses saved in consequence of the buyer's breach.

"(2) If the measure of damages provided in subsection (1) is inadequate to put the seller in as good a position as performance would have done then the measure of damages is the profit (including reasonable overhead) which the seller would have made from full performance by the buyer, together with any incidental damages provided in this Article (Section 2–710), due allowance for costs reasonably incurred and due credit for payments or proceeds of resale."

Prior to the Uniform Commercial Code the law was the same. [Citations.] In both of these cases it is stated that for a breach of contract for the sale of personal chattel, yet to be manufactured, the vendor is entitled to recover the difference between the selling price and the market value at the time and place of delivery.

Appellant seeks to avoid the application of this rule by a contention that the proof of the market price of similar yarn was lacking in the particular that the place where the price of $1.90 per pound prevailed was not established. This argument was not advanced in the court below nor was it discussed by the lower court in its opinion. Although it should not be considered by us at this time, we note that in the complaint the market price was alleged to be $1.95 "at the time and place of tender", which allegation was not sufficiently denied in appellant's answer. We conclude that the only variance between the allegata and the probata was in the price ($1.95 as alleged and $1.90 as proved), not in the time or place factor. From what appears before us, no objection was made on account of this variation; there-

fore, any objection to it must be considered to have been waived.

Section 2–723 of the Uniform Commercial Code as amended October 2, 1959, P.L. 1023, § 2, 12A P.S. § 2–723, contains the following provisions for establishing market price:

"Proof of Market Price: Time and Place— (1) If an action based on anticipatory repudiation comes to trial before the time for performance with respect to some or all of the goods, any damages based on market price (Section 2—708 or Section 2—713) shall be determined according to the price of such goods prevailing at the time when the aggrieved party learned of the repudiation.

"(2) If evidence of a price prevailing at the times or places described in this Article is not readily available the price prevailing within any reasonable time before or after the time described or at any other place which in commercial judgment or under usage of trade would serve as a reasonable substitute for the one described may be used, making any proper allowance for the cost of transporting the goods to or from such other place.

"(3) Evidence of a relevant price prevailing at a time or place other than the one described in this Article offered by one party is not admissible unless and until he has given the other party such notice as the court finds sufficient to prevent unfair surprise."

We are of the opinion that this provision was complied with. Appellant did not contend either surprise or lack of notice and did not offer any evidence to refute the fact that the market price of similar yarn at the time and place of tender, or within a reasonable distance from such point, was a price other than $1.90 per pound.

In view of our conclusion that appellant properly based its measure of damages on the difference between the contract price and the current market price and satisfactorily established the proper market price, there is no need to engage in any further discussion of appellant's other contentions, other than to refer to the case of C. P. Mayer Brick Company v. D. J. Kennedy Company, 230 Pa. 98, 79 A. 246 (1911), which was relied on heavily by appellant. We find that case to be in accord with our views as previously stated. The measure of damages in the Mayer case was the difference between the contract price and the cost of manufacturing the brick because there was no market price proved in that case. * * * An existing market price was proved in the present case.

Judgment affirmed.

PETERSON MERCURY, INC. v. LOMBARDO

(1961) 259 Minn. 281, 107 N.W.2d 221.

MAGNEY, COMM. Peterson Mercury, Inc., brought this action against J. P. Lombardo to recover on a check. Plaintiff appeals from the judgment entered against it.

Plaintiff is a Minneapolis distributor of Mercury automobiles. On January 11, 1958, defendant signed a purchase order for a new Mercury. The order provided for a trade-in of a 1953 car at $1,600 and payment of $2,300 in cash. Defendant delivered a check in that amount to plaintiff. An attempt by plaintiff 2 days later to have the check certified failed because of insufficient funds. Plaintiff then ordered a car conforming to defendant's specifications from the factory. Upon being notified by plaintiff of the arrival of the car, defendant refused to bring in his old car or accept the new one. In the meantime he had purchased a new Buick. Plaintiff deposited the $2,300 check, which was returned, defendant having stopped payment. The new car was held for defendant for some time. It was then put on the floor and sold. There is no claim that plaintiff tendered defendant another car. Plaintiff does claim that it was at all times ready,

willing, and able to make delivery of a car in accordance with the contract. The court found that up to February 10, 1958, the date when the check was returned unpaid to plaintiff, and for some considerable but undetermined period of time thereafter, plaintiff was ready, able, and willing to deliver the Mercury to defendant but did not do so because of defendant's refusal to accept it; that thereafter plaintiff sold the car on some undetermined date and at some undetermined price but never thereafter renewed the tender of that car or an identical or similar one. The action was dismissed with prejudice, and plaintiff appeals from the judgment entered.

* * *

The chattel here involved was not unique and was readily resalable for a reasonable price by the seller. The seller does not complain that the car was not readily resalable. In fact, it was resold without difficulty. In such situations, the seller's only remedy, where the buyer neglects and refuses to accept and pay for the goods, is an action for damages as set out in § 512.64.

Plaintiff, here, is bringing an action to recover on the $2,300 check which was delivered to it by defendant at the time the purchase order was given. In the order, the $2,300 is listed as "BALANCE DUE." It is quite apparent that the payment of the price and the delivery of the car were to be concurrent acts.

We then have a situation where, after the buyer has refused to accept or pay for a car, a chattel which is not unique and is readily resalable, the seller disposes of the car at an undisclosed but probably satisfactory price and then brings an action on the check which represents the balance due on the purchase price. The action amounts to an attempt at specific performance of a contract involving an ordinary chattel. The check sued on is an unconditional order on the bank to pay $2,300. [Citations.]

Plaintiff, as we have indicated, could not recover the purchase price of the car in a direct action but would be limited to an action for breach of contract. The check represents the balance due on the purchase price so in effect this is an action to recover the purchase price. Plaintiff has already received the proceeds from the sale of the car. If permitted to recover here, it would also receive the greater part of the purchase price of the car. The law does not sanction such a result. Under all the facts and circumstances here disclosed, plaintiff's only remedy lies in an action for breach of contract, and the trial court properly disposed of the case.

Judgment affirmed.

CUMMINGS v. JACK HURWITZ, INC.

(1964 D.C.App.) 204 A.2d 332.

Hood, C. J. Early in the year 1962 Mr. and Mrs. Cummings conferred with appellee regarding draperies and wall-to-wall carpeting for their apartment. It was finally agreed that appellee would furnish custom-made carpeting of a particular color not available in regular carpeting at a cost of $2,327.50. The carpet was laid in June 1962 and final payment thereon was made on July 2d. A week or two thereafter Mrs. Cummings noticed marks in the carpeting and she called appellee's representative. He went to the apartment and saw the lines or marks in the carpet which he described as "pass marks." A representative from the manufacturer, who examined the carpet at appellee's request, also testified that the lines were "pass marks" and that "pass marks" are inherent in any custom-made carpet which must be made on a small loom. At some time (the date is not made clear by the record), Mrs. Cummings asked appellee to take back the carpeting and replace it, but she was told this could not be done. On January 12, 1963, an attorney for Mr. and Mrs. Cummings wrote appellee, requesting that appellee remove the carpet and refund the full purchase price. This request was refused, and in October 1963 Mr. and Mrs. Cummings brought his action.

The complaint alleged a "breach of contract resulting from unsatisfactory goods" and sought recovery of the full purchase price. At the conclusion of the trial the court, sitting without a jury, made no finding as to whether the contract had been breached, but ruled that plaintiffs were required to elect between an action for breach of contract and one for rescission of contract. The court further ruled that if plaintiffs relied on breach of contract, they had failed to prove damages, and if they relied on rescission they had lost that right by failure to act within a reasonable time. Accordingly, finding and judgment were entered for appellee.

The only point made on this appeal is that the plaintiffs (now appellants) exercised their right to rescind within a reasonable time. The general rule, recognized by appellants, is that one who seeks to rescind a contract must act within a reasonable time after discovery of the facts justifying rescission. [Citation.] Determination of what constitutes a reasonable time depends upon the particular facts of the case and ordinarily is a question of fact, though in extreme cases it may be one of law. [Citation.] The evidence here presented a question of fact and we cannot hold that the trial court was in error in finding that appellants lost their right of rescission, if they had such a right, by an unreasonable delay in asserting it.

Affirmed.

KEYSTONE DIESEL ENGINE COMPANY
v. IRWIN

(1963) 411 Pa. 222, 191 A.2d 376.

EAGEN, J. This is an appeal from the order of the court below striking off a counterclaim filed in an action in assumpsit.

The plaintiff, Keystone Diesel Engine Company, Inc., (Keystone) is a dealer in diesel engines, and the defendant, Floyd T. Irwin, (Irwin) operates tractor-trailers as a contract carrier. Some time prior to July 1960, Keystone sold Irwin a diesel engine for approximately $3000. which was subsequently installed in a tractor. The engine did not function properly and the plaintiff Keystone performed certain modifications and repairs to the engine at its own expense. Subsequent repairs were required and the plaintiff performed the additional work allegedly based upon an oral contract with the defendant whereby the defendant agreed to pay the plaintiff for the additional work. The defendant refused to pay for the last mentioned repairs and the plaintiff brought this action in assumpsit to recover the amount due of $623.08. Defendant filed a counterclaim for loss of profits totalling $5150. The basis for this latter claim was the inability of the defendant to use the tractor for 27 days because of various breakdowns of the engine furnished by the plaintiff, all in contravention of an implied warranty of merchantability.

The lower court struck off the counterclaim on the basis that the claim for loss of profit was too speculative to permit recovery. For the purpose of this appeal, we must assume that all allegations of the defendant are true, and determine whether or not the counterclaim was properly stricken as a matter of law.

Where a contract is breached without legal justification, the injured party is entitled to recover (absent contrary provisions in the contract) whatever damages he suffered, provided 1) they were such as would naturally and ordinarily follow from the breach; 2) they were reasonably foreseeable and within the contemplation of the parties at the time they made the contract; 3) they can be proved with reasonable certainty. [Citations.] There is no doubt that in a contract of this nature a breach causing malfunction of the engine would produce a halt in productive capacity and some damage could flow therefrom. Moreover, there would be no difficulty in measuring these damages with reasonable accuracy. The real issue to be determined is whether the damages sought for loss of profit were within the contemplation of the parties to the contract here in dispute.

The Uniform Commercial Code provisions which are appropriate in the instant case read as follows:

"The measure of damages for breach of warranty is the difference at the time and the place of acceptance between the value of the goods accepted and the value they would have had if they had been as warranted, unless *special circumstances* show proximate damages of a different amount."

"In a proper case any incidental and consequential damages under the next section may also be recovered."

"Consequential damages *resulting from the seller's breach* include (a) any loss resulting from general or particular requirements and needs of which the seller at the time of contracting had reason to know and which could not reasonably be prevented by cover or otherwise."

"Special circumstances" entitling the buyer to damages in excess of the difference between the values as warranted and the value as accepted exist where the buyer has communicated to the seller at the time of entering into the contract sufficient facts to make it apparent that the damages subsequently claimed were within the reasonable contemplation of the parties. [Citation.]

The language in Globe Refining Co. v. Landa Cotton Oil Co., 190 U.S. 540, at 545 (1903), 23 S.Ct. 754 at 756, 47 L.Ed. 1171, gives the rationale of the foregoing rule as follows: " '[O]ne of two contracting parties ought not to be allowed to obtain an advantage which he has not paid for * * *. If [a liability for the full profits that might be made by machinery which the defendant was transporting * * *] had been presented to the mind of the ship owner at the time of making the contract, as the basis upon which he was contracting, he would at once have rejected it. * * * The knowledge must be brought home to the party sought to be charged, under such circumstances that he must know that the person he contracts with reasonably believes that he accepts the contract with the special condition attached to it.' "

In the case at bar, no facts are alleged that would put the plaintiff on guard to the fact that the defendant would hold the plaintiff responsible for any loss of profit arising from the inability to use the engine in question. Following the defendant's theory to its logical conclusion, whenever a motor vehicle is sold for use in a profit motivated enterprise and the seller warrants that the vehicle will function properly, the seller will be liable in damages for a breach of warranty to the extent of profits lost on completely unrelated business contracts, where those profits are lost due to the vehicle malfunctioning.

In Macchia v. Megow, 355 Pa. 565, 569, 50 A.2d 314, 316 (1947), the rule was stated, " 'Parties, when they enter into contracts, may well be presumed to contemplate the ordinary and natural incidents and consequences of performance or nonperformance; but they are not supposed to know the conditions of each other's affairs, nor to take into consideration any existing or contemplated transactions, not communicated nor known, with other persons. Few persons would enter into contracts of any considerable extent as to subject-matter or time if they should thereby incidentally assume the responsibility of carrying out, or be held legally affected by, other arrangements over which they have no control and the existence of which are [sic] unknown to them': Sutherland on Damages, 4th ed. vol. 1, p. 182, § 47." Anticipated profits are not recoverable unless within the contemplation of the parties when the contract was made: Macchia v. Megow, supra. Clearly, the claim for loss of profits in the instant case was not within the contemplation of the parties to this contract.

The order of the court below is affirmed.

PROBLEMS

1. A contracts to sell 1,000 bushels of wheat to B at $1.00 per bushel. Just prior to the time A was to deliver the wheat, B notified him that he would not receive or accept the wheat. A sold the wheat for 90 cents per bushel, the market price, and, later, sued B for the difference of $100. B claims he was not notified by A of the resale and, hence, not liable. Decision?

2. On December 15, 1965, A wrote a letter to B stating that he would sell to B all of the mine run coal that B might wish to buy during the calendar year 1966 for use at B's factory, delivered at the factory at a price of $4.50 per ton. B immediately replied by letter to A stating that he accepted the offer and that he would need 200 tons of coal during the first week in January, 1966. During the months of January, February, and March, 1966, A delivered to B a total of 700 tons of coal for all of which B made payment to A at the rate of $4.50 per ton. On April 10, 1966, B ordered 200 tons of mine run coal from A who replied to B on April 11, 1966, that he could not supply A with any more coal except at a price of $5.00 per ton delivered. B thereafter purchased elsewhere at the market price namely $5.00 per ton, all of the requirements of his factory of mine run coal for the remainder of the year 1966, amounting to a total of 2,000 tons of coal. B now brings an action against A to recover damages at the rate of 50¢ per ton for the coal thus purchased amounting to $1,000. What judgment?

3. On January 10, B, of Emanon, Missouri, visited the show rooms of the X Piano Company in St. Louis and selected a piano. A sales memorandum of the transaction signed both by B and by the salesman of the X Piano Company read as follows: "Sold to B one new Andover piano, factory number 46832, price $1,300 to be shipped to the buyer at Emanon, Missouri, freight prepaid, before February 1. Prior to shipment seller will stain the case a darker color in accordance with buyer's directions and will make the tone more brilliant." On January 15, B repudiated the contract by letter to the X Piano Company. The Company subsequently stained the case, made the tone more brilliant, and offered to ship the piano to B on January 26. B persisted in his refusal to accept the piano. In an action by the X Piano Company against B to recover the contract price, what judgment?

4. Sims contracted in writing to sell Blake 100 electric motors at a price of $100 each, freight prepaid to Blake's warehouse. By the contract of sale Sims expressly warranted that each motor would develop 25 brake horse power. The contract provided that the motors would be delivered in lots of 25 per week beginning January 2, that Blake should pay by draft for each lot of 25 motors as delivered; but that Blake was to have right of inspection upon delivery.

Immediately upon delivery of the first lot of 25 motors on January 2, Blake forwards Sims a draft for $2,500, but upon testing each of the 25 motors Blake determines that none of the 25 motors will develop more than 15 brake horse power.

State all of the remedies available to Blake under the Uniform Commercial Code.

5. A Co., of Chicago, contracted to sell a carload of certain goods to B in Detroit on 60 days' credit. A Co. shipped the carload, consigned to B, and forwarded the bill of lading to B. Upon the arrival of the car at Detroit, B presented the bill of lading to the carrier, paid the freight charges and reconsigned the car to C at Boston, to whom he had previously contracted to sell the goods. While the car was in transit to Boston, B was adjudged a bankrupt. A Co. was informed of this at once and immediately wired the carrier to withhold delivery of the goods. What should the carrier do?

6. A and B entered into a written contract whereby A agreed to sell and B agreed to buy a certain automobile for $3,500. A drove the car to B's residence and properly parked it on the street in front of B's house where he tendered it to B and requested payment of the price. B refused to accept the car or pay the price. A informed B that he would hold him to the contract and before A had time to enter the car and drive it away, a fire truck, answering a fire alarm and traveling at a high speed, crashed into the car and demolished it. A brings an action against B to recover the price of the car. Who is entitled to judgment? Would there be any difference in result if A were a dealer in automobiles?

7. A sells and delivers to B on June 1 certain goods and receives from B at the time of delivery B's check in the amount of $900 for the goods. The following day B is petitioned into bankruptcy and the check is dishonored by the drawee bank. On June 5, A serves notice upon B and the trustee in bankruptcy that he reclaims the goods. The trustee is in possession of the goods and refuses to deliver them to A. What are the rights of the parties? Would it make any difference in result if, on June 1 at the time of delivery of the goods, A accepted B's check dated June 15 in payment of the price?

8. The ABC Company, located in Chicago, contracted to sell a carload of television sets to Dodd in St. Louis, Missouri, on 60 days' credit. ABC Company shipped the carload, consigned to Dodd and forwarded the bill of lading to Dodd. Upon arrival of the car at St. Louis, Dodd presented the bill of lading to XYZ Railroad Company, paid the freight charges and reconsigned the car to Hines at Little Rock, Arkansas, to whom he had previously contracted to sell the television sets. While the car was in transit to Little Rock, Dodd was adjudged a bankrupt. ABC Company was informed of this at once and immediately telegraphed XYZ Railroad Company to withhold delivery of the television sets. What should the XYZ Railroad Company do?

9. In March A contracted in writing to sell 100 crates of oranges to B at $4 a crate, to be delivered July 1. On June 15, A gave notice that he would not go through with the contract. B replied that he considered the contract as subsisting and in full force and effect. Afterwards, the market price of oranges dropped to $2.50 a crate and, on July 1, A tendered delivery of 100 crates of oranges, which B refused to accept. A then sued B for damages for breach of contract. Decision?

CHAPTER 23

WARRANTIES

Introductory. The concept of warranty as an obligation of the seller to the buyer with respect to the title, quality, quantity, state, or past or future performability of goods sold or to be sold, is an ancient one. Historically, the remedy of the buyer for breach of warranty was an action in tort for deceit. The law of warranty is much older than the law of assumpsit upon which the modern law of contracts is based. However, today the liability of a seller for breach of warranty is universally recognized as contractual.

Conditions and Warranties. A condition precedent is an operative event the happening of which gives rise to a cause of action. Conversely stated, it is an event the non-happening of which may operate as an excuse for non-performance of a contractual promise. Strictly speaking, a condition is not a promise, but an event the happening of which affects the duty of performance of a promise.

The term "warranty" is employed in a different sense in the law of insurance than in the law of sales. In applications for insurance policies, a warranty by the insured operates as a condition to the liability of the insurer. For instance, the insured warrants in an application for a policy of health insurance that he has never been treated for cancer or heart disease. If this warranty is untrue, the insurance company is not liable to the insured for breach of contract. The consequence of breach of such warranty is to relieve the insurance company from its duty to pay under the policy, and not to impose any duty upon the insurer. In the law of sales, a warranty creates a duty on the part of the seller for breach of which the buyer may recover a judgment against the seller for damages.

An example of a warranty which operates both as a condition to performance and as a contractual undertaking is the warranty given by a ship owner under a charter party contract. Under the law applicable to charter party contracts, pursuant to which a person desiring to ship goods charters a ship from the ship owner, a warranty by the owner of the ship that it is seaworthy or that it is at a given place at a given time is both a condition to the obligation of the charterer to take the ship and a contractual promise upon which the ship owner is liable for damages in the event of breach.

Definition of Warranty. Although the word "warranty" has different meanings as used in other branches of the law, a warranty under the law of sales is an obligation imposed by law upon the seller with respect to the goods. Warranties arise out of (1) the mere fact that the transaction is a sale of goods, as a warranty of title; (2) affirmations of fact or promises by the seller to the buyer, which are express warranties; or (3) circumstances under which the sale is made, as in the case of implied warranties of merchantability and of fitness for the buyer's particular purpose. Implied warranties are obligations of the seller which he has not assumed by express language.

A seller is not required to warrant the goods, and in every case by appropriate words he may exclude, negate, or modify a particular warranty or even all warranties. He may carefully refrain from making an express warranty. With respect to implied warranties he must act affirmatively, and in the manner prescribed by the Code in order effectively to disclaim liability. The seller will be guided in each case by his personal honesty, business judgment, the sales resistance of the particular customer, and his earnestness and desire to make the sale.

A seller who does not wish to make an implied warranty must use additional words to negate such warranty. An implied warranty arises out of the situation of the parties, the type of contract or sale, and the circumstances of the case. It has been developed by the law, not as something to which the parties have agreed, but as a departure from the early rule of *caveat emptor,* let the buyer beware. In its early formative period of development, the law of sales has undoubtedly been influenced more by the pressures and demands of sellers as a class rather than those of buyers as a class. However, in the field of implied warranties, the law has been more solicitous of the buyer and has provided him with rights unless his contract with the seller expressly stipulates against them.

Warranty of Title. Under the early English common law, there was no implied warranty of title by the seller. The principle applied was that of *caveat emptor.* A seller was held liable for fraud where he knew that he did not have title and concealed this fact from the buyer, but otherwise he assumed no risk as to title unless he made an express warranty. The law subsequently developed to the point where a seller in possession of the goods impliedly warranted title, but if he were not in possession at the time of the contract or sale, it was to be assumed that he was merely selling such interest in the goods, if any, as he might have.

Later the common law developed and enforced an implied warranty of title and implied warranty of quiet possession regardless of the location of the goods at the time of the sale.

The Code abolishes the implied warranty of quiet possession and imposes upon the seller the obligation of a warranty of title without designating it either as express or implied. Disturbance of quiet possession is merely one way in which a breach of warranty of title may be shown. The Code provides in Section 2–312:

> (1) Subject to subsection (2) there is in a contract for sale a warranty by the seller that
>
>> (a) the title conveyed shall be good, and its transfer rightful; and
>>
>> (b) the goods shall be delivered free from any security interest or other lien or encumbrance of which the buyer at the time of contracting has no knowledge.
>
> (2) A warranty under subsection (1) will be excluded or modified only by specific language or by circumstances which give the buyer reason to know that the person selling does not claim title in himself or that he is purporting to sell only such right or title as he or a third person may have.

A seller may disclaim a warranty of title under Section 2–312, although it should be noted that the disclaimer provisions of Section 2–316 with respect to implied warranties do not apply to warranty of title.

The disclaimer must be either (a) by specific language or (b) by circumstances under which the buyer should reasonably know that the seller does not claim that he has title but is selling only such right or interest as he or a third person may have in the goods.

Specific disclaimer language is a statement by the seller that he is transferring only such rights as he may have in the goods, such as "all my right, title, and interest."

Circumstances which indicate to a buyer that the seller is purporting to sell only a limited or unknown right are those attending a judicial sale or sales by sheriffs, executors, or foreclosing lienors. In such cases the seller is manifestly offering to sell only such right or title as he or a third person might have in the goods, as it is apparent that the goods are not the property of the person selling them.

Warranty against Infringement. A seller who is a merchant makes an additional warranty in sales of goods of the kind in which he regularly deals that such goods shall be delivered free of the rightful claim of any third person by way of infringement of any existing patent. Section 2–312(3).

This warranty does not run in favor of a buyer who furnishes specifications to the seller. In such case it is the buyer who must hold the seller harmless against any claim of infringement by a third person arising out of the seller's compliance with the specifications.

If the buyer is sued for infringement by a third person he must notify the seller within a reasonable time after he receives notice of the litigation or be barred from any remedy against the seller by reason of any liability established by the litigation. Section 2–607 (3) (b).

The same requirement of notice applies to the seller with respect to the obligation of the buyer to hold the seller harmless against claims for infringement. Section 2–607(6).

Express Warranties. The Code enumerates in Section 2–313 three methods by which express warranties are created, namely:

(1) Express warranties by the seller are created as follows:

    (a) Any affirmation of fact or promise made by the seller to the buyer which relates to the goods and becomes part of the basis of the bargain creates an express warranty that the goods shall conform to the affirmation or promise.

    (b) Any description of the goods which is made part of the basis of the bargain creates an express warranty that the goods shall conform to the description.

    (c) Any sample or model which is made part of the basis of the bargain creates an express warranty that the whole of the goods shall conform to the sample or model.

An express warranty is an explicit undertaking by the seller with respect to the quality, description, condition, or performability of the goods. The Code does not require that affirmations of fact or promises by the seller be relied upon by the buyer but only that they constitute a part of the basis of the bargain. If they are basic to the bargain, reliance by the buyer is implicit.

Affirmations of fact by the seller with respect to the goods are usually a part of the description of the goods. The seller expressly warrants that the goods shall conform to the description. The use of a sample or model is a means of describing the goods, and the seller expressly warrants that the entire lot of goods sold shall conform to the sample or model.

In order to create an express warranty it is not necessary that the seller have a specific intention to make a warranty or use formal words such as "warrant" or "guarantee". Statements or promises made by the seller to the buyer long prior to the sale may be express warranties, as they may form a part of the basis of the bargain just as much as statements made at the time of the sale. Each case presents a question of fact whether statements of the seller made some time prior to the formation of the contract should reasonably be considered as basic to the bargain.

At common law statements or promises by the seller made subsequent to the contract or sale are not binding on the seller in the absence of new consideration from the buyer. Such statements were regarded not only as unsupported by consideration from the buyer but also as not inducing the contract or sale because it had already taken place.

Under the Code, statements or promises made by the seller subsequent to the contract or sale may become express warranties even though no new consideration is given. Section 2–209(1) provides that, "An Agreement modifying a contract within this Article needs no consideration to be binding."

Thus, a statement, or promise, or assurance with respect to the goods made by the seller to the buyer at the time of delivery may be a binding modification of the prior contract of sale and held to be an express warranty as basic to the bargain. It requires no consideration from the buyer to be binding on the seller.

Statements of Value or Opinion. The Code provides that a mere affirmation of the value of the goods or a statement purporting merely to be the seller's opinion or commendation of the goods does not create a warranty. Section 2–313(2). Such statements do not deceive the ordinary buyer. They are accepted merely as opinions or as puffing statements. If the seller genuinely believes the goods to be more valuable than the price at which he is willing to sell them, he probably would not sell. However, a statement of value may be an express warranty where the seller states the price at which the goods were purchased from a former owner, or where he gives market figures relating to sales of similar goods. These are affirmations of facts. They are statements of events and not mere opinions, and the seller is liable for breach of warranty in the event they are untrue.

It is not necessary that a seller have knowledge of the falsity of a statement made by him in order to be liable for breach of express warranty. The seller may be acting in good faith and relying upon second-hand inaccurate information. To be liable for fraud, a person must make a misrepresentation of fact with knowledge of its falsity.

While ordinarily a statement of opinion by the seller is not a warranty, if the seller is an expert and gives his opinion as such, he may be liable for breach of warranty. Thus, an art expert who states that in his opinion a certain painting is a genuine Rem-

brandt, thereby inducing the buyer to purchase it from him, warrants the accuracy of his opinion.

A seller may also be liable if he misrepresents his opinion. Thus, a seller may say, "This horse is sound," or he may say, "In my opinion, this horse is sound." In the first instance he has made an express warranty of the soundness of the horse. In the second, he has made no warranty if he actually believed the horse to be sound. But if he knew that the horse was unsound at the time of stating his opinion to the contrary, he has misrepresented his opinion as a factual matter. This is not only fraud, but also a breach of warranty.

Another manner in which a statement of opinion may become an affirmation of fact is illustrated by Section 539 of the Restatement of Torts:

> "A statement of opinion in a business transaction upon facts not disclosed or otherwise known to the recipient may reasonably be interpreted as an implied statement that the maker knows of no fact incompatible with his opinion."

Implied Warranty of Merchantability. A seller who is a merchant impliedly warrants the merchantability of goods that are of the kind in which he deals.

At early common law a seller was not held to any implied warranty as to the quality of the goods, particularly in the case of a sale of specific goods. The rule was that of *caveat emptor* (let the buyer beware). In a contract to sell goods by description, the courts held that the seller was under a duty to furnish goods of fair, average, merchantable quality corresponding to the description.

The implied warranty of merchantability is an obligation of the merchant-seller that the goods are reasonably fit for the general purpose for which they are manufactured and sold, and also that they are of fair, average, merchantable quality.

The Code defines the minimum requirements of merchantability in detail. Section 2–314 provides:

(1) Unless excluded or modified (Section 2–316), a warranty that the goods shall be merchantable is implied in a contract for their sale if the seller is a merchant with respect to goods of that kind. Under this section the serving for value of food or drink to be consumed either on the premises or elsewhere is a sale.

(2) Goods to be merchantable must be at least such as

(a) pass without objection in the trade under the contract description; and

(b) in the case of fungible goods, are of fair average quality within the description; and

(c) are fit for the ordinary purposes for which such goods are used; and

(d) run, within the variations permitted by the agreement, of even kind, quality and quantity within each unit and among all units involved; and

(e) are adequately contained, packaged, and labeled as the agreement may require; and

(f) conform to the promises or affirmations of fact made on the container or label if any.

(3) Unless excluded or modified (Section 2–316) other implied warranties may arise from course of dealing or usage of trade.

The above definition of merchantability in the Code does not exclude possible meanings of the word which may arise from course of dealing between the parties or usage of trade.

The term "merchantable" has come to mean fair, average, medium quality. The seller is not required to supply the finest or highest quality of goods, nor is the buyer obliged to accept the lowest quality or dregs of goods which comply with the description. Between the two extremes is a medium or average quality. The nature and extent of a seller's warranty of merchantability may de-pend upon the price at which the sale is closed in relation to the market for goods of that description. If the goods described in the contract have a brand name, they must have the quality of that brand which is fairly salable. To be merchantable the goods must be of such quality as to pass in the market without objection and be honestly resalable by the buyer in the normal course of business.

Implied Warranty of Fitness for Particular Purpose. Any seller, whether or not he is a merchant, impliedly warrants that the goods are reasonably fit for the particular purpose of the buyer for which the goods are required, if at the time of contracting the seller has reason to know such particular purpose and that the buyer is relying upon the seller's skill and judgment. Section 2–315 provides:

Where the seller at the time of contracting has reason to know any particular purpose for which the goods are required and that the buyer is relying on the seller's skill or judgment to select or furnish suitable goods, there is unless excluded or modified under the next section an implied warranty that the goods shall be fit for such purpose.

A particular purpose of the buyer differs from the ordinary purpose for which the goods are usually purchased. A particular purpose may be a specific use peculiar to the business of the buyer or relate to a special situation in which the buyer intends to use the goods. Thus, if the seller has reason to know that the buyer is purchasing a pair of shoes for mountain climbing and that the buyer is relying upon the seller's judgment to furnish suitable shoes for this purpose, a sale of shoes suitable only for ordinary walking purposes would be a breach of this implied warranty.

Fitness for the buyer's particular purpose may be the same as merchantability. Thus, in the sale of foodstuffs at a grocery store or supermarket, both the particular purpose of the buyer and the ordinary purpose for which such goods are sold is human consumption. In such a sale both implied warranties exist.

The mere fact that the goods have a patent or trade name does not defeat an implied warranty of fitness for the buyer's particular purpose. If the seller recommends such an article as adequate for the particular purpose of the buyer, the warranty attaches. However, if the buyer asks for or insists upon a particular brand of goods, or goods bearing a patent or trade name, there is no implied warranty of fitness as the buyer is not relying upon the seller's skill or judgment but upon his own. This is also the case where the buyer has furnished the seller with technical specifications of the goods.

The buyer need not specifically inform the seller of his particular purpose. It is sufficient if the seller has reason to know it. However, the buyer must rely upon the seller's skill or judgment in selecting or furnishing suitable goods in order that this implied warranty exist.

In a case in which the plaintiff, a 67-year-old woman, purchased a new household stepladder from defendant drug store, the stepladder collapsed while in use causing the plaintiff to fall and sustain personal injuries. The Court held that there was no implied warranty of merchantability as this was not a sale of goods by description as the plaintiff had an opportunity to examine the stepladder in the drug store at the time she purchased it. The Court however found there was an implied warranty of fitness for the buyer's particular purpose. This purpose was considered to have been impliedly made known to the seller by the very nature of the article sold. Kirk v. Stineway Drug Store Co., 38 Ill.App.2d 415, 187 N.E.2d 307 (1963).

Buyer's Examination of the Goods. If the buyer inspects the goods, an express warranty does not apply to obvious defects which are apparent upon a casual examination.

Thus, if the seller warrants a horse to be sound, and the blind condition of the horse is evident to the buyer who inspects it, the express warranty will not be held to extend to the blind condition. However, if the seller tells the buyer that the horse merely has a temporary eye infection which will last only a few days, he is liable on his express warranty. The buyer is not required to make a detailed or expert examination of the horse but is justified in relying upon the seller's representations.

Where the seller makes an express warranty, and the buyer does not inspect the goods although an inspection would have readily revealed that the seller's representations were false, the seller is liable as the buyer is justified in taking the seller at his word.

Where the buyer has examined the goods, there is no implied warranty as to defects which his examination ought to have revealed. In such case, the buyer is not relying on the judgment of the seller as to the goods. This rule is codified in Section 2–316(3) (b) of the Code which provides:

> When the buyer before entering into the contract has examined the goods or the sample or model as fully as he desired or has refused to examine the goods there is no implied warranty with regard to defects which an examination ought in the circumstances to have revealed to him.

The rule does not apply to latent defects. Thus, if a meat shop has twenty or more dressed chickens on display for sale, a buyer who after examination selects one of them and purchases it, is exercising judgment as to the size, weight, color of skin, and firmness of meat, but not as to its fitness for human consumption. If the chicken thus inspected and selected by the buyer is contaminated, the seller has breached both his implied warranty of fitness and of merchantability.

Buyer's Refusal to Examine the Goods. It may be noted that Section 2–316(3) (b) provides not only that there is no implied warranty as to defects which an examination ought to have revealed where the buyer has examined the goods as fully as he desired, but also where the buyer has refused to examine the goods.

A mere failure or omission to examine the goods is not a refusal to examine them. It is not enough that the goods were available for inspection and the buyer did not see fit to inspect them.

In order for the buyer to have "refused to examine the goods" the seller must have first made a demand upon the buyer that he examine them. Such demand is necessary. It serves to notify the buyer that he is assuming the risk of defects which an examination ought to reveal.

Trade Usage. If a well-recognized trade usage or custom exists, of which both of the parties to a contract or sale have knowledge, in the absence of evidence of a contrary intention, the law will regard the parties as having intended the usage to apply to their contract or sale, and they are bound by the trade usage.

Thus, where the seller of a new automobile failed to lubricate it before delivery to the buyer, and the evidence established that it was the regular custom and usage of new car dealers to do so, the seller was held liable to the buyer for the resulting damages to the automobile in an action for breach of implied warranty. (Davis Motors, Dodge & Plymouth Co. v. Avett, 294 S.W.2d 882, Texas Civ. App.1956).

The Code in Section 2–314(3) expressly provides that implied warranties may arise from course of dealing or usage of trade.

An implied warranty can also be excluded or modified by course of dealing or course of performance or usage of trade. Section 2–316(3) (c).

Disclaimer or Modification of Warranties. Exclusion or modification of warranties under the Code may be summarized as follows:

(1) Warranty of title may be excluded or modified only by specific language or by certain circumstances. Section 2–312(2).

(2) Express warranties may be excluded upon the seller carefully refraining from making any promise or affirmation of fact relating to the goods, or description of the goods, or a sale by means of a sample or model. Section 2–313. The seller may also negate an express warranty by clear, specific, unambiguous language in the contract to that effect. Section 2–316(1).

(3) To exclude an implied warranty of merchantability, the language of disclaimer must mention merchantability and in the case of a writing must be conspicuous. Section 2–316(2), subject to 2–316(3).

(4) To exclude an implied warranty of fitness for the particular purpose of the buyer, the language of disclaimer must be in writing and conspicuous. Section 2–316(2), subject to 2–316(3).

(5) Notwithstanding the express requirements of Section 2–316(2) all implied warranties, unless the circumstances indicate otherwise, are excluded by expressions like "as is", "with all faults", or other language plainly calling the buyer's attention to the exclusion of warranties. Section 2–316(3) (a). They may also be excluded by the buyer's examination of the goods or by his refusal to examine them. Section 2–316(3) (b); or by course of dealing, course of performance, or usage of trade. Section 2–316 (3) (c).

The provisions of Section 2–316 of the Code on disclaimer or modification of warranties are not simple and uncomplicated. Subsection 1 calls for a reasonable construction of words or conduct tending to negate or limit warranties. The plain requirements of subsection 2 are eroded by subsection 3. In addition, subsection 4 provides that remedies and recovery of damages for breach of warranty may be contractually limited under Sections 2–718 and 2–719.

It is important for the businessman not only to know the kinds of warranties that exist, and how they are created, but also the manner in which they may be disclaimed or modified. The Code makes clear that the seller should not rely upon a time-honored formula of words or expect to obtain a disclaimer which may go unnoticed by the buyer. Disclaimers should be positive, explicit, unequivocal, and conspicuous.

In the sale of a used European-based helicopter for $225,000, the written contract contained an express warranty of title followed by the statement: "The foregoing warranty is given and accepted in lieu of any and all other warranties, expressed or implied, arising out of the sale of the helicopter." The Court held this was not an effective disclaimer of the implied warranties of merchantability and fitness for the buyer's particular purpose in that (1) it was not clear, definite, precise, and specific; and (2) it was in the same size and color of the other typewritten provisions of the contract and therefore not "conspicuous" as required by Section 2–316 of the Code. A judgment in favor of the buyer in the amount of $180,295 was affirmed. Boeing Airplane Company v. O'Malley, 329 F.2d 585 (C.A.8, 1964).

Cumulation and Conflict of Warranties. In a contract for the sale of goods it is possible to have both express warrranties and implied warranties. All warranties are to be construed as consistent with each other and cumulative, unless such construction is unreasonable.

The intention of the parties is controlling, and in ascertaining that intention the Code sets forth the following rules: (a) Exact or technical specifications displace an inconsistent sample, or model, or general language of description; (b) A sample from an existing bulk displaces inconsistent general language of description; and (c) Express warranties displace inconsistent implied warranties other than an implied warranty of fitness for a particular purpose. Section 2–317.

Requirement of Notice of Breach. Where the buyer has accepted a tender of goods which are warranted by the seller, he is required to notify the seller of any breach of warranty, express or implied, as well as any other breach, within a reasonable time after he has discovered or should have discovered it.

The Code provides that if the buyer fails to notify the seller of any breach within such time, the buyer shall be barred from any remedy against the seller. Section 2–607(3) (a).

Privity of Contract. By reason of the association of warranties with contracts, a principle of law became established in the nineteenth century whereby recovery for breach of warranty would not be allowed unless the plaintiff was in a contractual relationship with the defendant. This relationship is known as privity of contract.

A warranty made by seller A to buyer B who resold and similarly warranted the goods to C affords C no right against A. In the event of breach of warranty, C may recover only from B who in turn may recover from A.

Suppose A sells a horse to B with a warranty that it is sound. B resells the horse to C with no warranty. The horse is not sound. C has no cause of action against A because there is no contractual relation or privity of contract between C and A, and the warranty does not run with the horse.

One reason for the rule which requires privity of contract is that by merely selling goods the seller does not thereby necessarily also intend that the buyer shall be a transferee of a right of action which he may have against the person from whom he had previously bought the goods. Thus, B buys a horse from A with a warranty of soundness. The horse is not sound. B has both the horse and a cause of action against A for breach of warranty. These are both assets of B and he may wish to sell one and not the other. The fact that he sells the horse to C does not mean that he is also selling to C his cause of action against A. He could assign this cause of action to C or to any one.

A second reason for the rule is that a warranty is similar to a personal indemnity. An accrued right of action for breach of warranty is assignable, but to permit the buyer to assign the warranty itself would be an enlargement of the scope of the seller's undertaking to include the indemnification of persons to whom it was not made.

The requirement of privity of contract may have had some merit in an economy where the retailers of goods were the sole source of representations as to the quality of the goods purchased by users and consumers. A century ago it was common practice for retailers to purchase goods in bulk and upon resale to package or bag separately for each customer the desired quantity purchased. The retailer had an opportunity to become familiar with the condition, quality, and purity of the merchandise which he sold to the public. However, where the retailer buys and resells goods which are packaged by the manufacturer, and he has no control over the products that he sells except as distributor, the advertising of the goods and representations made to purchasers to induce their purchase come not from the retailer, but from the manufacturer directly to the consumer through the media of mass communication.

Today the affirmations, promises, and representations with respect to goods are made directly to retail purchasers by persons remote in the distributive chain through widespread use of television, radio, newspapers,

magazines, and direct mail. There is no privity of contract between the person making the representations and the person induced thereby to purchase the goods. As a result many courts, including those in leading commercial States such as New York, New Jersey, Ohio, Michigan, Illinois, and California, have abolished the requirement of privity of contract. Other courts in States where the rule is still in effect, except for cases within Section 2–318 of the Code, express no sympathy for the rule but feel bound by *stare decisis* to apply it, stating that a change in the law is for the legislature.

It may be noted that even in States where the requirement of privity is still in force, it has long been held not to apply to sales of food for human consumption. Most States hold a manufacturer of food liable on an implied warranty of merchantability and fitness to purchasers and consumers with whom the manufacturer has no privity of contract. This has been stated as an exception to the rule.

Third Party Beneficiaries of Warranties. The Code relaxes the requirement of privity of contract to the extent of permitting recovery on a seller's warranty to members of the family or household of the buyer or guests in his home. Section 2–318 provides:

> A seller's warranty whether express or implied extends to any natural person who is in the family or household of his buyer or who is a guest in his home if it is reasonable to expect that such person may use, consume or be affected by the goods and who is injured in person by breach of the warranty. A seller may not exclude or limit the operation of this section.

This limited extension of the seller's liability applies to a class of users or consumers who are not subpurchasers of the buyer or purchasers at all. They occupy a family or guest relationship to the buyer, and are not in privity of contract with any one. Consequently, except for Section 2–318 they would have no rights on any warranty at all.

It is not the avowed purpose of the Code to hasten the demise of the requirement of privity of contract. Developing case law is attending to that. The Official Comment to Section 2–318 states:

> This section expressly includes as beneficiaries within its provisions the family, household, and guests of the purchaser. Beyond this, the section is neutral and is not intended to enlarge or restrict the developing case law on whether the seller's warranties, given to his buyer who resells, extend to other persons in the distributive chain.

It has been held that Section 2–318 does not include among third party beneficiaries an employee of the buyer, Hochgertel v. Canada Dry Corporation, page 516; nor the fiancée of the buyer, Wood v. Hub Motor Co., 190 Ga.App. 101, 137 S.E.2d 674 (1964); nor a guest injured while riding in the buyer's automobile, since it is not the buyer's home, Thompson v. Reedman, 199 F.Supp. 120 (D.C.E.D.Pa.1961).

This section extends the seller's warranty only to natural persons (not corporations or domestic pets) and limits their rights to recover damages for personal injuries, not property damage. Their rights are further limited to the seller's warranty which may possibly contain disclaimers, exclusions, or modifications. Although a seller is prohibited from excluding or limiting the operation of Section 2–318, he may substantially reduce the scope and content of the warranty upon which it operates as permitted by Section 2–316.

It is not clear from the language of Section 2–318 or the Official Comment whether the rights afforded the third party beneficiaries extend only to the warranties which the buyer has received from his immediate seller or whether they extend to warranties of remote vendors. In a jurisdiction where the rule of privity of contract is enforced, the rights of the buyer are limited to his immediate seller. It would seem that the rights of the benefici-

aries would be similarly limited as they should not transcend those of the buyer. The question is also unresolved in a jurisdiction where the requirement of privity has been abolished. The language of Section 2–318 is *"A seller's warranty * * * extends to * * * person * * * in the family * * * of his buyer * * * or * * * a guest in his home."* These words could be construed as restricting the rights of the beneficiaries to the warranty of the buyer's immediate seller, although the buyer himself might have in addition, by reason of no privity requirement, rights against remote vendors.

Contributory Negligence. Historically the origin of liability for warranty is in tort based upon the idea of a deceit practised upon the buyer. However, as warranties pertained to sales of goods based upon contracts, the remedy for breach of warranty was allowed in an action for breach of contract.

By reason of the development of warranty liability in the law of sales and contracts, contributory negligence of the buyer is no defense to an action against the seller for breach of warranty. Contributory negligence belongs in the field of tort law and not contract law.

However, if the buyer after discovery of a defect in the goods which may cause injury, and being aware of the danger, nevertheless proceeds to make use of the goods, he will not be permitted to recover damages from the seller for the injuries caused by such use. This is not strictly contributory negligence, but voluntary assumption of a known risk.

In a case in which the plaintiff had broken off a front tooth as a result of biting into a hard-roll sandwich purchased by him from defendant, one of the defenses was that the plaintiff's tooth was weak as three years previously it had been desensitized by removal of the nerve. The Court held the defendant liable on the ground of breach of implied warranty of fitness of the roll for human consumption, stating: "The suggested hypothesis that the cause of the injury was the plaintiff's weak tooth avails the defendant nothing. It took the plaintiff as it found him." Scanlon v. Food Crafts, Inc., 2 Conn. Cir. 3, 193 A.2d 610 (1963).

No Warranty of Goods Supplied Incidental to a Service. As previously indicated, a warranty is part and parcel of a sale or contract to sell. Express warranties must be part of the basis of the bargain which is the contract of sale. Both at common law and under the Code, a sale is defined as the passing of title to goods from the seller to the buyer for a price. Section 2–106.

In certain transactions goods are used up or consumed. A question arises whether title has passed to the user and the use or consumption is a sale or whether the goods are merely incidental to a service being furnished.

Although the early common law regarded an innkeeper as "uttering" rather than selling the meals or victuals served to patrons for consumption on the premises, it has long been held at common law that the serving of food, including water for which no charge was made, by a hotel or restaurant to paying guests is a sale and therefore subject to implied warranty obligations. This rule is codified in the Code which expressly provides that the serving for value of food or drink to be consumed on the premises or elsewhere is a sale. Section 2–314(1).

The courts have not treated a blood transfusion performed in a hospital as a sale of blood to the patient but rather as a service necessary and incidental to his care and treatment. Thus, implied warranties do not apply to a transfer of blood plasma whether supplied by the hospital or by an independent blood bank. Balkowitsch v. Minneapolis Memorial Blood Bank, Inc., page 526.

It has been held that a person who sustained injuries, including dermatitis and loss of hair as the result of application of certain cosmetic products in the course of a beauty treatment, could not recover from either the operator of the beauty parlor or the manufacturers of the products for the reason that the transaction did not involve a sale of goods or any warranty as the plaintiff was not purchasing goods but was receiving a treatment in which the use of the cosmetics was incidental. Epstein v. Giannattasio, 25 Conn. Sup. 109, 197 A.2d 342 (1963).

No Warranty Before Existence of Contract or Sale. In a self-service store the usual practice is for the customer to enter through a turnstile, select from open shelves the goods he wishes to buy, and take them to the cashier to whom payment is made. The transaction is a cash sale. No contract is formed by the customer taking the goods from the shelves. He may return them to the shelves at any time before paying for them, and he is not obligated to buy them. Title to the merchandise selected passes to the buyer when he pays for them.

If a buyer is injured by goods selected by him in a self-service store before he has paid for them, it has been held that he may not recover damages from the seller for breach of any implied warranty. In the absence of a contract of sale or a sale, the seller makes no warranty. Thus, a customer in such a store selected a bottle of carbonated beverage described as a "tonic." Before she could place the bottle in a basket preliminary to taking it to the cashier and paying for it, the bottle exploded causing her severe injuries. The court held that she could not recover damages from the store, as there was no negligence on the part of the store, and there was no implied warranty because there was no contract or sale. (Lasky v. Economy Grocery Stores, 319 Mass. 224, 163 A.L.R. 235, 65 N.E.2d 305 (1946).)

CASES

STAN CROSS BUICK, INC. v.
CONCORD AUTO
AUCTION, INC.

(1965) — Mass. —, 212 N.E.2d 862.

SPIEGEL, J. This is an action of contract to recover damages for an alleged breach of a warranty of title. A judge of the Superior Court made a "finding" constituting an order for judgment for the defendant from which the plaintiff appeals.

The action was tried on an "agreed statement of facts." Commercial Credit Corporation (Commercial), the owner of a certain 1957 Ford automobile, stored the vehicle on the premises of one Lloyd, an automobile dealer in Maine. Lloyd brought the automobile to the defendant Concord Auto Auction, Inc. (Concord) in Massachusetts and paid Concord $10 to "cry" the vehicle. On April 15, 1958, the automobile was sold and delivered to the plaintiff Stan Cross Buick, Inc. (Stan Cross) which "paid one thousand six hundred eighty dollars ($1,680.00) to said Robert Lloyd and paid five dollars ($5.00) to defendant corporation, Concord Auto Auction, Inc." Concord furnished a form bearing the caption, "Title Warranty and Bill of Sale" which was signed by Lloyd as seller, by Stan Cross as buyer, and by Concord as the guarantor of the buyer's title. The following day Stan Cross sold the car to a third party for $1,780. Two weeks later Commercial learned of the sale to Stan Cross and requested Stan Cross and Concord to return the automobile. On February 4, 1959, Commercial brought an action of tort for conversion against Stan Cross and Concord. In accordance with the decision of this court in Commercial Credit Corp. v. Stan Cross Buick, Inc., 343 Mass. 622, 180 N.E.2d 88, a judgment was entered for Commercial in the amount of $2,489.35 as against Stan

Cross and a judgment was entered for Concord. The judgment not being satisfied, on a petition filed by Commercial, a receiver was appointed for Stan Cross. Concord was not notified of this proceeding. "Stan Cross * * * has not satisfied in any part the judgment held by Commercial * * * against it."

Stan Cross contends that Concord is liable for breach of its agreement which reads in part: "The undersigned Auction Company * * * guarantees the title to the above described vehicle to be as shown herein." Concord argues that its "only liability can be as guarantor that it will pay if the primary debtor does not, after a reasonable attempt has been made to recover against him and the guarantor's chance of recovery, if it pays, has not been prejudiced."

We note that the agreement refers to "the Title Warranty of the named Auction Company," and makes provision for the subrogation of the buyer's claim against the seller "[o]n payment of any claim arising under this Warranty, either by the Auction Company or its insurer." The agreement guarantees the title; it does not guarantee payment by the seller if the title is defective. Consequently, we are of opinion that the guaranty constituted a warranty on which the buyer could sue directly. [Citation.]

Stan Cross also contends that Concord is liable for the $2,489.35 judgment entered against it. Concord argues that because Stan Cross made no payments on the judgment it did not sustain any actual loss and therefore there can be no recovery. We do not agree. "Where damages include indemnity against expense occasioned by a wrong * * * a plaintiff may recover for obligations incurred whether he has satisfied them or not." Arwshan v. Meshaka, 288 Mass. 31, 34, 192 N.E. 162, 163. [Citation.]

Concord also argues that "it was necessary that * * * [it] be informed when the receivership proceedings were instituted by Commercial against the plaintiff," since a term of the agreement required notification "[i]n case any claim is made by any person regarding any lien or otherwise affecting the title to this vehicle, whether by suit or otherwise." This argument is not tenable, because the receivership proceeding was merely to collect on a judgment and did not affect the title to the automobile.

Finally, Concord argues that the judge was warranted in ordering judgment for it because this action was instituted more than fifty months after the date of the sale of the car. In support of this contention Concord refers to the title warranty provision that "The liability of the Auction Company named on the face of this Title Warranty and Bill of Sale shall be limited to the sale price of the vehicle, and the amount payable hereunder shall be reduced on account of depreciation by deducting from the sale price 2% thereof on the first of each month following the sale date as shown on the face of this instrument; and this Warranty will expire and become void fifty months after said date."

We perceive nothing in this provision limiting the time when an action must be brought. The contract provision merely guarantees the title for a period of fifty months. Title to the automobile was defective when the sale was made and therefore there was an immediate breach of the warranty. Concord knew of this breach within two weeks from the date of the sale by reason of the true owner's request of both Stan Cross and Concord for the return of the car.

From the foregoing it is clear that Concord is liable on its warranty. This obligation, however, is expressly "limited to the sale price of the vehicle." Accordingly, the order for judgment is reversed and an order for judgment is to be entered for the plaintiff in the sum of $1,680.

(Judgment for Plaintiff.)

LENTZ v. OMAR BAKING CO.

(1934) 125 Neb. 861, 252 N.W. 410.

DAY, J. This was an action to recover damages for personal injuries received by plaintiff [Lentz] by reason of a breach of a warranty by the defendant in the sale of a horse. The defendant appeals from a judgment in favor of plaintiff for $3,989.35.

The plaintiff, a cripple by reason of an affliction to his hips, walked slowly, awkwardly, and with difficulty. He purchased a horse from the defendant. The defendant's agents were told about his physical condition, his age, sixty-nine years, and his need for a gentle horse. The defendant assured the plaintiff that the horse in question was such an animal. In fact, the evidence discloses that the horse was used on a bakery wagon for several years, going over the route without hitching while the driver went into various houses to serve customers for bakery goods. When the plaintiff with the help of others first hitched the horse to a buggy and got in, the horse without warning ran away, broke the side of the barn, a part of the fence, caught the buggy on a heavy post and broke loose from it and ran away.

Both of the plaintiff's legs were broken in this event. Thereafter, the horse was sold by the plaintiff to a man who used him upon a garbage wagon, where again he walked over his route without being tied while the driver was calling at various houses. So far as the record discloses, the incident when the horse ran away with the plaintiff is this horse's only deviation from the character of a safe and gentle horse. It is difficult to understand, but the fact is undisputed that upon this one occasion he did not behave as a gentle horse suitable for the plaintiff to drive.

There is no explanation in the record as to the cause of the runaway except that he was not gentle. It seems he ran away without apparent cause.

There was much conversation between the daughter of the plaintiff and employees of defendant in negotiating the sale. It was thoroughly understood that plaintiff was a cripple and his necessity required a horse of unquestioned gentleness. It is apparent under the circumstances that the plaintiff must have been induced to purchase the horse by the express warranty of the defendant. The evidence supports a finding that there was an express warranty as to this horse. The horse so warranted did not prove to be gentle and as a result the plaintiff was injured.

Where seller makes an affirmation of fact or promise, the natural tendency of which induces buyer to purchase, relying thereon, it is an express warranty. Comp.St.1929, sec. 69-412. The defendant was not entitled to a directed verdict in this case, as contended.

It is not necessary to prove seller's knowledge of the evil propensities of a horse where there is an express warranty, to recover for breach. This is not a tortious action but contractual, and negligence is not involved. Therefore the common-law rule of scienter is not applicable. * * *

The verdict in this case was for $3,989.35. The plaintiff was a cripple before the accident. He was sixty-nine years old. The hospital expenses were $395.35 and doctor's bills were $300. He could walk after a fashion before and take care of chickens and other chores. At the time of the trial, he had to be "taken care of like a baby and could not get out of bed." The evidence as to much pain and suffering is convincing. However, the plaintiff, due to his advanced age and previous crippled condition, did not have a large loss of future earnings under the circumstances of his case. For this reason, the verdict seems excessive, and we have reached the conclusion that the verdict should be reduced to $3,195.35. If the plaintiff files a remittitur of all in excess of this amount within 20 days, the judgment will be affirmed. Otherwise it is reversed and remanded.

Affirmed on condition.

STRAUSS v. WEST

(R.I.1966) 216 A.2d 366.

POWERS, J. This is an action of assumpsit to recover the agreed consideration for the sale of a race horse which, after delivery, the defendant rejected for an alleged breach of warranty. The case was tried to a superior court justice, sitting without a jury, and resulted in a decision for the plaintiff. It is before us on the defendant's exceptions to the decision and to an evidentiary ruling.

The uncontradicted evidence discloses that plaintiff was the owner of a race horse stabled at Belmont Park, a race track located in New York, when on April 27, 1962 it was purchased by defendant and at the latter's request was shipped over the road for delivery at Suffolk Downs in Massachusetts.

On the day of the sale defendant was accompanied by John D. Canzano, a professional horse trainer with twenty-three years' experience, who assisted him in negotiating the purchase. The horse was shown to them by Lawrence Gieger, a public horse trainer who was acting as agent for plaintiff.

Mr. Gieger refused to have the horse galloped for the reason that it had raced the previous day, but he assured defendant and his agent that the horse was sound. The horse was brought from the stable, walked in the presence of defendant and his trainer, and examined by the latter who found nothing wrong with the animal.

The plaintiff's agent accepted defendant's check in the sum of $1,800 payable to plaintiff, whereupon the parties agreed title passed to defendant.

Thereafter, pursuant to defendant's request, plaintiff's trainer made arrangements to ship the horse by motor van which left on the evening of April 28, 1962 and arrived at Suffolk Downs, a distance of some 215 miles, about six o'clock the following morning.

The defendant's trainer testified that within an hour and a half after the horse arrived, he had it saddled and mounted to observe how it galloped, and that when it started to gallop it almost fell down. After some adjustments another attempt was made but again, after a shorter gallop, the horse almost fell.

He further testified that he then examined the horse's front legs and found a bowed tendon in the left leg, and that on April 29 and April 30 he made seven or eight telephone calls to New York in an unsuccessful effort to speak to the trainer Gieger. Thereupon on May 1, 1962, defendant stopped payment on the check and on May 3, trainer Canzano shipped the horse back to New York.

The plaintiff's trainer testified that there were several possible ways by which a horse might sustain a bowed tendon and included traveling in a van for a considerable distance as one of them.

The trial justice found as a fact that the horse was sound at the time it was purchased and rendered decision for plaintiff in the sum of $1,800 with interest.

In support of his exception to the decision, defendant argues that the case is controlled by the provisions of the Uniform Commercial Code, G.L.1956, §§ 6A–2–313, 6A–2–513 and 6A–2–601. These sections set forth the conditions on which a warranty is established, the buyer's right to inspect and his right to reject for breach of warranty, respectively.

He contends that the facts in the instant case disclose an express warranty, an inspection of the horse on delivery, and rejection thereof within a reasonable time after it was discovered that the horse was not sound as warranted. In support of this contention he cites several Rhode Island cases. These are of no assistance to defendant, however, for the facts on which they rest are not present here.

Here the trial justice found that the horse was sound as warranted when purchased by defendant and delivered to him in New York. That it was found to have a bowed tendon subsequent to delivery was immaterial. There was no breach of warranty, if the trial justice's finding that the horse was sound when purchased can be supported by the evidence on which such finding was made. * * * [Citations.]

All of the defendant's exceptions are overruled, and the case is remitted to the superior court for entry of judgment on the decision.

Judgment for plaintiff affirmed.

PICKER X–RAY CORP. v. GENERAL MOTORS CORP.

(1962 D.C.Mun.App.) 185 A.2d 919.

MYERS, J. Corporate appellant sought recovery from appellee manufacturer for breach of implied warranty in the sale of a new automobile through a retail dealer. Three months after its purchase, while being operated by appellant's employee, the vehicle was damaged when it left the roadway, allegedly due to a defective steering mechanism. Appellant sued both the manufacturer and the dealer, alleging as to each negligence and breach of implied warranty of fitness. Appellee manufacturer moved to dismiss the warranty count on the ground there was no privity between it and the purchaser. From the granting of this motion, this appeal followed.

Since we must assume the allegations in the complaint to be true, the only question before us is whether a purchaser can sue a manufacturer for breach of an implied warranty of the fitness of its product bought through a retail outlet.

Historically, an action based upon warranty originated as a tort similar to an action for deceit, but by accident warranty came to be associated with contractual actions and thus assumed some aspects of tort, such as the measure of damages, and some aspects of contract, such as the requirement of privity. The latter requirement was imported into the law from a dictum in Winterbottom v. Wright, 10 M. & W. 109, 11 L.J.Ex. 415, 152 Eng.Rep. 402, and was followed by courts in most jurisdictions which prohibited any suit by a consumer against a manufacturer of a defective product, either on the basis of negligence or for breach of warranty, in the absence of a contractual relationship between them. As to negligence, the requirement of privity was ruled out by Justice Cardozo in MacPherson v. Buick Motor Co., 217 N.Y. 382, 111 N.E. 1050, L.R.A.1916F 696, but it has persisted principally in warranty actions.

In the recent trend where privity has no longer been required, the courts have given numerous reasons for their rulings to ameliorate the harshness of the doctrine. Judicial opinions have relied upon concepts of agency, assignment and third party beneficiary. Then a more functional approach to the problem was taken by some courts which simply dispensed with the rule itself, holding that the warranty "runs with the product," while others have relied frequently upon public policy.

Methods of commerce have drastically changed in the twentieth century. Now the retailer has little control over the products he sells because they are packaged or built before they reach him. He can neither protect his purchaser from harm nor himself from liability, yet he is liable to the immediate purchaser for breach of warranty. The only justification for holding the innocent retailer, and not the manufacturer, liable to the purchaser is that the former can recoup his loss by suing the manufacturer. Hence, a disclaimer of warranties or some other break in the chain can fasten liability on an innocent party, while the manufacturer, who is in better position to protect the consumer, goes free from liability. Moreover, even if successful, subsequent recoupment actions by retailers are an unnecessary burden upon the courts and litigants alike, add to congested trial calendars and delay the conclusion of litigation. More important, by reason of the tremendous increase in national advertising methods and programs, prospective purchasers no longer rely upon representations or warranties by retailers. Modern advertising by manufacturers on a large scale stresses trademarks and trade names and the superior qualities and benefits of their products and induces purchasers to ask for products by name because they have been represented as reliable and fit for the specific purpose and better than other similar products on the market. Lavishly-presented publicity programs by TV, radio and the press cultivate public favor and are major inducements in the consumer's final decision to buy. Thus, the advertising runs from the manufacturer to the ultimate consumer, and the manufacturer should not be permitted to shield himself from liability on the technical ground of lack of privity with the consumer or user, or for lack of foreseeable injury to the latter.

The courts have begun to disassociate contract from warranty and to recognize that a warranty is a duty imposed by law for protection of the buying public, regardless of the consent of the parties. The nineteenth-century policy of protecting young manufacturers is now giving way to one of protecting innocent consumers from unexpected injuries or losses due to defective products over which they have no control. Manufacturers should properly assume those burdens incident to the cost of doing business. Liability should no longer be dependent upon any contractual relationship between the manufacturer and the ultimate consumer or user.

We are aware that in this jurisdiction the United States Court of Appeals for the District of Columbia Circuit decided in 1932 that "according to the great weight of authority, a manufacturer of food is not liable to third persons under an implied warranty, because there is no privity of contract between them." Connecticut Pie Co. v. Lynch, 61 App.D.C. 81, 57 F.2d 447. This ruling was followed in another food case, Hanback v. Dutch Baker Boy, Inc., 70 App.D.C. 398, 107 F.2d 203.

Ordinarily we would feel bound to apply this principle of law to the present case. However, from a study of recent decisions on the question of privity in implied warranty cases involving food products as well as manufactured articles, we note that there is a distinct trend to repudiate this doctrine entirely. The more recent authorities, in cases involving both food and defectively-manufactured products which would be dangerous to life or limb, have eliminated the requirement of privity between the maker and the reasonably-expected ultimate consumer or user and have ruled that, in keeping with modern methods of commerce and sales, an implied warranty runs between the manufacturer or wholesaler and the consumer who buys his product through a retail outlet. * * *

In state courts, requirement of privity has been generally abandoned in food product actions based upon implied warranty violations where the food products are shown to be in the same condition as when they left the control of the manufacturer. Numerous other state decisions have eliminated the requirement in nonfood cases. * * *

There seems to be some confusion in understanding the nature of implied warranty liability. In the first place, concepts of negligence and fault, as defined by negligence standards, have no place in warranty recovery cases. Proof of negligence is unnecessary to liability for breach of implied warranty and the lack of it is immaterial to defense thereof. Since the warranty is *implied*, either in fact or in law, no express representations or agreements by the manufacturer are needed. Implied warranty recovery is based upon two factors: (a) The product or article in question has been transferred from the manufacturer's possession while in a "defective" state, more specifically, the product fails either to be "reasonably fit for the particular purpose intended" or of "merchantable quality," as these two terms, separate but often overlapping, are defined by the law; and (b) as a result of being "defective," the product causes personal injury or property damage.

Appellee contends that the Uniform Sales Act codified the doctrine of privity and that any change must come from legislation. This argument has been rejected often by the courts. Moreover, the Uniform Commercial Code, the most comprehensive proposed legislation on the subject, expressly leaves questions concerning privity to the judiciary.

There seems to be no sound reason at this date for permitting recovery in food cases upon implied warranty and denying it in nonfood cases. A defectively manufactured, potentially-dangerous instrumentality like an automobile, which will travel at high speeds on crowded highways and in congested areas, is far more dangerous to its driver, its passengers, and the public at large than is a contaminated food product in a can or package.

We are of the opinion that, regardless of the lack of contractual privity, the implied warranty of fitness and merchantability runs to the ultimate consumer for whose use the article or personal property had been purchased. The policy of protecting the public from injury, physical or pecuniary, resulting from misrepresentation, outweighs allegiance to a rule of law which, if observed, might produce great injustice. It is a new obligation attendant upon a new era, which dictates that the manufacturer should be held responsible to the consumer public for representations made for the purpose of promoting the sale of the product. Irrespective of the early rulings in this jurisdiction upon the requirement of privity *in food cases*, we are convinced that the buying public in the District of Columbia is better protected by eliminating the requirement for contractual privity in suits brought by the user against the manufacturer for breach of implied warranty resulting from a defectively manufactured product.

We express no views as to the existence of any defect in the present case, or of the sufficiency of proof to establish breach of implied warranty against the manufacturer. We rule that appellant should be allowed to proceed to trial on the alleged violation of the implied warranty rule in the absence of privity between them.

Reversed.

INGLIS v. AMERICAN MOTORS CORP.

(1965) 3 Ohio St.2d 132, 209 N.E.2d 583.

HERBERT, J. * * *

The question here may be stated in this language:

"Is privity of contract essential in an action based on breach of warranty where the purchaser of an automobile relies upon representations made in advertising of the manufacturer of the automobile in mass communications media to the effect that its automobiles are trouble-free, economical in operation and built and manufactured with a high quality of workmanship, and the purchaser suffers damage in the form of diminution of value of the automobile attributable to latent defects not readily ascertainable at the time of the purchase?"

The defendants' demurrer to the petition admits as true all facts properly pleaded. It follows, therefore, that the automobile manufactured and sold by the defendants to the plaintiff was defective as alleged in the petition to the extent that its value, instead of being $2,700—the price paid for it by the purchaser—was $1,200 thereby causing a pecuniary loss to the plaintiff in the sum of $1,500. There was no privity of contract between the defendant manufacturer and the plaintiff.

Rogers v. Toni Home Permanent Co., 167 Ohio St. 244, 147 N.E.2d 612, 75 A.L.R.2d 103, is a landmark case in the development of the law of products liability. It is widely recognized and the reasoning therein is generally respected. The syllabus reads:

"1. Originally, an action grounded on breach of warranty sounded in tort rather than contract.

"2. An express war.... affirmation of fact by the seller as to ... duct or commodity to induce the purchase thereof, on which affirmation the buyer relies in making the purchase.

"3. Under modern merchandising practices, where the manufacturer of a product in his advertising makes representations as to the quality and merit of his product aimed directly at the ultimate consumer and urges the latter to purchase the product from a retailer, and such ultimate consumer does so in reliance on and pursuant to the inducements of the manufacturer and suffers harm in the use of such product by reason of deleterious ingredients therein, such ultimate consumer may maintain an action for damages immediately against the manufacturer on the basis of express warranty, notwithstanding that there is no direct contractual relationship between them."

The distinguishing feature between Toni, supra, and the case at bar is that in Toni the purchaser of the "permanent" suffered some physical injuries to her hair and scalp by reason of using the product. In the case at bar there was not any personal injury or property damage—the loss being that of a pecuniary nature.

*   *   *

The most recent case that we have been able to find that is squarely in point with the case at bar is Santor v. A & M Karagheusian, Inc. (1964), 82 N.J.Super. 319, 197 A.2d 589, reversed by the Supreme Court (44 N.J. 52, 207 A.2d 305) on February 17, 1965.

Santor, the plaintiff, purchased approximately 100 square yards of what was claimed by the seller to be excellent carpeting. Within a few months the carpet showed streaks and the plaintiff was told that they would disappear. The streaks in the carpet became more marked and offensive and finally it was conceded that the carpet was practically worthless.

Action was brought against the manufacturer for the purchaser's financial loss by reason of the defective worthless carpet. This carpet was widely advertised. Plaintiff Santor was aware of this advertising. He brought an action for breach of warranty against the manufacturer. The plaintiff was awarded a judgment for pecuniary loss in the trial court. This judgment was reversed in the Appellate Division, but upon appeal to the Supreme Court of New Jersey the appellate judgment was likewise reversed and the judgment of the trial court reinstated.

The Appellate Division stated its conception of the law in this language:

" *   *   * It is clear to us that as of this writing, absent personal injury or damage to health consequent upon use of the product in question, there is no action in this State on the part of a purchaser of goods for breach of warranty in respect of their quality or fitness for use except as against the party from whom he has purchased them. *   *   * " 82 N.J.Super., at page 322, 197 A.2d, at page 591. However the Supreme Court of New Jersey disagreed and stated the law as follows:

"There is no doubt that the great mass of warranty cases imposing liability on the manufacturer regardless of lack of privity were concerned with personal injuries to the ultimate consumer. *   *   * [Citation of authorities]. But we see no just cause for recognition of the existence of an implied warranty of merchantability and a right to recovery for breach thereof regardless of lack of privity of the claimant in the one case and the exclusion of recovery in the other simply because loss of value of the article sold is the only damage resulting from the breach.

"The manufacturer is the father of the transaction. He makes the article and puts it in the channels of trade for sale to the public. No one questions the justice of a rule which holds him liable for defects arising out of the design or manufacture, or other causes while the product is under his control. After completion the article may pass through a series of hands, such as distributor and wholesaler, before reaching the dealer at the point of ultimate intended sale. The dealer is simply a way station, a conduit on its trip from manufacturer to consumer. For these reasons in the recent past the courts of many jurisdictions, in an endeavor to achieve justice for the ultimate consumer, have imposed an implied warranty of reasonable fitness on the person responsible for the existence of the article and the origin of the marketing process. From the standpoint of principle, we perceive no sound reason why the implication of reasonable fitness should be attached to the transaction and be actionable against the manufacturer where the defectively-made product has caused personal injury, and not actionable when inadequate manufacture has put a worthless article in the hands of an innocent purchaser who has paid the required price for it. * * * "

* * *

The case at bar is one of first impression in Ohio. Ohio has already contributed one landmark case—Rogers v. Toni Permanent Co., supra, that is respected and followed widely in the field of products liability. It was an instance of Ohio leadership in a mass of difficult legal questions. The principle laid down in Toni has been a strong arm of the law in its development to keep pace with the remarkable economic growth of our country during the past one-half century.

We cannot overestimate the importance of a sound administration of justice in these days of ever growing, economic and social problems and challenges. The protection of the defenseless consumer has proven its value as a cornerstone in the structure of our national administration of justice. We believe that justice requires that the consumer who has been caused to suffer substantial pecuniary losses by national advertising of false claims should be protected regardless of the lack of privity.

Judgment affirmed (for plaintiff).

HOCHGERTEL v. CANADA DRY CORPORATION

(1963) 409 Pa. 610, 187 A.2d 575.

EAGEN, J. The plaintiff, a bartender on duty in the clubhouse quarters of a fraternal organization, was injured by flying glass fragments, when an unopened bottle of carbonated soda water exploded as it was standing on the counter behind the bar. The soda water was previously bottled, sold and delivered by the defendant to plaintiff's employer. The plaintiff sued the defendant bottler manufacturer in assumpsit, charging a breach of implied warranties, namely: (1) That the soda water was of merchantable quality; (2) That it was fit and safe for the purposes for

which it was sold. The court below sustained preliminary objections to the complaint in the nature of a demurrer. This appeal followed, challenging the legal correctness of this order.

There is no doubt that when the defendant manufacturer sold the bottle of soda water to the fraternal lodge involved, it impliedly warranted *to the purchaser* that the contents of the bottle were fit for the purposes intended. [Citations.]

Two interesting questions are posed by this appeal: (1) Did this implied warranty extend to the plaintiff, an employee of the purchaser? (2) Did the warranty cover the container as well as the contents of the bottle? Our answer to the first question is determinative of the case.

Pennsylvania was the first state to adopt the Uniform Commercial Code (Code). See, Act of April 6, 1953, P.L. 3, as amended, 12A P.S. § 1–101 et seq. Clearly the Code gives no basis for the extension of the existing warranty to an *employee* of the purchaser. The pertinent provision, Section 2–318, is as follows:

"A seller's warranty whether express or implied extends to any natural person who is in the family or household of his buyer or who is a guest in his home if it is reasonable to expect that such person may use, consume or be affected by the goods and who is injured in person by breach of the warranty. A seller may not exclude or limit the operation of this section."

Comment 2, which follows this provision of the Code states:

"The purpose of this section is to give the buyer's family, household and guests the benefit of the same warranty which the buyer received in the contract of sale, thereby freeing any such beneficiaries from any technical rules as to 'privity.' It seeks to accomplish this purpose without any derogation of any right or remedy resting on negligence. It rests primarily upon the merchant-seller's warranty under this Article that the goods sold are merchantable and fit for the ordinary purposes for which such goods are used rather than the warranty of fitness for a particular purpose. Implicit in this section is that any beneficiary of a [breach of] warranty may bring a direct action for breach of warranty against the seller whose warranty extends to him."

Comment 3 then states:

"This section expressly includes as beneficiaries within its provisions the family, household, and guests of the purchaser. Beyond this, the section is neutral and is not intended to enlarge or restrict the developing case law on whether the seller's warranties, given to his buyer who resells, extend to other persons in the distributive chain."

It is clear from the language used that in order to qualify as a person (not a buyer), who is within the protection of the warranty, one must be a member of the buyer's family, his household or a guest in his home. An employee is definitely in none of these categories. * * *

Since the Code was not intended to restrict the case law in this field (see, § 2–318, Comment 3, supra), a study of pertinent Pennsylvania authorities is also necessary for the purposes of this decision.

The general rule in the United States is that the mere resale of a warranted article does not give a subpurchaser the right to sue the manufacturer in assumpsit, on the basis of breach of warranty, for damages incurred by him due to a defect in the quality of the goods. Pennsylvania decisions are in accord with this general proposition. The warranty is personal to the immediate or original buyer, and he alone may avail himself of the benefit thereof. This limitation is based on the rule of privity of contract. [Citations.]

However, nearly a third of the American jurisdictions, including Pennsylvania, have broken away from the rule of "privity of contract" in cases involving food, beverages and like goods for human consumption, and have for various stated reasons permitted a *subpurchaser* to sue the manufacturer directly in assumpsit for breach of an implied warranty that the food was wholesome and fit to eat. [Citations.]

* * *

In no case in Pennsylvania has recovery against the manufacturer for breach of an implied warranty been extended beyond *a purchaser* in the distributive chain. In fact, the inescapable conclusion from Loch v. Confair, 361 Pa. 158, 63 A.2d 24 (1949), is that no warranty will be implied in favor of one who is not in the category of a purchaser.

Despite arguments to the contrary, we see no impelling meritorious reason why the warranty should be extended to an employee of a purchaser. He is a complete stranger to any contractual transaction involved. His cause of action is basically one of tort and should stand or fall thereon. To grant such an extension of the warranty, as urged herein, would in effect render the manufacturer a guarantor of his product and impose liability in all such accident cases even if the utmost degree of care were exercised. This would lead to harsh and unjust results.

Further, in express warranties the purchaser or subpurchaser can rely thereon, for they are considered a part of the consideration for the purchase and are meant to be relied upon by the purchaser. [Citation.] So also the basis for recovery upon an implied warranty, absent a specific statutory exception such as contained in the Uniform Commercial Code, must be that the implied warranty forms a part of the consideration for the contract, and flows from manufacturer to subpurchaser through the conduit of a contractual chain.

Plaintiff has an adequate remedy in trespass, * * *.

Order affirmed.

WEBSTER v. BLUE SHIP TEA ROOM, INC.

(1964) 347 Mass. 421, 198 N.E.2d 309.

REARDON, J. This is a case which by its nature evokes earnest study not only of the law but also of the culinary traditions of the Commonwealth which bear so heavily upon its outcome. It is an action to recover damages for personal injuries sustained by reason of a breach of implied warranty of food served by the defendant in its restaurant. An auditor, whose findings of fact were not to be final, found for the plaintiff. On a retrial in the Superior Court before a judge and jury, in which the plaintiff testified, the jury returned a verdict for her. The defendant is here on exceptions to the refusal of the judge (1) to strike certain portions of the auditor's report, (2) to direct a verdict for the defendant, and (3) to allow the defendant's motion for the entry of a verdict in its favor under leave reserved.

The jury could have found the following facts: On Saturday, April 25, 1959, about 1 P.M., the plaintiff, accompanied by her sister and her aunt, entered the Blue Ship Tea Room operated by the defendant. The group was seated at a table and supplied with menus.

This restaurant, which the plaintiff characterized as "quaint," was located in Boston "on the third floor of an old building on T Wharf which overlooks the ocean."

The plaintiff, who had been born and brought up in New England (a fact of some consequence), ordered clam chowder and crabmeat salad. Within a few minutes she received tidings to the effect that "there was no more clam chowder," whereupon she ordered a cup of fish chowder. Presently, there was set before her "a small bowl of fish chowder." She had previously enjoyed a breakfast about 9 A.M. which had given her no difficulty. "The fish chowder contained haddock, potatoes, milk, water and season-

ing. The chowder was milky in color and not clear. The haddock and potatoes were in chunks" (also a fact of consequence). "She agitated it a little with the spoon and observed that it was a fairly full bowl * *. It was hot when she got it, but she did not tip it with her spoon because it was hot * * but stirred it in an up and under motion. She denied that she did this because she was looking for something, but it was rather because she wanted an even distribution of fish and potatoes." "She started to eat it, alternating between the chowder and crackers which were on the table with * * * [some] rolls. She ate about 3 or 4 spoonfuls then stopped. She looked at the spoonfuls as she was eating. She saw equal parts of liquid, potato and fish as she spooned it into her mouth. She did not see anything unusual about it. After 3 or 4 spoonfuls she was aware that something had lodged in her throat because she couldn't swallow and couldn't clear her throat by gulping and she could feel it." This misadventure led to two esophagoscopies at the Massachusetts General Hospital, in the second of which, on April 27, 1959, a fish bone was found and removed. The sequence of events produced injury to the plaintiff which was not insubstantial.

We must decide whether a fish bone lurking in a fish chowder, about the ingredients of which there is no other complaint, constitutes a breach of implied warranty under applicable provisions of the Uniform Commercial Code, the annotations to which are not helpful on this point. As the judge put it in his charge, "Was the fish chowder fit to be eaten and wholesome? * * * [N]obody is claiming that the fish itself wasn't wholesome. * * * But the bone of contention here—I don't mean that for a pun—but was this fish bone a foreign substance that made the fish chowder unwholesome or not fit to be eaten?"

* * *

The defendant asserts that here was a native New England eating fish chowder in a "quaint" Boston dining place where she had been before; that "[f]ish chowder, as it is served and enjoyed by New Englanders, is a hearty dish, originally designed to satisfy the appetites of our seamen and fishermen"; that "[t]his court knows well that we are not talking of some insipid broth as is customarily served to convalescents." We are asked to rule in such fashion that no chef is forced "to reduce the pieces of fish in the chowder to miniscule size in an effort to ascertain if they contained any pieces of bone." "In so ruling," we are told (in the defendant's brief), "the court will not only uphold its reputation for legal knowledge and acumen, but will, as loyal sons of Massachusetts, save our world-renowned fish chowder from degenerating into an insipid broth containing the mere essence of its former stature as a culinary masterpiece." Notwithstanding these passionate entreaties we are bound to examine with detachment the nature of fish chowder and what might happen to it under varying interpretations of the Uniform Commercial Code.

Chowder is an ancient dish preëxisting even "the appetites of our seamen and fishermen." It was perhaps the common ancestor of the "more refined cream soups, purées, and bisques." [Citation.] The word "chowder" comes from the French "chaudière," meaning a "cauldron" or "pot." "In the fishing villages of Brittany * * * 'faire la chaudière' means to supply a cauldron in which is cooked a mess of fish and biscuit with some savoury condiments, a hodge-podge contributed by the fishermen themselves, each of whom in return receives his share of the prepared dish. The Breton fishermen probably carried the custom to Newfoundland, long famous for its chowder, whence it has spread to Nova Scotia, New Brunswick, and New England." [Citation.] Our literature over the years abounds in references not only to the delights of chowder but also to its manufacture. A namesake of the plaintiff, Daniel Webster, had a recipe for fish chowder which has survived into a number of modern cookbooks and in which the removal of fish bones is not mentioned at all. One old time recipe recited in the New English Dictionary study defines chowder as "A dish made of fresh fish (esp. cod) or clams, stewed with slices of pork or bacon, onions, and biscuit. 'Cider and champagne are sometimes added.'" Hawthorne, in The House of the Seven Gables (Allyn and Bacon, Boston, 1957) p. 8, speaks of "[a] codfish of sixty pounds, caught in the bay, [which] had been dissolved into the rich liquid of a chowder." A chowder variant, cod "Muddle," was made in Plymouth in the 1890s by taking "a three or four pound codfish, head added. Season with salt and pepper and boil in just enough water to keep from burning. When cooked, add milk and piece of butter." The recitation of these ancient formulae suffices to indicate that in the construction of chowders in these parts in other years, worries about fish bones played no role whatsoever. This broad outlook on chowders has persisted in more modern cookbooks. "The chowder of today is much the same as the old chowder * * *." [Citation.] The all embracing Fannie Farmer states in a portion of her recipe, fish chowder is made with a "fish skinned, but head and tail left on. Cut off head and tail and remove fish from backbone. Cut fish in 2-inch pieces and set aside. Put head, tail, and backbone broken in pieces, in stewpan; add 2 cups cold water and bring slowly to boiling point * * *." The liquor thus produced from the bones is added to the balance of the chowder. Farmer, The Boston Cooking School Cook Book (Little Brown Co., 1937) p. 166.

Thus, we consider a dish which for many long years, if well made, has been made generally as outlined above. It is not too much to say that a person sitting down in New

England to consume a good New England fish chowder embarks on a gustatory adventure which may entail the removal of some fish bones from his bowl as he proceeds. We are not inclined to tamper with age old recipes by any amendment reflecting the plaintiff's view of the effect of the Uniform Commercial Code upon them. We are aware of the heavy body of case law involving foreign substances in food, but we sense a strong distinction between them and those relative to unwholesomeness of the food itself, e. g., tainted mackerel [citation], and a fish bone in a fish chowder. Certain Massachusetts cooks might cavil at the ingredients contained in the chowder in this case in that it lacked the heartening lift of salt pork. In any event, we consider that the joys of life in New England include the ready availability of fresh fish chowder. We should be prepared to cope with the hazards of fish bones, the occasional presence of which in chowders is, it seems to us, to be anticipated, and which, in the light of a hallowed tradition, do not impair their fitness or merchantability. While we are buoyed up in this conclusion by Shapiro v. Hotel Statler Corp., 132 F.Supp. 891 (S.D.Cal.), in which the bone which afflicted the plaintiff appeared in "Hot Barquette of Seafood Mornay," we know that the United States District Court of Southern California, situated as are we upon a coast, might be expected to share our views. We are most impressed, however, by Allen v. Grafton, 170 Ohio St. 249, 164 N.E. 2d 167, where in Ohio, the Midwest, in a case where the plaintiff was injured by a piece of oyster shell in an order of fried oysters, Mr. Justice Taft (now Chief Justice) in a majority opinion held that "the possible presence of a piece of oyster shell in or attached to an oyster is so well known to anyone who eats oysters that we can say as a matter of law that one who eats oysters can reasonably anticipate and guard against eating such a piece of shell * * *."

Thus, while we sympathize with the plaintiff who has suffered a peculiarly New England injury, the order must be

Exceptions sustained.

Judgment for the defendant.

HENNINGSEN v. BLOOMFIELD MOTORS, INC.

(1960) 32 N.J. 358, 161 A.2d 69.

[Action by purchaser of automobile and his wife against retail dealer and manufacturer of a defective automobile to recover damages for injuries sustained by the wife while driving the car shortly after its purchase. A warranty by the manufacturer to make good defective parts at its factory was stated to be "expressly in lieu of all other warranties express or implied." Judgment in favor of the plaintiffs and against the defendants was affirmed.]

FRANCIS, J. * * *

The Effect of the Disclaimer and Limitation of Liability Clauses on the Implied Warranty of Merchantability.

Judicial notice may be taken of the fact that automobile manufacturers, including Chrysler Corporation, undertake large scale advertising programs over television, radio, in newspapers, magazines and all media of communication in order to persuade the public to buy their products. As has been observed above, a number of jurisdictions, conscious of modern marketing practices, have declared that when a manufacturer engages in advertising in order to bring his goods and their quality to the attention of the public and thus to create consumer demand, the representations made constitute an express warranty running directly to a buyer who purchases in reliance thereon. The fact that the sale is consummated with an independent dealer does not obviate that warranty. [Citations.]

In view of the cases in various jurisdictions suggesting the conclusion which we have now reached with respect to the implied warranty of merchantability, it becomes apparent that manufacturers who enter into promotional activities to stimulate consumer buying may incur warranty obligations of either or both the express or implied character. These developments in the law inevitably suggest the inference that the form of express warranty made part of the Henningsen purchase contract was devised for general use in the automobile industry as a possible means of avoiding the consequences of the growing judicial acceptance of the thesis that the described express or implied warranties run directly to the consumer.

In the light of these matters, what effect should be given to the express warranty in question which seeks to limit the manufacturer's liability to replacement of defective parts, and which disclaims all other warranties, express or implied? In assessing its significance we must keep in mind the general principle that, in the absence of fraud, one who does not choose to read a contract before signing it, cannot later relieve himself of its burdens. [Citation.] And in applying that principle, the basic tenet of freedom of competent parties to contract is a factor of importance. But in the framework of modern commerical life and business practices, such rules cannot be applied on a strict, doctrinal basis. The conflicting interests of the buyer and seller must be evaluated realistically and justly, giving due weight to the social policy evinced by the Uniform Sales Act, the progressive decisions of the courts engaged in administering it, the mass production methods of manufacture and distribution to the public, and the bargaining position occupied by the ordinary consumer in such an economy. This history of the law shows that legal

doctrines, as first expounded, often prove to be inadequate under the impact of later experience. In such case, the need for justice has stimulated the necessary qualifications or adjustments. [Citations.]

In these times, an automobile is almost as much a servant of convenience for the ordinary person as a household utensil. For a multitude of other persons it is a necessity. Crowded highways and filled parking lots are a commonplace of our existence. There is no need to look any farther than the daily newspaper to be convinced that when an automobile is defective, it has great potentiality for harm.

*   *   *

What influence should these circumstances have on the restrictive effect of Chrysler's express warranty in the framework of the purchase contract? As we have said, warranties originated in the law to safeguard the buyer and not to limit the liability of the seller or manufacturer. It seems obvious in this instance that the motive was to avoid the warranty obligations which are normally incidental to such sales. The language gave little and withdrew much. In return for the delusive remedy of replacement of defective parts at the factory, the buyer is said to have accepted the exclusion of the maker's liability for personal injuries arising from the breach of the warranty, and to have agreed to the elimination of any other express or implied warranty. An instinctively felt sense of justice cries out against such a sharp bargain. But does the doctrine that a person is bound by his signed agreement, in the absence of fraud, stand in the way of any relief?

*   *   *

The warranty before us is a standardized form designed for mass use. It is imposed upon the automobile consumer. He takes it or leaves it, and he must take it to buy an automobile. No bargaining is engaged in with respect to it. In fact, the dealer through whom it comes to the buyer is without authority to alter it; his function is ministerial —simply to deliver it. The form warranty is not only standard with Chrysler but, as mentioned above, it is the uniform warranty of the Automobile Manufacturers Association. Members of the Association are: General Motors, Inc., Ford, Chrysler, Studebaker-Packard, American Motors, (Rambler), Willys Motors, Checker Motors Corp., and International Harvester Company. Automobile Facts and Figures (1958 Ed., Automobile Manufacturers Association) 69. Of these companies, the "Big Three" (General Motors, Ford, and Chrysler) represented 93.5% of the passenger-car production for 1958 and the independents 6.5%. Standard & Poor (Industrial Surveys, Autos, Basic Analysis, June 25, 1959) 4109. And for the same year the "Big Three" had 86.72% of the total passenger vehicle registrations. Automotive News, 1959 Almanac (Slocum Publishing Co., Inc.) p. 25.

The gross inequality of bargaining position occupied by the consumer in the automobile industry is thus apparent. There is no competition among the car makers in the area of the express warranty. Where can the buyer go to negotiate for better protection? Such control and limitation of his remedies are inimical to the public welfare and, at the very least, call for great care by the courts to avoid injustice through application of strict common-law principles of freedom of contract. Because there is no competition among the motor vehicle manufacturers with respect to the scope of protection guaranteed to the buyer, there is no incentive on their part to stimulate good will in that field of public relations. Thus, there is lacking a factor existing in more competitive fields, one which tends to guarantee the safe construction of the article sold. Since all competitors operate in the same way, the urge to be careful is not so pressing. See

"Warranties of Kind and Quality," 57 Yale L.J. 1389, 1400 (1948).

Although the courts, with few exceptions, have been most sensitive to problems presented by contracts resulting from gross disparity in buyer-seller bargaining positions, they have not articulated a general principle condemning, as opposed to public policy, the imposition on the buyer of a skeleton warranty as a means of limiting the responsibility of the manufacturer. They have endeavored thus far to avoid a drastic departure from age-old tenets of freedom of contract by adopting doctrines of strict construction, and notice and knowledgeable assent by the buyer to the attempted exculpation of the seller. [Citations.]

*   *   *

It is undisputed that the president of the dealer with whom Henningsen dealt did not specifically call attention to the warranty on the back of the purchase order. The form and the arrangement of its face, as described above, certainly would cause the minds of reasonable men to differ as to whether notice of a yielding of basic rights stemming from the relationship with the manufacturer was adequately given. The words "warranty" or "limited warranty" did not even appear in the fine print above the place for signature, and a jury might well find that the type of print itself was such as to promote lack of attention rather than sharp scrutiny. The inference from the facts is that Chrysler placed the method of communicating its warranty to the purchaser in the hands of the dealer. If either one or both of them wished to make certain that Henningsen became aware of that agreement and its purported implications, neither the form of the document nor the method of expressing the precise nature of the obligation intended to be assumed would have presented any difficulty.

But there is more than this. Assuming that a jury might find that the fine print referred to reasonably served the objective of directing a buyer's attention to the warranty on the reverse side, and, therefore, that he should be charged with awareness of its language, can it be said that an ordinary layman would realize what he was relinquishing in return for what he was being granted? Under the law, breach of warranty against defective parts or workmanship which caused personal injuries would entitle a buyer to damages even if due care were used in the manufacturing process. Because of the great potential for harm if the vehicle was defective, that right is the most important and fundamental one arising from the relationship. Difficulties so frequently encountered in establishing negligence in manufacture in the ordinary case make this manifest. [Citations.] Any ordinary layman of reasonable intelligence, looking at the phraseology, might well conclude that Chrysler was agreeing to replace defective parts and perhaps replace anything that went wrong because of defective workmanship during the first 90 days or 4,000 miles of operation, but that he would not be entitled to a new car. It is not unreasonable to believe that the entire scheme being conveyed was a proposed remedy for physical deficiencies in the car. *In the context* of this warranty, only the abandonment of all sense of justice would permit us to hold that, as a matter of law, the phrase "its obligation under this warranty being limited to making good at its factory any part or parts thereof" signifies to an ordinary reasonable person that he is relinquishing any personal injury claim that might flow from the use of a defective automobile. Such claims are nowhere mentioned. The draftsmanship is reflective of the care and skill of the Automobile Manufacturers Association in undertaking to avoid warranty obligations without drawing too much attention to its effort in that regard. No one can doubt that if the will to do so were present, the ability to inform the buying public of the intention to disclaim liability for injury claims arising from breach of warranty would present no problem. * * *

Public policy at a given time finds expression in the Constitution, the statutory law and in judicial decisions. In the area of sale of goods, the legislative will has imposed an implied warranty of merchantability as a general incident of sale of an automobile by description. The warranty does not depend upon the affirmative intention of the parties. It is a child of the law; it annexes itself to the contract because of the very nature of the transaction. [Citation.] The judicial process has recognized a right to recover damages for personal injuries arising from a breach of that warranty. The disclaimer of the implied warranty and exclusion of all obligations except those specifically assumed by the express warranty signify a studied effort to frustrate that protection. True, the Sales Act authorizes agreements between buyer and seller qualifying the warranty obligations. But quite obviously the Legislature contemplated lawful stipulations (which are determined by the circumstances of a particular case) arrived at freely by parties of relatively equal bargaining strength. The lawmakers did not authorize the automobile manufacturer to use its grossly disproportionate bargaining power to relieve itself from liability and to impose on the ordinary buyer, who in effect has no real freedom of choice, the grave danger of injury to himself and others that attends the sale of such a dangerous instrumentality as a defectively made automobile. In the framework of this case, illuminated as it is by the facts and the many decisions noted, we are of the opinion that Chrysler's attempted disclaimer of an implied warranty of merchantability and of the obligations arising therefrom is so inimical to the public good as to compel an adjudication of its invalidity. See 57 Yale L.J., supra, at pp. 1400–1404; proposed Uniform Commercial Code, 1958 Official Text, § 202.

* * * [Judgments for plaintiff buyer and wife affirmed.]

MINIKES v. ADMIRAL CORPORATION

((1966) D.C. Nassau County, N.Y.) 266 N.Y.S.2d 461.

JOHN S. LOCKMAN, J. Defendant Newmark & Lewis, as seller, moves for summary judgment dismissing a purchaser's complaint which alleges a breach of contract because the merchandise, a refrigerator, did not comply with the implied warranties of merchantability and fitness set forth in Sections 2–314 and 2–315 of the Uniform Commercial Code (U.C.C.).

The defendant contends that Section 2–316 U.C.C. permits a disclaimer of implied warranties and exhibited the purchase order to show that it had disclaimed. Although the prelude to the disclaimer stating: "All orders accepted are subject to the following:" was in larger type, the disclaimer was in five point type and smaller than the type on the rest of the "purchase order".

The burden of preparing an effective disclaimer is heavy. It is one of the hazards of business. Before a merchant can disqualify for the implied warranties the public has become accustomed to, it must show that the customer was clearly placed on notice. [Citation]. A reading of Section 2–316 relied upon by the defendant indicates that any written disclaimer must be *conspicuous*. Conspicuous is defined in Section 1–201 U.C.C.

"General Definitions: * * * (10) 'Conspicuous': A term or clause is conspicuous when it is so written that a reasonable person against whom it is to operate ought to have noticed it. A printed heading in capitals (as: Non-Negotiable Bill of Lading) is conspicuous. Language in the body of a form is 'conspicuous' *if it is in larger or other con-*

trasting type or color. But in a telegram any stated term is 'conspicuous'. Whether a term or clause is 'conspicuous' or not is for decision by the court." (Emphasis added.)

Since the disclaimer is smaller, not larger, than the rest of the purchase order, it is not conspicuous. Accordingly, defendant's motion for summary judgment dismissing the complaint is denied.

Whether the conduct or conversation constituted a disclaimer under Section 2–316 is an issue of fact to be determined at the trial.

Short form order entered.

FIRST NATIONAL BANK OF ELGIN v. HUSTED

(1965) 57 Ill.App.2d 227, 205 N.E.2d 780.

DAVIS, J. This is an appeal from an Order entered by the Circuit Court denying defendants' motion to open a judgment in the sum of $672.18, confessed against them on January 27, 1964, by plaintiff, First National Bank of Elgin.

The judgment was based on a Retail Installment Contract entered into by defendants, as buyers, and Reed Motors, Inc., as seller, in connection with the sale of a 1958 Ford. The customary warrant of attorney and confession clause were on the reverse side of the contract, under the heading "Covenants and Conditions", along with the "Dealer's Assignment", whereby said contract was assigned to plaintiff, without recourse.

* * *

The Retail Sales Contract was dated August 29, 1963, and was assigned to plaintiff August 30, 1963. Defendants, by said contract, acknowledged notice of intended assignment of the contract, and agreed to make all payments to assignee, and their answer admitted said assignment. The contract, on its face, provided that payments were to be made at the First National Bank of Elgin.

The motion to open the judgment, and to file answer, and the affidavit in support thereof, alleged that defendants purchased the Ford in question on August 29, 1963, from Reed Motors Inc., upon warranty that it was in good operating condition; that on September 1, 1963, defendants observed that the car did not operate properly, and that it became inoperative, and was damaged by fire; that thereafter, on September 2, 1963, Reed Motors Inc., promised to repair the car upon delivery thereof to it; that said car was delivered to Reed Motors Inc., but was never repaired, and was later sold by Reed Motors Inc., or plaintiff; and that neither Reed Motors Inc., nor plaintiff, its assignee, sold said car until December 2, 1963, which sale was not within a reasonable time after the retaking, and hence there was an election of remedies under section 23 of the Retail Installment Sales Act, (Ill.Rev.Stat.1963, Chap. 121½, section 247) and thereby defendants have been released from any obligations to Reed Motors Inc., or plaintiff. Defendants' affidavit also charged lack of notice of the assignment and failure of consideration.

*   *   *

Defendants further charge that plaintiff was not a holder in due course of the Retail Installment Contract, and, therefore, the defenses which they have asserted are available against the plaintiff. However, the contract provided: "Buyer agrees to settle all claims against Seller directly with Seller and will not set up any such claims against Seller as defense, counterclaim, set off, cross complaint or otherwise in any action for the purchase price or possession brought by any assignee of this contract."

The Uniform Commercial Code, provides:
"(1) Subject to any statute or decision which establishes a different rule for buyers of consumer goods, an agreement by a buyer that he will not assert against an assignee any claim or defense which he may have against the seller is enforceable by an assignee who takes his assignment for value, in good faith and without notice of a claim or defense, except as to defenses of a type which may be asserted against a holder in due course of a negotiable instrument under the Article on Commercial Paper. (Article 3). A buyer who as part of one transaction signs both a negotiable instrument and a security agreement makes such an agreement.

"(2) When a seller retains a purchase money security interest in goods the Article on Sales (Article 2) governs the sale and any disclaimer, limitation or modification of the seller's warranties."

(Ill.Rev.Stat.1963, Chap. 26, Sec. 9–206).

*   *   *

The defenses which may be asserted against a holder in due course are:
"(a) infancy, to the extent that it is a defense to a simple contract; and
"(b) such other incapacity, or duress, or illegality of the transaction, as renders the obligation of the party a nullity; and
"(c) such misrepresentation as has induced the party to sign the instrument with neither knowledge nor reasonable opportunity to obtain knowledge of its character or its essential terms; and
"(d) discharge in insolvency proceedings; and
"(e) any other discharge of which the holder has notice when he takes the instrument."

Ill.Rev.Stat.1963, Chap. 26, Par. 3–305 (2).

Thus, a buyer may contractually waive, as against an assignee, any defenses except those enumerated in Articles 3–305(2) and 9–206(2). The defenses which defendants, as buyers, seek to assert against plaintiff are: failure of consideration; lack of notice of assignment; breach of express and implied warranties; subsequent promises and failure to repair the car, and an election to retain the car arising by failure to resell it within a reasonable time after the re-taking. In absence of allegation in defendants' affidavit that plaintiff did not take the assignment for value, in good faith, and without notice of claim or defense, and in view of the date of the contract and assignment, we believe that plaintiff is an assignee for value, in good faith, and without notice of claim or defense.

The buyers' defenses of failure of consideration, and subsequent promise and failure to repair the car were waived, as against the plaintiff, assignee, under Article 9–206 of the Uniform Commercial Code.

*   *   *

The Retail Installment Sales Act contains no provisions relative to warranties. The exclusion and modification of warranties is governed by Article 2–316 of the Uniform Commercial Code (Ill.Rev.Stat.1963, Chap. 26, par. 2–316). Its purpose is to protect the buyer from unbargained language of disclaimer by denying effect to such language when inconsistent with the contract language of express warranty, and it permits the exclusion of implied warranties by conspicuous language in the contract. It provides that "all implied warranties are excluded by expressions like 'as is', 'with all faults' or other language which in common understanding calls the buyer's attention to the exclusion of warranties and makes plain that there is no implied warranty." It also provides that there is no implied warranty where "the buyer before entering into the contract has examined the goods or the sample or model as fully as he desired or has refused to examine the goods *   *   *."

The contract in question, immediately beneath the names of the parties, in language printed in the size type of all of the words of the paragraphs of the contract, provided: "Buyer acknowledges delivery, examination and acceptance of said car in its present con-

dition." The "Covenants and Conditions" of the contract contained the following language, printed in the same size type: "This agreement constitutes the entire contract and no waivers or modification shall be valid unless written upon or attached to this contract, and said car is accepted without any express or implied warranties, agreements, representations, promises or statements unless expressly set forth in this contract at the time of purchase." The contract contained no express warranties pertaining to the car.

We believe that the words "in its present condition" are similar to the words "as is" or "with all faults", and have the effect of excluding implied warranties. Further, the buyer acknowledged examination of the car and this precludes an implied warranty. Consequently, the defenses of express and implied warranties were not available to the defendants.

*   *   *

Judgment affirmed.

BALKOWITSCH v. MINNEAPOLIS WAR MEMORIAL BLOOD BANK, INC.

(1965) 270 Minn. 151, 132 N.W.2d 805.

MURPHY, J. This is an appeal from a summary judgment for defendant in an action by which plaintiff Marie A. Balkowitsch sought to recover damages for personal injuries sustained when she contracted the disease of serum hepatitis from a transfusion of impure blood supplied by defendant, Minneapolis War Memorial Blood Bank, Inc. Plaintiff John Balkowitsch sought recovery based upon his derivative rights as the husband of Marie Balkowitsch. The claim is predicated upon a breach of implied warranty under a contractual sales-act theory as well as strict liability in tort.

The facts may be briefly stated. Between March 20 and March 29, 1958, quantities of whole blood were administered by transfusion to Mrs. Balkowitsch, hereinafter called plaintiff, while she was a patient at St. Mary's Hospital in Minneapolis. The blood she received was furnished by the defendant, the Minneapolis War Memorial Blood Bank, Inc. The transfusions were ordered by her physician. Prior to the receipt of the blood, ownership of it remained in the defendant. Payment was based upon the amount of blood received and was made directly by plaintiff to defendant. It does not seem to be disputed that the blood was contaminated and produced the disability from which plaintiff suffered. Neither is it claimed that defendant was negligent in the processing or distribution of the blood. Plaintiffs assert that defendant "sold" the blood to her, impliedly warranting its fitness and merchantable quality; that the blood was not as warranted in that it contained the virus; and as a consequence plaintiff sustained damages.

In considering the merits of plaintiffs' case, it is necessary to examine the function of defendant's activities and the nature of the service in which it is engaged. Defendant is a nonprofit public service corporation engaged in the collection and storage of whole blood which is used for transfusion purposes. The process by which human blood is grouped and stored for use involves an advanced science which employs complex and elaborate facilities. The blood must be obtained, processed, stored, and transported so that it is immediately available in sufficient quantities, and carefully labeled as to group, RH factor, and other pertinent data. Science has perfected storage techniques with the result that whole blood may be stored safely up to 21 days and blood derivatives, such as plasma, may be stored for longer periods of time. This program is carried on largely through the activities of the American Red Cross and 923 regional blood banks, of which defendant is one, and their branch banks. In addition to these, there are one national and five district "clearing house" offices which

accomplish the interbank transfers of blood; five central and 18 regional reference laboratories; a central file of rare donors and a special bank of extremely rare blood. The blood-bank arrangement provides an accessible place where sufficient quantities of all kinds of blood are readily available and from which people may obtain needed blood at actual cost.

In spite of the great advancements which have been made in the collection and storage of blood, there remain certain risks which medical science has been unable to eliminate. A few diseases may be communicated from person to person by blood transfusions. Some of these are susceptible to tests whereby their presence in the blood may be ascertained. But this is not so in respect to serum hepatitis, a virus disease which is also referred to in medical literature as homologous serum hepatitis or homologous serum jaundice or simply as SH virus. * * * These decisions illustrate the inability of medical science, despite all due care, to detect serum hepatitis in the blood. They recognize that since the medical profession is aware of the risk inherent in transfusions, due care does not impose on those who provide the blood a duty to warn the profession. It is a matter of medical judgment to determine whether in a particular case the benefits outweigh the risk.

* * * In Perlmutter v. Beth David Hospital, 308 N.Y. 100, 123 N.E.2d 792, the complaint alleged that while plaintiff was a paying patient in defendant hospital she purchased a blood transfusion for $60; that plaintiff relied upon the skill and judgment of the hospital and the implied warranty that the blood was "fit" for the intended purpose and was of "merchantable quality" and was not impure or contaminated. The sole question on defendant's motion for a dismissal was whether or not the transaction constituted a sale under the New York Sales Act— whether there was a vendor-vendee relation-

ship between the hospital and the patient. In holding that the blood transfusion did not constitute a sale, and hence carried with it no warranties of fitness or merchantability, the court described the relationship between a hospital and its patients in these words (308 N.Y. 104, 123 N.E.2d 794):

"* * * The essence of the contractual relationship between hospital and patient is readily apparent; the patient bargains for, and the hospital agrees to make available, the human skill and physical materiel of medical science to the end that the patient's health be restored.

"Such a contract is clearly one for services, and, just as clearly, it is not divisible. Concepts of purchase and sale cannot separately be attached to the healing materials—such as medicines, drugs or, indeed, blood—supplied by the hospital for a price as part of the medical services it offers. That the property or title to certain items of medical material may be transferred, so to speak, from the hospital to the patient during the course of medical treatment does not serve to make each such transaction a sale. ' "Sale" and "transfer" are not synonymous', and not every transfer of personal property constitutes a sale. [Citations.] As Benjamin put it in his work on Sale (p. 166), 'a contract of sale is not constituted merely by reason that the property in the materials is to be transferred * * *. If they are simply accessory to work and labour, the contract is for work, labour and materials. Such is the case of medicine supplied by a medical man to a patient, * *'."

* * *

From these authorities it is apparent that courts have rejected the sales analogy by which liability in blood-transfusion cases might be imposed on the theory of implied warranty. We agree with those courts which hold that the furnishing of blood is more in the nature of a service than in the sale of goods. It is our view that the law expressed in the Perlmutter case applies here.

Plaintiffs seek to distinguish the Perlmutter case on the basis that the defendant here is not a hospital as it was there. But we cannot concede that defendant, which is a nonprofit corporation, should be treated differently than a hospital or that it should be characterized as a commercial business which offers its products for sale in the market place in competition with others for the sole motive of making a profit. The acts performed by the hospital in the Perlmutter case are not so unrelated to those performed by the defendant in the case before us as to justify a different result.

* * * We find it difficult to give literal application of principles of law designed to impose strict accountability in commercial transactions to a voluntary and charitable activity which serves a humane and public health purpose. The activities involved in the transfusion of whole blood, a component of the living body, from one human being to another may be characterized as sui generis in that the sequence of events involve acts common to legal concepts of both a sale and a service. Moreover, it seems to us that under the facts in the case before us it would be unrealistic to hold that there is an implied warranty as to qualities of fitness of human blood on which no medical or scientific information can be acquired and in respect to which plaintiffs' physician has the same information, knowledge, and experience as the supplier.

Affirmed.

———

PROBLEMS

1. A stole merchandise and sold it to B, who did not know of the theft. B sold the merchandise to C who was likewise ignorant of how A obtained the property. The bill of sale by B to C contained no warranty of any kind. Subsequent to delivery of the merchandise to C, D sued C and proved that he, D, was the owner. Judgment was rendered in D's favor and D obtained possession of the

merchandise. Thereafter, C sues B for breach of warranty. Decision?

2. B examined a race horse which A had for sale for $2,500, and decided to buy it. While the parties were preparing the written contract, B said he thought the horse appeared to be slightly lame. A replied, in good faith, that this was because the horse had not been exercised for a few days, and that he warranted the horse to be sound in every respect. A and B then signed the contract, and B took the horse away. It turned out that the horse was actually lame, and that B had to pay $350 to cure the lameness. B now sues A for $350 damages for breach of warranty. Decision?

3. A Co. sold B a Beverly tractor, B having informed A Co. as to the particular kind of work for which he wanted it. The printed contract contained this provision: "No warranties have been made in reference to said motor vehicle by the seller to the buyer unless expressly written hereon at the date of purchase." None were written thereon. As the parties were signing the contract, the A Co. representative stated to B that the tractor was exactly fit for the purpose which B had stated. The tractor turned out to be wholly unsuitable for B's purpose and he refuses to pay for it. A Co. sues B. Has B any defense?

4. B purchased face powder from the A company containing two aniline dyes which are irritants to some people, but not to the average person. A rash, diagnosed as dermatitis, appeared on B's face shortly after she applied the face powder. She had never used this particular brand of powder before and had never had a similar rash on her face. B sues A company for breach of implied warranty of fitness of the face powder. Decision?

5. The X Company, manufacturer of a widely advertised and expensive perfume, sold a quantity of this product to Y, a retail druggist. A and B visited the store of Y, and A, desiring to make a gift to B, purchased from Y a bottle of this perfume, asking for it by its trade name. Y wrapped up the bottle so purchased and handed it directly to B. The perfume contained an injurious foreign chemical substance which, upon the first use of the perfume by B, severely burned the face of B and caused a permanent facial disfigurement. What are the rights of B, if any, against A, Y, and the X Company, respectively?

6. A was the manufacturer of Xcello dog food. The dog food was sold to the Y Department store. M bought some of the dog food for his trained pointer. The dog ate the food and soon became violently ill as a result of the food being very poorly packed. M could not use his pointer during the pheasant season, and he had to spend $350 to cure the dog of his illness. (a) M sues A for breach of warranty. Decision? (b) If M did not sue for breach of warranty, what other theory, if any, could he use in a suit against A?

7. B brings an action to recover for injuries suffered while eating a dinner purchased and served on January 15, at a restaurant owned and operated by A. B alleges that as part of the dinner A furnished for drinking purposes water that was contaminated with bacteria and unfit for human consumption. He further alleges that he drank the water and became ill therefrom. At the trial it was established that A had employed ordinary and reasonable care in obtaining the water from a faucet through which the water was supplied by the city, and that A had no knowledge, nor by the exercise of due care could have had knowledge, that the water was contaminated. What judgment?

8. Lee was shopping in the XYZ self-service market. A bottle of soft drink, which he took from a shelf, exploded in his hand. He sued Better Beverage Company which had bottled the drink to recover damages upon the theory that there had been a breach of warranty arising from the sale of food. Decision?

9. A route salesman for Ideal Milk Company delivered a one-half gallon glass jug of milk to Allen's home. The next day when Allen grasped the milk container by its neck to take it out of his refrigerator, it shattered in his hand and caused serious injury. Allen paid Ideal on a monthly basis for the regular delivery of milk. Ideal's milk bottles each contained the legend "Property of Ideal—to be returned" and the route salesman would pick up the empty bottles when he delivered milk. Allen brought an action against Ideal Milk Company, charging breach of warranty. Decision?

10. On October 1 X rented a car to Y for two months at $30 per month. On October 8 after Y took possession, Z forced the lock on Y's garage and stole the car. On October 10, Z sold the car to P who paid full value and had no knowledge of the theft. Z assured P that the car

was in "A-1 condition in every way" and this induced P, who wouldn't know a differential from a Hubbard squash, to buy the car. On October 15, as P was driving to town, he ran the car into T's truck. The accident resulted from the sudden failure of the steering mechanism which had been badly worn and which X knew when he rented the car to Y. As a result of the accident, P pays T $200 for damage to the truck. $100 of damage is done to the car's fenders, and P decides to wait until spring to fix this, but he spends $50 to fix the steering mechanism. Upon filing the accident report on October 22, all facts come to light.

(a) Can P recover for breach of warranty? If so, from whom and for breach of what warranty? (b) Who is entitled to immediate possession of the car? (c) What damages may Y recover from Z? (d) May P recover the $50 for repairs? From whom? (e) If the $100 damage to the fender had resulted from P's negligence and not from faulty brakes, who would be entitled to the $100 recovered in a joint action by X and Y against P?

CHAPTER 24

PRODUCTS LIABILITY

Introductory. The preceding chapter on warranties opens the door to the interesting subject of products liability and invites this more extended treatment.

This chapter deals with the liability of manufacturers and vendors of goods and chattels to users and consumers on a much broader basis that that of express or implied warranty.

The recent and rapid development of the case law in this field is almost phenomenal. An impetus to the extension of liability has been the modern practice whereby the retailer serves principally as a conduit of pre-packaged goods in sealed containers which are widely advertised by the manufacturer or distributor on television and radio, in newspapers, magazines, brochures, and by direct mail. The retailer remains liable to his purchaser on express and implied warranties with respect to goods which he may be unable to examine before reselling. The extension of products liability to manufacturers of goods has not lessened the exposure of the immediate vendor to liability to the user or consumer. It has, rather, broadened and extended the base of liability by the development and application of new principles of law.

The requirement of privity of contract is rapidly disappearing as the result of these developments in the law. Fifty years ago the liability of a manufacturer to the user of his product with whom he had no contractual relationship was novel. Today it is commonplace.

In a landmark case decided in 1916, the manufacturer of an automobile was held liable for personal injuries sustained by the plaintiff who had purchased it from a retail dealer and while driving it was injured as the result of the collapse of a wheel due to the crumbling of the spokes which had been made of defective wood. The wheels had been purchased by the automobile manufacturer from a third person who was not a defendant in the case. The basis of liability was negligence of the automobile manufacturer and its duty to foresee that the finished product, if negligently constructed or built of defective component parts, would be inherently or imminently dangerous. Mac-Pherson v. Buick Motor Co., 217 N.Y. 382, 111 N.E. 1050 (1916).

Products liability has become firmly established as a separate and distinct field of law, combining and enforcing rules and principles of contract, sales, warranty, negligence, and tort law.

The most recent development, and one which is likely to have far reaching effect, is the imposition of liability upon manufacturers and assemblers of products based upon the principle of strict liability in tort. This rule has been applied with respect to an airplane in Goldberg v. Kollman Instrument Corp., 12 N.Y.2d 432, 240 N.Y.S.2d 592, 191 N.E.2d 81 (1963); a power tool in Greenman v. Yuba Power Products, Inc., 59 Cal.2d 57, 27 Cal.Rptr. 697, 377 P.2d 897 (1965); and a tractor-trailer with defective brakes in Suvada v. White Motor Co., 32 Ill.2d 612, 210 N.E.2d 182 (1965), page 544.

The rule was formulated in the Restatement of the Law of Torts, 2d, in May, 1964, as Section 402A "Special Liability of Seller of Product for Physical Harm to User or Consumer" and will be considered more fully later in this chapter.

The law of products liability is in a state of rapid development and the trend in the case law toward imposition of both an extended and a strict liability is clearly discernable.

Bases of Liability. The liability of manufacturers and sellers of goods by reason of a defect or condition in a product, or its failure to perform adequately, may be based upon one or more of the following: (1) express warranty; (2) implied warranty; (3) fraudulent misrepresentation; (4) non-fraudulent misrepresentation; (5) negligence; (6) violation of statutory duty; (7) strict liability in tort. These several grounds of liability will be considered in order.

Liability Based on Express Warranty. This type of liability is predicated upon a promise, affirmation of fact, or description of the goods made by the vendor to his vendee. It is covered in Section 2–313 of the Code, and discussed in the preceding chapter.

Liability Based on Implied Warranty. Except for implied warranties arising from course of dealing or usage of trade, the three warranties imposed upon the seller by the Code, unless properly disclaimed, are (1) warranty of title, Section 2–312; (2) implied warranty of merchantability, Section 2–314; (3) implied warranty of fitness for the buyer's particular purpose, Section 2–315.

The vendor's warranty of title does not extend beyond liability to his immediate vendee. However, the Code extends a seller's warranty, express or implied, to members of the buyer's family or household, or persons who are guests in his home, if it is reasonable to expect that such persons may use, consume or be affected by the goods and are injured in person by breach of the warranty. Section 2–318.

In the trial of an action against a manufacturer of cigarettes to recover damages for wrongful death resulting from lung cancer allegedly caused by the decedent having smoked from one to three packages of Lucky Strike cigarettes a day for thirty years, the jury in answer to four special interrogatories

found as facts: (1) the decedent had primary cancer in his left lung; (2) this cancer was one of the causes of his death; (3) the decedent's smoking of the cigarettes was a proximate cause of the development of the lung cancer; and (4) the defendant manufacturer could not have known by the reasonable application of human skill and foresight that the users of such cigarettes by inhalation of the smoke would be endangered of contracting cancer of the lung. On the basis of the answer to the fourth interrogatory, the court entered judgment for the defendant which was affirmed on appeal. Green v. American Tobacco Co., 304 F.2d 70 (C.A. 5, 1962). Upon rehearing, as the case was governed by Florida law, the Court of Appeals certified to the Supreme Court of Florida the following question of law:

> "Does the law of Florida impose on a manufacturer and distributor of cigarettes absolute liability, as for breach of implied warranty, for death caused by using such cigarettes from 1924 or 1925 until February 1, 1956, and the death occurring February 25, 1958, when the defendant manufacturer and distributor could not, on or prior to February 1, 1956, by the reasonable application of human skill and foresight have known that the users of such cigarettes would be endangered, by the inhalation of the main stream smoke from such cigarettes of contracting cancer of the lung?"

In response to this question, the opinion of the Supreme Court of Florida stated:

> "Upon the critical point, our decisions conclusively establish the principle that a manufacturer's or seller's actual knowledge or opportunity for knowledge of a defective or unwholesome condition is wholly irrelevant to his liability on the theory of implied warranty, and the question certified must therefore be answered in the affirmative."

Based upon this statement of the Florida law by the highest court in the State, the Court of Appeals reversed the judgment for defendant and remanded the case for a new trial at which the parties would be bound by the answers of the jury to the four interrogatories. Green v. American Tobacco Co., 325 F.2d 673 (C.A.5, 1963).

Fraudulent Misrepresentation. Fraud is available as a remedy to the injured user or consumer of a product to whom a misrepresentation of fact has been made to induce action and who in reliance thereon has sustained loss and damage. Fraud may consist either of intentional misrepresentation, such as the mislabeling of packaged drugs or cosmetics, or concealment of defects as where a wooden stepladder is made of defective wood and the defects are concealed by paint.

Non-fraudulent Misrepresentation. The Restatement of the Law of Torts provides for liability on the part of a person engaged in the business of selling goods who makes to the public a misrepresentation as to the character or quality of the goods, even though such misrepresentations are not made fraudulently or negligently and even though there is no privity of contract.

The Restatement of the Law of Torts, Second, § 402B, provides:

> One engaged in the business of selling chattels who, by advertising, labels, or otherwise, makes to the public a misrepresentation of a material fact concerning the character or quality of a chattel sold by him is subject to liability for physical harm to a consumer of the chattel caused by justifiable reliance upon the misrepresentation, even though
>
> > (a) it is not made fraudulently or negligently, and
> >
> > (b) the consumer has not bought the chattel from or entered into any contractual relation with the seller.

This rule is one of strict liability in tort for personal injuries sustained by a consumer resulting from a misrepresentation of the goods even though innocently made.

Thus, A, a manufacturer of automobiles, advertises in newspapers, magazines and an illustrated brochure that the glass in its cars is "shatter-proof". B reads this advertising and in reliance thereon purchases from a retail dealer an automobile manufactured by A. While B is driving the car, a pebble impelled by a passing truck strikes the windshield and shatters it, causing a splinter of glass to penetrate B's eye. A is subject to strict liability to B. Baxter v. Ford Motor Co., 168 Wash. 456, 12 P.2d 409, 88 A.L.R. 521 (1932).

Liability Based upon Negligence. Conduct involving an unreasonable or foreseeable risk of harm is negligence. The failure to exercise reasonable care under the circumstances which proximately causes loss or damage to the person or property of another is the basis of liability for negligence. A manufacturer or assembler of goods must exercise due care to make his product safe for the purpose for which it is intended to be used. This requires care in the design of the product, selection of materials, selection and fabrication of component parts, inspection and testing, and may require an adequate warning of dangers in the use of the product of which the ordinary person might not be aware. The duty of the manufacturer extends to inspection and testing of products fabricated by others and incorporated into his product.

Recoveries have been sustained against manufacturers of motor cars on behalf of buyers, users, passengers and bystanders, based upon negligence, for damages and injuries resulting from defective steering apparatus, wheels, axles, brakes, tires, and other operating components.

A right of action based upon negligence does not require privity of contract between the injured plaintiff and the negligent defendant manufacturer or seller.

The Restatement of the Law of Torts, Second, § 395 provides:

> A manufacturer who fails to exercise reasonable care in the manufacture of a chattel, which, unless carefully made, he should rec

ognize as involving an unreasonable risk of causing substantial bodily harm to those who lawfully use it for a purpose for which it is manufactured and to those whom the supplier should expect to be in the vicinity of its probable use, is subject to liability for bodily harm caused to them by its lawful use in a manner and for a purpose for which it is manufactured.

Violation of Statutory Duty. State and Federal statutes impose duties upon manufacturers of food, drugs, cosmetics, flammable materials, and toxic substances, with respect to branding, labeling, description of contents, advertising, and the selling or offering for sale of adulterated, contaminated or unwholesome products. Included among these statutes are The Federal Food, Drug and Cosmetics Act, 15 U.S.C.A. §§ 301–392; Federal Flammable Fabrics Act, 15 U.S.C.A. §§ 1191–1200; Federal Hazardous Substances Labeling Act, 15 U.S.C.A. §§ 1261–1273; Federal Insecticide, Fungicide and Rodenticide Act, 7 U.S.C.A. §§ 135–135(k).

These statutes provide for enforcement by criminal sanctions, seizure of goods, and injunctions. They do not expressly impose civil liability based upon injuries to the user or consumer of a product which has been sold in violation of the statute. However, in a civil action for damages, a violation of statutory duty may be alleged and if established by evidence many courts hold that it constitutes negligence *per se*.

In an action to recover damages for destruction of property resulting from fire caused by installation of faulty electrical wiring which did not comply with the requirements of the North Carolina Building Code, the Court stated:

> "It is well settled law in this jurisdiction, that when a statute imposes upon a person a specific duty for the protection of others, a violation of such statute is negligence *per se*. Of course, to make out a case of actionable negligence the additional essential element of proximate cause is required." Lutz

Industries v. Dixie Home Stores, 242 N.C. 332, 88 S.E.2d 333 (1955).

A wholesale seed merchant who sold mislabelled seed to a retailer who resold it in the original package to a farmer for planting, was held liable in damages to the farmer. The label on the seed was false and misleading in violation of a Florida statute which provided penal sanctions but no civil remedies for breach. The Supreme Court of Florida reversed a judgment in favor of the wholesale merchant stating:

> "Where one violates a penal statute imposing upon him a duty designed to protect another he is negligent as a matter of law, therefore responsible for such damage as is proximately caused by his negligence." Hoskins v. Jackson Grain Co., 63 So.2d 514 (Fla.1953).

A non-statutory safety code may impose a duty of care upon a manufacturer of goods. In a case in which the plaintiff was injured by a fall resulting from the breaking of a stepladder while using it, the evidence showed that the defendant manufacturer had adopted the American Standard Safety Code for Portable Wood Ladders sponsored by the American Ladder Institute and two other national associations and that the construction of the stepladder did not comply with this Safety Code. In affirming a judgment for the plaintiff the Court stated:

> "The voluntary adoption of a safety code as the guide to be followed for protection of the public is at least some evidence that a reasonably prudent person would adhere to the requirements of the code." Wilson v. Lowe's Asheboro Hardware, Inc., 259 N.C. 660, 131 S.E.2d 501 (1963).

Strict Liability in Tort. As previously stated, the most recent, significant, and far-reaching development in the field of products liability is that of strict liability in tort. It imposes liability only upon a person who is in the business of selling the product involved; applies to any product in a defective condition, and extends both to personal injuries and property damage suffered by the ultimate user or consumer of the product. It does not apply to an occasional seller who is not in the business of selling the product, such as a person who trades in his used car, or who sells his lawn mower to a neighbor. It is similar in this respect to the implied warranty of merchantability under Section 2–314 of the Code which applies only to sales by a merchant with respect to goods of the type in which he deals. It also does not apply to sales of the stock of merchants not in the usual course of business, such as execution sales, bankruptcy sales, and bulk sales. Subject to the foregoing, it applies to all sellers engaged in business including manufacturers, wholesalers, distributors, retailers, and operators of restaurants.

Section 402A of the Restatement of the Law of Torts, 2d, defines this strict liability in tort but before discussing the necessary elements of the liability, it may be well to consider the two preceding Sections, 401 and 402.

Section 401 provides:

> A seller of a chattel manufactured by a third person who knows or has reason to know that the chattel is, or is likely to be, dangerous when used by a person to whom it is delivered or for whose use it is supplied, or to others whom the seller should expect to share in or be endangered by its use, is subject to liability for bodily harm caused thereby to them if he fails to exercise reasonable care to inform them of the danger or otherwise to protect them against it.

This liability applies to any seller of a chattel manufactured by a third person. The chattel does not have to be in a defective condition. The seller must have "reason to know" and is not under a duty to ascertain unknown facts. This duty is less strict than one imposed by the words "should know". The liability is based upon the dangerous character of the product and the duty is to exercise reasonable care to inform the purchaser or user of the danger or otherwise to protect him against it. The extent of the liability is for damages resulting from personal injuries.

Section 402 excuses from liability the seller of goods manufactured by a third person who neither knows nor has reason to know of their dangerous character, for failure to inspect or test the goods before selling them, and provides:

> A seller of a chattel manufactured by a third person, who neither knows nor has reason to know that it is, or is likely to be, dangerous, is not liable in an action for negligence for harm caused by the dangerous character or condition of the chattel because of his failure to discover the danger by an inspection or test of the chattel before selling it.

This section protects a retailer who sells goods that are pre-packaged or placed in sealed containers by the manufacturer, from liability based upon negligence. The retailer, however, may be liable upon express or implied warranties to his purchaser or to a member of the family or household, or guest in the home, of the purchaser.

Thus, A, a wholesale distributor, sells to B, a retail dealer, a defective gas heater manufactured by X, a reputable manufacturer, which both A and B believe to be in perfect condition, although neither of them have inspected it. C purchases the gas heater from B and is injured by reason of the emission of poisonous fumes. Neither A nor B is liable to C for negligence although B may be liable to C upon an implied warranty of merchantability or fitness for the buyer's purpose.

Section 402A, imposing strict liability in tort, provides:

> (1) One who sells any product in a defective condition unreasonably dangerous to the user or consumer or to his property is subject to liability for physical harm thereby

caused to the ultimate user or consumer, or to his property, if

    (a) the seller is engaged in the business of selling such a product, and

    (b) it is expected to and does reach the user or consumer without substantial change in the condition in which it is sold.

  (2) The rule stated in Subsection (1) applies although

    (a) the seller has exercised all possible care in the preparation and sale of his product, and

    (b) the user or consumer has not bought the product from or entered into any contractual relation with the seller.

This liability is imposed by law as a matter of public policy and does not depend upon contract either express or implied. It does not require reliance by the injured user or consumer upon any statements made by the manufacturer or seller. The liability is not limited to persons in a relationship of buyer and seller. No notice of defect is required to have been given by the injured user or consumer. The liability is not subject to disclaimer, exclusion, or modification by contractual agreement. The liability is strictly in tort and arises out of the common law announced in recent judicial decisions. It is not governed by the provisions of the Uniform Commercial Code.

It is to be emphasized that negligence is not the basis of this liability which applies although "the seller has exercised all possible care in the preparation and sale of his product." However, the seller is not an insurer of the goods which he manufactures or sells and the essential requirements for this type of liability are: (1) that the product was in a defective condition; (2) that the defective condition was one which made the product unreasonably dangerous to the user or consumer or to his property; (3) that the defect in the product existed at the time it left the hands of the defendant; (4) that the

plaintiff sustained physical harm or property damage by use or consumption of the product; and (5) that the defective condition was the proximate cause of such injury or damage.

In an action against a defendant manufacturer or seller to recover damages under the rule of strict liability in tort, the plaintiff must prove a defective condition in the product, but he is not required to prove how or why or in what manner the product became defective. On the issue of liability, the reason or cause of the defect is not material as it would be in an action based upon negligence. The plaintiff, however, must show that at the time he was injured the condition of the product was not substantially changed from what it was at the time it was sold by the defendant manufacturer or seller.

The reasons asserted in support of imposing strict liability in tort upon manufacturers and assemblers of products are: (1) maximum protection should be given consumers against dangerous defects in products; (2) manufacturers are in the best position to prevent or reduce the hazards to life and health in defective products; (3) manufacturers realize the most profit from the total sales of their goods and are best able to carry the financial burden of such liability by distributing it among the public as a cost of doing business; (4) manufacturers utilize wholesalers and retailers merely as conduits in the marketing of their products and should not be permitted to avoid liability simply because they have no contract with the user or consumer; and (5) since the manufacturer is liable to his vendee who may be a wholesaler who in turn is liable to the retailer who in turn is liable to the ultimate purchaser, time and expense would be saved by making the liability a direct one rather than a chain reaction.

Duty to Warn of Danger. The duty of a manufacturer or seller of a product to warn the user or consumer of potential dangers or hazards in connection with its use arises out of the duty of ordinary or reasonable care which is the basis of liability for negligence. The essential elements of this duty are contained in the Restatement of Law of Torts, Second, § 388:

> One who supplies directly or through a third person a chattel for another to use is subject to liability to those whom the supplier should expect to use the chattel with the consent of the other or to be endangered by its probable use, for physical harm caused by the use of the chattel in the manner for which and by a person for whose use it is supplied, if the supplier
>
> > (a) knows or has reason to know that the chattel is or is likely to be dangerous for the use for which it is supplied, and
> >
> > (b) has no reason to believe that those for whose use the chattel is supplied will realize its dangerous condition, and
> >
> > (c) fails to exercise reasonable care to inform them of its dangerous condition or of the facts which make it likely to be dangerous.

Almost any product may be used or misused in a manner which involves danger of physical harm. The blow of a poorly-aimed hammer may crush a thumb. The inhaling of a feather may damage a lung. The use of a sled on a busy street may endanger the child using it. The excessive drinking of liquor is dangerous. Allowing children to play with fire arms is also dangerous. These hazards arise out of the use of products in a manner or to the extent that they were not intended by the supplier to be used, and no duty is imposed upon the manufacturer or seller to give warning against the possible dangers that might arise from such misuse of the product.

The duty to give a warning arises out of a foreseeable danger of physical harm arising out of the normal use or probable use of the product and the likelihood that unless warned, the user or consumer will not ordinarily be aware of such danger or hazard.

In Spruill v. Boyle-Midway Incorporated, 308 F.2d 79 (C.A.4, 1962), the defendants were manufacturers and distributors of furniture polish, containing 98% mineral seal oil, the remaining ingredients consisting of cedar oil, a trace of turpentine, and some red dye. The label on the bottle in which the product was sold stated in red letters about ⅛ inch in height "CAUTION, COMBUSTIBLE MATERIAL". Beneath this in red letters 1⁄16 inch in height were the words "DO NOT USE NEAR FIRE OR FLAME". This warning was followed by seven lines of directions printed in letters about 1⁄32 inch in height following which was a statement in letters of the same height "Contents refined petroleum distillate, may be harmful if swallowed, especially by children."

A baby, 14 months old, died as the result of chemical pneumonia caused by swallowing a small quantity of this furniture polish. The mother of the child had been using the product to polish furniture and had left the bottle on a bureau near the baby's crib for four or five minutes when she was called out of the room. During that period of time the baby pulled the bottle into the crib and swallowed a small portion of its contents.

In an action to recover damages for wrongful death of the infant, a judgment of $20,000 was entered in favor of all of the plaintiffs other than the child's mother. The court held that the defendant manufacturer had not given adequate warning of the poisonous nature of the product by reason of its containing a petroleum distillate. The testimony showed that mineral seal oil is a toxic substance, a petroleum distillate, and that one teaspoon of this product would kill a small child. The warning against combustibility made almost inconspicuous the warning against the toxic nature of the product.

In Sylvania Electric Products Inc. v. Barker, 228 F.2d 842 (C.A.1, 1955), the Court states:

> "In Massachusetts the rule seems to be that every manufacturer is presumed to know the nature and qualities of his products. [Citations.] Thus, once a plaintiff establishes in a Massachusetts court that a manufacturer-defendant's product is dangerous in its ordinary use, and that no warning of its danger was given, a presumption of the defendant's knowledge of the danger arises, and this presumption with, of course, proof of causation and injury, completes the plaintiff's *prima facie* case. Hence in Massachusetts it is up to a manufacturer-defendant to come forward, if it can, with exculpatory evidence of its faultless ignorance of the dangers of its product to those who might use it."

Liability of Supplier of Component Parts. The defective condition of a product may be traceable to a component part which was supplied to the manufacturer by a third person. In an action to recover damages by an injured user or consumer of the product, the manufacturer of the finished product and of the component part may both be liable.

The rule of strict liability in tort applies to the manufacturer of a defective component part which has been incorporated into the larger product where no essential change has been made in it by the manufacturer of the finished product. This was the holding with respect to a defective braking system incorporated in a used reconditioned tractor unit in Suvada v. White Motor Co., page 544.

The manufacturer of the finished product is not excused from liability by reason of a defective condition resulting exclusively from a defective component part. The manufacturer of the defective component part is not excused from liability by reason of the failure of the manufacturer of the finished product to discover the defect by testing or inspection.

Liability of Intermediate Party or Distributor. The rationale underlying the rule of strict liability in tort does not apply to an intermediate party such as a wholesaler of the product who has purchased it from the manufacturer and who resells it in the same condition.

Although the rule does not require proof of negligence of the manufacturer, and there is seldom any negligence attributable to the middle man or wholesaler with respect to the character or condition of the product, the exemption of the wholesaler from tort liability is not based upon freedom from negligence, but upon the difference in his position in the distributive chain with respect to the marketing of the goods. Ordinarily he is not aware of a defective condition of the goods unless it is obvious. He relies upon the manufacturer to produce non-defective merchandise to properly describe and label it, and to provide in an adequate manner all necessary warnings of danger.

In an action by a retail purchaser of a defective new Ford tractor, the court entered judgment against the retail seller but not against the wholesaler, stating that absent privity of contract and fault, the wholesaler should not be held liable simply because he happens to be in the stream of commerce. Price v. Gatlin, page 548.

A retail druggist who properly fills the prescription of a medical doctor with an unadulterated drug is also not subject to strict liability in tort. While he is a merchant selling the drugs used in compounding the prescription, he is acting under the direction of a physician, and is selling goods prepared according to exact specifications at the request of the buyer. He therefore makes no implied warranty of fitness for the buyer's particular purpose and his position is such that he should not be subject to strict liability in tort.

The retail druggist filling a prescription is liable only by reason of his failure to compound the proper drugs and in the proportion prescribed, by his failure to use due and proper care in the compounding process, or by his use of adulterated drugs. McLeod v. W. S. Merrell Co., Division of Richardson-Merrell, page 549.

Liability of Lessors of Chattels. Although liability for personal injuries caused by the defective condition of goods which makes them unreasonably dangerous is usually associated with warranties in connection with sales of goods, such liability also exists with respect to leases of such good or chattels.

The extension of liability to lessors of chattels is not surprising in view of the rationale developed by the courts in imposing strict liability in tort upon manufacturers of products and component parts. The danger to which the public is exposed by defectively manufactured cars and trucks traveling on the highways is not greatly different from the hazards of defectively maintained cars and trucks leased to operators.

The Restatement of the Law of Torts, Second, § 408, provides:

> One who leases a chattel as safe for immediate use is subject to liability to those whom he should expect to use the chattel, or to be endangered by its probable use, for physical harm caused by its use in a manner for which and by a person for whose use, it is leased, if the lessor fails to exercise reasonable care to make it safe for such use or to disclose its actual condition to those who may be expected to use it.

In a case in which the plaintiff, a passenger and employee of the lessee of a truck, was injured due to the defendant lessor's failure to maintain the vehicle in a safe operating condition, the Court held that the leasing agreement gave rise to "a continuing implied promissory warranty that the leased trucks would be fit for plaintiff's employer's use for the duration of the lease." The Court also applied the rule of strict liability in tort and held that the plaintiff had a cause of action. Cintrone v. Hertz Truck Leasing & Rental Service, 45 N.J. 434, 212 A.2d 769 (1965).

Assumption of Risk. Contributory negligence of the plaintiff is a bar to his recovery at common law in an action based upon negligence of the defendant.

However, as strict liability in tort is not based upon negligence, the failure of an injured user or consumer of the product to use reasonable care in connection with the discovery of the defect in the product or guarding against the possibility of its existence is no defense. Contributory negligence, therefore, is not available to the defendant in an action based upon strict liability in tort.

However, the user or consumer of a product who voluntarily and unreasonably proceeds to use it in the face of danger which he knows or should know exists, will be barred from recovery against the manufacturer or seller of the product. The user or consumer will be denied recovery because he has voluntarily assumed the risk of danger, as in a situation where he discovers the defect, is aware of the danger, but nevertheless proceeds to make use of the product, and is injured thereby.

The defense of assumption of risk is not the same as contributory negligence.

CASES

MITCHELL v. MILLER

(1965) 26 Conn.Sup. 142, 214 A.2d 694.

KLAU, J. The defendant General Motors Corporation demurs to the third count of the complaint on the ground that no cause of action for breach of the warranty may lie against this defendant, as no privity exists between the plaintiff's decedent and said defendant.

This is an action for damages arising from injuries which resulted in the death of Burnell R. Mitchell, the decedent of the plaintiff executrix, allegedly caused by the defendants Nancy Backman, her father, Horace G. Miller, Wallingford Country Club, Inc., and General Motors Corporation. The allegations of the first count are based on the negligence of the defendants Wallingford Country Club, Horace G. Miller and Nancy Backman. In substance, the first count sets forth that the defendant Nancy Backman had parked a car upon the parking area of the defendant Wallingford Country Club, which parking area overlooks the seventeenth fairway of the golf course of said defendant country club. The car, a 1962 Buick automobile, had been manufactured by defendant General Motors and was parked on a slope overlooking said fairway and so left there by defendant Backman, who was driving the car as a family car of the defendant Horace G. Miller. In parking the car, the defendant Backman placed the hydromatic transmission gearshift lever in the area designated "park" on the indicator and locked all of the doors to the car. Despite the fact that the automobile hydromatic gearshift mechanism was placed in the area marked "park" on the indicator, the shifts were not locked therein and the transmission was only partially engaged. Being parked on an incline, the transmission became disengaged, and the shift lever slipped into the "neutral" position, thereby allowing the automobile to roll. The car so parked rolled down the incline, striking the plaintiff's decedent, Burnell R. Mitchell, while he was playing golf upon the seventeenth fairway, with such force as to cause injuries from which he died.

The second count against the defendant General Motors Corporation solely alleges acts of negligence in manufacturing and in selling, through its authorized dealer, a defective automobile to the defendant Horace G. Miller, which defect, by reason of the aforementioned failure of the transmission to lock when parked, rendered the car inherently and imminently dangerous to the public and to the plaintiff's decedent and resulted in injuries which caused his death.

The third count alleges that the defendant General Motors Corporation, as a manufacturer, through extensive advertisements by means of radio, television, newspapers, etc., impliedly and expressly warranted to the defendant Miller, to the public generally, and to the decedent Mitchell as a member of the public that the said 1962 Buick automobile purchased by Miller was safe and fit for its intended use and safe operation, and contained no defects, dangerous tendencies or characteristics which would endanger the public, including the plaintiff's decedent, and in reliance thereon, said automobile was purchased by the defendant Miller; and the count further alleges that the unsafe and dangerous tendency and characteristics of the hydromatic gearshift mechanism in slipping from a "park" locking to a neutral position constituted breach of warranty to the plaintiff's decedent, and that he suffered severe injuries from which he died as a result of said breach.

The demurrer of the defendant General Motors attacks the cause of action alleged in this third count. From the allegations of the third count, it is obvious that no privity existed between the plaintiff's decedent, Mitchell, and the defendant General Motors Corporation. It is further clear from the allegations of this count that the deceased Mitchell was not within the distributive chain of any sale originating from the manufacturer of the automobile, nor could he reasonably have been anticipated by this defendant to have been one who would use, occupy or service the operation of the automobile. It is clear from the allegations of the count that the deceased Mitchell was not a user but, on the contrary, a victim of an automobile which was defectively manufactured by the defendant, since the demurrer admits the allegations of the count which are well pleaded, and such facts are clearly to be drawn from the allegations. There being no sale, therefore, to trace back the decedent's connection with the chattel to the defendant General Motors Corporation, the question is whether liability can be imposed upon the basis of an implied warranty of a reasonable fitness for use from the defendant General Motors Corporation to the plaintiff's decedent, Burnell Mitchell, in the absence not only of privity between the parties but of a sale of the chattel upon which to base such a warranty.

Although the concept of warranty founded on contract is to be found in the Uniform Sales Act and the Uniform Commercial Code, the recent development of the law of product liability has re-established the common-law action of breach of warranty sounding in tort rather than in contract. "The recognition of such a right of action rested on the public policy of protecting an innocent buyer from harm rather than on the ensuring of any contractual rights." Hamon v. Digliani, 148 Conn. 710, 716, 174 A.2d 294, 296. * * *

In imposing liability upon manufacturers to ultimate consumers in terms of implied warranty even though no privity exists, the courts have used a convenient legal fiction to accomplish this result. Ordinarily, there is no contract in a real sense between a manufacturer and an expected ultimate consumer of his product. As a matter of public policy, the law has imposed on all manufacturers a duty to consumers irrespective of contract or of privity relationship between them. The search for correct principles to delineate manufacturers' responsibility to consumers has found expression in the doctrine of tort and strict liability. The "strict tort liability" doctrine is "surely a more accurate phrase" than breach of implied warranty of suitability for use. [Citation.]

The second Restatement of the Law of Torts adopts the basis of strict liability, in the case of the seller of products, for occasioning physical harm to a user or consumer. See Restatement (Second), 2 Torts § 402A. The rule is one of strict liability, making the seller subject to liability to the user or consumer even though the seller has exercised all possible care in the preparation and sale of the product. The product, of course, must be not only defective but unreasonably dangerous to the user or consumer.

The question, then, is whether strict liability ought to be extended to one who is not in the category of one who is a user or consumer of the product, or whether it is to be confined solely to commercial transactions where injury results only to the user or ultimate consumer. In a caveat, the American Law Institute in its second Restatement of the Law of Torts expresses no opinion as to whether the rules stated in § 402A may not apply to harm to persons other than users or consumers. In commenting upon this caveat, the Restatement states: "Thus far the courts, in applying the rule stated in this Section, have not gone beyond allowing recovery to users and consumers, as those terms are defined in Comment l. Casual bystanders, and others who may come in contact with the product, as in the case of employees of the retailer, or a passer-by injured by an exploding bottle, or a pedestrian hit by an automobile, have been denied recovery. There may be no essential reason why such plaintiffs should not be brought within the scope of the protection afforded, other than that they do not have the same reasons for expecting such protection as the consumer who buys a marketed product; but the social pressure which has been largely responsible for the development of the rule stated has been a consumers' pressure, and there is not the same demand for the protection of casual strangers. The Institute expresses neither approval nor disapproval of expansion of the rule to permit recovery by such persons."

Restatement (Second), 2 Torts § 402A, comment o.

In the only reported case involving an injury to a nonuser in this state, the court refused to find that a cause of action, based on a warranty of fitness, existed, as against the used-car dealer from whom the car was purchased, in favor of a pedestrian who was injured as a result of a defect in the car existing at the time of the sale. The court, as a matter of public policy was unwilling to extend the doctrine of strict liability in favor of a pedestrian against a used-car dealer. See Kuschy v. Norris, 25 Conn.Sup. 383, 206 A.2d 275. Since the decision in the Kuschy case, the Michigan Supreme Court has applied the doctrine of strict liability in favor of an innocent bystander who was injured when the barrel of a shotgun being fired by another party exploded because of a defective shell. Piercefield v. Remington Arms Co., 375 Mich. 85, 133 N.W.2d 129.

The trend toward applying the doctrine of strict liability in the case of an injury arising from the manufacture of a product which may be unreasonably dangerous and from which the likelihood of injury arising from its use is reasonably foreseeable is expanding. Foreseeable or reasonable anticipation of injury from the defect is becoming the test. Reliance on representations or notice of injury are no longer absolute conditions precedent. * * *

A defective automobile manufactured as alleged in this complaint by the defendant General Motors constitutes a real hazard upon the highway. [Citation.] The likelihood of injury from its use exists not merely for the passengers therein but for the pedestrian upon the highway. The public policy which protects the user and consumer should also protect the innocent bystander. In the instant case, an innocent bystander, while playing golf, was killed by a car defectively manufactured, insofar as the allegations of the

complaint go, by the defendant automobile corporation. There seems to be no sound public policy to bar a trial upon the issues raised in the complaint. Accordingly, the demurrer of the General Motors Corporation to the third count of the complaint is overruled.

_____

PRITCHARD v. LIGGETT & MYERS TOBACCO CO.

(1965 C.A.3d) 350 F.2d 479.

SMITH, C. J. The plaintiff brought this action for personal injury alleging that he contracted lung cancer as a result of having smoked Chesterfield cigarettes for many years. The claims for relief, stated in separate counts of the complaint, alleged negligence and breach of warranty as the bases of liability. The defendant, admittedly the manufacturer of the cigarettes, denied the allegations of the complaint and pleaded assumption of risk as an affirmative defense to each of the claims. The jurisdiction of the court below was invoked on the ground of diversity of citizenship and therefore under the facts of the case the law of Pennsylvania was applicable.

* * * The present appeal is from a judgment entered on a jury verdict in favor of the defendant. * * *

The plaintiff, who was 63 years old at the time of the second trial, admittedly smoked cigarettes since he was 15 years of age. He was an habitual cigarette smoker for several years prior to 1924, when he began smoking Chesterfields for the first time. Thereafter, and during the critical period, between sometime in 1924 and the latter part of 1953, he smoked Chesterfields regularly, consuming "at least a carton" per week. There was ample evidence in the record from which the jury could have found, as it did, that the smoking of Chesterfields was a cause of the lung cancer, which was diagnosed and removed in 1953. This finding is not an issue on this appeal.

The alleged warranties were contained in a series of advertisements published periodically in both newspapers and magazines. These advertisements featured in bold type such factual affirmations as the following: "Chesterfields Are Best For You"; "Chesterfields Are As Pure As The Water You Drink And The Food You Eat"; "A Good Cigarette Can Cause No Ills"; "Nose, Throat And Accessory Organs Not Adversely Affected By Smoking Chesterfields"; "Play Safe Smoke Chesterfields." (See also the earlier opinion of this Court). Many of the advertisements contained assurances that the affirmations were based upon extensive research and the opinions of medical specialists. There was implicit in these assurances a strong suggestion that while other brands of cigarettes might be harmful, Chesterfields were not.

This Court stated in its earlier opinion: "The evidence compellingly points to an express warranty, for the defendant, by means of various advertising media, not only repeatedly assured plaintiff that smoking Chesterfields was absolutely harmless, but in addition the jury could very well have concluded that there were express assurances of no harmful effect on the lungs."

The issues were submitted to the jury on a series of special interrogatories, Fed.Rules Civ.Proc., rule 49(a), 28 U.S.C.A., all of which, except one, were answered adversely to the plaintiff. The jury found: (1) the smoking of Chesterfield cigarettes by the plaintiff was "the cause, or one of the causes," of the cancer; (2) the defendant was not chargeable with negligence; (3) the defendant made no "express warranties upon which the plaintiff relied and by which he was induced to purchase" the cigarettes; and (4) the plaintiff assumed the risk of injury by his smoking the cigarettes. A judgment for

the defendant in accord with the special findings was entered.

* * *

* * * If a manufacturer extends to the public an express warranty that his product is harmless and thereafter a purchaser suffers personal injury as a result of its breach, the manufacturer cannot disclaim liability on the ground that there was no reliance on the warranty. The express warranty is an integral part of the contract of sale and may not be disaffirmed, after a breach has occurred, on the ground that the purchaser did not actually rely on it.

Assumption of risk in its secondary sense is ordinarily synonymous with contributory negligence and involves a failure to exercise reasonable care for one's own safety. Under this concept recovery is barred because of the plaintiff's departure from the standard of reasonable conduct and notwithstanding the misconduct of the defendant. [Citations.] Assumption of risk in its primary and strict sense involves voluntary exposure to an obvious or known danger which negates liability. Under this concept recovery is barred because the plaintiff is assumed to have relieved the defendant of any duty to protect him.

* * *

We are of the view, and so hold, that since contributory negligence is not available as a defense in an action for personal injury based on breach of warranty, assumption of risk in the sense of contributory negligence is likewise not available. However, if a consumer uses a product for a purpose not intended by the manufacturer and suffers an injury as a result, he may not recover because such misuse is beyond the scope of the warranty. [Citations.]

It is the law of Pennsylvania that a person who voluntarily exposes himself to a danger of which he has knowledge, or has had notice, assumes the attendant risk. He may not recover for personal injuries sustained as the result of the exposure, because under the circumstances the person responsible for the danger is relieved of any duty to protect the injured person. [Citations.] It is clear from these cases that assumption of risk, in its primary and strict sense, is available as a defense in an action for personal injuries based upon negligence. It follows as a matter of logic that the same defense is apposite in an action based on breach of express warranty.

The defense of assumption of risk rested solely on the testimony of the plaintiff which, viewed in the light most favorable to the defendant, was clearly insufficient. There was no evidence upon which the jury could have predicated a determination that the plaintiff either knew or had notice of the harmful effects of Chesterfields. Absent such evidence, the defense of assumption of risk failed.

There was overwhelming evidence that many of the defendant's advertisements carried factual affirmations, professedly based on medical research, that Chesterfields were safe and smoking them could have no adverse effect on "the nose, throat and accessory organs." These advertisements were calculated to overcome any fears the potential consumers might have had as to the harmful effects of cigarettes, and particularly Chesterfields. Under the circumstances it is difficult to perceive how the plaintiff, a cabinetmaker with no scientific background, could have been charged with notice or knowledge of a danger, which the defendant, with its professed superior knowledge, extensively advertised did not exist. We should emphasize that the medical researchers engaged by the defendant in 1952, apparently failed to detect the danger.

As hereinabove noted, assumption of risk was apposite as a defense in the action based upon breach of express warranty but only in its primary sense. However, the issue raised by the defense was submitted to the jury on general instructions which were inadequate and confusing in that they failed to differentiate between the primary and secondary concepts; in the instructions these concepts were treated as equivalent. Absent such a differentiation, the instructions as given did not correctly relate the law to the issue and were therefore erroneous. [Citations.] It was also error to submit the issue to the jury in the absence of evidence to support the defense.

* * *

The judgment of the court below will be reversed and the action will be remanded with the direction that a new trial be had.

Reversed.

SUVADA v. WHITE MOTOR CO.

(1965) 32 Ill.2d 612, 210 N.E.2d 182.

HOUSE, J. * * * The plaintiffs Steven Suvada and John Konecnik are partners engaged in the business of buying, selling and distributing milk in Cook County. On February 11, 1957, they purchased a used reconditioned tractor unit from defendant White Motor Company. The brake system for the tractor was manufactured by defendant Bendix-Westinghouse Automotive Air Brake Company and installed by White. On June 24, 1960, the brake system failed and the tractor collided with a Chicago Transit Authority bus causing a number of injuries to the bus passengers and considerable damage to the bus and the plaintiffs' tractor-trailer milk truck.

On June 21, 1962, plaintiffs filed this action against White and Bendix to recover the costs they incurred in repairing their tractor-trailer unit, repairing the bus and in their settlement of personal injury claims by the bus passengers. Included in the damages for settling the personal injury claims are the costs of legal services and investigation.

The trial court held that plaintiffs had stated causes of action for damages to their tractor-trailer unit against White on the basis of breach of implied warranty and negligence and against Bendix on the basis of negligence, but dismissed the counts for damage to the bus, personal injury claims and expenses. On appeal by the plaintiffs the Appellate Court held that plaintiffs had stated causes of action for all elements of damage pleaded against White and Bendix on the basis of breach of an implied warranty. (Suvada v. White Motor Co., 51 Ill.App.2d 318, 201 N.E. 2d 313.) Only Bendix seeks review of this holding.

The theory advanced by Bendix is essentially: (1) That any warranty as to its product runs to White and that plaintiffs cannot recover for a breach of this warranty because they are not in privity with Bendix. (2) That any liability of Bendix to plaintiff must therefore be based on its negligence, but it cannot be held liable to plaintiff for the costs of settling the injury claims because: (a) If Bendix was solely negligent in manufacturing the brake system, then plaintiffs were not responsible for the accident and they acted as volunteers in settling the injury claims and the damage claim for the bus; (b) if, on the other hand, Bendix was negligent and plaintiffs were also responsible for the accident, it would be because plaintiffs were also negligent; thus, Bendix and plaintiffs would be joint tort-feasors and plaintiffs cannot seek contribution from their joint tort-feasor.

"If there is any question of law which can truly be called characteristic of products liability litigation it is the question of privity of contract—that is, whether there can be recovery for injury caused by a product against a manufacturer or seller who had sold the product, where the person who suffered the injury was not a party to the sale and hence is not in privity of contract with the manufacturer or seller sought to be held liable." [Citation.] * * * The three recognized

exceptions to the rule requiring privity were also adopted, namely, (1) where the negligence of a manufacturer or vendor is with reference to an article imminently dangerous to human life or health, (2) where an owner's negligence causes injury to one invited on the premises, and (3) where one knowing the qualities of an article which are imminently dangerous to life or health sells the article without notice of these qualities.

* * *

Although this court has held that an action for breach of warranty is an action *ex contractu* and can only be maintained by a party to the contract, [Citation.] we have recognized that privity of contract is not essential in an action for breach of implied warranty in the sale of food. [Citation.]

* * *

Recognizing that public policy is the primary factor for imposing strict liability on the seller and manufacturer of food in favor of the injured consumer, we come to the crucial question in this case, namely, is there any reason for imposing strict liability in food cases and liability based on negligence in cases involving products other than food. Arguments advanced to support the imposition of strict liability in food cases have been: (1) The public interest in human life and health demands all the protection the law can give against the sale of unwholesome food. [Citation.] (2) The manufacturer solicits and invites the use of his product by packaging advertising or otherwise, representing to the public that it is safe and suitable for use. Having thus induced use of the product, the law will impose liability for the damage it causes. [Citation.] (3) The losses caused by unwholesome food should be borne by those who have created the risk and reaped the profit by placing the product in the stream of commerce. [Citation.] Without extended discussion, it seems obvious that public interest in human life and health, the invitations and solicitations to purchase the product and the justice of imposing the loss on the one creating the risk and reaping the profit are present and as compelling in cases involving motor vehicles and other products, where the defective condition makes them unreasonably dangerous to the user, as they are in food cases.

* * *

We note that the views herein expressed coincide with the position taken in section 402A of the American Law Institute's revised Restatement of the Law of Torts approved in May 1964. The section provides:

"(1) One who sells any product in a defective condition unreasonably dangerous to the user or consumer or to his property is subject to liability for physical harm thereby caused to the ultimate user or consumer, or to his property, if

"(a) the seller is engaged in the business of selling such a product, and

"(b) it is expected to reach the user or consumer in the condition in which it is sold.

"(2) The rule stated in subsection (1) applies although

"(a) the seller has exercised all possible care in the preparation and sale of his product, and

"(b) the user or consumer has not bought the product from or entered into any contractual relation with the seller".

(The rapid development of the law on this subject is typified by the development of section 402A. The original Restatement of Torts had no provision for strict liability. In April 1961, Tentative Draft No. 6 recommended adoption of a new section, section 402A, which recognized a seller's strict liability for food for human consumption. In April 1962, Tentative Draft No. 7 expanded the coverage of the section to products intended for intimate bodily use. Tentative Draft No. 10 applies to all products and expanded coverage to property damages as well as bodily harm.)

The Appellate Court imposed strict liability on the theory of an implied warranty and held that lack of privity between plaintiffs and Bendix is no defense. Bendix has argued that lack of privity is a defense and cites in support of its position section 2–318 of the Uniform Commercial Code (Ill.Rev.Stat. 1963, chap. 26, par. 2–318.) That section provides, "A seller's warranty whether express or implied extends to any natural person who is in the family or household of his buyer or who is a guest in his home if it is reasonable to expect that such person may use, consume or be affected by the goods and who is injured in person by breach of the warranty. A seller may not exclude or limit the operation of this Section." It is argued that this section codifies the common-law requirement of privity in a breach-of-warranty action except as to those persons specifically excluded in the section and that this court had no power to enlarge the class of persons excluded from the privity requirement.

Our holding of strict liability in tort makes it unnecessary to decide what effect section 2–318 has on an action for breach of implied warranty. * * *

Bendix argues that the imposition of strict liability, in effect, requires it to guarantee both White's and Suvada's use of the brake system. Such liability does not, of course, make Bendix an absolute insurer. The plaintiffs must prove that their injury or damage resulted from a condition of the product, that the condition was an unreasonably dangerous one and that the condition existed at the time it left the manufacturer's control. [Citation.]

It is also argued that the rule of strict liability in tort should not apply to the maker of a component part. It appears that White did not make any change in the brake system manufactured by Bendix but merely installed it into the tractor unit. Under these circumstances we see no reasons why Bendix should not come within the rule of strict liability. See Comment q, section 402A, Tentative Draft No. 10, Restatement of the Law, Second, Torts (1964).

*   *   *

The judgment of the Appellate Court is affirmed.

Judgment affirmed.

O'BRIEN v. COMSTOCK FOODS, INC.

(1965) 125 Vt. 158, 212 A.2d 69.

HOLDEN, C. J. The plaintiff Ursula O'Brien presents two complaints for personal injuries which she claims were caused by eating a piece of glass, contained in a can of string beans packed by the defendant. Her first complaint is founded on an alleged breach of warranty; the second charges negligence in the packing of the product. Her husband seeks redress for similar injuries and he, too, resorts to actions in contract and tort to recover his damage.

*   *   *

Since ancient times, the purveyors of food and drink have been held to special responsibilities. As early as the thirteenth century dealers in food products and beverages were subjected to criminal penalties for trafficking in "corrupt" commodities. Civil liability in the common law followed the same pattern. According to Blackstone, "in contracts for provisions it is always implied that they are wholesome. * * *" [Citations.]

The invitation of the manufacturer or originator of the product, referred to some fifty years ago in the MacPherson case, has become more extensive and persuasive by way of modern packaging and advertising techniques. "Today when so much of our food is bought in packages it is not just or sensible to confine the warranty's protection to the individual buyer. At least as to food

and household goods, the presumption should be that the purchase was made for all the members of the household." [Citations.]

*   *   *

The illogic and injustice of applying the rule of privity to the immediate buyer has equivalent effect when applied to restrict liability to the immediate seller. The inducement of the sale, in modern economic society, generally comes from the producer of the food product. The middlemen in the chain of distribution, are, for the most part silent so far as the consumer is concerned. [Citations.]

For the same reasons of logic and fairness, Connecticut has overruled earlier decisions founded on the doctrine of caveat emptor and requirements of privity. The Court held that a manufacturer or producer who markets his product in a sealed container impliedly warrants to the ultimate consumer that the product is reasonably fit for the purpose intended and that it does not contain any harmful or deleterious substance of which due and ample warning has not been given. Where the product fails to conform to that undertaking, and an ultimate consumer sustains injury from that source, the lack of privity furnishes no bar to his action against the manufacturer. [Citation.]

We are not restrained by any precedent in this jurisdiction where the requirement of privity has been applied to products liability. We must find the applicable law as it has developed and grown in other jurisdictions. These sources summon us to hold that whether the food producer's undertaking is referred to as a duty or an implied warranty is of little consequence. His responsibility to the injured consumer is the same. Once causation is established, want of privity will not relieve the legal obligation.

Order dismissing actions reversed. (For plaintiff).

PRICE v. GATLIN

(1965) 241 Or. 315, 405 P.2d 502.

GOODWIN, J. This is an action for damages for economic loss resulting from the defective manufacture of a tractor. A jury found that because a new Ford tractor had failed to perform adequately the plaintiff had suffered $4,500 in damages to his business. Judgment was entered against the retail seller, but not against the wholesaler. (The manufacturer was not sued.) The purchaser appeals the judgment in favor of the wholesaler.

The only issue in this case is whether a purchaser of a defectively manufactured product, who is not in privity with the wholesaler, may recover for economic loss against a wholesaler through whose hands the product (or papers representing it) may have passed en route from the manufacturer to the retailer.

A purchaser, or even a stranger, who has sustained personal injuries may maintain an action for damages against a manufacturer whose defective work causes bodily harm. Such a plaintiff is unembarrassed by a lack of contract privity, whether or not he must allege and prove negligence. See, e. g., Wights v. Staff Jennings, Inc., Or., 405 P.2d 624 (September 9, 1965). [Citation.]

This court has not yet held that a non-privity purchaser may maintain an action against a manufacturer for economic loss, as distinguished from personal injury, caused by defective workmanship. That issue is not now before us, and we express no opinion upon the matter. This plaintiff is seeking to hold a wholesaler liable for innocently passing along a defective product. This he may not do.

The plaintiff alleges no fault or misrepresentation upon the part of the wholesaler. The plaintiff is frankly searching for a solvent defendant, in this state, whose liability is to be grounded solely upon the fact that he shares in the profits generated by the distribution of merchandise. The plaintiff argues that because the wholesaler makes a profit, even though he is free from fault, he should share in the economic burdens caused by the manufacturer's sale of a defective product.

If both privity and fault are irrelevant, the wholesaler would be liable, not for a duty he failed to perform, nor for the breach of a contract he never made, but because he happens to lie in the stream of commerce. Wholesalers in this state have had no reason to believe that they would be held liable to strangers, in unlimited amounts, when they are without fault. By whatever name it is called, this kind of liability is enterprise liability. We do not believe that the case at bar is a proper one in which to impose this new form of liability upon wholesalers.

We are not unaware of the authority which has been marshaled in support of the plaintiff's theory. We believe, however, that the social and economic reasons which courts elsewhere have given for extending enterprise liability to the victims of physical injury are not equally persuasive in a case of a disappointed buyer of personal property. [Citation.]

We hold that a purchaser may not recover against a nonprivity seller, who is not alleged to be at fault in connection with the loss, for economic losses caused by a third party's defective workmanship.

Affirmed.

HOLMAN, J. (specially concurring). Causes of action brought by the consumer on the basis of the strict liability of manufacturers and wholesalers for damages resulting from the sale of goods of unmerchantable quality should be limited to those situations where the use of the defective product results in physical harm to persons or property. [Citation.] In the past, the attaching of liability where there is no privity has been primarily for the benefit of persons physically injured by the defect. This is so whether responsibility was attached on the theory of enterprise liability, implied negligence through the doctrine of res ipsa loquitur, or implied warranty. Seldom has it been for solely economic loss.

What is the basis for distinguishing between the two? At first there seems to be no logical basis to distinguish them when they have resulted from the same thing— the defective product. Probably the reason is social rather than legal, if the two can be distinguished. In establishing liability in personal injury cases courts have been motivated to overlook any necessity for privity because the hazard to life and health is usually a personal disaster of major proportions to the individual both physically and financially and something of minor importance to the manufacturer or wholesaler against which they can protect themselves by a distribution of risk through the price of the article sold. There has not been the same social necessity to motivate the recovery for strictly economic losses where the damaged person's health, and therefore his basic earning capacity, has remained unimpaired. To enforce strict liability for personal injuries because of such necessity and then to allow recovery for purely economic losses because they arise from the same defect is to apply the doctrine of strict liability when the original motivating factor therefor is not present. I doubt that it is wise to swing the door open to all who are disappointed with their purchase. They should be left for that kind of recovery to the one with whom they dealt.

For the reason stated above, I concur in the result of JUSTICE GOODWIN's opinion.

McLEOD v. W. S. MERRELL CO., DIV. OF RICHARDSON-MERRELL

(1965 Fla.) 174 So.2d 736.

THORNAL, J. * * * We must decide whether a retail druggist who properly fills a prescription of a medical doctor with an unadulterated drug is liable to the patient-purchaser for breach of an implied warranty of fitness or merchantability if the drug produces harmful effects on such purchaser.

Petitioner McLeod's physician prescribed for his use a drug known as "Mer/29". It had been advertised as a commodity for controlling body cholesterol. The drug was manufactured by W. S. Merrell Co. It was sold by the manufacturer to the respondents International Pharmacies, Inc. and James Drug Shop, Inc., for resale to the public only on prescriptions of medical doctors. The respondents International and James filled the prescriptions presented to them by petitioner McLeod. The prescriptions were filled strictly in accordance with instructions of the doctor.

It was stipulated that Merrell had prepared the drug and that the retail druggist respondents had received it in the original sealed packets; that the drug was sold at retail to McLeod in the original unbroken containers without analysis by the druggists; that the use of the drug had been prescribed for the petitioner McLeod by his personal physician.

By a three-count complaint, McLeod, as plaintiff in the trial court, sued Merrell, the manufacturer, and the two respondent retail druggists. The retailers were named only in the third count. It was alleged that although intended as a remedial control of cholesterol, the drug "Mer/29" actually exposed the user to a grave risk of harm when used in ordinary dosages, by causing severe side effects, such as the formation of cataracts and other eye damage. There was no warning by any of the respondents suggesting a possible inherent danger in the use of the drug.

The third count of the complaint charged the three defendants, the manufacturer and the two retailers, with breaches of implied warranties, of (1) reasonable fitness for the intended purpose; (2) merchantability; and (3) wholesomeness or reasonable fitness for human consumption. The third count was dismissed as to the respondent retail drug stores. The trial judge had the view that a retail druggist does not warrant the inherent fitness of drugs he sells on prescription. * * * The instant suit does *not* involve: (1) an action against a manufacturer; (2) adulteration of a commodity by spoilation or the presence of a foreign substance; (3) a product for human consumption available indiscriminately to the public generally; and, (4) a purchase for a particular purpose with reliance upon the druggist to supply a commodity fit for such purpose.

It may be well to note also that we are not here dealing with a complaint grounded in negligence.

By contrast to the foregoing, we should examine the instant record within a narrow orbit circumscribed by the salient facts, which are: (1) an action against a retail druggist; (2) the drug was available only to a limited segment of the public who could present a medical doctor's prescription therefor; (3) the prescription was filled precisely in accordance with its directions, and even then, in the manufacturer's original packet; (4) there was no adulteration; (5) both the patient-purchaser and the retail druggist relied upon the doctor's prescription, rather than upon the druggist's judgment.

An implied warranty of fitness for a particular purpose is conditioned upon the buyer's reliance on the skill and judgment of the seller to supply a commodity suitable for the intended purpose. [Citation.] The warranty of merchantability applies when goods are offered for consumption by the public generally. Therefore, in order to be merchantable the goods must be fit for ordinary uses for which such goods are sold. [Citations.]

In the instant case the commodity, "Mer/ 29", was not available to the general public

in the sense that it could be purchased by any customer who entered the store and paid the price. Actually, it was available only to a very limited segment of the public who had previously been seen by their personal physicians and who presented their doctor's prescription directing that the drug be supplied. Obviously, the patient-purchaser did not rely upon the judgment of the retail druggist in assuming that the drug would be fit for its intended purpose. This confidence had been placed in the physician who prescribed the remedy. Supposedly, he in turn had placed his reliance on the representations of the manufacturer.

The petitioner insists that his position is sustained by our opinion in Green v. The American Tobacco Co., Fla., 154 So.2d 169. There are several distinguishing elements. Green was a suit against a manufacturer. It involved a commodity which was available indiscriminately to the public generally. Green can be summarized as a case which applied a rule of absolute or strict liability to the manufacturer of a commodity who had placed it in the channels of trade for consumption by the public generally. The case before us is lacking in many of these significant elements.

In effect, the petitioner McLeod is asking us to impose upon these retail prescription druggists an absolute, strict liability without fault in an action in tort. While the claim of the petitioner is presented in the posture of an alleged breach of implied warranties, actually, the real theory upon which we are invited to rely is the rapidly evolving concept of strict liability without fault. [Citations.] The obvious effect of the application of this concept, were we to accept it, would be to convert the retail prescription druggists into insurers of the safety of the manufactured drug. We are asked to do this despite the absence of any basis for implying a warranty.

* * *

The concept of strict liability without fault should not be applied to the prescription druggists in the instant situation. Rather, it appears to us, that the rights of the consumer can be preserved, and the responsibilities of the retail prescription druggist can be imposed, under the concept that a druggist who sells a prescription warrants that (1) he will compound the drug prescribed; (2) he has used due and proper care in filling the prescription (failure of which might also give rise to an action in negligence); (3) the proper methods were used in the compounding process; (4) the drug has not been infected with some adulterating foreign substance. [Citations.] It is unnecessary to reach respondent's claim that the retail druggists, in filling a prescription, are rendering a "service" instead of supplying a commodity.

When measured by the foregoing standards, we find no breach of implied warranty in the case at bar.

Judgment for defendants affirmed.

*

PART FIVE
COMMERCIAL PAPER

CHAPTER 25

COMMERCIAL PAPER—FORM AND CONTENT

NEGOTIABILITY

Introductory. Just as no business could be operated without the use of contracts, modern business could not be conducted without the use of commercial paper—checks, drafts, promissory notes. Rare indeed is the transaction that does not involve the writing of one or more checks. Drafts, of which checks are a specialized form, perform an important monetary and credit function in the business world, both within and without the banking system. Promissory notes are commonplace items, not only in areas of high finance, but at the level of the small businessman and consumer as well. The term "instrument" is frequently used to describe any kind of commercial paper when differentiation among types is not important.

The various forms of commercial paper, while in many respects resembling an ordinary contract, may (but need not) also possess the unique characteristic known as negotiability. The rules applicable to drafts and promissory notes grew up in the mercantile courts and were part of the Lex mercatoria or the "law merchant." After centuries of independent development, these principles were assimilated into the common law during the eighteenth and nineteenth centuries and finally became the subject of statutory enactment, first in England in 1882 with the Bills of Exchange Act; later in the United States with the State by State adoption of the Uniform Negotiable Instruments Law commencing in 1896; and finally with the widespread adoption of the Uniform Com-

mercial Code, commencing in 1953. The Code draftsmen specifically recognized the continued validity of the law merchant, however, stating at Section 1–103:

> Unless displaced by the particular provisions of this Act, the principles of law and equity, including the law merchant * * * shall supplement its provisions.

Negotiability Defined. The concept of negotiability as developed under the law merchant and refined by the common law and by statute will be treated subsequently in this chapter. An introduction to the definition of negotiability, however, requires an understanding of the term "holder in due course": a person who acquires an instrument for value, in good faith and without notice that it is overdue, or that payment has been refused or that there is a defense against or claim to it on the part of any person. The commercial utility of negotiability lies in the fact that in the hands of a person with the rights of a holder in due course a negotiable instrument may be enforced against any person obligated on it despite any defenses (with certain limited exceptions) which he might otherwise have.

The difference between the rights of a holder in due course of a negotiable instrument and the rights of an assignee of an ordinary contract claim for money are readily apparent. Absent negotiability, a person obligated on a contract may assert any defense he may have, e. g., failure of consideration, not only against the original party to whom the obligation ran, but also against anyone to whom the claim might be assigned. Add negotiability to the instrument evidencing the obligation, give the transferee the rights of a holder in due course, and the defense may no longer be interposed: the claim may be enforced. The person thus required to pay may then, of course, bring an independent action in contract to recover from the person against whom the defense actually existed. The holder in due course obtains his money promptly and the dispute between the original parties to the contract must be settled between them.

It is obvious that the element of negotiability vastly increases the merchantability of an instrument. It may pass readily through the channels of commerce without a taker being required to check back on possible defenses available to prior parties.

Negotiable Instruments as a Substitute for Money. Because of the extraordinary concept of negotiability, negotiable instruments payable on demand (that is, whenever the holder wishes payment, e. g., a check is payable whenever the holder presents it at the drawee bank) are treated by the commercial community as a substitute for money. Checks greatly augment our currency supply, and merchants regard them as money equivalents because in 996 cases out of 1,000, as determined by a survey, they will be paid when presented to the bank upon which they are drawn. In the other four cases the merchant is not necessarily out-of-pocket. He has recourse against the parties who have signed the check, and the procedural advantages, cut-off protection, and the like flowing from the concept of negotiability give him a substantial chance to recoup his money.

Occasionally, of course, someone takes a loss upon a "bad check" or some other negotiable instrument. When this happens the merchant learns anew that while negotiable instruments are regarded as substitutes for money, they are not money. They are not issued by the government, or under govern-

mental authority, as official media of exchange. Negotiable instruments are redeemable in money; they are not themselves money. The holder always runs the risk that the instrument is not genuine or that the parties to it lack capacity to contract or will become insolvent. These risks, which will be considered in detail at a later point, are not so substantial that they deter the use of negotiable paper, and demand instruments are by far the most common medium of payment now utilized. In a very real sense, negotiable instruments are a "substitute for money."

Negotiable Instruments as Credit Devices. Negotiable instruments originated in ancient times as a "substitute for money." It was not until the Middle Ages that they came to be used as credit instruments as well. This development occurred when it was discovered that negotiable instruments did not have to be made payable on demand; they could be made payable at future dates. When such an instrument was executed, the payee at first was expected to wait until the maturity date to collect it. It was a credit instrument with the payee supplying the credit. Subsequently, means were discovered of finding out the commercial reputation of the maker and other parties who had signed the paper, and then these instruments became salable assets prior to maturity. Of course, the face amount of the instrument would not be paid. It would be discounted, the purchaser paying a price which took into account an interest charge, a risk charge, and a charge for administering the transaction. The discounting process enabled payees to raise immediate cash on instruments calling for future payment, and it shifted credit responsibilities from merchants to banks. The credit aspects of negotiable instruments are now as important as their "money" aspects.

Negotiability. We have seen that one function of negotiable instruments is to supplement the supply of currency by being a "substitute for money." Another function is to represent the future payment of money. These functions are quite different from those of the simple contract, and the consequences of using simple contracts differ radically from those which attend negotiable instruments. Therefore, some method had to be devised to distinguish one from the other. To keep the cost of administering the paper low, and to eliminate the risk of getting non-negotiable paper where a negotiable instrument was intended, business men and banks have insisted that the negotiability of an instrument should be determinable by merely inspecting it, and this insistence has resulted in a custom that negotiability is a matter of form. All contracts which comply with a particular form are negotiable; all others are non-negotiable.

TYPES OF COMMERCIAL PAPER

There are two basic categories of commercial paper: drafts and notes. Although each of these categories includes a wide variety of instruments, the U.C.C. specifically defines only one variant of each: checks, which are the most widely used type of draft, and certificates of deposit, which are in fact a specialized type of note.

Drafts. A draft is an instrument whereby one party, called the drawer, orders a second party, called the drawee, to pay a stated sum of money to a third party, called the payee. Thus, a draft is an instrument involving three parties, or, more precisely, parties in three distinct capacities, since the same party may appear in more than one capacity, (e. g., drawer and payee) and more than one party may appear in a single capacity (e. g., joint payees).

Drafts may be either "time" or "sight." A time draft is one payable at a specified future date, whereas a sight draft is payable immediately upon presentation to the drawee.

A form of time draft known as a trade acceptance is frequently used as a credit device in a commercial transaction. For example, assume that Ben Buyer wishes to purchase goods from Sam Seller. Seller needs cash immediately, but Buyer cannot pay for the goods until he has resold them, or processed and sold them, which may take a long period of time. Therefore, Seller draws a draft on Buyer ordering Buyer to pay the amount of the purchase price to the order of Seller at a specified future date. Seller presents this draft to Buyer, who "accepts" it thereby agreeing to make payment according to its terms. At this point, Seller has the following instrument:

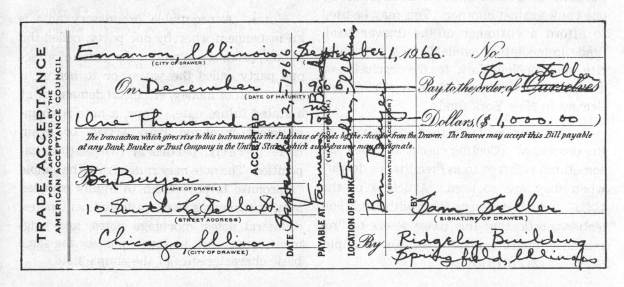

Seller may then indorse and discount the instrument at his bank. On the due date the bank or any subsequent holder of the instrument will collect it from Buyer.

A frequent use of the sight draft is in connection with the shipment and delivery of goods. In the foregoing example, assume that Buyer had been able to pay cash immediately, but Seller wished to assure himself of payment before Buyer received delivery of the goods. Seller would ship the goods, obtain an order bill of lading from the carrier and prepare a sight draft on Buyer to which he would attach the bill of lading. These items would then be forwarded to a bank in Buyer's city, which would notify Buyer of their arrival. Buyer would pay the draft on presentation to him, thereby obtaining the bill of lading, whereupon the bank would then remit the payment to Seller, thus concluding the transaction. The draft involved in this transaction would be of the following type:

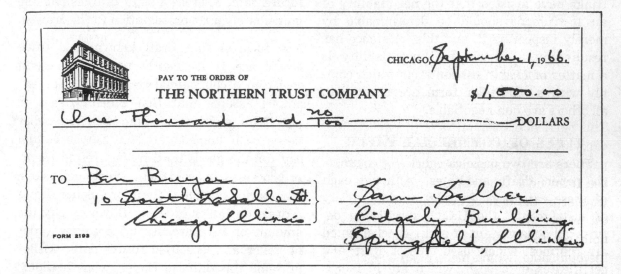

Another function of the draft is to effect a transfer of funds. Frequently this takes the form of a bank draft—a draft drawn by one bank against another. This may be used to afford a customer of the drawer bank funds immediately available in a particular city, such as New York, for the conclusion of a business transaction there requiring settlement in New York funds.

Bank drafts are also used extensively in the process of collecting checks and they are sometimes referred to as "remittance drafts" when they are so used. Article 4 of the U.C.C., which concerns itself with bank collections, reflecting this usage refers to "remittance instruments." See, for example, Section 4–211(3)(a).

Checks. Checks are merely drafts drawn on a bank and payable on demand. They are, of course, the most common form of draft.

Notes. A negotiable promissory note is an instrument whereby one party, called the maker, promises to pay to the order of a second party called the payee, or to bearer, a stated sum of money, either on demand or at a stated future date. Thus, a note is an instrument involving two parties, or again more precisely, parties in two distinct capacities. The note may range from the simple "I promise to pay" form to highly complex legal instruments such as installment notes, collateral notes, mortgage notes, and judgment notes. All, however, possess the same basic characteristics of the simple note.

Examples and descriptions of some of these follow.

1. *Simple Promissory Note.* In its simplest form, the promissory note may read as follows:

ACCOUNT NO.	CODE	OFFICER	DIV.	NL R	RATE

No._____   Chicago, Ill. *October 1,* 19*66*

DEMAND NOTE

ON DEMAND, *the undersigned, for value received, promise(s) to pay to the order of*

THE NORTHERN TRUST COMPANY

One Thousand and ^no^ *Too* ————————————DOLLARS,

at its office in Chicago, Illinois, together with interest thereon from the date hereof until paid at the rate of 5½ *per cent, per annum.*

Daniel Debtor

Address *111 West Monroe Street*
2249 (5-21-6?) *Chicago, Illinois*

This particular example is of a demand note, carrying interest at the rate stated until paid. Simple promissory notes may also take the form of a time note, payable at a fixed time after the date of issue at a stated interest rate. See, for example, the collateral note set forth below. A third type is the discount note, which merely requires the repayment of a stated sum. That sum, however, will represent both the amount borrowed and the interest payable to date of maturity. Thus, if the borrower receives $1,000, payable in six months at 6% interest, he will sign a six month note for $1,030.90, which represents the principal plus interest at that rate: Six per cent interest for six months on $1,000 equals $30.00, but since the $30.00 is in effect also being borrowed at that time, 6 per cent is also charged on that, accounting for the additional 90 cents added to the amount of the note. The example of an installment note set forth below is typical of a note issued on a discounted basis.

2. *Collateral Notes.* To understand a collateral note, it is necessary to understand the meaning of "pledge." A pledge is a bailment of personal property as a security for a debt. If the debt is paid, the personal property is returned to the debtor or pledgor; if the pledgor defaults in payment of his debt, the pledgee may, after the giving of necessary notice, sell the personal property at public sale, applying the proceeds to payment of the debt. A collateral note is one that is secured by the pledging of personal property or, as it is commonly called, "collateral security." The security is "collateral" because it is subsidiary to the principal debt, running parallel with it or collateral to it. The ordinary collateral note is secured by the pledging of stocks, bonds, or other securities, but it may be secured by delivering to the creditor or pledgee any personal property such as a contract, a policy of insurance, a lease, a note of a third party, a mortgage, a book account, a bill of lading, a warehouse receipt, or any other personal property. Delivery of possession of the pledged property to the

pledgee is essential in connection with a collateral note.

An example of a time collateral note is as follows:

ACCOUNT NO.	CODE	OFFICER	DIV.	NL R	DAYS	RATE	$

No._____ Due *December 1, 1966* Chicago, Ill., *September 1,* _____ 19*66*

Ninety - one Days _____ after date, the undersigned, for value received, promise(s) to pay to the order of **THE NORTHERN TRUST COMPANY** (hereinafter called the "Bank") *One Thousand and no/100* _____ DOLLARS, at its office in Chicago, Illinois, together with interest thereon from the date hereof until paid at the rate of *5½* per cent, per annum, payable *at maturity.* _____.

To secure payment of this note and of all other liabilities of the undersigned (hereinafter called the "Maker") to the holder hereof, howsoever created, whether now existing or hereafter arising, whether direct or indirect, whether absolute or contingent, and whether due or to become due (this note and all such other liabilities being hereinafter called the "Obligations"), the Maker pledges to the Bank and grants to the Bank a security interest in all property of the Maker of any kind, now or at any time hereafter assigned, transferred or delivered to or left in the possession of the Bank by or for the account of the Maker, including but without limitation all property described in receipts for collateral from time to time issued by the Bank to or for the account of Maker and in all dividends and distributions on, other rights in connection with and all substitutions for such property (hereinafter called the "Collateral").

TIME NOTE

If the holder should at any time be of the opinion that the Collateral is not sufficient or has declined or may decline in value or should the holder deem itself insecure, then the holder may call for additional security satisfactory to the holder, and the Maker promises to furnish such additional security forthwith. The call for additional security may be oral or by telegram or by United States mail addressed to the last address for the Maker shown on the holder's records.

At the option of the holder, all Obligations shall become immediately due and payable without notice or demand upon the occurrence of any of the following events of default:

(a) Failure of any Maker to comply with any of the promises contained in this note or to pay or perform any other Obligation of the Maker to the holder; or

(b) Death, dissolution, termination of existence, insolvency, failure to pay debts as they mature, business failure, appointment of a receiver of any part of the property of, assignment for the benefit of creditors by, or the commencement of any proceedings under any bankruptcy or insolvency laws by or against, any Maker, indorser, or guarantor hereof.

Upon the occurrence of any such event of default, and at any time thereafter, the holder shall have the rights and remedies of a secured party under the Uniform Commercial Code of Illinois, including without limitation thereto, the right to sell or otherwise dispose of any or all of the Collateral. If any notification of intended disposition of any of the Collateral is required by law, such notification, if mailed, shall be deemed reasonably and properly given if mailed at least five days before such disposition, postage prepaid, addressed to the Maker either at the address shown below, or at any other address of the Maker appearing on the records of the holder. Any proceeds of the disposition of any of the Collateral may be applied by the holder to the payment of reasonable expenses incurred in connection therewith, including reasonable attorneys' fees and legal expenses, and any balance of such proceeds may be applied by the holder toward the payment of such of the Obligations and in such order of application as the holder may from time to time elect.

The right is expressly granted to the holder at its option to transfer at any time into the name of the holder or its nominee any Collateral pledged hereunder, to thereafter exercise, at its option, all of the rights of a registered owner with respect thereto, including voting rights, and to receive the income

on the Collateral and hold the same as security herefor, or apply it on the principal or interest due hereon or due on any Obligation secured hereby.

At any time any deposit or other indebtedness credited by or due from the holder to any Maker may be set off against and applied in payment of any Obligations, whether due or not, and such deposits or other indebtedness may at all times be held and treated as collateral security for the payment of the Obligations.

The holder may at its option, whether or not this note is due, demand, sue for, collect, or make any compromise or settlement it deems desirable with reference to Collateral held hereunder. The holder shall not be bound to take any steps necessary to preserve any rights in the Collateral against prior parties, which the Maker hereby assumes to do.

No delay or omission on the part of the holder in exercising any right hereunder or under any other agreement pertaining to the Collateral shall operate as a waiver of such right or of any other right. A waiver on any one occasion shall not be construed as a bar to or waiver of any such right and/or remedy on any future occasion.

Every Maker, indorser and guarantor of this note, or the obligation represented hereby, expressly waives presentment, protest, demand, notice of dishonor or default, and notice of any kind with respect to this note or any guaranty of this note or the performance of the obligations under this note or any guaranty of this note. No renewal or extension of this note, whether or not longer than the original period, no release or surrender of any Collateral or other security for this note or any guaranty of this note, no release of any person, primarily or secondarily liable on this note (including any Maker, indorser or guarantor), no delay in the enforcement of payment of this note or any guaranty of this note, and no delay or omission in exercising any right or power under this note or any guaranty of this note shall affect the liability of any Maker, indorser or guarantor of this note.

Whenever an event of default exists Maker agrees to pay on demand all expenses of collection of this note and enforcement of rights under any of the Collateral, including reasonable attorneys' fees and legal expenses.

As herein used the word "holder" shall mean the payee or other indorsee of this note, who is in possession of it, or the bearer hereof, if this note is at the time payable to the bearer. As used herein the word "Maker" shall mean each of the undersigned.

ADDRESS *111 West Monroe Street*   *Daniel Debtor*   SIGN HERE
Chicago, Illinois
TELEPHONE NUMBER

The foregoing example contains the usual recital of the holder's right to sell the collateral on default. His rights in this regard are governed by Article 9 of the U.C.C., Secured Transactions, discussed in Chapter 44. In the event of a sale, any surplus remaining is returned to the maker. If the proceeds of the sale are insufficient to satisfy the indebtedness, the maker remains liable to the holder of the note for the amount of the deficiency.

3. *Installment Notes.* An installment note is simply one in which the principal is

payable in specified installments at specified times, together with interest on the unpaid balance, until the note is paid in full. Installment notes usually contain a so-called "acceleration" clause or provision, which permits the holder of the note, at his election or option to declare the entire principal amount and all accrued interest on the note payable immediately upon default by the maker in the payment of any installment of either principal or interest, unless the note is on a discounted basis, in which case the installments will be of principal only. An example of a discount installment note is as follows:

THE NORTHERN TRUST COMPANY

INSTALLMENT NOTE

$ *1,500.00*

Chicago, Illinois

September 1, 19*66*

The undersigned, for value received, hereby promise(s) to pay to the order of THE NORTHERN TRUST COMPANY (hereinafter called the "Bank") at its office in Chicago, Illinois, the sum of *Fifteen Hundred and no/100* ——————————————Dollars in *36* ——installments as follows: $ *41.67* on *October 1*, 19*66*, and the same amount on the same day of each successive *month* thereafter (except that the last installment shall be the unpaid balance) until paid in full, together with interest after maturity on all unpaid principal amounts at the rate of seven per cent (7%) per annum.

At the option of the holder hereof, this note and all other liabilities of the undersigned (hereinafter called the "Maker") to the holder howsoever created, whether now existing or hereafter arising and whether due or to become due (this note and all such other liabilities being hereinafter called the "Obligations"), shall become immediately due and payable without notice or demand upon the occurrence of any of the following events of default:

(a) Failure of any Maker to comply with any of the promises contained in this note or to pay or perform any other Obligation of the Maker to the holder; or

(b) Death, dissolution, termination of existence, insolvency, failure to pay debts as they mature, business failure, appointment of a receiver of any part of the property of, assignment for the benefit of creditors by, or the commencement of any proceedings under any bankruptcy or insolvency laws by or against, any Maker, indorser, or guarantor hereof; or

(c) Any warranty, representation or statement made or furnished to the Bank by or on behalf of the Maker in connection with this note or to induce the Bank to make a loan to the Maker proves to have been false in any material respect when made or furnished.

To further secure the payment of said amount, each Maker and each and every indorser and guarantor hereby jointly and severally irrevocably authorizes and empowers any attorney or attorneys of any Court of Record to appear for each Maker and each and every indorser and guarantor, or either or any of them, in such court at any time after maturity of this note (either by its terms or at the option of the holder as provided herein), in term time or vacation, and to confess judgment without process against them, or any one or more of them, jointly or severally, in favor of the holder of this note, for such sum as may appear to be unpaid and owing hereon, together with interest and costs (including reasonable attorneys' fees), and to waive and release all errors which may intervene in such proceeding, and to consent to immediate execution upon such judgment or judgments, hereby ratifying and confirming all that said attorney or attorneys may do by virtue hereof, and further agrees that the confession of any such judgment against any one or more, but less than all, of the Makers, indorsers and guarantors shall not preclude the confession of judgment against any other of the Makers, indorsers and the guarantors.

At any time any deposit or other indebtedness credited by or due from the holder to any Maker may be set off against and applied in payment of any Obligations, whether due or not, and such deposits or other indebtedness may at all times be held and treated as collateral security for the payment of the Obligations.

No delay or omission on the part of the holder in exercising any right hereunder shall operate as a waiver of such right or of any other right under this note. A waiver on any one occasion shall not be construed as a bar to or waiver of any such right and/or remedy on any future occasion.

Every Maker, indorser and guarantor of this note, or the obligations represented hereby, expressly waives presentment, protest, demand, notice of dishonor or default, and notice of any kind with respect to this note or any guaranty of this note or the performance of the obligations under this note or any guaranty of this note. No renewal or extension of this note, no release or surrender of any collateral or other security for this note or any guaranty of this note, no release of any person, primarily or secondarily liable on this note (including any Maker, indorser or guarantor), no delay in the enforcement of payment of this note or any guaranty of this note, and no delay or omission in exercising any right or power under this note or any guaranty of this note shall affect the liability of any Maker, indorser or guarantor of this note.

Delinquency charges: The Maker agrees to pay a delinquency and collection charge on each installment in default for a period of more than 10 days in an amount equal to five percent (5%) of the installment or five dollars ($5) whichever is less.

The Maker will pay on demand all costs of collection, legal expenses, and attorneys' fees incurred or paid by the holder in collecting and/or enforcing this note on default.

As herein used the word "holder" shall mean the payee or other indorsee of this note, who is in possession of it, or the bearer hereof, if this note is at the time payable to the bearer. As used herein the word "Maker" shall mean each of the undersigned. If this note is signed by more than one person, it shall be the joint and several liabilities of such persons.

On any loan of eight-hundred dollars or less, the undersigned agrees to pay a service charge of five dollars ($5) in addition to the interest, which will be collected when the loan is made.

ADDRESS

1 North La Salle Street
Chicago, Illinois

SIGNATURE

Daniel Debtor

The foregoing installment note is also an example of a judgment note, that is, one in which the maker authorizes the immediate entry of a judgment against him, in the event of his default on the note, by a court proceeding without service of summons on him, without other notice to him, and without a trial of the case. As an express provision of the note, the maker gives a power or warrant of attorney to "any attorney" to appear on his behalf and confess judgment against him on the note. Many States have abolished or restricted the granting of a power to confess judgment as being against public policy. Where legal, such a clause may appear in any type of promissory note. In any event, a confession of judgment clause will render an instrument non-negotiable under Section 3–112 (1) (d) unless it is specifically made operable only at or after maturity.

4. *Real Estate Mortgage Notes.* A real estate mortgage note is a note secured by a mortgage on specific real property of the maker. A real estate mortgage note usually recites that "the payment of this note is secured by a trust deed, bearing even date herewith, to A, as Trustee, on real estate in the [name of County and State]." Such a note is negotiable if it contains all of the requisites of negotiability.

5. *Certificates of Deposit.* A certificate of deposit is essentially a note issued by a bank acknowledging receipt of money and engaging to repay it upon the terms stated. Except for one special situation involving the Statute of Limitations, the U.C.C. treats certificates of deposit as if they were notes, and for economy of exposition, they will be so treated in this book except in that connection.

Other Negotiable Instruments Having Some Degree of Negotiability. In addition to commercial paper, the negotiability of which is treated under Article 3 of the U.C.C., there are other types of instruments which are negotiable, although perhaps not in precisely the same sense.

1. *Bonds.* Although the word "bond" is used in a broad sense to refer to all types and kinds of bonds, it is more ordinarily used as a shorthand expression for "mortgage bond." A mortgage bond is a written promise to pay money, issued by individuals, partnerships, and public and private corporations, and secured by a mortgage of property. A bond is one of a series of similar instruments, usually but not necessarily for the same amount and with the same maturity. Bonds issued by corporations are generally secured by a mortgage deed or trust indenture conveying title to all or a specified part of the corporate assets to a designated trustee, usually a trust company, as security for the payment of the bonds. When the bonds are paid, title to the mortgaged property reverts back to the corporation by release of the mortgage or trust indenture. The bond itself invariably refers to the mortgage deed and embodies some of its terms.

Bonds generally and also stock certificates, meet the requirements of a "Security" under Section 8–102 of the Code, and as such are negotiable, Section 8–105.

2. *Stocks.* Stock certificates were never regarded as subject to the Negotiable Instruments Law, but they were accorded a degree of negotiability under the Uniform Stock Transfer Act. Ownership could be transferred by mere indorsement and delivery and ownership claims could be cut off by due negotiation.

Stocks are governed by Article 8 of the Uniform Commercial Code, Investment Securities.

3. *Bills of Lading and Warehouse Receipts.* Before the adoption of the U.C.C., transfers of bills of lading and warehouse receipts were governed, respectively, by the Uniform Bills of Lading Act, the Uniform Warehouse Receipts Act, and, to a lesser extent by the Uniform Sales Act. While such instruments, commonly referred to as documents of title, were never regarded as subject to the Negotiable Instruments Law, they were negotiable in some respects. They are analogous to the promissory note: they may contain a negotiable promise by a bailee (carrier or warehouseman) to deliver goods to the holder of the document. A "delivery order" is analogous to the draft: it contains an order by one who is entitled to possession of goods in the hands of a bailee directing the bailee to deliver them to a third party.

4. *Other U.C.C. Provisions Applicable.* It was against this background that the draftsmen of the U.C.C. made their most important change in the law of negotiable instruments; they decided to treat investment securities and documents of title separately from commercial paper. Accordingly, Article 8 of the U.C.C. was drafted to cover investment paper, such as bonds, debentures, stock, interim certificates and the like, Article 7, to cover documents of title, and Article 3, to cover short-term notes, drafts, checks and certificates of deposit.

Only instruments taking a particular form qualify for coverage under Article 3. Article 8, on the other hand, uses a functional test. Instruments qualify for coverage under that article if they are "commonly dealt in upon security exchanges * * * or commonly recognized * * * as a medium for investment." Section 8–102. It would be possible for an instrument to meet both the formal test of Article 3 and the functional test of Article 8. To prevent the possibility that two separate and, in most respects, different

articles of the U.C.C. might happen to govern a particular negotiable instrument, a provision was made that in case of overlap Article 8 rather than Article 3 should apply. Section 8–102(1) (b).

By removing investment securities from Article 3, the draftsmen of the U.C.C. were able to set out rigorous rules designed to promote certainty in the case of commercial paper (notes, drafts, checks) without risking damage to documents commonly traded on security exchanges.

Similarly, Article 7 confers a degree of negotiability on documents of title which meet its tests. Again, there is no conflict with the more exacting provisions of Article 3.

The U.C.C. now governs all types of instruments referred to above, and the Uniform Acts formerly controlling have been repealed. For all practical purposes, negotiability is now entirely controlled by the rules established under the U.C.C.

THE FORM OF NEGOTIABLE INSTRUMENTS

In order for negotiable instruments to perform their function in the business community effectively, they must be capable of passing from hand to hand freely. This is made possible because negotiability is wholly a matter of form. Within the four corners of the instrument is all the information required to determine whether it is negotiable. No reference to any other sources is required.

The formal requirements which an instrument must satisfy if it is to be negotiable are set forth in Section 3–104(1) as follows:

> Any writing to be a negotiable instrument within this Article must
>
> (a) be signed by the maker or drawer; and
>
> (b) contain an unconditional promise or order to pay a sum certain in

money and no other promise, order, obligation or power given by the maker or drawer except as authorized by this Article; and

(c) be payable on demand or at a definite time; and

(d) be payable to order or to bearer.

For a full understanding of the meaning of these formal requisites of negotiability, each aspect must be considered in detail, much of which is supplied by explanatory provisions of the U.C.C.

1. *The Instrument Must be a Writing.* It is obvious that to pass through the channels of commerce, an instrument must have physical existence, but the requirement that it be a writing is quite broadly construed. Printing, typewriting or any other intentional reduction to tangible form is sufficient to satisfy the requirement. Section 1–201(46). Pen, pencil or paint are equally valid.

Nor has there been any attempt to limit the materials upon which the writing is made. Most negotiable instruments, of course, are written on paper, but this is not required. There may be some theoretical limits on the kind of materials on which a negotiable instrument may be written, because a negotiable instrument to serve its function must be capable of circulating. This would tend to indicate that a negotiable instrument should not be prepared on a non-movable object. And, since negotiable instruments are designed to serve a credit and currency function, it would seem that they must be prepared on a material capable of retaining the writing, thus permitting them to remain outstanding for a period of time. For these reasons it may be doubted whether a negotiable instrument could be written on a cake of ice or on the side of a barn. Occasionally, however, oddly drawn checks are presented to and paid by banks, (e. g., a check carved on a watermelon to signal the start of National Watermelon Week).

2. *The Instrument Must be Signed.* A note must be signed by the maker; a draft or check must be signed by the drawer. As in the case of a writing, however, extreme latitude is granted in determining what constitutes a signature. Any symbol executed or adopted by a party with present intention to authenticate a writing is sufficient. Section 1–201(39). It may be printed, stamped or typed, although it would behoove the recipient of the instrument to insist on a written signature as a matter of proof of genuineness or authority. It may consist of any word or mark used in lieu of a written signature (Section 3–401(2)), such as initials, an X or a thumb print. It may be a trade name or assumed name (Section 3–401(2)), however false or fictitious. Parol evidence is admissible to identify the signer, and when he is identified, the signature is effective. It may be made on behalf of the maker or drawer by an agent or other representative. Section 3–403(1).

Even the location of the signature on the document is unimportant. Normally a maker or drawer signs in the lower right hand corner of the instrument, but this is not required. A statement in the body of the instrument such as: "I, John Doe, promise to pay * * *" is sufficient. A billhead or letterhead on which the instrument is written has been held to be sufficient.

Present intention to authenticate is the key to determining the effectiveness of the signature.

3. *A Negotiable Instrument Must Contain a Promise to Pay, in Case of a Note, or an Order to Pay in Case of a Draft or Check.* This requirement is based on the principle that a negotiable instrument must evidence an absolute intention that the money be paid in all events.

A promise is an undertaking to pay and must be more than the acknowledgment of an obligation. Section 3–102(1) (c).

An order is a direction to pay and must be more than an authorization or request and it must identify the person to pay with reasonable certainty. Section 3–102(1) (b).

The demarcation line dividing promises from acknowledgments and orders from requests is not easy to draw in some cases, but in most no trouble has ensued. The so-called "due bill" or "I. O. U." is not a promise, but a mere acknowledgment of indebtedness. Accordingly, an instrument reciting, "due Adam Brown $100" or "I. O. U., Adam Brown, $100" is not negotiable. Similarly, it was held in a celebrated case that the following request did not amount to an order, and hence the instrument was not negotiable: "Mr. Little—Please let the bearer have seven pounds and place it to my account, and you will oblige your humble servant R. Slackford." Little v. Slackford, Moody & M. 171 (1828).

Where there is doubt, the use of words of negotiability ("order" or "bearer") often tips the balance toward a finding that the words used fairly import a promise or order. Thus, while "I. O. U. Adam Brown, $100" is not promissory, the language "due Adam Brown, or order, $100" might make the instrument negotiable, the theory being that the use of promissory words indicates an intention to create a negotiable instrument, and from this it is fair to imply a promise to pay rather than a bare acknowledgment of debt. Some courts, however, have shown hostility to "hazy," oddly-drawn instruments, and this disposition is often implemented by finding them to be non-negotiable. Well-drafted notes use the word "promise" and well-drafted drafts use the word "pay" to fairly import a promise to pay in the case of a note and an order to pay in the case of a draft. Any other usage simply invites trouble. Words of courtesy, in a draft, however, such as "Please pay" or "Kindly pay" are permissible and will not be regarded as converting the direction to a mere request.

4. *The Promise or Order Must be Unconditional.* A further step in carrying forward the principle that a negotiable instrument must evidence an absolute intention that the money be paid in all events is the requirement that the promise or order be unconditional. The currency and credit functions of such instruments would be defeated by conditions limiting the promise, since costly and time consuming investigations would become necessary. Moreover, if the holder had to take an instrument subject to certain conditions his risk factor would be substantial and this would lead to high discounting. Substitutes for money must be capable of rapid circulation at minimum risks and credit instruments are feasible only when low discounting prevails. Obviously, then, negotiable instruments must be unconditional to serve the purposes for which they are designed.

A promise or order may be expressly subject to a condition as "I promise to pay, if, but only if, the television set for which this note is given proves entirely satisfactory to me." Such an instrument is clearly non-negotiable.

A promise or order also becomes conditional, thereby destroying negotiability of the instrument involved, under two basic sets of facts: (a) Where the instrument states that it is subject to or governed by any other agreement; and (b) Where the instrument states that it is to be paid only out of a particular fund or source. Section 3–105(2). In an effort to define what provisions an instrument may contain without running afoul of these rules, the drafters of the U.C.C. included some very specific language in Section 3–105(1).

(a) *Reference to Other Agreements.* The controlling consideration is whether the holder of an instrument must look to something outside the four corners of the instrument to determine whether the person obligated is required to pay.

A statement in a note such as:

> "This note is given in partial payment for a T.V. set to be delivered two weeks from date in accordance with a contract of this date between the payee and the maker"

does not impair negotiability. It merely constitutes a description of the transaction giving rise to the note, and describes the consideration. It does not place any restriction or condition on the maker's obligation to pay. The holder does not have to concern himself with the question of whether the payee in fact delivers the T.V. set on the date specified. In other words, the promise is not affected by any implied or constructive conditions. They must be expressly stated in the instrument as:

> "and in the event such set is not delivered, then the maker's obligation hereunder shall be null and void."

If such a condition were contained in the underlying contract, but not in the note, it would not affect the negotiability of the note. On the other hand, if the note said:

> "in accordance with a contract of this date between the payee and the maker and subject to such contract"

it would not be negotiable, no matter what the underlying contract provided, because a subsequent holder would have to examine the contract before knowing what the maker's obligation was. Terms such as "As per our contract, I promise to pay   .   .   ." or "In accordance with our contract, I promise to pay   .   .   ." are not regarded as making the instrument subject to the contract, and hence do not affect negotiability. Section 3–105(1) (b).

Reference to the fact that an instrument is secured, whether by real estate mortgage, conditional sale contract, pledge of securities or otherwise, will not affect negotiability. In fact, such terms, if anything, increase the marketability of the instrument since it then becomes more than an unsupported promise or order to pay. The security agreement augments the holder's prospects of recovery. It does not condition the promise to pay.

Thus, a distinction is to be made between a mere recital of the *existence* of a separate agreement (this does not destroy negotiability) and a recital which shows that the executing parties intended the instrument to be *burdened* with the terms of another agreement (this does destroy negotiability). Whether a recital merely refers to a separate agreement or burdens the promise with its terms is a fact question which no code or statute can resolve in every case, and doubtful provisions will continue to cause difficulties, which will have to be resolved by the courts.

(b) *The Particular Fund Doctrine.* An order or promise to pay out of a particular fund is conditional and destroys negotiability, because payment is qualified by the existence and sufficiency of the particular fund. The holder would be required to check into this before having any assurance he would be paid. On the other hand, an unconditional promise or order to pay, coupled with a mere indication of a particular fund out of which reimbursement is to be made, or a particular account to be debited with the amount, does not destroy negotiability, since the drawer's or maker's general credit is relied upon and the charging of a particular account is merely a bookkeeping direction to be followed after payment. Thus there is a difference between a recital which says: "Sixty days after date pay to the order of John Jones $500 out of the proceeds of the sale of the contents of freight car No. 1234" and "Sixty days after date pay to the order of John Jones $500 and charge to proceeds of sale of the contents of freight car No. 1234." In the first case, payment would be made only if such contents were sold and the proceeds were sufficient. In the second case, the instrument is interpreted as creating a general obligation, with merely bookkeeping instructions to the drawee of the draft.

The U.C.C. creates two exceptions to this rule, however, in the interest of promoting marketability of instruments: The first exception is aimed at permitting governmental agencies to draw short-term commercial paper in which payment is restricted to a particular fund. Statutes in many States and municipalities authorize the issuance of instruments to pay for public improvements, and these instruments are generally payable only out of funds raised from special assessments of the property benefited. To aid municipalities and States, and to prevent investors from disappointment, Section 3–105(1)(g) makes an exception to the particular fund doctrine by providing that an instrument is not rendered non-negotiable solely because payable out of a particular fund "if the instrument is issued by a government or governmental agency or unit."

The other exception is in favor of persons and organizations generally regarded in commercial circles as separate business entities, although in fact they may not be from a technical legal point of view. Trustees, executors and administrators commonly limit payment to the assets of the trust or estate they are administering. Partners tend to limit payment to the assets of the partnership. Other unincorporated organizations such as associations, joint stock companies and Massachusetts Trusts or business trusts issue instruments limited to payment from the assets of the organization, expressly providing that the members are not to be personally liable thereon. Section 3–105(1)(h) of the U.C.C. specifies that none of these limitations impair negotiability of an instrument despite the fact that its payment is limited to a particular fund. In fact, the limitation is no more than that present where a corporation is the party involved: the entire assets committed to the business enterprise are made available to support the obligation under the instrument.

5. *The Payment Required Must be of a Sum Certain in Money.* The holder must be able to determine from the face of the instrument the amount which he will receive in all events, so that he can ascertain the present and future value of the instrument, a process indispensable to discounting.

"Money" Defined. The term "money" means a medium of exchange authorized or adopted by a domestic or foreign government as part of its currency. Section 1–201(24). Consequently, even though local custom may make gold dust, uncut diamonds, beaver pelts or cigarettes media of exchange, an instrument payable in such commodities would be non-negotiable because of the lack of governmental sanction of such media. On the other hand, the fact that an instrument states the sum payable in French francs, German marks or Japanese yen, would not affect its negotiability. Unless otherwise specified, however, such an instrument may be satisfied by payment of the dollar equivalent of such foreign currency on the date the instrument is payable, or, if payable on demand, on the day of demand. An instrument payable in "currency" or "current funds" is deemed to be payable in money. Section 3–107.

"Sum Certain" Defined. The requirement of payment of a "sum certain" must be considered from the point of view of the holder, not the obligor, under the philosophy evident in Section 3–106. The holder must be assured of a determinable minimum payment, although certain provisions of the instrument may augment the recovery under certain circumstances. Thus, a frequent provision of a note is that the maker will pay, in addition to the face amount and specified interest, if any, costs of collection or attorney's fees or both upon default in payment. Such a provision is designed to make the paper more attractive without lessening the certainty of the amount due.

For example, an instrument payable in the amount of $100 and containing no interest clause and no attorney-fee clause might be thought to contain an absolutely fixed "sum certain." But the amount of money the holder can recover on the instrument is by no means fixed. If the obligor (maker or drawee) refuses to pay the item when it becomes due, what will be the holder's ultimate net recovery? He might have to pay an attorney $25 or $30 to collect the instrument, and there may be other costs. Depending upon conditions beyond his control, the holder may net anywhere from $50 to $100 on the instrument. If, on the other hand, the instrument contains a clause in which the obligor promises to pay collection charges, including attorney's fees, in addition to the $100, the instrument might be regarded as not fixed as to "sum," especially when viewed from the position of the obligor. But it is fixed from the point of view of the holder, because he is assured that his ultimate (net) recovery will be $100. In short, the auxiliary clauses do not affect the sum certain due on the instrument; they simply shift the costs of collection and other risks.

An instrument payable with a stated rate of interest is an obligation for a sum certain. The rates may be different before and after default, or before and after a specified date. In fact, if the instrument merely provides that the principal amount is payable "with interest," the statutory legal rate of interest applies. (This is not to be confused with the maximum rate of interest which may legally be charged: e. g., in Illinois the statutory legal rate is 5% but the maximum allowable is 7%.) But if interest is payable "at the current rate," (which means current banking rate) it is non-negotiable because this is not a matter that can be determined without reference to any outside source.

Where no date is specified from which interest is to run, interest accrues from the date of the instrument, and if the instrument is undated, from the time the possession of it is first transferred to the payee or the first holder.

A sum payable is a sum certain, even though it is payable in installments, or with a fixed discount if paid before maturity or a fixed addition if paid thereafter. Again, the minimum sum receivable is ascertainable, although additional amounts may be added in the event the instrument is not paid before or at maturity. In addition, it is always possible to make the necessary computations from the face of the instrument to determine the amount due at any given time.

The U.C.C. does not render any of these provisions legal where they would otherwise be illegal under State law, such as a statute with respect to usury. It merely provides that any such provision does not affect negotiability.

One matter left in some doubt is whether a promise to pay taxes levied on an instrument, in addition to the principal sum, would render it non-negotiable. It would appear that the philosophy of Section 3–106 would indicate that such a provision would not impair negotiability, but until courts pass on the matter, a definitive answer is not possible.

6. *The Instrument may Contain No Other Promise or Order.* A negotiable instrument must contain a promise or order to pay money, but it may not contain any other promise, order, obligation or power given by the maker or drawer, except as otherwise specifically authorized under Section 3–104 (1) (b).

Accordingly, if an instrument contains an order or promise to do an act in addition to the payment of money, it is not negotiable. For example, a promise to pay $100 "and a ton of coal" would be non-negotiable. The reason for the limitation is obvious. The concept of negotiability requires that an instrument be made payable in money because this makes it possible to determine its present value. Where the promise requires something in addition to money, its present value is more difficult to compute, and such promises, therefore, are not suitable in instruments which must be highly certain as to present value to serve the credit and currency functions for which they are created.

In view of this reason for the rule, it is not strange to see courts drawing a distinction between "additional" acts which destroy certainty of present value, thereby rendering the instrument non-negotiable, and those acts, though technically additional to the payment of money, which better secure the payment of the debt but do not render the instrument non-negotiable. In the case of First Nat. Bank of Bridgeport v. Blackman, 249 N.Y. 322, 164 N.E. 113 (1928), the New York Court of Appeals put the matter this way:

> "The question in every case is not whether the act is technically 'additional' to the payment of money but whether it is substantively so. If its real purpose is to aid the holder to secure the payment of money and protect him from the risks of insolvency, if it steadies the value of the note, and makes it circulate more readily, then it should not be fatal to negotiability."

Accepting this idea, the draftsmen of the U.C.C. set out in Section 3–112 a list of terms and provisions which may be included in instruments without adversely affecting negotiability. Among these are: a promise or power to maintain, protect or increase collateral and to sell it in case of default in payment of principal or interest on the instrument; a term authorizing confession of judgment on the instrument if it is not paid when due; a term purporting to waive the benefit of any law intended for the advantage or protection of any obligor, such as a homestead exemption; and a term in a draft providing that the payee, by indorsing or cashing it acknowledges full satisfaction of an obligation of the drawer.

It is important to note that the U.C.C. does not render any of these terms legal or effective, it merely provides that their inclusion will not affect negotiability. For example, so-called "judgment notes" are illegal in many States, and the U.C.C. does not purport to validate them. And as pointed out above even in States where they are legal, they will be negotiable only when confession of judgment is authorized if the note is not paid when due. If judgment may be taken by confession under any other circumstances, negotiability is affected. Similarly, many States forbid waiver of laws for the protection of debtors. In such a State, a waiver in the instrument would be ineffective, but it would not affect negotiability.

The rule that the instrument may contain no promise, order, obligation or power other than for the payment of money does not prevent incorporation of such matters into a separate agreement, so long as the instrument is not made subject to such agreement. The terms of such other agreement, however, while binding on the parties thereto cannot limit the rights of a holder in due course who takes without notice of the limitation. Section 3–119. For example, a separate agreement may provide that upon maturity of a note, the maker shall be entitled to extend it for a year. As between the original parties, this is all part of one transaction, and binding on them. If a holder in due course takes the instrument, even with notice that there is a separate agreement but without knowledge of its terms, he is not bound, and may enforce the note when due. If, on the other hand, he knew of the maker's right of extension when he took the instrument, he must grant the extension if the maker requests it.

7. *The Instrument Must be Payable on Demand or at a Definite Time.* Not only must a negotiable instrument contain an unconditional promise or order, but it must also be payable at a time which is certain. This requirement, like the other formal requisites of negotiability, is designed to promote cer-

tainty in ascertaining the present value of a negotiable instrument. In determining the value of an instrument, it is necessary to know when the obligor can be compelled to pay, when the obligations of secondary parties will arise, and when the Statute of Limitations will start to run. Without this information, interest and discount rates cannot be fixed and credit risks cannot be properly assessed. The present value of an instrument cannot be determined unless its time of payment is fixed and certain.

Section 3–104(1) (c) of the U.C.C. accordingly requires, for purposes of negotiability, that the instrument "be payable on demand or at a definite time."

(a) *Demand Paper*. Demand paper always has been considered sufficiently certain as to time of payment to satisfy the requirements of negotiability, because it is the holder who makes the demand and thus sets the time of payment. The discount rate of demand paper can be determined, because the holder himself can plan on a presentment to be made at a particular time. Indeed, demand paper is very valuable to holders, because it gives them an opportunity to present at an earlier time than they had planned, if the obligor shows signs of financial weakness.

An instrument qualifies as being payable on demand if it is payable "at sight" or "on presentation," or if, as in the case of a check, no time for payment is stated. Section 3–108.

(b) *Time Paper*. Instruments payable at a definite time, other than on demand, are called "time paper." When the date of payment is stated, discounts and risks may be evaluated with that in mind. Such paper is thus clearly consistent with the concept of negotiability.

Various types of provisions which may be regarded as fixing a definite time for payment of an instrument are detailed in Section 3–109 and will be considered separately.

(1) *"On or before" Clauses*. Section 3–109(1) (a) provides that an instrument is payable at a definite time if it is payable "on or before a stated date." Obligors, with bargaining strength, frequently insist on the use of the "on or before" clause. For example, a maker wants to borrow money and plans to repay it on September 1, 1968. There is a possibility that he might be able to repay it sooner, and he would like to have the legal right to do so in order to reduce interest charges. He therefore insists that the promissory language of the note he signs to evidence the loan take the following form: "On or before September 1, 1968, I promise to pay to the order of * * *" The holder is thus assured that he will have his money, at the latest, by the maturity date of September 1, 1968, although he may receive it sooner. This right of anticipation enables the maker to pay the note in advance of the stated maturity date and thereby stop the further accrual of interest. It constitutes sufficient certainty to prevent negotiability from being impaired.

(2) *At a Fixed Period after a Stated Date*. Frequently, instruments are made payable at a fixed period after a stated date. For example, the instrument may be made payable "thirty days after date." This means it is payable thirty days after the date of issuance which is recited on the instrument. Such an instrument is payable at a definite time, for its exact maturity date can be reckoned by simple arithmetic. It is consistent with negotiability.

An undated instrument payable "thirty days after date" is not payable at a definite time, since the date of payment cannot be determined from its face. It is therefore non-negotiable. It is, however, an incomplete instrument, and, according to rules hereinafter considered, will meet the payable at a definite time standard when completed as authorized, or, in the hands of a holder in due course, when completed even in an unauthorized manner. Sections 3–115; 3–407.

(3) *At a Fixed Period after Sight.* This clause is frequently used in a trade acceptance. As noted above, the trade acceptance is a draft, drawn by the seller of goods on the purchaser of such goods, and accepted by the purchaser. Usually the draft is accompanied by a bill of lading ("bill of lading with draft attached") and the purchaser is not given the bill of lading until he accepts the draft. If he accepts the draft, the bill of lading will be delivered to him, and this enables him to obtain the goods. The accepted draft makes the drawee primarily liable, and he plans to sell the goods and raise sufficient money to pay it when it becomes due. The seller thus extends credit to the buyer where a trade acceptance is used. The credit period is fixed by the sales contract, but it is reflected in the draft which accompanies the bill of lading. If the time of maturity of the draft is "60 days after sight," this means that a 60-day credit period has been given the purchaser, for "60 days after sight" means sixty days after the drawee accepts.

Clearly an instrument payable a fixed period after sight is negotiable, for the instrument, with a slight arithmetic calculation, makes the maturity date certain.

(4) *At a Definite Time Subject to Any Acceleration.* It has been observed that a demand instrument is payable at a time definite enough for purposes of negotiability. So far as this formal requisite is concerned, an instrument payable at a fixed time subject to acceleration should also be satisfactory. Indeed, such an instrument would seem to have a more certain maturity date than a demand instrument, because it at least states a definite time beyond which it cannot run. For this reason, the U.C.C. specifies that such a provision does not adversely affect the certainty of the time of payment.

Acceleration may be authorized under various sets of circumstances. For example, at the maker's option: "On or before January 31, 1967, I promise to pay * * *". Or upon the occurrence of some event, whether certain or uncertain to happen: "On January 31, 1967, or at such time before then as I shall sell my car, I promise to pay * * *". Or upon the failure of the maker to perform some collateral undertaking, such as one to pay taxes on real estate securing the note, or to furnish additional collateral when required.

The most frequent basis for acceleration, of course, is the failure of the maker to make payment of interest or installments of principal as specified in the note. On the other hand, the U.C.C. also sanctions the inclusion in a negotiable note with a fixed payment date of a provision such as:

"Should the holder of this note deem himself insecure, he may demand payment at any time and this note shall thereupon become immediately due and payable."

Such a term, authorizing acceleration at the holder's option would appear to be subject to abuse, but the U.C.C. regards this as a matter related to good faith rather than to negotiability. Thus, Section 1–208 provides:

A term providing that one party or his successor in interest may accelerate payment or performance or require collateral or additional collateral "at will" or "when he deems himself insecure" or in words of similar import shall be construed to mean that he shall have power to do so only if he in good faith believes that the prospect of payment or performance is impaired. The burden of establishing lack of good faith is on the party against whom the power has been exercised.

Consequently, the danger of a capricious exercise of such power of acceleration is minimized.

(5) *At a Definite Time, Subject to Extension.* A similar provision permitting an

acceptor of a draft to extend the payment date to a further definite time is also unexceptionable. Extension clauses, it will be observed with little reflection, are simply the other side of the acceleration-clause coin. Thus a maker may make a note payable in one year, but with the right to pay it after six months. The same transaction might take the form of the note being made payable in six months, with the maker given the right to extend it to one year. The first situation involves acceleration; the second involves extension. They are treated the same, and neither impairs negotiability.

Of course if the maker is given an option to extend the note for an indefinite period of time, his promise is illusory and there is no certainty of time of payment. Such a note is clearly non-negotiable. If, however, the maker's right to extend is limited to a further definite time, the extension clause is no more objectionable than an acceleration clause, which, of course, has an outside time limit. Hence, extension clauses which are so limited do not impair negotiability. Section 3–109(1) (d).

No time limit is needed when the extension is at the option of the holder. A holder can in effect extend any obligation by mere inaction, and consequently an extension clause gives him no rights, except that it permits him to extend and still hold secondary parties liable. In this regard, however, he is limited by Section 3–118(f) which provides:

> Unless otherwise specified consent to extension authorizes a single extension for not longer than the original period. A consent to extension, expressed in the instrument, is binding on secondary parties and accommodation makers. A holder may not exercise his option to extend an instrument over the objection of a maker or acceptor or other party who in accordance with Section 3–604 tenders full payment when the instrument is due.

The last sentence of the section prohibits a holder from extending a "good" note (so as to collect interest) if the maker is insistent that it be paid at its initial maturity date. Neither this matter, nor the matter of releasing secondary parties, goes to the problem of negotiability, and the extension clause, under the U.C.C., whatever its other limitations, does not adversely affect the negotiability of the instrument containing it.

Finally, extension may be made automatic upon or after a specified act or event, provided a definite time limit is stated. An example of such an extension clause is, "I promise to pay to the order of John Doe the sum of $2,000 on December 1, 1967, but it is agreed that if the crop of sections 25 and 26 of Twp. 145 is below eight bushels per acre for the 1967 season, this note shall be extended for one year." (State Bank of Halsted v. Bilstad, 162 Iowa 433, 136 N.W. 204 (1912).)

(6) *An Instrument Payable Only upon an Act or Event Uncertain as to Time of Occurrence is Not Payable at a Definite Time.* If an instrument provided: "Upon the sale of my house, I promise to pay * * *" a holder would have no certainty as to whether it would ever become payable. If it provided: "Six weeks after the death of my Uncle George Doe, I promise to pay * * *" the holder would be sure that the note would become payable, but the time when payment would be due could not be ascertained with sufficient accuracy.

Hence, both instruments are denied negotiability by the U.C.C. as not payable at a definite time, despite the fact that they constitute valid obligations of the maker within the time limitations indicated. Since it is also necessary that the negotiability of an instrument be determinable from its face, the fact that the act or event specified has occurred will not confer negotiability upon an instrument tainted with this fault at the outset.

Notes designed to anticipate an inheritance by being payable at a stated period after the death of a relative are not the type of instrument normally used in business transactions, and denying them negotiability does not adversely affect commerce. It is interesting to note, however, that it would appear possible to circumvent the limitations of this provision of the U.C.C. by use of an authorized acceleration clause. Thus, if the instrument were drawn, "I promise to pay 100 years from date, but payment shall be accelerated by the death of my Uncle George Doe to a point of time six months after his death," it would seem that the time would be certain enough to satisfy the requirements of the Code. This matter, however, has not been settled definitely.

8. *The Instrument Must be Payable to Order or to Bearer.* A negotiable instrument must contain words indicating that the maker or drawer intends that it may pass into the hands of someone other than the person to whom it was originally issued. This requires language clearly providing either that it will be paid to such party as the person to whom it was issued may direct or order, or that it will be paid to any person who presents it for payment—i. e., the bearer. The "magic words" are thus "to the order of" or "to bearer," but other words which are clearly equivalent to these may be regarded as fulfilling this requirement. In the case of doubt of equivalence, however, the decision may well be against negotiability. The use of synonyms only invites trouble.

(a) When an Instrument is Payable to Order. Section 3–110 clarifies the meaning of "payable to order." In addition to the eminently correct "Pay to the order of John Jones," the maker or drawer may state: "Pay to John Jones or his order;" or "Pay to John Jones or his assigns." Furthermore, the U.C.C. specifically provides that this requirement is met by a conspicuous designation of an instrument on its face as "exchange" or the like, so long as it names a payor. Presumably, then, a conspicuous provision on the face of an instrument "This note is negotiable" would satisfy the requirement that it be payable to order. On the other hand, a statement frequently found on certificates of deposit: "payable upon return of this instrument properly indorsed" does not render it payable to order. It means merely that the maker or drawee is entitled to have the payment of the instrument receipted by indorsement.

Interestingly enough, an indorsement reading merely "Pay John Jones" or even "Pay John Jones only" has the effect of making the instrument payable to the order of John Jones. Section 3–206(1). Such an indorsement leaves the instrument fully negotiable thereafter, and the formal requirements imposed with respect to the body of the instrument itself do not apply.

In every instance, the person to whose order the instrument is to be payable must be designated with reasonable certainty. Within this limitation, a broad range of payees is possible. It may be payable to the order of:

(1) The maker or drawer, in which case he will have to indorse it to negotiate it;

(2) The drawee, who will then pay himself, presumably by transfer from the drawer's account with this drawee to the drawee's own individual account;

(3) Two or more payees, and if they are named in the alternative, it is payable to any one of them and may be negotiated, discharged or enforced by any of them who has possession of it, but if they are not named in the alternative, it is payable only to all of them and may be negotiated, discharged or enforced only by all of them (Section 3–116);

(4) An office, such as "The Swedish Consulate";

(5) A named person with the addition of words describing him as an agent or officer, by his title such as "Treasurer

of the City Club," or "County Collector of Cook County", in either of which cases the instrument is payable to his principal, but the agent or officer named, or the incumbent of the office, when unnamed, may act as if he were the holder (Section 3–117);

(6) A named person with the addition of words describing him as a fiduciary (other than an officer or agent) for a specified person or purpose, in which case the instrument is payable to him and may be negotiated, discharged or enforced by him, but he remains liable for any breach of his obligation as a fiduciary, and a holder who takes with knowledge of such a breach is not a holder in due course (Section 3–117);

(7) An estate, trust or fund, even though not a legal entity; it is deemed to be payable to the representative thereof, such as the executor, trustee or administrator or his successors;

(8) A partnership or unincorporated association, in which case it is payable to the partnership or association and may be indorsed or transferred by any person thereto authorized;

(9) A named person with the addition of words describing him in any manner other than as a fiduciary for a specified person or purpose such as "John Doe, Attorney" or "Richard Roe, President", in which case the additional words are of no effect on subsequent parties. Section 3–117.

(b) *When an Instrument is Payable to Bearer.* Section 3–111 states that an instrument fulfills the requirements of being payable to bearer if it is payable,

(1) to bearer;

(2) to the order of bearer, a phraseology which usually results from filling the word "bearer" in a printed form designed to be payable to order;

(3) to the order of a specified person or "bearer";

(4) to "cash" or to the order of "cash" or any other indication which does not purport to designate a specific payee, such as "Pay bills payable" or "Pay to the order of one keg of nails."

It should be noted, however, that Section 3–110(3) provides that an instrument made payable to order and to bearer is payable to order unless the bearer words are handwritten or typewritten. This Section is primarily designed to cover the situation where a drawer has filled in a payee's name on a printed form without noticing it is payable to bearer.

9. *Interpretation of Instruments.* Frequently the negotiability of an instrument will be questioned because of the omission of certain provisions or other peculiarities. Problems also arise in connection with interpretation of instruments whether or not negotiability is called into question. The U.C.C. undertakes to provide specific answers covering some of the more frequently encountered matters of this sort.

(a) *Absence of a Statement of Consideration.* Just as consideration is required to support a contract at common law, so is it necessary for the creation of a negotiable instrument which would be enforceable in the hands of any holder. Section 3–408 provides that want or failure of consideration is a defense, although through the magic of negotiability, such defense is cut off as against a person with the rights of a holder in due course. An exception to the requirement of consideration is made in favor of an instrument given in payment of or as security for any debt already owed by the party giving it or by a third person. In particular it should be noted that this would permit the giving of an instrument in satisfaction of a liquidated obligation of a greater amount. Without more, these exceptions would not constitute consideration at common law.

It is not necessary, however, that an instrument contain a statement of the consideration supporting it, and Section 3–112(1) (a) provides that the omission of such a statement does not affect negotiability. The giving of consideration is presumed, and want or failure thereof must be raised as an affirmative defense by the person obligated. If the holder proves he is a holder in due course, however, the defense cannot prevail. If he is not, it then becomes incumbent upon him to prove that consideration was given through the introduction of affirmative evidence.

(b) *Absence of Statement of Where the Instrument is Drawn or Payable.* To determine what law will control on questions related to the issuance and form of an instrument, the place of issue must be known. To determine the law applicable to matters of payment, the place of payment must be known. But the omission of a statement of either of these on the face of the instrument will not affect its negotiability. Section 3–112(1) (a). These matters may be shown by other evidence. But if a place is stated, it is conclusive in favor of a holder in due course, irrespective of the facts.

(c) *Sealed Instruments.* The fact that an instrument is under seal has no effect on its negotiability, whatever other effect the seal might have under common law. Section 3–113.

(d) *The Dating of the Instrument.* The negotiability of an instrument is not affected by the fact that it is undated, antedated or postdated. (Section 3–114.)

If the instrument is antedated, that is, carries a date prior to its actual issue, the stated date controls. Hence if it is dated October 1, 1966, payable thirty days after date, and is issued on November 1, 1966, it is due and payable the day before its issue. This would prevent anyone from becoming a holder in due course (Section 3–302(1) (c)), because it could not be negotiated before maturity, and it would deprive any indorser of the right to require presentment, notice of dishonor or protest before he could be held liable on the instrument. Section 3–501(4).

If the instrument is postdated, that is, carries a date later than the date on which it was issued, again the date stated is conclusive. A demand instrument is thus converted into a time instrument, for demand is not proper prior to the date of issue. In this fashion, a postdated check is a time instrument, for payment by the bank on which it is drawn will not be made until the date shown. Similarly, a time instrument, payable thirty days from date may be made payable sixty days from date of issue through the medium of postdating.

The undated instrument, particularly one payable at a fixed time "after date" is uncertain as to time of payment, and therefore is non-negotiable. But since it is an incomplete instrument, its completion is governed by the rules considered immediately below.

(e) *The Incomplete Instrument.* On occasion, a party will sign a paper, the contents of which show that it is intended to become an instrument, but which, either by intention or through oversight, is incomplete in some necessary respect, such as the promise or order, the designation of the payee, the amount payable or the time of payment. Section 3–115 makes such a paper unenforceable until it has been completed. If it is completed in accordance with authority given, it is effective as completed. If it is completed without authorization, the unauthorized completion is a defense against anyone except a holder in due course who may enforce the instrument as completed. Section 3–407(3).

If an undated instrument is issued on November 1, 1966, payable "thirty days after date," the person to whom it is issued has an implied authority to fill in "November 1, 1966." Until he does so, however, the instrument is not negotiable because it is not payable at a definite time. In the event he fills in "October 1, 1966," the instrument appears to be immediately due and payable. Since completion in this fashion was not authorized, however, he cannot enforce it as though issued on October 1, 1966, if the maker or drawer can sustain the burden of establishing the improper completion.

If a thief steals a signed check on which both the amount and the payee are blank, and fills in his own name and any amount he sees fit, the check is enforceable in the hands of a holder in due course to whom the thief may have negotiated it. This result is equitable, since it is the general policy of the law to impose a loss which one of two innocent parties must sustain upon the party whose negligence contributed to such loss. Certainly the drawer was guilty of negligence in leaving a signed, incomplete instrument where it could fall into improper hands.

Even if the holder in due course knew that the instrument was incomplete, and perhaps watched his transferor complete it, he may enforce the instrument as completed unless he had reason to know that the completion was unauthorized. The fact that the instrument was incomplete does not raise any presumption, in and of itself, that a completion is unauthorized.

(f) *The Ambiguous Instrument.* Rather than commit the parties to the use of parol evidence to establish the interpretation of an instrument, Section 3–118 of the U.C.C. establishes fixed rules to resolve some common ambiguities. This tends to promote negotiability by providing a degree of certainty to the holder which would otherwise be lacking.

Where there is doubt whether the instrument is a draft or a note, the holder may

treat it as either and present it for payment to the drawee or the person signing it. A draft drawn on the drawer is, of course, effective as a note. For example, an instrument reading

> "To X: On demand I promise to pay $50 to the order of Y
>
> "/s/Z"

may be presented for payment to X as a draft or to Z as a note. On the other hand, an instrument which named no drawee, but states:

> "On demand, please pay $50 to the order of Y
>
> "/s/Z"

would be in the form of a draft, but would be treated as a note and presented to Z for payment.

Instruments are frequently drawn by filling in printed forms by typewriter, by handwriting, or by both. Since in using a pre-prepared form, some elements of the text may go unnoticed and be contradicted by the material filled in, the rule is that handwritten terms control typewritten and printed terms, and typewritten control printed. Thus, if a printed note provides for interest at 4 per cent in the text, but at the bottom there appears in handwriting, "Interest at 6 per cent," the note will bear interest at the latter rate.

Another frequent area of conflict is between the words and figures on an instrument. The words may show "One Hundred Dollars," whereas the figures may show "$10.00" or "$1,000." In such event, the words will control, since it is conclusively presumed that the maker or drawer would have been more conscious of what he was doing when he wrote the words. On the other hand, if the instrument read "Three Sixty Five Dollars" in words and "$365" or "$3.65" in figures, the figures control because of the rule that figures control if the words are ambiguous. If both the words and figures are ambiguous, no rules can help, and the parties must be put to their proof.

Another matter which may require interpretation is the rate of interest on an instrument which merely specifies that it is "payable with interest." The parties may always by specific provision fix the interest at any rate, or combination of rates before and after maturity permissible under applicable State law, or by omission of any such term cause the instrument to be non interest bearing until maturity. Where the ambiguous term, "payable with interest" appears, without more, the rule is that interest at the judgment rate at the place of payment runs from the date of the instrument or, if it is undated, from the date of its issue.

A problem of interpretation may arise where an instrument phrased in the singular is signed by two or more persons as part of the same transaction. For example, a note may read "I promise to pay * * *" and be signed by two makers. Such signatures may also be in the capacity of drawer, acceptor or indorser. In any such event, the parties are jointly and severally liable in the capacity in which they signed.

A problem of ambiguity may also arise in the interpretation of the capacity in which an individual signed an instrument. Normally, the capacity in which an individual signs is clear: If John Doe signs "I, John Doe, promise to pay * * *" he is signing only as the maker. If he signs "John Doe, witness" he has no liability. Where a drawee signs in an unusual place, and if no other reason for his signing is determinable from the instrument, it is logical to assume he is signing as an acceptor. A signature in the lower right hand corner, by custom and usage, is deemed to be that of the maker or drawer. But occasionally a signature will not indicate in any way the obligation of the signatory. Section 3–402 covers this situation by providing that any signature not clearly made in another capacity is an indorsement.

CASES

HAGGARD v. MUTUAL OIL & REFINING CO.

(1924) 204 Ky. 209, 263 S.W. 745.

[Action by Rodney Haggard against Mutual Oil & Refining Company. Judgment for defendant, and plaintiff appeals.]

CLARKE, J. The single question presented by this appeal is whether or not the following check is a negotiable instrument:

"$2,500.00. Winchester, Ky., July 10, 1920.

"The Winchester Bank, of Winchester, Ky.: Pay to Arco Refinery Construction Company twenty-five hundred and no/100 dollars, for a/c constructing refinery, switch, and loading racks, Win. Ky.

"Mutual Oil & Refining Co.,
"By C. L. Bell, Pres."

Subdivision 4 of section 3720b, which is the Negotiable Instruments Act [citation], § 1, provides that:

"An instrument to be negotiable must conform to the following requirements: * * * (4) Must be payable to the order of a specified person or to bearer."

Since, as the check itself shows, and as is admittedly true, the maker, in issuing the check, drew a line through the printed words "or bearer," we need only to examine it to ascertain whether or not it was "payable to the order of a specified person," for unless so, it lacked one of the essentials prescribed for negotiability.

Section 8 of the act [citation] defines when an instrument is payable to order as follows:

"The instrument is payable to order where it is drawn payable to the order of a specified person or to him or his order."

It will be noticed that the above check is not payable to the order of the payee, nor to the payee or its order, but is payable simply to the payee. It therefore seems to us too clear for dispute that this check is not payable to order, and is therefore, as the lower court held, not negotiable.

In other words, we think it is clear that subsection 8 means, as it says, that the instrument must be payable either (1) to the order of the payee, or (2) to the payee or order, and that it does not permit of the construction that the instrument may be payable (1) to the order of the payee, (2) or to the payee, or (3) to his order.

To give the section the latter of these two constructions rather than the former makes the first and third alternatives identical, and this plainly was never intended. Not only is this conclusion unavoidable from a consideration simply of the language of the section, but it has uniformly been so construed by this and other courts. [Citations.]

In England and Canada the rule is otherwise, but this is due to the fact that the Bills of Exchange Act expressly provides that a bill or note is payable to order where expressed to be payable to a particular person and not containing words prohibiting transfer or indicating an intention that it should not be transferable. [Citation.]

Counsel for appellant concede that this section has been construed by this court and others in the above cases to require the use of the words "order or bearer" or other words of similar legal import in order to make a note or other bill negotiable, but they insist that there is such a material difference between a note and a check as that these cases are not applicable to one in which, as here, the bill is a check.

But in this they are clearly mistaken. Section 185 of the act [citation], expressly declares that a check is a bill of exchange payable on demand, and that, except as otherwise therein provided, the provisions of the act applicable to a bill of exchange payable on demand shall apply to a check, and, as it is not otherwise therein provided, it is clear that sections 1 and 8 of the act apply to a check as well as to any other bill of exchange, and to be negotiable it also must employ some such words as "order" or "bearer" indicating negotiability.

It results, therefore, that a check, just as any other bill of exchange that is made payable simply to the payee and not to his order or to bearer, is not negotiable, and that appellant, to whom this check was assigned by the payee, took same subject to all defenses which were available between the original parties.

The lower court therefore did not err in overruling appellant's demurrer to appellee's answer pleading want of consideration, etc., or in dismissing his petition upon his refusal to reply thereto.

Judgment affirmed.

D'ANDREA v. FEINBERG

(1965) 45 Misc.2d 270, 256 N.Y.S.2d 504.

DILLON, J. The plaintiffs as holders in due course of a promissory note in the face amount of $4,000. have moved for summary judgment under CPLR 3213. The maker of the note is Sain Builders, Inc. and the note is executed on behalf of the maker by Samuel Feinberg as President. The note is endorsed by Samuel Feinberg in his capacity as President of the corporation and individually. The action was commenced against the corporation and against Samuel Feinberg individually. The note was duly presented for payment, was dishonored and protested. The corporate defendant is involved in bankruptcy proceedings in the Federal District Court and in connection therewith an order has been signed staying all actions against it until a final decree has been entered in the bankruptcy proceedings. Accordingly, the motion for summary judgment as against the corporation is denied.

On behalf of the individual defendant, it is urged that plaintiffs are not holders in due course because at the time they acquired the note they were aware of the existence of a contract between the corporate defendant and the payee of the note. This fact cannot be disputed because the note itself has endorsed thereon, in the lower left hand corner the legend "as per contract." It is argued that the endorser should not be held liable on the note until such time as the primary obligation between the maker and the payee has been resolved. The court is thus faced with two questions: (1) whether the note is a negotiable instrument; and (2) whether the plaintiffs are holders in due course.

The note meets all the requirements of section 3–104 of the U.C.C. with the possible exception that it does not contain an unconditional promise because of the legend "as per contract." Section 3–105(1) (c) expressly states that an unconditional promise "is not made conditional by the fact that the instrument * * * (c) refers to or states that it arises out of a separate agreement or refers to a separate agreement for rights as to prepayment or acceleration."

The official comment on the above quoted provision [citation] is that it was "intended to resolve a conflict, and to reject cases in which a reference to a separate agreement was held to mean that payment of the instrument must be limited in accordance with the terms of the agreement, and hence was conditioned by it." The court is satisfied that the legend "as per contract" does not affect the negotiability of an instrument as would a statement that the instrument "is subject to or governed by any other agreement" (Uniform Commercial Code, Sec. 3–105(2) (a); [citation].

The court determines that the note being sued upon is a negotiable instrument and that the plaintiffs are holders in due course. Since a cause of action against "an indorser of any

instrument accrues upon demand following dishonor of the instrument," (Uniform Commercial Code, Sec. 3–122(3) it is clear that the plaintiffs need not first recover judgment against the maker as the individual defendant urges.

Accordingly, the action is severed and plaintiffs are awarded summary judgment as prayed for against the individual defendant.

UNITED STATES v. FARRINGTON

(1959 U.S.D.C.Mass.) 172 F.Supp. 797.

ALDRICH, D. J. This is an action for the balance due on two promissory notes of which the maker, Davis Aircraft Engineering, Inc., is in bankruptcy and substantially in default. The transactions were entered into in Massachusetts. Most of the facts were stipulated, and I find in accordance with the stipulation. Certain oral evidence was offered, which I will deal with subsequently. The payee was a bank. On the face of each note, which was on a printed form, appeared the following, the italicized portions being in ink and inserted between the printing, in lined, blank spaces provided therefor:

"* * * having deposited with this obligation as Collateral Security, * * *

Assigned Government Contracts

This note evidences a borrowing made under and is subject to the terms of loan agreement dated Jan. 3, 1952 between the undersigned and the payee thereof and should the market value of the same, in the judgment of the holder or holders hereof, decline, *we* promise to furnish satisfactory additional collateral on demand * * *."

On the back of the notes, over their typed names but without any other writing, are the signatures of Davis, one Atkinson, and the defendant. By restrictive endorsements of the payee, under these signatures, the notes became payable to the plaintiff, a holder for value.

The loan agreement established a revolving credit arrangement for the benefit of Davis Aircraft. It also contained a number of protective provisions and recited the borrower's various obligations with respect to security, one of the paragraphs being the following:

"V., 3. All borrowings under this credit are to be personally endorsed or guaranteed by Daniel E. Davis, Donald T. Atkinson and Phillips Farrington."

Davis and Atkinson, but not Farrington, signed this agreement on behalf of the company. Reference was made in the loan agreement to a "Guarantee Agreement" between the bank and the Department of the Army, "annexed hereto and made a part hereof * * *." This agreement on its first page contained the following typewritten words as part of a description of "the terms and conditions" of the loan being guaranteed: "The loan shall be personally endorsed or guaranteed by Daniel E. Davis, Donald T. Atkinson and Phillips Farrington."

There is no evidence that either the payee or the plaintiff had any notice of any infirmity in the instruments, and with the exception of the oral evidence about to be referred to there is no claim of infirmity. The defendant testified that in 1950 he was a young man just out of college, with some inherited money, but no experience; that he obtained employment with Davis Aircraft Engineering, Inc., and was "given an opportunity," of which he availed himself, of acquiring most of the preferred stock of the company; that all the common stock was held equally by Davis and Atkinson; that beginning in January, 1952 he was put in charge of personnel, and at or about this time heard talk that the company was obtaining substantial loans in connection with some government contracts; that through the winter and spring of 1952 Davis presented to him a series of promissory notes, of which those in suit are two, and asked him to sign on the

back thereof, which in each instance he did; that at the time Davis made the first request, which apparently did not involve either of the notes being sued upon, he asked Davis why his signature was wanted; and was told that it was in connection with a loan and the only reason for signing was that the payee bank wanted assurance that the stockholders of the company knew "what was transpiring"; that nothing was ever stated with relation to his incurring obligations as a result of his signature, and that he did not intend to incur any. With respect to the recitation in the loan agrement which would have contradicted what Davis allegedly told defendant, the defendant stated that he never saw the loan agreement or the guarantee agreement, and had no knowledge of what was in them.

While it is difficult to credit such a state of business naivete, the circumstances of the defendant's original investment in this company tend to confirm it, and I accept his story. The plaintiff had a chance to ask Davis to deny its accuracy and did not do so. Also, the fact that Davis and Atkinson signed these instruments themselves, and their size, would have tended to corroborate Davis' explanation. It is perhaps easier to think that the defendant believed what Davis is said to have told him than to believe that he intentionally incurred these additional obligations, very many times greater than his original investment.

If these notes were negotiable there is no defense; the defendant is liable as an endorser. [Citations.] He contends that they were not negotiable because making the obligation subject to the terms of the loan agreement caused it to lack "certainty." Mass.G.L. c. 107, § 23(2),* provides that for an instrument to be negotiable it "Must * * contain an unconditional promise or order to pay a sum certain in money." Defendant

* Now M.G.L.A. c. 106 § 3–104(1).

does not and cannot point to anything in the loan agreement which would have, in fact, imposed any contingency upon the obligation had the terms of the loan agreement been included on the face of the note itself. [Citation.] His position is that as a matter of law an instrument is conditional if it incorporates by reference a separate document making it impossible to know whether the obligation is certain or not until that document is examined. The Massachusetts cases upon which defendant relies, with the possible exception of Costelo v. Crowell, 127 Mass. 293, all involved separate agreements that in fact imposed contingencies when read into the instrument. Whether the instrument becomes non-negotiable because on its face it is subject to an agreement which may impose contingencies even though in actual fact it does not, is quite a different matter, leading to policy questions of large compass. Although this precise question is often left undiscussed by the cases, [citation] there is a considerable body of authority to the effect that if the instrument contains the phrase, "subject to" the terms of another document, or words to that effect, the reference is fatal to negotiability regardless of the actual provisions of the other document. [Citations.]

*   *   *3

In the case at bar it could be argued from the placement of the handwritten words that the note was described as subject to the loan agreement for the purpose of indicating the circumstances under which it was executed, and setting forth more fully the undertaking with respect to collateral security, and not in order to limit the promise to pay. However, I believe this is not the only and necessary interpretation, and that the am-

biguity can be resolved only by examination of the loan agreement. It is true that inspection of this agreement will resolve the ambiguity in favor of the plaintiff, but I rule that that is not enough to make the instrument negotiable.

*   *   *

It is not open to the defendant to claim that he was defrauded by Davis. As against an innocent third party, either the payee or the plaintiff, he must be ruled to have acted too negligently to permit him to use such fraud as a shield. The defendant admitted that he knew that loans to the Company were being arranged, that he "probably did know" that the instruments he was signing were notes, and that he was being asked to indicate his knowledge as a stockholder of "what was transpiring." He must be charged with knowledge that his signature had all the appearance of being an endorsement or subjecting him to liability in some manner, or at the least was capable of being so construed. [Citations.] It would be expected for the bank to assume a knowledge of the loan agreement on his part as it was an integrated part of the transaction with which he understood the bank wanted him to be acquainted. Since at the least the loan agreement resolves an ambiguity for which defendant must be charged, I rule under the circumstances that he is liable on the instrument even though it is not negotiable.

The amounts due have been stipulated.

Judgment is ordered for plaintiff in the amount of $350,683.35.

ROSE CHECK CASHING SERVICE v. CHEMICAL BANK N.Y. TRUST CO.

(1964) 43 Misc.2d 679, 252 N.Y.S.2d 100.

HOFSTADTER, J. A comparatively recently introduced banking service—designated a "Personal Money Order"—is the subject of

---

3. Such would also seem to be the meaning of the Uniform Commercial Code, Mass.G.L.A. c. 106, § 3–105(2) (a). See Massachusetts Commercial Code Comment (appearing in M.G.L.A.) and particularly the Uniform Commercial Code Comment No. 8, stating that "an instrument is not negotiable unless the holder can ascertain all of its essential terms upon its face."

this appeal. Except for a single 1963 case, also decided in the Civil Court [citation], the legal issues are novel.

The facts were stipulated in the court below. The decision of Judge Baer, who heard the case without a jury, is included in a carefully written extended opinion.

The instrument in suit, prepared by defendant and bearing its name and address and impressed bank seal, contains, in four places, the words "Personal Money Order." It is dated November 21, 1962. Its printed serial number is that of the bank. The form provides that it is "Not valid Over $250.00." By check writing machine, defendant inserted the amount for which it was issued, namely $40.00. Otherwise blank, it was then issued to one James L. Witzelberger in exchange for a check in like amount drawn on his special checking account in another of defendant's branches plus a nominal fee. The instrument made provision for insertion of the name of a payee on a line prefixed with the words "Pay to the order of" and for the subscription of the signature and address of the purchaser.

Witzelberger completed the instrument by making it payable to "Cash", subscribed his name and address, and cashed it with plaintiff, a licensed check cashing corporation. When presented by plaintiff to the bank, it was not paid—and was stamped "Payment stopped by the bank"—because there were insufficient funds in Witzelberger's special checking account to meet the check he had delivered to defendant.

We are called upon, then, to fix this new form into the law merchant and the Negotiable Instruments Law—to ascertain the intent of the bank when issuing it—to declare its character—to find who, between the parties, must in law bear the loss.

* * *

The instrument before this Court is not a check drawn on a regular or special checking account, where continuity is a factor and an account designated to the depositor is opened in each case.

Rather it is akin to a cashier's check or a traveler's check drawn by the issuing bank upon itself.

"A cashier's check is a check of the bank's cashier on his or another bank. It is in effect a bill of exchange drawn by a bank on itself, and accepted in advance by the act of its issuance; and in substance is an order or direction to the bank to pay the payee from its funds, a written promise of the issuing bank to pay on demand. It is not a receipt, but is a negotiable instrument." (10 C.J.S. Bills and Notes § 5, pp. 409–410)

* * *

"Traveler's checks, intended to be signed by the purchaser in the seller's presence at the time of sale are essentially cashier's checks in the nature of bills of exchange drawn by the issuing bank upon itself." (10 C.J.S. Bills and Notes § 5, p. 410)

* * *

Differences in detail there are—but essentially the intent here is the same.

The Appellate Division of this Department has said (Matter of Bank of United States, 243 App.Div. 287, 291, 277 N.Y.S. 96):

"A cashier's check issued by a bank * * is not an ordinary draft. * * * It is the primary obligation of the bank which issues it [citation] and constitutes its written promise to pay upon demand [citation]. It has been said that a cashier's check is a bill of exchange drawn by a bank upon itself, accepted in advance by the very act of issuance. (citing cases) Such being the nature of the obligation which was accepted in exchange for the claimant's check, it seems clear to us that it created an unconditional credit in favor of the National City Bank which was reflected by appropriate entries on the books of the Bank of United States. (citing case) The Bank of United States remained the debtor, and the only debtor, to the holder of its cashier's check for the amount of the deposit."

If the instrument is ambiguous, it may be treated by plaintiff as a note. [Citation.]

In Legniti v. Mechanics & Metals Nat. Bank, 230 N.Y. 415, pp. 419–420, 130 N.E. 597, 16 A.L.R. 185, Judge Crane, thereafter Chief Judge, observed:

"It has long been an established custom among banks and financial institutions to sell credit usually represented by draft or check. * * * The draft is a direction to pay. It is not, itself, money or credit. It is simply used as such. The money paid the bank by the purchaser of the draft becomes the bank's money. The transaction is that of purchase and sale. No trust relationship is established.

" * * * The thing sold is the same in the case of the cable or wireless transaction as in the case of the draft or check. It is the credit of the bank or seller. The means of establishing or transmitting the credit is simply an incident of the transaction."

So also in the case before us. For a consideration accepted as adequate by defendant, Witzelberger purchased the credit of the bank [citations]. The means of establishing or transmitting that credit was the "Personal Money Order" issued by the bank. As between the bank and plaintiff, it was, in legal effect, the same as a certificate of deposit or certified check [citations]. Once issued to the purchaser, it was no longer revocable by the bank [citation].

Under long settled rules, Witzelberger was authorized to fill in the blanks in the money order [citations]. In form negotiable, defenses otherwise available against Witzelberger, may not be asserted against plaintiff, a holder in due course [citation].

The argument is of the amicus that the instrument is a check merely because it does not bear the written signature of the bank is without merit. The authenticity of the instrument is not questioned; and the printed name of the bank verified by its seal impressed at the time of the sale is sufficient to evidence the bank's intent to be bound thereunder.

The judgment is affirmed, with $25 costs.

FERRI v. SYLVIA

(1965) — R.I. —, 214 A.2d 470.

JOSLIN, J. This action of assumpsit based upon a promissory note was tried before a justice of the superior court sitting without a jury and resulted in a decision for the plaintiff of $2,600. The defendants prosecute their exceptions to evidentiary rulings and to the decision.

The note, which is dated May 25, 1963, obligates defendants to pay to plaintiff or her order $3,000 "within ten (10) years after date." The trial justice determined that the maturity of the note was uncertain, admitted testimony of the parties as to both their intentions and prior agreements, and premised upon such extrinsic evidence found that plaintiff "could have the balance that may be due at any time she needed it and that she could call for and demand the full payment of any balance that may be due or owing her at the time of her demand."

The question is whether the note is payable at a fixed or determinable future time. If the phrase "within ten (10) years after date" lacks explicitness or is ambiguous then clearly parol evidence was admissible for the purpose of ascertaining the intention of the parties. [Citations.] Moreover, if it was apparent from an inspection of the note that it did not include the entire agreement of the parties then it was permissible to accept extrinsic evidence of their prior agreements relative to its due date in supplementation and explanation of the writing; provided, however, that the collateral terms were consistent therewith and such as would normally have been excluded by the parties from the note. [Citations.] While the trial justice in admitting and accepting the extrinsic evidence apparently relied on these principles, neither is applicable because the payment provisions of the note are not uncertain nor are they incomplete.

At the law merchant it was generally settled that a promissory note or a bill of exchange payable "on or before" a specified date fixed with certainty the time of payment. [Citations.] The same rule has been fixed by statute first under the negotiable instruments law, G.L.1956, § 6–18–10, subd. 2, and now pursuant to the uniform commercial code. The code in § 6A–3–109(1) reads as follows: "An instrument is payable at a definite time if by its terms it is payable (a) on or before a stated date or at a fixed period after a stated date * * *."

The courts in the cases we cite were primarily concerned with whether a provision for payment "on or before" a specified date impaired the negotiability of an instrument. Collaterally, of course, they necessarily considered whether such an instrument was payable at a fixed or determinable future time for unless it was, an essential prerequisite to negotiability was lacking.

They said that the legal rights of the holder of an "on or before" instrument were clearly fixed and entitled him to payment upon an event that was certain to come, even though the maker might be privileged to pay sooner if he so elected. They held, therefore, that the due date of such an instrument was fixed with certainty and that its negotiability was unaffected by the privilege given the maker to accelerate payment. Professor Chafee referred to it as providing "the simplest form of acceleration provision," 32 Harv.L.Rev. 747, 757, and Judge Cooley in Mattison v. Marks, 31 Mich. 421, observing that notes of this kind were common in commercial transactions, said 31 Mich. at page 423:

"It seems to us that this note is payable at a time certain. It is payable certainly, and at all events, on a day particularly named; and at that time, and not before, payment might be enforced against the maker. * * * The legal rights of the holder are clear and certain; the note is due at a time fixed, and it is not due before. True, the maker may pay sooner if he shall choose, but this option, if exercised, would be a payment in advance of the legal liability to pay, and nothing more."

On principle no valid distinction can be drawn between an instrument payable "on or before" a fixed date and one which calls for payment "within" a stipulated period. This was the holding in Leader v. Plante, 95 Me. 339, where the court said at page 341, 50 A. 54:

" 'Within' a certain period, 'or or before' a day named and 'at or before' a certain day, are equivalent terms, and the rules of construction apply to each alike."

See also General Mortgage & Loan Corp. v. Dickey, 274 Mass. 207, 174 N.E. 176, where the note provided that "said principal sum shall be paid in or within in the following manner * * *."

We follow the lead of the Maine court and equate the word "within" with the phrase "on or before." So construed it fixes both the beginning and the end of a period, and insofar as it means the former it is applicable to the right of a maker to prepay, and insofar as it means the latter it is referable to the date the instrument matures. We hold that the payment provision of a negotiable instrument payable "within" a stated period is certain as well as complete on its face and that such an instrument does not mature until the time fixed arrives.

For the foregoing reasons it is clear that the parties unequivocally agreed that the plaintiff could not demand payment of the note until the expiration of the ten-year period. It is likewise clear that any prior or contemporaneous oral agreements of the parties relevant to its due date were so merged and integrated with the writing as to prevent its being explained or supplemented by parol evidence. [Citations.]

The defendants' exception to the trial justice's decision is sustained, and on November 29, 1965 the plaintiff may appear in this court to show cause, if any she has, why the case should not be remitted to the superior court with direction to enter judgment for the defendants.

RESERVE PLAN, INC. v. SCHLEIDER

(1955) 208 Misc. 805, 145 N.Y.S.2d 122.

BENNETT, J. It appears that the action was brought to recover the unpaid balance of an alleged promissory note. The plaintiff contends that it is a holder for value in due course and that as such the defenses of general denial, breach of warranty and breach of agreement are not available against it. The instrument on which the action is predicated was executed by the defendant on May 5, 1954 and was given to secure payment for dental work to be performed by the payee. These payments were to be made in monthly installments of $20 each beginning June 5, 1954 for a total sum of $480. Two days after the execution of said instrument the same was negotiated to the plaintiff.

The defendant contends that the payee did not perform his agreement and that he still is in serious need of dental care which the payee has neglected and refused to furnish him; that he was not informed that the instrument he signed was a negotiable document but only a contract for installment payments.

The question arises as to whether the agreement is in fact a negotiable instrument. If it is then the defenses asserted would not be available against this plaintiff. However, if the instrument does not conform to the requirements of the Negotiable Instruments

Law of the State of New York, such defenses may be asserted against the present holder.

Section 20 of the said Negotiable Instruments Law provides in subdivision 2 thereof as follows: "Must contain an unconditional promise or order to pay a sum certain in money", in setting forth the elements of a promissory note.

Examination of the instrument in suit discloses that the same contains this proviso, "In case of death of maker all payments not due at date of death are cancelled". Can it then be said that the form of the instrument sets forth an unconditional promise to pay a sum certain? It appears to this Court that such essential element is definitely lacking.

* * *

It is obvious * * * that the document herein does not meet the required standards * * * for although the sum specified as payable is stated to be $480, such payment would be contingent on the maker continuing to live during the twenty-four months during which the installments were payable. By the terms of the said agreement, the contingency was always present during the said twenty-four months that a lesser amount would be payable in the event of death of the maker.

For the foregoing reasons the Court finds that the instrument does not constitute a negotiable promissory note and that the defendant is entitled to assert his defenses which raise issues of fact that can only be determined by a trial. Accordingly the motion is denied.

UNIVERSAL C. I. T. CREDIT CORP. v. INGEL

(1964) 347 Mass. 119, 196 N.E.2d 847.

SPIEGEL, J. This is an action of contract on a promissory note by the assignee of the payee against the maker. * * * Upon conclusion of the evidence the court allowed a motion by the plaintiff for a directed verdict to which the defendants excepted. They also excepted to the exclusion of certain evidence.

At the trial the plaintiff introduced in evidence the note,[1] a completion certificate signed by the defendants, and the District Court's finding for the plaintiff. The defendants admitted the authenticity of the signatures on the note and the completion certificate. As a witness for the defendants, one Charles D. Fahey testified that he was the plaintiff's Boston branch manager at the time the defendants' note was purchased, and that the plaintiff purchases instalment contracts regarding automobile and property improvement purchases. He described the procedures by which purchases of commercial paper are arranged by the plaintiff; these procedures included a credit check on the "customer," i. e., the maker of the note which the plaintiff is planning to purchase. The defendants attempted to introduce through Fahey a credit report obtained by the plaintiff on Allied Aluminum Associates, Inc. (Allied), the payee of the note. The defendants excepted to the exclusion of this evidence. They offered to prove that the excluded report, which was dated "3-31-59," contained the following statement: "The subject firm is engaged in the sale of storm windows, doors, roofing, siding,

---

1. [Footnotes by the Court.]

"This Is A Negotiable Promissory Note

$1890.00   Fitchburg, Mass., 6/22, 1959
(Total Amount of Note)   (City, State)   (Date)

I/WE JOINTLY AND SEVERALLY PROMISE TO PAY TO ALLIED ALUMINUM ASSOCIATES, INC. OR ORDER THE SUM OF EIGHTEEN HUNDRED NINETY DOLLARS IN 60 SUCCESSIVE MONTHLY INSTALMENTS OF $31.50 EACH, EXCEPT THAT THE FINAL INSTALMENT SHALL BE THE BALANCE THEN DUE ON THIS NOTE. COMMENCING THE 25 DAY OF JULY, 1959, AND THE SAME DATE OF EACH MONTH THEREAFTER UNTIL PAID, with interest after maturity at the highest lawful rate, and a reasonable sum (15% if permitted by law) as attorney's fees, if this note is placed in the hands of any attorney for collection after maturity. Upon non-payment of any instalment at its maturity, all remaining instalments shall at the option of the holder become due and payable forthwith. Charges for handling late payments, of 5¢ per $1 (maximum $5), are payable on any instalment more than 10 days in arrears. * * * *Notice of Proposed Credit Life Insurance:* Group credit life insurance will be obtained by the holder of this instrument, without additional charge to customer, subject to acceptance by the insurer, Old Republic Life Insurance Company, Chicago, Illinois. Such insurance will cover only the individual designated and signing below as the person to be insured (who must be an officer if customer is a corporation, a partner if partnership), except that no individual 65 years of age or older on the date the indebtedness is incurred will be eligible for such insurance. Such insurance will become effective, upon acceptance by the insurer, as of the date the indebtedness is incurred, and will terminate when the indebtedness terminates or upon such default or other event as terminates the insurance under the terms of the group policy. The amount of such insurance will be equal to the amount of customer's indebtedness hereunder at any time but not to exceed $10,000; proceeds will be applicable to reduction or discharge of the indebtedness. The provisions of this paragraph are subject to the terms of the group policy and the certificate to be issued.

PLEASE PRINT MAILING ADDRESS

Customer acknowledges receipt of a completed copy
of this promissory note, including above Notice.
ALBERT T. INGEL
Customer (Person on whose life group credit life
insurance will be obtained, if applicable.)
DORA INGEL
(Additional Customer, if any)
ORIGINAL"

and bathroom and kitchen remodeling work. The firm engages a crew of commission salesmen and it is reported they have been doing a good volume of business. They are reported to employ high pressure sales methods for the most part. They have done considerable advertising in newspapers, on radio, and have done soliciting by telephone. They have been criticized for their advertising methods, and have been accused of using bait advertising, and using false and misleading statements. The Boston Better Business Bureau has had numerous complaints regarding their advertising methods, and have reported same to the Attorney General. *FHA has had no complaints other than report of this from Better Business Bureau and have warned the firm to stop their practice."*

* * *

I.

The defendants contend that the note was nonnegotiable as a matter of law and, therefore, any defence which could be raised against Allied may also be raised against the plaintiff. They argue that the note contained a promise other than the promise to pay, failed to state a sum certain, and had been materially altered.

It appears that the note was a form note drafted by the plaintiff. The meaning of Fahey's general testimony that the note and the completion certificate were "together" when given by the plaintiff to Allied is unclear. However, we see nothing in this testimony to justify the inference urged upon us by the defendants that in this case the note and completion certificate were "part of the same instrument" and that an additional obligation in the completion certificate rendered the note nonnegotiable under G.L. c. 106, § 3–104(1) (b).[3] Similarly, we are not concerned with any variance between the written contract (entered into by Allied and the defendants) and the note, since there is nothing in the note to indicate that it is subject to the terms of the contract. We are equally satisfied that the insurance clause in the note does not affect negotiability under § 3–104 (1) (b) since it is clear that the "no other promise" provision refers only to promises by the maker.

The provision in the note for "interest after maturity at the highest lawful" rate does not render the note nonnegotiable for failure to state a sum certain as required by § 3–104(1) (b). We are of opinion that after maturity the interest rate is that indicated in G.L. c. 107 § 3,[4] since in this case there is no agreement in writing for any other rate after default. This being the case, we do not treat this note differently from one payable "with interest." The latter note would clearly be negotiable under G.L. c. 106, § 3–118(d).[5]

The note in question provides that payment shall be made "commencing the 25 day of July, 1959." It appears that there is an alteration on the face of the note in that "July" was substituted for "June," the "ly" in the former word being written over the "ne" in the latter. The alteration has no effect in this case, where the defendants admitted that they had paid a particular sum on the note and where the sum still owing

3. "Any writing to be a negotiable instrument within this Article must * * * contain an unconditional promise or order to pay a sum certain in money and no other promise, order, obligation or power given by the maker or drawer except as authorized by this Article."

4. "If there is no agreement or provision of law for a different rate, the interest of money shall be at the rate of six dollars on each hundred for a year, but, except as provided in sections seventy-eight, ninety, ninety-two, ninety-six and one hundred of chapter one hundred and forty, it shall be lawful to pay, reserve or contract for any rate of interest or discount. No greater rate than that before mentioned shall be recovered in a suit unless the agreement to pay it is in writing."

5. "Unless otherwise specified a provision for interest means interest at the judgment rate at the place of payment from the date of the instrument, or if it is undated from the date of issue."

(assuming the note to be enforceable on its face) is not in dispute. [Citation.]

We thus conclude that the note in question is a negotiable instrument.[6]

II.

The finding of the District Court which the plaintiff offered in evidence is, under G.L. c. 231, § 102C, prima facie evidence upon such matters as are put in issue by the pleading at the trial in the Superior Court. [Citation.] The defendants' answer denies that the plaintiff is "a holder in due course" of the note on which the action is brought; accordingly, this must be regarded as a matter "put in issue by the pleadings." We are satisfied that the finding of the District Court was prima facie evidence that the plaintiff took the note for value and without notice, and notwithstanding the provisions of G.L. c. 106, § 3–307(3),[7] the burden was on the defendants to rebut the plaintiff's prima facie case. [Citation.]

* * *

Exceptions overruled.

SMITH v. LENCHNER

(1964) 204 Pa.Super. 500, 205 A.2d 626.

WRIGHT, J. We are here concerned with an appeal by Martin B. Smith from an order of the Court of Common Pleas of Allegheny County making absolute a rule to open a judgment entered by confession on a note.

The note in question is dated July 6, 1962, in amount of $1,200.00 payable on demand, and is under seal. The petition for the rule alleges that the maker of the note is not

indebted to the payee, and requests that the judgment be opened because (a) the note was given "under duress of a threat made by the plaintiff to maliciously and falsely interfere with and disrupt a business transaction which petitioner was then negotiating"; and (b) no consideration was received for the execution and delivery of the note. Appellant's answer denies that the note was given under duress of a threat, and avers to the contrary that the note was voluntarily negotiated as "the result of a good-faith, arms-length business transaction". The answer further denies want of consideration, and alleges to the contrary (1) that the presence of the seal imports consideration and (2) that the transaction which gave rise to the note "was a sale of stock by plaintiff to defendant". Depositions were taken of both parties, and also of the attorney for the maker of the note.

* * *

We perceive no merit in appellee's contention that he was under duress when he executed and delivered the note in question.

* * *

Appellee also contends that he may raise his alleged defense of want of consideration despite the fact that the note was executed under seal. Reliance is placed upon Section 3–113 of the Uniform Commercial Code, which reads as follows: "An instrument otherwise negotiable is within this Article even though it is under a seal". It is argued that the Code Comment under this section, as well as the Pennsylvania Bar Association Notes, indicate that the defense of want of consideration is now available despite the presence of a seal. This question was raised but expressly not decided in Thomasik v. Thomasik, 413 Pa. 559, 198 A.2d 511. Howbeit, the note in the instant case is not "an instrument otherwise negotiable" because it authorizes confession of judgment as of any term. Prior to the enactment of the Code, a note containing a warrant of attorney to confess judgment at any time was held to be

---

6. By G.L. c. 255, § 12C, inserted by St.1961, c. 595, certain notes given in connection with the sale of consumer goods were made nonnegotiable.

7. "After it is shown that a defense exists a person claiming the rights of a holder in due course has the burden of establishing that he or some person under whom he claims is in all respects a holder in due course."

a non-negotiable instrument: [Citation]. This rule was applied to a demand note: [Citation]. The same result has been reached in cases subsequent to the enactment of the Code. [Citations.] Since the instant note is non-negotiable, it follows that the seal imports consideration.

We should perhaps here mention that Section 3–112(1) of the Code provides that the negotiability of a note "is not affected by * * * (d) a term authorizing a confession of judgment on the instrument if it is not paid when due". The Pennsylvania Bar Association Notes under this section point out that most judgment notes in use in this Commonwealth are not negotiable because judgment may be entered before the amount is due. To the same effect is the Code Comment that "paragraph (d) is intended to mean that a confession of judgment may be authorized only if the instrument is not paid when due, and that otherwise negotiability is affected". The Code did not change prior law in this respect: [Citation].

Appellee contends finally that appellant may not rely upon the seal because he affirmatively pleaded independent consideration. It is argued that appellant "should now be estopped from relying upon the seal as a substitute for consideration". The doctrine of estoppel has no application in the instant case. We perceive no reason which would prevent appellant from utilizing both theories.

Order reversed.

GUTHRIE v. NATIONAL HOMES CORPORATION

(1965 Tex.) 394 S.W.2d 494.

POPE, J. National Homes Corporation sued N. E. Guthrie, Jr. and John D. Crow and recovered judgment upon a jury verdict against both for $780.00, owing upon what it alleged was a negotiable promissory note. The Court of Civil Appeals affirmed. 387 S.W.2d 158. Guthrie alone has appealed and he has done so without bringing forward a statement of facts. He urges that he is not liable on a negotiable instrument on which his name nowhere appears, and also that the note contains a variance between the figures and the unambiguous written words that state the amount payable, in which case the courts below should have given controlling effect to the written words. It is our opinion that the instrument sued upon was not a negotiable instrument, and Guthrie is bound by the jury finding that he ratified it. We sustain Guthrie's contention that the unambiguous written words control the figures.

The instrument sued upon is as follows:

"$5780.00   Electra   Texas   3/8   1962
"Ninety (90) Days after date for Value Received I Promise To Pay to the Order of NATIONAL HOMES CORPORATION Five Thousand Eighty and 00/100 Dollars at Earl Avenue at Wallace, Lafayette, Indiana
It is hereby understood that $1000. overpayments will be made on future house deliveries until this obligation is paid.
With Interest at 6.5% per annum after date. All parties to this note, including endorsers and guarantors thereof, hereby waive presentment and demand for payment, protest, and notice of dishonor.
No. _____ Due _____ /s/ John D. Crow Crow Construction Co."

The instrument is non-negotiable. These words were written in longhand on the face of the note, "It is hereby understood that $1000. (sic) overpayments will be made on future house deliveries until this obligation is paid." Goldman v. Blum and Heidenheimer Bros., 58 Tex. 630 (1883) says: " * * * though the agreement or written instrument may have to some extent the form of a promissory note, and may use in its body the conventional terms that ordinarily invest such instruments with the character of negotiability, but if, by a stipulation in the body of the instrument, these elements which give it negotiability are limited and qualified, the negotiability of the instrument is destroyed * * *." [Citation.] The additional terms written into the note burden it with the conditions of an extrinsic agreement and render it non-negotiable. [Citations.]

* * *

The trial court admitted parol evidence concerning the agreement between National Homes Corporation and Crow with respect to the amount payable. The jury found that the principal amount they agreed upon was $5780 as evidenced by the figures instead of $5080 as evidenced by the written words in the note. The jury also found that there was an unpaid balance of $780. In other words $5000 had been paid on the note. Guthrie contends, however, that the written words "Five Thousand Eighty and 00/100 * * * Dollars" are unambiguous and that they prevail over the figures as a matter of law. That is the rule applicable to negotiable instruments. [Citations.] It is our opinion that the reasons for the rule are sound and that the same rule applies and should apply to non-negotiable instruments. [Citations.] When there is a variance between unambiguous written words and figures the written words control, and the trial court erred in giving judgment based upon the figures. The amount payable was therefore "Five Thousand Eighty and 00/100 * * * Dollars" and according to the jury $5,000 has been paid. National Homes Corporation should have judgment for only eighty dollars.

The judgments of the trial court and the Court of Civil Appeals are accordingly reformed so that National Homes Corporation shall have judgment for the sum of eighty dollars.

————

PROBLEMS

1. State whether the following provisions in a note, draft, or certificate of deposit or other instrument, impair negotiability, the instrument in each instance being otherwise in proper form. Answer each statement with either the word "Negotiable" or "Non-negotiable." If you so desire, you may explain your answer to each statement by no more than three lines.

(a) A note for $2,000 payable in twenty monthly installments of $100 each, providing: "In case of death of maker all payments not due at date of death are cancelled."

(b) A note stating, "this note is secured by a chattel mortgage of even date herewith on personal property located at 351 Maple Street, Smithton, Illinois."

(c) A certificate of deposit reciting, "John Jones has deposited in the Citizens Bank of Emanon, Illinois, Two Thousand Dollars, to the credit of himself, payable upon the return of this instrument properly indorsed, with interest at the rate of $4\frac{3}{4}\%$ per annum from date of issue upon 90 days written notice."

(d) An instrument reciting "I.O.U., Mark Noble, $1,000.00."

(e) A note stating "In accordance with our contract of December 13, 1966, I promise to pay to the order of Sam Stone $100 on March 13, 1967."

(f) A draft drawn by Brown on the Acme Publishing Company for $500, payable to the order of the Sixth National Bank of Erewhon, directing the bank to "Charge this draft to my royalty account."

(g) A note executed by Pierre Janvier, a resident of Chicago, for $2,000, payable in Swiss francs.

(h) An undated note for $1,000 payable "six months after date."

(i) A note for $500 payable to the order of Ray Rodes six months after the death of Albert Olds.

(j) A note for $500 payable to the assigns of Levi Lee.

2. State whether the following provisions in a note impair negotiability, the instrument in

each instance being otherwise in proper form. Answer each statement with either the word "Negotiable" or "Non-negotiable." If you so desire, you may explain your answer to each statement by no more than three lines.

(a) A note signed by Henry Brown in the trade name of the Quality Store.

(b) A note for $450, payable to the order of TV Products Company, "If, but only if, the color television set for which this note is given proves entirely satisfactory to me."

(c) A note executed by Adams, Burton and Cady Company, a partnership, for $1000, payable to the order of Davis, payable only out of the assets of the partnership.

(d) A note promising to pay $500 to the order of Leigh and to deliver ten tons of coal to Leigh.

(e) A note for $10,000 executed by Eaton payable to the order of the First National Bank of Emanon in which Eaton promises to give additional collateral if the bank deems itself insecure and demands additional security.

(f) A note reading, "I promise to pay to the order of Richard Roe $1000 on January 31, 1967, but it is agreed that if the crop of Blackacre falls below ten bushels per acre for the 1966 season, this note shall be extended indefinitely."

(g) A note payable to the order of Ray Rogers 50 years from date but providing that payment shall be accelerated by the death of Silas Hughes to a point of time four months after his death.

(h) A note for $4000 calling for payments of installments of $250 each and stating, "In the event any installment hereof is not paid when due this note shall immediately become due at the holder's option."

(i) An instrument dated September 17, 1966, in the handwriting of John Henry Brown which reads in full: "Sixty days after date, I, John Henry Brown, promise to pay to the order of William Jones $500."

(j) A note reciting: "I promise to pay Ray Reed $100 on December 24, 1966."

3. On March 10, 1965, Tolliver Tolles, also known as Thomas Towle, delivered to Alonzo Craig and Abigail Craig the following instrument, written by him in pencil:

"For value received, I, Thomas Towle, promise to pay to the order of Alonzo Craig or Abigail Craig One Thousand Seventy-Five ($1,000.75) six months after I shall become the legal owner of Blackacre, Fayette County, Kentucky, conveyed to me by my mother, Alma Tolles, reserving to herself a life estate in the land conveyed, with interest at the rate of five per cent from date to maturity and after maturity at the rate of six per cent. I hereby waive the benefit of all laws exempting real or personal property from levy or sale."

Alma Tolles died on February 10, 1966, and, on April 21, 1966, Alonzo Craig indorsed the instrument to John Hughes, an innocent purchaser, who paid $950 for it. Tolles refused to pay the instrument when presented to him for payment on August 10, 1966. Hughes sues Tolles for $1,075 and interest. Assume that the liability of Tolles depends upon whether or not the quoted instrument is a negotiable instrument. Decision?

4. Henry Hughes, who operates a department store, executed the following instrument:
"$2,600　　　　　　　Chicago, March 5, 1966

"On July 1, 1966, I promise to pay Daniel Dalziel, or order, the sum of Twenty-six Hundred Dollars, for the privilege of one framed advertising sign, size 24 × 36 inches, at one end of each of two hundred sixty motor coaches of the New Omnibus Company for a term of three months, from May 15, 1966.

Henry Hughes."

Dalziel indorsed the instrument to Silas Kenney, for value, on the day of its execution. Before the time when the privilege of advertising was to commence, Dalziel forfeited any right he may have acquired to use the motor coaches in the manner indicated and the privilege specified never was furnished Hughes. Kenney had no notice that payment depended upon a condition precedent to be performed by Dalziel other than contained in the instrument itself. Hughes refused to pay the instrument when it matured, and Kenney sues Hughes for $2,600. Hughes denies liability. Decision?

5. A note in every other respect possessing the formal requisites of negotiability contains the following language: "This note secured by G. W. Davis note copy of contract hereto attached and made a part of this note. Negotiable and payable at Southeast Missouri Trust Company." The payee of the note indorses and delivers it for value to a purchaser in good faith before maturity. The maker of the note does not pay it at maturity, and in a suit brought by the purchaser of the note against the maker, the latter defends

on the ground that the note and contract were obtained through fraud in the inducement practiced by the payee. What judgment?

6. P agreed to lend M $500. Thereupon M made and delivered his note for $500 payable to P or order "ten days after my marriage." P, however, made no part of the agreed loan to M. Shortly thereafter M was married. Before M's marriage P indorsed and sold the note to H, an innocent purchaser for value. Ten days after M's marriage H presented the note for payment to M, who refused to pay it. H then sues M on the note. Decision?

7. On June 1, A executed a note for $500 payable to the order of B, which contained the clause: "This note is payable when this year's corn crop is harvested." The note was delivered to B for a consideration which subsequently failed. On September 1, and before the corn crop matured, B sold the note for $450 to C who had no knowledge of the failure of consideration. On the following January 1, after the corn crop matured, C sued A for the amount of the note and interest. Decision?

8. M employs A to work for him for one year from January 1, 1966, to December 31, 1966 at a salary of $500 a month payable monthly. On January 2, M delivers to A twelve promissory notes in otherwise negotiable form, maturing respectively on the last day of successive calendar months throughout the year 1966. On the first note there is the statement "For January 1966 salary"; on the second note "For February 1966 salary"; and so on for each note. On January 3, 1966, A sells and indorses the twelve notes to XYZ Bank and on January 4, 1966, quits work. XYZ Bank sues M on these notes as they fall due. Is the bank entitled to recover?

9. On March 2, Dale and his wife, Deborah, executed their negotiable promissory note payable to the order of Tolles Mortgage Company, Inc., of Pinckard, for $8,000, payable in installments over a period of seven years, with interest payable semi-annually at the rate of 6% per annum, and secured the note by executing a deed of trust upon an improved parcel of real estate in Pinckard. The note contained this provision: "Upon breach of any promise made in this note or in the deed of trust securing it, at the option of the holder the entire indebtedness hereby evidenced shall become due then or thereafter as the holder may elect regardless of the date of maturity. Notice of the exercise of such option is hereby expressly waived."

The parties contemplated that Valiant Life Insurance Company would purchase the note since its inspector had agreed to recommend it. With respect to negotiating loans, Tolles Mortgage Company was the agent of the borrower and not of the insurance company. On March 26, the insurance company wrote Tolles Mortgage Company that it did not desire to purchase the note. In the meantime, on March 5, Tolles Mortgage Company borrowed $8,000 from Citizens Bank of Pinckard, for which it gave its note, with the Dale note attached as collateral. Dale was not advised of this transaction, but, on the contrary, was told from time to time by the mortgage company that the matter was still being considered by the insurance company.

On July 14, Tolles, president of the company, died, and it developed that the company was insolvent. Upon learning of this situation, Dale and his wife, never having received any money for their note, brought an action to enjoin the bank from foreclosing the deed of trust securing the note. Decision?

CHAPTER 26

TRANSFER AND NEGOTIATION

Introductory. Whether an instrument has the necessary form and content to render it negotiable is of significance only if it is designed to be transferred to a party other than the one to whom it was issued. As between the original parties, ordinary contract rules of rights and liabilities apply, whether or not the instrument is negotiable in form or even, in other than Statute of Frauds situations, whether an instrument exists at all.

Even though an instrument is fully negotiable in form, the rights of the transferee depend in part upon the method of transfer. Assignment, for example, continues the application of ordinary contract rules permitting assertion of defenses against assignees, whereas transfer by negotiation is one of the factors necessary to the creation of holder in due course status, whereupon defenses are cut off.

Rights Conferred on Transferees. Perhaps the most important rule applicable to transfers in general, whether by assignment or negotiation, is that, with a specified exception, the transfer of an instrument vests in the transferee such rights as the transferor has therein. Section 3–201(1). The transferor may not be the owner of the instrument: he may have only a security interest in it as the result of its being pledged as collateral. When he transfers the instrument, he transfers whatever rights he has. The transfer need not be for value: if the instrument is transferred as a gift, the donee acquires whatever rights the donor had. If the donor was a holder in due course, the donee acquires the rights of a holder in due course, and he in turn may transfer such rights to another transferee.

Insofar as this principle applies to the transfer of the rights of a holder in due course, it is sometimes referred to as the "shelter" provision. Superficially this rule seems to be an unfair concession to purchasers who are not themselves holders in due course but who were fortunate enough to buy from one who was. The rule, however, was not designed to aid the purchaser but to aid the holder in due course. This is explained in the case of Kost v. Bender, 25 Mich. 515 (1872):

> "It is perfectly true as a general rule, that the bona fide holder of negotiable paper has a right to sell the same, with all the rights and equities attaching to it in his own hands to whoever may see fit to buy of him, whether such purchaser was aware of the original infirmity or not. Without this right, he would not have the full protection which the law merchant designs to afford him, and negotiable paper would cease to be a safe and reliable medium for the exchange of commerce. For, if one can stop the negotiability of paper against which there is no defense, by giving notice that a defense once existed while it was held by another, it is obvious that an important element is taken away."

The rule thus carries out the policy of the U.C.C. to promote free transferability by assuring the holder in due course of a free market for his paper. Thus, if P induces M by fraud to make an instrument payable to the order of P, P may negotiate the instrument to A in such a fashion that A becomes a holder in due course. After the instrument is overdue, A gives it to B, who has notice of the fraud. B cannot be a holder in due course, since he takes the instrument when it is overdue, he does not pay value for it, and he has notice of M's defense against it. Nonetheless, through the operation of the shelter provision, B acquires A's rights as a holder in due course, and M cannot successfully assert his defenses against B.

591

There is an exception to the operation of this rule having a sound basis in logic and fair play: A transferee who has himself been a party to any fraud or illegality affecting the instrument or who as a prior holder (without having the rights of a holder in due course) had notice of a defense or claim against it cannot wash the paper clean by passing it into the hands of a holder in due course and then repurchasing it.

For example, P may induce M by fraud to make an instrument payable to the order of P. If P negotiates it to A, a holder in due course, and then repurchases it from him, P does not succeed to A's rights as a holder in due course, and remains subject to the defense of fraud. If, however, A had had notice of the fraud he could not have become a holder in due course upon acquisition of the instrument from P. Although he might then negotiate it to H, a holder in due course, and repurchase it from him, the instrument in his hands would remain subject to the defense of fraud: he will likewise not be permitted to improve his position by taking from a holder in due course.

Transferee's Right to Indorsement. Unless the parties otherwise agree, any transfer for value of an instrument not then payable to bearer gives the transferee the specifically enforceable right to have the unqualified indorsement of the transferor. Section 3–201(3).

The parties may, of course, agree that the transfer is to be an assignment rather than a negotiation, and consequently that no indorsement will be supplied. Absent such agreement, however, in the case of the ordinary transfer for value it is presumed that negotiation was intended, and therefore that any indorsement necessary to the transferee's title should be supplied. Where the transfer is not for value, the transaction is normally not commercial in nature, and such a presumption is not appropriate. And where the instrument is payable to bearer either as is-

sued, or, if indorsed, by virtue of a blank indorsement, no indorsement is necessary to a holder's title, and therefore is not required by the U.C.C.

The right to indorsement in an appropriate case conferred by Section 3–201(3) is made specifically enforceable, since an action at law for damages would not appear to furnish the prompt and adequate relief to which the transferee should be entitled. In addition, unless otherwise agreed, the indorsement required must be a general one, without qualification. It is reasonable to assume that if anything less than an unqualified indorsement had been intended, the parties would have specifically so provided.

Until the necessary indorsement has been supplied, however, the transferee has nothing more than the rights of an assignee. Negotiation takes effect only when the indorsement is made. If, before indorsement, the maturity date of the instrument passes or the transferee receives notice of a defense, he cannot become a holder in due course, even though the instrument is subsequently properly indorsed. On the other hand, under the shelter provision, if his transferor was a holder in due course, he acquires the rights of such a holder even though the indorsement is never supplied.

Negotiation of an Instrument. "Negotiation" is the name given to the special type of transfer of an instrument by which the transferee becomes a "holder" as that term is defined in Section 1–201(20) of the U.C.C.:

> "Holder" means a person who is in possession of * * * an instrument * * * drawn, issued or indorsed to him or to his order or to bearer or in blank.

Such a person has a prima facie right to enforce the instrument according to its terms. He acquires the rights of his transferor under the shelter provision of Section 3–201 (1) and, in addition, may become a holder in due course if he fulfills the other requirements for that status. The mechanics of negotiation are defined in Section 3–202.

If an instrument is payable to bearer, it is negotiated by delivery, which means a voluntary transfer of possession. A theft, therefore, does not constitute a negotiation of the instrument to the thief, and he does not become a holder.

In the absence of any special agreement, no one is under an obligation to become a transferee of commercial paper. Consequently, a proposed transferee may condition his acceptance as he may see fit. In the case of bearer paper, the transferee quite usually will require the indorsement of his transferor so as to increase the value of the instrument by adding the transferor's liability as an indorser. This practice is commercially acceptable and rarely results in any controversy.

If an instrument is payable to the order of a named person (or entity), not only delivery, but also the indorsement of such person (or entity) is a necessary element to a valid negotiation.

How Indorsements are Made. An indorsement must be written on the instrument or on a paper (called an allonge) so firmly affixed to the instrument as to become a part thereof. A purported indorsement on a separate piece of paper, clipped or pinned to the instrument is not valid. The use of an allonge is required when there are so many indorsements that there is no room for more. It is normally firmly pasted to the instrument.

Customarily, indorsements are made on the back of an instrument, starting at the top and continuing down the back. The order of their indorsement (and of their liability, unless otherwise agreed) is presumed to be the order in which their signatures appear. Section 3–414(2). Occasionally, however, a signature may appear on an instrument in such a way that it is impossible to tell with certainty the capacity in which it was made. In such an event, Section 3–402 specifies that the signer is to be treated as an indorser. In keeping with the rule that a transferee must be able to determine his rights from the face of the instrument, the person who signed in an ambiguous capacity may not introduce parol evidence to establish that he intended to be something other than an indorser.

An indorsement may be complex or simple. It may be dated but frequently is not. It may indicate where it is made, but frequently does not. Neither date nor place need be shown. The simplest type is merely the signature of the indorser. Since the indorser undertakes certain obligations, as will be explained later, an indorsement consisting of merely a signature may be said to be the shortest contract known to the law.

On occasion a person other than the holder may choose to lend his credit to the instrument by adding his indorsement, but the indorsement necessary to the negotiation of the instrument must be made by or on behalf of the holder. Hence, a forged or otherwise unauthorized signature is wholly inoperative and thus breaks the chain of title to the instrument. Section 3–404(1).

If the instrument is payable to the order of the holder under a misspelled name or one other than his own, as for example, a trade name, he may indorse the instrument in that name or his own or both. Section 3–203. A check payable to "Crescent Pizza Palace", which happens to be a sole proprietorship, may thus be quite properly indorsed by the owner in either his own name, John Doe, or that of his business, Crescent Pizza Palace. To assure the highest degree of security and to facilitate subsequent negotiation by removal of doubts, a person paying or giving value for the instrument may wish to require an indorsement in both names, and the U.C.C. authorizes him to do so.

In keeping with the general legal principle that a cause of action cannot be split, an indorsement which conveys less than the entire instrument (or the entire unpaid residue thereon) is ineffective as a negotiation. Section 3–202(3). An indorsement containing a direction to pay A "one-half of the within note" or "$500 of the within note", or to pay "two-thirds to A, one-third to B" consequently constitutes only an assignment in whole or in part, as the case may be. But an indorsement "to A and B" is effective since it transfers the entire interest to A and B as tenants in common.

On the other hand, words such as "I hereby assign all my right, title and interest in the within note" are sufficient to support a negotiation, and will not cause the transfer to be regarded as a mere assignment. Section 3–202(4). Too frequently a layman with a little knowledge (a dangerous thing) will phrase his indorsement in this fashion out of an excess of caution and a desire to indicate formally that the instrument is being conveyed, rather than with any intent to limit the effect of his signature. Recognizing this fact, the U.C.C. gives his language its intended interpretation and effect. Similarly, a layman, trying to spell out his conception of an indorser's liability may add: "I guarantee payment." Although this may affect his liability as provided in Section 3–416, it will not restrict the character of the indorsement.

Effectiveness of Negotiation. In keeping with the policy of promoting free negotiability by making it unnecessary for a transferee to look beyond the four corners of the instrument, Section 3–207 provides that a negotiation is effective even though the transaction involved is voidable or even void under the laws of contract. While retaining his rights to avoid or set aside the transaction, the transferor loses all rights in the instrument itself until he recovers it. If, in the meantime, the transferee negotiates it to

a holder in due course, the void or voidable transaction may no longer be rescinded, and the original transferor is relegated to his other rights against his transferee under the laws of contract. The holder in due course is fully protected.

This rule applies whether the transaction could be set aside because of the incapacity of the person negotiating: a minor, a corporation exceeding its powers, or any other person without capacity; manner in which the negotiation was obtained: through fraud, duress or mistake of any kind; illegality of the transaction; or breach of duty by an agent or other fiduciary.

Where the instrument has not come into the hands of a holder in due course, the transferor has those remedies normally available in the case of a void or voidable transaction, such as rescission of the transaction, declaration of a constructive trust, replevin of the instrument and enjoining its enforcement, collection or negotiation.

Types of Indorsements. The type of indorsement used in negotiating an instrument affects its subsequent negotiation. Every indorsement is either special or blank (Section 3–204), and either restrictive or nonrestrictive (Section 3–205 and Section 3–206).

A third method of categorizing indorsements, qualified and unqualified, is reserved for consideration in a subsequent chapter because it deals with the character of the indorser's contract and in no way affects the subsequent negotiation of the instrument. A qualified indorsement is one in which the indorsement is accompanied by the words "without recourse," or language of similar import.

These indorsements are not mutually exclusive. Indeed, all indorsements must be sorted into three of these six pigeonholes. This is true because all indorsements disclose three things: (1) The method to be employed in making subsequent negotiations. This depends upon whether the indorsement is blank or special. (2) The type of interest being transferred. This depends upon whether the indorsement is restrictive or non-restrictive. (3) The liability of the indorser. This depends upon whether the indorsement is qualified or unqualified.

Thus, an indorser merely signing his name on the back of an instrument is a blank, non-restrictive, unqualified indorser. Courts seldom give three names to an indorsement, because the problems before them usually do not require so great a breakdown. The name given to the indorser or indorsement is related to the problem at hand.

Examples of the various kinds of indorsements are:

(1) "John Doe"—Blank—unqualified—non-restrictive

(2) "Pay to Richard Roe, John Doe"—Special—unqualified—non-restrictive

(3) "Without recourse, John Doe"—Blank—qualified—non-restrictive

(4) "Pay to Richard Roe, without recourse, John Doe"—Special—qualified—non-restrictive

(5) "John Doe, without recourse, for collection only"—Blank—qualified—restrictive

(6) "Pay to XYZ Bank for collection and deposit only, without recourse on me, John Doe"—Special—qualified—restrictive

Special Indorsements. A special indorsement specifies the person to whom or to whose order the instrument is payable. Thus, if M makes a note payable to bearer and delivers it to P, P may convert it from a bearer instrument to an order instrument by indorsing it: "Pay to the order of A." If A delivers the note to B without indorsing it, B does not become a holder, despite the fact that on its face the instrument is payable to bearer. He must first obtain A's indorsement. This is appropriate because P, as the owner of the instrument, should have the

right to direct the payment and require the indorsement of his indorsee as evidence of the satisfaction of P's obligation to A.

Blank Indorsements. Just as a bearer instrument may be converted into an order instrument by the form of the indorsement, so also may an order instrument be changed to bearer paper. This is effected by a blank indorsement, which is one specifying no particular indorsee. The usual form of blank indorsement is merely the name of the holder. An instrument indorsed in blank is transferable in the manner of cash: it may be negotiated from hand to hand without further indorsement. Hence, the holder must treat it with the same care as cash. He may protect himself, however, by converting the blank indorsement to a special indorsement by writing over the signature of the indorser any contract consistent with the character of the indorsement.

Restrictive Indorsements. As the term implies, a restrictive indorsement restricts the rights of the indorsee in some fashion designed to protect the rights of the indorser. The U.C.C. recognizes four types of restrictive indorsements (Section 3–205), each of which will be considered separately.

1. *Conditional Indorsements.* A conditional indorsement is one by which the indorser makes the rights of the indorsee subject to the happening of a certain event. Suppose that M makes a note payable to P's order. P indorses it "Pay A, but only if the good ship Jolly Jack arrives in Chicago harbor by May 15, 1966." If M had used this language in the instrument, it would be non-negotiable, because his promise to pay must be unconditional to satisfy the formal requisites of negotiability. But indorsers are permitted to condition the rights of their indorsees without destroying negotiability.

If the good ship Jolly Jack does not arrive in Chicago harbor by May 15, 1966, A has no rights in the instrument. If he presents the instrument to M for payment, M must dishonor the instrument or be forced to pay it again to P. Under Section 3–603(1) (b), M is not discharged when he pays an instrument which has been restrictively indorsed, unless he pays in a manner consistent with the indorsement. Since the Jolly Jack did not arrive in port by May 15, 1966, it would be inconsistent with P's restrictive indorsement to pay to A or his order the amount due on the instrument.

The same rule would apply if A had negotiated the instrument to B. He, too, would be under a duty to pay or apply any value given by him for the instrument consistently with the indorsement. To the extent he does so, he becomes a holder for value, but not otherwise.

2. *Indorsements Prohibiting Further Transfer.* Under Section 3–104(1) (d), to be negotiable, an instrument not payable to bearer must be payable to the order of the payee. If the instrument reads merely "Pay A" it is not negotiable and the only method of transfer would be by assignment. No such restriction is imposed upon indorsements, however. An indorsement reading "Pay A" or even "Pay A only" is interpreted as meaning "Pay to the order of A." Such indorsements, or any other purporting to prohibit further transfer, are designed to be a restriction on the rights of the indorsee. As a practical matter, however, further negotiation is normally contemplated, if only for bank collection. The indorsee clearly becomes a holder, and the indorsement itself gives no notice to subsequent parties of any defense or claim of the indorser. To remove any doubt as to the effect of such a provision, Section 3–206(1) provides that no restrictive indorsement prevents further transfer or negotiation of the instrument. The net result of this provision is that any indorsement which merely purports to prohibit further transfer is given the same effect as an unrestricted indorsement. Subsequent holders of

the instrument, if they otherwise qualify, may become holders in due course.

3. *Indorsements for Deposit or Collection.* The most frequently used form of restrictive indorsement is that designed to lodge the instrument in the banking system for deposit or collection. Indorsements of this type include those "for collection," "for deposit" and "pay any bank." Such an indorsement would put all non-banking persons on notice as to who has the real interest in the paper. Thus, if the instrument goes outside of the bank collection chain, any person buying it would have to see to it that the money he expended was applied consistently with the indorsement. This might mean that such a person would have to pay twice: once when he acquired the paper, and later when the restrictive indorser proved that the paper was not collected in such a way that he received the proceeds.

4. *Indorsements in Trust.* Another common kind of restrictive indorsement is that in which the indorser creates a trust for the benefit of himself or a third person. If an instrument is indorsed "Pay T in trust for B" or "Pay T for B" or "Pay T for account of B" or "Pay T as agent for B", whether B is the indorser or a third person, T is a fiduciary, subject to liability for any breach of his obligation. Trustees of course commonly and legitimately sell trust assets, and as a consequence, a trustee has power to negotiate an instrument and make the transferee a holder in due course. When T negotiates the instrument to C, however, C must pay or apply any value given by him consistently with the indorsement, or risk having to pay twice. But in the case of an indorsement in trust, the obligation to see that payment is made consistently with a restrictive indorsement does not extend beyond the transferee taking the instrument from the fiduciary. Therefore, a subsequent taker without notice of any negotiation in breach of fiduciary duty may be a holder in due course. The fact that the in-

dorsements clearly show that a prior transfer was by a fiduciary does not constitute notice of negotiation in breach of duty.

A distinction is thus drawn between the intermediate indorsee of paper restrictively indorsed by way of condition and the intermediate indorsee of paper restrictively indorsed in trust or for the benefit of the indorser or a third party. Where the paper is indorsed "conditionally" all intermediate indorsers, except banks, and all primary parties making payments, except banks, must see to it that money paid is applied consistently with the condition. Where the restrictive indorsement is for the benefit of the indorser or a third party, but not conditioned, responsibility is imposed more narrowly.

5. *Duty of Banks in the Case of Restrictive Indorsements.* Since banks must handle checks and other instruments rapidly and in great volume, at certain stages in the collection process it is impractical to require examination of each indorsement before processing is completed and the check continued on its journey. Consequently, the U.C.C. makes certain exceptions in order to facilitate the flow of commerce. In every case, a bank receiving an item for deposit to an account of its customer must honor restrictive indorsements in accordance with the foregoing rules. A bank to which the item is transferred by another bank for collection or payment, however, need concern itself only with the indorsement of its immediate transferor, and may disregard any other restrictive indorsements. Section 3–206(2).

Reacquisition of an Instrument. Sometimes an instrument, in the course of its journey through commercial channels, is reacquired by a party who had previously negotiated it. When this occurs, any person whose indorsement follows that of the reacquiring party is discharged as against the reacquiring party and subsequent holders not in due course. Section 3–208. This follows from the fact that if the reacquirer attempted to enforce the instrument against the intervening indorsers, they in turn could enforce it against him. The reacquirer may also cancel any of the intervening indorsements, thereby discharging the indorser against subsequent holders in due course as well.

Suppose the indorsements on an instrument read: P, A, B, C, A, D. In the event A were held liable on the instrument, he could not recover from B or C. If before renegotiating the instrument A had cancelled B's indorsement, B would not be liable to D even though the latter was a holder in due course.

The problem is the effect the cancellation would have on C's rights in the event D sought to recover from him. It would appear that C should be discharged under Section 3–606(1) (a) because A had impaired C's right of recourse against B. Since C in all probability depended in very large part on B's credit when he took the instrument, no subsequent holder may be permitted to deprive C of this right if he is to continue liable on the instrument.

Another matter not wholly clear under the U.C.C. is whether the discharge of B and C in the above example should be permitted as against A and D if A's first indorsement was made "without recourse", which would mean that for many purposes A (under his "without recourse" indorsement) could not be sued by subsequent holders such as B and C.

CASES

WATERTOWN FEDERAL SAVINGS & LOAN ASS'N v. SPANKS

(1963) 346 Mass. 398, 193 N.E.2d 333.

CUTTER, J. The plaintiff (the bank) seeks to recover from the defendants, husband and wife, upon a promissory note, dated June 24, 1959, payable to "Greenlaw & Sons Roofing & Siding Co.," indorsed to Colony Distributors, Inc. (Colony), by an indorsement signed "Greenlaw & Sons by George M. Greenlaw," and then indorsed by Colony to the bank. The defendants denied the genuineness of their purported signatures and of all indorsements and filed a declaration in set-off to recover their payments to the bank on the note.

At the trial, the defendants admitted signing the note and also a completion certificate which they had given to the bank. This certificate recited that the siding material, paid for by the note, had been attached to the defendants' house and that the work was satisfactory. The bank presented evidence of the balance due on the note.

The defendants requested the trial judge to rule that their "demand for proof * * * of their supposed signatures and of the supposed endorsements * * * is constructively broad enough to come within" G.L. c. 106, § 3—203.[1] The judge denied this request "not because as an abstract statement of law it may not be correct, but because, upon the facts as found by me * * * it has no bearing." Apart from an offer of proof

[1.] [Footnote by the Court.] As inserted by St.1957, c. 765, § 1 (the Uniform Commercial Code), § 3–203 reads, "Where an instrument is made payable to a person under a misspelled name or one other than his own he may indorse in that name or his own or both; but signature in both names may be required by a person paying or giving value for the instrument."

mentioned later in this opinion, the defendants offered no evidence.

The trial judge found for the bank both as plaintiff and as defendant in set-off. The case is here on the defendants' bill of exceptions.

1. The trial judge correctly denied the defendants' requested ruling as immaterial. It does not appear that Greenlaw & Sons and Greenlaw & Sons Roofing & Siding Co. are not the same company. The indorsement by Greenlaw was not shown to have been in a name other than his own, nor is it shown that the name of the payee, as stated in the note, was not a name under which Greenlaw individually did business, identifiably repeated in the indorsement. Section 3—203 purports to give only an indorsee for value, and not the maker of a note, the power to require indorsement in both names in the circumstances stated in the section. No evidence was introduced with respect to the indorsement. It comes within G.L. c. 106, § 3—307 (and see the official comments on that section), which reads in part, "(1) * * * When the effectiveness of a signature is put in issue (a) the burden of establishing it is on the party claiming under the signature; but (b) the signature is presumed to be genuine or authorized [with an exception not here pertinent]. (2) When signatures are * * * established, production of the instrument entitles a holder to recover on it unless the defendant establishes a defense." There was no evidence whatsoever to counter the presumption of the indorsement's regularity existing under § 3—307(1) (b). Thus the signature of Greenlaw was established under § 3—307(2), and the bank, as the holder of the note, see G.L. c. 106, § 1—201(20), is entitled to recover.

* * *

Exceptions overruled.

COULTER v. STEWART

(1963) 93 Ariz. 242, 379 P.2d 910.

UDALL, VICE CHIEF JUSTICE. Appeal was taken from a summary judgment for plaintiff in an action on a promissory note. Suit was brought in Maricopa County Superior Court.

The promissory note was executed in the state of Colorado by Richard L. and Rebecca H. Sardou to Clyde H. and Caroline Harvey for the amount of $54,271.47. The Harveys were the original appellants on this appeal. (Subsequent to the bringing of this appeal Clyde H. Harvey died and Rufus C. Coulter, Jr., as ancillary administrator with the will annexed of the estate of Clyde H. Harvey, was substituted as an appellant in the place of Clyde H. Harvey.) September 10, 1956, at Colorado Springs, Colorado, Clyde H. and Caroline Harvey transferred the note to W. O. Stewart, the appellee, by use of the following statement on the back of the note:

"September 10, 1956

"FOR VALUABLE CONSIDERATION, we hereby assign all of our right, title and interest in the within installment note to W. O. STEWART.

　　　　　"/s/　　Clyde H. Harvey
　　　　　"/s/　　Caroline Harvey"

Payments on the note became delinquent and a foreclosure proceeding in Colorado on certain security resulted in the reduction of principal to $43,499.36. Stewart then brought this action against the Sardous, the makers, who were not served and whose residence was alleged in the complaint to be unknown, and against the Harveys as endorsers of the note. The suit resulted in a summary judgment against the Harveys. From this the appeal is taken upon the following assignments of error:

"1. The complaint fails to state a claim upon which relief can be granted; and

"2. The motion for summary judgment and the supporting affidavits (considered with the appellants' controverting affidavit) are wholly insufficient to warrant the granting of the summary judgment here upon appeal."

The transfer of the instrument from the Harveys to the appellee occurred in Colorado. Therefore, the law of that state should govern the effect of the transaction. * * * The parties base their arguments upon Colorado Revised Statutes, § 95–1–38 (1953) which * * * reads:

"A qualified [e]ndorsement constitutes the [e]ndorser a mere assignor of the title to the instrument. It may be made by adding to the [e]ndorser's signature the words *'without recourse' or any words of similar import.* Such an [e]ndorsement does not impair the negotiable character of the instrument." (Emphasis supplied.) [A.R.S. 44–438 employs this identical language.]

In other jurisdictions where similar language is found in the statutes the courts have disagreed on whether the words "assign all our right, title and interest," the words used in the transfer which we are called upon to consider, are words of "similar import" to the words "without recourse". We are asked to take the difficult position of deciding what the Colorado courts would do if they were themselves confronted with this problem. However, in the absence of an interpretation of the statute by the Colorado courts we will adopt a construction we deem most reasonable. [Citations.]

We are of the view that the language used to transfer the note in the case at bar is not language of limitation and the signers are merely general endorsers. The principal reason for this position is found in the Uniform Negotiable Instruments Law § 63 which has the same wording as A.R.S. § 44–463 and Colorado Revised Statutes § 95–1–63 (1953). It reads:

"A person placing his signature upon an instrument otherwise than as maker, drawer or acceptor, is deemed to be an [e]ndorser, unless he clearly indicates by appropriate words his intention to be bound in some other capacity."

This section should be read in conjunction with Uniform Negotiable Instruments Law § 38, which is the same wording as A.R.S. § 44–438 and Colorado Revised Statutes § 95–1–38 (1953), supra. By doing so we conclude that words used in this transaction are not words of "similar import" to the words "without recourse" and do not convey clearly that the Harveys meant to be bound as mere assignors. The words "We assign all our right, title and interest" are not appropriate words that clearly indicate an intention by the signers to be bound in some other capacity than that of an endorser.

It was said in Prichard v. Strike, 66 Utah 394, 243 P. 114, 117, 44 A.L.R. 1348 (1926) where statutes identical to those we are considering were in force:

" * * * (W)e think that one [e]ndorsing a negotiable promissory note and desiring to disclaim the responsibilty of an [e]ndorser must, by appropriate words, clearly indicate such an intention or an intention to be bound in some other capacity, and that he does not do so by language as here assigning and delivering all his right, title, and interest in the note *which is nothing more than what the law implies from a blank or general [e]ndorsement* without words creating the implication, and hence is but the expression of a clause which the law implies, and works nothing." (Emphasis supplied.)

See also McCullough v. Stepp, 91 Ga.App. 103, 85 S.E.2d 159, 160 (1954) where it was said:

"The words, 'I hereby transfer my right to this note over to W. E. McCullough,' are not words of similar import to 'without recourse.' "

Furthermore, the view we take more adequately insures the free circulation of negotiable paper. This is of vital importance to the commercial world and any language likely to hamper it must be strictly construed. [Citations.]

We conclude that appellee had a cause of action against the Harveys, and since no dispute over the facts existed the trial judge properly granted the motion for summary judgment. [Citations.] The appellants' arguments that the intent of the parties and contemporaneous circumstances surrounding the transaction should be considered on this appeal are without merit. As a matter of law the Harveys were mere endorsers and neither their intentions nor the contemporaneous circumstances could change it.

 * * *

Judgment affirmed.

NORTHEAST FACTOR & DISC. CO. v. MORTGAGE INVEST., INC.

(1963) 107 Ga.App. 705, 131 S.E.2d 221.

Northeast Factor & Discount Company, formerly Northeast Investment Corporation, brought suit against Mortgage Investments, Inc. of Georgia in the Civil and Criminal Court of DeKalb County upon a promissory note signed by Guy Smith as maker, payable to Mortgage Investment Company, Inc. on demand, and which carried on the reverse side the entry "for value received transferred to Dealers Discount & Investment Company" which was dated April 6, 1960 and signed Mortgage Investments Inc. of Georgia, by D. D. Dominey, Pres.

A general demurrer to the petition was sustained with leave to amend, and by amendment plaintiff alleged that Dealers Discount & Investment Company, the transferee, had reduced the note to judgment by bringing suit against Guy Smith, the maker, in Clayton Superior Court, and that thereafter Dealers Discount had been adjudged to be insolvent and a receiver appointed for its affairs, that plaintiff had purchased the execution based upon the judgment and the note from the receiver, and that title thereto had been transferred to him by a bill of sale from the receiver duly approved by an order of court. Neither the bill of sale nor the order of approval was attached. Plaintiff further alleged that it was a holder of the note in due course.

The demurrer to the petition was renewed to it in its amended form and additional demurrers were interposed. All demurrers were sustained without leave to amend, the petition was dismissed, and the plaintiff here excepts.

EBERHARDT, J.

1. (a, b) *Did the form of the transfer here amount to a general indorsement, a special indorsement, or an assignment only?*

While there is a hopeless conflict of authority as to the effect of a transfer in the form used here, the majority rule both before and after adoption of the Negotiable Instruments Law has been and is that the effect is that of a general or commercial indorsement. [Citations.] Prior to the adoption of NIL [1] the majority rule had been adopted in Georgia. [Citations.] The only case dealing with the matter after adoption of the NIL that we have found is McCullough v. Stepp, 91 Ga. App. 103, 85 S.E.2d 159. While it is stated in the body of that opinion that such a transfer constitutes a *special indorsement*, a reading of the record and the full opinion reveals that the question before the court was whether it amounted to a *qualified* indorsement or whether it could be shown by parol evidence that the intention of the parties was that it be a qualified indorsement. The court properly held that it neither was nor could be shown to be a qualified indorsement.

We need not here determine whether the form of transfer used is an assignment, for even if it is "[t]he general rule is that a writing on the back of a bill or note with the intention of transferring title is an indorsement, although it is in terms an assignment * * *." 10 C.J.S. Bills & Notes § 208, p. 695; Beutel's Brannan, Negotiable Instrument Law, § 31, p. 601. Of course, if the transfer had not been entered on the note itself we should be confronted with a different situation.

But it would not matter whether we followed the majority rule giving the transfer the status of a general indorsement, or the minority rule giving it that of a special indorsement, in reaching our conclusion here. In either situation the transferor engages to pay the note, for the only manner in which that might have been avoided was to negative it specifically by use of the words "without recourse," or words of similar import, as provided by NIL § 38 (Code § 14–409). This was implicit in McCullough. Unless one who places his name upon an instrument wishes to be bound as an indorser he must clearly indicate the contrary by appropriate words. NIL § 63 (Code § 14–604). The words of the transfer "are to be construed as strongly as their sense will allow against those using them." 1 Daniel, Neg. Inst. § 688c (6th Ed.), cited approvingly in Prichard v. Strike, 66 Utah 394, 243 P. 114, 44 A.L.R. 1348, 1351.

There can be no question here but that Mortgage Investments was an indorser with the attendant liability of one in that position.

But even if it be conceded that the indorsement was special, retaining the character of the note as order paper, it does not follow that since no further indorsement appears by the transferee as required by § 34 (Code § 14–405) the plaintiff did not acquire legal title in purchasing from the receiver, and can not maintain this suit at law in its own name.

1. [Footnote by the Court.] Repealed by Uniform Commercial Code (Code Ann. § 109A–10–103), which, however, does not become effective until January 1, 1964. (Ga.Laws 1963, p. 188). With some clarifying changes the NIL is basically carried forward in Article 3 of the Commercial Code. See Code Ann. §§ 109A–3–101, et seq.

Prior to the adoption of NIL this contention would have been meritorious. [Citations.] But § 49 of NIL (Code § 14–420) changed that. It is now settled that a transfer for value, without indorsement, vests in the transferee such title as the transferor had, and the transferee may bring suit thereon in his own name. * * *

Judgment reversed.

EASTERN ACCEPTANCE CORP.
v. KAVLICK

(1950) 10 N.J.Super. 253, 77 A.2d 49.

JACOBS, S. J. A. D. This is an appeal from a judgment for defendants entered in the Camden County District Court.

Under date of January 10, 1948 the defendants executed and delivered a promissory note in the sum of $590.04 to the order of J. Rothman, Contractors. The note was endorsed and delivered to the plaintiff before maturity and for value. The endorsement was in the following form:

"Pay to the order of
Eastern Acceptance Corporation
Without Recourse

except that the undersigned indorser warrants that the undersigned has furnished and installed all articles and materials and has fully completed all work which constitutes the consideration for which this note was executed and delivered by the maker.

J. Rothman, Contractors
By J. Rothman
(Dealer)
Title Owner"

The District Court found that there had been a failure of consideration between the payee and the makers of the note but also found that when the plaintiff purchased the note "it had no notice or knowledge of the defenses of the defendants." Nevertheless it entered judgment for the defendants on the ground that since the note had been transferred to the plaintiff by a qualified endorsement it remained subject to all defenses between the payee and the makers.

It is well recognized that an endorsement "without recourse" is not restrictive under section 36 of the Uniform Negotiable Instruments Act (R.S. 7:2–36, N.J.S.A.) but is a qualified endorsement which, under section 38 (R.S. 7:2–38, N.J.S.A.), does not impair the negotiable character of the instrument. [Citation.] Its purpose is simply to exempt the endorser from liability for payment of the instrument in the event it is dishonored at maturity and its presence does not indicate that the endorser's title may be defective. [Citations.] * * *

In the light of the authorities we are satisfied that the plaintiff was not precluded from becoming a holder in due course of the note because the endorsement was without recourse. The remaining question is whether there were any other circumstances which constituted notice to the plaintiff of any infirmity or defect. [Citations.] The note represented payment to the contractor of the purchase price of heating equipment installed by him; however, under the prevailing view, mere knowledge of that fact or the possibility that the contractor might later default in his stipulated performance would be immaterial. [Citations.] * * *

We have concluded that the plaintiff was a holder in due course and that the District Court's ruling to the contrary was erroneous. [Citation.] As a holder in due course it was not subject to the defense of failure of consideration available between the payee and makers. [Citations.]

Reversed, and with direction that judgment for plaintiff be entered in the District Court.

FULTZ v. FIRST NATIONAL BANK IN GRAHAM

(1965 Tex.) 388 S.W.2d 405.

STEAKLEY, J. This suit was brought by W. B. Fultz, Petitioner here, against the First National Bank in Graham, Respondent, to recover the sum of $13,060.00 representing "less cash" sums, in amounts ranging between $50.00 and $300.00, paid by the bank to Mrs. Fern McCoy, an employee of Fultz, in "for deposit only" transactions to the account of Fultz over a period of time between February, 1960, and April, 1963. The sums so paid to Mrs. McCoy were misappropriated to her personal use. Mrs. McCoy had not signed a signature card at the bank and was not authorized by Fultz either to check on his account or to withhold cash amounts from the deposits made for him. The full endorsement which was stamped on each of the checks read: "Pay to the order of the First National Bank, Graham, Texas—For deposit only— W. B. Fultz."

Both parties moved for summary judgment and the trial court granted the motion of Fultz. The Court of Civil Appeals held that the alleged negligence on the part of Fultz in not examining his bank statements and other records and discovering the defalcations so as to notify the bank would, if found to be true, constitute a defense to his suit against the bank. Consequently, that Court held that in these respects there were issues of fact to be determined by the trier of facts and the summary judgment for Fultz was improper. * * * We reverse the judgment of the Court of Civil Appeals and affirm that of the trial court.

The key to the first problem is the undisputed fact that the bank violated the written instructions of Fultz, and hence breached its deposit contract with him in each deposit transaction. In the exercise of care by Fultz, all of the checks which were deposited were endorsed "For Deposit Only." This was an unqualified direction to the bank to place the full amount of the checks to the account of Fultz. This instruction was violated when part of the amount of the checks was paid to Mrs. McCoy in cash. The bank had knowledge of its acts in violation of the instruction. Fultz as the depositor had the right to rely on the bank to honor the "For Deposit Only" instructions he had established as the regular deposit routine for his employee and the bank to follow; he was under no duty to exercise further care to ascertain if the bank had followed his instructions, and it is not asserted that Fultz had actual knowledge that the bank had not done so. The instruction carried in the restricted endorsement, "For Deposit Only," if followed, afforded absolute protection to both the bank and the depositor in the check deposit transactions and would have rendered the misappropriations impossible. The bank was in no way misled. Fultz had not filed a signature card for his defalcating employee and had not authorized his employee to sign checks on his account or make cash withdrawals in connection with deposits to his account. The "For Deposit Only" endorsements in the latter transactions were positively to the contrary.

The decisions which consider the question of the liability of a bank for the payment of forged checks recognize the principle stated by the Supreme Court of the United States in Leather Manufacturers' National Bank v. Morgan, 117 U.S. 96, 6 S.Ct. 657, 29 L.Ed. 811 (1885), and quoted with approval in Southwest National Bank of Dallas v. Underwood, 120 Tex. 83, 36 S.W.2d 141 (1931), that "If the bank's officers, before paying forged or altered checks, could by proper care and skill have detected the forgeries, then it cannot receive a credit for the amount of these checks, even if the depositor omitted all examination of his account."

So it is here. The Respondent bank had only to exercise proper care by following the specific instructions of Fultz, the depositor; the doing of this required no skill. Its course of action in failing to do so resulted in liability to Fultz "even if" he "omitted all examination of his account." This distinguishes the decisions in the cases which are premised upon a duty of the depositor to examine his statements from the bank, which examination would have revealed the defalcations. [Citations.]

Another rule of general acceptance, quoted with approval by this Court in Liberty State Bank v. Guardian Savings & Loan Assn., 127 Tex. 311, 94 S.W.2d 133 (1936), is that "[T]he duty imposed upon the depositor to examine his pass book and vouchers does not extend to an examination of the signatures of the payees on the returned vouchers." This rule is bottomed upon the premise that "it is the duty of the bank to determine the genuineness of a payee's indorsement, and the depositor is not expected to know his signature." By analogy, it was the clear and simple duty of the bank in the case here to honor the "For Deposit Only" endorsement, and Fultz was not expected to know that the bank had not done so, or to anticipate that the bank might not do so, or to take measures to determine if the bank had done so.

Further, as recognized in Liberty State Bank, since Fultz owed no duty to the bank to examine his bank statements and other records, he was, for that reason, not guilty of negligence in not doing so, and in not discovering the defalcations of his employee. For the same reason he is not estopped to assert the liability of the bank. There existed no genuine issue of fact between the parties in such respects.

The judgment of the Court of Civil Appeals is reversed and that of the trial court is affirmed.

SPARKS v. BANK OF GEORGIA

(1964) 110 Ga.App. 198, 138 S.E.2d 86.

[Action against a bank for conversion of a check which had been endorsed by plaintiff for deposit to plaintiff's account and was thereafter stolen and the proceeds thereof credited by defendant bank to an account opened by thief who thereafter withdrew most of the proceeds of the check.]

RUSSELL, J. 1. "Whoever takes and carries away the property of another without his consent is not absolved from liability as for a conversion by his own good faith in the transaction and although he may take the property by the consent of one whom he mistakenly believes to be the owner, he still may be held as for a conversion, where he refuses on demand to surrender the property to the true owner. [Citations.]

2. "Where the requirements of law are otherwise met a trover action will lie, although the property has been disposed of by the defendant prior to the date of demand and the filing of the suit." Scoggins v. General Finance & Thrift Corp., 80 Ga.App. 847 (3), 57 S.E.2d 686.

3. "[A] restrictive indorsement puts subsequent parties on notice that the indorser retains ownership of the instrument. * * Kirstein Leather Co. v. Deitrick (C.C.A.Mass. 1936) 86 F.2d 793; and Nordin v. Eagle Rock State Bank (1934) 139 Cal.App. 584, 34 P.2d 490." [Citations.] A holder of a check containing such a restrictive endorsement is not a holder in due course and does not have title to the instrument; it is therefore in his hands subject to the same defenses and only those pertaining to a nonnegotiable instrument. [Citations.]

4. (a) The plaintiff Wynona Sparks received a check from Sabco Investments, Inc. drawn on the Florida National Bank at Lakeland, Florida in the sum of $6,000. She endorsed it "Mrs. Wynona T. Sparks for deposit

only, Acct. of Wynona Sparks", placed it in a "Bank-by-mail envelope addressed to the First National Bank, Atlanta, Georgia, where she kept her account, and placed it over a tier of mailboxes in her apartment house along with other letters to be picked up by the mailman the following day. The check was stolen. The thief then went to the defendant Bank of Georgia, where plaintiff was unknown, represented herself to be Mrs. Wynona T. Sparks, opened an account in that name and deposited $60 in cash. The same day or the next $40 was withdrawn and the check in question was deposited. It was forwarded for collection, duly paid, and thereafter the imposter cashed a $2,500 check on the account with the defendant and purchased a cashier's check for $2,000 which she also cashed. This left $1,520 in the account. On the trial the plaintiff sought a money judgment for the value of the check; the trial judge hearing the case without the intervention of a jury found for the defendant, and the plaintiff moved for a new trial on the general grounds.

(b) Applying the foregoing law to these facts, the evidence demanded a finding that the defendant had converted the check in question. The check was stolen, it had not become bearer paper, and it was not negotiable. Title remained in the plaintiff subject to only that which might legally be done under the endorsement—that is, collection of the proceeds and turning them over to the true owner. The bank was guilty of a conversion when it took and used the check, although innocently, for a different purpose. The bank credited the proceeds of the check to the account of Wynona Sparks, true; but it did not credit it to the account of the plaintiff since it intended that the funds be placed at the disposition of another person who represented herself to be Wynona Sparks but was not in fact the plaintiff, and payment was made on the checks drawn by this imposter to the very person whom the bank intended

to receive the money, and who had no right or title thereto. This was an unauthorized exercise of dominion over the property of another in defiance of the owner's right, and it did not matter whether such dominion was exercised for its own use or for the use of such other. [Citations.]

5. (a) It is contended however that the plaintiff's loss was occasioned by her own negligence, first in placing the envelope with the check in a place where it might easily be stolen, and second in not checking soon enough with the First National Bank in which it had been deposited to see that it had reached its destination safely. This raises the question of whether negligence of the plaintiff may be a defense to a trover suit where stolen property is involved. In the first place, a bank has a duty to see that funds are not paid over to an improper party, and if the plaintiff gave an opportunity to the thief by placing the check in a location where it might be stolen, the bank also gave the thief an opportunity to complete her design by failing to check the residence address, business address and references of the imposter which she gave when the account was opened on the very day, or at least within 24 hours of the time she deposited the check, all of which information was false as would have been discovered by making a telephone call to any of the places listed. Negligence short of estoppel will not bar the plaintiff in a trover action. [Citations.]

(b) The defendant in error also insists that the plaintiff's negligence here exists and also constitutes a true estoppel such as to bar her from recovery as a matter of law. First observing that the plaintiff did nothing to deceive or mislead the defendant (as in Roberts v. Davis, 72 Ga. 819(1), and Southern Discount Co. v. Elliott, 86 Ga.App. 50, 70 S. E.2d 605) it is well stated: "It certainly is not a general rule of law that a person can be deprived of his property by an unauthorized transfer thereof, simply because he has not exercised ordinary care to prevent such transfer." Schmidt v. Garfield National Bank, 64 Hun 298, 19 N.Y.S. 252, 257. * *

The trial court erred in overruling the motion for a new trial.

Judgment reversed.

SNYDER v. TOWN HILL MOTORS, INC.

(1960) 193 Pa.Super. 578, 165 A.2d 293.

MONTGOMERY, J. This was an action of assumpsit in which minor appellant sought to recover $1,000.00 from appellees on three theories, viz., (a) fraud perpetrated by appellees upon him, (b) the right of rescission of a minor's contract, and (c) the right of an infant to rescind the negotiation of an instrument under § 3–207 of the Uniform Commercial Code of 1953, April 6, P.L. 3 (12A P.S. § 3–207). The jury returned a verdict for defendants (appellees) and appellant's motions for judgment n. o. v. and a new trial were refused.

The following relevant facts are established from the stipulation filed in lieu of printing the notes of testimony:

The minor (Snyder) contracted with his friend, Rhea, to purchase the latter's 1955 Chrysler automobile for $1,000 and the trade of his 1946 Pontiac automobile. Thereafter they went to the place of business of the Town Hill Motors, Inc. (hereinafter referred to as Motor Company), where Rhea negotiated with Abbamondi, the Motor Company's salesman, for the purchase of a Lincoln automobile. Thereupon, Rhea instructed Snyder to assign the title of the Pontiac to the Motor Company and to endorse and deliver to it the check for $1,000 made to Snyder's order and in his possession, as the down payment by Rhea on the Lincoln. Snyder intended to use the check in payment for the Chrysler. Snyder complied with Rhea's instructions, delivered the check and title to Abbamondi as agent for the Motor Company, and demanded a receipt from Rhea, who gave it in the following form:

"Received of Richard Snyder one-thousand dollars and 1946 Pontiac Coupe * * * in exchange for a 1955 Chrysler Windsor. * * *"

Snyder accepted delivery of the Chrysler; but one month or more later he returned it to the Motor Company and, contending that the amount of an encumbrance on the Chrysler was more than Rhea had represented it to be, demanded the return of the Pontiac and $1,000. Having deposited the check and received the proceeds thereof, the Motor Company refused Snyder's demand. Rhea disposed of the Chrysler and applied the proceeds of the sale on the encumbrance.

The lower court refused to submit the issue of fraud to the jury and stated in its opinion that, if any fraud existed, it had been committed by Rhea and not by the appellees. The only alleged misrepresentation was made by appellee Abbamondi and was an opinion expressed by him concerning Snyder's right to drive the Chrysler before receiving the title, which at that time was in the hands of the holder of the encumbrance. This statement was made after consummation of the contract between Snyder and Rhea and does not meet the standard set forth in Gerfin v. Colonial Smelting & Refining Company, Inc., 374 Pa. 66, 97 A.2d 71, wherein it is stated that evidence of fraud must be clear and convincing to justify the submission of the question of fraud to the jury. We find no error in the action of the lower court in this regard.

On the question, with which of the parties did appellant contract, the jury found that the appellant had contracted with Rhea and not with appellees. There is sufficient competent evidence to sustain this finding. Nevertheless, appellant now argues that appellee Motor Company was a third party beneficiary to that contract. We find nothing in either the contract or the evidence to establish that fact. A third party beneficiary to a contract comes into existence when it appears in the contract itself that both parties to the contract intend that the third party benefit thereby. [Citations.] In the present case there were two separate contracts, one between Snyder and Rhea and the other between Rhea and the Motor Company. The Motor Company was not a party to the first contract and became, as a result of Rhea's directions to Snyder, merely a transferee of the consideration passing to Rhea.

Appellant's third theory is, likewise, without merit. The rescission of a negotiable instrument by an infant against a subsequent holder in due course is not permitted by § 3–207 of the Uniform Commercial Code, on which appellant relies. Having received the instrument by negotiation from Rhea for value, in good faith, and without notice that it was overdue or had been dishonored or that there was any defense against it, the Motor Company was a subsequent holder in due course. Section 3–302 of the Code. The jury has found that there were no dealings between Snyder and the appellees.

Appellant's argument that the Motor Company was not a "subsequent" holder in due course is not supported by the evidence. The fact that the check was not manually transferred from Snyder to Rhea and then to the Motor Company would be immaterial under the definition of "delivery" contained in § 191 of the Negotiable Instruments Law of 1901, Act of May 16, 1901, P.L. 194, 56 P.S. § 491 et seq., which provides that transfer of possession may be actual or constructive. Although the Uniform Commercial Code repealed the Negotiable Instruments Law, it nevertheless did not prescribe any new definition of the term delivery. We are of the opinion, therefore, that the established definition should prevail. The generally recognized meaning of "delivery" set forth in Corpus Juris Secundum is as follows: "What constitutes delivery depends largely on the intent of the parties. It is not necessary that delivery should be by manual transfer. A constructive delivery is sufficient if made with the intention of transferring the title, and this rule is recognized by the definition of delivery in Negotiable Instruments Act § 191 as the transfer of possession, 'actual or constructive.'" 10 C.J.S. Bills and Notes § 78d.

The facts previously stated show clearly the intention of these parties. Together, Snyder and Rhea took the check to the Motor Company, where it was exhibited and where Rhea exercised dominion over it by directing Snyder to hand it over to the Motor Company. Snyder agreed to this and accepted Rhea's receipt, which acknowledged that Rhea had received the proceeds of the check. This was sufficient to constitute constructive delivery from Snyder to Rhea and "subsequently" from Rhea to the Motor Company.

Orders affirmed.

————

PROBLEMS

1. A employed B, an attorney, who obtained a judgment for A against C. In payment of the judgment C handed B his check drawn on the X Bank payable to the order of "A, judgment creditor, and B, attorney for judgment creditor." B informed A that he had this check, and asked A to sign a receipt and a document stating that the judgment had been paid. A signed both and handed them to B, who indorsed the check "A, judgment creditor; B, attorney for judgment creditor; B". When B presented the check, X Bank paid it to him. B took the money and spent it. A brought an action against X Bank for damages for the wrongful payment of the check. Decision?

2. A note payable to Brown or order is indorsed "Pay to Henry Jones for collection" over Brown's signature. It is then indorsed "Pay to William Johnson" over Jones' signature. Johnson collects the amount of the note from the maker. To whom does the money belong?

3. A negotiable promissory note executed and delivered by B to C passes in due course to and is indorsed in blank by C, D, E and F. G is the last holder and strikes out D's indorsement. What is the liability of D, E and F on their indorsements?

4. Answer each of the following statements with either the word "True" or "False." Explain your answer to each statement by no more than three lines.

(a) A qualified indorsement of a negotiable instrument bars later holders from being holders in due course.

(b) An indorsement "Pay to A for collection" is a restrictive indorsement.

(c) The words, "I hereby assign all my right, title and interest in this note to F in full," constitute a qualified indorsement.

(d) The words "Pay to the Southern Trust Company" constitute a special indorsement.

(e) "Pay to the order of the Farmers Bank of Nicholasville for deposit only" is a restrictive indorsement.

5. Max Moe executed and delivered to Allan and Anna Brown a promissory note, negotiable in form, for $1,500, dated March 1, 1965, payable to their order one year after date. On April 1, 1965, Allan Brown indorsed the note in blank and delivered it to Henry Hale in partial payment of a used automobile. Henry Hale immediately negotiated the note to Mark Hale by delivery only. Mark Hale paid Henry Hale $1,400 for the note. Before the indorsement and delivery to Henry Hale, Allan Brown had procured R. S. Tate, Sr., to sign as a joint maker, the signing being actually done by Allan Brown, R. S. Tate, Sr., being unable to write his name. R. S. Tate, Sr., was induced to consent to the placing of his name on the note by Allan Brown's fraudulent representation that R. S. Tate, Jr., had requested it. On September 1, 1966, Mark Hale brought an appropriate action on the note against R. S. Tate, Sr., seeking to recover $1,500, interest and costs. On December 1, 1966, Anna Brown indorsed the note in blank. The defendant, R. S. Tate, Sr., pleaded and proved fraud in the inducement and lack of consideration. Decision?

6. Adams, by fraudulent representations, induced Barton to purchase 100 shares of the capital stock of the Evermore Oil Company. The shares were worthless. Barton executed and delivered to Adams a negotiable promissory note for $5,000 dated May 5, in full payment of the shares, due six months after date. On May 20, Adams indorsed and sold the note to Cooper for $4,800. On October 21, Barton, having learned that Cooper now held the note, notified Cooper of the fraud and stated he would not pay the note. On December 1, Cooper negotiated the note to Davis who, while not a party to had full knowledge of the fraud perpetrated on Barton. Upon refusal of Barton to pay the note, Davis sues Barton for $5,000. Decision?

7. Roy Rand executed and delivered to Seth Sims the following note: "Chicago, Illinois, June 1, 1966. I promise to pay to the order of Seth Sims or bearer, on or before July 1, 1966, the sum of $2,000. This note is given in consideration of Sims transferring to the undersigned title to his 1965 Buick automobile. (signed) Roy Rand." Rand and Sims agreed that delivery of the car be deferred to July 1, 1966. On June 15, Sims sold and delivered the note to Karl Kaye, an innocent purchaser for value, for $1,750. On June 21, Sims's automobile was stolen and he was unable to make delivery of the car to Rand. On July 1, Rand refused to pay Kaye, informing him of the non-delivery of the automobile and pointed out that Sims had failed to indorse the note when he sold it to Kaye. On July 5, Kaye demanded and obtained Sims's indorsement. On July 6, 1966 Kaye brought an appropriate action on the note against Rand to recover $2,000. Decision?

CHAPTER 27

HOLDER IN DUE COURSE

Introductory. The concept of the holder in due course is the unique aspect of the law of commercial paper. Negotiability is significant only to the extent a holder in due course evolves; the rights of a holder other than in due course are only those of an assignee. A holder in due course, however, takes an instrument free of all claims of ownership in other parties, and free of all defenses to the instrument except for a very limited number specifically set forth in Section 3–305.

A "holder" is a person who is in possession of an instrument drawn, issued or indorsed to him or to his order or to bearer or in blank. Section 1–201(20). He need not have given value for it; he may, but need not, be a holder in due course.

Whether or not the holder is the owner of the instrument, he may transfer it, negotiate it, or (with certain exceptions specified in Section 3–603, to be treated later) discharge it or enforce payment in his own name. Section 3–301.

To be a holder in due course, however, the holder must take the instrument for value, in good faith, and without notice that it is overdue or has been dishonored or that any person has a defense against it or a claim to it. Section 3–302(1). These requirements will be analyzed separately.

1. *The Requirement of Value.* The law requires a holder in due course to *have given* value. The holder in due course occupies a preferred position and to "earn" it he must have parted with value for the instrument.

The obvious case of failure to give value is the one in which the holder, who does not possess the rights of a holder in due course, makes a gift of the instrument to a third party. For example, assume M executed a note

payable to the order of P in payment for goods to be delivered later. P, however, failed to make the delivery, but in the meantime, gave the note to his fiancee, W. After their marriage, when the note became due, M refused to pay, asserting the defense of failure of consideration. Since W had not given value for the note, she was not a holder in due course and the defense was available against her.

The concept of value in the law of negotiable instruments is not the same as that of consideration under the law of contracts. An executory promise, clearly valid consideration to support a contract, is not the giving of value to support a holder in due course status. A purchaser of a note or draft who has not yet given value may rescind the transaction and avoid it if a defense becomes known to him. A person who has given value, however, needs and deserves the protection given to a holder in due course. For example, suppose that M makes a $1,000 note payable to the order of P. P negotiates the note to H who promises to pay P for it a month later. During the month, H learns that M has a defense against P. H can rescind (cancel) the deal with P and return or tender the note back to P. This makes him whole. He has no need to cut off M's defense. Assume, on the other hand, that H has paid P for the note before he learns of M's defense. It may not be possible for H to recover his money from P. H then needs the holder-in-due-course protection which permits him to recover on the instrument from M.

Section 3–303(a) establishes this principle by providing in part that a holder takes an instrument for value only to the extent that agreed consideration has been performed.

Assume that in the foregoing case, H had agreed to pay P $900 for the note. If H had paid P $600, he could be a holder in due course only to the extent of $600, and if a defense were available, it would be valid against him to the extent of the balance. When H completed the payment of $900 to P, however, he would become a holder in due course as to the full $1,000 value of the note. A holder in due course, to give value, is not required to pay the face amount of the instrument, but only the amount he agreed to pay. In the example, then, when H paid the remaining $300 of the agreed price, he could gain holder in due course protection for an additional $400—the balance of the principal of the note. If otherwise he qualified as a holder in due course, he could collect the full $1,000, despite M's defense and despite the fact he paid only $900. Unless a party has a defense, it is of no concern to him what price has been paid by the holder for the instrument being enforced.

A rule similar to that in the case of partial payment of agreed consideration prevails in the case of an instrument given as security for an obligation. The taker is regarded as having given value to the extent of his security interest. Suppose, for example, that M makes a note in the amount of $1,000 payable to the order of P. P does not want to sell the note to H, but wants to borrow money from H who requests M's note to secure repayment of the loan. The parties agree, and H lends P $700, taking M's note as security. Since H has advanced $700, he has given value to this extent and with respect to the requirement of value qualifies as a holder in due course to this extent. If P cannot repay the loan, H can foreclose on the note by collecting it from M. Suppose M has a personal defense against P. In such case, H is free and clear of the defense to the extent of $700; with respect to the balance, the defense may be asserted. This is the rule announced by Section 3–302(4): "A purchaser of a limited interest can be a holder in due course only to the extent of the interest purchased."

The requirement that a holder in due course must give value does not mean that the holder of an antecedent claim, who gives it up in exchange for the instrument, has not given "value." He has, although this would not constitute consideration under ordinary contract law. Thus, if P owes H $1,000, and M makes and delivers a note to the order of P in the amount of $1,000, which P negotiates to H in return for a discharge of the original debt, H thereby meets the value requirement of a holder in due course. Section 3–303(b). The claim given up may be one against any person, not just one against the transferor of the instrument.

Still another question in determining whether a holder has given value: Does H have to pay for an instrument in cash to give value, or may he pay for it with another negotiable instrument, i. e., a check? For example, suppose that M makes a note in the amount of $1,000 payable to the order of P. P sells the note to H who pays P by giving him a check in the amount of $1,000 drawn on XYZ Bank. Before P takes the check to the bank for collection, H learns of a defense which M has against P. H does not stop payment of his check. Section 3–302 requires that a holder in due course give value *before* he learns of any defenses or claims against the instrument. Has H met this requirement? The answer is in the affirmative. H gave value when he gave P his check; not when the check was finally paid. Section 3–303(c). It would not be desirable to condition H's status on what had happened to his check at the time he received notice of the defense. The check itself might well have passed into the hands of a holder in due course, a fact which H could not ascertain. In effect, he has irrevocably parted with control of the check, and if he stopped payment on it at his bank, he might be forced to pay in any event by a holder in due course. The same rule of "value" applies when H has made any other irrevocable commitment, if such commitment runs to a third party rather than to P. To this extent making an executory contract can constitute the giving of value. An example of such a commitment is the issuance by a bank of a letter of credit, under which it agrees to pay amounts advanced to the person to whom it is issued, up to a stated amount. The bank has no way of stopping payment on such a letter.

Another aspect of the concept of "value" deserves mention. Suppose that P has $1,000 on deposit in his account in XYZ Bank. He receives a check drawn by D upon the Bigtown Bank in the amount of $1,000, which he deposits to his account in XYZ Bank, receiving a provisional credit therefor. The next day P deposits another $1,000 in cash to his account, and the following day he withdraws $2,000. Has XYZ Bank given value for D's check so as to constitute itself a holder in due course? Under the theory that the first money in is the first money out (FIFO), the bank would be deemed to have paid value to P for the check drawn by D, thus making itself eligible for a holder-in-due-course status.

2. *The Requirement of Good Faith.* All civilized legal systems require a good faith taking before the transferee may qualify as a holder in due course.

While the "good faith" requirement of a holder in due course is universal in application, different countries define the element in different ways. The American concept of good faith has been largely influenced by its English antecedents. The earliest English rule measured good faith "subjectively." Under this rule, if the purchaser actually was innocent, he bought in good faith, even though a prudent man would have known that something was wrong with the paper. Subsequently, in England the rule was changed to a "suspicious circumstances" test:

if the holder bought the paper under "suspicious circumstances," he could not claim good faith even though his actual state of mind may have been one of innocence. Under this test, for example, a person buying a $10,000 note from an obvious tramp could not be said to be a good faith purchaser, even though he may have bought in innocence. The circumstances militate against a finding of good faith under these circumstances. Later on, the English changed the rule again. They rejected the "suspicious circumstances" test in favor of a "prudent man" test. If a prudent man, defined as a reasonably knowledgeable and careful person, would reasonably regard the paper free of defenses and defects, then the purchaser could be said to have bought it in good faith.

Survivals of all three English rules took root in the United States, and, as a result, American courts became widely divided over the definition of "good faith." The U.C.C. attempts to settle this matter by defining good faith as "honesty in fact in the conduct or transaction concerned." Section 1–201 (19). This appears to be an adoption of the subjective test of the early English cases, an interpretation which is borne out by the rules specified to determine whether a transferee takes without notice.

3. *The Requirement of Lack of Notice.* To become a holder in due course, a transferee must take the instrument without notice of certain specified matters. "Notice" is defined in Section 1–201(25) as follows: "A person has 'notice' of a fact when (a) he has actual knowledge of it; or (b) he has received a notice or notification of it; or (c) from all the facts and circumstances known to him at the time in question he has reason to know that it exists." The last part of this Section sounds like the suspicious circumstance test, but it is not. The purchaser must be aware of the suspicious circumstances to make the rule operative; the fact that suspicious circumstances are present

does not adversely affect the purchaser, unless *he knows* of them. Thus, the test is subjective: it measures good faith by what the purchaser knows or believes. He may be empty-headed, but if his heart is pure, he can pass muster on good faith grounds.

(a) Notice of a Claim or Defense. There may be some limitations imposed on the "pure-heart-and-empty-head" test of good faith, however, by the rules of Section 3–304 which spell out in considerable detail when a purchaser is deemed to have notice of a claim or defense. Section 3–304(1) (a) provides that "The purchaser has notice of a claim or defense if the instrument is so incomplete, bears such visible evidence of forgery or alteration, or is otherwise so irregular as to call into question its validity, terms or ownership or to create an ambiguity as to the party to pay."

Suppose that the drawer draws a check on the XYZ National Bank for $100, payable to the order of the payee. Suppose the payee crudely raises the amount of the check to $1,000 and sells it to a holder. Is the holder a holder in due course? The U.C.C. would answer in the negative. He has not bought in good faith. He is charged with information which he can learn from the instrument. The instrument is so irregular, and there is such a clear indication that it has been raised that it cannot be conceded that the holder is a holder in due course.

Suppose, on the other hand, that there is an obvious change in the instrument which would not indicate wrongdoing or excite suspicion. For example, the date might be changed from January 2, 1965, to January 2, 1966, under circumstances in which it might be reasonable to assume that the drawer, out of force of habit, wrote "1965" rather than "1966" (this frequently happens in January). The holder could be a holder in due course of such an instrument. Irregularity is a fact question, to be tested in each case by its tendency to indicate to the purchaser that something is wrong.

Section 3–304(1) (b) provides that "The purchaser has notice of a claim or defense if the purchaser has notice that the obligation of any party is voidable in whole or in part, or that all parties have been discharged."

Under the first part of the rule, if the holder knows, for example, that the maker of a note has a defense against the payee which entitles him to avoid the obligation, the holder is not a holder in due course if he purchases the instrument. No one can be said to have taken an instrument in good faith when he knows that a party to the instrument has a defense which permits him to avoid his obligation as to some prior party.

The fact that the holder knows that one party has been discharged, however, should not have the same consequences as knowledge of other defenses. For example, indorsers on demand paper are discharged unless the instrument is presented within a reasonable time after they become liable on it. Suppose M makes a demand note in January payable to the order of P who indorses it and delivers it to A at the same time that he receives it. If A proposes to sell the note to B the following December, B would know that he could not hold the payee P. But if B bought the note with A's indorsement, he should be able to hold A if he presents it within a reasonable time. The fact that the holder knows that P is discharged does not prevent him from holding A, and Section 3–503 provides that seven days after the indorsement is a reasonable time. If, on the other hand, all parties are discharged, there is no one liable on the instrument, and if B takes with notice of this, he of course takes nothing.

With respect to claims only, Section 3–304 (2) provides:

> The purchaser has notice of a claim against the instrument when he has knowledge that a fiduciary has negotiated the instrument in

payment of or as security for his own debt or in any transaction for his own benefit or otherwise in breach of duty.

Section 3–304(4) (e), on the other hand, provides:

> Knowledge of the following facts does not of itself give the purchaser notice of a defense or claim * * * (e) that any person negotiating the instrument is or was a fiduciary.

The Sections are easily reconcilable. Suppose M makes a note payable to the order of "T, as trustee for the estate of Z." The instrument itself shows that T does not own the instrument, but holds it in a fiduciary (trust) capacity. If the purchaser from T knows that T is using the instrument for his own personal use or pleasure and not for trust business (e. g., he negotiates it at the race track), he has knowledge of T's rascality which prevents him from being a good faith purchaser and deprives him of the status of holder in due course.

On the other hand, trustees normally have the right to sell trust assets. The fact that the purchaser knows that the asset (the note in question) is being sold by the trustee does not of itself apprise him that anything is wrong. Where the sale is made in the ordinary course of affairs, the purchaser can take in good faith and thus be a holder in due course, even if it is subsequently proved that the trustee's dealing was a breach of his fiduciary duty. In short, it is only where the purchaser knows that the trustee is acting contrary to his trust that he is deprived of the status of good faith holder. Consistent with this rule is the provision of Section 3–206(4) that only the first taker under an indorsement for the benefit of another person must see that value given is properly applied and later holders are not required to check this fact if they have no knowledge of any improper action.

Other matters, knowledge of which does not of itself give the purchaser notice of a defense or claim, are specified in the other subparagraphs of Section 3–304(4). Subparagraph (a) so classifies knowledge of the fact that the instrument is antedated or postdated. This accords with the provision of Section 3–114(1) that antedating or postdating does not affect negotiability.

Subparagraph (b) of Section 3–304(4) provides that the mere fact that the purchaser of an instrument knows that it was originally given for an executory promise or was accompanied by a separate agreement does not destroy his good faith position, unless he knows that the promise has not been kept. In such case, he would have knowledge that the instrument was voidable, and this would prevent him from being a holder in due course. For example, suppose M makes and delivers a note to the order of P, and the note recites that it was given "As per our contract of even date." This recital does not destroy negotiability, because it does not burden the note with the extraneous contract. Section 3–105(b). But the recital does notify prospective purchasers of the note that it was given pursuant to a contract which may or may not have been performed. This knowledge would not prevent them from taking in good faith, because every negotiable instrument, whether it contains such a recital or not, must necessarily either be a gift or the result of a business transaction, and, therefore, subject to some possibility of defense. The fact that a defense is possible does not give notice that a claim of defense exists.

Subparagraph (c) states that mere knowledge of the fact that one party has signed for the accommodation of another does not give the purchaser notice of any claim or defense. Suppose that M makes a note payable to the order of P and that W also signs as maker to accommodate M. If a purchaser of the note from P knows the relationship between M and W he has knowledge of a *possible defense*; but he does not know of any defense and he is not deprived of the status of holder in due course.

Subparagraph (d) provides that knowledge of the fact that an incomplete instrument has been completed does not constitute notice of a defense or claim unless the purchaser has notice of the fact that the completion was improper. This rule is consistent with the principles applicable to completion of incomplete instruments set forth in Sections 3–115 and 3–407. For example, suppose M makes a note payable to the order of P, leaving the amount of the instrument blank. P proposes to sell the instrument to H, and, in H's presence, writes "$1,000.00" in the space reserved for the amount. Can H be a holder in due course? He knows the possibility of a defense—that P has exceeded his authority in filling in the blank space in the instrument. But H does not know as a fact that P has exceeded his authority, and, hence, he may be a holder in due course. Only if H knew that P in fact had exceeded his authority would he be precluded from this position.

Subparagraph (f) states a well-established rule that knowledge that the obligor has defaulted in the payment of interest does not defeat the purchaser's good faith. However, knowledge that there has been a default in the payment of principal or an uncured default in the payment of another instrument of the same series does prevent a finding that the purchaser took in good faith.

Section 3–304(5) also states the established rule that "constructive notice" of a defense does not prevent the purchaser from acquiring the instrument in good faith. Suppose that M makes a note payable to the order of P and secures it with the execution of a mortgage on his land. The note refers to the mortgage; the mortgage is recorded or filed with a county official; and the mortgage instrument reveals a defense which M has against P. Is H bound to check the records? The answer is, no. The concept of negotiability requires rapid circulation at minimum risks. If potential holders were constructively notified (bound by what was re-

corded), the concept of negotiability would be seriously impaired. In Foster v. Augustanna College, 92 Okl. 96, 218 P. 335 (1923) the court said: "The doctrine of constructive notice is applicable only to a person who is dealing with the land itself, and since the purchaser of a negotiable promissory note secured by a mortgage is not dealing in land, there is no field for operation of the registry laws in cases of this kind." While this rationale is frequently used, the real reason that constructive notice cannot operate to defeat the good faith status of the purchaser is that such a rule would adversely affect— perhaps to a fatal degree—the concept of negotiability.

Section 3–304(6) deals with the interesting question of a prospective holder learning of a defense before he has purchased the instrument, but the knowledge comes too late for him to act upon it. The old rule that a purchaser must have a "pure" heart as of the time of purchase worked some hardship in the situation, especially in view of the realities of modern commercial life. Suppose that the bank upon which a check is drawn is notified one minute before the teller cashes it that payment should be stopped because of fraud. Does the acquisition of this notice prevent the bank from being a holder in due course? The U.C.C. answers in the negative. Section 3–304(6) provides:

> To be effective, notice must be received at such time and in such manner as to give a reasonable opportunity to act on it.

(b) Notice an Instrument is Overdue. To be a holder in due course the purchaser must take the instrument without notice that it is overdue. This requirement is closely related to the requirement that he take the instrument in "good faith," because it is based on the idea that overdue paper conveys a suspicion that something is wrong. If the "suspicious circumstance" test of good faith had remained in the law, the requirement under consideration might have been as-

similated by it. Since "good faith" is measured subjectively, a separate requirement is needed to cover the suspicious circumstance attending overdue paper.

Under this requirement, the holder is bound to know what the instrument itself reveals. Thus, if an instrument is payable on July 1, a purchaser cannot become a holder in due course by buying it on July 2. The instrument would give him notice that it was overdue.

In the case of an installment note, or of several notes issued as part of the same transaction with successive maturity dates, there is a natural question as to the effect of notice of default in payment of an installment or of a note in the same series. Section 3–304(3) (a) answers this by providing that the purchaser has notice that an instrument is overdue if he has reason to know that any part of the principal amount is overdue or that there is an uncured default in payment of another instrument of the same series.

Demand paper, however, is different. Section 3–304(3) (c) provides that it is not overdue for purposes of preventing one from becoming a holder in due course unless the purchaser has notice that he is taking it after demand has been made, or until it has been outstanding an unreasonable length of time. Usually, in the case of a demand note, this means about 60 days. The time is somewhat shorter for drafts, and is considerably shorter for checks. With regard to checks, Section 3–304(3) (c) also provides that a reasonable time is presumed to be thirty days. But the facts of the particular case, business custom, and the like, are important factors in making the determination, and no hard-and-fast rules are possible. The courts are content to use the flexible "reasonable time" rule.

Acceleration clauses have also caused trouble. Section 3–109 broadly validates acceleration provisions. If an instrument's maturity date has been automatically ac-

celerated, the holder may be unaware that it is past due. A prospective purchaser may similarly be unaware of this fact. Section 3–304(3) (b) provides that the latter can be a holder in due course, unless he has reason to know that the acceleration has occurred.

(c) Notice an Instrument has been Dishonored. If a transferee has notice that an instrument has been dishonored by the refusal of a party to pay or accept it, he obviously cannot become a holder in due course. He knows the instrument will not be paid.

4. *A Payee may be a Holder in Due Course.* Section 3–302(2) provides that "A payee may be a holder in due course." At first blush, it might be thought that a payee could not be a holder in due course, because he is an immediate party with actual notice of defenses and claims. There are a number of situations, however, in which the payee is not an immediate party. For example, a remitter, upon purchasing goods from P, obtains a bank draft payable to the order of P and forwards it to P, who takes it for value and without any knowledge that the remitter has defrauded the bank into issuing the draft. In such a case, the payee, P, is held to be a holder in due course, free and clear of the defense.

There are a number of other ways in which a payee may be a holder in due course, but they are rather infrequent. In every instance, however, there are three parties involved in the transaction, and the defense exists between the parties other than the payee. The payee is innocent, for otherwise he could not fulfill the "without notice" requirement.

5. *Special Circumstances Denying Holder in Due Course Status.* In keeping with the theory that the purpose of negotiability is to facilitate the flow of commerce, when an instrument is acquired in a way other than the ordinary flow of commerce, there is no reason to accord the transferee holder in due course

status. Section 3–302(3) defines the situations in which this rule applies as follows:

> A holder does not become a holder in due course of an instrument:
> - (a) by purchase of it at judicial sale or by taking it under legal process; or
> - (b) by acquiring it in taking over an estate; or
> - (c) by purchasing it as a part of a bulk transaction not in regular course of business of the transferor.

In each of these situations, the transferee takes under unusual circumstances which indicate he is merely a successor in interest to a prior holder. As such, he should acquire no better rights. But if his transferor was a holder in due course, under the shelter provision of Section 3–201, he would acquire the rights of such a holder.

6. *Defenses Available Against a Holder in Due Course.* Section 3–305 sets forth succinctly the rights of a holder in due course: He takes the instrument free from all claims to it on the part of any person and free from all defenses of any party with whom he has not dealt except for a limited number, to be discussed later, which render the instrument null and void. Such defenses, since they are available against everyone, including a holder in due course, are frequently referred to as "real" defenses as opposed to defenses which are cut off as against a holder in due course and which are on occasion described as "personal defenses."

Defenses to an instrument may arise in many ways, either at the time of its issuance or later. In general, defenses to liability on a negotiable instrument are those which would be available in the case of simple contract. Their number are legion. Section 3–306 provides that they are available against any holder of the instrument unless he has the rights of a holder in due course. The defenses which are available against a holder in due course are those listed in Section 3–305(2), and forgery and material alteration.

Among the "personal" defenses which are available against any holder except a holder in due course are: (a) lack of consideration; (b) failure of consideration; (c) breach of contract; (d) fraud in the inducement; (e) illegality which does not, by local statute, render the transaction a nullity; (f) duress or undue influence; (g) set-off or counterclaim; (h) discharge; (i) non-delivery of an instrument, whether complete or incomplete; (j) unauthorized completion of an incomplete instrument; and (k) lack of authority of a corporate officer or an agent or partner as to the particular instrument, where such officer, agent or partner had general authority to issue negotiable paper for his principal or firm.

These eleven situations are the most common examples, but others exist. Indeed, the U.C.C. does not attempt to detail defenses which may be cut off. It is content to state that a holder in due course takes free and clear of all defenses except those listed in Section 3–305(2) and forgery and material alteration, which are separately covered in Section 3–404 and 3–407.

A few illustrations may suffice. Suppose that M gives P a note in payment for a television set. P indorses and delivers the note to H, a holder in due course. None of the following possible defenses are available against H: (1) The set does not work; (2) The set is not as represented; (3) P induced the sale to M by threatening to boycott him if he did not buy; (4) M paid P but failed to take up the note; (5) M refused to deliver the note to P, and P snatched it from him; (6) M delivered an incomplete instrument to P who filled it in and exceeded his authority in doing so; (7) P made the sale to M on Sunday, in violation of a local law prohibiting goods from being sold on that day; (8) M delivered the note to P on condition that P would deliver the television set to M by Friday. P did not deliver the set at all.

Defenses (1) and (2) are examples of failure of consideration or breach of contract. These defenses could be asserted by M to defeat P. But they cannot be asserted against a holder in due course.

Defense (3) illustrates "duress" or "undue influence". These consist of exercising such pressure as to overcome the will of another party, thereby inducing him to do an act he would not otherwise do. If P threatens to boycott M, M may have a defense which could be asserted against P but duress of this type would make the contract voidable rather than void. The defense would be cut off by negotiation to a holder in due course.

Defense (4) illustrates that discharge is not a defense available against a holder in due course. When a negotiable instrument is paid, the indebtedness which it represents is discharged. Usually payment is not made until the maturity date, and after maturity it is difficult for one to become a holder in due course, because no one can acquire such a status if he has reason to know that the instrument is overdue. If the instrument is payable on demand, however, it could be paid at a relatively early date. If it were not taken up by the primary party or marked "Paid" a subsequent purchaser could become a holder in due course, and, in such a case, the defense of payment would not prevail against him.

By the same token, a cancelled instrument is discharged, and usually cancellation prevents anyone from becoming a holder in due course, because it puts one on notice that something is wrong. Where the cancellation, however, does not put the purchaser on notice that there is an irregularity, the purchaser can be a holder in due course cutting off the defense. In Ingham v. Primrose, 7 C.B. (N.S.) 82, 141 Eng.Rep. 745 (1859), the instrument was torn up by the primary party and thrown into the street. It was picked up and pasted together so carefully that a reasonable inspection would not reveal that it

had been destroyed. It was sold to the plaintiff in this condition. The court held that the plaintiff was a holder in due course, cutting off the defense of cancellation (discharge).

Similarly, an indorser to whom notice of dishonor is not given usually is discharged. An instrument is generally not dishonored until maturity, and thereafter no one can be a holder in due course. However, a demand instrument may be purchased within a reasonable time after issue, even after dishonor upon presentment and notice thereof and demand upon indorser for payment. If the purchaser takes such an instrument in good faith and without knowledge of the dishonor, he can be a holder in due course free of the indorser's defense of discharge.

In accordance with these rules, Section 3–602 provides:

> No discharge of any party provided by this Article is effective against a subsequent holder in due course unless he has notice thereof when he takes the instrument.

A holder in due course may have notice that one indorser has been discharged, but no knowledge that a second indorser has been discharged. The notice with respect to the first indorser does not prevent him from being a holder in due course regarding the second indorser. That is the meaning of the last part of Section 3–602.

Defense (5) illustrates the defense of lack of delivery. Every negotiable instrument is revocable by its maker or drawer until the instrument has been delivered to the payee. Delivery, of course, is a possessory concept. It means the transfer of possession from one person to another. If the transfer of possession from the maker or drawer to the payee is not intended to give the latter rights, such as where he wrongfully takes the instrument, the instrument may be "delivered" in a technical sense, but it has not been "issued". "Issue" means to deliver with the intention of giving the transferee rights. A negotiable instrument can be revoked prior to issuance.

Failure to issue the instrument is a defense which can be cut off by negotiation to a holder in due course. Thus, where the payee forcibly takes the instrument from the drawer, the drawer has a defense against him. If the payee negotiates the instrument to a holder in due course, the defense is cut off.

Defense (8), where M delivered the note to P on condition that P would deliver the television set by Friday, and P did not deliver the set at all, involves the personal defense of a "conditional delivery". Since the condition upon which the delivery of the note to P was not met, the delivery is revocable, and the instrument is said not to be issued after the condition is broken. This means that M has a defense against P. It is a defense to which a holder in due course is not subject.

Defense (6), where M delivered an incomplete instrument to P who filled in the blanks in an unauthorized way, may not be asserted against a holder in due course.

Defense (7), in which P made a sale of the television to M on Sunday, taking in return for it P's promissory note, pleads a "blue law" prohibiting transactions of this kind on Sunday, but this defense normally is cut off by negotiation to a holder in due course. "Blue laws" do not render the obligation a nullity, and hence the obligation is only voidable at best.

Because of the commercial desirability of protecting a holder in due course from ordinary contract defenses such as the foregoing, the U.C.C. provides that such a holder takes the instrument free from all such defenses. Overriding public policy dictates, however, that certain types of defenses should be available even though the rights of a holder in due course are thereby affected. These defenses, which are detailed in Sections 3–305(2), 3–404 and 3–407, are sometimes referred to as "real" defenses and will be treated separately herein. Some may bear a resemblance to one or more of those discussed above but they are in fact distinguishable.

(a) Minority. All States have a firmly entrenched public policy of protecting minors from persons who might take advantage of them through contractual dealings. The exact manifestation of this policy may differ from State to State, but it exists in all. In recognition of this fact, the U.C.C. provides that minority—technically referred to as "infancy"—is a defense available against a holder in due course to the extent it is a defense to a simple contract under the laws of the State involved. No other defense based on voidability of a contract may be asserted against a holder in due course.

(b) Void Obligations. Where the obligation on an instrument originates in such a way that under the law of the State involved it is void from the beginning, the U.C.C. authorizes the interposition of this defense against a holder in due course. This follows from the fact that where the party was never obligated, it is unreasonable to permit an event over which he has no control—negotiation to a holder in due course—to convert a nullity into a valid claim against him. The purchaser has bought a valueless item and should look to his transferor for reimbursement.

Incapacity, other than minority, duress and illegality of the transaction are defenses which may render the obligation of a party voidable or void, depending upon the law of the State involved as applied to the facts of a transaction. To the extent the obligation is rendered void, the defense may be asserted against a holder in due course. To the extent it is voidable only, the defense is cut off.

Contractual incapacity may be based upon mental incapacity of an individual, such as insanity or, in the case of a corporation, lack of legal capacity to execute the instrument based on some statutory or constitutional requirement. An example of this is an instrument executed by a governmental unit. If the State constitution, for example, prohibits towns of certain size from making promissory notes, the town should not be able to avoid this limitation by making such notes and having them come into the hands of holders in due course. If the holder in due course could take free of this limitation, the division of powers in our government would be upset. To prevent an unconstitutional act from having legal effect through the concept of negotiability, therefore, the governmental unit is given a defense when it exceeds its own authority which it can assert even against a holder in due course.

The type of duress which would render an obligation void is a matter of degree and may vary from State to State. Certainly an instrument signed at the point of a gun would be void in any State. But one signed on the basis of a threat to prosecute the maker's son, or to boycott the drawer or maker, as described above, would be merely voidable in most States. In that case the defense would not be available against the holder in due course. Again, State law is determinative.

Closely related to these situations of contractual incapacity and duress are cases in which the relevant State, for reasons of its own public policy, makes void certain kinds of transactions. Gaming statutes, for example, may provide that any contract made pursuant to a gambling transaction is void. Suppose that D draws a check in such a State to pay his gambling debt. It is void. Usury statutes are another common example of laws which in some States make the underlying transaction and instrument void. The most stringent usury statutes make unenforceable any instrument or contract containing an usurious agreement. Under such a law, if M made a note carrying an excessive rate of interest, not even a holder in due course could enforce the instrument. In other States, however, usury may not be a defense sufficient to prevent collection of the principal of the note, and in others it may render the note voidable rather than void. In such States, the defense could not be as-serted against a holder in due course. Similarly, blue laws usually render obligations voidable rather than void.

In certain States, statutes may declare other obligations void because of illegality of the transaction. These are matters primarily of local concern and local policy, but the U.C.C. honors them by making all instruments which are void for illegality unenforceable even by holders in due course.

(c) Fraud in the Execution. Fraud in the execution of the instrument is another defense which renders the instrument void and, therefore, constitutes a defense even against a holder in due course. Section 3–305 (2) (c) describes it as such misrepresentation as has induced the party to sign the instrument with neither knowledge nor reasonable opportunity to obtain knowledge of its character or its essential terms. For example, suppose that M is asked to sign a receipt. He does so, not realizing that his signature is being transmitted by highly sensitive carbon paper to a promissory note which is concealed under the receipt. In this case, M's signature appears on the note, and, in a sense, he has signed it. But a signature procured under these circumstances does not involve a consent to the instrument upon which it appears, and the courts treat it as no consent and no contract.

A more common example of fraud in the execution arises where an illiterate is asked to sign a receipt or some other paper, and he puts his signature on a negotiable instrument which is pushed before him. Here he has directly signed the instrument reasonably thinking it was a receipt. If he had no way to find out the true nature of the instrument that he signed, the instrument is void as to him.

The test of the availability of the defense of fraud in the execution is whether the signer's ignorance of the contents of the writing was excusable. Not only must he have had no such knowledge, but he must also have had no reasonable opportunity to obtain such knowledge. Relevant factors include the signer's age, sex, intelligence, education, business experience, ability to read or understand English, the necessity for acting promptly and similar pertinent evidentiary matters.

(d) Forgery and the Unauthorized Signature. Closely akin to the defense of void obligation is the defense of unauthorized signature. A party's signature to an instrument is unauthorized when it is made without actual, implied or apparent authority, and includes a forgery. Where in all probability the party whose unauthorized signature appears on the instrument has never seen it or been aware of its existence, the magic of negotiation to a holder in due course cannot convert it into a valid claim against him.

For example, if the maker's signature is forged to a note, he cannot be held liable on it, in the absence of estoppel, even if the instrument is negotiated to a holder in due course. The maker has not made a contract. There is no basis upon which he can be held. Similarly, if A's signature were forged to the back of an instrument, A could not be held as an indorser, even assuming the holder satisfied the conditions precedent to liability by presenting the instrument and giving A prompt notice of dishonor. A has not made a contract. There is no basis upon which he can be held. In keeping with these principles, Section 3–404 provides that any unauthorized signature is wholly inoperative as that of the person whose name is signed unless he ratifies it or is precluded from denying it.

A party with a valid defense may nonetheless be precluded from asserting it under the legal doctrine of estoppel. It is well settled that one may be estopped (precluded) from asserting a defense, because his own conduct

in the matter would make it unconscionable for him to do so. Suppose D's son forges D's name to a check which the drawee bank cashes. When the returned check reaches D he learns of the forgery. Rather than subject his son to trouble, possibly criminal prosecution, D says nothing. Thereafter, D's son continues to forge checks and cashes them at the drawee bank. The bank may be suspicious of the signature, but the fact that D has not complained may induce it to believe that the signatures are all right. Finally, D does complain. Can he now compel the bank to re-credit his account for all the forged checks? The answer is, no. He is precluded by his own conduct from such a right.

(e) Material Alteration. Just as an unauthorized signature cannot create liability, even in favor of a holder in due course, so alteration of an instrument cannot change or increase the obligation of a party thereto. A holder in due course of an altered instrument may enforce it according to its original terms, but the alteration is a complete defense insofar as any greater or different liability is involved. Section 3–407(3). Although unauthorized completion of an incomplete instrument is defined as a material alteration under Section 3–407(1), as has been indicated above, it cannot be asserted as a defense against a holder in due course. The maker or drawer, by leaving the blank, must bear the responsibility for making the unauthorized completion possible. Section 3–406. This follows the generally recognized principle of law that as between two innocent parties, the one who was negligent must bear the loss.

(f) Discharge in Insolvency Proceedings. If a party becomes bankrupt and is discharged in bankruptcy proceedings, he has a defense to his negotiable instrument obligations. The purpose of bankruptcy law is to give the bankrupt an opportunity to wipe the slate clean and to start afresh. This purpose would be partially frustrated if holders in

due course could compel the bankrupt to pay debts which have been discharged. To implement the policy of the Bankruptcy Act, and other insolvency proceedings, the discharged party is accorded a defense on his negotiable instruments, good against all parties including a holder in due course.

7. *Claims or Equities of Ownership.* Claims or equities of ownership are similar to defenses, except that the alleged owner uses them affirmatively rather than defensively. Suppose that M makes and delivers a note payable to the order of P; P indorses the note in blank; the note, in this form, is stolen from P and negotiated to H. If H sues P on the indorsement contract, P will set up the defense that he did not deliver the note. This defense will not defeat an action by H, a holder in due course. P, however, might not wait for H to sue him. In such a case P would be asserting a "claim of ownership" or an "equity of ownership"; in the first situation he is asserting a defense based on lack of delivery.

Such claims of ownership are treated like defenses other than those which are specifically excepted as discussed above. They are defeated by holders in due course. If H is a holder in due course, P cannot compel him to return the note to P. The note belongs to H. His holder-in-due-course status cuts off the ownership rights that others might have had in the instrument.

8. *Jus Tertii.* *Jus tertii* defenses are those not possessed by the defender but possessed by a third party. Suppose that M makes and delivers a note payable to the order of P; P indorses and delivers the note to H, in return for which H undertakes certain contractual obligations to P. H does not perform these obligations. P thereupon directs M not to pay the note when H presents it. M has no defense of his own. If H sues M on the note, may he assert P's defense? This is the question which lawyers call "the question of *jus tertii.*"

At common law the courts were divided on the question whether the defense of *jus tertii* could be successfully asserted by a party to a negotiable instrument. Section 3–306(d) resolves this question. It denies the right of *jus tertii*, except where the instrument has been stolen or restrictively indorsed by providing:

> Unless he has the rights of a holder in due course any person takes the instrument subject to * * * (d) the defense that he or a person through whom he holds the instrument acquired it by theft, or that payment or satisfaction to such holder would be inconsistent with the terms of a restrictive indorsement. The claim of any third party to the instrument is not otherwise available as a defense to any party liable thereon unless the third person himself defends the action for such party.

Of course, the *jus tertii* situation seldom arises where the plaintiff is a holder in due course as the defense is a personal one and not available against such a holder. Where H is not a holder in due course, he may nevertheless be able to recover against M, where M does not have a defense of his own but asserts a defense which P would have in an action by H against P. Under the U.C.C., M cannot set up P's defenses against H. P must intervene in the action and assert his own defense. P might be prompted to intervene by way of asserting an equitable claim of ownership to the note upon rescission of his contract with H for non-performance by H. P would ask that H take nothing in his suit against M and that judgment be entered in favor of P against M on the note.

9. *Procedure in Recovering on Instrument.* A frequent misconception is that only a holder in due course may recover on an instrument and that the plaintiff's lack of holder-in-due-course status is a defense. Nothing could be further from the truth.

In the normal law suit in which recovery on an instrument is attempted, the question of whether the plaintiff is a holder in due course may never arise. Section 3–307 describes the step by step procedure.

When the holder files suit to collect, he relies upon Section 3–301, which provides that the holder of an instrument, whether or not he is a holder in due course, may, among other things, enforce payment in his own name. Upon filing of suit, it is assumed that all signatures are valid and effective unless the defendant denies this. Even at this point it is not pertinent whether the plaintiff is a holder in due course, since the defense of unauthorized signature is valid against any holder.

If the signatures are admitted, or proved valid, the plaintiff is entitled to recover merely upon production of the instrument unless the defendant alleges a defense. Up to this point there has been no occasion for the plaintiff to allege that he is a holder in due course. If no defense is asserted, he obtains judgment without more. If the defense asserted is one of those which is effective against a holder in due course, the suit goes to trial without the matter ever being mentioned.

Only if the defense raised is one which is cut off as against a holder in due course does it behoove the plaintiff to allege and prove his status. If he fails, the defense must be tried on its merits. If he succeeds, however, the defendant is denied the right to prove his defense, since it is irrelevant. It is toward this single objective that the whole law of commercial paper with its unique concept of the holder in due course is directed.

CASES

KORZENIK v. SUPREME RADIO, INC.

(1964) 347 Mass. 309, 197 N.E.2d 702.

WHITTEMORE, J. The plaintiffs, as indorsees, brought an action in the District Court of Western Hampden to recover $1,900 on two "note[s] in the form of * * * trade acceptance[s]" given by Supreme Radio, Inc. (Supreme), to Southern New England Distributing Corporation (Southern), dated October 16, 1961, and due, respectively, on November 1, 1961, and December 1, 1961. The plaintiffs are partners in the practice of law. The trade acceptances in suit and others, all of a total face value of about $15,000, were transferred to them on October 31, 1961, by their client Southern "as a retainer for services to be performed" by the plaintiff Korzenik. The trade acceptances in suit and two others given by Supreme had been obtained by fraud. Southern had retained Korzenik on October 25, 1961, in connection with certain anti-trust litigation. Korzenik did some legal work between October 25 and October 31, but there was no testimony as to the value of the services and the trial judge was unable to determine their value. He found for the defendant. Korzenik did not know that the acceptances were obtained by fraud. "He has paid co-counsel retained in the anti-trust case part of the money he has collected" on the assigned items.

The Appellate Division dismissed the report of the trial judge.

Decisive of the case, as the Appellate Division held, is the correct ruling that the plaintiffs are not holders in due course under G.L. c. 106, § 3–302; they have not shown to what extent they took for value under § 3–303. That section provides: "A holder takes the instrument for value (a) to the extent that the agreed consideration has been performed or that he acquires a security interest in or a lien on the instrument otherwise than by legal process; or (b) when he takes the instrument in payment of or as security for an antecedent claim against any person whether or not the claim is due; or (c) when he gives a negotiable instrument for it or makes an irrevocable commitment to a third person."

Under clause (a) of § 3–303 the "agreed consideration" was the performance of legal services. It is often said that a lawyer is "retained" when he is engaged to perform services, and we hold that the judge spoke of "retainer" in this sense. The phrase that the judge used, "retainer *for services*" (emphasis supplied), shows his meaning as does the finding as to services already performed by Korzenik at the time of the assignments. Even if the retainer had been only a fee to insure the attorney's availability to perform future services [citation] there is no basis in the record for determining the value of this commitment for one week.

The Uniform Laws Comment to § 3–303 points out that in this article "value is divorced from consideration" and that except as provided in paragraph (c) "[a]n executory promise to give value is not * * * value * * * The underlying reason of policy is that when the purchaser learns of a defense * * * he is not required to enforce the instrument, but is free to rescind the transaction for breach of the transferor's warranty."

General Laws c. 106, § 3–307(3), provides: "After it is shown that a defense exists a person claiming the rights of a holder in due course has the burden of establishing that he or some person under whom he claims is in all respects a holder in due course." The defence of fraud having been established this section puts the burden on the plaintiffs. The plaintiffs have failed to show "the extent * * * [to which] the agreed consideration * * * [had] been performed."

The only other possible issue under § 3–303 is whether, because of or in connection with taking the assignments, Korzenik made "an irrevocable commitment to a third person." There is no evidence of such a commitment. The finding as to a payment to cocounsel shows only that some of the proceeds of other assigned items have been expended by Korzenik.

Order dismissing report affirmed.

FIRST PENNSYLVANIA BANKING & TRUST CO. v. DE LISE

(1958) 186 Pa.Super. 398, 142 A.2d 401.

GUNTHER, J. This appeal is from an order of the court below discharging defendants' rule to open judgment.

The First Pennsylvania Banking and Trust Company confessed judgment against the defendants. The negotiable judgment note in question was made to Babco Aluminum Products Co., Inc., a home improvement contracting corporation, as payee and endorsed to the plaintiff blank.

A petition to open the judgment was filed setting forth the following grounds:

1. The Babco Aluminum Products Co., Inc., obtained defendants' signature by fraud;

2. The consideration for the note failed;

3. The plaintiff bank had notice of dishonor before negotiation;

4. The plaintiff bank had notice that a valid defense existed before endorsement.

An answer was filed denying the above allegations and depositions were taken. The record discloses that on September 7, 1955, Babco Aluminum Products and defendants entered into an agreement for certain alterations to the house of the defendants, stipulating that defendants execute a promissory note to the order of Babco Aluminum Products in the amount of $2,320.66. The note was endorsed for value to the First National Bank of Philadelphia, predecessor to plaintiff.

Defendants, in their petition, claim that they were induced to sign the note by false representations as to the nature of the instrument by Babco Aluminum Products Co., Inc. It was also averred that plaintiff's predecessor in title had notice of dishonor prior to the date of the negotiation of the note.

Plaintiff denied any misrepresentations; it also denied receipt of notice of dishonor.

At the time of the taking of the depositions, it was stipulated that the plaintiff was a holder in due course except as to notice of dishonor and notice that a valid defense existed against the note.

Defendants testified that it was their impression that the legal size paper which they signed concerned the repairs only. They did not, according to their version, suspect that they were signing a judgment note. It was not until after Babco Aluminum Products Co., Inc., began the work that the defendants were advised that the legal size paper was a judgment note. The note in question is dated October 10, 1955, for $2,320.25 payable in thirty-six monthly installments of $64.46 each, beginning November 15, 1955. Defendants contend that they notified the bank that they would not honor the note because the repairs were not being made in a workmanlike manner and assert that the notice to the bank took place during the first week of October, 1955.

The bank, however, maintains that it first received notice from Mrs. DeLise, one of the defendants, on December 15, 1955, when she complained that the repairs were not satisfactory. Mr. Hanson, the bank supervisor, testified that the next time he heard from the defendants was on March 2, 1956, when Mr. DeLise complained that the work was unfinished. As to the instrument itself, the reverse side contains the following printed matter: "Pay to the Order of The First National Bank of Phila., Pa. Without Recourse except that the undersigned endorser warrants that the undersigned has furnished and installed all articles and materials and has fully completed all work which constitutes the consideration for which this note was executed and delivered by the maker. Babco Aluminum Products Co., Inc. Abe S. Mendelson."

The plaintiff bank introduced no testimony as to the date or circumstances of purchase of the note. There is evidence, however, that about the 9th or 10th of September the note was signed and that a few days later, when some disagreement arose over the straightening of the floor, Mrs. DeLise was requested to call the bank and informed the bank that she was not going to pay for the repairs unless the kitchen would be fixed the way it was promised.

* * * On July 11, 1957, the rule to open judgment was discharged * * *. It is from this decree that the defendants filed the appeal.

It is our opinion that the judgment should be opened and defendants be allowed to present their defense. A holder in due course is a holder who takes the instrument without notice that it is overdue or has been dishonored or of any defense against it. Uniform Commercial Code, Act of April 6, 1953, P.L. 3, section 3–302, 12A P.S. section 3–302. Defendants contend that they were induced to sign the note by fraud and misrepresentation and that they notified the bank that they would not pay the note which Babco either intended to or did assign. Section 3–307(3) of the Uniform Commercial Code, supra, provides that after evidence of a defense has been introduced a person claiming the rights of a holder in due course has the burden of establishing that he or some person under whom he claims is in all respects a holder in due course. Since the plaintiff introduced no testimony as to the circumstances under which the note was negotiated and since the endorsement is not dated, plaintiff has not met the burden placed upon it. [Citation.] Where the makers of a negotiable instrument testify that it was fraudulently executed and used for a purpose not intended, a breach of faith is sufficiently established to require the endorsee to assume the burden of proving that he is a holder in due course. Here, evidence of a defense has been shown and the holder has the burden placed upon him by the Code.

Had plaintiff bank introduced evidence to the effect that it received the note for value before maturity and without notice of any claim or defense, a refusal to open judgment would have been warranted. However, the telephone call from Mrs. DeLise to the bank, advising it of her refusal to pay unless certain things were done, was sufficient. Notice may be given in any reasonable manner. It may be oral or written and in any terms which identify the instrument and states that it has been dishonored. Uniform Commercial Code, supra, section 3–508(3). As to the date of the notice, a question of fact has been raised, and this question is solely for the determination of the jury.

The other point in the appeal involves the question of fraud. The testimony of the defendants reveals that the Babco representatives gave them the impression that the instrument they were signing dealt with the matter of repairs only. Defendants aver that they never intended to sign a judgment note or any other negotiable instrument. On September 7, 1955, they entered into an agreement for repairs to be made in a workmanlike manner and to execute a promissory note at the completion thereof. Two days later Babco representatives called upon them to complete the details of repairs but instead had them execute a judgment note. This, if true, was an illegal imposition of liability on defendants. This misrepresentation induced them to sign the instrument without reasonable opportunity to obtain knowledge of its character.

It is urged, however, that some five months after the notice given to the bank, defendants voluntarily began payments on the note and continued to do so until October, 1956, operated as a waiver of rights accruing from the notice of dishonor. The testimony of defendants show that payments were made only after threats of foreclosure and sheriff's sale of their property were made. Such payments, under duress, cannot be considered as a waiver of anything nor a ratification of their acts. The relevant factors and circum-stances surrounding execution of the judgment note lead us to conclude that justice will be served in opening the judgment and allowing the question to be determined by a jury.

The order of the court below is reversed.

PAZOL v. CITIZENS NATIONAL BANK OF SANDY SPRINGS

(1964) 110 Ga.App. 319, 138 S.E.2d 442.

[The Citizens National Bank of Sandy Springs brought an action against Sidney Pazol to recover $49,600, the amount of a check drawn by him on the Fulton National Bank of Atlanta, payable to the order of Eidson & Seiden Construction & Development Co., Inc. Plaintiff, in its petition, alleged that the check was dated January 4, 1964, (the check was actually dated January 4, 1963,) and delivered to the payee on the day named; that on January 9, 1964, the payee caused the check to be indorsed "For deposit" and deposited it in its checking account with Citizens National Bank, which credited its account with the amount of the check upon its deposit and, on January 9 and 10, prior to receipt of any notice of dishonor of the check, permitted the payee-depositor to withdraw the full amount of the check. Citizens National Bank presented the check for collection to the drawee bank, Fulton National Bank of Atlanta, but the check was dishonored by that bank, conformably to Pazol's stop payment order and was returned to Citizens National Bank on January 13, 1964. Plaintiff, Citizens National Bank, alleged that it had taken the check in good faith, before it was overdue or had been dishonored and without notice of any defense against or claim to it by any person. Pazol refused to pay Citizens National Bank the amount of the check upon proper demand. Pazol filed a general demurrer to plaintiff's petition, the demurrer was overruled, and defendant Pazol excepted.]

FELTON, C. J. 1. Prior to the enactment of the Uniform Commercial Code (Ga.L.1962, p. 156 et seq.; Code Title 109A), the law in this State with regard to the present situation was expressed in Pike v. First National Bank of Rome, 99 Ga.App. 598(1) 109 S.E.2d 620, as follows: "The deposit by a customer in a bank of a check to the credit of the depositor gives rise to the presumption, as between the parties, that the bank is the collecting agency of the depositor. And even though there is an express agreement to that effect, where, however, it is the custom of the bank to credit such deposits to the account of the customer and to permit him to draw against it, and where the depositor does in fact draw out substantially the entire proceeds of the checks before collection thereof by the bank and before any notice of any infirmity in such checks, the bank by such action gives value and becomes a holder in due course of the instruments sued on, with the privilege of collecting the proceeds of the checks in its own name in an action against the drawer thereof, and without being subject to any defenses which might have been urged against the original payee." [Citations.]

An examination of the provisions of the U.C.C. (Code Title 109A) and a comparison of it with the law prior to its passage reveal that the adoption of the U.C.C. has not changed the result under the present alleged factual situation. The plaintiff bank is at least a holder, as defined by Code Ann. § 109 A–1–201(20), i. e., "a person who is in possession of a document of title or an instrument or an investment security drawn, *issued or indorsed* to him or to his order or to bearer or in blank." (Emphasis supplied.) The petition alleges that the payee delivered the check to the plaintiff and "caused the same to be endorsed for deposit." Even if this is construed to mean that the payee did not personally indorse the instrument, as indeed the copy of the check attached as an exhibit shows to be the case, it was issued to the plaintiff. Code Ann. § 109A–3–202(2) provides that "[a]n indorsement must be written by *or on behalf of* the holder," which holder may be the payee under Code Ann. § 109A–3–302(2). Code Ann. § 109A–4–205(1) provides as follows: "A depositary bank which has taken an item for collection may supply any indorsement of the customer which is necessary to title unless the item contains the words 'payee's indorsement required' or the like. In the absence of such a requirement a statement placed on the item by the depositary bank to the effect that the item was deposited by a customer or credited to his account is effective as the customer's indorsement." The comment of the National Conference of Commissioners on Uniform State Laws and the American Law Institute pertaining to this particular section explains that this subsection "is designed to speed up collections by eliminating any necessity to return to a *non-bank depositor* any items he may have failed to indorse." (Emphasis supplied.) 1962 Official Text of the Uniform Commercial Code, p. 389. The phrase "non-bank depositor" means a depositor which is not a bank, rather than one depositing in something other than a bank, as is contended by the plaintiff in error. Under the provisions of Code Ann. § 109A–3–301, "[t]he holder of an instrument whether or not he is the owner may transfer or negotiate it and, except as otherwise provided in 109A–3–603 on payment or satisfaction discharge it or *enforce payment in his own name*." (Emphasis supplied.) There being no provisions in Code Ann. § 109A–3–603 which apply to the case sub judice, the plaintiff, being a holder of the check, could, under the above Code sections, enforce payment in its own name against the drawer.

Furthermore, under the allegations of the petition, the plaintiff was a holder in due course as defined by Code Ann. § 109A–3–302 (1), which requires that the holder take the instrument "(a) for value; and (b) in good faith; and (c) without notice that it is overdue or has been dishonored or of any defense against or claim to it on the part of any person." Regarding requirement (a), Code § 109A–4–209 provides as follows: "For purposes of determining its status as a holder in due course, the bank has given value *to the extent that it has a security interest in an item* provided that the bank otherwise complies with the requirements of 109A–3–302 on what constitutes a holder in due course." (Emphasis supplied.) Code Ann. § 109A–208(1) provides that "[a] bank has a security interest in an item * * * (a) in case of an item deposited in an account to the extent to which credit given for the item has been withdrawn or applied." Code Ann. § 109A–3–303 also provides that a holder takes an instrument for value to the extent that he acquires a security interest in the instrument. Code Ann. § 109A–3–205 defines a restrictive indorsement as one which "(c) includes the words 'for collection,' 'for deposit,' 'pay any bank,' or *like terms signifying a purpose of deposit or collection.*" (Emphasis supplied.) Code Ann. § 109A–3–206(3) provides that the transferee of an instrument with such an indorsement" * * * must pay or apply any value given by him for or on the security of the instrument consistently with the indorsement and to the extent that he does so he becomes a *holder for value.* In addition such transferee is a *holder in due course* if he otherwise complies with the requirements of 109A–3–302 on what constitutes a holder in due course." (Emphasis supplied.) By causing the check to be indorsed "for deposit," as alleged, the payee signified its purpose of deposit and the plaintiff bank, by applying the value given consistently with this indorsement by crediting the payee-depositor's account with the amount of the check, became a holder for value.

Regarding requirement (b) of a holder in due course (Code Ann. § 109A–3–302(1)), there is nothing on the face of the petition to indicate a lack of good faith on the part of the plaintiff in accepting the check. Good faith is presumed until questioned by appropriate pleadings.

The liability of the drawer to pay the amount of his dishonored check is established by Code Ann. § 109A–3–413(2): "The drawer engages that upon dishonor of the draft and any necessary notice of dishonor or protest he will pay the amount of the draft to the holder or to any indorser who takes it up. * * *" Under Code Ann. § 109A–3–511(2), notice or protest is entirely excused when "(b) such party has himself dishonored the instrument or has countermanded payment or otherwise has no reason to expect or right to require that the instrument be accepted or paid."

* * *

2. Regarding requirement (c) of a holder in due course, the fact that the copy of the check attached as an exhibit to the petition bears a date more than one year prior to the time the instrument was alleged to have been transferred to the plaintiff bank does not subject the petition to a general demurrer on the ground that the petition shows that the bank had notice that the check was overdue. While it is true that "[w]here the instrument or any signature thereon is dated, the date is presumed to be correct," Code Ann. § 109A–3–114(3) (Ga.L.1962, pp. 156, 244), this presumption is not conclusive, and may be overcome by parol evidence that it was in fact made on another date, Mutual Fertilizer Co. v. Henderson, 18 Ga.App. 495(1), 89 S.E. 602; this evidence not being inadmissible as seeking to vary the contents of the instrument. [Citations.] It is alleged that the plaintiff gave credit for the check prior to receiving any knowledge or notice of its having been dishonored and without notice of any defense against or claim to it on the part of any person. This allegation is sufficient as against a general demurrer to allege compliance with requirement (c) of a holder

in due course. The petition therefore alleges the plaintiff to be a holder in due course, with the rights incident thereto as set out in Code Ann. § 109A–3–305.

The court did not err in its judgment overruling the general demurrer to the petition.

Judgment affirmed.

HOWARD v. BIGGS

(1963 Okl.) 378 P.2d 306.

BERRY, J. In September, 1956, defendant in error, hereafter referred to as "defendant", owned and operated a drive-in restaurant in Bartlesville, Oklahoma. During said month, W. B. Cunningham, hereafter referred to as "vendor", and defendant entered into a contract in writing by the terms of which vendor agreed to sell and install and defendant agreed to buy for an agreed consideration of $3,405.00 a communication system for use by patrons of the restaurant in ordering food. The name applied to the system was "Ordermatic".

Following installation of the system, defendant, on November 26, 1956, executed and delivered to vendor a chattel mortgage which granted to vendor a lien on the system. In drafting the mortgage a printed form was used. As evidenced by the form it was intended to apply to automobiles only. However, verbiage which vendor caused to be written upon the form showed that the mortgage was applicable to the system. A copy of the mortgage was filed of record December 17, 1956.

The bottom of the mentioned form consisted of a printed form of promissory note. Vendor caused blanks on this form to be filled in so as to show that on November 26, 1956, defendant promised to pay vendor $2400.00 (balance owing on the purchase price of the system) in monthly installments of $100.00 each month beginning January 15, 1957. In the blank space re-

lating to the rate of interest the word "no" was inserted. While defendant executed both the chattel mortgage and note, he testified that he intended only to execute the mortgage and did not realize that he also executed the note. With the exception of the date and name of the payee which were typewritten, the blank spaces were filled in by using a pen.

In December, 1956, vendor sold and assigned with recourse the mortgage and note to plaintiff in error, hereafter referred to as "plaintiff". As of date of sale, the note had been detached from the mortgage. However, a copy of the mortgage was delivered to plaintiff. The copy showed this: "90 day service warranty 12 months parts warranty from date of this contract (mortgage)".

In the fall of 1957, no payments having been made on the note, plaintiff for the first time demanded payment of past-due installments. Defendant refused to pay. His refusal was based upon the proposition that vendor had agreed to service the system; that vendor breached the agreement and that the system would not operate properly. Plaintiff in turn contended that prior to maturity the note was transferred to him for a valuable consideration; that as of date of transfer he was without knowledge of alleged failure of consideration or of any facts which gave him notice of any alleged infirmities in the note.

Following repeated refusals on defendant's part to pay in accordance with the tenor of the note, plaintiff instituted this action.

As indicated, the basic issue presented by the pleadings and evidence was whether plaintiff was a holder in due course of the note. By verdict of the jury to whom the case was tried and judgment of the trial court thereon, this issue was resolved against plaintiff. We add, at the conclusion of the trial plaintiff moved for a directed verdict, which motion was denied.

From order denying plaintiff's motion for new trial which was directed to the judgment, plaintiff appealed.

As pointed out, prior to due date of the first installment, plaintiff for a valuable consideration purchased the note. The only notice that he had of the terms and conditions of the sale that resulted in execution of the note or of any infirmities in the note, were statements set forth in the mortgage relative to vendor's agreement to service the system for 90 days and his warranty of the parts used therein for 12 months. If vendor had in fact breached said conditions prior to the transfer, there is no evidence showing that plaintiff then had notice of the breach. As a general rule, knowledge that a note was given in consideration of an executory agreement of the payee, which has not been performed, will not deprive a holder of the note of the character of a bona fide holder, unless he had knowledge as of time of transfer of same that the agreement had been breached. [Citations.]

Defendant testified that while vendor advised him that he would call to service the system about every two weeks, following execution of the mortgage and note, vendor failed to service the system; that during and following rains the system would not function properly; that the system gradually deteriorated; that he dismantled the system in 1960 and stored it in the attic of his home. There is no evidence that defendant ever offered to return the system to vendor. While defendant testified that he was unable to locate vendor following execution of the mortgage and note, it appears that defendant caused vendor's deposition to be taken. The deposition was not introduced in evidence. Defendant's testimony as to malfunction of the system was corroborated.

Defendant contends that the evidence shows that in purchasing the note, plaintiff acted in bad faith and for said reason the jury properly found that plaintiff was not a holder in due course. In support of this contention defendant alludes to that portion of 48 O.S.1961 § 122 to the effect that "a holder in due course is a holder who [had] taken the instrument under the following conditions: * * * 4. That at the time it was negotiated to him he had no notice of any infirmity in the instrument or defect in the title of the person negotiating it;" to Sec. 126, same title, to the effect that "To constitute notice of an infirmity in the instrument or defect in the title of the person negotiating the same, the person to whom it is negotiated must have had actual knowledge of the infirmity or defect, or knowledge of such facts that his action in taking the instrument amount to bad faith," and quotes the third paragraph of the syllabus to Commercial Nat. Bank of Muskogee v. Ahrens, 117 Okl. 65, 245 P. 557, to the effect that "While suspicion of defect of title, or the knowledge of circumstances which would excite such suspicion in the mind of a prudent man, or of circumstances sufficient to put him upon inquiry, will not defeat the title of a holder, and that result can be produced only by bad faith of the holder, yet the jury—or the court, in the absence of the jury—may find bad faith therefrom."

Facts and circumstances showing bad faith on plaintiff's part are asserted to be these: Plaintiff only paid 75 per cent of the face value of the note. "The note was partly handwritten, but the name of payee (vendor) and the date were typewritten." The note was attached to a chattel mortgage designed to grant a mortgage on an automobile. The mortgage showed that vendor had agreed to service the equipment. Vendor endorsed the note "with recourse". Plaintiff did not demand payment until some ten months after he acquired it. Plaintiff did not sue to foreclose the mortgage.

The fact that plaintiff paid but 75 per cent of the face value of the note did not prevent him from becoming a holder in due course [citation], nor under the evidence did the fact that the date thereof and name of the payee may have been filled in after same was executed or that vendor endorsed the note with recourse operate to destroy the negotiability of note [citations]; nor did plaintiff's knowledge of the warranty provisions set forth in the mortgage affect his alleged status as a holder in due course [citation]. Defendant has cited no authority sustaining his suggestion that any of the other matter that he has pointed out affected the negotiability of the note or showed that plaintiff was guilty of bad faith in purchasing it.

We are convinced that the evidence wholly fails to show that plaintiff was guilty of bad faith in purchasing the note; that under the evidence he must be considered a holder in due course of the note and for said reason the defenses that defendant seeks to urge are not available against the plaintiff. * *

The only defense resting on defendant being the one herein discussed, plaintiff's motion for a directed verdict should have been sustained.

Reversed with directions to enter judgment for plaintiff.

CITY OF NEW YORK v. NIC HOMES, INC.

(1964) 44 Misc.2d 440, 253 N.Y.S.2d 926.

PICARIELLO, J.   This consolidated action was tried by the Court without a jury.

The cause is one to recover against the corporate defendant, as maker of the subject check, and the heirs of the deceased payee of said check under the provisions of Article 7 of the Decedent Estate Law.

The decisive facts are not in dispute.

The subject check is dated October 23, 1959, was made by the corporate defendant, signed and issued by the decedent as maker's president, made payable to him, and endorsed over by said decedent to the plaintiff as a deposit payment on a sale at auction by the plaintiff of two lots purchased by a third party.

It is plaintiff's contention that the circumstances under which it became possessed of the check renders it a holder in due course against whom the interposed defenses, even if provable and substantiated, will not prevail.

* * *

The maker takes the position that the appearance of the check itself and the circumstances surrounding its negotiation to the plaintiff gave notice of a sufficient fact and invoked inquiry to ascertain payee's title thereto and his right to negotiate the same; and the failure to conduct such inquiry renders plaintiff not a holder in due course and therefore subjects it to all provable and substantiated defenses of the maker against the payee.

It is elementary that if plaintiff is a holder in due course it holds the instrument free of any defenses available to prior parties among themselves. [Citation.] It is also fundamental that the burden is on the plaintiff to prove that it is a holder in due course. [Citation.]

It may be true that the existence of merely suspicious circumstances does not, *without more*, amount to notice of an infirmity in a negotiable instrument or defect in title of person negotiating it [citation] and that the same does not constitute bad faith and destroy the status of a holder in due course [citations].

However, "good faith" necessary to make one a holder in due course of a note cannot be proved simply by showing that value was paid for property, even though such a presumption follows [citation]. In determining the existence or nonexistence of "good faith" one must look at all the circumstances in the case [citation].

The principal fact or event, viz., the "good faith" of the holder of the note, being the object of investigation, the circumstances [citation] consist of all the related or accessory facts or occurrences which attend upon it, which closely precede or follow it, which surround and accompany it, which depend upon it, or which support or qualify it.

What are these facts and circumstances in this case?

Plaintiff is conducting a sale by auction of real estate. Nothing in the record discloses who did the bidding for the property, but the same resulted in the negotiation of the subject check to the plaintiff as "earnest money." The check constituted an obligation of the defendant corporate maker, was signed by the deceased as its president, was made payable to the deceased and was endorsed over by the deceased to the plaintiff as "earnest money," deposited on this purchase of real estate by a third party.

While the plaintiff was not bound to be on the watch for facts which would put a very cautious man on his guard, it was bound to act in good faith. [Citations.] And even if plaintiff's actual good faith is not questioned, if the facts known to it should have led it to inquire, and by inquiry it could have discovered the real situation, in a commercial sense it acted in bad faith and the law will withhold from it the protection that it would otherwise have extended.

The Court can conceive of no standard of commercial rectitude that should have more intensely excited the plaintiff to suspect the authority of the payee to negotiate the check for the purposes intended thereby than the circumstances under which this check was negotiated. The check itself gave notice of a suspicious fact and invoked inquiry in relation thereto. One who suspects, or ought to suspect, is bound to inquire, and

the law presumes that he knows whatever proper inquiry would disclose. While the courts are careful to guard the interests of commerce by protecting the negotiation of commercial paper, they are also careful to guard against fraud by defeating titles taken in bad faith, when regarded from a commercial standpoint. In the case of Cheever v. Pittsburgh, etc., R. R. Co., 150 N.Y. 59, 67, 44 N.E. 701, 703, wherein an officer of a corporation made the corporate obligation payable to himself and then attempted to deal with it for his own benefit, the Court held, "When paper of that character is presented by the officer or agent of the corporation, it bears upon its face sufficient notice of the incapacity of the officer or agent to issue it."

The subject check, when read and considered in the light of the facts surrounding its negotiation, was notice to the plaintiff that it was apparently accepting money from one to whom it did not belong, and this cast upon plaintiff the duty of inquiring into the matter so as to ascertain whether the facts were in accord with the appearances; for if they were, it knew that it could not honestly accept the check. [Citation.]

The plaintiff, having accepted from an officer of the corporate maker the subject check as "earnest money," on the purchase of real estate by a third party, at its own peril, the Court finds prima facie the act to be unlawful, and, unless the check was actually authorized, the plaintiff is deemed to have accepted it with notice of the rights of the corporate maker.

Under the circumstances, the Court concludes that plaintiff is not a holder in due course within the meaning and intent of the statute, as the same has been construed by the courts, and that it accepted the check subject to the defenses of the immediate parties.

* * *

There can be no question and the Court is convinced on the record, however, that there was no consideration running from the payee to the maker of the check. This defense is therefore sustained and plaintiff's complaint is dismissed as against the corporate defendant.

Section 170 of the Decedent Estate Law authorizes actions against legatees and others to enforce a liability for decedent's debt. The action authorized by this section is, in form, one against the estate of the deceased debtor, but in substance is against decedent's property which has come into possession of heirs, legatees or next of kin [citation]. The purpose of the statute was to remove the strict and unjust limitations of the common law. [Citation.]

The only argument presented by the individual defendants is that the phrase in the stated section, to wit, "for a debt of the decedent," is not intended to apply to an obligation such as the one sought to be enforced herein.

* * *

The Court finds that deceased's liability to the plaintiff by virtue of his endorsement of the subject check is one for which he could undoubtedly have been held to account had he survived the litigation. Under the circumstances, the debt is of such a nature that an action against decedent's distributees to enforce payment thereof to the extent only in which they participated in the distribution of the assets of decedent's estate is proper and permissible under the Statute.

* * *

Settle judgment in accordance with the above on three days' notice.

RUSSELL v. UNIVERSAL ACCEPTANCE CORPORATION

(1965 D.C.App.) 210 A.2d 834.

QUINN, ASSOCIATE JUDGE: Appellee [Universal Acceptance Corporation] instituted this action to recover the balance due on a promissory note executed by appellant [Russell] for the purchase of a wig and services from Wigtyme, Inc. Appellant answered alleging that she was not indebted to appellee since there had been a failure of consideration. The trial court found, however, that appellee was a holder in due course and awarded judgment for the amount in default. Appellant challenges the decision of the court.

Appellant purchased the wig in March 1963. The price was $336 and included Wigtyme's promise to provide forty-eight "servicings" over a four-year period. As payment, she executed a promissory note payable in twenty-four monthly installments of $14 each. The note was subsequently transferred to appellee on April 2, 1963, pursuant to a contract which the two companies had signed the previous February. Under this contract Wigtyme was to sell appellee notes such as appellant's for $270, $120 of which was to be credited to a reserve account held by appellee against possible losses. It further provided that when a note was paid in full appellee would retain $20 of the reserve and remit the balance to the wig company or hold it against future losses. The result was that appellee agreed to purchase Wigtyme's $336 notes at a discount of $86, although only $150 would actually change hands at the time of the transfer. The agreement left Wigtyme free to sell its notes to other purchasers, and appellee was not obligated to buy the notes proffered by Wigtyme. The evidence established that some notes were refused by appellee and that some were sold elsewhere.

After the transfer of the note to appellee, appellant received a notice from one United Securities Corporation that it was the holder of her note, and she made several payments to that company. The evidence established, and the trial court found, that United Securities Corporation and appellee were one and the same company. It is clear from the record that the note was transferred to appellee,

Universal Acceptance Corporation, which has held it ever since. Payments made in the name of United Securities Corporation were credited to appellant's account on its books. There is thus no merit to her contention that appellee is not the holder of the note.

In October 1963 Wigtyme went out of business and it became impossible for appellant to obtain the wig "servicings" for which she had contracted. After that occurrence she made no further payments on her note, contending that this failure of consideration is a good defense against appellee's claim for the amount in default. It is well settled that failure of consideration is no defense against a holder in due course even if it would have been against the payee of the note. [Citations.] This is true even if the purchaser of the note had full knowledge at the time of the purchase that the consideration for it was executory and had not yet been performed, so long as he had no knowledge of any breach thereof. [Citations.] Thus, unless appellee is found not to be a holder in due course, it is entitled to the full amount due on the note.

Appellant alleges that appellee could not have the status of a holder in due course because it either took her note in bad faith or was a party to her original contract with Wigtyme. She contends that the entire transaction was actually a mask for a usurious loan similar to that found in Beatty v. Franklin Investment Company, 115 U.S.App. D.C. 311, 319 F.2d 712 (1963). In that case, the maker of the note was charged $150 to finance a cash balance of $301, and the finance company was found not to be a holder of the note in due course because it had notice that usury was embraced therein. That is not the situation here, however. Wigtyme's contract provided for only one price, and whether appellant had paid in one payment or over a two-year period, the price would have been the same; no finance charge was included.

It is true that a notation "F. C. 66" was written on one of appellee's records, but the court was not required to find, as appellant urges, that this established a usurious finance charge. Whether a transaction is a bona fide sale or a loan and a cloak for usury is largely a factual question, and we cannot find that the trial court's determination was erroneous. [Citations.]

The purchase of a negotiable note at a high discount has been held to be evidence tending to show bad faith or fraud on the part of the purchaser, especially when tied in with other suspicious circumstances. [Citation.] However, the discount at which appellee bought appellant's note, about twenty-five percent, was not so high as to prevent it from becoming a holder in due course. [Citations.] The record does not support appellant's contention that the discount was actually fifty-five percent. She alleges that the $120 reserve fund was a sham and not part of the purchase price of the note. However, such reserves against losses are not uncommon and serve to facilitate the negotiability of financial paper, encouraging finance companies to provide merchants with ready cash. Moreover, the United States Internal Revenue Service placed a levy on the reserve fund as an asset of Wigtyme and appellee acknowledged to the government that the funds in its possession did belong to the wig company.

Appellant attempts to demonstrate that such a close association between appellee and Wigtyme existed as to make the former a party to the contract with her and thus subject to the defense of failure of consideration. She shows that appellee's president was acquainted with two of the incorporators of Wigtyme and that in July 1963 these three persons formed another wig company. She further claims that the contractual relationship between appellee and Wigtyme and the fact that the note was payable at appellee's office establish that appellee was not a holder in due course. While it is true that these circumstances may create some suspicion of fraud, more than suspicion was needed to upset the proof offered by appellee that it was a holder in due course. "[A]n endorsee's bad faith or fraud in acquiring a negotiable note can never be assumed but must be shown by clear and unequivocal testimony * * *." Wilson v. Gorden, 91 A.2d at 330; [Citation]. Unless such clear proof is shown there is no reason to prevent merchants and finance companies from establishing their relationship prior to the making of notes to be negotiated or to prevent them from providing that the notes should be payable at the finance company's office. * * *

The trial court's finding that there had been no proof of bad faith on the part of appellee so as to keep it from being a holder in due course will not be disturbed.

Affirmed.

BURCHETT v. ALLIED CONCORD FINANCIAL CORP. (DEL.)

(1965) 74 N.M. 575, 396 P.2d 186.

[Kelly represented himself as selling Kaiser aluminum siding for a firm named Consolidated Products of Roswell, New Mexico. Kelly talked with John Burchett and his wife, Tinnie, and Harol Beevers and his wife, Marie, at their homes offering to install aluminum siding on their houses for a stipulated price in exchange for their permission to allow their houses to be used for advertising purposes as "show houses," in order to promote other sales of aluminum siding. The two couples neither knew nor had seen Kelly previously. Kelly told them they would receive a credit of $100 on each aluminum siding contract sold within a 25-mile radius of Clovis, and that this credit would be applied toward the contract debt, being the cost of the installation of the siding on their own houses. The two couples under-

stood that by this method they would receive the improvements for nothing. They agreed to the offers and Kelly handed each couple a form of a printed contract to read. While they were reading the contract, Kelly was occupied filling out blanks in other forms. After they had read the form of the contract submitted to them, they signed, without reading, the form or forms filled out by Kelly, assuming them to be the same as those which they had read and also which Kelly assured them they would receive. The contracts clearly stated on the same pages which bore the signatures of the purchasers:

"No one is authorized on behalf of this company to represent this job to be 'A Sample Home or a Free Job.'"

What the couples signed were notes and mortgages on their property to cover the cost of the aluminum siding, and contracts containing no mention of credits for advertising or other sales.

Within a few days after the contracts were signed, the aluminum siding was installed, although the jobs were not completed to the satisfaction of the purchasers. Shortly afterwards, the Burchetts and the Beevers received letters from Allied Concord Financial Corporation, informing them that it had purchased the notes and mortgages which had been issued in favor of Consolidated Products and that they were delinquent in their first payments. Upon discovering that mortgages had been recorded against their property, the Burchetts and the Beevers brought appropriate actions to have the notes and mortgages held by Consolidated Products cancelled and declared void. The cases were consolidated. Defendant Consolidated Products appeals from judgments voiding the instruments.]

CARMODY, JUSTICE. * * * In both cases, the trial court found that the notes and mortgages, although signed by the appellees, were fraudulently procured. The court also found that the appellant paid a valuable consideration for the notes and mortgages, although at a discount, and concluded as a matter of law that the appellant was a holder in due course. The findings in both of the cases are substantially the same, with the exception that the court found in the Burchett case that the Burchetts were not guilty of negligence in failing to discover the true character of the instruments signed by them. There is no comparable finding in the Beevers case.

*   *   *

The trial court's decisions are grounded upon two propositions, *   *   * (2) that fraud in their inception rendered the notes and mortgages void for all purposes.

*   *   * The only real question in the case is whether, *   *   * appellees, by substantial evidence, satisfied the provisions of the statute relating to their claimed defense as against a holder in due course.

In 1961, by enactment of ch. 96 of the session laws, our legislature adopted, with some variations, the Uniform Commercial Code. The provision of the code applicable to this case appears as § 50A–3–305(2) (c), N.M.S.A.1953, Replacement Volume 8, Part 1, which, so far as material, is as follows:

"To the extent that a holder is a holder in due course he takes the instrument free from

" *   *   *

"(2) all defenses of any party to the instrument with whom the holder has not dealt except

" *   *   *

"(c) such misrepresentation as has induced the party to sign the instrument with neither knowledge nor reasonable opportunity to obtain knowledge of its character or its essential terms; and

" *   *   *."

Although fully realizing that the official comments appearing as part of the Uniform Commercial Code are not direct authority for the construction to be placed upon a section of the code, nevertheless they are persuasive and represent the opinion of the National Conference of Commissioners on Uniform State Laws and the American Law Institute. The purpose of the comments is to explain the provisions of the code itself, in an effort to promote uniformity of interpretation. We believe that the official comments following § 3–305(2) (c), Comment No. 7, provide an excellent guideline for the disposition of the case before us. We quote the same in full:

"7. Paragraph (c) of subsection (2) is new. It follows the great majority of the decisions under the original Act in recognizing the defense of 'real' or 'essential' fraud, sometimes called fraud in the essence or fraud in the factum, as effective against a holder in due course. The common illustration is that of the maker who is tricked into signing a note in the belief that it is merely a receipt or some other document. The theory of the defense is that his signature on the instrument is ineffective because he did not intend to sign such an instrument at all. Under this provision the defense extends to an instrument signed with knowledge that it is a negotiable instrument, but without knowledge of its essential terms.

"The test of the defense here stated is that of excusable ignorance of the contents of the writing signed. The party must not only have been in ignorance, but must also have had no reasonable opportunity to obtain knowledge. In determining what is a reasonable opportunity all relevant factors are to be taken into account, including the age and sex of the party, his intelligence, education and business experience; his ability to read or to understand English, the representations made to him and his reason to rely on them or to have confidence in the person making them; the presence or absence of any third person who might read or explain the instrument to him, or any other possibility of obtaining independent information; and the apparent necessity, or lack of it, for acting without delay.

"Unless the misrepresentation meets this test, the defense is cut off by a holder in due course."

We observe that the inclusion of subsection (2) (c) in § 3–305 of the Uniform Commercial Code was an attempt to codify or make definite the rulings of many jurisdictions on the question as to the liability to a holder in due course of a party who either had knowledge, or a reasonable opportunity to obtain the knowledge, of the essential terms of the instrument, before signing. Many courts were in the past called upon to determine this question under the Uniform Negotiable Instruments Law. Almost all of the courts that were called upon to rule on this question required a showing of freedom from negligence, in order to constitute a good defense against a bona fide holder of negotiable paper.

One of the clearest statements of the rule under the Negotiable Instruments Law, which has received widespread approval, appears in United States v. Castillo (D.N.M. 1954), 120 F.Supp. 522, as follows:

"Although a holder in due course holds an instrument such as the instant one free from any defect of title, and free from defenses available to prior parties among themselves insofar as a voidable instrument is concerned, where fraud in the inception is present, such as here, such fraud makes the instrument an absolute nullity and not merely voidable. However, to completely invalidate the enforceability of a negotiable promissory note the fraud perpetrated must be such as to induce the maker of the note to execute the same under the mistaken belief that the instrument being signed is something other than a promissory note and must come about as a direct result of misrepresentation on the part of the payee or his agent. Naturally, the maker cannot be guilty of negligence in signing a written instrument and then defend upon the ground of lack of knowledge where in the exercise of reasonable prudence the attempted fraud could be discovered; and, generally it is no defense to the enforcement of an obligation like the instant one to insist that a fraud has been wrought where the maker does not take the care to read the instrument being signed, inasmuch as such an omission generally constitutes negligence. If such were not the general rule, where a person is of average intelligence and is qualified to read, then every negotiable instrument would be clouded with the possible defense that the maker did not read the instrument prior to signing it. However, the failure to read an instrument is not negligence per se but must be considered in light of all surrounding facts and circumstances with particular emphasis on the maker's intelligence and literacy."

We recognize that, in Castillo, the United States District Court for New Mexico found the instrument to be void, and properly so under the facts of that case. It is worthy of note, however, that the rule with respect to negligence has been applied in rejecting the defense of the maker in the Pennsylvania decisions subsequent to that state's adoption of the Uniform Commercial Code, [citations]; as well as in the appellate courts of states which had not on the date of the decisions adopted the Uniform Commercial Code. * *

The reason for the rule, both as it was applied under the Negotiable Instruments Law and as is warranted under the Uniform Commercial Code, is that when one of two innocent persons must suffer by the act of a third, the loss must be borne by the one who enables the third person to occasion it.

We believe that the test set out in Comment No. 7 above quoted is a proper one and should be adhered to by us. (By giving approval to this Comment, we do not in any sense mean to imply that we thereby are expressing general approval of all the Comments to the various sections of the Uniform

Commercial Code.) Thus the only question is whether, under the facts of this case, the misrepresentations were such as to be a defense as against a holder in due course.

The facts and circumstances surrounding each particular case, both under the Negotiable Instruments Law and the Uniform Commercial Code, require an independent determination. [Citations.]

Applying the elements of the test to the case before us, Mrs. Burchett was 47 years old and had a ninth grade education, and Mr. Burchett was approximately the same age, but his education does not appear. Mr. Burchett was foreman of the sanitation department of the city of Clovis and testified that he was familiar with some legal documents. Both the Burchetts understood English and there was no showing that they lacked ability to read. Both were able to understand the original form of contract which was submitted to them. As to the Beevers, Mrs. Beevers was 38 years old and had been through the ninth grade. Mr. Beevers had approximately the same education, but his age does not appear. However, he had been working for the same firm for about nine years and knew a little something about mortgages, at least to the extent of having one upon his property. Mrs. Beevers was employed in a supermarket, and it does not appear that either of the Beevers had any difficulty with the English language and they made no claim that they were unable to understand it. Neither the Beevers nor the Burchetts had ever had any prior association with Kelly and the papers were signed upon the very day that they first met him. There was no showing of any reason why they should rely upon Kelly or have confidence in him. The occurrences took place in the homes of appellees, but other than what appears to be Kelly's "chicanery," no reason was given which would warrant a reasonable person in acting as hurriedly as was done in this case. None of the appellees attempted to obtain any independent information either with respect to Kelly or Consolidated Products, nor did they seek out any other person to read or explain the instruments to them. As a matter of fact, they apparently didn't believe this was necessary because, like most people, they wanted to take advantage of "getting something for nothing." There is no dispute but that the appellees did not have actual knowledge of the nature of the instruments which they signed, at the time they signed them. Appellant urges that appellees had a reasonable opportunity to obtain such knowledge but failed to do so, were therefore negligent, and that their defense was precluded.

We recognize that the reasonable opportunity to obtain knowledge may be excused if the maker places reasonable reliance on the representations. The difficulty in the instant case is that the reliance upon the representations of a complete stranger (Kelly) was not reasonable, and all of the parties were of sufficient age, intelligence, education, and business experience to know better. In this connection, it is noted that the contracts clearly stated, on the same page which bore the signatures of the various appellees, the following:

"No one is authorized on behalf of this company to represent this job to be 'A SAMPLE HOME OR A FREE JOB.' "

* * * In our opinion, the appellees here are barred for the reasons hereinabove stated.

Although we have sympathy with the appellees, we cannot allow it to influence our decision. They were certainly victimized, but because of their failure to exercise ordinary care for their own protection, an innocent party cannot be made to suffer.

The cases before us are surprisingly similar to the Oregon case of Amato v. Fullington, 1958, 213 Or. 71, 322 P.2d 309, which involved a contract for the installation of siding and roofing on dwelling houses, and there the Supreme Court of Oregon, referring to the question of negligence on the part of the maker of a negotiable note, stated:

" * * * Here the plaintiff, although a man of quite limited education, was able to read English, and, by his own testimony, knew the risk he ran in signing a blank printed form. Nevertheless he signed it. Clearly this was negligence. * * * And it was negligence which enabled Napco's representatives to perpetrate a fraud on the defendants, so that the rule might well be applied that, whenever one of two innocent persons must suffer by the acts of a third party, he who has enabled the third party to occasion the loss must sustain it. * * * "

The Amato case, although decided before Oregon adopted the Uniform Commercial Code, in actuality amounts to a rule of decision which has now become statutory law by the enactment of § 3–305(2) (c) of the Uniform Commercial Code.

The finding of the trial court that Burchetts were not guilty of negligence is not supported by substantial evidence and must fall. We determine under these facts as a matter of law that both the Burchetts and the Beevers had a reasonable opportunity to obtain knowledge of the character or the essential terms of the instruments which they signed, and therefore appellant as a holder in due course took the instruments free from the defenses claimed by the appellees.

* * *

The judgments will be reversed and the cause is remanded to the district court with directions to dismiss appellees' complaints. It is so ordered.

PARK STATE BANK v. ARENA AUTO AUCTION, INC.

(1965) 59 Ill.App.2d 235, 207 N.E.2d 158.

PETERSEN, J. This case comes into Court by reason of certain mistakes made by employees of the involved parties following the normal routine of customary business details so characteristic of the rapidly changing society and world in which we live.

Defendant-Appellant, Arena Auto Auction, Inc., created the problem brought to court by the issuance of its check dated December 17, 1963, and by the mailing of it to Plunkett Auto Sales, Rockford, Illinois. For clarity's sake, we will refer to the Rockford Plunkett and the Alabama Plunkett by these geographic designations rather than by their corporate names which, to this Court, are almost identical. Rockford Tom Plunkett might well have felt, upon receiving said check, that he was the recipient of some giveaway or promotional scheme, for it later appears that he had sold no merchandise, a fact of which he was well aware, to the Defendant-Appellant. We might visualize Rockford Tom Plunkett as a fast-thinking, old-time horse trader, now engaged in the business of buying and selling used automobiles. He, being well known to the Plaintiff-Appellee Bank by reason of his borrowing and having cashed one previous check of the Defendant-Appellant, after holding his check from December 17th or 18th until January 3rd, 1964, and after due reflection on his part, signed his name to the check and presented it for payment to Charlotte Parish, head teller, who, promptly and without question, turned over to him the check-designated sum of $1,435.00.

On January 9, 1964, the said check was returned to the Plaintiff-Appellee Bank by reason of a stop-payment order by the maker, and came into the hands of the Assistant Vice-President, Mr. Marconi, whose duties are to assist in the operation of a financial institution, to know its customers, and equally, to earn a profit for the Plaintiff-Appellee. Vice-President Marconi promptly called his personal friend, Jack Clark of the Arena Auto Auction, Inc., who, to cover the shortcomings of his secretary, called at the Plaintiff-Appellee Bank on January 10, 1964, to make explanation. Now, Jack Clark, being in the business of operating an automobile auction and using the speed of their operation to explain the error, commented thus: "This guy here (meaning Rockford Tom Plunkett) wasn't supposed to get the check. It was another Plunkett in Alabama. But Alabama Plunkett wasn't on our books, so that's why our gals sent the check to Rockford Plunkett, and that's why we stopped payment on our check."

But, to put the frosting on the cake, or as Counsel put it, to add insult to injury, Defendant-Appellant, Arena Auto Auction, Inc., issued their second check in the same amount to the same payee, and again sent the check to Rockford Tom Plunkett. Again we can visualize quick-thinking Rockford Tom Plunkett's surprise, for this truly must come from the money tree. He loses no time in going to the same financial institution as before. Not so fortunate on this second occasion, poor Rockford Tom Plunkett, as he tendered the second check, is questioned as to why payment was stopped on the first one. In his effort to secure quick payment he stated, "This check is to replace the first. Cash this check, give me back the first one, and I will return it to the Arena Auto Auction."

Mindful of the first experience, the Vice-President was reluctant to follow this advice and informed poor Tom that he was in difficulty. Rockford Tom Plunkett, seeing that the Vice-President could be right, promptly left the State of Illinois and established his abode in a more sunny climate. This is verified by Vice-President Marconi, who stated that he held a telephone conversation with Mr. Plunkett who was then in a restaurant in Amory, Mississippi. Despite the Vice-President's appeal to Tom to come home and correct his mistake, which is again borne out by the testimony as follows: "All I can tell you is you'd better come up here and make

this good." It was to no avail. Rockford Tom Plunkett said, "You will never find me." Sad, but true; Vice-President Marconi tried: "Rockford Tom Plunkett wasn't there and I don't know where he is now."

So now we find the Plaintiff-Appellee Bank in the embarrassing position of having cashed a check and having had payment of that check stopped. Desirous of not losing money, they start suit to recover from the Arena Auto Auction. Judge Dusher of the Circuit Court of Winnebago decided in favor of the Plaintiff and against the Arena Auto Auction, Inc., who appeals to this Court.

From a purely legal point of view, there are two questions raised. First, did Rockford Tom Plunkett commit a forgery by signing his own name to a check ostensibly issued to him. Without passing on the very technical question of whether or not these facts constitute a forgery, this is apparently admitted by all parties concerned, for they cite cases in the Trial Court and in this Court, holding that a forgery passes no title by which one can recover as a bar to the Plaintiff-Appellee recovering. The Plaintiff-Appellee Bank relies upon Chapter 26, Illinois Revised Statutes, 1963, Section 3–406; which, being a new section of our Commercial Code, is as follows:

"Any person who by his negligence substantially contributes to a material alteration of the instrument or to the making of an unauthorized signature is precluded from asserting the alteration or lack of authority against a holder in due course or against a drawee or other payor who pays the instrument in good faith in accordance with the reasonable commercial standards of the drawee's or payor's business."

Hence, we may have a case of first impression in construing the latter section of our statutory law.

Without repeating the various errors previously recited, it appears to this Court presumptuous on the part of Arena Auto Auction, Inc., Defendant-Appellant, to insist that they did nothing for which they should be held accountable. We point out the interval of lapsed time before they, in their fast-thinking, fast-operating business, decide first to stop payment.

Secondly, bearing in mind the erroneous sending of a second check to the same payee, and considering the custom of the trade as set forth by the testimony of the several gentlemen of the financial world as to the routine handling of checks in banking institutions, it is our considered conclusion that to require the recipient Bank to stop and question persons known to that Bank and presenting checks in routine business and issued by makers likewise known to the Bank, would be placing cogs in the wheels of business, which, in turn, would bring those wheels of the banking business to an astounding and abrupt halt. This, as we see it, was neither the intent nor the purpose of our legislators in passing the section in our Commercial Code to which reference was made.

We, therefore and accordingly, do conclude that the Trial Court was correct in holding that the Defendant-Appellant, by their own negligence, substantially assisted in making it possible that an unauthorized person's signature passed title to the funds represented by said check.

Judgment of the Trial Court is affirmed.

_____

NATIONAL CURRENCY EXCHANGE, INC. #3 v. PERKINS

(1964) 52 Ill.App. 215, 201 N.E.2d 668.

KLUCZYNSKI, J. This is an action on a check drawn May 14, 1960 and dated May 16, 1960. Prior to the due date of the check, on May 14, the payee, John Stauropoulos, endorsed and cashed the check at plaintiff's currency exchange. The drawer, defendant Perkins, instructed drawee bank, Commercial National Bank of Chicago, to stop payment on the check on May 16. The plaintiff presented the check to the drawee bank for payment but it was dishonored. Plaintiff secured a default judgment against Stauropoulos, the payee therein, which judgment remains unsatisfied. Consequently, plaintiff brought the instant action against the defendant, the drawer thereof. The trial court found against defendant, and entered judgment on the instrument.

The sole question presented to this court, which is one of first, and perhaps last, impression in this State is whether one who purchases for value and in good faith a postdated check before its maturity or due date is a holder in due course and does not take the check subject to whatever defenses are available as between the original parties.

The facts are uncontroverted. The defendant, Perkins, is engaged primarily in the distribution of amusement machines. On May 14 he was contacted by a customer and restaurant owner, John Stauropoulos, who informed defendant of his intention to open a second restaurant. In return for permitting defendant to install an amusement machine in his proposed restaurant, Stauropoulos asked defendant to lend him $450.00.

Desiring to obtain this business, defendant issued the check, postdating it for the purpose of investigating Stauropoulos' representations and background. Upon discovering that Stauropoulos was insolvent and about to close his one restaurant, and that he had no intention of opening a second one, defendant, at the opening of business Monday morning, May 16, instructed his bank to stop payment on the check.

On May 14, Stauropoulos and another man entered plaintiff's currency exchange, and presented the check for cashing. Stauropoulos was known to the cashier, Mrs. Ross, who testified that since the amount of the check was over $250, she first cleared it with her employer, and determined that defendant's company existed. She then cashed the check. Her further testimony was that postdating would not enter into consideration in cashing a check, and that in the instant case she did not notice that the check was in fact post-dated. Mrs. Ross also stated that the man accompanying Stauropoulos represented himself as being from defendant's company, and showed credentials and assured her that the check was genuine, though upon cross-examination she could not recall the type or nature of the credentials.

Plaintiff deposited the check in its account at the Exchange National Bank, but it was returned with the notation that payment had been stopped on May 16.

To sustain his position defendant argues that a postdated check is irregular within the meaning of sec. 72 of the Negotiable Instruments Law (Chap. 98, sec. 72, Ill.Rev. Stat. (1959)). That section in part reads:

"72. [Who is a holder in due course] § 52. A holder in due course is a holder who has taken the instrument under the following conditions:

"1. That the instrument is complete and regular upon its face. * * * "

* * *

In 21 A.L.R. 234, the annotation following the case of Wilson v. Mid-West State Bank, 193 Iowa 311, 186 N.W. 891, 21 A.L.R. 229 (1922), cited by the defendant, the annotator states:

"From the foregoing review of the cases, it appears to be the uniform opinion that the mere fact that a postdated check is negotiated before the date it bears, does not prevent the transferee from becoming a bona fide holder. * * *

"The Negotiable Instruments Law is not clear in the matter. In Section 12 (sec. 32 of Chap. 98, Ill.Rev.Stat.1959) it is provided: 'The instrument is not invalid for the reason only that it is antedated or postdated, pro-

vided this is not done for an illegal or fraudulent purpose. The person to whom an instrument so dated is delivered acquires the title thereto as to the date of delivery.' In the cases decided under the act the check has been held a negotiable instrument prior to the date borne thereby. [Citations.]"

In attempting to find further support for his theory, defendant urges that a postdated check is not payable on demand with the drawee bank, and an action cannot be brought on it until the maturity date arrives. But, arguendo, it does not follow that the check is not negotiable, nor that it is invalid. Indeed, the contrary is true. Section 32 of the Negotiable Instruments Law (Chap. 98, sec. 32, Ill.Rev.Stat. (1959)) states as follows:

"The instrument is not invalid for the reason only that it is antedated or post-dated, proving this is not done for an illegal or fraudulent purpose. The person to whom an instrument so dated is delivered acquires the title thereto as of the date of delivery."

* * *

The weight of authority is that the mere fact that a postdated check is negotiated prior to the date it bears, does not prevent the transferee from becoming a holder in due course. [Citations.] The decisions also hold that the date on the paper is not notice of defenses, and while the question of regularity has not received serious consideration heretofore, the results of the cases are consistent with the rule that postdated checks are complete and regular. [Citations.]

The question posed by this appeal is not one dealt with by any specific provision of the N.I.L. and the instant decision is, perhaps, best rendered by weighing the policy consideration attendant to the problem presented. Though inapplicable to the instant case because the situation arose prior to the effective date of the Uniform Commercial Code (Chap. 26, et seq. Ill.Rev.Stat. (1963)), sec.

3–304(4) (a) thereof addresses itself to the question before us. That section reads:

"(4) Knowledge of the following facts does not of itself give the purchaser notice of a defense or claim

"(a) that the instrument is antedated or postdated."

The comments relating to this section in the Smith-Hurd Annotated Statutes state:

"Section 12 of the NIL provided that an instrument was not invalid if antedated or postdated unless this was done for an illegal or fraudulent purpose. Although no Illinois case is directly in point, it was generally accepted that knowledge of postdating or antedating [would] not make the holder one not in due course on grounds that instrument was not complete and regular as required by § 52(1) of the NIL. * * *"

Based upon the above authorities, though sparse, we do not believe sec. 72 of the Negotiable Instruments Law (Chap. 98, sec. 72, Ill.Rev.Stat.1959) should be read so as to regard postdating of a check a material alteration or irregularity of such a nature as to indicate wrongdoing, and thereby charging a purchaser for value and in good faith, with notice of defenses, or to cast upon him a duty of inquiry where the instrument is taken before the due date. Otherwise, it would destroy the good faith position of a purchaser who knows of the postdating, but who does not have actual knowledge that possibly someone may be able to assert a defense. It is a purchaser who knows at the time of the purchase of an asserted defense, or of facts or circumstances which may create a defense who is precluded from being a holder in due course, and then on the theory of "bad faith." The rule announced here not only favors negotiability but is consistent with sound commercial practice and experience, as evidenced by the relevant provisions quoted above from the recently enacted Uniform Commercial Code, now the law in Illinois. Therefore, the judgment of the lower court finding plaintiff to be a holder in due course and entitled to recover on the instrument is affirmed.

Affirmed.

PROBLEMS

1. On March 1, Martin borrowed and received $500 from Price, and gave Price his negotiable promissory note for $500, payable September 1. Price in order to assist his brother, Henry Price, indorsed the note and delivered it to him as a gift on September 14. Upon Martin's refusal to pay, Henry Price sued Martin on the note for $500. Martin defended upon the ground that Henry Price was not a holder in due course. Decision?

2. On September 1, 1965, Simeon Sharpe executed a negotiable promissory note for $1,500, due March 1, 1966, with interest at five per cent from date, payable to the order of Ben Bates. On December 1, 1965, Sharpe paid Bates $200 and obtained a receipt therefor. On January 10, 1966, Bates sold the note to Carl Cady, indorsing as follows: "Pay to the order of Carl Cady. Ben Bates." Cady paid Bates $1,200 for the note. Subsequently, the note was stolen while in Cady's possession by Timothy Tate. At maturity, Tate presented the note to Sharpe, stating that he represented Cady who would settle for $1,000 in cash. Sharpe paid $1,000 in currency to Tate and received his note. Upon discovering the facts stated, Cady brought an appropriate action against Sharpe for $1,500 and interest. Decision?

3. Worth executed and delivered to Brooks a note for $4,500, dated November 1, 1965, payable to the order of Brooks "Four (4) .... after date." A mortgage securing the note, executed contemporaneously, described the note as payable "four (4) months from date." The note and mortgage were on separate sheets of paper unattached. The blank in the note was not filled before its acquisition by Reliance Acceptance Corporation for value on February 1, 1966.

Worth brings an action to cancel the note and mortgage, and to enjoin the negotiation of the note and the foreclosure of the mortgage. He alleges that the consideration failed; that the note and mortgage were delivered conditionally and that the condition was never fulfilled. Reliance Acceptance Corporation answered, claiming to be a holder of the note and mortgage in due course. Decision?

4. On December 2, 1965, Miles executed and delivered to Proctor a negotiable promissory note for $1,000, payable to Proctor or order, due March 2, 1966, with interest at 5% from maturity, in partial payment of a used automobile. January 3, 1966, Proctor, in need of ready cash, indorsed and sold the note to Hughes for $800. Hughes paid $600 in cash to Proctor on January 3 and agreed to pay the balance of $200 one week later, namely, on January 10. On January 6, Hughes learned that Miles claimed a breach of warranty by Proctor and, for this reason, intended to refuse to pay the note when it matured. On January 10, Hughes paid Proctor $200, conformably to their agreement of January 3. Following Miles's refusal to pay the note on March 2, 1966, Hughes sues Miles for $1,000. Decision?

5. Morton signed his name to a blank form of promissory note and left it in his desk at his office in Chicago. Bain stole the note and completed it by dating it July 7, 1965, filling in the amount of $500 in words and figures, an interest rate of 5% from date, and making it payable to the order of Bain on January 7, 1966. On July 19 Bain indorsed and sold the note to Carter for $375. On December 24, Carter gave the note to his sister, Caroline, as a Christmas present. On February 4, 1966, Caroline Carter indorsed and sold the note to Drake for $350. Upon refusal of Morton to pay the note, Drake sues Morton for $500. Decision?

6. Bremrandt borrowed $2,000 from Hume. Hume became disturbed about Bremrandt's solvency and demanded that he either pay or give security for the debt. Bremrandt was unable to pay, but as security he indorsed and delivered to Hume a note from Marsh for $2,400, which was payable to Bremrandt's order in twelve equal monthly installments. The note did not contain an acceleration clause, but it did recite that the consideration for the note was Bremrandt's promise to paint Marsh's portrait. At the time Bremrandt transferred the note to Hume, the first installment on the note was overdue and unpaid. Hume was unaware of this fact. Shortly thereafter Bremrandt committed suicide. Marsh did not pay any of the installments on the note which he had given to Bremrandt. When the last installment came due, Hume presented the note to Marsh for payment. Marsh refused to pay upon the ground that Bremrandt had never painted his portrait. Bremrandt was hopelessly insolvent at his death. What are Hume's rights, if any, against Marsh on the note?

7. X fraudulently represented to D that he would obtain for him a new car for $2,800 from P Motor Company. D thereupon executed his promissory note for $2,800, due in 30 days, payable to the order of P Motor Company, and delivered the note to X, who immediately delivered it to the Motor Company in payment of his own prior indebtedness. The Motor Company had no knowledge of the representations made by X to D. P Motor Company now brings an action on the note against D, who defends on the ground of failure of consideration. Decision?

8. Adams reads with difficulty. He arranged to borrow $200 from Bell. Bell prepared a note which Adams read laboriously. As Adams was about to sign it, Bell diverted Adams's attention and substituted the following paper, which was identical with the note Adams had read except that the amounts were different:

"On June 1, 1966 I promise to pay Ben Bell or order Two Thousand Dollars with interest from date at 4%. This note is secured by certificate No. 13 for 100 shares of stock of Brookside Mills, Inc."

Adams did not detect the substitution, signed as maker, handed the note and stock certificate to Bell, and received from Bell $200. Bell indorsed and sold the paper to Fore, a holder in due course, who paid him $2,000. Fore presented the note at maturity to Adams who refused to pay. Fore gave notice of dishonor to Bell. What are Fore's rights, if any, against Adams?

9. On January 2, 1966, A executes and delivers to B an undated negotiable note, payable six months after date. B inserts "September 13, 1965," as the date on which the note was executed, and on January 16, 1966, negotiates the note to C, a bona fide purchaser for value without notice that there is anything wrong with the note. (a) What is the effect of the insertion with respect to the maturity of the note as to C? (b) Does it avoid the instrument in his hands?

10. On September 8, 1965, Acton executed and delivered to Boone a negotiable promissory note for $500, payable to "Boone or bearer," due January 8, 1966, with interest at five per cent from maturity, in partial payment of a used automobile. On September 15, Boone negotiated the note to Cooper without indorsing it. On October 15, Cooper sold the note to Davis without indorsing it. On December 6, the note came into the hands of Evans, a holder in due course, as a note for $5000, the alteration not being apparent on the face of the instrument. Follow-

ing Acton's refusal to pay the note on January 8, 1966, Evans sues Acton for $5,000. Decision?

11. Abner Ames executed and delivered to Roy Rowe the following note: "August 1, 1966, Thirty days from date, I promise to pay Roy Rowe or bearer $1,000 in payment of a 1961 Continental to be delivered to me on August 20, 1966, and guaranteed by Rowe. (signed) Abner Ames." On August 12, Rowe, without indorsing the note, delivered it to Walter Wood for $450. Rowe told Wood that he would probably not be able to deliver the automobile. On August 20, Ames demanded the car from Rowe. Rowe told him he was not going to let him have the car and refused to say who had the note. On August 23, Wood indorsed the note, "Pay to Roger Rice," and gave it to Rice, his nephew, as a gift. The next day, Rice, without indorsing the note delivered it to Henry Hay, who was not aware of any of the facts stated, in exchange for Hay's note for $800 and his promise to deliver a certain painting to Rice on September 10. On August 31, Ames refused to pay Hay, claiming failure of consideration. On September 3, 1966, Hay brings an appropriate action on the note against Ames to recover $1,000. Decision?

CHAPTER 28

LIABILITY OF PARTIES

Introductory. The key to liability on commercial paper is the party's signature. No person is liable on an instrument unless his signature appears thereon. Section 3–401 (1).

A corollary to this rule has already been noted: An unauthorized signature is wholly inoperative as that of the person whose name is signed and he has a defense valid against all parties, including a holder in due course. (Section 3–404(1).)

As was pointed out in the discussion of the form of a negotiable instrument, a signature may take many forms, such as a mark, a word, a trade name or an assumed name. It may be written, typed, printed or made in any other manner.

An important question to determine is, what is the effect of a signature when one signs, purportedly on behalf of another?

Effect of Signature of Authorized Representative. Negotiable instruments are frequently executed by agents or other representatives with a view to binding their principals only. Where the execution is done skillfully (for example "P, principal, by A, agent") the courts have had no difficulty. In such cases, if the agent is authorized to execute the instrument, the principal is liable and the agent is not liable. Occasionally, however, the agent, although fully authorized, uses a careless form of signature, and holders or prospective holders may be mislead as to the identity of the party to be held. Who should be liable in such a case? Section 3–403 provides the answers.

Careless forms of signatures by agents are myriad, but they can be conveniently sorted into three groups. The first is where the agent signs his own name to an instrument intending to bind his principal, but neither the fact that the agent is signing in a representative capacity nor the name of the principal is revealed. For example, Adams, the agent of Prince, makes a note on behalf of Prince but signs it "Adams." The signature does not indicate that Adams has signed in a representative capacity or that he has made the instrument on behalf of Prince. In this situation the courts have universally held the agent alone is liable on the instrument. The holder can hold Adams; he cannot hold Prince on the instrument. Prince may be liable to Adams or to a third party, but not on the instrument. His liability sounds in quasi contract and not under law merchant rules now incorporated into the U.C.C. This holding accords with the ancient law of negotiable instruments, restated in Section 3–401(1), that one whose name does not appear on a negotiable instrument cannot be held liable on it. The concept of negotiability requires that holders be able to tell at a glance who is liable. Adams appears to be the maker. Holders have taken the instrument relying on his sole signature. He should not be permitted to disappoint their expectations—and thus weaken the concept of negotiability—by being allowed to exonerate himself from liability upon proof of his agency status.

The second class of careless signatures is that in which the authorized agent indicates that he is signing in a representative capacity, but does not disclose the name of his principal. For example, Adams, executing an instrument on behalf of Prince, merely signs it "Adams, agent," but does not indicate for whom he is an agent. No place on the instrument does the name "Prince" appear.

As between the immediate parties to the instrument, if the payee knows that Adams represents Prince, Prince is liable. As to any subsequent party, however, Prince is not liable and Adams alone is personally obligated on the instrument.

The third type of careless signatures involves signatures by agents which reveal their principal's name, but do not indicate that the agent has signed in a representative capacity. For example, Adams, signing an instrument on behalf of Prince, signs it "Adams and Prince." A holder might well think that Adams and Prince were co-makers, and it would be unfair to let Adams exonerate himself from liability as against remote parties. Consequently, he is fully liable as to them. If the immediate party who dealt with Adams knew he was acting on behalf of Prince, however, it would be unfair for him to hold Adams personally. Therefore, Adams may prove this fact by parol evidence and exonerate himself from liability as to this immediate party.

It should be noted that the principal cannot be held in the first two classes of cases, because his name does not appear on the instrument. But since Adams was authorized to put Prince's name on the instrument in the third situation, Prince could be held.

To reiterate, under the rule that no person is liable on an instrument unless his signature appears thereon, where Adams merely signs his own name to the instrument, Prince is not liable on it. Also, where Adams signs his own name, indicating a representative capacity but not the person he represents, Prince is not liable on the instrument, because his name does not appear thereon. But where Adams with authority to do so signs Prince's name on the instrument along with his own, but without indicating his representative capacity, Prince is liable. But Adams is personally obligated in all three cases.

The U.C.C. gives Adams a clear-cut way of avoiding personal liability where he rep-

resents a corporation or other organization. Section 3–403(3) provides:

> Except as otherwise established the name of an organization preceded or followed by the name and office of an authorized individual is a signature made in a representative capacity.

The appropriate method of signing would thus be:

> XYZ Corporation
> By Adams, Agent.

The XYZ Corporation would be liable, Adams would not. When signing for an individual, the same type of signature would be appropriate:

> Prince
> By Adams, Agent.

Also of the same effect would be the simple signature, "Prince," executed by Adams.

The foregoing discussion assumes that Adams was fully authorized to sign on behalf of his principal. Suppose, however, a purported agent lacks authority to bind his principal, but executes a negotiable instrument in the name of the principal and clearly reveals his own representative capacity. For example, suppose Adams, without authority, signs Prince's name to an instrument, "Prince, by Adams, agent." Who is liable on such an instrument? Clearly not Prince. As to him, an unauthorized signature is no more binding than a forgery. Indeed, courts often liken an unauthorized signature to a forgery.

Section 3–404(1) provides the answer:

> Any unauthorized signature * * * operates as the signature of the unauthorized signer in favor of any person who in good faith pays the instrument and takes it for value.

Under this Section the unauthorized agent is liable, just as a forger would be. Notice the rule is broad enough to make him liable whether or not his own name appears on the instrument. Thus, if Adams, without authority, merely signed Prince's name to an instrument, Adams would be liable on the instrument. The rule represents, therefore, an exception to the principle that only those whose names appear on a negotiable instrument can be liable thereon. But the rule is consistent with the principle that someone must be liable on a negotiable instrument, a principle which would be defeated if a forger or unauthorized agent were permitted to escape liability on the instrument simply because his name did not appear on it. Surely no social policy is violated in holding such a person personally liable on the instrument, and the rule has the advantage of supporting the concept of negotiability, for a holder at least has the assurance of knowing that someone will be liable on the instrument. It is consistent with this policy, however, that the liability runs only in favor of a person who in good faith pays the instrument and takes it for value. There is no occasion for protecting a person who has not given value, or who has taken it in bad faith.

Liability of Parties in General. Unless they disclaim liability, all parties whose signatures appear on a negotiable instrument incur certain contractual obligations. Only a promissory note fully reveals the contract, and it does so only with respect to the maker who assumes an absolute obligation to pay according to the tenor of the note at the time of his engagement.

Drawers of drafts and checks order a drawee to pay their instruments without indicating their own liability in the event of non-payment. Indorsers may merely sign their names on the back of negotiable instruments, and these signatures, standing alone, do not fully reveal the indorsement contract.

When a check or other draft is issued, the drawee has no liability on it whatsoever in favor of the payee or subsequent parties: His signature is not on it. The payee may not sue a bank for non-payment of a check drawn on it, whether the drawer has money on deposit or not. The check or draft does not operate as an assignment of any funds in the hands of the drawee, and until he accepts it, he is in no way liable on it. Section 3–409(1). He may indicate his acceptance by merely signing his name across the face of the instrument. Such an acceptance does not show the nature or extent of the drawee's liability in so many words.

By the rules of the law merchant, however, the contractual obligations of the drawer, the indorser and the acceptor were as well understood as those of the maker, and these rules are now codified as part of the U.C.C. Drawers and indorsers do not promise to pay the instrument; their expectation is that the drawee or maker will pay it. But they engage that they will pay it if the maker, drawee or acceptor, as the case may be, dishonors it upon due presentment, provided notice of dishonor is given to them promptly. Thus their liability is *secondary*, because it is subject to the conditions of presentment, dishonor and notice of dishonor.

The maker and acceptor, however, are said to be *primarily* liable because they are unconditionally committed.

LIABILITY OF PRIMARY PARTIES

In General. There is a primary party on every note: the maker. No one is primarily liable on a draft as issued. The drawer, the payee if he indorses it, and other indorsers are only secondarily liable. Section 3–102(d). The drawee, as such, is not liable on the instrument. He is free to pay it or accept it as he sees fit, although by refusing to do so he may be liable to the drawer for breach of contract to pay. His refusal to pay or accept the draft causes the drawer to become liable on the instrument upon receiving prompt notice of dishonor.

The drawee may become a primary party, however, by accepting the draft (Section 3–409(1)), after which event he is known as the acceptor. Acceptance is the drawee's signed engagement to honor the draft as presented to him. (Section 3–410(1)).

(a) The Contract of Primary Parties. The maker or acceptor engages that he will pay the instrument according to its tenor at the time of his engagement (Section 3–413(1)) and if he does not, he may be sued by the holder.

Suppose, however, a maker executes an incomplete note or a drawee accepts an incomplete draft, and the instruments are subsequently completed. What is the liability of the primary parties in such a case? If the instrument is completed after it leaves the maker or acceptor, it should be enforceable against them as completed, at least by holders in due course. This is the rule which Section 3–413 promulgates by incorporating by reference Section 3–115.

Of course, neither the maker nor the acceptor is obligated to pay beyond his initial engagement. If the drawee accepts an instrument which is in the amount of $1,000, or the maker signs a note in this amount, neither could be compelled to pay $5,000 if the note were subsequently altered so as to appear to be made payable in such larger amount. The limiting language "at the time of his engagement" found in Section 3–413 makes this quite clear.

A new dimension is added, however, if the maker or acceptor should pay an instrument which has been altered after primary liability has been fixed, e. g., after a bank certifies a check in the amount of $1,000, it is raised to $5,000 and the bank pays the holder $5,-000. Since the primary party should know the amount of his own liability, it has been thought that he is negligent in paying an item so altered after he became liable on it. The maker of a note, for example, should remember that his note was in the amount of $1,000; he is careless if he pays $5,000 on it. The same is true of the acceptor. Therefore, under Section 3–417(1), neither the maker nor the acceptor is able to recover anything from a holder in due course who has received payment of a raised note or draft.

(b) Method of Acceptance. The holder of a sight draft ordinarily has no occasion to have the draft accepted by the drawee: when it is presented, it is due for payment. The holder of a time draft, on the other hand, is entitled to the assurance of the drawee that it will be paid when due, and it is in this situation that acceptance is most common. In fact, some drafts specifically require presentation for acceptance a stated period before payment may be required. In any event, refusal to pay or accept a draft constitutes dishonor. Section 3–507(1).

Checks may also be accepted by the drawee bank. This process is called certification. Section 3–411(1). It is the bank's promise to honor the check when subsequently presented for payment. Since it is in essence a sight draft, however, the bank has no obligation to certify it: the order upon the bank is to pay, and refusal to certify is therefore not dishonor of the check.

Section 3–410 provides that an acceptance must be written on the draft. No writing separate from the draft, and no oral statement or conduct of the drawee will convert a drawee into an acceptor.

Acceptance may take many forms. It may be printed on the face of the draft, ready for the drawee's signature. It may consist of a rubber stamp, with the signature of the drawee added. It may be the drawee's signature, preceded by a word or phrase such as "Accepted," "Certified" or "Good." It may consist of nothing more than the drawee's signature. There is no possibility for misinterpretation, since there is no other reason for the drawee's signature to appear on the draft. Normally, but by no means necessarily, an acceptance is written vertically across the face of the draft.

The acceptance becomes operative when completed by delivery, or by notification to the holder, in which case delivery is not required. Once the acceptance becomes operative, the acceptor becomes the primary party, and his obligation is identical with that of the maker of a note.

It follows from this that an acceptance is effective although the draft has not been signed or is otherwise incomplete or is overdue or has been dishonored. Section 3–410 (2). It is as though the draft became a note and the acceptor, the maker. How he recovers from the purported drawer, if at all, becomes his problem.

Also consistent with this is the rule of Section 3–411 that where a check is certified either at the request of the holder or by the bank itself before returning it for lack of proper indorsement, the drawer and all prior indorsers are discharged. At that point the bank will segregate from the drawer's account sufficient funds to cover the check. Since the bank then has the funds and the drawer does not, the discharge is reasonable and the bank becomes primarily liable. Where the holder elects to have a check certified, he in effect elects to rely on the credit of the bank, and since he could then have received cash, prior indorsers are discharged along with the drawer. The liability of indorsers subsequent to certification is not affected.

Certification at the request of the drawer does not relieve him of secondary liability on the instrument, although the bank then becomes primarily liable. For example, the drawer may have a check certified before using it to close a business transaction such as the purchase of a house. The seller requires that a bank be primarily liable, but since the drawer is then obtaining the benefit of the transaction, he should bear the risk of the bank's credit, rather than the payee.

(c) The Liability of Primary Parties for Interest. Since the maker of a note and the acceptor of a draft are primarily liable, presentment (that is, a demand for payment) is not a condition to the right of the holder to sue them. While the holder necessarily must make a demand before he can actually receive his money, there is nothing preventing him from holding on to a "good" instrument for a long period of time, thus accumulating interest. The maker has no way to pay the instrument so as to avoid liability for the interest which is accruing, for he cannot claim discharge or excuse by the failure of the holder to present, because presentment is not a condition precedent to his liability—he is liable absolutely. Of course, if he could find the holder he could "tender" payment. A tender is an offer to do what the obligor is bound to do, and it results in terminating future interest and other costs. The difficulty, however, is that the maker may be unable to locate the holder, particularly if the instrument has been negotiated many times.

Section 3–604 provides relief in such a situation. Tender of payment to a holder when or after the instrument is due stops the running of interest, as well as liability for costs and attorney's fees. If the note or draft is so-called "domiciled" paper, that is, payable at a special place, and the maker or acceptor is able and ready to pay at such place when the instrument is due, he is treated as having made tender of payment, and the running of interest is stopped. The holder, of course, can thereafter collect the principal, but he loses the interest which otherwise would have accrued after the date of maturity. The rule was stated in the leading case of Adler v. Interstate Trust & Banking Co., 166 Miss. 215, 146 So. 197, 87 A.L.R. 347 (1933) as follows: "If the money for payment of a note awaits the holder at the time and place of payment, this is equivalent to a tender by the maker, but it does not follow that, if the holder fails to present his note for payment, he forfeits the principal or the indebtedness and accrued interest. He only forfeits the unearned interest * * *."

When is an instrument payable at a "special place" for purposes of this rule? It is clear the place must be limited in its geographic size so that the holder can locate the maker in it. Thus, an instrument payable in "Chicago" or "New York" would not be payable at a special place. On the other hand, an instrument payable at "Edgely, North Dakota" was held payable at a special place in the case of Engen v. Medberry Farmers' Equity Elevator Co., 52 N.D. 410, 203 N.W. 182, 39 A.L.R. 915 (1925). Usually, instruments are made payable at a particular bank (e. g., "Payable at the Tenth National Bank of Bigtown"). While such instruments clearly are "domiciled," for purposes of the rule, this does not necessarily mean that the holder can look to the bank for payment, because in some States, at least, an instrument payable at a bank does not authorize the bank to pay it; the instrument simply sets the place of payment. In other States, the instrument payable at a bank is deemed to carry with it an implied authorization for the bank to make payment.

The draftsmen of the U.C.C. did not want to change bank practices with regard to instruments made payable at banks, and therefore, in preparing Section 3–121 the enacting State was given its option in this matter. New York, for example, adopted Alternative "A" which provides:

> A note or acceptance which states that it is payable at a bank is the equivalent of a a draft drawn on the bank payable when it falls due out of any funds of the maker or acceptor in the current account or otherwise available for such payment.

Illinois, for example, on the other hand, adopted Alternative "B" which provides:

> A note or acceptance which states that it is payable at a bank is not of itself an order or authorization to the bank to pay it.

Under Alternative A, when an instrument domiciled at a bank is presented, the bank is authorized to pay it. Under Alternative B, when an instrument is domiciled at a bank, the latter's only function is to notify the maker or acceptor that the instrument has been presented and to ask for instructions. In both cases, the instrument is payable at a special place and the interest stops running at maturity if the obligor is then and there ready, willing and able to make payment.

Suppose the maker executes his note payable at a bank and leaves in his account an amount sufficient to pay it when it becomes due. Although this procedure stops the running of interest at maturity it raises another problem. If the bank becomes insolvent before the holder presents the instrument, who incurs the loss with respect to the money deposited to cover the domiciled note. Logically, the loss should be on the maker, because the holder is under no duty to make a presentment. On the other hand, the maker can argue that this is not a situation which should be controlled by strict logic; that his loss is due to the slowness of the holder; that the holder's failure to present promptly should shift the risk of insolvency to the holder. The U.C.C. accepts the latter argument. Section 3–502(1) (b). Where presentment is without excuse delayed beyond the time when it is due, the risk of the solvency of the bank is assumed by the holder. The maker, drawer or acceptor may discharge his liability by assigning to the holder his rights to the funds maintained with the bank for payment of the instrument.

(d) The Statute of Limitations and the Liability of Primary Parties. Since presentment is not necessary to charge persons who are primarily liable on negotiable instruments, the Statute of Limitations starts to run in favor of the maker of a promissory note or the acceptor of a draft or check the moment these instruments mature. In the case of a demand instrument, the Statute of

Limitations starts to run in favor of the primary parties at the moment of issue, because no demand for payment is needed to charge the maker on a demand note, or the acceptor of a demand draft or check. "A demand is not necessary with respect to a note where the maturity is definitely specified, and neither is a demand necessary where the instrument recites that it is payable 'on demand', since the latter phrase has, by mercantile custom and long usage, come to mean that the instrument is due, payable, and matured when made and delivered." Gregg v. Middle States Utilities Co. of Delaware, 228 Iowa 933, 293 N.W. 66, 132 A.L.R. 415 (1940).

Of course, a demand and refusal are conditions precedent to the right of a depositor to sue a bank upon a savings deposit account, and, consequently, the Statute of Limitations does not start to run on such an account until the depositor has asked for payment. Theoretically, the certificate of deposit is different from a simple deposit account (which takes the form of a non-negotiable passbook). A certificate of deposit is an instrument issued by a bank in which it acknowledges receipt of a specific sum of money and promises to pay such sum to the named depositor or his order, with or without interest, upon return of the certificate properly indorsed. This instrument may take the form of a demand promissory note and be used in a savings-account transaction. Suppose Jones deposits $1,000 in his savings account with the expectation of leaving it there for twenty years. The bank gives him a demand certificate of deposit. Twenty years later Jones brings it in and demands his money. Can the bank set up the Statute of Limitations barring the depositor on this stale claim? If so, this would have the unfortunate effect of barring a depositor's right to his "savings account" simply because he was thrifty and did not withdraw it within the period of the Statute of Limitations.

To avoid this undesirable result, the draftsmen of the U.C.C. made an exception to the generally sound principle that no demand is necessary to charge a primary party. The exception applies only to the certificate of deposit. Section 3–122(2) sets it out:

> A cause of action against the obligor of a demand or time certificate of deposit accrues upon demand, but demand on a time certificate may not be made until on or after the date of maturity.

LIABILITY OF SECONDARY PARTIES

In General. We have noted that the drawer of a draft or check and the indorsers of all negotiable instruments are normally "secondary parties," and are said to be "secondarily liable." By this is meant that there are conditions precedent to their liability. The conditions precedent are presentment, notice of dishonor and, in some situations, protest. If the instrument is not paid and these conditions are satisfied, and if the secondary party had not disclaimed such liability by drawing or indorsing without recourse, he must pay. The drawer engages that he will pay the amount of the draft to the holder or any indorser who takes it up unless he disclaims this liability by drawing without recourse. Section 3–413(2). The indorser engages that he will pay the instrument according to its tenor at the time of his indorsement to the holder or any subsequent indorser who takes it up. Section 3–414(1).

To know when these contractual engagements become effective, it is necessary to understand the meaning of the terms "presentment," "notice of dishonor" and "protest".

(a) Presentment. Presentment is a demand for acceptance or payment made upon the maker, acceptor or drawee by the holder. Section 3–504. If there are two or more makers, acceptors or drawees, presentment to one is sufficient. The holder is entitled to expect that any one of the named parties will pay or accept. He should not be re-

quired to go to the trouble and expense of making separate presentments to each.

Presentment may be made in any reasonable fashion. The only specific requirement is that a draft accepted or a note made payable at a bank in the United States must be presented at such bank. Section 3–504(4). Otherwise, presentment may be made by mail, through a clearing house in a proper case, or at the place specified in the instrument, or if there be none, at the place of business or residence of the party to accept or pay. Section 3–504(2).

When presentment is to be made is set forth in detail in Section 3–503. An instrument showing the date on which it is payable is due for presentment on that date. In any other case the standard of "a reasonable time" determines the date presentment is due: after acceleration; after date or issue in the case of an instrument payable after sight; after a party becomes secondarily liable thereon. What is "a reasonable time" depends upon all the facts of the particular case, including the nature of the instrument and any usage of banking or trade.

In the case of an uncertified check, Section 3–503(2) is specific: a reasonable time for presentment for payment or to initiate the bank collection process is presumed to be:

> (i) with respect to the liability of the drawer, thirty days after date or issue, whichever is later; and
> (ii) with respect to the liability of an indorser, seven days after his indorsement.

The discharge of one indorser, of course, does not mean that all are discharged. Assume that D draws a check payable to the order of P on March 1. P indorses it to A on March 3 and A indorses it to B on March 6. B must present the check by the 10th to hold P, but if he presents by the 13th he can hold A. If he waits until after the 13th, both parties are discharged unless B, who is now unaided by the presumption can show by af-

firmative evidence that the presentment was within a reasonable time. B, however, has thirty days within which to present it in order to hold D liable, this period being presumptively reasonable as to the drawer. If he did not present the check for payment until after March 31, D would be discharged to the extent of any loss he might have suffered as the result of the delay, but not otherwise. P and A, on the other hand, would be completely discharged by B's failure to make presentment within a reasonable time, irrespective of lack of injury.

The difference in treatment as between indorsers and drawers is based upon the simple fact that the drawer always expects to have to pay the check and the indorser has no reason to expect that he will ever be called upon to do so. Consequently, the latter should be given prompt notice of dishonor so that he may take immediate steps to assert his rights against parties he may charge.

Presentments are of two types: presentment for acceptance and presentment for payment. Section 3–501(1).

Presentment of a draft for acceptance is necessary to charge secondary parties where the draft so provides, or is payable elsewhere than at the residence or place of business of the drawee, or its date of payment depends on such presentment, as in the case of a draft providing: "Seven days after acceptance pay . . . ." Presentment for acceptance is also authorized in the case of any other time draft, although it is not required. A refusal to accept in any of these cases constitutes a dishonor of the draft.

Presentment of any instrument for payment is necessary to charge any indorser, although an exception exists in the case of a draft previously dishonored when presented for acceptance. Failure to present for payment does not discharge the drawer, however, except to the extent, as indicated above, that there was unreasonable delay in presenting a draft to a bank where funds were available for its payment and the bank became insolvent in the interim. Assignment of such funds to the holder under such circumstances discharges the drawer. It is proper that the drawer should not be discharged otherwise, for he has had the benefit of the transaction in connection with which he issued the check. To discharge him would result in his unjust enrichment. Section 3–502(1) (b).

If, upon proper presentment, acceptance or payment, as the case may be, is refused, nothing more is required than to give notice of dishonor to parties secondarily liable. If, on the other hand, the drawee agrees to accept the instrument with some variation in its terms, the holder is presented with a choice. For example, the drawee of a time draft may agree to accept but only if the time for payment is extended for a specified period beyond that stated in the instrument. The holder may refuse the acceptance and treat the draft as dishonored, in which case the drawee is entitled to have his acceptance cancelled if he has theretofore accepted the draft with conditions. Section 3–412(1). On the other hand, if the holder is willing to rely on the credit of the drawee despite the variance in the terms of the draft, he may assent to such an acceptance, but if he does so, the drawer and indorsers are discharged unless they affirmatively agree to the variance. Their contract related only to the acceptance and payment of the draft as originally drawn. If the holder is willing to accept the drawee's contract to pay on a different basis, he, in effect, agrees to look to the drawee exclusively. The contingent liability of secondary parties is therefore discharged.

Although the drawee may be willing to accept the draft in strict accordance with its terms, he nevertheless has certain rights which he is entitled to exercise before he commits himself. These rights, the exercise of which in no sense constitutes a dishonor, are set out in Sections 3–505 and 3–506. Their principal purpose is to permit the drawee to assure himself that his acceptance would be proper. He may require exhibition of the instrument, its production at a proper place, reasonable identification of the person making presentment, and upon payment, a signed receipt, with surrender of the instrument if it is paid in full. Failure to comply with any of these requests invalidates the presentment, and consequently there can be no dishonor. The person making presentment is entitled to a reasonable opportunity to comply with any such requests, and the time for making presentment is extended accordingly.

Acceptance may be deferred until the close of the next business day following a proper presentment, thereby giving the drawee the opportunity to check back with the drawer or to take any other steps he may desire to assure himself of the propriety of acceptance. Conversely, the holder is authorized to allow postponement of acceptance for an additional business day in a good faith effort to obtain acceptance. For example, the drawee may refuse to accept without verification from the drawer and be unable to get in touch with him. He would either have to dishonor the instrument or ask the holder for an additional day. If the holder grants it, there is no dishonor and secondary parties are not discharged.

Payment of an instrument may be deferred without dishonor pending reasonable examination to determine whether the instrument is properly payable, but payment must be made in any event before the close of business on the day of presentment. The reason for the shorter period of time allowed in the case of presentment for payment is that in that situation, the holder is entitled to the use of his money on that day. In the case of presentment for acceptance, the only question at issue is whether the drawee will pay at a date in the future. The holder is not being deprived of the use of any funds to which he has a right.

(b) Notice of Dishonor. An instrument is dishonored when presentment has been duly made and acceptance or payment is refused or cannot be obtained within the prescribed time, or presentment is excused and the instrument is not duly accepted or paid. Section 3–507(1). Return for lack of a proper indorsement is not dishonor, however.

Upon dishonor, and subject to any necessary notice of dishonor and protest, the holder has an immediate right of recourse against drawers and indorsers upon giving them prompt notice of dishonor. Such notice is necessary to charge any indorser. It is also necessary in the case of any drawer or the acceptor of a draft payable at a bank or of the maker of a note payable at a bank, but failure to give such notice discharges them only to the same extent they would have been discharged for failure of presentment as discussed above. (Section 3–502(1) (b)).

Notice of dishonor, of course, is normally given by the holder or by an indorser who has himself received notice. Suppose, for example, M makes a note payable to the order of P; P indorses it to A; A indorses it to B; B indorses it to H, the last holder; H presents it to M, who refuses payment. H is entitled to give notice of dishonor to all secondary parties: P, A, and B. If he is satisfied that B will pay him, he may only notify B. B then must see to it that A or P is notified, or B will have no recourse. He may notify either or both. If he notifies A only, A will have to see to it that P is notified, or A will have no recourse.

If, in our hypothetical problem, H notifies P alone, A and B will be discharged. P cannot complain, because if every one does what he can to protect his own rights, P ultimately will be held liable. That is, H can push the loss onto B; B can push it onto A; A can push it onto P. P then must look to the maker alone. It cannot matter to P that he is compelled to pay H rather than A, and therefore subsequent parties are permitted to skip intermediate indorsers if they want to discharge them and are willing to look solely to prior indorsers or the payee for recourse.

Section 3–508(1) further permits any party who may be compelled to pay the instrument to notify any party who may be liable on it. Thus an indorser who has not himself received notice may give notice, and one may notify another who is not liable to him.

Section 3–508(2) provides that any necessary notice must be given by a bank before midnight on the next banking day following the banking day on which it receives notice of dishonor, and by any other person before midnight of the third business day after dishonor or receipt of notice of dishonor. Suppose that D draws a check on Y bank payable to the order of P; P indorses to A; A deposits it to his account in X bank; X bank presents it to Y bank, the drawee; Y bank dishonors it because the drawer, D, has insufficient funds on deposit to cover it. X bank has until midnight of the day after presentment to notify A of the dishonor. That is, if X received the dishonor on Monday, it would have until midnight of Tuesday to notify A. If it failed to notify him, it could not charge the item back to A. But A has until midnight of the third business day after dishonor or receipt of notice of dishonor to notify P. If he received notice on Tuesday, he would have until midnight on Friday to notify P.

Parties other than banks are given additional time to give notice of dishonor because they are normally not in the business of handling commercial paper, whereas banks are. Consequently, other parties are given additional time to find out what they need to do, and under most circumstances they will have time to take care of the matter by an ordinary business letter.

Frequently, notice of dishonor is given by returning the unpaid instrument with a stamp, ticket or memorandum attached stating that the item was not paid and requesting that the recipient make good on it. Section 3–508(3). But since the purpose of notice is to give knowledge of dishonor and to inform the secondary party that he may be held on the instrument, any kind of notice which accomplishes these things is sufficient. No formal requisites are imposed—notice may be given in any reasonable manner. An oral notice is sufficient, but it may be difficult to prove. Consequently, one is not advised to use it, and oral notification has little place in the business world, except as a mere preliminary to be followed by a more formal statement in writing. For example, the holder, out of courtesy, may call an indorser and tell him that an item has been dishonored. This oral notice is traditionally confirmed in writing.

If the person notified is not misled, a misdescription of the instrument should not defeat the notice, and Section 3–508(3) so provides. Thus, if a payee of a promissory note executed on January 3 by Mike Maker is told that the "note of January 5 made by Mike Maker" has been dishonored, this would constitute a sufficient notice if the recipient knew that the dishonor related to Mike Maker's note made January 3. Furthermore, notice operates for the benefit of all parties who have rights against the party notified. Section 3–508(8). It would be redundant and wasteful to require that a secondary party be notified more than once of the dishonor. Suppose, for example, that M makes a note payable to the order of P; P indorses it to A; A indorses it to H. H duly presents the note to M who dishonors it. H notifies both P and A of the dishonor, and then asks A to pay him. A does so. Can A now hold P? The answer is, yes. A does not have to notify P of the dishonor. P already has been notified of it. It would be a useless thing to

require A to notify him again. Since A has rights on the instrument against P, H's notice to P inures to the benefit of A.

(c) Protest. Until the adoption of the U. C.C., the somewhat expensive and formalistic procedure of protest was a standard aspect of fixing liability in the event of dishonor of a negotiable instrument. The U.C.C. eliminates this requirement except where the draft is drawn or payable outside the United States. If such an international draft is dishonored, protest is still required, the reason being that it is still required by the laws of foreign countries. Section 3–509.

In addition, any holder may, at his option make protest of any dishonor. Since protest is basically evidentiary in character, it may be a convenience, saving necessity for depositions and other expensive means of obtaining evidence.

A protest is a certificate of dishonor made under the hand and seal of a United States consul or vice consul or a notary public or other person authorized to certify dishonor by the law of the place where dishonor occurs. It may be made upon information satisfactory to such person. It must identify the instrument and certify either that due presentment has been made or the reason why it is excused and the instrument has been dishonored by nonacceptance or nonpayment. The protest may also certify that notice of dishonor has been given to all parties or to specified parties. Protest, or the noting for protest, must be made at a point of time proximate to the time of dishonor, so that the facts are fresh in the mind of the notary or the one making it. Therefore, subsections 3–509(4) and (5) require the protest to be made or noted within the time allowed for giving notice of dishonor.

The "noting-for-protest" procedure is usually to write the words "protested for nonpayment," or the like, on the instrument at the time of its dishonor. If this is done, the more formal protest can be made at a later time and antedated to the time of noting. The words "protested for nonpayment" written on the instrument by a notary along with the date thereof followed by the officer's signature, have been held a due noting of protest. Moreland's Adm'r v. Citizens' Sav. Bank, 114 Ky. 577, 71 S.W. 520 (1903).

The officer certifying the dishonor may act upon any evidence satisfactory to him. He may personally verify the facts or he may act upon the testimony of any person he regards as reliable. Thus, under some circumstances the protest may be based upon hearsay evidence, but nonetheless it is admissible in evidence to establish a presumption of dishonor and any notice thereof stated in the protest. Section 3-510.

Equivalent to protest for evidentiary purposes, however, in the case of an instrument other than an international draft is the stamp, ticket or other writing of a bank that acceptance or payment has been refused for reasons consistent with dishonor, such as insufficient funds, payment stopped, no account, or account closed. Section 3-510(b). Such reasons involve no question of the validity of the instrument, but rather constitute a refusal to pay. Reasons based on the invalidity of the claim such as forgery, alteration or indorsement missing are not consistent with dishonor, and consequently, evidence of refusal to pay for such reasons is not competent evidence of dishonor.

Proof of dishonor may also be made by introduction of bank records kept in the ordinary course of business showing that the instrument was dishonored. Section 3-510(c). This rule stems from the fact that records kept in such fashion may normally be assumed to be correct.

(d) When Presentment, Notice of Dishonor and Protest are Excused or Waived. Section 3-511(1) outlines two situations in which presentment, notice and protest are ex-

cused. The first excuses a delay where the holder does not have notice that the instrument is due. When would such a situation occur? An instrument may provide that its maturity shall be automatically accelerated upon the happening of a particular event. If the holder does not know that this event has happened, he is excused from presentment until he learns of the acceleration and the secondary parties are not discharged because of the delay. For example, suppose M makes a note payable on January 2, 1999, but payment is to be accelerated by the death of Uncle George to a point of time six weeks after his death. The note is negotiated by the payee to a holder. Uncle George dies, but because the holder does not learn of it, he does not present the note to M. The payee is not discharged. Presentment is excused. Once the holder learns of Uncle George's death, he must present the note within a reasonable time to hold the payee-indorser liable.

The second situation dealt with by Section 3-511(1) excuses the holder's delay where it is caused by circumstances beyond his control. For example, suppose the holder cannot present the instrument to the primary party because a storm has disrupted all means of communication and transportation. He should be excused, in such a case, until the storm is over, at which time he must exercise reasonable diligence to present it. How severe does the "circumstance" have to be to excuse the holder? This is a fact question which the courts have handled on a case-by-case basis, but the general rule was well stated in an early case, Polk v. Spinks, 45 Tenn. (5 Cold.) 431 (1868): "Obstacles of the kind which will excuse need not be of the degree or extent which make travel, intercourse, presentment, impossible. It is enough if they be of the degree and character which deter men of ordinary prudence, energy and courage from encountering them in the prosecution of business, in respect of which they owe an active and earnest duty, and feel an active and earnest interest."

Another situation in which presentment, notice, or protest, as the case may be, is excused is based on the notion that no one should be required to do a useless thing. If the drawee refuses to accept a draft upon a due presentment, there is every reason to think he will not pay it when it becomes due. The holder is therefore not required to present it for payment or to protest or serve notice of dishonor for nonpayment unless the drawee has in the meantime accepted the instrument.

Section 3–511(2) (b) entirely excuses the holder from presentment, notice or protest if the secondary party to be charged has himself dishonored the instrument or has countermanded payment or otherwise has no reason to expect the instrument to be accepted or paid. Suppose D draws a check payable to the order of P; P indorses the check to H. D then orders his bank to stop payment. Clearly, so far as D is concerned, H should not be required to present the check to the drawee bank for payment, since D, by his own act, has ordered the bank not to pay. Therefore, presentment is entirely excused with respect to D—D can be held liable without presentment. He can also be held liable even though H does not give him notice of dishonor, for D must know the check will be dishonored in view of his stop order. Of course, H is entirely excused only so far as D is concerned. If he wants to hold P, he will have to present and give notice of dishonor.

Similarly, if D draws a check on a bank with which he has no account, or has closed his account, he is not entitled to a due presentment and notice of dishonor. These matters are entirely excused so far as he is concerned. But they would have to be made to hold P, or other intermediate indorsers who did not have any reason to expect that the instrument would not be accepted or paid.

Subsection 3–511(2) (c) entirely excuses a presentment, notice or protest, as the case may be, if these things cannot be accomplished by reasonable diligence. For example, if the maker of a note has "departed for places unknown," the holder has no way of making a presentment to him. In such a case, presentment is entirely excused, and the holder should treat the instrument as dishonored and give notice of dishonor. If one of the indorsers cannot be located, notice of dishonor would not have to be given to him— it would be entirely excused.

Subsection 3–511(3) sets out some additional situations in which *presentment* is entirely excused. These situations do not excuse notice or protest.

Subsection 3–511(3) (a) entirely excuses presentment in situations where a holder might reasonably think that payment was an impossibility: Where the maker, acceptor or drawee of any instrument except a documentary draft is dead or in insolvency proceedings. This rule is based on the idea that no one should be required to do a useless thing. If the holder has good reason to think the primary party will not pay, then he should not have to present. The documentary draft is excluded, because often a buyer's personal representative will want to honor such a draft so as to take advantage of a favorable contract that has been made by the insolvent or decedent with the drawer. For example, seller makes a contract with buyer and draws a draft for the price. Seller attaches the draft to a bill of lading controlling the goods, thus making it impossible for the buyer to obtain the goods until the draft is paid or accepted. If the contract is favorable to the buyer, his representative in insolvency or decedent proceedings may want to proceed with it. There is no assurance that a documentary draft will be dishonored merely because the buyer (drawee) is dead or insolvent. Consequently, the holder is not entirely excused from making presentment in such a case.

Section 3–511(3) (b) provides that presentment is entirely excused when acceptance or payment is refused but not for want of proper presentment. The purpose of presentment is to determine whether or not the primary party will pay or accept the instrument. If the primary party refuses payment or acceptance for reasons not relating to presentment, it is clear that a subsequent presentment would be a useless ceremony. The question to which presentment addresses itself, namely, will the primary party pay or accept, has been answered once, and there is no reason to require a second determination of the same matter.

(e) Waiver of Presentment, Notice and Protest. Presentment, notice and protest may also be waived. A waiver of all these conditions makes the drawer and indorser almost indistinguishable from a primary party, such as a maker, who has no conditions precedent to his liability.

Waivers are of two types, express and implied. Express waivers have not caused much trouble. Usually, they are stated in terms such as, "Presentment, notice and protest waived" or "Protest waived". Where such language appears on the face of the instrument, it is deemed to bind all parties. Where it is written above the signature of an indorser, it binds him only. Section 3–511(6).

It is possible to waive all conditions or only some conditions. For example, an indorser could waive notice of dishonor, but require the holder to make a due presentment to hold him. Most of the trouble with express waivers has involved an interpretation of the language to determine which conditions have or have not been waived. The courts are divided on methods of construction, and are also divided as to the effect of particular waivers. For example, the courts do not agree as to

whether a waiver of presentment is also a waiver of notice. The strict approach is illustrated by the case of Hall v. Crane, 213 Mass. 326, 100 N.E. 554 (1913): "The liability of an indorser is conditional, the conditions being first, that at the maturity of the note there shall be a demand upon the maker for payment, and, second, that if the note be not then paid due notice thereof shall be given to the indorser. And these two conditions are distinct and independent of each other. Either can be waived and the other insisted upon. Neither upon principle nor by the great weight of authority is a waiver of one without more a waiver of the other as a matter of law." On the other hand, in Thompson v. Curry, 79 W.Va. 771, 91 S.E. 801 (1917) the court held that a waiver of notice of dishonor waives presentment as well.

Under Section 3–511(5) of the U.C.C. it is provided that a waiver of protest is also a waiver of presentment and of notice of dishonor even though protest is not required. This rule is based upon the common commercial understanding of the term "Protest waived." Most business men regard this as a waiver of presentment and notice of dishonor as well as protest, and the U.C.C. gives the term this meaning. While this provision is helpful, the U.C.C. does not resolve the other differences of opinion over whether a waiver of presentment also waives notice, or whether a waiver of notice also waives presentment, and these matters are left to common-law development.

(f) Disclaimer of Liability by Secondary Parties. Both drawers and indorsers may disclaim their normal secondary liability by drawing or indorsing instruments "without recourse". Sections 3–413(2), 3–414(1). The use of the words "without recourse" is understood in commercial circles to place purchasers on notice that they may not rely on the credit of the person using this language, but may look only to the other parties

to the instrument. A person drawing or indorsing an instrument in this manner does not incur the normal contractual liability of a drawer or indorser to pay the instrument to any holder or person who takes it up upon dishonor and any necessary notice or protest, but, as will appear later, he may be liable for breach of warranty under certain circumstances.

Needless to say, neither the drawee nor a subsequent holder is required to accept an instrument in which the liability of his transferor or any other party is so limited. He may, however, do so because of special circumstances, or because it is the best deal he can make.

Liability of Accommodation Parties. Accommodation parties are those who sign a negotiable instrument in any capacity for the purpose of lending their credit to another party to it. Section 3–415. They may be makers or co-makers, drawers or co-drawers, or indorsers. When an instrument has been taken for value before it is due, the accommodation party is liable in the capacity in which he signed. It is immaterial that the taker knew of the accommodation.

As an example of an accommodation arrangement, suppose M wants to borrow money from P, but P is not sure that M can repay the loan, and, therefore, asks M to request his friend, F, to sign a note along with M. Normally, M and F would sign as co-makers and P would occupy the position of payee. F would be liable to P if he signed the note, and P and subsequent holders could hold F as a maker. Since he signed as a maker, he would incur the liability of a primary party. If F were compelled to pay the note, he would have an action against M for reimbursement. On the other hand, if a holder compelled M to pay the note, M would have no action against F. As between M and F, M should pay the note since he received the value for which the note was issued. There is consideration to support F's promise,

because he bargained for a loan to be made to M, but F received none of the fruits of the deal, and M finally should have to pay the debt. Thus F, the accommodating party, can bring an action for reimbursement against M, the party accommodated, but M cannot bring an action for reimbursement against F.

Suppose P proposes that F sign the note as a maker and M sign the instrument on its back. The parties comply and P lends the money to M. What now is the relationship of the parties? Clearly, both F and M are liable to P, because this is their bargain. There is no legal problem in holding F, for he has signed as a maker and will be held as such; the payee has rights against the maker. P has a problem in establishing rights against M, however, for M has signed as an indorser, and thus appears to be subsequent to P. If P were to indorse the instrument to H, he might sign above or below M's signature. If he signed above M's signature, it would look as if M had rights against him. If he signed below M's signature, the indorsements would be "irregular," because there would be no way to explain them in terms of the chain of title of the instrument. However, oral evidence is admissible to explain the true order of liability. Section 3–414(2).

The situation is different as far as H is concerned. If P's indorsement is the first one and M's the second, H is entitled to hold the parties in this order. As far as H is concerned, P and M are indorsers and F is the maker, and they are liable to him accordingly.

M, being the accommodated party—the one who received the loan of money from the transaction—has no right to expect or to require F to pay the instrument. Hence, under the rule of Section 3–511(2) (b), discussed above, H could hold M even though no presentment or notice of dishonor were given.

If H collected on the instrument from F, F would have a right to bring a reimbursement action against M. This presents the curious spectacle of a maker holding an indorser liable.

The most common situation in which indorsers agree among themselves to be liable in a manner other than the order of their signing occurs when a number of persons are asked to indorse an instrument to accommodate one of the parties. Suppose M wants to borrow money from P, and P insists that M procure the signatures of A, B, C and D before the loan is made. M asks these parties to accommodate him, and, pursuant to the agreement with P, M makes the note and A, B, C and D sign their names on the back of it in that order. A, B, C and D are liable to P. M is liable to P and to A, B, C and D, if these accommodating parties pay the instrument. What is the liability among the accommodating indorsers themselves? Suppose M becomes insolvent, so that the reimbursement rights that A, B, C and D have against him are meaningless. Suppose P holds D liable. Can D pass the loss on to C? May C shift it to B? Would A ultimately be out-of-pocket simply because he signed first? Clearly, parol evidence would be admissible to show that the parties had agreed to share equally any loss, if that is the case. If the parties made no agreement at all, the presumption of liability-in-order-of-signature rule might be fatal to A but many courts would find an implicit understanding to exist among accommodating parties to share equally all losses. Accommodation parties are sureties, and the law of suretyship has long recognized the right of contribution among co-sureties.

Liability of Parties for Conversion. "Conversion" is a tort in which a party becomes liable to a second party in damages because he treated as his own certain property belonging to the second party. If the second party suffers loss as a result, he may recover in an action at law.

Section 3–419 provides that a conversion occurs in three situations: (a) when a drawee to whom a draft is delivered for acceptance refuses to return it on demand; (b) when any person to whom an instrument is delivered for payment refuses on demand either to pay or to return it; and (c) when an instrument is paid on a forged indorsement. Situations (a) and (b) involve a wilful action on the part of the party guilty of the conversion, whereas in situation (c) the payor's action was in all probability completely innocent. Nevertheless, the liability is the same in all three cases: good faith is completely immaterial.

Where the action in conversion is brought against the drawee, the measure of liability is the face amount of the instrument. In any other action for conversion of commercial paper, the measure of liability is presumed to be the face amount of the instrument, but the defendant may establish a lesser liability if he can.

Situations (a) and (b) involve a conversion as against the holder. Negligent loss or destruction of the instrument or any other unintentional failure to return is not a conversion. In such case the party may be liable in damages for negligence, but not for conversion. In addition, a lost, destroyed or stolen instrument may still be enforced by the owner upon proof of the facts, although a court may require security to indemnify the payor against loss by reason of possible further claims on the instrument. Section 3–804.

Where payment is made on a forged indorsement (situation (c)), the conversion is a wrong against the true owner, who was deprived of the instrument by the forgery. Since he is still the owner, he may recover from the payor, forcing him to pay twice unless he can recover from a prior party in an action in warranty, as hereinafter discussed.

Liability of Persons Dealing with Impostors or Employing Dishonest Agents. If a drawee pays a draft or check drawn on him, the drawer is under a duty to make reimbursement. Usually, the drawer has funds in the hands of the drawee, and the drawee honoring a draft or check reimburses himself immediately by charging the drawer's account or his funds. The drawee can be reimbursed, however, only if he acts in accordance with the drawer's order as it appears on the draft. Thus, if Davis draws a check to the order of Jones, the drawee bank to whom the instrument is addressed acquires no right of reimbursement by paying Roe, unless Jones has indorsed the check to Roe. In short, it is up to the drawee to determine whether the one presenting the item for payment or acceptance has rights in it, for if he pays the wrong party it is his loss and not the drawer's.

Two situations involving the above principles have been especially troublesome. The first relates to impostors. John Doe, falsely representing himself as Richard Roe, a creditor of Ray Davis, induces Davis to draw a check payable to the order of Richard Roe and to deliver it to him. Doe then forges Roe's name to the check and presents it to the drawee for payment. The drawee pays it. Subsequently, the drawer denies the drawee's right of reimbursement upon the ground that the drawee did not pay in accordance with his order: the drawer ordered payment to Roe, or to Roe's order. Roe did not order payment to anyone; therefore, the drawee would not acquire a right of reimbursement against the drawer Davis. This is the argument in favor of the drawer.

The second situation is similar, only it involves a faithless agent rather than an impostor. The drawer's agent falsely tells him that money is owed to X, and the drawer draws a check payable to the order of X and hands it to the agent for delivery to X. The agent forges X's name to the check and obtains payment from the drawee.

The drawer then denies the drawee's claim to reimbursement upon the ground that the latter did not comply with his order; that the drawer had ordered payment to X or order; that the drawee had not made payment according to this instruction, for X's indorsement, being a forgery, is wholly inoperative; that the drawee really paid in accordance with the scheme of the faithless agent, and did not comply with the drawer's order.

Who should take the loss in these two situations? There is probably a feeling, largely unarticulated, that the loss should be taken by the drawer. His employee caused it in the second situation, and his own failure to detect the impersonation of the impostor caused it in the first situation. Section 3–405 of the U.C.C. adopts this approach. It recognizes that the fraud of the faithless employee and the impostor cases present business risks which should be assumed by the party employing the agent or dealing with the impostor. The matter is handled in a straightforward way by making the indorsement of the impostor or the faithless agent effective as that of the named payee, thus permitting the drawee to pay in accordance with the drawer's order when it pays these items.

Liability Based on Warranty. (a) In General. A draft or note is not only the written evidence of contract liability, but it is a species of property, subject to sale. Since certain implied warranties attach to the sale of chattels, it is not surprising that certain implied warranties also attach to the sale of commercial paper.

The implied warranties which are present in the sale of chattels relate to title and quality. The implied warranties which accompany commercial paper also have to do with title and quality, though defects in quality are treated more appropriately in this field as matters of defense or claims of ownership.

Actually, these matters are qualitative in nature, for an instrument subject to defenses and infirmities lacks quality in a very real sense.

The matter of warranty sounds in contract, and it can be disclaimed. The warranty contract, however, does not exactly coincide with the indorsement contract. A qualified indorser (one who signs "without recourse"), for example, incurs no indorsement liability. But he is subject to liability upon a warranty. On the other hand, the indorsement contract may run in favor of parties who cannot claim on the warranties, and the damages for breach of warranty may be less than the damages for breach of the indorsement contract.

(b) Warranties on Transfer. Any person who transfers an instrument and receives value makes certain warranties. Section 3–417(2). The requirement that he receive value is intended to eliminate the warranty liability of an accommodation party. It is for this reason, among others, that Section 3–415 contains rules concerning what constitutes notice of the fact that a person is an accommodation party.

Warranties on transfer run to the immediate transferee only if transfer is by delivery alone, but if the transfer is made by indorsement, whether qualified or unqualified, the warranties run to "any subsequent holder who takes the instrument in good faith."

Section 3–417(2) (a)–(e) lists the warranties that are given, whether the indorsement is qualified or unqualified or the transfer is by mere delivery. Subsection (a) imposes a warranty that the transferor has a good title to the instrument or is authorized to obtain payment or acceptance on behalf of one who has a good title and the transfer is otherwise rightful. Under this rule, if M makes a note payable to the order of P, and it is stolen from the latter and the thief forges P's indorsement and sells the instrument to A, A

does not have good title. The break in the indorsement chain prevents him from acquiring title. If A indorses the instrument over to B for a consideration, B can hold A for breach of warranty. The warranty action is important to B, because it enables him to hold A liable, even if A has indorsed the note "without recourse."

In the foregoing situation the warranty imposed by subsection (b) would also be breached: That all signatures are genuine or authorized.

Subsection (c) provides a warranty against material alteration. Suppose that M makes a note payable to the order of the payee in the amount of $100. The payee, without authority, raises the note so that it appears to be drawn for $1,000 and negotiates the instrument to A, who buys it innocent of the alteration. A, indorsing "without recourse," negotiates the instrument to B for a consideration. B presents the instrument to M, who refuses to pay more than $100 on it. B can collect the difference from A. While A is not liable to B on the indorsement contract, he is liable to him upon the warranty.

Subsection (d) imposes a warranty that no defense of any party is good against the transferor. In the case of this subsection only, the transferor who indorses "without recourse" stands in a better position than an unqualified indorser: His warranty is only that he has no knowledge of any such defense. Section 3–417(3). Suppose that M, a minor, makes a note payable to bearer; P, the first holder, negotiates it to A by mere delivery; A qualifiedly ("without recourse") indorses it to B; B unqualifiedly indorses it to H. H cannot recover upon the instrument against M because of M's minority (a real defense). H therefore recovers against B on the indorsement contract, after giving him prompt notice of dishonor. B cannot recover against A upon A's qualified indorsement. Can B hold A for breach of warranty? Since A indorsed without recourse, he does not warrant that the instrument is defenseless; he only warrants that he knows of no defense which is good against him. Assuming that A did not know that M was a minor, B cannot hold A for breach of warranty. Can B hold P? Surely P is not liable as an indorser, because he did not indorse the instrument. While he must warrant that there are no defenses good against him, this warranty only extends to his immediate transferee, A. Therefore, B cannot hold P. This illustration shows the interplay between indorsement and warranty liability, and the relationship between the liability imposed under the various warranties and the individuals who can or cannot claim protection under a particular warranty.

All parties who transfer a negotiable instrument warrant that they have no knowledge of any insolvency proceedings instituted with respect to the maker or acceptor or the drawer of an unaccepted instrument. This rule is set out in Section 3–417(2) (e). Thus, if M makes a note payable to bearer, and the first holder, P, negotiates it by mere delivery to A, and A negotiates it by qualified indorsement to B, both P and A make a warranty that they do not know that M is in bankruptcy. However, B could not hold P for breach of warranty, since P's warranty runs only in favor of his immediate transferee, A. If B should hold A liable on his warranty, A could thereupon hold P, his immediate transferor, liable.

(c) Warranties of Presentment. The drawee bank agrees to pay checks as ordered by the depositor so long as his account is sufficient to cover them. If the bank pays other than pursuant to the depositor's order, it cannot charge the payment to the depositor's account. The point is well illustrated by the early case of Hall v. Fuller, 5 B. & C. 750, 108 Eng.Rep. 279 (1826). In that case the drawer drew a check for three pounds. A holder altered it so that it appeared to be drawn for two hundred pounds, and the bank paid out two hundred pounds when the instrument was presented for payment. It was held that the bank could charge only three pounds against the drawer's account. The court said: "The banker, as the depository of the customer's money, is bound to pay from time to time such sums as the latter may order. If, unfortunately, he pays money belonging to the customer upon an order which is not genuine, he must suffer, and to justify the payment, he must show that the order is genuine, not in signature alone, but in every respect."

This statement of the law, while directly applicable to a drawee bank, shows the responsibility to which all parties called upon to pay or accept are subject: they must pay strictly in compliance with the order given them.

If a drawee pays an instrument which has been forged or altered, he has the initial loss, for he cannot charge this amount to the drawer. May the drawee shift this loss to the party who received the payment (the presenting party)? The famous case of Price v. Neale, 3 Burr. 1354, 97 Eng.Rep. 871 (1762) answered in the negative with respect to instruments on which the drawer's signature had been forged. Later cases, however, limited the doctrine of Price v. Neale to situations involving a forgery of the drawer's signature, and held that the drawee could charge back against the presenting party any loss incurred because of a forged indorsement or an alteration of the instrument. For example, suppose D's name is forged to a check so as to make it appear that it was drawn by him. If the bank pays out this check, it cannot charge D's account. Similarly, if a drawee pays a draft, it cannot seek reimbursement from D, if D's signature is forged. The justification for the rule is that the drawee is supposed to know the drawer's signature. On the other hand, if D draws a check to P or order, and P's indorsement is forged, the bank does not follow D's order in paying such an item, and hence cannot charge his account (except in the impostor or faithless employee situations discussed above). The bank, however, can recover from the presenting party the payment made to him. Here it is thought that the bank should not have to take the ultimate loss, because it should not be required to know the signature of payees; it should know the signatures of its own customers (drawers). The same rationale applies to raised instruments. If D makes a check to P's order in the amount of $3 and it is raised so as to appear to be in the amount of $200, the bank cannot charge the $200 it pays out on such an item to the drawer's account. It can only charge the account to the extent of $3, because that is all the drawer ordered it to pay out. On the other hand, the bank can charge back the difference against the presenting party who received payment, upon the ground that the bank cannot be expected to know the amount in which every check will be drawn.

The examples to this point have all involved drawees. Suppose that it is the maker of a note who pays on a forged indorsement or an altered item. The maker, like the drawee, cannot know everyone's signature, and where the indorser's signature is forged, the maker cannot discharge the instrument by paying it, but he can recover back any money paid to the presenting party. The situation is different where the note has been raised. Suppose that the maker makes a note in the amount of $300 and it is raised to $2,000. If he pays this note, he is not permitted to recover back from an innocent presenting party, because the maker— unlike a drawee—has a way of knowing the original principal amount of the instrument. Similarly, suppose that a check or draft is raised *after* it has been accepted or certified by the drawee. If the drawee pays the raised amount to an innocent presenting party, it should not be able to charge it back to him,

because it has a way of knowing the proper amount of this item.

The rule of Price v. Neale and all its modifications and developments as described above have been incorporated in Section 3–417(1) as limitations on the warranties given to a party who in good faith pays or accepts an instrument. These warranties, as so limited, run not only from the person who obtains payment or acceptance, but also from any prior transferor.

Subsection (a) of Section 3–417(1) extends the same warranty of good title to persons who pay or accept as is granted to transferees under subsection (a) of Section 3–417 (2), discussed above. The warranty goes to the genuineness of the indorsements, not of the signature of the drawer or maker, in accord with Price v. Neale. A person who presents an instrument knowing that the signature of the maker or drawer is forged or unauthorized is committing an obvious fraud and consequently subsection (b) imposes a warranty that the presenter has no knowledge that the signature of the maker or drawer is unauthorized.

To protect a person who takes an instrument in good faith and later learns it was forged, and in keeping with Price v. Neale, certain exceptions to the warranty of subsection (b) are specified. A holder in due course acting in good faith does not give such a warranty to the maker of a note, to the drawer of a draft, even if he is also the drawee, or to the acceptor of a draft if such holder took the draft after acceptance or obtained the acceptance without knowledge of the unauthorized signature. Only a holder in due course can avail himself of these exceptions, however.

Subsection (c) imposes a warranty against material alteration, but again it is not given by a holder in due course to a maker, or drawer, whether or not the drawer is also the drawee. Further, the holder in due course does not give this warranty to the acceptor of a draft with respect to an alteration made prior to acceptance if such holder took after acceptance, even though the acceptance included a term such as "payable as originally drawn." The acceptor had the first opportunity to detect the alteration. To permit the acceptor to shift the responsibility for a prior material alteration to a subsequent party would defeat the entire purpose of acceptance and certification. An acceptance or certification must constitute a definite commitment to honor a definite instrument.

Of course this rule should not be confused with that which applies where the alteration is made *after* the acceptance or certification. In such a situation, the drawee knows the amount of the original acceptance or certification and he should not be able to charge back against an innocent party if he pays out more than that amount. Hence, a holder in due course does not warrant against post acceptance or certification alterations. The anomalous rule under consideration above deals with alterations which take place *before* the drawee certifies or accepts.

(d) Damages for Breach of Warranty. Suppose a party establishes that there has been a breach of warranty. How much can he recover from the party guilty of the breach? Usually, warranty damages equal the face amount of the instrument, but this is not necessarily true. Damages for breach of warranty are computed by determining the difference between the value of the instrument in its present state and the value it would have had if the warranty had not been breached.

Suppose, for example, that F forges M's name to a $1,000 note payable to the order of P and sells it to P. P indorses the note "without recourse" to A. Upon presentment, M refuses to pay A, setting up the defense of forgery. A cannot sue P on the indorsement contract, because it has been disclaimed by the qualified indorsement. The instrument is not genuine, however, and P has therefore breached his warranty of genuineness. A can recover $1,000 from P, because this represents the difference between the value of the note as it is (worthless) and the value it would have had if the warranty had not been breached—that is, the value it would have had if M's signature were genuine ($1,000).

Suppose, however, that M had been insolvent as of the time of presentment, so that, even if his signature had been genuine, A could only have collected $300 on it (M is able to pay only 30 cents on the dollar to creditors). How much can A collect from P in such a case? The answer is only $300. The point was well illustrated in the case of McNaghten Loan Co. v. Sandifer, 137 Kan. 353, 20 P.2d 523 (1933). The maker's signature had been forged in that case, and he subsequently became insolvent and could pay his creditors only part of their claims. The court refused to allow a holder to recover the full amount of the instrument against an indorser under the breach of warranty of genuineness, but limited recovery to the amount that the holder could have collected from the maker had the latter's signature not been forged.

TERMINATION OF LIABILITY

In General. Sooner or later, every commercial transaction must come to rest, with the potential liabilities of the parties thereto terminated. One aspect of this is covered by Section 3–418. Except for the presentment warranties, a holder in due course has no further liability to an acceptor or payor after acceptance or payment: The payment or acceptance is final. This Section thus follows the rule of Price v. Neale. The payor or acceptor cannot thereafter recover even though he discovers he has paid or accepted a forged instrument, or he has paid a check over a stop order or the drawer had insufficient funds on deposit.

The provisions of this Section also run in favor of a person who in good faith has changed his position in reliance on the payment or acceptance.

Finality in favor of other parties, however, is not necessary, for if there has been no change of position, or no value given the holder loses nothing if he is required to disgorge the payment or forego the acceptance. He is not entitled to profit at the expense of the drawee or maker. If he has given only an executory promise or credit, he can protect himself by refusal to perform.

The major aspect of termination of liability on the other hand is when the liability of a party, whether primary or secondary, or of all parties, is discharged. The means of discharge are detailed in Section 3–601, but it must be remembered that no discharge of any party is effective against a subsequent holder in due course unless he has knowledge thereof when he takes the instrument. Section 3–602.

(a) Payment or Satisfaction. The most obvious way for a party to discharge his liability on an instrument is to pay the holder. Section 3–603. Such a payment results in a discharge even though it is made with knowledge of the claim of another person to the instrument unless such other person either supplies adequate indemnity or obtains an injunction in a proceeding to which the holder is made a party. Reasonably enough, the person making payment is not required to decide at his peril whether the claim to the instrument is valid or not. Such a claim may arise, for example, where the prior holder contends the instrument was stolen from him.

The person making payment should, of course, take up the instrument so that it cannot pass into the hands of a subsequent holder in due course, as against whom his discharge would be ineffective. Only the liability of the paying party is discharged,

and if there are others liable to him, he may enforce the instrument against them.

(b) Tender of Payment. Any party liable on an instrument who makes tender of full payment to a holder when or after payment is due is discharged to the extent of all subsequent liability for interest, costs and attorney's fees. Section 3–604(1). He does not, however, relieve himself of his liability for the face amount of the instrument or any interest accrued thereon to that time. The principal importance of this rule lies in the fact discussed above that a maker or acceptor has no way of seeking out a holder so as to make tender to stop the running of interest. Subsection (3) of Section 3–604 solves this problem by providing that if such party is ready and able to pay a time instrument when it is due at every place of payment specified in the instrument, it is the equivalent of tender. This remedy is not available in the case of demand paper or paper which does not specify a place of payment.

Occasionally a holder will refuse a tender of payment for reasons known only to himself. It may be that he believes he has rights over and beyond the amount of the tender, or because he desires to enforce payment against another party. In any event, his refusal of the tender has the effect of wholly discharging every party who has a right of recourse against the party making tender. Section 3–604(2). For example, suppose a note executed by M in favor of P is negotiated by indorsement in order to A, B and H. If P tenders full payment to H and H refuses to accept it, desiring to collect from M, A and B are wholly discharged as far as H is concerned. A and B both would have rights of recourse against P if they were required to pay, and, hence, they are discharged.

(c) Cancellation and Renunciation. Section 3–605 provides that a holder may discharge the liability of any one or more parties to an instrument, or that of all parties, as he may see fit, in any manner apparent

on the face of the instrument or the indorsement, as the case may be. To do so he may cancel the instrument, or the signature of the party or parties to be discharged, by destruction or mutilation or by striking out the party's signature.

Since the instrument itself constitutes the obligation, intentional cancellation of it by the holder results in a full release of the obligation of all parties thereto. Accidental destruction of an instrument does not have such an effect, nor does cancellation in any form by anyone other than the holder.

If the holder wishes to discharge one, but not all parties, he may merely strike out that party's signature. He must be careful, however, that he does not discharge other parties as well by impairing their rights of recourse, as discussed below.

A holder may also renounce his rights by a writing signed and delivered, or by surrender of the instrument, to the party to be discharged. As in the case of other discharges, however, a written renunciation is of no effect as against a subsequent holder in due course who takes without knowledge of it.

Cancellation or renunciation is effective, even without consideration. This is in direct conflict with the common-law rule (now modified insofar as sales are concerned by Section 2–209) that an obligation cannot be discharged except with consideration, and the acceptance of a dollar amount less than the amount due upon a liquidated and undisputed debt is only a discharge to that extent.

(d) Impairment of Recourse or Collateral.
If the holder collects the amount of an instrument from an indorser, the latter normally has a right of recourse against parties primarily liable, prior indorsers, if any, the drawer, in the case of a draft, or any one or more of them, as the case may be. At the time such indorser accepted the instrument, he relied upon the credit of the prior parties, the strict nature of their liability, and, in

the case of an instrument secured by collateral, on the value of that collateral.

If any of these rights is adversely affected by the action or inaction of the holder, the indorser should not be required to pay the instrument, for when he thereafter seeks reimbursement, he will not possess the rights he bargained for at the time he accepted the instrument. The same rule should apply to an accommodation maker or acceptor known to the holder to be such.

Section 3–606 protects such a party to an instrument from the impairment of such rights by providing that he is discharged to the extent that without his consent the holder

1. Releases or agrees not to sue any person against whom such party, to the knowledge of the holder, has a right of recourse;

2. Agrees to suspend the right to enforce against such person the instrument or collateral;

3. Otherwise discharges such person; or

4. Unjustifiably impairs any collateral given by or on behalf of the party or any person against whom such party has a right of recourse.

As indicated above, striking out the signature of a prior indorser discharges subsequent indorsers who have a right of recourse against the indorser discharged.

Similarly, if the holder suspends the right to enforce the instrument, as by granting an unauthorized extension of time to pay, or by not liquidating collateral promptly, the subsequent indorsers are discharged. Their undertaking is only to pay if the maker or drawee does not pay on demand or on the date specified in a time instrument. They have not contracted for any extension of the time for payment. The discharge of the indorser is based upon principles of suretyship law.

The holder may, however, take any of the first three steps indicated above without discharging a party with a right of recourse if at the same time he expressly reserves his rights against such party. In so doing, he gives up his own rights to that extent, but he cannot, of course, impair any rights of recourse which such party may possess against others. For example, in the case where M executed a note in favor of P, and it was negotiated by indorsement and delivery consecutively to A, B and H, if H strikes P's indorsement, P would no longer be liable on the instrument, but A and B would be discharged because their right of recourse against P had been impaired. If H cancels P's indorsement but simultaneously notifies A and B he expressly reserves his rights against them, he may still sue and recover from them. If because of their insolvency or otherwise, he fails to recover, he is nonetheless barred as against P. But if he does recover from A or B, such party still has his right of recourse against P, despite the fact that H could not have held him liable.

(e) Other Methods of Discharge. Other methods by which a party's liability may be discharged have been discussed in connection with other matters. These include

1. Discharge of intervening parties upon reacquisition of an instrument by a prior holder. Section 3–208.

2. Fraudulent and material alteration. Section 3–407.

3. Discharge of the drawer and prior indorsers by certification procured by a holder. Section 3–411.

4. Acceptance varying a draft. Section 3–412.

5. Unexcused delay in presentment, notice of dishonor or protest. Section 3–502.

Any party may also be discharged as against another party by any act or agreement with such party which would discharge his simple contract for the payment of money.

CASES

UNIVERSAL LIGHTNING ROD, INC. v. RISCHALL ELECTRIC CO.

(1963) 24 Conn.Sup. 399, 192 A.2d 50.

HOLDEN, J. This is an action, brought against the defendant Harold M. Rischall, seeking to hold him personally liable on a promissory note, in the amount of $590, which is dated April 9, 1962. The question presented is whether he is liable personally on the note. He signed the note in manner and form as follows: "Rischall Electric Co., Inc., [and under this designation] Harold M. Rischall."

The Rischall Electric Company, Inc., was a corporation which had been in business for more than twenty years. In the course of its business, certain lightning rods were ordered from the plaintiff in order to fill a contract for electrical work in a low-cost housing project. The note in question was prepared at the direction of Harold M. Rischall, hereinafter called the defendant, and none of its terms were demanded or suggested by the plaintiff.

In the course of the trial, the question of interpretation of the word "we" as used in the note was raised. Objection was made that such evidence was inadmissible under the parol evidence rule. The objection was sustained, not for the reasons stated, but because any attempt to describe the meaning of the word "we" would be, at best, self serving. Where the parties have reduced their agreement to a writing, their intention is to be determined from its language and not on the basis of any intention either may have secretly entertained. [Citation.] Where a note contains the words, "I promise to pay," and is signed by two persons as makers, they are deemed to be and are jointly and severally liable thereon, and either of the makers is liable for the full amount of the note due and unpaid. [Citation.] Needless to say, the use of the word "we" would assess joint and several liability upon all makers. This interesting and academic question of semantics is not decisive of the issue.

The decision must be based upon the terms of § 42a–3–403 of the General Statutes, which is part of the commercial code enacted into law effective October 1, 1961. A liberal construction must be given to the sections of this law so as to secure to them a reasonable meaning and to effectuate the intention of its framers and make it workable and serviceable to the important business to which it relates. [Citation.] Section 42a–403 takes the place of § 39–21 (a section of the Negotiable Instruments Act, repealed) and states in part: "(2) An authorized representative who signs his own name to an instrument * * (b) except as otherwise established between the immediate parties, is personally obligated if the instrument names the person represented but does not show that the representative signed in a representative capacity." When the defendant executed the note in question, he did not indicate that he did so in any representative capacity.

* * *

For the reasons stated above, the issues are found for the plaintiff and the claim of the defendant that he is not personally liable is overruled. Interest has been expressly waived by the plaintiff. The note calls for the payment of a reasonable attorney's fee, and the sum of $168 is a reasonable fee.

Accordingly, judgment may enter for the plaintiff to recover from the defendant the sum of $590, damages, and a reasonable attorney's fee of $168, or a total to be recovered of $758 and its costs.

The suit against Rischall Electric Company, Inc., has been withdrawn and is not considered here.

LEAHY v. McMANUS

(1965) 237 Md. 450, 206 A.2d 688.

OPPENHEIMER, J. This appeal is from a judgment absolving the individual appellee from personal liability on a note of the corporate appellee, on the ground that the former signed in a representative capacity.

The note, dated April 15, 1957, reads: "—Four months after date we promise to pay to order of A. Hamilton Leahy—One Thousand and no/100—Dollars Payable at ———. Without defalcation, value received, with interest." There follows authority to confess judgment. The note bears the stamped name of Multi-Krome Color Process, Inc. (the corporation); immediately below are the signatures and seals of the individual appellee, C. E. McManus, Jr. (McManus) and C. E. Delauney (Delauney), without designation of any representative capacity. A. Hamilton Leahy (Leahy), the payee of the note, died on October 10, 1962, and suit on the note was brought in the Circuit Court for Baltimore County by his executrix, the appellant herein. Judgment by confession was entered against both the corporation and McManus; McManus filed a motion to vacate the judgment, stating under oath that he had signed the note solely as an officer of the corporation; testimony was taken on the motion, and Judge Turnbull vacated the judgment against McManus, setting the case to be heard on the merits.

Certain facts, adduced at the two hearings, are undisputed. The $1000 represented by the note went into the corporation's funds. At the time the note was executed, Leahy was a stockholder and director of the corporation. McManus was chairman of the Board, and Delauney was the corporation's treasurer. On October 24, 1956, when the corporation was in some financial difficulties, although not insolvent, the corporation's board of directors passed a resolution requiring the counter-signature on all the corporation's checks of either McManus or one Ralph Bolgiano, in addition to the already authorized signatures of the treasurer (Delauney), the president, or the vice-president. Delauney prepared the note here involved. The corporation, at the time of suit, had discontinued operations and was insolvent. Leahy never made demand on the corporation or McManus for payment of the note during his lifetime.

At the hearing on the motion to vacate, Bolgiano testified that the corporate resolution as to signing of checks was meant to and did apply to the signing of all corporate obligations. McManus testified to the same effect at the hearing on the merits. The resolution had not been prepared by the corporation's counsel. At the time of the second hearing, Bolgiano was deceased, as were all the other persons involved, other than McManus. McManus testified that he had made advances to the corporation, and that Leahy had lent money to Delauney, whose estate, at the time of his death, was insolvent. McManus also stated that he signed the note "as a result of the new set-up" of the corporation, under which he was authorized to sign for the corporation. He was not permitted to testify as to any conversations with Leahy about the note, because of the Dead Man's Statute, Code (1957) Art. 35, Section 3, but on cross-examination, stated that the "we" in the note referred to the corporation, as "a collective group", and that he signed in a representative capacity.

At the conclusion of the testimony, the lower court held that there was a *prima facie* case against McManus, but found that, on the evidence, Leahy knew that McManus and Delauney, were signing in representative capacities and accepted the note as the obliga-

tion of the corporation alone. The court's verdict was for McManus; the judgment against the corporation remained undisturbed.

* * *

The appellant's principal contention is that the lower court erred in finding that McManus signed the note only in a representative capacity. It is clear, as the appellant contends, that an endorsement can be written anywhere on the instrument; that a person may endorse a negotiable instrument in a representative capacity in such terms as to negative personal liability; and that, in the absence of such express negation, the endorser is liable to a holder for value. [Citations.] It has been held that ordinarily a corporation may validly sign an instrument by stamp. [Citations.] Even though no holder for value is here involved, absent permissible evidence that McManus signed only in a representative capacity, he would be liable as a maker or an endorser.

As between the parties, in this State, while a person who signed a note made by a corporation is *prima facie* liable to the payee, if there is conflict in the evidence relative to the circumstances, the individual who signed that note is not liable if he affirmatively shows an understanding between him and the payee that there was to be no personal liability. [Citation.] While the Uniform Commercial Code was not in effect at the time of the transaction here involved, the Code embodies this principle. Code (1957) Art. 95B, Sections 3–402, 3–403.

* * *

In this case, there was ample evidence of ambiguity in the evidence as to the circumstances under which the note was executed. While there was no testimony of conversations between Leahy and McManus, the relationship of Leahy to the company, the fact that Delauney who also signed the note, was one of the officers whose signature was required to bind the corporation, and Leahy's failure to attempt to hold McManus personally liable for over four years, were factors supporting McManus' contention of an understanding with Leahy that he, McManus, signed only in a representative capacity. We have considered all the evidence and do not find the judgment of the lower court was clearly erroneous. [Citation.]

* * *

Judgment affirmed.

LAWLESS v. TEMPLE

(1926) 254 Mass. 395, 150 N.E. 176, 48 A.L.R. 758.

PIERCE, J. This is an action by the payee of a bill of exchange against the drawee. The bill is as follows:

"Natick, Sept. 24, 1923.
"Maurice E. Temple
"Please pay to the order of Hazel Lawless $351.50/100 three hundred and fifty one dollars & 50/100

"Norris J. Temple
"Maurice E. Temple"

The answer raised the question of the sufficiency of the acceptance under G.L. c. 107, sec. 155, which is as follows: "The acceptance of a bill is the signification by the drawee of his assent to the order of the drawer. The acceptance must be in writing and signed by the drawee. It must not express that the drawee will perform his promise by any other means than the payment of money." The specific contention of the defendant is that the mere signature of the name of the drawee on the bill cannot fulfill the requirement of the statute that the signification of the assent of the drawee must be in writing and must also be signed. Before the passage of the negotiable instruments act, an oral acceptance of an existing bill of exchange was generally valid in this country and formerly was so in England. [Citation.] The reason for the adoption of the rule requiring acceptance in writing, like the underlying reason for the statute of frauds and similar statutes, "is that sound policy requires some substantial evidence of the contract and more reliable in its nature than the statement or recollection of witnesses." [Citations.]

The common practice before the act was to write the word "accepted" on the face of the bill, followed by the signature of the acceptor. [Citation.] But such was not necessary, as Sewall, J., said in Storer v. Logan, 9 Mass. 55 at page 59: "An acceptance entered upon a bill generally, or the blank endorsement of the name of the drawee, holds him absolutely as the acceptor; and no conditions or stipulations, which he may have connected with his acceptance, unless expressed upon the bill, will avail him against an endorsee or payee, to whom the bill has been negotiated, and who had received the bill as accepted, without notice of the conditions."

It was said by Cowen, J., in Spear v. Pratt, 2 Hill (N.Y.) 582, 38 Am.Dec. 600, in considering the legal valuation of the mere signature of the drawee on the bill, under a statute of New York which required the acceptance to be in writing and signed by the acceptor or his agent, "The acceptance in question was, as we have seen, declared by the law merchant to be a *writing* and a *signing*. The statute contains no declaration that it should be considered less. An endorsement must be *in writing* and *signed*; yet the name alone is constantly holden to satisfy the requisition." [Citations.]

* * *

We are of opinion that under G.L. c. 107, sec. 155, a drawee may be charged as acceptor although he writes merely his name upon the bill, and that any one taking the bill has the right to fill up a blank acceptance on the same principle that any holder may fill up a blank indorsement. [Citation.]

The instrument in question was legally accepted. It follows in accordance with the terms of the stipulation that judgment is to be "entered for the plaintiff for the full amount of the bill and interest thereon from the date of demand as set forth in the second count."

So ordered.

CORBETT v. ULSAKER PRINTING CO.

(1922) 49 N.D. 103, 190 N.W. 75, 24 A.L.R. 1047.

BIRDZELL, C. J. This is an action to foreclose a conditional sale of contract. The plaintiff (Corbett) recovered a judgment, and the defendant appeals. The facts are that the defendant, in August, 1920, purchased of the plaintiff a Mahlstedt Multi-Color Printing Press for the sum of $1,100, paying $175 in cash and agreeing to pay $175 September 5th following. The balance of $650 was covered by notes of $50 each, the first one due October 5th, 1920, and one falling due each month thereafter until the whole would be paid. The sale contract reserved title in the plaintiff until payment of all notes, and contained a provision that in case default should be made in the payment of any of them, the whole of the balance of the purchase price and the unpaid notes should become immediately due and payable. The notes were dated Fargo, North Dakota, August 17th, 1920, and each one was expressed to be payable to the order of the plaintiff "At Fargo, North Dakota." The notes falling due prior to April 5th, 1921, were paid, but that note and subsequent notes, with interest, were not paid when due. This action was begun by the service of summons and complaint in June, 1921. In the complaint the plaintiff declared an election to treat the whole of the balance as due. Judgment was entered for the full amount unpaid and special execution awarded.

The principal error argued on this appeal is that up to the time the action was brought there had been no default in the payment of the purchase price notes to justify the bringing of an action, or at any rate, the entry of a judgment covering the amount of the purchase price embraced in notes not yet matured. This contention is founded upon sec. 6955, Comp.Laws, 1913 (Sec. 70, Uniform Neg.Inst.Act) which provides that presentment for payment is not necessary in order to charge a person primarily liable on an instrument, but if the instrument is, "by its terms, payable at a special place and he is able and willing to pay it there at maturity, such ability and willingness are equivalent to a tender of payment upon his part." It is argued that as the note was payable "at Fargo, North Dakota," it was payable at a "special place" within the meaning of this statute, and, hence, that the trial court should have allowed the defendant to establish its ability and willingness to pay the notes as they fell due in order that it might be considered to have tendered payment; and, having in legal effect tendered payment, to have rendered inoperative the express condition in the contract authorizing the vendor to declare the balance due.

We are clearly of the opinion that the designation of a city in which the instrument is payable is not the designation of a "special place" within this provision of the statute. The purpose of the statute seems to us to be obvious. It subserves the convenience of both parties in that it contemplates the designation of a particular place where the holder of the instrument, on the one hand, may go with the expectation of receiving the amount due or of ascertaining that the instrument will not be met, thus obviating the necessity of seeking out the obligor; while, on the other hand, it enables the obligor to make provision against default or dishonor by having the funds at such place, thereby stopping interest and obviating costs. The clear purpose of the statute would not be carried out, in our opinion, by giving to the expression "a special place" a meaning which would make it coextensive with the borders of a city.

*   *   *

Where the payee has not agreed upon "a special place" and is content to seek redress against the primary party alone, he is under no duty to make presentment and the statute so declares. It is, therefore, incumbent upon the primary party to relieve such default by payment or tender. There being no specified place of payment in the notes involved here, the failure to pay at maturity was a default within the contract. We are, therefore, of the opinion that the main contention of the appellant must be denied. Such of the remaining specifications of error as have merit are dependent upon the principal contention hereinbefore discussed and require no additional consideration. The judgment appealed from must be affirmed. It is so ordered.

BATCHELDER v. GRANITE TRUST CO.

(1959) 339 Mass. 20, 157 N.E.2d 540.

SPALDING, J. The declaration in this action of contract alleges that the plaintiff was the holder of a promissory note which it placed in the defendant's hands for collection and that due to the defendant's failure to make proper presentment to the maker, the indorser, from whom the plaintiff would otherwise have been able to collect the amount of the note, was discharged. The case was heard by a judge on evidence and agreed facts, and he made a general finding for the defendant.

We summarize the pertinent evidence as follows: The defendant operates a bank in Quincy. The plaintiff for some time prior to 1946 had been the president, treasurer, and sole stockholder of C. H. Batchelder Co. In January, 1946, he entered into negotiations with one George E. Felton which resulted in the sale on April 1, 1946, of the major portion of the assets of C. H. Batchelder Co. (hereinafter called the company) to C. H. Batchelder Co., Inc., (hereinafter called the corporation), which was organized by Felton to continue the business of the company. Under the agreement of sale payment for the assets was to be partly in cash and partly by three interest bearing promissory notes, payable to the company, each in the amount of $5,000. The maturity dates of the notes were March 31, 1947, March 31, 1948, and March 31, 1949, respectively. Each note was signed on behalf of the corporation by Felton as chairman of its board of directors and each was indorsed by Felton individually. In this form they were delivered to the plaintiff. Thereafter the notes were indorsed by the company to the plaintiff and he in turn indorsed them in blank. In none of the notes was either the place of payment or the address of the maker specified. The defendant was not a party to any of the foregoing transactions.

On April 29, 1946, the plaintiff placed the three notes with the defendant for collection. The first note was paid at the defendant's bank on its due date March 31, 1947. The second note was not paid at maturity and was returned by the defendant to the plaintiff. Shortly thereafter it was paid by the corporation directly to the plaintiff. The third note —and this is the note involved in the present controversy—except for payments of interest down to March 31, 1948, remains unpaid.

The following was agreed to by the parties: "At all times material to this action, it was the practice and usage of * * * [the defendant], when holding a note for collection such as the notes * * * [here] to send a notice by mail to the maker about ten days before the due date, informing him that the bank held the note, that it would fall due on a date specified, and inquiring what disposition he wished to make of it. * * * The bank continued to hold the note at its office through banking hours on the date of maturity. If it was not paid by the close of banking hours, the bank turned it over to a notary public to make a demand at the bank and send out notices of protest to the maker, payee and all indorsers. It was not the custom of the bank to have someone take the note itself to the maker's place of business or residence." It was also agreed that this procedure was followed with respect to the three notes placed with the defendant by the plaintiff.

On March 31, 1949, the third note was turned over to one Cameron, a notary public, who was also employed by the defendant. Cameron stamped on the note "Protested for Non-payment, Mar. 31, 1949." Notices of protest properly addressed were sent by mail to the corporation, to the company, and to Felton. The third note was returned to the plaintiff on April 21, 1949.

The maker of the third note (the corporation) was duly adjudged bankrupt on April 18, 1949, upon an involuntary petition filed on April 15, 1949.

Felton, "the indorser of the third note, is a man of means and would have been able to pay any judgment which might have been entered against him * * * as such indorser * * *."

The questions for decision arise out of exceptions taken by the plaintiff to certain rulings on evidence and to the denial of his fourth request for ruling.

The fourth request asked the judge to rule that the defendant did not make proper presentment of the third note. Inasmuch as the facts relating to presentment were agreed this presents a question of law. The request was rightly denied.

Since this case arose prior to the adoption of the Uniform Commercial Code the rights of the parties must be governed by the negotiable instruments law, G.L. c. 107, §§ 94–97. [Now M.G.L.A. c. 106 §§ 3–503 to 3–505.] Section 96 of that statute provides

that "Where no place of payment is specified, and no address is given" "[p]resentment for payment is made at the proper place" when "the instrument is presented at the usual place of business or residence of the person to make payment." And § 97 requires that the instrument must be exhibited at the time payment is demanded. The plaintiff argues that this case is governed by these provisions, and since the defendant did not strictly comply with them, it failed to make proper presentment.

Prior to the adoption of the negotiable instruments law in 1898, it was well settled in this Commonwealth in situations similar to this that a written demand mailed by a bank to the maker of a note to pay the note at the bank on the due date was sufficient to make the offices of the bank the place of payment. [Citations.] And it has been said that "such previous notice to the promisor, and neglect on his part to pay the note at the bank, are a conventional demand and refusal, amounting to a dishonor of the note." Mechanics' Bank at Baltimore v. Merchants' Bank, 6 Metc. 13, 24; President, etc., of Warren Bank v. Parker, 8 Gray 221. A physical exhibition of the note was not required. [Citations.] We are not aware of any case decided since 1898 which holds that the language of G.L. c. 107, §§ 96, 97, either approves or disapproves the earlier practices sanctioned by our common law.

* * *

It could be argued that a strict construction of § 96 would call for different presentment procedure than that employed by the defendant. But we are not disposed to construe that section as abrogating a rule which has been so deeply embedded in our law. Our common law rule arose from the custom of merchants, the development of which was described by Chief Justice Shaw in these terms: " * * * the custom of the banks of Massachusetts, of sending a notice to the maker of a note to come to the bank and pay it, and treating his neglect to do so during bank hours, on the last day of grace, as a dishonor, and all parties acquiescing in, and consenting to, such neglect as a dishonor, has become so universal and continued so long, that it may well be doubted, whether it ought not now to be treated as one of those customs of merchants, of which the law will take notice, so that every man, who is sufficiently a man of business to indorse a note, may be presumed to be acquainted with it, and assent to it, at least, until the contrary is expressly shown." Grand Bank v. Blanchard, 23 Pick. 305, 306. See Mechanics' Bank of Baltimore v. Merchants' Bank, 6 Metc. 13, 23–24. If conformity to custom need be shown, it was not lacking. The bank followed its usual practice in dealing with this note. Its practice was similar to that of the other local banks. The payee, maker and indorsers of this note were acquainted with this practice, since it was followed in making demand for payment of the two earlier notes, and they acquiesced in its use with regard to them.

It is worthy of note that the Uniform Commercial Code, which became law in this Commonwealth on October 1, 1958, although not applicable here, would sanction the presentment procedure followed by the defendant. See G.L. c. 106, §§ 3–504, 4–210, inserted by St.1957, c. 765, § 1.

General Laws c. 106, § 4–210(1), provides: "Unless otherwise instructed, a collecting bank may present an item not payable by, through or at a bank by sending to the party to accept or pay a written notice that the bank holds the item for acceptance or payment. The notice must be sent in time to be received on or before the day when presentment is due and the bank must meet any requirement of the party to accept or pay under section 3–505 by the close of the bank's next banking day after it knows of the requirement."

Exceptions overruled.

ROLLER v. JAFFE

(1957) 387 Pa. 501, 128 A.2d 355.

BELL, J. Plaintiff instituted an action in assumpsit on a promissory note, not under seal, in the principal amount of $10,000. The note was executed on January 2, 1951, by the two defendants, Isadore and Lenor Jaffe, who are husband and wife. The note reads as follows:

"$10,000.00   January 2—1951
. . . . after date I promise to pay to the order of   Caroline Roller
———— ten thousand ————xx Dollars at   if requested after January 2—1952. Without defalcation, for value received with interest at . . . . per annum.
No. . . . . Due Jan. 2—1952.
            Lenor Cutting Jaffe
            Isadore H. Jaffe"

Plaintiff in her amended complaint averred that three payments totaling $3,000 were made by the defendants and that these payments were on account of principal and interest. Plaintiff further averred that on June 28, 1955, demand for payment of the note was made by her, but the demand was refused by defendants.

Defendants admitted the execution of the note and the receipt of the $10,000 by the husband-defendant, Isadore Jaffe. The wife-defendant, however, averred under "New Matter" that she never received any consideration for the note and that no consideration was ever intended to pass from the plaintiff to her. The wife-defendant contends that for this reason there is no legal obligation upon her. The wife-defendant admitted that she executed the note as accommodation maker for the accommodation of her husband. The husband-defendant, on the other hand, admitted liability for $10,000 less the $3,000 paid on account of principal, but admitted liability for interest only from the date on which payment of the principal was demanded by plaintiff.

Plaintiff in her reply to "New Matter" averred that the money was loaned to both defendants at the request of both defendants and that the money was loaned to them only after both defendants executed the note. Plaintiff further averred that if the wife-defendant, Lenor Jaffe, had not signed the note, plaintiff would not have loaned the money to defendants. No replication was filed to plaintiff's reply.

Plaintiff filed a Motion for Judgment on the Pleadings which was overruled by the lower Court. The lower Court based its action on two grounds: (1) the pleadings raised factual questions requiring a jury trial, and (2) the wife-defendant's plea of want of consideration raised an adequate defense to a suit on an unsealed note. We do not agree with this conclusion; the plea of want of consideration was not a legal defense to the note.

The general rule is that when two or more persons execute a promissory note, they are jointly and severally liable. Negotiable Instruments Law of May 16, 1901, P.L. 194, Ch. 1, Art. 1, § 17, 56 P.S. § 22; Uniform Commercial Code of April 6, 1953, P.L. 3, § 3–118, 12A P.S. § 3–118(e). * * *

Ch. 1, Art. II, § 29 of the Negotiable Instruments Law of 1901, supra, 56 P.S. § 67, provides with respect to an accommodation maker: "Such a person is liable on the instrument to a holder for value, notwithstanding such holder at the time of taking the instrument knew him to be only an accommodation party." In Delaware County Trust, Safe Deposit & Title Ins. Co. v. Haser, 199 Pa. 17, at page 25, 48 A. 694, at page 696, this Court stated:

"It may now be considered as well settled in this state that one who signs a note as maker, though he does it merely for the accommodation of the payee or the indorser, thereby places himself in the situation of a principal and will not be allowed to escape the consequences of his action by subsequently alleging that he was but a surety. * * * The relation created by the maker is that of principal debtor, and his rights and liabilities are the same whether the accommodation is for the payee in the note or for a third person. The liability of the maker does not depend upon the person for whose accommodation the note is made, but upon the situation in which the maker has placed himself by assuming the position of a principal debtor."

The defense of "accommodation maker" is no longer available to a married woman. * * *

On the question of interest, defendants' position is equally untenable. The note clearly specifies that it is payable "with interest". Unless the note provides otherwise, interest is due on a promissory note, not from the due date, but from the date of execution. Section 17(2) of the Negotiable Instruments Law of 1901, supra, provides:

"2. Where the instrument provides for the payment of interest, without specifying the date from which interest is to run, the interest runs from the date of the instrument, and if the instrument is undated from the issue thereof." [The Code has a similar provision: Uniform Commercial Code of April 6, 1953, P.L. 3, § 3–118(d) 12A P.S. § 3–118(d).]

Order reversed. The record is remanded to the lower Court with directions to enter judgment on the pleadings in favor of the plaintiff and against the defendants in the sum of $8,955.98 with interest from April 30, 1954.

PHILADELPHIA TITLE INS. CO. v. FIDELITY–PHILADELPHIA TRUST CO.

(1965) 419 Pa. 78, 212 A.2d 222.

COHEN, J. This is an appeal in an action in assumpsit brought by plaintiff-appellant, Philadelphia Title Insurance Company, against defendant-appellee, Fidelity-Philadelphia Trust Company, to recover the sum of $15,640.82 which was charged against the Title Company's account with Fidelity in payment of a check drawn by the Title Company on Fidelity. The complaint alleged that the endorsement of one of the payees had been forged and that, therefore, Fidelity should not have paid the check. Fidelity joined the Philadelphia National Bank as an additional defendant claiming that if Fidelity were liable to plaintiff, PNB was liable over to Fidelity for having guaranteed the endorsements. PNB joined the Penn's Grove National Bank and Trust Company as a second additional defendant claiming that if PNB were liable to Fidelity, Penn's Grove was liable to PNB for having cashed the check and guaranteed the endorsements. By way of defense all of the banks asserted that none of them were liable because the issuance of the check by the Title Company was induced by an impostor and delivered by the Title Company to a confederate of the impostor thereby making the forged endorsement effective.

The case was tried before the lower court sitting without a jury. The trial judge found in favor of the Title Company. Exceptions to said finding were sustained unanimously by the court en banc and judgment was entered against the Title Company and in favor of the banks. The judgment must be affirmed.

The pertinent facts are stated by the lower court:

"Edmund Jezemski and Paula Jezemski were husband and wife, estranged and living apart. Edmund Jezemski was administrator and sole heir of his deceased mother's estate, one of the assets of which was premises 1130 North Fortieth Street, Philadelphia. Mrs. Jezemski, without her husband's knowledge, arranged for a mortgage to be placed on this real estate. This mortgage was obtained for Mrs. Jezemski through John M. McAllister, a member of the Philadelphia Bar, and Antho-

ny DiBenedetto, a real estate dealer, and was to be insured by Philadelphia Title Insurance Company, the plaintiff. Shortly before the date set for settlement at the office of the title company, Mrs. Jezemski represented to McAllister and DiBenedetto that her husband would be unable to attend the settlement. She came to McAllister's office in advance of the settlement date, accompanied by a man whom she introduced to McAllister and DiBenedetto as her husband. She and this man, in the presence of McAllister and DiBenedetto, executed a deed conveying the real estate from the estate to Edmund Jezemski and Paula Jezemski as tenants by the entireties and also executed the mortgage, bond and warrant which had been prepared. McAllister and DiBenedetto, accompanied by Mrs. Jezemski, met at the office of the title company on the date appointed for settlement, the signed deed and mortgage were produced, the mortgagee handed over the amount of the mortgage, and the title company delivered its check to Mrs. Jezemski for the net proceeds of $15,640.82, made payable, as we have already mentioned, to Mr. and Mrs. Jezemski individually and Mr. Jezemski as administrator of his mother's estate."

* * * * * *

"[The Title Company's] settlement clerk, in the absence of Edmund Jezemski at the settlement, accepted the word of McAllister and DiBenedetto that the deed and mortgage had been signed by Jezemski; he himself, though he had not seen the signatures affixed, signed as a witness to the signatures on the mortgage; he also signed as a witness to the deed, and in his capacity as a notary public he acknowledged its execution."

* * * * * *

" * * * Paula Jezemski, one of the payees, * * * presented [the check], with purported endorsements of all the payees, at the Penns Grove National Bank and Trust Company in Penns Grove, New Jersey, for cash. Edmund Jezemski received none of the proceeds, either individually or as administrator of the estate of Sofia Jezemski; and it is conceded that the endorsements purporting to be his were forged. The Penns Grove bank negotiated the check through the Philadelphia National Bank, and it was eventually paid by Fidelity-Philadelphia Trust Company, which charged the amount of the check against the deposit account of plaintiff."

* * * * * *

"There is no question that the man whom Mrs. Jezemski introduced to McAllister and DiBenedetto was not Edmund Jezemski, her husband. It was sometime later that Edmund Jezemski, when he tried to convey the real estate, discovered the existence of the mortgage. When he did so he instituted an action in equity which resulted in the setting aside of the deed and mortgage and the repayment of the fund advanced by the mortgagee."

The parties do not dispute the proposition that as between the payor bank (Fidelity-Philadelphia) and its customer (Title Company), ordinarily, the former must bear the loss occasioned by the forgery of a payee's endorsement (Edmund Jezemski) upon a check drawn by its customer and paid by it. [Citations.] Uniform Commercial Code—Commercial Paper, Act of April 6, 1953, P.L. 3, § 3–404, as amended, 12A P.S. § 3–404. The latter provides, inter alia, that "(1) Any unauthorized signature [Edmund Jezemski's] is wholly inoperative as that of the person whose name is signed unless he ratifies it or is precluded from denying * * *."

However, the banks argue that this case falls within an exception to the above rule, making the forged indorsement of Edmund Jezemski's name effective so that Fidelity-Philadelphia was entitled to charge the account of its customer, the Title Company, who was the drawer of the check. The exception asserted by the banks is found in § 3–405(1) (a) of the Uniform Commercial Code—Commercial Paper which provides:

"An indorsement by any person in the name of a named payee is effective if (a) an impostor by use of the mails or otherwise has induced the maker or drawer to issue the instrument to him or his confederate in the name of the payee; * * *."

The lower court found and the Title Company does not dispute that an imposter appeared before McAllister and DiBenedetto, impersonated Mr. Jezemski, and, in their presence, signed Mr. Jezemski's name to the deed, bond and mortgage; that Mrs. Jezemski was a confederate of the impostor; that the drawer, Title Company, issued the check to Mrs. Jezemski naming her and Mr. Jezemski as payees; and that some person other than Mr. Jezemski indorsed his name on the check. In effect, the only argument made by the Title Company to prevent the applicability of Section 3–405(1) (a) is that the impostor, who admittedly played a part in the swindle, *did not "by the mails or otherwise" induce the Title Company* to issue the check within the meaning of Section 3–405(1) (a). The argument must fail.

Outside the Uniform Commercial Code, the impostor doctrine has taken many forms and been based on numerous theories, see Annotation 81 A.L.R.2d 1365 (1962), all of which, when applicable, place the loss on the "innocent" duped drawer of the check rather than the "innocent" duped drawee or payor. Although one form of the doctrine had existed in Pennsylvania for at least fifty-three years before the adoption of the Commercial Code, see Land Title and Trust Company v. Northwestern National Bank, 196 Pa. 230, 46 A. 420 (1900), no case has been found which decided whether or not the pre-Code doctrine would have applied to the instant factual situation—when the impostor, rather than communicating directly with the drawer, brings his impersonation to bear upon the drawer through the medium of the representations of third persons upon whom the drawer relies, in part, in issuing the check. But, regardless of the pre-Code form of the impostor doctrine and its applicability to the instant factual situation, the matter must be decided by statutory construction and application of the impostor doctrine as it now appears in Section 3–405(1) (a) of the Code.

Both the words of Section 3–405(1) (a) and the official Comment thereto leave no doubt that the impostor can induce the drawer to issue him or his confederate a check within the meaning of the section even though he does not carry out his impersonation before the very eyes of the drawer. Section 3–405(1) (a) says the inducement might be by "the mails or otherwise." The Comment elaborates:

"2. Subsection (1) (a) is new. It rejects decisions which distinguish between face-to-face imposture and imposture by mail and hold that where the parties deal by mail the dominant intent of the drawer is to deal with the name rather than with the person so that the resulting instrument may be negotiated only by indorsement of the payee whose name has been taken in vain. The result of the distinction has been under some prior law, to throw the loss in the mail imposture forward to a subsequent holder or to the drawee. Since the drawer believes the two to be one and the same, the two intentions cannot be separated, and the 'dominant intent' is a fiction. The position here taken is that the loss, regardless of the type of fraud which the particular impostor has committed, should fall upon the drawer."

Moreover, the Legislature's use of the word "otherwise" and the Comment, which suggests that results should not turn upon "the type of fraud which the particular impostor committed," indicates that the Legislature did not intend to limit the applicability of the section to cases where the impostor deals directly with the drawer (face-to-face, mails, telephone, etc.). Naturally, the Legislature could not have predicted and expressly included all the ingenious schemes designed and carried out by impostors for the purpose of defrauding the makers or drawers of negotiable instruments. Something had to be left for the courts by way of statutory construction. For purposes of imposing the loss on one of two "innocent" parties, either the drawer who was defrauded or the drawee bank which paid out on a forged endorsement, we see no reason for distinguishing between the drawer who is duped by an impersonator communicating directly with him through the mails and a drawer who is duped by an impersonator communicating indirectly with him through third persons. Thus, both the language of the Code and common sense dictates that the drawer must suffer the loss in both instances.

The parties have argued at length respecting the effect that should be given to the "negligence" of the Title Company's settlement clerk. While ascertaining the negligence in each case used to play a significant role in the application of the impostor doctrine, [citations] such an approach is no longer warranted under the Commercial Code's version of the imposter doctrine. [Citations.] On the other hand, the Code does include a separate provision, § 3–406, wherein the drawer's or maker's negligence is quite material to his right to recover. However, it is unnecessary to decide whether that section applies here to defeat the Title Company's recovery since recovery is precluded by reason of the applicability of § 3–405.

Judgment affirmed.

STONE & WEBSTER ENG. CORP. v. FIRST NATIONAL BANK & TRUST CO.

(1962) 345 Mass. 1, 184 N.E.2d 358.

[Between January 1 and May 15, 1960, Stone & Webster Engineering Corporation (Stone & Webster) was indebted from time to time to Westinghouse Electric Corporation (Westinghouse) for goods and services furnished to it by Westinghouse. To pay the indebtedness, Stone & Webster drew three checks within the period on its checking account in the First National Bank of Boston (First National), payable to the order of Westinghouse in the aggregate amount of $64,755.44. Before delivery of the checks to Westinghouse, an employee of Stone & Webster in possession of the checks, forged the indorsement of Westinghouse and presented the checks to the First National Bank & Trust Company of Greenfield (Greenfield Bank), which cashed them and delivered the proceeds to the employee who devoted the proceeds to his own use. Greenfield Bank forwarded the checks to First National and received from it the full amounts thereof. First National charged Stone & Webster's account with the full amounts of the checks. The first two checks were indorsed in typewriting "For Deposit Only: Westinghouse Electric Corporation, By O. D. Costine, Treasury Representative" followed by an ink signature "O. D. Costine." The third check was indorsed in typewriting "Westinghouse Electric Corporation, By (Sgd.) O. D. Cosdine, Treasury Representative." All three checks bore an indorsement by rubber stamp: "Pay to the order of any bank, banker or trust company, prior indorsements guaranteed * * *. (date) The First National Bank & Trust Company of Greenfield, Mass." Each check bore the stamped indorsement of the Federal Reserve Bank of Boston and on its face the paid stamp of First National.

Upon refusal of Stone & Webster's demand to recredit its checking account, it brought an appropriate action against Greenfield Bank to recover $64,755.44. The first count is in contract. Count 2, also in contract, is on an account annexed for money owed, namely, $64,755.44, the proceeds of the checks of Stone & Webster "cashed" by Greenfield Bank on the forged indorsements. Counts 3 and 4 are for conversion of the checks and for negligence in "cashing" the checks with forged indorsements. Defendant Greenfield Bank's demurrer was sustained, and plaintiff appealed.

Upon appeal, the court stated the questions argued concern the rights of the drawer against a collecting bank which "cashed" checks for an individual who had forged the payee's indorsement on the checks, which were never delivered to the payee.

WILKINS, C. J. 1. Count 1, the plaintiff contends, is for money had and received. We shall so regard it. "An action for money had and received lies to recover money which should not in justice be retained by the defendant, and which in equity and good conscience should be paid to the plaintiff." [Citations.]

The defendant has no money in its hands which belongs to the plaintiff. The latter had no right in the proceeds of its own check payable to Westinghouse. Not being a holder or an agent for a holder, it could not have presented the check to the drawee for payment. Uniform Commercial Code, enacted by St.1957, c. 765, § 1, G.L. c. 106, §§ 3–504 (1), 1–201(20). See Am.Law Inst. Uniform Commercial Code, 1958 Official Text with comments, § 3–419, comment 2: "A negotiable instrument is the property of the holder." [Citations.] The plaintiff contends that "First National paid or credited the proceeds of the checks to the defendant and charged the account of the plaintiff, and consequently, the plaintiff was deprived of a credit, and the defendant received funds or a credit which 'in equity and good conscience' belonged to the plaintiff."

In our opinion this argument is a non sequitur. The plaintiff as a depositor in First National was merely in a contractual relationship of creditor and debtor. [Citations.] The amounts the defendant received from First National to cover the checks "cashed" were the bank's funds and not the plaintiff's. The Uniform Commercial Code does not purport to change the relationship. See G.L. c. 106, §§ 1–103, 4–401 to 4–407. Section 3–409(1) provides: "A check or other draft does not of itself operate as an assignment of any funds in the hands of the drawee available for its payment, and the drawee is not liable on the instrument until he accepts it." This is the same as our prior law, which the Code repealed. [Citations.] Whether the plaintiff was rightfully deprived of a credit is a matter between it and the drawee, First National.

* * *

The plaintiff relies upon the Uniform Commercial Code, G.L. c. 106, § 3–419, which provides, "(1) An instrument is converted when * * * (c) it is paid on a forged indorsement." This, however, could not apply to the defendant, which is not a "payor bank," defined in the Code, § 4–105(b), as "a bank by which an item is payable as drawn or accepted." See Am.Law Inst. Uniform Commercial Code, 1958 Official Text with comments, § 4–105, comments 1–3; G.L. c. 106, §§ 4–401, 4–213, 3–102(b).

A conversion provision of the Uniform Commercial Code which might have some bearing on this case is § 3–419(3).[3] This section implicitly recognizes that, subject to defences, including the one stated in it, a collecting bank, defined in the Code, § 4–105(d), may be liable in conversion. In the case at bar the forged indorsements were "wholly inoperative" as the signatures of the payee,

Code §§ 3–404(1), 1–201(43), and equally so both as to the restrictive indorsements for deposits, see § 3–205(c), and as to the indorsement in blank, see § 3–204(2). When the forger transferred the checks to the collecting bank, no negotiation under § 3–202 (1) occurred, because there was lacking the necessary indorsement of the payee. For the same reason, the collecting bank could not become a "holder" as defined in § 1–201(20), and so could not become a holder in due course under § 3–302(1). Accordingly, we assume that the collecting bank may be liable in conversion to a proper party, subject to defences, including that in § 3–419(3). [Citation.] But there is no explicit provision in the Code purporting to determine to whom the collecting bank may be liable, and consequently, the drawer's right to enforce such a liability must be found elsewhere. Therefore, we conclude that the case must be decided on our own law, which, on the issue we are discussing, has been left untouched by the Uniform Commercial Code in any specific section.

In this Commonwealth there are two cases (decided in 1913 and 1914) the results in which embrace a ruling that there was a conversion, but in neither was the question discussed and, for aught that appears, in each the ruling seems to have been assumed without conscious appreciation of the issue here considered. * * *

The authorities are hopelessly divided. We think that the preferable view is that there is no right of action. Jurisdictions denying such right are [citations]. Expressing a contrary view, but not all on the ground of conversion, are [citations].

We state what appears to us to be the proper analysis. Had the checks been delivered to the payee Westinghouse, the defendant might have been liable for conversion to the payee. The checks, if delivered, in the hands of the payee would have been valuable property which could have been transferred for

---

3. [Footnotes are by the Court.] "Subject to the provisions of this chapter concerning restrictive indorsements a representative, including a depositary or collecting bank, who has in good faith and in accordance with the reasonable commercial standards applicable to the business of such representative dealt with an instrument or its proceeds on behalf of one who was not the true owner is not liable in conversion or otherwise to the true owner beyond the amount of any proceeds remaining in his hands." See Code §§ 1–201(35); 4–201(1).

value or presented for payment; and, had a check been dishonored, the payee would have had a right of recourse against the drawer on the instrument under § 3–413(2). Here the plaintiff drawer of the checks, which were never delivered to the payee [citations] had no valuable rights in them. Since, as we have seen, it did not have the right of a payee or subsequent holder to present them to the drawee for payment, the value of its rights was limited to the physical paper on which they were written, and was not measured by their payable amounts. [Citations.]

The enactment of the Uniform Commercial Code opens the road for the adoption of what seems the preferable view. An action by the drawer against the collecting bank might have some theoretical appeal as avoiding circuity of action. [Citations.] It would have been in the interest of speedy and complete justice had the case been tried with the action by the drawer against the drawee and with an action by the drawee against the collecting bank. [Citation.] So one might ask: If the drawee is liable to the drawer and the collecting bank is liable to the drawee, why not let the drawer sue the collecting bank direct? We believe that the answer lies in the applicable defences set up in the Code.[4]

The drawer can insist that the drawee recredit his account with the amount of any unauthorized payment. Such was our common law. [Citations.] This is, in effect, retained by the Code §§ 4–401(1),[5] 4–406(4). But the drawee has defences based upon the drawer's substantial negligence, if "contributing," or upon his duty to discover and report unauthorized signatures and alterations. §§ 3–406, 4–406. As to unauthorized indorsements, see § 4–406(4).[6] Then, if the

drawee has a valid defence which it waives or fails upon request to assert, the drawee may not assert against the collecting bank or other prior party presenting or transferring the check a claim which is based on the forged indorsement. § 4–406(5).[7] See Am. Law Inst. Uniform Commercial Code, Official Text with comments, § 4–406, comment 6, which shows that there was no intent to change the prior law as to negligence of a customer. [Citations.] If the drawee recredits the drawer's account and is not precluded by § 4–406(5), it may claim against the presenting bank on the relevant warranties in §§ 3–417 and 4–207, and each transferee has rights against his transferor under those sections.

If the drawer's rights are limited to requiring the drawee to recredit his account, the drawee will have the defences noted above and perhaps others; and the collecting bank or banks will have the defences in § 4–207(4)[8] and § 4–406(5), and perhaps others. If the drawer is allowed in the present case to sue the collecting bank, the assertion of the defences, for all practical purposes, would be difficult. The possibilities of such a result

---

4. Cases where a payee has acquired rights in an instrument may stand on a different footing.

5. "As against its customer, a bank may charge against his account any item which is otherwise properly payable from that account * * *."

6. "Without regard to care or lack of care of either the customer or the bank a customer who does not

within one year from the time the statement and items are made available to the customer (subsection [1]) discover and report his unauthorized signature or any alteration on the face or back of the item or does not within three years from that time discover and report any unauthorized indorsement is precluded from asserting against the bank such unauthorized signature or indorsement or such alteration."

7. "If under this section a payor bank has a valid defense against a claim of a customer upon or resulting from payment of an item and waives or fails upon request to assert the defense the [drawee] may not assert against * * * [a] collecting bank or other prior party presenting or transferring the item a claim based upon the unauthorized signature or alteration giving rise to the customer's claim."

8. "Unless a claim for breach of warranty under this section is made within a reasonable time after the person claiming learns of the breach, the person liable is discharged to the extent of any loss caused by the delay in making claim."

would tend to compel resort to litigation in every case involving a forgery of commercial paper. It is a result to be avoided.

The demurer to count 1 was rightly sustained.

2. The second count, the plaintiff states, is for money had and received to the plaintiff's use and is covered by the argument as to count 1. We accept this interpretation of the allegations. As no new point is argued, we hold that the demurrer to the second count was also rightly sustained.

3. Count 3 is a brief count resembling the suggestion in G.L.(Ter.Ed.) c. 231, § 147, Form 11, and is for the conversion of "checks which were the property of the plaintiff in the total sum of $64,755.44." Supplementing these allegations with such information as may be gleaned from the checks, we again note that the plaintiff is the drawer, that there are apparent indorsements by the payee (not alleged to be forged), and indorsements by the defendant, which is not the drawee bank. No right of ownership in the plaintiff is apparent.

The demurrer was rightly sustained as to count 3.

4. Count 4 alleges that "on divers dates between January 1, 1960, and May 15, 1960, the defendant by reason of its negligence in cashing checks with forged indorsements thereon damaged the plaintiff in the full amount of said checks, to wit $64,755.44. Wherefore, the plaintiff prays judgment against the defendant in the sum of $64,755.-44, with interest." From the checks, we observe that, wholly apart from any duty on the part of the defendant toward the plaintiff [citation] there is no allegation of legal damage. When the defendant "cashed" checks with its own funds, no legal harm befell the plaintiff. From what we have said in respect of counts 1 and 3, there would be difficulty in making such an allegation. The harm which befell the plaintiff was the

charging of its account by the drawee bank. As has been noted above, the drawer has a cause of action, possibly subject to defences, against that bank. It does not appear that this right is impaired.

There was no error in sustaining the demurrer to count 4.

Order sustaining demurrer affirmed.

PRICE v. NEALE

(1762) 3 Burrow's 1355 (Court of King's Bench).

This was a special case reserved at the sittings at Guildhall after Trinity term 1762, before Lord Mansfield.

It was an action upon the case brought by Price against Neale; wherein Price declares that the defendant Edward Neale was indebted to him in 80 pounds for money had and received to his the plaintiff's use; and damages were laid to 100 pounds. The general issue was pleaded; and issue joined thereon.

It was proved at the trial, that a bill was drawn as follows—"Leicester, 22d November 1760. Sir, Six weeks after date pay Mr. Rogers Ruding or order forty pounds, value received for Mr. Thomas Ploughfor; as advised by, Sir, your humble servant Benjamin Sutton. To Mr. John Price in Bush-lane Cannon-street, London;" indorsed "R. Rudding; Antony Topham, Hammond and Laroche. Received the contents, James Watson and son: witness Edward Neale."

That this bill was indorsed to the defendant for a valuable consideration; and notice of the bill left at the plaintiff's house, on the day it became due. Whereupon the plaintiff sent his servant to call on the defendant, to pay him the said sum of 40 pounds and take up the said bill: which was done accordingly.

That another bill was drawn as follows— "Leicester, 1st February 1761. Sir, Six weeks after date pay Mr. Rogers Ruding or order forty pounds, value received for Mr. Thomas Ploughfor; as advised by, Sir, your humble servant Benjamin Sutton. To Mr. John Price in Bush-lane, Cannon-street, London." That this bill was indorsed, "R. Ruding, Thomas Watson and son. Witness for "Smith, Right and Co." That the plaintiff accepted this bill, by writing on it, "accepted John Price:" and that the plaintiff wrote on the back of it.—"Messieurs, Freame and Barclay, pray pay forty pounds for John Price."

That this bill being so accepted was indorsed to the defendant for a valuable consideration, and left at his bankers for payment; and was paid by order of the plaintiff, and taken up.

Both these bills were forged by one Lee, who has been since hanged for forgery.

The defendant Neale acted innocently and bona fide, without the least privity or suspicion of the said forgeries or of either of them; and paid the whole value of those bills.

The jury found a verdict for the plaintiff; and assessed damages 80 pounds and costs 40 shillings subject to the opinion of the court upon this question—

"Whether the plaintiff, under the circumstances of the case, (a) can recover back, from the defendant, the money he paid on the said bills, or either of them."

Mr. Stowe, for the plaintiff, argued that he ought to recover back the money, in this action; as it was paid by him by mistake only, on supposition "that these were true genuine bills;" and as he could never recover it against the drawer, because in fact no drawer exists; nor against the forger, because he is hanged.

He owned that in a case at Guild-hall, of Jenys v. Fawler et al, (an action by an indorsee of a bill of exchange brought against the acceptor,) Lord Raymond would not admit the defendants to prove it a forged bill, by calling persons acquainted with the hand of the drawer, to swear "that they believed

it not to be so:" and he even strongly inclined, "that actual proof of forgery would not excuse the defendants against their own acceptance, which had given the bill a credit to the indorsee."

But he urged, that in the case now before the court, the forgery of the bill does not rest in belief and opinion only; but has been actually proved, and the forger executed for it.

Thus it stands even upon the accepted bill. But the plaintiff's case is much stronger upon the other bill which was not accepted. It is not stated "that that bill was accepted before it was negotiated;" on the contrary, the consideration for it was paid by the defendant, before the plaintiff had seen it. So that the defendant took it upon the credit of the indorsers, not upon the credit of the plaintiff; and therefore the reason, upon which Lord Raymond grounds his inclination to be of opinion "that actual proof of forgery would be no excuse," will not hold here.

Mr. Yates, for the defendant, argued that the plaintiff was not entitled to recover back this money from the defendant.

He denied it to be a payment by mistake: and insisted that it was rather owing to the negligence of the plaintiff; who should have inquired and satisfied himself "whether the bill was really drawn upon him by Sutton, or not." Here is no fraud in the defendant; who is stated "to have acted innocently and bona fide, without the least privity or suspicion of the forgery; and to have paid the whole value for the bills."

Lord Mansfield stopped him from going on; saying that this was one of those cases that could never be made plainer by argument.

It is an action upon the case, for money had and received to the plaintiff's use. In which action, the plaintiff can not recover the money, unless it be against conscience in the defendant, to retain it: and great liberality is always allowed, in this sort of action.

But it can never be thought unconscientious in the defendant, to retain this money, when he has once received it upon a bill of exchange indorsed to him for a fair and valuable consideration, which he had bona fide paid, without the least privity or suspicion of any forgery.

Here was no fraud: no wrong. It was incumbent upon the plaintiff, to be satisfied "that the bill drawn upon him was the drawer's hand," before he accepted or paid it: but it was not incumbent upon the defendant, to inquire into it. Here was notice given by the defendant to the plaintiff of a bill drawn upon him: and he sends his servant to pay it and take it up. The other bill he actually accepts; after which acceptance, the defendant innocently and bona fide discounts it. The plaintiff lies by, for a considerable time after he has paid these bills; and then found out "that they were forged:" and the forger comes to be hanged. He made no objection to them, at the time of paying them. Whatever neglect there was, was on his side. The defendant had actual encouragement from the plaintiff himself, for negotiating the second bill, from the plaintiff's having without any scruple or hesitation paid the first: and he paid the whole value, bona fide. It is a misfortune which has happened without the defendant's fault or neglect. If there was no neglect in the plaintiff, yet there is no reason to throw off the loss from one innocent man upon another innocent man: but, in this case, if there was any fault or negligence in any one, it certainly was in the plaintiff, and not in the defendant.

Per Cur'.

Rule—That the postea be delivered to the Defendant.

THE UNION BANK v. MOBILLA

(1959 Pa.) 43 Erie 45.

LAUB, J. This is a complaint in assumpsit for breach of warranty to which the defendant filed an answer containing new matter and a counterclaim. The plaintiff filed a reply, then moved for judgment on the pleadings. It is this latter action which is before us now.

On January 15, 1958, the defendant, a used car dealer, represented to the plaintiff bank that he had sold a used Ford automobile to one Theresa Piotrowski of 650 East 24th Street. For finance purposes, he exhibited an installment sales contract and a judgment note allegedly signed by Theresa Piotrowski as maker. There was nothing on the face of either instrument to indicate that the signatures had not been placed there by the maker or that either had been signed by someone else acting in the maker's behalf. The note which was payable to defendant was endorsed by him "without recourse", and the security agreement, which was in defendant's favor as a seller of a chattel, was assigned to the bank. Both instruments, as well as the title to the vehicle in question, were turned over to the bank as part of the finance transaction.

The installment sales contract called for monthly payments of $72.18, and during the months of February, March and April someone paid the bank the installments due for those periods. The debt went into default on May 15, 1958, and no further payments have been made thereon, the unpaid balance being $1,396.97 with interest. After default the bank importuned both the purported maker and the defendant to discharge the obligation but without avail, the maker having denied executing either document or having bought the vehicle from the defendant. In consequence, plaintiff instituted this action, alleging that defendant is guilty of a breach of warranty, and as part of its action, alleging a written warranty in the security agreement "that the above instrument is genuine and in all respects what it purports to be". Plaintiff also claims upon an implied warranty of the genuineness of the note.

The defendant in his answer admits that he endorsed the note and assigned the security agreement to the plaintiff. He also admits that the maker did not sign either document. It is his defense, however, that Theresa Piotrowski's signature was affixed by an authorized agent named Edward Rogalia and that he (the defendant) is not liable in any event because his endorsement of the note was "without recourse". He also contends that plaintiff may not recover, as an item of damage, the fifteen per cent collection or attorney's fees provided for in the warrant to confess judgment.

We can see no merit whatever in the defenses offered and consider that plaintiff is entitled to the judgment which it seeks. The defendant's conception of the litigation as being a suit against an endorser who signed "without recourse", misses the point. Plaintiff is not suing on the note, but, as noted above, is claiming upon a breach of warranty. If it were true that the suit was against the defendant on the sole basis that he was an endorser, there might be some value to the defenses offered, but the pleadings reveal an entirely different situation. As the pleadings now stand, it is admitted on the record that the defendant in writing warranted the security agreement to be all that it purported to be, and it is clear that it was not. Further, the admission that defendant endorsed the note as part of his finance dealings with the plaintiff and that the note was not signed by the maker is a clear admission of a breach of the implied warranty which accompanies situations of this character. While no statute is required to establish the common sense conclusion that one who presents a document for discount or otherwise, impliedly warrants its genuineness when he accepts a considera-

tion for its transfer, the Uniform Commercial Code has such a provision. In Section 3–417 (2) (a) of that Act (Act 1953, April 6, P.L. 3, 12A P.S. 3–417(2) (a)) it is provided that the transferor of an instrument for consideration warrants, among other things, that all signatures are genuine or authorized. This certainly does not imply that a transferor, with knowledge that a signature is not that of the person it purports to belong to and there is no qualifying or descriptive language indicating that the signature was made by someone other than the maker, may remain silent and suppress such knowledge to the detriment of the transferee.

* * *

[Judgment for plaintiff.]

PROBLEMS

1. A who is indebted to B in the amount of $300 for goods sold and delivered, draws a check upon the X National Bank in Detroit for the sum of $300, payable to the order of B, and delivers the check to B who takes it to the drawee bank and has it properly certified. B then indorses the check to C, a creditor of B, and mails the check so indorsed to C in San Francisco. C deposits the check in a San Francisco bank, and about a week later the check is returned to C for the reason that the drawee bank had become insolvent and had closed its doors before the check was presented for payment. In an action by C against A and against B on the check, what judgment?

2. M gave his negotiable note to P for goods purchased, payable at the Mechanics Bank, Chicago. P negotiated it to H, a holder in due course. H forgot about the note until two weeks after its maturity. Shortly thereafter, H negotiated it to T for value. Next day, T presents the note to M for payment. M refuses to pay the note because (1) it was not presented for payment at the bank at maturity, when funds were on hand to pay it; and (2) T is not a holder in due course. Is M correct?

3. C, having received B's check for $1,000 in payment of a debt, indorsed it to the order of D, who on the same day procured its certification by the drawee bank. (a) What is the ob-

ligation, if any, assumed by the bank upon certifying? (b) What effect, if any, does such certification have upon the liability of B and C on the check?

4. A was indorser on a promissory note which was not paid when due. Notice of dishonor and protest was mailed to him at 500 Fifth Avenue, New York City, where he was in the habit of receiving his mail, although he resided and also received mail at suburban Westchester. He did not receive the notice and was sued on his indorsement. Decision?

5. A, a depositor in the C Bank, did an extensive business, had many customers and issued many checks. The regular routine followed in the issuing of checks was that the checks were made out on a typing machine according to instructions given to the typist by M, A's chief clerk; then a carbon copy of each check was initialed by M, after which the check bearing M's "o. k." was passed on to another desk to be signed by two other employees, who were authorized by A to sign all checks bearing M's "o. k." without further investigation. Fifty checks were thus drawn and signed according to this routine payable to seven different customers of A, to none of whom A owed anything. M intercepted these checks and forged the indorsements of the payees. The checks were cashed through banks other than the C Bank, were subsequently paid by the C Bank and charged to A's account. M disappeared and A sued the C Bank for the amount of the checks. Decision?

6. C drew a check on the A bank payable to the order of B. An employee of C stole the check before delivery to B, erased B's name, skillfully inserted his own name as payee, obtained the certification of the A bank and then negotiated it to the D bank, the latter obtaining payment from the accepting A bank. The accepting A bank then sued the D bank to recover the money so paid on the altered check. Decision?

7. A drew and delivered a check on the B bank for $50 payable to the order of James Hill. Hill had an employee named James Hall. Hall stole this check, and skillfully changed the name from Hill to Hall, and also raised the amount of the check to $500. He then had the check certified by the B bank. He next purchased a car from H, and indorsed and delivered the check to H, a holder in due course,

in payment thereof. H duly collected the check from the B bank. At the end of the month the alteration is discovered.

(a) Can the bank charge A's account with the amount of this check or any part thereof?

(b) Can the bank recover the $500 from H?

8. The Howland Dairy Company, a depositor of the Woodford National Bank, had in its employ a bookkeeper, George Travers, whose duties included the preparation of vouchers and the drawing of checks which he submitted to the president of the company for signature. Between June, 1963, and November, 1966, Travers prepared 92 false vouchers with checks attached in favor of 45 different payees to some of whom the dairy company was not indebted. Travers had the company president sign the checks, forged the payees' indorsements and then cashed the checks among acquaintances. All the checks were charged to the dairy company's account with the drawee bank. The dairy company received a statement and cancelled checks from the bank each month. In 1962, about a year after Travers was employed by the dairy company, the president learned that he had been "involved" previously in a financial difficulty as an employee of another company and had "made a settlement" of a shortage in cash, after which he left that company. The dairy company brings an action against the drawee bank to recover for losses sustained from the cashing of the checks bearing the forged indorsements. Decision?

9. A gave B his promissory note for money won by B in a game of cards. A statute of the State made notes given for gambling debts void. B indorsed the note in due course and for value to the C Bank. After due presentment and notice of dishonor the C Bank sues B for the amount of the note. B interposes the defense that the note was given for an amount won in a gambling transaction. Decision?

10. M, nineteen years of age, bought a motorcycle from P. M executed and delivered to P his negotiable promissory note for $550, representing the amount of the purchase price, due ninety days after date, and payable to "P or Bearer." P negotiated the note to A by mere delivery. A, who did not know of M's minority, indorsed the note "Without recourse" and sold it to B. B indorsed the note "Pay to H, B" and sold it to H.

Upon the maturity of the note, H presented it to M for payment. M refused to pay the instrument. Compliance with all notice requirements, presentment and necessary proceedings on dishonor was made. What is the liability, if any, of M, P, A and B, respectively, to H?

11. A, having a note executed by M, tears it up with the idea of releasing M. Later, A changes his mind and sues M. M defends on the ground that A had torn up the note. A replies that this was done without any consideration. What judgment?

CHAPTER 29

BANK DEPOSITS AND COLLECTIONS

Introductory. In our society, goods and services are typically sold and paid for with some form of credit and without a physical transfer of "money." Sales where immediate payment in currency takes place represent a smaller percentage of total sales each year and are limited for the most part to small consumer items. Even in this area, the wide acceptance of the credit card, charge accounts and various deferred payment plans have made the cash sale increasingly rare. But even credit sales must ultimately be settled. On the day of reckoning, cash is seldom the form of payment. Rather, a check is the vehicle by which payment is typically accomplished. By check, credit of the buyer on the books of his bank is transferred to the books of the seller's bank for his use. Should the parties to a sales transaction happen to do business at the same bank, this transfer of credit is easily accomplished. In the vast majority of cases, the parties do business at different banks, and the check must journey from the payee's bank (depositary bank) to the drawer's bank (payor bank), frequently passing through one or more other banks (intermediary banks) in the process, so that it may be collected and the appropriate entries recorded.

Our banking system has developed a network to handle the collection of checks and other instruments. The twelve Federal Reserve Banks located across the country form the main arteries of this system. When a check is drawn on a bank in one Federal Reserve district and is deposited at a bank in another, it customarily is routed through the "Fed." And traffic is heavy. For example, the Fed. of Chicago alone handled almost 842 million checks in 1965, having a total dollar value of over $281,000,000,000. To handle more local traffic, banks in the major cities have formed clearing house associations. Through such a clearing house, a member bank is able to obtain payment for checks deposited by its customers drawn on other banks in the metropolitan area and to receive in one package checks drawn by its depositors which have been deposited with other banks in the area. Only one settlement is made by a clearing bank for all checks handled on a given day. If the total amount of checks drawn on such member bank exceeds the total of all checks it is collecting from other members, it pays a sum to the clearing house equal to the difference. Conversely, if a member's collections total more than its payables, it receives the difference from the clearing house. In 1965, the Chicago Clearing House handled checks having a total value of $82,000,000,000.

Still another method of collecting checks is through the so-called "correspondent bank" arrangement. Larger banks in major urban centers have accounts on their books from many other banks, primarily those located in smaller communities in the area. An item received for deposit by such an outlying or "country" bank may be forwarded to its big city correspondent, which will then collect it through a clearing house, a correspondent of its own, or by sending it directly to the payor bank. In reverse, an item drawn on a country bank may be collected through its big city correspondent. In either case, settlement is made through appropriate adjustment to the account of the country bank on the books of the city bank.

Despite the tremendous volume of traffic and the intricacies of the bank collection system, it has proved most efficient and has operated without undue legal problems for many years. Perhaps for this reason there has been no uniform statutory law controlling the rights and duties of the various parties involved in the bank collection process, although the model Bank Collection Code promulgated by the American Bankers Association did have some limited acceptance. Article 4 of the Uniform Commercial Code, "Bank Deposits and Collections," is designed to fill the void in this area of statutory law by providing a uniform statement of the principal rules of the modern bank collection process with ample provision for flexibility so that future changes in procedure can be accommodated without the necessity of revising the statute on each occasion.

Since items in the bank collection process are essentially those covered by Article 3, "Commercial Paper," and to a much lesser extent, by Article 8, "Investment Securities," some accommodation between these Articles is necessary in case of conflict. This need is supplied by Section 4–102(1), which provides that in the event of conflict the provisions of Article 4 govern those of Article 3 but the provisions of Article 8 govern those of Article 4. The difference stems from the fact that investment securities enter the bank collection system only rarely—largely in the case of collection of bonds and bond coupons —and hence the rules of Article 4 should be secondary to those of Article 8. The lifeblood of the bank collection process, however, is commercial paper and it is that very process which gives such items a large measure of their value. Hence the provisions of Article 4 should be dominant.

On the other hand, hard and fast rules established by Article 4 could tend to freeze the collection process in its present form, choking off any prospect of changes resulting from improved techniques and technological developments. Progress in this regard has been almost unbelievable in the past. There is no reason to think it will not continue into the future. To preserve the degree of flexibility necessary to meet the requirements of change, Section 4–103 provides that the effect of the provisions of Article 4 may be varied by agreement. Therefore, to the extent a deposit agreement, for example, between a bank and its customer printed on a deposit ticket or signature card departs from the provisions of Article 4, it is effective.

More particularly, however, Section 4–103 (2) specifically provides that Federal Reserve regulations and operating letters, clearing house rules, and the like are the equivalent of agreements for this purpose. It is from such sources, of course, that major developments in the bank collection process may be expected.

Certain limitations based on public policy are imposed upon the type of agreements authorized. No agreement can disclaim a bank's responsibility for its own lack of good faith or failure to exercise ordinary care, nor can such agreement limit the measure of damages in the case of such lack or failure. Section 4–103(1). The measure of damages for failure to exercise ordinary care in handling an item, in the absence of bad faith, can be no more than the amount of the item. Section 4–103(5). In fact, if it can be established that the full amount of the item could not have been realized in any event, as in the case of insolvency of a drawer or insufficient funds in his account, the amount of damages will be limited to the amount which would have been recoverable by the use of ordinary care. Where there is bad faith, however, not only may the amount of the item be recovered, but also recovery may be had of the amount of any other loss which the party may have suffered as a result of the lack of good faith as, for example, the profit on a deal.

1. *Collection of Items—Depositary and Collecting Banks.* Except as it involves the relationship of a bank with its own customers, to be considered later, Article 4 does not concern itself with the situation in which

Customer A deposits a check on the account of Customer B of the same bank. In that case, upon making the deposit, Customer A receives a credit to his account. It is not final, and is subject to being reversed if the check, for some reason, cannot be charged to Customer B's account. Thus, the credit to Customer A's account is characterized as "provisional." Normally, a bank will not permit a customer to draw against a provisional credit, although it may do so in the case of a valued and reliable customer. When the check has passed through the bank's internal bookkeeping process and been charged to the account of Customer B, the drawer, the credit to Customer A's account becomes final and the transaction is closed.

If the check is not paid for any reason, such as a stop payment order or insufficient funds in Customer B's account, the provisional credit to Customer A's account is reversed, his account is debited for that amount, and the check is returned to him with a statement of the reason for nonpayment. If, in the meantime, he has been permitted to draw against the provisional credit, the bank will recover the payment from him in whatever manner is most feasible.

In the case just described, the bank involved was both the "depositary bank"—the first bank to which the item was transferred for collection (Section 4–105(a))—and the "payor bank"—the bank by which the item was payable. Section 4–105(b). It is only where the depositary and payor banks are different that the bank collection aspects of Article 4 come into play. Where the depositary and payor banks are different, it is necessary for the item to pass from one to the other, either directly, through a clearing house, if both are members, or through one or more "intermediary banks," which is the term applied to any bank in the collection chain other than the depositary or payor bank. In the usual situation, the depositary bank gives a provisional credit to its customer, transfers the item to the next bank in the chain, receiving a provisional credit or "settlement" from it, and so on to the payor bank, which gives a provisional settlement to its transferor. When the item is paid, all the provisional settlements given become final and the particular transaction has been completed. No adjustment is necessary on the books of any of the banks involved. The reason this procedure has been adopted by the banking system and Article 4 is that the vast majority of items are paid, and thus the bookkeeping processes of all the banks involved are simplified because only one entry is necessary if the item is paid.

But all items are not paid. Checks may be dishonored by the payor bank for a number of reasons, including stop payment orders, insufficient funds in the drawer's account, and legal proceedings that have the effect of attaching the drawer's balance in the hands of the payor bank. If an item is not paid by the payor, it is returned from whence it came and each collecting bank reverses the provisional settlement or credit previously given by it to its forwarding bank. Ultimately, the depositary bank will charge the account of its customer that deposited the item, and he must seek recovery from the indorsers or the drawer.

A settlement may be effected by a payment in cash, by the efficient, but somewhat complicated, process of the adjustment and offsetting of balances through a clearing house, by debit or credit entries in accounts between banks, by the forwarding of one of the various types of remittance instruments or otherwise as instructed. Section 4–104 (1) (j). Settlements may be either provisional or final, depending on whether they are subject to being reversed.

(a) *Agency Status of Collecting Banks.* A collecting bank (any bank handling the item for collection other than the payor bank —Section 4–105(d)) is an agent or subagent of the owner of the item until the settlement which it gave the owner becomes final. Section 4–201(1). Clearly, then, unless otherwise provided, any credit given for the item initially is provisional. Once it is firmed up into a final settlement, the agency relationship changes to one of debtor-creditor.

The effect of this agency rule is that the risk of loss remains with the owner and any chargebacks go to him, not to the collecting bank. On the other hand, as discussed below, the fact that he remains the owner gives him certain preferential rights in the case of insolvency of a bank in the collection chain.

(b) *Responsibility for Collection.* A collecting bank must use ordinary care in handling an item transferred to it for collection. Section 4–202(1). Of particular importance are the steps it takes in presenting an item or sending it for presentment. It must act within a reasonable time after receipt of the item, and must choose a reasonable method of forwarding the item for presentment. It is also responsible for using care in the selection of the routing of the item to the payor bank: Should it be sent through the Federal Reserve System, through correspondent banks, and if so, which ones, or should it be presented directly? Usually a bank will have established procedures which have stood the test of usage, and continued adherence to such procedures in the absence of change of circumstances will normally be deemed to comply with the requirements of use of ordinary care.

Section 4–204 further simplifies the task of the collecting bank by specifying certain rules concerning methods of sending and presenting items. The bank must adopt a reasonably prompt method, taking into consideration any relevant instructions from its transferor, the nature of the item, the number of items on hand, the cost of collection involved and its own usage and customs, as well as those of the banking system as a whole. But more specifically, a collecting bank is authorized to send any item directly to the payor bank by direct mail, express, messenger or the like. This method is now in widespread use because of the need for speed, the general responsibility of banks, Federal Deposit Insurance protection and other reasons.

Normally, items payable by makers or drawees which are not banks are not sent to them because non-bank payors are of unknown responsibility. To the extent a bank chooses without authorization to make presentment in this manner, it must take the risk of any loss which may result. Authorization for direct presentment may be granted by the transferor of the item if he is willing to assume that risk. In addition, in some cities, it has long been the practice under clearing house procedures to forward directly to non-bank payors certain types of items such as insurance loss drafts drawn by field agents on home offices. To permit growth of such practices, Section 4–204(2) (c) approves sending any item other than a documentary draft to a non-bank payor if authorized by Federal Reserve regulation or operating letter, clearing house rule or the like. The exception for documentary drafts —drafts with bill of lading or warehouse receipt attached—is included because the very purpose in forwarding a documentary draft is to assure the drawer that payment will be made before papers entitling the drawee to the goods are delivered to him. To deliver the draft and the documents to him before payment would defeat the security character of the transaction.

The proper method of presenting an item on a non-bank payor is in person, by a representative of the collecting bank. To simplify procedures and save time, it is specified by Section 4–210 that unless otherwise instructed, the collecting bank may send a written notice to the drawee or maker that the bank holds the item for acceptance or payment. Notice with respect to a time item must be sent so that it is received on or before the day when presentment is due. The drawee or maker may require the collecting bank to comply with any of the requirements specified under Section 3–505, such as exhibiting the item or establishing its authority to present it. Upon receipt of such a request the bank must meet such requirement by the close of its next banking day. When presentment has been made by notice and neither honor nor request for compliance with a requirement under Section 3–505 is received by the close of business on the day after maturity in the case of a time item, or by the close of business on the third banking day after notice was sent, in the case of a demand item, the presenting bank may treat the item as dishonored and charge secondary parties by sending appropriate notice.

Ordinary care must also be observed by a collecting bank in settling for an item when the bank itself receives a final settlement, and in taking appropriate steps in the event an item is dishonored, lost or delayed in transit.

Where a collecting bank has exercised ordinary care, as, for example, in the case of selection of intermediary banks, it is not liable for the insolvency, neglect, misconduct, mistake or default of another bank or person or for loss or destruction of an item in transit or in the possession of others. Section 4–202(3).

(c) *Duty to Act Seasonably.* Closely related to the collecting bank's duty of care is its duty to act seasonably. For an understanding of what constitutes seasonable action, it is necessary to understand the concept of the "midnight deadline" introduced by Article 4. Whether action was taken before a bank's midnight deadline is an important element in determining liability in numerous situations. It means midnight on a bank's next banking day following the banking day on which it receives the relevant item or notice. Section 4–104(1) (h). In other words, when the time for a bank to

take action of some sort commences to run on a given banking day, such as Monday, the midnight deadline applicable is midnight of the next banking day, or Tuesday in this example. A banking day means that part of any day on which a bank is open to the public for carrying on substantially all of its banking functions. Section 4–104(1) (c). If the bank is open for only limited functions, as for example on a Friday evening or a Saturday to receive deposits and cash checks, but with loan, bookkeeping and other departments closed, it is not part of a banking day.

A further problem is presented by the fact that it necessarily takes time to process an item through a bank, whether it be the depositary, an intermediary or the payor. If the various steps in connection with a day's transaction are to be completed without overtime work, either the bank must close early or it must fix a cutoff time for the day's work. Recognizing this problem, Section 4–107 provides that for the purpose of allowing time to process items, prove balances and make the necessary entries on its books to determine its position for the day, a bank may fix an afternoon hour of 2:00 P.M. or later as a cutoff hour for the handling of money and items and the making of entries on its books. Application of this rule permits a bank to extend its banking day until a much later hour without penalty as to the beginning of the running of time for various purposes.

Items received after the cutoff hour so fixed or after the close of the banking day may be treated as having been received at the opening of the next banking day, and the time for taking action and for determining the bank's midnight deadline with respect to the item involved begins to run from that point.

Most rules specified under the U.C.C. for determining whether a bank has acted seasonably relate to its midnight deadline. But cutting across all such rules are the provisions of Section 4–108. Recognizing that if an item is not paid, everyone involved will be greatly inconvenienced, that Section provides that unless otherwise instructed, a collecting bank in a good faith effort to secure payment may, in the case of specific items, waive, modify or extend the time limits specified in Article 4 for not in excess of one additional banking day. Such an extension may be made without the approval of the parties involved, and, despite the provisions of Article 3, without discharging secondary parties. The application of this provision is limited to a specific instance in which a collecting bank in good faith believes a particular item will be paid if an additional day is granted. The Section also authorizes delay in the case of interruption of communications, as by blizzard, flood, hurricane or other disaster or "Act of God," suspension of payments by another bank, war, emergency conditions or other circumstances beyond the control of the bank. Delay for such causes will be excused only if the bank exercises such diligence as the circumstances require. All provisions of Article 4 relating to the time in which an act must be performed must be regarded as modified by this Section.

A collecting bank acts seasonably in any event if it takes proper action, such as forwarding or presenting an item before its midnight deadline following receipt of the item, notice or payment, as the case may be. Section 4–202(2). If the bank adheres to this standard, the timeliness of its action cannot be challenged. If Article 4 fails to specify a time within which a particular action must be taken, and the action is delayed beyond the midnight deadline, the bank has the burden of establishing that it acted within a reasonable time in view of all the facts and circumstances. For example, in the case of a time draft, action after the midnight deadline, but sufficiently in advance of maturity for proper presentation is within such a reasonably longer time as to be regarded as seasonable.

(d) *Indorsements.* When an item is restrictively indorsed with words such as "pay any bank," it is locked into the bank collection system and only a bank may acquire the rights of a holder until the item has been either (a) returned to the customer initiating the collection, whereupon, under Section 3–208, he may cancel all indorsements subsequent to his own, or (b) specially indorsed by a bank to a person who is not a bank. Section 4–201(2). Consequently, such an indorsement by a customer initiating collection protects his ownership rights in the item by making it impossible for anyone outside the banking system to acquire legitimate rights to the item. If a bank specially indorses the item to a person not a bank, the indorsing bank would be liable for any loss resulting therefrom if the transfer was in bad faith or with lack of ordinary care.

When a bank forwards an item for collection, it normally indorses it "pay any bank," irrespective of the type of indorsement, if any, which the item carried at the time of receipt. This serves to protect the collecting bank by making it impossible for the item to stray from regular collection channels.

If the item had no indorsement when received by the depositary bank, it may supply any indorsement of its customer which is necessary to title unless the item contains the words "payee's indorsement required" or the like, as is the case with certain government, pension and insurance checks. Section 4–205(1). This rule speeds up the collection process by eliminating the necessity of returning checks for indorsement where the depositary bank knows they came from their customers. The usual form of such an indorsement reads "Deposited to the account of the within named payee." This will be followed by the bank's own "pay any bank" indorsement. Each intermediary bank will in turn place a similar restrictive indorsement on the item, since no bank in the collection chain other than a depositary bank is given notice or otherwise affected by the restrictive indorsement of any person except its immediate transferor. Sections 4–205 (2) and 3–206. This rule is necessary to keep the collection process moving smoothly and rapidly. The depositary bank has the responsibility of examining the item for prior restrictive indorsements. Subsequent transferors need check only one indorsement, and are authorized in relying on the fact that the depositary bank performed its required function. It would be unnecessarily time consuming to require each bank to examine all the indorsements on each item.

Section 4–206 permits collecting banks to dispense with the more formal requirements of Section 3–202 in transferring items to another bank. It provides that any agreed method which identifies the transferor is sufficient. Since the responsibilities of banks are fixed by Articles 3 and 4, it is not necessary to incorporate them in a long, detailed indorsement. For example, Section 4–207, on warranties, gives every indorsement of a customer or collecting bank the same effect as an indorsement specifically stating "All prior indorsements guaranteed." Thus, such language is no longer required, and Section 4–206 would appear to authorize agreement on the effectiveness of a simple indorsement "Pay any bank" followed by identification of the indorsing bank, even by transit number only.

(e) *Warranties.* Section 4–207 provides that customers and collecting banks give substantially the same warranties as those given by parties under Article 3, Sections 3–417 and 3–414, upon presentment and transfer. Consequently, a detailed discussion of those warranties at this point would be unduly repetitive.

A claim for breach of any of the warranties under Section 4–207 must be made within a reasonable time after the person claiming becomes aware of the breach, or the person liable will be discharged to the extent of any loss caused by the delay in making claim. For example, if upon prompt notice of breach of warranty the person liable could have recovered from a prior party who subsequently became insolvent, such person would be discharged to the extent of the amount not recoverable because of the insolvency. If, on the other hand, the insolvency occurred before the breach of warranty became known to the person claiming, there would be no discharge resulting from the delay.

(f) *Settlements.* As has been indicated previously, as an item passes through the bank collection system, the normal procedure is for a transferee, whether it be the payor bank, an intermediary bank or a non-bank payor, to give a settlement to its transferor bank. Section 4–211(1) specifies certain types of settlements which a collecting bank may accept without liability in the event of ultimate nonpayment of an item.

The first type of settlement authorized is a check on some bank other than the bank making the settlement (the remitting bank). The check may be drawn by the remitting bank or by another. The reason it must be on a bank other than the remitting bank is that the latter already owes the money and its liability would in no sense be altered by a check issued on itself. This rule is modified where both the remitting and collecting banks are either members of, or clear through a member of, the same clearing house. In that special situation, a cashier's check or similar primary obligation of the remitting bank is approved. The check may then be collected through the clearing house in the normal course of events.

If the item is drawn on or payable by a person other than a bank, Section 4–211 approves the established custom of acceptance of a cashier's check, certified check or other check or obligation on any bank.

Another frequently used approved method of settlement is an authorization given to the collecting bank to charge the amount of the remittance against an account which either the remitting bank or another bank carries on the books of the collecting bank.

The foregoing situations involve a remittance—the sending of something back to the collecting bank. In no sense does this imply disapproval of other methods of settlement, such as through a clearing house or merely by debits and credits in accounts between correspondent banks. In fact, the latter two methods are those used in the settlement of the large majority of items moving through the bank collection system.

The type of handling which a collecting bank must accord remittance instruments and authorizations to charge is as provided in subsections (2) and (3) of Section 4–211. The provisions of those subsections may be summarized as follows:

(i) When a collecting bank receives a remittance check or authorization to charge on itself, which can properly be dishonored, it must take such action prior to its midnight deadline.

(ii) When the remittance instrument is one of or on another bank, and is of a kind approved by subsection (1) of Section 4–211, the collecting bank is not liable to prior parties in the event the instrument is dishonored if it presents the instrument or forwards it for collection before its midnight deadline. Not until the instrument is finally paid by such other bank does the remittance become a final settlement.

(iii) When the remittance instrument is of a type which is not approved by subsection (1), and the collecting bank has not authorized the use of such a remittance medium, such bank has two courses of action open to it. It may either refuse the instru-

ment and return it to the remitting bank, or present or forward it for collection before the collecting bank's midnight deadline. In neither case does the collecting bank incur any liability to prior parties. Usually it will be to the interest of all concerned for the collecting bank to present or forward the item rather than return it, since in most instances it will be paid. The collecting bank will not be deemed to have received a final settlement until the item has in fact been paid.

(iv) If a collecting bank receives a remittance of the type discussed in paragraphs (i), (ii) and (iii) above, but fails to take appropriate action prior to its midnight deadline, it is deemed to have received a final settlement as of such time, and to have become fully liable to its transferor and other prior parties for the amount involved: any provisional settlement it has given its transferor becomes final. Unless the bank is then able to collect on the instrument or from its transferee, it must stand the loss.

(v) In the event the collecting bank has authorized a type of remittance not approved by subsection (1), the collecting bank is deemed to have received a final settlement and to have become fully liable to prior parties upon receipt of such unapproved remittance instrument, whether or not it ultimately collects on the instrument or from the remitting bank.

When a collecting bank which has given a provisional settlement to its customer receives a final settlement for an item, the transaction is completed, the provisional settlement becomes final and the credit becomes withdrawable as of right as soon as the bank has had a reasonable time to learn that the settlement has become final. Sections 4–213(3) and (4) (a).

On the other hand, if the collecting bank has given a provisional settlement to its customer, and itself fails by reason of dishonor, suspension of payments by a bank or otherwise, to receive a final settlement for an item, it may revoke the provisional settlement given to its customer. Section 4–212(1). If the customer's account has sufficient funds, the amount of the item may be charged back to the account. Otherwise the collecting bank will be required to seek reimbursement by other means. It is for this reason that banks normally do not permit withdrawals of "uncollected funds."

(g) *Final Payment.* The provisional settlements made in the collection chain are all pointed toward final payment of the item by the payor bank. This is one terminus of the collection process—the turn-around point from which the proceeds of the item begin the return flow, and the initiation of the process of firming provisional settlements into final ones. For example, a customer of the California Country State Bank may deposit a check on the State of Maine Country National Bank. The check may then take a course such as follows: to a correspondent bank in San Francisco, to the Federal Reserve Bank of San Francisco, to the Federal Reserve Bank of Boston, to the payor bank. At each step, provisional settlements were made. When the payor bank finally paid the item, the proceeds technically began a return flow over the same course. In fact, however, the provisional settlements became final, one after another by mere passage of time, and no further action was required by any party.

The critical question is the point in time when the item has been finally paid by the payor bank, since this not only commences the payment process but also has a major bearing on questions of priority between the item on the one hand and things such as the filing of a stop order against the item or some notice with respect to the item or legal process or setoff affecting the amount available in the drawer's account. It is clear that final payment occurs at some moment during the processing of the item by the payor bank. This moment is difficult to ascertain.

An item may be received by a bank in many ways: over the counter, through the mail from a customer, in a collection letter from another bank or through a clearing house. Under some of these circumstances a receipt may be given or an entry made in a passbook. The item then normally moves through the sorting and proving departments. Still later it goes to the bookkeeping department, where it is examined for form and signature. It is then matched against the ledger for the customer's account to see if funds are sufficient or whether there is a stop order or some other reason why the item should not be paid from the account. If everything is in good order, the item will be posted to the drawer's account either then or later. The item will be stamped or punched "Paid" and filed with the other items paid from the customer's account. When did final payment occur?

Section 4–213 establishes rules for determining when that point in time has been reached.

Traditionally, when a bank pays an item in cash, it is deemed to have made a final payment. This rule is reaffirmed in subsection (1) (a) of Section 4–213.

Equivalent to cash payment in making final payment is a final settlement for the item. If the payor bank has not reserved the right to revoke the settlement, or does not have such right through agreement, statute or clearing house rule, final payment has been made. Section 4–213(1) (b).

A provisional settlement also becomes a final payment if the payor bank does not revoke it in the time and manner permitted by statute, clearing house rule or agreement. Section 4–213(1) (d).

More importantly, however, final payment is made when the payor bank has completed the process of posting the item to the account of the drawer or maker. Section 4–213(1) (c). Essentially, this means the point in time when the decision is made to pay the item. The question then arises: when is the process of posting completed?

Not so many years ago, demand deposit accounting was largely a manual operation at most commercial banks. When a check was posted, i. e., charged to the indicated account of the drawer on the books of the bank, the bank had previously conducted its investigation as to the sufficiency of funds, stop payments, and garnishments, and determined to pay the item. The courts, therefore, adopted the act of posting the item to the account of the drawer as an indication of its decision to honor and to cut off the right of the bank thereafter to reverse the entry and return the item. Today, commercial banks make use of high-speed data processing equipment in the handling of their demand deposit accounting. Without these machines it would be virtually impossible to handle the volume of checks involved in the bank collection process. In this system, the account record of a depositor is merely an internal record within the computer. One of the first things that happens when an item is processed by the payor bank is that the appropriate account record is charged with the amount of that item. If there are reasons such as stop payment orders that would dictate that this item should not be paid, the machine which stores this information will prepare a special listing relative to the account involved. If the account supervisor who reviews this listing determines that a paid item should not be paid, a reversing entry is made, i. e., a credit for the amount of the check is made to the account.

To clarify the steps legitimately involved in posting an item, Section 4–109 provides as follows:

> The "process of posting" means the usual procedure followed by a payor bank in determining to pay an item and in recording the payment including one or more of the

following or other steps as determined by the bank:

> (a) verification of any signature;
> (b) ascertaining that sufficient funds are available;
> (c) affixing a "paid" or other stamp;
> (d) entering a charge or entry to a customer's account;
> (e) correcting or reversing an entry or erroneous action with respect to the item.

Normally, all of these steps must be completed before the "process of posting" has been completed, and an item may be regarded as finally paid.

Once final payment has been made in any of the ways specified above, the payor bank becomes accountable for the amount of the item, and, under Section 4–213, various results follow. Provisional settlements for the items, whether through a clearing house or by debits and credits to accounts between banks, become final. The customer of the depositary bank has an absolute right to withdraw the credit as soon as the bank has had time to learn of the settlement. If the depositary bank is also the payor bank, however, unless the item is not finally paid, the depositor has a right to withdraw the amount of the item at the opening of the bank's second banking day following receipt of the item.

It would appear that when a deposit is made in cash, the customer should be entitled to draw against it immediately. Since the bookkeeping process takes time, Section 4–213(5) establishes the rule that although the deposit is final, nevertheless it does not become available for withdrawal as of right until the opening of the bank's next banking day.

(h) *Rights on Insolvency of a Bank.* Much controversy as to the rights of parties in the event a collecting or payor bank suspends payments will be avoided by the application of Section 4–214. When a bank suspends payments, items in its possession are in various stages of processing. Some have not yet been paid. Others have been paid and final settlements have been given. Between these two extremes are items which have been paid but final settlements have not been given. The stage of processing reached is of major importance because it establishes the rights of the owner of the item.

In the event the item has not been paid when payments are suspended, whether by a payor or collecting bank, the item must be returned to the presenting bank or the closed bank's customer, as the case may be. It is as though the item had never been deposited or forwarded for collection, and the owner retains all his rights against the other parties to the instrument.

The problem arises when an item has been finally paid by a bank before it suspends payment. If a final settlement has been given, the funds are out of the hands of the insolvent bank and prior parties are unaffected. Settlement has been made. If, on the other hand, a payor bank has paid the item but has made no settlement which is or becomes final, a debtor creditor relationship arises and the owner of the item has a creditor's claim against the payor bank. Subsection (2) of Section 4–214, however, gives this claim a preferred status, so that the holder will be entitled to payment before general creditors of the bank.

A preferred status is also granted the owner of an item as against a collecting bank if the latter receives a final settlement for such item but suspends payment before making a final settlement with its customer. Again, the debtor creditor relationship arises, but the owner has a preferred claim.

If a payor or collecting bank has given a provisional settlement for an item and then suspends payments, the suspension does not prevent or interfere with the settlement becoming final if such finality occurs auto-matically upon the lapse of time or the happening of certain events. In that case the money is out of the insolvency proceeding and it is as though the final settlement had been made before insolvency.

If finality depends upon some affirmative act such as the dispatch of a remittance, however, the provisional settlement will not become final and the owner of the item will have to take the status of a preferred creditor.

2. *Collection of Items—Payor Banks.* In recent years, with the tremendous increase in volume of bank collections as well as the improved methods of processing items by payor banks, it has become necessary to adopt production line methods for handling checks to assure an even flow of items on a day to day basis. This is necessary if work is to be conducted without abnormal peak loads and overtime. The solution has been the institution of deferred posting procedures whereby items are sorted and proved on the day of receipt, but are not posted to customers' accounts or returned until the next banking day. Part 3 of Article 4 of the U.C. C. not only gives approval to this procedure, but sets up specific standards to govern its application to the actions of payor banks.

When a payor bank which is not a depository bank receives a demand item other than a documentary draft otherwise than for immediate payment over the counter, it must either return the item or give its transferor a provisional settlement before midnight of the banking day on which the item is received. Otherwise it becomes liable to its transferor for the amount of the item unless it has a valid defense. Section 4–302(a).

If it gives the provisional settlement as required, it then has until its midnight deadline to return the item or, if it is held for protest or is otherwise unavailable for return, to send written notice of dishonor or nonpayment. Section 4–301(1). Upon so doing, it is entitled to revoke the settlement and recover any payment made.

A payor bank, which is the depositary bank as well, also has until its midnight deadline to return or send notice of dishonor of such an item and may thereupon revoke any credit given or recover the amount thereof from its customer if the credit has been withdrawn. Section 4–301(2).

If the payor bank, whether or not it is the depositary bank, fails to return the item or send notice before its midnight deadline, it becomes accountable for the amount of the item unless it has a valid defense for its inaction. Section 4–302(a).

There are innumerable reasons why a bank may dishonor an item and return it or send notice where appropriate. Among these are, of course, ones such as that the drawer or maker either has no account or has insufficient funds to cover the item; that the signature on the item is forged; or that payment of the item has been stopped by the drawer or maker.

Certain reasons for dishonor, including some of those just mentioned, are the result of the occurrence of events which affect the payor bank's right or duty to pay items. For example, a bank may receive either actual knowledge or legal notice affecting the item or the bank's right to pay it, such as knowledge or notice that the drawer has filed a petition in bankruptcy. The bank's customer may have filed a stop order directing the bank not to pay the item. The bank may have been served with legal process such as an attachment, garnishment or a tax or other lien against the account from which the item would otherwise be payable. The bank itself may have exercised its right of setoff against the account to cover an unpaid obligation of the customer to the bank.

When such an event occurs at or about the time the bank is obligated to pay or settle for an item or return it unpaid, a question of priority may develop. Which takes precedence against the customer's account: the item or the event affecting the account? Section 4–303 supplies the rules to remove the payor bank from the horns of this dilemma. Such knowledge, notice, stop order or legal process comes too late to affect the bank's right or duty to pay the item if it is received or served and a reasonable time for the bank to act upon it expires (or the right of setoff is exercised) after the bank has accepted or certified the item, made a final payment for it as provided in Section 4–213(1), discussed above, or become accountable for it to its transferor by reason of a failure to return or send notice as provided in Section 4–302.

As to priority between items, however, where the customer's account is not sufficient to pay them all, the bank may charge them against the account in any order it deems convenient. Items against an account may reach the bank in several different ways on the same day. It would be unreasonable to require the bank to determine their order of arrival. Items received at the same time, but passing through different channels may be posted to the customer's account hours apart. Consequently, a person presenting an item to a payor bank may not object that the bank paid other items received the same day and left his unpaid. He is properly relegated to seeking his remedy against the maker, drawer or other secondary parties. The owner of the account from which the item was payable also has no basis for complaint that one item, rather than another, was paid. It is his responsibility to have enough funds on deposit to pay all items chargeable to his account at any time.

3. *Relationship between Payor Bank and Its Customer.* (a) *The Payor Bank's Right or Duty to Pay an Item.* When a payor bank receives an item properly payable from a customer's account but there are insufficient funds in the account to pay it, the bank may dishonor the item and return it as discussed

above. It is under no duty to do so, however. It may instead pay the item and charge its customer's account even though an overdraft is created as a result. Section 4–401(1). The item authorized or directed the bank to make the payment, and hence carries with it an enforceable implied promise to reimburse the bank.

It has been noted that under Section 3–409 the holder of a check or draft has no right to require the bank to pay, whether or not there are sufficient funds in the drawer's account. But if an item is presented to a payor bank and the bank refuses to pay it, it will incur a liability to its customer from whose account the item should have been paid. Section 4–402. If the item is not more than six months old and regular in form, if the customer had adequate funds on deposit and there is no other valid basis for the refusal to pay, the bank is liable to its customer for any reasonably expectable damages which the customer may incur. Such damages may include, for example, damages for arrest or prosecution under a statute which makes the issuance of a check against insufficient funds a deceptive practice punishable by fine or imprisonment.

As indicated above, a payor bank is under no obligation to its customer to pay an uncertified check which is over six months old. Section 4–404. This rule reflects the usual banking practice of consulting a depositor before paying a stale item on his account. The bank is not required to dishonor such an item, however, and if its payment is made in good faith, it may charge the amount of the item to its customer's account.

(b) *Stop Payment Orders.* A check drawn on a bank is an order to pay a sum of money and an authorization to charge the amount to the drawer's account. The drawer may countermand this order, however, by means of a stop payment order. If such order does not come too late under the rule of Section 4–303 discussed above, the bank is bound by

it and must assume the risk of loss. An oral stop order is binding on the bank for only fourteen calendar days. Therefore, the normal practice is for a customer to confirm an oral stop order in writing, and such an order is effective for six months, and may be renewed in writing.

The fact that a drawer has filed a stop payment order does not automatically relieve him of liability. If the bank honors the stop payment order and returns the check, the holder may file suit against the drawer. If the holder qualifies as a holder in due course, personal defenses that the drawer might have to such a suit would be of no avail.

If the holder is not a holder in due course, the drawer would be required to establish a valid defense to avoid payment of the check, and then he would be successful only to the extent his defense would operate.

If the bank inadvertently pays a check over a valid stop order, it is prima facie liable to the customer, but only to the extent of the customer's loss resulting from the payment. Further, the burden of establishing the fact and amount of loss is on the customer. Otherwise unjust enrichment of the customer would result: Suppose he had purchased some goods and given a check for them. He later decided he did not like the goods, so he stopped payment on the check. If the bank pays the check in error, the seller has been paid and the customer has the goods and has paid nothing for them. He would thus be unjustly enriched at the expense of the bank. Section 4–407 spells out in some detail other rules to prevent unjust enrichment in the case of payment of an item over a stop payment order. The payor bank may, by subrogation, obtain the following rights:

1. The rights of any holder in due course of the item against the drawer or maker. If the holder qualified as a holder in due course, this would mean that the payor bank would be

able to enforce payment of the item against its customer in most circumstances; and

2. The bank may elect to succeed to the rights of the payee or of any other holder of the item against the drawee or maker, either on the item or on the underlying transaction. For example, the bank may be entitled to collect the fair market value of whatever goods or services were furnished to the drawer; and

3. The bank may elect to take the rights of its customer against the payee or any other holder of the item in respect to the underlying transaction. For example, the bank could sue the vendor of the goods for breach of contract and recover damages to the same extent as if it had been the contracting purchaser.

(c) *Effect of Death or Incompetence of a Customer.* The general rule is that death or incompetence revokes all agency agreements. Furthermore, adjudication of incompetency by a court is regarded as notice to the world of that fact. Actual notice is not required. Section 4–405 modifies these stringent rules with respect to bank deposits and collections in several ways.

First, a payor bank's authority to accept, pay or collect an item or to account for proceeds of its collection is not rendered ineffective by the incompetence of a customer of either bank at the time the item is issued or its collection undertaken if the bank does not in fact know of the adjudication of incompetence. The item may be paid without the bank incurring any liability.

Second, neither death nor adjudication of incompetence of a customer revokes such authority until the bank knows of it and has a reasonable opportunity to act on such knowledge. In view of the tremendous volume of bank collections and the general duty to pay

imposed by Section 4–402, no other rule would be equitable.

Finally, even though a bank knows of the death of its customer, it may for ten days after the date of his death pay or certify checks drawn by the customer unless a person claiming an interest in the account, such as an heir, legatee or executor or administrator of his estate, orders the bank to stop making such payments. This rule facilitates matters for all concerned. There is almost never any reason why such checks should not be paid and if there is, the personal representative of the deceased customer would have a claim against the person receiving payment. If the check is not paid, the holder will be required to file a claim in the probate proceeding and the personal representative will have the duty of processing it for payment.

(d) *Customer's Duty to Discover and Report Unauthorized Signature or Alteration.* In order to terminate a bank's open liability for paying an item with a forged signature or indorsement or an item which has been altered, Section 4–406 imposes certain affirmative duties on bank customers and fixes time limits within which they must assert their rights. The duties arise and the time starts to run from the time the bank either sends or makes available to its customer a statement of account accompanied by the items paid against the account. The customer is required to exercise reasonable care and promptness to examine the statement and items to discover his unauthorized signature or any alteration on an item. Since he is not presumed to know the signatures of payees or indorsers, this duty of prompt and careful examination applies only to the customer's own signature and alterations, both of which he should be able to detect immediately. If he discovers an unauthorized signature or an alteration, he must notify the bank promptly.

If the customer fails to discharge those duties of prompt examination and notice, Section 4–406(2) precludes him from asserting against the bank his unauthorized signature and alteration if the bank establishes that it suffered a loss by reason of such failure.

Furthermore, he will lose his rights in a potentially more important situation. Occasionally a forger will embark upon a series of transactions involving the account of the same individual. Perhaps he is an employee who has access to his employer's check book. He may forge one or more checks each month until he is finally detected. The bank, on the other hand, having paid one or more such signatures without objection, may be lulled into a false sense of security. Suddenly the forgery is detected by the customer after many months or even years. Is the bank to be held liable for all such items? Section 4–406(2) answers this in the negative. The bank is liable on all items with unauthorized signatures or alterations by the same wrongdoer which accompany the statement with which the first such item is returned. The customer had no way of knowing such items were being cashed. But once the statement and items become available to him, he must examine them within a reasonable period, which in no event may exceed fourteen calendar days, but may, under the circumstances, be less, and notify the bank. Any alterations or unauthorized signatures on instruments by the same wrongdoer paid by the bank during that period will still be the responsibility of the bank, but any paid thereafter but before the customer notifies the bank may not be asserted against it. This rule is based on the proposition that the loss involved is directly traceable to the customer's negligence and, as a result, he should stand the loss.

The two rules under Section 4–406(2) depend on the bank exercising ordinary care in paying the items involved. If it does not, it properly loses its right to require prompt action on the part of its customer. But whether the bank exercised due care or not, the customer must in all events report an alteration or his own unauthorized signature within one year from the time the statement and items were made available to him or lose his right to do so. Section 4–406(4). Any unauthorized indorsement must be asserted within three years from such time.

CASES

CITIZENS NAT. BANK OF ENGLE-WOOD v. FORT LEE S. & L. ASS'N

(1965) 89 N.J.Super. 43, 213 A.2d 315.

BOTTER, J. S. C. Citizens National Bank of Englewood has moved for summary judgment to recover monies advanced against a check which was deposited with the bank for collection but was later dishonored. The issue is whether the bank should be protected for advances made to its depositor before the check cleared. The summary judgment is sought against the drawer and payee-indorser who stopped payment on the check.

On August 27, 1963, George P. Winter agreed to sell a house in Fort Lee, New Jersey to defendant Jean Amoroso and her husband. On the same day Amoroso requested her bank, Fort Lee Savings and Loan Association (Fort Lee Savings), to issue the bank's check to her order for $3,100 to be used as a deposit on the contract for sale. Fort Lee Savings complied by drawing the check against its account with the Fort Lee Trust Company. Later that day Amoroso indorsed and delivered the check to Winter, and he deposited the check in his account at the plaintiff bank. At that time he had a balance of $225.33. After the $3,100 check was deposited the bank cashed a $1,000 check for him against his account. In addition, on August 27 or August 28, the bank cleared and charged Winter's account with four other checks totaling $291.76.

The next day Amoroso discovered that Winter had previously sold the property to a third party by agreement which had been recorded in the Bergen County Clerk's Office. Amoroso immediately asked Winter to return her money. She claims that he admitted the fraud and agreed to return the deposit. But when Mrs. Amoroso and her husband reached Winter's office they learned that he had attempted suicide. He died shortly thereafter.

Upon making this discovery, in the afternoon of August 28, the Amorosos went to Fort Lee Savings to advise it of the fraud and request it to stop payment on the check. The bank issued a written stop payment order which was received by the Fort Lee Trust Company, the drawee, on the following day, August 29. In the meantime the $3,100 check was sent by plaintiff through the Bergen County Clearing House to the Fort Lee Trust Company. By then the stop payment order had been received. Notice of nonpayment was thereafter transmitted to plaintiff.

Plaintiff contends that, under the Uniform Commercial Code, N.J.S. 12A:1–101 et seq., N.J.S.A., it is a holder in due course to the extent of the advances made on Winter's account and is entitled to recover these moneys from the drawer and payee-indorser of the check. Plaintiff's claim against the drawee, Fort Lee Trust Company, was voluntarily dismissed by plaintiff at the pretrial conference.

The central issue is whether plaintiff bank is a holder in due course, since a holder in due course will prevail against those liable on the instrument in the absence of a real defense. Of course, it must first be determined that plaintiff is a "holder" if plaintiff is to

be declared a holder in due course. Amoroso contends that plaintiff bank does not own the check because it is only an agent of its depositor Winter for collection purposes and, consequently, plaintiff is not a "holder." It is true that a collecting bank is presumed to be an agent of the owner of the item unless a contrary intention appears, or until final settlement. N.J.S. 12A:4–201(1), N.J.S.A. Assuming that the bank was at all times an agent in this case, it does not follow that the bank cannot also be a holder. On the contrary, a collecting bank may be a holder whether or not it owns the item. [Citations.] The definition of "holder" includes a person who is in possession of an instrument indorsed to his order or in blank. N.J. S. 12A:1–201(20), N.J.S.A. It is clear that the bank is a holder of the check notwithstanding that it may have taken the check solely for collection and with the right to charge back against the depositor's account in the event the check is later dishonored. [Citations.]

To be a holder in due course one must take a negotiable instrument for value, in good faith and without notice of any defect or defense. N.J.S. 12A:3–302(1), N.J.S.A. Amoroso contends that plaintiff did not act in good faith or is chargeable with notice because it allowed Winter to draw against uncollected funds at a time when his account was either very low or overdrawn. Winter's account was low in funds. However, this fact, or the fact that Winter's account was overdrawn, currently or in the past, if true, would not constitute notice to the collecting bank of an infirmity in the underlying transaction or instrument and is not evidence of bad faith chargeable to the bank at the time it allowed withdrawal against the deposited check. N.J. S. 12A:1–201(19) and (25); N.J.S. 12A:3–304, N.J.S.A. See United States Cold Storage Corp. v. First Nat'l Bank of Fort Worth, 350 S.W.2d 856 (Tex.Civ.App.1961), declaring the bank a holder in due course where it applied a deposited check against a large overdraft of its depositor, the court specifically holding that lack of good faith was not shown merely by the fact that the bank knew the depositor was considerably overdrawn in his account. As stated in First Nat'l Bank of Springfield v. DiTaranto, 9 N.J.Super. 246, 253, 75 A.2d 907, 911 (App.Div.1950):

"Evidence of fraud, not merely suspicious circumstances, must have been brought home to the Bank as a holder for value whose rights had accrued before maturity, in order to defeat its recovery upon the ground of fraud in the inception of the negotiable note or between the parties to it. Hudson County Nat. Bank v. Alexander Furs, Inc., supra [133 N.J.L. 256, 44 A.2d 73]. To constitute notice to the Bank of the alleged infirmity in the note or defect in the title of Tidey who negotiated it, the Bank must have had actual knowledge of the infirmity or defect or knowledge of such facts that the action amounted to bad faith."

Moreover, a depositary bank may properly charge an account by honoring a check drawn by a depositor even though it creates an overdraft. N.J.S. 12A:4–401(1), N.J.S.A. It would be anomalous for a bank to lose its status as a holder in due course merely because it has notice that the account of its depositor is overdrawn.

Lacking bad faith or notice of a defect or defense, plaintiff will be deemed a holder in due course if one additional element is satisfied, namely, the giving of value for the instrument. Prior to the adoption of the Uniform Commercial Code the general rule was that a bank does give value and is a holder in due course to the extent that it allows a depositor to draw against a check given for collection notwithstanding that the check is later dishonored. * * * The cases clearly hold that this rule applies even though the item is received for collection only under an agreement with the bank that gives the bank the right to charge back

against the depositor's account the amount of any item which is not collected. It is sometimes said that the contract of conditional credit is changed when the bank honors the deposit by allowing a withdrawal, and the bank then becomes the owner of or holder of a lien on the item to the extent of value given. [Citations.] See Bath Nat'l Bank v. Ely N. Sonnenstrahl, supra, 249 N.Y. at p. 394, 164 N.E. at p. 328, where the New York Court of Appeals said that the bank becomes a holder in due course in these circumstances and, "At least it may then hold the instrument as collateral security."

This result is continued by provisions of the Uniform Commercial Code which give plaintiff a security interest in the check and the monies represented by the check to the extent that credit given for the check has been withdrawn or applied. N.J.S. 12A:4–208 and 209, N.J.S.A. See also N.J.S. 12A:4–201, N.J.S.A. and U.C.C. Comment 5 thereunder.

N.J.S. 12A:4–208, N.J.S.A., provides in part as follows:

"(1) A bank has a security interest in an item and any accompanying documents or the proceeds of either

(a) in case of an item deposited in an account to the extent to which credit given for the item has been withdrawn or applied;

(b) in case of an item for which it has given credit available for withdrawal as of right, to the extent of the credit given whether or not the credit is drawn upon and whether or not there is a right of charge-back; or

(c) if it makes an advance on or against the item."

N.J.S. 12A:4–209, N.J.S.A., is as follows:

"For purposes of determining its status as a holder in due course, the bank has given value to the extent that it has a security interest in an item provided that the bank otherwise complies with the requirements of 12A:3–302 on what constitutes a holder in due course."

The New Jersey Study Comment under N.J.S. 12A:4–209, N.J.S.A., includes the following:

"Because the bank is a holder of the item in most cases, it is possible for it to be a holder in due course if it otherwise qualifies by its good faith taking, prior to maturity, for value. See, U.C.C. sec. 3–302; N.I.L. sec. 52 (N.J.S.A. 7:2–52). It is important for a bank to be a holder in due course when the depositor fails, for this status enables it to prevail over the obligor (drawer or maker) of the instrument even though the obligor has some personal defense against the payee (depositor)."

It would hinder commercial transactions if depositary banks refused to permit withdrawal prior to clearance of checks. Apparently banking practice is to the contrary. It is clear that the Uniform Commercial Code was intended to permit the continuation of this practice and to protect banks who have given credit on deposited items prior to notice of a stop payment order or other notice of dishonor. N.J.S. 12A:4–208 and 209, N.J.S.A., supra [citations].

It is also contended that liability on the check is excused because N.J.S. 12A:4–403, N.J.S.A. gives Fort Lee Savings the right to order Fort Lee Trust Company to stop payment on the check. However, U.C.C. comment 8 under this section makes it clear that the stop payment order cannot avoid liability to a holder in due course. "The payment can be stopped but the drawer remains liable on the instrument to the holder in due course * * *." [Citation.]

Finally, Amoroso attempts to raise the fraud perpetrated by Winter against Amoroso as a defense to plaintiff's claim. Plaintiff's status as a holder in due course insulates it from all personal defenses of any party to the instrument with whom it has not dealt, although real defenses may still be asserted. N.J.S. 12A:3–305, N.J.S.A. The defense raised here is fraud in inducing Amoroso to enter into the contract. There is no suggestion that either defendant signed the check without knowledge of "its character or its essential terms." N.J.S. 12A:3–305(2) (c), N.J.S.A. Therefore the fraud is a personal defense available only against Winter and cannot be asserted against plaintiff. [Citations.]

Accordingly both Fort Lee Savings as drawer and Amoroso as indorser of the check are liable to plaintiff. N.J.S. 12A:3–413(2) and 12A:3–414(1), N.J.S.A., defining the liability of a drawer and indorser of a negotiable instrument to a holder in due course.

The motion for summary judgment will be granted in the sum of $1,066.43, plus interest. The amount of the judgment represents advances made on Winter's account before notice of dishonor, $1,291.76, less the existing balance of $225.33 in Winter's account. This opinion will not deal with the disposition of claims between Amoroso and Fort Lee Savings. By reason of the stop payment order Fort Lee Savings has on hand sufficient funds which were charged against Amoroso's account to meet plaintiff's judgment, and part of these funds, representing the difference between the potential judgment and the $3,100 retained, has been refunded to Amoroso pursuant to the pretrial order.

UNIVERSAL C. I. T. CREDIT CORPORATION v. GUARANTY BANK AND TRUST COMPANY

(1958 D.C.D.Mass.) 161 F.Supp. 790.

WYZANSKI, DISTRICT JUDGE. This case, falling within this Court's diversity jurisdiction, arises under that version of the Negotiable Instruments Law now embodied in Mass. G.L.(Ter.Ed.), c. 107. The only problem of any difficulty is whether under Massachusetts law as it now stands, that is, before the effective date of what is commonly called the Commercial Code, adopted by c. 765 of the Massachusetts Acts of 1957 effective October 1, 1958, when a bank receives from its depositor a check endorsed without restriction but deposited pursuant to the usual deposit slip wherein the bank agrees merely to act as a collection agent, but nonetheless, the bank, before collecting the check allows the depositor to draw from the bank an amount equivalent to both his entire balance and the amount of that uncollected check, the bank is a holder for value of that uncollected check.

An abbreviated statement of the facts will suffice in view of what this Court concludes are the governing principles of law.

C. I. T. (more fully described as Universal C. I. T. Credit Corporation, a New York corporation, plaintiff herein) had an account with Guaranty (more fully described as Guaranty Bank and Trust Company, a Massachusetts corporation, defendant and third-party plaintiff herein). McCarthy (more fully described as McCarthy Motor Sales, Inc., a Massachusetts corporation, not a party to this case) had an account with Worcester (more fully described as Worcester County Trust Company, a Massachusetts corporation, third-party defendant.)

On October 1, 1955 C. I. T. drew on Guaranty payable to the order of McCarthy two checks (hereinafter called A and B) in the amounts respectively of $10,886 and $880 (or a total of $11,766). The same day McCarthy deposited in Worcester these checks endorsed without restriction but accompanied by and in accordance with the usual bank deposit slip reciting that the item was received by the bank for collection only. At 9:10 a. m. October 2, 1956 C. I. T.'s representative presented to Guaranty a written stop-payment order covering checks A and B. Nonetheless, at the clearing later that same day when Worcester presented to Guaranty checks A and

B for payment, Guaranty gave Worcester a final credit for the $11,766 stated therein. Later Guaranty asked Worcester to take back checks A and B, but Worcester refused. Guaranty debited C. I. T.'s account for $11,766. C. I. T. claims that this was an unauthorized debit.

On October 1, 1956 McCarthy's balance at Worcester was $18.22. After McCarthy on October 1, 1956 had deposited checks A and B, before Guaranty sought to return to Worcester checks A and B, and before Worcester had any reason to know that checks A and B would be subject to any difficulties, Worcester during business hours on October 2, 1956 paid or settled at the clearing a check drawn on September 24, 1956 by McCarthy on Worcester payable to C. I. T. in the amount of $11,297.04 (hereinafter called check X) together with other checks which in combination exhausted both McCarthy's October 1 cash balance of $18.22 and the provisional credit of $11,766, attributable to checks A and B.

Upon the foregoing facts, the initial question relates to the effect of C. I. T.'s order to Guaranty to stop payment upon checks A and B. C. I. T., as the drawer of the checks, had an absolute right to order payment stopped; Guaranty, the drawee bank making payment thereon, acted at its peril. Since a check is merely an order to a bank to make payment in the manner set forth, the customer has the right to revoke such order before it is carried out. That was the rule of the common law. [Citations.] It is the present rule under the Massachusetts version of the N. I. L. [Citations.] It will be the law when the Commercial Code becomes effective in Massachusetts. Mass.G.L.(Ter.Ed.) c. 106, § 4–403. [Citation.] And reference to this code is appropriate because the Massachusetts court regards it less as a novel enactment than as largely a restatement and clarification of existing law which has the approval of American scholars. [Citation.]

But although under the principles just stated C. I. T. has established against Guaranty a claim arising out of the unauthorized debiting by Guaranty of C. I. T.'s account in the amount of $11,766, the next issues are whether Worcester was a holder in due course of checks A and B amounting to $11,766, and whether, to avoid circuity of action, Guaranty is subrogated to Worcester's claim against C. I. T.

Unquestionably under presently effective Massachusetts law, Worcester did not become a holder for value of checks A and B merely by taking those checks for collection only, even if simultaneously Worcester gave McCarthy a provisional credit based thereon. [Citations.]

But Worcester went further than to enter a provisional credit. Worcester, though it was not required so to do, allowed McCarthy to draw to the full amount of the credit before it had been collected. As is noted in 20 Columbia Law Review 351, there are at least three possible constructions of this action. "In the absence of any express intention between the parties, some courts view such a transaction as a loan on the personal credit [of the depositor] and allowed as a convenience * * *. Other cases maintain that an advance by the bank against an uncollected deposited check terminates the principal-agent relationship and becomes an act of purchase of the check * * * And still others while not giving the bank title indicate that a lien is created in its favor for any debt due it from the depositor by virtue of such advances."

That Massachusetts would follow the third of these choices is indicated by a case that preceded the adoption of the N. I. L. Shawmut National Bank v. Manson, 168 Mass. 425, 47 N.E. 196. The N. I. L. was not designed to alter that rule. For, as stated in Mass.G. L.(Ter.Ed.) c. 107, § 50, it provides that "where the holder has a lien on the instru-

ment, arising either from contract or by operation of law, he is deemed a holder for value to the extent of his lien." Cf. Mass.G.L.(Ter. Ed.) c. 107, § 18 definition of "value" and § 82.

Indeed, the majority of courts have ruled, pursuant either to the N. I. L. or to the common law, that a bank in Worcester's position is a holder in due course to the extent of its advances. [Citations.] The commentators have approved these rulings. [Citations.] So have the draftsmen of the (as yet inoperable in Massachusetts) provisions of the Commercial Code. § 4–208(a) thereof will provide:

"§ 4–208. Security Interest of Collecting Bank in Items, Accompanying Documents and Proceeds.

"(1) A bank has a security interest in an item and any accompanying documents or the proceeds of either

"(a) in case of an item deposited in an account to the extent to which credit given for the item has been withdrawn or applied;"

The comment on that subsection states:

"1. Subsection (1) states a rational rule for the interest of a bank in an item. The customer of the depositary bank is normally the owner of the item and the several collecting banks are his agents (Section 4–201). A collecting agent may properly make advances on the security of paper held by him for collection, and when he does acquires at common law a possessory lien, for his advances. Subsection (1) applies an analogous principle to a bank in the collection chain which extends credit on items in the course of collection. The bank has a security interest to the extent stated in this section. To the extent of its security interest it is a holder for value (Sections 3–303, 4–209) and a holder in due course if it satisfies the other requirements for that status. (Section 3–302.) Subsection (1) does not derogate from the banker's general common-law lien or right of set-off against indebtedness owing in deposit accounts. See Section 1–103. Rather subsection (1) specifically implements and extends the principle as a part of the bank collection process."

And § 4–209 will provide:

"§ 4–209. When Bank gives Value for Purposes of Holder in Due Course.

"For purposes of determining its status as a holder in due course, the bank has given value to the extent that it has a security interest in an item provided that the bank otherwise complies with the requirements of section 3–302 on what constitutes a holder in due course. (1957, 765, § 1; effective Oct. 1, 1958.)"

Authority apart, there is fairness in this majority rule to the effect that there is a presumption that where a bank advances credit to a customer on his drawings after that customer has deposited with the bank for collection a check endorsed unrestrictively both parties intend that the bank may look to the collection item for security up to the amount of the bank's advances. In this country it is unusual for a bank to allow a customer to draw except against funds theretofore deposited or upon a formally established credit. Where the bank allows a customer to draw against an uncollected item, particularly in the face of a contract recognizing that the depositor has no right to demand such a privilege, both parties would ordinarily view this allowance not as an unsecured loan upon the customer's general credit but as a bank loan buttressed by the security of the uncollected item. This view is strengthened when, as in the case at bar, the bank's allowance to the customer is within the financial limits of the face amount of the uncollected item. In short, barring some clear agreement by both parties that the bank will not claim any such security rights, when the bank gives the customer the exceptional privilege of of drawing against an uncollected item, a privilege to which under his contract the depositor has no right, the bank, while not purchasing the item is entitled to security to the extent of its advances, and is to that extent a holder in due course —that is, a person who has given value.

The only obstacles to a conclusion that Worcester was a holder in due course to the amount of its advances (which in the case at bar precisely equalled the total of checks A and B) are the relatively recent decision in Agricultural Insurance Co. v. Andrade, D.C.Mass., 146 F.Supp. 893, and the decisions in Boston Continental National Bank v. Hub Fruit Co., 285 Mass. 187, 189 N.E. 89; Grower's Marketing Service v. Webster & Atlas Nat. Bk., 318 Mass. 496, 62 N.E. 2d 225, and Kirstein Leather Co. v. Dietrick, 1 Cir., 86 F.2d 793 on which it purports to be bottomed.

There is no difficulty in distinguishing the last two of these cited cases. In each of them, as in American Barrel Co. v. Commissioner of Banks, 290 Mass. 174, 179, lines 14–15, 195 N.E. 335, the depositor had not drawn against the uncollected funds and so the original depositary bank had not given value and so was not a holder in due course on account of funds advanced.

However, in the Boston Continental National Bank the depositor had drawn against an uncollected item. But as a fact in that particular case the trial judge had found that the depositary bank had nonetheless not given value for that item. The trial judge regarded as significant the fact that the depositor had endorsed the check "for deposit only to the credit of" the depositor and the further fact that the deposit slip stated in the usual form that the bank took the item for collection only and for provisional credit. He evidently regarded those facts as constituting a contract between the depositor and the bank to the effect that the bank neither bought the item nor took it as security for future advances. The Supreme Judicial Court merely held that such a finding was permissible (285 Mass. at pages 189–191, 189 N.E. 89).

Perhaps Justice Donahue's opinion is explicable on the narrow ground that the depositor had endorsed the item "for collection only", and that a trial judge could find that in taking such an item the bank agreed not to become a holder in due course. If that be the ground, it does not apply to this case or to the Agricultural Insurance Co., case. And, in any event, that ground was doubtful under the existing Massachusetts law. It certainly does not state what will be the law in Massachusetts when the Commercial Code becomes effective. See § 4–201(1). The second sentence of that subdivision recognizes that "any rights of the [depositor as] owner to proceeds of the item are subject to rights of the collecting bank such as those resulting from outstanding advances on the item." See also § 4–208(1) (a) and § 4–209, quoted earlier in this opinion.

In Agricultural Insurance Co. v. Andrade Judge Aldrich found as a fact in that particular case that the depositary bank had allowed the depositor to draw on an uncollected item on the basis that he was "a well known resident * * * customer". But, from the learned judge's own statement it appears that the depositary bank also relied on the item it took as an agent for collection. Thus it would appear that the court should have held that the bank gave value for the item, was a holder in due course, and held a valid interest to the extent of the advances or drawings allowed. Insofar as that Court reached a different result this Court declines to follow the ruling in the Agricultural Insurance Co. case. [146 F.Supp. 895.]

This Court having concluded that under Massachusetts law, as indeed under the law in most other states, under the N. I. L., and under the Commercial Code, Worcester was a holder in due course for the amount of its advances, which were in fact the same as the amount of checks A and B, it follows that Guaranty, (in responding to C. I. T.'s claim that Guaranty could not properly have debit-

ed C. I. T.'s account for checks A and B which were covered by C. I. T.'s timely order to stop payment,) is subrogated to Worcester's rights against C. I. T. on checks A and B. [Citations.] It is usually said that to avoid circuity of action, C. I. T. is not allowed to recover from Guaranty. But perhaps, (see comment to Commercial Code § 4–407,) a sounder way of stating the matter is that C. I. T. is not allowed to recover because it has not borne its burden of showing that it suffered loss from Guaranty's disregard of the stop payment order; C. I. T. suffered no loss because it would have been liable to Worcester as a holder in due course in any event. Whichever form of statement is used, judgment must enter for defendant Guaranty in the action brought against it by C. I. T. Guaranty having prevailed against C. I. T., Guaranty's third-party action against Worcester is without foundation, and in that third-party action judgment must enter for Worcester.

CLARKE v. CAMDEN TRUST CO.

(1964) 84 N.J.Super. 304, 201 A.2d 762.

PASCOE, J. C. C. (temporarily assigned). Plaintiff, a member of the New Jersey Bar, maintained two demand checking accounts in defendant bank. One account was an attorney's account (general account) and the other was a trust account (for clients). Defendant Isabelle Denning, plaintiff's secretary, forged his signature to checks drawn on defendant bank during the period August 1957 through August 1961. Plaintiff notified the bank of the forgeries on November 3, 1961 following the mysterious disappearance of Miss Denning.

The present suit is to recover $12,403.07 for some 41 checks bearing plaintiff's forged signature. At the pretrial conference it was agreed that the two-year limitation provided in N.J.S.A. 17:9A–226 was applicable to 33 of the 41 checks, and the pretrial order provided for an amendment of the demand which reduced the claim to $4,525. A default judgment was entered against defendant Isabelle Denning, so that the remaining question for this court to determine is the liability of the bank.

The facts are that although plaintiff received monthly statements charging his accounts with the forged checks, nevertheless the criminal acts of Miss Denning went undiscovered over the years. She would draw a check to her own order on plaintiff's printed checks and forge his signature. Her ordinary duties included making deposits, drawing checks for signature, and periodically making reconciliations of bank statements. From August 16, 1957 to May 22, 1958 Miss Denning possessed a power of attorney to withdraw funds from the attorney's account on her own signature.

Plaintiff left the reconciliation of bank statements to his trusted secretary and only conducted superficial spot checks personally. He stated that he was only concerned with whether the bank balance was in reasonable shape, and the few checks he did examine were recognized by him. He did not attempt to balance his books against the bank statements. Responding to an internal audit by the bank, plaintiff confirmed his balance as of March 31, 1961, although he did not know whether the balance was correct.

The vice-president in charge of the bank's record-keeping department testified that the bookkeepers did not take every check and compare the signature with the depositor's signature card. Such comparison was made only when there was something about the signature which caused it to be questioned. The bank's bookkeepers relied upon their recollection of the appearance of the signature.

The accounts for regular checking accounts were broken down into alphabetical segments. A bookkeeper was assigned to each segment. This person would sort the checks in complete alphabetical sequence and examine each check for date, formality, alterations, signature and endorsements. If satisfactory, the bookkeeper would post the check to the related account.

Each bookkeeper had a partner who worked on the adjacent section of the alphabet. After posting, the partners would exchange checks and repeat the entire process of posting as a safeguard against errors. This system of bookkeeping is called dual posting, as opposed to a single posting by only one bookkeeper.

As noted, the only time there is an actual comparison of signature is where the bookkeeper questions the validity of the signature or whether the correct number of signatures appears.

A handwriting expert testified that the ordinary person could not detect the forgeries involved in this case. This would be true even if the person compared the signatures on the checks with the master signature card.

A vice-president of the First Pennsylvania National Bank and Trust Company and a retired bank examiner testified that the procedures used by defendant bank during the period in question were in accord with the general usage and practice in similar banks. Indeed, the bank examiner mentioned that it had been 35 to 40 years since banks made a comparison of signature on every check. The reason for this procedure is rather obvious when one considers that each bookkeeper handles approximately 1,000 checks a day— a figure which, according to various banking experts, is a normal volume of work per bookkeeper.

The law dealing with a bank's liability to its depositor when forgery of the depositor's signature results in honoring the forged check is well defined. A bank, to the extent that it pays a check bearing the forged signature of its depositor, pays out of its own fund and cannot charge the forged check to the depositor's account. A bank is bound to know the signatures of its depositors, and the payment of a forged check, however skillful the forgery, cannot be debited against the depositor if he is wholly free from neglect or fault. [Citations.]

The bank is relieved from this strict liability where its payment of forged checks is caused by the negligence of its depositor and where the bank is free from negligence. [Citations.]

R.S. 7:2–23, N.J.S.A., provides:

"Where a signature is forged or made without the authority of the person whose signature it purports to be, it is wholly inoperative, and no right to retain the instrument, or to give a discharge therefor, or to enforce payment thereof against any party thereto, can be acquired through or under such signature, unless the party, against whom it is sought to enforce such right, is precluded from setting up the forgery or want of authority."

The term "precluded" as used in this statute includes the negligence of the depositor in failing reasonably to examine returned checks and vouchers. [Citations.]

A depositor violates the duty he owes a bank when he neglects to do those things dictated by ordinary business customs and prudence and fair dealing toward a bank, and which, if done, would have prevented the wrongdoing. [Citations.]

Each month, from 1957 to 1961, defendant bank sent to plaintiff a statement of his account. On each printed statement there was the following direction:

"Please examine at once—if no error is reported within ten days the account will be considered correct."

In addition, there is to be found on the signature card signed by plaintiff,

"I hereby agree to the Rules and Regulations of Camden Trust Company."

The depositor must examine his cancelled checks and statements received from the bank and notify the bank promptly of any irregularities. If this is omitted by the depositor, any further losses occurring as a result of such omission must be borne by the depositor unless the bank itself is guilty of contributory negligence. [Citations.]

In Stumpp v. Bank of New York, 212 App.Div. 608, 209 N.Y.S. 396 (Sup.Ct.1925), the depositor was required to take at least three steps in reconciliating the bank statement with his own records: (1) compare vouchers returned by the bank with check stubs in his stub book; (2) compare balance entered in statement or passbook with balance in stub book, and (3) compare returned vouchers with list of checks entered in statement or check list.

The depositor's duty of verification and reconciliation of returned check vouchers can be delegated to an employee who has proven himself competent and trustworthy. The majority rule is that a depositor cannot be charged with knowledge which the employee has, when that same employee is the forger. However, any information which would have come to light if the employee was unconnected with the forgery and a reasonable examination conducted, is chargeable to the depositor. [Citations.]

The mere fact that the forgery was committed by a confidential employee or agent of the depositor does not enable the bank to shift the loss of the depositor, in the absence of some circumstances raising an estoppel against the depositor. [Citations.]

While the bank must also use reasonable and proper methods to detect the forgeries, the tellers and bookkeepers of the bank are not held to a degree of expertness which a handwriting expert possesses. [Citations.]

* * *

An account stated may always be impeached for mistake. It is only *prima facie* evidence of its correctness. [Citations.]

It is the contention of defendant bank that plaintiff is estopped from asserting a claim against it because of his negligence in failing to discover the forgeries through a reasonable examination of returned checks and vouchers. [Citation.] Miss Denning was the sole person who reconciled the cancelled checks with plaintiff's books and records fully. Plaintiff's supervision was only on a spot check basis and was inadequate for the purposes of N.J.S.A. 17:9A–226(C).

Under the ruling in Pannonia B. & L. Asso. v. West Side Trust Co., 93 N.J.L. 377, 108 A. 240; First Nat. Bank of Birmingham v. Allen, 100 Ala. 476, 14 So. 335, 27 L.R.A. 426 (Sup.Ct. 1893), and First National Bank of Richmond v. Richmond Electric Co., 106 Va. 347, 56 S.E. 152, 7 L.R.A.,N.S., 744 (Sup. Ct.App.1907), if a depositor assigns the duty of examining the returned checks and vouchers to the employee who committed the forgery, the employee is the agent of the depositor in examining the vouchers and the depositor is chargeable with the agent's knowledge of the fraud.

This is the minority rule and differs from the so-called majority view in that the depositor is bound in most jurisdictions by the knowledge that a competent and honest employee should have acquired. [Citations.]

Under either rule plaintiff did not meet the required standard of care under the reconciliation procedures used by him and his employee. Any competent and honest employee would have discovered in any kind of reasonable examination that there were no vouchers or office records that justified payment of the forged checks. The yearly audit made for income tax purposes by plaintiff's accountants did not satisfy the requirements of a reasonable bank reconciliation.

Defendant bank has not only proven the negligence of plaintiff but also has shown that there was no negligence on its part in honoring the forged checks. Each check was regular on its face, and each forged signature was a reasonable facsimile of the genuine signature. Plaintiff would have this court require the banks of this country to bear absolute liability as the alternative to costly procedures of comparing the signature on each instrument with the signature card. The court finds that this procedure would result in prohibitive costs to defendant bank and should not be required.

The court finds the checks sued upon were forged and were improperly paid by the bank. However, the depositor was guilty of negligence in his methods of reconciliation of bank statements and cannot recover against the bank. The bank, on its part, used proper care in its bookkeeping procedures and is not guilty of negligence.

Judgment for defendant bank.

ROCK ISLAND AUCTION SALES v. EMPIRE PACKING CO.

(1965) 32 Ill.2d 269, 204 N.E.2d 721.

SCHAEFER, J. This case presents issues concerning the construction and validity of section 4—302 of the Uniform Commercial Code. Ill.Rev.Stat.1963, chap. 26, par. 4—302.

The facts were admitted or stipulated. On Monday, September 24, 1962, the plaintiff, Rock Island Auction Sales, Inc., sold 61 head of cattle to Empire Packing Co., Inc. and received therefor Empire's check in the sum of $14,706.90. The check was dated September 24, 1962, and on that day the plaintiff deposited it in the First Bank and Trust Company of Davenport, Iowa. It was received by the payor bank, Illinois National Bank and Trust Company of Rockford, Illinois, on Thursday, September 27, 1962. Empire's balance was inadequate to pay the check, but the payor bank, relying upon Empire's assurances that additional funds would be deposited, held the check until Tuesday morning, October 2, 1962. It then marked the check "not sufficient funds", placed it in the mail for return to the Federal Reserve Bank of Chicago and sent notice of dishonor by telegram to the Federal Reserve Bank. The depositary bank, the First Trust and Savings Bank of Davenport, received the check on October 4, 1962. The check was never paid. On November 7, 1962, bankruptcy proceedings were instituted against Empire and on December 13, 1962, it was adjudicated a bankrupt.

On February 15, 1963, the plaintiff instituted this action against Illinois National Bank and Trust Company of Rockford, Empire Packing Co., Inc., and Peter Cacciatori, the officer of Empire who had signed the check. Cacciatori was not served with process, and no further action was taken against Empire after a stay order was issued by the United States District Court in the bankruptcy proceeding. The plaintiff's case against Illinois National Bank and Trust Company of Rockford, (hereafter defendant) rests squarely on the ground that as the payor bank it became liable for the amount of the check because it held the check without payment, return or notice of dishonor, beyond the time limit fixed in section 4—302 of the Uniform Commercial Code. Ill.Rev.Stat. 1963, chap. 20, par. 4—302.

The defendant relies upon several alternative defenses. It first asserts that section 4—302, properly construed, does not make it liable for the face amount of the check, and that if the section is construed to impose that liability it violates the principle of separation of powers, and deprives the defendant of due process of law and equal protection of the laws. It then asserts that section 4–214(4) of the Code is invalid because it attempts to provide for preferred claims against national banks, and it contends that the asserted invalidity of that section renders the entire article 4 of the Code void. It relies also upon certain conduct of the plaintiff, which will be described, as establishing defenses by way of waiver and estoppel. The trial court entered judgment for the plaintiff for the face amount of the check, and the defendant has appealed directly to this court because the case involves questions arising under the Constitution of the United States and of this State.

Section 4—302 of the Uniform Commercial Code provides: "In the absence of a valid defense such as breach of a presentment warranty (subsection (1) of Section 4—207), settlement effected or the like, if an item is presented on and received by a payor bank the bank is accountable for the amount of (a) a demand item * * * if the bank * * * retains the item beyond midnight of the banking day of receipt without settling for it or * * * does not pay or return the item or send notice of dishonor until after its midnight deadline; * * *." Section 4—104(h) of the Code defines the "midnight deadline" of a bank as midnight on the banking day following the day on which it received the item.

The important issues in the case involve the construction and validity of section 4—302. The defendant argues that the amount for which it is liable because of its undenied retention of the check beyond the time permitted by section 4—302 is not to be determined by that section, but rather under section 4—103(5) which provides that "[t]he measure of damages for failure to exercise ordinary care in handling an item is the amount of the item reduced by an amount which could not have been realized by the use of ordinary care * * *." To support this argument it points out that other provisions of article 4 use the words "liable" "must pay" and "may recover." Its position is that the word "accountable" in section

4—302 means that "the defendant must account for what it actually had (which is zero because there were not funds on deposit sufficient to pay the check) plus the damages (as measured by Section 4—103(5)) sustained by the plaintiff as the result of the failure to meet the deadline, but for no more."

But the statute provides that the bank is accountable for the amount of the item, and not for something else. "Accountable" is synonymous with "liable", (Webster's New Twentieth Century Dictionary Unabridged, Second Edition; Webster's Dictionary of Synonyms,) and section 4—302 uses the word in that sense. The word "accountable" appears to have been used instead of its synonym "liable" in order to accommodate other sections of article 4 of the Code which relate to provisional and final settlements between banks in the collection process, and to bar the possibility that a payor bank might be thought to be liable both to the owner of the item and to another bank. The circuit court correctly held that the statute imposes liability for the amount of the item.

This construction does not create an irrational classification and so cause the statute to violate constitutional limitations. Defendant's contention to the contrary is based upon the proposition that section 4—302 is invalid because it imposes a liability upon a payor bank for failing to act prior to its midnight deadline that is more severe than the liability which section 4—103(5) imposes upon a depositary bank or a collecting bank for the same default. Of course there are no such separate institutions as depositary, collecting and payor banks. All banks perform all three functions. The argument thus comes down to the proposition that the failure of a bank to meet its deadline must always carry the same consequence, regardless of the function that it is performing.

But the legislature may legitimately have concluded that there are differences in function and in circumstance that justify different consequences. Depositary and collecting banks act primarily as conduits. The steps that they take can only indirectly affect the determination of whether or not a check is to be paid, which is the focal point in the collection process. The legislature could have concluded that the failure of such a bank to meet its deadline would most frequently be the result of negligence, and fixed liability accordingly. The role of a payor bank in the collection process, on the other hand, is crucial. It knows whether or not the drawer has funds available to pay the item. The legislature could have considered that the failure of such a bank to meet its deadline is likely to be due to factors other than negligence, and that the relationship between a payor bank and its customer may so influence its conduct as to cause a conscious disregard of its statutory duty. The present case is illustrative. The defendant, in its position as a payor bank, deliberately aligned itself with its customer in order to protect that customer's credit and consciously disregarded the duty imposed upon it. The statutory scheme emphasizes the importance of speed in the collection process. A legislative sanction designed to prevent conscious disregard of deadlines can not be characterized as arbitrary or unreasonable, nor can it be said to constitute a legislative encroachment on the functions of the judiciary.

* * *

On October 4, 1964, an officer of the defendant asked the plaintiff to re-present the check for payment. The plaintiff did not do so. Later Empire Packing Company offered to pay the plaintiff $5,000 in cash and the balance of the amount of the check in equal installments. The plaintiff rejected this offer. From the failure to re-present or to agree to extend credit the defendant attempts to distill a waiver or estoppel that would bar the plaintiff from asserting its rights under section 4—302. But the plaintiff did not induce the defendant to act nor was it guilty of any deception. The facts relied upon to constitute waiver or estoppel were legally insufficient and the trial court did not err in striking those defenses.

The judgment of the circuit court of Rock Island County is affirmed.

Judgment affirmed.

PROBLEMS

1. On December 9, John Jones writes a check for $500 payable to Ralph Rodgers in payment for goods to be received later in the month. Before the close of business on the 9th John notifies the bank by telephone to stop payment on the check. On the 19th of December Ralph gives the check to Bill Briggs for value and without notice. On the 20th Bill deposits the check in his account at Bank A. On the 21st Bank A sends the check to its correspondent Bank B. On the 22nd Bank B presents the check through the clearing house to Bank C. On the 23rd Bank C presents the check to Bank P, the payor bank. On the 28th of December the payor bank makes payment of the check final. John Jones sues the payor bank. Decision?

2. Howard Harrison, a long time customer of Western Bank, operates a small department store, Harrison's Store. Since his store has few experienced employees, Harrison frequently travels throughout the United States on buying trips, although he also runs the financial operations of the business. On one of his buying trips Harrison purchased a gross of sport shirts from Well-Made Shirt Company and paid for the transaction with a check on his store account with Western Bank in the amount of $1,000. Adams, an employee of Well-Made who deposits its checks in Security Bank, raised the amount of the check to $10,000 and indorsed the check, "Pay to the order of Adams from Pension Plan Benefits, Well-Made Shirt Company by Adams". He cashes the check and cannot be found. The check is processed and paid by the Western Bank and is sent to Harrison's Store with the monthly statement. After brief examination of the statement, Harrison leaves on another buying trip for three weeks.

(a) Assuming the bank acted in good faith and the alteration is not discovered and reported to the bank until an audit con-

ducted 13 months after the statement was received by Harrison's Store, who must bear the loss on the raised check?

(b) Assuming that Harrison, because he was unable to examine his statement promptly due to his buying trips, left instructions with the bank to notify him of any item over $5,000 to be charged to his account and the bank paid the item anyway in his absence, who bears the loss if the alteration is discovered one month after the statement was received by Harrison's Store?

3. John Jones of Chicago, Illinois, purchased from Frank Reynolds of southern California some merchandise on January 1. In accordance with the contract agreement John Jones issued a note for $150 payable to Reynolds on May 30. May 25, Reynolds gave the note to his bank, Bank X, for collection, at which time Bank X made an agreement that it was only liable up to $100 on the note if some negligence occurred within the bank. Several weeks later Reynolds learned that only $100 was credited to his account, because the collecting bank misplaced the note and after intensive search could not find it. Because of the agreement limiting the bank's liability it refused to pay the additional $50. What recourse does Reynolds have?

4. Tom Jones owed Bank Y $10,000 on a note due November 17, with 1% interest due the bank for each day delinquent in payment. Tom Jones issued a check to Bank Y and delivered it via night vault the evening of November 17. Several days later he received a letter saying he owed one day's interest on the payment because of one day delinquency in payment on the original $10,000. Jones refused because he said he had put it in the vault on the 17th of November. What action?

5. Assume that D draws a check on Y Bank payable to the order of P; that P indorses to A; that A deposits it to his account in X Bank; that X Bank presents it to Y Bank, the drawee; that Y Bank dishonors it because of insufficient funds. X Bank has until midnight of the day after presentment to notify A of the dishonor. That is, if X Bank received the dishonor on Monday, it would have until midnight of Tuesday to notify A. Assume that X Bank, because of an interruption of communication facilities, fails to notify A by midnight Tuesday, is A, the secondary liable party, now discharged?

6. A presented a check for $1000 to B Bank. A was not a customer of the bank. There was an agreement that B Bank would take the check and send it through for collection and that A could come back, to receive his cash or the check if it was dishonored, in five days. B Bank maintains its account with C Bank, and at the close of each business day sends its checks to C Bank by railway. B Bank sent its checks together with A's collection item in this usual manner that same evening. Due to a derailment the item was delayed one day before finally reaching the payor bank. The B Bank had not received any notice whether the check had been paid or dishonored within the time set. A came back to B Bank on the agreed day and demanded his money or the check.

Would A be able to hold B Bank to the agreement?

7. Jones, a food wholesaler whose company carries an account with B Bank in New York City, is traveling in California on business. He comes upon a particularly attractive offer and decides to buy a carload of oranges for delivery in New York. He gives S, the seller, his company's check for $25,000 to pay for the purchase. S places the check, with others he received that day, with his bank, the C Bank. C Bank sends the check to D Bank in Los Angeles which, in turn, deposits with the Los Angeles Federal Reserve Bank. The L. A. Fed. sends the check, with others, to the N. Y. Fed. The N. Y. Fed. forwards the check to B Bank, Jones's bank for collection.

(a) Is B Bank a depository bank? A collecting bank? A payor bank?

(b) Is C Bank a depository bank? A presenting bank?

(c) Is the N. Y. Fed. a remitting bank? An intermediary bank?

(d) Is D Bank a collecting bank? A remitting bank?

*

PART SIX
PARTNERSHIPS

CHAPTER 30

DEFINITION AND GENERAL NATURE OF PARTNERSHIP

Introductory. A business enterprise may be operated or conducted by a sole proprietor, a partnership, a corporation or by some other form of business organization. The selection of the particular form of business unit to be employed is a matter for the owner or owners of the enterprise to determine at the inception. It is not unusual for a business to have a small beginning as a sole proprietorship, later expand into a partnership, and ultimately be incorporated. Where a new enterprise is started as a fairly large operation, various factors will affect the decision to use one medium rather than another, not the least of which will be the current or prospective incidence of Federal or State income tax laws.

As distinguished from the conduct of a business by a single individual, a partnership is generally defined as the association of two or more persons for the purpose of carrying on a business as co-owners for profit. In a partnership the members of the firm have a proprietary interest in the business. In a corporation the shareholders, although not owners of the corporate assets, are the ultimate owners of the enterprise. In a business trust, another type of business unit, the holders of certificates of beneficial interest in the trust are the real owners of the business and entitled to the profits during the life of the trust and to a distribution of the assets upon its termination. Other less common business devices are joint ventures, syndicates, pools, limited partnerships and joint stock companies.

References to "U. P. A." or to the "Uniform Act" refer to the Uniform Partnership Act.

Partnership Defined. A partnership, or copartnership, as it is sometimes called, has been variously defined, although the best definition is that contained in Section 6 of the Uniform Partnership Act. Other definitions are added for comparison.

> "A partnership is an association of two or more persons to carry on as co-owners a business for profit." (Section 6, U.P.A.)
> "Partnership is the relation which subsists between persons carrying on a business in common with a view of profit." (Section 1, English Partnership Act of 1890.)

> "Partnership, often called co-partnership, is usually defined to be a voluntary contract between two or more competent persons to place their money, effects, labor and skill, or some or all in lawful commerce or business, with the understanding that there shall be a communion of the profits thereof between them." Story, on Partnerships, (2d Ed.) p. 1.

> "Partnerships may be tentatively defined as a legal relation, based upon the express or implied agreement of two or more persons whereby they unite their property, labor or skill in carrying on some lawful business as principals for their joint profit."

Mechem, Elements of Partnership, (2d Ed.) p. 1.

Entity Theory. An entity is anything which possesses the quality of oneness and may therefore be regarded collectively or otherwise as a single unit. A legal person or legal entity is such a unit which has the recognized capacity of possessing legal rights and being subject to legal duties. A legal entity may acquire, own and dispose of property. It may enter into contracts, commit wrongs, sue and be sued. It is a juristic person. Each human being is a legal entity of natural origin. Each business corporation is a legal entity created by the act of a law making body or legislature. The common law however does not recognize a partnership as a legal entity.

A partnership is a relationship or association of persons which has the quality of oneness but legally is regarded not as an entity but as an aggregation of individuals. Unlike a corporation, a partnership is not an artificial person having a distinct legal existence separate from its members. This was the prevailing theory at common law and is the view adopted by the Uniform Partnership Act. As a result of the legal characterization of a partnership as an association of individuals, it necessarily follows that, in the absence of a permissive statute, a partnership can neither sue nor be sued in the firm name. Since a partnership is not a legal entity, the debts of the partnership are the debts of the individual partners, and any one partner may be held liable for the partnership's entire indebtedness.

A partnership is not a legal entity, but it is nevertheless an entity and clearly recognized as such in the following respects:

(1) For bookkeeping purposes, the assets, liabilities, and business transactions of the firm are treated as those of a business unit and are considered separate and distinct from the individual assets, liabilities and non-partnership business transactions of the members.

(2) In the marshalling of assets, the assets and liabilities of the firm and of the respective individual members are considered separate and distinct, and the partnership creditors have a prior right to partnership assets, while creditors of the individual members have a prior right, respectively, to the separate assets of the individual debtors.

(3) Title to real estate may be acquired by a partnership in the partnership name, and if so acquired can be conveyed only in the partnership name, as provided in section 8(c) of the Uniform Partnership Act.

(4) In certain States by statute, and in the Federal courts, a partnership may sue and be sued in the partnership name.

(5) A partnership, including a limited partnership, may be adjudicated a bankrupt either separately or jointly with one or more or all of its general partners, and a bankruptcy proceeding may involve the partnership without involving the individual separate assets of the members of the firm, as provided in Section 5 of the Federal Bankruptcy Act.

It may therefore be observed that a partnership is a unit and in ordinary transactions is regarded as a business unit distinct from each of its component members. It is manifest that a partnership could be endowed by the law with full legal personality and become a legal entity. It is so regarded by the law of Louisiana and of certain foreign countries.

The rule in Louisiana, which differs from the common law rule, is that a commercial partnership is a legal entity and the partners are not owners of the partnership property but are regarded as owners of the residuum of the partnership property after all obligations of the partnership have been discharged. Henderson's Estate v. Commissioner, 155 F.2d 310, 164 A.L.R. 1030 (C.A.5, 1946).

A 1965 New Hampshire statute provides that every non-resident or foreign partnership desiring to do business in that State shall file an application for authority to do business, pay a fifty dollar registration fee, and continuously maintain in the State a registered office and registered agent. Upon desiring to withdraw from doing business in New Hampshire, the statute requires the foreign partnership to file a formal statement with the Secretary of State which alleges that it surrenders its authority to do business in the State. This statute imposes on foreign partnerships requirements similar to those imposed on foreign corporations. It treats a foreign partnership as an entity. Inasmuch as a partnership is not a legal entity at common law, it may violate rights of non-residents who seek to do business in New Hampshire as a partnership which are guaranteed by the privileges and immunities clause and the equal protection clause of the Fourteenth Amendment of the United States Constitution.

Income Tax Aspects of Partnership. As a partnership is not a legal entity it is not required to pay a Federal income tax although it must file each year an informational return which sets forth the income or profits realized, whether received or not, by each of the partners who are individually required to report and to pay a tax thereon.

Since the amendment to the Internal Revenue Code in 1948 which gave to married persons throughout the United States the tax benefits previously enjoyed by residents of States having community property laws, namely, that of permitting the husband and wife to make a joint return of their total income and to compute the tax of each upon one-half of the adjusted total, there has been no incentive for a husband and wife to form a partnership for the purpose of tax mitigation.

Partnerships between parent and child have sometime been formed for the purpose, among others, of accomplishing a reduction in the amount of income tax payable. In such cases the courts have carefully scrutinized the facts to determine whether the parties had a genuine intention to form a partnership and whether an actual contribution of capital or services was made or intended to be made by each of the parties involved. In 1951 a new section was added to the Internal Revenue Code dealing expressly with income derived from family partnerships which are defined by the statute to include a husband or wife, ancestor, lineal descendants, and any trust for the primary benefit of such persons.

Delectus Personae. A partnership is manifestly a highly personal relationship. Each partner has a right to take part in the management of the business, to handle the partnership assets for partnership purposes, and to act as agent of the partnership. Accordingly, a partner, by his negligence, injudiciousness or dishonesty, may bring financial loss or ruin to his co-partners. Because of the close relationship involved, partnerships must necessarily be founded on mutual trust and confidence. While occasionally a person may be chosen as a partner because of his ability to make a needed capital contribution, the mutual choice of partners is based largely on desirable personal traits such as business ability, good health, experience, sound judgment, good reputation and integrity. All this finds expression in the term delectus personae, which means literally choice of the person and indicates the right one has to choose or select his partners. This principle finds expression in Section 18(g) of the Uniform Partnership Act, which provides: "No person can become a member of a partnership without the consent of all the partners."

Tests of Partnership Existence. The existence of a community of interest for business purposes is one of the fundamental tests of the existence of a partnership. By this is meant a community of interest in the capital employed in the business, a community of interest in profits and losses, and a community of authority to conduct the business operations.

In the typical contract of partnership, the parties expressly agree to become partners and co-owners of a business for profit, to contribute certain capital to their mutual enterprise, to devote their personal services to the conduct of the business, and to share the profits and losses in stated proportions. Occasionally, persons become associated in the conduct of a business with only an informal or incomplete agreement as to the extent of their rights and duties and the nature of their relationship. In other situations, the express contract between the parties may purport to be a loan, a lease, or a contract of employment and yet contain certain elements of a partnership.

Co-ownership alone does not establish a partnership. The co-ownership must relate to a business. Conversely, granting the existence of a business, a person financially interested in or participating in the operation of the business is not a partner unless his interest in participation in the enterprise is that of a co-owner of the business. The existence of a business being relatively easy to ascertain, most of the tests of the partnership relation pertain to the issue of co-ownership. In this connection the incidents of partnership, such as the sharing of profits, the sharing of losses, and the right to manage and control the business, are helpful in determining the element of co-ownership.

Section 7(2) of the Uniform Partnership Act provides that joint tenancy, tenancy in common, tenancy by the entireties, joint property, common property or part-ownership does not of itself establish a partnership, even though the co-owners share the profits made by the use of the property. In addition to property there must be a business. An intention to acquire profits being essential to the conduct of a business enterprise, it is clear that an unincorporated non-profit association, such as a gun club, literary society, or fraternal or political organization, is not a business and, therefore, not a partnership. Where persons are associated together for mutual financial gain on a temporary or limited basis involving a single transaction or a relatively few isolated transactions, no partnership results because the parties are not engaged in a continuous series of commercial activities necessary to constitute a business. Thus, a contract between four farmers whereby they purchase a threshing machine for their mutual use and agree to rent the machine to others and divide the profits does not create a partnership. Co-ownership of the means or instrumentality of accomplishing a single business transaction or a limited series of transactions may result in a joint venture but not a general partnership.

To illustrate: A and B are joint owners of shares of the capital stock of a corporation, have a joint bank account, and have inherited or purchased real estate as joint tenants or tenants in common. They share the dividends paid on the stock, the interest on the bank account, and the net proceeds from the sale or lease of the real estate. A and B are not partners. Although they are co-owners and share profits, they are not engaged in the carrying on of a business, and, hence, no partnership results. On the other hand, if A and B were engaged in continuous transactions of buying and selling real estate over a period of time and were carrying on the business of trading in real estate, a partnership relation would exist between them, irrespective of whether they regarded one another as partners.

A, B and C each inherit an undivided one-third interest in a hotel and instead of selling the property decide, by an informal and incomplete agreement, to continue operation of the hotel. The operation of a hotel is a business, and, as co-owners of a hotel business, A, B and C are partners and are subject to all of the rights, duties and incidents arising from the partnership relation.

The receipt by a person of a share of the profits of a business is prima facie evidence that he is a partner in the business, but Section 7(4) of the Uniform Partnership Act further provides that no inference of the existence of a partnership relation shall be drawn where the profits are received in payment:

(1) of a debt by installments or otherwise;

(2) of wages of an employee or rent to a landlord;

(3) of an annuity to a widow or representative of a deceased partner;

(4) of interest on a loan, though the amount of payment vary with the profits of the business, or

(5) as consideration for the sale of the good-will of a business or other property by installments, or otherwise.

Because the payment of money or the transfer of title to property may be either the capital contribution of a partner or a loan or sale on credit by a creditor, it is important that courts have some criteria for distinguishing between the two situations. Outside of the usual incidents of a loan or a sale on credit, the test more frequently employed in doubtful situations is whether an obligation has been created to pay for goods received or to repay money advanced in any event. If the party sought to be charged as a partner is entitled at some time to receive payment for the money or property which he advanced, he is generally not a co-owner or partner but a creditor.

Two other tests of co-ownership of a business may be touched upon briefly. They are: (1) an agreement to share in or contribute to the losses of a business, and (2) the exercise of the power of management and control. Both afford strong evidence of an ownership interest, especially an undertaking to

share in the losses. Evidence as to participation in the management or control of a business, standing alone, does not constitute conclusive proof of a partnership relation. A voice in management and control of a business may be accorded, in a limited degree, to an employee, a lessor, or a creditor. On the other hand, one who is actually a partner may take no active part in the affairs of the firm and, indeed, may, by agreement with his co-partners, forego all right to exercise any control over the ordinary affairs of the business.

Partnership by Estoppel. As previously stated, partnership is a voluntary relationship. It is founded upon contract, express or implied. This contractual aspect of partnership is emphasized by the doctrine of delectus personae. No person can become a member of a firm without the consent of all of the other partners, and no person can be forced into the partnership relationship against his will. The meaning sought to be conveyed by the term "partnership by estoppel" is not that a partnership may be created by any other method than by contract but, rather, that persons not actually partners as to one another may be treated as partners and a partnership liability imposed upon them as to third persons by reason of words or conduct which estop or preclude them from asserting that in truth no partnership exists.

Partnership by estoppel has no bearing on the relations of actual or assumed partners among themselves. It pertains solely to the duties and liabilities of persons not partners in fact to third persons who have changed their position in reasonable reliance upon an assumed partnership existence. As such, it constitutes an exception to the general rule that persons who are not partners as to one another are not partners as to third persons. This exception was well known to the common law and finds expression in Section 16 of the Uniform Partnership Act. The substance of the exception is that a person not actually a partner is liable as a partner where by his words, acts, conduct or acquiescence he has held himself out, or knowingly suffered others to represent him, as a partner with one or more persons not actually his partners. This liability extends to any person to whom such representation has been made who, acting reasonably and in good faith, has given credit to the actual or apparent partnership in reliance upon such holding out or representation.

It is immaterial whether a person represents himself to be a partner or whether he knowingly permits himself to be held out as a partner by others. Liability will attach in either case. For example, A and B are partners. C states to T that he is a member of the firm and, in reliance upon C's statement, T sells goods to A and B believing that he is selling to A, B and C as co-partners. Upon the failure of the actual partners to pay for the goods, T can hold A, B and C liable as partners. By his statement to T, C is estopped from denying that he is a member of the partnership. The same result would obtain if A introduced C as a member of the firm to T and C made no objection. C's failure to disavow A's statement as to his membership in the firm is conduct reasonably calculated to instill in T's mind the belief that C is a partner. Thus, in an action by T against A, B and C as partners, C could not successfully defend upon the ground that A's statement was false and that he was in fact not a partner.

In order to create partnership liability by estoppel, there must be actual reliance upon the representation of a partnership. Where T has positive knowledge that C is not a member of the firm of A and B, despite the fact that A or B hold out C as a partner with C's consent, T cannot impose a partnership liability on C. Except where the representation of membership in a firm has been made in a public manner, no person is entitled to

rely upon a representation of partnership unless it is made directly to him. For example: B tells C that he is a member of the firm of A and Company, and C casually relays this information to T. If, without anything further, T thereafter enters into a contract with A and Company, T cannot hold B responsible as a partner. T had no right to rely upon B's representation made privately to C alone. Where, however, B knowingly permits his name to appear in the firm name or list of partners or permits it to be displayed at the firm place of business or used in announcements and advertisements of the firm, he becomes liable as a partner to any member of the general public dealing with the firm in reliance upon the representations thus made. Such a person is not a partner in fact, but he is held liable to third persons as a partner by estoppel. It should be observed that a partnership by estoppel exists only for the purpose of working out justice in favor of the third party who relied on the holding out in the particular instance. It is not a true partnership. Estoppel does not create a partnership but only the duties incident thereto. A partnership can only be created by contract, express or implied.

Types of Partners. A real partner is one who is associated with one or more other persons as the co-owner of a business for profit. He is an actual partner, a partner both in law and in fact. He may be active or inactive in partnership affairs, and his membership in the firm may or may not be known to the general public.

As ostensible partner is one who has consented to be held out as a partner whether he is a real partner or not. The term is more commonly and correctly applied to one who is a nominal partner or a partner by estoppel, that is, one who is not a real partner but by his conduct allows himself to be held out as a partner. Although not a real partner, he is liable as an actual partner to those who, in good faith, have extended credit on the assumption that he was a partner in fact.

A general partner is one whose liability for partnership indebtedness is unlimited. In addition to being a real partner, he is usually an active partner and known as such.

A special or limited partner is one who, as a member of a limited partnership, is liable for firm indebtedness only to the extent of the capital which he has contributed or agreed to contribute.

A silent partner is a real partner who has no voice, and takes no part, in the partnership business.

A secret partner is a real partner whose membership in the firm is not disclosed to the public.

A dormant partner is a real partner who is both a silent and a secret partner.

A sub-partner is one who is not a partner at all but has a contractual arrangement with a partner which entitles him to a share of the profits realized by such partner. The relationship calls for no continuous acts or the performance of any duty by the sub-partner. He is not a co-owner of the assets or the property of the partnership, and the sharing of income with the party who is a partner may not properly be considered as carrying on a business. The sub-partner is therefore not a member of any partnership, but merely an assignee of a portion of the interest of the assigning member in the partnership. As an equitable assignee he is entitled to an accounting from the partnership after dissolution.

Limited Partnership. A limited partnership is one composed of one or more general partners and one or more limited partners. It is sometimes called a special partnership in contrast to a general partnership. It differs from a general partnership in several respects, two of which are basic. First, it can be formed only under statutory authority, and, second, the liability of the limited partners for partnership debts is limited to the extent of the capital which they have contributed or have agreed to contribute.

The Uniform Limited Partnership Act provides, as to the formation of a limited partnership, that two or more persons desiring to form such a partnership shall sign and swear to a certificate, which shall state: the name of the partnership; the character of the business; the location of the principal place of business; the name and place of residence of each member, general and limited partners being respectively designated; the term for which the partnership is to exist; the amount of cash and a description, and the agreed value, of any other property contributed by each limited partner; the additional contributions, if any, to be made by each limited partner and the times at which or events on the happening of which they shall be made; the time, if agreed upon, when the contribution of each limited partner is to be returned; the share of the profits or the other compensation by way of income which each limited partner is entitled to receive; the right, if given, of a limited partner to substitute an assignee as contributor in his place, and the terms and conditions of the substitution; the right, if given, of the partners to admit additional limited partners; the right, if given, of one or more limited partners to priority over other limited partners, as to contributions or to compensation by way of income, and the nature of such priority; the right, if given, of the remaining general partner or partners to continue the business on the death, retirement or insanity of a general partner, and the right, if given, of a limited partner to demand and receive property other than cash in return for his original contribution.

This certificate must be filed or caused to be recorded in the office of a designated public official, usually in the county in which the principal office of the limited partnership is located. In some States there is the further requirement that a copy of the certificate shall be published in some newspaper for a designated period, and that proof of such publication be evidenced by an affidavit of the publisher filed with the original certificate. On substantial compliance in good faith with the statutory requirements, a limited partnership is formed.

The contribution of a limited partner may be cash or other property but not services. The inclusion of the surname of a limited partner in the partnership name is prohibited unless it is also the surname of a general partner. A violation of this provision renders the limited partner liable as a general partner to any creditor who did not know that he was a limited partner. A limited partner is also liable as a general partner if he takes part in the control of the business. If the certificate contains a false statement, any one who suffers loss by reliance on such statement may hold liable any party to the certificate who knew the statement to be false.

A limited partner may assign his interest. If he does so, the assignee may become a substituted limited partner if all the others consent, or if the assigning partner, having such power as provided in the certificate, gives the assignee this right. Upon the death of a limited partner, his executor or administrator has all the rights of such partner for the purpose of settling his estate, and such power as the deceased partner had to constitute his assignee a substituted limited partner.

A limited partner occupies a position similar in some respects to that of a shareholder in a corporation. He is primarily an investor. Except at the risk of incurring unlimited liability, he can take no part in the management or operation of the business. He is not an agent of the partnership. Unlike a general partner, he knows in advance the exact extent of his possible loss.

Joint Stock Company. A joint stock company, or joint stock association, as it is sometimes called, is technically a form of general partnership having some of the attributes of a corporation yet differing in several important respects from the ordinary partnership. It is dissimilar to a partnership in that its capital is divided into shares represented by certificates which are transferable; its business and affairs are managed by directors or managers elected by the members, and who alone have the authority to represent and bind it; its members as such are not its agents; and a transfer of shares by a member, or his death, insanity or other incapacity, does not dissolve it or afford a ground for dissolution. It is similar to a partnership, and, unlike a corporation, it is formed by contract and not by State authority; it is not a legal entity, and its members are each under unlimited liability with respect to obligations incurred by it during the period of their membership.

Joint Venture. A joint venture or joint adventure is a form of temporary partnership organized to carry out a single or isolated business enterprise for profit, and usually, although not necessarily, of short duration. It is an association of persons who combine their property, money, efforts, skill and knowledge for the purpose of carrying out a single business operation for profit. An example is a securities underwritings syndicate. Another is a syndicate formed to acquire a certain tract of land for subdivision and resale. A joint venture, however, is not necessarily confined to a syndicate and may comprise any type of single business deal or undertaking. It differs in a practical way from an ordinary partnership in that the latter is formed to carry on a business involving a continuous series of activities over a considerable or indefinite period of time. It also differs legally in several respects from the ordinary partnership. In the latter, each partner is an agent of the partnership with the right and authority to represent and bind his co-partners in the usual course of its business. A joint venturer, as such, is not an agent of his co-venturers and does not necessarily have authority to bind them, although in a given case a joint venturer may have real or apparent authority to bind his co-venturers. Usually the management and operation of the enterprise is placed by agreement in the hands of one member designated as manager. The death of a partner dissolves the partnership automatically, while the death of a joint venturer does not necessarily dissolve the joint venture. A partner cannot sue a co-partner or the firm at law, but must go into equity for relief. On the other hand, a court of law will take jurisdiction over disputes between joint venturers. Except for these principal differences between a joint venture and a partnership, a joint venture is generally governed by the law of partnerships.

Mining Partnerships. A mining partnership is an association of the several owners of the mineral rights in land for the purpose of operating a mine and extracting minerals of economic value for their mutual profit. Although mining partnerships are governed to a considerable extent by the law of general partnerships, there are certain important differences between them. A mining partner has the right to sell his interest in the partnership to anyone who is willing to buy his share. In some cases transferable certificates are issued to the partners representing their respective interests in the firm. Upon the transfer of a partner's interest, whether by sale or by death, the purchaser or devisee, as the case may be, becomes a member of the firm. Neither the sale of a partner's interest nor the death of a partner operates to dissolve a mining partnership. In addition, mere membership in a mining partnership does not constitute a partner an agent of the firm, and in consequence a mining partner ordinarily has no actual or apparent authority to represent or bind the partnership. Frequently, one of the partners is designated as manager of the enterprise, and he alone has authority to bind the partnership on contracts made in the usual and ordinary course of the business. Mining partners are subject to unlimited liability for partnership debts and obligations. It may be observed that in some of the western States these partnerships are regulated by special statutes.

Limited Partnership Associations. This form of business unit, known as a limited partnership association, is permitted by statute in certain States. It is a legal hybrid. Although called a partnership association, it closely resembles a corporation. In its organization, regulation, status and liability it has practically all the attributes of a corporation. It is governed by statute and is a legal entity separate and distinct from its members. The members of the association are not personally responsible for its debts, their liabilities being limited to their capital contribution, except in the event of violation of some statutory provision. To the end that creditors may be put on notice of the limited liability of the members of the association, the statutes of the several States require the inclusion of the word "limited" in the association name. The only important difference between this type of association and a corporation pertains to the transfer of shares. Although the shares in a limited partnership association are freely transferable by the members, the transferee does not, however, become a member in the association unless so elected by the other members. If membership is refused, he may recover the value of his shares from the association. It is significant that the States which sanction partnership associations, although commercially important, are few in number.

Trading and Non-Trading Partnerships. The primary business of a trading or commercial partnership consists of buying and selling for profit. A non-trading or non-commercial partnership, while it may buy or sell incidentally, is one whose chief activity is rendering a service or performing an employment. Examples of non-trading pursuits include the practice of a profession, such as law, accounting, medicine and dentistry, all the building and construction trades, repair work of all kinds, laundry, dry cleaning and dyeing, warehousing, transportation, farming, mining, printing and publishing, photography, and the operation of barber and beauty shops, hotels, theaters and other places of amusement.

Business Trusts. A trust is a transfer of the legal title to certain specific property to one person for the use and benefit of another. Where an express trust results from contract, the agreement is commonly known as a declaration of trust which customarily sets forth a designation of the property or trust res, the duration of the trust, the exact functions and duties of the trustees with respect to the management of the property, the persons to whom the income of the trust is to be paid and the share to be received by each, the method of winding up the trust, and the person or persons entitled to share in the trust property upon termination.

Although trusts are almost as old as the law of equity itself, it was not until late in the nineteenth century that lawyers and business men perceive that the trust concept was capable of being utilized as a method of conducting a commercial enterprise. The business trust, otherwise known as a Massachusetts trust, was devised to avoid the burdens of corporate regulation, and particularly the formerly widespread prohibition denying to corporations the power to own and deal in real estate. Like an ordinary trust between living persons, a business trust may be created by a voluntary agreement without the necessity of any authorization or consent of the State.

Founded on a trust agreement, a business trust is essentially an arrangement whereby the grantors, usually several in number, transfer legal title to certain property and assets to certain trustees to be held and managed by them for designated business uses and purposes for the benefit of such persons as may, from time to time, be the holders of transferable certificates representing units of beneficial interest in the trust. The distinguishing characteristics of the business trust are three in number. First, the trust estate is devoted to the conduct of a business. Secondly, by the terms of the agreement each beneficiary is entitled to a certificate evidencing his ownership of a proportional interest in the trust which he is free to sell or otherwise transfer. Thirdly, the trustees must have the exclusive right to manage and control the business free from the control of the beneficiaries, otherwise the trust may fail and the beneficiaries become personally liable for the obligations of the business as partners.

As the legal owners of the business, with complete control over the management of its property and affairs, the trustees are personally liable for the debts of the business unless, in entering into contractual relations with others, it is expressly stipulated or definitely understood between the parties that the obligation is incurred solely upon the responsibility of the trust estate. The trustee, in order to escape personal liability on the contractual obligations of the business, must obtain the agreement or consent of the other contracting party to look solely to the assets of the trust. The personal liability of the trustees for their own torts or the torts of their agents and servants employed in the operation of the business stands on a different footing. While this liability cannot be avoided, the risk involved may be reduced substantially or eliminated altogether by insurance.

Unincorporated Associations. Voluntary associations formed for social, political purposes, or as trade associations, are not partnerships. The property rights and legal liabilities of the members, as between themselves, depend upon the association's constitution and by-laws. With respect to third persons, the members are liable as though they were partners and it is immaterial that their interests in the property of the association are represented by certificates, or that they call themselves shareholders, or believe that their liability for losses is limited to the amount which they have invested. Every member is regarded by the law as authorizing whatever action is taken by the majority of the members although taken in his absence or contrary to his vote, and his only escape from liability is to protest the action and promptly terminate his membership.

CASES

MORRISON'S ESTATE

(1941) 343 Pa. 157, 22 A.2d 729.

[Frank Morrison and Francis Hanson operated a gasoline station as partners under the firm name of F. Hanson and Company. Failing to receive gasoline taxes collected by the partnership, the State obtained a judgment against the partners. Subsequently Morrison died leaving liabilities in excess of his assets. From an award allowing the State a priority against the estate, Morrison's other creditors appeal, on the theory, among others, that the judgment obtained by the State is not a lien on the individual property of Morrison.]

PARKER, J. * * * The final position of the appellants is that even if the Commonwealth has a valid judgment, it is only a lien upon partnership property owned by F. Hanson and Company as such, and that at least it was not a lien upon the separate property of Frank Morrison as against another judgment creditor. They argue that the 12th section of the Liquid Fuels Tax Act of 1927 provided that "all taxes collected by a dealer shall be a lien on the franchise or property, both real and personal, of any dealer", that property of the *dealer* means property used by the partnership, and that the meaning cannot be extended so as to cover property of the individual partners not used in the partnership business.

Our problem is to determine what is meant by the phrase "property of any dealer", and the natural inquiry is first as to the sense in which the word "dealer" is used. Is the dealer F. Hanson and Company, or Frank Morrison and F. Hanson, doing business as F. Hanson and Company? Section 1(b) of the Liquid Fuels Tax Act states that "the word 'dealer' shall include any person, firm, copartnership. * * *" There the legislature recognized that "dealer" might possibly connote an individual and, to remove all question, was attempting only to make it clear that it meant to include all forms of business organization, though for convenience the word "dealer" was used throughout the statute. We deem it to be the law in Pennsylvania and the approved opinion in most other jurisdictions that a partnership is not recognized as an entity like a corporation, that it is not a legal entity having as such a domicile or residence separate and distinct from that of the individuals who compose it. It is rather a relation or status between two or more persons who unite their labor or property to carry on a business for profit. This is subject to an apparent exception, for while a partnership as such is not a person, it, as a matter of fact, is treated by a legal fiction as a quasi person or entity for such purposes as keeping of partnership accounts and marshaling assets. It is so treated under the law of this Commonwealth and under the Federal

Bankruptcy Act. We have held that while it is customary for a partnership to adopt a name in which a business is conducted, a partnership may exist as such without being designated by any name. [Citation.] Until the promulgation of Pa.R.C.P. 2128, a partnership could not be sued in its firm name, and even yet, under Pa.R.C.P. 2127, partners must be named individually in actions by a partnership. We are here dealing with the extent of a statutory lien on real estate which has ripened into a judgment, and there is not involved a marshaling of assets. Since under our law F. Hanson and Company is not a separate entity, it would appear that it was F. Hanson and Frank Morrison who were the dealers and that it was therefore their property which was subject to a lien entered by virtue of the Liquid Fuels Tax Act of 1927, whether such property was used in the partnership business or individually owned.

* * *

The decree of the court below is affirmed.

PETERSON v. EPPLER

(1946 Sup.) 67 N.Y.S.2d 499.

BOTEIN, J. Although the agreement upon which plaintiff bases his present action for an accounting of the alleged partnership between himself and the defendants states that plaintiff was to be a "junior partner," it expressly provides for a fixed monthly payment "as salary" in addition to a fixed percentage of the net profits derived by the firm from its accountancy practice. In addition the agreement definitely stipulates that plaintiff was to have no other financial interest in the firm or its property or profits and that he was to have no right or authority to participate in the management and conduct of the firm's affairs except as the "capital partners" might authorize from time to time.

The Partnership Law defines a partnership as "an association of two or more persons to carry on as co-owners a business for profit." § 10. It is clear from the express provisions of the contract between the parties that plaintiff was not to be a co-owner of the business. He was limited to a salary and a share of the profits from certain business and was not even entitled to a share in the profits of all the business or income of the firm. Section 40 of the Partnership Law provides that "all partners have equal rights in the management and conduct of the partnership business." The agreement, however, excluded plaintiff from any such right. It is also to be noted, although it may not be determinative, that there is no provision for plaintiff's sharing in the losses of the firm. In the light of the foregoing the court is constrained to hold that the plaintiff was only an employee of the firm, entitled to receive a fixed salary and a specified percentage of the net profits from some of its business. Although the fact that parties to an agreement may refer to their relationship as one of partnership is a circumstance entitled to great weight, it is by no means conclusive. The parties cannot by using the word "partnership" create such a relationship when the contract between them clearly provides that there was to be no community of interest in the business as such and no right to participate in the management of the business. [Citations.]

It follows that plaintiff is not entitled to an accounting in equity from the defendants and that his remedy, if any, is in an action at law. The motion to dismiss is granted with leave to serve an amended complaint on the law side of the court.

HACKNEY CO. v. LEE HOTEL, 156 Tenn. 243, 300 S.W. 1 (1927). *Cook, J.* * * * The contract, in express terms, created the relation of landlord and tenant and fixed the rent charge at a sum equal to five per cent the first year and six per cent thereafter based upon Lockmiller's investment, and an additional charge, dependent upon the result of the use of the property, of half the net profits. Without more a partnership could not be inferred. It is contended, however, that Lockmiller reserved such control over Jerow's operations as to authorize the inference that he joined as a partner in operating the hotel.

The provisions of the lease relied on to sustain that insistence are substantially as follows: A limitation upon Jerow's personal use of rooms in the hotel; the provision of a deduction of $200 a month, Jerow's salary as manager of the hotel among the other deductions to be made in the process outlined to determine net profits; the requirement that Jerow should give his personal attention to the management of the hotel, and not substitute another without Lockmiller's consent in writing; the requirement that Jerow render to Lockmiller a daily statement of rooms occupied, and a daily statement as well as a monthly statement of the business, and an auditor's statement once a year; that complainant should have the right to inspect the books of the hotel; that Jerow carry his account at the Citizens National Bank; that the hotel be operated on a cash basis, and the further provision that failure to comply with the terms imposed or to pay the rent as stipulated would result in a forfeiture of the lease upon thirty days' notice.

These provisions were intended to prevent wasteful methods in the conduct of the leased premises and to enable the landlord to determine whether the operation of the hotel produced a profit in excess of the fixed consideration from which the additional contingent consideration might be drawn. The insertion of such provisions, giving the lessor the means of ascertaining contingent profits and intended to facilitate payment of his share, would not change the lease to a partnership. * * *

O'CONNOR v. SHERLEY, 107 Ky. 70, 52 S.W. 1056 (1899). *Burnam*, J. * * * We can not concur in these conclusions, as Sherley never was in any sense a partner of the firm of O'Connor & McCulloch. He only agreed to divide the profits or share the losses which McCulloch might sustain in the prosecution of the business of that firm. The law is well settled that:

"If several persons are partners, and one of them agrees to share the profits derived by him with a stranger, this agreement does not make the stranger a partner in the original firm. The result of such an agreement is to constitute what is called a 'Subpartnership,' but in no way affects the other members of the principal firm; nor is there any authority for saying that, because the stranger shares the profits of that firm, he can be made liable to persons dealing with it as if he were a partner therein." (See Coll. Part., P. 45.) And in ex parte Barrow, Lord Eldon puts the law on this subject in this way: "I take it," he says, "to have been long since established that a man may become a partner with A, where A and B were partners, and yet not be a member of that partnership which existed between A and B. In the case of Sir Charles Raymond, a banker in the city, a Mr. Fletcher agreed with Sir Charles Raymond that he should be interested so far as to receive a share of his profits of the business, and which share he had a right to draw out from the firm of Raymond & Co. But it was held that he was no partner in that partnership, had no demand against it, had no account in it, and that he must be satisfied with a share of the profits arising and given to Sir Charles Raymond."

PUMP–IT, INC. v. ALEXANDER

(1950) 230 Minn. 564, 42 N.W.2d 337.

GALLAGHER, J. * * * The law governing the doctrine of ostensible partnership is clear. M.S.A. § 323.15, subd. 1, provides:

"When a person, * * * consents to another representing him to any one, as a partner in an existing partnership or with one or more persons not actual partners, he is liable to any such person to whom such representation has been made, who has, on the faith of such representation, given credit to the actual or apparent partnership, * * *."

Plainly, this statute declares that a person representing himself as a partner may be equitably estopped to deny that relationship as to those who have in good faith relied on the representation to their detriment. [Citation.] The rule as stated in 5 Dunnell, Dig. § 7348, is as follows: "Persons not partners inter se may render themselves liable as such, as to third persons, by holding themselves out to be partners; and, on the principle of estoppel, this may be by words spoken or written, or by conduct leading to the belief that they are partners. The person seeking to enforce such a liability must have acted in reliance on such holding out. Parties are held prima facie to be partners as to creditors, upon slighter proof than is necessary to establish that relation among themselves. Evidence of representations, conduct, and circumstances calculated to induce the belief in the existence of a partnership is admissible, and ordinarily the question is for the jury."

The principal basis for the estoppel in the case before us is the representations contained in the Dun & Bradstreet reports (plaintiff's exhibits W and RR). One making statements to an agency dealing in commercial information must know that the information will be communicated to his prospective creditors, who are its subscribers, and such communication is accordingly deemed to be made with his knowledge and consent. [Citations.] Clearly, then, proper proof that Ferris made representations of partnership to Dun & Bradstreet, Inc., would amply sustain the judgment. In this connection, Ferris complains of the exclusion of

testimony of himself and Edward as to what representations were made to Theyson during the course of the interview. Inasmuch as Edward had testified previously that he had not been present during the interview, there could be no material error in excluding any testimony which he might offer on that subject.

* * *

On the other hand, there is no apparent reason why a disinterested representative of a reputable commercial agency should misrepresent or color the truth. The salability of his employer's service and his position depend upon the accuracy of the reports. These reports are compiled by a regular procedure and enjoy a good reputation in the business community. [Citation.] This, coupled with the statement containing representations of partnership, the signing of which was admitted by Ferris, conclusively indicates that the representations were made as claimed. * * *

MILLARD v. NEWMARK & COMPANY

(1966) 24 A.D.2d 333, 266 N.Y.S.2d 254.

STEVENS, J.: Defendants appeal from an order entered July 8, 1965, insofar as such order denied defendants' motion to dismiss the complaint and each cause of action therein, and to strike certain allegations thereof, and further denying defendants' motion for reargument.

Plaintiffs are 32 limited partners, or approximately 30% of a total of about 100 such partners, of Terrace Associates, Ltd. (hereinafter Terrace). They bring this action individually and as limited partners on behalf of themselves and all others similarly situated, and in the right of Terrace.

The individual defendants Maurice S. Handler, Horodas and Karpas are general partners of Terrace. Defendant Newmark & Company (Newmark) is a New York partnership composed of six of the individual defendants, not including the three persons above named, though there is alleged to be a degree of relationship between at least two of them and certain members of the partnership. Defendant Austin Newmark, Inc. (Austin Newmark) is a New York corporation largely owned by Newmark.

On or about October 24, 1957, Newmark contracted to purchase the Terrace Motor Hotel (the Motel) in Austin, Texas. The contract was assigned to defendants Maurice S. Handler and Karpas who, as landlords, entered into a fifteen-year lease of the Motel with Newmark as tenant, at an annual base rental of $330,000. The contract of purchase was assigned to Terrace which took title to the Motel in May 1958. At some point the lease was taken over by the Sheraton interests (Sheraton) which operated thereunder until about July 1959, when it discontinued operations and transferred the lease to Austin Newmark. A prospectus was issued to the public in January 1958 by Newmark, a real estate syndication of the Motel was worked out, and these plaintiffs and others became limited partners in the venture. Sometime about May 1964 the venture failed and there was a foreclosure of the Terrace partnership property by the mortgagee.

This action was commenced in July 1964. The complaint sets forth five causes of action charging false misrepresentations, fraud and misconduct by the general partners and others, and sought restitution of assets to Terrace; damages for wrongs done to Terrace and damages for wrongs done to plaintiffs as investors. Plaintiffs purport to bring a class action on behalf of all the limited partners, including those not named or joined. The false representations were allegedly contained in the printed prospectus. Defendants moved to dismiss the representative and derivative phases of the complaint alleging lack of capacity, and also contending certain parts of the first three causes of action were time

barred. Defendants also sought an amended complaint with causes separately stated and numbered.

Without attempting to analyze in detail the various charges, basic to the disposition of this appeal is resolution of the question— may the limited partners maintain this action as a class action?

Limited partnerships were unknown to the common law. They are solely creatures of statute [citations]. " '[T]he object to be accomplished * * * is to protect the special partner, and exempt him from a general liability, and to place his capital alone at the peril of the business.' [Citations.] "[L]imited partners as such shall not be bound by the obligations of the partnership" (Partnership Law § 90), and they have only such rights, duties, obligations, etc., as the statute may provide (Partnership Law [Limited Partnership] §§ 90–115). It should be noted that a limited partner is expressly given "(1) the same rights as a general partner to (a) [h]ave the partnership books kept at the principal place of business of the partnership, and at all times to inspect and copy any of them. (b) Have on demand true and full information of all things affecting the partnership, *and a formal account of partnership affairs* whenever circumstances render it just and reasonable, and (c) Have dissolution and winding up by decree of court. (2) A limited partner shall have the right to receive a share of the profits or other compensation by way of income, and to the return of his contribution as provided in sections one hundred and four and one hundred and five of this article" (Partnership Law § 99, emphasis supplied). Section one hundred and four deals with the compensation of a limited partner, while section one hundred and five deals with the question of withdrawal or reduction of a limited partner's contribution.

From the foregoing it is obvious that a limited partner is not in the hopeless position where he must only suffer in silence when an alleged wrong occurs. He has a right of full and free access to information contained in the partnership books, and of all things affecting the partnership, as well as a right to a formal accounting. Even a stockholder has no right to an accounting but must have recourse to a derivative action on behalf of and for the benefit of the corporation. Of course a limited partner, unlike a stockholder, has no right to a counsel fee if he prevails in the action. A limited partner also has a right to dissolution in addition to his rights as an individual against third parties. In brief, a limited partner has such rights and only such rights as the law and his contract affords [citation].

Section 115, Partnership Law, which provides "[a] contributor, unless he is a general partner, is not a proper party to proceedings by or against a partnership, except where the object is to enforce a limited partner's right against or liability to the partnership." It does not restrict or limit the rights enumerated in Section 99. It relates to claims by or against the partnership, and declares the circumstances under which a limited partner may be or may become a necessary or proper party to litigation. Even though a limited partnership may be regarded as a distinct entity for the purposes of pleading [citation], and CPLR 1025 provides, in part, "[t]wo or more persons conducting business as a partnership may sue or be sued in the partnership name," there is no right in a limited partner to sue in a derivative capacity on behalf of the partnership (Partnership Law [Limited Partnership] § 115). Nor does a limited partner "become liable as a general partner unless, in addition to the exercise of his rights and powers as a limited partner, he takes part in the control of the business" [citations].

Upon withdrawal or reduction of his contribution, "In the absence of any statement in the certificate to the contrary or the consent of all members, a limited partner, irrespective of the nature of his contribution, has only the right to demand and receive cash in return for his contribution" (Partnership Law § 105(3); see also §§ 99, 112, 115). Only a general partner is authorized to act in behalf of the partnership [citations].

While a limited partner has been compared to a shareholder of a corporation (Klebanow v. New York Produce Exchange, 2 Cir., 344 F.2d 294) and has been characterized as having "quasi-shareholder status" [citation] the fact remains that the legislature has not seen fit to endow him with the status of a shareholder, or to confer upon him the rights, powers and obligations of a shareholder. It is not part of the judicial function to do so. For an extensive discussion of the Klebanow case and the status of limited partners see "Standing of Limited Partners to Sue Derivatively", 65 Columbia Law Review, 1463. The writer discusses the analogy of a limited partner as a creditor as well as the contrasting view of a limited partner as a stockholder or trust beneficiary. He asserts, however, "the limited partner is perhaps most aptly analogized to the holder of preferred stock whose capacity to sue derivatively has been widely accepted" (p. 1479). However, it should be borne in mind, as previously pointed out, that the legislature which created the limited partnership took great care to enumerate the rights, privileges and benefits accruing to a limited partner. While allowing certain economic advantages to such partner, he is not at the same time exposed to the unlimited liability of a general partner. In the corporate form the corporation is an entity recognized by law for the purpose of bringing or defending an action as distinct from the individuals who comprise it. New York has long recognized the right of shareholders to maintain a derivative action. The contention that the limited partnership should be recognized as analogous to the corporate entity by a similar right in the contributor or limited partner to maintain a derivative action is presumably based on an equitable concept in positive law. The rights of the limited partner are increased but there is no corresponding increase in responsibility or potential liability.

The rights of a limited partner have been defined with precision in the Partnership Law heretofore referred to. CPLR 1005 has neither extended nor limited those rights. Each limited partner has a right to any share of the profits and to a return of his contribution (Partnership Law § 99). In the case before us plaintiffs seek general damages for all limited partners (not a right or incident of the relationship), the return of their investment, an accounting, and expenses. The nature of the action precludes any conclusion that the "question is one of a common or general interest" (CPLR 1005(a)) or that the interests of each and every limited partner is common or identical so as to authorize a single common action [citations]. If there was wrongdoing each limited partner suffered a separate wrong and has a separate cause of action.

The basis for the alleged misrepresentations as the inducing cause for investment is the prospectus which was circulated publicly. Aside from the fact that such prospectus need not have been the inducing cause for each and every one of the limited partners or influenced each to the same extent, there is grave doubt that a class action for fraud could be premised thereon [citation]. If there was fraud in the inducement, the wrong done was to each limited partner individually, and his cause of action is separate and individual [citations].

* * *

Accordingly, the order appealed from is reversed on the law and the motion to dismiss the complaint granted, with leave to replead, and with costs and disbursements to appellants.

Reversed.

PROBLEMS

1. Clark owned a vacant lot. Bird was engaged in building houses. An oral agreement was entered into between Clark and Bird whereby Bird was to erect a house on the lot. Upon the sale of the house and lot, Bird was to have his money first. Clark was then to have the agreed value of the lot, and the profits were to be equally divided. Did a partnership exist?

2. A and B are joint owners of shares of stock of a corporation, have a joint bank account and have purchased and own as tenants in common a piece of real estate. They share equally the dividends paid on the stock, the interest on the bank account, and the rent from the real estate. Without the knowledge of A, B makes a trip to inspect the real estate and on his way runs over X. X sues A and B for his personal injuries, joining A as defendant on the theory that A was B's partner. Is A liable?

3. Smith, Jones and Brown were creditors of White, who operated a grain elevator known as White's Elevator. White was heavily involved and was about to fail when the three creditors mentioned agreed to take a conveyance of his elevator property and pay all the debts. It was also agreed that White should continue as manager of the business at a salary of $500 per month and that all profits of the business were to be paid to Smith, Jones and Brown. It was further agreed that they could dispense with White's services at any time and he was also at liberty to quit when he pleased. White accepted the proposition and continued to operate the business as before, buying and selling grain, incurring obligations and borrowing money at the bank in his own name for the business. He did, however, tell the banker of the transaction with Smith, Jones and Brown and other former creditors of the business knew of it. It worked successfully and for several years paid substantial profits,—enough so that Smith, Jones and Brown had received back nearly all that they had originally advanced. Were Smith, Jones and Brown partners?

4. X, Y and Z formed a partnership for the purpose of betting on boxing matches. X and Y would become friendly with various boxers and offer them bribes to lose certain bouts. Z would then place large bets, using money contributed by all three, and would collect the winnings. After Z had accumulated a large sum of

money, X and Y demanded their share but Z refused to make any split. X and Y then brought suit in a court of equity to compel Z to account for the profits of the partnership. What decision?

5. A, B and C agree that A and B will form and conduct a partnership business and that C will become a partner in two years. C agrees to lend the firm $5,000 and take 10% of the profits in lieu of interest. Without C's knowledge A and B tell X that C is a partner and X, relying on C's sound financial status, gives the firm credit. Later the firm becomes insolvent and X seeks to hold C liable as a partner. Should X succeed?

6. S refuses an invitation to become a partner of P and R in the retail grocery business. Nevertheless, P inserts an advertisement in the local newspaper representing S as their partner. S takes no steps to deny the existence of a partnership between them. X, who extended credit to the firm, seeks to hold S liable as a partner. Decision?

7. John Palmer and Henry Morrison formed the partnership of Palmer & Morrison for the management of the Huntington Hotel. The partnership agreement provided that Palmer would contribute $10,000 and be a general partner and Morrison would contribute $5,000 and be a limited partner. Palmer was to manage the dining and cocktail rooms and Morrison was to manage the rest of the hotel. Nanette, a popular French singer, who knew nothing of the partnership affairs, appeared for four weeks in the Blue Room at the hotel and was not paid her salary of $8,000. Subsequently, Palmer and Morrison had a difference of opinion and Palmer bought Morrison's interest in the partnership for $3,000. Palmer later went into bankruptcy. Nanette sued Morrison for $8,000. For how much, if anything, is Morrison liable?

CHAPTER 31

FORMATION, FIRM NAME, AND PARTNERSHIP PROPERTY

Introductory. The formation of a partnership is very simple and may be done consciously or unconsciously. Needless to say, a partnership has a greater likelihood of success when it is formed consciously and carefully. The association of two or more persons as co-owners in carrying on a business enterprise may result from an oral or written agreement between the parties, or it may be such an informal arrangement that the agreement is not definitely articulated but left to subsequent expression. Persons become partners by associating themselves in business together as co-owners. Whether their agreement is simple or elaborate, definite or indefinite, cleancut and fair or obscure and productive of discord, is of importance principally to the partners. The existence of the relationship depends upon the agreement and the association in business, not upon the degree of care, intelligence, study or investigation which may have preceded the making of the agreement.

Articles of Partnership. In the interest of a better understanding of the terms and scope of the partnership agreement, it is preferable to have the contract between the parties reduced to writing. The written agreement creating the partnership is referred to as the articles of partnership, and among the more important items usually contained therein are:

(1) The firm name and the identity of the partners;

(2) The nature and scope of the partnership business;

(3) Duration of the partnership;

(4) The capital contributions of each partner and whether in money or property;

(5) The division of profits and sharing of losses;

(6) The amount of time that each partner agrees to devote to the business and the duties of each partner in the management;

(7) A provision for salaries and drawing accounts of partners, if desired;

(8) Restrictions, if any, upon the authority of particular partners to bind the firm;

(9) The right, if desired, of a partner to withdraw from the firm and the terms, conditions and notice requirements in the event of such withdrawal;

(10) A provision for continuation of the business by the remaining partners, if desired, in the event of the death of a partner or dissolution otherwise caused, and a statement of the method or formula for appraisal and payment of the interest of the deceased or former partner.

Articles of partnership are not necessary to the formation or existence of a partnership, but the advantage of having a written contract tailored to meet the requirements of a particular situation and encompassing the full understanding and agreement of the partners is obvious. It serves to minimize, if not entirely eliminate, a common cause of friction, namely, disputes as to the precise terms of the agreement between the partners.

Who May Become Partners. Any natural person having full contractual capacity may enter into a partnership. Inasmuch as a minor has capacity to act as principal or agent, he may become a partner, although he has the privilege of disaffirming the partnership agreement at any time before reaching majority and of avoiding all personal liability to partnership creditors. Upon disaffirmance and withdrawal from the partnership, the minor is entitled to the return of his capital contribution and his share in the profits, unless the remaining assets of the partnership are insufficient to pay all of the debts and obligations of the firm. In such case, the minor is not entitled to his capital contribution but only to such portion thereof as may remain after partnership creditors have been paid or provision made for their payment. A disaffirming minor does not share pari passu with partnership creditors.

The position of an insane person who enters into a partnership is substantially the same as that of a minor except that his insanity may afford his co-partners a ground for seeking dissolution by court decree as provided in Section 32 of the Uniform Act (Appendix B). The contract of a person who has been declared or adjudicated insane in a judicial proceeding is void, and such person may therefore not become a partner. A partnership agreement with an enemy alien is also void.

A married woman by virtue of the statute removing her common-law disabilities has legal capacity to enter into a business partnership. In Texas, however, a married woman before acquiring the capacity to become a partner is first required to obtain the removal of the disabilities of coverture by compliance with certain statutory formalities.

A trust estate as distinguished from a trustee is incapable of becoming a partner. This is because a trust estate is not a person.

A corporation is defined as a "person" in Section 2 of the Uniform Act and is therefore legally capable of entering into a partnership. This means that the law of partnerships does not disenable a corporation from becoming a partner. However, the law of corporations must also be considered, and the general rule is that, in the absence of express charter and statutory authorization, a corporation cannot enter into a partnership. A corporation is a creature of limited powers, and, by statute, the business and affairs of a corporation are managed by a board of directors elected by its shareholders. As a member of a partnership, a corporation would find itself in a situation where its property and affairs would be subject to direction and control by its co-partners and not by its directors and officers, contrary to the public policy of the State of incorporation. It should be noted that a corporation may engage in a joint venture.

Incidence of Statute of Frauds. The Statute of Frauds does not expressly apply to a contract for the formation of a partnership, and therefore no writing is required in order to create the relationship. The promise of an incoming partner to assume existing debts incurred in the prior operation of the business is not within Section 4 of the Statute as a promise to answer for the debt or default of another, because such promise is made not to the creditors but to the debtor or debtors. It is a third party creditor beneficiary type of contract. However, a contract to form a partnership to continue for a period longer than one year is within the statute and requires a writing in order to be enforceable. To the extent that such an oral agreement is acted upon, the partners have formed a partnership at will terminable at any time by either or any party.

A contract for the transfer of an interest in real estate to or by a partnership, or by a member or prospective member thereof, is governed by the Statute of Frauds and requires a writing to be enforceable. However, the statute does not bar an accounting suit brought by a partner to recover his share of the proceeds of fully consummated transactions in real estate carried on pursuant to an orally constituted partnership or joint venture.

With respect to the applicability of Section 17 of the Statute to an agreement by a partner to assign to co-partners or to third parties his interest in the partnership, such an interest is a chose in action and is not within the term "goods, wares and merchandise." If the pertinent statute does not include choses in action, an agreement to assign an interest in the partnership is not within the statute.

Firm Name. In the interest of acquiring and retaining good will a partnership should have a firm name. It is more desirable for the partners to provide their business enterprise with a name than to wait for the public to do this for them. The name selected by the partners should not be identical with or deceptively similar to the name of any other existing business concern. It may be the name of the partners or of any one of them, followed by the words "and Company," as "Smith, Jones and Company" or "William Smith and Company." It may simply be the names of the partners, as "Anderson, O'Connor and Goldsmith." The partners may decide to operate the business under a fictitious name, such as "The Atomic Restaurant," or "Gem Theater," or "Peerless Tailors." In certain States it is unlawful for an individual or partnership to conduct a business under a name ending with the word "Company" or an abbreviation thereof unless followed by the words "Not Incorporated," or "Unincorporated," or "Not Inc.," or some similar indication that the company is not a corporation. A partnership may not use a name which would represent it to be a corporation.

Assumed Name Statutes. Forty-five States have enacted statutes which require any person or persons conducting or transacting any business under an assumed or fictitious name to file in a designated public office a certificate setting forth the name under which the business is conducted and the true or real names and addresses of all persons conducting the business as partners or proprietors. The purpose of such a statute is to disclose and make available to the public the real names of all parties who see fit to deal or trade with the public under an assumed or fictitious name. The statutes are generally penal in nature and provide penalties of fine or imprisonment, or both, for violations. In California, Colorado, Oklahoma, Oregon, and Pennsylvania, no action upon contract can be maintained by an individual or a partnership who has failed to comply with the statute. In other States, namely, Arizona, Michigan, Minnesota, Montana, South Dakota, Vermont and Washington the failure to file the required certificate may be cured, with respect to the right to institute a suit, provided that the certificate is filed prior to the institution of suit even though it was not filed at the time the cause of action arose.

Where a partnership is conducted under an assumed or fictitious name and one of the partners withdraws the partnership is thereby dissolved, and if a new partnership continues to operate under an assumed name a new certificate must be filed. This rule applies also to the addition of a member to an existing partnership being conducted under an assumed name. Ordinarily, it is the duty of a new partnership to file a new certificate. However, in some States the retiring partner is required by statute to file a certificate evidencing his withdrawal.

Partnership Capital. The sum total of the money and property contributed by the partners and dedicated to permanent use in the enterprise is the partnership capital. Except upon dissolution no partner may withdraw any part of his capital contribution without the consent of all the partners. Partnership property is the sum of all of the partnership assets including capital contributions, and may vary in amount from day to day or even from hour to hour, while partnership capital is a fixed amount.

A partner, by the terms of the agreement, may contribute no capital but only his skill and services, or a partner may contribute the use of certain property rather than the property itself. For example, a partner who owns a store building may contribute to the partnership the use of the building but not the building itself. The building is therefore not partnership property, and the amount of capital contributed by this partner is the capitalized value of the reasonable annual rental of the building for the duration of the partnership agreement or for the remaining economic life of the building, whichever is the lesser.

Although in accounting practice, partnership profits or surplus are frequently included in the capital account, a clear differentiation should be made between them. Likewise, a loan by a partner to the firm should be distinguished from capital. A partner is entitled to his share of the profits and to repayment of money advanced as a loan without any new agreement with his co-partners, but a withdrawal of capital requires a new agreement. Furthermore, upon dissolution, a debt owing to a partner by the partnership has priority over the rights of partners to return of capital.

Tenancy in Partnership. As provided in Section 24 of the Uniform Act, the property rights of a partner are (1) his rights in specific partnership property, (2) his interest in the partnership, and (3) his right to participate in the management. By definition, partners must be co-owners of partnership property. The proper description of this type of co-ownership is tenancy in partnership. A partner's ownership interest in any specific item of partnership property is not that of an outright owner, joint tenant, or tenant in common but is that of a tenant in partnership. (Section 25, Uniform Act.) This species of ownership exists only in a partnership, and the principal characteristics of a tenancy in partnership are:

(1) Each partner has an equal right with his co-partners to possess partnership property for partnership purposes, and he has no right to possess it for any other purpose without the consent of his co-partners.

(2) A partner may not make an individual assignment of his right in specific partnership property.

(3) A partner's interest in specific partnership property is not subject to attachment or execution at the instance of his individual creditors. It is subject to attachment or execution only on a claim against the partnership.

(4) None of the partners may assert any claim to specific partnership property under the homestead or exemption laws.

(5) Upon the death of a partner, his right in specific partnership property vests in the surviving partner or partners. Upon the death of the last surviving partner, his right in such property vests in his legal representative.

(6) A partner's right in specific partnership property is not subject to dower, curtesy, or allowances to widows, heirs or next of kin.

In addition to owning as a tenant in partnership every specific item of partnership property, each partner has an interest in the partnership which is defined as his share of the profits and surplus, and is expressly stated to be personal property. (Section 26, Uniform Act.)

Possession of Partnership Property. Under Section 25(2) (a) of the Uniform Act, unless otherwise provided in the partnership agreement, each partner has an equal right with his co-partners to possess specific partnership property for partnership purposes. In certain partnerships the right to possession and management is by agreement especially given to a managing partner or partners. Although a partner may wrongfully obtain or retain possession of specific partnership property, his co-partners may not maintain against him a possessory action, such as replevin, to recover such property.

The exclusive remedy is an accounting suit in equity. Such suit is ordinarily brought in connection with or to effect a dissolution and winding up of the affairs of the partnership.

Acquisition of Title to Real Estate. At common law a deed of conveyance of real estate in which the grantee was the assumed or fictitious name of a partnership did not pass legal title to the real estate for the reason that a partnership is not a legal entity. If the name of the grantee included the surname of a partner such partner became vested with legal title to the real estate which he held as trustee for the partnership.

Under Section 8(3) of the Uniform Act a conveyance of real estate may be made to a partnership in the partnership name. Real estate so conveyed may be subsequently transferred by the partnership only by a deed wherein the partnership so named is the grantor.

Title to real estate which is properly a partnership asset, as where purchased with partnership funds or specifically made a capital contribution, may stand in the name of an individual partner or a third party. Under the doctrine of a resulting trust or a constructive trust, the partnership is the equitable owner of such real estate.

A question may arise whether real estate owned by a partner before formation of the partnership and used in the partnership business shall be deemed a capital contribution and asset of the partnership. The mere fact that legal title to the land remains unchanged is not conclusive evidence that it has not become a partnership asset. The ownership of the property may be determined by the partnership agreement, or if not expressly covered by the agreement, by evidence of the intention of the parties. An intention that real estate is partnership property may be inferred from any of the following facts: (1) the property was improved with partnership funds; (2) the property was carried on the books of the partnership as an asset; (3) taxes, liens or expenses, such as insurance, were paid by the partnership; (4) income or proceeds of the property were treated as partnership funds; (5) admissions or declarations by the partners.

Equitable Conversion. In order to avoid the application of certain well-established rules of real property law to real estate owned by a partnership, the courts invented the fiction that partnership real estate is personal property. This is known as the doctrine of equitable conversion. The law, of course, cannot change the nature of real estate but, by treating it as personal property, the widow of a deceased partner does not have dower rights in partnership real estate, nor does title to the property descend to his heirs at law. This convenient fiction solved a practical difficulty and has been adopted by the Uniform Act (Sections 25, 26, 31, 38). For purposes of winding up the affairs of a dissolved partnership, real estate belonging to the partnership is treated as though it were personal property. For equitable purposes, it is converted into personal property.

CASES

SMITH v. HENSLEY

(1962 Ky.) 354 S.W.2d 744, 98 A.L.R.2d 340.

STANLEY, COMMISSIONER. The action is by Clyde Hensley, one of eight partners constituting the firm of Mary Gail Coal Company, against all the partners, including himself by name, to recover damages for the value of a motor truck owned individually by the plaintiff, which he alleges was destroyed by the negligence of employees of the partnership.

* * *

On June 10, 1958, plaintiff's driver had filled his gasoline tank preparatory to hauling a load of coal to the tipple when gasoline became ignited and fire destroyed the truck. The plaintiff alleged this was caused by the defendants' negligently permitting gasoline to be spilled from the pumps and to remain exposed on the ground. The defendants pleaded sole or contributory negligence of the plaintiff's driver or that the loss was an unavoidable casualty. Upon a verdict judgment for $4,000 was entered for the plaintiff against his seven partners.

The defendants have contended that the plaintiff may not maintain the action against his co-partners. Specifically, they say the manager and other employees of the mining partnership were agents of the plaintiff as well as agents of the defendants, and their negligence, if any, was imputable to the plaintiff as well as to the defendants. The record fails to disclose the articles or contract of partnership, but we may assume that it was a general, ordinary partnership, without limitations or reservations inter se.

The situation presents a novel question in the field of partnership law.

Various legalistic concepts could be invoked as a basis for denying a right of recovery to the plaintiff. One would be that a partner cannot sue the partnership because a litigant cannot sue himself. Another would be that if negligence of the partnership employees is to be imputed to the defendant partnership to establish a basis for liability, by the same token the negligence must be imputed to the plaintiff so as to bar recovery.

It is our opinion, however, that under a realistic approach, seeking to achieve substantial justice, the plaintiff should be held entitled to maintain the action.

It is true that an action at law *ordinarily* is not maintainable between a partner and his firm. [Citations.] But the situation here presented is not an ordinary one. The law is

well settled that a partner who has paid an obligation of the firm out of his own funds may obtain contribution from his copartners. [Citation.] Also, a partner is entitled to reimbursement from the firm for losses suffered by him in the ordinary and proper course of the firm affairs. [Citations.]

*   *   *

The law is well settled that if one partner negligently damages the property of another partner, the latter may recover from the former. [Citation.] Thus there is no basic public policy or rule of law to the effect that a partner who uses his own property in connection with the partnership business does so completely at his own risk. Why then, should he be held to assume the sole risks when the damage is done by a partnership *employee* rather than by another member of the partnership? It is a common practice for partnerships to carry on their business through employes. The practical realities of the business world dictate that the partners should share the loss of damage to property resulting from the negligence of the partnership employees, regardless of who owns the property.

If it be considered, as appears actually to have been the case here, that the use of the plaintiff's truck was not *in* the partnership business but was a collateral use in connection with an independent contract between the plaintiff and the partnership, then there is more reason to impose a duty on the partners to share the loss, because there is no basis upon which it could be said that the plaintiff contributed his truck to the use of the partnership with an intent of the parties that he would assume all risk of loss.

We hold the action is maintainable.

*   *   *

The judgment is against the plaintiff's seven co-partners by name "doing business as Mary Gail Coal Company." This recognizes that the liability was that of the partnership firm, even though the plaintiff was a partner. [Citation.] The negligence was that of the firm's employees, acting within the scope of their employment. The partners, who are liable jointly and severally (KRS 362.220(1)) for obligations of the firm should bear their respective proportionate shares as may be determined by the contract of partnership. [Citation.] The plaintiff, Hensley, must bear his part. So the judgment should provide that satisfaction be out of the assets of the partnership, as an "association" (KRS 362.175), before resorting to the individual members thereof. [Citations.]

The judgment may be so modified and as modifed it is affirmed.

CENTRAL TRUST & SAFE CO. v. RESPASS

(1902) 112 Ky. 606, 66 S.W. 421, 56 L.R.A. 479.

[Action for the settlement of partnership accounts by J. B. Respass against the trust company, as executor of the will of his deceased partner, S. L. Sharp. The partners owned and managed a racing stable and, in addition, were engaged in book making, or accepting wagers on race horses. At the time Sharp died, $4,724, representing the undistributed profits of the book making business, was on deposit in Sharp's personal bank account. The trial court held that Respass was entitled to one-half of the profits from the bookmaking business and the executor appeals.]

DURELLE, J. * * * A closer question is presented by the claim for a division of the "bank roll." This $4,724 was, as found by the chancellor, earned by the firm composed of Respass and Sharp in carrying on an illegal business—that of "bookmaking"—in the State of Illinois. But though this amount

had been won upon horse races in Chicago, it is claimed that, though secured illegally, "the transaction has been closed, and the appellee Respass is only seeking his share from the realized profits from the illegal contracts, if they are illegal." On the other hand, it is claimed for appellant, the executor, that, as to the bank roll, this proceeding is a bill for an accounting of profits from the business of gambling.

It does not seem to be seriously contended that the business of "bookmaking," whether carried on in Chicago or in this Commonwealth, was legal, for by the common law of this country all wagers are illegal. [Citation.] One of the most interesting cases upon this subject is that of Everet v. Williams —the celebrated Highwaymen's Case—an account of which is given in 9 Law Quart.Rev., 197 [England]. That was a bill for an accounting of a partnership in the business of highwaymen, though the true nature of the partnership was veiled in ambiguous language. The bill set up the partnership between defendant and plaintiff, who was "skilled in dealing in several sorts of commodities;" that they "proceeded jointly in the said dealing with good success on Hounslow Heath, where they dealt with a gentleman for a gold watch;" that defendant had informed plaintiff that Finchley "was a good and convenient place to deal in," such commodities being "very plenty" there, and if they were to deal there "it would be almost all gain to them;" that they accordingly "dealt with several gentlemen for divers watches, rings, swords, canes, hats, cloaks, horses, bridles, saddles, and other things, to the value of £200 and upwards;" that a gentleman of Blackheath had several articles which defendant thought "might be had for a little or no money in case they could prevail on the said gentleman to part with the said things;" and that, "after some small discourse with the said gentleman," the said things were dealt for "at a very cheap rate."

The dealings were alleged to have amounted to £2,000 and upward. This case, while interesting, from the views it gives of the audacity of the parties and their solicitors, sheds little light upon the legal questions involved, for the bill was condemned for scandal and impertinence; the solicitors were taken into custody, and "fyned" £50 each for "reflecting upon the honor and dignity of this court;" the counsel whose name was signed to the bill was required to pay the costs; and both the litigants were subsequently hanged, at Tyburn and Maidstone, respectively; while one of the solicitors was transported. [Citations.] * * *

In Watson v. Fletcher, 7 Grat., 1, the business of the firm had been the operation of a faro bank. One of the partners having died, the survivor sought an accounting of profits earned. The syllabus reads: "A court of equity will not lend its aid for the settlement and adjustment of the transactions of a partnership for gambling. Nor will it give relief to either partner against the other, founded on transactions arising out of such partnership, whether for profits, losses, expenses, contribution, or reimbursement." * * *

We conclude that in this country, in the case of a partnership in a business confessedly illegal, whatever may be the doctrine where there has been a new contract in relation to, or a new investment of, the profits of such illegal business, and whatever may be the doctrine as to the rights or liabilities of a third person who assumes obligations with respect to such profits, or by law becomes responsible therefor, the decided weight of authority is that a court of equity will not entertain a bill for an accounting.

The judgment of the chancellor is therefore reversed, and the cause remanded, with directions to enter a judgment in accordance with this opinion.

STATE v. PETERSON

(1957) 232 La. 931, 95 So.2d 608.

HAMLIN, J. The State of Louisiana appeals from a judgment of the trial court sustaining a motion to quash the information filed against the defendant.

By amended bill of information, the defendant, Eric Peterson, was charged with the theft of $7,000 from the Baton Rouge Millworks, a partnership composed of Eric Peterson and Herman Green. He applied for a bill of particulars, praying for the following information:

1. Was the money in the possession of Herman Green?

2. Under what circumstances did he take or come into possession of the money?

3. If money was not in the possession of Green, in what bank and under whose name was it deposited?

4. What business relationship existed between Green and defendant prior to the alleged theft?

5. Was the partnership agreement written or oral, and when was the partnership formed and when was it dissolved?

The State answered that the partnership was formed on February 20, 1956, by oral agreement of the partners, Eric Peterson and Herman Green; that the money was deposited in the Capital Bank and Trust Company, Baton Rouge, Louisiana, in the names of Eric Peterson and Herman Green; that the alleged theft, consisting of one misappropriation from the Capital Bank and Trust Company, occurred on or about May 18, 1956; and, that there had been no accounting or dissolution of the partnership.

* * *

LSA–Revised Statutes 14:67 provides:

"Theft is the misappropriation or taking of anything of value which belongs *to another,* either without the consent of the other to the misappropriation or taking, or by means of fraudulent conduct, practices or representations. An intent to deprive the other permanently of whatever may be the subject of the misappropriation or taking is essential." (Italics ours.) * * *

It is incumbent that we decide whether the word "another", employed in the above statute, includes a commercial partnership of which the accused is a partner. * * *

It is the contention of the State that since a partnership is a legal entity, it necessarily follows that a person—in this particular case, Eric Peterson—can commit a theft from a partnership. It argues that under LSA–Revised Statutes 14:2 a partnership falls under the definition of the word "another".

Partnerships are divided, as to their object, into commercial partnerships and ordinary partnerships. LSA–Civil Code, Article 2824.

LSA–Civil Code, Article 2872, set forth the extent of liability of partners as follows:

"Ordinary partners are not bound in solido for the debts of the partnership, and no one of them can bind his partners, unless they have given him power so to do, either specially or by the articles of partnership.

"Commercial partners are bound in solido for the debts of the partnership."

* * *

Although the liability of the individual partners of a commercial partnership comes into existence and becomes enforceable after the dissolution of the partnership, it follows that they are still eventually liable for unpaid partnership debts. Since the liability is in solido, any commercial partner is faced with the eventual obligation of having to pay all outstanding claims against a dissolved partnership. Therein lies the difference between a partner of a commercial partnership and a stockholder of a corporation whose liability is limited (LSA–C.C., Article 437).

Therefore, if a man can be held liable for an entire debt of a commercial partnership of which he is a member, the commercial partnership cannot be classed as "another" apart from himself.

* * *

A member of a partnership, who believes that his co-partner is withdrawing partnership funds and appropriating them to his own use, has his remedy by bringing a suit for an accounting and a dissolution of the partnership; or, in certain exceptional cases, by direct action against his partner. [Citations.] His recourse is not by instigating a criminal prosecution against one who can be held equally liable with him on any partnership obligation. [Citations.] His remedy is specifically provided for in the LSA–Civil Code, Book 3, Chapter 3, Sec. 1—Of The Obligations of Partners Towards Each Other—Articles 2858, 2859, 2860, 2861, 2862, and 2865.

For the reasons assigned, the judgment of the trial court, sustaining the motion to quash and discharging the defendant, is affirmed.

JOHNSON v. HILL

(1965) 1 Ariz.App. 290, 402 P.2d 225.

KRUCKER, C. J. This appeal involves a dispute arising out of a medical partnership. The appellant (plaintiff below), Dr. Johnson, sought an accounting for his share of the net worth of the partnership from the defendants, Doctors Holbrook, Stephens, Hill and Goodin. The lower court, sitting without a jury, found for the defendants. * * *

In 1934, Dr. Holbrook entered into a medical partnership with Dr. Hill in Tucson, Arizona. Dr. Stephens was admitted into the partnership in 1946. In 1950, Dr. Johnson, the plaintiff, was employed on salary by the then existing partnership. In 1960, Dr. Johnson became the fourth member in the partnership. Articles of partnership were drawn up, giving Dr. Johnson a 23.5% share of net profits. Dr. Goodin was made a partner on January 1, 1961, by oral agreement with the unanimous consent of the other partners. It was this oral agreement that caused the dispute in the settling of accounts when Dr. Johnson left the partnership. Plaintiff contends that this oral agreement revoked the written articles, and therefore he is entitled to a percentage of the net worth of the partnership. * * *

Two provisions of the articles of partnership of 1960 are of importance in this case:

"Article III—Contingencies

1. With the unanimous consent of the then existing partners, new partners may be admitted into the partnership at any time. Each new partner shall adopt and subscribe to these Articles by affixing his signature to "Schedule A—Partnership Interests" (hereunto annexed and by reference made a part hereof, and shall adopt and subscribe to any other terms and conditions which may then be imposed.

2. * * * Upon such withdrawal, he shall be entitled to receive, and there shall be assigned to him forthwith in full payment for his interest in the partnership, only such policy or policies of life insurance as is or are then being carried on his life by the partnership, * * *."

On January 1, 1961, when Dr. Goodin was unanimously accepted as a partner, he did not sign the articles of 1960, nor were they ever signed by him. Plaintiff thus contends that as of January 1, 1961, there was a new partnership based on the oral agreement, and the formation of this new partnership revoked the written articles of partnership. * * *

It is a well-established general rule than an existing partnership is dissolved and a new partnership is formed whenever a partner retires or a new one is admitted. In other words, every change in the personnel of a firm works a dissolution. [Citation.] This general rule would apply unless something in the agreement provides otherwise. The written agreement in this case did provide for admission of new partners, but said provision was not complied with.

This leads us to the conclusion that upon Dr. Goodin's admittance the old partnership of January 1, 1960 to January 1, 1961, consisting of Doctors Holbrook, Hill, Stephens, and Johnson, was terminated as a matter of law. [Citations.] Thereafter, a new partnership was formed consisting of Doctors Holbrook, Hill, Stephens, Johnson, and Goodin. There is no argument that a partnership may be formed by oral agreement, [citation] in absence of statutory regulation.

The question therefore remains, was there evidence at the trial to show that the new partnership by oral agreement was to exist and abide by the written articles of the terminated partnership.

* * *

In the present case, the plaintiff, Dr. Johnson, testified that the written agreement was not discussed at the meeting in which Dr. Goodin was admitted to the partnership. He also testified that there was no conversation that under the oral agreement they would operate according to the provisions of the written agreement. He testified that a new paper was handed around but that he only noticed the new percentages.

In contrast, Dr. Goodin testified that a new written agreement (after Dr. Johnson had departed) was the same as they had always been under as far as he knew. Dr. Holbrook testified that he brought a copy of the old written agreement to the meeting to point out that under the new arrangement they would continue to operate under the written agreement. Doctors Stephens and Hill corroborated Dr. Holbrook in that the latter did have a copy of the written agreement with him. They also testified that all the old partners were to bring their copy in so that Dr. Goodin could sign them.

It is thus apparent to the Court that there is conflicting evidence as to the Doctors' intention concerning the written Articles. The lower court chose to believe the defendants. Upon a reading of the transcript of testimony, we find ample evidence to support the finding of the lower court.

* * *

The judgment of the lower court is affirmed.

CULTRA v. CULTRA

(1949) 188 Tenn. 506, 221 S.W.2d 533.

BURNETT, J. This case presents the question of whether or not the real estate owned by a partnership, purchased by said partnership with partnership funds for partnership purposes, and not needed to pay partnership debts, descends to the heirs of a deceased partner or continues to be personalty and subject to the laws of distribution.

The cause was heard below on bill, answer and on a stipulation of facts. It is shown, and was found by the chancellor, that four people (Cultra's) were partners doing business under the trade name "Morning Star Nursery," the interest being ⅓ in one of the four and ⅔ in the other three. These partners for the purpose of the partnership acquired three tracts of land. Two of these tracts of land were acquired in the name of the four partners, "Trading and doing business as Morning Star Nursery," while the third tract was merely acquired in the names of the individuals, the trade name not being inserted in the deed. It is shown though without question that this third tract was acquired by the partnership out of partnership funds and for partnership purposes.

Two of the partners have died. The question here is raised by the after-born child of one of these partners. This child through her guardian ad litem takes the position that the property descends as realty to her to the exclusion of the widow, that is, the interest

of her deceased father. The chancellor held that this property, all having been acquired with partnership funds and for the use of the partnership, upon the death of the partners, their interest therein was to be disposed of as personalty and that the surviving partners had a right to sell this land and then distribute the proceeds thereof as other partnership property.

Prior to the enactment of the Uniform Partnership Law in 1917, Chapter 140 of the Public Acts of that year which is now carried in the Code as Sections 7841–7882 inclusive, the courts of this State have uniformly held that it is a rule of property that real estate of a partnership is held as personalty for the purposes of the partnership but where not needed for such purposes it descends, as other real estate, to the heirs. Williamson v. Fontain, Ex'r, 66 Tenn. 212.

In thus holding the courts of this State were in line with the majority of the cases in the United States. These cases hold that the real estate, in equity, is regarded as personal property so long as it was necessary to use the real estate in settling and paying debts of the partnership and in adjusting the equities between the partners, but after this was done, any real estate remaining descends as real estate and was subject to laws of descent and distribution. See the full and copious Annotation 25, A.L.R. 389, 414, where cases from practically every state in the Union are cited and many are digested, setting forth the respective rules as adopted by various states.

Since the adoption of the Uniform Partnership Act, above referred to, the courts of this State have not passed upon the question. One case, Marks v. Marks, 1 Tenn.App. 436, apparently held that the passage of this Act did not affect the previous law, but in deciding that case, the court more or less went off on the proposition that the facts of the case did not show that it was the intent of the partnership to use the realty for partnership purposes or in other words, they held that the interested parties failed to carry the burden of showing that that intent appeared. We, therefore, do not consider this case as an authority upon the question here presented. It is true that in the Marks case, the court there cited Williamson v. Fontain, supra, but in citing it, the court merely said this was the established law in this State.

Courts of other states, in construing the Uniform Partnership Act, adopt the rule of "out and out" conversion, that is, that when the property is acquired by the partnership, from the partnership fund, for partnership purposes, it becomes personalty for all purposes. The most notable of these cases is Wharf v. Wharf, 306 Ill. 79, 137 N.E. 446, 449.

These cases, and the holdings last above referred to, in effect adopt the English rule. This rule is that partnership realty must be regarded as personalty for all purposes, including descent and distribution. Real estate purchased and used for partnership purposes is an "out and out" conversion to personalty so that it will be distributed as such. [Citation.]

In Tiffany Real Property, 3rd Edition, Vol. 2, at section 445, it is said: "A conveyance to the partners for partnership purposes makes them, in England, in accordance with the general rule there prevailing, joint tenants as regards the legal title, with the right of survivorship, and the same view might, it seems, be adopted in those states in which trustees take as joint tenants, since the partners are, in such case, trustees. This appears also to be the purpose and effect of the Uniform Partnership Act."

Those courts that have considered the Uniform Partnership Act in reference to realty, used and purchased for partnership purposes, have considered the same with reference "to the sections of the Act to the effect that: (1) The title to the firm realty vests in the surviving partner and, if there is none, in the personal representative of the deceased partner, (Code Section 7864(2)(d)); (2) a partner's interest is only a share in the profits and surpluses, the same being personal property; (Code Section 7865); (3) a partner's interest in specific partnership property is not subject to dower, curtesy, or allowance to the next of kin; (Code Section 7864(2)(e)); and (4) the debts of the partnership are to be paid and the surplus paid in cash to the partners. (Code Section 7877(1))." 16 Tenn.Law Review, 886.

The Supreme Court of Illinois in Wharf v. Wharf, supra, in commenting on these various sections of the Uniform Partnership Act (the Act of Illinois being identical with that of Tennessee) said: "It seems that the legislative intention was to adopt the English rule that real estate which becomes personal property for the purposes of a partnership remains personal property for the purpose of distribution."

It is true that in the Wharf case the partnership was solely for the purpose of dealing in real estate and that the general rule is that real estate partnerships are considered as personalty, and must be distributed as such. [Citation.] We consider the reasoning in the Wharf case, that is, that the rule is changed as to all partnerships, by reason of the passage of the Uniform Partnership Act, is the most reasonable rule and is one that we should adopt and do adopt as the applicable rule in this State.

In this construction and application of the Uniform Partnership Act we are meeting and reaching the intent of the Legislature in passing this Act. By so doing the conversion of real estate into personalty for certain purposes and then when those purposes have been met, reconverting the real estate back into realty is done away with by this Act. By this construction when a partnership once acquires real estate, with partnership funds and for partnership purposes, it then becomes personalty for all purposes and can be conveyed according to the terms of the Act as other partnership property. This seems a sound rule to apply and we are applying it here.

From what has been said above, it results that the decree of the Chancellor must be affirmed.

PROBLEMS

1. A, a minor, enters into a partnership with two adults, B and C. A contributes $5,000 and agrees to contribute an additional $5,000 within five years. B and C each contribute $5000. At the end of one year's operation, the firm has assets totalling $15,000, and is indebted to creditors in the total amount of $20,000. A demands the return of the $5,000 that he contributed. Levying creditors refuse to permit this and insist that A make good his promise to contribute an additional $5,000. What are the rights of the parties?

2. A, B and C were partners in a retail furniture business, trading under the name of A and Company. They owned certain real estate and the store in which the business was conducted, and also a stock of goods. The business was not paying expenses. A executed and acknowledged an instrument under seal purporting to convey the real estate, signing the firm name and the name of each of the partners, and delivered the instrument to a purchaser for adequate consideration. Did the purchaser obtain a good title to the real estate?

3. A and B engaged in the grocery business as partners. In one year they earned considerable money and at the end of the year, after due deliberation they decided to and did invest a part of the profits in oil land. Title to the land was taken in their names as tenants in common. The investment was fortunate for oil was discovered near the land and its value increased many times. A died, leaving a wife and one child. At the time of A's death both he and the partnership were heavily involved financially and there was a contest between his creditors and the partnership creditors for a prior claim against the oil land. Which should succeed?

4. A and B are partners in a taxicab business. They own 25 second-hand automobiles which are used in the business. One day while A is out of town, B sells and delivers the entire lot of 25 cars to X, a bona fide purchaser for value. Upon A's return, he wishes to set aside the sale. What are the rights of the parties?

5. (a) The partnership of A and B has no assets except real property. Is A's proprietary interest in the firm, as a partner, real or personal property? (b) On May 2, 1966, the three partners in the firm of A, B and C signed a dissolution agreement whereby the firm's affairs were to be liquidated as of July 15, 1966. On May 15, B without the knowledge or consent of A or C procured for himself a five-year lease of the premises occupied by the firm to run from the following July 17, and on July 17 B sold this lease at a profit. Have A and C a legal right to share in B's profit?

6. Five brothers, as partners, owned and operated a traveling carnival consisting of numerous sideshows and exhibits. In 1965, poor business and competitive conditions reduced the profits greatly and an opportunity was presented to sell the entire business to a rival organization which submitted a written agreement to purchase the carnival for $75,000. This agreement was dated December 1, 1965, and provided for the payment of the purchase price and the delivery of the carnival properties on January 25, 1966. Three brothers favored the sale and signed the contract. The other two brothers refused to sign the contract and notified the purchaser that they were opposed to the sale. On January 25, 1966, the three brothers who signed the contract tendered the carnival properties to the purchaser and demanded the purchase price. Is the purchaser obligated to pay?

7. A, B, C and D, residents of the State of X, were partners doing business under the trade name of Morning Glory Nursery. A owned a one-third interest and B, C and D, two-ninths each. The partners acquired three tracts of land in the State of X for the purpose of the partnership. Two of the tracts were acquired in the names of the four partners, "trading and doing business as Morning Glory Nursery." The third tract was acquired in the names of the individuals, the trade name not appearing in the deed. This third tract was acquired by the partnership out of partnership funds and for partnership purposes. B died intestate, survived by his wife, Beulah, and their son, B Junior, as his only heirs-at-law. B's widow and his son bring an appropriate action seeking a declaration that the interest of B in the property descended as real property to them.

Decision? Give reasons.

CHAPTER 32

RELATIONS AMONG PARTNERS AND WITH
THIRD PERSONS

Introductory. The rights and duties of partners to one another and their rights and duties with respect to third persons are distinct and separate. On partnership obligations all of the partners are liable, either jointly, or jointly and severally, to creditors of the firm and to persons wronged by the firm, although rights of contribution or indemnity may exist within the partnership. The rules which govern the internal affairs of the partnership and the relations of the partners among themselves generally do not concern third persons or outsiders.

RELATIONS AMONG PARTNERS

Partners are Fiduciaries. A fiduciary relationship exists among the members of a partnership based upon the high standard of trust and confidence which they have a right to repose in one another. Each partner owes a duty of good faith and utmost loyalty to his co-partners, and it is only upon such basis that so intimate a business relationship could function. The requirement in the ordinary agency relationship that the agent shall not make a profit other than his agreed compensation, and shall not compete with his principal, or otherwise profit from the relationship at the expense of his principal, appears in partnership law as the accountability of each partner by reason of the fiduciary duty which he owes to his co-partners. Section 21 of the Uniform Act provides that every partner must account to the partnership for any benefit, and hold as trustee for it any profits derived by him without the consent of the other partners from any transaction connected with the formation, conduct, or liquidation of the partnership or from any use by him of its property. This rule also applies to the representatives of a deceased partner engaged in the liquidation of the affairs of the partnership as the personal representative of the last surviving partner. A partner may not deal at arm's length with his co-partners. He may not prefer himself over the firm. His duty is one of undivided and continuous loyalty to his co-partners.

Right to Share in Profits. As a partnership is an association to carry on a business for profit, each partner is entitled to a share in the profits, and conversely, must contribute toward the losses (Section 18(a)). In the absence of an agreement among the partners with regard to division of profits, the partners share the profits equally, regardless of the ratio of their financial contributions and advancements or the degree of their participation in the management. Unless the partnership agreement provides otherwise, the partners bear losses in the same proportion in which they share profits. The agreement may, however, validly provide for bearing losses in some different ratio than that in which profits are shared.

Right to Return of Capital. Subject to the rights of the partnership creditors, upon termination of the firm each partner is entitled to be repaid his contribution by way of capital. Unless otherwise agreed, a partner is not entitled to interest on his capital contribution. His share of the profits of the partnership may be considered as the earnings on his investment of capital. However, if there is a delay in return of his capital contribution, he is entitled to interest at the legal rate from the date when it should have been paid.

A partner may also make advancements from time to time over and above his agreed capital contribution, and with respect to such advancements or loans he is, in effect, a creditor of the firm. He is entitled to repayment of the loan plus interest thereon (Section 18 (d)). His position as a creditor of the firm is subordinate to the claims of creditors who are not partners. A partner who has reasonably incurred personal liabilities in the ordinary and proper conduct of the business of the firm or who has made payments on behalf of the partnership is entitled to indemnification or repayment (Section 18(b)). However, if the liability is occasioned by the partner's own negligence or wrongdoing, he may not recover from the partnership.

Right to Compensation. The Uniform Act provides that, unless otherwise agreed, no partner is entitled to remuneration for acting in the partnership business (Section 18 (f)). This represents the common-law viewpoint that whatever a partner does for the partnership, he is doing for himself. If the partnership agreement contemplates that one partner shall perform a substantial or disproportionate share of the work of conducting the business, such partner may, by agreement among all of the partners, receive a salary or, in lieu of salary, an increased percentage of the profits. In the absence of agreement, he is entitled to no salary but only his share of the profits.

Even where the services are extraordinary in nature and not contemplated by the parties at the time the agreement was made, the partner rendering such services is not entitled to compensation therefor. The only exception to the rule is that provided in Section 18(f) of the Act whereby a surviving partner is entitled to reasonable compensation for his services in winding up the partnership affairs.

Right to Participate in Management. The strength of a partnership, with respect to its operating efficiency and business management, may lie in full utilization of the complementary talents of its members. The members often perform different functions.

One may keep the books or supervise the bookkeeping; another may have charge of the sales and personnel, while a third partner who is technically trained may devote his energies exclusively to production. Although each of the partners may carve out for himself or have delegated to him a certain sphere of activity within the business, each of them has an absolute right to know how the business is operated in its entirety and has an equal voice in its management.

When a difference of opinion develops, the majority prevails, both at common law and under the Uniform Act (Section 18(h)). There is conflict among the authorities as to what should be done in the event of an equal division of opinion resulting in a stalemate. Some decisions hold that, in such case, a partner may go ahead and deal with third parties with impunity to his own relations within the partnership. Others hold to the contrary. Unanimous agreement of the partners is necessary if a matter involves contravention of any agreement between the partners. Impliedly, this would include the addition of a new business activity or the dropping of an old one, changing the location of the business, compromising a firm debt, agreeing to an arbitration, or a disposition of so much of the firm's assets that it would be impossible to continue the business.

Right to Information and Inspection of the Books. Each partner is entitled to full information on all partnership matters upon demand at any time, and each has a duty to supply such information as he may possess. The right to demand information extends also to the legal representative of a deceased partner for a reasonable time following the dissolution of the partnership (Section 20).

Unless the partners agree otherwise, the books of the partnership are to be kept at the principal place of business at all times, and each partner has an absolute right to have access to them, to inspect them, and to copy any of them. This right may be exercised by a duly authorized attorney or accountant on behalf of a partner. The right continues after dissolution of the partnership, although the courts are loath to require that the records be maintained for an extended period with the attendant expense after the partnership no longer has a place of business.

Right to Choose Associates. No partner may be forced to accept another as a partner whom he does not choose. This is essentially because of the fiduciary relationship between the parties. The courts refuse to impose so personal a relation upon the parties regardless of what other equities may be involved. When a partner sells his interest to another, the purchaser does not become a partner and is not entitled to participate in the management. He is entitled only to receive the profits accruing to the share which he has bought. If the purchaser is admitted to the firm as a partner by agreement of all of the parties, the old partnership is ended and a new one has been formed.

No partner has to acquiesce in the efforts of his partners to bring a new partner into the business. He may choose to dissolve the partnership, and, if this is necessary because of the insistence of the others, he may be entitled to an accounting for damages against them. On the other hand, the partners cannot prevent a partner withdrawing if he chooses to do so, as a court will not decree specific performance of a partnership contract. The wrongfully withdrawing partner is subject to damages in a suit against him by his co-partners for breach of the partnership contract.

It is common in partnership agreements for provision to be made that the partners shall not indorse certain types of commercial paper, become a surety for another, or otherwise place themselves in a precarious position with respect to their personal financial situations. While such actions may not directly concern the partnership when such liability is assumed, they may imperil its continuance later if the financial integrity of the individual partner is affected. In the absence of such an agreement, however, there are no restrictions upon the manner in which the partners may conduct their personal affairs.

Right to an Accounting. At common law and under the Uniform Act, a partner is entitled to an accounting and may invoke the power of a court of equity to decree an accounting whenever he is wrongfully excluded from the partnership business or possession of its property by his co-partners, or whenever other circumstances render it just and reasonable (Section 22). A partner may not be permitted to sue the partnership at law, as he would be suing himself, but he may sue in equity in an action for an accounting. The suit will be against his co-partners individually, as there is no legal entity involved.

Rights of Partners Upon Expiration of Agreed Term. Where the members of a partnership continue operation of the business after the expiration of the specified term for which the partnership was formed, or after the accomplishment of the particular purpose for which it was formed, the rights and duties of the partners remain the same as they were at such termination, so far as they are consistent with a partnership at will (Section 23.) A continuation of the business by the partners as they habitually acted during the agreed term, without any settlement or liquidation of the partnership affairs, is prima facie evidence of a continuation of the partnership.

Rights Among Limited Partners. Since limited partnerships are organized pursuant to statute, the rights of the parties usually are set forth with relative clarity in the articles.

It should be specially noted that there are certain differences in the relations between limited and general partners. A limited partner, in order to preserve his status as such, must not actively engage in the management of the business, and his name may not be included in the firm name except where it is also the same as the name of a general partner. He may advise the other partners as to the prudent conduct of the business. He also is entitled to demand full and true information of all things affecting the partnership and to an accounting in the same manner as general partners.

RELATIONS BETWEEN PARTNERS AND THIRD PERSONS

Agency is Basis of Liability. The law of partnership is a branch of the law of agency and therefore most of the problems arising out of the relation between partners and third persons involve application of the general principles of agency law. These problems usually attend an assertion of partnership liability either in contract or in tort.

Partners as Agents. Each partner is an agent of (1) the partnership as such and (2) every other partner, and, consequently each partner is the principal of every other partner. Thus, the act of every partner binds the partnership. This agency relation is naturally limited to transactions within the scope of the partnership business or, as described in the Uniform Partnership Act, is confined to acts for carrying on in the usual way the business of the partnership.

A partner's authority may be:

1. Express actual authority, such as specifically set forth in the partnership agreement or in a collateral agreement between the partners, written or oral.

2. Implied actual authority, such as authority which is neither expressly granted nor expressly denied but is reasonably deduced from the nature of the partnership, the terms of the partnership agreement, and the relations of the partners.

3. Apparent authority, which may or may not be actual, but is such authority as may, in view of the circumstances and the conduct of the parties, be reasonably considered to

exist by a third person who has no knowledge or notice of the lack of actual authority. Apparent authority is based upon the principle of estoppel.

A partner may bind the partnership by his act (1) if he has actual authority, express or implied, to perform the act; or (2) if he has apparent authority to perform the act, his lack of actual authority being unknown to the third person, and the act apparently carries on in the usual way the business of the partnership. If the act is not apparently within the scope of the partnership business, then the partnership is bound only where the partner has actual authority, and the third person dealing with the partner assumes the risk of the existence of such actual authority.

The Uniform Partnership Act (Section 9) provides that the following acts do not bind the partnership unless performed (1) by all of the partners, or (2) by one partner with actual authority from all of the others:

1. Assignment of partnership property in trust for creditors.
2. Disposal of the good-will of the business.
3. Any act which would make it impossible to carry on the ordinary business of the partnership.
4. Confession of a judgment.
5. Submission of a partnership claim or liability to arbitration or reference.

In addition to the foregoing, a partner who does not have actual authority from each of his co-partners may not bind the partnership by any of the following acts inasmuch as they are clearly outside of the scope of the partnership under ordinary circumstances: (1) execution of contracts of guaranty and suretyship in the firm name; (2) sale of partnership property not held for sale in the usual course of business, and (3) payment of individual debts out of partnership assets.

The members of a trading partnership have much wider apparent authority than do the members of a non-trading partnership.

A trading partnership is one which in the ordinary course of its business buys and sells goods, wares, merchandise, or other property. A non-trading partnership is one which does not purchase and sell commodities in the ordinary course of its business, such as a law firm or accounting firm. Partners in a trading firm have apparent authority to borrow money and to execute negotiable instruments, while partners in a non-trading firm do not.

A third person may not rely upon apparent authority in any situation where he is put on notice or has knowledge that the partner does not, or may not, have actual authority. In such case, the third person must ascertain the actual authority of the partner or assume the risk of the absence of such authority.

Conveyance of Real Estate. At common law, real estate, unlike personal property, could not be conveyed to a partnership in the partnership name, and therefore a conveyance had to be made to one or more or all of the partners. When the partnership wished to convey title to partnership real estate to a third person, the partners who were the nominal owners were required to sign the deed of conveyance. Section 8 of the Uniform Act permits title to real estate to be conveyed to a partnership in the partnership name, and Section 10 permits title to any such real estate to be conveyed by any partner by a deed executed in the partnership name. This changes the common law.

Under Section 10 of the Uniform Act:

1. Where the title to real property is in the names of all the partners, a conveyance executed by all the partners passes all their rights in such property.

2. Where title is in the partnership, any partner may:

    (a) Convey title by a conveyance executed in the partnership name, subject to recovery by the partnership unless the partnership is bound because of the actual or apparent authority of the partner or unless the property has subsequently been conveyed to a holder for value without knowledge that the partner lacked authority, or

    (b) Transfer the equitable interest of the partnership by a conveyance executed in his own name, provided that he has actual or apparent authority.

3. Where title is in the name of one or more, but not all, of the partners:

    (a) The partners in whose name the title stands may convey title, subject to recovery by the partnership unless the partnership is bound because of the actual or apparent authority of the partners or unless the purchaser or his assignee is a holder for value without knowledge of the partnership's interest.

    (b) Any partner may transfer the equitable interest of the partnership by a conveyance executed in the partnership name or his own name provided that he has actual or apparent authority.

In the above instances where the grantee in the conveyance acquires an equitable interest, he may compel the partnership or its authorized agents to transfer to him the legal title to the real estate.

Admissions of a Partner. An admission or representation by any partner concerning partnership affairs, within the scope of his authority, is evidence against the partnership. An admission by one person that a partnership exists does not prove its existence. But once the partnership is established by competent evidence, the admission of one partner may be used against the partnership provided the partner is acting within the scope of the partnership business.

Notice to and Knowledge of One Partner. Section 12 of the Uniform Act provides, as follows:

"Notice to any partner of any matter relating to partnership affairs, and the knowledge of the partner acting in the particular matter acquired while a partner or then present to his mind, and the knowledge of any other partner who reasonably could and should have communicated it to the acting partner, operate as notice to or knowledge of the partnership, except in the case of a fraud on the partnership committed by or with the consent of that partner."

A demand upon one partner as representative of the firm constitutes a demand upon the partnership.

At common law, service of process in a lawsuit predicated upon a partnership obligation must be made upon all partners within the jurisdiction of the court. Service of a summons upon one partner does not give the court jurisdiction over the partnership or over any partner not served. Certain States have statutes permitting service upon a representative of the partnership, but even in those States a judgment for the plaintiff will not stand as a personal judgment against any partner not served with summons.

Contract Liability of Partners. The Uniform Act provides (Section 15) that partners are jointly liable on all debts and contract obligations of the partnership. The distinction between joint liability and joint and several liability consists generally of the following:

1. In a suit upon a joint obligation, each living joint obligor must be made a party defendant to the action. Where an obligation is joint and several, the obligors may all be joined as defendants in one suit or they may each be sued in separate suits.

2. A judgment based upon a joint obligation must be against all of the obligors or none. The death of an obligor terminates his liability. A judgment against all of the joint obligors served with summons, some not being served as outside the jurisdiction or as secret partners whose identity is unknown to the plaintiff obligee, will generally bar further action in a separate suit against those who were not served with summons.

A judgment upon a joint and several obligation against one of the obligors, until and unless satisfied, does not release the others nor bar a subsequent suit against them.

3. A release of one joint obligor releases all. In some jurisdictions, the release of one joint and several obligor releases all, but the majority view is that a release of a single joint and several obligor releases only that one. A covenant not to sue may be given to one of several joint obligors and will have the effect of releasing that one while preserving rights against the others.

In certain States, the distinction between joint and joint and several obligations has been eliminated by statute. However, a statute providing that "all joint obligations and covenants shall be taken and held to be joint and several obligations and covenants" has been held not to apply to partnership obligations which are joint as provided in Section 15 of the Uniform Partnership Act.

It should be noted that once judgment has been entered against a partner, whether upon a joint or a joint and several partnership obligation, it may be satisfied out of partnership assets or out of the individual assets of the partner.

Tort Liability of Partners. The liability of partners for a tort committed by any partner or by an employee of the firm in the course of partnership business is joint and several. The rules with reference to joint and several obligations apply to partnership liability for tort. All of the partners may be sued jointly in an action based upon tort liability, or separate actions may be maintained against each of them and separate judgments obtained. However, payment of any one of the judgments operates as a satisfaction of all of them.

Under general agency principles, a partner is liable for the torts of his co-partner only if the latter is acting within the scope or course of the partnership business.

Liability for Holding Oneself Out as a Partner. If a person represents himself or consents to have another person represent him as a partner in an existing partnership, (1) he is liable to any person who gives credit to the actual or apparent partnership in reliance upon such representation, and (2) if the representation is made in a public manner, he is liable to any person who gives credit to the actual or apparent partnership, whether the representation has or has not been made or communicated to such person by or with the knowledge of the apparent partner. When a partnership liability results, he is liable as though he were a member of the partnership. When no partnership liability results, he is liable jointly with such persons who may have consented either to the contract or to the representation.

A person who holds himself out as a partner is the agent of those who consent to or acquiesce in such representation. Where all the members of an existing partnership consent to the representation, all of them are liable. Where less than all of the partners consent to the holding out of another person as a partner, the liability attaches only to the person who permits himself to be represented as a partner and to those partners who consent thereto.

Liability of Incoming Partner. A person admitted as a partner into an existing partnership is liable for all of the obligations of the partnership arising before his admission as though he had been a partner when such obligations were incurred, although this liability may be satisfied only out of partnership property, as provided in Section 17 of the Uniform Partnership Act. In substance, the liability of an incoming partner upon antecedent debts and obligations of the firm is limited to his capital contribution. This restriction does not apply, of course, to obligations arising subsequent to his admission into the partnership as to which his liability is unlimited.

CASES

OLIVIER v. ULEBERG

(1946) 74 N.D. 453, 23 N.W.2d 39, 165 A.L.R. 974.

[George Olivier, plaintiff, brought an action to dissolve his partnership with Carl Uleberg, defendant. A dissolution was decreed and an accounting had. With regard to one item in the accounting, the trial court held that, under the terms of the oral partnership agreement of twenty-eight years standing, it was incumbent upon each partner to devote his whole time to the partnership business; that for a period of eighteen months prior to the decree of dissolution Olivier had failed to perform any services for the partnership; that the services which Olivier thus failed to perform were of the value of $300 per month; that, as a consequence of the breach of the partnership agreement, the partnership had a valid claim against Olivier for $5,400; that in the accounting Olivier should be debited in the amount of $5,400; and that, the partners being equal partners and the $5,400 being the same as any other assets of the firm, Olivier and Uleberg should each be credited with one-half, or $2,700. The net result of this ruling was to increase Uleberg's share upon liquidation by $2,700 and to reduce Olivier's share by a like amount. From this item in the accounting Olivier appeals.]

CHRISTIANSON, C. J. * * * Plaintiff's counsel invokes the rule embodied in § 45-0112, N.D.Rev. Codes 1943, which reads: "A partner is not entitled to any compensation for services rendered by him to the partnership." "This section is a declaration of the common law on the subject." Wisner v. Field, 11 N.D. 257, 260, 91 N.W. 67. Under this rule "a partner is not entitled to receive compensation for services rendered in the prosecution of the partnership business merely by reason of any inequality of services rendered by him, as compared with those rendered by his copartners." 40 Am. Jur. 214, Partnership, § 123. [Citations.] This rule, however, does not preclude the parties from making their own agreements so as to adjust the respective equities of the partners. But, in the absence of agreement (express or implied) for compensation, unequaled services will be presumed to have been rendered without expectation of reward. [Citation.]

"The relationship of partners is fiduciary and imposes upon them an obligation of the utmost good faith and integrity in their dealings with one another with respect to partnership affairs." 40 Am.Jur. 217, Partnership. [Citation.] And where "partners agree among themselves what duties each will perform in the common business, and one wilfully fails to perform his agreed part, an allowance should be made to the one who performs that part. Also, it has been held that a partner who neglects and refuses, without reasonable cause, to perform the services which he has stipulated to render the partnership is liable to account to the firm for the value of the services in the settlement of partnership accounts, and that such an allowance is not precluded by the rule denying a partner compensation for individual or unequal services." 40 Am.Jur. 216, Partnerhip. In Rowley's work on the law of partnership, it is said: "If one partner refuses without good cause to perform the services to which he has agreed, the other will usually be given an allowance therefor, or a deduction will be made from the share of the partner who did not perform his agreed service." 1 Rowley, Modern Law of Partnership, p. 415, § 356. [Citations.] In Lay v. Emery, 8 N.D. 515, 79 N.W. 1053, this court held: "In an action for an accounting between partners, where it appears that one of the partners contracted to devote his entire time to the management of the partnership business, and that he has retained from the firm funds compensation

for his entire time, when in fact he devoted only a portion of it, a court of equity, upon a final adjustment of the partnership accounts, may make deduction for the value of the portion of time not so employed."

On this appeal it stands undisputed that the partnership agreement provided that each of the partners should devote his full time to the partnership business; also that the agreement provided for a division of duties, which was recognized and adhered to for more than twenty-eight years. The evidence clearly shows that the plaintiff Olivier was absent from the place of business of the partnership since December 16, 1942, and subsequent to that date failed to perform the work which, under the partnership agreement he had agreed to perform. That subsequent to December 16, 1942, he performed labor only for a few days, and that after April 20, 1943, he performed no work of any kind for the partnership.

The defendant Uleberg testified that the value of the services of Olivier, which he thus failed to perform and of which the partnership was deprived, was $350 per month. This testimony stands uncontradicted. The court placed a value of $300 per month on such services.

While the record shows there was some disagreement between the partners, we are unable to see where the evidence shows any reasonable ground for the plaintiff abandoning his position and failing to perform the work which the partnership agreement obligated him to perform. Whatever difficulties existed, there is nothing to show that Uleberg in any manner interfered with Olivier performing his work. The mere fact that strained relations had grown up between the partners did not relieve either of them from his duties and obligations under the partnership agreement. [Citation.] * * *

In its memorandum opinion the trial court said: "By the well-settled law of partnership, both at common law and under our statute, partners are not entitled to compensation for their services, however unequal in value or amount. However, the Court herein is not allowing partner Uleberg any compensation for services rendered to the partnership during the time that Olivier was absent therefrom. The Court is simply charging Olivier, as a partner, for a total breach of his contractual obligation * * *

"Marsh's Appeal, 69 Pa. 30, 8 Am.Rep. 206, reads as follows: (commencing at page 209) 'The plaintiffs are not seeking compensation for the services they rendered the partnership. They are simply seeking to charge the defendant with the loss occasioned the partnership by his refusal to render the services which he agreed to perform. If the partnership has suffered by his breach of the agreement, why should he not make good the loss, and put the firm in the same condition it would have been if he had not broken the agreement? If the defendant is compelled to make good the loss, each member of the firm, including himself, will receive his proportion of the amount in the distribution of the partnership assets, and in no just sense can this be regarded as compensation for the services individually rendered.' " * * *

Judgment affirmed.

LEVY v. LEAVITT, 257 N.Y. 461, 178 N.E. 758 (1931). *Lehman*, J. * * * We consider first whether a charge may be made for services rendered. In Bradford v. Kimberly (3 Johns. Ch. 431) Chancellor Kent stated the rule: "In the case of joint partners, the general rule is, that one is not entitled to charge against another, a compensation for his more valuable or unequal services bestowed on the common concern, without a special agreement; for it is deemed a case of voluntary management." The rule has been often stated in different form, but no authority, judicial or extra-judicial, has seriously questioned its substance. In the

ordinary course of business affairs, services are usually rendered with expectation of reward, and silent acceptance of such services may justify, or at times, even dictate, the inference of an implied promise to pay the reasonable value of such services. The basis for such inference is lacking when circumstances point to the conclusion that the services were rendered voluntarily and without reasonable expectation of payment. [Citation.]

In the business of a partnership the services of a partner are rendered for the common benefit in the performance of an obligation created by the partnership agreement, and the resultant benefit is divided pro rata as provided in the partnership contract. Those profits constitute, in the absence of other agreement, the stipulated reward for services to be rendered, and there is no right to other compensation based on the reasonable value of the services actually rendered. Inequality in the value of services rendered, even the fact that the services were extraordinary and that, at the time the contract was made, the parties did not contemplate that such services would be required in the course of the partnership business, would not alone justify the award of compensation outside the share of profits accruing to the partner rendering the services.

UNITED BROKERS CO. v. DOSE

(1933) 143 Or. 283, 22 P.2d 204.

[Action by United Brokers Co., plaintiff, against Dose, defendant, who filed a counterclaim. The parties entered into a joint venture, the profits to be divided equally. The profits were collected by the defendant and plaintiff alleges that the defendant did not pay to plaintiff its proper share of the profits. Defendant claims that he was entitled to compensation for his services. He also contended that he was entitled to contribution from plaintiff in respect to money paid by defendant to a person injured by defendant while driving a car in connection with the business of the joint venture. Judgment for plaintiff and defendant appeals.]

BELT, J. * * * Relative to the claim of compensation for services rendered by defendant, it is clear that the court was right in denying the same. There is no evidence of any express agreement that defendant was to receive compensation for his services. The rule applicable is thus stated in 20 R.C.L. 877: "The general rule is that a partner is not entitled to compensation for services in conducting the partnership business beyond his share of the profits unless there is a stipulation to that effect, and that he has no right by implication to claim anything extra by reason of any inequality of services rendered by him, as compared with those rendered by his copartners."

The second counter-claim arose out of an automobile accident which occurred while defendant Dose was driving to Washington to inspect some potatoes. The trip was made with the knowledge and consent of the plaintiff. Dan Schuler, who accompanied Dose, was injured as a result of the latter's negligence. Schuler threatened to bring an action. Dose thereupon, without the knowledge or consent of the plaintiff, paid to Schuler, in settlement of his claim, the sum of $2,000. The further sum of $1,214.60 was paid by Dose to cover hospital bills for Schuler and himself. The liability of the partnership to a third person for the negligence of one of the partners while acting within the scope of the partnership business is not involved. * * *

The law of partnership is the law of agency. Each partner is the agent of the other and impliedly agrees that he will exercise reasonable care and diligence in the operation of the partnership business. When a loss is paid by a partnership, there is a right of indemnity against the party whose negligence caused the loss. [Citations.] It is the same rule where the principal is held liable for the negligent act of his agent. Upon payment of the loss, the principal may bring action against his agent to be indemnified for the loss sustained: 2 C.J. 721. As stated in Rowley's "Modern Law of Partnership" Vol. 2, sec. 983, "Losses caused wholly by the negligence or misconduct of one party must be borne by him." In "The Law of Partnership" by Shumaker (2d Ed.) 160, it is said, "A partner has no right to charge the firm with losses or expenses caused by his own negligence or want of skill * * *".

In Carlin v. Donegan, 15 Kan. 495, Mr. Justice Brewer, speaking for the court in an action brought by one partner against his copartner for an accounting, approved an instruction that each partner would be "held responsible for fraud, negligence, etc.," and that "the degree of care and diligence that partners are generally held to between themselves is such care and diligence about any transaction as men generally of common or average care and prudence would exercise." It was also declared by the court that "The omission of such ordinary care and prudence, is ordinary negligence; and a partner is responsible for losses resulting from ordinary negligence."

In Kiffer v. Bienstock, 128 Misc. 451, 218 N.Y.S. 526, it was held that where a judgment was recovered against a partner individually by a person injured by a partner's sole negligence in operating a partnership automobile in firm business the partner was not entitled to contribution by his copartner on dissolution of the partnership. * * *

The decree of the lower court is affirmed.

BOTSIKAS v. YARMARK

(1965 Fla.) 172 So.2d 277.

HORTON, J. Plaintiff-appellant brought a bill in equity against the administratrix of decedent's estate, his widow, and heirs at law, praying that the court declare (1) a partnership between appellant and decedent, or (2) the imposition of an involuntary or constructive trust as to certain properties, and an accounting.

In substance, the amended complaint alleges, inter alia, that a confidential relationship existed between appellant and the decedent; that they lived together in the relationship of husband and wife although the deceased had a living undivorced wife; that they entered into a partnership for life to acquire property, etc.; that appellant contributed capital from her own resources and in addition operated, managed and supervised hotel properties acquired by the partnership, all in furtherance of the alleged partnership activity; that certain properties were purchased for the partnership but taken in the name of the deceased only or in the names of certain corporations; and that appellant is entitled to her interest in the properties and profits thereof either as a partner or upon the theory of a constructive trust. The defendant-appellees' motions to dismiss for failure to state a cause of action were sustained, giving rise to this appeal.

Upon a review of the material allegations of the amended complaint, we conclude that they are sufficient to state a cause of action for recovery upon the theory of the existence of a constructive trust. We also conclude that the amended complaint fails to state sufficient facts, which if proven would warrant a court of equity in finding that a legal partnership existed between the appellant and the deceased. Mutual promises to live together in a meretricious or illegal relationship are not sufficient consideration to support an agreement of partnership. It is true the allegations of the amended complaint do not allege such relationship to be the consideration for the agreement; nevertheless no other consideration is alleged. When all the allegations are considered, the conclusion that the

illegal relationship was the consideration for the partnership is not an unreasonable one.

* * *

Appellant has alleged that she contributed property and funds for the acquisition of properties allegedly obtained for the benefit of both the deceased and herself, but that title to these properties was in fact placed in the name of the deceased or in corporations. She has further alleged that these contributions were as the result of the confidence placed by her in the deceased, and failure to grant her interest therein would be an abuse of the confidential relationship and amount to unjust enrichment of decedent's estate. * * Compensation for services rendered by the appellant during the existence of the meretricious relationship of course would not be recoverable.

Accordingly, the order appealed is reversed, and the cause is remanded for further proceedings not inconsistent herewith.

Reversed and remanded.

DECOTIS v. D'ANTONA

(1966) — Mass. —, 214 N.E.2d 21.

SPALDING, J. The objective of this bill in equity is to impose a constructive trust for the benefit of the plaintiff and the defendant as partners on a parcel of real estate alleged to have been acquired by the defendant in violation of a fiduciary duty owed to the plaintiff.

The case was referred to a master whose findings included the following: The plaintiff and the defendant first met in December, 1960, and thereafter became friends. On several occasions they talked about going into business together. They discussed the liquor and the motel business and the possibility of financing and building a bowling alley. Subsequently they got in touch with a broker named Bucchiere and instructed him to bring to their attention "any good leads in land sites, restaurants, liquor lounges, motel sites, and bowling alley sites" as they were "going to be partners." About this time the defendant, with Bucchiere, looked at two restaurants which were for sale. In January, 1961, the plaintiff and the defendant, with another broker, looked at business sites in Peabody, Georgetown and Haverhill, but nothing was ever done to acquire any of these properties.

In August, 1961, one Pitman, who owned a motel on Route 1, Saugus, known as Saugus Pines, authorized Bucchiere to produce a buyer for the property. Bucchiere told the plaintiff that Saugus Pines was for sale, and the plaintiff informed the defendant of this fact. The plaintiff and the defendant discussed the possibility of developing the property, and the defendant told the plaintiff that he desired to look at it. The plaintiff told him "to go ahead but not to talk with anyone as Bucchiere was the agent for it." After viewing the property, the defendant talked with the plaintiff about purchasing it together "and * * * going in business * * * as partners." The defendant agreed to give the plaintiff a check for $2,500 to be used for a down payment and "they would go fifty-fifty on the deal."

The Saugus Pines property included a motel and a diner. The plaintiff and the defendant "agreed they would pay $110,000 or $115,000 for all the property or $75,000 or $85,000 for everything excluding the Diner." The plaintiff, in the defendant's presence, told Bucchiere to try to get the property at these prices, preferably at the lower amounts. Subsequently, the defendant asked the plaintiff if "he [would] mind if he bought the place alone." The plaintiff replied, "Look, now, I called you on the deal. We agreed to be partners. Now leave the thing alone because Mr. Bucchiere has got the check to buy the place and you know that and just leave it alone, stay out of my business." Later, upon learning that the defendant was negotiating to buy the property, the plaintiff called him on the telephone and said, "[S]tay out of my business because I am buying the place * * *. I was good enough to call you and now you don't want to be my partner. I am going to buy it alone."

The plaintiff went to Saugus Pines with Bucchiere and subsequently Bucchiere submitted to Pitman (the owner) an offer of $90,000 for the property, exclusive of the diner, and told him that he would make a deposit of $5,000. The deposit was not accepted.

In August or September, Bucchiere learned that Saugus Pines had been purchased by the defendant. Shortly thereafter Bucchiere met the defendant who told him that he did not want to be regarded as a "dirty double crosser" but that the property was a "terrific buy and he wanted to grab it [for] himself."

The final paragraph of the master's report reads: "I find that because of the oral agreement between the parties that they would buy the property as partners there was a relationship of 'trust and confidence' between them; that there was a breach of this relationship when * * * [the defendant] secretly purchased the property himself; and that * * * [the defendant] holds the Saugus Pines property upon a constructive trust for the benefit of himself and * * * [the plaintiff]."

There were numerous objections (now exceptions) by the defendant to the master's report. The judge entered an interlocutory decree in which he sustained exceptions 1, 3 and 4, overruled the rest and confirmed the report with the last paragraph struck. A final decree was entered dismissing the bill. From the interlocutory and final decrees the plaintiff appealed.

The decrees were right.

There can be doubt that the plaintiff and the defendant originally intended to embark on a business enterprise in which they would be either partners or joint adventurers. Whether the relationship would have been one or the other need not concern us, for in either case their duties to each other, so far as here material, would be the same. "While the enterprise continues, joint adventurers, like partners, owe to one another the utmost good faith and loyalty." [Citation.] If during the existence of either relationship one of the members of the enterprise acquired property for himself that he was under a duty to obtain for the enterprise he would hold the property on a constructive trust. [Citations.]

On the facts found by the master no partnership or joint adventure existed at the time the defendant acquired Saugus Pines. That relationship, if there was one, had been terminated. When the plaintiff learned that the defendant was seeking to purchase the property for himself, the plaintiff told him unequivocally that the arrangement between them was at an end, and that he proposed to buy the property "alone." Thereafter each was free to acquire the property for himself. The plaintiff could not have it both ways. He could not repudiate the arrangement and thus buy the property for himself and at the same time treat the arrangement as subsisting in order to hold the defendant accountable in the event he bought the property first.

The subsidiary facts found by the master did not support his ultimate finding to the effect that the defendant acquired the property in breach of a duty of trust and confidence owed to the plaintiff. The judge, therefore, rightly struck this finding from the report. With this finding eliminated, the plaintiff's case fails. Cardullo v. Landau, 329 Mass. 5, 105 N.E.2d 843.

This is the opinion of a majority of the court.

Interlocutory decree affirmed.

Final decree affirmed.

LEE v. DAHLIN

(1965) 399 Pa. 50, 159 A.2d 679, 81 A.L.R.2d 442.

COHEN, J. Dahlin Bros. Coal Mining Company was a partnership owned by A. Vern Dahlin and George T. Dahlin, which mined coal in Clearfield County. At the death of George T. Dahlin on May 31, 1951, the partnership was dissolved, but A. V. Dahlin, the surviving partner, continued to operate the mine for eighteen months, after which time he gradually began to liquidate the partnership. A. V. Dahlin died on January 8, 1956, and because the partnership still had not been fully liquidated, a receiver was appointed.

The receiver filed a complaint in equity against the Estate of A. V. Dahlin for a full accounting of the partnership affairs and liquidation from the date of the death of the first deceased partner. The administrator of the estate filed a partial accounting which was not satisfactory and the court directed the receiver to investigate and make a report. After the receiver filed his account and the court below filed an adjudication to which exceptions were made, a decree was entered finding the estate liable to the receiver for $7,221.44. This is an appeal by the administrator of the estate from this final decree.

* * *

The appellant next contends that A. V. Dahlin was entitled to compensation as a surviving partner. The Uniform Partnership Act of March 26, 1915, P.L. 18, Part IV, § 18(f), 59 P.S. § 51, provides that a partner is not entitled to compensation "except that a surviving partner is entitled to *reasonable* compensation for his services in winding up the partnership affairs." (Emphasis supplied.) At common law in Pennsylvania a liquidating partner was entitled to compensation only for *extraordinary* services performed in the liquidation. In Murdock v. Murdock, 1930, 300 Pa. 280, 289–290, 150 A. 599,

603, the court held that "though partners, in the absence of special agreement, receive no compensation, yet 'a surviving partner is entitled to reasonable compensation for his services in winding up the partnership affairs.'" There is no question that ordinarily A. V. Dahlin would have been entitled to some compensation; however, on the facts of this case, he has forfeited this right. A surviving partner is in a fiduciary capacity as regards the estate of his deceased partner. [Citation.] Since the death of one partner leaves the survivor in a position of absolute control with only the duty to account, it is apparent that the survivor must proceed with utmost caution and use the highest degree of care in the liquidation of the partnership. This was not done. There is ample evidence on the record that A. V. Dahlin, after the death of George Dahlin, took a truck belonging to the partnership for which he failed to account; used partnership funds for personal expense and failed to account to George Dahlin's estate even after a lapse of approximately five years. A trustee who breaches his fiduciary duty with a resultant loss to the estate forfeits his rights to compensation. [Citation.] For this reason it is evident that A. V. Dahlin was not entitled to the monies which he withdrew from the partnership as compensation, and the final decree of the court below requiring its return is correct.

Decree affirmed at appellant's cost.

SCHUMACHER V. SUMNER TELEPHONE CO., (1913) 161 Iowa 326, 142 N.W. 1034. *Weaver*, C. J. * * * In nontrading partnerships and unincorporated associations the authority of partners to involve each other in financial obligations is much more limited than in trading organizations. While in the latter the authority to borrow money for the real or professed use of the partnership is ordinarily recognized, in the former it is quite as universally denied. According to the great weight of authority, it is not within the power of a nontrading partnership or association to borrow money or make negotiable paper and charge with individual liability partners or members not assenting thereto. * * * Stated in substantially the same form it has been said that in the case of a nontrading concern the burden is upon the plaintiff to prove either express authority, or circumstances from which such authority can be fairly implied, in the partner executing the note. [Citations.] Indeed, the rule as indicated by the authorities cited is no more than an application of the doctrine which is applied to partnerships in general that the authority of the partners to bind each other by their contracts is limited to contracts made within the scope of the business for which they are associated. [Citation.] The borrowing of money and the giving of negotiable paper is not a necessary or an ordinary incident of the business of a non-trading association, and when it happens that such a concern does desire to borrow or a member or officer proposes to give or tenders a promissory note in its name, it is no hardship upon the lender or creditor to require him to look into the authority of one who proposes to bind others who are not present or consenting. * * *

PHILLIPS v. COOK

(1965) 239 Md. 215, 210 A.2d 743.

MARBURY, J. This is an appeal by Daniel Phillips individually, and trading as "Dan's Used Cars", one of the defendants below, from a judgment in favor of Delores Cook and Marshall Cook, her husband, plaintiffs below, entered upon the verdict of a jury in favor of the plaintiffs against the defendants, Isadore Harris and Daniel Phillips, individually and as co-partners trading as Dan's Used Cars, in the Superior Court of Baltimore City. The verdict was rendered in an action by the Cooks to recover damages for injuries sustained by them as a result of a collision involving a partnership automobile operated by Harris and bearing dealer plates issued to Dan's Used Cars by the Department of Motor Vehicles.

The Cooks sued Harris and Phillips, individually, and as co-partners trading as Dan's Used Cars. The accident in question occurred on January 7, 1960, at about 6:50 p. m., when a partnership automobile operated by Harris struck the rear of a vehicle driven by one Smith, which in turn hit an automobile operated by Delores Cook, at the intersection of Reisterstown Road and Quantico Avenue in Baltimore. Harris was on his way home from the used car lot when the accident occurred. He was using the most direct route from the partnership lot and was only five blocks from his home at the time of the incident.

In October 1959, Harris and Phillips entered into a partnership on an equal basis under the name of "Dan's Used Cars" for the purpose of buying and selling used automobiles. * * * This partnership agreement was oral and it was agreed between the partners that each would have an equal voice in the conduct and management of the business.

Neither of the partners owned a personal automobile or had one titled in his individual name. It was agreed as a part of the partnership arrangement that Harris would use a partnership vehicle for transportation to and from his home. Under this agreement, he was authorized to demonstrate and sell such automobiles, call on dealers for the purpose of seeing and purchasing used cars, or go to the Department of Motor Vehicles on partnership business after leaving the lot in the evening and before returning the next day. Both Harris and Phillips could use a partnership automobile as desired. Such vehicles were for sale at any time during the

day or night and at various times and places they had "for sale" signs on the windshields. Harris had no regular hours to report to the used car lot but could come and go as he saw fit. Phillips testified that it was essential that Harris have a partnership automobile for his transportation to and from his home, and that it was the most practical way to operate. * * *

In a case involving a partnership, the contract of partnership constitutes all of its members as agents of each other and each partner acts both as a principal and as the agent of the others in regard to acts done within the apparent scope of the business, purpose and agreement of the partnership or for its benefit. It is clear that the partnership is bound by the partner's wrongful act if done within the scope of the partnership's business. Code (1957), Article 73A, Section 13 provides:

"Where, by any wrongful act or omission of any partner acting in the ordinary course of the business of the partnership, or with the authority of his copartners, loss or injury is caused to any person, not being a partner in the partnership, or any penalty is incurred, the partnership is liable therefor to the same extent as the partner so acting or omitting to act."

The test of the liability of the partnership and of its members for the torts of any one partner is whether the wrongful act was done within what may reasonably be found to be the scope of the business of the partnership and for its benefit. The extent of the authority of a partner is determined essentially by the same principles as those which measure the scope of an agent's authority. [Citation.] Partnership cases may differ from principal and agent and master and servant relationships because in the non-partnership cases, the element of control or authorization is important. This is not so in the case of a partnership for a partner is also a principal, and control and authorization are generally within his power to exercise.

* * *

Here, the fact that the defendant partners were in the used car business; that the very vehicle involved in the accident was one of the partnership assets for sale at all times, day or night, at any location; that Harris was on call by Phillips or customers at his home—he went back to the lot two or three times after going home; that he had no set time and worked irregular hours, coupled with the fact that he frequently stopped to conduct partnership business on the way to and from the lot; drove partnership vehicles to the Department of Motor Vehicles, and to dealers in Baltimore to view and buy used cars while on his way to or from his home; that one of the elements of the partnership arrangement was that each partner could have full use of the vehicles; that the use of the automobile by Harris for transportation to and from his home was admittedly "essential" to the partnership arrangement and the most practical and convenient way to operate; and that Harris conducted partnership business both at the used car lot and from his home requires that the question of whether the use of the automobile at the time of the accident was in the partnership interest and for its benefit be submitted to the jury. * * *

The appellant next complains that the lower court committed reversible error in charging the jury that the burden of proof was upon the defendants to show that the vehicle was not at the time being operated on partnership business. * * *

* * * We have held that in a collision caused by an automobile operated by the servant of the owner, there is a reasonable presumption that the servant was acting in the scope of his employment and upon the business of his master, and the burden of overcoming this presumption is upon the master by showing that the servant was em-

ployed in business other than his employer's. [Citations.] Here, where it was shown that a vehicle was owned by the partnership for resale and operated by one of the partners at the time of the accident, there arose the presumption that the car was upon partnership business. It was incumbent at that time for the defendants to show otherwise. * * *

Judgment affirmed.

ELLINGSON v. WALSH, O'CONNOR & BARNESON

(1940) 15 Cal.2d 673, 104 P.2d 507.

GIBSON, C. J.　This is an action against a partnership and its members for rent due under a written lease. The case was submitted upon an agreed statement of facts. Judgment was rendered against the partnership and all general partners, and from this judgment Lionel T. Barneson, one of the general partners, appeals. Appellant admits his liability for rent, but contends that the obligation therefor arose before his admission to the partnership, and that under section 2411 of the Civil Code this liability must be satisfied only out of partnership property. * * *

The issue in this case is not the liability of the partnership as such, nor the liability of its assets. There is no doubt whatever that the plaintiff may satisfy his claim against the partnership out of any of its properties. The sole question is whether the appellant's liability as an incoming partner may be satisfied by resort to his personal assets.

Section 2411 of the Civil Code (sec. 17 of the Uniform Partnership Act) provides: "A person admitted as a partner into an existing partnership is liable for all the obligations of the partnership arising before his admission as though he had been a partner when such obligations were incurred, except that this liability shall be satisfied only out of partnership property." It is this section upon which appellant relies, and the interpretation urged by appellant is the sole basis of his case. Appellant contends that since the lease was executed before he became a partner, the obligation of the lease arose before his admission, and therefore his liability can only be satisfied out of partnership property.

This contention would be sound if the only obligation of the partnership in this transaction was one which arose prior to appellant's admission to the firm. For example, if a promissory note had been executed by the partnership for a consideration then passing to it, the obligation would have arisen at the time of execution of the note and the case would plainly be within the statute. But appellant's contention overlooks the fact that a tenant of real property is not liable for rent solely by reason of the contract of lease. Tenancies in property need not necessarily be created by valid leases. One may become a tenant at will or a periodic tenant under an invalid lease, or without any lease at all, by occupancy with consent. Such tenancies carry with them the incidental obligation of rent, and the liability therefore arises not from contract but from the relationship of landlord and tenant. The tenant is liable by operation of law. Where there is a lease the liability of the tenant arising by operation of law is not superseded by the contractual obligation. Both liabilities exist simultaneously. The lease has a dual character; it is a conveyance of an estate for years, and a contract between lessor and lessee. The result is that dual obligations arise,—contractual obligations from the terms of the lease, and obligations under the law from the creation of the tenancy. * * *

Under the above principles, the first partnership, which did not include appellant as a member, was bound by these dual obligations; that is, having expressly assumed the obligations of the lease, it was bound in contract and also by reason of its tenancy. When appellant became a member, the first partnership was, in legal theory, dissolved and a new partnership came into being composed of the old members and appellant. This second partnership did not expressly assume the obligations of the lease, but it occupied the premises. Whether it was liable contractually on the lease is immaterial; it became liable for rent as a tenant. Strangers coming in with consent and occupying the premises would be liable; tenants would be liable even if there were no lease at all; and this second partnership and all its members were liable regardless of any lack of assumption of the obligations of the lease. If this were not true, then the second partnership could have been ousted despite its asserted right to occupy the premises under the existing lease. No one has suggested that the admission of appellant as a partner would have permitted the lessor to terminate the lease. But if the new partnership could not be ousted, it was a tenant and was liable for rent. And with respect to the liability of a tenant during this period, appellant's position is identical with that of any other member of the new partnership formed when he entered the old association. * * *

The judgment is affirmed.

PROBLEMS

1. A, B, and C, were partners in the business of painting and wallpapering. C went to the bank one day and borrowed $5,000 in the name of the firm and executed a promissory note for that amount. This action was not authorized by A and B and was unknown to them as C had spent the money in paying off the mortgage debt on C's home. When the note became due, the bank demanded payment from the partnership, and, upon nonpayment, brought suit against A, B, and C as partners. What decision?

2. A and B are partners in the dry goods business. A, without the knowledge of B, becomes a member of the firm of A, X and Company, in the same city, doing the same kind of business in competition with A and B. "A, X and Company" make a large profit. Is the A and B firm entitled to any of this profit?

3. A and B are partners, A having contributed $25,000 and B, his time and skill. (a) Can A change the nature of the business over B's objection? (b) On dissolution, after paying all firm debts, the assets are $20,000. B claims that he is entitled to $10,000. Is he correct?

4. Price and Brown organized a partnership to operate a hotel. The partnership was operating a rooming house in an apartment building which was leased by the partnership. Brown purchased with his own funds and without Price's knowledge, the apartment building in which the partnership was operating the rooming house, and he also purchased the adjacent apartment building. Is Price entitled to a partnership interest in the property purchased by Brown?

5. A and B were partners engaged in the business of operating a hardware store. B was a very lazy individual, spending considerable time in the summers on the golf course and most of the winters in Florida or California. All that B did in the partnership was to collect his share of the profits. In order to carry on the business successfully, A hired X to do B's work.

    (a) When the time came to divide up the profits, A deducted X's salary from B's share of the profits. B sued A to recover the amount of the salary paid to X out of B's share. The court dismissed the suit. Why? Could B collect in any court proceeding? If so, how?

    (b) Assume that A died, and that B returned and did a good job of winding up the partnership affairs. Could B recover compensation for these services?

6. A and B formed a partnership to buy and sell real estate, and particularly commercial locations. The normal procedure was for the partnership to follow up "leads" as to possible purchases that might come to the notice of one or the other of the partners. While the partnership was in force, there was brought to the attention of A because of his business, but in the course of a social affair at his golf club, that a certain commercial corner could be acquired cheaply. The partnership had sufficient funds available to make the purchase but since the two partners had been quarreling for some time A, anticipating a probable early dissolution of the partnership, arranged for C, his son-in-law, to effect the purchase for the account of A with personal funds of A advanced for the purpose.

No mention of the transaction was made to B. Sometime thereafter, the partnership was dissolved. Later, B learned of the above facts and, the property in question having been sold, sued A for an accounting and share of the profits which had been turned over to A by C. Decision?

7. In 1956, Constantine and Nicholas entered into a partnership for the conduct of a restaurant business. In the course of the partnership they established a number of restaurants, leasing various properties for this purpose. Early in 1966, at a time when the lease of one of the restaurants had a year or two more to run, Constantine, without the knowledge of Nicholas, purchased as a personal investment the real estate and building in which the leased restaurant premises were situated, using his own funds for that purpose. On July 1, 1966, the partnership was terminated by mutual consent. Thereafter, on learning of the purchase, Nicholas sued Constantine for a partnership accounting and claimed that the real estate purchased by Constantine should be treated as a partnership asset and the partnership accounts adjusted accordingly after crediting Constantine with the amount paid for the purchase price. Decision?

8. A and B were brothers and partners operating a large farm, Blackacre. The brothers encountered financial complications in the operation of the farm and became heavily indebted. A and B agreed to terminate the partnership farm operation and agreed that A would convey his one-half interest in Blackacre to B so that B could mortgage the farm and pay off the indebtedness. It was also agreed that B would continue to operate the farm for the purpose of paying off the indebtedness, and that when the indebtedness was paid that B would reconvey the one-half interest to A. Soon after the conveyance was made, farm values and farm income greatly increased to the extent that B was able to pay off the indebtedness. A then demanded that B reconvey to him the one-half interest in Blackacre. Upon the refusal of B to reconvey, A brought an appropriate action against B to compel the reconveyance. Decision?

9. A, B and C composed a trading partnership doing business under the name of the Fulton Lumber Company. A and B withdrew from the firm by mutual consent, C assuming the debts of the firm which he afterwards paid, and continuing the business at the same place and under the same name. No formal notice of dissolution was given. Subsequently, P had dealings

with C under the firm of Fulton Lumber Company. P had never dealt with the firm before dissolution and had no knowledge of the persons constituting it either before dissolution or at the time of the dealings in question. Could he hold the retired members responsible for a firm liability arising out of his dealings with C?

10. A, B, and C composed a partnership which operated the Bijou Theater. C was a secret partner. C retired from the firm upon an agreement with A and B whereby A and B paid him $10,000 for his interest and further agreed to pay all of the debts of the firm. At that time X was a creditor of the firm. After C's retirement X brings an action against A, B, and C, doing business as the Bijou Theater. Can C escape liability by pleading: (1) that he was a secret partner; (2) that he has retired from the firm; and (3) that A and B have assumed and agreed to pay the debt owing to X?

11. A and B, co-partners, hired a truck for two weeks from T for use in the firm business. On the following Sunday, B, with A's knowledge and consent, used the truck to move his furniture to his new house. While so using the truck, and due to his negligence B collided with P's car. As a result, both the truck and the car were severely damaged.

(a) P sues A and B, as partners for the damage to his car. Decision?

(b) T sues A and B, as partners for the damage to his truck. Decision?

12. Hanover leased a portion of his farm to Brown and Black, doing business as the "Colorite Hatchery." Brown went upon the premises to remove certain chicken sheds which they had placed there for hatchery purposes. Hanover thought Brown intended to remove certain other sheds which were his property, and an altercation occurred between them. Brown, wilfully struck Hanover and knocked him down. Thereafter, Brown ran to the Colorite truck which he had previously loaded with chicken coops and proceeded to drive back to the hatchery. Upon his return trip, he picked up George, who was hitchhiking to the city to look for a job. Brown was in a hurry and was driving at seventy miles per hour down the highway. At an open intersection with another highway, Brown ran a stop sign, striking another vehicle at the intersection, the collision causing severe injuries to George. Immediately thereafter, the partnership was dissolved; Brown was insolvent. Hanover and George each bring separate actions against Black as co-partner for the alleged tort committed by Brown against each.

What judgment as to each?

CHAPTER 33

DISSOLUTION AND WINDING UP

Introductory. There are three steps leading to the extinguishment of a partnership: (1) dissolution; (2) winding up or liquidation, and (3) termination. The Uniform Partnership Act defines dissolution as the change in the relation of the partners caused by any partner ceasing to be associated in the carrying on, as distinguished from the winding up, of the business. (Section 29.) Upon dissolution, the partnership is not terminated. It continues until the winding up of the partnership affairs is completed. (Section 30.)

Between dissolution and termination there is a twilight period, called winding up or liquidation, during which the business affairs are put in order, receivables collected, accountings had, payments made to creditors according to their respective contractual preferences, and distribution made of the remaining assets to the partners as provided in Section 40 of the Uniform Act.

As a partnership is a personal relationship, a partner always has the power to dissolve a partnership, but whether he has the right to do so is determined by the particular case. Reasonable notice is required to be given to the other partners.

Dissolution may be brought about (1) by act of the parties, or (2) by operation of law. Recourse to the courts is not necessary during winding up and liquidation, but court action may be sought by a partner or by creditors. The courts, upon application by a partner, may order dissolution upon any of the grounds set forth in Section 32 of the Uniform Act.

Dissolution by Act of the Parties. A partnership is dissolved by the act of the parties when (1) they expressly agree to dissolve the partnership, as the parties may contract for dissolution just as they contract for creation of the partnership; (2) a partner withdraws from the firm or a partner is added, as the partnership ends whenever its membership changes for any reason; (3) the partners indicate by conduct that they clearly do not intend to continue the partnership; (4) a partner violates the partnership agreement, although the other partners may choose to ignore the violation and thereby continue the relationship, or by failure to dissolve the partnership may be held to have waived their right to do so; (5) the award of an arbitrator dissolves the partnership, in the event the partners have provided by agreement that an arbitrator shall determine any differences between them, or (6) the period of time provided in the agreement as the term of the partnership expires, or the purpose for which the partnership was formed has been accomplished.

Dissolution by Operation of Law. A partnership is dissolved by operation of law upon (1) the death of a partner; (2) the bankruptcy of a partner or of the partnership; (3) subsequent illegality of the partnership, or (4) the entry of a decree or order of court upon any of the grounds contained in Section 32 of the Uniform Act.

Dissolution by Court Order. When controversies develop between partners which they are unable to settle by agreement, one of the partners usually petitions a court of equity for an accounting. This brings the matter before the court, which may decide as a matter of fact that the parties have by their own acts dissolved the partnership. The court will thereupon supervise liquidation, and, after all creditors have been paid or provision has been made for payment, will determine a proper accounting between the parties.

Upon application by a partner, a court will order a dissolution if it finds that (1) a partner is insane or suffers some other incapacity preventing him from functioning as a partner; (2) a partner is guilty of conduct prejudicial to the business or has wilfully and persistently breached the partnership agreement; (3) the business can only be carried on at a loss, or (4) other circumstances render it inequitable for the partnership to continue. (Section 32, Uniform Act.)

Effect of Dissolution. Except with respect to winding up the partnership affairs, including the completion of unfinished transactions commenced prior to dissolution, the authority of a partner to bind the partnership is terminated upon dissolution so far as the rights of the partners against one another are concerned. (Section 33.) Dissolution does not discharge the existing liability of any partner. (Section 36.)

When dissolution is caused by the death or retirement of a partner, and the business is continued by the surviving partner or partners or by them with one or more third persons, without liquidation of the partnership affairs, the creditors of the dissolved partnership are also creditors of the new partnership continuing the business. However, the liability of incoming new partners to creditors of the dissolved partnership is limited to the property of the partnership. (Section 41(7).)

When a partner dies or retires and the business is continued by the surviving partner or partners with or without third persons as new partners, and without any settlement of accounts with the retired partner or the legal representative of the deceased partner, the retired partner or such legal representative is entitled to have the value of his interest as of the date of the dissolution ascertained and to be paid the amount thereof as an ordinary creditor of the partnership. In addition, he is entitled to receive interest on this amount, or at his option, in lieu of interest, the profits of the business attributable to the use of his right in the property of the dissolved partnership. His rights, however, are subordinate to those of creditors of the dissolved partnership. (Section 42.)

Dissolution Upon Application of a Third Party. A partner may sell or assign his interest in the partnership, but this does not necessarily cause dissolution. The new owner does not become a partner, does not succeed to the partner's rights to participate in the management, and does not have access to the information available to a member of the firm as a matter of right. He is merely entitled to receive, in accordance with his contract, the profits to which the assigning partner would otherwise be entitled. He may not wish to force a dissolution, since the value of the interest assigned to him might greatly diminish during a winding up and liquidation. However, he may make application to a court for a dissolution.

Another instance of application to the courts by third parties is that of a creditor who has charged the interest of a partner with a judgment debt and applies for the appointment of a receiver. (Section 28, Uniform Act.) The court may appoint a receiver for the partner's interest who will receive and hold for the benefit of the creditor the share of profits which ordinarily would be paid to the partner. Dissolution does not necessarily result, and may not be desired by the other partners who are not at fault in any way and who might suffer needless loss upon dissolution and liquidation. Neither the judgment creditor nor the receiver is entitled to participation in the management or to have access to information except that relating to the partnership agreement and the extent of the profits. If the debt cannot be paid from the partner's share of profits, the next step is a foreclosure of the debtor's interest, and dissolution will result.

Dissolution Wrongfully Caused. Because of the personal element in a partnership, courts will not decree specific performance of a partnership agreement. They will not order a partner who has wrongfully withdrawn to return to the partnership. Such a wrongdoing partner is entitled to an accounting and to realize his interest in the partnership subject to the damages which the other partners may have sustained as the result of his breach of the agreement. The other partners are entitled to a lien upon his interest in the partnership until their claims against him are satisfied.

A partner who has been wrongfully expelled from the partnership is entitled to an accounting for his full interest in the partnership, including a share of the value of good will. However, one who has wrongfully withdrawn is entitled only to his interest, which may be computed without reference to the good will of the business. In addition, the remaining partners are entitled, if they so desire, to use the capital contributions of the wrongdoing partner for the unexpired period of the partnership agreement. They must however indemnify the former partner against further loss. This arrangement does not constitute in any way a continuance of the old partnership. The withdrawal has effected a dissolution of it, and a new partnership has been formed by the remaining partners who may hold their former partner's capital as an integral part of the business for the remainder of the period of time originally agreed upon.

Appointment of a Receiver upon Dissolution. Where the partnership agreement contains no provision for winding up the affairs of the partnership upon dissolution and the partners are unable to agree upon control, management, and procedures during the winding up period, a court upon the petition of a partner may appoint a receiver of all of the property and assets of the partnership with authority to operate the business subject to the direction of the court for such time as may be reasonably necessary. The receiver will not hold or administer any property individually owned by the partners.

The appointment of a receiver is discretionary with the court and its discretion may be exercised upon any of the following grounds:

1. Waste, fraud, misconduct or other breach of duty by a partner.

2. Conversion or misappropriation of property by a partner.

3. Exclusion of a partner by his co-partner from the business or premises of the partnership.

4. Refusal of a partner to render an account or to allow his co-partner access to partnership books and records.

5. Dissension and lack of confidence or harmony among the partners.

6. Mental incompetence of one or more of the partners.

7. Insolvency of the partnership.

8. The fact that a partner has become an enemy alien or non-resident of the State.

9. The fact that the partner requesting the receivership has contributed all or a greater portion of the funds and property invested in the partnership.

10. Material breach by a partner of the terms of a dissolution agreement.

Rights of Creditors With Respect to a Reconstituted Partnership. Whenever a partnership undergoes any change in membership, it is dissolved, and a new partnership is formed even though a majority of the old partners are present in the new combination. This is true whether the change consists in dropping one or more members, adding one or more members, or both. The creditors of the old partnership have claims against the new partnership and may also proceed to hold personally liable all of the members of the dissolved partnership. If a withdrawing partner has made arrangements with those who continue the business whereby they assume and pay all debts and obligations of the firm, and the accounting between the partners has reflected this undertaking, the withdrawing partner is nevertheless liable to creditors whose claims arose prior to the dissolution. His position is that of a surety. Upon being compelled to pay such debts, he immediately has a right of action against his former partners who agreed to pay them but failed to do so.

If a new partner is added to the firm, the partnership as formerly constituted is likewise dissolved, although there is no winding up or liquidation, and the business continues apparently without interruption. However, a new partnership has been formed. The new partner is liable for all of the obligations arising before his admission to the firm, although his liability on such pre-existing obligations may be satisfied only out of partnership property. (Section 17, Uniform Act.)

A withdrawing partner may protect himself against liability upon contracts which were entered into by the firm subsequent to his withdrawal by giving notice that he is no longer a member of the firm. Otherwise, he is liable for debts thus incurred and due and owing to a creditor who had no notice or knowledge of the partner having severed his association with the firm. Actual notice is required to be given to the persons with whom the partnership regularly does business, while notice by newspaper publication will be sufficient for the general business community. (Section 35, Uniform Act.) The basis of liability is estoppel. In the absence of notice, the outgoing partner is estopped to deny his membership in the firm in an action at law against him by a creditor who sold merchandise to the firm in the reasonable belief that he was still a member.

If the partnership is insolvent, the partners individually are obliged to contribute their respective share of the losses in order to make the creditors whole. If one or more of the partners is insolvent or bankrupt or, being out of the jurisdiction, refuses to contribute, the other partners are obliged to contribute the additional amount necessary to pay the firm's liabilities, in the relative proportions in which they share the profits. (Section 40, Uniform Act.) When any partner has paid an amount in excess of his proper share of the losses, he has a right of contribution against the other partners who have not paid their share.

Marshalling of Assets. The doctrine of marshalling of assets arose in equity. It is applicable only where the assets of a partnership and of its respective members are being administered by a court of equity or in bankruptcy. Marshalling means segregating and considering separately the assets of the partnership and the respective assets of the individual partners, as well as the respective liabilities of the partnership and of the several partners. Partnership creditors are entitled to be satisfied first out of partnership assets. To the extent that their claims are not satisfied out of partnership property, they have a right to recover the deficiency out of the individually owned assets of the partners, subordinate however to the rights of non-partnership creditors to those assets.

Conversely, the non-partnership creditors have first claim to the individually-owned assets of their respective debtors, and a claim junior to that of partnership creditors to participate in partnership assets to the extent of the interest therein of their individual debtors.

The cardinal principle of creditors' rights with respect to a partnership and its individual members, when it appears that the firm and several or all of the partners are insolvent, is that the partnership creditors are entitled to prior participation in the partnership assets and non-partnership creditors are entitled to participate first in individually owned assets. When a partner is insolvent or has become bankrupt, the order of distribution of his assets is, as follows: (1) debts and liabilities owing to non-partnership creditors; (2) debts and liabilities owing to partnership creditors, and (3) contributions owing to other partners with respect to payments by them to partnership creditors in excess of their respective share of the liabilities of the firm.

Settlement of Partners' Accounts. Section 18(a) of the Uniform Act provides that in the absence of any contrary agreement each partner shall "share equally in the profits and surplus remaining after all liabilities, including those to partners, are satisfied; and must contribute towards the losses, whether of capital or otherwise, sustained by the partnership according to his share in the profits."

Assume that A, B and C form the ABC Company, a partnership, with A contributing $6,000 capital, B contributing $4,000 capital, and C contributing services but no capital. There is no agreement as to the proportions in which profits and losses are to be shared. After a few years of operations, the partnership is liquidated and partnership liabilities to creditors are found to exceed partnership assets by $8,000. The aggregate loss of $18,000 must be borne equally by A, B and C. A's capital contribution of $6,000 is equal to his one-third share of the total loss. B must pay an additional $2,000 to make good his share of the loss, and C must pay $6,000 in order to equalize the loss and make the partnership creditors whole. In California, however, the rule appears to be that C would not be obligated to contribute to the loss. See Kovacik v. Reed, 49 Cal.2d 166, 315 P.2d 314 (1957).

The proportion in which the parties bear losses, whether of capital or otherwise, does not depend upon their relative capital contributions. It is determined by their agreement, and absent agreement, losses are borne in the same proportion in which profits are shared.

In the event that each of the partners, as well as the partnership itself, is insolvent, the claims of partnership creditors, under the facts above stated will be unpaid to the extent of $8,000. However, if any one of the partners individually is solvent, the partnership creditors may require him to pay the full amount of their claims.

Section 40(d) of the Uniform Act provides in part that "if any, but not all, of the partners are insolvent, or, not being subject to process, refuse to contribute, the other partners shall contribute their share of the liabilities, and, in the relative proportions in which they share the profits, the additional amount necessary to pay the liabilities."

In the case above stated, if both the ABC Company and A individually are insolvent, the results would not be changed since A had contributed $6,000 at the time of the formation of the partnership. However, if A and B were solvent and C were insolvent, A and B must contribute equally, since that is the ratio in which they share profits, the amount of C's share of the loss. As C's share of the loss is $6,000, A and B must each contribute $3,000 in addition to their own share of the loss. A would be obliged to pay an additional $3,000 and B an additional $5,000 in order to satisfy the unpaid claims of partnership creditors.

Assume now that the ABC Company, A individually, and C individually, are insolvent. B would be required to pay the entire balance of $8,000 due to partnership creditors, representing his unpaid share of the loss plus a contribution of the full amount of C's unpaid share of the liabilities.

Section 40 of the Uniform Act sets forth the rules to be observed in settling accounts between the parties after dissolution. As provided in Section 40(b), the order in which the liabilities of a partnership are ranked for payment out of partnership assets is as follows:

I. Amounts owing to creditors other than partners;

II. Amounts owing to partners other than for capital and profits;

III. Amounts owing to partners in respect of capital.

IV. Amounts owing to partners in respect of profits.

CASES

McCLENNEN v. COMMISSIONER OF INTERNAL REVENUE

(1943 C.C.A.1st) 131 F.2d 165, 144 A.L.R. 1127.

[George R. Nutter, a partner in the law firm of Nutter, McClennen & Fish, was entitled to eight per cent of the net profits. The partnership agreement also contained the following provision: "On the retirement of a partner or on his death—the others continuing the business—the retiring partner or his estate in the case of his death shall, in addition to his percentage of net profits of the Firm received by it in cash up to the date of such death or retirement, also receive the same percentage of net profits of the Firm received by it in cash until the expiration of the eighteen (18) calendar months next after such retirement, or death, and this shall be in full of the retiring or deceasing member's interest in the capital, the assets, the receivables, the possibilities and the good will of the Firm." Following Nutter's death in February, 1937, the surviving partners continued the business. During the course of the next eighteen months, eight per cent of the profits, amounting to $34,069.99, were paid over to the executors of Nutter's will. In filing a Federal estate tax return the only item included pertaining to the partnership was the sum of $6,136.21, representing Nutter's share in undistributed profits of the firm as of date of death. Beyond this nothing was included with respect to the value of decedent's interest in the partnership.]

MAGRUDER, J. * * * In his notice of deficiency the Commissioner determined that $34,069.99 should have been included in the gross estate as the value of decedent's "interest in partnership Nutter, McClennen & Fish." The Board has upheld the Commissioner in this determination. We think the Board was right.

In the absence of a controlling agreement in the partnership articles the death of a partner dissolves the partnership. The survivors have the right and duty, with reasonable dispatch, to wind up the partnership affairs, to complete transactions begun but not then finished, to collect the accounts receivable, to pay the firm debts, to convert the remaining firm assets into cash, and to pay in cash to the partners and the legal representative of the deceased partner the net amounts shown by the accounts to be owing to each of them in respect of capital contributions and in respect of their shares of profits and surplus. The representative of a deceased partner does not succeed to any right to specific partnership property. In substance the deceased partner's interest, to which his representative succeeds, is a chose in action, a right to receive in cash the sum of money shown to be due him upon a liquidation and accounting. These substantive results may be rationalized upon a theory of the partnership "entity". [Citation.] The same substantive results are reached under the Uniform Partnership Act which, in form at least, proceeds on the aggregate theory. [Citation.] That act, which is law in Massachusetts, conceives of the partner as a "co-owner with his partners of specific partnership property holding as a tenant in partnership"; but provides that on the death of a partner "his right in specific partnership property vests in the surviving partner or partners". Another enumerated property right of a partner, "his interest in the partnership", is described as "his share of the profits and surplus, and the same is personal property", regardless of whether the firm holds real estate or personalty or both. [Citations.] * * *

In the case at bar, if there had not been the controlling provision in the partnership articles, above quoted, or if the survivors had not come to some agreement otherwise with the executors of Mr. Nutter, the survivors would have had to proceed to wind up the affairs of the partnership, to conclude all unfinished legal business on hand at the date of the death, to realize upon all of the assets of the firm, tangible or intangible, to pay the debts, to return to Mr. Nutter's estate his contribution of capital, if any, and to pay to his estate in cash the amount shown to be due in respect of his "interest in the partnership", that is, his "share of the profits and surplus", as determined upon an accounting. Among other things to be taken into account, "the earned proportion of the unfinished business" would have had "to be valued to determine the decedent's interest in the partnership assets". [Citations.]

To obviate the necessity of a liquidation, or to eliminate accounting difficulties in determining the value of the deceased partner's interest, partners often make specific provision in the partnership articles.

Sometimes the partnership agreement merely provides for the postponement of liquidation, say, to the end of the term for which the partnership was created. Thus, a partnership agreement between A, B and C might provide that "should any partner die during the term of said co-partnership the firm shall not be dissolved thereupon, but the business shall be continued by the survivors until the expiration of said partnership term, the estate of the deceased partner to bear the same share in profits and losses as would have been received and borne by the deceased partner had he lived". Under such an agreement, if A dies, B and C do not buy out A's interest in the partnership. Unless more appears, A's executor does not become personally liable as a general partner. [Citation.] Nor is A's general estate in the executor's hands liable as a partner for new debts created by B and C in continuing the business. [Citation.] For the remainder of the term, A's share already embarked in the business remains in, subject to the risks of the business. It would seem not improper to describe the continuing business as now being owned by B and C as general partners, with A's estate (or A's executor as trustee under the will of A) as a limited partner therein, sharing in the profits, but not liable beyond the amount or interest already embarked in the business.

In the case at bar the partnership agreement contains another familiar arrangement, whereby no liquidation and final accounting will ever be necessary in order to satisfy the claim of the deceased partner. In place of the chose in action to which Mr. Nutter's executor would have succeeded in the absence of specific provision in the partnership articles, that is, a right to receive payment in cash of the amount shown to be due the deceased partner upon a complete liquidation and accounting, a different right is substituted, a right of the estate to receive a share of the net profits of the firm for 18 calendar months after the partner's death.

The language of the partnership agreement in the present case is couched in terms of a purchase of the deceased partner's interest. What the estate is to receive "shall be in full of the retiring or deceasing member's interest in the capital, the assets, the receivables, the possibilities and the good will of the Firm". There is to be an extinguishment of the decedent's interest in the totality of the firm assets, tangible and intangible, as they stood at the moment of death, and the interests therein of the surviving partners are to be correspondingly augmented. Decision in the estate tax case now before us does not turn on the question whether the effect of the partnership agreement may be characterized with entire accuracy as a "purchase" and "sale" of the deceased partner's interest in the partnership.

The decision of the Board of Tax Appeals is affirmed.

GIANAKOS v. MAGIROS

(1965) 238 Md. 178, 208 A.2d 718.

[Executor of wife of deceased partner brought action against administrator of estate, who was also son and copartner of deceased, asking that accounting of partnership assets be made, that executor be permitted to elect between profits of partnership earned after partner's death or interest on deceased partner's capital account from his death, and that receiver be appointed to take over partnership assets. Decree in favor of defendant, executor appeals.]

OPPENHEIMER, J. * * * The court below found that it was entirely proper, under the circumstances, for Thomas to operate the restaurant as an individual proprietorship after George's death, subject only to the admitted obligation to account to George's estate as a creditor for George's interest. The Executor contends that this conclusion was incorrect on the grounds that under The Uniform Partnership Act, Code (1957), Art. 73A (the Act), Thomas as sole surviving partner was under the duty to wind up the affairs of the partnership, and that Thomas, acting as legal representative of the deceased partner, was without legal capacity to elect to stand as an ordinary creditor.

Under the Act, one of the causes of dissolution of a partnership is the death of a partner. § 31. On dissolution, the partnership is not terminated but continues until the winding up of partnership affairs is completed. § 30. On the death of a partner (when he is not the last surviving partner) his right in the specific partnership property vests in the surviving partner. § 25(2)(d). Under § 37, unless otherwise agreed, the surviving partner has the right to wind up the partnership affairs, provided, however, that any partner or his legal representative, upon cause shown, may obtain winding up by the court. Under § 41(1), (2) and (3), the surviving partner may continue the business without liquidation of the partnership affairs if he has the consent of the representative of the deceased partner and if there is no agreement to the contrary. The rights of the legal representatives of the deceased partner, in such case, are to have the value of the deceased partner's interest ascertained as of the date of dissolution, which was the date of death of the deceased partner; and to receive that amount as an ordinary creditor.

There was no agreement between the partners, George and Thomas, as to what should happen upon the death of either partner. Thomas, as administrator of George's estate, therefore, by reason of his appointment, had to make the election as to whether the business should be continued by himself in his individual capacity as surviving partner with the interest of George's estate therein valued as of the date of dissolution; or whether to ask the court to wind up the partnership affairs, in which case, George's estate would receive one-half of the net proceeds of the eventual liquidation.

Absent any breach of fiduciary relationship, it is clear under the Act that Thomas, as surviving partner, had the right to continue the business without liquidation of the partnership affairs, under Section 41(2) of the Act with his own consent as representative of the deceased partner (George's estate of which Thomas was administrator); that such consent was given, although not in formal terms, by Thomas as administrator to Thomas as surviving partner; that by virtue thereof, under § 41(3), Thomas, as surviving partner, had the same rights as if a formal assignment had been made; and that, there being no agreement to the contrary, under § 42 of the Act, Thomas' rights as George's administrator were to receive as an ordinary creditor the value of George's interest in the dissolved partnership, with legal interest, or at Thomas' option, as George's representative, instead of interest on the claim, the profits attributable to the use of the right of George's estate in the property of the dissolved partnership. [Citation.]

The Executor contends that the provisions of the Act to which reference has been made do not apply because they are predicated upon the continuance of the business. He argues that Thomas did not continue the partnership business because he closed out the partnership books and operated the business as an individual proprietorship subject to the obligation as surviving partner to account to George's estate as creditor for George's one-half interest in the dissolved partnership. However, the Act does not require that the business be continued as a partnership. The statutory reference to continuation of the business, under the circumstances, clearly refers to continuation of the business by the survivor in his own right. Under the provisions of the Act, Thomas, as administrator of George's estate, consented to the continuation of the business of the dissolved partnership and, therefore, Thomas, as the legal representative of George's estate, had the right to have the value of George's one-half interest ascertained at the date of dissolution, and to receive the amount thereof as an ordinary creditor, unless he was precluded from exercising the choice which the statute

gives because of his dual relationship as administrator and surviving partner.

It is this choice which Thomas made as administrator of his father's estate which the Executor claims he did not have the right to make. Apart from the provisions of the Act which by its terms, as has been seen, gives the administrator of an estate the right to make the election here considered, the Executor claims that under general equitable principles Thomas was precluded from taking any action in which the interest of the beneficiaries under his position as administrator and his own personal interest as surviving partner may conflict.

*   *   *

In this case, under the Act, it was inherent in Thomas' position as administrator that he elect, for the estate, either to receive the value of George's interest in the dissolved partnership as an ordinary creditor, or under Section 30, to have the partnership continue until the winding up of partnership affairs is completed, with the right to an accounting for the deceased partner's interest, under Section 43. If an administrator is properly appointed by the court having jurisdiction, he is not disqualified by the filing of a personal claim against the estate; nor, as administrator, is he required to avail himself of a defense of limitations against such a claim. [Citation.] By reason of his court appointment, in the absence of proof of wrongdoing, he is authorized to take action which might, under other circumstances, constitute a conflict between his personal position and his fiduciary capacity. He is, of course, liable under his bond as administrator for any breach of his duty in that capacity. In this case, Sophie, the wife, did not protest Thomas' appointment as administrator, and the Executor expressly disclaims any request for his removal. No intentional wrongdoing by Thomas is claimed.

*   *   *

In this case, Thomas accounted for George's partnership interest by including in the inventory of the assets of George's estate a one-half interest in the partnership assets at the value set by the Orphans' Court appraisers. There is a difference of opinion as to whether the partnership interest of the deceased partner should be accounted for by filing an inventory or a list of debts. * * * It is undisputed that the interest of George in the partnership assets was included by Thomas in the inventory of George's estate. While exceptions were filed to that account, the record does not disclose what the exceptions were or what the inventory was or, indeed, that the inventory was not correct. The record does affirmatively show that all requests of the Executor to Thomas for information in connection with the partnership business were answered.

* * *

What has been said as to the Executor's request for an accounting is also applicable to his request for appointment of a receiver. Admittedly, the appointment of a receiver in a case of this kind is discretionary with the court. [Citation.] The Executor contends that the refusal of the lower court to appoint a receiver in this case was a clear abuse of discretion. We disagree. On the facts as disclosed by the record, we find nothing to indicate that the appointment of a receiver is necessary for the protection of the interests of the parties. There is no showing that George's estate will not receive what may be determined to be due him or that the safety of the estate requires that Thomas as surviving partner be divested of his control of the business. The refusal of the court below to appoint a receiver, in our opinion, was not erroneous but, on the contrary, was justified by the facts in the case.

Decree affirmed; costs to be paid by the appellant.

FISHER v. FISHER

(1965) — Mass. —, 212 N.E.2d 222.

SPIEGEL, J. This is a bill in equity for dissolution of a partnership and a partnership accounting. The defendants filed a counterclaim for breach of the partnership agreement. The case was referred to a master. The plaintiff filed objections (treated as exceptions) to the master's report. An interlocutory decree was entered overruling the plaintiff's exceptions and confirming the master's report, from which decree the plaintiff appealed.

After this interlocutory decree was entered the plaintiff moved to have the report recommitted to the master. Another interlocutory decree was entered recommitting the report to the master "for the sole purpose of determining the amount of the complainant's share of the profits from October 1, 1962." The plaintiff appealed from this decree "only in so far as said Decree failed to recommit to the master the issue of the amount of the Plaintiff's drawing account from January 1, 1963, to the date of the master's additional report." The master filed a supplementary report to which the plaintiff filed objections.

No decree was entered regarding the objections or the confirmation of the master's supplementary report. A final decree was entered dismissing the plaintiff's bill from which the plaintiff appealed.

The master found the following facts.

In 1897 George E. Fisher established George E. Fisher & Co. Over a period of years, from 1919 to around 1930, he took into his business as partners his brother Carlos (plaintiff) and sons Allen, George Ellis, and Donald (defendants). When George E. Fisher died, his widow was taken in as a nominal partner until her death in 1956.

The parties operated under ten year term partnership agreements covering business in insurance, real estate and mortgage loans. However, their last agreement, made in 1960, covered only insurance business. Under the 1960 agreement the plaintiff was to work half time and to draw $65 per week plus an auto allowance, life insurance premiums, and one quarter of the net profits. Provision was made for the payment of specified sums on death or withdrawal of a partner. All of the agreements required each partner to contribute to the partnership fifteen per cent of all fees and commissions received for acting in any fiduciary capacity. In April of 1961 the defendants discovered that Carlos had been receiving moneys for which he failed to properly account to the partnership. An accountant's report showed that the plaintiff owed about $380 to the partnership for money received after execution of the 1960 partnership agreement and several thousand dollars for money received on earlier dates. The defendants suspended the plaintiff from the partnership as of May 1, 1961, and stopped his drawing account, auto allowance, and insurance premiums. The plaintiff wrote a letter protesting the stopping of his drawing account and claiming his rights as a partner. On June 23, 1961, the plaintiff was notified that he was "permanently suspended" from the partnership because of his failure to account to the partnership. In October, 1961, be brought this bill for a partnership accounting.

The master also found that if Carlos was wrongfully excluded from the partnership, he was entitled to $34,469.51 on liquidation, and he should be charged for $4,983.03 withheld from the firm. On recommittal on the issue of the plaintiff's share of the profits after October 1, 1962, the master found the plaintiff's share to be $4,682.80.

The plaintiff contends that he is not barred from maintaining this suit by his conduct toward the partnership. "The doctrine of clean hands is not one of absolutes. It is to be so applied as to accomplish its purpose." [Citation.] Its purpose is to prevent a party from benefiting by his dishonesty. In the instant case the plaintiff's claims do not arise out of his improper conduct. "A partner does not lose his rights in the accrued profits of a firm by reason of breaches of the partnership articles, whether or not committed in bad faith, although of course he will be subject to charges for all unexcused breaches in the final accounting." [Citations.]

The defendants argue that by his actions the plaintiff withdrew from the partnership and the provisions of the partnership agreement on withdrawal govern him. There is no provision in the agreement or in the Uniform Partnership Act that a breach is equivalent to withdrawal from the partnership, and we will not imply one. This bill cannot be construed as a withdrawal, since the plaintiff had already been excluded from the partnership.

The plaintiff's failure to properly account to the partnership for moneys received by him constituted a breach of the agreement. This breach furnished grounds for the defendants to seek a decree of dissolution of the partnership under the provisions of G.L. c. 108A, § 32(1) (d). Instead of following the procedure under the statute and without any provision in the agreement authorizing what the defendants called a "permanent suspension," they ousted the plaintiff from the partnership and divided his interest in the partnership among themselves. This wrongful action furnished the plaintiff with grounds to obtain dissolution under the same provisions of the statute.

We believe that in justice to the defendants they should not be required to continue to pay the plaintiff moneys beyond June 23, 1961, the date the plaintiff was notified in writing that he was suspended from the partnership because of his failure to account to the partnership. Equity and the furtherance of justice (see G.L. c. 211, § 3) require that the partnership be dissolved as of June 23, 1961. Such a decree may be entered nunc pro tunc. [Citation.]

It follows, therefore, that the plaintiff is entitled to receive from the partnership such sums as may be determined to be due him if the partnership had been dissolved as of June 23, 1961, in accordance with the provisions of G.L. c. 108A, § 38, with interest from that date.

* * *

The interlocutory and final decrees are reversed and the case is remanded to the Superior Court for further proceedings in accordance with this opinion.

So ordered.

ELLIOT v. ELLIOT

(1964) 88 Idaho 81, 396 P.2d 719.

TAYLOR, J. Defendant (appellant) in partnership with his brother, Gordon Elliot, began farming in 1951. The partners leased lands from their father and uncle by oral lease upon a year to year basis. Of this leased land 378 acres was farm land and 320 acres grazing land. In 1952 they expanded their operation to include 130 acres of Indian farm land. * * *

In the fall of 1957 Gordon Elliot withdrew from the partnership and separated from his wife, the plaintiff (respondent) in this action. The plaintiff and Gordon Elliot were married in January, 1940. They lived together on the leased farm land during the existence of the partnership. Defendant Philip Elliot during that time was unmarried. Plaintiff and Gordon were divorced April 30, 1958. By the decree of divorce Gordon's interest in the partnership assets was awarded to plaintiff. The court in this case found that the partnership

was dissolved by Gordon's withdrawal October 15, 1957. Thereafter, Philip conducted the farming operations as before. In the fall of 1957 after Gordon's departure, plaintiff advised defendant of her intention to procure renewal of the leases on the Indian lands in her own name, or in the name of Gordon Elliot. Defendant then requested plaintiff to allow him to procure new leases in his name, and assured her the interests of plaintiff and her children would be safeguarded. Accordingly defendant procured new leases in his own name, which were executed January 22, 1958. These leases were for five years and expired December 31, 1962. In the fall of 1957, after Gordon's departure, plaintiff requested defendant to render an accounting of the partnership business and assets, and offered to settle with him for a stated amount without an accounting. This the defendant refused to do and advised plaintiff that Gordon had no interest to settle.

In March, 1959, plaintiff commenced this action for an accounting, and to recover the interest of Gordon Elliot in the assets of the partnership.

* * *

As to the leases, the court found that defendant continued to farm the leased lands, during the five years subsequent to dissolution, in the same manner as before; continued to use the partnership equipment in that activity; and refused to wind up the affairs of the partnership or to render any accounting to plaintiff.

Gordon's withdrawal effected a dissolution of the partnership. I.C. § 53–331.

"The dissolution of a partnership is the change in the relation of the partners caused by any partner ceasing to be associated in the carrying on as distinguished from the winding up of the business." I.C. § 53–329.

"On dissolution the partnership is not terminated, but continues until the winding up of partnership affairs is completed." [Citations.]

Plaintiff did not become a partner by virtue of the divorce decree, but she did thereby become the successor in interest of Gordon Elliot in the assets of the partnership, subject to dissolution and the payment of its existing obligations. She became in effect Gordon's assignee.

"In case of a dissolution of the partnership, the assignee is entitled to receive his assignor's interest and may require an account from the date only of the last account agreed to by all the partners." I.C. § 53–327 (2).

Upon the dissolution it became defendant's duty to wind up the affairs of the partnership. His refusal to limit his subsequent activities to the performance of that duty rendered defendant liable to account to plaintiff for the subsequent use of partnership assets. The leases had not expired at the date of the dissolution, and crops had been planted upon the leased lands in the fall of 1957 for the production of crops to be harvested in 1958. In view of the statute I.C. § 53–330, defendant's refusal to wind up the partnership affairs and his continuance of the partnership business, and refusal to account, justified the court's finding that the successive renewals of the leases were partnership assets. The value thereof as fixed by the court was modest and amply supported by the evidence.

* * *

Judgment affirmed.

FARMERS' & MECHANICS' NAT. BANK v. RIDGE AVENUE BANK

(1916) 240 U.S. 498, 36 S.Ct. 461, 60 L.Ed. 767.

WHITE, C. J. The essential facts stated in the certificate of the court below are these: The firm of William Gray & Sons and its three partners, William J. Gray, Peter Gray and Alexander J. Gray, were adjudged bankrupts. The same person was appointed trustee of the four estates. It resulted from charging separately against each estate the mere necessary and unquestioned expenses of administration that there was nothing whatever in the estate either of the partnership, of that of William J. Gray or of Peter Gray,—indeed in the latter there was nothing to defray the expenses of administration. As to the estate of Alexander J. Gray, after charging the expenses of administration there remained $1,597.26. Creditors of the firm proved their debts against it, the Ridge Avenue Bank of Philadelphia being among the number, while only one creditor, the Farmers' & Mechanics' National Bank of Philadelphia, proved a debt against the individual estate of Alexander J. Gray, that debt exceeding the total sum of the estate. No creditor proved against the individual estate of William J. Gray or that of Peter Gray. Under these conditions the dispute which arose was whether the estate of Alexander J. Gray was to go wholly to the Farmers' & Mechanics' National Bank, the individual creditor, or was to be proportionately applied to the individual and firm creditors because of the absence of any firm estate for distribution. The District Court directed the funds to be distributed between the Farmers' & Mechanics' National Bank, the creditor of the individual estate, and the creditors of the firm, and the question of law which the court below propounds to enable it to review this action of the District Court, is as follows:

"When a partnership as such is insolvent and when each individual member is also insolvent, and when the only fund for distribution is produced by the individual estate of one member, are the individual creditors of such member entitled to priority in the distribution of the fund?"

The solution of this question primarily depends upon an interpretation of subsection f of sec. 5 of the Bankruptcy Act of 1898, and secondarily upon a consideration of all the pertinent subsections of the section, indeed, of all the relevant provisions of the context of the act. Subsection f is as follows:

"f. The net proceeds of the partnership property shall be appropriated to the payment of the partnership debts, and the net proceeds of the individual estate of each partner to the payment of his individual debts. Should any surplus remain of the property of any partner after paying his individual debts, such surplus shall be added to the partnership assets and be applied to the payment of the partnership debts. Should any surplus of the partnership property remain after paying the partnership debts, such surplus shall be added to the assets of the individual partners in the proportion of their respective interests in the partnership." * * *

It follows that the question propounded will be answered, Yes.

And it is so ordered.

PROBLEMS

1. Simmons, Hoffman, and Murray were partners doing business under the firm name of Simmons & Co. The firm borrowed money from a bank and gave the bank the firm's note for the loan. In addition, each partner guaranteed the note individually. The firm became insolvent and a receiver was appointed. The bank claims that it has a right to file its claim as a firm debt and also that it has a right to participate in the distribution of the assets of the individual partners before partnership creditors receive any payment from such assets.

(a) Explain the principle involved in this case.

(b) Is the bank correct?

2. A, B and C form a partnership, A contributing $10,000, B, $5,000, and C his time and skill. Nothing was said as to the division of profits. The firm becomes insolvent, and after payment of all firm debts, the remaining assets realize $6,000. A claims that he is entitled to the entire $6,000. B contends that the distribution is $4,000 to A and $2,000 to B. C claims the $6,000 should be divided equally between the partners. Who is correct?

3. A, B and C were partners under a written agreement made in 1959 that it should continue for 10 years. During 1965, C being indebted to X sold and conveyed his interest in the partnership to X. A and B paid X $5,000 as C's share of the profits for the year 1965, but refused X permission to inspect the books or to come into the managing office of the partnership. X brings an action setting forth the above facts and asks for an accounting and an order to inspect the books and to participate in the management of the partnership business.

(a) Does C's action dissolve the partnership?

(b) To what is X entitled with respect (1) partnership profits, (2) inspection of partnership books, (3) accounting by the partnership and (4) participation in the partnership management?

(c) In case of a dissolution to what is X entitled with respect to C's interest and accounting?

4. The articles of partnership of the firm of Wilson and Company provide:

"William Smith to contribute $50,000; to receive interest thereon at 7% per annum, and to devote such time as he may be able to give; to receive 30% of the profits."

"John Jones to contribute $50,000; to receive interest on same at 7% per annum; to give all of his time to the business, and to receive 30% of the profits."

"Henry Wilson to contribute all of his time to the business, and to receive 20% of the profits."

"James Brown to contribute all of his time to the business, and to receive 20% of the profits." There is no provision for sharing losses. After six years of operations, the firm has assets of $400,000 and liabilities to creditors of $420,000. Upon dissolution and winding up, what are the rights of the respective parties?

5. Indicate which of the following statements are true and which are false:

(a) Creditors having claims based upon torts committed by partners in the course of business of the partnership are preferred over creditors with claims based upon contracts.

(b) Partners who wish to continue the business have a prior right to purchase the assets;

(c) In the absence of a contract providing otherwise, the distribution to partners of accrued profits should be in equal parts regardless of the fact that the partners had contributed to the firm unequally.

(d) Advances in the nature of loans made by the various partners to the partnership share in the firm assets on the same basis as debts due other creditors.

(e) As between the partners the assets of the partnership must be applied to pay the claims of partners in respect of capital ahead of the claims of partners in respect to profits.

(f) Debts owing to partners (other than for the capital and profits) rank ahead of debts owing to partners in respect to capital and profits.

(g) The capital contributed by a limited partner must be repaid before any other claims or debts are paid out of partnership assets.

6. Harold Warner and Tom Clardy were co-partners in the operation of a cattle raising partnership. Warner and Clardy were both killed as the result of a common disaster. Mary Warner, the widow of Harold Warner, took charge of the partnership business and spent considerable time and effort in winding up the partnership business. In a suit brought for an accounting, Mary Warner made a claim for a reasonable allowance for services rendered in winding up the affairs of the partnership. The partnership agreement contained no provision for payment for services rendered in connection with the winding up of partnership affairs.

What decision?

*

PART SEVEN

CORPORATIONS

CHAPTER 34

GENERAL NATURE, FORMATION, AND POWERS OF CORPORATIONS

Introductory. A corporation is a body established by law and existing separate and distinct from the individuals whose contributions of initiative, property, and continuing control make it possible for it to function. In the language of Chief Justice Marshall of the United States Supreme Court in Dartmouth College v. Woodward, 4 Wheat. (U. S.) 518, 636, 4 L.Ed. 629 (1819):

"A corporation is an artificial being, invisible, intangible, and existing only in contemplation of law. Being the mere creature of law, it possesses only those properties which the charter of its creation confers upon it, either expressly or as incidental to its very existence. These are such as are supposed best calculated to effect the object for which it was created. Among the most important are immortality, and, if the expression may be allowed, individuality; properties by which a perpetual succession of many persons are considered as the same, so that they may act as a single individual. A corporation manages its own affairs, and holds property without the hazardous and endless necessity, of perpetual conveyances for the purpose of transmitting it from hand to hand. It is chiefly for the purpose of clothing bodies of men, in succession, with these qualities and capacities, that corporations were invented, and are in use. By these means, a perpetual succession of individuals are capable of acting for the promotion of the particular object, like one immortal being."

A corporation, therefore, should be distinguished from the individuals who compose it and those who control it as well as from the property which it owns. A corporation is merely the medium or device through which its shareholders as investors, and its officers and directors, as management, carry on a particular business enterprise. While the corporation is artificial, invisible, and intangible, its proprietors and management are human beings, and its property is real, personal, tangible, and frequently substantial. Use of the corporation as an instrument of commercial enterprise has made possible the vast purposive concentrations of wealth and capital which have largely transformed this country from an agrarian to an industrial economy.

785

Partnerships and Corporations Contrasted. The essential differences between a partnership and a corporation may be summarized, as follows:

	Partnership	Corporation
Creation	By agreement of the parties	By statutory authorization
Entity	Not a legal entity	A legal entity
Duration	Dissolved by death, bankruptcy, or withdrawal of a partner	May be perpetual
Limitation of Liability	Partners are subject to unlimited liability upon the contracts, debts and torts of the partners	Shareholders are not liable for the contracts, debts, or torts of the corporation
Transferability of Interest	Interest of a partner in a partnership is not transferable without the consent of all of the other partners	Shares of stock in a corporation are freely transferable
Management and Control	Each partner is entitled to an equal voice in the management and control of the business and affairs of the partnership	The business of the corporation is managed by a board of directors elected by the shareholders
Agency	Each partner is both a principal and an agent of his co-partners	A shareholder is neither a principal nor an agent of the corporation
Suits by and Against	In actions brought by the partnership, all partners are parties plaintiff; in suits against the partnership on contracts or debts, all partners are necessary parties defendant	May sue and be sued in the name of the corporation

---

A Corporation must have a Franchise. In order to obtain the advantages of conducting a business enterprise in corporate form, a charter or franchise granted by the legislative branch of the government is indispensable. Prior to the middle of the nineteenth century, it was not uncommon for the legislatures of the several States and for the English Parliament to pass special acts creating corporations. The early railroad companies in this country were formed under special acts of the legislature of their respective States of incorporation. It would be an intolerable burden today upon the law-making branch of the government if each corporation were required to be the subject of a special statute. It would also, obviously, make incorporation more difficult and less speedy of accomplishment and reduce the corporate birth rate. The number of business corporations in existence in the United States is in the hundreds of thousands. A large number of States have provisions in their constitutions prohibiting the creation of corporations by special act of the legislature. The legislature therefore enacts a general law pursuant to which the Secretary of State or other designated State official may issue a charter or certificate of incorporation to those persons who comply with its provisions. A corporation is still a creature of the legislature, but it is permitted to be formed by the provisions of a general statute rather than by special act.

The charter is a contract between the corporation and the State of its origin. Under the Federal constitution, no State legislature may enact a statute which impairs the obligation of contract, and, consequently, as held by the Supreme Court of the United States in the Dartmouth College case, a State, after creating a corporation, may not, by subsequent legislation, infringe upon any of its rights or any of the rights of its shareholders or members. In order to avoid the impact of this decision, practically every general incorporation law contains a provision, which reserves to the legislature the power to amend, repeal or modify the statute at its pleasure. This section of the statute is part and parcel of the charter of every corporation organized under it and is a valid and material part of the contract between the corporation and the State. It causes every corporation organized under a general statute to be subject to any amendment or modification of the statute.

A Corporation is a Legal Entity. A corporation is a legal entity separate and apart from its members or shareholders, with rights and liabilities entirely distinct from theirs. It may sue, or be sued by, or contract with, any one of its members, although an individual cannot sue himself or contract with himself. A transfer of stock in the corporation from one individual to another has no effect upon the legal existence of the corporation. Even where a single individual owns all of the stock in the corporation and no other person has any interest in the cor-

poration whatever, the shareholder and the corporation are not the same but continue their separate and distinct existences. Title to corporate property belongs not to such a shareholder but to the corporation.

Piercing the Corporate Veil. The corporate entity will be disregarded whenever it is used to defeat public convenience, justify wrong, protect fraud, promote crime, or circumvent the law. This is frequently referred to as piercing the corporate veil or going behind the corporate entity and holding accountable the individuals who are attempting to utilize the entity to insulate themselves from the consequences of their wrongdoing. The courts are not blind and are quick to pierce the corporate veil where deemed necessary to promote the ends of justice. Thus, where a substantial shareholder and creditor of a corporation set fire to an insured building owned by the corporation, the insurance company was held not liable on the fire insurance policy which it issued to the corporation covering the building thus destroyed.

The Corporation as a Person. A corporation is a person within the meaning of the fifth and fourteenth amendments to the constitution of the United States, which provide, in part, that no "person" shall be deprived of "life, liberty, or property without due process of law." A corporation is also a person within the provision of the fourteenth amendment which provides that no State shall "deny to any person within its jurisdiction the equal protection of the laws."

While a corporation is frequently considered a person whenever that word is used in a constitution or statute, there are instances where it is not so considered. For example, a corporation is not considered as a person within that clause of the fifth amendment to the constitution which protects a "person" against self-incrimination. The rule of construction to be applied in determining whether corporations are within the term "persons" as used in a particular statute depends upon the legislative history of the statute, and especially upon its aim, purpose and intendment.

A corporation is not a person within the meaning of statutes which license a "person" to practice a profession such as law, medicine or dentistry and require personal qualifications relating to competence and integrity. In every State, the laws which provide for the licensing of persons to practice these professions preclude a corporation from obtaining a license. In a few States, the courts have held, or the legislatures have determined by statute, that optometry, auditing, chiropody, engineering, and architecture are professions the practice of which is prohibited to corporations. It has been ruled that a corporation may not have for its name "Credit Adjustment Company," inasmuch as adjusting debts is the function of one who practices law and a corporate name may not indicate or imply a purpose or undertaking which it may not legally fulfill.

A Corporation as a Citizen. A corporation is not a citizen as the term is used in that part of the fourteenth amendment to the constitution of the United States which provides, "No state shall make or enforce any law which shall abridge the privileges or immunities of citizens of the United States."

A corporation, however, is regarded as a citizen of the State of its incorporation, or of the State in which it has its principal office, for the purpose of determining diversity of citizenship as a basis for jurisdiction of the Federal courts of an action at law or suit in equity to which the corporation is a party. For example, a lawsuit involving $10,-000 or more may be brought against the X Company, a Delaware corporation, by anyone who is not a citizen of Delaware or incorporated therein, in the Federal court in any Federal district in which summons may be served upon the X Company. Such a suit may not be brought in a Federal court against the X Company where the requisite diversity of citizenship between the parties to the suit is lacking. The Federal Judicial Code provides that for this purpose a corporation shall be deemed to be a citizen of the State wherein it has its principal place of business, as well as of the State of its incorporation.

Classification of Corporations. Corporations have been classified as aggregate and sole; public and private; profit and nonprofit; domestic and foreign; de jure and de facto.

Blackstone, who apparently first classified corporations as aggregate and sole, defined aggregate corporations as those which "consist of many persons united together in one society, and maintained by a perpetual succession of members, so as to continue forever." On the other hand, sole corporations "consist of one person only and his successors, in some particular station, incorporated by law, in order to give them some legal capacities and advantages, particularly that of perpetuity, which in their persons, they could not have had. The king is a corporation sole; so is a bishop, and every parson and vicar."

A public corporation is one created by the State for political purposes to act as an agency in the administration of civil government, such as a county, city, town, village, school district, park district, sanitation district, or to operate and conduct a public business, such as the Reconstruction Finance Corporation, Tennessee Valley Authority, or the Chicago Transit Authority. Public corporations are sometimes called political corporations and more frequently municipal corporations. A private corporation is one consisting of private individuals and formed for business purposes, as distinguished from governmental purposes.

Corporations which are formed under business corporation statutes are sometimes referred to as profit corporations to distinguish them from the non-profit or charitable corporations organized under a separate statute referred to as the not-for-profit-corporation statute. Instances of non-profit corporations are educational institutions, athletic clubs, library groups, fraternities, sororities, hospitals, and organizations which have exclusively a charitable purpose.

A corporation is said to be domestic with reference to the State of its incorporation or domicile. It is regarded as foreign in every jurisdiction other than the State of its incorporation.

Formation of Corporation. The formation of a corporation under a general incorporation statute requires the performance of several acts by various groups, individuals and State officials. Among the various steps in the procedure to organize such a corporation are:

(1) the existence of a general statute passed by the legislature of the State permitting the issuance of a charter to a group of persons upon compliance with its terms;

(2) the promotion of the proposed corporation by its organizers, who are sometimes referred to as promoters, including the procurement of offers by interested persons known as subscribers to buy stock in the corporation when created, and the preparation of the necessary incorporation papers;

(3) the execution of the articles of incorporation by the incorporators, who are usually required to be subscribers;

(4) the filing of the incorporation papers and the issuance of the charter or certificate of incorporation by the Secretary of State;

(5) the holding of organization meetings by incorporators, stockholders and directors immediately upon the issuance of the charter, and

(6) the recording of the certificate of incorporation in the public recorder's office.

All of the States have general incorporation laws which permit a group of persons to obtain a charter by complying with the requirements therein contained. Such laws delegate to a State executive official, ordinarily the Secretary of State, the duty of determining whether the general law has been complied with and, if so, of issuing a charter to the applying group. Under modern corporation acts, the incorporators are required to execute and to deliver to the Secretary of State "articles of incorporation," which are, in effect, an application for a charter. If the Secretary of State determines that the articles are adequate and in proper form, he permits them to be filed and issues and returns to the incorporators a "certificate of incorporation," which includes the duplicate executed copy of the articles and is the corporation's charter. The creation of the corporate entity occurs on the day the Secretary of State files the articles in his office and issues the certificate. On that day, corporate existence begins.

Prior to the actual incorporation, the organization procedure is in the hands of the promoters, subscribers, and incorporators. The functions of each of these groups may be performed by the same persons. For example, A, B and C may form a small corporation and each one be a promoter, subscriber, and incorporator. On the other hand, it is possible for the promoters, subscribers, and incorporators to be different persons, except in those States which require that all incorporators be subscribers.

After incorporation, the promoters' task is finished; the incorporators may be required in some States to call a shareholders' meeting or participate in an incorporators' meeting, and thereafter they cease to function. Upon incorporation, by the law of most States, the subscribers immediately become shareholders. After incorporation and the post-incorporation organization meetings, the life of the corporation is in the hands of its shareholders, and its business and affairs are managed by its board of directors and by its officers. At this point, the corporation, alive and mature, takes its place among the business population.

Selecting a State for Incorporation. Ordinarily, a corporation is incorporated in the State in which it is intended that it transact all or the principal part of its business. However, it is possible for a corporation to be created in one State, by meeting that State's requirements for incorporation, and to transact all or most of its business in another State or States by qualifying or obtaining a license, to do business in such other State or States. The principal criteria for determination of the State in which a particular corporation is to be formed are:

(1) Fees and taxes, including organization fees, annual franchise taxes, corporate income taxes, inheritance taxes on shares held by non-residents, stamp taxes on transfer of shares, and taxes on intangible values.

(2) Voting rights and restrictions thereon (in Illinois, for example, the constitution and statute require that each share of stock be entitled to vote).

(3) Restrictions on the declaration of dividends.

(4) Provisions of State Securities Acts or Blue Sky Laws.

(5) Requirements for amending articles of incorporation.

(6) Powers of shareholders and directors in internal management.

(7) Consideration for shares and standards employed in the valuation of property received as consideration.

(8) Liabilities imposed upon shareholders and directors.

Organization Procedure. Although the procedure varies to some extent under the different State incorporation laws, generally the steps required to be taken to organize a corporation are, as follows (sections of the Model Business Corporation Act, Appendix D, are indicated where applicable):

(1) Preparation of the articles of incorporation. (Section 48.)

(2) Signing of the articles by the required number of qualified incorporators and, generally, acknowledgment of the signatures before a notary public. (Section 47.)

(3) Delivery of the articles to the Secretary of State, and payment of the required organizational fees. (Section 49.)

(4) Filing of the articles by the Secretary of State and the issuance by him of the certificate of incorporation. (Section 49.)

(5) Recording of the certificate and articles of incorporation with the recorder of deeds, county clerk, or other county official of the county in which the registered office or principal office of the corporation is located.

(6) In a few States the articles must be published or must be approved by a court or commissioner.

(7) Holding the directors' first or organization meeting at the call of the directors to adopt the by-laws, elect officers, and transact other business. (Section 52.)

(8) In some States a permit or license to do business is required.

(9) Qualification of the corporation's stock under the State securities law in the event that no exemption is available.

(10) Registration of the corporation's stock under the Federal Securities Act of 1933 in the event that no exemption is available.

(11) Issuance of stock and receipt of payment therefor.

(12) Procurement of corporate seal and minute book.

(13) Commencement of business.

Articles of Incorporation. Under modern business corporation acts, the incorporators are required to prepare the articles of incorporation. Although the requirements differ in the several States, the Model Business Corporation Act requires the articles of incorporation to set forth the following (Section 48, Appendix D):

(1) Name of the corporation.

(2) Address of the corporation's registered office and the name of its registered agent, whose address must be identical with that of the registered office, such agent to be an agent for service of process, notice or demand upon the corporation.

(3) Duration, which may be perpetual or for a limited period of time.

(4) Names and addresses of the incorporators, consisting of three or more subscribers who are natural persons of the age of twenty-one years or more.

(5) Purpose or purposes for which the corporation is formed, which may be any lawful purpose except banking, insurance, or the operation of railroads.

(6) Number of authorized shares of stock and the par value of each share or a statement that the shares are without par value.

(7) If the shares are to be divided into classes, the designation, preferences, limitations, and relative rights in respect of the shares of each class.

(8) Number of shares to be issued before the corporation commences business, and the consideration to be received therefor, which must not be less than one thousand dollars.

(9) Number of directors constituting the initial board of directors, and the names and addresses of those who are to serve as directors until the first meeting of shareholders.

(10) Any provision which the incorporators may choose to insert limiting or denying to shareholders the pre-emptive right to acquire additional shares of the corporation,

such right existing unless specifically limited or denied in the articles of incorporation.

(11) Any provision which the incorporators may choose to insert for the regulation of the internal affairs of the corporation.

Name. A corporation must have a name and, as Blackstone stated, "by that name alone it must sue and be sued, and do all legal acts, though a very minute variation therefrom is not material. Such name is the very being of its constitution, without which it could not perform its corporate functions."

The general incorporation laws in the various States have differing provisions in regard to the corporate name. Some laws provide that the name must be expressed in English letters or characters. Most acts require that the name contain a word or words which clearly indicate that it is a corporation, such as "corporation," "company," "incorporated," "limited," "Corp.," "Co.," "Inc.," or "Ltd." Other permissive words in some states are "Association," "Society," "Institute," "Club," "Union," and "Syndicate." In most States, certain other words must not be included in corporate names, such as "Bank," "Insurance," or words indicating an improper purpose. In some States, it is required that "Company" not be preceded by "and" lest a partnership be implied.

Practically every incorporation statute provides that no corporate name shall be the same as, or deceptively similar to, the name of an existing corporation doing business within the State.

Incorporators. The "incorporators," or "corporators" as they are sometimes called, are the persons who execute the articles of incorporation. They are usually required to be natural persons, twenty-one years or more of age, and subscribers to the stock of the corporation to be organized. Most modern business corporation acts require three or more incorporators, although one or two acts provide for "any number," which would apparently be satisfied by one incorporator. Ordinarily, the incorporators need not be residents of the State of incorporation. New York and Pennsylvania provide, however, that two-thirds of the incorporators must be citizens of the United States. Most of the statutes require that the incorporators be "natural persons," which would prevent corporations from acting as incorporators, and even in those States where the statute is silent, it is doubtful whether a corporation may lawfully act as an incorporator without express statutory authority and express power in its charter to do so. The Michigan statute provides expressly that a corporation may act as an incorporator. Most acts require that the incorporators be twenty-one years old, or "of legal age" or "adults" and, in the absence of an express restriction, a similar one would be implied since the charter is a contract and a minor lacks full capacity to contract. Most of the acts require incorporators to be subscribers to the stock, although this restriction does not seem to be of great importance since an incorporator may transfer his shares of stock to another person immediately following incorporation.

Ordinarily, the incorporators must hold an organization meeting, although certain States dispense with this requirement. Such meeting may be held anywhere, except where the statute specifies that it must be held in the State of incorporation. At this meeting, the first board of directors is elected, and the future activities of the corporation are turned over to the directors, whereupon the incorporators as such cease to have any further function. In certain States, the individuals composing the first board of directors are named in the articles of incorporation. In Illinois, the incorporators call a shareholders' meeting instead of holding a meeting of the incorporators.

De Jure and De Facto Corporations. A de jure corporation, or a corporation by law or by right, is one formed in strict compliance with the general corporation statute in accordance with the organization procedure heretofore outlined. A de jure corporation is entitled to exist and operate for the period named in its charter or perpetually, if so provided, and such existence may not be challenged by anyone, not even by the State in a direct proceeding commenced for this purpose.

However, it occasionally happens that, although the incorporators intend and attempt to create a de jure corporation, they fail to comply with every necessary requirement of the controlling statute. If the circumstances reveal (1) the existence of a general corporation law, (2) a bona fide attempt to comply with that law and to organize a corporation thereunder, and (3) an actual exercise of corporate powers in the belief that a corporation has been created, then a de facto corporation, or corporation in fact, results. The existence of a de facto corporation can be questioned only by the State in a direct attack challenging such existence. This means that a de facto corporation has the same rights and privileges as a de jure corporation insofar as any person or entity, other than the State is concerned. The de facto corporation may sue and be sued, may make contracts, may acquire and transfer property, and perform every other act which a de jure corporation may perform. If a de facto corporation commences a lawsuit to collect a debt owing to it, it is no defense to such suit that the plaintiff corporation is not de jure. In fact, not even the State can *collaterally* question de facto corporate existence in a proceeding involving another issue. The State must bring an independent suit for the express purpose of challenging corporate existence and of ousting the corporation.

Example: A, B and C, believing they have organized a corporation known as the ABC Company, cause the company to enter into a contract under its own name with T, a third party. Because of the failure to comply or even attempt to comply with the general incorporation law, neither a de jure nor de facto corporation has been created. Actually, there is no corporate existence, but if T deals and contracts with A, B and C as a corporation he thereby admits that they are a corporation, and as between the parties there is a "corporation by estoppel" for the purpose of this contract only. In a suit by the ABC Company against T for breach of contract, T is estopped to deny that the ABC Company is a corporation.

Many statutes prohibit private inquiry into irregularities of organization. The Illinois Act, which is illustrative, provides that "a certificate of incorporation shall be conclusive evidence, except against the State, that all conditions precedent required to be performed by the incorporators have been complied with and that the corporation has been incorporated under this Act." (Compare Model Act, section 50, Appendix D.)

Subscribers and Subscriptions. A subscription is an offer to purchase capital stock in a corporation yet to be formed. The offeror is called a "subscriber." Sometimes the term subscription is used loosely to include a contract to purchase stock in an existing corporation, but, strictly speaking, this latter type of agreement is an executory contract of purchase and sale rather than a subscription. The distinction is important since a subscriber becomes a shareholder, with all of the rights and liabilities attached thereto as soon as his offer is accepted, whereas a purchaser of stock does not become a shareholder until the certificate of stock is issued to him. For example, if ABC Corporation becomes insolvent and its assets are delivered into the hands of a trustee in bankruptcy, the trustee may collect the consideration for unpaid stock from subscriber X but not from purchaser Y, assuming that neither X nor Y had received his certificate of stock prior to the bankruptcy. The reason is that subscriber X became a shareholder and liable

for payment of his stock simultaneously with the acceptance of his subscription, regardless of the fact that his certificate had not been delivered, while purchaser Y would not become a shareholder until his certificate was issued to him, an act which became impossible of performance when the ABC Corporation became bankrupt. Whether any particular transaction is a subscription or a purchase agreement depends upon ascertaining the intention of the parties, and the usual rules of interpretation of contracts are applicable. Use of the words "subscribe" or "subscription," or "purchase" or "sale" may be considered but these words, taken alone, are not determinative.

Courts have viewed subscriptions in two ways. The majority regards a subscription as a continuing offer to purchase stock from a non-existing entity, which is incapable of accepting the offer until it shall have been created. Under this view, a subscription may be revoked at any time prior to its acceptance. A minority of jurisdictions treat a subscription as a contract between the various subscribers and therefore irrevocable except with the consent of all of the subscribers. Almost all courts agree that the subscription is accepted by the corporation immediately upon its coming into existence. Very few courts require an express acceptance, but even where required, express acceptance is found in any act of recognition by the corporation of the subscriber as a shareholder, such as entering his name in the records as a shareholder or issuing a certificate of stock in his name, and the corporation is not required to notify the subscriber of its acceptance. The general common-law rule is that a subscription may be revoked by the subscriber at any time prior to the incorporation of the corporation but may not be revoked thereafter.

Any element of doubt as to the status of a subscription has been removed, however, by modern incorporation acts. Under the

Model Act, for example, a subscription is irrevocable for a period of six months, unless otherwise provided in the subscription agreement, or unless all of the subscribers consent to the revocation of the subscription. (Section 16.)

Although it is not the general rule, there is some justification for considering a subscription as a contract among the various subscribers. It is certainly true that many subscribers sign a subscription agreement primarily because of the character and standing of the other persons whose names appear on the agreement. Consequently, there exists a source of temptation for promoters to procure the names of influential and reputable persons on the subscription agreement, and often this has been done by representing to such persons that they may rescind the agreement at any time they wish to do so. In such cases, the courts have enforced payment by these persons of the consideration for the stock on the theory that the collateral agreement permitting rescission was invalid as a fraud upon other subscribers, as well as creditors of the corporation. A subscription agreement may be released or rescinded only upon the unanimous consent of all of the subscribers and for sufficient consideration. Nevertheless, in cases where promoters have fraudulently procured subscriptions, upon misrepresentations or otherwise, and the subscriber was not a party to the fraud, he has been permitted to rescind the subscription after formation of the corporation.

Payment by Subscribers. By the terms of the subscription agreement, the subscriber agrees to furnish certain consideration for the shares of stock which he is to receive. The statutes generally set forth requirements as to the sufficiency and nature of the consideration. The Model Act provides that shares having a par value may not be issued for less than par. (Section 17.) Shares without par value may be issued for such consideration as may be fixed from time to time by the board of directors or shareholders. (Section 17.) Under this Act it would not be lawful for par value stock to be issued as a gift or as a bonus with the purchase of other stock. However, treasury stock, that is, stock once validly issued and re-acquired by the corporation, may be sold for any consideration.

The Model Act further provides that payment for shares must be made either in money, in other property, tangible or intangible, or in labor or services actually performed. (Section 18.) Neither promissory notes nor future services constitute payment for shares. Most Corporation Laws have similar provisions.

The time for payment of the consideration is usually set forth in the subscription agreement, but if not, the time is determined by the board of directors upon making a call or assessment.

In most States, a corporation must not commence business until a stated minimum amount of consideration, usually one thousand dollars, has been paid in, and if the corporation commences business contrary to this requirement, the directors of the corporation are personally liable up to such amount.

Promoters' Contracts. In addition to procuring subscriptions and preparing the incorporation papers, promoters often enter into contracts in anticipation of the creation of the corporation. The contracts may be ordinary agreements necessary for the eventual operation of the business, such as leases, purchase orders, employment contracts, and sales contracts, or the promoter may obtain a particularly advantageous contract outside of the routine business requirements of the incipient corporation, such as a valuable selling franchise. If these contracts are executed by the promoter in his own name and there is no further action, the promoter is liable on such contracts, and the corporation, when created, is not liable. A pre-incorporation contract made by promoters does not bind the corporation even though made in the name of the corporation and in its behalf, except where so provided by statute as in Michigan. The promoter, in executing such contracts, may do so in the corporate name although incorporation has not yet taken place. Prior to its formation, a corporation has no capacity to enter into contracts or to employ agents or representatives. Upon being formed, it is not liable at common law upon any prior contract, even one made in its name, unless it adopts or ratifies the contract expressly, impliedly, or by knowingly accepting benefits under it.

Promoters' Fiduciary Duty. Promoters occupy a fiduciary relationship to subscribers, shareholders and the corporation itself, and are under a duty to account for any secret profit made at the expense of those to whom the fiduciary duty is owing.

Since a promoter is prohibited only from gaining secret profits there is nothing to prevent him from lawfully obtaining profits known and assented to by all of the persons interested in the corporation at the time of its formation. Thus, if the promoters themselves subscribe to all of the capital stock, or if they inform and obtain the consent of all of the original subscribers in regard to their profit, no one can complain, even though the original stock may be subsequently transferred to innocent investors who have no knowledge of the profit.

By-Laws. The by-laws of a corporation are the rules and regulations adopted by the corporation for its internal management. They are subject to, and must be consistent with, the constitution and statutes of the State of incorporation and the charter of the corporation. In the absence of a specified power to adopt by-laws in the general law or in the charter of the corporation, this power resides in the shareholders. The Mod-

el Business Corporation Act (Section 25, Appendix D) provides that "The power to alter, amend or repeal the by-laws or adopt new by-laws shall be vested in the board of directors unless reserved to the shareholders by the articles of incorporation".

The Model Act further provides that "The by-laws may contain any provisions for the regulation and management of the affairs of the corporation not inconsistent with law or the articles of incorporation." This is the general rule.

Qualification of Stock under Blue Sky Laws and the Securities Act of 1933. In 1911, the first statute was enacted in this country by the Kansas legislature providing regulation for the issuance and sale of corporate stock and other securities. This law and similar statutes in effect in every State except Nevada, Delaware, and Alaska, are popularly known as "Blue Sky Laws." In 1933, Congress passed the first Federal statute providing regulation of securities offered for sale and sold through the use of the mails or instrumentalities of interstate commerce. This statute often called the "Truth in Securities Act," is administered by the Securities and Exchange Commission. It is a disclosure type of statute, and the Commission does not examine into the merits of the security proposed to be offered but only into the truthfulness, accuracy, and completeness of the information given and required to be given in a registration statement and prospectus.

Regulation of the issuance and sale of securities is contained in statutory anti-fraud provisions and in requirements for registration of broker-dealers, agents, and investment advisers, and for registration of securities. There is no uniformity among the State Blue Sky Laws although concerted efforts may be expected in this direction since the approval of the Uniform Securities Act on August 25, 1956, by the National

Conference of Commissioners on Uniform State Laws.

The State laws are administered by different departments in various States, such as the Attorney General (Alabama, Maryland, New Jersey, New York); the Corporation Commission (Arizona, California, Oregon, Virginia); the Bank Commissioner (Arkansas, Connecticut, Kentucky, Louisiana, Nebraska); the Securities Commissioner (Colorado, Florida, Kansas, Oklahoma, Pennsylvania, South Dakota, Texas); the Commissioner of Insurance (Iowa, New Hampshire, South Carolina) and the Secretary of State (Georgia, Illinois, Mississippi, North Carolina).

Certain State statutes are of the licensing or qualification type and others are of the notification or description type. The Blue Sky Law in Illinois which was completely revised and modernized in 1953, provides for three types of registration of non-exempt securities: (1) registration by notification, in the case of seasoned securities which have been effectively registered with the S.E.C.; (2) registration by description, in the case of unseasoned securities or those issued by a newly formed corporation with no record of earnings, which have, however, been effectively registered with the S.E.C.; and (3) registration by qualification, in the case of securities which have not been effectively registered with the S.E.C. The effect of these provisions is to simplify and facilitate the registration of a security in Illinois which has previously been qualified for sale under the Federal statute by means of an effective registration statement and prospectus on file with the Securities and Exchange Commission.

In no case does any State by qualifying an issue of stock or other security for sale, nor the S.E.C. by permitting a registration statement to become effective, thereby give any endorsement of the merits of the security.

Corporations which are issuing a relatively small amount of stock, or a substantial amount to relatively few persons have an exemption from qualification under the Blue Sky Laws of most States and the Securities Act of 1933. In certain cases, it is necessary to comply with the rules formulated by the Securities and Exchange Commission or by the appropriate State agency in order to gain an exemption from registration of a stock issue. If no exemption is available, a corporation issuing or offering for sale its stock or other securities, as well as any person selling such securities, is subject to injunction, possible criminal prosecution, as well as civil liability to the person to whom the securities are sold in violation of the Blue Sky Law of any State or the Securities Act of 1933.

CORPORATE POWERS

In General. A corporation derives its existence and all of its powers from the State and, therefore, has only such powers as the State has conferred upon it. Power is used here to mean the legal capacity to execute and fulfill the objects and purposes for which the corporation was created, and the source of this power is the charter and the statute under which the corporation was organized. Unless carefully defined, the term may cause confusion inasmuch as a corporation may, by its duly authorized agents, engage in and perform acts which are beyond its corporate powers. To declare these acts null and void is merely to deal with the effect of them and not to dispute their existence. Such acts are ultra vires, yet the corporation did them. While the absence of power ordinarily connotes inability, it has never been denied that a corporation has the physical ability to engage in activities or transactions which transgress the limits of its charter or statutory powers. To say that a corporation did not do a certain act because such act was legally impossible inasmuch as it was not legally authorized is to confuse physical occurrence and legal effect. Properly considered, ultra vires does not mean without power. It does not refer to the unauthorized act of an officer or agent of the corporation; nor does it refer to an act of a corporation which is illegal because of the nature of the subject-matter and would be so considered if done by an individual or partnership. Ultra vires simply refers to acts, activities, and transactions of a corporation which are beyond the scope of those which are legally authorized, namely, the type of acts which it has not been legally created and empowered to perform.

Statutory Powers. Every corporation organized under a general statute has all of the general powers granted by the statute, which may include, as provided in Section 4 of the Model Business Corporation Act (Appendix D), the following powers:

(1) To have perpetual succession or a shorter duration of life as stated in the articles of incorporation.

(2) To sue and be sued in the corporate name.

(3) To have a corporate seal.

(4) To buy, lease or otherwise acquire and own, hold and use real and personal property.

(5) To sell, convey, mortgage, pledge, lease and otherwise dispose of all or part of its property and assets.

(6) To lend money to its employees, other than its officers and directors.

(7) To buy, subscribe for or otherwise acquire, own, hold, vote, use, sell, mortgage, pledge or otherwise dispose of shares, interests in, or obligations of other corporations, associations, partnerships or individuals.

(8) To make contracts, incur liabilities and issue notes, bonds or other obligations.

(9) To invest surplus funds.

(10) To conduct its business and carry on its operations within or without the State of incorporation.

(11) To elect or appoint officers and agents, define their duties and fix their compensation.

(12) To make and alter by-laws for the administration and regulation of its affairs.

(13) To lend money to the State or Federal government for war purposes.

(14) To have and exercise all powers necessary or convenient to effect any or all of the purposes for which the corporation is formed.

(15) To cease its corporate activities and surrender its corporate franchise.

In addition to the above enumerated general powers, the statutes usually provide that a corporation has power to:

(1) Acquire its own shares.

(2) Deal in real estate to the extent provided in the articles of incorporation.

(3) Change its registered agent and registered office.

(4) Create and issue shares of stock, as provided in the articles of incorporation.

(5) Allocate part of the consideration received for its shares to stated capital and part to paid-in surplus.

(6) Fix a record date for the purpose of determining the shareholders entitled to notice, to vote, or to receive a dividend.

(7) Declare and pay dividends.

(8) Amend its articles of incorporation.

(9) Effect a reduction of stated capital or paid-in surplus.

(10) Effect a merger or consolidation with one or more other corporations.

A corporation is not authorized generally to contribute corporate funds to charity, as this is a form of vicarious generosity. The law generally regards a corporation as existing solely for the purpose of making money for its stockholders, and only such expenditures as contribute to this purpose are within its powers. Certain States have enacted statutes which permit a corporation to make donations to community funds to be used for the improvement of social and economic conditions in the community in which the corporation is doing business. The Federal government permits corporations to take as deductions gifts to recognized charities for income tax purposes. The giving of free passes or reduced transportation rates to ministers of the Gospel or persons engaged in eleemosynary or charitable work, as permitted by statute, has been upheld against attack by a shareholder of a railroad corporation. State ex rel. Spillman v. Chicago, B. & Q. R. R., 112 Neb. 248, 199 N.W. 534 (1924).

Providing pensions to old and infirm employees, sick benefits, hospitalization, recreational facilities, vacations with pay, and performing humane acts of kindness and care for employees are regarded as within the powers and duties of the corporation. As stated by one court, "The reasonable care of its employees * * * is merely transacting the business of the corporation." The contribution of funds for scientific research or to assist colleges and universities in specific projects is also permissive where a possible advantage to the corporation is not too remote.

Express Charter Powers. The objects or purposes for which a corporation is formed are expressly stated in its articles of incorporation, which delineate in general language the type of business activities in which the corporation proposes to engage. This serves (1) to advise the shareholders of the nature and kind of particular business activity in which their investment is being risked, (2) to guide the officers, directors and management as to the extent of the corporation's authority to act, and (3) to inform any person who may contemplate dealing with the cor-

poration of the extent of its legally authorized power.

The express powers must relate to a legitimate business activity or industry within the purview of the general statute, such as manufacturing, mining, milling, merchandising, management of real estate, operation of transmission lines, local transportation, water, gas and electric utilities, or the performance of services. A bank, insurance company or railroad company may not be organized under a general corporation law but may be organized under a separate statute, and, therefore, an express power to engage in any of these businesses will not be granted to a corporation formed under the general statute. A corporation may not be organized to practice law, medicine or dentistry as public policy restricts to individuals the right to engage in the practice of these and other professions.

Implied Powers. A corporation has the authority to do any act which is necessary or conveniently adapted to and consistent with the execution of any of its express powers and the operation of the business which it was formed to conduct. This power exists by implication and is based not upon express language in the charter or statute but upon reasonable inference as to the proper scope and content of such language, taking into consideration the facts and circumstances of the particular case. Thus, a railroad corporation is not ordinarily authorized to operate a hotel, but at a junction point of two of its intersecting lines a particular railroad company was held to have the implied power to build, own and manage a hotel to accommodate its transfer passengers who would otherwise be without such facilities.

The express powers of a corporation may and should be stated in general language, and it is not necessary to set forth in detail every particular type of act which the corporation is empowered to perform. A general statement of corporate purpose or object is sufficient to give rise to all of the powers necessary, incidental or convenient to the effectuation of that purpose. For instance, a corporation organized expressly "to buy and sell goods, wares and merchandise" has implied power to (1) purchase or lease store premises, (2) employ salesmen, (3) to buy or rent trucks or delivery wagons, (4) spend money for advertising, (5) open and manage a bank account, (6) employ buyers and pay their salaries and traveling expenses and (7) purchase insurance on the lives of officers or substantial debtors, and, in addition, to perform numerous other acts which bear a logical relation to the proper execution of the power expressly granted. Implied powers are closely akin to express powers from which they are derived by implication.

Liability for Torts and Crime. A corporation is liable for the torts and crimes committed by its agents in the course of their employment. The doctrine of ultra vires even in those jurisdictions where it is permitted as a defense, has no application to wrongdoing by the corporation. The doctrine of respondeat superior imposes full liability upon a corporation for the torts of its agents and employees while engaged in company business.

Example: X, a truck driver employed by the ABC Corporation, while on a business errand, negligently runs over Y, a pedestrian. Both X and the ABC Corporation are fully liable to Y in an action by him to recover damages for the injuries sustained.

A corporation may also be found guilty of fraud, false imprisonment, malicious prosecution, libel and other torts.

One of the essential elements of most crimes is a guilty mind or criminal intent, and it has been argued that since a corporation is artificial, intangible and incorporeal, it cannot have either a mind or a soul and is therefore incapable of committing a crime. This is a tenuous argument and overlooks the fact that a corporation never acts except through the minds, eyes, and hands of human agents, and that some corporations command and are commanded by the finest executive minds in this country. As a juristic fiction, a corporation is theoretically immortal. It may not have a soul to save, but the absence of a soul in its incorporeal body does not noticeably inhibit or prevent a corporation from transgressing the laws of man which exist for the welfare and safety of the community and the State. Corporations do not go to heaven because no business is transacted there. Corporations are amenable to the criminal law for violations of which they may be indicted and punished. The punishment necessarily is by fine and not imprisonment.

Defense of Ultra Vires. Since a corporation has authority to act only within the limitations of its charter and statutory powers, any contract is invalid where made by it in the purported exercise of authority beyond those powers. This is the early view of the courts and is modified today by statute. Even where not modified, a majority of the courts give full effect to the defense of ultra vires only where the contract is executory on both sides. If the corporation has received full performance from the other party to the contract, it is not usually permitted to escape liability by a plea of ultra vires, and, conversely, if the corporation has fully performed the contract on its side and is suing the other party for failure to perform, a defense that the plaintiff corporation has exceeded its powers is generally unavailing.

Section 6 of the Model Business Corporation Act abolishes the defense of ultra vires by providing:

"No act of a corporation and no conveyance or transfer of real or personal property to or by a corporation shall be invalid by reason of the fact that the corporation was without capacity or power to do such act or to make or receive such conveyance or transfer."

Effect of Ultra Vires Activities. While ultra vires under modern statutes may no longer be used defensively as a shield against liability, corporate activities which are ultra vires may be redressed in any of the three following ways as provided in Section 6 of the Model Act:

(1) In an injunction proceeding brought by a shareholder against the corporation to restrain and enjoin the further commission of ultra vires acts.

(2) In a suit by the corporation acting directly or through a receiver, trustee or other legal representative or through shareholders in a representative suit against the officers or directors of the corporation.

(3) In a proceeding by the Attorney General of the State of incorporation to dissolve the corporation or to enjoin it from the further transaction of unauthorized business.

It should be noted that officers or directors are not liable for causing the corporation to do any act or engage in any activity in excess of its powers where they act in good faith. An honest mistake of judgment, an oversight, or a calculated program undertaken upon advice of counsel, may possibly involve the corporation in ultra vires activities for which the officers and directors would not be individually liable. However, where the officers and directors manifest utter disregard for charter limitations and apply corporate funds to unauthorized purposes, they become individually liable for any loss thereby sustained by the corporation.

Model Business Corporation Act. In 1946 a committee of the American Bar Association after careful study and research submitted a draft of a Model for State Business Corporation Act patterned largely upon the Illinois Business Corporation Act which had been adopted in that State in 1933. The Model Act has been constantly revised and improved and is the product of the best thinking of leading practitioners of corporation law in the United States.

The Model Act consists of 145 sections, the first 53 of which are in general devoted to substantive provisions and the next 45 to procedures of various types. Nineteen sections are devoted to foreign corporations, 10 to annual reports, fees, franchise taxes, and various charges payable to the State, and 18 to penalties, administrative authority, and miscellaneous matters.

The Model Act has been adopted in whole, or in part, in 23 jurisdictions. It is being considered for adoption in numerous other States. All States have felt its influence, and many have adopted various sections of the Model Act while not adopting the Act in its entirety.

The Model Act as revised to 1964 is set forth in Appendix D. It is valuable both as a source and as a guide to the statutory law of business corporations.

CASES

MARSH v. GENERAL GRIEVANCE COMMITTEE OF THE LAKE ERIE AND WESTERN DISTRICT OF THE BROTHERHOOD OF LOCOMOTIVE FIREMEN AND ENGINEMEN

(1965) 1 Ohio St.2d 165, 205 N.E.2d 571.

[The plaintiff, who had performed services and incurred expenses for autonomous committee of unincorporated association, brought action against the committee to recover for services and expenses incurred. The Court of Appeals for Allen County reversed the judgment of the Court of Common Pleas and entered final judgment for the committee. The cause came before the Supreme Court for review.]

HERBERT, J. * * * Is the appellee committee severable from the Brotherhood of Locomotive Firemen and Enginemen to adjudicate such issues as are raised in the case at bar?

The brotherhood embraces firemen and enginemen employed on railroads throughout the United States and Canada, whereas the appellee is composed of three members chosen from three lodges comprising a district of the brotherhood. Neither the brotherhood nor the appellee is incorporated. Appellant is no longer a member of the brotherhood.

One of the members of the appellee committee, J. W. Jennings,—called to testify on behalf of the committee—testified as follows relative to the appellee committee:

" * * *

"A. Well, the general grievance committee on this railroad being composed of three men, is somewhat an oddity in the brotherhood. We have general grievance committees on certain larger carriers that are composed of 30, 40 local chairmen—have that many lodges in some of the larger railroads, but again I say that the local chairman conducts all his business of his own up to a point. Now, in the composition of these committees, our own brotherhood law provides that we will meet as a committee; we will elect a chairman, a vice chairman. On many of the bigger properties, we have more than one vice chairman. We have several. We have a secretary-treasurer of that committee. I think, as outlined in cross-examination here the other day, *the only way that you can pay the expenses of a general grievance committee on any property is by levying of assessments upon the members of that particular committee.* The committee itself has the right to determine how much it costs to operate this committee. If they deem it ad-

visable to assess every member one dollar a month, this they do. If the expenses get to the point where it is deemed advisable to add to that one dollar, then this is done to pay all the expenses that might arise." (Emphasis added.)

The appellee committee appears to be an autonomous body elected by and responsible to three lodges, one at Lima, Ohio, one at Peru, Indiana, and the other at Frankfort, Indiana, comprising the district known as the Lake Erie and Western District of the Brotherhood of Locomotive Firemen and Enginemen. Each of the three lodges had one member on the committee. The committee deposited its funds in a bank of its own choosing and in the name of the committee, appellee here. It is authorized to adopt or amend its own bylaws.

The chairman and secretary-treasurer of the appellee committee determines the amount of assessments upon members of the three lodges, necessary to meet all expenses of the committee and levies and collects such assessments. A lodge failing to collect and forward this assessment "shall stand suspended."

* * *

It is quite clear that the appellee is an entity within the brotherhood, with complete autonomy in matters and issues raised here. Appellee levies and collects assessments to pay the expenses of members of the committee in the performance of their duties. It selects the banks or bank for the deposit of its funds. Its duties and responsibilities are set out clearly in the constitution of the brotherhood. Grievance committees are known and respected as essential independent entities throughout the railroad industry. The appellee in the case at bar is composed of members chosen from the three lodges comprising the district. It has its own funds to pay its expenses and a method to replenish such funds from time to time as the occasion may require. These three lodges, together with the appellee committee, are an unincorporated association created and maintained for certain specified purposes, both fraternal and economic. The remedy provided in Section 1745.01 et seq., Revised Code, is available to the appellant as a remedy in his cause. * * *

Judgment reversed.

LYONS v. AMERICAN LEGION POST NO. 650 REALTY CO.

(1961) 172 Ohio St. 331, 175 N.E.2d 733, 92 A.L.R.2d 492.

[Action against, inter alia, individual members of unincorporated association, which was not itself made party defendant. The Supreme Court, held that the individual members could be held liable.]

ZIMMERMAN, J. * * * Or stating it in another way, "In the absence of an enabling statute, a voluntary association cannot be sued by its association name. It has no legal existence, and the persons composing it must be joined individually." [Citations.]

Then, effective on September 30, 1955, the General Assembly enacted legislation which is now Sections 1745.01 through 1745.04, Revised Code. Section 1745.01 provides:

"Any unincorporated association may contract or sue in behalf of those who are members and, in its own behalf, be sued as an entity under the name by which it is commonly known and called."

Section 1745.02 reads:

"All assets, property, funds, and any right or interest, at law or in equity, of such unincorporated association shall be subject to judgment, execution and other process. A money judgment against such unincorporated association shall be enforced only against the association as an entity and shall not be enforceable against the property of an individual member of such association."

* * *

Is it the purpose and intent of the statutes quoted and referred to above to limit actions solely against unincorporated associations as entities in the names they commonly use, as determined by the two lower courts herein, or may the individual members of such associations still be sued as under the former practice? We think the new statutes are no more than cumulative and do not abrogate the right to sue the members of the associations if the suitor chooses to proceed in that way. It is to be noted that Section 1745.01, Revised Code, uses the permissive word, "may," and that, under Section 1745.02, Revised Code, when a suitor does take advantage of the enabling statutes by suing an unincorporated association by the name it uses, the collection of any judgment obtained against such association must be satisfied out of its property alone and the property of its members is immune from seizure. Surely, had the General Assembly intended to eliminate actions against the individuals composing an unincorporated association, it would have so expressed itself.

* * * Thus, in 7 C.J.S. Associations § 36, p. 91, the following statement is made:

"It has been said that it is only by virtue of statute that an unincorporated association may be sued as an entity. In some states statutes have been enacted which expressly or impliedly authorize the bringing of actions against unincorporated associations in their common name * * *."

And at page 92, ibid., it is stated that such statutes do "not take away the right previously existing at common law. The individuals composing such an association do not, by force of such statutes, acquire any immunity from individual liability, and it is optional with a creditor to sue either the association as such or the individuals composing it."

* * *

However, a recognized difference exists between an unincorporated association organized for the transaction of business and one organized for fraternal or social purposes. This is illustrated in Azzolina v. Order of Sons of Italy, Conte Luigi Cadorna, No. 440, 119 Conn. 681, 691, 179 A. 201, 204, where it is stated in the opinion:

"In the case of a voluntary association formed for the purpose of engaging in business and making profits, its members are liable, as partners, to third persons upon contracts which are within its scope and are entered into with actual or apparent authority, and a joint judgment against them is justified. * * * But when, as here, the purpose of the association is not business or profit, the liability, if any, of its members is not in its nature that of partners but that arising out of the relation of principal and agent, and only those members who authorize or subsequently ratify an obligation are liable on account of it."

The same principle is recognized in relation to torts. In Thomas, Potentate v. Dunne, 131 Colo. 20, 30, 279 P.2d 427, 432, the following language is found in the course of the opinion:

"We cannot subscribe to the proposition that one who becomes a member of an unincorporated association such as a fraternal organization, a veterans organization or any one of numerous other societies which might be mentioned, subjects himself to liability for injuries sustained in ceremonies held under the auspices of that organization, in the absence of any allegation in the complaint against him that he took an active part in the act resulting in the injury or in some manner had knowledge of the proposed initiation rites or 'stunts' to be employed and gave assent or encouragement to the use thereof."

* * *

In the instant case the petition alleges that the defendants, American Legion Post No. 650 Realty Co., Inc., and the individual members of American Legion Post No. 650 "jointly and severally, conducted or caused to be conducted within said building a social affair known as a fish fry for which they charged each person attending the sum of one dollar ($1.00)," and that "defendants, and each of them, were negligent in failing to provide a safe heating system in the building; in equipping and maintaining the building with a defective heating system; in failing to adequately inspect said heating system; in failing to provide proper ventilation in the building; and in failing to warn invitees in the building, including decedent, of the presence of carbon monoxide fumes therein."

Such petition probably states causes of action good as against demurrer so that defendants should plead to conserve their interests, but on the trial of the action to establish liability on the part of individual defendants evidence would have to be produced linking them as active participants in the affair resulting in plaintiff's decedent's alleged injuries, and, furthermore, that they knew or in the exercise of ordinary care should have known of the defective condition of the instrumentality claimed to have caused the injury. And, of course, the other elements necessary to support recovery would have to be proved.

* * *

Judgment sustaining demurrer reversed.

PEOPLES PLEASURE PARK CO. v. ROHLEDER

(1907) 109 Va. 439, 61 S.E. 794.

[Action by Rohleder, plaintiff, against Peoples Pleasure Park Co., a corporation, defendant, to annul a conveyance of certain lands to defendant. The land in question was part of a tract known as Fulton Park, which had been subdivided into 1330 lots. In 1904, plaintiff purchased three of those lots improved with a house, and some other lots were sold to other individuals. Later, Fulton Park, excepting the lots already sold, was sold to the Revere Beach County Fair and Musical Co. In all the deeds making the above conveyances were the covenants, conditions or stipulations in these words: "The title to this land never to vest in a person or persons of African descent;" or "The title to this land never to vest in a colored person or persons." The lands owned by the Revere Company were ultimately acquired by one Fulton, who, in 1906, conveyed them to the defendant. Defendant was a corporation composed exclusively of colored persons. Defendant's demurrer to plaintiff's bill was overruled, and a decree entered for plaintiff. Defendant appeals.]

CALDWELL, J. * * * Aside from the question, whether or not appellee [plaintiff] could obtain the relief she asks against appellants—that is, an annulment of the conveyance to appellant, Peoples Pleasure Park Co., Inc.—on the ground that the restriction on the right of alienation of any of the Fulton Park land to "a person or persons of African descent" or "colored person" had been violated by a sale of a part of the land to said appellant, the bill fails to allege facts showing a violation of the restriction, and should have been dismissed upon the demurrers thereto. Such a conveyance, by no rule of construction, vests the title to the property conveyed in "a person or persons of African descent." Although a copy of the charter to the grantee is filed as an exhibit with the bill and made a part thereof, and which sets out that the object for which the corporation is formed is "to establish and develop a pleasure park for the amusement of colored people," a contemplated sale of the property to "a person or persons of African descent" is not even alleged, but only a contemplated use of the property as a place of amusement for colored persons, which the restriction relied on neither expressly, nor by implication, prohibits.

"A corporation is an artificial person, like the State. It has a distinct existence—an existence separate from that of its stockholders and directors." I Cook on Corp. (4th ed.), sec. 1. * * *

In Green's Brice, Ultra Vires (2nd Am. ed.), secs. 1, 2, it is said that "a corporation is a person which exists in contemplation of law only, and not physically," The same author, in commenting on Kyd's definition, says: "But sufficient stress is not laid upon that which is its real characteristic in the eye of the law, viz., its existence separate and distinct from the individual or individuals composing it. * * * This is the one important fact. The members of a corporation aggregate, and the one individual who is constituted a corporation sole, may, from their connection with such, have rights and privileges, and be under obligations and duties, over and above those affecting them in their private capacity; but they get them by reflection, as it were, from the corporation. They individually are not the corporation—cannot exercise the corporate powers, enforce the corporate rights, or be responsible for the corporate acts." * * *

For the above reasons, we are of opinion that the decree complained of is erroneous, and it will be set aside and annulled, the demurrers of appellants to the bill sustained, and the bill dismissed.

FELSENTHAL CO. v. NORTHERN ASSURANCE CO., LTD.

(1918) 284 Ill. 343, 120 N.E. 268.

[Action by plaintiff, D. I. Felsenthal Company, against defendant, the Northern Assurance Company, Ltd. of London, on a fire insurance policy issued in favor of plaintiff. Defendant resisted liability on the grounds, among others, that gasoline kept on the premises was fraudulently, knowingly and purposely ignited by plaintiff, its officers, agents and employees in such manner as to cause the fire and for the purpose of causing the fire and destroying the property. Judgment rendered on the verdict in favor of defendant. The Appellate Court affirmed the judgment. The cause is here upon a certificate of importance granted by the Appellate Court.

Plaintiff was an Illinois corporation capitalized at $15,000. The corporation was engaged in the wholesale business of dealing in tailors' clippings, and had its warehouse and assorting rooms in leased buildings located at 902–904 South Morgan street, Chicago, consisting of a three-story brick building with a small barn in the rear. Morris L. Fox was the beneficial owner of practically all of the 150 shares of capital stock, was its president, a director and, also, a creditor of the company in the amount of approximately $30,000—a sum greater than the total loss caused by the fire. March 7, 1912, about three or four o'clock A.M., plaintiff's property, consisting of loose and bailed tailors' clippings, was destroyed or damaged by fire. The total amount of insurance then carried on the property was $31,500; the total cash value of the property $30,721.42; the total loss and damage $29,471.73.

Evidence adduced by defendant tended strongly to prove, in substance, that Fox and David I. Felsenthal, about two months prior to the fire, went to the saloon of Moe Rosenberg, and from there went with Rosenberg into the restaurant adjoining the saloon and had dinner. Fox and Felsenthal told Rosenberg they were going out of business and were planning to have a fire at their place. Fox had known Rosenberg from his early boyhood. Rosenberg told them that Ben Fink, who was in the saloon with him, was in the business of firing and destroying buildings and property insured. Rosenberg saw Fink for them and gave them his terms for firing the building and its contents, namely, ten per cent of the amount of insurance collected from the insurance company, $500 to be paid in advance. They told Rosenberg they had $32,000 or $33,000 of insurance; that they had shipped out some of the stock but had not cancelled any of the insurance, and that they did not know whether any of the policies would hold. Rosenberg then told them he would take up the matter with Fink and have Fink, in turn, take it up with Nathan Spira, an insurance adjuster, and who was at the fire when it occurred and afterwards appeared as a representative of the plaintiff in adjusting the loss. The burning of the building was agreed to upon these terms and about ten days later Fox paid Rosenberg $500 advance deposit. The agreement was carried out.

Upon the basis of the facts narrated, the Supreme Court observed that the jury was warranted in finding that the building was destroyed at the instigation of Fox beyond all reasonable doubt, and that the loss by the fire was the loss of Fox himself as every dollar of insurance money recovered would ultimately be paid to Fox.]

DUNCAN, C. J. * * * It is true, as contended by appellant [plaintiff], that the general rule of law is that the willful burning of property by a stockholder in a corporation is not a defense against the collection of the insurance by the corporation, and that the corporation cannot be prevented from collecting the insurance because its agents willfully set fire to the property without the participation or authority of the corporation or of all of the stockholders of the corporation. When, however, the beneficial owner of practically all of the stock in a corporation, and who has the absolute management and control of its affairs and its property and is its president and a director, sets fire to the property of a corporation or causes it to be done, there is no sound reason to support the contention of appellant that the corporation should be allowed to recover on a policy for the destruction of the corporate property by a fire so occasioned. Every principle of insurance law and sound reasoning would seem to be against such contention. * * *

It certainly cannot be said that a corporation can recover on a fire insurance policy where the property insured is destroyed by a fire at the instance of all of the stockholders and of all of the creditors of the corporation. That is substantially the fact found by the jury as disclosed by this record, as Fox is sole creditor and equitable owner, and the trial court held, and so instructed the jury, that the charge of incendiarism must be proved beyond a reasonable doubt. * * *

No matter from what angle this case may be viewed, to allow appellant (plaintiff) to recover in this case would be to go against the established rule of law that the assured may not profit by his own criminal act, which is at the same time an act committed with a criminal intent to defraud the insurance company. While the money collected from appellee (defendant) on this insurance policy would not be paid directly to Fox, still, ultimately, the amount collected would all go, under the showing in this record, in the settlement of the affairs of the corporation to Fox. It is therefore certainly good law to hold that an incendiary cannot by a circuity of action recover from an insurance company a loss occasioned by his own willful conduct, which loss he could not recover by a direct suit against the company on a policy made direct to him. We cannot allow the corporation in this case to be used as a cloak to protect Fox and to aid him in his designs to defraud the insurance company and at the same time to profit by his own wrong or fraud. * * *

Judgment affirmed.

MULL v. COLT CO.

(1962 D.C.S.D.N.Y.) 31 F.R.D. 154.

EDELSTEIN, D. J. This is an action arising out of an accident in which plaintiff sustained serious injuries when he was pinned between the rear of his car and the front of a taxicab. Jurisdiction is predicated on diversity of citizenship. Plaintiff is a resident of New Jersey and defendants are, with the exception of Ford Motor Company, all residents of New York. Ford Motor Company is a resident of Michigan. The moving defendants are Edwin Ackerman, Janith Ackerman, Samuel T. Goodman and Marion Goodman, the controlling shareholders of the various cab corporations; a group of corporations which own and operate taxicabs in the City of New York; Ford Motor Company, the manufacturer of the taxicab involved in the instant action; and King Ford Motors, Inc., which sold the taxicab to one of the companies of the taxicab fleet involved herein. * * * The facts as they appear from the papers before the court present a somber picture of human tragedy, framed against a backdrop of corporate machinations.

Plaintiff's car was parked on Madison Avenue in front of his employer's office on the Sunday morning of December 21, 1958. Plaintiff had driven into New York City from his home in New Jersey for the purpose of picking up some office furniture and supplies which had been given to him by his employer. After carrying down a number of packages and placing them on the curb, plaintiff stepped into the street directly behind his parked vehicle, opened the trunk, and proceeded to arrange the contents of the trunk to receive the packages which he had brought down from the office. It was while in this position that he was struck by a taxicab being operated by defendant, Max Fermaglick. Fermaglick was driving a taxicab, registered in the name of Colt Company, Inc., in a southerly direction along Madison Avenue on the morning of December 21, 1958. As he approached the intersection of Madison Avenue and 41st Street, the pace of traffic caused him to reduce the speed of the cab. As he moved the gear shift lever from high to a lower gear, the lever jammed, causing the car to stall. Fermaglick got out of the car, opened the hood, ascertained that he was unable to correct the jammed gears, closed the hood, returned to the cab and attempted to move it to the curb to avoid blocking traffic. Since the gears were jammed, Fermaglick attempted to move the vehicle by using the accelerator and starter of the cab, a process known as "bucking." While Fermaglick was so engaged, the hood flew up in front of the windshield, blocking his vision. Undaunted, defendant Fermaglick did not stop the cab, but proceeded blindly with his maneuvers to bring it to the curb. It was then that the cab struck the plaintiff, pinning him between the two vehicles.

In his affidavit, plaintiff's counsel alleges that the plaintiff sustained extremely serious injuries. There is little or no doubt that he was indeed severely injured. His right leg has been amputated and his left leg was badly shattered. Plaintiff spent 209 days in the hospital immediately following the accident and underwent approximately twenty surgical operations. Up until the time the motion was argued, plaintiff had incurred approximately $30,000 in medical and other expenses resulting from this injury. Since the date of the accident, he has been unable to work.

The Colt Company carries the minimum allowable insurance for taxicabs. At the time of the accident, this amount was fixed by statute at $5,000 for injury to one person. [Citation.] * * * The complaint alleges that the Colt Company is dominated and controlled by the Ackermans and the Goodmans, who have incorporated 100 corporations, each having two cabs registered in the corporate name and each carrying the same minimum amount of insurance.

The assets of the driver, Max Fermaglick, are miniscule. The only real assets of the Colt Company are the aforementioned minimal insurance and two used taxicabs. It would appear that if plaintiff were to prevail in this action, any award reasonably calculated to compensate him for his loss could not be satisfied out of the available assets of the driver and the Colt Company. Faced with the sobering realization that success at trial may be no more than a pyrrhic victory, plaintiff has joined as defendants a large group of the individual taxicab corporations and the individuals in control of this complex, seeking to pierce the corporate veil for the purpose of holding the entire economic entity liable. Additionally, plaintiff has joined as defendants the manufacturer of the cab and the dealer who sold the cab, seeking recovery on the theories of negligence and breach of warranty.

* * *

The situation existing in New York City with respect to taxicab fleets and their responsibilities to those unfortunate enough to be injured in accidents involving their operations merits some general observations before proceeding to consider the respective motions herein. The problems involved in cases arising out of injuries inflicted by negligently operated and negligently maintained taxicabs are not unique. They have come before the courts of New York in various forms during the past few years. Attempts by injured plaintiffs to pierce the corporate veil in order to reach those who are financially responsible have met with less than complete success. The courts have morally condemned the obvious devices, artifices and stratagems engaged in by owners of large fleets to deny injured plaintiffs a fair and just measure of compensation for injuries sustained.

"It is common knowledge that owners of large fleets of taxicabs, for the purpose of limiting the amount of a possible recovery with respect to any accident, have developed a method of continuing to operate those large fleets of many hundreds and perhaps a thousand taxicabs, and yet maintaining the ownership of such taxicabs in the fleet in the names of many corporations. It is also common knowledge that no more than three or perhaps four taxicabs are registered in the name of any one corporation * * *." [Citation.] * * *

Multiple shell incorporations designed to exploit the minimum statutory insurance clearly perverts the legislative intent. The purpose underlying the enactment of compulsory insurance provisions for taxicabs was to protect the riding public and to provide means of recovery to those who suffered from the negligence of insolvent owners. [Citations.] This enactment by the Legislature was never intended to provide a shield for the evasion of public responsibility through the ingenious employment of the corporate fiction.

It is to be hoped for that the legislature will take effective action to remedy these shocking conditions. It is indeed an unfortunate fact of life that taxicabs roam the streets like predators, preying upon an unsuspecting public which heavily relies upon this form of transportation and believes that the same high degree of care and responsibility obtains in this industry as is customary in every other public utility. Unaware that this industry, clearly vested with a public interest, has fortified itself by various devious devices against discharging its obligations, except in some small measure, the public proceeds to use taxicabs day in and day out, feeling secure in the erroneous belief that it is adequately protected in the event of harm suffered thereby. The industry generally has demonstrated an appalling lack of concern for the public and has been guilty of so shameful an exercise in immorality that it almost defies description. Although legislative action is desirable, this does not mean that the plaintiff cannot be afforded relief under the law as presently constituted.

* * * Therefore, on this aspect of the motions before me, I hold that the complaint states a claim against the individual defendants which falls within one of the exceptions for piercing the corporate veil as set forth by Judge Metzner.

* * * The rule is well established that where corporations are organized, controlled and utilized so as to make them merely instrumentalities, agencies or conduits of another corporation, the corporate entity will be disregarded. [Citations.] "When one corporation controls another, and uses it as the means, agency, and instrumentality by which the former carries out and performs its business, it is liable for the torts of the latter." [Citation.]

Plaintiff is seeking to hold liable the entire taxicab operation garaged at one location as a single economic entity. The complaint alleges that defendants organized a group of corporations to hold title to two cabs each, which were garaged, maintained and operated centrally. Furthermore, it is alleged that these subsidiary corporations were shams and fictions and that they were so completely dominated and controlled as to negate a separate existence of their own. Manifestly, these allegations of agency, dominion and control are sufficient to sustain the complaint as to the defendant cab companies. * * *

Plaintiff has attached another string to his bow in an effort to sustain his complaint as against the various motions to dismiss. Plaintiff contends that where a corporation is organized and operated with insufficient capital to accomplish the purposes for which it was incorporated, courts will pierce the corporate veil. Defendants have not addressed themselves specifically to this argument, being content, it would seem, to rest on their general position that the instant case does not present the proper circumstances for disregarding the various corporate entities. The complaint alleges that the one hundred individual cab corporations were inadequately capitalized as measured by the nature, extent and conduct of their business and that the purpose of this device of undercapitalization was to defraud the public.

The rule that inadequate capitalization can serve as a basis for disregarding the corporate entity has been gaining support in the decisions. "An obvious inadequacy of capital, measured by the nature and magnitude of the corporate undertaking, has frequently been an important factor in cases denying stockholders their defense of limited liability." [Citations.] "It is coming to be recognized as the policy of the law that shareholders should in good faith put at the risk of the business unincumbered capital reasonably adequate for its prospective liabilities. If the capital is illusory or trifling compared with the business to be done and the risks of loss, this is a ground for denying the separate entity privilege." [Citation.] Cases in other jurisdictions have come increasingly to accept inadequate capitalization as a factor in piercing the corporate veil. [Citations.]

* * *

To permit the creation of an inadequately capitalized corporation as a separate entity is incompatible with the concepts underlying an independent existence. Where it is sought on the one hand to make available to general or tort creditors only an illusory amount compared with the size of the business and the public responsibility inherent in its very nature, while on the other hand advancing necessary expenses through secured devices, it would be a gross inequity to allow such a flimsy organization to provide a shield for personal liability. Courts will not tolerate

arrangements which throw all the risks on the public and which enable stockholders to reap profits while being insulated against losses. Plaintiff will not be denied the opportunity to prove inadequate capitalization as a factor to be considered in disregarding the facade of the various and sundry taxicab corporations.

Based upon all of the foregoing, the plaintiff has stated a claim upon which relief may be granted. The complaint alleges more than enough to permit plaintiff to hold the individual and cab company defendants liable if he can prove that the individuals and corporations are inextricably interwoven as a single economic entity. * * *

Accordingly, all the motions to dismiss the complaint are denied. It is so ordered.

STEWART REALTY CO. v. KELLER

(1962) 118 Ohio App. 49, 193 N.E.2d 179.

GUERNSEY, P. J. This is an appeal and cross-appeal on questions of law in an action for damages brought by the plaintiff, as vendor in a contract for the sale of real estate, against Gerald D. Keller, who the plaintiff claims is personally liable on the contract.

The vendee named in the contract, "Avon Brand, Inc., an Ohio corporation," was never organized in accordance with the representations of Keller. The contract was signed, "Avon Brand, Inc., by Gerald D. Keller, Pres." It is undisputed in evidence that the contract was executed by plaintiff with full knowledge that Avon Brand, Inc., did not have any corporate existence at the time, *de jure* or *de facto,* and that Keller expressly declined to execute any contract naming him as a party individually. * * *

Nevertheless, there is a more fatal defect in plaintiff's proof. The action was on the contract for the sale of real estate, and to prevail it was necessary that plaintiff prove that the defendant was personally liable under the contract. The defendant was in the category of a promoter, and as stated in 18 C.J.S. Corporations § 132, p. 533, "[p]romoters are not personally liable on contracts made in the name and solely on the credit of the future corporation, and not on an express or implied representation that there is an existing corporation, where such intention is known to the other contracting party * * *. Whether or not a contract was made by the promoters personally or on the credit of the corporation only, may be a question of fact or one of law according to circumstances." [Citation.]

Considering the contract herein in its entirety, there is nothing on the face thereof which indicates, as a matter of either fact or law, that it was anything other than a contract to bind plaintiff and the corporation named therein. There were no promises made in the contract by defendant as an individual or any benefits to be received by him individually under the provisions of the contract. As to the knowledge of the plaintiff that the corporation only was to be bound and not the defendant personally, plaintiff proved this by its own witnesses, in particular plaintiff's attorney, and offered no evidence of any probative value to the contrary.

* * *

There being no evidence of any probative value of defendant's personal liability on the contract, the plaintiff was not entitled to judgment as a matter of law. Plaintiff's cross-appeal is, therefore, entirely without merit.

* * *

Judgment reversed in part and affirmed in part.

PALMER v. SCHEFTEL

(1919) 183 App.Div. 77, 170 N.Y.S. 588.

[Action by Palmer, as trustee in bankruptcy of the Cypress Knitting Mills, Inc., against the defendant, Scheftel, to recover an amount claimed to be due and unpaid upon the defendant's subscription. The defendant and two others organized the corporation on September 6, 1912, and were the sole incorporators. The defendant subscribed for 70 shares, Einsetler for 70 shares, and Buehler for 40 shares, each of the par value of $50; the authorized capital being $10,000. The corporation was organized and the subscriptions were made pursuant to a prior agreement between the three subscribers, whereby, as affecting the defendant, it was agreed that, in consideration of his paying to the corporation $200 in cash and transferring to it his interest in a certain knitting machine, of the value of $800, "and in further consideration of the defendant acting as president and director of said Cypress Knitting Mills, Incorporated, for a period of one year from and after its incorporation, the defendant would be entitled to and would receive 70 shares of the capital stock of the said Cypress Knitting Mills, Incorporated, which said stock was to be full-paid and nonassessable." Apparently the agreement contained a similar provision as to each of the other incorporators, for the resolution authorizing the issue of the stock to each refers to such an agreement.

At the first meeting of the incorporators, held September 14, 1912, the three incorporators, who also constituted the entire board of directors, resolved to accept the offers made by themselves, and adjudged and declared that the contributions referred to were of the fair and reasonable value stated in the resolution of themselves as stockholders, that the same were necessary for the business of the company, and authorized the issue of the shares as "full-paid and nonassessable." Accordingly, on or about September 14, 1912, the cash contributions were paid to the corporation, the interest in the knitting machine was transferred to it, and the defendant was elected president and director, and acted as such continuously for more than one year thereafter, and in consideration of the payment of $200 and the transfer of defendant's interest in the knitting machine, "and in further consideration of the defendant's said agreement to act as president and director of said corporation for said period of time" (one year), the corporation issued to the defendant "seventy shares of its capital stock, full-paid and non-assessable." From a judgment for defendant, plaintiff appeals.]

SHEARN, J. The case of this bankrupt corporation presents in aggravated form the evil of permitting capital stock to be issued for "services." Notwithstanding the fact that the statute authorizes capital stock to be issued in consideration of labor actually performed for the benefit of the corporation, and despite the seeming liberality recently manifested in interpreting the statute (Morgan v. Bon Bon Co., 222 N.Y. 22, 118 N.E. 205), this record exhibits such a palpable attempt to evade the statute as to merit condemnation, if the facts can be fairly distinguished from those in the case referred to. * * *

Stock Corporation Law, sec. 55, provides: "No corporation shall issue either stock or bonds except for money, labor done or property actually received for the use and lawful purposes of such corporation."

It was therefore a violation of law to issue to the defendant the 70 shares of stock before he had performed his alleged services. But it will be at once said we are not concerned with the validity of the issue of the stock in this action, but are solely concerned with whether it has been paid for; the action being to recover the amount unpaid. It is plausibly argued that it would be illegal for a corporation to issue its stock for promissory notes; but, if the notes were paid, such payment would constitute payment for the stock and discharge the subscription. Therefore, it is said, as the stipulated facts

show that the services were rendered, it must be held that this stock was paid for. This argument might be difficult to meet, had the defendant and his codirectors not violated another well-settled rule of law, which may be availed of to protect the creditors of this corporation.

The "services" rendered in this case, and claimed to constitute part payment of the defendant's stock subscription, consisted in defendant's acting as a director and president of the corporation. The general rule is that directors and officers of corporations, such as president, vice president, secretary, treasurer, etc., presumptively serve without compensation, and that they are entitled to no compensation for performing the usual and ordinary duties pertaining to the office, in the absence of some express provision therefor by statute, charter, or by-laws, or by an agreement to that effect, and unless such provision or agreement was made or entered into before the services were rendered. Thompson on Corporations (2d Ed.) secs. 1715, 1728.

No statute, charter, or by-law authorized the defendant to be paid for serving as a director or officer. There was an agreement, but the agreement was invalid. The only authority for the agreement was a resolution adopted solely by the votes of the directors who were the direct beneficiaries, and who not only fixed their own compensation, but determined the value to the corporation of their contemplated services, and who decided that the duties, which are presumptively rendered without compensation, were in their own case worth several thousand dollars. It is almost universally held that directors, acting as such at their meetings, have no power to vote themselves salaries or compensation for their services, either before or after such services have been rendered. [Citations.]

While it has been said that corporate agreements made on the authority of resolutions adopted by the vote of directors who are the beneficiaries are voidable at the instance of the corporation, the agreement with which we are dealing was void. It was void, because it not only contemplated, but actually provided, that something should be done which is prohibited by law, namely, the issuing of stock for services before any services were rendered. The agreement was therefore not only voidable, but, being unlawful, was void, and affords no legal basis for treating the defendant's performance of his duties as director and president of the corporation as payment for his stock subscription. If the court sanctioned such practices as are here disclosed, there would be little security in dealing with corporations. Not only would creditors suffer, but grave injury would be done to corporations that are lawfully and properly conducted. * * *

Judgment reversed, and a new trial ordered.

A. P. SMITH MFG. CO. v. BARLOW

(1953) 13 N.J. 145, 98 A.2d 581, 39 A.L.R.2d 1179.

JACOBS, J. The Chancery Division, in a well-reasoned opinion by Judge Stein, determined that a donation by the plaintiff The A. P. Smith Manufacturing Company to Princeton University was intra vires. Because of the public importance of the issues presented, the appeal duly taken to the Appellate Division has been certified directly to this court under Rule 1:5–1(a).

The company was incorporated in 1896 and is engaged in the manufacture and sale of valves, fire hydrants and special equipment, mainly for water and gas industries. Its plant is located in East Orange and Bloomfield and it has approximately 300 employees. Over the years the company has contributed regularly to the local community chest and on occasions to Upsala College in East Orange and Newark Uni-

versity, now part of Rutgers, the State University. On July 24, 1951 the board of directors adopted a resolution which set forth that it was in the corporation's best interests to join with others in the 1951 Annual Giving to Princeton University, and appropriated the sum of $1,500 to be transferred by the corporation's treasurer to the university as a contribution towards its maintenance. When this action was questioned by stockholders the corporation instituted a declaratory judgment action in the Chancery Division and trial was had in due course.

Mr. Hubert F. O'Brien, the president of the company, testified that he considered the contribution to be a sound investment, that the public expects corporations to aid philanthropic and benevolent institutions, that they obtain good will in the community by so doing, and that their charitable donations create favorable environment for their business operations. In addition, he expressed the thought that in contributing to liberal arts institutions, corporations were furthering their self-interest in assuring the free flow of properly trained personnel for administrative and other corporate employment. Mr. Frank W. Abrams, chairman of the board of the Standard Oil Company of New Jersey, testified that corporations are expected to acknowledge their public responsibilities in support of the essential elements of our free enterprise system. He indicated that it was not "good business" to disappoint "this reasonable and justified public expectation," nor was it good business for corporations "to take substantial benefits from their membership in the economic community while avoiding the normally accepted obligations of citizenship in the social community." Mr. Irving S. Olds, former chairman of the board of the United States Steel Corporation, pointed out that corporations have a self-interest in the maintenance of liberal education as the bulwark of good government. He stated that "Capitalism and free enterprise owe their survival in no small degree to the existence of our private, independent universities" and that if American business does not aid in their maintenance it is not "properly protecting the long-range interest of its stockholders, its employees and its customers." Similarly, Dr. Harold W. Dodds, President of Princeton University, suggested that if private institutions of higher learning were replaced by governmental institutions our society would be vastly different and private enterprise in other fields would fade out rather promptly. Further on he stated that "democratic society will not long endure if it does not nourish within itself strong centers of nongovernmental fountains of knowledge, opinions of all sorts not governmentally or politically originated. If the time comes when all these centers are absorbed into government, then freedom as we know it, I submit, is at an end."

* * *

During the first world war corporations loaned their personnel and contributed substantial corporate funds in order to insure survival; during the depression of the '30s they made contributions to alleviate the desperate hardships of the millions of unemployed; and during the second world war they again contributed to insure survival. They now recognize that we are faced with other, though nonetheless vicious, threats from abroad which must be withstood without impairing the vigor of our democratic institutions at home and that otherwise victory will be pyrrhic indeed. More and more they have come to recognize that their salvation rests upon sound economic and social environment which in turn rests in no insignificant part upon free and vigorous nongovernmental institutions of learning. It seems to us that just as the conditions prevailing when corporations were originally created required that they serve public as well as private interests, modern conditions require that corporations acknowledge and discharge social as well as private responsibilities as members of the communities within which they operate. Within this broad concept there is no difficulty in sustaining, as incidental to their proper objects and in aid of the public welfare, the power of corporations to contribute corporate funds within reasonable limits in support of academic institutions. But even if we confine ourselves to the terms of the common-law rule in its application to current conditions, such expenditures may likewise readily be justified as being for the benefit of the corporation; indeed, if need be the matter may be viewed strictly in terms of actual survival of the corporation in a free enterprise system. The genius of our common law has been its capacity for growth and its adaptability to the needs of the times. Generally courts have accomplished the desired result indirectly through the molding of old forms. Occasionally they have done it directly through frank rejection of the old and recognition of the new. But whichever path the common law has taken it has not been found wanting as the proper tool for the advancement of the general good. [Citations.]

* * *

In the light of all of the foregoing we have no hesitancy in sustaining the validity of the donation by the plaintiff. There is no suggestion that it was made indiscriminately or to a pet charity of the corporate directors in furtherance of personal rather than corporate ends. On the contrary, it was made to a pre-eminent institution of higher learning, was modest in amount and well within the limitations imposed by the statutory enactments, and was voluntarily made in the reasonable belief that it would aid the public welfare and advance the interests of the plaintiff as a private corporation and as part of the community in which it operates. We find that it was a lawful exercise of the corporation's implied and incidental powers under common-law principles and that it came within the express authority of the pertinent state legislation. As has been indicated, there is now widespread belief throughout the nation that free and vigorous non-governmental institutions of learning are vital to our democracy and the system of free enterprise and that withdrawal of corporate authority to make such contributions within reasonable limits would seriously threaten their continuance. Corporations have come to recognize this and with their enlightenment have sought in varying measures, as has the plaintiff by its contribution, to insure and strengthen the society which gives them existence and the means of aiding themselves and their fellow citizens. Clearly then, the appellants, as individual stockholders whose private interests rest entirely upon the well-being of the plaintiff corporation, ought not be permitted to close their eyes to present-day realities and thwart the long-visioned corporate action in recognizing and voluntarily discharging its high obligations as a constituent of our modern social structure.

Affirmed.

PROBLEMS

1. A State statute provided that any person or persons doing business under an assumed or fictitious name should file their true names in the office of the public recorder. A, B and C owned all the stock of the Star Sales Company, a duly organized corporation. The State prosecutes A, B and C for failing to register their names under this statute. Decision?

2. A, B, and C petitioned for a corporate charter for the purpose of conducting a retail show business. All the statutory provisions were complied with, except that they failed to have their charter recorded. This was an oversight on their part, and they felt that they had fully complied with the law. They operated the business for three years, after which time it became insolvent. The creditors desire to hold the members liable as partners. May they do so?

3. The AB Corporation has outstanding 20,000 shares of common stock without par value, of which 19,000 are owned by Peter B. Arson, 500 shares are owned by Elizabeth Arson, his wife, and 500 shares are owned by Joseph Q. Arson, his brother. These three individuals are the officers and directors of the corporation. The AB Corporation obtained a $10,000 fire insurance policy covering a certain building owned by it. Thereafter, Peter B. Arson set fire to the building which was wholly destroyed by the fire. The corporation now brings an action against the fire insurance company to recover on the $10,000 fire insurance policy. What judgment?

4. The board of directors of the Landis Construction Company, a corporation created to carry on a general construction business, has voted to enter into a partnership agreement with Manners, a heating contractor, to carry on the business of industrial heating installation. The articles of incorporation of the corporation are silent as to the right of the corporation to act as a partner.

Noble, a minority shareholder of Landis Construction Company, brings suit to enjoin the directors and officers from executing the agreement.

What result?

5. After part of the shares of a proposed corporation had been successfully subscribed, A, the promoter, hired a carpenter to repair a building. The promoters subsequently secured subscriptions to the balance of the shares, and completed the organization, but the corporation declined to use the building or pay the carpenter for the reason that it was not suitable to the purposes of the company, whereupon the carpenter brought suit against it for the amount agreed to be paid him by the promoter. Was the corporation liable?

6. C. A. Nimocks was a promoter engaged in effecting the organization of the Times Printing Company. On September 12, on behalf of the proposed corporation, he made a contract with McArthur for his services as comptroller for the period of one year beginning October 1. The Times Printing Company was incorporated October 16, and at that date McArthur commenced his duties as comptroller. No formal action with reference to his employment was taken by the board of directors or by any officer, but all the shareholders, directors and officers knew of the contract made by Nimocks. On December 1,

McArthur was discharged without cause. Has he a cause of action against the Times Printing Company?

7. A and B obtained an option upon a building which had been used for manufacturing pianos. They acted as the promoters for a corporation and turned over the building to the new corporation for $100,000 worth of stock. As a matter of fact, their option on the building called for a purchase price of only $60,000. The other shareholders desire to have $40,000 of the common stock cancelled. Can they succeed in an action to have it cancelled?

8. Ames, Bard and Cate, residents of the State of X and men of considerable personal wealth, decide to organize a corporation, Tots Toys, Inc., for the purpose of conducting a business of manufacturing children's toys. The Articles of Incorporation prepared at a pre-incorporation meeting provided that initial capital of the corporation was to be $6,000 and its capital stock 600 shares without par value. Ames, Bard and Cate designated themselves directors and officers of the corporation and each subscribed for 200 shares of stock, agreeing to pay $10 per share. Ames and Bard signed the Articles and had their signatures properly acknowledged. In this form the Articles were given to Cate for his signature. Cate, thinking the Articles were complete and ready for filing, did not sign and mailed the Articles to the Secretary of State, together with the required fees and taxes. The Secretary of State filed the Articles, returning a certified copy to Ames. Ames, Bard and Cate, after paying in the specified minimum capital, immediately held an organizational meeting at which they adopted by-laws and authorized the purchase of a truck and a small toy manufacturing plant.

On the third day of the plant's operation, Day, an employee of Tots Toys, Inc., while driving a load of supplies to the factory in the corporation's truck, negligently ran over a pedestrian, Pace, causing him serious personal injuries. You may assume that Pace has a legally enforceable claim for $50,000. Because of the corporation's limited assets, Pace brings an action against Ames, Bard and Cate to recover damages in the amount of $50,000. Decision?

9. A corporation is formed for the purpose of manufacturing, buying, selling and dealing in drugs, chemicals and similar products. In 1966, the corporation, under authority of its board of directors, contracted to purchase the land and building occupied by it as a factory and store. S, a shareholder, sues in equity to restrain the corporation from completing the contract, claiming that as the certificate of incorporation contained no provision authorizing the corporation to purchase real estate, the contract was ultra vires. Decision?

10. The D Company, a corporation engaged in manufacturing shoes, operated a motor bus between its plant and the railroad stations in a city two miles distant. A regular charge was made for transportation of passengers. P, while a passenger on the bus, sustained personal injuries through the negligence of the driver, and sued the D Company for damages. On the trial, it appeared from the evidence that the D Company exceeded its corporate authority in operating the motor bus, and that such operation was clearly ultra vires. Can P recover?

CHAPTER 35

CAPITAL STOCK AND DIVIDENDS

Introductory. Probably no term in the law of corporations has caused so much confusion and misunderstanding as the phrase "capital stock." In the decisions and in commercial usage, the terms "capital stock," "capital" and "stock" are sometimes treated as synonymous. Likewise, the words "stock" and "shares" are used interchangeably to indicate the same concept. Aside from the variety of divergent definitions which may be found in the cases, the fundamental idea of capital stock is that it is the property or consideration which the corporation has obtained from its shareholders, whether in the form of cash, services rendered, or property, which is dedicated to use in the business and represented by outstanding certificates for a specific number of shares. While capital stock may be authorized by the charter but not issued, the term has little practical significance except where applied to shares of stock which have been sold and issued. Where par value stock has been sold at a premium, that is, at a price greater than par, the amount of the premium or excess over par is allocated to a paid-in surplus account rather than to capital stock. It is sometimes referred to as capital surplus.

Capital stock should not be confused with the assets of a corporation nor, on the other hand, with the certificates representing shares of capital stock. The value of corporate assets and the aggregate value of shares outstanding may fluctuate from day to day, or they may have different values attributed to them at any given time, depending upon the purpose for which the valuation is sought. Capital stock, however, has a fixed and predetermined stated value as fixed by the charter or by the directors or shareholders in accordance with the charter and the laws of the State of incorporation. This dollar amount attributed to the capital stock cannot be changed except in compliance with the charter and, in the last analysis, in a manner prescribed by law.

The term "capital stock" has caused so much misunderstanding that the corporation laws of certain States have discarded the term altogether and have adopted in its place phraseology which is more precise. Thus, the Model Business Corporation Act uses "stated capital" instead of "capital stock." (Section 2). "Stated capital" stands for the same idea as capital stock, as above defined, but rightly implies an arbitrary and legal concept and thereby avoids the different meanings which might be attributed to "capital stock."

Shares of capital stock are property, but they are, unlike the certificates by which they are represented, intangible and incorporeal and cannot be seized or reduced to physical possession. Shares are a method of describing a proportionate interest in a corporate enterprise, and they do not in any way vest their owner with any title to the property of the corporation.

Classes of Shares

Corporations are generally authorized to issue two or more classes of stock which differ according to their respective rights and interests. Thus, classes may vary with respect to their rights to dividends, their voting rights, and their right to share in the assets of the corporation upon dissolution. The power of a corporation to issue a variety of classes of stock is generally derived from the statute, and the most usual and principal classification is into common and preferred.

Common Stock. By definition, common stock is that class of stock which does not have any special contract rights or preferences. It is generally true that common stock, the most frequent type of corporate security, carries with it all the risks of the business. If the venture is a success, its holders may receive the largest dividends, while, if the venture fails, they must absorb the initial and the heaviest burden of the losses. In return, the common shareholders generally have the predominant voice in management.

Preferred Stock. Although, it is usual, when talking about capital stock other than common, to refer to it as "preferred stock," the phrase itself hardly covers the great variety of contractual arrangements between the corporation and the shareholder which may exist within that broad classification. Preferred shares, unlike common, are interests in the corporation which have certain special contractual rights or powers, and because these rights or powers generally give the holder a prior claim of some sort over the holder of common stock, either as to dividends or the assets of the corporation on liquidation, or other interest of the corporation, they are referred to as being preferred. Obviously, the description is relative or comparative, and the extent of the preferences can only be determined, first, by the terms of the contract (certificate) itself; secondly, by the charter or possibly the by-laws of the corporation under which the preferred shares are issued, and, finally, by the provisions of the statute from which the corporation derives its power to issue capital stock with special rights or preferences. Since the variations and combinations of contract rights which find expression in preferred stock are limited principally by the extent of man's ingenuity, it is not surprising that there has been a great amount of litigation over the rights of the holders of stock of this description.

The most common incidents of preferred shares are the right to receive a stated dividend before any dividends are paid to the holders of common shares and the right to receive a specified sum of money upon liquidation before any assets are distributed to the holders of common stock. Depending upon the terms of the contract between the corporation and the preferred shareholder, the latter may be entitled to cumulative dividends. In other words, if a preferred dividend is passed, no dividend on the common stock may be paid until all arrearages on the preferred stock shall have been paid. A not uncommon provision is that preferred shares shall be "participating." Although this term may cover a multitude of different arrangements, such a description usually means that the preferred is entitled to share equally with the common shareholders in any distribution of earnings for a given year *after* the common shares shall have received a dividend equal to the prior dividend payable to the preferred.

The corporation may attach certain conditions or limitations upon the preferred shares, if so authorized by its charter. Preferred stock may be redeemable at the election of the corporation, or it may be convertible into shares of another class. Sometimes preferred shares are expressly denied voting rights. The constitutions of certain States, as in Illinois, prohibit the denial of voting rights to any class of stock. Any attempt to alter or change the rights of the holders of preferred shares raises problems relative to the impairment of vested contract rights, as noted hereafter in the discussion of cancellation and redemption.

Notwithstanding the special rights and preferences which distinguish preferred from common, preferred stock, similar to the common, represents a contribution of capital. Preferred stock is no more a debt than is common, and, until a dividend is declared, the holder of preferred shares is not a creditor of the corporation. Preferred shareholders do not have liens on specific corporate assets or priorities over creditors. Their rights are subordinate to the rights of all of the creditors of the corporation.

Par Value and No Par Value Stock

The practice of placing a par value on a share of stock has been criticized as misleading. The issuance of watered or fictitiously paid up stock is abetted by the appearance of full value lent by the dollar amount printed on the face of the certificate. Even if no fraud were involved, the par value may mislead shareholders who assume that the market value or the book value of their interest is the same as the par value recited on the face of the certificate.

In an effort to correct this situation, many States, with New York taking the lead in 1912, authorized the issuance of stock without par value. In the case of no par shares the "stated value" assigned to the shares is determined by the directors or the shareholders. This amount may represent the entire consideration paid for the shares, or a nominal value may be allocated to the shares and the balance credited to the paid-in surplus account. One court has illustrated the purported advantage of no par stock by observing that "if the assets received are one thousand dollars in money, it is of no consequence whether five shares or ten shares, or one thousand shares are given for it. Each share has its one-fifth or one-tenth or one one-thousandth aliquot part of the thousand dollars as the case may be, and no one is damaged because everyone knows that under each share is simply its proportionate part of the total assets, unexpressed in terms of money." Bodell v. General Gas & Electric Corporation, 15 Del.Ch. 119, 130, 132 A. 442.

Amount and Issuance. In the case of par value shares, the amount of the capital stock or stated capital is the aggregate par value of all the issued shares. In the case of no

par stock, it is the consideration received by the corporation for all the no par shares which have been issued, except such part thereof as may have been allocated otherwise than to capital stock or stated capital in a manner permitted by law. This excess would generally be credited to an account designated as capital surplus or paid-in surplus. Without further issuance or cancellation of shares, stated capital may be increased or reduced by adjustments between that account and the paid-in surplus account if such adjustments are made in a manner permitted by law.

The amount of capital stock to be initially issued is determined by the promoters or incorporators and is generally governed by practical business considerations and financial exigencies. Once the amount which the corporation is *authorized* to issue has been established and specified in the charter, this cannot be increased or decreased without obtaining an amendment to the charter. This means that the shareholders have the residual authority over increases or decreases in the amount of authorized capital stock. It is a frequent practice to authorize initially more capital stock than is immediately to be issued, which may have very practical consequences with respect to control over the affairs of the corporation. The directors alone may have the power to issue additional shares if all the authorized shares are not already issued and outstanding. In such case, if the shareholders' pre-emptive rights are denied or abridged by the charter, the directors have the power to change the proportionate interests of shareholders by issuing additional shares without obtaining the consent of the shareholders or offering such shares to them.

With respect to the issuance of capital stock, there are two paramount questions: (a) What type of consideration may be validly accepted in payment for shares, and (b) who shall determine whether valid consideration has been paid and what limits are placed upon the discretion of those making the decision?

With very few exceptions, and in the absence of any charter or statutory limitation, cash, property, and services are generally accepted as valid consideration for the issuance of shares (Camden v. Stuart, 144 U.S. 104, 12 S.Ct. 585, 36 L.Ed. 363), and this general rule has been recognized by statute. Section 18, Model Act, Appendix D. Because the capital of a corporation is looked upon as the ultimate source for payment of corporate debts, the courts have frequently refused to accept as "property" certain items which for other purposes might be so considered. In most jurisdictions, promissory notes or future services are not acceptable in payment for the issuance of shares, and this rule has been adopted by the Model Act (Section 18). Patents, good will, merchandise, leases and the assets of a business are acceptable consideration for shares of stock. The good will of a business which has been operating at a loss, or an unpatented formula, however, have been held not to constitute adequate payment.

In general, a corporation may accept in payment for its shares such property as it is authorized to acquire in the conduct of its business. An example of the limits which may be imposed by restrictions in the charter of the corporation is the power to acquire shares of stock in another corporation. If a corporation is authorized to hold stock in another corporation, it has the power to accept such shares in payment for its own shares, otherwise not.

The determination of the value to be placed on property which is exchanged for shares is the responsibility of the directors. The ultimate consequence of issuing stock for over-valued property may be to impose liability upon the shareholder to creditors or to other shareholders even though the stock purports to be fully paid and non-assessable. Certain jurisdictions hold that notwithstand-

ing good faith and the absence of fraud in the valuation, a subscriber is liable for the difference between the actual value of the property and the stated or par value of the shares issued. Other jurisdictions, and probably the majority, hold that valuation is a matter of opinion and that, if the parties making the valuation have exercised good faith and no actual fraud is present in the transaction, the shareholder is not liable even though the actual value of the property proves to be considerably less than the dollar amount of the stock issued in exchange for it.

Section 18 of the Model Business Corporation Act provides: "In the absence of fraud in the transaction, the judgment of the board of directors or the shareholders, as the case may be, as to the value of the consideration received for shares shall be conclusive."

What constitutes "actual fraud" depends, of course, upon the facts and circumstances of the particular case. Evidence of gross undervaluation alone may be enough to permit a court to find that there was fraud. Payment for shares having an aggregate par value of $999,800 by a patent worth not over $50,500 has been held to constitute a fraudulent over-valuation. On the other hand, no fraud was found where a long-established business with a record of annual earnings between $25,000 and $50,000 was exchanged for $150,000 of stock even though recent earnings had declined and actual losses were experienced. Where a going business is exchanged for shares of stock, a wide divergence of honest opinion as to value is not unusual.

Redemption, Cancellation and Acquisition of Its Own Shares by a Corporation. Shares of common stock ordinarily are not subject to redemption. Preferred shares, however, are frequently redeemable by the corporation at a call price stated in the certificate. This power is not to be implied from the mere existence of preferred shares; it must be provided for in the articles of incorporation, pursuant to authorization in the applicable statute. The redemption or call price must be specified in the charter along with all of the other special rights or limitations of the preferred shares.

Redemption of preferred shares when the business is in financial straits may be harmful to those who extended credit in reliance upon the capital represented by such shares. Generally, however, creditors are held to have no right to complain as the redemption provisions are recited in the charter. In an effort to insure against injury to creditors or to the holders of other classes of preferred shares, in some States there are statutory restrictions upon redemption which are superior to the terms of the contract.

The power of a corporation to effect changes in an issue of its preferred stock depends upon the contract with the preferred shareholders and the applicable law. No change may be made which will impair vested contractual rights because any State statute or action taken thereunder which impairs the right of contract is violative of the Constitution of the United States. However, the statute in effect at the time of the issuance of the preferred stock is considered part and parcel of the contract, and therefore subsequent changes in the redemption, dividend rate, or other rights of the preferred shareholders which are effected strictly in accordance with the statute are binding upon all of the shareholders.

A provision in the charter of a corporation whereby a prescribed majority of the shareholders, voting by classes, have the power to alter or change the "rights and preferences" of preferred stock has been held to be a material part of the shareholders' contract and to afford a proper basis for the cancellation of unpaid arrearages of dividends on cumulative preferred stock, notwithstanding the objections of a dissenting preferred shareholder.

It has long been recognized that a corporation may acquire its own shares by purchase, gift or otherwise without complying with the usual statutory requirements regulating the reduction of capital stock. Shares of its own stock lawfully acquired by a corporation and not cancelled are referred to as treasury shares. The power of a corporation to acquire and hold its own shares has usually been subject to the qualification that the rights of creditors should not thereby be injured. In some jurisdictions, under the trust fund theory, it is improper for a corporation to purchase its own shares if its remaining net assets are less than the par value of all of the issued shares including those held in the treasury.

Example: In 1909, R, the owner of 500 shares of preferred stock of the Fishel Company, sold his stock to the Fishel Company for $50,000 and received as consideration the promissory note of the company for $50,000 due in 1911. At maturity, the note was not paid, and a renewal note in the same amount due in 1912 was given by the Company to R. At the time of the sale of the stock in 1909, the Fishel Company was solvent, but in 1912 it had become insolvent, was adjudicated bankrupt, and there was no surplus or profits with which to pay the note. The $50,000 note was therefore disallowed as a creditor's claim, and allowed only as a claim based upon preferred stock in this amount. In re Fechheimer Fishel Co., 212 F. 357 (C.A. 2d, 1914).

More recently, some statutes have set out formulae which determine the power of a corporation to purchase its own shares. The effect of the Illinois statutory provision is to permit purchase of shares only out of earned surplus. The stock of a corporation upon being re-acquired either through gift or purchase by the issuing corporation is not thereby extinguished or cancelled. The corporation may resell it at market value or issue it as a stock dividend, and no liability attaches to the purchaser or holder to pay up to the par value of the stock. Treasury stock cannot be voted, no dividends of any kind are payable upon it, and no pre-emptive rights of shareholders exist with respect to it.

Shares acquired by outright purchase or by donation may be cancelled or retired in the manner provided by law, and a corporation may be required by its charter to cancel shares which have been redeemed. The effect is to reduce the stated capital or capital stock to the extent of the shares so cancelled. A reduction of the stated capital or capital stock by retirement and cancellation of shares requires affirmative action by the shareholders of each class of stock outstanding.

DIVIDENDS

In General. The objective of every private business corporation is to operate profitably, and it is the fundamental right of shareholders, subject to certain limitations, to share in the profits through the receipt of dividends. Although profits or net earnings are not synonymous with dividends, the two concepts are so fundamentally linked in corporate law that the dividend is sometimes identified with the source from which it is usually paid which, in certain instances, may not be profits or earnings but may be a legitimate return of all or part of the original investment in the business.

The conditions under which the earnings of a business may be paid out in the form of dividends will depend upon the contractual rights of the holders of the particular shares involved, the provisions in the charter or by-laws of the corporation, and the basic statute of the State of incorporation which is generally designed to protect creditors and shareholders from dissipation of corporate assets. Finally, as a practical matter dividend policy is greatly influenced by the income tax laws which apply both to the corporation and the shareholder.

Types of Dividends. The most customary type of dividend is the cash dividend declared and paid at regular intervals depending in amount upon the financial success of the enterprise during the preceding fiscal period. References to "regular" dividends in a charter or contract are considered as referring to a distribution of the earned surplus in the form of a portion of the cash assets of a corporation. While dividends are almost invariably paid in cash, in a few instances a distribution of earnings has been made to shareholders in the form of property. On one occasion, a distillery declared and paid a dividend in bonded whiskey.

A stock dividend is a ratable distribution of additional shares of the capital stock of the corporation to its shareholders. It is reflected on the books of the corporation by a reduction in the surplus account equal to the amount of the stock dividend and a corresponding increase in the capital account. The practical and legal significance of a dividend payable in shares of capital stock differs greatly from a dividend payable in cash or property from the point of view of both the corporation and the shareholder. Following the payment of a stock dividend, the assets of the corporation are no less than they were before, and the shareholder does not have any greater relative interest in the net worth of the corporation than he had before except possibly where the dividend is paid in shares of a different class. His shares will each represent a smaller proportionate interest in the assets of the corporation, but by reason of the increase in the number of shares his total investment will remain the same. The declaration and payment of a stock dividend means that surplus which may have been previously available for distribution or other uses is thereafter frozen in the capital account.

The power to pay dividends in the form of shares of capital stock may be authorized by statute, as it is, for example, in Wisconsin and Illinois, but in the absence of any specific statutory prohibition such as exists in Massachusetts with respect to trust companies, there is no legal objection to a stock dividend as such.

A stock dividend should not be confused with a stock split. By the latter, each of the issued and outstanding shares is simply broken up into a greater number of shares, each representing a proportionately smaller interest in the corporation. A stock split is frequently accomplished in an effort to increase the marketability of the shares and the number of shareholders by lowering the unit price. After splitting, the stated or par value of each of the shares is considerably reduced, but no change is effected in the aggregate dollar amount of stock outstanding or in the surplus account. Where there is more than one class of shares outstanding it is possible for either a stock dividend or a stock split to alter materially the relative voting strength of the different classes.

While dividends ordinarily are identified with the distribution of profits, a distribution of capital assets to shareholders upon termination of the business is considered a form of dividend and is referred to as a liquidating dividend. A distribution to common shareholders of paid-in surplus or capital surplus, or a distribution to shareholders of funds taken from a proper reserve for depreciation of assets, is also a liquidating dividend and must be specifically identified as such. The statute requires that the stockholder be informed that the dividend he receives is a liquidating dividend. It is not taxable to the recipient as income but as a return of capital.

The rights, powers, and obligations of the corporation and shareholder vary with respect to each type of dividend and can best be considered in the light of the particular facts of each case.

Source of Dividends. In almost all instances cash dividends on common stock may be paid only out of current earnings or accumulated surplus. Surplus has been defined, for dividend purposes, as "an excess in the aggregate value of all assets of a corporation over the sum of its entire liabilities, including capital stock." Branch v. Kaiser, 291 Pa. 543, 140 A. 498, 500. In Illinois this general rule is reflected in the provision that no dividends may be declared and paid if the net assets are, or would, as a result of the dividend become, less than the stated capital. The Illinois provision means that no dividend may be paid, even if there were a profit for the current year, where there is an existing deficit. In some jurisdictions, notably Delaware, dividends may be paid out of current earnings even where the sum of the net assets is less than the amount of the capital stock. Under a statute such as exists in Illinois, a deficit may be eliminated by a reduction in paid-in surplus or by a reduction of stated capital. In such a case, current earnings would then be available for dividends. Under this statute, dividends are not only prohibited if the corporation is insolvent or its net assets are less than its stated capital, but also if the payment of the dividend would render the corporation insolvent or reduce its net assets below its stated capital.

A surplus may be produced by means other than the accumulation of profits and may be shown on the books of the corporation as a result of an allocation of part of the consideration received for no-par shares or by a reappraisal upward of certain corporate assets. Were a dividend paid out of such surplus, it would constitute a return to the shareholders of a part of their original investment, a fact of which they would probably be unaware, and would also impair the invested capital of the corporation even though, technically, its capital stock or stated capital would not be reduced below its net book assets. To guard against this possibility, certain jurisdictions prohibit the declaration of dividends out of paid-in surplus except as to shares having a preferential claim to dividends, and provide that only a stock dividend may be declared or paid out of surplus arising from unrealized appreciation or revaluation of assets.

A dividend paid out of paid-in surplus, created by a reduction of stated capital, or otherwise created, is generally referred to as a dividend "in partial liquidation." No such dividend may be paid if the corporation is insolvent, or if there are arrearages of accrued cumulative dividends on the preferred stock, or if such dividend would reduce the remaining net assets below the aggregate preferential amount payable to preferred shareholders in the event of liquidation. Unlike dividends paid out of earnings, any such dividend must be authorized not only by the board of directors but by the affirmative vote of the holders of at least two-thirds of the outstanding shares of stock of each class. A careful balance should be maintained between protecting shareholders and creditors from dissipation of corporate assets and the occasional necessity or advisability of such a distribution of capital by a going business.

Since, in most instances, dividends may only be paid out of the excess of assets over liabilities, including capital stock, the proper valuation of assets is sometimes a troublesome problem. An overvaluation of assets due to inadequate depreciation charges, insufficient reserve for bad debts, unjustified appraisal of questionable accounts receivable, or unrealized appreciation of fixed assets, might cause a dividend to constitute an illegal invasion of the capital investment. The care with which this danger is anticipated is reflected generally in the rule that those responsible for the declaration of dividends must likewise be responsible for a bona fide valuation of the assets. The rule that only stock dividends may be paid out of surplus resulting from an unrealized appreciation or revaluation of assets has been applied even in the absence of a statutory provision. Berks

Broadcasting Co. v. Craumer, 356 Pa. 620, 52 A.2d 571.

The declaration and payment of a stock dividend may be more restricted than a cash dividend where substantially all of the authorized shares of the corporation are outstanding. In such a case, an amendment to the charter increasing the authorized capital is a prerequisite to the declaration and payment of a stock dividend.

Nimble Dividends. Although dividends are properly payable only out of earnings or earned surplus and are generally not payable when the corporation has an accrued earned deficit, the statutes of Delaware, Maryland, Virginia and Wyoming permit payment of dividends out of earnings of the current or next preceding year notwithstanding the existence of such deficit.

This does not permit the declaration or payment of dividends which impair capital, but permits a board of directors by timely action to declare a dividend in a year when the corporation has no earnings, provided it had earnings for the year immediately preceding. Because of the time limitation within which such dividends must be declared, they are sometimes called "nimble dividends."

Declaration and Payment. The declaration of dividends is the responsibility of the directors of the corporation. This duty cannot be delegated, and an attempt by shareholders to usurp the power is ineffective, although, in some instances, informal distribution of corporate profits has been sustained where all shareholders consent and no creditors are injured. It is well settled that there can be no discrimination in the declaration of dividends among shareholders of the same class.

Once properly declared, a cash dividend is considered a debt owing by the corporation to the shareholders, and in the event of failure to pay or insolvency, the shareholder may prosecute his claim as an unsecured creditor in a court of law or in a bankruptcy court. In rare instances, a separate fund may be established at the time of declaration out of which the dividend is to be paid, and, in such a case, the courts have regarded the fund as having the characteristics of a trust to which the shareholders have a preferential claim. There has been some suggestion, not generally accepted, that the declaration of a cash dividend must be made public or otherwise brought to the attention of the shareholders before a debtor-creditor relationship is created.

It follows from the debtor-creditor relationship created by the declaration of a cash dividend that once declared it cannot be rescinded as against non-assenting shareholders. However, a stock dividend may be revoked unless actually distributed.

The time, place and manner of payment are in the discretion of the directors. It is not uncommon for the resolution declaring a dividend to fix a cut-off date, namely, to provide that the dividend shall be paid to the shareholders of record at the close of business on a specified future date, usually about two weeks earlier than the date fixed for payment. The directors may also attach certain conditions precedent, such as the requirement that specific creditors be paid in full before payment is made of the dividend.

Whether preferred shares have the right to cumulative dividends will, naturally, be governed by the intent of the parties as evidenced by their contract. In the absence of any evidence of intent that the shares are to be non-cumulative, the courts generally hold that they are cumulative. Where dividends on preferred stock are expressly stated to be non-cumulative, the question arises whether they should nevertheless be cumulative to the extent earned in a given year. The Supreme Court of the United States has held that even where earnings in a particular year

are adequate, the holders of non-cumulative preferred are not entitled to a dividend in that year unless the directors declare one. Wabash Railway Co. v. Barclay, 280 U.S. 197, 50 S.Ct. 106, 74 L.Ed. 368. This is the majority rule. On the other hand, the Supreme Court of New Jersey has held that dividends on non-cumulative preferred are cumulative to the extent earned, and although dividends on the preferred were not declared for the year in which they were earned, they nevertheless constitute a charge for that year which is prior to the rights of the holders of the common stock. See Sanders v. Cuba Railroad Co. page 839.

Dividends are sometimes said to be guaranteed. Any contract by the corporation which purports to bind it to pay dividends under all circumstances runs counter to the principle that dividends must come out of net earnings and generally cannot be enforced in the absence of such earnings. Ordinarily, such a guaranty, although absolute in form is construed to mean that dividends will be paid if the proper funds are on hand. A promise by a director that he will vote to declare dividends may impinge upon the independence of his judgment in the management of the corporation, and on the grounds of public policy would be of questionable validity. A corporation may occasionally guarantee the declaration and payment of the dividends of another corporation with which it has some relationship, and such guaranty is enforceable if the guarantor-corporation has the requisite authority. It is not unlawful for an individual, such as the vendor of shares, to guarantee the payment of dividends. As to a guaranty by a corporation of dividends on its own shares, the test is whether the corporate managers have committed themselves or the corporation in a manner which conflicts with the rights of other shareholders or creditors. It is possible, of course, for a guaranty by a corporation to create, in effect, an interest-bearing debt security which should be properly classified as such.

Because of the negotiable characteristics of most certificates of stock, the problem frequently arises as to which of two successive owners of shares is entitled to a particular dividend. The general rule is that, in the absence of a special agreement, the owner of the shares at the time the dividend is declared is entitled to the dividend even though prior to the time for payment the ownership has changed hands. Where the resolution declaring a dividend fixes a cut-off date, the owner of record as of that date is entitled to the dividend. Sales of stock between the cut-off date and the date of payment are said to be "ex-dividend."

A pledgee of stock does not ordinarily receive any cash dividends on the pledged stock, although as holder of legal title to the shares he could effect the issuance of a new certificate in his name and thereby perfect his right to cash dividends. In order to prevent a dilution of the security, the pledgee is entitled to all stock dividends declared on the pledged stock.

Wrongful or Illegal Dividends. Section 43 of the Model Business Corporation Act imposes joint and several liability upon the directors of a corporation who vote for or assent to the declaration of a dividend or the distribution of corporate assets (a) when the corporation is insolvent or when its net assets are less than its stated capital, or (b) when the declaration of such a dividend would render the corporation insolvent or reduce its net assets below its stated capital. The measure of damages in the first instance is the amount of the dividend, whereas in the second instance the directors are liable only to the extent that the corporation is rendered insolvent or its net assets are reduced below its stated capital.

The imposition of liability upon directors for the wrongful declaration of dividends ap-pears in most statutes, and, in the absence of statutory provision, liability has been imposed upon directors on the grounds of negligence or breach of trust. A common statutory provision is that a director shall not be liable for a dividend which impairs the capital if he relies in good faith upon a balance sheet and profit and loss statement which is represented to him to be correct by the president or officer of the corporation having charge of its books of account or by an independent public or certified public accountant (Section 43, Model Act, Appendix D). A director cannot, however, escape liability by a delegation of his responsibility:

"We believe that a corporate director participates in a dividend, that is, declares or assents to a dividend, under the statute, if he votes to give such an executive committee the power to declare a dividend and this is done, if he himself is an active member of the executive committee which declares a dividend or if he approves, ratifies or assents to a declaration of the executive committee." DeMet's, Inc. v. Insull, 122 F.2d 755, 757, C. A. 7.

The liability of directors is generally to the corporation or to its creditors. The Model Act expressly provides that the directors who vote for or assent to an illegal dividend are jointly and severally liable to the corporation, thus facilitating a ratable distribution of the amounts recovered.

Where an illegal dividend has been declared but not yet paid, a shareholder or creditor may by speedy action obtain a court injunction against the payment. Where the directors have improperly discriminated between various classes of stock in the declaration of a dividend, a shareholder may likewise by prompt action restrain the payment.

The obligation of a shareholder who has received payment of an illegally declared dividend to repay depends upon a variety of factors which may include the good or bad faith on the part of the shareholder in accepting the dividend, his knowledge of the facts, the solvency or insolvency of the corporation, and, in some instances, special statutory provisions. The existence of a statutory liability on the part of directors does not relieve shareholders from the duty to make repayment. A shareholder who receives illegal dividends either as a result of his own fraudulent act or with knowledge of their unlawful character, is under a duty to refund them to the corporation.

Where the corporation is insolvent, a dividend may not be retained by the stockholder even though received by him in good faith. This rule stems from the doctrine that the capital stock is a trust fund for creditors under the rules relating to fraudulent conveyances and the basic common law concept that a person must be just before he can be generous. The shareholders do not have the status of innocent purchasers.

Where an unsuspecting shareholder receives an illegal dividend from a solvent corporation, the majority rule is that he cannot be compelled to make a refund. The Maryland Supreme Court has rationalized this doctrine, as follows:

"We are disposed to follow the federal decisions as being more in accord with modern conditions and with the realities of life. In these days stocks of corporations are so widely held that it would be practically impossible for stockholders generally to know whether each semi-annual dividend paid in regular course was earned. Whatever their position may be theoretically, practically they are in no better position than creditors to know the condition of the company, and it would be an unfair and unreasonable burden to require them to pay back, years after they have been spent, dividends received in good faith from a solvent corporation in regular course of business." Bartlett v. Smith, 162 Md. 478, 482, 160 A. 440, 441.

In the event that the shareholder recipient of an illegal dividend is held liable to make restitution, the party or parties to whom the refund is owing depends in part upon the theory of liability. If an innocent shareholder is obliged to make a refund because the capital is regarded as a trust fund, the creditors of the corporation are the logical claimants, and this doctrine has in some cases been extended to grant relief even to creditors whose claims arose after the illegal payment. However, even where the statute expressly gives creditors the right to recover, it has been held that the corporation itself may hold the shareholder liable on the theory that the illegal dividends constitute property of the corporation unlawfully in the possession of the shareholders.

CASES

DOYLE v. CHLADEK

(1965 Or.) 401 P.2d 18.

HOLMAN, J. Plaintiff is receiver for the Senior Citizens Land and Development Co., an insolvent Oregon corporation. This suit is brought to recover on subscriptions to the capital stock of the corporation which plaintiff claims are owed by the defendants. * *

Senior Citizens Land and Development Co. was formed for the purpose of furnishing housing for the elderly. At first it was intended that this be done with new housing, but that intent was abandoned and equities in two older hotel properties were purchased. * * *

The corporation was organized in October of 1960. * * *

In November of 1960 both of the defendants subscribed in writing for 30,000 shares of capital stock at 50 cents per share. Both were subsequently elected to the board of directors. * * *

The business was operated for a little more than a year. It steadily lost money from its inception. * * *

By this time the die was cast. In the trial of this case in circuit court the trial judge analyzed the situation as follows: "The company was underfinanced because of the failure of stock subscribers to pay for their stock. As is to be expected, the house of cards has collapsed."

* * *

This suit was brought by the receiver on the stock subscription rather than the note. The defendant Kring, in his first affirmative defense, pleads that he paid the corporation $2,500 in cash and delivered to it his promissory note for the sum of $12,500. We interpret this as an attempt to plead the defense of payment so that Kring would no longer be liable upon his stock subscription though he might be on his note.

There is considerable controversy as to whether a corporation can accept notes in payment of stock subscriptions. Some courts have held that notes may not be so received. Many states have prohibited it by statute. Section 18 of the Model Business Corporation Act specifically prohibits it.

In Oregon it would appear that it is proper for a corporation to receive the note of a stock subscriber. When section 18 of the Model Act was adopted by the legislature (ORS 57.106), that part prohibiting the payment of stock subscriptions by the giving of notes was deleted. It now reads that the consideration for the issuance of shares may be the giving of property tangible or intangible. The articles of incorporation issued by the state to the corporation authorized the receipt of notes in payment for stock. [Citation.]

This does not necessarily mean that a corporation must sue on the note and that the debt on the stock subscription is extinguished. The law in Oregon as demonstrated by a long series of cases, is that the giving of a note does not extinguish the debt for which it was given unless the parties have intended or agreed that this be so. [Citations.]

* * *

Prima facie, the giving of the note did not extinguish the obligation on the stock subscription. It is therefore necessary to examine the facts to see whether there are other circumstances sufficient to overcome the case for conditional payment. There is no testimony which throws any light on the question one way or the other except the showing that the stock was issued by the corporation to Kring.

It is contended that the giving of the note must have been intended as absolute and unconditional payment as otherwise the corporation had no power to issue the stock because of ORS 57.121(4) which is as follows:

"No certificate shall be issued for any share until such share is fully paid."

We might be a little more impressed with the argument if we did not have before us many illustrations of the corporate officers grossly disregarding the law and the niceties of authorized corporate procedure and authority. An illustration would be the issuance of $15,-000 worth of stock to the defendant Huston for which he gave nothing—not even a note. Under these circumstances the delivery of the stock to Kring was not very meaningful.

We see no reason, in this case, why the legal implications of the giving of a note for the issuance of shares of stock should be any different than if it were given for the purchase and delivery of a cow. The corporation, in taking the note, received only another promise to pay for the stock.

This case is being brought for the benefit of creditors of the corporation against its president on his stock subscription. We are not inclined to stretch any points in favor of the president relative to the intention of the parties concerning a transaction between him and the corporation when we have a history of utter disregard for the niceties of corporate authority and procedure and there can be serious doubt that he at all times dealt at arm's length with the corporation.

* * *

It is our finding that there is no evidence sufficient to overcome the prima facie case for conditional payment only. The note being past due, the receiver may sue on either the underlying debt on the stock subscription or the note, as he chooses.

The decree of the trial court is modified in that judgment will be given in favor of plaintiff and against the defendant Huston in the sum of $15,000 and against the defendant Kring in the sum of $12,500.

REILLY v. SEGERT

(1964) 31 Ill.2d 293, 201 N.E.2d 444.

SCHAEFER, J. Prior to the enactment of the Business Corporation Act of 1933, it was settled that a shareholder of a corporation who sold his stock to the corporation while it was insolvent was liable to an injured creditor of the corporation for the amount paid to the shareholder for his stock. [Citations.] This liability was based upon the adverse effect of the transaction upon creditors, and not upon the guilt or innocence of the shareholder, who was held liable even though there was no evidence of fraud. [Citation.] The question for decision in this case is whether or not this liability was repealed by section 42 of the Business Corporation Act. (Ill.Rev.Stat.1959, chap. 32, par. 157.42.) The circuit court of Lake County held that it was, the Appellate Court affirmed (44 Ill. App.2d 343, 194 N.E.2d 544), and we allowed leave to appeal.

The plaintiffs are George L. Reilly, the receiver of Deerfield Lumber & Fuel Co., Inc.

and three creditors of that company. The defendants are the directors of the company and five shareholders. The complaint alleged that the directors authorized purchases of stock from the defendant shareholders at a time when the corporation was insolvent and had no earned surplus. The directors defaulted, and judgments were entered against them for the amounts paid to the defendant shareholders for their stock. No appeal was taken from the judgments so entered, and we are not concerned with them.

Those counts of the complaint, however, that asserted liability against the defendant shareholders, were dismissed upon motion, and final judgments were entered against the plaintiffs on those counts. The judgments thus entered were based upon the proposition that section 42 of the Business Corporation Act affords the only remedy available, and that it does not authorize an action directly against shareholders.

The portions of section 42 that are relied upon to support the judgment are as follows:

"In addition to any other liabilities imposed by law upon directors of a corporation:

"(a) Directors of a corporation who vote for or assent to the declaration of any dividend or other distribution of the assets of a corporation to its shareholders shall be jointly and severally liable to the corporation for the amount of such dividend which is paid or the value of such assets which are distributed if, at the time of such payment or distribution, the corporation is insolvent or its net assets are less than its stated capital.

"(b) The directors of a corporation who vote for or assent to the declaration of any dividend or other distribution of assets of a corporation to its shareholders which renders the corporation insolvent or reduces its net assets below its stated capital shall be jointly and severally liable to the corporation for the amount of such dividend which is paid or the value of such assets which are distributed, to the extent that the corporation is thereby rendered insolvent or its net assets are reduced below its stated capital.

*   *   *   *   *   *

"Any director against whom a claim shall be asserted under or pursuant to this section for the improper declaration of a dividend or other distribution of assets of a corporation and who shall be held liable thereon, shall be entitled to contribution from the shareholders who knowingly accepted or received any such dividend or assets, in proportion to the amounts received by them respectively."

In our opinion section 42 does not preclude this action against the shareholders. Even as to the liability of directors, its language makes it clear that it was not designed to provide an exclusive remedy, for the liabilities with which it deals are expressly stated to be "[i]n addition to any other liabilities imposed by law upon directors of a corporation." In the absence of this specific disclaimer, the result would be the same. "Where a liability is imposed upon an officer of [sic] a director by a state statute, his common-law liability for misfeasance and negligence in the performance of his duties is not thereby excluded." [Citation.]

In this case, moreover, we are concerned with the direct liability of shareholders, a subject with which section 42 does not purport to deal. The existence of a statutory provision dealing with the liability of directors does not preclude a non-statutory liability on the part of shareholders. * * *

The judgment of the Appellate Court is reversed, and the cause is remanded to the circuit court of Lake County for further proceedings not inconsistent with this opinion.

Reversed and remanded.

ROBINSON v. WANGEMANN

(1935 C.A.5th) 75 F.2d 756.

[In the bankruptcy proceeding of Reichardt-Abbott Company, Inc., the executrix of the will of Arthur Wangemann, deceased, filed a claim as a general creditor for $35,000 representing the balance due on a purchase by the company of 500 shares of its own stock from Arthur Wangemann. The district court upheld an order of the referee in bankruptcy allowing the claim. The trustee in bankruptcy appeals.]

FOSTER, J. This is an appeal from a judgment affirming an order of the referee allowing a claim against the estate of Reichardt-Abbott Company, Inc., bankrupt, based on a note given by the corporation in payment for shares of its own stock purchased by it.

The facts are not in dispute. In October, 1922, Arthur Wangemann, who was its president and a large stockholder in Wangemann-Reichardt Company, Inc., sold 500 shares of its own stock owned by him to the corporation at $110 per share, a total of $55,000. The purchase was authorized by a meeting of stockholders and the company's note, due January 1, 1923, bearing 7 per cent. interest from October 1, 1922, was delivered to him in payment. At that time the corporation was solvent and its surplus in cash, over and above its liabilities, was more than $55,000. The note, due January 1, 1923, was not paid. From time to time, renewal notes were issued and the debt was reduced to $35,000. The name of the corporation was changed to Reichardt-Abbott Company, Inc., and under that name it was adjudicated bankrupt. Its assets are not sufficient to pay creditors in full. The claim of appellee is based on one of the renewal notes for $30,000, due January 1, 1933, and four notes each for $500, given in payment of interest on said note, together with interest on all the said notes. Appellee holds said notes as executrix under his will and sole legatee of Arthur Wangemann.

The referee held that the corporation had the right to purchase its own stock, relying upon the cases of San Antonio Hardware Co. v. Sanger (Tex.Civ.App.) 151 S.W. 1104; Medical Arts Bldg. Co. v. Southern Finance & Development Co. (C.C.A.) 29 F.2d 969, that the transaction was in good faith, and, as the corporation had sufficient surplus out of which the stock could have been paid for at the time it was purchased, without prejudice to creditors, appellee was entitled to prove her claim and participate equally with the other creditors in the distribution of the assets.

It may be conceded that if Arthur Wangemann had received cash for his stock at the time he relinquished it the transaction would have been valid, but that is not the case here presented.

We will not attempt to review all the authorities cited by the parties. In the two cases relied upon by the referee the controversies were between the corporations and the noteholders and no creditors were complaining. They are not in point as applied to the facts in this case. Arthur Wangemann loaned no money to the corporation. The note he accepted for his stock did not change the character of the transaction nor did the renewals have that effect. A transaction by which a corporation acquires its own stock from a stockholder for a sum of money is not really a sale. The corporation does not acquire anything of value equivalent to the depletion of its assets, if the stock is held in the treasury, as in this case. It is simply a method of distributing a proportion of the assets to the stockholder. The assets of a corporation are the common pledge of its creditors, and stockholders are not entitled to receive any part of them unless creditors are paid in full. When such a transaction is had, regardless of the good faith of the par-

ties, it is essential to the validity that there be sufficient surplus to retire the stock, without prejudice to creditors, at the time payment is made out of assets. In principle, the contract between Wangemann and the corporation was executory until the stock should be paid for in cash. It is immaterial that the corporation was solvent and had sufficient surplus to make payment when the agreement was entered into. It is necessary to a recovery that the corporation should be solvent and have sufficient surplus to prevent injury to creditors when the payment is actually made. This was an implied condition in the original note and the renewals accepted by Arthur Wangemann.

As the assets of the bankrupt are not sufficient to pay the creditors in full and there is no surplus out of which the note could be paid, appellee, who is in no better position than the original holder of the notes, cannot be permitted to share with the other unsecured creditors in the distribution of the assets of the bankrupt estate. She may be permitted to file her claim, but it is subordinate to the claims of the other creditors. * * *

Reversed and remanded.

SHERMAN v. PEPIN PICKLING CO.

(1950) 230 Minn. 87, 41 N.W.2d 571.

PETERSON, J. Action by a preferred stockholder of defendant corporation, hereinafter referred to as defendant, to recover the par value of 33 shares of cumulative preferred stock of $100 par value and accumulated dividends at seven percent per annum. The defense was that, pursuant to statutes in force when the stock was issued and when defendant subsequently amended its articles of incorporation, defendant by such an amendment canceled not only the stock held by plaintiff by issuing in lieu thereof new preferred stock having a par value of $70 per share and entitled to dividends at five percent per annum beginning January 1, 1936, but also the accumulated undeclared and unpaid dividends on plaintiff's stock.

The questions for decision are:

(1) Whether, under statutes (G.S.1913, §§ 6185 and 6193 [M.S.A. §§ 300.45 and 300.54]) providing that (a) a corporation may amend its articles of incorporation so as to increase or decrease its capital stock, to change the number and par value of the shares of the capital stock, or in respect of any other matter which an orignal certificate (articles of incorporation) of a corporation of the same kind might lawfully have contained, and (b) a corporation by its original articles of incorporation or amendment thereof may issue preferred and common stock and give such preference as it deems best to such preferred stock, a corporation organized and amending its articles of incorporation when such statutes were in force has the power as against a nonassenting preferred stockholder to amend its articles of incorporation so as to substitute for cumulative preferred stock having a par value and entitled to dividends at a stipulated rate new noncumulative preferred stock having less par value and entitled to dividends at a lesser rate; and

(2) Whether, in such a case, the corporation has the power by such an amendment to cancel dividends on the old stock, which at the time of the amendment had accrued by the lapse of time, but had not been declared.

It was in effect conceded upon the argument that if these questions stated were answered in favor of defendant it was entitled to decision here. Accordingly, the facts will be stated only insofar as they are material to these questions.

Defendant was incorporated in 1917 with a capital stock of $100,000, consisting of 500 shares of common stock with a par value of $100 and 500 shares of cumulative seven per-

cent preferred stock with a par value of $100. The articles of incorporation provided that the preferred stock should be entitled to receive cumulative dividends at the rate of seven percent annually payable on January 1 of each year; that it should be retired at the time therein mentioned by payment therefor of its par value and accumulated dividends; and that such stock should have, upon default of payment of the stipulated dividends, certain voting and other rights. On March 26, 1934, defendant amended its articles of incorporation so as to provide, among other things, that its stock should consist of 3,000 shares, of which 1,000 shares should be common stock with no par value and 2,000 shares should be preferred stock of the par value of $70 entitled to five percent dividends annually commencing January 1, 1936, with certain voting, redemption, and retirement rights. There was no provision that the dividends should be cumulative. At the trial below and upon the argument here, it was assumed for purposes of decision that the effect of the amendment of the articles of incorporation was an attempt to cancel the seven percent cumulative preferred stock of $100 par value and all accrued but undeclared and unpaid dividends thereon and to substitute therefor the new five percent preferred stock of $70 par value.

Plaintiff is the owner of 33 shares of the seven percent cumulative preferred stock of $100 par value issued to him or his assignors between January 26, 1918, and February 26, 1927. The 1934 amendment of the articles of incorporation was passed over plaintiff's express objection. Neither plaintiff nor his assignors ever assented thereto. On the contrary, they have repeatedly and consistently claimed and demanded their rights to the stock originally issued to them. * * *

As a consequence of business reverses, defendant during the years from about 1933 to 1945 not only failed to earn any profits, but operated at a large deficit, part of which represented an unpaid bank loan. Its credit was impaired, and apparently it had become practically insolvent. Its bankers advised that it was impossible for defendant to operate in its then condition or to borrow any more money, and that some kind of reorganization should take place. In order to get into a sound condition, defendant thereupon reduced the book value of its inventory, carried its common stock at no value, and reduced the book value of its outstanding preferred stock to that fixed by the amendment of the articles of incorporation. The trial court found, as stipulated facts, that as of and prior to the amendment of the articles of incorporation in 1934, defendant was unable to retire the seven percent cumulative preferred stock plus accrued dividends "without jeopardizing the financial structure of the defendant corporation and without prejudice to its creditors"; that between the date of the amendment and June 30, 1945, it also was unable to do so; and that after the last-mentioned date it was able to do so. Plaintiff in his brief concedes that defendant was unable to pay dividends when it defaulted in the payment thereof.

Briefly, plaintiff claims that his rights to the face value of the old stock and accumulated dividends thereon are contractual; that such rights are vested; and that the amendment substituting for such stock other preferred stock of less par value and entitled to a lesser rate of dividend and canceling accrued dividends on the old stock is invalid as impairing such vested rights. Defendant contends that statutes in force when the corporation was organized and when it amended its articles of incorporation, authorizing it by amendment to change the preference rights of its stockholders, became part of plaintiff's contractual rights as a stockholder and qualified and conditioned them as subject to corporate action pursuant to such statutory authorization.

1. Preferred stock of a corporation is, as the words indicate, corporate stock having preference rights. It represents a contribution to the capital of the corporation and is in no sense a loan of money. Because preferred stock is stock and not a loan, preferred stockholders' rights are governed by the rules of law governing those of stockholders having preference rights and not by those governing the rights of money lenders. As said in Booth v. Union Fibre Co., 137 Minn. 7, 8, 162 N.W. 677: " * * * By general definition preferred stock is stock entitled to a preference over other kinds of stock in the payment of dividends. The dividends come out of earnings and not out of capital. Unless there are net earnings there is no right to dividends. The stockholder is still a stockholder and not a creditor. He makes a contribution to capital and not a loan. The corporation is not his debtor." [Citation.]

In the Booth case, the question was raised whether the stock certificate evidenced preferred stock or a loan. Here, there is no such question. It is undisputed that plaintiff's securities are preferred stock—it was so alleged in the complaint, and the litigation both below and here has proceeded upon the assumption that they were such in fact.

2. A dividend is a portion of the profits of a corporation declared by the board of directors of the corporation, or other governing body thereof, to be set apart and paid to the stockholders ratably according to their respective interests. The declaration of a dividend involves segregating it from the property of the corporation so as to become the property of the stockholders distributively. [Citation.] The declaration of dividends involves not only the consideration of earnings, but also the business needs of the corporation. [Citations.] Because a corporate dividend depends upon a declaration thereof by the board of directors of the corporation, an undeclared dividend is in no sense a debt. The effect of a provision in the articles of in-

corporation for accumulated dividends is to restrict the corporation from declaring dividends on other classes of stock until the cumulative dividends have been declared and paid. While the preferential right is a valuable one, it has no existence apart from the stock and cannot be either alienated or devised. Mere lapse of time creates no dividend rights. "No preferred stockholder has a right to demand that dividends be paid him merely because a period of time has elapsed." McNulty v. W. & J. Sloane, 184 Misc. 835, 842, 54 N.Y.S.2d 253, 260. According to the undisputed facts here, there was no duty on the part of defendant, through its board of directors, when the articles of incorporation were amended and when dividends were not declared and paid, to declare and pay any dividend, for the obvious reason that defendant had no earnings, accumulated or otherwise, out of which to pay them. On the contrary, defendant was then engaged in a struggle for its very existence, which reorganization and improved business operations alone made possible.

3. At the outset of the consideration of the question whether preferred stockholders' rights may be altered, we should remember that the sole basis for the rule of law that stockholders' rights among themselves may not be altered is the rule of the Dartmouth College case, Trustees of Dartmouth College v. Woodward, 4 Wheat. 518, 17 U.S. 518, 4 L.Ed. 629, to the effect that such rights are contractual in nature. But in that case Mr. Justice Story suggested that, where the right to amend or alter such rights is reserved, that very thing may be done. Accordingly, the common practice ever since has been to make such a reservation either by general statute or in some other manner. Where a statute authorizes the formation of a corporation upon compliance with its provisions and the statute contains provisions reserving the right to alter by amendment the rights of stockholders, the statute becomes part of the

articles of incorporation (the corporate charter) and of any stock issued thereunder as effectively as if printed therein at length, and it operates not only to confer upon the corporation reserved power to alter by amendment the rights of stockholders, but also to notify them of such reserved power. In other words, where the right to so amend is reserved, the contract between the corporation and its stockholders and among the stockholders themselves, arising from their stock ownership, is not an unconditional one, but is rather one subject to the condition that it may be changed or altered in the manner authorized by the statute. [Citations.] * *

In conclusion, we hold that the statutes, G.S.1913, §§ 6185, 6193, M.S.A. §§ 300.45, 300.54, in effect when defendant was incorporated and when the amendment of the articles of incorporation was adopted reserved power to defendant to amend its articles in the respects which it did and that the amendment is valid. Because that is true, defendants are entitled to judgment and a reversal here.

Reversed with directions to enter judgment for defendants.

DODGE v. FORD MOTOR CO.

(1919) 204 Mich. 459, 170 N.W. 668.

[Action in equity by John F. and Horace E. Dodge, plaintiffs, against the Ford Motor Company and its directors to compel the declaration of dividends and for an injunction restraining a contemplated expansion of the business. The complaint was filed in November, 1916. Since 1909, the capital stock of the company had been $2,000,000, divided into 20,000 shares of the par value of $100 each of which plaintiffs held 2,000. As of the close of business of July 31, 1916, the end of the company's fiscal year, the surplus above capital was $111,960,907.53 and the assets included cash on hand of $52,550,771.-92.

For a number of years the company had paid regularly quarterly dividends equal to sixty per cent annually on the capital stock of $2,000,000. In addition, from December, 1911, to October, 1915, inclusive, eleven special dividends totalling $41,000,000 had been paid and in November, 1916, after this action was commenced, a special dividend of $2,000,000 was paid.

Plaintiffs' complaint alleged that Henry Ford, president of the company and a member of its board of directors, had declared it to be the settled policy of the company not to pay any special dividends in the future, but to put back into the business all future earnings in excess of the regular quarterly dividend. Plaintiffs sought an injunction restraining the carrying out of the alleged declared policy of Henry Ford and a decree requiring the directors to pay a dividend of at least seventy-five per cent of the accumulated cash surplus.

In December, 1917, the trial court entered a decree requiring the directors to declare and pay a dividend of $19,275,385.96 and enjoining the corporation from usings its funds for a proposed smelting plant and certain other planned projects. From this decree, defendants have appealed.]

OSTRANDER, J. * * * The case for plaintiffs must rest upon the claim, and the proof in support of it, that the proposed expansion of the business of the corporation, involving the further use of profits as capital, ought to be enjoined because inimical to the best interests of the company and its shareholders, and upon the further claim that in any event the withholding of the special dividend asked for by plaintiffs is arbitrary action of the directors requiring judicial interference.

The rule which will govern courts in deciding these questions is not in dispute. * * *

In 1 Morawetz on Corporations (2d Ed.), sec. 447, it is stated:

"Profits earned by a corporation may be divided among its shareholders; but it is not a violation of the charter if they are allowed to accumulate and remain invested in the company's business. The managing agents of a corporation are impliedly invested with a discretionary power with regard to the time and manner of distributing its profits. They may apply profits in payment of floating or funded debts, or in development of the company's business; and so long as they do not abuse their discretionary powers, or violate the company's charter, the courts cannot interfere.

"But it is clear that the agents of a corporation, and even the majority, cannot arbitrarily withhold profits earned by the company, or apply them to any use which is not authorized by the company's charter. The nominal capital of a company does not necessarily limit the scope of its operations; a corporation may borrow money for the purpose of enlarging its business, and in many instances it may use profits for the same purpose. But the amount of the capital contributed by the shareholders is an important element in determining the limit beyond which the company's business cannot be extended by the investment of profits. If a corporation is formed with a capital of $100,-000 in order to carry on a certain business, no one would hesitate to say that it would be a departure from the intention of the founders to withhold profits, in order to develop the company's business, until the sum of $500,000 had been amassed, unless the company was formed mainly for the purpose of accumulating the profits from year to year. The question in each case depends upon the use to which the capital is put, and the meaning of the company's charter. If a majority of the shareholders or the directors of a corporation wrongfully refuse to declare a dividend and distribute profits earned by the company, any shareholder feeling aggrieved may obtain relief in a court of equity.

"It may often be reasonable to withhold part of the earnings of a corporation in order to increase its surplus fund, when it would not be reasonable to withhold all the earnings for that purpose. The shareholders forming an ordinary business corporation expect to obtain the profits of their investment in the form of regular dividends. To withhold the entire profits merely to enlarge the capacity of the company's business would defeat their just expectations. After the business of a corporation has been brought to a prosperous condition, and necessary provision has been made for future prosperity, a reasonable share of the profits should be applied in the payment of regular dividends, though a part may be reserved to increase the surplus and enlarge the business itself."
* * *

When plaintiffs made their complaint and demand for further dividends the Ford Motor Company had concluded its most prosperous year of business. The demand for its cars at the price of the preceding year continued. It could make and could market in the year beginning August 1, 1916, more than 500,000 cars. Sales of parts and repairs would necessarily increase. The cost of materials was likely to advance, and perhaps the price of labor, but it reasonably might have expected a profit for the year of upwards of $60,000,000. It had assets of more than $132,000,000, a surplus of almost $112,000,000, and its cash on hand and municipal bonds were nearly $54,000,000. Its total liabilities, including capital stock, was a little over $20,000,000. It had declared no special dividend during the business year except the October, 1915, dividend. It had been the practice, under similar circumstances, to declare larger dividends. Considering only these facts, a refusal to declare and pay further dividends appears to be not an exercise of discretion on the part of the directors, but an arbitrary refusal to do what the circumstances required to be done. These facts and others call upon the directors to justify their action, or failure or refusal to act. In justification, the defendants have offered testimony tending to prove, and which does prove, the following facts. It had been the policy of the corporation for a considerable time to annually reduce the selling price of cars, while keeping up, or improving, their quality. As early as in June, 1915, a general plan for the expansion of the productive capacity of the concern by a practical duplication of its plant had been talked over by the executive officers and directors and agreed upon, not all of the details having been settled and no formal action of directors having been taken. The erection of a smelter was considered, and engineering and other data in connection therewith secured. In consequence, it was determined not to reduce the selling price of cars for the year beginning August 1, 1915, but to maintain the price and to accumulate a large surplus to pay for the proposed expansion of plant and equipment, and perhaps to build a plant for smelting ore. It is hoped, by Mr. Ford, that eventually 1,000,000 cars will be annually produced. The contemplated changes will permit the increased output.

The plan, as affecting the profits of the business for the year beginning August 1, 1916, and thereafter, calls for a reduction in the selling price of cars. * * * In short, the plan does not call for and is not intended to produce immediately a more profitable business but a less profitable one; not only less profitable than formerly but less profitable than it is admitted it might be made. The apparent immediate effect will be to diminish the value of shares and the returns to shareholders.

It is the contention of plaintiffs that the apparent effect of the plan is intended to be the continued and continuing effect of it and that it is deliberately proposed, not of record and not by official corporate declaration, but nevertheless proposed, to continue the corporation henceforth as a semi-eleemosynary institution and not as a business institution. In support of this contention they point to the attitude and to the expressions of Mr. Henry Ford.

Mr. Henry Ford is the dominant force in the business of the Ford Motor Company. No plan of operations could be adopted unless he consented, and no board of directors can be elected whom he does not favor. One of the directors of the company has no stock. One share was assigned to him to qualify him for the position, but it is not claimed that he owns it. A business, one of the largest in the world, and one of the most profitable, has been built up. It employs many men, at good pay.

"My ambition", said Mr. Ford, "is to employ still more men, to spread the benefits of this industrial system to the greatest possible number, to help them build up their lives and their homes. To do this we are putting the greatest share of our profits back in the business." * * *

The record, and especially the testimony of Mr. Ford, convinces that he has to some extent the attitude towards shareholders of one who has dispensed and distributed to them large gains and that they should be content to take what he chooses to give. His testimony creates the impression, also, that he thinks the Ford Motor Company has made too much money, has had too large profits, and that although large profits might still be earned, a sharing of them with the public, by reducing the price of the output of the company, ought to be undertaken. We have no doubt that certain sentiments, philanthropic and altruistic, creditable to Mr. Ford, had large influence in determining the policy to be pursued by the Ford Motor Company—the policy which has been herein referred to. * * *

These cases, after all, like all others in which the subject is treated, turn finally upon the point, the question, whether it appears that the directors were not acting for the best interests of the corporation. * * The difference between an incidental humanitarian expenditure of corporate funds for the benefit of the employees, like the building of a hospital for their use and the employment of agencies for the betterment of their condition, and a general purpose and plan to benefit mankind at the expense of others, is obvious. * * * A business corporation is organized and carried on primarily for the profit of the stockholders. The powers of the directors are to be employed for that end. The discretion of directors is to be exercised in the choice of means to attain that end and does not extend to a change in the end itself, to the reduction of profits or to the nondistribution of profits among stockholders in order to devote them to other purposes. * * *

We are not, however, persuaded that we should interfere with the proposed expansion of the business of the Ford Motor Company. In view of the fact that the selling price of products may be increased at any time, the ultimate results of the larger business cannot be certainly estimated. The judges are not business experts. It is recognized that plans must often be made for a long future, for expected competition, for a continuing as well as an immediately profitable venture. The experience of the Ford Motor Company is evidence of capable management of its affairs. * * *

Defendants say, and it is true, that a considerable cash balance must be at all times carried by such a concern. But, as has been stated, there was a large daily, weekly, monthly, receipt of cash. The output was practically continuous and was continuously, and within a few days, turned into cash. Moreover, the contemplated expenditures were not to be immediately made. The large sum appropriated for the smelter plant was payable over a considerable period of time. So that, without going further, it would appear that, accepting and approving the plan of the directors, it was their duty to distribute on or near the first of August, 1916, a very large sum of money to stockholders.

* * *

The decree of the court below fixing and determining the specific amount to be distributed to stockholders is affirmed. In other respects, except as to the allowance of costs, the said decree is reversed.

TENNANT v. EPSTEIN

(1934) 356 Ill. 26, 189 N.E. 864, 98 A.L.R. 1515.

[The Grayslake Gelatin Corporation was organized with capital stock of $160,000, consisting of 30,000 shares of seven per cent cumulative preferred and 2,000 shares of common stock, all of the par value of $5. Tennant owned 2,000 shares of preferred and 500 shares of common stock. Harry, Anna and Chester Epstein owned all the remaining stock. Dividends on the preferred had been paid annually during the seven year period since the corporation was organized in 1922. No dividends having previously been declared on the common stock, the corporation, in 1929, paid a forty-nine per cent dividend on such stock. Subsequently a stock dividend of one share of common for each share of preferred or common outstanding was paid and $160,000 of the surplus was capitalized. Thereafter cash dividends were paid on all common stock.

Tennant brought an action in equity against the other shareholders and the corporation for the cancellation of the stock dividend and the repayment of dividends paid on such new shares on the theory that the preferred stock was not entitled to participate in any dividends, whether of cash or in stock, in excess of the expressed preference of seven per cent. The articles of incorporation and the by-laws simply provided that "the preferred stock shall be seven per

cent (7%) cumulative dividend preferred". Plaintiff appeals from a decision of the intermediate appellate court reversing a decree in his favor entered in the trial court.]

FARTHING, J. * * * The question presented by this record is whether the holders of a preferred stock in this company have a right to share in a stock dividend to be paid for out of the undivided earnings and surplus in addition to the seven per cent annual cash dividend. The preference which preferred stock enjoys over common stock as to dividends is entirely a matter of contract. The contract is generally set forth in the charter or articles of incorporation, by-laws or stock certificates. * * *

It is elementary that the statute in force when the contract between the shareholders was made is a part of their contract. Where no statute exists the contract itself is all that need be looked to to determine the preferential rights of preferred stockholders. [Citation.] At the time the contract contained in the articles of incorporation in this case was entered into between the parties to this suit, the act in force was the act of 1919 as amended in 1921. (Smith's Stat.1931, p. 745.) Sections 6 and 31 provide, respectively, what shall be included in the articles of incorporation and stock certificates. Paragraph 4 of section 6 provides that each corporation organized under the act shall, subject to the conditions and limitations prescribed by the act, have the following powers, rights and privileges: "To have a capital stock of such an amount, and divided into shares with a par value, or without a par value, and to divide such capital stock into such classes, with such preferences, rights, values and interests as may be provided in the articles of incorporation," etc. Section 31 provides: "Shares of stock having a par value shall be represented by certificates which shall state the number of shares represented thereby, the par value thereof, the name of the holder, the relative rights, interests and preference (if any) of such shares," etc. These provisions of the statute clearly limit the rights, preferences and interest of preferred as well as common shareholders to what is set out in the articles of incorporation and the stock certificates. In addition to statutory provisions, the rule of construction has been generally adhered to that *expressio unius est exclusio alterius*. [Citations.] * * *

We think the results reached in Stone v. United States Envelope Co., 119 Me. 394, 111 A. 536, Niles v. Ludlow Valve Manf. Co., 202 F. 141, id., 231 U.S. 748, 34 S.Ct. 320, 58 L. Ed. 465, and Will v. United Lankat Plantations Co. [1914] A.C. 11, 67 A.L.R. 775, are more nearly in accord with business usage and the expectation of investors when they purchase preferred shares of stock. In Will v. United Lankat Plantations Co., supra, Earl Loreburn, speaking for the House of Lords, said that a general assumption is well founded that where preference shares are given and a definite preferential dividend is fixed, "that impliedly negatives any right to take any further dividend." It was contended that the rights of preference shareholders ought not to be cut down except where something is found which negatives the right to any further share in the profits. He remarked that people taking the preference shares would doubtless have been surprised to learn that they were to receive the "almost boundless additional advantages which have been held out to them in the arguments we have been hearing," and that it was really an attempt to add to the terms of the contract "by screwing something out of the articles which the framers of the contract, I do not believe, ever thought of." In Stone v. United States Envelope Co., supra, it was said: "The other theory, which we believe to be the better and supported by the weight of authority, is, that in receiving the greater security of his preferential rights the preferred stockholder impliedly agrees to ac-

cept such rights in leiu of equal participation. The maxim *expressio unius,* etc., applies to this case and is decisive. The parties by a contract embodied in the by-laws have provided for the preferred stockholders a seven per cent preferential dividend, and in case of liquidation one hundred per cent. This excludes other participation." We think the reasoning of these cases applies here. The preferences stated in the stock certificates are a delimitation of the rights of the preferred stockholders.

Another act adverse to appellees' contention is found in the payment of the forty-nine per cent dividend on the value of the 2000 shares of common stock in 1929 and the payment of but the limited seven per cent on the value of 30,000 shares of preferred stock in that year prior to the stock dividend. Appellees contend that by payment of this "equalizing" dividend the case of Stone v. United States Envelope Co., supra, is rendered inapplicable, but cite Englander v. Osborne, 261 Pa. 366, 104 A. 614, where it is said: "We find nothing limiting the right of the preferred stockholders to the six per cent dividend regardless of the earnings of the company, and in absence of such limitation the general rule is that such stockholders are entitled to share with the holders of the common stock all profits distributed after the latter have received in any year an amount equal to the dividends on the preferred stock." If this rule of law quoted by appellees is correct, the preferred stock should have had a dividend in 1929 of forty-nine per cent instead of seven per cent "and no more," as provided in the stock certificates. What was paid on the preferred stock shows the interpretation by the parties of their rights and privileges as expressed in the articles of incorporation.

The position of the appellees is that the preferred stockholders are as much parties to the business venture as the common stockholders and are entitled to all the rights of the common stockholders except as modified by statute and contract. [Citation.] In other words, they say that the preferences contained in the articles and the stock certificates are merely delimitations of the preferences and not of the rights of the stockholders. The effect of this would be to make the preferred shares participating when no mention of such a right or interest is contained in the articles of incorporation. The parties had the duty, under the law, to provide for this additional right if they intended to create it. * * *

Appellate Court reversed, circuit court affirmed.

SANDERS v. CUBA RAILROAD CO.

(1956) 21 N.J. 78, 120 A.2d 849.

Jacobs, J. In the Chancery Division the parties made cross-motions for summary judgment; the defendant's motion was granted and the plaintiffs' motion was denied. The plaintiffs appealed to the Appellate Division and we certified under R.R. 1:10–1(a).

The plaintiffs (excluding Joseph P. Sanders who has disposed of his stockholdings) are the holders of 750 shares of the 6% non-cumulative preferred stock of the defendant The Cuba Railroad Company, a New Jersey corporation. The company has outstanding 100,000 shares of the preferred stock and 700,000 shares of common stock with no par value. All of the common stock is held by Consolidated Railroads of Cuba, a Cuban corporation; the New Jersey corporation and the Cuban corporation have the same directors. Since 1933 no dividends have been paid on the preferred stock although annual earnings were in excess of $600,000 in each year from 1941 through 1948 and in 1951 and 1952. The net income for the aforementioned years was reserved by the defendant's board of directors as

working capital and was apparently used in the business of the corporation. At the end of the fiscal year 1953 the defendant's earned surplus was in excess of $15,000,000; since then it has declined and its published annual report for 1955 indicates its earned surplus to be $12,225,000.

* * * In their complaint the plaintiffs set forth the foregoing and sought judgment: (a) determining and declaring the rights of the plaintiffs and the other preferred stockholders, and the extent of such rights to accumulated dividends and their equity in earned surplus in preference to the common stock, and (b) fixing the amount now due to the preferred stockholders for accumulated dividends and ordering the defendant to pay such amount into court for distribution to the plaintiffs and other preferred stockholders.

* * *

The rights of the holders of the non-cumulative preferred stock rest generally (apart from statutory restrictions) upon the terms of the defendant's certificate of incorporation. [Citation.] Those terms conferred priority rights over common stockholders when there were annual net profits from which dividends could properly be declared. [Citation.] If there were no such profits in a given year, then no dividends could be paid to the preferred stockholders with respect to that year, then or thereafter. If, however, there were such profits the board of directors still had broad discretionary power to withhold any declaration of dividends and retain the profits as part of the corporation's working capital. If during a later year the corporation earned net profits and its board of directors wished to declare dividends to both the non-cumulative preferred stockholders and the common stockholders, the question would then be presented as to whether the preferred stockholders were entitled to receive the earlier dividends (which were passed though they could have been paid from the annual net profits) before the common stockholders received any dividends. This question finds neither a clear nor a specific answer in the defendant's certificate of incorporation, and its determination, in an appropriate case, will involve full consideration of the precise language of the certificate and the present scope and effect of New Jersey's so-called "Cast Iron Pipe Doctrine" or dividend credit rule. [Citations.]

It may be acknowledged that New Jersey's dividend credit rule has not generally been accepted by the other states or in the federal courts. [Citations.] Judge Frank expressed the view that nothing in the terms of the ordinary non-cumulative preferred stock contract points to "a contingent or inchoate right to arrears of dividends" and that the contrary notion is an invention "stemming from considerations of fairness, from a policy of protecting investors in those securities." There seems to be little doubt that equitable factors did play a significant part in the development of New Jersey's doctrine. * * *

The contention has been made that recent judicial expressions indicate that we have limited our dividend credit doctrine to instances where the undistributed profits have been retained in a cash or other readily convertible account and that it is not to be applied where they have been turned into working capital and have actually been used in the corporation's normal business operations. [Citations.] However, in none of the New Jersey cases was the issue involved and we do not believe that it should be determined abstractly in the instant proceeding. * * *

The cited New Jersey decisions which dealt with the dividend credit rule were injunctive proceedings in which allegedly improper dividends were about to be distributed. In the instant matter there is no suggestion that any dividends are about to be

declared or distributed nor is any injunction or other coercive relief sought; the sole relief which the plaintiffs seek (as expressed in the concluding paragraph of their brief in this court) is that the judgment in the Chancery Division be modified "to provide that summary judgment be granted in favor of plaintiffs as to their preferential dividend rights over the common stockholders and that the amount of such preference is $9,535,000," subject to a possible offset and adjustment. We agree with the Chancery Division that the plaintiffs are not entitled to any declaratory judgment as to the "value of their equity in the present surplus of the defendant company." That surplus is ever changing and has been considerably reduced since the institution of the Chancery Division proceeding; indeed, it may be wiped out entirely and no proper purpose would now be served by speculating as to the inchoate rights of the non-cumulative preferred stockholders in profits which may thereafter be accumulated. [Citations.] * * *

Affirmed.

WOOD v. CITY NAT. BANK

(1928 C.C.A.2d) 24 F.2d 661.

[Action by Wood, ancillary receiver of the Stanton Oil Company, a Delaware corporation, to recover from the defendants, stockholders in the corporation, dividends paid to them in the years 1917, 1918 and 1919. The plaintiff alleged that at the time the dividends were declared the corporation "was in fact insolvent and unable to pay its debts, and had not then, nor had it ever had, any reserve over and above its capital stock, or any surplus or net profits of any kind, and each and all of the said dividends were paid wholly from and out of the capital of said corporation". On motion of defendants, the complaint was dismissed for insufficiency on its face and plaintiff appeals.]

L. HAND, Jr., J. * * * We have not to do with the liability commonly imposed by statute, because, whatever that may be in Delaware, the plaintiff does not invoke it here. He depends upon the fact that the directors have paid, and the defendants received, dividends when the corporation was insolvent. Merely because this impairs the capital stock, it is commonly regarded as a wrong to creditors on the directors' part, and it is often made such by statute. We may, without discussion, assume that it would be a wrong in the case at bar. Even so, it is primarily only the wrong of those who commit it, like any other tort, and innocent participants are not accomplices to its commission. Hence it has been settled, at least for us, that, when the liability is based merely on the depletion of the capital, a stockholder must be charged with notice of that fact. McDonald v. Williams, 174 U.S. 397, 19 S.Ct. 743, 43 L.Ed. 1022. This has become a thoroughly fixed principle in the federal courts. [Citations.]

It is apparent that this result could not have been reached if the capital of the corporation were regarded as a trust fund for its creditors, because a stockholder is not a purchaser, but a donee, and his bona fides would not protect him, in the absence of some further equity, in detaining the proceeds of a trust. So it became necessary to decide that the capital was not such a fund, and McDonald v. Williams did expressly so decide. The so-called "trust fund" doctrine had, indeed, earlier been repudiated by the Supreme Court, [citation]; but it was a hardy weed and would not die at the first uprooting. It is apparent, therefore, that the bill does not set forth a cause of suit based upon the impairment of the capital, because the stockholders are not alleged to have been privy to the directors' tort. This is not a defense which must be pleaded, like that of bona fide purchaser; it is necessary positively to allege the stockholders' complicity in the wrong to set forth any case at all.

However, there is quite another theory, and quite another liability, if the payments not only impair the capital, but are taken out of assets already too small to pay the existing debts. The situation then strictly is not peculiar to corporation law, but merely an instance of a payment from an insolvent estate. Since, as we have said, a stockholder is a donee, he receives such payments charged with whatever trust they were subject to in the hands of the corporation. In that situation it can indeed be said with some truth that the corporate assets have become a "trust fund." [Citation.] Hence it has never been doubted, so far as we can find, at least in any federal court, that if the dividends are paid in fraud of creditors the stockholder is so liable. [Citations.] * * *

If the bill be regarded as presenting only an instance of a payment in fraud of creditors, the question arises whether it is enough merely to allege that the payment was made while the corporation was insolvent. It is agreed with substantial unanimity that, when an insolvent makes a voluntary payment out of his assets, it is regarded as at least presumptively in fraud of his creditors. [Citations.] We shall assume, for argument, in accordance with the language of some of the foregoing decisions, that such a transfer is fraudulent per se. In Hayden v. Williams, (C.C.A.2) 96 F. 279, no more is mentioned than that the corporation was insolvent, and apparently no more was thought necessary. Even so, the bill is bad, because, when the invalidity of the gift depends only upon the fact of the donor's insolvency, regardless of his intent, it is voidable only at the demand of creditors existing when it is made. [Citations.] Hummell v. Harrington, 92 Fla. 87, 109 So. 320, if holding otherwise, is an exception; it probably meant no more than that, if there be actual intent to defraud subsequent creditors, they also may avoid the gift.

[Citation.] In the case at bar the bill does not allege that any of the creditors in existence when the receiver was appointed were creditors when the dividends were declared. Only in case the bill had alleged this, would the question arise whether insolvency per se avoids the gift. For this reason, and this alone, the decree was right.

[Decree affirmed without prejudice to file an amended complaint alleging the dividends were paid in fraud of creditors and that some of the present creditors were also creditors when the dividends were paid.]

PROBLEMS

1. On May 1, A entered into a subscription agreement for ten shares of a corporation to be formed under the Model Business Corporation Act and agreed to pay $100 per share. Others also subscribed for stock in this corporation. On August 1, A advised the others that he revoked his subscription and would not purchase the stock when called upon to do so. On October 1, the certificate of incorporation was issued by the Secretary of State, and subsequently the corporation called upon A to pay for the subscribed stock. Is A liable to pay for this stock?

2. The XYZ Corporation was duly organized on July 10. Its certificate of incorporation provides for a total authorized capital of $100,000, consisting of 1,000 shares of common stock, par value $100 per share. The corporation issues for cash a total of 50 certificates, numbered 1 to 50 inclusive, representing various amounts of shares in the names of various individuals. Payment for the shares having been made in advance, the certificates are all dated and mailed on the same day to the individuals, respectively, whose names appear thereon. The 50 certificates of stock represent a total of 1,050 shares. Certificate No. 49 for 30 shares was issued to John Smith. Certificate No. 50 for 25 shares was issued to William Jones. Is there any question concerning the validity of any of the stock thus issued? What are the rights of the shareholders?

3. D subscribed for 200 shares of 8 per cent cumulative, participating, redeemable, convertible, preferred shares of the X Hotel Company of the par value of $100 per share. The subscription agreement provided that he was to receive

a bonus of one share of common stock of $100 par value for each share of preferred stock. D fully paid his subscription agreement of $20,000 and received the aforementioned 200 shares of preferred and the bonus stock of 200 shares of the par value common. Subsequently, the X Hotel Co. becomes insolvent. R the receiver of the corporation, brings suit for $20,000, the par value of the common stock. What judgment?

4. Frank McAnarney and Joseph Lemon entered into an agreement to promote a corporation to engage in the manufacture of farm implements. Prior to the organization of the corporation McAnarney and Lemon solicited subscriptions to the stock of the corporation and presented a written agreement for signatures of the subscribers.

The agreement provided that subscribers pay $100 per share for stock in the corporation in consideration of McAnarney's and Lemon's agreement to organize the corporation and advance the pre-incorporation expenses. Thomas Jordan signed the agreement making application for 100 shares of stock. Subsequent to the filing of the articles of incorporation with the Secretary of State, but prior to the issuance of a charter to the corporation, Jordan died. The administrator of Jordan's estate notified McAnarney and Lemon that the estate would not honor Jordan's subscription.

After the formation of the corporation, Franklin Adams signed a subscription agreement making application for 100 shares of stock. Before acceptance by the corporation Adams advised the corporation that he was cancelling his subscription.

(a) The corporation brings an appropriate action against Jordan's estate to enforce Jordan's stock subscription. Decision?

(b) The corporation brings an appropriate action to enforce Adams's stock subscription. Decision?

5. The Bel-Aire Corporation was incorporated with a capitalization of 10,000 shares of common stock with a par value of $10 per share and 1,000 shares of preferred stock with a par value of $100 per share. Davis, Evans and Foster, the incorporators, each subscribed and paid for one share of common stock. Davis, the president, was a former advertising executive who specialized in television productions. In order to sell shares the following plan was devised by Davis and two of his nominees who constituted the board of direc-

tors: each purchaser of preferred shares was entitled to one share of common stock free with the purchase of each share of preferred stock and the 8th, 16th, 32nd and 64th purchasers of common shares were entitled to a 50% discount on the purchase price.

Foster brought an action to enjoin the sale of any shares pursuant to this plan. What result? Do not give any consideration to Federal or State securities legislation.

6. X Corporation, organized under the Model Business Corporation Act, has an earned deficit of $100,000 at the end of 1964. During 1965 the corporation earns a net profit of $50,000 after taxes. Out of this net profit the directors declare a dividend aggregating $10,000 to the holders of the common stock. Is this a lawful dividend?

7. The Ace Corporation declared a dividend on May 1, payable May 21 to shareholders of record on May 15. X purchased 100 shares of Ace Corp. from W on May 12 but failed to notify the corporation of his purchase until May 18. The corporation paid the dividend to W, whereupon X immediately filed suit against the corporation for the amount of the dividend. What decision?

8. A owns 100 shares of stock of the X Steel Corporation. At a meeting of the board of directors held in January, a dividend was declared, payable April 1 to shareholders of record March 1. A died on March 15, leaving a will under which everything that he owned at the time of his death was left in trust, the income thereof only to be paid to his wife during her life. When the dividend was paid to the executors of A's will on April 1, was it proper to treat it as part of the trust estate or as income payable to the wife?

9. Paul Bunyan is the owner of non-cumulative eight per cent preferred stock in the Broad-view Corporation which had no earnings or profits in 1964. In 1965 the corporation had large profits and a surplus from which it might properly have declared dividends. The directors refused to do so, but used the surplus to purchase goods necessary for their expanding business.

In view of the large profits made in 1965, the directors declared a ten per cent dividend on the common stock and an eight per cent dividend on the preferred stock, without paying preferred dividends for 1964 and 1965.

(a) Is Bunyan entitled to dividends for 1964 and 1965?

(b) Could Bunyan have compelled the directors to declare dividends in 1964 and 1965?

10. A corporation has outstanding 400 shares of $100 par value common stock which has been issued and sold at $105 per share for a total of $42,000. At a time when the assets of the corporation amount to $65,000, and the liabilities to creditors total $10,000, the directors learn that S, who holds 100 of the 400 shares of stock, is planning to sell his shares on the open market for $10,500. Considering that this will not be to the best interest of the corporation, the directors enter into an agreement with S whereby S sells to the corporation itself the 100 shares in exchange for a corporate note for $10,500, payable one year from date. About six months later, when the assets of the corporation have decreased to $50,000 and its liabilities, exclusive of its liability to S, have increased to $20,000, the directors use $10,000 to pay a dividend to all of the shareholders. Subsequently, the corporation becomes insolvent.

(a) Is the corporation liable to S on the note for $10,500?

(b) Was the payment of the $10,000 dividend proper?

CHAPTER 36

MANAGERIAL AND FIDUCIARY DUTIES OF OFFICERS AND DIRECTORS

Introductory. A corporation, being invisible, intangible and artificial, must act through human instrumentalities. Its business and affairs are managed by a board of directors elected by the shareholders. A director is sometimes referred to as an agent, and sometimes as a trustee. Strictly speaking, he is neither. Although as a board the directors, like agents, act for and on behalf of another and are not liable on contracts of the corporation which they negotiate within the scope of their authority, the directors control the corporation in a way such as no agent controls his principal. The directors not only act for and on behalf of the corporation, but without a board of directors, or some similarly functioning authority, the corporation is powerless to act. Directors and officers, by reason of the domination and control which they exercise over the corporation and their access to inside information, occupy positions of trust and confidence. They are fiduciaries. They are not strictly trustees, since they do not own or hold title to any property for the use and benefit of another, as does a trustee. The corporation as a legal entity holds the title to its own property, while the directors and officers control, manage and direct the disposition and the manner and extent to which that property is utilized.

Directors occupy a position of responsibility. It is the duty of the board to appoint the officers of the corporation, and in some instances a business manager or general manager who may not be an officer. These, in turn, employ subordinates, agents, salesmen, employees, workmen, and all of the operating personnel the sum of whose efforts represents the work carried on by the corporation. Directors are not ordinarily expected to devote their full time to the affairs of the corporation. The board therefore has broad authority to delegate power to officers and agents. The by-laws of the corporation set forth the duties of each of the officers, and the appointment by the board of a person to a certain office necessarily gives such person the powers requisite and incident to the performance of those duties. The usual officers are a president, one or more vice-presidents, a secretary and a treasurer. In addition to these officers designated by statute, the by-laws may provide for other officers, such as a comptroller, cashier, auditor or general counsel, or may provide for the office of assistant to the president, assistant secretary or assistant treasurer. A person may hold more than one office, except that one person may not at the same time be both president and secretary.

Qualifications of Directors. The statute of the State in which the corporation is formed, its articles of incorporation and by-laws determine the qualifications which individuals must possess in order to serve as its directors. There are no common-law requirements. A not infrequent requirement is that directors be shareholders and residents of the State of incorporation. These requirements are not imposed by the more modern statutes, but may be provided by the articles or by-laws. It is relatively easy to comply with the stock-ownership requirement by a transfer to the director of one or two shares of stock, which are called qualifying shares. This may defeat the principal purpose of the requirement which is to minimize the disassociation of management and ownership, yet it has been upheld by the courts as sufficient compliance. With respect to a corporation owning and operating substantial properties whose share-holders are numerous and scattered through many States, the requirement that its direc-tors reside in the State of incorporation is of doubtful value. Such a requirement need not apply to an entire board. In New York, for example, only one member of the board need be a citizen and resident of the State. An alien may be a director, as may a married woman or an infant. In Illinois, the incor-porators, who must be not less than three in number, are required by statute to be sub-scribers to shares and not less than 21 years of age. There is no such requirement of directors. The New York statute requires all directors to be at least 21 years of age.

Number and Tenure in Office. Directors are elected at the annual meeting of the shareholders to hold office for one year or until their successors are elected. If the number of shares represented at a meeting in person or by proxy is not sufficient to con-stitute a quorum, the old board continues in office as "hold over" directors until an elec-tion is held at a proper meeting. A board may consist of a minimum of three members. There is no stated maximum. Where the board consists of nine or more, the by-laws may provide for a division of the directors into two or three classes, to be as nearly equal in number as possible, and the election of the members of each class once a year. (Section 35, Model Act.) This permits one-third of the board to be elected annually for a three-year term, or one-half of the board to be elected annually for a two-year term, and thus provides an element of continuity of membership where the board is large. How-ever, such classification has been held invalid in Illinois as an abridgement of the constitu-tionally guaranteed right of cumulative vot-ing. Wolfson v. Avery, 6 Ill.2d 78, 126 N. E.2d 701.

A board of directors is a governing body which acts independently of the shareholders, who generally have no authority to discharge or remove a director during his term of office. A contract or agreement or understanding whereby a director subordinates his will and judgment to the dictates of a shareholder or group of shareholders is contrary to public policy and illegal. The law does not recog-nize a "dummy" or sterile board of directors. Except where the board has such power, a vacancy occurring in the board by reason of the death or resignation of a member is filled by vote of the shareholders at an annual meeting or at a special meeting called for that purpose.

Vacancies and Removal of Director. Di-rectors are ordinarily elected for a term of one year at the annual meeting of the share-holders. Where classification of directors is permitted, a class of directors may be elected for a two-year or a three-year term. Except for death or resignation, a director remains in office until his successor is duly elected or until he is removed.

The Model Act provides that a vacancy in the board may be filled by the affirmative vote of a majority of the remaining direc-tors (Section 36). The director so elected shall hold office for the unexpired term of his predecessor. A directorship to be filled by reason of an increase in the number of directors requires election by the sharehold-ers at an annual or special meeting.

Twenty-three States have no statutory pro-vision for removal of directors, although a common law rule permits removal for cause by action of the shareholders.

The Model Act is liberal in permitting re-moval of one or more of the directors, or of the entire board by the shareholders with or without cause at a special meeting called for that purpose. (Section 36A).

The New York statute authorizes judicial removal of a director *for cause* despite un-willingness of the other directors or a ma-jority of the shareholders to act. A suit for this purpose may be maintained by the Attorney-General or by the holders of 10% of the outstanding stock.

Meetings of Directors. Directors do not by reason of their office have the power to act as individuals, but only as a board. A director who is president or other officer or agent has the power to bind the corporation when he acts singly and within the scope of his authority, but at such time he is not acting as a director. When he acts as a director, it is at a meeting with other directors and by formal resolutions of the board adopted at such meeting. For example, all of the directors of the X corporation, acting separately and not as a board, executed a deed to certain real estate owned by the corporation. In a suit brought by shareholders to have the deed cancelled, the court held that the deed was void, as the directors could not bind the corporation by their separate and individual action.

However, a statute in Delaware provides that, unless restricted by the certificate of incorporation or by-laws any action which may be taken at any meeting of the board of directors or of any committee thereof may be taken without a meeting, if prior to such action a written consent thereto is signed by all of the members of the board or of the committee, as the case may be, and this written consent is filed with the corporate minutes Section 141(g), Delaware General Corporation Law. Action by the directors without a meeting is also provided in Optional Section 39A of the Model Act (Appendix D).

The board of directors is presumably representative of the shareholders. Its members usually are men of experience in various fields of business, including professional men, lawyers, bankers, and financiers, who may represent and speak for diverse interests among the shareholders. A minority interest having representation on the board is entitled to have its viewpoint presented and considered by the board in meeting assembled. Discussion, deliberation, interchange of ideas,

and consideration of a problem or policy in the light of the wisdom and experience of all the members acting in combination rather than separately is the objective sought by the requirement that the directors act as and in a body. Unlike shareholders, directors may not vote by proxy.

Example: A, B, C, and D owned all of the stock of the X Company. B, C and D each gave A a proxy to vote their stock. A thereupon proceeded to elect himself, B and C as the directors of the corporation. At a directors' meeting, at which A alone was present, with the aid of the proxies of the other two directors, A elected himself president and treasurer. In a suit testing A's right to hold these offices, it was held that A was not legally elected president or treasurer, as no director of a corporation can vote at a meeting of the board by proxy.

Meetings are held either regularly at a time and place fixed in the by-laws, or specially or periodically as they may be called. Notice of meetings must be given to each director as prescribed in the by-laws. Attendance of a director at any meeting is a waiver of such notice, unless the director attends for the express purpose of objecting to the transaction of any business on the ground that the meeting is not lawfully called or convened. Most modern statutes provide that meetings of the board, either regular or special, may be held either within or without the State.

A majority of the members of the board of directors constitutes a quorum, the minimum number of members necessary to be present at a meeting in order to transact business. The articles of incorporation or by-laws may, however, require a number greater than a simple majority for the quorum. If a quorum is present at any meeting, the act of a majority of the directors in attendance at such meeting is the act of the board. For instance, the attendance of three directors at a properly called meeting of a five-man board would constitute a quorum, and the vote of any two of them would be the act of the board.

Powers of the Board of Directors. A summary of the statutory powers of a typical board of directors may be obtained from an examination of the Model Business Corporation Act. Under this Act the board has power to:

(1) Authorize a change of the registered office or registered agent. (Section 12.)

(2) If expressly authorized by the articles, divide special or preferred stock into series and fix the rights and preferences of the shares of any series. (Section 15.)

(3) Determine the method of payment of subscriptions for shares, whether in full or in installments, and the terms thereof. (Section 16.)

(4) Fix the selling price of newly issued par value shares at not less than par. (Section 17.)

(5) Fix the stated value and selling price of no par shares, unless the power to do so is reserved to the shareholders by the articles. (Section 17.)

(6) Determine the value of the consideration in the form of property, or labor or services actually performed, received by the corporation in payment for shares issued. (Section 18.)

(7) Determine, subject to statutory limitations, what part of the consideration received by the corporation for its newly issued shares shall be stated capital and what part shall be paid-in surplus. (Section 19.)

(8) Increase stated capital by transfer of all or a part of paid-in or other surplus, and allocate the increased amount of stated capital to any designated class of shares. (Section 19.)

(9) Direct the issuance of scrip or other evidence of ownership of fractional shares, and impose a condition that the scrip shall become void if not exchanged for share certificates within a specified time, or a condition whereby the corporation may sell the shares for which the scrip is exchangeable and distribute the proceeds thereof to the holders of the scrip. (Section 22.)

(10) Make, alter, amend or repeal the by-laws, unless this power is reserved to the shareholders by the articles. (Section 25.)

(11) Provide for closing of stock transfer books, and fix a record date for the purpose of determining the shareholders who are entitled to receive notice, to vote, or to receive a dividend. (Section 28.)

(12) Manage the business and affairs of the corporation. (Section 33.)

(13) Elect a director to fill a vacancy occurring in the board of directors. (Section 36.)

(14) Declare dividends, subject to statutory limitations. (Section 40.)

(15) Remove any officer or agent of the corporation at any time, without prejudice, however, to the contracts rights, if any, of the person so removed. (Section 45.)

(16) Apply any part or all of the paid-in surplus to the reduction or elimination of a deficit. (Section 64.)

(17) Initiate proceedings to amend the articles of incorporation. (Section 54.)

(18) Initiate proceedings to reduce the stated capital. (Section 63.)

(19) Initiate proceedings for merger or consolidation. (Sections 65–66.)

(20) Sell, lease, exchange or mortgage assets of the corporation in the usual and regular course of business. (Section 71.)

(21) Initiate proceedings for the sale, lease, exchange or mortgage of assets of the corporation other than in the usual and regular course of business. (Section 72.)

(22) Initiate proceedings to dissolve the corporation. (Section 77.)

As the officers and directors are subject to the by-laws of the corporation, a summary of the typical objectives which may be accomplished through the by-laws by statutory authorization is helpful. Under the Model Business Corporation Act, the by-laws may provide for:

(1) Penalties for failure to pay installments or calls on subscriptions for shares. (Section 16.)

(2) The place of shareholders' meetings. (Section 26.)

(3) The calling of special meetings of shareholders by the president, the board of directors, the holders of not less than one-tenth of the outstanding shares of stock, entitled to vote, or by such officer or person as the by-laws may provide. (Section 26.)

(4) The qualifications of directors. (Section 33.)

(5) An increase or decrease in the number of directors, except for the number to be elected at the first meeting of shareholders, which is fixed by the articles. (Section 34.)

(6) Classification of directors. (Section 35.)

(7) The number of directors necessary for a quorum, not less than a majority. (Section 37.)

(8) An executive committee of the board of directors. (Section 38.)

(9) The notice to be given for meetings of the board of directors. (Section 39.)

(10) The duties of each of the officers, and what officers there shall be, if any, in addition to the president, vice-president, secretary, and treasurer. (Section 44.)

(11) The number of vice-presidents, if there is to be more than one. (Section 44.)

(12) The number of offices, other than those of president and secretary, which may be held by the same person. (Section 44.)

The by-laws may contain provisions other than those above enumerated. However, nothing contained in the by-laws may be contrary to or inconsistent with any provision in the statute or in the articles of incorporation, and nothing in the articles may be repugnant to the statute.

Example: The directors of the Chicago City Railway Company, without consulting or seeking the approval of the shareholders or obtaining an amendment of the articles of incorporation, resolved to increase the capital stock of the corporation from $1,250,000 to $1,500,000. A shareholder filed a bill in equity to enjoin the proposed increase. The directors relied upon a provision in the charter that "all the corporate powers of said corporation shall be vested in and exercised by a board of directors." An injunction was granted on the ground that a change so organic and fundamental as an increase in the capital stock beyond the limit fixed by the charter could not be accomplished by the board of directors. Chicago City Railway Co. v. Allerton, 18 Wall. (U.S.) 233, 21 L.Ed. 902.

Liability of Directors. The losses sustained by a corporation by reason of the poor business judgment, or honest mistake of judgment, of its directors may be severe, but no legal liability therefor is imposed upon the directors. It is a corporation's good fortune if its directors are intelligent, conscientious, industrious men possessed of business acumen, and its misfortune if they prove to be mediocre or worse. The directors are not insurers of business success. They are required only to be honest, loyal, and reasonably careful. The shareholders have only themselves to blame if the directors are dull, stupid, and unimaginative. In the discharge of their duties, directors must exercise ordinary care and prudence—"the same degree of care and prudence that men prompted by self-interest generally exercise in their own affairs." Hun v. Cary, 82 N.Y. 65. Directors and officers are permitted to entrust important work to others, and, if employees have been selected with care, are not liable for the negligent acts or willful wrongs of such employees. A reasonable amount of supervision is required, and an officer or director will be held liable for the losses resulting from an employee's carelessness, theft, or peculations if he knew or ought to have known or suspected that such losses were being incurred. A reasonable amount of supervisory attentiveness is required.

In one case, a director of a bank, who in the five and a half years that he had been on the board had never attended a board meeting or made any examination of the books and records, was held liable for approximately $20,000 because of the losses resulting from the unsupervised acts of the president and cashier who had made various improper loans and had permitted large overdrafts. The court said with respect to this director:

"He seems to have been a man of affairs and standing in the community, and in the best of faith accepted a directorship in the Salmon Bank, and after his election was content to trust entirely to the officers of the bank, and did nothing himself in the performance of any duty incident to his directorship. Mr. Bowerman failed to keep himself advised of even general conditions, and was not even sufficiently actively interested to make inquiry of any kind about the affairs of the bank until it was found that those immediately in charge had, through gross mismanagement, brought the bank to failure, and that as a result the directors would be called upon to answer for losses. Let it be conceded that the inattention of a director situated as was Bowerman has been brought about without any evil intention on his part, and that it may therefore work some hardship to hold him liable for the losses due directly to the positive negligence of the president and loan committee. * * * The fact that Mr. Bowerman lived 200 miles away is not an excuse for him." McCormick v.

King, 241 F. 737, 744–745; affirmed Bowerman v. Hamner, 250 U.S. 504, 39 S.Ct. 549, 63 L.Ed. 1113.

In addition to civil liability for negligence and mismanagement, directors may also be liable for losses which the corporation may incur through engaging in ultra vires activities. When the directors or officers permit assets of the corporation to be diverted to purposes and objectives that are not within the charter or statutory powers, express or implied, they may not only be enjoined from a continuation of such activities, but must answer in damages to a receiver or trustee appointed for the corporation or to the shareholders in a representative suit.

Directors are also liable for issuing shares of the corporation at a discount and for declaring a dividend which is paid when the corporation is insolvent or when its net assets are, or by the payment of the dividend become, less than its stated capital. They are liable for any distribution of the assets to shareholders, after the filing of a statement of intent to dissolve, without adequate provision for the payment of all of the debts and obligations of the corporation. They are also liable for voting or assenting to any loan of corporate funds to any officer or director until the loan is repaid. Directors are liable to any known creditor for failure to mail a notice of the filing of a statement of intent to dissolve, and, also, for all debts incurred after the filing of such statement in the carrying on of the corporation's business otherwise than as may be necessary for the winding up of its affairs.

Directors who vote for or assent to any of the transactions mentioned in the preceding paragraph are jointly and severally liable. If a director is present at a meeting of the board at which action on any corporate matter is taken, he is conclusively presumed to have assented to such action unless in addition to dissenting therefrom he (1) has his dissent entered of record in the minutes of the meeting, or (2) files his written dissent to such action with the person acting as secretary before the meeting adjourns, or (3) forwards his written dissent by registered mail to the secretary of the corporation immediately after the adjournment of the meeting. A director who has been held liable for assenting to an improper transaction and has satisfied such liability is entitled to ratable contribution from the other directors who are similarly liable thereon. A director is not liable if, in determining the amount available for a dividend, he in good faith regarded the assets of the corporation to be equal to their book value.

In addition to incurring civil liability, directors who vote for or assent to the declaration of a dividend prohibited by statute or to the making of any loan of corporate assets to an officer or director of the corporation may be deemed guilty of conspiracy and are subject to criminal prosecution. Criminal liability also attaches to any officer or director who fails or refuses to answer truthfully and fully interrogatories which may be propounded to him by the Secretary of State, or who knowingly signs any false report or statement filed with the Secretary of State.

Compensation of Officers and Directors. Directors do not receive salaries for their services as directors. It is usual for them to be paid a small fee, or honorarium, of $25 or $50 for attendance at meetings, as provided in the by-laws, and it is customary to provide necessary transportation and traveling expenses for out-of-town members who attend meetings. The reason for the rule prohibiting salaries is succinctly stated in a New York case:

"It is the general rule that a director, assuming office as such without any agreement as to compensation, is presumed to render his official services gratuitously, for he assumes thereby, in a sense, a trust relation towards the company, and it would be against sound policy to permit him to assert claims for services which were within the line of his duties." Bagley v. Carthage R. R. Co., 165 N. Y. 179, 192, 58 N.E. 895.

A director who occupies the position of an officer may properly be paid the salary of such officer. The amount of the salary is usually fixed by the resolution of the board appointing the individual to the office. If not, and the duties of the office are nominal, the individual is entitled to no salary unless the by-laws so provide. If, however, the duties are such that the person devotes his full time to them, or even a substantial part of his working time, he is entitled under an implied contract to receive the reasonable value of his services where compensation therefor was or should have been reasonably intended.

Example: B, a director of a railroad company, was appointed consulting engineer by a resolution of the board which did not fix any salary for the position. Later, B was elected secretary of the corporation. He continued to render services as consulting engineer. In a suit to recover for services rendered, the Court held that the fact that B was a director and officer did not preclude him from recovering the reasonable value of his services as consulting engineer.

If a director is appointed to a salaried position by a resolution of the board, and his vote is required in order to carry the resolution, or his presence at the meeting at which the resolution is passed is necessary in order to have a quorum, the appointment is invalid and the director is not entitled to receive the salary voted him.

"Stockless" Stock Bonus Plan. A deferred compensation plan for officers and key employees of a corporation may provide the financial benefits of participating in earnings of the company and appreciation in value of its stock without stock ownership. Such a plan is similar to a stock option plan but does not require the issuance of stock.

In 1956 the shareholders of Koppers Company, Inc., approved this type of plan whereby 100,000 units each representing one share of common stock were created. A committee of five directors, who were ineligible to participate in the plan, awarded the units to various officers and employees. The value of each unit as of the date of issue was that of one share of common stock of the corporation on the same date. The employees to whom units were assigned were required to agree to remain in the employ of the corporation at least five years, or until retirement, not to compete with Koppers, and not to become an employee of a competitor of Koppers. As dividends were declared on the stock, a credit equal thereto was given to the units as assigned. Upon termination of employment, the employee was entitled to receive his total dividend credit plus the excess market value of the units, i. e., the difference between the assigned value of the units at time of issue and the market value of the stock at time of termination. The Court held this plan valid as designed to achieve the legitimate business purpose of retaining qualified executive personnel in the employ of the corporation. No question of excessive compensation was involved. Lieberman v. Becker, 38 Del.Ch. 540, 155 A.2d 596 (1959).

Fiduciary Duties of Officers and Directors. A person who occupies a position of trust and confidence is a fiduciary. The officers and directors of a corporation are therefore fiduciaries and owe a fiduciary duty to the corporation and to its shareholders. The essence of a fiduciary duty is the subordination of self-interest to the interest of the person or persons to whom the duty is owing. It requires constant loyalty on the part of officers and directors to the corporation which they both serve and control. It prohibits an officer or director from making secret profits for himself or for others in whom he has an interest by the use of inside information which is available to him by reason of his position. It prohibits such a person from accepting bribes or secret favors even though it may not be demonstrated that the judgment of the officer or director was thereby influenced in the slightest degree. As Bowen, C. J., stated in Archer's Case, 1892, 1 Ch. at 341: "The director is really a watch dog, and the watch dog has no right, without the knowledge of his master, to take a sop from a possible wolf."

An officer or director is required to make full disclosure to the corporation of any possible interest which he may have in any transaction to which the corporation is a party. This is a corollary to the rule which forbids fiduciaries from making secret profits. He is also precluded from engaging in any business which is in competition with that of the corporation. His business conduct must at all times be calculated to benefit the corporation, and he may not avail himself of opportunities to advance his personal interest at the expense of the corporation. He may not represent conflicting interests, and when he competes with the corporation his personal self-interest is in direct conflict with his duty of strict allegiance to the corporation.

In Meinhard v. Salmon, 249 N.Y. 458, 464, 164 N.E. 545, 546, Justice Cardozo states:

"Many forms of conduct permissible in a work-a-day world for those acting at arms length are forbidden to those bound by fiduciary ties. A trustee is held to something stricter than the morals of the market place. Not honesty alone, but the punctilio of an honor, the most sensitive, is then the standard of behavior. As to this there has developed a tradition that is unbending and inveterate. Uncompromising rigidity has been the attitude of courts of equity when petitioned to undermine the rule of undivided loyalty by the 'disintegrating erosion' of particular exceptions. [Citation.] Only thus has the level of conduct for fiduciaries been kept at a level higher than that trodden by the crowd. It will not consciously be lowered by any judgment of this court."

The remedy for breach of fiduciary duty is a suit in equity by the corporation, or more often a derivative suit instituted by a shareholder, to require the fiduciary to pay to the corporation the secret profits which he has obtained through breach of his fiduciary duty. It need not be shown that the corporation could otherwise have made the profits which the fiduciary has realized. The object of the rule is to discourage breaches of duty by a fiduciary and this is achieved by taking from the fiduciary all of the profits he has made. The enforcement of the rule may result in a windfall to the corporation, but this is an incidental consequence. Where there is absence of loyalty or full devotion on the part of officers and directors to the interests of the corporation, it is impossible to recast the situation and to determine at some later time what the position of the corporation might have been if these fiduciaries had been faithful.

Contracts Between Directors and the Corporation. A contract between an officer or a director and the corporation is not void, but voidable. A rule which would preclude such a contract would be unreasonable because it would prevent directors from giving financial assistance to the corporation in time of need when possibly no other help would be available. Therefore, if such a contract is honest and fair, it will be upheld. In such case, the officer or director is not making a secret profit from his dealing with the corporation, but all of the facts and circumstances are known to both parties to the contract.

Contracts Between Corporations Having Common Directors. In the case of contracts between corporations having an interlocking directorate or having one or more persons who are members of both boards of directors, the courts subject the contracts to the severest scrutiny and are quick to set them aside unless the transaction is shown to have been entirely fair and entered into in good faith. The Supreme Court of the United States has aptly stated the rule in Geddes v. Anaconda Copper Mining Co., 254 U.S. 590, 599, 41 S. Ct. 209, 212, 65 L.Ed. 425:

"The relation of directors to corporations is of such a fiduciary nature that transactions between boards having common members are regarded as jealously by the law as are personal dealings between a director and his corporation; and where the fairness of such transactions is challenged, the burden is upon those who would maintain them to show their entire fairness; and where a sale is involved the full adequacy of the consideration. Especially is this true where a common director is dominating in influence or in character. This court has been consistently emphatic in the application of this rule, which, it has declared, is founded in soundest morality, and we now add, in the soundest business policy."

Corporate Opportunity. An officer or director of a corporation which has extensive properties and substantial operations is frequently confronted with an opportunity to use his position of trust and confidence to self-advantage and thereby reap huge profits for himself. Officers and directors are managing property and operating a business which belongs to others, and they are entrusted with power and responsibility because of their presumed integrity. When they exercise this power for selfish purposes, the courts uniformly hold that they must account for all the profits which they have thereby realized.

For example: A is president, director and the dominant figure in the affairs of the ABC Company, a corporation which has 500 shares of capital stock outstanding, of which A owns 300 shares. The remaining 200 shares are owned in various small lots by individuals not connected with the management. X is interested in purchasing all of the stock of the company and enters into negotiations with

A.   X is unwilling to pay more than $360,000 for all of the stock, which amounts to $720 per share.   A is unwilling to sell his shares for less than $1,000 each, or a total of $300,-000.   A enters into a contract with X whereby X agrees to purchase the 300 shares of stock owned by A for $300,000 provided A can obtain for X the remaining 200 shares at a price of $300 per share.   A thereupon writes to the other shareholders telling them that X "wants to buy all of the stock of the corporation, and is willing to pay $300 a share for the stock" and requesting them to deposit their stock with A if they wish to sell it at this price.   This is the only information the minority stockholders have of the transaction.   They deposit their stock with A, and X pays A a total of $360,000 for the stock, of which A receives $300,000 for his 300 shares, and the minority stockholders receive $60,-000 for their 200 shares.   Upon later learning the facts, the minority stockholders sue A to recover the difference between the amount which they actually received and the amount they would have received if they had been paid $720 per share.   In this suit, A is liable to the minority shareholders, and a court of equity will decree that he pay each of them the amount of such difference.

A further example of corporate opportunity is that of Arnold, Bennett and Cobden, who each owned one-third of the capital stock of ABC Company, a corporation.   The company was engaged in the construction of industrial plants for private corporations.   With the outbreak of World War II, the opportunity presented itself of entering into building contracts with the Government on a cost-plus basis.   Arnold and Bennett proceeded to organize a new corporation called the Ajax Construction Company, each owning one-half of its capital stock.   As orders and bids for construction developed, Arnold and Bennett turned over the bids for private construction to the ABC Company and the Government contracts to Ajax Company.   Upon learning of this, Cobden brought a suit seeking to have one-third of the stock of the Ajax Construction Company awarded to him and to have an accounting made of all of the profits realized by Arnold and Bennett through their stock holding in that corporation.   The court in this case would hold that Cobden is entitled to subscribe to one-third of this stock and to be paid one-third of the profits realized from the Government contracts.

In a frequently cited case, Sonora Products Corporation had an option to acquire $100,-000 of stock in another corporation which controlled patent rights that were useful to Sonora.   Certain directors of Sonora exercised the option and purchased the stock in their individual behalf.   They attempted to excuse this action on the ground that Sonora was finally unable to buy the stock.   The court held this excuse inadequate.   The directors as well as others who had profited by participation in the transaction with knowledge of the directors' breach of fiduciary duty were held accountable.   Irving Trust Co. v. Deutsch, 73 F.2d 121 (C.A.2d 1934)

Purchases and Sales of Stock by Insiders. Officers and directors occupy a position whereby they have inside advance information not available to the public which may affect the future market value of the shares of the corporation.   This position gives them a trading advantage.   If the information indicates an unpublicized loss, or a reduction in dividends, or reflects adversely on prospective earnings, the officer or director may sell his shares through a broker in the open market, or even sell the stock short.   Conversely, if the information pertains to some potential profit or lucrative contract in the offing or unpublicized substantial earnings, the officer or director may purchase stock in the open market or approach a shareholder and negotiate a purchase of his stock on the basis of current market quotations without disclosure of the factors which will increase the market value of the shares upon becoming public knowledge.

In the event of a sale of stock, the officer or director can hardly be regarded as owing a fiduciary to the purchaser who may have no prior interest in the corporation. However, in buying stock the officer or director is acquiring it from an existing shareholder to whom he may be held to owe a fiduciary duty. It is manifest that in these purchases or sales the corporation sustains no loss. The person who buys stock which soon declines in value or who sells stock which thereafter quickly depreciates in value, is the one who incurs the loss. The majority view of the courts is that the officer or director in this situation is under no fiduciary duty to the shareholder, and if he refrains from making any fraudulent misrepresentation about the stock, he may retain any profit that he realizes from such purchase.

A strong and growing minority view is that he is under a fiduciary duty to make disclosure to the person from whom he buys the stock, and particularly where there are special circumstances or "special facts" as in the case of Taylor vs. Wright, p. 865. Where a fiduciary duty is held to exist a failure of the officer or director to disclose to the selling shareholder, the special facts which relate to possible future appreciation in the value of the shares results in liability for the profits that the officer or director may realize as a result of the purchase.

Statutes have defined and extended the liability of officers and directors who purchase shares of stock of their corporation without adequate disclosure of all material facts in their possession that may affect the value or potential value of the stock. Under the Securities Exchange Act of 1934, the Securities and Exchange Commission adopted Rule X–10 B–5 which requires disclosure in such purchases of stock listed on the Na-

tional Stock Exchange and also unlisted stock where use has been made of the mails or an instrumentality of interstate commerce, such as the telephone or telegraph.

Short-Swing Speculations. Section 16(b) of the Securities and Exchange Act of 1934 adopts the so-called "six months rule" with respect to purchases and sales by a director, officer, or person owning ten percent or more of the stock of a corporation, if the stock is listed on a national securities exchange or registered with the S.E.C. under the 1964 Amendments of the Act. Under this statute, the corporation, or any shareholder thereof suing on its behalf, if the corporation fails to take action, may recover in the Federal court the amount of profits which have been made by any of its officers, directors, or person owning ten percent or more of its outstanding stock, by reason of the sale of its stock within a period of six months after the stock was purchased, or by reason of a purchase within six months after a sale of the stock. The rule applies either to a "long" or to a "short" position in the market. Its purpose is to prevent short-swing speculation in stocks by insiders, namely, officers, directors, or persons having a substantial stock ownership. Officers, directors, and persons owning ten percent or more of the stock of a listed or registered corporation are required to report periodically to the Securities and Exchange Commission their purchases and sales of stock of the corporation. In this way trading by insiders in the stock of the corporation is made available to the public.

The 1964 amendment to the Securities and Exchange Act of 1934 has extended the reporting and disclosure requirements and the liability of insiders for short-swing profits within the "six months rule" of Section 16 (b) to any corporation with total assets exceeding $1,000,000 and any class of stock held of record by 500 or more persons.

CASES

STOTT v. STOTT REALTY CO.

(1929) 246 Mich. 267, 224 N.W. 623.

[Bill by Stott, plaintiff, against the Stott Realty Company, defendant, to enjoin the removal of the secretary of the defendant corporation. The president and secretary of the company were directed by the board of directors to sign certain mortgage papers. Julia Stott Orloff, secretary, (and also a director) of the company, refused to sign them. Shortly thereafter she was removed from the office of secretary at a full meeting of the board of directors, and T. P. Danahey was appointed to fill the vacancy. From a decree dismissing the bill plaintiff appeals.]

FELLOWS, J. * * * Cases will be found holding that the board of directors may remove fellow directors, but the weight of authority is against the proposition. Mrs. Orloff was continued as director. The office of secretary is a ministerial office, may be filled by one not a director, and its occupant, unless a director, has nothing to say about the management of the company. The selection is made by the board of directors (section 5, chap. 1, pt. 2, Act No. 335, Pub.Acts 1927). This distinction between a director and a secretary should be kept in mind. The director, being selected by the stockholders, may only be removed by them, while the secretary, being selected by the directors, may be removed by them. The rule is thus stated in 3 Thompson on Corporations (3d Ed.) sec. 1926:

"Below the grade of director and such other officers as are elected by the corporation at large, the general rule is that the officers of private corporations hold their offices during the will of the directors, and are hence removable by the directors without assigning any cause for the removal, except so far as their power may be restrained by contract with the particular officer,—just as any other employer may discharge his employee. Speaking generally, it may be said that the power to appoint carries with it the power to remove. * * * Applying the foregoing principles, it has been held that the directors, unless specially authorized, have no power to remove an officer or agent elected or employed by the stockholders; and that the president has no power to remove an officer appointed by the board of directors. The ordinary ministerial and other lesser officers, however, hold their offices during the pleasure of the directors and may be removed at will, without assigned cause. Of this class of officers and agents are the secretary and treasurer of the corporation."

Without quoting from them, the text-writers generally state the same rule although in different language. * * *

The removal of Mrs. Orloff as secretary of the company was validly accomplished, and we have left only the question of the validity of the election of Mr. Danahey as her successor. The board has power under the by-laws of the company to fill vacancies. Mr. Danahey was a member of the board of directors. We need not consider whether he could validly vote for himself, as there was a quorum present without him, and a majority of that quorum voted for his election. With his vote he received a majority of the full board; without it he received the vote of a majority of the quorum which was present after Mrs. Orloff had left the meeting. The rule is recognized by this court and elsewhere that a quorum may act, and a majority vote of such quorum binds the corporation.

Decree affirmed.

MODEL, ROLAND & CO. v. INDUSTRIAL ACOUSTICS CO. INC.

(1965) 16 N.Y.2d 703, 261 N.Y.S.2d 896, 209 N.E.2d 553.

MEMORANDUM: Order of the Appellate Division directing judgment for the plaintiff-respondent affirmed. Defendant-appellants are correct in their contention that the provisions of article VIII of the corporate by-laws are ineffective to the extent that they require a two-thirds majority shareholder vote to amend certain of the by-laws—in particular the by-law which sets the number of directors on the board. The Business Corporation Law clearly provides that a simple majority vote of the shareholders is sufficient to amend the by-laws, unless the certificate of incorporation provides otherwise. [Citations.] The two-thirds majority vote provision here involved would have been valid were it placed in the certificate of incorporation, but as a by-law it is invalid. [Citation.]

However, the single question submitted under CPLR 3222 to the Appellate Division was whether or not a simple majority resolution of the stockholders, increasing the number of directors from four to five, was valid and effective. This question was correctly answered in the negative by that court. Subdivision (b) of section 702 of the Business Corporation Law provides that the shareholders may change the number of directors (1) by an amendment to the by-laws embodying the change, or (2) by a simple resolution, *if* there is a by-law in effect which provides for the change by such a resolution. In either case the change is effected by means of a by-law. Here the shareholders acted by resolution alone, and not under the provisions of a by-law. It is clear, therefore, that, even though a simple shareholder vote could have effected a change in the number of directors if such a by-law had been adopted authorizing such a vote, their naked resolution to do so cannot be enforced.

Affirmed.

———

BATES v. DRESSER

(1920) 251 U.S. 524, 40 S.Ct. 247, 64 L.Ed. 388.

HOLMES, J. This is a bill in equity, brought by the receiver of a national bank, to charge its former president and directors with the loss of a great part of its assets through the thefts of an employee of the bank while they were in power. The case was sent to a master, who found for the defendants; but the district court entered a decree against all of them. 229 F. 772. The circuit court of appeals reversed this decree, dismissed the bill as against all except the administrator of Edwin Dresser, the president, cut down the amount with which he was charged, and refused to add interest from the date of the decree of the district court. 162 C.C.A. 541, 250 F. 525. Dresser's administrator and the receiver both appeal, the latter contending that the decree of the district court should be affirmed with interest and costs.

The bank was a little bank at Cambridge, with a capital of $100,000 and average deposits of somewhere about $300,000. It had a cashier, a bookkeeper, a teller, and a messenger. Before and during the time of the losses Dresser was its president and executive officer, a large stockholder, with an inactive deposit of from $35,000 to $50,000. From July, 1903, to the end, Frank L. Earl was cashier. Coleman, who made the trouble, entered the service of the bank as messenger in September, 1903. In January, 1904, he was promoted to be bookkeeper, being then not quite eighteen, but having studied bookkeeping. In the previous August an auditor employed on the retirement of a cashier had reported that the daily balance book was very much behind, that it was impossible to prove the deposits, and that a competent bookkeeper should be employed upon the work immediately. Coleman kept the deposit ledger, and this was the work that fell into his hands. There was no cage in the bank, and in 1904 and 1905 there were some small shortages in the accounts of three successive tellers that were not accounted for, and the last of them, Cutting, was asked by Dresser to resign on that ground. Before doing so he told Dresser that someone had taken the money, and that if he might be allowed to stay he would set a trap and catch the man, but Dresser did not care to do that, and thought that there was nothing wrong. From Cutting's resignation on October 7, 1905, Coleman acted as paying and receiving teller, in addition to his other duty, until November, 1907. During this time there were no shortages disclosed in the teller's accounts. In May, 1906, Coleman took $2,000 cash from the vaults of the bank, but restored it the next morning. In November of the same year he began the thefts that come into question here. Perhaps in the beginning he took the money directly. But as he ceased to have charge of the cash in November, 1907, he invented another way. Having a small account at the bank, he would draw checks for the amount he wanted, exchange checks with a Boston broker, get cash for the broker's check, and, when his own check came to the bank through the clearing house, would abstract it from the envelope, enter the others on his book, and conceal the difference by a charge to some other account or a false addition in the column of drafts or deposits in the depositors' ledger. He handed to the cashier only the slip from the clearing house that showed the totals. The cashier paid whatever appeared to be due and thus Coleman's checks were honored. So far as Coleman thought it necessary, in view of the absolute trust in him on the part of all concerned, he took care that his balances should agree with those in the cashier's book.

By May 1, 1907, Coleman had abstracted $17,000, concealing the fact by false additions in the column of total checks, and false balances in the deposit ledger. Then for the moment a safer concealment was effected by charging the whole to Dresser's account. Coleman adopted this method when a bank examiner was expected. Of course when the fraud was disguised by overcharging a depositor it could not be discovered except by calling in the pass books, or taking all the deposit slips and comparing them with the depositors' ledger in detail. By November, 1907, the amount taken by Coleman was $30,100, and the charge on Dresser's account was $20,000. In 1908 the sum was raised from $33,000 to $49,671. In 1909 Coleman's activity began to increase. In January he took $6,829.26; in March, $10,833.73; in June, his previous stealings amounting to $83,390.94, he took $5,152.06; in July, $18,050; in August, $6,250; in September $17,350; in October, $47,277.08; in November, $51,847; in December, $46,956.44; in January, 1910, $27,395.53; in February, $6,473.97; making a total of $310,143.02, when the bank closed on February 21, 1910. As a result of this the amount of the monthly deposits seemed to decline noticeably and the directors considered the matter in September, but concluded that the falling off was due in part to the springing up of rivals, whose deposits were increasing, but was parallel to a similar decrease in New York. An examination by a bank examiner in December, 1909, disclosed nothing wrong to him.

In this connection it should be mentioned that in the previous semiannual examinations by national bank examiners nothing was discovered pointing to malfeasance. The cashier was honest and everybody believed that they could rely upon him, although in fact he relied too much upon Coleman, who also was unsuspected by all. If Earl had opened the envelopes from the clearing house, and had seen the checks, or had examined the deposit ledger with any care, he would have found out what was going on. The scrutiny of anyone accustomed to such details would have discovered the false additions and other indicia of fraud that were on the face of the book. But it may be doubted whether anything less than a continuous pursuit of the figures through pages would have done so except by a lucky chance.

The question of the liability of the directors in this case is the question whether they neglected their duty by accepting the cashier's statement of liabilities and failing to inspect the depositors' ledger. The statements of assets always were correct. A by-law that had been allowed to become obsolete or nearly so is invoked as establishing their own standard of conduct. By that a committee was to be appointed every six months "to examine into the affairs of the bank, to count its cash, and compare its assets and liabilities with the balances on the general ledger, for the purpose of ascertaining whether or not the books are correctly kept, and the condition of the bank in a sound and solvent condition." Of course, liabilities as well as assets must be known to know the condition, and, as this case shows, peculations may be concealed as well by a false understatement of liabilities as by a false show of assets. But the former is not the direction in which fraud would have been looked for, especially on the part of one who, at the time of his principal abstractions, was not in contact with the funds. A debtor hardly expects to have his liability understated. Some animals must have given at least one exhibition of dangerous propensities before the owner can be held. This fraud was a novelty in the way of swindling a bank, so far as the knowledge of any experience had reached Cambridge before 1910. We are not prepared to reverse the finding of the master and the circuit court of appeals that the directors should not be held answerable for taking the cashier's statement of liabilities to be as correct as the statement of assets always was. If he had not been negligent without their knowledge it would have been. Their confidence seemed warranted by the semiannual examinations by the government examiner, and they were encouraged in their belief that all was well by the president, whose responsibility as executive officer, interest as large stockholder and depositor, and knowledge, from long daily presence in the bank, were

greater than theirs. They were not bound by virtue of the office gratuitously assumed by them to call in the pass books and compare them with the ledger, and, until the event showed the possibility, they hardly could have seen that their failure to look at the ledger opened a way to fraud. [Citations.] We are not laying down general principles, however, but confine our decision to the circumstances of the particular case.

The position of the president is different. Practically he was the master of the situation. He was daily at the bank for hours, he had the deposit ledger in his hands at times, and might have had it at any time. He had had hints and warnings in addition to those that we have mentioned,—warnings that should not be magnified unduly, but still that, taken with the auditor's report of 1903, the unexplained shortages, the suggestion of the teller, Cutting, in 1905, and the final seeming rapid decline in deposits, would have induced scrutiny but for an invincible repose upon the status quo. In 1908 one Fillmore learned that a package containing $150 left with the bank for safekeeping was not to be found, told Dresser of the loss, wrote to him that he could but conclude that the package had been destroyed or removed by someone connected with the bank, and in later conversation said that it was evident that there was a thief in the bank. He added that he would advise the president to look after Coleman, that he believed that he was living at a pretty fast pace, and that he had pretty good authority for thinking that he was supporting a woman. In the same year, or the year before, Coleman, whose pay was never more than $12 a week, set up an automobile, as was known to Dresser and commented on unfavorably to him. There was also some evidence of notice to Dresser that Coleman was dealing in copper stocks. In 1909 came the great and inadequately explained seeming shrinkage in the deposits. No doubt plausible explanations of his conduct came from Coleman and the notice as to speculations may have been slight, but, taking the whole story of the relations of the parties, we are not ready to say that the two courts below erred in finding that Dresser had been put upon his guard. However little the warnings may have pointed to the specific facts, had they been accepted, they would have led to an examination of the depositors' ledger, a discovery of past and a prevention of future thefts.

We do not perceive any ground for applying to this case the limitations of liability ex contractu adverted to in Globe Ref. Co. v. London Cotton Oil Co., 190 U.S. 540, 23 S.Ct. 754, 47 L.Ed. 1171. In accepting the presidency Dresser must be taken to have contemplated responsibility for losses to the bank, whatever they were, if chargeable to his fault. Those that happened were chargeable to his fault, after he had warnings that should have led to steps that would have made fraud impossible, even though the precise form that the fraud would take hardly could have been foreseen. We accept with hesitation the date of December 1, 1908, as the beginning of Dresser's liability, but think it reasonable that interest should be charged against his estate upon the sum found by the circuit court of appeals to be due. It is a question of discretion, not of right [citations]; but to the extent that the decree of the district court was affirmed [citations], it seems to us just, upon all the circumstances, that it should run until the receiver interposed a delay by his appeal to this court. [Citation.] Upon this, as upon the other points, our decision is confined to the specific facts.

Decree modified by charging the estate of Dresser with interest from February 1, 1916, to June 1, 1918, upon the sum found to be due, and affirmed.

WAGNER TRADING CO. v. BATTERY PARK NAT. BANK

(1920) 228 N.Y. 37, 126 N.E. 347, 9 A.L.R.2d 340.

[Action by plaintiff corporation against defendant bank upon checks payable to the order of plaintiff, indorsed by its president as such, and deposited in the president's personal account at the bank. Judgment for plaintiff.]

ELKUS, J. The plaintiff is a New York corporation. It was incorporated in April, 1910, at which time it acquired all the assets and business formerly conducted by one Christopher J. Wagner, who became its president, which office he held during the time of all the transactions here in question. * * *

Section 4 of article 3 of plaintiff's by-laws provides:

"The treasurer shall have the care and custody of all the funds and securities of the corporation and shall deposit the same in the name of the corporation in such bank, banks, or trust companies as the directors may elect. He may sign checks, drafts or orders for the payment of money, but all checks and notes of the corporation signed by him shall be countersigned by such persons as may be designated for that purpose by the board of directors."

By article 3, section 2, of the by-laws the president was authorized to sign and execute contracts in the name of the company when authorized to do so by the board of directors, and also to sign checks, drafts and orders for the payment of money, but all checks and notes of the corporation, signed by him, shall also be countersigned by persons designated for that purpose by the board of directors.

In pursuance of this by-law, on April 7, 1910, the board of directors adopted a resolution, providing that checks might be signed by the president, vice president, secretary, or treasurer, but that such checks shall be countersigned by one Leggett or one Sloane, or by any officer of the corporation.

The plaintiff had its bank account with the Chatham & Phœnix Bank, but had no account with the defendant or any other bank.

A portion of the plaintiff's business was exporting merchandise to South America. Drafts were drawn by the plaintiff on the South American customer, and sent to the Bank of New York for collection, and in some cases advances were made by the Bank of New York upon these drafts while in process of collection. The proceeds of these drafts were paid and some advances thereon were made by cashier's checks of the Bank of New York to the order of Wagner Trading Company. These checks, to the number of 15, were indorsed, "Wagner Trading Company, C. J. Wagner, Pres.," the signature of "C. J. Wagner" being in the handwriting of C. J. Wagner, the president of the plaintiff corporation, the remainder of the indorsement being a rubber stamp impression. The first of these checks was dated May 17, 1915, and indorsed May 25, 1915. The last check was dated October 30, 1916, and indorsed October 31, 1916.

It is stipulated that no part of the "proceeds of said checks, to wit, $14,117.29, has been received by the plaintiff except the sum of $85.37."

C. J. Wagner had a personal account with the defendant. In this account he deposited, among others, 36 checks, representing salary paid to him by the plaintiff between February 2, 1914, and April 3, 1916. These checks were drawn on the Chatham & Phœnix National Bank to the order of "C. J. Wagner," signed "Wagner Trading Company, C. J. Wagner, Pres." On the left margin of the check appears in print "Wagner Trading Company . . . . Countersigned," with the signature in ink of W. H. Leggett, Jr., above

the word "Countersigned." These checks were indorsed by C. J. Wagner, and collected through the New York Clearing House in the usual course of banking business. This statement shows the relation of the parties.

Wagner, having indorsed the 15 checks made payable by the Bank of New York to the Wagner Trading Company, in the manner described, deposited them to the credit of his personal account with the defendant, which collected the proceeds in the usual course of banking, and held same for Wagner, and as his agent "paid out the proceeds thereof on the personal checks of Christopher J. Wagner," to use the exact words of the stipulation of the parties. The action is for conversion.

The facts showing the conversion are complete. Wagner had authority to indorse the checks, although no by-law or resolution is in evidence to that effect, but only for the purposes of the corporation's business, and not to transfer the checks to himself personally or for his personal use. The defendant endeavored to prove estoppel and negligence of the plaintiff. The trial court rightly excluded all such evidence. The plaintiff had no relations with and owed no special duty to the defendant. It was not a depositor of the defendant. When the defendant accepted the deposit of Wagner and became his banking agent, the defendant was in complete control of its relations with Wagner. It could, to safely protect itself in its dealing with Wagner, inquire as to his relations with the plaintiff, the authority he possessed, and could insist upon an examination of the plaintiff's by-laws and minutes if it thought that necessary to protect itself. When it accepted the checks payable to the plaintiff and indorsed by Wagner as president of the plaintiff for deposit to the account of Wagner himself, it did so at its peril to ascertain whether Wagner had authority to indorse them and by his indorsement transfer the money to be paid thereon to his personal account. [Citations.] If Wagner had no such authority, title to the money in question never passed to the defendant, and, if it received it, it did so without authority, and must account and make payment to the owner. [Citations.]

The transaction and decision are not affected by the fact that, relying upon the funds it supposed were deposited by Wagner, the defendant paid out funds upon Wagner's personal check drawn upon it. To do so would be to charge the plaintiff because of transactions with which it had no connection.

The rule governing this case is well stated in Standard S. S. Co. v. Corn Exchange Bank, 220 N.Y. 478, 481, 116 N.E. 386, 387 (L.R. A.1918B, 575), where Pound, J., says:

"Any person taking checks made payable to a corporation which can act only by agents does so at his peril, and must abide by the consequences if the agent who indorses the same is without authority, unless the corporation is negligent * * * or is otherwise precluded by its conduct from setting up such lack of authority in the agent. * * *

"If the original indorsement was authorized, the diversion of the funds after indorsement would not make it a forgery; but, if the original indorsement was unauthorized, parties dealing with the wrongdoer and innocent parties alike were bound to know the lack of the agent's authority to convey title away from the true owner to any one."

Assuming, as we do, that Wagner had general authority to indorse checks for the plaintiff's corporate purposes, this clearly does not authorize him to indorse checks to his own order and appropriate the money to his own personal use, and the nature of this transaction was such as to warn defendant that the checks were being diverted from usual business channels.

* * *

The courts are careful to guard the interests of commerce and to protect and strengthen its great medium, commercial paper, but they are also careful to defeat titles taken in bad faith or with knowledge, actual or imputed, which amounts to bad faith. [Citations.]

The evidence offered was immaterial as to this tort-feasor and his agent, and would not have influenced the verdict. Wagner, having no authority to indorse in behalf of the corporation for the purpose of applying the proceeds of these checks to his own account, could not transfer any greater right than he possessed to his agent for collection, the bank. [Citation.] There was no offer of proof of express ratification by the plaintiff, with full knowledge of the facts.

Judgment affirmed.

PEPPER v. LITTON

(1939) 308 U.S. 295, 60 S.Ct. 238, 84 L.Ed. 281.

[In a bankruptcy proceeding the District Court disallowed either as a secured or as an unsecured claim, a judgment by confession obtained by the dominant shareholder of the bankrupt corporation on alleged salary claims. The Court of Appeals for the Fourth Circuit reversed the District Court. Certiorari was granted.]

DOUGLAS, J. * * * The mere fact that an officer, director, or stockholder has a claim against his bankrupt corporation or that he has reduced that claim to judgment does not mean the bankruptcy court must accord it pari passu treatment with the claims of other creditors. Its disallowance or subordination may be necessitated by certain cardinal principles of equity jurisprudence. A director is a fiduciary. [Citation.] So is a dominant or controlling stockholder or group of stockholders. [Citation.] Their powers are powers in trust. [Citation.] Their dealings with the corporation are subjected to rigorous scrutiny and where any of their contracts or engagements with the corporation is challenged the burden is on the director or stockholder not only to prove the good faith of the transaction but also to show its inherent fairness from the viewpoint of the corporation and those interested therein. [Citation.] The essence of the test is whether or not under all the circumstances the transaction carries the earmarks of an arm's length bargain. If it does not, equity will set it aside. While normally that fiduciary obligation is enforceable directly by the corporation, or through a stockholder's derivative action, it is, in the event of bankruptcy of the corporation, enforceable by the trustee. For that standard of fiduciary obligation is designed for the protection of the entire community of interests in the corporation-creditors as well as stockholders.

As we have said, the bankruptcy court in passing on allowance of claims sits as a court of equity. Hence, these rules governing the fiduciary responsibilities of directors and stockholders come into play on allowance of their claims in bankruptcy. In the exercise of its equitable jurisdiction the bankruptcy court has the power to sift the circumstances surrounding any claim to see that injustice or unfairness is not done in administration of the bankrupt estate. And its duty so to do is especially clear when the claim seeking allowance accrues to the benefit of an officer, director, or stockholder. That is clearly the power and duty of the bankruptcy courts under the reorganization sections. In Taylor v. Standard Gas & Electric Co., 306 U.S. 307, 59 S.Ct. 543, 83 L.Ed. 669, this Court held that the claim of Standard against its subsidiary (admittedly a claim due and owing) should be allowed to participate in the reorganization plan of the subsidiary only in subordination to the preferred stock of the subsidiary. This was based on the equities of the case—the history of spoliation, mismanagement, and faithless stewardship of the affairs of the subsidiary by Standard to the detriment of the public investors. Simi-

lar results have properly been reached in ordinary bankruptcy proceedings. Thus, salary claims of officers, directors, and stockholders in bankruptcy of "one-man" or family corporations have been disallowed or subordinated where the courts have been satisfied that allowance of the claims would not be fair or equitable to other creditors. And that result may be reached even though the salary claim has been reduced to judgment. It is reached where the claim is void or voidable because the vote of the interested director or stockholder helped bring it into being or where the history of the corporation shows dominancy and exploitation on the part of the claimant. It is also reached where on the facts the bankrupt has been used merely as a corporate pocket of the dominant stockholder, who, with disregard of the substance or form of corporate management, has treated its affairs as his own. And so-called loans or advances by the dominant or controlling stockholder will be subordinated to claims of other creditors and thus treated in effect as capital contributions by the stockholder not only in the foregoing types of situations but also where the paid-in capital is purely nominal, the capital necessary for the scope and magnitude of the operations of the company being furnished by the stockholder as a loan.

*　*　*

On such a test the action of the District Court in disallowing or subordinating Litton's claim was clearly correct. Litton allowed his salary claims to lie dormant for years and sought to enforce them only when his debtor corporation was in financial difficulty. Then he used them so that the rights of another creditor were impaired. Litton as an insider utilized his strategic position for his own preferment to the damage of Pepper. Litton as the dominant influence over Dixie Splint Coal Company used his power not to deal fairly with the creditors of that company but to manipulate its affairs in such a manner that when one of its creditors came to collect her just debt the bulk of the assets had disappeared into another Litton company. Litton, though a fiduciary, was enabled by astute legal manoeuvring to acquire most of the assets of the bankrupt not for cash or other consideration of value to creditors but for bookkeeping entries representing at best merely Litton's appraisal of the worth of Litton's services over the years.

This alone would be a sufficient basis for the exercise by the District Court of its equitable powers in disallowing the Litton claim. But when there is added the existence of a "planned and fraudulent scheme," as found by the District Court, the necessity of equitable relief against that fraud becomes insistent. No matter how technically legal each step in that scheme may have been, once its basic nature was uncovered it was the duty of the bankruptcy court in the exercise of its equity jurisdiction to undo it. Otherwise, the fiduciary duties of dominant or management stockholders would go for naught; exploitation would become a substitute for justice; and equity would be perverted as an instrument for approving what it was designed to thwart. * * *

[Judgment of the Court of Appeals reversed and that of the District Court affirmed.]

GUTH v. LOFT, INC.

(1939) 16 Del.Ch. 255, 5 A.2d 503.

[Suit by Loft, Inc. against Charles G. Guth and others to impress a trust in favor of the plaintiff on all shares of stock of the Pepsi-Cola Company registered in the name of the defendants, to secure a transfer of those shares to the plaintiff, and for an accounting. From a decree in favor of the plaintiff, defendants appeal.]

LAYTON, C. J. * * * Corporate officers and directors are not permitted to use their position of trust and confidence to further their private interests. While technically not trustees, they stand in a fiduciary relation to the corporation and its stockholders. A public policy, existing through the years, and derived from a profound knowledge of human characteristics and motives, has established a rule that demands of a corporate officer or director, peremptorily and inexorably, the most scrupulous observance of his duty, not only affirmatively to protect the interests of the corporation committed to his charge, but also to refrain from doing anything that would work injury to the corporation, or to deprive it of profit or advantage which his skill and ability might properly bring to it, or to enable it to make in the reasonable and lawful exercise of its powers. The rule that requires an undivided and unselfish loyalty to the corporation demands that there shall be no conflict between duty and self-interest. The occasions for the determination of honesty, good faith and loyal conduct are many and varied and no hard and fast rule can be formulated. The standard of loyalty is measured by no fixed scale.

If an officer or director of a corporation, in violation of his duty as such, acquires gain or advantage for himself, the law charges the interest so acquired with a trust for the benefit of the corporation, at its election, while it denies to the betrayer all benefit and profit. The rule, inveterate and uncompromising in its rigidity, does not rest upon the narrow ground of injury or damage to the corporation resulting from a betrayal of confidence, but upon a broader foundation of a wise public policy that, for the purpose of removing all temptation, extinguishes all possibility of profit flowing from a breach of the confidence imposed by the fiduciary relation. Given the relation between the parties, a certain result follows; and a constructive trust is the remedial devise through which precedence of self is compelled to give way to the stern demands of loyalty. [Citations.]

The rule, referred to briefly as the rule of corporate opportunity, is merely one of the manifestations of the general rule that demands of an officer or director the utmost good faith in his relation to the corporation which he represents. * * *

Duty and loyalty are inseparably connected. Duty is that which is required by one's station or occupation; is that which one is bound by legal or moral obligation to do or refrain from doing; and it is with this conception of duty as the underlying basis of the principle applicable to the situation disclosed, that the conduct and acts of Guth with respect to his acquisition of the Pepsi-Cola enterprise will be scrutinized. Guth was not merely a director and the president of Loft. He was its master. It is admitted that Guth manifested some of the qualities of a dictator. The directors were selected by him. Some of them held salaried positions in the company. All of them held their positions at his favor. Whether they were supine merely, or for sufficient reasons entirely subservient to Guth, it is not profitable to inquire. It is sufficient to say that they either wilfully or negligently allowed Guth absolute freedom of action in the management of Loft's activities, and theirs is an unenviable position whether testifying for or against the appellants.

* * *

It is urged by the appellant that Megargel offered the Pepsi-Cola opportunity to Guth personally, and not to him as president of Loft. The Chancellor said that there was no way of knowing the fact, as Megargel was dead, and the benefit of his testimony could not be had; but that it was not important, for the matter of consequence was how Guth received the proposition.

It was incumbent upon Guth to show that his every act in dealing with the opportunity presented was in the exercise of the utmost good faith to Loft; and the burden was cast upon him satisfactorily to prove that the of-

fer was made to him individually. Reasonable inferences, drawn from acknowledged facts and circumstances, are powerful factors in arriving at the truth of a disputed matter, and such inferences are not to be ignored in considering the acts and conduct of Megargel. He had been for years engaged in the manufacture and sale of a cola syrup in competition with Coca-Cola. He knew of the difficulties of competition with such a powerful opponent in general, and in particular in the securing of a necessary foothold in a new territory where Coca-Cola was supreme. * *

Although the facts and circumstances disclosed by the voluminous record clearly show gross violations of legal and moral duties by Guth in his dealings with Loft, the appellants make bold to say that no duty was cast upon Guth, hence he was guilty of no disloyalty. The fiduciary relation demands something more than the morals of the market place. Meinhard v. Salmon, 249 N.Y. 458, 164 N.E. 545, 62 A.L.R. 1. Guth's abstractions of Loft's money and materials are complacently referred to as borrowings. Whether his acts are to be deemed properly cognizable in a civil court at all, we need not inquire, but certain it is that borrowing is not descriptive of them. A borrower presumes a lender acting freely. Guth took without limit of stint from a helpless corporation, in violation of a statute enacted for the protection of corporations against such abuses, and without the knowledge or authority of the corporation's Board of Directors. Cunning and craft supplanted sincerity. Frankness gave way to concealment. He did not offer the Pepsi-Cola opportunity to Loft, but captured it for himself. He invested little or no money of his own in the venture, but commandeered for his own benefit and advantage the money, resources and facilities of his corporation and the services of its officials. He thrust upon Loft the hazard, while he reaped the benefit. His time was paid for by Loft. The use of the Grace plant was not essential to the enterprise. In such manner he acquired for himself and Grace ninety one percent of the capital stock of Pepsi, now worth many millions. A genius in his line he may be, but the law makes no distinction between the wrong doing genius and the one less endowed.

Upon a consideration of all the facts and circumstances as disclosed we are convinced that the opportunity to acquire the Pepsi-Cola trademark and formula, goodwill and business belonged to the complainant, and that Guth, as its President, had no right to appropriate the opportunity to himself.

* * *

[Affirmed.]

TAYLOR v. WRIGHT

(1945) 69 Cal.App.2d 371, 159 P.2d 980.

[Action by Emma F. Taylor against Marie A. Wright and Allen J. Wright, mother and son, directors of Commonwealth Acceptance Corporation, to recover damages sustained by reason of defendants buying stock of the Corporation from the plaintiff at less than its fair value. From a judgment for plaintiff, defendants appeal.]

PETERS, P. J. * * * On these facts, the first question of law to be determined is whether directors and officers of a company owe any duty at all to stockholders in relation to transactions whereby the officers and directors buy for themselves shares of stock from the stockholders. On this subject there are three rules—the so-called majority rule, the so-called "special facts" rule, and the so-called minority rule. These three rules were exhaustively discussed in the case of American Trust Co. v. California, etc. Ins. Co., 15 Cal.2d 42, 98 P.2d 497. The so-called majority rule is frequently stated to be that directors and officers owe no fiduciary duty at all to stockholders, but may deal with them

at arm's length. No duty of disclosure of facts known to the director or officer exists. Nondisclosure cannot constitute constructive fraud. At page 56 of 15 Cal.2d, at page 504 of 98 P.2d in the American Trust case, supra, the court states the so-called majority rule to be " * * * that a corporation director owes no fiduciary obligation to the stockholder, as such, but only to the corporation. Hence * * * nondisclosure * * * was not fraudulent because there was no duty to disclose.

"The doctrine upon which appellants rely, which is said to be the majority rule, is in substance that a director is a fiduciary with respect to the corporation as an entity, and not to the stockholders as individuals. Otherwise expressed, it is that in dealings with or for the corporation, the director is exercising a corporate function, and is subject to the usual fiduciary duty to disclose all material facts; but that in personal dealings with stockholders he is not exercising a corporate function, and is free to deal with them at arms' length. Nearly all of the cases applying the rule are concerned with transactions for the purchase of stock between director and stockholder, and they hold that the director need not disclose to the stockholder his special knowledge affecting the value of the shares." * * *

The so-called majority rule is predicated on the theory that the corporation—the collective stockholders—is a separate and distinct legal entity, an artificial personality, to whom the director owes his duty. The legal writers above referred to and the more recent cases adopting the minority view, have pointed out the fallacy of this reasoning. These authorities logically point out that the detailed information a director has of corporate affairs is in a very real sense property of the corporation, and that no director should be permitted to use such information for his own benefit at the expense of his stockholders. The so-called majority rule permits a director to secure for himself profits rightfully belonging to all. Such a rule offends the moral sense, and is contrary to our modern concept of the duty of a director towards those he represents.

Although the numerical weight of authority is in favor of the so-called majority rule, the harshness and obvious unfairness of that rule has lead many of the states that originally aligned themselves with the majority rule to adopt an exception to that rule to ameliorate its harshness. This exception is referred to as follows in the American Trust Company case, supra, 15 Cal.2d at page 57, 98 P.2d at page 504: "Conceding the absence of a fiduciary relationship in the ordinary case, they (some of the states that have adopted the so-called majority view) nevertheless hold that where special circumstances or facts are present which make it inequitable for the director to withhold information from the stockholder, the duty to disclose arises, and concealment is fraud." The leading case adopting this "Special facts" exception to the so-called majority rule is Strong v. Repide, 213 U.S. 419, 29 S.Ct. 521, 53 L.Ed. 853. That case differs from the present one in many respects, but it is significant that the United States Supreme Court there held that, among other things there present, it was fraudulent for a director to buy from a shareholder without disclosing his identity. "Concealing his identity when procuring the purchase of the stock, by his agent, was in itself strong evidence of fraud." 213 U.S., at page 432, 29 S.Ct. at page 525, 53 L.Ed. 853.

The exact rule that exists in this state is somewhat uncertain. The cases of Ryder v. Bamberger, 172 Cal. 791, 158 P. 753; Robbins v. Pacific Eastern Corp., 8 Cal.2d 241, 65 P.2d 42; McCord v. Martin, 47 Cal.App. 717, 191 P. 89, and Bacon v. Soule, 19 Cal.App. 428, 126 P. 384, contain some language that supports the advocates of the so-called majority rule. These cases were analyzed at length by the Supreme Court in the American Trust Company case, supra. It was there held that what was said in these cases on the subject was dicta. At page 61 of 15 Cal.2d at page 507 of 98 P.2d, the court concluded as follows: "In this connection, we may observe that the question is still open in this state as to whether we shall follow the majority rule, the majority rule as modified by the 'special facts' doctrine, or the minority rule; and a decision on this question would be immaterial here."

In the present case the trial court instructed on the so-called "special facts" doctrine, and no challenge is made as to the form of the instruction. Whether this rule, or the so-called minority rule, is ultimately to be adopted in this state need not now be decided. No reasonable argument can be advanced against the adoption of at least the "special facts" limitation to the majority rule. A fair reading of the American Trust Company case, supra, indicates that the Supreme Court, although not directly deciding the point, has indicated a disapproval of the so-called majority rule, and that when the point is directly presented to it, it will adopt either the "special facts" doctrine or the minority rule.

Assuming that the "special facts" doctrine, at least, is applicable in this state, there can be no reasonable doubt but that the appellants, under the facts, owed respondent a duty, and violated that duty to her damage. The stock here involved was not sold or traded on any exchange. The appellants actively and successfully concealed their identity as the purchasers. The appellants, by reason of their position as directors, had full knowledge of the actual value of the stock. The appellants were active in inducing the sale. They sought out the respondent and made no effort to tell her the real value of her stock, but kept that knowledge, which they had acquired as directors, to themselves. Moreover, the appellants knew they were buying pledged stock, and that the loan for which the stock was pledged was "distressed". They knew that the bank's primary interest was to secure enough for the stock to put the loan in a sound condition. They knew that respondent would find it difficult to resist their offer should the bank deem it acceptable. Obviously, both the respondent and the bank would have been suspicious had they known who the true purchasers were. Under such circumstances the implied findings of the jury that appellants were guilty of fraud within the meaning of the "special facts" rule are amply supported by the evidence.

Appellants make much of the fact that there is no legal requirement that they disclose the market value of the securities to the stockholders, and that setting forth security values at cost in the financial statements is an approved accounting practice. That is undoubtedly true, but we are here dealing with a corporation which was largely controlled by two men who had intimate and detailed knowledge of the market value of the company. They knew as practical men that none of the stockholders had that knowledge. When Wright actively solicited a sale from respondent he was, under the facts, under a duty to speak fully, fairly and honestly. This he did not do. * * *

Affirmed.

PROBLEMS

1. A is a director but not a shareholder of X Corporation, B is both a shareholder and director and C is a shareholder but not a director of the corporation. E, an employee of the corporation, while in the course of his employment, negligently runs over and injuries P, who sues A, B, C, X Corporation, and E, jointly, to recover damages for his injuries. Against whom is P entitled to obtain judgment?

2. Brown was the president and director of a corporation engaged in owning and operating a chain of motels. Brown was advised, upon what seemed to be good authority, that a super-highway was to be constructed through the town of X,

which would afford a most desirable location for a motel. Brown represented these facts to the board of directors of the motel corporation and recommended that the corporation build a motel in the town of X at the location described. The board of directors agreed, and the new motel was constructed. It developed that the superhighway plans were changed after the motel was constructed. The highway was never built. Later, a packing house was built on property adjoining the motel and as a result the corporation sustained a considerable loss.

The shareholders brought an appropriate action against Brown charging that his representation had caused a substantial loss to the corporation.

What decision?

3. A, B, C, D, and E constituted the board of directors of the X Corporation. While D and E were out of town, A, B, and C held a special meeting of the board. Just as the meeting began, C became ill. He then gave a proxy to A and went home. A resolution was then adopted directing and authorizing the purchase by the X Corporation of an adjoining piece of land, owned by S, as a site for an additional factory building. A and B voted for the resolution, and A, as C's proxy, cast C's vote in favor of the resolution. A contract was then made by the X Corporation with S for the purchase of the land. Upon the return of D and E, another special meeting of the board was held, with all five directors present. A resolution was then unanimously adopted to cancel the contract with S. S was so notified, and now sues X Corporation for damages for breach of contract. Decision?

4. Bernard Koch was president of United Corporation, a close corporation. Koch, James Trent, and Henry Phillips comprised the three man board of directors. At a meeting of the board of directors, Trent was elected president, replacing Koch. At the same meeting, Trent attempted to have the salary of the president increased. He was unable to obtain board approval of the increase because, while Phillips voted for the increase, Koch voted against it. Trent was disqualified from voting.

As a result the directors, by a two-to-one vote, amended the by-laws to provide for the appointment of an executive committee, composed of three reputable business men, to pass upon and fix all matters of salary for employees of the corporation. Subsequently, the executive committee consisting of John Jones, James Black and William Johnson, increased the salary of the president.

Koch brought an appropriate action against the corporation, Trent and Phillips, to enjoin them from paying the increased compensation to the president above that fixed by the board of directors.

What decision?

5. Promoters A, B and C organized Theatre Corporation. Its stock was sold to the public, and an independent board of directors, not including A, B, or C, was elected. Shortly after, the same promoters organized Management Corporation, in which they own all the stock in equal shares. A management contract was then executed, under which Management Corporation agreed to manage the business of Theatre Corporation in return for a specified percentage of the net profits of the latter. Management Corporation, in addition to the general right to manage the business, was given the right to hire employees on behalf of Theatre Corporation, to direct it to sign checks as necessary, and to decide its "entertainment policy." Due to the managerial ability of A, B and C, Theatre Corporation has been highly successful. The promoters have amassed personal fortunes, and the shareholders have received large dividends.

The articles of incorporation of Theatre Corporation state: "The Board of Directors shall have control of the business affairs of the corporation, with power to select and appoint such employees and agents necessary to carry on the business of the corporation and to make such other contracts as may be deemed for the best interests of the corporation."

Discuss the validity of this management arrangement and advise A, B, and C and the Theatre Corporation what corrective steps, if any, are desirable.

Decision?

6. Zenith Steel Company operates a prosperous business. Its president, Roe, who is also a director, in January of 1966, was voted a $100,000 bonus by the board of directors for his valuable services to the company in 1965. Roe receives an annual salary of $25,000 from the company. In January, 1966, the board of directors also voted to spend $20,000,000 of the surplus funds of the company to purchase a majority of the stock of two other companies—the Green Insurance Company and the Blue Trust Company. The Green

Insurance Company is a thriving business whose stock is an excellent investment at the price at which it will be sold to Zenith Steel Company. The principal reasons for the purchase of the Green Insurance stock by the Steel Company are as an investment of surplus funds and as a diversification of its business. The Blue Trust Company owns a controlling interest in Zenith Steel Company. The main purpose for the purchase of the Blue Trust Company stock by Zenith Steel Company is to enable the present management and directors of Zenith Steel Company to perpetuate their management of the company.

Black, a minority shareholder in Zenith Steel Company, brings an appropriate action to enjoin any payment by the company of the $100,000 bonus to its president, Roe, and to enjoin the purchase by Zenith Steel Company of the stock of either the Green Insurance Company or of the Blue Trust Company.

You may assume that the articles of incorporation and the applicable statute authorize the purchase of shares in another corporation, and that Black has standing to bring the action.

Decision? Give reasons.

7. (a) Smith, a director of the Sample Corporation, sells a piece of vacant land to the Sample Corporation for $5,000, which land cost him $3,700.

(b) Jones, a shareholder of the Sample Corporation, sells a used truck to the Sample Corporation for $800, which truck was worth $750.

Raphael, a minority shareholder of the Sample Corporation, claims that the above sales are void and should be annulled. Is he correct?

8. A, a member of the board of directors of the XYZ Oil Corporation, was the owner of several choice filling station locations. The corporation desired to expand its activities and to acquire additional filling station locations. The board of directors passed a resolution authorizing the purchase of the filling station locations owned by A. The price paid to A for the real estate was in excess of the fair market value of the property. The corporation was solvent, the property purchased was valuable and necessary for the future growth and expansion of the corporation. The shareholders brought an action to set aside the sale. A defends on the ground that while the sale was in excess of the fair market value of the property it was a sale beneficial to the corporation, the transaction enabling the

corporation to increase its profit by reason of the acquisition of the additional outlets.

What decision?

9. The Crown Corporation had ample funds and was seeking investment opportunities. Allyn Rittenhouse was president of the corporation and a member of the board of directors, which he dominated. He had been offered the opportunity of purchasing stock of the Monarch Corporation and also certain patents belonging to it, in his individual capacity. Subsequent to this offer, he presented the opportunity to the board of directors of the Crown Corporation. The board of directors voted to purchase the stock but rejected the offer of the patents. Rittenhouse did not vote at the board meeting.

After the board rejected the offer of the patents Rittenhouse purchased the patents for himself. Later, Rittenhouse sold the patents to several of his friends. George Donnelly, a shareholder, brought an appropriate action against Rittenhouse for an accounting of the profits on the patents. What decision?

10. A, who is president and a director of the X Corporation, offered to buy at a slight premium over market value the shares of stock held by B, a stranger, in the X Corporation. B inquired of A how the business of the corporation was in general, and A replied that it was fair without disclosing that he had recently signed lucrative contracts with the government which were expected to double the net profits of the corporation for the current year. Upon later discovering these facts, B tenders to A the amount of the purchase price that he had received and demands the return of the shares of stock. A refuses to return the stock, and B files a suit to rescind the sale. What decision?

CHAPTER 37

RIGHTS, POWERS, AND REMEDIES OF SHAREHOLDERS

Introductory. The shareholders of a corporation, as owners of the equity or risk capital, feel more quickly than any other class of investor the vicissitudes of its business. The market value of stock will proportionately advance more in times of prosperity and decline more in times of adversity and do either more speedily, than will the market value of bonds, debentures, or any other type of debt security. The shareholders of a corporation are its primary reason for existence, a fact which is sometimes apparently ignored by a self-centered management, overly aggressive labor interests, and certain administrative agencies of government. There are occasions when it would appear that it is the shareholder who is regarded as an "artificial, invisible, intangible creature, existing only in contemplation of law."

Shareholders, however, have definite established rights. Among them are (1) the right to have their ownership of shares evidenced by a tangible stock certificate, (2) the pre-emptive right to subscribe ratably to subsequent issues of stock, (3) the right to vote, (4) the right to inspect the books and records of the corporation, (5) the right to receive a dividend, and (6) the right to participate in the assets of the corporation upon dissolution.

Right to a Certificate. A share of stock is intangible personal property, and exists independently of a stock certificate. The name and address of the owner is usually recorded on the books of the corporation or of a transfer agent employed by the corporation, but these records are not determinative of ownership. The loss or destruction of a certificate of stock does not deprive the owner of his title to the shares of stock represented by the certificate, although it does prevent the owner from making an effective transfer or pledge of the shares. The stock certificate is more than mere evidence of the shares. It is the best evidence, and by commercial usage is closely associated with the shares which it represents. In order to sell or otherwise dispose of his shares of stock, a shareholder must have possession of the certificate and must indorse and deliver it to the transferee. It is uniformly held that a shareholder has the right to demand a certificate from the corporation representing the shares of which he is the owner. A shareholder has the right to have his name and address entered on the records of the corporation so that he may receive dividends, notices of meetings, and the reports of operations and financial condition which the corporation distributes to its shareholders.

So long as the corporate records reflect his ownership of stock, a shareholder does not need a certificate for the purpose of receiving notices or dividends or in order to vote or execute a proxy. He has a right to a certificate in order to be in a position to make a transfer of the title to his shares. If his certificate of stock has been accidentally lost or destroyed, the shareholder is entitled to have a new certificate issued to him by the corporation upon furnishing the corporation an indemnity bond to protect it against the possibility of loss in the event the certificate should reappear at some future date in the hands of a bona fide purchaser.

Pre-emptive Rights. At common law, a shareholder has the right to purchase a pro rata share of every offering of stock by the corporation in order to preserve his proportionate interest in the equity. This right may be denied or limited by the articles of incorporation, as permitted by statute, or it may be subject to a statutory right of the corporation to make an offering of stock to its employees without first offering the stock to its shareholders. In the absence of a pre-emptive right, a shareholder may be unable to prevent a dilution of his ownership interest in the corporation.

For example: X owns 200 shares of stock of the ABC Company, which has a total of 1,000 shares outstanding. Through cumulative voting this enables him to elect one of the five directors of the corporation. The company determines to increase its capital stock to 2,000 shares. If X has pre-emptive rights, he and every other shareholder will be offered one share of the newly issued stock for every share they own. Upon accepting the offer and buying the stock, he will have 400 shares out of a total of 2,000 outstanding, and his relative interest in the corporation will be unchanged. However, without pre-emptive rights, he may have only 200 out of the 2,000 shares outstanding and, instead of owning twenty percent of the stock, would own ten percent. With this diluted interest, he would not be able to elect a director and would lose his voice in the management.

Stock Warrants. Where pre-emptive rights exist, a corporation issuing additional shares of its stock gives each shareholder a stock purchase warrant entitling him to buy, within a limited period of time, usually two weeks, at a price stated in the warrant, a given number of shares or scrip for a fractional share. The offering price to the shareholder is ordinarily fixed at less than the prevailing market for the stock in order to give value to the warrants. It may not be less than the par value of the stock but may be such amount in excess of par as the board of directors determine. The warrants are trans-

ferable, and if a shareholder does not wish to exercise the warrant and purchase the additional stock which he is entitled to buy, he may sell his stock warrant for such value as it may have. The value of the stock purchase warrant will obviously be the differential between the prevailing market price of the stock and the offering price to the shareholder. If the offering is one of considerable size it is common practice for the corporation to enter into a contract with an underwriter to purchase all unsubscribed shares upon the expiration of the time within which the warrants are required to be exercised.

Right to Vote. In the early development of corporations each shareholder was entitled to one vote. In most States today a shareholder is entitled to one vote for each share of stock that he owns. The constitutions of certain States, including Illinois, prohibit the issuance of non-voting stock, but where no constitutional obstacle exists, the statutes may, as in Delaware, permit the issuance of one or more classes of non-voting stock. The denial of a right to vote is occasionally found in an issue of preferred stock, not infrequently coupled with a provision that upon the happening of a certain condition such as the omission of dividends or the failure to maintain a specified working capital ratio, the holders of the preferred stock shall be permitted to vote and to elect a majority of the directors, where voting by classes is also permitted.

It should be noted that Section 216(12) of Chapter X of the Bankruptcy Act, as amended, provides that the charter of a corporation reorganized under the Act shall contain a prohibition against the issuance of non-voting stock. The purpose of this provision is to preserve the shareholder's voting franchise and in this way assure corporate democratization.

Non-voting shares may be useful in stabilizing control in a close corporation. In a New Jersey case, a will provided that a certain business be incorporated and that three designated persons receive each one-third of the shares but that the stock should be arranged so that A and B would never take advantage of C. The court ordered that a corporation be organized to issue 100 shares of voting stock and 50 shares of non-voting stock; that the voting stock be distributed 25 shares each to A and B, and 50 shares to C, and that the non-voting stock 25 shares each to A and B.

In this manner each shareholder received 50 shares but A and B combined could not outvote C. Clausen v. Leary, 113 N.J.Eq. 324, 166 A. 623 (1933).

Voting Trusts. All or part of the stock of a corporation may, by agreement among the shareholders, be issued to a trustee or trustees who thereupon hold legal title to the stock and have all of the voting rights possessed by the stock. The voting trustee or trustees issue to the former shareholders certificates of beneficial interest which represent units, comparable to shares, of the equitable and beneficial ownership of the stock. A voting trust differs from a proxy in that a proxy is revocable at any time and ordinarily expires at the end of eleven months in any event. The holder of the proxy does not have title to the stock nor possession of the stock certificates, as do the voting trustees. A voting trust is not terminable except as provided in the voting trust agreement.

Voting trusts have been sometimes used for wrongful purposes, and their validity has been successfully attacked where the object of the trust was to mobilize voting strength in a few persons who thereby obtained control of the management and utilized this control for their individual benefit. Certain early decisions held that voting trusts were illegal regardless of their purpose, but the general view today at common law is that if the purpose is not unlawful, the voting trust will be sustained. In many States, voting trusts have received the sanction of a statute. The Illinois Business Corporation Act limits the duration of a voting trust of shares of stock to a maximum of ten years, and gives to the holders of the certificates of beneficial interest the same right to examine the books and records of the corporation which shareholders possess.

Right to Examine Books and Records. The right of a shareholder to inspect the books and records of the corporation, in person or by his attorney, agent or accountant, and to make transcriptions therefrom, is provided by statute in practically every State. At common law, the right also existed where the request for inspection was made at a proper time and for a proper purpose. By examination of the books and records, a shareholder may determine the financial condition of the corporation, the profits realized or loss sustained, the propriety of certain items reflected in the profit and loss statement or balance sheet, the amount of executive salaries and administrative overhead, and the possible existence of causes of action based upon fraud or breach of fiduciary duty by officers or directors. The shareholder may also learn the names and addresses of other shareholders and whether officers or directors have made purchases or sales of stock of the corporation. The right of inspection is therefore a valuable one and may be enforced by an action of mandamus. However, it is subject to abuse and will be denied to any shareholder whose purpose is to embarrass or cause loss to the corporation or its shareholders, to make improper use of the information sought, or to obtain a list of shareholders in order to offer it for sale.

Where the purpose of inspection is not improper, any officer or agent of the corporation who refuses to allow a shareholder to examine and make extracts from its books and records of account, minutes, and records of shareholders, is liable to a penalty recoverable by the shareholder in a civil action.

Under the Model Act, the penalty is ten percent of the value of the shares owned by the person who has been denied the right to inspect the books and records of the corporation. (Section 46, Appendix D.)

Right to a Dividend. A shareholder may not maintain an action at law against the corporation to recover a dividend until and unless the dividend has been formally declared by resolution of the board of directors. A proper dividend so declared becomes a debt of the corporation, and enforceable at law as any other debt.

Where the directors decline or omit to declare a dividend, the propriety of their action may be the subject of a suit in equity brought against them and the corporation by a shareholder seeking a mandatory injunction requiring the directors to meet and declare a dividend. Courts of equity are reluctant to order an injunction of this kind and will not do so where it involves merely substituting the business judgment of the court for that of the directors elected by the shareholders. A court of equity will grant an injunction and require the directors to declare a dividend where (1) a demand has been made upon the directors before commencement of the suit; (2) corporate earnings or surplus are available out of which a dividend may be declared; (3) the earnings or surplus is in the form of available cash and not in accounts receivable, inventory, goods in process of manufacture, or other non-liquid assets, and (4) the directors are acting so unreasonably in withholding a dividend that their conduct clearly amounts to an abuse of discretion. If the corporation has adequate reserves for every legitimate contingency, and the directors permit profits to accumulate year after year without any program or policy to employ the accumulated surplus in plant expansion, new equipment, legitimate experimentation or research, or other proper corporate purpose, such an arbitrary attitude on the part of the board not to distribute to share-holders by way of a dividend some of the available profits or surplus would be unreasonable and entitle a shareholder to invoke the powers of a court of equity to compel the directors to declare an appropriate dividend.

The existence of a large accumulated surplus will not alone justify compelling the directors to distribute funds which, in their opinion, should be retained for plant expansion, experimentation, or other bona fide corporate purposes. Relief has been denied a shareholder although the corporation had never declared a dividend in the thirty years of its existence, had a surplus of $161,000, and had outstanding capital stock of only $75,000. Where the evidence shows noncorporate motives or personal animosity as the basis for a refusal to declare dividends, a court may require the directors to distribute what appears to be a reasonable portion of the earnings. Thus, personal philanthropic convictions are no basis for refusal to pay out substantial amounts of earned surplus (Dodge v. Ford Motor Co., page 833.); and testimony that the chairman of the board and controlling shareholder had sworn he would never pay a dividend as long as he lived suggests other than proper business reasons for retaining all the earnings of a corporation.

The fact that a preferred shareholder has prior rights with respect to dividends does not make his position different from that of the holder of common shares with respect to the discretion of the directors as to the declaration of dividends. The holders of preferred stock, in the absence of special contract or statute, must likewise abide by the decision of the directors, although provisions for management control in an issue of preferred stock in the event dividends are passed may go a long way to insure the declaration of dividends to the holders of stock of such issue.

Rights Upon Dissolution. When a corporation is dissolved and the claims of all of its creditors are satisfied, the remaining assets are distributable pro rata among its shareholders. The holders of preferred stock will have priority to the extent of their contractual preferences. In the event that the preferred stock is given no express preference upon liquidation or dissolution, the preferred and common stock share ratably in the remaining assets. If the corporation which is dissolved voluntarily by act of all of the shareholders or by act of the corporation, or involuntarily by decree of court at the instance of the Attorney General, has assets which are not sold, levied upon by creditors, or distributed to shareholders, the title to such assets passes to the shareholders after the corporation has ceased to exist. In the event that the dissolved corporation owns real estate which before or after dissolution has not been sold, transferred, or seized by creditors, the shareholders of the corporation at the time of dissolution own such real estate as tenants in common.

Rights of Defrauded Shareholders. Where a shareholder has been induced to subscribe for stock or to purchase his stock from the corporation by means of fraudulent misrepresentations, he has the same remedies which the law provides for any person who has been defrauded. If he has not paid for the stock, he may plead the fraud defensively in a suit by the corporation against him to recover the amount of the subscription price. If, however, he has paid for the stock, he may elect to rescind the stock subscription contract or purchase contract and recover the amount of money he has paid for the stock.

In England, the law is settled that all relief from a stock subscription contract upon the ground of fraud is cut off by the insolvency of the corporation. The weight of American authority, contrary to the English rule, permits the defrauded shareholder to rescind even after the corporation has become insolvent or bankrupt, provided he repudiates the subscription contract promptly after discovering the fraud, and provided, further, that the rights of creditors of the corporation are not thereby impaired.

While the American decisions permit rescission after the corporation has become insolvent or bankrupt, they do not allow the claim of a defrauded shareholder to rank on a parity with claims of unsecured creditors of the corporation. The position of the rescinding shareholder with respect to participation in the assets of the corporation is subordinate to that of creditors but prior to that of non-rescinding shareholders.

Right to Receivership and Dissolution. A minority shareholder is not required to sit idly by and suffer a board of directors dominated by the majority to misapply or waste the assets of the corporation, or to permit a deadlock in the management to cause or threaten irreparable injury to the corporation. A minority shareholder may apply to a court of equity, which has full power to appoint a receiver and to liquidate the assets and business of a corporation in an action instituted by any shareholder when it appears (1) that the directors are deadlocked in the management of the corporate affairs and the shareholders are unable to break the deadlock, and that irreparable injury to the corporation is being suffered or is threatened by reason thereof; (2) that the acts of the directors or those in control of the corporation are illegal, oppressive, or fraudulent, or (3) that the corporate assets are being misapplied or wasted. (Section 90, Model Act.)

CASES

WAGONER v. MAIL DELIVERY SERVICE, INC.

(1964) 193 Kan. 470, 394 P.2d 119.

SCHROEDER, J. This is an action to recover the face value of stock certificates or the actual value thereof upon the defendant corporation's refusal and neglect to issue stock certificates or recognize the plaintiff as a stockholder of the corporation. Appeal has been duly perfected from an order of the trial court sustaining a demurrer to the petition.

The only question is whether the petition states a cause of action.

The petition alleges that Mail Delivery Service, Inc. (defendant-appellee) is a Kansas corporation operating under and by virtue of the laws of the state of Kansas with its resident office in Topeka, Kansas. It further alleges that Warren W. Wagoner (plaintiff-appellant) acquired stock certificates representing ten shares of $100 par value per share in the appellee corporation on July 13, 1962; that the appellant subsequently surrendered said stock certificates, each of which was properly signed and endorsed by the owner thereof, to the corporation and made request upon it to reissue said stock to the appellant, and to make the corporate records available to the appellant for his inspection; and for the corporation to notify the appellant of stockholder meetings and board of director meetings; that notwithstanding such demands upon the corporation, it has refused and neglected to issue its stock certificate representing ten shares of stock to the appellant and has refused and neglected to allow the appellant to inspect the corporate records and books, and has refused and neglected to notify the appellant of stockholder meetings and board of director meetings.

The petition further alleges damages and prays for judgment to recover the face value of the stock certificates or the actual value thereof, together with interest and costs.

* * *

The petition alleges in effect that the corporation accepted surrender of the appellant's stock certificate and thereafter refused and neglected to reissue a certificate, representing the appellant's interest in the corporation, to the appellant. At no time did the corporation recognize the appellant as a stockholder or interest holder in the corporation. Liberally construed, the acts and failure to act on the part of the corporation and its refusal to recognize the appellant as a *bona fide* stockholder of the corporation, as alleged, constituted a conversion of the appellant's stock by the corporation. By reason of such conduct, if proved, the appellant is entitled to recover the value of the stock.

Accordingly, the judgment of the lower court is reversed.

G. S. & M. CO. v. DIXON

(1964) 220 Ga. 329, 138 S.E.2d 662.

GRICE, J. * * * Petitioner, a bona fide stockholder, has requested the right to inspect the books of the corporation, including its bylaws, its minute books, and its financial records. Although his counsel has been allowed a limited examination of its financial records, the corporation has persistently refused to allow him to examine such minute books or bylaws.

The examination was asked in good faith for a specific and honest purpose, and not to gratify curiosity or for speculative or vexatious purposes. The purpose is germane to petitioner's interest as a stockholder, is proper and lawful in character, and is not inimical to the interest of the corporation. He has asked that such inspection be allowed during reasonable business hours at the corporation's principal office in a named Georgia county.

A stockholders' meeting has been called for a specified date and place in the State of New York. The corporate charter does not provide that stockholders' meetings may be held outside the State of Georgia.

Petitioner has made persistent and repeated efforts to examine the corporation's books, records, and bylaws in order to ascertain the legality of such meeting, to determine the worth of the decedent's share for inventory and estate tax purposes, to ascertain whether the corporation's assets have been properly administered, and for other proper and legitimate purposes. But the corporation has refused to allow such examination.

* * *

The basis of this right is simple and logical: "The basis of the right of stockholders to inspect the books and records is the ownership of the corporate property and assets through ownership of shares; as owners, they have the right to inform themselves as to the management of their property by the directors and officers who are their trustees in direct charge of the property." [Citation.]

This right is not dependent upon the amount of stock held. It is " * * * immaterial whether a stockholder asserting a right of inspection holds a few shares or many." [Citations.]

* * * The purposes of the desired inspection are proper. The petitioner alleged that he desires the right to inspect the books and records of the company in order that he may ascertain the legality of the stockholders' meeting, determine the worth of the shares of the decedent for inventory and estate tax purposes, ascertain whether the assets of the corporation have been properly administered, and for other proper and legitimate purposes. It alleged that the examina-

tion was asked in good faith and not to gratify curiosity, speculate or vex; that his purposes are germane to his interest as a stockholder and not inimical to the interest of the corporation; and that his request was reasonable as to time and place. Thus, the petition sufficiently shows that the stockholder has the right to inspect and has been denied it.

We, therefore, hold that the trial court properly overruled the general demurrers to the petition and denied the oral motion to dismiss.

Judgment affirmed.

STULL v. BELLEFONTE STONE PRODUCTS CORPORATION

(1964) 205 Pa.Super. 40, 205 A.2d 677.

ERVIN, J. This appeal is concerned with the right of a president of a corporation to recover unpaid salary from stockholders of the corporation. The court below, by its order, entered judgment for Harold R. Stull, president of Bellefonte Stone Products Corporation, against the defendants, E. R. Scheuner and Joseph Mills, two stockholders of the corporation, in the respective amounts of $2,574.00 and $3,332.00, with interest, for unpaid salary due to Stull as president of the corporation. The two stockholders have appealed.

The Act of May 5, 1933, P.L. 364, 15 P.S. § 2852–514, provides: "A. A shareholder of a business corporation shall not be personally liable for any debt or liability of the corporation, except salaries and wages due and owing to its laborers and employees, for services rendered to the corporation. In such event, every shareholder shall be personally liable in an amount equal to the value of the shares of the corporation owned by him * * *."

The appellants argue that the above provision does not "apply to the chief executive officer who has complete control of the corporation."

The Act of June 25, 1864, P.L. 947, § 7, provided for individual liability of the stockholders "for debts due mechanics, workmen and laborers employed" by the company. By the Act of April 29, 1874, P.L. 73, § 14, the liability of shareholders was limited to "all work or labor done to carry on the operations of each of said corporations." Section 514 of the Business Corporation Law of 1933, above quoted, enlarged the language theretofore used by the use of the phrase "*salaries* and wages due and owing to its laborers and *employes*." (Emphasis supplied) The word "wages" is commonly used with reference to pay of laborers and workmen, whereas the word "salary" may be used with reference to the pay of any employe, no matter how big his position or how large his pay. We are of the opinion that the legislature intended, by the 1933 law, to include any employe of the company, whether he be president or common laborer.

While the 1933 act does not expressly include officers, we believe their inclusion is implicit from the words "salaries" and "employes." Construing the words in their popular sense, the inference to be made is that salaried employes include officers of the corporation.

* * *

Judgment affirmed.

_____

CHADWICK v. CROSS, ABBOTT CO.

(1964) 124 Vt. 325, 205 A.2d 416.

SHANGRAW, J. This is an appeal by the defendant from a judgment of the Orange County Court entered in a civil action tried by court. By its brief the defendant attacks certain findings of fact, and the judgment of $4,882.70 with interest, rendered in favor of the plaintiff.

On November 23, 1959, the parties to this action caused a corporation, known as Randolph Red & White, Inc., to be organized under the laws of the State of Vermont.

This corporation at the time of organization issued 1000 shares of common stock, of which the plaintiff as minority stockholder held 490 shares, and the defendant as majority stockholder held 510 shares.

* * *

The plaintiff, the minority stockholder, decided to withdraw from the corporation as of January 2, 1962, and so notified the defendant in accordance with Article 18 of the By-laws. At this time the stock ownership of the corporation remained the same as when the stock was first issued. Article 18, in so far as here material, reads:

"In the event the minority stockholders decide to withdraw from the Corporation for any reason, they shall first ascertain the book value of their minority shares of stock as of the date of their notice to withdraw which notice shall be in writing to the majority shareholders. They shall notify the majority shareholders, in writing at the time of their notice to withdraw, of the said book value which shall be the purchase price for said shares of stock. Said book value shall be determined from the books of said Corporation and according to sound and accepted accounting rules and practice. The above notice to withdraw to the said majority shareholders shall be accompanied by a written opinion of a Certified Public Accountant in substance that said book value is correct and accurate to the best of his knowledge and belief. Within thirty (30) days after said notice to withdraw the majority shareholders shall tender or deliver to the minority stockholders at their home address, cash or certified or cashier's check payable to them in the amount of said book value as stated in the notice or information accompanying said notice. * * * For the purposes of carrying out the provisions of this Article, the majority stockholders shall cooperate with the minority stockholders to ascertain the book value of the shares in question."

The plaintiff engaged a firm of certified public accountants to determine the book value of his stock. In the notice to withdraw from the corporation the notice stated that plaintiff had ascertained the book value of his shares of stock as of the date of his notice to withdraw, as determined from the books of the corporation, according to sound and accepted accounting rules and practice. The book value therein stated was $114.67456 per share, a total of $56,190.53 for the 490 shares. This was accompanied by a written opinion from the firm of accountants certifying in substance that said book value of $114.67456 per share was correct and accurate.

* * *

The defendant claims that the book value of plaintiff's minority stock was $106.43307 per share, a total of $52,150.70 for plaintiff's 490 shares. This book value was determined by the defendant by the use of the so-called double declining method of computing depreciation expense.

$52,150.70 was paid the plaintiff. In this action he seeks to recover the difference between the two appraisals, together with interest on $56,190.43 computed from the date of notice of withdrawal, January 2, 1962 through April 1, 1962 at $842.87, a total of $4,882.70 reflected in the judgment order.

This controversy arises by reason of the different methods adopted by the parties in determining the book value of plaintiff's stock—more particularly the approach to depreciation write-off. Generally speaking book value of stock represents the difference between the assets and liabilities of a corporation—that is the value of the net assets.

Depreciation, under generally accepted accounting principles, is charged in such manner and in such amount as to recover the original cost of each asset over its estimated useful life and in proportion to the actual annual decrease in value of such asset. The four factors which enter into the computation of depreciation expense are:—original cost, the life in years, the salvage value, and the method chosen to write off the cost of depreciable assets.

Under the straight line method of depreciation used by the plaintiff an equal amount is charged off as expense during each year of the life of an asset. This method of depreciation allocates the cost of the asset equally over its life.

Randolph Red & White, Inc., in its bookkeeping, had used the double declining method of depreciation which was adopted by the defendant in determining the book value of plaintiff's stock. By the double declining method of depreciation a larger portion of depreciation expense accruable over the life of an asset is charged as expense in the first year, and lesser amounts in the following years. This method was sanctioned by the Internal Revenue Code of 1954, 26 U.S.C.A. (I.R.C.1954) § 167. In addition the defendant used the arbitrary extra depreciation allowances permitted under the Internal Revenue Code for newly purchased assets. This allowance was 20 percent in the first year. Defendant increased its depreciation $2000.00 by the use of this arbitrary method alone.

* * *

* * * It is not disputed that the depreciation method adopted by the defendant may have been proper for some purpose, such as income tax accounting. The purpose of Article 18 was to permit plaintiff to arrive at the just and actual value of his stock. Whether plaintiff's or defendant's method is preferable is not the point. By Article 18 plaintiff was given the choice of methods to be employed provided his determination of book value was determined from the books of the corporation, which was done, and according to sound and accepted accounting rules and practice. The evidence reveals that the straight line method of depreciation is a sound and accepted accounting practice, and by its use reflected a realistic and sound value of plaintiff's stock.

As bearing upon plaintiff's adherence to Article 18, the trial court made the following finding.

"17. The Court further finds that the plaintiff observed every requirement under Article 18 of the By-laws of the Corporation at the time of his withdrawal from the same in the ascertaining of the book value of his stock according to sound and accepted accounting principles."

This finding is amply supported by the evidence.

*   *   *

Judgment affirmed.

GALLER v. GALLER

(1965) 32 Ill.2d 16, 203 N.E.2d 577.

UNDERWOOD, JUSTICE. Plaintiff, Emma Galler, sued in equity for an accounting and for specific performance of an agreement made in July, 1955, between plaintiff and her husband, of one part, and defendants, Isadore A. Galler and his wife, Rose, of the other.

*   *   *

There is no substantial dispute as to the facts in this case. From 1919 to 1924, Benjamin and Isadore Galler, brothers, were equal partners in the Galler Drug Company, a wholesale drug concern. In 1924 the business was incorporated under the Illinois Business Corporation Act, each owning one half of the outstanding 220 shares of stock. In 1945 each contracted to sell 6 shares to an employee, Rosenberg, at a price of $10,500 for each block of 6 shares, payable within 10 years. They guaranteed to repurchase the shares if Rosenberg's employment were terminated, and further agreed that if they

sold their shares, Rosenberg would receive the same price per share as that paid for the brothers' shares. Rosenberg was still indebted for the 12 shares in July, 1955, and continued to make payments on account even after Benjamin Galler died in 1957 and after the institution of this action by Emma Galler in 1959. Rosenberg was not involved in this litigation either as a party or as a witness, and in July of 1961, prior to the time that the master in chancery hearings were concluded, defendants Isadore and Rose Galler purchased the 12 shares from Rosenberg. A supplemental complaint was filed by the plaintiff, Emma Galler, asserting an equitable right to have 6 of the 12 shares transferred to her and offering to pay the defendants one half of the amount that the defendants paid Rosenberg. The parties have stipulated that pending disposition of the instant case, these shares will not be voted or transferred. For approximately one year prior to the entry of the decree by the chancellor in July of 1962, there were no outstanding minority shareholder interests.

In March, 1954, Benjamin and Isadore, on the advice of their accountant, decided to enter into an agreement for the financial protection of their immediate families and to assure their families, after the death of either brother, equal control of the corporation. In June, 1954, while the agreement was in the process of preparation by an attorney-associate of the accountant, Benjamin suffered a heart attack. Although he resumed his business duties some months later, he was again stricken in February, 1955, and thereafter was unable to return to work. During his brother's illness, Isadore asked the accountant to have the shareholders' agreement put in final form in order to protect Benjamin's wife, and this was done by another attorney employed in the accountant's office. On a Saturday night in July, 1955, the accountant brought the agreement to Benjamin's home, and 6 copies of it were executed there by the two brothers and their wives. The accountant then collected all signed copies of the agreement and informed the parties that he was taking them for safe keeping. Between the execution of the agreement in July, 1955, and Benjamin's death in December, 1957, the agreement was not modified. Benjamin suffered a stroke late in July, 1955, and on August 2, 1955, Isadore and the accountant and a notary public brought to Benjamin for signature two powers of attorney which were retained by the accountant after Benjamin executed them with Isadore as a witness. The plaintiff did not read the powers and she never had them. One of the powers authorized the transfer of Benjamin's bank account to Emma and the other power enabled Emma to vote Benjamin's 104 shares. Because of the state of Benjamin's health, nothing further was said to him by any of the parties concerning the agreement. It appears from the evidence that some months after the agreement was signed, the defendants Isadore and Rose Galler and their son, the defendant, Aaron Galler sought to have the agreements destroyed. The evidence is undisputed that defendants had decided prior to Benjamin's death they would not honor the agreement, but never disclosed their intention to plaintiff or her husband.

On July 21, 1956, Benjamin executed an instrument creating a trust naming his wife as trustee. The trust covered, among other things, the 104 shares of Galler Drug Company stock and the stock certificates were endorsed by Benjamin and delivered to Emma. When Emma presented the certificates to defendants for transfer into her name as trustee, they sought to have Emma abandon the 1955 agreement or enter into some kind of a noninterference agreement as a price for the transfer of the shares. Finally, in September, 1956, after Emma had refused to abandon the shareholders' agreement, she did agree to permit defendant Aaron to become

president for one year and agreed that she would not interfere with the business during that year. The stock was then reissued in her name as trustee. During the year 1957 while Benjamin was still alive, Emma tried many times to arrange a meeting with Isadore to discuss business matters but he refused to see her.

Shortly after Benjamin's death, Emma went to the office and demanded the terms of the 1955 agreement be carried out. Isadore told her that anything she had to say could be said to Aaron, who then told her that his father would not abide by the agreement. He offered a modification of the agreement by proposing the salary continuation payment but without her becoming a director. When Emma refused to modify the agreement and sought enforcement of its terms, defendants refused and this suit followed.

During the last few years of Benjamin's life both brothers drew an annual salary of $42,000. Aaron, whose salary was $15,000 as manager of the warehouse prior to September, 1956, has since the time that Emma agreed to his acting as president drawn an annual salary of $20,000. In 1957, 1958, and 1959 a $40,000 annual dividend was paid. Plaintiff has received her proportionate share of the dividend.

The July, 1955, agreement in question here, entered into between Benjamin, Emma, Isadore and Rose, recites that Benjamin and Isadore each own 47½% of the issued and outstanding shares of the Galler Drug Company, an Illinois corporation, and that Benjamin and Isadore desired to provide income for the support and maintenance of their immediate families. No reference is made to the shares then being purchased by Rosenberg. The essential features of the contested portions of the agreement are substantially as set forth in the opinion of the Appellate Court: (2) that the bylaws of the corporation will be amended to provide for a board of four directors; that the necessary quorum shall be three directors; and that no directors' meeting shall be held without giving ten days notice to all directors. (3) The shareholders will cast their votes for the above named persons (Isadore, Rose, Benjamin and Emma) as directors at said special meeting and at any other meeting held for the purpose of electing directors. (4, 5) In the event of the death of either brother his wife shall have the right to nominate a director in place of the decedent. (6) Certain annual dividends will be declared by the corporation. The dividend shall be $50,000 payable out of the accumulated earned surplus in excess of $500,000. If 50% of the annual net profits after taxes exceeds the minimum $50,000, then the directors shall have discretion to declare a dividend up to 50% of the annual net profits. If the net profits are less than $50,000, nevertheless the minimum $50,000 annual dividend shall be declared, providing the $500,000 surplus is maintained. Earned surplus is defined. (9) The certificates evidencing the said shares of Benjamin Galler and Isadore Galler shall bear a legend that the shares are subject to the terms of this agreement. (10) A salary continuation agreement shall be entered into by the corporation which shall authorize the corporation upon the death of Benjamin Galler or Isadore Galler, or both, to pay a sum equal to twice the salary of such officer, payable monthly over a five-year period. Said sum shall be paid to the widow during her widowhood, but should be paid to such widow's children if the widow remarries within the five-year period. (11, 12) The parties to this agreement further agree and hereby grant to the corporation the authority to purchase, in the event of the death of either Benjamin or Isadore, so much of the stock of Galler Drug Company held by the estate as is necessary to provide sufficient funds to pay the federal estate tax, the Illinois inheritance tax and other administrative expenses of the estate. If as a result of such purchase from the estate of the decedent the amount of dividends to be received by the heirs is reduced, the parties shall nevertheless vote for directors so as to give the estate and heirs the same representation as before (2 directors out of 4, even though they own less stock), and also that the corporation pay an additional benefit payment equal to the diminution of the dividends. In the event either Benjamin or Isadore decides to sell his shares he is required to offer them first to the remaining shareholders and then to the corporation at book value, according each six months to accept the offer.

The Appellate Court found the 1955 agreement void because "the undue duration, stated purpose and substantial disregard of the provisions of the Corporation Act outweigh any considerations which might call for divisibility" and held that "the public policy of this state demands voiding this entire agreement".

* * *

The power to invalidate the agreements on the grounds of public policy is so far reaching and so easily abused that it should be called into action to set aside or annul the solemn engagement of parties dealing on equal terms only in cases where the corrupt or dangerous tendency clearly and unequivocally appears upon the face of the agreement itself or is the necessary inference from the matters which are expressed, and the only apparent exception to this general rule is to be found in those cases where the agreement, though fair and unobjectionable on its face, is a part of a corrupt scheme and is made to disguise the real nature of the transaction. [Citation.]

* * *

At this juncture it should be emphasized that we deal here with a so-called close corporation. Various attempts at definition of the close corporation have been made. [Citation.] For our purposes, a close corporation is one in which the stock is held in a few hands, or in a few families, and wherein it is not at all, or only rarely, dealt in by buying or selling. [Citation.] Moreover, it should be recognized that shareholder agreements similar to that in question here are often, as a practical consideration, quite necessary for the protection of those financially interested in the close corporation. While the shareholder of a public-issue corporation may readily sell his shares on the open market should management fail to use, in his opinion, sound business judgment, his counterpart of the close corporation often has a large total of his entire capital invested in the business and has no ready market for his shares should he desire to sell. He feels, understandably, that he is more than a mere investor and that his voice should be heard concerning all corporate activity. Without a shareholder agreement, specifically enforceable by the courts, insuring him a modicum of control, a large minority shareholder might find himself at the mercy of an oppressive or unknowledgeable majority. Moreover, as in the case at bar, the shareholders of a close corporation are often also the directors and officers thereof. With substantial shareholding interests abiding in each member of the board of directors, it is often quite impossible to secure, as in the large public-issue corporation, independent board judgment free from personal motivations concerning corporate policy. For these and other reasons too voluminous to enumerate here, often the only sound basis for protection is afforded by a lengthy, detailed shareholder agreement securing the rights and obligations of all concerned. For a discussion of these and other considerations, see Note, "A Plea for Separate Statutory Treatment of the Close Corporation", 33 N.Y.U.L.Rev. 700 (1958).

As the preceding review of the applicable decisions of this court points out, there has been a definite, albeit inarticulate, trend toward eventual judicial treatment of the close corporation as *sui generis*. Several shareholder-director agreements that have technically "violated" the letter of the Business Corporation Act have nevertheless been upheld in the light of the existing practical circumstances, i. e., no apparent public injury, the absence of a complaining minority interest, and no apparent prejudice to creditors. However, we have thus far not attempted to limit these decisions as applicable only to close corporations and have seemingly implied that general considerations regarding judicial supervision of all corporate behavior apply.

* * *

The Appellate Court correctly found many of the contractual provisions free from serious objection, and we need not prolong this opinion with a discussion of them here. That court did, however, find difficulties in the stated purpose of the agreement as it relates to its duration, the election of certain persons to specific offices for a number of years, the requirement for the mandatory declaration of stated dividends (which the Appellate Court held invalid), and the salary continuation agreement.

Since the question as to the duration of the agreement is a principal source of controversy, we shall consider it first. The parties provided no specific termination date, and while the agreement concludes with a paragraph that its terms "shall be binding upon and shall inure to the benefits of" the legal representatives, heirs and assigns of the parties, this clause is, we believe, intended to be operative only as long as one of the parties is living. It further provides that it shall be so construed as to carry out its purposes, and we believe these must be determined from a consideration of the agreement as a whole. Thus viewed, a fair construction is that its purposes were accomplished at the death of the survivor of the parties. While these life spans are not precisely ascertainable, and the Appellate Court noted Emma Galler's life expectancy at her husband's death was 26.9 years, we are aware of no statutory or public policy provision against stockholder's agreements which would invalidate this agreement on that ground. * * While limiting voting trusts in 1947 to a maximum duration of 10 years, the legislature has indicated no similar policy regarding straight voting agreements although these have been common since prior to 1870. In view of the history of decisions of this court generally upholding, in the absence of fraud or prejudice to minority interests or public policy, the right of stockholders to agree among themselves as to the manner in which their stock will be voted, we do not regard the period of time within which this agreement may remain effective as rendering the agreement unenforceable.

The clause that provides for the election of certain persons to specified offices for a period of years likewise does not require invalidation. * * *

We turn next to a consideration of the effect of the stated purpose of the agreement upon its validity. The pertinent provision is: "The said Benjamin A. Galler and Isadore A. Galler desire to provide income for the support and maintenance of their immediate families." Obviously, there is no evil inherent in a contract entered into for the reason that the persons originating the terms desired to so arrange their property as to provide post-death support for those dependent upon them. Nor does the fact that the subject property is corporate stock alter the situation so long as there exists no detriment to minority stock interests, creditors or other public injury.

* * *

The terms of the dividend agreement require a minimum annual dividend of $50,000, but this duty is limited by the subsequent provision that it shall be operative only so long as an earned surplus of $500,000 is maintained. It may be noted that in 1958, the year prior to commencement of this litigation, the corporation's net earnings after taxes amounted to $202,759 while its earned surplus was $1,543,270, and this was increased in 1958 to $1,680,079 while earnings were $172,964. The minimum earned surplus requirement is designed for the protection of the corporation and its creditors, and we take no exception to the contractual dividend requirements as thus restricted. [Citation.]

The salary continuation agreement is a common feature, in one form or another, of corporate executive employment. It requires that the widow should receive a total benefit, payable monthly over a five-year period, aggregating twice the amount paid her deceased husband in one year. This requirement was likewise limited for the protection of the corporation by being contingent upon the payments being income tax-deductible by the corporation. The charge made in those cases which have considered the validity of payments to the widow of an officer and shareholder in a corporation is that a gift of its property by a noncharitable corporation is in violation of the rights of its shareholders and *ultra vires*. Since there are no shareholders here other than the parties to the contract, this objection is not here applicable, and its effect, as limited, upon the corporation is not so prejudicial as to require its invalidation.

* * *

Accordingly, the judgment of the Appellate Court is reversed except insofar as it relates to fees, and is, as to them affirmed.

* * *

Affirmed in part and reversed in part, and remanded with directions.

PROBLEMS

1. Gore had been the owner of one per cent of the outstanding shares of the Webster Company, a corporation, since its organization in

1951. Ratliff, the president of the Company, was the owner of seventy per cent of the outstanding shares. In May, 1966, Ratliff used the shareholders' list to submit to the shareholders an offer of $50 per share for their stock. Gore, upon receiving the offer, called Ratliff and told him that the offer was inadequate and advised that he was willing to offer $60 per share, and for that purpose demanded a shareholders' list. Ratliff was informed that Gore was willing and able to supply the funds necessary to purchase the stock but he nevertheless refused to supply the list to Gore. Further, he did not offer to transmit Gore's offer to the shareholders of record. Gore then filed a petition for mandamus to compel the corporation to make the shareholders' list available to him.

What decision?

2. (a) May shareholders of a corporation at their meeting restrict the directors in the management of the corporation. May the shareholders, by vote, compel the directors to declare a dividend?

(b) A owns stock in the X corporation. Upon his death, B is appointed A's executor. Can B vote the stock without having a certificate issued in his name as executor?

(c) What is a voting trust of corporate stock?

3. Discuss briefly the validity of the following by-laws, the charter being silent on the matters involved.

(a) That no shareholder owning less than ten shares of capital stock shall be allowed to vote at the annual meeting of shareholders.

(b) That no shareholder shall sell or transfer his stock, except by will or inheritance, without first offering it to the corporation at its market value.

(c) Shareholders may inspect the corporate books at the annual meeting only and at no other time.

4. In each of the following statements may the shares be voted at a regular meeting of shareholders, and if so, by whom?

1. Shares of its own stock belonging to a corporation.

2. A transferee of shares, the transfer not being registered on the books of the corporation.

3. Shares of a deceased shareholder who died testate.

4. The holder of a legal proxy, not coupled with an interest, where the owner of the shares is present and attempts to vote.

5. Shares of an owner, who is a candidate for director, on the election of directors.

5. The Acme Corporation held 1,000 shares of its own stock in its treasury. This stock had been previously issued and later purchased by the corporation. The board of directors adopted a resolution authorizing the sale of this stock on the open market. A, a shareholder, immediately filed suit to restrain such action contending that as a shareholder, he had the right to purchase his proportionate share of such stock before it was placed on the market. What decision?

6. Union Corporation is capitalized for $75,000, represented by 750 shares of capital stock at the par value of $100 each, of which Smith owns 250 shares. At a properly called shareholders' meeting, the owners of the other 500 shares vote, over Smith's objections, to amend the articles of incorporation by increasing the capital stock to 1,000 shares and further vote to sell the new shares, at par value, to Jones, a person not previously interested in the corporation. Smith now seeks an injunction to restrain the corporation from issuing the new shares over his objection as a minority shareholder. There is no provision in the charter or by-laws of the corporation concerning the issuance of additional shares of stock and it is conceded by all parties that par value is a fair price for the shares. What result?

7. Fore, a minority shareholder of Middlesboro Iron Works Corporation, brought an appropriate action seeking to have four by-laws adjudged invalid and to restrain the other shareholders from doing anything inconsistent therewith. The by-laws provided (a) that no action should be taken by the shareholders except upon their unanimous vote but that, if thirty days' notice of the meeting had been given, unanimous vote of the shareholders present in person or by proxy should be sufficient; (b) that the directors should be the three persons receiving the shareholders' unanimous vote at the annual meeting; (c) that no action should be taken by the directors except by unanimous vote of all of them; and (d) that the by-laws should not be amended except by unanimous vote of all of the shareholders.

Discuss and decide the validity of each of these by-laws.

8. In 1961, at a duly called meeting of the shareholders of Commerce Corporation, the hold-

ers of a majority of the outstanding stock adopted a by-law prohibiting any shareholder from selling or transferring his stock without first giving the corporation a thirty-day option to purchase such stock at its book value. Nothing further was done to implement the by-law.

In 1965 Karl Boone, a shareholder, without first offering his stock to the company, sold and assigned his certificate of stock to Fred Marberry who was not a shareholder. Marberry bought Boone's stock at par, although the book value was considerably below par value. Commerce Corporation refused to transfer the stock to Marberry on its books. Marberry brought an appropriate action against Commerce Corporation to compel the corporation to transfer the stock to him.

What decision?

9. In 1962, Sayre learned that Adams, Boone, and Chase were planning to form a corpo- ration for the purpose of manufacturing and marketing a line of novelties to wholesale outlets. Sayre had patented a self-lock gas tank cap, but lacked the financial backing to market it profita- bly. He negotiated with Adams, Boone and Chase, who agreed to purchase the patent rights for $5,000 in cash and 200 shares of $100 par value preferred stock in a corporation to be formed.

The corporation was formed and Sayre's stock issued to him in 1962 but the corporation has refused to be bound by the agreement for the cash payment. It has refused to declare dividends, although the business has been very profitable due to the value of Sayre's patent, and has a sub- stantial earned surplus with a large cash balance on hand. It is selling the remainder of the origi- nally authorized issue of preferred shares, ignor- ing Sayre's demand to purchase a proportionate share of the stock so sold. What are Sayre's rights, if any?

CHAPTER 38

TRANSFER OF SHARES

Introductory. A share of corporate stock, like the corporation itself, is intangible, invisible, and incorporeal. Although it exists independently of a certificate, the shareholder has a right to have his stock evidenced by a stock certificate. He has the further right to transfer such stock just as he has the inherent right to transfer any other property he may own. He may transfer by way of sale, gift, or pledge the legal title to a specific number of shares by delivering possession of the certificate which is either indorsed or accompanied by an executed stock power. The right to transfer shares of stock is a valuable one, and the ease with which it may be done adds to their value and marketability. The availability of a ready market for any stock affords liquidity and makes the stock attractive to investors and useful as collateral.

In the absence of a statutory provision, by-law, or agreement, a corporation has no lien upon outstanding shares of its stock to secure a debt due to the corporation from the stockholder. Where authorized by statute, a by-law provision requiring a shareholder to offer his stock to the corporation before selling it to someone else will be upheld. However, no lien in favor of the corporation or any restriction upon the transfer of shares of stock, even where authorized, is effective unless "noted conspicuously" upon the certificate as provided in Section 8–103 of the Uniform Commercial Code.

The statutory rules applicable to transfers of shares of stock are contained in the Code, Article 8—Investment Securities.

Article 8 of the Code applies not only to certificates of stock but also to bonds, debentures, voting trust certificates, certificates of beneficial interest in business trusts, and any other instrument of a "class or series", in "bearer or registered form", and "issued or dealt in as a medium for investment", which "evidences a share, participation or other interest in property or in an enterprise or evidences an obligation of the issuer." Section 8–102. A certificate of stock is within the definition of a "security" in Section 8–102.

Manner of Transfer. At common law, a share of stock, as in the case of other items of personal property, could be sold and title transferred by a bill of sale or by sufficient evidence of an intention to effect a transfer, without delivery of the certificate.

Under the Code, a transfer of shares of stock is made by delivery of the certificate alone if it is in bearer form or indorsed in blank or, if in registered form, which is more usual, by delivery of the certificate with either (1) the indorsement thereof by "an appropriate person", or (2) a separate document of assignment and transfer, usually called a stock power, signed by "an appropriate person". The term "appropriate person", as defined in Section 8–308, includes the person specified in the certificate or entitled to it by special indorsement, their successors in interest, or the authorized agent of a person so specified or entitled.

The purpose and effect of a requirement that a transfer of shares must be made on the books of the corporation or by a registrar or transfer agent is to enable a corporation to be currently informed as to the identity of its shareholders. The corporation is therefore protected, in the absence of actual knowledge of an unrecorded transfer, in according only to shareholders of record the right (1) to vote, (2) to receive dividends, (3) to receive notices of shareholders' meetings and annual reports or periodic statements of earnings and financial condition, and (4) to participate in the assets upon dissolution. However, legal title to shares of stock passes to the transferee upon delivery of the properly indorsed certificate independently of any registration on books of record. The certificate is regarded as representative of the shares, and a transfer on the books is analogous to recording a deed of conveyance of real estate in that it merely serves to memorialize an already accomplished fact.

Section 8–207 of the Code provides:

(1) Prior to due presentment for registration of transfer of a security in registered form the issuer or indenture trustee may treat the registered owner as the person exclusively entitled to vote, to receive notifications and otherwise to exercise all the rights and powers of an owner.

(2) Nothing in this Article shall be construed to affect the liability of the registered owner of a security for calls, assessments or the like.

The delivery of an unindorsed certificate by the owner with the intention of transferring title thereto gives the intended transferee as against the transferor complete rights in the certificate and in the shares represented thereby, including the right to compel indorsement. He becomes a bona fide purchaser of the shares, however, only as of the time the indorsement is supplied. The person making such a transfer is under a duty, in the absence of an agreement to the contrary, to indorse the certificate and thereby complete the transfer. Having parted with possession of the certificate, he is powerless to effect a transfer of legal title to the shares to any other person. This duty to make an indorsement upon the certificate may be specifically enforced in a court of equity. Section 8–307.

Negotiability of Stock Certificate. Shares of corporate stock, like commercial paper, are extensively traded and have acquired through development of the common law of estoppel certain attributes of negotiability. The Supreme Court of the United States, in First National Bank of South Bend v. Lanier, 11 Wall. 369, 377, 20 L.Ed. 172 (1871), observed:

"It is no less the interest of the shareholder, than the public, that the certificate representing his stock should be in a form to secure public confidence, for without this he could not negotiate it to any advantage. It is in obedience to this requirement that stock certificates of all kinds have been constructed in a way to invite the confidence of business men, so that they have become the basis of commercial transactions in all the large cities of the country, and are sold in open market the same as other securities. Although neither in form or character negotiable paper, they approximate it as nearly as practicable."

Section 8–105(1) of the Code goes all the way. It provides: "Securities governed by this Article are negotiable instruments."

Negotiation of a stock certificate is accomplished by delivery of the certificate properly indorsed or accompanied by a properly signed stock power. The effect of negotiation is to enable the transferee to take title to the shares of stock free of adverse claims.

Unlike commercial paper, the indorser of a stock certificate assumes no obligation other than the warranties of a transferor. Sections 8–308(4), and 8–306(2).

The Code defines a "purchase" as taking by "sale, discount, negotiation, mortgage, pledge, lien, issue or re-issue, gift or any other voluntary transaction creating an interest in property." Section 1–201(32).

A "purchaser" is defined as "a person who takes by purchase." Section 1–201(33).

The Code defines a bona fide purchaser in Section 8–302:

A "bona fide purchaser" is a purchaser for value in good faith and without notice of any adverse claim who takes delivery of a security in bearer form or of one in registered form issued to him or indorsed to him or in blank.

Bearing these definitions in mind, the negotiation or transfer of a certificate of stock to a bona fide purchaser creates title in the transferee free of all adverse claims. The bona fide purchaser from a thief, finder, or other unauthorized person, is protected.

Section 8–301 of the Code provides:

(1) Upon delivery of a security the purchaser acquires the rights in the security which his transferor had or had actual authority to convey except that a purchaser who has himself been a party to any fraud or illegality affecting the security or who as a prior holder had notice of an adverse claim cannot improve his position by taking from a later bona fide purchaser. "Adverse claim" includes a claim that a transfer was or would be wrongful or that a particular adverse person is the owner of or has an interest in the security.

(2) A bona fide purchaser in addition to acquiring the rights of a purchaser also acquires the security free of any adverse claim.

(3) A purchaser of a limited interest acquires rights only to the extent of the interest purchased.

Section 8–304 of the Code provides:

(1) A purchaser (including a broker for the seller or buyer but excluding an intermediary bank) of a security is charged with notice of adverse claims if

(a) the security whether in bearer or registered form has been indorsed "for collection" or "for surrender" or for some other purpose not involving transfer; or

(b) the security is in bearer form and has on it an unambiguous statement that it is the property of a person other than the transferor. The mere writing of a name on a security is not such a statement.

(2) The fact that the purchaser (including a broker for the seller or buyer) has notice that the security is held for a third person or is registered in the name of or indorsed by a fiduciary does not create a duty of inquiry into the rightfulness of the transfer or constitute notice of adverse claims. If, however, the purchaser (excluding an intermediary bank) has knowledge that the proceeds are being used or that the transaction is for the individual benefit of the fiduciary or otherwise in breach of duty, the purchaser is charged with notice of adverse claims.

The Code has specific rules on delivery of a stock certificate in Section 8–313:

(1) Delivery to a purchaser occurs when

(a) he or a person designated by him acquires possession of a security; or

(b) his broker acquires possession of a security specially indorsed to or issued in the name of the purchaser; or

(c) his broker sends him confirmation of the purchase and also by book entry or otherwise identifies a specific security in the broker's possession as belonging to the purchaser; or

(d) with respect to an identified security to be delivered while still in the possession of a third person when that person acknowledges that he holds for the purchaser.

(2) Except as specified in subparagraphs (b) and (c) of subsection (1) the purchaser is not the holder of securities held for him by his broker despite a confirmation of purchase and a book entry and other indication that the security is part of a fungible bulk held for customers and despite the customer's acquisition of a proportionate property interest in the fungible bulk.

Forged or Unauthorized Signature on Issue of Stock. If the face of a certificate of stock bears the forged signature of an officer of the issuing corporation, it is spurious and does not represent shares of stock in the corporation. However, the unauthorized signature of the president or other employee of the issuer or of the registrar or transfer agent, while ineffective generally, is effective in favor of a bona fide purchaser for value and without notice of the lack of authority of the party signing the certificate. Section 8–205 provides:

> An unauthorized signature placed on a security prior to or in the course of issue is ineffective except that the signature is effective in favor of a purchaser for value and without notice of the lack of authority if the signing has been done by
>
>> (a) an authenticating trustee, registrar, transfer agent or other person entrusted by the issuer with the signing of the security or of similar securities or their immediate preparation for signing; or
>>
>> (b) an employee of the issuer or of any of the foregoing entrusted with responsible handling of the security.

The signature of an authenticating trustee, registrar, or transfer agent, carries certain warranties as provided in Section 8–208:

> (1) A person placing his signature upon a security as authenticating trustee, registrar, transfer agent or the like warrants to a purchaser for value without notice of the particular defect that
>
>> (a) the security is genuine and in proper form; and
>>
>> (b) his own participation in the issue of the security is within his capacity and within the scope of the authorization received by him from the issuer; and
>>
>> (c) he has reasonable grounds to believe that the security is within the amount the issuer is authorized to issue.
>
> (2) Unless otherwise agreed, a person by so placing his signature does not assume responsibility for the validity of the security in other respects.

Forged or Unauthorized Indorsement. The owner of shares of stock represented by a certificate is not deprived of his title by a transfer of the certificate bearing a forged or unauthorized indorsement.

An innocent purchaser of a certificate of stock bearing a forged indorsement who re-

sells and transfers the certificate to a bona fide purchaser is liable to such purchaser for the value of the stock by reason of the implied warranty that the seller has the legal right to transfer it. In this situation neither party has a legal right to the shares represented by the certificate, as title cannot be transferred through a forged indorsement.

Although the buyer of a certificate bearing a forged indorsement does not acquire title to shares of stock, he has a cause of action against the seller for breach of warranty. Section 8–306(2) provides:

> A person by transferring a security to a purchaser for value warrants only that
>
>> (a) his transfer is effective and rightful; and
>>
>> (b) the security is genuine and has not been materially altered; and
>>
>> (c) he knows no fact which might impair the validity of the security.

For this reason, where a certificate of stock is in "street name," that is, in the name of some person frequently unknown to either seller or buyer and not necessarily intended to have any interest in the stock, and indorsed by such person in blank, it is important both to the seller and the buyer that the indorsement be the authentic or genuine signature of the person in whose name the stock was issued. It is common if not universal practice, particularly when the stock is in "street name," to have the signature of the indorser guaranteed by some reputable bank or trust company.

Warranties. The person who guarantees the signature of an indorser on a certificate of stock also assumes certain warranty obligations. Section 8–312 provides:

> (1) Any person guaranteeing a signature of an indorser of a security warrants that at the time of signing
>
>> (a) the signature was genuine; and
>>
>> (b) the signer was an appropriate person to indorse (Section 8–308); and

(c) the signer had legal capacity to sign. But the guarantor does not otherwise warrant the rightfulness of the particular transfer.

(2) Any person may guarantee an indorsement of a security and by so doing warrants not only the signature (subsection 1) but also the rightfulness of the particular transfer in all respects. But no issuer may require a guarantee of indorsement as a condition to registration of transfer.

(3) The foregoing warranties are made to any person taking or dealing with the security in reliance on the guarantee and the guarantor is liable to such person for any loss resulting from breach of the warranties.

There is a significant difference between guaranteeing the signature of an indorser and guaranteeing the indorsement of the stock certificate. The guarantor of the signature of an indorser merely certifies that the signature is genuine and does not warrant that the particular transfer is rightful. On the other hand, the guarantor of an indorsement not only warrants that the signature of the indorser is genuine but also that the particular transfer is rightful in all respects.

The issuing corporation or transfer agent may require a guarantee of the signature of the indorser before issuing a new stock certificate. Section 8–402(1) (a). However, the issuer may not require a guarantee of indorsement before issuance of a new certificate representing the shares being transferred. Section 8–312(2).

The Code fully protects a bona fide purchaser for value of shares represented by a certificate bearing a forged or unauthorized indorsement who in good faith receives in exchange for it a new or re-registered certificate from the issuer on registration of transfer. Prior to such re-registration the bona fide purchaser is not protected. The issuer is of course liable for the improper registration.

Section 8–311 of the Code provides:

Unless the owner has ratified an unauthorized indorsement or is otherwise precluded from asserting its ineffectiveness

(a) he may assert its ineffectiveness against the issuer or any purchaser other than a purchaser for value and without notice of adverse claims who has in good faith received a new, reissued or re-registered security on registration of transfer; and

(b) an issuer who registers the transfer of a security upon the unauthorized indorsement is subject to liability for improper registration (Section 8–404).

Section 8–306(1) provides:

A person who presents a security for registration of transfer or for payment or exchange warrants to the issuer that he is entitled to the registration, payment or exchange. But a purchaser for value without notice of adverse claims who receives a new, reissued or re-registered security on registration of transfer warrants only that he has no knowledge of any unauthorized signature (Section 8–311) in a necessary indorsement.

Example: A loses by theft or otherwise his unindorsed certificate of stock. X, a thief or finder, forges A's signature on the reverse side of the certificate or signs A's name by X, his agent, when such authority to sign as agent is lacking. X thereafter sells and delivers the certificate to B, a bona fide transferee who pays value and takes the certificate without knowledge of the theft or loss or of the forged or unauthorized indorsement. A is still the owner of the shares, and B is liable to A for their value. If B surrenders the certificate to the issuing corporation which recognizes B as the owner, cancels the certificate, and issues a new one in B's name, under the Code (Section 8–311) B is now the owner of the shares represented by the new certificate registered in his name. A has a right against the corporation to receive a new certificate for the same number of shares. Section 8–404(2). If the corporation is unable to acquire such shares by purchase, and has all of its authorized shares outstanding so that any newly issued shares would be illegal as an overissue of stock, Section 8–104 applies:

> (1) The provisions of this Article which validate a security or compel its issue or reissue do not apply to the extent that validation, issue or reissue would result in overissue; but
>
>> (a) if an identical security which does not constitute an overissue is reasonably available for purchase, the person entitled to issue or validation may compel the issuer to purchase and deliver such a security to him against surrender of the security, if any, which he holds; or
>>
>> (b) if a security is not so available for purchase, the person entitled to issue or validation may recover from the issuer the price he or the last purchaser for value paid for it with interest from the date of his demand.
>
> (2) "Overissue" means the issue of securities in excess of the amount which the issuer has corporate power to issue.

The rights of the owner of shares against a purchaser based upon a wrongful transfer of the stock are set forth in Section 8–315:

> (1) Any person against whom the transfer of a security is wrongful for any reason, including his incapacity, may against anyone except a bona fide purchaser reclaim possession of the security or obtain possession of any new security evidencing all or part of the same rights or have damages.
>
> (2) If the transfer is wrongful because of an unauthorized indorsement, the owner may also reclaim or obtain possession of the security or new security even from a bona fide purchaser if the ineffectiveness of the purported indorsement can be asserted against him under the provisions of this Article on unauthorized indorsements (Section 8–311).
>
> (3) The right to obtain or reclaim possession of a security may be specifically en-

forced and its transfer enjoined and the security impounded pending the litigation.

Duty of Issuer to Register Transfer of Stock. The issuing corporation is under a firm duty to register transfers of stock and to issue new certificates representing the shares to the new owner or purchaser. The owner or purchaser is entitled to be registered in order to vote, receive dividends, and notices. He is entitled to a new certificate because the only way that he can sell or pledge or dispose of the shares is by a transfer of the certificate which represents them.

Section 8–401 of the Code provides:

> (1) Where a security in registered form is presented to the issuer with a request to register transfer, the issuer is under a duty to register the transfer as requested if
>
>> (a) the security is indorsed by the appropriate person or persons (Section 8–308); and
>>
>> (b) reasonable assurance is given that those indorsements are genuine and effective (Section 8–402); and
>>
>> (c) the issuer has no duty to inquire into adverse claims or has discharged any such duty (Section 8–403); and
>>
>> (d) any applicable law relating to the collection of taxes has been complied with; and
>>
>> (e) the transfer is in fact rightful or is to a bona fide purchaser.
>
> (2) Where an issuer is under a duty to register a transfer of a security the issuer is also liable to the person presenting it for registration or his principal for loss resulting from any unreasonable delay in registration or from failure or refusal to register the transfer.

If the issuer, when a certificate of stock is presented to it for register of transfer, has written notice of an adverse claim to the shares, it is under a duty of inquiry. Section 8–403 provides that the issuer may discharge this duty by notice to the adverse claimant by registered or certified mail that the transfer will be registered within 30 days unless such claimant (1) obtains an injunction or court order restraining the transfer, or (2) provides the issuer with an indemnity bond sufficient to protect it from any loss it may suffer by complying with the adverse claim.

Sale of Stock Through Broker. Most transactions in shares of stock are made through licensed brokers and on stock exchanges. Section 8–314 of the Code provides:

> (1) Unless otherwise agreed where a sale of a security is made on an exchange or otherwise through brokers
>
>> (a) the selling customer fulfills his duty to deliver when he places such a security in the possession of the selling broker or of a person designated by the broker or if requested caused an acknowledgment to be made to the selling broker that it is held for him; and
>>
>> (b) the selling broker including a correspondent broker acting for a selling customer fulfills his duty to deliver by placing the security or a like security in the possession of the buying broker or a person designated by him or by effecting clearance of the sale in accordance with the rules of the exchange on which the transaction took place.
>
> (2) Except as otherwise provided in this Section and unless otherwise agreed, a transferor's duty to deliver a security under a contract of purchase is not fulfilled until he places the security in form to be negotiated by the purchaser in the possession of the purchaser or of a person designated by him or at the purchaser's request causes an acknowledgment to be made to the purchaser that it is held for him. Unless made on an exchange a sale to a broker purchasing for his own account is within this subsection and not within subsection (1).

Section 8–306(5) of the Code provides:

> A broker gives to his customer and to the issuer and a purchaser the warranties provided in this section and has the rights and privileges of a purchaser under this section. The warranties of and in favor of the broker acting as an agent are in addition to applicable warranties given by and in favor of his customer.

Broker Not Liable in Conversion by Good Faith Delivery. At common law a securities broker who receives from a customer certificates of stock bearing a forged or unauthorized indorsement and sells them for the customer's account is liable to the owner for conversion of the stock.

This rule is changed by the Code which provides that an agent or bailee who in good faith, including the observance of reasonable commercial standards if he is a broker, has received securities and sells, pledges, or delivers them according to the instructions of his principal, is not liable for conversion as for participation in breach of fiduciary duty although the principal had no right to dispose of them. Section 8–318.

Lost, Destroyed, or Stolen Certificates. Where a certificate of stock has been lost, apparently destroyed, or wrongfully taken, the shareholder is entitled to a new certificate to replace the missing one provided he (1) requests it before the issuer has notice that the "missing" certificate has been acquired by a bona fide purchaser, and (2) files with the issuer a sufficient indemnity bond, and (3) satisfies other reasonable requirements of the issuer such as furnishing a sworn statement of the facts in connection with the loss. Section 8–405(2).

If the owner fails to notify the issuer of the loss of the certificate within a reasonable time after learning of it, he is precluded from asserting a claim against the issuer and from claiming a new certificate to replace the lost one. Section 8–405(1).

Attachment of Stock. At common law, a share of stock was not subject to attachment or levy at the instance of a creditor of the shareholder since it was intangible and similar in this respect to a chose in action. The creditor's remedy was by way of garnishment proceedings against the corporation or by filing a creditor's bill in equity. In most jurisdictions if, at the time of the garnishment or institution of the equity suit, the stock had been previously transferred but the transfer not recorded on the books of the corporation, the transferee was allowed to prevail over the creditor. However, where it was provided that a valid transfer could be effected only by registry of the new ownership on the books of the corporation, certain jurisdictions held that the creditor in the garnishment action had priority over the transferee.

Under Section 8–317 of the Code, no attachment or levy may be made upon shares of stock except by the actual seizure of the outstanding certificate by the officer making the attachment or levy. Section 8–317 provides:

> (1) No attachment or levy upon a security or any share or other interest evidenced thereby which is outstanding shall be valid until the security is actually seized by the officer making the attachment or levy but a security which has been surrendered to the issuer may be attached or levied upon at the source

> (2) A creditor whose debtor is the owner of a security shall be entitled to such aid from courts of appropriate jurisdiction, by injunction or otherwise, in reaching such security or in satisfying the claim by means thereof as is allowed at law or in equity in regard to property which cannot readily be attached or levied upon by ordinary legal process.

The procedure by a creditor's bill in equity available to the judgment creditor of a shareholder who has been unable to obtain physical possession of the debtor's stock certificate is discussed in the case of Parkhurst v. Almy, page 898.

CASES

TURNBULL v. LONGACRE BANK

(1928) 249 N.Y. 159, 163 N.E. 135.

LEHMAN, J. The plaintiffs are stockbrokers and dealers in securities. In the course of their business they deliver securities to other brokers within the city of New York. On the 11th day of November, 1924, the plaintiffs telephoned to the Wall Street Messenger Co. to send a messenger to the plaintiff's office, for the purpose of delivering securities to certain other brokers. When the messenger came to the plaintiffs' office, he was handed certificates of corporate securities of the Freed-Eiseman Radio Corporation, the Lehigh Valley Coal Company, and the Standard Oil Company (Indiana), with instructions to deliver them to other brokers. All the certificates were indorsed in blank and transferable by delivery. The messenger stole the certificates.

The stolen certificates came into the possession of the defendant Brinkman. By him, they were used as collateral security for a loan of $13,000, which he obtained from the defendant Longacre Bank on the 17th day of November, 1924. The loan was renewed by the bank, but has never been paid. In making and renewing the loan, the bank acted without negligence, honestly, and in good faith.

The plaintiffs upon discovery of the theft gave notice thereof to the corporations which had issued the certificates. Beginning on January 6, 1925, the plaintiffs published in the New York Times a notice of the theft one day in each week for five successive weeks. Thereafter the corporations issued new certificates to the plaintiffs upon the application of the plaintiffs and upon receipt of indemnity bonds issued by the National Surety Company of New York.

Thereafter the plaintiffs learned that the stolen securities were in the possession of the Longacre Bank. Then they brought this action.

The prayer of the complaint is that the defendant Longacre Bank be restrained from transferring, selling, or assigning the securities, or from seeking in any manner to have the said securities transferred, upon the books of the corporations which issued the securities. Incidental to this relief, the plaintiffs ask that these corporations be restrained from transferring the securities upon their books, and that the Longacre Bank be directed to deliver the securities to the plaintiffs for the purpose of canceling the same upon the books of the said corporations. The foreign corporations appeared voluntarily in the action, and a restraining order was issued pendente lite as prayed for in the complaint. * * *

It is unnecessary for us to decide whether at common law the defendant bank might retain the stolen certificates as pledgee. Elements of negotiability of certificates of corporate stock, lacking at common law, have been supplied by article 6 of the Personal Property Law (Consol.Laws, c. 41) the Uniform Stock Transfer Act. Title to a certificate may be transferred by delivery of the certificate indorsed in blank (section 162). It is provided by section 166 that—

"The delivery of a certificate to transfer title in accordance with the provisions of section one hundred and sixty-two is effectual, except as provided in section one hundred and sixty-eight, though made by one having no right of possession and having no authority from the owner of the certificate or from the person purporting to transfer the title."

Section 168 provides that—

"If the delivery of a certificate was made (c) without authority from the owner, * * the possession of the certificate may be reclaimed and the transfer thereof rescinded, unless: (1) The certificate has been transferred to a purchaser for value in good faith without notice of any facts making the transfer wrongful. * * *"

Here the evidence and findings establish that the Longacre Bank is a purchaser for value and without notice of any facts making the transfer wrongful. It is evident that under the provisions of the Personal Property Law the possession of an innocent purchaser for value of certificates of stock indorsed in blank is fully protected. In that respect, though delivery was made by one who, being a thief, had himself neither right of possession nor authority to transfer title, such certificate possesses the attributes of negotiable instruments. The bank has acquired title to the certificates as pledgee. The plaintiffs may reclaim the certificates only by payment of the debt for which they are security. * * *

From the time that the bank filed its answer, these corporations knew that the bank claimed title to the certificates issued by it as a purchaser for value, and, except as restrained by order of the court, demanded transfer of the certificates upon the corporate books and payment of dividends which had accrued or might thereafter accrue. Ordinarily, a corporation may continue to pay dividends to the person registered on its books as the owner of the stock. Personal Property Law, Sec. 164. It may not do so after a transferee from the registered owner has not only given notice of such transfer but has demanded that new certificates be issued to him. The rights of the actual owner of the stock to dividends are not altered by the injunction which precluded such a demand for a change on the corporate registry of stock ownership. The purpose of the injunction pendente lite was to maintain the existing status until the courts might pass upon the disputed ownership of the stock. The corporations were not compelled because of the injunction to continue to pay dividends to the plaintiffs after they had notice, not only of the claim of the bank, but also of the fact that litigation was then pending to determine the validity of that claim. The bank is therefore entitled to dividends payable on its securities after the answer containing its counterclaim was served on the corporations which issued the certificates.

We think that the Appellate Division went too far in also allowing the bank to recover dividends payable on the securities from the date that the corporations received notice of the loss or theft of the securities. Notice of loss or theft is not notice that the securities were transferred wrongfully to an innocent purchaser for value. Until the corporations received notice that an innocent purchaser had obtained good title against the original owner, and that such purchaser claimed from the corporations the right to dividends, which is incidental to ownership of the corporate stock, the corporations might continue to recognize the exclusive right of the person registered on its books as the owner of shares to receive dividends. [Citation.]

[Judgment for defendant bank modified by limiting the award of dividends to the period beginning with the date of the service of the bank's answer upon the plaintiffs.]

MILLER v. SILVERMAN

(1928) 247 N.Y. 447, 160 N.E. 910.

KELLOGG, J. This action, in replevin, was brought to recover the possession of certain securities which were in the possession of Edward A. New at the time of his death. The plaintiff, in her complaint, made no allegation as to the facts constituting her acquisition of title. She was content to assert that she was, at all the times mentioned in the complaint, and now is, the owner of the securities and entitled to the possession thereof. This allegation was denied by the defendant. On the trial, at the conclusion of the evidence, each side moved for the direction of a verdict. The trial judge directed a verdict for the plaintiff. The Appellate Division reversed and dismissed the action.

The securities were found, after the death of Edward A. New, in a safe deposit box in the vaults of a certain safe deposit company. An envelope containing certificates of stock in various corporations, issued to Edward A. New, was discovered in the box. Upon the outside of the envelope there had been written by New the words: "All in envelope belong to Anna C. Miller." Anna C. Miller is the plaintiff. Within the envelope there was a slip of paper upon which New had written: "Whatever is in this envelope belongs to Miss Anna C. Miller." There were also two packages of bonds in the safe deposit box. One contained bonds of the Baltimore & Ohio Railroad Company, payable to bearer. Attached thereto was a slip bearing words, written by New, reading: "These bonds of B. & O. belong to Anna C. Miller. Edw. A. New." The other package contained bonds of the Tennessee Electric Power Company, payable to bearer. Attached was a slip bearing the words, in New's handwriting: "These bonds Tenn. Elect. belong to Anna C. Miller. Edw. A. New."

The safe deposit box had been rented by Edward A. New in November, 1925. Prior to that time the plaintiff, Anna C. Miller, had a deposit box in the same safe deposit company. Frequently she and New had visited the vaults of the company; had removed the plaintiff's box; had retired to a booth to open it; had handled the securities therein contained. After New had leased a box for himself, the two had pursued the same course of action in reference to that box and the securities in question which were contained therein.

In Govin v. De Miranda, 140 N.Y. 474, 35 N.E. 626, there was considered the case of a testator who left certain bonds in an envelope upon which there appeared a declaration by him that they belonged to the plaintiffs in the action. The court held that the ownership of the plaintiffs had been proven thereby. It said:

"We must infer from the language that they came to the ownership of the plaintiffs in some legal way—by purchase or gift from some one; and if there was nothing else in the paper qualifying the declaration no one would dispute that it furnished absolute evidence of their ownership of the bonds."

In our case, as in the Govin Case, the plaintiff is contending, not that the memoranda were in themselves sufficient instruments of transfer, but that they constituted evidence that all acts, necessary to the vesting of title in her, had been performed. There can be no doubt of the correctness of the contention. If other evidence indicated that Edward A. New had originally owned the securities, then the memoranda proved all the facts of a lawful transfer. If a transfer by gift was indicated, then they evidenced delivery as well as intention to give. The certificates of stock, which were issued in the name of New, although unindorsed by him, as well as the bonds, which were payable to bearer, were susceptible of transfer by a manual delivery with intention to give. [Citations.] Moreover, there was ample opportunity to make the gift when the plaintiff and New made their visits to the vaults of the safe deposit company and jointly handled the securities in question. In Gallagher v. Brewster, 153 N.Y. 364, 47 N.E. 450, the court considered a writing wherein a testator had declared his financial obligation to the plaintiff. It said:

"But as an admission it was competent evidence, although the testator retained it in his possession. An entry or memorandum made by a deceased person against his interest, found in his books or papers, is in general admissible against his estate in favor of a party seeking to establish the fact stated. They are presumably truthful."

It may well be that in our case a trier of fact might consider that the declarations, as evidence of the plaintiff's title, were outweighed by evidence of other facts, such as the fact that the securities were purchased by New, the fact that dividends and interest moneys upon the securities were received by New, and the fact that no other person than New possessed the key to the safe deposit box which held the securities. However this may be, the fact remains that no trier of fact, as yet, has ever so held. The Appellate Division made no findings of fact. It dismissed the action as a matter of law. We think that in the face of substantial evidence to the effect that the securities belonged to the plaintiff, the dismissal was error.

The judgment should be modified by granting a new trial, and, as modified, affirmed, with costs to abide the event.

Judgment accordingly.

IN RE DAVIS' ESTATE

(1953) 95 Ohio App. 452, 120 N.E.2d 907.

COLLIER, J. This case is in this court on an appeal on questions of law from a judgment of the Probate Court of Jackson County, sustaining exceptions to certain items contained in the inventory and appraisement of the estate of Margaret Parry Davis, deceased.

The exceptor, Frank Delay, is the administrator of the estate of E. Stanton Davis, deceased, who was the surviving spouse of Margaret Parry Davis, deceased. Margaret Parry Davis, the wife, died on March 31, 1949, and E. Stanton Davis, the husband, died on July 13, 1949. For the purpose of brevity, we shall refer to them as the husband and the wife.

The exceptor claims that certain certificates of stock of the Oak Hill Savings Bank and the Cambria Clay Products Company, a U. S. Government check dated May 11, 1949, in the sum of $61.40, and a dividend check of such bank for $10, dated July 7, 1949, are not the property of the wife's estate, but belong to the husband's estate.

The executor of the estate of the wife claims title to the certificates of stock by reason of a separate blank assignment stapled to the certificates, which were found after her death in a safe-deposit box of the Oak Hill Savings Bank. The deposit box, at the time of the wife's death, stood in her name alone. The assignments of all the certificates are in blank, except for the signatures of the husband and one Bruney, a witness thereto. The assignments do not contain the names of the corporations issuing the stock; there is no number of the certificates, no number of shares, no name of the transferee and no date when the assignments were signed by the husband. A blank form of assignment was used with none of the blank spaces filled in.

There is no evidence that the husband ever delivered the certificates to the wife with intention to transfer title to her. The only evidence explaining the assignment is the testimony of the witness, Bruney, who said that the husband signed the blank form of assignments to make the certificates negotiable. The only basis for the claim of the executor of the wife's estate to ownership is the separate blank assignment attached to the certificates, and the further fact they were found after her death in the safe-deposit box which stood in her name. The evidence shows that from September 1, 1941, until December 22, 1948, this box, number 145, was rented by the husband with right of access thereto by his wife as his deputy; that the husband had owned the stock for many years prior to the death of either of them; and that it was after the husband sustained an injury on December 22, 1948, and

was confined to his home, that the box was rerented in the name of the wife.

The one question for determination under these facts and circumstances is whether the certificates of stock belong to the estate of the wife or to the estate of the husband. Since the enactment in this state of the Uniform Stock Transfer Act in 1911, 102 Ohio Laws, 500, such certificates may be transferred only as prescribed by the provisions of the General Code. There is no exception for the transfer of stock in an Ohio corporation.

Subdivision (b) of Section 8673–1, General Code, sets forth the necessary steps to transfer such certificates by separate document, and provides:

"By delivery of the certificate and a separate document containing a written assignment of the certificate or a power of attorney to sell, assign, or transfer the same or the shares represented thereby signed by the person appearing by the certificate to be the owner of the shares represented thereby."

Two essential requirements of this statute are, first, that there must be a delivery of the certificate and, second, that there must be a separate document describing the certificate so that it may be identified, neither of which has been established in this case. A different rule applies where the assignment is written on the certificate. Section 8673–20, General Code, provides for a blank indorsement on the certificate. [Citation.]

In the case of Bolles v. Toledo Trust Co., 132 Ohio St. 21, 4 N.E.2d 917, our Supreme Court has established the quantum of proof required in a case of this kind. In that case, where the facts are very similar to the facts involved in the instant case, it is held that to place title in the wife, the transfer from the husband must be shown by clear and convincing proof. The single fact that the certificates were found in the deposit box is not sufficient to give rise to the presumption of ownership.

It follows for the same reasons that the dividend check is the property of the husband's estate. He being the owner of the stock at the time of his death, his estate is entitled to the dividends thereon.

The United States Government check in question was issued May 11, 1949, sometime after the death of the wife but while the husband was still living, in payment of an income tax refund on a joint tax return made by the husband and wife. The evidence shows that almost all income reported represented the salary of the husband. We are unable to see how the executor of the wife's estate has any legal claim to this check.

We find no substantial error in the ruling and judgment of the Probate Court, and the judgment of that court is affirmed.

Judgment affirmed.

PARKHURST v. ALMY

(1915) 222 Mass. 27, 109 N.E. 733.

[Bill in equity to reach and apply in payment of a judgment certain shares of corporate stock standing in the name of the defendant. A decree for the plaintiff was sustained, subject to modification.]

LORING, J. A corporation has no right to make an overissue of its capital stock, and a court has no power to give it a right to do so. A decree in the form set forth in the report seems to undertake to proceed upon that basis in providing that upon the issue of certificates to a special master in lieu of the certificates now standing in the name of William F. Almy "such corporations shall be discharged and released from all liability by reason of the outstanding certificates in the name of said William F. Almy," provided that plaintiffs give to each of the corporations a bond "conditioned to hold such corporations harmless from all claims of any person or corporation establishing by and

through the outstanding certificates in the name of William F. Almy a title legally and equitably paramount to the title obtained by the purchaser of the certificates sold by the special master hereunder."

If it were established that Almy was now the owner of the shares which stand on the books of the corporation in his name, and also that no one could become entitled to them hereafter, there would be no objection to the clause in the decree which provides that upon the issue of certificates to the special master in lieu of the certificates now outstanding in the name of William F. Almy, "such corporations shall be discharged and released from all liability by reason of the outstanding certificates in the name of said William F. Almy." But neither one of these two propositions is established. If the certificates for these shares have been transferred already to a bona fide purchaser for value without notice the title to the shares is in the transferee of these certificates. [Citations.] Even if title to these shares is now in Almy it would pass from him if certificates for these shares are hereafter transferred by him to a bona fide purchaser for value without notice. [Citations.]

As we construe the decree it (in effect) takes away these shares from the true owners of them (in case the certificates for them already have been or shall be hereafter transferred by Almy to a bona fide purchaser for value without notice) and it substitutes for the shares rights of action against the corporations. But that is something which the court has no power to do. A court has no power to take away from the owner his property in shares in the capital stock of a corporation and substitute for that property a right of action against the corporation. It has no more power to take away shares belonging to a bona fide purchaser of Almy's certificates on substituting therefor a right of action against the corporation (even although the right of action is made good by a bond with sufficient sureties) than it has to take away from the owner of them his property in other shares in the capital stock of a corporation. * * *

How then can a creditor of a holder of shares in the capital stock of a corporation reach and apply in satisfaction of the debt due to him the property of his debtor in shares standing in the debtor's name on the books of the corporation? If the creditor should procure certificates for an equal number of shares and should put these certificates in trust to be surrendered to the corporation in case it should turn out that the certificates standing in the debtor's name on the books of the corporation already had or thereafter should come to the hands of a bona fide transferee for value, objection to a possible overissue of its capital stock by the corporation and the objection that the ownership of shares standing in the debtor's name might not now, or (if now) might not thereafter be the property of the debtor, would be avoided.

In the ordinary case it would seem to be possible for the creditor to procure shares to be thus put in trust by borrowing from an owner the necessary number of shares in the capital stock of the corporation. If the creditor should borrow a like number of shares and should hypothecate them for the protection of the corporation and a possible purchaser of the debtor's certificates, the course of proceedings would be as follows: New certificates for the debtor's shares would be issued to the special master and the special master would then sell them, the proceeds being applied to the debt owed by the debtor to the creditor. At the sale by the special master the creditor is safe in bidding (up to the amount of the debt due him from the debtor) for the shares sold by the master, because the money paid by the creditor to the master is immediately returned by the master to the creditor. For that reason it would seem to be possible for the creditor to

procure by borrowing them the shares which have to be put in trust before the certificates are issued to the special master to protect the corporation and possible transferees without notice of the debtor's certificates. After the creditor has bought in the shares sold by the commissioner, he can return the shares bought in satisfaction of the shares borrowed. After this has been done the creditor has the proceeds of the sale of the certificates issued to the master. In addition he has the shares hypothecated for the indemnity of the corporation and the possible bona fide purchaser of the debtor's certificates subject to that hypothecation. If ultimately it turns out that no transfer to a bona fide purchaser of the debtor's certificates has taken place the shares hypothecated for the protection of the corporation and the possible bona fide transferee of the debtor's certificates belong to the creditor absolutely. The net result of the whole transaction in that event is that the creditor ultimately gets the proceeds of the sale of the debtor's shares in the corporation. If, on the other hand, there is a transfer of the debtor's certificates to a bona fide purchaser for value without notice, and the shares hypothecated for the protection of the corporation and the bona fide purchaser of the debtor's certificates are applied to that purpose, the result is that the creditor gets nothing. And in that event it is right that he should get nothing, for in that event the shares sold were not the shares of the debtor but were the shares of the transferee for value without notice of the debtor's certificates. * * *

PROBLEMS

1. Brown, in the excitement of a railroad accident, lost four stock certificates indorsed in blank which he had been carrying in a brief case. These were found by another passenger who made no attempt to ascertain or find the loser but two weeks later sold the certificates to Jones, who paid full value and had no knowledge of Brown's

loss. Did Jones become the legal owner of the certificates?

2. A has a certificate of stock in X Company reciting that he is the owner of 10 shares. He indorses the power of attorney and form of transfer on the back and puts it in his pocket. A pickpocket steals it from him and sells and delivers the certificate to B, an innocent purchaser for value. As between A and B who is shareholder in X Company?

3. X owned five shares of the Western Union Telegraph Company. On the back of each share was printed a blank form of transfer and power of attorney. X kept the certificates in his bank box. Some person gained access to the box, took the certificates, forged X's name to the transfer and to the power of attorney and obtained a transfer of the shares on the books of the company. X commenced a suit in equity against the company to compel it to replace in his name the shares and to issue to him the proper certificates for the same. Should X succeed?

4. S, borrowing money from L, pledges certificate No. 50 of the X Corporation which recites that he is the owner of 100 shares of its stock. On the back of the certificate is the usual blank form for use in case of transfer. S signs this in blank, so that if the stock is sold, the name of the transferee can be written above his signature. L sells this stock in violation of his rights, S not being in default. The purchaser supposes L to be the owner, and the certificate so signed by S is delivered to him. As between S and the purchaser, who is the owner?

5. A certificate for 100 shares of stock of General Motors Corporation was issued to Jones & Co. The certificate was misappropriated from the portfolio of Jones & Co. by X who by forged indorsement transferred and delivered it for value to Y, a bona fide purchaser. Y subsequently delivered the certificate to his stock broker, Bond & Share Co., with instructions to sell the shares represented thereby. Bond & Share Co. sold it upon the open market, remitting the proceeds of the sale to Y less the usual brokerage commission. Jones & Co. learns the facts, and brings an action in conversion against Bond & Share Co. to recover the value of the shares. What judgment?

6. What does the Uniform Commercial Code provide with respect to:

(a) A recital in a certificate of stock that the shares represented thereby shall be transferable only on the books of the corporation?

(b) The indorsement and delivery of a certificate of stock to a bona fide purchaser for value?

(c) Implied warranties on the part of a transferor for value of a certificate of stock?

(d) Attachment or levy upon shares of stock represented by an outstanding certificate?

(e) A lien in favor of a corporation upon the shares represented by a certificate of stock issued by it?

7. A by-law of Betma Corporation provides that no shareholder can sell his shares unless he first offers them for sale to the corporation or its directors. The by-law also states that this restriction shall be printed or stamped upon each stock certificate and will thereupon bind all present or future owners or holders. Betma Corporation did not comply with this latter provision. Shaw, having knowledge of the by-law restriction, purchased 20 shares of the corporation's stock from Rice, but these shares were not first offered for sale to the corporation or its directors by Shaw or Rice. When Betma Corporation refused to effectuate a transfer of the shares to him, Shaw sued to compel a transfer and the issuance of a new certificate to him.

Decision?

8. Ray, a shareholder in Swanson Company, a corporation, delivered his stock certificate indorsed in blank to Turpin, a purchaser for value. The following day, Ray died. His executor, believing that the certificate was lost, applied to the corporation for a new certificate, which was issued and the shares transferred to the executor's name on the books. The executor sold the new certificate to Upson, an innocent purchaser, delivering the certificate to him, indorsed to his name, three weeks after Ray's death. Two days later, Turpin presented the original certificate to the corporation, asking that appropriate action be taken to reflect his ownership of the shares. The request was refused.

Turpin brings an action against Swanson Company, demanding that he be adjudged the owner of the stock, that Swanson Company be required to issue a new certficate in his name, and that he be paid a dividend which had accrued since the certificate was transferred to him. Upson is not a party to the action.

(a) Decision? Give reasons.

(b) What are the rights, if any, of Upson?

CHAPTER 39

RIGHTS AND REMEDIES OF CREDITORS

Introductory. Persons who have advanced money to a corporation, who have sold to it property or services, who have unpaid salary or wages due from it, who have a right of action or have obtained a judgment against it, or who have purchased its bonds, notes or other evidences of indebtedness, are its creditors. The Government is also a creditor to the extent of unpaid taxes of any kind. The rights of creditors of a corporation do not differ substantially from the rights of creditors on an individual. A corporation is liable for breach of contract or commission of a tort and may be sued in an action at law. Upon the entry of a judgment against it, a writ of execution is issued thereon, and a levy or attachment may be made upon its property which is sold at a judicial sale and the net proceeds of the sale credited upon the judgment. Garnishment proceedings against persons who are indebted to the judgment debtor may also be used to effect collection of the judgment.

These are the ordinary remedies of an unsecured creditor. In an action against a corporation to recover a debt, the corporation may not plead usury as a defense. A corporation also does not have the advantage or benefit of any homestead or exemption laws.

A secured creditor is one whose claim against the corporation is enforceable not only against the general assets of the corporation but is also a lien upon certain specific property. The holder of a first mortgage bond not only has the contractual promise of the corporation to pay the face amount of the bond but also, as security for the performance of this promise, has a lien upon certain real estate which is prior to the claim of any other class of creditor except a claim for taxes. Likewise, a creditor who is a vendor under a conditional sales contract or who holds a chattel mortgage, equipment trust certificate, pledge of accounts receivable, bill of lading, or warehouse receipt, is also a secured creditor and, with respect to the corporation and all of its other creditors, enjoys the prior right to have his claim first satisfied out of the specific property to which his lien or security attaches. The secured creditor in order to have priority over claims of third persons must perfect his security interest as provided in Article 9 of the U.C.C. See Chapter 44. Realization upon the security is usually accomplished by foreclosure, sale, or repossession of the property.

Trust Fund Doctrine. In the case of Wood v. Drummer, Fed.Case No. 17,944, 3 Mason 308 (1824), Judge Story, by way of hyperbole, stated that "the capital stock of banks is to be deemed a pledge or trust fund for the payment of the debts contracted by the bank." This language was unnecessary to the decision in the case but nevertheless has been so often repeated in subsequent opinions that it has become almost regarded as axiomatic. It is not true that the capital stock of a bank or any other corporation is a trust fund for its creditors. The assets of a corporation represented by its capital stock are owned by it completely and entirely. It does not hold legal title to its assets in trust for its creditors, as would be the situation if a trust fund existed. It is not merely an equitable or beneficial owner of its property but has, particularly while solvent, as complete a power of disposition of its assets that are not subject to mortgage or lien as does any individual who may have assets and likewise have creditors.

However, the idea that the assets of a corporation are a trust fund for its creditors has a partial validity which serves to give nourishment and continued circulation to the expression of Judge Story. In the case of an insolvent corporation, its assets are not sufficient to satisfy the claims of its creditors and there is no equity or value in these assets for the shareholders. The officers and directors, who are responsible to the shareholders, are therefore managing property in which the shareholders have no interest. The equitable owners of the enterprise are not the shareholders but the creditors. A transfer of assets of the corporation for inadequate consideration in this situation would hinder and defeat the claims of creditors and amount to a fraudulent conveyance. A payment made by an insolvent corporation to one of its creditors is an unlawful preference and voidable if made within four months prior to the filing of a petition in bankruptcy by or against the corporation. In the event of bankruptcy or receivership, the assets of a corporation constitute a trust estate administered under court auspices primarily for the benefit of creditors and, if the corporation is not insolvent, for the benefit of its shareholders also. It is not inappropriate to refer to the assets of an insolvent corporation or assets in the hands of a court trustee or receiver as a trust fund.

Rights of Creditors to Participate in Management. Creditors have no standing to object to the manner in which the business of a corporation is operated. They have no voice in the management. Their only right is to have their just claims satisfied out of corporate assets. If the directors of a corporation cause it to adopt a certain policy, to undertake certain operations, or to execute a long-term lease which from the point of view of a particular creditor is disadvantageous to the corporation, the only action which the creditor may take is to restrict his line of credit, insist upon adequate security, or proceed to enforce his claim by legal action. He cannot interfere with the judgment of the board of directors, as he has no responsibility for management.

It has been held at common law that a by-law which purported to give voting rights to bondholders is void and could not even be sustained on the theory that it was a contract between the shareholders and the bondholders. By statute, however, bondholders may be given a right to vote in certain instances, but such a statute is unusual, and bondholders must comply strictly with its provisions in order to have or exercise any voting rights. The Delaware law (Section 29) permits a corporation to provide by its charter that its bondholders shall have the right to vote in respect to corporate affairs in the same manner as shareholders.

The New York Business Corporation Law (Revised to July 23, 1965) provides, Section 518(c):

> A corporation may, in its certificate of incorporation, confer upon the holders of any bonds issued or to be issued by the corporation, rights to inspect the corporate books and records and to vote in the election of directors and on any other matters on which shareholders of the corporation may vote.

Remedies of Employees. By statute in some States employees of corporations are extended rights that other creditors of the corporation do not have. Generally the rights are to recover from shareholders unpaid wages and salaries owing to them by the corporation.

The New York statute (Section 630) provides that the ten largest shareholders, as determined by the fair value of their beneficial interest in the corporation, shall be jointly and severally personally liable for all debts, wages, or salaries due and owing to any of the laborers, servants or employees other than contractors, for services performed by them for the corporation. Shareholders of corporations whose shares are listed on a national securities exchange or regularly quoted in an over-the-counter market are exempt from this liability.

Remedies of Secured Creditors. The financing of a corporation is sometimes partially accomplished by conditional sales contracts, equipment trust certificates, trust receipts, chattel mortgages, real estate mortgages, or trust indentures in the nature of a mortgage. The rights and remedies of a secured creditor are usually set forth at length in the document which creates his security. Rights and remedies in Secured Transactions under the Code are discussed in Chapter 44. The bondholders of a corporation are secured by a conveyance of legal title to certain property, usually real estate, equipment or rolling stock, to an indenture trustee pursuant to the terms of a trust indenture. Enforcement of the rights of bondholders by foreclosure is in the hands of the trustee, and a common provision in trust indentures is one which denies to an individual bondholder the right to institute foreclosure proceedings. The duties of an indenture trustee are greater in the event of default by the corporate obligor than prior to such default. Indentures securing issues of bonds in the amount of $1,000,000 or more are subject to the provisions of the Trust Indenture Act of 1939 which is administered by the Securities and Exchange Commission.

Creditors' Rights with Respect to Unpaid Stock Subscriptions. An unpaid balance due upon a stock subscription is an asset of the corporation. In the event of bankruptcy of the corporation, this asset passes to the trustee in bankruptcy, who may properly bring an action at law against the subscriber and obtain judgment for the balance due. If there is no bankruptcy, a creditor of the corporation who has exhausted his legal remedies by reducing his claim to judgment and having an execution issued thereon and returned not satisfied, may proceed by a bill in equity on behalf of himself and other creditors against those shareholders who owe a

balance upon their respective stock subscriptions. A transferee of stock is also liable for call or assessments on the stock until the par value of the stock has been fully paid, unless the certificate transferred to him recites that it is fully paid and non-assessable. The liability of the shareholders is several, not joint, and all of them who may have balances due and owing upon their respective subscriptions need not be made defendants in the creditor's bill. The corporation, however, is a necessary party to the suit.

If a shareholder who owes a balance due upon his subscription is also a creditor of the corporation, he may not, where the corporation is insolvent, set off the amount due to him from the corporation against his liability upon the unpaid stock subscription. He is required to pay the full amount due upon his stock subscription and is permitted as a creditor to share pro rata therein with other creditors. The reason for this rule is that the capital stock of a corporation is the basis of credit extended to the corporation. It would also amount to an unlawful preference to allow the claim of the shareholder as a creditor to be paid in full by permitting it to be set off against his shareholder's liability.

Likewise, a corporation may not defeat the claims of creditors by releasing subscribers from their obligations to pay a balance due upon stock subscriptions. For example: ABC Company is a corporation with $50,000 of stated capital. B and C each subscribed for $25,000 of the stock. C paid only $10,000 and promised to pay the remainder of his subscription upon call. The ABC Company subsequently released C from any and all liability upon this stock. In a creditors' bill against C, the release would be held fraudulent as to creditors and C would be liable for the remaining $15,000 due upon his subscription or so much thereof as would be needed to pay the claims of creditors of the corporation.

Creditors' Rights with Respect to Watered Stock. A corporation is said to have issued bonus or watered stock when it issues fully paid up shares upon receiving no consideration therefor or consideration worth less than the par or stated value of the shares. In the case of bonus stock where no consideration is received for the shares, or in the case of shares sold at a cash discount, it is easy to discern both the existence and extent of the water in the stock. However, when stock is issued in exchange for property or for services rendered, and the board of directors or shareholders have fixed a value for the property or services equivalent to the value of the stock, a determination that the stock is watered depends upon whether the property or services have been over-valued.

In certain jurisdictions, the courts apply the true value rule whereby the actual value of the property received by, or the services rendered to, the corporation must not be less than the par or stated value of the shares issued by the corporation in consideration therefor. In other jurisdictions where the good faith rule is followed, a more lenient standard is applied, and if the board of directors or shareholders do not act fraudulently in placing a valuation upon the consideration received by the corporation for its shares, their judgment as to such valuation is conclusive. The Model Business Corporation Act (Section 18) adopts the good faith rule.

The liability of shareholders on bonus or watered stock is enforceable by a creditor's bill in equity. At common law, persons who became creditors of the corporation before the issuance of the bonus or watered stock have no ground for complaint, as they obviously did not extend credit in reliance upon the stock being outstanding and the corporation having received full consideration therefor. Also, a creditor who participated in the issuance of bonus or watered stock, consented thereto, or who dealt with the corporation with full knowledge thereof, had no standing to maintain a suit against the persons to whom such stock was issued. The common-law rule has been changed by statutes in certain States which impose liability upon shareholders who have received bonus or watered stock without regard to any distinction between prior and subsequent creditors, or between creditors with knowledge and those without.

By the weight of authority, a corporation is bound to the terms upon which its shares have been issued and may not maintain suit against the holders of bonus or watered stock. Under this view, the liability of the shareholder is not regarded as an asset of the corporation. In the minority jurisdictions where the liability of holders of bonus or watered stock is enforceable by the issuing corporation, a trustee in bankruptcy succeeds to the right of the corporation and may enforce the liability for the benefit of the creditors. Under the majority view, which does not regard such liability as an asset of the corporation but as enforceable only at the instance of subsequent creditors who relied upon the representation that the capital stock was fully paid when in fact it was not, the trustee in bankruptcy cannot maintain suit against the holders of bonus or watered stock.

Creditors' Rights to a Receivership. Apart from the rights of bondholders or secured creditors to have a receiver appointed for property of the corporation in connection with the foreclosure of a mortgage, any creditor of a corporation may, pursuant to statute, maintain a suit in equity for the appointment of a receiver of the property of the corporation and for the purpose of having the assets and business of the corporation liquidated upon a showing that (1) the corporation has become unable to pay its debts and obligations as they mature in the regular course of its business, and (2) the creditor has reduced his claim to a judgment and has had an execution issued upon the judgment and returned unsatisfied, or the corporation has admitted in writing that the claim of the creditor is due and owing. (Section 90, Model Business Corporation Act, Appendix D.)

CASES

HOLLINS v. BRIERFIELD COAL & IRON CO.

(1893) 150 U.S. 371, 14 S.Ct. 127, 37 L.Ed. 1113.

MR. JUSTICE BREWER. * * * The plaintiffs were simple contract creditors of the company; their claims had not been reduced to judgment, and they had no express lien by mortgage, trust deed, or otherwise. It is the settled law of this court that such creditors cannot come into a court of equity to obtain the seizure of the property of their debtor, and its application to the satisfaction of their claims; and this, notwithstanding a statute of the State may authorize such a proceeding in the courts of the State. The line of demarcation between equitable and legal remedies in the Federal courts cannot be obliterated by state legislation. [Citations.] Nor is it otherwise in case the debtor is a corporation, and an unpaid stock subscription is sought to be reached. [Citations.] Nor is this rule changed by the fact that the suit is brought in a court in which at the time is pending another suit for the foreclosure of a mortgage or trust deed upon the property of the debtor. Doubtless in such foreclosure suit the simple contract creditor can intervene, and if he has any equities in respect to the property, whether prior or subsequent to those of the plaintiff, can secure their determination and protection; and here, by the express language of the bill filed by the trustee, all claimants and creditors were invited to present their claims and have them adjudicated. These plaintiffs did not intervene,

though, as shown by the allegations of their bill, they knew of the existence of the foreclosure suit; neither did they apply for a consolidation of the two suits. On the contrary, the whole drift and scope of their suit was adverse to that brought by the trustee, and in antagonism to the rights claimed by him. They obviously intended to keep away from that suit, and maintain, if possible an independent proceeding to have the property of the debtor applied to the satisfaction of their claims. But this, as has been decided in the cases cited, cannot be done. * * *

In the case of Hawkins v. Glenn, 131 U.S. 319, 332, 9 S.Ct. 739, 33 L.Ed. 184, which was an action brought by the trustee of a corporation against certain of its stockholders to recover unpaid subscriptions, and in which the defence of the statute of limitations was pleaded, Chief Justice Fuller referred to this matter in these words: "Unpaid subscriptions are assets, but have frequently been treated by courts of equity as if impressed with a trust sub modo, upon the view that, the corporation being insolvent, the existence of creditors subjects these liabilities to the rules applicable to funds to be accounted for as held in trust, and that, therefore, statutes of limitation do not commence to run in respect to them until the retention of the money has become adverse by a refusal to pay upon due requisition."

These cases negative the idea of any direct trust or lien attaching to the property of a corporation in favor of its creditors, and at the same time are entirely consistent with those cases in which the assets of a corporation are spoken of as a trust fund, using the term in the sense that we have said it was used.

The same idea of equitable lien and trust exists to some extent in the case of partnership property. Whenever, a partnership becoming insolvent, a court of equity takes possession of its property, it recognizes the fact that in equity the partnership creditors have a right to payment out of those funds in preference to individual creditors, as well as superior to any claims of the partners themselves. And the partnership property is, therefore, sometimes said, not inaptly, to be held in trust for the partnership creditors, or, that they have an equitable lien on such property. Yet, all that is meant by such expressions is the existence of an equitable right which will be enforced whenever a court of equity, at the instance of a proper party and in a proper proceeding, has taken possession of the assets. It is never understood that there is a specific lien, or a direct trust. * *

[Suit dismissed.]

RHODE v. DOCK–HOP CO.

(1920) 184 Cal. 367, 194 P. 11.

OLNEY, J. This is an action by the judgment creditor of a corporation against certain of its stockholders, seeking to collect from them what are claimed to be unpaid balances on the par value of their shares. The plaintiff had judgment, and the defendants appeal.

No contention is made that the plaintiff's claim against the corporation is not valid. The sole point in the case is as to whether or not the defendants are required, because of that claim, to make up any difference which may exist between what was actually paid in on their stock and its par value. Upon this point, the complaint alleged simply that the defendants were subscribers and stockholders of the corporation in amounts specified and that only 25 cents on the dollar had been paid in on the par value of their shares. The answers of the defendants, in addition to some other defenses, denied that they were either subscribers or stockholders, or that the full par value of their stock had not been paid.

* * *

It is apparent that, when one accepts partially paid stock, which does not purport to be anything else, he does so, or must be taken to do so, upon the understanding that it is answerable upon call for the unpaid balance upon it, and that he as its owner must respond to such a call. When he enters into relationship with the corporation as one of its stockholders owning stock of that character, he assumes as an incident of the relationship, the obligation to respond to calls upon him for further contributions to the capital of the company until such capital is fully paid in. [Citations.]

But where a person accepts the ownership of stock which purports to be fully paid, a very different situation is presented. It cannot be said of him for a moment that he accepts the stock and enters upon the relation of stockholder to the corporation upon any understanding that his stock is liable for further calls on capital account, or that he, as an incident of his ownership and consequent relationship, assumes any such obligation. On the contrary, it is evident that he accepts the ownership of the stock and enters upon the relationship of stockholder with just the contrary understanding. What then, is the principle upon which the holder of watered stock is, under any circumstances, obligated to supply substance instead of water, to make good what it is pretended the corporation received but did not? The answer to this question is not in doubt. The stockholder is held upon the principle that one giving credit to a corporation is entitled to rely upon its ostensible capitalization as the basis for the credit given, and that, when the corporation issues watered stock and thereby assumes an ostensible capitalization in excess of its real assets, the transaction necessarily involves the misleading of subsequent creditors, and, whether done with that purpose actually in mind or not, is at least a constructive fraud upon such creditors. In other words the essence of the right of the creditor to brush aside the issuance of the stock as fully paid, and to show that it was not such and to compel the payment of the balance upon it, is that its issuance as fully paid was as to him a fraud. This is now the view generally accepted in this country. [Citation.]

It must be taken, then, that the right of a creditor of a corporation, which knowingly issued shares as fully paid when they are not, to compel payment on them in full, proceeds upon the ground of fraud. This ground is entirely different from the ground upon which proceeds his right in the case of shares only partially paid up and issued as such, and it follows that a recovery may be had in the latter case, when it cannot be in the former. In the case of partially paid shares issued as such, the stockholder does so, as we have said, upon the condition that his shares are subject to call for the unpaid balance upon them, and that he, as their owner, will respond to such call. This obligation is an asset of the corporation which it may enforce, and which, if it does not itself do so, its unpaid creditors may themselves enforce if it be necessary for the full discharge of their debt. It makes no difference, therefore, in such a case, whether any particular stockholder against whom a recovery is sought was a party to the original transaction whereby the stock was issued or is only a transferee of some such party. He is liable simply as the owner of the stock and because of the relationship with the corporation which he voluntarily assumed when he accepted such ownership.

Such, however, is not the situation of the stockholder owning shares ostensibly fully paid but not so in fact. He owes the corporation no duty to make good the difference, and there is no obligation on his part which is an asset of the corporation or which the corporation may enforce. [Citation.] He is liable only because of the original transaction whereby the stock was issued for a fictitious consideration, and then only to those

who were defrauded thereby. His liability, in other words, is not based upon his relationship to the corporation as a stockholder but upon a fraudulent transaction. Upon the plainest principles, therefore, he cannot be held liable unless he was either a party to the transaction in the first instance or has in effect in some manner made himself a party since. It is not sufficient to justify a recovery against him that it be pleaded, proven, and found only that he be a stockholder owning watered stock. Upon those facts alone the full elements necessary to make a cause of action against him do not appear. * * *

Judgment reversed.

DOGGRELL v. GREAT SOUTHERN BOX CO., INC. OF MISSISSIPPI

(1953 C.A.6th) 206 F.2d 671.

MARTIN, J. Judgment for $3,332.47, with interest, was entered against appellant Frank E. Doggrell, Jr., and W. G. Konz, in an action brought by the appellee in the United States District Court for Western Tennessee. Appellant was one of the three original incorporators and also an original stockholder in Forrest City Wood Products, Inc., an organization attempted to be created in the spring of 1948 as a corporation under the laws of Arkansas. Concededly, at the time the debt was incurred upon which the instant action is grounded, the corporate organization had not been completed in compliance with the requirements of section 64–103, Arkansas Statutes, Annotated, 1947, which provides that the "corporate existence shall begin" upon filing the Articles of Incorporation with the Secretary of State; provided, however, "a set of the Articles of Incorporation * * shall be filed for record with the County Clerk of the County in which the corporation's principal office or place of business in this State is located."

The corporate charter was not filed for record with the County Clerk of St. Francis County, the principal place of business of the corporation, or in any other county in Arkansas, until March 19, 1951, nearly three years after the issuance of the charter by the Secretary of State of Arkansas. During this period, the debt in controversy was incurred while Forrest City Wood Products was conducting a furniture manufacturing business at Forrest City, Arkansas. The instant action of appellee against appellant and Konz was brought to recover the invoice price of merchandise which, pursuant to contract made in the fall of 1950, it had sold and shipped to Forrest City Wood Products, Inc. The latter organization was in bankruptcy at the time the suit was filed.

The district court held that appellant and Konz, as incorporators and stockholders of Forrest City Wood Products, Inc., were liable as partners jointly and severally for the debts, including the one involved in this case, incurred by that organization. Konz has not appealed from the judgment. In his oral opinion, the United States District Judge rested his decision upon the authority of three opinions of the Supreme Court of Arkansas: Whitaker v. Mitchell Mfg. Co., 1952, 219 Ark. 779, 244 S.W.2d 965; Gazette Publishing Co. v. Brady, 204 Ark. 396, 162 S.W. 2d 494, and Garnett v. Richardson, 35 Ark. 144. * * *

We think that undoubtedly the district judge construed the Arkansas opinions correctly. The Whitaker case, supra, is directly in point. There, the State of Arkansas' Supreme Court passed upon the legality of the incorporation of Forrest City Wood Products, Inc., at the time the debt in issue herein was incurred. Whitaker was the third incorporator of Forrest City Wood Products, Inc., and was directly responsible for the failure to record the corporate charter in St. Francis County, Arkansas, before the debts were incurred. He was president and gen-

eral manager of the purported corporation in which both appellant and Konz were inactive. They had not even been aware that Whitaker had not filed the certificate as required by law before engaging in business and creating the corporate debt for which they were sued as partners. * * *

We think that, under the "full faith and credit" clause of the Federal Constitution, where the Arkansas statute upon which liability in the instant case is grounded is not penal in the sense that it cannot be enforced in the forum of another state, the courts of Tennessee, including a United States District Court sitting in that state, are bound to apply to the existing factual situation the pertinent Arkansas statute as construed by the Supreme Court of that state. [Citations.] * * *

The final contention of appellant, and also the second ground of the decision by the Tennessee Chancellor in Turner Brass Works v. Doggrell, supra, is that even if the liability should be conceded to be contractual in nature and therefore enforceable according to the laws of Arkansas, Whitaker is a necessary party to the litigation in the United States District Court in Tennessee. In support of this argument, it was said by the chancellor that, under the provisions of the Uniform Partnership Law, effective in both Tennessee and Arkansas, "the obligation sought to be created by the Arkansas corporation laws against the incorporators as partners must be held to be a joint liability only"; and that, therefore, Whitaker was a necessary and indispensable party.

Appellant cites Rule 19(a) of the Federal Rules of Civil Procedure, 28 U.S.C.A., to the point that persons having a joint interest in a litigation must be made parties and joined on the same side as plaintiffs or defendants. It is contended that, upon the authority of State of Washington v. United States, 9 Cir., 87 F.2d 421, it was indispensable to join Whitaker as a defendant in the instant case, for he was "the party who alone was most familiar with the subject matter of the controversy, and most responsible for the alleged liability." It is urged that, under the Uniform Partnership Act, operative in both Tennessee and Arkansas, Williams Tenn. Code, Ann., section 7854, and Arkansas Statutes, Ann.1947, section 65–115, the liability of the partners for all debts and obligations of a corporation of the character here involved is *joint*, and *not joint and several*. * *

The contention of appellant that the obligation with which we are here concerned is governed by the Uniform Partnership Laws effective in both Arkansas and Tennessee is unsound, for the reason that, in Whitaker v. Mitchell Manufacturing Co., supra, decided more than ten years after the enactment of the Arkansas Uniform Partnership Law, the Supreme Court of Arkansas held the incorporators of the incompletely organized corporation to be individually liable as partners.

Certain existing statutes in both Tennessee and Arkansas make joint obligations joint and several. The Arkansas Statute, section 27–810, provides: "Joint obligations shall be construed to have the same effect as joint and several obligations, and may be sued on, and recoveries had thereon in like manner." In Tennessee, the same official Code of 1931, which contains the section of the Uniform Partnership Law defining the nature of a partner's liability, section 7854, also contains section 8613, which provides: "All joint obligations and promises are made joint and several, * * *."

So, even if the Uniform Partnership Law of each of the two states makes partners jointly liable for a debt of the character here concerned the foregoing statute in each state makes that joint liability *joint and several*. Therefore, it was not necessary that Whitaker be made a party defendant to the instant action in order to hold Doggrell and

Konz individually liable as partners for the debts of the defectively organized corporation, Forrest City Wood Products, Inc.

The judgment of the district court is affirmed.

————

PAPER PRODUCTS CO. v. DOGGRELL

(1953) 195 Tenn. 581, 261 S.W.2d 127, 42 A.L.R.2d 651.

TOMLINSON, J. Appellees, Doggrell and Konz, together with one Van E. Whitaker, Jr., were the sole stockholders in an Arkansas corporation formed by them under the name of Forrest City Wood Products, Inc. with principal office to be located in St. Francis County, Arkansas.

The Arkansas statute requires the articles of incorporation to be filed (1) with the Secretary of State and (2) thereafter in the office of the County Clerk of the County in which the corporation's principal place of business is to be located.

Doggrell and Konz, Tennessee residents, left the management of the corporation entirely to the third stockholder, Whitaker, a resident of Arkansas. The lawyer in Memphis who prepared the charter directed Whitaker to file it with the Secretary of State and then with the Clerk of the County Court of St. Francis County, Arkansas. Whitaker did file it with the Arkansas Secretary of State, but inadvertently failed to file it with the Clerk of the County Court of St. Francis County. It was not filed with this clerk until after the account which gave rise to this suit had been made. Neither Doggrell nor Konz were aware of the fact that the charter had not been filed in St. Francis County as required by the Arkansas statute. Neither has received any dividends or profits or remuneration from the corporation.

Under the decisions of the Arkansas Court of last resort the stockholders of a corporation are liable as partners when the charter is not filed as required by the Arkansas statute in the county where the principal office of the corporation is to be maintained. Based on those decisions of the Arkansas Supreme Court, Whitaker, the third stockholder in the aforementioned corporation, has been adjudged by the Arkansas Court liable for a debt made by this corporation before this charter was filed in St. Francis County. Whitaker v. Mitchell Manufacturing Co., 219 Ark. 779, 244 S.W.2d 965. The Arkansas Court rendered no judgment in that case against Doggrell and Konz because no service had been had on these Tennessee residents.

Whitaker who operated and managed the business of the corporation purchased goods in the name of the corporation from Paper Products Company and issued the company's note payable in thirty days. Paper Products Company in this transaction dealt with the Forrest City Wood Products, Inc. as such and not through the personal credit of Doggrell and Konz. These two stockholders knew nothing whatever about the account in question.

Forrest City Wood Products, Inc. became bankrupt. A substantial balance of its note issued to Paper Products Company remains unpaid. Accordingly, Paper Products Company instituted this suit in Shelby County, Tennessee Circuit Court against Doggrell and Konz. It seeks a recovery against them individually because of the Arkansas law holding stockholders personally liable as partners for the accounts made by a corporation whose charter has not been filed in the County where its principal office is located.

It was the judgment of the Shelby County Circuit Court that Doggrell and Konz are not liable individually, or as partners, for this obligation of Forrest City Wood Products, because this Arkansas rule "is penal in its nature, and will not be enforced in the State Courts of Tennessee". Paper Products Company has appealed and insists that (1) the

Arkansas rule is not penal in nature and (2) under the law of comity the Arkansas rule should be applied to this case.

Under Tennessee decisions, the liability of a stockholder for the debts of his corporation is determined by the law of the State in which that corporation is domiciled unless such law is contrary to the legislation or public policy of Tennessee, or is penal in nature. Under these circumstances such law of a sister State will not be enforced in Tennessee. [Citation.]

When a Tennessee Court is called upon to enforce the civil law of a sister jurisdiction it will determine whether such law is penal in nature or contrary to the public policy of the law of Tennessee in which it is sought to be enforced. [Citation.] Whether the aforementioned law of Arkansas, therefore, is contrary to our public policy or penal in nature is a matter to be determined in this case by the Tennessee Court since it is in that Court that it is sought to enforce this Arkansas rule.

The Arkansas statute heretofore referred to provides that "Upon the filing with the Secretary of State of articles of incorporation, *the corporate existence shall begin.*" Ark.Stats. § 64–103. (Emphasis supplied.) It follows that the corporate existence of Forrest City Wood Products, Inc. had begun prior to the inadvertent failure of Whitaker to file the corporation's charter in the office of the County Court of St. Francis County, Arkansas. The Arkansas rule, therefore, is that an inadvertent failure to comply with some detail in a bona fide effort to comply with the law chartering corporations is a failure which makes the stockholders liable in Arkansas for those debts of the corporation made prior to the compliance with such required detail.

This Arkansas rule is contrary to the public policy of Tennessee, wherein the rule is that the stockholders are not liable for the debts of their corporation in a case where there has been "made a bona fide effort to comply with the provisions of law", but "have inadvertently failed in some particular, and in good faith have exercised the franchises of such corporation." [Citation.] It is a commonly known fact that one of the purposes of organizing a corporation for the carrying on of a business is to relieve stockholders of individual liability for the debts of the corporation. That fact is well known to those dealing with corporations. The Tennessee rule forwards the accomplishment of that purpose.

In ascertaining whether the Arkansas statute is penal in nature it is well to observe again that under the Arkansas rule the stockholders of the corporation are liable as partners for the mere failure, after the commencement of corporate existence, to file its charter in the Arkansas County of its principal office. This liability is imposed without regard to the fact that a creditor is not prejudiced by the failure to comply with this detail and was not misled thereby. There is no escape from the conclusion, therefore, that this rule prescribes a penalty in order to enforce a compliance with the law of Arkansas as to the registering of a charter in the county where the principal office of the corporation is maintained. "Penalties prescribed by one state to enforce a compliance with its laws will not be enforced by the courts of another state." Brower v. Watson, 146 Tenn. 626, 636, 244 S.W. 362, 365, 26 A.L.R. 991.

A case directly in point is Woods v. Wicks, 75 Tenn. 40, cited in appellees' brief. A statute of Kentucky was involved in that suit. That statute required the directors of a corporation to file and record within a specified time in a certain office a certificate stating the amount of the capital stock fixed and paid in. Stockholders were arbitrarily made liable in double the amount of their stock for failure to file such certificate. The Tennes-

see Court refused to hold such stockholders liable for the failure to file such certificate. In rejecting such a suit our Court said that "no court of another sovereignty can be expected to enforce such a penalty". 75 Tenn. at page 50. * * *

The judgment must be affirmed with costs taxed to Paper Products Company and its surety.

On Petition to Rehear.

The case of Doggrell v. Great Southern Box Company, Inc., was decided by the United States Court of Appeals for the 6th Circuit on July 9, 1953. 206 F.2d 671. It came to that Court by appeal from the Federal District Court for the Western District of Tennessee. That case involved the identical Arkansas law and question decided by this Court in the instant case on July 17, 1953.

Preceded by well considered remarks unnecessary here to detail, the conclusion of the United States Court of Appeals in that case is that the Arkansas law in question is not penal within the meaning of the full faith and credit clause of our Federal Constitution, Article 4, § 1; hence, that "the courts of Tennessee, including a United States District Court sitting in that state, are bound" to give effect to this Arkansas law in proceedings brought by a creditor of the Arkansas corporation to recover a personal money judgment against some of the stockholders of that Arkansas corporation. In the instant case this Court reached the opposite conclusion. Judge McAllister, in a dissenting opinion in the Federal case, reached the same conclusion as that reached by this Court with reference to the penal nature of this Arkansas law.

Because of the majority opinion of the United States Court of Appeals in its case, supra, Paper Products Company, appellant in the instant case, has filed in the instant case its petition to rehear. * * *

The expression Arkansas "law," rather than Arkansas "statute", is used by this Court because it is a decision of the Arkansas Supreme Court as to the effect which must be given a failure to comply with the Arkansas statute requiring a copy of the corporation's charter to be filed in the office of the County Court Clerk of the county in which the corporation's principal place of business is located. Its decision is that such failure, ipso facto, renders each stockholder of such Arkansas corporation liable for every debt incurred by that corporation prior to such filing in such county, notwithstanding the fact that such charter had been filed with the Arkansas Secretary of State, whereby, under the express language of the statute, its "corporate existence shall begin." [Citation.]

This Court was of the opinion that the instant case fell within the ruling of Woods v. Wicks, 75 Tenn. 40, wherein this Court refused to give effect to a very similar Kentucky statute because of its penal nature. The United States Court of Appeals thought its case to be distinguishable from Woods v. Wicks because the incorporation of the Kentucky organization had been completed whereas such incorporation of the Arkansas organization lacked completion, so it is said, to the extent that a copy of its charter had not been filed in the Arkansas county of its principal office.

Apparently, in considering material such above stated distinction between the Kentucky and Arkansas organizations, the United States Court of Appeals inadvertently failed to give effect to the fact that in Tennessee the stockholders of a de facto corporation are not liable for its debts, and that corporations de facto are "those which have made a bona fide effort to comply with the provisions of law and have inadvertently failed in some particular, and in good faith have exercised the franchises of such corporation." [Citations.] * * *

As heretofore stated, this Court thinks that there is no escape from the conclusion that the sole purpose of the Arkansas law in question is to procure a compliance with its statute as to a formal or technical requirement. But, pursuing further the immediately above stated test furnished by Huntington v. Attrill, 146 U.S. 657, 13 S.Ct. 224, 36 L.Ed. 1130, there is particularly applicable the statement in Judge McAllister's dissenting opinion in Doggrell v. Great Southern Box Company, supra [206 F.2d 682], that:—"There was no wrong committed against any individual in not filing the articles with the County Clerk. To subject an innocent party, who happens to be an incorporator or original stockholder, to what may prove great financial losses or ruin, in being obliged to pay personally all the debts of the corporation merely because someone who should have complied with this technical requirement failed to do so, seems to me to subject appellant to a liability that is clearly penal in its nature."

On principle, as well as under the test pronounced by the United States Supreme Court, this Court is of the opinion that the penal nature of the Arkansas law in question is such that the Tennessee Court is not required by the full faith and credit clause of our Federal Constitution to give it effect.

The rule of comity does not apply because the Arkansas law is contrary to the law and public policy of this State. Woods v. Wicks, supra, 75 Tenn. 40, 46.

The petition to rehear must be denied.

DOGGRELL v. SOUTHERN BOX CO.

(1953 C.A.6th) 208 F.2d 310.

McAllister, J. For the reasons stated in the dissenting opinion heretofore filed, and because of the decisions of the Supreme Court of Tennessee in the cases of Paper Products Co. v. Doggrell, 195 Tenn. 581, 261 S.W.2d

127; and Turner Brass Works, a Corporation, The Meyercord Company, a Corporation v. Frank E. Doggrell, Jr., and W. G. Konz (Decided July 17, 1953), unreported, as well as the decision and opinion of the Supreme Court of Tennessee on the petition for rehearing of Paper Products Co. v. Doggrell, 195 Tenn. 581, 261 S.W.2d 130, all filed during the pendency of a motion for rehearing in the above entitled cause, in which it was held that the provision of the Arkansas statute in question was a penal statute and would not be enforced by the courts of Tennessee, and that appellant was a stockholder in a *de facto* corporation and, according to the law of Tennessee, would not be individually liable for the payment of the debts of the Arkansas corporation, I am of the opinion that the petition for rehearing should be granted; that the opinion heretofore filed should be set aside; and that a judgment should be entered in favor of appellant.

MILLER, J. Although I am not in agreement with the recent opinion of the Supreme Court of Tennessee in the case of Paper Products Co. v. Doggrell, 195 Tenn. 581, 261 S.W. 2d 127, rehearing denied October 9, 1953, Tenn.Sup., 261 S.W.2d 130, I am of the opinion that under the authority of Erie R. Co. v. Thompkins, 304 U.S. 64, 58 S.Ct. 817, 82 L.Ed. 1188; Vandenbark v. Owens-Illinois Glass Co., 311 U.S. 538, 61 S.Ct. 347, 85 L.Ed. 327; Klaxon Co. v. Stentor Co., 313 U.S. 487, 61 S.Ct. 1020, 85 L.Ed. 1477, and Guaranty Trust Co. v. York, 326 U.S. 99, 109–110, 65 S.Ct. 1464, 89 L.Ed. 2079, the ruling in that case is controlling in this case, with the result that the petition for rehearing should be granted and the judgment of the District Court be reversed.

PROBLEMS

1. A corporation issues a certificate of stock reciting that it is fully paid for. The holder sells it to X, who has no knowledge of the fact that it is not fully paid for. (a) Can the corporation hold X to make the payment thereon that will constitute full payment? (b) Can a creditor upon insolvency of the corporation compel full payment from X?

2. A, who was a promoter of a corporation, was issued fully paid up shares for services and property that were greatly overvalued. He transferred these shares to B, who knew nothing of the overvaluation. The corporation and its creditors now seek to recover the difference between the value of the property and the value of the shares from B. Decision? What if B knew of the overvaluation, but relied on the statement on the face of the stock certificate that it was "fully paid and nonassessable" in purchasing it?

3. John Brown paid $10,000 for 100 shares of the preferred stock of Y Corporation of a par value of $100 per share. The corporation in accordance with its usual practice delivered to him as a bonus one share of common stock of the par value of $100 for each share of preferred purchased. As a result of business recession, the corporation became insolvent and a suit on behalf of creditors was instituted against Brown under the statute in force in the State of incorporation to compel payment by him of "the unpaid portion of his stock." Brown interposed the defense that he had never contracted to pay anything for the common stock; that there was no evidence of its value; that therefore there was no basis on which to determine the amount of the unpaid portion of his stock; and that, accordingly, there could be no recovery. Decision?

4. A, the president of the B Corporation, indorsed checks payable to the corporation and deposited them in his personal account in the C bank. The bank collected the proceeds and paid them out on the personal checks of A. The B Corporation sues the C bank for the proceeds of the checks deposited by A, its president. Can the corporation recover?

5. A, B, and C organized the Wistful Vista Corporation for the purpose of subdividing and selling 100 acres of land located on the outskirts of a certain city. The authorized capital of the corporation consisted of 2,000 shares of common stock of $100 par value. A conveyed to the corporation in exchange for 500 shares of stock 50 acres of land which he had purchased for $5,000.

B conveyed to the corporation in exchange for 400 shares of stock 25 acres of land for which he had paid $4,000. C conveyed to the corporation in exchange for 300 shares of stock 25 acres of land for which he had paid $3,000. The remaining 800 shares of stock were sold to the public at par for a total of $80,000. After two years of unsuccessful operations the corporation has spent the $80,000, and has incurred debts aggregating $50,000. What are the rights of its creditors?

CHAPTER 40

CONSOLIDATION, MERGER, AND DISSOLUTION

Introductory. In certain situations, it may be desirable for a corporation to enlarge its plant, increase its properties, and extend its operations. In doing so, the corporation may wish to acquire the assets, and possibly the good will, of another corporation or corporations, and combine them with its own. This may be accomplished by (1) purchase of such assets, (2) lease of such assets, (3) merger, (4) consolidation, or (5) purchase of a controlling interest in the stock of such other corporation or corporations. The procedure with reference to the first four of these methods is set forth in each State's general Corporation Act. The fifth method presents the familiar situation of parent and subsidiary corporation. Public utilities and quasi public corporations, in addition to the necessary corporate action, require approval or certification by a State or Federal regulatory agency or commission before consummating any such program. The discussion which follows does not relate to this type of corporation but only to the general business corporation.

Purchase or Lease by One Corporation of All of the Assets of Another. When one corporation purchases or leases all, or substantially all, of the assets of another corporation, no change is effected in the legal personality of either corporation. The purchaser or lessee corporation simply has acquired ownership or control of more physical assets, and the selling or lessor corporation has, in lieu of its physical properties, a sum of cash or a stipulated rental, which may be a fixed sum or a percentage of income, for a term of years. Each corporation continues its separate existence with only the form or extent of its assets altered. However, the selling or leasing corporation, by liquidating all of its assets or placing them beyond its control, has substantially changed its position and perhaps its ability to carry on the business contemplated by its charter. For this reason, such a sale or lease must not only be approved by its board of directors, but also by the affirmative vote of the holders of at least two-thirds of its outstanding stock at a meeting of the shareholders duly called for this purpose. (Section 72, Model Act, Appendix D.) A dissenting shareholder of the selling corporation may demand and insist upon being paid by the corporation the fair value of his stock.

Merger. A merger of two or more corporations is the combination of all of their total assets, title to which is vested in one of them, known as the surviving corporation. The other party or parties to the merger, known as the merged corporation or corporations, go out of existence. All of their debts and other liabilities of all kinds become the liabilities of the surviving corporation. Their shareholders receive stock or other securities issued by the surviving corporation, as provided in the plan of merger. A merger requires the approval of the boards of directors of each of the corporations involved, as well as the affirmative vote of the respective holders of at least two-thirds of the outstanding stock of each of the corporations party to the merger at meetings of the shareholders, respectively, duly called for this purpose. A dissenting shareholder of any corporation which is a party to the merger may demand and insist upon receiving from the surviving corporation the fair value of his stock.

Consolidation. A consolidation of two or more corporations is the combination of all of their total assets, title to which is taken by a newly created corporation known as the

915

consolidated corporation. Each of the constituent corporations goes out of existence, and all of their debts and liabilities of every kind are assumed by the new corporation. The shareholders of each of the constituent corporations receive stock or other securities, not necessarily of the same class, issued to them by the new corporation in exchange for their old stock pursuant to the provisions of the plan of consolidation. A consolidation requires the approval of the boards of directors of each of the constituent corporations, as well as the affirmative vote of the respective holders of at least two-thirds of the outstanding stock of each of such corporations, at meetings of the shareholders, respectively, duly called for this purpose. A dissenting shareholder of any corporation which is a party to the consolidation may demand and insist upon receiving from the new corporation the fair value of his stock.

Parent and Subsidiary Corporation. When one corporation acquires all of the stock or a controlling interest in the stock of another corporation, no change is wrought in the legal existence of either corporation. The acquiring corporation acts through its board of directors, while the corporation which becomes a subsidiary does not act at all as the sale of stock is by its shareholders. There is no statutory procedure to be followed except for public utility or quasi-public corporations. The capital structure of the subsidiary remains unchanged, and that of the parent need not be altered unless some change is required in connection with financing the acquisition of the stock of the subsidiary.

Rights of Dissenting Shareholders. It may be noted that while the consent of creditors is not requisite to a merger, consolidation, or sale or lease of all of the assets of a corporation, the affirmative consent of shareholders owning at least two-thirds of the outstanding stock is usually required. A shareholder is not obliged to consent or to become an owner of shares in some new or different corpora-

tion. If he dissents, he is entitled to be paid the fair value of his stock, provided he follows closely the statutory procedure.

In order to perfect his right to payment for his stock, a dissenting shareholder of a corporation which is a party to a merger or consolidation, as provided in Section 74 of the Model Act, must:

(1) File with the corporation a written objection to the proposed merger or consolidation prior to or at the meeting of the shareholders at which the plan of merger or consolidation is submitted.

(2) Abstain from voting in favor of the proposed merger or consolidation, either in person or by proxy.

(3) Make a written demand upon the surviving or new corporation, within 10 days after the merger or consolidation has been authorized by the requisite shareholders' vote, for the payment of the fair value of his shares as of the day prior to the date on which the vote was taken.

Unless written demand is made within the 10-day period, the dissenting shareholder is bound by the terms of the proposed corporate action.

Example: A is the owner of 10 per cent of the outstanding stock of the X Corporation which has proposed a merger or consolidation with the Y Corporation. At the meeting of the shareholders, A files written objections, makes a vehement speech in opposition to the proposed merger or consolidation, and casts a dissenting vote. However, the holders of two-thirds of the outstanding stock vote in favor of it. Thereafter, at every opportunity A loudly proclaims his disagreement and dissent. Nevertheless, he forgets and fails to file a written demand for payment within the 10-day period. Despite his protests to the contrary, A has legally assented to the merger or consolidation and is bound by the terms thereof. A is in precisely the same position as if he had favored the merger or consolidation from the start and had voted in favor of it.

The obvious purpose of the statute is to fix a date not too remote at which time the corporation may be apprised of the number of shares for which it is required to pay cash in order to carry through the merger or consolidation. If the minority dissenting shareholders in sufficient numbers perfect their right to be paid, the lack of sufficient cash or the inability of the surviving or new corporation to raise funds for this purpose may defeat, at this stage, the merger or consolidation. The rights of dissenting shareholders cease whenever the corporation at any time abandons the merger or consolidation.

The procedure to be followed by a shareholder dissenting from a proposed sale, lease, exchange, or mortgage of all, or substantially all, of the corporation's assets, in order to preserve his right to be paid the fair value of his stock, is, in general, similar to that with respect to a merger or consolidation.

Dissolution. The life of a corporation is terminated by dissolution which may be brought about in any of the following ways:

(1) Act of the legislature of the State of incorporation.

(2) Expiration of the period of time for which the corporation was formed.

(3) Voluntary action on the part of all of the holders of all of the outstanding shares of stock.

(4) Voluntary action by the corporation, pursuant to a resolution of the board of directors which is approved by the affirmative vote of the holders of at least two-thirds of the outstanding shares of stock at a meeting of the shareholders duly called for this purpose.

(5) Decree of a court of equity at the instance of the Attorney General of the State of incorporation when it appears that the corporation has failed to file its annual report or to pay its annual franchise tax, or that the charter of the corporation was procured through fraud practiced upon the State, or that the corporation has continued to exceed or abuse its corporate powers or to violate any section of the criminal code after a demand to discontinue was made upon it by the Secretary of State.

Upon dissolution, the assets of a corporation are liquidated and used first to pay its creditors according to their respective contract or lien rights, and any remainder is distributed to shareholders ratably according to their respective contract rights, preferred stock having priority over common.

Unless, upon dissolution, the assets and property of a corporation are liquidated and distributed, title to the assets and property becomes vested in the shareholders as tenants in common. These assets, however, are subject to the claims of creditors of the corporation for a period fixed by the statute, usually two years following the date of dissolution, during which time suit may be brought by any creditor against the corporation and in the corporate name. (Section 98, Model Act, Appendix D.)

CASES

RATH v. RATH PACKING CO.

(1965) — Iowa —, 136 N.W.2d 410.

GARFIELD, C. J. The question presented is whether an Iowa corporation may carry out an agreement with another corporation, designated "Plan and Agreement of Reorganization," which amounts to a merger in fact of the two without approval of holders of two thirds of its outstanding shares, as provided by section 496A.70, Code 1962, I. C.A., and its articles of incorporation. The question is one of first impression in Iowa. We must disagree with the trial court's holding this may be done.

Plaintiffs, minority shareholders of Rath, brought this action in equity to enjoin carrying out the agreement on the ground, so far as necessary to consider, it provides for a merger in fact with Needham Packing Co., which requires approval of two thirds of the holders of outstanding Rath shares and that was not obtained. The trial court adjudicated law points under rule 105, Rules of Civil Procedure, in favor of defendants Rath and its officers, and entered judgment of dismissal on the pleadings. It held approval of the plan by holders of a majority of Rath shares was sufficient. Plaintiffs appeal.

Plaintiffs own more than 6000 shares of Rath Packing Co., an Iowa corporation with its principal plant in Waterloo, Iowa, existing under Code 1962, chapter 496A, I.C.A. (Iowa Business Corporation Act). Rath has 993,185 shares outstanding held by about 4000 owners. It is engaged in meat packing and processing, mostly pork and allied products. Its yearly sales for the last five years were from about $267,000,000 to $296,000,-000. Its balance sheet as of January 2, 1965, showed assets of about $56,500,000, current liabilities of about $20,600,000, and long-term debt of about $7,000,000.

Needham Packing Co. is a corporation organized in 1960 under Delaware law with its principal plant in Sioux City, Iowa. Its total shares outstanding, including debentures and warrants convertible into stock, are 787,907, held by about 1000 owners. Both Rath and Needham stock is traded on the American Stock Exchange. Needham is also engaged in meat packing, mostly beef. Its annual sales were from about $80,000,000 to $103,000,000. Its balance sheet as of December 26, 1964, showed assets of $10,300,-000, current liabilities of $2,262,000, and long-term debt of $3,100,000.

Pursuant to authority of Rath's board prior to April 2, 1965, it entered into the questioned agreement with Needham, designated "Plan and Agreement of Reorganization," under which Rath agreed to: (1) amend its articles to double the number of shares of its common stock, create a new class of preferred shares and change its name to Rath-Needham Corporation; (2) issue to Needham 5.5 shares of Rath common and two shares of its 80-cent preferred stock for each five shares of Needham stock in exchange for all Needham's assets, properties, business, name and good will, except a fund not exceeding $175,000 to pay expenses in carrying out the agreement and effecting Needham's dissolution and distribution of the new Rath-Needham stock to its shareholders, any balance remaining after 120 days to be paid over to Rath; (3) assume all Needham's debts and liabilities; and (4) elect two Needham officers and directors to its board.

Under the plan Needham agreed to: (1) transfer all its assets to Rath; (2) cease using its name; (3) distribute the new Rath-Needham shares to its stockholders, liquidate and dissolve; and (4) turn over to Rath its corporate and business records.

If the plan were carried out, assuming the new preferred shares were converted into common, the thousand Needham shareholders would have about 54 per cent of the outstanding common shares of Rath-Needham and the four thousand Rath shareholders would have about 46 per cent.

Under the plan the book value of each share of Rath common stock, as of January 2, 1965, would be reduced from $27.99 to $15.93, a reduction of about 44 per cent. Each share of Needham common would be increased in book value, as of December 26, 1964, from $6.61 to $23.90, assuming conversion of the new Rath-Needham preferred.

In the event of liquidation of Rath-Needham, Needham shareholders would be preferred to Rath's under the plan, by having a prior claim to the assets of Rath-Needham to an amount slightly in excess of the book value of all Needham shares. Needham shareholders are also preferred over Rath's under the plan in distribution of income by the right of the former to receive preferred dividends of 80 cents a share—about five per cent of Needham's book value. Shortly prior to the time terms of the plan were made public Rath and Needham shares sold on the American Exchange for about the same price. Almost immediately thereafter the price of Needham shares increased and Rath's decreased so the former sold for 50 per cent more than the latter.

At a meeting of Rath shareholders on April 26, 1965, 60.1 per cent of its outstanding shares, 77 per cent of those voted, were voted in favor of these two proposals: (1) to amend the articles to authorize a class of 80 c preferred stock and increase the authorized common from 1,500,000 shares ($10 par) to 3,000,000 shares (no par); and (2) upon acquisition by Rath of the assets, properties, business and good will of Needham to change Rath's name to Rath-Needham Corporation and elect as its directors Lloyd and James Needham. Holders of 177,000 shares voted against these proposals and 218,000 shares were not voted. The plan was not approved by the shareholders except as above stated.

Rath officers vigorously solicited proxies for the meeting by personal travel, telephone and through a professional proxy soliciting agency. This action was commenced five days prior to the meeting and four days thereafter a supplement and amendment to the petition were filed.

I. We will summarize the provisions of Code chapter 496A, I.C.A., so far as material to the appeal.

Section 496A.74 provides that a foreign corporation and a domestic one may merge if permitted by laws of the state where the former is organized and "1. Each domestic corporation shall comply with the provisions of this chapter with respect to the merger * * * of domestic corporations * * *."

Section 496A.68 states that two or more domestic corporations may merge pursuant to a plan approved in the manner provided in this chapter. The board of each corporation shall approve a plan setting forth: (1) the names of the merging corporations and the survivor; (2) terms of the merger; (3) manner of converting shares of each merging corporation into shares of the survivor; (4) any changes in the articles of incorporation of the survivor; (5) other provisions of the merger deemed necessary or desirable.

Section 496A.70 provides for approval of the plan of merger by the shareholders of each merging corporation and "[a]t each such meeting, a vote of the shareholders shall be taken on the proposed plan * * *. * * * The plan * * * shall be approved upon receiving the affirmative vote of the holders of at least two-thirds of the outstanding shares of each such corporation, * * *."

Section 496A.71 states that upon such shareholder approval articles of merger shall be executed by each corporation setting forth: (1) the plan of merger; (2) the number of shares of each corporation outstanding; (3) as to each corporation, the number of shares voted for and against the plan. The articles shall be filed with the secretary of state and county recorder and a certificate of merger shall be issued by the former.

Section 496A.73 provides that upon issuance of the certificate the merger shall be effected and (1) the merging corporations shall be a single corporation—the one designated in the plan as the survivor; (2)

the separate existence of the merging corporations, except the survivor, shall cease; (3) the survivor shall have all the powers and be subject to the same duties as a corporation organized under chapter 496A; (4) the survivor shall have all the rights, franchises and properties of the merging corporations; (5) the survivor shall be liable for all obligations of the merging corporations; (6) the articles of incorporation of the survivor shall be deemed amended to the extent that changes therein are stated in the plan of merger.

Section 496A.77 states that any shareholder shall have the right to dissent from any merger to which the corporation is a party.

Section 496A.78 gives a dissenting shareholder, by following the procedure there outlined, the right to be paid the fair value of his shares as of the day prior to that on which the corporate action was approved.

The above sections are those on which plaintiffs rely. They contend these statutes specifically provide for effecting a merger and the same result cannot legally be attained at least without approval of the holders of two thirds of the shares and according to dissenters "appraisal rights"—i. e., the right to receive the fair value of their stock by compliance with the specified procedure.

Defendants contend and the trial court held compliance with the above sections was not required and defendants could legally proceed under other sections of chapter 496A which merely authorize amendments to articles of incorporation and issuance of stock. The sections just referred to provide (section 496A.55) that a corporation may amend its articles in any respects desired and in particular: change its name, change the number of shares of any class, change shares having a par value to those without par and create new classes of shares with preferences over shares then authorized.

Section 496A.56 states articles may be amended by giving shareholders notice of a meeting at which the amendments are to be considered, with a summary of the proposed changes, and upon receiving the affirmative vote of holders of a majority of the stock entitled to vote. The articles of amendment shall be filed with the secretary of state and county recorder (496A.59) and be effective upon issuance by the former of the certificate of amendment (496A.60).

Section 496A.17 provides that shares, with or without par, may be issued for such consideration as the board fixes.

Section 496A.18 states that shares may be paid for in money or property, tangible or intangible, and in the absence of fraud the judgment of the board as to value of the consideration received shall be conclusive.

II. The principal point of law defendants asked to have adjudicated under rule 105, R.C.P., is that the provisions of chapter 496A last referred to are legally independent of, and of equal dignity with, those relating to mergers and the validity of the action taken by defendants is not dependent upon compliance with the merger sections under which the same result might be attained. The trial court accepted this view.

* * *

We may also observe that the trial court "concluded the 'safeguards' written into the codes of most states, including Iowa and Delaware, with respect to rights of dissenting shareholders in connection with mergers are based on outmoded concepts of economic realities, particularly in the case of an enterprise such as Rath which is regularly traded on the American Exchange and has a diversified stock ownership with over 4000 shareholders. The court cites especially in this regard articles of Professor Manning, 72 Yale Law Journal 223, and Professor Folk, 49 Virginia Law Review 1261."

If the soundness of this view were admitted, the statutory safeguards should of course be removed by legislative, not judicial action. Our 1959 legislature evidently had a purpose in enacting what we may call the merger sections of chapter 496A as well as those relating to amending articles and issuing stock. We have frequently pointed out it is not the province of courts to pass upon the policy, wisdom or advisability of a statute. * * *

If, as we hold, this agreement provides for what amounts to a merger of Rath and Needham, calling it a Plan and Agreement of Reorganization does not change its essential character. A fundamental maxim of equity, frequently applied, is that equity regards substance rather than form. * * *

At common law no merger could take place without unanimous consent of the stockholders. However, statutes in all jurisdictions now authorize mergers upon a vote of less than all stockholders. A shareholder who dissents to a merger may obtain the value of his stock if the right thereto is provided by statute, if procedure is established therefor and is followed by him. * * *

"It is an old and familiar principle * * that where there is in the same statute a specific provision, and also a general one which in its most comprehensive sense would include matters embraced in the former, the particular provision must control, and the general provision must be taken to effect only such cases within its general language as are not within the provisions of the particular provision. Additional words of qualification needed to harmonize a general and a prior special provision in the same statute should be added to the general provision, rather than to the special one." 20 Am.Jur., Statutes, section 367.

* * *

It is apparent that if the sections pertaining to amending articles and issuing stock are construed to authorize a merger by a majority vote of shareholders they conflict with the sections specifically dealing with the one matter of mergers which require a two-thirds vote of shareholders. The two sets of sections may be harmonized by holding, as we do, that the merger sections govern the matter of merger and must be regarded as an exception to the sections dealing with amending articles and issuing stock, which may or may not be involved in a merger.

* * *

As indicated at the outset, Article XI of Rath's articles of incorporation provides: "The corporation shall not merge with or consolidate into any other corporation * * except upon obtaining the vote in favor thereof of the holders of record of two-thirds (⅔) of the shares of common stock * *." Article XII requires the affirmative vote of the holders of two thirds of the shares of common stock to amend Article XI.

* * *

We hold entry of judgment of dismissal on the pleadings was error, that defendants should be enjoined from carrying out the "Plan and Agreement of Reorganization" until such time, if ever, as it is approved by the holders of at least two thirds of the outstanding shares of Rath and in the event of such approval plaintiffs, if they dissent to such plan and follow the procedure provided by Code section 496A.78, I.C.A., shall be entitled to be paid the fair value of their shares in Rath. For decree in harmony with this opinion the cause is—Reversed and remanded.

AHLENIUS v. BUNN & HUMPHREYS, INC.

(1934) 358 Ill. 155, 192 N.E. 824.

[The plaintiff, R. O. Ahlenius, the owner of 150 shares of the common stock of J. F. Humphreys & Co., filed a petition in the circuit court of McLean county against the defendant, Bunn & Humphreys, Inc., successor by consolidation to the former company and to John W. Bunn & Co., by which he sought the determination of the fair value of his shares of stock and their purchase by the consolidated corporation. The cause was tried by the court without a jury and judgment for $12,842.72 and costs was rendered in favor of the plaintiff and against the defendant. Upon appeal, the Appellate Court found (1) that Ahlenius was a stockholder of J. F. Humphreys & Co. before and at the time of its consolidation with John W. Bunn & Co.; (2) that he objected to the consolidation; (3) that the fair value of the shares of stock owned by him at the time of the consolidation was $17,470.50; (4) that the two named corporations were consolidated September 21, 1928; (5) that the interest on the principal debt from that day to the date of the rendition of the former judgment amounted to $2673.50 and (6) that the total damages due Ahlenius from Bunn & Humphreys, Inc., at that time were $20,144. Accordingly, the Appellate Court reversed the judgment of the circuit court and rendered judgment for $20,144 and costs in plaintiff's favor. The Supreme Court granted a writ of certiorari for a further review.]

PER CURIAM. * * * It does not appear that the method of appraisal of the shares of dissenting stockholders has received consideration by this court. In other jurisdictions the question presented has arisen under similar statutes in a relatively small number of cases. The value of shares of corporate stock has been held to mean not merely the market price, if the stock is traded in by the public, but its intrinsic value, to determine which all the assets and liabilities of the corporation must be ascertained. [Citation.] The value of the stock of a corporation, it also has been decided, must be determined by the fair market value of the corporate property as an established and going business.

[Citation.] Precise rules for determining the value, whatever the descriptive term used, cannot be laid down. [Citation.] The very nature of most cases precludes proof of value and damage with the precision of mathematical computation. A situation is presented which calls for the exercise of judgment upon consideration of every relevant evidential fact and circumstance entering into the value of the corporate property and reflecting itself in the worth of corporate stock. [Citation.] Among the factors which have been considered in analogous cases are earning capacity [citation]; the investment value of the stock which is largely determined by the rate of dividends, the regularity with which they have been paid, the possibility that they will be increased or diminished, the selling price of stocks of like character, the amount of preferred stock in comparison with the common stock, the size of the accumulated surplus applicable to dividends, the record of the corporation and its prospects for the future [citation], and good will [citation].

Mere book value should not govern in determining the value of the shares of objecting stockholders [citation], and appraisal values are not necessarily controlling. [Citation.] The use of book values, especially, to measure the value of corporate shares, owing to the multifarious uses for which they are employed, is generally condemned as unsound. "Remedies of Dissenting Stockholders under Appraisal Statutes," Prof. Norman D. Lattin, 45 Harvard L.R. p. 233; "Dissenting Shareholders: Their Rights to Dividends and the Valuation of Their Shares," Benjamin M. Robinson, 32 Columbia L.R. p. 60. The Circuit Court of Appeals for the Second Circuit, in Borg v. International Silver Co., 11 F.2d 147, observed: "The suggestion that the book value of the shares is any measure of their actual value is clearly fallacious. It presupposes, first, that book values can be realized on liquidation, which is practically never the case; and, second, that liquidation values are a measure of present values. Everyone knows that the value of shares in a commercial or manufacturing company depends chiefly on what they will earn, on which balance sheets throw very little light. When all is said, value is nothing more than what people will pay for the shares, given as wide an opportunity for bidders to come in as is reasonably possible." * * *

If it be conceded that the evidence shows the book value of each of the shares exchanged by Humphreys was $116.47, it does not follow that it corresponded with their fair value. * * * Proof that the fair and the book values of the assets received by Rogers Humphreys for a part of his stock were the same is wanting. The Appellate Court's finding of fact that the fair value of the stock owned by the defendant in error at the time of the consolidation was $17,470.50 is, therefore, without foundation.

Judgment of Appellate Court reversed.

Judgment of Circuit Court affirmed.

SCHMITT REALTY & INV. CO.
v. MONKS

(1929) 32 Ohio App. 405, 168 N.E. 213.

[Action by Mable B. Monks and Thomas E. Monks for dissolution of the Schmitt Realty & Inv. Co., as owners of one-third or more of the capital stock of the corporation pursuant to the provisions of the Ohio Corporation Act. Judgment for plaintiff. Defendants appeal.]

LEVINE, J. The parties appear here in an order the reverse of that occupied in the trial court. This action was commenced in the common pleas court by Mable B. Monks and Thomas E. Monks for dissolution of the Schmitt Realty & Inv. Company, as owners of one-third or more of the capital stock of the corporation, under favor of section 11938,

General Code (72 Ohio Laws, p. 138). This section has since been repealed and has been replaced by section 8523–86, General Code (112 Ohio Laws, p. 43), as part of the new Corporation Act. Section 11938 reads:

"When * * * stockholders representing not less than one-third of the capital stock of a corporation, * * * deem it beneficial to the interests of the stockholders that the corporation be dissolved * * * they may apply by petition to the Common Pleas Court * * * for its dissolution pursuant to the provisions of this chapter."

The court found from the evidence that dissolution of the corporation would be beneficial to the stockholders and not injurious to the public interest. There was no claim of insolvency on any of the other grounds set forth in the statute. The sole issue in the case, the one which the common pleas court decided, was whether the situation presented by the evidence showed that the dissolution of the corporation would be beneficial to the stockholders. The trial court held that it would be beneficial to the stockholders, and ordered a dissolution accordingly. Plaintiffs in error contend that the court committed error in so finding and in decreeing a dissolution.

The record discloses that the company was organized in 1915 to deal in real estate; that its operations were profitable until about the beginning of 1926, at which time they ceased to be profitable, and that since that time its sole business has been confined to the maintenance and care of the properties theretofore acquired. The net worth of the company is approximately $400,000. Its assets, in addition to cash, accounts receivable and certain stocks in other corporations, consist entirely of real property. The total outstanding capital stock of the company consists of 500 shares, of which 304 shares are owned by defendants Theodore Schmitt, Emma Schmitt, his wife, Walter J. Schmitt, his son, and Frank Hauschke, an employe. The remainder, to wit, 196 shares, are owned by the defendants in error herein. Prior to 1920 the company paid no dividends on the common stock and paid no salaries. In 1920, upon advice of counsel, the policy of the company was changed. Beginning in 1920, and continuing until the beginning of 1927, there was paid to Theodore Schmitt $300 per month, to Thomas E. Monks $300 per month, and to Walter J. Schmitt $400 per month. These sums, paid as salaries, were determined in proportion to the amount of stock held by the various parties, except that Walter J. Schmitt was allowed an extra $100 per month for collecting the rents. A reading of the record leads us to the conclusion that these sums paid to the various parties, while paid in the form of salaries, were in fact in lieu of common stock dividends, and totaled about $1,000 per month. Until 1926 the Monks and the Schmitts were on friendly terms. When the company started, it was through Mr. Schmitt's solicitation that Mr. Monks invested his services in the company for the first stock that he received, and he thereby became interested in the company. While the harmonious relations existed the company made progress and was highly successful.

In 1926 discord and strife began to arise between the Monks and the Schmitts. The parties lost confidence in each other, and their respective judgments concerning the operation of the company came into serious conflict. In the latter part of 1926 the affairs of the corporation were taken over by the rental department of the Guardian Trust Company, and Walter Schmitt lost his job. This incident increased the discord between the parties. In January, 1927, at a regular meeting the Schmitt interests voted a discontinuance of Mr. Monks' salary of $300 per month, paid in lieu of dividends, increased Walter Schmitt's salary by that amount, and voted an alleged salary of $25 per month to Frank Hauschke, so that thereafter the

Monks received nothing from the company, whereas Theodore Schmitt received $300 per month, and Walter Schmitt received $700 per month, and Frank Hauschke, $25. In other words, since January 1927, the Schmitts have been receiving from the company $12,300 per year on their shares of stock, while the Monks received nothing. It is not straining the record to state that this expenditure of $12,300 per year under the circumstances, which reveal that the activities of the company are confined to the maintenance and care of the property heretofore acquired, and to the collection of rents, is far in excess of what would be required by a rental agency. There is considerable conflict between counsel as to whether or not since 1926 the company operated at a substantial loss. This much, however, must be considered, namely, that it made no profit; that, in so far as the stockholders are concerned, the affairs of the company showed no profit from which dividends in the form of salaries could be paid; that this is but one of the incidents which led to the strained relation between the parties. The trial court found from all the evidence that the relationship of the minority stockholders to the majority stockholders is such that there can be no reasonable hope of future harmonious co-operation; that, because of the lack of harmonious co-operation between the parties, and their workings to opposite ends and purposes, the property and assets of the company are bound to depreciate and diminish, and that therefore it will be beneficial to all the stockholders that the company be dissolved. * * *

The mere ability of the minority stockholders to resort to the process of injunction by way of remedying some of the abuses will not bridge the gap now existing between the contending factions; nor will it bring about future harmonious co-operation; nor does it furnish a more favorable view of the company's prospects. Quite the contrary is true.

Litigation of the character suggested intensifies the feeling between the parties, and makes their relations even more strained. It is the common experience of the business world that embittered litigation between factions in a corporation tends to reduce the value of the corporation's assets. It has a destructive and depreciating effect, which in some cases leads to utter disorganization.

* * *

Affirmed.

KRUGER v. GERTH

(1964) 22 App.Div.2d 916, 255 N.Y.S.2d 498.

MEMORANDUM BY THE COURT. In an action by minority stockholders of the defendant corporation, in which the complaint alleges: (a) one cause of action to compel the individual defendants, who are two of the corporation's three directors, to dissolve the corporation; and (b) two causes of action to enjoin, as waste, the payment by the corporation of certain bonuses to the defendant Arthur A. Gerth and two other employees of the corporation, and to recover such bonus payments as have been made, the individual defendants appeal from so much of a judgment of the Supreme Court, Nassau County, entered May 19, 1964 upon the court's decision after a nonjury trial, as directed them "forthwith to take all steps and procedures provided by Article 10 of the Business Corporation Law to cause the [corporation] to be dissolved," and as awarded costs to the plaintiffs.

* * * No appeal has been taken from the court's dismissal of the second and third causes of action relating to the payment of the bonuses.

* * *

During the relevant period of time in issue, the defendant Arthur A. Gerth was the only party to the action in the corporation's employ; he owned 53% of the corporation's common stock and half of its preferred stock; his brother, defendant Harry J. Gerth, owned 1% of its common stock; and plaintiffs owned the remainder of its common and preferred stock. The corporation is in the retail lumber business.

The gist of the first cause of action to compel dissolution of the corporation is that Arthur A. Gerth has dominated and controlled the affairs of the corporation; that he has taken salaries and bonuses in such amounts as to leave little net profit annually; that no dividends have ever been paid on the common stock; that the dividend payments on the preferred stock, which began only in 1958, gave plaintiffs a meagre return for their capital interest in the corporation; that, because of various conditions that affect the business of the corporation, the corporation cannot be operated so as to increase its profits; that the said Gerth has a personal interest in continuing the business of the corporation, namely, to provide himself with employment, at substantial salaries and bonuses, and thereby has been exploiting the corporation to the detriment of the other stockholders.

The corporation's net profit in each of the years 1958 to 1961, both inclusive, has been less than $2,000, before provision for income taxes. In each of the first three of those years Arthur A. Gerth's salary was $9,000; and in 1961 it was $9,374.94. His bonus for each of the four years was, respectively, $5,857.20, $7,153.20, $6,480 and $6,120. Throughout these years the corporation has had a net worth of substantially more than $100,000 and total annual sales ranging from about $245,000 to about $275,000.

More is required to sustain an action to compel the dissolution of a corporation than to sustain a derivative stockholder's action for waste. Dissolution will not be compelled unless it be found that the dominant stockholders or directors have been "looting" the corporation's assets and impairing the corporation's capital or maintaining the corporation for their own special benefit, thereby enriching themselves at the expense of the minority stockholders; and the fact that the corporation is operating profitably or that the complaining stockholders may have a right to relief by way of derivative suits or otherwise is not in itself a bar to compelling dissolution [citations.]

In the instant case there was no evidence from which it could be found that there was any looting and impairment of capital or maintenance of the corporation for the special purpose of the individual defendants at the expense of the other stockholders. The plaintiffs acquired their stock in a bequest under the last will and testament of Henry M. Kruger, who died in August 1961. In 1950 both he and Arthur A. Gerth were employees of the corporation, receiving equal salaries of $6,000. In that year the said Kruger became ill and retired from active participation in the business. Thereupon, the only stockholder in active participation in the business carrying the responsibilities of the business was Arthur A. Gerth, but he had to employ another person to replace Henry M. Kruger. Nevertheless, said Kruger continued to receive a salary from the corporation for about eleven years, that is, from 1950 to 1961, when he died.

In 1951 Arthur A. Gerth's salary was increased to $7,500; and he began taking a bonus. Since then there have been increases in his salary and bonus. There was no evidence that anyone complained that the said Gerth did not deserve the salaries and bonuses he received during the eleven years up to August 1961 during which he operated the business while Kruger remained on the sidelines. There was no material difference between the total of Gerth's salaries and bonuses annually from 1955 to 1961, both years inclusive. As a matter of fact, at the conclusion of the trial, plaintiffs' counsel expressly admitted that no proof had been offered to

the effect that Gerth's salaries had been excessive.

In sum, plaintiffs' claim rests only on the fact that the amount of the bonus for each of the four years up to and including 1961, though varying from year to year, served so to reduce the net profit as to leave an insufficient amount to provide a fair return to plaintiffs on their stock in the corporation. We have found no case in which dissolution of a corporation was directed on such a meagre showing. * * *

Indeed, plaintiffs' own motives in prosecuting this action are doubtful and suspect; and their motives bear upon the issue of whether defendant Arthur A. Gerth has taken unfair advantage of his position. The plaintiff Henry L. Kruger in his testimony admitted that he had been employed by the corporation from the time of its creation in 1924 until November 1946, when he resigned to operate his own business; that he and his brother, plaintiff Sydney F. Kruger, have operated their own business since January 1946; that their personal business is in competition with the business of the defendant corporation; and that their personal business would profit should the business of the defendant corporation cease.

(Judgment reversed).

AMERICAN RAILWAY EXPRESS CO. v. COMMONWEALTH

(1920) 190 Ky. 636, 228 S.W. 433.

CARROLL, C. J. The purpose of this suit, which was brought in July, 1919, by the commonwealth of Kentucky was to make the American Railway Express Company liable for certain judgments amounting in round numbers to $4,000, obtained by the commonwealth against the Adams Express Company in the Harlan circuit court. The lower court gave judgment for the amount asked against the American Railway Express Company, and to have a reversal of that judgment it prosecutes this appeal. * * *

On this evidence the outstanding facts in this case may be stated in this way: (a) There was no merger or consolidation of the two companies. The American simply bought, and paid for in its stock, all of the property of every kind, character, and description employed by the Adams in the express business, and took its place as an express company; the transaction being untainted by actual fraud of any description. (b) The American did not pay to the Adams any consideration except the issual of its stock to the Adams to the amount of $8,000,-000, and this stock although delivered to the Adams Company, was delivered to it, as we will assume, to be held by it as trustee for the use and benefit of its stockholders, or to be delivered by it to the stockholders in proportion to their respective rights. (c) Before the sale the Adams had ample tangible property, including real estate, in this state, out of which the judgment could have been satisfied, and after the sale it had in this state no property of any kind or character that could be subjected to the satisfaction of the judgment; nor were any of its stockholders residents of this state. (d) The Adams had in New York, or some other state, after the sale, assets sufficient in value to satisfy the judgment, but whether these assets could be subjected to its payment is not certain, nor is it material whether this could or not be done. (e) Immediately upon the sale the Adams ceased to do business as an express company, leaving no agent in the state for the service of process, but retained its corporate identity merely for the purpose of winding up its affairs. (f) The sale and transfer simply had the effect of putting the American Company, in consideration of its stock, in the possession of all the property used by the Adams and other express companies in the conduct of their business, and it continued to carry on the express business just as the selling companies had carried it on before the sale. We may also here state that, under our Constitution and statutes, the Adams, although a joint-stock company organized under the laws of New York, is to be treated in this state as a corporation. Whether its stockholders are personally liable for its debts, as in the case of a partnership, we are not able to say, as we are not advised concerning the statutes of New York or the articles of association under which it was organized. And so, under these circumstances, we will treat it as a corporation.

On these facts, the precise question before us is: Will a purchasing corporation that has paid the full purchase price to the selling corporation by the issual of its stock to it be responsible in law, to the extent of the value of the property received, for the debts or liabilities, whether liquidated or unliquidated, or sounding in contract or tort, that were outstanding against the selling corporation at the time of the sale, when the effect of the sale is to leave the selling corporation without any property in the state in which the liability accrued to satisfy it, although except for the sale it would have been subjected to the payment of the liability, and may have property in some other state that could be subjected to the payment of the liability? * * *

All the cases also hold that where there is a merger, or consolidation, or reincorporation, or reorganization, and a continuance of the business under a new name, the corporation taking over the assets and property of the corporation extinguished for all practical purposes will be liable for its debts, and, as before said, in virtually all this class of cases the corporation that went out of business was paid for its property in stock of the new corporation.

Keeping these rulings in mind, it is difficult to find any substantial difference between the methods of absorption often employed, as in the case of a merger or reincorporation or reorganization, and a straight-out sale, like the one here in question, when the selling corporation gets nothing but stock in the purchasing one. It is true there is no direct evidence that the stockholders of the Adams received, or will receive, in exchange for their stock, the stock of the American that was delivered, as shown by the evidence to the Adams; but it is fair to, and we will, assume that this stock was turned over to the Adams for distribution to its stockholders as their rights may appear, because they owned the whole beneficial interest in the property that was given up for this stock, and the clear inference is that the Adams, as a corporate entity, holds this stock in trust for its shareholders or to be delivered to them.

* * *

Of course, a corporation may sell its property and all of it of every kind, just as any natural person may, and when it does this, and receives its fair value in money to pay its debts, or property that the creditor can subject to the payment of its debts, a purchaser, in the absence of a contract obligation, cannot be held for the debts and liabilities of the selling corporation. But when the selling corporation disposes of all its property and takes for it shares of stock in the purchasing corporation, and both the buyer and seller refuse to pay the debts of the seller, it is perfectly plain that the rights of creditors of the seller have been prejudiced by the sale; as to them the sale is constructively fraudulent, and for this reason courts will hold the purchasing corporation liable for the debts of the selling one. * * *

When the American bought the Adams, that company had for years been engaged in an extensive business throughout the United States and the American must have known that it had liabilities; but no provision whatever was made for their payment, and it now says to the creditors of the Adams in Kentucky, "If you want your money, go to the state of New York and try to get it." We will not give our sanction to a scheme like this, and the conclusion we have reached is supported by abundant authority. * * *

In considering this case we have not thus far noticed the authorities relied on by counsel for the American Company, the principal one being McAlister v. American Railway Express Co., 179 N.C. 556, 103 S.E. 129. In that case, as in this, the American Company took over the business and property of the Southern Express Co. at the same time and for the same reason and under the same circumstances that it took over the property and business of the Adams Company. McAlister in that case sought to make the American liable for a claim he had against the Southern. The facts of the two cases are as nearly alike as the facts of two cases could well be, but the North Carolina court reached the conclusion that the American Company was not liable, putting its decision upon the ground that the purchasing company, in the absence of contract obligation, or fraud, cannot be held liable for the debts of the selling corporation when there has been no merger or consolidation, and the selling corporation does not become extinct and retains sufficient property to pay its debts.

We do not, however, find ourselves willing to agree with the North Carolina court, although its decision finds some support in the authorities. We are well satisfied that the great weight of modern authority, as well as the right of the case, supports the conclusion we have reached.

Judgment affirmed.

PROBLEMS

1. The stock in Hotel Management, Inc., a hotel management corporation, was divided equally between two families. For several years the two families had been unable to agree or cooperate in the management of the corporation. As a result of this dissension no meeting of shareholders or directors had been held for five years.

There had been no withdrawal of profits for five years and the hotel had been operated at a loss for the year prior to the suit. While the corporation was not insolvent such a state was imminent due to the fact that the business was poorly managed and its properties in need of repair. As a result the owners of one-half of the stock brought an action in equity for dissolution of the corporation.

What decision?

2. (a) A merger is effected by the A, B and C corporations.

(b) The X, Y and Z corporations consolidate.

(c) The D Corporation, duly authorized by the shareholders, sells its entire assets to the E Corporation.

   (1) State the effect of these transactions on the legal existence of the respective business units involved.

   (2) State the effect, if any, of these transactions on the rights of the creditors of the respective business units involved.

3. (a) When may a corporation sell, lease, exchange, mortgage, or pledge all, or substantially all, of its assets in the usual and regular course of its business?

(b) When may a corporation sell, lease, exchange, mortgage, or pledge all, or substantially all, of its assets otherwise than in the usual and regular course of its business?

(c) What are the rights of a shareholder who dissents from a proposed sale or exchange of all or substantially all, of the assets of a corporation otherwise than in the usual and regular course of its business?

4. The X Company was duly merged into the Y Company. S, a shareholder of the former X Company, having paid in only one-half of his subscription, is now sued by the Y Company for the balance of such subscription. S, who took no part in the merger proceedings, denied liability on the ground that inasmuch as the X Company no longer exists, all his rights and obligations in connection with the X Company have been terminated. Decision?

5. The Federal government brought a criminal proceeding charging that the Slave Driver Corporation had violated certain provisions of the Fair Labor Standards Act. The corporation filed a motion to quash service of process. Accompanying the motion was an affidavit stating that the corporation had been organized under the laws of Delaware but had been dissolved eighteen months prior to service of process "by appropriate proceedings pursuant to the laws of that State." The Delaware statute provided that:

"All corporations, whether they expire by their own limitation, or are otherwise dissolved, shall nevertheless be continued for the term of three years from such expiration or dissolution bodies corporate for the purpose of prosecuting and defending suits by or against them, and of enabling them gradually to settle and close their business, to dispose of and convey their property, and to divide their capital stock but not for the purpose of continuing the business for which said corporation shall have been established; provided, however, that with respect to any action, suit or proceeding begun or commenced by or against the corporation prior to such expiration or dissolution and with respect to any action, suit or proceeding begun or commenced by or against the corporation within three years after the date of such expiration or dissolution, such corporation shall only for the purpose of such actions, suits or proceedings so begun or commenced be continued corporate bodies beyond said three year period and until any judgments, orders or decrees therein shall be fully executed."

The district court sustained the motion and dismissed the proceeding. Was the decision of the district court correct?

6. Smith, while in the course of his employment with the Bee Corporation, negligently ran the company's truck into X, injuring him very severely. Subsequently, the Bee Corporation, and the Sea Corporation, consolidated, forming the SeaBee Corporation. X filed suit against the SeaBee Corporation for damages and the SeaBee Corporation interposed the defense that the injuries sustained by X were not caused by any of SeaBee's employees, that the SeaBee was not even in existence at the time of the injury, and that, therefore, the SeaBee Corporation was not liable. What decision?

7. The Business Corporation Act of the State of X, after prescribing the procedure for the consolidation of two or more corporations, provides that "such surviving or new corporation shall thenceforth be responsible and liable for all the liabilities and obligations of each of the corporations so merged or consolidated."

(a) The A Company, a corporation organized under the laws of the State of X, duly authorized by the shareholders, sold its entire assets to the

B Company, also an X Corporation. T, an unpaid creditor of the A Company, sues the B Company upon his claim. Decision?

(b) The Z Company also incorporated under the laws of the State of X was duly merged into the Y Company. S, a shareholder of the former Z Company, having paid in only one-half of his subscription, is now sued by the Y Company for the balance of such subscription. S, who took no part in the merger proceedings, denies liability upon the ground that since the Z Company no longer exists, all his rights and obligations in connection with Z Company have been terminated. Decision?

CHAPTER 41

FOREIGN CORPORATIONS

Introductory. The earlier treatment of problems of corporate creation, existence, structure, and function has impliedly assumed uniform application of the law to all corporate entities. No consideration has been given to corporations which owe their existence not to local franchise but to the laws of other jurisdictions. Under the American Federal system, each State has sovereign authority to create corporations which as artificial creatures or instrumentalities of the State of incorporation are foreign in any other jurisdiction.

Except for acts in interstate commerce, a corporation may not transact business in a State other than the State of its incorporation without the permission and authorization of such State. Every State, however, provides for the issuance to foreign corporations of a certificate to do business within its borders.

Status and Rights Generally. Corporate existence is a privilege granted by the sovereign upon compliance with specified conditions. It is axiomatic that any such franchise cannot be operative outside of the jurisdiction of the granting power except as other jurisdictions may be willing to permit. In the United States, each corporation derives all of its powers from the State of incorporation and, subject to the rights it may have under the Federal constitution, the privilege to enter any other jurisdiction depends upon basic notions of comity, public policy and the legislation of such State. The powers or rights which a corporation may exercise outside of the State of incorporation will be found either expressly or by implication in its charter, in the statutes of the State of incorporation, and in the local laws of the foreign State wherein it seeks to do business.

Shareholders' or directors' meetings held outside the State of incorporation have no validity unless authorized by statute of the State which granted the charter. However, the trade which a corporation may carry on through its agents in other States will depend not only upon its original powers but also upon the rights granted to it by such other jurisdictions.

A foreign corporation must comply with those local laws which are expressly designed to regulate foreign corporations. A problem occasionally arises whether local statutes relating to corporations in general apply to foreign as well as to domestic corporations. Where the statutes relate to internal corporate acts, they will not be held to apply to foreign corporations. Statutes governing the rights of shareholders or the consequences of insolvency will be applied exclusively to domestic corporations, while those relating primarily to commerce or trade, such as local usury laws, will be applicable both to foreign and domestic corporations.

In the absence of express statutory prohibition, foreign corporations are generally accorded the fundamental commercial rights extended to domestic corporations with regard to contracts, commercial paper, and the acquisition of property or interests therein. This general right may be specifically denied or limited in instances where public policy reflects an intent to restrict certain powers to organizations more amenable to local sanction. Thus, it is not uncommon for foreign corporations to be denied the power to act as trustees or in other fiduciary capacities.

A matter of importance is the location of the domicile, residence, or habitat of a corporation which engages in business in numerous jurisdictions. The domicile of a natural person, depending in part upon intention, is sometimes very difficult of ascertainment. At an early date, it was determined that a corporation, irrespective of its roving commercial capabilities, could have only one domicile, and that its domicile was the State of its incorporation. Bank of Augusta v. Earle, 13 Pet. (U.S.) 519, 10 L.Ed. 274. Modern commerce has of necessity caused certain adjustments in the temper of the law since Chief Justice Taney of the United States Supreme Court observed that a corporation "must dwell in the place of creation and cannot migrate to another sovereignty." It is now recognized that a corporation may have a "residence" or be "located" in jurisdictions other than the State of incorporation. The question of domicile may be of great importance in many circumstances. Federal statutes relating to venue may turn upon domicile, and substantial business interests may be affected by the application of this technical concept. The jurisdiction of a particular State over a foreign corporation may depend upon whether the corporation had so established itself by maintaining a place of business in the State as to become resident therein. Local statutes distinguishing between natural persons, and residence by a foreign corporation may thus have additional and significant practical consequences.

Statutory Regulation of Foreign Corporations. An obvious corollary to the rule that a State may refuse to permit a foreign corporation to transact any intrastate business within its borders is that the State may impose reasonable conditions precedent to the granting of permission to carry on such business.

In order to protect its citizens in their dealings with foreign corporations and, incidentally, to obtain additional revenue, every State has provided by statute that foreign corporations must obtain a license or certificate of authority before they may transact intrastate business or have access to the lo-

cal courts to enforce rights arising out of such business. Conditions are imposed in connection with the granting of the certificate of authority to do business within the State. Since a corporation is not considered a citizen under the privileges and immunities clause of the Federal constitution, foreign corporations may not object, at least upon this ground, to conditions which are more onerous than those imposed on domestic corporations. The courts have also recognized that inherent differences between corporations and individuals may justify the imposition of more severe requirements on the former than would be permitted against the latter by the due process clause or the equal protection clause of the Federal constitution. Nevertheless, a State cannot by statute require as a condition anything which would arbitrarily interfere with the rights guaranteed a corporation by the Federal constitution. An example of an invalid requirement is one which would require a corporation as a prerequisite to doing business to agree to waive its right where there is diversity of citizenship to resort to the Federal courts.

Most jurisdictions require that foreign corporations designate a local registered agent upon whom service of summons and other notices may be had. An additional requirement is the filing of annual reports which will give some evidence of financial condition and also afford a basis for the imposition of whatever franchise or license taxes may be levied by the State. The State may, in order to protect domestic corporations, restrict the use of certain corporate names or, on the grounds of local public policy, the type of business in which a foreign corporation may engage.

A few jurisdictions go so far as to require the posting of bond by a foreign corporation to insure performance of its contracts, and certain States require a foreign corporation to comply with standards of financial responsibility before a certificate of authority to transact intrastate business will be issued.

A State may specify conditions under which a license or certificate of authority shall be revoked. Upon revocation, the foreign corporation is denied the right to transact further local business in the State. In general, the statutes provide that a failure to pay taxes, file reports, or maintain a registered agent will justify revocation of a license by the State. The power to evict is implied from the power to refuse admission, and insofar as the permission to do business is a mere license, it has been said that consent by the State may be withdrawn at any time with or without cause. Fidelity & D. Co. v. Tafoya, 270 U.S. 426, 46 S.Ct. 331, 70 L.Ed. 664. This dictum, although repeated and restated in many cases, has been limited by more fundamental constitutional rights in cases where substantial investments have been made in reliance upon local law and vested rights are threatened. In such cases, the State may be said to have waived its sovereign power of expulsion.

Doing Business. The question of whether a corporation is or is not present in a State other than the State of incorporation is generally raised in connection with local statutes imposing obligations upon foreign corporations which invariably provide that they apply to foreign corporations "doing business" or "transacting business" within the State. Although the phrase "doing business" is so common as to have become almost a term of art, it is a term for which no satisfactory general definition can be given for the reason that whether or not a foreign corporation is doing business in a particular State is essentially a question of fact. Approximately a dozen jurisdictions have attempted to define the phrase in their statutes and the necessity of litigating each new set of facts has not been noticeably lessened by statutory definitions.

These statutory definitions have no consistent pattern. Section 17–506 of the corporation statute of Kansas requiring qualification provides:

"Every corporation organized under the laws of another state, territory or foreign country that has an office or place of business within this State, or a distributive point herein, or that delivers its wares or products to resident agents for sale, delivery or distribution, shall be held to be doing business in this State."

California has a sweeping definition for the purpose of the local franchise tax. Section 5 of its Bank and Corporation Franchise Tax Act reads:

"The term 'doing business' as herein used, means actively engaged in any transaction for the purpose of financial or pecuniary gain or profit."

No two jurisdictions may necessarily agree upon whether a given set of facts constitutes doing business. The problem is further complicated by the different meanings attached to the phrase in the same jurisdiction, depending upon the particular local regulation which is sought to be imposed upon the foreign corporation. There are at least three principal types of statutes which apply to a foreign corporation within the State:

1. Statutes requiring foreign corporations to qualify or register and to subject themselves to regulations pertaining to their operations in the State.

2. Statutes imposing taxes upon foreign corporations.

3. Statutes providing for service of process upon foreign corporations.

What may constitute doing business as to subject a corporation to valid service of process may not be sufficient to constitute doing business to the extent that the foreign corporation must obtain a certificate of authority from the State. Furthermore, the qualifying statutes are limited in their application by the constitutional provision that commerce among the States shall be regulated by the Congress of the United States. The problem of a foreign corporation doing business to the extent that process may be served upon one of its agents is not primarily a question of interference with commerce among the States but a question of due process of law under the fourteenth amendment to the Federal constitution.

Although it is fundamental that a State may not impose regulations which constitute a burden upon or interference with interstate commerce, it is not always clear when a particular course of corporate action is solely intrastate or local in character and when it affects interstate commerce. The shipment of goods into a State to fill an order solicited in the State and accepted only at the home office outside of the State is generally considered to be interstate commerce, and a local statute regulating corporations which do business in the State would not apply to foreign corporations making such shipments. More difficult problems arise where goods are shipped into the State, stored there, and after an interval of time are sold to local customers. If later offered for sale to the general public, the usual rule is that they have lost their interstate status. If, however, they are later sold pursuant to the original contract between the foreign corporation and a local buyer, the transaction remains interstate in character.

Similar problems arise when a contract provides not only for the sale of goods but for the performance locally of installation services by the foreign vendor. The contract may be held to be separable and the sale to be in interstate commerce, whereas the installation is local and subjects the corporation to local control without impinging upon its constitutional rights. The line of demarcation is illustrated by two Illinois decisions involving correspondence schools. In one, the school maintained a local distributing office and was held to have been doing an intrastate business not within the protection of the commerce clause. In a later case where no local distributing office was maintained, the school was held to have been engaged in interstate commerce.

It is considerably easier to say what does not constitute doing business than to say what does, and this negative approach is reflected in the statutes, the textbooks, and the welter of judicial decisions dealing with the subject. In nearly every jurisdiction, an isolated transaction of the type generally engaged in by the foreign corporation will not constitute doing business so as to subject it to local qualification statutes. The courts have held that acts preliminary to the commencement of business, or acts solely for the purpose of winding up the corporation's affairs, do not constitute doing business within the state. The holding of title to real estate does not of itself constitute doing business, and in a few States this has been recognized by statute. Isolated sales of goods, although not interstate in character, have been held not to amount to doing business. The presence of traveling salesmen or drummers soliciting orders within the State does not subject the employer foreign corporation to the provisions of a statute imposing franchise taxes upon foreign corporations doing business in the State.

A series of acts each insufficient by itself to constitute doing business may bring a foreign corporation within the jurisdiction of the State where they are performed. Thus, maintenance of a sales force, a local office listed in the telephone directory, a local bank account, and a warehouse would undoubtedly constitute doing business within a State, while each taken separately might not.

The extent to which the business of a foreign corporation is adapted to local requirements may depend upon the severity of the penalties for failing to qualify if the corporation is found to be "doing business." One of the most common penalties is to deny the corporation access to local courts and, until recently, to treat any contract between the corporation and a resident as unenforceable by the corporation. In many instances the foreign corporation was not permitted to enforce a contract made prior to obtaining a certificate of authority to do business. Recent statutes have considerably mollified the consequences of doing business without qualifying. Section 117 of the Model Act reflects the prevailing current view that qualification is primarily a matter between the State and the foreign corporation and that a failure to obtain a certificate of authority to transact business in the State does not invalidate a contract entered into by the corporation. This section provides that an unlicensed foreign corporation doing business in the State shall not be entitled to maintain a suit in the State courts until such corporation shall have obtained a certificate of authority, but that the failure to obtain a license does not invalidate any contract of such corporation. This less stringent attitude is a recognition that the complexity and extent of modern commercial transactions, in conjunction with the unsatisfactory state of the law on the subject of doing business, make bona fide errors of opinion probable if not inevitable.

Internal Affairs. It is a common and accepted principle that local courts will not interfere with the internal affairs of a foreign corporation. This principle may have developed because of the obvious difficulties in attempting to enforce a judgment in cases where the books, records and principal officers may be outside the jurisdiction or because of general considerations of public policy and comity. Whatever the rationale behind the rule, a court of any State other than the State of incorporation almost invariably refuses relief when the issues involved are solely matters of administrative or managerial policy.

There is no clear line of demarcation between the internal affairs and the other affairs of a corporation. Litigation raising questions of shareholders' right is generally considered outside the province of a foreign jurisdiction. Contests over the election of directors or officers or the issuance of capital stock should also be brought before a court of the State of incorporation. However, courts have ordered a foreign corporation to transfer shares of stock on its books and to permit inspection of its books and records by a shareholder. Where a corporation has its principal office and principal assets in a State in which it is not incorporated and its directors, officers, and most of its agents reside in such State, the reluctance of a local court to inquire into its internal affairs may be tempered by a recognition that the corporation is domesticated if not domestic.

CASES

CONKLIN LIMESTONE CO. v. LINDEN

(1964) 22 A.D.2d 63, 253 N.Y.S.2d 578.

TAYLOR, J. The primary question presented by this appeal is whether or not plaintiff, a foreign corporation, concededly not having qualified to do business here may maintain an action to recover for goods sold and delivered to defendant between March 20, 1960 and September 8, 1960. [Citation.]

Finding that the action was barred by statute the County Court of Columbia County dismissed the complaint. From the resultant judgment plaintiff appeals. * * *

The facts are not in dispute. Plaintiff, a Connecticut corporation, has been engaged for some years in the business of crushing limestone for agricultural use at its plant located in Canaan in that State. Some part of the output is packaged in bags and sold to retail dealers. The major portion, however, is sold in bulk and transported in vehicles equipped with a spreading device by means of which trained corporate employees apply the ground limestone in measured quantities directly to the farmlands of purchasers for fertilization purposes. In 1960 plaintiff received 351 orders directly from customers residing in New York State or from retail dealers engaged in business therein in response to which it delivered within this State 7,500 tons of the lime which represented about 30% of its total sales. Gross income approximating $60,000 derived from such corporate activities. It appears that between 1957 and 1960 plaintiff under a contract with the Columbia County Soil Conservation Committee agreed to participate in the furnishing of conservation materials and services to farmers for use in carrying out a Federal Conservation Program. Although appellant employed no salesmen, an officer of the corporation occasionally examined a regional farm, at its owner's request, to determine the spreadability of the bulk lime. It maintained no office here. Upon appeal plaintiff does not contest the trial court's finding that the contract sued on was made in New York.

Whether the local activities engaged in by an unauthorized corporation sufficiently make out the transaction of business in this State within the meaning of the statute must be determined on the particular facts of each case. [Citation.] A showing of business conduct, regular and continuous, is essential to bring a foreign corporate plaintiff within it operative provisions. [Citations.]

Applying this test to the present record we find ample evidence to support the conclusion of the court below that plaintiff was, within the purview of the statute, doing business in this State.

Appellant's position that the interstate features of its transactions with defendant

brought it within the protection of the commerce clause of the Federal Constitution is untenable. The spreading of the lime over extensive farm acreage from especially equipped motor vehicles was strictly a local activity exclusively within the State's regulatory statute. [Citation.]

Judgment affirmed.

GOLDEN DAWN FOODS, INC. v. CEKUTA

(1964) 1 Ohio App.2d 464, 205 N.E.2d 121.

JONES, J. This case comes on for appeal from a judgment entry dated October 2, 1963, wherein defendants' motion for a directed verdict was sustained by the court and judgment entered thereon.

*   *   *

At the conclusion of the plaintiff's presentation, defendants moved for judgment on the basis that the evidence showed that the plaintiff was a foreign corporation doing business in Ohio without having registered with the Secretary of State as provided by law, and, therefore, that it could not maintain an action in Ohio courts.

*   *   *

The first issue to pass upon, as raised by assignment of error one, is whether Golden Dawn Foods, Inc., a foreign corporation, was doing business in the state of Ohio at the time suit was commenced. Since it is an agreed fact that Golden Dawn Foods, Inc., was a Pennsylvania corporation, not licensed to do business in Ohio, then, if this question is answered in the affirmative, they have no right to maintain an action in Ohio. This is so, as Section 1703.03, Revised Code, provides:

"No foreign corporation not excepted from Sections 1703.01 to 1703.31, inclusive, of the Revised Code, shall transact business in this state unless it holds an unexpired and uncancelled license to do so issued by the secretary of state. * * *."

Section 1703.29, Revised Code, provides:

"(A) The failure of any corporation to obtain a license under Sections 1703.01 to 1703.31, inclusive, of the Revised Code, does not affect the validity of any contract with such corporation, but no foreign corporation which should have obtained such license shall maintain any action in any court until it has obtained such license. * * *."

* * *

Was Golden Dawn Foods, Inc., doing business in the state of Ohio, pursuant to the law at the time suit was filed? From the state of the bill of exceptions, we think not. The only testimony is that Golden Dawn Foods, Inc., is a corporation organized and doing business under the laws of the commonwealth of Pennsylvania; that it is a wholesale grocery company which processes, buys, and sells foods and other products for sale on a wholesale basis to independent retail outlets; that it sells to some fifty stores in Ohio and about one hundred stores in Pennsylvania; that it owns no real estate in Ohio, nor is it the lessee or lessor of any property in Ohio; that its warehouses are all located in Pennsylvania; and that its salesmen are dispatched out of the Pennsylvania office.

Because of plaintiff's ownership of some stock in McVeigh store in Ohio, defendants claim that plaintiff is doing business in Ohio. The Gates and McVeigh Store, a corporation which has been operating in Warren, Ohio, for more than sixteen years, encountered financial difficulties. As a temporary arrangement during these difficulties, the Golden Dawn Foods Store, Inc., became an owner of a portion of the stock of Gates and McVeigh. The daily operation of the store was in the hands of Jack Gates and Stanley McVeigh. They controlled the buying and selling policies of that store. It can hardly be said that ownership of stock of the corpo-

ration in Ohio would qualify such owner as doing business in the state of Ohio.

* * *

The state of the record indicates nothing more or less than sales of merchandise to Ohio outlets by Golden Dawn Foods, Inc. There is no mention in the record of advertising devices or services or other assistance given to the retail outlets in Ohio carrying the name, "Golden Dawn Foods." * * *

We, therefore, conclude that prior to and at the time of suit, Golden Dawn Foods, Inc., was engaged solely in interstate commerce and as such had the right to maintain suit in the state of Ohio. The first assignment of error is, therefore, well taken.

* * *

This case is remanded for further proceedings according to law.

TERRAL v. BURKE CONSTRUCTION CO.

(1922) 257 U.S. 529, 42 S.Ct. 188, 66 L.Ed. 352.

TAFT, C. J. This is an appeal by Terral, defendant, from the District Court under sec. 238 of the Judicial Code, in a case in which the law of a State is claimed to be in contravention of the Constitution of the United States.

The Burke Construction Company, a corporation organized under the laws of the State of Missouri, filed its bill against Terral, Secretary of State of Arkansas, averring that it had been licensed to do business in the State of Arkansas under an act of the Arkansas Legislature approved May 13, 1907; that it was organized for the purpose of doing construction work, and carrying on interstate commerce, and was actually so engaged in Arkansas; that the right to do business in the State was a valuable privilege, and the revocation of the license would greatly injure it; that it had brought an original suit in the federal court of Arkansas and had removed a suit brought against it to the same federal court; that the Secretary of State was about to revoke the license because of such suit and such removal, acting under the requirement of sec. 1 of the Act of the Legislature of Arkansas of May 13, 1907, reading as follows:

"If any company shall, without the consent of the other party to any suit or proceeding brought by or against it in any court of this State, remove said suit or proceeding to any Federal court, or shall institute any suit or proceeding against any citizen of this State in any Federal court, it shall be the duty of the Secretary of State to forthwith revoke all authority to such company and its agents to do business in this State, and to publish such revocation in some newspaper of general circulation published in this State; and if such corporation shall thereafter continue to do business in this State, it shall be subject to the penalty of this Act for each day it shall continue to do business in this State after such revocation."

The penalty fixed is not less than $1,000 a day. The Construction Company avers that this act is in contravention of sec. 2, Article III, i. e., the judiciary article of the Federal Constitution, and of sec. 1 of the Fourteenth Amendment. * * *

The sole question presented on the record is whether a state law is unconstitutional which revokes a license to a foreign corporation to do business within the State because, while doing only a domestic business in the State, it resorts to the federal court sitting in the State.

The cases in this court in which the conflict between the power of a State to exclude a foreign corporation from doing business within its borders, and the federal constitutional right of such foreign corporation to resort to the federal courts has been considered, can not be reconciled. [Citations.]

The principle established by the more recent decisions of this court is that a State may not, in imposing conditions upon the privilege of a foreign corporation's doing business in the State, exact from it a waiver of the exercise of its constitutional right to resort to the federal courts, or thereafter withdraw the privilege of doing business because of its exercise of such right, whether waived in advance or not. The principle does not depend for its application on the character of the business the corporation does, whether state or interstate, although that has been suggested as a distinction in some cases. It rests on the ground that the Federal Constitution confers upon citizens of one State the right to resort to federal courts in another, that state action, whether legislative or executive, necessarily calculated to curtail the free exercise of the right thus secured is void because the sovereign power of a State in excluding foreign corporations, as in the exercise of all others of its sovereign powers, is subject to the limitations of the supreme fundamental law. It follows that the cases of Doyle v. Continental Insurance Co., 94 U.S. 535, 24 L.Ed. 148, and Security Mutual Life Insurance Co. v. Prewitt, 202 U.S. 246, 26 S.Ct. 619, 50 L.Ed. 1013, 6 Ann.Cas. 317, must be considered as overruled and that the views of the minority judges in those cases have become the law of this court. The appellant in proposing to comply with the statute in question and revoke the license was about to violate the constitutional right of the appellee. In enjoining him the District Court was right, and its decree is

Affirmed.

BRYANT v. FINNISH NATIONAL AIRLINE

(1965) 15 N.Y.2d 426, 260 N.Y.S.2d 625, 208 N.E.2d 439.

DESMOND, C. J. * * * Plaintiff is a resident of New York. The complaint in this suit alleges that at an airport in Paris plaintiff, an employee of Trans World Airlines, was injured through the negligence of defendant Finnish National Airline when she was struck by a baggage cart blown against her by an excessive blast of air produced by one of defendant's aircraft which was moving across the airfield to a parking spot. The question is whether within the statute and cases defendant was "doing business" in New York State so as to subject it to personal jurisdiction here. The Appellate Division, reversing Special Term, answered that question in the negative.

The Appellate Division majority opinion in these words summarized the facts set forth in the affidavits as to the kind and amount of business done by defendant Finnish National Airline in New York City: "The defendant is a foreign corporation organized under the laws of Finland, with its principal operating base, its head executive and administrative offices located in Helsinki, Finland, and is not registered in the United States. None of its stockholders, directors or officers are citizens or residents of the United States and defendant has not qualified to do business in the State of New York. All of Finnair's flights begin and end outside of the United States. It operates no aircraft within the United States and, according to Rosenberg, the office in New York does not sell tickets even for its own flights and receives no payment of fares for defendant's flights at its New York office. Defendant maintains a one-and-a-half room office at 10 East 40th Street, New York, staffed with three full-time and four part-time employees, none of whom is an officer or director of defendant. Its principal function is to receive from international air carriers or travel agencies reservations for travel on Finnair in Europe which it transmits to defendant's space control office in Europe. Upon occasion the New York office will transmit information concerning a reservation from the international air carrier or travel agency to defendant's space control office in Europe and relay the conformation or reply, when received, to such airline or agency. The New York office does some information and publicity work for defendant, and places a certain amount of advertising regarding Finnair's European services in connection with its publicity work. None of the New York office employees has authority to bind the defendant and contracts in connection with such office activities must be sent to the office in Helsinki for approval. Finnair maintains a bank account in which, according to Rosenberg, the average balance is less than $2000 and out of which is paid the salaries of the employees, the rent and normal operating expenses of the New York office." (22 A.D.2d, pp. 19–20, 253 N.Y.S.2d at p. 219.)

* * * The test for "doing business" is and should be a simple pragmatic one, which leads us to the conclusion that defendant should be held to be suable in New York. The New York office is one of many directly maintained by defendant in various parts of the world, it has a lease on a New York office, it employs several people and it has a bank account here, it does public relations and publicity work for defendant here including maintaining contacts with other airlines and travel agencies and, while it does not make reservations or sell tickets, it transmits requests for space to defendant in Europe and helps to generate business. These things should be enough.

The order appealed from should be reversed and the motion to dismiss the complaint denied, with costs in this court and in the Appellate Division.

DALE ELECTRONICS, INC. v. COPYMATION, INC.

(1965) 178 Neb. 239, 132 N.W.2d 788.

SPENCER, J. The sole question involved in this appeal is whether the district court erred in sustaining a special appearance filed by Copymation, Inc., an Illinois corporation.

The appellant, Dale Electronics, Inc., hereinafter referred to as Dale, brought this action against Copymation, Inc., hereinafter referred to as Copymation, and Standard Blueprint Company, a Nebraska corporation, hereinafter referred to as Standard, to recover damages for alleged breach of warranty of fitness of use of a copy machine manufactured by Copymation and sold to Dale by Standard. * * *

Copymation is engaged in the business of manufacturing and distributing certain jobbed items in the technical reproduction field. It has never qualified and is not licensed to do business in Nebraska as a foreign corporation, and has never appointed a resident agent or designated a registered office in the state. Copymation sells copy machines which it manufactures to users as well as to retail dealers who in turn sell them to users. It maintains a sales force on both the east and west coasts and in the southwest, but does business in the midwest only through dealers to whom it sells at wholesale. Standard is such a dealer in the State of Nebraska. Copymation maintains no office of any nature in Nebraska. Its salesmen do not call on Standard or on any prospective user in Nebraska. It has never had a show, exhibition, or demonstration of its products in Nebraska. The only advertising it does is through trade publications on a national basis. It does not participate in any advertising on a local level anywhere in the country, by sharing expenses, or otherwise.

The copy machine which is the subject of this litigation was sold to Dale at Columbus, Nebraska, by a Standard salesman on a Standard sales order. Standard, which is located in Omaha, then sent a purchase order on its own form to Copymation, with directions to ship the machine direct to Dale at Columbus. The machine was shipped by common carrier, as per instructions. When it arrived at Columbus, Standard was notified, and the machine was installed for Dale under the direction of an employee of Standard. Standard paid Copymation the wholesale price for the machine and billed Dale for the agreed price. Payment to Copymation was in no way dependent upon collection. In the event Dale did not pay Standard, the latter was still obligated to pay Copymation.

Once a machine is sold to a dealer, Copymation maintains no control over the resale of such machine at retail, and has no connection or responsibility for its installation. The Standard employee who installed the machine had spent 5 days at the Copymation factory school to familiarize himself with the product. His transportation to the factory was paid by Standard but his expenses at the factory were paid by Copymation. This, however, is a purely voluntary service provided by Copymation to familiarize dealer servicemen with the operation and construction of its machines. Copymation exercises no control of any nature over the servicemen.

Standard does not maintain a stock of Copymation equipment, nor has it ever displayed any Copymation machines or any placards or signs pertaining to Copymation. Standard has never advertised Copymation products in the newspapers. Standard salesmen are fulltime Standard employees, and sell copy machines made by other manufacturers as well as those of Copymation. They also sell all other items handled by Standard, including materials for copy machines. They have no connection with and receive no remuneration of any nature from Copymation. The copy machine sold to Dale was only the second sale of a Copymation machine in the State of Nebraska.

We have detailed the course of dealings at length to show that the transaction involved herein is a sale by a dealer or jobber who purchased a machine from Copymation after the dealer or jobber had found a purchaser. Does this type of transaction constitute doing business in Nebraska on the part of Copymation sufficient to authorize service of process under section 21–1201, R.R.S.1943?

* * *

In Brown v. Globe Laboratories, Inc., 165 Neb. 138, 84 N.W.2d 151, we held: "Before any state can subject a foreign corporation to the jurisdiction of that state such corporation must have either expressly consented to such jurisdiction or must have done sufficient business therein to constitute a submission to such jurisdiction.

"No all-embracing rule can be laid down as to just what constitutes the doing of sufficient business in a state by a foreign corporation in order to subject it to process of that jurisdiction. Each case must necessarily be determined by its own facts."

* * *

The relation of Standard to this transaction is that of an independent contractor and not as an agent of Copymation. Standard was in business for itself. It could buy Copymation machines at wholesale, but was under no obligation to buy or to sell the products of Copymation. In dealing with Dale, Standard was dealing on its own account. We do not feel that the filling of orders solicited by an independent contractor brings Copymation within the orbit of doing business in Nebraska sufficient to warrant service of process under section 21–1201, R.R.S.1943.

It does seem, as a minimal requirement, that the manner and extent of doing business in this state must be such as to warrant the inference of an actual as distinguished from a merely fictitious or constructive presence in the state, and such that it may be said that the corporation itself, through the representative capacity of its agents, is in the state. To hold that a foreign corporation is doing business in Nebraska merely because it fills an order received by mail from a Nebraska resident without more appearing, is to extend the doctrine of doing business in the state for the purpose of constructive service too far.

There was no proper service of process on Copymation. Its special appearance was properly sustained, and the order sustaining it is affirmed.

Affirmed.

WRIGHT v. POST

(1929) 268 Mass. 126, 167 N.E. 278.

WAIT, J. The plaintiffs appeal from an interlocutory decree of the Superior Court sustaining demurrers to their bill in equity, and from a final decree dismissing the bill entered after the plaintiffs had had opportunity to amend their bill but had filed no amendment.

The allegations of the bill, which is very long, need not be stated in detail. They disclose the pendency of controversy with regard to the plaintiffs' claim to be the legally chosen directors of the Triplex Gold Mines, Limited, a corporation organized under the laws of the Province of Ontario in the Dominion of Canada, and with regard to the legality of a meeting of alleged shareholders held at Worcester on June 2, 1928. They disclose further, that litigation in which the corporation and others of the parties herein are parties, begun in 1922, is pending in the courts of said Province affecting rights as shareholders of the parties plaintiff and defendant, or some of them, material to the issues of this bill, which would be in issue were this bill to be heard on its merits; and that matters vitally affecting Triplex Gold Mines, Limited, and its management by one body or another of persons whose status as stockholders has not been finally ascertained by any court, are involved, which depend, in part at least, upon the corporation laws of said Province. The bill, among other things, seeks from courts of Massachusetts an adjudication that the plaintiffs are the duly elected directors of Triplex Gold Mines, Limited, and orders placing the books and control of its business in their hands, restraining the prosecution of litigation in the courts of Ontario, restraining action by the defendant Post in obedience to orders made by courts of Ontario or elsewhere, and establishing alleged rights of Triplex Gold Mines, Limited, against certain defendants. In substance it asks the court of Massachusetts to interfere with pending litigation in the courts of Ontario and to adjudicate with regard to the internal affairs of a foreign corporation.

The bill was filed August 9, 1928. Defendant Heslor demurred on August 23. The corporation on August 22 filed a plea to the jurisdiction, alleging it had no usual place of business in Massachusetts and was not engaged in doing business within the jurisdiction of the Commonwealth. An order of notice to show cause why a temporary injunction should not issue was heard on or about August 25; and, on August 25, the Superior Court restrained temporarily defendants either as stockholders, officers or employees of Triplex Gold Mines, Limited, from calling any adjourned meeting of the meeting of June 2, 1928, for the purpose of casting any cloud on action taken at the meeting of June 2, or for the purpose of electing officers or directors of Triplex Gold Mines, Limited, for the year beginning June 2, 1928. On September 4, the remaining defendants filed a demurrer. Sometime prior to October 5, the demurrers were argued and sustained on the grounds that the proper remedy in a contested corporate election was mandamus; that the bill was multifarious; and that jurisdiction should be declined because the controversy ought to be settled in the courts of the domicil of the corporation.

No extended discussion is necessary. The law is settled that the courts of this Commonwealth may properly refuse to pass upon a controversy relating in substance to the internal management and control of a foreign corporation, even if individual officers or stockholders are domiciled in Massachusetts.

[Citations.] It is especially fitting that they so refuse where litigation, dealing in large part with matters likely to be in issue in the proceedings sought to be instituted here is already pending in the courts of the corporation's domicil; see Kimball v. St. Louis & San Francisco Ry. Co., 157 Mass. 7, 31 N.E. 697, 34 Am.St.Rep. 250, and, above all, where they are asked to forbid obedience to orders of the courts of the domicil. Andrews v. Mines Corporation Limited, 205 Mass. 121, 91 N.E. 122, 137 Am.St.Rep. 428, presents utterly different considerations, and is not controlling.

The action of the Superior Court in granting a temporary injunction at a date before complete pleadings were required by rule or order of the court, is not such assumption of jurisdiction to retain and try the merits of the bill of complaint, that the court may not, at any later time refuse jurisdiction.

Decree affirmed.

PROBLEMS

1. X Corporation, organized under the laws of State S, sends travelling salesmen into State M to solicit orders which are accepted only at the Home Office of X Corporation in State S. D, a resident of State M, places an order which is accepted by X Corporation and the goods are shipped to D from the office of X Corporation in State S. The Corporation Act of State M provides that "no foreign corporation transacting business in this state without a certificate of authority shall be permitted to maintain an action in any court of this state until such corporation shall have obtained a certificate of authority." D fails to pay for the goods and when X Corporation sues D in a court of State M, D defends on the ground that X Corporation has never had such a certificate of authority from State M. Result?

2. The Emanon Corporation was a Delaware corporation having its executive office in Philadelphia, Pa. Jones, its vice-president was served with a summons in Trenton, N. J. The corporation had not procured a license to do business in New Jersey. It appeared that Jones had an

office in Trenton in which he devoted his time to research work on matters affecting the Emanon Corporation, to the editing of printed literature for the corporation, and to the training of employees for it. Do these facts constitute doing business within New Jersey to such an extent as to give the courts of the State jurisdiction of the Emanon Corporation?

3. The X Company, of Pennsylvania, manufactures articles and merchandise used all over the United States. Its business in Massachusetts was handled through the A Company, a large jobbing house, which purchased from the X Company in Pennsylvania and resold to retailers in Massachusetts. The X Company maintained no office in Massachusetts, was never licensed to do business in Massachusetts and paid no taxes to that State. Four times a year salesmen from the home office of the X Company canvassed the retail trade in Massachusetts, educating the trade in the use of the X Company's products and taking orders. Such orders were immediately turned over to the A Company by the salesmen, the A Company filling the orders from its own stock, purchased from the X Company. The State of Massachusetts levied taxes against the X Company on the business thus done and added heavy penalties on the ground that the X Company was doing business in Massachusetts without having obtained the necessary license. Decision?

4. (a) X Corporation was an Illinois corporation. The Illinois legislature passed a statute exempting all stock in Illinois corporations from personal property tax. Y Corporation was a foreign corporation doing 75% of its business in the State of Illinois. As a result of the tax savings made possible by the above statute to persons owning stock in Illinois corporations, Y Corporation was at a great disadvantage in securing proper financing through stock sales. In a proper suit, Y Corporation challenged the constitutionality of the statute.

(b) Illinois likewise passed a tax law providing that a personal property tax shall be levied on *all* the railroad cars owned by a railroad corporation, operating in Illinois, whether such cars ever come into Illinois or not. About 5% of X Railroad Corporation's cars were operated in Illinois. In a proper suit the X Railroad Corporation challenged the constitutionality of the statute.

Decide the issues involved in the above fact situations.

5. Corporation A sued corporation B in Illinois for breach of contract and defendant filed an answer setting up the following defenses, to wit: (1) plaintiff was a Michigan corporation not authorized to or doing business in Illinois; (2) defendant was a West Virginia corporation, not doing business in Illinois and having no officer or agent there upon whom legal service could be had. Which, if any, or either of the defenses were good?

6. The A corporation, organized under the laws of New Jersey, has its general office and factory in New York and opens up a branch office in Illinois, from which contracts are closed and goods are delivered to purchasers. It also has a traveling salesman in Massachusetts who solicits orders and sends them in to be approved and filled. It also purchases land in Ohio, and then, deciding not to open an office there, resells the land and takes back a mortgage. In which of these States must it comply with the foreign corporation law?

PART EIGHT

UNFAIR COMPETITION, BANKRUPTCY, SECURED TRANSACTIONS

CHAPTER 42

UNFAIR COMPETITION AND TRADE REGULATION

Introductory. The economic community is best served in normal times by free competition in trade and industry. It is in the public interest that quality, price, and service, in an open competitive market for goods and services be determining factors in the business rivalry for the customer's dollar.

Practices such as imitation of a competitor's trade mark, passing or palming off one's product as that of another, betrayal of trade secrets, disloyalty of employees, interference with contracts, false advertising, and product disparagement, are injurious to free and fair competition in business. To preserve fairness and to protect freedom of competition by preventing businessmen from taking unfair advantage of their competitors, certain rules and principles have been developed by the courts. Generally referred to as the law of unfair competition, they are basically rules of fair play, the rules of the game applied to the world of business.

Enterprises such as power companies, water companies, railroads, airlines and other common carriers, telephone and telegraph companies, banks, and insurance companies, are extensively regulated by statute in the public interest. They are public utilities or enterprises vested with a public interest and to a certain extent occupy a protected monopoly position. They are subject to a much greater degree of regulation than the ordinary business enterprise, and are responsible to administrative agencies, boards, and commissions. Governmental supervision is so close and watchful that there is usually little latitude for unfair competition by public utilities.

Trade regulation embraces more than unfair competition. In a generic sense, the law of unfair competition is a part of trade regulation which usually refers to regulation of business by statutes that not only impose civil liability, but are enforceable by direct governmental action and sanctions of suspensions, injunctions, fines, and imprisonment.

Palming off Goods. One of the earliest forms of unfair competition is the fraudulent marketing of one person's goods as those of another. This unlawful practice is sometimes referred to as "passing off" or "palming off". It may involve infringement of another's trademark or appropriation of another's trade name, or a conscious imitation of the physical appearance of another's goods deceptive to the purchaser. It is basically a "cashing in" on the good will, good name, and reputation of a competitor and of his products. It results in deception of the public and loss of trade by honest businessmen.

Misuse of Trade Secrets. Every business has secret information including lists of customers, contracts with suppliers and customers. Some have secret formulas, processes, and methods used in the production of goods that are vital to successful operation of the business. These are sometimes designated as "trade secrets", involving information received and held in confidence by employees which they are required to have in order to perform their duties.

An employee is under a duty of loyalty to his employer which includes the non-disclosure of trade secrets to competitors. It is wrongful for a competitor to obtain vital secret trade information of this type from an employee by bribery or otherwise. The faithless employee also commits a tort by divulging secret trade information. Contracts of employment frequently contain restrictive covenants whereby the employee agrees that for a stated period of time and within a specific territory he will not directly or indirectly engage in competition with his former employer, or become employed by a competitor of his former employer. These restrictive agreements, if reasonable with respect to time and area limitations, are enforced by the courts, although in some jurisdictions enforcement depends upon the employee having acquired trade secrets of his employer during the course of his employment.

In the absence of contract restriction, an employee is under no duty upon termination of his employment to refrain from competing or working for a competitor of his former employer. During the period of employment he is under such a duty whether or not provided by contract. An example of unfair competition would be the inducement by one company of employees of another company possessed of certain unique technical skills, and secret knowledge acquired by them in the course of such employment, to terminate their employment and to use such skills and secret information for its benefit. Thus A and B, who have been employees of the X Company for 15 years, have developed in the course of their employment highly specialized knowledge and skills in the manufacture of space suits for astronauts. There are few, if any, persons who have equivalent skill and knowledge. Y Company, desirous of obtain-ing a contract with the government for the manufacture of space suits, approaches A and B and offers them employment. There is no contract which prohibits A and B from leaving the X Company and going to work for the Y Company. However, if they do so, the X Company is entitled to an injunction restraining A, B, and the Y Company from the use of trade secrets and methods for manufacturing space suits which were developed by A and B while in the employ of the X Company.

Trade-Marks. A trade-mark is a distinctive mark, word, letter, number, design, picture or combination thereof in any form of arrangement which is affixed to goods and is adopted or used by a person identifying goods which he manufactures or sells. Generic and descriptive designations cannot be used as trademarks. Thus, a word which is descriptive of the ingredients, quality, purpose, function, or uses of a product, may not be monopolized by a person as his proprietary trademark. The word "Plow" cannot be a trade-mark for plows, although it may be a trade-mark for shoes.

A geographical name may be used as a trade-mark unless the name is not likely to be understood as representing that the goods were produced or processed in the place designated by the name, or that they are of the same distinct kind or quality as goods produced, processed, or used in that place; or, unless the person using the name is the owner, or acts with the consent of the owner of the geographical place, or is the sole source of supply of goods originated in the place indicated by the name.

At common law a trade-mark was required to be affixed to the goods it identified. The Lanham Act, Trade-Mark Act of 1946, relaxes this requirement by permitting trade-mark registration and protection of a mark placed "on the goods or their containers or the displays associated therewith or on the tags or labels affixed thereto."

Trade-marks may be registered in the United States Patent Office. If infringed, the owner is entitled to injunctive relief and damages.

Service Marks, Certification Marks, Collective Marks. Similar in function to the trade-mark which identifies tangible goods and products, a service mark is used to identify and distinguish the services of one person from those of others. A service mark need not be affixed to goods and when registered in the Patent Office is entitled to the same protection as a registered trade-mark. Service marks were not registerable prior to the Lanham Act of 1946.

A certification mark is a mark used upon or in connection with goods or services of one or more persons other than the owner of the mark to certify regional or other origin, material, mode of manufacture, quality, accuracy, or other characteristics of the goods or services, or that the work or labor in the goods or services were performed by members of a union or other organization.

A collective mark is a distinctive mark or symbol used to identify, or indicate membership in a trade union, trade association, fraternal society, or other organization.

Trade-marks, service marks, certification marks, and collective marks, are protected against misuse or infringement by injunctive relief and a right of action for damages against the infringer. An infringement is a form of passing off one's goods or services as those of the owner of the mark, is deceptive of the public, and amounts to unfair competition.

Trade Names. A trade name, like a trade-mark, is serviceable as an identification of the product of a particular manufacturer or distributor. It may also designate a service or be the name under which a business is conducted. Trade names, therefore, have broader scope than trade-marks which only identify goods.

Descriptive and generic words, and personal and generic names, although not proper trademarks, may become protected as trade names upon acquiring a special significance in the trade. This special significance is frequently referred to as a "secondary meaning" of the name acquired as the result of continuing extended use in connection with specific goods or services whereby the name has lost its primary meaning to a substantial number of purchasers or users of the goods or services. A trade name for a product may be coined, such as "Kodak" or "Nylon", or it may be a popularly accepted nickname as "Coke".

Trade names are protected, and a person who palms off his goods or services by using the trade name of another is liable in damages and also may be enjoined from doing so.

Copyright. A copyright is the exclusive right to print, reprint, publish, copy, and sell books, periodicals, newspapers, dramatic and musical compositions, lectures, works of art, photographs, pictorial illustrations, and motion pictures, for a period of 28 years from the date of first publication.

Applications for copyright are filed with the Register of Copyrights, Copyright Office, Library of Congress, Washington, D. C.

The right is protected by the Federal Copyright Act, and infringements are remediable in the Federal Courts.

Patents. A patent is the grant by the government of a monopoly right to an inventor to exclude others from making, using, or selling his invention for a period of 17 years.

The owner of the patent may also profit by licensing others to use the invention on a royalty basis. A patent is issued by the United States Patent Office upon the basis of an application containing specific claims relating to the invention, process, product, or design.

Before granting a patent, the Patent Office makes a careful and thorough examination of the prior art and determines that the submitted invention has novelty and does not conflict with a prior pending application or a previously issued patent. An application for a patent is confidential and its contents will not be divulged by the Patent Office. This confidentiality ends upon granting of the patent.

The granting of a patent is no guaranty of exclusive rights to make, use, or sell the alleged invention. The Patent Office is not a court and does not determine the rights of holders of patents. It may be necessary for the patentee to bring an action in the Federal court for infringement in order to determine the validity of his patent. If the court finds that the idea or invention is not novel, or is fully covered by the prior art, or that someone else had reduced the idea to practice before conception date by the patentee, the patent may be ruled invalid.

The Supreme Court has held that the Copyright and Patent laws have pre-empted their respective fields and that in the absence of a copyright or patent, no State law of unfair competition may provide a cause of action for reproducing uncopyrighted material or imitating unpatented product designs except for the tort of "palming off" or mislabeling. Sears Roebuck & Co. v. Stiffel Co., 376 U.S. 225, 84 S.Ct. 784, 11 L.Ed.2d 661 (1964) page 964.

Disparagement of Another's Property. An unprivileged statement which is untrue and disparaging to the title or quality of another's property, and which adversely affects the conduct of a third person as prospective purchaser or lessee of the property, subjects the person making the statement to liability. He is liable to the person whose property is disparaged even though he did not intend to influence the conduct of a third person, and although he neither knew nor believed that the disparaging matter was false.

Disparagement is defined as statements intended by the party making them to be understood, or which are reasonably understood, as casting doubt upon the title or quality of another's property, if the statements are so understood by the person to whom made.

Thus, A, while contemplating the purchase of a stock of merchandise which belongs to B, reads an advertisement in a newspaper in which C falsely asserts he has a lien upon the merchandise. C has disparaged B's property in the goods.

A person who publishes disparaging matter is liable for loss sustained by the owner of the property disparaged as a result of repetition of the disparaging matter by a third person if the repetition was either authorized or reasonably foreseeable. For instance, Jones makes an offer to purchase Smith's farm which has been represented free and clear of encumbrances. Tattle tells Mrs. Jones that the farm is mortgaged up to its full value. Mrs. Jones, as she is privileged to do, repeats this to her husband who withdraws his offer for the farm. Tattle is liable to Smith.

An untrue expression of opinion, dishonestly made, which is disparaging, is wrongful and actionable. However, no action lies to recover damages resulting from an honest statement of opinion, one actually held by the party making it, and clearly expressed as such.

The pecuniary loss which may be recovered by an injured person is that which directly and immediately results from impairment of the marketability of the property disparaged. Thus, A publishes an untrue statement in a magazine that cranberries grown during the current season in a particular area are unwholesome. B is a jobber who has contracted to buy the entire output of cranberries grown in this area. B's business falls off 50%. If there are no other facts which account for this falling off of B's business, B is entitled to recover the amount of his loss from A.

Unfair Sales Acts. Certain States have enacted statutes to prevent the advertising or sale of merchandise by either a retailer or wholesaler at less than cost. These statutes are aimed at "loss leaders" whereby a brand product is advertised at a price lower than cost and lower than its ordinary retail price. The purpose is to attract customers to the store. The merchant may have very few of the advertised items in stock and they are quickly sold. No advertisement is ever made by the merchant that his supply of such merchandise has been exhausted.

These statutes generally define the term "cost to the retailer" as including freight charges, transportation costs, taxes, and a mark up to cover a proportionate part of the cost of doing business. The Unfair Sales Act of Oklahoma provides for a 6% mark up in the absence of proof of a lesser cost. Diehl v. Magic Empire Grocers Ass'n of Oklahoma, 399 P.2d 460 (1965) p. 963.

Anti-Trust Statutes. The common law has traditionally favored free and open competition in the market place and has held illegal and unenforceable agreements and contracts in restraint of trade. Implementing this policy are Anti-Trust statutes adopted in most of the States to prohibit local anti-competitive practices. There is no Federal common law against restraint of trade, but only statutory law enacted by the Congress. In the latter half of the 19th century, it became apparent that concentrations of economic power in the form of "trusts" and "combinations" were too powerful and widespread to be effectively curbed and controlled by State action. This prompted the Congress in 1890 to enact the first Federal statute in this field known as the Sherman Anti-trust Act.

Section 1 of the Sherman Act provides: "Every contract, combination in the form of trust or otherwise, or conspiracy, in restraint of trade or commerce among the several States, or with foreign nations, is declared to be illegal." Section 2 provides: "Every person who shall monopolize, or attempt to monopolize, or combine or conspire with any other person or persons, to monopolize any part of the trade or commerce among the several States, or with foreign nations, shall be deemed guilty of a misdemeanor." Violators of either section are subject to fine or imprisonment, or both. The Federal district courts are empowered to issue injunctions restraining violations, and anyone injured by a violation is entitled to recover in a civil action treble damages, three times the amount of his actual loss sustained. It is the duty of United States district attorneys, under the supervision of the Attorney General, and of the Federal Trade Commission, to institute appropriate enforcement proceedings other than treble damage actions.

The object of the Sherman Act, as stated by the United States Supreme Court, is the prohibition of all "contracts or acts which it was considered had a monopolistic tendency, especially those which were thought to unduly diminish competition," and of acts "producing or tending to produce the consequences of monopoly." The Act has resulted in an enormous amount of both civil litigation and criminal prosecutions. Perhaps the most significant case is a 1911 decision of the United States Supreme Court which established the so-called "rule of reason" doctrine, declaring that only those contracts or combinations which impose unreasonable restraints upon trade and commerce are proscribed by the Act. Standard Oil Co. of New Jersey v. United States, 221 U.S. 1, 31 S.Ct. 502 (1911).

Certain combinations and agreements in restraint of trade have been held by the Supreme Court to be *per se* violations of the Anti-Trust Statutes. They do not come within the "rule of reason" and when proved cannot be justified on any reasonable basis.

Among these *per se* violations are (1) the sale of an unpatented product tied to a patented article; (2) territorial allocation of markets; (3) group boycotts or refusals to deal; (4) horizontal price fixing; and (5) vertical price fixing unless lawful under a Fair Trade Act.

The Clayton Act. In 1914 Congress strengthened the Sherman Act by adopting the Clayton Act which was expressly designed "to supplement existing laws against unlawful restraints and monopolies." Section 2 as amended in 1936, prohibits price discrimination, and is commonly referred to as the Robinson-Patman Act.

Section 3 of the Clayton Act prohibits "tying contracts," exclusive selling and leasing arrangements preventing purchasers from dealing with the seller's competitors, where the effect is to substantially lessen competition or tend to create a monopoly. A lease of patented machines for dispensing industrial salt tablets but conditioned on the lessee's purchase of the lessor's salt was held to be a violation of this section.

Section 7 of the Clayton Act, as amended, prohibits the acquisition by a corporation of stock in another corporation or assets of another corporation where the effect may be to substantially lessen competition or tend to create a monopoly. Interlocking directorates in competing corporations engaged in interstate commerce (except banks, banking associations, trust companies and common carriers) where the aggregate capitalization is a million dollars or more, are prohibited by Section 8.

The Clayton Act exempts labor, agricultural and horticultural organizations from anti-trust laws. Section 6.

The Federal Trade Commission. In 1914 the Congress enacted the Federal Trade Commission Act creating the Federal Trade Commission and charging it with the duty to prevent "unfair methods of competition in

commerce, and unfair or deceptive acts or practices in commerce." To this end the five member Commission is empowered to conduct appropriate investigations and hearings. It may issue "cease and desist" orders against violators enforceable in the Federal courts. Its broad power has been described as follows by the United States Supreme Court:

> "The 'unfair methods of competition,' which are condemned by * * * the Act, are not confined to those that were illegal at common law or that were condemned by the Sherman Act * * *. It is also clear that the Federal Trade Commission Act was designed to supplement and bolster the Sherman Act and the Clayton Act * * * *to stop in their incipiency acts and practices which, when full blown, would violate those Acts.*" F. T. C. v. Motion Picture Adv. Service Co., 344 U.S. 392, 73 S.Ct. 361, 97 L.Ed. 426 (1953). (Emphasis supplied).

Complaints may be instituted by the Commission which after a hearing may enter a cease and desist order having the effect of an injunction. Appeals may be taken from orders of the Commission to United States Courts of Appeals which have exclusive jurisdiction "to enforce, set aside, or modify, orders of the Commission."

The work of the Federal Trade Commission includes not only investigation of possible violations of the anti-trust laws but also unfair methods of competition such as false and misleading advertisements, false or inadequate labeling of products, passing or palming off goods as those of a competitor, lotteries, gambling schemes, discriminatory offers of rebates and discounts, false disparagement of a competitor's goods, false or misleading descriptive names of products, use of false testimonials, and other unfair trade practices.

Illustrative of price advertising which the Federal Trade Commission considered deceptive is the case of a manufacturer and distributor of paint sold under the trade name of "Mary Carter." This company in advertising its product stated: "Buy one, get one free;" "Every Second Can Free of Extra Cost;" "Every Second Can Free". While this might not deceive a sophisticated purchaser, the Commission found that inasmuch as the manufacturer had no history of selling single cans of paint but was marketing twins, its allocation of what in fact was the price of two cans to one can, and calling one "free", was a misrepresentation. The Commission entered a cease and desist order. The Court of Appeals reversed the Commission, 333 F. 2d 654, (C.C.A.5, 1964), but was reversed by the Supreme Court. Federal Trade Commission v. Mary Carter Paint Co., 382 U.S. 46, 86 S.Ct. 219, 15 L.Ed. 128 (1965).

The Robinson-Patman Act. In 1936 the Congress amended Section 2 of the Clayton Act by adopting the Robinson-Patman Act which prohibits price discrimination in interstate commerce of commodities of like grade and quality. In order to constitute a violation, the price discrimination must substantially lessen competition or tend to create a monopoly, or injure, disturb, or prevent competition with any person who either grants or knowingly receives the benefit of such discrimination, or with customers of either the party claiming or receiving a price discrimination.

The Federal Trade Commission is empowered after due investigation and hearing, to establish quantity limits as to particular commodities where it finds that available purchasers in greater quantities are so few as to render differentials on account of quantities allotted to customers unjustly discriminatory or promoting monopoly.

Under this Act sellers of goods are prevented from granting discounts to buyers and from making any payments or furnishing any services or facilities connected with the processing, handling, sale, or offering for sale of commodities, including allowances for radio and newspaper advertising, counter displays and samples, unless offered to all other purchasers on proportionately equal terms. The Act also outlaws other types of discounts, rebates, and allowances and makes it unlawful to sell goods at unreasonably low prices for the purpose of destroying competition or eliminating a competitor. The Act makes it unlawful for one knowingly to "induce or receive" an illegal discrimination in price, thus creating buyer, as well as seller, liability.

Fair Trade Acts. Except for a permissive statute, resale price maintenance, sometimes referred to as "vertical price fixing", would violate the Sherman Act. Contracts between a manufacturer of proprietary medicines and its customers to maintain prices fixed by the manufacturer for all sales of its product, both at wholesale and retail, were held by the Supreme Court to violate the Anti-Trust statute in Dr. Miles Medical Co. v. John D. Parke & Sons Co., 220 U.S. 373, 31 S.Ct. 376, 55 L.Ed. 502 (1911).

In the early years of the depression commencing in 1930, trade associations of retailers lobbied for legislation in the various States which would permit manufacturers or distributors of products with a brand name or trade name to fix their minimum retail price. The legislation was aimed at the widespread practice of certain retailers to cut prices and to advertise well known brand name products as "loss leaders". The first statute of this type was enacted in California in 1931. The great majority of States thereafter adopted similar statutes commonly referred to as Fair Trade Acts.

In 1936 the constitutionality of the Fair Trade Act of Illinois was upheld by the United States Supreme Court against attack on the ground that it was a denial of due process of law and of equal protection of the laws in violation of the Fourteenth Amendment to the Federal Constitution. The Court held that the Illinois Act was not an unlawful delegation of the power of private persons to control the property of others where such control existed by reason of contract between the parties. Old Dearborn Distributing Co. v. Seagrams Distillers Corp., 299 U.S. 183, 57 S.Ct. 139, 81 L.Ed. 109, 106 A.L.R. 1476 (1936).

In 1937 Congress enacted the Miller-Tydings Act by amendment of the Sherman Act which exempted contracts or agreements fixing minimum prices for the resale of trade-marked commodities provided they were lawful as intrastate transactions under local law.

A problem confronting manufacturers and distributors desirous of maintaining retail prices was that the chief offenders were retailers who refused to sign contracts to maintain minimum prices. In one way or another they would acquire trade name products and undersell retailers who had signed agreements. These retailers complained bitterly to the manufacturers and distributors that they were held to a minimum resale price while their competitors were not. This led to inclusion in the Fair Trade Acts of a non-signer clause, a unique provision whereby one contract made between a manufacturer and a retailer fixing the minimum resale price of a commodity became binding upon any person, although not a party to the contract, who wilfully and knowingly advertised, offered for sale or sold such commodity at less than the price stipulated in the contract. Such a statutory provision is known as a non-signer clause.

It should be noted that resale price maintenance permitted under Fair Trade Acts does not validate price maintenance agreements between producers, between wholesalers, or between retailers. Any price fixing agreement between persons who are engaged in business at the same distributional level is "horizontal price fixing", illegal, violative of the Sherman Anti-Trust Act, and not permitted by any statute.

In 1951 the Supreme Court held invalid the Louisiana Fair Trade Act containing a non-signer clause on the ground that although the Miller-Tydings Act authorized contracts or agreements prescribing minimum resale prices, it did not authorize price fixing by compulsion on persons who were not parties to the contracts or agreements. Schwegmann Bros. v. Calvert Distillers, 341 U.S. 384, 71 S.Ct. 745, 95 L.Ed. 1035, 19 A.L.R.2d 1119 (1951).

In order to change the result in the Schwegmann case, the Congress in 1952 passed the McGuire Act which validated non-signer provisions providing they were lawful as applied to intrastate transactions under local law. This removed non-signer provisions from prohibition by Federal law. Under the McGuire Act, the United States Court of Appeals for the Fifth Circuit in 1953 sustained the validity of the Louisiana Fair Trade Law. Schwegmann Bros. Giant Super Marts v. Eli Lilly & Co., C.A.5th, 205 F.2d 788 (1953), certiorari denied 346 U.S. 856, 74 S.Ct. 71, 98 L.Ed. 369.

The State courts of last resort are in hopeless conflict with respect to the validity of non-signer clauses under their respective State constitutions.

As stated by the Supreme Court of Rhode Island in United States Time Corp. v. Ann & Hope Factory Outlet, Inc., —— R.I. ——, 205 A.2d 125 (1964):

"Fair trade acts have been enacted at one time or another in all but four of the states and have been construed by the courts of last resort in thirty-eight of them. The judicial box score as to the constitutional validity of nonsigner provisions is a constantly changing one. Illustrative is the action of the court of appeals in New York which found the act unconstitutional, Doubleday, Doran & Co. v. R. H. Macy & Co., 269 N.Y. 272, 199 N.E. 409, 103 A.L.R. 1325, and then reversed itself in Bourjois Sales Corp. v. Dorfman, 273 N.Y. 167, 7 N.E.2d 30, 110 A.L.R. 1411. In Pennsylvania the reverse was the case. Burche Co. v. General Electric Co., 382 Pa. 370, 115 A. 2d 361; Olin Mathieson Chemical Corp. v. White Cross Stores, Inc., No. 6, 414 Pa. 95, 199 A.2d 266. In Ohio the court first found a constitutional violation and then upon amendment of the act ruled otherwise. Union Carbide & Carbon Corp. v. Bargain Fair, Inc., 167 Ohio St. 182, 147 N.E.2d 481; Hudson Distributors, Inc. v. Upjohn Co., 174 Ohio St. 487, 190 N.E.2d 460."

Exclusive Supply Contracts. A contract or undertaking between a manufacturer and independent dealers whereby the latter agree to purchase all of their requirments from the manufacturer and not handle competing products may be a violation of the Anti-Trust statutes as provided in Section 3 of the Clayton Act:

> "It shall be unlawful for any person engaged in commerce, in the course of such commerce, to lease or make a sale or contract for sale of goods, wares, merchandise, machinery, supplies or other commodities, whether patented or unpatented, for use, consumption, or resale within the United States * * * on the condition, agreement or understanding that the lessee or purchaser thereof shall not use or deal in the goods * * * of a competitor or competitors of the * * * seller, where the effect of such lease, sale, or contract for sale or such condition, agreement or understanding may be to substantially lessen competition or tend to create a monopoly in any line of commerce."

For violation of this Section the court enjoined Standard Oil Company of California and its subsidiary, Standard Stations, Inc., from enforcing or entering into exclusive supply contracts with independent dealers in petroleum products and automobile accessories. Approximately 6000 independent stations, or 16% of the retail gasoline outlets in seven western States, were involved. Some had agreed with Standard not to sell competitive gasoline or other petroleum products only. Others had agreed not to handle any competing line of tires, tubes, and batteries. The Supreme Court held that the effect was such that it might substantially lessen competition. The injunction, of course, did not apply to retail stations or outlets owned by Standard Oil and operated by its agents. Standard Oil Co. of California v. United States, 337 U.S. 293, 69 S.Ct. 1051, 93 L.Ed. 1371 (1948).

CASES

CARL A. COLTERYAHN DAIRY, INC. v. SCHNEIDER DAIRY

(1964) 415 Pa. 276, 203 A.2d 469.

JONES, J. This is an appeal challenging the validity of a decree of the Court of Common Pleas of Allegheny County which enjoined for a four month period (1) four individuals from (a) divulging the names or soliciting the patronage of customers of their former employer and (b) diverting any business of their former employer or attempting to persuade customers of their former employer from continuing their patronage, and (2) a corporation from (a) soliciting the patronage of customers of the plaintiff-appellee who became known to the individual defendants through a previous employment and (b) entering into new business relationships with such customers.

On January 26, 1964, following competitive bidding, Baldwin Dairy, [Baldwin], which operated eight (8) retail milk routes in the South Hills area of Allegheny County, was purchased by Carl A. Colteryahn Dairy, Inc. [Colteryahn]. The Schneider Dairy, [Schneider], had submitted a bid which was subsequently withdrawn. Colteryahn and Schneider are two of thirteen major dairies which maintain milk routes in the South Hills area.

For some time prior to the date of the sale, Ronald Yochum, Richard Rump, Albert Eltringham and Wayne Herman had been employed by Baldwin as driver-salesmen on certain specified retail routes. Shortly after the sale, these men gave Colteryahn seven (7) days notice of their intention to leave its employ, admittedly giving false reasons for relinquishing their jobs, and went to work on February 3, 1964, for Schneider. Immediately after assuming employment with Schneider, they began to solicit the business of their former Baldwin customers.

Colteryahn promptly instituted an equity action in the Court of Common Pleas of Allegheny County against Schneider and the four individual employees seeking both injunctive relief and damages. The action averred that Schneider was maliciously interfering with the business relations of Colteryahn and that Yochum, Rump, Eltringham and Herman were soliciting their old customers of Baldwin and, in some instances, making false and misleading statements to them. After an extensive hearing, the court below granted injunctive relief. It is from that preliminary decree that this appeal has been taken.

* * *

It is clear that an employee, absent an agreement to the contrary, has no duty not to compete with a former employer upon severance of their relationship: [Citation]. However, we have long recognized that the use of confidential material obtained by an employee from a position of trust and confidence may not be used in later competition to the prejudice of his employer. [Citations.] Colteryahn's position here is that the customer lists and information retained by the individual appellants constitute trade secrets and that the use thereof in Schneider's employ is prohibited. Our inquiry is to ascertain whether the names, addresses and other information concerning customers constitute such confidential material as to entitle Coltryahn to protection against its competitive use.

* * *

Generally, in the absence of an express contract to the contrary, solicitation of a former employer's customers, on behalf of another in competition with his former employer, will not be enjoined. This rule has been recognized by numerous text writers and courts. However, even in the absence of such an express agreement an employer is entitled to equitable protection against the competitive use of confidential and secret information obtained as a result of the trust and confidence of previous employment. [Citations.]

We are here concerned with the use of customer names and addresses retained solely by the mental processes and, admittedly, the major part of such information was obtained from Baldwin during the time of employment. Numerous jurisdictions have held that the above-noted exception does not apply where the knowledge is carried in the memory of the former employees even where it was at least partially obtained from lists furnished during employment. This concept is also recognized by the Restatement (2d), Agency, § 396, which provides: "Unless otherwise agreed, after the termination of the agency, the agent: * * * (b) has a duty to the principal not to use or to disclose to third persons, on his own account or on account of others, in competition with the principal or to his injury, trade secrets, written lists of names, or other similar confidential matters given to him only for the principal's use or acquired by the agent in violation of duty. *The agent is entitled to use general information concerning the method of business of the principal and the names of the customers retained in his memory, if not acquired in violation of his duty as agent.*" (Emphasis supplied.) An analysis of the present facts leads us to the conclusion that, by their actions, the appellants violated no duty owed Colteryahn.

Once handed the customer list by Baldwin the responsibility for the route rested with the driver-salesman. His cultivation of a working relationship with the customers was imperative to his survival in this phase of the dairy business. For expeditious operation of the route, and indeed the result of daily repetition, the names, addresses and orders were quickly memorized. Thus, even though the route books were returned when leaving Colteryahn's employ, the facts here involved remained imbedded in the mental processes of the individual drivers. No fraud or deception was used to obtain this knowledge. It was merely the result of the performance of their job. * * * As this Court stated in Spring Steels, Inc. v. Molloy, 400 Pa. 354, 363, 162 A.2d 370, 375: "Nor is the fact that the new company may acquire some of the plaintiff's former customers contrary to law. It is not a phenomenal thing in American business life to see an employee, after a long period of service, leave his employment and start a business of his own or in association with others. And it is inevitable in such a situation, where the former employee has dealt with customers on a personal basis that some of those customers will want to continue to deal with him in his new association. This is natural, logical and part of human fellowship, that an employer who fears this kind of future competition must protect himself by a preventive contract with his employee, unless, of course, there develops a confidential relationship which of itself speaks for non-disclosure and non-competition in the event the employer and employee separate. There is nothing of that in this case."

    * * *

There was some testimony that the drivers, in soliciting their former customers, made false and misleading representations as to the circumstances under which they left the employ of Colteryahn and such representations were made to play on the sympathies of the customers and influence them so that they could be obtained by Schneider. Allowing this type of conduct is to countenance unfair competition. Equity will prevent unjustified interference with contractual relations: [Citation]. We believe that the decree of the court below should be modified to enjoin only this type of improper solicitation and conduct on the part of the individual appellants.

The decree, as modified in accordance with this opinion, is affirmed. Each party to bear own costs.

BANCROFT–WHITNEY CO. v. GLEN

(1966) 49 Cal.Rptr. 825, 411 P.2d 921.

MOSK, J. This is an action for breach of fiduciary duty by a corporate officer and for unfair competition. Plaintiff, Bancroft-Whitney Company, engaged in publishing lawbooks, is a California corporation with its principal place of business in San Francisco. Defendants are Judson B. Glen, the former president and a director of plaintiff, Matthew Bender & Co., a New York corporation which also publishes lawbooks (hereinafter called Bender Co.), and John T. Bender (hereinafter referred to as Bender), the president of Bender Co., who is sued individually and in his official capacity. The complaint alleges as follows:

Over the years plaintiff has spent large sums of money to develop a highly skilled staff of legal researchers and editors and, as of December 1, 1961, it employed more than 50 persons in these capacities in San Francisco. In July 1961 Glen, while ostensibly serving as president of plaintiff, and defendants Bender and Bender Co. commenced negotiations for the purpose of establishing a western division of Bender Co.

During November 1961, Glen, without resigning or giving notice to plaintiff or its officers, directors, or shareholders, signed a contract with Bender Co. to become president of the contemplated western division, commencing on or about January 1, 1962. Beginning in July 1961 and thereafter, defendants joined in a concerted effort to obtain a staff of editor and other personnel for the proposed new western division and, using misrepresentations and half-truths, intentionally interfered with plaintiff's advantageous contractual relationships and surreptitiously sought to entice away carefully selected members of plaintiff's executive staff and working force. Using to full advantage the inside knowledge and confidential business information provided by Glen, who continued to occupy a position of trust with plaintiff, defendants solicited more than 20 officers, directors, and trained employees of plaintiff. On and subsequent to December 15, 1961, more than 15 persons, including officers, directors, researchers, and editors left plaintiff's employ without notice and entered the employ of the newly created western division of Bender Co. When the company qualified to do business as a foreign corporation in California on January 5, 1962, the great majority, if not all, of its employees were persons who had just previously worked for plaintiff under the supervision of Glen.

The publishing schedules, including proposed formats, types, and titles of publications, dates of publication, planned future publications, as well as customer lists, relative value of customers, and other methods and techniques of doing business are closely kept secrets of lawbooks publishers, and Glen, as the once-trusted fiduciary of plaintiff, became acquainted with its trade secrets and confidential business information. At the request of the other two defendants, Glen disclosed this valuable information to them, to the damage of plaintiff.

It is further alleged that the acts of Glen, including the enticement away of plaintiff's officers, directors, and trained employees, and the disclosure of trade secrets and confidential business information of plaintiff to its competitors, violated the fiduciary duties owed to plaintiff by him as an officer or director and that these acts were done for the purpose of crippling or destroying plaintiff and to provide advantage to defendants at the expense of plaintiff. The acts of the other two defendants, in subverting trusted officers and directors of plaintiff and using them and confidential and secret information provided by them to raid plaintiff's staff and entice away plaintiff's employees constitute unfair competition and were performed for the purpose of crippling and destroying plaintiff.

It is also alleged that defendants acted with malice, fraud, and oppression, and the complaint prays for general damages, punitive damages, and an injunction to restrain defendants from further approaching plaintiff's employees for the purpose of inducing them to leave plaintiff's employ and from disclosing trade secrets or confidential business information to Bender Co.

After a lengthy trial, the court, sitting without a jury, found in favor of defendants. It refused injunctive relief and held that Glen did not breach his fiduciary duties, that defendants were not guilty of unfair competition, and that no trade secrets or confidential business information were disclosed by Glen or used by the other defendants. It also found that defendants were not guilty of any of the specific wrongful acts alleged in the complaint.

It may be helpful at the outset of this long and complex chronicle of events to describe the issues involved in the controversy. Plaintiff does not seriously contend that Glen acted improperly in seeking employment with Bender Co. or that the other defendants are liable because they hired Glen, and no damages are sought for the departure of Glen from plaintiff's employ. It is contended, however, that Glen breached his fiduciary duties by his conduct leading up to the employment of the other persons who resigned from positions with plaintiff, and the gravamen of the action against Bender and Bender Co. relates to their role in cooperating in Glen's breach for the purpose of obtaining the employment of these persons by Bender Co. We hold, for the reasons hereinafter stated, that the evidence shows as a matter of law that Glen violated his duties to plaintiff and that the other defendants, having co-operated in and reaped the fruits of his violation, are guilty of unfair competition.

The record in this case consists of several thousand pages. The facts leading up to the employment by Bender Co. of Glen and Gordon Baker, plaintiff's sales manager, form the backdrop against which the employment of plaintiff's other personnel occurred.
* * *

The majority of the stock of plaintiff corporation is owned by the Lawyer's Co-Operative Publishing Co. (LCP), whose principal place of business is Rochester, New York. Glen was employed by the parent company as an editor from 1938 until 1949, and in 1949 he became the editor-in-chief of plaintiff. From 1958 until his resignation on December 15, 1961, he was also president of plaintiff, chairman of the executive committee of plaintiff, and chairman of the product planning committee of LCP. In April 1960, Thomas Gosnell became president of LCP and exercised direct control and domination over much of the actual business operations of plaintiff. Glen and Baker thereafter became dissatisfied with their employment.
* * *

In analyzing the legal principles applicable in this case, it should be repeated that we are not concerned with the simple right of one competitor to offer the employees of another a job at more favorable terms than they presently enjoy or the right of an employee (or an officer of a corporation) to seek a better job. The question here is whether the president of a corporation is liable for the breach of his fiduciary duty because of the conduct described above relating to other employees of the corporation and whether, under these facts, those who hire the employees are guilty of unfair competition for acting in concert with the president.

The general rules applicable to the duties of a corporate officer have been frequently stated. In the leading case of Guth v. Loft (1939) 23 Del. ch. 255, 5 A.2d 503, 510, these obligations were cogently described as follows: "Corporate officers and directors are not permitted to use their position of trust and confidence to further their private interests. While technically not trustees, they stand in a fiduciary relation to the corporation and its stockholders. A public policy, existing through the years, derived from a profound knowledge of human characteristics and motives, has established a rule that demands of a corporate officer or director, peremptorily and inexorably, the most scrupulous observance of his duty, not only affirmatively to protect the interests of the corporation committed to his charge, but also to refrain from doing anything that would work injury to the corporation, or to deprive it of profit or advantage which his skill and ability might properly bring to it, or to enable it to make in the reasonable and lawful exercise of its powers." Section 820 of the Corporations Code provides that an officer must exercise his powers in good faith, with a view to the interests of the corporation.

There are only a few cases cited by the parties which involve the specific question whether an officer may offer employees of his corporation jobs with a competing enterprise he is preparing to join. These cases are not consistent in their results and appear to rest on general principles relating to the obligations of a fiduciary. [Citations.] The mere fact that the officer makes preparations to compete before he resigns his office is not sufficient to constitute a breach of duty. It is the nature of his preparations which is significant. No ironclad rules as to the type of conduct which is permissible can be stated, since the spectrum of activities in this regard is as broad as the ingenuity of man itself.

The parties hereto have emphasized the issue whether an officer must disclose to the corporation his acts preparatory to entering into competition with it. This question is not identical with the issue whether the officer must reveal that he is negotiating for his own employment with a prospective employer, although, obviously, the two problems overlap since it is impossible for the officer to disclose his activities relating to the formation of a competing enterprise without also disclosing his own plans to join the competitor.

*   *   *

There is no requirement that an officer disclose his preparations to compete with the corporation in every case, and failure to disclose such acts will render the officer liable for a breach of his fiduciary duties only where particular circumstances render nondisclosure harmful to the corporation. [Citations.] Conversely, the mere act of disclosing his activities cannot immunize the officer from liability where his conduct in other respects amounts to a breach of duty. The significant inquiry in each situation is whether the officer's acts or omissions constitute a breach under the general principles applicable to the performance of his trust.

In our view, the conduct of Glen in the present case, when assessed by the standards set forth above, amounts to a breach of his fiduciary duties to plaintiff as a matter of law. The undisputed evidence shows a consistent course of conduct by him designed to obtain for a competitor those of plaintiff's

employees whom the competitor could afford to employ and would find useful. If Glen while still president of plaintiff had performed these acts on behalf of Bender Co. without also obligating himself to join the company, there could be no doubt that he would have violated his duties to plaintiff. Surely his position in this regard cannot be improved by the fact that he was also to be employed by Bender Co. and was to share in the profits of the new western division. In carrying out his design, Glen misled Gosnell into believing there was no danger that Bender Co. would attempt to hire plaintiff's personnel, suggested a two-step salary increase without informing Gosnell that he had solicited some editors and that he or Bender Co. would solicit others if they successfully consummated their negotiations, and disclosed confidential information regarding salaries to Bender in order to facilitate the solicitation. Ultimately, positions at higher salaries than plaintiff was paying were offered either by Glen or Bender Co. to the treasurer of plaintiff, three of its four managing editors, one or two of the four assistant managing editors, three of the four indexers, and approximately 10 other editors. We need not decide whether any of these acts would constitute a breach of fiduciary duty, taken alone, since there can be little doubt that, in combination, they show a course of conduct which falls demonstrably short of "the most scrupulous observance" of an officer's duty to his corporation.

The conclusion is inescapable that Glen deliberately misled Gosnell regarding the possibility of a raid by Bender Co. on plaintiff's editorial staff and that his suggestion to Gosnell that half of the proposed salary increases for the editors be postponed until after January 1, 1962, without informing Gosnell of his plan to offer them positions, directly or indirectly, with Bender Co. at higher salaries if his own negotiations with Bender were successful, amounts at the very least to a deliberate and inexcusable failure to inform Gosnell of a matter of vital interest to plaintiff. * * *

Another significant aspect of Glen's activities on behalf of Bender relates to the list of employees and their salaries compiled at Carmel. It is beyond question that a corporate officer breaches his fiduciary duties when, with the purpose of facilitating the recruiting of the corporation's employees by a competitor, he supplies the competitor with a selective list of the corporation's employees who are, in his judgment, possessed of both ability and the personal characteristics desirable in an employee, together with the salary the corporation is paying the employee and a suggestion as to the salary the competitor should offer in order to be successful in recruitment. This conclusion is inescapable even if the information regarding salaries is not deemed to be confidential. No case has been cited or found considering the question whether a list of salaries paid by a corporation to its employees is confidential. We are of the view, however, that such an unpublished list does constitute confidential information and that an officer of a corporation violates his trust if he reveals it to a competitor for the purpose of enabling the solicitation of the corporation's employees by the competitor.

* * *

The assistance given by Glen to the solicitation of the editors on the list is also to be condemned as a breach of his fiduciary duty. As we have seen, Glen not only provided the list on which the recruiting was based, but he suggested certain tactics to be followed in discussions with the editors, supplied a picture of the new organization's quarters for use by Billo, discussed the persons on the list with Billo during the recruiting campaign, and, in Glen's own words in his letter to Bender, Billo was to keep in touch with him so that "he and we here can cooperate to full advantage." * * *

It is clear from the evidence set forth above that Bender was aware of or ratified Glen's breach of his fiduciary duties in all but a few respects, that he cooperated with Glen in the breach, and that he received the benefits of Glen's infidelity. It cannot be said here, as was stated in another context by Justice Pitney in International News Serv. v. Associated Press (1918) 248 U.S. 215, 239, 39 S.Ct. 68, 72, 63 L.Ed. 211, that Bender Co. did not "reap where it has not sown." Under all the circumstances, Bender and Bender Co. must be held liable for their part in Glen's breach of his fiduciary duties. [Citations.] They encouraged the sowing and reaped the benefit. They cannot now disclaim the burden.

* * *

Defendants argue that even if we conclude that Glen breached his fiduciary duty and that the other defendants are guilty of unfair competition, we cannot award any damages for this wrongdoing because plaintiff has failed to show that the departure of the employees was proximately caused by defendants' actions. They admit that the primary reason the employees left was that they were offered higher salaries by Bender Co. As recounted above, it was Glen's breach that enabled Bender to determine the amount of salary which would induce these persons to leave plaintiff's employ. Under these circumstances there is no merit in defendants' contention. The causal relationship between Glen's violation of duty and Bender's persuasive inducement to the plaintiff's personnel is crystal clear.

* * *

The trial court's conclusion that Bender and Bender Co. were not activated by malice in their actions finds support in the record. The cause of action for punitive damages does not survive Glen's death (Prob.Code, § 573).

The judgment is reversed with directions to the trial court to retry the issue of general damages and enter judgment for plaintiff. [Reversed.]

TISCH HOTELS, INC. v. AMERICANA INN, INC.

(1965 C.A.7th) 350 F.2d 609.

KILEY, C. J. This appeal presents the question whether plaintiffs are entitled to injunctive relief based on alleged trademark infringement and unfair competition by reason of defendants' adoption and use, without consent, of plaintiffs' registered service mark "Americana". The district court's findings and judgment were against plaintiffs. We reverse.

Plaintiffs own and operate a number of hotels, three of them bearing the name "Americana". They began construction of the Miami Beach, Florida Americana in May 1955 and opened that hotel in December 1956. The Americana of New York opened in September 1962 and the Americana of San Juan, Puerto Rico began operations in November 1962. These are large luxury hotels in the highest price class, catering chiefly to the resort and large convention trade. Defendants own and operate two motels in the Chicago area. Their Americana Motel opened in March 1957 and their Americana Inn opened in April 1961. These motels cater chiefly to businessmen and to families, at moderate rates, and have facilities for sales meetings and small conventions.

Late in 1960 plaintiffs learned of defendants' use of the word "Americana" in connection with hotel services. In February 1961 plaintiffs applied to the Patent Office for registration of Service Mark No. 177,926, consisting of the word "americana", in lower case type, superimposed on a hemispheric background of North and South America. Regis-

tration on the Principal Register was granted on September 11, 1962. In August 1961 plaintiffs wrote to defendants complaining of the latter's infringement of the trademark "Americana" and demanded cessation of its use. Defendants rejected this demand.

On September 7, 1962 plaintiffs applied for registration of Service Mark No. 152,729 consisting of the word "Americana" in connection with hotel, restaurant, banquet and catering services. Defendant rejected a second demand by plaintiffs in January 1963 that they cease use of the name, and plaintiffs filed this suit in March 1963. Registration on the Principal Register of the service mark "Americana" was granted on September 17, 1963 and plaintiffs subsequently amended their complaint to add a claim of infringement of this mark. There were no prior registrations of the name in connection with hotel services and no evidence of any such use of the name prior to plaintiffs' adoption of the name.

The district court dismissed the suit upon the merits after finding that plaintiffs' mark was "weak" and entitled only to narrow protection; that plaintiffs had not proved secondary meaning in the name "Americana"; that there was "negligible" evidence of actual or probable confusion; and that plaintiffs had unduly delayed filing suit after being put on notice of defendants' use of their mark. The court concluded ultimately that there was no infringement and that plaintiffs were guilty of laches precluding them from equitable relief. We think that certain of the findings are clearly erroneous and that the conclusions are erroneous.

The court erred in concluding that "since 'Americana' is a widely used common word, rather than a coined or fanciful name, it is a weak trademark and is only entitled to narrow, restricted protection". The word "Americana", as applied to hotel and related services, is, in our opinion, an arbitrary mark since it in no way suggests or describes hotel services, and it cannot be said that it is weak and entitled to little protection. [Citations.]

Under the Lanham Trade-Mark Act the test of infringement is likelihood of confusion. [Citations.] The test of actual confusion, followed by this court in Rytex Co. v. Ryan, 126 F.2d 952 (7th Cir. 1942), is no longer the law. [Citation.] Likelihood of confusion can be proved without any evidence of actual confusion, [citations], * * *

Plaintiffs do not contend that they and defendants are in direct competition or that there is a likelihood that a traveler will become confused and register at defendants' motel in Chicago thinking it is the Miami Beach Americana. Their position is that a prospective patron seeing the "americana" mark on defendants' motel would be likely to confuse it with the same mark used by plaintiffs, and that, being confused as to the source of the services, if the patron is dissatisfied with defendants' services, plaintiffs would suffer, since their "reputation is no longer within [their] own control and there is an injury, unless there is a clear distinction between the marks." [Citations.] "The question is, are the uses related so that they are likely to be connected in the mind of a prospective purchaser." We conclude, "as our reactions persuade us," [citation], that there was, and is, this likelihood.

After adopting the name in 1955, plaintiffs spent about $500,000 in a pre-opening promotion for their Miami Beach hotel in order to identify the mark in the public mind with luxurious hotel service. They sent out 50,-000 21-page brochures to travel agents and prospective patrons and advertised and received free publicity throughout the country. Much of this activity was carried on in Chicago, which is one of plaintiffs' largest markets. During the opening week at the Miami Beach Americana in December 1956 the hotel was host for the convention of the National Broadcasting Company, and a number of network television shows, including the Per-

ry Como and Steve Allen "Tonight" shows, were televised from the hotel, all prominently featuring the hotel and pictures of its distinctive sign. In all of this promotion, publicity and advertising, the name "americana" was used, in lower case letters, with a five-point star over the "i" and usually with a white line running through the first "a". There is no evidence that anyone else had ever given these distinctive notes to the common word.

Three months after the opening of the Miami Beach Americana defendants adopted the name "Americana" and have used it in the identical style employed extensively by plaintiffs. * * *

The district court found as a fact and concluded that defendants acted in good faith in adopting the name "Americana", "without intending to exploit the reputation or good will of Plaintiffs * * *." A finding of fraudulent intent or bad faith is not essential to the award of an injunction for trademark infringement where likelihood of confusion exists. [Citations.] But we think that defendants adopted plaintiffs' name deliberately with a view to obtaining some advantage from plaintiffs' investments in promotion and advertising. The inference of likelihood of confusion is therefore readily drawn because the adoption itself indicates that defendants expected that likelihood to their profit. [Citations.] A comparison of plaintiffs' and defendants' marks shown above clearly discloses the copying. Defendants knew of plaintiffs' mark and should have taken reasonable precautions to avoid the likelihood of confusion. [Citations.]

* * *

The fact that the word "americana" is used in connection with numerous other businesses, enterprises and products is irrelevant. Uses of the name outside the hotel field could not possibly cause confusion with plaintiffs' mark. [Citations.]

Because of our conclusion that plaintiffs' mark is not descriptive and that there is likelihood of confusion in this case, we need not consider whether plaintiffs' mark has acquired secondary meaning. [Citations.]

* * *

For the reasons given, the judgment is reversed and the cause remanded with instructions to enter an injunction in accordance with the views expressed herein.

Reversed and remanded.

INTERNATIONAL SILVER CO. v. ROGER CHROMEWARE, INC.

(1964 D.C.E.D.N.Y.) 235 F.Supp. 216.

BRUCHHAUSEN, D. J. The plaintiff moves for a preliminary injunction restraining the defendants from using the name "Roger" allegedly infringing plaintiff's mark Rogers.

* * *

The plaintiff claims that the use of the mark "Roger" by the defendants will tend to confuse the public in believing that the defendants' wares are those of the plaintiff or that the plaintiff has authorized the defendants to sell this named merchandise and that the plaintiff will sustain irreparable damage in that its reputation, developed by it during the period of more than a century, will be destroyed. The defendants' merchandise is chrome-plate.

It is common knowledge that the name "Rogers" is associated with fine silverware. The plaintiff has over the years developed an excellent reputation in this field. It is well settled that appropriation of a portion of a well known name constitutes infringement. [Citations.]

The Court in Lincoln Restaurant Corp. v. Wolfies Rest., Inc., D.C., 185 F.Supp. 454, affirmed 291 F.2d 302, at page 303, 2 Cir., 1961 held in part:

"All this evidence lends solid support to Judge Byers' finding that defendant's adoption of the name 'Wolfies' is compatible with nothing but 'a purpose to capitalize in Brooklyn upon the trade name "Wolfies" first adopted by the plaintiffs in Miami Beach.' Thus intent to trade on plaintiffs' reputation and plaintiffs' name was specifically found, and we see no distinction between this and ordinary 'palming off' in a products case. As this court has recently recognized, 'a court of equity will restrain such practices as constitute palming off, actual deception or appropriation of another's property' even absent proof of secondary meaning." See cases cited.

The Court, after careful examination and consideration of the affidavits, briefs and argument, concludes that a preliminary injunction is warranted.

The plaintiff will post a bond in the sum of $1,000.

VOLKSWAGENWERK AKTIENGESELL-SCHAFT v. VOLKS CITY, INC.

(1965 C.A.3d) 348 F.2d 659.

GANEY, C. J. The defendant is engaged in the business of selling and servicing new and used automobiles, including Volkswagens, in East Orange, New Jersey. Plaintiff, the manufacturer of Volkswagen vehicles, brought an action to restrain the defendant from trade-mark infringement and unfair competition. The main purpose of the action is to prevent defendant from holding itself out as an authorized franchised Volkswagen Dealer; no attempt is being made to prevent defendant from selling or servicing Volkswagen products. The parties agreed that the district court dispose of plaintiff's motion for a preliminary injunction on the basis of affidavits and the testimony of a defendant witness. The court found, among other facts, that defendant had inserted in the Evening News a six by eight inch advertisement which stated, "Do You Want a Brand-New 1964 Volkswagen * * * Then You've Got it." and offering "a brand-new factory-fresh Volkswagen"; that later on in the same newspaper, it offered for sale Volkswagens described as "Just arrived from Wolfsburg, Germany" (plaintiff's well-known headquarters and principal manufacturing point), and numerous other advertisements clearly intended to convey the impression of affiliation with the plaintiff. The court therefore concluded that "defendant's use of plaintiff's registered mark 'Volkswagen' * * * in connection with the sale, offering for sale and advertising of goods and services was likely to cause confusion, mistake or deception and therefore constitutes trade mark infringement under 15 U.S.C. § 1114 (1), as amended." and that the injury to plaintiff's good will by defendant's conduct was irreparable. It therefore issued a preliminary injunction enjoining defendant from using, among other designations such as "Volkswagen Dealer" or "Dealer in Volkswagens", the trade names "Volks City", "Volkswagen City", "Wagen City", "Wagon City", "Beetle City" or any other name commonly associated with Volkswagen products, "Except in conjunction with the legend 'Not a Franchised Volkswagen Dealer' in the same size lettering and type face as any such name." Defendant has appealed.

* * *

The order of the District Court will be affirmed.

DIEHL v. MAGIC EMPIRE GROCERS ASS'N

(1965 Okl.) 399 P.2d 460.

WILLIAMS, J. The question for our determination in this appeal is whether the judgment of the trial court permanently enjoining defendant from violating the Unfair Sales Act in the advertising, offering for sale and selling of groceries should be reversed as being clearly against the weight of the evidence. Our decision is that it should not.

* * *

Defendant argues that: "The real issue in this appeal goes to the sufficiency of the evidence constituting a prima facie case on behalf of the trade association entitling it to injunctive relief as provided by Section 598.5 of the Act. The Defendant argues in this appeal that the Plaintiff did not prove all of the elements of a prima facie case in that (1) there was no evidence that a sale was ever made at reduced prices by the Defendant; (2) there was no evidence the handbills were ever distributed by anyone nor that anyone ever read the handbills, and (3) there was no evidence as to the actual price paid by the Defendant for articles sold and (4) there was no evidence as to the amount of the markup allowed; (5) there was no evidence that the groceries purchased from the Hale Halsell Grocery Company were the same groceries which had been allegedly advertised for sale; (6) there was no evidence as to what other grocers, if any, were affected by the sale of groceries below cost by the Defendant."

Under the Unfair Sales Act, it was not necessary for plaintiff to show that a sale was made by defendant at unlawfully reduced prices. Title 15 O.S.1961 § 598.3 provides:

"It is hereby declared that any *advertising,* offer to sell, or sale of any merchandise, either by retailers or wholesalers, at less than cost as defined in this Act with the intent and purpose of inducing the purchase of other merchandise or of unfairly diverting trade from a competitor or otherwise injuring a competitor, impair and prevent fair competition, injure public welfare, are unfair competition and contrary to public policy and the policy of this Act, where the result of such advertising, offer or sale is to tend to deceive any purchaser or prospective purchaser, or to substantially lessen competition, or to unreasonably restrain trade, or to tend to create a monopoly in any line of commerce." (Emphasis ours.)

* * *

It is to be noted that sub-section (a) of the second section (598.2) of the Act in question defines "cost to the retailer" as including freight charges, cartage costs, taxes "and (4) a markup to cover a proportionate part of the cost of doing business, which markup, in the absence of proof of a lesser cost, shall be six per cent (6%) of the cost of the retailer as herein set forth after adding thereto freight charges and cartage but before adding thereto a markup."

Section 598.5 paragraph (c) of the Unfair Sales Act provides:

"Evidence of advertisement, offering to sell, or sale of merchandise by any retailer or wholesaler at less than cost to him, shall be prima facie evidence of intent to injure competitors and to destroy or substantially lessen competition."

* * *

Plaintiff's evidence further showed that in the circulars for January 12th through January 16th, it advertised certain items for sale at approximately the prices it had paid Hale-Halsell for them. This resulted in an advertised price below the 6% markup required by the Oklahoma Uniform Sales Act, supra, on the following articles: Milnot, Home Maid Biscuits, Vigo, Jello and Miracle Whip. For the period of January 19th through January 23rd, Vigo, Miracle Whip, Jello and Milnot were advertised in such circulars for sale at prices approximating the cost and below the required markup. For the period of January 26th through the 30th, the same was true as to the items of Jello, Milnot, Vigo and Northern Tissue.

* * *

From the above recitation, we determine that there was evidence of effect that defendant, through advertising circulars, of-

fered for sale certain items above-enumerated in violation of the Unfair Sales Act, supra; that such circulars were distributed to prospective purchasers in the areas served by defendant's respective stores; that it was not necessary for plaintiff to prove that the identical groceries purchased from Hale-Halsell were the ones advertised for sale in view of the fact that the brands of the items offered for sale in violation of the Unfair Sales Act were identical to the brands purchased from Hale-Halsell and that such purchases were made immediately prior to the distribution of the circulars. For example, Northern Tissue was purchased from Hale-Halsell and Northern Tissue was offered for sale. The same applies to Home Maid Biscuits, Vigo, Milnot, Jello, C & H Sugar and Miracle Whip.

* * *

Judgment affirmed.

SEARS, ROEBUCK & CO. v. STIFFEL CO.

(1964) 376 U.S. 225, 84 S.Ct. 784, 11 L.Ed.2d 661.

BLACK, J. The question in this case is whether a State's unfair competition law can, consistently with the federal patent laws, impose liability for or prohibit the copying of an article which is protected by neither a federal patent nor a copyright. The respondent, Stiffel Company, secured design and mechanical patents on a "pole lamp"—a vertical tube having lamp fixtures along the outside, the tube being made so that it will stand upright between the floor and ceiling of a room. Pole lamps proved a decided commercial success, and soon after Stiffel brought them on the market Sears, Roebuck & Company put on the market a substantially identical lamp, which it sold more cheaply, Sears' retail price being about the same as Stiffel's wholesale price. Stiffel then brought this action against Sears in the United States District Court for the Northern District of Illinois, claiming in its first count that by copying its design Sears had infringed Stiffel's patents and in its second count that by selling copies of Stiffel's lamp Sears had caused confusion in the trade as to the source of the lamps and had thereby engaged in unfair competition under Illinois law. There was evidence that identifying tags were not attached to the Sears lamps although labels appeared on the cartons in which they were delivered to customers, that customers had asked Stiffel whether its lamps differed from Sears', and that in two cases customers who had bought Stiffel lamps had complained to Stiffel on learning that Sears was selling substantially identical lamps at a much lower price.

The District Court, after holding the patents invalid for want of invention, went on to find as a fact that Sears' lamp was "a substantially exact copy" of Stiffel's and that the two lamps were so much alike, both in appearance and in functional details, "that confusion between them is likely, and some confusion has already occurred." On these findings the court held Sears guilty of unfair competition, enjoined Sears "from unfairly competing with [Stiffel] by selling or attempting to sell pole lamps identical to or confusingly similar to" Stiffel's lamp, and ordered an accounting to fix profits and damages resulting from Sears' "unfair competition."

The Court of Appeals affirmed. 313 F.2d 115. That court held that, to make out a case of unfair competition under Illinois law, there was no need to show that Sears had been "palming off" its lamps as Stiffel lamps; Stiffel had only to prove that there was a "likelihood of confusion as to the source of the products"—that the two articles were sufficiently identical that customers could not tell who had made a particular one. Impressed by the "remarkable sameness of appearance" of the lamps, the Court of Appeals upheld the trial court's findings of likelihood of confusion and some actual confusion, find-

ings which the appellate court construed to mean confusion "as to the source of the lamps." The Court of Appeals thought this enough under Illinois law to sustain the trial court's holding of unfair competition, and thus held Sears liable under Illinois law for doing no more than copying and marketing an unpatented article. We granted certiorari to consider whether this use of a State's law of unfair competition is compatible with the federal patent law. [Citation.]

* * *

The grant of a patent is the grant of a statutory monopoly; indeed, the grant of patents in England was an explicit exception to the statute of James I prohibiting monopolies. Patents are not given as favors, as was the case of monopolies given by the Tudor monarchs, [citation], but are meant to encourage invention by rewarding the inventor with the right, limited to a term of years fixed by the patent, to exclude others from the use of his invention. During that period of time no one may make, use, or sell the patented product without the patentee's authority. 35 U.S.C. § 271. But in rewarding useful invention, the "rights and welfare of the community must be fairly dealt with and effectually guarded." [Citation.] To that end the prerequisites to obtaining a patent are strictly observed, and when the patent has issued the limitations on its exercise are equally strictly enforced. To begin with, a genuine "invention" or "discovery" must be demonstrated "lest in the constant demand for new appliances the heavy hand of tribute be laid on each slight technological advance in an art." [Citations.] Once the patent issues, it is strictly construed, [citation], it cannot be used to secure any monopoly beyond that contained in the patent, [citation], the patentee's control over the product when it leaves his hands is sharply limited, [citation], and the patent monopoly may not be used in disregard of the antitrust laws. [Citations.] Finally, and especially relevant here, when the patent expires the monopoly created by it expires, too, and the right to make the article—including the right to make it in precisely the shape it carried when patented—passes to the public. [Citations.]

Thus the patent system is one in which uniform federal standards are carefully used to promote invention while at the same time preserving free competition. Obviously a State could not, consistently with the Supremacy Clause of the Constitution, extend the life of a patent beyond its expiration date or give a patent on an article which lacked the level of invention required for federal patents. To do either would run counter to the policy of Congress of granting patents only to true inventions, and then only for a limited time. Just as a State cannot encroach upon the federal patent laws directly, it cannot, under some other law, such as that forbidding unfair competition, give protection of a kind that clashes with the objectives of the federal patent laws.

In the present case the "pole lamp" sold by Stiffel has been held not to be entitled to the protection of either a mechanical or a design patent. An unpatentable article, like an article on which the patent has expired, is in the public domain and may be made and sold by whoever chooses to do so. What Sears did was to copy Stiffel's design and to sell lamps almost identical to those sold by Stiffel. This it had every right to do under the federal patent laws. That Stiffel originated the pole lamp and made it popular is immaterial. "Sharing in the goodwill of an article unprotected by patent or trade-mark is the exercise of a right possessed by all—and in the free exercise of which the consuming public is deeply interested." [Citation.] To allow a State by use of its law of unfair competition to prevent the copying of an article which represents too slight an advance to be patented would be to permit the State to block off from the public something which federal law has said belongs to the public. The result would be that while federal law grants only 14 or 17 years' protection to genuine inventions, see 35 U.S.C. §§ 154, 173, States could allow perpetual protection to articles too lacking in novelty to merit any patent at all under federal constitutional standards. This would be too great an encroachment on the federal patent system to be tolerated.

Sears has been held liable here for unfair competition because of a finding of likelihood of confusion based only on the fact that Sears' lamp was copied from Stiffel's unpatented lamp and that consequently the two looked exactly alike. Of course there could be "confusion" as to who had manufactured these nearly identical articles. But mere inability of the public to tell two identical articles apart is not enough to support an injunction against copying or an award of damages for copying that which the federal patent laws permit to be copied. Doubtless a State may, in appropriate circumstances, require that goods, whether patented or unpatented, be labeled or that other precautionary steps be taken to prevent customers from being misled as to the source, just as it may protect businesses in the use of their trademarks, labels, or distinctive dress in the packaging of goods so as to prevent others, by imitating such markings, from misleading purchasers as to the source of the goods. But because of the federal patent laws a State may not, when the article is unpatented and uncopyrighted, prohibit the copying of the article itself or award damages for such copying. [Citation.] The judgment below did both and in so doing gave Stiffel the equivalent of a patent monopoly on its unpatented lamp. That was error, and Sears is entitled to a judgment in its favor.

Reversed.

HUDSON DISTRIBUTORS INC. v. ELI LILLY & CO.

(1964) 377 U.S. 386, 84 S.Ct. 1273, 12 L.Ed.2d 394.

MR. JUSTICE GOLDBERG delivered the opinion of the Court.

These appeals raise the question of whether the McGuire Act, 66 Stat. 631, 15 U.S.C. § 45(a) (1)–(5), permits the application and enforcement of the Ohio Fair Trade Act against appellant in support of appellees' systems of retail price maintenance. For the reasons stated below, we hold that the Ohio Act, as applied to the facts of these cases, comes within the provisions of the McGuire Act exempting certain resale price systems from the prohibitions of the Sherman Act, 26 Stat. 209, 15 U.S.C. § 1 et seq.

The two appeals, one involving The Upjohn Co. and one involving Eli Lilly & Co., were considered together in the Ohio courts. For simplicity we state only the facts of the Lilly case. Appellant, Hudson Distributors, Inc., owns and operates a retail drug chain in Cleveland, Ohio. Appellee, Eli Lilly & Co., manufactures pharmaceutical products bearing its trademarks and trade names. Lilly sells its products directly to wholesalers and makes no sales to retailers. Hudson purchases Lilly brand products from Regal D. S., Inc., a Michigan wholesaler.

In June 1959, the Ohio Legislature enacted a new Fair Trade Act, Ohio Revised Code §§ 1333.27–1333.34. Subsequently Lilly sent letters to all Ohio retailers of Lilly products, including Hudson, to notify them of Lilly's intention to establish minimum retail resale prices for its trademarked products pursuant to the new Ohio Act and to invite the retailers to enter into written fair-trade contracts. More than 1,400 Ohio retailers of Lilly products (about 65% of all the retail pharmacists in Ohio) signed fair-trade contracts with Lilly. Hudson, however, refused to enter into a written contract with Lilly and ignored the specified minimum resale prices. Lilly formally notified Hudson that the Ohio Act required Hudson to observe the minimum retail resale prices for Lilly commodities. Hudson, nevertheless, continued to purchase and then to resell Lilly products at less than the stipulated minimum retail resale prices.

Hudson thereupon filed a petition in the Court of Common Pleas for Cuyahoga County, Ohio, for a judgment declaring the Ohio Act invalid under the State Constitution and federal law. Lilly answered and cross-petitioned for enforcement of the Ohio Act against Hudson. The Court of Common Pleas held the Ohio Act unconstitutional under the State Constitution. On appeal, the Court of Appeals for Cuyahoga County, after discussing the federal and state legislation, 117 Ohio App. 207, 176 N.E.2d 236, reversed the trial court and entered a judgment declaring that the Ohio Act was not "in violation of the Constitution of the State of Ohio nor of the Constitution of the United States * * *." The court remanded the case "for further proceedings according to law with respect to the cross-petition * * *." On further appeal, the Supreme Court of Ohio affirmed the judgment of the Court of Appeals. [Citations.] * * * Section 2 of the McGuire Act provides in pertinent part as follows:

"Nothing contained in this section or in any of the Antitrust Acts shall render unlawful any contracts or agreements prescribing minimum or stipulated prices, * * * when contracts or agreements of that description are lawful as applied to intrastate transactions under any statute, law, or public policy now or hereafter in effect in any State * * *."

Section 3 of the McGuire Act reads as follows:

"Nothing contained in this section or in any of the Antitrust Acts shall render unlawful the exercise or the enforcement of any right or right of action created by any statute, law, or public policy now or hereafter in effect in any State, Territory, or the District of Columbia, which in substance provides that willfully and knowingly advertising, offering for sale, or selling any commodity at less than the price or prices prescribed in such contracts or agreements whether the person so advertising, offering for sale, or selling is or is not a party to such a contract or agreement, is unfair competition and is actionable at the suit of any person damaged thereby."

Before the enactment of the McGuire Act, this Court in 1951 in Schwegmann Bros. v. Calvert Distillers Corp., 341 U.S. 384, 71 S.Ct. 745, 95 L.Ed. 1035, 19 A.L.R.2d 1119, considered whether the Miller-Tydings Act, 50 Stat. 693, 15 U.S.C. § 1, removed from the prohibition of the Sherman Act, 26 Stat. 209, 15 U.S.C. § 1 et seq., a state statute which authorized a trademark owner, by notice, to require a retailer who had not executed a written contract to observe resale price maintenance. Respondents in that case argued that since the Sherman Act outlawed "contracts" in restraint of trade and since the Miller-Tydings amendment to the Sherman Act excepted "contracts or agreements prescribing minimum prices for the resale" of a commodity where such contracts or agreements were lawful under state law, the Miller-Tydings Act therefore immunized all arrangements involving resale price maintenance authorized by state law. 341 U.S. at 387, 71 S.Ct. at 747, 95 L.Ed. at 1044. After examining the history of the Miller-Tydings Act, the Court concluded that Congress had intended the words "contracts or agreements" as contained in that Act to be used "in their normal and customary meaning," id., at 388, 95 L.Ed. at 1045, and to cover only arrangements whereby the retailer voluntarily agreed to be bound by the resale price restrictions. The Court held therefore that the state resale price maintenance law could not be applied to nonsigners—"recalcitrants * * * dragged in by the heels and

compelled to submit to price fixing." Id., 341 U.S. at 390, 71 S.Ct. at 748, 95 L.Ed. at 1045. The Court stated that:

"It should be remembered that it was the state laws that the federal law was designed to accommodate. Federal regulation was to give way to state regulation. When state regulation provided for resale price maintenance by both those who contracted and those who did not, and the federal regulation was relaxed only as respects 'contracts or agreements,' the inference is strong that Congress left the noncontracting group to be governed by preexisting law." [Citation.]

Shortly after the Schwegmann decision, Congress passed the McGuire Act, 66 Stat. 631, 15 U.S.C. § 45(a) (1)–(5). The Report of the House Committee on Interstate and Foreign Commerce, which accompanied the McGuire Act, declared that:

"The primary purpose of the [McGuire] bill is to reaffirm the very same proposition which, in the committee's opinion, the Congress intended to enact into law when it passed the Miller-Tydings Act * * *, to the effect that the application and enforcement of State fair-trade laws—including the nonsigner provisions of such laws—with regard to interstate transactions shall not constitute a violation of the Federal Trade Commission Act or the Sherman Antitrust Act. This reaffirmation is made necessary because of the decision of a divided Supreme Court in Schwegmann v. Calvert Distillers Corporation (341 U.S. 384, [71 S.Ct. 745, 95 L.Ed. 1035, 19 A.L.R.2d 1119] May 21, 1951). In that case, six members of the Court held that the Miller-Tydings Act did not exempt from these Federal laws enforcement of State fair trade laws with respect to nonsigners. Three members of the Court held that the Miller-Tydings Act did so apply.

"The end result of the Supreme Court decision has been seriously to undermine the effectiveness of the Miller-Tydings Act and, in turn, of the fair-trade laws enacted by 45

States. H.R. 5767, *as amended, is designed to restore the effectiveness of these acts by making it abundantly clear that Congress means to let State fair-trade laws apply in their totality; that is, with respect to non-signers as well as signers."* (Emphasis added.) [Citation.]

This authoritative report evinces the clear intention of Congress that, where sanctioned by a state fair-trade act, a trademark owner such as Lilly could be permitted to enforce, even against a nonsigning retailer such as Hudson, the stipulated minimum prices established by written contracts with other retailers.

Without disputing this interpretation of the McGuire Act, Hudson argues that the Ohio Act as interpreted by the Ohio courts reaches beyond the exemptive terms of the federal Act by permitting the maintenance of resale prices "by notice alone" where no contract has been entered into between the owner of the trademark and any retailer. Hudson emphasizes that the Ohio courts sustained the Ohio Act under the State Constitution on the theory that Hudson, simply by acquiring Lilly's products with notice of the stipulated prices, impliedly contracted to observe the minimum prices. This implied contract theory was deemed necessary by the Ohio Legislature and by the Ohio courts to satisfy the State Constitution which had recently been held to invalidate the enforcement of resale prices against nonsigners. [Citation.] Whatever merit there may be in the argument that the logic of the Ohio implied contract theory would apply to prices set by notice alone and without any conventional or express contracts, on the facts of the present case we need not and do not consider whether a state statute so applied would involve "contracts or agreements" in the sense in which those terms are used in the McGuire Act. The undisputed facts show that Lilly had established a system of resale price maintenance involving written contracts with

some 1,400 Ohio retailers. Section 1333.29 (A) of the Ohio Act authorizes the establishment of minimum prices through such contracts. Under these circumstances the fact that the Ohio law, as construed for purposes of assessing its validity under the State Constitution, regards Hudson as a "contractor" (or "implied contractor") rather than as a nonsigner does not control the application and effect of the federal statute—the McGuire Act. Section 3 of the federal Act plainly upholds "any right or right of action created by any statute * * * in effect in any State * * * which in substance" permits enforcement of resale prices prescribed in contracts whether or not the violating seller was a party to those contracts. For the purposes of § 3 of the McGuire Act, therefore, it is clear that these cases involve the requisite contracts with retailers, that, regardless of whether Hudson itself entered into "contracts" within the meaning of the McGuire Act, Hudson was at least a nonsigner, and that under such circumstances Congress plainly intended "to let State fair-trade laws apply * * * with respect to nonsigners as well as signers." H.R.Rep. No. 1437, 82d Cong. 2d Sess. at 2. Accordingly we hold that the Ohio Act, as applied to the facts of these cases, comes within the terms of the McGuire Act.

*   *   *

The price fixing authorized by the Ohio Fair Trade Act and involving goods moving in interstate commerce would be, absent approval by Congress, clearly illegal under the Sherman Act, 26 Stat. 209, 15 U.S.C. § 1 et seq. Dr. Miles Medical Co. v. John D. Park & Sons Co., 220 U.S. 373, 31 S.Ct. 376, 55 L. Ed. 502. "Fixing minimum prices, like other types of price fixing, is illegal per se." Schwegmann Bros. v. Calvert Distillers Corp., supra, 341 U.S. at 386, 71 S.Ct. at 746, 95 L.Ed. at 1043. Congress, however, in the McGuire Act has approved state statutes sanctioning resale price maintenance schemes such as those involved here. Whether it is good policy to permit such laws is a matter for Congress to decide. Where the statutory language and the legislative history clearly indicate the purpose of Congress that purpose must be upheld. We therefore affirm the judgments of the Supreme Court of Ohio.

Affirmed.

PROBLEMS

1. Discuss the validity and effect of each of the following:

   (a) An agreement between two or more manufacturers of radios to sell their products at the same prices.

   (b) An agreement between a distiller and a retail liquor dealer fixing a minimum retail price for the distiller's products.

   (c) An agreement between two manufacturers of the same type of products to allocate territories whereby neither will sell its products in the area allocated to the other.

   (d) An agreement between a manufacturer and distributor not to sell to a dealer a particular product or parts necessary for repair of the product.

   (e) An agreement between two or more dealers not to purchase the products of a particular manufacturer.

   (f) An agreement between a manufacturer and an independent dealer whereby the latter agrees to purchase for re-sale the products of the manufacturer exclusively, and not to deal in any competing product.

   (g) An agreement between an automobile manufacturer and a dealer allowing discounts on purchases of new cars which are not allowed to other dealers in the area.

2. A conceived a secret process for the continuous freeze drying of food stuffs and related products and constructed a small pilot plant which practiced the process. A lacked the financing necessary to develop the commercial potential of the process and in hopes of obtaining a contract for its development and the payment of royalties, disclosed it in confidence to B, a coffee manufacturer, who signed an agreement not to disclose it to anyone else. At the same time, A signed an agreement not to disclose the process to any other person as long as A and B were considering a contract for its development. Upon disclosure, B became extremely interested and offered to pay A the sum of $1,750,000 if, upon further development, the process proved to be commercially feasible. While negotiations between A and B were in progress, C, a competitor of B, learned of the existence of the process and requested a disclosure from A who informed C that the process could not be disclosed to anyone unless negotiations with B were broken off. C offered to pay A $2,500,000 for the process provided it met certain defined objective performance criteria. A contract was prepared and executed between A and C on this basis without any prior disclosure of the process to C. Upon the making of this contract, A rejected the offer of B. The process was thereupon disclosed to C and demonstration runs of the pilot plant in the presence of representatives of C were conducted under varying conditions. After three weeks of experimental demonstrations, compiling of data and analyses of results, C informed A that the process did not meet the performance criteria in the contract and that for this reason C was rejecting the process. Two years later C placed on the market freeze-dried coffee which resembled in color, appearance and texture the product of A's pilot plant. What are the rights of the parties?

3. B, a chemist, was employed by A, a manufacturer, to work on a secret process for A's product under an exclusive three-year contract. C, a salesman, was employed by A on a week-to-week basis. B and C resigned the employment with A and accepted employment in their respective capacities with D, a rival manufacturer. C began soliciting patronage from A's former customers whose names he had memorized. What are the rights of the parties in (1) a suit by A to enjoin B from working for D; and (2) a suit by A to enjoin C from soliciting A's customers?

4. P entered into an exclusive franchise agreement with D, a brewery, to become the exclusive wholesale distributor of D's beer, in X County for five years. In reliance upon the contract, P entered into a lease of office and warehouse space and made heavy investments in motor trucks and equipment. D repudiated the agreement with P

and appointed C his exclusive distributor in X County. In an action by P against C and D to enjoin C from selling D's beer in X County, and to obtain damages from D, what decree? What would be the difference in result if the franchise agreement between P and D contained no time limit but provided that it could be terminated with or without cause by either party upon 10 days written notice?

5. George McCoy of Florida has been manufacturing and distributing a cheese cake for over five years, labeling his product with a picture of a cheese cake which serves as a background for a Florida bathing beauty under which is written the slogan "McCoy All Spice Florida Cheese Cake". George McCoy has not registered his trade mark. Subsequently, Leo McCoy of California begins manufacturing a similar product on the West coast using a label in appearance similar to that of George McCoy, containing a picture of a Hollywood star, and the words "McCoy's All Spice Cheese Cake." Leo McCoy begins marketing his products in the Eastern United States, using labels with the word "Florida" added as in George McCoy's label. Leo McCoy has registered his product under the Federal Trademark Law. To what relief, if any, is George McCoy entitled?

6. R, a professional baseball player, contracted to play for the C Club exclusively for two years. After six months, R demanded an increase in salary which was denied. R therefore refused to play any longer and threatened to play for a team in a neighboring city. What are the the rights of the C Club?

7. P seeks an injunction to restrain D, a former employee, from soliciting business from customers of P with whom D had dealt while working for P. D had never agreed that he would not compete with P or solicit P's customers. After leaving P's employ D solicited customers of P on behalf of X, a competitor of P. What decree?

8. X, having filed locally an affidavit required under the "Assumed Name" statute has been operating and advertising his exclusive toy store for 20 years in Centerville, Illinois. His advertising has consisted of large signs on his premises reading "The Toy Mart". B, after operating a store in Chicago under the name of "The Chicago Toy Mart" relocated in Centerville, Illinois, and erected a large sign reading "TOY MART" with the word "Centerville" being written underneath in substantially smaller letters. Thereafter, the sales of X declined, and many of X's customers patronized B's store thinking it to be a branch of B's business. What are the rights of the parties?

CHAPTER 43

BANKRUPTCY—CORPORATE REORGANIZATION

Introductory. A debt is a specific sum of money owed by one person to another. A debt exists because one person has given another person something of value at one time and has not required from the other person payment for it until a later time. The person owing the money and under an obligation to pay it is the *debtor*. The person to whom the money is owed and who has a right to enforce payment is the *creditor*. The creditor has given credit to, or has put his trust, faith and belief in the debtor and his promise to pay at a later date.

Practically every person is a debtor at almost any particular moment of his existence since it is customary for everyone to accept something of value before making payment. A debt is created when A's wife purchases a loaf of bread on a charge account from the local grocer on January 3, and the debt is not satisfied until A pays the monthly bill on February 7. A debt exists for electricity and gas and other utilities consumed in the home from day to day and until the following month's statement is paid. A passenger boarding a commuter train is a debtor in relation to the railroad company until the conductor collects his fare. Similarly, the average person is a creditor much of the time since most persons are involved in transactions where they give something of value before receiving payment. A wage earner who is paid on Friday for the week's work is a creditor of his employer from Monday to Friday. A person who accepts a check or a promissory note is a creditor of the drawer or maker until the instrument is paid. A person engaged in any profession, occupation or business where he performs services or gives up a product before receiving payment is a creditor.

In the ordinary course of commercial life, the great majority of debts are eventually satisfied by payment. However, a comparatively few debts are not paid and these give rise to a significant field of business law broadly characterized as "Creditors' Rights and Debtor Relief," the most important phase of which is bankruptcy.

Creditors' Rights and Debtor Relief. When a debt is not paid it may be due to the debtor's desire not to pay or to his inability to pay. In either case, the creditor usually takes the following steps in this order: (1) writes, telegraphs, telephones or personally sees the debtor and attempts to enforce collection; (2) turns the matter over to his lawyer, who then writes, telegraphs, telephones or personally sees the debtor and attempts to enforce collection; (3) authorizes his lawyer to file a lawsuit and obtain a judgment against the debtor. At this point, the reluctant debtor as distinguished from the debtor with no, or insufficient, assets, usually pays the judgment and the matter is closed.

If the judgment is not satisfied by payment, the creditor, who has now become a "judgment creditor," can take out a writ of execution, directing the sheriff to seize the debtor's property and creating a lien upon the debtor's real property; or, by means of a garnishment action, can seize the debtor's property in the hands of third parties, or, by means of a creditor's bill in equity, can seize equitable interests of the debtor not subject to legal process. If any of the debtor's property is located and seized, that property will be sold and applied to satisfaction of the judgment.

If, however, the debtor has no property the creditor will receive nothing in payment, or, if the aggregate of the debtor's debts exceeds his total assets, the creditor will probably receive nothing if another creditor is more diligent in seizing the property. At this point, two conflicting policies or theories of justice clash head-on. On the one hand, the creditors have just claims and are entitled to payment. The kindly creditor who has held back from seizing the debtor's property is entitled to payment as well as the diligent creditor who has seized all of the insufficient assets. On the other hand, the debtor who has, with or without fault, contracted debts beyond his ability to pay is entitled to relief from what might otherwise be a lifetime burden tending to destroy him and his family, provided he is willing to give up all of his present assets.

Out of this conflict between creditors' rights and debtor relief have come various compromises, some of which are non-legal in form, such as those effected by the hundreds of credit agencies and adjustment bureaus. Of the legal compromises, some are founded in common law and involve simple contract and trust principles, such as compositions and assignments; others are statutory, such as statutory assignments. Some involve the intervention of a court and its officers, such as equity receiverships, and others do not. The most important method of compromising creditor rights and debtor relief is the Federal Bankruptcy Act, which is largely statutory and involves court intervention.

Compositions. A common-law or non-statutory composition is an ordinary contract or agreement between the debtor on the one hand and his creditors on the other, whereby the creditors receive pro rata a part, but not the whole amount, of their claims and the debtor is discharged from the balance of the claims, since the whole amount is deemed satisfied by payment of the part.

As a contract, it requires the formalities of a contract, such as offer, acceptance and consideration. For example, debtor D owing debts of $5,000 to A, $2,000 to B, and $1,000 to C, offers to compose these claims by paying $4,000 to A, B and C. If A, B and C accept the offer, a composition results with A receiving $2,500, B $1,000, and C $500. The consideration for the promise of A to forgive the balance of his claim, consists of the promises of B and C to forgive parts of their claims. All the creditors benefit since a race of diligence among creditors to obtain the debtor's limited assets is avoided. Thus, a composition differs from an accord and satisfaction, involving a single debtor and a single creditor, in which case some additional consideration from D is necessary before the balance of a liquidated debt will be deemed satisfied by payment of only a part of it.

It should be noted, however, that, in accordance with fixed contract principles, the debtor in a composition is discharged from liability for only the claims of creditors who voluntarily consent to the composition and thereby voluntarily release the balance of their claims. If, in the illustration, C refused to accept the offer of composition and refused to take the $500, he could later attempt to collect the full $1,000 claim. Likewise, if D owed additional debts to X, Y and Z, these creditors would not be bound by the agreement between D and A, B and C. Another disadvantage of the composition is the fact that any creditor can attach the assets of the debtor during the usual period of bargaining and negotiation which precedes the execution of the composition agreement. For instance, once D advised A, B and C that he was offering to compose the claims, any one of the creditors could seize D's property.

Assignments for Benefit of Creditors. A common-law or non-statutory assignment for the benefit of creditors or general assignment, as it is sometimes called, is a voluntary transfer by the debtor of some or all of his property to an assignee in trust, or trustee, who applies the property to the payment of all of the debtor's debts. Debtor D transfers title to his property to trustee T, who converts the property into money and pays it to all of the creditors on a pro rata basis.

The advantage of the assignment over the composition is that it immunizes the debtor's assets from attachment and execution, and it halts the race of diligent creditors to attach. On the other hand, the common-law assignment does not require the consent of the creditors and payment by the trustee of part of the claims does not discharge the debtor from the balance of them. Thus, even after T pays A $2,500, B $1,000 and C $500 (and appropriate payments to all other creditors), nevertheless A, B and C and the other creditors may still attempt to collect the balance of their claims.

Statutory Assignments. Because of the benefit to creditors of assignments by immunizing the debtor's assets from attachments, there have been many statutory attempts to retain the idea of the assignment and, at the same time, to give a corresponding benefit to the debtor by discharging him from the balance of his debts. Since the Federal constitution prohibits a State from impairing the obligation of a contract between private citizens, it is impossible for a State to force all creditors to discharge a debtor upon a pro rata distribution of assets, although, as pointed out hereafter, the Federal government *does* have such power and exercises it in the Bankruptcy Act. Accordingly, the States have generally enacted two different types of assignment statutes, one type providing that any person who voluntarily accepts a dividend (or part payment) *automatically* discharges the debtor from the balance of the claim, the creditor having the privilege of refusing to participate and retaining his claim in full, and the other type permitting the debtor to exact *voluntary* releases of the balance of claims from creditors who accept part payments, thus combining the advantages of common-law compositions and assignments. Statutes of the first type have generally been superseded by the Federal Bankruptcy Act but statutes of the second type continue in effect.

Equity Receiverships. One of the oldest remedies in equity is the appointment of a receiver by the court. The receiver is a disinterested person who receives and preserves the debtor's assets and the income therefrom, and disposes of the assets and income at the direction of the court which appointed him.

A receiver will not be appointed upon the petition of the debtor himself nor upon the petition of an unsecured simple contract creditor or group of creditors. In proper cases, a receiver will be appointed upon the petition (1) of a secured creditor seeking foreclosure of his security; (2) of a judgment creditor bringing a creditors' bill in equity after exhausting legal remedies to satisfy the judgment, or (3) of a shareholder of a corporate debtor where it appears that the assets of the corporation will be dissipated by fraud or mismanagement, as distinguished from mere differences of opinion or errors of judgment. The appointment of a receiver always rests within the sound discretion of the court. Insolvency, in the equity sense of inability by the debtor to meet his obligations as they become due, is one of the factors considered by the court in appointing a receiver but, generally, something more than mere insolvency, such as dissipation of assets, must be shown before a receiver is appointed.

Once the receiver is appointed and takes over the possession of the debtor's assets all of his future actions are governed by the court of appointment which may instruct him either (1) to liquidate the assets by public or private sale; (2) to operate the business as a going concern temporarily; or (3) to conserve the assets until final disposition of the matter before the court. A receiver has been aptly described as a liquidator, manager and custodian.

History of Bankruptcy. The word "bankrupt" is derived from the Latin *banque,* meaning bench or table, and *ruptus,* meaning broken. There is some authority for the legend that, upon bankruptcy, the distinguishing trademark of a merchant, his bench or table, was literally broken. In any event, it was figuratively broken since bankruptcy meant commercial failure.

The idea of bankruptcy goes far back into history, taking such various forms among the civilizations of antiquity, according to Blackstone, as "imprisoning the debtor's person in chains, subjecting him to stripes and hard labor, at the mercy of his rigid creditors, and sometimes selling him, with his wife and children, into perpetual foreign slavery," or the form "whereby the creditors might cut the debtor's body into pieces, and each take his proportionate share." The Christian emperors of Rome introduced a lenient bankruptcy law which permitted a debtor to yield all of his property to his creditors and thereby to become immune from personal seizure.

The first English Bankruptcy Act in 1542 applied only to traders since, quoting Blackstone, "that class of men are, generally speaking, the only persons liable to accidental losses, and to an inability to pay their debts, without any fault of their own," whereas "if persons in other situations of life run into debt, they must take the consequences of their own indiscretion." Until the passage of the English Bankruptcy Act of 1861, the English acts applied only to traders or merchants, that is, persons who bought and re-sold merchandise.

The constitution of the United States provides that "The Congress shall have power * * * to establish * * * uniform Laws on the subject of Bankruptcies throughout the United States." (Article I, Section 8, clause 4.) The first American Bankruptcy Act of 1800 (repealed after three years) applied only to traders, but the second Act of 1841 (repealed after two years) and the third Act of 1867 applied to persons other than merchants, which is true at the present time. The Act of 1867 was repealed in 1878 and the fourth act was passed on July 1, 1898. Between 1878 and 1898, there was no Federal Bankruptcy Act and, during that period, many States passed Insolvency Acts, which were generally similar to Statutory Assignment Statutes, discussed heretofore. The Bankruptcy Act was completely overhauled and revised by the Congress in 1938 by the passage of the Chandler Act.

Purpose of Bankruptcy. Bankruptcy legislation serves a dual purpose: (1) to effect an equitable distribution of the debtor's property among his creditors and (2) to discharge the debtor from his debts and enable him to rehabilitate himself and start afresh. Other subsidiary purposes are to regulate uniformly credit transactions, to preserve existing business relations, to stabilize commercial usages, and to effect a speedy, as well as equitable, distribution of the debtor's assets.

The Bankruptcy Act, as amended by the Chandler Act, contains several specialized kinds of bankruptcy proceedings:

	Proceedings	Chapter		Sections	
1.	Ordinary bankruptcy	I–VII	1	through	72
2.	Agricultural compositions and extensions	VIII	75		
3.	Railroad reorganizations	VIII	77		
4.	Compositions for taxing agencies	IX	81	through	84
5.	Corporate reorganizations	X	101	through	276
6.	Arrangements	XI	301	through	399
7.	Real property arrangements	XII	401	through	526
8.	Wage earners' plans	XIII	601	through	686
9.	Maritime Commission liens	XIV	701	through	703
10.	Railroad adjustments	XV	700,	705 through	755

Straight bankruptcy (Chapters I through VII) provides for liquidation and termination of the business of the bankrupt, whereas most of the other procedures provide for reorganization and continuance of the business of the bankrupt.

Straight bankruptcy and Chapter XI, providing for the settlement or extension of unsecured debts, apply to *both* individuals and corporations. (Sections 4a and 306(3).) Chapter X applies *only* to corporations (Section 106(5)) and Section 77 applies only to railroad corporations. (Section 77(a).) Section 75 applies *only* to individual farmers (Section 75(r)), Chapter XIII applies only to individual wage-earners (Section 606(8)), and Chapter XII, relating to plans for the alteration of rights of creditors holding debts secured by real property applies to individual persons only. (Section 406(6).)

Chapters X, XI, XII, and XIII provide that the provisions of straight bankruptcy (Chapters I through VII) apply to these special proceedings also, unless the ordinary provisions are inconsistent with the special provisions, in which case the latter will, of course, prevail. (Sections 102, 302, 402, 602.)

Who May Become a Bankrupt. A bankrupt is a person (1) who has filed a *voluntary* petition in bankruptcy, or (2) against whom an *involuntary* petition in bankruptcy has been filed, or (3) who has been adjudged a bankrupt. (Section 1(4).) To be adjudged a bankrupt by a bankruptcy court, the debtor must have had his principal place of business, or have resided or have had his domicile within the jurisdiction of the bankruptcy court for a longer portion of the six months immediately preceding the filing of the petition than in any other jurisdiction. (Section 2a(1).)

Voluntary Bankruptcy. Any person may become a voluntary bankrupt by filing a petition on his own behalf. (Sections 4a and 59a.) A "person" includes natural persons, corporations and partnerships (Section 1 (23)), but does not include municipal, railroad, insurance or banking corporations, or building and loan associations. (Sections 4a and 4b.) A person need not be insolvent to file a voluntary petition in bankruptcy, nor is it necessary that he has committed an "act of bankruptcy," which is described hereafter.

Involuntary Bankruptcy. An involuntary petition in bankruptcy may be filed *by* (1) any three or more creditors who have provable claims at the time of the filing against the debtor, which claims are fixed as to liability and liquidated as to amount and total in the aggregate $500 or more, or, (2) if all of the creditors of the debtor are less than twelve in number, then, by one of such creditors whose claim equals $500 or more. (Section 59b.)

An involuntary petition may be filed *against* (1) any natural person or any moneyed, business or commercial corporation (Section 4b), (2) owing debts to the amount of $1,000 or more (Section 4b), (3) who has committed an "act of bankruptcy" (Section 3b), (4) within four months prior to the filing of the petition. (Section 3b.)

An involuntary petition may be filed against any natural person except a wage earner, who is defined as a person who works for wages, salary or hire at a rate of compensation not exceeding $1,500 per year (Section 1(32)), or a farmer. Thus, ordinary bankruptcy proceedings exclude the great majority of persons engaged in commercial enterprise and conforms the Bankruptcy Act somewhat to the original idea of applying only to traders and merchants. Chapter XIII of the Bankruptcy Act, entitled "Wage Earners' Plans," applies to wage earners but, for the purposes of that chapter, a wage earner is defined as a person who works for wages, salary or hire at a rate of compensation which does not exceed $5,000 per year when added to all of his other income. Section 75 of Chapter VIII of the Bankruptcy Act applies to farmers and permits agricultural compositions and extensions. An involuntary petition may not be filed against a municipal, railroad, insurance or banking corporation or against a building and loan association. (Sections 4a and 4b.)

Acts of Bankruptcy. Section 3a of the Bankruptcy Act sets forth the following six acts of bankruptcy:

1. *Fraudulent Conveyance:* Conveying, transferring, concealing, removing or permitting to be concealed or removed any part of a debtor's property, with intent to hinder, delay or defraud his creditors or any of them;

2. *Preference:* Transferring, *while insolvent,* any portion of a debtor's property to one or more of his creditors with intent to prefer such creditors over his other creditors;

3. *Permitting Creditor to Obtain Lien:* Suffering or permitting, *while insolvent,* any creditor to obtain a lien upon any of a debtor's property through legal proceedings and not having vacated and having discharged such lien within thirty days from the date thereof or within five days of the date before any sale or disposition of property;

4. *General Assignment:* Making a general assignment for the benefit of a debtor's creditors;

5. *Permitting Appointment of Receiver: While insolvent or unable to pay his debts as they may mature,* procuring, permitting or suffering voluntarily or involuntarily the appointment of a receiver or trustee to take charge of a debtor's property; or

6. *Admission in Writing:* Admitting in writing by a debtor of his inability to pay his debts and his willingness to be judged a bankrupt.

Insolvency. Insolvency, for the purpose of the Bankruptcy Act, exists whenever the aggregate of property owned by the debtor is not sufficient in amount to pay his debts (Section 1(19)), as distinguished from the equity meaning of inability to pay debts as they mature. Before the amendment of the

Bankruptcy Act by the Chandler Act in 1938, an involuntary petition could not be brought against a debtor unless he was insolvent *at the time of the filing of the petition.* Since the Chandler Act amendments, however, insolvency is not required in every case. It is required *at the time of committing* the second and third acts of bankruptcy, and insolvency under the Bankruptcy Act or inability to pay debts as they mature is required *at the time of committing* the fifth act.

Furthermore, solvency *at the time of filing a petition* is a defense under the first act of bankruptcy (Section 3c) and the burden of proving solvency is upon the debtor. In the case of the second, third and fifth acts of bankruptcy, the burden of proving the insolvency of the debtor is upon the creditor unless the debtor fails to appear and submit to an examination, in which latter case the burden is upon the debtor to prove solvency (Section 3d). Solvency is not required either at the time of filing the petition or at the time of committing the fourth and sixth acts of bankruptcy.

Fraudulent Conveyances. Broadly speaking, a fraudulent conveyance is a transfer of property without adequate consideration and with the intent that the transferee will hold the property for the benefit of the transferor, returning it when requested, so as to defraud creditors who could otherwise seize the property in payment of their debts. For example, A, who is in debt, transfers title to his home to B, his father, without any payment by B to A and with the understanding that, when the home is no longer in danger of seizure by creditors, B will reconvey it to A. This differs from a preference, which is a transfer of property in payment of an antecedent debt by a debtor to one creditor at a time when other creditors of like standing will not be paid in full. Debtor A while insolvent pays creditor C, an old friend, but does not pay creditors D, E, or F. This is a preference, not a fraudulent conveyance.

Fraudulent transfers are defined in Sections 67 and 70 of the Act and constitute acts of bankruptcy under Section 3a (1). Section 67d(2) provides that every transfer made and every obligation incurred by a debtor within *one year* prior to the filing of the petition is fraudulent:

1. As to creditors existing at the time of transfer, if made without fair consideration by an insolvent debtor, without regard to actual intent;

2. As to then existing creditors and as to other persons who become creditors during the continuance of a business, if made without fair consideration by a debtor engaged in such business, for which the remaining property is an unreasonably small capital, without regard to actual intent;

3. As to then existing and future creditors if made without fair consideration by a debtor who intends to incur debts beyond his ability to pay as they mature; and

4. As to then existing and future creditors, if made with actual intent, as distinguished from intent presumed in law, to hinder, delay, or defraud creditors. (Section 67d(2).)

A fraudulent transfer is null and void. (Section 67d(6).) Consideration given for the property or obligation of a debtor is "fair" (1) when, in good faith, in exchange and as a fair equivalent therefor, property is transferred or an antecedent debt is satisfied, or (2) when such property or obligation is received in good faith to secure a present advance or antecedent debt in an amount not disproportionately small as compared with the value of the property or obligation obtained. (Section 67d(1).)

These provisions of the Bankruptcy Act incorporate the like provisions of the Uniform Fraudulent Conveyances Act.

Preferences. A preference is (1) a transfer (2) of any of the property of a debtor (3) to or for the benefit of a creditor (4) for or on account of an antecedent debt, (5) made or suffered by the debtor while insolvent (6) and within four months before the filing by or against him of a petition in bankruptcy, (7) the effect of which transfer will be to enable the creditor to obtain a greater percentage of his debt than some other debtor of the same class. (Section 60 a.)

In order for a preference to be an act of bankruptcy, there must be the additional element of intent *by the debtor* to prefer one creditor over another. (Section 3a(2).) If such intent on the part of the debtor were not required, any payment, however small or routine and whether in full payment or merely on account, of a debt due any general creditor would be an act of bankruptcy, provided that the debtor was insolvent and the payment was made within four months before the petition was filed.

A preference or preferred payment to a creditor may be avoided by the trustee in bankruptcy if the creditor receiving it thereby had, at the time when the transfer was made, reasonable cause to believe that the debtor was insolvent. (Section 60b.) Thus, for a preference to be an act of bankruptcy, the *debtor* must have intended to prefer; for a preference to be voidable, the *creditor* must have had knowledge of the debtor's insolvency. Where the preference is voidable, the trustee may recover the property or, if it has been converted, its value from any person who has received or converted such property, except a bona-fide purchaser for value. (Section 60b.)

A partial payment to a creditor by a debtor who is insolvent, but who is capable of paying the same proportion to all of his other creditors, is a preference if the other creditors are not actually paid.

Liens. Every lien against the property of an insolvent person obtained by attachment, judgment, levy, or other legal or equitable process within four months before the filing of a bankruptcy petition is not only an act of bankruptcy (Section 3a(3)), but is also deemed null and void if such lien was sought and permitted in fraud of the provisions of the Bankruptcy Act. (Section 67a(1).) The property affected by any lien deemed null and void is discharged from the lien and passes to the trustee in bankruptcy. (Section 67a(3).)

Bankruptcy Courts. The District Courts of the United States, which are trial courts with general jurisdiction in law and equity over all Federal matters, are also bankruptcy courts or "courts of bankruptcy" (Section 1(10)), with exclusive original jurisdiction over bankruptcy proceedings. (Section 2a.) In bankruptcy proceedings, the word "court," as distinguished from "bankruptcy court," refers to the judge of the bankruptcy court, who is the District Judge, or to the referee of the bankruptcy court, who is discussed hereafter. (Section 1(9).) An involuntary bankrupt is entitled to a jury trial with respect to the questions of insolvency and the commission of an act of bankruptcy (Section 19a), and the right to a trial by jury as to other matters in controversy in bankruptcy proceedings is preserved. (Section 19c.)

Section 2a of the Bankruptcy Act sets forth twenty-one express jurisdictional powers of bankruptcy courts. The Supreme Court of the United States has held that "courts of bankruptcy are essentially courts of equity, and their proceedings inherently proceedings in equity." Thus, the District Courts, when functioning as bankruptcy courts, primarily administer the bankruptcy statute and secondarily exercise equitable powers to further bankruptcy proceedings in all matters not expressly covered by the bankruptcy statute.

Referees. The Bankruptcy Act provides for referees (Section 33), who are appointed by the judge or judges of the bankruptcy court for six-year terms (Section 34). Full-time referees with a maximum salary of $22,500 per year are generally appointed, but, where a full-time referee is not necessary because of the small volume of bankruptcy cases, part-time referees with a maximum salary of $11,000 are appointed. (Sections 37, 40.)

A referee must (1) be competent; (2) not hold a public office for profit; (3) not be related to judges of the bankruptcy courts or Federal appellate courts; (4) be resident within the territorial limits of the bankruptcy court and maintain an office therein, and (5) be a member in good standing at the bar of the Federal District Court in which he is appointed. (Section 35.) A referee must not (1) act in cases in which he is directly or indirectly interested or (2) purchase, directly or indirectly, any property of an estate in bankruptcy. Furthermore, full-time referees must not engage in the practice of law and part-time referees must not engage in the practice of bankruptcy law. (Section 39b.)

A general reference of a bankruptcy proceeding to a referee gives him the authority to conduct all necessary proceedings. A special reference limits the referee's authority to the special matters set forth in the order of reference. In either case, the referee's actions are subject to review by the judge of the bankruptcy court. (Sections 2a(10), 38.) The referee files a report with the judge of his proposed findings of fact and conclusions of law, and the judge must accept the findings of fact, "unless clearly erroneous" (General Order in Bankruptcy 47). The judge, after hearing, may adopt the report, or may modify it, or may reject it in whole or in part, or may receive further evidence, or may recommit it to the referee with instructions.

In addition to exercising bankruptcy jurisdiction, subject to review by the judge (Section 38), the referee performs many routine duties necessary to bankruptcy administration, such as sending out notices, keeping records and so forth. (Section 39.)

Receivers. The bankruptcy court may appoint, upon the application of parties in interest, receivers or the United States marshal to take charge of the property of the bankrupt and to protect the interests of creditors during the period after the filing of the bankruptcy petition and until the petition is dismissed or until the trustee is appointed and qualified to act. (Section 2a(3).) The bankruptcy court may authorize the receiver to conduct pending litigation or to commence any suit on behalf of the estate (Section 2a (3)), and may also authorize the receiver (or the marshal or trustee) to carry on the business of the bankrupt for a limited period. (Section 2a(5).)

Adjudication. A decree of adjudication in bankruptcy is simply a judicial pronouncement that a person is bankrupt. It is the jurisdictional basis for the court's administration of the affairs of the bankrupt, the taking over and liquidation of his assets, and distribution of dividends to creditors. Ordinarily it is the first order entered in the proceedings. In the case of a voluntary petition other than a petition on behalf of a partnership by fewer than all of the partners no order of adjudication is necessary. An amendment to the Bankruptcy Act in 1959 provides that the filing of such a petition shall be deemed an adjudication in bankruptcy with the same force and effect of a decree of adjudication. Where a voluntary petition is filed on behalf of a partnership by less than all of the partners, or in the case of an involuntary petition, the court after a hearing on the petition and any answer that may be filed enters either a decree of adjudication or an order dismissing the petition.

Meetings of Creditors. The first meeting of the creditors of the bankrupt is held not less than ten nor more than thirty days after the adjudication. (Section 55a.) The judge or referee presides and allows or disallows claims of creditors there presented and publicly examines the bankrupt or permits creditors to examine him. (Section 55b.)

The court calls subsequent meetings of creditors whenever one-fourth or more in number of creditors who have proved their claims file a written request. (Section 55d.) Whenever the affairs of the estate are ready to be closed, a final meeting is called, except that a no-asset case can be closed without a final meeting. (Section 55e.)

Creditors pass upon matters submitted to their meetings by a majority vote in number and amount of claims of all creditors whose claims have been allowed and who are present. (Section 56a.) Claims of $50 or less are not counted in computing the number of creditors voting or present at creditors' meetings, but are counted in computing the amount. (Section 56c.) Creditors holding claims which are secured or have priority are not entitled to vote; nor are such claims counted in computing the number of creditors or the amount of their claims. (Section 56b.)

Trustees. The Bankruptcy Act creates the office of trustee. (Section 33.) The creditors of a bankrupt at their first meeting appoint a trustee or three trustees. If the creditors fail to make the appointment, the court appoints a trustee. (Section 44a.) The creditors may also appoint a creditors' committee of not less than three creditors to consult and advise with the trustee. (Section 44b.)

Trustees perform the following duties (Section 47):

> 1. Collect and reduce to money the property of the estates for which they are trustees, under the direction of the court, and close up the estates as expeditiously as is compatible with the best interests of the parties in interest;

2. Deposit all money received by them in designated depositories;

3. Account for and pay over to the estates under their control all interest received by them upon funds belonging to such estates;

4. Disburse money only by check or draft on such depositories;

5. Keep records and accounts showing all amounts and items of property received and from what sources, all amounts expended and for what purposes and all items of property disposed of;

6. Set apart the bankrupts' exemptions allowed by law, if claimed, and report the items and estimated value thereof to the courts as soon as practicable after their appointment;

7. Examine the bankrupts (a) at the first meetings of creditors or at other meetings specially fixed for that purpose, unless they shall already have been fully examined by the referees, receivers, or creditors, and (b) upon the hearing of objections, if any, to their discharges, unless otherwise ordered by the court;

8. Examine all proofs of claim and object to the allowance of such claims as may be improper;

9. Oppose at the expense of estates the discharges of bankrupts when they deem it advisable to do so;

10. Furnish such information concerning the estates of which they are trustees and their administration as may be requested by parties in interest;

11. Pay dividends within ten days after they are declared by the referees;

12. Report to the courts in writing the condition of the estates, the amounts of money on hand, and such other details as may be required by the courts, within the first month after their appointment and every two months thereafter, unless otherwise ordered by the courts;

13. Make final reports and file final accounts with the courts fifteen days before the days fixed for the final meetings of the creditors; and

14. Lay before the final meetings of the creditors detailed statements of the administration of the estates.

Trustee's Title to Bankrupt's Property. A bankrupt must surrender all of his property, except that exempt by law, for the benefit of his creditors. The trustee appointed by the creditors, upon his appointment and qualification, is vested by operation of law with whatever title the bankrupt had, as of the date of the filing of the petition, in all property except that exempt by law. (Section 70a.) As to all property in the possession or under the control of the bankrupt, the trustee is vested with the rights, remedies and powers of a creditor holding a lien, and, as to all other property, the trustee is vested with the rights, remedies and power of a judgment creditor holding an execution duly returned unsatisfied. (Section 70c.)

Exemptions of Bankrupts. The bankrupt may retain title to such of his property as is exempted by the laws of the United States or by State laws in force at the time of the filing of the petition. (Section 6.) In Illinois, every householder having a family is entitled to an estate of homestead to the extent in value of $2,500 in real estate occupied by him as a residence (Ill.Rev.Stat.1965, chapter 52, § 1) and every debtor is entitled to the following exemptions:

First—The necessary wearing apparel, bible, school books, and family pictures of every person; and

Second—For one year after the receipt thereof all money received by any person a resident of this State as a pension, adjusted or additional compensation or a bonus from the United States Government or from the State of Illinois on account of military or naval service, whether the same shall be in the actual possession of such person or deposited or loaned; and

Third—One hundred dollars' worth of household furniture and, in addition, when the debtor is the head of a family and resides with the same, three hundred dollars' worth of other household furniture, in lieu thereof, or,

Fourth—One hundred dollars' worth of property, to be selected by the debtor, and in addition, when the debtor is the head of a family and resides with the same, three hundred dollars worth of other property, to be selected by the debtor. (Ill.Rev.Stat. 1965, chapter 52, § 13.)

Fifth—Net cash value of all life insurance, endowment policies, and annuity contracts, and proceeds payable to wife or husband of insured, or child, parent, or other person dependent on the insured. (Ill.Rev. Stat.1965, chapter 73, § 850.)

Claims. A debt or demand owned by a creditor may be the basis for a *claim* against the bankrupt's estate, and, if the claim is *proved* and *allowed,* the creditor will share pro rata with other creditors in the bankrupt's estate, if any, and the bankrupt will eventually be discharged from such debt in full.

Proof of Claims. Any creditor who owns a debt or demand against the bankrupt must make a claim therefor by filing in the bankruptcy court within six months after the first meeting of creditors (Section 57n) a *proof of claim,* consisting of a statement under oath, in writing and signed by the creditor, setting forth (1) the claim; (2) the consideration therefor; (3) whether any and, if so, what securities are held therefor; (4) whether any and, if so, what payments have been made thereon, and (5) that the claim is justly owing from the bankrupt to the creditor. (Section 57a.) Whenever a claim is founded upon an instrument in writing, such instrument must be filed with the proof of claim. (Section 57b.)

Provable Claims. Claims may be proved and allowed if founded upon (Section 63a):

1. Fixed liability, as evidenced by a judgment or an instrument in writing, absolutely owing at the time of the filing of the bankruptcy petition, whether then payable or not.

2. Costs taxable against a bankrupt in a proceeding where the bankrupt was the plaintiff and the trustee in bankruptcy declines to prosecute.

3. Claim for taxable costs incurred by a creditor, before the filing of the petition, in an action to recover a provable debt.

4. Open account, or contract, express or implied.

5. Provable debts reduced to judgment after the filing of the petition and before the consideration of the bankrupt's application for a discharge.

6. Award of an industrial [Workmen's Compensation] commission in case of injury or death from injury, if such injury occurred prior to adjudication.

7. Right to recover damages in any action for negligence instituted prior to and pending at the time of the filing of the petition in bankruptcy.

8. Contingent debts and contingent contractual liabilities.

9. Claims for anticipatory breach of contracts, executory in whole or in part, including unexpired leases of real or personal property.

These nine classes of debts are called "provable" claims, and a debt not falling within any of these classes may not be proved.

Future Rent Claims. Prior to the Chandler Act, a landlord's claim for future rent was not provable since a lease was viewed, not as a contract, but as an estate in real property under which claims for damages could arise only in connection with continued use and occupation of the premises. The Chandler Act added to the classes of provable claims those based on unexpired leases. However, the present act limits those claims by providing that a landlord's claim for damages for injury resulting from the rejection of an unexpired lease of real estate shall not exceed the lease rental for one year after the surrender of the premises plus unpaid rent then accrued. (Section 63a(9).)

Allowance of Claims. Provable claims which have been duly proved shall be *allowed* when presented to the court, unless objection is made by a party in interest, in which case the claim shall be determined by the court. (Section 57d.) The court will allow such a claim if it is shown to be valid and well-founded and not subject to any set-offs or defenses, such as the Statute of Limitations. When a claim is proved and allowed, the creditor may then participate with the other creditors in the distribution of the bankrupt's property.

Contingent Claims. Contingent claims were added to the classes of provable claims by the Chandler Act, but the Act also provides that an unliquidated or contingent claim is not allowable unless liquidated or the amount thereof estimated in the manner and within the time directed by the court. The claim shall not be allowed if the court shall determine that it is not capable of liquidation, or of reasonable estimation, or that such liquidation or estimation would unduly delay the administration of the estate. (Section 57d.)

Priority of Claims. Certain classes of claims have a priority, which means that they must be paid in full out of the bankrupt's estate before any dividends, or part payments, are paid to other creditors. The prior claims and the order of their payment are as follows (Section 64a):

1. *Expenses of administration* of the bankrupt estate, including the expenses of preserving the estate subsequent to filing the petition in bankruptcy; the filing fees paid by creditors in involuntary cases; the expenses of creditors in recovering concealed assets for the benefit of the bankrupt's estate; the trustee's expenses in opposing the bankrupt's discharge; the fees and mileage payable to witnesses; reasonable attorney's fees for professional services actually rendered to the petitioning creditors in involuntary cases and to the bankrupt in voluntary and involuntary cases, as the court may allow.

2. *Wages,* not to exceed $600 to each claimant, which have been earned within three months before the date of the commencement of the proceeding, due to workmen, servants, clerks, or traveling or city salesmen on salary or commission basis, whole or part time, whether or not selling exclusively for the bankrupt.

3. Where the confirmation of an arrangement or wage earner plan or the bankrupt's discharge has been refused, revoked, or set aside upon the objection and through the efforts and at the cost and expense of one or more creditors, or, where through the efforts and at the cost and expense of one or more creditors, evidence shall have been adduced resulting in the conviction of any person of an offense under the Bankruptcy Act, the *reasonable costs and expenses* of such creditors.

4. *Taxes* legally due and owing by the bankrupt to the United States or any State or any subdivision thereof.

5. *Debts* owing to any person who by the laws of the United States is *entitled to priority, and rent owing to a landlord who is entitled to priority* by State law, *provided,* however, that rent priority shall be restricted to rent due for actual use and occupancy which accrued within three months before the date of bankruptcy.

These priorities are statutory priorities fixed by the Bankruptcy Act. Bankruptcy Act priorities supersede State priorities and to a certain extent supersede statutory liens. Statutory liens on personal property not accompanied by possession of the property and liens of distress for rent are postponed in payment to priorities (1) and (2), administrative costs and wage claims. (Section 67c.) The bankruptcy court can control statutory liens by virtue of the fact that a claim based upon a lien must be disallowed unless the lien is surrendered. (Section 57 g.)

Secured Claims. In addition to statutory priorities, lawful priorities can be established by contract between debtor and creditor, as in the case where the creditor takes possession of the security for payment of the debt. The secured creditor has two courses open to him upon the bankruptcy of his debtor: (1) he can waive his security, prove his claim *for the full amount,* and participate in the assets on an equal footing with unsecured creditors; or (2) he can convert his security into money (under the control of the bankruptcy court), credit the amount of such money against the debt, and prove his claim *for the balance* of the debt. (Section 57h.)

A secured creditor cannot realize upon the security and then participate in the assets upon his entire claim, even though under such an arrangement he would not be paid the entire debt. For example, assume that bankrupt B owes creditor C $1,000; that C holds as security for the debt stock now worth $200, and that general creditors of B will receive 50 per cent of their claims. Thus, C could sell the stock and realize $200 and, if he were permitted to share in the assets of B, he would receive $500, or a total of $700. However, he cannot do this. He must either (1) realize $200 on the security and receive 50 per cent of $800, or $400, from the bankrupt estate, thus receiving a total of $600, or (2) turn the security over to the bankrupt estate and receive 50 per cent of $1,000, or $500, from the estate.

It can be seen that, in effect, the secured credit has an absolute priority on the security, that this priority is created by the original contract between the secured creditor and debtor, and that it does not depend upon the statutory priorities.

Subordination of Claims. In addition to statutory and contract priorities, the bankruptcy court itself can, in its discretion in proper cases, apply equitable priorities. This is accomplished through the doctrine of subordination of claims, whereby, assuming two claims of equal statutory priority, the bankruptcy court declares that one claim must be paid in full before the other claim can be paid anything. Subordination is applied in cases where, to allow a claim in full would be unfair and inequitable to other creditors, such as to allow the inflated salary claims of officers in family or closed corporations. In such cases, the court does not disallow the claim but merely orders it paid after all other claims are paid in full.

The claim of a parent corporation against its bankrupt subsidiary corporation may be subordinated to the claims of other creditors of the subsidiary in cases where the parent has been guilty of mismanaging the subsidiary to the detriment of its innocent creditors in a manner so unconscionable as to preclude the parent from seeking the aid of a bankruptcy court. For example, assume that corporation ABC owns all of the capital stock of corporation XYZ. Assume further that whenever XYZ shows a profit, such profit is taken out of XYZ and into ABC by means of questionable intercorporate transactions; whenever XYZ shows a loss and ABC is required to put some money back into XYZ, it does so by "lending" the money to XYZ. Over a period of time, ABC takes $500,000 out of XYZ and puts $100,000 back. When XYZ goes into bankruptcy, ABC has a claim of $100,000, and other creditors have claims aggregating $100,000. If the assets total $100,000, ABC will receive $50,000 and the other creditors $50,000. Since ABC has already received $500,000, it is obviously unfair for it to receive an additional $50,000 at the expense of the other creditors. The bankruptcy court can exercise its equity power of subordinating claims and subordinate ABC's claim to that of the other creditors. Thereupon, the other creditors will receive the entire $100,000 and ABC will receive nothing unless the prior claims are paid in full.

Declaration and Payment of Dividends. Dividends of an equal per cent are declared and paid on all allowed claims, except claims which have priority or are secured. (Section 65a.)

The first dividend must not include more than fifty per cent of the money in the estate in excess of the amount necessary to pay debts which have priority. Subsequent dividends are declared as often as the amount of the dividend equals ten per cent or more and upon closing the estate. (Section 65b.)

Dividends unclaimed for sixty days are paid into the bankruptcy court by the trustee and, if unclaimed for one year, are distributed to the creditors whose claims have been allowed but not paid in full, and, after such claims are paid in full, the balance is paid to the bankrupt. (Section 66a, b.)

Discharges. The adjudication of any individual person as a bankrupt operates as an automatic application for a discharge. A corporation may, within six months after its adjudication, file an application for a discharge. (Section 14a.) A discharge means the release of the bankrupt from all of his debts which are provable in bankruptcy, whether allowable in full or in part, except those debts expressly made immune from discharge and discussed hereafter. (Section 1 (15), Section 17a.)

After the bankrupt has been examined concerning his acts, conduct and property, the bankruptcy court fixes a time for filing objections to the bankrupt's discharge. If no objection is filed, the bankrupt is discharged. If objection is made by the trustee, the creditors, or the United States district attorney, the court hears such objection (Section 14b) and grants the discharge, unless satisfied that the bankrupt (Section 14c):

(1) Committed an offense punishable by imprisonment under the Bankruptcy Act;

(2) Destroyed, falsified, concealed or failed to keep books of account and records;

(3) Obtained money or property on credit by making materially false statements in writing respecting his financial condition;

(4) Transferred, removed, destroyed or concealed any of his property with intent to hinder, delay or defraud his creditors within twelve months preceding the filing of the bankruptcy petition;

(5) Has, within six years prior to bankruptcy been granted a discharge or had a composition confirmed under the Bankruptcy Act;

(6) Refused to obey any lawful order of, or to answer any material question approved by, the court in the course of bankruptcy proceedings; or

(7) Has failed to explain satisfactorily any losses of assets or deficiency of assets to meet his liabilities.

If, upon a hearing of an objection to a discharge, the objector shows to the satisfaction of the court that there are reasonable grounds for believing that the bankrupt has committed any of the above acts, then the burden of proving that he has not committed such acts rests upon the bankrupt. (Section 14c.) If the bankrupt fails to submit himself to examination at the first meeting of creditors, at any meeting specially called for his examination, or at the hearing upon his application for a discharge, he is deemed to have waived his right to a discharge. (Section 14d.)

Debts Not Discharged. Debts which are not provable are not dischargeable. The following debts are expressly made immune from discharge (Section 17):

1. Taxes;
2. Legal liabilities
   a. For obtaining money or property by false pretenses or false representations.
   b. For wilful and malicious injuries to the person or property of another (that is, intentional torts but not negligent torts);
   c. For alimony;
   d. For support of wife or child;

    e. For seduction of an unmarried female, for breach of promise of marriage accompanied by seduction, or for criminal conversation;

    3. Debts not scheduled, unless the creditor knew of the bankruptcy;

    4. Debts created by the fraud or embezzlement of the bankrupt while acting in a fiduciary capacity;

    5. Wages earned within three months before commencement of bankruptcy proceedings; and

    6. Moneys of an employee received by his employer to secure the faithful performance by the employee of the terms of a contract of employment.

CORPORATE REORGANIZATION

If an adequately capitalized corporation has wise, capable, and honest management, and its business is operated efficiently, economically and profitably, it will probably never need a reorganization. However, a pressing need for reorganization is not always caused by poor or faulty management. A widespread economic depression, local disruption of trade, a catastrophe, unexpected and undue obsolescence of equipment or product, legislation requiring a drastic changeover in business or method of operation, or the maturing of a bond issue too large to be readily refunded, may also be factors which cause a corporation to become either insolvent or unable to meet its debts as they mature, or both.

Reorganization is the means by which a business enterprise and its value as a going concern are preserved through the correction or elimination of those factors which brought about its distress. If the business of a corporation is such that it cannot be expected to operate profitably, there is little or no going concern value to be preserved. Such a corporation should not be reorganized; its operations should be terminated and its assets liquidated. The sooner this is done and current operating losses ended, the more assets it will have available for ultimate distribution to its creditors, and, if it is solvent, to its shareholders. Liquidation means death to the enterprise, either absolutely or so far as its instant owners are concerned, while reorganization means continued life. The going concern value of a business which is kept alive is almost always greater than the total amount which may be realized upon a piecemeal sale and liquidation of its assets. Creditors and shareholders are both interested in realizing the greatest possible value out of the corporate assets.

The earliest reorganizations through court proceedings were in equity receiverships. While the assets were in the hands of an operating receiver and in the custody of the court, a creditors' committee would formulate a plan of reorganization. A judicial sale was necessary in order to satisfy the interests of those creditors or bondholders who dissented from the plan and desired only their ratable share of the cash proceeds of a foreclosure sale. The assenting bondholders would receive securities issued by a newly formed corporation which had acquired the properties of the old debtor corporation at the judicial sale.

On June 8, 1934, the Congress enacted Section 77B of the Bankruptcy Act, which permitted reorganization without the cumbersome machinery of a sale and the requirement of raising cash to pay off dissenters. This section gave to a two-thirds majority of the creditors of each class the power to bind the minority to the terms of a fair and feasible plan of reorganization. However, Section 77B lent itself to abuses and otherwise proved to be inadequate, and after a comprehensive study conducted by the Securities and Exchange Commission, the Congress, on June 22, 1938, amended the Bankruptcy Act by passing the Chandler Act. Chapter X of the Bankruptcy Act, as thus amended, deals with the reorganization of corporations and supersedes former Section 77B.

Chapter X Proceedings. Reorganization of a corporation under Chapter X of the Bankruptcy Act is commenced by the filing of a petition in the United States District Court. The petition may be a voluntary one filed by the debtor corporation, or it may be an involuntary one filed by the indenture trustee acting on behalf of the bondholders or by three or more creditors who have claims totalling $5,000 or more which are liquidated as to amount and not contingent as to liability. Shareholders of a corporation do not have the right to file a petition seeking its reorganization under Chapter X. A voluntary petition requires authorization by resolution of the board of directors of the debtor.

If the judge finds that the petition is properly filed in good faith, he will enter an order approving it and either appoint a trustee or permit the debtor to remain in possession of its assets. If the liabilities of the debtor exceed $250,000, the judge is required, under the statute, to appoint a disinterested trustee for the debtor.

The Disinterested Trustee. The trustee, upon his appointment and qualification, is vested with title to all the assets of the debtor and is charged with the conduct and operation of its business. He is selected by the court for his integrity, competence and business judgment and, to be eligible, must be disinterested. Section 158 of Chapter X provides that a person shall not be deemed disinterested if he is a creditor or shareholder of the debtor; if he is or was within two years prior to the filing of the petition a director, officer, employee, or attorney of the debtor or of an underwriter of any securities of the debtor; if he is or was any such underwriter within five years prior to the filing of the petition; if he has any other direct or indirect relationship or connection with the debtor or such underwriter, or if he has any interest materially adverse to the interest of any class of creditors or shareholders. The purpose of these qualifications is to assure utmost impartiality and independence on the part of the trustee.

The trustee usually endeavors to retain the operating business organization and payroll of the debtor. He may employ officers of the debtor at rates of compensation approved by the court. He may adopt or reject leases or executory contracts of the debtor with the permission of the court. It is his duty to prepare and file a list of the names and addresses of the creditors of each class and shareholders of each class and, also, to conduct an investigation of the property, liabilities and financial condition of the debtor, the operation of its business and the desirability of its continuance.

The trustee prepares a report of his investigation and submits it to all of the creditors and shareholders, to the Securities and Exchange Commission, and to such other persons as the judge may designate. He is also required to notify the creditors and shareholders that they may submit to him suggestions for the formulation of a plan of reorganization or proposals in the form of a plan. It is, however, the duty of the trustee to formulate a plan of reorganization.

The disinterested trustee has the primary responsibility of investigation, development and enforcement of causes of action, if any, against officers and directors of the debtor.

For the purpose of operating the business and managing the property of the debtor, the judge may, if he so desires, appoint as an additional trustee a person who is a director, officer or employee of the debtor. The duties of such additional trustee are limited to operation and management, and he does not participate in the preparation of the plan of reorganization.

Plan of Reorganization. The main objective of a reorganization proceeding is to develop and consummate a fair, equitable, and feasible plan of reorganization. After a plan has been prepared and filed, a hearing is held before the court to determine whether or not it shall be approved. Notice is given to all the creditors, shareholders and interested parties of this hearing, and any of them may interpose objections to any provision in the plan.

Before approving a plan, the court must find that it is fair and equitable, which means that it must preserve the absolute priorities of the respective contractual rights of the interested parties. The holders of bonds secured by a first mortgage must be given full priority over the holders of junior liens or equity interests in all of the property covered by the mortgage.

A hearing on a plan of reorganization necessarily involves a determination of the value of all of the assets of the debtor. If, upon a proper valuation of these assets, the total indebtedness is found to exceed such valuation, the debtor is insolvent and any plan is unfair which accords participation to shareholders of any class unless they contribute cash or new value of some kind commensurate with such participation. Conversely, where an equity is found to exist for the shareholders, a plan which excludes them from participation would be unfair.

In addition to fairness, the court must find the plan feasible, which means that it must be workable and practicable. The reorganized corporation must have adequate working capital, sufficient earning power to meet fixed lien charges, fairly good credit prospects, ability to retire or refund its proposed debt over the period of extended maturity, must be soundly capitalized with no disproportionate ratio of debt to total value of assets, and must have assurance of reasonably good management. The essence of feasibility is that the reorganized entity will be able to operate economically and efficiently, will be able to compete upon fairly equal terms with other companies within the in-

dustry, and is not likely to require a second reorganization within the foreseeable future.

The cornerstone of the fairness and feasibility of a plan of reorganization is a proper valuation of the debtor's assets. A valuation for reorganization purposes does not mean physical appraisal, book value, original cost less depreciation, reproduction cost less depreciation, reimbursement cost, or aggregate current market prices of outstanding security issues, but means going concern value. The proper method of determining this value is by ascertaining the reasonably prospective earnings of the reorganized corporation and by applying to these prospective earnings a proper rate of capitalization which will reflect all of the elements of risk inherent in the ability of the reorganized entity to realize the estimated earnings.

For example: The ABC Corporation is a manufacturing company in reorganization under Chapter X. Its liabilities are: $100,000 due the Federal government for income tax; $1,000,000 principal amount of outstanding first mortgage bonds; $200,000 due general unsecured creditors; $300,000 of 6 per cent cumulative preferred stock upon which no dividends have been paid for ten years, and $500,000 of common stock. The average annual net earnings of the company after all charges except interest on bonds and Federal income tax are $200,000, which also appears to be the reasonably prospective earnings after adequate provision for maintenance and depreciation of fixed assets. The working capital requirements of the company are $250,000, and its net current assets $350,000. All of the assets of the company except the excess working capital of $100,000 are necessary to produce the earnings estimated. Upon the assumption that a proper rate of capitalization is 12½ per cent, or eight times earnings, the capitalized value of the company's assets is $1,600,000. To this sum should be added the excess working capital, making the total valuation $1,700,-

000. The total liabilities, excluding common stock and including dividend arrearages on the preferred stock, amount to $1,780,000. The plan of reorganization should therefore provide for payment of income tax and participation only by the first mortgage bondholders, general unsecured creditors, and preferred shareholders. The holders of the common stock will not participate, nor will they vote on the plan, as there is no equity for them after making provision for the creditors and preferred shareholders who occupy a position senior to the common stock. The valuation of the debtor's assets is the controlling factor.

A plan of reorganization may provide for a completely altered capital structure of the debtor corporation. It may call for a scaling down or elimination of bonded debt, a change of interest rate or sinking fund requirements or extension of maturity of any or all of the outstanding bond issues of the debtor, or the exchange of bonds for either preferred stock or common stock or both. It may provide for an extremely simple capital structure with no debt but only common stock. In such case, if junior issues also participate, the holders of senior securities must be accorded additional stock to compensate for the step down in position. The charter of the reorganized corporation must contain a prohibition against the issuance of non-voting stock. A plan of reorganization may provide for the sale of all or any part of the debtor's property at not less than a fair upset price.

Approval and Confirmation. After the court has found a plan of reorganization to be fair, equitable, and feasible and has approved it, the plan, together with a summary, is transmitted by the trustee to the creditors and shareholders for their acceptance.

If the indebtedness exceeds $3,000,000, before the plan is submitted to creditors and shareholders, the court is required to send it to the Securities and Exchange Commission for an advisory report. In the event that the Commission files such a report, a copy thereof or a summary prepared by the Commission must also be submitted to the creditors and shareholders so that they may be fully informed of the analysis of the plan made by this expert administrative agency and of the conclusions and recommendations of the Commission before they reach a decision to accept or reject the plan.

The solicitation of acceptances of a plan before it is approved by the court and transmitted to creditors and shareholders is prohibited by Section 176, and any such acceptance of a plan in advance of approval is invalid unless the consent of the court has been obtained. Before the plan may be confirmed, it must receive the written acceptances of creditors holding two-thirds in amount of the claims filed and allowed of each class, and if the debtor has not been found to be insolvent, the written acceptances of the holders of a majority of the stock of each class of which proofs have been filed and allowed. Notice of the hearing on confirmation is required to be given creditors and shareholders, and any creditor or shareholder is entitled to appear and to be heard on his objection to confirmation. Upon the entry of an order of confirmation, the plan is ready for consummation and is ordinarily placed in operation within a reasonably short period of time.

Allowances of Compensation. After a plan of reorganization has been confirmed and where the proceedings are nearing termination, an order is usually entered by the court directing the trustee and all parties, and their attorneys, to file their respective applications for allowance of compensation and reimbursement of expenses within a time fixed by the court. After the applications are filed, notice of a hearing thereon is given to all creditors, shareholders, and parties in interest.

Any party to the proceedings or attorney whose services were beneficial in the administration of the estate or which contributed to the confirmed plan of reorganization or to the disapproval of any unfair plan is entitled to receive from the estate of the debtor reasonable compensation for those services.

Section 249 of Chapter X provides that any person acting in the proceedings in a representative or fiduciary capacity is absolutely barred from any allowance of compensation for services or reimbursement for expenses if he has traded in any of the securities of the debtor since assuming to act in such capacity. The courts have held that the statute requires denial of compensation even though the purchase and sale of such securities has involved a loss to the applicant. Attorneys, committee members, and trustees in a reorganization proceeding are also denied all compensation if at any time during the proceeding they represented conflicting interests. The court does not inquire in such case whether any harm or evil resulted or whether there was actual fraud or wrongdoing. The mere showing that a person has represented interests which are conflicting is sufficient to require denial of all compensation. This rule is prophylactic in character and may work hardship, but its enforcement insures undeviating loyalty and a single-minded interest on the part of those who serve in a representative or fiduciary capacity in a reorganization proceeding.

Effect of Reorganization. The reorganized debtor or the new corporation succeeding to the debtor's properties emerges from the proceedings and begins life anew with only such obligations as are imposed upon it by the plan. It is entitled to injunctive relief to insure its freedom of all prior debts, obligations and duties of every kind except those which have been preserved in the plan. Upon the entry of a final decree closing the proceedings, the debtor, as provided in Section 228, is discharged from all of its debts and liabilities. All persons who are entitled to participate in the plan of reorganization have a period of not less than five years from the date of the final decree within which to exchange their old securities for the new as provided in the plan.

It should be observed that the liability of a surety or guarantor of any of the outstanding indebtedness of the debtor corporation is not altered or affected by a plan of reorganization, and an action at law by a creditor against such surety or guarantor will not be enjoined.

CASES

BANK OF MARIN v. ENGLAND

(1965 C.A.9th) 352 F.2d 186.

HAMLEY, C. J. Bank of Marin appeals from a district court judgment affirming an order of a referee in bankruptcy holding the bank and Eureka Fisheries, Inc., jointly liable to a trustee in bankruptcy for the sum of $2,312.-82. The sole question presented is whether a bank which honored checks of a depositor after the depositor had filed a voluntary petition in bankruptcy is liable to the trustee in bankruptcy for the amount of the checks paid where the bank had no notice of the bankruptcy proceeding.

The relevant facts are not in dispute. Between August 27, 1963, and September 17, 1963, Marin Seafoods drew and delivered five checks in favor of Eureka Fisheries upon its commercial account with Bank of Marin, San Rafael, California. The total amount of the checks was $2,318.82. On September 26, 1963, before these checks had been presented to the bank for payment, Marin Seafoods filed a voluntary petition in bankruptcy. The petition was filed in the United States District Court for the Northern District of California, Southern Division. John M. England was appointed as receiver and so acted until October 20, 1963, at which time he became trustee for the bankrupt.

On the date of the filing of the petition, sums of money in excess of $3,200 were due and owing Marin Seafoods from customers for merchandise previously delivered. Beginning on the day after the filing of the petition, and continuing for several days, Marin Seafoods, through its principal officer, collected portions of these outstanding accounts receivable and deposited them in the company's commercial account at the bank. On October 2, 1963, the checks which Marin Seafoods had drawn and delivered to Eureka Fisheries prior to the filing of the petition, were duly presented to the bank by Eureka Fisheries for payment, and were paid.

At the time the bank paid these checks it had received no notice, and had not otherwise obtained knowledge of the filing of the petition in bankruptcy. The bank was not informed of the pending bankruptcy proceeding until October 3, 1963, when it received a letter, dated October 2, 1963, from the receiver. This was one day after the bank had honored the checks referred to above.

Proceeding under section 2, sub. a of the Bankruptcy Act (Act), 52 Stat. 842 (1938), as amended, 11 U.S.C. § 11, sub. a (1964), the trustee applied to the referee for a turnover order. The trustee sought to require the bank to pay over to the trustee a sum of money equivalent to the sum paid by the bank to Eureka Fisheries on October 2, 1963. In the alternative he sought relief against Eureka Fisheries. A show cause proceeding ensued, resulting in the entry of an order by the referee, supported by findings of fact and conclusions of law. The referee determined that the bank and Eureka Fisheries were jointly liable to the trustee for the sum of $2,312.82, the amount paid by the bank to Eureka Fisheries.

In so ruling, the referee held that the bank's lack of knowledge of the filing of the voluntary petition in bankruptcy by its depositor Marin Seafoods, afforded the bank no protection. Eureka Fisheries paid the total amount of $2,312.82 to the trustee and then filed with the bankruptcy court, and served upon the bank, a demand for contribution. The bank petitioned for a review of the referee's order, and on such review, that order was affirmed. This appeal by Bank of Marin followed.

In seeking recovery of the stated amount from the bank, the trustee relied upon section 70, sub. a of the Act, 52 Stat. 879 (1938), as amended, 11 U.S.C. § 110, sub. a (1964). This section provides, in pertinent part, that, upon his appointment and qualification, a trustee in bankruptcy shall be vested "by operation of law" with the title of the bankrupt as of the date of the filing of the petition initiating a proceeding in bankruptcy, with exceptions not here material, to describe kinds of property wherever located. Among the kinds of property so described, the statute includes:

" * * * (5) property, including rights of action, which prior to the filing of the petition he [bankrupt] could by any means have transferred or which might have been levied upon and sold under judicial process against him, or otherwise seized, impounded, or sequestered: *Provided*, * * * [not here material]."

This provision of the Act, considered by itself, would appear to support the trustee's application for a turnover order against the bank. The bank, however, contends that notwithstanding this statute, it should be held that a bank is not liable to a trustee in bankruptcy when, in good faith, and without actual knowledge of the bankruptcy proceedings, it honors the checks of a bankrupt depositor in the regular course of business after the adjudication of bankruptcy.

* * *

Upon considering the respective arguments, we think the bank makes out a strong case for hardship and impracticability insofar as the timely discovery of bankruptcy proceedings involving depositors is concerned. We are not as certain that the problem is one which threatens great and unprotectible financial liability. The fact that our case, and Rosenthal (139 F.Supp. 730) appear to be the only reported cases dealing with this particular problem is some indication that it is not one which will frequently confront banks. Moreover, it would seem that the risk, such as it is, may ordinarily be taken into account as a cost of the business and financed as such.

* * *

The California Bankers Association, appearing in this court as *amicus curiae*, joins the bank in all of the contentions discussed above. It also presents the additional argument that the failure of the trustee to revoke the bankrupt's order for the payment of funds on deposit with the Bank of Marin bars the trustee from recovery against the bank.

The gist of this argument is as follows: (1) under section 70, sub. a (5) of the Act, a trustee in bankruptcy succeeds only to such rights as the bankrupt possessed at the time of the bankruptcy petition, and is subject to all defenses and equities which might have been asserted against the bankrupt but for the filing of that petition; (2) in California an ordinary depositor does not have title to any specific funds deposited in a bank, the relationship of bank and depositor, founded upon contract, being that of debtor and creditor; (3) under that contract, a bank has both the right and duty to honor checks of its depositors properly drawn and duly presented, unless the depositor provides the bank with notice of the revocation of his order for payment prior to the time his checks are accepted by the bank; (4) absent the giving of a timely "stop payment" order such payment operates to discharge the bank's obligation, and the depositor has no right to recover the amounts paid; and (5) under the

premise set forth at the outset, the trustee is subject to the same defense.

The bankruptcy of a drawer operates as a revocation of the drawee's authority. Such revocation is not dependent upon or subject to notice to the drawee, since the trustee is immediately vested with the title of the bankrupt by operation of law. The parties to a depositor's contract with a bank are chargeable with knowing this when they enter into the contract. These circumstances constitute an implied exception to the contractual obligation of the bank to honor checks unless and until a "stop payment" notice is received. The asserted bank defense based upon lack of a "stop payment" notice is therefore not available against a trustee in bankruptcy in the case of the bankruptcy of the drawer.

* * *

Congress may not proceed in complete disregard of the property rights of those dealing in good faith with bankrupts. It may, however, enact legislation balancing bankruptcy objectives with the interests of those dealing in good faith with a bankrupt. Section 70(d) of the Act, we believe, demonstrates that Congress has, in this balancing process, taken into account the latter interests and has accommodated them to the extent deemed feasible having in view the desirability of speedy, economical and effective bankruptcy administration.

In our opinion, the order under discussion does not offend the due process clause, insofar as notice to the bank is concerned.

This brings us to the second facet of the Constitutional argument presented by the bank and *amicus curiae*. This is the contention that the due process clause prohibits imposing liability upon the bank because to do so would require the bank to pay a single debt twice. There is a strong Constitutional policy against requiring the double payment of the same debt. [Citation.]

The argument for the bank is premised upon these propositions: the relationship of a bank to its depositor is that of debtor and creditor; the bank is obligated to discharge its indebtedness by honoring checks drawn by depositors; and failure to honor such checks results in liability to the depositor. These propositions are not challenged by the trustee for they are well established. Next the bank argues that in honoring the checks drawn by the bankrupt, it discharged its indebtedness in accordance with its obligation to its depositor. From this, the conclusion is drawn that to require a second payment now to the trustee is a violation of the Fifth Amendment.

As we have already seen, at the time the checks were honored, title to the deposits was vested in the trustee by virtue of section 70, sub. a. From the moment of filing the petition, the bank's duty with regard to the deposits was owed to the trustee, not to the bankrupt and not to the payee of the checks. We have already held that, in legal contemplation, the filing was sufficient notice to those subsequently dealing with the bankrupt's assets. Accordingly, and regardless of actual notice, the bank's obligation to honor the checks disappeared before it paid them. Therefore, in paying the checks when presented by Eureka Fishcries, the bank was not paying a debt for which it was obligated. It follows that if as a result of this judgment, the bank pays any part of the checks, it will not be paying the same debt twice.

* * *

Affirmed.

Judgment of the Court of Appeals reversed by the Supreme Court of the United States in Bank of Marin v. England, —— U.S. ——, 87 S.Ct. 274, 17 L.Ed.2d 197 (Nov. 21, 1966), Harlan, J., dissenting. The Supreme Court opinion per Douglas, J., contains this statement:

"Yet we do not read these statutory words [Section 70(d) of the Bankruptcy Act] with the ease of a computer. There is an overriding consideration that equitable principles govern the exercise of bankruptcy jurisdiction."

HOUSEHOLD FINANCE CORP. v. ALTENBERG

(1966) 5 Ohio St.2d 190, 214 N.E.2d 667.

MATTHIAS, J. The sole question raised by this appeal is whether a plaintiff must prove fraud under Section 35(2), Title 11, U.S. Code, by clear and convincing evidence. Both the courts below have so held.

Section 35(2), Title 11, U.S.Code, a part of the Bankruptcy Act, reads, in pertinent part:

"A discharge in bankruptcy shall release a bankrupt from all of his provable debts, whether allowable in full or in part, except such as * * * (2) are liabilities * * * for obtaining money or property on credit or obtaining an extension or renewal of credit in reliance upon a materially false statement in writing respecting his financial condition made or published or caused to be made or published in any manner whatsoever with intent to deceive * * *."

A debt discharged by bankruptcy is not extinguished. However, the debtor has a perfect defense to any action upon the debt, unless an exception is applicable. Section 35(2), Title 11, U.S.Code, provides such an exception. Therefore, a discharge in bankruptcy does not relieve a defendant from liability on his promissory note, where the debt for which the note was given was created in reliance upon a materially false statement in writing made by such defendant for the purpose of obtaining such credit from plaintiff.

Plaintiff herein has asserted just such an occurrence in its petition. In so doing it has set forth a cause of action of fraud, and by so doing must bear the burden of proving fraud by the requisite degree.

"Fraud is a civil wrong" (Place v. Elliott, 147 Ohio St. 499, 503, 72 N.E.2d 103), and "there is no doctrine of the law settled more firmly than the rule which authorizes issues of fact in civil cases to be determined in accordance with the preponderance or weight of the evidence." [Citations.]

Defendant, however, maintains that the fraud alleged by plaintiff must be firmly established by a higher degree of evidence, evidence that is clear and convincing. In support of this, defendant cites many cases so holding. Without indulging in detail, suffice it to say that such a degree of evidence has indeed been required by this court in many instances where fraud was alleged. However, upon closer examination, it becomes apparent that in the vast majority of such instances the cause of action involved was an equitable one to set aside or rescind a written document. In that class of cases, a court does require clear and convincing evidence as a prerequisite to granting a decree dissolving the legal effect of a solemnly executed written document.

In the instant case, plaintiff indeed relies upon a written document, a financial statement signed by defendant. However, plaintiff does not seek to rescind or reform this document as defendant contends. This case is a civil action for money only. It does not fall into the category of equitable actions discussed above. * * *

* * * More specifically, we approve paragraph one of the syllabus in Severns, Exr., v. Boylan, 75 Ohio App. 15, 60 N.E.2d 521, wherein Judge Matthews stated for a unanimous court:

"In an action for equitable relief, such as to set aside or reform a written contract, or to remove a cloud on the ground of fraud, it seems that clear and convincing evidence of the fraud is required, but in the ordinary action at law based on fraud only a preponderance is required." See, also, Place v. Elliott, supra, where, in a civil action for money only, plaintiff alleged that defendant cheated and defrauded him with a check returned because of insufficient funds. The trial court charged that "the burden of proof is upon the plaintiff in this case to prove such

fraud and *by a preponderance* of the evidence" (emphasis added), and this court held that such charge was correct. * * *

Therefore, we hold that in a cause of action to recover money loaned in reliance upon a materially false statement in writing respecting the financial condition of the borrower, the degree of evidence required in proving fraud pursuant to Section 35(2), Title 11, U.S.Code, is by a preponderance of the evidence.

The judgment of the Court of Appeals is reversed, and the cause remanded for further proceedings according to law.

Judgment reversed.

SECURITIES AND EXCHANGE COMMISSION v. AMERICAN TRAILER RENTALS CO.

(1965) 379 U.S. 594, 85 S.Ct. 513, 13 L.Ed.2d 510.

MR. JUSTICE GOLDBERG delivered the opinion of the Court.

The issue in this case is whether respondent's attempted corporate rehabilitation under the Bankruptcy Act, materially affecting the rights of widespread public investor creditors, may be conducted under Chapter XI of the Bankruptcy Act, 52 Stat. 905, as amended, 11 U.S.C. § 701 et seq. (1958 ed.), or whether dismissal or, in effect, transfer to proceedings under Chapter X of that Act, 52 Stat. 883, as amended, 11 U.S.C. § 501 et seq. (1958 ed.), is required upon motion by the Securities and Exchange Commission or any other party in interest, pursuant to Bankruptcy Act § 328, 66 Stat. 432, 11 U.S.C. § 728 (1958 ed.).

Respondent, American Trailer Rentals Company, was organized in 1958 to engage in the automobile-trailer rental business. The business was financed largely through the sale of trailers to investors and their simultaneous leaseback. From 1959 to 1961 hundreds of small investors, scattered throughout the entire western part of the United States, purchased and leased back a total of 5,866 trailers, paying an aggregate price of $3,587,437 (approximately $600 per trailer). Under the usual form of lease-back agreement, the trailer owners were to receive a set 2% of their investment per month for 10 years.

The trailers sold to investors and then leased back are of the general utility type that are attached to the rear bumper of automobiles. They were placed by respondent at gasoline stations, the operators of which acted as respondent's rental agents, without the investors ever having seen them. Respondent had about 700 such service station operators in December 1961, although the number had declined to about 500 by the time the petition for an arrangement was filed a year later.

*   *   *

At the time of filing its Chapter XI petition, respondent stated its total assets as $685,608, of which $500,000 represented the stated estimated "value" of its trailer-rental system, an intangible asset. It stated in its petition that its trailer-rental system (which then consisted of arrangements with some 500 service station operator agents) "was built by respondent at an estimated cost of $500,000," despite the fact that respondent's balance sheet in 1961 showed the cost of establishing a system of 700 stations as only $33,750, and that in 1961 respondent had estimated that cost of establishing an additional 800 rental stations would be only $56,000. The total liabilities were stated at $1,367,890, of which $710,597 was owed to trailer owners under their leasing agreements; $200,677 was owed to the investors who had paid for trailers that had never been manufactured; $71,805 was owed to trade and other general creditors; and $285,277 was owed to respondent's officers and directors.

Under the proposed plan of arrangement submitted by respondent the investor-trailer owners were to exchange their entire interests (their rights in the trailers as well as the amounts owed them under the rental agreements) for stock of Capitol on the basis of one share of stock for each $2 of "remaining capital investment in the trailers," which sum was to be determined by deducting from the original purchase price of the trailers the amount, if any, which the owners had received as rental payments. Respondent's officers and directors, as well as trade and other general creditors, were to receive one share of stock for each $3.50 of their claims. Respondent, itself, in exchange for transferring to Capitol its trailer-rental system, was to receive 107,000 shares which it would then distribute to its stockholders. Finally, obligations to two banks, totaling $55,558, although clearly unsecured, were to be paid in full, presumably because the officers and directors of respondent would otherwise have been liable as guarantors of these obligations.

If this plan were approved and all of the investment-trailer owners participated, a total of approximately 866,000 shares of Capitol's stock would be issued to them, but approximately 81,500 shares would be issued directly to the officers and directors of respondent, 22,400 to trade and other general creditors, and 107,000 to respondent itself to be distributed to its stockholders. More than 60% of respondent's stock was held by eight men; seven of whom are officers and directors and the eighth one of the original promoters of the venture.

*   *   *

Before passage, in 1934, of § 77B of the Bankruptcy Act, 48 Stat. 911, 912, bankruptcy procedures offered no facilities for corporate rehabilitation, which, therefore, were left to equity receiverships, with their attendant paraphernalia of creditors' and security holders' committees, and of rival plans of reorganization. Lack of judicial control of the conditions attending formulation of the plans, inadequate protection of widely scattered security holders, frequent adoption of plans which favored management at the expense of other interests and which afforded the corporation only temporary respite from financial collapse, so often characteristic of equity receivership reorganizations, led to the enactment of § 77B. [Citation.] As does the present Chapter X, § 77B permitted the adjustment of all interests in the debtor, secured creditors, unsecured creditors, and stockholders.

The day following the enactment of § 77B, Congress created the Securities and Exchange Commission as a special agency charged with the function of protecting the investing public, 48 Stat. 885, as amended, 15 U.S.C. § 78d. At the urging of, and based on extensive studies by the SEC, § 77B was, in 1938, revised and enacted in changed form as Chapter X. The aims of Chapter X as thus revised were to afford greater protection to creditors and stockholders by providing greater judicial control over the entire proceedings and impartial and expert administrative assistance in corporate reorganizations through appointment of a disinterested trustee and the active participation of the SEC. The trustee in a Chapter X proceeding is required to make a thorough examination and study of the debtor's financial problems and management, § 167(3), (5), and then transmit his independent report to the creditors, stockholders, the SEC, and others. Following this, the trustee gives notice to all creditors and stockholders to submit to him proposals for a plan of reorganization. § 167(5), (6). The trustee then formulates a plan of reorganization which he presents to the court. If the court finds the plan worthy of consideration, it may refer it to the SEC for its opinion and must so refer it where the debtor's liabilities exceed $3,000,-000. § 172. When the proposed plan, after approval by the court, is finally submitted to

the debtor's creditors and stockholders, it is accompanied by the advisory report of the SEC, as well as the opinion of the judge who approved the plan. § 175. The plan must receive the approval of two-thirds in each class of creditors and stockholders whose rights it modifies, § 216, and becomes effective upon final confirmation by the court, based on a finding, *inter alia*, that "the plan is fair and equitable." § 221.

As part of the same Act in which Chapter X was enacted Congress also, in 1938, enacted Chapter XI. Chapter XI is a statutory variation of the common-law composition of creditors and, unlike the broader scope of Chapter X, is limited to an adjustment of unsecured debts. It was sponsored by the National Association of Credit Men and other groups of creditors' representatives whose experience had been in representing trade creditors in small and middle-sized commercial failures. [Citation.] The contrast between the provisions of Chapter X, carefully designed to protect the creditor and stockholder interests involved, and the summary provisions of Chapter XI is quite marked. The formulation of the plan of arrangement, and indeed the entire Chapter XI proceeding, for all practical purposes is in the hands of the debtor, subject only to the requisite consent of a majority in number and amount of unsecured creditors, § 362, and the ultimate finding by the court that the plan is, *inter alia*, "for the best interests of the creditors," § 366. "The process of formulating an arrangement and the solicitation of consent of creditors, sacrifices to speed and economy every safeguard, in the interest of thoroughness and disinterestness, provided in Chapter X." [Citation.] The debtor generally remains in possession and operates the business under court supervision, § 342. A trustee is only provided in the very limited situation where a trustee in bankruptcy has previously been appointed, § 332. There is no requirement for a receiver, but the Court "may" appoint one if it finds it to be "necessary," § 332. The plan of arrangement is proposed by, and only by, the debtor, §§ 306 (1), 323, 357, and creditors have only the choice of accepting or rejecting it. Acceptances may be solicited by the debtor even before filing of the Chapter XI petition and, in fact, must be solicited before court review of the plan, § 336(4). There are no provisions for an independent study by the court or a trustee, or for advice by them being given to creditors in advance of the acceptance of the arrangement. In short, Chapter XI provides a summary procedure whereby judicial confirmation is obtained on a plan that has been formulated and accepted with only a bare minimum of independent control or supervision. This, of course, is consistent with the basic purpose of Chapter XI: to provide a quick and economical means of facilitating simple compositions among general creditors who have been deemed by Congress to need only the minimal disinterested protection provided by that Chapter.

In enacting these two distinct methods of corporate rehabilitations, Congress has made it quite clear that Chapters X and XI are not alternate routes, the choice of which is in the hands of the debtor. Rather, they are legally, mutually exclusive paths to attempted financial rehabilitation. A Chapter X petition may not be filed unless "adequate relief" is not obtainable under Chapter XI, § 146(2). Likewise, a Chapter XI petition is to be dismissed, or in effect transferred, if the proceedings "should have been brought" under Chapter X, § 328.

* * *

Applying the above principles, it is obvious that Chapter X is the appropriate proceeding for the attempted rehabilitation of respondent in this case. Here public debts are being adjusted. The investors are many and widespread, not few in number intimately connected with the debtor, and the adjustment is quite major and certainly not minor.

These facts alone would require Chapter X proceedings under the above-stated principles. In addition there is here, as we have previously pointed out, substantial evidence of misappropriation of assets, and not only is there a need for a complete corporate reorganization, it is obvious that the proposed plan of arrangement is just that. The trailer owners are exchanging their entire interests, including a sale of their trailers, in exchange for stock in a new corporation, in which other creditors of respondent, including respondent's officers and directors, as well as respondent itself will have substantial interests.

* * *

Indeed, the facts of this case aptly demonstrate the need for Chapter X protection as a general rule on the above-stated principles. There is clearly a need for a study by a disinterested trustee to make a thorough examination of respondent's financial problems and management and submit a full report to the public-investor creditors. Respondent has never operated profitably, has always been in precarious financial condition, and apparently was hopelessly insolvent, in both the bankruptcy and equity sense, when the arrangement was proposed. At an earlier period its management apparently misappropriated substantial corporate funds. Most of the trailers were purchased from an affiliated company; a large number of them, although paid for, were either not manufactured or, if manufactured, were not delivered. The affiliated company is bankrupt. Only approximately two-thirds of the $3,587,437 contributed by the public investors for the purchase of trailers was used for that purpose; the balance apparently having been drained off in high commissions taken by the management on the sale of the trailers to the public. Portions of these commissions on new trailer sales were, in turn, used by the management to pay prior purchasers of trailers the rentals which they had been promised. When respondent filed its petitition for an arrangement, its stated liabilities of $1,367,890 were approximately double its stated assets of $685,608; with even most of the latter ($500,000) representing the alleged "estimated" value of the trailer-rental system, *i. e.*, the debtor's arrangements with the service station operators. The District Court itself recognized that "there may be in this situation need for new management, and there certainly is some question as to whether or not the management that is presently * * * operating it, would continue to do so for the best interests of the investors." I did not find, however, that Chapter X was necessary since this need for new management had "not been clearly established yet." One of the purposes of Chapter X is to give the independent trustee the opportunity to conduct a searching inquiry so as to "clearly establish" whether or not new management is necessary, when there is, as here, a substantial basis for such a belief. * * * We also reject respondent's further argument that the time and expense of a Chapter X proceeding would be so great that the ultimate result might be straight bankruptcy liquidation, which, respondent contends, "would mean probable total loss for [the] trailer owners." In addition to the above answers to respondent's general time and expense argument, we feel compelled to point out, without indicating any opinion as to the ultimate outcome of the attempted financial rehabilitation in this case, that it must be recognized that Chapters X and XI were not designed to prolong—without good reason and at the expense of the investing public— the corporate life of every debtor suffering from terminal financial ills. [Citation.]

Applying the above-stated principles, it is clear that in this case the motion by the SEC to dismiss, or, in effect, to transfer the proceedings to Chapter X, should have been granted. Therefore, the judgment of the Court of Appeals is reversed and the case re-manded to that court for proceedings consistent with this opinion.

Reversed and remanded.

PROBLEMS

1. (a) B goes into bankruptcy. His estate has no assets. Are B's taxes discharged by the proceedings?

(b) B obtains property from A on credit by representing he is solvent when in fact he knows he is insolvent. Is B's debt to A discharged by B's discharge in bankruptcy?

2. B goes into bankruptcy owing $5,000 as wages to his employees. There is enough in his estate to pay all costs of administration and enough to pay his employees but nothing will then be left for general creditors. Do the employees take all the estate? Under what conditions? If the general creditors received nothing at all would these debts be discharged?

3. A person occupying premises under a ten-year lease is adjudicated an involuntary bankrupt. The lease has five years remaining. Can the landlord treat the lease cancelled or discharged by operation of law or is the trustee entitled to possession of the premises? If the trustee elects not to take possession, has the landlord any remedy?

4. A debtor went through bankruptcy and received his discharge. Which of the following debts were completely discharged and which remain debts against him in the future:

(a) Claims of $900 each by X and Y for wages earned within three months immediately prior to bankruptcy.

(b) A judgment of $3,000 against the bankrupt by C for breach of contract.

(c) Sales taxes of $1,800.

(d) $1,000 in past alimony and support money owed to his divorced wife for herself and their child.

(e) A judgment of $4,000 for injuries received because of the bankrupt's negligent operation of an automobile.

5. Rosinoff and his wife, who were business partners, were adjudged bankrupt. Objection

was made to their discharge in bankruptcy by a creditor, Baldwin, on the grounds that:

    (a) The partners had obtained credit from Baldwin on the basis of a false financial statement;

    (b) The partners had failed to keep books of account and records from which their financial condition would be ascertained;

    (c) Rosinoff had falsely sworn that he had taken $7 from the partnership account when the correct amount was $700.

Were the bankrupts entitled to a discharge?

6. X Corporation is a debtor in corporate reorganization proceedings under Chapter X of the Bankruptcy Act. By fair and proper valuation its assets are worth $100,000. The indebtedness of the corporation is $105,000, it has outstanding preferred stock of the par value of $20,000 and common stock of the par value of $75,000. The plan of reorganization submitted by the trustees would eliminate the common shareholders, give bonds of the face amount of $50,000 to the creditors and common stock in the ratio of 84% to the creditors and 16% to the preferred shareholders. Should this plan be approved?

CHAPTER 44

SECURED TRANSACTIONS UNDER THE UNIFORM COMMERCIAL CODE

Introductory. Secured transactions arise basically in two ways: somebody wants to borrow some money and cannot get it without giving collateral to secure repayment, or perhaps giving collateral will result in a lower rate of interest; or a purchaser of goods does not have the full purchase price and the seller will not sell the goods on open credit but insists on retaining a security interest in the property. In either case you have a debtor (the borrower or the buyer) and secured party (the lender or the seller), and you have collateral (for example, stock, jewelry, or the goods sold).

Historically, various separate devices were used to make secured transactions possible. These devices range from the simple pledge through chattel mortgages and conditional sales to trust receipts and factor's liens. Each device had certain kinds of transactions for which it was appropriate, and there might be competition between the various possibilities. The array of concepts in the field of secured financing is explainable only on the basis of historical accident, and for the first time in our history the multiplicity of devices is unified in the Uniform Commercial Code. The Code abolishes distinctions based solely on the "form" of the transaction in favor of differentiations arising from the kind of collateral and the status of the debtor. There is a difference between the requirements of consumer financing and those of commercial financing, and the Code recognizes this, where under pre-Code law if a chattel mortgage were used, for example, the same rules would apply whether the secured loan were for $100 or $10,000,000.

Financing patterns which were successfully used before the Code may still be used. These patterns have grown up for sufficient reasons in various fields, such as automobile financing and furniture financing, and they may be continued. Under the Code the same general business arrangements could be continued, although there might be differences in mechanical aspects of perfecting security interests and in some of the legal concepts involved.

Article 9, Secured Transactions, of the Uniform Commercial Code applies to any transaction, regardless of its form, which is intended to create a security interest in personal property. It applies to security interests created by contract, "including pledge, assignment, chattel mortgage, chattel trust, trust deed, factor's lien, equipment trust, conditional sale, trust receipt, other lien or title retention contract and lease or consignment intended as security." We will examine the traditional devices, look at the problems involved in using them, and then note how they are treated under the Code.

PRE-CODE SECURITY DEVICES

Pledges and Chattel Mortgages. The simplest kind of secured transaction is the pledge. It is as old as recorded history. A pledge is simply a transfer of the physical possession of personal property to secure the repayment of a debt. While a written agreement is not necessary, one is customary and desirable. The agreement may be embodied in the note evidencing the loan or it may be in a separate document.

A simple pledge situation is this. George wishes to borrow $1,000 from his friend Richard, and he has a painting, appraised at $2,000, to offer as security. George executes a note for $1,000 payable to Richard's order, setting forth the interest rate and terms of payment; he executes a simple loan agreement stating that he is pledging the particular painting with Richard to secure the repayment of the note, and stating Richard's right on default to dispose of the painting; and possession of the painting is transferred to Richard.

Under pre-Code law, this transaction could have been handled as a chattel mortgage instead of a pledge. If it were done in that way, a document would be recorded stating that the mortgagor conveyed his interest in the painting to the mortgagee as security for the loan, but that possession was to remain with the mortgagor; and the mortgage would be recorded to give public notice of the mortgagee's rights.

In form, the mortgage would probably purport to transfer "title" to the painting from the mortgagor to the mortgagee, but it might not have that effect in fact; it might, and usually would, create only a "lien." A lien is simply an interest in property which secures repayment of a debt. The lien is said to be general if it is against all of the debtor's assets, and it is specific if it affects specific property, as the described painting. While a great deal of metaphysical learning has been devoted to liens, the only significant effect a lien has is to give a creditor the right to proceed against certain property to satisfy a debt. This is true whether we are talking about a mortgage lien on a house, a chattel mortgage lien on a painting, or a mechanic's lien on real estate for labor which adds to the value of the property.

In the simple example of a chattel mortgage on a painting, several problems are apparent. If the debtor retains possession of the painting and can continue to enjoy it, he may have less incentive to repay the loan. He may need more money and, despite the mortgage, he may sell the painting to a buyer with no actual knowledge of the mortgage. While a recorded mortgage is constructive notice to the world that a lien exists, and the mortgagee can legally recover the property from a purchaser, there is the very practical problem of finding the purchaser and the painting. Or the painting might be burned or stolen, and there might be no insurance. No matter what happens to the painting, the debt is not extinguished until it is paid, but presumably a lender has a purpose in mind in taking collateral in the first place. He wants to be sure that if the debt is not paid in the ordinary course of events, it can be satisfied out of the collateral. The case of the painting is one example where a pledge is more satisfactory, for very practical reasons, than a chattel mortgage, or the equivalent under the Uniform Commercial Code.

Another common but uncomplicated pledge situation arises when a borrower pledges stock to secure a bank loan. An assignment of the named owner's interest in the stock certificate will be given to the bank, so that if a default occurs the bank can sell the stock. Any excess proceeds over the amount of the unpaid loan will be remitted to the borrower.

Next to the pledge, the chattel mortgage is the oldest security device. The chattel mortgage could be used where security was needed but the collateral was to remain with the mortgagor-debtor. The mortgage was recorded to give public notice that there was a security interest in property which the debtor might otherwise be assumed to own free of encumbrances. This notice presumably would warn other potential creditors not to rely on the mortgaged assets to satisfy their loans, if they extended credit.

Chattel mortgages could be used where the property could be reasonably identified and where it was plainly intended that the mortgagor retain possession of the chattels. A chattel mortgage on a merchant's stock in trade would generally have been a nullity as to third parties because the collateral was intended to be sold in the ordinary course of trade and it would be a fraud on both buyers and other creditors for a mortgagee to be able to claim a lien on the stock which would follow the property after sale. Moreover, the problem of describing the property, which would be constantly changing, was almost insuperable.

In most States a chattel mortgage was the only possible security device where the debtor already owned the chattels available for security and did not want to lose possession. If you owned an automobile and wanted to use it for security, a chattel mortgage could be given to the lender; in this case the security interest would often be noted on the certificate of title rather than recorded locally, as was ordinarily required of chattel mortgages.

The reason for local filing or recording is historical. When chattel mortgages were first devised, there would have been no other place to record them except in a local governmental office, and such recording in small communities would once have served as actual, as well as constructive, notice of the lien. A local filing system is still adequate for secured loans to consumers, but it does not meet business needs. The recording requirements for chattel mortgages varied among the States, but usually recording was required in the county of the debtor's residence and also in the county or counties where the property was located, both at the time the mortgage was made and at the time it was recorded. A chattel mortgage on a refrigerator used in the mortgagor's home did not present a recording problem, but consider a chattel mortgage covering 1,000 liquefied petroleum gas tanks, where the tanks were in North Dakota when the mortgage was made but were subsequently shipped to a borrower in Illinois for use by gas consumers in Illinois, Wisconsin, and Iowa. It was not always simple to ascertain the residence of a corporate borrower, perhaps a Delaware corporation doing business in Illinois, or perhaps an Illinois corporation whose registered office is in Kane County but whose principal place of business is in Cook County. There were similar problems with partnerships, where the partners resided in different counties. Moreover under the Illinois chattel mortgage law, a mortgage had to be recorded within 20 days after its execution and it had to comply with numerous statutory technicalities or else it was not effective against third parties regardless of whether they knew of the mortgage. That is, a mortgage recorded 21 days after its execution would not be considered notice to third parties; it would be of no validity as far as they were concerned. This attitude reflected a nineteenth century abhorrence of consumer credit and has been found to be unrealistic for the present day.

Conditional Sales. Chattel mortgages were sometimes used in purchase money transactions: the seller of chattels transferred their title to the buyer and took back a mortgage to secure the unpaid balance of the purchase price. But the most common form of purchase money security was the conditional sale. Under this plan the seller reserved the title to the goods until the buyer had paid the purchase price, usually in installments, while the buyer had possession of the goods and the risk of loss. In States having the Uniform Conditional Sales Act, public notice of these transactions was given by filing. In other States, conditional sales were actually secret liens; that is, the apparent owner of property (the buyer) was not the owner in fact, and there was no public means to discover this situation.

Since a conditional sale is not the loan or forbearance of money, the credit charge is not governed by State usury laws. Unless prohibited by legislation, the seller of goods can charge a different price when he sells on time, the difference between the cash price and the time price being called the time price differential. The time price differential has often been so large that so-called retail installment sales acts now commonly set a maximum amount which can be charged and in other ways regulate the terms of the contract of sale. The purpose of this legislation is to protect consumers. Since time price problems have sometimes been most acute in the automobile field, some of the retail installment sales acts regulate only automobile sales, and the allowable time price differential varies with the age of the automobile sold. Regulatory legislation, such as usury laws, consumer credit laws, and retail installment sales acts are not displaced by the Uniform Commercial Code.

Chattel Paper Financing. The secured seller of goods, whether the transaction was cast as a conditional sale or as a purchase money chattel mortgage, might in turn need financing. There is often a continuing arrangement between a seller and a financial institution, by which the seller transfers his chattel paper to the financer. ("Chattel paper" is the term used in the Uniform Commercial Code for a writing which evidences both a monetary obligation and a security interest in goods, such as a conditional sale contract or a note and chattel mortgage.) This chattel paper is in itself collateral. Usury must be considered in this kind of financing, but frequently State statutes provide that corporations cannot plead usury as a defense, so if the seller-borrower is a corporation, the problem may not arise.

The chattel paper may be sold by the borrower-seller to the financer, with or without recourse, or it may simply be assigned to secure an obligation of the seller. The future collections may be made either by the seller or by the financer. Where the seller continues to make collections and his debtors are not notified of the security interest involved, if the seller becomes involved in financial difficulty, problems may arise because of the seller's dominion over the collateral, and these problems will be discussed subsequently. This kind of financing is carried on under the Code in approximately the same way it was handled in pre-Code days. The legal problems involved in not policing collections and other collateral or proceeds of collateral are thought to be solved by the Code; the business risks remain, of course.

Whether the chattel paper is sold or assigned, the seller will be required to warrant that the facts of the sale, as the seller represents them, are true: that the buyer has made the stipulated down payment, that the goods are not otherwise encumbered, that the seller has not previously assigned the paper, that no express or implied sales warranties have been breached to the seller's knowledge and that if any have been breached the seller will be responsible for making them good.

If a financer makes a loan against chattel paper, it will be for less than the amount owing on the paper. The seller-borrower will receive, say, 90% of the unpaid balance of the paper assigned. This loan will be evidenced by a note executed by the borrower, who is primarily liable for repayment. The assigned chattel paper is simply security. The unpaid principal balances on the assigned notes include the time price differential which is collected as each installment is paid. It is not uncommon for the financer to apply a percentage, usually 5%, of the amounts received on the assigned installment notes to a "dealer's reserve account" as additional security for all outstanding balances due from the borrower dealer. These reserve or holdback accounts may be used by the financer as cushions to cover delinquencies and defaults, or they may be periodically paid over to the borrower, if no defaults exist; or the excess over a certain amount may be paid over, with the secured party retaining an agreed reserve.

Accounts Receivable Financing. In many sales, whether by merchants to consumers or by manufacturers to distributors or dealers, no security is involved; the sales are simply "on account." These accounts receivable are not represented by documents like conditional sales contracts or notes and chattel mortgages; they are simply recorded in ledger records.

Accounts receivable financing has long been prevalent in the textile industry, but its use in more wide-spread commercial transactions is relatively recent. One inhibiting factor in the growth of this kind of financing was lack of any legislation spelling out the rights of assignees and third parties. A particularly acute problem at common law was the matter of double assignments of the same accounts. In the absence of any statutory regulation, what rights did the first assignee acquire as against the second assignee of the account? Some States protected the first assignee only if he had notified the account debtor. Others protected the first assignee with a written assignment which fully described the account, without notification to the debtor, on the ground that the assignor had nothing he could assign to a second assignee. A third rule was that the first assignee was protected unless the second had collected the account in good faith, or reduced his claim to judgment, or obtained a direct obligation of the debtor.

Statutory regulation has been of various kinds. Some have required "book-marking," by which assigned accounts are stamped as such on the assignor's books; many financers require this as a business precaution regardless of any statute. Other statutes have required the filing of public notice to evidence that the parties intend to engage in accounts receivable financing. A third group of States has had so-called validation statutes, by which written assignments are validated without notifying the account debtor and without public filing of notice of the financing. Obviously, rather complex problems can arise where the assignee-financer is in one State, the assignor is in another, and the account

debtors are in many States. In general, the law of the State where the assignor keeps his account records is applicable; this is the solution adopted by the Code.

Many of the problems discussed under chattel paper recur in accounts receivable financing: notification or non-notification of the account debtor; recourse or non-recourse by the assignee against the assignor; outright sale of accounts or merely an advance by a financer on the security of the assignment. Probably every assignment, whether by way of sale or security, will require a warranty by the assignor that the account is genuine, that the account debtor had capacity to contract, that the account has not been previously assigned, and that the assignor has authority to assign the account. A breach of any warranty will give the assignee a right of recourse against the assignor; this would be so even in cases where the accounts had been sold and the assignee assumed the credit risk of collection. Of course, the detailed contractual arrangement between the parties is a matter of negotiation. Statutes prescribe no more than rules for perfecting an assignment against subsequent assignees and creditors, including trustees in bankruptcy.

An acute problem in accounts receivable financing, although it has broader application, is the matter of how much "dominion" the financer can allow his debtor to maintain over the collateral. In a very famous case, Benedict v. Ratner, 268 U.S. 353, 45 S. Ct. 566, 69 L.Ed. 991 (1925), Mr. Justice Brandeis announced that under the law of New York "a transfer of property as security which reserves to the transferer the right to dispose of the same, or to apply the proceeds thereof, for his own uses, is, as to creditors, fraudulent in law and void." That this case announced an interpretation of State law has often been forgotten, but since such was the fact, the rule can be abrogated by

State statute and it has in fact been abolished by the Code.

There were always ways to get around the rule of Benedict v. Ratner in those States which adhered to it. The procedures were often cumbersome and costly to the debtor, but they were usually legally foolproof. The debtor would be required to remit all collections every day, usually in the form in which they were received with indorsements where necessary. These collections might be used to reduce the debt, or the financer could pay over the cash to the debtor under a revolving credit arrangement. Or special bank accounts might be maintained for the deposit of collections received. Business judgment might, indeed, require some of the precautions, regardless of any legal problems. Financers are not likely to allow their debtors to compromise accounts without strict accounting, or to accept returned merchandise without a segregation of the goods and a settlement in due time. In those States which adhered to the Benedict rule, the failure of the financer to police the debtor meant not merely the loss of the security of only the few accounts in which the procedures had been questionable; if the debtor exercised too much dominion in any case, the entire security arrangement was void as to other creditors, and the financer was merely a general creditor in bankruptcy. He would have a claim for the amount owing him, but the security would not be his; it would go to the enlargement of the bankrupt's estate for all general creditors, of which the former secured party would simply be one.

Warehouse Receipts. The Uniform Warehouse Receipts Act, which is in force in those States where the Code is not yet effective, provides a simple means for a financer to achieve a security interest in adaptable collateral. The borrower stores his goods in a warehouse and secures a warehouse receipt for them. The receipt may be negotiable, in which case it will be negotiated to the finan-

cer, or it may be non-negotiable, in which case it will be issued in the name of the financer.

A receipt is negotiable if it states that the goods will be delivered to the bearer of the receipt or if the goods are deliverable to the order of the person in whose name the receipt is issued. A negotiable receipt is said to represent the goods, while a non-negotiable receipt merely evidences an ordinary bailment.

Whether a negotiable or a non-negotiable receipt is used depends on the kind of collateral and the business considerations involved. Where a negotiable receipt is issued, it must be presented when withdrawals of goods are made and the withdrawals are noted on it. If large quantities of goods are stored and they are to be withdrawn in small lots, the negotiable receipt is not satisfactory from the lender's point of view. In such a case, a non-negotiable receipt works very well, for if the warehouseman has issued such a receipt to the financer, the financer may give a withdrawal order to the warehouseman whenever the borrower has paid for or is entitled to any of the goods, and the original receipt need not be presented. The same considerations continue under the Code.

Field Warehousing. If a manufacturer needs financing to acquire raw materials which will be turned into finished products, it may be inconvenient and expensive to use a public warehouse for storage. In such circumstances field warehousing is a possible financing device. Here an independent warehouseman, a specialist in such transactions, sets up a warehouse on the debtor's premises. The warehouseman leases suitable space from the debtor and partitions it off from the rest of the premises. The goods are then stored in such warehouse, receipts are issued, and the financer is enabled to make a loan to the debtor with the goods as security. The goods may be released by the financer's order to the warehouseman when the debtor makes an appropriate payment or substitutes other collateral. The same procedure may be used under the Code.

Factor's Liens. If neither warehouse receipts nor field warehousing financing were suitable, a manufacturer's inventory could be financed by complying with a factor's lien statute, if the jurisdiction involved had one. These statutes have taken many forms, since there is no uniform act in this field, and largely came into existence after 1942. In general, they allow a financer to acquire a lien on a manufacturer's raw materials, work in process, finished goods, and the proceeds arising from the sale of finished goods. Notice of the lien had to be publicly filed.

Trust Receipts. The concept of trust receipt financing grew up as a common-law development, but only after the promulgation of the Uniform Trust Receipts Act in the early 1930's did this form of financing become wide-spread. It was used primarily for the financing of "hard goods," such as refrigerators or automobiles, in the hands of wholesale or retail sellers. The financer, called the entruster, who had acquired title to or a security interest in the collateral, entrusted it to the debtor, called the trustee, who normally held the collateral for sale, and after sale the security interest attached to the proceeds. Under Section 1 of the Uniform Trust Receipts Act the entruster had to be someone who had actually financed the goods, such as a bank, and could not be a manufacturer who allowed a retail seller to acquire his products for ultimate sale.

In a trust receipt transaction involving goods, the entruster and trustee entered into an agreement stating the terms of the transaction between them, and a brief statement was filed to give public notice that the financing was being engaged in. The statement had to accurately describe the goods to be financed, and it was effective to protect financing of the type described in it for a period of one year from the date of filing. The

Act also protected transactions which took place within 30 days before the filing, but as a practical matter, the pre-filing protection could be for no more than 21 days because of a limitation in Section 60 of the Federal Bankruptcy Act.

Summary of Pre-code Security Devices. While the types of secured transactions briefly discussed above were not the only types available before the Uniform Commercial Code, they were the principal ones. They grew up at common law or were enacted by statute to meet specific needs, and some of them have worked quite well. There was, however, no coordination between them. Some of the terminology and practices were confusing to all but specialists in the kinds of transactions involved. Because of a lingering judicial antipathy toward secured financing, or perhaps borrowing in general, some of the older kinds of secured transactions were heavily burdened with highly technical rules which have never prevented the extension of secured credit but have only made its extension more expensive to debtors.

Where pre-Code patterns of financing have worked successfully, those patterns may be continued under the Code. The terminology will, however, be different, and this fact alone may well cause a re-examination of the structure of secured financing. The content and not the form of the financing will now be of paramount importance.

SECURED TRANSACTIONS UNDER THE UNIFORM COMMERCIAL CODE

General Concepts. Article 9 of the Uniform Commercial Code covers every consensual security interest in personal property and fixtures which the law of the Code States is permitted to govern, except for those transactions specifically excluded. The principal exclusions are these: security interests perfected under a Federal statute, to the extent that such statute governs the rights of the parties to the transaction and third parties;

wage assignments; equipment trusts covering railway rolling stock; transfers of claims under insurance policies; transfers of deposit, savings, and like accounts maintained with a bank, savings and loan association, credit union, or like organization.

If the Code applies, it applies without regard to where "title" to the property is located and without regard to the "form" the transaction is given. That is, before the Code it made a considerable difference whether the form of the transaction was that of a conditional sale, where the seller retained title, or a chattel mortgage, where the mortgagor was usually said to have title subject to the mortgagee's lien. Under the Code, such distinctions are immaterial. The distinctions which the Code makes among the various kinds of collateral are principally related to the method of perfecting the security interest and are based on the kind of collateral involved and its use.

In addition to security interests in personal property, Article 9 also applies to sales of accounts, contract rights, and chattel paper. Article 9 does not, however, displace regulatory legislation such as a usury act, a consumer finance act, or a retail installment sales act (except to the extent Article 9 governs remedies available on the default of the buyer under a sale subject to such an act, if the act's default provisions have been repealed when the Code is enacted).

For the old terminology, which varied according to the device used, Article 9 substitutes a simple uniform set of terms:

secured party replaces mortgagee, conditional seller, entruster, factor, assignee (of accounts);

debtor replaces mortgagor, conditional buyer, trustee, assignor (of accounts);

security interest replaces mortgage, "title" in conditional sales, trust receipts, factor's lien, and assignment of accounts;

security agreement states the arrangement between the parties;

financing statement is the instrument filed to give public notice;

collateral is the subject of the security agreement (or sale).

Attachment of the Security Interest. Three events, which may occur in any order, are necessary for the creation of a security interest: there must be an agreement, the secured party must give "value," and the debtor must have "rights" in the collateral. (Section 9–204(1).) When these events have occurred, the security interest is said to "attach."

The security agreement may be oral in a case where collateral is pledged with the secured party, but otherwise it must be in writing and signed by the debtor to be enforceable against the debtor or third parties. (Section 9–203.) This requirement is in the nature of a Statute of Frauds. Since "legal" security interests are so simple to create under the Code, "equitable" interests, often held to arise under informal arrangements under pre-Code law, are prohibited. The security agreement may be as long or as short as the parties wish, but it must contain a description of the collateral, and when the security interest covers crops or oil, gas, or minerals to be extracted, or timber to be cut, the land involved must also be described.

Except where the Code's requirements are explicit and cannot be waived, a security agreement is effective according to its terms between the parties, against purchasers of the collateral, and against creditors.

Perfection of the Security Interest. In order to have a security interest which is good against third parties—other secured parties, attaching creditors, a trustee in bankruptcy—the security interest must be "perfected." Depending on the kind of collateral involved, a security interest may be perfected when it attaches, as in the case of a purchase money security interest in consumer goods other than fixtures or automobiles; or perfection may require a transfer of possession of the collateral from the debtor to the secured party, as in the case of a pledge of stock certificates; or filing may be necessary to achieve perfection, and this is the usual situation.

When filing or a transfer of possession is necessary for perfection, that act may occur before other events necessary for the attachment of the security interest have occurred, so perfection is accomplished when the last of the events necessary for attachment and perfection has occurred. Since the Code adopts a system of "notice filing," similar to that used under the Uniform Trust Receipts Act, there may be great advantages to the secured party who is the first to file, when there are conflicting security interests in the same collateral, so filing may well take place before the secured party gives value or the debtor has rights in the collateral.

It is obvious that "perfection" is used in several different ways in the Code, and it should be noted that a perfected security interest is not necessarily good against all the world. There may, in fact, be conflicting perfected security interests in the same collateral, and it is a great merit of the Code that, for the first time, definite rules governing priorities among conflicting interests are clearly set out in the Act. As a simple example, a consumer may buy a refrigerator on time from a dealer who retains a purchase money security interest, and this interest is perfected when it attaches. Presently the consumer needs money and secures a loan from a financer, using the refrigerator as collateral, and since this is a nonpurchase money security interest in consumer goods, filing is required for perfection. (The first transaction is the usual conditional sale and the second is a typical chattel mortgage case.) Since the seller of the refrigerator had a perfected purchase money security in-

terest, he would prevail over the conflicting interest under the rule in Section 9–312(4) of the Code.

In connection with the attachment of a security interest, it should be noted that a debtor has no "rights" in crops until they are planted or in the young of livestock until they are conceived; nor in fish until caught, oil, gas, or minerals until extracted, timber until cut; nor in a contract right until the contract has been made; nor in an account until it comes into existence.

It is possible to provide in a security agreement that after-acquired collateral will secure all obligations covered by the security agreement, except that such a clause will not be effective in the case of consumer goods (other than accessions) unless they are acquired by the debtor within ten days after the secured party gives value, and an after-acquired property clause will not attach to crops which become such more than a year after the security agreement is executed unless it is given in connection with a real estate transaction such as a lease or mortgage. (Section 9–204.)

The Code validates a security interest in constantly changing collateral. This kind of a lien has been called at various times a floating lien, a lien on a shifting stock, an inventory lien, a free-handed mortgage, and a floating charge. The Code provides in Section 9–205 that a security interest is not invalid or fraudulent by reason of liberty in the debtor to use, commingle, or dispose of all or part of the collateral, or to collect or compromise accounts, contract rights, or chattel paper, or to use, commingle, or dispose of proceeds, or by reason of the failure of the secured party to require the debtor to account for proceeds or to replace collateral. This section removes the basis for the rule of Benedict v. Ratner, 268 U.S. 353, 45 S.Ct. 566, 69 L.Ed. 991 (1925).

The so-called "floating lien" of the Code is made possible by the after-acquired property clause and the Section validating the security interest even though the debtor may use or dispose of the collateral without accounting for it, together with the first-to-file priority rule and the system of notice filing. The floating lien may be used only with respect to inventory or accounts receivable, but of course it may be used to tie up all of a debtor's assets, a security arrangement which can now be achieved through one piece of paper instead of through the use of a multitude of devices in pre-Code law. The floating lien, using the term in its broadest sense, has been subject to considerable criticism, but in practice it seems not to be used to tie up all of a debtor's collateral, and in fact it could not be used too successfully for such a purpose. In any event, the concept is a highly useful one in inventory and accounts receivable financing. Its use is more a matter of business judgment than a matter of law.

Filing. Where filing is required to perfect a security interest, the document filed is called a "financing statement." It need contain only the names, addresses, and signatures of the debtor and the secured party, and a description of the types or items of collateral covered; but if crops or fixtures are covered, the real estate concerned must be described, and if the products or proceeds of collateral are claimed, this must be stated. (Section 9–402.) Products may be claimed when raw materials of a manufacturer are financed, as in the case where chocolate is financed for a candy manufacturer, and proceeds may be claimed where the inventory of a dealer is financed.

The financing statement requires no formalities such as an aknowledgment or an affidavit of good faith. It simply gives notice that secured financing has occurred or may occur in the future. Interested persons must get details from the debtor. This is somewhat analogous to a recorded memorandum of a lease of real estate; the memorandum gives notice to third parties that the lessee

has certain rights in the property, but the details of the lease are not publicly disclosed, except perhaps for its term of years.

Under the Code, any description of personal property or real estate is sufficient, whether or not it is specific, if it reasonably identifies what is described. This does away with requirements for detailed property descriptions found in some old chattel mortgage cases, the so-called "serial number" test, where a failure to be extremely exact resulted in invalidation of the lien even though no one was actually misled as to the property covered.

The Code provides for three alternative filing systems, but there have been local variations beyond the suggestions of the Code's draftsmen. The suggested alternatives are these: (A) (1) local filing where the goods are or are to become fixtures, (2) central filing in all other cases; (B) (1) local filing where the goods are or are to become fixtures, (2) local filing for consumer goods and farm-connected collateral, (3) central filing in all other cases; and (C) the same as (B) with local filing in addition to central filing in (3) where the debtor has a place of business in only one county, in such county; or if the debtor has no place of business but resides in the State, in the county where he resides, as the case may be. (Section 9–401.) The basic idea is to provide local filing for transactions of essentially local interest.

A filed financing statement which states a maturity of five years or less is effective until such maturity date plus sixty days. If no maturity date is stated in the financing statement, or if the date is one in excess of five years, the statement is effective for five years. The secured party may file a "continuation statement" within six months before or sixty days after a stated maturity date of five years or less, and otherwise within six months before the expiration of the five year period. This will continue the the effectiveness for five years. (Section 9–

403.) There is no limit on the number of continuation statements that may be filed. On a failure to file a continuation statement, the effectiveness of the financing statement lapses and the security interest becomes unperfected.

Kinds of Collateral. 1. *Goods.* Goods are divided into four different classes, "consumer goods," "equipment," "farm products," and "inventory," depending upon their use, and their use at the time the security interest attaches determines the method of perfection of the security interest. The same goods may, at one time or another, come under different classifications. For instance, a refrigerator may be inventory if held by a manufacturer or dealer, equipment if held by a physician for use in his office for storing medicines, and consumer goods if purchased for use in the physician's home.

We will now examine the classes of goods and how security interests in them are perfected.

Consumer Goods. Goods are consumer goods if they are used or bought for use primarily for personal, family, or household use. (Section 9–109(1).) A security interest in a motor vehicle is perfected by notation on the certificate of title, in those States having statutes providing for it. Interests in fixtures are filed with real estate mortgage records. In the case of non-purchase money financing, the financing statement is filed locally (assuming filing alternative B or C, as given above, is adopted by the Code State) if the debtor is a resident, and if he is a non-resident, filing is in the county where the goods are kept. In the case of purchase money financing, no filing is required for perfection, but if the secured party does not file, a buyer will take free of the security interest if he buys without knowledge of it, for value, and for personal or household use. (Section 9–307.) In other words, filing is not required to protect a purchase money financer from every third party except an in-nocent neighbor who buys the goods for his own use.

A purchase money security interest under the Code arises either where the seller retains a security interest or where a financer advances funds which are in fact used by the debtor to purchase property. (Section 9–107.)

Equipment. Goods are equipment if they are used or bought for use primarily in business (including farming or a profession) or by a debtor who is a non-profit corporation or governmental subdivision or agency, or if the goods are not included in definitions of inventory, farm products, or consumer goods. (Section 9–109(2).) This is a catch-all definition.

Perfection of security interests in equipment is generally by central filing, with exceptions for motor vehicles (where there is certificate of title notation), fixtures (where filing is with local real estate mortgage records), and farm equipment (local filing). In connection with purchase money interests in farm equipment, there is an exception similar to the one for purchase money interests in consumer goods: no filing is required for perfection when the cost of the farm equipment is below a specified amount ($2,500 in the Official Text of the Code), and a buyer without knowledge of the security interest, for value, and for farming use will take free of an unfiled security interest.

The Code does not, however, apply to all goods coming within the definition of equipment. Equipment trusts covering railway rolling stock are excluded from the Code, although conditional sales of the rolling stock are covered, and where a Federal act provides a means of filing or registration for the perfection of security interests in equipment, such as the Ship Mortgage Act of 1920, that act governs, although the Code will supply any deficiencies.

While the Code naturally applies to security interests in personal property located within the Code State, it also applies to interests in mobile equipment normally used in more than one jurisdiction such as road building equipment, commercial harvesting equipment, and construction equipment, if the chief place of business of the debtor is in the Code State. If these goods are classified as equipment or as inventory by reason of their being leased by the debtor to others, central filing is required in the State of the debtor's chief place of business. (Section 9–103.)

Aside from goods normally used in more than one jurisdiction, if personal property already subject to a security interest is brought into a Code State, the validity of the security interest is determined by the law of the jurisdiction where the property was located when the interest attached, unless the parties intended at that time that the goods be brought to the Code State and this happened within thirty days, in which case the law of the latter State governs. Foreign security interests continue to be valid in a Code State for only four months unless they are perfected in the Code State, which may be accomplished by the filing of a financing statement signed only by the secured party.

Farm Products. Goods are farm products if they are crops or livestock or supplies used or produced in farming operations, or they are products of crops or livestock in their unmanufactured states (such as ginned cotton, wool-clip, maple syrup, milk and eggs), and if they are in the possession of a debtor engaged in raising, fattening, grazing, or other farming operations. If goods are farm products, they are neither equipment nor inventory. (Section 9–109(3).) In most Code States, local filing is required to perfect security interests in farm products, and also in accounts and contract rights arising from the sale of farm products and in equipment, with the exception of a purchase money interest in lower priced farm equipment as mentioned above.

Inventory. Goods are inventory if they are held by a person who holds them for sale or lease, or to be furnished under contracts of service or if he has so furnished them, or if they are raw materials, work in process, or materials used or consumed in a business. (Section 9–109(4).) This definition covers a merchant's stock in trade as well as a manufacturer's raw materials, work in process, finished goods, and the crates or boxes in which the finished goods are shipped. It also covers goods held for lease. Central filing for perfection is provided for in the Code, subject to any local variations.

As a general rule, a security interest continues in collateral despite sale or disposition, unless the debtor's action was authorized, but in the case of inventory, a "buyer in ordinary course of business" takes free of the security interest even though it is perfected and the buyer knows of it, provided the buyer does not actually know that the sale violates the terms of the security agreement. (Section 9–307(1).) It is inherent in the usual inventory financing that the goods should be sold and that a good faith purchaser who pays value should acquire the goods unencumbered by the security interest. While leased goods are classified as inventory under the Code, it is unlikely, as a practical matter, that there could be a buyer of them in the ordinary course of business, so as to cut off the security interest, since such a buyer must, by definition, buy from a person in the business of selling the kind of goods involved. (Section 1–201(9).)

Proceeds. While a security interest may continue in collateral after it is disposed of without authority, the security interest also continues in any identifiable proceeds arising from the disposition. The term "proceeds" includes whatever is received when collateral or proceeds is sold, exchanged, collected or otherwise disposed of. Money, checks, and the like are "cash proceeds." All other proceeds are "non-cash proceeds."

(Section 9–306(1).) A sale may be partly for cash with turned-in property representing the balance, or a portion or all of the price may be financed by a time payment arrangement. In any case, whatever the seller receives on a sale is proceeds.

The security interest in proceeds is continuously perfected if the interest in the original collateral was perfected, but it ceases to be perfected ten days after receipt by the debtor unless a filed financing statement covering the original collateral also covers proceeds or the security interest in proceeds is perfected within ten days, which the secured party may accomplish by filing a financing statement. (Section 9–306(3).) The proceeds received on a sale may be considered as substitute collateral, replacing the sold goods, and thus included under the original security agreement, or proceeds may be the subject of independent financing.

2. *Collateral Involving "Indispensable Paper."* Three kinds of collateral involve rights evidenced by an "indispensable paper": chattel paper, instruments, and documents.

"Chattel paper" means a writing or writings which evidence both a monetary obligation and a security interest in or a lease of specific goods. (Section 9–105(1) (b).) The term covers the usual conditional sale contract or a note and chattel mortgage, and the Code covers both loans on and purchases of chattel paper.

Chattel paper may arise on the sale of inventory by a merchant, and it might be covered as proceeds by a financing statement covering inventory, or it might be financed independently.

A security interest in chattel paper may be perfected either by filing or by taking physical possession of the paper. The dual methods of perfection are designed to conform to business practices. In the field of automobile financing, it is customary for the financer, who has been assigned the seller's interest in the contract of sale, to take possession of the paper, notify the buyer, and make direct collection of the payments due. In the furniture field, the financer-assignee does not usually notify the buyer that an assignment has been made, and the buyer continues to pay the seller-assignor, who in turn remits collections to the financer. In the automobile financing case, since the assignee has taken possession of the chattel paper, no filing is required for perfection, while in the case of furniture financing filing will be required for perfection, since the assignor retains possession of the paper.

Even though a security interest in chattel paper has been perfected by filing, where the paper is left with the assignor, certain purchasers of the paper will take priority over the interest of the assignee. Where the paper is claimed merely as proceeds by an inventory financer, a purchaser of the chattel paper who gives new value and takes possession of the paper in the ordinary course of business will take priority over the inventory financer's claim although the purchaser knows that the specific paper is subject to an earlier security interest. Even though a financer has a security interest in the paper which has been perfected by filing, a purchaser of the paper who gives new value and takes possession in the ordinary course of business, will take priority over the earlier interest if he buys without knowledge of it. (Section 9–308.) Of course the first financer, if he wishes to protect himself against this contingency, may stamp the paper he leaves with the debtor so that no purchaser could buy the paper without knowledge of the earlier interest.

The term "instrument" includes negotiable instruments, stocks, bonds, and other investment securities. (Section 9–105(1) (g).) This is the kind of paper which is always accepted as being self-sufficient; that is, the paper itself evidences the rights involved.

With two exceptions, the only means of perfecting an interest in instruments is by taking possession of them. Filing does not constitute notice of the security interest to bona fide purchasers or holders in due course. The two exceptions are these: where a security interest in instruments arises for new value under a written security agreement, the interest is perfected without filing or taking possession for 21 days from the time it attaches; and if the interest has been perfected by taking possession, it continues to be perfected for 21 days where the secured party delivers the instruments to the debtor for sale or exchange, or presentation, collection, renewal or registration of transfer. (Section 9–304.) The Uniform Trust Receipts Act had a similar provision. There are legitimate business reasons for allowing the debtor to have the collateral for short periods. It would serve no particular purpose to require filing for short-term transactions, and in long-term transactions it is the universal custom for the secured party to take possession of the collateral. However, where the secured party does not have possession of the instruments, even though his interest is temporarily perfected, a holder in due course of a negotiable instrument or a bona fide purchaser of a security will take priority over the security interest. (Section 9–309.)

The term "document" includes bills of lading and warehouse receipts. (Sections 9–105 (1) (e), 1–201(15).) These documents may be either negotiable or non-negotiable. A document of title is negotiable if by its terms the goods it covers are to be delivered to bearer or to the order of a named person, and any other document is non-negotiable. (Section 7–104.) A security interest in goods represented by a negotiable document is perfected by perfecting an interest in the document. If a bailee in possession of the goods has not issued a negotiable document, then a security interest in the goods is perfected either by the issuance of a document in the name of the secured party, or by notifying the bailee of the secured party's interest, or by filing as to the goods. (Section 9–304(3).) This provision covers the traditional area of field warehousing.

A security interest in a negotiable document may be perfected either by filing or by taking possession of the document. However, filing is not notice to a holder to whom a negotiable document has been duly negotiated. There are similar 21-day "trust receipt privileges" as in the case of "instruments" discussed above, where the security interest is temporarily perfected without filing or taking possession, but again the secured party runs the risk that the debtor will duly negotiate the document to a bona fide purchaser, who will take priority over the secured party. (Sections 9–304, 9–309.)

3. *Intangible Collateral.* The Code recognizes three kinds of collateral which are neither goods nor "paper" collateral: accounts, contract rights, and general intangibles. This intangible collateral is not evidenced by any indispensable paper, such as a stock certificate or a negotiable bill of lading.

The term "account" means a right to payment for goods sold or leased or for services rendered which is not evidenced by an instrument or chattel paper; and "contract right" means any right to payment under a contract not yet earned by performance and not evidenced by an instrument or chattel paper. (Section 9–106.) The Code covers both loans on and purchases of accounts and contract rights.

Perfection of a security interest in accounts and contract rights is by filing, and in most Code States the filing will be central, except for accounts and contract rights arising from the sale of farm products by a farmer, where filing is local. However, no filing is required where the assignment is of an insignificant part of the assignor's accounts or contract rights, such as an assignment of a few accounts for collection, and no filing is required where the assignment is in connection with the sale of the business out of which the accounts arose. (Sections 9–104 (f), 9–302(e).) Since the financing of accounts and contract rights generally involves a number of transactions in many States, the Code provides for filing a financing statement in the Code State, if the assignor keeps his records in that State; otherwise the validity and perfection of the security interest and the place of filing are regulated by the law of the jurisdiction where such records are kept. (Sections 9–103(1), 9–401.)

Accounts arise where goods are sold without any security interest in them. They are simply sold on "open account," and the evidence of the seller's right to payment is contained in a ledger record. A contract right exists, for example, under a construction contract where the contractor's right to payment arises as construction is completed, periodically, probably monthly. Contract rights become accounts as performance takes place and the right to payment is earned.

The term "general intangibles" means any personal property (including things in action) other than goods, accounts, contract rights, chattel paper, documents, and instruments. (Section 9–106.) This is a catch-all category for interests not otherwise covered or specifically excluded. It leaves room for the utilization of new kinds of collateral for financing purposes. It could include good will, literary rights, rights to performance, and interests in patents, trademarks, and copyrights to the extent they are not regulated by Federal statute. Since there is no indispensable paper which evidences rights in general intangibles, perfection is by filing a financing statement, if the debtor maintains his chief place of business in a Code State. There is probably no means of perfecting a security interest in such collateral if the debtor's chief place of business is in a non-Code State.

Priorities. The problem of conflicting security interests in the same collateral is given rather detailed treatment in the Code.

A purchase money security interest in inventory has priority over a conflicting security interest, if the purchase money interest was perfected when the debtor received the collateral, if the purchase money secured party notified prior secured parties who had filed or were otherwise known to him that the financing was to take place before the debtor received the collateral, and if the notice stated that a purchase money security interest was about to be acquired, describing the inventory by item or type. (Section 9–312(3).) This provision is necessary for a number of reasons, but one is that it prevents a single financer from tying up all of a debtor's financing, and for another it provides a method by which after-acquired inventory will not automatically be included under a filed financing statement if the proper steps are taken; but an inventory financer who has filed first may continue to give value as new collateral is acquired and he will be protected by the inclusion of such collateral as security in the absence of a notice of new purchase money financing covering the same kind of inventory he is financing.

In the case of a purchase money security interest in inventory, the security interest must be perfected when the debtor receives possession of the collateral for the financer to prevail over prior secured parties. In the case of any other collateral, a purchase money security interest has priority over a conflicting security interest if it is perfected when the debtor gets possession of the collateral or within ten days thereafter. (Section 9–312(4).) There is a similar grace period for purchase money interests in any collateral if the secured party files before or within ten days after the debtor gets the collateral, as against transferees in bulk and lien creditors (including a trustee in bankruptcy) whose rights arise between the time the security interest attaches and the time of filing. (Section 9–301(2).) If the priorities among conflicting security interests are not governed by the rules above, the priority is determined in the order of filing, if both are perfected by filing; or in the order of perfection if both are not perfected by filing; and in the order of attachment if neither is perfected. (Section 9–312(5).)

It is obvious that purchase money security interests are given a preferred position throughout Article 9. This was usually true under pre-Code law, although the methods by which the ends were achieved were sometimes devious, and no statute governed priorities among conflicting kinds of interests.

The subject of priorities is difficult. Except in extreme cases the problem of priorities does not arise. But of course it is in anticipation of difficulty that security interests are taken, and conflicts between them can happen. Some simple examples may illustrate some of the problems and their resolution.

Suppose A files a financing statement with respect to the debtor on March 1 and B files with respect to the same debtor on April 1. Then B makes a non-purchase money advance against certain collateral on May 1, and A makes an advance against the same collateral on June 1. A takes priority over B, even though B made his advance first and it was perfected when it was made. Both interests here were perfected by filing, and the first party to file prevails. This solution is inherent in a notice filing system, which the Code adopts. B can protect himself against this contingency in a number of ways, but the first financer to file is not obligated to check the files continually before making advances. Of course, if B's advance created a purchase money security interest in collateral other than inventory, B would prevail over A, and if the purchase money advance was against inventory, B would prevail

if he gave A notice in advance that this particular financing was about to occur.

Now suppose A and B make non-purchase money advances against the same collateral and neither interest is perfected when the advance is made. Whichever secured party first perfects his interest, either by filing or by taking possession of the collateral, will prevail. He will take priority over the other financer whether or not he knows of the conflicting interest when he perfects his own security interest.

It should be noted that if a security interest in goods is perfected before the goods become fixtures, the security interest takes priority over both prior and subsequent real estate claims. (Section 9–313.) The determination of what goods become fixtures, and when, is left to local law except that, in general, goods such as bricks and glass which are incorporated into a structure cannot be fixtures. If the secured party has priority over all claims based on interests in the real estate, the fixtures may be removed on default without regard to any loss of value in the real estate, if the secured party reimburses any encumbrancer or owner of the real estate (other than the debtor) for repairing the injury to the property. A person entitled to reimbursement may refuse permission to remove until adequate security is given for performance of the obligation to repair.

Default. After default, the rights and remedies of the parties are governed by the security agreement and by the applicable provisions of Article 9. In general, the secured party may reduce his claim to judgment, foreclose or otherwise enforce the security interest by any available judicial procedure. (Section 9–501.) Unless the parties have agreed otherwise, the secured party may take possession of the collateral on default, without judicial process if it can be done without a breach of the peace. Without removing it, the secured party may render equipment unusable and dispose of it on the debtor's premises. (Section 9–503.) The secured party may sell, lease, or otherwise dispose of any collateral in its existing condition or following commercially reasonable preparation or processing. The debtor is entitled to any surplus and, unless otherwise agreed, the debtor is liable for any deficiency, except that these provisions are not applicable in the case of a sale of accounts, contract rights, or chattel paper unless the security agreement so provides. (Section 9–504(1), (2).)

The collateral may be disposed of at public or private sale, so long as all aspects of the disposition are "commercially reasonable." Unless the collateral is perishable or threatens to decline speedily in value or is of a type customarily sold on a recognized market, reasonable notice of a public sale or of the time after which a private disposition will be made must be sent to the debtor and, except in the case of consumer goods, to other secured parties who have filed or are known by the secured party to have security interests in the collateral. The secured party may buy at a public sale, and he may buy at a private sale if the collateral is customarily sold in a recognized market or is the subject of widely distributed standard price quotations. (Section 9–504(3).)

With exceptions in the case of consumer goods, noted hereafter, the secured party may, after default, send written notice to the debtor and, except in the case of consumer goods, to other secured parties that he proposes to retain the collateral in satisfaction of the obligation, and if no objection is received within thirty days, the secured party may so retain the collateral; if objection is received, the collateral must be disposed of pursuant to the Code's provisions. In the case of consumer goods, if the debtor has paid sixty per cent of the obligation and has not, after default, signed a statement renouncing his rights, the secured party who has taken possession of the collateral must

dispose of it within ninety days or the debtor may recover in conversion or under a provision of the Code authorizing a recovery of not less than the credit service charge plus ten per cent of the principal amount of the debt or the time price differential plus ten per cent of the cash price. (Sections 9–505, 9–507(1).)

Unless the debtor has waived his rights in the collateral after default, he has a right of redemption at any time before the secured party has disposed of the collateral or entered into a contract to dispose of it. (Section 9–506.)

CASES

INDUSTRIAL PACKAGING PROD. CO. v. FORT PITT PACK. INTERNATIONAL, INC.

(1960) 399 Pa. 643, 161 A.2d 19.

BENJAMIN R. JONES, J. The Provident Trust Company of Pittsburgh, pursuant to Sec. 9–403 of the Uniform Commercial Code (Act of April 6, 1953, § 9–403, 12A P.S. § 9–403) filed the following financing statement in the office of the Prothonotary of Allegheny County on August 18, 1955:

"15110 of 1955
"Financing Statement

"This financing statement is presented to a filing officer for filing pursuant to the Uniform Commercial Code.

"1. Debtor (or assignor)—Fort Pitt Packaging Co., Inc., 5615 Butler Street, Pittsburgh 1, Pa.

"2. Secured Party (or assignee)—Provident Trust Co., 900 East Ohio St., Pittsburgh 1, Pa.

"3. Maturity date of obligation _____.

"4. The financing statement covers the following types of property: All present and future accounts receivable submitted.

"Fort Pitt Packaging Co., Inc.

"Leo A. Levy, Treas.

"Provident Trust Company

"A. W. Charlton

"Executive Vice Pres."

Under Sec. 9–403 of the Code such a statement remains effective for a period of five years. On August 19, 1955, Provident Trust Company filed a similar statement in the office of the Secretary of the Commonwealth in Harrisburg.

On February 4, 1957, Fort Pitt Packaging International Inc. entered into a written contract with the United States Government for the maintenance, repair and overhaul of vehicles. On March 26, 1957, Fort Pitt entered into a contract with Empire Commercial Corporation wherein Empire agreed to lend Fort Pitt $140,000, and Fort Pitt agreed to assign to the Provident Trust Company as Empire's agent its contract with the United States Government and any and all payments due or to become due thereunder. On the same day, March 26, Fort Pitt sold and assigned to the Provident Trust Company, the payments due or which may become due under the governmental contract. Notice of the assignment was given to the Contracting Officer of the Department of the Army, pursuant to the provisions of the Federal Assignment of Claims Act of 1940, as amended, 31 U.S.C.A. § 203.

One year later, on March 27, 1958, Fort Pitt was placed in receivership and on May 27, 1958, upon petition of creditors, Robert Mellin, Esquire, was appointed receiver. On June 10, 1958, the said receiver petitioned the Court of Common Pleas of Allegheny County for a rule upon Empire to show cause why the assignments of the proceeds for Fort Pitt's services performed under the government contracts should not be declared null, void and ineffective as against the receiver. After hearing held and argument, the court below dismissed the receiver's petition. From that order this appeal was taken.

Empire contends that the laws of New York should govern because under paragraph 16 of Fort Pitt's letter to Empire dated March 26, 1957,—the contract between them—, it is provided "that [the] agreement and performance thereof shall in all respects be governed by and in accordance with the laws of the state of New York." Empire cites Sec. 1–105(6) of the Uniform Commercial Code which provides "whenever a contract, instrument, document, security or transaction bears a reasonable relationship to one or more states or nations in addition to this state the parties may agree that the law of any such other state or nation shall govern their rights and duties. In the absence of an agreement which meets the requirements of this subsection, this Act governs." However, the Uniform Commercial Code also provides, in Sec. 9–103, "if the office where the assignor * * keeps his records * * * is in this state, the validity and perfection of a security interest * * * is governed by this Article." We agree with the court below that "as between parties it is lawful for them to agree as to what law shall apply; but where, as here, we are dealing with the rights of creditors in the property of one of the contracting parties, then the law of the state of such party's domicile or place of business shall apply. Otherwise, it would be possible for two parties to render nugatory as to third parties an act of Assembly passed for the benefit of such third parties." The laws of Pennsylvania, not New York, governs this controversy.

Appellant Mellin contends that the filing of the financing statement in 1955 was not sufficient to secure the amounts due under Fort Pitt's contract with the United States Government which was executed in 1957. The filing of the financing statement pursuant to Sec. 9–403 was entirely proper. The

Uniform Commercial Code does not require that the secured party as listed in such statement be a principal creditor and not an agent. In this case, apparently, the Provident Trust Company filed the financing statement as a principal creditor, but in 1957, it became the collecting agent for the Empire Commercial Corporation. Neither the Provident Trust Company nor Empire had any reason to believe that it would be necessary to file a second financing statement which would in all respects duplicate the 1955 statement with the exception that the Provident Trust Company would be listed as an agent for Empire. The purpose of filing this financing statement is to give notice to potential future creditors of the debtor or purchasers of the collateral. It makes no difference as far as such notice is concerned whether the secured party listed in the filing statement is a principal or an agent, and no provision in the Uniform Commercial Code draws such a distinction.

The financing statement covered "all present and future accounts receivable submitted." Section 9–110 of the Uniform Commercial Code provides that "for the purposes of this Article any description is sufficient whether or not it is specific if it reasonably identifies the thing described." There is no doubt that the description in the financing statement reasonably identifies the collateral security. It is difficult under the circumstances to imagine how the description could be more complete without filing new and amended descriptions each time a new account receivable falls within the purview of the financing statement. Nowhere in the Uniform Commercial Code is such a requirement set forth.

Section 9–204(3) provides that "except as provided in subsection (4) [which deals with crops and consumer goods] *a security agreement may provide that collateral, whenever acquired, shall secure any* advances made or other *value given at any time* pursuant to the security agreement." (Emphasis added.)

In the 1957 agreement between Fort Pitt and Empire, Fort Pitt agreed to assign to Provident Trust Company all payments to be received as they became due from the United States Government under Fort Pitt's contract of February 4, 1957 with the Government. These amounts due fell within the clause "future accounts receivable submitted" contained in the 1955 financing statement filed by Provident Trust Company. Comment 2 to Sec. 9–303 of the Code states that the "secured party is entitled to have his security interest recognized in insolvency proceedings instituted against the debtor." Therefore, the interest of the secured party, Provident Trust Company is superior to that of the receiver in bankruptcy and any funds which have been placed in the hands of Provident Trust Company pursuant to the assignment by Fort Pitt need not be turned over to the receiver. These funds are properly being held by the Provident Trust Company for the benefit of its principal, Empire Commercial Corporation.

Order affirmed.

NATIONAL CASH REGISTER CO. v. FIRESTONE & CO.

(1963) 346 Mass. 255, 191 N.E.2d 471.

WILKINS, C. J. In this action of tort for conversion of a cash register there was a finding for the plaintiff. The Appellate Division dismissed a report, and the defendant appealed.

The case was heard on a case stated. The underlying question is the relative standing of two security interests. On June 15, 1960, the plaintiff, a manufacturer of cash registers, and one Edmund Carroll, doing business in Canton as Kozy Kitchen, entered into a conditional sale contract for a cash register. On November 18, 1960, the defendant, which was in the financing business, made a loan to Carroll, who conveyed certain personal property to the defendant as collateral under a security agreement. The defendant filed a financing statement with the Town Clerk of Canton on November 18, 1960, and with the Secretary of State on November 22, 1960. Between November 19 and November 25 the plaintiff delivered a cash register to Carroll in Canton. On November 25, the contract of June 15 was canceled and superseded by a new contract for the same cash register but providing for different terms of payment. The plaintiff filed a financing statement with respect to this contract with the Town Clerk of Canton on December 20 and with the Secretary of State on December 21. Carroll subsequently became in default both on the contract with the plaintiff and on the security agreement with the defendant. In December the defendant took possession of the cash register, and although notified on January 17, 1961, of the plaintiff's asserted right sold it at auction on the following day.

The defendant's security agreement recites that Carroll in consideration of $1,911 paid by it does "hereby grant, sell, assign, transfer and deliver to Grantee the following goods, chattels, and automobiles, namely: The business located at and numbered 574 Washington Street, Canton, Mass. together with all its good-will, fixtures, equipment and merchandise. The fixtures specifically consist of the following: *All contents of lunch-eonette including equipment such as: booths and tables; stand and counter; tables; chairs; booths; steam tables; salad unit; potato peeler; U. S. Slicer; range; case; fryer; compressor; bobtail; milk dispenser; silex; 100 Class air conditioner; signs; pastry case; mixer; dishes; silverware; tables; hot fudge; Haven Ex.; 2 door stationwagon 1957 Ford A57R107215* together with all property and articles now, and which may hereafter be, used or mixed with, added or attached to, and/or substituted for, any of the foregoing described property."

In the defendant's financing statement the detailed description of the "types (or items) of property" is the same as the words in supplied italics in the security agreement. There is no specific reference to a cash register in either document, and no mention in the defendant's financing statement of property to be acquired thereafter.

Under the Uniform Commercial Code, enacted by St.1957, c. 765, § 1, after-acquired property, such as this cash register, might become subject to the defendant's security agreement when delivered, G.L. c. 106, § 9–204(3); and likewise its delivery under a conditional sale agreement with retention of title in the plaintiff would not, in and of itself, affect the rights of the defendant. G.L. c. 106, § 9–202. Although the plaintiff could have completely protected itself by perfecting its interest before or within ten days of the delivery of the cash register to Carroll, it did not try to do so until more than ten days after delivery. Thus the principal issue is whether the defendant's earlier security interest effectively covers the cash register.

The trial judge gave no reasons for his ruling. The Appellate Division rested its decision upon the mere statement of the omission of the defendant's financing statement to refer to after-acquired property or to the cash register specifically. * * *

Contrary to the plaintiff's contention, we are of opinion that the security agreement is broad enough to include the cash register, which concededly did not have to be specifically described. The agreement covers "All contents of luncheonette including equipment such as," which we think covers all those contents and does not mean "equipment, to wit." There is a reference to "all property and articles now, and which may hereafter be, used * * * with, [or] added * * * to * * * any of the foregoing described property." * * *

We now come to the question whether the defendant's financing statement should have mentioned property to be acquired thereafter before a security interest in the cash register could attach. The Code G.L. c. 106, § 9–402(1), reads in part: "A financing statement is sufficient if it is signed by the debtor and the secured party, gives an address of the secured party from which information concerning the security interest may be obtained, gives a mailing address of the debtor and contains a statement indicating the types, or describing the items, of collateral."

In the official comment to this section appears the following: "2. This Section adopts the system of 'notice filing' which has proved successful under the Uniform Trust Receipts Act. What is required to be filed is not, as under chattel mortgage and conditional sales acts, the security agreement itself, but only a simple notice which may be filed before the security interest attaches or thereafter. The notice itself indicates merely that the secured party who has filed may have a security interest in the collateral described. Further inquiry from the parties concerned will be necessary to disclose the complete state of affairs. Section 9–208 provides a statutory procedure under which the secured party, at the debtor's request, may be required to make disclosure. Notice filing has proved to be of great use in financing transactions involving inventory, accounts and chattel paper, since it obviates the necessity of refiling on each of a series of transactions in a continuing arrangement where the collateral changes from day to day. Where other types of collateral are involved, the alternative procedure of filing a signed copy of the security agreement may prove to be the simplest solution." [Citation.]

The framers of the Uniform Commercial Code, by adopting the "notice filing" system, had the purpose to recommend a method of protecting security interests which at the same time would give subsequent potential creditors and other interested persons information and procedures adequate to enable the ascertainment of the facts they needed to know. In this respect the completed Code reflects a decision of policy reached after several years' study and discussion by experts. We conceive our duty to be the making of an interpretation which will carry out the intention of the framers of uniform legislation which already has been enacted in twenty-five States. That the result of their policy decision may be asserted to favor certain types of creditors as against others or that a different policy could have been decided upon is quite beside the point.

The case at bar is, for all practical purposes, one of first impression under the Code. There seem to be no decisions anywhere which specifically deal with the situation presented to us.

* * *

The words, "All contents of luncheonette," including, as we have held, all equipment, were enough to put the plaintiff on notice to ascertain what those contents were. This is not a harsh result as to the plaintiff, to which, as we have indicated, § 9–312(4) made available a simple and sure procedure for completely protecting its purchase money security interest.

The order of the Appellate Division is reversed. Judgment for the defendant.

IN RE WHEATLAND ELECTRIC PRODUCTS CO.

(1964 D.C.W.D.Pa.) 237 F.Supp. 820.

MILLER, D. J. * * * Burroughs Corporation, on December 27, 1960, had leased to Wheatland Electric Products Company a Burroughs Style No. F–1503 machine for a term of one year and to continue on a month to month basis until terminated. In that lease, the list price of the machine was established at $8,025.00 and the monthly rental was set at $241.00. The lease contained a purchase option provision, granting Wheatland the right to purchase the machine at the list price at any time during the term of the lease or within thirty days after its termination and further providing that 75% of the rentals paid prior to the purchase date would be applied to the list price up to but not exceeding 75% of that price. On May 16, 1962, a new lease for the same equipment was entered into for one year at a monthly rental of $197.50. Also executed at that time was a purchase option rider, granting Wheatland the option to buy the equipment at the list price. That option was to be exercised within thirty-six months of the commencement of the original lease or to terminate automatically if not exercised. The termination date of said option was December 27, 1963. By the terms of the option rider, 75% of the rentals paid prior to its exercise were to be credited if exercised within one year of the original lease and 70% of the rentals were to be applied to the purchase price up to but not exceeding 75% of that price if exercised after one year from the date of the original lease.

* * *

Wheatland filed a Petition for Arrangement under Chapter XI of the Bankruptcy Act on February 5, 1964. The Trustee appointed in these proceedings paid the monthly rental due in March 1964. Thereafter Wheatland was in default on its rental payments and Burroughs filed a Petition for Reclamation. That Petition was refused by the Referee in Bankruptcy on the ground that the lease, being a security agreement under the terms of the Uniform Commercial Code, 12A P.S. § 1–201(37), had not been filed as required by the Code, 12A P.S. § 9–302, and was therefore invalid against the Trustee.

The question presented by the Petition for Review is whether the lease was intended as security and is to be determined by the facts of the case. In determining the intent of the parties, we may look only to the language of the lease itself, which provided that "there are no understandings, agreements, representations or warranties, express or implied, not specified herein, respecting this lease or the equipment or service hereinabove described." (12A P.S. § 2–202)

The Code provides that "the inclusion of an option to purchase does not of itself make the lease one intended for security." It further provides that "an agreement that upon compliance with the terms of the lease the lessee shall become or has the option to become the owner of the property for no additional consideration or for a nominal consideration does make the lease one intended for security." [12A P.S. § 1–201(37)]

This language of the Code describes what was formerly known in Pennsylvania as a bailment lease, a security device by which one desiring to purchase an article of personal property, but not wishing to pay for it immediately, could secure possession of it with the right to use and enjoy it as long as the rental was paid and with the further right to become the owner, upon completing the installment payments, by the payment of an additional nominal sum. [Citation.]

The Courts, in referring to the term "nominal consideration", frequently use it interchangeably with the sum of $1.00 or some other small amount. [Citations.]

In the instant case, the additional amount which Wheatland was to pay to secure ownership of the machinery should it choose to exercise the option was a minimum of 25% of the list price, or $2,006.25. That amount is not a nominal consideration for the right to become the owner of the equipment, but represents a substantial proportion of the purchase price. In the case of In re Royer's

Bakery, Inc., 56 Berks County Law Journal 48 (1963), the Referee held that an agreement was intended as security when it provided that 80% of the rental payments previously made could be applied to the purchase price. But that provision differed from the instant one in that the credit could be applied up to but not exceeding the list price, so that upon compliance with the terms the lessee could become the owner without paying any additional consideration.

With regard to a lease intended as security, the law recognizes that the ultimate intent of the agreement is a sale, to take effect and become operative only upon compliance with the provisions of the lease. Here considerably more than completion of the rental payments provided for in the lease was required to give Wheatland ownership of the machinery. A further indication that this lease was not intended for security by the parties is the fact that in May 1963, when the lease was extended, the purchase option rider was not likewise extended, although the option would terminate if not exercised, before the end of the term of the extended lease. On February 5, 1964, when Wheatland filed its petition for arrangement, the only agreement in effect between it and Burroughs was the lease, the purchase option rider having expired on December 27, 1963, because Wheatland failed to exercise it.

Because we find that the leasing agreement between Burroughs and Wheatland was not one intended for security within the terms of the Uniform Commercial Code, Burroughs was not required to file a financing statement to perfect its interest and to maintain its right to reclamation. For this reason, the Order of the Referee in Bankruptcy filed July 22, 1964, will be reversed and the case remanded to the Referee for proceedings consistent with this Opinion.

Order reversed.

PROBLEMS

1. Under the Uniform Commercial Code:
   (1) What three conditions must exist in order for a security interest to attach to specific collateral?
   (2) What is meant by perfecting a security interest?
   (3) What are the requirements of a financing statement?
   (4) When is a security interest perfected?

2. Under the Uniform Commercial Code:
   (1) Name and describe each of the four classes of goods which are used as collateral in security agreements.
   (2) Define and describe field warehousing.
   (3) What is a "floating lien"? To what kinds of collateral may it attach?

3. A sells to B a refrigerator under a conditional sales contract for $400 payable in monthly installments of $20 for 20 months. The refrigerator is installed in the kitchen of B's apartment. There is no filing of any financing statement. Assume that after B has made the first three monthly payments:
   (1) B moves from his apartment and sells the refrigerator in place to the new occupant for $250 cash. What are the rights of A?
   (2) B is adjudicated bankrupt, and his trustee in bankruptcy claims the refrigerator. What are the rights of the parties?

4. On May 1 A lends B $10,000 and receives from B his promissory note for this amount due in two years and secured by a chattel mortgage on the machinery and equipment in B's factory. A proper financing statement is filed with respect to this mortgage. On August 1, upon A's request B executes an addendum to the chattel mortgage covering after acquired machinery and equipment in B's factory. A second financing statement is filed covering the addendum. In September B acquires $5,000 worth of new equipment which he installs in his factory. In December C, a judgment creditor of B, causes an attachment to issue against the new equipment. What are the rights of the parties?

5. A and B are residents of Chicago, Illinois. On March 15 A lends $5,000 to B who executes and delivers a three-year note and security agreement creating a security interest

in a yacht owned by B. A financing statement covering the transaction is properly executed and filed with the Secretary of State of Illinois. On June 1 B moves to Cleveland, Ohio, and takes the yacht with him. A who has been in Europe all summer returns in September and learns for the first time that B has removed the yacht to Ohio. A writes a letter to B on September 10 requesting B to execute a new financing statement for filing in Ohio. B replies on September 13 that he will be pleased to do so, but no action is taken. On October 15 C obtains a judgment against B in Ohio for $8,000 and causes a writ of execution to issue and a levy made against the yacht in Cleveland. What are the rights of the parties?

6. On January 16 A sells certain goods to B on credit. On January 17 A delivers the goods to B. On January 20 an involuntary petition in bankruptcy is filed against B who is insolvent. On January 21 A takes the necessary steps to rescind the sale and reclaim the goods under Section 2–702 of the Uniform Commercial Code which is in effect. The trustee in bankruptcy claims the property for general creditors under Section 70(c) of the Bankruptcy Act. Who prevails?

*

PART NINE
PROPERTY

CHAPTER 45

GENERAL NATURE OF PROPERTY—
PERSONAL PROPERTY

Introductory. In a democratic and enterprising society such as the United States the concept of "property" has an importance second only if not equal to the idea of "liberty." While a large part of our rules of property stems directly from English law, property, in America, occupies a unique status because of the protection expressly granted it by the Federal constitution as well as by most State constitutions. The fifth amendment to the Federal constitution provides, in part, that "No person shall be * * deprived of life, liberty, or property, without due process of law; nor shall private property be taken for public use, without just compensation." A similar injunction is incorporated into the fourteenth amendment: "No State shall * * * deprive any person of life, liberty, or property, without due process of law." Under the American constitutional system, all laws are subject to the superior and overriding authority of the constitution. It follows, therefore, that the ownership of property—whatever form it may take—is a right vested with enormous prerogatives and protected by the highest sanctions that can be granted by our legal system.

Because of this unique place accorded property by the American constitution, it might be hoped that the term would be easily defined. However, this is not so. Perhaps no term has been subject to as much uncertainty. This should not be surprising: the term "property" includes almost every *right,* exclusive of personal liberty, that the law will

protect. Land is valuable only because our law provides that certain consequences follow from the ownership of it. The right to use the land, to sell it, and to say to whom it shall pass on death, are all included within the term "property." In this sense, property is not so much a thing capable of being reduced to physical possession as it is an interest, or group of interests, that will, at any given time, be honored by society.

When a person speaks of "owning property" he may have two separate ideas in mind. He may refer to the *thing* itself, as when a home owner says, "I just bought a piece of property in Oakland," or when a corporation president reports to the board of directors that the company "has acquired a site in Bridgeport." In each of these cases, outright and complete ownership of a physically identifiable object usually is implied.

"Property" may, on the other hand, refer to one of many interests in a physical object, each of which may be less than full ownership, and none of which may be capable of reduction to *physical* possession. A tenant under a lease for years owns property in the land leased. The holder of a mortgage has a property interest in the mortgaged premises although the legal ownership may be in the person who secured a debt by mortgaging the property. A person who has a right-of-way over the land of another has a property interest in the land even though he does not "own" the land. It is apparent, then, that any one physical object is really made up of a group of rights or interests that may belong to one person or to a number of persons. In this sense, "property" might be conceived of as a bundle of faggots each representing an interest the law will protect and each of which may be retained or disposed of. If A says he "owns a farm," he probably means that he has all the faggots. But A, as owner, may give B a lease of the land. A thereby gives up one faggot: the right to exclusive possession. A may make a written agreement with C, a neighboring landowner, that C may cross over A's land. A still "owns" the land but he has given up another of the faggots. A may then make and deliver a deed to D of all title to the land to take effect upon A's death. A then has an interest only for life. He has thus parted with another, the right to transmit the property on his death. A, B, C and D all have property interests in the same land. Had A not dealt in such fashion with his land he would, in effect, have retained the full bundle of faggots or interests. Thus, in this manner, "property" in any given physical object may be contracted or expanded.

Property includes many things or ideas in addition to land and the rights incident thereto. The "good will" of a business has a very definite status in modern commerce, and, although accountants and economists dispute its exact meaning, the law recognizes it as property and, consequently, damages are given for injury to good will. The law of unfair competition that prohibits the misleading use of a name is based upon the idea that a name may be valuable property entitled to protection. The law of patents is based upon the theory that an idea may, upon proper application, be property.

Classification of Property. Many attempts have been made to effect a logical catalog of types of property. It should be apparent from the wide scope of the term that any formal classification is difficult and certainly of little practical advantage. For our purposes, property will be considered from the standpoint of its classification as: (1) Tangible or Intangible Property, and (2) Real or Personal Property.

1. *Tangible and Intangible Property.* A 40-acre farm, a chair, and a household pet are *tangible* property. The group of rights or interests referred to as "title" or "ownership" are embodied in each of these physical objects. On the other hand, a stock certificate, a promissory note, and a deed granting X a right-of-way over the land of Y are *intangible* property. Each is nothing but a piece of paper with little value except as it represents and stands for certain rights that are not capable of reduction to physical possession, but that have a *legal* reality in the sense that they will be protected. The same item may be the object of both tangible and intangible property rights. Suppose A purchases a book published by B. On the first page, there is the statement "Copyright, 1966, by B." A owns the volume he purchased. He has the right to exclusive physical possession and use of that particular copy. It is a *tangible* piece of property of which he is the owner. B, however, has the exclusive right to publish copies of the book. This is a right granted him by the copyright laws. The courts will protect this *intangible* property of B as effectively as they will guard A's right to the particular volume he has in his library.

This distinction between "tangible" and "intangible" property can have significant consequences. The courts have frequently been called upon to decide the classification of things for the purpose of retail sales tax laws levying taxes upon "tangible personal property." Several States have exempted the sale of gas and electrical energy from these laws because they are not "tangible" personal property. Other States have included both these sources of power within the definition of taxable property.

2. *Real and Personal Property.* The most significant practical distinction between types of property is the classification into things real and things personal. A simple definition would be to say that land and all interests therein are real property and every other thing or interest identified as property is personal.

For most purposes this easy description is adequate although certain physical objects that are personal property under most circumstances may, because of their attachment to land or their use in connection with land, become real property. Although this volatile characteristic may be important in certain relations such as that existing between landlord and tenant, most property always remains either real or personal.

The importance of the distinction between real and personal property stems primarily from very practical legal consequences that follow from the distinction. There are at least three of these consequences. They are:

(a) *Transfer of property during life.* The transfer of real property during life can only be accomplished by a written instrument known as a deed and is usually accompanied by formal and even ritualistic acts reflecting the unique character of real property. Personal property, on the other hand, may be transferred with relative simplicity and informality. Title to cash or a suit of clothes is so readily transferred that we hardly are aware of the acts the law holds necessary to effect such a transfer.

(b) *Devolution of title on death.* One hoary doctrine of property that still has considerable vitality today is the almost universal rule that if a person dies without directing by will how his property shall pass, title to his real property passes directly to whomever the law declares to be his heirs while title to his personal property passes to the decedent's personal representative who, in turn, must distribute it as the law directs.

A widow's right to dower in her deceased husband's property was, by the common law, limited to a specified interest in his *real* property and even where the old right of dower has been abolished or modified, the widow will generally be allowed a different percentage of the real property than of the personal property of her deceased husband.

(c) *The applicable law.* Although all laws in the fifty States are subject to the provisions of the Federal constitution, there is ample room for variation among the States as to the rules governing rights in property within the constitutional limits referred to at the beginning of this chapter. It is possible, although increasingly unlikely, that the legal consequences of the same set of facts may be different in each State. There are, in spite of a growing tendency toward uniformity, many rules that vary from State to State. It is for this reason that the following rule has considerable practical consequence: The governing law with respect to real property is the law of its location or situs whereas the governing law with respect to personal property is frequently the domicile of the owner, regardless of where the personal property or the evidence of the property is located. Thus, suppose A, a resident of Illinois, dies without a will, leaving real estate in Indiana and stocks and bonds in Wisconsin. Each State has its own laws prescribing who shall receive what interest in the estate of a person who dies without a will. The Indiana real estate will be distributed in accordance with the laws of Indiana, not of Illinois. The stocks and bonds, however, will be distributed according to Illinois law, not the law of Wisconsin.

ACQUISITION OF TITLE TO PERSONAL PROPERTY

Introductory. Title to personal property is acquired and transferred with relative ease and with a minimum of form. The facility with which personal property may be acquired and transferred is due also to the demands of a society based upon commerce. Trade and industry concern themselves with personal property. Profits depend upon the rapid turnover of personal property. Stocks, bonds, merchandise and, indeed, ideas must frequently be sold with a minimum of delay in a free economy. It is only natural that the law will reflect these mercantile needs. If the sale of a share of stock or a suit of clothes required the ritual accompanying a sale of land, the present extent of our daily transactions in commerce would be impossible.

Much of the law of personal property has been standardized to meet the particular needs of this or that phase of commerce. A whole body of the law deals with the sale of goods and is commonly referred to as the law of sales. Nearly all of the States have enacted the Uniform Commercial Code which now includes the law of sales as well as the law governing the acquisition and transfer of title to commercial paper such as promissory notes. An important part of the Code states the rules governing the purchase and sale of certificates of stock. These particular branches of the law of personal property constitute part of the general field of the law of personal property. A few of the less "commercial" aspects of the law respecting the acquisition of title to personal property will be noted.

Title by Gift. A gift is a transfer of property from one person to another without consideration. The lack of any consideration is the basic distinction between a gift and a contract. Because, by definition, there is no compensation or consideration, a gift to be effective must be executed or actually made. A gratuitous promise to make a gift in the future is not binding. A will be bound if he delivers a painting to B intending to make a gift of it. A will not be bound if he tells B that he intends to make B a gift of the painting "next month."

Delivery is absolutely necessary to a valid gift. The term "delivery" has a very special meaning including of course, but not limited to, manual transfer of the item to the recipient, or "donee," as he is called. There can be "delivery" of a gift sufficient to make it irrevocable if the item is turned over to a third person with instructions to give it to the donee. Frequently, an item, because of its size or location, is incapable of immediate manual delivery. In such case, an irrevocable gift may be effected by delivery of something symbolic of dominion over the item. This may be referred to as constructive delivery. If A declares that he gives an antique desk and all its contents to B and hands B the key to the desk, in many States a valid gift has been made.

The law is clear that there must, in any event, be an *intent* on the part of the donor to make a present gift of the property. Thus, if A leaves a packet of stocks and bonds with B, B may or may not have a good title thereto, depending upon whether A intended to make a gift of them or simply to place them in B's hands for safekeeping. A voluntary, uncompensated delivery with intent to give the recipient title immediately constitutes a gift. If these conditions are met, the donor has no further claim to the property.

It is possible for a person to make a gift of property while still retaining the right to the income therefrom during his life. A person can make a valid present gift of shares of stock and, at the same time, reserve the right to receive the dividends therefrom during his life. The retention of any interest in the object may, however, be evidence that a gift was not intended.

Inter Vivos Gifts and Gifts Causa Mortis. In most instances, a valid gift is made during lifetime and takes effect immediately and irrevocably upon the delivery of the property. These are inter vivos gifts and the foregoing rules apply to such gifts.

Sometimes a gift is made in apprehension or contemplation of death. This apprehension may arise from a serious illness or the expectation of impending peril. Such gifts are frequently referred to by their Latin name, donatio causa mortis. The principal distinction between inter vivos gifts and gifts causa mortis is that the latter are revocable in the event that the would-be donor does not die. If A, about to undergo a serious surgical operation, gives B his collection of Royal Doulton china, this is a gift causa mortis, and should A, to the surprise of all concerned, effect a complete recovery, he can claim back his china.

Tax Incidence of Gifts. Perhaps the most practical current problems surrounding gifts result from the application of the Federal income and estate tax laws. Inter vivos gifts are subject to taxes but at substantially lower rates than the tax upon transfer of property at death. It is also possible to make substantial gifts every year without being subject to any gift tax. More and more frequently, persons desiring to lessen the tax burden upon their estates at death by taking advantage of the gift tax exemptions, make inter vivos gifts of property to their children or spouses. If, however, the gift is made within three years of death, the law presumes that the gift was made "in contemplation of death" and is therefore subject to the higher death taxes, and the burden is placed upon the estate to prove that the gift was not made in contemplation of death.

Another major issue involves the question of whether a transfer of property is "income" to the recipient. If A gives B $1,000, this is not income to B and is not subject to the income tax. But, suppose A, a creditor of B, voluntarily and without payment, cancels a $10,000 promissory note of B's. B has certainly received property. Is this a non-taxable gift, or is it taxable income to B? If in this non-business transaction no consideration passed to A for his forgiveness, the cancellation of the debt probably will be a gift, in which case A will have to file a gift tax return, but B will not report the amount of the cancelled note as income. But, if A agrees to cancel the note without payment if B performs other services for him, the amount of the cancelled debt is taxable income to B as compensation for his services. Much will depend upon the relationship of the parties.

Where the indebtedness is assumed by an individual in connection with the purchase or acquisition of property which is *used in his trade* or *business,* and its cancellation would otherwise have constituted income to the debtor, the Internal Revenue Code gives the debtor an option either to treat the cancelled debt as income in the year of its cancellation or to consent, instead, to a reduction in the cost basis of such property. If the debtor consents to a reduction in basis, which he must do on a special form provided for this purpose, the gain will be taxed in the form of a larger spread between basis and selling price (if the property is subsequently sold) and in the form of smaller depreciation allowances until the property is sold or fully depreciated. Prior to 1954, the same treatment was given to cancellation of any indebtedness incurred by a corporation. The Code has continued this treatment for corporations and, as we have seen, has extended it to individual indebtedness incurred in connection with property used in a trade or business.

Accession. Many of the practical problems surrounding the title to personal property stem from its principal characteristic: movability. One of these problems is identified by the phrase "title by accession" and another by the term "title by confusion."

"Accession," in its strict sense, means the right of the owner of property to any increase thereof, whether caused by natural or man-made means. The more practical problems arising under this term involve the rights between the owner of a chattel and the owner of another item of property which is attached to or made a part of the chattel when the attachment or conversion is without the consent of the owner of the item attached or converted. A takes lumber belonging to B and without B's consent builds it into a wagon. Or, A takes a silver loving cup belonging to B and without B's consent melts it down into a tray. To whom does the "new" product belong? The material, or part of it, was originally the property of B. The labor and skill necessary to create the new product were A's.

The law has evolved a set of rules to decide these and similar problems. In any case where there is a dispute concerning accession, the relative rights are measured in terms of two principles:

1. Was the taking or conversion wilful or unintentional? Did the taker know the item was not his?

2. What is the relative importance of the labor of the taker and the property taken? This standard may be expressed in any one of three ways:

    (a) What is the relative value of the property taken and the "new" item?

    (b) Is the property taken still identifiable?

    (c) Is the property taken easily severable or "reconverted" from the new item?

Whatever the outcome under these tests, the owner of the converted item will be entitled to one of two forms of relief. He will either be entitled to a return of the item or to damages. Which of these two forms of relief he can claim will depend upon how the facts of the case fit into the foregoing tests.

If a taking was deliberate and with knowledge that the item was the property of another, the law has little interest in the increase in value due to the applied labor. Where property is wilfully converted, the general rule is that the original owner can have the property returned to him except in a case where the identity has been hopelessly lost or the value of the new item is almost entirely the result of the labor of the taker and this value is far greater than the value of the original item. If A knowingly takes a piece of canvas belonging to B and on it creates a masterpiece in oil, B probably cannot claim title to the painting but, because the taking was wilful, B will be entitled to damages based upon the increase in value of the canvas. Except in such a rare instance, a wilful taking will not pass title and the owner of the taken item will be able to claim title to it or to the new property of which it forms an integral part.

The more difficult and frequent problems arise where the taking is without knowledge that the property belongs to another. In this case, the law is not aided by a sense of punishing a wrongdoing. The law must attempt to reconcile two innocent parties without injuring either. One rule is that if there is an innocent taking and the identity of the converted item has changed, then title passes to the person who applied the labor. The original owner is only able to obtain damages for the *original* value of the converted article. This rule simply moves the issue up a peg where the meaning of the phrase "change of identity" must be determined. It has been held that cloth does not lose its identity when converted into a coat nor timber when it is converted innocently into planks. It is apparent, however, in most cases that title passes to the innocent converter if the value of the labor is greater than the value of the converted material in its original form. In such a case, the original owner will not be entitled to the new item; his only remedy will be an award of money damages for the value of the original article.

Applicability of the Uniform Commercial Code. Rules substantially the same as those for fixtures, which will be considered hereafter, apply to accessions, such as a new motor in an old car. If the secured party is entitled to priority, he has a right of removal. (Sections 9–313(5), 9–314(4)). Section 9–314 has no application to goods which are so commingled in a manufacturing process that their original identity is lost. That type of situation is covered by Section 9–315.

If there is a perfected security interest in goods and subsequently they become part of a product or mass, the security interest continues in the product or mass if (a) the goods are so manufactured, processed, assembled or commingled that their identity is lost in the product or mass; or (b) a financing statement covering the original goods also covers the product into which the goods have been manufactured, processed or assembled. (Section 9–315(1)). In cases to which paragraph (b) applies, no separate security interest may be claimed under Section 9–314 dealing with accessions. When, under subsection (1), several security interests attach to the product or mass, they rank equally according to the ratio that the cost of the goods subject to each interest bears to the cost of the total product or mass. (Section 9–315 (2)).

Under Section 9–315 the security interest continues in the resulting mass or product in the cases stated in subsection (1). This Section applies not only to cases where flour, sugar and eggs are commingled into cake mix or cake, but also to cases where components are assembled into a machine. In the latter case a secured party is put to an election at the time of filing by the last sentence of subsection (1), whether to claim under Section 9–315 or to claim a security interest in one component under Section 9–314.

Title by Confusion. The basic problem here is much the same as in the case of title by accession. Hereford cattle belonging to B are mixed with Hereford cattle belonging to A and neither man's herd can be specifically identified; or grain of X is mixed with grain of Y. The problem arises only where the goods are identical. Thereby arises the "confusion." The confusion may result from accident, mistake, wilful act or agreement of the parties. If the goods can be apportioned, each owner proving his share of the whole, each will receive his share even if the confusion was by the wilful act of one of the parties. If, however, the confusion results from the wilful and wrongful act of one of the parties, he will lose his entire interest if he cannot prove his share. Frequently, the real problem arises not because the original interest cannot be proved but because there is not enough left to distribute a full share to each owner. In such a case, if the confusion was due to mistake, accident or agreement, the loss will be borne by each, proportionate to his share. If caused by an intentional and unauthorized act, the wrongdoer will first bear any loss.

Where, as is frequently the case, the confusion is caused by acts of a third party, his liability will depend not only upon the character of his act, as in the foregoing instance, but also upon whether his responsibility was assumed gratuitously or for a consideration. The third party is generally referred to as a "bailee."

Title to Lost or Misplaced Personal Property. Suppose X, the owner of an apartment hotel, leases a kitchenette apartment to Y. One night, Z, who happens to be Y's mother-in-law, is invited to sleep in the Murphy bed in the living room. In the course of preparing the bed, Z finds an emerald ring caught on the springs under the mattress. The ring is turned over to the police but diligent inquiry does not turn up the true owner. Who is entitled to the ring? The law insists, as a theoretical proposition, that title be in someone and, anyway, as a very practical matter,

X, Y and Z will each insist that he or she has title. Z will be entitled to the ring. The law says that a "finder" is entitled to lost property as against the whole world except the true owner. It might be argued that calling Z the "finder" simply begs the question. X owned the property on (or in) which the lost article was located. Was not he thereby the "finder"? Suppose that X buys an old trunk because he believes it contains some letters written by Benjamin Franklin. He does not locate the letters, but, while Y is repairing the trunk at the bequest of X, Y comes across the correspondence in a secret compartment. In this case, X as owner of the trunk, will probably have a superior claim to the lost items. Here, it is said that, since X purchased the trunk with the intention of claiming the items, he is the "finder." The general superior right of the one who first takes physical hold of the goods is limited by some courts where the object is discovered by an employee in the course of employment. If, instead of Y's mother-in-law, the maid employed to clean the apartment had found the emerald ring, then the owner of the apartment would have had a stronger claim to the property.

A different rule applies when the lost property is in the ground. Here, the owner of the land has a claim superior to that of the finder. X employs Y to excavate a lateral sewer. Y uncovers old Indian relics. X, not Y, has the superior claim. There is, of course, no logic to this distinction between something found in a building and something found in the ground. The building is as much a part of the real estate as is the land. The only exception to the rule granting superior rights to the landowner when the property is buried is the rule governing "treasure trove." In some jurisdictions, the person who discovers bullion or coin in the soil has a claim superior to that of the owner of the land. This exception probably stems from the traditional rule that the sovereign had a right to a share of any treasure trove, and a rule encouraging discovery had a distinct financial advantage to the crown.

There is a further exception to the rule giving the "finder" first claim against all but the true owner. Most decisions hold that if property has been mislaid, not lost, then the owner of the premises, not the "finder," has first claim if the true owner is not discovered. This doctrine is involved frequently in cases where items are found on trains. The true owner, it is said, did not lose the parcel of banknotes, he simply mislaid them. Barber shops and restaurants are a common focal point for litigation over mislaid articles. The owner of the premises has superior title if the articles were mislaid.

FIXTURES

Introductory. It is not always easy to decide whether a particular thing is real property or personal property. Land and things affixed to the land are real property. Personal property may be defined as any kind of property which is not real estate. Personal property which is brought onto the land for the purpose of being used in the construction of a building will remain personal property until so used. Thus, materials for a building are clearly personal property. But, worked into a building as its construction progresses from the foundation up, they become real property because buildings are part of the land.

Even this simple illustration bristles with problems. Buildings are generally part of the land, but are all buildings always part of the land? What is meant by materials worked into a building? Would plumbing be correctly described as "materials worked into a building"?

Consider the following list of things which, at one stage, are clearly personal property but which are used in connection with buildings: heating, lighting and air conditioning systems; ranges, refrigerators, television antennae, bathroom and kitchen cabinets, mantels, fire places, dishwashers, disposals, door mirrors, venetian blinds, shades, window screens, awnings, storm windows, window boxes, storm doors, screen doors and mail boxes. These items may be so firmly affixed to the land or building that they have lost their character as personal property, or they may have retained this character as fixtures.

While the question whether these various items are personal property or real property may in certain instances be difficult to answer, it is only by obtaining the answer that conflicting claims to the ownership of such things may be determined.

The conflict may arise between the landlord and his tenant. One tenant may have built a garage on the leased premises which he intends and expects to be able to remove when the lease expires. Another may have installed heating and lighting systems in the landlord's building, expecting to take them with him when he leaves. In each case the landlord may successfully contend that these things have become part of the real estate and are no longer the property of the tenant.

The conflict may arise between the vendor and the purchaser of a house. The vendor may think that the sale did not include the refrigerator, range, venetian blinds, and screens, while the purchaser thinks otherwise.

The conflict may also arise between the equity owner of an apartment building and the mortgagee. The mortgagee may regard the new refrigerators and gas stoves installed subsequent to the execution of the mortgage as part of his security, yet the owner contends that these are items which he bought with fresh capital and are not subject to the mortgage. Even more troublesome is the conflict between a conditional vendor (or chattel mortgagee) of these types of items

and the subsequent purchaser of the building, or the prior or subsequent mortgagee of the building.

General Rules. One accepted general rule is that as between parties to a valid agreement, the intention of the parties as expressed in the agreement will control. This rule removes many conflicts between the well advised landlord and tenant, and between the well advised vendor and purchaser. As between themselves, these parties may expressly provide, in the lease or in the contract of sale, with respect to the ownership of each item of property.

Thus, in a lease it may be provided that the tenant shall have the right to remove all items of property, including buildings, placed on the leased premises by him. For this reason, it may not be accurate to say that all buildings always become part of the realty. A similar provision may be included in a contract between the vendor and purchaser of real estate.

As between landlord and tenant, a presumption obtains that the tenant is entitled to all of the fixtures installed by him, provided that they may be removed without material injury to the landlord's property. But, if the lease specifically enumerates the fixtures which the tenant may remove, the presumption as to all fixtures not specifically enumerated operates in favor of the landlord.

It is important that the lease provide when the fixtures may be removed. Unless the lease is of uncertain duration, the right of the tenant to remove his fixtures ceases the same moment his leasehold interest expires. Where the lease is of uncertain duration, it is generally held that, upon its termination, since its termination cannot be easily foreseen by the tenant, the tenant has a reasonable time to remove the fixtures.

Suppose a lease containing carefully drafted provisions as to fixtures is later renewed by a new lease which contains no provisions as to fixtures. In such a situation the tenant will lose the right to remove those fixtures, such as buildings which he would not have had the right to remove except for the special agreement in the prior lease. Furthermore, the tenant may lose, and many courts have held that he does lose, the right to remove all fixtures, even those which he had the right to remove without a special agreement in the prior lease. The reason given is that his right to remove the fixtures expired with the prior lease and the fixtures thereupon became the property of the landlord.

The sale of real estate usually involves two stages, the first of which is the contract for sale, and the second, the delivery and acceptance of the deed. Unless the contract specifically provides otherwise, the second stage, the delivery and acceptance of the deed, constitutes a complete discharge of the contract. That is, acceptance of the deed may terminate all of the purchaser's rights under the contract. From the purchaser's point of view, an important feature of the contract is that it gives him the right to refuse to accept the deed until the vendor has complied with all of the provisions of the contract.

Any provision as to fixtures in the contract for sale will be of little value to the purchaser if he accepts a deed which makes no reference to fixtures. If the purchaser desires to be protected he must not only take care that the contract contain adequate provisions as to fixtures but also that the deed incorporates such provisions.

The provisions of an agreement designed to obviate problems with regard to fixtures are, in general, effective only between the parties to it. Thus, the agreement between a conditional seller of a fixture and the owner of the realty to which it is to be attached, will control as between them, but it does not solve the problem as between the conditional seller of the fixture and a subsequent bona fide purchaser of the realty who purchases for value and without notice of the agreement.

Apart from the fact that many leases and contracts for sale of realty do not include provisions as to fixtures, there are important areas in which such agreements do not solve the problem because the conflict is between parties who could not have anticipated the conflict and who have not entered into an agreement with one another. Where there is such a conflict, and where the resolution of it is not, or could not be, governed by an agreement, it becomes necessary to decide whether any particular item is part of the realty and therefore belongs to the owner of the land, or whether it has retained its identity and character as personal property and therefore belongs to someone else.

Absent the binding force of an agreement, the following guides are helpful in determining whether any particular item is part of the realty, and thus belongs to the landowner or person having the title or right to the realty: (1) the physical relationship of the item to the land; (2) the intention of the person who places the item upon the land; (3) the purpose served by the item in relation to the land and in relation to the person who brought it there; and (4) the interest of that person in the land.

Although physical attachment is significant, a more important test is whether the item can be removed without material injury to the land or building on the land. If it cannot be so removed, it is generally held that the item has become part of the realty. The converse is also true but to a lesser degree. Where the item may be removed without material injury to the land or building, it is generally held that it has not become part of the realty. This test, however, is not conclusive.

In the converse situation the courts have searched for the answer in the intention of the person who brought the item upon the realty and attached it thereto. The tests of intention are objective. One of the tests developed has been to inquire into the purpose or use of the item in relation to the land and in relation to the person who brought it there. If the use or purpose of the item is unusual for the type of realty involved (e. g., small crane in the backyard of a country house) or peculiar to the particular individual who brought it there, then it may be reasonably concluded that the individual intended to remove the item when he leaves.

The converse of this test is not true. An item is not regarded as part of the realty merely because its use or purpose is usual for the type of realty involved. For example, it is usual to have beds and dressers in the bedrooms, and dining tables in the dining rooms, but these items are not part of the realty. The test of purpose or use becomes operative only if the item both (a) is affixed to the realty in some way, and (b) can be removed without material injury to the realty. In such a situation, if the use or purpose of the item is peculiar to the particular owner or occupant of the premises the courts will tend to let him remove the item when he leaves.

While it has been said that the test of purpose or use becomes operative only if the item is affixed to the realty, it does not follow that all items which are not affixed definitely remain personal property. Some buildings, such as metal frame-corrugated iron constructions, may not be affixed to a foundation but may merely be resting on the ground. It *cannot be said* that they are definitely personal property, and it would be difficult to establish, assuming that such a structure is erected on an unimproved lot, that its use or purpose is usual for the type of realty involved.

The courts, in searching for the intention of the person bringing such items upon the land, have looked to his interest in the realty. The courts have found it much easier to find an intention to remove such items on the part of occupants with a limited interest in the real estate, such as lessees, and more difficult to find such an intention on the part of absolute owners of the real estate.

Different Conflicting Interests.

(1) *Landlord and Tenant.*

(a) If an item is brought onto the land by a tenant and is *not affixed* thereto, it may always be removed by him either before or after the expiration of the lease.

(b) If an item is brought onto the land by a tenant and *is affixed* thereto, it may always be removed by him before the expiration of the lease, provided (1) it may be removed without material injury to the realty, and (2) its use or purpose on the premises is peculiar to the tenant. Whether the tenant may remove the item, if its use is not peculiar to him and is usual for the realty involved, is less certain but the general view is that he may, if the removal will not result in material injury to the realty.

Accordingly, in the law of landlord and tenant, it is settled that the tenant may remove "trade fixtures," i. e., items used in connection with his trade, provided that this can be done without material injury to the realty. This is merely another way of saying that he may remove items whose use on the premises is peculiar to him.

If the item is a building which is merely resting on the land, the tenant may have no right to remove it merely because it is not firmly affixed to or embedded in the land. The reason for this is that buildings, of whatever kind, are traditionally regarded as realty. In view of this tradition, it is extremely doubtful that a tenant would be permitted to remove a building if it is not a "trade fixture," that is, if its use on the *premises is not peculiar to the tenant's trade.* These various uncertainties show why it is important that the tenant, who anticipates making substantial improvements on the premises, should insist that his rights of ownership and of removal be expressly recited in the lease agreement.

(2) *Vendor and Purchaser.* This discussion pertains to a vendor of real estate who is parting with his absolute ownership in the property. Such a vendor is not in as favorable a position, with regard to fixtures brought onto the realty by him, as a tenant would be. Courts find it more difficult to hold that an absolute owner of realty intended to remove the fixtures, at some future date, when he placed them on his property. Applying the general rules previously stated, in the context of the vendor and purchaser relationship, the results may be summarized as follows:

(a) If an item was brought onto the land by the vendor and was *not affixed* thereto, it may always be removed by him as against the purchaser, unless it is a building which merely rests upon the ground.

(b) If an item was brought onto the land by the vendor and *was affixed* thereto then he may not remove it *unless both* (1) it can be removed without material injury to the land, and (2) its use or purpose on the premises is so peculiar to the particular vendor that a reasonable purchaser would not expect it to be included with the realty.

The difference between the vendor's position and that of a tenant is that the vendor is presumed to have sold all fixtures which usually go with the type of property involved, whereas the tenant may generally remove any of his fixtures which are removable without material injury to the property.

(3) *Owner and Mortgagee.* If a mortgagee ever becomes the owner of the mortgaged realty, he does so by two stages which are usually many years apart. The first stage is when he takes the mortgage; the second is when he forecloses upon default by the mortgagor, and becomes a buyer of the property at the foreclosure sale. If we look only to the time of foreclosure it can be said that the mortgagee is then in much the same position as a purchaser and takes all of the fixtures which a purchaser would take at that time. The majority of the courts hold this to be the proper test, and rule that the mortgagee has a security interest not only in those fixtures which would have passed to a purchaser at the time of the making of the mortgage but, also, in those fixtures which would pass to a purchaser at the time of the foreclosure sale. The mortgagee's security interest is allowed to attach to fixtures which have become a part of the mortgaged property after the date of the making of the mortgage.

There is a respectable minority, however, which considers this view unfair. The mortgagee, they observe, has made a loan based upon a valuation of the property in the condition in which it was at the time he took the mortgage. There is no reason, therefore, for allowing the mortgagee's security interest to be enchanced to the extent of the value of fixtures added after the date of the mortgage. The minority view that the mortgagee's security interest does not attach to after-acquired fixtures is qualified, however, by the rule that the owner will not be permitted to remove such fixtures if this will damage the mortgaged property, as this would lessen the value of the mortgagee's original security.

In connection with this minority view, it may be noted that the so called "package mortgage" is becoming increasingly popular. The lender-mortgagee includes in his loan a sum intended to cover the purchase of household appliances and specifically provides in the mortgage instrument that such appliances shall be part of his security. This provision in the mortgage, as to those fixtures which it expressly enumerates, is effective to change the result obtained under the minority view, at least as between the mortgagor and mortgagee.

(4) *Persons Holding Security Interests in the Fixture; Subsequent Purchasers of the Realty; and Security Holders of the Realty.* In conditional sales, as between the conditional vendor and conditional vendee of an item which is to be affixed to the vendee's land, the item remains personal property, and may be removed by the conditional seller upon default by the buyer. As between the conditional seller and purchaser, their agreement will govern, and such agreement invariably provides that the seller may repossess the item upon default by the conditional vendee.

The position of the conditional seller of a fixture when the real estate to which it has become affixed is sold by the conditional purchaser before payment of all the installments of the price may be unfortunate. Can the conditional seller, in the event of default, repossess the fixture from a bona fide purchaser of the real estate who paid value for the property and took it without notice of the conditional vendor's lien? The answer to this question depends upon whether the fixture has become a part of the realty so as to pass to the bona fide purchaser under the deed.

(a) If the fixture is of the type which, if owned outright by the vendor of the realty, *would not* pass to a purchaser of the realty in a case where the deed does not mention fixtures, the conditional seller can certainly repossess as against the new owner of the realty. Assume, however, that the deed specifically includes the item which is subject to the conditional sales contract. In such case the new owner of the realty takes the item as would any other purchaser of personal property, and in jurisdictions where the reserved title of the conditional vendor is protected, he would not obtain title, unless the conditional vendor in some manner by conduct should be precluded or estopped from asserting his reserved title.

(b) If the fixture is of the type which, if owned outright by the vendor of the realty, *would pass* to a purchaser of the realty, then the conditional seller may not repossess as against the new owner of the realty unless the purchaser took title to the real estate with notice, actual or constructive, of the conditional sale. In this situation, some authorities hold that the conditional seller may not repossess the fixture from a purchaser of the realty who had notice of the conditional sale, unless the fixture may be removed without material injury to the realty. This is the rule adopted in Section 7 of the Uniform Conditional Sales Act. The theory is that although the new owner has no title to the fixture, he does have the right to preserve his realty intact. In this situation, while the conditional vendor may not repossess, he may be entitled to recover damages against the new owner who, in turn, may recover from the vendor of the real estate for breach of warranty of title.

The new owner of the realty, since he took with notice of the conditional sale, ought to have anticipated that the conditional seller might want to remove it in the event of default. The law might provide the conditional seller, in such a case, the right to remove the fixture upon indemnifying the new owner for any damage to his realty. This is the solution advanced in Section 9–313 of the Uniform Commercial Code.

With respect to the rights of the conditional seller of the fixture in relation to the rights of the mortgagee of the realty, there are two possible situations:

(a) O (Owner of a house) purchases a fixture from CS (conditional seller), his time payments to extend over 24 months. O installs the fixture in his house. Within the 24 months, O mortgages his house to M (mortgagee) who has no notice of CS's contract with O. Who has the better interest in the fixture, CS or M?

(b) O mortgages his house to M. During the term of the mortgage, he purchases a fixture from CS, under a conditional sale, and installs it in his house. Who has the better interest in the fixture, CS or M?

In situation (a), if the fixture is of the sort which would be regarded as part of the realty if owned outright by O, M will have the better interest in it because he has no notice of the contract between CS and O, and because the fixture was in the house when M took his mortgage. In situation (a), if the fixture is of the sort which would not be regarded as part of the realty if owned outright by O, then, clearly, CS has the better interest in it, since M's security interest attaches only to the realty and to such items as are regarded as part of the realty.

In situation (b), if the fixture is of the sort which would be regarded as part of the realty if owned outright by O, the majority view is that CS will be protected because it was attached to the realty *after* M took his security in the realty. This view is sometimes qualified by the rule that CS may not remove the fixture as against M if such removal would damage the realty. This qualification is modified in Section 9–313 of the Uniform Commercial Code, which provides, that CS may remove the fixture, in this situation, on condition that he indemnify against damage to the realty.

The majority view as to the rights of CS and M, in situation (b), appears to be inconsistent with the majority view as to the rights of O and M discussed earlier under the caption "(3) Owner and Mortgagee." However, an owner who adds fixtures to the realty, after he has mortgaged it, should not be surprised if the mortgagee claims such fixtures as part of his original security, whereas a conditional seller, who sells a fixture to the owner, after the owner has mortgaged the realty, does not expect to be deprived of his security interest in the fixture by someone who loaned money on the security of the realty when it was without such fixture.

Priority of Security Interests in Fixtures under the Code. The Code recognizes security interests in fixtures but leaves it to other law to determine whether and when chattels become fixtures. Section 9–313(1), however, specifically excludes from its application goods which are incorporated into a structure in the manner of lumber, bricks, tile, cement, glass, metal work and the like, unless the structure remains personal property under the applicable law.

The Code's provisions govern the separate financing of fixtures, which will almost always be purchase money financing. It is extremely rare for a lender to lend money against the security of fixtures in place. Where fixtures are financed as a part of the real estate, they may be included in a real estate mortgage and a separate Code filing is not required.

A security interest which attaches to goods before they become fixtures takes priority as to the goods over prior claims based upon an interest in the real estate. If the interest has attached but is not perfected before affixation, the secured party has priority over prior real estate claims but not over (a) a subsequent purchaser for value of any interest in the real estate; or (b) a creditor with a lien on the real estate subsequently obtained by judicial proceedings; or (c) a creditor with a prior encumbrance of record on the real estate to the extent that he makes subsequent advances, if the interests of these parties arose without actual knowledge of the security interest and before it was perfected. (Section 9–313(4).)

A purchaser at a foreclosure sale, other than an encumbrancer purchasing at his own foreclosure sale, is a subsequent purchaser for the purposes of this provision. (Section 9–313(4).)

If the security interest attaches to goods after they become fixtures, it is valid against all persons, subsequently acquiring interests in the real estate except as stated in Section 9–313(4), but it is invalid against any person with an interest in the real estate at the time the security interest attaches to the goods who has not in writing consented to the security interest or disclaimed an interest in the goods as fixtures. (Section 9–313(3).)

When a secured party has priority over the claims of all persons who have interests in the real estate, i. e., the security interest attached and was perfected before the goods were affixed to the realty, he may, on default, remove his collateral from the real estate but he must reimburse any encumbrancer or owner of the real estate, who is not the debtor and who has not otherwise agreed, for the cost of repair of any physical injury, but not for any diminution in value of the real estate caused by the absence of the goods removed or by any necessity for replacing them. The secured party may be required to give adequate security for the performance of his obligation to repair before a person entitled to reimbursement gives permission to remove the fixtures. (Section 9–313(5).)

CASES

THRASHER v. CITY OF ATLANTA

(1934) 178 Ga. 514, 173 S.E. 817.

[Suit for injunction to restrain flight of airplanes at low altitudes over plaintiff's land that was adjacent to municipal airport. The plaintiff's petitions were dismissed, and he appeals.]

BELL, J. * * * The allegations with reference to flights over the land and the complaints against low flying are now to be considered. In paragraph 13 the petition averred: "That there have been frequent occasions of low flying by pilots, who have permission to arrive and depart at the said field and whose names are unknown to petitioner, but are acting by permit and under license of the defendant, City of Atlanta, and other defendants named in the bill, who arrive and depart, who have been guilty of low flying, that such low flights over adjacent property is a trespass and is a violation of the constitutional rights of plaintiff and other property owners, and that such low flying has been so frequent as to be a nuisance and is dangerous to plaintiff and his family and others in the community." * * *

The Civil Code (1910), sec. 3617, declares that "the right of an owner of lands extends downward and upward indefinitely." In section 4477 it is stated that "the owner of realty having title downwards and upwards indefinitely, an unlawful interference with his rights, below and above the surface, alike gives him a right of action." These statements as to ownership above the surface are based upon the common-law maxim, cujus est solum ejus est usque ad coelum,—who owns the soil owns also to the sky. These provisions of the code should therefore be construed in the light of the authoritative content of the maxim itself. As a matter of fact, the language of the code that the title to land extends upwards indefinitely would seem to be a limitation upon the ad coelum doctrine, indicating by implication that the title will include only such portions of the upper space as may be seized and appropriated by the owner of the soil. Such a construction of the code provisions would materially minimize the difficulties in the present case; but even if the code was intended to express the ad coelum theory in its entirety, and this we assume in the present case, it remains true that the maxim can have only such legal signification as it brings from the common law.

What is the sky? Who can tell where it begins or define its meaning in terms of the law? When can it be said that a plane is above the sky or below it? How can there be an unqualified tangible right in a thing so indeterminate and elusive? What and where is the res of which a court may assume jurisdiction in a case involving a private claim of title? Possession is the basis of all ownership [citation], and that which man can never possess would seem to be incapable of being owned. [Citations.] In order to recover for a trespass it is necessary to show title or actual possession. [Citation.] The space in the far distance above the earth is in the actual possession of no one, and, being incapable of such possession, title to the land beneath does not necessarily include title to such space. The legal title can hardly extend above an altitude representing the reasonable possibility of man's occupation and dominion, although as respects the realm beyond this the owner of the land may complain of any use tending to diminish the free enjoyment of the soil beneath. The maxim to which reference has been made is a generalization from old cases involving the title to space within the range of actual occupation, and any statement as to title beyond was manifestly a mere dictum. For instance, a court in dealing with the title to space at a given distance above the earth could make no authoritative decision as to the title at higher altitudes, the latter question not being involved. The common-law cases from which the ad coelum doctrine emanated were limited to facts and conditions close to earth and did not require an adjudication on the title to the mansions in the sky. Accordingly, the maxim imported from the ancient past consists in large measure of obiter dicta, and to that extent can not be taken as an authentic statement of any law. It follows that the literal terms of the code sections referred to must be discounted or qualified in like measure. * * *

But the space is up there, and the owner of the land has the first claim upon it. If another should capture and possess it, as by erecting a high building with a fixed overhanging structure, this alone will show that the space affected is capable of being possessed, and consequently the owner of the soil beneath the overhanging structure may be entitled to ejectment or to an action for trespass. However, the pilot of an airplane does not seize and hold the space or stratum of air through which he navigates, and can not do so. He is merely a transient, and the use to which he applies the ethereal realm does not partake of the nature of occupation in the sense of dominion and ownership. So long as the space through which he moves is beyond the reasonable possibility of possession by the occupant below, he is in free territory,—not as every or any man's land, but rather as a sort of "no man's land." As stated above, however, the occupant of the soil is entitled to be free from danger or annoyance by any use of the super-incumbent space, and for any infringement of this right he may apply to the law for appropriate redress or relief. * * *

[The court held that the plaintiff's allegations were insufficient to show that the flights constituted a trespass.]

GRACE v. KLEIN

(1966) —— W.Va. ——, 147 S.E.2d 288.

CAPLAN, PRESIDENT. In this action instituted in the Circuit Court of Cabell County the plaintiff, Abbie Grace, seeks an award of certain funds which are on deposit in the Guaranty National Bank of Huntington, situate in Huntington, West Virginia. These funds are in a savings account and a checking account on deposit in said bank in the name of the plaintiff's sister, Anna E. Boggs, now deceased. Upon the refusal of Charles C. Klein, Administrator, C. T. A. of the estate of Anna E. Boggs, to deliver these funds to the plaintiff she instituted this action.

The case was submitted to the trial court for decision upon the pleadings and exhibits filed therein and upon oral arguments of counsel. The court having entered judgment for the plaintiff, the defendant prosecutes this appeal.

Anna E. Boggs, during her lifetime, had on deposit in the Guaranty National Bank of Huntington certain sums of money, namely, $4,234.00 in a checking account and $11,048.-46 in a savings account. It is these sums of money which are the subject of the controversy. By her will dated March 13, 1961, Anna E. Boggs, after directing that her just debts be paid, bequeathed all of the residue of her estate, of every kind and character, whatsoever and wheresoever situate, to her son Raymond Robert Ward and to each of his children, Phyllis, Grace, Walter, Bobby and Bryan, share and share alike.

On April 29, 1962, Mrs. Boggs, during a serious illness, from which she died on July 4, 1962, signed and apparently delivered to the plaintiff the following letter, which is attached to the complaint as an exhibit:

> "Chesapeake, Ohio
> R.F.D. No. 1
> April 29, 1962
>
> The Guaranty National Bank
> Huntington, W. Va.
> Gentlemen:
>
> I Anna E. Boggs sister of Abbie Grace request that if I should die *befor* my sister you transfer both savings and checking accounts to my sister, Abbie Grace, on her presentation of certificate of my death.
> Thank you.
> ANNA E. BOGGS
>
> Witnesses:
> GEORGE D. WARD
> MARY A. WARD"

This letter was not written by Mrs. Boggs but, as indicated above, was signed by her. Furthermore, it is readily admitted that Mary A. Ward did not sign this document as a witness in the presence of Mrs. Boggs.

Shortly after the death of Anna E. Boggs, who at that time was a resident of Lawrence County, Ohio, Abbie Grace presented the above letter for probate to the Probate Court of said Lawrence County, claiming that such letter constituted a valid testamentary disposition of the funds in the accounts referred to therein. After due consideration the Probate Court of Lawrence County, Ohio entered a final decree which concluded as follows: "It, therefore, is ordered that such instrument be denied admission to probate and a final entry is hereby ordered refusing to probate such instrument as a Codicil to the Last Will and Testament of Anna E. Boggs, deceased."

It is the position of the plaintiff in this proceeding that the letter of April 29, 1962 constitutes a valid gift *causa mortis* and that by reason thereof she is entitled to the funds in the aforesaid bank accounts. The defendants, on the other hand, contend that the Boggs letter is testamentary in character; that, not being executed in accordance with the law pertaining to wills, it could not effect a testamentary disposition of the funds involved; and that the letter does not constitute a gift *causa mortis* for the reason that it did not effect a present transfer of the bank accounts to the plaintiff.

* * *

The sole question to be decided in this case is whether the Boggs letter of April 29, 1962 constitutes a valid gift *causa mortis*. In making this decision we must determine whether the essential attributes or constituent elements of a gift *causa mortis,* as defined by law, exist by virtue of such letter. Only personal property may be transferred by such gift. The donor must make the gift in contemplation of death, either in his last illness or while he is in other imminent peril; he must give up all dominion and control over the subject of the gift so that it may belong to the donee presently, as his own property; the donor must make an actual delivery of the thing given or a delivery of the means of getting immediate possession and enjoyment of the gift. A gift *causa mortis* may be revoked by the donor during his lifetime. [Citations.]

Although courts do not generally favor gifts *causa mortis,* such gifts will be given legal effect if made in compliance with the above named requirements. It has been held that the doctrine should not be extended beyond its present limits and that evidence of such gift will be regarded with suspicion and scrutinized with care. This caution is prompted by the fact that a gift *causa mortis* presents a chance for fraud and perjury. [Citations.] In view of the manner in which a gift *causa mortis* is regarded, it is imperative that every element essential to such gift exists before such gift is afforded legal effect.

Although the plaintiff, in the Ohio court, contended that the Boggs letter constituted a testamentary disposition of the subject funds, she made no such contention in the trial of this case or upon this appeal. Whether or not that document is testamentary in character, it is sufficient to note that it was not executed in accordance with the requirements of law pertaining to disposition of property by will and therefore could not effect a conveyance as a will.

We come now to the consideration of whether the Boggs letter contains the elements essential to a valid gift *causa mortis.* The funds in bank accounts, being personal property, constitute proper subject matter for such gift. [Citations.] It is undisputed that Mrs. Boggs signed the letter purportedly making a gift in contemplation of death and during her last illness. These elements are essential to a valid gift causa mortis. However, before a donor can successfully convey the subject of a gift in this manner

the other essential elements must be found to exist.

In order to make an effective gift, whether it be *inter vivos* or *causa mortis,* the donor must consummate the transfer as a present gift to the donee, thereby giving such donee the present right to immediate possession of the gift and divesting the donor of possession and all dominion and control over the thing given. This is distinguishable from a gift to be made in the future which connotes a testamentary disposition. [Citations.]

The foregoing principle is succinctly stated in Harrison on Wills and Administration, Second Edition, Gifts Causa Mortis, § 83, as follows: "* * * It has been repeatedly decided that where a gift has no effect until after the death of the donor, the donor retaining the dominion and control over the property, it cannot be sustained as a valid gift either *inter vivos* or *causa mortis* but such a gift is testamentary and all the provisions of the testamentary law must be complied with to make it effective. Thus, the broad distinction between all forms of gifts and testamentary dispositions. A gift testamentary in character cannot have any effect until after death. A gift not testamentary must take effect at once."

In Seabright v. Seabright, et al., 28 W.Va. 412, this Court quoted from Basket v. Hassell, 107 U.S. 602, 2 S.Ct. 415, 27 L.Ed. 500, as follows: "A *donatio mortis causa* must be completely executed, precisely as required in the case of gifts *inter vivos* subject to be diverted by the happening of any of the conditions subsequent; that is upon actual revocation by the donor, or by the donor's surviving the apprehended peril, or outliving the donee, or by the occurrence of a deficiency of assets necessary to pay the debts of the deceased donor and if the gift does not take effect as an executed and complete transfer to the donee of possession and *title* either legal or equitable, during the life of the donor, it is a testamentary disposition, good only if made and proved as a will. * * *".

Demonstrating further that a valid *causa mortis* gift must be effective upon the delivery thereof and not in the future is the following statement in 38 C.J.S. Gifts § 99. "A bank deposit may be the subject of a valid gift causa mortis when the gift is fully executed by such a delivery as is sufficient to confer on the donee a present right to the fund. * * * The delivery must be as a gift in praesenti, and not for the purpose of making a future disposal of it under the directions of the donor."

Delivery of the gift by the donor is an essential element of a valid gift causa mortis, not the mere possession thereof by the donee. Such delivery must take place while the donor is alive. This is well illustrated by the language of Point 9 of the Syllabus of Dickeschied v. Bank, 28 W.Va. 340, which reads as follows: "If such actual delivery to the donee do not take place during the lifetime of the donor, the authority of such third person to deliver the gift is revoked by the donor's death; the property does not pass to the donee but remains in the donor, and goes to his executor or administrator."

Applying these principles to the Boggs letter in the instant case, we find that Mrs. Boggs requested the Guaranty National Bank, at some time in the future and if she should precede her sister in death, to "transfer both savings and checking accounts to my sister, Abbie Grace, on her presentation of certificate of my death". Here the intended donor directed the bank to transfer her funds to her sister, not at that time, but at some time in the future. This was not a present gift. It was to have no effect until after the death of the donor. Furthermore, the donor did not relinquish all dominion and control over the subject of the gift. In these circumstances the plaintiff was not the recipient of a fully executed and complete transfer of the funds. She obtained neither possession of such funds nor the means of gaining such possession at the time of the delivery of the letter. Mrs. Boggs, by her letter, did not confer upon the plaintiff a present right to the funds but merely gave directions as to the future disposition thereof.

In this posture the letter of April 29, 1962, which had no effect until after the death of the purported donor, was testamentary in character. It could not, therefore, constitute a valid gift *causa mortis*. Consequently, the subject letter, being neither a valid will nor a valid gift *causa mortis*, must fail in its endeavor to transfer the funds in the bank accounts to the plaintiff.

It is urged on behalf of the plaintiff that the words "if I should die *befor* my sister" are a mere restatement of one of the requirements of a valid gift *causa mortis* and therefore should not be considered such condition as would destroy the gift. While it is essential to the validity of this type of gift that the donor must predecease the donee, it is nonetheless essential that the donor make a present gift as discussed above. This was not done in this case.

The plaintiff further asserts that Mrs. Boggs, by her letter, did all that was required to perfect a gift *causa mortis* to the plaintiff. Although it appears that she did intend to convey the funds in her bank accounts to the plaintiff, such conveyance must have been accomplished in accordance with the methods prescribed by law. Mrs. Boggs could have effected such transfer by a lawfully executed will. She also could have made a gift of such funds by making a present transfer thereof. Mrs. Boggs did neither.

For the reasons stated herein, the judgment of the Circuit Court of Cabell County is reversed and the case is remanded to that court for such further proceedings, consistent with this opinion, as may be proper.

Reversed and remanded.

JACKSON v. STEINBERG

(1948) 186 Or. 129, 200 P.2d 376.

[Plaintiff, a chambermaid in a hotel owned by defendant, found eight one hundred dollar bills under paper lining of a dresser drawer in a room. She was cleaning the room at the time. She turned the money over to the defendant who attempted unsuccessfully to locate the true owner. The plaintiff then demanded the return of the money but he refused. The trial court gave a judgment for plaintiff. Defendant appeals.]

HAY, J. * * * Lost property is defined as that with the possession of which the owner has involuntarily parted, through neglect, carelessness, or inadvertence. [Citation.] It is property which the owner has unwittingly suffered to pass out of his possession, and of the whereabouts of which he has no knowledge. [Citation.]

Mislaid property is that which the owner has voluntarily and intentionally laid down in a place where he can again resort to it, and then has forgotten where he laid it. [Citations.]

Abandoned property is that of which the owner has relinquished all right, title, claim, and possession, with the intention of not reclaiming it or resuming its ownership, possession or enjoyment. [Citations.]

"Treasure trove consists essentially of articles of gold and silver, intentionally hidden for safety in the earth or in some secret place, the owner being unknown." Brown: Personal Property, sec. 13. The foregoing is a modern definition, sufficient for the purposes of the present discussion. Another is: "Money or coin, gold, silver, plate, or bullion found hidden in the earth or other private place, the owner thereof being unknown." Black, Law Dict. [Citations.]

From the manner in which the bills in the instant case were carefully concealed beneath the paper lining of the drawer, it must be presumed that the concealment was affected intentionally and deliberately. The bills, therefore, cannot be regarded as abandoned property. [Citation.]

With regard to plaintiff's contention that the bills constituted treasure trove, it has been held that the law of treasure trove has been merged with that of lost goods generally, at least so far as respects the rights of the finder. [Citations.] Treasure trove, it is said, may, in our commercial age, include the paper representatives of gold and silver. [Citation.]

The natural assumption is that the person who concealed the bills in the case at bar was a guest of the hotel. Their considerable value, and the manner of their concealment, indicate that the person who concealed them did so for the purposes of security, and with the intention of reclaiming them. They were, therefore, to be classified not as lost, but as misplaced or forgotten property [Citation], and the defendant, as occupier of the premises where they were found, had the right and duty to take them into his possession and to hold them as a gratuitous bailee for the true owner. [Citations.]

The decisive feature of the present case is the fact that plaintiff was an employee or servant of the owner or occupant of the premises, and that, in discovering the bills and turning them over to her employer, she was simply performing the duties of her employment. She was allowed to enter the guest room solely in order to do her work as chambermaid, and she was expressly instructed to take to the desk clerk any mislaid or forgotten property which she might discover. It is true that, in the United States, the courts have tended to accede to the claims of servants to the custody of articles found by them during the course of their employment, where the articles are, in a legal sense, lost property. [Citation.] * * * In the case at bar, however, the bills were not lost property. * * *

The position of the defendant in the case at bar is fortified by the fact that, as an innkeeper, he is under common law and statutory obligations in respect of the found bills.

* * *

Where money is found in an inn on the floor of a room common to the public, there being no circumstances pointing to its loss by a guest, the finder, even if an employee of the innkeeper, is entitled to hold the money as bailee for the true owner. [Citation.] It would seem that, as to articles voluntarily concealed by a guest, the very act of concealment would indicate that such articles have not been placed "in the protection of the house" (Brown: Personal Property, section 14), and so, while the articles remain concealed, the innkeeper ordinarily would not have the responsibility of a bailee therefor. Upon their discovery by the innkeeper or his servant, however, the innkeeper's responsibility and duty as bailee for the owner becomes fixed.

* * *

The plaintiff in the present case is to be commended for her honesty and fair dealing throughout the transaction. Under our view of the law, however, we have no alternative other than to reverse the judgment of the lower court. It will be reversed accordingly.

GARRISON GENERAL TIRE SERVICE, INC. v. MONTGOMERY

(1965) 75 N.M. 321, 404 P.2d 143.

COMPTON, J. On May 2, 1962, the plaintiff, a foreign corporation, commenced this action against the defendant in the district court of Lincoln County, New Mexico, to recover on a money judgment obtained in Texas. On the same date it filed an attachment bond, a writ of attachment and summons, and a notice of lis pendens describing, insofar as this appeal is concerned, a cabin situate on the E½ of Lot 2, Block "CC," Singing Pines Subdivision, Ruidoso, New Mexico. The Lincoln County Sheriff filed the notice of levy for record in the office of the Clerk of the District Court. * * *

On January 25, 1963, Kenneth Peeler intervened in the action alleging that the defendant executed to him a bill of sale to the cabin and its contents in Midland, Texas, on April 12, 1962, and that at the time of the levy of the writ of attachment the cabin was his separate property. * * *

The trial court entered a money judgment only in favor of the plaintiff. From a judgment entered in favor of the intervenor declaring him to be the owner of the cabin, the plaintiff appeals.

Appellant contends (a) that the cabin was real estate, and (b) that the cabin was a fixture, hence real estate, and that the doctrine of lis pendens applied. The facts may be summarized as follows: In October, 1960, the defendant executed his promissory note to the Midland 66 Oil Company, Inc., of which intervenor is an officer, in an amount in excess of $15,000.00, representing past indebtedness. Because this note was in default, and pursuant to prior negotiations between them, on April 12, 1962, the defendant executed to the intervenor a bill of sale to the cabin for $4,900.00, this amount being credited on his note as of that date. After its execution in Texas, the bill of sale was retained by the defendant for mailing to the county clerk of Lincoln County, New Mexico, where it was recorded on June 8, 1962. Thereafter it was sent to and received by the intervenor on June 12, 1962, at which time he had knowledge of the commencement of this action.

The land on which the cabin is situated has been for a number of years, and is now, owned by the Ruidoso Realty Company, Inc. It was leased to the defendant on July 14, 1960, for a term of 15 years. The unrecorded lease provided that upon either cancellation or expiration thereof the lessee, if all rentals due lessor had been paid, could remove all structures which had been placed on the premises by the lessee. The cabin rested on the land by means of pine posts or footing. It was wired and plumbed. At the time of the execution of the bill of sale the defendant agreed to assign his lease to the intervenor. On July 26, 1962, a new lease for 13 years, the remainder of time under the original lease, was entered into between Ruidoso Realty and intervenor. This was the lessor's usual procedure with respect to assignments of their leases.

The appellant bases his position that the cabin is real property upon two grounds. One, that it falls within the definition of real estate as that term is used in § 70–1–1, N.M. S.A., 1953 Comp., and two, that it is a fixture under the laws of this state.

Section 70–1–1, supra, provides:

"The term, real estate, as used in this chapter, shall be so construed as to be applicable to lands, tenements and hereditaments, including all real movable property."

The appellant asserts this definition clearly establishes that under our law the cabin in question is realty. This statute appears in the chapter dealing with conveyances and general provisions pertaining to real estate. We find no merit to appellant's first ground. In State ex rel. Truitt v. District Court of Ninth Judicial Dist., Curry County, 44 N.M. 16, 96 P.2d 710, 126 A.L.R. 651, we held that this section does not attempt to convert what was personal property at common law into real estate, but only to bring leasehold estates within the compass of the conveyancing statutes. [Citations.]

The appellant next contends that if the cabin is not real estate as that term is commonly employed or as used in the statutory definition, then it is a fixture under New Mexico law and should be treated as real estate. This contention likewise has no merit. This court has long subscribed to the three general tests to be applied in determining whether an article used in connection with realty is to be considered a fixture. First, annexation to the realty, either actual or constructive; second, adaptation or application to the use or purpose to which that part of the realty to which it is connected is appropriated; and, third, intention to make the article a permanent accession to the freehold. [Citation.] And, we have held that in determining whether personal property loses or retains its identity as a chattel by being placed on land, the general intention of the parties is a controlling factor. [Citations.] The case of Taylor v. Shaw, 48 N.M. 395, 151 P.2d 743, cited by the appellant, is distinguishable on the facts. There, the improvements were permanently annexed to the land, intended to be permanently enjoyed with the land, and those things not so permanently affixed were intended by the parties to be used and enjoyed in conjunction with the permanent fixtures.

The undisputed evidence is that the owner-lessor of the land and the defendant, the original lessee thereof, recognized the cabin in question as the personal property of the lessee and intended it to so remain, expressly providing in the lease for its removal upon the expiration or termination thereof. It is also undisputed that this had been the established practice of the community and of the owner-lessor for many years. Where the lessor and lessee expressly so agree, structures placed on leased premises by a lessee remain the personal property of the lessee. [Citations.]

* * *

The judgment should be affirmed. It is so ordered.

———

COX v. STATE FARM FIRE & CASUALTY CO.

(1966) 240 Ark. 60, 398 S.W.2d 60.

GEORGE ROSE SMITH, J. This is an action by the appellants upon a fire insurance policy issued by the appellee. The policy provided coverage of $10,000 upon the appellants' dwelling and $4,000 upon unscheduled personal property. The dwelling and its contents were damaged by fire in 1964. The insurer paid the full limit of its liability for unscheduled personal property and paid $5,220.-14 for damage to the dwelling.

The only item now in dispute is damage of $335.01 to a wall-to-wall carpet. The homeowners contend that the carpet was a fixture, so that its loss falls within the coverage upon the dwelling. The trial court held, however, that the carpet was personal property, for the loss of which the insurance company had discharged its maximum possible liability of $4,000.

All the facts were stipulated. When the plaintiffs bought the house the downstairs floors were covered with wall-to-wall carpeting that had worn out. About a month before the fire the plaintiffs moved this carpeting upstairs and replaced it with new carpeting downstairs. The new carpet was specially cut to fit the house; its effect in enhancing the value of the house was greater than its resale value. It was attached to the floor with tacks around the edges and could have been removed without damage to the house.

The hardwood floor under the carpet had been patched with unfinished boards. It was stipulated that the plaintiffs (if permitted to do so) would have testified: (a) That if they had removed the carpet to use the bare floor they would have relaid and refinished parts of the floor; (b) that in laying the carpet they meant for it to become part of the house; and (c) that if they should sell the house it would be their intention to sell the carpeting along with the building.

The case was tried by the court sitting without a jury. Even though there was an agreed statement of facts the court's judgment has the binding effect of a jury verdict if there were inferences and conclusions to be drawn from the stipulated proof. [Citation.] Thus the question is whether it must be said as a matter of law that the wall-to-wall carpeting was a fixture. In many cases we have held such an issue about an asserted fixture to be one for the jury. [Citations.]

Here the question was plainly one of fact. It is agreed that the carpeting could have been removed without any damage to the floors. Such ready removability supports the conclusion that the article is not a fixture. [Citation.] On the other hand, the carpeting was cut to fit this particular house —a circumstance that led the plaintiffs to regard it as so much a part of the dwelling that they would only have sold the house and carpeting as a unit. This determination on their part is clearly not conclusive of the issue. Bookcases, tables, cabinets, and other pieces of stationary furniture are often constructed to fit a particular wall or corner in a particular room. Nevertheless, if they merely stand in place without being permanently attached to the house they are certainly not fixtures as a matter of law, no matter how sincere the owner may be in his determination not to sell the house apart from such custom-built furniture.

Whether wall-to-wall carpeting is a fixture has been considered in a number of other states. The decided majority of the cases have concluded that such carpeting is not a fixture. [Citations.]

As an alternative argument the appellants contend that, regardless of its character as a fixture, the carpeting should be held to fall within this language in the insurance policy: "This policy covers: dwelling building described in the Declarations, including its additions and extensions, building equipment, fixtures and outdoor equipment pertaining to the service of the premises (if the property of the owner of the dwelling), while located on the premises of the described dwelling or temporarily elsewhere, and all materials and supplies on such premises or adjacent thereto incident to the construction, alteration or repair of such dwelling."

The appellants stress this part of the quoted clause: " * * * dwelling building described in the Declarations, including its * * * fixtures * * * while located on the premises of the described dwelling or temporarily elsewhere." It is argued that the reference to the "dwelling building" is in itself sufficient to encompass everything that is defined by the law as a fixture. Hence, the appellants insist, the further reference to "fixtures" indicates an intention on the part of the parties to refer to something in addition to what the law regards as a fixture. We are cited to the case of Cosgrove v. Troescher, 62 App.Div. 123, 70 N.Y.S. 764 (1901), where the court said that "carpets, window shades, and *gas fixtures* are movables, and not *fixtures*." (Emphasis supplied.)

This argument does not reach the situation presented here. It is true that one may refer, in everyday speech, to an electrical fixture or to a gas fixture without intending to employ the technical legal definition of a fixture. Hence if this case involved such a removable electrical or gas appliance the appellants' argument might be persuasive. But we are not aware of any usage in everyday speech that refers to a "carpet fixture" or to a "wall-to-wall carpet fixture." A carpet could at best be called a fixture only in the legal sense, and, as we have seen, the record does not compel us to reach that conclusion of fact.

Affirmed.

COBB, J., not participating.

PROBLEMS

1. A, being fatally ill in the Good Samaritan Hospital, told his nurse to take his wallet which contained $1,000 and hand it over to his friend B as a last gift. B came in later to see A, who was then unconscious. The nurse gave B the wallet as directed by A. A died without regaining consciousness. While walking down the hall to the elevator, the wallet slipped from B's pocket to the floor, where it was found a few minutes later by a doctor. B was never heard of again. The executor of A's will and the hospital demand the wallet from the doctor, each claiming title. Decision?

2. Decide each of the following problems.

(a) A chimney sweep found a jewel and took it to a goldsmith whose apprentice took the stone out and refused to return it. The chimney sweep sues the goldsmith.

(b) One of several boys walking along a railroad track found an old stocking. All started playing with it until it burst in the hands of its discoverer revealing several hundred dollars. The original discoverer claims it all; the other boys claim it should be divided equally.

(c) A traveling salesman notices a parcel of bank notes on the floor of a store as he is leaving. He picks them up and gives them to the owner of the store to keep for the true owner. After three years they have not been reclaimed, and the salesman sues the storekeeper.

(d) F is hired to clean out the swimming pool at the country club. He finds a diamond ring on the bottom of the pool. The true owner can not be found. The country club sues F.

(e) A customer found a pocketbook lying on a barber's table. He gave it to the barber to hold for the true owner who failed to appear. The customer sues the barber.

3. Jones had 50 crates of oranges about equally divided between grades A, B and C, grade A being the highest quality and C the lowest quality. Smith had 1000 crates of oranges, about 90 per cent of which were of grade A, but some of them grade B and C, the exact quantity of each being unknown. Smith wilfully mixed Jones's crates with his own so that it was impossible to identify any particular crate. Jones seized the whole lot. Smith demanded 900 crates of grade A and 50 each of grades B and C. Jones refused to give them up unless Smith could identify particular crates. This, Smith could not do. Smith brought an action against Jones to recover what he demanded or the value of the same. Judgment for whom, and why?

4. A, the owner and operator of Blackacre, decided to cease farming operations and liquidate his holdings. A sold 50 head of yearling Merino

sheep to B and sold Blackacre to C. He executed and delivered to B a bill of sale for the sheep and was paid $40 each for the 50 sheep. It was understood that B would send a truck for the sheep within a few days. At the same time, A executed a warranty deed conveying Blackacre to C. C took possession of the farm and brought along 100 head of his yearling Merino sheep and turned them into the pasture, not knowing the sheep A sold B were still in the pasture. After the sheep were mixed, it was impossible to identify the 50 head belonging to B. After proper demand, B sued C to recover the 50 head of sheep. Decision?

5. Smith indorsed his name and the name of his son John Jr. as assignee on the back of a certificate for 100 shares of the Smith Company. Smith told John of his generosity, but retained the certificate in his safe deposit box. Dividend checks uncashed were also placed in the box. The United States claims that income tax is due it from Smith on account of these dividends. Smith says his son owes the tax. Result of controversy?

6. A rented vacant lots from B for a filling station under an oral agreement and placed thereon a lightly constructed building bolted to a concrete slab and storage tanks laid on the ground in a shallow excavation. Later, a lease was prepared by A, providing that A might remove the equipment at the termination of the lease. This lease was not executed, having been rejected by B because of a renewal clause it contained, but several years later another lease was prepared which A and B signed. This lease did not mention removal of the equipment. At the termination of this lease A removed the equipment and B brought an action of replevin. What judgment?

7. A sold a parcel of real estate describing it by its legal description and making no mention of any improvements or fixtures thereon. The land had upon it a residence, a barn, a rail fence, a stack of hay, some growing corn, a wind mill; and the residence had a mirror built into the panel, a heating system consisting of a furnace and steam pipes and coils; in the house were chairs, beds, tables, and other furniture. On the house was a lightning rod. In the basement were screens for the windows. State which of these things passed by the deed and which did not.

8. Elmer Woods was the owner and operator of a large office building. He gave a mortgage upon the building to the State-National Bank which was promptly recorded. Subsequently, Woods purchased from the Cool Company an air conditioning unit to cool the entire building. The unit was installed in the basement and consisted of a large compressor and a blower to operate into the existing fresh air cooling system. The compressor and blower were attached to a concrete foundation in the basement. The air conditioning equipment was purchased under a conditional sales contract.

Woods defaulted in the mortgage payments to the State-National Bank but was not in default in his installment payments to the Cool Company. The bank foreclosed its mortgage upon the building and purchased the property at the foreclosure sale.

Upon default by Woods to the Cool Company, the Cool Company brought an appropriate action against the bank to recover the air conditioning equipment. Decision?

9. Abbott was a silversmith who enjoyed birdwatching. Belmont permitted Abbott to use his farm for this hobby. While engaged in birdwatching on Belmont's farm, Abbott discovered a buried chest containing silver bars of unknown origin, worth $1,000. Saying nothing to Belmont, Abbott appropriated the bars and, after months of labor, fashioned a chalice worth $5,000.

Subsequently, Abbott contracted a rare disease and, on being told that he might not recover, he called his grandson, Charles, to his bedside. Pointing to the chalice on the table by the bed, he said in the presence of the doctor: "Boy, you may have the chalice. Keep it to remember me by." Charles took the chalice and still has it.

Abbott recovered from the rare disease but he was so weakened that he died six week later from a heart attack. He never asked Charles to return the chalice but his will left all of his property to his widow, Anne. The chalice is now claimed by Anne, as executor and sole legatee under the will; by Belmont; and by Charles.

What are the rights of each?

10. A buys a house on installments, with the provision that on failure of payment, he may be declared in default, and a forfeiture declared. Before default, he had some storm doors put on the house, removable by merely lifting off the same hinges used for the screens in summer time. Has he a right to these doors if he forfeits his title?

CHAPTER 46

REAL PROPERTY—FREEHOLD ESTATES, FUTURE INTERESTS, LANDLORD AND TENANT

In general. Among all the variety of estates in real property the most valuable, generally speaking, are those which combine the enjoyment of immediate possession with ownership at least for life. These estates are either estates in fee simple of one form or another, or estates for life.

Fee Simple Estate. When a person says that he has "bought" a house or a corporation advises its shareholders that it has "purchased" an industrial site, the property is generally held in fee simple. That is, the property is owned absolutely (possibly subject to a mortgage) and it can be sold or passed on at will to heirs or successors. The absolute right of alienability and of transmitting by inheritance are basic characteristics of a fee simple estate. The estate signifies full dominion over the property. If estates are measured by the quantity of the rights possessed in the property the fee simple signifies the greatest quantity of possible rights.

At common law, specific language was essential in a deed or a will to create an estate in fee simple. If A wanted to pass absolute title to Blackacre to B he had to convey "to B *and his heirs.*" If A simply conveyed "to B," B had title only for his life. Even a deed "to B to have and hold forever" would not give B absolute title forever. Indeed, the desire of the feudal system to obstruct free and absolute alienation of land was so great it was said that the pronoun before "heirs" was essential to create a fee simple, and that "to B and heirs" was not enough. In nearly all jurisdictions, all such technicalities are now dispensed with. A fee simple is created by any words which indicate an intent to convey absolute ownership. "To

B in fee simple" will accomplish just that. "To B forever" means legally just what the grantor said. The general presumption is that a conveyance is intended to convey full and absolute title in the absence of a clear intent to the contrary.

A practical consequence of a fee simple title is that it may not only be voluntarily alienated but it also may be levied upon and sold at the instance of judgment creditors. A fee simple estate is subject to the dower rights of a wife.

Base or Qualified Fee Estate. It is possible to convey or will property to a person to enjoy absolutely, subject to being taken away if a certain event takes place. The estate thus created is known as a base or qualified fee. A may provide in his will that his widow is to have his house and lot in "fee simple forever so long as she does not remarry." If his widow dies without remarrying, the property is inherited as though she owned it absolutely since the condition did not take place. Such a condition was bound to occur, if at all, during the life of the taker of the property. A condition in a deed which conveys land "to A and if he dies without children then to revert" to the grantor and his heirs, must also occur, if at all, within A's lifetime. A limitation on a fee simple may, on the other hand, survive the life of the first taker. "To A until Birnam wood to high Dunsinane hill shall come," or "to A as long as no commercial buildings are erected thereon," imposes a qualification which limits the fee through subsequent purchasers from A.

Whether the qualification is of the first or second type, in the event of the occurrence of the qualifying event, the property will revert to the grantor or, if he is no longer alive, to his descendants. The limitation in either type of base or qualified fee followed any transfer by the taker during his lifetime. In effect, such limitations impose substantial restraints on the marketability of land. If land is left to A forever so long as she does not remarry, and A first sells the land to B and then remarries, B thereby loses his title to the land and it reverts to the heirs of the grantor.

Fee Tail. At one time, it was not uncommon to convey property to a person and his lineal descendants to the exclusion of his heirs in general. Thus, a conveyance instead of being "to A and his heirs" might read "to A and the heirs of his body", or, with greater restriction "to A and the heirs male of his body" or "to A and the heirs male of his body on Mary." Each of these estates was known as a fee tail and, in varying extent, narrowed the right of absolute inheritance characteristic of a full fee simple estate. If the grantee died without any heirs of the named class the property reverted to the grantor or his heirs. Such restraints were not popular. Fee tail estates have generally been abolished by statute. The usual statutory provisions automatically convert an attempted fee tail into a fee simple in the first taker ("A" in our examples), or into a life estate in the first taker with a remainder in fee simple to the next taker or takers. Thus, in the above examples A would either take a fee simple estate or a life estate with a remainder in fee simple to those members of the entail who are the next takers upon A's death.

Life Estates. By tradition, life estates are generally divided into two major classes, (1) conventional life estates or those created by voluntary act and (2) those established by law, the most significant example of which is a wife's dower right in the property of her husband.

(1) *Conventional Life Estates.* A grant or a devise "to A for life" creates in A an estate which terminates on his death. Such a provision may stand alone in which case the property will revert to the grantor and his heirs or, as is more likely, it will be followed by a subsequent grant to another party such as "to A for life and then to B and his heirs." A is the life tenant and B is generally described as the "remainderman." A's life may not be the measure of his life estate, as where an estate is granted "to A for the life of B." Upon B's death, A's interest terminates and, if A dies before B, A's interest passes to his heirs or as he directs in his will for the remainder of B's life.

No particular words are necessary to create a life estate. It is always a matter of determining the intent of the grantor.

Life estates arise most frequently in connection with the creation of trusts, a subject considered in Chapter 50. A man may leave his property upon death to trustees who are instructed to pay the income from the property to the widow during her life, and, upon her death, to distribute the property itself to the children. The widow has what is known as an equitable life estate. Or, a man may convey property to trustees who are instructed to pay the income therefrom to him during his life and, upon his death, to distribute it in a particular manner. The grantor has thereby reserved a life estate in the property to himself. Occasionally, life estates are created with the power given to the tenant to dispose of the proceeds as he may direct in his will. Thus, A may leave his property to trustees "to pay the net income to my wife during her life and to distribute the principal as she may direct in her will." Since the widow cannot dispose of the property during her lifetime, she does not enjoy a fee simple estate. Nevertheless, this "power of appointment" has important practical consequences. Under Federal estate tax law, a "marital deduction" up to fifty per cent of the value of the estate is allowed on all property left to the surviving spouse of the decedent. If, for example, a widow has only a life estate in a trust of $100,000 with the principal going to her children on her death, the marital deduction is not allowed as to the $100,000. If, however, she has also a power of appointment by will over the $100,000 it is said that she has a sufficient dominion over the property to qualify the gift for the marital deduction.

The other practical issue raised by a life estate relates to the rights and duties of the life tenant vis-a-vis the person who is entitled to the property at the end of the life estate. If a ranch is left "to A for life and on his death to B," certainly A cannot sell the ranch, but what limits are there upon his use of it? No over-all rule can be formulated but, as a general proposition, A may make such reasonable use of the property as is consistent with the right of B to receive it upon A's death in good condition. Failure to care properly for the property will constitute "waste." The failure to make repairs on a building, the unreasonable cutting of timber or the neglect of an adequate conservation policy may subject the life tenant to an action for damages by the person entitled to the property at the termination of the life estate. Where land is involved, a life tenant can generally use the property to the extent it was being used by the former owner. Similar problems arise where the property is in the form of securities. If A, the life tenant, has a right to the income during his life and B is to receive the securities outright upon A's death, there is a probability of a conflict of interests. A will want the capital invested in securities which realize a high return. B, on the other hand, is obviously concerned only that the capital be unimpaired when it passes to him. Since these two conditions are not usually found in the same investment, the opportunity for dispute is apparent. Where the property is under the direction of a trustee the attempt to maintain a reasonable balance between these two extremes is one of his most difficult tasks. In case of doubt, the safest policy is to protect the capital even at a sacrifice of the return to the holder of the life estate.

The life tenant is obligated to pay the general taxes on the property but he may demand contribution from the remainderman to pay any special assessment or tax which results in a permanent improvement.

A conveyance by the life tenant passes only his interest. The life tenant and the remainderman may, however, join in a conveyance to pass the entire fee to the property, or the life tenant may terminate his interest by conveying it to the remainderman.

(2) *Dower.* Dower is a life estate which a wife surviving her husband has in one-third of all the real property of the husband owned during the marriage. It arises by operation of law and exists irrespective of the intent or wishes of the parties. Property sold by the husband before his marriage is not subject to dower.

A valid marriage is, of course, prerequisite to dower. It is also essential that the wife survive the husband. Until the death of the husband, the wife's dower is contingent or "inchoate." During his life she cannot transfer or sell her dower interest. Since dower arises out of property of the husband which he owns at his death, it can only exist in fee simple estates or in an estate that, for practical purposes, is equivalent to a fee simple estate. There is no dower in a life estate since it is not an estate of inheritance. Likewise, although a widow has dower in property which the husband owned as a tenant in common, because each tenant's interest passes by inheritance, there is no dower in property held in joint tenancy since the survivor of the joint tenants is entitled to the entire property.

Although the widow does not realize her dower unless she survives her husband, her right in this respect is protected during the marriage. If the husband sells his property after he marries, the purchaser takes subject to the inchoate right of dower even though the purchaser did not know the seller was married. In a few States, by statute, this inability of the husband to bar dower during marriage has been modified but in no event is the husband permitted to convey his property for an inadequate consideration so as to defraud the wife of her dower. Generally, to bar dower during marriage, it is necessary that the wife expressly waive her dower and, since dower is an interest in land, such a release must be in writing. Generally, the husband is required to join in the release. In most jurisdictions, the wife can bar her dower simply by joining in a conveyance with her husband.

A common problem which arises upon the death of the husband is the relative priority of the widow's dower and the claims of creditors of the husband. Dower takes precedence over any claims against his estate which were not reduced to judgment or made a lien against his property before marriage. If property is mortgaged before marriage, or if the wife joins in a mortgage, the mortgage is superior to dower and, upon foreclosure after the husband's death, the widow will be entitled to dower computed only on the surplus over the amount of the lien. She has dower in the equity of redemption. If, however, the husband executes a mortgage in which the wife does not join she will be entitled to her one-third in the gross value of the property.

To this rule, the purchase money mortgage is an exception. A purchase money mortgage is a mortgage on property purchased either in whole or in part with the proceeds of the loan which it secures. Thus, H, husband, purchases a house from V, vendor, for $25,000. He pays $10,000 down and gives V a mortgage on the house for the balance. The mortgage is a purchase money mortgage. Again, H purchases a house from V for $25,000. H pays $25,000 which sum includes a $15,000 loan from First Bank secured by a mortgage on the house. First Bank's mortgage is a purchase money mortgage. The rule is that whether or not H's wife joins in the purchase money mortgage, the mortgage is superior to her dower rights.

The incidents of dower at common law have been substantially modified by statute in most jurisdictions and most particularly is this the case with respect to statutory alternatives to dower.

In some States, the widow may elect whether to take common-law dower or an alternative amount given her by statute. Under such statutes, the widow is given a period of time within which to elect between dower and her statutory portion. In many jurisdictions, dower has been abolished and a statutory share of the husband's property is substituted in lieu thereof. Under common law, the one-third life interest was to be taken out of each parcel of real property. By statute in some States, the total value of the widow's share may be taken out of one parcel. Not infrequently the present value of the dower right is paid in cash. This involves a computation of the present value of the widow's right to receive during her life one-third of the rents and profits of the husband's dowable property and requires reference to mortality tables to determine the life expectancy of the widow.

If the husband makes provision for the widow in his will he may intend his gift to be in lieu of dower. Even if the gift is clearly intended as an alternative to dower the widow still may elect whether to accept the gift or take dower.

Divorce generally bars dower although this is not the case in some States if the divorce is obtained by reason of the fault of the husband. It is possible to bar dower by antenuptial contract between the husband and wife if adequate consideration has been given the wife in exchange for her release and if she enters into the agreement with an understanding of the meaning of her rights to dower.

Curtesy. The surviving husband, at common law, had a life estate in the real property of his wife akin to, if not identical with, the widow's dower. This estate, known as curtesy, required a valid marriage and the death of the wife before the husband. It existed only in estates of inheritance. There was no curtesy in a life estate. Unlike dower, curtesy did not exist unless a child were born of the marriage. The child need not survive the wife. But, like dower, the wife could not alienate the husband's claim to curtesy without his written waiver. In many States, the estate of curtesy has been substantially modified or entirely abolished and in lieu thereof the husband is given a statutory share in the estate of his wife.

FUTURE INTERESTS

Introductory. Not all interests in property are subject to immediate use and possession even though the right and title to the interest are absolute. Thus, where property is conveyed or left by will "To A during his life and then to B and his heirs," B has a definite present *interest* in the property but he is not entitled to immediate *possession*. Such and similar rights are generically referred to as future interests.

Remainders. A remainder is an estate in property which will take effect in possession, if at all, upon the termination of a prior estate created by the same instrument. A gift to "A for his life and then to B and his heirs" creates a remainder in B. Upon the natural determination of the life estate, B will be entitled to possession as remainderman. A gift to A for 10 years and then to B will give B

an estate to use and possess *after* the occurrence of the event that terminates A's estate. B takes his title not from A but from the original grantor.

Thus, if H, in his will, provides that W, his wife, is to enjoy the income from property during her life and upon her death the property to go to the children, an inheritance tax is payable by the children upon the death of H on the computed value of their remainder interest but not upon the death of W because the transfer to the children is considered as coming from H, under his will, and not from W.

The primary classification of remainders has been into *vested* remainders and *contingent* remainders. Although many of the earlier technical distinctions relating to future interests have been abolished by statute, there are still important practical consequences resulting from the vested rather than the contingent character of a remainder. The tax incidence may vary according to the nature of a remainder.

(1) *Vested Remainders.* A remainder is vested when the only contingency to the possession by the remainderman is the termination of the preceding estate. When B has a remainder in fee, subject only to a life estate in A, the only obstacle to the right of immediate possession by B or his heirs is A's life. A's death, no more, no less, is sufficient and necessary to place B in possession. The law considers this vested remainder as a fixed *present* interest but to be enjoyed in the future. It is property just as much as the preceding estate in possession; and it is characteristic of a vested remainder that the owner of the preceding estate can do nothing to defeat the remainder. If X makes a will leaving securities to his wife, Y, "for her life and then to my daughter Z for her life and then to my nephew, A, and his heirs," upon the death of X, A has at that instant a vested remainder although it may be many years before he or his heirs will enjoy possession. If the re-

mainder is vested in fee simple the vesting does not depend upon the named remainder-man surviving the owner of the intervening estate. In 1961, X dies leaving his farm to Y for life and then to Z and his heirs. Two years later, Z dies and, in 1966, Y dies. The widows of X, Y and Z are all living in 1966 and are the only heirs-at-law of the three decedents. The farm will belong to the widow of Z since the remainder was vested in Z and his heirs at the death of X.

(2) *Contingent Remainders.* A remainder is contingent if the right to possession is dependent or conditional upon some event *in addition to* the termination of the preceding estate. The remainder may be conditioned upon the existence of some person not yet in being or upon the happening of some event which may never occur. A contingent remainder, by definition and unlike a vested remainder, is *not* ready to take immediate possession simply upon the termination of the preceding estate. A provision in a will "to A for life and then to his children but if he has no children then to B" creates contingent remainders both as to the children and as to B. If A marries and has a child, the remainder then vests in that child and B's expectancy is closed out. If A dies without having fathered a child, then and only then will an estate vest in B. It is, of course, possible for a contingent remainder to become vested while possession is still in the preceding life estate as evidenced by the birth of a child to A in the foregoing illustration.

A remainder may be contingent on some uncertain event. "To A for life and then to B and his heirs if B then be living in Chattanooga" will give B an estate only if he meets the condition. Under such a case, it is impossible to determine whether the remainder will be vested until the termination of the preceding life estate. A gift to X "until Y returns from Mexico and then to Z" is another illustration of a remainder (to Z) contingent upon an event which may never take place. It is

not always easy to decide whether a remainder is contingent or is actually vested "subject to being divested" by a condition subsequent. If X, by his will, leaves his property to his wife for her life with the power to dispose of it by her will but, in the absence of such disposition, to their children, he creates a vested remainder in the children upon the death of X, subject to being divested by the exercise of the power. To the uninitiated in technical rules of property this remainder to the children would seem just as "contingent" as any of the previous illustrations. The difference, however, between the less complex examples of vested and contingent remainders is clear. In one sense, both are contingent but there is an important distinction between the nature of the contingency. The grant "to A for life and then to B and his heirs" is contingent only as to the exact time when B will be entitled to possession. A grant "to A for life and then to B and his heirs if B is then a bachelor" is contingent upon the qualification of B, not just upon the death of A.

The Rule in Shelley's Case. At common law, in order to create a fee simple, it was necessary to follow a gift to A with the phrase "and his heirs." In an early English case, it was first held that the use of "heirs" not only was necessary to a fee simple but absolutely created a fee in A, regardless of the intention of the grantor. Thus, the grantor might intend to give only a life estate to A, with a remainder to whomever might be his heirs at his death. Under the Rule in Shelley's case, a conveyance to "A for life, remainder to the heirs of A," created a fee simple estate in A. The word "heirs" simply describes the estate given A and does not create any interest in his heirs except as they may take by inheritance if A does not dispose of the property during his life. In order to give A only a life estate, it was necessary to use a more explicit phrase such as "to A and then to his children," or "to A and then to his issue." Under a deed "to A and his heirs," the heirs took nothing by the conveyance. The arbitrary rule facilitated the alienability of property by vesting the full fee one generation earlier than would otherwise be the case but it was frequently and strictly applied in clear disregard of the grantor's intentions. In many States, the Rule in Shelley's case has been abrogated by statute, giving the first taker only a life estate with a remainder to whomever are his heirs on his death.

Reversions and Possibility of Reverter. Under the common law, the fee interest in property always had to be in someone. If A conveyed property "to B for life" and made no disposition of the remainder of the estate, A holds the reversion. This result is not as apparent when A conveys property "to B for life and then to my heirs." It is arguable that there is a remainder in the grantor's next-of-kin. The common-law doctrine, however, was that such a reference to the heirs of the grantor placed a reversion in *him*, and his heirs took nothing except as they might inherit the reversion. This technical rule has important practical consequences where it has not been changed by statute. It means that the reversion may be attached by the grantor's creditors or it may be sold by him or devised by his will and, in any of such events, his heirs receive nothing.

Assume that H devises a life estate in farm land to his wife, W "and then to the legal heirs of my body," and that he devises the residue of his estate to W. H and W had no children, and H died without heirs of his body. The remainder to H's unborn children being necessarily limited on an event which may happen before or after, or at or after, the termination of the particular estate was contingent. Since there was no one in being to take the remainder when H died, a reversion was created by operation of law. W took this reversion which H had devised to her.

A "possibility of reverter," as the phrase suggests, exists where property may return to the grantor because of the happening of an event upon which a fee simple estate was to terminate. It is the possibility of a reversion that is present in the grant of a conditional fee discussed in this chapter. Thus, A has a possibility of reverter if he dedicates property to a public use "so long as it is used as a park." If, in one hundred years, the city ceases to use the property for a park the persons who are the heirs of A will be entitled to the property. Unlike a reversion that is a present estate to be enjoyed in the future, a possibility of reverter is simply an expectancy.

The Rule Against Perpetuities. A contingent estate is void unless, by the terms of its creation, it must vest within a life or lives in being and twenty-one years thereafter. Its purpose is to encourage the easy transfer of property by prohibiting the clouding of the title with future interests dependent upon uncertain contingencies which may not take place for a long period of time. A gift in a will by C to the first son of B who reaches the age of 30 years is void if B had no son at the death of C because a son might be born who would not reach the age of 30 until longer than 21 years after B's death, B being the "life in being" under the rule. If, on the other hand, the gift had been to the first child of B who reaches 21 years of age the gift is valid since such an event must take place, if at all, within 21 years of B's death. A "life in being" may be anyone named by the donor and need not be connected in any way with the property. Any number of persons may be the lives in being as long as the death of the last survivor can be determined. Thus, a gift to the children of B who are living upon the death of the last survivor of the present living descendants of Queen Victoria is valid. The fact that it is probable the contingent gift will vest, if at all, within the required period is not enough to avoid the rule. The rule is a strict rule which is not always governed by what appears reasonable in view of general human experience.

Vested interests are not within the rule against perpetuities. If a future interest is vested it is not prohibited by the rule against perpetuities no matter how long it may be before the possession will be enjoyed. A grant to X for 999 years and then to Z and his heirs creates a present vested interest in Z and his interest is not therefore subject to the rule. Thus, in any problem of future interests, the first question is always: Is the gift vested? If it is vested, the rule against perpetuities has no application. If the future interest is not vested, the second question is: Must it vest, if at all, within a named life or lives in being and twenty-one years thereafter.

Accumulation of Income. The law does not favor the indefinite accumulation of income. If a trust were established whereby the trustees were to collect and reinvest the income forever without distributing it, an ad terrorem argument could be made that, eventually, enormous amounts of capital and resources would be concentrated in a few hands. As a consequence, in most States income cannot be accumulated for a period longer than a life or lives in being and twenty-one years. In other States, the law provides that the accumulation must be limited to one of four periods; namely, during the life of the donor, during twenty-one years after the death of the donor, during the minority of anyone who is living at the donor's death, or during the minority of a person who is entitled to the income.

LANDLORD AND TENANT

Introductory. A lease is both a contract and a grant of an estate in land. It is a contract by which the owner of the fee or of a lesser estate in land, the landlord, grants to another, the tenant, an exclusive right to use and possession of the land for a definite

or ascertainable period of time or term. The possessory term thus granted is an estate in land. The principal characteristics of this estate are that it continues for a definite or ascertainable term and that it carries with it the obligation upon the part of the tenant to pay rent to the landlord.

Creation of the Leasehold Estate. By statute, in most jurisdictions, leases for a term longer than a specified period of time must be in writing. This period is fixed at one year in some jurisdictions; in others it is three years.

Tenant's Obligation to Pay Rent. While the leasehold estate carries with it an implied obligation upon the part of the tenant to pay reasonable rent, the contract of lease almost always contains an express promise, known as a covenant, by the tenant to pay rent in specified amounts at specified times. There are several reasons for this. The most obvious is that, in the absence of such express covenant providing the amount of rental and the times for payment, the rent is a *reasonable* amount and is *payable only at the end of the term.*

Aside from the economic advantage of settling the amount of the rent without recourse to the courts and of obtaining its payment in stated installments, the tenant's express covenant to pay rent serves other useful functions.

Most leases contain a provision to the effect that breach by the tenant of any of his covenants in the lease will entitle the landlord to declare the lease at an end, and will give him the right to regain possession of the premises. The tenant's express undertaking to pay rent thus becomes one of the covenants upon which this provision can operate. At common law, where there is no such provision in the lease, the tenant's failure to pay rent when due gives the landlord only the right to recover a judgment for the amount of such rent; it gives him no right to oust the tenant from the premises. This is a direct result of the common-law doctrine that the mutual covenants in a lease are independent of one another, unless the lease contains an express provision to the contrary. If the tenant breaches his covenant to pay rent, or fails to perform any of the other covenants in the lease, the landlord is not thereby relieved of his covenant to provide the tenant with quiet enjoyment of the premises. While the landlord at common law could successfully maintain against the tenant an action for breach of contract, he could not treat that breach as an excuse for non-performance by the landlord.

In many jurisdictions today the foregoing rule has been changed by statute, to the extent that the landlord is given a right to dispossess the tenant for non-payment of rent although there is no provision for this in the lease. However, such statutes give the landlord a meaningful remedy only where the lease contains an express covenant to pay rent in stated installments or in advance. Rent which is not expressly made payable in advance or in stated installments becomes payable only at the end of the term.

Termination of the Tenant's Obligation to Pay Rent

Assignment of the Lease. The implied obligation to pay reasonable rent, because it arises in and out of the leasehold estate, ceases as soon as the estate is transferred by assignment. Thus, when the tenant assigns a lease which does not contain an express agreement to pay rent, the implied obligation to pay reasonable rent passes to the assignee. This is not true where the lease contains an express agreement of the tenant to pay rent. The tenant remains liable under this express covenant despite the fact that he has assigned the leasehold estate to another, unless the landlord releases him from the obligation. The assignee is also liable to the landlord for the stipulated rent. Note that the assignee of a lease which contains an express covenant to pay rent is li-

able for the *stipulated* rent—not for the reasonable rent. This result is obtained under the theory that certain covenants in the lease, of which the covenant to pay rent is one, *run with the land*. Such covenants pass to and obligate the assignee of the lease as if they were attached to the land covered by the lease. Covenants which have this quality of "running with the land" are covenants which "touch and concern" the land. The idea of covenants "touching and concerning" the land is an old one and is not easy of application. The following covenants have been held to "touch and concern" the land and thus to "run" with it: covenants to pay rent, covenants to pay taxes, options to renew, options to purchase, covenants to repair and restore, and covenants to keep the premises insured but only if coupled with covenants to repair and restore.

Under this doctrine, the covenant to pay rent passes to and obligates the assignee of the lease so long as he remains in possession of the leasehold estate. Although the assignee of the lease is thus bound to pay rent, the original tenant is not relieved of his contractual obligation to pay rent. Should the assignee fail to pay the stipulated rent, the original tenant will have to pay it. He will, of course, have a right to be reimbursed by the assignee.

Absent specific restrictions in the lease, leases are freely assignable. Many leases, however, prohibit assignment without the landlord's written consent. If the tenant assigns without such written consent, the assignment is not void, but it may be avoided by the landlord. If, however, the landlord accepts rent from the assignee he will be held to have waived the restriction. The restriction, once waived, cannot be revived by the landlord upon subsequent assignments.

Sublease. A sublease differs from an assignment in that it involves the transfer, by the tenant to another, of less than all the tenant's rights in the lease. For example,

T, is a tenant under a lease which is to terminate on December 31, 1972. He enters into an agreement with S L, captioned "Assignment of Lease." The agreement provides that T "hereby assigns all his right, title and interest in the above lease to" S L, for a stated sum of money, and provides further that S L "undertakes to pay the rent reserved in the lease" to T's landlord and that if S L fails to do so "then and in that event T reserves the right to reenter the said premises." Most courts hold that even though this agreement is labeled "Assignment of Lease," T has not, in fact, assigned the lease but has merely subleased. The reason is that T has reserved a right of re-entry, that is, he has in fact transferred less than his whole interest in the lease. Most subleases are easily recognizable as such. The typical sublease would arise in the foregoing example if T leased the premises to S L for a shorter period than that covered by his own lease, e. g., until December 30, 1972, at a stated rental payable to T—not to T's landlord.

The legal effects of a sublease are entirely different from those of an assignment. In a sublease the sublessee, S L in the example, has no obligation to T's landlord. S L's obligations run solely to T, the original tenant. T is not relieved of any of his obligations under the lease. The doctrine that certain covenants run with the land has no application to a sublease. Thus, T's landlord has no right of action against T's sublessee S L, under any covenants contained in the original lease between him and T, because that lease has not been assigned to S L. T, of course, remains liable for the rent reserved, and upon all of the other covenants of the lessee, in the original lease between him and his landlord.

Effect of Destruction of the Premises upon the Tenant's Obligation to Pay Rent

The dual character of a lease as a contract and as a grant of an estate in land is particularly evident when we consider the common-law rule governing the destruction of the premises by fire or other fortuitous cause.

Where the tenant leases property together with a building and the building is destroyed by fire, or other fortuitous cause, the common law does not relieve him of his obligation to pay rent nor does it permit him to terminate the lease. The reason for this rule is that the common law regards the tenant's obligation to pay rent as given in exchange for the *estate* in land. The "estate" is a possessory term. The concept of an estate at common law is divorced from the economic benefits which go with it. Thus, while the destruction of a building may very well deprive the tenant of the entire economic benefit of his lease, the common law does not permit him to argue that the destruction of the building in fact amounted to a destruction of his "estate."

The common-law rule has been modified in some States by statute, e. g., New York Real Property Law, § 227, and in most States it is not applied to tenants who occupy only a portion of the building and have no interest in the building as a whole, e. g., apartment tenants. Most courts take the view that it would be stretching the concept of an "estate" too far to say that a tenant occupying a few rooms in a house is left with his "estate" in return for which he must pay rent, despite the total destruction of the building or his rooms.

Most leases contain clauses covering the fortuitous destruction of the premises. A typical clause provides that, upon damage by fire or other fortuitous cause, the landlord will repair and restore, and that if the premises are wholly untenantable the tenant's obligation to pay rent will be suspended until the premises are restored, but that if the landlord decides to demolish and reconstruct the premises the lease will terminate.

This standard clause has several disadvantages to the business tenant. If the landlord elects to repair, the tenant remains bound under the lease although his business may be suspended long enough to cause a substantial loss of profit. Moreover, the tenant remains liable for the full rent if the premises, though partially destroyed, are not "wholly untenantable."

Effect of Public Controls and Condemnation upon Tenant's Obligation to Pay Rent. This subject is dealt with more fully in Chapter 49. A tenant proposing to make a particular business use of the premises should be careful to check the applicable zoning ordinances before he enters into a lease. An existing zoning ordinance prohibiting the very use which the tenant has in mind when he enters into the lease will not relieve him of the obligation to pay rent. An exception may be made, however, in the case where the lease specifically restricts the tenant's use to a use which is subsequently outlawed by a zoning ordinance. In such cases, the doctrine of commercial frustration is frequently applied by the courts to relieve the tenant of his obligations under the lease. A recent decision goes so far as to hold that an existing zoning restriction, prohibiting the very use to which the property was expressly limited under the terms of the lease, does not relieve the tenant of his obligations under the lease.

Total condemnation of the fee in the premises for public use terminates the lease and relieves the tenant from all obligations under it. Partial condemnation, however, does not relieve the tenant from his obligation to pay rent. For example, where T leases an office building for five years, and, in the first year a portion of the building is condemned for the construction of a road, T must continue to pay full rent to his landlord for the remainder of the term. He is entitled, however, to so much of the condemnation award as represents the rent he would be required to pay to the landlord for the portion con-demned for the remainder of the term. Because this computation has the tendency to exhaust a substantial portion of the condemnation award, landlords prefer to insert a clause in the lease providing for a proportionate reduction of the rent, reserving to themselves the right to claim the entire condemnation award.

Effect of Eviction upon the Tenant's Obligation to Pay Rent

(a) *Dispossession by Landlord for Breach of Covenant.* When the tenant breaches one of the covenants in his lease, such as the covenant to pay rent, and the landlord evicts or dispossesses him pursuant to an express provision in the lease or under statute authorizing him to do so, the lease is terminated. Because the breach of the covenant to pay rent does not involve any injury to the premises and because the landlord's action in evicting the tenant terminates the lease, the tenant is not liable to the landlord for any future installments of the rent after such eviction. However, most long term business leases contain a "survival clause" providing that the eviction of the tenant for non-payment of rent will not relieve him of liability for damages measured by the difference between the rent reserved in the lease and the rent the landlord is able to obtain upon a reletting. Such a survival clause alone is not adequate protection to the landlord. It has generally been held that, because the tenant's liability is one in damages, the landlord is not entitled to sue him until the day on which the lease would have terminated if it had not been broken. This could mean that the landlord would have to wait twenty years to recover damages if that was the unexpired term of the lease. For this reason, landlords, in addition to inserting the "survival clause" mentioned, also insert a clause to the effect that the damages recoverable under it will accrue "at such times as the rent would have accrued under this lease." Such provisions have been upheld by the courts.

(b) *Wrongful Abandonment by Tenant.* If the tenant wrongfully abandons the premises before the expiration of the term of the lease and the landlord re-enters the premises or relets them to another, a majority of the courts hold that the tenant's obligation to pay rent terminates. The landlord, if he desires to hold the tenant to his obligation to pay rent, must either leave the premises vacant, or he must have available in the lease another "survival clause" covering this situation. Such survival clauses generally provide that, upon wrongful abandonment by the tenant, the landlord may relet the premises "as agent for the tenant;" and that the tenant will remain liable to the landlord for the difference between the rent reserved in the lease and the rent obtained upon such reletting minus costs of reletting. Under such a clause the tenant remains liable for the rent, the lease is not terminated as in the case of eviction, and the landlord may sue him on the dates when installments of rent become due and payable under the original lease.

(c) *Wrongful Eviction by Landlord.* If the tenant is wrongfully evicted by the landlord his obligations under the lease are terminated. The landlord is bound to provide for the tenant quiet and peaceful enjoyment. This duty arises by implication, and is known as the landlord's covenant of "quiet enjoyment." It is the only covenant in a lease which, if breached, has the effect of terminating the lease without any express provision to this effect. The landlord breaches this covenant whenever he wrongfully evicts the tenant. He is also regarded as having breached this covenant if the tenant is evicted by someone having a better title than the landlord. The landlord is not responsible, however, for the wrongul acts of third parties unless they are done with his assent and under his direction.

(d) *The Doctrine of Construcive Eviction and the Landlord's Obligations.* Absent express provisions in the lease, the landlord, under the common law, has few obligations to his tenant. At the inception of the lease he must give the tenant a right to possession, but, under the majority rule, he is not required to give the tenant actual possession. Thus, if the previous tenant wrongfully holds over and refuses to move out, the landlord must bring dispossession proceedings to oust him, but he is not responsible to the new tenant for the delay thus occasioned and the new tenant is not relieved of the obligation to pay rent from the inception of his lease. The tenant who fears that such a situation may arise may guard against it in the lease by inserting a provision that, if through no fault of his own, he is kept out of possession, his obligation to pay rent will be suspended. It is wise, also, to provide that if the delay is longer than a specified time the lease shall become void.

Once the tenant enters into possession the landlord may not do anything to disturb him in that possession but he is not responsible for the wrongful acts of others unless done by his direction or with his consent.

Unless there is a specific undertaking in the lease, the landlord is under no obligation to maintain the premises in a tenantable condition or to make them fit for any purpose. There is an exception to this rule in the case of furnished apartments. Where the lease is of a furnished apartment, the majority of the courts hold that the landlord must maintain it in a tenantable condition.

In a few States there are statutes requiring landlords, specifically apartment landlords, to keep the premises fit for occupation. Zoning ordinances and health and safety regulations may also impose certain duties upon the landlord.

In the absence of an express provision in the lease, or statutory duty, no obligation rests upon the landlord to repair or restore the premises. The landlord does have, however, a duty to maintain, repair, and keep in safe condition, those portions of the premises which remain under his control.

While, at common law, the landlord is under no duty to repair, restore, or keep the premises in a tenantable condition, he may and often does assume those duties in the lease. When he does, the question presents itself whether breach by him of any of his undertakings under the lease entitles the tenant to abandon the premises and refuse to pay rent. Unless an express provision in the lease gives the tenant this right, the common law gives him only an action for damages. The reason for this rule is the same as the reason for the rule that a landlord has no right to dispossess the tenant for the breach of any of his covenants. The common law regards the mutual covenants in the lease as independent of one another. Thus, a breach by the landlord of any of his covenants does not operate to excuse the tenant from the duty to abide by his covenants, and vice versa. The only exception to this rule, noted earlier, is the landlord's covenant for quiet enjoyment.

In some States, statutes have changed this rule in favor of the landlord by giving him a right to evict the tenant for non-payment of rent. In practice, most leases contain express provisions giving the landlord the right to evict the tenant for breach of any of his covenants. Very few leases, however, give the tenant a correlative right. The inequality manifest in this situation has led the courts to develop the doctrine of *constructive eviction.* Under this doctrine, a failure by the landlord in any of his undertakings under the lease, which causes a substantial and lasting injury to the tenant's beneficial enjoyment of the premises, is regarded as being, in effect, an eviction of the tenant. Under such circumstances, the courts permit the tenant to abandon the premises and thereby terminate the lease.

The Obligation to Repair and Restore. The tenant is under no duty to make any repairs to the demised premises, unless the lease expressly so provides. He is not obliged to repair or restore substantial or extraordinary damage occurring without his fault, nor to repair damage caused by ordinary wear and tear. If damage occurs, the tenant continues to pay rent and to enjoy the use of the unrepaired premises.

The landlord, likewise, is under no duty to repair and maintain premises which he has wholly leased to another, unless the lease expressly so provides. However, he is under a duty to repair and maintain any portion of the premises which remain under his control. For example, an apartment house owner who controls the stairways, elevators and other common areas is liable for their maintenance and repair and is responsible for injuries occurring as a result of his failure to do so. In respect to apartment buildings, the presumption obtains that any portion of the premises which is not expressly leased to the tenants remains under the landlord's control. Thus, the landlord, in such cases, is liable to make external repairs, including repairs to the roof.

In some States and in many cities, the duties of certain types of landlords, particularly the lessors of units in apartment buildings or multiple dwellings, are regulated by statute and local ordinances, and those duties may include keeping the apartments in good repair.

The obligations to repair and to restore the premises are usually covered by the provisions of the lease. A tenant's covenant to "repair" has been interpreted by the majority of the courts as including an obligation to restore the premises after destruction by fire or other fortuitous cause. The same result has been reached in the case of the landlord's covenant to "repair." A tenant or landlord who does not wish to undertake such a duty should be careful to qualify his duty to "repair" with the clause "reasonable wear and tear or damage by the elements excepted." Care should be taken when using printed forms to avoid any ambiguity on this point. Failure to do so sometimes presents the situation of a lease, which contains a standard clause dealing with destruction by fire or other fortuitous cause, coupled with a provision requiring the tenant to "repair" and ending with a clause "at the expiration of this lease the tenant shall return the premises in as good condition as they now are, reasonable wear and tear or damage by the elements excepted." While the standard clause dealing with destruction by fire and requiring the landlord to restore, is not inconsistent with the final clause, the clause requiring the tenant to "repair" without qualification is obviously inconsistent with the other two. Such oversights in draftsmanship usually lead to litigation.

Expiration of the Lease

Definite Term. A lease for a definite term expires at the end of the term by virtue of its own limitation. No notice to terminate is required.

Periodic Tenancy. A periodic tenancy is a definite term to be held over and over in indefinite succession. To illustrate, a lease "to T from month to month" or "from year to year" creates a periodic tenancy. Periodic tenancies arise frequently by implication. L leases to T without stating any term in the lease. This creates a tenancy at will, discussed in the next section. If T pays rent to L at the beginning of each month, and L accepts such payments, most courts hold that the tenancy at will has been transformed into a tenancy from month to month. A periodic tenancy may also arise where the tenant holds over after the expiration of his lease. A periodic tenancy may be terminated by either party at the expiration of any one period but only upon adequate notice to the other party.

A periodic tenancy may be terminated by either party at the expiration of any one pe-

riod but only upon adequate notice to the other party. In the absence of express agreement in the lease, the common law requires six months' notice in tenancies from year to year. However, this period has been shortened in some jurisdictions by statute. In periodic tenancies involving periods of less than one year, the notice required at common law is one full period in advance, but, again, this may be subject to regulation by statute.

Tenancy at Will. A lease containing a provision that either party may terminate at will creates a tenancy at will. So does a lease which does not specify any duration. At common law such tenancies were terminable without any notice but many jurisdictions now have statutes requiring a notice to terminate, usually thirty days.

Tenancy at Sufferance. One who is in possession without a valid lease is a tenant at sufferance. The most common case of a tenancy at sufferance arises when a tenant fails to vacate the premises at the expiration of the lease. A tenant at sufferance is technically a trespasser and the landlord owes him no duties except to the extent that, under the common law, no landowner has a right wilfully to injure a trespasser.

Holdover Tenant. A tenant who fails to vacate the premises when his lease expires, whether by its own limitation or by notice, is a tenant at sufferance—a technical trespasser. The common law gives the landlord the right to elect either to dispossess such tenant or to hold him for another term. If the expired lease was one for a year or more, or from year to year, the landlord can hold the holdover tenant for another full year. If the expired lease was for less than a year, or from month to month, the landlord can hold the holdover tenant for another full month. In the absence of express agreement, the holdover tenancy is a periodic tenancy, that is, it must be terminated by proper notice. The strict common-law rule is that the landlord may elect to hold the tenant for another full period regardless of the fact that the tenant's failure to vacate on time was wholly without fault. Most courts today attempt to avoid this result if at all possible, and the rule has not been applied where the tenant's holdover is for a comparatively short time and is due to sickness or death of one of the members of his household.

If the landlord decides not to hold the tenant for another full term, he may dispossess him. Furthermore, if the tenant's failure to vacate is wilful, by statute in many jurisdictions, the landlord is given the additional right to double the rent for the period during which he was kept out of possession by the tenant's wilful failure to vacate the premises.

The statutory right to sue a wilful holdover tenant for double rent and the common-law right to hold the holdover tenant for an additional term are mutually exclusive, and the landlord must elect between them.

CASES

GRIFFIN v. MOON

(1965) 238 Ark. 692, 384 S.W.2d 243.

HOLT, J. This case requires the interpretation of a will. The appellees instituted an action against the appellants seeking specific performance of their written agreement to purchase certain realty. The appellants' refusal to purchase was based upon their assertion that appellees did not have a merchantable title because of the ambiguous terms in a will devising the property to the appellees. The chancellor decreed specific performance of appellants' contract to purchase the lands. On appeal appellants' sole contention is that the trial court erred in finding that appellees' title to the land in question is marketable.

The appellants argue that the correctness of the decision of the chancellor depends upon the construction of a portion of the will which reads as follows:

"I give all the residue of my estate comprising a farm of twenty-four (24) acres and one lot, where I now reside, in Miller County, State of Arkansas, after fulfilling the foregoing legacies, to my wife, with the remainder thereof on her decease or marriage, to my said children and their children, respectively, share and share alike".

The testator was survived only by his widow, Maggie J. Moon, and his four sons, Ivor, Erbert, Loy and Fred Moon. These parties and the wives of the four sons are the appellees. The testator's widow is living and has never remarried. Each of his sons now has children, however, his sons had no children when the testator died. The appellants reject the title as unmarketable upon the contention that the remainder interest does not finally vest in the testator's children until the death or remarriage of the life tenant, the testator's widow. Further, that the testator's grandchildren, born and unborn, eventually would be entitled to an interest as remaindermen. We do not agree with the appellants and find no merit in either contention.

The real issue to be determined is whether the testator's four sons, the appellees, took a vested or contingent remainder upon the death of their father. If they took a vested remainder, then they can join with their mother, the life tenant, and convey a merchantable title; if they took only a contingent remainder, then they cannot. [Citation.] We are of the view that the questioned provisions of the will created a vested remainder in the testator's sons upon his death.

In the early case of Booe v. Vinson, 104 Ark. 439, 149 S.W. 524, we said:

"It is also a well-established principle that the law favors the vesting of estates, and, in the absence of a contrary intention of the testator appearing from the will, the estate will vest at the time of his death; and if a will is susceptible of a dual construction, by one of which the estate becomes vested, and by the other it remains contingent, the construction which vests the estate will be adopted."

In McKinney v. Dillard & Coffin Co., 170 Ark. 1181, 283 S.W. 16, the devise involved principles applicable to the case at bar. In that case the father devised realty to his daughter for her natural life and at her death the lands were devised to her children in equal portions and if at the time of her death "any of her children be dead, leaving children, then such child or children is to have the same interest in said lands that said parent would have had, if alive." In that case we held that the remainder vested in the daughter's children as soon as born and before the death of the daughter. Further, that such vested interest, upon partition of the lands by the consent of the life tenant and vested remaindermen, was subject to a valid and enforceable mortgage. [Citations.]

In the very recent case of Gibson v. Lowry, 235 Ark. 234, 357 S.W.2d 531, we held that where a will gave a life estate to the testator's mother and stepfather and provided that at their death the farm should vest absolutely in the testator's brother, a vested remainder and not a contingent remainder was created in the brother. There we said that the interest vested "at the same instant and by the same grant as the life estate" and that although "the enjoyment of the possession of this interest was postponed until the termination of the life estate, still this right, * * * was presently fixed, and was in no wise dependent upon the happening of any event. [Citation.]"

Thus, in the case at bar, appellants' contention that under the terms of the will the remainder is not vested in the testator's four sons until the death or remarriage of the life tenant is without merit. We hold that the testator's four sons now have a vested re-

mainder and it is not subject to the happening of any future event. Their remainder interest vested at the same time that the life estate vested. [Citations.]

It is well settled that where both the life tenant and vested remaindermen join in a deed the entire estate in fee is passed to the grantee. Therefore, it follows that in the case at bar a deed by the appellees conveys a merchantable title.

The decree of the chancellor ordering specific performance of the contract is affirmed.

MILLER v. ROGERS

(1965) 246 S.C. 468, 144 S.E.2d 485.

Bussey, J. This action sought construction of the last will and testament of Winston J. Rogers, as well as certain incidental relief. The appeal is from an order of the circuit court, confirming the construction given to said will by the special referee. No question of incidental relief is here involved.

The testator, a resident of Darlington County, was apparently possessed of a substantial estate, though the total value of such estate does not appear in the record. He died testate on October 5, 1932, his will being dated September 30, 1929. Testator was twice married, having by this first wife six children and by his second wife none. In 1929, when his will was executed, five of his children were still living; one, Neva Rogers Garden, had died on November 12, 1912, leaving surviving her an only child, J. D. Garden. On the date of the will, testator's second wife, Mary D. Rogers, was fifty years of age. Testator's age does not appear in the record, but other facts therein would clearly indicate that testator was considerably older than his second wife. In his will he made substantial, though not equal, provision for each of his children, as well as his grandson, J. D. Garden, and his wife Mary D. Rogers. All of testator's children living at the time of the execution of the will were still living at the time of his death, but between that date and the death of his widow, Mary D. Rogers, in January 1962, three more of his children died, one of them childless and unmarried.

The instant controversy arises out of item II of the will which reads as follows:

"I give, devise and bequeath unto my beloved wife, Mary D. Rogers, my plantation on which I now reside, containing 245 acres, more or less, for and during the term of her natural life and at her death, I direct that said plantation be sold by my Executors, or the survivor of them, hereinafter named and the proceeds of said sale to be divided between my living children and the children of any deceased child, share and share alike."

It is contended by the respondents, and was held by the lower court, that under the foregoing language the children of the testator living at the date of his death and his grandson, J. D. Garden, took a vested interest in remainder in the proceeds of the sale of the tract of land in question. Under that construction either a per capita or per stirpes distribution of the proceeds would reach the same result.

The appellants contend that this construction is incorrect; that the children of the testator living at his death took only a contingent remainder, as opposed to a vested remainder, and that it was the intention of the testator that the proceeds be divided, on a per capita basis, between his children who were still living upon the death of the life tenant and the children of any deceased child or children of the testator.

The conclusion of the special referee was predicated, primarily though not solely, on the rule that the law favors the vesting of estates at the earliest time possible, not inconsistent with the intent of the testator. This rule was stated and discussed, correct-

ly we think, in Faber v. Police, 10 S.C. 376, 386, as follows:

"Questions of this kind are involved in no little difficulty and uncertainty, owing mainly, as we think, to the efforts which the Courts have made to construe limitations so as to constitute vested instead of contingent remainders, the rule being, as stated by Kent (4 Com. 203), that 'the law favors vested estates and no remainder will be construed to be contingent which may, *consistently with the intention,* be deemed vested.' This rule, by its very terms, admits, as it should do, the paramount importance of the intention of the testator which must necessarily override every other rule and be the governing principle, otherwise the Court instead of the testator would make the will." (Emphasis added.)

It is fundamental and well established in this state that, while there are certain rules of construction to be followed in seeking the intent of a testator, they are all subservient to the paramount consideration of determining what was meant or intended by the terms used in the will, the cardinal rule of construction being to ascertain and effectuate the intention of the testator, unless that intention contravenes some well settled rule of law or public policy.

It seems to us the controlling question here is what the testator meant by the terms "my living children" as used in item II of his will. The testator used the word "living" to qualify the word "children", and the conclusion of the referee apparently did not fully take into consideration the intent or meaning of the quoted words, as used by the testator.

* * *

While the modifying word here is "living" rather than "surviving", we think that the two terms are equivalent, at least in the context here used, and applying the rationale of the Roundtree decision [Roundtree v. Roundtree,] 26 S.C. 450, 2 S.E. 474, to the language of the instant case, it would appear that the testator intended that his children who were to share in the proceeds of the remainder would be only those children who were living at the death of the life tenant, and hence, his children, at the time of his death, did not take a vested remainder interest.

Here, * * * the language used could appertain to only one of three dates: the date of the will, the death of the testator, or the death of the life tenant. The first date is clearly excluded here because the testator included in the division "the children of any deceased child", and on the date of the will he had only a single grandson by a predeceased child. If the testator intended the second period, the date of his death, the word "living" would have been surplusage, * * *. If he intended his children living at the date of his death to take a vested interest immediately, he did not need to use the modifying word "living" and would have accomplished that result by the use of the word "children", without any modifying adjective. Here, the testator's mind was directed to the division of that portion of his estate which, according to his scheme, could not possibly take place until some future, indefinite time, and while his mind was so directed to that period, he used the term "my living children."

The disposition thus apparently intended and made by the testator is, we think, not at all unreasonable or unnatural in view of the facts of the instant case and the scheme of testator's will as a whole. As pointed out above, he was substantially older than his wife and he was making substantial provision for each of his children living at the time of the will, as well as his grandson by a predeceased daughter. When the testator considered disposing of the remainder interest in the real estate here involved, it should be borne in mind that the greater portion of his estate was being otherwise finally disposed of by the terms of his will. In view of the normal life expectancy of his wife,

her life tenancy in the tract of land would not likely terminate for quite a number of years. Testator could not know which, if any, of his children might still be living at that probably distant date, and, under these circumstances, we think it not at all unnatural that he should conclude that the proceeds of the ultimate, but probably distant, sale of the tract of land should be divided, share and share alike, between those of his children who might, perchance, then still be living, and the children of any deceased child or children.

For the foregoing reasons, we think that the conclusion of the referee, to the effect that the children of the testator, living at the time of his death, took a vested interest in remainder, is erroneous and not in accord with the intent of the testator. We conclude that under a proper construction of the will the proceeds of the sale of the tract of land should be equally divided on a per capita basis between such of the children of the testator as were living upon the death of the life tenant and the children of the deceased children of testator.

The judgment of the lower court is, accordingly, reversed and the cause remanded for further proceedings consistent with the views herein expressed.

Reversed and remanded.

SELLERS v. ARCHER

(1961) 8 Ill.2d 371, 134 N.E.2d 264.

HERSHEY, C. J. This appeal from the circuit court of Cook County raises a narrow future interest question—whether the grant of a life estate to an unmarried boy of 15, with remainder over to "the heirs of his body," violates the rule against perpetuities.

The issue arose on complaint for partition by certain collateral heirs of Frost Sellers, the testator. They asked the court to construe the following provisions of his will and to declare void the remainder interests therein created:

"Second: I give, devise and bequeath unto my stepdaughter, Hazel Tabb Jackson, now past the age of her majority and married, a life estate in and to all of my property real, personal and mixed.

"Third: I give, devise and bequeath unto my stepdaughter, Hazel Tabb Jackson, the premises known and described as: [here the legal description of two parcels was inserted], for her natural life and at her death to James Phil Robinson, her son, for his natural life, and at his death, to the heirs of his body."

At the time of the testator's death in August, 1953, the beneficiaries, Hazel Tabb Jackson and James Phil Robinson, were living, the latter then being 15 years old and unmarried.

On motion of defendant Hazel Tabb Jackson, the trial court dismissed the complaint.

The plaintiffs' position on this appeal is summarized in the following quotation from their brief: "A grant of a life estate to an unmarried boy of 15, with remainder over to 'the heirs of his body,' is void in that it violates the rule against accumulation and the rule or statute against *perpetities,* for the reason that at the time the estate was created —the date the will was admitted to probate— he had no 'heirs of his body' and the likelihood of the estate not vesting within a life or lives in being and 21 years thereafter is great, for he may never marry and consequently will never have any 'heirs of his body.' "

As regards the plaintiffs' reference to the rule against accumulations, it is sufficient to note that neither clause of the will requires any income to be accumulated. Hence, there obviously could be no violation of the statute against accumulations.

Nor is there a violation of the rule against perpetuities. The remainder interests will vest, if at all, no later than the death of a life in being, James Phil Robinson. But the plaintiffs speculate that "he may never marry and consequently will never have any 'heirs of his body.' " That possibility has no bearing upon the application of the rule against perpetuities. Indeed, in every case where the interest is not presently vested, there is some uncertainty as to whether it will ever become vested. The rule against perpetuities is designed merely to insure that the vesting in title, if and when it happens, takes place within the time fixed by the rule.

For the reasons stated, the action of plaintiffs in asking for partition was premature, and the trial court properly dismissed their complaint. [Citation.]

The decree of the circuit court of Cook County is affirmed.

Decree affirmed.

ERNST v. CONDITT

(1965) 54 Tenn.App. 328, 390 S.W.2d 703.

CHATTIN, J. Complainants, B. Walter Ernst and wife, Emily Ernst, leased a certain tract of land in Davidson County, Tennessee, to Frank D. Rogers on June 18, 1960, for a term of one year and seven days, commencing on June 23, 1960.

Rogers went into possession of the property and constructed an asphalt race track and enclosed the premises with a fence. He also constructed other improvements thereon such as floodlights for use in the operation of a Go-Cart track.

We quote those paragraphs of the lease pertinent to the question for consideration in this controversy:

"3. Lessee covenants to pay as rent for said leased premises the sum of $4,200 per annum, payable at the rate of $350 per month or 15% of all gross receipts, whether from sales or services occurring on the leased premises, whichever is the larger amount. The gross receipts shall be computed on a quarterly basis and if any amount in addition to the $350 per month is due, such payment shall be made immediately after the quarterly computation. All payments shall be payable to the office of Lessors' agent, Guaranty Mortgage Company, at 316 Union Street, Nashville, Tennessee, on the first day of each month in advance. Lessee shall have the first right of refusal in the event Lessors desire to lease said premises for a period of time commencing immediately after the termination date hereof.

*   *   *   *   *   *

"5. Lessee shall have no right to assign or sublet the leased premises without prior written approval of Lessors. In the event of any assignment or sublease, Lessee is still liable to perform the covenants of this lease, including the covenant to pay rent, and nothing herein shall be construed as releasing Lessee from his liabilities and obligations hereunder.

*   *   *   *   *   *

"9. Lessee agrees that upon termination of this contract, or any extensions or renewals thereof, that all improvements above the ground will be moved at Lessee's expense and the property cleared. This shall not be construed as removing or digging up any surface paving; but if any pits or holes are dug, they shall be leveled at Lessors' request."

Rogers operated the business for a short time. In July, 1960, he entered into negotiations with the defendant, A. K. Conditt, for the sale of the business to him. During these negotiations, the question of the term of the lease arose. Defendant desired a two-year lease of the property. He and Rogers went to the home of complainants and negotiated an extension of the term of the lease which resulted in the following amendment to the lease, and the sublease or assignment of the lease as amended to Conditt by Rogers:

"By mutual consent of the parties, the lease executed the 18th day of June 1960,

between B. Walter Ernst and wife, Emily H. Ernst, as Lessors, and Frank G. Rogers as Lessee, is amended as follows:

"1. Paragraph 2 of said lease is amended so as to provide that the term will end July 31, 1962 and not June 30, 1961.

"2. The minimum rent of $350 per month called for in paragraph 3 of said lease shall be payable by the month and the percentage rental called for by said lease shall be payable on the first day of the month following the month for which the percentage is computed. In computing gross receipts, no deduction or credit shall be given the Lessee for the payment of sales taxes or any other assessments by governmental agencies.

"3. Lessee agrees that on or prior to April 1, 1961, the portion of the property covered by this lease, consisting of about one acre, which is not presently devoted to business purposes will be used for business purposes and the percentage rent called for by paragraph 3 of the original lease will be paid on the gross receipts derived therefrom. In the event of the failure of the Lessee to devote the balance of said property to a business purpose on or before April 1, 1961, then this lease shall terminate as to such portion of the property.

"4. Lessee agrees to save the Lessor harmless for any damage to the property of the Lessor, whether included in this lease or not, which results from the use of the leased property by the Lessee or its customers or invitees. Lessee will erect or cause to be erected four (4) 'No Parking' signs on the adjoining property of the Lessor not leased by it.

"5. Lessor hereby consents to the subletting of the premises to A. K. Conditt, but upon the express condition and understanding that the original Lessee,

Frank D. Rogers, will remain personally liable for the faithful performance of all the terms and conditions of the original lease and of this amendment to the original lease.

"Except as modified by this amendment, all terms and conditions of the original lease dated the 18th day of June, 1960, by and between the parties shall remain in full force and effect.

"In witness whereof the parties have executed this amendment to lease on this the 4 day of August, 1960.

> B. Walter Ernst
> Emily H. Ernst
> Lessors
> Frank D. Rogers
> Lessee

"For value received and in consideration of the promise to faithfully perform all conditions of the within lease as amended, I hereby sublet the premises to A. K. Conditt upon the understanding that I will individually remain liable for the performance of the lease.

"This 4 day of Aug, 1960.

> Frank D. Rogers
> Frank D. Rogers

"The foregoing subletting of the premises is accepted, this the 4 day of Aug, 1960.

> A. K. Conditt
> A. K. Conditt."

Conditt operated the Go-Cart track from August until November, 1960. He paid the rent for the months of August, September and October, 1960, directly to complainants. In December, 1960, complainants contacted defendant with reference to the November rent and at that time defendant stated he had been advised he was not liable to them for rent. However, defendant paid the basic monthly rental of $350.00 to complainants in June, 1961. This was the final payment received by complainants during the term of the lease as amended. The record is not clear whether defendant continued to operate the business after the last payment of rent or abandoned it. Defendant, however, remained in possession of the property until the expiration of the leasehold.

On July 10, 1962, complainants, through their Attorneys, notified Conditt by letter the lease would expire as of midnight July 31, 1962; and they were demanding a settlement of the past due rent and unless the improvements on the property were removed by him as provided in paragraph 9 of the original lease; then, in that event, they would have same removed at his expense. Defendant did not reply to this demand.

On August 1, 1962, complainants filed their bill in this cause seeking a recovery of $2,404.-58 which they alleged was the balance due on the basic rent of $350.00 per month for the first year of the lease and the sum of $4,200.-00, the basic rent for the second year, and the further sum necessary for the removal of the improvements constructed on the property.

The theory of the bill is that the agreement between Rogers, the original lessee, and the defendant, Conditt, is an assignment of the lease; and, therefore, defendant is directly and primarily liable to complainants.

The defendant by his answer insists the agreement between Rogers and himself is a sublease and therefore Rogers is directly and primarily liable to complainants.

* * *

The Chancellor found the instrument to be an assignment. A decree was entered sustaining the bill and entering judgment for complainants in the sum of $6,904.58 against defendant.

Defendant has appealed to this Court and has assigned errors insisting the Chancellor erred in failing to hold the instrument to be a sublease rather than an assignment.

To support his theory the instrument is a sublease, the defendant insists the amendment to the lease entered into between Rogers and complainants was for the express purpose of extending the term of the lease and obtaining the consent of the lessors to a "subletting" of the premises to defendant. That by the use of the words "sublet" and "subletting" no other construction can be placed on the amendment and the agreement of Rogers and the acceptance of defendant attached thereto.

Further, since complainants agreed to the subletting of the premises to defendant "upon the express condition and understanding that the original lessee, Frank D. Rogers, will remain personally liable for the faithful performance of all the terms and conditions of the original lease and this amendment to the original lease," no construction can be placed upon this language other than it was the intention of complainants to hold Rogers primarily liable for the performance of the original lease and the amendment thereto. And, therefore, Rogers, for his own protection, would have the implied right to re-enter and perform the lease in the event of a default on the part of the defendant. This being true, Rogers retained a reversionary interest in the property sufficient to satisfy the legal distinction between a sublease and an assignment of a lease.

*   *   *

As stated in complainants' brief, the liability of defendant to complainants depends upon whether the transfer of the leasehold interest in the premises from Rogers is an assignment of the lease or a sublease. If the transfer is a sublease, no privity of contract exists between complainants and defendant; and, therefore, defendant could not be liable to complaints on the covenant to pay rent and the expense of the removal of the improvements. But, if the transfer is an assignment of the lease, privity of contract does exist between complainants and defendant; and

defendant would be liable directly and primarily for the amount of the judgment. [Citations.]

The general rule as to the distinction between an assignment of a lease and a sublease is an assignment conveys the whole term, leaving no interest nor reversionary interest in the grantor or assignor. Whereas, a sublease may be generally defined as a transaction whereby a tenant grants an interest in the leased premises less than his own, or reserves to himself a reversionary interest in the term.

The common law distinction between an assignment of a lease and a sublease is succinctly stated in the case of Jaber v. Miller, 219 Ark. 59, 239 S.W.2d 760:

"If the instrument purports to transfer the lessee's estate for the entire remainder of his term it is an assignment, regardless of its form or of the parties' intention. Conversely, if the instrument purports to transfer the lessee's estate for less than the entire term— even for a day less—it is a sublease, regardless of its form or of the parties' intention."

*   *   *

In Southern R. Company v. Bacon, 128 Tenn. 169, 159 S.W. 602, it is said:

"Contracts must be construed with reference to the situation and surroundings of the parties, the nature of the business in which they are engaged and to which the contract relates, and also with reference to the subject-matter."

It is our opinion under either the common law or modern rule of construction the agreement between Rogers and defendant is an assignment of the lease.

*   *   *

It results the assignments are overruled and the decree of the Chancellor is affirmed with costs.

WILLIAMSON v. GRIZZARD

(1965) 215 Tenn. 544, 387 S.W.2d 807.

WHITE, J. The complainants, appellants here, in his case are the Trustees and the Manse Committee of the Cumberland Presbyterian Church at Goodlettsville. The appellees, defendants below, are two of the heirs at law of R. W. Grizzard and wife, Annie E. Grizzard, as well as some of the heirs at law of L. Hinton Grizzard and wife, Elizabeth Grizzard. The unknown heirs of both R. W. Grizzard and wife, and L. Hinton Grizzard and wife were made parties defendant to the suit.

This suit concerns a provision of a deed by which, many years ago, R. W. Grizzard and wife conveyed certain described property to the Cumberland Presbyterian Church at Goodlettsville. The provision reads as follows:

"To have and told [and to hold] said lot with the improvements and everything pertaining thereto to the said church forever. Provided the following conditions are complied with, said lot of land with improvements thereon is to be used by said church as a parsonage and to be known as L. Linton [Hinton] and Elizabeth Grizzard Memorial Parsonage. Should said property cease to be needed as a parsonage for said Church, said property may be rented or leased and the proceeds realized therefrom may be applied to the support of a pastor or pulpit supply for said church. Should said property be used for any other purpose than above specified or should it cease to be used for the purposes above specified for a period of five consecutive years, then this conveyance to said church will be null and void and title to said property will become vested in the heirs at law of the said L. Hinton Grizzard, deceased, or their legal representatives."

The bill alleges that the property in question had been used for a church manse or parsonage for many years. The church parsonage had previously been located in a residential area, however, it is now surrounded by purely commercial property which makes it unsuited for the intended use, i. e., a church manse.

Appellants seek to have the property sold free of the aforesaid provision with the express understanding that the proceeds of the sale be re-invested in another manse or parsonage for the Goodlettsville Cumberland Presbyterian Church to be known as the L. Hinton and Elizabeth Grizzard Memorial Parsonage, which new parsonage would be located in a more desirable residential district, the deed to such parsonage to contain the same provisions as to reversion as does the deed in question.

A demurrer was filed to the bill by the appellees (defendants), which was sustained by the chancellor. * * *

Errors to the action of the chancellor have been assigned which present the basic question for our determination, i. e., whether, in light of the habendum provision of the deed, the law permits the sale of the described land with its restrictions and reversionary interests, and the subsequent reinvestment in a new tract of land which would be used for the same purposes and contain the same reversionary interests which the present deed contains.

It is the well accepted rule in this State that in attempting to determine the estate conveyed in a deed, we must examine the deed to determine the intention of the parties, or in this case the intention of the grantors. [Citations.]

We think it is clear that the intention of the grantors in this case was to give their property to the church so long as it was used for church purposes and, then, when not so used, the property was to revert to the grantors, or their heirs. The language of the deed is that

" * * * should said property be used for any other purpose than above specified

* * * then this conveyance to said church will be null and void and title to said property will become vested in the heirs at law of the said L. Hinton Grizzard, deceased, or their legal representatives."

Thus, it appears that the deed by which the described property was conveyed did not create an absolute title in fee simple. The provisions of the deed clearly show that the church's estate was and is limited, and might be termed a determinable fee or fee simple on condition subsequent, both of which estates are recognized by the property law of this State. [Citations.]

Of course, the result is the same in this case whether the estate created constituted a determinable fee or a fee simple on condition subsequent. If the deed created a determinable fee, it left in the heirs of the grantors a possibility of reverter. If it conveyed a fee simple on condition subsequent, it left in the grantors a right of re-entry. The only distinction between the two future interests is, in a determinable fee, upon the happening of the condition, the grantee's estate automatically terminates and the entire fee simple title reverts to the grantors or their heirs. If the estate created is a fee simple on a condition subsequent, some act of re-entry on the part of the grantors or their heirs is necessary upon the happening of the condition, to re-vest title in the grantors or their heirs. [Citation.]

It is the contention of the appellants that under their proposal the conditional aspects of the habendum clause of the deed would not be disregarded or ignored. The proposal is merely to substitute a new parcel of land which would have the same conditions and reversionary interests as the original deed. Thus, so the appellants reason, the grantors' charitable purpose could be fulfilled and at the same time the appellants would retain their reversionary interests in a tract of land of equal value.

* * *

Our interpretation of the grantors' intent is that they wished the church to use the land so long as it had a use for it, and then desired thereafter that their heirs receive the benefit therefrom. It appears from the bill that the described land may have served its usefulness to the church, and we conclude that the heirs should receive the land in accordance with the clear, intent and wish of the grantors, provided, of course, the church fails to use the land for the purposes specified in the deed.

We think the chancellor was eminently correct in relying on the case of Mountain City Missionary Baptist Church v. Wagner, 193 Tenn. 625, 249 S.W.2d 875, in sustaining the demurrer. In that case the grantor conveyed to the trustees of a church certain property to be used for church purposes, with a clause limiting the estate in much the same language as is found in the case at bar. The trustees of the church filed a bill to eliminate the condition of the deed so that the church might erect a new building and borrow money thereon. The Court held the estate created was a determinable fee, refused to overlook the conditional limitations of the deed.

* * *

We think the above case is controlling in this matter. Appellants, however, seek to distinguish this case contending that it is not their intention to destroy the possibility of reverter, but merely to sell the present land and re-invest in other property and to which the reversionary interests of appellees would be transferred.

Appellants' position is untenable. The practical effect of such a plan would be to severely limit the reversionary rights of the appellees. And also, the reversionary interest of the appellees was created in the particular tract of land described in the deed. A substitute parcel of land might be much less desirable to them in the event of an exercise of the reversionary rights, and it would be an obvious usurpation of the appellees' rights to permit the substitution.

Likewise, if the law allows the substitution, the church might, in subsequent years, sell and re-invest again, and again. In so doing, the probability of the appellees coming into their reversionary interests would be greatly reduced, if not done away with.

Such reasoning, in effect, would be to completely ignore the conditional aspect of the deed, and we are unwilling to do so. The intention of the grantors is clear and should not be deviated from. If the property ceases to be used for the purposes set forth in the deed, then the property reverts to the heirs of the grantors as expressly provided in the deed.

The chancellor is affirmed.

LEO v. SANTAGADA

(1964) 45 Misc.2d 309, 256 N.Y.S.2d 511.

FISCHLER, J. Plaintiffs-tenants and defendant-landlord entered into a lease for the basement apartment in defendant-landlord's building. The building contained two other apartments. On the 5th day of August, 1964, plaintiffs-tenants moved into said premises at 10 P.M. with their child. The husband, one of the plaintiffs, left to purchase some groceries. He returned at 10:45 P.M. whereupon he testified that he saw approximately twelve (12) cockroaches. His wife testified that while her husband was gone she did not see any cockroaches. Upon his return at 10:45 P.M., the plaintiff-tenants claim they saw the roaches and took their child and left the premises. They seek by way of a constructive eviction to recover the deposit of $35.00.

As a general rule, the presence of great numbers of rats, vermin, and other like pests, or the stench or discomfort caused by them in a building rented to several tenants, where the landlord retains control—may constitute such a nuisance as to justify a tenant in abandoning the demised premises. [Cita-

tions.] However, the intolerable condition must be such that the tenant neither caused nor can cope with it in his own portion of the premises. [Citations.]

Every deprivation of the beneficial enjoyment of the demised premises does not necessarily amount to a constructive eviction. The deprivation must be "substantial and effectual." Bromberger v. Empire Flashlight Co. (S Ct BxCo. 1930) 138 Misc. 754, 246 N.Y.S. 67. If the acts complained of, can be readily remedied by the tenant, it has been held that such acts are not sufficiently material as to constitute a constructive eviction. [Citations.] A tenant would not be justified in vacating premises because on some particular occasion he was deprived of their beneficial enjoyment by an act of omission or commission on the part of the landlord. He would, however, if such act continued or were persisted in for an unreasonable time. [Citation.]

If a tenant is able to show that, during his occupation, his landlord was guilty of affirmative acts causing a nuisance, of a nature dangerous to life or health and against which the tenant is remediless by the performance of any acts called for by his own covenants this is evidence of a constructive eviction. [Citation.]

The landlord may create a nuisance from stench arising upon the landlord's property and because of the landlord's repeated neglect. If through the fault of the landlord, the premises are rendered unfit for occupation, the tenant is justified in abandoning them. [Citation.]

The law is well settled, the condition must be such that the tenant neither caused or can cope with it. The landlord must also have the opportunity to remedy the situation. The plaintiff-tenants made no attempt to help themselves by using what an ordinary housewife would use under the same circumstances nor did they notify defendant-landlord to afford him an opportunity to remedy the situation.

Decision for defendant-landlord.

Defendant has interposed by way of counterclaim an action for balance due on rent, which was set at $75.00 for said premises.

The law as it relates to contracts is well settled. "The law" said Pound, J., "wisely imposes upon a party subjected to injury from the breach of a contract the active duty to make reasonable efforts to render the injury as light as possible." Losei Realty Corp. v. City of New York (1930) 254 N.Y. 41, 47, 171 N.E. 899, 902.

However, it is well established that the usual obligation in the law of contracts to reduce damages has no application to a contract of leasing, and a landlord is under no obligation or duty to his tenant to relet, or attempt to relet, abandoned premises in order to minimize his damages. [Citations.] If the landlord does relet, after the tenants' abandonment, without the tenants' express or implied consent to relet on his behalf, such reletting may operate as a surrender by operation of law, and thereby release the tenants from further liability for the balance of the rent. "It is a well-established principle that the right to relet after abandonment by the tenant rests in contract, and does not flow from the mere relation of landlord and tenant. * * * The rule, applicable to certain classes of contracts, requiring a party complaining of a breach to minimize the resultant damage, has no applicability to contracts of lease. * * * He may accept or refuse to accept the surrender, but, if he relets without the sanction of an agreement, the tenant cannot be held liable for future rent." Gaffney v. Paul (AT 1819) 29 Misc. 642, 644, 61 N.Y.S. 173, 174.

In the instant case the court finds that the plaintiffs have surrendered said premises and the defendant-landlord had accepted same by reletting within 5 days from said surrender thereby relieving the plaintiffs from further liability for future rent.

Plaintiffs' motion to dismiss the counterclaim granted on the law.

LANGEMEIER, INC. v. PENDGRAFT

(1965) 178 Neb. 250, 132 N.W.2d 880.

FLORY, J. This is an action by plaintiff, Langemeier, Inc., a corporation, against defendant Robert Pendgraft to recover unpaid rent on two gasoline stations in Norfolk, Madison County, Nebraska. Both leases provided for fixed monthly rentals and in addition thereto defendant was to pay for gasoline sold by him, which was purchased from the plaintiff, every week. One of the stations operated 24 hours a day. The defendant admitted owing plaintiff certain sums of rent and gasoline payments but denied that he was in default when the action was commenced due to plaintiff's previous course of conduct in accepting late rental payments, and cross-petitioned against the plaintiff for damages for wrongful eviction by plaintiff. A jury trial was had. After the evidence of both parties was adduced the trial court directed a verdict for plaintiff and against the defendant for the amount admittedly owing by defendant and submitted the defendant's cross-petition against the plaintiff to the jury. The jury returned a verdict for defendant against the plaintiff for damages. Plaintiff moved for judgment notwithstanding the verdict on defendant's cross-petition or in the alternative for a new trial. From the order overruling that motion this appeal was taken by plaintiff.

Evidence adduced by both plaintiff and defendant was undisputed that defendant was chronically late in monthly rental payments; that in late January or early February, 1963, Roy Langemeier, president of plaintiff, had told defendant he would like to have the rent caught up; that during the night of February 27, 1963, defendant left the city of Norfolk taking with him his automobile, a motorcycle, some clothes, a case of oil, some of his tools, and $500 from his business; and that he told no one where he was going but told his wife he would be gone for a week or 10 days. Defendant's wife testified that she expected him back the next day and when he did not return, she contacted the county attorney; and on March 4, 1963, reported him as a missing person to the Nebraska Highway Patrol, subsequently making several inquiries as to its success in locating him. On February 28, 1963, plaintiff learned of the situation and that night took possession of the stations without objection, and filed this action on March 1, 1963. No word was had of or contact made with the defendant until March 19, 1963, when a telephone contact was made in the State of Illinois. Defendant was also indebted to Roy Langemeier, president of plaintiff and his wife in the approximate amount of $2,600 which was secured by a chattel mortgage on equipment. Defendant's wife had taken care of the books of the business but had not worked around the stations. Defendant testified that he intended to return and that he did not worry about the stations too much.

"Where the tenant has actually abandoned the premises, the landlord is entitled to reënter and take charge and possession; and, even where he acts too hastily, *but in good faith and under circumstances justifying a belief that the premises have been abandoned*, he is guilty only of a technical violation of the tenant's contractual rights under the lease. The question of whether a lease has been abandoned so as to confer a right of reëntry is one of fact to be determined from the acts and intentions of the parties." (Emphasis supplied.) 52 C.J.S. Landlord and Tenant, § 717, p. 581.

* * *

Considering the facts and circumstances of this case we hold that there was an abandonment by the defendant so that the plaintiff was within its rights in making a reëntry and taking possession of the stations; and that the trial court should have sustained plaintiff's motion for judgment notwithstanding the verdict on defendant's cross-petition. The judgment is therefore affirmed as to the directing of a verdict for plaintiff against the defendant and reversed in accordance with the above holding, and the cause remanded with directions to the trial court to dismiss defendant's cross-petition.

Affirmed in part, and in part reversed and remanded.

PROBLEMS

1. Under the will of X, a farm was devised to Y, to have and to hold for and during his life and upon his death to Z. Y went into possession on the death of X. Some years thereafter, oil was discovered in the vicinity. Y thereupon made an oil and gas lease and the oil company set up its machinery to commence drilling operations. Z thereupon filed suit to enjoin the operations. Assuming an injunction to be the proper form of remedy, what decision?

2. George Cook conveyed Blackacre, as follows:

"I convey and warrant to my daughter, Jane Cook, and her bodily heirs and assigns forever, all of the following described premises [legal description]."

When the deed was delivered, Jane Cook was seven years of age. Later George Cook died, at which time Jane was married and the mother of two children. After her father's death, another child was born to Jane. Subsequently, Jane conveyed all of her right, title and interest in the premises to Brooks. Brooks now contends that he is the owner in fee simple of the premises. After the conveyance to Brooks, a fourth child was born to Jane.

Determine and explain the estate created by the conveyance and the interests, if any, of the children in the premises.

3. S owned Blackacre in fee simple. In section 3 of a properly executed will, S devised

Blackacre as follows: "I devise my farm Blackacre to my son D so long as it is used as a farm." Sections 5 and 6 made testamentary gifts to persons other than D. The last and residuary clause of S's will provided: "All the residue of my real and personal property not disposed of heretofore in this will, I devise and bequeath to the A B C University."

S died in 1966, survived by his son D. S's estate has been administered. D has been offered $100,000 for Blackacre if he can convey title to it in fee simple.

What interests in Blackacre were created by S's will?

4. By his validly executed will John Stone provided: "I give and bequeath to my son, Ray Stone, my farm known as Blackacre to have and enjoy the use thereof during his natural life and upon his death said real estate shall be divided in equal parts among his children." Ray Stone, recently married to a young wife, survived his father as did the only children of his first marriage, Jack and Jill, 22 and 24 years of age, respectively.

Shortly after the probate of John Stone's will had been completed, Ray and his two children had an opportunity to sell Blackacre to William Todd provided they could grant a fee simple title. Can they convey a fee simple title?

5. By the seventh section of his will, validly executed, Guy Golden directed that his seven farms be sold and the proceeds placed in a "fund from which my grandchildren are to receive an education as high as their abilities may acquire" and that "each of them are to share alike". Golden was survived by two married daughters, an unmarried daughter and a married son, their ages and those of their spouses ranging from 21 to 34 years. Each of the married couples had one child. Golden hoped for and expected other grandchildren.

The executors of Golden's will brought an appropriate action to construe section 7 of the will. Decision?

6. John Brown died testate. His will provided, in part, as follows: "I give, devise and bequeath to my wife, Mary Brown, the full use and control of the following described real estate (describing it) during her natural life, to use and occupy as she sees fit. At the death of said Mary Brown, said lands are to be equally divided among our children, Elizabeth Brown, George Brown

and Henry Brown." Subsequent to the death of the testator and prior to the death of the widow, George Brown died intestate, leaving him surviving as his sole heir-at-law a son, William. After the death of the widow, Mary Brown, the son of George Brown, William, claimed that, as heir to his father, he was entitled to one-third of the estate under the will of John Brown. Henry and Elizabeth claimed that William was not entitled to anything under the will because his father George did not survive the widow, Mary Brown. Discuss the relative rights of the parties.

7. On September 1, 1963, A, the owner of a 160-acre farm leased it to B. The terms of the lease provided that the lease should continue from year to year and could be terminated upon a 60-day notice. B remained in possession for three years, paying the agreed rental. A desired to terminate the lease and, on June 1, 1966, gave the required 60-day notice to B, that he had elected to terminate the lease at the end of the tenant year, being September 1, 1966. On June 15, 1966, B planted a corn crop, cultivated the same and on September 1, 1966, delivered possession of the premises to A. On October 1, 1966, B returned to harvest the matured corn crop and was prevented from entering the land by A. B brought an action against A for the value of his share of the corn crop.

What decision?

8. A leased a house to B from May 1, 1965, to April 30, 1966, at $200 per month. On April 10, 1966, A told B that if he wished to renew the lease, the rent would be $220 a month. B, without signing a new lease, remained in possession after April 30, 1966, and now contends that inasmuch as A failed to give him 60 days' written notice, he is entitled to remain in possession for another year at $200 per month. Is B correct?

9. A leased to B for a term of ten years beginning May 1, 1965, certain premises located at 527–529 Main Street in the city of X. The premises were improved with a 3-story building, the first floor being occupied by stores and the upper stories by apartments. On May 1, 1966, B leased one of the apartments to C for one year. On July 5, 1966, a fire destroyed the second and third floors of the building. The first floor was not burned but was rendered untenantable. Neither the lease from A to B, nor the lease from B to C contained any provision in regard to the fire loss. Discuss the liability of B and C to continue to pay rent.

10. Ames leased an apartment to Boor at $150 a month payable the last day of each month. The term of the written lease was from January 1, 1965, through April 30, 1966. On March 15, 1965, Boor moved out, telling Ames that he disliked all the other tenants. Ames replied: "Well, you are no prize as a tenant; I probably can get more rent from someone more agreeable than you." Ames and Boor then had a minor physical altercation in which neither was injured. Boor sent the keys to the apartment to Ames by mail. Ames wrote Boor, "It will be my pleasure to hold you for every penny you owe me. I am renting the apartment in your behalf to Clay until April 30, 1966, at $135 a month." Boor had paid his rent through February 28, 1965. Clay entered the premises on April 1, 1965.

How much rent, if any, may Ames recover from Boor? Explain.

CHAPTER 47

REAL PROPERTY—CONCURRENT OWNERSHIP, EASEMENTS—NATURAL RIGHTS

Introductory. If the title to real or personal property is concurrently in two or more persons they are generally referred to as co-tenants, each entitled to an undivided interest in the entire item and neither of them claiming any specific portion of it. Each may have equal undivided interests or one may have a larger share than the other. Concurrent ownership may have different consequences depending upon the nature of its origin, or the subsequent acts of the parties, or operation of law, but regardless of the particular relationships between the co-tenants, in all instances this form of ownership must be carefully distinguished from the separate ownership of specific parts of an item of property by different persons. Thus, it is possible, for example, for A, B and C to each own distinct and separate parts of Blackstone Manor or they may each own an undivided one-third interest in all of Blackstone Manor. Whether they are co-tenants or owners of specific portions will depend upon the manner and form in which they acquired their interests.

There are two major classifications of concurrent ownership, tenancy in common and joint tenancy. They have in common the characteristic of undivided interest in the whole, a right in both tenants to possession and the power of alienability during life of his interest by either tenant thereby terminating the original relationship. The differences, however, between these two principal classes of co-tenancy are more marked than their similarities.

Joint Tenancy. The most significant incident of joint tenancy is the right of survivorship. Upon the death of either co-owner, title to the entire property passes by operation of law to the survivor. The heirs-at-law of the deceased joint tenant have no claim to his interest; nor can a joint tenant transfer his interest by will.

The undivided interest of a joint tenant is not an "estate of inheritance" so that where a husband holds property in joint tenancy with someone other than his wife, his wife cannot claim dower in her husband's interest as against the surviving joint tenant. However, by far the most common joint tenancy is that between husband and wife. In some States, where the common-law tenancy by entireties has not been abolished by statute, the husband and wife hold jointly in tenancy by the entireties.

Because of the right of survivorship, the attractive feature of a joint tenancy or tenancy by the entireties between husband and wife is that, upon the death of either spouse, the joint tenancy property will go to the survivor by operation of law without recourse to a will and the necessity, together with the attendant delay, of probate. For this reason, joint tenancies between husband and wife or between other members of a family, have, on occasion, been referred to as the "poor man's will."

Tax considerations, however, often make this form of ownership inadvisable as a substitute for a will. While the following observations are not exhaustive of the problems created by joint tenancy, consideration of them should show that even in the case of the smaller estate, use of the joint tenancy in substitution for a will should not be lightly undertaken without benefit of counsel.

(1) Creation of Joint Tenancy in Real Property. At common law, a joint tenancy between A and B, or a tenancy by the entireties where A and B are husband and wife, would arise under a conveyance "to A and B and their heirs." By statute, in most States, those words would not, today, be sufficient to create a joint tenancy in real property. Some of those statutes, e. g., New York Real Property Law, § 66, provide that a grant of an estate to two or more persons in their own right "shall be a tenancy in common, unless expressly declared to be in joint tenancy." Other statutes, e. g., Illinois Revised Statutes, 1965, chapter 76, paragraph 1, add that the deed of conveyance must expressly state that the estate is granted "not in tenancy in common but in joint tenancy." While the courts have striven to avoid results which would defeat the grantor's intention, it is not safe to assume that, under this type of statute, which creates a presumption that a tenancy in common was intended, any form of words showing a contrary intention will suffice.

An inexpertly drafted deed of conveyance in joint tenancy, should it result in a tenancy in common, will wholly fail in its purpose where it is intended that it act in substitution for a will. This is so because there is no right of survivorship in a tenancy in common. Instead, assuming that the deceased tenant in common leaves no will, (as may be the case where reliance was placed upon the existence of a joint tenancy) his undivided interest will descend to his heirs-at-law under the statutes of descent.

Under the rules of intestate succession, an undivided interest of a deceased tenant in *common* will not always go wholly to the survivor even where the survivor is the spouse of the deceased. Thus, even as between husband and wife who believe that they owned certain property in joint tenancy but who, because of inept draftsmanship, held it as tenants in common under the above statutes, the surviving spouse, in some States, if there are no children surviving, will take only one half of the deceased spouse's interest, the remaining one half going to other relatives of the deceased spouse. This result is entirely different from that which the parties intended.

There is one other important case which, because of the technical rules surrounding the creation of joint tenancy, may result in a mere tenancy in common, with all the unintended consequences in terms of succession.

To sustain a joint tenancy the common law requires the presence of what is known as the "four unities" of time, title, interest and possession. (1) The unity of time means that the interest of all tenants must vest at the same time; (2) the unity of title means that all tenants must acquire title by the same instrument or by a joint adverse possession; (3) the unity of interest means that all tenants must have identical interests as to duration and scope; (4) the unity of possession means that all the tenants have the same right of possession and enjoyment. The absence of any one of these four unities will prevent the creation of a joint tenancy. Failure of any one of the first three unities will result in the creation of a tenancy in common. The only unity required of a tenancy in common is the unity of possession.

The most important unity is that of time. Most would-be joint tenancies are created by the same instrument (unity 2) and purport to grant identical interests as to duration and scope (unity 3). The failure of the unity of time, however, has resulted in many disappointed expectations. Assume that H owns Blackacre. H marries W. H and W decide that they should hold all real property as joint tenants so as to assure succession between them without recourse to a will. Accordingly, H conveys Blackacre "to H and W as joint tenants and not as tenants in common." H dies and W claims Blackacre by right of survivorship. Under the common law, W's claim will not be sustained because when H conveyed Blackacre to H and W as joint tenants his interest in Blackacre was already in existence—he owned Blackacre. W's interest came into existence at a later time than H's. Because of the failure of the unity of time, H and W held as tenants in common and W takes only such interest in Blackacre as will come to her under the rules of intestate succession. Statutes in some States have changed this rule, but its existence must be borne in mind when creating a joint tenancy. In the absence of such a statute, H should convey Blackacre to a "dummy," who reconveys "to H and W as joint tenants and not as tenants in common."

The requirement of unity of interest would prevent a joint tenancy from arising if a deed conveyed the title to H to ¾ and W to ¼ as joint tenants. However, a joint tenancy may exist in the ownership of a single parcel of real estate, and the shares held by the joint tenants need not be equal. Assume that H and W, as joint tenants, own an undivided ¾ interest in Blackacre, and A and B, as joint tenants, own the other ¼ interest in the property. The right of survivorship would exist between H and W only with respect to their joint tenancy, and between A and B in their joint tenancy, and the two groups hold as tenancy in common toward each other. Accordingly, if A and B should both die, H and W would not acquire any interest in their one-fourth, which would pass to the heirs of the survivors of A and B.

(2) Severance. One important rule of joint tenancies, not generally anticipated by laymen who think of the joint tenancy as a substitute for a will, is that any joint tenant may sever the joint tenancy by conveying or mortgaging his interest to a third party. The interest of either co-tenant is subject to levy and sale upon execution. The mere entry of a judgment against one of the joint tenants does not sever the joint tenancy. However, where a judgment has been entered

against one of the joint tenants, the judgment creditor may reach his interest and a sale under execution will sever the joint tenancy. "Sever" here means that the right of survivorship is lost and the tenancy becomes a tenancy in common as between the remaining joint tenant and the grantee, mortgagee or execution purchaser. In those States which still recognize tenancy by the entireties between husband and wife, a conveyance by either of the spouses does not defeat the surviving spouse's right of survivorship. Except in those States, however, a joint tenancy between husband and wife as a substitute for a will may, because of the rule permitting severance, defeat the expectations of either party.

The will of one of the joint tenants devising his interest in the joint tenancy property to a third person does not effect a severance. A will does not become effective until the death of the testator. Upon the death of a joint tenant the entire estate automatically vests in the surviving joint tenant by operation of law. Accordingly, there is no property for the will in such a case to operate upon.

(3) Tax Considerations. In the case of larger estates, the use of the joint tenancy as a substitute for a will may result in serious tax loss. Indeed, even where no estate tax considerations are involved the joint tenancy may present tax problems.

Under the Internal Revenue Code where title is taken by two or more persons in joint tenancy and one of the joint tenants has furnished the entire consideration for the purchase of such property, that joint tenant is deemed to have made a taxable gift to the other joint tenants in the amount of the cost attributable to their interests.

The Code, however, makes an exception to this rule in favor of the husband and wife who take property in joint tenancy or tenancy by the entireties. The Code provides that the spouse furnishing the consideration for such property may elect either to pay the gift tax immediately or to postpone it until the date of the severance of joint ownership, if any.

Thus, where H purchases land for $60,000 and causes title to be conveyed to himself and his wife W as joint tenants with right of survivorship, a gift tax would normally be due on a gift of $30,000, but H may postpone it until severance. It should be remembered in this connection that there is an annual exclusion of $3,000 and a cumulative lifetime exemption of $30,000, provided for under the gift tax provisions of the Internal Revenue Code. The Code provides for a marital deduction of one half of the gift between husband and wife. Assuming that H has exhausted his cumulative exemption by previous gifts, he would be subject to a gift tax on $12,000. There is a similar provision relating to the Federal estate tax, to equalize the treatment given to spouses living in community property States. As will appear, in the community property States, husband and wife are deemed to be co-owners of all real and personal property acquired by either so that any gift or inheritance between husband and wife in these States is only one half of its gross amount, and the tax is payable on one half, only.

The right of the husband, H in our example, to elect to pay or not to pay the gift tax upon the creation of the joint tenancy may involve very special problems when it is anticipated that the property purchased will later be sold. Suppose that, in our example, oil is discovered under the land which H purchased for $60,000 so that now the property is worth $200,000. H and W want to sell the property. If H had elected to pay the gift tax when the joint tenancy was created he would have paid a tax on $12,000 (we are assuming that H has exhausted his cumulative exemption). When the property is sold for $200,000 and H and W each re-

ceive $100,000, no further gift tax is due from H.

But suppose that H had elected to postpone the gift tax. Upon the sale of the property for $200,000 and the distribution of the proceeds equally between H and W, the Internal Revenue Code provides that H shall be deemed to have made a gift to the extent that the proportion of the total consideration furnished by H multiplied by the proceeds of the sale exceeds the value of such proceeds received by H.

Thus, failure to elect to pay the gift tax at the time of creation of the joint tenancy, in this situation renders H liable for a gift tax on $47,000 (one half of $100,000 minus annual exclusion of $3,000), instead of a tax upon $12,000 as would have been the case had he elected to pay the gift tax at the time of the creation.

Assume that H and W do not sell the appreciated property and that H dies when the property is worth $200,000, leaving W and several children surviving. The entire value of the property will now be included in H's gross estate. This will be so even if H had elected to pay the gift tax upon the creation of the joint tenancy. Under the Internal Revenue Code, this is immaterial so long as H originally furnished all the consideration for the joint property. The gift tax will, of course, be a credit against the estate tax but, in the nature of things, because the estate tax is computed upon H's entire estate, the estate tax attributable to the joint tenancy property is generally larger than the gift tax paid at its creation.

If W dies more than ten years after H and leaves all her property, including the subject property, to the children the same property will be taxed in W's estate. Reliance upon the joint tenancy for succession has thus resulted in subjecting the property to two separate estate taxes in one generation. Without going into the computation of such tax, assuming that the property is the principal asset of H's estate, the total estate taxes required to be paid upon the property before it reaches the children of H and W will be approximately $36,000.

Suppose, however, that H had bought the land in his own name and had left it by will, one half to W outright (to take advantage of the marital deduction) and one half to W for life, with remainder to the children, the total estate taxes required to be paid on the property before it reaches the children will be approximately $9,600.

Thus, the use of the joint tenancy as a form of ownership where the gross estate of any joint tenant can be anticipated to exceed $60,000 (the Federal Estate Tax exemption) may result in serious tax loss in the context of the entire estate plan.

Joint Tenancy in Bank Accounts. Joint tenancies may be created in personal property and, unlike joint tenancies in real property, they may be created by parol. The statutes which require an affirmative expression of intention to create a joint tenancy apply to transfers of personal property, so that failing such an expression of intention, either by parol or in writing, a tenancy in common will result.

The most common case of joint tenancy in personal property is the joint bank account. The formalities attending the creation of a joint bank account are governed by the banking laws of the different States.

Joint bank accounts, payable to the depositor or a third party with the right of survivorship, have become increasingly popular. Their popularity is probably due to the fact that the depositors are seeking to make a testamentary disposition without incurring the expense of drafting a will or the delay incident to probate proceedings.

The deposit agreement signed by both parties usually reads: "As joint tenants, with right of survivorship and not as tenants in common." In some States, the statutes provide that deposits made payable to either depositor or survivor create a presumption of joint tenancy which is rebuttable during the lives of the depositors but becomes conclusive upon the death of either. In other States, parol evidence has been held admissible to contradict a written form, generally used by banks in connection with joint accounts, declaring the account payable to either depositor or the survivor. A joint tenancy in a bank account may, in some States, be created by making the account payable to either depositor without mention of survivorship.

A recurring question is whether an interest in joint tenancy with the right of survivorship has actually been created. A majority of jurisdictions apply the law of gifts to the joint and surviving account. The courts which employ the gift theory have refused to apply contract law upon the ground that there is no consideration to support a contract between the depositor and the donee. The minority view is that the execution of the deposit agreement creates and vests equal rights, with survivorship in all the parties. Since the contract is fully executed, no consideration is required. Other courts regard the deposit of funds with the bank as sufficient consideration to support an agreement between the bank, the depositor and the donee. Under the law of gifts, parol evidence is admissible to determine the deceased depositor's intent, while under the law of contracts the deposit agreement, signed by both of the parties, is considered as conclusive evidence of their rights, absent fraud, duress, or mistake.

A few States have abolished the right of survivorship in joint tenancies of personal property altogether. An attempted creation of a joint tenancy of personal property in such States creates a tenancy in common. Other States, e. g., Illinois, have abolished the right of survivorship in joint tenancies of personal property except where the joint tenancy is created by an instrument in *writing* expressly providing for survivorship. Also, many States, have statutes exonerating the banks from any liability for paying out the entire fund of a joint account to the survivor.

The joint bank account presents difficulties of proof for purposes of the Federal estate tax. The entire account is included in the decedent's gross estate unless the survivor can show that part of such fund was deposited by him. The Regulations under the Internal Revenue Code provide that there is no gift upon the creation of a joint bank account but the gift takes place when one joint tenant draws upon the fund in excess of the amount deposited by him.

Joint Tenancy in Securities. An obvious advantage of owning securities such as shares of stock as joint tenants with the right of survivorship is the ease of transfer upon the death of one of the co-owners. The necessity for probate of such property is obviated and the usual delays attending administration of estates are not present. Advantages of this nature may be outweighed by both Federal and State tax consequences. There is but little, if any, advantage, under the Federal Estate Tax Law in joint ownership. Under the Federal law the entire value of property owned in joint tenancy is includible in the gross estate of the decedent, unless the survivor can prove that he or she contributed some part or all of the cost of the property. As a practical matter, this proof is often difficult to establish, particularly when the death of one of the co-owners occurs many years after acquisition of the property. Where a husband and wife own property as joint tenants, the result frequently is to subject the property to unnecessarily large Federal estate taxation. Assume that H and W, husband and wife, have an estate of $240,000, all jointly owned but all purchased by the husband. The property will qualify for the Federal marital deduction so that only half, or $120,000,

is taxable upon the death of H, who dies first. There would be a tax of $9,500. Upon the death of W, the whole estate would be taxable at approximately $41,850. If, however, the same property is owned individually and H and W each have carefully drawn wills, the total tax liability could be reduced to about $19,000 for a saving of $32,350.

In many instances the purchase of securities in joint names results in a liability for a gift tax, or at least a duty to file a gift tax return, at a time when the parties may be unaware of such obligation. A special rule for United States Savings Bonds obtains, a rule which provides that the gift takes place and the liability for the tax is incurred when the bonds are redeemed. Otherwise, when one person buys securities and has them registered in the names of joint tenants, a legal obligation to file a gift tax return arises at the time of purchase. Even though a gift tax is paid when securities are purchased in joint names, the property may still be subject to Federal estate tax when one of the co-owners dies.

Tenancy in Common. Tenants in common are persons who hold undivided interests in the same property, each having the right to possession but neither claiming any specific portion of the property. There is no right of survivorship and, also unlike joint tenants, the only prerequisite is the so-called unity of possession. One tenant may have acquired his interest by conveyance a year ago from one person and the other may have acquired his interest through the will of another party ten years before. Persons may become tenants in common by operation of law as well as by the intention of a party. Thus, when grain belonging to several individuals is commingled in a single elevator, all the owners are said to be tenants in common, each having an undivided interest proportionate to the original amount placed in storage by him.

A conveyance to two or more parties, "share and share alike," is a frequent method of establishing tenancy in common and, by statute in many States, a conveyance to two or more persons will be presumed to create a tenancy in common. A tenancy in common may result from the unskilled attempt to create a joint tenancy. The relationship will also arise when an owner conveys a fractional interest in his property to another person as, for example, a conveyance of a one-tenth interest in a coal mine or an oil lease.

Tenancy in common may be terminated either by transfer of all co-interests to one person or by partition of the property among the tenants, making each the exclusive owner of a specific part of the entire item.

Partition is a device recognized and regulated by law for changing undivided interests into several and exclusive interests proportionate to the former undivided shares. Because of the obvious practical difficulty of making an equitable division of most real estate, the usual consequence of a partition suit instituted by a co-owner of real property is not partition at all but a sale of the entire tract by order of court with each co-owner receiving a share of the proceeds equivalent to his undivided interest in the property.

Community Property. In Arizona, California, Idaho, Louisiana, Nevada, New Mexico, Texas and Washington, any property acquired by the efforts of either the husband or wife belongs one-half to each spouse. This system known as "community property" originated in the civil law of continental Europe but it has been modified and affected by the common law in this country. Since each State has varied the attributes of this marital system and in each jurisdiction the system is statutory, only general observations can be made regarding it.

In most instances, the only property which belongs separately to either spouse is that acquired prior to the marriage or subsequent thereto by gift or devise. Upon the death of either spouse, one-half the community property belongs outright to the survivor and the interest of the deceased spouse in the other half may go to the heirs of the decedent or as directed by will, although, under some conditions in a few jurisdictions, the surviving spouse may also claim an interest in the decedent's one-half share of the property.

Community property is said to be liable for all "community debts," being those debts incurred by the husband after marriage and not for his own separate benefit. It is also generally liable for the ante-nuptial debts of both husband and wife. Formerly, the husband had control over all such property during his lifetime but this doctrine has been substantially modified.

Tenancy by the Entireties. This form of concurrent ownership, less common today than formerly, was created only by a conveyance to a husband and wife and was distinguished from joint tenancy by the inability of either spouse to convey separately his or her interest during life and thus destroy the right of survivorship. Likewise, the interest of either spouse could not be attached by creditors. In some States, statutes giving the wife the right to convey her property have been construed as abolishing this form of concurrent ownership, but, in other jurisdictions, a conveyance to a husband and wife is still presumed to create a tenancy by the entireties unless a joint tenancy or a tenancy in common is clearly indicated. By the nature of the tenancy, a divorce terminates the relationship and partition would then be available as a method of creating separate interests in the property.

Rights and Duties of Co-owners. As a rule of general application, each co-tenant is entitled to the use of any or all of the property subject only to a similar right in his co-tenants. As a practical matter, the most common problems between co-tenants arise from the exclusive use of the property by one of the co-tenants. In such cases, the issues are

(1) the extent of the duty of the possessor to account to his co-tenants for the rents or profits and (2) the extent of the duty of the co-tenants to contribute to the costs of maintaining the common property. In some instances, a third problem—that of waste—may arise due to the use of the land by the co-tenant who is in possession.

The duty of one co-tenant to account for rents and profits over and above his fair (proportionate) share was established by statute in England at an early date. In most jurisdictions, this duty to account is only for the rents or profits actually received and not for a fair return on the property except where the possessing tenant has ousted the other tenants from the property. Thus, if A, by common consent, lives in and manages an apartment building owned jointly by himself, B and C, on which the 1960 rents still prevail, he will not be liable to B and C for more than two-thirds of the rent received even though it is evident that, in general, rents have subsequently risen for similar properties.

Non-possessing co-tenants are obligated to contribute to such costs as repairs and taxes if they have not been restrained from using the property, and if the possessing tenant has incurred the expenses in good faith and they have mutually benefited all the owners. There is more doubt as to the liability of co-tenants to contribute to major or capital improvements even though the improvement may benefit the property and thus increase the value of each co-tenant's interest.

The doctrine of waste which exists with respect to life tenants, remaindermen, and landlord and tenant has application among concurrent owners. Whether or not waste has been committed by a co-tenant will depend not only upon the extent of the use but upon the nature of the property. Thus, the cutting of timber may be waste while the mining of coal would not be. The former may constitute an unreasonable use of the land while the latter would be a natural use.

It is sometimes said that co-owners share a fiduciary obligation to each other. By this, the courts generally mean that such owners cannot deal with each other as they might with strangers driving whatever bargain circumstances permit. Thus, a person must account to his co-tenants if he bids on the common property at a judicial or tax sale and they, in turn, if they wish to reacquire an interest in the property, must contribute to the bid price.

Parties dealing with co-owners must recognize the limits upon the powers of any individual co-tenant. While he can sell, mortgage or lease his undivided interest, that is all with which he can deal. One co-owner cannot dispose of or encumber any specific portion of the common property. All must act to deal effectively with the entire property. For example, A, one of several tenants in common, gives a lease to B of all the property. Later, A and all the others lease the entire tract to C who has knowledge of the lease to B. Under these circumstances, B has the right to use only A's interest while C has the right to the use of the entire remaining interest.

_____

EASEMENTS

In General. An easement may be defined as a limited right to make use of the land of another in a specific manner, created by the acts of the parties or by operation of law, and having all the attributes of an estate in the land itself. A typical easement exists where A sells a part of his land to B and expressly provides in the same or a separate document that B, as the adjoining landowner, shall have a right-of-way over a strip of A's remaining parcel of land. B's land is said to be the *dominant* parcel and A's land, which is subject to the easement, is the *servient* parcel. Easements may, of course, include a multitude of different types of uses as, for example, a right to run a ditch across another's land, to lay pipe under the surface, to erect power lines or, in the case of adjacent buildings, to use a stairway or a common or "party" wall.

Easements fall into two classes, easements *appurtenant* and easements *in gross*. Appurtenant easements are by far the more common type and, as the name indicates, the rights and duties created by such easements pertain to the land itself and not to the particular individuals who may have created them. Thus, in the foregoing illustration, if A conveys his servient parcel to C who has actual notice of the easement for the benefit of B's land or constructive notice by means of the local recording act, C takes the parcel subject to the easement. Likewise, if B conveys his dominant parcel to D, it is not necessary to refer specifically to the easement in the deed from B to D in order to give to D, as the new owner of the dominant parcel, the right to use the right-of-way over the servient parcel. Since B does not then own the dominant parcel he has no further right to use the right-of-way. B could not, however, transfer the benefit of the easement to a party who did not acquire an interest in the dominant parcel of land. Most frequently, a deed conveying the land "together with all appurtenances" is sufficient to transfer the easement. This characteristic of an appurtenant easement is described by the statement that both the burden and the benefit of an appurtenant easement pass with the land.

The second class of easements are those which are said to be in gross or personal to the particular individual who received the right. They do not depend upon the ownership of land and, in effect, amount to little more than an irrevocable license.

Creation of Easements. (1) *Easements Created by Express Grant, Reservation or Exception.* When A conveys part of his land to B, he may, in the same deed, expressly grant an easement to B over A's remaining property. Alternatively, A may grant an easement to B in a separate document. This document must comply with all the formalities of a deed. An easement is an interest in land subject to the Statute of Frauds. Like other instruments granting interests in land, it must be recorded, otherwise it will not be binding upon anyone who acquires A's remaining property for value and without notice of B's easement.

In the example given, A may want to "reserve" an easement in favor of the land retained by himself over the land granted to B. A may do this by express words to that effect in the deed of conveyance to B. Alternatively, A may "except" an easement right over the land granted to B in favor of the land retained by himself. At one time, the "reservation" of an easement by A required express words of grant "to A and his heirs," because it was thought that, having conveyed his entire interest in the land to B, A must obtain his easement, if at all, by way of re-grant from B. An "exception," on the other hand, was thought of merely as a retention by A of a part of his existing interest in the land conveyed to B. No words indicating a re-grant of an easement by B to A were necessary. These distinctions have largely disappeared today but cautious conveyancers still adhere to them.

(2) *Easements by Implication.* (a) *Implied easement as a survival of an existing use.* Suppose A owns two adjacent lots, Nos. 1 and 2. There is a house on each lot. Behind each of the houses is a garage. A has constructed a driveway along the medial line between the two lots, partly on lot 1 and partly on lot 2, which leads from the street in front of the houses to the two garages in the rear. A conveys lot 2 to B without any mention of the driveway. A is held to have *impliedly granted* an easement to B over that portion of the driveway which lies on A's lot 1, and he is held to have *impliedly re-*

served an easement over that portion of the driveway which lies on B's lot 2.

Easements by implied grant or implied reservation arise whenever an owner of adjacent properties establishes an *apparent* and *permanent* use, in the nature of an easement, and then conveys one of the properties without mention of any easement. The law causes the apparent and permanent use (commonly known as a quasi-easement) to survive the conveyance by implying a grant or a reservation of such easement in the conveyance. In the example given, there was both an implied grant and an implied reservation when A conveyed lot 2 to B because the driveway was partly on lot 1 and partly on lot 2.

(b) *Implied easements by necessity.* If A conveys part of his land to B, and the part conveyed to B is so situated that B would have no access to it except across A's remaining land, the law implies a grant by A to B of a right-of-way across A's remaining land. An easement by necessity does not depend upon the prior existence of an apparent and permanent roadway across A's remaining land; on the other hand, the circumstances which will give rise to a way by necessity must be more than mere convenience. A way by necessity will not usually arise if an alternative but circuitous approach to B's land is available. It should be noted that a way by necessity can be established only over the land of one who has conveyed the landlocked property. Thus, where A conveys a parcel of land to B which is wholly landlocked by the properties of C, D and E, no way by necessity can be established against C, D or E. A way by necessity may, however, arise by implied reservation. This would be the case where A conveys part of his land to B and A's remaining property would be wholly landlocked unless he is given a right-of-way across the land conveyed to B.

(c) *Implied easements in subdivisions.* When an owner of land subdivides it into lots and records the plan or plat of the subdivision, he is held, both by common law and now more frequently by statute, to have dedicated *to the public* all of the streets, alleys, parks, playgrounds and beaches shown on the plat. In addition, when the subdivider sells the lots by reference to the plat, it is now generally recognized that the purchasers acquire easements by implication over the areas shown dedicated to the public.

Thus, if the municipal authority does not accept some of the streets shown on the plat and the streets are never improved, the lot owners in the subdivision will continue to have a right, a private easement right, to use the strips shown as streets on the plat. This is particularly important in connection with beaches and parks shown on the plat. Frequently, disputes arise between the lot owners who have purchased lots facing a beach and those who have purchased lots in the heart of the subdivision. The owners of the lots facing the beach are tempted to claim that the beach is private. They are sometimes encouraged to do so by representations made to them by the subdivider at the time of purchase. Again, if the municipal authority does not accept a park in the subdivision, the subdivider sometimes attempts to build more houses in the area shown as a park on the plat. It is now generally recognized that the other lot owners are entitled to have the beaches and parks shown on the plat kept open and accessible, on the theory that when they purchased their lots by reference to the plat, they acquired private rights in such areas.

(3) *Easements by Prescription.* Finally, easements may arise by prescription where the owner, or the successive owners, of a parcel of land make use, in some manner, of an adjacent parcel for a substantial period of time. This period varies from State to

State but, in most instances, it is the same period as is necessary in the particular jurisdiction to establish ownership by adverse possession. Twenty years is a common statutory period. Thus, the pollution of a stream for the statutory period of years by one riparian owner may give him an easement which cannot be restricted by other adjacent landowners. Similarly, the use of a cow path by the owner of one tract of land over the land of another for the prescriptive period may establish the cow path as an easement by prescription.

Substantially the same rules govern easements by prescription as control the acquisition of fee interests in land by adverse possession, and the practical difficulty of establishing such an adverse interest is equally applicable to easements as to other interests. To obtain an easement by prescription, the use must be open, adverse, and uninterrupted. Thus, a subsurface pipe line would not give rise to such an easement unless there were actual knowledge of the pipe line on the part of the owner of the land or there were pumps or other fittings above the surface. Very little is required in the way of exercise of dominion by the owner of the land to break off the "uninterrupted" adverse user and start the period running again from the beginning. One common practice in cases of paths or private roads is for the owner to block the passage for a day. Little more than symbolic assertion of ownership appears to be required.

Consider the following situation: A, the owner of a farm, orally agreed with B, the owner of an adjoining farm, to allow B to use a right-of-way over A's farm jointly with A so long as A lived. The right-of-way was so used by A and B for 40 years. A then threatened to prevent B from using the right-of-way. B has not acquired a right-of-way by prescription. The acquiescence of A in the use by B for a statutory period is not sufficient, alone, to create a prescriptive easement. In order that a way may be establish-

ed by prescription, the use of the way must be not only with the knowledge and lack of consent of the owner of the land over which it is claimed to extend for the period of 20 years, but must, in addition thereto, be adverse, exclusive, uninterrupted and under a claim of right for that period. A verbal permission to pass over the lands of another cannot ripen into a prescriptive right regardless of the length of time such permissive use is enjoyed. It must originate under a claim of right and not under a mere permission. The permissive use may be rescinded at any time.

It is generally recognized that where two adjacent lot owners agree to improve a common driveway located on part of each of the two lots and expend money on the improvement, each may acquire a right to the other's half of the driveway by prescription. While the original parties to the agreement continue to own the adjoining lots, neither can prevent the other from using his half of the driveway without becoming liable in damages, since each has given consideration for the agreement. If, after twenty years of common use, one of the lots is sold, the new purchaser will not be permitted to interfere with the long continued use of the driveway by his neighbor.

Use and Maintenance of Easements. In the case of easements established by grant, the extent of the use which can be made of the easement will depend not only upon the terms of the grant but, also, upon the circumstances surrounding the transaction. A right-of-way general in its terms may validly be used for automobiles even though only horse-drawn carriages were in style at the time of its creation. On the other hand, a way intended as access to one parcel of land may not be extended so as to afford access to other land although, as a practical matter, such invalid and excessive user is often difficult to establish. If a grant is for a specific purpose, the dominant owner has no right to use it for other purposes. Thus, an easement for a pipe line does not permit the establishment of a power line nor a roadway although the owner of the easement will, of course, be entitled to have reasonable access to the pipe line for repair and maintenance.

Since the title to the servient parcel remains in the owner of the entire servient tract, he may make any use of, or allow others the use of, the tract which does not interfere with the easement. Thus, crops may be grown over an easement for a pipe line but livestock could not be pastured on an easement for a driveway. Although it is the duty of the owner of the servient parcel not to interfere with the use of the easement, it is generally the responsibility of the owner of the dominant parcel to maintain and keep in repair the easement. Conversely, the owner of the servient parcel does not have an affirmative duty to keep the property in proper condition for the use of the easement.

Since an easement is considered as benefiting all the dominant parcel, the right to use the easement will generally pass to each owner upon the sale of portions of the dominant parcel, unless the additional use is excessive to a degree not reasonably anticipated at the time the easement was created.

Extinction of Easements. Easements may be extinguished by (1) express release, (2) merger of the dominant and servient parcels, (3) abandonment, (4) misuser or change of the dominant property and (5) destruction of the servient property.

Although easements may, of course, be removed by express release by the owner of the dominant property, there are numerous circumstances under which easements will be extinguished without any executed document in the nature of a transfer of an interest in land. For this reason companies which issue policies to buyers of land guaranteeing the title will rarely agree to guarantee an easement appurtenant to the land.

When title to the servient and dominant tract become united in one owner, the easement is extinguished since the right formerly enjoyed by the dominant parcel becomes an ordinary incident to the ownership of the entire tract of land. The ownership of both parcels must be identical in quantity and quality, however, to affect an extinguishment. If the owner of the servient parcel acquires a lease of the dominant parcel, or if he acquires an estate for years, or holds title as trustee, the easement will not be extinguished.

It is possible that an easement may be extinguished by abandonment. A right to draw water for a mill may cease if the mill is destroyed and the use abandoned for a long period of time. Mere non-user, however, is not equivalent to abandonment. Nor is a declaration that the use is abandoned necessarily sufficient to accomplish the extinguishment of the easement. Abandonment is a question of fact in each case to be determined by all the circumstances, no one of which may be controlling. As noted, misuser or change in the character of the dominant parcel may overburden the servient parcel. This excessive user may be sufficient to terminate the easement. Finally, destruction of the servient property does not impose any duty upon its owner to rebuild and an easement which depended upon the existence of a structure on the servient estate is thereby extinguished. If the servient structure is rebuilt, however, it is generally held that the easement is thereby re-established.

PROFITS A PRENDRE

The grant by B to A, an adjoining landowner, of the right to remove coal or fish or timber from B's land or to graze his cattle on B's land (thereby "removing" the grass) is said to create in A a profit a prendre in B's land. It is a right to remove the produce of another's land. Like an easement, a profit may arise by prescription but, if by act of the parties, it must be created with all the formalities of a grant of an estate in real property. Unless the right is clearly designated as exclusive, it is always subject to a similar use by the owner of the land. The right to take profits is frequently held independent of the ownership of other land. Thus, A may have a right to remove crushed gravel from B's acreage even though A lives in another part of the county. Indeed, in order for profits to be appurtenant to a dominant tenement and pass with it, the right must directly benefit the dominant parcel.

Profits are subject to extinguishment in much the same manner as easements, by release, merger or, under some circumstances, improper use.

LICENSES

It is not always easy to distinguish such real interests in property as easements or profits from an equally common power of use designated as a license. Permission to make use of one's land generally constitutes a license which creates no interest in the property and is, in most circumstances, exercised only at the will of and subject to revocation by the owner at any time. If A tells B he may cut across A's land to pick hickory nuts, B has nothing but a license subject to revocation at any time. It is possible that, upon the basis of a license, B may expend funds to exercise the right and the courts may prevent A from revoking the license simply because, under the circumstances, it would be unfair to penalize B. In such a case, B's interest is practically indistinguishable from an easement.

The usual illustration of a typical license is a theater ticket or the use of a hotel room. No interest is acquired in the premises; simply a right to use for a given length of time, subject to good behavior. No formali-ty is required to create a license; a shopkeeper licenses persons to enter his establishment merely by being open for business.

NATURAL RIGHTS

Introductory. The ownership of land in itself carries with it certain rights in neighboring land, irrespective of any transfer of an interest by the adjoining landowner. Because these "rights" and the correlative duties are imposed by operation of law without regard to the intent of the parties, they are referred to as "natural rights." Without these "rights," a landowner might be effectively deprived of the use of his land because of the acts of his neighbor. In their operation, if not their origin, these rights are similar to easements, and, because they operate to restrict the use of land, they are occasionally and loosely termed "negative easements."

These rights take many forms. The most common are, (1) Right of lateral support, (2) Right of riparian ownership, and (3) Right to unpolluted air.

Right of Lateral Support. The enjoyment and use of land depends upon the lateral support it receives from adjacent land, and every landowner is entitled to expect that his land, in its natural condition, will receive this support. If A excavates upon his land and fails to provide adequate artificial support for the adjoining land of B, the latter may recover for any damages to the soil. There are, of course, limits upon this right of support. The general rule is that this right does not extend to land which has buildings or other structures on it. At least, damages will not usually be granted for injury to buildings caused by the excavation of adjacent land if there would have been no damage were the land unimproved by structures. An owner is entitled only to such support as will hold up the land in its natural condition. Thus, if X digs a well near the boundary of Y's land and a building on Y's land is damaged but the land is not substantially affected, Y will have no claim for damages. Obviously, it is frequently difficult to establish whether land improved with buildings would or would not have collapsed in its natural state.

This doctrine is altered in some jurisdictions by statute. Thus, under statute, the question sometimes may not be one of absolute liability for removing support but whether the landowner used reasonable care in excavating and giving the adjoining property owner notice in order that he might take necessary precautions.

Riparian Rights. The presence of water adjacent to, upon or under land, raises special problems and creates certain rights and duties in the owner of the land irrespective of any agreement between individuals. These rights and duties that are peculiar to land on which there is water are referred to as "riparian." A riparian right is a term used to describe the interest which a landowner has, for example, in a stream which flows through his property. It is not surprising that, as a general rule, it is said that a riparian landowner may make whatever use he chooses of the water provided he does not materially interfere with the rights of other riparian owners to do the same. A, living upstream from B, may appropriate the water for use in a mill, provided he does not substantially diminish the flow through B's land. A may not, however, divert the stream out of its natural course so that it no longer flows through B's land. In some jurisdictions, it is the law that if A's use is for domestic uses or for watering his livestock, his use, if reasonably necessary for these purposes may exhaust the supply without giving the lower riparian owners any valid cause for complaint. And, in some States in the western sections of the United States, where water is a vital and not always abundant natural resource, the doctrine of "first come-first

served" is reflected in the rule that he who makes a prior appropriation of the water is entitled to as much as he wants regardless of the consequences to later settlers along the river or stream. What is a "reasonable use" in a semi-arid region may be entirely different than in a region of abundant supply.

The same reasons are equally applicable to action by a riparian owner downstream who, by damming the stream, causes the water to inundate property upstream. Each owner is entitled to have the free flow of a stream through the land, except where the aforesaid doctrine of "prior appropriation" applies.

Surface water, as distinguished from streams or lakes, has its own rules. The problem usually arises where one landowner drains surface water off his land causing it to flow on adjoining land or where an owner constructs walls or abutments causing surface water to back up onto adjoining property. The freedom of the landowner to do so varies in different jurisdictions.

Subsurface water has a substantial body of law governing rights and duties of landowners through whose property the subteranean flow passes. If the flow is not in a regular channel any landowner may appropriate all of it. A may sink a well drawing off percolating water, thereby causing a spring on B's land to dry up without being liable to B. If the subsurface water flows in a definite channel, the rules governing use are substantially the same as those affecting streams.

Right to Unpolluted Air. Even in the absence of local ordinance or statute, a person will not be able to establish a rendering plant on a fifty-foot lot in a residential neighborhood. The adjacent landowner has the right to clean air. Fumes, vapor or dust caused by a use of adjacent land will give the suffering property owner a cause of action. If the offensive use is extensive, it will give rise to a right of complaint on the part of the general public and will probably be regulated by local ordinance. Whether the damage is limited to a private neighbor or is offensive to the entire community, it is generally designated as a "nuisance." The nature of "public nuisances" and the limitations of the law of nuisances are considered in Chapter 49. Zoning law has developed primarily because of the inadequacy of the common-law rules governing this natural right of property owners to be protected against offensive odors, noise and dirt.

CASES

RICHARDSON v. RICHARDSON

(1951) 121 Ind.App. 523, 98 N.E.2d 190.

ACHOR, J. This was an action filed by appellant, Maxine J. Richardson, (plaintiff in the court below) against the appellees herein. Appellants William Dale Richardson and Richard Dale Richardson were made defendants to the cross-complaint of the appellees in the court below. In this action appellant Maxine J. Richardson claimed to be the owner of a one-fourth interest as tenant in common pursuant to the will of William Dale Richardson, her deceased husband.

The deed by which the said William Dale Richardson acquired title with the appellees herein contained the following words of conveyance in its premises or granting clause:

"Convey and Warrant to Ray M. Richardson, W. Dale Richardson, Lavon Richardson and Lena Richardson, in equal proportions and in case of the death of any one or more of the said grantees, his or her interest in said land shall go to the other surviving grantees then living in equal proportions."

The question before this court is, does the above provision of conveyance create a joint tenancy, as maintained by the appellees, or does it create a tenancy in common, as contended by appellants? The court below found "That said deed vested title in Ray M. Richardson, Lavon Richardson, Lena Richardson and W. Dale Richardson, as joint tenants." Pursuant to this conclusion of law judgment was rendered for the appellees against the appellants.

The statute of this state applicable to the creation of joint tenancies and tenancies in common is as follows, § 56–111, Burns' 1943 Replacement: "All conveyances and devises of lands, or of any interest therein, made to two (2) or more persons, except as provided in the next following section, shall be construed to create estates in common and not in joint tenancy, unless it shall be expressed therein that the grantees or devisees shall hold the same in joint tenancy and to the survivor of them, or it shall manifestly appear, from the tenor of the instrument, that it was intended to create an estate in joint tenancy."

By reason of this statute appellant correctly asserts that, whereas joint tenancies were favored under the common law, that the opposite presumption now prevails under our statute. [Citation.]

Appellant contends that the granting clause in the new deed is severable in two parts: that the first part being "Convey and Warrant to Ray M. Richardson, W. Dale Richardson, Lavon Richardson and Lena Richardson, in equal proportions * * *" with the remainder of the sentence constituting a separate, limited, ambiguous, repugnant habendum thereto. Appellant charges that the second part of the sentence is ambiguous in that it does not contain the words "joint," "jointly," or "joint tenancy," and that it is repugnant in that it attempts to control the "inheritance" of the real estate after that right had already been vested absolutely under the previous clause. They maintain that under our statute, § 56–115, Burns' 1943 Repl. the words "conveys and warrants" conveyed title in fee simple to all the named grantees, and that the fee simple title having been once vested, the remaining clause regarding survivorship, being ambiguous and repugnant thereto, is to be given no effect. [Citations.] * * *

However, the rule seems well established, 16 Am.Jur. § 239, page 573, " * * * *that where, by statutory provision, the use in the granting clause of words of inheritance is rendered unnecessary neither the use of such words nor the fact that the fee might pass to the grantee under the statute will render subsequent clauses limiting the estate void for repugnance.* * * *"* (Our Italics.) [Citations.]

Appellees, on the other hand, contend that the deed before the court is distinguishable from those cited in the cases by appellants in that there is no habendum separate from the "granting clause," as was true in the cases cited. That in the case at bar there is only a single granting clause which consisted of one single and complete sentence. That this sentence is to be considered in its entirety and is not to be subjected to rhetorical surgery in order to consider its member parts separately and thereby arrive at a result opposite to that which is obviously intended from the sentence as a whole. As to this contention we concur with appellees.

Furthermore, appellees maintain that appellant fails to give proper emphasis to the second clause of the statute, § 56–111, Burns' 1943 Repl., supra, which clearly provides that the manifest intention of the deed should prevail where " * * * it shall manifestly appear, from the tenor of the instrument, that it was intended to create an estate in joint tenancy." And in determining "the manifest intention of the deed" appellees assert that the deed must be taken as a whole and that when this rule is applied to the deed in controversy a clear intention is expressed to create an estate of joint tenancy, the distinguishing feature of which is a quality of survivorship. [Citations.]

It is our observation that the "estate" here in controversy contains not only a quality of survivorship but also the other distinguishing features of joint tenancy. These features are set forth in the case of Case v. Owen, 139 Ind. at pages 22 and 23, 38 N.E. at page 395:

"An estate in joint tenancy is an estate held by two or more tenants jointly, with an equal right in all to share in the enjoyment of the land during their lives. Upon the death of any one of the tenants, his share vests in the survivors. Four requisites must exist to constitute a joint tenancy, viz.: *First.* The tenants must have one and the same interest. *Second.* The interests must accrue by one and the same conveyance. *Third.* The interests must commence at one and the same time. *Fourth.* It must be held by one and the same undivided possession. 6 Am. and Eng.Enc.Law, 891. A joint tenancy can be created in no other way than by purchase, and its distinguishing feature is that of survivorship."

The tenancy now in controversy was created by purchase; the tenants had one and the same interest; the interest accrued by one and the same conveyance; commenced at one and the same time, had the quality of survivorship and was held by one and the same undivided possession.

We concur with the conclusion of law stated by the trial court "that the deed vested title in Ray M. Richardson, W. Dale Richardson, Lena Richardson and Lavon Richardson, as joint tenants."

Judgment affirmed.

WILKINSON v. WITHERSPOON

(1965) 206 Va. 297, 142 S.E.2d 478.

CARRICO, J. This controversy is between John W. Witherspoon, the complainant, and Nancy Eugenia Wilkinson, the defendant. The litigation arose when the complainant, individually and as co-executor under the will of Oscar O. Hewitt, deceased, filed a bill of complaint against the defendant, individually and as co-executor of the estate.

The bill of complaint sought the advice and guidance of the court in the settlement of the estate. Specifically, the bill was directed to the ascertainment of the ownership of a savings account in the Franklin Federal Savings and Loan Association of Richmond. The account was in the names of the testator, Oscar O. Hewitt, and the defendant, as joint tenants with the right of survivorship. The prayer of the bill was that the court determine whether the balance of $9,703.88 in the account belonged to the estate or to the defendant.

The chancellor heard the case ore tenus and ruled that the savings account belonged to the estate. A final decree was entered directing delivery of the funds to the executors and the defendant, individually, was granted an appeal.

The evidence shows that the complainant and the defendant are brother and sister and were, respectively, the nephew and niece of Oscar O. Hewitt.

Mr. Hewitt was, for more than fifty years, employed as a staff accountant with A. M. Pullen and Company, a public accounting firm of Richmond.

Mr. Hewitt's wife died in December of 1961. On February 1, 1962, he executed his will, dividing his estate equally between the complainant and the defendant and appointing them as co-executors.

On March 2, 1962, the savings account now in dispute was opened by Mr. Hewitt.

Mr. Hewitt retired from his employment in April of 1962. His first entry into the hospital, in connection with his fatal illness, was on September 30, 1962, and he died on November 17, 1962, at the age of 79.

While the evidence discloses that Mr. Hewitt's relationship with his nephew, the complainant, was "pleasant", it shows that his relationship with his niece, the defendant, was close and personal.

* * *

This close relationship continued through the years but, after the death of his wife, Mr. Hewitt appeared to rely more heavily upon the defendant for companionship and comfort. * * *

On September 30, 1962, when Mr. Hewitt was to enter the hospital for an operation, he telephoned the defendant so to inform her and she and her daughter took him to the hospital. * * *

When Mr. Hewitt was discharged from the hospital on October 27, the defendant took him to her home and cared for him for two weeks. * * *

While Mr. Hewitt was in the hospital, the defendant visited him every day and took care of his personal needs. During the week after he returned home and before he died, the defendant visited him and telephoned him. In that final week, he wrote a letter to a relative stating that the defendant and her husband "have been wonderful to me, and I can never repay them for what they have done."

The savings account in question was opened by Mr. Hewitt, entirely with his own funds, on March 2, 1962, subsequent to the execution of his will and prior to his retirement. In the eight and one-half months following the opening of the account and preceding his death, Mr. Hewitt made fourteen deposits and no withdrawals.

The account was opened with a signature card executed by Mr. Hewitt and the defendant. The latter testified that, pursuant to Mr. Hewitt's request, she visited him one evening at his home; that he presented her with the card and told her to sign it; that she asked him what the card was for and "he kind of giggled, or laughed, and he said, well, who knows, someday somebody may want to pay some bills"; that she signed the card and left it with him, and that no other discussion about the matter ever took place between them.

The defendant had no knowledge of the existence of the savings account until after Mr. Hewitt's death. * * * One month and a half after Mr. Hewitt's death, the defendant withdraw the full balance in the account and placed the funds in a new savings account in the savings and loan association in her own name.

The signature card, which is the focal point of this controversy, was, so far as is pertinent here, in the following language:

" * * * Hewitt, Oscar O. * * * and Wilkinson, Nancy Eugenia * * * as joint tenants with right of survivorship and not as tenants in common, and not as tenants by the entirety, the undersigned hereby apply for membership and a savings account in the Franklin Federal Savings and Loan Association and for the issuance of evidence thereof in their joint names described as aforesaid. You are directed to act pursuant to any one or more of the joint tenants' signatures, shown below; it is agreed that any one or more such person(s) so authorized shall have power to act in all matters related to this account, including, but without limiting the generality of the foregoing, the withdrawal in whole or in part of this account, and the pledging of this account in whole or in part as security for any loan made by you to one or more of the undersigned. Any such pledge shall not operate to sever or terminate either in whole or in part the joint tenancy estate and relationship reflected in or established by this contract. It is agreed by the signatory parties with each other and by the parties with you that any funds placed in or added to the account by any one of the parties *is and shall be conclusively intended to be a gift and delivery* at that time of such funds to the other signatory party or parties

to the extent of his or their pro rata interest in the account.

    *   *   *   *   *   *

"Note: The correct way to establish a common law joint tenancy or its equivalent in any state is to use 'and' in joining tenants' names on all evidence of the account. All tenants should sign this card. * * * " (The italicized language was so emphasized in the signature card itself.)

The sole question to be decided is whether the balance in the savings account belongs to the defendant or to the estate of Oscar O. Hewitt, deceased.

* * * At the threshold of our discussion, however, we note that never before, in the cases coming before us, have we encountered language in a signature card as comprehensive as in that signed by Mr. Hewitt and the defendant.

    *   *   *

[I]t appears that the golden thread of decision running through these cases is that the intention of the depositor is the all-important consideration. Where there was, in the terms of the deposit, a clear expression of an intention that the survivor should become the owner of the account upon the death of the depositor, * * * the intention was upheld. Where such an intention was not fully disclosed by the terms of the deposit but clearly appeared when the terms were considered along with other evidence, * * * effect was given to the intention. But where a contrary intention was shown to exist, * * * the court did not hesitate to exclude the pretended rights of the survivor.

The case before us has only one element in common with those cases in which the survivors' rights were denied. The language, "as joint tenants with right of survivorship", in the signature card signed by Mr. Hewitt and the defendant, was similar to the terms of the deposits in the other cases. But here the similarity ceases. The signature card now before us, unlike the terms of the deposits in those cases, is fully descriptive of the rights of the parties and contains this crucial language:

" * * * It is agreed by the signatory parties with each other and by the parties with you that any funds placed in or added to the account by any one of the parties *is and shall be conclusively intended to be a gift and delivery* at that time of such funds to the other signatory party or parties to the extent of his or their pro rata interest in the account. * * * " (Emphasis included in the signature card itself.)

The complainant contends that this language is insufficient, in view of the circumstances surrounding the deposit, to constitute the transaction between Mr. Hewitt and the defendant as a gift *inter vivos*. There is lacking, the complainant says, the essential elements of acceptance by the defendant and divesting of control by Mr. Hewitt.

* * *

We hold that the rights of the parties are to be determined, not by principles applicable to gifts *inter vivos*, but by rules pertaining to the interpretation of contracts. Those rules require us to search for, and give effect to, the intention of the parties. Accordingly, the provisions of the signature card come eloquently into play. That signature card constituted a contract made with the savings and loan association and controlled the terms of the account.

It is here that attention must be given to two statutory provisions which touch upon the question under consideration. Code, § 55–20 abolishes survivorship as between joint tenants. But Code, § 55–21 specifically provides that § 55–20 shall not apply "to an estate conveyed or devised to persons in their own right when it manifestly appears from the tenor of the instrument that it was intended the part of the one dying should then belong to the others." And it has been held

that the provisions of Code, § 55–21 apply to bank accounts. [Citation.]

The contract here made with the savings and loan association manifested a clear intention on the part of Mr. Hewitt that the savings account should, upon his death, belong to the defendant. That intention resulted in the creation of an express right of survivorship in the defendant, in accordance with the saving features of Code, § 55–21.

In so deciding, we do not overlook what has been said in our previous cases that, in situations similar to the one before us, there arises a presumption that the account was opened for the convenience of the depositor. Here, any such presumption pales in the light of the language of the deposit contract and the circumstances surrounding its execution.

* * *

Mr. Hewitt was a trained accountant with long experience, versed in the intricacies of bank and savings and loan accounts. He was obviously well informed concerning the disposition of estates. A copy of his will is found in the record. Written entirely by his own hand, it is a model of testamentary perfection. It would be eminently unfair to infer that Mr. Hewitt did not know what he was about when he created the survivorship account with the defendant.

On the other hand, it is entirely fair to draw from the evidence the conclusion that Mr. Hewitt deliberately intended to favor his niece, the defendant, over his nephew, the complainant, in the distribution of his worldly goods upon his death. His close attachment to her and her long devotion to him establish abundant reason for his action. And it is significant that the opening of the savings account followed, and not preceded, the execution of his will which, without the opening of the account, would have resulted in an equal division of his estate between his niece and nephew.

* * *

* * * The account here was so fixed that the defendant was entitled to its proceeds upon the death of Mr. Hewitt, in accordance with his declared intention, an intention undimmed by any evidence in the case.

The decree appealed from will be reversed and a final decree will be entered here declaring the defendant to be the true owner of the balance, as of November 17, 1962, of the funds in the savings account opened by Mr. Hewitt on March 2, 1962, in the Franklin Federal Savings and Loan Association.

Reversed and final decree.

MITCHELL v. HOUSTLE

(1958) 217 Md. 259, 142 A.2d 556.

PRESCOTT, J. The Chancellor decreed that the appellants must cease using a certain sewer pipe that runs under the land of the appellees from the appellants' lot to the public sewer. The appellants and appellees are the owners of contiguous lots in Baltimore City that are bounded on the north by Sulgrave Avenue; on the east by Lochlea Road; and on the south by South Road. South Road and Sulgrave Avenue are parallel streets. The appellees' lot (unimproved) lies north of the appellants' lot (improved by a dwelling), and has frontage on both Sulgrave Avenue and Lochlea Road; the appellants' parcel lies immediately south of the appellees' land and has frontage on South Road and Lochlea Road.

Both properties were from 1916 until 1947 part of a larger tract under unified ownership. In 1947, the property was divided approximately in half, with the southern portion passing by mesne conveyances to the appellants (Mitchells) and the northern portion, also by mesne conveyances, to the appellees (Houstles). The lots slope sharply downward to the north, and as a result the sewer line was laid in the bottom of Sulgrave

Avenue. There is no sewer line in South Road, as the street level is higher than the ground level of most of the houses on South Road. It was stipulated that the sewer line from the appellants' residence was laid in 1929 when both lots were owned by the same person; and there is nothing in the land records which would show the existence of such an easement. The sewer pipe extended from the appellants' present residence northerly on the appellees' lot to Sulgrave Avenue. As before stated, the lots in question remained under unified ownership until 1947. In February of that year, the then owner conveyed to the predecessor in title of the Mitchells that portion of the whole tract which the Mitchells now own. The first question for our determination is whether, at the time of this conveyance, an easement was created. If this question be answered in the affirmative, we would then be required to answer the further question of whether the easement inured to the benefit of the present owners, the Mitchells. The appellants contend that an implied easement was created for the benefit of the property they now own and they are entitled to the said easement for the purposes of carrying their sewer pipe to the public sewer line. They argue that said easement contained all of the essential characteristics of being continuous, reasonably necessary for the enjoyment of their property, and that it was "visible" as there were two clean-out fittings located on the Houstle lot that extended from 6 to 8 inches above the ground. The appellants claim further that the appellees were put on notice of said easement by the Plumbing Code of Baltimore City which required clean-outs every 100 feet, the original application with reference to the sewerage for the appellants' property which was in the health department, and also by a statement made by a spectator when the appellees purchased, at public auction in 1956, their portion of the property. The appellees contend that their property is not subject to any implied easement and that they had no notice, actual or constructive, concerning the fact that the sewer line had been laid under their property.

The question as to what easements are, or are not, created by implied grant or implied reservation has been before this Court on many occasions. From a very early date, a distinction has been made between an implied grant and an implied reservation; with the rule being much more strict when called upon to create an easement by implied reservation, than to create one by implied grant. [Citation.] * * *

See * * * McConihe v. Edmonston, 157 Md. 1, 145 A. 215, where many of the earlier cases are cited and analysed. It will be noted from these cases that the use made of the property must be such that the easement resulting from it would be of the kind known as (1) continuous, (2) apparent, and (3) necessary for the reasonable enjoyment of the property conveyed, determined as of the time of the severance of the tenement. The appellants maintain that they have met the burden of proof placed upon them and shown that the purported easement has all three of the essential qualities just named. We shall lay aside the other two necessary characteristics and confine our discussion as to whether or not it was "apparent."

There are at least two good reasons to support the rule that one of the necessary characteristics of a *quasi* easement, which is to ripen into an easement by implication and pass with a conveyance of the dominant estate, is that it be "apparent." First, the basis of an implied easement is the implied intention of the parties that an easement be created; if the easement be not apparent, it could hardly form the basis for an implied intention to grant the same. Second, if such a *quasi* easement be not visible, it would not come to the knowledge of a prospective purchaser of either the dominant or servient estate, and if an innocent purchaser of a ser-

vient estate were required to accept his title subject to easements that were not apparent, it would create chaos in the field of land purchases, and work hardships never contemplated by the law. [Citations.]

* * *

The only evidence in the present case with reference to the alleged easement being "apparent" was that there were two clean-out pipes from the sewer pipe across the appellees' property that were about five inches in diameter and extended out of the ground eight to ten inches. The appellees contended the lot was completely covered by weeds and brush, and they did not discover the clean-out pipes until after their purchase of the property.

The chancellor found that the claimed easement was not "apparent," and we see no good reason to disturb his decision. * * * With the burden of proof being upon the appellants, as it was, to show that the claimed easement was "apparent," we concur with the chancellor that they failed to prove that the claimed easement was visible, or such as would necessarily come to the knowledge of a prospective purchaser by such an examination of the premises as is ordinarily made by one desiring to purchase.

* * *

The appellants make as their final and unusual contention that the appellees have an adequate remedy at law, in that they have a right to a refund of the purchase price they paid for their property, and their remedy is at law against their grantor. This argument fails from every approach taken to it. The right to this remedy at law would be dependent upon whether a valid easement existed or did not exist. If a valid easement exists, it constitutes a complete defense for the appellants in this suit, and they would have no interest in whether the appellees were entitled to a refund of their purchase money or not. If an easement does not exist, and we hold that it does not, then the appellees would not be entitled to a return of their purchase money from their grantor, so the argument fails from this angle also. Furthermore, the doctrine that equity will grant no relief when there is an adequate remedy at law is limited to cases in which there is an adequate legal remedy against the defendants that are before the court. [Citations.]

Decree affirmed.

SHANKS v. FLOOM

(1955) 162 Ohio St. 479, 124 N.E.2d 416.

The appellants, hereinafter referred to as plaintiffs, are the successors in title to a property on the south side of West Maple Street in North Canton, Ohio, formerly owned by Austin Schiltz. Schiltz purchased this property in 1910 and erected a house on it in 1911. At the same time, he constructed a driveway from West Maple Street to the rear of his lot. A few years later, William Floom purchased the vacant lot adjacent to the Schiltz property on the west and built a house on it. For four or five years thereafter, both Floom and his family and Schiltz used this unimproved driveway on the Schiltz property.

About 1924 or 1925, Schiltz and Floom, pursuant to an oral agreement, constructed a cement driveway, seven feet wide and 110 feet long, between and on their two properties, each owner bearing one-half the cost thereof. Cement aprons from the common driveway to the respective garages were constructed at the same time. Each owner continued to use the common driveway until the year 1948 when Schiltz sold his property to the plaintiffs, and the appellees, hereinafter referred to as defendants, inherited their property from William Floom, who died in that year.

Shortly after the acquisition of their respective properties, difficulties arose between the present owners. On July 26, 1951, plaintiffs commenced an action in the Court of Common Pleas of Stark County, seeking to enjoin the defendants' use of the common driveway and to quiet the title of the plaintiffs against any claims of the defendants. The Common Pleas Court denied the injunction, holding that nothing had occurred to alter the obligation of each party to recognize the right of the other to use the driveway.

On appeal to the Court of Appeals on questions of law and fact, that court quieted the title of the plaintiffs as to the west line of their property, and held that both properties are subject to an easement for driveway purposes, where the cement drive is now located, by reason of more than 21 years of adverse use.

The cause is now before this court pursuant to allowance of a motion to certify the record.

BELL, J. The agreement which resulted in the construction of the driveway came about, according to the testimony of Austin Schiltz, as follows:

"A. One evening Mr. Floom said, 'Aust, how about making this drive in the center; you pay half and I'll pay half' and I said, 'O. K.' and it was done and I paid my share and he paid his."

It is conceded by defendants that if their use of the driveway, and that of their predecessors in title, pursuant to this agreement, was permissive only such use under the law of Ohio could not ripen into an easement. [Citations.] Defendants' contention is that there was an adverse use under a claim of right which ripened into an easement after 21 years.

This precise question is before this court for the first time. However, the case of Rubinstein v. Turk, 29 Ohio Law Abst. 653, decided by the Court of Appeals for the Eighth Appellate District, presented the identical problem. In that case, the parties' predecessors in title acquired adjoining sublots in

1909. Both sublots were improved with dwellings. Shortly afterwards, the owners of the two lots agreed to construct a driveway for their joint use, substantially one-half of which was to be on each lot. The agreement was not in writing. Pursuant to the agreement, the driveway was constructed and the owner of each lot paid one-half of the cost of construction. More than 21 years later, differences arose between the owners and defendant attempted to construct a fence across the driveway. In granting an injunction to the plaintiff, the majority of the Court of Appeals held:

"When * * * the owners * * * constructed a joint driveway by agreement between themselves, each owner thereafter claimed the right of an easement in the part of the driveway on his neighbor's lot, in consideration of having given his neighbor a similar easement on his own lot. Thereafter * * * the 'possession and use' of each owner was under a 'claim of right' and therefore adverse. This adverse possession continued for more than 21 years and therefore ripened into a prescriptive right."

The reasoning of the Court of Appeals was based largely on the definition of "hostile use" set out as follows by this court in Kimball v. Anderson, 125 Ohio St. 241, 244, 181 N.E. 17, 18:

"To establish hostility it is not necessary to show that there was a heated controversy, or a manifestation of ill will, or that the claimant was in any sense an enemy of the owner of the servient estate; the facts which prove hostility might greatly differ in different cases, and it has been held in many cases that it is sufficient if the use is inconsistent with the rights of the title owner and not subordinate or subservient thereto. Hostile use is sometimes described as possession and use under a claim of right."

The Kimball case also involved a driveway between two lots. It differs from the present case, however, in that the driveway there was constructed by a single owner of the two lots, followed by a sale of one lot by warranty deed without a reservation of that part used for the driveway. This court held that the warranty deed did not prevent the grantor's subsequent use of the driveway from being adverse. * * *

The facts set out as follows in Johnson v. Whelan, 171 Okl. 243, 42 P.2d 882, 98 A.L. R. 1096, appear to be almost identical with those of the present case:

"Plaintiff and defendant own adjacent lots in Oklahoma City. Plaintiffs own the west lot and defendant the east lot. Both lots face the north, and in 1908 were improved with substantial residential buildings on the northerly portion and smaller buildings to the rear on the south. In 1908 one Binns owned the west lot and one Collet the east lot. These owners jointly constructed a concrete paved driveway on their medial line, from the street on the north to small buildings on rear, each furnishing half of the expense. Apparently each intended to furnish half the ground for the seven-foot driveway. However, a survey in 1931 showed some six or nine inches more on the east than on the west lot. No writing was executed by either owner, nor by subsequent owners, granting to the other any rights or privileges in the lot of the other.

" * * * At all times the driveway has been used jointly by the occupants of the two lots. In 1931 defendant built an additional strip of pavement on her side, and threatened to construct a wall or fence along the lot line, which would have left insufficient room for a driveway between the house of the plaintiffs and the property line. Plaintiffs brought this suit to enjoin the defendant from interfering with their use of the driveway."

The Supreme Court of Oklahoma, in granting the injunction, held:

"While the mere permissive use of a way over the land of another will not ripen into an easement, yet one who joins his adjacent landowner in the construction of a paved private way over and along the medial line has given such adjacent owner more than a mere license. Each owner, by use of the driveway, is continuously asserting an adverse right in the portion of the way on the other's lot. And from such use for 15 years the law raises a presumption of the grant of an easement."

Similar conclusions have been reached in cases in Arkansas, Georgia, Iowa, Kentucky, Maryland, Massachusetts, Minnesota. Nebraska, New Jersey, New York and South Carolina. [Citations.] * * *

We believe it is unreasonable to assume that the owners of these properties, at the time this driveway was constructed and the use thereof began, each felt that he was using his half as a matter of right and the other's half merely by permission. On the contrary, the nature and permanence of the improvement, that it was constructed of concrete, and that it was constructed on what the owners considered to be the boundary line between their properties are more consistent with a claim of right on the part of each than with a day-to-day permissive use. We hold therefore, that the use in this case was under a claim of right and as such was adverse and not permissive. Such use being for more than 21 years, it follows that an easement for the common use of this driveway has been acquired by both parties. * * *

The judgment of the Court of Appeals is hereby affirmed.

Judgment affirmed.

AMPAGOOMIAN v. ATAMIAN

(1948) 323 Mass. 319, 81 N.E.2d 843.

SPALDING, J. The plaintiff brought this suit in equity in the Land Court to determine the extent of an easement appurtenant to her land. She also sought to restrain the defendants from interfering with a use, herein-

after described, which she was making of the easement. [Citation] The evidence is not reported, but the judge made findings of facts.

The facts may be summarized as follows: In 1916 the defendants named in the bill, Atam Atamian and Marta Atamian, acquired by deed an undivided one-half interest in a certain parcel of land and the buildings thereon in that part of Northbridge known as Whitinsville. At the same time and by the same deed the remaining undivided one half interest in this parcel was conveyed to one Garabed Jigarjian. In September, 1922, Jigarjian conveyed his interest in a portion of this property to the Atamians. By this conveyance the Atamians became the sole owners, subject to an easement presently to be mentioned, of a parcel which was bounded on the north by East Church Street. The deed contained the following provision: "The strip of land fifteen feet wide on the easterly side of the granted premises is to forever be maintained as a driveway." In June, 1926, the Atamians conveyed to Jigarjian their interest in the remaining portion of the original parcel. The deed, after describing the property, recited "Together with a right of way over the grantors' adjoining land, from said East Church Street, southeasterly." By this deed Jigarjian became the sole owner of a lot which was bounded on the north by East Church Street and on the west by the lot owned by the Atamians. Both lots ran back the same distance from the street. In 1937 Jigarjian conveyed a portion of his land in the rear to the plaintiff "together with a right of way over the adjoining land of Atam Atamian et ux from said East Church Street southeasterly." On the plaintiff's lot there is a house, as there is on the lot owned by Jigarjian. These houses "were there in 1916." There is also a house on the Atamian's lot which was built in 1922 or 1923. It was agreed by the parties "that water pipes had been laid from East Church

Street throughout the length of the fifteen foot driveway" and that these "supplied the plaintiff's house with water." In August of 1944 the Worcester Gas Light Company at the plaintiff's request "laid gas pipes in the fifteen foot driveway from East Church Street up to the plaintiff's house." Upon learning of this Marta Atamian (hereinafter called the defendant) objected, and it was agreed between her and the gas company that the pipes might remain in the driveway, but not connected, "pending the adjudication of this case." "When the conveyance was made (and) the driveway was created, there was no gas in Whitinsville." No question was raised "as to the right of the plaintiff to use the fifteen foot driveway for ingress and egress to her land, and the defendant admitted at the trial that no question was raised as to the use of the land in said driveway for the water pipes." The sole question for decision in the court below was whether the plaintiff's easement was broad enough to include the right to lay gas pipes under the driveway for the purpose of conveying gas to her house. The judge ruled that it was not, and ordered the bill dismissed. From a final decree dismissing the bill the plaintiff appealed.

The decree was right.

It is not disputed that the plaintiff had, as appurtenant to her land, an easement of way over the defendant's land. "When an easement or other property right is created, every right necessary for its enjoyment is included by implication." [Citations.] But it cannot be said that the laying of gas pipes beneath the driveway was necessary to the enjoyment of the plaintiff's right of passage over it. The defendant as owner of the servient estate retained the use of her land for all purposes except such as were inconsistent with the plaintiff's easement. [Citations.] The use of the way to which the plaintiff claims to be entitled was not included either expressly or by implication in the

grant creating the easement. It has generally been held that a right of way over the land of another, even though, as here, it be granted in general terms does not include the right to lay pipes or to erect structures in or upon the way. * * *

The contention of the plaintiff that the judge erred in failing to decide that she had a right to maintain the water pipes in the driveway is without merit. In view of the pleadings and the fact that the defendant admitted at the trial that no question was raised as to the use of the driveway for this purpose, this question was not before the judge, and, on this record, we are in no position to decide it.

It follows that the entry must be

Decree affirmed.

MOORE v. CENTER

(1964) 124 Vt. 277, 204 A.2d 164.

HOLDEN, C. J. The plaintiffs instituted this action for injunctive relief to protect an easement in lands of the defendant in the town of Sudbury. The easement claimed by the plaintiffs was created by the common predecessors in title to the lands of both parties in this controversy.

After making extensive findings of fact, the chancellor denied equitable relief to the plaintiffs, but issued an order forbidding the plaintiffs access to the lands of the defendant. The plaintiffs appeal.

The plaintiffs are the owners of an island on Lake Hortonia. To gain access to the lake on the mainland from Highway 141 that extends along the north and west shores, they acquired a narrow strip of land extending from the highway to the low water mark. This parcel was conveyed to them by warranty deed of Horace W. and Nettie C. Tupper, dated July 13, 1949.

In addition to conveying the fee to the access strip, the Tupper grant makes provision for the grantees' use of other lands of the grantors on both sides of the highway. The provision as to the use of land on the westerly side of the road is: "And granting further to said grantees, their heirs and assigns, the right and privilege of parking their automobile and removing same, on other lands of the grantors located on the westerly side of the highway, at such place as may from time to time be mutually agreed upon." The plaintiffs caused the deed, including the provision quoted, to be recorded in the land records of the town of Sudbury on July 27, 1949.

As to this aspect of the grant, the chancellor found—

"That on July 13, 1949, immediately after the execution and delivery of the deed in question, Plaintiffs made inquiry of the said Horace W. Tupper and Nettie C. Tupper concerning the area where it would be agreeable to Horace W. Tupper and Nettie C. Tupper that the Plaintiffs exercise their rights of parking their automobile as set forth in the deed of July 13, 1949; that Horace W. Tupper and Nettie C. Tupper then and there indicated an area northeasterly of the dwelling house then occupied by them, near a power pole and on the lands now owned by the Defendant Center; and that the Plaintiffs forthwith moved their car to the point so designated and have continuously used the same until excluded therefrom by the acts of the Defendants—."

Horace Tupper died shortly after these events. His widow, in her own behalf and presumably as successor to the interest of her deceased husband, conveyed lands northwest of Highway 141, including the area designated for parking, to the defendant on January 17, 1950. The conveyance to the defendant failed to mention the interest granted the plaintiffs by the prior deed of July, 1949. The deed from Mrs. Tupper warranted the premises free from every encumbrance. This instrument was recorded in the Sudbury land records January 27, 1950.

The plaintiffs continued to use the parking area during the years 1950 through 1956. The court found, however, that during this time the defendant was absent from his property and had no knowledge of this use.

In 1957 the defendant complained to the plaintiffs about their parking on his land. At this time the plaintiffs made known their claim to the easement as a matter of right.

In the fall of the year 1960, the defendant constructed a garage, driveway and retaining wall on his property. The findings state that the continued use of the parking lot by the plaintiffs in the area originally designated will encroach on the 1960 improvements and will deprive the defendant of his free and unencumbered use of his property. This situation resulted in the defendant's excluding the plaintiffs from the land. There has been no relocation of the parking area by mutual agreement.

The chancellor concluded that the defendant had no actual or constructive notice of the plaintiffs' easement. Accordingly, he dismissed the plaintiffs' complaint and prohibited them from further parking their automobile on the lands and premises of the defendant.

Although the deed from Horace and Nettie Tupper did not locate the easement afforded the plaintiff, it effectively created a right and interest in the lands retained. The particular area upon which the plaintiffs' right was to be exercised was competently left to subsequent agreement. [Citations.]

The findings tell us that the grantors availed themselves of this choice. And it can be inferred from the facts reported that the area selected was one which would accommodate the convenience of both the dominant and servient estates. [Citation.]

These acts were performed according to the dictates of the deed. When the area became fixed by agreement and continued use, it could not be disturbed nor relocated without the combined consent of the owners of both estates. [Citations.]

The fact that the improvements made in 1960 resulted in increasing the burden of the parking area beyond that experienced in prior years, is not attributable to the plaintiffs. It was done by the defendant's own hand after the plaintiffs had asserted their right to use the area in 1957 by virtue of the easement previously granted.

On that occasion, the findings report the defendant disclaimed any knowledge of the plaintiffs' easement since it was not mentioned in defendant's deed from Mrs. Tupper. He now contends the plaintiffs' easement was extinguished since he purchased the property in 1950 without notice. He argues that the plaintiffs' grant concerns other lands of the common grantors which are outside his chain of title, and the recording of the deed of July 13, 1949 is not constructive notice of the easement created in that instrument.

The argument is unsound. It is based on the erroneous notion that since the title to the fee of the dominant estate is not a part of the defendant's tract, the easement created in favor of that estate is outside the defendant's line.

To be sure, the lands acquired by the plaintiffs, if considered apart from the beneficial interest created by the defendant's predecessor, was not taken from the defendant's tract. However, its appurtenant easement was established on the defendant's parcel. The instrument which granted the plaintiffs' easement imposed a correlative burden by way of a servitude which stands as an encumbrance of record on the lands retained. The plaintiffs' interest was carved out of the very lands which the defendant subsequently acquired. It was in derogation of that grant.

"In such a case at common law, the purchaser would take subject to easement pre-viously created, as being a legal interest, irrespective of whether he has notice thereof, and the rule in this respect could not well be regarded as changed by the adoption of the recording law, as applied to a case in which the grant of the easement does appear of record, though in connection with other lands, to which the easement is made appurtenant." 2 Tiffany, Real Property, p. 2188 (1920 Ed.). [Citations].

The grantors of the plaintiffs' easement were not strangers to the defendant's title. Nettie C. Tupper, one of the grantors of the right, was the defendant's immediate predecessor in the servient estate.

The content of the Sudbury land records discloses that the deed of July 13, 1949 directly affected the premises which the defendant subsequently acquired. The record of that instrument constituted constructive notice of the true state of the defendant's title on January 17, 1950. It afforded notice to the grantee of the servitude against the defendant's parcel, since that encumbrance was imposed by the very persons who are the source of his grant. [Citations.]

The plaintiffs' interest in the defendant's premises is not impaired by the fact that the subsequent conveyance in the defendant's chain of title failed to mention it. The clause in the deed from the Tuppers to the Moores constituted notice of the easement and its corresponding burden on the land which the defendant acquired. [Citations.]

Until that burden is lifted or modified by mutual agreement of the owners of both estates, the plaintiffs are entitled to have their interest in the defendant's land protected. On the facts found, it was error to dismiss the complaint and to enjoin the plaintiffs from further enjoyment of their prior right.

Decree reversed and cause remanded for further proceedings according to the decision.

PROBLEMS

1. Hubert Watson and his wife, Wilma, were owners in joint tenancy of a tract of vacant property which they had contracted to sell to Samuel Stone. Hubert subsequently died and Wilma continued to collect the payments under the terms of the contract and refused to turn over any part of the proceeds to Barnes, who was the administrator of Hubert's estate. Barnes brought an action to collect one-half of the proceeds arising out of the real estate contract from Wilma. Decision?

2. In 1950, Roy Martin and his wife, Alice, their son, Hiram, and the latter's wife, Myrna, acquired title to a 240-acre farm. The deed ran to Roy Martin and Alice Martin, the father and mother, as joint tenants, with the right of survivorship, and to Hiram Martin and Myrna Martin, the son and his wife, as joint tenants, with the right of survivorship. Alice Martin died in 1960, and in 1963 Roy Martin married Agnes Martin. By his will, Roy Martin bequeathed and devised his entire estate to Agnes Martin. When Roy Martin died in 1965, Hiram and Myrna Martin assumed complete control of the farm.

State the interest in the farm, if any, of Agnes, Hiram and Myrna Martin, immediately upon the death of Roy Martin.

3. A and B, who are husband and wife, acquired Redacre by a warranty deed which contained the following clause, ". . . convey and warrant to A and B with full rights of survivorship and not as tenants in common. . ." A executed a mortgage upon his interest to C, which he subsequently paid. A died intestate, leaving as his only heirs-at-law, his widow, B and and his son, D.

(a) What is the interest, if any, of B in Redacre?

(b) What is the interest, if any of D in Redacre?

4. Robert Dudley died leaving a will in which he devised Blackacre to his sisters, Anne, Belle and Celia in joint tenancy. Anne, by quitclaim deed, conveyed all her interest in the property to Belle. Anne died the following year. Bell died five years later, and by her will she devised whatever interest she had in the realty to four nieces. The latter instituted an action to partition the property. Their complaint and Celia's answer were based upon diametrically opposing theories. The complaint of the nieces alleged that Anne's deed entirely severed the joint tenancies existing among the three sisters; that thereafter Belle owned an undivided two-thirds interest in the property and Celia an undivided one-third interest as tenants in common; and that the nieces, as successors to Belle's interest, each owned an undivided one-sixth interest as tenants in common with Celia, who owned an undivided one-third. Celia's answer averred that the nieces each owned an undivided one-twelfth interest as tenants in common with Celia, who owned an undivided two-thirds. Who is correct?

5. Henry Thornburn and Mary Thornburn, husband and wife, acquired vacant lands by warranty deed. The deed recited, ". . . do convey and warrant to Henry Thornburn and Mary Thornburn as joint tenants the (legal description)." Shortly thereafter, marital discord developed and Henry conveyed his one-half interest in the premises to his brother Jim. Mary did not join in the conveyance. Henry died intestate in 1966 leaving his widow, Mary, and no children.

What is the interest of Mary, if any, in the real estate?

6. T, having no relatives, died testate. His will granted a life estate to A in certain real estate, with remainder to B and C in joint tenancy. All the residue of T's estate was left to the X College. While going to T's funeral, the car in which A, B and C were driving was wrecked. B was killed, C died a few minutes later, and A died on his way to the hospital. Who is entitled to the real estate in question?

7. Watson owned three adjoining lots, numbered 16, 17 and 18. He erected a separate brick apartment building on each lot, but the building on lot 17 encroached about one foot over on lot 16. He constructed a driveway on the common boundary line between lots 17 and 18. He then sold lot 16 to Young and lot 18 to Zemon, giving each grantee a warranty deed describing the lot involved and nothing further. Later, Young brought an action against Watson to remove the encroachment. Watson brought another action against Zemon to enjoin his use of the driveway inasmuch as it involved movement over lot 17.

What decisions?

8. X, the owner of two adjoining lots, conveyed one of them, on which stood a photograph studio, to B, a photographer. The remaining lot was vacant, and subsequently X commenced the erection of a large building on it which, if completed, would obstruct the light to the build-

ing occupied by B, and render it useless for purposes of photography. B brought suit for injunction to restrain X from erecting his building on the ground that he (B) had an implied easement for light. Should the injunction be granted?

9. Otis Olson, the owner of two adjoining city lots, A and B, built a house on each. He laid a drainpipe from lot B across lot A to the main sewer pipe under the alley beyond lot A. Olson then sold and conveyed lot A to Fred Ford. The deed, which made no mention of the drainpipe, was promptly recorded. Ford had no actual knowledge or notice of the drainpipe although it would have been apparent to anyone making an inspection of the premises, having been only partially imbedded. Later, Olson sold and conveyed lot B to Luke Lane. This deed, which likewise made no reference to the drainpipe, was also promptly recorded.

A few weeks thereafter, Ford discovered the drainpipe across lot A and removed it. Did he have the right to do so?

10. A proposed to place a building on his lot which would require an excavation of a large area to the depth of eighteen feet. Adjoining A's lot on the west was an unimproved lot owned by B and left in its natural condition for use as a playground for his children. Adjoining A's lot on the east was a lot owned by C and improved with a large brick residence. Adjoining A's lot on the north was a building owned by D and having a party wall, built by agreement between A and D, with the center line along the boundary line dividing the lot owned by A from the lot owned by D, and with its foundations extending to a depth of twelve feet. A notified B, C and D of the proposed excavation and warned them to take proper precautions. B, C and D in turn each noticed A making his own excavation but stopped short of taking measures to support any of the adjoining property. As a consequence—

(a) The lot of B caved in, leaving a deep depression—

(b) The residence of C settled with resulting cracks in the ceilings, jammed doors, etc.—and

(c) The party wall of D's building likewise settled and the joists of D's building had to be re-set.

B, C and D thereupon sued A for the damages to their respective properties. What judgment in each suit?

CHAPTER 48

DEEDS AND CONVEYANCING

Introductory. The law has always been and is today extremely cautious with respect to the transfer of title to real estate. Personal property may, for the most part, be readily and informally passed from owner to owner but real property, occupying a position of uniqueness and singularity, can only be transferred in compliance with a variety of formalities.

The modern deed as authorized in American jurisdictions is a somewhat simplified version of an early English deed known as a "grant." Originally, a grant was used to transfer intangible interests in land but its use was gradually expanded to include transfer of any type of interest in land.

Types of Modern Deeds

(1) *Warranty Deed*. By a warranty deed, the seller (grantor) promises the buyer (grantee) that he has a valid title to the property and, expressly or impliedly, under such a deed, the grantor obliges himself to make the grantee whole if the latter suffers any damage because the grantor's title was defective. In most jurisdictions, a form of warranty deed is set out in the statute and the words necessary to create such a deed are specified.

Aside from the liability of the grantor for any defects in his title, a distinct characteristic of the warranty deed is that it will convey an after-acquired title. On January 30, A conveys Blackacre by warranty deed to B. On January 30, A's title to Blackacre is defective but by February 14th, A has acquired a good title. Without more, B has good title under the deed.

(2) *Special Warranty Deed*. Whereas a warranty deed contains a general warranty of title, a special warranty deed is one which warrants only that the title has not been impaired, encumbered or rendered defective by reason of any act or omission of the grantor. The grantor merely warrants the title so far as acts or omissions of the grantor are concerned. He does not warrant that the title may not be defective by reason of the acts or omissions of others.

(3) *Quitclaim Deed*. By a quitclaim deed, the grantor says no more, in effect, than "I make no promise as to what interest I do have in this land but whatever it be I convey it to you." Quitclaim deeds are used most frequently when it is desired to have persons who appear to, or may, have an interest in land release their interest. If one tenant in common offers to buy his co-tenant's interest a quitclaim deed is customarily the method of transfer. If, through some error in a legal description in a prior deed, A, the owner of a parcel, has innocently acquired some interest in an adjoining parcel of land belonging to B, A will be asked to execute a quitclaim deed in order to clear up B's title.

Form and Requirements. Any transfer of an interest in land is within the Statute of Frauds if it is an interest of more than a limited duration and must be in writing. Originally, leases for less than three years were excepted from this requirement. Today, in some jurisdictions, a lease for more than a year has to be in writing to create more than a tenancy at will.

Nearly all deeds, whatever the type, follow substantially the same pattern and most of the essential characteristics of deeds can be considered by analyzing the component parts of the usual deed. These parts are:

1. Names of parties
2. Consideration
3. Words of conveyance
4. Description of the land conveyed
5. Exceptions or reservations
6. Quantity of the estate conveyed
7. Covenants of title
8. Execution

Items 1 through 5 are referred to as the *premises,* and item 6 is the *habendum.*

(1) *Names of Parties.* The omission of the name of the grantor from a deed is generally not as serious a flaw as the omission of the grantee's name since the grantor's signature will appear at the bottom. Omission of the grantee's name is said to void a deed but generally it can be filled in, provided it is done before delivery and with the oral authority of the grantor. A deed from a man and wife will usually read "Tom Jones and Mary Jones, his wife."

(2) *Consideration.* In most instances, the law does not require consideration for a valid deed. A grantor may be bound by his gift of land if the deed is properly executed and delivered. It is, however, the custom to specify nominal consideration in deeds, presumably to protect the grantee not only from the allegation that he holds the property under a resulting trust for the grantor but also to protect him from third parties with adverse interests in the land who might allege that he was not an innocent purchaser for value. The usual practice of reciting a consideration of ten dollars even though the actual price may be many times this amount probably is due partly to custom and partly to a wish to conceal the actual sale price from those who might inspect the public records. Whatever the recited consideration, the Federal documentary stamps required on the face of all deeds will be based upon the true consideration although, in some cases, the desire to mislead subsequent purchasers as to the actual sale price has led to the use of a larger amount of these stamps than was required by law. A deed executed by a trustee will generally recite the full consideration to avoid the charge that the trustee neglected his obligation to the beneficiaries by selling the property at less than its fair value.

(3) *Words of Conveyance.* The statutory forms of deeds prescribed by statute in most States suggest certain operative words of conveyance. The words used will, of course, vary depending upon whether the instrument is a warranty deed or a quitclaim deed. A common phrase for a warranty deed is "convey and warrant" although, in a number of States the phrase "grant, bargain and sell" is used together with a covenant by the seller later in the deed that he will "warrant and defend the title." A quitclaim deed will generally provide that the grantor "conveys and quitclaims" or, more simply, "quitclaims all interest" in the property. Whatever the recommended statutory form, generally any words which substantially evidence the intent of the grantor will be sufficient.

(4) *Description of the Land Conveyed.* The primary requirement of any description is that it be sufficiently clear and certain to permit identification of the property conveyed. The test is frequently applied in terms of whether a subsequent purchaser or a surveyor employed by him could mark off the land from the description. This does not mean that any particular method is necessary to a valid conveyance. There is a great variety to be found in legal descriptions of property. A conveyance of "all my land in McHenry County" is sufficient, provided all the grantor's land is determinable from other records. The conveyance of "my house" will pass title to the lot although a description in a conveyance by street number is risky be-

cause of the chance of revisions in the street numbers.

Such informal descriptions may be sufficiently clear to validly convey property; this is not, however, the usual method. Customary descriptions generally fall into three major classes, (a) Description by reference to monuments and courses; (b) Description by reference to Rectangular Survey System; and (c) Description by reference to recorded plat.

(a) *By Reference to Monuments and Courses.* One of the oldest methods of describing property is by reference to its boundaries in terms of physical objects. These may be metal or stone markers placed there for the specific purpose of identifying the boundary or they may be natural or man-made objects such as trees, rivers, fences or highways. The description will state the "course" of a boundary, the direction in which the line runs in terms of the compass and the line may then be described as running a certain distance or as running between two designated monuments.

Where there is a conflict between monuments, on the one hand, and courses or distances, the former will generally prevail since they represent more or less permanent objects on the site while a course or distance is simply someone's judgment as to the direction or length of a line.

The use of monuments is, of course, subject to the risk that they may disappear or be changed and, where alternative methods of description are feasible, description by monuments and courses is not preferred.

(b) *By Reference to Rectangular Survey System.* Most of the continental United States west of the Allegheny Mountains is included in a survey made by the Federal government and known as the Rectangular Survey System. Land in this great area is generally conveyed by use of a description which, in its entirety or in part, refers to this comprehensive system. The survey has for its points of beginning lines running parallel to longitudinal and latitudinal bases. A line conforming to a parallel of latitude is referred to as a "base" line and a series of lines running due North and South at right angles to the base line are called "Principal Meridians." Lines running due East and West drawn at intervals of six miles both North and South of the base line are designated as Township lines. Similar lines drawn at six-mile intervals East and West of the Principal Meridians and running due North and South are designated as Range lines. The six-mile strips of the Township lines and Range lines are numbered consecutively, extending from the base line and Principal Meridian, respectively. The six-mile square areas formed by the intersection of range and township lines are "townships" and these, in turn, are divided into thirty-six "Sections" containing one square mile and numbered consecutively from one to thirty-six. A normal section contains 640 acres but, due to the convergence of the range lines running true north, in some instances a section may contain less than 640 acres. Fractional sections may also result from natural boundaries which cut into the land.

The breakdown of a Section is shown on the following chart:

A SECTION OF LAND — 640 ACRES

	80 rods.	10 chains.	330 ft.	
A rod is 16½ feet.			5 acres.	5 acres.
A chain is 66 feet or 4 rods.				
A mile is 320 rods, 80 chains or 5,280 ft.		20 acres.	8 chs.	20 rods.
A square rod is 272¼ square feet.				
An acre contains 43,560 square feet.				

A rod is 16½ feet.
A chain is 66 feet or 4 rods.
A mile is 320 rods, 80 chains or 5,280 ft.
A square rod is 272¼ square feet.
An acre contains 43,560 square feet.
 "   "   "   160 square rods.
 "   "   is about 208¾ feet square.
 "   "   is 8 rods wide by 20 rods long.
    or any two numbers (of rods) whose
    product is 160.
25x125 feet equals .0717 of an acre.

80 rods.

80 acres.

10 chains.   330 ft.

5 acres.   5 acres.

20 acres.   8 chs.   20 rods.

40 rods

10 acres.

660 feet.   10 chains.

80 acres.

40 acres

80 rods.

660 feet.

CENTER   20 chains.   1,320 feet.

OF SECTION ·

Sectional Map of a Township with adjoining Sections.

36	31	32	33	34	35	36	31
1	6	5	4	3	2	1	6
12	7	8	9	10	11	12	7
13	18	17.	16	15	14	13	18
24	19	20	21	22	23	24	19
25	30	29	28	27	26	25	30
36	31	32	33	34	35	36	31
1	6	5	4	3	2	1	6

160 acres.

40 chains, 160 rods or 2,640 feet.

[Provided by the Chicago Title and Trust Company, Chicago, Illinois.]

Although the Section is the smallest official unit of the Survey, for the purpose of conveyancing, each section may be divided into quarters of 160 acres and each quarter, in turn, may be quartered into 40-acre tracts. Thus, property may be described as "the Northwest Quarter of the Southeast Quarter of Section 12, Township 3 North, Range 2 West of the 3rd Principal Meridian." Frequently, even smaller parcels are described as follows:

"The North half of the Southwest Quarter of the Northeast Quarter of Section 11— being 20 acres more or less."

or

"The Northwest Quarter of the Southeast Quarter of the Northwest Quarter of Section 12 * * *."

(c) *By Reference to Recorded Plat.* A third method of describing property in a deed is by reference to a survey of a larger tract which includes the parcel to be conveyed and which has been filed for record in the county in which the land is located. Sellers may thereby avoid a lengthy description by monuments or reference only to the government survey and, instead, refer to the property as "Lot 1" or "Lot 12" in an identified plat. This method is used where, under authorization of statute, an owner has had his land surveyed and subdivided into blocks, lots and streets. In most cases, the seller is required to convey or "dedicate" the streets to the local government for public use. In most cities, villages and incorporated towns, reference to a plat is the common method of describing property. Thus, such a deed might describe the land as "Lot 1 in Block 7 of McGuire's Subdivision in the village of Bull Creek, Iowa, being part of Section 1, Township 4 North, Range 28 West of the 4th Principal Meridian."

When the boundary of a tract is described by reference to a body of water or to a street or highway, additional problems of identification may arise. Where the stream bed does not belong to the State, it is a general rule that the owner of the land "bounded by" a stream is entitled to the bed to the center of the stream, in the absence of a clear indication in the description that the grantee was only to take to the edge of the water. Similarly, unless the State owns the fee to a roadbed a description of land as bounded "by" a street will be sufficient to pass title to the center of the street. An intention to exclude the road bed to the center line must be clearly indicated.

It was noted in Chapter 47 that a conveyance of land will convey easements or other rights appurtenant thereto without further reference.

(5) *Exceptions or Reservations.* Immediately following the description of the property conveyed, the grantor will usually provide for any exceptions or reservations which are to be excluded from the grant. One illustration would be a deed conveying "The East one half of the Northwest Quarter of Section 11 * * * excepting therefrom one acre square in the Northeast corner of the Northeast Quarter of said Northwest Quarter." Another example would be a deed conveying "Lots 2, 3 and 4 of Laurence's Subdivision in Section 1 * * * reserving, however, to the grantors, his heirs and assigns forever, the minerals upon and underneath said land."

An exception or reservation in a deed cannot create any interest in a stranger to the transaction. A warranty deed contained the following language:

> "Grantors, Mary Brown and John Brown, her husband, of the City of Chicago, County of Cook and State of Illinois, for $10.00 and other valuable consideration convey and warrant the following described property (here follows property description) unto William Smith of the City of Chicago, County of Cook and State of Illinois, excepting a life estate for William White and Helen White, father and mother of grantor Mary Brown."

The father and mother of Mary Brown acquired nothing by the deed. The effect of the language was to reserve to the grantor, Mary Brown, presumed to be the owner, an interest for the lifetime of her father and mother and the grantee took title subject thereto.

(6) *Quantity of the Estate Conveyed.* After the property has been described, the deed will state "to have and to hold" and then proceed to describe the *quantity* of estate conveyed to the grantee. Thus, either "to have and to hold to himself and his heirs forever" or "to have and to hold in fee simple" would vest the grantee with absolute title to the land. This part of a deed is called the *habendum* and is distinguished from the parts which come before it (and have been previously discussed) which are called the *premises.*

There is the possibility that in a carelessly prepared deed there will be a conflict between the size of estate granted in the premises and the quantity described in the habendum. One technical rule is that the estate described in the granting clause takes precedence over that described in the habendum. A more reasonable rule is that the larger estate will prevail whether it appears in the granting clause of the premises or in the habendum.

(7) *Covenants of Title.* It is the practice in deeds for the grantor to make certain promises concerning his title to the land. If any one of these promises or covenants is breached the grantee will be indemnified. There are a number of these covenants, the most usual of which are of title, against incumbrances, of quiet enjoyment, and of warranty. These various covenants of title add up to an assurance that the grantee will have undisturbed possession and will, in turn, be able to transfer the land without adverse claims of right by third parties. In many States, these covenants, or many of them, are implied from the words of conveyance

themselves such as "warrants" or "grant, bargain and sell."

(8) *Execution.* Deeds are generally concluded by the signature of the grantor, a seal and an acknowledgment before a notary public or other official authorized to attest to the authenticity of documents. The signature can be made by a person other than the grantor himself as his attorney or agent if such party has written authority from the grantor in a form required by law. The seal today has lost a great deal of its former significance and in those jurisdictions where it is required, the seal is sufficient if the word "Seal" or the letters "L. S." appear next to the signature.

Although the acknowledgment may not be required to bind the parties to the deed, it is generally a prerequisite to recording the deed and without an acknowledgment a deed may not be effective as against third parties. In most jurisdictions, a special form of acknowledgment for deeds is specified by statute. A simple and usual notary's statement that a party "subscribed and was sworn" may not be sufficient.

Delivery of Deeds. A deed does not transfer title to land until it is delivered. "Delivery" means an *intent* that the deed shall take effect and will be evidenced by the acts or statements of the grantor. Manual or physical transfer of the deed is usually the best evidence of this intent but is not necessary to effect "delivery." Thus, the act of the grantor in placing a deed in a safe deposit box may or may not constitute delivery depending upon many facts such as whether the grantee did or did not have access to the box and whether the grantor deals with the deed as though the property were the grantee's. A deed conceivably may be "delivered" even when kept in the possession of the grantor just as it would be possible that physical delivery of the deed to the grantee would not transfer title. A deed is frequently turned over to a third party to

hold until the performance of certain conditions by the grantee. This is spoken of as an escrow and the third party is the escrow agent. Upon the performance of the condition, the escrow agent is obliged to turn the deed over to the grantee. If, after delivery to the escrow agent, the grantor should die or become incompetent the "delivery" is said to "date back" to the time the deed was placed with the escrow agent. In this way, the subsequent incapacity of the grantor is circumvented. If a grantor dies subsequent to the execution of a deed, it is possible that questions will be raised as to whether there was "delivery" before death. This will depend upon whether the evidence shows an intent on his part to divest himself of dominion over the property and to give control to the named grantee.

Upon the following facts, one court held that a deed was invalid because it had not been delivered before the death of the grantor. K had three sons. He owned considerable real estate. He expressed to his good friend, E, a desire that his (K's) sons should have the benefit of some of this real estate and told E that he proposed to convey it to them, but that he did not wish the conveyance placed on record. He duly executed a warranty deed to Harry, one of his sons, as trustee for himself and his two brothers. This deed was handed to Harry and by him given to E. During the remainder of his lifetime, K continued in the possession, management and control of the property, paid all the taxes, made repairs and in every way treated the property as his own. All of this was done with the knowledge and acquiescence of Harry. The day after K's death, E handed the deed to Harry, who immediately caused it to be recorded. Until handed to Harry at the time, it had been continuously in the possession of E and never recorded.

This is an arguable case and it illustrates the uncertainties which arise when the intent of a deceased person is the deciding factor.

It is indispensable to the delivery of a deed that the grantor should part with control over it with the intention that it will immediately become operative to convey the estate described in it. If the grantor retains any dominion and control over the deed, it is ineffectual as a conveyance. In this case, the court felt that the mere placing of a deed in the hands of a grantee momentarily did not constitute delivery because the grantor did not so intend as evidenced by his expressed wishes and his subsequent acts of ownership.

ADVERSE POSSESSION

It is a possible although very rare event that title to land may be transferred *involuntarily* without any deed or other formality. Such an occurrence results from what the law calls "adverse possession" and, although the landowner should be aware of this peculiar risk, its infrequency calls for only a brief comment.

In most States, if a person openly and continuously occupies or exerts dominion over the land of another for a period of twenty years, that person will gain title to the land. The possession must be actual and not merely constructive. Living on land, farming it, or building and maintaining fences on it have been held sufficient to constitute possession. It is necessary, however, that the possession be *adverse*. By this, it is meant that any act of dominion by the true owner during the twenty years will stop the period from running. His entry on the land or the assertion of ownership by him will break the period. In such event, the period will have to commence anew from that time.

The purchasers or heirs of one occupying adversely may "tack on" the period during which the vendor or ancestor possessed the land to establish the necessary period of time. So long as the persons occupied continuously without break and had some continuity by

virtue of inheritance or contract, it is not necessary that the same person remain for twenty years.

In some jurisdictions, shorter periods of adverse possession have been established by statute where there is not only possession but also some other claim such as the payment of taxes for seven years and at least a colorable claim of title.

Unless provided by statute, adverse possession cannot be asserted against the United States or against a State.

CONVEYANCING

Introductory. A transfer of land for valuable consideration invariably involves two steps: (1) A contract for the sale of land and (2) the delivery of the deed and payment of the agreed consideration.

There are good reasons why the two-step system has become firmly established in the law of conveyancing. Except in cases of fraud, the acceptance of a deed is an irrevocable step. Thereafter, if it should appear that the vendor's title is defective or that he has no title at all, the purchaser's sole remedy is an action for damages based upon the covenants in the deed, if any. The rule in most jurisdictions is that the damages recoverable on account of failure of title may not, in any case, exceed the purchase price paid plus the costs of defending a bad title.

Obviously, most purchasers want some assurance that they can keep the property they are about to purchase. Such assurance may be obtained only from a thorough and competent title search. This may involve (a) a search of all the relevant records conducted by the purchaser's attorney himself; (b) an examination by the purchaser's attorney of an abstract of such a search prepared by an abstract company and furnished by the vendor; or (c) a guaranty policy issued by a title insurance company, which, in addition to assuring recovery of loss due to title defects, shows, indirectly, that the title search made by the insurance company has failed to unearth any defects except those noted upon the face of the policy. Clearly, a party will not undertake the expense of a title search unless he has a contract assuring him that the transaction will be consummated.

Even where no title search is contemplated, there are obvious reasons why a conveyance of land for a valuable consideration will be preceded by a contract for its sale. Although in the case of a gift of land one might expect no antecedent agreement, in a sale for valuable consideration, the parties will mutually desire to reach an agreement before the deed is prepared. Since an oral agreement will not be enforceable under the Statute of Frauds, the vendor, if he wants to be assured that the deed will be accepted, must reduce the agreement to writing and have it signed by the purchaser. The simplest agreement should contain (1) the names and addresses of the parties; (2) a description of the property to be conveyed; (3) the time for the conveyance; (4) the type of deed to be given, and (5) the price, and manner of payment. To avoid dispute, and to assure adequate protection of the rights of both parties, there are many other points which should be covered by a contract for the sale of land.

Statute of Frauds. Binders and Memoranda of Sale. Most real estate brokers require the purchaser to sign a binder or memorandum of sale even before the formal agreement is prepared. The law developed under the Statute of Frauds requires that such binders contain the essential terms of the contract. The courts have not been in agreement as to the details which must be covered to render such binders enforceable by action.

Contract of Sale: (1) Vendor's Obligation to Convey Marketable Title. It is firmly es-

tablished in the law of conveyancing that a contract for the sale of land carries with it an implied obligation upon the part of the vendor to convey marketable title. A marketable title is one which is free from (a) encumbrances, such as mortgages, easements, liens, and restrictive covenants; (b) defects in the chain of title appearing in the land records, such as a prior recorded conveyance of the same property by the vendor or by one of his predecessors in title showing that title is in a stranger; (c) any defects which, while they are not sufficient to amount to encumbrances, may yet subject the purchaser to the inconvenience of having to defend his title in court. This third category of defects comes under an oft repeated principle that "no purchaser should be forced to buy a lawsuit."

Two important exceptions to this rule should be noted. (1) Most courts hold that the vendor's implied or express obligation to convey marketable title does not require him to convey free from existing zoning restrictions. The reasons given are (a) the buyer is charged with notice of the existing law and (b) the zoning restriction being beneficial to the community as a whole, in effect, benefits rather than encumbers the property involved. The time for a purchaser to check for zoning restrictions is *before* he signs a contract to purchase, *not after*. (2) Some courts also hold that the vendor's implied or express obligation to convey marketable title does not require him to convey free from open and visible public rights of way or easements such as public roads and sewers.

Except in those two instances, however, the purchaser's *knowledge* or constructive knowledge of an encumbrance or other title defect *never* operates to diminish the vendor's obligation to convey marketable title. In all such cases, it is conclusively presumed that by the contract of sale the vendor has undertaken to remove such defects before the date set for the delivery of the deed known as the "closing date."

It can be seen, therefore, that if the vendor desires to establish any exceptions to this very strict duty he must do so by express language in the contract of sale.

(2) Customary Exceptions. It is common practice for the contract of sale to provide that the vendor shall convey marketable title subject only to: (1) special taxes or assessments for improvements not yet completed; (2) installments not due at the date thereof of any special tax or assessment for improvements theretofore completed; (3) general taxes for a stated year and for subsequent years; (4) building, building line and use or occupancy restrictions, conditions and covenants of record; (5) zoning and building laws or ordinances; (6) roads and highways, if any.

If there are any existing leases not expiring before the date of closing or if there are any outstanding mortgages, subject to which the purchaser is undertaking to take the property, these must be included in the foregoing list.

The purpose of exceptions (1) and (2) is to avoid the failure of the vendor's title because of a lien for special taxes or assessments which he cannot remove because the time for payment has not yet arrived. The lien generally attaches when the improvements are first authorized by the local authority. Exception (3) avoids a similar situation in the case of general taxes, the lien of which customarily attaches at the beginning of the tax year but payment of which cannot be made until a later date when the tax bills have been prepared, which is subsequent to the closing date. Exceptions (5) and (6) are usually inserted through an abundance of caution.

(3) Apportionment of Charges. Since, by virtue of the customary exceptions (1) (2) and (3), the purchaser undertakes to accept a conveyance subject to existing liens for taxes and assessments which have not and cannot be paid at the time of closing, the contract must provide for an apportionment of those charges between vendor and purchaser so that each may pay the proportion of the entire charge which is attributable to his period of ownership. Suppose that, under the applicable law, the lien for general taxes attaches on April 1, 1965, but that the amount of the taxes is not ascertained or payable until May 1, 1966. The contract calls for closing on June 1, 1965. If the taxes for 1965 are not excepted from the vendor's obligation to convey marketable title, he will not be able to convey marketable title until May 1, 1966. If they are excepted, then the purchaser will be required to pay the entire tax for 1965. It follows that such an exception should be coupled with a clause prorating the tax on the basis of the most recent available tax bill, requiring the vendor to pay so much as is attributable to the period before June 1, 1965, and the purchaser to pay the remainder.

The same situation exists in the case of advance payments of rent where the purchaser has agreed to take subject to outstanding leases. Suppose the leases require payment of rent yearly in advance on January 1 of each year. Assume that the rent for 1965 has already been paid to the vendor. At common law, rents are not apportionable. Accordingly, unless the contract of sale provides for a credit to the purchaser by prorating the rent he will receive no rent from June 1, 1965, the date of the conveyance, until the next advance payment becomes due, i. e., January 1, 1966.

(4) Further Assurances of Title. It has been noted that the purchaser will want greater title protection than the assurance of a right of action for damages based upon the covenants in the deed. This is provided by the title search. The significance of the vendor's obligation to convey marketable

title is that if the title search reveals any flaw which has not been made an express exception to that obligation, the purchaser may refuse to take the conveyance on the date set for closing, and may sue and recover damages from the seller unless the title defect is promptly remedied.

The title search may take several forms. In some localities and in some States it is still customary for the purchaser's attorney to conduct a search of all the relevant records. This search is aided by the recording acts which provide, in general, that any instrument affecting title which is not recorded will have no effect against subsequent purchasers who take the property for value and without notice of such an instrument. Without going further into the law surrounding the recording acts, the importance to the purchaser of recording the deed of conveyance to him *immediately* after delivery, cannot be overemphasized.

It may be seen that the title searcher can rely largely upon the instruments of record to determine whether the vendor's title is good. There are, however, many encumbrances which will not appear of record and which are not required to be recorded. Thus, easements by implication and inchoate dower interests of spouses who are not mentioned in any conveyance in the chain of title will not appear of record, yet the purchaser will take subject to them despite his good faith and lack of notice. This is also true of the rights of persons in possession of the premises. It is possible, however, to procure title guaranty policies to cover such defects.

While the individual title search is still common, the growing practice is to rely upon searches made by abstract companies or upon title guaranty policies. The abstract or the preliminary report of title furnished by the title insurance company must still be examined by the purchaser's attorney to determine, in the one case, whether the abstract reveals any title defects and, in the other, whether the title guaranty which the title insurance company is willing to issue will cover all the defects and encumbrances that are not assumed by the purchaser.

Whichever method of title assurance is adopted, the contract of sale must contain careful provisions for it and should, among other things, provide which party is to bear the expense.

It is customary to include a clause in the contract of sale giving the vendor a stated period of time in which to remove such defects as may be revealed in the course of title examination, or shown on a preliminary report on title furnished by the title insurance company. Such clauses may contain a provision exonerating the vendor from liability for damages on account of any defect which renders the title unmarketable. The purchaser should, therefore, be careful to include in the contract words to the effect that the vendor must, during such period of time, use diligent effort to remove any and all defects revealed by the title search, as, otherwise, the vendor may do nothing and the purchaser find himself compelled to decide either not to take the property or to take it subject to the discovered defects of title without recourse against the vendor.

The Torrens System. In a number of States, it is possible to register land with the local government and make the condition of the title determinable by reference to the certificate of registration alone. This method of title registration is known as the Torrens System after its original sponsor, Sir Robert Torrens, who introduced it into Australia about the middle of the nineteenth century. Under the Torrens System, an owner of land files a petition in court to have his land registered and, after careful investigation, a certificate is issued by direction of the court confirming the owner's title and noting thereon any outstanding interests or encumbrances. One copy of the certificate is filed in the registration office; one goes to the owner. Upon subsequent sale, the owner executes his deed and delivers his duplicate copy of the certificate to the buyer. The buyer may inform himself as to the state of the seller's title by inspecting the certificate on file in the registrar's office. The buyer is absolutely protected against any liens or outstanding interests which have not been noted on the certificate. He does not need an abstract or a guaranty policy. The statute provides that the certificate is conclusive as to all but a very few interests. If a judgment creditor of the seller has failed to note his lien on the certificate the buyer takes the land clear of the claim. The title vests in the buyer not upon the execution of the deed but upon the delivery of the new certificate by the appropriate division of the local government.

It is apparent that, in theory at least, the Torrens System represents a great improvement over the older methods of giving buyers further assurances as to the seller's title. Under the Torrens System, there is no need to make or pay for a careful search of the history of the parcel because the certificate is conclusive evidence of the present state of the title. There have been many disputes as to why the Torrens System has not always worked better than was hoped for by its proponents. It has not as yet claimed wide adoption in this country and even in the States where it is authorized by statute it has not made serious inroads upon the abstract or guaranty policy systems.

Risk Between Contract and Closing Date. Except in a few jurisdictions which have adopted the Uniform Vendor and Purchaser Risk Law, a majority of the jurisdictions adhere to the common-law rule that, *after the contract, the risk of loss or destruction of the property is upon the purchaser.* The reason for the rule is that a contract for the sale of land is specifically enforceable in a court of equity, and therefore at the time of making the contract the purchaser is regarded as the equitable or beneficial owner of the land. It is important, therefore, to make provision in the contract that, upon payment of the purchase price, the purchaser will be entitled to the proceeds of any insurance held by the vendor. It is not advisable for the vendor to assign his policy of insurance on the date of the contract for the reason that, if the purchaser thereafter defaults and becomes insolvent, the vendor may not be able to reach the proceeds in the hands of the purchaser. A solution to the problem is to secure an indorsement of the policy making it payable to either the vendor or the purchaser "as his interest may appear." If such an indorsement cannot be secured, the purchaser usually obtains an insurance policy on his own behalf protecting his interest in the property.

The contract of sale may, of course, provide that the risk of loss or destruction shall remain upon the vendor until conveyance to the purchaser, or it may provide that the vendor shall restore any structures destroyed before closing.

Description of the Property—Fixtures. In addition to the obvious requirement of an adequate description of the premises to be conveyed, the contract should contain careful provisions as to any and all fixtures intended to be included in the sale.

Escrow Agreements. The value of an escrow in title closing may be illustrated by the following example: P desires to purchase a house from V. To do so, he must obtain a loan from Second Bank to be secured by a first mortgage upon the property. The house is now subject, however, to a mortgage in favor of First Bank. V does not have the funds to pay off that mortgage indebtedness, so as to secure its release before title closing, and wishes to use, for this purpose, a portion of the purchase money to be paid by P. However, Second Bank will not advance the money which it has agreed to lend to P until the first mortgage is released, as its agreement entitles it to have a prior lien on the property as security for the new loan. First Bank will not release its mortgage until it has obtained payment of the indebtedness secured thereby. The transaction may be carried out through an escrow agent. Both First Bank and Second Bank will be satisfied if a financially stable and dependable third person, as escrowee, will undertake to handle the funds and the documents and to make payment of the money and delivery of the documents in accordance with written instructions signed by both banks and by the contracting parties. In this way the escrow agent uses the proceeds of the new mortgage loan to pay off the old mortgage.

CASES

STERLING v. PARK

(1907) 129 Ga. 309, 58 S.E. 828, 13 L.R.A.,N.S., 298.

Evans, J. The various assignments of error raise but one question: Is it essential that a person who signs, seals and delivers a deed should be mentioned in the body of the deed, to be bound by it, and to make it an operative conveyance of his estate in the land? The case in hand was complaint for land, and one of the plaintiff's muniments of title was a deed in which M. C. Huntley was named as grantor, and R. E. Park as grantee, and which purported to convey, for a valuable consideration, a described lot of land, in fee simple. The deed was signed and sealed by M. C. Huntley, W. H. Huntley, and the defendant. Neither W. H. Huntley nor the defendant was named in it as grantor. At the time the deed was executed the title to the land was in M. C. Huntley for life, with remainder to the others who signed the deed. The plaintiff's contention is that the deed is operative and effective as a conveyance of the estate which

each maker-signer had in the land; while on the other hand, the defendant contends that as she was not named in the deed as grantor, it is not an operative conveyance of her estate in remainder.

The point in the case has been before many courts of last resort, and there is much contrariety of opinion on the subject. We believe the true rule to be that one who signs, seals, and delivers a deed, in which he is not named as grantor, is nevertheless bound by these acts as a grantor. We think an examination into the origin and reason of the contrary doctrine will demonstrate the correctness of our conclusion. At common law a deed is defined to be a writing, sealed and delivered by the parties. Coke's Lit. 171; 2 Bl.Com. 295. Lord Coke said: "There have been eight formal or orderly parts of a deed of feofment, viz.: 1 the premises of the deed implied by Littleton; 2 the habendum, whereof Littleton here speaketh; 3 the tenendum, mentioned by Littleton; 4 the reddendum; 5 the clause of warrantie; 6 the in cujus rei testimonium, comprehending the sealing; 7 the date of the deed, containing the day, the month, the yeare and stile of the King, or the yeare of our Lord; lastly, the clause of his testibus . . . The office of the premises of the deed is twofold: first rightly to name the feofor and the feofee; and secondly to comprehend the certaintie of the lands or tenements to be conveyed by the feofment either by express words or which may by reference be reduced to a certaintie." 1 Coke's Inst. 6a. Signing was not necessary to make a deed valid as such, at common law, and Sir William Blackstone says that "It was held in all our books that sealing alone was sufficient to authenticate a deed: and so the common form of attesting deeds—'sealed and delivered'—continues to this day notwithstanding the statute 29 Car. II, c. 3," which requires deeds to be signed by the maker. 2 Bl.Com. 307. Not only could any seal be used, but "a stick or any

such like thing which doth make a print."
Shep.Touch. 57. "In Termes de la Ley s. v.
'Fait,' reference is made to a charter of Edward III, of which the last two lines run in
the English translation thus:

'And in witness that it was sooth
He bit the wax with his foretooth.' "
Norton on Deeds, 6.

Thus it will be seen, from the conditions
prevailing at common law, the prime importance of the grantor's name appearing in
the body of the deed was to identify the deed
as the act of a particular grantor. Without
signature, and executed with a seal indented
by the prick of a pin, or imprint of a tooth,
the deed could not disclose the identity of the
grantor, except by mention of his name in
the grant. From the very necessity of the
case grew the rule that the name of the
grantor should appear in connection with apt
words indicating that the deed was his grant.
But even at common law a deed could be
made in a very informal manner. Says Lord
Coke: "I have tearmed the said parts of the
deed formall or orderly parts, for that they
be not of the essence of a deed of feofment;
for if such a deed be without premises, habendum, tenendum, the clause of in cujus rei
testimonium, the date, and the clause of hiis
testibus, yet the deed is good. For if a man
by deed give lands to another, and to his
heires, without more saying, this is good, if
he put his seale to the deede, deliver it and
make lievry accordingly." 1 Coke's Inst. 7a.
Thus it would seem that the requirement of a
deed made before the statute of frauds was,
not that the grantor's name should appear in
formal context, but if the writing should
identify the grantor, the deed would be considered his grant. * * *

Text writers now very generally discard as
unsound the proposition that the grantor
should be named as such in the deed, and
approve those cases which hold that the conveyance is operative when signed by the
grantor, though his name be omitted from
the body of the instrument. [Citations.]

The requisites of a deed under the code are,
that it must be in writing, signed by the
maker, attested by at least two witnesses,
and delivered to the purchaser, or some one
for him, and be made on a valuable or good
consideration. No prescribed form is essential to the validity of a deed, and the instrument will be deemed sufficient if it make
known the transaction. [Citation.] We
think that the deed under discussion measures up to these statutory essentials, and is
effective as a conveyance of the defendant
and her coremainderman, though their
names are not mentioned in the body of the
installment. [Citation.]

Judgment affirmed.

RITCHIE v. DAVIS

(1965) 26 Wis.2d 636, 133 N.W.2d 312.

Action of ejectment by plaintiff Gordon
Ritchie, Jr., against defendant Lorraine E.
Davis (hereinafter "Mrs. Davis") to recover
possession of certain real estate and damages
equivalent to the reasonable rental value of
said property during the time it was alleged
to have been wrongfully withheld from plaintiff. Certain other persons were later impleaded as parties defendant. * * *

On June 7, 1955, Edwin J. Davis, who was
then single, executed a warranty deed to Andrew P. Cotter, Gladys D. Cotter, his wife,
and plaintiff Ritchie, as joint tenants. Cotter was a practicing attorney in Montello
who had done legal work for Davis in the
past, and Ritchie was a second cousin and
favorite relative of Davis. This deed conveyed an undivided one-third interest in a 40-
acre parcel of land (hereinafter referred to
as the "tree farm") which Cotter had apparently agreed to purchase from Davis, and all
of another parcel of land situated in the city
of Montello on which was located the Davis

Hotel. The instant action is concerned only with the hotel property, not the tree farm. The deed was properly witnessed and notarized. * * *

The deed was handed by Davis to Cotter sometime in the late summer or early fall of 1955 with instructions that he did not wish the deed recorded "while he [Davis] was around." About two days later Cotter gave Davis a written receipt for the deed. At that time Cotter told Davis that he did not like to have "my property tied up with his" and would prefer to have a separate deed to the tree farm. Davis replied that this was the very reason he had done it because he wanted "it" (the hotel property) tied in with Cotter's affairs. Cotter suggested the possibility that he might predecease Davis, to which Davis replied, "I know I won't have any trouble with your wife." Neither Davis nor Cotter ever informed Mrs. Cotter or plaintiff Ritchie of the existence of the deed until after the death of Davis which occurred October 24, 1963, who was then sixty years of age.

On November 17, 1956, Davis married the defendant after a three-month courtship. The marriage proved to be a happy and compatible one. After the marriage Mr. and Mrs. Davis did extensive remodeling and repairing of the hotel building. Mrs. Davis testified that she used approximately $10,000 or more of her own money in making these improvements. Two notes were introduced in evidence from an Illinois bank dated respectively February 28, 1957, and March 15, 1957, in the respective amounts of $3,500 and $2,500, which had been signed by Mr. and Mrs. Davis and collateralized by stocks owned by Davis. Mrs. Davis further testified that her funds paid off both notes.

About a month after the marriage Cotter drafted a joint will for Mr. and Mrs. Davis whereby each bequeathed and devised a life interest to the survivor with remainder to Daniel G. Priske, son of Mrs. Davis by a prior marriage, with a gift over to his children in the event he predeceased the survivor. At the time Davis spoke to Cotter about drafting such will, Cotter inquired as to whether Davis had told Mrs. Davis of the existence of the deed. Davis replied, "What she doesn't know won't bother her." This is the last conversation which took place between Davis and Cotter with respect to the deed. * * * The will was executed by both Mr. and Mrs. Davis on January 2, 1957.

At the time of the marriage and the making of the will Davis owned the personal property in the hotel, and stocks worth about $8,000 and had about $200 on deposit in his checking account. Mrs. Davis owned a double flat in the city of Princeton worth about $12,000 and had approximately $12,000 in cash, a new Oldsmobile automobile, and some life insurance.

In 1959, Davis told his longtime friend, Marvin Hook, that Mrs. Davis was doing the remodeling of the hotel and stated, "She enjoys doing it and eventually it will belong to her anyway." A similar statement was made by Davis to another longtime friend, Miss Curran, in the summer of 1958 or 1959. In 1963, while Mr. and Mrs. Davis were on a visit to California, Davis told Carl Carstensen, another friend, that he had left his real and personal property to Mrs. Davis in his will.

Following the death of Davis on October 24, 1963, Cotter and his wife executed a quitclaim deed to plaintiff Ritchie covering the hotel property, and both the warranty deed of June 7, 1955, and this quitclaim deed were recorded in the office of the register of deeds on November 5, 1963.

Trial was had to the court without a jury. The trial court filed an exhaustive memorandum decision in which it found and determined: That there was an intent on Davis' part to pass title at the time of the execution of the deed and delivery to Cotter; that the deed took effect as of the date of the delivery; having once taken effect it was not changed by any subsequent conduct or remarks of Davis; and that $240 per month was the reasonable rental value of the premises during the time possession was withheld from the plaintiff by Mrs. Davis. * * * Judgment on behalf of plaintiff was rendered June 25, 1964, ejecting defendant from the premises and awarding plaintiff $1,800 damages for wrongfully withholding possession of the property. Defendant and all impleaded defendants, except Cotter and his wife, have appealed from this judgment.

CURRIE, C. J. Appellants' brief states that the sole issue on this appeal is whether the June 7, 1955, deed from Davis to the two Cotters and to Ritchie constituted an irrevocable conveyance or an attempted testamentary disposition. It is appellants' contention that the delivery to Cotter was as agent for Davis, was revocable, and, therefore, was an ineffective testamentary disposition. The trial court, however, found it was Davis' intent at the time of delivery of the deed to Cotter that title then pass to the grantees.

There are many cases which have been decided in this and other jurisdictions involving the delivery of a deed by the grantor to a third person with instructions to deliver it to the grantee or to record it after the death of the grantor. Here, however, we have the unusual circumstance that the person to whom the grantor made the delivery was also named as one of the grantees. We will first consider the problem as if the plaintiff Ritchie had been the sole grantee. It was clearly Davis' intention that Ritchie should have the hotel property after Davis' death and the naming of Cotter and his wife as co-grantees was merely a device which Davis thought would insure that result.

The general rule is that the deposit of a deed with a third person for delivery to the grantee on the grantor's death will operate as a valid transfer as of the time of the first delivery, provided the grantor intends irrevocably to vest title in the grantee and surrenders control over the deed. [Citations.] Wisconsin cases which have applied this general rule and have found the deed was effective as of the time of delivery to the third person are: [Citations.] However, where it is agreed that the third person custodian is to hold the deed subject to the control of the grantor, title does not pass at the time of deposit with the custodian. [Citation.]

* * *

The test of whether the deed is effective upon delivery to the third person is not whether the grantor has retained possession or control of the property, but rather, whether he has retained possession or control of the deed. [Citation.] Therefore, it is immaterial that the grantor continues in possession and control of the conveyed real estate, as did Davis, from the time of delivery of the deed to the third person until the grantor's death. The deed operates as a conveyance *in praesenti* although the enjoyment is postponed until the grantor's death. [Citations.] Some courts hold that the grantor retains an implied reserved life estate in the premises. [Citations.] It was held in the inheritance tax case of Estate of Ogden (1932), 209 Wis. 162, 168, 244 N.W. 571, that an effective life estate may be reserved by the grantor by oral agreement even though the deed is absolute on its face and has been delivered to the grantee.

The intention of the grantor at the time he makes the delivery of the deed to the third person controls as to whether the deed is revocable or irrevocable. There are several facts in the instant case which tend to establish that Davis intended an irrevocable conveyance. Nothing was said between Davis and Cotter at the time of the delivery of the deed to Cotter. This in itself is more consistent with an intention that the deed was irrevocable rather than revocable. Davis made no attempt thereafter to revoke the delivery. When the subject of the joint will was discussed between Davis and Cotter, Davis remarked to Cotter, "What she [Mrs. Davis] doesn't know won't bother her." This tends to support the inference that he considered the deed an accomplished fact and not something he could change at will. The inclusion in the deed of the third interest in the tree farm, which Cotter was apparently entitled to receive immediately, shows intent of irrevocable delivery.

Appellants strongly rely upon the statements which Davis made to his friends Hook, Curran, and Carstensen, that Mrs. Davis would receive the hotel after he died. Concededly it is difficult to reconcile these statements with the other facts which point so strongly to the conclusion that the delivery of the deed was irrevocable. However, * * *, once the deed takes effect as of date of delivery, subsequent conduct or remarks of the grantor cannot operate retroactively to change such effect.

We now turn to the legal significance of Cotter having been named as one of the grantees in the deed. Chaudoir v. Witt (1920), 170 Wis. 556, 170 N.W. 932, 174 N.W. 925, is directly in point with respect to this aspect of the case. There a grantor, while seriously ill, executed a deed in which his wife joined in conveying a store building in which he and his family lived to one Suelflow, a real estate and insurance man. Suelflow and his wife then executed a deed to the same property to grantor's wife. Suelflow, who had possession of both deeds briefly, then delivered both to grantor's wife. It was understood between grantor and Suelflow that these two deeds were only to be effective in case grantor died of his then illness and that the deeds were not to be recorded until after grantor's death. Grantor recovered and lived for 36 more years. After his death an action was commenced to set aside the two deeds on the

ground that they were testamentary in character and had never been delivered so as to be effective as deeds. This court held that a delivery in escrow or upon condition cannot be made to a grantee. Mr. Chief Justice Winslow in his opinion stated (at p. 563, 174 N.W. at p. 925):

"No court has more positively or consistently held that there cannot be a conditional delivery of a deed to the grantee himself than this court."

Likewise in George Williams College v. Williams Bay (1943), 242 Wis. 311, 320, 7 N.W.2d 891, this court declared, "Furthermore, as a matter of law there cannot be a conditional delivery of a deed to a grantee: in such a case the delivery becomes absolute." Delivery of a deed to one of several grantees, in the absence of evidence to the contrary, is generally regarded as a delivery in favor of all grantees. [Citations.]

It necessarily follows that the judgment of the circuit court must be affirmed. First, the finding that it was the intent of Davis that the delivery of the deed to Cotter was irrevocable is not against the great weight and clear preponderance of the evidence. Secondly, because Cotter was named as a co-grantee, there could not be a conditional delivery as to him as a matter of law, and, in the absence of any expressed intention to the contrary, delivery to Cotter was effective as to his co-grantee Ritchie.

* * *

Judgment affirmed.

STILL v. STILL

(1965) 239 Ark. 865, 394 S.W.2d 733.

ROBINSON, J. The appellant, Andrew Still, is the owner of a small farm in Searcy County, lying immediately south and adjacent to the Marion-Searcy County line. The appellee, Archie Still, owns 60 acres immediately north and adjacent to the Marion-Searcy

County line and directly across from appellant's farm. In 1944, appellant, along with Roy Still, the then owner of appellee's property, caused a survey to be made in order to establish the true location of the Marion-Searcy County line. At the completion of the survey, fences were erected along the boundaries set out by the surveyor. Upon their agreement, however, Roy Still permitted appellant to erect a fence which deviated from the boundary so as to include about 1¼ acre of the Marion County land within appellant's fences. This was done in order to keep Roy Still's cattle away from appellant's home and barn and away from appellant's cattle.

Appellee, Archie Still, acquired the Marion County tract in 1961. Since that time he and appellant, Andrew Still, have continually disagreed as to the ownership of the 1¼ acre tract. Appellee finally filed suit for its possession in the Marion County Circuit Court. The cause was removed to equity, which court confirmed title in appellee, subject only to an easement in favor of appellant extending from appellant's home and property to the county road. Since no cross-appeal was taken as to the Chancellor's finding regarding the easement, the only question before this court is whether the Chancellor's finding that appellant's possession of the land was permissive and not adverse, is against the preponderance of the evidence.

Appellant relies on his original agreement with Roy Still and his subsequent use of the land for the required statutory period in order to establish title by adverse possession. We agree with the court below that no such title was established here. The testimony of several witnesses, along with the testimony of appellant himself, clearly indicates that appellant's possession was permissive. When asked to relate the basis of his agreement with Roy Still, appellant testified: "* * * when I would go to feed my stock, his stock would come over and give

me lots of trouble and he gave me permission to build the fence there for both our conveniences." Appellant's wife testified: "* * * we have it in our possession to use, that was the agreement." Appellant's uncle, Charlie Still, telling about his recollection of the agreement stated that: "He gave him permission to use that land, that is all." It is well settled that the holding of land by permission can not ripen into an adverse or hostile right until notice is brought home to the owner and holding has continued thereafter for the statutory period. [Citations.] A preponderance of the evidence does not show that appellant ever brought home such notice to Roy Still, or any other holder of record title. Appellant asserts that at one time in 1955 he forced appellee off the property, but the record shows that appellee did not acquire title until 1961.

The preponderance of the evidence supports the conclusions of the Chancellor that appellant's possession was permissive and not adverse. The decree is accordingly affirmed.

TREMBLAY v. AYCOCK

(1965) 263 N.C. 626, 139 S.E.2d 898.

This is an action for land.

On 5 January 1921 C. E. Lee conveyed to Lemon Lee by deed of bargain and sale, recorded in Book 197 at page 115, Registry of Harnett County, a one-third undivided interest in three tracts of land, containing 100 acres, 28⅘ acres and 5 acres, respectively. Only the one-third interest in the 100-acre tract is involved in this action, and this 100-acre tract has apparently been divided and the one-third herein involved has been set off as a 34-acre tract.

The following provisions of the deed are pertinent.

(1). Naming clause—"* * * to Lemon Lee and the heirs of his body * * *."

(2). Granting clause—"* * * to said Lemon Lee and the heirs of his body * * *."

(3). *Habendum* clause—"* * * to the said Lemon Lee and the heirs of his body to their only use and behoof forever."

(4). Warranty clause—"* * * with said Lemon Lee and the heirs of his body, if any * * *."

(5). Following the description and preceding the *habendum* clause—"The intent and purpose of this deed is to convey to Lemon Lee a life estate in ⅓ of the described lands in this deed, and at his death a fee simple estate to the heirs of his body if any, and in the event he has no heirs of his body in that event then to be equally divided among his brothers."

At the time of the execution of the above deed on 5 January 1921 Lemon Lee was unmarried and had no children; he had two living brothers. In 1924 he married Maude Pollard and one child was born to this union. Maude Pollard Lee died in 1929, and Lemon Lee thereafter married Viola Parrish who bore him five children. The six children of Lemon Lee are the plaintiffs in this action. Lemon Lee died in 1959.

Defendant Rachel Aycock White is in possession of the *locus in quo* and claims title thereto by *mesne* conveyances from Lemon Lee and wife, Viola Lee. The instruments in Mrs. White's chain of title are sufficient to vest in her a fee simple title unless plaintiffs, by virtue of the provisions of the deed from C. E. Lee to Lemon Lee, have a superior title. At the time of the trial Mrs. White was the only defendant "having a real interest in this cause." (She is hereafter the defendant.)

The cause was heard by the court below upon an agreed statement of facts, and judgment was entered declaring "that the defendant Rachel A. (Aycock) White is the owner

of the * * * lands in fee." Plaintiffs appeal.

Moore, J. Determination of the ownership of the *locus in quo* requires interpretation of the provisions of the deed of 5 January 1921 from C. E. Lee to Lemon Lee.

We pass over, for the present, the paragraph immediately following the description. According to the naming, granting and *habendum* clauses the conveyance was "to Lemon Lee and the heirs of his body." This provision, standing alone, vested in Lemon Lee an estate tail, which was converted to a fee simple by statute, G.S. 41–1. [Citations.] The covenants of warranty are "with Lemon Lee and the heirs of his body, if any." The words, "if any," do not affect the character of the estate, since there is no limitation over. [Citation.]

Lemon Lee had no children at the time of the conveyance, and if the words "heirs of his body," as used in the naming, granting, *habendum* and warranty clauses, could be construed to mean "children," the estate of Lemon Lee would still have been a fee simple. "It is settled law with us that when a conveyance is made to A and his children, if A has children when the deed is executed, he and they take as tenants in common. [Citation.] But if A has no children when the deed is executed, he takes an estate tail which, under our statute, is converted into a fee. [Citations.]" Davis v. Brown, 241 N.C. 116, 84 S.E.2d 334. However, we have found no case, in which the conveyance is merely to A and the heirs of his body, and A has children at the time, that "heirs of the body" has been construed to mean "children." [Citations.]

This brings us to a consideration of the provisions of the deed set out following the description and preceding the *habendum* clause: "The intent and purpose of this deed is to convy to Lemon Lee a life estate in ⅓ of the described lands in this deed, and at his death a fee simple estate to the heirs of his body if any, and in the event he has no heirs of his body in that event then to be equally divided among his brothers." Plaintiffs insist and contend that this language should be given effect, the words "heirs of his body" in this connection are not used in a technical sense, they mean "children," Lemon Lee acquired only a life estate, and plaintiffs having survived him acquired the remainder in fee. [Citations.] On the other hand, the defendant contends that said provisions following the description are repugnant to the estate created by the granting and *habendum* clauses and are surplusage and of no effect. She also contends that, if these provisions are given effect, Lemon Lee took a defeasible fee, and, issue having survived him, the fee became absolute and she is the owner. [Citations.]

* * *

An interpretation of the language of the paragraph following the description is not necessary to a determination of the question involved. "When the granting clause in a deed to real property conveys an unqualified fee and the *habendum* contains no limitation on the fee thus conveyed and a fee simple title is warranted in the covenants of title, any additional clause or provision repugnant thereto and not by reference made a part thereof, inserted in the instrument as a part of, or following the description of the property conveyed, or elsewhere other than in the granting or *habendum* clause, which tends to delimit the estate thus conveyed, will be deemed mere surplusage without force or effect." [Citations.] The granting and *habendum* clauses vested in Lemon Lee an unqualified fee, and the fee simple title is warranted. If plaintiffs' construction of the language following the description is correct, it is repugnant to the fee simple estate of Lemon Lee and tends to delimit it. That language is not by reference made a part of the granting, *habendum* or warranty clause. It is, therefore, surplusage without force or effect, if plaintiffs' interpretation of the provisions is correct. If defendant's interpretation is correct Lemon Lee had a fee simple title in any event. When rules of construction have been settled they should be observed and enforced. [Citation.]

* * *

Affirmed.

HOUCK v. DARLING

(1964) 238 Or. 484, 395 P.2d 445.

LUSK, J. This is a suit to cancel a deed to real property, described as follows:

"The West 12 ft. of Lot 4, and the East 30.5 ft. of the South ½ of Lot 5, all in Block 26, Caruthers Addition to the City of Portland, in the County of Multnomah, State of Oregon."

The plaintiff alleged in his amended complaint that on August 31, 1960, the defendants, acting through one of them, Cecil H. Russell, "by fraud, duress and artifice, obtained an acknowledged and purported deed of conveyance" to the real property in question from the plaintiff; that a notary public was obtained to execute a form of acknowledgment on the deed, whereas in fact the plaintiff never acknowledged the deed before the notary public, and that the defendants, acting through Russell, caused the deed to be placed of record in the deed records of Multnomah County, Oregon.

The case was put at issue and after trial the court entered a decree denying the relief sought and declaring the deed valid. The plaintiff has appealed.

The plaintiff made his home on the property in question. The defendants, who are the children of his second wife (whom he married in June, 1961), are the grantees in the deed. The deed reserves a life estate in the grantor.

No facts constituting fraud, duress or artifice, are alleged in the amended complaint, and there is no evidence to support the charge, or that the plaintiff lacked capacity to make a deed. The plaintiff signed and delivered the deed freely and voluntarily, and the court below was right in denying the relief of cancellation of the deed.

It is shown, however, without dispute, that the acknowledgment is false, as the grantor never appeared before the notary public who signed it. [Citation.] Such an abuse of the notarial authority is not to be passed by in silence. An acknowledgment is not essential to the validity of a deed as between the parties [citations]; its purpose is to entitle the deed to be recorded [citation] and a record of a deed bearing a false acknowledgment should be stricken. [Citation.]

The amended complaint contains a prayer for general relief, and the allegations of the pleading are sufficient to support a decree expunging the record of the deed. [Citation.] It is so ordered.

With this modification, the decree is affirmed.

BARRETT v. CARNEY

(1958) 337 Mass. 466, 150 N.E.2d 276.

CUTTER, J. The plaintiff on February 1, 1957, made an oral agreement to purchase certain land of the defendants on Mossdale Road in West Roxbury. On February 6, a written purchase and sale agreement was executed.

This agreement provided that the land was to be "conveyed together with the right to use Mossdale Road * * * for all purposes for which public streets are * * * or may * * * be commonly used in * * * Boston * * * provided, however, that the Grantor * * * may take such actions as may be necessary to cause said Mossdale

Road to become a public way * * *." The agreement further provided that if the defendants "shall be unable to give title or to make conveyance as above stipulated, any payments made under this agreement shall be refunded, and all other obligations of either party * * * shall cease." The premises were to be conveyed subject to 1957 taxes and applicable zoning laws "on or before March 1, 1957 by a * * * quitclaim deed * * * conveying a good and clear title to the same, free from all incumbrances." Neither the plaintiff nor the defendants knew that the city of Boston on October 15, 1956, had made a street betterment assessment on the land. This had been recorded, although no bills had been sent out by the city.

The plaintiff, who owned other land in the neighborhood, brought this bill for specific performance. The defendants filed a counterclaim alleging injury to the land by the plaintiff.

The trial judge (a) found the material facts indicated above; (b) found that there was a mutual mistake of fact about the existence of the betterment assessment; (c) ruled that the plaintiff was not entitled to specific performance and that the parties were entitled to rescission of the agreement; and (d) found that the defendants were not entitled to any damages by way of counterclaim. A final decree was entered denying specific performance and ordering rescission. The plaintiff has appealed. The evidence is not reported.

1. The betterment assessment as a lien was an encumbrance. See G.L. c. 80, § 12 (as amended through St.1955, c. 194). [Citations.] Although the defendants could have removed the lien by paying the betterment assessment, the agreement contained no provision requiring the defendants to remove or to use reasonable efforts (compare Widebeck v. Sullivan, 327 Mass. 429, 433, 99 N.E.2d 165) to remove any defect in title. In the

absence of such a provision, or of fault on the part of the vendors (see Fisher v. Sneierson, 330 Mass. 48, 50, 110 N.E.2d 838), the defendants were under no obligation to remove the lien as a defect in title and, accordingly the provision for cessation of obligations and refund of the deposit became operative. [Citations.] Under the provisions of this agreement, specific performance could not be compelled, even if the plaintiff were willing (which his counsel stated at the argument he was not) to pay the full purchase price without any deduction for the lien. "The defendants therefore have a right to be entirely excused from performance if they can prove [as they have here] a defect in the title existing before the contract was made which prevents them from conveying a good and clear title free from all encumbrances as agreed." [Citation.]

2. The provision of the contract, already quoted, with respect to Mossdale Road afforded some basis for the conclusion that the parties made their agreement in the mutually mistaken belief that Mossdale Road was a private way, and that no public taking of rights in it had been made. In view, however, of our conclusion that the defendants were excused from performance under the agreement itself, there is no occasion for considering whether there was such mutual mistake of fact as would justify the rescission of the agreement.

3. The decree in form must be revised and, therefore, is reversed. A new decree is to be entered dismissing the bill and the defendants' counterclaim.

So ordered.

ELIASON v. WILBORN

(1930) 281 U.S. 457, 50 S.Ct. 382, 74 L.Ed. 962.

HOLMES, J. The appellants had been holders of a certificate of title under the Torrens Act of Illinois. As a result of negotiations they entrusted this certificate to one Napletone, who is alleged to have presented it together with a forged conveyance to himself to the Registrar and by those means to have obtained from the Registrar a new certificate of title in Napletone, on May 19, 1926. Napletone a few days later sold and conveyed to the Wilborns, appellees, whose good faith is not questioned. After the Wilborns had bought but before a new certificate was issued to them, they had notice of the appellants' claim and the appellants notified the Registrar of the forgery and demanded a cancellation of the deeds and certificates to Napletone and the Wilborns and the issue of a certificate to themselves. The Registrar refused and this petition is brought to compel him to do what the appellants demand. It was dismissed on demurrer by the Circuit Court of the State, and the judgment was affirmed by the Supreme Court. 335 Ill. 352, 167 N.E. 101. The Supreme Court construed the statutes as giving title to the Wilborns, who purchased in reliance upon the certificate held by Napletone. Whether we are bound to or not we accept that construction and its result. The petitioners appealed to this Court on the ground that the statute, construed as it was construed below, deprived the appellants of their property without due process of law contrary to the Constitution of the United States, by making the certificate of title issued by the Registrar upon a forged deed without notice to them conclusive against them. * * *

The appellants seem to claim a constitutional right to buy land that has been brought under the Torrens Act free from the restrictions that that Act imposes. But they have no right of any kind to buy it unless the present owner assents, and if, as in this case, the owner from whom the appellants bought, offered and sold nothing except a Torrens title we do not perceive how they can complain that that is all that they got. Even if the restrictions were of a kind that was open to constitutional objection, the appellants bought knowing them and got what they paid for, and knew that they were liable to lose their title without having parted with it and without being heard. Even if they had been the original holders under the Torrens Act and had attempted to save their supposed rights by protest the answer would be that they were under no compulsion when they came into the system, that an elaborate plan was offered of which the provisions objected to were an important part, and that they could take it as it was or let it alone. There are plenty of cases in which a man may lose his title when he does not mean to. If he entrusts a check indorsed in blank to a servant or friend he takes his chance. So when he entrusts goods to a bailee under some factors' acts that are well known. So, more analogous to the present case, a man may be deprived of a title by one who has none; as when an owner who has conveyed his property by a deed not yet recorded executes a second deed to another person who takes and records the later deed without notice of the former. There are few constitutional rights that may not be waived.

But there is a narrower ground on which the appellants must be denied their demand. The statute requires the production of the outstanding certificate, as a condition to the issue of a new one. The appellants saw fit to entrust it to Napletone and they took the risk. They say that according to the construction of the act adopted the Registrar's certificate would have had the same effect even if the old certificate had not been produced. But that, if correct, is no answer. Presumably the Registrar will do his duty, and if he does he will require the old certificate to be handed in. It does not justify the omission of a precaution that probably would be sufficient, to point out that a dishonest official could get around it. There is not the slightest reason to suppose that Napletone would have got a certificate on which the Wilborns could rely without the delivery of the old one by the appellants. As between two innocent persons one of whom must suffer the consequence of a breach of trust the one who made it possible by his act of confidence must bear the loss.

Decree affirmed.

PROBLEMS

1. Dickerson executed a warranty deed transferring the title in fee simple to a farm he owned to Graham, subject to a life estate in himself, for good and valuable consideration. The deed was delivered to Dickerson's attorney with the following instrument:

"I herewith place in your hands for absolute delivery a warranty deed which I have executed conveying my farm to Graham. I have surrendered full possession and control of this deed and I give you full authority to hold said deed and upon my death to have the deed recorded."

Upon Dickerson's death the deed was caused to be recorded by the attorney. Dickerson's heirs-at-law bring suit to set aside the deed and to partition the farm.

What result, and why?

2. G, a bachelor, living in the State of X, owned in fee simple two tracts of land which he wished to give to his two nephews, A and B, who resided in different States. He accordingly executed two deeds, each properly describing one of the tracts, naming as grantees A and B, respectively. Each deed was subscribed and duly acknowledged by G.

(a) Deed No. 1, in favor of A, was recorded by G, who then enclosed it addressed to A, and placed the envelope in a tray in his office in which outgoing mail was kept. Before the office-boy came to collect the mail, G removed the envelope from the tray and destroyed the deed. A learned of the transaction later from the notary public who had read the deed.

(b) Deed No. 2, in favor of B, was handed by G to X, who was then starting for a vacation in B's city, and instructed X to deliver the deed to B on B's birthday, about one month in the future. When X reached Denver for a stopover, he received from G a wire directing him to return the deed to G. X did so and then notified B of the facts.

In regard to the respective deeds, what are the rights of A and B?

3. A, for a valuable consideration, executed and delivered to B a warranty deed conveying a lot improved with a bungalow. The deed was delivered on January 15. B did not record this deed, but took possession and moved into the bungalow on February 1. C, who held A's note for $1,000 which was due January 2, obtained a judgment on the note against A on February 3, and on February 4th, took out an execution and placed it in the hands of the sheriff. Did C acquire a lien on the premises?

4. Robert was the holder of the legal title of record by deed to the N½ of the SE¼ of Section 5. The legal title of record by deed to the N½ of the SW¼ of Section 5 was in Stanley.

Stanley fenced his 80 acres in 1942. He placed his east fence fifteen feet east of the east line of th N½ of the SW¼ of Section 5. Thereafter, he was in possession of this fifteen foot strip of land lying in the N½ of the SE¼ of Section 5 and kept it fenced and cultivated continuously until possession thereof was delivered by him to Nathan on March 1, 1947. Nathan took possession under deed from Stanley by which Stanley conveyed to Nathan the N½ of the SW¼ of Section 5. Nathan continued possession and cultivation of the fifteen-foot strip until May 27, 1966, when Robert, having on several occasions strenuously objected to Nathan's possession, brought suit against Nathan for trespass.

What decision?

5. A owned a farm in fee simple, together with the grain growing thereon. A conveyed the farm to C by warranty deed. A entered upon the farm and harvested the grain when ripe and carried it away. C sued A for the value of the grain. A defended, claiming that the grain belonged to him. What judgment?

6. A, a widower and the owner of Brown Acre, was the father of four bachelor sons, B, C, D and E. A died intestate. B conveyed an undivided one-half interest in Brown Acre by warranty deed to F. C and D died intestate, never having married. B died testate never having married and left all of his property, real and personal, to his brother, E.

E filed his suit for partition against F asking for a division of Brown Acre.

What is the interest of E in Brown Acre?

7. A owns a farm being the S. E. ¼ of the S. E. ¼ of the N. W. ¼ in Section 1, Township 2 North, Range 2, East of the Third Principal Meridian. Show by drawing the exact location of the farm. How many acres does it contain?

8. A owns a farm, the legal description of which is as follows: "The North Half (N½) of the Northeast Quarter (NE¼) of the Southwest Quarter (SW¼), Section 16, Township 34 North, Range 15 East of the Third Principal Meridian."

(a) Show by a drawing of a *section* the exact location of A's farm.

(b) How many acres does A's farm contain?

(c) What is the distance from the east boundary line of A's farm to the third principal meridian? Explain how you arrive at your answer.

(d) What is the distance from the north boundary line of A's farm to the base line? Explain how you arrive at your answer.

9. On January 1, 1965, A and B owned Blackacre as tenants in common. On July 1, 1965, A made a written contract to sell Blackacre to C for $25,000. Pursuant to this contract, C paid A $25,000 on August 1, 1965, and A executed and delivered to C a warranty deed to Blackacre. On May 1, 1966, B quitclaimed his interest in Blackacre to A. C brings an action against A for breach of warranty of title. What judgment?

10. John Doe, for a valuable consideration, agreed to convey to Richard Roe 80 acres of land. He delivered a deed, the material portions of which read:

"I, John Doe, grant and convey to Richard Roe 80 acres of land, [legal description]: To have and to hold unto Richard Roe, his heirs and assigns forever.

"I, John Doe, convenant to warrant and defend the premises hereby conveyed against all persons claiming the same or any part thereof by or through me."

Thereafter, Roe conveyed "all my right, title and interest" in the 80 acres to Paul Poe. It develops that Doe had no title to the land when he conveyed to Roe. Subseqently, Doe inherited an undivided one-half interest in the property.

What rights, if any, does Poe have against Doe and Roe? Explain.

CHAPTER 49

PUBLIC RIGHTS IN PRIVATE PROPERTY—PRIVATE RESTRICTIONS UPON LAND USE

EMINENT DOMAIN

The power to take private property for public use, the power of eminent domain, is recognized as one of the inherent powers of government. It is recognized in the Federal constitution and in the constitutions of the individual States, at the same time it is carefully circumscribed and controlled. The fifth amendment to the Federal constitution provides: "Nor shall private property be taken for public use without just compensation." Similar or identical provisions are to be found in the constitutions of the States. There is, therefore, a direct constitutional prohibition against taking private property without just compensation and an implicit prohibition against taking private property for other than public use.

Moreover, under both Federal and State constitutions the individual is entitled to due process of law in connection with the taking. A Kansas statute providing for the determination of just compensation at a hearing of which notice was to be given only by publication in a newspaper was held unconstitutional upon the ground that due process requires that the property owner be served with personal notice of such hearing. Under most statutes regulating the exercise of the power, condemnation involves a judicial proceeding in a court of law, and a trial by jury upon issues of fact is available to the same extent as in other judicial proceedings. It is generally recognized that the property owner is entitled to receive the fair market value of the property as determined by a jury.

Public Use. As has been noted, there is an implicit constitutional prohibition against taking private property for other than pub-
lic use. "Public use," here, has been interpreted to mean the same thing as "public purpose." Thus, it was early established that the power of eminent domain may be delegated to railroad and public utility companies. The reasonable exercise of this power by such companies, to enable them to offer continued and improved service to the public was upheld as being for a public purpose. As society grows more complex other public purposes are found and are accepted as legitimate grounds for exercise of the power of eminent domain.

One area in which the expansion of the concept of public purpose has been most noticeable is in the area of urban renewal. Most States now have legislation permitting the establishment of housing authorities with power to condemn slum, blight and vacant areas, and to finance, construct and maintain low rental housing projects.

Two types of legislation have been adopted under this heading. The first sets up public authorities to plan and assemble, by condemnation or purchase, areas found to be slum, blight or vacant and unproductive, and authorizes such public authorities to lease or sell the property to private developers who must undertake to carry out the provisions of the plan. Federal aid is authorized for this type of development to the extent of two thirds of the net cost of the project.

A second type of legislation, known as Redevelopment Corporation Laws, relies entirely upon private enterprise. It authorizes the formation of private corporations to undertake the task of planning, assembling and redeveloping the area. Public control is exercised through a Redevelopment Commission, a public body, whose duty is to determine that the area covered by the private plan is slum or blight and that the plan meets certain requirements for the re-development of the community as a whole. Once the plan is approved, the redevelopment corporation is invested with the power of eminent domain, subject, however, to one important limitation. The redevelopment corporation may use its power of eminent domain only after it has acquired a specified percentage (usually sixty percent) of the land in the area through voluntary purchase agreements.

Both types of legislation, designed to encourage the use of private enterprise for urban renewal, have come under sharp constitutional attack. Their constitutionality has been upheld in the State courts upon the ground that the elimination of slum and blight areas is a public purpose in itself, even though the property is used thereafter by the private redevelopers for their own purposes. The Supreme Court of the United States has held the first type of legislation constitutional in Berman v. Parker, 348 U.S. 26 (1954).

Who is Entitled to Compensation. The compensation award goes to holders of vested interests in the condemned property. Future contingent interests are not compensated. For instance, a wife is not entitled to compensation for her inchoate dower interest in her husband's land. It is possible she might predecease her husband.

Difficult problems arise upon condemnation as between landlord and tenant. Suppose L (landlord) leases certain unimproved property to T (tenant) for a period of twenty years. T is to erect a garage upon the property and the lease provides that, upon its termination, T can remove all his fixtures except the garage building which is to become L's property. It is settled that if the fee, i. e., the absolute ownership in the property, is condemned, the lease is extinguished. Putting aside, for the moment, the question raised by the garage building, T loses the benefit of the unexpired term of his lease but is relieved from the obligation to pay rent. Upon condemnation of the fee, T loses the difference, if any, between the fair worth of the unexpired term of the lease and the rent he would have been required to pay had not condemnation intervened. The courts have held that T is entitled to this amount, which is to be paid to him out of the total condemnation award. The danger of this computation lies in the fact that the total condemnation award is based upon the market value of the property condemned. This figure may or may not include the margin between the fair worth of the unexpired term of the lease and the rent reserved. The result is that T's award may very easily be allowed to reduce L's legitimate compensation. For this reason, it is sound practice, in entering into a long term lease, for the landlord to insist upon a clause, substantially as follows:

> "If all or substantially all of the demised premises shall be taken by condemnation, the lease hereby created shall terminate upon such taking by the acquiring authority and the rent and other charges shall be apportioned accordingly. No part of any award, however, shall belong to the tenant."

What of the garage building under the lease we have supposed? If the building is condemned along with the fee is L entitled to that portion of the condemnation award which represents the value of the building? The lease provides that, upon its expiration, L will be entitled to the building. But T, in agreeing to this clause, anticipated twenty years of use during which period he would amortize the construction cost of the building. If the condemnation takes place in the fifth year of the lease, an award going entirely to L would seem unfair.

Since the lease provides that the garage is to become the property of L upon the "expiration" of the lease—it is possible that the courts would hold that "expiration" is not the same thing as extinguishment by condemnation. For this reason, the tenant entering into a long term lease should insist upon clauses protecting his interest in fixtures which would otherwise become the landlord's property upon the expiration of the lease. No problem is raised by fixtures which the tenant has a right to remove under the lease, for if they are condemned along with the real estate their value will be awarded to him.

Sometimes, especially in the case of the Federal Government, the condemnation sought is only of a possessory interest for a number of years. If this period is less than the unexpired term of the lease, the tenant is not only entitled to the entire award but he is also entitled to the cost of removal from the premises as a separate item of damage. If the period extends beyond the term of the lease, while the tenant is entitled to his proportionate share of the entire award, he is not entitled to removal costs for the reason that he would have had these costs in any event, namely, at the time of the expiration of his lease.

In either case, the tenant is not relieved of his obligation to pay rent to the landlord. In the law of property the tenant's covenant to pay rent is given in return for the conveyance to him of a leasehold estate by the landlord. The tenant's inability to retain possession relieves him from the obligation to pay rent only where his landlord causes him to be evicted, actually or constructively. The landlord does not cause the condemnation proceedings. Accordingly, the tenant is not relieved from his obligation to pay rent where his possessory interest is condemned. The different rule which applies where the fee is condemned results from the operation of such condemnation to extinguish the entire estate, including the leasehold estate which supports the covenant to pay rent.

POLICE POWER, CITY PLANNING AND ZONING

The police power, the power to provide for the public health, safety, morals, and welfare, like the power of eminent domain, is one of the inherent powers of government. It is a basic *power* of the government, all other governmental powers being incidental or ancillary to it. The Federal constitution nowhere provides for its exercise but neither does it prohibit it. It is one of the powers which is neither delegated to the United States by the Federal constitution, nor prohibited by it to the States; it is, therefore by article X of the constitution "reserved to the States * * *, or to the people."

The first thing to be noted about the police power in this connection is that its legitimate exercise does not require payment of compensation to the property owner affected by such exercise. From this, it follows that the exercise of the police power may not result in a condemnation or "taking" of private property.

Police power can be used only to *regulate* private property, never to "take" it. It is firmly established that regulation which has no reasonable relation to public health, safety, morals, or welfare is unconstitutional as being contrary to due process of law.

Zoning. The power to zone, which involves the exercise of the State's police power, is delegated to local city and village authorities by statutes known as "enabling" statutes. A typical "enabling" statute will grant the following powers to the municipalities: (1) to regulate and limit the height and bulk of buildings thereafter to be erected; (2) to establish, regulate and limit the building or setback lines on or along any street, traffic way, drive or parkway; (3) to regulate and limit the intensity of the use of lot areas, and to regulate and determine the area of open spaces, within and surrounding buildings; (4) to classify, regulate and restrict the location of trades and industries and the location of buildings designated for specified industrial, business, residential and other uses; (5) to divide the entire municipality into districts of such number, shape, area, and such different classes as may be deemed best suited to carry out the purposes of the Act; and (6) to fix standards to which buildings or structures shall conform.

The enabling statute will also provide that the foregoing powers are to be exercised only "To the end that adequate light, pure air, and safety from fire and other dangers may be secured; that the taxable value of land and buildings throughout the municipality may be conserved; that congestion in the public streets may be lessened and avoided, and that the public health, safety, comfort, morals, and welfare may be otherwise promoted." Many enabling statutes provide, in addition, that "such regulation shall be in accordance with a comprehensive plan."

Under these powers the local authorities may enact zoning ordinances which consist of a map and a text. The map involves an exercise of the fourth and fifth powers enumerated above, that is, it divides the municipality into districts which are designated principally as industrial, commercial, or residential, with possible sub-classification.

A well drafted zoning ordinance will carefully define the uses permitted in each area. If a proposed use does not appear anywhere in the ordinance and its classification is doubtful, it is not safe for the property owner to rely upon an opinion of the zoning authorities or upon the issuance of a building permit, because it is well settled that a municipality is not estopped from later maintaining that the use is unlawful in the particular area. The property owner may, however, rely upon a variation granted pursuant to the provisions of the zoning ordinance.

The division of a municipality into areas of permitted use is familiar to the layman. However, comprehensive zoning ordinances include regulations regarding the height and bulk of buildings, establish set-back lines and often prescribe spacing and minimum lot size for residential areas. Some courts have held that an ordinance which does not include such provisions is not "comprehensive," and that an ordinance which is not "comprehensive" in this sense cannot possibly bear a reasonable relation to public health, safety, morals, and welfare, and, accordingly, is invalid. There is a marked tendency to adopt this view in those States in which the enabling statute provides that "such regulation (i. e., zoning) shall be in accordance with a comprehensive plan." In every case the constitutional validity of a zoning ordinance is tested by its relation to public health, safety, morals, and welfare.

METHODS OF FREEING PROPERTY FROM ZONING RESTRICTIONS

The property owner who finds that he cannot use his property for the purpose desired has several possible remedies:

(1) He may be able to show that the zoning ordinance is invalid as a whole either because (a) it bears no reasonable relation to public health, safety, morals, or welfare, or (b) it involves an exercise of powers not granted to the municipality by the "enabling" act. Assume that A owns a parcel of property located in a district which is zoned "Residence A." The ordinance provides that "Every dwelling hereafter erected or placed in a Residence A District shall have a living-floor space, as herein defined: of not less than 768 square feet for a one-story dwelling; of not less than 1,000 square feet for a two-story dwelling." A intends to build a housing development on his property and is convinced that there will be a greater demand for residential housing of smaller liv-

ing-floor space than that required by the ordinance.

(a) A may be able to convince the courts that the ordinance is unreasonable and that it bears no relation to public health, safety, morals, or welfare. His argument may be that the minimum floor space requirement is not tied in to occupancy, that is, it is impossible to state whether 768 square feet for a one-story dwelling is conducive to health, safety, or morals unless one knows how many persons will live in the dwelling. He may be able to show that the only purpose of the ordinance is to prevent poorer families from living within the municipality and that, if such ordinances become common throughout the country, poorer families may not be able to purchase housing at all. The question of the validity of minimum floor requirements is not fully settled.

(b) A may be able to show that the "enabling" statute does not authorize the adoption of such an ordinance. The enabling statute should be considered to see whether such an ordinance would be authorized under it.

(2) The second method of freeing property from zoning restrictions is by application to the zoning authorities for a variance. All enabling statutes provide that the zoning authorities shall have power to grant variances in cases of "particular hardship." There are two difficulties connected with this method of freeing property from unwanted restrictions: (a) there is considerable authority to the effect that the power to vary is the power to vary only the strict letter of the zoning ordinance, that is, if the owner's proposed use can be carried on only by changing the classification of his property from "residential" to "commercial," the zoning authorities may not have statutory power to make such a change under the guise of a variance. The statutory grant of such power raises a constitutional problem of delegation of legislative power to administrative officials. Moreover, a variance which makes

such a major change for the benefit of one owner encounters the constitutional prohibition against spot zoning.

(b) A variance is not available except in cases of "particular hardship." Mere failure to make a profit is not enough. It must affirmatively appear that the property as presently zoned cannot yield a reasonable return upon the owner's investment therein.

(3) The third method of freeing property from zoning restrictions is to show that the ordinance is invalid as applied to this particular property, either because (a) it is unreasonable as so applied, or (b) it results in a confiscation or a "taking" of property without compensation.

(a) The test of unreasonableness in application is difficult to state. The property owner may be able to show that classification of his property as "residential" is unreasonable in the light of the character and use of the area immediately contiguous to his property. Thus, he may argue that the classification of property located on one side of the street as "residential" while property located on the other side is not only classified but built up as "industrial" is unreasonable. Part of his argument would be that the classification deprives him of any beneficial use of the property since there is very little incentive to build or purchase a residence opposite a factory. In most cases, the contrast and its effects are not too obvious. A powerful deterrent to the acceptance of this form of attack is to be found in the argument that if a parcel of property falling within an area zoned "residential" is to be freed from the restriction merely because it happens to front upon some commercial establishments the next parcel will also have to be freed when the first parcel is built up as commercial. In other words, the snowball effect of freeing one parcel of property is a powerful deterrent to the acceptance of this form of attack upon the ordinance.

(b) A more successful form of attack is to show that the restrictions amount to confiscation or a "taking." For this purpose, it is not sufficient for the owner to show that he will sustain a financial loss if the restriction is not lifted. In this connection, the courts have stated that what is good for the entire community cannot be bad for a particular owner. Other courts merely say that the private interest must give way to the public good. But where the property owner can show that the restriction makes it impossible for him to use the property for any beneficial purpose, he will prevail. Deprivation of a property owner of all beneficial use is confiscation.

Suppose A owns a small lot in a residential area. The city adopts an official map which locates a proposed street through the middle of A's lot. The Official Map Statute provides that one who builds in the bed of a proposed street will not be entitled to compensation for such building when his property is condemned for a street. The street may never be built. Meanwhile, A is effectively prevented from making any use of his property for residential purposes. This is confiscation. Other less obvious forms of confiscation have resulted in ordinances being held invalid. The test in each case is whether the owner has been effectively prevented from making any beneficial use of his property—if so, the ordinance is confiscatory of his property and invalid.

Non-conforming Uses. It is generally agreed that a zoning ordinance may not immediately terminate a lawful use existing prior to its enactment. Such use must be permitted to continue as a non-conforming use—at least for a reasonable time. Some ordinances provide that non-conforming uses must be discontinued within a specified time. Such ordinances are subject to attack by owners who maintain that the specified time is unreasonable as applied to their property.

Most ordinances provide for the elimination of non-conforming uses (a) when the use is discontinued, (b) when a non-conforming structure is destroyed or substantially damaged or (c) when a non-conforming structure has been permitted to exist for the period of its useful life as fixed by municipal authorities. The last provision constitutes a sound method of eliminating non-conforming structures but it cannot be utilized in cases of non-conforming uses such as junk yards and parking lots which have no ascertainable useful life.

Subdivision Control. A growing municipality has a special interest in regulating new housing developments so that they will harmonize with the rest of the community; that roads within the development are integrated with other existing roads or planned roads; that adequate provision is made for open spaces for traffic, recreation, light and air, and that adequate provision is made for water, drainage and sanitary facilities. Accordingly, in most States there is legislation enabling local authorities to require municipality approval of every land subdivision plat. These "enabling" statutes provide penalties for failure to secure such approval where required by local ordinance. Some statutes make it a criminal offense to sell lots by reference to unrecorded plats, and provide that such plats may not be recorded unless approved by the local planning board. Other statutes provide that building permits will not be issued unless the plat is approved and recorded.

Planning Laws and the Purchaser of Real Property. All purchasers of real property, and particularly those who intend to carry on certain business or manufacturing activities, should be advised of the importance of zoning. This is so because an existing zoning restriction is not regarded as an encumbrance and does not render title unmarketable. A contract for the sale of land usually obligates the vendor to convey marketable title to the purchaser. Since the courts hold that an existing zoning restriction does not render title unmarketable, the time for the purchaser to inquire whether his proposed use is permissible is before he signs a contract to purchase the property, not after. If he signs the contract first, and then discovers that he is not permitted to make use of the property for the purpose he had in mind, he will not be able to rescind the contract, unless the vendor has fraudulently represented that the intended use is permissible. The vendor is not required to inform the purchaser of restrictions—he may remain silent—as the purchaser is presumed to know the law.

It may not be safe for the purchaser to rely upon the fact that the vendor is currently using the property for the same purpose as that intended by the purchaser. If the vendor's use is unlawful, i. e., constitutes a violation of the zoning or building ordinances, his title is unmarketable and, accordingly, the purchaser may refuse to take the conveyance, or sue the vendor for breach of covenant against encumbrances, if such is given in the deed. But the vendor's use may be a lawful non-conforming use which has almost reached a termination date. Furthermore, the vendor's existing use may be based upon a variance. A purchaser who relies upon the fact that his vendor is currently using the property for the same purpose as that which he intends, may find to his dismay that he is not entitled to rely upon the vendor's variance. A variance is, as observed, based on "particular hardship" to the person who obtained it. There is authority to the effect that no one may buy his way into another's hardship. However, one who purchases property which is subject to a zoning restriction is not deprived of the right to challenge the validity or constitutionality of the restriction.

PRIVATE RESTRICTIONS UPON LAND USE

Introductory. Suppose X owns a lot in a residential subdivision of a suburban community. On the lot there are a house and a garage, and the remainder of the subdivision is either similarly improved or still vacant. X decides to enlarge his living room and to extend the front of the house to within twenty feet of the front line of the lot. He knows that this is not prohibited by the zoning ordinance and that there is no limitation in the deed from his seller limiting the area of the house. He will, indeed, be astounded when a neighbor, observing the excavation, informs him that he, X cannot build to within twenty feet of the front line. He will be only slightly less surprised to hear that the reason he cannot do so is because of a provision in the recorded deed from the original subdivider to the original purchasers of lots in the subdivision requiring front yards of at least thirty feet depth.

X will discover upon further investigation that the entire subdivision has been subjected to a general building plan designed to benefit all the lots and any lot owner in the subdivision has the right to enforce the restriction against a purchaser whose title descends from a grantor common to both lots.

In such a case, the owners of lots are said to be subject to restrictive covenants which, if actually brought to the attention of subsequent purchasers, or recorded by original deed, or by means of a recorded plat or separate agreement, will bind those purchasers as though a special restriction had been inserted in their own deed.

Nature of Restrictive Agreements. Restrictive covenants of the foregoing type do not fit into any established pigeonhole of the common law. They are, in a sense, easements—or at least *negative* easements—to the extent that they impose a limitation on the use of the land in favor of other land.

Yet, unlike most easements they are not directly based upon any formal grant, and the ability of any number of property owners to enforce them does not suggest the usual easement that normally is enforceable by an adjoining landowner.

Restrictive covenants are a consequence of the untechnical notion that a person should not, as noted in a leading case, "be permitted to use the land in a manner inconsistent with the contract entered into by his vendor, and with notice of which he purchased." If there is a clear intent that a restriction is intended to benefit an entire tract, the fact that the covenant is not formally executed will not prevent it being enforced against a subsequent purchaser of one of the lots in the tract. Indeed, some cases have held that the restriction need not appear in the deeds at all if the intent to establish a general building scheme is evident from a plat recorded at the time of the original formation of the subdivision. As long as two requirements are met the restriction will be enforced: First, that it is apparent that the restriction was intended to benefit the purchaser of any lot in a tract, and, second, that the restriction appeared somewhere in the chain of title under which he claims.

Type and Construction of Restrictive Covenants. There are many types of restrictive covenants. The more common types limit the use of property to residential purposes or restrict the area of the lot on which a structure can be built or provide for a special type of architecture as, for example, the requirement that all houses must be of Early American Colonial design. Frequently, a subdivider will specify a minimum cost for each house, attempting thereby to maintain a minimum standard in the neighborhood.

A provision prohibiting the sale of intoxicating liquor is a common covenant which will be enforced for the benefit of owners of other lots derived from one original tract.

One difficult problem in construing these covenants is the meaning of words describing the restriction. "Dwelling," "business use" and "trade purposes" are not certain in their application. Generally, a covenant restricting the use to "private dwellings" excludes apartments. On the other hand, a doctor's or dentist's office incidental to a private residence will not violate a covenant against "business or trade use." Billboards have been held prohibited by a covenant restricting property to residential use, but the sale of intoxicating liquor in the original package by a grocer has been held not to violate a covenant against the sale of liquor. A building line restriction is not violated by a fire escape that encroaches on the minimum space and a porch may or may not constitute a violation of a minimum front yard restriction, depending upon whether its construction substantially blocks the view.

Termination of Restrictive Covenants. In the example of X and his enlarged living room, it may turn out that he will be advised to proceed with his plans and ignore the complaints of his neighbor. If so, such advice may be based on the belief that the character of the neighborhood has so changed that the original purpose of the covenant (in this case, to provide front yards of considerable depth) has no further application to present circumstances. If, during the last decade, houses, apartment buildings and even stores have been constructed in disregard of the building line restriction, X may successfully maintain that the character of the area has so changed as to no longer justify the enforcement of the covenant against him. And, in this, he may succeed if the court is convinced that the circumstances which gave rise to the covenant no longer exist. Typical of this "abandonment" of restrictive covenants is the once fine residential area which has gradually deteriorated into a neighborhood of boarding houses and small shops. In such a case, a court will probably refuse to enforce a covenant restricting use to single-family houses. Evidence of changed conditions may be found either within the tract covered by the original covenant or in the area adjacent to or surrounding the tract.

One principal reason for the deterioration of a neighborhood originally subject to building restrictions is acquiescence by neighbors in previous violations of the covenant. Aside from the obvious failure of the original purpose of the covenant in such cases, the courts consider it unreasonable to have the covenant suddenly enforced after years of indifference to violations. Acquiescence in one or two isolated violations in the entire tract will not, however, be a defense to a complaint against a violation.

Validity of Restrictive Covenants. Although restrictions upon the use of land have never been popular in the law, if it appears that the restriction will operate to the general benefit of all the land intended to be affected, the restriction, as indicated, will be enforced. The usual method of enforcing such agreements is by seeking an injunction to restrain a violation.

There is one type of restrictive covenant the validity of which has been challenged for many years. That is the covenant which restricts the use to members of a certain race. The issue raised by such covenants illustrates in a classic manner the way in which established rules of the law of property become involved in American constitutional law. For many decades, the United States Supreme Court took the position that *private* racial restrictive agreements, regardless of their moral status, did not infringe any rights guaranteed by the Federal constitution. It has been the law for many years, however, that a State or municipality could not, under the fourteenth amendment to the Federal constitution, impose any such restrictions by statute or ordinance. In 1947,

the United States Supreme Court held that private racial restrictive covenants could not be enforced by State courts since the courts were an arm of the State government and were, therefore, by the provisions of the fourteenth amendment to the constitution, prohibited from lending their aid to such covenants.

CASES

BELOVSKY v. REDEVELOPMENT AUTHORITY

(1947) 357 Pa. 329, 54 A.2d 277, 172 A.L.R. 953.

[Plaintiff filed a bill to enjoin the Redevelopment Authority of the City of Philadelphia from entering upon any activities pursuant to the Urban Redevelopment Law and the Redevelopment Cooperation Act of 1945. The trial court dismissed the complaint. Plaintiff appeals.]

STERN, J. * * * The Urban Redevelopment Law * * * declares it to be "the policy of the Commonwealth of Pennsylvania to promote the health, safety and welfare of the inhabitants thereof by the creation of bodies corporate and politic to be known as Redevelopment Authorities, which shall exist and operate for the public purposes of acquiring and replanning such areas and of holding or disposing of them in such manner that they shall become available for economically and socially sound redevelopment. Such purposes are hereby declared to be public uses for which public money may be spent, and private property may be acquired by the exercise of the power of eminent domain." * * *

The act creates for each city and county of the Commonwealth a so-called "Redevelopment Authority", which is not in any way to be deemed to be an instrumentality of the city or county or engaged in the performance of a municipal function. No Authority shall transact business or otherwise become operative until the governing body of the city or county shall find and declare that there is need for it to function; upon such declaration being made the mayor or the board of county commissioners, as the case may be, shall appoint the members of the Authority. An Authority "shall constitute a public body, corporate and politic, exercising public powers of the Commonwealth as an agency thereof", and shall have all the powers necessary or appropriate to effectuate the purposes and provisions of the act,—among them the power to acquire property whether by purchase, gift or eminent domain; to own, hold, improve and manage such property; to sell, lease or otherwise transfer, subject to approval by the local governing body, any development area, either as an entirety to a single redeveloper or in parts to several redevelopers; and to borrow from private lenders or from the State or Federal Government funds necessary for its operation and work.

The scheme of redevelopment proceeds under the act as follows:—The local planning commission makes a "redevelopment area plan" designating an area which it finds to be blighted because of the existence of the conditions enumerated in the act and containing recommendations for the redevelopment of such area. * * * Thereupon the Authority prepares a "redevelopment proposal" for the redevelopment of all or part of such area, including the proposed redevelopment contract and the selection of the redeveloper, and submits this proposal to the planning commission for review. The proposal, together with the planning commission's recommendations thereon, are then certified to the governing body, which, after a public hearing, approves or rejects the proposal and the redevelopment contract; in the event of the proposal being approved the Authority is empowered to execute the contract and to take such action as may be necessary to carry it out. The contract provides for the amount of the consideration to be paid by the redeveloper to the Authority and for the necessary continuing controls. Any deed or lease to a redeveloper in furtherance of the contract must contain such provisions as the Authority may deem desirable to run with the land in order to effectuate the purposes of the act. The Authority is granted the right of eminent domain and title to any property thus acquired shall be an absolute or fee simple title unless a lesser title shall be designated in the eminent domain proceedings. The Authority may issue bonds for any of its corporate purposes, the principal and interest of which are payable from its revenues generally; such bonds may be secured by a pledge of any of its revenues or by a mortgage of any of its property; the bonds and the income therefrom shall at all times be free from taxation for State or local purposes. Neither the bonds nor any other obligations of the Authority shall be a debt of any municipality or of the Commonwealth, nor shall any municipality or the Commonwealth nor any revenues or any property of any municipality or of the Commonwealth be liable therefor.
* * *

Legislation similar to these Pennsylvania statutes has been adopted in 23 other States.
* * *

The present attack upon the constitutionality of the Urban Redevelopment Law centers largely upon the grant therein made to the Redevelopment Authorities of the power to exercise the right of eminent domain. It is contended that the taking of property under the act is not for a public purpose and therefore cannot constitutionally be effected by resort to the power of eminent domain.

Dornan v. Philadelphia Housing Authority, 331 Pa. 209, 200 A. 834, may be regarded as the prototype of the present case since all the arguments not presented on this subject were there fully considered. The Urban Redevelopment Law closely parallels the provisions of the "Housing Authorities Law" of May 28, 1937, P.L. 955, with which the Dornan case was concerned. The fundamental purpose of both these acts was the same, namely, the clearance of slum areas, although the Housing Authorities Law aimed more particularly at the elimination of undesirable dwelling houses whereas the Urban Redevelopment Law is not so restricted. But the Housing Authorities Law had an important additional objective in that, as ancillary to the slum clearances, there were to be provided "decent, safe, and sanitary urban or rural dwellings, apartments or other living accommodations for persons of low income"; these were to be constructed and acquired by the Housing Authorities and leased out by them to the class of tenants for whose use such accommodations were designed. In the case of the Urban Redevelopment Law the operation of clearing and rehabilitating the "slums", now called "blighted areas", is not to be followed by a continuing ownership of properties by the Redevelopment Authorities for any such further and ulterior social-welfare purpose as that of providing low rental homes for persons in moderate circumstances. In this additional feature of the Housing Authorities Law there was implicit the modern recognition of an enlarged social function of government which called for an advance over previous legal conceptions of what constitutes a public use justifying the exercise of the power of eminent domain, but this court sustained the constitutionality of that act, and the courts of numerous other States have, without exception, upheld similar legislation. In the case of the Urban Redevelopment Law, therefore, the justification of the grant of the power of eminent domain is even clearer than in the case of the Housing Authorities Law, there being in the present act only the one major purpose of the elimination and rehabilitation of the blighted sections of our municipalities, and that purpose certainly falls within *any* conception of "public use" for nothing can be more beneficial to the community as a whole than the clearance and reconstruction of those substandard areas which are characterized by the evils described in the Urban Redevelopment Law. It has long been clear that those evils cannot be eradicated merely by such measures, however admirable in themselves, as tenement-house laws, zoning laws and building codes and regulations; these deal only with future construction, not with presently existing conditions. Nor, as experience has shown, is private enterprise adequate for the purpose. The legislature has therefore concluded—and the wisdom of its conclusion is for it alone—that public aid must accompany private initiative if the desired results are to be obtained. * * *

One of the objections urged against the constitutionality of the Urban Redevelopment Act is the feature of the "redevelopment project" which contemplates the sale by the Authority of the property involved in the redevelopment, it being claimed that thereby the final result of the operation is to take property from one or more individuals and give it to another or others. Nothing, of course, is better settled than that property cannot be taken by government without the owner's consent for the mere purpose of devoting it to the private use of another, even though there be involved in the transaction an incidental benefit to the public. But plaintiff misconceives the nature and extent of the public purpose which is the object of this legislation. That purpose, as before pointed out, is not one requiring a continuing ownership of the property as it is in the case of the Housing Authorities Law in order to carry out the full purpose of that act, but is directed solely to the clearance, reconstruction and rehabilitation of the blighted area, and after that is accomplished the public purpose is completely realized. When, therefore, the need for public ownership has terminated, it is proper that the land be re-transferred to private ownership, subject only to such restrictions and controls as are necessary to effectuate the purposes of the act. It is not the object of the statute to transfer property from one individual to another; such transfers, so far as they may actually occur, are purely incidental to the accomplishment of the real or fundamental purpose. * * * Nor does the taking lose its public character merely because there may exist in the operation some feature of private gain, for if the public good is enhanced it is immaterial that a private interest also may be benefited. * * *

Decree dismissing the bill affirmed.

CITY OF BUFFALO v. MICHAEL

(1965) 16 N.Y.2d 88, 262 N.Y.S.2d 441, 209 N.E.2d 776.

FULD, J. In this condemnation proceeding, a tenant, having a lease of roof space for the maintenance of a sign, claims that it is entitled to compensation for the value of the sign which it had placed there.

On October 22, 1959, under its program for the clearance and rehabilitation of certain substandard areas within the Ellicott Redevelopment Project in the City of Buffalo, the plaintiff city served upon the defendant landlord a resolution of its Common Council appropriating the latter's apartment building. Permanently annexed to the roof of that building was an advertising sign, 15 feet high and 40 feet long, owned by the tenant Whitmier & Ferris Co. (hereafter referred to as either tenant or claimant). The sign, attached to the roof and walls by steel beams and supports, could not be removed without damage to the building. For the use of the roof space, the tenant paid an annual rent of $250 under a lease which ran from year

to year and gave the tenant a right to remove the sign at its expiration. The claimant's customers rented the roof sign, denominated a "spectacular" in the trade, for $4,800 a year. The lease which the claimant had with the landlord expired on April 1, 1960. Prior to that time, and solely because of the city's condemnation of the building, the landlord had notified the claimant that the lease would not be renewed.[1]

Following a trial, the Supreme Court awarded the landlord $47,250 for the land and building. It made no award to the tenant for the sign because, in the court's view, it retained the characteristics of personal property and, consequently, was not a "compensable" fixture. The Appellate Division reversing the trial court's judgment, held that the tenant was entitled to compensation for the sign and directed a new trial "to establish damage, if any, by reason of the appropriation" (19 A.D.2d 853, 244 N.Y.S.2d 30). Upon such new trial, the court found that the value of the sign, after deductions for depreciation and salvaged items, was $4,926 and awarded the claimant that amount, with interest. The city appeals from this determination.

It is settled that a tenant is entitled to compensation in condemnation proceedings for fixtures annexed to real property "whenever the city in taking the real property destroys the leasehold interest of the tenant", even though they may remain, in consequence of an agreement between the parties, the personal property of the tenant with a right in the latter to remove them upon termination of the lease. [Citations.] For the rule to apply, the annexation must, of course, be such that the fixtures "would have become part of the real property if they had been in-

1. [Footnote by the Court.] Claimant removed the sign, at the landlord's request, on July 15, 1960; the city, under a resolution of its Common Council dated April 19, 1960, took title to the property and on April 26 it went into possession.

stalled permanently by the owner of the fee" [citation] and, indeed, it has recently been held, signs and billboards permanently affixed to land or buildings are compensable fixtures. [Citations.]

In the light of the cases, the sign with which we are concerned was such a fixture. On the one hand, because it was permanently and firmly annexed to the roof and walls of the condemned building, it was not personalty which a public body might except from its appropriation. [Citation.] On the other hand, although not removable without causing some injury to the freehold, it had not "lost its identity by becoming a structural part of a building". [Citations.] Quite properly, therefore, its value was not included in the valuation placed upon the building, and the tenant was entitled to a separate award. [Citation.] The award to the owner of the building, it is quite true, included compensation based on the rental value of the roof for sign-bearing purposes but that award did not in any way duplicate the award to the claimant; the landlord was allowed nothing for the value of the sign itself.

Nor does anything turn on the circumstance that the claimant's lease expired on April 1, 1960, some weeks before the city took title to and possession of the property. The significant facts are that the condemnation proceeding was begun in October of 1959, by service of a resolution of the Common Council; that the proceeding thus commenced was tried in February, 1960; and that the decision of the trial court was rendered on March 28, 1960, all before the end of the lease term. It was solely because of the city's initiation of the proceeding that the landlord had notified the tenant that the lease would not be renewed and requested it to remove the sign. By thus forcing the premature removal of the claimant's fixture, the city effectively destroyed the value of the tenant's sign except for the salvageable portions. [Citations.] In short, as this court recently wrote in the Marraro case (12 N.Y.2d 285, 291, 239 N.Y. S.2d 105, 108, 189 N.E.2d 606, 609, supra), "although the tenant * * * loses his right to compensation for his leasehold, he does not lose the right to be paid for his removable fixtures. * * * [T]he parties might have chosen to preserve the value of the fixtures 'either by renewal of the lease or by transfer of title to the fixtures from the tenant to the owner of the fee. Choice lay with the tenant and landlord, and how that choice would have been exercised rests in speculation which does not concern the courts in this jurisdiction.' (256 N.Y., p. 249, 176 N.E., p. 381.)"

The judgment appealed from should be affirmed.

Judgment affirmed.

FRANKLIN PLANNING & ZONING COMMISSION v. SIMPSON COUNTY LBR. CO.

(1965 Ky.) 394 S.W.2d 593.

HILL, J. This appeal concerns the propriety of a judgment interpreting the rights of these litigants under a planning and zoning ordinance of the City of Franklin.

Appellee Desford Potts for about seven years owned a six-acre tract of land within the corporate limits of Franklin. It lies between Railroad and Morris Streets. During this period, Potts maintained a livestock barn on the tract in which was stored lumber and other building materials. Outside, and mostly to the rear of the barn, brick was stored in stacks four or five feet high. In 1959 the City of Franklin passed a zoning ordinance by virtue of which Potts' lot was classified as residential (R–2) property.

Shortly before this suit was instituted, Potts moved some saw logs onto his lot back of the barn where he had recently had a bulldozer level the lot. The city complained.

Potts sued to enjoin interference by the city. The chancellor decided in favor of Potts.

The city contends the continued use by Potts of his property for storage of building materials is a "nonconforming" use, and under the law cannot be enlarged by storing saw logs thereon. Potts contends it is not an enlargement of the "nonconforming" use and therefore not in violation of the zoning ordinance. We should say here that a "nonconforming use" means simply a use which does not conform to the classification provided for in the ordinance, residential in this instance.

The applicable portion of the ordinance is as follows:

"Section 33, Continuance of Non-Conforming Uses. Any use of land or structure existing at the time of enactment or subsequent amendment of this ordinance, but not in conformity with its use provisions may be continued * * *."

Regardless of our sadness at seeing the elimination of the "spreading chestnut tree", and the village smith, it must be admitted that in the interest of progress the law favors the gradual elimination of "nonconforming" uses of property in our cities. [Citation.] It naturally follows that such nonconforming uses as are tolerated under the law cannot be enlarged. [Citations.]

So, our question is whether the storage of saw logs on Potts' lot is an enlargement of the "nonconforming use" he enjoyed previously. The chancellor found as a matter of fact the use was not enlarged. We have numerous photographs of the stored logs, and they appear to be stacked higher than the brick, perhaps eight feet high; but it cannot be said they are unsightly, obnoxious, or a health hazard.

Admitting the saw logs were stacked higher than the brick and not so symmetrically, unless they obstruct the view or impede the natural flow of air we cannot see wherein

their storage back of the barn is materially different from the storage of the stacks of brick. Accordingly, we agree with the chancellor that the "nonconforming use" by Potts of his property has not been enlarged by the storage of saw logs on the property. There is no contention Potts plans a sawmill. It goes without saying that a sawmill in such a residential community would be such an enlargement as appellants oppose.

The judgment is affirmed.

———

TRAYLOR v. HOLLOWAY

(1965) 206 Va. 257, 142 S.E.2d 521.

BUCHANAN, J. Eloise Randolph Traylor and Harry E. Traylor, Jr., Trustees, referred to herein as complainants, filed their bill for injunction against Benjamin D. Holloway and Joan B. Holloway, defendants, to require them to remove from their premises a building which the complainants alleged violated a restrictive covenant in defendants' deed. The court below refused the injunction, dismissed the bill and the complainants have appealed.

The suit was heard on the bill, the answer of defendants, a stipulation of facts and issues, and the testimony of one witness heard *ore tenus* by the court, all of which presented the following case:

The complainants are trustees in a deed of trust by which there was conveyed to them a tract of 147.246 acres of land in Chesterfield county for the purposes set out therein, which include authority to subdivide the property into residential lots subject to such restrictions as they deemed advisable. Pursuant thereto the complainants proceeded to divide part of the tract into a subdivision called Traylor Estates, as shown on a map which was duly recorded; and by a declaration of restrictions duly executed and recorded on April 4, 1958, the lots in Section A of the subdivision were made subject to certain restrictions, designed to create a select residential area. Paragraphs 1 and 2 of said restrictions are set out in the margin.[1] Similar restrictive covenants have been placed on all of the other sections of Traylor Estates.

By deed dated March 16, 1959, duly recorded, the complainants conveyed Lot 4, Block C, Section A, to the defendants Holloway, who are husband and wife. The deed was expressly made "subject to the restrictive covenants and conditions of 'Traylor Estates Section A,' " as stated above.

According to the stipulation of facts and issues, "without any submission to the architectural committee, the defendants constructed on their lot a structure 12' x 12', of which approximately 8' x 12', is enclosed, which structure is used as a playhouse for the children of the defendants and their friends;" and the issue for decision is whether complainants have proved that the structure is a "building" within the meaning of the restrictions, and whether the restrictions should be so construed as to require the removal of the structure.

The stipulation also contains the statement that the subdivision "has been developed into a fine residential section."

The only witness to testify was O. L. Hopkins, a real estate broker who developed the Traylor Estates and is agent for the sale of the lots. He testified as to his efforts to make this a high-class subdivision; that he drew up the restrictions with that in view and after careful study, and that he explained to each purchaser of a lot as to the restrictions and what they required. Pictures showing the kind and quality of the homes that had been built on the lots in Section A were introduced. Defendants' counsel conceded that the subdivision "is very high quality." Hopkins described the structure on the Holloway lot as "just a small building with a little overhanging porch in front of it." Pictures were presented showing the front, sides and rear of the structure. Hopkins testified that he had received objections to this particular house on this lot.

The court below was of opinion, as stated in its decree, "that a reasonable and proper interpretation of the restrictive covenants here involved does not prohibit the erection and maintenance of the subject playhouse upon the rear lot of the defendants."

From the evidence and the pictures it is quite clear that this structure is a building. It has four walls and a front porch, all under one roof. The entire structure, including the porch, is 12 feet by 12 feet. The four walls enclose a space 12 feet by 8 feet and the open porch extends four feet beyond the enclosed portion.

Defendants do not assert that the structure is not a building. They argue that it is not a building "within the meaning of the restrictive covenants," and that the meaning of the covenants should be determined by what the parties intended when they agreed that no building should be erected, and by "the evil sought to be avoided."

The parties are agreed that covenants restricting the free use of land are not favored and must be strictly construed. The burden is on the person who seeks to enforce such

---

1. 1. No lot shall be used except for residential purposes. No building shall be erected, altered, placed, or permitted to remain on any lot other than one detached single-family dwelling not to exceed two stories in height and a private garage for not more than two cars.

2. No building shall be erected, placed, or altered on any lot until the construction plans and specifications thereof and a plan showing the location thereof shall have been approved by the architectural committee hereinafter established as to quality and types of materials, harmony of external design with existing structures, and location with respect to topography and finish grade elevation. No fence or wall not constituting part of a building shall be erected, placed, or altered on any lot nearer to any street than the minimum building setback line unless similarly approved. The approval aforesaid shall be as provided in paragraphs 9 and 10.

covenants to establish that the thing objected to is within their terms. [Citations.]

* * *

According to the evidence in the present case the circumstances were that the complainants proposed to make of the property a high-class subdivision where attractive homes would be built and attractive grounds maintained. To secure this result restrictions were prepared and made applicable to all lots, placed on record, referred to in each deed, and explained to each purchaser. These covenants included the provision that

" * * * No building shall be erected, altered, placed, or permitted to remain on any lot other than one detached single-family dwelling not to exceed two stories in height and a private garage for not more than two cars."

They included the further provision that no building should be erected, placed, or altered on any lot until the construction plans and specifications and its location were approved by the architectural committee.

There is no ambiguity in these restrictions. They are stated in plain words. They were made to apply to all the lots, and the uncontradicted evidence is that what they were and what they required were explained to every person who purchased a lot. While the fact that the structure on this lot is used as a children's playhouse makes it desirable to the defendants, it does not create an exception to the terms of the restrictions. The restrictions made part of the defendants' deed apply to the type of the structure. They make no exception in favor of the use made of it. If the restrictions are to be construed as permitting structures other than those specified, because they are desirable, the result could readily be to nullify the restrictions and to make a contract different from the one made by the parties. As suggested in University Gardens Property Owners Assn. v. Solomon, Sup., 88 N.Y.S.2d 789, " * * * There is a danger in disregarding

the violation of such agreements; the first departure from such agreement is usually of a minor character but by gradual small infringement a substantial impairment or destruction of the whole scheme may gradually result."

* * *

" * * * It is well settled that where the grantor has clearly restricted the use of the land granted, and the restriction itself is not illegal, the covenant creates a trust which, in a proper case, courts of equity will enforce by means of an injunction against an inconsistent use. * * * " [Citations.]

Spilling v. Hutcheson, 111 Va. 179, 68 S. E. 250, involved an application for an injunction to require the removal of a part of a building which encroached on a restriction in the defendant's deed. The defendant urged that the enforcement of the restriction inflicted an unnecessary hardship and that the plaintiff should be left to an action at law for damages. But this court said the correct rule in such case was stated in Doherty v. Allman, 3 H.L.App.Cas. 720, as follows:

" '* * * If parties, for valuable consideration, with their eyes open, contract that a particular thing shall not be done, all that a court of equity has to do is to say by way of injunction that which the parties have already said by way of covenant—that the thing shall not be done, and in such case the injunction does nothing more than give the sanction of the process of the court to that which already is the contract between the parties. It is not, then, a question of convenience or inconvenience, or of the amount of damage or injury. It is the specific performance, by the court, of that negative bargain which the parties have made, with their eyes open, between themselves.' " 111 Va. at 182, 68 S.E. at 251.

We hold that the structure complained of violates Paragraphs 1 and 2 of the restrictions set out above, and that the complainants are entitled to have the structure removed.

*   *   *

The decree appealed from is accordingly reversed and the cause is remanded to the Circuit Court with direction to issue a mandatory injunction requiring the defendants to remove the structure from their lot.

Reversed and remanded.

VOYLES v. KNIGHT

(1964) 220 Ga. 305, 138 S.E.2d 565.

Syllabus Opinion by the Court

DUCKWORTH, C. J.   1. As a general rule, the owner of land in fee has the right to use the property for any lawful purpose, and any claim that there are restrictions upon such use must be clearly established, and such limitations of use will be strictly construed, as limitations thereon by implication are not favored. [Citations.] Indeed, any doubt as to the restrictions on use will be construed in favor of the grantee. [Citations.]

2. The restrictive instrument was signed by all the owners, witnessed and recorded. It provided that these covenants shall run with the land and shall be binding on all parties and all persons claiming under them until January 1, 1979. The first paragraph listed the owners of the land, and the second clause is, "The said subdivision is intended for residential purposes only." Then it recites that in consideration of "the foregoing and the benefits flowing to the present and future owners" the following protective and/or restrictive covenants which shall be applicable to all subdivided lots shown on the plat referred to shall be imposed. Thereafter, it provides that: "All lots in the tract shall be known and described as residential lots. No structure shall be erected, altered, placed or permitted to remain on any residential building plot other than one single-family dwelling house not to exceed 2½ stories in height." Other restrictions in the instrument are irrelevant here.

Thus is presented a duly executed and recorded restrictive instrument made by the owners of the land. The words residence and residential relate solely to use. No structure could become a residence or residential in the absence of its use by people residing therein. At precisely the time when people fail to live therein it ceases to be a residence. Put another way to fit the facts of this case, irrespective of its former use, or the nature of the structure, when the building here involved ceased to be a residence and became exclusively "a day nursery," it was no longer a residence, and the clause of the covenant, to wit: "No structure shall be erected, altered, placed or *permitted to remain* on any residential building plot" comes into operation. And by its terms such structure shall not be "permitted to remain." We are convinced that the foregoing references to the covenant leave no reasonable doubt but that its intent is to prohibit any use other than as residence of any lot. This manifest intent being the cardinal rule of construction will control over the above mentioned rule of strict construction against restrictions. If the intent is plainly manifest no ambiguity exists, and it is only in cases of ambiguity that the rule of strict construction applies.

*   *   *

3. The evidence showing that the "day nursery" is to be operated in the vacant dwelling house adjacent to the residence of the defendant, the lower court erred in refusing to grant the temporary injunction to prevent the defendant from using said property for any purpose other than a residential purpose.

Judgment reversed.

SHELLEY v. KRAEMER

(1947) 334 U.S. 1, 68 S.Ct. 836, 92 L.Ed. 1161, 3 A.L.R.2d 441.

[Suits were commenced in Missouri and Michigan to enjoin violations of covenants in deeds restricting the use and occupancy of real estate to persons of the Caucasian race. The Supreme Courts of both States upheld the covenants, and the two cases were joined upon certiorari being granted by the United States Supreme Court.]

VINSON, C. J. * * * Whether the equal protection clause of the Fourteenth Amendment inhibits judicial enforcement by state courts of restrictive covenants based on race or color is a question which this Court has not heretofore been called upon to consider. * * *

It is well, at the outset, to scrutinize the terms of the restrictive agreements involved in these cases. In the Missouri case, the covenant declares that no part of the affected property shall be "occupied by any person not of the Caucasian race, it being intended hereby to restrict the use of said property * * * against the occupancy as owners or tenants of any portion of said property for resident or other purpose by people of the Negro or Mongolian Race." Not only does the restriction seek to proscribe use and occupancy of the affected properties by members of the excluded class, but as construed by the Missouri courts, the agreement requires that title of any person who uses his property in violation of the restriction shall be divested. The restriction of the covenant in the Michigan case seeks to bar occupancy by persons of the excluded class. It provides that "This property shall not be used or occupied by any person or persons except those of the Caucasian race."

It should be observed that these covenants do not seek to proscribe any particular use of the affected properties. Use of the properties for residential occupancy, as such, is not forbidden. The restrictions of these agreements, rather, are directed toward a designated class of persons and seek to determine who may and who may not own or make use of the properties for residential purposes. The excluded class is defined wholly in terms of race or color; "simply that and nothing more."

It cannot be doubted that among the civil rights intended to be protected from discriminatory state action by the Fourteenth Amendment are the rights to acquire, enjoy, own and dispose of property. * * *

But the present cases, unlike those just discussed, do not involve action by state legislatures or city councils. Here the particular patterns of discrimination and the areas in which the restrictions are to operate, are determined, in the first instance, by the terms of agreements among private individuals. Participation of the State consists in the enforcement of the restrictions so defined. The crucial issue with which we are here confronted is whether this distinction removes these cases from the operation of the prohibitory provisions of the Fourteenth Amendment.

Since the decision of this Court in the Civil Rights Cases, 109 U.S. 3, 3 S.Ct. 18, 27 L.Ed. 835 (1883), the principle has become firmly embedded in our constitutional law that the action inhibited by the first section of the Fourteenth Amendment is only such action as may fairly be said to be that of the States. That Amendment erects no shield against merely private conduct, however discriminatory or wrongful.

We conclude, therefore, that the restrictive agreements standing alone cannot be regarded as violative of any rights guaranteed to petitioners by the Fourteenth Amendment. So long as the purposes of those agreements are effectuated by voluntary adherence to their terms, it would appear clear that there has been no action by the State and the provisions of the Amendment have not been violated. [Citation.]

But here there was more. These are cases in which the purposes of the agreements were secured only by judicial enforcement by state courts of the restrictive terms of the agreements. * * *

We hold that in granting judicial enforcement of the restrictive agreements in these cases, the States have denied petitioners the equal protection of the laws and that, therefore, the action of the state courts cannot stand. We have noted that freedom from discrimination by the States in the enjoyment of property rights was among the basic objectives sought to be effectuated by the framers of the Fourteenth Amendment. That such discrimination has occurred in these cases is clear. Because of the race or color of these petitioners they have been denied rights of ownership or occupancy enjoyed as a matter of course by other citizens of different race or color. The Fourteenth Amendment declares "that all persons, whether colored or white, shall stand equal before the laws of the States, and, in regard to the colored race, for whose protection the amendment was primarily designed, that no discrimination shall be made against them by law because of their color." Strauder v. West Virginia, 100 U.S. 303, at 307, 25 L.Ed. 664. * * *

Upon full consideration, we have concluded that in these cases the States have acted to deny petitioners the equal protection of the laws guaranteed by the Fourteenth Amendment. Having so decided, we find it unnecessary to consider whether petitioners have also been deprived of property without due process of law or denied privileges and immunities of citizens of the United States.

For the reasons stated, the judgment of the Supreme Court of Missouri and the judgment of the Supreme Court of Michigan must be reversed.

PROBLEMS

1. (a) The city council of Urbania enacted a zoning ordinance which limited the use of A's land to residential. At the time of the enactment of the ordinance A owned and operated a tavern upon the premises in question. Urbania's building commissioner arrested A for violating the ordinance. What defenses, if any, are available to A upon his trial?

(b) As a member of Urbania's city council, could you suggest anything to alleviate the problems suggested? Would your suggestions withstand an attack based upon constitutional grounds?

2. A, the owner of several lots in an area zoned for commercial and residential uses, conveyed one of his lots to B "so long as B shall use the said premises for private dwelling purposes only." Ten years later B sold the property to C, who proposed constructing a multi-office building on the lot. By this time the area was about 40% residential and 60% commercial. When A learned of C's plans he brought an action to enjoin C from proceeding with those plans. What decision?

3. Z, owner of a meat packing plant situated in an industrial area of the city where other packing plants are located, develops a new process for making glue which, although efficient, gives off an unusually unpleasant odor. Packing plants and other concerns in the area sue Z to enjoin the use of this odor producing process. They are able to show at the trial that 90% of their employees are made ill from the odor to the extent that their working efficiency is reduced 20%. Result of suit?

4. B operated a retail bakery, D a drug store, F a food store, G a gift shop and H a hardware store in adjoining locations along one side of a single suburban village block. As the population grew the business section developed at the other end of the village and the establishments of B, D, F, G and H were surrounded for at least a mile in each direction solely with residences. A zoning ordinance with the usual provisions was adopted by the village and the area including the five stores was declared to be a "residential district for single-family dwellings." Thereafter, B tore down the frame building which housed the bakery and commenced to construct a modern brick bakery. D found his business increasing to such an extent that he began to build an addition upon the drug store in order to extend it to the rear

alley. F's building was destroyed by fire and he started to reconstruct it in order to restore it to its former condition. G changed the gift shop into a sporting goods store and after six months of operation has decided to go back into the gift shop business. H sold his hardware store to X.

The village building commissioner brings an action under the zoning ordinance to enjoin the construction work of B, D and F and to enjoin the carrying on of any business by G and X. Assume the ordinance is valid.

What result?

PART TEN
TRUSTS, MORTGAGES, INSURANCE, WILLS

CHAPTER 50

TRUSTS AND MORTGAGES

Trusts Defined. The legal title to property is frequently held by one person while the right to the use and the benefit of the same property is enjoyed by another. This situation may arise by a voluntary and express act of a person or this separation of title and enjoyment may be decreed by law; in either event, the relationship created is generally described as a "trust."

The Creation of the Trust; Formalities. Each trust has (1) a creator or "settlor," (2) a trustee and (3) a beneficiary. Except for the requirement that a sole beneficiary cannot be the sole trustee, these offices may be held by the same person. A may convey in trust to B for the benefit of C; or A may declare himself trustee for the benefit of C; or A may convey in trust to B for the benefit of himself, A.

Although there are many varieties of trusts, all trusts may be divided into two major groups, express and implied. The implied trusts, which are imposed upon property by courts, are known as either "constructive" or "resulting" trusts and these two special types are explained later.

The express trust is, as the name indicates, a trust established by voluntary action and is represented by a written document or, under some conditions, an oral statement. In a majority of jurisdictions, an express trust of real property must be in writing to meet the requirements of the Statute of Frauds. No particular words are necessary to create a trust, provided that the intent of the settlor

to establish a trust is unmistakable. A not uncommon provision is "to X, as Trustee, to have and hold upon the trusts and uses hereinafter set forth."

Trusts are widely employed in wills as a means of conserving property for the benefit of widows and children. They are frequently established by individuals during their lifetime in which case they are referred to as inter vivos trusts. Such living trusts frequently are employed as a method of avoiding taxes by taking advantage of lower Federal tax rates upon gifts during lifetime than upon transfers at death, or by transferring the income from property owned by a parent in a high income tax bracket to a child in a comparatively low tax bracket.

Consideration is not esssential to an enforceable trust. In this respect, a trust is more akin to a conveyance than a contract. It is not, however, always clear whether a person has by his actions created a trust or simply *promised* to create a trust. Since consideration is necessary to enforce such a promise, the practical importance of distinguishing between an actual declaration of trust and a statement of intent to create a trust in the future is apparent. Although it is said that there must be "delivery" of a trust to make it binding, the term is misleading since it is used in a highly technical sense and means only that an intent to have the instrument take effect is necessary.

Any person legally capable of making a contract can create a trust.

Subject Matter. One of the chief characteristics which sets a trust apart from other relationships is the requirement that the subject matter of the trust must be definite and specific. A trust cannot be created of property not yet in existence or to be acquired at a later date. In 1964, A organized a corporation and executed a trust instrument declaring he held the future dividends in trust for his children. When dividends were declared in 1965, A could keep them or set them aside as trust property. His declarations in 1964 did not oblige him to hold the *future* unrealized profits in trust. In each succeeding year, a declaration would be necessary in order to impose the character of a trust upon the dividends. If X informs Y that he has left Y $100,000 in his will, a declaration of trust by Y during X's lifetime covering this expectancy is of no effect to bind Y upon the death of X. On the other hand, the need of a definite and certain subject matter is met when A provides in his will that he leaves to B, as trustee, sufficient funds to pay $200 a month to C.

A definite subject matter frequently distinguishes a trustee-beneficiary relationship from a debtor-creditor relationship, and this distinction has many important consequences in business affairs, particularly where an obligor has become insolvent. If A owes B $1,000 and A becomes insolvent, B will share ratably with A's other creditors. If, on the other hand, A opens a bank account as "A, Trustee for B," deposits the $1,000 and then becomes insolvent, B will be able to collect the full amount due him under the trust. When money is paid over to one person for the use of another, as in the case of rents paid to an agent for the owner of the premises or the purchase price paid to a commission agent for goods sold, the earmarking of the proceeds or the maintenance of a separate credit by the agent generally establishes him as a trustee, not a debtor. When a corporation declares a dividend, it becomes a debtor to the shareholders of record. If, in addition to a declaration, it sets funds aside in a special bank account to pay the dividend, it will be considered a trustee and in the event of its subsequent insolvency, the shareholders will, so far as that fund is concerned, share ahead of the corporation's general creditors. In most of these cases, the crucial issue is whether there is an identifiable subject matter separate and distinct from the obligor's other assets.

The Trustee; His Duties and Powers. Anyone legally capable of dealing with property may be a trustee. A corporation may act as trustee within the limits of its authorized powers; a public institution may act as a trustee. A substantial trust business is carried on by many banks, a function limited primarily by the statutory provision in most States that only local institutions are qualified to act as corporate trustees. The lack of a trustee will not, however, destroy the trust. If the settlor neglects to appoint one, or if a named trustee does not qualify, the court, upon request, will appoint an individual or institution to act as trustee.

A trustee can, of course, decline to serve, and before the property will vest in him it is necessary that he accept the trust. Acceptance is often inferred from the acts of the trustee indicative of an intent to exercise dominion over the trust estate. It is a common statutory requirement that a trustee must post a bond for the honest administration of his duties and, in the absence of statute, the court, in its discretion may require the trustee to post bond.

There are three primary duties of any trustee:

1. To carry out the purposes of the trust.

2. To act with prudence and care in the administration of the trust.

3. To exercise a high degree of loyalty toward the beneficiary.

The first of these duties needs little comment. It is obvious that the trustee is charged with following the direction of the settlor as to the manner of administration of the estate and the distribution of the property to the beneficiaries.

The second responsibility, that of using prudence and care in administration, is not as easily defined. No special skills are required of a trustee under ordinary circumstances. What constitutes the prudence of a "prudent man" is, of course, not easy to classify in any particular case. In those cases involving disastrous investments by the trustee the advantages of hindsight often obscure the fact that, at the time of the investment, the general business community looked upon a particular security as a good risk. Generally, a trustee follows a safe course if he makes the conservation of capital his main goal and the realization of income a policy to be followed only insofar as it is consistent with the continued security of the capital entrusted to him.

The third duty of the trustee, that of loyalty, arises out of and illustrates the fiduciary character of the relationship between the trustee and the beneficiary. The trustee in all his dealings with the trust property, the beneficiary and third parties, must always act in the exclusive interest of the beneficiary. Indeed, the trustee, to protect himself from liability for misfeasance, must lean over backward to avoid any suggestion of personal advantage from the trust. He cannot act as though the beneficiary were a stranger with whom he could deal at arms length. Lack of loyalty may arise from palpable self-dealing or it may be entirely innocent; in either event the trustee can be charged with lack of loyalty. The cases are full of illustrations of this principle. The sale of his own property to a trust or the purchase of trust property at a sale conducted by himself as trustee are common instances of a violation of this fiduciary duty. The loan of trust

funds by a trustee to himself or the loan of such funds to a corporation of which he is a principal shareholder would constitute a breach of this duty. The fact that the transaction is carried on through a "dummy" will not prevent a court from setting aside such a transaction. The fact that no harm may be done the trust does not excuse the transaction. It is a prophylactic rule designed to discourage temptation regardless of the outcome of any particular transaction.

A beneficiary can require that the disloyal trustee restore the status quo. A beneficiary who is legally competent may, on the other hand, ratify the disloyal act and be prevented from later charging the trustee with disloyalty. In such a case, the beneficiary would be estopped, however, only if full disclosure of the entire transaction had been made by the trustee.

The powers of a trustee are determined by (1) the rules of law in the jurisdiction in which the trust is established and (2) the authority granted him by the settlor in the instrument creating the trust. State laws affecting the powers of trustees have their greatest impact upon the investments a trustee may make with trust funds. Most States prescribe a list of types of securities qualified for trust investment. In some jurisdictions this list is permissive; in others it is mandatory. If the list is permissive, the trustee may invest in unlisted types of securities although he carries the burden of showing that he made a prudent choice. If the list is mandatory, it would appear that the trustee must confine himself to the listed types regardless of the "prudence" of an unlisted investment. Those investments usually approved, in the order of their general preference, are (1) obligations of the United States, (2) bonds of States and municipalities which meet certain standards, (3) first mortgages, if the security is adequate and, occasionally, (4) the secured-debt securities of triple-A corporations, generally limited to public utilities. If a security does not fall within these classes, its purchase by a trustee will be disapproved except in extraordinary cases. Such improper investments would include unsecured loans, investments in a small business, loans secured by second mortgages and other junior liens and, in most instances, common and preferred stocks. In some States, statutes or court decisions have relaxed the rule insofar as certain stocks are concerned.

It is within the power of the settlor to give the trustee wide discretion as to investments and, in such an event, the trustee is not bound to adhere to the list deemed advisable under the statute. Thus, if a statute does not include the preferred stock of industrial corporations a trustee may so invest if given the authority by the settlor. It is not uncommon for a settlor to specifically direct the trustee to retain the stock in a family corporation and the trustee may do so whereas, otherwise, he would undoubtedly be obliged to dispose of the securities within a reasonable time. Wide discretion in a trust instrument does not, nevertheless, relieve a trustee from the general duty of prudence and care referred to before.

In the absence of specific directions, the trustee normally has the power and, indeed, sometimes the duty, to sell or exchange securities left in trust. He may also select a depositary for the funds and do those other things impliedly necessary to carry out satisfactorily the purpose of the trust. But, in the absence of specific authority, there are many incidents of ownership normally exercised by the average person that a cautious trustee would hesitate to undertake. It is for this reason that an adequate trust will grant very broad powers to the trustee.

The Beneficiary. There are very few restrictions on who (or what) may be a beneficiary. Dogs, cats, horses and a multitude of pets limited only by the imaginative attachments of humans have at one time or another been held to be the proper objects of a settlor's bounty. Charitable uses are a common purpose of trusts and, if the settlor's object does not outrage public policy or morals, almost any purpose which happens to strike the fancy of a settlor will be upheld. A corporation or a public institution may be a beneficiary. The settlor not infrequently makes himself beneficiary and, if this does not defraud his creditors, such action is perfectly valid.

In the absence of restrictive provisions in the trust instrument, a beneficiary's interest may be attached by his creditors, the beneficiary may sell his interest and, upon his death, if he held more than a life estate in the trust, his estate will pass to his heirs where the corpus of the trust is real estate or to his personal representative if the trust consists of personal property.

Termination of Trust. Unless the power of revocation is reserved by the settlor, the general rule is that a trust, once validly created, is irrevocable. Not infrequently, such power of revocation is reserved in which case the trust can end at the discretion of the settlor. Parents occasionally create living trusts for children and reserve a power of revocation to insure proper filial respect for parental discipline. Under present tax laws, however, the income from a trust is taxable to the settlor if, directly or indirectly, he reserves a power of revocation, a fact which has somewhat dampened former enthusiasm for the revocable family trust.

Normally, a trust has a termination date in the instrument and the trust ends simply and without complication. A period of years may be specified or the settlor may provide that the trust shall continue for the life of a named individual. The death of the trustee or beneficiary does not terminate the trust if neither of their lives is the measure of the duration of the trust. Occasionally, the purpose for which a trust has been established ends before the specified termination date. In such a case, a court will occasionally, upon request by all interested parties, decree the termination of the trust. A court will usually decree a trust terminated if the beneficiary also acquires the legal title, but most courts will not order the termination of a trust simply because all the beneficiaries petition the court to do so. The court will be governed by the purposes set out by the settlor, not the wishes of the beneficiaries.

Types of Trusts. The trust relationship can take a variety of forms. Some of them have distinguishing characteristics which merit special attention. The following types of trusts are neither mutually exclusive nor are they properly classified together but they are listed herein for simplicity of identification. They are:

1. Implied Trusts

    (a) Constructive Trusts

    (b) Resulting Trusts

2. Charitable Trusts

3. Spendthrift Trusts

4. Precatory Trusts

(1) *Implied Trusts.* In some cases, the courts, in the absence of any expressed trust intent, will impose a trust upon property because the acts of the parties appear to call for such a construction. An implied trust owes its existence to the law. Customarily, these implied trusts are divided into two classes, constructive trusts and resulting trusts. Although the line between these two subclasses is frequently blurred, a constructive trust is said to cover those instances where the court will impose a trust upon property to rectify a fraud or to prevent unjust enrichment.

A constructive trust exists where a confidential relation, and the subsequent abuse of the confidence reposed are sufficient to establish such trust, or where actual fraud is considered as equitable ground for raising the trust. While, as a general rule, a donee

by deed who has received real property, under an oral promise to hold it for the donor or another may rely on the Statute of Frauds, an exception prevails where a confidential relation exists between grantor and grantee. The mere existence of such relationship prohibits the one trusted from seeking any selfish benefit for himself during the course of the relationship and affords a basis for fastening a constructive trust upon the property in his hands, irrespective of his oral promise to use it for the benefit of another. In general, a fiduciary or confidential relation exists where trust and confidence are reposed by one person in another, who, as a result, gains an influence and superiority over the first. Specifically, a confidential relation exists where, by reason of kinship, business or association, disparity in age, or physical or mental condition, or other reason, the grantee occupies an especially intimate position with regard to the grantor and the latter reposes a high degree of trust and confidence in the former. Where a fiduciary relation exists, the burden rests upon the grantee or beneficiary of an instrument executed during the existence of such relationship to prove, by clear and convincing proof, the fairness of the transaction, that it was equitable and just, that it did not proceed from undue influence, and that he exercised good faith and did not betray the confidence reposed in him, irrespective of whether he was instrumental in causing the conveyance to be made. It is not essential that the undue influence vitiating the transfer be deemed fraudulent. It is sufficient if the influence arises out of the fiduciary or confidential relation.

Business and personal affairs are full of examples of *constructive* trusts. If a person obtains money or other property by fraud or duress, equity may treat him as a trustee. A director of a corporation who makes an undisclosed profit in a deal with the corporation will be treated as a trustee for the corporation to the extent of the profit. A trustee under an express trust who permits a lease held by the trust to expire and then acquires a new lease in his individual capacity will be required to hold the new lease in trust for the beneficiary. If an agent who is given money by his principal to purchase property in the name of the principal instead uses the funds to acquire title in himself, most courts will treat him as a trustee for the principal.

A *resulting* trust is said to be distinguished from a constructive trust in that, while the latter is designed to rectify fraud, the former serves to carry out the true intent of the parties in those cases where the intent was inadequately expressed. The most common example of a resulting trust is where A pays the purchase price for property and title is taken in the name of B. The presumption here is that the parties intended B to hold the property for the benefit of A, and B will be treated as a trustee. The difficulty is that, in many cases, it would be equally reasonable to presume that A intended to make a gift to B, and, in the cases where the payor is a husband or a parent, a gift is generally the more favored presumption.

A resulting trust does not depend on contract or agreement but is founded on a presumed intent which arises out of the acts of the parties. Since a resulting trust is created by implication and operation of law, it need not be evidenced by writing. The trust arises, if at all, in the same transaction in which the legal title vests, on consideration advanced before or at that time and not on acts arising thereafter. It is, of course, always possible to prove that a trust was not intended. A resulting trust is only a presumption based upon human behavior, and courts generally require very careful proof to establish a resulting trust. The burden of proof rests on the parties seeking to es-

tablish a resulting trust and the evidence, to be effective for such purpose, must be clear, strong, unequivocal, unmistakable, and so convincing as to lead to but one conclusion. If a reasonable explanation of the evidence may be made upon any theory other than the existence of a resulting trust, a trust will not be declared and enforced.

(2) *Charitable Trusts.* The legal meaning of charity is broader than that usually attributed to the word by the layman. It includes substantially any *public* purpose which will contribute to education, the advancement of science and knowledge in general. Almost any trust which has for its purpose the improvement of mankind, or a class of mankind, will be classified as charitable, provided it is not so vague and indefinite as to be incapable of enforcement. Gifts for public museums, upkeep of parks, propagation of a particular political doctrine or religious belief have been upheld as "charitable" in character. An unusual trust was provided for in the will of a wealthy man who devised and bequeathed the larger part of his substantial estate "To organize a farmers' home for worthy, honest, respectable, law-abiding, American citizens to be named the Adam B. Carter Home and is to be known as a charity Home." An attack against this provision of the will was rejected, the court holding that it created a valid charitable trust.

There are practical differences in the law depending upon whether a trust is for charitable or private purposes. In general, the rule against perpetuities does not apply to charitable trusts. For example, it is valid to provide for a gift in trust to the Middlesex Hospital with a provision that if the hospital ceased to maintain free wards the property should go to the Town of Middlesex for care of the poor. If the trust had been for a private purpose the contingent gift to the town would have violated the rule against perpetuities.

Secondly, the cy pres doctrine is applicable only to charitable trusts. This doctrine reflects the traditional sympathy of courts toward charitable motives and it means that when it is impossible or impracticable to carry out a charitable bequest exactly as directed by the settlor, a court will apply the funds to a charity as similar as possible in purpose to that specified. One of the famous cases illustrating the doctrine of cy pres involved two trusts, one providing funds to create sentiment favoring the abolition of slavery and the second establishing a fund to aid runaway slaves. The Emancipation Proclamation abolished slavery soon after the death of the settlor and the court authorized the use of the first trust fund for Negro education and the second for the aid of needy Negroes in the town where the settlor had lived. There must, however, be a general charitable intent in order to apply cy pres. A trust to encourage the propagation of a particular religious cult could not, if the cult disbanded, be applied for use by any other religion unless there was a definite indication of a non-sectarian religious purpose on the part of the settlor.

(3) *Spendthrift Trusts.* A settlor frequently does not believe that a beneficiary can be relied upon to preserve even the limited rights granted him as beneficiary. He will then provide that the beneficiary cannot, by assignment, or otherwise, impair his rights to receive principal or income and that creditors of the beneficiary cannot attach the fund or the income. The term "spendthrift", as used in connection with spendthrift trusts, merely means one on whose behalf, or for whose support, a fund is provided in such a way as to be removed from the beneficiary's control and disposition and from liability for his individual debts. Of course, once the income actually is received by the beneficiary, creditors may seize it or the beneficiary may do with it as he pleases.

Spendthrift provisions are generally valid. A typical provision follows:

> "Payments and distributions to all the beneficiaries hereunder, except to minors and persons under disability, shall be made only to such beneficiaries in person or upon their personal receipt, and no interest of any beneficiary in the income or principal of the Trust Estate shall be assignable in anticipation of payment, either by the voluntary or involuntary act of such beneficiary or by operation of law, or be liable in any way for the debts of such beneficiary."

(4) *Precatory Trusts.* It is not always easy to tell whether a settlor really intended to create a trust. Sometimes, words of request or recommendation are used in connection with a gift implying that the gift should be used for the purpose referred to by the request or recommendation. Thus, instead of leaving property "to X for the benefit and use of Y," a settlor may leave property to X "in full confidence and with hope that he will care for Y." Such a "precatory expression" may be so definite and certain as to impose a trust upon the property for the benefit of Y. Whether it creates a trust or is nothing more than a guide or gratuitous wish will depend on whether the court believes from all the facts that the settlor really intended a trust. More frequently, courts are viewing such words as "request," "hope" and "rely" as creating no legal obligation upon the recipient of the gift.

MORTGAGES

History and Nature. A mortgage is security for a promise to pay a debt or to perform some other act and, generally, it is in the form of a lien upon property, the charge being represented by a document transferring an interest in the property to the creditor or obligee. The debtor is referred to as the "mortgagor;" the creditor is the "mortgagee." The term "mortgage" covers a variety of security transactions and the history of the mortgage is one of the most ancient and complex in the common law of property.

In the early development of the common law of England, the forerunner of the modern mortgage, far from being a transaction to secure a debt, was in form and in fact an outright conveyance by the debtor-mortgagor to the creditor-mortgagee, subject to the condition that the former could repossess the property upon payment of the debt on the due date. Failure to make payment on the exact date gave the creditor unconditional title to the property.

The patent hardship to the debtor under this requirement of payment on an exact date and strict compliance therewith afforded the courts of equity an opportunity to relieve the debtor by permitting him to recover the land even after the due date upon payment of the debt. This right or "equity of redemption" naturally placed a cloud upon the conditional title of the creditor and it was not long before the courts provided that the right of redemption had to be exercised within a specified time after the due date, or the right of the debtor would be foreclosed, an indefeasible title going to the creditor.

Once the doctrine of the equity of redemption was established the courts would not permit the waiver of this right by the mortgagor and the phrase "once a mortgage, always a mortgage" was applied most frequently in cases where an attempt to deny this fundamental right was prevented by the courts. Except as limited by the decree of strict foreclosure, the equity of redemption became an inherent characteristic of the mortgage and remains so today.

The notion that the transaction was primarily a conveyance with a defeasible legal title in the mortgagee prevailed generally long after equity had undertaken to alter other early characteristics of the mortgage and, indeed, in some jurisdictions the doctrine that a mortgage is a conveyance of the legal title still prevails. In most jurisdictions today, however, by statute or court decision, the established concept of equity that a mortgage is a security transaction has been accepted and the rule is that the mortgagor retains both legal and equitable title to the property while the mortgagee has simply a lien to secure the payment of the debt.

This distinction between the "title" and "lien" theory of a mortgage does result in occasional variations in the application of some rules relating to mortgages but, for the most part, does not substantially affect the basic rights and duties of the mortgagor and mortgagee.

Form of Mortgage. Even though the lien theory of a mortgage now generally prevails, the instrument creating a mortgage still remains in form a conveyance with all the necessary requirements for such documents, namely, adequate description of the property, seal and acknowledgment, and delivery. In most jurisdictions, a simple and concise form is recognized by statute but the transaction remains the same whether it is a one-page document covering a house and lot or a 350-page book covering substantially all the property of an interstate railroad company.

Because the mortgage is simply the security for a promise (usually a debt), it is accompanied by a second instrument which most frequently is a promissory note from the mortgagor to the mortgagee expressly secured by the mortgage.

The usual mortgage will differ from an outright conveyance of the property by virtue of a provision in the instrument for the "reconveyance" of the property (or, more practically, the release of the mortgage) upon the performance of his promise by the mortgagor. This condition is referred to as the "defeasance," and, while normally it appears on the face of the mortgage, it may be in a separate document. If evidence indicates that an instrument which purports to be an outright conveyance is actually a security transaction, defeasance will be implied.

The conception of a mortgage as a lien upon property as security for the performance of a promise applies with equal force to transactions under a different name which may take a different form. A *trust deed* is fundamentally identical with a mortgage, the most striking difference being that, under a trust deed, the property is conveyed not to the creditor but to a third person as a trustee for the benefit of the creditor. Trust deeds are frequently employed where the amount borrowed is substantial and has been obtained from a large number of creditors. The creditors will then receive bonds or certificates evidencing their interest in the trust. The trust deed creates rights substantially similar to those created by a mortgage.

Property which can be Mortgaged. Almost any interest in property can be mortgaged. Rents, life estates, vested remainders and even, in some instances, options, have been held to be proper subjects of a mortgage.

At common law, it was the general rule that property not yet acquired or not in existence could not be mortgaged since there could be no present conveyance under such circumstances. Under this rule, mortgage clauses seeking to subject after-acquired property to a mortgage were void. The majority of the jurisdictions today recognize the validity of such clauses in equity on the theory that the mortgage attaches to the property when acquired.

After-acquired property clauses are commonly used in connection with the "package mortgage," which has become increasingly popular as a means of financing the purchase of household appliances together with a new house. Under a package mortgage, the lender-mortgagee provides funds for the house and the household appliances, and specifically provides in the mortgage instrument that such appliances shall be part of the security.

The appliances covered by such a mortgage may be expected to wear out and to require replacement before the mortgage debt is paid. In most instances, the value of the realty itself generally provides adequate security for the loan. Nevertheless, the after-acquired property clause in package mortgages generally includes replacements of the appliances which were part of the original security. With time, as more appliances are considered indispensable in the modern home the after-acquired property clauses in package mortgages covering such appliances will assume greater importance. It should be noted that the after-acquired property clause affects only property to which the mortgagor subsequently acquires absolute title. Accordingly, the after-acquired property clause will not cover a replacement appliance purchased by the mortgagor subject to a purchase money security interest, until the price is paid and complete ownership shall have vested in the mortgagor.

Rights and Duties of Mortgagor. The correlative rights and duties of the parties to a mortgage may depend upon whether the transaction is viewed as a lien or as passing legal title to the mortgagee. In the "lien" theory States, the mortgagor, even in the absence of any stipulation in the mortgage, is entitled to possession of the premises to the exclusion of the mortgagee and this is true even in case of default by the mortgagor. Only by foreclosure or sale can the right of possession be taken away from the mortgagor. In this respect the law in these jurisdictions has reversed the common-law rule that gave the right of possession to the mortgagee, a rule which is still the law in those few jurisdictions which cling to the "title" theory of a mortgage. Even in these latter States, however, in most cases, as a practical matter, the mortgagor retains possession because the mortgagee has little interest in possession as such until default.

In the "lien" States, the mortgagor is, for practical purposes, the owner of the property and he may lease, sell, give away, or transfer by will his interest, subject only to the claim of the mortgage. Dower exists in the mortgagor's interest. The mortgagor's interest is subject to execution by his judgment creditors. In these cases, it is, in effect, the mortgagor's equity of redemption that, voluntarily or involuntarily, is being dealt with. If a house and lot have a market value of $35,000 and are subject to a mortgage of $25,000, the mortgagor's "equity" is $10,000 and it is this margin with which he may deal.

If the mortgagor is in possession he is entitled to the rents and profits from the land. His obligation to the mortgagee is to pay the interest and principal when due. It is occasionally stipulated, however, that the rents and profits shall be assigned to the mortgagee as additional security for the debt. The notion that the mortgagor is the true owner has been so firmly established that, in some jurisdictions, a mortgagor has been permitted to sue the mortgagee for illegal interference with his use just as any owner might sue a stranger having no interest in the property.

Even though the mortgagor be entitled to possession and to many of the attributes of unfettered ownership, he has a responsibility to deal with the property in such a manner as not to impair the security which it represents to the mortgagee. The general rules as to waste applying between landlord and tenant or life tenant and remainderman are modified to some extent, however, in the direction of allowing greater freedom to the mortgagor who is in possession. This is particularly true in the "lien" theory States. Indeed, the mortgagor is frequently allowed to deal with the property at his pleasure, so long as the security of the mortgagee is not rendered insufficient.

In most instances, "waste" (impairment of the security) results from the failure of the mortgagor to prevent the action, or threatened action, of third parties against the land. Thus, a failure by the debtor to pay taxes or to discharge a prior lien may seriously impair the security of the creditor. In such cases, the creditor is generally permitted to pay the obligation and add it to his claim against the mortgagor. Similarly, although a mortgagor is not obligated to insure the premises in the absence of an agreement to do so, if he does promise to insure and fails to do so, the mortgagee may insure and charge the expense to the mortgagor.

Whether a mortgage is viewed as giving the mortgagee a legal title or simply a lien may also affect the rights of the mortgagee against third parties. In States that consider the legal title to be in the mortgagee, he does, of course, have all the remedies incident to ownership. Where he is looked upon as having only a lien, he is, nevertheless, regarded as having a sufficient interest to obtain an injunction against damage to the property although he will not always be permitted to maintain an action at law for damages.

Some of the most troublesome problems relate to the rights and duties of the mortgagee vis-a-vis a lessee of the mortgagor. A mortgage made subsequent to a lease of the premises cannot interfere with the right of the tenant to use the property for the term of the lease, but once a mortgage has been placed on the property no subsequent lease by the mortgagor will bind the mortgagee. Thus, if A rents a farm to C on January 1 and later mortgages the same land to B, upon default by A in paying the mortgage debt any subsequent foreclosure by B cannot disturb C's right to use of the land under his lease. But, if B holds a mortgage on A's farm and A later leases the land to C, upon foreclosure (and in the absence of any power in the mortgage to lease) B may either eject C or elect to treat him as the tenant. If C is ejected, he will have a right to sue A for breach of a covenant in the lease for quiet enjoyment.

Transfer of the Interests Under the Mortgage. The interests of the original mortgagor and mortgagee are capable of being transferred and the rights and obligations of the assignees will depend primarily upon (1) the agreement of the parties to the assignment and (2) the rules of law designed to protect the interests of the original party who did not participate in the transfer.

If the mortgagor conveys the land, the purchaser (of the equity of redemption) is not personally liable for the mortgage debt which the mortgagor promised to pay although the land may be foreclosed to pay or contribute towards payment of the debt. Frequently, a transfer of mortgaged property is made "subject to" the mortgage. This, alone, will not make the transferee personally liable, although his subsequent actions may make him personally liable for the debt.

If the transferee expressly assumes personal liability for the debt, he is directly liable to the mortgagee although the latter can still hold the original mortgagor on his promise to pay, in the absence of an agreement to the contrary.

Since, at common law, the mortgage placed legal title in the mortgagee there could be no assignment of the mortgage except by formal conveyance. Today, in many States, particularly where the lien theory is accepted, an assignment of the *debt*, whether formal or not, effects an assignment of the mortgage. This follows from the basic principle of the lien theory that the transaction is basically a debt with security and not a conditional conveyance of property.

Because, many times, the debt secured by a mortgage is evidenced by a series of promissory notes, it is possible that there may be assignments of the debt to more than one person. If, for example, the outstanding and assigned notes secured by a mortgage have a face value of $40,000 and the property on foreclosure realizes $30,000, the relative priority of each note is important. There are two major rules for determining priority. Under one rule, if the notes mature at different times, the assignees share in order of their due dates. In the foregoing case, if there were five notes for $8,000 each maturing six months apart, the first three notes would be paid in full, the fourth would receive $6,000 and the last note would be entitled to nothing. The alternative rule, applied in some jurisdictions, provides that the assignees share according to their proportionate interests, regardless of the date of maturity. In this same case, under this rule, each of the five notes would be entitled to $6,000.

It is important, as a practical matter, that an assignee have his assignment recorded to prevent loss of his rights to persons who subsequently deal with the mortgage without knowledge that it has been assigned. Failure to record an assignment may cause an assignee of a mortgage note to lose his security. For example, A buys land from B, relying upon a release executed and recorded by the mortgagee, C. C, however, had previously assigned the mortgage to D who had failed to have his assignment recorded. In the absence of actual knowledge on the part of A of the assignment by C, D has no claim against the property.

An assignee who does cause his assignment to be recorded is, of course, protected against prior assignees who neglected to record their interests. The recording of an assignment does not, nevertheless, constitute notice to the mortgagor. This means that X, a mortgagor without actual notice of a recorded assignment, may discharge his debt by payment to Y, the original mortgagee, in spite of the fact that Y, by virtue of an assignment, may have absolutely no interest in the property at the date he is paid.

Payment, Redemption and Discharge of Mortgage. It was previously observed that the right of the mortgagor to pay the debt and relieve the property from the lien is inherent to a mortgage. This right of redemption is the most obvious characteristic of a mortgage and it cannot be extinguished except by operation of law. The right to redeem naturally carries with it the obligation to make payment of the debt, and payment in full with interest is a prerequisite to redemption.

At early common law, even though the mortgagee was looked upon as possessing legal title, payment of the debt in full on the due date was all that was necessary to place title in the borrower. If, however, payment were delayed beyond the due date, the mortgagee's title became indefeasible and, upon payment, a reconveyance was necessary. Under the more modern lien theory, payment simply discharges the lien on the land, title to which had always remained in the borrower. It is, nevertheless, a practical necessity for the mortgagor to receive a release from the mortgagee and record it in order to show an unencumbered title in the owner. It does not follow from the right of the mortgagor to pay the debt and redeem the property on or after the maturity of the debt that he may make payment and redeem before maturity. Unless the creditor consents, the mortgagor cannot pay off the debt before the due date.

The mortgagor is not the only person with a right to redeem. Any person with an interest that is affected by the mortgage may discharge the mortgage. He will then generally be subrogated to the rights of the mortgagee; he will, in other words, be entitled to claim the security and other rights formerly belonging to the mortgagee. If A, one of three tenants in common with equal interests in a property on which there is a $30,000 mortgage, pays the debt in full, he will be entitled to contribution from his co-tenants to the extent of $10,000 each and he will have a lien on their respective undivided interests to that extent.

Foreclosure. The mortgagor's right to redeem the property from the lien of his personal obligation is limited in all jurisdictions by the right of foreclosure. Usually, the mortgagee's right to foreclose arises when the mortgagor fails to pay the debt. By stipulation in the mortgage, the mortgagor's default on other conditions in the mortgage may give the mortgagee this right. Thus, a mortgage may provide that failure of the mortgagor to pay taxes will permit foreclosure. It is a common provision of mortgages that default on an installment of the debt makes the entire obligation due, permitting foreclosure for the entire amount.

Foreclosure has historically taken three principal forms:

1. *Strict Foreclosure.* By the time equity had developed the right of the mortgagor to redeem after his obligation had matured, it became apparent that there had to be a time limit upon the exercise of this right. The practice arose of providing by judicial decree that this right would be "foreclosed" within a specified time. Upon the expiration of this period, an indefeasible title to the property vested in the mortgagee. This was known as "strict foreclosure" and, in effect, meant that the consequences, under early common law, of failure to discharge the debt on the exact due date were merely postponed for the period of redemption. Although this method of foreclosure is still possible in one or two States, it had all the unpopular consequences of early common-law mortgages (e. g., the acquisition by the mortgagee of property the value of which in many cases greatly exceeded the debt) and this practice is no longer permitted in most jurisdictions.

2. *Foreclosure by Judicial Sale.* The most general method of cutting off the right to redeem is by a bill in equity to obtain a judicial decree directing the sale of the property by an officer of the court, the debt being paid out of the proceeds of the sale and the excess, if any, going to the mortgagor. In

some jurisdictions, the mortgagor is given a statutory right to redeem from the sale within a specified period of time. This right is, in effect, a second "right of redemption" and should not be confused with the customary right of redemption before foreclosure. In most jurisdictions, the sale is subject to approval by the court. During the depression of the 'thirties, this power of judicial supervision was frequently extended to permit a court to reject a sale if the purchase price was ridiculously low. Otherwise, a mortgagee, directly or through an agent, might, for example, purchase land formerly worth $15,-000 for one-fourth its value and still have a claim for the balance of the debt not satisfied by the sale of his security. In such cases, an appraisal to establish a "fair value" was a device occasionally employed to protect mortgagors.

3. *Power of Sale in Mortgage.* In States where foreclosure is not limited to a sale under judicial decree, a clause is inserted in most mortgages permitting the mortgagee to foreclose by a sale without obtaining an order of court. This power of sale is considerably more expedient than a judicial proceeding. In most cases, a power of sale must provide for a public auction with published notice thereof, and not infrequently the mortgagee is forbidden by statute to purchase at the sale on the theory that he occupies a fiduciary relation to the mortgagor that would be breached by him buying in at a sale conducted by himself.

Whether the foreclosure is by sale under judicial proceeding or by grant of the power in the mortgage itself, the transaction retains its character of a procedure to apply a lien to the satisfaction of a personal debt. If the proceeds are insufficient to satisfy this debt, the debtor-mortgagor still faces the problem of payment of the balance of the debt. Generally, the mortgagee will obtain a deficiency judgment for the unsatisfied balance of the debt and may then proceed to collect this

amount out of other assets of the mortgagor. A discharge in bankruptcy may, of course, make this remedy worthless.

Mechanics' Liens. At common law, the person who furnished material or labor for the erection or repair of a building or structure had no lien against the property. Today, in nearly all States, the laborer or materialman has, by statute, a direct lien upon the property on which he worked or for which he supplied materials, *provided* he takes the required legal steps within the time specified in the statute to "perfect" his claim. The statute gives protection to both prime contractors and subcontractors and any builder should always demand waivers or releases of all liens upon final payment for the work done on his property.

A mechanic's lien, once perfected in the manner required by statute, may be asserted against a purchaser of the property, and it takes precedence over subsequent mortgages. A mortgage executed *and recorded* before the attaching of a mechanic's lien takes precedence over the lien. In some jurisdictions, however, a mechanic's lien perfected *after* a mortgage will be entitled to a prior claim only to the extent of the value of the improvement or repair for which the lien is asserted.

CASES

IN RE PETRALIA'S ESTATE

(1965) 32 Ill.2d 134, 204 N.E.2d 1.

HERSHEY, J. In 1948 Antonio Petralia opened a savings account in the First National Bank of Chicago, naming himself as "trustee" for the benefit of his daughter, Domenica Di Maggio, to whom the balance in the account at his death was to be paid. After Petralia's death, Dominica Di Maggio, plaintiff herein, instituted a citation proceeding against the defendant administrator of the estate of Antonio Petralia in the probate court of Cook County in which she claimed title to the account. The probate court held that a valid trust had been created and that under the terms thereof the plaintiff was entitled to the balance of $17,189.15 in the account. The Appellate Court affirmed, and we granted leave to appeal.

This is the first occasion on which we have been called upon to consider the validity of savings bank or "Totten" trusts. The defendant urges the court to reverse the judgments below on two grounds: (1) that the execution of the signature card was insufficient to establish an intent on the part of Antonio Petralia to create a trust; and (2) "that the form of trust attempted to be executed by the savings accounts trusts is an attempt at a testamentary disposition and not operative, due to the failure to conform with the Statute of wills."

The record indicates that for a number of years prior to 1948 Antonio Petralia was the sole owner of a regular savings account which he had opened in his name at the First National Bank of Chicago. On November 8, 1948, he closed the account and transferred all the funds therein to the savings account trust which is the subject of this litigation. The new account was entitled "Tony Petralia, Trustee," and on the first side of the signature card appeared the signature "Tony Petralia" with the word "trustee" written beneath. On the reverse side of the card was the following language:

"All deposits in this account are made for the benefit of Domenica Di Maggio To whom or to whose legal representative said deposits or any part thereof, together with the interest thereon, may be paid in the event of the death of the undersigned Trustee."

The signature "Tony Petralia" again appeared below the language on a line designated "trustee". Beneath the signature was written "Mrs. Domenica Di Maggio", "July 29, 1909" and "Daughter."

Introduced in evidence were facsimile ledger sheets of the First National Bank which showed that from the date the account was opened to the date of his death, Antonio Petralia alone made numerous deposits to and infrequent withdrawals from the account. The balance in the account steadily increased.

In support of his contention that the execution of the signature card was insufficient to show an intent to create a trust, the administrator emphasizes the fact that the printed agreement on the card provided that the bank "may", rather than "shall", pay the balance to the plaintiff at his death. The use of the word "may" is said to show a lack of intent that the plaintiff was definitely to receive the benefit of the account.

The reason for the inclusion of the word "may" in the agreement is not clear. Due to the similarity of the language on the signature card to the statutory provision for nonliability of banks for death taxes in certain situations [citation.], it may be that the wording was used to follow the statutory language for some reason. Whatever the reason for the use of the word "may", however, we think that the general tenor of the agreement indicates an intent to create a trust and that the settlor intended that the funds be paid to his daughter at his death. This conclusion is confirmed by the fact that the settlor changed his regular savings account to a savings account in trust form, an act which would have been unnecessary if he intended to maintain the account solely for his own benefit. We think it significant also that Antonio Petralia did not in fact withdraw the funds in the account and use them for his own benefit during his lifetime but instead followed a regular pattern of making deposits, thereby steadily increasing the size of the account, apparently for the benefit of his daughter. Although there was testimony by Antonio Petralia's nephew that Petralia had told him the account was opened so that his daughter could make deposits for him, the fact that Petralia alone made all deposits greatly discredits the persuasiveness of such evidence. We think there was ample evidence to support the trial court's finding that Antonio Petralia intended to create a trust.

This brings us to a consideration of the defendant's contention that the trust was invalid as an attempted testamentary disposition without compliance with the Statute of Wills. Since the trust agreement was not executed in accordance with the formalities required by the Statute of Wills, the determinative issue becomes whether a valid *inter vivos* trust was created. One of the requirements for the establishment of a valid *inter vivos* trust is that the beneficiary acquire a present interest during the lifetime of the settlor. [Citations.] The defendant argues that since the settlor alone retained the power to withdraw interest and principal from the account during his lifetime, the trust was illusory and testamentary in that the beneficiary never obtained any present interest during the settlor's lifetime.

It is true that Antonio Petralia, as settlor and trustee, retained extensive control over the savings account trust which he established. However, in this respect it is not significantly different in substance from other revocable *inter vivos* trusts which have been held valid in this and other jurisdictions. [Citations.] The nature of the beneficiary's present interest under such trusts is well stated in 1 Scott, The Law of Trusts, 353–354: "The declaration of trust immediately creates an equitable interest in the beneficiaries although the enjoyment of the interest is postponed until the death of the settlor, and although the interest may be divested by the exercise of the power of

revocation." The fact that the beneficiary's actual enjoyment of the trust is contingent on Antonio Petralia's death without first having revoked the trust by withdrawing the balance in the account does not negate the existence of a present interest in the plaintiff during her father's lifetime, even though that interest may have been highly destructible.

We conclude that the instrument executed by Antonio Petralia on November 8, 1948, was sufficient to create a valid and enforceable *inter vivos* savings account trust. In so holding we accept the position adopted by the American Law Institute in § 58 of the Restatement (Second) of Trusts: "Where a person makes a deposit in a savings account in a bank or other savings organization in his own name as trustee for another person intending to reserve a power to withdraw the whole or any part of the deposit at any time during his lifetime and to use as his own whatever he may withdraw, or otherwise to revoke the trust, the intended trust is enforceable by the beneficiary upon the death of the depositor as to any part remaining on deposit on his death if he has not revoked the trust."

The judgment of the Appellate Court affirming the order of the probate court of Cook County is affirmed.

Judgment affirmed.

DOUGHERTY v. DUCKWORTH

(1965 Mo.) 388 S.W.2d 870.

WELBORN, COMMISSIONER. This is an action to establish a purchase money resulting trust in 120 acres of real estate located in Jefferson County, Missouri. (We will refer to the parties as they appeared in the trial court.) The plaintiffs, William P. Dougherty and William L. Smith, claim to have furnished the money for payment of the purchase price of the property. Title to the property was taken in the names of the defendants John R. Duckworth and Rosemary Duckworth, his wife. Defendant Emma Wenzel is the grantee of a subsequent deed to the property by the Duckworths. In addition to seeking a declaration of a resulting trust in their favor, plaintiffs sought to set aside the deed to Wenzel and to quiet title to the property in themselves. The trial court found a resulting trust for the benefit of plaintiffs in a three-fourths interest in the property. The remaining one-fourth interest was found to be in the Duckworths. The plaintiffs have appealed from the decree, contending that they should be declared the owners of the entire beneficial interest in the property. The defendants have appealed on the grounds that the evidence does not support a finding of a resulting trust in favor of the plaintiffs for any interest in the property. * * * [Citation.]

Plaintiff Dougherty, a 43-year-old plant superintendent, became acquainted with defendant John Duckworth at some unspecified time when Duckworth stopped at Dougherty's house to see about remodeling the house and chicken house into an apartment. The exact nature of Duckworth's business does not appear, but the inference from the testimony is that he was a builder or a contractor.

Subsequently Dougherty and Duckworth discussed the possibility of constructing a retirement center. After "several discussions at my kitchen table, over coffee," Dougherty and Duckworth decided that the latter should look for some property which might be developed for this purpose. Dougherty told Duckworth he could get enough money together to finance the project.

Duckworth located the 120-acre tract here in question. He and Dougherty went out to examine it. Dougherty told Duckworth to offer the owner, Pete Miller, $17,500 for the property and to give Miller a $50 check for earnest money "because that was all I had in the bank." The next day Duckworth told

Dougherty that he had given a $200 check as earnest money because he wanted to acquire the property for his own use. However, a week or two later Duckworth told Dougherty he could not handle the purchase himself and that he needed $200 to cover the check he had given because he did not have that amount on deposit in the bank on which the check was drawn.

At sometime, whether after or before the locating of the property does not appear, Dougherty had interested plaintiff Smith and Clyde Elrod in the retirement center idea. Smith was apparently at that time a foreman in the same plant in which Dougherty was employed. * * * Smith told Dougherty that he had $1,000 to put up as earnest money to purchase the land. Eventually Dougherty called upon Smith for this amount, which Dougherty received and turned over to Duckworth.

Again the sequence of events is not entirely clear, but at some stage of the project the idea of a joint enterprise took shape in which Dougherty, Smith and Elrod would supply the purchase price of the land and Duckworth would supervise the construction of the necessary facilities thereon in return for which each participant would have a one-fourth interest in the enterprise. The arrangement was never reduced to writing.

The purchase of the land was completed and the transaction closed in July, 1961. The contract of sale was not introduced in evidence. Dougherty testified that the sale price was $17,000 or "might have been $17,500." Smith's $1,000, $3,200 contributed by Dougherty and $3,000 by Elrod were turned over to Duckworth and applied on the purchase price. In addition, a loan of $10,000 was made from the Webster Groves Trust Company secured by a deed of trust on the property. The proceeds of the loan were used to pay the balance of the purchase price. Title was taken in the name of the Duckworths and they also executed the note or notes for the $10,000 indebtedness and the deed of trust given to secure it. Plaintiffs testified that Duckworth put no money into the purchase.

The plaintiffs' explanation for placing the title in Duckworth's name was that, since he had signed the sale contract, the plaintiffs thought that more time might be required in order to change the transaction into the name of the four individuals, so they went through with the purchase and placed the property in Duckworth's name. * * *

Subsequent to the transfer of the property Smith, from August 10, 1961 to March 5, 1962, issued nine checks in the amount of $85 each, payable to Dougherty, who in turn endorsed them to Duckworth who in turn applied the proceeds in payment of monthly installments on the $10,000 indebtedness. When some problem arose about Duckworth's making the payments, Smith issued checks directly to the Webster Groves Trust Company. Nineteen such checks were issued from April 11, 1962 through November 15, 1963, each in the amount of $85.75. Apparently this was the correct amount of the monthly payments. There is some intimation that Duckworth made up the 75¢ deficiency in the $85 checks delivered to him. There is also some intimation that Duckworth paid one monthly payment, although Smith made a remittance to pay the obligation falling due in the same month. * * *

Dougherty agreed with defendants' counsel's statement that the retirement center project "never got off the ground." * * *

* * * There was some discussion about "buying out" Duckworth, but no agreement with him was reached. Smith did "buy out" Elrod, paying the latter $2,200 for his share of the enterprise.

In April, 1963, the Duckworths, without prior notice to the plaintiffs, transferred the property to Emma Wenzel. Wenzel had been employed as a secretary in a law office with which the Duckworth's attorney had formerly been associated. This action followed, the petition being filed April 16, 1963.

The Duckworths and Wenzel as appellants contend that the decree of the trial court establishing a resulting trust in favor of the plaintiffs for three-fourths interest is unsupported by the evidence. They contend that the testmony regarding the proposal that each of the four original parties to the transaction should become the owner of one-fourth interest in the real estate is unenforceable by reason of the statute of frauds. [Citation.] They further contend that the evidence does not show that Dougherty, Smith and Elrod contributed a share of the purchase price sufficient to warrant the finding of a one-fourth interest in them. They contend that there is no evidence to show that the contributions of each of them equalled one-fourth of the purchase price and therefore no resulting trust of that share may be found. They also contend that the plaintiffs failed to show that they are entitled to a resulting trust in any part of the property because they fail to show what proportion of the purchase price the plaintiffs actually contributed. This contention is based on the theory that the plaintiffs' evidence failed to establish the purchase price for the property and therefore no proportionate share may be computed.

Plaintiffs on the other hand contend that the evidence established a purchase money resulting trust, that the evidence showed that the plaintiffs either paid or obligated themselves to pay the full purchase price and that Duckworth, having breached the agreement by endeavoring to transfer the property without the consent of the plaintiffs, forfeited his right to any share in the real estate. Therefore, according to the plaintiffs, the trial court should have found them owners of the entire beneficial interest of the property.

" 'Where a transfer of property is made to one person and the purchase price is paid by another, a resulting trust arises in favor of the person by whom the purchase price is paid, except as stated in §§ 441, 442, and 444.'" 2 Restatement, Trusts, 2d, Sec. 440, p. 393. [Citation.]

"We have recently stated that ' "a resulting trust must arise, if at all, at the instant the deed is taken. Unless the transaction is such that the moment the title passes the trust results from the transaction itself, then no trust results. It cannot be created by subsequent occurrences." Bender v. Bender, 281 Mo. 473, 220 S.W. 929, 930 * * *. "A resulting trust, as distinguished from an express trust, is one implied by law from the acts and conduct of the parties and the facts and circumstances which at the time exist and attend the transaction out of which it arises." Little v. Mette, 338 Mo. 1223, 93 S.W.2d 1000, 1009(8); [citation]. "As between strangers, a purchase-money resulting trust arises against the grantee of real property in favor of the payor of the purchase money unless it was the payor's intent that no such trust should arise; but the presumption of a resulting trust is rebuttable. * * * This presumption is based upon the sound principle that, absent evidence to the contrary, it is not the intent of any such payor to make a gift to the grantee." Ferguson v. Stokes, Mo.Sup., 269 S.W.2d 655, 659.' [Citation.] It is also well settled that the evidence required to establish a resulting trust must be clear, cogent and convincing. [Citation.] If a resulting trust is established in a case where a person pays only a part of the purchase price the person so paying acquires a pro tanto interest in the real estate. [Citation.] Isenman v. Schwartz, Mo.Sup., 335 S.W.2d 112, 116(2–7).

The plaintiffs' evidence, although essentially uncontroverted, is somewhat vague and indefinite. However, it does warrant the conclusion that Dougherty, Smith and Elrod contributed $7,200 to the purchase price of the property prior to its acquisition. There being no testimony on behalf of the defend-

ants to rebut the presumption of the resulting trust arising from such payment, such trust would have arisen in the proportion which the amount so contributed bore to the purchase price.

* * * In our opinion this testimony is insufficient to show that the advance of the $7,200 was intended as a loan to Duckworth. In fact, Dougherty's declining a note indicates that the payor did not intend the advance as a loan and his intention is the significant factor in a case such as this. [Citation.]

The trial court found that, according to the agreement among the parties, the plaintiffs were to supply all the money "that is to purchase the real estate and furnish the materials for the construction of the Center." * * * The court further found that the plaintiffs supplied the monthly payments on the mortgage. However, the testimony regarding any agreement or understanding relative to the payment on the mortgage was extremely vague. In his testimony Dougherty stated, with respect to the purchase price, that he was to advance one-fourth, Elrod one-fourth and "Smith was going to put in $1,000 plus making monthly payments." In another place Dougherty stated: "Bill (Smith) would be making the monthly payments, * * * I'd be making a portion of the monthly payments and John Duckworth would work out his ¼ interest."

We find in this testimony no evidence of an agreement among the plaintiffs and the Duckworths that the plaintiffs were to make the monthly payments and that the Duckworths were to be relieved of any liability on the indebtedness in their names. The plaintiffs point to no evidence in this regard. They merely state that the plaintiffs "obligated themselves" to pay the monthly installments on the indebtedness. They point to no specific testimony as evidencing such obligation and apparently rely on the fact that money for the payments was supplied by Smith.

There is no evidence that Duckworth was in any manner a party to an agreement whereby the plaintiffs were to make the monthly payments. There is no showing of any dealings with the lender of the money and no evidence that the bank understood it was to look to the plaintiffs for the monthly payments. In fact, although there is some indication that the source of the money for such purpose was timber which he cut from the land, Duckworth, according to the plaintiffs, paid one installment on the indebtedness which would appear to be inconsistent with an unconditional obligation to pay by the plaintiffs. In addition, although the amount is minor, Duckworth apparently made up the difference between the amount Smith furnished and the amount due on the first nine payments. We conclude that the plaintiffs have failed to establish the facts necessary to show a resulting trust arising by reason of the payments on the indebtedness. [Citation.] "Where the transferee undertakes an obligation to the vendor to pay the purchase price, and another person at the time of the purchase does not agree with the transferee to pay the purchase price to the vendor, or to contribute to the payment, a resulting trust does not arise in favor of the other even though he subsequently pays the purchase price or assumes an obligation to pay it." 2 Restatement, Trusts, 2d, Sec. 456, Comment h, pp. 431–432.

Therefore, the only resulting trust established by the plaintiffs' evidence was that which arose by reason of their contribution to the cash payment applied toward the purchase of the property prior to the time of its acquisition. There is no evidence to support a finding that such contribution equalled or exceeded one-fourth of the purchase price. The oral arrangement that Dougherty, Smith and Elrod were each to have a one-fourth interest in the property is unenforceable by reason of the statute of frauds. [Citations.] Therefore, plaintiffs are entitled to a result-

ing trust only in the proportion that their contribution bore to the total purchase price. [Citation.]

* * *

Ordinarily we would formulate the decree to be entered in this case. However, because the plaintiffs' evidence of the purchase price is indefinite, tending to support three different figures, $17,000, $17,200 and $17,500, we are unable properly to calculate the plaintiffs' interests. There must be better evidence available to establish the purchase price than that which the plaintiffs presented. We, therefore, will remand the cause to permit additional evidence to be presented to establish the purchase price. Upon the proof thereof, Dougherty will be entitled to a resulting trust in the proportion which his $3,200 contribution bears to the purchase price. Smith will be entitled to a resulting trust in the proportion which the $4,000 he and Elrod combined contributed bears to the entire price. * * *

No objection having been made to the portion of the judgment setting aside the deed from Duckworth to Wenzel, that portion of the judgment is affirmed. The remainder of the judgment is reversed and the cause remanded for further proceedings in accordance with this opinion and the entry of a new judgment thereafter as herein directed.

IN RE BLETSCH'S ESTATE

(1964) 25 Wis.2d 40, 130 N.W.2d 275.

The testator, Jack Bletsch, died in December, 1962, leaving an estate of over $150,000. A will, dated October 6, 1960, was admitted to probate in the Milwaukee county court. The will provided that his entire estate was to go to his wife, or, if she did not survive him, to his daughter. In the event that neither his wife nor daughter survived him, the testator left his estate to the "Masonic Home for Crippled Children of the State of Illinois."

When the testator died in 1962, both his wife and daughter had predeceased him. The appellant, a cousin of the testator, is the only living heir at law of the testator. It was found, upon investigation, that there is no "Masonic Home for Crippled Children of the State of Illinois."

The probate court heard evidence and found that the intent of the testator was to help crippled children and that the organization whose operations closely reflected such intent was the "Shriners' Hospital for Crippled Children" located in Chicago, Illinois. The latter institution is incorporated in the state of Colorado. Several other organizations with generally related names were brought to the attention of the trial court. Disclaimers were filed by such institutions. The word "crippled" did not appear in the name of any of the institutions except the respondent.

At the hearing, there was testimony that the testator's only daughter was crippled in that she suffered from a spinal deformity. She was described as a "hunchback." In his testimony, Mr. Otto Koerner explained the history of the testator's residuary gift. Mr. Koerner and the testator were close friends and business associates.

In 1945, Mr. Koerner had made a will, and the testator had asked Mr. Koerner what he had arranged to do with his estate if his family predeceased him. Mr. Koerner replied that he had picked out the "Masonic Home for Crippled Children." The testator is then purported to have said that he would use it also. There was evidence that both Mr. Koerner and the testator used the same attorney for drafting their wills.

GORDON, J. The trial court analyzed the evidence and determined that the testator's purpose was "to help crippled children through Masonic charitable organizations of the state of Illinois." The following conclusion of law was entered:

"That the only organization whose operations closely reflect the intent of the deceased is in the 'Shriners Hospital for Crippled Children' located in Chicago, Illinois."

The designated beneficiary in the instant case is non-existent; this gave rise to a latent ambiguity which made it appropriate to examine the extrinsic evidence. In Estate of Gibbs (1961), 14 Wis.2d 490, 496, 111 N.W.2d 413, this court explained that there are two classes of latent ambiguity:

"One, where there are two or more persons or things exactly measuring up to the description in the will; the other where no person or thing exactly answers the declarations and descriptions of the will, but two or more persons or things answer the description imperfectly. Extrinsic evidence must be resorted to under these circumstances to identify which of the parties, unspecified with particularity in the will, was intended by the testator."

The trial court had before it the testimony of Mr. Koerner, who described the origins of the language which was later used by the testator in his will. The extrinsic evidence also included a description of the physical disability of the testator's daughter.

The appellant urges that the instant case is controlled by Tharp v. Seventh Day Adventist Church (1923), 182 Wis. 107, 195 N.W. 331. There the gift was to the "Seventh Day Adventist Church" for use in publishing and distributing literature of the church. Evidence was received in that case which demonstrated that the Seventh Day Adventists constituted a religious denomination with numerous "conferences." Although there were two incorporated "conferences" in Wisconsin holding title to church property, the testator was not a member of either. The court held that it was impossible to determine which group the testator had in mind, and therefore the bequest failed. Similarly, in the instant case, appellant argues that it is impossible to determine which group Jack Bletsch intended to benefit.

The findings of the trial court in the case at bar are different from those in the Tharp Case. Here the trial court found that there was a distinct charitable purpose on the part of the testator and, using the will and the extrinsic evidence adduced, it found that the Shriners' Hospital for Crippled Children was the only one which closely reflected the testator's plan. In our opinion, this finding is not against the great weight or clear preponderance of the evidence.

The trial court applied the *cy pres* doctrine. That doctrine, as defined in Saletri v. Clark (1961), 13 Wis.2d 325, 329, 108 N.W.2d 548, 550, is this:

"Very briefly stated, when a charitable purpose cannot be fulfilled according to its terms, equity will attempt to do the next best similar charitable thing. That is the *cy pres* doctrine."

* * *

In England, at common law, there were two doctrines of *cy pres*. One was judicial *cy pres;* the other was known as prerogative *cy pres*. Under the latter doctrine, the king, in the exercise of his prerogative power, could, in certain cases, ignore a testator's intention and dispose of a man's property as the king wished. There was no duty on the part of the king (other than moral) to honor the testator's wishes. It is this prerogative doctrine of *cy pres* which has been disavowed in the United States.

The distinction between prerogative *cy pres* and judicial *cy pres* is signficant because in the former the purposes to which the king might apply the property could be diametrically contrary to the intentions of the decedent; however, in judicial *cy pres* the court's principal burden was to effectuate as closely as possible the testator's plan. We doubt that

the courts of Wisconsin ever truly intended to disavow judicial *cy pres*.

* * *

Although it was not so denominated, judicial *cy pres* was, in effect, applied by the court in Estate of Briggs (1926), 189 Wis. 524, 208 N.W. 247. * * * That the *cy pres* concept was tacitly followed in the Briggs Case is implicit from the following portion, at page 529, 208 N.W. at page 249:

"While it may be conceded that a bequest to a particularly denominated hospital might ordinarily be deemed lapsed where such hospital is in fact nonexistent (which would also be true as to a given church or school, under the same circumstances), nevertheless, if from all the surrounding facts and circumstances it can reasonably be gathered that the object of the testator was centered, not in the aims of one hospital or one church or one school, but upon a general scheme to promote a given *cause,* then such named hospital, church, or school may be deemed a mere agency for administrative purposes, and, if the agency fails, a chancellor will not permit the purpose to fail, but will supply a new agency, in the form of a trustee, to carry out the testator's intention."

* * *

The doctrine of *cy pres* is preserved in the American Law Institute's Restatement of Trusts. Restatement, 2 Trusts, p. 1208, sec. 399. [Citation.]

While most of the descriptions of *cy pres* confine its operation to charitable "trusts," there is no sound reason for the requirement that there be a formal trust, as such. In our opinion, it is sufficient if there is a bequest to a charity. In a sense, it can perhaps be said that a charity always receives the gift in trust for its purposes. In Estate of Briggs (1926), 189 Wis. 524, 208 N.W. 247, there was a gift to the "Young Women's Christian Association of Wisconsin." Although no express trust was created, the court treated the matter as a charitable trust. Instead of saying that gifts to charities are necessarily in trust, we deem it better to rule that the doctrine of judicial *cy pres* is available when there is a gift to a charity—without requiring that there be a formal trust.

The Wisconsin legislature, in 1933, enacted sec. 231.11(7), (d), Stats. This subsection reflects a legislative intention both to preserve the *cy pres* doctrine and also to apply it even though the gift to the charity is not expressly in trust. This subsection provides as follows:

"Where the fulfillment of the special purpose expressed in a trust or other gift for charitable or public purposes is or becomes impracticable, impossible or unlawful, it shall be the duty of the courts by a liberal construction of the trust or gift to ascertain the general purpose of the donor and to carry it into effect in the nearest practicable manner to the expressed special purpose; provided, however, that the right of visitation of a living donor shall not be held to be impaired by anything contained in this subsection."

We do not believe that a bequest to a charity must fail when those purposes are clearly evidenced and there is in existence an identifiable beneficiary whose charitable or public program and goals are reasonably close to those expressed by or attributable to the testator. *Cy pres* remains a sound and useful doctrine. * * *

Judgment affirmed.

IN RE DUFF'S WILL

(1965) 45 Misc.2d 970, 258 N.Y.S.2d 598.

KEANE, SURROGATE. John R. Duff was a kind, beloved and respected high school teacher for many years in Binghamton. While confined to the hospital in midsummer of 1964, for abdominal surgery, he wrote in his own hand the document which shortly thereafter was admitted to probate as his last will and testament. While some legal ques-

tions have arisen concerning this document, the contents in general show the depth of generosity of John R. Duff.

His gross estate was just over $100,000.00. He gave $5,000.00 to a first cousin, his only living relative; $1,000.00 to a minor son of an employee who had been of assistance to him in his work; $1,000.00 to his elderly landlady; $1,000.00 to a friend who was named as one of the executors, and $1,000.00 to two other friends for the education of their minor daughter. The balance of his estate was left to two churches, one in Binghamton and one in Buffalo, of which he had been a member during his lifetime.

In the preparation of his will and its execution, John R. Duff did not have the benefit of legal counsel. As a result, this Court must determine what was meant when he directed his executors:

" * * * to leave * * *

"3. An amount of $1000.00 to Mr. and Mrs. Howard G. Roe to be used in the education of their daughter Carol."

Another question related to this clause exists because Howard G. Roe and (Mrs.) Kathryn Roe were witnesses to the will, as well as J. Edgar Hyatt, a friend, to whom he left $1,000.00. Finally, he named Mr. Roe and Mr. Hyatt as his executors.

The will was admitted to probate on the testimony of Howard G. Roe and (Mrs.) Kathryn Roe, but the question of the legacy to J. Edgar Hyatt depends on the disposition of this construction proceeding.

This is no time for the Court to indulge in one of those speculative inquiries concerning, "What did the draftsman intend?" When a will is prepared by an attorney, the Court ordinarily can assume that he comprehended the meaning of the language used. Here the Court must ascertain what the lay draftsman meant as he penned these four letter sized sheets in a strong firm hand prior to his operation which turned out to be terminal.

John R. Duff had no difficulty in making absolute bequests. One bequest of $1,000.00 was to a minor absolutely, the son of an employee who had been helpful to him in his work. Had he intended to do this for Carol Roe, he could have done so. Therefore, the bequest made by the language quoted above is not an absolute bequest to Carol Roe. In deciding that the bequest is not absolute, there is ruled out the possibility that Mr. and Mrs. Howard G. Roe are to receive the funds as the donees of a power in trust for the benefit of Carol Roe.

Being a high school teacher, John R. Duff knew well the advantages of an education beyond high school. It is clear to this Court that his intent was to have the sum of $1,000.-00 available for the education of Carol Roe beyond high school. This Court finds that the testator intended to create a trust for the benefit of Carol Roe for the purpose of her education beyond high school. The trustees are Howard G. Roe and Kathryn Roe. Before appointment, they will have to qualify pursuant to statute.

Authority for this determination is found in Matter of Babbage's, Estate, 21 Misc. 750, 106 N.Y.S.2d 332 (1951). There the language of the will read as follows:

"I give and bequeath the sum of thirty thousand dollars ($30,000.00) to Louise Sanford Pierson, to be used by her in promoting the welfare of her children, Victoria, Laura Louise and Theodore."

Mr. Surrogate Collins experienced no difficulty in determining that the testatrix therein intended to create a trust. So, too, this Court experiences no difficulty in determining that a trust has been created for the benefit of Carol Roe. It is true that the will states no period for duration of a trust for the purposes of a trust in detail. Since the will speaks of using the money for education, this Court determines that the purpose is sufficiently clear.

Since education beyond the high school level is usually terminated at or shortly after attainment of 21 years of age, the Court finds that the trust shall continue during the lifetime of Carol Roe, or until she reaches 21 years of age. Because of the limited amount involved, the Court advises that Mr. and Mrs. Howard G. Roe can use both income and principal for the education of Carol Roe beyond high school without application to the Court. They will always be subject to accountability at the termination of the trust. The Court believes that this disposition fills those lacunae existing because John R. Duff did not have the benefit of legal counsel to formulate proper language to implement his wishes.

In the corollary matter, the two subscribing witnesses, Howard G. Roe and (Mrs.) Kathryn Roe, take no beneficial interest under the will as the trustees for the trust above. As a result, the legacy payable to J. Edgar Hyatt, who is a legatee and a subscribing witness, is a valid bequest since the will was capable of proof without his testimony.

Submit decree in accord with decision.

LIGHTCAP v. BRADLEY

(1900) 186 Ill. 510, 58 N.E. 221.

[H. W. Lightcap brought an ejectment action against Lydia Bradley. Defendant, to defend her claim, proved that one of the grantors in plaintiff's chain of title had made a trust deed of the land to defendant to secure promissory notes payable to her and that this deed had been foreclosed and she had received a deed from the trustee's heirs. It was agreed that the trust deed conveyed the fee to the trustee with only the equitable right on the part of the mortgagor to redeem. Judgment for defendant, and plaintiff appeals.]

CARTWRIGHT, J. * * * Leaving out of consideration the effect of a mortgage in the statutory form, it is true that a mortgage or trust deed like the one in question here, which purports to convey title, does, as between the mortgagor and mortgagee, convey such title; but it is only a qualified conveyance of the land, and the mortgagor parts with the title only as security to his creditor and during the existence of his debt or obligation. In the development of the law of real estate mortgages in England the mortgage was at first a pledge of land, usually requiring a judgment to complete the transfer of title and to vest it in the mortgagee. Afterward, a form of mortgage came into use which vested title of itself, and the pledge changed into an estate in fee without judicial foreclosure upon the mortgagor's default. This mortgage vested absolute title in the mortgagee upon condition broken. Courts of equity, however, recognizing the purpose of the mortgage as merely a pledge to secure a debt, established a right of the mortgagor to redeem. They created a new estate in the form of the equity of redemption and a remedy for the creditor to cut off this estate. A proceeding was devised to extinguish the mortgagor's right to redeem and to vest title in the mortgagee, and this was the proceeding now known as strict foreclosure. [Citation.] Equity assumed jurisdiction to relieve the mortgagor against a fortfeiture upon default, and he was relieved from it on payment of the debt. [Citation.] Courts of law, following the lead of courts of equity, have adopted many equitable principles as to the titles of the respective parties, and at law the title of the mortgagee can be used only for the purpose of securing his equitable rights under it. "As to all persons except the mortgagee and those claiming under him, it is everywhere the established modern doctrine that a mortgagor in possession is at law, both before and after breach of the condition, the legal owner." (1 Jones on Mortgages, sec. 11.) In many of the States a mortgage confers no title or estate upon the mortgagee, and it is nothing but a mere security for a debt or obligation. This State has adhered to the rule that at law a title vests in the mortgagee, but only for the protection of his interests. For the purpose of protecting and enforcing his security the mortgagee may enter and hold possession by virtue of his title and take the rents and profits in payment of his mortgage debt. He may maintain the possessory action of ejectment on the strength of such title, but the purpose and effect of the action are not to establish or confirm title in him, but, on the contrary, to give him the rents and profits which undermine and destroy his title. [Citation.] When the rents and profits have paid the mortgage debt, both the title and right of possession of the mortgagee are at an end. The mortgagor's interest in the land may be sold upon execution; his widow is entitled to dower in it; it passes as real estate by devise; it descends to his heirs, by his death, as real estate; he is a freeholder by virtue of it; he may maintain an action for the land against a stranger and the mortgage cannot be set up as a defense. The mortgagee has no such estate as can be sold on execution; his widow has no right to dower in it; upon his death the mortgage passes to his personal representatives as personal estate, and it passes by his will as personal property. [Citation.] The title of the mortgagee, even after condition broken, is not an outstanding title of which a stranger can take advantage, but it is available only to the mortgagee or one claiming under him. [Citation.] The mortgagor may sell and convey his title or mortgage it to successive mortgagees, and his grantee or mortgagee will succeed to his estate and occupy his position subject to the encumbrance.

* * *

The mortgagee is the legal owner for only one purpose, while, at the same time, the mortgagor is the owner for every other purpose and against every other person. The title of the mortgagee is anomalous, and exists only between him and the mortgagor and for a limited purpose. * * * The title is never out of the mortgagor, except as between him and the mortgagee and as an incident of the mortgage debt, for the purpose of obtaining satisfaction. When the debt is barred by the Statute of Limitations the title of the mortgagee or trustee ceases at law as well as in equity. When the debt, the principal thing, is gone, the incident, the mortgage, is also gone. [Citation.] The mortgagor's title is then freed from the title of the mortgagee, and he is the owner of the premises, not by any new title, but by the title was he always had. Statutes of limitation do not transfer title from one to another, and a statute of limitations which would have the effect of transferring the legal title back from the mortgagee to the mortgagor would be unconstitutional. [Citation.] The title of the mortgagor becomes perfect because the title of the mortgagee is measured by the existence of the mortgage debt or obligation and terminates with it. [Citation.] * * *

Reversed and remanded.

WEST ROXBURY CO–OP BANK v. BOWSER

(1949) 324 Mass. 489, 87 N.E.2d 113.

[Action upon a promissory note, secured by a mortgage of real estate, to recover a deficiency after a foreclosure sale. Defendants, original makers of the note, set up a number of defenses, among which was the averment that plaintiff-mortgagee had not shown good faith at the foreclosure sale in attempting to find a bona fide buyer for the property but had purchased the property itself at an unreasonably low price. Verdict for defendants, and plaintiff brings exceptions.]

SPALDING, J. * * * The plaintiff contends that there was no evidence of lack of good faith on its part in connection with the foreclosure of the mortgage and that the judge erred in submitting this issue to the jury. This point was raised by the plaintiff's third request which asked for an instruction that "the only consideration for the jury is —has the plaintiff proved that the note is a witnessed note." This request was refused, subject to the plaintiff's exception, the judge stating that it was covered by the charge and given in substance. But an examination of the charge, which is before us, reveals that this instruction was not given in substance and that the judge submitted the issue of bad faith to the jury. Indeed, the major portion of the charge was devoted to a discussion of that issue. This exception must be sustained.

The evidence bearing on that issue is as follows: The note and mortgage were delivered to the plaintiff by the defendants in 1927 in consideration of a loan of $4,500. "The note * * * is the co-operative bank type mortgage note, secured by co-operative bank shares." In 1929 the defendants transferred the property which was the subject of the mortgage to James and Olga Challoner and "took a second mortgage for $500." The Challoners, it seems, owned the equity in the property when the mortgage was foreclosed. At that time, February 19, 1935, the mortgage was in default and the amount due on the note was $4,942.80. "The property was advertised for sale under the power of sale" contained to the mortgage. Representatives of the plaintiff (but apparently nobody else) attended the sale and it was sold to the plaintiff, the highest bidder, for $3,000. One Deming, an assistant treasurer of the plaintiff who was also a licensed auctioneer, conducted the sale. Deming testified that "he did not know if the bank or anyone else sent any notice" of the foreclosure to the defendants. He did not make an inspection of the property to determine its fair market value. In answer to a question whether he went "out anywhere and attempt(ed) to get anybody to buy" the property, Deming replied that he did not.

It is familiar law that a mortgagee in exercising a power of sale in a mortgage must act in good faith and must use reasonable diligence to protect the interests of the mortgagor. [Citations.] The burden is on the mortgagor (the defendants here) to prove that the mortgagee has failed in that duty. [Citations.] When, as was the fact here, "a mortgagee * * * is both seller and buyer, his position is one of great delicacy. Yet, when he has done his full duty to the mortgagor in his conduct of the sale under the power, and the bidding begins, in his capacity as bidder a mortgagee may buy as cheaply as he can, and owes no duty to bid the full value of the property as that value may subsequently be determined by a judge or a jury." Cambridge Savings Bank v. Cronin, 289 Mass. 379, 383, 194 N.E. 289, 290. On this record it cannot be said that there was any evidence which would warrant the jury in finding bad faith on the part of the plaintiff. No contention is made that the foreclosure proceedings were not in compliance with the power of sale contained in the mortgage. If we assume in favor of the defendants that it could have been found that the price at which the property was sold was inadequate (although there was no evidence as to what the fair market value of the property was at the time of the sale), that fact, without more, would not show bad faith or lack of diligence. [Citations.] That the plaintiff advertised the property in accordance with law is not disputed. It was not required to advertise it more extensively. [Citations.] And the fact, standing alone, that no one other than representatives of the plaintiff was present at the sale, was not proof of bad faith. [Citation.] * * The judge ought not to have submitted this issue to the jury and his refusal to grant the plaintiff's third request was prejudicial error. * * *

Exceptions sustained. [Decision for plaintiff.]

PROBLEMS

1. In each of the following situations state whether or not a trust is created.

(a) A declares himself trustee of "the bulk of my securities" in trust for B.

(b) A, the owner of Blackacre, purports to convey to B in trust for C "a small part" of Blackacre.

(c) A orders B, a stockbroker, to buy a thousand shares of American Steel or any part thereof at par. After the broker has bought five hundred shares but before A knows whether any shares have been bought for him, A declares himself trustee for C of such shares of American Steel as A has bought.

(d) A owns ten bonds. He declares himself trustee, for B, of such five of the bonds as B may select at any time within a month.

(e) A deposits $1000 in a savings bank. He declares himself trustee of the deposit in trust to pay B $500 out of the deposit, reserving the power to withdraw from the deposit any amounts not in excess of $500.

2. In 1951, A executed a trust agreement providing that the trust corpus of $100,000 was to be held by B, as trustee, for the benefit of A's children, C and D, aged 7 and 9, respectively. The agreement further provided that B was to invest the corpus in stocks and bonds and accumulate all income from those investments until C and D reached age 25, at which time the trust was to terminate and the property distributed to C and D, share and share alike. In 1965 B dies. D who was then 23 years of age and madly in love with Neromina, a dancer, brought an action to terminate the trust and to obtain his share of the trust. His complaint alleged that the trust must terminate because of B's death and because of the prohibition against accumulations of income. Decision?

3. A, a married man, purchased a house for $24,000 and paid cash for the same from his own funds. Before the purchase was consummated it was agreed between A and his wife, B, that

title should be taken in B's name and that she should hold the same as a joint homestead for herself and her husband during their lives, and that during her life B would make a will devising the property at her death, to A, or, in case of his death prior to B's death, then to the two children of A, by a former marriage. The deed was taken in B's name. A and B lived on the property and A made improvements and the two children spent money and labor on the property improving the premises. B died shortly after A's death, without making a will, and the two children of A claimed the fee to the premises as against the claim of B's heirs-at-law. Decision?

4. The following provision was in A's will: "To the Solid Trust Company with the sure knowledge that it will expend the funds for the maintenance, education and comfort of my grand-niece Sally."

The Solid Trust Co. brings a suit to have the will construed to determine whether or not a valid trust is established. Decision?

5. D in his will gives his estate to T as trustee to hold the estate in trust to pay the income to A during A's life and after A's death to transfer the estate to B. In the trust estate there are some bonds worth 90% of par. These bonds increase in value to par. Who is entitled to the increase as between A and B? If A dies between interest days, will the interest be apportioned?

6. Testator gives property to T in trust for B's benefit, providing that B cannot anticipate the income by assignment or pledge. B borrows money from L, assigning his future income under the trust for a stated period. Can L obtain any judicial relief to prevent B from collecting this income?

7. X owned Blackacre which was worth about $35,000, subject to a mortgage debt of $5,000 which was due in 1966. The mortgage debt bore interest at the rate of 6% per annum, payable semi-annually, on March 1st and September 1st. In 1958, X conveyed the farm to Y for life with remainder to Z and his heirs. The income from the farm was about $5,000 per year and the annual real estate tax is $500. Y failed to pay the interest on the mortgage debt in 1959 and 1960 and did not pay the taxes due for those years. Neither would he pay anything on the mortgage debt. Does Z have any relief?

8. A, the owner of Redacre, executed a real estate mortgage to the Shawnee Bank and Trust Company for $5,000. After the execution and recording of the mortgage, A constructed a dwelling on the premises and planted a corn crop. After default in the payment of the mortgage debt, the bank proceeded to foreclose the mortgage. At the time of the foreclosure sale, the corn crop was mature and unharvested. A contends: (a) the value of the dwelling should be credited to him and (b) he is entitled to the corn crop. Decision?

9. A owns a house and lot worth $10,000. He borrows $5,000 from M, due in five years, and gives M a mortgage on the house and lot. Two years later, A sells and conveys the property to B for $10,000, subject to the mortgage, B paying $5,000 cash. What difference, if any, may it make to B whether the deed from A to B states "Subject to a mortgage indebtedness of $5,000," or "Subject to a mortgage indebtedness of $5,000 which said indebtedness the grantee herein (B) assumes and agrees to pay?"

CHAPTER 51

INSURANCE

What is Insurance? An insurance contract is a promise by one person (the "insurer") to pay a sum of money or to give something of value to another (the "insured" or a "beneficiary") upon the happening of a contingency or fortuitous event which is beyond the control of the contracting parties and in which the promisee has an interest apart from the contract. It is normally a unilateral contract, in that the promisor's obligation becomes enforceable only when the promisee gives a consideration (the "premium") which he is not contractually obligated to do.

The modern concept of insurance is not limited to what is popularly considered as insurance. If a manufacturer gives a warranty (or a guarantee, as it is sometimes called) of its goods which is so broad that it extends beyond those contingencies which are within the manufacturer's control, it will be considered insurance. If a warranty of an electric shaver manufacturer promises repair or replacement for damage to the shaver from any cause for a period of one year from date of sale, it is insurance and subject to State regulation; because dropping the shaver and breaking its case, for example, is a fortuitous event beyond the control of the maker. A one-year warranty against defects in material and workmanship would not be insurance, since those potential defects are within the control of the maker.

State Regulation of Insurance. Insurance affects everyone in the United States, directly or indirectly, and in view of the public interest involved, the industry has long been regulated by the States. In 1944 the Supreme Court of the United States decided, in United States v. South-Eastern Underwriters Association, 322 U.S. 533, that interstate insurance was interstate commerce which was subject to Federal regulation, but the McCarran Act (*Public Law 15*), enacted in 1945, left the regulation of insurance to the States, with several exceptions not material here.

Each State has its own statutes regulating its domestic insurance companies as well as setting forth standards which foreign insurance companies must meet in order to do business within the State. Most of the State legislation relates to the incorporation, licensing, supervision, and liquidation of insurers, and to licensing and supervision of agents and brokers.

Classification of Companies. Since there is a great difference between life insurance and other kinds of insurance, life insurance companies do not generally write other lines. In Illinois, for example, all companies are classified according to the classes of insurance they are authorized to write, and three classes are recognized: (1) Life (including endowments and annuities) and Accident and Health; (2) Casualty, Fidelity and Surety (including accident and health, vehicle, liability, workmen's compensation, burglary and forgery, glass, fidelity and surety, and various miscellaneous kinds); and (3) Fire and Marine (including fire, elements, war, riot and explosion, marine and transportation, vehicle, property damage, sprinkler leakage and crop, and other miscellaneous risks). Companies which write the types of insurance described in both Class 2 and Class 3 are called "multiple-line" companies.

Forms of Organization. Perhaps the oldest kind of insurance organization is the fraternal society, which existed in many ancient civilizations. There are still many fraternal benefit societies which write insurance only for members of their groups.

The oldest continuously operating form of insurer is Lloyd's of London. While originally Lloyd's was restricted to marine insurance, the organization now writes every form of insurance except ordinary life, and the form of organization remains basically unchanged; the insurance is written by syndicates of individuals who are personally liable to the extent of the risk they have assumed. An American Lloyds is recognized by statute in Illinois and Kentucky, but this plan whereby individuals act through an attorney-in-fact is not widely used.

The first insurance corporations in England were chartered by Parliament in 1720, and they were granted monopolies, as corporations, in insuring ships and cargoes. These companies were not very successful as marine insurers, and they gradually turned to fire and life insurance, leaving most of the marine insurance to individual insurers. Their monopoly in this field was not broken until 1824, when a company organized by Nathan Rothschild was chartered and the repeal of the grant of monopoly was approved.

Similar in pattern to American Lloyds are the reciprocals or interinsurance exchanges. Here, the participants act through an attorney-in-fact, as in Lloyds, but the distinguishing feature is that each participant is both insurer and insured. This operation is necessarily limited in scope, but it is occasionally beneficial to aggregations of businesses which might individually have to pay rather large premiums for needed insurance, where, by means of this device, if a surplus exists at the end of the policy period, it is credited to the subscribers.

Most insurance is written either by mutual corporations or by stock corporations. In theory, mutual corporations are aggregations of individuals each of whom is both insurer and insured; if there is a surplus, it is divided among the members by way of a dividend; and if there is insolvency, the members are required to contribute their appropriate shares. The contribution requirement may be restricted by statute, of course, so that a member's liability is limited and may not exist at all.

Stock insurance corporations are organized along the lines of ordinary corporations and are intended to make a profit for their shareholders, although many stock life insurance companies issue participating policies by which the surplus is shared with the policyholders. There is no call, however, on policyholders for contribution in the event of insolvency. Stock companies generally operate through agents who are paid commissions on insurance sold, whereas mutual companies often operate through salaried employees. As is generally true in corporation law, when we speak of a *domestic* insurance corporation, we mean one organized under the laws of the particular State of which we are speaking; while a *foreign* insurer is one organized under the laws of any other State; and, an *alien* insurer is organized under the laws of a foreign country.

Kinds of Insurance. Life Insurance might be more accurately called "death insurance," since it is a contract between an insurer and an insured by the terms of which the insurer will pay a specified sum of money upon the death of the insured, provided the required premiums have been paid. The payment is made either to a named beneficiary, ordinarily a third-party donee or creditor, or to the estate of the deceased. The naming of a beneficiary is a privilege of the insured, but unless the right to do so is reserved in the policy, the insured has no right to change the beneficiary, without the consent of the beneficiary. Most modern policies as part of the standard form give to the insured the express right to change beneficiaries. Ordinary life insurance is often considered a form of saving or investment, since the insured has a right to borrow from the insurer an amount not to exceed the cash surrender value of the policy, which value increases the longer the policy is in force. Such a loan bears a reasonable interest rate and is secured by an assignment to the insurer of the policy proceeds to the extent necessary to pay the loan in the event of death, with the remainder going to the beneficiary.

"Ordinary" life insurance requires the payment of premiums until death, unless the policy is converted into a different type of policy by agreement, whereas "term" life insurance is issued for a limited number of years with premiums payable during the period of coverage. "Limited-payment" life policies require the payment of premiums only for a fixed number of years, thus eliminating the duty of paying premiums through the later years of life when such payments may be burdensome. Term insurance is the least expensive form of life insurance because it is in effect only for a specified period, and death may not occur during this period. It builds up no cash surrender or loan values. Term policies are especially useful to young married men, who cannot afford to purchase permanent insurance. Such policies may contain provisions for later renewal or for conversion to ordinary life or other types of insurance. Term policies generally contain a right to convert to a permanent plan of insurance (ordinary life, limited-payment life, or endowment) upon payment of the premium applicable at the time of conversion; or, by suitable payment, the policyholder may elect to convert as of the date of the original policy. Usually, the conversion right must be exercised within a limited time after issuance of the policy, as during the first three years of a five-year term, to reduce the possibility of adverse selection. There are numerous variations in individual policies.

If the insured under an ordinary life policy is unable to continue making premium payments, he does not lose all the money he has already paid. Policies contain various non-forfeiture provisions which give the in-

sured at least three alternatives: (1) the cash surrender value of the policy; (2) "extended term" insurance in the face amount of the policy for whatever period the cash surrender value will purchase; or (3) a reduced amount of "paid-up" insurance which can be purchased by the cash surrender value. The policy may provide that one of the alternatives is automatically chosen by the insured unless he notifies the insurer of a different election within a certain period of time, such as sixty days after the due date of the premium in default.

Endowment Contracts and *Annuities* are also written by life insurance companies. Either one may contain various provisions which are customarily found in life insurance contracts, but basically an endowment contract is an agreement by the insurer to pay a lump sum of money to the insured when he reaches a certain age or to a beneficiary in the event of premature death, and an annuity contract is an agreement by the insurer to pay fixed sums to the insured at periodic intervals after the insured reaches a designated age. Strictly speaking, an annuity policy is not an insurance contract, but most annuity contracts contain various life insurance features, which subject them to regulation by State insurance departments. A modern version of the annuity is called the Variable Annuity. The Variable Annuity is an agreement by the company to pay to the annuitant a variable sum depending on the effect of inflation or deflation on the company's equity investments. The formula used in computing the annuitant's interest is complex, but the principle is designed as a hedge against inflation. In the usual annuity contract, the company agrees to pay fixed sums periodically, and these sums are based on the return the company can expect to receive on a conservative investment of the premiums paid by the annuitant.

Tontine Insurance is a form of life insurance in which a group of policyholders agree to accumulate earnings for a period of years, with a distribution to the survivors at the end of the period. There are many variations on this general theme, but the original idea was conceived by Lorenzo Tonti, an Italian of the seventeenth century. The scheme is revived periodically, under one guise or another, but it is always frowned upon and is often forbidden by State statute or judicial decision.

Industrial Life Insurance is the name applied to life insurance policies restricted to low principal sums, such as $1,000, where the premiums are payable weekly or sometimes monthly.

Some provisions which once appeared in life insurance contracts are now prohibited by statute, and other provisions, once unknown, are now required. One provision which is now commonly required is that if the applicant for insurance misstates his age, the amount of insurance is reduced to that sum which the premiums paid would have purchased at the insured's correct age.

Another provision which is found in some life insurance contracts provides for the recovery of "double indemnity," or twice the face amount of the policy, in the event of accidental death or death which results "directly and independently of all other causes from bodily injuries sustained solely from external, violent, and accidental means." These accidental death provisions are worded in various ways and have given rise to much litigation, frequently involving the question whether a death which resulted from the unexpected consequences of an intentional act was an accidental death. The cases cannot be reconciled, but it has been held that a death resulting from an infection following the intentional pulling of a hair from the nose was accidental death, whereas death resulting from sunstroke, due to voluntary but unintentional overexposure to the sun, was not. Death as a result of playing Russian roulette has been held not to be accidental, under a double indemnity clause.

Accident and Health Insurance is really insurance against losses due to accidents and sickness, and it provides for the payment of certain benefits or the reimbursement of specified expenses in the event of illness or accidental injury, within the limits set forth in the policies.

Fire Insurance protects the owner (and possibly a creditor or mortgagee) of real or personal property against loss resulting from damage to or destruction of the property by fire and certain related perils. These policies are normally written for periods of one, three, or five years.

Fire insurance policies are standardized in the United States, either by statute or by order of the State insurance departments, but their coverage is frequently enlarged by an "endorsement" or "rider" to include other perils or to benefit the insured in ways not provided in the standard form. Co-insurance is common in fire policies and is a means of sharing the risk between insurer and insured, with a reduction in premium. Instead of taking a policy for the full insurable value of a building, the owner may take a policy with an eighty per cent co-insurance clause. If the value of the building is $10,000, then the policy should be in the amount of $8,000, with the insured bearing $2,000 of the risk. If the property is under-insured, as it would be if the policy were, for example, $6,000, then the insurer will pay only that proportion of the loss which the insurance carried bears to eighty per cent of the value of the property; that is, if the property were fifty per cent destroyed, the loss would be $5,000, of which the insurer would pay $3,750, which is seventy-five per cent (or 6000/8000) of $5,000. On a total loss the recovery could not, of course, exceed the face amount of the policy.

Casualty Insurance is a term of broad and indefinite scope, but it clearly covers loss due to the damage or destruction of personal property by various causes other than fire and the elements, and it is sometimes applied to personal injury or death due to accident.

Collision Insurance protects the owner of an automobile against the risk of loss or damage due to contact with other objects.

Credit Insurance protects creditors against loss due to the insolvency of their debtors. *Credit Life Insurance* protects the creditor and the debtor by providing for the payment of an indebtedness of the insured in the event of his death before the indebtedness shall have been fully liquidated by the time payments which the debtor has contracted to make.

Fidelity Insurance protects an employer against loss due to the dishonesty or defalcation of employees.

Group Insurance covers a number of individuals, having some common interest, under a blanket or single policy. This insurance is usually either life or accident and health insurance.

Liability Insurance provides indemnification against loss or liability to the insured due to injuries to another's person or property. While this kind of insurance is most generally thought of in connection with automobiles, where it is often of greater interest to the injured person than to the driver who caused the injury, it is customarily carried by owners and lessees of real property to protect against liability for injuries arising on the premises owned or leased.

Marine Insurance originally was restricted to destruction of vessels or cargo due to the perils of the sea. While it is sometimes divided into ocean marine and inland marine, the distinction is not always made, and marine insurance covers transportation risks generally, as well as personal property floater risks and other personal property coverages of almost all kinds. A floating or floater policy is one which is variable as to the property covered, as in a personal property floater policy in which the property covered is not specifically identified at the time the policy is written.

Reinsurance. Reinsurance may be thought of as an insurance policy for insurance companies. This is not strictly true, but it is the basic idea. Reinsurance is a contract whereby one insurer, for a consideration, agrees to indemnify another, wholly or partially, against loss or liability arising under a separate policy of insurance which such other insurer has issued to a third party.

A reinsurance treaty is an agreement between two insurance companies whereby one agrees to cede and the other agrees to accept reinsurance business under the terms specified in the treaty.

A reinsurance compact is an agreement between two or more insurance companies by the terms of which each agrees in advance to reinsure any policies written in certain lines by the others, in an amount equal to a fixed percentage of such lines or in the amount by which a risk exceeds a particular sum.

Surplus Line Insurance is the one exception to the requirement that insurance can be written within a particular State only by companies licensed by that State. If an Illinois applicant, for instance, wants a form of insurance coverage (other than life) which a broker or agent after diligent search is unable to place with a company authorized to do business in Illinois, the insurance may be placed with an unlicensed company, provided the agent or broker fulfills certain requirements. This is called surplus line insurance and it is the source of much of the American business given to Lloyd's of London.

Title Insurance provides indemnity against loss arising from defects in the title to real estate or due to liens or encumbrances thereon. Title insurance companies are organized under statutes different from those under which other insurance companies are organized. An owner's title insurance policy is issued in the amount of the purchase price of the property and guarantees the owner against any loss due to defects in the title to the property, or due to liens or encumbrances except for those stated in the policy as existing at the time the policy is issued. Such policies may be issued to mortgagees or to tenants of property to protect their interests. This form of insurance is not available everywhere in the United States but it is written in all major metropolitan areas. In some cities the Torrens system of land registration, which is operated by the local government, is competitive with the private title insurance business.

There are many other kinds of private insurance not specifically mentioned here, as well as insurance programs operated by the State and Federal governments, such as the National Service Life Insurance and the Federal Deposit Insurance Corporation.

Premiums. Life insurance companies receive premiums from their insureds over long periods of years. These premiums are fixed in amount and are such that the company will be able to pay the principal sum when the policy matures upon the death of the insured, through the accumulation of reserves. Company funds are invested to bring as high a return as the company is able to secure, commensurate with security of principal and compliance with State investment laws. Barring catastrophes, a life company can estimate quite accurately how many policyholders will die during a particular period. Some will die prematurely and some will live longer than expected, but the company can operate efficiently on actuarial averages. This enables a life com-

pany to invest its funds in long-term loans, such as mortgages and corporate bonds and debentures.

Life insurance premiums are calculated on the basis of (1) mortality, (2) interest, and (3) expense.

Mortality tables are constructed on the basis of the experience which companies have accumulated in the past, and they show the experienced rate of death. There are many mortality tables, constructed on various bases. The most famous is the "American Experience Table of Mortality," published in 1868 and standard until 1948, when it was replaced by the "Commissioners' 1941 Standard Ordinary Mortality Table," which was based on the experience of sixteen companies between 1930 and 1940. The C.S.O. table shows, for each age, the number of persons living, the number dying, and the rate of mortality per thousand lives. The number of persons living at age one is arbitrarily taken as 1,000,000. Since, in fact, the mortality rate is determined first and the other columns are based on it, we see that the mortality rate for persons between age one and age two is 5.77 per thousand and therefore the number of deaths during that year is 5770, so that at the beginning of the second year of life, there are 994,230 still living of the 1,000,000 lives we assumed at the beginning of age one. Other mortality tables are in use. However, while premiums may be set by one table, the use of another table may be required by a State in the valuation of policy reserves.

Almost all life insurance is written on the level-premium plan, which means that the annual premium payable during the life of the insured is a fixed amount. The company will earn interest on the premiums over a period of years, and while the earned interest rate may fluctuate, the company must assume a constant rate of interest which will be sufficient, when added to the principal held in reserve, to equal the total required death payments at the assumed mortality rate.

In these calculations companies use compound, not simple, interest, because as interest is returned to the companies through their investments, this money is reinvested and in turn bears interest. Simple interest on $1,000 for two years at five per cent would be $100, or $50 at the end of the first year and $50 at the end of the second. Actually, the $50 received at the end of the first year would be reinvested and, assuming the same five per cent rate, would earn $2.50 during the second year. Therefore, compound interest on $1,000 for two years at five per cent would be $102.50. The total amount of interest and principal at the end of two years would thus be $1,102.50; or $1,000 is said to be the "present value" of $1,102.50 due in two years at five per cent compound interest.

Premiums are calculated on the present value of future claims; that is, premiums are such amounts as will be sufficient, if invested at an assumed compound interest rate, to pay future claims as they become due, the number of claims being estimated on the basis of mortality tables. $100 is the present value of $200 payable in twenty-three years, assuming a three per cent interest rate, since $100 invested at three per cent interest, compounded annually, will double itself in twenty-three years.

The mortality and interest items just discussed enter into the calculation of the "net" premiums. These items add up to the amount necessary to pay claims without any provision for expenses or adverse contingencies, and will be the same for all companies using the same mortality and interest bases.

In order to compute the gross premium, which the policyholder actually pays, an amount to cover expenses and contingencies called "loading" must be added to the net premium. A company must pay for a medical examination of the applicant, a commission or salary to the agent who brought in the business, and for the book work and office expense in setting up the policy on company records. Some of the expenses involved are just as great in writing a policy for $1,000 as one for $100,000, and certain companies therefore allow what may be called a "quantity discount," or a reduction in premium for larger amounts of insurance. Some companies include in the premium a larger expense charge than is estimated to be necessary and then return the overage to policyholders through dividends.

Under the level premium plan of life insurance, a policyholder pays more during the earlier period of the policy than the actual cost of insurance, just as he pays less than the actual cost during later years, and the excess payments which the company receives are accumulated as the "reserve." This fund is a liability on the company's books and is not a surplus in any conventional accounting sense.

The calculations involved in determining a premium are more complicated than this discussion indicates. The same is true in connection with policy reserves, but basically reserves are the funds on hand at the beginning of an accounting year (the "net" premiums received plus, after the first year, accrued interest thereon), plus interest on this fund during the year, less death claims paid.

Casualty insurance policies are written only for periods of a few years at most. Long continued liability on this type of policy is the exception rather than the rule. Most casualty company investments must be such that they can quickly be converted into cash to pay losses, for the risks assumed are often very large and will occur within a short time, if at all. It is the business of the underwriters to determine whether a particular risk can or should be assumed, and, if so, to set the premium. Some casualty or multiple-line companies are adventurous in the varieties of risks against which they will insure. If the event to be insured against is very likely to happen, the premium may be prohibitive, but, so long as the chances of occurrence are less than even, in most cases an underwriter may be found who is willing to issue a policy.

The rates which may be charged for fire and various kinds of casualty insurance are regulated by State law. The regulatory authorities are under a duty to require that the companies' rates be reasonable, not unfairly discriminatory, and neither excessively high nor inadequately low. The solvency of the companies must be maintained for the benefit of the policyholders.

Life insurance rates are not regulated but the mortality tables which companies may use are subject to approval.

The terms "assurance" and "assured" are synonomous with "insurance" and "insured," although in the United States they are usually used only in conection with life insurance.

Investments of Insurance Companies. Insurance companies, through premium collection and the accumulation of reserves, have large financial resources. These funds are continuously invested and reinvested.

The New York statutes, passed after the famous Hughes investigation in 1905, restricted life company investments to public debt obligations, adequately secured corporate bonds, first mortgages on real estate having a value of at least twice the amount loaned, and such real estate as the company needed for its own use and occupancy. Real estate acquired through mortgage foreclosure was required to be disposed of within five years unless the insurance department granted an extension of time because of hardship or market conditions. Investments

were forbidden in common stocks, unsecured corporate obligations, or obligations of unincorporated associations or individuals unless secured by mortgages or by collateral in which investments could be made directly. Other States passed even more restrictive legislation.

The effect of this legislation was to correct existing abuses, but it also unduly restricted the scope of permissible investments, and in later years many liberalizing changes in the statutes were made.

It might seem that an insurance company would not need to be concerned about the investment restrictions of any State other than the State of its incorporation. This is sometimes true, although New York requires that companies doing business in that State must comply in substance with New York's restrictions, so interstate insurers doing business in New York are subject to the burden of multiple compliance.

It is customary for each State to levy a tax on foreign or alien companies doing business within the State, based on a percentage of the premiums collected on business written there. In the case of fire insurance, this premium tax is primarily for the benefit of local fire departments.

Agents and Brokers. A corporation, such as an insurance company, can act only through agents, from the president down to the salesman, and it is the local selling agent most persons mean when they refer to an insurance agent. This particular kind of agent must be appointed by the company for which he acts and must be licensed by the insurance department of the State in which he works. Licensing requirements vary from the perfunctory to written examinations and educational standards.

Brokers are required to be licensed in approximately two-thirds of the States, and the requirements for a broker's license are generally higher than those for an agent's license. A broker occupies a somewhat anomalous position in that he is usually the agent for the insured to procure insurance, yet his compensation is paid by commissions from the insurance companies. To illustrate the function of a broker, the X Corporation which needs a number of kinds of insurance —automobile liability insurance covering a fleet of company cars, collision insurance, fire and extended coverage insurance for real estate owned, rent loss insurance for real estate rented, public liability and property damage insurance covering office locations, workmen's compensation, and fidelity bonds—calls upon a broker to place the insurance. The broker selects the companies which can write the policies which X needs and negotiates with them to secure the desired coverages. The policies are delivered to the broker for transmission to X, and the broker will be the agent of the insurer for the purpose of collecting the premiums.

The usual rules of agency law are applicable to local agents of insurance companies in their dealings with applicants and insureds. An agent binds his principal when he acts within the scope of his authority. That authority may be express, implied, or apparent, and beyond that point there is always the possibility that a company will ratify an agent's unauthorized acts or else will be estopped to deny the authority of a local agent because of the particular circumstances involved in a given case. An agent is not personally liable on a contract made in the name of the principal where the agent had any kind of authority to make the contract; but if the agent had no authority but represented that he did, the agent is liable to third parties who relied upon his representations.

Local agents of an insurance company do not always act as the company officials may desire, but the knowledge which agents receive through the exercise of their authority is usually imputed to the principal, and the principal often is bound by an agent's waiver of certain conditions in an insurance contract. Policies may have clauses in them stating that no waiver of any provision will be effective unless it is in writing and attached to the policy, but the effect which courts give to this clause varies considerably. If all agents were honest, the problems of the companies would be less, as would those of insureds. The company does not ordinarily discover that an agent has waived a condition until there has been a loss under the policy. It is often difficult to determine whether the insured (or beneficiary) is telling the truth about the agent's conduct, and it is highly unlikely that the insured would admit having read in the policy that an agent could not waive compliance with an express condition upon the waiver of which the insured's recovery depends. In the event that there has been provable collusion between a local agent and an applicant or insured with the intention of defrauding an insurance company, the knowledge of the agent will not be imputed to the principal, nor will his conduct bind the company.

Nature of Insurance Contracts. The basic principles of contract law are applicable to insurance contracts, but whereas most contracts contemplate a fairly even exchange between the parties, insurance contracts are aleatory. The insurer's promise to pay involves a far larger sum than it is receiving in premiums from the insured, and its promise to pay is enforceable only under certain conditions. Those conditions probably will not occur (or in the case of life insurance, probably will not occur prematurely) or else the insurance would not be written. Since insurance companies do a large volume of business over wide areas, their policies are standardized and in some cases standardization is required by State law. This method of business operation usually means that the insured must accept a given policy or do without insurance, and for this reason insurance contracts are sometimes said to be contracts of adhesion.

Insurable Interest. The concept of insurable interest has been developed over many years, primarily to eliminate gambling and to reduce what is called the moral hazard. If one were free to take out an enforceable insurance policy on the life of another, or a fire insurance policy on property which he did not own or in which he had no interest, he would be in a position to profit by the loss of such person's life or the destruction of the property. A fire policy may not be purchased by one having no insurable interest in the property, for a fire policy is a policy of indemnification against loss. The extent of a loss due to fire is ascertainable, whereas the loss due to the death of an individual is not. Life insurance policies are in a fixed amount and may only be taken out by the person whose life is involved or by a limited group of persons who, because of their relationship to the insured, would sustain direct loss by reason of his death. In some States the insurer and the insured are permitted to agree in advance upon the value of the property insured (a "valued policy") and in the event of total loss, the agreed value will be paid. In general, an insurable interest is some relationship between the insured and a specified contingency, such that the happening of the contingency will cause a substantial loss or injury to the insured.

In property insurance, ownership of the fee creates an insurable interest in the property, whether the ownership is sole, or by joint tenants or tenants in common. In some instances, shareholders in corporations have been held to have an insurable interest in the corporation's property. Lessees of property have interests which are insurable as do holders of security interests, such as mortgagees or conditional sellers.

In life insurance, those who may take out insurance on another's life are practically limited to close relatives, creditors, and business associates or employers, depending generally on the particular facts involved. The insurable interest need exist only at the time the policy is taken out and not at the time of death (except possibly in Texas). In property insurance, the interest must exist at the time the loss occurs and probably need not exist at the time the insurance is procured, although the latter is sometimes said to be necessary. In life insurance, except for that written by fraternal benefit societies, an insured may take out a policy on his own life and name any one he chooses as beneficiary, although that particular beneficiary may have no insurable interest in the insured's life. An insured may assign the life policy proceeds to a third person who has no insurable interest. Fire insurance policies are not assignable before loss occurs.

In fire insurance policies, the recovery is usually the replacement value of the property, minus depreciation, except in the case of a valued policy, where the agreed value is the recovery on a total loss. An owner or lessee of property may take out rent loss or business interruption insurance to protect himself against loss during the time that the property is unusable.

Offer and Acceptance. Insureds often know the names of the life insurance companies in which they have policies, but do not know the names of the fire or casualty companies which insure them. One reason which has been advanced for this situation is that life policies are generally solicited by company agents, whereas those who desire fire or casualty insurance usually call an insurance agent or broker, and leave the selection of the company to him.

No matter how assiduously a life insurance agent has solicited a person to take out a policy, it is generally true that it is the applicant who makes the offer, and the contract is created when that offer is accepted by the company. The company's acceptance may be conditioned, for instance, upon payment of the premium or delivery of the policy while the insured is in good health. If the company writes a policy which differs from the application, then it is the company which makes a counter-offer which the applicant may or may not choose to accept. This situation arises most frequently where the company is unwilling to write the policy which the agent proposed, because of the results of a physical examination of the applicant, but is willing to write a different policy based on the particular risk involved. Some companies will not intentionally insure persons who have had certain physical ailments or a history of disease, while other companies will write such life insurance for a premium which they consider appropriate to the risk.

Binding Receipts and Binders. Life insurance agents cannot bind the company to a contract with the insured, although on occasion a "binding receipt" may be issued by an authorized agent, acknowledging payment of the premium and providing for the issuance of a standard policy effective from the date of the medical examination, so long as the company has no bona fide reason to reject the application. In fire and casualty insurance, agents often have authority to make the insurance effective immediately, when needed, by means of a "binder." In the event of a loss before the company has actually issued a policy, the binder will be effective on the same terms and conditions the policy would have had if it had been issued.

Representations. A representation is a statement made by or on behalf of an applicant for insurance to induce an insurer to enter into a contract. The representation is not a part of the insurance contract, and if the application containing the representation is incorporated by reference into the contract, as in liability or burglary insurance, the representation becomes a warranty. For a representation to have legal consequences, it must have been relied upon by the insurer as an inducement to enter into the contract, and it must have been substantially false when made or it must have become so, to the insured's knowledge, before the contract was created. The principal remedy of the insurer, on discovery of misrepresentation, is rescission of the contract. To rescind the contract, the insurer must tender to the insured all premiums which have been paid, since a rescission restores the parties to the same position they were in before the contract was made. Rescission may or may not be available to the life insurer, however, because of the "incontestable clause" which makes the policy incontestable by the insurer after a specified period of time, such as one or two years after the policy has been in effect during the lifetime of the insured. To be effective, rescission must be made as soon as possible after discovery of the misrepresentation.

An innocent misrepresentation of a material fact (not opinion) is a sufficient ground for avoidance of a policy by the insurer, unless it is substantially true. Whether the fact is material or not depends, generally, upon whether the policy would have been issued had the truth been known. An immaterial misrepresentation, even though fraudulently made, is not a ground for avoidance of the policy.

Warranties. Representations are inducements made by the applicant to the insurer to enter into the contract but are not part of the contract itself. If they are incorporated into the contract, they become "warranties." By statute in many States, representations cannot be converted into warranties in life insurance policies by incorporating the application into the policy by reference.

Warranties are of great importance in insurance contracts because they state conditions which must exist before the contract is effective or before the insurer's promise to pay is enforceable. Failure of the condition to exist or to occur relieves the insurer from any obligation to perform its promise. Broadly speaking, a condition is simply an event the happening of which or failure to happen will change an existing legal relationship. Conditions are either precedent or subsequent; for example, payment of the premium is a condition precedent to the enforcement of the insurer's promise, as is the happening of the insured event. A condition subsequent is an operative event the happening of which terminates an existing duty to perform. A provision in a policy to the effect that the insured shall not be liable unless suit is brought within twelve months from the date of the occurrence of the loss operates as a condition subsequent.

Usually, those statements in policies which the insurer looks upon as express warranties can be identified by the use of the words "warrant" or "on condition that" or "provided that" or words of similar import. Other statements which are important to the risk assumed, as a building address may be in the case where personal property at a particular location is insured against fire, are sometimes held to be informal warranties. Generally, the trend is away from allowing an insurer to avoid liability on the policy for *any* breach of a warranty by an insured; the breach must usually be "material" to have such an effect.

The effect of warranties is frequently regulated by statute. The New York statute provides that all statements made by an applicant for life insurance shall be deemed representations and not warranties, regardless of what the policy or application may state.

Affirmative warranties state conditions which must exist at the time the insurance contract is made, while promissory warranties are undertakings to do or cause something to be done during the period of the policy. A statement in a fire insurance policy that the premises are used as a grocery store probably will be considered an affirmative warranty which need be true only at the time the policy is issued. Unless the character of use is changed to such an extent that there is a substantial increase in the hazard, the policy will remain enforceable. A statement in a burglary policy that a watchman will be on duty at all times is a promissory warranty.

Concealment. While rarely relied upon in life insurance, the doctrine of concealment has vitality in other fields of insurance. Concealment is simply the failure of an applicant for insurance to disclose material facts which the insurer does not know. For example, if an applicant telephoned an insurance company agent for a policy protecting against damage by windstorm, effective immediately, and at the same time was watching a tornado approach, he could hardly complain if the insurer objected to settling for a total loss. The non-disclosure must normally be fraudulent as well as material to invalidate the policy; that is, (1) did the applicant have reason to believe the fact was material, and (2) would its disclosure have affected the acceptance of the risk by the insurer?

Waiver and Estoppel. There are instances when an insurer would normally be entitled to deny liability under a policy because of a misrepresentation or breach of condition or concealment, but because of other facts, the insurer is said to be "estopped" to take advantage of the defense or else to have "waived" the right to rely on it.

The distinctions between "waiver" and "estoppel" are usually only verbal. The terms are used interchangeably, although by definition they are not synonomous. As generally defined, waiver is the intentional relinquishment of a known right, and estoppel means that a person is precluded by his own conduct from asserting a position which is inconsistent with his acts which have been relied upon by another with justification.

Since a corporation, such as an insurance company, can act only by agents, situations involving waiver always find root in an agent's conduct. The higher the agent's position in the company organization, the more likely his conduct is to bind the company, since an agent acting within the scope of his authority binds the principal. Insureds have the right to rely on representations made by the insurer's employees and where such representations induce or cause a change of position by the insured, or prevent the insured from causing a condition to occur, the insurer may not assert the failure of the condition to occur, whether the term applied to this situation be waiver or estoppel. Companies have tried in many ways to limit the authority of local selling agents to bind the company through waiver or estoppel, but this is most difficult to do effectively.

As a general rule, when a local agent delivers a policy with knowledge of the non-occurrence of a condition precedent to the company's liability which would make the policy void or voidable at the company's option, the condition is waived. While there is always a question whether the agent had authority to waive the condition, most courts will find an effective waiver even though the condition is a delivery-in-good-health clause or the medical-treatment clause in a life insurance policy. Such clauses provide that a life insurance policy shall not take effect unless it is delivered to the applicant during his lifetime while his insurability or good health continues, and also the policy shall not take effect if the applicant has been treated by a physician or has been hospitalized between the date of the application and the date of delivery of the policy.

Performance and Termination. Most contracts of insurance are performed according to their terms, and due performance termi-

nates the insurer's obligation. In life insurance contracts, the insurer pays the principal sum due on death, and the contract is thereby performed and discharged. In other insurance contracts, there may be a dispute over the amount due upon the happening of the insured event, but when the conflict is resolved and the agreed sum is paid, the insurer has performed its obligation.

Cancellation of an insurance contract by mutual consent is one way of terminating it. Cancellation by the insurer alone means that the insurer is liable according to the terms of the policy until such time as the cancellation is effective. This is not always a right which is available to insurers, but where available, it is sometimes mistakenly used where rescission is preferable, from the insurer's point of view. If an insurer under an accident policy elects to cancel after the occurrence of an insured event, where a right of rescission existed because of material misrepresentation, this will be taken as an admission of liability for events occurring before cancellation. To cancel a policy, the insurer must tender the unearned portion of the premium to the insured. To effect a rescission, all premiums received by the insurer must be returned to the insured.

Occasionally, a life insurance company will decline to pay a death benefit because of a material misrepresentation by the insured. In a suit by the beneficiary against the insurer, the company may be faced with facts pointing to waiver or estoppel due to the actions of a local agent, and this problem will ordinarily be resolved by a jury. In the event the insurer learns of a material misrepresentation during the lifetime of the insured, the proper remedy is rescission of the contract. Because of the incontestable clause in life insurance policies, the insurer's rights to rescind are restricted, but an insured may cancel the policy and recover the cash surrender value at any time. The minimum cash surrender value payable on cancellation by the insured is determined by calculations specified in the non-forfeiture statute, but, in general, this value will approximate the reserve on the policy, at least after the policy has been in effect long enough to amortize certain expenses incurred in writing the policy.

The 1943 New York standard fire insurance policy gives the insured the right to cancel at any time and the insurer must refund the "excess of the paid premium above the customary short rates for the expired time." The company has a right to cancel at any time (with or without cause) by giving five days' written notice to the insured "with or without tender of the excess of paid premium above the pro rata premium for the expired time, which excess, if not tendered, shall be refunded on demand," and the notice must so state, if a tender is not made. If the loss is payable to a designated mortgagee, the mortgagee is entitled to ten days' notice. When a fire policy is cancelled, the company is entitled to retain a portion of the premium in payment for the protection which the insured has received when the policy was in force. Upon cancellation by the company the premium retention is only that proportion of the premium paid which the time the policy was in effect bears to the time the total premium covered; whereas, upon cancellation by the insured the "short rates" apply whereby the company is entitled to retain a larger proportion of the premium paid to cover reasonable expenses incurred in writing the policy.

After the occurrence of the insured event, the insured is required to give notice to the insurer and, in the case of property insurance, proof of loss within a specified time, such as 60 days for fire insurance. In liability policies the requirement of immediate notice is construed by the courts as notice within a "reasonable" time. The period within which an insured may commence suit against the insurer upon a fire policy is limit-

ed by the policy, usually to one year. Automobile liability policies required that the insured immediately notify the insurer of any accident or occurrence which may involve liability as well as notify the insurer of the institution of suit and forward any summons or process served upon him. These notice requirements are conditions precedent to the insurer's contractual liability, but all of them may be waived by the insurer. If an insured under an automobile liability policy fails to forward a summons to the insurer and a judgment by default is entered, the insurer loses the opportunity to defend the suit, due to the delay. The insured's breach of condition will give the insurer a defense in any action brought to enforce the policy. Delay of only a few days, even though "immediate" notice is required, may not prejudice the insurer at all.

The proper procedure is for the insured to give notice as promptly as possible after the happening of an insured event and to furnish a proof of loss, if required, within the time allowed. If the terms of the policy are complied with, it is beneficial to both insured and insurer. An insurance company will rarely rely upon a strict construction of notice provisions unless the company has been prejudiced by the insured's delay, but these provisions are in policies for sufficient reasons and failure to perform a condition in a contract normally excuses performance by the other party.

CASES

LIBERTY NATIONAL LIFE INSURANCE CO. v. WELDON

(1958) 267 Ala. 171, 100 So.2d 696, 61 A.L.R.2d 1346.

LAWSON, J. This is a suit by Gaston Weldon, who sues as the father of Shirley Dianne Weldon, deceased, his minor daughter, under

§ 119, Title 7, Code 1940, the so-called homicide statute, against Liberty National Life Insurance Company, a corporation; National Life & Accident Insurance Company, a corporation; and Southern Life & Health Insurance Company, a corporation.

We will sometimes hereafter refer to Gaston Weldon as the plaintiff, to his deceased child as Shirley, and to the defendant insurance companies as Liberty National, National Life and Southern Life.

Shirley died on May 1, 1952, when she was approximately two and one-half years of age. Prior to her death each of the defendant insurance companies had issued a policy wherein Shirley's life was insured. The policy of Liberty National in the amount of $500 was issued on December 1, 1951. National Life's policy in the amount of $1,000 was issued on or about April 23, 1952. The policy of Southern Life in the amount of $5,000 was issued in the latter part of March, 1952. Each of those policies was issued on an application of Mrs. Earle Dennison, who was an aunt-in-law of Shirley, that is, she was the widow of a brother of Shirley's mother. Each of the policies provided that the death benefits be paid to Mrs. Dennison. * * *

The theory on which plaintiff seeks to recover damages from the defendants is that Mrs. Dennison had no insurable interest in Shirley's life and that the defendants knew or should have known that fact; and, that by reason of the wrongful and negligent issuance of the "illegal" policies of insurance Mrs. Dennison murdered Shirley with the hope of collecting the insurance proceeds.

* * *

There were verdict and judgment for the plaintiff in the amount of $75,000. The motions for new trial filed by each of the defendant insurance companies having been overruled, each of them has appealed to this court. * * *

The evidence in this case shows beyond peradventure that Shirley was murdered by Mrs. Dennison. * * *

The evidence is also clear to the effect that Mrs. Dennison murdered the child in order to collect insurance benefits payable to her upon the child's death. We will not undertake to set out all of the evidence which tends to support that statement, for the defendants do not contend that such was not the case. We simply call attention to one incident which we think clearly shows why Mrs. Dennison poisoned the child. Mrs. Dennison was a nurse in the hospital to which Shirley was admitted and she was directed by the doctor in charge of Shirley to administer aid to the patient. By late afternoon when it was apparent that Shirley was dying, Mrs. Dennison left the hospital and drove approximately twelve miles to the home of an insurance agent to pay the premium on the Liberty National policy which was about to lapse.

So it is clear that the harm which came to plaintiff's little girl was not caused by the direct act of any of the defendants, but by the intervening act of Mrs. Dennison, who has paid with her life for her horrible crime. * * *

The plaintiff has proceeded against these defendants on the theory that Mrs. Dennison did not have an insurable interest in the life of Shirley and hence the policies involved were illegal and void as against public policy; that the defendants were negligent in the issuance of the policies in that they knew there was no such interest or failed to exercise reasonable diligence to ascertain that fact before issuing the policies, although there was a duty upon them to do so; and that the failure to perform that duty was in fact the proximate cause of the child's death.

The evidence was sufficient to show a lack of insurable interest. In the brief filed here on behalf of appellants reference is made to the case of National Life & Accident Ins. Co.

v. Davis, 179 Ark. 621, 17 S.W.2d 312, which holds, in effect, that the relationship of aunt and niece, standing alone, is sufficient to provide an insurable interest. But such is not the law of this state. We have held to the contrary. [Citation.] * * *

Since the jury was authorized under the evidence to find that Mrs. Dennison had no insurable interest in the life of Shirley, a finding that the policies of insurance were illegal and void as repugnant to public policy naturally followed. * * *

The conclusions which we have reached above, namely, that the evidence was sufficient to show that Shirley was murdered and the policies were void because of lack of insurable interest and were, in effect, negligently issued do not, of course, determine the liability of th defendants. For all negligence is not actionable. To be actionable it must be the breach of a duty which the defendant owed the plaintiff as an individual or one of a class [Citation] and the plaintiff must not only show causal connection between the negligent breach of the duty but that such negligence was the proximate cause of the injury. [Citation.]

The defendants below, the appellants here, assert with considerable emphasis in briefs filed in this court that there was no duty on them to determine whether Mrs. Dennison at the time the policies were issued had an insurable interest in the life of the plaintiff's minor daughter. Of course, if there was no such duty the defendants were entitled to the general affirmative charge with hypothesis, as requested.

Does a life insurance company have the duty to use reasonable care not to issue a policy of life insurance in favor of a beneficiary who has no interest in the continuation of the life of the insured?

No case has come to our attention where this specific question has been considered by any court. But we are of the opinion that such a duty exists, for there is a duty upon all to exercise reasonable care not to injure another. [Citations.]

The position of the defendants seems to be that if murder results the insurance companies are, of course, sorry that the insured met with such a fate, but they have no liability if there is no insurable interest although they can treat such policies as completely void. If an early death from natural causes makes the policy unprofitable, the defendants can and do refuse to pay the beneficiary for the reason that such policies are void. In other words, the defendants seem to be of the opinion that the insurable interest rule is to protect insurance companies. We do not agree. The rule is designed to protect human life. Policies in violation of the insurable interest rule are not dangerous because they are illegal; they are illegal because they are dangerous.

As we have shown, it has long been recognized by this court and practically all courts in this country that an insured is placed in a position of extreme danger where a policy of insurance is issued on his life in favor of a beneficiary who has no insurable interest. There is no legal justification for the creation of such a risk to an insured and there is no social gain in the writing of a void policy of insurance. Where this court has found that such policies are unreasonably dangerous to the insured because of the risk of murder and for this reason has declared such policies void, it would be an anomaly to hold that insurance companies have no duty to use reasonable care not to create a situation which may prove to be a stimulus for murder.

* * *

We come now to the contention of the appellants that they were entitled to the affirmative instruction presently under consideration for the reason that the plaintiff failed to meet the burden which was upon him to present some evidence tending to show that the defendants' acts were the proximate cause of Shirley's death. In their brief the defendants say that the evidence shows that "in the instant case, the *separate, independent, superseding, wilful, malicious, crime of murder* became 'the responsible cause' of the death of Shirley Dianne Weldon."

Persons who perpetrate torts are, as a rule, responsible and only responsible for the proximate consequences of the wrongs they commit. In other words, unless the tort be the proximate cause of the injury complained of, there is no legal accountability. * * *

Here we have an intervening cause, the criminal act of Mrs. Dennison. The many decisions of this court dealing with negligence as the proximate cause, when some agency has intervened and has been the immediate cause of the injury, hold the party guilty of negligence in the first instance is not responsible, unless at the time of the original negligence the act of the agency could have been reasonably foreseen. If the act of the intervening agency could have been reasonably foreseen the causal chain is not broken. But if the injury results from an independent, intervening, efficient cause, not reasonably to be anticipated, to wit, the act of a third person, the negligence shown, if any, is not the proximate cause of the injury. [Citations.] * * *

We cannot agree with the defendants in their assertion that we should hold as a matter of law that the murder of the young girl was not reasonably foreseeable. They created a situation of a kind which this court and others have consistently said affords temptation to a recognizable percentage of humanity to commit murder. We quote again from the case of Helmetag's Adm'r v. Miller, 76 Ala. 183: "The reason of the law which vitiates wager policies is the pecuniary interest which the holder has in procuring the death of the subject of insurance, *thus opening a wide door by which a constant tempta-*

tion is created to commit for profit the most atrocious of crimes." (Emphasis supplied.)

The question of proximate cause was properly left for the jury's determination. * * *

We hold that the trial court did not err in overruling those grounds of the motion for new trial which are argued here as having been well taken. * * *

The judgment of the circuit court is affirmed.

FIDELITY & GUARANTY INS. UNDERWRITERS, INC. v. GREGORY

(1965 Ky.) 387 S.W.2d 287.

DAVIS, COMMISSIONER. Appellee recovered $7,000, the face amount of a fire insurance policy issued to him by appellant, based upon the total destruction by fire of the appellee's residence.

Appellant's defense, and its contentions of reversible error, are based on the admitted failure of appellee to file written proof of loss as provided by the insurance policy. For the appellee it is maintained that the policy provision requiring proof of loss was effectively waived. Appellant also presents claimed error in the instruction to the jury and in the admission of certain evidence.

Fire destroyed appellee's dwelling on August 2, 1962, while a fire insurance policy issued by appellant was in force. The loss was total; the face value of the policy was $7,000. The policy is a "valued policy" within the purview of KRS 304.905.

Appellee was out of Kentucky when the fire occurred. When he returned the next day he learned of the fire and reported it to the insurance agent from whom he had obtained the policy. That agent, Pruett, transmitted the information to appellant forthwith.

Under date August 6, 1962, appellant's general agent referred the fire loss to General Adjustment Bureau at the latter's Madisonville office. A copy of the transmittal letter from the general agent to General Adjustment was furnished Pruett, and is in evidence. The letter to the adjustment agency, on a prepared printed form, contained this language. "We have received notice of loss in connection with the above [the instant claim] and are taking the following action: Referring loss to you for adjustment. Forward completed loss papers to this office."

Shortly after receiving the adjustment instructions General Adjustment Bureau sent its employee, Wedding, to investigate the matter. Wedding met with the appellee at the fire scene, and made certain measurements. Wedding asked appellee to furnish a photograph of the residence as it had appeared before the fire; appellee did mail to Wedding such a photograph. Indeed, it is conceded that appellee fully "cooperated" with Wedding.

Wedding testified that he concluded that "as the fire was of undetermined origin and the house was vacant—and appeared to be over insured I made a report to Mr. Bracey." (Bracey is employed by the National Board of Fire Underwriters.) Wedding said that Bracey investigated the fire, as did an investigator for the State Fire Marshal.

Wedding further said that when the investigation came within the investigative jurisdiction of the Fire Marshall "there was nothing I could do until they were through." Accordingly, Wedding said that about two weeks after the fire he informed appellee that the matter was in the hands of the Fire Marshal, and that Wedding could do nothing until the Marshal's investigation had been concluded. Wedding testified that "the proof of loss was never mentioned" as between him and the appellee.

Appellee made one further communication with his own insurance broker, Pruett, at which time he indicated to Pruett that the claim had not been settled. On October 15, 1962, appellee consulted and retained Raymond Dycus as his attorney to enforce payment on the policy. The attorney testified that on that date he had a telephone conversation with adjuster Wedding, and that Wedding said that the insurance company had waived proof of loss. In his testimony Wedding specifically denied making such statement, and further asserted that he had no such authority.

When no response was forthcoming from the insurance company, the present suit was filed on October 25, 1962. The insurance company made an affirmative plea in avoidance that appellee had failed to furnish the written proof of loss. The pertinent terms of the insurance policy are:

" * * * and within sixty days after the loss, unless such time is extended in writing by this Company, the insured shall render to this Company a proof of loss, signed and sworn to by the insured, stating the knowledge and belief of the insured as to the following: the time and origin of the loss, the interest of the insured and of all others in the property, the actual cash value of each item thereof and the amount of loss thereto, all encumbrances thereon, all other contracts of insurance, whether valid or not, covering any of said property, any changes in the title, use, occupation, location, possession or exposures of said property since the issuing of this policy, by whom and for what purpose any building herein described and the several parts thereof were occupied at the time of loss and whether or not it then stood on leased ground * * *

"No suit or action on this policy for the recovery of any claim shall be sustainable in any court of law or equity unless all the requirements of this policy shall have been complied with, and unless commenced within twelve months next after inception of the loss."

By a reply, the appellee-plaintiff reaffirmed his contention that the company had waived the filing of proof of loss and, in the alternative, pleaded: " * * * in the event it should be determined that this plaintiff has not furnished proof of loss as required * * and that the company has not waived this * * * then * * * plaintiff's complaint should be dismissed without prejudice and plaintiff permitted to tender such proof." The company's motion to strike the reply was overruled. So far as is disclosed by the record, no specific ruling of the trial court was sought or made with respect to the alternative pleading.

Our cases recognize the validity of provisions of insurance policies requiring proof of loss. In some instances the cases have dealt with such clauses which incorporate a provision for forfeiture of the insurance claim; in others, as in the present case, the provision does not impose forefeiture but makes the proper filing a condition precedent to maintenance of a suit upon the policy. [Citations.]

It is well established also that the filing of proof of loss may be waived. [Citations.]

We have held that an adjuster may waive such proof of loss. [Citation.]

We believe the insurance company is estopped here to rely on failure to file proof of loss. As noted, the company specifically directed General Adjustment to "Forward completed loss papers to this office." Adjuster Wedding did ask appellee to furnish a photograph of the residence, and this was done. Wedding told appellee, during the sixty-day period, that since the matter had been taken under consideration by the Fire Marshal, there was nothing more he could do pending that investigation. The inference is clear, we think, from Wedding's conversation with appellee, that after the Fire Marshal's investigation had been finished, Wedding would resume action looking toward adjustment of the claim. Wedding did not ask for proof of loss, although the company asked him to forward it.

The insurance company can become bound by the activities of its agent, even though it may be said that the agent lacked actual authority to waive the filing of the proof of loss. We consider sound the statement made in 45 C.J.S. Insurance § 982(6), p. 1201: "As a general rule, one who is intrusted by the company with apparent power to adjust the loss ordinarily has authority to waive notice or proofs of loss." We hold that Wedding's actions, in the sixty-day period, were sufficient as a matter of law to estop the appellant company from insisting on a proof of loss. [Citation.]

It is our view that Wedding's conduct, without respect to what he may or may not have said to attorney Dycus, was of that nature as "would naturally induce delay or lead an ordinarily prudent person to believe that the requirement of the policy respecting proof was waived by the company." [Citation.]

* * *

The judgment is affirmed.

YOUSE v. EMPLOYERS FIRE INS. CO. BOSTON, MASS.

(1951) 172 Kan. 111, 238 P.2d 472.

PRICE, J. This was an action to recover for the loss and damage to a star sapphire ring caused by fire. Plaintiff insured prevailed in the court below and defendant company has appealed.

For convenience, the parties will be referred to as the insured and the company.

Both parties state the sole question for determination to be: "Is the loss resulting from damage to jewelry, by a fire intentionally kindled in and confined to a place where fire was intended to be, insured against under the terms of the fire insurance policy in question?"

The facts, which are not in dispute, are as follows:

On an occasion while the policy in question was in force the wife of insured was carrying her ring wrapped in a handkerchief in her purse. Upon arriving at her home she placed the handkerchief, together with some paper cleansing tissues. (Kleenex), on the dresser in her bedroom. Later her maid, in cleaning the room, inadvertently picked up the handkerchief containing the ring, together with the cleansing tissues, and threw them into a wastebasket. Still later, another servant emptied the contents of the wastebasket, along with other trash, into a trash burner at the rear of the premises and proceeded to burn the trash so deposited. The trash burner was intended for that purpose, the fire was intentionally lighted by the servant, and was confined to the trash burner. About a week later the ring was found in the trash burner. It had been damaged to the extent of $900.

The policy, a standard form, insured household goods and personal property, usual or incidental to the occupancy of the premises as a dwelling, belonging to insured or a member of his family while contained on the premises, " * * * against all direct loss or damage by fire, except as hereinafter provided, * * *" in an amount not exceeding $2,000. The parties agree that the "exceptions" contained in the policy are immaterial to the issues in this case.

The insured also carried a "floater policy" in another company (not a party to this action) by the terms of which the ring was insured to the extent of $250. The company issuing the "floater policy" offered to pay that amount to insured, but as of the time of trial of this action such offer had not been accepted.

In the court below the company offered no evidence and elected to stand on its demurrer to insured's evidence, which established the facts as hereinbefore related. Judgment was rendered in favor of insured in the amount of $650 (being the amount of the loss less the "floater policy" coverage), and for attorney fees in the amount of $300, to be collected as costs. * * *

The company contends here, as it did in the court below, that the quoted insuring clause of the policy, "against all direct loss or damage by fire" covers only loss or damage resulting from a "hostile" fire as distinguished from a "friendly" fire; that here, the fire being intentionally lighted in and confined to a place or receptacle where it was intended to be, was not a hostile fire within the usual and well-established meaning of the term and therefore no recovery can be had.

The insured argues that he purchased and paid for *fire insurance*—not just for fire insurance to cover loss resulting only from so-called "hostile" fires; that the direct loss and damage to the ring by fire is undisputed; that the company would have the court write into the policy an unauthorized and unreasonable restriction; that there is no ambiguity in the terms of the policy and therefore it should be enforced according to its literal terms; and that even though there were some uncertainty as to its meaning the court is bound to construe the policy strictly against the company and favorably to the insured. [Citations.] * * *

A friendly fire is defined as being a fire lighted and contained in a usual place for fire, such as a furnace, stove, incinerator, and the like, and used for the purposes of heating, cooking, manufacturing, or other common and usual everyday purposes.

A hostile fire is defined as being a fire unexpected, unintended, not anticipated, in a place not intended for it to be and where fire is not ordinarily maintained, or as one which has escaped in the usual and ordinary sense of the word. A fire originally friendly, by escaping, becomes hostile, and ordinarily recovery may be had for loss or damage resulting thereby. * * *

Words employed in contracts of insurance are to be construed according to the meaning of the terms used, and are to be taken and understood in their plain, ordinary and peculiar sense, so as to give effect to the intention of the parties. [Citation.] See also G.S.1949, 77–201, second, relating to statutory construction which, among other things, provides that such words and phrases as may have acquired a peculiar and appropriate meaning in law shall be construed according to such peculiar and appropriate meaning. In applying the rule the test is not what the insurer intended the words to mean but what a reasonable person in the position of an insured would have understood them to mean. [Citation.]

We think it cannot be denied that in common parlance and everyday usage one has not "had a fire" so long as it has burned only in the place where it was intended to burn, and where fire ordinarily is maintained. By way of illustration, when a person maintains a fire in his furnace, cookstove or fireplace, or when he burns trash in his incinerator, he has not "had a fire" in the ordinary, common acceptation of the term. On the other hand, if a fire on the roof results from sparks from fire in the furnace, cookstove or fireplace, if sparks from the latter should burn a rug or furniture or if the fire in the trash burner escapes therefrom and sets fire to the garage or fence, such person has "had a fire" for which recovery can be had, notwithstanding the fire was originally friendly.

We think it is quite true to say that when one purchases standard fire insurance he does so with the idea in mind of protecting himself from loss or damage resulting from what the law defines as a "hostile" fire, and that the word "fire," as used in fire insurance policies, has, in common parlance, such well-understood meaning * * *

In our opinion there can be no question but that the fire which damaged or destroyed the sapphire ring was what in law is known as a "friendly" fire. It was intentionally lighted, was for the usual and ordinary purpose of burning trash, and was at all times confined to the place where it was intended, and did not escape.

We are not concerned here with the provisions of a "floater policy," and neither are we concerned with the question of the negligence or inadvertence of insured's servant in throwing the ring into the trash burner, which latter fact, according to insured's argument, made the fire a "hostile" fire so far as insured is concerned. Negligence or inadvertence of an insured or of one of his employees of course ordinarily would not bar recovery—*provided* the fire causing the loss or damage is what is known in law as a *hostile* fire. True, here the loss was occasioned by fire—but, it was a *friendly* fire, and under such circumstances no recovery may be had.

It follows that the court erred in overruling the demurrer to the evidence and in rendering judgment in favor of insured. The judgment of the lower court is therefore reversed.

PROBLEMS

1. Lile, an insurance broker, handled all insurance for X Co. Lile purchased a fire policy from Insurance Company insuring X Co.'s factory against fire in the amount of $100,000. Before the policy was delivered to X Co. and while it was in Lile's hands, X Co. advised Lile to cancel the policy. Prior to cancellation, X Co. suffered a loss and makes claim against Insurance Company on the policy. The premium had been billed to Lile but was unpaid at the time of

loss. In an action by X Co. against Insurance Company, what judgment?

2. On July 15, 1966, A purchased in Chicago a 1963 Buick Sedan intending to drive it that day to St. Louis, Missouri. He telephoned a friend X who was in the insurance business and told him that he wished public liability insurance on the automobile limited in amount to $50,000 for injuries to one person and $100,000 for any one accident. X took the order and told A over the telephone that he was covered and that his policy would be written by the Y Insurance Company. Later that same day and before X had advised the Y Insurance Company of A's application, A negligently operated the automobile on the public highway and seriously injured B who brings suit against A. Is A protected by public liability insurance?

3. A owns a building having a fair market value of $10,000. He takes out a fire insurance policy in the B Company for $6,000, the policy containing an eighty (80) percent co-insurance clause. The building is damaged by fire to the extent of $4,000. How much insurance is A entitled to collect?

4. The B Automobile Insurance Company issues to A, owner of a Mercury automobile, a liability policy, $10,000–$20,000 limits. June 3, 1966, as the result of A's negligent operation of his car, C, D and E are injured in a collision. C, D and E sue A and recover judgments of $15,000, $3,000 and $2,000, respectively. To what extent is the B Company liable?

5. Arthur Heartburn, having knowledge of a bad heart condition, arranges to have his friend Ira Imposter, represent himself as Heartburn to the medical examiner of the Taken Life Insurance Company. Imposter, posing as Heartburn, is found to be physically sound; and the Insurance Company issues a $50,000 life insurance policy to Heartburn. The policy contains a two-year incontestable clause. Twenty-six months after the issuance of the policy Heartburn suffers a heart attack and dies. Before paying off the claim of Heartburn's widow, the beneficiary under the policy, the Insurance Company learns about Imposter's actions in helping Heartburn procure the policy. When the Taken Insurance Company refuses to pay the claim, the widow files suit on the policy. What decision?

6. Jones buys a contract of life insurance and states in the application that his age is 45 when actually he is 47. It is stated in the application that all statements made by the insured in the application are to be construed as warranties. Jones dies and the company denies liability upon the ground of breach of warranty. In a suit by Jones's beneficiary against the insurance company, what judgment?

7. A fire policy provides that no recovery shall be had thereon if the property becomes vacant. The insured vacates the property and this becomes known to the insurance company through one of its inspectors. About ten days later the building burns. The company in the meantime has taken no action. After the loss the company notifies the insured that it will not pay because of his violation of the provision.

Is the insured entitled to recover?

8. A fire policy provides that no agent of the company may waive any provisions therein. The insured calls up a general agent of the company and notifies him of a condition of affairs which is forbidden to exist by the policy. The agent says: "We will waive that point." A fire occurs. Is the insured entitled to recover?

9. Wiley, an insurance salesman, induces Glutz to purchase a $10,000 life insurance policy on the life of his best friend Doe and at the same time sells a policy to Doe insuring Glutz's life. After ten years Doe dies, and on due proof of death, the insurance company denies liability. Glutz sues the company. Decision?

CHAPTER 52

TRANSFER BY WILL—INTESTATE SUCCESSION AND ADMINISTRATION OF ESTATES

Introductory. The concept of private property does not greatly antedate the principle that a man should be able to exercise some control over the transfer of his property at his death.

Hand in hand with the principle of control at death over what was possessed during life has developed the competing doctrine that the sovereign might limit this testamentary power in accordance with what appeared, from time to time, to be socially desirable or politically expedient. This doctrine was strongly indicated during feudal England when the voluntary transfer of land at death was all but forbidden, and it is evident today not only in the general statutory regulation of the manner and power to make a will but, also, in the substantial taxes imposed upon the transfer of property at death.

There is one major characteristic of a will which sets it apart from other transactions such as deeds and contracts: A will is revocable at any time during life. There is no such thing as an irrevocable will. If a document is binding during life it may be a contract (such as a promise to make a will) or a deed (conveying a vested remainder after a life estate in the grantor) but it is not a will. A will takes effect only upon and not until the death of the testator.

Whether a will is looked upon as an inalienable right or a privilege granted by society the fact remains that the execution of a will is, in a large sense, a moral responsibility and it is one that is too frequently ignored or forgotten by persons who own property. It is indeed a strange fact that persons who exercise the most extreme caution over their affairs during life neglect to execute a will, thereby allowing the State, by default, to direct who shall inherit their property.

Capacity and Power to Will Property. Not every person can make a valid disposition of property at death. Two types of qualifications are necessary and these are described by the statement that, to make a valid will, the testator must have both the "power" and the "capacity" to do so. Both of these terms refer to restrictions imposed by statute or court decision but each has a distinct and separate meaning. The power to make a will is granted by the State to persons who are of a class believed generally able intelligently to handle their affairs without regard to personal limitations. Thus, in most States, children under a certain age cannot make valid wills. In Illinois, for example, a person must be eighteen years of age at the time of executing a will to have it recognized and enforced by a court. Prior to the general legal emancipation of married women they were frequently denied the power to make a will, regardless of the degree of intelligence and acumen demonstrated during life.

The capacity to make a will refers to the limits placed upon particular persons in the class generally granted the power to make wills because of personal mental deficiencies. The will of an insane adult is invalid because he did not have the capacity to make a will. Since capacity is a personal matter it is not easy to set down any test which will, in all cases, measure this qualification. A person adjudged insane can, in a lucid period, make a valid will. An aged and enfeebled octogenerian may have the capacity to execute a will. If one rule appears clear, it is that it takes less in the way of mental qualities to meet the test of capacity to make a will than is required for the independent management of one's affairs during lifetime. A deed from X to Y may be set aside because of the incompetence of X although X may validly leave the same property to Y by will. Proof that the testator held beliefs not accepted by society in general will not impinge upon his capacity. A firm conviction in reincarnation or a devotion to the precepts of Zoroaster is not of itself inconsistent with the capacity to make a will.

Underlying the notion of capacity is the premise that, in order to be valid, a testator must *intend* a document to be his will. This requisite intent will be lacking if he is insane or suffers from delusions just as intent is presumed to be lacking in persons below the age at which persons generally are given the power to make wills.

Formalities of a Will. By statute, today, in all jurisdictions, a will to be valid must comply with certain formalities. These are necessary not only to indicate that the testator understood what he was doing but, also, to help prevent fraud.

(1) *Writing.* A basic requirement to any valid will is that it be in writing. The only notable exceptions to this rule are found in statutes permitting oral wills by soldiers and sailors and, less frequently, in statutes validating oral wills of personal property made on death bed or in extremis.

The writing may be informal so long as the basic formalities required by the statute are substantially met. Pencil, ink, and mimeograph are equally valid methods and valid wills have been made on scratch paper or on an envelope.

It is also valid to incorporate into a will by reference another document which in itself is not a will for lack of proper execution. To incorporate a memorandum in a will by reference, the following four conditions must exist: (1) it must be in writing; (2)

it must be in existence when the will is executed; (3) it must be adequately described in the will; and (4) it must be described in the will as being in existence. Assume that T dies leaving a will which leaves the residue of his substantial estate in trust "to be delivered by the trustee to such charities" as T "shall designate to his trustee." No charities are named in the will. Upon this fact situation, it has been observed: "The memorandum in the present case was not in existence at the time the will was made, nor was it described in the will as being in existence, but was described as something to be described in the future." Phelps v. La Moille, 52 Ill.App.2d 164, 201 N.E.2d 634. The court held that the intended trust failed. In short, although a memorandum could be used to define and make certain beneficiaries already named in the will, it could not be used as evidence to supply the omitted beneficiaries. A memorandum, not a part of the will, cannot be used to establish the terms and conditions and the requirements of a trust not set forth in the will itself.

(2) *Signature.* A will must be signed by the testator. The signature indicates that the will has been executed and it is a fundamental requirement in almost all jurisdictions. What constitutes a valid signature will vary with local custom and from case to case. The initials "A. H." or "father" at the end of a will is valid if the signature was intended as an execution. On the other hand, a person who makes a couple of strokes of the pen and then stops saying "I can't sign it now" has not made a valid signature.

Most statutes require the signature to be at the end of the will and, even in jurisdictions where this is not specified, careful draftsmanship will so provide to avoid the charge that the portions of a will coming after a signature were written subsequent to the execution and, therefor, without the necessary formality of a signature. Fortunately, legibility is not a prerequisite to a valid signature.

(3) *Attestation*. With the exception of a few isolated types of wills noted later that are valid in a limited number of jurisdictions, a written will must be attested by witnesses. The number and qualification of witnesses and the manner of attestation are generally set out by statute. Usually two and sometimes three witnesses are required. It is good practice to have a will attested by one more than the legal minimum number to increase the likelihood that at least two will be available at the time the will is offered for probate. Similarly, although a witness generally need not be a resident of or domiciled in the jurisdiction of the testator it is not expedient to have witnesses who will not be easily available at probate. Age is no barrier to a witness, provided he is generally competent although, again, for obvious reasons, an elderly person may be a risky witness from an actuarial point of view.

The function of witnesses is to acknowledge that the testator did execute the will and that he had the requisite intent and capacity. It is important, therefore, that the testator sign first in the presence of all the witnesses and it is usually essential that they attest in his presence and the presence of each other.

The most common restriction on a qualified witness is that he must not have any interest in the will he witnesses. This requirement takes at least two forms under statutes. One type of statute disqualifies a witness who is also a beneficiary under the will. The other type voids the share of the interested witness thereby making him a disinterested and qualified witness. What constitutes an "interest" sufficient to disqualify a witness is not always easily defined. The spouse of a beneficiary under a will has been held to be "interested" and thus not qualified. Generally, a person is not disqualified simply because he is named as executor in the will.

The attorney who drafts the will is generally a qualified witness because his function as attorney for the executor will depend entirely upon the free choice of the executor. Nor is usually a member of a church named as a beneficiary nor a shareholder of a corporate executor or trustee under a will so "interested" as to be disqualified. In all cases, however, caution should dictate that the witnesses have not the slightest connection with persons or institutions entitled to share under a will.

(4) *Publication*. It is sometimes said that a testator must declare that a document is his Last Will and Testament and that this should take the form of an oral declaration to the witnesses. This idea stems from the concept that there must be "publication" of a will. It is generally an unnecessary formality.

Undue Influence, Fraud and Mistake. The requisite testamentary intent must always be present in order to create a valid will. Any document purporting to be a will that is the creature of an intent other than the testator's is not a valid will. This is the basis for the rule that a will which transmits property as a result of undue influence or a fraud is no will at all. What constitutes "undue influence" cannot be generally defined. Certainly, a wife can urge her husband to leave all his property to her and, out of love and affection, he will probably accede. This influence is not "undue." Nor is a general influence over the testator sufficient to make a case of improper pressure. The influence must be directed specifically to the act of making the will. Most frequently, the charge of undue influence is made when a testator leaves his property to a person who is not a blood relative, such as a friend who took care of the testator in his last illness or during his last years.

If the evidence demonstrates that the beneficiary under the will was in close contact with the testator and that natural objects of his bounty are ignored in the will, there is a suggestion of undue influence.

The charge of fraud is similar. A dies leaving all his property to B upon the representation by B that he is A's long lost son. B in fact is not A's son. In such a case, the will may be set aside because the misrepresentation was made with the intent that A rely upon it. Fraud sufficient to set aside a will exists where a mother dies willing all her property to one of two daughters because the daughter who takes under the will falsely represented to the mother that the other daughter was scheming to have the mother committed to an institution. The burden of proving undue influence and fraud rests with those who make the allegation, and where a will is in proper form, signed and attested, either of these charges may, as a practical matter, be extremely difficult to establish.

The law is generally not as ready to invalidate or partially revise a will because of mistake as it is to adjust a contract based on an error. A mistake as to the identity of the instrument voids a will. But a stenographic error or a mistake in drafting such as the phrase "40 acres" when the testator meant "80 acres" would not invalidate the bequest or devise.

Revocation. By definition, a will is revocable at the choice of the testator up to the time of his death. Under certain circumstances, a will may be revoked by operation of law. This does not mean that certain formalities are not necessary to effect a revocation. In most jurisdictions, the methods by which a will is revoked are specified by statute. These methods of revocation fall into the following classes:

(1) *Destruction or Alteration of the Will.* Tearing, burning, or otherwise destroying a will is a strong sign that the testator intended to revoke it and, in the absence of a showing that the destruction was inadvertent, this is an effective way of revoking a will. In some States, partial revocation of a will may be accomplished by erasure or obliteration of a part thereof. In no case, however, will a substituted or additional bequest by interlineation be effective without re-execution and re-attestation.

(2) *Later Will.* The execution of a second will does not in itself constitute a revocation of an earlier will. To the extent that the second will is inconsistent, however, with the former will, the first will is revoked. The most certain manner of revocation is the execution of a later will which contains a declaration that all former wills are revoked. In some but not all jurisdictions, a will may be revoked by a written declaration to this effect in a subsequent document such as a letter, even though the document does not meet the formal requirements of a will.

(3) *Operation of Law.* A marriage generally revokes a will executed prior to the marriage. This rule of law is based partly on the reasonable presumption that a person's wishes with respect to his property change with marriage, even though he may neglect to alter a prior will, and partly on the belief that marriage imposes new moral obligations which should not be impaired by a will executed before marriage. Divorce does not necessarily revoke a provision in the will of one of the parties for the benefit of the other party.

Some statutes specifically cover these situations. For example, one State statute provides: "Unless the will expressly provides to the contrary: (1) marriage of the testator revokes a will executed by the testator before the date of the marriage; and (2) divorce or annulment of the marriage of the testator revokes every beneficial devise, legacy, or interest given to the testator's former spouse in a will executed before the entry of the decree of divorce or annulment, and the will shall take effect in the same manner as if the former spouse died before the testator."

(4) *After-Born Children.* The birth of a child after execution of a will may revoke a will at least as far as that child is concerned if it appears that the testator forgot to make a provision for the child. It is for this reason that, occasionally, a nominal sum will be left to a child whom the testator intends to disinherit.

Statutory provisions are frequently to the effect that unless provision is made in a will for a child of the testator born after the will is made or unless it appears by the will that it was the intention of the testator to disinherit the child, the child is entitled to receive the portion of the estate to which he would be entitled if the testator had died intestate, and all devises and legacies shall be shared proportionately thereafter.

Renunciation by Spouse. Statutes provide for a right of renunciation of the will by a surviving spouse and set forth the method of accomplishing it. The purpose of such statutory provisions is to enable the spouse to elect which method of taking, e. g., under the will or under the Statute of Descent, would be most advantageous to him or her. Where a spouse dies owning real and personal property, the surviving spouse has an interest in the decedent's estate which cannot be divested by will, or otherwise, without his consent. The right to renounce a will may be exercised only by persons designated by the statute, and the right conferred on the surviving spouse is personal. A surviving spouse must execute and file a written renunciation of the will within the time prescribed. The right is absolute; and approval of the renunciation or its filing is not required. Upon renunciation of the will, the law determines the share of the estate taken by the survivor.

Ademption and Abatement. In his will, A leaves $5,000 to B, $5,000 to C and "my faithful Collie, Rex" to D. At the time of A's death, after payment of his debts, there is only $5,000 in his estate and a Siamese cat by the name of Queenie, faithful Rex having been disposed of after biting his master. B and C will each receive $2,500 and D will receive nothing, Queenie going to whomever takes the residue of A's estate. The gifts to B and C are said to have abated while the gift to D, not being in existence at the time of A's death, has "adeemed."

Abatement is an occurrence generally resulting from a reduction in the value of the estate of the testator after the execution of his will. It can have serious implications. The first items which abate in a will are all the residue or remainder after provisions for specific devises and legacies. These specific gifts must be satisfied first. Thus, if John, a widower, after making specific gifts, leaves "all the rest, residue and remainder of my estate to my daughter, Mary," Mary may receive a great deal less than her deceased father intended. For example, suppose at the time John executes his will he estimates his worth at $150,000. He leaves $20,000 to his church and $20,000 to the Salvation Army and he assumes that Mary will receive approximately $110,000. John dies five years later without changing his will but having suffered substantial business and market reverses. His executor reports that there is only $50,000 in the estate. Mary will receive $10,000 less than each of the charitable bequests and only a fraction of what her father expected her to enjoy. Unless the specific bequests are small or the testator has confidence in the stability of his estate, specific bequests to persons outside his family or to institutions should be based on a percentage of the net estate of the decedent.

Ademption may not be as serious as abatement but the consequences may be regrettable. It occurs when a testator neglects to change his will after changed circumstances have rendered impossible of performance a provision in the will. X buys a farm "Blackacre" and wants it to go on his death to a favorite nephew who is studying agronomy at college. After so providing in his will, he sells "Blackacre" and, with the purchase price, buys "Greenacre." The general rule is that the nephew will not be entitled to Greenacre. More difficult problems can be easily imagined. Ademption is always a question of trying to determine the testator's intent. Did he want the legatee or devisee to have *that* particular item and no other? If X leaves "my 200 shares of General Motors stock" to Y and at his death he has no such securities, his executor will not be authorized to purchase 200 shares and give them to Y. But, if X leaves "my 100 shares of Southern Commonwealth stock" to Y and, upon his death, he has only 50 shares of Eastern Commonwealth, Southern having merged therewith and a 1 for 2 stock reorganization having transpired, Y will be entitled to the 50 shares.

Capacity to Take Under a Will. The power of the sovereign to restrict the right to dispose of property at death is exercised not only by affirmative regulations governing the method of passing property at death but also by imposing limits upon the receipt of such property.

Special Types of Wills. (1) *Nuncupative Wills.* A nuncupative will is an oral declaration made before witnesses without any writing. In the jurisdictions where authorized, generally it can only be made when the testator is in his last illness. Under most statutes permitting nuncupative wills only personal property may be passed by such a will. An abortive attempt to make a written will in which the testator gives oral directions generally will not be recognized as a nuncupative will. The intent must be to make a nuncupative will.

(2) *Holographic Wills.* In some jurisdictions, a will entirely in the handwriting of the testator is a valid testamentary document notwithstanding the fact that the will is not witnessed. Such an instrument is referred to as a holographic will. Printing of any kind on the paper will invalidate such a will. Thus, a holographic will cannot be written on hotel stationery or on a pad of paper that has even part of a date printed on it if dating is essential to a valid will in the jurisdiction. A holographic will must comply strictly with the statutory requirements for such wills.

(3) *Soldiers' and Sailors' Wills.* In the case of soldiers on active service and sailors while at sea most statutes relax the formal requirements surrounding wills and permit a valid testamentary disposition regardless of the informality of the document. In most jurisdictions, however, such a will cannot pass title to real estate.

(4) *Conditional Wills.* A contingent or conditional will is one which takes effect as a will only on the happening of a specified contingency which is a condition precedent to the operation of the will. If a contingency is referred to in a will as a reason for making the particular disposition that is provided for, and the disposition and the contingency are so related that the one is dependent on the other, the will is contingent, but the language must clearly show an intention to make a will which will operate only during a certain period or until a certain emergency has passed, and whether a particular will is conditional or is unconditional is largely dependent upon the factual situation presented. For example, X executed an instrument, properly witnessed, at 2:00 A.M., reading: "I am leaving for New York State this morning, and if anything should happen to me I request that everything I own, both personal and real, be given to my sister, Z." The will was held to be unconditional.

(5) *Joint Wills—Mutual or Reciprocal Wills.* A joint will is one where the same instrument is made the will of two or more persons and is signed by them jointly. Mutual or reciprocal wills are the separate instruments of two or more persons, the terms being reciprocal and by which each testator

makes testamentary disposition in favor of the other.

Codicil. A codicil is an addition to or revision of a will, generally by a separate instrument, in which the will is expressly referred to and, in effect, incorporated into the codicil, by reference. Generally, codicils must be executed with all the formal solemnities of a will. The most frequent and difficult problem raised by codicils is the extent to which their terms, if not absolutely clear, revoke or alter provisions in the will. For the purpose of determining the testator's intent, the codicil and the will are regarded as a single instrument.

Intestate Succession and Administration of Estates. When a person dies the title to his property must pass to someone; the law insists that the title to property be somewhere. If the decedent leaves a valid will, property will pass as he directs, subject only to certain limitations imposed by the State, such as the widow's right to dower. If, however, no valid will has been executed, the decedent is said to have died "intestate" and the State prescribes who shall be entitled to the property.

The rules set forth in statutes for determining, in case of intestacy, to whom the decedent's property shall descend and be distributed not only assure an orderly transfer of title to property but, also, purport to carry out what would probably be the wishes of the decedent.

The fact that the rules of descent are statutory reflects the dominant principle recognized in most jurisdictions that inheritance is a privilege granted by the sovereign and may, therefore, be regulated by it. The State may, at any time, change the rules. If A expects to be the heir of B upon the latter's death, it is within the constitutional power of the State to change the rules *before* B's death in such a way that A would not fall within the class designated as heirs. Until the death

of B, A has no vested property right that the constitution will protect. Similarly, it would be legally possible, no matter how unlikely, that a State might provide that, after the payment of the debts of a decedent, all his intestate property should be public property, or that intestate property should pass to persons other than the next of kin.

Personal Property and Real Property. As noted in Chapter 45, one distinction between real and personal property is the manner of its descent upon death. This distinction is likewise statutory and varies from State to State. It used to be, under the common law, that title to the personal property of an intestate passed immediately to his personal representative while his real estate descended directly to his heirs. This distinction no longer has much practical significance and, in some States, by statute, it has been eliminated. The important difference between the two is that, in most States, the debts of the decedent must be first satisfied out of his personal property and, in some instances, this is the rule even where a debt is secured by a mortgage on real estate.

Property which Descends. Any present vested interest in property will descend to heirs. A vested remainder which is not reduced to possession because the remainderman dies before the life tenant will nevertheless pass to the heirs of the former and may be possessed by such heirs when the life tenant dies.

Course of Descent. The rules of descent vary widely from State to State but, as a general rule, and always excepting the specific statutory or dower rights of the widow, the intestate property passes in equal shares to each child of the decedent. One method is to provide that, if A dies intestate leaving a widow and children, the widow will receive one-third of the real estate (in fee or for life) and one-half the personal property, and all the rest of the real and personal property passes to the children equally. If the widow does not survive A, all the property goes to the children. If A dies leaving two children, B and C, and grandchildren D_1 and D_2 the children of a predeceased child D, the estate will go one-third to B, one-third to C and one-sixth each to D_1 and D_2, the grandchildren dividing equally their parent's equal share. This result is legally described by the statement that lineal descendants take property per stirpes or that lineal descendants of predeceased children take by representation of their parent. If, in the example, A had executed a will, he might have provided that all his lineal descendants, regardless of generation, would share equally. In that case, given the above example, A's estate would have been divided into four equal parts and the descendants would be said to take per capita.

If no children but only the widow and other relatives survive the decedent, a larger share is generally allotted the widow. She may then receive all the personal property and one-half the real estate or, in some States, all the real estate.

Regardless of who the other relatives are, whether children, brothers, parents or cousins of the deceased, the surviving widow cannot, without her consent, be cut off from her dower or statutory share.

At common law, property could not lineally ascend; parents of an intestate decedent did not, in any event, share in his estate. Today, in many States, if there are no lineal descendants, the statute provides that parents are the next to share.

Most statutes make some provision for brothers and sisters in the event no spouse, parents or children survive the decedent. These, together with nieces, nephews, aunts and uncles are termed collateral heirs. Beyond these limits most statutes provide that, if there are no survivors of the named classes, the property shall be distributed equally among the next of kin in equal degree.

The common law did not consider a step-child as an heir or next of kin; that is, as one to whom property would descend by operation of law, and this rule prevails today in nearly all jurisdictions. Legally adopted children are, however, recognized as lawful heirs of their adopting parents.

These generalities should be accepted as such; few fields of the law of property are so strictly a matter of statute, and the rights of heirs cannot be reasonably predicted without a knowledge of the exact terms of the applicable statute.

The one impression that the layman should take with him from even a brief glance at the law of intestate succession is the complete abdication of his control over disposition of his property that results from the failure to execute a will. In some cases, intestacy may result from an intelligent analysis of the consequences, but most frequently when a person dies without a will he has left to the State the decision as to who shall receive his estate.

ADMINISTRATION OF ESTATES

Introductory. Whether a man dies intestate or leaves a valid will it is obvious that an efficient and impartial method must exist to protect his creditors and to carry out his testamentary instructions or determine who is entitled to his property under the applicable rules of descent. The rules and procedures controlling the management of the estate of a deceased are statutory and therefore vary in some respect from State to State. In all jurisdictions, the estate is managed and finally disbursed under the supervision of a court. The procedure of managing the estates of decedents is referred to as "probate" and not infrequently the court which supervises the procedure is designated as the Probate Court.

The Executor and the Administrator. The first legal step after death is usually to determine whether or not the deceased left a will. His personal attorney may have the will or may know that one was executed; sometimes the existence or absence of a will is not determined until after a careful search of the safe deposit box and personal papers of the deceased.

If a will exists, it is probable that in it the testator named his widow, a friend or a trust company as his executor.

If there is no will, or if there is a will which fails to name an executor, the court will, upon petition, appoint an administrator. The closest adult relative who is a resident of the State is entitled to such office. In the event there is no one else who qualifies as administrator, the public administrator may fill the office.

An administrator or executor is required to post a bond to insure the faithful performance of his duties, although, if a testator directs that the executor need not post bond, this will be accepted by the court in most cases. Usually, this bond is an amount in excess of the estimated value of the personal estate of the decedent. Once approved or appointed by the court, it is the executor or administrator who holds title to all the personal property of the deceased and who accounts to the creditors and the beneficiaries. The estate is his responsibility.

Preliminary Steps in Probate. If there is a will, it must be proved before the court by the witnesses. They will usually testify as to the mental condition of the testator. If the witnesses are dead, proof of their handwriting is necessary. If the court is satisfied that the will is proved, a formal decree will be entered admitting the will to probate.

Proof of heirship is required whether there is a will or whether the decedent died intestate. This step requires testimony by any relative who is acquainted with the genealogy of the family as to the heirs of the decedent. This testimony is obviously necessary where

there is no will in order to establish those entitled under law to the property of the decedent. If there is a will, proof of heirship is required so that heirs may be notified in order to protect their interests. By custom, in most jurisdictions, the proof of heirship is made up partly of first-hand knowledge and partly of hearsay.

Soon after the admission of the will to probate or the issuance of letters of administration, the personal representative of the decedent (i. e., the executor or administrator) must file an inventory of the estate. Frequently, independent appraisers must be appointed to value the personal assets.

A bank account will be opened in the name of the estate, and the personal representative will commence his duties of collecting the assets, paying the debts and disbursing the remainder. In his position the executor or administrator occupies a fiduciary position not unlike that of a trustee and his responsibility for investing proceeds and otherwise managing the estate is equally demanding.

Creditors; Widow's Award. One of the first duties of the personal representative is to publish a notice that all claims against the decedent's estate must be filed and proved within a certain period of time. It is the duty of the personal representative to demand proof of the claims and pay those which are valid. In most jurisdictions, certain claims are entitled to priority over the general creditors of the decedent. At the top of these preferred claims are estate and inheritance taxes which are discussed hereafter. By statute, the widow is entitled to a cash allowance pending final disposition of the estate and this "widow's award" is regarded as a preferred debt of the estate. After settlement of these obligations and the funeral expenses, the general creditors of the decedent will be satisfied before any amounts are paid to beneficiaries or heirs.

Assets. Corporate securities, government obligations, and items of personal use are all part of the assets of the decedent which pass into the hands of the personal representative. The personal representative may exercise the same powers incident to the ownership of such property as the decedent might have exercised during his life. Thus, the personal representative may vote stock owned by the decedent or exercise conversion privileges attached to such securities.

Insurance on the life of the decedent passes directly to the named beneficiary and does not go into his estate unless payable to his executor or the estate itself. Thus, insurance will not be available to pay the debts of the decedent if it is payable directly to a named beneficiary other than the personal representative.

Estate and Inheritance Taxes. Taxes are imposed at death by both the Federal government and the State. It is the responsibility of the executor or administrator to pay these taxes. It is also his responsibility to file an income tax return and pay the tax not only for the partial year immediately preceding the death of the testator or intestate but also on the income received by the estate during its administration.

(1) *Federal Estate Tax.* The Federal government imposes a tax upon the total value of the estate, less a specific exemption of $60,-000, the valid debts and the expenses of administration of the estate. This is a tax upon the estate itself, not upon the beneficiaries, and it is not generally affected by the character of a bequest or the relationship of the beneficiary to the decedent except in two important respects: A gift to a charity recognized as such by the Treasury Department will be deductible from the total estate for tax purposes. Secondly, an amount not to exceed fifty per cent of the adjusted gross estate will be allowed as a marital deduction and not be subjected to estate tax provided the decedent

left at least such amount to his or her surviving spouse. Thus, if X bequeaths or leaves to his wife his entire estate valued at $120,-000, the marital deduction of one-half of the estate and the $60,000 Federal estate tax exemption applied to the other half leaves no taxable estate. If the estate after providing for claims and expenses were valued at $200,-000, upon taking the marital deduction and the specific exemption, the amount of the taxable estate would be $40,000 to which the prevailing rates would apply to determine the amount of tax payable. The "marital deduction" allows to residents of all of the States for tax purposes the benefits of the doctrine of community property which is law in some of the western and southwestern States. It applies only between spouses. If, in the above example X were unmarried at the time of his death and left an estate of $120,000 after payment of all allowed claims and expenses, upon applying the exemption, $60,000 would be subject to an estate tax. If the amount of X's estate were $200,000, and X died unmarried, his taxable estate would be $140,000.

(2) *State Inheritance Tax.* The inheritance tax imposed by the State is imposed upon the *recipient* of a bequest or legacy and not upon the estate itself. The tax rate is graduated according to the relationship of the beneficiary to the decedent, a close member of decedent's family paying less than a stranger. Thus, in one jurisdiction, assuming two bequests of $50,000, with exemptions but no deductions, one to the wife and one to a family friend, the wife would pay $600 inheritance tax, and the friend, $5,588.

The inheritance tax is in addition to the Federal estate tax. It is not unusual, however, for the testator to provide that all taxes, including the inheritance tax, shall be paid by his estate, thus permitting the recipient of a specified sum of money to receive and retain the entire amount of the bequest.

CASES

IN RE COSGROVE'S ESTATE

(1939) 290 Mich. 258, 287 N.W. 456, 125 A.L.R. 410.

CHANDLER, J. On October 6, 1937, Augustus M. Cosgrove called at the office of Willamena Young, manager of Michigan Title Company abstract office in the city of Grand Haven. He carried with him a six page document written by himself in pencil. Except for signature, attestation clause and subscription of witnesses, the document was in form a will by the terms of which the testator's real and personal property were to be distributed.

Mr. Cosgrove said: "Miss Young, will you copy this will for me?" and she replied, "Yes, I will." He then gave her his tax receipts and requested that she check the property descriptions in the will against the descriptions in the abstract office records. When she indicated that she was too busy to typewrite the will that day, he told her to do it at her own time and added that he was going to Ohio. Miss Young asked, "Would you like to sign this will in case anything should happen?" Mr. Cosgrove answered, "Yes, I would, Miss Young, and that is a good suggestion." Thereupon, he signed the instrument before Miss Young and another woman, and the latter persons subscribed their names as witnesses thereto. In Mr. Cosgrove's presence, Miss Young filled in the date in ink and wrote the attestation clause, whereupon Mr. Cosgrove left the office.

Subsequently, Miss Young made a typewritten copy of the will. After Mr. Cosgrove returned from Ohio, he informed her that he would come to her office and sign the typewritten copy of the will, but before having done so, he became ill and died on November 15, 1938.

The pencil draft of the will was admitted to probate in the probate court against the ob-jections of the heirs at law. The heirs at law now appeal from the decision of the circuit court, which also admitted the document for probate as the last will and testament of Augustus M. Cosgrove, deceased.

The decisive question is whether Mr. Cosgrove intended at the time he executed the document in question for it to operate as a testamentary disposition of his property.

It is the theory of the contestants that the document which the deceased executed was not intended by him to be his will, but was merely to serve as a memorandum for the guidance of Miss Young in typing the will in final form. Although this may have been his original intention, from the record it seems clear that at the time the deceased executed the instrument, he did so with testamentary intent. * * *

The record shows that the deceased handed Miss Young the paper in question with a request that she check the real estate descriptions therein and then typewrite a copy of the same for his signature. This document was entitled "Will" and began as follows:

"I, August M. Cosgrove of the city of Grand Haven in the county of Ottawa and State of Michigan, being of sound mind and memory and understanding do make my last will and testament in manner and form following."

It cannot be argued that the document did not contain the provisions he desired to have therein. It was written in his own handwriting and was complete in form except for signature, attestation, and the name of the executor. But it is claimed that Mr. Cosgrove did not intend this specific document to operate as his will. The testimony of Miss Young indicates that he signed the document at her suggestion because he was going away before the final draft would be prepared, just in case "anything should happen." No fraud or undue influence in procuring the testator's signature is alleged and Mr. Cosgrove stated that signing the will was "a good suggestion."

In our opinion the signature by the testator of his pencil draft and the attestation of witnesses in his presence indicated a change of purpose by him to have the draft operate as his last will and testament pending execution of the typewritten copy. * * *

The judgment is affirmed.

IN RE ESTATE OF WILLIAMS

(1965 Fla.) 182 So.2d 10.

O'CONNELL, J. The District Court of Appeal, Third District, has certified to us, as passing upon a question of great public interest, its decisions in In re Williams Estate, Fla.App.1965, 172 So.2d 464, and In re Estate of Zarkey, Fla.App.1965, 172 So.2d 465.

In each of these cases the county judge refused to admit to probate a will signed by the testator with a mark, similar to an X, on the ground that the making of a mark was not sufficient signing of the will under the provisions of F.S. Section 731.07, F.S.A. On appeal the district court affirmed the county judge in each case. The factual circumstances in both cases are so similar as to require no discussion.

The single issue for decision is whether, under the wording of Sec. 731.07, a testator may execute his will by making his mark, as distinguished from writing his alphabetical name. The county judges and the district court held that a will could not be validly executed in this manner. We cannot agree.

The pertinent portions of the controlling statute read:

"731.07 Execution of Wills.—Every will, other than a nuncupative will, must be in writing and must be executed as follows:

"(1) The testator must sign his will at the end thereof, or some other person in his presence and by his direction must subscribe the name of the testator thereto.

"(2) The testator, in the presence of at least two attesting witnesses present at the same time, must sign his will or cause his name to be signed as aforesaid or acknowledge his signature thereto."

We are here concerned only with the requirement that the "testator must sign his will at the end thereof * * *." The county judges and the district court were of the view that in order to "sign" the testator must write his alphabetical name. The respondents, of course, agree with this, while the petitioners argue that one may "sign" by making his mark.

In the construction of any statute it is always our duty to give effect to the legislative intent where such is ascertainable. However, we find nothing in the statute itself which gives support to either of the definitions urged to be given the word "sign."

This being so, we think we must then decide in that way which gives effect to the will of the testators involved unless some countervailing factor of public policy prevents.

We are surprised that the question here presented is one of first impression in this state. The only Florida case dealing with the question of signing by mark is Bruner v. Hart, 1910, 59 Fla. 171, 51 So. 593, in which this court held that a witness to a deed could subscribe as a witness by affixing his mark, rather than by writing his alphabetical name. In so holding this court stated that a person could witness by mark unless such method was forbidden by statute and noted that the applicable statute did not forbid a witness "subscribing his name by making his mark." A witness to a will is now required to actually sign his name to the will. [Citation.]

It is interesting to note that in Bruner v. Hart, supra, the two grantors also signed the questioned deed by mark. Surprisingly the deed was not attacked on this ground. This would seem to indicate that the parties in that case conceded that a grantor could "sign" by mark, but questioned only whether a witness could "subscribe" by mark. It is not unreasonable to assume that a like and widely held concession that a testator could sign his will by mark may account for the fact that no case in point has previously been presented to the appellate courts of this state.

We have carefully read the three cases cited by this court in support of the holding in Bruner v. Hart that a witness could subscribe by mark. Two of the cited cases decided that a witness to a will could subscribe as an attesting witness by mark. Garrett v. Heflin, 1893, 98 Ala. 615, 13 So. 326; and Pridgen v. Pridgen's Heirs, 1852, 13 Ired. 259, 35 N.C. 259. In the Pridgen case that court discussed the early English cases and statutes dealing with the execution of wills, explained that the word "signum" (from which our word sign is derived) meant no more than a mark, and expressed the view that sign and subscribe meant essentially the same thing when used in a statute. This seems to be the prevailing view in this country.

There can be no doubt that the effect of this court's decision in Bruner v. Hart is that a person can meet the statutory mandate of subscribing his name by making his mark rather than writing his alphabetical name. If there is a difference in meaning in the words "sign" and "subscribe" it is that "subscribe" is more limited than "sign." This logically leads to the conclusion that if one can subscribe by making his mark he can certainly sign by the same means. We so hold.

The great majority of the courts which have dealt with cases like these involving similar statutes hold as we do here, that a mark made by the testator at the proper place on his will with the intent that it constitute his signature and evidence his assent to the will is sufficient to satisfy the statutory requirement that he "sign" his will. [Citations.]

We have not ignored respondent's contention that public policy, which is to protect testators and their heirs from fraud, would be best served by refusing to accept as properly executed under the statute a will signed by the testator with only his mark. In support of this contention respondents argue that it is impossible for handwriting experts to determine the authenticity of a mark as might be done with a handwritten alphabetical name. They also argue that if a testator cannot write his name and is not permitted to sign by mark, he will be forced to have another person subscribe his name for him. This they say will be added protection because a person requested to sign the name of another will not be likely to do so without first determining the identity of the purported testator.

It is true that even a handwriting expert would have difficulty determining who made a mark in the absence of distinguishing characteristics by which certain comparisons can reasonably be made. If proof of the execution of a will rested entirely upon the identification of the mark or signature of the testator the respondents' argument would be difficult to overcome. But such is not the case. The greatest protection against fraud, and the greatest aid in proof that a testator did in any manner sign his will as his, is furnished by the statutory requirement that it be done in the presence of, or acknowledged in the presence of, at least two attesting witnesses.

Furthermore, the alternative method for the execution of a will, by which some other person may subscribe the testator's name, really seems to offer even less protection than the testator's mark.

This is so because the statute does not require the person signing for the testator to be identified in the document. True, a careful lawyer supervising the execution of a will would see that such person's identity was reflected in some manner at the end of the will. Nevertheless, the statute does not require it nor does it prescribe how it shall be made known that the testator's name was subscribed by another or how such person is to be identified in the document.

Therefore, we fail to see how fraud on testators would be prevented in any meaningful way by a holding that our statute requires that a person must either subscribe his alphabetical name or have another person to do so for him. Rather, we hold, as do most jurisdictions, that a testator may "sign" his will by making a mark. It is a matter of fact to be proved in proper proceedings whether the testator made the mark with the intention that it evidence his assent to the document.

If this cause accomplishes nothing more than to call attention to the inadequacies of Section 731.07(1) and (2) it will have served a useful purpose. We have no doubt that the appropriate committees of The Florida Bar and the Legislature will give attention to making the changes which are necessary to make clear whether a person should be able to sign his will by mark, and to prescribe the formalities to be followed and recorded as a part of the will when the testator signs by mark or another person subscribes the name of the testator at the testator's direction.

For the reasons given above the decisions of the district court are reversed and the cause remanded for further proceedings consistent herewith.

It is so ordered.

CHAMBERS v. YOUNES

(1966) 240 Ark. 428, 399 S.W.2d 655.

JOHNSON, J. This appeal is from denial of a petition to set aside probate of a will.

On September 24, 1962, Boyd Ruff died leaving surviving his wife, no issue, three brothers and a sister. After his funeral Mrs. Ruff found in his wallet a blank check on the back of which was written a purported holographic will. On March 13, 1964, Modene Ruff, the widow, filed a petition in Searcy Probate Court for admission of the instrument to probate as a will, nominating appellee Rex Younes as administrator with will annexed. On March 14th instrument was admitted to probate and letters of administration issued to appellee on March 19, 1964.

On September 11, 1964, appellant Lois R. Chambers, sister of decedent, filed a petition to set aside the will on the grounds that (1) on its face it was not a valid holographic will, (2) it did not show a valid intent to make a will, and (3) that it did not show it was executed with the lawful testamentary intent, and prayed for dismissal of probate and distribution of the estate according to the laws of descent and distribution. Decedent's three brothers did not join in this contest.

At trial the court admitted extrinsic evidence in support of the will over the objection of appellant. From the decree of May 12, 1965, finding the instrument to be a valid holographic will and the last will and testament of Boyd Ruff, and dismissing appellant's petition, comes this appeal.

Appellant has prefaced her argument with the statement that it is not disputed that the words written on the instrument were in the handwriting of the decedent, nor is it disputed that the handwriting was proven in accordance with the applicable statute on proving holographic wills, and further, there is no question of competency or undue influence.

The instrument in controversy reads simply as follows:

"I Boyd Ruff request that all I own in the way of personal or real estate property to be my wife Modene.

"Boyd Ruff"

The statute on holographic wills is Ark. Stat.Ann. § 60–404 (Supp.1965):

"Where the entire body of the will and the signature thereto shall be written in the proper handwriting of the testator, such will may be established by the evidence of at least three credible disinterested witnesses to the handwriting and signature of the testator, notwithstanding there may be no attesting witnesses to such will."

The statute on testimony to prove a will is Ark.Stat.Ann. § 62–2117 (Supp.1965):

"A will shall be proved as follows:

*   *   *

b.   A holographic will:

By the testimony of at least three credible disinterested witnesses proving the handwriting and signature of the testator, and such other facts and circumstances as would be sufficient to prove a controverted issue in equity."

For reversal appellant urges that the trial court erred in admitting extrinsic evidence to prove testamentary intent.

This precise question has not been directly answered by this court in any of the multitude of cases on Arkansas holographic wills. A section in 94 C.J.S. Wills § 203, p. 1038, however, discusses our holdings and reflects our persuasion:

"Testamentary intent is necessary to the validity of a holographic will. [Citations.] No particular words are necessary to manifest the animo testandi; thus, the paper need not refer to itself as a will. * * * The fact that the holographic instrument concerns itself with matters other than the disposition of property will not nullify its effect as a will, but it may be considered in determining the intent of the writer [Cartwright v. Cartwright, 158 Ark. 278, 250 S.W. 11]. *Inquiry may be made into all relevant circumstances where the existence of testamentary intent is in doubt*." [Emphasis ours.]

Review of our cases clearly indicates that our courts have customarily admitted extrinsic testimony to establish testamentary intent, without considering whether the statute on proof of a holographic will (§ 62–2117, *supra*) expressly permits such testimony. Perusal of Arendt v. Arendt, 80 Ark. 204, 96 S.W. 982, and Weems v. Smith, 218 Ark. 554, 237 S.W.2d 880, and the letters therein held to be valid holographic wills, it is apparent that extrinsic testimony was necessary to fortify the finding of existence of testamentary intent. We think this is proper. As was said in Arendt v. Arendt, supra:

"This will is in the form of a letter from William Arendt to his wife. But, to quote the language of a distinguished author, 'the law has not made requisite to the validity of a will that it should assume any particular form, or be couched in language technically appropriate to its testamentary character. It is sufficient that the instrument, however irregular in form or inartificial in expression, discloses the intention of the maker respecting the posthumous destination of his property; and, if this appear to be the nature of its contents, any contrary title or designation which he may have given to it will be disregarded.' 1 Jarman on Wills (6 Ed.) 21; Whyte v. Pollack, 7 Appeal Cases, 409."

"There are many decisions that illustrate this rule of law. The Supreme Court of California held that a writing in the following language was a will, and admitted it to probate: 'Dear Old Nance: I wish to give you my watch, two shawls, and also five thousand dollars. Your old friend, E. A. Gordon.' Clarke v. Ransom, 50 Cal. 595.

"So the Supreme Court of North Carolina held the following unattested writing to be a will: 'It is my wish and desire that my good friend and relative, Dr. Joseph B. Outlaw, have all my property of every description. David Outlaw.' Outlaw v. Hurdle, 46 N.C. [1 Jones, Law] 150. The same court in a much more recent case held that a letter from the testator to his sister, in which he said: 'If I die or get killed in Texas, the place must belong to you, and I would not want you to sell it,' was a valid will. Alston v. Davis, 118 N.C. 202, 24 S.E. 15.

"There are many other cases to the same effect. [Citations.]

"The evidence proves that William Arendt was sincerely attached to his wife, and the language of this letter to her, written under the shadow of impending death, shows in our opinion, that it was testamentary in character and intended to direct the disposition of his property after his death, and we are of the opinion that the circuit court properly so held."

Appellant's second point urged for reversal is that the instrument, on its face, fails to show that it was testamentary in character and executed with testamentary intent. Our ruling on the first point, i. e., that inquiry may be made into all relevant circumstances where the existence of testamentary intent is in doubt, disposes also of this point.

Appellant's final point is that the evidence of the circumstances surrounding the execution of the instrument is insufficient to show that the instrument was testamentary in character or that it was executed with the necessary testamentary intent. The probate court found decedent had a serious coronary condition which he knew about, and was aware that his life might be terminated on pretty short order, that the parties had been married for many years, had no children, lived together and got along well, the decedent's wife was the natural object of his bounty, and that the will was executed within a fairly short time prior to his death following another severe heart attack, and, finally, that the instrument was the valid and last will of decedent. Review of the record reveals no testimony which fails to support these findings, and judgment of the trial court is therefore affirmed.

STELLY v. STELLY

(1965 La.App.) 175 So.2d 829.

SAVOY, J. Appellants have appealed to this Court from a judgment of the district court decreeing the last will and testament of Cloma Stelly to be valid.

Cloma Stelly departed this life at her domicile in Vermilion Parish, Louisiana, on January 6, 1964, leaving surviving her only collateral heirs. Her will was duly probated in Vermilion Parish, Louisiana, * *. Shortly thereafter, appellants filed the instant suit to have the will declared invalid because (1) of the mental incapacity of the testatrix at the time of the confection of the will; (2) the will was obtained through fraudulent practices by appellees; (3) the will was not written in the form prescribed by law, in that same is typewritten rather than in writing, and also because of the improper declaration as to the reason for the testatrix not signing said will and testament.

There was no showing that fraud was practiced on the testatrix in order to have her execute the will in question.

Appellants took the deposition of Dr. Charles A. Barne, Jr., a medical doctor, who treated the testatrix during her last illness shortly before her death. In summary, the doctor testified he was of the opinion that she was of sound mind and was able to make a will and testament. He stated that although she had suffered a stroke, she had progressed well until shortly prior to her death; and, except for the infirmities which go with old age, she was approximately 77 when he first saw her and 79 years of age when she died, she was mentally alert.

Mr. I. P. Saal, Jr., Notary Public and attorney at law, testified without objection that he was called to the testatrix's house on the night the will was executed; that he went there with his secretary and brought along his typewriter and legal size blank paper. Prior to preparing the will, he asked the testatrix to sign her name, and she stated that because of her illness she was unable to write her name legibly. This was done in the presence of one of the witnesses to the will.

The notary then assembled in the testatrix's room with the witnesses and proceeded to prepare a will by nuncupative act. He ended the will with the following declaration:

"The Testator, Cloma Stelly, declared that she knows how to read and write, but at the present time she is unable to sign her name for the reason that she is ill, and her signature would be illegible if she attempted to sign her name."

Counsel for appellants have abandoned all of their reasons for declaring the will invalid except two, namely, that the requirements of LSA–C.C. Article 1578 have not been complied with, and that the above declaration in the will does not satisfy the requirements of LSA–C.C. Article 1579.

Articles 1578 and 1579 of the Louisiana Civil Code state:

"Art. 1578. Nuncupative testament by public act, formalities

"Art. 1578. The nuncupative testaments by public act must be received by a notary public, in presence of three witnesses residing in the place where the will is executed, or of five witnesses not residing in the place.

"This testament must be dictated by the testator, and written by the notary as it is dictated.

"It must then be read to the testator in presence of the witnesses.

"Express mention is made of the whole, observing that all those formalities must be fulfilled at one time, without interruption, and without turning aside to other acts."

"*   *   *   *   *   *

"Art. 1579. Nuncupative testament by public act, signature of testator

"Art. 1579. This testament must be signed by the testator; if he declares that he knows not how, or is not able to sign, express mention of his declaration, as also of the cause that hinders him from signing, must be made in the act."

As to the invalidity of the will because of non-compliance with LSA–C.C. Art. 1578, counsel state that Mr. Saal, the notary to the will, did not test the ability of the testatrix to sign her name in the presence of all the witnesses as required by that Civil Code article. * * *

There is no showing in the record that the portion of the will in contest was not written, dated, read and signed at one and the same time without interruption as required by LSA–C.C. Article 1578.

As to the nullity of the will because of non-compliance with LSA–C.C. Article 1579, counsel for appellants cite the cases of Succession of Davis v. Richardson, 226 La. 887, 77 So.2d 524, and Succession of Watson, (La. App., 4 Cir., 1963), 157 So.2d 612. Both of these cases involved contested wills. In each case the testament recited that the testatrix signed the will by making her mark with an "X" and also stated that she could not sign because of physical disability. Both wills were declared valid. The appellate courts in both cases stated that they were cognizant of decisions interpreting LSA–C.C. Article 1579 which indicated that it was desirable to state the exact nature of the testator's disability, but found that the courts had uniformly declared said wills containing such a declaration of physical disability sufficient to satisfy the codal requirement.

In our opinion, the testatrix's statement in the nuncupative act that she was unable to sign due to illness is a sufficient compliance with the civil code's requirement for an express statement of the cause of the testatrix's inability to sign the testament. We are cited to no authority to the contrary.

For the reasons assigned, the judgment of the district court is affirmed.

Affirmed.

LAMB v. FORD

(1965) 239 Ark. 339, 389 S.W.2d 419.

McFADDIN, J. This appeal challenges two rulings of the Probate Court made in the administration of the estate of A. R. Ford, who died testate on February 2, 1963. He was survived by his wife, Viva Lamb Ford, and by four children of a former marriage. We will separately discuss the two questions presented.

I.

Dower. The first question relates to the dower claim. Mr. Ford had executed a will on May 25, 1962, when he was a widower. Viva Lamb Ford was not mentioned in the will. He left his entire estate to his four children. Mr. Ford and Viva Lamb Ford were married on December 22, 1962, but he never changed his will. After Mr. Ford's death (which occurred on February 2, 1963) his children met with their stepmother, Viva Lamb Ford, on one or two occasions in an effort to induce her to take one-fifth of the estate in fee rather than her dower interest in the estate. Mrs. Viva Lamb Ford had the matter under consideration, but had given no definite answer, when she was killed in an automobile collision on February 6, 1963. Jones Lamb (appellant) was appointed administrator of her estate, and as such administrator he sought to claim the dower interest of Viva Lamb Ford in the estate of A. R. Ford, deceased. Appellee J. R. Ford, executor of the estate of A. R. Ford, resisted the claim of dower. Trial in the Probate Court resulted in a judgment against the estate of Viva Lamb Ford and this appeal resulted.

We thus have a factual situation wherein: (a) a man made a will which did not mention the lady that he subsequently married; (b) he married; (c) he died; and

(d) then she died without having elected to claim her dower. It is conceded that we do not have a case with a factual situation on all fours with the one at bar. Regardless of how our statutory law and case law may have indicated views prior to the adoption of the Probate Code (being Act No. 140 of 1949), we nevertheless reach the conclusion that, under the provisions of the said Probate Code, the judgment of the Probate Court on this dower matter must be affirmed.

When Mr. Ford executed his will on May 25, 1962, he was a widower and Viva Lamb Ford was not mentioned in his will. His subsequent marriage to Viva Lamb Ford did not operate as a revocation of his will because § 23 of Act No. 140 of 1949 (now found in Ark.Stat.Ann. § 60–407 [Supp. 1963]) reads:

"Change in circumstances; marriage or divorce. If after making a will the testator is divorced, all provisions in the will in favor of the testator's spouse so divorced are thereby revoked. With this exception, no will or any part thereof shall be revoked by any change in the circumstances, condition or marital status of the testator; subject, however, to the provisions of Section 33."

In the above section reference is made to Section 33 of the Act No. 140 of 1949, which may now be found in Ark.Stat.Ann. § 60–501 (Supp.1963); and that section reads:

"When surviving spouse may elect to take against the will.—When a married man dies testate as to any part of his estate, or when a married woman dies leaving as her last will one executed prior to her marriage, the surviving spouse shall have the right to elect to take against the will and to take such part of the property as he or she would have taken had the deceased spouse died intestate."

Furthermore, Section 37 of Act No. 140 of 1949 (as now found in Ark.Stat.Ann. § 60–505 [Supp.1963]) reads:

"Right of election personal to surviving spouse.—The right of election of the surviving spouse is personal. It is not transferable and does not survive the surviving spouse. * * *"

Thus, it is clear that the will of A. R. Ford was not revoked by his subsequent marriage and that Viva Lamb Ford had the right to take against that will, if she so elected; but the right was personal to her and did not survive her. The fact that she died before making any election does not give her estate the right to subsequently make an election: the right of election ended when she died. Her stepchildren met with her on one or two occasions after the death of A. R. Ford to see if she would take a child's part of the estate (that is, one-fifth in fee), rather than her dower part. They evidently assumed—as was perfectly natural to do—that she would elect to take against the will, since she received nothing under the will; and the children were, in effect, offering to trade her a one-fifth fee interest for her dower interest when and if she elected to take dower. But all this intended trade was dependent on her election to take against the will; and she died without ever having made any such election.

Even before the Probate Code (Act No. 140 of 1949), this Court held in Barnes v. Cooper, 204 Ark. 118, 161 S.W.2d 8, that when the wife outlived her husband only thirty minutes, nevertheless her estate could not claim her statutory allowances because she had failed to claim the same in her lifetime. After the adoption of the Code, we held in Jeffcoat v. Harper, 224 Ark. 778, 276 S.W.2d 429, that the right to take against the will was personal. It is argued in the briefs that it was unnecessary for Viva Lamb Ford to make her selection because she would take nothing under the will. Even so, she

would have been required, under our statutes as previously quoted, to take steps in the Probate Court to claim her dower. She never did this, and the right, being personal as fixed by statute, died with her and her estate cannot claim dower in the estate of A. R. Ford. So we affirm the decree of the Probate Court which denied Viva Lamb Ford's estate any dower in the estate of A. R. Ford.

* * *

The judgments of the Probate Court are affirmed on both direct appeal and cross appeal.

IN RE WILL OF BONNER

(1966) 17 N.Y.2d 9, 266 N.Y.S.2d 971, 214 N.E.2d 154.

FULD, J. Merritt Bonner died on October 2, 1963 and, a short time thereafter, a 1959 will which had been cut in two was found among his papers. It was contained in an envelope (bearing the legend "Last Will and Testament of Merritt Bonner") also cut in two, and it seems clear that both will and envelope had been severed at the same time. The separate pieces were enclosed in a larger envelope which, though not produced, bore—according to the legatee-executrix who found it—the words, "My Will", in the decedent's handwriting. The executors named in the instrument offered it for probate. Their petition was opposed by the decedent's father on the ground, among others, that it had been revoked.

Despite objections voiced by the contestant, the proponents were permitted at the hearing to adduce the testimony of two witnesses to the effect that about a year before he died the decedent had stated that he had cut his will by mistake while cutting up old insurance papers. One of these witnesses, the decedent's aunt, assured him that, since he had a copy of the document, its validity remained unimpaired, and, the lady stated, he appeared satisfied with this advice. On the other hand, another witness, called by the contestant, declared that Bonner had repeatedly spoken of his intention to change his will and, in fact, mentioned that he had actually cut it.

The Surrogate, noting that he was attaching no weight to the decedent's reported declarations, concluded, nevertheless, that the will had not been revoked and that it should be admitted to probate. The Appellate Division affirmed without opinion; however, two justices dissented on the ground that the mutilated condition of the will gave rise to a presumption of revocation which was not overcome by evidence of the manner in which the decedent had kept the pieces.

There can be no dispute about the governing rule of law. If a will had been in the custody of the testator and is found among his personal effects, after his death, cut or otherwise mutilated in any of the modes prescribed by statute [citation], there is a presumption that the cutting or mutilation was effected by the testator *animo revocandi*. [Citations.] This presumption may, of course, be overcome by adequate proof to the contrary but such proof does not include the declarations of the decedent designed to establish the continued existence of the will, unless they were made "in connection with some act, under such circumstances as to become a part of the *res gestae*". (Matter of Kennedy's Will, 167 N.Y. 163, 172, 60 N.E. 442, 444.) As we wrote in the Kennedy case, 167 N.Y., at p. 170, 60 N.E. at p. 444, "The whole course of legislation in this state from the earliest times to the present day, concerning the execution and revocation of wills, discloses a clear purpose to * * * sweep away all parol proof of testamentary intentions, and, hence, to exclude statements or declarations of the deceased." [Citations.] Were the rule otherwise, it has been said,

"there would be apt to arise a contest in regard to the number and character of conflicting declarations of the deceased which he could neither deny nor explain, and in the course of which contest great opportunities for fraud and perjury would exist. The statutes as to wills were passed, as we believe, for the very purpose of shutting out all contests of such a character." (Matter of Fox, 9 N.Y.2d, at p. 406, 214 N.Y.S.2d at p. 411, 174 N.E.2d at p. 503, quoting from Throckmorton v. Holt, 180 U.S. 552, 581, 21 S.Ct. 474.)

We adhere to our long-settled rule and, like the courts below, refrain from considering the conflicting reports of the decedent's oral declarations. With such testimony out of the case, the only remaining evidence is that the two pieces of the document were found in an envelope on which he had written the words "My Will". Obviously, such evidence is highly equivocal. The decedent may have kept the will as a record of its provisions or, perhaps, as a model for future testamentary disposition; or, after cutting it in two to effect a revocation, he may have had a change of heart and placed the pieces in the outer envelope with the idea—futile, of course, absent compliance with the statutory requirements [citations]—of reviving the instrument. In short, the proof in the record before us that the decedent retained in an envelope the will which he had cut in two is insufficient, as a matter of law, to overcome the presumption that the mutilation was an act of revocation.

The order of the Appellate Division should be reversed, with costs in all courts to appellant payable out of the estate, and the matter remitted to the Surrogates' Court of New York County for further proceedings in accordance with this opinion.

Order reversed, etc.

IN RE WRIGHT'S WILL

(1960) 7 N.Y.2d 365, 165 N.E.2d 561.

FULD, J. The question posed by this appeal involves the doctrine of ademption. Is a specific legacy adeemed if, although the item bequeathed is missing at the time of the testator's death, its value has been paid to the estate by an insurance carrier?

Claire Wright died in May of 1956. By her will, executed the year before, she bequeathed all her "furs and jewelry, both costume and precious", to Helen Erskine. The testatrix had in 1954 taken out a policy insuring her against the loss of jewelry and furs and in a schedule attached to the policy 27 items were listed, including a diamond ring valued at $4,920 and a gold fountain pen, valued at $75. About a month after the testatrix' death, her executors, following a search of her effects, concluded that the ring and pen were "missing" and some time later filed a proof of loss for those articles. The insurance carrier, accepting the claim, paid the executors $4,920 on account of the ring.

In their account of proceedings, the executors requested instructions as to the disposition to be made of the insurance proceeds. Objections to the accounting were raised by both Helen Erskine and the testatrix' mother, Mary Robinson, one of the residuary legatees. The former claimed, in effect, that the insurance proceeds should be treated as a "specific legacy" and paid to her, while Mrs. Robinson urged that the bequest of the ring had been adeemed and that the insurance moneys constitute part of the residuary estate.

The Surrogate's Court sustained Helen Erskine's objection; reasoning that she was "vested with ownership" of the missing ring, the Surrogate decided that the insurance proceeds belonged to her. Upon an appeal taken by Mrs. Robinson, the Appellate Division took a different view, holding that the specific bequest failed and that the insurance moneys became part of the residuary estate.

As indicated above, we deal with the problem of ademption. Although, in the early days of our law, ademption was based on the intention of the testator, today in New York, as well as in many other jurisdictions, intention has nothing to do with the matter; the bequest fails and the legatee takes nothing if the article specifically bequeathed has been given away, lost or destroyed during the testator's lifetime. [Citations.]

Thus, wrote the court in Matter of Brann, 219 N.Y. 263, 268, 114 N.E. 404, 405, supra, "It was once thought that ademption was dependent on intention, and 'it was, therefore, held in old days that when a change was effected by public authority, or without the will of the testator, ademption did not follow. But for many years, that has ceased to be law' [case cited] * * * What courts look to now is the fact of change. That ascertained, they do not trouble themselves about the reason for the change." The thing given is gone, and a court is not privileged to substitute something else for it. How unimportant the element of intention is, may be gleaned from Matter of Ireland's Estate, 257 N.Y. 155, 177 N.E. 405, 406, supra, where certain stock specifically bequeathed was held to have been adeemed, even though the stock had been sold by the testator's committee after he had become incompetent. This court, after noting that the Appellate Division had declared that "the intention of the testator was the governing factor in the case, and that, as he had become incompetent to change or modify his will, his committee had no power to dispose of his property * * * so as to work an ademption of the legacy", went on to say (257 N.Y. at page 158, 177 N. E. at page 406): "The rule as it existed at common law, and still exists, admits of no such exception. * * * The exact thing which was given by the will could not physically be passed on to the legatee. From the very nature of the case and of the gift, the legacy became extinct. In the absence of statute, there is no power in the courts to change a specific into a general legacy or turn over the balance of the proceeds derived from the sale of the specific property to the legatee in place of the particular thing intended to be given."

What is significant, therefore, is the fact that the precise thing given by the will is not available for disposition at the time of the testator's death, and it matters not whether this came to pass because of an intentional and voluntary act on the part of the testator, such as abandonment, sale or gift, or because of an occurrence involuntary and unintended, such as condemnation, fire or theft. [Citations.]

* * *

As to the further contention advanced by the appellant that the ring was actually a part of the testatrix' estate at the time of her death, it is necessary merely to observe, first, that the burden of proving that is on the person making the claim [citations] and, second, that the appellant failed to meet that burden in this case. In point of fact, not only is there not a word of testimony in the record before us that the ring was held by the testatrix or was among her effects when she died, but there is ample basis for concluding, as the Surrogate himself assumed, that the ring was either lost or stolen prior to her death. Payment of the loss by the insurance company established nothing more than that the carrier was satisfied that the policy covered the ring and that article was missing.

Order affirmed.

McGUINNESS v. BATES

(1963) 345 Mass. 632, 189 N.E.2d 212.

REARDON, J. This is an appeal by four of the legatees under the will of William A. Conley from a decree of the Probate Court for Worcester County. The decree was entered upon a petition for instructions on the distri-

bution of 381 shares of the common stock of American Telephone and Telegraph Company, hereinafter called American. The judge made a report of material facts. The facts are these: The testator executed a will on November 26, 1957. At that time he owned 127 shares of American which was all the stock he had. In early 1959 American split its common stock on a three to one basis and then issued to the testator a certificate representing 254 shares thus making a total of 381 shares held by him until his death.

In his will the testator, after stating in the preamble his desire "to direct how all my property shall be disposed of after my death," made disposition of a portion of his stock in American to ten legatees including the four appellants. The provisions of the will affecting the four appellants and the respondent Rev. Harold F. Conley read as follows: "Fifth. I give, devise, and bequeath to Hannah Kallio three (3) shares of A T & T stock. Sixth. I give, devise, and bequeath to Annie H. Bates twelve (12) shares of A T & T stock." "Eighth. I give, devise, and bequeath to Abel J. Bates six (6) shares of A T & T stock. Ninth. I give, devise, and bequeath to David Kallio six (6) shares of A T & T stock." "Thirteenth. The rest, residue and remainder of my estate whether real, personal or mixed, wheresoever situated I give, devise, and bequeath to my nephew, Rev. Harold F. Conley."

The total number of shares of American bequeathed in the above and other provisions of the will excluding clause Thirteenth was forty-five.

The judge ruled that the bequests of American stock were general legacies and that the additional shares, the product of the "so-called split," fell within the residue. The appellants contend that the legacies to them were specific and that they are entitled to two shares of American in addition to each share left to them respectively in the several clauses of the will. We do not agree. Ordinarily a gift of stock is general. Desoe v. Desoe, 304 Mass. 231, 234, 23 N.E.2d 82. A testator's intent to make a gift specific must prevail "if it can be ascertained from the language of the whole will read in the light of the circumstances known to the testator at the time of its execution, and no positive rule of law forbids." Desoe v. Desoe, supra, 234, 23 N.E. 2d 83. Igoe v. Darby, 343 Mass. 145, 177 N.E.2d 676, is a recent example of the application of that concept, in a determination that gifts of stock made by the testatrix were specific. However, as has been argued by respondent appellee, the testatrix in the Igoe case bequeathed the exact number of shares owned by her at the time of the execution of her will and coupled with each bequest of stock a gift of personal property which was clearly specific. In view of those circumstances, we ruled that each share so bequeathed (also American common stock) became entitled to the additions made available by the stock split. The facts obtaining in the Igoe case are distinguishable from those presented here.

In some situations the use of the word "my" in connection with bequests of stock actually owned by a testator at the time the will is executed might be sufficient to make the legacy specific. [Citations.] But such is not the case here where the testator used the word "my" only in the preamble of the will, and only in reference to the generic term "property." The number of shares he bequeathed represented merely a fraction of the total number he owned when he executed his will. He did not clearly specify except by quantity which shares he intended to bequeath. In sum, reading the will in the light of all the circumstances known to the testator at the time of its execution, the probate judge justifiably and properly concluded that he intended more probably than otherwise to make general rather than specific legacies of his American stock.

Decree affirmed.

KAUFMAN v. KAUFMAN'S ADM'R

(1942) 292 Ky. 351, 166 S.W.2d 860, 144 A.L.R. 866.

[Suit by heirs against administrator of estate of a deceased and his sureties. The defendant had qualified as administrator of estate of his father although he was a farmer with little schooling or experience in financial affairs. He reluctantly agreed to be administrator upon the understanding that he would employ an attorney who would do most of the work. Funds of the estate were entrusted to the attorney, a man of good reputation up to that time, and the funds were embezzled by the attorney. The heirs now seek to hold the administrator and his sureties liable. Judgment for plaintiffs, and defendants appeal.]

STANLEY, COMMISSIONER. * * * The honesty and good faith of the administrator are not questioned. His inexperience and reliance upon the dishonest lawyer is what got him into trouble. Kaufman kept no records or bank account as administrator, but turned everything over to Doolan, including collections he made himself. The attorney deposited the funds in his individual account and gave personal checks for disbursements, including some to the heirs. * * * From time to time he [the administrator] and some of the others asked Doolan about a settlement and he gave some plausible excuse and said the money was drawing interest. Judge Gilbert Burnett, as attorney for one of the heirs, talked with Doolan several times over a period of three years before his exposure and was told that the estate was complicated, requiring the collection of a number of lien notes, which Judge Burnett realized did take time. He testified he and everyone else had confidence in Doolan and his investigation showed the administrator to have a sound surety and he so advised his client. Thus, Doolin lulled the administrator, the heirs, and the attorneys of one of them into inaction for five years.

It is not always easy to describe or discern the liability of executor or administrator or other fiduciary for loss resulting from the negligence or fault of agents or attorneys properly employed or retained by him. The question is essentially one of good faith and reasonable diligence. Where that appears, the acts are treated with indulgence. Mistaken judgment is not enough to impose liability. There is a vague distinction, in general, between the functions and duties of an executor or administrator and a trustee. Bogert on Trusts and Trustees, Sec. 12. But in relation to conditions like the present, there appears to be no distinction within the limitations of fiducial duties of a personal representative. [Citation.] Those duties are to collect and distribute the estate among creditors and heirs in accordance with the statutes or will. The administration involves all that may be done rightfully in the collection and preservation of the assets and the management of the same, with that prudence and diligence which is observed in regard to private affairs by men of reasonable prudence and fair, average capacity. [Citations.] For losses resulting from the failure to exercise that care the representative is personally liable. [Citation.] But this degree of prudence obviously calls for the exercise of administrative discretion, which, in turn, often requires the use of agents and assistants, particularly in the performance of duties of a ministerial nature or of a type the executor or administrator could not reasonably be expected to perform personally. In the instant case there is no doubt that prudence and discretion required the employment of a lawyer as counselor, and, in respect to some of the assets, to his services as an attorney to collect and reduce the same to cash. And it is the generally accepted view that an administrator is not personally liable for loss through his lawyer's misconduct, negligence or non-feasance if he exercised due prudence in the selection of the lawyer.

[Citation.] But this necessary authority cannot extend to the surrender of all the duties of the trust or the delegation of all functions without becoming responsible to distributees for any loss sustained. [Citations.] "The trustee is under a duty to the beneficiary not to delegate to others the doing of acts which the trustee can reasonably be required personally to perform. Thus, he cannot properly commit the entire administration of the trust to an agent or other person unless he is permitted to do so by the terms of the trust." Restatement of Law of Trusts, A. L. I., Sec. 171. If he does that without such permission and loss results he is responsible for it.

Under similar states of fact, it is generally held that an administrator permitting an attorney to retain for several years money of the estate collected by him without any effort to recover it from the attorney is liable for its loss to the estate. [Citations.] It was held to be gross negligence, with consequent liability, in Re Estate of Skeer, 236 Pa. 404, 84 A. 787, 42 L.R.A., N.S., 170, for an administratrix to permit an attorney in fact to handle an estate for nine years without an accounting and settlement, during which time he misappropriated the funds.

*   *   *

The negligence is not confined simply to the act of employing the attorney to collect the notes but in permitting him to assume exclusive control and retain the proceeds and other funds and then by reason of the administrator's supine inaction apply the money to his own use. It is the administrator's course of conduct or the negative violation of his duty in remaining passive and in letting the attorney handle the funds of the estate, commingled with his own, as if they were his own property, and not requiring an accounting and settlement. While Kaufman was not familiar with his duties in respect to managing and settling the estate himself, and rested upon his confidence in the lawyer, he is to be judged by the standard of the average prudent and diligent man in handling his personal affairs. We cannot conceive of such man going along for five years without requiring an accounting from anyone. We concur in the chancellor's decision that the administrator did not, in the language of his bonds, "faithfully perform and discharge all the duties" of his trust. The failure to make the accounting is the essential liability. The defense was properly adjudged insufficient. * * *

[Judgment affirmed except as to certain issues not involved in the foregoing excerpt.]

PROBLEMS

1. George Jones executed a will by which he gave one-third of his entire estate to Arthur Jones, his grandson, and two-thirds of his estate to Grace Brown. The will was attested by William Johnson, the attorney who drew the will, and who, after the will was executed and before the testator's death, married Grace Brown. The will was also attested by Robert Jones, the father of Arthur Jones. The applicable statute provides that every will shall be attested by two or more credible witnesses. Is this will entitled to be admitted to probate?

2. William Brown executed his will, which was duly attested, and which contained the following provision: "I give, devise and bequeath all of my property, real, personal and mixed, to my brothers, George Brown and Henry Brown, and my sisters, Mary Brown and Sarah Jones." After this will was executed, William Brown decided that he did not want his brother, George Brown, to have any interest in his estate so he sent for the two witnesses who had attested the will and told them that he did not want George Brown to have anything and in their presence crossed out with ink the name of George Brown. (a) Should this will be admitted to probate? (b) If admitted to probate, did George Brown take anything under this will?

3. A executed a one-page will, wherein he devised his farm to B. Later, as the result of a quarrel with B, A wrote the words "I hereby cancel and revoke this will /s/A," and nothing more, in the margin of the will, but did not

destroy the will. A then executed a deed to the property, naming C as grantee, and placed the deed and will in his safe. Shortly afterwards, A married D, by whom he had one child, E. Thereafter, A died and the deed and will were found in his safe. B, C, and E claim the fee to the farm and D claims dower. Discuss the validity of each claim.

4. One item of T's will read: "I give to my nephew, B, the note which I now hold in the sum of $5000, payable to my order and signed by C." Before T's death, C's note fell due, and he voluntarily paid it to T, who deposited the money in his bank. At T's death, to what is B entitled under this item?

5. T, a bachelor, made a will giving all of his property to his brother, B. Later, T married C. T died, leaving C, his wife, and D, his only child. T's will was found among his papers at his death. Is this will entitled to probate?

6. The following instrument was offered for probate: "I give, devise and bequeath all of my property, both real and personal, which I may have a right to dispose of at my death, unto my sister, Mary Strong, for life and after her death said property to go to and become vested in the heirs of her body when they reach the age of twenty-five years.

                John Smith (seal)"

"Witnesses:
W. C. Jones
R. C. Brown"

At the hearing on the probate of the will, the two witnesses were called and testified but Mary Strong, who was the only heir-at-law of the testator, objected to the probate of the will for the following reasons: (1) there was nothing on the face of the instrument signed by the witnesses to show that the testator acknowledged said instrument as his will before them or that they saw him sign it, or that they believed him to be of sound mind at the time he signed; (2) it made no provision for the payment of the testator's debts; (3) it did not name an executor. Decide each objection.

7. A obtained a divorce from his wife, B, because she deserted him and their only child, C. He was awarded the custody of C. Later, he married D, a widow with one son, E. A and D had another child, F. A legally adopted G, the child of a deceased friend. E later married and had a son, J. A died intestate, leaving all of the above surviving him except E, who died earlier.

His parents and a brother also survived A. He left a large estate comprising both real and personal property. Who will share in his estate and what fractional interest will they take?

8. Elmer Owens made and executed his will in 1963. At the time of the execution of the will, he had two sons, John and William. His wife had predeceased him. His will provided, among other things, that "the entire estate be divided equally between my sons, John and William, share and share alike." The will was witnessed by his son, John, and by Henry Wentworth. William Owens died intestate in 1964 leaving as his only heir, his daughter, Mary Owens. Henry Wentworth died in 1965. Elmer Owens died in 1966. The will was offered for probate.

(a) Should the will be admitted to probate?

(b) What is the interest of John Owens, if any?

(c) What is the interest of Mary Owens, if any?

9. John owned a 1966 Chriscraft boat, valued at $7,000. In a will dated June 1, 1966, one of many dispositive clauses gave the boat to Peter. During a violent storm on the 4th of July the boat overturned and sank, and John was drowned.

John carried insurance on the boat to the extent of $5,000.

The duly appointed Executor of John's will received the $5,000 from the insurance company. Should he give the money to Peter or consider it as an asset of the estate?

10. The validly executed will of John Dane contained the following provision: "I give and devise to my daughter, Mary, Redacre for and during her natural life and, at her death the remainder to go to Wilmore College." The will also provided that the residue of his estate should go to Wilmore College. Thereafter, Dane sold Redacre and then added a validly executed codicil to his will, "Due to the fact that I have sold Redacre which I previously gave to my daughter, Mary, I now give and devise Blackacre to Mary in place and instead of Redacre."

Another clause of the codicil provided: "I give my one-half interest in the oil business which I own in common with William Steele to my son, Henry." Subsequently, Dane acquired all of the interest in the oil business from his partner, Steele, and, at the time of his death, Dane owned the entire oil business. The will and codicil have been admitted to probate.

(a) What interest, if any, does Mary acquire in Blackacre? Explain.

(b) What is the interest, if any, of Henry in the oil business? Explain.

*

APPENDIX A

THE UNIFORM COMMERCIAL CODE

(Adopted in 49 jurisdictions: Alabama, Alaska, Arkansas, California, Colorado, Connecticut, Delaware, District of Columbia, Florida, Georgia, Hawaii, Illinois, Indiana, Iowa, Kansas, Kentucky, Maine, Maryland, Massachusetts, Michigan, Minnesota, Mississippi, Missouri, Montana, Nebraska, Nevada, New Hampshire, New Jersey, New Mexico, New York, North Carolina, North Dakota, Ohio, Oklahoma, Oregon, Pennsylvania, Rhode Island, South Carolina, South Dakota, Tennessee, Texas, Utah, Vermont, Virginia, Virgin Islands, Washington, West Virginia, Wisconsin, Wyoming.)

The Code consists of 10 Articles as follows:

Art.

1. General Provisions
2. Sales.
3. Commercial Paper
4. Bank Deposits and Collections
5. Letters of Credit
6. Bulk Transfers
7. Warehouse Receipts, Bills of Lading and Other Documents of Title
8. Investment Securities
9. Secured Transactions: Sales of Accounts, Contract Rights and Chattel Paper
10. Effective Date and Repealer

1962 OFFICIAL TEXT

ARTICLE 1

GENERAL PROVISIONS

PART 1

SHORT TITLE, CONSTRUCTION, APPLICATION AND SUBJECT MATTER OF THE ACT

§ 1—101. Short Title.

This Act shall be known and may be cited as Uniform Commercial Code.

§ 1—102. Purposes; Rules of Construction; Variation by Agreement.

(1) This Act shall be liberally construed and applied to promote its underlying purposes and policies.

(2) Underlying purposes and policies of this Act are

(a) to simplify, clarify and modernize the law governing commercial transactions;

(b) to permit the continued expansion of commercial practices through custom, usage and agreement of the parties;

(c) to make uniform the law among the various jurisdictions.

(3) The effect of provisions of this Act may be varied by agreement, except as otherwise provided in this Act and except that the obligations of good faith, diligence, reasonableness and care prescribed by this Act may not be disclaimed by agreement but the parties may by agreement determine the standards by which the performance of such obligations is to be measured if such standards are not manifestly unreasonable.

(4) The presence in certain provisions of this Act of the words "unless otherwise agreed" or words of similar import does not imply that the effect of other provisions may not be varied by agreement under subsection (3).

(5) In this Act unless the context otherwise requires

    (a) words in the singular number include the plural, and in the plural include the singular;

    (b) words of the masculine gender include the feminine and the neuter, and when the sense so indicates words of the neuter gender may refer to any gender.

§ 1—103. Supplementary General Principles of Law Applicable.

Unless displaced by the particular provisions of this Act, the principles of law and equity, including the law merchant and the law relative to capacity to contract, principal and agent, estoppel, fraud, misrepresentation, duress, coercion, mistake, bankruptcy, or other validating or invalidating cause shall supplement its provisions.

§ 1—104. Construction Against Implicit Repeal.

This Act being a general act intended as a unified coverage of its subject matter, no part of it shall be deemed to be impliedly repealed by subsequent legislation if such construction can reasonably be avoided.

§ 1—105. Territorial Application of the Act; Parties' Power to Choose Applicable Law.

(1) Except as provided hereafter in this section, when a transaction bears a reasonable relation to this state and also to another state or nation the parties may agree that the law either of this state or of such other state or nation shall govern their rights and duties. Failing such agreement this Act applies to transactions bearing an appropriate relation to this state.

(2) Where one of the following provisions of this Act specifies the applicable law, that provision governs and a contrary agreement is effective only to the extent permitted by the law (including the conflict of laws rules) so specified:

Rights of creditors against sold goods. Section 2—402.

    Applicability of the Article on Bank Deposits and Collections. Section 4—102.

    Bulk transfers subject to the Article on Bulk Transfers. Section 6—102.

    Applicability of the Article on Investment Securities. Section 8—106.

    Policy and scope of the Article on Secured Transactions. Sections 9—102 and 9—103.

§ 1—106. Remedies to Be Liberally Administered.

(1) The remedies provided by this Act shall be liberally administered to the end that the aggrieved party may be put in as good a position as if the other party had fully performed but neither consequential or special nor penal damages may be had except as specifically provided in this Act or by other rule of law.

(2) Any right or obligation declared by this Act is enforceable by action unless the provision declaring it specifies a different and limited effect.

§ 1—107. Waiver or Renunciation of Claim or Right After Breach.

Any claim or right arising out of an alleged breach can be discharged in whole or in part without consideration by a written waiver or renunciation signed and delivered by the aggrieved party.

§ 1—108. Severability.

If any provision or clause of this Act or application thereof to any person or circumstances is held invalid, such invalidity shall not affect other provisions or applications of the Act which can be given effect without the invalid provision or application, and to this end the provisions of this Act are declared to be severable.

§ 1—109. Section Captions.

Section captions are parts of this Act.

PART 2

GENERAL DEFINITIONS AND PRINCIPLES OF INTERPRETATION

§ 1—201. General Definitions.

Subject to additional definitions contained in the subsequent Articles of this Act which are applicable to specific Articles or Parts thereof, and unless the context otherwise requires, in this Act:

(1) "Action" in the sense of a judicial proceeding includes recoupment, counterclaim, set-off, suit in equity and any other proceedings in which rights are determined.

(2) "Aggrieved party" means a party entitled to resort to a remedy.

(3) "Agreement" means the bargain of the parties in fact as found in their language or by implication from other circumstances including course of dealing or usage of trade or course of performance as provided in this Act (Sections 1—205 and 2—208). Whether an agreement has legal consequences is determined by the provisions of this Act, if applicable; otherwise by the law of contracts (Section 1—103). (Compare "Contract".)

(4) "Bank" means any person engaged in the business of banking.

(5) "Bearer" means the person in possession of an instrument, document of title, or security payable to bearer or indorsed in blank.

(6) "Bill of lading" means a document evidencing the receipt of goods for shipment issued by a person engaged in the business of transporting or forwarding goods, and includes an airbill. "Airbill" means a document serving for air transportation as a bill of lading does for marine or rail transportation, and includes an air consignment note or air waybill.

(7) "Branch" includes a separately incorporated foreign branch of a bank.

(8) "Burden of establishing" a fact means the burden of persuading the triers of fact that the existence of the fact is more probable than its non-existence.

(9) "Buyer in ordinary course of business" means a person who in good faith and without knowledge that the sale to him is in violation of the ownership rights or security interest of a third party in the goods buys in ordinary course from a person in the business of selling goods of that kind but does not include a pawnbroker. "Buying" may be for cash or by exchange of other property or on secured or unsecured credit and includes receiving goods or documents of title under a pre-existing contract for sale but does not include a transfer in bulk or as security for or in total or partial satisfaction of a money debt.

(10) "Conspicuous": A term or clause is conspicuous when it is so written that a reasonable person against whom it is to operate ought to have noticed it. A printed heading in capitals (as: NON-NEGOTIABLE BILL OF LADING) is conspicuous. Language in the body of a form is "conspicuous" if it is in larger or other contrasting type or color. But in a telegram any stated term is "conspicuous". Whether a term or clause is "conspicuous" or not is for decision by the court.

(11) "Contract" means the total legal obligation which results from the parties' agreement as affected by this Act and any other applicable rules of law. (Compare "Agreement".)

(12) "Creditor" includes a general creditor, a secured creditor, a lien creditor and any representative of creditors, including an assignee for the benefit of creditors, a trustee in bankruptcy, a receiver in equity and an executor or administrator of an insolvent debtor's or assignor's estate.

(13) "Defendant" includes a person in the position of defendant in a cross-action or counterclaim.

(14) "Delivery" with respect to instruments, documents of title, chattel paper or securities means voluntary transfer of possession.

(15) "Document of title" includes bill of lading, dock warrant, dock receipt, warehouse receipt or order for the delivery of goods, and also any other document which in the regular course of business or financing is treated as adequately evidencing that the person in possession of it is entitled to receive, hold and dispose of the document and the goods it covers. To be a document of title a document must purport to be issued by or addressed to a bailee and purport to cover goods in the bailee's possession which are either identified or are fungible portions of an identified mass.

(16) "Fault" means wrongful act, omission or breach.

(17) "Fungible" with respect to goods or securities means goods or securities of which any unit is, by nature or usage of trade, the equivalent of any other like unit. Goods which are not fungible shall be deemed fungible for the purposes of this Act to the extent that under a particular agreement or document unlike units are treated as equivalents.

(18) "Genuine" means free of forgery or counterfeiting.

(19) "Good faith" means honesty in fact in the conduct or transaction concerned.

(20) "Holder" means a person who is in possession of a document of title or an instrument or an investment security drawn, issued or indorsed to him or to his order or to bearer or in blank.

(21) To "honor" is to pay or to accept and pay, or where a credit so engages to purchase or discount a draft complying with the terms of the credit.

(22) "Insolvency proceedings" includes any assignment for the benefit of creditors or other proceedings intended to liquidate or rehabilitate the estate of the person involved.

(23) A person is "insolvent" who either has ceased to pay his debts in the ordinary course of business or cannot pay his debts as they become due or is insolvent within the meaning of the federal bankruptcy law.

(24) "Money" means a medium of exchange authorized or adopted by a domestic or foreign government as a part of its currency.

(25) A person has "notice" of a fact when

(a) he has actual knowledge of it; or

(b) he has received a notice or notification of it; or

(c) from all the facts and circumstances known to him at the time in question he has reason to know that it exists.

A person "knows" or has "knowledge" of a fact when he has actual knowledge of it. "Discover" or "learn" or a word or phrase of similar import refers to knowledge rather than to reason to know. The time and circumstances under which a notice or notification may cease to be effective are not determined by this Act.

(26) A person "notifies" or "gives" a notice or notification to another by taking such steps as may be reasonably required to inform the other in ordinary course whether or not such other actually comes to know of it. A person "receives" a notice or notification when

(a) it comes to his attention; or

(b) it is duly delivered at the place of business through which the contract was made or at any other place held out by him as the place for receipt of such communications.

(27) Notice, knowledge or a notice or notification received by an organization is effective for a particular transaction from the time when it is brought to the attention of the individual conducting that transaction, and in any event from the time when it would have been brought to his attention if the organization had exercised due diligence. An organization exercises due diligence if it maintains reasonable routines for communicating significant information to the person conducting the transaction and there is reasonable compliance with the routines. Due diligence does not require an individual acting for the organization to communicate information unless such communication is part of his regular duties or unless he has reason to know of the transaction and that the transaction would be materially affected by the information.

(28) "Organization" includes a corporation, government or governmental subdivision or agency, business trust, estate, trust, partnership or association, two or more persons having a joint or common interest, or any other legal or commercial entity.

(29) "Party", as distinct from "third party", means a person who has engaged in a transaction or made an agreement within this Act.

(30) "Person" includes an individual or an organization (See Section 1—102).

(31) "Presumption" or "presumed" means that the trier of fact must find the existence of the fact presumed unless and until evidence is introduced which would support a finding of its nonexistence.

(32) "Purchase" includes taking by sale, discount, negotiation, mortgage, pledge, lien, issue or re-issue, gift or any other voluntary transaction creating an interest in property.

(33) "Purchaser" means a person who takes by purchase.

(34) "Remedy" means any remedial right to which an aggrieved party is entitled with or without resort to a tribunal.

(35) "Representative" includes an agent, an officer of a corporation or association, and a trustee, executor or administrator of an estate, or any other person empowered to act for another.

(36) "Rights" includes remedies.

(37) "Security interest" means an interest in personal property or fixtures which secures payment or performance of an obligation. The retention or reservation of title by a seller of goods notwithstanding shipment or delivery to the buyer (Section 2—401) is limited in effect to a reservation of a "security interest". The term also includes any interest of a buyer of accounts, chattel paper, or contract rights which is subject to Article 9. The special property interest of a buyer of goods on identification of such goods to a contract for sale under Section 2—401 is not a "security interest", but a buyer may also acquire a "security interest" by complying with Article 9. Unless a lease or consignment is intended as security, reservation of title thereunder is not a "security interest" but a consignment is in any event subject to the provisions on consignment sales (Section 2—326). Whether a lease is intended as security is to be determined by the facts of each case; however, (a) the inclusion of an option to purchase does not of itself make the lease one intended for security, and (b) an agreement that upon compliance with the terms of the lease the lessee shall become or has the option to become the owner of the property for no additional consideration or for a nominal consideration does make the lease one intended for security.

(38) "Send" in connection with any writing or notice means to deposit in the mail or deliver for transmission by any other usual means of communication with postage or cost of transmission provided for and properly addressed and in the case of an instrument to an address specified thereon or otherwise agreed, or if there be none to any address reasonable under the circumstances. The receipt of any writing or notice within the time at which it would have arrived if properly sent has the effect of a proper sending.

(39) "Signed" includes any symbol executed or adopted by a party with present intention to authenticate a writing.

(40) "Surety" includes guarantor.

(41) "Telegram" includes a message transmitted by radio, teletype, cable, any mechanical method of transmission, or the like.

(42) "Term" means that portion of an agreement which relates to a particular matter.

(43) "Unauthorized" signature or indorsement means one made without actual, implied or apparent authority and includes a forgery.

(44) "Value". Except as otherwise provided with respect to negotiable instruments and bank collections (Sections 3—303, 4—208 and 4—209) a person gives "value" for rights if he acquires them

   (a) in return for a binding commitment to extend credit or for the extension of immediately available credit whether or not drawn upon and whether or not a charge-back is provided for in the event of difficulties in collection; or

   (b) as security for or in total or partial satisfaction of a pre-existing claim; or

   (c) by accepting delivery pursuant to a pre-existing contract for purchase; or

   (d) generally, in return for any consideration sufficient to support a simple contract.

(45) "Warehouse receipt" means a receipt issued by a person engaged in the business of storing goods for hire.

(46) "Written" or "writing" includes printing, typewriting or any other intentional reduction to tangible form.

§ 1—202. Prima Facie Evidence by Third Party Documents.

A document in due form purporting to be a bill of lading, policy or certificate of insurance, official weigher's or inspector's certificate, consular invoice, or any other document authorized or required by the contract to be issued by a third party shall be prima facie evidence of its own authenticity and genuineness and of the facts stated in the document by the third party.

§ 1—203. Obligation of Good Faith.

Every contract or duty within this Act imposes an obligation of good faith in its performance or enforcement.

§ 1—204. Time; Reasonable Time; "Seasonably".

(1) Whenever this Act requires any action to be taken within a reasonable time, any time which is not manifestly unreasonable may be fixed by agreement.

(2) What is a reasonable time for taking any action depends on the nature, purpose and circumstances of such action.

(3) An action is taken "seasonably" when it is taken at or within the time agreed or if no time is agreed at or within a reasonable time.

§ 1—205. Course of Dealing and Usage of Trade.

(1) A course of dealing is a sequence of previous conduct between the parties to a particular transaction which is fairly to be regarded as establishing a common basis of understanding for interpreting their expressions and other conduct.

(2) A usage of trade is any practice or method of dealing having such regularity of observance in a place, vocation or trade as to justify an expectation that it will be observed with respect to the transaction in question. The existence and scope of such a usage are to be proved as facts. If it is established that such a usage is embodied in a written trade code or similar writing the interpretation of the writing is for the court.

(3) A course of dealing between parties and any usage of trade in the vocation or trade in which they are engaged or of which they are or should be aware give particular meaning to and supplement or qualify terms of an agreement.

(4) The express terms of an agreement and an applicable course of dealing or usage of trade shall be construed wherever reasonable as consistent with each other; but when such construction is unreasonable express terms control both course of dealing and usage of trade and course of dealing controls usage of trade.

(5) An applicable usage of trade in the place where any part of performance is to occur shall be used in interpreting the agreement as to that part of the performance.

(6) Evidence of a relevant usage of trade offered by one party is not admissible unless and until he has given the other party such notice as the court finds sufficient to prevent unfair surprise to the latter.

§ 1—206. Statute of Frauds for Kinds of Personal Property Not Otherwise Covered.

(1) Except in the cases described in subsection (2) of this section a contract for the sale of personal property is not enforceable by way of action or defense beyond five thousand dollars in amount or value of remedy unless there is some writing which indicates that a contract for sale has been made between the parties at a defined or stated price, reasonably identifies the subject matter, and is signed by the party against whom enforcement is sought or by his authorized agent.

(2) Subsection (1) of this section does not apply to contracts for the sale of goods (Section 2—201) nor of securities (Section 8—319) nor to security agreements (Section 9—203).

§ 1—207. Performance or Acceptance Under Reservation of Rights.

A party who with explicit reservation of rights performs or promises performance or assents to performance in a manner demanded or offered by the other party does not thereby prejudice the rights reserved. Such words as "without prejudice", "under protest" or the like are sufficient.

§ 1—208. Option to Accelerate at Will.

A term providing that one party or his successor in interest may accelerate payment or performance or require collateral or additional collateral "at will" or "when he deems himself insecure" or in words of similar import shall be construed to mean that he shall have power to do so only if he in good faith believes that the prospect of payment or performance is impaired. The burden of establishing lack of good faith is on the party against whom the power has been exercised.

ARTICLE 2

SALES

PART 1

SHORT TITLE, CONSTRUCTION AND SUBJECT MATTER

§ 2—101. Short Title.

This Article shall be known and may be cited as Uniform Commercial Code—Sales.

§ 2—102. Scope; Certain Security and Other Transactions Excluded From This Article.

Unless the context otherwise requires, this Article applies to transactions in goods; it does not apply to any transaction which although in the form of an unconditional contract to sell or present sale is intended to operate only as a security transaction nor does this Article impair or repeal any statute regulating sales to consumers, farmers or other specified classes of buyers.

§ 2—103. Definitions and Index of Definitions.

(1) In this Article unless the context otherwise requires

(a) "Buyer" means a person who buys or contracts to buy goods.

(b) "Good faith" in the case of a merchant means honesty in fact and the observance of reasonable commercial standards of fair dealing in the trade.

(c) "Receipt" of goods means taking physical possession of them.

(d) "Seller" means a person who sells or contracts to sell goods.

(2) Other definitions applying to this Article or to specified Parts thereof, and the sections in which they appear are:

"Acceptance". Section 2—606.

"Banker's credit". Section 2—325.
"Between merchants". Section 2—104.
"Cancellation". Section 2—106(4).
"Commercial unit". Section 2—105.
"Confirmed credit". Section 2—325.
"Conforming to contract". Section 2—106.
"Contract for sale". Section 2—106.
"Cover". Section 2—712.
"Entrusting". Section 2—403.
"Financing agency". Section 2—104.
"Future goods". Section 2—105.
"Goods". Section 2—105.
"Identification". Section 2—501.
"Installment contract". Section 2—612.
"Letter of Credit". Section 2—325.
"Lot". Section 2—105.
"Merchant". Section 2—104.
"Overseas". Section 2—323.
"Person in position of seller". Section 2—707.
"Present sale". Section 2—106.
"Sale". Section 2—106.
"Sale on approval". Section 2—326.
"Sale or return". Section 2—326.
"Termination". Section 2—106.

(3) The following definitions in other Articles apply to this Article:
"Check". Section 3—104.
"Consignee". Section 7—102.
"Consignor". Section 7—102.
"Consumer goods". Section 9—109.
"Dishonor". Section 3—507.
"Draft". Section 3—104.

(4) In addition Article 1 contains general definitions and principles of construction and interpretation applicable throughout this Article.

§ 2—104. Definitions: "Merchant"; "Between Merchants"; "Financing Agency".

(1) "Merchant" means a person who deals in goods of the kind or otherwise by his occupation holds himself out as having knowledge or skill peculiar to the practices or goods involved in the transaction or to whom such knowledge or skill may be attributed by his employment of an agent or broker or other intermediary who by his occupation holds himself out as having such knowledge or skill.

(2) "Financing agency" means a bank, finance company or other person who in the ordinary course of business makes advances against goods or documents of title or who by arrangement with either the seller or the buyer intervenes in ordinary course to make or collect payment due or claimed under the contract for sale, as by purchasing or paying the seller's draft or making advances against it or by merely taking it for collection whether or not documents of title accompany the draft. "Financing agency" includes also a bank or other person who similarly intervenes between persons who are in the position of seller and buyer in respect to the goods (Section 2—707).

(3) "Between merchants" means in any transaction with respect to which both parties are chargeable with the knowledge or skill of merchants.

§ 2—105. Definitions: Transferability; "Goods"; "Future" Goods; "Lot"; "Commercial Unit".

(1) "Goods" means all things (including specially manufactured goods) which are movable at the time of identification to the contract for sale other than the money in which the price is to be paid, investment securities (Article 8) and things in action. "Goods" also includes the unborn young of animals and growing crops and other identified things attached to realty as described in the section on goods to be severed from realty (Section 2—107).

(2) Goods must be both existing and identified before any interest in them can pass. Goods which are not both existing and identified are "future" goods. A purported present sale of future goods or of any interest therein operates as a contract to sell.

(3) There may be a sale of a part interest in existing identified goods.

(4) An undivided share in an identified bulk of fungible goods is sufficiently identified to be sold although the quantity of the bulk is not determined. Any agreed proportion of such a bulk or any quantity thereof agreed upon by number, weight or other measure may to the extent of the seller's interest in the bulk be sold to the buyer who then becomes an owner in common.

(5) "Lot" means a parcel or a single article which is the subject matter of a separate sale or delivery, whether or not it is sufficient to perform the contract.

(6) "Commercial unit" means such a unit of goods as by commercial usage is a single whole for purposes of sale and division of which materially impairs its character or value on the market or in use. A commercial unit may be a single article (as a machine) or a set of articles (as a suite of furniture or an assortment of sizes) or a quantity (as a bale, gross, or carload) or any other unit treated in use or in the relevant market as a single whole.

§ 2—106. Definitions: "Contract"; "Agreement"; "Contract for Sale"; "Sale"; "Present Sale"; "Conforming" to Contract; "Termination"; "Cancellation".

(1) In this Article unless the context otherwise requires "contract" and "agreement" are limited to those relating to the present or future sale of goods. "Contract for sale" includes both a present sale of goods and a contract to sell goods at a future time. A "sale" consists in the passing of title from the seller to the buyer for a price (Section 2—401). A "present sale" means a sale which is accomplished by the making of the contract.

(2) Goods or conduct including any part of a performance are "conforming" or conform to the contract when they are in accordance with the obligations under the contract.

(3) "Termination" occurs when either party pursuant to a power created by agreement or law puts an end to the contract otherwise than for its breach. On "termination" all obligations which are still executory on both sides are discharged but any right based on prior breach or performance survives.

(4) "Cancellation" occurs when either party puts an end to the contract for breach by the other and its effect is the same as that of

"termination" except that the cancelling party also retains any remedy for breach of the whole contract or any unperformed balance.

§ 2—107. Goods to Be Severed From Realty: Recording.

(1) A contract for the sale of timber, minerals or the like or a structure or its materials to be removed from realty is a contract for the sale of goods within this Article if they are to be severed by the seller but until severance a purported present sale thereof which is not effective as a transfer of an interest in land is effective only as a contract to sell.

(2) A contract for the sale apart from the land of growing crops or other things attached to realty and capable of severance without material harm thereto but not described in subsection (1) is a contract for the sale of goods within this Article whether the subject matter is to be severed by the buyer or by the seller even though it forms part of the realty at the time of contracting, and the parties can by identification effect a present sale before severance.

(3) The provisions of this section are subject to any third party rights provided by the law relating to realty records, and the contract for sale may be executed and recorded as a document transferring an interest in land and shall then constitute notice to third parties of the buyer's rights under the contract for sale.

PART 2

FORM, FORMATION AND READJUSTMENT OF CONTRACT

§ 2—201. Formal Requirements; Statute of of Frauds.

(1) Except as otherwise provided in this section a contract for the sale of goods for the price of $500 or more is not enforceable by way of action or defense unless there is some writing sufficient to indicate that a contract for sale has been made between the parties and signed by the party against whom enforcement is sought or by his authorized agent or broker. A writing is not insufficient because it omits or incorrectly states a term agreed upon but the contract is not enforceable under this paragraph beyond the quantity of goods shown in such writing.

(2) Between merchants if within a reasonable time a writing in confirmation of the contract and sufficient against the sender is received and the party receiving it has reason to know its contents, it satisfies the requirements of subsection (1) against such party unless written notice of objection to its contents is given within ten days after it is received.

(3) A contract which does not satisfy the requirements of subsection (1) but which is valid in other respects is enforceable

(a) if the goods are to be specially manufactured for the buyer and are not suitable for sale to others in the ordinary course of the seller's business and the seller, before notice of repudiation is received and under circumstances which reasonably indicate that the goods are for the buyer, has made either a substantial beginning of their manufacture or commitments for their procurement; or

(b) if the party against whom enforcement is sought admits in his pleading, testimony or otherwise in court that a contract for sale was made, but the contract is not enforceable under this provision beyond the quantity of goods admitted; or

(c) with respect to goods for which payment has been made and accepted or which have been received and accepted (Sec. 2—606).

§ 2—202. Final Written Expression: Parol or Extrinsic Evidence.

Terms with respect to which the confirmatory memoranda of the parties agree or which are otherwise set forth in a writing intended by the parties as a final expression of their agreement with respect to such terms as are included therein may not be contradicted by evidence of any prior agreement or of a contemporaneous oral agreement but may be explained or supplemented

(a) by course of dealing or usage of trade (Section 1—205) or by course of performance (Section 2—208); and

(b) by evidence of consistent additional terms unless the court finds the writing to have been intended also as a complete and exclusive statement of the terms of the agreement.

§ 2—203. Seals Inoperative.

The affixing of a seal to a writing evidencing a contract for sale or an offer to buy or sell goods does not constitute the writing a sealed instrument and the law with respect to sealed instruments does not apply to such a contract or offer.

§ 2—204. Formation in General.

(1) A contract for sale of goods may be made in any manner sufficient to show agreement, including conduct by both parties which recognizes the existence of such a contract.

(2) An agreement sufficient to constitute a contract for sale may be found even though the moment of its making is undetermined.

(3) Even though one or more terms are left open a contract for sale does not fail for indefiniteness if the parties have intended to make a contract and there is a reasonably certain basis for giving an appropriate remedy.

§ 2—205. Firm Offers.

An offer by a merchant to buy or sell goods in a signed writing which by its terms gives assurance that it will be held open is not revocable, for lack of consideration, during the time stated or if no time is stated for a reasonable time, but in no event may such period of irrevocability exceed three months; but any such term of assurance on a form supplied by the offeree must be separately signed by the offeror.

§ 2—206. Offer and Acceptance in Formation of Contract.

(1) Unless otherwise unambiguously indicated by the language or circumstances

    (a) an offer to make a contract shall be construed as inviting acceptance in any manner and by any medium reasonable in the circumstances;

    (b) an order or other offer to buy goods for prompt or current shipment shall be construed as inviting acceptance either by a prompt promise to ship or by the prompt or current shipment of conforming or nonconforming goods, but such a shipment of non-conforming goods does not constitute an acceptance if the seller seasonably notifies the buyer that the shipment is offered only as an accommodation to the buyer.

(2) Where the beginning of a requested performance is a reasonable mode of acceptance an offeror who is not notified of acceptance within a reasonable time may treat the offer as having lapsed before acceptance.

§ 2—207. Additional Terms in Acceptance or Confirmation.

(1) A definite and seasonable expression of acceptance or a written confirmation which is sent within a reasonable time operates as an acceptance even though it states terms additional to or different from those offered or agreed upon, unless acceptance is expressly made conditional on assent to the additional or different terms.

(2) The additional terms are to be construed as proposals for addition to the contract. Between merchants such terms become part of the contract unless:

    (a) the offer expressly limits acceptance to the terms of the offer;

    (b) they materially alter it; or

    (c) notification of objection to them has already been given or is given within a reasonable time after notice of them is received.

(3) Conduct by both parties which recognizes the existence of a contract is sufficient to establish a contract for sale although the writings of the parties do not otherwise establish a contract. In such case the terms of the particular contract consist of those terms on which the writings of the parties agree, together with any supplementary terms incorporated under any other provisions of this Act.

§ 2—208. Course of Performance or Practical Construction.

(1) Where the contract for sale involves repeated occasions for performance by either party with knowledge of the nature of the performance and opportunity for objection to it by the other, any course of performance accepted or acquiesced in without objection shall be relevant to determine the meaning of the agreement.

(2) The express terms of the agreement and any such course of performance, as well as any

course of dealing and usage of trade, shall be construed whenever reasonable as consistent with each other; but when such construction is unreasonable, express terms shall control course of performance and course of performance shall control both course of dealing and usage of trade (Section 1—205).

(3) Subject to the provisions of the next section on modification and waiver, such course of performance shall be relevant to show a waiver or modification of any term inconsistent with such course of performance.

§ 2—209. **Modification, Rescission and Waiver.**

(1) An agreement modifying a contract within this Article needs no consideration to be binding.

(2) A signed agreement which excludes modification or rescission except by a signed writing cannot be otherwise modified or rescinded, but except as between merchants such a requirement on a form supplied by the merchant must be separately signed by the other party.

(3) The requirements of the statute of frauds section of this Article (Section 2—201) must be satisfied if the contract as modified is within its provisions.

(4) Although an attempt at modification or rescission does not satisfy the requirements of subsection (2) or (3) it can operate as a waiver.

(5) A party who has made a waiver affecting an executory portion of the contract may retract the waiver by reasonable notification received by the other party that strict performance will be required of any term waived, unless the retraction would be unjust in view of a material change of position in reliance on the waiver.

§ 2—210. **Delegation of Performance; Assignment of Rights.**

(1) A party may perform his duty through a delegate unless otherwise agreed or unless the other party has a substantial interest in having his original promisor perform or control the acts required by the contract. No delegation of performance relieves the party delegating of any duty to perform or any liability for breach.

(2) Unless otherwise agreed all rights of either seller or buyer can be assigned except where the assignment would materially change the duty of the other party, or increase materially the burden or risk imposed on him by his contract, or impair materially his chance of obtaining return performance. A right to damages for breach of the whole contract or a right arising out of the assignor's due performance of his entire obligation can be assigned despite agreement otherwise.

(3) Unless the circumstances indicate the contrary a prohibition of assignment of "the contract" is to be construed as barring only the delegation to the assignee of the assignor's performance.

(4) An assignment of "the contract" or of "all my rights under the contract" or an assignment in similar general terms is an assignment of rights and unless the language or the circumstances (as in an assignment for security) indicate the contrary, it is a delegation of performance of the duties of the assignor and its acceptance by the assignee constitutes a promise by him to perform those duties. This promise is enforceable by either the assignor or the other party to the original contract.

(5) The other party may treat any assignment which delegates performance as creating reasonable grounds for insecurity and may without prejudice to his rights against the assignor demand assurances from the assignee (Section 2—609).

PART 3

GENERAL OBLIGATION AND CONSTRUCTION OF CONTRACT

§ 2—301. **General Obligations of Parties.**

The obligation of the seller is to transfer and deliver and that of the buyer is to accept and pay in accordance with the contract.

§ 2—302. **Unconscionable Contract or Clause.**

(1) If the court as a matter of law finds the contract or any clause of the contract to have been unconscionable at the time it was made

the court may refuse to enforce the contract, or it may enforce the remainder of the contract without the unconscionable clause, or it may so limit the application of any unconscionable clause as to avoid any unconscionable result.

(2) When it is claimed or appears to the court that the contract or any clause thereof may be unconscionable the parties shall be afforded a reasonable opportunity to present evidence as to its commercial setting, purpose and effect to aid the court in making the determination.

§ 2—303. Allocation or Division of Risks.

Where this Article allocates a risk or a burden as between the parties "unless otherwise agreed", the agreement may not only shift the allocation but may also divide the risk or burden.

§ 2—304. Price Payable in Money, Goods, Realty, or Otherwise.

(1) The price can be made payable in money or otherwise. If it is payable in whole or in part in goods each party is a seller of the goods which he is to transfer.

(2) Even though all or part of the price is payable in an interest in realty the transfer of the goods and the seller's obligations with reference to them are subject to this Article, but not the transfer of the interest in realty or the transferor's obligations in connection therewith.

§ 2—305. Open Price Term.

(1) The parties if they so intend can conclude a contract for sale even though the price is not settled. In such a case the price is a reasonable price at the time for delivery if

    (a) nothing is said as to price; or

    (b) the price is left to be agreed by the parties and they fail to agree; or

    (c) the price is to be fixed in terms of some agreed market or other standard as set or recorded by a third person or agency and it is not so set or recorded.

(2) A price to be fixed by the seller or by the buyer means a price for him to fix in good faith.

(3) When a price left to be fixed otherwise than by agreement of the parties fails to be fixed through fault of one party the other may at his option treat the contract as cancelled or himself fix a reasonable price.

(4) Where, however, the parties intend not to be bound unless the price be fixed or agreed and it is not fixed or agreed there is no contract. In such a case the buyer must return any goods already received or if unable so to do must pay their reasonable value at the time of delivery and the seller must return any portion of the price paid on account.

§ 2—306. Output, Requirements and Exclusive Dealings.

(1) A term which measures the quantity by the output of the seller or the requirements of the buyer means such actual output or requirements as may occur in good faith, except that no quantity unreasonably disproportionate to any stated estimate or in the absence of a stated estimate to any normal or otherwise comparable prior output or requirements may be tendered or demanded.

(2) A lawful agreement by either the seller or the buyer for exclusive dealing in the kind of goods concerned imposes unless otherwise agreed an obligation by the seller to use best efforts to supply the goods and by the buyer to use best efforts to promote their sale.

§ 2—307. Delivery in Single Lot or Several Lots.

Unless otherwise agreed all goods called for by a contract for sale must be tendered in a single delivery and payment is due only on such tender but where the circumstances give either party the right to make or demand delivery in lots the price if it can be apportioned may be demanded for each lot.

§ 2—308. Absence of Specified Place for Delivery.

Unless otherwise agreed

    (a) the place for delivery of goods is the seller's place of business or if he has none his residence; but

    (b) in a contract for sale of identified goods which to the knowledge of the parties at the time of contracting are in some other place, that place is the place for their delivery; and

(c) documents of title may be delivered through customary banking channels.

§ 2—309. Absence of Specific Time Provisions; Notice of Termination.

(1) The time for shipment or delivery or any other action under a contract if not provided in this Article or agreed upon shall be a reasonable time.

(2) Where the contract provides for successive performances but is indefinite in duration it is valid for a reasonable time but unless otherwise agreed may be terminated at any time by either party.

(3) Termination of a contract by one party except on the happening of an agreed event requires that reasonable notification be received by the other party and an agreement dispensing with notification is invalid if its operation would be unconscionable.

§ 2—310. Open Time for Payment or Running of Credit; Authority to Ship Under Reservation.

Unless otherwise agreed

(a) payment is due at the time and place at which the buyer is to receive the goods even though the place of shipment is the place of delivery; and

(b) if the seller is authorized to send the goods he may ship them under reservation, and may tender the documents of title, but the buyer may inspect the goods after their arrival before payment is due unless such inspection is inconsistent with the terms of the contract (Section 2—513); and

(c) if delivery is authorized and made by way of documents of title otherwise than by subsection (b) then payment is due at the time and place at which the buyer is to receive the documents regardless of where the goods are to be received; and

(d) where the seller is required or authorized to ship the goods on credit the credit period runs from the time of shipment but post-dating the invoice or delaying its dispatch will correspondingly delay the starting of the credit period.

§ 2—311. Options and Cooperation Respecting Performance.

(1) An agreement for sale which is otherwise sufficiently definite (subsection (3) of Section 2—204) to be a contract is not made invalid by the fact that it leaves particulars of performance to be specified by one of the parties. Any such specification must be made in good faith and within limits set by commercial reasonableness.

(2) Unless otherwise agreed specifications relating to assortment of the goods are at the buyer's option and except as otherwise provided in subsections (1) (c) and (3) of Section 2—319 specifications or arrangements relating to shipment are at the seller's option.

(3) Where such specification would materially affect the other party's performance but is not seasonably made or where one party's cooperation is necessary to the agreed performance of the other but is not seasonably forthcoming, the other party in addition to all other remedies

(a) is excused for any resulting delay in his own performance; and

(b) may also either proceed to perform in any reasonable manner or after the time for a material part of his own performance treat the failure to specify or to cooperate as a breach by failure to deliver or accept the goods.

§ 2—312. Warranty of Title and Against Infringement; Buyer's Obligation Against Infringement.

(1) Subject to subsection (2) there is in a contract for sale a warranty by the seller that

(a) the title conveyed shall be good, and its transfer rightful; and

(b) the goods shall be delivered free from any security interest or other lien or encumbrance of which the buyer at the time of contracting has no knowledge.

(2) A warranty under subsection (1) will be excluded or modified only by specific language or by circumstances which give the buyer reason to know that the person selling does not

claim title in himself or that he is purporting to sell only such right or title as he or a third person may have.

(3) Unless otherwise agreed a seller who is a merchant regularly dealing in goods of the kind warrants that the goods shall be delivered free of the rightful claim of any third person by way of infringement or the like but a buyer who furnishes specifications to the seller must hold the seller harmless against any such claim which arises out of compliance with the specifications.

§ 2—313. Express Warranties by Affirmation, Promise, Description, Sample.

(1) Express warranties by the seller are created as follows:

(a) Any affirmation of fact or promise made by the seller to the buyer which relates to the goods and becomes part of the basis of the bargain creates an express warranty that the goods shall conform to the affirmation or promise.

(b) Any description of the goods which is made part of the basis of the bargain creates an express warranty that the goods shall conform to the description.

(c) Any sample or model which is made part of the basis of the bargain creates an express warranty that the whole of the goods shall conform to the sample or model.

(2) It is not necessary to the creation of an express warranty that the seller use formal words such as "warrant" or "guarantee" or that he have a specific intention to make a warranty, but an affirmation merely of the value of the goods or a statement purporting to be merely the seller's opinion or commendation of the goods does not create a warranty.

§ 2—314. Implied Warranty: Merchantability; Usage of Trade.

(1) Unless excluded or modified (Section 2—316), a warranty that the goods shall be merchantable is implied in a contract for their sale if the seller is a merchant with respect to goods of that kind. Under this section the serving for value of food or drink to be con-

sumed either on the premises or elsewhere is a sale.

(2) Goods to be merchantable must be at least such as

(a) pass without objection in the trade under the contract description; and

(b) in the case of fungible goods, are of fair average quality within the description; and

(c) are fit for the ordinary purposes for which such goods are used; and

(d) run, within the variations permitted by the agreement, of even kind, quality and quantity within each unit and among all units involved; and

(e) are adequately contained, packaged, and labeled as the agreement may require; and

(f) conform to the promises or affirmations of fact made on the container or label if any.

(3) Unless excluded or modified (Section 2—316) other implied warranties may arise from course of dealing or usage of trade.

§ 2—315. Implied Warranty: Fitness for Particular Purpose.

Where the seller at the time of contracting has reason to know any particular purpose for which the goods are required and that the buyer is relying on the seller's skill or judgment to select or furnish suitable goods, there is unless excluded or modified under the next section an implied warranty that the goods shall be fit for such purpose.

§ 2—316. Exclusion or Modification of Warranties.

(1) Words or conduct relevant to the creation of an express warranty and words or conduct tending to negate or limit warranty shall be construed wherever reasonable as consistent with each other; but subject to the provisions of this Article on parol or extrinsic evidence (Section 2—202) negation or limitation is inoperative to the extent that such construction is unreasonable.

(2) Subject to subsection (3), to exclude or modify the implied warranty of merchantability or any part of it the language must mention merchantability and in case of a writing

must be conspicuous, and to exclude or modify any implied warranty of fitness the exclusion must be by a writing and conspicuous. Language to exclude all implied warranties of fitness is sufficient if it states, for example, that "There are no warranties which extend beyond the description on the face hereof."

(3) Notwithstanding subsection (2)

(a) unless the circumstances indicate otherwise, all implied warranties are excluded by expressions like "as is", "with all faults" or other language which in common understanding calls the buyer's attention to the exclusion of warranties and makes plain that there is no implied warranty; and

(b) when the buyer before entering into the contract has examined the goods or the sample or model as fully as he desired or has refused to examine the goods there is no implied warranty with regard to defects which an examination ought in the circumstances to have revealed to him; and

(c) an implied warranty can also be excluded or modified by course of dealing or course of performance or usage of trade.

(4) Remedies for breach of warranty can be limited in accordance with the provisions of this Article on liquidation or limitation of damages and on contractual modification of remedy (Sections 2—718 and 2—719).

§ 2—317. Cumulation and Conflict of Warranties Express or Implied.

Warranties whether express or implied shall be construed as consistent with each other and as cumulative, but if such construction is unreasonable the intention of the parties shall determine which warranty is dominant. In ascertaining that intention the following rules apply:

(a) Exact or technical specifications displace an inconsistent sample or model or general language of description.

(b) A sample from an existing bulk displaces inconsistent general language of description.

(c) Express warranties displace inconsistent implied warranties other than an implied warranty of fitness for a particular purpose.

§ 2—318. Third Party Beneficiaries of Warranties Express or Implied.

A seller's warranty whether express or implied extends to any natural person who is in the family or household of his buyer or who is a guest in his home if it is reasonable to expect that such person may use, consume or be affected by the goods and who is injured in person by breach of the warranty. A seller may not exclude or limit the operation of this section.

§ 2—319. F.O.B. and F.A.S. Terms.

(1) Unless otherwise agreed the term F.O.B. (which means "free on board") at a named place, even though used only in connection with the stated price, is a delivery term under which

(a) when the term is F.O.B. the place of shipment, the seller must at that place ship the goods in the manner provided in this Article (Section 2—504) and bear the expense and risk of putting them into the possession of the carrier; or

(b) when the term is F.O.B. the place of destination, the seller must at his own expense and risk transport the goods to that place and there tender delivery of them in the manner provided in this Article (Section 2—503);

(c) when under either (a) or (b) the term is also F.O.B. vessel, car or other vehicle, the seller must in addition at his own expense and risk load the goods on board. If the term is F.O.B. vessel the buyer must name the vessel and in an appropriate case the seller must comply with the provisions of this Article on the form of bill of lading (Section 2—323).

(2) Unless otherwise agreed the term F.A.S. vessel (which means "free alongside") at a named port, even though used only in connection with the stated price, is a delivery term under which the seller must

(a) at his own expense and risk deliver the goods alongside the vessel in the manner usual in that port or on a dock designated and provided by the buyer; and

(b) obtain and tender a receipt for the goods in exchange for which the carrier is under a duty to issue a bill of lading.

(3) Unless otherwise agreed in any case falling within subsection (1) (a) or (c) or subsection (2) the buyer must seasonably give any needed instructions for making delivery, including when the term is F.A.S. or F.O.B. the loading berth of the vessel and in an appropriate case its name and sailing date. The seller may treat the failure of needed instructions as a failure of cooperation under this Article (Section 2—311). He may also at his option move the goods in any reasonable manner preparatory to delivery or shipment.

(4) Under the term F.O.B. vessel or F.A.S. unless otherwise agreed the buyer must make payment against tender of the required documents and the seller may not tender nor the buyer demand delivery of the goods in substitution for the documents.

§ 2—320. C.I.F. and C. & F. Terms.

(1) The term C.I.F. means that the price includes in a lump sum the cost of the goods and the insurance and freight to the named destination. The term C. & F. or C.F. means that the price so includes cost and freight to the named destination.

(2) Unless otherwise agreed and even though used only in connection with the stated price and destination, the term C.I.F. destination or its equivalent requires the seller at his own expense and risk to

(a) put the goods into the possession of a carrier at the port for shipment and obtain a negotiable bill or bills of lading covering the entire transportation to the named destination; and

(b) load the goods and obtain a receipt from the carrier (which may be contained in the bill of lading) showing that the freight has been paid or provided for; and

(c) obtain a policy or certificate of insurance, including any war risk insurance, of a kind and on terms then current at the port of shipment in the usual amount, in the currency of the contract, shown to cover the same goods covered by the bill of lading and providing for payment of loss to the order of the buyer or for the account of whom it may concern; but the seller may add to the price the amount of the premium for any such war risk insurance; and

(d) prepare an invoice of the goods and procure any other documents required to effect shipment or to comply with the contract; and

(e) forward and tender with commercial promptness all the documents in due form and with any indorsement necessary to perfect the buyer's rights.

(3) Unless otherwise agreed the term C. & F. or its equivalent has the same effect and imposes upon the seller the same obligations and risks as a C.I.F. term except the obligation as to insurance.

(4) Under the term C.I.F. or C. & F. unless otherwise agreed the buyer must make payment against tender of the required documents and the seller may not tender nor the buyer demand delivery of the goods in substitution for the documents.

§ 2—321. C.I.F. or C. & F.: "Net Landed Weights"; "Payment on Arrival"; Warranty of Condition on Arrival.

Under a contract containing a term C.I.F. or C. & F.

(1) Where the price is based on or is to be adjusted according to "net landed weights", "delivered weights", "out turn" quantity or quality or the like, unless otherwise agreed the seller must reasonably estimate the price. The payment due on tender of the documents called for by the contract is the amount so estimated, but after final adjustment of the price a settlement must be made with commercial promptness.

(2) An agreement described in subsection (1) or any warranty of quality or condition of the goods on arrival places upon the seller the risk of ordinary deterioration, shrinkage and the like in transportation but has no effect on the place or time of identification to the contract for sale or delivery or on the passing of the risk of loss.

(3) Unless otherwise agreed where the contract provides for payment on or after arrival of the goods the seller must before payment allow such preliminary inspection as is feasible; but if the goods are lost delivery of the documents and payment are due when the goods should have arrived.

§ 2—322. Delivery "Ex-Ship".

(1) Unless otherwise agreed a term for delivery of goods "ex-ship" (which means from the carrying vessel) or in equivalent language is not restricted to a particular ship and requires delivery from a ship which has reached a place at the named port of destination where goods of the kind are usually discharged.

(2) Under such a term unless otherwise agreed

(a) the seller must discharge all liens arising out of the carriage and furnish the buyer with a direction which puts the carrier under a duty to deliver the goods; and

(b) the risk of loss does not pass to the buyer until the goods leave the ship's tackle or are otherwise properly unloaded.

§ 2—323. Form of Bill of Lading Required in Overseas Shipment; "Overseas".

(1) Where the contract contemplates overseas shipment and contains a term C.I.F. or C. & F. or F.O.B. vessel, the seller unless otherwise agreed must obtain a negotiable bill of lading stating that the goods have been loaded on board or, in the case of a term C.I.F. or C. & F., received for shipment.

(2) Where in a case within subsection (1) a bill of lading has been issued in a set of parts, unless otherwise agreed if the documents are not to be sent from abroad the buyer may demand tender of the full set; otherwise only one part of the bill of lading need be tendered. Even if the agreement expressly requires a full set

(a) due tender of a single part is acceptable within the provisions of this Article on cure of improper delivery (subsection (1) of Section 2—508); and

(b) even though the full set is demanded, if the documents are sent from abroad the person tendering an incomplete set may nevertheless require payment upon furnishing an indemnity which the buyer in good faith deems adequate.

(3) A shipment by water or by air or a contract contemplating such shipment is "overseas" insofar as by usage of trade or agreement it is subject to the commercial, financing or shipping practices characteristic of international deep water commerce.

§ 2—324. "No Arrival, No Sale" Term.

Under a term "no arrival, no sale" or terms of like meaning, unless otherwise agreed,

(a) the seller must properly ship conforming goods and if they arrive by any means he must tender them on arrival but he assumes no obligation that the goods will arrive unless he has caused the non-arrival; and

(b) where without fault of the seller the goods are in part lost or have so deteriorated as no longer to conform to the contract or arrive after the contract time, the buyer may proceed as if there had been casualty to identified goods (Section 2—613).

§ 2—325. "Letter of Credit" Term; "Confirmed Credit".

(1) Failure of the buyer seasonably to furnish an agreed letter of credit is a breach of the contract for sale.

(2) The delivery to seller of a proper letter of credit suspends the buyer's obligation to pay. If the letter of credit is dishonored, the seller may on seasonable notification to the buyer require payment directly from him.

(3) Unless otherwise agreed the term "letter of credit" or "banker's credit" in a contract for sale means an irrevocable credit issued by a financing agency of good repute and, where the shipment is overseas, of good international repute. The term "confirmed credit" means that the credit must also carry the direct obli-

gation of such an agency which does business in the seller's financial market.

§ 2—326. Sale on Approval and Sale or Return; Consignment Sales and Rights of Creditors.

(1) Unless otherwise agreed, if delivered goods may be returned by the buyer even though they conform to the contract, the transaction is

(a) a "sale on approval" if the goods are delivered primarily for use, and

(b) a "sale or return" if the goods are delivered primarily for resale.

(2) Except as provided in subsection (3), goods held on approval are not subject to the claims of the buyer's creditors until acceptance; goods held on sale or return are subject to such claims while in the buyer's possession.

(3) Where goods are delivered to a person for sale and such person maintains a place of business at which he deals in goods of the kind involved, under a name other than the name of the person making delivery, then with respect to claims of creditors of the person conducting the business the goods are deemed to be on sale or return. The provisions of this subsection are applicable even though an agreement purports to reserve title to the person making delivery until payment or resale or uses such words as "on consignment" or "on memorandum". However, this subsection is not applicable if the person making delivery

(a) complies with an applicable law providing for a consignor's interest or the like to be evidenced by a sign, or

(b) establishes that the person conducting the business is generally known by his creditors to be substantially engaged in selling the goods of others, or

(c) complies with the filing provisions of the Article on Secured Transactions (Article 9).

(4) Any "or return" term of a contract for sale is to be treated as a separate contract for sale within the statute of frauds section of this Article (Section 2—201) and as contradicting the sale aspect of the contract within the provisions of this Article on parol or extrinsic evidence (Section 2—202).

§ 2—327. Special Incidents of Sale on Approval and Sale or Return.

(1) Under a sale on approval unless otherwise agreed

(a) although the goods are identified to the contract the risk of loss and the title do not pass to the buyer until acceptance; and

(b) use of the goods consistent with the purpose of trial is not acceptance but failure seasonably to notify the seller of election to return the goods is acceptance, and if the goods conform to the contract acceptance of any part is acceptance of the whole; and

(c) after due notification of election to return, the return is at the seller's risk and expense but a merchant buyer must follow any reasonable instructions.

(2) Under a sale or return unless otherwise agreed

(a) the option to return extends to the whole or any commercial unit of the goods while in substantially their original condition, but must be exercised seasonably; and

(b) the return is at the buyer's risk and expense.

§ 2—328. Sale by Auction.

(1) In a sale by auction if goods are put up in lots each lot is the subject of a separate sale.

(2) A sale by auction is complete when the auctioneer so announces by the fall of the hammer or in other customary manner. Where a bid is made while the hammer is falling in acceptance of a prior bid the auctioneer may in his discretion reopen the bidding or declare the goods sold under the bid on which the hammer was falling.

(3) Such a sale is with reserve unless the goods are in explicit terms put up without reserve. In an auction with reserve the auctioneer may withdraw the goods at any time until he announces completion of the sale. In an auction without reserve, after the auctioneer calls for bids on an article or lot, that article or lot cannot be withdrawn unless no bid is made within a reasonable time. In either case a bidder may retract his bid until the auction-

eer's announcement of completion of the sale, but a bidder's retraction does not revive any previous bid.

(4) If the auctioneer knowingly receives a bid on the seller's behalf or the seller makes or procures such a bid, and notice has not been given that liberty for such bidding is reserved, the buyer may at his option avoid the sale or take the goods at the price of the last good faith bid prior to the completion of the sale. This subsection shall not apply to any bid at a forced sale.

PART 4

TITLE, CREDITORS AND GOOD FAITH PURCHASERS

§ 2—401. Passing of Title; Reservation for Security; Limited Application of This Section.

Each provision of this Article with regard to the rights, obligations and remedies of the seller, the buyer, purchasers or other third parties applies irrespective of title to the goods except where the provision refers to such title. Insofar as situations are not covered by the other provisions of this Article and matters concerning title became material the following rules apply:

(1) Title to goods cannot pass under a contract for sale prior to their identification to the contract (Section 2—501), and unless otherwise explicitly agreed the buyer acquires by their identification a special property as limited by this Act. Any retention or reservation by the seller of the title (property) in goods shipped or delivered to the buyer is limited in effect to a reservation of a security interest. Subject to these provisions and to the provisions of the Article on Secured Transactions (Article 9), title to goods passes from the seller to the buyer in any manner and on any conditions explictly agreed on by the parties.

(2) Unless otherwise explicitly agreed title passes to the buyer at the time and place at which the seller completes his performance with reference to the physical delivery of the goods, despite any reservation of a security interest and even though a document of title is to be delivered at a different time or place; and in particular and despite any reservation of a security interest by the bill of lading

    (a) if the contract requires or authorizes the seller to send the goods to the buyer but does not require him to deliver them at destination, title passes to the buyer at the time and place of shipment; but

    (b) if the contract requires delivery at destination, title passes on tender there.

(3) Unless otherwise explicitly agreed where delivery is to be made without moving the goods,

    (a) if the seller is to deliver a document of title, title passes at the time when and the place where he delivers such documents; or

    (b) if the goods are at the time of contracting already identified and no documents are to be delivered, title passes at the time and place of contracting.

(4) A rejection or other refusal by the buyer to receive or retain the goods, whether or not justified, or a justified revocation of acceptance revests title to the goods in the seller. Such revesting occurs by operation of law and is not a "sale".

§ 2—402. Rights of Seller's Creditors Against Sold Goods.

(1) Except as provided in subsections (2) and (3), rights of unsecured creditors of the seller with respect to goods which have been identified to a contract for sale are subject to the buyer's rights to recover the goods under this Article (Sections 2—502 and 2—716).

(2) A creditor of the seller may treat a sale or an identification of goods to a contract for sale as void if as against him a retention of possession by the seller is fraudulent under any rule of law of the state where the goods are situated, except that retention of possession in good faith and current course of trade by a merchant-seller for a commercially reasonable time after a sale or identification is not fraudulent.

(3) Nothing in this Article shall be deemed to impair the rights of creditors of the seller

(a) under the provisions of the Article on Secured Transactions (Article 9); or

(b) where identification to the contract or delivery is made not in current course of trade but in satisfaction of or as security for a pre-existing claim for money, security or the like and is made under circumstances which under any rule of law of the state where the goods are situated would apart from this Article constitute the transaction a fraudulent transfer or voidable preference.

§ 2—403. Power to Transfer; Good Faith Purchase of Goods; "Entrusting".

(1) A purchaser of goods acquires all title which his transferor had or had power to transfer except that a purchaser of a limited interest acquires rights only to the extent of the interest purchased. A person with voidable title has power to transfer a good title to a good faith purchaser for value. When goods have been delivered under a transaction of purchase the purchaser has such power even though

(a) the transferor was deceived as to the identity of the purchaser, or

(b) the delivery was in exchange for a check which is later dishonored, or

(c) it was agreed that the transaction was to be a "cash sale", or

(d) the delivery was procured through fraud punishable as larcenous under the criminal law.

(2) Any entrusting of possession of goods to a merchant who deals in goods of that kind gives him power to transfer all rights of the entruster to a buyer in ordinary course of business.

(3) "Entrusting" includes any delivery and any acquiescence in retention of possession regardless of any condition expressed between the parties to the delivery or acquiescence and regardless of whether the procurement of the entrusting or the possessor's disposition of the goods have been such as to be larcenous under the criminal law.

(4) The rights of other purchasers of goods and of lien creditors are governed by the Articles on Secured Transactions (Article 9), Bulk Transfers (Article 6) and Documents of Title (Article 7).

PART 5

PERFORMANCE

§ 2—501. Insurable Interest in Goods; Manner of Identification of Goods.

(1) The buyer obtains a special property and an insurable interest in goods by identification of existing goods as goods to which the contract refers even though the goods so identified are non-conforming and he has an option to return or reject them. Such identification can be made at any time and in any manner explicitly agreed to by the parties. In the absence of explicit agreement identification occurs

(a) when the contract is made if it is for the sale of goods already existing and identified;

(b) if the contract is for the sale of future goods other than those described in paragraph (c), when goods are shipped, marked or otherwise designated by the seller as goods to which the contract refers;

(c) when the crops are planted or otherwise become growing crops or the young are conceived if the contract is for the sale of unborn young to be born within twelve months after contracting or for the sale of crops to be harvested within twelve months or the next normal harvest season after contracting whichever is longer.

(2) The seller retains an insurable interest in goods so long as title to or any security interest in the goods remains in him and where the identification is by the seller alone he may until default or insolvency or notification to the buyer that the identification is final substitute other goods for those identified.

(3) Nothing in this section impairs any insurable interest recognized under any other statute or rule of law.

§ 2—502. Buyer's Right to Goods on Seller's Insolvency.

(1) Subject to subsection (2) and even though the goods have not been shipped a buyer who has paid a part or all of the price of goods in which he has a special property under the provisions of the immediately preceding section may on making and keeping good a tender of any unpaid portion of their price recover them from the seller if the seller becomes insolvent within ten days after receipt of the first installment on their price.

(2) If the identification creating his special property has been made by the buyer he acquires the right to recover the goods only if they conform to the contract for sale.

§ 2—503. Manner of Seller's Tender of Delivery.

(1) Tender of delivery requires that the seller put and hold conforming goods at the buyer's disposition and give the buyer any notification reasonably necessary to enable him to take delivery. The manner, time and place for tender are determined by the agreement and this Article, and in particular

(a) tender must be at a reasonable hour, and if it is of goods they must be kept available for the period reasonably necessary to enable the buyer to take possession; but

(b) unless otherwise agreed the buyer must furnish facilities reasonably suited to the receipt of the goods.

(2) Where the case is within the next section respecting shipment tender requires that the seller comply with its provisions.

(3) Where the seller is required to deliver at a particular destination tender requires that he comply with subsection (1) and also in any appropriate case tender documents as described in subsections (4) and (5) of this section.

(4) Where goods are in the possession of a bailee and are to be delivered without being moved

(a) tender requires that the seller either tender a negotiable document of title covering such goods or procure acknowledgment by the bailee of the buyer's right to possession of the goods; but

(b) tender to the buyer of a non-negotiable document of title or of a written direction to the bailee to deliver is sufficient tender unless the buyer seasonably objects, and receipt by the bailee of notification of the buyer's rights fixes those rights as against the bailee and all third persons; but risk of loss of the goods and of any failure by the bailee to honor the non-negotiable document of title or to obey the direction remains on the seller until the buyer has had a reasonable time to present the document or direction, and a refusal by the bailee to honor the document or to obey the direction defeats the tender.

(5) Where the contract requires the seller to deliver documents

(a) he must tender all such documents in correct form, except as provided in this Article with respect to bills of lading in a set (subsection (2) of Section 2—323); and

(b) tender through customary banking channels is sufficient and dishonor of a draft accompanying the documents constitutes non-acceptance or rejection.

§ 2—504. Shipment by Seller.

Where the seller is required or authorized to send the goods to the buyer and the contract does not require him to deliver them at a particular destination, then unless otherwise agreed he must

(a) put the goods in the possession of such a carrier and make such a contract for their transportation as may be reasonable having regard to the nature of the goods and other circumstances of the case; and

(b) obtain and promptly deliver or tender in due form any document necessary to enable the buyer to obtain possession of the goods or otherwise required by the agreement or by usage of trade; and

(c) promptly notify the buyer of the shipment.

Failure to notify the buyer under paragraph (c) or to make a proper contract under paragraph (a) is a ground for rejection only if material delay or loss ensues.

§ 2—505. Seller's Shipment Under Reservation.

(1) Where the seller has identified goods to the contract by or before shipment:

(a) his procurement of a negotiable bill of lading to his own order or otherwise reserves in him a security interest in the goods. His procurement of the bill to the order of a financing agency or of the buyer indicates in addition only the seller's expectation of transferring that interest to the person named.

(b) a non-negotiable bill of lading to himself or his nominee reserves possession of the goods as security but except in a case of conditional delivery (subsection (2) of Section 2—507) a non-negotiable bill of lading naming the buyer as consignee reserves no security interest even though the seller retains possession of the bill of lading.

(2) When shipment by the seller with reservation of a security interest is in violation of the contract for sale it constitutes an improper contract for transportation within the preceding section but impairs neither the rights given to the buyer by shipment and identification of the goods to the contract nor the seller's powers as a holder of a negotiable document.

§ 2—506. Rights of Financing Agency.

(1) A financing agency by paying or purchasing for value a draft which relates to a shipment of goods acquires to the extent of the payment or purchase and in addition to its own rights under the draft and any document of title securing it any rights of the shipper in the goods including the right to stop delivery and the shipper's right to have the draft honored by the buyer.

(2) The right to reimbursement of a financing agency which has in good faith honored or purchased the draft under commitment to or authority from the buyer is not impaired by subsequent discovery of defects with reference to any relevant document which was apparently regular on its face.

§ 2—507. Effect of Seller's Tender; Delivery on Condition.

(1) Tender of delivery is a condition to the buyer's duty to accept the goods and, unless otherwise agreed, to his duty to pay for them. Tender entitles the seller to acceptance of the goods and to payment according to the contract.

(2) Where payment is due and demanded on the delivery to the buyer of goods or documents of title, his right as against the seller to retain or dispose of them is conditional upon his making the payment due.

§ 2—508. Cure by Seller of Improper Tender or Delivery; Replacement.

(1) Where any tender or delivery by the seller is rejected because non-conforming and the time for performance has not yet expired, the seller may seasonably notify the buyer of his intention to cure and may then within the contract time make a conforming delivery.

(2) Where the buyer rejects a non-conforming tender which the seller had reasonable grounds to believe would be acceptable with or without money allowance the seller may if he seasonably notifies the buyer have a further reasonable time to substitute a conforming tender.

§ 2—509. Risk of Loss in the Absence of Breach.

(1) Where the contract requires or authorizes the seller to ship the goods by carrier

(a) if it does not require him to deliver them at a particular destination, the risk of loss passes to the buyer when the goods are duly delivered to the carrier even though the shipment is under reservation (Section 2—505); but

(b) if it does require him to deliver them at a particular destination and the goods are there duly tendered while in the possession of the carrier, the risk of loss passes to the buyer when the goods are there duly so tendered as to enable the buyer to take delivery.

(2) Where the goods are held by a bailee to be delivered without being moved, the risk of loss passes to the buyer

(a) on his receipt of a negotiable document of title covering the goods; or

(b) on acknowledgment by the bailee of the buyer's right to possession of the goods; or

(c) after his receipt of a non-negotiable document of title or other written direction to deliver, as provided in subsection (4) (b) of Section 2—503.

(3) In any case not within subsection (1) or (2), the risk of loss passes to the buyer on his receipt of the goods if the seller is a merchant; otherwise the risk passes to the buyer on tender of delivery.

(4) The provisions of this section are subject to contrary agreement of the parties and to the provisions of this Article on sale on approval (Section 2—327) and on effect of breach on risk of loss (Section 2—510).

§ 2—510. Effect of Breach on Risk of Loss.

(1) Where a tender or delivery of goods so fails to conform to the contract as to give a right of rejection the risk of their loss remains on the seller until cure or acceptance.

(2) Where the buyer rightfully revokes acceptance he may to the extent of any deficiency in his effective insurance coverage treat the risk of loss as having rested on the seller from the beginning.

(3) Where the buyer as to conforming goods already identified to the contract for sale repudiates or is otherwise in breach before risk of their loss has passed to him, the seller may to the extent of any deficiency in his effective insurance coverage treat the risk of loss as resting on the buyer for a commercially reasonable time.

§ 2—511. Tender of Payment by Buyer; Payment by Check.

(1) Unless otherwise agreed tender of payment is a condition to the seller's duty to tender and complete any delivery.

(2) Tender of payment is sufficient when made by any means or in any manner current in the ordinary course of business unless the seller demands payment in legal tender and gives any extension of time reasonably necessary to procure it.

(3) Subject to the provisions of this Act on the effect of an instrument on an obligation (Section 3—802), payment by check is conditional and is defeated as between the parties by dishonor of the check on due presentment.

§ 2—512. Payment by Buyer Before Inspection.

(1) Where the contract requires payment before inspection non-conformity of the goods does not excuse the buyer from so making payment unless

(a) the non-conformity appears without inspection; or

(b) despite tender of the required documents the circumstances would justify injunction against honor under the provisions of this Act (Section 5—114).

(2) Payment pursuant to subsection (1) does not constitute an acceptance of goods or impair the buyer's right to inspect or any of his remedies.

§ 2—513. Buyer's Right to Inspection of Goods.

(1) Unless otherwise agreed and subject to subsection (3), where goods are tendered or delivered or identified to the contract for sale, the buyer has a right before payment or acceptance to inspect them at any reasonable place and time and in any reasonable manner. When the seller is required or authorized to send the goods to the buyer, the inspection may be after their arrival.

(2) Expenses of inspection must be borne by the buyer but may be recovered from the seller if the goods do not conform and are rejected.

(3) Unless otherwise agreed and subject to the provisions of this Article on C.I.F. contracts (subsection (3) of Section 2—321), the buyer is not entitled to inspect the goods before payment of the price when the contract provides

(a) for delivery "C.O.D." or on other like terms; or

(b) for payment against documents of title, except where such payment is due only after the goods are to become available for inspection.

(4) A place or method of inspection fixed by the parties is presumed to be exclusive but un-

less otherwise expressly agreed it does not postpone identification or shift the place for delivery or for passing the risk of loss. If compliance becomes impossible, inspection shall be as provided in this section unless the place or method fixed was clearly intended as an indispensable condition failure of which avoids the contract.

§ 2—514. When Documents Deliverable on Acceptance; When on Payment.

Unless otherwise agreed documents against which a draft is drawn are to be delivered to the drawee on acceptance of the draft if it is payable more than three days after presentment; otherwise, only on payment.

§ 2—515. Preserving Evidence of Goods in Dispute.

In furtherance of the adjustment of any claim or dispute

(a) either party on reasonable notification to the other and for the purpose of ascertaining the facts and preserving evidence has the right to inspect, test and sample the goods including such of them as may be in the possession or control of the other; and

(b) the parties may agree to a third party inspection or survey to determine the conformity or condition of the goods and may agree that the findings shall be binding upon them in any subsequent litigation or adjustment.

PART 6

BREACH, REPUDIATION AND EXCUSE

§ 2—601. Buyer's Rights on Improper Delivery.

Subject to the provisions of this Article on breach in installment contracts (Section 2—612) and unless otherwise agreed under the sections on contractual limitations of remedy (Sections 2—718 and 2—719), if the goods or the tender of delivery fail in any respect to conform to the contract, the buyer may

(a) reject the whole; or

(b) accept the whole; or

(c) accept any commercial unit or units and reject the rest.

§ 2—602. Manner and Effect of Rightful Rejection.

(1) Rejection of goods must be within a reasonable time after their delivery or tender. It is ineffective unless the buyer seasonably notifies the seller.

(2) Subject to the provisions of the two following sections on rejected goods (Sections 2—603 and 2—604),

(a) after rejection any exercise of ownership by the buyer with respect to any commercial unit is wrongful as against the seller; and

(b) if the buyer has before rejection taken physical possession of goods in which he does not have a security interest under the provisions of this Article (subsection (3) of Section 2—711), he is under a duty after rejection to hold them with reasonable care at the seller's disposition for a time sufficient to permit the seller to remove them; but

(c) the buyer has no further obligations with regard to goods rightfully rejected.

(3) The seller's rights with respect to goods wrongfully rejected are governed by the provisions of this Article on Seller's remedies in general (Section 2—703).

§ 2—603. Merchant Buyer's Duties as to Rightfully Rejected Goods.

(1) Subject to any security interest in the buyer (subsection (3) of Section 2—711), when the seller has no agent or place of business at the market of rejection a merchant buyer is under a duty after rejection of goods in his possession or control to follow any reasonable instructions received from the seller with respect to the goods and in the absence of such instructions to make reasonable efforts to sell them for the seller's account if they are perishable or threaten to decline in value speedily. Instructions are not reasonable if on demand indemnity for expenses is not forthcoming.

(2) When the buyer sells goods under subsection (1), he is entitled to reimbursement from the seller or out of the proceeds for reasonable expenses of caring for and selling them, and if the expenses include no selling commission then to such commission as is usual in the trade or if there is none to a reasonable sum not exceeding ten per cent on the gross proceeds.

(3) In complying with this section the buyer is held only to good faith and good faith conduct hereunder is neither acceptance nor conversion nor the basis of an action for damages.

§ 2—604. Buyer's Options as to Salvage of Rightfully Rejected Goods.

Subject to the provisions of the immediately preceding section on perishables if the seller gives no instructions within a reasonable time after notification of rejection the buyer may store the rejected goods for the seller's account or reship them to him or resell them for the seller's account with reimbursement as provided in the preceding section. Such action is not acceptance or conversion.

§ 2—605. Waiver of Buyer's Objections by Failure to Particularize.

(1) The buyer's failure to state in connection with rejection a particular defect which is ascertainable by reasonable inspection precludes him from relying on the unstated defect to justify rejection or to establish breach

    (a) where the seller could have cured it if stated seasonably; or

    (b) between merchants when the seller has after rejection made a request in writing for a full and final written statement of all defects on which the buyer proposes to rely.

(2) Payment against documents made without reservation of rights precludes recovery of the payment for defects apparent on the face of the documents.

§ 2—606. What Constitutes Acceptance of Goods.

(1) Acceptance of goods occurs when the buyer

    (a) after a reasonable opportunity to inspect the goods signifies to the seller that the goods are conforming or that he will take or retain them in spite of their nonconformity; or

    (b) fails to make an effective rejection (subsection (1) of Section 2—602), but such acceptance does not occur until the buyer has had a reasonable opportunity to inspect them; or

    (c) does any act inconsistent with the seller's ownership; but if such act is wrongful as against the seller it is an acceptance only if ratified by him.

(2) Acceptance of a part of any commercial unit is acceptance of that entire unit.

§ 2—607. Effect of Acceptance; Notice of Breach; Burden of Establishing Breach After Acceptance; Notice of Claim or Litigation to Person Answerable Over.

(1) The buyer must pay at the contract rate for any goods accepted.

(2) Acceptance of goods by the buyer precludes rejection of the goods accepted and if made with knowledge of a non-conformity cannot be revoked because of it unless the acceptance was on the reasonable assumption that the non-conformity would be seasonably cured but acceptance does not of itself impair any other remedy provided by this Article for nonconformity.

(3) Where a tender has been accepted

    (a) the buyer must within a reasonable time after he discovers or should have discovered any breach notify the seller of breach or be barred from any remedy; and

    (b) if the claim is one for infringement or the like (subsection (3) of Section 2—312) and the buyer is sued as a result of such a breach he must so notify the seller within a reasonable time after he receives notice of the litigation or be barred from any remedy over for liability established by the litigation.

(4) The burden is on the buyer to establish any breach with respect to the goods accepted.

(5) Where the buyer is sued for breach of a warranty or other obligation for which his seller is answerable over

(a) he may give his seller written notice of the litigation. If the notice states that the seller may come in and defend and that if the seller does not do so he will be bound in any action against him by his buyer by any determination of fact common to the two litigations, then unless the seller after seasonable receipt of the notice does come in and defend he is so bound.

(b) if the claim is one for infringement or the like (subsection (3) of Section 2—312) the original seller may demand in writing that his buyer turn over to him control of the litigation including settlement or else be barred from any remedy over and if he also agrees to bear all expense and to satisfy any adverse judgment, then unless the buyer after seasonable receipt of the demand does turn over control the buyer is so barred.

(6) The provisions of subsections (3), (4) and (5) apply to any obligation of a buyer to hold the seller harmless against infringement or the like (subsection (3) of Section 2—312).

§ 2—608. Revocation of Acceptance in Whole or in Part.

(1) The buyer may revoke his acceptance of a lot or commercial unit whose non-conformity substantially impairs its value to him if he has accepted it

(a) on the reasonable assumption that its non-conformity would be cured and it has not been seasonably cured; or

(b) without discovery of such non-conformity if his acceptance was reasonably induced either by the difficulty of discovery before acceptance or by the seller's assurances.

(2) Revocation of acceptance must occur within a reasonable time after the buyer discovers or should have discovered the ground for it and before any substantial change in condition of the goods which is not caused by their own defects. It is not effective until the buyer notifies the seller of it.

(3) A buyer who so revokes has the same rights and duties with regard to the goods involved as if he had rejected them.

§ 2—609. Right to Adequate Assurance of Performance.

(1) A contract for sale imposes an obligation on each party that the other's expectation of receiving due performance will not be impaired. When reasonable grounds for insecurity arise with respect to the performance of either party the other may in writing demand adequate assurance of due performance and until he receives such assurance may if commercially reasonable suspend any performance for which he has not already received the agreed return.

(2) Between merchants the reasonableness of grounds for insecurity and the adequacy of any assurance offered shall be determined according to commercial standards.

(3) Acceptance of any improper delivery or payment does not prejudice the aggrieved party's right to demand adequate assurance of future performance.

(4) After receipt of a justified demand failure to provide within a reasonable time not exceeding thirty days such assurance of due performance as is adequate under the circumstances of the particular case is a repudiation of the contract.

§ 2—610. Anticipatory Repudiation.

When either party repudiates the contract with respect to a performance not yet due the loss of which will substantially impair the value of the contract to the other, the aggrieved party may

(a) for a commercially reasonable time await performance by the repudiating party; or

(b) resort to any remedy for breach (Section 2—703 or Section 2—711), even though he has notified the repudiating party that he would await the latter's performance and has urged retraction; and

(c) in either case suspend his own performance or proceed in accordance with the provisions of this Article on the seller's right to identify goods to the contract notwithstanding breach or to salvage unfinished goods (Section 2—704).

§ 2—611. Retraction of Anticipatory Repudiation.

(1) Until the repudiating party's next performance is due he can retract his repudiation unless the aggrieved party has since the repudiation cancelled or materially changed his position or otherwise indicated that he considers the repudiation final.

(2) Retraction may be by any method which clearly indicates to the aggrieved party that the repudiating party intends to perform, but must include any assurance justifiably demanded under the provisions of this Article (Section 2—609).

(3) Retraction reinstates the repudiating party's rights under the contract with due excuse and allowance to the aggrieved party for any delay occasioned by the repudiation.

§ 2—612. "Installment Contract"; Breach.

(1) An "installment contract" is one which requires or authorizes the delivery of goods in separate lots to be separately accepted, even though the contract contains a clause "each delivery is a separate contract" or its equivalent.

(2) The buyer may reject any installment which is non-conforming if the non-conformity substantially impairs the value of that installment and cannot be cured or if the non-conformity is a defect in the required documents; but if the non-conformity does not fall within subsection (3) and the seller gives adequate assurance of its cure the buyer must accept that installment.

(3) Whenever non-conformity or default with respect to one or more installments substantially impairs the value of the whole contract there is a breach of the whole. But the aggrieved party reinstates the contract if he accepts a non-conforming installment without seasonably notifying of cancellation or if he brings an action with respect only to past installments or demands performance as to future installments.

§ 2—613. Casualty to Identified Goods.

Where the contract requires for its performance goods identified when the contract is made, and the goods suffer casualty without fault of either party before the risk of loss passes to the buyer, or in a proper case under a "no arrival, no sale" term (Section 2—324) then

    (a) if the loss is total the contract is avoided; and

    (b) if the loss is partial or the goods have so deteriorated as no longer to conform to the contract the buyer may nevertheless demand inspection and at his option either treat the contract as avoided or accept the goods with due allowance from the contract price for the deterioration or the deficiency in quantity but without further right against the seller.

§ 2—614. Substituted Performance.

(1) Where without fault of either party the agreed berthing, loading, or unloading facilities fail or an agreed type of carrier becomes unavailable or the agreed manner of delivery otherwise becomes commercially impracticable but a commercially reasonable substitute is available, such substitute performance must be tendered and accepted.

(2) If the agreed means or manner of payment fails because of domestic or foreign governmental regulation, the seller may withhold or stop delivery unless the buyer provides a means or manner of payment which is commercially a substantial equivalent. If delivery has already been taken, payment by the means or in the manner provided by the regulation discharges the buyer's obligation unless the regulation is discriminatory, oppressive or predatory.

§ 2—615. Excuse by Failure of Presupposed Conditions.

Except so far as a seller may have assumed a greater obligation and subject to the preceding section on substituted performance:

    (a) Delay in delivery or non-delivery in whole or in part by a seller who complies with paragraphs (b) and (c) is not a breach of his duty under a contract for sale if performance as agreed has been made impracticable by the occurrence of a contingency the non-occurrence of which was a basic assumption on which the contract was made or by compliance in good faith with any applicable foreign or domestic governmental regulation or order whether or not it later proves to be invalid.

(b) Where the causes mentioned in paragraph (a) affect only a part of the seller's capacity to perform, he must allocate production and deliveries among his customers but may at his option include regular customers not then under contract as well as his own requirements for further manufacture. He may so allocate in any manner which is fair and reasonable.

(c) The seller must notify the buyer seasonably that there will be delay or non-delivery and, when allocation is required under paragraph (b), of the estimated quota thus made available for the buyer.

§ 2—616. Procedure on Notice Claiming Excuse.

(1) Where the buyer receives notification of a material or indefinite delay or an allocation justified under the preceding section he may by written notification to the seller as to any delivery concerned, and where the prospective deficiency substantially impairs the value of the whole contract under the provisions of this Article relating to breach of installment contracts (Section 2—612), then also as to the whole,

(a) terminate and thereby discharge any unexecuted portion of the contract; or

(b) modify the contract by agreeing to take his available quota in substitution.

(2) If after receipt of such notification from the seller the buyer fails so to modify the contract within a reasonable time not exceeding thirty days the contract lapses with respect to any deliveries affected.

(3) The provisions of this section may not be negated by agreement except in so far as the seller has assumed a greater obligation under the preceding section.

PART 7

REMEDIES

§ 2—701. Remedies for Breach of Collateral Contracts Not Impaired.

Remedies for breach of any obligation or promise collateral or ancillary to a contract for sale are not impaired by the provisions of this Article.

§ 2—702. Seller's Remedies on Discovery of Buyer's Insolvency.

(1) Where the seller discovers the buyer to be insolvent he may refuse delivery except for cash including payment for all goods theretofore delivered under the contract, and stop delivery under this Article (Section 2—705).

(2) Where the seller discovers that the buyer has received goods on credit while insolvent he may reclaim the goods upon demand made within ten days after the receipt, but if misrepresentation of solvency has been made to the particular seller in writing within three months before delivery the ten day limitation does not apply. Except as provided in this subsection the seller may not base a right to reclaim goods on the buyer's fraudulent or innocent misrepresentation of solvency or of intent to pay.

(3) The seller's right to reclaim under subsection (2) is subject to the rights of a buyer in ordinary course or other good faith purchaser or lien creditor under this Article (Section 2—403). Successful reclamation of goods excludes all other remedies with respect to them.

§ 2—703. Seller's Remedies in General.

Where the buyer wrongfully rejects or revokes acceptance of goods or fails to make a payment due on or before delivery or repudiates with respect to a part or the whole, then with respect to any goods directly affected and, if the breach is of the whole contract (Section 2—612), then also with respect to the whole undelivered balance, the aggrieved seller may

(a) withhold delivery of such goods;

(b) stop delivery by any bailee as hereafter provided (Section 2—705);

(c) proceed under the next section respecting goods still unidentified to the contract;

(d) resell and recover damages as hereafter provided (Section 2—706);

(e) recover damages for non-acceptance (Section 2—708) or in a proper case the price (Section 2—709);

(f) cancel.

§ 2—704. Seller's Right to Identify Goods to the Contract Notwithstanding Breach or to Salvage Unfinished Goods.

(1) An aggrieved seller under the preceding section may

(a) identify to the contract conforming goods not already identified if at the time he learned of the breach they are in his possession or control;

(b) treat as the subject of resale goods which have demonstrably been intended for the particular contract even though those goods are unfinished.

(2) Where the goods are unfinished an aggrieved seller may in the exercise of reasonable commercial judgment for the purposes of avoiding loss and of effective realization either complete the manufacture and wholly identify the goods to the contract or cease manufacture and resell for scrap or salvage value or proceed in any other reasonable manner.

§ 2—705. Seller's Stoppage of Delivery in Transit or Otherwise.

(1) The seller may stop delivery of goods in the possession of a carrier or other bailee when he discovers the buyer to be insolvent (Section 2—702) and may stop delivery of carload, truckload, planeload or larger shipments of express or freight when the buyer repudiates or fails to make a payment due before delivery or if for any other reason the seller has a right to withhold or reclaim the goods.

(2) As against such buyer the seller may stop delivery until

(a) receipt of the goods by the buyer; or

(b) acknowledgment to the buyer by any bailee of the goods except a carrier that the bailee holds the goods for the buyer; or

(c) such acknowledgment to the buyer by a carrier by reshipment or as warehouseman; or

(d) negotiation to the buyer of any negotiable document of title covering the goods.

(3) (a) To stop delivery the seller must so notify as to enable the bailee by reasonable diligence to prevent delivery of the goods.

(b) After such notification the bailee must hold and deliver the goods according to the directions of the seller but the seller is liable to the bailee for any ensuing charges or damages.

(c) If a negotiable document of title has been issued for goods the bailee is not obliged to obey a notification to stop until surrender of the document.

(d) A carrier who has issued a non-negotiable bill of lading is not obliged to obey a notification to stop received from a person other than the consignor.

§ 2—706. Seller's Resale Including Contract for Resale.

(1) Under the conditions stated in Section 2—703 on seller's remedies, the seller may resell the goods concerned or the undelivered balance thereof. Where the resale is made in good faith and in a commercially reasonable manner the seller may recover the difference between the resale price and the contract price together with any incidental damages allowed under the provisions of this Article (Section 2—710), but less expenses saved in consequence of the buyer's breach.

(2) Except as otherwise provided in subsection (3) or unless otherwise agreed resale may be at public or private sale including sale by way of one or more contracts to sell or of identification to an existing contract of the seller. Sale may be as a unit or in parcels and at any time and place and on any terms but every aspect of the sale including the method, manner, time, place and terms must be commercially reasonable. The resale must be reasonably identified as referring to the broken contract, but it is not necessary that the goods be in existence or that any or all of them have been identified to the contract before the breach.

(3) Where the resale is at private sale the seller must give the buyer reasonable notification of his intention to resell.

(4) Where the resale is at public sale

(a) only identified goods can be sold except where there is a recognized market for a public sale of futures in goods of the kind; and

(b) it must be made at a usual place or market for public sale if one is reasonably available and except in the case of goods which are perishable or threaten to decline in value speedily the seller must give the buyer reasonable notice of the time and place of the resale; and

(c) if the goods are not to be within the view of those attending the sale the notification of sale must state the place where the goods are located and provide for their reasonable inspection by prospective bidders; and

(d) the seller may buy.

(5) A purchaser who buys in good faith at a resale takes the goods free of any rights of the original buyer even though the seller fails to comply with one or more of the requirements of this section.

(6) The seller is not accountable to the buyer for any profit made on any resale. A person in the position of a seller (Section 2—707) or a buyer who has rightfully rejected or justifiably revoked acceptance must account for any excess over the amount of his security interest, as hereinafter defined (subsection (3) of Section 2—711).

§ 2—707. "Person in the Position of a Seller".

(1) A "person in the position of a seller" includes as against a principal an agent who has paid or become responsible for the price of goods on behalf of his principal or anyone who otherwise holds a security interest or other right in goods similar to that of a seller.

(2) A person in the position of a seller may as provided in this Article withhold or stop delivery (Section 2—705) and resell (Section 2—706) and recover incidental damages (Section 2—710).

§ 2—708. Seller's Damages for Non-acceptance or Repudiation.

(1) Subject to subsection (2) and to the provisions of this Article with respect to proof of market price (Section 2—723), the measure of damages for non-acceptance or repudiation by the buyer is the difference between the market price at the time and place for tender and the unpaid contract price together with any incidental damages provided in this Article (Section 2—710), but less expenses saved in consequence of the buyer's breach.

(2) If the measure of damages provided in subsection (1) is inadequate to put the seller in as good a position as performance would have done then the measure of damages is the profit (including reasonable overhead) which the seller would have made from full performance by the buyer, together with any incidental damages provided in this Article (Section 2—710), due allowance for costs reasonably incurred and due credit for payments or proceeds of resale.

§ 2—709. Action for the Price.

(1) When the buyer fails to pay the price as it becomes due the seller may recover, together with any incidental damages under the next section, the price

(a) of goods accepted or of conforming goods lost or damaged within a commercially reasonable time after risk of their loss has passed to the buyer; and

(b) of goods identified to the contract if the seller is unable after reasonable effort to resell them at a reasonable price or the circumstances reasonably indicate that such effort will be unavailing.

(2) Where the seller sues for the price he must hold for the buyer any goods which have been identified to the contract and are still in his control except that if resale becomes possible he may resell them at any time prior to the collection of the judgment. The net proceeds of any such resale must be credited to the buyer and payment of the judgment entitles him to any goods not resold.

(3) After the buyer has wrongfully rejected or revoked acceptance of the goods or has failed to make a payment due or has repudiated

(Section 2—610), a seller who is held not entitled to the price under this section shall nevertheless be awarded damages for non-acceptance under the preceding section.

§ 2—710. Seller's Incidental Damages.

Incidental damages to an aggrieved seller include any commercially reasonable charges, expenses or commissions incurred in stopping delivery, in the transportation, care and custody of goods after the buyer's breach, in connection with return or resale of the goods or otherwise resulting from the breach.

§ 2—711. Buyer's Remedies in General; Buyer's Security Interest in Rejected Goods.

(1) Where the seller fails to make delivery or repudiates or the buyer rightfully rejects or justifiably revokes acceptance then with respect to any goods involved, and with respect to the whole if the breach goes to the whole contract (Section 2—612), the buyer may cancel and whether or not he has done so may in addition to recovering so much of the price as has been paid

  (a) "cover" and have damages under the next section as to all the goods affected whether or not they have been identified to the contract; or

  (b) recover damages for non-delivery as provided in this Article (Section 2—713).

(2) Where the seller fails to deliver or repudiates the buyer may also

  (a) if the goods have been identified recover them as provided in this Article (Section 2—502); or

  (b) in a proper case obtain specific performance or replevy the goods as provided in this Article (Section 2—716).

(3) On rightful rejection or justifiable revocation of acceptance a buyer has a security interest in goods in his possession or control for any payments made on their price and any expenses reasonably incurred in their inspection, receipt, transportation, care and custody and may hold such goods and resell them in like manner as an aggrieved seller (Section 2—706).

§ 2—712. "Cover"; Buyer's Procurement of Substitute Goods.

(1) After a breach within the preceding section the buyer may "cover" by making in good faith and without unreasonable delay any reasonable purchase of or contract to purchase goods in substitution for those due from the seller.

(2) The buyer may recover from the seller as damages the difference between the cost of cover and the contract price together with any incidental or consequential damages as hereinafter defined (Section 2—715), but less expenses saved in consequence of the seller's breach.

(3) Failure of the buyer to effect cover within this section does not bar him from any other remedy.

§ 2—713. Buyer's Damages for Non-Delivery or Repudiation.

(1) Subject to the provisions of this Article with respect to proof of market price (Section 2—723), the measure of damages for non-delivery or repudiation by the seller is the difference between the market price at the time when the buyer learned of the breach and the contract price together with any incidental and consequential damages provided in this Article (Section 2—715), but less expenses saved in consequence of the seller's breach.

(2) Market price is to be determined as of the place for tender or, in cases of rejection after arrival or revocation of acceptance, as of the place of arrival.

§ 2—714. Buyer's Damages for Breach in Regard to Accepted Goods.

(1) Where the buyer has accepted goods and given notification (subsection (3) of Section 2—607) he may recover as damages for any non-conformity of tender the loss resulting in the ordinary course of events from the seller's breach as determined in any manner which is reasonable.

(2) The measure of damages for breach of warranty is the difference at the time and place of acceptance between the value of the goods accepted and the value they would have had if they had been as warranted, unless special circumstances show proximate damages of a different amount.

(3) In a proper case any incidental and consequential damages under the next section may also be recovered.

§ 2—715. Buyer's Incidental and Consequential Damages.

(1) Incidental damages resulting from the seller's breach include expenses reasonably incurred in inspection, receipt, transportation and care and custody of goods rightfully rejected, any commercially reasonable charges, expenses or commissions in connection with effecting cover and any other reasonable expense incident to the delay or other breach.

(2) Consequential damages resulting from the seller's breach include

(a) any loss resulting from general or particular requirements and needs of which the seller at the time of contracting had reason to know and which could not reasonably be prevented by cover or otherwise; and

(b) injury to person or property proximately resulting from any breach of warranty.

§ 2—716. Buyer's Right to Specific Performance or Replevin.

(1) Specific performance may be decreed where the goods are unique or in other proper circumstances.

(2) The decree for specific performance may include such terms and conditions as to payment of the price, damages, or other relief as the court may deem just.

(3) The buyer has a right of replevin for goods identified to the contract if after reasonable effort he is unable to effect cover for such goods or the circumstances reasonably indicate that such effort will be unavailing or if the goods have been shipped under reservation and satisfaction of the security interest in them has been made or tendered.

§ 2—717. Deduction of Damages From the Price.

The buyer on notifying the seller of his intention to do so may deduct all or any part of the damages resulting from any breach of the contract from any part of the price still due under the same contract.

§ 2—718. Liquidation or Limitation of Damages; Deposits.

(1) Damages for breach by either party may be liquidated in the agreement but only at an amount which is reasonable in the light of the anticipated or actual harm caused by the breach, the difficulties of proof of loss, and the inconvenience or nonfeasibility of otherwise obtaining an adequate remedy. A term fixing unreasonably large liquidated damages is void as a penalty.

(2) Where the seller justifiably withholds delivery of goods because of the buyer's breach, the buyer is entitled to restitution of any amount by which the sum of his payments exceeds

(a) the amount to which the seller is entitled by virtue of terms liquidating the seller's damages in accordance with subsection (1), or

(b) in the absence of such terms, twenty per cent of the value of the total performance for which the buyer is obligated under the contract or $500, whichever is smaller.

(3) The buyer's right to restitution under subsection (2) is subject to offset to the extent that the seller establishes

(a) a right to recover damages under the provisions of this Article other than subsection (1), and

(b) the amount or value of any benefits received by the buyer directly or indirectly by reason of the contract.

(4) Where a seller has received payment in goods their reasonable value or the proceeds of their resale shall be treated as payments for the purposes of subsection (2); but if the seller has notice of the buyer's breach before reselling goods received in part performance, his resale is subject to the conditions laid down in this Article on resale by an aggrieved seller (Section 2—706).

§ 2—719. Contractual Modification or Limitation of Remedy.

(1) Subject to the provisions of subsections (2) and (3) of this section and of the preceding section on liquidation and limitation of damages,

(a) the agreement may provide for remedies in addition to or in substitution for those provided in this Article and may limit or alter the measure of damages recoverable under this Article, as by limiting the buyer's remedies to return of the goods and repayment of the price or to repair and replacement of non-conforming goods or parts; and

(b) resort to a remedy as provided is optional unless the remedy is expressly agreed to be exclusive, in which case it is the sole remedy.

(2) Where circumstances cause an exclusive or limited remedy to fail of its essential purpose, remedy may be had as provided in this Act.

(3) Consequential damages may be limited or excluded unless the limitation or exclusion is unconscionable. Limitation of consequential damages for injury to the person in the case of consumer goods is prima facie unconscionable but limitation of damages where the loss is commercial is not.

§ 2—720. Effect of "Cancellation" or "Rescission" on Claims for Antecedent Breach.

Unless the contrary intention clearly appears, expressions of "cancellation" or "rescission" of the contract or the like shall not be construed as a renunciation or discharge of any claim in damages for an antecedent breach.

§ 2—721. Remedies for Fraud.

Remedies for material misrepresentation or fraud include all remedies available under this Article for non-fraudulent breach. Neither rescission or a claim for rescission of the contract for sale nor rejection or return of the goods shall bar or be deemed inconsistent with a claim for damages or other remedy.

§ 2—722. Who Can Sue Third Parties for Injury to Goods.

Where a third party so deals with goods which have been identified to a contract for sale as to cause actionable injury to a party to that contract

(a) a right of action against the third party is in either party to the contract for sale who has title to or a security interest or a special property or an insurable interest in the goods; and if the goods have been destroyed or converted a right of action is also in the party who either bore the risk of loss under the contract for sale or has since the injury assumed that risk as against the other;

(b) if at the time of the injury the party plaintiff did not bear the risk of loss as against the other party to the contract for sale and there is no arrangement between them for disposition of the recovery, his suit or settlement is, subject to his own interest, as a fiduciary for the other party to the contract;

(c) either party may with the consent of the other sue for the benefit of whom it may concern.

§ 2—723. Proof of Market Price: Time and Place.

(1) If an action based on anticipatory repudiation comes to trial before the time for performance with respect to some or all of the goods, any damages based on market price (Section 2—708 or Section 2—713) shall be determined according to the price of such goods prevailing at the time when the aggrieved party learned of the repudiation.

(2) If evidence of a price prevailing at the times or places described in this Article is not readily available the price prevailing within any reasonable time before or after the time described or at any other place which in commercial judgment or under usage of trade would serve as a reasonable substitute for the one described may be used, making any proper allowance for the cost of transporting the goods to or from such other place.

(3) Evidence of a relevant price prevailing at a time or place other than the one described in this Article offered by one party is not admissible unless and until he has given the other party such notice as the court finds sufficient to prevent unfair surprise.

§ 2—724. Admissibility of Market Quotations.

Whenever the prevailing price or value of any goods regularly bought and sold in any established commodity market is in issue, reports in official publications or trade journals or in newspapers or periodicals of general circulation published as the reports of such market shall be admissible in evidence. The circumstances of the preparation of such a report may be shown to affect its weight but not its admissibility.

§ 2—725. Statute of Limitations in Contracts for Sale.

(1) An action for breach of any contract for sale must be commenced within four years after the cause of action has accrued. By the original agreement the parties may reduce the period of limitation to not less than one year but may not extend it.

(2) A cause of action accrues when the breach occurs, regardless of the aggrieved party's lack of knowledge of the breach. A breach of warranty occurs when tender of delivery is made, except that where a warranty explicitly extends to future performance of the goods and discovery of the breach must await the time of such performance the cause of action accrues when the breach is or should have been discovered.

(3) Where an action commenced within the time limited by subsection (1) is so terminated as to leave available a remedy by another action for the same breach such other action may be commenced after the expiration of the time limited and within six months after the termination of the first action unless the termination resulted from voluntary discontinuance or from dismissal for failure or neglect to prosecute.

(4) This section does not alter the law on tolling of the statute of limitations nor does it apply to causes of action which have accrued before this Act becomes effective.

ARTICLE 3

COMMERCIAL PAPER

PART 1

SHORT TITLE, FORM AND INTERPRETATION

§ 3—101. Short Title.

This Article shall be known and may be cited as Uniform Commercial Code—Commercial Paper.

§ 3—102. Definitions and Index of Definitions.

(1) In this Article unless the context otherwise requires

(a) "Issue" means the first delivery of an instrument to a holder or a remitter.

(b) An "order" is a direction to pay and must be more than an authorization or request. It must identify the person to pay with reasonable certainty. It may be addressed to one or more such persons jointly or in the alternative but not in succession.

(c) A "promise" is an undertaking to pay and must be more than an acknowledgment of an obligation.

(d) "Secondary party" means a drawer or endorser.

(e) "Instrument" means a negotiable instrument.

(2) Other definitions applying to this Article and the sections in which they appear are:

"Acceptance".   Section 3—410.
"Accommodation party".   Section 3—415.
"Alteration".   Section 3—407.
"Certificate of deposit".   Section 3—104.
"Certification".   Section 3—411.
"Check".   Section 3—104.
"Definite time".   Section 3—109.
"Dishonor".   Section 3—507.
"Draft".   Section 3—104.
"Holder in due course".   Section 3—302.
"Negotiation".   Section 3—202.
"Note".   Section 3—104.
"Notice of dishonor".   Section 3—508.
"On demand".   Section 3—108.
"Presentment".   Section 3—504.
"Protest".   Section 3—509.

"Restrictive Indorsement". Section 3—205.

"Signature". Section 3—401.

(3) The following definitions in other Articles apply to this Article:

"Account". Section 4—104.

"Banking Day". Section 4—104.

"Clearing house". Section 4—104.

"Collecting bank". Section 4—105.

"Customer". Section 4—104.

"Depositary Bank". Section 4—105.

"Documentary Draft". Section 4—104.

"Intermediary Bank". Section 4—105.

"Item". Section 4—104.

"Midnight deadline". Section 4—104.

"Payor bank". Section 4—105.

(4) In addition Article 1 contains general definitions and principles of construction and interpretation applicable throughout this Article.

§ 3—103. Limitations on Scope of Article.

(1) This Article does not apply to money, documents of title or investment securities.

(2) The provisions of this Article are subject to the provisions of the Article on Bank Deposits and Collections (Article 4) and Secured Transactions (Article 9).

§ 3—104. Form of Negotiable Instruments; "Draft"; "Check"; "Certificate of Deposit"; "Note".

(1) Any writing to be a negotiable instrument within this Article must

(a) be signed by the maker or drawer; and

(b) contain an unconditional promise or order to pay a sum certain in money and no other promise, order, obligation or power given by the maker or drawer except as authorized by this Article; and

(c) be payable on demand or at a definite time; and

(d) be payable to order or to bearer.

(2) A writing which complies with the requirements of this section is

(a) a "draft" ("bill of exchange") if it is an order;

(b) a "check" if it is a draft drawn on a bank and payable on demand;

(c) a "certificate of deposit" if it is an acknowledgment by a bank of receipt of money with an engagement to repay it;

(d) a "note" if it is a promise other than a certificate of deposit.

(3) As used in other Articles of this Act, and as the context may require, the terms "draft", "check", "certificate of deposit" and "note" may refer to instruments which are not negotiable within this Article as well as to instruments which are so negotiable.

§ 3—105. When Promise or Order Unconditional.

(1) A promise or order otherwise unconditional is not made conditional by the fact that the instrument

(a) is subject to implied or constructive conditions; or

(b) states its consideration, whether performed or promised, or the transaction which gave rise to the instrument, or that the promise or order is made or the instrument matures in accordance with or "as per" such transaction; or

(c) refers to or states that it arises out of a separate agreement or refers to a separate agreement for rights as to prepayment or acceleration; or

(d) states that it is drawn under a letter of credit; or

(e) states that it is secured, whether by mortgage, reservation of title or otherwise; or

(f) indicates a particular account to be debited or any other fund or source from which reimbursement is expected; or

(g) is limited to payment out of a particular fund or the proceeds of a particular source, if the instrument is issued by a government or governmental agency or unit; or

(h) is limited to payment out of the entire assets of a partnership, unincorporated association, trust or estate by or on behalf of which the instrument is issued.

(2) A promise or order is not unconditional if the instrument

    (a) states that it is subject to or governed by any other agreement; or

    (b) states that it is to be paid only out of a particular fund or source except as provided in this section.

§ 3—106. Sum Certain.

(1) The sum payable is a sum certain even though it is to be paid

    (a) with stated interest or by stated installments; or

    (b) with stated different rates of interest before and after default or a specified date; or

    (c) with a stated discount or addition if paid before or after the date fixed for payment; or

    (d) with exchange or less exchange, whether at a fixed rate or at the current rate; or

    (e) with costs of collection or an attorney's fee or both upon default.

(2) Nothing in this section shall validate any term which is otherwise illegal.

§ 3—107. Money.

(1) An instrument is payable in money if the medium of exchange in which it is payable is money at the time the instrument is made. An instrument payable in "currency" or "current funds" is payable in money.

(2) A promise or order to pay a sum stated in a foreign currency is for a sum certain in money and, unless a different medium of payment is specified in the instrument, may be satisfied by payment of that number of dollars which the stated foreign currency will purchase at the buying sight rate for that currency on the day on which the instrument is payable or, if payable on demand, on the day of demand. If such an instrument specifies a foreign currency as the medium of payment the instrument is payable in that currency.

§ 3—108. Payable on Demand.

Instruments payable on demand include those payable at sight or on presentation and those in which no time for payment is stated.

§ 3—109. Definite Time.

(1) An instrument is payable at a definite time if by its terms it is payable

    (a) on or before a stated date or at a fixed period after a stated date; or

    (b) at a fixed period after sight; or

    (c) at a definite time subject to any acceleration; or

    (d) at a definite time subject to extension at the option of the holder, or to extension to a further definite time at the option of the maker or acceptor or automatically upon or after a specified act or event.

(2) An instrument which by its terms is otherwise payable only upon an act or event uncertain as to time of occurrence is not payable at a definite time even though the act or event has occurred.

§ 3—110. Payable to Order.

(1) An instrument is payable to order when by its terms it is payable to the order or assigns of any person therein specified with reasonable certainty, or to him or his order, or when it is conspicuously designated on its face as "exchange" or the like and names a payee. It may be payable to the order of

    (a) the maker or drawer; or

    (b) the drawee; or

    (c) a payee who is not maker, drawer or drawee; or

    (d) two or more payees together or in the alternative; or

    (e) an estate, trust or fund, in which case it is payable to the order of the representative of such estate, trust or fund or his successors; or

    (f) an office, or an officer by his title as such in which case it is payable to the principal but the incumbent of the office or his successors may act as if he or they were the holder; or

    (g) a partnership or unincorporated association, in which case it is payable to the partnership or association and may be indorsed or transferred by any person thereto authorized.

(2) An instrument not payable to order is not made so payable by such words as "payable upon return of this instrument properly indorsed."

(3) An instrument made payable both to order and to bearer is payable to order unless the bearer words are handwritten or typewritten.

§ 3—111. Payable to Bearer.

An instrument is payable to bearer when by its terms it is payable to

(a) bearer or the order of bearer; or

(b) a specified person or bearer; or

(c) "cash" or the order of "cash", or any other indication which does not purport to designate a specific payee.

§ 3—112. Terms and Omissions Not Affecting Negotiability.

(1) The negotiability of an instrument is not affected by

(a) the omission of a statement of any consideration or of the place where the instrument is drawn or payable; or

(b) a statement that collateral has been given to secure obligations either on the instrument or otherwise of an obligor on the instrument or that in case of default on those obligations the holder may realize on or dispose of the collateral; or

(c) a promise or power to maintain or protect collateral or to give additional collateral; or

(d) a term authorizing a confession of judgment on the instrument if it is not paid when due; or

(e) a term purporting to waive the benefit of any law intended for the advantage or protection of any obligor; or

(f) a term in a draft providing that the payee by indorsing or cashing it acknowledges full satisfaction of an obligation of the drawer; or

(g) a statement in a draft drawn in a set of parts (Section 3—801) to the effect that the order is effective only if no other part has been honored.

(2) Nothing in this section shall validate any term which is otherwise illegal.

§ 3—113. Seal.

An instrument otherwise negotiable is within this Article even though it is under a seal.

§ 3—114. Date, Antedating, Postdating.

(1) The negotiability of an instrument is not affected by the fact that it is undated, antedated or postdated.

(2) Where an instrument is antedated or postdated the time when it is payable is determined by the stated date if the instrument is payable on demand or at a fixed period after date.

(3) Where the instrument or any signature thereon is dated, the date is presumed to be correct.

§ 3—115. Incomplete Instruments.

(1) When a paper whose contents at the time of signing show that it is intended to become an instrument is signed while still incomplete in any necessary respect it cannot be enforced until completed, but when it is completed in accordance with authority given it is effective as completed.

(2) If the completion is unauthorized the rules as to material alteration apply (Section 3—407), even though the paper was not delivered by the maker or drawer; but the burden of establishing that any completion is unauthorized is on the party so asserting.

§ 3—116. Instruments Payable to Two or More Persons.

An instrument payable to the order of two or more persons

(a) if in the alternative is payable to any one of them and may be negotiated, discharged or enforced by any of them who has possession of it;

(b) if not in the alternative is payable to all of them and may be negotiated, discharged or enforced only by all of them.

§ 3—117. Instruments Payable With Words of Description.

An instrument made payable to a named person with the addition of words describing him

(a) as agent or officer of a specified person is payable to his principal but the agent or officer may act as if he were the holder;

(b) as any other fiduciary for a specified person or purpose is payable to the payee and may be negotiated, discharged or enforced by him;

(c) in any other manner is payable to the payee unconditionally and the additional words are without effect on subsequent parties.

§ 3—118. Ambiguous Terms and Rules of Construction.

The following rules apply to every instrument:

(a) Where there is doubt whether the instrument is a draft or a note the holder may treat it as either. A draft drawn on the drawer is effective as a note.

(b) Handwritten terms control typewritten and printed terms, and typewritten control printed.

(c) Words control figures except that if the words are ambiguous figures control.

(d) Unless otherwise specified a provision for interest means interest at the judgment rate at the place of payment from the date of the instrument, or if it is undated from the date of issue.

(e) Unless the instrument otherwise specifies two or more persons who sign as maker, acceptor or drawer or indorser and as a part of the same transaction are jointly and severally liable even though the instrument contains such words as "I promise to pay."

(f) Unless otherwise specified consent to extension authorizes a single extension for not longer than the original period. A consent to extension, expressed in the instrument, is binding on secondary parties and accommodation makers. A holder may not exercise his option to extend an instrument over the objection of a maker or acceptor or other party who in accordance with Section 3—604 tenders full payment when the instrument is due.

§ 3—119. Other Writings Affecting Instrument.

(1) As between the obligor and his immediate obligee or any transferee the terms of an instrument may be modified or affected by any other written agreement executed as a part of the same transaction, except that a holder in due course is not affected by any limitation of his rights arising out of the separate written agreement if he had no notice of the limitation when he took the instrument.

(2) A separate agreement does not affect the negotiability of an instrument.

§ 3—120. Instruments "Payable Through" Bank.

An instrument which states that it is "payable through" a bank or the like designates that bank as a collecting bank to make presentment but does not of itself authorize the bank to pay the instrument.

§ 3—121. Instruments Payable at Bank.

Note: *If this Act is introduced in the Congress of the United States this section should be omitted.*
(States to select either alternative)

Alternative A—

A note or acceptance which states that it is payable at a bank is the equivalent of a draft drawn on the bank payable when it falls due out of any funds of the maker or acceptor in current account or otherwise available for such payment.

Alternative B—

A note or acceptance which states that it is payable at a bank is not of itself an order or authorization to the bank to pay it.

§ 3—122. Accrual of Cause of Action.

(1) A cause of action against a maker or an acceptor accrues

(a) in the case of a time instrument on the day after maturity;

(b) in the case of a demand instrument upon its date or, if no date is stated, on the date of issue.

(2) A cause of action against the obligor of a demand or time certificate of deposit accrues upon demand, but demand on a time certificate may not be made until on or after the date of maturity.

(3) A cause of action against a drawer of a draft or an indorser of any instrument accrues

upon demand following dishonor of the instrument. Notice of dishonor is a demand.

(4) Unless an instrument provides otherwise, interest runs at the rate provided by law for a judgment

(a) in the case of a maker, acceptor or other primary obligor of a demand instrument, from the date of demand;

(b) in all other cases from the date of accrual of the cause of action.

PART 2

TRANSFER AND NEGOTIATION

§ 3—201. Transfer: Right to Indorsement.

(1) Transfer of an instrument vests in the transferee such rights as the transferor has therein, except that a transferee who has himself been a party to any fraud or illegality affecting the instrument or who as a prior holder had notice of a defense or claim against it cannot improve his position by taking from a later holder in due course.

(2) A transfer of a security interest in an instrument vests the foregoing rights in the transferee to the extent of the interest transferred.

(3) Unless otherwise agreed any transfer for value of an instrument not then payable to bearer gives the transferee the specifically enforceable right to have the unqualified indorsement of the transferor. Negotiation takes effect only when the indorsement is made and until that time there is no presumption that the transferee is the owner.

§ 3—202. Negotiation.

(1) Negotiation is the transfer of an instrument in such form that the transferee becomes a holder. If the instrument is payable to order it is negotiated by delivery with any necessary indorsement; if payable to bearer it is negotiated by delivery.

(2) An indorsement must be written by or on behalf of the holder and on the instrument or on a paper so firmly affixed thereto as to become a part thereof.

(3) An indorsement is effective for negotiation only when it conveys the entire instrument

or any unpaid residue. If it purports to be of less it operates only as a partial assignment.

(4) Words of assignment, condition, waiver, guaranty, limitation or disclaimer of liability and the like accompanying an indorsement do not affect its character as an indorsement.

§ 3—203. Wrong or Misspelled Name.

Where an instrument is made payable to a person under a misspelled name or one other than his own he may indorse in that name or his own or both; but signature in both names may be required by a person paying or giving value for the instrument.

§ 3—204. Special Indorsement; Blank Indorsement.

(1) A special indorsement specifies the person to whom or to whose order it makes the instrument payable. Any instrument specially indorsed becomes payable to the order of the special indorsee and may be further negotiated only by his indorsement.

(2) An indorsement in blank specifies no particular indorsee and may consist of a mere signature. An instrument payable to order and indorsed in blank becomes payable to bearer and may be negotiated by delivery alone until specially indorsed.

(3) The holder may convert a blank indorsement into a special indorsement by writing over the signature of the indorser in blank any contract consistent with the character of the indorsement.

§ 3—205. Restrictive Indorsements.

An indorsement is restrictive which either

(a) is conditional; or

(b) purports to prohibit further transfer of the instrument; or

(c) includes the words "for collection", "for deposit", "pay any bank", or like terms signifying a purpose of deposit or collection; or

(d) otherwise states that it is for the benefit or use of the indorser or of another person.

§ 3—206. Effect of Restrictive Indorsement.

(1) No restrictive indorsement prevents further transfer or negotiation of the instrument.

(2) An intermediary bank, or a payor bank which is not the depositary bank, is neither given notice nor otherwise affected by a restrictive indorsement of any person except the bank's immediate transferor or the person presenting for payment.

(3) Except for an intermediary bank, any transferee under an indorsement which is conditional or includes the words "for collection", "for deposit", "pay any bank", or like terms (subparagraphs (a) and (c) of Section 3—205) must pay or apply any value given by him for or on the security of the instrument consistently with the indorsement and to the extent that he does so he becomes a holder for value. In addition such transferee is a holder in due course if he otherwise complies with the requirements of Section 3—302 on what constitutes a holder in due course.

(4) The first taker under an indorsement for the benefit of the indorser or another person (subparagraph (d) of Section 3—205) must pay or apply any value given by him for or on the security of the instrument consistently

with the indorsement and to the extent that he does so he becomes a holder for value. In addition such taker is a holder in due course if he otherwise complies with the requirements of Section 3—302 on what constitutes a holder in due course. A later holder for value is neither given notice nor otherwise affected by such restrictive indorsement unless he has knowledge that a fiduciary or other person has negotiated the instrument in any transaction for his own benefit or otherwise in breach of duty (subsection (2) of Section 3—304).

§ 3—207. Negotiation Effective Although It May Be Rescinded.

(1) Negotiation is effective to transfer the instrument although the negotiation is

(a) made by an infant, a corporation exceeding its powers, or any other person without capacity; or

(b) obtained by fraud, duress or mistake of any kind; or

(c) part of an illegal transaction; or

(d) made in breach of duty.

(2) Except as against a subsequent holder in due course such negotiation is in an appropriate case subject to rescission, the declaration of a constructive trust or any other remedy permitted by law.

§ 3—208. Reacquisition.

Where an instrument is returned to or reacquired by a prior party he may cancel any indorsement which is not necessary to his title and reissue or further negotiate the instrument, but any intervening party is discharged as against the reacquiring party and subsequent holders not in due course and if his indorsement has been cancelled is discharged as against subsequent holders in due course as well.

PART 3

RIGHTS OF A HOLDER

§ 3—301. Rights of a Holder.

The holder of an instrument whether or not he is the owner may transfer or negotiate it and, except as otherwise provided in Section 3—603 on payment or satisfaction, discharge it or enforce payment in his own name.

§ 3—302. Holder in Due Course.

(1) A holder in due course is a holder who takes the instrument

(a) for value; and

(b) in good faith; and

(c) without notice that it is overdue or has been dishonored or of any defense against or claim to it on the part of any person.

(2) A payee may be a holder in due course.

(3) A holder does not become a holder in due course of an instrument:

    (a) by purchase of it at judicial sale or by taking it under legal process; or

    (b) by acquiring it in taking over an estate; or

    (c) by purchasing it as part of a bulk transaction not in regular course of business of the transferor.

(4) A purchaser of a limited interest can be a holder in due course only to the extent of the interest purchased.

§ 3—303. Taking for Value.

A holder takes the instrument for value

    (a) to the extent that the agreed consideration has been performed or that he acquires a security interest in or a lien on the instrument otherwise than by legal process; or

    (b) when he takes the instrument in payment of or as security for an antecedent claim against any person whether or not the claim is due; or

    (c) when he gives a negotiable instrument for it or makes an irrevocable commitment to a third person.

§ 3—304. Notice to Purchaser.

(1) The purchaser has notice of a claim or defense if

    (a) the instrument is so incomplete, bears such visible evidence of forgery or alteration, or is otherwise so irregular as to call into question its validity, terms or ownership or to create an ambiguity as to the party to pay; or

    (b) the purchaser has notice that the obligation of any party is voidable in whole or in part, or that all parties have been discharged.

(2) The purchaser has notice of a claim against the instrument when he has knowledge that a fiduciary has negotiated the instrument in payment of or as security for his own debt or in any transaction for his own benefit or otherwise in breach of duty.

(3) The purchaser has notice that an instrument is overdue if he has reason to know

    (a) that any part of the principal amount is overdue or that there is an uncured default in payment of another instrument of the same series; or

    (b) that acceleration of the instrument has been made; or

    (c) that he is taking a demand instrument after demand has been made or more than a reasonable length of time after its issue. A reasonable time for a check drawn and payable within the states and territories of the United States and the District of Columbia is presumed to be thirty days.

(4) Knowledge of the following facts does not of itself give the purchaser notice of a defense or claim

    (a) that the instrument is antedated or postdated;

    (b) that it was issued or negotiated in return for an executory promise or accompanied by a separate agreement, unless the purchaser has notice that a defense or claim has arisen from the terms thereof;

    (c) that any party has signed for accommodation;

    (d) that an incomplete instrument has been completed, unless the purchaser has notice of any improper completion;

    (e) that any person negotiating the instrument is or was a fiduciary;

    (f) that there has been default in payment of interest on the instrument or in payment of any other instrument, except one of the same series.

(5) The filing or recording of a document does not of itself constitute notice within the provisions of this Article to a person who would otherwise be a holder in due course.

(6) To be effective notice must be received at such time and in such manner as to give a reasonable opportunity to act on it.

§ 3—305. Rights of a Holder in Due Course.

To the extent that a holder is a holder in due course he takes the instrument free from

(1) all claims to it on the part of any person; and

(2) all defenses of any party to the instrument with whom the holder has not dealt except

    (a) infancy, to the extent that it is a defense to a simple contract; and

    (b) such other incapacity, or duress, or illegality of the transaction, as renders the obligation of the party a nullity; and

    (c) such misrepresentation as has induced the party to sign the instrument with neither knowledge nor reasonable opportunity to obtain knowledge of its character or its essential terms; and

    (d) discharge in insolvency proceedings; and

    (e) any other discharge of which the holder has notice when he takes the instrument.

§ 3—306. Rights of One Not Holder in Due Course.

Unless he has the rights of a holder in due course any person takes the instrument subject to

    (a) all valid claims to it on the part of any person; and

    (b) all defenses of any party which would be available in an action on a simple contract; and

    (c) the defenses of want or failure of consideration, nonperformance of any condition precedent, non-delivery, or delivery for a special purpose (Section 3—408); and

    (d) the defense that he or a person through whom he holds the instrument acquired it by theft, or that payment or satisfaction to such holder would be inconsistent with the terms of a restrictive indorsement. The claim of any third person to the instrument is not otherwise available as a defense to any party liable thereon unless the third person himself defends the action for such party.

§ 3—307. Burden of Establishing Signatures, Defenses and Due Course.

(1) Unless specifically denied in the pleadings each signature on an instrument is admitted. When the effectiveness of a signature is put in issue

    (a) the burden of establishing it is on the party claiming under the signature; but

    (b) the signature is presumed to be genuine or authorized except where the action is to enforce the obligation of a purported signer who has died or become incompetent before proof is required.

(2) When signatures are admitted or established, production of the instrument entitles a holder to recover on it unless the defendant establishes a defense.

(3) After it is shown that a defense exists a person claiming the rights of a holder in due course has the burden of establishing that he or some person under whom he claims is in all respects a holder in due course.

PART 4

LIABILITY OF PARTIES

§ 3—401. Signature.

(1) No person is liable on an instrument unless his signature appears thereon.

(2) A signature is made by use of any name, including any trade or assumed name, upon an instrument, or by any word or mark used in lieu of a written signature.

§ 3—402. Signature in Ambiguous Capacity.

Unless the instrument clearly indicates that a signature made in some other capacity it is an indorsement.

§ 3—403. Signature by Authorized Representative.

(1) A signature may be made by an agent or other representative, and his authority to make it may be established as in other cases of representation. No particular form of appointment is necessary to establish such authority.

(2) An authorized representative who signs his own name to an instrument

(a) is personally obligated if the instrument neither names the person represented nor shows that the representative signed in a representative capacity;

(b) except as otherwise established between the immediate parties, is personally obligated if the instrument names the person represented but does not show that the representative signed in a representative capacity, or if the instrument does not name the person represented but does show that the representative signed in a representative capacity.

(3) Except as otherwise established the name of an organization preceded or followed by the name and office of an authorized individual is a signature made in a representative capacity.

§ 3—404. Unauthorized Signatures.

(1) Any unauthorized signature is wholly inoperative as that of the person whose name is signed unless he ratifies it or is precluded from denying it; but it operates as the signature of the unauthorized signer in favor of any person who in good faith pays the instrument or takes it for value.

(2) Any unauthorized signature may be ratified for all purposes of this Article. Such ratification does not of itself affect any rights of the person ratifying against the actual signer.

§ 3—405. Impostors; Signature in Name of Payee.

(1) An indorsement by any person in the name of a named payee is effective if

(a) an impostor by use of the mails or otherwise has induced the maker or drawer to issue the instrument to him or his confederate in the name of the payee; or

(b) a person signing as or on behalf of a maker or drawer intends the payee to have no interest in the instrument; or

(c) an agent or employee of the maker or drawer has supplied him with the name of the payee intending the latter to have no such interest.

(2) Nothing in this section shall affect the criminal or civil liability of the person so indorsing.

§ 3—406. Negligence Contributing to Alteration or Unauthorized Signature.

Any person who by his negligence substantially contributes to a material alteration of the instrument or to the making of an unauthorized signature is precluded from asserting the alteration or lack of authority against a holder in due course or against a drawee or other payor who pays the instrument in good faith and in accordance with the reasonable commercial standards of the drawee's or payor's business.

§ 3—407. Alteration.

(1) Any alteration of an instrument is material which changes the contract of any party thereto in any respect, including any such change in

(a) the number or relations of the parties; or

(b) an incomplete instrument, by completing it otherwise than as authorized; or

(c) the writing as signed, by adding to it or by removing any part of it.

(2) As against any person other than a subsequent holder in due course

(a) alteration by the holder which is both fraudulent and material discharges any party whose contract is thereby changed unless that party assents or is precluded from asserting the defense;

(b) no other alteration discharges any party and the instrument may be enforced according to its original tenor, or as to incomplete instruments according to the authority given.

(3) A subsequent holder in due course may in all cases enforce the instrument according to its original tenor, and when an incomplete instrument has been completed, he may enforce it as completed.

§ 3—408. Consideration.

Want or failure of consideration is a defense as against any person not having the rights of a holder in due course (Section 3—305), except that no consideration is necessary for an instrument or obligation thereon given in payment of or as security for an antecedent obligation of any kind. Nothing in this section shall be taken to displace any statute outside this Act under which a promise is enforceable notwithstanding lack or failure of consideration. Partial failure of consideration is a defense pro tanto whether or not the failure is in an ascertained or liquidated amount.

§ 3—409. Draft Not an Assignment.

(1) A check or other draft does not of itself operate as an assignment of any funds in the hands of the drawee available for its payment, and the drawee is not liable on the instrument until he accepts it.

(2) Nothing in this section shall affect any liability in contract, tort or otherwise arising from any letter of credit or other obligation or representation which is not an acceptance.

§ 3—410. Definition and Operation of Acceptance.

(1) Acceptance is the drawee's signed engagement to honor the draft as presented. It must be written on the draft, and may consist of his signature alone. It becomes operative when completed by delivery or notification.

(2) A draft may be accepted although it has not been signed by the drawer or is otherwise incomplete or is overdue or has been dishonored.

(3) Where the draft is payable at a fixed period after sight and the acceptor fails to date his acceptance the holder may complete it by supplying a date in good faith.

§ 3—411. Certification of a Check.

(1) Certification of a check is acceptance. Where a holder procures certification the drawer and all prior indorsers are discharged.

(2) Unless otherwise agreed a bank has no obligation to certify a check.

(3) A bank may certify a check before returning it for lack of proper indorsement. If it does so the drawer is discharged.

§ 3—412. Acceptance Varying Draft.

(1) Where the drawee's preferred acceptance in any manner varies the draft as presented the holder may refuse the acceptance and treat the draft as dishonored in which case the drawee is entitled to have his acceptance cancelled.

(2) The terms of the draft are not varied by an acceptance to pay at any particular bank or place in the United States, unless the acceptance states that the draft is to be paid only at such bank or place.

(3) Where the holder assents to an acceptance varying the terms of the draft each drawer and indorser who does not affirmatively assent is discharged.

§ 3—413. Contract of Maker, Drawer and Acceptor.

(1) The maker or acceptor engages that he will pay the instrument according to its tenor at the time of his engagement or as completed pursuant to Section 3—115 on incomplete instruments.

(2) The drawer engages that upon dishonor of the draft and any necessary notice of dishonor or protest he will pay the amount of the draft to the holder or to any indorser who takes it up. The drawer may disclaim this liability by drawing without recourse.

(3) By making, drawing or accepting the party admits as against all subsequent parties including the drawee the existence of the payee and his then capacity to indorse.

§ 3—414. Contract of Indorser; Order of Liability.

(1) Unless the indorsement otherwise specifies (as by such words as "without recourse") every indorser engages that upon dishonor and any necessary notice of dishonor and protest he will pay the instrument according to its tenor at the time of his indorsement to the holder or to any subsequent indorser who takes it up, even though the indorser who takes it up was not obligated to do so.

(2) Unless they otherwise agree indorsers are liable to one another in the order in which they indorse, which is presumed to be the order in which their signatures appear on the instrument.

§ 3—415.   **Contract of Accommodation Party.**

(1) An accommodation party is one who signs the instrument in any capacity for the purpose of lending his name to another party to it.

(2) When the instrument has been taken for value before it is due the accommodation party is liable in the capacity in which he has signed even though the taker knows of the accommodation.

(3) As against a holder in due course and without notice of the accommodation oral proof of the accommodation is not admissible to give the accommodation party the benefit of discharges dependent on his character as such.   In other cases the accommodation character may be shown by oral proof.

(4) An indorsement which shows that it is not in the chain of title is notice of its accommodation character.

(5) An accommodation party is not liable to the party accommodated, and if he pays the instrument has a right of recourse on the instrument against such party.

§ 3—416.   **Contract of Guarantor.**

(1) "Payment guaranteed" or equivalent words added to a signature mean that the signer engages that if the instrument is not paid when due he will pay it according to its tenor without resort by the holder to any other party.

(2) "Collection guaranteed" or equivalent words added to a signature mean that the signer engages that if the instrument is not paid when due he will pay it according to its tenor, but only after the holder has reduced his claim against the maker or acceptor to judgment and execution has been returned unsatisfied, or after the maker or acceptor has become insolvent or it is otherwise apparent that it is useless to proceed against him.

(3) Words of guaranty which do not otherwise specify guarantee payment.

(4) No words of guaranty added to the signature of a sole maker or acceptor affect his liability on the instrument.   Such words added to the signature of one of two or more makers or acceptors create a presumption that the signature is for the accommodation of the others.

(5) When words of guaranty are used presentment, notice of dishonor and protest are not necessary to charge the user.

(6) Any guaranty written on the instrument is enforcible notwithstanding any statute of frauds.

§ 3—417.   **Warranties on Presentment and Transfer.**

(1) Any person who obtains payment or acceptance and any prior transferor warrants to a person who in good faith pays or accepts that

(a) he has a good title to the instrument or is authorized to obtain payment or acceptance on behalf of one who has a good title; and

(b) he has no knowledge that the signature of the maker or drawer is unauthorized, except that this warranty is not given by a holder in due course acting in good faith

(i) to a maker with respect to the maker's own signature; or

(ii) to a drawer with respect to the drawer's own signature, whether or not the drawer is also the drawee; or

(iii) to an acceptor of a draft if the holder in due course took the draft after the acceptance or obtained the acceptance without knowledge that the drawer's signature was unauthorized; and

(c) the instrument has not been materially altered, except that this warranty is not given by a holder in due course acting in good faith

(i) to the maker of a note; or

(ii) to the drawer of a draft whether or not the drawer is also the drawee; or

(iii) to the acceptor of a draft with respect to an alteration made prior to the acceptance if the holder in due course took the draft after the acceptance, even though the acceptance provided "payable as originally drawn" or equivalent terms; or

    (iv) to the acceptor of a draft with respect to an alteration made after the acceptance.

(2) Any person who transfers an instrument and receives consideration warrants to his transferee and if the transfer is by indorsement to any subsequent holder who takes the instrument in good faith that

    (a) he has a good title to the instrument or is authorized to obtain payment or acceptance on behalf of one who has a good title and the transfer is otherwise rightful; and

    (b) all signatures are genuine or authorized; and

    (c) the instrument has not been materially altered; and

    (d) no defense of any party is good against him; and

    (e) he has no knowledge of any insolvency proceeding instituted with respect to the maker or acceptor or the drawer of an unaccepted instrument.

(3) By transferring "without recourse" the transferor limits the obligation stated in subsection (2) (d) to a warranty that he has no knowledge of such a defense.

(4) A selling agent or broker who does not disclose the fact that he is acting only as such gives the warranties provided in this section, but if he makes such disclosure warrants only his good faith and authority.

§ 3—418. Finality of Payment or Acceptance.

Except for recovery of bank payments as provided in the Article on Bank Deposits and Collections (Article 4) and except for liability for breach of warranty on presentment under the preceding section, payment or acceptance of any instrument is final in favor of a holder in due course, or a person who has in good faith changed his position in reliance on the payment.

§ 3—419. Conversion of Instrument; Innocent Representative.

(1) An instrument is converted when

    (a) a drawee to whom it is delivered for acceptance refuses to return it on demand; or

    (b) any person to whom it is delivered for payment refuses on demand either to pay or to return it; or

    (c) it is paid on a forged indorsement.

(2) In an action against a drawee under subsection (1) the measure of the drawee's liability is the face amount of the instrument. In any other action under subsection (1) the measure of liability is presumed to be the face amount of the instrument.

(3) Subject to the provisions of this Act concerning restrictive indorsements a representative, including a depositary or collecting bank, who has in good faith and in accordance with the reasonable commercial standards applicable to the business of such representative dealt with an instrument or its proceeds on behalf of one who was not the true owner is not liable in conversion or otherwise to the true owner beyond the amount of any proceeds remaining in his hands.

(4) An intermediary bank or payor bank which is not a depositary bank is not liable in conversion solely by reason of the fact that proceeds of an item indorsed restrictively (Sections 3—205 and 3—206) are not paid or applied consistently with the restrictive indorsement of an indorser other than its immediate transferor.

PART 5

PRESENTMENT, NOTICE OF DISHONOR AND PROTEST

§ 3—501. When Presentment, Notice of Dishonor, and Protest Necessary or Permissible.

(1) Unless excused (Section 3—511) presentment is necessary to charge secondary parties as follows:

   (a) presentment for acceptance is necessary to charge the drawer and indorsers of a draft where the draft so provides, or is payable elsewhere than at the residence or place of business of the drawee, or its date of payment depends upon such presentment. The holder may at his option present for acceptance any other draft payable at a stated date;

   (b) presentment for payment is necessary to charge any indorser;

   (c) in the case of any drawer, the acceptor of a draft payable at a bank or the maker of a note payable at a bank, presentment for payment is necessary, but failure to make presentment discharges such drawer, acceptor or maker only as stated in Section 3—502(1) (b).

(2) Unless excused (Section 3—511)

   (a) notice of any dishonor is necessary to charge any indorser;

   (b) in the case of any drawer, the acceptor of a draft payable at a bank or the maker of a note payable at a bank, notice of any dishonor is necessary, but failure to give such notice discharges such drawer, acceptor or maker only as stated in Section 3—502(1) (b).

(3) Unless excused (Section 3—511) protest of any dishonor is necessary to charge the drawer and indorsers of any draft which on its face appears to be drawn or payable outside of the states and territories of the United States and the District of Columbia. The holder may at his option make protest of any dishonor of any other instrument and in the case of a foreign draft may on insolvency of the acceptor before maturity make protest for better security.

(4) Notwithstanding any provision of this section, neither presentment nor notice of dishonor nor protest is necessary to charge an indorser who has indorsed an instrument after maturity.

§ 3—502. Unexcused Delay; Discharge.

(1) Where without excuse any necessary presentment or notice of dishonor is delayed beyond the time when it is due

   (a) any indorser is discharged; and

   (b) any drawer or the acceptor of a draft payable at a bank or the maker of a note payable at a bank who because the drawee or payor bank becomes insolvent during the delay is deprived of funds maintained with the drawee or payor bank to cover the instrument may discharge his liability by written assignment to the holder of his rights against the drawee or payor bank in respect of such funds, but such drawer, acceptor or maker is not otherwise discharged.

(2) Where without excuse a necessary protest is delayed beyond the time when it is due any drawer or indorser is discharged.

§ 3—503. Time of Presentment.

(1) Unless a different time is expressed in the instrument the time for any presentment is determined as follows:

   (a) where an instrument is payable at or a fixed period after a stated date any presentment for acceptance must be made on or before the date it is payable;

   (b) where an instrument is payable after sight it must either be presented for acceptance or negotiated within a reasonable time after date or issue whichever is later;

   (c) where an instrument shows the date on which it is payable presentment for payment is due on that date;

   (d) where an instrument is accelerated presentment for payment is due within a reasonable time after the acceleration;

(e) with respect to the liability of any secondary party presentment for acceptance or payment of any other instrument is due within a reasonable time after such party becomes liable thereon.

(2) A reasonable time for presentment is determined by the nature of the instrument, any usage of banking or trade and the facts of the particular case. In the case of an uncertified check which is drawn and payable within the United States and which is not a draft drawn by a bank the following are presumed to be reasonable periods within which to present for payment or to initiate bank collection:

(a) with respect to the liability of the drawer, thirty days after date or issue whichever is later; and

(b) with respect to the liability of an indorser, seven days after his indorsement.

(3) Where any presentment is due on a day which is not a full business day for either the person making presentment or the party to pay or accept, presentment is due on the next following day which is a full business day for both parties.

(4) Presentment to be sufficient must be made at a reasonable hour, and if at a bank during its banking day.

§ 3—504. How Presentment Made.

(1) Presentment is a demand for acceptance or payment made upon the maker, acceptor, drawee or other payor by or on behalf of the holder.

(2) Presentment may be made

(a) by mail, in which event the time of presentment is determined by the time of receipt of the mail; or

(b) through a clearing house; or

(c) at the place of acceptance or payment specified in the instrument or if there be none at the place of business or residence of the party to accept or pay. If neither the party to accept or pay nor anyone authorized to act for him is present or accessible at such place presentment is excused.

(3) It may be made

(a) to any one of two or more makers, acceptors, drawees or other payors; or

(b) to any person who has authority to make or refuse the acceptance or payment.

(4) A draft accepted or a note made payable at a bank in the United States must be presented at such bank.

(5) In the cases described in Section 4—210 presentment may be made in the manner and with the result stated in that section.

§ 3—505. Rights of Party to Whom Presentment Is Made.

(1) The party to whom presentment is made may without dishonor require

(a) exhibition of the instrument; and

(b) reasonable identification of the person making presentment and evidence of his authority to make it if made for another; and

(c) that the instrument be produced for acceptance or payment at a place specified in it, or if there be none at any place reasonable in the circumstances; and

(d) a signed receipt on the instrument for any partial or full payment and its surrender upon full payment.

(2) Failure to comply with any such requirement invalidates the presentment but the person presenting has a reasonable time in which to comply and the time for acceptance or payment runs from the time of compliance.

§ 3—506. Time Allowed for Acceptance or Payment.

(1) Acceptance may be deferred without dishonor until the close of the next business day following presentment. The holder may also in a good faith effort to obtain acceptance and without either dishonor of the instrument or discharge of secondary parties allow postponement of acceptance for an additional business day.

(2) Except as a longer time is allowed in the case of documentary drafts drawn under a letter of credit, and unless an earlier time is agreed to by the party to pay, payment of an instrument may be deferred without dishonor

pending reasonable examination to determine whether it is properly payable, but payment must be made in any event before the close of business on the day of presentment.

§ 3—507. Dishonor; Holder's Right of Recourse; Term Allowing Re-Presentment.

(1) An instrument is dishonored when

(a) a necessary or optional presentment is duly made and due acceptance or payment is refused or cannot be obtained within the prescribed time or in case of bank collections the instrument is seasonably returned by the midnight deadline (Section 4—301); or

(b) presentment is excused and the instrument is not duly accepted or paid.

(2) Subject to any necessary notice of dishonor and protest, the holder has upon dishonor an immediate right of recourse against the drawers and indorsers.

(3) Return of an instrument for lack of proper indorsement is not dishonor.

(4) A term in a draft or an indorsement thereof allowing a stated time for re-presentment in the event of any dishonor of the draft by nonacceptance if a time draft or by nonpayment if a sight draft gives the holder as against any secondary party bound by the term an option to waive the dishonor without affecting the liability of the secondary party and he may present again up to the end of the stated time.

§ 3—508. Notice of Dishonor.

(1) Notice of dishonor may be given to any person who may be liable on the instrument by or on behalf of the holder or any party who has himself received notice, or any other party who can be compelled to pay the instrument. In addition an agent or bank in whose hands the instrument is dishonored may give notice to his principal or customer or to another agent or bank from which the instrument was received.

(2) Any necessary notice must be given by a bank before its midnight deadline and by any other person before midnight of the third business day after dishonor or receipt of notice of dishonor.

(3) Notice may be given in any reasonable manner. It may be oral or written and in any terms which identify the instrument and state that it has been dishonored. A misdescription which does not mislead the party notified does not vitiate the notice. Sending the instrument bearing a stamp, ticket or writing stating that acceptance or payment has been refused or sending a notice of debit with respect to the instrument is sufficient.

(4) Written notice is given when sent although it is not received.

(5) Notice to one partner is notice to each although the firm has been dissolved.

(6) When any party is in insolvency proceedings instituted after the issue of the instrument notice may be given either to the party or to the representative of his estate.

(7) When any party is dead or incompetent notice may be sent to his last known address or given to his personal representative.

(8) Notice operates for the benefit of all parties who have rights on the instrument against the party notified.

§ 3—509. Protest; Noting for Protest.

(1) A protest is a certificate of dishonor made under the hand and seal of a United States consul or vice consul or a notary public or other person authorized to certify dishonor by the law of the place where dishonor occurs. It may be made upon information satisfactory to such person.

(2) The protest must identify the instrument and certify either that due presentment has been made or the reason why it is excused and that the instrument has been dishonored by nonacceptance or nonpayment.

(3) The protest may also certify that notice of dishonor has been given to all parties or to specified parties.

(4) Subject to subsection (5) any necessary protest is due by the time that notice of dishonor is due.

(5) If, before protest is due, an instrument has been noted for protest by the officer to make protest, the protest may be made at any time thereafter as of the date of the noting.

§ 3—510. Evidence of Dishonor and Notice of Dishonor.

The following are admissible as evidence and create a presumption of dishonor and of any notice of dishonor therein shown:

(a) a document regular in form as provided in the preceding section which purports to be a protest;

(b) the purported stamp or writing of the drawee, payor bank or presenting bank on the instrument or accompanying it stating that acceptance or payment has been refused for reasons consistent with dishonor;

(c) any book or record of the drawee, payor bank, or any collecting bank kept in the usual course of business which shows dishonor, even though there is no evidence of who made the entry.

§ 3—511. Waived or Excused Presentment, Protest or Notice of Dishonor or Delay Therein.

(1) Delay in presentment, protest or notice of dishonor is excused when the party is without notice that it is due or when the delay is caused by circumstances beyond his control and he exercises reasonable diligence after the cause of the delay ceases to operate.

(2) Presentment or notice or protest as the case may be is entirely excused when

(a) the party to be charged has waived it expressly or by implication either before or after it is due; or

(b) such party has himself dishonored the instrument or has countermanded payment or otherwise has no reason to expect or right to require that the instrument be accepted or paid; or

(c) by reasonable diligence the presentment or protest cannot be made or the notice given.

(3) Presentment is also entirely excused when

(a) the maker, acceptor or drawee of any instrument except a documentary draft is dead or in insolvency proceedings instituted after the issue of the instrument; or

(b) acceptance or payment is refused but not for want of proper presentment.

(4) Where a draft has been dishonored by nonacceptance a later presentment for payment and any notice of dishonor and protest for nonpayment are excused unless in the meantime the instrument has been accepted.

(5) A waiver of protest is also a waiver of presentment and of notice of dishonor even though protest is not required.

(6) Where a waiver of presentment or notice or protest is embodied in the instrument itself it is binding upon all parties; but where it is written above the signature of an indorser it binds him only.

PART 6

DISCHARGE

§ 3—601. Discharge of Parties.

(1) The extent of the discharge of any party from liability on an instrument is governed by the sections on

(a) payment or satisfaction (Section 3—603); or

(b) tender of payment (Section 3—604); or

(c) cancellation or renunciation (Section 3—605); or

(d) impairment of right of recourse or of collateral (Section 3—606); or

(e) reacquisition of the instrument by a prior party (Section 3—208); or

(f) fraudulent and material alteration (Section 3—407); or

(g) certification of a check (Section 3—411); or

(h) acceptance varying a draft (Section 3—412); or

(i) unexcused delay in presentment or notice of dishonor or protest (Section 3—502).

(2) Any party is also discharged from his liability on an instrument to another party by

any other act or agreement with such party which would discharge his simple contract for the payment of money.

(3) The liability of all parties is discharged when any party who has himself no right of action or recourse on the instrument

    (a) reacquires the instrument in his own right; or

    (b) is discharged under any provision of this Article, except as otherwise provided with respect to discharge for impairment of recourse or of collateral (Section 3—606).

§ 3—602. Effect of Discharge Against Holder in Due Course.

No discharge of any party provided by this Article is effective against a subsequent holder in due course unless he has notice thereof when he takes the instrument.

§ 3—603. Payment or Satisfaction.

(1) The liability of any party is discharged to the extent of his payment or satisfaction to the holder even though it is made with knowledge of a claim of another person to the instrument unless prior to such payment or satisfaction the person making the claim either supplies indemnity deemed adequate by the party seeking the discharge or enjoins payment or satisfaction by order of a court of competent jurisdiction in an action in which the adverse claimant and the holder are parties. This subsection does not, however, result in the discharge of the liability

    (a) of a party who in bad faith pays or satisfies a holder who acquired the instrument by theft or who (unless having the rights of a holder in due course) holds through one who so acquired it; or

    (b) of a party (other than an intermediary bank or a payor bank which is not a depositary bank) who pays or satisfies the holder of an instrument which has been restrictively indorsed in a manner not consistent with the terms of such restrictive indorsement.

(2) Payment or satisfaction may be made with the consent of the holder by any person including a stranger to the instrument. Surrender of the instrument to such a person gives him the rights of a transferee (Section 3—201).

§ 3—604. Tender of Payment.

(1) Any party making tender of full payment to a holder when or after it is due is discharged to the extent of all subsequent liability for interest, costs and attorney's fees.

(2) The holder's refusal of such tender wholly discharges any party who has a right of recourse against the party making the tender.

(3) Where the maker or acceptor of an instrument payable otherwise than on demand is able and ready to pay at every place of payment specified in the instrument when it is due, it is equivalent to tender.

§ 3—605. Cancellation and Renunciation.

(1) The holder of an instrument may even without consideration discharge any party

    (a) in any manner apparent on the face of the instrument or the indorsement, as by intentionally cancelling the instrument or the party's signature by destruction or mutilation, or by striking out the party's signature; or

    (b) by renouncing his rights by a writing signed and delivered or by surrender of the instrument to the party to be discharged.

(2) Neither cancellation nor renunciation without surrender of the instrument affects the title thereto.

§ 3—606. Impairment of Recourse or of Collateral.

(1) The holder discharges any party to the instrument to the extent that without such party's consent the holder

    (a) without express reservation of rights releases or agrees not to sue any person against whom the party has to the knowledge of the holder a right of recourse or agrees to suspend the right to enforce against such person the instrument or collateral or otherwise discharges such person, except that failure or delay in effecting any required presentment, protest or notice of dishonor with respect to any such person does not discharge any party as to whom presentment, protest or notice of dishonor is effective or unnecessary; or

(b) unjustifiably impairs any collateral for the instrument given by or on behalf of the party or any person against whom he has a right of recourse.

(2) By express reservation of rights against a party with a right of recourse the holder preserves

(a) all his rights against such party as of the time when the instrument was originally due; and

(b) the right of the party to pay the instrument as of that time; and

(c) all rights of such party to recourse against others.

PART 7

ADVICE OF INTERNATIONAL SIGHT DRAFT

§ 3—701. Letter of Advice of International Sight Draft.

(1) A "letter of advice" is a drawer's communication to the drawee that a described draft has been drawn.

(2) Unless otherwise agreed when a bank receives from another bank a letter of advice of an international sight draft the drawee bank may immediately debit the drawer's account and stop the running of interest pro tanto. Such a debit and any resulting credit to any account covering outstanding drafts leaves in the drawer full power to stop payment or otherwise dispose of the amount and creates no trust or interest in favor of the holder.

(3) Unless otherwise agreed and except where a draft is drawn under a credit issued by the drawee, the drawee of an international sight draft owes the drawer no duty to pay an unadvised draft but if it does so and the draft is genuine, may appropriately debit the drawer's account.

PART 8

MISCELLANEOUS

§ 3—801. Drafts in a Set.

(1) Where a draft is drawn in a set of parts, each of which is numbered and expressed to be an order only if no other part has been honored, the whole of the parts constitutes one draft but a taker of any part may become a holder in due course of the draft.

(2) Any person who negotiates, indorses or accepts a single part of a draft drawn in a set thereby becomes liable to any holder in due course of that part as if it were the whole set, but as between different holders in due course to whom different parts have been negotiated the holder whose title first accrues has all rights to the draft and its proceeds.

(3) As against the drawee the first presented part of a draft drawn in a set is the part entitled to payment, or if a time draft to acceptance and payment. Acceptance of any subsequently presented part renders the drawee liable thereon under subsection (2). With respect both to a holder and to the drawer payment of a subsequently presented part of a draft payable at sight has the same effect as payment of a check notwithstanding an effective stop order (Section 4—407).

(4) Except as otherwise provided in this section, where any part of a draft in a set is discharged by payment or otherwise the whole draft is discharged.

§ 3—802. Effect of Instrument on Obligation for Which It Is Given.

(1) Unless otherwise agreed where an instrument is taken for an underlying obligation

(a) the obligation is pro tanto discharged if a bank is drawer, maker or acceptor of the instrument and there is no recourse on the instrument against the underlying obligor; and

(b) in any other case the obligation is suspended pro tanto until the instrument is due or if it is payable on demand until its presentment. If the instrument is dishonored action may be maintained on either the instrument or the obligation; discharge of the underlying obligor on the instrument also discharges him on the obligation.

(2) The taking in good faith of a check which is not postdated does not of itself so extend the time on the original obligation as to discharge a surety.

§ 3—803. Notice to Third Party.

Where a defendant is sued for breach of an obligation for which a third person is answerable over under this Article he may give the third person written notice of the litigation, and the person notified may then give similar notice to any other person who is answerable over to him under this Article. If the notice states that the person notified may come in and defend and that if the person notified does not do so he will in any action against him by the person giving the notice be bound by any determination of fact common to the two litigations, then unless after seasonable receipt of the notice the person notified does come in and defend he is so bound.

§ 3—804. Lost, Destroyed or Stolen Instruments.

The owner of an instrument which is lost, whether by destruction, theft or otherwise, may maintain an action in his own name and recover from any party liable thereon upon due proof of his ownership, the facts which prevent his production of the instrument and its terms. The court may require security indemnifying the defendant against loss by reason of further claims on the instrument.

§ 3—805. Instruments Not Payable to Order or to Bearer.

This Article applies to any instrument whose terms do not preclude transfer and which is otherwise negotiable within this Article but which is not payable to order or to bearer, except that there can be no holder in due course of such an instrument.

ARTICLE 4

BANK DEPOSITS AND COLLECTIONS

PART 1

GENERAL PROVISIONS AND DEFINITIONS

§ 4—101. Short Title.

This Article shall be known and may be cited as Uniform Commercial Code—Bank Deposits and Collections.

§ 4—102. Applicability.

(1) To the extent that items within this Article are also within the scope of Articles 3 and 8, they are subject to the provisions of those Articles. In the event of conflict the provisions of this Article govern those of Article 3 but the provisions of Article 8 govern those of this Article.

(2) The liability of a bank for action or non-action with respect to any item handled by it for purposes of presentment, payment or collection is governed by the law of the place where the bank is located. In the case of action or non-action by or at a branch or separate office of a bank, its liability is governed by the law of the place where the branch or separate office is located.

§ 4—103. Variation by Agreement; Measure of Damages; Certain Action Constituting Ordinary Care.

(1) The effect of the provisions of this Article may be varied by agreement except that no agreement can disclaim a bank's responsibility for its own lack of good faith or failure to ex-

ercise ordinary care or can limit the measure of damages for such lack or failure; but the parties may by agreement determine the standards by which such responsibility is to be measured if such standards are not manifestly unreasonable.

(2) Federal Reserve regulations and operating letters, clearing house rules, and the like, have the effect of agreements under subsection (1), whether or not specifically assented to by all parties interested in items handled.

(3) Action or non-action approved by this Article or pursuant to Federal Reserve regulations or operating letters constitutes the exercise of ordinary care and, in the absence of special instructions, action or non-action consistent with clearing house rules and the like or with a general banking usage not disapproved by this Article, prima facie constitutes the exercise of ordinary care.

(4) The specification or approval of certain procedures by this Article does not constitute disapproval of other procedures which may be reasonable under the circumstances.

(5) The measure of damages for failure to exercise ordinary care in handling an item is the amount of the item reduced by an amount which could not have been realized by the use of ordinary care, and where there is bad faith it includes other damages, if any, suffered by the party as a proximate consequence.

§ 4—104. Definitions and Index of Definitions.

(1) In this Article unless the context otherwise requires

(a) "Account" means any account with a bank and includes a checking, time, interest or savings account;

(b) "Afternoon" means the period of a day between noon and midnight;

(c) "Banking day" means that part of any day on which a bank is open to the public for carrying on substantially all of its banking functions;

(d) "Clearing house" means any association of banks or other payors regularly clearing items;

(e) "Customer" means any person having an account with a bank or for whom a bank has agreed to collect items and includes a bank carrying an account with another bank;

(f) "Documentary draft" means any negotiable or nonnegotiable draft with accompanying documents, securities or other papers to be delivered against honor of the draft;

(g) "Item" means any instrument for the payment of money even though it is not negotiable but does not include money;

(h) "Midnight deadline" with respect to a bank is midnight on its next banking day following the banking day on which it receives the relevant item or notice or from which the time for taking action commences to run, whichever is later;

(i) "Properly payable" includes the availability of funds for payment at the time of decision to pay or dishonor;

(j) "Settle" means to pay in cash, by clearing house settlement, in a charge or credit or by remittance, or otherwise as instructed. A settlement may be either provisional or final;

(k) "Suspends payments" with respect to a bank means that it has been closed by order of the supervisory authorities, that a public officer has been appointed to take it over or that it ceases or refuses to make payments in the ordinary course of business.

(2) Other definitions applying to this Article and the sections in which they appear are:

"Collecting bank"	Section 4—105.
"Depositary bank"	Section 4—105.
"Intermediary bank"	Section 4—105.
"Payor bank"	Section 4—105.
"Presenting bank"	Section 4—105.
"Remitting bank"	Section 4—105.

(3) The following definitions in other Articles apply to this Article:

"Acceptance"	Section 3—410.
"Certificate of deposit"	Section 3—104.
"Certification"	Section 3—411.
"Check"	Section 3—104.
"Draft"	Section 3—104.
"Holder in due course"	Section 3—302.
"Notice of dishonor"	Section 3—508.

"Presentment"   Section 3—504.
"Protest"   Section 3—509.
"Secondary party"   Section 3—102.

(4) In addition Article 1 contains general definitions and principles of construction and interpretation applicable throughout this Article.

§ 4—105. "Depository Bank"; "Intermediary Bank"; "Collecting Bank"; "Payor Bank"; "Presenting Bank"; "Remitting Bank".

In this Article unless the context otherwise requires:

(a) "Depository bank" means the first bank to which an item is transferred for collection even though it is also the payor bank;

(b) "Payor bank" means a bank by which an item is payable as drawn or accepted;

(c) "Intermediary bank" means any bank to which an item is transferred in course of collection except the depositary or payor bank;

(d) "Collecting bank" means any bank handling the item for collection except the payor bank;

(e) "Presenting bank" means any bank presenting an item except a payor bank;

(f) "Remitting bank" means any payor or intermediary bank remitting for an item.

§ 4—106. Separate Office of a Bank.

A branch or separate office of a bank [maintaining its own deposit ledgers] is a separate bank for the purpose of computing the time within which and determining the place at or to which action may be taken or notices or orders shall be given under this Article and under Article 3.

Note: *The brackets are to make it optional with the several states whether to require a branch to maintain its own deposit ledgers in order to be considered to be a separate bank for certain purposes under Article 4. In some states "maintaining its own deposit ledgers" is a satisfactory test. In others branch*

banking practices are such that this test would not be suitable.

§ 4—107. Time of Receipt of Items.

(1) For the purpose of allowing time to process items, prove balances and make the necessary entries on its books to determine its position for the day, a bank may fix an afternoon hour of two P.M. or later as a cut-off hour for the handling of money and items and the making of entries on its books.

(2) Any item or deposit of money received on any day after a cut-off hour so fixed or after the close of the banking day may be treated as being received at the opening of the next banking day.

§ 4—108. Delays.

(1) Unless otherwise instructed, a collecting bank in a good faith effort to secure payment may, in the case of specific items and with or without the approval of any person involved, waive, modify or extend time limits imposed or permitted by this Act for a period not in excess of an additional banking day without discharge of secondary parties and without liability to its transferor or any prior party.

(2) Delay by a collecting bank or payor bank beyond time limits prescribed or permitted by this Act or by instructions is excused if caused by interruption of communication facilities, suspension of payments by another bank, war, emergency conditions or other circumstances beyond the control of the bank provided it exercises such diligence as the circumstances require.

§ 4—109. Process of Posting.

The "process of posting" means the usual procedure followed by a payor bank in determining to pay an item and in recording the payment including one or more of the following or other steps as determined by the bank:

(a) verification of any signature;

(b) ascertaining that sufficient funds are available;

(c) affixing a "paid" or other stamp;

(d) entering a charge or entry to a customer's account;

(e) correcting or reversing an entry or erroneous action with respect to the item.

PART 2

COLLECTION OF ITEMS: DEPOSITARY AND COLLECTING BANKS

§ 4—201. **Presumption and Duration of Agency Status of Collecting Banks and Provisional Status of Credits; Applicability of Article; Item Indorsed "Pay Any Bank".**

(1) Unless a contrary intent clearly appears and prior to the time that a settlement given by a collecting bank for an item is or becomes final (subsection (3) of Section 4—211 and Sections 4—212 and 4—213) the bank is an agent or sub-agent of the owner of the item and any settlement given for the item is provisional. This provision applies regardless of the form of indorsement or lack of indorsement and even though credit given for the item is subject to immediate withdrawal as of right or is in fact withdrawn; but the continuance of ownership of an item by its owner and any rights of the owner to proceeds of the item are subject to rights of a collecting bank such as those resulting from outstanding advances on the item and valid rights of setoff. When an item is handled by banks for purposes of presentment, payment and collection, the relevant provisions of this Article apply even though action of parties clearly establishes that a particular bank has purchased the item and is the owner of it.

(2) After an item has been indorsed with the words "pay any bank" or the like, only a bank may acquire the rights of a holder

   (a) until the item has been returned to the customer initiating collection; or

   (b) until the item has been specially indorsed by a bank to a person who is not a bank.

§ 4—202. **Responsibility for Collection; When Action Seasonable.**

(1) A collecting bank must use ordinary care in

   (a) presenting an item or sending it for presentment; and

   (b) sending notice of dishonor or non-payment or returning an item other than a documentary draft to the bank's transferor [or directly to the depositary bank under subsection (2) of Section 4—212] (*see note to Section 4—212*) after learning that the item has not been paid or accepted as the case may be; and

   (c) settling for an item when the bank receives final settlement; and

   (d) making or providing for any necessary protest; and

   (e) notifying its transferor of any loss or delay in transit within a reasonable time after discovery thereof.

(2) A collecting bank taking proper action before its midnight deadline following receipt of an item, notice or payment acts seasonably; taking proper action within a reasonably longer time may be seasonable but the bank has the burden of so establishing.

(3) Subject to subsection (1) (a), a bank is not liable for the insolvency, neglect, misconduct, mistake or default of another bank or person or for loss or destruction of an item in transit or in the possession of others.

§ 4—203. **Effect of Instructions.**

Subject to the provisions of Article 3 concerning conversion of instruments (Section 3—419) and the provisions of both Article 3 and this Article concerning restrictive indorsements only a collecting bank's transferor can give instructions which affect the bank or constitute notice to it and a collecting bank is not liable to prior parties for any action taken pursuant to such instructions or in accordance with any agreement with its transferor.

§ 4—204. **Methods of Sending and Presenting; Sending Direct to Payor Bank.**

(1) A collecting bank must send items by reasonably prompt method taking into consideration any relevant instructions, the nature of the item, the number of such items on hand, and the cost of collection involved and the method generally used by it or others to present such items.

(2) A collecting bank may send

    (a) any item direct to the payor bank;

    (b) any item to any non-bank payor if authorized by its transferor; and

    (c) any item other than documentary drafts to any non-bank payor, if authorized by Federal Reserve regulation or operating letter, clearing house rule or the like.

(3) Presentment may be made by a presenting bank at a place where the payor bank has requested that presentment be made.

§ 4—205. Supplying Missing Indorsement; No Notice from Prior Indorsement.

(1) A depositary bank which has taken an item for collection may supply any indorsement of the customer which is necessary to title unless the item contains the words "payee's indorsement required" or the like. In the absence of such a requirement a statement placed on the item by the depositary bank to the effect that the item was deposited by a customer or credited to his account is effective as the customer's indorsement.

(2) An intermediary bank, or payor bank which is not a depositary bank, is neither given notice nor otherwise affected by a restrictive indorsement of any person except the bank's immediate transferor.

§ 4—206. Transfer Between Banks.

Any agreed method which identifies the transferor bank is sufficient for the item's further transfer to another bank.

§ 4—207. Warranties of Customer and Collecting Bank on Transfer or Presentment of Items; Time for Claims.

(1) Each customer or collecting bank who obtains payment or acceptance of an item and each prior customer and collecting bank warrants to the payor bank or other payor who in good faith pays or accepts the item that

    (a) he has a good title to the item or is authorized to obtain payment or acceptance on behalf of one who has a good title; and

    (b) he has no knowledge that the signature of the maker or drawer is unauthorized, except that this warranty is not given by any customer or collecting bank that is a holder in due course and acts in good faith

       (i) to a maker with respect to the maker's own signature; or

       (ii) to a drawer with respect to the drawer's own signature, whether or not the drawer is also the drawee; or

       (iii) to an acceptor of an item if the holder in due course took the item after the acceptance or obtained the acceptance without knowledge that the drawer's signature was unauthorized; and

    (c) the item has not been materially altered, except that this warranty is not given by any customer or collecting bank that is a holder in due course and acts in good faith

       (i) to the maker of a note; or

       (ii) to the drawer of a draft whether or not the drawer is also the drawee; or

       (iii) to the acceptor of an item with respect to an alteration made prior to the acceptance if the holder in due course took the item after the acceptance, even though the acceptance provided "payable as originally drawn" or equivalent terms; or

       (iv) to the acceptor of an item with respect to an alteration made after the acceptance.

(2) Each customer and collecting bank who transfers an item and receives a settlement or other consideration for it warrants to his transferee and to any subsequent collecting bank who takes the item in good faith that

    (a) he has a good title to the item or is authorized to obtain payment or acceptance on behalf of one who has a good title and the transfer is otherwise rightful; and

    (b) all signatures are genuine or authorized; and

(c) the item has not been materially altered; and

(d) no defense of any party is good against him; and

(e) he has no knowledge of any insolvency proceeding instituted with respect to the maker or acceptor or the drawer of an unaccepted item.

In addition each customer and collecting bank so transferring an item and receiving a settlement or other consideration engages that upon dishonor and any necessary notice of dishonor and protest he will take up the item.

(3) The warranties and the engagement to honor set forth in the two preceding subsections arise notwithstanding the absence of indorsement or words of guaranty or warranty in the transfer or presentment and a collecting bank remains liable for their breach despite remittance to its transferor. Damages for breach of such warranties or engagement to honor shall not exceed the consideration received by the customer or collecting bank responsible plus finance charges and expenses related to the item, if any.

(4) Unless a claim for breach of warranty under this section is made within a reasonable time after the person claiming learns of the breach, the person liable is discharged to the extent of any loss caused by the delay in making claim.

§ 4—208. Security Interest of Collecting Bank in Items, Accompanying Documents and Proceeds.

(1) A bank has a security interest in an item and any accompanying documents or the proceeds of either

(a) in case of an item deposited in an account to the extent to which credit given for the item has been withdrawn or applied;

(b) in case of an item for which it has given credit available for withdrawal as of right, to the extent of the credit given whether or not the credit is drawn upon and whether or not there is a right of charge-back; or

(c) if it makes an advance on or against the item.

(2) When credit which has been given for several items received at one time or pursuant to a single agreement is withdrawn or applied in part the security interest remains upon all the items, any accompanying documents or the proceeds of either. For the purpose of this section, credits first given are first withdrawn.

(3) Receipt by a collecting bank of a final settlement for an item is a realization on its security interest in the item, accompanying documents and proceeds. To the extent and so long as the bank does not receive final settlement for the item or give up possession of the item or accompanying documents for purposes other than collection, the security interest continues and is subject to the provisions of Article 9 except that

(a) no security agreement is necessary to make the security interest enforceable (subsection (1) (b) of Section 9—203); and

(b) no filing is required to perfect the security interest; and

(c) the security interest has priority over conflicting perfected security interests in the item, accompanying documents or proceeds.

§ 4—209. When Bank Gives Value for Purposes of Holder in Due Course.

For purposes of determining its status as a holder in due course, the bank has given value to the extent that it has a security interest in an item provided that the bank otherwise complies with the requirements of Section 3—302 on what constitutes a holder in due course.

§ 4—210. Presentment by Notice of Item Not Payable by, Through or at a Bank; Liability of Secondary Parties.

(1) Unless otherwise instructed, a collecting bank may present an item not payable by, through or at a bank by sending to the party to accept or pay a written notice that the bank holds the item for acceptance or payment. The notice must be sent in time to be received on or before the day when presentment is due and the bank must meet any requirement of the party to accept or pay under Section 3—505 by the close of the bank's next banking day after it knows of the requirement.

(2) Where presentment is made by notice and neither honor nor request for compliance

with a requirement under Section 3—505 is received by the close of business on the day after maturity or in the case of demand items by the close of business on the third banking day after notice was sent, the presenting bank may treat the item as dishonored and charge any secondary party by sending him notice of the facts.

§ 4—211. Media of Remittance; Provisional and Final Settlement in Remittance Cases.

(1) A collecting bank may take in settlement of an item

(a) a check of the remitting bank or of another bank on any bank except the remitting bank; or

(b) a cashier's check or similar primary obligation of a remitting bank which is a member of or clears through a member of the same clearing house or group as the collecting bank; or

(c) appropriate authority to charge an account of the remitting bank or of another bank with the collecting bank; or

(d) if the item is drawn upon or payable by a person other than a bank, a cashier's check, certified check or other bank check or obligation.

(2) If before its midnight deadline the collecting bank properly dishonors a remittance check or authorization to charge on itself or presents or forwards for collection a remittance instrument of or on another bank which is of a kind approved by subsection (1) or has not been authorized by it, the collecting bank is not liable to prior parties in the event of the dishonor of such check, instrument or authorization.

(3) A settlement for an item by means of a remittance instrument or authorization to charge is or becomes a final settlement as to both the person making and the person receiving the settlement

(a) if the remittance instrument or authorization to charge is of a kind approved by subsection (1) or has not been authorized by the person receiving the settlement and in either case the person receiving the settlement acts seasonably before its midnight deadline in presenting, forwarding for collection or paying the instrument or authorization,—at the time the remittance instrument or authorization is finally paid by the payor by which it is payable;

(b) if the person receiving the settlement has authorized remittance by a non-bank check or obligation or by a cashier's check or similar primary obligation of or a check upon the payor or other remitting bank which is not of a kind approved by subsection (1) (b),—at the time of the receipt of such remittance check or obligation; or

(c) if in a case not covered by sub-paragraphs (a) or (b) the person receiving the settlement fails to seasonably present, forward for collection, pay or return a remittance instrument or authorization to it to charge before its midnight deadline,—at such midnight deadline.

§ 4—212. Right of Charge-Back or Refund.

(1) If a collecting bank has made provisional settlement with its customer for an item and itself fails by reason of dishonor, suspension of payments by a bank or otherwise to receive a settlement for the item which is or becomes final, the bank may revoke the settlement given by it, charge back the amount of any credit given for the item to its customer's account or obtain refund from its customer whether or not it is able to return the items if by its midnight deadline or within a longer reasonable time after it learns the facts it returns the item or sends notification of the facts. These rights to revoke, charge-back and obtain refund terminate if and when a settlement for the item received by the bank is or becomes final (subsection (3) of Section 4—211 and subsections (2) and (3) of Section 4—213).

[(2) Within the time and manner prescribed by this section and Section 4—301, an intermediary or payor bank, as the case may be, may return an unpaid item directly to the depositary bank and may send for collection a draft on the depositary bank and obtain reimbursement. In such case, if the depositary bank has received provisional settlement for the item, it must reimburse the bank drawing the draft and any provisional credits for the item between banks shall become and remain final.]

Note: *Direct returns is recognized as an innovation that is not yet established bank practice, and therefore, Paragraph 2 has been bracketed. Some lawyers have doubts whether it should be included in legislation or left to development by agreement.*

(3) A depositary bank which is also the payor may charge-back the amount of an item to its customer's account or obtain refund in accordance with the section governing return of an item received by a payor bank for credit on its books (Section 4—301).

(4) The right to charge-back is not affected by

(a) prior use of the credit given for the item; or

(b) failure by any bank to exercise ordinary care with respect to the item but any bank so failing remains liable.

(5) A failure to charge-back or claim refund does not affect other rights of the bank against the customer or any other party.

(6) If credit is given in dollars as the equivalent of the value of an item payable in a foreign currency the dollar amount of any charge-back or refund shall be calculated on the basis of the buying sight rate for the foreign currency prevailing on the day when the person entitled to the charge-back or refund learns that it will not receive payment in ordinary course.

§ 4—213. **Final Payment of Item by Payor Bank; When Provisional Debits and Credits Become Final; When Certain Credits Become Available for Withdrawal.**

(1) An item is finally paid by a payor bank when the bank has done any of the following, whichever happens first:

(a) paid the item in cash; or

(b) settled for the item without reserving a right to revoke the settlement and without having such right under statute, clearing house rule or agreement; or

(c) completed the process of posting the item to the indicated account of the drawer, maker or other person to be charged therewith; or

(d) made a provisional settlement for the item and failed to revoke the settlement in the time and manner permitted by statute, clearing house rule or agreement.

Upon a final payment under subparagraphs (b), (c) or (d) the payor bank shall be accountable for the amount of the item.

(2) If provisional settlement for an item between the presenting and payor banks is made through a clearing house or by debits or credits in an account between them, then to the extent that provisional debits or credits for the item are entered in accounts between the presenting and payor banks or between the presenting and successive prior collecting banks seriatim, they become final upon final payment of the item by the payor bank.

(3) If a collecting bank receives a settlement for an item which is or becomes final (subsection (3) of Section 4—211, subsection (2) of Section 4—213) the bank is accountable to its customer for the amount of the item and any provisional credit given for the item in an account with its customer becomes final.

(4) Subject to any right of the bank to apply the credit to an obligation of the customer, credit given by a bank for an item in an account with its customer becomes available for withdrawal as of right

(a) in any case where the bank has received a provisional settlement for the item,—when such settlement becomes final and the bank has had a reasonable time to learn that the settlement is final;

(b) in any case where the bank is both a depositary bank and a payor bank and the item is finally paid,—at the opening of the bank's second banking day following receipt of the item.

(5) A deposit of money in a bank is final when made but, subject to any right of the bank to apply the deposit to an obligation of the customer, the deposit becomes available for withdrawal as of right at the opening of the bank's next banking day following receipt of the deposit.

§ 4—214. Insolvency and Preference.

(1) Any item in or coming into the possession of a payor or collecting bank which suspends payment and which item is not finally paid shall be returned by the receiver, trustee or agent in charge of the closed bank to the presenting bank or the closed bank's customer.

(2) If a payor bank finally pays an item and suspends payments without making a settlement for the item with its customer or the presenting bank which settlement is or becomes final, the owner of the item has a preferred claim against the payor bank.

(3) If a payor bank gives or a collecting bank gives or receives a provisional settlement for an item and thereafter suspends payments, the suspension does not prevent or interfere with the settlement becoming final if such finality occurs automatically upon the lapse of certain time or the happening of certain events (subsection (3) of Section 4—211, subsections (1) (d), (2) and (3) of Section 4—213).

(4) If a collecting bank receives from subsequent parties settlement for an item which settlement is or becomes final and suspends payments without making a settlement for the item with its customer which is or becomes final, the owner of the item has a preferred claim against such collecting bank.

PART 3

COLLECTION OF ITEMS: PAYOR BANKS

§ 4—301. Deferred Posting; Recovery of Payment by Return of Items; Time of Dishonor

(1) Where an authorized settlement for a demand item (other than a documentary draft) received by a payor bank otherwise than for immediate payment over the counter has been made before midnight of the banking day of receipt the payor bank may revoke the settlement and recover any payment if before it has made final payment (subsection (1) of Section 4—213) and before its midnight deadline it

(a) returns the item; or

(b) sends written notice of dishonor or nonpayment if the item is held for protest or is otherwise unavailable for return.

(2) If a demand item is received by a payor bank for credit on its books it may return such item or send notice of dishonor and may revoke any credit given or recover the amount thereof withdrawn by its customer, if it acts within the time limit and in the manner specified in the preceding subsection.

(3) Unless previous notice of dishonor has been sent an item is dishonored at the time when for purposes of dishonor it is returned or notice sent in accordance with this section.

(4) An item is returned:

(a) as to an item received through a clearing house, when it is delivered to the presenting or last collecting bank or to the clearing house or is sent or delivered in accordance with its rules; or

(b) in all other cases, when it is sent or delivered to the bank's customer or transferor or pursuant to his instructions.

§ 4—302. Payor Bank's Responsibility for Late Return of Item.

In the absence of a valid defense such as breach of a presentment warranty (subsection (1) of Section 4—207), settlement effected or the like, if an item is presented on and received by a payor bank the bank is accountable for the amount of

(a) a demand item other than a documentary draft whether properly payable or not if the bank, in any case where it is not also the depositary bank, retains the item beyond midnight of the banking day of receipt without settling for it or, regardless of whether it is also the depositary bank, does not pay or return the item or send notice of dishonor until after its midnight deadline; or

(b) any other properly payable item unless within the time allowed for acceptance or payment of that item the bank either accepts or pays the item or returns it and accompanying documents.

§ 4—303. When Items Subject to Notice, Stop-Order, Legal Process or Set-off; Order in Which Items May Be Charged or Certified.

(1) Any knowledge, notice or stop-order received by, legal process served upon or setoff exercised by a payor bank, whether or not effective under other rules of law to terminate, suspend or modify the bank's right or duty to pay an item or to charge its customer's account for the item, comes too late to so terminate, suspend or modify such right or duty if the knowledge, notice, stop-order or legal process is received or served and a reasonable time for the bank to act thereon expires or the setoff is exercised after the bank has done any of the following:

(a) accepted or certified the item;

(b) paid the item in cash;

(c) settled for the item without reserving a right to revoke the settlement and without having such right under statute, clearing house rule or agreement;

(d) completed the process of posting the item to the indicated account of the drawer, maker or other person to be charged therewith or otherwise has evidenced by examination of such indicated account and by action its decision to pay the item; or

(e) become accountable for the amount of the item under subsection (1) (d) of Section 4—213 and Section 4—302 dealing with the payor bank's responsibility for late return of items.

(2) Subject to the provisions of subsection (1) items may be accepted, paid, certified or charged to the indicated account of its customer in any order convenient to the bank.

PART 4

RELATIONSHIP BETWEEN PAYOR BANK AND ITS CUSTOMER

§ 4—401. When Bank May Charge Customer's Account.

(1) As against its customer, a bank may charge against his account any item which is otherwise properly payable from that account even though the charge creates an overdraft.

(2) A bank which in good faith makes payment to a holder may charge the indicated account of its customer according to

(a) the original tenor of his altered item; or

(b) the tenor of his completed item, even though the bank knows the item has been completed unless the bank has notice that the completion was improper.

§ 4—402. Bank's Liability to Customer for Wrongful Dishonor.

A payor bank is liable to its customer for damages proximately caused by the wrongful dishonor of an item. When the dishonor occurs through mistake liability is limited to actual damages proved. If so proximately caused and proved damages may include damages for an arrest or prosecution of the customer or other consequential damages. Whether any consequential damages are proximately caused by the wrongful dishonor is a question of fact to be determined in each case.

§ 4—403. Customer's Right to Stop Payment; Burden of Proof of Loss.

(1) A customer may by order to his bank stop payment of any item payable for his account but the order must be received at such time and in such manner as to afford the bank a reasonable opportunity to act on it prior to any action by the bank with respect to the item described in Section 4—303.

(2) An oral order is binding upon the bank only for fourteen calendar days unless confirmed in writing within that period. A written order is effective for only six months unless renewed in writing.

(3) The burden of establishing the fact and amount of loss resulting from the payment of an item contrary to a binding stop payment order is on the customer.

§ 4—404. Bank Not Obligated to Pay Check More Than Six Months Old.

A bank is under no obligation to a customer having a checking account to pay a check, other than a certified check, which is presented more than six months after its date, but it may charge its customer's account for a payment made thereafter in good faith.

§ 4—405. Death or Incompetence of Customer.

(1) A payor or collecting bank's authority to accept, pay or collect an item or to account for proceeds of its collection if otherwise effective is not rendered ineffective by incompetence of a customer of either bank existing at the time the item is issued or its collection is undertaken if the bank does not know of an adjudication of incompetence. Neither death nor incompetence of a customer revokes such authority to accept, pay, collect or account until the bank knows of the fact of death or of an adjudication of incompetence and has reasonable opportunity to act on it.

(2) Even with knowledge a bank may for ten days after the date of death pay or certify checks drawn on or prior to that date unless ordered to stop payment by a person claiming an interest in the account.

§ 4—406. Customer's Duty to Discover and Report Unauthorized Signature or Alteration.

(1) When a bank sends to its customer a statement of account accompanied by items paid in good faith in support of the debit entries or holds the statement and items pursuant to a request or instructions of its customer or otherwise in a reasonable manner makes the statement and items available to the customer, the customer must exercise reasonable care and promptness to examine the statement and items to discover his unauthorized signature or any alteration on an item and must notify the bank promptly after discovery thereof.

(2) If the bank establishes that the customer failed with respect to an item to comply with the duties imposed on the customer by subsection (1) the customer is precluded from asserting against the bank

(a) his unauthorized signature or any alteration on the item if the bank also establishes that it suffered a loss by reason of such failure; and

(b) an unauthorized signature or alteration by the same wrongdoer on any other item paid in good faith by the bank after the first item and statement was available to the customer for a reasonable period not exceeding fourteen calendar days and before the bank receives notification from the customer of any such unauthorized signature or alteration.

(3) The preclusion under subsection (2) does not apply if the customer establishes lack of ordinary care on the part of the bank in paying the item(s).

(4) Without regard to care or lack of care of either the customer or the bank a customer who does not within one year from the time the statement and items are made available to the customer (subsection (1)) discover and report his unauthorized signature or any alteration on the face or back of the item or does not within three years from that time discover and report any unauthorized indorsement is precluded from asserting against the bank such unauthorized signature or indorsement or such alteration.

(5) If under this section a payor bank has a valid defense against a claim of a customer upon or resulting from payment of an item and waives or fails upon request to assert the defense the bank may not assert against any collecting bank or other prior party presenting or transferring the item a claim based upon the unauthorized signature or alteration giving rise to the customer's claim.

§ 4—407. Payor Bank's Right to Subrogation on Improper Payment.

If a payor bank has paid an item over the stop payment order of the drawer or maker or otherwise under circumstances giving a basis for objection by the drawer or maker, to prevent unjust enrichment and only to the extent necessary to prevent loss to the bank by reason of its payment of the item, the payor bank shall be subrogated to the rights

(a) of any holder in due course on the item against the drawer or maker; and

(b) of the payee or any other holder of the item against the drawer or maker either on the item or under the transaction out of which the item arose; and

(c) of the drawer or maker against the payee or any other holder of the item with respect to the transaction out of which the item arose.

PART 5

COLLECTION OF DOCUMENTARY DRAFTS

§ 4—501. Handling of Documentary Drafts; Duty to Send for Presentment and to Notify Customer of Dishonor.

A bank which takes a documentary draft for collection must present or send the draft and accompanying documents for presentment and upon learning that the draft has not been paid or accepted in due course must seasonably notify its customer of such fact even though it may have discounted or bought the draft or extended credit available for withdrawal as of right.

§ 4—502. Presentment of "On Arrival" Drafts.

When a draft or the relevant instructions require presentment "on arrival", "when goods arrive" or the like, the collecting bank need not present until in its judgment a reasonable time for arrival of the goods has expired. Refusal to pay or accept because the goods have not arrived is not dishonor; the bank must notify its transferor of such refusal but need not present the draft again until it is instructed to do so or learns of the arrival of the goods.

§ 4—503. Responsibility of Presenting Bank for Documents and Goods; Report of Reasons for Dishonor; Referee in Case of Need.

Unless otherwise instructed and except as provided in Article 5 a bank presenting a documentary draft

(a) must deliver the documents to the drawee on acceptance of the draft if it is payable more than three days after

presentment; otherwise, only on payment; and

(b) upon dishonor, either in the case of presentment for acceptance or presentment for payment, may seek and follow instructions from any referee in case of need designated in the draft or if the presenting bank does not choose to utilize his services it must use diligence and good faith to ascertain the reason for dishonor, must notify its transferor of the dishonor and of the results of its effort to ascertain the reasons therefor and must request instructions.

But the presenting bank is under no obligation with respect to goods represented by the documents except to follow any reasonable instructions seasonably received; it has a right to reimbursement for any expense incurred in following instructions and to prepayment of or indemnity for such expenses.

§ 4—504. Privilege of Presenting Bank to Deal With Goods; Security Interest for Expenses.

(1) A presenting bank which, following the dishonor of a documentary draft, has seasonably requested instructions but does not receive them within a reasonable time may store, sell, or otherwise deal with the goods in any reasonable manner.

(2) For its reasonable expenses incurred by action under subsection (1) the presenting bank has a lien upon the goods or their proceeds, which may be foreclosed in the same manner as an unpaid seller's lien.

ARTICLE 5

LETTERS OF CREDIT

§ 5—101. Short Title.

This Article shall be known and may be cited as Uniform Commercial Code—Letters of Credit.

§ 5—102. Scope.

(1) This Article applies

  (a) to a credit issued by a bank if the credit requires a documentary draft or a documentary demand for payment; and

  (b) to a credit issued by a person other than a bank if the credit requires that the draft or demand for payment be accompanied by a document of title; and

  (c) to a credit issued by a bank or other person if the credit is not within subparagraphs (a) or (b) but conspicuously states that it is a letter of credit or is conspicuously so entitled.

(2) Unless the engagement meets the requirements of subsection (1), this Article does not apply to engagements to make advances or to honor drafts or demands for payment, to authorities to pay or purchase, to guarantees or to general agreements.

(3) This Article deals with some but not all of the rules and concepts of letters of credit as such rules or concepts have developed prior to this act or may hereafter develop. The fact that this Article states a rule does not by itself require, imply or negate application of the same or a converse rule to a situation not provided for or to a person not specified by this Article.

§ 5—103. Definitions.

(1) In this Article unless the context otherwise requires

  (a) "Credit" or "letter of credit" means an engagement by a bank or other person made at the request of a customer and of a kind within the scope of this Article (Section 5—102) that the issuer will honor drafts or other demands for payment upon compliance with the conditions specified in the credit. A credit may be either revocable or irrevocable. The engagement may be either an agreement to honor or a statement that the bank or other person is authorized to honor.

  (b) A "documentary draft" or a "documentary demand for payment" is one honor of which is conditioned upon the presentation of a document or documents. "Document" means any paper including document of title, security, invoice, certificate, notice of default and the like.

  (c) An "issuer" is a bank or other person issuing a credit.

  (d) A "beneficiary" of a credit is a person who is entitled under its terms to draw or demand payment.

  (e) An "advising bank" is a bank which gives notification of the issuance of a credit by another bank.

  (f) A "confirming bank" is a bank which engages either that it will itself honor a credit already issued by another bank or that such a credit will be honored by the issuer or a third bank.

  (g) A "customer" is a buyer or other person who causes an issuer to issue a credit. The term also includes a bank which procures issuance or confirmation on behalf of that bank's customer.

(2) Other definitions applying to this Article and the sections in which they appear are:

"Notation of Credit". Section 5—108.
"Presenter". Section 5—112(3).

(3) Definitions in other Articles applying to this Article and the sections in which they appear are:

"Accept" or Ac-
  ceptance". Section 3—410.
"Contract for sale". Section 2—106.
"Draft". Section 3—104.
"Holder in due
  course". Section 3—302.
"Midnight deadline". Section 4—104.
"Security". Section 8—102.

(4) In addition, Article 1 contains general definitions and principles of construction and interpretation applicable throughout this Article.

§ 5—104. Formal Requirements; Signing.

(1) Except as otherwise required in subsection (1) (c) of Section 5—102 on scope, no particular form of phrasing is required for a credit. A credit must be in writing and signed by the issuer and a confirmation must be in writing and signed by the confirming bank. A modification of the terms of a credit or confirmation must be signed by the issuer or confirming bank.

(2) A telegram may be a sufficient signed writing if it identifies its sender by an authorized authentication. The authentication may be in code and the authorized naming of the issuer in an advice of credit is a sufficient signing.

§ 5—105. Consideration.

No consideration is necessary to establish a credit or to enlarge or otherwise modify its terms.

§ 5—106. Time and Effect of Establishment of Credit.

(1) Unless otherwise agreed a credit is established

    (a) as regards the customer as soon as a letter of credit is sent to him or the letter of credit or an authorized written advice of its issuance is sent to the beneficiary; and

    (b) as regards the beneficiary when he receives a letter of credit or an authorized written advice of its issuance.

(2) Unless otherwise agreed once an irrevocable credit is established as regards the customer it can be modified or revoked only with the consent of the customer and once it is established as regards the beneficiary it can be modified or revoked only with his consent.

(3) Unless otherwise agreed after a revocable credit is established it may be modified or revoked by the issuer without notice to or consent from the customer or beneficiary.

(4) Notwithstanding any modification or revocation of a revocable credit any person authorized to honor or negotiate under the terms of the original credit is entitled to reimbursement for or honor of any draft or demand for payment duly honored or negotiated before receipt of notice of the modification or revocation and the issuer in turn is entitled to reimbursement from its customer.

§ 5—107. Advice of Credit; Confirmation; Error in Statement of Terms.

(1) Unless otherwise specified an advising bank by advising a credit issued by another bank does not assume any obligation to honor drafts drawn or demands for payment made under the credit but it does assume obligation for the accuracy of its own statement.

(2) A confirming bank by confirming a credit becomes directly obligated on the credit to the extent of its confirmation as though it were its issuer and acquires the rights of an issuer.

(3) Even though an advising bank incorrectly advises the terms of a credit it has been authorized to advise the credit is established as against the issuer to the extent of its original terms.

(4) Unless otherwise specified the customer bears as against the issuer all risks of transmission and reasonable translation or interpretation of any message relating to a credit.

§ 5—108. "Notation Credit"; Exhaustion of Credit.

(1) A credit which specifies that any person purchasing or paying drafts drawn or demands for payment made under it must note the amount of the draft or demand on the letter or advice of credit is a "notation credit".

(2) Under a notation credit

    (a) a person paying the beneficiary or purchasing a draft or demand for payment from him acquires a right to honor only if the appropriate notation is made and by transferring or forwarding for honor the documents under the credit such a person warrants to the issuer that the notation has been made; and

    (b) unless the credit or a signed statement that an appropriate notation has been made accompanies the draft or demand for payment the issuer may delay honor until evidence of notation has been procured which is satisfactory to it but its obligation and that of its customer continue for a reasonable time not exceeding thirty days to obtain such evidence.

(3) If the credit is not a notation credit

(a) the issuer may honor complying drafts or demands for payment presented to it in the order in which they are presented and is discharged pro tanto by honor of any such draft or demand;

(b) as between competing good faith purchasers of complying drafts or demands the person first purchasing has priority over a subsequent purchaser even though the later purchased draft or demand has been first honored.

§ 5—109. Issuer's Obligation to Its Customer.

(1) An issuer's obligation to its customer includes good faith and observance of any general banking usage but unless otherwise agreed does not include liability or responsibility

(a) for performance of the underlying contract for sale or other transaction between the customer and the beneficiary; or

(b) for any act or omission of any person other than itself or its own branch or for loss or destruction of a draft, demand or document in transit or in the possession of others; or

(c) based on knowledge or lack of knowledge of any usage of any particular trade.

(2) An issuer must examine documents with care so as to ascertain that on their face they appear to comply with the terms of the credit but unless otherwise agreed assumes no liability or responsibility for the genuineness, falsification or effect of any document which appears on such examination to be regular on its face.

(3) A non-bank issuer is not bound by any banking usage of which it has no knowledge.

§ 5—110. Availability of Credit in Portions; Presenter's Reservation of Lien or Claim.

(1) Unless otherwise specified a credit may be used in portions in the discretion of the beneficiary.

(2) Unless otherwise specified a person by presenting a documentary draft or demand for payment under a credit relinquishes upon its honor all claims to the documents and a person by transferring such draft or demand or causing such presentment authorizes such relinquishment. An explicit reservation of claim makes the draft or demand non-complying.

§ 5—111. Warranties on Transfer and Presentment.

(1) Unless otherwise agreed the beneficiary by transferring or presenting a documentary draft or demand for payment warrants to all interested parties that the necessary conditions of the credit have been complied with. This is in addition to any warranties arising under Articles 3, 4, 7 and 8.

(2) Unless otherwise agreed a negotiating, advising, confirming, collecting or issuing bank presenting or transferring a draft or demand for payment under a credit warrants only the matters warranted by a collecting bank under Article 4 and any such bank transferring a document warrants only the matters warranted by an intermediary under Articles 7 and 8.

§ 5—112. Time Allowed for Honor or Rejection; Withholding Honor or Rejection by Consent; "Presenter".

(1) A bank to which a documentary draft or demand for payment is presented under a credit may without dishonor of the draft, demand or credit

(a) defer honor until the close of the third banking day following receipt of the documents; and

(b) further defer honor if the presenter has expressly or impliedly consented thereto.

Failure to honor within the time here specified constitutes dishonor of the draft or demand and of the credit [except as otherwise provided in subsection (4) of Section 5—114 on conditional payment].

Note: *The bracketed language in the last sentence of subsection (1) should be included only if the optional provisions of Section 5—114(4) and (5) are included.*

(2) Upon dishonor the bank may unless otherwise instructed fulfill its duty to return the draft or demand and the documents by holding them at the disposal of the presenter and sending him an advice to that effect.

(3) "Presenter" means any person presenting a draft or demand for payment for honor under a credit even though that person is a confirming bank or other correspondent which is acting under an issuer's authorization.

§ 5—113. Indemnities.

(1) A bank seeking to obtain (whether for itself or another) honor, negotiation or reimbursement under a credit may give an indemnity to induce such honor, negotiation or reimbursement.

(2) An indemnity agreement inducing honor, negotiation or reimbursement

    (a) unless otherwise explicitly agreed applies to defects in the documents but not in the goods; and

    (b) unless a longer time is explicitly agreed expires at the end of ten business days following receipt of the documents by, the ultimate customer unless notice of objection is sent before such expiration date. The ultimate customer may send notice of objection to the person from whom he received the documents and any bank receiving such notice is under a duty to send notice to its transferor before its midnight deadline.

§ 5—114. Issuer's Duty and Privilege to Honor; Right to Reimbursement.

(1) An issuer must honor a draft or demand for payment which complies with the terms of the relevant credit regardless of whether the goods or documents conform to the underlying contract for sale or other contract between the customer and the beneficiary. The issuer is not excused from honor of such a draft or demand by reason of an additional general term that all documents must be satisfactory to the issuer, but an issuer may require that specified documents must be satisfactory to it.

(2) Unless otherwise agreed when documents appear on their face to comply with the terms of a credit but a required document does not in fact conform to the warranties made on negotiation or transfer of a document of title (Section 7—507) or of a security (Section 8—306) or is forged or fraudulent or there is fraud in the transaction

    (a) the issuer must honor the draft or demand for payment if honor is demanded by a negotiating bank or other holder of the draft or demand which has taken the draft or demand under the credit and under circumstances which would make it a holder in due course (Section 3—302) and in an appropriate case would make it a person to whom a document of title has been duly negotiated (Section 7—502) or a bona fide purchaser of a security (Section 8—302); and

    (b) in all other cases as against its customer, an issuer acting in good faith may honor the draft or demand for payment despite notification from the customer of fraud, forgery or other defect not apparent on the face of the documents but a court of appropriate jurisdiction may enjoin such honor.

(3) Unless otherwise agreed an issuer which has duly honored a draft or demand for payment is entitled to immediate reimbursement of any payment made under the credit and to be put in effectively available funds not later than the day before maturity of any acceptance made under the credit.

[(4) When a credit provides for payment by the issuer on receipt of notice that the required documents are in the possession of a correspondent or other agent of the issuer

    (a) any payment made on receipt of such notice is conditional; and

    (b) the issuer may reject documents which do not comply with the credit if it does so within three banking days following its receipt of the documents; and

    (c) in the event of such rejection, the issuer is entitled by charge back or otherwise to return of the payment made.]

[(5) In the case covered by subsection (4) failure to reject documents within the time specified in sub-paragraph (b) constitutes acceptance of the documents and makes the payment final in favor of the beneficiary.]

> **Note:** *Subsections (4) and (5) are bracketed as optional. If they are included the bracketed language in the last sentence of Section 5—112(1) should also be included.*

§ 5—115. Remedy for Improper Dishonor or Anticipatory Repudiation.

(1) When an issuer wrongfully dishonors a draft or demand for payment presented under a credit the person entitled to honor has with respect to any documents the rights of a person in the position of a seller (Section 2—707) and may recover from the issuer the face amount of the draft or demand together with incidental damages under Section 2—710 on seller's incidental damages and interest but less any amount realized by resale or other use or disposition of the subject matter of the transaction. In the event no resale or other utilization is made the documents, goods or other subject matter involved in the transaction must be turned over to the issuer on payment of judgment.

(2) When an issuer wrongfully cancels or otherwise repudiates a credit before presentment of a draft or demand for payment drawn under it the beneficiary has the rights of a seller after anticipatory repudiation by the buyer under Section 2—610 if he learns of the repudiation in time reasonably to avoid procurement of the required documents. Otherwise the beneficiary has an immediate right of action for wrongful dishonor.

§ 5—116. Transfer and Assignment.

(1) The right to draw under a credit can be transferred or assigned only when the credit is expressly designated as transferable or assignable.

(2) Even though the credit specifically states that it is nontransferable or nonassignable the beneficiary may before performance of the conditions of the credit assign his right to proceeds. Such an assignment is an assignment of a contract right under Article 9 on Secured Transactions and is governed by that Article except that

(a) the assignment is ineffective until the letter of credit or advice of credit is delivered to the assignee which delivery constitutes perfection of the security interest under Article 9; and

(b) the issuer may honor drafts or demands for payment drawn under the credit until it receives a notification of the assignment signed by the beneficiary which reasonably identifies the credit involved in the assignment and contains a request to pay the assignee; and

(c) after what reasonably appears to be such a notification has been received the issuer may without dishonor refuse to accept or pay even to a person otherwise entitled to honor until the letter of credit or advice of credit is exhibited to the issuer.

(3) Except where the beneficiary has effectively assigned his right to draw or his right to proceeds, nothing in this section limits his right to transfer or negotiate drafts or demands drawn under the credit.

§ 5—117. Insolvency of Bank Holding Funds for Documentary Credit.

(1) Where an issuer or an advising or confirming bank or a bank which has for a customer procured issuance of a credit by another bank becomes insolvent before final payment under the credit and the credit is one to which this Article is made applicable by paragraphs (a) or (b) of Section 5—102(1) on scope, the receipt or allocation of funds or collateral to secure or meet obligations under the credit shall have the following results:

(a) to the extent of any funds or collateral turned over after or before the insolvency as indemnity against or specifically for the purpose of payment of drafts or demands for payment drawn under the designated credit, the drafts or demands are entitled to payment in preference over depositors or other general creditors of the issuer or bank; and

(b) on expiration of the credit or surrender of the beneficiary's rights under it unused any person who has given such funds or collateral is similarly entitled to return thereof; and

(c) a charge to a general or current account with a bank if specifically consented to for the purpose of indemnity against or payment of drafts or demands for payment drawn under the designated credit falls under the same rules as if the funds had been drawn out in cash and then turned over with specific instructions.

(2) After honor or reimbursement under this section the customer or other person for whose account the insolvent bank has acted is entitled to receive the documents involved.

ARTICLE 6

BULK TRANSFERS

§ 6—101. Short Title.

This Article shall be known and may be cited as Uniform Commercial Code—Bulk Transfers.

§ 6—102. "Bulk Transfer"; Transfers of Equipment; Enterprises Subject to This Article; Bulk Transfers Subject to This Article.

(1) A "bulk transfer" is any transfer in bulk and not in the ordinary course of the transferor's business of a major part of the materials, supplies, merchandise or other inventory (Section 9—109) of an enterprise subject to this Article.

(2) A transfer of a substantial part of the equipment (Section 9—109) of such an enterprise is a bulk transfer if it is made in connection with a bulk transfer of inventory, but not otherwise.

(3) The enterprises subject to this Article are all those whose principal business is the sale of merchandise from stock, including those who manufacture what they sell.

(4) Except as limited by the following section all bulk transfers of goods located within this state are subject to this Article.

§ 6—103. Transfers Excepted From This Article.

The following transfers are not subject to this Article:

(1) Those made to give security for the performance of an obligation;

(2) General assignments for the benefit of all the creditors of the transferor, and subsequent transfers by the assignee thereunder;

(3) Transfers in settlement or realization of a lien or other security interest;

(4) Sales by executors, administrators, receivers, trustees in bankruptcy, or any public officer under judicial process;

(5) Sales made in the course of judicial or administrative proceedings for the dissolution or reorganization of a corporation and of which notice is sent to the creditors of the corporation pursuant to order of the court or administrative agency;

(6) Transfers to a person maintaining a known place of business in this State who becomes bound to pay the debts of the transferor in full and gives public notice of that fact, and who is solvent after becoming so bound;

(7) A transfer to a new business enterprise organized to take over and continue the business, if public notice of the transaction is given and the new enterprise assumes the debts of the transferor and he receives nothing from the transaction except an interest in the new enterprise junior to the claims of creditors;

(8) Transfers of property which is exempt from execution.

Public notice under subsection (6) or subsection (7) may be given by publishing once a week for two consecutive weeks in a newspaper of general circulation where the transferor had its principal place of business in this state an advertisement including the names and addresses of the transferor and transferee and the effective date of the transfer.

§ 6—104. Schedule of Property, List of Creditors.

(1) Except as provided with respect to auction sales (Section 6—108), a bulk transfer subject to this Article is ineffective against any creditor of the transferor unless:

    (a) The transferee requires the transferor to furnish a list of his existing creditors prepared as stated in this section; and

(b) The parties prepare a schedule of the property transferred sufficient to identify it; and

(c) The transferee preserves the list and schedule for six months next following the transfer and permits inspection of either or both and copying therefrom at all reasonable hours by any creditor of the transferor, or files the list and schedule in (*a public office to be here identified*).

(2) The list of creditors must be signed and sworn to or affirmed by the transferor or his agent. It must contain the names and business addresses of all creditors of the transferor, with the amounts when known, and also the names of all persons who are known to the transferor to assert claims against him even though such claims are disputed. If the transferor is the obligor of an outstanding issue of bonds, debentures or the like as to which there is an indenture trustee, the list of creditors need include only the name and address of the indenture trustee and the aggregate outstanding principal amount of the issue.

(3) Responsibility for the completeness and accuracy of the list of creditors rests on the transferor, and the transfer is not rendered ineffective by errors or omissions therein unless the transferee is shown to have had knowledge.

§ 6—105. Notice to Creditors.

In addition to the requirements of the preceding section, any bulk transfer subject to this Article except one made by auction sale (Section 6—108) is ineffective against any creditor of the transferor unless at least ten days before he takes possession of the goods or pays for them, whichever happens first, the transferee gives notice of the transfer in the manner and to the persons hereafter provided (Section 6—107).

[§ 6—106. Application of the Proceeds.

In addition to the requirements of the two preceding sections:

(1) Upon every bulk transfer subject to this Article for which new consideration becomes payable except those made by sale at auction it

is the duty of the transferee to assure that such consideration is applied so far as necessary to pay those debts of the transferor which are either shown on the list furnished by the transferor (Section 6—104) or filed in writing in the place stated in the notice (Section 6—107) within thirty days after the mailing of such notice. This duty of the transferee runs to all the holders of such debts, and may be enforced by any of them for the benefit of all.

(2) If any of said debts are in dispute the necessary sum may be withheld from distribution until the dispute is settled or adjudicated.

(3) If the consideration payable is not enough to pay all of the said debts in full distribution shall be made pro rata.]

Note: *This section is bracketed to indicate division of opinion as to whether or not it is a wise provision, and to suggest that this is a point on which State enactments may differ without serious damage to the principle of uniformity.*

In any State where this section is omitted, the following parts of sections, also bracketed in the text, should also be omitted, namely:

Section 6—107(2)(e).
6—108(3)(c).
6—109(2).

In any State where this section is enacted, these other provisions should be also.

Optional Subsection (4)

[(4) The transferee may within ten days after he takes possession of the goods pay the consideration into the (specify court) in the county where the transferor had its principal place of business in this state and thereafter may discharge his duty under this section by giving notice by registered or certified mail to all the persons to whom the duty runs that the consideration has been paid into that court and that they should file their claims there. On motion of any interested party, the court may order the distribution of the consideration to the persons entitled to it.]

Note: *Optional subsection (4) is recommended for those states which do not have a general statute providing for payment of money into court.*

§ 6—107. The Notice.

(1) The notice to creditors (Section 6—105) shall state:

  (a) that a bulk transfer is about to be made; and

  (b) the names and business addresses of the transferor and transferee, and all other business names and addresses used by the transferor within three years last past so far as known to the transferee; and

  (c) whether or not all the debts of the transferor are to be paid in full as they fall due as a result of the transaction, and if so, the address to which creditors should send their bills.

(2) If the debts of the transferor are not to be paid in full as they fall due or if the transferee is in doubt on that point then the notice shall state further:

  (a) the location and general description of the property to be transferred and the estimated total of the transferor's debts;

  (b) the address where the schedule of property and list of creditors (Section 6—104) may be inspected;

  (c) whether the transfer is to pay existing debts and if so the amount of such debts and to whom owing;

  (d) whether the transfer is for new consideration and if so the amount of such consideration and the time and place of payment; [and]

  [(e) if for new consideration the time and place where creditors of the transferor are to file their claims.]

(3) The notice in any case shall be delivered personally or sent by registered or certified mail to all the persons shown on the list of creditors furnished by the transferor (Section 6—104) and to all other persons who are known to the transferee to hold or assert claims against the transferor.

§ 6—108. Auction Sales; "Auctioneer".

(1) A bulk transfer is subject to this Article even though it is by sale at auction, but only in the manner and with the results stated in this section.

(2) The transferor shall furnish a list of his creditors and assist in the preparation of a schedule of the property to be sold, both prepared as before stated (Section 6—104).

(3) The person or persons other than the transferor who direct, control or are responsible for the auction are collectively called the "auctioneer". The auctioneer shall:

  (a) receive and retain the list of creditors and prepare and retain the schedule of property for the period stated in this Article (Section 6—104);

  (b) give notice of the auction personally or by registered or certified mail at least ten days before it occurs to all persons shown on the list of creditors and to all other persons who are known to him to hold or assert claims against the transferor; [and]

  [(c) assure that the net proceeds of the auction are applied as provided in this Article (Section 6—106).]

(4) Failure of the auctioneer to perform any of these duties does not affect the validity of the sale or the title of the purchasers, but if the auctioneer knows that the auction constitutes a bulk transfer such failure renders the auctioneer liable to the creditors of the transferor as a class for the sums owing to them from the transferor up to but not exceeding the net proceeds of the auction. If the auctioneer consists of several persons their liability is joint and several.

§ 6—109. What Creditors Protected; [Credit for Payment to Particular Creditors].

(1) The creditors of the transferor mentioned in this Article are those holding claims based on transactions or events occurring before the bulk transfer, but creditors who become such after notice to creditors is given (Sections 6—105 and 6—107) are not entitled to notice.

[(2) Against the aggregate obligation imposed by the provisions of this Article concerning the application of the proceeds (Section 6—106 and subsection (3) (c) of 6—108) the transferee or auctioneer is entitled to credit for sums paid to particular creditors of the transferor, not exceeding the sums believed in good faith at the time of the payment to be properly payable to such creditors.]

§ 6—110. Subsequent Transfers.

When the title of a transferee to property is subject to a defect by reason of his non-compliance with the requirements of this Article, then:

(1) a purchaser of any of such property from such transferee who pays no value or who takes with notice of such non-compliance takes subject to such defect, but

(2) a purchaser for value in good faith and without such notice takes free of such defect.

§ 6—111. Limitation of Actions and Levies.

No action under this Article shall be brought nor levy made more than six months after the date on which the transferee took possession of the goods unless the transfer has been concealed. If the transfer has been concealed, actions may be brought or levies made within six months after its discovery.

Note to Article 6: *Section 6—106 is bracketed to indicate division of opinion as to whether or not it is a wise provision, and to suggest that this is a point on which State enactments may differ without serious damage to the principle of uniformity.*

In any State where Section 6—106 is not enacted, the following parts of sections, also bracketed in the text, should also be omitted, namely:

Sec. 6—107(2)(e).
6—108(3)(c).
6—109(2).

In any State where Section 6—106 is enacted, these other provisions should be also.

ARTICLE 7

WAREHOUSE RECEIPTS, BILLS OF LADING AND OTHER DOCUMENTS OF TITLE

PART 1

GENERAL

§ 7—101. Short Title.

This Article shall be known and may be cited as Uniform Commercial Code—Documents of Title.

§ 7—102. Definitions and Index of Definitions.

(1) In this Article, unless the context otherwise requires:

(a) "Bailee" means the person who by a warehouse receipt, bill of lading or other document of title acknowledges possession of goods and contracts to deliver them.

(b) "Consignee" means the person named in a bill to whom or to whose order the bill promises delivery.

(c) "Consignor" means the person named in a bill as the person from whom the goods have been received for shipment.

(d) "Delivery order" means a written order to deliver goods directed to a warehouseman, carrier or other person who in the ordinary course of business issues warehouse receipts or bills of lading.

(e) "Document" means document of title as defined in the general definitions in Article 1 (Section 1—201).

(f) "Goods" means all things which are treated as movable for the purposes of a contract of storage or transportation.

(g) "Issuer" means a bailee who issues a document except that in relation to an unaccepted delivery order it means the person who orders the possessor of goods to deliver. Issuer includes any person for whom an agent or employee purports to act in issuing a document if the agent or employee has real or apparent authority to issue documents, notwithstanding that the issuer received no goods or that the goods were misdescribed or that in any other respect the agent or employee violated his instructions.

(h) "Warehouseman" is a person engaged in the business of storing goods for hire.

(2) Other definitions applying to this Article or to specified Parts thereof, and the sections in which they appear are:

"Duly negotiate". Section 7—501.

"Person entitled under the document". Section 7—403(4).

(3) Definitions in other Articles applying to this Article and the sections in which they appear are:

"Contract for sale". Section 2—106.

"Overseas". Section 2—323.

"Receipt" of goods. Section 2—103.

(4) In addition Article 1 contains general definitions and principles of construction and interpretation applicable throughout this Article.

§ 7—103. Relation of Article to Treaty, Statute, Tariff, Classification or Regulation.

To the extent that any treaty or statute of the United States, regulatory statute of this State or tariff, classification or regulation filed or issued pursuant thereto is applicable, the provisions of this Article are subject thereto.

§ 7—104. Negotiable and Non-Negotiable Warehouse Receipt, Bill of Lading or Other Document of Title.

(1) A warehouse receipt, bill of lading or other document of title is negotiable

(a) if by its terms the goods are to be delivered to bearer or to the order of a named person; or

(b) where recognized in overseas trade, if it runs to a named person or assigns.

(2) Any other document is non-negotiable. A bill of lading in which it is stated that the goods are consigned to a named person is not made negotiable by a provision that the goods are to be delivered only against a written order signed by the same or another named person.

§ 7—105. Construction Against Negative Implication.

The omission from either Part 2 or Part 3 of this Article of a provision corresponding to a provision made in the other Part does not imply that a corresponding rule of law is not applicable.

PART 2

WAREHOUSE RECEIPTS: SPECIAL PROVISIONS

§ 7—201. Who May Issue a Warehouse Receipt; Storage Under Government Bond.

(1) A warehouse receipt may be issued by any warehouseman.

(2) Where goods including distilled spirits and agricultural commodities are stored under a statute requiring a bond against withdrawal or a license for the issuance of receipts in the nature of warehouse receipts, a receipt issued for the goods has like effect as a warehouse receipt even though issued by a person who is the owner of the goods and is not a warehouseman.

§ 7—202. Form of Warehouse Receipt; Essential Terms; Optional Terms.

(1) A warehouse receipt need not be in any particular form.

(2) Unless a warehouse receipt embodies within its written or printed terms each of the following, the warehouseman is liable for damages caused by the omission to a person injured thereby:

(a) the location of the warehouse where the goods are stored;

(b) the date of issue of the receipt;

(c) the consecutive number of the receipt;

(d) a statement whether the goods received will be delivered to the bearer, to a specified person, or to a specified person or his order;

(e) the rate of storage and handling charges, except that where goods are stored under a field warehousing arrangement a statement of that fact is sufficient on a non-negotiable receipt;

(f) a description of the goods or of the packages containing them;

(g) the signature of the warehouseman, which may be made by his authorized agent;

(h) if the receipt is issued for goods of which the warehouseman is owner, either solely or jointly or in common with others, the fact of such ownership; and

(i) a statement of the amount of advances made and of liabilities incurred for which the warehouseman claims a lien or security interest (Section 7—209). If the precise amount of such advances made or of such liabilities incurred is, at the time of the issue of the receipt, unknown to the warehouseman or to his agent who issues it, a statement of the fact that advances have been made or liabilities incurred and the purpose thereof is sufficient.

(3) A warehouseman may insert in his receipt any other terms which are not contrary to the provisions of this Act and do not impair his obligation of delivery (Section 7—403) or his duty of care (Section 7—204). Any contrary provisions shall be ineffective.

§ 7—203. Liability for Non-Receipt or Misdescription.

A party to or purchaser for value in good faith of a document of title other than a bill of lading relying in either case upon the description therein of the goods may recover from the issuer damages caused by the non-receipt or misdescription of the goods, except to the extent that the document conspicuously indicates that the issuer does not know whether any part or all of the goods in fact were received or conform to the description, as where the description is in terms of marks or labels or kind, quantity or condition, or the receipt or description is qualified by "contents, condition and quality unknown", "said to contain" or the like, if such indication be true, or the party or purchaser otherwise has notice.

§ 7—204. Duty of Care; Contractual Limitation of Warehouseman's Liability.

(1) A warehouseman is liable for damages for loss of or injury to the goods caused by his failure to exercise such care in regard to them as a reasonably careful man would exercise under like circumstances but unless otherwise agreed he is not liable for damages which could not have been avoided by the exercise of such care.

(2) Damages may be limited by a term in the warehouse receipt or storage agreement limiting the amount of liability in case of loss or damage, and setting forth a specific liability per article or item, or value per unit of weight, beyond which the warehouseman shall not be liable; provided, however, that such liability may on written request of the bailor at the time of signing such storage agreement or within a reasonable time after receipt of the warehouse receipt be increased on part or all of the goods thereunder, in which event increased rates may be charged based on such increased valuation, but that no such increase shall be permitted contrary to a lawful limitation of liability contained in the warehouseman's tariff, if any. No such limitation is effective with respect to the warehouseman's liability for conversion to his own use.

(3) Reasonable provisions as to the time and manner of presenting claims and instituting actions based on the bailment may be included in the warehouse receipt or tariff.

(4) This section does not impair or repeal . . .

> **Note:** *Insert in subsection (4) a reference to any statute which imposes a higher responsibility upon the warehouseman or invalidates contractual limitations which would be permissible under this Article.*

§ 7—205. Title Under Warehouse Receipt Defeated in Certain Cases.

A buyer in the ordinary course of business of fungible goods sold and delivered by a warehouseman who is also in the business of buying and selling such goods takes free of any claim under a warehouse receipt even though it has been duly negotiated.

§ 7—206. Termination of Storage at Warehouseman's Option.

(1) A warehouseman may on notifying the person on whose account the goods are held and any other person known to claim an inter-

est in the goods require payment of any charges and removal of the goods from the warehouse at the termination of the period of storage fixed by the document, or, if no period is fixed, within a stated period not less than thirty days after the notification. If the goods are not removed before the date specified in the notification, the warehouseman may sell them in accordance with the provisions of the section on enforcement of a warehouseman's lien (Section 7—210).

(2) If a warehouseman in good faith believes that the goods are about to deteriorate or decline in value to less than the amount of his lien within the time prescribed in subsection (1) for notification, advertisement and sale, the warehouseman may specify in the notification any reasonable shorter time for removal of the goods and in case the goods are not removed, may sell them at public sale held not less than one week after a single advertisement or posting.

(3) If as a result of a quality or condition of the goods of which the warehouseman had no notice at the time of deposit the goods are a hazard to other property or to the warehouse or to persons, the warehouseman may sell the goods at public or private sale without advertisement on reasonable notification to all persons known to claim an interest in the goods. If the warehouseman after a reasonable effort is unable to sell the goods he may dispose of them in any lawful manner and shall incur no liability by reason of such disposition.

(4) The warehouseman must deliver the goods to any person entitled to them under this Article upon due demand made at any time prior to sale or other disposition under this section.

(5) The warehouseman may satisfy his lien from the proceeds of any sale or disposition under this section but must hold the balance for delivery on the demand of any person to whom he would have been bound to deliver the goods.

§ 7—207. Goods Must Be Kept Separate; Fungible Goods.

(1) Unless the warehouse receipt otherwise provides, a warehouseman must keep separate the goods covered by each receipt so as to permit at all times identification and delivery of those goods except that different lots of fungible goods may be commingled.

(2) Fungible goods so commingled are owned in common by the persons entitled thereto and the warehouseman is severally liable to each owner for that owner's share. Where because of overissue a mass of fungible goods is insufficient to meet all the receipts which the warehouseman has issued against it, the persons entitled include all holders to whom overissued receipts have been duly negotiated.

§ 7—208. Altered Warehouse Receipts.

Where a blank in a negotiable warehouse receipt has been filled in without authority, a purchaser for value and without notice of the want of authority may treat the insertion as authorized. Any other unauthorized alteration leaves any receipt enforceable against the issuer according to its original tenor.

§ 7—209. Lien of Warehouseman.

(1) A warehouseman has a lien against the bailor on the goods covered by a warehouse receipt or on the proceeds thereof in his possession for charges for storage or transportation (including demurrage and terminal charges), insurance, labor, or charges present or future in relation to the goods, and for expenses necessary for preservation of the goods or reasonably incurred in their sale pursuant to law. If the person on whose account the goods are held is liable for like charges or expenses in relation to other goods whenever deposited and it is stated in the receipt that a lien is claimed for charges and expenses in relation to other goods, the warehouseman also has a lien against him for such charges and expenses whether or not the other goods have been delivered by the warehouseman. But against a person to whom a negotiable warehouse receipt is duly negotiated a warehouseman's lien is limited to charges in an amount or at a rate specified on the receipt or if no charges are so specified then to a reasonable charge for storage of the goods covered by the receipt subsequent to the date of the receipt.

(2) The warehouseman may also reserve a security interest against the bailor for a maximum amount specified on the receipt for charges other than those specifed in subsection (1), such as for money advanced and interest. Such a security interest is governed by the Article on Secured Transactions (Article 9).

(3) A warehouseman's lien for charges and expenses under subsection (1) or a security interest under subsection (2) is also effective against any person who so entrusted the bailor with possession of the goods that a pledge of them by him to a good faith purchaser for value would have been valid but is not effective against a person as to whom the document confers no right in the goods covered by it under Section 7—503.

(4) A warehouseman loses his lien on any goods which he voluntarily delivers or which he unjustifiably refuses to deliver.

§ 7—210. Enforcement of Warehouseman's Lien.

(1) Except as provided in subsection (2), a warehouseman's lien may be enforced by public or private sale of the goods in bloc or in parcels, at any time or place and on any terms which are commercially reasonable, after notifying all persons known to claim an interest in the goods. Such notification must include a statement of the amount due, the nature of the proposed sale and the time and place of any public sale. The fact that a better price could have been obtained by a sale at a different time or in a different method from that selected by the warehouseman is not of itself sufficient to establish that the sale was not made in a commercially reasonable manner. If the warehouseman either sells the goods in the usual manner in any recognized market therefor, or if he sells at the price current in such market at the time of his sale, or if he has otherwise sold in conformity with commercially reasonable practices among dealers in the type of goods sold, he has sold in a commercially reasonable manner. A sale of more goods than apparently necessary to be offered to insure satisfaction of the obligation is not commercially reasonable except in cases covered by the preceding sentence.

(2) A warehouseman's lien on goods other than goods stored by a merchant in the course of his business may be enforced only as follows:

(a) All persons known to claim an interest in the goods must be notified.

(b) The notification must be delivered in person or sent by registered or certified letter to the last known address of any person to be notified.

(c) The notification must include an itemized statement of the claim, a description of the goods subject to the lien, a demand for payment within a specified time not less than ten days after receipt of the notification, and a conspicuous statement that unless the claim is paid within the time the goods will be advertised for sale and sold by auction at a specified time and place.

(d) The sale must conform to the terms of the notification.

(e) The sale must be held at the nearest suitable place to that where the goods are held or stored.

(f) After the expiration of the time given in the notification, an advertisement of the sale must be published once a week for two weeks consecutively in a newspaper of general circulation where the sale is to be held. The advertisement must include a description of the goods, the name of the person on whose account they are being held, and the time and place of the sale. The sale must take place at least fifteen days after the first publication. If there is no newspaper of general circulation where the sale is to be held, the advertisement must be posted at least ten days before the sale in not less than six conspicuous places in the neighborhood of the proposed sale.

(3) Before any sale pursuant to this section any person claiming a right in the goods may pay the amount necessary to satisfy the lien and the reasonable expenses incurred under this section. In that event the goods must not be sold, but must be retained by the warehouseman subject to the terms of the receipt and this Article.

(4) The warehouseman may buy at any public sale pursuant to this section.

(5) A purchaser in good faith of goods sold to enforce a warehouseman's lien takes the goods free of any rights of persons against whom the lien was valid, despite noncompliance by the warehouseman with the requirements of this section.

(6) The warehouseman may satisfy his lien from the proceeds of any sale pursuant to this section but must hold the balance, if any, for delivery on demand to any person to whom he would have been bound to deliver the goods.

(7) The rights provided by this section shall be in addition to all other rights allowed by law to a creditor against his debtor.

(8) Where a lien is on goods stored by a merchant in the course of his business the lien may be enforced in accordance with either subsection (1) or (2).

(9) The warehouseman is liable for damages caused by failure to comply with the requirements for sale under this section and in case of willful violation is liable for conversion.

PART 3

BILLS OF LADING: SPECIAL PROVISIONS

§ 7—301.   Liability for Non-Receipt or Misdescription; "Said to Contain"; "Shipper's Load and Count"; Improper Handling.

(1) A consignee of a non-negotiable bill who has given value in good faith or a holder to whom a negotiable bill has been duly negotiated relying in either case upon the description therein of the goods, or upon the date therein shown, may recover from the issuer damages caused by the misdating of the bill or the non-receipt or misdescription of the goods, except to the extent that the document indicates that the issuer does not know whether any part or all of the goods in fact were received or conform to the description, as where the description is in terms of marks or labels or kind, quantity, or condition or the receipt or description is qualified by "contents or condition of contents of packages unknown", "said to contain", "shipper's weight, load and count" or the like, if such indication be true.

(2) When goods are loaded by an issuer who is a common carrier, the issuer must count the packages of goods if package freight and ascertain the kind and quantity if bulk freight. In such cases "shipper's weight, load and count" or other words indicating that the description was made by the shipper are ineffective except as to freight concealed by packages.

(3) When bulk freight is loaded by a shipper who makes available to the issuer adequate facilities for weighing such freight, an issuer who is a common carrier must ascertain the kind and quantity within a reasonable time after receiving the written request of the shipper to do so. In such cases "shipper's weight" or other words of like purport are ineffective.

(4) The issuer may by inserting in the bill the words "shipper's weight, load and count" or other words of like purport indicate that the goods were loaded by the shipper; and if such statement be true the issuer shall not be liable for damages caused by the improper loading. But their omission does not imply liability for such damages.

(5) The shipper shall be deemed to have guaranteed to the issuer the accuracy at the time of shipment of the description, marks, labels, number, kind, quantity, condition and weight, as furnished by him; and the shipper shall indemnify the issuer against damage caused by inaccuracies in such particulars. The right of the issuer to such indemnity shall in no way limit his responsibility and liability under the contract of carriage to any person other than the shipper.

§ 7—302.   Through Bills of Lading and Similar Documents.

(1) The issuer of a through bill of lading or other document embodying an undertaking to be performed in part by persons acting as its agents or by connecting carriers is liable to anyone entitled to recover on the document for any breach by such other persons or by a connecting carrier of its obligation under the document but to the extent that the bill covers an undertaking to be performed overseas or in territory not contiguous to the continental United States or an undertaking including matters other than transportation this liability may be varied by agreement of the parties.

(2) Where goods covered by a through bill of lading or other document embodying an undertaking to be performed in part by persons other than the issuer are received by any such person, he is subject with respect to his own performance while the goods are in his possession to the obligation of the issuer. His ob-

ligation is discharged by delivery of the goods to another such person pursuant to the document, and does not include liability for breach by any other such persons or by the issuer.

(3) The issuer of such through bill of lading or other document shall be entitled to recover from the connecting carrier or such other person in possession of the goods when the breach of the obligation under the document occurred, the amount it may be required to pay to anyone entitled to recover on the document therefor, as may be evidenced by any receipt, judgment, or transcript thereof, and the amount of any expense reasonably incurred by it in defending any action brought by anyone entitled to recover on the document therefor.

§ 7—303. Diversion; Reconsignment; Change of Instructions.

(1) Unless the bill of lading otherwise provides, the carrier may deliver the goods to a person or destination other than that stated in the bill or may otherwise dispose of the goods on instructions from

    (a) the holder of a negotiable bill; or

    (b) the consignor on a non-negotiable bill notwithstanding contrary instructions from the consignee; or

    (c) the consignee on a non-negotiable bill in the absence of contrary instructions from the consignor, if the goods have arrived at the billed destination or if the consignee is in possession of the bill; or

    (d) the consignee on a non-negotiable bill if he is entitled as against the consignor to dispose of them.

(2) Unless such instructions are noted on a negotiable bill of lading, a person to whom the bill is duly negotiated can hold the bailee according to the original terms.

§ 7—304. Bills of Lading in a Set.

(1) Except where customary in overseas transportation, a bill of lading must not be issued in a set of parts. The issuer is liable for damages caused by violation of this subsection.

(2) Where a bill of lading is lawfully drawn in a set of parts, each of which is numbered and expressed to be valid only if the goods have

not been delivered against any other part, the whole of the parts constitute one bill.

(3) Where a bill of lading is lawfully issued in a set of parts and different parts are negotiated to different persons, the title of the holder to whom the first due negotiation is made prevails as to both the document and the goods even though any later holder may have received the goods from the carrier in good faith and discharged the carrier's obligation by surrender of his part.

(4) Any person who negotiates or transfers a single part of a bill of lading drawn in a set is liable to holders of that part as if it were the whole set.

(5) The bailee is obliged to deliver in accordance with Part 4 of this Article against the first presented part of a bill of lading lawfully drawn in a set. Such delivery discharges the bailee's obligation on the whole bill.

§ 7—305. Destination Bills.

(1) Instead of issuing a bill of lading to the consignor at the place of shipment a carrier may at the request of the consignor procure the bill to be issued at destination or at any other place designated in the request.

(2) Upon request of anyone entitled as against the carrier to control the goods while in transit and on surrender of any outstanding bill of lading or other receipt covering such goods, the issuer may procure a substitute bill to be issued at any place designated in the request.

§ 7—306. Altered Bills of Lading.

An unauthorized alteration or filling in of a blank in a bill of lading leaves the bill enforceable according to its original tenor.

§ 7—307. Lien of Carrier.

(1) A carrier has a lien on the goods covered by a bill of lading for charges subsequent to the date of its receipt of the goods for storage or transportation (including demurrage and terminal charges) and for expenses necessary for preservation of the goods incident to their transportation or reasonably incurred in their sale pursuant to law. But against a purchaser for value of a negotiable bill of lading a carrier's lien is limited to charges stated in

the bill or the applicable tariffs, or if no charges are stated then to a reasonable charge.

(2) A lien for charges and expenses under subsection (1) on goods which the carrier was required by law to receive for transportation is effective against the consignor or any person entitled to the goods unless the carrier had notice that the consignor lacked authority to subject the goods to such charges and expenses. Any other lien under subsection (1) is effective against the consignor and any person who permitted the bailor to have control or possession of the goods unless the carrier had notice that the bailor lacked such authority.

(3) A carrier loses his lien on any goods which he voluntarily delivers or which he unjustifiably refuses to deliver.

§ 7—308.   Enforcement of Carrier's Lien.

(1) A carrier's lien may be enforced by public or private sale of the goods, in bloc or in parcels, at any time or place and on any terms which are commercially reasonable, after notifying all persons known to claim an interest in the goods. Such notification must include a statement of the amount due, the nature of the proposed sale and the time and place of any public sale. The fact that a better price could have been obtained by a sale at a different time or in a different method from that selected by the carrier is not of itself sufficient to establish that the sale was not made in a commercially reasonable manner. If the carrier either sells the goods in the usual manner in any recognized market therefor or if he sells at the price current in such market at the time of his sale or if he has otherwise sold in conformity with commercially reasonable practices among dealers in the type of goods sold he has sold in a commercially reasonable manner. A sale of more goods than apparently necessary to be offered to ensure satisfaction of the obligation is not commercially reasonable except in cases covered by the preceding sentence.

(2) Before any sale pursuant to this section any person claiming a right in the goods may pay the amount necessary to satisfy the lien and the reasonable expenses incurred under this section. In that event the goods must not be sold, but must be retained by the carrier subject to the terms of the bill and this Article.

(3) The carrier may buy at any public sale pursuant to this section.

(4) A purchaser in good faith of goods sold to enforce a carrier's lien takes the goods free of any rights of persons against whom the lien was valid, despite noncompliance by the carrier with the requirements of this section.

(5) The carrier may satisfy his lien from the proceeds of any sale pursuant to this section but must hold the balance, if any, for delivery on demand to any person to whom he would have been bound to deliver the goods.

(6) The rights provided by this section shall be in addition to all other rights allowed by law to a creditor against his debtor.

(7) A carrier's lien may be enforced in accordance with either subsection (1) or the procedure set forth in subsection (2) of Section 7—210.

(8) The carrier is liable for damages caused by failure to comply with the requirements for sale under this section and in case of willful violation is liable for conversion.

§ 7—309.   Duty of Care; Contractual Limitation of Carrier's Liability.

(1) A carrier who issues a bill of lading whether negotiable or non-negotiable must exercise the degree of care in relation to the goods which a reasonably careful man would exercise under like circumstances. This subsection does not repeal or change any law or rule of law which imposes liability upon a common carrier for damages not caused by its negligence.

(2) Damages may be limited by a provision that the carrier's liability shall not exceed a value stated in the document if the carrier's rates are dependent upon value and the consignor by the carrier's tariff is afforded an opportunity to declare a higher value or a value as lawfully provided in the tariff, or where no tariff is filed he is otherwise advised of such opportunity; but no such limitation is effective with respect to the carrier's liability for conversion to its own use.

(3) Reasonable provisions as to the time and manner of presenting claims and instituting actions based on the shipment may be included in a bill of lading or tariff.

PART 4

WAREHOUSE RECEIPTS AND BILLS OF LADING: GENERAL OBLIGATIONS

§ 7—401. Irregularities in Issue of Receipt or Bill or Conduct of Issuer.

The obligations imposed by this Article on an issuer apply to a document of title regardless of the fact that

   (a) the document may not comply with the requirements of this Article or of any other law or regulation regarding its issue, form or content; or

   (b) the issuer may have violated laws regulating the conduct of his business; or

   (c) the goods covered by the document were owned by the bailee at the time the document was issued; or

   (d) the person issuing the document does not come within the definition of warehouseman if it purports to be a warehouse receipt.

§ 7—402. Duplicate Receipt or Bill; Overissue.

Neither a duplicate nor any other document of title purporting to cover goods already represented by an outstanding document of the same issuer confers any right in the goods, except as provided in the case of bills in a set, overissue of documents for fungible goods and substitutes for lost, stolen or destroyed documents. But the issuer is liable for damages caused by his overissue or failure to identify a duplicate document as such by conspicuous notation on its face.

§ 7—403. Obligation of Warehouseman or Carrier to Deliver; Excuse.

(1) The bailee must deliver the goods to a person entitled under the document who complies with subsections (2) and (3), unless and to the extent that the bailee establishes any of the following:

   (a) delivery of the goods to a person whose receipt was rightful as against the claimant;

   (b) damage to or delay, loss or destruction of the goods for which the bailee is not liable [, but the burden of establishing negligence in such cases is on the person entitled under the document];

Note: *The brackets in (1)(b) indicate that State enactments may differ on this point without serious damage to the principle of uniformity.*

   (c) previous sale or other disposition of the goods in lawful enforcement of a lien or on warehouseman's lawful termination of storage;

   (d) the exercise by a seller of his right to stop delivery pursuant to the provisions of the Article on Sales (Section 2—705);

   (e) a diversion, reconsignment or other disposition pursuant to the provisions of this Article (Section 7—303) or tariff regulating such right;

   (f) release, satisfaction or any other fact affording a personal defense against the claimant;

   (g) any other lawful excuse.

(2) A person claiming goods covered by a document of title must satisfy the bailee's lien where the bailee so requests or where the bailee is prohibited by law from delivering the goods until the charges are paid.

(3) Unless the person claiming is one against whom the document confers no right under Sec. 7—503(1), he must surrender for cancellation or notation of partial deliveries any outstanding negotiable document covering the goods, and the bailee must cancel the document or conspicuously note the partial delivery thereon or be liable to any person to whom the document is duly negotiated.

(4) "Person entitled under the document" means holder in the case of a negotiable document, or the person to whom delivery is to be made by the terms of or pursuant to written instructions under a non-negotiable document.

§ 7—404. No Liability for Good Faith Delivery Pursuant to Receipt or Bill.

A bailee who in good faith including observance of reasonable commercial standards has received goods and delivered or otherwise disposed of them according to the terms of the document of title or pursuant to this Article is not liable therefor. This rule applies even though the person from whom he received the goods had no authority to procure the document or to dispose of the goods and even though the person to whom he delivered the goods had no authority to receive them.

PART 5

WAREHOUSE RECEIPTS AND BILLS OF LADING: NEGOTIATION AND TRANSFER

§ 7—501. Form of Negotiation and Requirements of "Due Negotiation".

(1) A negotiable document of title running to the order of a named person is negotiated by his indorsement and delivery. After his indorsement in blank or to bearer any person can negotiate it by delivery alone.

(2) (a) A negotiable document of title is also negotiated by delivery alone when by its original terms it runs to bearer.

(b) When a document running to the order of a named person is delivered to him the effect is the same as if the document had been negotiated.

(3) Negotiation of a negotiable document of title after it has been indorsed to a specified person requires indorsement by the special indorsee as well as delivery.

(4) A negotiable document of title is "duly negotiated" when it is negotiated in the manner stated in this section to a holder who purchases it in good faith without notice of any defense against or claim to it on the part of any person and for value, unless it is established that the negotiation is not in the regular course of business or financing or involves receiving the document in settlement or payment of a money obligation.

(5) Indorsement of a non-negotiable document neither makes it negotiable nor adds to the transferee's rights.

(6) The naming in a negotiable bill of a person to be notified of the arrival of the goods does not limit the negotiability of the bill nor constitute notice to a purchaser thereof of any interest of such person in the goods.

§ 7—502. Rights Acquired by Due Negotiation.

(1) Subject to the following section and to the provisions of Section 7—205 on fungible goods, a holder to whom a negotiable document of title has been duly negotiated acquires thereby:

(a) title to the document;

(b) title to the goods;

(c) all rights accruing under the law of agency or estoppel, including rights to goods delivered to the bailee after the document was issued; and

(d) the direct obligation of the issuer to hold or deliver the goods according to the terms of the document free of any defense or claim by him except those arising under the terms of the document or under this Article. In the case of a delivery order the bailee's obligation accrues only upon acceptance and the obligation acquired by the holder is that the issuer and any indorser will procure the acceptance of the bailee.

(2) Subject to the following section, title and rights so acquired are not defeated by any stoppage of the goods represented by the document or by surrender of such goods by the bailee, and are not impaired even though the negotiation or any prior negotiation constituted a breach of duty or even though any person has been deprived of possession of the document by misrepresentation, fraud, accident, mistake, duress, loss, theft or conversion, or even though a previous sale or other transfer of the goods or document has been made to a third person.

§ 7—503. Document of Title to Goods Defeated in Certain Cases.

(1) A document of title confers no right in goods against a person who before issuance of the document had a legal interest or a perfected security interest in them and who neither

    (a) delivered or entrusted them or any document of title covering them to the bailor or his nominee with actual or apparent authority to ship, store or sell or with power to obtain delivery under this Article (Section 7—403) or with power of disposition under this Act (Sections 2—403 and 9—307) or other statute or rule of law; nor

    (b) acquiesced in the procurement by the bailor or his nominee of any document of title.

(2) Title to goods based upon an unaccepted delivery order is subject to the rights of anyone to whom a negotiable warehouse receipt or bill of lading covering the goods has been duly negotiated. Such a title may be defeated under the next section to the same extent as the rights of the issuer or a transferee from the issuer.

(3) Title to goods based upon a bill of lading issued to a freight forwarder is subject to the rights of anyone to whom a bill issued by the freight forwarder is duly negotiated; but delivery by the carrier in accordance with Part 4 of this Article pursuant to its own bill of lading discharges the carrier's obligation to deliver.

§ 7—504. Rights Acquired in the Absence of Due Negotiation; Effect of Diversion; Seller's Stoppage of Delivery.

(1) A transferee of a document, whether negotiable or nonnegotiable, to whom the document has been delivered but not duly negotiated, acquires the title and rights which his transferor had or had actual authority to convey.

(2) In the case of a non-negotiable document, until but not after the bailee receives notification of the transfer, the rights of the transferee may be defeated

    (a) by those creditors of the transferor who could treat the sale as void under Section 2—402; or

    (b) by a buyer from the transferor in ordinary course of business if the bailee has delivered the goods to the buyer or received notification of his rights; or

    (c) as against the bailee by good faith dealings of the bailee with the transferor.

(3) A diversion or other change of shipping instructions by the consignor in a non-negotiable bill of lading which causes the bailee not the deliver to the consignee defeats the consignee's title to the goods if they have been delivered to a buyer in ordinary course of business and in any event defeats the consignee's rights against the bailee.

(4) Delivery pursuant to a non-negotiable document may be stopped by a seller under Section 2—705, and subject to the requirement of due notification there provided. A bailee honoring the seller's instructions is entitled to be indemnified by the seller against any resulting loss or expense.

§ 7—505. Indorser Not a Guarantor for Other Parties.

The indorsement of a document of title issued by a bailee does not make the indorser liable for any default by the bailee or by previous indorsers.

§ 7—506. Delivery Without Indorsement: Right to Compel Indorsement.

The transferee of a negotiable document of title has a specifically enforceable right to have his transferor supply any necessary indorsement but the transfer becomes a negotiation only as of the time the indorsement is supplied.

§ 7—507. Warranties on Negotiation or Transfer of Receipt or Bill.

Where a person negotiates or transfers a document of title for value otherwise than as a mere intermediary under the next following section, then unless otherwise agreed he warrants to his immediate purchaser only in addition to any warranty made in selling the goods

    (a) that the document is genuine; and

(b) that he has no knowledge of any fact which would impair its validity or worth; and

(c) that his negotiation or transfer is rightful and fully effective with respect to the title to the document and the goods it represents.

§ 7—508. Warranties of Collecting Bank as to Documents.

A collecting bank or other intermediary known to be entrusted with documents on behalf of another or with collection of a draft or other claim against delivery of documents warrants by such delivery of the documents only its own good faith and authority. This rule applies even though the intermediary has purchased or made advances against the claim or draft to be collected.

§ 7—509. Receipt or Bill: When Adequate Compliance With Commercial Contract.

The question whether a document is adequate to fulfill the obligations of a contract for sale or the conditions of a credit is governed by the Articles on Sales (Article 2) and on Letters of Credit (Article 5).

PART 6

WAREHOUSE RECEIPTS AND BILLS OF LADING: MISCELLANEOUS PROVISIONS

§ 7—601. Lost and Missing Documents.

(1) If a document has been lost, stolen or destroyed, a court may order delivery of the goods or issuance of a substitute document and the bailee may without liability to any person comply with such order. If the document was negotiable the claimant must post security approved by the court to indemnify any person who may suffer loss as a result of non-surrender of the document. If the document was not negotiable, such security may be required at the discretion of the court. The court may also in its discretion order payment of the bailee's reasonable costs and counsel fees.

(2) A bailee who without court order delivers goods to a person claiming under a missing negotiable document is liable to any person injured thereby, and if the delivery is not in good faith becomes liable for conversion. Delivery in good faith is not conversion if made in accordance with a filed classification or tariff or, where no classification or tariff is filed, if the claimant posts security with the bailee in an amount at least double the value of the goods at the time of posting to indemnify any person injured by the delivery who files a notice of claim within one year after the delivery.

§ 7—602. Attachment of Goods Covered by a Negotiable Document.

Except where the document was originally issued upon delivery of the goods by a person who had no power to dispose of them, no lien attaches by virtue of any judicial process to goods in the possession of a bailee for which a negotiable document of title is outstanding unless the document be first surrendered to the bailee or its negotiation enjoined, and the bailee shall not be compelled to deliver the goods pursuant to process until the document is surrendered to him or impounded by the court. One who purchases the document for value without notice of the process or injunction takes free of the lien imposed by judicial process.

§ 7—603. Conflicting Claims; Interpleader.

If more than one person claims title or possession of the goods, the bailee is excused from delivery until he has had a reasonable time to ascertain the validity of the adverse claims or to bring an action to compel all claimants to interplead and may compel such interpleader, either in defending an action for nondelivery of the goods, or by original action, whichever is appropriate.

ARTICLE 8

INVESTMENT SECURITIES

PART 1

SHORT TITLE AND GENERAL MATTERS

§ 8—101. Short Title.

This Article shall be known and may be cited as Uniform Commercial Code—Investment Securities.

§ 8—102. Definitions and Index of Definitions.

(1) In this Article unless the context otherwise requires

(a) A "security" is an instrument which

    (i) is issued in bearer or registered form; and

    (ii) is of a type commonly dealt in upon securities exchanges or markets or commonly recognized in any area in which it is issued or dealt in as a medium for investment; and

    (iii) is either one of a class or series or by its terms is divisible into a class or series of instruments; and

    (iv) evidences a share, participation or other interest in property or in an enterprise or evidences an obligation of the issuer.

(b) A writing which is a security is governed by this Article and not by Uniform Commercial Code—Commercial Paper even though it also meets the requirements of that Article. This Article does not apply to money.

(c) A security is in "registered form" when it specifies a person entitled to the security or to the rights it evidences and when its transfer may be registered upon books maintained for that purpose by or on behalf of an issuer or the security so states.

(d) A security is in "bearer form" when it runs to bearer according to its terms and not by reason of any indorsement.

(2) A "subsequent purchaser" is a person who takes other than by original issue.

(3) A "clearing corporation" is a corporation all of the capital stock of which is held by or for a national securities exchange or association registered under a statute of the United States such as the Securities Exchange Act of 1934.

(4) A "custodian bank" is any bank or trust company which is supervised and examined by state or federal authority having supervision over banks and which is acting as custodian for a clearing corporation.

(5) Other definitions applying to this Article or to specified Parts thereof and the sections in which they appear are:

"Adverse claim".	Section 8—301.
"Bona fide purchaser".	Section 8—302.
"Broker".	Section 8—303.
"Guarantee of the signature".	Section 8—402.
"Intermediary Bank".	Section 4—105.
"Issuer".	Section 8—201.
"Overissue".	Section 8—104.

(6) In addition Article 1 contains general definitions and principles of construction and interpretation applicable throughout this Article.

§ 8—103. Issuer's Lien.

A lien upon a security in favor of an issuer thereof is valid against a purchaser only if the right of the issuer to such lien is noted conspicuously on the security.

§ 8—104. Effect of Overissue; "Overissue."

(1) The provisions of this Article which validate a security or compel its issue or reis-

sue do not apply to the extent that validation, issue or reissue would result in overissue; but

  (a) if an identical security which does not constitute an overissue is reasonably available for purchase, the person entitled to issue or validation may compel the issuer to purchase and deliver such a security to him against surrender of the security, if any, which he holds; or

  (b) if a security is not so available for purchase, the person entitled to issue or validation may recover from the issuer the price he or the last purchaser for value paid for it with interest from the date of his demand.

(2) "Overissue" means the issue of securities in excess of the amount which the issuer has corporate power to issue.

§ 8—105. Securities Negotiable; Presumptions.

(1) Securities governed by this Article are negotiable instruments.

(2) In any action on a security

  (a) unless specifically denied in the pleadings, each signature on the security or in a necessary indorsement is admitted;

  (b) when the effectiveness of a signature is put in issue the burden of establishing it is on the party claiming under the signature but the signature is presumed to be genuine or authorized;

  (c) when signatures are admitted or established production of the instrument

entitles a holder to recover on it unless the defendant establishes a defense or a defect going to the validity of the security; and

  (d) after it is shown that a defense or defect exists the plaintiff has the burden of establishing that he or some person under whom he claims is a person against whom the defense or defect is ineffective (Section 8—202).

§ 8—106. Applicability.

The validity of a security and the rights and duties of the issuer with respect to registration of transfer are governed by the law (including the conflict of laws rules) of the jurisdiction of organization of the issuer.

§ 8—107. Securities Deliverable; Action for Price.

(1) Unless otherwise agreed and subject to any applicable law or regulation respecting short sales, a person obligated to deliver securities may deliver any security of the specified issue in bearer form or registered in the name of the transferee or indorsed to him or in blank.

(2) When the buyer fails to pay the price as it comes due under a contract of sale the seller may recover the price

  (a) of securities accepted by the buyer; and

  (b) of other securities if efforts at their resale would be unduly burdensome or if there is no readily available market for their resale.

PART 2

ISSUE—ISSUER

§ 8—201. "Issuer."

(1) With respect to obligations on or defenses to a security "issuer" includes a person who

  (a) places or authorizes the placing of his name on a security (otherwise than as authenticating trustee, registrar, transfer agent or the like) to evidence that it represents a share, participation or other interest in his property or in an enterprise or to evidence his

duty to perform an obligation evidenced by the security; or

  (b) directly or indirecting creates fractional interests in his rights or property which fractional interests are evidenced by securities; or

  (c) becomes responsible for or in place of any other person described as an issuer in this section.

(2) With respect to obligations on or defenses to a security a guarantor is an issuer

to the extent of his guaranty whether or not his obligation is noted on the security.

(3) With respect to registration of transfer (Part 4 of this Article) "issuer" means a person on whose behalf transfer books are maintained.

§ 8—202. Issuer's Responsibility and Defenses; Notice of Defect or Defense.

(1) Even against a purchaser for value and without notice, the terms of a security include those stated on the security and those made part of the security by reference to another instrument, indenture or document or to a constitution, statute, ordinance, rule, regulation, order or the like to the extent that the terms so referred to do not conflict with the stated terms. Such a reference does not of itself charge a purchaser for value with notice of a defect going to the validity of the security even though the security expressly states that a person accepting it admits such notice.

(2) (a) A security other than one issued by a government or governmental agency or unit even though issued with a defect going to its validity is valid in the hands of a purchaser for value and without notice of the particular defect unless the defect involves a violation of constitutional provisions in which case the security is valid in the hands of a subsequent purchaser for value and without notice of the defect.

(b) The rule of subparagraph (a) applies to an issuer which is a government or governmental agency or unit only if either there has been substantial compliance with the legal requirements governing the issue or the issuer has received a substantial consideration for the issue as a whole or for the particular security and a stated purpose of the issue is one for which the issuer has power to borrow money or issue the security.

(3) Except as otherwise provided in the case of certain unauthorized signatures on issue (Section 8—205), lack of genuineness of a security is a complete defense even against a purchaser for value and without notice.

(4) All other defenses of the issuer including nondelivery and conditional delivery of the security are ineffective against a purchaser for value who has taken without notice of the particular defense.

(5) Nothing in this section shall be construed to affect the right of a party to a "when, as and if issued" or a "when distributed" contract to cancel the contract in the event of a material change in the character of the security which is the subject of the contract or in the plan or arrangement pursuant to which such security is to be issued or distributed.

§ 8—203. Staleness as Notice of Defects or Defenses.

(1) After an act or event which creates a right to immediate performance of the principal obligation evidenced by the security or which sets a date on or after which the security is to be presented or surrendered for redemption or exchange, a purchaser is charged with notice of any defect in its issue or defense of the issuer

(a) if the act or event is one requiring the payment of money or the delivery of securities or both on presentation or surrender of the security and such funds or securities are available on the date set for payment or exchange and he takes the security more than one year after that date; and

(b) if the act or event is not covered by paragraph (a) and he takes the security more than two years after the date set for surrender or presentation or the date on which such performance became due.

(2) A call which has been revoked is not within subsection (1).

§ 8—204. Effect of Issuer's Restrictions on Transfer.

Unless noted conspicuously on the security a restriction on transfer imposed by the issuer even though otherwise lawful is ineffective except against a person with actual knowledge of it.

§ 8—205. Effect of Unauthorized Signature on Issue.

An unauthorized signature placed on a security prior to or in the course of issue is ineffective except that the signature is effective in favor of a purchaser for value and without notice of the lack of authority if the signing has been done by

    (a) an authenticating trustee, registrar, transfer agent or other person entrusted by the issuer with the signing of the security or of similar securities or their immediate preparation for signing; or

    (b) an employee of the issuer or of any of the foregoing entrusted with responsible handling of the security.

§ 8—206. Completion or Alteration of Instrument.

(1) Where a security contains the signatures necessary to its issue or transfer but is incomplete in any other respect.

    (a) any person may complete it by filling in the blanks as authorized; and

    (b) even though the blanks are incorrectly filled in, the security as completed is enforceable by a purchaser who took it for value and without notice of such incorrectness.

(2) A complete security which has been improperly altered even though fraudulently remains enforceable but only according to its original terms.

§ 8—207. Rights of Issuer With Respect to Registered Owners.

(1) Prior to due presentment for registration of transfer of a security in registered form the issuer or indenture trustee may treat the registered owner as the person exclusively entitled to vote, to receive notifications and otherwise to exercise all the rights and powers of an owner.

(2) Nothing in this Article shall be construed to affect the liability of the registered owner of a security for calls, assessments or the like.

§ 8—208. Effect of Signature of Authenticating Trustee, Registrar or Transfer Agent.

(1) A person placing his signature upon a security as authenticating trustee, registrar, transfer agent or the like warrants to a purchaser for value without notice of the particular defect that

    (a) the security is genuine; and

    (b) his own participation in the issue of the security is within his capacity and within the scope of the authorization received by him from the issuer; and

    (c) he has reasonable grounds to believe that the security is in the form and within the amount the issuer is authorized to issue.

(2) Unless otherwise agreed, a person by so placing his signature does not assume responsibility for the validity of the security in other respects.

PART 3

PURCHASE

§ 8—301. Rights Acquired by Purchaser; "Adverse Claim"; Title Acquired by Bona Fide Purchaser.

(1) Upon delivery of a security the purchaser acquires the rights in the security which his transferor had or had actual authority to convey except that a purchaser who has himself been a party to any fraud or illegality affecting the security or who as a prior holder had notice of an adverse claim cannot improve his position by taking from a later bona fide purchaser. "Adverse claim" includes a claim that a transfer was or would be wrongful or that a particular adverse person is the owner of or has an interest in the security.

(2) A bona fide purchaser in addition to acquiring the rights of a purchaser also acquires the security free of any adverse claim.

(3) A purchaser of a limited interest acquires rights only to the extent of the interest purchased.

§ 8—302. "Bona Fide Purchaser."

A "bona fide purchaser" is a purchaser for value in good faith and without notice of any adverse claim who takes delivery of a security in bearer form or of one in registered form issued to him or indorsed to him or in blank.

§ 8—303. "Broker."

"Broker" means a person engaged for all or part of his time in the business of buying and selling securities, who in the transaction concerned acts for, or buys a security from or sells a security to a customer. Nothing in this Article determines the capacity in which a person acts for purposes of any other statute or rule to which such person is subject.

§ 8—304. Notice to Purchaser of Adverse Claims.

(1) A purchaser (including a broker for the seller or buyer but excluding an intermediary bank) of a security is charged with notice of adverse claims if

(a) the security whether in bearer or registered form has been indorsed "for collection" or "for surrender" or for some other purpose not involving transfer; or

(b) the security is in bearer form and has on it an unambiguous statement that it is the property of a person other than the transferor. The mere writing of a name on a security is not such a statement.

(2) The fact that the purchaser (including a broker for the seller or buyer) has notice that the security is held for a third person or is registered in the name of or indorsed by a fiduciary does not create a duty of inquiry into the rightfulness of the transfer or constitute notice of adverse claims. If, however, the purchaser (excluding an intermediary bank) has knowledge that the proceeds are being used or that the transaction is for the individual benefit of the fiduciary or otherwise in breach of duty, the purchaser is charged with notice of adverse claims.

§ 8—305. Staleness as Notice of Adverse Claims.

An act or event which creates a right to immediate performance of the principal obligation evidenced by the security or which sets a date on or after which the security is to be presented or surrendered for redemption or exchange does not of itself constitute any notice of adverse claims except in the case of a purchase

(a) after one year from any date set for such presentment or surrender for redemption or exchange; or

(b) after six months from any date set for payment of money against presentation or surrender of the security if funds are available for payment on that date.

§ 8—306. Warranties on Presentment and Transfer.

(1) A person who presents a security for registration of transfer or for payment or exchange warrants to the issuer that he is entitled to the registration, payment or exchange. But a purchaser for value without notice of adverse claims who receives a new, reissued or re-registered security on registration of transfer warrants only that he has no knowledge of any unauthorized signature (Section 8—311) in a necessary indorsement.

(2) A person by transferring a security to a purchaser for value warrants only that

(a) his transfer is effective and rightful; and

(b) the security is genuine and has not been materially altered; and

(c) he knows no fact which might impair the validity of the security.

(3) Where a security is delivered by an intermediary known to be entrusted with delivery of the security on behalf of another or with collection of a draft or other claim against such delivery, the intermediary by such delivery warrants only his own good faith and authority even though he has purchased or made advances against the claim to be collected against the delivery.

(4) A pledgee or other holder for security who redelivers the security received, or after payment and on order of the debtor delivers that security to a third person makes only the warranties of an intermediary under subsection (3).

(5) A broker gives to his customer and to the issuer and a purchaser the warranties provided in this section and has the rights and privileges of a purchaser under this section.

The warranties of and in favor of the broker acting as an agent are in addition to applicable warranties given by and in favor of his customer.

§ 8—307. Effect of Delivery Without Indorsement; Right to Compel Indorsement.

Where a security in registered form has been delivered to a purchaser without a necessary indorsement he may become a bona fide purchaser only as of the time the indorsement is supplied, but against the transferor the transfer is complete upon delivery and the purchaser has a specifically enforceable right to have any necessary indorsement supplied.

§ 8—308. Indorsement, How Made; Special Indorsement; Indorser Not a Guarantor; Partial Assignment.

(1) An indorsement of a security in registered form is made when an appropriate person signs on it or on a separate document an assignment or transfer of the security or a power to assign or transfer it or when the signature of such person is written without more upon the back of the security.

(2) An indorsement may be in blank or special. An indorsement in blank includes an indorsement to bearer. A special indorsement specifies the person to whom the security is to be transferred, or who has power to transfer it. A holder may convert a blank indorsement into a special indorsement.

(3) "An appropriate person" in subsection (1) means

(a) the person specified by the security or by special indorsement to be entitled to the security; or

(b) where the person so specified is described as a fiduciary but is no longer serving in the described capacity,—either that person or his successor; or

(c) where the security or indorsement so specifies more than one person as fiduciaries and one or more are no longer serving in the described capacity,—the remaining fiduciary or fiduciaries, whether or not a successor has been appointed or qualified; or

(d) where the person so specified is an individual and is without capacity to act by virtue of death, incompetence, infancy or otherwise,—his executor, administrator, guardian or like fiduciary; or

(e) where the security or indorsement so specifies more than one person as tenants by the entirety or with right of survivorship and by reason of death all cannot sign,—the survivor or survivors; or

(f) a person having power to sign under applicable law or controlling instrument; or

(g) to the extent that any of the foregoing persons may act through an agent,—his authorized agent.

(4) Unless otherwise agreed the indorser by his indorsement assumes no obligation that the security will be honored by the issuer.

(5) An indorsement purporting to be only of part of a security representing units intended by the issuer to be separately transferable is effective to the extent of the indorsement.

(6) Whether the person signing is appropriate is determined as of the date of signing and an indorsement by such a person does not become unauthorized for the purposes of this Article by virtue of any subsequent change of circumstances.

(7) Failure of a fiduciary to comply with a controlling instrument or with the law of the state having jurisdiction of the fiduciary relationship, including any law requiring the fiduciary to obtain court approval of the transfer, does not render his indorsement unauthorized for the purposes of this Article.

§ 8—309. Effect of Indorsement Without Delivery.

An indorsement of a security whether special or in blank does not constitute a transfer until delivery of the security on which it appears or if the indorsement is on a separate document until delivery of both the document and the security.

§ 8—310. Indorsement of Security in Bearer Form.

An indorsement of a security in bearer form may give notice of adverse claims (Section

8—304) but does not otherwise affect any right to registration the holder may possess.

§ 8—311. Effect of Unauthorized Indorsement.

Unless the owner has ratified an unauthorized indorsement or is otherwise precluded from asserting its ineffectiveness

(a) he may assert its ineffectiveness against the issuer or any purchaser other than a purchaser for value and without notice of adverse claims who has in good faith received a new, reissued or re-registered security on registration of transfer; and

(b) an issuer who registers the transfer of a security upon the unauthorized indorsement is subject to liability for improper registration (Section 8—404).

§ 8—312. Effect of Guaranteeing Signature or Indorsement.

(1) Any person guaranteeing a signature of an indorser of a security warrants that at the time of signing

(a) the signature was genuine; and

(b) the signer was an appropriate person to indorse (Section 8—308); and

(c) the signer had legal capacity to sign. But the guarantor does not otherwise warrant the rightfulness of the particular transfer.

(2) Any person may guarantee an indorsement of a security and by so doing warrants not only the signature (subsection 1) but also the rightfulness of the particular transfer in all respects. But no issuer may require a guarantee of indorsement as a condition to registration of transfer.

(3) The foregoing warranties are made to any person taking or dealing with the security in reliance on the guarantee and the guarantor is liable to such person for any loss resulting from breach of the warranties.

§ 8—313. When Delivery to the Purchaser Occurs; Purchaser's Broker as Holder.

(1) Delivery to a purchaser occurs when

(a) he or a person designated by him acquires possession of a security; or

(b) his broker acquires possession of a security specially indorsed to or issued in the name of the purchaser; or

(c) his broker sends him confirmation of the purchase and also by book entry or otherwise identifies a specific security in the broker's possession as belonging to the purchaser; or

(d) with respect to an identified security to be delivered while still in the possession of a third person when that person acknowledges that he holds for the purchaser.

(e) appropriate entries on the books of a clearing corporation are made under Section 8—320.

(2) The purchaser is the owner of a security held for him by his broker, but is not the holder except as specified in subparagraphs (b), (c) and (e) of subsection (1). Where a security is part of a fungible bulk the purchaser is the owner of a proportionate property interest in the fungible bulk.

(3) Notice of an adverse claim received by the broker or by the purchaser after the broker takes delivery as a holder for value is not effective either as to the broker or as to the purchaser. However, as between the broker and the purchaser the purchaser may demand delivery of an equivalent security as to which no notice of an adverse claim has been received.

§ 8—314. Duty to Deliver, When Completed.

(1) Unless otherwise agreed where a sale of a security is made on an exchange or otherwise through brokers

(a) the selling customer fulfills his duty to deliver when he places such a security in the possession of the selling broker or of a person designated by the broker or if requested causes an acknowledgment to be made to the selling broker that it is held for h' n; and

(b) the selling broker including a correspondent broker acting for a selling customer fulfills his duty to deliver by placing the security or a like security in the possession of the buying broker or a person designated by him or by effecting clearance of the sale in accordance with the rules of the exchange on which the transaction took place.

(2) Except as otherwise provided in this section and unless otherwise agreed, a transferor's duty to deliver a security under a contract of purchase is not fulfilled until he places the security in form to be negotiated by the purchaser in the possession of the purchaser or of a person designated by him or at the purchaser's request causes an acknowledgment to be made to the purchaser that it is held for him. Unless made on an exchange a sale to a broker purchasing for his own account is within this subsection and not within subsection (1).

§ 8—315. Action Against Purchaser Based Upon Wrongful Transfer.

(1) Any person against whom the transfer of a security is wrongful for any reason, including his incapacity, may against any one except a bona fide purchaser reclaim possession of the security or obtain possession of any new security evidencing all or part of the same rights or have damages.

(2) If the transfer is wrongful because of an unauthorized indorsement, the owner may also reclaim or obtain possession of the security or new security even from a bona fide purchaser if the ineffectiveness of the purported indorsement can be asserted against him under the provisions of this Article on unauthorized indorsements (Section 8—311).

(3) The right to obtain or reclaim possession of a security may be specifically enforced and its transfer enjoined and the security impounded pending the litigation.

§ 8—316. Purchaser's Right to Requisites for Registration of Transfer on Books.

Unless otherwise agreed the transferor must on due demand supply his purchaser with any proof of his authority to transfer or with any other requisite which may be necessary to obtain registration of the transfer of the security but if the transfer is not for value a transferor need not do so unless the purchaser furnishes the necessary expenses. Failure to comply with a demand made within a reasonable time gives the purchaser the right to reject or rescind the transfer.

§ 8—317. Attachment or Levy Upon Security.

(1) No attachment or levy upon a security or any share or other interest evidenced thereby which is outstanding shall be valid until the security is actually seized by the officer making the attachment or levy but a security which has been surrendered to the issuer may be attached or levied upon at the source.

(2) A creditor whose debtor is the owner of a security shall be entitled to such aid from courts of appropriate jurisdiction, by injunction or otherwise, in reaching such security or in satisfying the claim by means thereof as is allowed at law or in equity in regard to property which cannot readily be attached or levied upon by ordinary legal process.

§ 8—318. No Conversion by Good Faith Delivery.

An agent or bailee who in good faith (including observance of reasonable commercial standards if he is in the business of buying, selling or otherwise dealing with securities) has received securities and sold, pledged or delivered them according to the instructions of his principal is not liable for conversion or for participation in breach of fiduciary duty although the principal had no right to dispose of them.

§ 8—319. Statute of Frauds.

A contract for the sale of securities is not enforceable by way of action or defense unless

(a) there is some writing signed by the party against whom enforcement is sought or by his authorized agent or broker sufficient to indicate that a contract has been made for sale of a stated quantity of described securities at a defined or stated price; or

(b) delivery of the security has been accepted or payment has been made but the contract is enforceable under this provision only to the extent of such delivery or payment; or

(c) within a reasonable time a writing in confirmation of the sale or purchase and sufficient against the sender under paragraph (a) has been received by the party against whom enforcement is sought and he has failed to send written objection to its contents within ten days after its receipt; or

(d) the party against whom enforcement is sought admits in his pleading, testimony or otherwise in court that a contract was made for sale of a stated quantity of described securities at a defined or stated price.

§ 8—320. Transfer or Pledge within a Central Depository System.

(1) If a security

(a) is in the custody of a clearing corporation or of a custodian bank or a nominee of either subject to the instructions of the clearing corporation; and

(b) is in bearer form or indorsed in blank by an appropriate person or registered in the name of the clearing corporation or custodian bank or a nominee of either; and

(c) is shown on the account of a transferor or pledgor on the books of the clearing corporation;

then, in addition to other methods, a transfer or pledge of the security or any interest therein may be effected by the making of appropriate entries on the books of the clearing corporation reducing the account of the transferor or pledgor and increasing the account of the transferee or pledgee by the amount of the obligation or the number of shares or rights transferred or pledged.

(2) Under this section entries may be with respect to like securities or interests therein as a part of a fungible bulk and may refer merely to a quantity of a particular security without reference to the name of the registered owner, certificate or bond number or the like and, in appropriate cases, may be on a net basis taking into account other transfers or pledges of the same security.

(3) A transfer or pledge under this section has the effect of a delivery of a security in bearer form or duly indorsed in blank (Section 8—301) representing the amount of the obligation or the number of shares or rights transferred or pledged. If a pledge or the creation of a security interest is intended, the making of entries has the effect of a taking of delivery by the pledgee or a secured party (Sections 9—304 and 9—305). A transferee or pledgee under this section is a holder.

(4) A transfer or pledge under this section does not constitute a registration of transfer under Part 4 of this Article.

(5) That entries made on the books of the clearing corporation as provided in subsection (1) are not appropriate does not affect the validity or effect of the entries nor the liabilities or obligations of the clearing corporation to any person adversely affected thereby.

PART 4

REGISTRATION

§ 8—401. Duty of Issuer to Register Transfer.

(1) Where a security in registered form is presented to the issuer with a request to register transfer, the issuer is under a duty to register the transfer as requested if

(a) the security is indorsed by the appropriate person or persons (Section 8—308); and

(b) reasonable assurance is given that those indorsements are genuine and effective (Section 8—402); and

(c) the issuer has no duty to inquire into adverse claims or has discharged any such duty (Section 8—403); and

(d) any applicable law relating to the collection of taxes has been complied with; and

(e) the transfer is in fact rightful or is to a bona fide purchaser.

(2) Where an issuer is under a duty to register a transfer of a security the issuer is also liable to the person presenting it for registration or his principal for loss resulting from any unreasonable delay in registration or from failure or refusal to register the transfer.

§ 8—402. Assurance that Indorsements Are Effective.

(1) The issuer may require the following assurance that each necessary indorsement (Section 8—308) is genuine and effective

(a) in all cases, a guarantee of the signature (subsection (1) of Section 8—312) of the person indorsing; and

(b) where the indorsement is by an agent, appropriate assurance of authority to sign;

(c) where the indorsement is by a fiduciary, appropriate evidence of appointment or incumbency;

(d) where there is more than one fiduciary, reasonable assurance that all who are required to sign have done so;

(e) where the indorsement is by a person not covered by any of the foregoing, assurance appropriate to the case corresponding as nearly as may be to the foregoing.

(2) A "guarantee of the signature" in subsection (1) means a guarantee signed by or on behalf of a person reasonably believed by the issuer to be responsible. The issuer may adopt standards with respect to responsibility provided such standards are not manifestly unreasonable.

(3) "Appropriate evidence of appointment or incumbency" in subsection (1) means

(a) in the case of a fiduciary appointed or qualified by a court, a certificate issued by or under the direction or supervision of that court or an officer thereof and dated within sixty days before the date of presentation for transfer; or

(b) in any other case, a copy of a document showing the appointment or a certificate issued by or on behalf of a person reasonably believed by the issuer to be responsible or, in the absence of such a document or certificate, other evidence reasonably deemed by the issuer to be appropriate. The issuer may adopt standards with respect to such evidence provided such standards are not manifestly unreasonable. The issuer is not charged with notice of the contents of any document obtained pursuant to this paragraph (b) except to the extent that the contents relate directly to the appointment or incumbency.

(4) The issuer may elect to require reasonable assurance beyond that specified in this section but if it does so and for a purpose other than that specified in subsection 3(b) both requires and obtains a copy of a will, trust, indenture, articles of co-partnership, by-laws or other controlling instrument it is charged with notice of all matters contained therein affecting the transfer.

§ 8—403. Limited Duty of Inquiry.

(1) An issuer to whom a security is presented for registration is under a duty to inquire into adverse claims if

(a) a written notification of an adverse claim is received at a time and in a manner which affords the issuer a reasonable opportunity to act on it prior to the issuance of a new, reissued or re-registered security and the notification identifies the claimant, the registered owner and the issue of which the security is a part and provides an address for communications directed to the claimant; or

(b) the issuer is charged with notice of an adverse claim from a controlling instrument which it has elected to require under subsection (4) of Section 8—402.

(2) The issuer may discharge any duty of inquiry by any reasonable means, including notifying an adverse claimant by registered or certified mail at the address furnished by him or if there be no such address at his residence or regular place of business that the security has been presented for registration of transfer by a named person, and that the transfer will be registered unless within thirty days from the date of mailing the notification, either

(a) an appropriate restraining order, injunction or other process issues from a court of competent jurisdiction; or

(b) an indemnity bond sufficient in the issuer's judgment to protect the issuer and any transfer agent, registrar or other agent of the issuer involved, from any loss which it or they may suffer by complying with the adverse claim is filed with the issuer.

(3) Unless an issuer is charged with notice of an adverse claim from a controlling instrument which it has elected to require under subsection (4) of Section 8—402 or receives notification of an adverse claim under subsection (1) of this section, where a security presented for registration is indorsed by the appropriate person or persons the issuer is under no duty to inquire into adverse claims. In particular

(a) an issuer registering a security in the name of a person who is a fiduciary or who is described as a fiduciary is not bound to inquire into the existence, extent, or correct description of the fiduciary relationship and thereafter the issuer may assume without inquiry that the newly registered owner continues to be the fiduciary until the issuer receives written notice that the fiduciary is no longer acting as such with respect to the particular security;

(b) an issuer registering transfer on an indorsement by a fiduciary is not bound to inquire whether the transfer is made in compliance with a controlling instrument or with the law of the state having jurisdiction of the fiduciary relationship, including any law requiring the fiduciary to obtain court approval of the transfer; and

(c) the issuer is not charged with notice of the contents of any court record or file or other recorded or unrecorded document is in its possession and even though the transfer is made on the indorsement of a fiduciary to the fiduciary himself or to his nominee.

§ 8—404. Liability and Non-Liability for Registration.

(1) Except as otherwise provided in any law relating to the collection of taxes, the issuer is not liable to the owner or any other person suffering loss as a result of the registration of a transfer of a security if

(a) there were on or with the security the necessary indorsements (Section 8—308); and

(b) the issuer had no duty to inquire into adverse claims or has discharged any such duty (Section 8—403).

(2) Where an issuer has registered a transfer of a security to a person not entitled to it the issuer on demand must deliver a like security to the true owner unless

(a) the registration was pursuant to subsection (1); or

(b) the owner is precluded from asserting any claim for registering the transfer under subsection (1) of the following section; or

(c) such delivery would result in overissue, in which case the issuer's liability is governed by Section 8—104.

§ 8—405. Lost, Destroyed and Stolen Securities.

(1) Where a security has been lost, apparently destroyed or wrongfully taken and the owner fails to notify the issuer of that fact within a reasonable time after he has notice of it and the issuer registers a transfer of the security before receiving such a notification, the owner is precluded from asserting against the issuer any claim for registering the transfer under the preceding section or any claim to a new security under this section.

(2) Where the owner of a security claims that the security has been lost, destroyed or wrongfully taken, the issuer must issue a new security in place of the original security if the owner

(a) so requests before the issuer has notice that the security has been acquired by a bona fide purchaser; and

(b) files with the issuer a sufficient indemnity bond; and

(c) satisfies any other reasonable requirements imposed by the issuer.

(3) If, after the issue of the new security, a bona fide purchaser of the original security presents it for registration of transfer, the insurer must register the transfer unless registration would result in overissue, in which event the issuer's liability is governed by Section 8—104. In addition to any rights on the indemnity bond, the issuer may recover the new security from the person to whom it was issued or any person taking under him except a bona fide purchaser.

§ 8—406. Duty of Authenticating Trustee, Transfer Agent or Registrar.

(1) Where a person acts as authenticating trustee, transfer agent, registrar, or other agent for an issuer in the registration of transfers of its securities or in the issue of new securities or in the cancellation of surrendered securities

    (a) he is under a duty to the issuer to exercise good faith and due diligence in performing his functions; and

    (b) he has with regard to the particular functions he performs the same obligation to the holder or owner of the security and has the same rights and privileges as the issuer has in regard to those functions.

(2) Notice to an authenticating trustee, transfer agent, registrar or other such agent is notice to the issuer with respect to the functions performed by the agent.

ARTICLE 9

SECURED TRANSACTIONS; SALES OF ACCOUNTS, CONTRACT RIGHTS AND CHATTEL PAPER

PART 1

SHORT TITLE, APPLICABILITY AND DEFINITIONS

§ 9—101. Short Title.

This Article shall be known and may be cited as Uniform Commercial Code—Secured Transactions.

§ 9—102. Policy and Scope of Article.

(1) Except as otherwise provided in Section 9—103 on multiple state transactions and in Section 9—104 on excluded transactions, this Article applies so far as concerns any personal property and fixtures within the jurisdiction of this state

    (a) to any transaction (regardless of its form) which is intended to create a security interest in personal property or fixtures including goods, documents, instruments, general intangibles, chattel paper, accounts or contract rights; and also

    (b) to any sale of accounts, contract rights or chattel paper.

(2) This Article applies to security interests created by contract including pledge, assignment, chattel mortgage, chattel trust, trust deed, factor's lien, equipment trust, conditional sale, trust receipt, other lien or title retention contract and lease or consignment intended as security. This Article does not apply to statutory liens except as provided in Section 9—310.

(3) The application of this Article to a security interest in a secured obligation is not affected by the fact that the obligation is itself secured by a transaction or interest to which this Article does not apply.

Note: *The adoption of this Article should be accompanied by the repeal of existing statutes dealing with conditional sales, trust receipts, factor's liens where the factor is given a non-possessory lien, chattel mortgages, crop mortgages, mortgages on railroad equipment, assignment of accounts and generally statutes regulating security interests in personal property.*

Where the state has a retail installment selling act or small loan act, that legislation should be carefully examined to determine what changes in those acts are needed to conform them to this Article. This Article primarily sets out rules defining rights of a secured party against persons dealing with the debtor; it does not prescribe regulations and controls which may be necessary to curb abuses arising in the small loan business or in the financing of consumer purchases on credit. Accordingly, there is no intention to repeal existing regulatory acts in those fields. See Section 9—203(2) and the Note thereto.

§ 9—103. Accounts, Contract Rights, General Intangibles and Equipment Relating to Another Jurisdiction; and Incoming Goods Already Subject to a Security Interest.

(1) If the office where the assignor of accounts or contract rights keeps his records concerning them is in this state, the validity and perfection of a security interest therein and the possibility and effect of proper filing is governed by this Article; otherwise by the law (including the conflict of laws rules) of the jurisdiction where such office is located.

(2) If the chief place of business of a debtor is in this state, this Article governs the validity and perfection of a security interest and the possibility and effect of proper filing with regard to general intangibles or with regard to goods of a type which are normally used in more than one jurisdiction (such as automotive equipment, rolling stock, airplanes, road building equipment, commercial harvesting equipment, construction machinery and the like) if such goods are classified as equipment or classified as inventory by reason of their being leased by the debtor to others. Otherwise, the law (including the conflict of laws rules) of the jurisdiction where such chief place of business is located shall govern. If the chief place of business is located in a jurisdiction which does not provide for perfection of the security interest by filing or recording in that jurisdiction, then the security interest may be perfected by filing in this state. [For the purpose of determining the validity and perfection of a security interest in an airplane, the chief place of business of a debtor who is a foreign air carrier under the Federal Aviation Act of 1958, as amended, is the designated office of the agent upon whom service of process may be made on behalf of the debtor.]

(3) If personal property other than that governed by subsections (1) and (2) is already subject to a security interest when it is brought into this state, the validity of the security interest in this state is to be determined by the law (including the conflict of laws rules) of the jurisdiction where the property was when the security interest attached. However, if the parties to the transaction understood at the time that the security interest attached that the property would be kept in this state and it was brought into this state within 30 days after the security interest attached for purposes other than transportation through this state, then the validity of the security interest in this state is to be determined by the law of this state. If the security interest was already perfected under the law of the jurisdiction where the property was when the security interest attached and before being brought into this state, the security interest continues perfected in this state for four months and also thereafter if within the four month period it is perfected in this state. The security interest may also be perfected in this state after the expiration of the four month period; in such case perfection dates from the time of perfection in this state. If the security interest was not perfected under the law of the jurisdiction where the property was when the security interest attached and before being brought into this state, it may be perfected in this state; in such case perfection dates from the time of perfection in this state.

(4) Notwithstanding subsections (2) and (3), if personal property is covered by a certificate of title issued under a statute of this state or any other jurisdiction which requires indication on a certificate of title of any security interest in the property as a condition of perfection, then the perfection is governed by the law of the jurisdiction which issued the certificate.

[(5) Notwithstanding subsection (1) and Section 9—302, if the office where the assignor of accounts or contract rights keeps his records concerning them is not located in a jurisdiction which is a part of the United States, its territories or possessions, and the accounts or contract rights are within the jurisdiction of this state or the transaction which creates the security interest otherwise bears an appropriate relation to this state, this Article governs the validity and perfection of the security interest and the security interest may only be perfected by notification to the account debtor.]

Note: *The last sentence of subsection (2) and subsection (5) are bracketed to indicate optional enactment. In states engaging in financing of airplanes of foreign carriers and of international open accounts receivable bracketed language will be of value. In other states not engaging in financing of this type,* *the bracketed language may not be considered necessary.*

§ 9—104. Transactions Excluded From Article.

This Article does not apply

(a) to a security interest subject to any statute of the United States such as the Ship Mortgage Act, 1920, to the extent that such statute governs the rights of parties to and third parties affected by transactions in particular types of property; or

(b) to a landlord's lien; or

(c) to a lien given by statute or other rule of law for services or materials except as provided in Section 9—310 on priority of such liens; or

(d) to a transfer of a claim for wages, salary or other compensation of an employee; or

(e) to an equipment trust covering railway rolling stock; or

(f) to a sale of accounts, contract rights or chattel paper as part of a sale of the business out of which they arose, or an assignment of accounts, contract rights or chattel paper which is for the purpose of collection only, or a transfer of a contract right to an assignee who is also to do the performance under the contract; or

(g) to a transfer of an interest or claim in or under any policy of insurance; or

(h) to a right represented by a judgment; or

(i) to any right of set-off; or

(j) except to the extent that provision is made for fixtures in Section 9—313, to the creation or transfer of an interest in or lien on real estate, including a lease or rents thereunder; or

(k) to a transfer in whole or in part of any of the following: any claim arising out of tort; any deposit, savings, passbook or like account maintained with a bank, savings and loan association, credit union or like organization.

§ 9—105. Definitions and Index of Definitions.

(1) In this Article unless the context otherwise requires:

(a) "Account debtor" means the person who is obligated on an account, chattel paper, contract right or general intangible;

(b) "Chattel paper" means a writing or writings which evidence both a monetary obligation and a security interest in or a lease of specific goods. When a transaction is evidenced both by such a security agreement or a lease and by an instrument or a series of instruments, the group of writings taken together constitutes chattel paper;

(c) "Collateral" means the property subject to a security interest, and includes accounts, contract rights and chattel paper which have been sold;

(d) "Debtor" means the person who owes payment or other performance of the obligation secured, whether or not he owns or has rights in the collateral, and includes the seller of accounts, contract rights or chattel paper. Where the debtor and the owner of the collateral are not the same person, the term "debtor" means the owner of the collateral in any provision of the Article dealing with the collateral, the obligor in any provision dealing with the obligation, and may include both where the context so requires;

(e) "Document" means document of title as defined in the general definitions of Article 1 (Section 1—201);

(f) "Goods" includes all things which are movable at the time the security interest attaches or which are fixtures (Section 9—313), but does not include money, documents, instruments, accounts, chattel paper, general intangibles, contract rights and other things in action. "Goods" also include the unborn young of animals and growing crops;

(g) "Instrument" means a negotiable instrument (defined in Section 3—104), or a security (defined in Section 8—

102) or any other writing which evidences a right to the payment of money and is not itself a security agreement or lease and is of a type which is in ordinary course of business transferred by delivery with any necessary indorsement or assignment;

(h) "Security agreement" means an agreement which creates or provides for a security interest;

(i) "Secured party" means a lender, seller or other person in whose favor there is a security interest, including a person to whom accounts, contract rights or chattel paper have been sold. When the holders of obligations issued under an indenture of trust, equipment trust agreement or the like are represented by a trustee or other person, the representative is the secured party.

(2) Other definitions applying to this Article and the sections in which they appear are:

"Account".	Section 9—106.
"Consumer goods".	Section 9—109(1).
"Contract right".	Section 9—106.
"Equipment".	Section 9—109(2).
"Farm products".	Section 9—109(3).
"General intangibles".	Section 9—106.
"Inventory".	Section 9—109(4).
"Lien creditor".	Section 9—301(3).
"Proceeds".	Section 9—306(1).
"Purchase money security interest".	Section 9—107.

(3) The following definitions in other Articles apply to this Article:

"Check".	Section 3—104.
"Contract for sale".	Section 2—106.
"Holder in due course".	Section 3—302.
"Note".	Section 3—104.
"Sale".	Section 2—106.

(4) In addition Article 1 contains general definitions and principles of construction and interpretation applicable throughout this Article.

§ 9—106. Definitions: "Account"; "Contract Right"; "General Intangibles".

"Account" means any right to payment for goods sold or leased or for services rendered which is not evidenced by an instrument or chattel paper. "Contract right" means any right to payment under a contract not yet earned by performance and not evidenced by an instrument or chattel paper. "General intangibles" means any personal property (including things in action) other than goods, accounts, contract rights, chattel paper, documents and instruments.

§ 9—107. Definitions: "Purchase Money Security Interest".

A security interest is a "purchase money security interest" to the extent that it is

(a) taken or retained by the seller of the collateral to secure all or part of its price; or

(b) taken by a person who by making advances or incurring an obligation gives value to enable the debtor to acquire rights in or the use of collateral if such value is in fact so used.

§ 9—108. When After-Acquired Collateral Not Security for Antecedent Debt.

Where a secured party makes an advance, incurs an obligation, releases a perfected security interest, or otherwise gives new value which is to be secured in whole or in part by after-acquired property his security interest in the after-acquired collateral shall be deemed to be taken for new value and not as security for an antecedent debt if the debtor acquires his rights in such collateral either in the ordinary course of his business or under a contract of purchase made pursuant to the security agreement within a reasonable time after new value is given.

§ 9—109. Classification of Goods; "Consumer Goods"; "Equipment"; "Farm Products"; "Inventory".

Goods are

(1) "consumer goods" if they are used or bought for use primarily for personal, family or household purposes;

(2) "equipment" if they are used or bought for use primarily in business (including farming or a profession) or by a debtor who is a non-profit organization or a governmental subdivision or agency or if the goods are not in-

cluded in the definitions of inventory, farm products or consumer goods;

(3) "farm products" if they are crops or livestock or supplies used or produced in farming operations or if they are products of crops or livestock in their unmanufactured states (such as ginned cotton, wool-clip, maple syrup, milk and eggs), and if they are in the possession of a debtor engaged in raising, fattening, grazing or other farming operations. If goods are farm products they are neither equipment nor inventory;

(4) "inventory" if they are held by a person who holds them for sale or lease or to be furnished under contracts of service or if he has so furnished them, or if they are raw materials, work in process or materials used or consumed in a business. Inventory of a person is not to be classified as his equipment.

§ 9—110. Sufficiency of Description.

For the purposes of this Article any description of personal property or real estate is sufficient whether or not it is specific if it reasonably identifies what is described.

§ 9—111. Applicability of Bulk Transfer Laws.

The creation of a security interest is not a bulk transfer under Article 6 (see Section 6—103).

§ 9—112. Where Collateral Is Not Owned by Debtor.

Unless otherwise agreed, when a secured party knows that collateral is owned by a person who is not the debtor, the owner of the collateral is entitled to receive from the secured party any surplus under Section 9—502(2) or under Section 9—504(1), and is not liable for the debt or for any deficiency after resale, and he has the same right as the debtor

(a) to receive statements under Section 9—208;

(b) to receive notice of and to object to a secured party's proposal to retain the collateral in satisfaction of the indebtedness under Section 9—505;

(c) to redeem the collateral under Section 9—506;

(d) to obtain injunctive or other relief under Section 9—507(1); and

(e) to recover losses caused to him under Section 9—208(2).

§ 9—113. Security Interests Arising Under Article on Sales.

A security interest arising solely under the Article on Sales (Article 2) is subject to the provisions of this Article except that to the extent that and so long as the debtor does not have or does not lawfully obtain possession of the goods

(a) no security agreement is necessary to make the security interest enforceable; and

(b) no filing is required to perfect the security interest; and

(c) the rights of the secured party on default by the debtor are governed by the Article on Sales (Article 2).

PART 2

VALIDITY OF SECURITY AGREEMENT AND RIGHTS OF PARTIES THERETO

§ 9—201. General Validity of Security Agreement.

Except as otherwise provided by this Act a security agreement is effective according to its terms between the parties, against purchasers of the collateral and against creditors. Nothing in this Article validates any charge or practice illegal under any statute or regulation thereunder governing usury, small loans, retail installment sales, or the like, or extends the application of any such statute or regulation to any transaction not otherwise subject thereto.

§ 9—202. Title to Collateral Immaterial.

Each provision of this Article with regard to rights, obligations and remedies applies whether title to collateral is in the secured party or in the debtor.

§ 9—203. Enforceability of Security Interest; Proceeds, Formal Requisites.

(1) Subject to the provisions of Section 4—208 on the security interest of a collecting bank and Section 9—113 on a security interest arising under the Article on Sales, a security interest is not enforceable against the debtor or third parties unless

(a) the collateral is in the possession of the secured party; or

(b) the debtor has signed a security agreement which contains a description of the collateral and in addition, when the security interest covers crops or oil, gas or minerals to be extracted or timber to be cut, a description of the land concerned. In describing collateral, the word "proceeds" is sufficient without further description to cover proceeds of any character.

(2) A transaction, although subject to this Article, is also subject to ....*, and in the case of conflict between the provisions of this Article and any such statute, the provisions of such statute control. Failure to comply with any applicable statute has only the effect which is specified therein.

*Note: At * in subsection (2) insert reference to any local statute regulating small loans, retail installment sales and the like.*

The foregoing subsection (2) is designed to make it clear that certain transactions, although subject to this Article, must also comply with other applicable legislation.

This Article is designed to regulate all the "security" aspects of transactions within its scope. There is, however, much regulatory legislation, particularly in the consumer field, which supplements this Article and should not be repealed by its enactment. Examples are small loan acts, retail installment selling acts and the like. Such acts may provide for licensing and rate regulation and may prescribe particular forms of contract. Such provisions should remain in force despite the enactment of this Article. On the other hand if a Retail Installment Selling Act contains provisions on filing, rights on default,
etc., such provisions should be repealed as inconsistent with this Article.

§ 9—204. When Security Interest Attaches; After-Acquired Property; Future Advances.

(1) A security interest cannot attach until there is agreement (subsection (3) of Section 1—201) that it attach and value is given and the debtor has rights in the collateral. It attaches as soon as all of the events in the preceding sentence have taken place unless explicit agreement postpones the time of attaching.

(2) For the purposes of this section the debtor has no rights

(a) in crops until they are planted or otherwise become growing crops, in the young of livestock until they are conceived;

(b) in fish until caught, in oil, gas or minerals until they are extracted, in timber until it is cut;

(c) in a contract right until the contract has been made;

(d) in an account until it comes into existence.

(3) Except as provided in subsection (4) a security agreement may provide that collateral whenever acquired, shall secure all obligations covered by the security agreement.

(4) No security interest attaches under an after-acquired property clause

(a) to crops which become such more than one year after the security agreement is executed except that a security interest in crops which is given in conjunction with a lease or a land purchase or improvement transaction evidenced by a contract, mortgage or deed of trust may if so agreed attach to crops to be grown on the land concerned during the period of such real estate transaction;

(b) to consumer goods other than accessions (Section 9—314) when given as additional security unless the debtor acquires rights in them within ten days after the secured party gives value.

(5) Obligations covered by a security agreement may include future advances or other

value whether or not the advances or value are given pursuant to commitment.

§ 9—205. Use or Disposition of Collateral Without Accounting Permissible.

A security interest is not invalid or fraudulent against creditors by reason of liberty in the debtor to use, commingle or dispose of all or part of the collateral (including returned or repossessed goods) or to collect or compromise accounts, contract rights or chattel paper, or to accept the return of goods or make repossessions, or to use, commingle or dispose of proceeds, or by reason of the failure of the secured party to require the debtor to account for proceeds or replace collateral. This section does not relax the requirements of possession where perfection of a security interest depends upon possession of the collateral by the secured party or by a bailee.

§ 9—206. Agreement Not to Assert Defenses Against Assignee; Modification of Sales Warranties Where Security Agreement Exists.

(1) Subject to any statute or decision which establishes a different rule for buyers or lessees of consumer goods, an agreement by a buyer or lessee that he will not assert against an assignee any claim or defense which he may have against the seller or lessor is enforceable by an assignee who takes his assignment for value, in good faith and without notice of a claim or defense, except as to defenses of a type which may be asserted against a holder in due course of a negotiable instrument under the Article on Commercial Paper (Article 3). A buyer who as part of one transaction signs both a negotiable instrument and a security agreement makes such an agreement.

(2) When a seller retains a purchase money security interest in goods the Article on Sales (Article 2) governs the sale and any disclaimer, limitation or modification of the seller's warranties.

§ 9—207. Rights and Duties When Collateral Is in Secured Party's Possession.

(1) A secured party must use reasonable care in the custody and preservation of collateral in his possession. In the case of an instrument or chattel paper reasonable care includes taking necessary steps to preserve rights against prior parties unless otherwise agreed.

(2) Unless otherwise agreed, when collateral is in the secured party's possession

    (a) reasonable expenses (including the cost of any insurance and payment of taxes or other charges) incurred in the custody, preservation, use or operation of the collateral are chargeable to the debtor and are secured by the collateral;

    (b) the risk of accidental loss or damage is on the debtor to the extent of any deficiency in any effective insurance coverage;

    (c) the secured party may hold as additional security any increase or profits (except money) received from the collateral, but money so received, unless remitted to the debtor, shall be applied in reduction of the secured obligation;

    (d) the secured party must keep the collateral identifiable but fungible collateral may be commingled;

    (e) the secured party may repledge the collateral upon terms which do not impair the debtor's right to redeem it.

(3) A secured party is liable for any loss caused by his failure to meet any obligation imposed by the preceding subsections but does not lose his security interest.

(4) A secured party may use or operate the collateral for the purpose of preserving the collateral or its value or pursuant to the order of a court of appropriate jurisdiction or, except in the case of consumer goods, in the manner and to the extent provided in the security agreement.

§ 9—208. Request for Statement of Account or List of Collateral.

(1) A debtor may sign a statement indicating what he believes to be the aggregate amount of unpaid indebtedness as of a specified date and may send it to the secured party with a request that the statement be approved or corrected and returned to the debtor. When the security agreement or any other record kept by the secured party identifies the collateral a debtor may similarly request the secured

party to approve or correct a list of the collateral.

(2) The secured party must comply with such a request within two weeks after receipt by sending a written correction or approval. If the secured party claims a security interest in all of a particular type of collateral owned by the debtor he may indicate that fact in his reply and need not approve or correct an itemized list of such collateral. If the secured party without reasonable excuse fails to comply he is liable for any loss caused to the debtor thereby; and if the debtor has properly included in his request a good faith statement of the obligation or a list of the collateral or both the secured party may claim a security interest only as shown in the statement against persons misled by his failure to comply. If he no longer has an interest in the obligation or collateral at the time the request is received he must disclose the name and address of any successor in interest known to him and he is liable for any loss caused to the debtor as a result of failure to disclose. A successor in interest is not subject to this section until a request is received by him.

(3) A debtor is entitled to such a statement once every six months without charge. The secured party may require payment of a charge not exceeding $10 for each additional statement furnished.

PART 3

RIGHTS OF THIRD PARTIES; PERFECTED AND UNPERFECTED SECURITY INTERESTS; RULES OF PRIORITY

§ 9—301. Persons Who Take Priority Over Unperfected Security Interests; "Lien Creditor".

(1) Except as otherwise provided in subsection (2), an unperfected security interest is subordinate to the rights of

(a) persons entitled to priority under Section 9—312;

(b) a person who becomes a lien creditor without knowledge of the security interest and before it is perfected;

(c) in the case of goods, instruments, documents, and chattel paper, a person who is not a secured party and who is a transferee in bulk or other buyer not in ordinary course of business to the extent that he gives value and receives delivery of the collateral without knowledge of the security interest and before it is perfected;

(d) in the case of accounts, contract rights, and general intangibles, a person who is not a secured party and who is a transferee to the extent that he gives value without knowledge of the security interest and before it is perfected.

(2) If the secured party files with respect to a purchase money security interest before or within ten days after the collateral comes into possession of the debtor, he takes priority over the rights of a transferee in bulk or of a lien creditor which arise between the time the security interest attaches and the time of filing.

(3) A "lien creditor" means a creditor who has acquired a lien on the property involved by attachment, levy or the like and includes an assignee for benefit of creditors from the time of assignment, and a trustee in bankruptcy from the date of the filing of the petition or a receiver in equity from the time of appointment. Unless all the creditors represented had knowledge of the security interest such a representative of creditors is a lien creditor without knowledge even though he personally has knowledge of the security interest.

§ 9—302. When Filing Is Required to Perfect Security Interest; Security Interests to Which Filing Provisions of This Article Do Not Apply.

(1) A financing statement must be filed to perfect all security interests except the following:

(a) a security interest in collateral in possession of the secured party under Section 9—305;

(b) a security interest temporarily perfected in instruments or documents without delivery under Section 9—304 or in proceeds for a 10 day period under Section 9—306;

(c) a purchase money security interest in farm equipment having a purchase price not in excess of $2500; but filing is required for a fixture under Section 9—313 or for a motor vehicle required to be licensed;

(d) a purchase money security interest in consumer goods; but filing is required for a fixture under Section 9—313 or for a motor vehicle required to be licensed;

(e) an assignment of accounts or contract rights which does not alone or in conjunction with other assignments to the same assignee transfer a significant part of the outstanding accounts or contract rights of the assignor;

(f) a security interest of a collecting bank (Section 4—208) or arising under the Article on Sales (see Section 9—113) or covered in subsection (3) of this section.

(2) If a secured party assigns a perfected security interest, no filing under this Article is required in order to continue the perfected status of the security interest against creditors of and transferees from the original debtor.

(3) The filing provisions of this Article do not apply to a security interest in property subject to a statute

(a) of the United States which provides for a national registration or filing of all security interests in such property; or

Note: *States to select either Alternative A or Alternative B.*

Alternative A—

(b) of this state which provides for central filing of, or which requires indication on a certificate of title of, such security interests in such property.

Alternative B—

(b) of this state which provides for central filing of security interests in such property, or in a motor vehicle which is not inventory held for sale for which a certificate of title is required under the statutes of this state if a notation of such a security interest can be indicated by a public official on a certificate or a duplicate thereof.

(4) A security interest in property covered by a statute described in subsection (3) can be perfected only by registration or filing under that statute or by indication of the security interest on a certificate of title or a duplicate thereof by a public official.

§ 9—303. When Security Interest Is Perfected; Continuity of Perfection.

(1) A security interest is perfected when it has attached and when all of the applicable steps required for perfection have been taken. Such steps are specified in Sections 9—302, 9—304, 9—305 and 9—306. If such steps are taken before the security interest attaches, it is perfected at the time when it attaches.

(2) If a security interest is originally perfected in any way permitted under this Article and is subsequently perfected in some other way under this Article, without an intermediate period when it was unperfected, the security interest shall be deemed to be perfected continuously for the purposes of this Article.

§ 9—304. Perfection of Security Interest in Instruments, Documents, and Goods Covered by Documents; Perfection by Permissive Filing; Temporary Perfection Without Filing or Transfer of Possession.

(1) A security interest in chattel paper or negotiable documents may be perfected by filing. A security interest in instruments (other than instruments which constitute part of chattel paper) can be perfected only by the secured party's taking possession, except as provided in subsections (4) and (5).

(2) During the period that goods are in the possession of the issuer of a negotiable document therefor, a security interest in the goods is perfected by perfecting a security interest in the document, and any security interest in the goods otherwise perfected during such period is subject thereto.

(3) A security interest in goods in the possession of a bailee other than one who has issued a negotiable document therefor is perfect-

ed by issuance of a document in the name of the secured party or by the bailee's receipt of notification of the secured party's interest or by filing as to the goods.

(4) A security interest in instruments or negotiable documents is perfected without filing or the taking of possession for a period of 21 days from the time it attaches to the extent that it arises for new value given under a written security agreement.

(5) A security interest remains perfected for a period of 21 days without filing where a secured party having a perfected security interest in an instrument, a negotiable document or goods in possession of a bailee other than one who has issued a negotiable document therefor

    (a) makes available to the debtor the goods or documents representing the goods for the purpose of ultimate sale or exchange or for the purpose of loading, unloading, storing, shipping, transshipping, manufacturing, processing or otherwise dealing with them in a manner preliminary to their sale or exchange; or

    (b) delivers the instrument to the debtor for the purpose of ultimate sale or exchange or of presentation, collection, renewal or registration of transfer.

(6) After the 21 day period in subsections (4) and (5) perfection depends upon compliance with applicable provisions of this Article.

§ 9—305. When Possession by Secured Party Perfects Security Interest Without Filing.

A security interest in letters of credit and advices of credit (subsection (2) (a) of Section 5—116), goods, instruments, negotiable documents or chattel paper may be perfected by the secured party's taking possession of the collateral. If such collateral other than goods covered by a negotiable document is held by a bailee, the secured party is deemed to have possession from the time the bailee receives notification of the secured party's interest. A security interest is perfected by possession from the time possession is taken without relation back and continues only so long as possession is retained, unless otherwise specified in this Article. The security interest may be otherwise perfected as provided in this Article before or after the period of possession by the secured party.

§ 9—306. "Proceeds"; Secured Party's Rights on Disposition of Collateral.

(1) "Proceeds" includes whatever is received when collateral or proceeds is sold, exchanged, collected or otherwise disposed of. The term also includes the account arising when the right to payment is earned under a contract right. Money, checks and the like are "cash proceeds". All other proceeds are "non-cash proceeds".

(2) Except where this Article otherwise provides, a security interest continues in collateral notwithstanding sale, exchange or other disposition thereof by the debtor unless his action was authorized by the secured party in the security agreement or otherwise, and also continues in any identifiable proceeds including collections received by the debtor.

(3) The security interest in proceeds is a continuously perfected security interest if the interest in the original collateral was perfected but it ceases to be a perfected security interest and becomes unperfected ten days after receipt of the proceeds by the debtor unless

    (a) a filed financing statement covering the original collateral also covers proceeds; or

    (b) the security interest in the proceeds is perfected before the expiration of the ten day period.

(4) In the event of insolvency proceedings instituted by or against a debtor, a secured party with a perfected security interest in proceeds has a perfected security interest

    (a) in identifiable non-cash proceeds;

    (b) in identifiable cash proceeds in the form of money which is not commingled with other money or deposited in a bank account prior to the insolvency proceedings;

    (c) in identifiable cash proceeds in the form of checks and the like which are not deposited in a bank account prior to the insolvency proceedings; and

    (d) in all cash and bank accounts of the debtor, if other cash proceeds have been commingled or deposited in a bank account, but the perfected security interest under this paragraph (d) is

(i) subject to any right of set-off; and

(ii) limited to an amount not greater than the amount of any cash proceeds received by the debtor within ten days before the institution of the insolvency proceedings and commingled or deposited in a bank account prior to the insolvency proceedings less the amount of cash proceeds received by the debtor and paid over to the secured party during the ten day period.

(5) If a sale of goods results in an account or chattel paper which is transferred by the seller to a secured party, and if the goods are returned to or are repossessed by the seller or the secured party, the following rules determine priorities:

(a) If the goods were collateral at the time of sale for an indebtedness of the seller which is still unpaid, the original security interest attaches again to the goods and continues as a perfected security interest if it was perfected at the time when the goods were sold. If the security interest was originally perfected by a filing which is still effective, nothing further is required to continue the perfected status; in any other case, the secured party must take possession of the returned or repossessed goods or must file.

(b) An unpaid transferee of the chattel paper has a security interest in the goods against the transferor. Such security interest is prior to a security interest asserted under paragraph (a) to the extent that the transferee of the chattel paper was entitled to priority under Section 9—308.

(c) An unpaid transferee of the account has a security interest in the goods against the transferor. Such security interest is subordinate to a security interest asserted under paragraph (a).

(d) A security interest of an unpaid transferee asserted under paragraph (b) or (c) must be perfected for protection against creditors of the transferor and purchasers of the returned or repossessed goods.

§ 9—307. Protection of Buyers of Goods.

(1) A buyer in ordinary course of business (subsection (9) of Section 1—201) other than a person buying farm products from a person engaged in farming operations takes free of a security interest created by his seller even though the security interest is perfected and even though the buyer knows of its existence.

(2) In the case of consumer goods and in the case of farm equipment having an original purchase price not in excess of $2500 (other than fixtures, see Section 9—313), a buyer takes free of a security interest even though perfected if he buys without knowledge of the security interest, for value and for his own personal, family or household purposes or his own farming operations unless prior to the purchase the secured party has filed a financing statement covering such goods.

§ 9—308. Purchase of Chattel Paper and Non-Negotiable Instruments.

A purchaser of chattel paper or a non-negotiable instrument who gives new value and takes possession of it in the ordinary course of his business and without knowledge that the specific paper or instrument is subject to a security interest has priority over a security interest which is perfected under Section 9—304 (permissive filing and temporary perfection). A purchaser of chattel paper who gives new value and takes possession of it in the ordinary course of his business has priority over a security interest in chattel paper which is claimed merely as proceeds of inventory subject to a security interest (Section 9—306), even though he knows that the specific paper is subject to the security interest.

§ 9—309. Protection of Purchasers of Instruments and Documents.

Nothing in this Article limits the rights of a holder in due course of a negotiable instrument (Section 3—302) or a holder to whom a negotiable document of title has been duly negotiated (Section 7—501) or a bona fide purchaser of a security (Section 8—301) and such holders or purchasers take priority over an earlier security interest even though perfected. Filing under this Article does not constitute notice of the security interest to such holders or purchasers.

§ 9—310. Priority of Certain Liens Arising by Operation of Law.

When a person in the ordinary course of his business furnishes services or materials with respect to goods subject to a security interest, a lien upon goods in the possession of such person given by statute or rule of law for such materials or services takes priority over a perfected security interest unless the lien is statutory and the statute expressly provides otherwise.

§ 9—311. Alienability of Debtor's Rights: Judicial Process.

The debtor's rights in collateral may be voluntarily or involuntarily transferred (by way of sale, creation of a security interest, attachment, levy, garnishment or other judicial process) notwithstanding a provision in the security agreement prohibiting any transfer or making the transfer constitute a default.

§ 9—312. Priorities Among Conflicting Security Interests in the Same Collateral.

(1) The rules of priority stated in the following sections shall govern where applicable: Section 4—208 with respect to the security interest of collecting banks in items being collected, accompanying documents and proceeds; Section 9—301 on certain priorities; Section 9—304 on goods covered by documents; Section 9—306 on proceeds and repossessions; Section 9—307 on buyers of goods; Section 9—308 on possessory against nonpossessory interests in chattel paper or non-negotiable instruments; Section 9—309 on security interests in negotiable instruments, documents or securities; Section 9—310 on priorities between perfected security interests and liens by operation of law; Section 9—313 on security interests in fixtures as against interests in real estate; Section 9—314 on security interests in accessions as against interest in goods; Section 9—315 on conflicting security interests where

goods lose their identity or become part of a product; and Section 9—316 on contractual subordination.

(2) A perfected security interest in crops for new value given to enable the debtor to produce the crops during the production season and given not more than three months before the crops become growing crops by planting or otherwise takes priority over an earlier perfected security interest to the extent that such earlier interest secures obligations due more than six months before the crops become growing crops by planting or otherwise, even though the person giving new value had knowledge of the earlier security interest.

(3) A purchase money security interest in inventory collateral has priority over a conflicting security interest in the same collateral if

(a) the purchase money security interest is perfected at the time the debtor receives possession of the collateral; and

(b) any secured party whose security interest is known to the holder of the purchase money security interest or who, prior to the date of the filing made by the holder of the purchase money security interest, had filed a financing statement covering the same items or type of inventory, has received notification of the purchase money security interest before the debtor receives possession of the collateral covered by the purchase money security interest; and

(c) such notification states that the person giving the notice has or expects to acquire a purchase money security interest in inventory of the debtor, describing such inventory by item or type.

(4) A purchase money security interest in collateral other than inventory has priority over a conflicting security interest in the same collateral if the purchase money security interest is perfected at the time the debtor receives possession of the collateral or within ten days thereafter.

(5) In all cases not governed by other rules stated in this section (including cases of purchase money security interests which do not qualify for the special priorities set forth in

subsections (3) and (4) of this section), priority between conflicting security interests in the same collateral shall be determined as follows:

(a) in the order of filing if both are perfected by filing, regardless of which security interest attached first under Section 9—204(1) and whether it attached before or after filing;

(b) in the order of perfection unless both are perfected by filing, regardless of which security interest attached first under Section 9—204(1) and, in the case of a filed security interest, whether it attached before or after filing; and

(c) in the order of attachment under Section 9—204(1) so long as neither is perfected.

(6) For the purpose of the priority rules of the immediately preceding subsection, a continuously perfected security interest shall be treated at all times as if perfected by filing if it was originally so perfected and it shall be treated at all times as if perfected otherwise than by filing if it was originally perfected otherwise than by filing.

§ 9—313. Priority of Security Interests in Fixtures.

(1) The rules of this section do not apply to goods incorporated into a structure in the manner of lumber, bricks, tile, cement, glass, metal work and the like and no security interest in them exists under this Article unless the structure remains personal property under applicable law. The law of this state other than this Act determines whether and when other goods become fixtures. This Act does not prevent creation of an encumbrance upon fixtures or real estate pursuant to the law applicable to real estate.

(2) A security interest which attaches to goods before they become fixtures takes priority as to the goods over the claims of all persons who have an interest in the real estate except as stated in subsection (4).

(3) A security interest which attaches to goods after they become fixtures is valid against all persons subsequently acquiring interests in the real estate except as stated in subsection (4) but is invalid against any person with an interest in the real estate at the time the security interest attaches to the goods who has not in writing consented to the security interest or disclaimed an interest in the goods as fixtures.

(4) The security interests described in subsections (2) and (3) do not take priority over

(a) a subsequent purchaser for value of any interest in the real estate; or

(b) a creditor with a lien on the real estate subsequently obtained by judicial proceedings; or

(c) a creditor with a prior encumbrance of record on the real estate to the extent that he makes subsequent advances

if the subsequent purchase is made, the lien by judicial proceedings is obtained, or the subsequent advance under the prior encumbrance is made or contracted for without knowledge of the security interest and before it is perfected. A purchaser of the real estate at a foreclosure sale other than an encumbrancer purchasing at his own foreclosure sale is a subsequent purchaser within this section.

(5) When under subsections (2) or (3) and (4) a secured party has priority over the claims of all persons who have interests in the real estate, he may, on default, subject to the provisions of Part 5, remove his collateral from the real estate but he must reimburse any encumbrancer or owner of the real estate who is not the debtor and who has not otherwise agreed for the cost of repair of any physical injury, but not for any diminution in value of the real estate caused by the absence of the goods removed or by any necessity for replacing them. A person entitled to reimbursement may refuse permission to remove until the secured party gives adequate security for the performance of this obligation.

§ 9—314. Accessions.

(1) A security interest in goods which attaches before they are installed in or affixed to other goods takes priority as to the goods installed or affixed (called in this section "accessions") over the claims of all persons to the whole except as stated in subsection (3) and subject to Section 9—315(1).

(2) A security interest which attaches to goods after they become part of a whole is valid against all persons subsequently acquir-

ing interests in the whole except as stated in subsection (3) but is invalid against any person with an interest in the whole at the time the security interest attaches to the goods who has not in writing consented to the security interest or disclaimed an interest in the goods as part of the whole.

(3) The security interests described in subsections (1) and (2) do not take priority over

(a) a subsequent purchaser for value of any interest in the whole; or

(b) a creditor with a lien on the whole subsequently obtained by judicial proceedings; or

(c) a creditor with a prior perfected security interest in the whole to the extent that he makes subsequent advances

if the subsequent purchase is made, the lien by judicial proceedings obtained or the subsequent advance under the prior perfected security interest is made or contracted for without knowledge of the security interest and before it is perfected. A purchaser of the whole at a foreclosure sale other than the holder of a perfected security interest purchasing at his own foreclosure sale is a subsequent purchaser within this section.

(4) When under subsections (1) or (2) and (3) a secured party has an interest in accessions which has priority over the claims of all persons who have interests in the whole, he may on default subject to the provisions of Part 5 remove his collateral from the whole but he must reimburse any encumbrancer or owner of the whole who is not the debtor and who has not otherwise agreed for the cost of repair of any physical injury but not for any diminution in value of the whole caused by the absence of the goods removed or by any necessity for replacing them. A person entitled to reimbursement may refuse permission to remove until the secured party gives adequate security for the performance of this obligation.

§ 9—315. Priority When Goods Are Commingled or Processed.

(1) If a security interest in goods was perfected and subsequently the goods or a part thereof have become part of a product or mass, the security interest continues in the product or mass if

(a) the goods are so manufactured, processed, assembled or commingled that their identity is lost in the product or mass; or

(b) a financing statement covering the original goods also covers the product into which the goods have been manufactured, processed or assembled.

In a case to which paragraph (b) applies, no separate security interest in that part of the original goods which has been manufactured, processed or assembled into the product may be claimed under Section 9—314.

(2) When under subsection (1) more than one security interest attaches to the product or mass, they rank equally according to the ratio that the cost of the goods to which each interest originally attached bears to the cost of the total product or mass.

§ 9—316. Priority Subject to Subordination.

Nothing in this Article prevents subordination by agreement by any person entitled to priority.

§ 9—317. Secured Party Not Obligated on Contract of Debtor.

The mere existence of a security interest or authority given to the debtor to dispose of or use collateral does not impose contract or tort liability upon the secured party for the debtor's acts or omissions.

§ 9—318. Defenses Against Assignee; Modification of Contract After Notification of Assignment; Term Prohibiting Assignment Ineffective; Identification and Proof of Assignment.

(1) Unless an account debtor has made an enforceable agreement not to assert defenses or claims arising out of a sale as provided in Section 9—206 the rights of an assignee are subject to

(a) all the terms of the contract between the account debtor and assignor and any defense or claim arising therefrom; and

(b) any other defense or claim of the account debtor against the assignor which accrues before the account debtor receives notification of the assignment.

(2) So far as the right to payment under an assigned contract right has not already become an account, and notwithstanding notification of the assignment, any modification of or substitution for the contract made in good faith and in accordance with reasonable commercial standards is effective against an assignee unless the account debtor has otherwise agreed but the assignee acquires corresponding rights under the modified or substituted contract. The assignment may provide that such modification or substitution is a breach by the assignor.

(3) The account debtor is authorized to pay the assignor until the account debtor receives notification that the account has been assigned and that payment is to be made to the assignee. A notification which does not reasonably identify the rights assigned is ineffective. If requested by the account debtor, the assignee must seasonably furnish reasonable proof that the assignment has been made and unless he does so the account debtor may pay the assignor.

(4) A term in any contract between an account debtor and an assignor which prohibits assignment of an account or contract right to which they are parties is ineffective.

PART 4

FILING

§ 9—401. **Place of Filing; Erroneous Filing; Removal of Collateral.**

First Alternative Subsection (1)

(1) The proper place to file in order to perfect a security interest is as follows:

   (a) when the collateral is goods which at the time the security interest attaches are or are to become fixtures, then in the office where a mortgage on the real estate concerned would be filed or recorded;

   (b) in all other cases, in the office of the [Secretary of State].

Second Alternative Subsection (1)

(1) The proper place to file in order to perfect a security interest is as follows:

   (a) when the collateral is equipment used in farming operations, or farm products, or accounts, contract rights or general intangibles arising from or relating to the sale of farm products by a farmer, or consumer goods, then in the office of the ...... in the county of the debtor's residence or if the debtor is not a resident of this state then the office of the ...... in the county where the goods are kept, and in addition when the collateral is crops in the office of the ...... in the county where the land on which the crops are growing or to be grown is located;

   (b) when the collateral is goods which at the time the security interest attaches are or are to become fixtures, then in the office where a mortgage on the real estate concerned would be filed or recorded;

   (c) in all other cases, in the office of the [Secretary of State].

Third Alternative Subsection (1)

(1) The proper place to file in order to perfect a security interest is as follows:

   (a) when the collateral is equipment used in farming operations, or farm products, or accounts, contract rights or general intangibles arising from or relating to the sale of farm products by a farmer, or consumer goods, then in the office of the ...... in the county of the debtor's residence or if the debtor is not a resident of this state then in the office of the ...... in the county where the goods are kept, and in addition when the collateral is crops in the office of the ...... in the county where the land on which the crops are growing or to be grown is located;

   (b) when the collateral is goods which at the time the security interest attaches are or are to become fixtures, then in the office where a mortgage on the real estate concerned would be filed or recorded;

(c) in all other cases, in the office of the [Secretary of State] and in addition, if the debtor has a place of business in only one county of this state, also in the office of ...... of such county, or, if the debtor has no place of business in this state, but resides in the state, also in the office of ...... of the county in which he resides.

Note: *One of the three alternatives should be selected as subsection (1).*

(2) A filing which is made in good faith in an improper place or not in all of the places required by this section is nevertheless effective with regard to any collateral as to which the filing complied with the requirements of this Article and is also effective with regard to collateral covered by the financing statement against any person who has knowledge of the contents of such financing statement.

(3) A filing which is made in the proper place in this state continues effective even though the debtor's residence or place of business or the location of the collateral or its use, whichever controlled the original filing, is thereafter changed.

Alternative Subsection (3)

[(3) A filing which is made in the proper county continues effective for four months after a change to another county of the debtor's residence or place of business or the location of the collateral, whichever controlled the original filing. It becomes ineffective thereafter unless a copy of the financing statement signed by the secured party is filed in the new county within said period. The security interest may also be perfected in the new county after the expiration of the four-month period, in such case perfection dates from the time of perfection in the new county. A change in the use of the collateral does not impair the effectiveness of the original filing.]

(4) If collateral is brought into this state from another jurisdiction, the rules stated in Section 9—103 determine whether filing is necessary in this state.

§ 9—402. Formal Requisites of Financing Statement; Amendments.

(1) A financing statement is sufficient if it is signed by the debtor and the secured party, gives an address of the secured party from which information concerning the security interest may be obtained, gives a mailing address of the debtor and contains a statement indicating the types, or describing the items, of collateral. A financing statement may be filed before a security agreement is made or a security interest otherwise attaches. When the financing statement covers crops growing or to be grown or goods which are or are to become fixtures, the statement must also contain a description of the real estate concerned. A copy of the security agreement is sufficient as a financing statement if it contains the above information and is signed by both parties.

(2) A financing statement which otherwise complies with subsection (1) is sufficient although it is signed only by the secured party when it is filed to perfect a security interest in

(a) collateral already subject to a security interest in another jurisdiction when it is brought into this state. Such a financing statement must state that the collateral was brought into this state under such circumstances.

(b) proceeds under Section 9—30 if the security interest in the original collateral was perfected. Such a financing statement must describe the original collateral.

(3) A form substantially as follows is sufficient to comply with subsection (1):

Name of debtor (or assignor) ....
Address ....
Name of secured party (or assignee) ....
Address ....

1. This financing statement covers the following types (or items) of property:
    (Describe) ....

2. (If collateral is crops) The above described crops are growing or are to be grown on:
    (Describe Real Estate) ....

3. (If collateral is goods which are or to become fixtures) The above described goods are affixed or to be affixed to:
    (Describe Real Estate) ....

4. (If proceeds or products of collateral are claimed) Proceeds—Products of the collateral are also covered.
    Signature of Debtor (or Assignor) ....

Signature of Secured Party (or Assignee) ....

(4) The term "financing statement" as used in this Article means the original financing statement and any amendments but if any amendment adds collateral, it is effective as to the added collateral only from the filing date of the amendment.

(5) A financing statement substantially complying with the requirements of this section is effective even though it contains minor errors which are not seriously misleading.

§ 9—403. What Constitutes Filing; Duration of Filing; Effect of Lapsed Filing; Duties of Filing Officer.

(1) Presentation for filing of a financing statement and tender of the filing fee or acceptance of the statement by the filing officer constitutes filing under this Article.

(2) A filed financing statement which states a maturity date of the obligation secured of five years or less is effective until such maturity date and thereafter for a period of sixty days. Any other filed financing statement is effective for a period of five years from the date of filing. The effectiveness of a filed financing statement lapses on the expiration of such sixty day period after a stated maturity date or on the expiration of such five year period, as the case may be, unless a continuation statement is filed prior to the lapse. Upon such lapse the security interest becomes unperfected. A filed financing statement which states that the obligation secured is payable on demand is effective for five years from the date of filing.

(3) A continuation statement may be filed by the secured party (i) within six months before and sixty days after a stated maturity date of five years or less, and (ii) otherwise within six months prior to the expiration of the five year period specified in subsection (2). Any such continuation statement must be signed by the secured party, identify the original statement by file number and state that the original statement is still effective. Upon timely filing of the continuation statement, the effectiveness of the original statement is continued for five years after the last date to which the filing was effective whereupon it lapses in the same manner as provided in subsection (2) unless another continuation statement is filed prior to such

lapse. Succeeding continuation statements may be filed in the same manner to continue the effectiveness of the original statement. Unless a statute on disposition of public records provides otherwise, the filing officer may remove a lapsed statement from the files and destroy it.

(4) A filing officer shall mark each statement with a consecutive file number and with the date and hour of filing and shall hold the statement for public inspection. In addition the filing officer shall index the statements according to the name of the debtor and shall note in the index the file number and the address of the debtor given in the statement.

(5) The uniform fee for filing, indexing and furnishing filing data for an original or a continuation statement shall be $......

§ 9—404. Termination Statement.

(1) Whenever there is no outstanding secured obligation and no commitment to make advances, incur obligations or otherwise give value, the secured party must on written demand by the debtor send the debtor a statement that he no longer claims a security interest under the financing statement, which shall be identified by file number. A termination statement signed by a person other than the secured party of record must include or be accompanied by the assignment or a statement by the secured party of record that he has assigned the security interest to the signer of the termination statement. The uniform fee for filing and indexing such an assignment or statement thereof shall be $....... If the affected secured party fails to send such a termination statement within ten days after proper demand therefor he shall be liable to the debtor for one hundred dollars, and in addition for any loss caused to the debtor by such failure.

(2) On presentation to the filing officer of such a termination statement he must note it in the index. The filing officer shall remove from the files, mark "terminated" and send or deliver to the secured party the financing statement and any continuation statement, statement of assignment or statement of release pertaining thereto.

(3) The uniform fee for filing and indexing a termination statement including sending or delivering the financing statement shall be $......

§ 9—405. Assignment of Security Interest; Duties of Filing Officer; Fees.

(1) A financing statement may disclose an assignment of a security interest in the collateral described in the statement by indication in the statement of the name and address of the assignee or by an assignment itself or a copy thereof on the face or back of the statement. Either the original secured party or the assignee may sign this statement as the secured party. On presentation to the filing officer of such a financing statement the filing officer shall mark the same as provided in Section 9—403(4). The uniform fee for filing, indexing and furnishing filing data for a financing statement so indicating an assignment shall be $.......

(2) A secured party may assign of record all or a part of his rights under a financing statement by the filing of a separate written statement of assignment signed by the secured party of record and setting forth the name of the secured party of record and the debtor, the file number and the date of filing of the financing statement and the name and address of the assignee and containing a description of the collateral assigned. A copy of the assignment is sufficient as a separate statement if it complies with the preceding sentence. On presentation to the filing officer of such a separate statement, the filing officer shall mark such separate statement with the date and hour of the filing. He shall note the assignment on the index of the financing statement. The uniform fee for filing, indexing and furnishing filing data about such a separate statement of assignment shall be $.......

(3) After the disclosure or filing of an assignment under this section, the assignee is the secured party of record.

§ 9—406. Release of Collateral; Duties of Filing Officer; Fees.

A secured party of record may by his signed statement release all or a part of any collateral described in a filed financing statement. The statement of release is sufficient if it contains a description of the collateral being released, the name and address of the debtor, the name and address of the secured party, and the file number of the financing statement. Upon presentation of such a statement to the filing officer he shall mark the statement with the hour and date of filing and shall note the same upon the margin of the index of the filing of the financing statement. The uniform fee for filing and noting such a statement of release shall be $.......

§ 9—407. Information From Filing Officer.

[(1) If the person filing any financing statement, termination statement, statement of assignment, or statement of release, furnishes the filing officer a copy thereof, the filing officer shall upon request note upon the copy the file number and date and hour of the filing of the original and deliver or send the copy to such person.

(2) Upon request of any person, the filing officer shall issue his certificate showing whether there is on file on the date and hour stated therein, any presently effective financing statement naming a particular debtor and any statement of assignment thereof and if there is, giving the date and hour of filing of each such statement and the names and addresses of each secured party therein. The uniform fee for such a certificate shall be $...... plus $...... for each financing statement and for each statement of assignment reported therein. Upon request the filing officer shall furnish a copy of any filed financing statement or statement of assignment for a uniform fee of $...... per page.]

Note: *This new section is proposed as an optional provision to require filing officers to furnish certificates. Local law and practices should be consulted with regard to the advisability of adoption.*

PART 5

DEFAULT

§ 9—501. Default; Procedure When Security Agreement Covers Both Real and Personal Property.

(1) When a debtor is in default under a security agreement, a secured party has the rights and remedies provided in this Part and except as limited by subsection (3) those provided in the security agreement. He may reduce his claim to judgment, foreclose or otherwise enforce the security interest by any available judicial procedure. If the collateral is documents the secured party may proceed either as to the documents or as to the goods covered thereby. A secured party in possession has the rights, remedies and duties provided in Section 9—207. The rights and remedies referred to in this subsection are cumulative.

(2) After default, the debtor has the rights and remedies provided in this Part, those provided in the security agreement and those provided in Section 9—207.

(3) To the extent that they give rights to the debtor and impose duties on the secured party, the rules stated in the subsections referred to below may not be waived or varied except as provided with respect to compulsory disposition of collateral (subsection (1) of Section 9—505) and with respect to redemption of collateral (Section 9—506) but the parties may by agreement determine the standards by which the fulfillment of these rights and duties is to be measured if such standards are not manifestly unreasonable:

    (a) subsection (2) of Section 9—502 and subsection (2) of Section 9—504 insofar as they require accounting for surplus proceeds of collateral;

    (b) subsection (3) of Section 9—504 and subsection (1) of Section 9—505 which deal with disposition of collateral;

    (c) subsection (2) of Section 9—505 which deals with acceptance of collateral as discharge of obligation;

    (d) Section 9—506 which deals with redemption of collateral; and

    (e) subsection (1) of Section 9—507 which deals with the secured party's liability for failure to comply with this Part.

(4) If the security agreement covers both real and personal property, the secured party may proceed under this Part as to the personal property or he may proceed as to both the real and the personal property in accordance with his rights and remedies in respect of the real property in which case the provisions of this Part do not apply.

(5) When a secured party has reduced his claim to judgment the lien of any levy which may be made upon his collateral by virtue of any execution based upon the judgment shall relate back to the date of the perfection of the security interest in such collateral. A judicial sale, pursuant to such execution, is a foreclosure of the security interest by judicial procedure within the meaning of this section, and the secured party may purchase at the sale and thereafter hold the collateral free of any other requirements of this Article.

§ 9—502. Collection Rights of Secured Party.

(1) When so agreed and in any event on default the secured party is entitled to notify an account debtor or the obligor on an instrument to make payment to him whether or not the assignor was theretofore making collections on the collateral, and also to take control of any proceeds to which he is entitled under Section 9—306.

(2) A secured party who by agreement is entitled to charge back uncollected collateral or otherwise to full or limited recourse against the debtor and who undertakes to collect from the account debtors or obligors must proceed in a commercially reasonable manner and may deduct his reasonable expenses of realization from the collections. If the security agreement secures an indebtedness, the secured party must account to the debtor for any surplus, and unless otherwise agreed, the debtor is liable for any deficiency. But, if the underlying transaction was a sale of accounts, contract rights, or chattel paper, the debtor is entitled to any surplus or is liable for any deficiency only if the security agreement so provides.

§ 9—503. Secured Party's Right to Take Possession After Default.

Unless otherwise agreed a secured party has on default the right to take possession of the collateral. In taking possession a secured party may proceed without judicial process if this can be done without breach of the peace or may proceed by action. If the security agreement so provides the secured party may require the debtor to assemble the collateral and make it available to the secured party at a place to be designated by the secured party which is reasonably convenient to both parties. Without removal a secured party may render equipment unusable, and may dispose of collateral on the debtor's premises under Section 9—504.

§ 9—504. Secured Party's Right to Dispose of Collateral After Default; Effect of Disposition.

(1) A secured party after default may sell, lease or otherwise dispose of any or all of the collateral in its then condition or following any commercially reasonable preparation or processing. Any sale of goods is subject to the Article on Sales (Article 2). The proceeds of disposition shall be applied in the order following to

(a) the reasonable expenses of retaking, holding, preparing for sale, selling and the like and, to the extent provided for in the agreement and not prohibited by law, the reasonable attorneys' fees and legal expenses incurred by the secured party;

(b) the satisfaction of indebtedness secured by the security interest under which the disposition is made;

(c) the satisfaction of indebtedness secured by any subordinate security interest in the collateral if written notification of demand therefor is received before distribution of the proceeds is completed. If requested by the secured party, the holder of a subordinate security interest must seasonably furnish reasonable proof of his interest, and unless he does so, the secured party need not comply with his demand.

(2) If the security interest secures an indebtedness, the secured party must account to the debtor for any surplus, and, unless otherwise agreed, the debtor is liable for any deficiency. But if the underlying transaction was a sale of accounts, contract rights, or chattel paper, the debtor is entitled to any surplus or is liable for any deficiency only if the security agreement so provides.

(3) Disposition of the collateral may be by public or private proceedings and may be made by way of one or more contracts. Sale or other disposition may be as a unit or in parcels and at any time and place and on any terms but every aspect of the disposition including the method, manner, time, place and terms must be commercially reasonable. Unless collateral is perishable or threatens to decline speedily in value or is of a type customarily sold on a recognized market, reasonable notification of the time and place of any public sale or reasonable notification of the time after which any private sale or other intended disposition is to be made shall be sent by the secured party to the debtor, and except in the case of consumer goods to any other person who has a security interest in the collateral and who has duly filed a financing statement indexed in the name of the debtor in this state or who is known by the secured party to have a security interest in the collateral. The secured party may buy at any public sale and if the collateral is of a type customarily sold in a recognized market or is of a type which is the subject of widely distributed standard price quotations he may buy at private sale.

(4) When collateral is disposed of by a secured party after default, the disposition transfers to a purchaser for value all of the debtor's rights therein, discharges the security interest under which it is made and any security interest or lien subordinate thereto. The purchaser takes free of all such rights and interests even though the secured party fails to comply with the requirements of this Part or of any judicial proceedings

(a) in the case of a public sale, if the purchaser has no knowledge of any defects in the sale and if he does not buy in collusion with the secured party, other bidders or the person conducting the sale; or

(b) in any other case, if the purchaser acts in good faith.

(5) A person who is liable to a secured party under a guaranty, indorsement, repurchase

agreement or the like and who receives a transfer of collateral from the secured party or is subrogated to his rights has thereafter the rights and duties of the secured party. Such a transfer of collateral is not a sale or disposition of the collateral under this Article.

§ 9—505. Compulsory Disposition of Collateral; Acceptance of the Collateral as Discharge of Obligation.

(1) If the debtor has paid sixty per cent of the cash price in the case of a purchase money security interest in consumer goods or sixty per cent of the loan in the case of another security interest in consumer goods, and has not signed after default a statement renouncing or modifying his rights under this Part a secured party who has taken possession of collateral must dispose of it under Section 9—504 and if he fails to do so within ninety days after he takes possession the debtor at his option may recover in conversion or under Section 9—507(1) on secured party's liability.

(2) In any other case involving consumer goods or any other collateral a secured party in possession may, after default, propose to retain the collateral in satisfaction of the obligation. Written notice of such proposal shall be sent to the debtor and except in the case of consumer goods to any other secured party who has a security interest in the collateral and who has duly filed a financing statement indexed in the name of the debtor in this state or is known by the secured party in possession to have a security interest in it. If the debtor or other person entitled to receive notification objects in writing within thirty days from the receipt of the notification or if any other secured party objects in writing within thirty days after the secured party obtains possession the secured party must dispose of the collateral under Section 9—504. In the absence of such written objection the secured party may retain the collateral in satisfaction of the debtor's obligation.

§ 9—506. Debtor's Right to Redeem Collateral.

At any time before the secured party has disposed of collateral or entered into a contract for its disposition under Section 9—504 or before the obligation has been discharged under Section 9—505(2) the debtor or any other secured party may unless otherwise agreed in writing after default redeem the collateral by tendering fulfillment of all obligations secured by the collateral as well as the expenses reasonably incurred by the secured party in retaking, holding and preparing the collateral for disposition, in arranging for the sale, and to the extent provided in the agreement and not prohibited by law, his reasonable attorneys' fees and legal expenses.

§ 9—507. Secured Party's Liability for Failure to Comply With This Part.

(1) If it is established that the secured party is not proceeding in accordance with the provisions of this Part disposition may be ordered or restrained on appropriate terms and conditions. If the disposition has occurred the debtor or any person entitled to notification or whose security interest has been made known to the secured party prior to the disposition has a right to recover from the secured party any loss caused by a failure to comply with the provisions of this Part. If the collateral is consumer goods, the debtor has a right to recover in any event an amount not less than the credit service charge plus ten per cent of the principal amount of the debt or the time price differential plus ten per cent of the cash price.

(2) The fact that a better price could have been obtained by a sale at a different time or in a different method from that selected by the secured party is not of itself sufficient to establish that the sale was not made in a commercially reasonable manner. If the secured party either sells the collateral in the usual manner in any recognized market therefor or if he sells at the price current in such market at the time of his sale or if he has otherwise sold in conformity with reasonable commercial practices among dealers in the type of property sold he has sold in a commercially reasonable manner. The principles stated in the two preceding sentences with respect to sales also apply as may be appropriate to other types of disposition. A disposition which has been approved in any judicial proceeding or by any bona fide creditors' committee or representative of creditors shall conclusively be deemed to be commercially reasonable, but this sentence does not indicate that any such approval must be obtained in any case nor does it indicate that any disposition not so approved is not commercially reasonable.

ARTICLE 10

EFFECTIVE DATE AND REPEALER

§ 10—101. Effective Date.

This Act shall become effective at midnight on December 31st following its enactment. It applies to transactions entered into and events occurring after that date.

§ 10—102. Specific Repealer; Provision for Transition.

(1) The following acts and all other acts and parts of acts inconsistent herewith are hereby repealed:

(Here should follow the acts to be specifically repealed including the following:

Uniform Negotiable Instruments Act
Uniform Warehouse Receipts Act
Uniform Sales Act
Uniform Bills of Lading Act
Uniform Stock Transfer Act
Uniform Conditional Sales Act
Uniform Trust Receipts Act
Also any acts regulating:
Bank collections
Bulk sales
Chattel mortgages
Conditional sales
Factor's lien acts
Farm storage of grain and similar acts
Assignment of accounts receivable)

(2) Transactions validly entered into before the effective date specified in Section 10—101 and the rights, duties and interests flowing from them remain valid thereafter and may be terminated, completed, consummated or enforced as required or permitted by any statute or other law amended or repealed by this Act as though such repeal or amendment had not occurred.

Note

Subsection (1) should be separately prepared for each state. The foregoing is a list of statutes to be checked.

§ 10—103. General Repealer.

Except as provided in the following section, all acts and parts of acts inconsistent with this Act are hereby repealed.

§ 10—104. Laws Not Repealed.

(1) The Article on Documents of Title (Article 7) does not repeal or modify any laws prescribing the form or contents of documents of title or the services or facilities to be afforded by bailees, or otherwise regulating bailees' businesses in respects not specifically dealt with herein; but the fact that such laws are violated does not affect the status of a document of title which otherwise complies with the definition of a document of title (Section 1—201).

[(2) This Act does not repeal ....
.... *, cited as the Uniform Act for the Simplification of Fiduciary Security Transfers, and if in any respect there is any inconsistency between that Act and the Article of this Act on investment securities (Article 8) the provisions of the former Act shall control.]

Note: *At * in subsection (2) insert the statutory reference to the Uniform Act for the Simplification of Fiduciary Security Transfers if such Act has previously been enacted. If it has not been enacted, omit subsection (2).*

*

APPENDIX B
UNIFORM PARTNERSHIP ACT

(Adopted in 43 jurisdictions: Alaska, Arizona, Arkansas, California, Colorado, Connecticut, Delaware, District of Columbia, Guam, Idaho, Illinois, Indiana, Kentucky, Maryland, Massachusetts, Michigan, Minnesota, Missouri, Montana, Nebraska, Nevada, New Jersey, New Mexico, New York, North Carolina, North Dakota, Ohio, Oklahoma, Oregon, Pennsylvania, Rhode Island, South Carolina, South Dakota, Tennessee, Texas, Utah, Vermont, Virginia, Virgin Islands, Washington, West Virginia, Wisconsin, and Wyoming.)

An Act to Make Uniform the Law of Partnerships
Be it enacted, etc.,

PART I

Preliminary Provisions

Sec. 1. (Name of Act.) This act may be cited as Uniform Partnership Act.

Sec. 2. (Definition of Terms.) In this act, "Court" includes every court and judge having jurisdiction in the case.

"Business" includes every trade, occupation, or profession.

"Person" includes individuals, partnerships, corporations, and other associations.

"Bankrupt" includes bankrupt under the Federal Bankruptcy Act or insolvent under any state insolvent act.

"Conveyance" includes every assignment, lease, mortgage, or encumbrance.

"Real property" includes land and any interest or estate in land.

Sec. 3. (Interpretation of Knowledge and Notice.) (1) A person has "knowledge" of a fact within the meaning of this act not only when he has actual knowledge thereof, but also when he has knowledge of such other facts as in the circumstances shows bad faith.

(2) A person has "notice" of a fact within the meaning of this act when the person who claims the benefit of the notice

(a) States the fact to such person, or

(b) Delivers through the mail, or by other means of communication, a written statement of the fact to such person or to a proper person at his place of business or residence.

Sec. 4. (Rules of Construction.) (1) The rule that statutes in derogation of the common law are to be strictly construed shall have no application to this act.

(2) The law of estoppel shall apply under this act.

(3) The law of agency shall apply under this act.

(4) This act shall be so interpreted and construed as to effect its general purpose to make uniform the law of those states which enact it.

(5) This act shall not be construed so as to impair the obligations of any contract existing when the act goes into effect, nor to affect any action or proceedings begun or right accrued before this act takes effect.

Sec. 5. (Rules for Cases Not Provided for in this Act.) In any case not provided for in this act the rules of law and equity, including the law merchant, shall govern.

PART II

Nature of Partnership

Sec. 6. (Partnership Defined.) (1) A partnership is an association of two or more persons to carry on as co-owners a business for profit.

(2) But any association formed under any other statute of this state, or any statute adopted by authority, other than the authority of this state, is not a partnership under this act,

unless such association would have been a partnership in this state prior to the adoption of this act; but this act shall apply to limited partnerships except in so far as the statutes relating to such partnerships are inconsistent herewith.

Sec. 7. (Rules for Determining the Existence of a Partnership.) In determining whether a partnership exists, these rules shall apply:

(1) Except as provided by Section 16 persons who are not partners as to each other are not partners as to third persons.

(2) Joint tenancy, tenancy in common, tenancy by the entireties, joint property, common property, or part ownership does not of itself establish a partnership, whether such co-owners do or do not share any profits made by the use of the property.

(3) The sharing of gross returns does not of itself establish a partnership, whether or not the persons sharing them have a joint or common right or interest in any property from which the returns are derived.

(4) The receipt by a person of a share of the profits of a business is prima facie evidence that he is a partner in the business, but no such inference shall be drawn if such profits were received in payment:

(a) As a debt by installments or otherwise,

(b) As wages of an employee or rent to a landlord,

(c) As an annuity to a widow or representative of a deceased partner,

(d) As interest on a loan, though the amount of payment vary with the profits of the business.

(e) As the consideration for the sale of a good-will of a business or other property by installments or otherwise.

Sec. 8. (Partnership Property.) (1) All property originally brought into the partnership stock or subsequently acquired by purchase or otherwise, on account of the partnership, is partnership property.

(2) Unless the contrary intention appears, property acquired with partnership funds is partnership property.

(3) Any estate in real property may be acquired in the partnership name. Title so acquired can be conveyed only in the partnership name.

(4) A conveyance to a partnership in the partnership name, though without words of inheritance, passes the entire estate of the grantor unless a contrary intent appears.

PART III

Relations of Partners to Persons Dealing with the Partnership

Sec. 9. (Partner Agent of Partnership as to Partnership Business.) (1) Every partner is an agent of the partnership for the purpose of its business, and the act of every partner, including the execution in the partnership name of any instrument, for apparently carrying on in the usual way the business of the partnership of which he is a member binds the partnership, unless the partner so acting has in fact no authority to act for the partnership in the particular matter, and the person with whom he is dealing has knowledge of the fact that he has no such authority.

(2) An act of a partner which is not apparently for the carrying on of the business of the partnership in the usual way does not bind the partnership unless authorized by the other partners.

(3) Unless authorized by the other partners or unless they have abandoned the business, one or more but less than all the partners have no authority to:

(a) Assign the partnership property in trust for creditors or on the assignee's promise to pay the debts of the partnership,

(b) Dispose of the good-will of the business,

(c) Do any other act which would make it impossible to carry on the ordinary business of a partnership,

(d) Confess a judgment,

(e) Submit a partnership claim or liability to arbitration or reference.

(4) No act of a partner in contravention of a restriction on authority shall bind the partnership to persons having knowledge of the restriction.

Sec. 10. (Conveyance of Real Property of the Partnership.) (1) Where title to real property is in the partnership name, any partner may convey title to such property by a conveyance executed in the partnership name; but the partnership may recover such property unless the partner's act binds the partnership under the provisions of paragraph (1) of section 9 or unless such property has been conveyed by the grantee or a person claiming through such grantee to a holder for value without knowledge that the partner, in making the conveyance, has exceeded his authority.

(2) Where title to real property is in the name of the partnership, a conveyance executed by a partner, in his own name, passes the equitable interest of the partnership, provided the act is one within the authority of the partner under the provisions of paragraph (1) of section 9.

(3) Where title to real property is in the name of one or more but not all the partners, and the record does not disclose the right of the partnership, the partners in whose name the title stands may convey title to such property, but the partnership may recover such property if the partners' act does not bind the partnership under the provisions of paragraph (1) of section 9, unless the purchaser or his assignee, is a holder for value, without knowledge.

(4) Where the title to real property is in the name of one or more or all the partners, or in a third person in trust for the partnership, a conveyance executed by a partner in the partnership name, or in his own name, passes the equitable interest of the partnership, provided the act is one within the authority of the partner under the provisions of paragraph (1) of section 9.

(5) Where the title to real property is in the names of all the partners a conveyance executed by all the partners passes all their rights in such property.

Sec. 11. (Partnership Bound by Admission of Partner.) An admission or representation made by any partner concerning partnership affairs within the scope of his authority as conferred by this act is evidence against the partnership.

Sec. 12. (Partnership Charged with Knowledge of or Notice to Partner.) Notice to any partner of any matter relating to partnership affairs, and the knowledge of the partner acting in the particular matter, acquired while a partner or then present to his mind, and the knowledge of any other partner who reasonably could and should have communicated it to the acting partner, operate as notice to or knowledge of the partnership, except in the case of a fraud on the partnership committed by or with the consent of that partner.

Sec. 13. (Partnership Bound by Partner's Wrongful Act.) Where, by any wrongful act or omission of any partner acting in the ordinary course of the business of the partnership or with the authority of his co-partners, loss or injury is caused to any person, not being a partner in the partnership, or any penalty is incurred, the partnership is liable therefor to the same extent as the partner so acting or omitting to act.

Sec. 14. (Partnership Bound by Partner's Breach of Trust.) The partnership is bound to make good the loss:

(a) Where one partner acting within the scope of his apparent authority receives money or property of a third person and misapplies it; and

(b) Where the partnership in the course of its business receives money or property of a third person and the money or property so received is misapplied by any partner while it is in the custody of the partnership.

Sec. 15. (Nature of Partner's Liability.) All partners are liable

(a) Jointly and severally for everything chargeable to the partnership under sections 13 and 14.

(b) Jointly for all other debts and obligations of the partnership; but any partner may enter into a separate obligation to perform a partnership contract.

Sec. 16. (Partner by Estoppel.) (1) When a person, by words spoken or written or by conduct, represents himself, or consents to another representing him to any one, as a partner in an existing partnership or with one or more persons not actual partners, he is liable to any such person to whom such representation has been made, who has, on the faith of such representation, given credit to the actual or apparent partnership, and if he has made such representation or consented to its being made in a public manner he is liable to such person, whether the representation has or has not been made or communicated to such person so giving credit by or with the knowledge of the apparent partner making the representation or consenting to its being made.

(a) When a partnership liability results, he is liable as though he were an actual member of the partnership.

(b) When no partnership liability results, he is liable jointly with the other persons, if any, so consenting to the contract or representation as to incur liability, otherwise separately.

(2) When a person has been thus represented to be a partner in an existing partnership, or with one or more persons not actual partners, he is an agent of the persons consenting to such representation to bind them to the same extent and in the same manner as though he were a partner in fact, with respect to persons who rely upon the representation. Where all the members of the existing partnership consent to the representation, a partnership act or obligation results; but in all other cases it is the joint act or obligation of the person acting and the persons consenting to the representation.

Sec. 17. (Liability of Incoming Partner.) A person admitted as a partner into an existing partnership is liable for all the obligations of the partnership arising before his admission as though he had been a partner when such obligations were incurred, except that this liability shall be satisfied only out of partnership property.

PART IV

Relations of Partners to One Another

Sec. 18. (Rules Determining Rights and Duties of Partners.) The rights and duties of the partners in relation to the partnership shall be determined, subject to any agreement between them, by the following rules:

(a) Each partner shall be repaid his contributions, whether by way of capital or advances to the partnership property and share equally in the profits and surplus remaining after all liabilities, including those to partners, are satisfied; and must contribute towards the losses, whether of capital or otherwise, sustained by the partnership according to his share in the profits.

(b) The partnership must indemnify every partner in respect of payments made and personal liabilities reasonably incurred by him in the ordinary and proper conduct of its business, or for the preservation of its business or property.

(c) A partner, who in aid of the partnership makes any payment or advance beyond the amount of capital which he agreed to contribute, shall be paid interest from the date of the payment or advance.

(d) A partner shall receive interest on the capital contributed by him only from the date when repayment should be made.

(e) All partners have equal rights in the management and conduct of the partnership business.

(f) No partner is entitled to remuneration for acting in the partnership business, except that a surviving partner is entitled to reasonable compensation for his services in winding up the partnership affairs.

(g) No person can become a member of a partnership without the consent of all the partners.

(h) Any difference arising as to ordinary matters connected with the partnership business may be decided by a majority of the partners; but no act in contravention of any agreement between the partners may be done rightfully without the consent of all the partners.

Sec. 19. (Partnership Books.) The partnership books shall be kept, subject to any agreement between the partners, at the principal place of business of the partnership, and every partner shall at all times have access to and may inspect and copy any of them.

Sec. 20. (Duty of Partners to Render Information.) Partners shall render on demand true and full information of all things affecting the partnership to any partner or the legal representative of any deceased partner or partner under legal disability.

Sec. 21. (Partner Accountable as a Fiduciary.) (1) Every partner must account to the partnership for any benefit, and hold as trustee for it any profits derived by him without the consent of the other partners from any transaction connected with the formation, conduct, or liquidation of the partnership or from any use by him of its property.

(2) This section applies also to the representatives of a deceased partner engaged in the liquidation of the affairs of the partnership as the personal representatives of the last surviving partner.

Sec. 22. (Right to an Account.) Any partner shall have the right to a formal account as to partnership affairs:

(a) If he is wrongfully excluded from the partnership business or possession of its property by his co-partners,

(b) If the right exists under the terms of any agreement,

(c) As provided by section 21,

(d) Whenever other circumstances render it just and reasonable.

Sec. 23. (Continuation of Partnership Beyond Fixed Term.) (1) When a partnership for a fixed term or particular undertaking is continued after the termination of such term or particular undertaking without any express agreement, the rights and duties of the partners remain the same as they were at such termination, so far as is consistent with a partnership at will.

(2) A continuation of the business by the partners or such of them as habitually acted therein during the term, without any settlement or liquidation of the partnership affairs, is prima facie evidence of a continuation of the partnership.

PART V

Property Rights of a Partner

Sec. 24. (Extent of Property Rights of a Partner.) The property rights of a partner are (1) his rights in specific partnership property, (2) his interest in the partnership, and (3) his right to participate in the management.

Sec. 25. (Nature of a Partner's Right in Specific Partnership Property.) (1) A partner is co-owner with his partners of specific partnership property holding as a tenant in partnership.

(2) The incidents of this tenancy are such that:

(a) A partner, subject to the provisions of this act and to any agreement between the partners, has an equal right with his partners to possess specific partnership property for partnership purposes; but he has no right to possess such property for any other purpose without the consent of his partners.

(b) A partner's right in specific partnership property is not assignable except in connection with the assignment of rights of all the partners in the same property.

(c) A partner's right in specific partnership property is not subject to attachment or execution, except on a claim against the partnership. When partnership property is attached for a partnership debt the partners, or any of them, or the representatives of a deceased partner, cannot claim any right under the homestead or exemption laws.

(d) On the death of a partner his right in specific partnership property vests in the surviving partner or partners, except where the deceased was the last surviving partner, when his right in such property vests in his legal representative. Such surviving partner or partners, or the legal representative of the last surviving partner, has no right to possess the partnership property for any but a partnership purpose.

(e) A partner's right in specific partnership property is not subject to dower, curtesy, or allowances to widows, heirs, or next of kin.

Sec. 26. (Nature of Partner's Interest in the Partnership.) A partner's interest in the partnership is his share of the profits and surplus, and the same is personal property.

Sec. 27. (Assignment of Partner's Interest.) (1) A conveyance by a partner of his interest in the partnership does not of itself dissolve the partnership, nor, as against the other partners in the absence of agreement, entitle the assignee, during the continuance of the partnership to interfere in the management or administration of the partnership business or affairs, or to require any information or account of partnership transactions, or to inspect the partnership books; but it merely entitles the assignee to receive in accordance with his contract the profits to which the assigning partner would otherwise be entitled.

(2) In case of a dissolution of the partnership, the assignee is entitled to receive his assignor's interest and may require an account from the date only of the last account agreed to by all the partners.

Sec. 28. (Partner's Interest Subject to Charging Order.) (1) On due application to a competent court by any judgment creditor of a partner, the court which entered the judgment, order, or decree, or any other court, may charge the interest of the debtor partner with payment of the unsatisfied amount of such judgment debt with interest thereon; and may then or later appoint a receiver of his share of the profits, and of any other money due or to fall due to him in respect of the partnership, and make all other orders, directions, accounts and inquiries which the debtor partner might have made, or which the circumstances of the case may require.

(2) The interest charged may be redeemed at any time before foreclosure, or in case of a sale being directed by the court may be purchased without thereby causing a dissolution:

(a) With separate property, by any one or more of the partners, or

(b) With partnership property, by any one or more of the partners with the consent of all the partners whose interests are not so charged or sold.

(3) Nothing in this act shall be held to deprive a partner of his right, if any, under the exemption laws, as regards his interest in the partnership.

PART VI

Dissolution and Winding up

Sec. 29. (Dissolution Defined.) The dissolution of a partnership is the change in the relation of the partners caused by any partner ceasing to be associated in the carrying on as distinguished from the winding up of the business.

Sec. 30. (Partnership Not Terminated by Dissolution.) On dissolution the partnership is not terminated, but continues until the winding up of partnership affairs is completed.

Sec. 31. (Causes of Dissolution.) Dissolution is caused: (1) Without violation of the of the agreement between the partners,

(a) By the termination of the definite term or particular undertaking specified in the agreement,

(b) By the express will of any partner when no definite term or particular undertaking is specified,

(c) By the express will of all the partners who have not assigned their interests or suffered them to be charged for their separate debts, either before or after the termination of any specified term or particular undertaking.

(d) By the expulsion of any partner from the business bona fide in accordance with such

a power conferred by the agreement between the partners;

(2) In contravention of the agreement between the partners, where the circumstances do not permit a dissolution under any other provision of this section, by the express will of any partner at any time;

(3) By any event which makes it unlawful for the business of the partnership to be carried on or for the members to carry it on in partnership;

(4) By the death of any partner;

(5) By the bankruptcy of any partner or the partnership;

(6) By decree of court under section 32.

Sec. 32. (Dissolution by Decree of Court.) (1) On application by or for a partner the court shall decree a dissolution whenever:

(a) A partner has been declared a lunatic in any judicial proceeding or is shown to be of unsound mind,

(b) A partner becomes in any other way incapable of performing his part of the partnership contract,

(c) A partner has been guilty of such conduct as tends to affect prejudicially the carrying on of the business,

(d) A partner wilfully or persistently commits a breach of the partnership agreement, or otherwise so conducts himself in matters relating to the partnership business that it is not reasonably practicable to carry on the business in partnership with him,

(e) The business of the partnership can only be carried on at a loss,

(f) Other circumstances render a dissolution equitable.

(2) On the application of the purchaser of a partner's interest under sections 27 or 28:

(a) After the termination of the specified term or particular undertaking,

(b) At any time if the partnership was a partnership at will when the interest was assigned or when the charging order was issued.

Sec. 33. (General Effect of Dissolution on Authority of Partner.) Except so far as may be necessary to wind up partnership affairs or to complete transactions begun but not then finished, dissolution terminates all authority of any partner to act for the partnership,

(1) With respect to the partners,

(a) When the dissolution is not by the act, bankruptcy or death of a partner; or

(b) When the dissolution is by such act, bankruptcy or death of a partner, in cases where section 34 so requires.

(2) With respect to persons not partners, as declared in section 35.

Sec. 34. (Right of Partner to Contribution From Copartners After Dissolution.) Where the dissolution is caused by the act, death or bankruptcy of a partner, each partner is liable to his copartners for his share of any liability created by any partner acting for the partnership as if the partnership had not been dissolved unless

(a) The dissolution being by act of any partner, the partner acting for the partnership had knowledge of the dissolution, or

(b) The dissolution being by the death or bankruptcy of a partner, the partner acting for the partnership had knowledge or notice of the death or bankruptcy.

Sec. 35. (Power of Partner to Bind Partnership to Third Persons After Dissolution.) (1) After dissolution a partner can bind the partnership except as provided in Paragraph (3)

(a) By any act appropriate for winding up partnership affairs or completing transactions unfinished at dissolution;

(b) By any transaction which would bind the partnership if dissolution had not taken place, provided the other party to the transaction

(I) Had extended credit to the partnership prior to dissolution and had no knowledge or notice of the dissolution; or

(II) Though he had not so extended credit, had nevertheless known of the partnership prior to dissolution, and, having no knowledge or notice of dissolution, the fact of dissolution had not been advertised in a newspaper of general circulation in the place (or in each place if more than one) at which the partnership business was regularly carried on.

(2) The liability of a partner under paragraph (1b) shall be satisfied out of partnership assets alone when such partner had been prior to dissolution.

(a) Unknown as a partner to the person with whom the contract is made; and

(b) So far unknown and inactive in partnership affairs that the business reputation of the partnership could not be said to have been in any degree due to his connection with it.

(3) The partnership is in no case bound by any act of a partner after dissolution

(a) Where the partnership is dissolved because it is unlawful to carry on the business, unless the act is appropriate for winding up partnership affairs; or

(b) Where the partner has become bankrupt; or

(c) Where the partner has no authority to wind up partnership affairs; except by a transaction with one who

(I) Had extended credit to the partnership prior to dissolution and had no knowledge or notice of his want of authority; or

(II) Had not extended credit to the partnership prior to dissolution, and, having no knowledge or notice of his want of authority, the fact of his want of authority has not been advertised in the manner provided for advertising the fact of dissolution in paragraph (1bII).

(4) Nothing in this section shall affect the liability under section 16 of any person who after dissolution represents himself or consents to another representing him as a partner in a partnership engaged in carrying on business.

Sec. 36. (Effect of Dissolution on Partner's Existing Liability.) (1) The dissolution of the partnership does not of itself discharge the existing liability of any partner.

(2) A partner is discharged from any existing liability upon dissolution of the partnership by an agreement to that effect between himself, the partnership creditor and the person or partnership continuing the business; and such agreement may be inferred from the course of dealing between the creditor having knowledge of the dissolution and the person or partnership continuing the business.

(3) Where a person agrees to assume the existing obligations of a dissolved partnership, the partners whose obligations have been assumed shall be discharged from any liability to any creditor of the partnership who, knowing of the agreement, consents to a material

alteration in the nature or time of payment of such obligations.

(4) The individual property of a deceased partner shall be liable for all obligations of the partnership incurred while he was a partner but subject to the prior payment of his separate debts.

Sec. 37. (Right to Wind Up.) Unless otherwise agreed the partners who have not wrongfully dissolved the partnership or the legal representative of the last surviving partner, not bankrupt, has the right to wind up the partnership affairs; provided, however, that any partner, his legal representative or his assignee, upon cause shown, may obtain winding up by the court.

Sec. 38. (Rights of Partners to Application of Partnership Property.) (1) When dissolution is caused in any way, except in contravention of the partnership agreement, each partner as against his co-partners and all persons claiming through them in respect of their interests in the partnership, unless otherwise agreed, may have the partnership property applied to discharge its liabilities, and the surplus applied to pay in cash the net amount owing to the respective partners. But if dissolution is caused by expulsion of a partner, bona fide under the partnership agreement and if the expelled partner is discharged from all partnership liabilities, either by payment or agreement under section 36(2), he shall receive in cash only the net amount due him from the partnership.

(2) When dissolution is caused in contravention of the partnership agreement the rights of the partners shall be as follows:

(a) Each partner who has not caused dissolution wrongfully shall have,

(I) All the rights specified in paragraph (1) of this section, and

(II) The right, as against each partner who has caused the dissolution wrongfully, to damages for breach of the agreement.

(b) The partners who have not caused the dissolution wrongfully, if they all desire to continue the business in the same name, either by themselves or jointly with others, may do so, during the agreed term for the partnership and for that purpose may possess the partnership property, provided they secure the payment by bond approved by the court, or pay to any partner who has caused the dissolution

wrongfully, the value of his interest in the partnership at the dissolution, less any damages recoverable under clause (2aII) of the section, and in like manner indemnify him against all present or future partnership liabilities.

(c) A partner who has caused the dissolution wrongfully shall have:

(I) If the business is not continued under the provisions of paragraph (2b) all the rights of a partner under paragraph (1), subject to clause (2aII), of this section,

(II) If the business is continued under paragraph (2b) of this section the right as against his co-partners and all claiming through them in respect of their interests in the partnership, to have the value of his interest in the partnership, less any damages caused to his co-partners by the dissolution, ascertained and paid to him in cash, or the payment secured by bond approved by the court, and to be released from all existing liabilities of the partnership; but in ascertaining the value of the partner's interest the value of the good-will of the business shall not be considered.

Sec. 39. (Rights Where Partnership is Dissolved for Fraud or Misrepresentation.) Where a partnership contract is rescinded on the ground of the fraud or misrepresentation of one of the parties thereto, the party entitled to rescind is, without prejudice to any other right, entitled,

(a) To a lien on, or right of retention of, the surplus of the partnership property after satisfying the partnership liabilities to third persons for any sum of money paid by him for the purchase of an interest in the partnership and for any capital or advances contributed by him; and

(b) To stand, after all liabilities to third persons have been satisfied, in the place of the creditors of the partnership for any payments made by him in respect of the partnership liabilities; and

(c) To be indemnified by the person guilty of the fraud or making the representation against all debts and liabilities of the partnership.

Sec. 40. (Rules for Distribution.) In settling accounts between the partners after dissolution, the following rules shall be observed, subject to any agreement to the contrary:

(a) The assets of the partnership are;

(I) The partnership property,

(II) The contributions of the partners necessary for the payment of all the liabilities specified in clause (b) of this paragraph.

(b) The liabilities of the partnership shall rank in order of payment, as follows:

(I) Those owing to creditors other than partners,

(II) Those owing to partners other than for capital and profits,

(III) Those owing to partners in respect of capital,

(IV) Those owing to partners in respect of profits.

(c) The assets shall be applied in the order of their declaration in clause (a) of this paragraph to the satisfaction of the liabilities.

(d) The partners shall contribute, as provided by section 18(a) the amount necessary to satisfy the liabilities; but if any, but not all, of the partners are insolvent, or, not being subject to process, refuse to contribute, the other parties shall contribute their share of the liabilities, and, in the relative proportions in which they share the profits, the additional amount necessary to pay the liabilities.

(e) An assignee for the benefit of creditors or any person appointed by the court shall have the right to enforce the contributions specified in clause (d) of this paragraph.

(f) Any partner or his legal representative shall have the right to enforce the contributions specified in clause (d) of this paragraph, to the extent of the amount which he has paid in excess of his share of the liability.

(g) The individual property of a deceased partner shall be liable for the contributions specified in clause (d) of this paragraph.

(h) When partnership property and the individual properties of the partners are in possession of a court for distribution, partnership creditors shall have priority on partnership property and separate creditors on individual property, saving the rights of lien or secured creditors as heretofore.

(i) Where a partner has become bankrupt or his estate is insolvent the claims against his separate property shall rank in the following order:

(I) Those owing to separate creditors,

(II) Those owing to partnership creditors,

(III) Those owing to partners by way of contribution.

Sec. 41. (Liability of Persons Continuing the Business in Certain Cases.) (1) When any new partner is admitted into an existing partnership, or when any partner retires and assigns (or the representative of the deceased partner assigns) his rights in partnership property to two or more of the partners, or to one or more of the partners and one or more third persons, if the business is continued without liquidation of the partnership affairs, creditors of the first or dissolved partnership are also creditors of the partnership so continuing the business.

(2) When all but one partner retire and assign (or the representative of a deceased partner assigns) their rights in partnership property to the remaining partner, who continues the business without liquidation of partnership affairs, either alone or with others, creditors of the dissolved partnership are also creditors of the person or partnership so continuing the business.

(3) When any partner retires or dies and the business of the dissolved partnership is continued as set forth in paragraphs (1) and (2) of this section, with the consent of the retired partners or the representative of the deceased partner, but without any assignment of his right in partnership property, rights of creditors of the dissolved partnership and of the creditors of the person or partnership continuing the business shall be as if such assignment had been made.

(4) When all the partners or their representatives assign their rights in partnership property to one or more third persons who promise to pay the debts and who continue the business of the dissolved partnership, creditors of the dissolved partnership are also creditors of the person or partnership continuing the business.

(5) When any partner wrongfully causes a dissolution and the remaining partners continue the business under the provisions of section 38(2b), either alone or with others, and without liquidation of the partnership affairs, creditors of the dissolved partnership are also creditors of the person or partnership continuing the business.

(6) When a partner is expelled and the remaining partners continue the business either

alone or with others, without liquidation of the partnership affairs, creditors of the dissolved partnership are also creditors of the person or partnership continuing the business.

(7) The liability of a third person becoming a partner in the partnership continuing the business, under this section, to the creditors of the dissolved partnership shall be satisfied out of partnership property only.

(8) When the business of a partnership after dissolution is continued under any conditions set forth in this section the creditors of the dissolved partnership, as against the separate creditors of the retiring or deceased partner or the representative of the deceased partner, have a prior right to any claim of the retired partner or the representative of the deceased partner against the person or partnership continuing the business, on account of the retired or deceased partner's interest in the dissolved partnership or on account of any consideration promised for such interest or for his right in partnership property.

(9) Nothing in this section shall be held to modify any right of creditors to set aside any assignment on the ground of fraud.

(10) The use by the person or partnership continuing the business of the partnership name, or the name of a deceased partner as part thereof, shall not of itself make the individual property of the deceased partner liable for any debts contracted by such person or partnership.

Sec. 42. (Rights of Retiring or Estate of Deceased Partner When the Business is Continued.) When any partner retires or dies, and the business is continued under any of the conditions set forth in section 41(1, 2, 3, 5, 6), or section 38(2b), without any settlement of accounts as between him or his estate and the person or partnership continuing the business, unless otherwise agreed, he or his legal representative as against such persons or partnership may have the value of his interest at the date of dissolution ascertained, and shall receive as an ordinary creditor an amount equal to the value of his interest in the dissolved partnership with interest, or, at his option or at the option of his legal representative, in lieu of interest, the profits attributable to the use of his right in the property of the dissolved partnership; provided that the creditors of the dissolved partnership as against the separate creditors, or the representative of the retired or deceased partner, shall have priority on any claim arising under this section, as provided by section 41(8) of this act.

Sec. 43. (Accrual of Actions.) The right to an account of his interest shall accrue to any partner, or his legal representative, as against the winding up partners or the surviving partners or the person or partnership continuing the business, at the date of dissolution, in the absence of any agreement to the contrary.

PART VII

Miscellaneous Provisions

Sec. 44. (When Act Takes Effect.) This act shall take effect on the ———— day of ———— one thousand nine hundred and ————.

Sec. 45. (Legislation Repealed.) All acts or parts of acts inconsistent with this act are hereby repealed.

APPENDIX C
UNIFORM LIMITED PARTNERSHIP ACT

(Adopted in 45 jurisdictions: Alaska, Arizona, Arkansas, California, Colorado, Connecticut, District of Columbia, Florida, Georgia, Hawaii, Idaho, Illinois, Indiana, Iowa, Maryland, Massachusetts, Michigan, Minnesota, Mississippi, Missouri, Montana, Nebraska, Nevada, New Hampshire, New Jersey, New Mexico, New York, North Carolina, North Dakota, Ohio, Oklahoma, Oregon, Pennsylvania, Rhode Island, South Carolina, South Dakota, Tennessee, Texas, Utah, Vermont, Virginia, Virgin Islands, Washington, West Virginia, Wisconsin.)

An Act to Make Uniform the Law Relating to Limited Partnerships

Be it enacted, etc., as follows:

Sec. 1. (Limited Partnership Defined.) A limited partnership is a partnership formed by two or more persons under the provisions of Section 2, having as members one or more general partners and one or more limited partners. The limited partners as such shall not be bound by the obligations of the partnership.

Sec. 2. (Formation.) (1) Two or more persons desiring to form a limited partnership shall

(a) Sign and swear to a certificate, which shall state

I. The name of the partnership,

II. The character of the business,

III. The location of the principal place of business,

IV. The name and place of residence of each member; general and limited partners being respectively designated.

V. The term for which the partnership is to exist,

VI. The amount of cash and a description of and the agreed value of the other property contributed by each limited partner,

VII. The additional contributions, if any, agreed to be made by each limited partner and the times at which or events on the happening of which they shall be made,

VIII. The time, if agreed upon, when the contribution of each limited partner is to be returned.

IX. The share of the profits or the other compensation by way of income which each limited partner shall receive by reason of his contribution,

X. The right, if given, of a limited partner to substitute an assignee as contributor in his place, and the terms and conditions of the substitution,

XI. The right, if given, of the partners to admit additional limited partners,

XII. The right, if given, of one or more of the limited partners to priority over other limited partners, as to contributions or as to compensation by way of income, and the nature of such priority,

XIII. The right, if given, of the remaining general partner or partners to continue the business on the death, retirement or insanity of a general partner, and

XIV. The right, if given, of a limited partner to demand and receive property other than cash in return for his contribution.

(b) File for record the certificate in the office of [here designate the proper office].

(2) A limited partnership is formed if there has been substantial compliance in good faith with the requirements of paragraph (1).

Sec. 3. (Business Which may be Carried On.) A limited partnership may carry on any business which a partnership without limited partners may carry on, except [here designate the business to be prohibited].

Sec. 4. (Character of Limited Partner's Contribution.) The contributions of a limited partner may be cash or other property, but not services.

Sec. 5. (A Name Not to Contain Surname of Limited Partner; Exceptions.) (1) The surname of a limited partner shall not appear in the partnership name, unless

(a) It is also the surname of a general partner, or

(b) Prior to the time when the limited partner became such the business had been carried on under a name in which his surname appeared.

(2) A limited partner whose name appears in a partnership name contrary to the provisions of paragraph (1) is liable as a general partner to partnership creditors who extend credit to the partnership without actual knowledge that he is not a general partner.

Sec. 6. (Liability for False Statements in Certificate.) If the certificate contains a false statement, one who suffers loss by reliance on such statement may hold liable any party to the certificate who knew the statement to be false.

(a) At the time he signed the certificate, or

(b) Subsequently, but within a sufficient time before the statement was relied upon to enable him to cancel or amend the certificate, or to file a petition for its cancellation or amendment as provided in Section 25(3).

Sec. 7. (Limited Partner Not Liable to Creditors.) A limited partner shall not become liable as a general partner unless, in addition to the exercise of his rights and powers as a limited partner, he takes part in the control of the business.

Sec. 8. (Admission of Additional Limited Partners.) After the formation of a limited partnership, additional limited partners may be admitted upon filing an amendment to the original certificate in accordance with the requirements of Section 25.

Sec. 9. (Rights, Powers and Liabilities of a General Partner.) (1) A general partner shall have all the rights and powers and be subject to all the restrictions and liabilities of a partner in a partnership without limited partners, except that without the written consent or ratification of the specific act by all the limited partners, a general partner or all of the general partners have no authority to

(a) Do any act in contravention of the certificate,

(b) Do any act which would make it impossible to carry on the ordinary business of the partnership,

(c) Confess a judgment against the partnership,

(d) Possess partnership property, or assign their rights in specific partnership property, for other than a partnership purpose,

(e) Admit a person as a general partner,

(f) Admit a person as a limited partner, unless the right so to do is given in the certificate,

(g) Continue the business with partnership property on the death, retirement or insanity of a general partner, unless the right so to do is given in the certificate.

Sec. 10. (Rights of a Limited Partner.) (1) A limited partner shall have the same rights as a general partner to

(a) Have the partnership books kept at the principal place of business of the partnership, and at all times to inspect and copy any of them,

(b) Have on demand true and full information of all things affecting the partnership, and a formal account of partnership affairs, whenever circumstances render it just and reasonable, and

(c) Have dissolution and winding up by decree of court.

(2) A limited partner shall have the right to receive a share of the profits or other compensation by way of income, and to the return of his contribution as provided in Sections 15 and 16.

Sec. 11. (Status of Person Erroneously Believing Himself a Limited Partner.) A person who has contributed to the capital of a business conducted by a person or partnership erroneously believing that he has become a limited partner in a limited partnership, is not, by reason of his exercise of the rights of a limited partner, a general partner with the person or in the partnership carrying on the business, or bound by the obligations of such person or partnership; provided that on ascertaining the mistake he promptly renounces his interest in the profits of the business, or other compensation by way of income.

Sec. 12. (One Person Both General and Limited Partner.) (1) A person may be a general partner and a limited partner in the same partnership at the same time.

(2) A person who is a general, and also at the same time a limited partner, shall have all the rights and powers and be subject to all the restrictions of a general partner; except that, in respect to his contribution, he shall have the rights against the other members which he would have had if he were not also a general partner.

Sec. 13. (Loans and Other Business Transactions with Limited Partner.) (1) A limited partner also may loan money to and transact other business with the partnership, and, unless he is also a general partner, receive on account of resulting claims against the partnership, with general creditors, a pro rata share of the assets. No limited partner shall in respect to any such claim

(a) Receive or hold as collateral security any partnership property, or

(b) Receive from a general partner or the partnership any payment, conveyance, or release from liability, if at the time the assets of the partnership are not sufficient to discharge partnership liabilities to persons not claiming as general or limited partners,

(2) The receiving of collateral security, or a payment, conveyance, or release in violation of the provisions of paragraph (1) is a fraud on the creditors of the partnership.

Sec. 14. (Relation of Limited Partners Inter Se.) Where there are several limited partners the members may agree that one or more of the limited partners shall have a priority over other limited partners as to the return of their contributions, as to their compensation by way of income, or as to any other matter. If such an agreement is made it shall be stated in the certificate, and in the absence of such a statement all the limited partners shall stand upon equal footing.

Sec. 15. (Compensation of Limited Partner.) A limited partner may receive from the partnership the share of the profits or the compensation by way of income stipulated for in the certificate; provided, that after such payment is made, whether from the property of the partnership or that of a general partner, the partnership assets are in excess of all liabilities of the partnership except liabilities to limited partners on account of their contributions and to general partners.

Sec. 16. (Withdrawal or Reduction of Limited Partner's Contribution.) (1) A limited partner shall not receive from a general partner or out of partnership property any part of his contribution until

(a) All liabilities of the partnership, except liabilities to general partners and to limited partners on account of their contributions, have been paid or there remains property of the partnership sufficient to pay them,

(b) The consent of all members is had, unless the return of the contribution may be rightfully demanded under the provisions of paragraph (2), and

(c) The certificate is cancelled or so amended as to set forth the withdrawal or reduction.

(2) Subject to the provisions of paragraph (1) a limited partner may rightfully demand the return of his contribution

(a) On the dissolution of a partnership, or

(b) When the date specified in the certificate for its return has arrived, or

(c) After he has given six months' notice in writing to all other members, if no time is specified in the certificate either for the return of the contribution or for the dissolution of the partnership,

(3) In the absence of any statement in the certificate to the contrary or the consent of all members, a limited partner, irrespective of the nature of his contribution, has only the right to demand and receive cash in return for his contribution.

(4) A limited partner may have the partnership dissolved and its affairs wound up when

(a) He rightfully but unsuccessfully demands the return of his contribution, or

(b) The other liabilities of the partnership have not been paid, or the partnership property is insufficient for their payment as required by paragraph (1a) and the limited partner would otherwise be entitled to the return of his contribution.

Sec. 17. (Liability of Limited Partner to Partnership.) (1) A limited partner is liable to the partnership

(a) For the difference between his contribution as actually made and that stated in the certificate as having been made, and

(b) For any unpaid contribution which he agreed in the certificate to make in the future at the time and on the conditions stated in the certificate.

(2) A limited partner holds as trustee for the partnership

(a) Specific property stated in the certificate as contributed by him, but which was not contributed or which has been wrongfully returned, and

(b) Money or other property wrongfully paid or conveyed to him on account of his contribution.

(3) The liabilities of a limited partner as set forth in this section can be waived or compromised only by the consent of all members; but a waiver or compromise shall not affect the right of a creditor of a partnership, who extended credit or whose claim arose after the filing and before a cancellation or amendment of the certificate, to enforce such liabilities.

(4) When a contributor has rightfully received the return in whole or in part of the capital of his contribution, he is nevertheless liable to the partnership for any sum, not in excess of such return with interest, necessary to discharge its liabilities to all creditors who extended credit or whose claims arose before such return.

Sec. 18. (Nature of Limited Partner's Interest in Partnership.) A limited partner's interest in the partnership is personal property.

Sec. 19. (Assignment of Limited Partner's Interest.) (1) A limited partner's interest is assignable.

(2) A substituted limited partner is a person admitted to all the rights of a limited partner who has died or has assigned his interest in a partnership.

(3) An assignee, who does not become a substituted limited partner, has no right to require any information or account of the partnership transactions or to inspect the partnership books; he is only entitled to receive the share of the profits or other compensation by way of income, or the return of his contribution, to which his assignor would otherwise be entitled.

(4) An assignee shall have the right to become a substituted limited partner if all the members (except the assignor) consent thereto or if the assignor, being thereunto empowered by the certificate, gives the assignee that right.

(5) An assignee becomes a substituted limited partner when the certificate is appropriately amended in accordance with Section 25.

(6) The substituted limited partner has all the rights and powers, and is subject to all the restrictions and liabilities of his assignor, except those liabilities of which he was ignorant at the time he became a limited partner and which could not be ascertained from the certificate.

(7) The substitution of the assignee as a limited partner does not release the assignor from liability to the partnership under Sections 6 and 17.

Sec. 20. (Effect of Retirement, Death or Insanity of a General Partner.) The retirement, death or insanity of a general partner dissolves the partnership, unless the business is continued by the remaining general partners

(a) Under a right so to do stated in the certificate, or

(b) With the consent of all members.

Sec. 21. (Death of Limited Partner.) (1) On the death of a limited partner his executor or administrator shall have all the rights of a limited partner for the purpose of settling his estate, and such power as the deceased had to constitute his assignee a substituted limited partner.

(2) The estate of a deceased limited partner shall be liable for all his liabilities as a limited partner.

Sec. 22. (Rights of Creditors of Limited Partner.) (1) On due application to a court of competent jurisdiction by any judgment creditor of a limited partner, the court may charge the interest of the indebted limited partner with payment of the unsatisfied amount of the judgment debt; and may appoint a receiver, and make all other orders, directions, and inquiries which the circumstances of the case may require.

In those states where a creditor on beginning an action can attach debts due the defendant before he has obtained a judgment against the defendant it is recommended that paragraph (1) of this section read as follows:

On due application to a court of competent jurisdiction by any creditor of a limited partner, the court may charge the interest of the indebted limited partner with payment of the unsatisfied amount of such claim; and may appoint a receiver, and make all other orders, directions, and inquiries which the circumstances of the case may require.

(2) The interest may be redeemed with the separate property of any general partner, but may not be redeemed with partnership property.

(3) The remedies conferred by paragraph (1) shall not be deemed exclusive of others which may exist.

(4) Nothing in this act shall be held to deprive a limited partner of his statutory exemption.

Sec. 23. (Distribution of Assets.) (1) In settling accounts after dissolution the liabilities of the partnership shall be entitled to payment in the following order:

(a) Those to creditors, in the order of priority as provided by law, except those to limited partners on account of their contributions, and to general partners,

(b) Those to limited partners in respect to their share of the profits and other compensation by way of income on their contributions,

(c) Those to limited partners in respect to the capital of their contributions,

(d) Those to general partners other than for capital and profits,

(e) Those to general partners in respect to profits,

(f) Those to general partners in respect to capital.

(2) Subject to any statement in the certificate or to subsequent agreement, limited partners share in the partnership assets in respect to their claims for capital, and in respect to their claims for profits or for compensation by way of income on their contributions respectively, in proportion to the respective amounts of such claims.

Sec. 24. (When Certificate Shall be Cancelled or Amended.) (1) The certificate shall be cancelled when the partnership is dissolved or all limited partners cease to be such.

(2) A certificate shall be amended when

(a) There is a change in the name of the partnership or in the amount or character of the contribution of any limited partner,

(b) A person is substituted as a limited partner,

(c) An additional limited partner is admitted,

(d) A person is admitted as a general partner,

(e) A general partner retires, dies or becomes insane, and the business is continued under section 20.

(f) There is a change in the character of the business of the partnership,

(g) There is a false or erroneous statement in the certificate,

(h) There is a change in the time as stated in the certificate for the dissolution of the partnership or for the return of a contribution,

(i) A time is fixed for the dissolution of the partnership, or the return of a contribution, no time having been specified in the certificate, or

(j) The members desire to make a change in any other statement in the certificate in order that it shall accurately represent the agreement between them.

Sec. 25. (Requirements for Amendment and for Cancellation of Certificate.) (1) The writing to amend a certificate shall

(a) Conform to the requirements of Section 2(1a) as far as necessary to set forth clearly the change in the certificate which it is desired to make, and

(b) Be signed and sworn to by all members, and an amendment substituting a limited partner or adding a limited or general partner shall be signed also by the member to be substituted or added, and when a limited partner is to be substituted, the amendment shall also be signed by the assigning limited partner.

(2) The writing to cancel a certificate shall be signed by all members.

(3) A person desiring the cancellation or amendment of a certificate, if any person designated in paragraphs (1) and (2) as a person who must execute the writing refuses to do so, may petition the [here designate the proper court] to direct a cancellation or amendment thereof.

(4) If the court finds that the petitioner has a right to have the writing executed by a person who refuses to do so, it shall order the [here designate the responsible official in the office designated in Section 2] in the office where the certificate is recorded to record the cancellation or amendment of the certificate; and where the certificate is to be amended, the court shall also cause to be filed for record in

said office a certified copy of its decree setting forth the amendment.

(5) A certificate is amended or cancelled when there is filed for record in the office [here designate the office designated in Section 2] where the certificate is recorded

(a) A writing in accordance with the provisions of paragraph (1), or (2) or

(b) A certified copy of the order of court in accordance with the provisions of paragraph (4).

(6) After the certificate is duly amended in accordance with this section, the amended certificate shall thereafter be for all purposes the certificate provided for by this act.

Sec. 26. (Parties to Actions.) A contributor, unless he is a general partner, is not a proper party to proceedings by or against a partnership, except where the object is to enforce a limited partner's right against or liability to the partnership.

Sec. 27. (Name of Act.) This act may be cited as The Uniform Limited Partnership Act.

Sec. 28. (Rules of Construction.) (1) The rule that statutes in derogation of the common law are to be strictly construed shall have no application to this act.

(2) This act shall be so interpreted and construed as to effect its general purpose to make uniform the law of those states which enact it.

(3) This act shall not be so construed as to impair the obligations of any contract existing when the act goes into effect, nor to affect any action on proceedings begun or right accrued before this act takes effect.

Sec. 29. (Rules for Cases Not Provided for in this Act.) In any case not provided for in this act the rules of law and equity, including the law merchant, shall govern.

Sec. 30.[1] (Provisions for Existing Limited Partnerships.) (1) A limited partnership formed under any statute of this state prior to the adoption of this act, may become a limited partnership under this act by complying with the provisions of Section 2; provided the certificate sets forth

(a) The amount of the original contribution of each limited partner, and the time when the contribution was made, and

(b) That the property of the partnership exceeds the amount sufficient to discharge its liabilities to persons not claiming as general or limited partners by an amount greater than the sum of the contributions of its limited partners.

(2) A limited partnership formed under any statute of this state prior to the adoption of this act, until or unless it becomes a limited partnership under this act, shall continue to be governed by the provisions of [here insert proper reference to the existing limited partnership act or acts], except that such partnership shall not be renewed unless so provided in the original agreement.

Sec. 31.[1] (Act [Acts] Repealed.) Except as affecting existing limited partnerships to the extent set forth in Section 30, the act (acts) of [here designate the existing limited partnership act or acts] is (are) hereby repealed.

---

[1] Sections 30, 31, will be omitted in any state which has not a limited partnership act.

APPENDIX D

MODEL BUSINESS CORPORATION ACT

Prepared by the
Committee on Corporate Laws (Section
of Corporation, Banking and Business Law)
of the
American Bar Association

(Incorporating all amendments by the Committee including those published in the 1964 Addendum)

(Adopted, in whole or in part, by 23 jurisdictions. The 20 which have adopted it substantially are: Alabama, Alaska, Arkansas, Colorado, District of Columbia, Illinois, Iowa, Mississippi, Missouri, Nebraska, North Dakota, Oregon, South Carolina, South Dakota, Texas, Utah, Virginia, Washington, Wisconsin, and Wyoming. Three States have adopted it partially, namely, Connecticut, Maryland, and North Carolina.)

§ 1. Short Title

This Act shall be known and may be cited as the "———— † Business Corporation Act."

† Insert name of state.

§ 2. Definitions

As used in this Act, unless the context otherwise requires, the term:

(a) "Corporation" or "domestic corporation" means a corporation for profit subject to the provisions of this Act, except a foreign corporation.

(b) "Foreign corporation" means a corporation for profit organized under laws other than the laws of this State for a purpose or purposes for which a corporation may be organized under this Act.

(c) "Articles of incorporation" means the original or restated articles of incorporation or articles of consolidation and all amendments thereto including articles of merger.

(d) "Shares" means the units into which the proprietary interests in a corporation are divided.

(e) "Subscriber" means one who subscribes for shares in a corporation, whether before or after incorporation.

(f) "Shareholder" means one who is a holder of record of shares in a corporation.

(g) "Authorized shares" means the shares of all classes which the corporation is authorized to issue.

(h) "Treasury shares" means shares of a corporation which have been issued, have been subsequently acquired by and belong to the corporation, and have not, either by reason of the acquisition or thereafter, been cancelled or restored to the status of authorized but unissued shares. Treasury shares shall be deemed to be "issued" shares, but not "outstanding" shares.

(i) "Net assets" means the amount by which the total assets of a corporation, excluding treasury shares, exceed the total debts of the corporation.

(j) "Stated capital" means, at any particular time, the sum of (1) the par value of all shares of the corporation having a par value that have been issued, (2) the amount of the consideration received by the corporation for all shares of the corporation without par value that have been issued, except such part of the consideration therefor as may have been allocated to capital surplus in a manner permitted by law, and (3) such amounts not included in clauses (1) and (2) of this paragraph as have been transferred to stated capital of the corporation, whether upon the issue of shares as a share dividend or otherwise, minus all reductions from such sum as have been effected in a manner permitted by law. Irrespective of the manner of designation thereof by the laws under which a foreign corporation is organized, the stated capital of a foreign corporation shall be determined on the same basis and in the same manner as the stated capital of a domestic corporation, for the purpose of computing fees, franchise taxes and other charges imposed by this Act.

(k) "Surplus" means the excess of the net assets of a corporation over its stated capital.

(l) "Earned surplus" means the portion of the surplus of a corporation equal to the balance of its net profits, income, gains and losses from the date of incorporation, or from the latest date when a deficit was eliminated by an application of its capital surplus or stated capital or otherwise, after deducting subsequent distributions to shareholders and transfers to stated capital and capital surplus to the extent such distributions and transfers are made out of earned surplus. Earned surplus shall include also any portion of surplus allocated to earned surplus in mergers, consolidations or acquisitions of all or substantially all of the outstanding shares or of the property and assets of another corporation, domestic or foreign.

(m) "Capital surplus" means the entire surplus of a corporation other than its earned surplus.

(n) "Insolvent" means inability of a corporation to pay its debts as they become due in the usual course of its business.

§ 3. Purposes

Corporations may be organized under this Act for any lawful purpose or purposes, except for the purpose of banking or insurance.

§ 4. General Powers

Each corporation shall have power:

(a) To have perpetual succession by its corporate name unless a limited period of duration is stated in its articles of incorporation.

(b) To sue and be sued, complain and defend, in its corporate name.

(c) To have a corporate seal which may be altered at pleasure, and to use the same by causing it, or a facsimile thereof, to be im-

pressed or affixed or in any other manner reproduced.

(d) To purchase, take, receive, lease, or otherwise acquire, own, hold, improve, use and otherwise deal in and with, real or personal property, or any interest therein, wherever situated.

(e) To sell, convey, mortgage, pledge, lease, exchange, transfer and otherwise dispose of all or any part of its property and assets.

(f) To lend money to its employees other than its officers and directors, and otherwise assist its employees, officers and directors.

(g) To purchase, take, receive, subscribe for, or otherwise acquire, own, hold, vote, use, employ, sell, mortgage, lend, pledge, or otherwise dispose of, and otherwise use and deal in and with, shares or other interests in, or obligations of, other domestic or foreign corporations, associations, partnerships or individuals, or direct or indirect obligations of the United States or of any other government, state, territory, governmental district or municipality or of any instrumentality thereof.

(h) To make contracts and guarantees and incur liabilities, borrow money at such rates of interest as the corporation may determine, issue its notes, bonds, and other obligations, and secure any of its obligations by mortgage or pledge of all or any of its property, franchises and income.

(i) To lend money for its corporate purposes, invest and reinvest its funds, and take and hold real and personal property as security for the payments of funds so loaned or invested.

(j) To conduct its business, carry on its operations, and have offices and exercise the powers granted by this Act in any state, territory, district, or possession of the United States, or in any foreign country.

(k) To elect or appoint officers and agents of the corporation, and define their duties and fix their compensation.

(l) To make and alter by-laws, not inconsistent with its articles of incorporation or with the laws of this State, for the administration and regulation of the affairs of the corporation.

(m) To make donations for the public welfare or for charitable, scientific or educational purposes; and in time of war to make donations in aid of war activities.

(n) In time of war to transact any lawful business in aid of the United States in the prosecution of the war.

(o) To indemnify any director or officer or former director or officer of the corporation, or any person who may have served at its request as a director or officer of another corporation in which it owns shares of capital stock or of which it is a creditor, against expenses actually and reasonably incurred by him in connection with the defense of any action, suit or proceeding, civil or criminal, in which he is made a party by reason of being or having been such director or officer, except in relation to matters as to which he shall be adjudged in such action, suit or proceeding to be liable for negligence or misconduct in the performance of duty to the corporation; and to make any other indemnification that shall be authorized by the articles of incorporation or by any by-law or resolution adopted by the shareholders after notice.

(p) To pay pensions and establish pension plans, pension trusts, profit-sharing plans, stock bonus plans, stock option plans and other incentive plans for any or all of its directors, officers and employees.

(q) To cease its corporate activities and surrender its corporate franchise.

(r) To have and exercise all powers necessary or convenient to effect any or all of the purposes for which the corporation is organized.

§ 5. Right of Corporation to Acquire and Dispose of Its Own Shares

A corporation shall have the right to purchase, take, receive or otherwise acquire, hold, own, pledge, transfer or otherwise dispose of its own shares, but purchases of its own shares, whether direct or indirect, shall be made only to the extent of unreserved and unrestricted earned surplus available therefor, and, if the articles of incorporation so permit or with the affirmative vote of the holders of at least two-thirds of all shares entitled to vote thereon, to the extent of unreserved and unrestricted capital surplus available therefor.

To the extent that earned surplus or capital surplus is used as the measure of the corpora-

tion's right to purchase its own shares, such surplus shall be restricted so long as such shares are held as treasury shares, and upon the disposition or cancellation of any such shares the restriction shall be removed pro tanto.

Notwithstanding the foregoing limitation, a corporation may purchase or otherwise acquire its own shares for the purpose of:

(a) Eliminating fractional shares.

(b) Collecting or compromising indebtedness to the corporation.

(c) Paying dissenting shareholders entitled to payment for their shares under the provisions of this Act.

(d) Effecting, subject to the other provisions of this Act, the retirement of its redeemable shares by redemption or by purchase at not to exceed the redemption price.

No purchase of or payment for its own shares shall be made at a time when the corporation is insolvent or when such purchase or payment would make it insolvent.

§ 6. Defense of Ultra Vires

No act of a corporation and no conveyance or transfer of real or personal property to or by a corporation shall be invalid by reason of the fact that the corporation was without capacity or power to do such act or to make or receive such conveyance or transfer, but such lack of capacity or power may be asserted:

(a) In a proceeding by a shareholder against the corporation to enjoin the doing of any act or acts or the transfer of real or personal property by or to the corporation. If the unauthorized acts or transfer sought to be enjoined are being, or are to be, performed or made pursuant to any contract to which the corporation is a party, the court may, if all of the parties to the contract are parties to the proceeding and if it deems the same to be equitable, set aside and enjoin the performance of such contract, and in so doing may allow to the corporation or to the other parties to the contract, as the case may be, compensation for the loss or damage sustained by either of them which may result from the action of the court in setting aside and enjoining the performance of such contract, but anticipated profits to be derived from the performance of the contract shall not be awarded by the court as a loss or damage sustained.

(b) In a proceeding by the corporation, whether acting directly or through a receiver, trustee or other legal representative, or through shareholders in a representative suit, against the incumbent or former officers or directors of the corporation.

(c) In a proceeding by the Attorney General, as provided in this Act, to dissolve the corporation, or in a proceeding by the Attorney General to enjoin the corporation from the transaction of unauthorized business.

§ 7.   Corporate Name

The corporate name:

(a) Shall contain the word "corporation," "company," "incorporated" or "limited," or shall contain an abbreviation of one of such words.

(b) Shall not contain any word or phrase which indicates or implies that it is organized for any purpose other than one or more of the purposes contained in its articles of incorporation.

(c) Shall not be the same as, or deceptively similar to, the name of any domestic corporation existing under the laws of this State or any foreign corporation authorized to transact business in this State, or a name the exclusive right to which is, at the time, reserved in the manner provided in this Act, or the name of a corporation which has in effect a registration of its corporate name as provided in this Act.

§ 8.   Reserved Name

The exclusive right to the use of a corporate name may be reserved by:

(a) Any person intending to organize a corporation under this Act.

(b) Any domestic corporation intending to change its name.

(c) Any foreign corporation intending to make application for a certificate of authority to transact business in this State.

(d) Any foreign corporation authorized to transact business in this State and intending to change its name.

(e) Any person intending to organize a foreign corporation and intending to have such corporation make application for a certificate of authority to transact business in this State.

The reservation shall be made by filing with the Secretary of State an application to reserve a specified corporate name, executed by the applicant. If the Secretary of State finds that the name is available for corporate use, he shall reserve the same for the exclusive use of the applicant for a period of one hundred and twenty days.

The right to the exclusive use of a specified corporate name so reserved may be transferred to any other person or corporation by filing in the office of the Secretary of State a notice of such transfer, executed by the applicant for whom the name was reserved, and specifying the name and address of the transferee.

§ 9.   Registered Name

Any corporation organized and existing under the laws of any state or territory of the United States may register its corporate name under this Act, provided its corporate name is not the same as, or deceptively similar to, the name of any domestic corporation existing under the laws of this State, or the name of any foreign corporation authorized to transact business in this State, or any corporate name reserved or registered under this Act.

Such registration shall be made by:

(a) Filing with the Secretary of State (1) an application for registration executed by the corporation by an officer thereof, setting forth the name of the corporation, the state or territory under the laws of which it is incorporated, the date of its incorporation, a statement that it is carrying on or doing business, and a brief statement of the business in which it is engaged, and (2) a certificate setting forth that such corporation is in good standing under the laws of the state or territory wherein it is organized, executed by the Secretary of State of such state or territory or by such other official as may have custody of the records pertaining to corporations, and

(b) Paying to the Secretary of State a registration fee in the amount of one dollar for each month, or fraction thereof, between the date of filing such application and December 31st of the calendar year in which such application is filed.

Such registration shall be effective until the close of the calendar year in which the application for registration is filed.

§ 10.   Renewal of Registered Name

A corporation which has in effect a registration of its corporate name, may renew such registration from year to year by annually filing an application for renewal setting forth the facts required to be set forth in an original application for registration and a certificate of good standing as required for the original registration and by paying a fee of ten dollars. A renewal application may be filed between the first day of October and the thirty-first day of December in each year, and shall extend the registration for the following calendar year.

§ 11.   Registered Office and Registered Agent

Each corporation shall have and continuously maintain in this State:

(a) A registered office which may be, but need not be, the same as its place of business.

(b) A registered agent, which agent may be either an individual resident in this State whose business office is identical with such registered office, or a domestic corporation, or a foreign corporation authorized to transact business in this State, having a business office identical with such registered office.

§ 12.   Change of Registered Office or Registered Agent

A corporation may change its registered office or change its registered agent, or both, upon filing in the office of the Secretary of State a statement setting forth:

(a) The name of the corporation.

(b) The address of its then registered office.

(c) If the address of its registered office be changed, the address to which the registered office is to be changed.

(d) The name of its then registered agent.

(e) If its registered agent be changed, the name of its successor registered agent.

(f) That the address of its registered office and the address of the business office of its registered agent, as changed, will be identical.

(g) That such change was authorized by resolution duly adopted by its board of directors.

Such statement shall be executed by the corporation by its president or a vice president, and verified by him, and delivered to the Secretary of State. If the Secretary of State finds that such statement conforms to the provisions of this Act, he shall file such statement in his office, and upon such filing the change of address of the registered office, or the appointment of a new registered agent, or both, as the case may be, shall become effective.

Any registered agent of a corporation may resign as such agent upon filing a written notice thereof, executed in duplicate, with the Secretary of State, who shall forthwith mail a copy thereof to the corporation at its registered office. The appointment of such agent shall terminate upon the expiration of thirty days after receipt of such notice by the Secretary of State.

If a registered agent changes his or its business address to another place within the same ....,† Insert appropriate designation of jurisdiction such as county, he or it may change such address and the address of the registered office of any corporations of which he or it is registered agent by filing a statement as required above except that it need be signed only by the registered agent and need not be responsive to (e) or (g) and must recite that a copy of the statement has been mailed to each such corporation.

§ 13.   Service of Process on Corporation

The registered agent so appointed by a corporation shall be an agent of such corporation upon whom any process, notice or demand required or permitted by law to be served upon the corporation may be served.

Whenever a corporation shall fail to appoint or maintain a registered agent in this State, or whenever its registered agent cannot with reasonable diligence be found at the registered office, then the Secretary of State shall be an agent of such corporation upon whom any such process, notice, or demand may be served. Service on the Secretary of State of any such process, notice, or demand shall be made by delivering to and leaving with him, or with any clerk having charge of the corporation department of his office, duplicate copies of such process, notice or demand. In the event any such process, notice or demand is served on the Secretary of State, he shall immediately cause one of the copies thereof to be forwarded by registered mail, addressed to the corporation at its registered office. Any service so had on the Secretary of State shall be returnable in not less than thirty days.

The Secretary of State shall keep a record of all processes, notices and demands served upon him under this section, and shall record therein the time of such service and his action with reference thereto.

Nothing herein contained shall limit or affect the right to serve any process, notice or demand required or permitted by law to be served upon a corporation in any other manner now or hereafter permitted by law.

§ 14. Authorized Shares

Each corporation shall have power to create and issue the number of shares stated in its articles of incorporation. Such shares may be divided into one or more classes, any or all of which classes may consist of shares with par value or shares without par value, with such designations, preferences, limitations, and relative rights as shall be stated in the articles of incorporation. The articles of incorporation may limit or deny the voting rights of or provide special voting rights for the shares of any class to the extent not inconsistent with the provisions of this Act.

Without limiting the authority herein contained, a corporation, when so provided in its articles of incorporation, may issue shares of preferred or special classes:

(a) Subject to the right of the corporation to redeem any of such shares at the price fixed by the articles of incorporation for the redemption thereof.

(b) Entitling the holders thereof to cumulative, noncumulative or partially cumulative dividends.

(c) Having preference over any other class or classes of shares as to the payment of dividends.

(d) Having preference in the assets of the corporation over any other class or classes of shares upon the voluntary or involuntary liquidation of the corporation.

(e) Convertible into shares of any other class or into shares of any series of the same or any other class, except a class having prior or superior rights and preferences as to dividends or distribution of assets upon liquidation, but shares without par value shall not be converted into shares with par value unless that part of the stated capital of the corporation represented by such shares without par value is, at the time of conversion, at least equal to the aggregate par value of the shares into which the shares without par value are to be converted.

§ 15. Issuance of Shares of Preferred or Special Classes in Series

If the articles of incorporation so provide, the shares of any preferred or special class may be divided into and issued in series. If the shares of any such class are to be issued in series, then each series shall be so designated as to distinguish the shares thereof from the shares of all other series and classes. Any or all of the series of any such class and the variations in the relative rights and preferences as between different series may be fixed and determined by the articles of incorporation, but all shares of the same class shall be identical except as to the following relative rights and preferences, as to which there may be variations between different series:

A.   The rate of dividend.

B.   Whether shares may be redeemed and, if so, the redemption price and the terms and conditions of redemption.

C.   The amount payable upon shares in event of voluntary and involuntary liquidation.

D.   Sinking fund provisions, if any, for the redemption or purchase of shares.

E.   The terms and conditions, if any, on which shares may be converted.

If the articles of incorporation shall expressly vest authority in the board of directors, then, to the extent that the articles of incorporation shall not have established series and fixed and determined the variations in the relative rights and preferences as between series, the board of directors shall have authority to divide any or all of such classes into series and, within the limitations set forth in this section and in the articles of incorporation, fix and determine the relative rights and preferences of the shares of any series so established.

In order for the board of directors to establish a series, where authority so to do is contained in the articles of incorporation, the board of directors shall adopt a resolution setting forth the designation of the series and fixing and determining the relative rights and preferences thereof, or so much thereof as shall not be fixed and determined by the articles of incorporation.

Prior to the issue of any shares of a series established by resolution adopted by the board of directors, the corporation shall file in the office of the Secretary of State a statement setting forth:

(a) The name of the corporation.

(b) A copy of the resolution establishing and designating the series, and fixing and determining the relative rights and preferences thereof.

(c) The date of adoption of such resolution.

(d) That such resolution was duly adopted by the board of directors.

Such statement shall be executed in duplicate by the corporation by its president or a vice president and by its secretary or an assistant secretary, and verified by one of the officers signing such statement, and shall be delivered to the Secretary of State. If the Secretary of State finds that such statement conforms to law, he shall, when all franchise taxes and fees have been paid as in this Act prescribed:

(1) Endorse on each of such duplicate originals the word "Filed," and the month, day, and year of the filing thereof.

(2) File one of such duplicate originals in his office.

(3) Return the other duplicate original to the corporation or its representative.

Upon the filing of such statement by the Secretary of State, the resolution establishing and designating the series and fixing and determining the relative rights and preferences thereof shall become effective and shall constitute an amendment of the articles of incorporation.

§ 16. Subscriptions for Shares

A subscription for shares of a corporation to be organized shall be irrevocable for a period of six months, unless otherwise provided by the terms of the subscription agreement or unless all of the subscribers consent to the revocation of such subscription.

Unless otherwise provided in the subscription agreement, subscriptions for shares, whether made before or after the organization of a corporation, shall be paid in full at such time, or in such installments and at such times, as shall be determined by the board of directors. Any call made by the board of directors for payment on subscriptions shall be uniform as to all shares of the same class or as to all shares of the same series, as the case may be. In case of default in the payment of any installment or call when such payment is due, the corporation may proceed to collect the amount due in the same manner as any debt due the corporation. The by-laws may prescribe other penalties for failure to pay installments or calls that may become due, but no penalty working a forfeiture of a subscription, or of the amounts paid thereon, shall be declared as against any subscriber unless the amount due thereon shall remain unpaid for a period of twenty days after written demand has been made therefor. If mailed, such written demand shall be deemed to be made when deposited in the United States mail in a sealed envelope addressed to the subscriber at his last post-office address known to the corporation, with postage thereon prepaid. In the event of the sale of any shares by reason of any forfeiture, the excess of proceeds realized over the amount due and unpaid on such shares shall be paid to the delinquent subscriber or to his legal representative.

§ 17. Consideration for Shares

Shares having a par value may be issued for such consideration expressed in dollars, not less than the par value thereof, as shall be fixed from time to time by the board of directors.

Shares without par value may be issued for such consideration expressed in dollars as may be fixed from time to time by the board of directors unless the articles of incorporation reserve to the shareholders the right to fix the consideration. In the event that such right be reserved as to any shares, the shareholders shall, prior to the issuance of such shares, fix the consideration to be received for such shares, by a vote of the holders of a majority of all shares entitled to vote thereon.

Treasury shares may be disposed of by the corporation for such consideration expressed in dollars as may be fixed from time to time by the board of directors.

That part of the surplus of a corporation which is transferred to stated capital upon the issuance of shares as a share dividend shall be deemed to be the consideration for the issuance of such shares.

In the event of a conversion of shares, or in the event of an exchange of shares with or without par value for the same or a different number of shares with or without par value, whether the same or a different class or classes, the consideration for the shares so issued in exchange or conversion shall be deemed to be (1) the stated capital then represented by the shares so exchanged or converted, and (2) that part of surplus, if any, transferred to stated capital upon the issuance of shares for the shares so exchanged or converted, and (3) any additional consideration paid to the corporation upon the issuance of shares for the shares so exchanged or converted.

§ 18. Payment for Shares

The consideration for the issuance of shares may be paid, in whole or in part, in money, in other property, tangible or intangible, or in labor or services actually performed for the corporation. When payment of the consideration for which shares are to be issued shall have been received by the corporation, such shares shall be deemed to be fully paid and nonassessable.

Neither promissory notes nor future services shall constitute payment or part payment, for shares of a corporation.

In the absence of fraud in the transaction, the judgment of the board of directors or the shareholders, as the case may be, as to the value of the consideration received for shares shall be conclusive.

[Optional] § 18A. Stock Rights and Options

Subject to any provisions in respect thereof set forth in its articles of incorporation, a corporation may create and issue, whether or not in connection with the issuance and sale of any of its shares or other securities, rights or options entitling the holders thereof to purchase from the corporation shares of any class or classes. Such rights or options shall be evidenced in such manner as the board of directors shall approve and, subject to the provisions of the articles of incorporation, shall set forth the terms upon which, the time or times within which and the price or prices at which such shares may be purchased from the corporation upon the exercise of any such right or option. If such rights or options are to be issued to directors, officers or employees as such of the corporation or of any subsidiary thereof, and not to the shareholders generally, their issuance shall be approved by the affirmative vote of the holders of a majority of the shares entitled to vote thereon or shall be authorized by and consistent with a plan theretofore approved by such a vote of shareholders and set forth or incorporated by reference in the instrument evidencing each such right or option. In the absence of fraud in the transaction, the judgment of the board of directors as to the adequacy of the consideration received for such rights or options shall be conclusive. The price or prices to be received for any shares having a par value, other than treasury shares to be issued upon the exercise of such rights or options, shall not be less than the par value thereof.

§ 19. Determination of Amount of Stated Capital

In case of the issuance by a corporation of shares having par value, the consideration received therefor shall constitute stated capital to the extent of the par value of such shares, and the excess, if any, of such consideration shall constitute capital surplus.

In case of the issuance by a corporation of shares without par value, the entire consideration received therefor shall constitute stated capital unless the corporation shall determine as provided in this section that only a part thereof shall be stated capital. Within a period of sixty days after the issuance of any shares without par value, the board of directors may allocate to capital surplus any portion of the consideration received for the issuance of such shares. No such allocation shall be made of any portion of the consideration received for shares without par value having a preference in the assets of the corporation in the event of involuntary liquidation except the amount, if any, of such consideration in excess of such preference.

If shares have been or shall be issued by a corporation in merger or consolidation or in acquisition of all or substantially all of the outstanding shares or of the property and assets of another corporation, whether domestic or foreign, any amount that would otherwise constitute capital surplus under the foregoing provisions of this section may instead be allocated to earned surplus by the board of directors of the issuing corporation except that its aggregate earned surplus shall not exceed the sum of the earned surpluses as defined in this Act of the issuing corporation and of all other corporations, domestic or foreign, that were merged or consolidated or of which the shares or assets were acquired.

The stated capital of a corporation may be increased from time to time by resolution of the board of directors directing that all or a part of the surplus of the corporation be transferred to stated capital. The board of directors may direct that the amount of the surplus so transferred shall be deemed to be stated capital in respect of any designated class of shares.

§ 20. Expenses of Organization, Reorganization and Financing

The reasonable charges and expenses of organization or reorganization of a corporation, and the reasonable expenses of and compensation for the sale or underwriting of its shares, may be paid or allowed by such corporation out of the consideration received by it in payment for its shares without thereby rendering such shares not fully paid or assessable.

§ 21. Certificates Representing Shares

The shares of a corporation shall be represented by certificates signed by the president or a vice president and the secretary or an assistant secretary of the corporation, and may be sealed with the seal of the corporation or a facsimile thereof. The signatures of the president or vice president and the secretary or assistant secretary upon a certificate may be facsimiles if the certificate is countersigned by a transfer agent, or registered by a registrar, other than the corporation itself or an employee of the corporation. In case any officer who has

signed or whose facsimile signature has been placed upon such certificate shall have ceased to be such officer before such certificate is issued, it may be issued by the corporation with the same effect as if he were such officer at the date of its issue.

Every certificate representing shares issued by a corporation which is authorized to issue shares of more than one class shall set forth upon the face or back of the certificate, or shall state that the corporation will furnish to any shareholder upon request and without charge, a full statement of the designations, preferences, limitations, and relative rights of the shares of each class authorized to be issued and, if the corporation is authorized to issue any preferred or special class in series, the variations in the relative rights and preferences between the shares of each such series so far as the same have been fixed and determined and the authority of the board of directors to fix and determine the relative rights and preferences of subsequent series.

Each certificate representing shares shall state upon the face thereof:

(a) That the corporation is organized under the laws of this State.

(b) The name of the person to whom issued.

(c) The number and class of shares, and the designation of the series, if any, which such certificate represents.

(d) The par value of each share represented by such certificate, or a statement that the shares are without par value.

No certificate shall be issued for any share until such share is fully paid.

§ 22. Issuance of Fractional Shares or Scrip

A corporation may, but shall not be obliged to, issue a certificate for a fractional share, and, by action of its board of directors, may issue in lieu thereof scrip in registered or bearer form which shall entitle the holder to receive a certificate for a full share upon the surrender of such scrip aggregating a full share. A certificate for a fractional share shall, but scrip shall not unless otherwise provided therein, entitle the holder to exercise voting rights, to receive dividends thereon, and to participate in any of the assets of the corporation in the event of liquidation. The board of directors may cause such scrip to be issued subject to the condition that it shall become void if not exchanged for certificates representing full shares before a specified date, or subject to the condition that the shares for which such scrip is exchangeable may be sold by the corporation and the proceeds thereof distributed to the holders of such scrip, or subject to any other conditions which the board of directors may deem advisable.

§ 23. Liability of Subscribers and Shareholders

A holder of or subscriber to shares of a corporation shall be under no obligation to the corporation or its creditors with respect to such shares other than the obligation to pay to the corporation the full consideration for which such shares were issued or to be issued.

Any person becoming an assignee or transferee of shares or of a subscription for shares in good faith and without knowledge or notice that the full consideration therefor has not been paid shall not be personally liable to the corporation or its creditors for any unpaid portion of such consideration.

An executor, administrator, conservator, guardian, trustee, assignee for the benefit of creditors, or receiver shall not be personally liable to the corporation as a holder of or subscriber to shares of a corporation but the estate and funds in his hands shall be so liable.

No pledgee or other holder of shares as collateral security shall be personally liable as a shareholder.

§ 24. Shareholders' Preemptive Rights

The preemptive right of a shareholder to acquire unissued or treasury shares of a corporation may be limited or denied to the extent provided in the articles of incorporation.

Unless otherwise provided by its articles of incorporation, any corporation may issue and sell its shares to its officers or employees or to the officers or employees of any subsidiary corporation, without first offering such shares to its shareholders, for such consideration and upon such terms and conditions as shall be approved by the holders of a majority of all shares entitled to vote thereon or by its board of directors pursuant to like approval of the shareholders.

Alternative § 24. Shareholders' Preemptive Rights

The shareholders of a corporation shall have no preemptive right to acquire unissued or treasury shares of the corporation, or obligations of the corporation convertible into such shares, except to the extent, if any, that such right is provided in the articles of incorporation.

§ 25. By-Laws

The initial by-laws of a corporation shall be adopted by its board of directors. The power to alter, amend or repeal the by-laws or adopt new by-laws shall be vested in the board of directors unless reserved to the shareholders by the articles of incorporation. The by-laws may contain any provisions for the regulation and management of the affairs of the corporation not inconsistent with law or the articles of incorporation.

[Optional] § 25A. By-Laws and Other Powers in Emergency

The board of directors of any corporation may adopt emergency by-laws, subject to repeal or change by action of the shareholders, which shall, notwithstanding any different provision elsewhere in this Act or in the articles of incorporation or by-laws, be operative during any emergency in the conduct of the business of the corporation resulting from an attack on the United States or any nuclear or atomic disaster. The emergency by-laws may make any provision that may be practical and necessary for the circumstances of the emergency, including provisions that:

(a) A meeting of the board of directors may be called by any officer or director in such manner and under such conditions as shall be prescribed in the emergency by-laws;

(b) The director or directors in attendance at the meeting, or any greater number fixed by the emergency by-laws, shall constitute a quorum; and

(c) The officers or other persons designated on a list approved by the board of directors before the emergency, all in such order of priority and subject to such conditions and for such period of time (not longer than reasonably necessary after the termination of the emergency) as may be provided in the emergency by-laws or in the resolution approving the list, shall, to the extent required to provide a quorum at any meeting of the board of directors, be deemed directors for such meeting.

The board of directors, either before or during any such emergency, may provide, and from time to time modify, lines of succession in the event that during such an emergency any or all officers or agents of the corporation shall for any reason be rendered incapable of discharging their duties.

The board of directors, either before or during any such emergency, may, effective in the emergency, change the head office or designate several alternative head offices or regional offices, or authorize the officers so to do.

To the extent not inconsistent with any emergency by-laws so adopted, the by-laws of the corporation shall remain in effect during any such emergency and upon its termination the emergency by-laws shall cease to be operative.

Unless otherwise provided in emergency by-laws, notice of any meeting of the board of directors during any such emergency may be given only to such of the directors as it may be feasible to reach at the time and by such means as may be feasible at the time, including publication or radio.

To the extent required to constitute a quorum at any meeting of the board of directors during any such emergency, the officers of the corporation who are present shall, unless otherwise provided in emergency by-laws, be deemed, in order of rank and within the same rank in order of seniority, directors for such meeting.

No officer, director or employee acting in accordance with any emergency by-laws shall be liable except for willful misconduct. No officer, director or employee shall be liable for any action taken by him in good faith in such an emergency in furtherance of the ordinary business affairs of the corporation even though not authorized by the by-laws then in effect.

§ 26. Meetings of Shareholders

Meetings of shareholders may be held at such place, either within or without this State, as may be provided in the by-laws. In the absence of any such provision, all meetings shall be held at the registered office of the corporation.

An annual meeting of the shareholders shall be held at such time as may be provided in the by-laws. Failure to hold the annual meeting at the designated time shall not work a forfeiture or dissolution of the corporation.

Special meetings of the shareholders may be called by the president, the board of directors, the holders of not less than one-tenth of all the shares entitled to vote at the meeting, or such other officers or persons as may be provided in the articles of incorporation or the by-laws.

§ 27. Notice of Shareholders' Meetings

Written notice stating the place, day and hour of the meeting and, in case of a special meeting, the purpose or purposes for which the meeting is called, shall be delivered not less than ten nor more than fifty days before the date of the meeting, either personally or by mail, by or at the direction of the president, the secretary, or the officer or persons calling the meeting, to each shareholder of record entitled to vote at such meeting. If mailed, such notice shall be deemed to be delivered when deposited in the United States mail addressed to the shareholder at his address as it appears on the stock transfer books of the corporation, with postage thereon prepaid.

§ 28. Closing of Transfer Books and Fixing Record Date

For the purpose of determining shareholders entitled to notice of or to vote at any meeting of shareholders or any adjournment thereof, or entitled to receive payment of any dividend, or in order to make a determination of shareholders for any other proper purpose, the board of directors of a corporation may provide that the stock transfer books shall be closed for a stated period but not to exceed, in any case, fifty days. If the stock transfer books shall be closed for the purpose of determining shareholders entitled to notice of or to vote at a meeting of shareholders, such books shall be closed for at least ten days immediately preceding such meeting. In lieu of closing the stock transfer books, the by-laws, or in the absence of an applicable by-law the board of directors, may fix in advance a date as the record date for any such determination of shareholders, such date in any case to be not more than fifty days and, in case of a meeting of shareholders, not less than ten days prior to the date on which the particular action, requiring such determination of shareholders, is to be taken. If the stock transfer books are not closed and no record date is fixed for the determination of shareholders entitled to notice of or to vote at a meeting of shareholders, or shareholders entitled to receive payment of a dividend, the date on which notice of the meeting is mailed or the date on which the resolution of the board of directors declaring such dividend is adopted, as the case may be, shall be the record date for such determination of shareholders. When a determination of shareholders entitled to vote at any meeting of shareholders has been made as provided in this section, such determination shall apply to any adjournment thereof.

§ 29. Voting List

The officer or agent having charge of the stock transfer books for shares of a corporation shall make a complete list of the shareholders entitled to vote at such meeting or any adjournment thereof, arranged in alphabetical order, with the address of and the number of shares held by each. Such list shall be produced and kept open at the time and place of the meeting and shall be subject to the inspection of any shareholder during the whole time of the meeting for the purposes thereof.

Failure to comply with the requirements of this section shall not affect the validity of any action taken at such meeting.

An officer or agent having charge of the stock transfer books who shall fail to prepare the list of shareholders, or produce and keep it open for inspection at the meeting, as provided in this section, shall be liable to any shareholder suffering damage on account of such failure, to the extent of such damage.

§ 30. Quorum of Shareholders

Unless otherwise provided in the articles of incorporation, a majority of the shares entitled to vote, represented in person or by proxy, shall constitute a quorum at a meeting of shareholders, but in no event shall a quorum consist of less than one-third of the shares entitled to vote at the meeting. If a quorum is present, the affirmative vote of the majority of the shares represented at the meeting and entitled to vote on the subject matter shall be the act of the shareholders, unless the vote of a greater number or voting by classes is re-

quired by this Act or the articles of incorporation or by-laws.

§ 31. Voting of Shares

Each outstanding share, regardless of class, shall be entitled to one vote on each matter submitted to a vote at a meeting of shareholders, except to the extent that the voting rights of the shares of any class or classes are limited or denied by the articles of incorporation as permitted by this Act.

Neither treasury shares, nor shares held by another corporation if a majority of the shares entitled to vote for the election of directors of such other corporation is held by the corporation, shall be voted at any meeting or counted in determining the total number of outstanding shares at any given time.

A shareholder may vote either in person or by proxy executed in writing by the shareholder or by his duly authorized attorney-in-fact. No proxy shall be valid after eleven months from the date of its execution, unless otherwise provided in the proxy.

(Either of the following prefatory phrases may be inserted here: "The articles of incorporation may provide that" or "Unless the articles of incorporation otherwise provide") . . . at each election for directors every shareholder entitled to vote at such election shall have the right to vote, in person or by proxy, the number of shares owned by him for as many persons as there are directors to be elected and for whose election he has a right to vote, or to cumulate his votes by giving one candidate as many votes as the number of such directors multiplied by the number of his shares shall equal, or by distributing such votes on the same principle among any number of such candidates.

Shares standing in the name of another corporation, domestic or foreign, may be voted by such officer, agent or proxy as the by-laws of such corporation may prescribe, or, in the absence of such provision, as the board of directors of such corporation may determine.

Shares held by an administrator, executor, guardian or conservator may be voted by him, either in person or by proxy, without a transfer of such shares into his name. Shares standing in the name of a trustee may be voted by him, either in person or by proxy, but no trustee shall be entitled to vote shares held by him without a transfer of such shares into his name.

Shares standing in the name of a receiver may be voted by such receiver, and shares held by or under the control of a receiver may be voted by such receiver without the transfer thereof into his name if authority so to do be contained in an appropriate order of the court by which such receiver was appointed.

A shareholder whose shares are pledged shall be entitled to vote such shares until the shares have been transferred into the name of the pledgee, and thereafter the pledgee shall be entitled to vote the shares so transferred.

On and after the date on which written notice of redemption of redeemable shares has been mailed to the holders thereof and a sum sufficient to redeem such shares has been deposited with a bank or trust company with irrevocable instruction and authority to pay the redemption price to the holders thereof upon surrender of certificates therefor, such shares shall not be entitled to vote on any matter and shall not be deemed to be outstanding shares.

§ 32. Voting Trust

Any number of shareholders of a corporation may create a voting trust for the purpose of conferring upon a trustee or trustees the right to vote or otherwise represent their shares, for a period of not to exceed ten years, by entering into a written voting trust agreement specifying the terms and conditions of the voting trust, by depositing a counterpart of the agreement with the corporation at its registered office, and by transferring their shares to such trustee or trustees for the purposes of the agreement. The counterpart of the voting trust agreement, so deposited with the corporation shall be subject to the same right of examination by a shareholder of the corporation, in person or by agent or attorney, as are the books and records of the corporation, and shall be subject to examination by any holder of a beneficial interest in the voting trust, either in person or by agent or attorney, at any reasonable time for any proper purpose.

§ 33. Board of Directors

The business and affairs of a corporation shall be managed by a board of directors. Directors need not be residents of this State or shareholders of the corporation unless the ar-

ticles of incorporation or by-laws so require. The articles of incorporation or by-laws may prescribe other qualifications for directors. The board of directors shall have authority to fix the compensation of directors unless otherwise provided in the articles of incorporation.

§ 34. Number and Election of Directors

The number of directors of a corporation shall be not less than three. Subject to such limitation, the number of directors shall be fixed by the by-laws, except as to the number constituting the initial board of directors, which number shall be fixed by the articles of incorporation. The number of directors may be increased or decreased from time to time by amendment to the by-laws, but no decrease shall have the effect of shortening the term of any incumbent director. In the absence of a by-law fixing the number of directors, the number shall be the same as that stated in the articles of incorporation. The names and addresses of the members of the first board of directors shall be stated in the articles of incorporation. Such persons shall hold office until the first annual meeting of shareholders, and until their successors shall have been elected and qualified. At the first annual meeting of shareholders and at each annual meeting thereafter the shareholders shall elect directors to hold office until the next succeeding annual meeting, except in case of the classification of directors as permitted by this Act. Each director shall hold office for the term for which he is elected and until his successor shall have been elected and qualified.

§ 35. Classification of Directors

When the board of directors shall consist of nine or more members, in lieu of electing the whole number of directors annually, the articles of incorporation may provide that the directors be divided into either two or three classes, each class to be as nearly equal in number as possible, the term of office of directors of the first class to expire at the first annual meeting of shareholders after their election, that of the second class to expire at the second annual meeting after their election, and that of the third class, if any, to expire at the third annual meeting after their election. At each annual meeting after such classification the number of directors equal to the number of the class whose term expires at the time of such meeting shall be elected to hold office until the second succeeding annual meeting, if there be two classes, or until the third succeeding annual meeting, if there be three classes. No classification of directors shall be effective prior to the first annual meeting of shareholders.

§ 36. Vacancies

Any vacancy occurring in the board of directors may be filled by the affirmative vote of a majority of the remaining directors though less than a quorum of the board of directors. A director elected to fill a vacancy shall be elected for the unexpired term of his predecessor in office. Any directorship to be filled by reason of an increase in the number of directors may be filled by the board of directors for a term of office continuing only until the next election of directors by the shareholders.

[Optional] § 36A. Removal of Directors

At a meeting called expressly for that purpose, directors may be removed in the manner provided in this section. The entire board of directors may be removed, with or without cause, by a vote of the holders of a majority of the shares then entitled to vote at an election of directors.

†If less than the entire board is to be removed,

†If cumulative voting is permissive, the sentence should begin with the phrase "In the case of a corporation having cumulative voting,".

no one of the directors may be removed if the votes cast against his removal would be sufficient to elect him if then cumulatively voted at an election of the entire board of directors, or, if there be classes of directors, at an election of the class of directors of which he is a part.

Whenever the holders of the shares of any class are entitled to elect one or more directors by the provisions of the articles of incorporation, the provisions of this section shall apply, in respect of the removal of a director or directors so elected, to the vote of the holders of the outstanding shares of that class and not to the vote of the outstanding shares as a whole.

§ 37. Quorum of Directors

A majority of the number of directors fixed by the by-laws, or in the absence of a by-law fixing the number of directors, then of the number stated in the articles of incorporation, shall constitute a quorum for the transaction of business unless a greater number is required by the articles of incorporation or the by-laws. The act of the majority of the directors present at a meeting at which a quorum is present shall be the act of the board of directors, unless the act of a greater number is required by the articles of incorporation or the by-laws.

§ 38. Executive and Other Committees

If the articles of incorporation or the by-laws so provide, the board of directors, by resolution adopted by a majority of the full board of directors, may designate from among its members an executive committee and one or more other committees each of which, to the extent provided in such resolution or in the articles of incorporation or the by-laws of the corporation, shall have and may exercise all the authority of the board of directors, but no such committee shall have the authority of the board of directors in reference to amending the articles of incorporation, adopting a plan of merger or consolidation, recommending to the shareholders the sale, lease, exchange or other disposition of all or substantially all the property and assets of the corporation otherwise than in the usual and regular course of its business, recommending to the shareholders a voluntary dissolution of the corporation or a revocation thereof, or amending the by-laws of the corporation. The designation of any such committee and the delegation thereto of authority shall not operate to relieve the board of directors, or any member thereof, of any responsibility imposed by law.

§ 39. Place and Notice of Directors' Meetings

Meetings of the board of directors, regular or special, may be held either within or without this State.

Regular meetings of the board of directors may be held with or without notice as prescribed in the by-laws. Special meetings of the board of directors shall be held upon such notice as is prescribed in the by-laws. Attendance of a director at a meeting shall constitute a waiver of notice of such meeting, except where a director attends a meeting for the express purpose of objecting to the transaction of any business because the meeting is not lawfully called or convened. Neither the business to be transacted at, nor the purpose of, any regular or special meeting of the board of directors need be specified in the notice or waiver of notice of such meeting unless required by the by-laws.

[Optional] § 39A.   Action by Directors Without a Meeting

Unless otherwise provided by the articles of incorporation or by-laws, any action required by this Act to be taken at a meeting of the directors of a corporation, or any action which may be taken at a meeting of the directors or of a committee, may be taken without a meeting if a consent in writing, setting forth the action so to be taken, shall be signed before such action by all of the directors, or all of the members of the committee, as the case may be. Such consent shall have the same effect as a unanimous vote.

§ 40.   Dividends

The board of directors of a corporation may, from time to time, declare and the corporation may pay dividends on its outstanding shares in cash, property, or its own shares, except when the corporation is insolvent or when the payment thereof would render the corporation insolvent or when the declaration or payment thereof would be contrary to any restrictions contained in the articles of incorporation, subject to the following provisions:

(a) Dividends may be declared and paid in cash or property only out of the unreserved and unrestricted earned surplus of the corporation, except as otherwise provided in this section.

(b) If the articles of incorporation of a corporation engaged in the business of exploiting natural resources so provide, dividends may be declared and paid in cash out of the depletion reserves, but each such dividend shall be identified as a distribution of such reserves and the amount per share paid from such reserves shall be disclosed to the shareholders receiving the same concurrently with the distribution thereof.

(c) Dividends may be declared and paid in its own shares out of any treasury shares that have been reacquired out of surplus of the corporation.

(d) Dividends may be declared and paid in its own authorized but unissued shares out of any

unreserved and unrestricted surplus of the corporation upon the following conditions:

(1) If a dividend is payable in its own shares having a par value, such shares shall be issued at not less than the par value thereof and there shall be transferred to stated capital at the time such dividend is paid an amount of surplus at least equal to the aggregate par value of the shares to be issued as a dividend.

(2) If a dividend is payable in its own shares without par value, such shares shall be issued at such stated value as shall be fixed by the board of directors by resolution adopted at the time such dividend is declared, and there shall be transferred to stated capital at the time such dividend is paid an amount of surplus equal to the aggregate stated value so fixed in respect of such shares; and the amount per share so transferred to stated capital shall be disclosed to the shareholders receiving such dividend concurrently with the payment thereof.

(e) No dividend payable in shares of any class shall be paid to the holders of shares of any other class unless the articles of incorporation so provide or such payment is authorized by the affirmative vote or the written consent of the holders of at least a majority of the outstanding shares of the class in which the payment is to be made.

A split-up or division of the issued shares of any class into a greater number of shares of the same class without increasing the stated capital of the corporation shall not be construed to be a share dividend within the meaning of this section.

§ 41.   Distributions from Capital Surplus

The board of directors of a corporation may, from time to time, distribute to its shareholders out of capital surplus of the corporation a portion of its assets, in cash or property, subject to the following provisions:

(a) No such distribution shall be made at a time when the corporation is insolvent or when such distribution would render the corporation insolvent.

(b) No such distribution shall be made unless the articles of incorporation so provide or such distribution is authorized by the affirmative vote of the holders of a majority of the outstanding shares of each class whether or not entitled to vote thereon by the provisions of the articles of incorporation of the corporation.

(c) No such distribution shall be made to the holders of any class of shares unless all cumulative dividends accrued on all preferred or special classes of shares entitled to preferential dividends shall have been fully paid.

(d) No such distribution shall be made to the holders of any class of shares which would reduce the remaining net assets of the corporation below the aggregate preferential amount payable in event of voluntary liquidation to the holders of shares having preferential rights to the assets of the corporation in the event of liquidation.

(e) Each such distribution, when made, shall be identified as a distribution from capital surplus and the amount per share disclosed to the shareholders receiving the same concurrently with the distribution thereof.

The board of directors of a corporation may also, from time to time, distribute to the holders of its outstanding shares having a cumulative preferential right to receive dividends, in discharge of their cumulative dividend rights, dividends payable in cash out of the capital surplus of the corporation, if at the time the corporation has no earned surplus and is not insolvent and would not thereby be rendered insolvent. Each such distribution, when made, shall be identified as a payment of cumulative dividends out of capital surplus.

§ 42. Loans

No loans shall be made by a corporation to its officers or directors, and no loans shall be made by a corporation secured by its shares.

§ 43. Liability of Directors in Certain Cases

In addition to any other liabilities imposed by law upon directors of a corporation:

(a) Directors of a corporation who vote for or assent to the declaration of any dividend or other distribution of the assets of a corporation to its shareholders contrary to the provisions of this Act or contrary to any restrictions contained in the articles of incorporation, shall be jointly and severally liable to the corporation for the amount of such dividend which is paid or the value of such assets which are distributed in excess of the amount of such dividend or distribution which could have been paid or distrib-

uted without a violation of the provisions of this Act or the restrictions in the articles of incorporation.

(b) Directors of a corporation who vote for or assent to the purchase of its own shares contrary to the provisions of this Act shall be jointly and severally liable to the corporation for the amount of consideration paid for such shares which is in excess of the maximum amount which could have been paid therefor without a violation of the provisions of this Act.

(c) The directors of a corporation who vote for or assent to any distribution of assets of a corporation to its shareholders during the liquidation of the corporation without the payment and discharge of, or making adequate provision for, all known debts, obligations, and liabilities of the corporation shall be jointly and severally liable to the corporation for the value of such assets which are distributed, to the extent that such debts, obligations and liabilities of the corporation are not thereafter paid and discharged.

(d) The directors of a corporation who vote for or assent to the making of a loan to an officer or director of the corporation, or the making of any loan secured by shares of the corporation, shall be jointly and severally liable to the corporation for the amount of such loan until the repayment thereof.

(e) If a corporation shall commence business before it has received at least one thousand dollars as consideration for the issuance of shares, the directors who assent thereto shall be jointly and severally liable to the corporation for such part of one thousand dollars as shall not have been received before commencing business, but such liability shall be terminated when the corporation has actually received one thousand dollars as consideration for the issuance of shares.

A director of a corporation who is present at a meeting of its board of directors at which action on any corporate matter is taken shall be presumed to have assented to the action taken unless his dissent shall be entered in the minutes of the meeting or unless he shall file his written dissent to such action with the person acting as the secretary of the meeting before the adjournment thereof or shall forward such dissent by registered mail to the secretary of the corporation immediately after the adjournment of the meeting. Such right to dissent shall not apply to a director who voted in favor of such action.

A director shall not be liable under subparagraphs (a), (b) or (c) of this section if he relied and acted in good faith upon financial statements of the corporation represented to him to be correct by the president or the officer of such corporation having charge of its books of account, or stated in a written report by an independent public or certified public accountant or firm of such accountants fairly to reflect the financial condition of such corporation, nor shall he be so liable, if in good faith in determining the amount available for any such dividend or distribution he considered the assets to be of their book value.

Any director against whom a claim shall be asserted under or pursuant to this section for the payment of a dividend or other distribution of assets of a corporation and who shall be held liable thereon, shall be entitled to contribution from the shareholders who accepted or received any such dividend or assets, knowing such dividend or distribution to have been made in violation of this Act, in proportion to the amounts received by them respectively.

Any director against whom a claim shall be asserted under or pursuant to this section shall be entitled to contribution from the other directors who voted for or assented to the action upon which the claim is asserted.

[Optional] § 43A. Provisions Relating to Actions by Shareholders

No action shall be brought in this State by a shareholder in the right of a domestic or foreign corporation unless the plaintiff was a holder of record of shares or of voting trust certificates therefor at the time of the transaction of which he complains, or his shares or voting trust certificates thereafter devolved upon him by operation of law from a person who was a holder of record at such time.

In any action hereafter instituted in the right of any domestic or foreign corporation by the holder or holders of record of shares of such corporation or of voting trust certificates therefor, the court having jurisdiction, upon final judgment and a finding that the action was brought without reasonable cause, may require the plaintiff or plaintiffs to pay to the parties named as defendant the reasonable expenses, including fees of attorneys, incurred by them in the defense of such action.

In any action now pending or hereafter instituted or maintained in the right of any domestic or foreign corporation by the holder or holders of record of less than five per cent of the outstanding shares of any class of such corporation or of voting trust certificates therefor, unless the shares or voting trust certificates so held have a market value in excess of twenty-five thousand dollars, the corporation in whose right such action is brought shall be entitled at any time before final judgment to require the plaintiff or plaintiffs to give security for the reasonable expenses, including fees of attorneys, that may be incurred by it in connection with such action or may be incurred by other parties named as defendant for which it may become legally liable. Market value shall be determined as of the date that the plaintiff institutes the action or, in the case of an intervenor, as of the date that he becomes a party to the action. The amount of such security may from time to time be increased or decreased, in the discretion of the court, upon showing that the security provided has or may become inadequate or is excessive. The corporation shall have recourse to such security in such amount as the court having jurisdiction shall determine upon the termination of such action, whether or not the court finds the action was brought without reasonable cause.

§ 44. Officers

The officers of a corporation shall consist of a president, one or more vice presidents as may be prescribed by the by-laws, a secretary, and a treasurer, each of whom shall be elected by the board of directors at such time and in such manner as may be prescribed by the by-laws. Such other officers and assistant officers and agents as may be deemed necessary may be elected or appointed by the board of directors or chosen in such other manner as may be prescribed by the by-laws. Any two or more offices may be held by the same person, except the offices of president and secretary.

All officers and agents of the corporation, as between themselves and the corporation, shall have such authority and perform such duties in the management of the corporation as may be provided in the by-laws, or as may be determined by resolution of the board of directors not inconsistent with the by-laws.

§ 45. Removal of Officers

Any officer or agent may be removed by the board of directors whenever in its judgment the best interests of the corporation will be served thereby, but such removal shall be without prejudice to the contract rights, if any, of the person so removed. Election or appointment of an officer or agent shall not of itself create contract rights.

§ 46. Books and Records

Each corporation shall keep correct and complete books and records of account and shall keep minutes of the proceedings of its shareholders and board of directors; and shall keep at its registered office or principal place of business, or at the office of its transfer agent or register, a record of its shareholders, giving the names and addresses of all shareholders and the number and class of the shares held by each.

Any person who shall have been a shareholder of record for at least six months immediately preceding his demand or who shall be the holder of record of at least five per cent of all the outstanding shares of a corporation, upon written demand stating the purpose thereof, shall have the right to examine, in person, or by agent or attorney, at any reasonable time or times, for any proper purpose, its books and records of account, minutes and record of shareholders and to make extracts therefrom.

Any officer or agent who, or a corporation which, shall refuse to allow any such shareholder, or his agent or attorney, so to examine and make extracts from its books and records of account, minutes, and record of shareholders, for any proper purpose, shall be liable to such shareholder in a penalty of ten per cent of the value of the shares owned by such shareholder, in addition to any other damages or remedy afforded him by law. It shall be a defense to any action for penalties under this section that the person suing therefor has within two years sold or offered for sale any list of shareholders of such corporation or any other corporation or has aided or abetted any person in procuring any list of shareholders for any such purpose, or has improperly used any information secured through any prior examination of the books and records of account, or minutes, or record of shareholders of such corporation or any other corporation,

or was not acting in good faith or for a proper purpose in making his demand.

Nothing herein contained shall impair the power of any court of competent jurisdiction, upon proof by a shareholder of proper purpose, irrespective of the period of time during which such shareholder shall have been a shareholder of record, and irrespective of the number of shares held by him, to compel the production for examination by such shareholder of the books and records of account, minutes, and record of shareholders of a corporation.

Upon the written request of any shareholder of a corporation, the corporation shall mail to such shareholder its most recent financial statements showing in reasonable detail its assets and liabilities and the results of its operations.

§ 47. Incorporators

One or more persons, or a domestic or foreign corporation, may act as incorporator or incorporators of a corporation by signing and delivering in duplicate to the Secretary of State articles of incorporation for such corporation.

§ 48. Articles of Incorporation

The articles of incorporation shall set forth:

(a) The name of the corporation.

(b) The period of duration, which may be perpetual.

(c) The purpose or purposes for which the corporation is organized.

(d) The aggregate number of shares which the corporation shall have authority to issue; if such shares are to consist of one class only, the par value of each of such shares, or a statement that all of such shares are without par value; or, if such shares are to be divided into classes, the number of shares of each class, and a statement of the par value of the shares of each such class or that such shares are to be without par value.

(e) If the shares are to be divided into classes, the designation of each class and a statement of the preferences, limitations and relative rights in respect of the shares of each class.

(f) If the corporation is to issue the shares of any preferred or special class in series, then the designation of each series and a statement of the variations in the relative rights and preferences as between series in so far as the same are to be fixed in the articles of incorporation, and a statement of any authority to be vested in the board of directors to establish series and fix and determine the variations in the relative rights and preferences as between series.

(g) A statement that the corporation will not commence business until consideration of the value of at least one thousand dollars has been received for the issuance of shares.

(h) Any provision limiting or denying to shareholders the preemptive right to acquire additional or treasury shares of the corporation.

(i) Any provision, not inconsistent with law, which the incorporators elect to set forth in the articles of incorporation for the regulation of the internal affairs of the corporation, including any provision restricting the transfer of shares and any provision which under this Act is required or permitted to be set forth in the by-laws.

(j) The address of its initial registered office, and the name of its initial registered agent at such address.

(k) The number of directors constituting the initial board of directors and the names and addresses of the persons who are to serve as directors until the first annual meeting of shareholders or until their successors be elected and qualify.

(*l*) The name and address of each incorporator.

It shall not be necessary to set forth in the articles of incorporation any of the corporate powers enumerated in this Act.

§ 49. Filing of Articles of Incorporation

Duplicate originals of the articles of incorporation shall be delivered to the Secretary of State. If the Secretary of State finds that the articles of incorporation conform to law, he shall, when all fees have been paid as in this Act prescribed:

(1) Endorse on each of such duplicate originals the word "Filed," and the month, day and year of the filing thereof.

(2) File one of such duplicate originals in his office.

(3) Issue a certificate of incorporation to which he shall affix the other duplicate original.

The certificate of incorporation, together with the duplicate original of the articles of incorporation affixed thereto by the Secretary of State, shall be returned to the incorporators or their representative.

§ 50. Effect of Issuance of Certificate of Incorporation

Upon the issuance of the certificate of incorporation, the corporate existence shall begin, and such certificate of incorporation shall be conclusive evidence that all conditions precedent required to be performed by the incorporators have been complied with and that the corporation has been incorporated under this Act, except as against this State in a proceeding to cancel or revoke the certificate of incorporation or for involuntary dissolution of the corporation.

§ 51. Requirement before Commencing Business

A corporation shall not transact any business or incur any indebtedness, except such as shall be incidental to its organization or to obtaining subscriptions to or payment for its shares, until there has been paid in for the issuance of shares consideration of the value of at least one thousand dollars.

§ 52. Organization Meeting of Directors

After the issuance of the certificate of incorporation an organization meeting of the board of directors named in the articles of incorporation shall be held, either within or without this State, at the call of a majority of the incorporators, for the purpose of adopting by-laws, electing officers and the transaction of such other business as may come before the meeting. The incorporators calling the meeting shall give at least three days' notice thereof by mail to each director so named, which notice shall state the time and place of the meeting.

§ 53. Right to Amend Articles of Incorporation

A corporation may amend its articles of incorporation, from time to time, in any and as many respects as may be desired, so long as its articles of incorporation as amended contain only such provisions as might be lawfully contained in original articles of incorporation at the time of making such amendment, and, if a change in shares or the rights of shareholders, or an exchange, reclassification or cancellation of shares or rights of shareholders is to be made, such provisions as may be necessary to effect such change, exchange, reclassification or cancellation.

In particular, and without limitation upon such general power of amendment, a corporation may amend its articles of incorporation, from time to time, so as:

(a) To change its corporate name.

(b) To change its period of duration.

(c) To change, enlarge or diminish its corporate purposes.

(d) To increase or decrease the aggregate number of shares, or shares of any class, which the corporation has authority to issue.

(e) To increase or decrease the par value of the authorized shares of any class having a par value, whether issued or unissued.

(f) To exchange, classify, reclassify or cancel all or any part of its shares, whether issued or unissued.

(g) To change the designation of all or any part of its shares, whether issued or unissued, and to change the preferences, limitations, and the relative rights in respect of all or any part of its shares, whether issued or unissued.

(h) To change shares having a par value, whether issued or unissued, into the same or a different number of shares without par value, and to change shares without par value, whether issued or unissued, into the same or a different number of shares having a par value.

(i) To change the shares of any class, whether issued or unissued, and whether with or without par value, into a different number of shares of the same class or into the same or a different number of shares, either with or without par value, of other classes.

(j) To create new classes of shares having rights and preferences either prior and superior or subordinate and inferior to the shares of any class then authorized, whether issued or unissued.

(k) To cancel or otherwise affect the right of the holders of the shares of any class to re-ceive dividends which have accrued but have not been declared.

(l) To divide any preferred or special class of shares, whether issued or unissued, into series and fix and determine the designations of such series and the variations in the relative rights and preferences as between the shares of such series.

(m) To authorize the board of directors to establish, out of authorized but unissued shares, series of any preferred or special class of shares and fix and determine the relative rights and preferences of the shares of any series so established.

(n) To authorize the board of directors to fix and determine the relative rights and preferences of the authorized but unissued shares of series theretofore established in respect of which either the relative rights and preferences have not been fixed and determined or the relative rights and preferences theretofore fixed and determined are to be changed.

(o) To revoke, diminish, or enlarge the authority of the board of directors to establish series out of authorized but unissued shares of any preferred or special class and fix and determine the relative rights and preferences of the shares of any series so established.

(p) To limit, deny or grant to shareholders of any class the preemptive right to acquire additional or treasury shares of the corporation, whether then or thereafter authorized.

§ 54. Procedure to Amend Articles of Incorporation

Amendments to the articles of incorporation shall be made in the following manner:

(a) The board of directors shall adopt a resolution setting forth the proposed amendment and directing that it be submitted to a vote at a meeting of shareholders, which may be either an annual or a special meeting.

(b) Written notice setting forth the proposed amendment or a summary of the changes to be effected thereby shall be given to each shareholder of record entitled to vote thereon within the time and in the manner provided in this Act for the giving of notice of meetings of shareholders. If the meeting be an annual meeting, the proposed amendment or such summary may be included in the notice of such annual meeting.

(c) At such meeting a vote of the shareholders entitled to vote thereon shall be taken on the proposed amendment. The proposed amendment shall be adopted upon receiving the affirmative vote of the holders of two-thirds of the shares entitled to vote thereon, unless any class of shares is entitled to vote thereon as a class, in which event the proposed amendment shall be adopted upon receiving the affirmative vote of the holders of two-thirds of the shares of each class of shares entitled to vote thereon as a class and of the total shares entitled to vote thereon.

Any number of amendments may be submitted to the shareholders, and voted upon by them, at one meeting.

§ 55. Class Voting on Amendments

The holders of the outstanding shares of a class shall be entitled to vote as a class upon a proposed amendment, whether or not entitled to vote thereon by the provisions of the articles of incorporation, if the amendment would:

(a) Increase or decrease the aggregate number of authorized shares of such class.

(b) Increase or decrease the par value of the shares of such class.

(c) Effect an exchange, reclassification or cancellation of all or part of the shares of such class.

(d) Effect an exchange, or create a right of exchange, of all or any part of the shares of another class into the shares of such class.

(e) Change the designations, preferences, limitations or relative rights of the shares of such class.

(f) Change the shares of such class, whether with or without par value, into the same or a different number of shares, either with or without par value, of the same class or another class or classes.

(g) Create a new class of shares having rights and preferences prior and superior to the shares of such class, or increase the rights and preferences of any class having rights and preferences prior or superior to the shares of such class.

(h) In the case of a preferred or special class of shares, divide the shares of such class into series and fix and determine the designation of such series and the variations in the relative rights and preferences between the shares of such series, or authorize the board of directors to do so.

(i) Limit or deny the existing preemptive rights of the shares of such class.

(j) Cancel or otherwise affect dividends on the shares of such class which have accrued but have not been declared.

§ 56. Articles of Amendment

The articles of amendment shall be executed in duplicate by the corporation by its president or a vice president and by its secretary or an assistant secretary, and verified by one of the officers signing such articles, and shall set forth:

(a) The name of the corporation.

(b) The amendment so adopted.

(c) The date of the adoption of the amendment by the shareholders.

(d) The number of shares outstanding, and the number of shares entitled to vote thereon, and if the shares of any class are entitled to vote thereon as a class, the designation and number of outstanding shares entitled to vote thereon of each such class.

(e) The number of shares voted for and against such amendment, respectively, and, if the shares of any class are entitled to vote thereon as a class, the number of shares of each such class voted for and against such amendment, respectively.

(f) If such amendment provides for an exchange, reclassification or cancellation of issued shares, and if the manner in which the same shall be effected is not set forth in the amendment, then a statement of the manner in which the same shall be effected.

(g) If such amendment effects a change in the amount of stated capital, then a statement of the manner in which the same is effected and a statement, expressed in dollars, of the amount of stated capital as changed by such amendment.

§ 57. Filing of Articles of Amendment

Duplicate originals of the articles of amendment shall be delivered to the Secretary of State. If the Secretary of State finds that the articles of amendment conform to law, he shall, when all fees and franchise taxes have been paid as in this Act prescribed:

(1) Endorse on each of such duplicate originals the word "Filed," and the month, day and year of the filing thereof.

(2) File one of such duplicate originals in his office.

(3) Issue a certificate of amendment to which he shall affix the other duplicate original.

The certificate of amendment, together with the duplicate original of the articles of amendment affixed thereto by the Secretary of State, shall be returned to the corporation or its representative.

§ 58. Effect of Certificate of Amendment

Upon the issuance of the certificate of amendment by the Secretary of State, the amendment shall become effective and the articles of incorporation shall be deemed to be amended accordingly.

No amendment shall affect any existing cause of action in favor of or against such corporation, or any pending suit to which such corporation shall be a party, or the existing rights of persons other than shareholders; and, in the event the corporate name shall be changed by amendment, no suit brought by or against such corporation under its former name shall abate for that reason.

§ 59. Restated Articles of Incorporation

A domestic corporation may at any time restate its articles of incorporation as theretofore amended, in the following manner:

(A) The board of directors shall adopt a resolution setting forth the proposed restated articles of incorporation and directing that they be submitted to a vote at a meeting of shareholders, which may be either an annual or a special meeting.

(B) Written notice setting forth the proposed restated articles shall be given to each shareholder of record entitled to vote thereon within the time and in the manner provided in this Act for the giving of notice of meetings of shareholders. If the meeting be an annual meeting, the proposed restated articles may be included in the notice of such annual meeting.

(C) At such meeting a vote of the shareholders entitled to vote thereon shall be taken on the proposed restated articles. The pro-posed restated articles shall be adopted upon receiving the affirmative vote of the holders of a majority of the shares entitled to vote thereon.

Upon such approval, restated articles of incorporation shall be executed in duplicate by the corporation by its president or a vice president and by its secretary or assistant secretary, and verified by one of the officers signing such articles, and shall set forth:

(a) The name of the corporation.

(b) The period of its duration.

(c) The purpose or purposes which the corporation is then authorized to pursue.

(d) The aggregate number of shares which the corporation has authority to issue; if such shares consist of one class only, the par value of each of such shares, or a statement that all of such shares are without par value; or, if such shares are divided into classes, the number of shares of each class, and a statement of the par value of the shares of each such class or that such shares are without par value.

(e) If the shares are divided into classes, the designation of each class and a statement of the preferences, limitations and relative rights in respect of the shares of each class.

(f) If the shares of any preferred or special class are issuable in series, the designation of each series and a statement of the variations in the relative rights and preferences as between series in so far as the same have been fixed, and a statement of any authority vested in the board of directors to establish series and fix and determine the variations in the relative rights and preferences as between series.

(g) Any existing provision limiting or denying to shareholders the preemptive right to acquire additional or treasury shares of the corporation.

(h) Any provisions, not inconsistent with law, which are then set forth in the articles of incorporation as theretofore amended, for the regulation of the internal affairs of the corporation.

(i) A statement that the restated articles of incorporation correctly set forth without change the corresponding provisions of the articles of incorporation as theretofore amended, and that the restated articles of incorporation supersede the original articles of incorporation and all amendments thereto.

Duplicate originals of the restated articles of incorporation shall be delivered to the Secretary of State. If the Secretary of State finds that such restated articles of incorporation conform to law, he shall, when all fees and franchise taxes have been paid as in this Act prescribed:

(1) Endorse on each of such duplicate originals the word "Filed," and the month, day and year of the filing thereof.

(2) File one of such duplicate originals in his office.

(3) Issue a restated certificate of incorporation to which he shall affix the other duplicate original.

The restated certificate of incorporation, together with the duplicate original of the restated articles of incorporation affixed thereto by the Secretary of State, shall be returned to the corporation or its representative.

Upon the issuance of the restated certificate of incorporation by the Secretary of State, the restated articles of incorporation shall become effective and shall supersede the original articles of incorporation and all amendments thereto.

[Optional] § 59A. Amendment of Articles of Incorporation in Reorganization Proceedings

Whenever a plan of reorganization of a corporation has been confirmed by decree or order of a court of competent jurisdiction in proceedings for the reorganization of such corporation, pursuant to the provisions of any applicable statute of the United States relating to reorganizations of corporations, the articles of incorporation of the corporation may be amended, in the manner provided in this section, in as many respects as may be necessary to carry out the plan and put it into effect, so long as the articles of incorporation as amended contain only such provisions as might be lawfully contained in original articles of incorporation at the time of making such amendment.

In particular and without limitation upon such general power of amendment, the articles of incorporation may be amended for such purpose so as to:

(a) Change the corporate name, period of duration or corporate purposes of the corporation;

(b) Repeal, alter or amend the by-laws of the corporation;

(c) Change the aggregate number of shares, or shares of any class, which the corporation has authority to issue;

(d) Change the preferences, limitations and relative rights in respect of all or any part of the shares of the corporation, and classify, reclassify or cancel all or any part thereof, whether issued or unissued;

(e) Authorize the issuance of bonds, debentures or other obligations of the corporation, whether or not convertible into shares of any class or bearing warrants or other evidences of optional rights to purchase or subscribe for shares of any class, and fix the terms and conditions thereof; and

(f) Constitute or reconstitute and classify or reclassify the board of directors of the corporation, and appoint directors and officers in place of or in addition to all or any of the directors or officers then in office.

Amendments to the articles of incorporation pursuant to this section shall be made in the following manner:

(a) Articles of amendment approved by decree or order of such court shall be executed and verified in duplicate by such person or persons as the court shall designate or appoint for the purpose, and shall set forth the name of the corporation, the amendments of the articles of incorporation approved by the court, the date of the decree or order approving the articles of amendment, the title of the proceedings in which the decree or order was entered, and a statement that such decree or order was entered by a court having jurisdiction of the proceedings for the reorganization of the corporation pursuant to the provisions of an applicable statute of the United States.

(b) Duplicate originals of the articles of amendment shall be delivered to the Secretary of State. If the Secretary of State finds that the articles of amendment conform to law, he shall, when all fees and franchise taxes have been paid as in this Act prescribed:

(1) Endorse on each of such duplicate originals the word "Filed," and the month, day and year of the filing thereof.

(2) File one of such duplicate originals in his office.

(3) Issue a certificate of amendment to which he shall affix the other duplicate original.

The certificate of amendment, together with the duplicate original of the articles of amendment affixed thereto by the Secretary of State, shall be returned to the corporation or its representative.

Upon the issuance of the certificate of amendment by the Secretary of State, the amendment shall become effective and the articles of incorporation shall be deemed to be amended accordingly, without any action thereon by the directors or shareholders of the corporation and with the same effect as if the amendments had been adopted by unanimous action of the directors and shareholders of the corporation.

§ 60. Restriction on Redemption or Purchase of Redeemable Shares

No redemption or purchase of redeemable shares shall be made by a corporation when it is insolvent or when such redemption or purchase would render it insolvent, or which would reduce the net assets below the aggregate amount payable to the holders of shares having prior or equal rights to the assets of the corporation upon involuntary dissolution.

§ 61. Cancellation of Redeemable Shares by Redemption or Purchase

When redeemable shares of a corporation are redeemed or purchased by the corporation, the redemption or purchase shall effect a cancellation of such shares, and a statement of cancellation shall be filed as provided in this section. Thereupon such shares shall be restored to the status of authorized but unissued shares, unless the articles of incorporation provide that such shares when redeemed or purchased shall not be reissued, in which case the filing of the statement of cancellation shall constitute an amendment to the articles of incorporation and shall reduce the number of shares of the class so cancelled which the corporation is authorized to issue by the number of shares so cancelled.

The statement of cancellation shall be executed in duplicate by the corporation by its president or a vice president and by its secretary or an assistant secretary, and verified by one of the officers signing such statement, and shall set forth:

(a) The name of the corporation.

(b) The number of redeemable shares cancelled through redemption or purchase, itemized by classes and series.

(c) The aggregate number of issued shares, itemized by classes and series, after giving effect to such cancellation.

(d) The amount, expressed in dollars, of the stated capital of the corporation after giving effect of such cancellation.

(e) If the articles of incorporation provide that the cancelled shares shall not be reissued, then the number of shares which the corporation has authority to issue, itemized by classes and series, after giving effect to such cancellation.

Duplicate originals of such statement shall be delivered to the Secretary of State. If the Secretary of State finds that such statement conforms to law, he shall, when all fees and franchise taxes have been paid as in this Act prescribed:

(1) Endorse on each of such duplicate originals the word "Filed," and the month, day and year of the filing thereof.

(2) File one of such duplicate originals in his office.

(3) Return the other duplicate original to the corporation or its representative.

Upon the filing of such statement of cancellation, the stated capital of the corporation shall be deemed to be reduced by that part of the stated capital which was, at the time of such cancellation, represented by the shares so cancelled.

Nothing contained in this section shall be construed to forbid a cancellation of shares or a reduction of stated capital in any other manner permitted by this Act.

§ 62. Cancellation of Other Reacquired Shares

A corporation may at any time, by resolution of its board of directors, cancel all or any part of the shares of the corporation of any class reacquired by it, other than redeemable shares redeemed or purchased, and in such event a statement of cancellation shall be filed as provided in this section.

The statement of cancellation shall be executed in duplicate by the corporation by its president or a vice president and by its secretary or an assistant secretary, and verified by one of the officers signing such statement, and shall set forth:

(a) The name of the corporation.

(b) The number of reacquired shares cancelled by resolution duly adopted by the board of directors, itemized by classes and series, and the date of its adoption.

(c) The aggregate number of issued shares, itemized by classes and series, after giving effect to such cancellation.

(d) The amount, expressed in dollars, of the stated capital of the corporation after giving effect to such cancellation.

Duplicate originals of such statement shall be delivered to the Secretary of State. If the Secretary of State finds that such statement conforms to law, he shall, when all fees and franchise taxes have been paid as in this Act prescribed:

(1) Endorse on each of such duplicate originals the word "Filed," and the month, day and year of the filing thereof.

(2) File one of such duplicate originals in his office.

(3) Return the other duplicate original to the corporation or its representative.

Upon the filing of such statement of cancellation, the stated capital of the corporation shall be deemed to be reduced by that part of the stated capital which was, at the time of such cancellation, represented by the shares so cancelled, and the shares so cancelled shall be restored to the status of authorized but unissued shares.

Nothing contained in this section shall be construed to forbid a cancellation of shares or a reduction of stated capital in any other manner permitted by this Act.

§ 63. Reduction of Stated Capital in Certain Cases

A reduction of the stated capital of a corporation, where such reduction is not accompanied by any action requiring an amendment of the articles of incorporation and not accompanied by a cancellation of shares, may be made in the following manner:

(A) The board of directors shall adopt a resolution setting forth the amount of the proposed reduction and the manner in which the reduction shall be effected, and directing that the question of such reduction be submitted to a vote at a meeting of shareholders, which may be either an annual or a special meeting.

(B) Written notice, stating that the purpose or one of the purposes of such meeting is to consider the question of reducing the stated capital of the corporation in the amount and manner proposed by the board of directors, shall be given to each shareholder of record entitled to vote thereon within the time and in the manner provided in this Act for the giving of notice of meetings of shareholders.

(C) At such meeting a vote of the shareholders entitled to vote thereon shall be taken on the question of approving the proposed reduction of stated capital, which shall require for its adoption the affirmative vote of the holders of a majority of the shares entitled to vote thereon.

When a reduction of the stated capital of a corporation has been approved as provided in this section, a statement shall be executed in duplicate by the corporation by its president or a vice president and by its secretary or an assistant secretary, and verified by one of the officers signing such statement, and shall set forth:

(a) The name of the corporation.

(b) A copy of the resolution of the shareholders approving such reduction, and the date of its adoption.

(c) The number of shares outstanding, and the number of shares entitled to vote thereon.

(d) The number of shares voted for and against such reduction, respectively.

(e) A statement of the manner in which such reduction is effected, and a statement, expressed in dollars, of the amount of stated capital of the corporation after giving effect to such reduction.

Duplicate originals of such statement shall be delivered to the Secretary of State. If the Secretary of State finds that such statement conforms to law, he shall, when all fees and franchise taxes have been paid as in this Act prescribed:

(1) Endorse on each of such duplicate originals the word "Filed," and the month, day and year of the filing thereof.

(2) File one of such duplicate originals in his office.

(3) Return the other duplicate original to the corporation or its representative.

Upon the filing of such statement, the stated capital of the corporation shall be reduced as therein set forth.

No reduction of stated capital shall be made under the provisions of this section which would reduce the amount of the aggregate stated capital of the corporation to an amount equal to or less than the aggregate preferential amounts payable upon all issued shares having a preferential right in the assets of the corporation in the event of involuntary liquidation, plus the aggregate par value of all issued shares having a par value but no preferential right in the assets of the corporation in the event of involuntary liquidation.

§ 64. Special Provisions Relating to Surplus and Reserves

The surplus, if any, created by or arising out of a reduction of the stated capital of a corporation shall be capital surplus.

The capital surplus of a corporation may be increased from time to time by resolution of the board of directors directing that all or a part of the earned surplus of the corporation be transferred to capital surplus.

A corporation may, by resolution of its board of directors, apply any part or all of its capital surplus to the reduction or elimination of any deficit arising from losses, however incurred, but only after first eliminating the earned surplus, if any, of the corporation by applying such losses against earned surplus and only to the extent that such losses exceed the earned surplus, if any. Each such application of capital surplus shall, to the extent thereof, effect a reduction of capital surplus.

A corporation may, by resolution of its board of directors, create a reserve or reserves out of its earned surplus for any proper purpose or purposes, and may abolish any such reserve in the same manner. Earned surplus of the corporation to the extent so reserved shall not be available for the payment of dividends or other distributions by the corporation except as expressly permitted by this Act.

§ 65. Procedure for Merger

Any two or more domestic corporations may merge into one of such corporations pursuant to a plan of merger approved in the manner provided in this Act.

The board of directors of each corporation shall, by resolution adopted by each such board, approve a plan of merger setting forth:

(a) The names of the corporations proposing to merge, and the name of the corporation into which they propose to merge, which is hereinafter designated as the surviving corporation.

(b) The terms and conditions of the proposed merger.

(c) The manner and basis of converting the shares of each merging corporation into shares or other securities or obligations of the surviving corporation.

(d) A statement of any changes in the articles of incorporation of the surviving corporation to be effected by such merger.

(e) Such other provisions with respect to the proposed merger as are deemed necessary or desirable.

§ 66. Procedure for Consolidation

Any two or more domestic corporations may consolidate into a new corporation pursuant to a plan of consolidation approved in the manner provided in this Act.

The board of directors of each corporation shall, by a resolution adopted by each such board, approve a plan of consolidation setting forth:

(a) The names of the corporations proposing to consolidate, and the name of the new corporation into which they propose to consolidate, which is hereinafter designated as the new corporation.

(b) The terms and conditions of the proposed consolidation.

(c) The manner and basis of converting the shares of each corporation into shares or other securities or obligations of the new corporation.

(d) With respect to the new corporation, all of the statements required to be set forth in articles of incorporation for corporations organized under this Act.

(e) Such other provisions with respect to the proposed consolidation as are deemed necessary or desirable.

§ 67. Approval by Shareholders

The board of directors of each corporation, upon approving such plan of merger or plan of consolidation, shall, by resolution, direct that the plan be submitted to a vote at a meeting of shareholders, which may be either an annual or a special meeting. Written notice shall be given to each shareholder of record, whether or not entitled to vote at such meeting, not less than twenty days before such meeting, in the manner provided in this Act for the giving of notice of meetings of shareholders, and, whether the meeting be an annual or a special meeting, shall state that the purpose or one of the purposes is to consider the proposed plan of merger or consolidation. A copy or a summary of the plan of merger or plan of consolidation, as the case may be, shall be included in or enclosed with such notice.

At each such meeting, a vote of the shareholders shall be taken on the proposed plan of merger or consolidation. The plan of merger or consolidation shall be approved upon receiving the affirmative vote of the holders of two-thirds of the shares entitled to vote thereon of each such corporation, unless any class of shares of any such corporation is entitled to vote thereon as a class, in which event, as to such corporation, the plan of merger or consolidation shall be approved upon receiving the affirmative vote of the holders of two-thirds of the shares of each class of shares entitled to vote thereon as a class and of the total shares entitled to vote thereon. Any class of shares of any such corporation shall be entitled to vote as a class if the plan of merger or consolidation, as the case may be, contains any provision which, if contained in a proposed amendment to articles of incorporation, would entitle such class of shares to vote as a class.

After such approval by a vote of the shareholders of each corporation, and at any time prior to the filing of the articles of merger or consolidation, the merger or consolidation may be abandoned pursuant to provisions therefor, if any, set forth in the plan of merger or consolidation.

§ 68. Articles of Merger or Consolidation

Upon such approval, articles of merger or articles of consolidation shall be executed in duplicate by each corporation by its president or a vice president and by its secretary or an assistant secretary, and verified by one of the officers of each corporation signing such articles, and shall set forth:

(a) The plan of merger or the plan of consolidation.

(b) As to each corporation, the number of shares outstanding, and, if the shares of any class are entitled to vote as a class, the designation and number of outstanding shares of each such class.

(c) As to each corporation, the number of shares voted for and against such plan, respectively, and, if the shares of any class are entitled to vote as a class, the number of shares of each such class voted for and against such plan, respectively.

Duplicate originals of the articles of merger or articles of consolidation shall be delivered to the Secretary of State. If the Secretary of State finds that such articles conform to law, he shall, when all fees and franchise taxes have been paid as in this Act prescribed:

(1) Endorse on each of such duplicate originals the word "Filed," and the month, day and year of the filing thereof.

(2) File one of such duplicate originals in his office.

(3) Issue a certificate of merger or a certificate of consolidation to which he shall affix the other duplicate original.

The certificate of merger or certificate of consolidation, together with the duplicate original of the articles of merger or articles of consolidation affixed thereto by the Secretary of State, shall be returned to the surviving or new corporation, as the case may be, or its representative.

[Optional] § 68A. Merger of Subsidiary Corporation

Any corporation owning at least ninety-five per cent of the outstanding shares of each class of another corporation may merge such other corporation into itself without approval by a vote of the shareholders of either corporation. Its board of directors shall, by resolution, approve a plan of merger setting forth:

(a) The name of the subsidiary corporation and the name of the corporation owning at least ninety-five per cent of its shares, which is hereinafter designated as the surviving corporation.

(b) The manner and basis of converting the shares of the subsidiary corporation into shares or other securities or obligations of the surviving corporation or the cash or other consideration to be paid or delivered upon surrender of each share of the subsidiary corporation.

A copy of such plan of merger shall be mailed to each shareholder of record of the subsidiary corporation.

Articles of merger shall be executed in duplicate by the surviving corporation by its president or a vice president and by its secretary or an assistant secretary, and verified by one of its officers signing such articles, and shall set forth:

(a) The plan of merger;

(b) The number of outstanding shares of each class of the subsidiary corporation and the number of such shares of each class owned by the surviving corporation; and

(c) The date of the mailing to shareholders of the subsidiary corporation of a copy of the plan of merger.

On and after the thirtieth day after the mailing of a copy of the plan of merger to shareholders of the subsidiary corporation or upon the waiver thereof by the holders of all outstanding shares duplicate originals of the articles of merger shall be delivered to the Secretary of State. If the Secretary of State finds that such articles conform to law, he shall, when all fees and franchise taxes have been paid as in this Act prescribed:

(1) Endorse on each of such duplicate originals the word "Filed," and the month, day and year of the filing thereof;

(2) File one of such duplicate originals in his office; and

(3) Issue a certificate of merger to which he shall affix the other duplicate original.

The certificate of merger, together with the duplicate original of the articles of merger affixed thereto by the Secretary of State, shall be returned to the surviving corporation or its representative.

§ 69. Effect of Merger or Consolidation

Upon the issuance of the certificate of merger or the certificate of consolidation by the Secretary of State, the merger or consolidation shall be effected.

When such merger or consolidation has been effected:

(a) The several corporations parties to the plan of merger or consolidation shall be a single corporation, which, in the case of a merger, shall be that corporation designated in the plan of merger as the surviving corporation, and, in the case of a consolidation, shall be the new corporation provided for in the plan of consolidation.

(b) The separate existence of all corporations parties to the plan of merger or consolidation, except the surviving or new corporation, shall cease.

(c) Such surviving or new corporation shall have all the rights, privileges, immunities and powers and shall be subject to all the duties and liabilities of a corporation organized under this Act.

(d) Such surviving or new corporation shall thereupon and thereafter possess all the rights, privileges, immunities, and franchises, as well of a public as of a private nature, of each of the merging or consolidating corporations; and all property, real, personal and mixed, and all debts due on whatever account, including subscriptions to shares, and all other choses in action, and all and every other interest of or belonging to or due to each of the corporations so merged or consolidated, shall be taken and deemed to be transferred to and vested in such single corporation without further act or deed; and the title to any real estate, or any interest therein, vested in any of such corporations shall not revert or be in any way impaired by reason of such merger or consolidation.

(e) Such surviving or new corporation shall thenceforth be responsible and liable for all the liabilities and obligations of each of the corporations so merged or consolidated; and any claim existing or action or proceeding pending by or against any of such corporations may be prosecuted as if such merger or consolidation had not taken place, or such surviving or new corporation may be substituted in its place. Neither the rights of creditors nor any liens upon the property of any such corporation shall be impaired by such merger or consolidation.

(f) In the case of a merger, the articles of incorporation of the surviving corporation shall be deemed to be amended to the extent, if any, that changes in its articles of incorporation are stated in the plan of merger; and, in the case of a consolidation, the statements set forth in the articles of consolidation and which are required or permitted to be set forth in the articles of incorporation of corporations organized under this Act shall be deemed to be the original articles of incorporation of the new corporation.

§ 70. Merger or Consolidation of Domestic and Foreign Corporations

One or more foreign corporations and one or more domestic corporations may be merged or consolidated in the following manner, if such merger or consolidation is permitted by the laws of the state under which each such foreign corporation is organized:

(a) Each domestic corporation shall comply with the provisions of this Act with respect to the merger or consolidation, as the case may be, of domestic corporations and each foreign corporation shall comply with the applicable provisions of the laws of the state under which it is organized.

(b) If the surviving or new corporation, as the case may be, is to be governed by the laws of any state other than this State, it shall comply with the provisions of this Act with respect to foreign corporations if it is to transact business in this State, and in every case it shall file with the Secretary of State of this State:

(1) an agreement that it may be served with process in this State in any proceeding for the enforcement of any obligation of any domestic corporation which is a party to such merger or consolidation and in any proceeding for the enforcement of the rights of a dissenting shareholder of any such domestic corporation against the surviving or new corporation;

(2) an irrevocable appointment of the Secretary of State of this State as its agent to accept service of process in any such proceeding; and

(3) an agreement that it will promptly pay to the dissenting shareholders of any such domestic corporation the amount, if any, to which they shall be entitled under the provisions of this Act with respect to the rights of dissenting shareholders.

The effect of such merger or consolidation shall be the same as in the case of the merger or consolidation of domestic corporations, if the surviving or new corporation is to be governed by the laws of this State. If the surviving or new corporation is to be governed by the laws of any state other than this State, the effect of such merger or consolidation shall be the same as in the case of the merger or consolidation of domestic corporations except in so far as the laws of such other state provide otherwise.

At any time prior to the filing of the articles of merger or consolidation, the merger or consolidation may be abandoned pursuant to provisions therefor, if any, set forth in the plan of merger or consolidation.

§ 71. Sale of Assets in Regular Course of Business and Mortgage or Pledge of Assets

The sale, lease, exchange, or other disposition of all, or substantially all, the property and assets of a corporation in the usual and regular course of its business and the mortgage or pledge of any or all property and assets of a corporation whether or not in the usual and regular course of business may be made upon such terms and conditions and for such consideration, which may consist in whole or in part of money or property, real or personal, including shares of any other corporation, domestic or foreign, as shall be authorized by its board of directors; and in any such case no authorization or consent of the shareholders shall be required.

§ 72. Sale of Assets Other Than in Regular Course of Business

A sale, lease, exchange, or other disposition of all, or substantially all, the property and assets, with or without the good will, of a corporation, if not in the usual and regular course of its business, may be made upon such terms and conditions and for such consideration, which may consist in whole or in part of money or property, real or personal, including shares of any other corporation, domestic or foreign, as may be authorized in the following manner:

(a) The board of directors shall adopt a resolution recommending such sale, lease, exchange, or other disposition and directing the submission thereof to a vote at a meeting of shareholders, which may be either an annual or a special meeting.

(b) Written notice shall be given to each shareholder of record, whether or not entitled to vote at such meeting, not less than twenty days before such meeting, in the manner provided in this Act for the giving of notice of meetings of shareholders, and, whether the meeting be an annual or a special meeting, shall state that the purpose, or one of the purposes is to consider the proposed sale, lease, exchange, or other disposition.

(c) At such meeting the shareholders may authorize such sale, lease, exchange, or other disposition and may fix, or may authorize the board of directors to fix, any or all of the terms and conditions thereof and the consideration to be received by the corporation therefor. Such authorization shall require the affirmative vote of the holders of two-thirds of the shares of the corporation entitled to vote thereon, unless any class of shares is entitled to vote thereon as a class, in which event such authorization shall require the affirmative vote of the holders of two-thirds of the shares of each class of shares entitled to vote as a class thereon and of the total shares entitled to vote thereon.

(d) After such authorization by a vote of shareholders, the board of directors nevertheless, in its discretion, may abandon such sale, lease, exchange, or other disposition of assets, subject to the rights of third parties under any contracts relating thereto, without further action or appproval by shareholders.

§ 73. Right of Shareholders to Dissent

Any shareholder of a corporation shall have the right to dissent from any of the following corporate actions:

(a) any plan of merger or consolidation to which the corporation is a party; or

(b) any sale or exchange of all or substantially all of the property and assets of the corporation not made in the usual and regular course of its business, including a sale in dissolution, but not including a sale pursuant to an order of a court having jurisdiction in the premises or a sale for cash on terms requiring that all or substantially all of the net proceeds of sale be distributed to the shareholders in accordance with their respective

interests within one year after the date of sale.

A shareholder may dissent as to less than all of the shares registered in his name. In that event, his rights shall be determined as if the shares as to which he has dissented and his other shares were registered in the names of different shareholders.

The provisions of this section shall not apply to the shareholders of the surviving corporation in a merger if such corporation is on the date of the filing of the articles of merger the owner of all the outstanding shares of the other corporations, domestic or foreign, which are parties to the merger.†

† If optional Section 68A is included, there should be added, "or if a vote of the shareholders of such corporation is not necessary to authorize such merger."

§ 74. Rights of Dissenting Shareholders

Any shareholder electing to exercise such right of dissent shall file with the corporation, prior to or at the meeting of shareholders at which such proposed corporate action is submitted to a vote, a written objection to such proposed corporate action. If such proposed corporate action be approved by the required vote and such shareholder shall not have voted in favor thereof, such shareholder may, within ten days after the date on which the vote was taken †

† If optional Section 68A is included, there should be inserted "or if a corporation is to be merged without a vote of its shareholders into another corporation, any of its shareholders may, within fifteen days after the plan of such merger shall have been mailed to such shareholders,".

make written demand on the corporation, or, in the case of a merger or consolidation, on the surviving or new corporation, domestic or foreign, for payment of the fair value of such shareholder's shares, and, if such proposed corporate action is effected, such corporation shall pay to such shareholder, upon surrender of the certificate or certificates representing such shares, the fair value thereof as of the day prior to the date on which the vote was taken approving the proposed corporate action, excluding any appreciation or depreciation in anticipation of such corporate action. Any shareholder failing to make demand within the ten day period shall be bound by the terms of the proposed corporate action. Any shareholder making such demand shall thereafter be entitled only to payment as in this section provided and shall not be entitled to vote or to exercise any other rights of a shareholder.

No such demand may be withdrawn unless the corporation shall consent thereto. If, however, such demand shall be withdrawn upon consent, or if the proposed corporate action shall be abandoned or rescinded or the shareholders shall revoke the authority to effect such action, or if, in the case of a merger, on the date of the filing of the articles of merger the surviving corporation is the owner of all the outstanding shares of the other corporations, domestic and foreign, that are parties to the merger, or if no demand or petition for the determination of fair value by a court shall have been made or filed within the time provided in this section, or if a court of competent jurisdiction shall determine that such shareholder is not entitled to the relief provided by this section, then the right of such shareholder to be paid the fair value of his shares shall cease and his status as a shareholder shall be restored, without prejudice to any corporate proceedings which may have been taken during the interim.

Within ten days after such corporate action is effected, the corporation, or, in the case of a merger or consolidation, the surviving or new corporation, domestic or foreign, shall give written notice thereof to each dissenting shareholder who has made demand as herein provided, and shall make a written offer to each such shareholder to pay for such shares at a specified price deemed by such corporation to be the fair value thereof. Such notice and offer shall be accompanied by a balance sheet of the corporation the shares of which the dissenting shareholder holds, as of the latest available date and not more than twelve months prior to the making of such offer, and a profit and loss statement of such corporation for the twelve months' period ended on the date of such balance sheet.

If within thirty days after the date on which such corporate action was effected the fair value of such shares is agreed upon between any such dissenting shareholder and the corporation, payment therefor shall be made within ninety days after the date on which such corporate action was effected, upon surrender of the certificate or certificates representing such shares. Upon payment of the agreed value the dissenting shareholder shall cease to have any interest in such shares.

If within such period of thirty days a dissenting shareholder and the corporation do not so agree, then the corporation, within thirty days after receipt of written demand from any dissenting shareholder given within sixty days after the date on which such corporate action was effected, shall, or at its election at any time within such period of sixty days may, file a petition in any court of competent jurisdiction in the county in this state where the registered office of the corporation is located praying that the fair value of such shares be found and determined. If, in the case of a merger or consolidation, the surviving or new corporation is a foreign corporation without a registered office in this state, such petition shall be filed in the county where the registered office of the domestic corporation was last located. If the corporation shall fail to institute the proceeding as herein provided, any dissenting shareholder may do so in the name of the corporation. All dissenting shareholders, wherever residing, shall be made parties to the proceeding as an action against their shares quasi in rem. A copy of the petition shall be served on each dissenting shareholder who is a resident of this state and shall be served by registered or certified mail on each dissenting shareholder who is a nonresident. Service on nonresidents shall also be made by publication as provided by law. The jurisdiction of the court shall be plenary and exclusive. All shareholders who are parties to the proceeding shall be entitled to judgment against the corporation for the amount of the fair value of their shares. The court may, if it so elects, appoint one or more persons as appraisers to receive evidence and recommend a decision on the question of fair value. The appraisers shall have such power and authority as shall be specified in the order of their appointment or an amendment thereof. The judgment shall be payable only upon and concurrently with the surrender to the corporation of the certificate or certificates representing such shares. Upon payment of the judgment, the dissenting shareholder shall cease to have any interest in such shares.

The judgment shall include an allowance for interest at such rate as the court may find to be fair and equitable in all the circumstances, from the date on which the vote was taken on the proposed corporate action to the date of payment.

The costs and expenses of any such proceeding shall be determined by the court and shall be assessed against the corporation, but all or any part of such costs and expenses may be apportioned and assessed as the court may deem equitable against any or all of the dissenting shareholders who are parties to the proceeding to whom the corporation shall have made an offer to pay for the shares if the court shall find that the action of such shareholders in failing to accept such offer was arbitrary or vexatious or not in good faith. Such expenses shall include reasonable compensation for and reasonable expenses of the appraisers, but shall exclude the fees and expenses of counsel for any experts employed by any party; but if the fair value of the shares as determined materially exceeds the amount which the corporation offered to pay therefor, or if no offer was made, the court in its discretion may award to any shareholder who is a party to the proceeding such sum as the court may determine to be reasonable compensation to any expert or experts employed by the shareholder in the proceeding.

Within twenty days after demanding payment for his shares, each shareholder demanding payment shall submit the certificate or certificates representing his shares to the corporation for notation thereon that such demand has been made. His failure to do so shall, at the option of the corporation, terminate his rights under this section unless a court of competent jurisdiction, for good and sufficient cause shown, shall otherwise direct. If shares represented by a certificate on which notation has been so made shall be transferred, each new certificate issued therefor shall bear similar notation, together with the name of the original dissenting holder of such shares, and a transferee of such shares shall acquire by such transfer no rights in the corporation other than those which the original dissenting shareholder had after making demand for payment of the fair value thereof.

Shares acquired by a corporation pursuant to payment of the agreed value therefor or to payment of the judgment entered therefor, as in

this section provided, may be held and disposed of by such corporation as in the case of other treasury shares, except that, in the case of a merger or consolidation, they may be held and disposed of as the plan of merger or consolidation may otherwise provide.

§ 75. Voluntary Dissolution by Incorporators

A corporation which has not commenced business and which has not issued any shares, may be voluntarily dissolved by its incorporators at any time within two years after the date of the issuance of its certificate of incorporation, in the following manner:

(A) Articles of dissolution shall be executed in duplicate by a majority of the incorporators, and verified by them, and shall set forth:

(a) The name of the corporation.

(b) The date of issuance of its certificate of incorporation.

(c) That none of its shares has been issued.

(d) That the corporation has not commenced business.

(e) That the amount, if any, actually paid in on subscriptions for its shares, less any part thereof disbursed for necessary expenses, has been returned to those entitled thereto.

(f) That no debts of the corporation remain unpaid.

(g) That a majority of the incorporators elect that the corporation be dissolved.

(B) Duplicate originals of the articles of dissolution shall be delivered to the Secretary of State. If the Secretary of State finds that the articles of dissolution conform to law, he shall, when all fees and franchise taxes have been paid as in this Act prescribed:

(1) Endorse on each of such duplicate originals the word "Filed," and the month, day and year of the filing thereof.

(2) File one of such duplicate originals in his office.

(3) Issue a certificate of dissolution to which he shall affix the other duplicate original.

The certificate of dissolution, together with the duplicate original of the articles of dissolution affixed thereto by the Secretary of State, shall be returned to the incorporators or their representative. Upon the issuance of such certificate of dissolution by the Secretary of State, the existence of the corporation shall cease.

§ 76. Voluntary Dissolution by Consent of Shareholders

A corporation may be voluntarily dissolved by the written consent of all of its shareholders.

Upon the execution of such written consent, a statement of intent to dissolve shall be executed in duplicate by the corporation by its president or a vice president and by its secretary or an assistant secretary, and verified by one of the officers signing such statement, which statement shall set forth:

(a) The name of the corporation.

(b) The names and respective addresses of its officers.

(c) The names and respective addresses of its directors.

(d) A copy of the written consent signed by all shareholders of the corporation.

(e) A statement that such written consent has been signed by all shareholders of the corporation or signed in their names by their attorneys thereunto duly authorized.

§ 77. Voluntary Dissolution by Act of Corporation

A corporation may be dissolved by the act of the corporation, when authorized in the following manner:

(1) The board of directors shall adopt a resolution recommending that the corporation be dissolved, and directing that the question of such dissolution be submitted to a vote at a meeting of shareholders, which may be either an annual or a special meeting.

(2) Written notice shall be given to each shareholder of record entitled to vote at such meeting within the time and in the manner provided in this Act for the giving of notice of meetings of shareholders, and, whether the meeting be an annual or special meeting, shall state that the purpose, or one of the purposes, of such meeting is to consider the advisability of dissolving the corporation.

(3) At such meeting a vote of shareholders entitled to vote thereat shall be taken on a resolution to dissolve the corporation. Such resolution shall be adopted upon receiving the affirmative vote of the holders of two-thirds of the shares of the corporation entitled to vote thereon, unless any class of shares is entitled to vote thereon as a class, in which event the resolution shall be adopted upon receiving the affirmative vote of the holders of two-thirds of the shares of each class of shares entitled to vote thereon as a class and of the total shares entitled to vote thereon.

(4) Upon the adoption of such resolution, a statement of intent to dissolve shall be executed in duplicate by the corporation by its president or a vice president and by its secretary or an assistant secretary, and verified by one of the officers signing such statement, which statement shall set forth:

(a) The name of the corporation.

(b) The names and respective addresses of its officers.

(c) The names and respective addresses of its directors.

(d) A copy of the resolution adopted by the shareholders authorizing the dissolution of the corporation.

(e) The number of shares outstanding, and, if the shares of any class are entitled to vote as a class, the designation and number of outstanding shares of each such class.

(f) The number of shares voted for and against the resolution, respectively, and, if the shares of any class are entitled to vote as a class, the number of shares of each such class voted for and against the resolution, respectively.

§ 78. Filing of Statement of Intent to Dissolve

Duplicate originals of the statement of intent to dissolve, whether by consent of shareholders or by act of the corporation, shall be delivered to the Secretary of State. If the Secretary of State finds that such statement conforms to law, he shall, when all fees and franchise taxes have been paid as in this Act prescribed:

(1) Endorse on each of such duplicate originals the word "Filed," and the month, day and year of the filing thereof.

(2) File one of such duplicate originals in his office.

(3) Return the other duplicate original to the corporation or its representative.

§ 79. Effect of Statement of Intent to Dissolve

Upon the filing by the Secretary of State of a statement of intent to dissolve, whether by consent of shareholders or by act of the corporation, the corporation shall cease to carry on its business, except in so far as may be necessary for the winding up thereof, but its corporate existence shall continue until a certificate of dissolution has been issued by the Secretary of State or until a decree dissolving the corporation has been entered by a court of competent jurisdiction as in this Act provided.

§ 80. Procedure After Filing of Statement of Intent to Dissolve

After the filing by the Secretary of State of a statement of intent to dissolve:

(a) The corporation shall immediately cause notice thereof to be mailed to each known creditor of the corporation.

(b) The corporation shall proceed to collect its assets, convey and dispose of such of its properties as are not to be distributed in kind to its shareholders, pay, satisfy and discharge its liabilities and obligations and do all other acts required to liquidate its business and affairs, and, after paying or adequately providing for the payment of all its obligations, distribute the remainder of its assets, either in cash or in kind, among its shareholders according to their respective rights and interests.

(c) The corporation, at any time during the liquidation of its business and affairs, may make application to a court of competent jurisdiction within the state and judicial subdivision in which the registered office or principal place of business of the corporation is situated, to have the liquidation continued under the supervision of the court as provided in this Act.

§ 81. Revocation of Voluntary Dissolution Proceedings by Consent of Shareholders

By the written consent of all of its shareholders, a corporation may, at any time prior to the issuance of a certificate of dissolution by the Secretary of State, revoke voluntary dissolution proceedings theretofore taken, in the following manner:

Upon the execution of such written consent, a statement of revocation of voluntary dissolution proceedings shall be executed in duplicate by the corporation by its president or a vice president and by its secretary or an assistant secretary, and verified by one of the officers signing such statement, which statement shall set forth:

(a) The name of the corporation.

(b) The names and respective addresses of its officers.

(c) The names and respective addresses of its directors.

(d) A copy of the written consent signed by all shareholders of the corporation revoking such voluntary dissolution proceedings.

(e) That such written consent has been signed by all shareholders of the corporation or signed in their names by their attorneys thereunto duly authorized.

§ 82. Revocation of Voluntary Dissolution Proceedings by Act of Corporation

By the act of the corporation, a corporation may, at any time prior to the issuance of a certificate of dissolution by the Secretary of State, revoke voluntary dissolution proceedings theretofore taken, in the following manner:

(1) The board of directors shall adopt a resolution recommending that the voluntary dissolution proceedings be revoked, and directing that the question of such revocation be submitted to a vote at a special meeting of shareholders.

(2) Written notice, stating that the purpose or one of the purposes of such meeting is to consider the advisability of revoking the voluntary dissolution proceedings, shall be given to each shareholder of record entitled to vote at such meeting within the time and in the manner provided in this Act for the giving of notice of special meetings of shareholders.

(3) At such meeting a vote of the shareholders entitled to vote thereat shall be taken on a resolution to revoke the voluntary dissolution proceedings, which shall require for its adoption the affirmative vote of the holders of two-thirds of the shares entitled to vote thereon.

(4) Upon the adoption of such resolution, a statement of revocation of voluntary dissolution proceedings shall be executed in duplicate by the corporation by its president or a vice

president and by its secretary or an assistant secretary, and verified by one of the officers signing such statement, which statement shall set forth:

(a) The name of the corporation.

(b) The names and respective addresses of its officers.

(c) The names and respective addresses of its directors.

(d) A copy of the resolution, adopted by the shareholders revoking the voluntary dissolution proceedings.

(e) The number of shares outstanding.

(f) The number of shares voted for and against the resolution, respectively.

§ 83. Filing of Statement of Revocation of Voluntary Dissolution Proceedings

Duplicate originals of the statement of revocation of voluntary dissolution proceedings, whether by consent of shareholders or by act of the corporation, shall be delivered to the Secretary of State. If the Secretary of State finds that such statement conforms to law, he shall, when all fees and franchise taxes have been paid as in this Act prescribed:

(1) Endorse on each of such duplicate originals the word "Filed," and the month, day and year of the filing thereof.

(2) File one of such duplicate originals in his office.

(3) Return the other duplicate original to the corporation or its representative.

§ 84. Effect of Statement of Revocation of Voluntary Dissolution Proceedings

Upon the filing by the Secretary of State of a statement of revocation of voluntary dissolution proceedings, whether by consent of shareholders or by act of the corporation, the revocation of the voluntary dissolution proceedings shall become effective and the corporation may again carry on its business.

§ 85. Articles of Dissolution

If voluntary dissolution proceedings have not been revoked, then when all debts, liabilities and obligations of the corporation have been paid and discharged, or adequate provision has been made therefor, and all of the

remaining property and assets of the corporation have been distributed to its shareholders, articles of dissolution shall be executed in duplicate by the corporation by its president or a vice president and by its secretary or an assistant secretary, and verified by one of the officers signing such statement, which statement shall set forth:

(a) The name of the corporation.

(b) That the Secretary of State has theretofore filed a statement of intent to dissolve the corporation, and the date on which such statement was filed.

(c) That all debts, obligations and liabilities of the corporation have been paid and discharged or that adequate provision has been made therefor.

(d) That all the remaining property and assets of the corporation have been distributed among its shareholders in accordance with their respective rights and interests.

(e) That there are no suits pending against the corporation in any court, or that adequate provision has been made for the satisfaction of any judgment, order or decree which may be entered against it in any pending suit.

§ 86. Filing of Articles of Dissolution

Duplicate originals of such articles of dissolution shall be delivered to the Secretary of State. If the Secretary of State finds that such articles of dissolution conform to law, he shall, when all fees and franchise taxes have been paid as in this Act prescribed:

(1) Endorse on each of such duplicate originals the word "Filed," and the month, day and year of the filing thereof.

(2) File one of such duplicate originals in his office.

(3) Issue a certificate of dissolution to which he shall affix the other duplicate original.

The certificate of dissolution, together with the duplicate original of the articles of dissolution affixed thereto by the Secretary of State shall be returned to the representative of the dissolved corporation. Upon the issuance of such certificate of dissolution the existence of the corporation shall cease, except for the purpose of suits, other proceedings and appropriate corporate action by shareholders, directors and officers as provided in this Act.

§ 87. Involuntary Dissolution

A corporation may be dissolved involuntarily by a decree of the ...... court in an action filed by the Attorney General when it is established that:

(a) The corporation has failed to file its annual report within the time required by this Act, or has failed to pay its franchise tax on or before the first day of August of the year in which such franchise tax becomes due and payable; or

(b) The corporation procured its articles of incorporation through fraud; or

(c) The corporation has continued to exceed or abuse the authority conferred upon it by law; or

(d) The corporation has failed for thirty days to appoint and maintain a registered agent in this State; or

(e) The corporation has failed for thirty days after change of its registered office or registered agent to file in the office of the Secretary of State a statement of such change.

§ 88. Notification to Attorney General

The Secretary of State, on or before the last day of December of each year, shall certify to the Attorney General the names of all corporations which have failed to file their annual reports or to pay franchise taxes in accordance with the provisions of this Act, together with the facts pertinent thereto. He shall also certify, from time to time, the names of all corporations which have given other cause for dissolution as provided in this Act, together with the facts pertinent thereto. Whenever the Secretary of State shall certify the name of a corporation to the Attorney General as having given any cause for dissolution, the Secretary of State shall concurrently mail to the corporation at its registered office a notice that such certification has been made. Upon the receipt of such certification, the Attorney General shall file an action in the name of the State against such corporation for its dissolution. Every such certificate from the Secretary of State to the Attorney General pertaining to the failure of a corporation to file an annual report or pay a franchise tax shall be taken and received in all courts as prima facie evidence of the facts therein stated. If, before action is filed, the corporation shall file its annual report or pay its franchise tax, together with all penalties thereon, or shall appoint or maintain a registered agent as provided in this Act, or shall file with the Secretary of State the required statement of change of registered office or registered agent, such fact shall be forthwith certified by the Secretary of State to the Attorney General and he shall not file an action against such corporation for such cause. If, after action is filed, the corporation shall file its annual report or pay its franchise tax, together with all penalties thereon, or shall appoint or maintain a registered agent as provided in this Act, or shall file with the Secretary of State the required statement of change of registered office or registered agent, and shall pay the costs of such action, the action for such cause shall abate.

§ 89. Venue and Process

Every action for the involuntary dissolution of a corporation shall be commenced by the Attorney General either in the ...... court of the county in which the registered office of the corporation is situated, or in the ...... court of ...... county. Summons shall issue and be served as in other civil actions. If process is returned not found, the Attorney General shall cause publication to be made as in other civil cases in some newspaper published in the county where the registered office of the corporation is situated, containing a notice of the pendency of such action, the title of the court, the title of the action, and the date on or after which default may be entered. The Attorney General may include in one notice the names of any number of corporations against which actions are then pending in the same court. The Attorney General shall cause a copy of such notice to be mailed to the corporation at its registered office within ten days after the first publication thereof. The certificate of the Attorney General of the mailing of such notice shall be prima facie evidence thereof. Such notice shall be published at least once each week for two successive weeks, and the first publication thereof may begin at any time after the summons has been returned. Unless a corporation shall have been served with summons, no default shall be taken against it earlier than thirty days after the first publication of such notice.

§ 90. Jurisdiction of Court to Liquidate Assets and Business of Corporation

The * * * courts shall have full power to liquidate the assets and business of a corporation:

(a) In an action by a shareholder when it is established:

(1) That the directors are deadlocked in the management of the corporate affairs and the shareholders are unable to break the deadlock, and that irreparable injury to the corporation is being suffered or is threatened by reason thereof; or

(2) That the acts of the directors or those in control of the corporation are illegal, oppressive or fraudulent; or

(3) That the sharholders are deadlocked in voting power, and have failed, for a period which includes at least two consecutive annual meeting dates, to elect successors to directors whose terms have expired or would have expired upon the election of their successors; or

(4) That the corporate assets are being misapplied or wasted.

(b) In an action by a creditor:

(1) When the claim of the creditor has been reduced to judgment and an execution thereon returned unsatisfied and it is established that the corporation is insolvent; or

(2) When the corporation has admitted in writing that the claim of the creditor is due and owing and it is established that the corporation is insolvent.

(c) Upon application by a corporation which has filed a statement of intent to dissolve, as provided in this Act, to have its liquidation continued under the supervision of the court.

(d) When an action has been filed by the Attorney General to dissolve a corporation and it is established that liquidation of its business and affairs should precede the entry of a decree of dissolution.

Proceedings under clause (a), (b) or (c) of this section shall be brought in the county in which the registered office or the principal office of the corporation is situated.

It shall not be necessary to make shareholders parties to any such action or proceeding unless relief is sought against them personally.

§ 91. Procedure in Liquidation of Corporation by Court

In proceedings to liquidate the assets and business of a corporation the court shall have power to issue injunctions, to appoint a receiver or receivers pendente lite, with such powers and duties as the court, from time to time, may direct, and to take such other proceedings as may be requisite to preserve the corporate assets wherever situated, and carry on the business of the corporation until a full hearing can be had.

After a hearing had upon such notice as the court may direct to be given to all parties to the proceedings and to any other parties in interest designated by the court, the court may appoint a liquidating receiver or receivers with authority to collect the assets of the corporation, including all amounts owing to the corporation by shareholders on account of any unpaid portion of the consideration for the issuance of shares. Such liquidating receiver or receivers shall have authority, subject to the order of the court, to sell, convey and dispose of all or any part of the assets of the corporation wherever situated, either at public or private sale. The assets of the corporation or the proceeds resulting from a sale, conveyance or other disposition thereof shall be applied to the expenses of such liquidation and to the payment of the liabilities and obligations of the corporation, and any remaining assets or proceeds shall be distributed among its shareholders according to their respective rights and interests. The order appointing such liquidating receiver or receivers shall state their powers and duties. Such powers and duties may be increased or diminished at any time during the proceedings.

The court shall have power to allow from time to time as expenses of the liquidation compensation to the receiver or receivers and to attorneys in the proceeding, and to direct the payment thereof out of the assets of the corporation or the proceeds of any sale or disposition of such assets.

A receiver of a corporation appointed under the provisions of this section shall have authority to sue and defend in all courts in his own name as receiver of such corporation. The court appointing such receiver shall have exclusive jurisdiction of the corporation and its property, wherever situated.

§ 92. Qualifications of Receivers

A receiver shall in all cases be a citizen of the United States or a corporation authorized to act as receiver, which corporation may be a domestic corporation or a foreign corporation authorized to transact business in this State, and shall in all cases give such bond as the court may direct with such sureties as the court may require.

§ 93. Filing of Claims in Liquidation Proceedings

In proceedings to liquidate the assets and business of a corporation the court may require all creditors of the corporation to file with the clerk of the court or with the receiver, in such form as the court may prescribe, proofs under oath of their respective claims. If the court requires the filing of claims it shall fix a date, which shall be not less than four months from the date of the order, as the last day for the filing of claims, and shall prescribe the notice that shall be given to creditors and claimants of the date so fixed. Prior to the date so fixed, the court may extend the time for the filing of claims. Creditors and claimants failing to file proofs of claim on or before the date so fixed may be barred, by order of court, from participating in the distribution of the assets of the corporation.

§ 94. Discontinuance of Liquidation Proceedings

The liquidation of the assets and business of a corporation may be discontinued at any time during the liquidation proceedings when it is established that cause for liquidation no longer exists. In such event the court shall dismiss the proceedings and direct the receiver to redeliver to the corporation all its remaining property and assets.

§ 95. Decree of Involuntary Dissolution

In proceedings to liquidate the assets and business of a corporation, when the costs and expenses of such proceedings and all debts, obligations and liabilities of the corporation shall have been paid and discharged and all of its remaining property and assets distributed to its shareholders, or in case its property and assets are not sufficient to satisfy and discharge such costs, expenses, debts and obliga-

tions, all the property and assets have been applied so far as they will go to their payment, the court shall enter a decree dissolving the corporation, whereupon the existence of the corporation shall cease.

§ 96. Filing of Decree of Dissolution

In case the court shall enter a decree dissolving a corporation, it shall be the duty of the clerk of such court to cause a certified copy of the decree to be filed with the Secretary of State. No fee shall be charged by the Secretary of State for the filing thereof.

§ 97. Deposit with State Treasurer of Amount Due Certain Shareholders

Upon the voluntary or involuntary dissolution of a corporation, the portion of the assets distributable to a creditor or shareholder who is unknown or cannot be found, or who is under disability and there is no person legally competent to receive such distributive portion, shall be reduced to cash and deposited with the State Treasurer and shall be paid over to such creditor or shareholder or to his legal representative upon proof satisfactory to the State Treasurer of his right thereto.

§ 98. Survival of Remedy After Dissolution

The dissolution of a corporation either (1) by the issuance of a certificate of dissolution by the Secretary of State, or (2) by a decree of court when the court has not liquidated the assets and business of the corporation as provided in this Act, or (3) by expiration of its period of duration, shall not take away or impair any remedy available to or against such corporation, its directors, officers, or shareholders, for any right or claim existing, or any liability incurred, prior to such dissolution if action or other proceeding thereon is commenced within two years after the date of such dissolution. Any such action or proceeding by or against the corporation may be prosecuted or defended by the corporation in its corporate name. The shareholders, directors and officers shall have power to take such corporate or other action as shall be appropriate to protect such remedy, right or claim. If such corporation was dissolved by the expiration of its period of duration, such corporation may amend its articles of incorporation at any time during such period of two years so as to extend its period of duration.

§ 99. Admission of Foreign Corporation

No foreign corporation shall have the right to transact business in this State until it shall have procured a certificate of authority so to do from the Secretary of State. No foreign corporation shall be entitled to procure a certificate of authority under this Act to transact in this State any business which a corporation organized under this Act is not permitted to transact. A foreign corporation shall not be denied a certificate of authority by reason of the fact that the laws of the state or country under which such corporation is organized governing its organization and internal affairs differ from the laws of this State, and nothing in this Act contained shall be construed to authorize this State to regulate the organization or the internal affairs of such corporation.

Without excluding other activities which may not constitute transacting business in this State, a foreign corporation shall not be considered to be transacting business in this State, for the purposes of this Act, by reason of carrying on in this State any one or more of the following activities:

(a) Maintaining or defending any action or suit or any administrative or arbitration proceeding, or effecting the settlement thereof or the settlement of claims or disputes.

(b) Holding meetings of its directors or shareholders or carrying on other activities concerning its internal affairs.

(c) Maintaining bank accounts.

(d) Maintaining offices or agencies for the transfer, exchange and registration of its securities, or appointing and maintaining trustees or depositaries with relation to its securities.

(e) Effecting sales through independent contractors.

(f) Soliciting or procuring orders, whether by mail or through employees or agents or otherwise, where such orders require acceptance without this State before becoming binding contracts.

(g) Creating evidences of debt, mortgages or liens on real or personal property.

(h) Securing or collecting debts or enforcing any rights in property securing the same.

(i) Transacting any business in interstate commerce.

(j) Conducting an isolated transaction completed within a period of thirty days and not in the course of a number of repeated transactions of like nature.

§ 100. Powers of Foreign Corporation

A foreign corporation which shall have received a certificate of authority under this Act shall, until a certificate of revocation or of withdrawal shall have been issued as provided in this Act, enjoy the same, but no greater, rights and privileges as a domestic corporation organized for the purposes set forth in the application pursuant to which such certificate of authority is issued; and, except as in this Act otherwise provided, shall be subject to the same duties, restrictions, penalties and liabilities now or hereafter imposed upon a domestic corporation of like character.

§ 101. Corporate Name of Foreign Corporation

No certificate of authority shall be issued to a foreign corporation unless the corporate name of such corporation:

(a) Shall contain the word "corporation," "company," "incorporated," or "limited," or shall contain an abbreviation of one of such words, or such corporation shall, for use in this State, add at the end of its name one of such words or an abbreviation thereof.

(b) Shall not contain any word or phrase which indicates or implies that it is organized for any purpose other than one or more of the purposes contained in its articles of incorporation or that it is authorized or empowered to conduct the business of banking or insurance.

(c) Shall not be the same as, or deceptively similar to, the name of any domestic corporation existing under the laws of this State or any foreign corporation authorized to transact business in this State, or a name the exclusive right to which is, at the time, reserved in the manner provided in this Act, or the name of a corporation which has in effect a registration of its name as provided in this Act.

§ 102. Change of Name by Foreign Corporation

Whenever a foreign corporation which is authorized to transact business in this State shall change its name to one under which a certificate of authority would not be granted to it on application therefor, the certificate of authority of such corporation shall be suspended and it shall not thereafter transact any business in this State until it has changed its name to a name which is available to it under the laws of this State.

§ 103. Application for Certificate of Authority

A foreign corporation, in order to procure a certificate of authority to transact business in this State, shall make application therefor to the Secretary of State, which application shall set forth:

(a) The name of the corporation and the state or country under the laws of which it is incorporated.

(b) If the name of the corporation does not contain the word "corporation," "company," "incorporated," or "limited," or does not contain an abbreviation of one of such words, then the name of the corporation with the word or abbreviation which it elects to add thereto for use in this State.

(c) The date of incorporation and the period of duration of the corporation.

(d) The address of the principal office of the corporation in the state or country under the laws of which it is incorporated.

(e) The address of the proposed registered office of the corporation in this State, and the name of its proposed registered agent in this State at such address.

(f) The purpose or purposes of the corporation which it proposes to pursue in the transaction of business in this State.

(g) The names and respective addresses of the directors and officers of the corporation.

(h) A statement of the aggregate number of shares which the corporation has authority to issue, itemized by classes, par value of shares, shares without par value, and series, if any, within a class.

(i) A statement of the aggregate number of issued shares itemized by classes, par value of shares, shares without par value, and series, if any, within a class.

(j) A statement, expressed in dollars, of the amount of stated capital of the corporation, as defined in this Act.

(k) An estimate, expressed in dollars, of the value of all property to be owned by the corporation for the following year, wherever located, and an estimate of the value of the property of the corporation to be located within this State during such year, and an estimate, expressed in dollars, of the gross amount of business which will be transacted by the corporation during such year, and an estimate of the gross amount thereof which will be transacted by the corporation at or from places of business in this State during such year.

(l) Such additional information as may be necessary or appropriate in order to enable the Secretary of State to determine whether such corporation is entitled to a certificate of authority to transact business in this State and to determine and assess the fees and franchise taxes payable as in this Act prescribed.

Such application shall be made on forms prescribed and furnished by the Secretary of State and shall be executed in duplicate by the corporation by its president or a vice president and by its secretary or an assistant secretary, and verified by one of the officers signing such application.

§ 104. Filing of Application for Certificate of Authority

Duplicate originals of the application of the corporation for a certificate of authority shall be delivered to the Secretary of State, together with a copy of its articles of incorporation and all amendments thereto, duly authenticated by the proper officer of the state or country under the laws of which it is incorporated.

If the Secretary of State finds that such application conforms to law, he shall, when all fees and franchise taxes have been paid as in this Act prescribed:

(1) Endorse on each of such documents the word "Filed," and the month, day and year of the filing thereof.

(2) File in his office one of such duplicate originals of the application and the copy of the articles of incorporation and amendments thereto.

(3) Issue a certificate of authority to transact business in this State to which he shall affix the other duplicate original application.

The certificate of authority, together with the duplicate original of the application affixed thereto by the Secretary of State, shall be returned to the corporation or its representative.

§ 105. Effect of Certificate of Authority

Upon the issuance of a certificate of authority by the Secretary of State, the corporation shall be authorized to transact business in this State for those purposes set forth in its application, subject, however, to the right of this State to suspend or to revoke such authority as provided in this Act.

§ 106. Registered Office and Registered Agent of Foreign Corporation

Each foreign corporation authorized to transact business in this State shall have and continuously maintain in this State:

(a) A registered office which may be, but need not be, the same as its place of business in this State.

(b) A registered agent, which agent may be either an individual resident in this State whose business office is identical with such registered office, or a domestic corporation, or a foreign corporation authorized to transact business in this State, having a business office identical with such registered office.

§ 107. Change of Registered Office or Registered Agent of Foreign Corporation

A foreign corporation authorized to transact business in this State may change its registered office or change its registered agent, or both, upon filing in the office of the Secretary of State a statement setting forth:

(a) The name of the corporation.

(b) The address of its then registered office.

(c) If the address of its registered office be changed, the address to which the registered office is to be changed.

(d) The name of its then registered agent.

(e) If its registered agent be changed, the name of its successor registered agent.

(f) That the address of its registered office and the address of the business office of its registered agent, as changed, will be identical.

(g) That such change was authorized by resolution duly adopted by its board of directors.

Such statement shall be executed by the corporation by its president or a vice president, and verified by him, and delivered to the Secretary of State. If the Secretary of State finds that such statement conforms to the provisions of this Act, he shall file such statement in his office, and upon such filing the change of address of the registered office, or the appointment of a new registered agent, or both, as the case may be, shall become effective.

Any registered agent of a foreign corporation may resign as such agent upon filing a written notice thereof, executed in duplicate, with the Secretary of State, who shall forthwith mail a copy thereof to the corporation at its principal office in the state or country under the laws of which it is incorporated. The appointment of such agent shall terminate upon the expiration of thirty days after receipt of such notice by the Secretary of State.

If a registered agent changes his or its business address to another place within the same
. . . . . .†

† Insert appropriate designation of jurisdiction such as county, he or it may change such address and the address of the registered office of any corporations of which he or it is registered agent by filing a statement as required above except that it need be signed only by the registered agent and need not be responsive to (e) or (g) and must recite that a copy of the statement has been mailed to each such corporation.

§ 108. Service of Process on Foreign Corporation

The registered agent so appointed by a foreign corporation authorized to transact business in this State shall be an agent of such corporation upon whom any process, notice or demand required or permitted by law to be served upon the corporation may be served.

Whenever a foreign corporation authorized to transact business in this State shall fail to appoint or maintain a registered agent in this State, or whenever any such registered agent cannot with reasonable diligence be found at the registered office, or whenever the certificate of authority of a foreign corporation shall be suspended or revoked, then the Secretary of State shall be an agent of such corporation upon whom any such process, notice, or demand may be served. Service on the Secretary of State of any such process, notice, or demand shall be made by delivering to and leaving with him, or with any clerk having charge of the corporation department of his office, duplicate copies of such process, notice or demand. In the event any such process, notice or demand is served on the Secretary of State, he shall immediately cause one of such copies thereof to be forwarded by registered mail, addressed to the corporation at its principal office in the state or country under the laws of which it is incorporated. Any service so had on the Secretary of State shall be returnable in not less than thirty days.

The Secretary of State shall keep a record of all processes, notices and demands served upon him under this section, and shall record therein the time of such service and his action with reference thereto.

Nothing herein contained shall limit or affect the right to serve any process, notice or demand, required or permitted by law to be served upon a corporation in any other manner now or hereafter permitted by law.

§ 109. Amendment to Articles of Incorporation of Foreign Corporation

Whenever the articles of incorporation of a foreign corporation authorized to transact business in this State are amended, such foreign corporation shall, within thirty days after such amendment becomes effective, file in the office of the Secretary of State a copy of such amendment duly authenticated by the proper officer of the state or country under the laws of which it is incorporated; but the filing thereof shall not of itself enlarge or alter the purpose or purposes which such corporation is authorized to pursue in the transaction of business in this State, nor authorize such corporation to transact business in this State under any other name than the name set forth in its certificate of authority.

§ 110. Merger of Foreign Corporation Authorized to Transact Business in This State

Whenever a foreign corporation authorized to transact business in this State shall be a party to a statutory merger permitted by the laws of the state or country under the laws of which

it is incorporated, and such corporation shall be the surviving corporation, it shall, within thirty days after such merger becomes effective, file with the Secretary of State a copy of the articles of merger duly authenticated by the proper officer of the state or country under the laws of which such statutory merger was effected; and it shall not be necessary for such corporation to procure either a new or amended certificate of authority to transact business in this State unless the name of such corporation be changed thereby or unless the corporation desires to pursue in this State other or additional purposes than those which it is then authorized to transact in this State.

§ 111. Amended Certificate of Authority

A foreign corporation authorized to transact business in this State shall procure an amended certificate of authority in the event it changes its corporate name, or desires to pursue in this State other or additional purposes than those set forth in its prior application for a certificate of authority, by making application therefor to the Secretary of State.

The requirements in respect to the form and contents of such application, the manner of its execution, the filing of duplicate originals thereof with the Secretary of State, the issuance of an amended certificate of authority and the effect thereof, shall be the same as in the case of an original application for a certificate of authority.

§ 112. Withdrawal of Foreign Corporation

A foreign corporation authorized to transact business in this State may withdraw from this State upon procuring from the Secretary of State a certificate of withdrawal. In order to procure such certificate of withdrawal, such foreign corporation shall deliver to the Secretary of State an application for withdrawal, which shall set forth:

(a) The name of the corporation and the state or country under the laws of which it is incorporated.

(b) That the corporation is not transacting business in this State.

(c) That the corporation surrenders its authority to transact business in this State.

(d) That the corporation revokes the authority of its registered agent in this State to accept service of process and consents that service of process in any action, suit or proceeding based upon any cause of action arising in this State during the time the corporation was authorized to transact business in this State may thereafter be made on such corporation by service thereof on the Secretary of State.

(e) A post-office address to which the Secretary of State may mail a copy of any process against the corporation that may be served on him.

(f) A statement of the aggregate number of shares which the corporation has authority to issue, itemized by classes, par value of shares, shares without par value, and series, if any, within a class, as of the date of such application.

(g) A statement of the aggregate number of issued shares, itemized by classes, par value of shares, shares without par value, and series, if any, within a class, as of the date of such application.

(h) A statement, expressed in dollars, of the amount of stated capital of the corporation, as of the date of such application.

(i) Such additional information as may be necessary or appropriate in order to enable the Secretary of State to determine and assess any unpaid fees or franchise taxes payable by such foreign corporation as in this Act prescribed.

The application for withdrawal shall be made on forms prescribed and furnished by the Secretary of State and shall be executed by the corporation by its president or a vice president and by its secretary or an assistant secretary, and verified by one of the officers signing the application, or, if the corporation is in the hands of a receiver or trustee, shall be executed on behalf of the corporation by such receiver or trustee and verified by him.

§ 113. Filing of Application for Withdrawal

Duplicate originals of such application for withdrawal shall be delivered to the Secretary of State. If the Secretary of State finds that such application conforms to the provisions of this Act, he shall, when all fees and franchise taxes have been paid as in this Act prescribed:

(1) Endorse on each of such duplicate originals the word "Filed," and the month, day and year of the filing thereof.

(2) File one of such duplicate originals in his office.

(3) Issue a certificate of withdrawal to which he shall affix the other duplicate original.

The certificate of withdrawal, together with the duplicate original of the application for withdrawal affixed thereto by the Secretary of State, shall be returned to the corporation or its representative. Upon the issuance of such certificate of withdrawal, the authority of the corporation to transact business in this State shall cease.

§ 114. Revocation of Certificate of Authority

The certificate of authority of a foreign corporation to transact business in this State may be revoked by the Secretary of State upon the conditions prescribed in this section when:

(a) The corporation has failed to file its annual report within the time required by this Act, or has failed to pay any fees, franchise taxes or penalties prescribed by this Act when they have become due and payable; or

(b) The corporation has failed to appoint and maintain a registered agent in this State as required by this Act; or

(c) The corporation has failed, after change of its registered office or registered agent, to file in the office of the Secretary of State a statement of such change as required by this Act; or

(d) The corporation has failed to file in the office of the Secretary of State any amendment to its articles of incorporation or any articles of merger within the time prescribed by this Act; or

(e) A misrepresentation has been made of any material matter in any application, report, affidavit, or other document submitted by such corporation pursuant to this Act.

No certificate of authority of a foreign corporation shall be revoked by the Secretary of State unless (1) he shall have given the corporation not less than sixty days notice thereof by mail addressed to its registered office in this State, and (2) the corporation shall fail prior to revocation to file such annual report, or pay such fees, franchise taxes or penalties, or file the required statement of change of registered agent or registered office, or file such articles of amendment or articles of merger, or correct such misrepresentation.

§ 115.   Issuance of Certificate of Revocation

Upon revoking any such certificate of authority the Secretary of State shall:

(1) Issue a certificate of revocation in duplicate.

(2) File one of such certificates in his office.

(3) Mail to such corporation at its registered office in this State a notice of such revocation accompanied by one of such certificates.

Upon the issuance of such certificate of revocation, the authority of the corporation to transact business in this State shall cease.

§ 116.   Application to Corporations Heretofore Authorized to Transact Business in This State

Foreign corporations which are duly authorized to transact business in this State at the time this Act takes effect, for a purpose or purposes for which a corporation might secure such authority under this Act, shall, subject to the limitations set forth in their respective certificates of authority, be entitled to all the rights and privileges applicable to foreign corporations procuring certificates of authority to transact business in this State under this Act, and from the time this Act takes effect such corporations shall be subject to all the limitations, restrictions, liabilities, and duties prescribed herein for foreign corporations procuring certificates of authority to transact business in this State under this Act.

§ 117.   Transacting Business Without Certificate of Authority

No foreign corporation transacting business in this State without a certificate of authority shall be permitted to maintain any action, suit or proceeding in any court of this State, until such corporation shall have obtained a certificate of authority. Nor shall any action, suit or proceeding be maintained in any court of this State by any successor or assignee of such corporation on any right, claim or demand arising out of the transaction of business by such corporation in this State, until a certificate of authority shall have been obtained by such corporation or by a corporation which has acquired all or substantially all of its assets.

The failure of a foreign corporation to obtain a certificate of authority to transact business in this State shall not impair the validity of any contract or act of such corporation, and shall not prevent such corporation from defending any action, suit or proceeding in any court of this State.

A foreign corporation which transacts business in this State without a certificate of authority shall be liable to this State, for the years or parts thereof during which it transacted business in this State without a certificate of authority, in an amount equal to all fees and franchise taxes which would have been imposed by this Act upon such corporation had it duly applied for and received a certificate of authority to transact business in this State as required by this Act and thereafter filed all reports required by this Act, plus all penalties imposed by this Act for failure to pay such fees and franchise taxes. The Attorney General shall bring proceedings to recover all amounts due this State under the provisions of this Section.

§ 118.   Annual Report of Domestic and Foreign Corporations

Each domestic corporation, and each foreign corporation authorized to transact business in this State, shall file, within the time prescribed by this Act, an annual report setting forth:

(a) The name of the corporation and the state or country under the laws of which it is incorporated.

(b) The address of the registered office of the corporation in this State, and the name of its registered agent in this State at such address, and, in the case of a foreign corporation, the address of its principal office in the state or country under the laws of which it is incorporated.

(c) A brief statement of the character of the business in which the corporation is actually engaged in this State.

(d) The names and respective addresses of the directors and officers of the corporation.

(e) A statement of the aggregate number of shares which the corporation has authority to issue, itemized by classes, par value of shares, shares without par value, and series, if any, within a class.

(f) A statement of the aggregate number of issued shares, itemized by classes, par value of shares, shares without par value, and series, if any, within a class.

(g) A statement, expressed in dollars, of the amount of stated capital of the corporation, as defined in this Act.

(h) A statement, expressed in dollars, of the value of all the property owned by the corporation, wherever located, and the value of the property of the corporation located within this State, and a statement, expressed in dollars, of the gross amount of business transacted by the corporation for the twelve months ended on the thirty-first day of December preceding the date herein provided for the filing of such report and the gross amount thereof transacted by the corporation at or from places of business in this State. If, on the thirty-first day of December preceding the time herein provided for the filing of such report, the corporation had not been in existence for a period of twelve months, or in the case of a foreign corporation had not been authorized to transact business in this State for a period of twelve months, the statement with respect to business transacted shall be furnished for the period between the date of incorporation or the date of its authorization to transact business in this State, as the case may be, and such thirty-first day of December. If all the property of the corporation is located in this State and all of its business is transacted at or from places of business in this State, or if the corporation elects to pay the annual franchise tax on the basis of its entire stated capital, then the information required by this subparagraph need not be set forth in such report.

(i) Such additional information as may be necessary or appropriate in order to enable the Secretary of State to determine and assess the proper amount of franchise taxes payable by such corporation.

Such annual report shall be made on forms prescribed and furnished by the Secretary of State, and the information therein contained shall be given as of the date of the execution of the report, except as to the information required by subparagraphs (g), (h) and (i) which shall be given as of the close of business on the thirty-first day of December next preceding the date herein provided for the filing of such report. It shall be executed by the corporation by its president, a vice president, secretary, an assistant secretary, or treasurer, and verified by the officer executing the report, or, if the

corporation is in the hands of a receiver or trustee, it shall be executed on behalf of the corporation and verified by such receiver or trustee.

§ 119. Filing of Annual Report of Domestic and Foreign Corporations

[Omitted.]

§ 120. Fees, Franchise Taxes and Charges to Be Collected by Secretary of State

[Omitted.]

§ 121. Fees for Filing Documents and Issuing Certificates

[Omitted.]

§ 122. Miscellaneous Charges

[Omitted.]

§ 123. License Fees Payable by Domestic Corporations

[Omitted.]

§ 124. License Fees Payable by Foreign Corporations

[Omitted.]

§ 125. Franchise Taxes Payable by Domestic Corporations

[Omitted.]

§ 126. Franchise Taxes Payable by Foreign Corporations

[Omitted.]

§ 127. Assessment and Collection of Annual Franchise Taxes

[Omitted.]

§ 128. Penalties Imposed Upon Corporations

[Omitted.]

§ 129. Penalties Imposed Upon Officers and Directors

[Omitted.]

§ 130. Interrogatories by Secretary of State

[Omitted.]

§ 131. Information Disclosed by Interrogatories

[Omitted.]

§ 132. Powers of Secretary of State

[Omitted.]

§ 133. Appeal from Secretary of State

[Omitted.]

§ 134. Certificates and Certified Copies to be Received in Evidence

[Omitted.]

§ 135. Forms to Be Furnished by Secretary of State

[Omitted.]

§ 136. Greater Voting Requirements

[Omitted.]

§ 137. Waiver of Notice

[Omitted.]

§ 138. Action by Shareholders Without a Meeting

Any action required by this Act to be taken at a meeting of the shareholders of a corporation, or any action which may be taken at a meeting of the shareholders, may be taken without a meeting if a consent in writing, setting forth the action so taken, shall be signed by all of the shareholders entitled to vote with respect to the subject matter thereof.

Such consent shall have the same effect as a unanimous vote of shareholders, and may be stated as such in any articles or document filed with the Secretary of State under this Act.

§ 139. Unauthorized Assumption of Corporate Powers

All persons who assume to act as a corporation without authority so to do shall be jointly and severally liable for all debts and liabilities incurred or arising as a result thereof.

§ 140. Application to Existing Corporations

[Omitted.]

§ 141. Application to Foreign and Interstate Commerce

[Omitted.]

§ 142. Reservation of Power

[Omitted.]

§ 143. Effect of Repeal of Prior Acts

[Omitted.]

§ 144. Effect of Invalidity of Part of This Act

[Omitted.]

§ 145. Repeal of Prior Acts

(Insert appropriate provisions) * * *.

APPENDIX E

DICTIONARY OF LEGAL TERMS

(Abridged and Adapted from Black's Law Dictionary.)

A

AB INITIO. Latin. From the beginning. E. g., void ab initio. An agreement is said to be "void ab initio" if it has at no time had any legal validity.

ABROGATE. To annul; to repeal. A statute may abrogate a rule of the common law.

ABSTRACT OF TITLE. A condensed history of the title to land, consisting of a synopsis or summary of the material or operative portion of all the conveyances, of whatever kind or nature, which in any manner affect said land, or any estate or interest therein, together with a statement of all liens, charges, or liabilities to which the same may be subject, and of which it is in any way material for purchasers to be apprised.

ACCEPTANCE. **In contracts and sales.** The act of a person to whom a thing is offered or tendered by another, whereby he receives the thing with the intention of retaining it, such intention being evidenced by a sufficient act.

In negotiable instruments. Acceptance of a bill of exchange. The act by which the person on whom a bill of exchange is drawn (called the "drawee") assents to the request of the drawer to pay it, or, in other words, engages, or makes himself liable to pay it when due. 2 Bl.Comm. 469. Under the negotiable Instruments Law, "the acceptance must be in writing and signed by the drawee."

ACCESSION. An addition to one's property by increase of the original property or by production from such property. Instances are: The growth of a tree on A.'s land, although the tree overhangs the land of B.; the birth of a calf to the cow of A.; the innocent conversion of B.'s material by A. into a thing of different kind, so that its former identity no longer exists, as where A. innocently converts the wheat of B. into bread.

ACCIDENT. An unusual event, not expected by the person affected by it.

In equity. "An occurrence in relation to a contract which was not anticipated by the parties when the same was entered into, and which gives an undue advantage to one of them over the other in a court of law. Jeremy, Eq. 358. This definition is objected to, because, as accidents may arise in relation to other things besides contracts, it is inaccurate in confining accidents to contracts; besides, it does not exclude cases of unanticipated occurrence resulting from the negligence or misconduct of the party seeking relief. In general, courts of equity will relieve a party who cannot obtain justice at law in consequence of an accident which will justify the interposition of a court of equity. The jurisdiction which equity exerts in case of accident is mainly of two sorts: Over bonds with penalties to prevent a forfeiture where the failure is the result of accident, as sickness, or where the bond has been lost, but, if the penalty be liquidated damages, there can be no relief; and, second, where a negotiable or other instrument has been lost, in which case no action lay at law, but where equity will allow the one entitled to recover upon giving proper indemnity. In some states it has been held that a court of law can render judgment for the amount, but requires the defendant to give a bond of indemnity. Relief against a penal bond can now be obtained in almost all common-law courts." Bouvier, Law Dict.

ACCOMMODATION PAPER. An accommodation bill or note is one to which the accommodating party, be he acceptor, drawer, or indorser, has put his name, without consideration, for the purpose of benefiting or accommodating some other party who desires to raise money on it and is to provide for the bill or note when due.

ACCORD AND SATISFACTION. An agreement between two persons, one of whom has a right of action against the other, that the latter should do or give, and the former accept, something in satisfaction of the right of action different from, and usually less than, what might be legally enforced. When the agreement is executed, and satisfaction has been made, it is called "accord and satisfaction." Accord and satisfaction is the substitution of another agreement between the parties in satisfaction of the former one, and execution of the latter agreement. Such is the definition of this sort of defense usually given. But a broader application of the doctrine has been made in later times, where one promise or agreement is set up in satisfaction of a prior one, unless it has been expressly accepted as such; as, where a new promissory note has been given in lieu of a former one, to have the effect of a satisfaction of the former, it must have been accepted on an express agreement to that effect.

ACCOUNT. A detailed statement of the mutual demands in the nature of debt and credit between parties, arising out of contracts or some fiduciary relation.

Account closed. An account to which no further additions can be made on either side, but which remains still open for adjustment and set-off, which distinguishes it from account stated.

Account current. An open or running or unsettled account between two parties.

Account rendered. An account made out by the creditor, and presented to the debtor for his examination and acceptance. When accepted, it becomes an account stated.

Account stated. The settlement of an account between the parties, with a balance struck in favor of one of them; an account rendered by the creditor, and by the debtor assented to as correct, either expressly or by implication of law from the failure to object.

ACKNOWLEDGMENT. In conveyancing. The act by which a party who has executed an instrument of conveyance as grantor goes before a competent officer, or court, and declares or acknowledges the same as his genuine and voluntary act and deed. The certificate of the officer on such instrument that it has been so acknowledged.

The term is also used of the act of a person who avows or admits the truth of certain facts which, if established, will entail a civil liability upon him. Thus, the debtor's acknowledgment of the creditor's demand or right of action will revive the enforceability of a debt barred by the statute of limitations.

ACTION. A lawsuit. A right of action; i. e., a right to bring suit.

ACT OF GOD. Any misadventure or casualty is said to be caused by the "act of God," when it happens by the direct, immediate, and exclusive operation of the forces of nature, uncontrolled and uninfluenced by the power of man, and without human intervention, and is of such a character that it could not have been prevented or escaped from by any amount of foresight or prudence, or by any reasonable degree of care or diligence, or by the aid of any appliances which the situation of the party might reasonably require him to use. Any accident produced by any physical cause which is irresistible, such as lightning, tempests, perils of the seas, inundations, earthquakes; and also the sudden death or illness of persons.

ADJUDICATION. The giving or pronouncing of a judgment in a case; also the judgment given. The term is principally used in bankruptcy proceedings; the adjudication being the order which declares the debtor to be a bankrupt.

ADMINISTRATION. The management and settlement of the estate of an intestate decedent.

ADMINISTRATOR. In the most usual sense, is a person to whom letters of administration—that is, an authority to administer the estate of a deceased person—have been granted by the proper court. He resembles an executor, but is appointed by the court, without any nomination by the deceased. An administrator of the estate is appointed, if the deceased has made no will, or has named no executor in his will.

ADMIRALTY. That system of law governing civil and criminal maritime cases.

ADVERSE POSSESSION. The actual, open, and notorious possession and enjoyment of real property, or of any estate lying in grant, continued for a certain length of time, held adversely and in denial and opposition to the title of another claimant, or under circumstances which indicate an assertion or color of right or title on the part of the person maintaining it, as against another person who is out of possession.

AFFIANT. The person who makes and subscribes an affidavit. The word is used, in this sense, interchangeably with "deponent." But the latter term should be reserved as the designation of one who makes a deposition.

AFFIDAVIT. A written or printed declaration or statement of facts, made voluntarily, and confirmed by the oath or affirmation of the party making it. taken before an officer having authority to administer such oath.

A FORTIORI. Latin. By a stronger reason.

AGENCY. A relation, created either by express or implied contracts or by law, whereby one party (called the principal) delegates the transaction of some lawful business or the power to do certain acts for him or in relation to his rights or property, with more or less discretionary power, to another person (called the agent, attorney in fact, or proxy) who undertakes to manage the affair and render him an account thereof.

AGENT. One who represents and acts for another under the relation of agency.

ALIAS. Latin. At other times.

In practice. An alias writ is one issued in a case wherein another writ the same in substance has been issued before. For instance, there may be an alias attachment, an alias summons, etc.

The word commonly precedes the assumed names under which a party to an action, usually a defendant in a criminal action, is known as the names are stated in the pleadings. For instance, "John Jones, alias John Smith," would indicate "John Jones, at other times known as John Smith."

ALIBI. Latin. Elsewhere. In criminal cases, the defendant frequently pleads that he was elsewhere at the time of the perpetration of the alleged crime. In such a case, he is said to plead an alibi.

Apparently through the ignorance of some of those persons reporting court news to the daily papers, the word has been often very incorrectly and inexcusably used to signify a justification or an excuse.

ALIENATION. The transfer of property from one person to another.

ALLEGATION. The assertion, declaration, or statement of a party to an action, made in a pleading, setting out what he expects to prove.

ALLEGE. To state, recite, assert, or charge; to make an allegation.

ANIMO CONTRAHENDI. Latin. With the intention of contracting.

ANIMUS TESTANDI. Latin. An intention to make a last will and testament.

ANNUL. To cancel; make void; destroy. To annul a judgment or judicial proceeding is to deprive it of all force and operation, either ab initio or prospectively as to future transaction.

ANSWER. In pleading. Any pleading setting up matters of facts by way of defense. In chancery pleading, the term denotes a defense in writing, made by a defendant to the allegations contained in a bill or information filed by the plaintiff against him. In pleading, under the Codes of Civil Procedure, the answer is the formal written statement made by a defendant setting forth the ground of his defense; corresponding to what, in actions under the common-law practice, is called the "plea."

ANTENUPTIAL CONTRACT. A contract made prior to marriage, usually between the prospective wife and the prospective husband, under which the wife gains certain advantages or suffers certain detriments. In some instances, the prospective wife, in consideration of the settling of a certain amount of real estate or of personalty upon her, gives up her right of dower in the property of the husband.

APPEAL. In civil practice. The complaint to a superior court of an injustice done or error committed by an inferior one, whose judgment or decision the court above is called upon to correct or reverse. The removal of a cause from a court of inferior to one of superior jurisdiction, for the purpose of obtaining a review and retrial.

APPEARANCE. A technical coming into court as a party to an action, as plaintiff or as defendant. The party may actually appear in court, or he may, by his attorney, enter his appearance by filing written pleadings in the case, or by filing a formal written entry of appearance. The term first came into use

at a time when the only appearance known was the actual physical appearance of a party in court.

APPELLANT. A party who takes an appeal from one court to another.

APPELLEE. The party in a cause against whom an appeal is taken; that is, the party who has an interest adverse to setting aside or reversing the judgment.

APPRAISE. In practice. To fix or set a price or value upon; to fix and state the true value of a thing, and, usually, in writing.

APPURTENANCES. Things that belong to another thing regarded as the principal thing. Things appurtenant pass as incident to the principal thing. Sometimes an easement consisting of a right of way over one piece of land will pass with another piece of land as being appurtenant to it.

ARBITRATION. In practice. The investigation and determination of a matter or matters of difference between contending parties, by one or more unofficial persons, chosen by the parties, and called "arbitrators," or "referees."

ARREST OF JUDGMENT. In practice. The act of staying a judgment, or refusing to render judgment in an action at law, after verdict, for some matter intrinsic appearing on the face of the record, which would render the judgment, if given, erroneous or reversible.

ASSUMPSIT. Latin. He undertook; he promised. A promise or engagement by which one person assumes or undertakes to do some act or pay something to another. It may be either oral or in writing, but is not under seal. It is express, if the promisor puts his engagement in distinct and definite language; it is implied, where the law infers a promise (though no formal one has passed) from the conduct of the party or the circumstances of the case.

In practice. A form of action which lies for the recovery of damages for the non-performance of a parol or simple contract, or a contract that is neither of record nor under seal.

The ordinary division of this action is into (1) common or indebitatus assumpsit, brought for the most part on an implied promise; and (2) special assumpsit, founded on an express promise.

The action of assumpsit differs from trespass and trover, which are founded on a tort, not upon a contract; from covenant and debt, which are appropriate where the ground of recovery is a sealed instrument, or special obligation to pay a fixed sum; and from replevin, which seeks the recovery of specific property, if attainable, rather than of damages.

ASSURANCE. In conveyancing. A deed or instrument of conveyance. The legal evidences of the transfer of property are in England called the "common assurances" of the kingdom, whereby every man's estate is assured to him, and all controversies, doubts, and difficulties are either prevented or removed.

ATTACHMENT. The act or process of taking, apprehending, or seizing a person's property, by virtue of a writ, and bringing the same into the custody of the law, used either for the purpose of bringing a person before the court, of acquiring jurisdiction over the property seized, to compel an appearance, to furnish security for debt or costs, or to arrest a fund in the hands of a third person who may become liable to pay it over. Also the writ or other process for the accomplishment of the purposes above enumerated, this being the more common use of the word.

ATTESTATION. The act of witnessing an instrument in writing, at the request of the party making the same, and subscribing it as a witness. Execution and attestation are clearly distinct formalities; the former being the act of the party, and the latter of the witnesses only.

Attestation clause. The clause commonly placed at the conclusion of an instrument, in which clause the witnesses certify that the instrument has been executed before them.

ATTESTING WITNESS. One who signs his name to an instrument as a witness thereto at the request of the parties, for the purposes of proof and identification.

ATTORNEY. In the most general sense, this term denotes an agent or substitute, or one who is appointed and authorized to act in the place or stead of another.

It is "an ancient English word, and signifieth one that is set in the turne, stead, or place of another; and of these some be private * * * and some be publike, as attorneys at law." Co. Litt. 51b.

One who is appointed by another to do something in his absence, and who has authority to act in the place and turn of him by whom he is delegated.

When used with reference to the proceedings of courts, the term always means "attorney at law."

AUCTION. A sale of property, conducted in public or after a notice to the general public, to the highest bidder.

AUCTIONEER. One who conducts an auction.

AUTHORITIES. Legislative enactments, judicial opinions, legal textbooks, and articles in law periodicals are recognized as authorities on the law. The weight given each of these classes of authorities is far from being equal to that given each of the others. Legislative enactments, if valid under the Constitution, represent the final word on what the present law is. Judicial opinions, until overruled, constitute another primary authority. Textbooks and legal articles, though important, are only secondary authorities, guiding into and interpreting the primary authorities, the statutes and decisions.

AWARD, v. To grant, concede, adjudge to. Thus, a jury awards damages; the court awards an injunction.

AWARD, n. The decision or determination rendered by arbitrators or commissioners, or other private or extrajudicial deciders, upon a controversy submitted to them; also the writing or document embodying such decision.

B

BAGGAGE. Such articles of necessity or convenience as are carried by passengers for their general use. It includes clothing, books of the student, tools of the workman, etc.

BAIL, v. To procure the release of a person from legal custody, by undertaking that he shall appear at the time and place designated and submit himself to the jurisdiction and judgment of the court.

BAIL, n. **In practice.** The sureties who procure the release of a person under arrest, by becoming responsible for his appearance at the time and place designated. Those persons who become sureties for the appearance of the defendant in court.

BAILEE. In the law of contracts, one to whom goods are bailed; the party to whom personal property is delivered under a contract of bailment.

BAILMENT. A delivery of goods or personal property, by one person to another in trust for the execution of a special object upon or in relation to such goods, beneficial either to the bailor or bailee or both, and upon a contract, express or implied, to perform the trust and carry out such object, and thereupon either to redeliver the goods to the bailor or otherwise dispose of the same in conformity with the purpose of the trust.

BAILOR. The party who bails or delivers goods to another, in the contract of bailment.

BANKRUPT. A person who has committed an act of bankruptcy; one who has done some act or suffered some act to be done in consequence of which, under the laws of his country, he is liable to be proceeded against by his creditors for the seizure and distribution among them of his entire property.

BARTER. A contract by which parties exchange goods or commodities for other goods. It differs from sale, in this: That in the latter transaction goods or property are always exchanged for money.

BATTERY. Any unlawful beating, or other wrongful physical violence or constraint, inflicted on a human being without consent.

BENEFICIARY. A person having the enjoyment of property of which a trustee, executor, etc., has the legal possession. The person to whom a policy of insurance is payable.

BEQUEATH. To give personal property by will to another.

BEQUEST. A gift by will of personal property; a legacy.

BID. An offer by an intending purchaser to pay a designated price for property which is about to be sold at auction.

BILL. A formal declaration, complaint, or statement of particular things in writing. As a legal term, this word has many meanings and applications, the more important of which are enumerated below.

BILL IN EQUITY. The first written pleading in a proceeding in equity. The complaint in a suit in equity.

BILL OF LADING. In common law. The written evidence of a contract for the carriage and delivery of goods sent by sea for a certain freight. A written memorandum, given by the person in command of a merchant vessel, acknowledging the receipt on board the ship of certain specified goods, in good order or "apparent good order," which he undertakes, in consideration of the payment of freight, to deliver in like good order (dangers of the sea excepted) at a designated place to the consignee therein named or to his assigns. The term is often applied to a similar receipt and undertaking given by a carrier of goods by land. A bill of lading is an instrument in writing, signed by a carrier or his agent, describing the freight so as to identify it, stating the name of the consignor, the terms of the contract for carriage, and agreeing or directing that the freight be delivered to the order or assigns of a specified person at a specified place.

BILL OF PARTICULARS. In practice. A written statement or specification of the particulars of the demand for which an action at law is brought, or of a defendant's set-off against such demand (including dates, sums, and items in detail), furnished by one of the parties to the other, either voluntarily or in compliance with a judge's order for that purpose.

BILL OF SALE. In contracts. A written agreement under seal, by which one person assigns or transfers his right to or interest in goods and personal chattels to another. An instrument by which, in particular, the property in ships and vessels is conveyed.

BONA FIDE. Latin. In good faith.

C

CAPITAL. Partnership. "The capital of a partnership is the aggregate of the sums contributed by its members to establish or continue the partnership business." Gilmore on Partnership, p. 132.

Corporations. In reference to a corporation, it is the aggregate of the sum subscribed and paid in, or secured to be paid in, by the shareholders, with the addition of all gains or profits realized in the use and investment of those sums, or, if loss have been incurred, then it is the residue after deducting such losses.

CAPITAL STOCK. The common stock or fund of a corporation. The sum of money raised by the subscriptions of the stockholders, and divided into shares. It is said to be the sum upon which calls may be made upon the stockholders, and dividends are to be paid.

CARRIER. One who carries passengers or the goods of another. See **Common Carrier; Private Carrier.**

CAUSE OF ACTION. Matter for which an action may be brought. The ground on which an action may be sustained. The right to bring a suit.

CAVEAT EMPTOR. Latin. Let the buyer take care. This maxim summarizes the rule that the purchaser of an article must examine, judge, and test it for himself, being bound to discover any obvious defects or imperfections.

CERTIFICATE OF DEPOSIT. In the practice of bankers. This is a writing acknowledging that the person named has deposited in the bank a specified sum of money, and that the same is held subject to be drawn out on his own check or order, or that of some other person named in the instrument as payee.

CERTIFICATE OF STOCK. A certificate of a corporation of joint-stock company that the person named is the owner of a designated number of shares of its stock; given when the subscription is fully paid and the "scrip certificate" taken up.

CESTUI QUE TRUST. Anglo-French. He who has a right to a beneficial interest in and out of an estate the legal title to which is vested in another. 2 Washb. Real Prop. 163. The person who possesses the equitable right to property and receives the rents, issues, and profits thereof, the legal estate of which is vested in a trustee. It has been proposed to substitute for this uncouth term the English word "beneficiary," and the latter, though still far from universally adopted, has come to be quite frequently used. It is equal in precision to the antiquated and unwieldy Norman phrase, and far better adapted to the genius of our language.

CHAMPERTY. A bargain made by a stranger with one of the parties to a suit, by which such third person undertakes to carry on the litigation at his own cost and risk, in consideration of receiving, if he wins the suit, a part of the land or other subject sought to be recovered by the action.

CHANCELLOR. In American law, this is the name given in some states to the judge (or the presiding judge) of a court of chancery. In England, besides being the designation of the chief judge of the Court of Chancery, the term is used as the title of several judicial officers attached to bishops or other high dignitaries and to the universities.

CHANCERY. Equity; equitable jurisdiction; a court of equity; the system of jurisprudence administered in courts of equity.

CHARTER. An instrument emanating from the sovereign power, in the nature of a grant, authorizing the formation of a corporation. Under modern statutes, a charter is usually granted by the state secretary of state, who acts under general statutory authority conferred by the state legislature.

CHARTER PARTY. A contract by which an entire ship, or some principal part thereof, is let to a merchant for the conveyance of goods on a determined voyage to one or more places.

CHATTEL. An article of personal property; any species of property not amounting to a freehold or fee in land.

CHATTEL MORTGAGE. An instrument of sale of personalty conveying the title of the property to the mortgagee with terms of defeasance; and, if the terms of redemption are not complied with, then, at common law, the title becomes absolute in the mortgagee.

CHECK. A draft or order upon a bank or banking house, purporting to be drawn upon a deposit of funds, for the payment at all events of a certain sum of money to a certain person therein named, or to him or his order, or to bearer, and payable instantly on demand.

CHOSE IN ACTION. A right to personal things of which the owner has not the possession, but merely a right of action for their possession. 2 Bl.Comm. 389, 397; 1 Chit.Pr. 99.

A right to receive or recover a debt, demand, or damages on a cause of action ex contractu, or for a tort connected with contract, but which cannot be made available without recourse to an action.

CHOSE IN POSSESSION. A thing in possession, as distinguished from a thing in action.

CIVIL. In contradistinction to "criminal," it indicates the private rights and remedies of men, as members of the community, in contrast to those which are public and relate to the government; thus, we speak of civil process and criminal process, civil jurisdiction and criminal jurisdiction.

CIVIL LAW. The "Roman law" and the "civil law" are convertible phrases, meaning the same system of jurisprudence; it is now frequently denominated the "Roman civil law."

CLIENT. A person who employs or retains an attorney, or counsellor, to appear for him in courts, advise, assist, and defend him in legal proceedings, and to act for him in any legal business.

CLOSE. A portion of land, as a field, inclosed, as by a hedge, fence, or other visible inclosure.

CODE. A collection or compendium of laws. A complete system of positive law, scientifically arranged, or promulgated by legislative authority.

COLLATERAL. By the side; at the side; attached upon the side. Not lineal, but upon a parallel or diverging line. Additional or auxiliary; supplementary; co-operating.

COLLATERAL SECURITY. A security given in addition to the direct security, and subordinate to it, intended to guarantee its validity or convertibility or insure its performance; so that, if the direct security fails, the creditor may fall back upon the collateral security. Collateral security, in bank phraseology, means some security additional to the personal obligation of the borrower.

COLOR. An appearance or semblance, as distinguished from a reality. Hence, color of title.

COMITY OF NATIONS AND STATES. The most appropriate phrase to express the true foundation and extent of the obligation of the laws of one nation within the territories of another. It is derived altogether from the voluntary consent of the latter; and it is inadmissible when it is contrary to its known policy, or prejudicial to its interest. In the silence of any positive rule affirming or denying or restraining the operation of foreign laws, courts of justice presume the tacit adoption of them by their own government, unless repugnant to its policy, or prejudicial to its interests. It is not the comity of the courts, but the comity of the nation, which is administered and ascertained in the same way and guided by the same reasoning, by which all other principles of the municipal law are ascertained and guided.

COMMERCIAL LAW. A phrase used to designate the whole body of substantive jurisprudence applicable to the rights, intercourse, and relation of persons engaged in commerce, trade, or mercantile pursuits. It is not a very scientific or accurate term. As foreign commerce is carried on by means of shipping, the term has come to be used occasionally as synonymous with "maritime law;" but, in strictness, the phrase "commercial law" is wider, and includes many transactions or legal questions which have nothing to do with shipping or its incidents.

COMMERCIAL PAPER. The term "commercial paper" means bills of exchange, promissory notes, bank checks, and other negotiable instruments for the payment of money, which, by their form and on their face, purport to be such instruments as are, by the law-merchant, recognized as falling under the designation of "commercial paper."

COMMISSION. A warrant or authority or letters patent, issuing from the government, or one of its departments, or a court, empowering a person or persons named to do certain acts, or to exercise jurisdiction, or to perform the duties and exercise the authority of an office (as in the case of an officer in the army or navy).

Also, in private affairs, it signifies the authority or instructions under which one person transacts business or negotiates for another.

In a derivative sense, a body of persons to whom a commission is directed. A board or committee officially appointed and empowered to perform certain acts or exercise certain jurisdiction of a public nature or relation; as a "commission of assize."

In commercial law. The recompense or reward of an agent, factor, broker, or bailee, when the same is calculated as a percentage on the amount of his transactions or on the profit to the principal. But in this sense the word often occurs in the plural.

COMMISSION MERCHANT. A factor.

COMMITTEE. A term applied, in some states, to the guardian of an insane person.

COMMODATUM. Latin. A loan of goods for use without pay, the goods to be returned in kind.

COMMON CARRIER. Of goods. "One who holds himself out to transport for hire the goods of such as choose to employ him." Goddard on Bailments and Carriers, § 191.

Of passengers. "Such as hold themselves out for hire to carry all persons indifferently who apply for passage." Id. § 317.

COMMON COUNTS. Certain general counts or forms inserted in a declaration in an action to recover a money debt not founded on the circumstances of the individual case, but intended to guard against a possible variance, and to enable the plaintiff to take advantage of any ground of liability which the proof may disclose within the general scope of the action. In the action of assumpsit, these counts are as follows: For goods sold and delivered, or bargained and sold; for work done; for money lent; for money paid; for money received to the use of the plaintiff; for interest, or for money due on an account stated.

COMMON LAW. As distinguished from the Roman law, the modern civil law, the canon law, and other systems, the common law is that body of law and juristic theory which was originated, developed, and formulated and is administered in England, and has obtained among most of the states and peoples of Anglo-Saxon stock.

As distinguished from law created by the enactment of legislatures, the common law comprises the body of those principles and rules of action, relating to the government and security of persons and property, which derive their authority solely from usages and customs of immemorial antiquity, or from the judgments and decrees of the courts recognizing, affirming, and enforcing such usages and customs, and in this sense, particularly the ancient unwritten law of England.

As distinguished from equity law, it is a body of rules and principles, written or unwritten, which are of fixed and immutable authority, and which must be applied to controversies rigorously and in their entirety, and cannot be modified to suit the peculiarities of a specific case, or colored by any judicial discretion, and which rests confessedly upon custom or statute, as distinguished from any claim to ethical superiority.

COMPLAINANT. The plaintiff in code pleading or in equity.

COMPLAINT. In civil practice. In those states having a Code of Civil Procedure, the complaint is the first or initiatory pleading on the part of the plaintiff in a civil action. It corresponds to the declaration in the common law practice.

In criminal law. A charge, preferred before a magistrate having jurisdiction, that a person named (or a certain person whose name is unknown) has committed a certain offense, with an offer to prove the fact, to the end that a prosecution may be instituted. It is a technical term, descriptive of proceedings before a magistrate.

COMPOSITION. An agreement, made upon a sufficient consideration between an insolvent or embarrassed debtor and his creditors, whereby the latter, for the sake of immediate payment, agree to accept a dividend less than the whole amount of their claims, to be distributed pro rata, in discharge and satisfaction of the whole.

COMPOS MENTIS. Latin. Sound of mind.

COMPOUNDING A FELONY. The offense committed by a person who, having been directly injured by a felony, agrees with the criminal that he will not prosecute him, on condition of the latter's making reparation, or on receipt of a reward or bribe not to prosecute.

The offense of taking a reward for forbearing to prosecute a felony; as where a party robbed takes his goods again, or other amends, upon an agreement not to prosecute.

COMPROMISE. An arrangement arrived at, either in court or out of court, for settling a dispute upon what appears to the parties to be equitable terms, having regard to the uncertainty they are in regarding the facts or the law and the facts together.

CONDITIONAL SALE. A sale under the terms of which the passage of title is made to depend upon the performance of a condition. Usually the condition precedent to the passage of title is payment of the purchase price by the purchaser.

CONFESSION OF JUDGMENT. The act of a debtor in permitting judgment to be entered against him by his creditor, for a stipulated sum, by a written statement to that effect or by warrant of attorney, without the institution of legal proceedings of any kind.

CONFLICT OF LAWS. An opposition, conflict, or antagonism between different laws of the same state or sovereignty upon the same subject-matter.

A similar inconsistency between the municipal laws of different states or countries, arising in the case of persons who have acquired rights or a status, or made contracts, or incurred obligations, within the territory of two or more states.

That branch of jurisprudence, arising from the diversity of the laws of different nations in their application to rights and remedies, which reconciles the inconsistency, or decides which law or system is to govern in the particular case, or settles the degree of force to be accorded to the law of a foreign country (the acts or rights in question having arisen under it), either where it varies from the domestic law, or where the domestic law is silent or not exclusively applicable to the case in point. In this sense it is more properly called "private international law."

CONNIVANCE. The secret or indirect consent or permission of one person to the commission of an unlawful or criminal act.

CONSANGUINITY. Kinship; blood relationship; the connection or relation of persons descended from the same stock or common ancestor.

CONSERVATOR. A guardian of an insane person's estate.

CONSIDERATION. The inducement to a contract. The cause, motive, price, or impelling influence which induces a contracting party to enter into a contract.

Any benefit conferred, or agreed to be conferred, upon the promisor, by any other person, to which the promisor is not lawfully entitled, or any prejudice suffered, or agreed to be suffered, by such person, other than such as he is at the time of consent lawfully bound to suffer, as an inducement to the promisor, is a good consideration for a promise.

CONSIGNEE. In mercantile law. One to whom a consignment is made. The person to whom goods are shipped for sale.

CONSIGNMENT. The act or process of consigning goods; the transportation of goods consigned; an article or collection of goods sent to a factor to be sold; goods or property sent, by the aid of a common carrier, from one person in one place to another person in another place.

CONSIGNOR. One who sends or makes a consignment. A shipper of goods.

CONSPIRACY. In criminal law. A combination or confederacy between two or more persons formed for the purpose of committing, by their joint efforts, some lawful or criminal act, or some act which is innocent in itself, but becomes unlawful when done by the concerted action of the conspirators, or for the purpose of using criminal or unlawful means to the commission of an act not in itself unlawful.

CONSTRUCTIVE. That which is established by the mind of the law in its act of construing facts, conduct, circumstances, or instruments; that which has not the character assigned to it in its own essential nature, but acquires such character in consequence of the way in which it is regarded by a rule or policy of law; hence, inferred, implied, made out by legal interpretation.

Constructive assent. An assent or consent imputed to a party from a construction or interpretation of his conduct; as distinguished from one which he actually expresses.

CONTRA. Latin. Opposite, contrary. Where a decision is said to be contra, it is on the opposite side of the question.

CONTRACT. "In its broadest sense, an agreement whereby one or more of the parties acquire a right, in rem or in personam, in relation to some person, thing, act, or forbearance." Clark on Contracts (3d Ed.) p. 1.

CONTRIBUTION. The sharing of a loss or payment among several. The act of any one or several of a number of codebtors, cosureties, etc., in reimbursing one of their number, who has paid the whole debt or suffered the whole liability, each to the extent of his proportionate share. In equity, a bill is brought by a surety that has paid the whole debt, for contribution by his cosureties. Such an action is also had at law.

CONVERSION. An unauthorized assumption and exercise of the right of ownership over goods or personal chattels belonging to another, to the alteration of their condition or the exclusion of the owner's rights.

Constructive conversion. An implied or virtual conversion, which takes place where a person does such acts in reference to the goods of another as amount in law to the appropriation of the property to himself.

CONVICT. Under the criminal law, to find guilty of an offense as charged in the indictment or information.

CORPORATION. An artificial person or legal entity, created by or under the authority of the laws of a state or nation, composed in same rare instances of a single person and his successors, being the incumbents of a particular office, but ordinarily consisting of an association of numerous individuals, who subsist as a body politic under a special denomination, which is regarded in law as having a personality and existence distinct from that of its several members, and which is, by the same authority, vested with the capacity of continuous succession, irrespective of changes in its membership, either in perpetuity or for a limited term of years, and of acting as a unit or single individual in matters relating to the common purpose of the association, within the scope of the powers and authorities conferred upon such bodies by law.

CORPOREAL PROPERTY. Such as affects the senses, and may be seen and handled by the body, as opposed to incorporeal property which cannot be seen or handled, and exists only in contemplation. Thus, a house is corporeal, but the annual rent payable for its occupation is incorporeal. Corporeal property is, if movable, capable of manual transfer; if immovable, possession of it may be delivered up. But incorporeal property cannot be so transferred, but some other means must be adopted for its transfer, of which the most usual is an instrument in writing.

CORPUS. Latin. Body.

CORPUS DELICTI. Latin. The body of the wrong; the essential fact of the crime. The general rule is that no one can be convicted of a crime unless the actual doing of the crime has been proved. Laymen are accustomed to regard the requirements of this general rule as being much more rigid than they really are, and some convictions are on record in which the proof of the corpus delicti, while not entirely absent, was comparatively slight.

COSTS. A pecuniary allowance, made to the successful party (and recoverable from the losing party), for his court costs in prosecuting or defending a suit or a distinct proceeding within a suit. Costs do not include attorney's fees, excepting where the parties have stipulated for them, or where a statute provides for their being included in costs.

COUNSEL. The one or more attorneys or counselors appearing for a party in a cause. Both theoretically and actually, attorneys are officers of the court, and, by virtue of their office, are expected to give advice to the court, through their briefs and arguments, as to the law involved in the case in hand. Thus they are, in a very real sense, counsel.

COUNT, n. In pleading. The different parts of a declaration, each of which, if it stood alone, would constitute a ground for action, are the counts of the declaration. Used also to signify the several parts of an indictment, each charging a distinct offense.

COUNTERCLAIM. A claim presented by a defendant in opposition to or deduction from the claim of the plaintiff. A species of set-off or recoupment introduced by the codes of civil procedure in several of the states, of a broad and liberal character.

COURT. In practice. An organ of the government, belonging to the judicial department, whose function is the application of the laws to controversies brought before it and the public administration of justice.

COURT ABOVE—COURT BELOW. In appellate practice, the "court above" is the one to which a cause is removed for review, whether by appeal, writ of error, or certiorari; while the "court below" is the one from which the case is being removed.

COVENANT. An agreement, convention, or promise of two or more parties, by deed in writing, signed, sealed, and delivered, by which either of the parties pledges himself to the other that something is either done or shall be done, or stipulates for the truth of certain facts. A promise contained in such an agreement.

COVERT. Covered, protected, sheltered. A pound covert is one that is closed or covered over, as distinguished from pound overt, which is open overhead. A feme covert is so called, as being under the wing, protection or cover of her husband.

COVERTURE. The condition or state of a married woman.

CRIME. A crime is an act committed or omitted, in violation of a public law, either forbidding or commanding it; a breach or violation of some public right or duty due to a whole community, considered as a community in its social aggregate capacity, as distinguished from a civil injury.

D

DAMAGE. Loss, injury, or deterioration, caused by the negligence, design, or accident of one person to another, in respect of the latter's person or property.

DAMAGES. 1. The plural of damage.
2. Compensation claimed or awarded in a judicial proceeding for damage or for the invasion of a legal right. Bauer on Damages, p. 1.

DEBT. A sum of money due to certain and express agreement; as by bond for a determinate sum, a bill or note, a special bargain, or a rent reserved on a lease, where the amount is fixed and specific, and does not depend upon any subsequent valuation to settle it.

DECEIT. A fraudulent and cheating misrepresentation, artifice, or device, used by one or more persons to deceive and trick another, who is ignorant of the true facts, to the prejudice and damage of the party imposed upon.

DECLARATION. The complaint in a civil proceeding at common law. It is the first pleading filed by the plaintiff upon beginning his action.

DECREE. In practice. The judgment of a court of equity or admiralty, answering to the judgment of a court of common law.

DEED. A sealed instrument, containing a contract or covenant, delivered by the party to be bound thereby, and accepted by the party to whom the contract or covenant runs.

DE FACTO. Latin. In fact; in deed; actually.

DEFENDANT. The party sued in an action. The person against whom the declaration or complaint is filed, and who is so named in such declaration or complaint.

DE JURE. Latin. Of right; legitimate; lawful; by right and just title.

DEL CREDERE. An agreement by which a factor, when he sells goods on credit, for an additional commission (called a "del credere commission"), undertakes that the purchase price will be paid the seller. The del credere factor is usually held to have undertaken a primary and absolute liability, but some cases hold that he is a mere surety.

DELICTUM. Latin. A tort.

DELIVERY. The physical or constructive transfer of an instrument or of goods from the hands of one person to those of another.

DEMISE. 1. A conveyance of an estate to another for life, for years, or at will; a lease.

2. Death or decease.

DEMURRER. In pleading. The formal mode of disputing the sufficiency in law of the pleading of the other side. In effect it is an allegation that, even if the facts as stated in the pleading to which objection is taken be true, yet their legal consequences are not such as to put the demurring party to the necessity of answering them or proceeding further with the cause.

An objection made by one party to his opponent's pleading, alleging that he ought not to answer it, for some defect in law in the pleading. It admits the facts, and refers the law arising thereon to the court.

It imports that the objecting party will not proceed, but will wait the judgment of the court whether he is bound so to do.

In equity. An allegation of a defendant, which, admitting the matters of fact alleged by the bill to be true, shows that as they are therein set forth they are insufficient for the plaintiff to proceed upon or to oblige the defendant to answer, or that, for some reason apparent on the face of the bill, or on account of the omission of some matter which ought to be contained therein, or for want of some circumstances which ought to be attendant thereon, the defendant ought not to be compelled to answer to the whole bill, or to some certain part thereof.

DE NOVO. Latin. Anew.

DEPONENT. One who makes oath to a written statement.

DEPOSIT. In banking law. The act of placing or lodging money in the custody of a bank or banker, for safety or convenience, to be withdrawn at the will of the depositor or under rules and regulations agreed on; also the money so deposited.

DEPOSITION. The testimony of a witness taken upon interrogatories, not in court, but intended to be used in court.

DEPOSITUM. Latin. A bailment having for its purpose that the bailee keep the goods for the bailor without reward.

DESCENT. Hereditary succession.

DESCRIPTIO PERSONÆ. Latin. Description of the person.

DETUR DIGNIORI. Latin. Let it be given to him who is more worthy.

DEVASTAVIT. Latin. He laid waste. The allegation, "He laid waste," in a suit brought against executor, administrator, guardian, or trustee, gave rise to the naming of the wrong "devastavit." In such a case, the defendant is alleged to have mismanaged and wasted assets of the estate intrusted to him and thereby caused a loss.

DEVISE. A testamentary disposition of land or realty; a gift of real property by the last will and testament of the donor.

DICTUM. Latin. The word is generally used as an abbreviated form of obiter dictum, "a remark by the way;" that is, an observation or remark made by a judge in pronouncing an opinion upon a cause, concerning some rule, principle, or application of law, or the solution of a question suggested by the case at bar, but not necessarily involved in the case or essential to its determination; any statement of the law enunciated by the court merely by way of illustration, argument, analogy, or suggestion.

DISCOUNT. In a general sense, an allowance or deduction made from a gross sum on any account whatever. In a more limited and technical sense, the taking of interest in advance. By the language of the commercial world and the settled practice of banks, a discount by a bank means a drawback or deduction made upon its advances or loans of money, upon negotiable paper or other evidences of debt payable at a future day, which are transferred to the bank.

DISHONOR. In mercantile law and usage. To refuse or decline to accept a bill of exchange, or to refuse or neglect to pay a bill or note at maturity.

DIVIDEND. A fund to be divided. The share allotted to each of several persons entitled to share in a division of profits or property. Thus, dividend may denote a fund set apart by a corporation out of its profits, to be apportioned among the shareholders, or the proportional amount falling to each. In bankruptcy proceedings, a dividend is a proportional payment to the creditors out of the insolvent estate.

DOMICILE. That place in which a man has voluntarily fixed the habitation of himself and family, not for a mere special or temporary purpose, but with the present intention of making a permanent home, until some unexpected event shall occur to induce him to adopt some other permanent home.

DORMANT PARTNER. See **Partners.**

DOWER. The provision which the law makes for a widow out of lands or tenements of her husband, for her support and the nurture of her children. Co. Litt. 30a. Dower is an estate for life of the widow in a certain portion of the estate of her husband, to which she has not relinquished her right during the marriage.

DRAWEE. A person to whom a bill of exchange is addressed, and who is requested to pay the amount of money therein named.

DRAWER. The person drawing a bill of exchange and addressing it to the drawee.

DUEBILL. A brief written acknowledgment of a debt. It is not made payable to order, like a promissory note.

DURESS. Unlawful constraint exercised upon a person, whereby he is forced to do some act against his will.

E

EARNEST. The payment of a part of the price of goods sold, or the delivery of part of such goods, for the purpose of binding the contract.

EASEMENT. A right in the owner of one parcel of land, by reason of such ownership, to use the land of another for a special purpose not inconsistent with a general property in the owner. 2 Washb. Real Prop. 25.

A private easement is a privilege, service, or convenience which one neighbor has of another, by prescription, grant, or necessary implication, and without profit; as a way over his land, a gateway, watercourse, and the like. Kitch. 105.

EJECTMENT. An action of which the purpose is to determine whether the title to certain land is in the plaintiff or is in the defendant.

ELECTION. The act of choosing or selecting one or more from a greater number of persons, things, courses, rights, or remedies.

EMANCIPATION. The act by which an infant is set at liberty from the control of parent or guardian and made his own master.

EMBEZZLEMENT. The fraudulent appropriation to his own use or benefit of property or money intrusted to him by another, by a clerk, agent, trustee, public officer, or other person acting in a fiduciary character.

EMBLEMENTS. The vegetable chattels called "emblements" are the corn and other growth of the earth which are produced annually, not spontaneously, but by labor and industry, and thence are called "fructus industriales."

EMINENT DOMAIN. Eminent domain is the right of the people or government to take private property for public use.

ENTIRETY. The whole, in contradistinction to a moiety or part only. When land is conveyed to husband and wife, they do not take by moieties, but both are seised of the entirety. Parceners, on the other hand, have not an entirety of interest, but each is properly entitled to the whole of a distinct moiety.

The word is also used to designate that which the law considers as one whole, and not capable of being divided into parts. Thus, a judgment, it is held, is an entirety, and, if void as to one of the two defendants, cannot be valid as to the other. So, if a contract is an entirety, no part of the consideration is due until the whole has been performed.

EO NOMINE. Latin. By that name.

EQUITABLE. Just, fair, and right. Existing in equity; available or sustainable only in equity, or only upon the rules and principles of equity.

EQUITABLE ASSIGNMENT. An assignment which, though invalid at law, will be recognized and enforced in equity; e. g., an assignment of a chose in action, or of future acquisitions of the assignor.

EQUITY. In one of its technical meanings, equity is a body of jurisprudence, or field of jurisdiction, differing in its origin, theory, and methods from the common law.

In a still more restricted sense, it is a system of jurisprudence, or branch of remedial justice, administered by certain tribunals, distinct from the common-law courts, and empowered to decree "equity" in the complex of well-settled and well-understood rules, principles, and precedents.

Equity also signifies an equitable right; i. e., a right enforceable in a court of equity. Hence a bill of complaint which did not show that the plaintiff had a right entitling him to relief was said to be demurrable for want of equity; and certain rights now recognized in all the courts are still known as "equities," from having been originally recognized only in the court of chancery.

EQUITY OF REDEMPTION. The right of the mortgagor of an estate to redeem the same after it has been forfeited, at law, by a breach of the condition of the mortgage, upon paying the amount of debt, interest and costs.

ERROR. A mistaken judgment or incorrect belief as to the existence or effect of matters of fact, or a false or mistaken conception or application of the law.

Such a mistaken or false conception or application of the law to the facts of a cause as will furnish ground for a review of the proceedings upon a writ of error; a mistake of law, or false or irregular application of it, such as vitiates the proceedings and warrants the reversal of the judgment.

"Error" is also used as an elliptical expression for "writ of error"; as, in saying that error lies; that a judgment may be reversed on error.

Assignment of errors. In practice. The statement of the plaintiff's case on a writ of error, setting forth the errors complained of; corresponding with the declaration in an ordinary action. A specification of the errors upon which the appellant will rely, with such fullness as to give aid to the court in the examination of the transcript.

Harmless error. In appellate practice. An error committed in the progress of the trial below, but which was not prejudicial to the rights of the party assigning it, and for which, therefore, the court will not reverse the judgment; as, where the error was neutralized or corrected by subsequent proceedings in the case, or where, notwithstanding the error, the particular issue was found in that party's favor, or where, even if the error had not been committed, he could not have been legally entitled to prevail.

Reversible error. In appellate practice. Such an error as warrants the appellate court in reversing the judgment before it.

ESCROW. The state or condition of a deed which is conditionally held by a third person, or the possession and retention of a deed by a third person pending a condition; as when an instrument is said to be delivered "in escrow."

ESTATE. The interest which any one has in lands, or in any other subject of property.

In another sense, the term denotes the property (real or personal) in which one has a right or interest; the subject-matter of ownership; the corpus of property.

In a wider sense, the term "estate" denotes a man's whole financial status or condition—the aggregate of his interests and concerns, so far as regards his situation with reference to wealth or its objects, including debts and obligations, as well as possessions and rights.

ESTOPPEL. A bar or impediment raised by the law, which precludes a man from alleging or from denying a certain fact or state of facts, in consequence of his previous allegation or denial or conduct or admission, or in consequence of a final adjudication of the matter in a court of law.

EVICTION. Dispossession by process of law; the act of depriving a person of the possession of lands which he has held, in pursuance of the judgment of a court.

EVIDENCE. Any species of proof, or probative matter, legally presented at the trial of an issue, by the act of the parties and through the medium of witnesses, records, documents, concrete objects, etc., for the purpose of inducing belief in the minds of the court or jury as to their contention.

EXCEPTION. In practice. A formal objection to the action of the court, during the trial of a cause, in refusing a request or overruling an objection; implying that the party excepting does not acquiesce in the decision of the court, but will seek to procure its reversal, and that he means to save the benefit of his request or objection in some future proceeding.

EXCHANGE. In conveyancing. A mutual grant of equal interests (in lands or tenements), the one in consideration of the other.

In commercial law. A negotiation by which one person transfers to another funds which he has in a certain place, either at a price agreed upon or which is fixed by commercial usage.

In law of personal property. Exchange of goods is a commutation, transmutation, or transfer of goods for other goods, as distinguished from "sale," which is a transfer of goods for money.

EX CONTRACTU. Latin. From or out of a contract. In both the civil and common law, rights and causes of action are divided into two classes—those arising ex contractu (from a contract); and those arising ex delicto (from a delict or tort).

EX DELICTO. Latin. From a delict, tort, fault, crime, or malfeasance. In both the civil and the common law, obligations and causes of action are divided into two great classes—those arising ex contractu (out of a contract) ; and those ex delicto.

EX DOLO MALO NON ORITUR ACTIO. Latin. Out of fraud no action arises ; fraud never gives a right of action. No court will lend its aid to a man who founds his cause of action upon an immoral or illegal act.

EXECUTED. Completed ; carried into full effect ; already done or performed ; taking effect immediately ; now in existence or in possession ; conveying an immediate right or possession. The opposite of executory.

EXECUTION. In contracts. (1) The signing of a contract not under seal, or the signing, sealing, and delivering of a contract under seal. (2) The doing or accomplishing of the things stipulated in a contract to be done.

In criminal law. The legal putting to death of a convict, in conformity with the terms of his sentence.

In civil practice. The writ in which the court authorizes and orders the sheriff or similar officer to put into effect the court's final decree or judgment.

"Final execution is one which authorizes the money due on a judgment to be made out of the property of the defendant." Bouvier's Law Dictionary.

EXECUTOR. A person appointed by a testator to carry out the directions and requests in his will, and to dispose of the property according to his testamentary provisions after his decease.

EXECUTORY. That which is yet to be executed or performed ; that which remains to be carried into operation or effect ; incomplete ; depending upon a future performance or event. The opposite of executed.

EXEMPLARY. Punitive, punitory, for punishment.

EXEMPLARY DAMAGES. Damages on an increased scale, awarded to the plaintiff over and above what will barely compensate him for his property loss, where the wrong done to him was aggravated by circumstances of violence, oppression, malice, fraud, or wanton and wicked conduct on the part of the defendant, and are intended to punish the defendant for his evil behavior.

EXEMPTION. A privilege allowed by law to a judgment debtor, by which he may hold property to a certain amount, or certain classes of property, free from all liability to levy and sale on execution or attachment.

EX GRATIA. Latin. Out of grace ; as a matter of favor or indulgence ; gratuitous.

EX MERO MOTU. Latin. Of his own mere motion ; of his own accord.

EXONERATION. Latin, exonere ; disburden ; take the load off of. The lifting of a burden from a person or property.

In administration of estates. The taking of the burden of a mortgage debt, in certain instances, from mortgaged real estate, and the placing of the burden upon personalty.

In suretyship. The right of exoneration is an equitable right of a surety to have the burden of the debt lifted from his shoulders and placed upon those of the principal debtor. When a surety is sued by the creditor, he has sometimes filed a bill in equity, asking that the creditor be enjoined from prosecuting the action at law against the surety before suing the principal, and offering a bond to indemnify the creditor against loss.

EX PARTE. Latin. On one side only ; by or for one party ; done for, in behalf of, or on the application of, one party only.

EXPRESS. Made known distinctly and explicitly, and not left to inference or implication. Declared in terms ; set forth in words. Manifested by direct and appropriate language, as distinguished from that which is inferred from conduct. The word is usually contrasted with "implied."

EX TURPI CONTRACTU NON ORITUR ACTIO. Latin. Out of an immoral or illegal contract an action does not arise. A contract founded upon an illegal or immoral consideration cannot be enforced by action. 2 Kent, Comm. 466.

F

FACTOR. A commercial agent, employed by a principal to sell merchandise consigned to him for that purpose, for and in behalf of the principal, but usually in his own name, being intrusted with the possession and control of the goods, and being remunerated by a commission.

FEE SIMPLE. In English law. A freehold estate of inheritance, absolute and unqualified. It stands at the head of estates as the highest in dignity and the most ample in extent ; since every other kind of estate is derivable thereout, and mergeable therein.

FEE TAIL. An estate of inheritance, descending only to a certain class or classes of heirs ; e. g., an estate is conveyed or devised "to A. and the heirs of his body," or "to A. and the heirs male of his body," or "to A., and the heirs female of his body." Such estates have been common in England, but never very common in the United States. State statutes have dealt variously with estates tail, some statutes converting them into estates in fee simple. The entire plan of the estate tail is contrary to the spirit of American progress, contemplating, as the plan does, the continuance of the tenure in one class of persons, regardless of the changes in ownership often required by the progress of the community as a whole.

FELONY. **In American law.** The term has no very definite or precise meaning, except in some cases where it is defined by statute. For the most part, the state laws, in describing any particular offense, declare whether or not it shall be considered a felony. Apart from this, the word seems merely to imply a crime of a graver or more atrocious nature than those designated as "misdemeanors."

FEME. L. Fr. A woman.

Feme covert. A married woman.

Feme sole. A single woman.

FICTION. An assumption or supposition of law that something which is or may be false is true, or that a state of facts exists which has never really taken place.

FIDUCIARY. As an adjective it means of the nature of a trust; having the characteristics of a trust; Analogous to a trust; relating to or founded upon a trust or confidence.

FINAL PROCESS. A writ of execution. Such process is final, as contrasted with earlier process in the action. Process prior to judgment is known as mesne process.

FINAL SETTLEMENT. The rendering of a final account by an executor or an administrator, at the closing of the business of the estate, approved by the probate court, and followed by the discharge of the executor or administrator.

FIRE INSURANCE. A contract under the terms of which the insurer agrees to indemnify the insured against loss caused by fire during a period specified in the contract.

FIXTURES. (Authorities differ so much in their definitions of this term that it is deemed best to include several definitions, presenting varying conceptions.)

"A fixture is a thing which, though originally a chattel, is, by reason of its annexation to land, regarded as a part of the land, partaking of its character and belonging to its owner. Whether a chattel annexed to land is, in a particular case, to be so regarded as a part thereof, is determined usually by the mode of its attachment to the land, and the character of the chattel, as indicating the presumed intention of the annexor." Tiffany on Real Property, c. 9 (IV).

"Personal chattels affixed to real estate, which may be severed and removed by the party who has affixed them, or by his personal representative, against the will of the owner of the freehold. There is much dispute among the authorities as to what is a proper definition." Bouvier's Law Dict.

F. O. B. Free on board. "If a quotation is f. o. b., the seller undertakes for the price named to deliver the goods on board car or ship at a designated place, free of charges to the buyer." Whitaker's Foreign Exchange, p. 335.

FORCIBLE DETAINER. The offense of violently keeping possession of lands and tenements, with menaces, force, and arms, and without the authority of law.

FORCIBLE ENTRY. An offense against the public peace, or private wrong, committed by violently taking possession of lands and tenements with menaces, force, and arms, against the will of those entitled to the possession, and without the authority of law.

FORECLOSURE. A proceeding by which the rights of the mortgagee of real property are enforced. This procedure varies greatly in different states. The property is commonly put up at public auction and sold to the highest bidder. The mortgagee gets out of the proceeds the amount of his debt, with costs. The remaining portion of the proceeds, if any, goes to the debtor, the mortgagor. If the property sells at a price less than the amount of the debt and costs, judgment is given against the mortgagor for the deficiency.

Foreclosure is now generally by court proceeding in the case of real estate mortgages, though formerly all mortgages were subject to "strict foreclosure"; i. e., foreclosure without judicial process.

FORFEITURE. **In bonds.** A bond is given as the absolute and sealed promise of the obligor to pay a certain sum of money, with a defeasance clause following the obligation. This clause states that, upon the happening of a certain event, such as the conveying of certain land or the faithful performance of the duties of a certain office during a specified term, the bond is to become null and void. If the condition subsequent stated in such defeasance clause does not occur, the obligor has forfeited his bond.

In insurance. In a fire insurance policy, it is often stated that the policy shall be forfeited upon the occurrence of a certain event, such as nonpayment of the premium, storage of gasoline on the premises, vacancy of the premises, etc. A life insurance policy usually provides that it shall be forfeited for nonpayment of premiums. In the event of the happening of such a condition subsequent in an insurance policy, the insurer may declare a forfeiture or may waive the forfeiture and permit the insurance to continue.

FORGERY. **In criminal law.** The falsely making or materially altering, with intent to defraud, any writing which, if genuine, might apparently be of legal efficacy or the foundation of a legal liability.

FORMS OF ACTION. Classes or kinds of action under the common law. "This term comprehends the various classes of personal action at common law, viz. trespass, case, trover, detinue, replevin, covenant, debt, assumpsit, scire facias, and revivor, as well as the nearly obsolete actions of account and annuity, and the modern action of mandamus. They are now abolished in England by Judicature Acts of 1873, and 1875, and in many of the states of the United States, where a uniform course of proceeding under codes of procedure has taken their place. But the principles regulating the distinctions between the common-law actions are still found applicable even where the technical forms are abolished." Bouvier's Law Dict.

FRANCHISE. A special privilege conferred by government upon an individual or corporation, and which does not belong to the citizens of the country generally, of common right.

FRAUD. Fraud consists of some deceitful practice or willful devise, resorted to with intent to deprive another of his right, or in some manner to do him an injury. As distinguished from negligence, it is always positive, intentional.

FREEHOLD. An estate in land or other real property, of uncertain duration; that is, either of inheritance or which may possibly last for the life of the tenant at the least (as distinguished from a leasehold), and held by a free tenure.

FRUCTUS INDUSTRIALES. Latin. Industrial fruits or fruits of industry. Those fruits of a thing, as of land, which are produced by the labor and industry of the occupant, as crops of grain; as distinguished from such as are produced solely by the powers of nature.

FRUCTUS NATURALES. Latin. Those products which are produced by the powers of nature alone; as wool, metals, milk, the young of animals.

FUNGIBLE THINGS. Movable goods, which may be estimated and replaced according to weight, measure, and number, things belonging to a class, which do not have to be dealt with in specie.

FUTURE ESTATE. An estate to begin in possession at or after the termination of the present estate; e. g., A. holds a life estate in a tract of land, and B. has a reversion therein, B.'s possession to begin on the termination of A.'s estate. B.'s reversion is one kind of future estate. The remainder is another common species of future estate.

G

GARNISH, v. To issue process of garnishment against a person.

GARNISHEE, n. One garnished.

GARNISHMENT. In the process of attachment. A warning to a person in whose hands the effects of another are attached not to pay the money or deliver the property of the defendant in his hands to him, but to appear and answer the plaintiff's suit.

GENERAL AND SPECIAL ISSUE. The former is a plea which traverses and denies, briefly and in general and summary terms, the whole declaration, indictment, or complaint, without tendering new or special matter.

GENERAL VERDICT. A verdict whereby the jury find either for the plaintiff or for the defendant in general terms; the ordinary form of verdict.

GRATIS DICTUM. Latin. A voluntary assertion; a statement which a party is not legally bound to make, or in which he is not held to precise accuracy.

GRAVAMEN. Latin. The burden or gist of a charge.

GUARANTY, n. A promise to answer for the payment of some debt, or the performance of some duty, in case of the failure of another person, who, in the first instance, is liable to such payment or performance.

GUARDIAN. A guardian is a person lawfully invested with the power, and charged with the duty, of taking care of the person and managing the property and rights of another person, who, for some peculiarity of status, or defect or age, understanding, or self-control, is considered incapable of administering his own affairs.

H

HEARSAY. A term applied to that species of testimony given by a witness who relates, not what he knows personally, but what others have told him, or what he has heard said by others.

HEIR. At common law. A person who succeeds, by the rules of law, to an estate in lands, tenements, or hereditaments, upon the death of his ancestor, by descent and right of relationship.

HEREDITAMENTS. Things capable of being inherited, be it corporeal or incorporeal, real, personal, or mixed, and including not only lands and everything thereon, but also heirlooms, and certain furniture which, by custom, may descend to the heir together with the land.

I

IMPLIED. This word is used in law as contrasted with "express"; i. e., where the intention in regard to the subject-matter is not manifested by explicit and direct words, but is gathered by implication or necessary deduction from the circumstances, the general language, or the conduct of the parties.

INCHOATE. Imperfect; unfinished; begun, but not completed; as a contract not executed by all the parties.

INCORPOREAL. Without body; not of material nature; the opposite of "corporeal."

INDEMNITY. An indemnity is a collateral contract or assurance, by which one person engages to secure another against an anticipated loss or to prevent him from being damnified by the legal consequences of an act or forbearance on the part of one of the parties or of some third person.

INDENTURE. A deed to which two or more persons are parties, and in which these enter into reciprocal and corresponding grants or obligations towards each other; whereas a deed poll is properly one in which only the party making it executes it, or binds himself by it as a deed, though the grantors or grantees therein may be several in number.

INDICIA. Latin. Signs; indications.

INDICTMENT. The formal written accusation of a crime, as presented by a grand jury. The indictment holds a place, in criminal pleading, analogous to the place held, in a civil case, by the declaration or complaint. The plaintiff, in a criminal case, is the state, and the proof introduced by the state must, in order to convict, sustain one or more of the counts named in the indictment, just as, in a civil case, the proof introduced by the plaintiff must sustain one or more counts in the declaration or complaint. In a criminal case, the state must sustain its case by proof beyond a reasonable doubt; in a civil case, the plaintiff need prove his case only by a preponderance of the evidence.

INDORSEE. The person to whom a bill of exchange, promissory note, bill of lading, etc., is assigned by indorsement, giving him a right to sue thereon.

INDORSEMENT. The act of a payee, drawee, accommodation indorser, or holder of a negotiable instrument in writing his name upon the back of same, with or without further words, whereby the property in same is transferred to another.

INDORSER. He who makes an indorsement.

INFANT. A person within age, not of age, or not of full age; a person under the age of twenty-one years; a minor.

INFORMATION. In the criminal law, an accusation made the basis of a prosecution for a crime, but not itself the result of a finding by a grand jury.

IN HÆC FŒDERA NON VENIMUS. Latin. We did not enter into these bonds; we did not make this contract.

IN INVITUM. Latin. Against an unwilling party.

INIQUUM EST INGENUIS HOMINIBUS NON ESSE LIBERAM RERUM SUARUM ALIENATIONEM. Latin. Literally, it is unjust to freeborn men that the alienation of their own property should not be free. A better and freer translation would be: It is unjust that freeborn men should be unable freely to alienate their own property. This maxim states a reason underlying the rule against restraints upon alienation.

INJUNCTION. A prohibitive writ issued by a court of equity, at the suit of a party complainant, directed to a party defendant in the action, or to a party made a defendant for that purpose, forbidding the latter to do some act, or to permit his servants or agents to do some act, which he is threatening or attempting to commit, or restraining him in the continuance thereof, such act being unjust and inequitable, injurious to the plaintiff, and not such as can be adequately redressed by an action at law.

INJURY. Any wrong or damage done to another, either in his person, rights, reputation, or property.

IN LIMINE. Latin. On or at the threshold; at the very beginning; preliminarily.

INNKEEPER. The proprietor or keeper of a hotel or inn.

IN PARI DELICTO. Latin. In equal fault; equally culpable or criminal.

In pari delicto, potior est conditio possidentis [defendentis]. In a case of equal or mutual fault (between two parties), the condition of the party in possession [or defending] is the better one. This maxim is often applied to cases in which a plaintiff seeks to procure, under an illegal contract, money or other property in the possession of the defendant, or to get a judgment or decree of any kind, under such a contract.

IN PERSONAM. Latin. Against the person. Actions or rights in personam are contrasted with actions or rights in rem, which are directed at specific property or at a specific right or status. A. sues B., in an action at law, for $100. This is one instance of an action in personam. All suits in equity were originally in personam, the bill and the decree being addressed directly to the person of the defendant and seeking to control his conduct.

IN RE. Latin. In the matter; e. g., "In re Jones" means "in the matter of Jones."

IN REM. Latin. Against a thing; against the status; directed at specific property, or at a specific right or status. An action in admiralty may be in rem, being against a certain vessel. A suit for the foreclosure of a mortgage is, in a sense, in rem, being directed against the property mortgaged. A divorce suit, while in a certain sense in personam, is actually directed against the status of marriage existing between the complainant and the respondent, and is therefore, in part, a suit in rem. It is usual to contrast rights or actions in rem with rights or actions in personam.

INSOLVENCY. The condition of a person who is insolvent; inability to pay one's debts; lack of means to pay one's debts. Such a relative condition of a man's assets and liabilities that the former, if all made immediately available, would not be sufficient to discharge the latter. Or the condition of a person who is unable to pay his debts as they fall due, or in the usual course of trade and business.

INSOLVENT. Latin, insolvens; not paying.

In bankruptcy. In the federal Bankruptcy Act the following rule is stated: "A person shall be deemed insolvent within the provisions of this act whenever the aggregate of his property, exclusive of any property which he may have conveyed, transferred, concealed or removed, or permitted to be concealed or removed, with intent to defraud, hinder or delay his creditors, shall not, at a fair valuation, be sufficient in amount to pay his debts." Section 1, cl. 15.

In sales. The Uniform Sales Act gives the following rule: "A person is insolvent within the meaning of this act who either has ceased to pay his debts in the ordinary course of business or cannot pay his debts as they fall due, whether he has committed an act of bankruptcy or not, and whether he is insolvent within the meaning of the federal bankruptcy law or not." Section 76.

IN SPECIE. Latin. In kind. Specific; specifically.

IN STATU QUO. Latin. In the condition or state (in which it was).

INSURABLE INTEREST. Such a real and substantial interest in specific property as will sustain a contract to indemnify the person interested against its loss. If the assured had no real interest, the contract would be a mere wager policy.

INSURANCE. A contract whereby, for a stipulated consideration, one party undertakes to compensate the other for loss on a specified subject by specified perils. The party agreeing to make the compensation is usually called the "insurer" or "underwriter"; the other, the "insured" or "assured"; the written contract, a "policy"; the events insured against, "risks" or "perils"; and the subject, right, or interest to be protected, the "insurable interest." Insurance is a contract whereby one undertakes to indemnify another against loss, damage, or liability arising from an unknown or contingent event. Civ. Code Cal. § 2527. It must be borne in mind, however, that, although the usual definition fits policies of fire and marine insurance, it does not apply strictly to policies of life insurance. Life insurance is not a contract of indemnity, but a contract to pay a speci-

fied sum upon the occurrence of a certain event; as, the death of the insured.

INSURED. In fire and other property insurance. The person whose property interest is insured.

In life insurance. The person whose life is insured.

INSURER. The underwriter or insurance company with whom a contract of insurance is made.

INTERPLEADER. When two or more persons claim the same thing (or fund) of a third, and he, laying no claim to it himself, is ignorant which of them has a right to it, and fears he may be prejudiced by their proceeding against him to recover it, he may file a bill in equity against them, the object of which is to make them litigate their title between themselves, instead of litigating it with him, and such a bill is called a "bill of interpleader."

INTER SE, or INTER SESE. Latin. Between or among themselves.

INTERSTATE COMMERCE COMMISSION. A commission appointed by the President of the United States by authority of the Interstate Commerce Act of 1887. The commission is not a court, and therefore has no sheriff or marshal to enforce its decisions. It is a corporate body, so that it may sue or be sued in the courts, and, by court action, its decisions, when valid, are enforced. Its work involves the rates and practices of interstate carriers.

INTERVENER. An intervener is a person who voluntarily interposes in an action or other proceeding with the leave of the court.

INTESTATE. Without making a will.

J

JOINT. United; combined; undivided; done by or against two or more unitedly; shared by or between two or more.

A "joint" bond, note, or other obligation is one in which the obligors or makers (being two or more in number) bind themselves jointly, but not severally, and which must therefore be prosecuted in a joint action against them all. A "joint and several" bond or note is one in which the obligors or makers bind themselves both jointly and individually to the obligee or payee, and which may be enforced either by a joint action against them all or by separate actions against any one or more at the election of the creditor.

JOINTLY. Acting together or in concert or cooperation; holding in common or interdependently, not separately. Persons are "jointly bound" in a bond or note when both or all must be sued in one action for its enforcement, not either one at the election of the creditor.

Jointly and severally. Persons who bind themselves "jointly and severally" in a bond or note may all be sued together for its enforcement, or the creditor may select any one or more as the object of his suit.

JOINT—STOCK COMPANY. A partnership with a capital divided into transferable shares. Gilmore on Partnership.

JOINT TENANCY. "Exists when a single estate in land is owned by two or more persons claiming under one instrument; its most important characteristic being that, unless the statute otherwise provides, the interest of each joint tenant, upon his death, inures to the benefit of the surviving joint tenant or tenants, to the exclusion of his own heirs, devisees, or personal representatives." Tiffany on Real Property, p. 368.

JUDGMENT. The official and authentic decision of a court of justice upon the respective rights and claims of the parties to an action or suit therein litigated and submitted to its determination.

JUDGMENT DEBTS. Debts, whether on simple contract or by specialty, for the recovery of which judgment has been entered up, either upon a cognovit or upon a warrant of attorney or as the result of a successful action.

JUDGMENT IN PERSONAM. A judgment against a particular person, as distinguished from a judgment against a thing or a right or status. The former class of judgments are conclusive only upon parties and privies; the latter upon all the world.

JUDGMENT IN REM. A judgment in rem is an adjudication, pronounced upon the status of some particular subject-matter, by a tribunal having competent authority for that purpose. It differs from a judgment in personam, in this: That the latter judgment is in form, as well as substance, between the parties claiming the right; and that it is so inter partes appears by the record itself.

JUDGMENT NOTE. A promissory note, embodying an authorization to any attorney, or to a designated attorney, or to the holder, or the clerk of the court, to enter an appearance for the maker and confess a judgment against him for a sum therein named, upon default of payment of the note.

JUDICIAL. Belonging to the office of a judge; as judicial authority.

JURAT. The clause written at the foot of an affidavit, stating when, where, and before whom such affidavit was sworn.

JURISDICTION. The power and authority constitutionally conferred upon (or constitutionally recognized as existing in) a court or judge to pronounce the sentence of the law, or to award the remedies provided by law, upon a state of facts, proved or admitted, referred to the tribunal for decision, and authorized by law to be the subject of investigation or action by that tribunal, and in favor of or against persons (or a res) who present themselves, or who are brought, before the court in some manner sanctioned by law as proper and sufficient.

JURY. (From the Latin jurare, to swear.) A body of persons selected and summoned by law and sworn to try the facts of a case and to find according to the law and the evidence. In general, the province of the jury is to find the facts in a case, while the judge passes upon pure questions of law. As a matter of fact, however, the jury must often pass upon mixed questions of law and fact in determining the case, and in all such cases the instructions of the judge as to the law become very important.

K

KIN. Relationship; relationship by blood or marriage. The term is sometimes restricted to relationship by blood.

KNOWLEDGE. Information. "Knowledge" is a broader term than "notice," including, not only facts of which one is put on notice, but also facts of which one gets knowledge by means other than notice.

L

LACHES. Negligence, consisting in the omission of something which a party might do, and might reasonably be expected to do, towards the vindication or enforcement of his rights. The word is generally the synonym of "remissness," "dilatoriness," "unreasonable or unexcused delay"; the opposite of "vigilance"; and means a want of activity and diligence in making a claim or moving for the enforcement of a right (particularly in equity) which will afford ground for presuming against it, or for refusing relief, where that is discretionary with the court.

LANDLORD. He of whom lands or tenements are holden. He who, being the owner of an estate in land, has leased the same for a term of years, on a rent reserved, to another person, called the "tenant."

LAPSE, n. **In the law of wills.** The failure of a testamentary gift in consequence of the death of the devisee or legatee during the life of the testator.

LARCENY. **In criminal law.** The wrongful and fraudulent taking and carrying away by one person of the mere personal goods of another from any place, with a felonious intent to convert them to his (the taker's) use, and make them his property, without the consent of the owner.

LAW MERCHANT. The system of rules, customs, and usages generally recognized and adopted by merchants and traders, and which either in its simplicity or as modified by common law or statutes, constitutes the law for the regulation of their transactions and the solution of their controversies.

LEASE. A conveyance of lands or tenements to a person for life, for a term of years, or at will, in consideration of a return of rent or some other recompense. The person who so conveys such lands or tenements is termed the "lessor," and the person to whom they are conveyed, the "lessee"; and when the lessor so conveys lands or tenements to a lessee, he is said to lease, demise, or let them.

LEASEHOLD. An estate in realty held under a lease; an estate for a fixed term of years.

LEGACY. A bequest or gift of personal property by last will and testament.

LEGAL TENDER. That kind of coin, money, or circulating medium which the law compels a creditor to accept in payment of his debt, when tendered by the debtor in the right amount.

LESSEE. He to whom a lease is made.

LESSOR. He who grants a lease.

LET, v. In conveyancing. To demise or lease. "To let and set" is an old expression.

LETTERS OF ADMINISTRATION. The formal instrument of authority and appointment given an administrator by the proper court, empowering him to enter upon the discharge of his duties as administrator.

LETTERS TESTAMENTARY. The formal instrument of authority and appointment given to an executor by the proper court, empowering him to enter upon the discharge of his office as executor.

LEVY, v. To raise; execute; exact; collect; gather; take up; seize. Thus, to levy (raise or collect) a tax; to levy (raise or set up) a nuisance; to levy (acknowledge) a fine; to levy (inaugurate) war; to levy an execution—i. e., to levy or collect a sum of money on an execution.

LIEN. A qualified right of property which a creditor has in or over specific property of his debtor, as security for the debt or charge or for performance of some act.

LIFE ESTATE. An estate whose duration is limited to the life of the party holding it, or of some other person; a freehold estate, not of inheritance.

LIFE TENANT. One who holds an estate in lands for the period of his own life or that of another certain person.

LIMITATION. In conveyances. A defining or limiting, either by express words or by implication of law, of the time during which the estate granted is to be enjoyed; e. g., "to A. and his heirs forever,"

limits an estate in fee simple to A.; "to B. for life, remainder to C. and his heirs," limits a life estate to B., with a remainder in fee simple to C.

In statutes of limitation. Under statutes of limitation, a certain limit of time is set, after the running of which, subsequent to the accruing of a cause of action, no action can be brought successfully, if the statute is pleaded.

LIMITED PARTNERSHIP. A partnership consisting of one or more general partners, jointly and severally responsible as ordinary partners, and by whom the business is conducted, and one or more special partners, contributing in cash payments a specific sum as capital to the common stock, and who are not liable for the debts of the partnership beyond the fund so contributed.

LIQUIDATED. Ascertained; determined; fixed; settled; made clear or manifest. Cleared away; paid; discharged.

LIQUIDATED ACCOUNT. An account whereof the amount is certain and fixed, either by the act and agreement of the parties or by operation of law; a sum which cannot be changed by the proof; it is so much or nothing; but the term does not necessarily refer to a writing.

LIQUIDATED AND UNLIQUIDATED DAMAGES. The former term is applicable when the amount of the damages has been ascertained by the judgment in the action, or when a specific sum of money has been expressly stipulated by the parties to a bond or other contract as the amount of damages to be recovered by either party for a breach of the agreement by the other.

LIS PENDENS. Latin. A suit pending; that legal process. in a suit regarding land, which amounts to legal notice to all the world that there is a dispute as to the title. In equity the filing of the bill and serving a subpœna creates a lis pendens, except when statutes require some record.

LOCATIO. Latin. A hiring of goods for a reward.

LOCUS PŒNITENTIÆ. Latin. A place for repentance; an opportunity for changing one's mind; a chance to withdraw from a contemplated bargain or contract before it results in a definite contractual liability. Also used of a chance afforded to a person, by the circumstances, of relinquishing the intention which he has formed to commit a crime, before the perpetration thereof.

LODGING HOUSE. A private house at which lodging is given for a consideration, as contrasted with a public house or inn or hotel.

L. S. An abbreviation for "locus sigilli," the place of the seal; i. e., the place where a seal is to be affixed, or a scroll which stands instead of a seal.

M

MAINTENANCE. An unauthorized and officious interference in a suit in which the offender has no interest, to assist one of the parties to it, against the other, with money or advice to prosecute or defend the action.

MALFEASANCE. The wrongful or unjust doing of some act which the doer has no right to perform, or which he has stipulated by contract not to do. It differs from "misfeasance" and "nonfeasance" (which titles see).

MALUM IN SE. Latin. A wrong in itself; an act or case involving illegality from the very nature of the transaction, upon principles of natural, moral, and public law. An act is said to be malum in se when it is inherently and essentially evil—that is, immoral in its nature and injurious in its consequences—without any regard to the fact of its being noticed or punished by the law of the state. Such are most or all of the offenses cognizable at common law (without the denouncement of a statute); as murder, larceny, etc.

MALUM PROHIBITUM. Latin. A wrong prohibited; a thing which is wrong because prohibited; an act which is not inherently immoral, but becomes so because its commission is expressly forbidden by positive law; an act involving an illegality resulting from positive law. Contrasted with malum in se.

MANDAMUS. Latin, we command. A legal writ compelling the defendant to do an official duty.

MANDATE. A bailment of property in regard to which the bailee engages to do some act without reward. Story, Bailm. § 137.

MATERIALMAN. One who furnishes materials to be used in the construction or repair of ships or houses.

MATURITY. In mercantile law. The time when a bill of exchange or promissory note becomes due.

MECHANIC'S LIEN. A species of lien created by statute in most of the states, which exists in favor of persons who have performed work or furnished material in and for the erection of a building. Their lien attaches to the land as well as the building, and is intended to secure for them a priority of payment.

MERGER. The fusion or absorption of one thing or right into another; generally spoken of a case where one of the subjects is of less dignity or importance than the other. Here the less important ceases to have an independent existence.

MESNE. Intermediate.

Mesne process. Process issued between the beginning of a suit and final process.

Mesne profits. Profits from the use of land during wrongful occupancy, recovered, in ejectment or trespass, by the owner from the defendant in the action.

MINOR. An infant or person who is under the age of legal competence. A term derived from the civil law, which described a person under a certain age as less than so many years. Minor viginti quinque annis, one less than twenty-five years of age.

MISDEMEANOR. In criminal law. A general name for criminal offenses of every sort, punishable by indictment or special proceedings, which do not in law amount to the grade of felony.

MISFEASANCE. A misdeed or trespass. The doing what a party ought to do improperly. The improper performance of some act which a man may lawfully do.

Misfeasance, strictly, is not doing a lawful act in a proper manner, omitting to do it as it should be done, while malfeasance is the doing an act wholly wrongful, and nonfeasance is an omission to perform a duty, or a total neglect of duty. But "misfeasance" is often carelessly used in the sense of "malfeasance."

MISREPRESENTATION. An intentional false statement respecting a matter of fact, made by one of the parties to a contract, which is material to the contract and influential in producing it.

MORTGAGE. An estate created by a conveyance absolute in form, but intended to secure the performance of some act, such as the payment of money, and the like, by the grantor or some other person, and to become void if the act is performed agreeably to the terms prescribed at the time of making such conveyance.

A conditional conveyance of land, designed as a security for the payment of money, the fulfillment of some contract, or the performance of some act, and to be void upon such payment, fulfillment, or performance.

A debt by specialty, secured by a pledge of lands, of which the legal ownership is vested in the creditor, but of which, in equity, the debtor and those claiming under him remain the actual owners, until debarred by judicial sentence or their own laches.

The foregoing definitions are applicable to the common-law conception of a mortgage. But in many states, in modern times, it is regarded as a mere lien, and not as creating a title or estate. It is a pledge or security of particular property for the payment of a debt, or the performance of some other obligation, whatever form the transaction may take, but is not regarded as a conveyance in effect, though it may be cast in the form of a conveyance.

MUTUUM. Latin. In the law of bailments. A loan for consumption; a loan of chattels, upon an agreement that the borrower may consume them, returning to the lender an equivalent in kind and quantity.

N

NEGLIGENCE. The omission to do something which a reasonable man, guided by those considerations which ordinarily regulate the conduct of human affairs, would do, or doing something which a prudent and reasonable man would not do. It must be determined in all cases by reference to the situation and knowledge of the parties and all the attendant circumstances.

Negligence, in its civil relation, is such an inadvertent imperfection, by a responsible human agent, in the discharge of a legal duty, as immediately produces, in an ordinary and natural sequence, a damage to another.

NEGLIGENCE VEL NON. (A phrase of mixed English and Latin.) Negligence or not.

NEGOTIABLE. An instrument embodying an obligation for the payment of money is called "negotiable" when the legal title to the instrument itself and to the whole amount of money expressed upon its face, with the right to sue therefor in his own name, may be transferred from one person to another without a formal assignment, but by mere indorsement and delivery by the holder or by delivery only.

NEMO PLUS JURIS AD ALIUM TRANSFERRE POTEST QUAM IPSE HABERET. Latin. No one can transfer to another more of right than he himself has. This maxim, like most maxims, must not be taken as true without any limitations. It is well known that the bona fide purchaser of real or personal property, or the holder in due course of a negotiable instrument, does in many cases take a greater right than his transferor has had.

NIL DEBET. Latin. He owes nothing. A plea that the defendant owes nothing.

NISI PRIUS. Latin. Literally, unless before. The expression has now so far departed from its original Latin signification as to mean substantially "at the trial." The words were originally words of some importance in the writ directing the sheriff to summon jurors. "A practice obtained very early, * * * in the trial of trifling causes, to continue the cause in the superior court from term to term, provided the justices in eyre did not sooner (nisi prius justiciari) come into the county where the cause of action arose, in which case they had jurisdiction when they so came." Bouvier's Law Dict.

NOMINAL AND SUBSTANTIAL DAMAGES. Nominal damages are a trifling sum awarded to a plaintiff in an action, where there is no substantial loss or injury to be compensated, but still the law recognizes a technical invasion of his rights or a breach of the defendant's duty, or in cases where, although there has been a real injury, the plaintiff's evidence entirely fails to show its amount.

NOMINAL PARTNER. A person who appears to be a partner in a firm, or is so represented to persons dealing with the firm, or who allows his name to appear in the style of the firm or to be used in its business, in the character of a partner, but who has no actual interest in the firm or business.

NON ASSUMPSIT. Latin. The general issue in the action of assumpsit, being a plea by which the defendant avers that "he did not undertake" or promise as alleged.

NON COMPOS MENTIS. Latin. Not sound of mind; insane.

NON EST FACTUM. Latin. It was not made.

NONFEASANCE. The neglect or failure of a person to do some act which he ought to do.

NONSUIT. Not following up the cause; failure on the part of a plaintiff to continue the prosecution of his suit. An abandonment or renunciation of his suit, by a plaintiff, either by omitting to take the next necessary steps, or voluntarily relinquishing the action, or pursuant to an order of the court. An order or judgment, granted upon the trial of a cause, that the plaintiff has abandoned, or shall abandon, the further prosecution of his suit.

NOTARY PUBLIC. A public officer whose function is to attest and certify, by his hand and official seal, certain classes of documents, in order to give them credit and authenticity in foreign jurisdictions; to take acknowledgments of deeds and other conveyances, and certify the same; and to perform certain official acts, chiefly in commercial matters, such as the protesting of notes and bills, the noting of foreign drafts, and marine protests in cases of loss or damage.

NUDUM PACTUM. Latin. A naked pact; a bare agreement; a promise or undertaking made without any consideration for it.

NUISANCE. That class of wrongs that arise from the unreasonable, unwarrantable, or unlawful use by a person of his own property, either real or personal, or from his own improper, indecent, or unlawful personal conduct, working an obstruction of or injury to the right of another or of the public, and producing such material annoyance, inconvenience, discomfort, or hurt that the law will presume a consequent damage.

O

OATH. An external pledge or asseveration, made in verification of statements made or to be made, coupled with an appeal to a sacred or venerated object, in evidence of the serious and reverent state of mind of the party, or with an invocation to a supreme being to witness the words of the party and to visit him with punishment if they be false.

OBITER DICTUM. Latin. A remark made, or opinion expressed, by a judge, in his decision upon a cause, "by the way"; that is, incidentally or collaterally, and not directly upon the question before him, or upon a point not necessarily involved in the determination of the cause, or introduced by way of illustration, or analogy or argument.

OMNIS RATIHABITIO RETROTRAHITUR ET MANDATO PRIORI ÆQUIPARATUR. Latin. Every ratification relates back and is equivalent to a prior authority. Broom, Max. 757, 871.

ORDINANCE. The term is used to designate the enactments of the legislative body of a municipal corporation.

OSTENSIBLE AGENCY. An implied or presumptive agency, which exists where one, either intentionally or from want of ordinary care, induces another to believe that a third person is his agent, though he never in fact employed him.

OSTENSIBLE PARTNER. A partner whose name is made known and appears to the world as a partner, and who is in reality such.

OUTLAWED. When applied to a promissory note, means debarred by the statute of limitations.

OYER. In modern practice. A copy of a bond or specialty sued upon, given to the opposite party, in lieu of the old practice of reading it.

P

PAR. In commercial law. Equal; equality. An equality subsisting between the nominal or face value of a bill of exchange, share of stock, etc., and its actual selling value. When the values are thus equal, the instrument or share is said to be "at par"; if it can be sold for more than its nominal worth, it is "above par"; if for less, it is "below par."

PARI PASSU. Latin. By an equal progress; ratably; without preference.

PARTICEPS. Latin. A participant; a sharer; anciently, a part owner, or parcener.

PARTICEPS CRIMINIS. Latin. A participant in a crime; an accomplice. One who shares or co-operates in a criminal offense, tort, or fraud.

PARTITION. The dividing of lands held by joint tenants, coparceners, or tenants in common, into distinct portions, so that they may hold them in severalty. And, in a less technical sense, any division of real or personal property between co-owners or co-proprietors.

PARTNERSHIP. A voluntary contract between two or more competent persons to place their money, effects, labor, and skill, or some or all of them, in lawful commerce or business, with the understanding that there shall be a proportional sharing of the profits and losses between them.

PART PERFORMANCE. The doing some portion, yet not the whole, of what either party to a contract has agreed to do.

PATENT, n. A grant of some privilege, property, or authority, made by the government or sovereign of a country to one or more individuals.

In English law. A grant by the sovereign to a subject or subjects, under the great seal, conferring some authority, title, franchise, or property; termed "letters patent" from being delivered open, and not closed up from inspection.

In American law. The instrument by which a state or government grants public lands to an individual.

A grant made by the government to an inventor, conveying and securing to him the exclusive right to make and sell his invention for a term of years.

PAWN, n. A bailment of goods to a creditor, as security for some debt or engagement; a pledge. Story, Bailm. art. 7.

PAYEE. The person in whose favor a negotiable instrument is made or drawn; the person to whom a negotiable instrument is made payable.

PAYER, or **PAYOR.** One who pays, or who is to make a payment; particularly the person who makes or is to make payment of a negotiable instrument.

PERFORM. To perform an obligation or contract is to execute, fulfill, or accomplish it according to its terms. This may consist either in action on the part of the person bound by the contract or in omission to act, according to the nature of the subject-matter; but the term is usually applied to any action in discharge of a contract other than payment.

PERFORMANCE. The fulfillment or accomplishment of a promise, contract, or other obligation according to its terms.

Part performance. The doing some portion, yet not the whole, of what either party to a contract has agreed to do.

Specific performance. Performance of a contract in the specific form in which it was made, or according to the precise terms agreed upon. This is frequently compelled by a bill in equity filed for the purpose. 2 Story, Eq. Pl. § 712 et seq. The doctrine of specific performance is that, where damages would be an inadequate compensation for the breach of an agreement, the contractor will be compelled to perform specifically what he has agreed to do. Sweet.

PERJURY. In criminal law. The willful assertion as to a matter of fact, opinion, belief, or knowledge, made by a witness in a judicial proceeding as **part**

of his evidence, either upon oath or in any form allowed by law to be substituted for an oath, whether such evidence is given in open court, or in an affidavit, or otherwise, such assertion being known to such witness to be false, and being intended by him to mislead the court, jury or person holding the proceeding.

PERPETUITY. "A future limitation, whether executory or by way of remainder, and of real or personal property, which is not to vest till after the expiration of, or which will not necessariy vest within, the period prescribed by law for the creation of future estates, and which is not destructible by the person for the time being entitled to the property subject to the future limitation, except with the concurrence of the person interested in the contingent event." Lewis, Perp. c. 12.

PER SE. Latin. By himself or itself; in itself; taken alone; inherently; in isolation; unconnected with other matters.

PERSONALTY. Personal property; movable property; chattels.

PERSONAL PROPERTY. See **Personalty.**

PIGNUS. Latin. A pledge. A collateral pledge.

PLAINTIFF. A person who brings an action; the party who complains or sues in a personal action and is so named on the record.

PLAINTIFF IN ERROR. The party who sues out a writ of error to review a judgment or other proceeding at law.

PLEA. In common-law practice. A pleading; any one in the series of pleadings. More particularly, the first pleading on the part of the defendant. In the strictest sense, the answer which the defendant in an action at law makes to the plaintiff's declaration, and in which he sets up matter of fact as defense, thus distinguished from a demurrer, which interposes objections on grounds of law.

In equity. A special answer showing or relying upon one or more things as a cause why the suit should be either dismissed or delayed or barred.

PLEAD. To make, deliver, or file any pleading; to conduct the pleadings in a cause. To interpose any pleading in a suit which contains allegations of fact; in this sense the word is the antithesis of "demur." More particularly, to deliver in a formal manner the defendant's answer to the plaintiff's declaration, or to the indictment, as the case may be.

PLEADING. The peculiar science or system of rules and principles, established in the common law, according to which the pleadings or responsive allegations of litigating parties are framed, with a view to preserve technical propriety and to produce a proper issue.

The process performed by the parties to a suit or action, in alternately presenting written statements of their contention, each responsive to that which precedes, and each serving to narrow the field of controversy, until there evolves a single point, affirmed on one side and denied on the other, called the "issue," upon which they then go to trial.

The act or step of interposing any one of the pleadings in a cause, but particularly one on the part of the defendant; and, in the strictest sense, one which sets up allegations of fact in defense to the action.

PLEDGE, n. A bailment of goods to a creditor, as security for some debt or engagement; a pawn. Story, Bailm. art. 7.

PLEDGEE. The party to whom goods are pledged, or delivered in pledge.

PLEDGOR. The party delivering goods in pledge; the party pledging.

POLICE POWER. The power vested in a state to establish laws and ordinances for the regulation and enforcement of public order and tranquillity. The power vested in the legislature to make, ordain, and establish all manner of wholesome and reasonable laws, statutes, and ordinances, either with penalties or without, not repugnant to the constitution, as they shall judge to be for the good and welfare of the commonwealth, and of the subjects of the same. The police power of the state is an authority conferred by the American constitutional system upon the individual states, through which they are enabled to establish a special department of police; adopt such regulations as tend to prevent the commission of fraud, violence, or other offenses against the state; aid in the arrest of criminals; and secure generally the comfort, health, and prosperity of the state, by preserving the public order, preventing a conflict of rights in the common intercourse of the citizens, and insuring to each an uninterrupted enjoyment of all the privileges conferred upon him by the laws of his country. It is true that the legislation which secures to all protection in their rights, and the equal use and enjoyment of their property, embraces an almost infinite variety of subjects. Whatever affects the peace, good order, morals, and health of the community comes within its scope; and every one must use and enjoy his property subject to the restrictions which such legislation imposes. What is termed the "police power" of the state, which, from the language often used respecting it, one would suppose to be be an undefined and irresponsible element in government, can only interfere with the conduct of individuals in their intercourse with each other, and in the use of their property, so far as may be required to secure these objects.

POLICY OF INSURANCE. A mercantile instrument in writing, by which one party, in consideration of a premium, engages to indemnify another against a contingent loss, by making him a payment in compensation, whenever the event shall happen by which the loss is to accrue.

POST–DATE. To date an instrument as of a time later than that at which it is really made.

POWER OF APPOINTMENT. A power or authority conferred by one person by deed or will upon another (called the "donee") to appoint, that is, to select and nominate, the person or persons who are to receive and enjoy an estate or an income therefrom or from a fund, after the testator's death, or the donee's death, or after the termination of an existing right or interest.

POWER OF ATTORNEY. An instrument authorizing a person to act as the agent or attorney of the person granting it.

PREFERENCE. The payment of money or the transfer of property to one creditor in preference to other creditors. Where the debtor is solvent, he may legally make such a preference. Under the federal Bankruptcy Act, a debtor is said to have made a preference if, being insolvent, he has made a transfer of any of his property and the effect of the enforcement of such transfer will be to enable any one of his creditors to obtain a greater percentage of his debt than any other of such creditors of the same class.

PREMIUM. The sum paid or agreed to be paid by an assured to the underwriter as the consideration for the insurance; being a certain rate per cent. on the amount insured.

PRESCRIPTION. The acquisition of incorporeal hereditaments by user or enjoyment for a very long time; i. e. "from time immemorial," or for a certain time set by a statute of limitations. For instance, A. continues to cross the land of B. by a certain path each day for twenty years, the period within which an action must be brought or other means taken to cause a discontinuance of A.'s user, under the laws of the state in which B.'s land lies. A. then has the right "by prescription" to continue to cross the land of B. His easement is complete.

PRESENTMENT. The production of a bill of exchange to the drawee for his acceptance, or to the drawer or acceptor for payment; or of a promissory note to the party liable, for payment of the same.

PRESUMPTION. An inference affirmative or disaffirmative of the truth or falsehood of any proposition or fact drawn by a process of probable reasoning in the absence of actual certainty of its truth or falsehood, or until such certainty can be ascertained.

PRIMA FACIE. Latin. At first sight; on the first apearance; on the face of it; so far as can be judged from the first disclosure; presumably.

A litigating party is said to have a prima facie case when the evidence in his favor is sufficiently strong for his opponent to be called on to answer it.

PRINCIPAL. In the law of agency. The employer or constitutor of an agent; the person who gives authority to an agent or attorney to do some act for him.

PRIVATE CARRIER. One who carries passengers or the goods of another without holding himself out to the general public as serving all persons that apply. The private carrier is contrasted with the common or public carrier.

PROBATE. The act or process of proving a will. The proof before an ordinary, surrogate, register, or other duly authorized person that a document produced before him for official recognition and registration, and alleged to be the last will and testament of a certain deceased person, is such in reality.

PROCEDURE. The method and mechanism, so to speak, by which proceedings in a court are conducted.

PROCESS. In practice. This word is generally defined to be the means of compelling the defendant in an action to appear in court.

PROCURATION. Agency; proxy; the act of constituting another one's attorney in fact; action under a power of attorney or other constitution of agency. Indorsing a bill or note "by procuration" (or per proc.) is doing it as proxy for another or by his authority.

PROMISSORY NOTE. A promise or engagement, in writing, to pay a specified sum at a time therein limited, or on demand, or at sight, to a person therein named, or to his order, or bearer.

PROMOTERS. In the law relating to corporations, those persons are called the "promoters" of a company who first associate themselves together for the purpose of organizing the company, issuing its prospectus, procuring subscriptions to the stock, securing a charter, etc.

PROSECUTE. To follow up; to carry on an action or other judicial proceeding; to proceed against a person criminally.

PRO TANTO. Latin. For so much; as far as it goes.

PROTEST. A notarial act, being a formal statement in writing made by a notary under his seal of office, at the request of the holder of a bill or note, in which such bill or note is described, and it is declared that the same was on a certain day presented for payment (or acceptance, as the case may be), and that such payment or acceptance was refused, and stating the reasons, if any, given for such refusal, whereupon the notary protests against all parties to such instrument, and declares that they will be held responsible for all loss or damage arising from its dishonor.

PROXY. A person who is substituted or deputed by another to represent him and act for him, particularly in some meeting or public body. Also the instrument containing the appointment of such person.

Q

QUA. Latin. As; in the character or capacity of. E. g., "the trustee qua trustee."

QUANTUM MERUIT. Latin. As much as he deserved.

In pleading. The common count in an action of assumpsit for work and labor, founded on an implied assumpsit or promise on the part of the defendant to pay the plaintiff as much as he reasonably deserved to have for his labor.

QUASI. Latin. As if; as it were; analogous to. This term is used in legal phraseology to indicate that one subject resembles another, with which it is compared, in certain characteristics, but that there are also intrinsic differences between them.

QUASI CONTRACT. In the civil law. A contractual relation arising out of transactions between the parties which give them mutual rights and obligations, but do not involve a specific and express convention or agreement between them.

QUIA EMPTORES. Latin. The English statute (18 Edw. I) prohibiting subinfeudation.

QUIET, v. To pacify; to render secure or unassailable by the removal of disquieting causes or disputes. This is the meaning of the word in the phrase "action to quiet title," which is a proceeding to establish the plaintiff's title to land by bringing into court an adverse claimant and there compelling him either to establish his claim or be forever after estopped from asserting it.

QUITCLAIM DEED. A deed of conveyance operating by way of release; that is, intended to pass any title, interest, or claim which the grantor may have in the premises, but not professing that such title is valid, nor containing any warranty or covenants for title.

QUO WARRANTO. Latin. By what warrant? A name commonly applied, in the United States, to an "information in the nature of a quo warranto," an action compelling the defendant to show by what warrant he exercises certain powers or privileges. The proceeding is used to test the right of a person to public office, or the right of a private or public corporation to exercise certain franchises.

R

RATIFICATION. The confirmation of a previous act done either by the party himself or by another; confirmation of a voidable act.

REAL ESTATE. See **Real Property.**

REALTY. See **Real Property.**

REAL PROPERTY. A general term for lands, tenements, and hereditaments; property which, on the death of the owner intestate, passes to his heir. Real property is either corporeal or incorporeal.

RECEIPT. A receipt is the written acknowledgment of the receipt of money, or a thing of value, without containing any affirmative obligation upon either party to it; a mere admission of a fact in writing.

Also the act or transaction of accepting or taking anything delivered.

RECEIVER. A receiver is an indifferent person between the parties appointed by the court to collect and receive the rents, issues, and profits of land, or the produce of personal estate, or other things which it does not seem reasonable to the court that either party should do; or where a party is incompetent to do so, as in the case of an infant. The remedy of the appointment of a receiver is one of the very oldest in the court of chancery, and is founded on the inadequacy of the remedy to be obtained in the court of ordinary jurisdiction.

RECOGNIZANCE. An obligation of record, entered into before some court of record, or magistrate duly authorized, with condition to do some particular act; as to appear at the assizes, or criminal court, to keep the peace, to pay a debt, or the like. It resembles a bond, but differs from it in being an acknowledgment of a former debt upon record.

RECOUPMENT. Recoupment is a right of the defendant to have a deduction from the amount of the plaintiff's damages, for the reason that the plaintiff has not complied with the cross-obligations or independent covenants arising under the same contract.

"Recoupment" differs from "set-off" in this respect: that any claim or demand the defendant may have against the plaintiff may be used as a set-off, while it is not a subject for recoupment unless it grows out of the very same transaction which furnishes the plaintiff's cause of action.

RECOVERY. The collection of a debt through an action at law.

Right of recovery. A plaintiff is said to have a right of recovery when he has a right of action under the facts of a given case.

REDEMPTION. (From the Latin, redemptio; a buying back.) A buying back of property from the original purchaser by the original seller. A mortgage purports to convey title to the mortgagee, subject to a right of redemption in the mortgagor; i. e., the mortgagor has an "equity of redemption" in the property. The mortgagor has a right and a power to defeat the efficacy of his mortgage as a complete conveyance of the title, by paying the amount of the debt secured by the mortgage, thus meeting the condition subsequent stated in the "defeasance clause" of the mortgage.

REIMBURSEMENT. The equitable and legal right of reimbursement of a surety is the surety's right to be reimbursed by his principal in the amount of the principal's debt paid by the surety.

RELATOR. The person upon whose complaint, or at whose instance, an information or writ of quo warranto is filed, and who is quasi the plaintiff in the proceeding.

RELEASE. The relinquishment, concession, or giving up of a right, claim, or privilege, by the person in whom it exists or to whom it accrues, to the person against whom it might have been demanded or enforced.

REMAINDER. An estate limited to take effect and be enjoyed after another estate is determined. As, if a man seised in fee-simple grants lands to A. for twenty years, and, after the determination of the said term, then to B. and his heirs forever, here A. is tenant for years, remainder to B. in fee.

REMAND. Where a decision of a trial court is reversed in an appellate court, it is frequently sent back or "remanded" to the trial court for a new trial. In some cases, as where the plaintiff has been given judgment on a state of facts that could not, in any view, justify such judgment, the appellate court may reverse the judgment without remanding.

REMEDIAL. Of or pertaining to the legal remedy, or to the form or procedural details of such remedy.

REMEDY. The means by which the violation of a right is prevented, redressed, or compensated. Though a remedy may be by the act of the party injured, by operation of law, or by agreement between the injurer and the injured, we are chiefly concerned with one kind of remedy, the judicial remedy, which is by action or suit.

REMITTITUR DAMNA. Latin. Usually shortened to **Remittitur.** An entry made on record, in cases where a jury has given greater damages than a plaintiff has declared for, remitting the excess.

RENT. The compensation, either in money, provisions, chattels, or labor, received by the owner of the soil from the occupant thereof.

REPLEVIN. A personal action ex delicto brought to recover possession of goods unlawfully taken (generally, but not only, applicable to the taking of goods distrained for rent), the validity of which taking it is the mode of contesting, if the party from whom the goods were taken wishes to have them back in specie, whereas, if he prefer to have damages instead, the validity may be contested by action of trespass or unlawful distress.

REPLEVIN BOND. A bond executed to indemnify the officer who executed a writ of replevin and to indemnify the defendant or person from whose custody the property was taken for such damages as he may sustain.

RESCISSION. Rescission, or the act of rescinding, is where a contract is canceled, annulled, or abrogated by the parties, or one of them.

RESIDENCE. Living or dwelling in a certain place permanently or for a considerable length of time. The place where a man makes his home, or where he dwells permanently or for an extended period of time.

RESIDUARY. Pertaining to the residue; constituting the residue; giving or bequeathing the residue; receiving or entitled to the residue.

RESIDUARY DEVISEE. The person named in a will, who is to take all the real property remaining over and above the other devises.

RESIDUARY ESTATE. The remaining part of a testator's estate and effects, after payment of debts and legacies; or that portion of his estate which has not been particularly devised or bequeathed.

RESIDUARY LEGATEE. The person to whom a testator bequeaths the residue of his personal estate, after the payment of such other legacies as are specifically mentioned in the will.

RESPONDEAT SUPERIOR. Latin. Let the master answer. This maxim means that a master is liable in certain cases for the wrongful acts of his servant, and a principal for those of his agent.

RESPONDENT. The party who makes an answer to a bill or other proceeding in chancery.

The party who appeals against the judgment of an inferior court is termed the "appellant"; and he who contends against the appeal, the "respondent."

REVERSE. An appellate court uses the term "reversed" to indicate that it annuls or avoids the judgment, or vacates the decree, of the trial court.

REVOCATION. The recall of some power, authority, or thing granted, or a destroying or making void of some deed that had existence until the act of revocation made it void. It may be either general, of all acts and things done before; or special, to revoke a particular thing.

RIGHT OF ACTION. The right to bring suit; a legal right to maintain an action, growing out of a given transaction or state of facts and based thereon.

RIGHT OF ENTRY. A right of entry is the right of taking or resuming possession of land by entering on it in a peaceable manner.

RIGHT TO REDEEM. The term "right of redemption" or "right to redeem," is familiarly used to describe the estate of the debtor when under mortgage, to be sold at auction, in contradistinction to an absolute estate, to be set off by appraisement. It would be more consonant to the legal character of this interest to call it the "debtor's estate subject to mortgage."

S

SATISFACTION. The act of satisfying a party by paying what is due to him (as on a mortgage, lien, or contract), or what is awarded to him, by the judgment of a court or otherwise. Thus, a judgment is satisfied by the payment of the amount due to the party who has recovered such judgment, or by his levying the amount.

SCIENTER. Latin. Knowingly.

SCINTILLA. Latin. A spark; a remaining particle; the least particle.

SCIRE FACIAS. Latin. You may cause to know. In practice, a judicial writ, founded upon some record, and requiring the person against whom it is brought to show cause why the party bringing it should not have advantage of such record, or (in the case of a scire facias to repeal letters patent) why the record should not be annulled and vacated.

The most common application of this writ is as a process to revive a judgment, after the lapse of a certain time, or on a change of parties, or otherwise to have execution of the judgment, in which cases it is merely a continuation of the original action.

SCROLL or SCRAWL. A mark intended to supply the place of a seal, made with a pen or other instrument of writing.

SEAL. An impression upon wax, wafer, or some other tenacious substance capable of being impressed.

SEISIN. Possession with an intent on the part of him who holds it to claim a freehold interest.

SET–OFF. A counterclaim or cross-demand; a claim or demand which the defendant in an action sets off against the claim of the plaintiff, as being his due, whereby he may extinguish the plaintiff's demand, either in whole or in part, according to the amount of the set-off.

SET UP. To bring forward or allege, as something relied upon or deemed sufficient; to propose or interpose, by way of defense, explanation, or justification; as, to set up the statute of limitations—i. e., offer and rely upon it as a defense to a claim.

SEVERANCE. The cutting of the crops, such as corn, grass, etc., or the separating of anything from the realty. Brown.

SHELLEY'S CASE, RULE IN. "That rule is that, where a life estate is given to A. with a future interest to A.'s heirs (the use of the particular word 'heirs' being necessary), the whole gift is construed as one 'to A. and his heirs,' at once giving an estate to A. in fee." Albert M. Kales, in 5 Am.Law & Proced. 105.

SILENT PARTNER. Popular name for dormant partners or special partners.

SIMPLE CONTRACT. A contract based upon consideration and not upon form.

SPECIAL INDORSEMENT. An indorsement in full, which specifically names the indorsee.

SPECIAL PARTNER. A member of a limited partnership, who furnishes certain funds to the common stock, and whose liability extends no further than the fund furnished.

SPECIAL PROPERTY. Property of a qualified, temporary, or limited nature; as distinguished from absolute, general, or unconditional property. Such is the property of a bailee in the article bailed, of a sheriff in goods temporarily in his hands under a levy, of the finder of lost goods while looking for the owner, of a person in wild animals which he has caught.

SPECIALTY. A writing sealed and delivered, containing some agreement.

SPECIAL VERDICT. A special finding of the facts of a case by a jury, leaving to the court the application of the law to the facts thus found.

SPOLIATION. In torts. Destruction of a thing by the act of a stranger, as the erasure or alteration of a writing by the act of a stranger, is called "spoliation." This has not the effect to destroy its character or legal effect.

SS. An abbreviation used in that part of a record, pleading, or affidavit, called the "statement of the venue." Commonly translated or read "to wit," and supposed to be a contraction of "scilicet."

STATUS. The status of a person is his legal position or condition.

STATUTE, n. An act of the legislature.

STATUTE OF FRAUDS. A celebrated English statute, passed in 1677, and which has been adopted, in a more or less modified form, in nearly all of the United States. Its chief characteristic is the provision that no action shall be brought on certain contracts unless there be a note or memorandum thereof in writing, signed by the party to be charged or by his authorized agent.

STATUTE OF LIMITATION. A statute prescribing limitations to the right of action on certain described causes of action; that is, declaring that no suit shall be maintained on such causes of action unless brought within a specified period after the right accrued.

STATUTORY UNDERTAKING. A penal bond, given, as required by statute, in connection with certain legal proceedings. "Common examples of statutory undertaking are: The bond given by a plaintiff in an injunction suit, as security to the defendant for damages caused by the issuance of an interlocutory injunction, such damages, within the amount of the penalty, to be collected by the defendant if the injunction is found to have been wrongfully issued; and the bond given for a very similar purpose in attachment or replevin." Bauer on Damages, p. 98, note.

STOCK. **In corporation law.** The capital or principal fund of a corporation or joint-stock company, formed by the contributions of subscribers or the sale of shares, and considered as the aggregate of a certain number of shares severally owned by the members or stockholders of the corporation; also the proportional part of the capital which is owned by an individual stockholder; also the incorporeal property which is represented by the holding of a certificate of stock, and in a wider and more remote sense, the right of a shareholder to participate in the general management of the company and to share proportionally in its net profits or earnings or in the distribution of assets on dissolution.

STOPPAGE IN TRANSITU. The act by which the unpaid vendor of goods stops their progress and resumes possession of them, while they are in course of transit from him to the purchaser, and not yet actually delivered to the latter.

STRICTISSIMI JURIS. Latin. Of the strictest right or law.

SUBAGENT. An under-agent; a substituted agent; an agent appointed by one who is himself an agent.

SUBINFEUDATION. Under the feudal system, an inferior lord sometimes carved out of an estate which he held of a superior lord, a part which he granted to an inferior tenant, whose lord he in turn became. This under-feudalizing, so to speak, used in order to evade restraints on alienation, was known as subinfeudation, and was prohibited by the Statute of Quia Emptores (St. 18 Edw. I).

SUBPŒNA. Latin. Sub, under, and pœna, punishment or penalty. In the Latin writs early used in England, one was commanded to appear "sub pœna," and these words have given the name to writs of those types in which they appeared.

Of a witness. A process commanding a witness to appear in court at a certain time to testify in a given cause.

In chancery practice. A process commanding a party or parties to a suit in equity to appear and answer matters alleged against them in the bill.

SUBROGATION. The substitution of one thing for another, or of one person into the place of another with respect to rights, claims, or securities.

Subrogation denotes the putting a third person who has paid a debt in the place of the creditor to whom he has paid it, so that he may exercise against the debtor all the rights which the creditor, if unpaid, might have done.

SUBSCRIBE. **In the law of contracts.** To write under; to write the name under; to write the name at the bottom or end of a writing.

SUBSTANTIVE LAW. The part of the law which the courts are established to administer, as opposed to the rules according to which the substantive law itself is administered. That part of the law which creates, defines, and regulates rights, as opposed to adjective or remedial law, which prescribes the method of enforcing rights or obtaining redress for their invasion.

SUI GENERIS. Latin. Of its own kind or class.

SUI JURIS. Latin. Of his own right; having legal capacity to manage his own affairs.

SUIT. "Suit" is a generic term, of comprehensive signification, and applies to any proceeding in a court of justice in which the plaintiff pursues, in such court, the remedy which the law affords him for the redress of an injury or the recovery of a right.

SUMMARY, adj. Immediate; peremptory; off-hand; without a jury; provisional; statutory.

SUMMON. **In practice.** To serve a summons; to cite a defendant to appear in court to answer a suit which has been begun against him; to notify the defendant that an action has been instituted against him, and that he is required to answer to it at a time and place named.

SUMMONS. **In practice.** A writ, directed to the sheriff or other proper officer, requiring him to notify the person named that an action has been commenced against him in the court whence the writ issues, and that he is required to appear, on a day named, and answer the complaint in such action.

SURETY. A surety is one who at the request of another, and for the purpose of securing to him a benefit, becomes responsible for the performance by the latter of some act in favor of a third person, or hypothecates property as security therefor.

T

TENANCY IN COMMON. A tenancy under which each cotenant has a distinct and several estate in the property. Under such a tenancy, the survivor from among the cotenants does not take the entire property as in the case of a joint tenancy.

TENANT. In the broadest sense, one who holds or possesses lands or tenements by any kind of right or title, whether in fee, for life, for years, at will, or otherwise. Cowell.

In a more restricted sense, one who holds lands of another; one who has the temporary use and occupation of real property owned by another person (called the "landlord"), the duration and terms of his tenancy being usually fixed by an instrument called a "lease."

TENDER. An offer of money; the act by which one produces and offers to a person holding a claim or demand against him the amount of money which he considers and admits to be due, in satisfaction of such claim or demand, without any stipulation or condition.

Also, there may be a tender of performance of a duty other than the payment of money.

TENOR. In pleading the "tenor" of a document is sometimes said to be shown when an exact copy is set out in the pleading. Also, the word is often used to denote the true meaning or purport of an instrument.

TENURE. In the law of public officers. The period during which an officer holds office.

In the law of real property. The legal mode in which one owns an estate in lands.

TERM. Of court. The word "term" when used with reference to a court, signifies the space of time during which the court holds a session. A "session" signifies the time during the term when the court sits for the transaction of business, and the session commences when the court convenes for the term, and continues until final adjournment, either before or at the expiration of the term. The "term" of the court is the time prescribed by law during which it may be in "session." The "session" of the court is the time of its actual sitting.

TESTATOR. One who makes or has made a testament or will; one who dies leaving a will.

TITLE. The means whereby the owner of lands or of personalty has the just possession of his property. See Co. Litt. 345; 2 Bl.Comm. 195.

TORT. Wrong; injury; the opposite of right. So called, according to Lord Coke, because it is "wrested," or crooked, being contrary to that which is right and straight. Co. Litt. 158b.

In modern practice, "tort" is constantly used as an English word to denote a wrong or wrongful act, for which an action will lie, as distinguished from a "contract." 3 Bl.Comm. 117.

A tort is a legal wrong committed upon the person or property independent of contract. It may be either (1) a direct invasion of some legal right of the individual; (2) the infraction of some public duty by which special damage accrues to the individual; (3) the violation of some private obligation by which like damage accrues to the individual. In the former case, no special damage is necessary to entitle the party to recover. In the two latter cases, such damage is necessary. Code Ga.1882, § 2951.

TORT–FEASOR. One who commits or is guilty of a tort.

TORTIOUS. Wrongful; of the nature of a tort. Formerly certain modes of conveyance (e. g., feoffments, fines, etc.) had the effect of passing not merely the estate of the person making the conveyance, but the whole fee simple, to the injury of the person really entitled to the fee; and they were hence called "tortious conveyances." Litt. par. 611; Co. Litt. 271b, note 1; 330b, note 1. But this operation has been taken away. Sweet.

TRANSITORY ACTION. An action that is personal—i. e., brought against the person of the defendant —and possible to be brought in any county in which service of process upon the defendant is obtained.

TRESPASS. Any misfeasance or act of one man whereby another is injuriously treated or damnified. 3 Bl.Comm. 208.

An injury or misfeasance to the person, property, or rights of another person, done with force and violence, either actual or implied by law.

In the strictest sense, an entry on another's ground, without a lawful authority, and doing some damage, however inconsiderable, to his real property. 3 Bl. Comm. 209.

In practice. A form of action, at the common law, which lies for redress in the shape of money damages for any unlawful injury done to the plaintiff, in respect either to his person, property, or rights, by the immediate force and violence of the defendant.

Trespass de bonis asportatis. (Trespass for goods carried away.) In practice. The technical name of that species of trespass for injuries to personal property which lies where the injury consists in carrying away the goods or property.

Trespass on the case. The form of action, at common law, adapted to the recovery of damages for some injury resulting to a party from the wrongful act of another, unaccompanied by direct or immediate force, or which is the indirect or secondary consequence of such act. Commonly called "case," or "action on the case."

Trespass quare clausum fregit. (Trespass wherefore he broke the close, or trespass for breaking the close.) The common-law action for damages for an unlawful entry or trespass upon the plaintiff's land.

TROVER. In common-law practice, the action of trover (or trover and conversion) is a species of action on the case, and originally lay for the recovery of damages against a person who had "found" another's goods and wrongfully converted them to his own use. Subsequently the allegation of the loss of the goods by the plaintiff and the finding of them by the defendant was merely fictitious, and the action became the remedy for any wrongful interference with or detention of the goods of another.

TRUST. An equitable or beneficial right or title to land or other property, held for the beneficiary by another person, in whom resides the legal title or ownership, recognized and enforced by courts of chancery.

TRUST DEED. An instrument in use in many states, taking the place and serving the uses of a common-law mortgage, by which the legal title to real property is placed in one or more trustees, to secure the repayment of a sum of money or the performance of other conditions.

TRUSTEE. The person appointed, or required by law, to execute a trust; one in whom an estate, interest, or power is vested, under an express or implied agreement to administer or exercise it for the benefit or to the use of another.

TRUSTEE PROCESS. The name given in the New England states, to the process of garnishment or foreign attachment.

U

ULTRA VIRES. Latin. Beyond the powers. A term used to express the action of a corporation which is beyond the powers conferred upon it by its charter, or the statutes under which it was instituted. 13 Am.Law Rev. 632.

UNDERTAKING. A promise, engagement, or stipulation. Each of the promises made by the parties to a contract, considered independently and not as mutual, may, in this sense, be denominated an "undertaking."

UNDERWRITER. The person who insures another in a fire or life policy; the insurer.

A person who joins with others in entering into a marine policy of insurance as insurer.

UNIFORM STATUTES. In general, statutes of substantially uniform substance, passed by various states, with the purpose of making the law of the subject uniform throughout the country. Such statutes have been drafted by the Commission on Uniform State Laws of the American Bar Association, and recommended for passage by the Legislatures of the various states. The most important of such statutes are the Negotiable Instruments Act, the Sales Act, and the Partnership Act, which have all been enacted in many of the states.

UNILATERAL. One-sided; ex parte; having relation to only one of two or more persons or things.

USURY. Unlawful interest; a premium or compensation paid or stipulated to be paid for the use of money borrowed or returned, beyond the rate of interest established by law. Webster.

V

VALID. Of binding force. A deed, will, or other instrument, which has received all the formalities required by law, is said to be valid.

VALIDITY. This term is used to signify legal sufficiency, in contradistinction to mere regularity.

VENDEE. A purchaser or buyer; one to whom anything is sold. Generally used of the transferee of real property, one who acquires chattels by sale being called a "buyer."

VENDITIONI EXPONAS. Latin. You may expose to sale. This is the name of a writ of execution, requiring a sale to be made, directed to a sheriff when he has levied upon goods under a fieri facias, but returned that they remained unsold for want of buyers; and in some jurisdictions it is issued to cause a sale to be made of lands, seized under a former writ, after they have been condemned or passed upon by an inquisition. Frequently abbreviated to "vend. ex."

VENDOR. The person who transfers property by sale, particularly real estate, "seller" being more commonly used for one who sells personalty.

VENIRE. Latin. To come; to appear in court. This word is sometimes used as the name of the writ for summoning a jury, more commonly called a "venire facias."

VENIRE FACIAS DE NOVO. Latin. A fresh or new venire, which the court grants when there has been some impropriety or irregularity in returning the jury, or where the verdict is so imperfect or ambiguous that no judgment can be given upon it, or where a judgment is reversed on error, and a new trial awarded.

VERDICT. The formal and unanimous decision or finding of a jury, impaneled and sworn for the trial of a cause, upon the matters or questions duly submitted to them upon the trial.

VESTED. Accrued; fixed; settled; absolute; having the character or giving the rights of absolute ownership; not contingent; not subject to be defeated by a condition precedent.

VINDICTIVE DAMAGES. Exemplary damages are damages on an increased scale, awarded to the plaintiff over and above what will barely compensate him for his property loss, where the wrong done to him was aggravated by circumstances of violence, oppression, malice, fraud, or wanton and wicked conduct on the part of the defendant, and are intended to solace the plaintiff for mental anguish, laceration of his feelings, shame, degradation, or other aggravations of the original wrong, or else to punish the defendant for his evil behavior or to make an example of him, for which reason they are also called "punitive" or "punitory" damages or "vindictive" damages, and (vulgarly) "smart money."

VOID. Null; ineffectual, nugatory; having no legal force or binding effect; unable, in law, to support the purpose for which it was intended.

VOIDABLE. That may be avoided, or declared void; not absolutely void, or void in itself. Most of the acts of infants are "voidable" only, and not absolutely void.

VOLUNTARY. Free; without compulsion or solicitation.

Without consideration; without valuable consideration; gratuitous.

VOLUNTEER. In conveyancing, one who holds a title under a voluntary conveyance; i. e., one made without consideration, good or valuable, to support it.

A person who gives his services without any express or implied promise of remuneration in return is called a "volunteer," and is entitled to no remuneration for his services, nor to any compensation for injuries sustained by him in performing what he has undertaken. Sweet. Also one who officiously pays the debt of another.

W

WAGER. A wager is a contract by which two or more parties agree that a certain sum of money or other thing shall be paid or delivered to one of them on the happening of an uncertain event or upon the ascertainment of a fact which is in dispute between them.

WAIVER. The renunciation, repudiation, abandonment, or surrender of some claim, right, privilege, or of the opportunity to take advantage of some defect, irregularity, or wrong.

WARD. An infant or insane person placed by authority of law under the care of a guardian.

WARRANT, v. In contracts. To engage or promise that a certain fact or state of facts, in relation to the subject-matter, is, or shall be, as it is represented to be.

WARRANT, n. A writ or precept from a competent authority in pursuance of law, directing the doing of an act, and addressed to an officer or person competent to do the act, and affording him protection from damage, if he does it.

WARRANTY. In real property law. A real covenant by the grantor of lands, for himself and his heirs, to warrant and defend the title and possession of the estate granted, to the grantee and his heirs, whereby either upon voucher, or judgment in the writ of warrantia chartæ, and the eviction of the grantee by paramount title, the grantor was bound to recompense him with other lands of equal value.

In sales of personal property. A warranty is a statement or representation made by the seller of goods, contemporaneously with and as a part of the contract of sale, though collateral to the express object of it, having reference to the character, quality, or title of the goods, and by which he promises or undertakes to insure that certain facts are or shall be as he then represents them.

A warranty is an engagement by which a seller assures to a buyer the existence of some fact affecting the transaction, whether past, present, or future.

In contracts. An undertaking or stipulation, in writing, or verbally, that a certain fact in relation to the subject of a contract is or shall be as it is stated or promised to be.

A warranty differs from a representation in that a warranty must always be given contemporaneously with, and as part of, the contract; whereas, a representation precedes and induces to the contract. And, while that is their difference in nature, their difference in consequence or effect is this: that, upon breach of warranty (or false warranty), the contract remains binding, and damages only are recoverable for the breach; whereas, upon a false representation, the defrauded party may elect to avoid the contract, and recover the entire price paid. Brown.

WILL. A will is the legal expression of a man's wishes as to the disposition of his property after his death.

An instrument in writing, executed in form of law, by which a person makes a disposition of his property, to take effect after his death.

WRIT OF ENTRY. A real action to recover the possession of land where the tenant (or owner) has been disseised or otherwise wrongfully dispossessed.

WRIT OF ERROR. A writ issued from a court of appellate jurisdiction, directed to the judge or judges of a court of record, requiring them to remit to the appellate court the record of an action before them, in which a final judgment has been entered, in order that examination may be made of certain errors alleged to have been committed, and that the judgment may be reversed, corrected, or affirmed, as the case may require.

A writ of error is defined to be a commission by which the judges of one court are authorized to examine a record upon which a judgment was given in another court, and, on such examination, to affirm or reverse the same, according to law.

Y

YEAR BOOKS. Books made up of reports of English cases from Edward II, 1292, to Henry VIII, early in the sixteenth century. They constitute an important source of information on the early English common law.

INDEX

References are to Pages

INDEX

INDEX